The Bud Collins
HISTORY OF TENNIS
An Authoritative Encyclopedia and Record Book

For Norma and Chuck,
No. 1 mixed team at
Half Moon Bay
Cheers!
Bud Collins
4-10-09

New Chapter Press

THE BUD COLLINS HISTORY OF TENNIS is published by New Chapter Press (www.newchapterpressmedia.com) and is distributed by the Independent Publishers Group (www.ipgbook.com)

ISBN: 978-0942257410

Photos in the Introduction (pages ix, xi, xii, xv, xvii) are courtesy of Bud Collins and Anita Klaussen.

Photos of Ernest and Willie Renshaw (page 1), Major Wingfield (page 3), James Dwight (page 7), R.D. Sears (page 9), Reggie Doherty (page 11) and Hazel Hotchkiss Wightman (page 14) from the Roots of the Game section, the Dwight Davis photo from the International Play section (page 483), the International Tennis Hall of Fame (page 525) and Jimmy van Alen (page 526) photos from the Biographies section and the Vinnie Richards (page 730) and Karel Kozeluh (page 731) photos from the Pro Tennis in the Pre-Open Era section are all courtesy of the International Tennis Hall of Fame.

The Guillermo Vilas photo in the 1977 chapter of the Year-by-Year Section (page 186) is courtesy of June Harrison.

The photos of Novak Djokovic from the Current Elite chapter (page 653), the Anna Kournikova photo from the They Also Served chapter in the Biographies section (page 662) and the Serena Williams photo (page 717) from the Other Big Events chapter in the Rankings, Tours and Other Championships section are courtesy of Chris Rogers.

The photo of World Team Tennis in 1978 with Chris Evert and Ilie Nastase (page 723) is courtesy of World Team Tennis.

All other interior photos are courtesy of Getty Images.

Cover images and spine image are all courtesy of Getty Images.

Back cover photo is courtesy of Walter Iooss.

New Chapter Press wants to express its thanks to Irene Tan, Simon Chong, McCarton Ackerman, Manfred Wenas, Ewing Walker, Gisela Walker, John George, Janey Marks, Chris Widmaier, Tim Curry, Jean Daly, Kat "Life Saver" Anderson, Emily Brackett, DeAnne McCaslin, Chris Rogers, Bill Mountford, Catherine O'Neal, Jack Mountford, Robert Geist, Greg Sharko, Rosie Crews and Blair Cummins.

Design by Visible Logic, Inc. Portland, Maine. www.visiblelogic.com

Printed in Canada

Dedication

For Barry "Orso" Lorge (1948–2008)

Great friend to me, and to all those who knew him—and to the readers who delighted in his stories on tennis as well as other sports and other subjects. A very kind bear of a man, whose touch on the keyboard made friends of strangers. Good humored and brave to the end, teaching us how it's done.

And For Anita Ruthling Klaussen,

Member of the International Packing Hall of Fame, Demon Editor and organizer without whose dedication this book would never have been finished as well as All-Star Roommate whose love and enthusiasm keeps me up and bright.

Acknowledgements

(Or, how could you get along without morsels of help and hope from your friends?)

Why produce this tome sweet tome?
　　I suppose it was self interest. In making the planetary tennis rounds I was weary of lugging an extra bag jammed with pertinent reference books. Why not just one volume covering everything a tennis junkie needed to know? This is it: the fourth or fifth edition—I can't remember. A tome to roam with, to comb for nuggets (it also makes a fine doorstop; a keepsake, marriage or divorce gift).

What hath Wingfield, winging it, wrought? That would be Major Walter Clopton Wingfield, the English sire who conceived the present-day game, patented it in 1874 and sent it on its globe-circling way to give so much fun to countless millions, whether Champions or Hackers, addicts or periodically interested.

Here's a toast to the major – and to numerous buddies, associates, inspirers, helpers to whom I owe thank-you's for softening my life:

The world has been my oyster in this stew with aid coming from historians par excellence—Frank Phelps and George Alexander; David Studham, librarian sensational of the Melbourne Cricket Club; indispensable Gringo Good Shoes (aka Randy Walker, publisher extraordinaire with endless patience, pride and caring).

Also supersearcher researchers Nick Imison, Mitzi Ingram, Neil Robinson of Barbara Travers' ITF gang; the Sharing-caring Shark of Ponte Vedra (Greg Sharko) and his school of ATP guppies, Nicola Arzani, Pete Holderman. The WTA's Vigilant Vani Vosburgh, Amy Binder, John "Who Gives a Damn!" Dolan, Gina Clement, Iz Hodge, Fern Kellmeyer. Tony Trabert, Mark Stenning, Kat Anderson, Linda Johnson, Mickey Riendeau, Mark Young of the International Tennis Hall of Fame.

Also Huzzahs to Janet Hopps Adkisson, Sunny Amatos, Arthur Ashe, "Hipster" Tucker Aufranc, Simon Barnes, John Barrett, Cugino "Breakfast" Basche, Fred Basilico, Bob Beach, Andrew Blauner, Peter Bodo, Ron Bookman, Bordes, Philippe Bouin, Brough & duPont, Jane Brown, Butch Buchholz, Mary Canfield, Mary Carillo, Rosebud Casals, Chris Clarey, Claudia and her cubs, Yannick Cochennec, Sarah Clarke, J. Spencer Courier, Bwana Piga Crawford, Matt Cronin, Joyce Comfort's Charlie, Sweet Caroline Davis, Dwight & Anne-Marie Davis, Alain Deflassieux, Frank Deford, D. Lundy Dell, Bones Dillard, Lisa Dillman, Vincenzo Doria, Joel Drucker, Bob Dunbar, Bill Dwyre, Judith Elian, Wendy Elkin, "Oh MY!" Enberg, Elizabeth Erbafina, Ashley Evans, C. Marie Evert, "Hurricane Donna" Fales, J. Brink Feinstein, Dee Dee Felich, Bobby Feller, Stefano Flink, Frosts, the Furgalians, Waltzing Robert Geist, Andrea Gerlin, Greg Harney, Neil Harman, Julie Hatfield, Harold Hecht, Ed Hickey, Snapper Iooss, Stan Isaacs, "Bizzy Bear" Jensen, Liz and David Kahn, Kamo & Miyagi, Arlen Kantarian, Bob Kelleher, Commissioner Kloss, Killius Kittens and Kin, Dorie Klissas, "Mother Freedom" BJ King, Chris and Harry Kirsch, Danielle Klaussen, Karl H.R. Klaussen, Knight Trainers Ant and Bev, Jack Kramer, Robertino Lacy, Muraling Marcelo, R. George Laver, Larry Lawrence, C.A. Timothy Leland, Michelino Lupica, Mauro and his Lusardi's gang, Capt. PMac, "Ohio Bear" MacKay, C. Gene Mako, Marvelous Martina, Ed "Fingers" Miller, Terry and "Emancipator" Marvin Miller, "One-more" Mullanes, Michael's Laura and Suzanna Mathews, Steve Mayer, Seth Mayeri, Mike McQuade, Paul Metzler, Sue Mott, Murray the Wrench and Susi the Wench, Roberto Nappo, Contessa Edith Nathanson, BSO Ace Jim Orleans, Barbara Paddock, Charlie Pasarell, Author Phillips, "String-along" Pilot, S.L. Price, Jamie Reynolds, Mickey Riendeau, John Roberts, Ted Robinson, Emily Rooney, Muscles Rosewall, Artist Brother Ford and his hummingbirds, Guillermo Salatino, Ronaldinho E.Y. Sampson, Ubaldo Scanagatta, Adam Scharff, Francisco Segura, Fred Sharf, Uncle Marty Shembrey, Sam Silverman, Jim Simpson, Ken Solomon, Jordan Sprechman, Joseph "Wood rackets forever!" Stahl, Mark Stenning, Nan St. Gore, Old Hacker Stolle, Bill Talbert, Rooms Tebbutt, Rino Tommasi, Alan Trengove, Candy & Jimmy Van Alen, Valiant Visser & Stoic Stockton, Sarah V. Wade, Judy Waligunda, Willie Weinbaum, Wineland "Jambo" Thomsons, Hazel Wightman, Midge Morrill Painter Whiting, Tiger Tom Winship, R.B.D.H. Wogan, Peggy and Ed Woolard, Helen Zimman.

Table of Contents

SECTION II – The Major Championships. 331

SECTION III – International Play 485

SECTION IV – Biographies 527

SECTION V – Tours, Rankings and Other Championships 699

Introduction

If the grass is greener on the other side of the sea, then we must be thinking of Wimbledon. God's own sod was, is—and always will be, I believe—the Wimbledonian stage for the game we chronicle and celebrate in this tome.

The United States in 1881, then Australia in 1905, followed in the English sneaker steps. But it wasn't until 1925 that the French sought, and gained, admission to what would become the exclusive major championships club. In a sort of Gallic "keep off the grass!" reaction, they preferred their lawn-shaving method of getting down and dirty and maintaining courts of crimson continental clay. By 1927 when France's "Four Musketeers" —Borotra, Brugnon, Cochet, Lacoste—lifted the Davis Cup from the U.S., the idea of the "big four," the only nations to capture the the tennis grail, was solidified.

This quartet of majors remains unchanged, although the U.S., abandoned greensward for a brief (1975-77) flirtation with clay,

then became addicted to the hard stuff, mean green pavement at a freshly-built complex, Flushing Meadow. A decade later, 1988, so did Australia at the new base, Melbourne Park. No longer green with envy of Wimbledon, the Americans dyed their courts blue in 2006, whereupon the Aussies did likewise in 2008.

So if the majors were to adopt a flag, it should be striped in red, green and blue.

Can a mere patch of grass in southwest London be a world of its own? This one is. A playground somberly walled in dull green and yet, surrounded by crowded galleries, it might remind the scribbler, Shakespeare, of his own playhouse, the Globe. Similarly open to the elements, it, too, is the scene of countless dramas—of kings and queens rising and falling.

It is called Centre Court, the planetary heart of a game known as tennis, in the precinct of Wimbledon—a territory often lamentably posing as the tropical rain forest of England. Although Shakespeare predated Wimbledon by centuries, he was acquainted with tennis, even penned a bit making fun of King Henry V in the play of that name.

In a sarcastic "Balls to you!" gesture, the Dauphin of France sends Henry a box of tennis balls, suggesting that the young king is more playboy than warrior. Henry responds by going on the road to break the dauphin's serve and France's nerve at the battle of Agincourt.

Though nothing as perilous as Agincourt takes place at Centre Court, the battles result in an afternoon's triumph or disaster, and become indelible in these pages. Unlike the Bard's, these dramas, played out in all corners of the earth, in one tournament or another, are unscripted. To be or not to be ain't known until the very end.

They can provoke unbearable suspense and passages of high tension, but not tragedy—unless you feel that label can be attached to a moment of elastic betrayal on Centre Court one afternoon in the 1920s. "Zing!" went the snapped waistband string, a prelude to the involun tary descent of the knickers (as that apparel is termed by Brits) belonging to future Hall of Famer Betty Nuthall, Betty, a jolly young thing, kept her chin up anyway, recovered, and would become in 1930 the first Englishwoman to win the U.S. championship.

She was not quite as open, as devil-may-care, on Centre as Melissa Johnson—a pale streak—decades later in the 1996 final. Actually as the overture to the final (contested by champ-to-be Richard Krajicek and MaliVai Washington), Melissa raced across the green fully unencumbered by attire. The resulting furor probably would have been considered much ado about nothingness by Shakespeare. He might have applauded it as an opening scene he wished he'd thought up, fashioning her as a sort of Godiva of the green.

Years before I'd ever sat at Centre Court, well before I was even aware of its existence, my own courts of dreams lay about 50 yards behind our house in a small Ohio town. Laid out on a bumpy, cracked, dirt flat, four of them, they belonged to the local college, set behind the sandstone gym whose lofty fire escape was my sky box. This was about the same time that something more harmful than knickers—German bombs—fell on Centre Court. The sounds of tennis—my summertime alarm clock—were explosive in their way: the PUH! PUH! PUH! of balls responding to swats, or jangling against wire fences.

It was a nice way to wake up, and I longed to play on those courts. Sometimes I did, but they were usually busy from daylight to dark with grown-ups. Kids squintingly struggled with dusk. Armed with hand-me-downs—bald, overly-abused balls, and rackets, not infrequently broken-stringed—we slashed and bashed at each other, and felt it was a pretty good game.

My favorite racket, borrowed from older neighbor Edith Reublin, was a wooden sky blue implement entitled, mysteriously, Onwentsia. Was that the name of a famed bygone champ? I coveted Edith's more valued Ellsworth Vines model, bearing the picture of Vines, once world No. 1, on the throat. (Sadly, the advent of open-throated rackets has eliminated personalized artwork, visages of such immortals as Jack Kramer, Alice Marble, Little Mo Connolly and Pancho Gonzalez.)

Edith wasn't letting Vines out of her sight. Still, I was happy with Onwentsia, which I learned, long after, was the name of a Chicago tennis club, not a Spanish or Italian Davis Cup hero.

Those courts became a tragedy, at least in my eyes, casualties of war: victims not of bombs, but a patriotic steam shovel! Baldwin-Wallace College, directed by the government to train naval officers during World War II, lacked a swimming pool. Somehow the War Department felt that knowing how to swim was more important to naval officers than a knowledge of tennis. Presto, change-o— the courts were gone, and so was my early rennis career. Hardly a loss to the game.

Not that I lost out entirely. Tennis survived as my lonely passion, played against myself by banging balls at a brick wall of the nearby elementary school. Sure, the wall always won. But,

without knowing it, I was hooked, afflicted by a jones, an addiction. Maybe we should pin this jones, this tennis dependency of mine—and innumerable others—on a Jones called Henry.

Dr. Henry Jones, a 19th century London M.D., may or may not have known much about obstetrics, but shouldn't we blame him for delivering this bouncing baby, baptized Lawn Tennis, which turned a healthy 134 in 2008. No, he wasn't the patriarch. That role belonged to a retired British army office, Major Walter Clopton Wingfield, patenting, in 1874, his outdoor variation on the ages-old tennis theme that Shakespeare alluded to in Henry V. It was also relished by "London Fats" himself, King Henry VIII, whose private playroom is yet in use at Hampton Court Palace.

Anyway, Dr. Jones, a founder of the All England Croquet Club in 1870, in the suburb of Wimbledon, fancying himself as an expert on games—he wrote about them for a popular publication called The Field—could see there was something to this diversion devised by Major Wingfield. It would go nicely on a croquet lawn. He sold fellow members on the idea of courts, and by 1877 there was enough interest so that he proposed a tournament for men: The Lawn Tennis Championships.

The name is unchanged, although that initial tournament at the club's Worple Road grounds soon became known as justplain Wimbledon, deferring to the location. As the wicket game took a back seat, the club rearranged its ID as the All England Lawn Tennis & Croquet Club.

Jones may never have written a prescription, but he wrote about tennis, helping to call attention to his tournament. Whether he ever played the game, Dr. Jones was spiritually in tune with a young physician in Boston, Dr. James Dwight. Neither let the practice of medicine interfere with his involvement in tennis.

Doc Dwight, truly the Father of American Tennis, may have been the first to play in America in 1874. If he wasn't the first, this Boston Brahmin was the most enthusiastic. He guided the structuring of the USNLTA (U.S. National Lawn Tennis Tennis Association at its founding, now the USTA) in 1881, competed in the earliest U.S. Championships (winning five doubles titles), presided over the national organization for 21 years, and laid the groundwork for the Davis Cup, launched in 1900.

Though I knew neither Jones nor Dwight, I was acquainted with Dr. Richard Dwight, the son of the Father, like his old man a member of Boston's Longwood Cricket Club. He played into his 90s, and died a very happy man in 1998 because he had—in a way—finally caught up with papa after 103 years, attaining a recognized singles ranking. Doc Dwight the elder was No. 3 in the U.S. in 1888, at 36. In 1991, Doc Dwight the Younger, 88, was No. 1 in New England in the super-seniors, the over-85 category. "I had to wait a while," he laughed, "but it made me feel good. My father wasn't very impressed by my tennis."

Neither was mine. A man who hadn't touched a racket for years, he beat me handily when I thought myself a hotshot, No. 1 on the high school team.

But he was impressed when the Boston Globe's superb editor-in-chief, Tom Winship, hired me away from the rival Herald and immediately shipped me to Australia to cover the 1963 Davis Cup challenge round, in Adelaide, a successful invasion by Yanks Chuck McKinley and Dennis Ralston. After a four-year

Bud Collins (right) interviews **Arthur Ashe.**

sojourn Down Under, the Cup was spirited back to the U.S. for a brief stay until the Aussies retrieved it in 1964.

Four years after that, a U.S. team spearheaded by Arthur Ashe returned to Adelaide to reclaim the Cup. Ashe, a lieutenant in the U.S. Army, had won the U.S. Amateur and Open titles of 1968. His blackness in a white sport, as well as his championship qualities in several directions, made Arthur a significant story.

"He's a horse you better ride," Winship suggested.

Luckily I did, a wonderful ride across five continents chronicling this humanitarian-with-racket, a rare blend of sensitivity and athleticism. The ride ended too soon, mournfully, at his Richmond, Virginia, graveside in 1993 as whites and blacks joined hands and sang, *We Shall Overcome.*

Arthur was one of those who made the transitional jump in 1968 from one era to the next at the uppermost level: amateurism to "opens," eventually shedding amateur status on his release from the U.S. Army to become a professional.

Like other professional sports that have succeeded with the public since World War II, tennis has come to be regarded as an entertainment and a business as much as a game. As the 2008 campaign began, the 40th anniversary of the advent of "opens" (the integration of amateurs and pros with cash payments offered on the basis of performance) more than $98 million was available throughout the world to male and $62.4 million for female professionals. The total for that seminal season of prize money was about $400,000.

Grandest financially of the 12 cautiously-approved open championships in the new-horizonal year was the U.S. Open at Forest Hills. A $100,000 pot held $14,000 and $6,000 as first prizes for champions Ashe and Virginia Wade respectively. (Arthur, unable to dip into the pot because of his Army-enforced amateur standing, came off with $20-a-day expenses. His final round victim, pro Tom Okker, collected the 14 grand.) By 2007, the purse had sweetened to $18,196,000, the singles first prize (the same for men and women since 1973) amounted to $1,400,000.

Despite all the gold, this diversion is yet a game that is sometimes raised to an art form—a competitive ballet—by the splendor in movement of such acrobatic zephyrs as Suzanne Lenglen, Henri Cochet, Fred Perry, Maria Bueno, Rod Laver, Ken Rosewall, Evonne Goolagong, Ilie Nastase, Martina Navratilova, John McEnroe, Steffi Graf, Andre Agassi, Martina Hingis, Pete Sampras, Roger Federer, the "Sisters Sledgehammer" (Venus and Serena Williams) and Justine Henin.

Often it is sublime drama. Never more so than on a chilly, grim October afternoon in Bucharest in 1972 when nationalism and personal pride, strength of character, and moral outlook were all wrapped up in a game of tennis between an American, Stan Smith, and a Romanian, Ion Tiriac, a menacing, Draculan figure right out of the Count D's stomping grounds.

Even though Smith was the best player in the world that year, he was out of his element. Slipping on the slow, crimson-colored European clay, he was assaulted by a canny, dark-haired grizzly, while a feverish crowd and unfailingly patriotic line judges gave him a thumbs-down treatment. Never mind the tennis match, Smith sometimes wondered whether he'd get out of town alive. At stake was the Davis Cup, that huge silver basin from which world conquerors have swilled victorious champagne since 1900. It is the most difficult bauble to win in tennis, a reward for the global team title, pursued each year by more than 120 countries. In 1972, the United States and Romania were the finalists. The Cup would be decided by the Smith-Tiriac match, and this fact made a boiling kettle of an intimate 7,000-seat wooden stadium that was hastily hammered together for what amounted to a state occasion in Romania.

Although Tiriac, a deceptively plodding and unstylish player, wasn't in Smith's league, he lifted himself as high as his native Carpathians with one thought—his tiny homeland, producer of few world-class players besides himself and teammate Ilie Nastase, could score a fantastic victory over the mighty U.S. if he beat Smith.

"I know only one way to play—to win. If I lose," Tiriac said, "then it is nothing. We don't win the Cup."

Ion orchestrated the chanting crowd and deferential line judges into a united front for himself and against Smith. He stalled, he emoted—and he played like a madman, forcing the excruciating match all the way into a fifth set. It seemed a morality play in short pants: the exemplary sportsman Smith, tall and fair-haired, against the scheming Tiriac, bearish and glaring. Somehow Smith held together amid chaos to play to his utmost, too, and win the last set in a run of six games, 4-6, 6-2, 6-4, 2-6, 6-0. Considering the adverse conditions and the magnitude of the prize, Smith's triumph was possibly the most extraordinary in the history of the game.

"I concentrated so hard I got a headache," he said.

That was the final, with the Cup at stake. However, Davis Cup, with all its nationalistic overtones, can grip you at any stage, even if it's not your own country enmeshed, and you have no rooting interest.

My heart never beat quicker for tennis than during three rainy May afternoons in Prague, 1971, a seeming ly insignificant Cup engagement between the Soviet Union and Czechoslovakia, neither of them contenders.

Insignificant? Not to the tormented folk of Czechoslovakia, under the thumbs of the USSR. Tuned in to TV throughout a tense, capricious weekend, they prayed for their own guys and cursed the white-costumed athletes representing the black-hearted invader whose tanks had echoed across those time-worn streets only three springs before. "Politics!" wailed Jan Kodes, the Czechs' main man, fresh from winning the French Open. "It isn't sport, it's politics, and my head aches from it because people want me to win so bad."

Those expectations made Jan tighter than Scarlett O'Hara's corset, and he was beaten by Alex Metreveli, who could feel the hatred directed at him by the jammed-in crowd of 5,000, most of them standing for hours. Dank silence greeted Metreveli's every point, no matter how brilliantly he might hit the ball. It was eerie. Wild, delighted cheers followed his errors plus anything good Kodes could do. Barbed whistles assailed the Soviets whenever they disputed a line call, many of which were very patriotic (a la Bucharest), in other words, against the Soviets, and well worth disputing.

"Yes, we screwed them on some calls," Kodes conceded, "but not as bad as they screwed us last year in Moscow."

Kafkaesque gloom descended after Metreveli beat Kodes. But obscure lefty Frantisek Pala saved the first day with his curlicue spins to defeat Vladimir Korotkov. So-called journalistic objectivity vanished in the drizzle. Sitting and soaking there, I became a Czech, chanting "Doe-tuh-hoe!"—"Come on!"—over and over as a member of the all-encompassing chorus.

Back and forth it went for three sodden days of nerve-quaking play wrapped around rain interruptions, days of hopes dashed and revived, dashed and revived again. "They don't like me much, do they?" Metreveli, a Georgian, observed with a wry smile. "Too much politics. I have nothing to do with that. I just do my job: play tennis."

Bud Collins (right) with **Alex Metreveli** (left) and **Marat Safin** (center).

But there was an unexpectedly happy ending. Kodes. Backboned by immense doubles partner Jan Kukal, pulled himself together, and the Czechs won. The hall porter at my hotel was ecstatic. "Tiny Czechoslovakia ... he held his hands about two inches apart. "Tiny Czechoslovakia ..." and then he spread them as far as possible, "beat giant Soviet Union!" Momentary bliss.

While Tiriac was chastised outside of Romania for a pragmatic approach to tennis, shunning accepted behavior, he was simply doing the best he could to seize a rare day for his homeland. It was only a game of tennis, but it had assumed a far greater significance for a few hours that afternoon.

The outlook had changed considerably since earlier days at Wimbledon, the 1889 all-comers final, for instance, when the six-time champ, Willie Renshaw, facing a match point against Harry Barlow, was engaged in a furious exchange—and fell, dropping his racket. Instead of stroking the ball out of Renshaw's reach, Barlow, in the words of the umpire, "elected to toss it amiably back," a soft shot so that Willie had a chance to get up, keep the point going, and win it. Willie saved five other match points, beat Barlow in five sets, and continued to beat his twin brother, Ernest, for a seventh title in the challenge round final.

But those were jolly good English blokes with no cash or computer points at stake. Times change, and the far-reaching significance, and the internationality is a source of much of the appeal of tennis. By this, of course, I mean the established worldwide tournament game to which this book is devoted.

The advance of the game since this form of tennis was set forth in London in 1874 by Major Wingfield, has been so complete that all continents are routinely represented in any tournament of consequence. Australians, Asians, Europeans, Africans, and North and South Americans populate a family of tournament players who work their way around the globe on an unending trek. They flit between Melbourne and Munich, Bombay and Buenos Aires, Johannesburg and Jacksonville as casually as suburbanite commuters.

The game may have been restricted to a 78-by-27-foot plot, but it has been is played worldwide on a variety of surfaces. Yet, regardless of how far tennis would stray from grass—to such exotic footing as dried cow dung in India, ant bed in Australia, carpet, ersatz grass (Astroturf) in numerous locations, as well as pavement, and plastic carpets for indoor play—the game was once and forever "lawn tennis" to the Brits, who would rather break their necks than tradition.

Lawn tennis or just-plain-tennis—whatever it is called, however the ball bounces on whichever surface— caught on in the U.S. more widely than anywhere else. Shortly after Wingfield started peddling his game, it reached the U.S. in 1874. In 1876, Doc Dwight won a baptismal tourney of sorts, a sociable get-together he arranged in the yard of the Appleton estate at Nahant, Massachusetts. However, nobody declared that tennis had landed in America. Or much noticed.

For many years afterwards, it was assumed, and written in several histories, that one Mary Outerbridge, of a prominent Staten Island (N.Y.) family, had planted the game in the U.S., on that island across from Manhattan, by bringing a set of tennis equipment home from Bermuda. Feminists may have been dis-

mayed in 1979 by English historian Tom Todd's assertion that it was Dwight—not Outerbridge—who introduced tennis to the States earlier that year. Founding mother or father? Both Outerbridge, longer hailed, and Dwight have their backers.

A century later (1974) an American historian, George Alexander, uncovered evidence of the first recorded play in the U.S. Not in New York or Massachusetts, but— holy half-volleys!—in the wilds of Apache country in the Arizona Territory, also 1874. And a brand new name enters the game's literature: Ella Wilkins Bailey. Was Ella, wife of a U.S. Army officer, the champ of Camp Apache? Unknown. But it has been documented that she played on the court there that year, possibly with her sister, Caroline Wilkins. Fair Ella may or may not have been the first American player. Doc Dwight the Elder and Fred Sears, his cousin, get this writer's nod.

But according to the thorough Alexander, Ella Wilkins Bailey is the first for whom a reliable reference has been found.

While some may keen, "Say it ain't so, Doc!" and charge Alexander and Todd with revisionism, Doc Dwight the Younger, ever, gracious, said before his death, "Even my father got mixed up as to the date when he later wrote about it. The main thing is that people did start to play and Mary Outerbridge was important in giving the push in New York. The fact seems to be that both my father and Outerbridge imported sets at about the same time, and nobody can be quite sure who was first."

Although tennis drifted across the country from Staten Island and Nahant and probably Newport, Philadelphia, San Francisco, and New Orleans (site of the New Orleans Tennis Club, the country's first, 1876), the power remained in the Northeast. Three decades after Dick Sears began his American championship dynasty in 1881, the American men's championship was still the property of an Ivy League crowd. Exceptions popped up among the women. Best known were Californians Marion Jones, U.S. champ in 1899 and 1902, May Sutton, champ in 1904 (a year prior to her butting into the homebodies' monopoly at Wimbledon), and Hazel Hotchkiss, 1909-11. But the Northeast's early stranglehold had actually been broken by Irishwoman Mabel Cahill (1891-92) and defied by Jones and Myrtle McAteer from Pittsburgh in 1900.

At least, in 1912, the men's U.S. Championships began to go truly national on the tail of the "California Comet," hyper-aggressive Maurice "Red" McLoughlin, and the general sporting public would soon become aware of tennis. Its evident appeal caused tennis to burst from the cloister of Newport as an amusement of the swells, and in 1915 the U.S. Championships for men moved to the metropolis, New York, and the West Side Tennis Club at Forest Hills. There would be a country club tinge right up to the present day of heavy money and professionalization, but at Forest Hills, tennis gained exposure to larger, more diverse crowds - and a national press.

Once peacetime arrived, following World War I, the press had a tennis hero to hype, and a heroine. Big Bill Tilden, the gangling Philadelphian with a blowtorch serve, and Suzanne Lenglen, a flying Frenchwoman, worked their respective sides of the Atlantic with irresistible flair and shotmaking. Not only were Tilden and Lenglen virtually invincible champions, they were also regal figures, draped in an air of mystery. Theirs was a magnetism that pulled crowds and sold tickets, and tennis became a commercial venture. With Tilden as strong man, the U.S. went on a record rampage of seven straight Davis Cups, and it was necessary to construct a 13,000-seat stadium at Forest Hills to hold the throngs eager to follow Davis Cup engagements and the U.S. Championships.

Because of Lenglen, never beaten in singles at Wimbledon, that citadel became too small for all the customers. Thus the All England Lawn Tennis & Croquet Club moved in 1922 to the present Wimbledon grounds where Centre Court accommodated nearly 14,000.

Tennis joined other sports as a business game, but, unfortunately, not as a profession. By 1926, it was apparent that the athletes who sold the tickets deserved to be paid. It was not apparent, however, to those volunteer, usually affluent, officials who controlled the game. For generations past its time, they would keep alive the fiction of "amateurism" at the game's upper level. Instead of prize money, the subsidy for careerists was "expenses," paid beneath the well-known table in proportion to a player's value as a gate attraction.

During the 1920s, Tilden made more real income out of tennis as an amateur than some of the better pros today. He earned it. But Tilden, a supreme individualist, showed neither gratitude nor obeisance to the amateur authorities and was eventually driven to the wilderness of outright professionalism in 1931, to take his place brilliantly on the treadmill of one-nighters. Until 1926, the only professionals were instructors, ineligible for customary tournaments. Occasionally they played small tournaments among themselves for pin money. Even though open tennis was discussed wistfully by progressives among players, officials and aficionados, such a sensible arrangement was well in the future.

Amateurs who traveled the world swinging at tennis balls, living and eating well, were called "tennis bums." This "shamateurism" was maintained until 1968. However, those who decided to accept money above the table were considered outlaws traveling under that dirty label, professionals. Forced to scrape for their living outside of the usual framework of private clubs, the pros appeared mainly in public arenas, moving constantly as nomads, folding their canvas court and jaunting to the next night's location.

This way of life began in October 1926 when La Belle Suzanne Lenglen defected from amateurism to roam North America with a troupe that included her nightly foe/pigeon, Mary K. Browne, the U.S. champion of 1912-14, and Vinnie Richards, the American second to Tilden. Their stopovers were regarded as exhibitions, but the pay was all right. Lenglen reportedly collected at feast $75,000, a fortune in 1927 dollars, for her four months on the road.

A few months after the debut of the original wandering pros, the first U.S. Pro Championships for men was thrown together at a small club in Manhattan in the summer of 1927 and won by Richards, whose reward was $1,000 from a purse of $2,000. His 1999 successor, at Boston's Longwood Cricket Club, the last champ before the tourney was abandoned, Marat Safin, won $46,000 from a pot of $325,000.

Prior to Open tennis, life as a pro meant barnstorming one-nighters. There wasn't enough money to support more than a handful of outlaws. Tournaments that mattered were restricted to amateurs, whose game had structure, continuity and the attention of the press and sporting public. Interest in amateur sport was high during the 1920s and 1930s, but after World War II that interest shifted to professional sport. While other sports gleamed in television's red eye, tennis languished away from the cameras.

Three events maintained an eminence: Wimbledon, Forest Hills, and the Davis Cup finale, which became the postwar preserve of the U.S. and Australia. As the 1950s dawned, a tidal wave swept from the Antipodes: it was the Aussies, the most dynastic force ever in tennis. Their muscle lasted for more than two decades, between the Davis Cup seizure by Frank Sedgman & Cohorts in 1950 and the Cup coup of John Newcombe and Rod Laver in 1973. In between were 16 Davis Cups and 14 Wimbledons for the men, two singles Grand Slams by Rod Laver, and a male record of 28 major titles by Roy Emerson (12 singles, 16 doubles), as well as the rise and fall of Lew Hoad, and the rise and rise of ageless Kenny Rosewall. Australian women were not as pervasive but one of them, Margaret Smith Court, rolled up a record 62 major titles in singles, doubles and mixed (24-19-19), including a Singles Grand Slam in 1970.

Midway through the 1960s, a period of rising acclaim for sport in general, tennis was sagging at both the amateur and professional levels. The best players were pros, but the best tournaments were amateur. Agitation for open play increased, especially in England, where Wimbledon officials, tiring of exorbitant expense payments to amateurs, sought to present the finest tennis. This was impossible as long as the professional elite—Laver, Rosewall, Pancho Gonzalez, Hoad, Butch Buchholz and Andres Gimeno—were off in limbo.

An impetus for the decisive move toward opens was provided startlingly in 1967 by a man unknown within tennis, Dave Dixon of New Orleans. Buoyed by Texas money supplied by Dallas petrocrat Lamar Hunt, his partner in a wildcat tennis venture, WCT (World Championship Tennis), Dixon signed up amateurs Newcombe, Tony Roche, Roger Taylor, Cliff Drysdale and Nikki Pilic plus pros Buchholz, Pierre Barthes and Dennis Ralston as his WCT Tennis troupe. Another promoter, American ex-Davis Cup captain George MacCall, founder of the NTL (National Tennis League), had enlisted amateur Emerson to blend with pros Laver, Gonzalez, Rosewall, Gimeno, Fred Stolle plus Rosie Casals, Billie Jean King, Ann Jones and Francoisc Durr. And so the amateur game was abruptly depleted of its top 10 players.

Aware that Dixon was lurking, Herman David, the Wimbledon chairman, realized that he and Wimbledon must follow their long smoldering desire to open up the game. First, he organized a test run, a three-day, pros-only tournament in August on the august Centre Court. Would the venerated turf wither beneath the feet of out-and-out outlaws (Laver, Rosewall, Gonzalez, Gimeno, Hoad, Stolle, Ralston, Buchholz)? Would the Big W's clientele even show up to watch the banished bad boys jousting for a then-record purse of $35,000?

The temple didn't crumble. It rumbled with applause as starved patrons filled Centre Court the second and third days.

Herman David and confreres came as close as All England Clubbies can come to grinning as Laver beat Rosewall in a terrific final, 6-2, 6-2, 12-10. David Gray wrote in The Guardian: "Having grown used to margarine, it was good to be reminded of the taste of butter."

There was no turning back. Confident of the British public and press' support, and with the backing of the nation's influential LTA (Lawn Tennis Association), Wimbledon announced that in 1968 it would be open to all players regardless of their status, amateur or pro. When that shot was fired, the U.S., led by enlightened USTA president Bob Kelleher, seconded the revolt, defying the International Tennis Federation. The rest of the world had no choice but to fall into line.

Bournemouth, England, was the scene of the first open, the British Hard Court (meaning clay) Championships in April 1968. Rosewall won the men's title, Virginia Wade the women's. Curly-headed Englishman Mark Cox wrote his footnote in sporting history as the first amateur to beat a pro at tennis. Cox, a left-hander, knocked off Pancho Gonzalez and Roy Emerson on successive afternoons to upstage all else on Britain's front pages.

The tennis epidemic to come in the 1970s had been set in motion, along with the venture into high-technology that would make wooden rackets obsolete. Ashe won his U.S. Amateur and Open titles with a split-shaft Head aluminum racket that he called "the snow-shoe." Billie Jean King and Rosie Casals, as well as teenager Jimmy Connors, were waving Wilson T-2000 "steelies" in the late 1960s. In 1971, Laver crossed the million-dollar mark in prize money after nine years as a pro. But by 1979, 15 other men and three women had followed, making their millions in shorter spans. And in 1977 Argentine's "Young Bull of the Pampas," Guillermo Vilas, had a year that would seem a splendid career for most athletes: $800,642. This was just walking-around money, as the upward-and-onward finances of the '80s and '90s and the first years of the new century would show. In 1990, 19-year-old Pete Sampras carted off a flabbergasting first prize of $2 million for winning the newly-contrived Grand Slam Cup tournament, and wound up the season with men's record winnings of $2,900,057. That mark wouldn't last long. He'd soon be in the $5-million-per-season class. In 1992, an 18-year-old Monica Seles set the female season record, $2,622,352, also perishable as Arantxa Sanchez Vicario was a few dollars shy of $3 million in 1994, Kim Cljisters earned $3,983,654 in 2005 with Justine Henin becoming the first woman to break $5 million earning $5,429,586 in 2007. Ivan Lendl retired in 1994 with the staggering prize-money record of $21,262,417, since hurdled by Sampras ($43,280,489 at his retirement at the end of 2002), Andre Agassi, Boris Becker and Yevgeny Kafelnikov. Martina Navratilova went out—she sort of—at about the same time with $20,337,902, a momentary record representing her 22 years of labor, eclipsed by Graf in her 14th professional season. While career millionaires weren't quite a dime a dozen, 393 men and over 150 women had earned that appellation by the close of 2007.

At first the boom in prize money benefitted principally the men. As in so many areas of life, the women were left behind. However, guided by brainy Gladys Heldman, publisher of World Tennis magazine, and inspired by the liberation-minded fire-

brand, Billie Jean King, the women divorced themselves from the conventional tournament arrangement they'd shared with the men. Top billing (and top dollars) had always gone to the men. Carrying the banner of Virginia Slims cigarettes, the women crusaded on a separate tour and made good artistically and economically. The Slims tour began haltingly in 1970 and picked up steam in 1971, when Billie Jean won $117,000, the first woman to earn more than 100 grand in prize money. The tour was solid by 1972, when ingénue Chrissie Evert won the first eight-woman playoff at the season's climax. In 1973, the women demanded and got equal prize money at the U.S. Open, one of the few remaining tournaments embracing both men's and women's events.

Television didn't rush to hug tennis when the Open era began, although network interest picked up. Two telecasts in particular aided in lifting the game to wide public notice: Rosewall's sensational 4-6, 6-0, 6-3, 6-7 (3-7), 7-6 (7-5), victory over Laver on NBC for the WCT title of 1972 in Dallas; and Billie Jean King's 6-4, 6-3, 6-3, put-down of 55-year-old Bobby Riggs on ABC's bizarre "Battle of the Sexes" at Houston's Astrodome in 1973

Also a constant, steady influence in the game's increasing popularity were the 1970s telecasts of PBS (no commercials, complete finals in singles and doubles), Monday night finals of the ATP summer circuit, and such events as the Davis Cup final 1978-79, the Masters, 1974-75-76, Greg Harney producing.

Bud Collins (right) with **Bobby Riggs** at the Longwood Cricket Club.

Tennis began to appear regularly on television, prize money accelerated for the stars, equipment sales and participation accelerated for the hackers. Construction of public courts as well as private clubs increased, particularly in the U.S., where the proliferation of indoor courts was a sporting phenomenon. Tennis was big business, and the pros, following the example of brethren in other sports, unionized to gain a stronger position in the management of their business. The male ATP (Association of Tennis Pros) and female WTA (Women's Tennis Association) were formed as player guilds, and two new governing bodies were also formed: the International Professional Tennis Councils for men (MIPTC) and women (WIPTC), containing representatives of the unions, the ITF, and the tournament promoters.

Those who thought the war was over when the forces of open tennis triumphed soon realized that strife would become a way of life in tennis. Revolution and evolution continued to change the face of the professional game. Athough for a long time the U.S. was the financial base, the stronghold for pro tennis, Europe caught up, and can Asia be far behind?

Interestingly it was another non-tennis figure, Hamilton Jordan, who launched a revolution on behalf of the ATP as Dave Dixon had done in founding WCT. Taking over as chief executive of the ATP in 1988, Jordan, former chief of staff for U.S. President Jimmy Carter, performed a political tour de force in bringing all the men's tourneys (except the four majors) under the umbrella of the ATP Tour in 1990.

This maneuver destroyed the MIPTC and the Grand Prix structure, which had embraced and administered the men's game for almost two decades, and, mercilessly, WCT as well. WCT, which had led the way into professionalization, operated its own circuit until absorbed by the Grand Prix. Nevertheless, WCT continued its annual championship playoff in Dallas, the event that had electrified the game with the $50,000 payoffs to Rosewall for his 1971 and 1972 victories over Laver. But after John McEnroe beat Brad Gilbert in the last of those in 1989, WCT sadly expired. The ATP also lost its original focus and function as a players' union, and may be challenged by players who feel they should have more influence in their own lives

As the brainchild of Hall of Famer Jack Kramer, the Grand Prix commenced in 1970, a points scheme linking men's tourneys and leading to a year-end show down, the Masters, for eight tour leaders. Cranked up in 1970 at Tokyo, the Masters had its most successful run at New York's Madison Square Garden, 1977-89, then moving to Germany (Frankfurt, 1990-95, Hannover, 1996-99.) Although the Masters continues in format, it was for 10 years (1990-99) re-billed as the ATP World Championship at Jordan's instigation. Wisely, the ATP, under the leadership of Mark Miles, successor to Jordan in 1990, restored the title as the Masters Cup in 2000 at Lisbon. The 2001-02 champ Lleyton Hewitt carted off $1.4 million. The Masters Series of nine prime tournaments (five in Europe, three in the U.S., one in Canada) is the backbone of the ATP Tour (re-branded Masters 1000 events in 2009).

Feeling threatened by the ATP's increased muscle, the ITF, principally Britain, the U.S., France and Australia, raised extraordinary prize money for their "Grand Slams"—Wimbledon and the U.S., French and Australian Opens. Furthermore, in 1990, the

ITF added to the usual confusion and overcrowded calendar by instituting the $6-million Grand Slam Cup, admitting the top finishers in those four tourneys, as the season's closing event. The obvious attempt was to upstage the ATP Championship by amassing a substantially richer purse. But after 10 years, the ITF showed some wisdom by making peace with the ATP to cooperate in one season-ending extravaganza.

Considerably more orderly, at least for a while, the women's tour has been generally easier to follow, underwritten by several sponsors (originally, longest and most successfully Virginia Slims, now Sony Ericsson). For 21 consecutive years, the WTA's season-ending Championships was held at New York's Madison Square Garden. Ill-considered were shifts to Munich in 2001, then Los Angeles in 2002, poorly attended financial disappointments. Since 1990, the WTA, unlike the ATP, has cooperated with the ITF to the extent that the four majors are part of the women's tour.

The U.S. has been a leader in all facets of the game's development, but tennis is truly universal and well received in pro tournament locations in more than 30 countries. The WTA has shown a willingness to explore new areas for its concluding championship, moving to Madrid in 2006-07, Doha, 2008. Growth continues and change has been constant. Venues are larger, less intimate, and, regrettably, grass and clay playing surfaces have largely given way to hard courts of asphalt. The Grand Slam route, once three-quarters turf, one-quarter clay (at Paris), is now more diverse. But more than 50 percent of professional tournaments are contested on unforgiving, body-unfriendly outdoor and indoor hard surfaces. Injuries are more prevalent.

Whatever the surface and wherever it is played, will the game ever be at peace? Probably not. Particularly with player agents behind the scenes, guiding the greed, and a practically perpetual season, over-cluttered with events. A genuine off-season (October-November-December) and reorganization of the hectic calendar is needed by all concerned to preserve the players' physical and emotional welfare. But who will have the sense— and guts—to bring about an unselfish ATP-WTA-ITF bonding on behalf of the game? Both the WTA and the ATP do seem committed to mercifully shortening the season.

War and Peace, the old Tolstoy story, could be the tennis theme. Count Leo Tolstoy, by the way, was an avid tennis player. He built a court on his estate at Yasnaya Polyana, one of the first in Russia, and put a tennis scene in his novel *Anna Karenina*. Did poor Anna throw herself in front of a train because she bungled a mixed doubles match with her lover, Vronsky? Stranger things have happened.

At best, tennis does deliciously evoke Kipling's iffy impostors, Triumph and Disaster. Obviously a Borg-McEnroe, Agassi-Sampras, Evert-Navratilova, Graf-Seles, Federer-Nadal, epic does—but a first-rounder between nobodies can be just as gripping. Tennis can twist you into knots.

But it remains a game, albeit at the professional level one that has been refined and polished, commercialized and subsidized well beyond the 19th-century imagination of the first proclaimed champion, Spencer W. Gore, triumphant at Wimbledon in 1877. The game has flourished and spread across the planet so incessantly that even I, the hopeless lover, am continually, pleas-

antly, startled. In my sixth decade as a two-way journalist (scribbler/babbler), I must admit that it does beat working for a living. Besides, would anybody else hire me?

Although my Uncle Studley swears that I covered the coming-out of Wimbledon with a quill pen, he's off by a few years. Still, I guess I could give you, treasured reader, a digest of the 135-years of tennis history, and it wouldn't take long:

1874—English gentleman with time on his hands, Major Wingfield, devises and patents the game, makes small change selling sets, and somebody—take your pick of claimants and candidates—starts it off in the U.S

1877—Wimbledon is launched (first, still foremost), and even shows a profit of a few pounds

1881 and 1887—Inaugural U.S. Championships for men, then women

1900—Harvard rich kid Dwight Davis donates sterling punch bowl for an international team competition, eventually known as Davis Cup. Davis with college pals beat Brits in leadoff finale. Only two countries interested then; more than 120 now

1905 and 1907—Californian May Sutton and Aussie Norman Brookes, respectively, are first alien winners of Wimbledon, a place no longer safe for the English homebodies

1919—France's Suzanne Lenglen wins Wimbledon, scandalously, showing thighs and unbeatable strokes. English are so shocked by her flaunting of female assets that the new [present] Wimbledon is built in 1922 to accommodate increasing hordes of offended ticket purchasers

1920—Big Bill Tilden, arrogant, artistic, all-conquering Philadelphian, dominates the game in the Twenties and makes U.S. tennis-conscious, inspiring construction of Forest Hills Stadium and keeping Davis Cup at home

1923—Unflappable "Little Miss Poker Face," Helen Wills, wins first of seven U.S. titles, succeeds Lenglen as dominatrix, and will win eight Wimbledons from baseline

1926—Lenglen goes for the dough, signs as first to tour professionally, opening job opportunities in an infant sport

1927—Four hands are finally better than one: the Four Musketeers—Rene Lacoste, Henri Cochet, Jean Borotra, Jacques Brugnon—bring down Tilden & Co., carting Davis Cup to France and necessitating the building of Stade Roland Garros in Paris

1932—English Davis Cupper Bunny Austin liberates male legs by showing up in shorts

1933—Last known Englishman—as far as many are concerned—to play tennis, Fred Perry, lifts Davis Cup from French and wins Wimbledon from 1934-36 before joining Tilden in the pro ranks

1938—Don Budge, having retrieved the Davis Cup, wins Australian, French, Wimbledon and U.S. titles, thus achieving the first-ever Grand Slam

1946—Jack Kramer spearheads the recovery of Davis Cup from Australia. In 1947, he's the first to win Wimbledon in shorts, also captures U.S. and turns pro to swipe that crown from Bobby Riggs.

1950—Frank Sedgman and Ken McGregor heist Davis Cup from U.S. to launch an Australian dynasty that will make Wimbledon and Forest Hills hostage to such Down Under-takers as Lew

Hoad, Ken Rosewall, Rod Laver, Neale Fraser, Roy Emerson, Fred Stolle, John Newcombe, and Tony Roche for a quarter-century

1953—Maureen "Little Mo" Connolly, 18, navigates first female Grand Slam

1956—New Yorker Althea Gibson, having hurdled the color rampart in 1950, wins the French, becoming first black to rule a major. She will follow with Wimbledon and U.S. titles in 1957-58

1961—Billie Jean Moffit, 17, wins Wimbledon doubles with Karen Hantze, 18, the first of B. J.'s record 20 titles at the Big W, six in singles

1962—Laver, after following Budge and Connolly as the third member of Grand Slam club, turns pro

1965—Jimmy Van Alen, father of the tie-breaker, shows it off at small Newport, R.I., pro tourney, but it won't be accepted until 1970

1968—Open tennis dawns. Tennis begins its metamorphosis from a sort-of-amateur sport to a big-business game. But amateur Arthur Ashe stunningly wins the first U.S. Open—the first black male to seize a major—and leads U.S. to Davis Cup success. Back from isolated life as outcast pros, Rosewall at French, Laver at Wimbledon, win the first major opens.

1969—Laver repeats as Grand Slammer, this time as a pro.

1970—Aussie Margaret Smith Court, all-time winner of major titles, 62 (24 in singles), goes Grand Slamming, the fourth member of club.

1971—Schoolgirl Christine Evert, 16, arrives at Forest Hills and coolly goes to semis to launch the Chrissie Craze with her two-handed backhand

1973—Labor problems. ATP boycotts Wimbledon. Most top men don't play, including Open era champs Laver, Newcombe, Stan Smith. Show goes on but ATP becomes a force. Billie Jean King beats Bobby Riggs in mixed singles schlockathon.

1974—"Lovebirds Double" at Wimbledon. Then affianced Chris Evert and Jimmy Connors triumph and begin cutting long championship swaths. They pay 33-to-1 with London bookies. Bjorn Borg, 18, wins French, and the three of them change the game, guiding the world to two-fisted backhandedness.

1976—High-tech rackets are here to stay, supplanting wood, as Howard Head puts the Prince Classic oversized club into play, drawing initial laughs, but commencing serious alteration of the game

1977—Borgiastic period is under way at Wimbledon's Centenary celebration as Bjorn wins second of five straight. But the show is stolen by last known Englishwoman—or so it seems—to play tennis. Virginia Wade, 32, accepts championship prize from the other queen in the house, Elizabeth II.

1978—Martina Navracilova beats Evert to win first of record nine Wimbledons, the last in 1990. U.S. Open flees Forest Hills, settling in Flushing.

1979—John McEnroe, 20, wins his first of four U.S. titles, while Tracy Austin, 16, becomes the youngest to rule her country.

1980—Borg holds off McEnroe to win a wowser of a Wimbledon, highlighted by the Battle of 18-16 (fabulous fourth-set tie-breaker). McEnroe will win the 1981 rematch.

1983—Yannick Noah sets off rejoicing across France when he becomes the first citizen in 37 years to win the French men's title.

Bud Collins (left) interviews **Martina Navratilova** after her Wimbledon victory in 1986.

1984—Ivan Lendl, from two sets back, beats McEnroe for the French title, establishing himself as a major figure who will win three U.S. titles.

1985—Daring volleyer, belly-flopping Boris Becker, 17, becomes the youngest and first unseeded Wimbledon victor.

1988—Steffi Graf, 19, not only becomes the fifth member of the Grand Slam club, but embellishes it with a gold medal as tennis returns to the Olympics. Australian Open bids farewell to grass (and rain-outs), opening a new complex in Melbourne with close-able roof stadium

1989—Drought-buster Michael Chang, 17, becomes first American guy in 34 years to win the French. Not only that but the youngest male champion of the majors.

1990—Cool summer for the callow: Monica Seles, 16, is the youngest winner of a major in 20th century, taking the French; Pete Sampras, 19, is the youngest U.S. champ.

1993—Seles, stabbed by loony Guenther Parche during match at Hamburg, will lose 26 months of a career already embracing seven major titles. Sampras wins first of seven Wimbledons, and will become Big W's Man of the Century, catching up with Willie Renshaw of the 1880s.

1995—Seles resurfaces to win Toronto and almost beats Graf in a splendid U.S. Open final, but Steffi, with fourth title, becomes only player to hold all four majors at least four times

1996—Winning a fifth French, seventh Wimbledon, fifth U.S., Steffi eclipses Evert and Navratilova (18), and Helen Wills (19), in major singles. At 21 titles, she's hot on the track of Margaret Court's 24

1997—Venus rising: 17-year-old Venus Williams, No. 66, unseeded in her first U.S. Open, glides to the final, losing to another 17-year-old, Swiss Martina Hingis, who has already won the Australian and Wimbledon crowns. Aussie revivalist Patrick

Rafter ends his island's 24-year dry spell in New York by winning the U.S. Open, and will repeat the following year.

1999—Andre Agassi joins a select society by winning the French, one of five guys capturing all four majors during their careers. The woman he will marry, Steffi Graf, also succeeds in Paris, for a sixth time, closing her career with a 22nd major. Little Sister, Serena Williams, beats Venus to the winner's circle by conquering the U.S. Open at 17, the first black to take a major since Ashe's Wimbledon of 1975

2000—Sampras' seventh Wimbledon title is his 13th major, eclipsing the 33-year-old record of Roy Emerson. Spain beats Australia, becoming the 10th country to win the Davis Cup. Venus and Serena collect Olympic gold, Venus winning the singles, following up on her Wimbledon and U.S. titles, and blending with Little Sister in the doubles. The good/bad Marat Safin falls on Sampras like a ton of Kremlin bricks as the first Russian to win the U.S. Open

2001—Wimbledon is stunned by Goran Ivanisevic's unique triumph as the lowest-ranked (No. 125), only wild-card champ. Lleyton Hewitt, a 20-year-old Aussie, beats Sampras to win the U.S. and finishes the year as youngest No. 1 man in tennis history

2002—Jennifer Capriati repeats as Australian Open champ, saving four match points to beat Hingis. But Serena takes over as No. 1, grabbing French, Wimbledon and U.S., uniquely beating Big Sister Venus in each final. Sampras concludes a miserable year brilliantly by downing Agassi for the U.S. title, his 14th major, and bids farewell. Mikail Youzhny, as a sub, lifts Russia to an exalted position as the 11th country in the Davis Cup Valhalla, winning the fifth match from two sets down over Paul-Henri Mathieu to beat France, 3-2.

2003—Serena keeps cooking—home cooking, burning Venus in the Australian final for Little Sister's fourth successive major title. She again? Navratilova overtakes ex-partner Billie Jean with 20th Wimbledon title, the mixed. A Swiss lad, named Federer begins to take over Wimbledon.

2004—No tears for Argentina with both finalists at French, unseeded Gaston Gaudio over Guillermo Coria. A 17-year-old chic chick, Maria Sharapova, lifts Wimbledon from Serena, and compatriot Svetlana Kuznetsova takes the U.S

2005—El Rey of Clay, Rafa Nadal, 19, starts French reign. Venus restores Wimbledon to the Williams family. Tiny Croatia pinches Davis Cup, beating U.S. on the way. Safin grabs Australian after beating Federer

2006—Navratilova, 49, says it (and apparently means it this time), "Adios!" after winning her 59th major, the U.S. mixed with Bob Bryan. Vive La France: Amelie Mauresmo wins Australian and Wimbledon

2007—Federer wins fifth straight Wimbledon, can't solve Nadal at French, but triples for third time, now has 12 majors. Sisters Long Shot: undertrained Serena, No. 81, seizes the Australian. Venus, though No. 31, pockets her fourth Wimbledon. The flying flyweight, Justine Henin, wings to the top again, No. 1 for a second straight year with French, U.S. titles.

Brisk enough? There's much, much more on the following pages. As the opium-loving writer, Thomas DeQuincey, would have said—and I second regarding my own form of dependency—once you've started, it's hard to stop.

How the game started is a delightful tale from Heiner Gillmeister's book, *Tennis: A Cultural History*. It concerns a 12th-century French cleric, Pierre, the Abbot of Morimond, who fell deathly ill. His soul was plucked by ball players from Hell, a devilish cast who, with their hands, batted it back and forth across a horridly steaming sulphorous valley. That's as good a theory about the creation of tennis as any. After all, it is a helluva game—with soul.

My hope is that you keep on hackin' as a player, and harkin' to the lore of this marvelous pastime/pleasure/passion.

—Bud Collins

Tennis Year-by-Year

Willie Renshaw (right) dominated at Wimbledon in the 1880s winning seven singles titles—including a record six in a row from 1881 to 1886—and seven doubles titles with twin brother **Ernest Renshaw** (left).

Leo Tolstoy was one of the wealthy Russian landowners in the 1870s who set up tennis courts. His novel, *Anna Karenina*, actually includes a tennis scene. He is photographed in this photo as early as 1896 on his court at Yasnaya Polyana.

Roots of the Game

Major Walter Wingfield was issued the patent for "A Portable Court of Playing Tennis," dated Feb. 23, 1874.

Why is that net in the way?

Although merely three-feet in height, it seems at times like the Great Wall of China or the Green Monster (the left field barrier at Boston's Fenway Park) to somebody desperately trying to hit a tennis ball over it—a wailing wall to the frustrated competitor.

Why? We can't say for sure when or where, but it has been an obstruction for eons, installed as the court centerpiece by someone who probably thought a net added a spicy challenge to those gamely knocking a ball back and forth. That's tennis, a pastime for the ages. Either the ball goes over that bloody net…or it doesn't. It had to start somewhere, well before a couple of gents named Gore and Marshall dueled at 25 paces or so on a strip of greensward, batting rubber balls at each other during a London summer afternoon in 1877. That occasion, Spencer Gore carrying the day, was the final of the introductory Wimbledon, recognized as the first tennis tournament. At least the original lawn tennis tournament.

But was it? Sort of. Yes and no.

Yes: It was a public launching of the present-day game with which we're familiar, having played it, seen it in person or on TV, and read about it—a convenient starting date for the innumerable tournaments that since have been played.

No: Tennis, as a game, pre-dates by centuries its patenting by an Englishman in 1874, and the unveiling of his version at Wimbledon three years later. That's the game we know, and what this book is about. But it's the offspring of an ancient sire.

Where does today's game come from? Surely, but mysteriously, from much deeper in history, a descendant of an old sport which evolved, was refined and continues to exist on its own as a separate pastime—played indoors in curiously conformed, concrete-walled courts—known variously as real tennis, royal tennis or court tennis. That game, sequestered in a few private clubs in the United Kingdom, United States, Australia and Continental Europe, dates back to 12th-century France. Or Italy? Or Spain?

Most likely tennis sprang—bounded?—from monastery cloisters in which off-duty monks were channeling their testosterone into batting a ball to and fro, and off the walls. First with their hands—*jeu de paume*. Eventually with rackets that appeared in the 16th century, possibly first in Italy, called *rachette*, to play a game called *gioco di rachette*.

Its precise origins remain shrouded in conjecture, contrasting notions and theories, and lack of documentation despite the diligent delving of historians

Even the mystery of the name—tennis—and the scoring terms, passed down from real tennis to our game (properly named lawn tennis because it began and prospered on grass) are unsolved. Nevertheless, the good brothers were onto something too good to keep cloistered in their backyards. It spread to commoners in outdoor courts as well as kings with their personal sanctums, evidence of which can be seen in European paintings of long, long ago. At one medieval time, a saying had it: "There are more tennis players in France than drunkards in England."

Terms of engagement? Love? Can you take seriously anything in which love means nothing? Maybe it derives from the French, *l'oeuf*: the old goose or duck egg. However, Heiner Gillmeister in his fascinating tome, *Tennis: A Cultural History*, puts forth a vote for the word *lof*. Gillmeister says it is, "the Dutch or Flemish equivalent of English 'honor.' It looks as if the English expression for a player's failure to score owes its existence to an expression used in the Low Countries, *omme lof spellen*—'to play for the honor.'"

The expression 'bagel' for zero would come much later, quite possibly from the lips of Eddie Dibbs, a leading American player during the 1970s and early '80s.

The quartered face of a clock seems the likely source of the game and point scores—15, 30—but why 40 instead of the original 45? Was it a cuckoo clock? It was probably shortened over time, an abbreviation like 5 instead of 15, common among hackers. Nobody really knows. Deuce is the clearest, from the French a *deux*.

'Tennis' itself? There are many theories which American historian George Alexander discusses, and have appeared elsewhere before, but not conclusively. George has his own idea, on 'tens' from the German, different from all the rest, as will be seen.

Lawn tennis reached an early high point of American national prestige during the presidency of Theodore Roosevelt (1901-09), who formed a "tennis cabinet." He ordered the White House's first court, clay, built on a site now occupied by the Oval Office. The players, headed by the vigorous president, were drawn from the younger administrators of, or just below, cabinet rank, and from foreign diplomats, led by the French ambassador, J. J. Jusserand. He was small, wiry and quick, and often a match for "Teddy" himself, the charging hero of San Juan Hill.

The ambassador was a serious player of both real tennis and lawn tennis and a student of the history of those games. Among the studies he undertook was the derivation of the English word 'tennis.' His was not the first search for the origin of the word, nor the last. Then, as now, the usual explanation was that "tennis" was derived from the French *tendere* meaning "to hold.'" Etymologists rationalized that the server called out *tendere* as a warning to his opponent just prior to serving. At first glance, this has an authentic ring, for it carries the approval of scholars of repute. The problem was that it did not make sense to Jusserand.

Jusserand made an extensive study of old French literature and he found much shouting by players—mostly profane—but no one ever seemed to have called out *tendere* or anything like it. Several studies on the subject made before and since the French ambassador have come to the same findings.

In 1878, Julian Marshall, in his monumental *Annals of Tennis*, addresses the matter, and he lists 10 spellings of tennis through the years. But he leaves the decision as to the origin of the word "tennis" to others, finding no answer that satisfied him.

In *Bailey's* magazine of August, 1918, C. E. Thomas offered a slightly more logical explanation. According to him, the derivation is from the French *tenez,* meaning "take it." Again a call of warning from the server. No one has come forth with evidence of such ever being done, let alone ever having been the custom.

Tennis Origins and Mysteries, by Malcolm Whitman, one of the pioneer Davis Cuppers, and U.S. champion (1898-1900), devotes a chapter to the subject and covers most of the theories that have been put forth through the years by tennis players with an interest in etymology. Most of these theories have a common root in French words that have "ten" as the start of words meaning, variously, "hold," "taut," "tense," "tendon," and several other similar words.

Two towns, widely separated, one on the Nile River in Egypt, the other in Northern France, having "Tennis" as their name, are thought to be possible origins of the name. Tennis in France was known for its lace; Tennis in Egypt for its fine long staple cotton. Since balls were often cloth bound (never in the 15th century), some have thought that was connection enough.

Alexander offers a more logical explanation. First, why was a new name for the game necessary when it came to England (some evidence indicates it came earlier to Scotland)? The French name then and now is *jeu de paume* (hand ball). By the time it reached the British Isles (the date not known with certainty), implements such as battledores, forerunners of rackets, were replacing the hand. Some of the French was retained, such as "deuce" and per-

haps "love," so no strong aversion to French words existed. This new pastime needed a name to differentiate the game of playing across a net from those played against a wall.

The root stem of "tens" has given us many words including those such as *tendere*, which is the often-listed parent of "tennis." One of the meanings of "tens" is the "weaver's shuttle" and other back-and-forth motions. Whitman had previously come across this, but he chose not to pursue it and he dropped it short of the shuttle meaning.

The naming of the game with a descriptive word is more logical than one requiring a tortured explanation. The logic of naming the game after some "shout" or ball material would have us call golf "fore" and the games of football "pigskin" and baseball "horsehide." The to-and-fro motion further lent its name to the missile that we know as the shuttlecock in badminton.

While the explanation may satisfy a few, more evidence is needed to support the theory, even though none has been offered to support the usually accepted *tendere*. It is like the unauthenticated, largely wishful, story of Mary Outerbridge introducing the game to the U.S.: once in place and repeated a few times, it takes on the position of presumed fact. But this is part of the intrigue of tennis.

Although the beginnings of tennis and many other sports and games are unknown and lost in the distant past, the history of modern (lawn) tennis is clearly documented. Its arrival was publicly announced on March 7, 1874, in two papers, the *Court Journal*, read by almost all of the British upper class as well as those who aspired to join, and the *Army & Navy Gazette*, read by the military, which was stationed worldwide—for them the sun truly never set on the vast British Empire.

These notices appeared after the British patent office issued to Major Walter Wingfield provisional letters of patent (No. 685) for "A Portable Court of Playing Tennis," dated Feb. 23, 1874. English-speaking sportsmen around the world who read *The Field* of March 21, 1874 were informed in detail of the new game, for it reproduced much of the information about the Major's game of lawn tennis. It contained a short history of tennis, instruction and notes for the "erection of the court," and the six rules of the game.

The game was an immediate success and spread throughout Great Britain and Ireland in a matter of weeks and around the English-speaking world soon thereafter. The equipment to play was sold by the inventor's agents, Messrs. French and Co., 46, Churton Street, London, S.W The price: Five guineas.

Sales literature noted that "the game is in a painted box, 36 x 12 x 6 inches and contains poles, pegs, and netting for forming the court, 4 tennis bats, by Jeffries and Mailings, a bag of balls, mallet, and brush and the instructive *The Book of the Game*."

The daily sales book for almost a year, July 6, 1874 to June 25, 1875, notes on July 15, 1874 that Major Rowan Hamilton settled his account for tennis sets he purchased in May "for Canada." Sets were bought for India and China. Sets were sold to Russia's royalty and to, of course, the Prince of Wales and many others, including 42 Lords, 44 Ladies and members of Parliament, among them agriculturist Ward Hunt, First Lord of the Admiralty, renowned for his girth which caused a semicircle to be cut from the Admiralty board table.

The records of French and Co. are not the complete list, for many sales went to unnamed parties and wholesale business was done with London retailers and, as so often happens, competing sets were soon on the market despite patent protection.

There were several reasons for this great and widespread success. There was a need for a game that afforded vigorous exercise for both sexes and all ages. That was how Wingfield described his new game. Croquet had been the fad during the 1860s and it inspired the construction of many well-rolled, level courts with close-clipped grass, made possible due to the invention of the lawn mower by Englishman Edwin Budding earlier in the century. The least standard croquet court measured 30 yards by 20 yards. Such courts were ubiquitous and were ready-made for lawn tennis, and "The ground need not even be turf; the only condition is that it must be level."

This was not exactly today's marvelous game, for it was quite simple. It used the scoring of 1, 2, 3, etc. of the game of rackets, but it bore the more refined name "tennis" rather than "rackets," which was associated with taverns and prisons. The game could also be played without buying the set, for items were sold separately. Rackets were 15 shillings, balls were five shillings a dozen, and *The Book of the Game* was six pence. People with rackets of other sports could easily try out the new game.

Wingfield learned, as have most inventors, to their dismay, that rather than receiving the thanks of grateful sportsmen, he was belittled. "Anyone could have invented his game," said numerous skeptics. Others came forth with claims for earlier games. Inventions almost always are based on other inventions, and (lawn) tennis obviously was based on (real/royal/court) tennis. This was acknowledged by Wingfield, as even the title of his patent and the game indicate. The major got another boost 14 years after the fact from another inventor, who also left his name to posterity but didn't profit from it. That was Charles Goodyear, who vulcanized rubber in 1860, leading to the bouncing ball, an innovation seized on by Germans to manufacture thin-walled balls. Wingfield's balls came from Germany.

Outdoor racket, ball and net play goes back to the time of Queen Elizabeth I. Earlier in England and France, a game called long tennis (*longue paume*) was played, and it is still played in France. Other similar games, at best neighborhood games, were without formal rules and they never traveled, soon dying out. The name Harry Gem is associated with such a game. He wrote in *The Field* of Nov. 28, 1874: "He (J.B. Perera) first introduced the game fifteen years ago, and it recently has received the name of Pelota..." After (lawn) tennis arrived, Gem wrote rules for "Pelota," which he sent to *The Field* and to his club, the Leamington Club, which added "Lawn Tennis" to its name.

Wingfield wrote to Gem in the fall of 1874 that he had worked on the game for a year and a half. After Wingfield's death, an acquaintance wrote that Wingfield's thoughts of a game went back to his service in India. He wrote in *The Book of the Game* that the game was "tested practically at several country houses during the past few months."

Since all five editions of the book are "dedicated to the party assembled at Nantclwyd [in Wales] in December 1873," it has been assumed that was where it was introduced. But there is no

evidence of that. The party was a housewarming given by the new owner of the estate Nantclwyd, Major Naylor-Leyland, for his friends in the area. It featured the presentation of two plays and a grand ball. The three-day affair was covered in detail by the *Wrexham Guardian* and makes no mention of lawn tennis or any athletic activity. Wingfield, his host and hostess and a great beauty of the day, Patsy Cornwallis-West, performed in the plays.

It would be reasonable that Onslow Hall, the main estate of his branch of the family, would be one of the test sites. It is more likely a test site than Wingfield's own Rhysnant Hall, which was at that time leased. The one country house that has a written record as a test site is Earnshill in Somerset. In May 1881, Wingfield's first cousin, R.T. Combe of Earnshill, wrote to the *Daily Telegraph*, "It is now some seven or eight years since Major Wingfield first put up a lawn tennis court here."

Several other places have been put forth as being sites of early play but confirming evidence is lacking. The first public exhibition occurred the Saturday following *The Field* announcement of May 4, 1874, which read in part, "It [lawn tennis] may be seen and played next week, on and after the opening of the Princes Cricket Ground, and also at the Polo Club, Lillie-bridge."

In the *Whitehall Review* (Nov. 14, 1896), Wingfield's good friend, Clement Scott, wrote in his column, 'Wheel of Life,' that the exhibition was in 1869. Such is an example of how fallible the human memory is and how important "the palest ink" is to true history

The closing of the Haymarket court tennis courts and the outdoor racket courts at taverns in several neighborhoods undoubtedly caused Wingfield to bring forth the new game.

Besides private homes with croquet lawns becoming places to play tennis, it immediately became a game played at public parks and other common lawns and the great clubs. Among the London clubs to take up the sport quickly were M.C.C.— The Marylebone Cricket Club (Lords)—Hurlingham Club and Princes Club, as well as many others throughout the land. A club that waited until 1875 to accept a rival sport was the then five-year-old All England Croquet Club, located off Worple Road in the London suburb, Wimbledon.

Henry Jones, the editor of the "Pastimes" section of *The Field*, which covered card games, Jones' forte, as well as lawn tennis, was a founder, along with his publisher, John Walsh, of the All England Croquet Club. Jones introduced lawn tennis to the club. He wrote under the nom de plume "Cavendish." Jones and Walsh were both doctors who had given up the practice of medicine to pursue their greater love, games and sports. Jones earned Wingfield's enmity by presuming to take over his game. It was Jones' nature to assume he had greater knowledge of all matters concerning games, and this included lawn tennis.

To Wingfield, the remarkable success of the game was evidence of the rightness of it, and that you should not change a winning game. However, in the fall of 1874 he issued a second edition of *The Book of the Game*. There were now twelve rules and a larger court, and it also made more use of the alternate name of *Sphairistike*, Greek for ball games. These changes and complications could be added, for now the game had taken root. By that time some confusion existed, at least on the pages of *The*

Field, because Perera's game, pelota, and a rival game, Germains Lawn Tennis, by J. H. Hale, with Jones' help, had been put forth. In reality nothing came of either; they were more complicated with no added redeeming features.

Through the winter, there was continued confusion. John Moyer Heathcote, who with his wife had introduced the Melton cloth-covered ball, wrote to Fitzgerald, secretary of M.C.C., suggesting a meeting of the factions. With the cooperation of Wingfield, the other interested parties agreed to a general meeting with the M.C.C.'s rules committee to establish rules for lawn tennis as they recently had done for real/royal/court tennis. This was done and the rules were announced in *The Field* of May 1875. There were now 25 rules and they appeared in subsequent editions of Wingfield's book.

Before the M.C.C. rules came out on May 2, 1875, Wingfield wrote Fitzgerald that he would execute any legal document "for the public good," canceling "en masse" his rules. A similar letter appeared in *The Field* a week after *The Field* published the M.C.C. rules. With the letter agreeing to the M.C.C. rules, Wingfield withdrew from the tennis scene.

In the spring of 1877, under the leadership of Henry Jones, the All England Club decided to hold a tennis tournament. The Field carried the announcement and a call for competitors and the promise "if entries are sufficiently numerous, prizes: Gold Champion Prize and the Silver Prize. Also a Silver Challenge Cup, value 25 guineas..."

The tournament committee was worried about infringing on Wingfield's patent. This was unnecessary, for Wingfield had allowed his patent to expire on Feb. 23, 1877, the patent's third anniversary, by not paying the £50 fee to extend the patent seven years. It was public information, being published in the *Official Journal (Patents)*. This was to the game's long-term benefit for it caused new rules to be drawn. These were written by a committee of Jones, Julian Marshall and Charles G. Heathcote. They established much of our present game.

The tournament, the original Wimbledon, was a success. Among 22 entries, Spencer Gore, a rackets player, beat William Marshall, a refugee from real tennis, in the final, 6-1, 6-2, 6-4.

The new rules used tennis scoring and a rectangular court (78 x 27 feet), dropping Wingfield's hourglass shape with baselines wider than the net and tapering to the net posts. Known as Wimbledon—it has been formally entitled The Lawn Tennis Championships from the beginning—the tournament became an annual fixture with Jones as referee. For several years, he adjusted the net height and the service line according to the total of points won and lost on service until 1882, when the net heights arrived at today's 3-1/2 feet at the posts and three feet at center with the service line at 21 feet from the net. Regulations then became essentially today's, except for two rules which were troublesome for several years. The changing-of-ends rule went through many alterations until the simple and fair alternating of sides after each odd game of each set was established in 1890. Foot-faulting, a problem even now as serving becomes increasingly dominant, probably should be further addressed in order to ground the leapers and diminish the strong advantage held by powerful, aggressive servers with high-tech rackets.

James Dwight rightfully became known as the father of American lawn tennis.

In the matter of tournament control, two improvements were brought forth. R.B. Bagnal-Wild of Bath in 1883 proposed the present system of having byes in the first round so as to have the number of remaining players be of a power of two. This prevented three players arriving in the semifinals as happened in the first Wimbledon. Such opening round byes were accepted for the 1885 Championships. The other improvement took longer. In 1883, none other than Charles L. Dodgson, a mathematician who wrote under the name of Lewis Carroll (*Alice in Wonderland*), issued a pamphlet, *Lawn Tennis Tournaments*—"The true method of assigning prizes, with proof of the fallacy of the present method." It was seeding that he envisioned, but he died before it was first permitted in the 1922 tournament.

In 1880, a Northern Lawn Tennis Association (of England) was founded and, in 1883, the formation of a Lawn Tennis Association was attempted, but it failed for want of All England Club cooperation. The All England Club became the premier organization in tennis, supplanting the M.C.C. in those matters, and has remained a powerful tennis body, as witness its ability to lead the world to "Open" tennis. The game owes much to the M.C.C. for its guidance and lending its name and prestige to the infant tennis during its early critical years.

On the courts, tennis made great strides in the 1880s. Progress in the level of play was led by the Renshaw twins. They had grown up with the game and were not handicapped with styles formed for rackets or real tennis. Willie Renshaw won the Wimbledon championships of 1881 through 1886 plus 1889. Ernest won in 1888. Herbert Lawford won in 1887 when Willie, laid up with the first well-known case of tennis elbow, did not defend his title. The Renshaws also dominated the doubles, winning seven of the first 10 titles.

Men's doubles was introduced in 1879, but played at Oxford until 1884, the year ladies' singles made the scene. Ladies' doubles and mixed doubles were added in 1913. The draws were small, only 16 players in 1887 for the men's tournament and six ladies in 1888, the all-time lows. Attendance grew from 200 in 1877 to 3,500 in 1885. This growth of tennis ended in 1890 with interest switching to bicycle activities that were much enhanced by the invention of the modern bicycle. The 1890s were also a time of recession in the business world.

With the cooperation of the A.E.C. (All England Club) the L.T.A. (Lawn Tennis Association) was formed in 1888. It was agreed that the A.E.C. and the L.T.A. would share the funds raised by the Championships. However, the decline in popularity of tennis brought small draws and reduced attendance. The tournament of 1895 was in the red, losing £35. By the turn of the century tennis regained favor and went on to greater crowds and more players.

It was natural that tennis would come quickly to North America for there were close relationships, both social and commercial, with the motherland. British periodicals, including *The Field*, came to many in the U.S. and Canada. The date the first set arrived is not known but its arrival was inevitable. Curiously, the earliest-found record of play is Oct. 8, 1874 in the then-remote Camp Apache, Arizona Territory, north of Tucson.

In Martha Summerhayes's book, *Vanished Arizona*, she reports tennis being played by an Army officer's wife, Ella Wilkins Bailey. Her husband's records confirm the date. The trip to Apache began in San Francisco on Aug. 6, 1874. Based on Major Hamilton's purchase in May 1874, Canada may have had its first taste of the game after he opened his "unpainted box."

Tennis certainly was on the East Coast in the summer of 1874, and who was first is of little importance, for it arrived independently at several places: Boston, Newport, New York and Philadelphia as well as New Orleans and San Francisco. The game did not spread from only one center.

While both Miss Mary Outerbridge of Staten Island, N.Y., and Dr. James Dwight of Boston have their adherents as 'the introducer' of the game to the United States, there is no definite certainty for either. It is certain that neither was trying to be first, and made no claim to that effect. However, leadership of the game in the U.S. clearly fell to Dr. Dwight, who became known rightfully as "the father of American lawn tennis."

He may also have been a "first" player, trying out the game with a cousin, Fred Sears, while summering at seaside Nahant outside of Boston in 1874. They marked out a court in the yard of the Appleton estate, and gave it a try. No date recorded. Regardless, he was associated with almost all important tennis events

during the first quarter century of tennis in the U.S. Doc Dwight did, undoubtedly, organize a tournament in 1876. With cousin Fred, he held a formal and handicapped round-robin tournament for 15 entries, Dwight beating Sears in the final. In 1878, the Nahant tournament used the A.E.C. rules. Two years later, Dwight played in the so-called "Nationals" at Staten Island Cricket and Baseball Club. Dwight's questioning of the balls used as not being proper was turned aside by the tournament officials by showing the word "Regulation" marked on each ball.

That unsatisfactory tourney caused the formation of the U.S. National Lawn Tennis Association in 1881. Dwight followed the first president, R.S. Oliver, as president, a position he held for 21 of the association's first 31 years. Under the direction of the new association, the first recognized national tournament was held at Newport and a 19-year-old Harvard student, Dick Sears, a Dwight cousin, was the winner, retaining the title through 1887. The "other guy" in that original final was an Englishman, William E. Glyn, who was 20 or 21, summered at Newport, and has pretty much been lost in history, not even being accorded celebrity as the first flop, 6-0, 6-3, 6-2. Was he also the first choker?

In the 1881 doubles, Sears and Dwight were surprised losers in the third round to Philadelphia's team of Clarence Clark and Fred Taylor, who went on to win the championship. Sears and Dwight won the doubles five of the next six years. In 1883, following matches between Dwight and Sears versus the winning Clark brothers, Clarence and Joe, the Clarks went off to England. There in an exhibition they lost to the Renshaws 6-4, 8-6, 3-6, 6-1, and a week later the Renshaws won in straight sets.

Later that year, following the U.S. Championships, Dwight went abroad and spent the fall, winter and spring competing against the best English players, including the Renshaws, playing indoors at Maida Vale in London and outdoors at Cannes. In 1885 he lost in the Wimbledon semifinals to the champion, Herbert Lawford, 6-2, 6-2, 6-3. As the most successful of the first Americans to play Wimbledon, in 1884 (he was joined by Dick Sears and Arthur Rives), Dwight was beaten in the second round of singles by the ambidextrous Herbert Chipp. Chipp had defeated Rives in the first round. Sears, kept out of the singles by injury, then joined Dwight to reach the doubles semifinals where they lost to the champion Renshaws, 6-0, 6-1, 6-2.

However, Dwight won the Northern England Championship in 1884, the first foreigner to take a title in the game's motherland, and with Willie Renshaw, the 1885, Buxton doubles tournament.

During these years, he ranked just below, the very best of England. He was much respected and through his instructional articles and two books, *Lawn Tennis* in 1886 and *Practical Lawn Tennis* in 1893, did much for the level of play in the U.S. His books were the standard instruction until 1920, when Bill Tilden's *The Art of Lawn Tennis* was published.

Tennis lost ground in the 1890s to both the bicycle and golf, but Dwight saw the game and the USLTA through those lean years. It was through his contacts with English players that the Davis Cup was launched in 1900 for which he drew up the rules. This helped restore the game to broad attention.

As the 20th century arrived, tennis had weathered its first recession and came back stronger than ever. It would not be

the last time the sport ebbed. By 1900, all the strokes, tactics and strategies had become part of the game. The Renshaws brought the net game; Lawford introduced topspin; and Holcombe Ward and Dwight Davis created the American twist serve (kicker). All these have been improved but a few, like the reverse twist serve, are no longer used.

Then, as now, most of the play took place on the public courts. This is not to gainsay the importance of the great tennis clubs. In the mid-1880s, Prospect Park in Brookyln, N.Y. had over 100 clubs using its facilities. Sports clubs have often been targeted as havens of snobs and bigots. Clubs, as other groups of people, have their share, but they have done much good for tennis and other sports. They established standards of play, deportment and facilities, which elevated the game everywhere. Almost all the greats of the game have started on the public courts, but they refined their games at clubs and colleges.

The year Doc Dwight organized the seminal tournament at Nahant, 1876, was also the year of the founding of the first tennis club in the U.S., the New Orleans Lawn Tennis Club. Founded in 1877, Boston's Longwood Cricket Club, then situated at the corner of Brookline and Longwood Avenues, near the plot where Fenway Park would rise in 1912, adopted lawn tennis in 1878. Longwood is another footnote alluding to the importance of Boston's Sears family in the evolution of the game. The property, a piece of his vast estate called Longwood after the manor in which the exiled Napoleon died on the isle of St. Helena, was rented from David Sears. His nephew, Dick, who won the first seven U.S. championships, was a Napoleon buff. Various other Searses made early marks, including Eleonora Sears, a Hall of Famer, and Evelyn Sears, U.S. champ in 1907.

The inaugural Wimbledon embraced only one event, the men's singles. An entry of 22 was received, and on Monday, July 9, 1877, a fine, sunny day, The Lawn Tennis Championships began. One entrant, C.F. Buller, was absent, so there were only 10 instead of the expected 11 matches. The 11 survivors were reduced to six on Tuesday, then to three on Wednesday. The notion of restricting byes to the first round was still eight years off. On Thursday, William Marshall had a free passage into the final while Spencer W. Gore beat Charles Heathcote. Advantage sets had not been adopted.

The title match was held over until the following Monday. Such delay had been indicated in the prospectus to allow for the Eton-Harrow cricket match at Lords. This was the ultimate sporting event so far as the fashionable London world was concerned, and lawn tennis, itself a fashionable sport, did not dream for many years of coming into conflict with that important fixture. Monday turned out wet, and the final was postponed until Thursday, July 19. That day was also damp, but rather than disappoint 200 spectators, each of whom had paid one shilling (then about 25 cents) to see Wimbledon's baptismal final, Gore and Marshall sportingly agreed to play. Gore came up to the net and volleyed. Whether this was entirely sporting was a matter of some debate, as was his striking the ball before it had crossed the net. He won, 6-1, 6-2, 6-4.

An old Harrovian of 27, Gore had played rackets at school and was a keen cricketer. He didn't think much of the new game. Defending his title the next year, he lost in the challenge round

to Frank Hadow, another old Harrovian on leave from coffee planting in Ceylon. Hadow thoughtfully circumvented Gore, the volleyer, by lobbing, a stroke not seen before. For Hadow, one shot—with high shots—at the title was enough. He didn't return until the Jubilee celebration in 1927.

Gore later wrote: "That anyone who has really played well at cricket, [real] tennis, or even rackets, will ever seriously give his attention to lawn tennis, beyond showing himself to be a promising player, is extremely doubtful; for in all probability the monotony of the game as compared with the others would choke him off before he had time to excel at it."

Those were the views of the world's first champion. Gore died in 1906, still an avid cricketer.

Competing in 1878 was a former Cambridge real tennis player, A. T. Myers. He, too, was an innovator, serving overhand. Yet it is obvious that at the time there was more of the vicarage lawn than athleticism about the infant game. In 1879, the Wimbledon champion was in fact a vicar, the Reverend John Hartley, yet another old Harrovian. He kept his title in 1880, and his ability to endlessly return the ball was notorious.

In 1881, the game took on a new dimension. Two wealthy young twins from Cheltenham, in the west of England, initiated a dominance that endured for nearly a decade. They were Willie and Ernest Renshaw. In that year, Willie won the first of his seven singles titles at Wimbledon. In the challenge round, he beat Hartley, 6-0, 6-1, 6-1, in an extraordinarily brief and devastating 37 minutes. Its brevity is partly explained by the fact that at that time players changed ends only after each set. It is also explained by the difference in style. Hartley was a gentle retriever. Renshaw served hard, volleyed hard, smashed hard and went for fast winners all round. He and Ernest created modern lawn tennis. Crowds flocked to see them play.

In winning six straight titles, a record, Willie had a streak of 12 matches, having to play only the challenge round for titles two through six against the winner of the all-comers final. That system was dropped in 1922. He missed 1887, then won two more matches before succumbing to "Ghost" Hamilton in the 1888 quarters, his winning string ending at 14. That was the tourney record for 48 years until countryman Fred Perry, champ in 1934-35-36, broke it with his 15th. Fred went on to establish a record of 21. Thirty-three years passed until that one fell to Aussie Rod Laver, who stretched the record to 31. Laver's mark endured just 11 years, falling to Bjorn Borg, who took it to 41 consecutive match wins.

Ernest Renshaw, overshadowed by his brother Willie, took only one Wimbledon singles title, 1888. But Ernest, who'd allowed the title to slip from the family in losing to Lawford in 1887, might have had another in 1889 if win-happy Willie hadn't made the first extraordinary comeback at the Big W—maybe the most extraordinary—in the all-comers final to beat Harry Barlow, 3-6, 5-7, 8-6, 10-8, 8-6. Willie resurrected himself from 2-5 in the fourth through six match points, and 0-5 in the fifth. Exhilarated by that, Willie beat Ernest in the fratricidal challenge round for his seventh and last title, a total equaled by Pete Sampras 111 years later.

The Scottish Championships in Edinburgh was inaugurated in 1878. The Irish Championships in Dublin, begun in 1879, was

Richard "Dick" Sears, the winner of the first U.S. Championships in 1881.

notable for initiating a women's singles as well as a mixed doubles event. The women's events, however, were restricted in some degree. While the main part of the tournament was played on courts prepared in Fitzwilliam Square and open to the public, the women were confined to the relative privacy of the Fitzwilliam Club itself. Only members and their guests were permitted the sight of well-turned ankles on display. The game's first woman champion of the world was 14-year-old May Langrishe, beating D. Meldon, 6-2, 0-6, 8-6.

The men's singles champion in the first Irish Championships was Vere "St. Leger" Goold. In the same year, he became finalist in the all-comers' singles at Wimbledon, losing to the gentle Hartley. Many years later, Goold wrote a unique, unsavory chapter for himself in the history of the game. Convicted of murder by a French court, he was sent to prison at Devil's Island where he died.

That spurious "Championship of America," staged in 1880, began on Sept. 1 on the courts at the Staten Island Cricket and Baseball Club. The prize was a silver cup valued at $100. Rackets scoring was used, with the results turning on the aggregate number of aces. An Englishman, Otway Edward Woodhouse, wrote from Chicago asking if he could enter. A member of the West Middlesex Club in Ealing, England, he had played that year at Wimbledon and reached the all-comers' final before losing to Lawford. Woodhouse's overhand service was a novelty to American players. With this advantage, he reached the final, where he beat a Canadian, J. F. Helmuth, 15-11, 14-15, 15-9, 10-15, victory based on a score of 54 points to 50. It was an unsatisfactory resolution.

In October of 1880, a tournament was played at Beacon Park, Boston. The winner was Dick Sears. Real tennis scoring was used. The non-standardization of the game, both in its equipment and scoring, brought increasing difficulties as it grew. Controversy about the correct way to play lawn tennis highlighted the need for fully accepted regulation. With that in mind, a meeting was arranged at the Fifth Avenue Hotel in New York on May 21, 1881, in the name of three prominent clubs: The Beacon Park Athletic Association of Boston, the Staten Island Cricket and Baseball Club of New York, and the All Philadelphia Lawn Tennis Committee.

Thirty-three clubs were represented, and the U.S. National Lawn Tennis Association, as it was then named, came into being. A constitution was drawn, the rules of the All England Club and the M.C.C. were adopted. R.S. Oliver of the Albany Lawn Tennis Club was elected president, and Clarence Clark as secretary-treasurer. A vice president and an executive committee of three were also chosen.

This was the first national association in the world, the doyen of such bodies. Apart from its standardization of the game, where the British example was followed, its other major decision was to inaugurate the National Championships of the United States (hereinafter called the U.S. Championships), embracing men's singles and doubles. The scene would be the Newport Casino at Newport, R.I., probably without equal at that time as the American resort of wealth and fashion.

It began on Aug. 31, 1881, with a singles entry of 26. Except for the final, the best of three sets (not five) was played. Sears, 19 years, 10 months old, won without losing a set. A U.S. champion with a remarkable career, he won seven times in all, playing through in both 1882 and 1883 without losing a set. In 1884, the challenge round was instituted, and in the title match Sears yielded a set for the first time, to Howard Taylor, 6-0, 1-6, 6-0, 6-2. After three further championships, he retired with a singular singles record: Matches played, 18; Matches won, 18.

From 1882 through 1887, Sears also won the doubles six times—five with James Dwight and once with Joseph Clark. Sears learned to volley in 1881, the same time that the Renshaw twins were introducing their arts of aggression in England. They did so independently of each other.

In 1884, the Wimbledon meeting was enlarged to include a women's singles and a men's doubles. The doubles cups were passed on from the tournament that had been staged, albeit with failing interest, at Oxford since 1879, and where originally the distance was over the best of seven sets.

The other new Wimbledon event, the women's singles, was staged at the same time. The first winner, from a field of 13 ambitious and progressive-minded young women, was Maud Watson. She was 19 years old, facing in the final her 26-year-old sister, Lilian. They were the daughters of the vicar of Berkswell, a village in the heart of England. Maud won, 6-8, 6-3, 6-3.

The losing semifinalist to Watson, Blanche Bingley (later Mrs. George Hillyard), became one of the most indefatigable champions of all time. She won the singles six times between 1886 and 1900 and played for the last time in 1913 when she was 49. Before winning at Wimbledon in 1884, Watson beat, in Dublin, the game's first female champion, May Langrishe, the Irish winner of 1879. There was coincidence in the deaths of the two women: Langrishe died in 1939 at a house called "Hammersmead" in Charmouth, a Devonshire, England seaside resort; seven years later Watson died in the same house.

The women's game, recognized first by the Irish in 1879, made its early efforts in England and Ireland in concert with the men. In the U.S., the women came forward on their own, at least in the beginning. In 1887, the first U.S. Women's Championship, held at the Philadelphia Cricket Club, was an outgrowth of the first (1886) Chestnut Hill Tennis Club Ladies Open. The second 'open' (amateurs nonetheless, but from any club) became the first U.S. Championships when the Wissahickon Inn offered the Wissahickon Cup as the singles prize. Arrangements for the 1886-87 tournaments were conducted by the Chestnut Hill T.C., and play was at the Philadelphia C.C. In 1888, the Cricket Club took over sponsorship of the national championships, and continued until the 1921 move to Forest Hills.

Seven women entered the singles in 1887, all from the greater Delaware Valley area. The champ, Ellen Hansell, a 6-1, 6-0, victor over Laura Knight, represented Philadelphia's Belmont Cricket Club. The 1888 tourney included New Yorkers Adeline Robinson and the Roosevelt sisters, Ellen and Grace (cousins to future U.S. President Franklin D. Roosevelt) but was won by another Philadelphian from the Belmont Club, Bertha Townsend.

On Feb. 9, 1889, the USNLTA carried a motion that "its protection be extended to the Lady Lawn Tennis players of the country." Ireland's Mabel Cahill won in 1892 and again one year later. She beat Elisabeth "Bessie" Moore in 1891. For eight of the next nine years the women played the best of five sets, but only in the all-comers finals and challenge rounds.

The growth of lawn tennis around the world was fast. Clubs were founded in Scotland, Brazil and India in 1875. It was played in Germany in 1876. In 1877, the Fitzwilliam Club was started in Dublin, Ireland, and the Decimal Club in Paris was the first in France. Australia, Sweden, Italy, Hungary and Peru had lawn tennis courts in 1878, and the first tournament in Australia was the Victorian Championship meeting in 1879. Denmark and Switzerland date their beginnings from 1880, Argentina from 1881. The first club in the Netherlands was in 1882; in Jamaica in 1883; and in 1885 in both Greece and Turkey. Lawn tennis came to Lebanon in 1889, to Egypt in 1890 and to Finland in the same year. South Africa's first championship was staged in 1891.

Wealthy Russian landowners were setting up courts in the late 1870s. One of them was the great author, Leo Tolstoy, whose

1878 novel, *Anna Karenina*, includes a tennis scene. An enthusiastic player himself, he was photographed playing as early as 1896 on his court at Yasnaya Polyana. The Lakhta Lawn Tennis Club outside of St. Petersburg was founded in 1888.

In 1879, a prize-money tournament was held at Duke Kinski's castle at Chocen, Bohemia (a sector of the Czech Republic). That year another Bohemian tourney was played on grass at Nove Benatsky involving a thirsty cast: First prize was a barrel of wine. The hungry were involved in the same area in an annual team match between the towns of Zbraslov and Rakovcnic: First prize, a gigantic cucumber. Like those remarkable cukes, the game just kept growing.

After the successful intervention of Britain's Otway Woodhouse, in that unofficial American championship of 1880, an Irishman, J.J. Cairnes, was refused entry to the 1881 Championships at Newport. But he was permitted to play in the Ladies Cup tourney there immediately afterwards, and Cairnes, a semifinalist in the initial Irish Championships of 1879, won the event easily, beating the newly crowned U.S. champ, Sears, in the final.

In 1889, Ernest Meets, a top British player, was one of the first overseas challengers at Newport. He lost in five sets to Oliver Campbell, 18. The following year Campbell became champion for the first time at the age of 19 years, six months, defeating Henry Slocum. He was the youngest champ for a century, until Sampras, 19 years, one month, in 1990. It was evidently a time that favored youth. One year later, in 1891, Wilfred Baddeley won the men's singles championship at Wimbledon at 19 years, six months, a record lowered by 17-year-old Boris Becker in 1985.

A "pro tour" of sorts even took brief form in 1889. George Kerr, billed as the Irish professional champ, came to the U.S. to battle Tom Pettit of Boston, the teaching pro at Newport Casino and regarded as the New World's leading professional. They played at Springfield, Mass., Boston and Newport, and Kerr was the victor in three of four matches.

In 1895, what almost amounted to a representative contest between the Americans and the British took the form of a round-robin tournament at the Neighborhood Club, West Newton, Mass. The British players were Ireland's Joshua Pim, the Wimbledon champion of 1893-94, and Harold Mahony, destined to become the champion in 1896. The Americans were Bill Larned, who later became a seven-time U.S. singles champion, Clarence Hobart, Fred Hovey and Malcolm Chace. Pim lost only to Hobart, while Mahony, unbeaten by Americans, lost only to Pim. The first prize went to Pim, the second to Mahony.

The British challenge at Newport in 1897 was formidable, comprising Mahony, Harold Nisbet and Wilberforce Eaves, who was Australian-born but living in England. The British spectators, if there were any among the wealthy and chic who came to the Newport Casino, must have held their heads high. Eaves and Nisbet made it an all-Empire final in the all-comers' singles. Eaves won and challenged Robert Wrenn, but American pride was restored. Wrenn won with difficulty, taking his fourth title. It was his second thwarting of a trans-Atlantic challenge.

For several years, "Doc" Dwight had been trying to stir up the Anglo-American rivalry into a team event instead of individual exercises. In 1900, his hopes reached fruition as his friend,

Reggie Doherty, along with his brother Laurie Doherty, starred for Britain in the early 1900s.

another Harvardian, undergraduate Dwight Davis, put up his famous bauble, the International Lawn Tennis Challenge Trophy, which soon became known as the Davis Cup. Davis had been inspired 12 months earlier by a tennis-playing tour he undertook with Holcombe Ward, Malcolm Whitman and Beals Wright, all keen players in their early 20s. Accompanied by George Wright, a famous baseball player and the father of Beals, they traveled some 8,000 miles, from the Atlantic Coast to the Pacific and up to British Columbia, and were met with friendship and cordial hospitality by fellow tennists along the way. If this sort of competition could generate such good feeling, Davis reasoned (and Dwight agreed), why couldn't it be as worthwhile and rewarding on an international basis.

The USLTA accepted Davis' offer and the International Lawn Tennis Challenge Trophy was offered to the world. They had the British primarily in mind and the Brits, despite the Boer War in South Africa, took up the challenge. Davis was named as the U.S. captain for the inaugural competition He was then 21 and had reached the all-comers' singles final at Newport in 1899. Whitman, 23, the champion of 1898-99, and Ward, 22, doubles partner of Davis, were the other members—Harvard men all. Their club, Longwood Cricket, at its original Boston site, was selected for the

showdown, and the matches were arranged for early August, well before the Newport meeting at the end of the month.

The British team—playing under the banner of the British Isles—comprised playing captain Arthur Gore, Ernest Black, and Herbert Roper Barrett. Gore, 32, with a lot of tennis life in him, had not yet won any of his three Wimbledon singles titles. The Scot, Black, never got as far as the quarters at Wimbledon. Roper Barrett was noted as a player of subtle abilities. It was not the best British team—the pre-eminent Doherty brothers were unavailable. It was selected not only on playing ability but also on a capacity to spare both the time and the money for the trip.

The British found the courts too soft, the grass too long and the Americans unexpectedly too tough. Roper Barrett would complain that the net "was a disgrace, the balls awful soft and mothery—and when served with the American twist came at you like an animated egg-plum. We never experienced this service before and it quite nonplussed us." The kicking serves, particularly those of Ward, bounding to the receiver's left, confounded them. But Roper Barrett thought the spectators "impartial" and "the female portion thereof not at all unpleasant to gaze upon."

The first two singles were played simultaneously on side-by-side courts. Whitman beat Gore easily and Davis beat Black. Black and Roper Barrett were helpless the following day against Ward and Davis, losing 6-4, 6-4, 6-4. On the last day, Davis was up, 9-7, 9-9, when rain intervened. The rest of the series was called off, and the U.S. had a 3-0 triumph.

Later, in the U.S. Championships by the sea at Newport, Gore and Black made an effort to retrieve British honor. They clashed in the quarterfinals and Gore won in straight sets only to lose to George Wrenn in the next round. Whitman was still the boss, thrusting back the challenge of Larned, 6-4, 1-6, 6-2, 6-2, to keep his title.

Anglo-American rivalry continued to be the international aspect of tennis for some years. There was no challenge for the Davis Cup in 1901, but in 1902 the British renewed their effort, sending Reggie and Laurie Doherty, the finest British players of the time, with two-time Wimbledon champ Pim. They played against Whitman, Davis and Larned at the Crescent Athletic Club in Brooklyn, N.Y. As in 1900, the two singles were played at the same time on adjacent courts. Fearful of Laurie's fitness, the British played Pim with Reggie Doherty in the singles. An opening afternoon split gave the Brits hope: Wimbledon champ Reggie defeated Larned to offset Whitman's victory over Pim. But when Larned brushed off Pim, 6-3, 6-2, 6-2, and Whitman beat Reggie, 6-1, 7-5, 6-4, the second day, it was all over. The doubles, scheduled to take place on the third day, was to unveil Laurie, well rested, but his and Reggie's expected victory over Davis and Ward was too late.

The classic powers of the Dohertys, which had captivated the crowds at Wimbledon and elsewhere in Britain, were again displayed to American audiences later in the month at Newport. The brothers reached the semifinals to play one another. Laurie gave a walkover to his elder brother and Reggie went on to beat Whitman in the all-comers final. Although he had beaten Larned in the Davis Cup, Reggie couldn't repeat his success with the U.S. title at stake and fell, 4-6, 6-2, 6-4, 8-6.

The year 1903 was a turning point and the British challenge in the U.S. was as effective as it was formidable. In the Davis Cup, where the British Isles was again the only challenger, the venue was again Longwood in Boston. Reggie and Laurie Doherty, put forward as a two-man side, made a gambling start, giving a match away. Because Reggie was the weaker physically and feeling unwell with a sore right shoulder, he defaulted his opening singles to Larned while Laurie beat Robert Wrenn. Then providence butted in—two days of rain. Reggie felt better and accompanied his brother to doubles victory over the Brothers Wrenn, Robert and George, 7-5, 9-7, 2-6, 6-3.

Thrilling but screwy was the decisive third day when both Dohertys won tight five-set matches, played side by side, that could have gone the other way. Larned's probably should have. In the confusion and tension of spectators, their cheers for one match sometimes interrupted the other as they tried to follow both. Anxiety was high in the stands and among the players as well as the two contests were neck-and-neck in the fifth. But Larned, up 15-40 against Laurie's serve, knocked a winning return and was announced as the leader, 5-4. Hold on. Laurie thought his serve had been a fault, long, and queried umpire Fred Mansfield. The umpire turned to the service linesman and ... beheld only an empty chair! That judge had disappeared. As the author of Cup regulations, and referee, Doc Dwight ruled the point replayed. Laurie won the point, the game, and the next two—thus the Cup, 6-4, 3-6, 6-4, 6-8, 7-5. Having paused to monitor the discussion, Reggie proceeded to finish off Wrenn, 6-4, 3-6, 6-3, 6-8, 6-4, and the Cup was to leave its homeland for the first time, 4-1. It stayed away, in London, as the Dohertys backboned their country to a four-year run.

In the 1905 prelims in London, the Souths Seas islanders and the Americans launched what would become the greatest of tennis feuds, fierce yet friendly. The Yanks beat the Australasians, 5-0, the first of 45 clashes (25-20, U.S.) through 2008.

Beals Wright beat Norman Brookes 12-10, 5-7, 12-10, 6-4; Bill Larned beat Tony Wilding 6-3, 6-2, 6-4; Holcombe Ward and Wright settled it winning the doubles over Brookes and Wilding 6-4, 7-5, 5-7, 6-2.

The Americans were no match for the Dohertys, however, bageled in the 1905-06 finales as Laurie won all four singles and, with Reggie, both doubles. The only close matches that counted were Ward's opposition to Laurie in the 1905 opener, 7-9, 4-6, 6-1, 6-2, 6-0, and the clinching doubles the next day over Ward and Wright, 8-10, 6-2, 6-2, 4-6, 8-6. Ward and Raymond Little made a fight of it in the clinching 1906 doubles, though the brothers handled it confidently, 3-6, 11-9, 9-7, 6-1.

By 1907, the Dohertys had retired and the boys from the Antipodes, Australasia, a two-nation blend in the persons of crafty left-handed Aussie Brookes and strapping, athletic New Zealander Wilding, had arrived. They spirited the Cup way down south and kept it until 1912. They were led by Brookes, 29, the first overseas entrant to win the Wimbledon men's singles. He piloted the Down Under-takers' seizure of their first of 27 Cups. It started with a 3-2 semifinal decision over the U.S. and ended with a 3-2 win over Britain.

Fresh from his Wimbledon triumph, and on the same ground,

Brookes led off against the Yanks, 6-4, 6-4, 6-2, over Wright, and Wilding made it 2-0 with difficulty over a man who would escape the *Titanic* five years hence, Karl Behr, 1-6, 6-3, 3-6, 7-5, 6-3. But Behr and Wright struck back over Brookes and Wilding, 3-6, 12-10, 4-6, 6-4, 6-3, to send it into a third day. There, Brookes halted Behr, 4-6, 6-4, 6-1, 6-2.

Even though the old boy Brits, Gore, 39, and Roper Barrett, 33, were left by the Dohertys to defend the Cup, they made a good show of it, right down to the fifth match, Brookes over Roper Barrett, 6-2, 6-0, 6-3. Their resistance, from 0-2 down, started with the doubles as the invaders came within points of locking it up, only to fall to Arthur and Herbert, 3-6, 4-6, 7-5, 6-2, 13-11. Gore pulled them even, beating Wilding, 3-6, 6-3, 7-5, 6-2.

U.S. champ Bill Larned beat Jim Parke, 6-3, 6-3, 7-5 to start a 1908 semis win over Britain, and assured the 4-1 victory the third day, 4-6, 6-3, 6-2, 6-3, over Josiah Richey. However, Bill didn't care to make the initial longest road trip for a U.S. team to the bottom of the world for the final. Still, the two-man American team of Beals Wright and Fred Alexander, the first Yanks to compete on Australian soil—after a journey of almost a month—made a battle of it in extreme 90 degree Melbourne heat. Lefty Wright beat both Wilding, 3-6, 7-5, 6-3, 6-1, and Brookes, 0-6, 3-6, 7-5, 6-2, 12-10, gamely hurdling two match points to make it 2-2. But Wilding made Australasia's first Cup defense a big hit, 6-3, 6-4, 6-1, over Alexander. Alexander nearly stunned the homeboy, Brookes, and the crowd, 5-7, 9-7, 6-2, 4-6, 6-3, the first day, and the visitors lost the tense doubles, 6-4, 6-2, 5-7, 2-6, 6-4. Alexander remained to win the Aussie title, the first American to do so, beating native Alf Dunlop, 3-6, 3-6, 6-0, 6-2, 6-3 in the final.

In 1909, same as '08, Larned mowed down Brits Charles Dixon 6-3, 6-2, 6-0, and Parke, 6-3, 6-2, 6-3, in a 5-0 Philadelphia semi, but No. 1 Bill said no-thanks again to the elongated voyage to Sydney for the final. That was the general attitude of American luminaries, so the greenest U.S. team ever—19-year-olds, Captain Maurice McLoughlin, and Melville Long—were packed off to Australia to absorb the worst 5-0 defeat. McLoughlin won their lone set, from Wilding when it no longer mattered. Brookes and Wilding toyed with the kids with only the doubles fairly interesting, 12-10, 9-7, 6-3.

Cup play was suspended for 1910, but in 1911 the U.S. varsity at last steeled themselves for the interminable boat ride after beating Britain again, 4-1 as Larned slipped past Dixon, 6-3, 2-6, 6-3, 3-6, 7-5, and clinched over Arthur Lowe, 6-3, 1-6, 7-5, 6-1. McLoughlin beat Lowe on the first day, 7-5, 6-1, 4-6, 6-3. But it was too late for the big guys, even though they got a huge break when Wilding opted out of the final, despite its staging in his hometown, Christchurch, New Zealand. Rod Heath, the initial Australian champ in 1905, replaced Wilding, and nailed Larned, 2-6, 6-1, 7-5, 6-2. Brookes felled Wright, 6-4, 2-6, 6-3, 6-3, then Brookes and Alf Dunlop beat McLoughlin and Wright, 6-4, 5-7, 7-5, 6-4, and the bagel was three-fifths toasted.

In 1912, the Brookes-Rodney Heath ticket couldn't withstand a challenge from Irishman Jim Parke and Charles Dixon, who reclaimed the Cup for Britain, 3-2, at Melbourne.

Tall, swift Parke shocked Melburnians by taking out their neighbor, Brookes, 8-6, 6-3, 5-7, 6-2, and Dixon raised the lead to

2-0, over Heath, 5-7, 6-4, 6-4, 6-4. But Brookes led a slow-down, winning the doubles with Dunlop over Alfred Beamish and Park, 6-4, 6-1, 7-5, and then beat Dixon, 6-2, 6-4, 6-4. However, Parke was ready for Heath, 6-2, 6-4, 6-4.

Failing to enter in 1912, the U.S. was back in the hunt—successfully—in 1913. Now it was the Australasian stars who backed away from the extended saltwater voyage. Their second raters were first-round losers, 4-1 at the West Side Tennis Club at Forest Hills, New York. McLoughlin ran over 39-year-old Horace Rice, 6-1, 6-3, 6-3, and clinched over Stanley Doust, 6-4, 6-4, 6-2. Rookie Dick Williams beat both of them, Doust, 6-4, 6-4, 1-6, 7-5, and Rice, 1-6, 4-6, 9-7, 6-1, 6-2, and was 6-1 for the campaign.

Thus the Yanks were off to England to shut out Germany, 5-0, and Canada, 3-0, and snatch the Cup from the Brits, 3-2, at Wimbledon, all within 19 days of July. "Miracle Man" Williams, only 14 months beyond his ordeal, swimming away from the doomed *Titanic*, saved the perilous first day that could have gone 2-0 to either side, beating Dixon, 8-6, 3-6, 6-2, 1-6, 7-5, after McLoughlin lost to Parke, 8-10, 7-5, 6-4, 1-6, 7-5. Then the McLoughlin took over. Collaborating with Harold Hackett in another squeeze over Roper Barrett and Dixon, 5-7, 6-1, 2-6, 7-5, 6-4, he then got the Cup-napping victory briskly, 8-6, 6-3, 6-2, over Dixon.

The Antipodeans, Brookes and Wilding, arriving in New York, had their eye on the 1914 Cup, but wondered if they'd ever play again. They had beaten Canada, 5-0 in Chicago, Germany, 5-0 in Pittsburgh and Britain, 3-0 in Boston. But World War I had just flared in August. Brookes and Wilding's countries were involved, and they soon would be, too.

Tragically for four-time Wimbledon champ Wilding, he was killed in action on May 9, 1915 during the Battle of Aubers Ridge at Neuve-Chapelle. France. He had opened the Cup final by cooling off Williams, 7-5, 6-2, 6-3. But McLoughlin wowed the very loud, very partisan witnesses—the crowds of 13,00 at the West Side Tennis Club at Forest Hills, New York were the largest to watch tennis at that time—with an epic starting set to defeat Brookes, 17-15, 6-3, 6-2. The redhead held to 9-9 from 0-40 with four of his 17 aces, and volleyed marvelously. The series would turn on the doubles, the invaders an iron wall at the net in a 6-3, 8-6, 9-7, decision over McLoughlin and Tom Bundy, who would sire a Hall of Famer, "Dodo" Cheney. Brookes then reclaimed the Cup over Williams, who got hot in the third, but lost his fire in the intermission and toppled, 6-1, 6-2, 8-10, 6-3.

The Cup went to Melbourne to sit out the war as a flower bowl in Brookes' home until 1920. Americans didn't see the gleaming basin again for six years when the two Bills, Tilden and Johnston, pried it from Brookes & Co. in Auckland.

After snatching the Cup in Boston in 1903, the Dohertys achieved something more in carting off, too, the U.S. Championships at Newport. Once again they were cast as foes in the quarterfinals. This time Laurie was given the walkover. He went on to reach the challenge round, where he relieved Larned of his title. The brothers also retained the doubles title.

Laurie, the first man to take the U.S. singles title overseas, was then 27, perhaps at his peak. Reggie, three years older, won four straight Wimbledon singles, 1897-1900. The more robust Laurie followed with a five-year sequence, 1902-06. Their classic skill

Hazel Hotchkiss Wightman, the woman who would become known as "Lady Tennis."

became a British legend and their impeccable sportsmanship a byword. In doubles, there was only one year between 1897 and 1905 that they missed out on the Wimbledon title.

If 1903 was a momentous year for the U.S. Championships, so was 1905 at Wimbledon. An American woman had entered for the first time in 1900. Marion Jones, then the U.S. champion, got as far as the quarterfinals. Five years later, a chubby, robust 18-year-old from California with an intimidating forehand made a memorable appearance. She was May Sutton and she, too, was the U.S. title-holder. As it happened, she was English-born at Plymouth, Devonshire, the daughter of a British naval captain who later took his family to California.

The staunch Sutton penetrated a citadel where the names of some women were already being spoken of reverently. Most venerated at that time was Lottie Dod, 15-year-old winner in 1887 of the first of her five championships, youngest ever to win a major singles. There was Blanche Hillyard, a six-time champion. Dorothea "Dolly" Douglass (later Mrs. Lambert Chambers) had, when

the uninhibited Sutton appeared, already won twice and was on the way to making herself a legend. But Sutton carved through all opposition and had the temerity to stop Douglass from winning for the third time, standing out as the first overseas player to take a Wimbledon championship.

Two years later, all three titles available left the country, another first. Brookes captured the men's singles and took the doubles as well with Wilding. May Sutton, (loser of her title to Dolly Chambers in 1906), regained it in a rematch, 6-1, 6-4. Women's doubles and mixed weren't yet on the card. The Brits would soon have to get used to such thefts.

In the U.S., the championships meeting at Newport settled back into American control after the Doherty sortie of 1903. Outstanding man of the first decade of the century was Larned. A New York stockbroker, he won the U.S. singles for the first time in 1901 over Wright at age 28, and would equal the record of Sears by taking it seven times, the last in 1911 over Maurice McLoughlin as the oldest of champs at 38. He played 73 singles in all and won 61. "Big" Bill Tilden, the last seven-time winner, did better (69-7). Larned had an unbroken sequence of 11 victories from 1907, when he played through and won, to his success in his last challenge round of 1911.

The popularity of the Newport singles reached unprecedented heights during Larned's career. The entries passed 128 for the first rime in 1908 and peaked at 202 in 1911, the last year of the challenge round. McLoughlin, a red-headed 21-year-old known as the "California Comet," took over for Larned, beating Wallace Johnson in 1912 and retaining in 1913. McLoughlin's dynamic serving brought a new dimension to the game and so did his background. He was the first public parks player to take a ride that had been dominated by club men from wealthy families.

In 1913, the year of McLoughlin's only appearance in England, he was an energetic factor in taking the Davis Cup from the homebodies, and leaving Wimbledon spectators awestruck by his serving—inspiring a new usage: "Cannonball." Before record crowds, he came through the all-comers' singles over Aussie Stanley Doust and challenged Wilding, the title-holder since 1910, for the crown. "The history of the match," it was written at the time, "may be succinctly stated by saying that McLoughlin ought to have won the first set and was very near to winning the third. He lost both of them, and the second into the bargain, and so Wilding retained the honors," 8-6, 6-3, 10-8.

Wilding's invincibility at Wimbledon was finally brought to an end in 1914 by his Davis Cup colleague, Brookes, who, at age 36, won his second Wimbledon singles. Not long afterward, they united to carry the Cup away from New York.

Three years earlier, in 1911, the West Side Tennis Club had staged its first Davis Cup. The famed, peripatetic club was put together in 1892 by 13 founding members who rented three clay courts on Central Park West between 88th and 89th Streets, Manhattan. By the end of that season, there were 43 members, five courts, and the initiation fee was $10, with a yearly subscription of the same amount. A move to a site near Columbia University at 117th Street between Morningside Drive and Amsterdam Avenue occurred in 1902. Six years later, another move took the club to 238th Street and Broadway, a site that had room for 12 grass

and 15 or more clay courts. The shift from Manhattan to Forest Hills in Queens was made in 1913.

In 1915, West Side became the grass court host to the U.S. Men's Singles Championship. Williams waved his racket and a farewell to Newport Casino's sod in 1914 by usurping McLoughlin's championship, 6-3, 8-6, 10-8, reversing the outcome of the 1913 final, won by "the Comet." The Casino, after 34 years as home of America's most prestigious event, had outlived that purpose, though it remains in the game as a pro tourney site and home of the International Tennis Hall of Fame. The age it represented, of wealth and fashion and leisure, was passing.

In 1921, West Side absorbed the U.S. Women's Championships as well, and New York became the country's tennis capital. Before that, the turf of the Philadelphia Cricket Club was the women's battleground. The most consistent champs had been Bessie Moore, four-time victor between 1896 and 1905, and Juliette Atkinson, capturing three between 1895 and 1898. Juliette prevailed in rare, five-set finals to win over Bessie in 1897, and Marion Jones in 1898. The women felt they had the physiques and moxie to play best-of-five finals just like the men, but timidly the USLTA soon wimped out on their behalf, settling on best-of-three to much distaff dismay and disagreement.

The champion of 1908, Maud Barger Wallach, took a special place in the roll of winners. A high-society lady who'd taken up the game at 30, she was 38 when she won the title over defender Evelyn Sears (the first left-handed champ). At 45, Maud was still ranked nationally at No. 5. However, Maud didn't have a chance at keeping her crown once a five-foot fireball, University of California student Hazel Hotchkiss, hit Philly. Hazel, who would go on to become known as "Lady Tennis," donated the Wightman Cup (as Mrs. George Wightman) for a team competition between the U.S. and Britain, and land in the Hall of Fame, swept Maud away in a tide of volleying, 6-0, 6-1. She recalled pitying her adversary: "Mrs. Barger Wallach didn't have a backhand. She looked 150 to young [22] me."

Hazel tripled that year, adding the doubles and mixed diadems, the first three of her record 45 U.S. adult championships. Ditto 1910 and 1911, a rare and unprecedented triple-triple—all nine U.S. titles in three years—before she settled in as a Boston housewife. Her only precarious singles victory was 1911 over one of the renowned Californian Sutton sisters, Florence. She was followed by yet another Californian triple-tripler Mary K. Browne, seizing all the silver in 1912-13-14.

Next into the winner's circle came the Norwegian-born strongwoman, Molla Bjurstedt, running four of her record eight titles between 1915 and 1918. Wightman grabbed one more singles, and after having a child, in 1919. Then it was Molla again (as Mrs. Franklin Mallory) for three more. Molla, raising the American level in the post-war years, didn't make her record exclusively as an American. An Olympian in Stockholm in 1912, she represented Norway, winning the bronze medal in singles on indoor courts.

Tennis was featured as part of the modern Olympic Games from the first in Athens in 1896 to the Paris event of 1924, then restored in 1988. At the pre-war Games, British players predomi-

nated except for those at St. Louis in 1904. Only men took part and the gold medalists were exclusively American, Wright taking one for the singles and, with Edgar Leonard, the doubles. Joseph Wear and Arthur Wear, whose nephew George Herbert Walker Bush became the 41st President of the United States, won bronze medals in doubles, but not with each other— Joseph partnering with Allen West and Arthur pairing with Clarence Gamble.

In international administration, 1913 was important, the year of the founding of the ILTF (International Lawn Tennis Federation), eventually shortened to the ITF. It was an idea proposed by Philadelphian Duane Williams, who didn't live to see it come into being. In 1912, he went down with the *Titanic*, from which his championship son, Dick Williams, swam to safety. Prior to this time, the world governing body, so far as there had been one, was the LTA (Lawn Tennis Association) of Britain. Its membership included clubs and associations from all around the world. In 1913, the LTA members included the associations of Australasia, Belgium, Bohemia, Ceylon, Chile, Finland, Hungary, Ireland, Jamaica, Mauritius, Netherlands, Norway, the Riviera, Russia, South Africa, Spain and Switzerland, as well as 26 individual clubs from 15 countries.

At the ITF's inaugural meeting in Paris on March 1, 1913, the founding members were Australasia, Austria, Belgium, the British Isles, Denmark, France, Germany, Netherlands, Russia, South Africa, Sweden and Switzerland. No U.S., which was only informally represented by one of the British delegates, H. Anthony Sabelli, secretary of the LTA. The absence resulted in the Davis Cup organization developing along different lines from the ITF, parallel but separate. (The merger didn't take place until 1978.) U.S. reluctance to join the ITF was occasioned by the allocation of various "World Championship" titles. Wimbledon was granted ("in perpetuity") "The World Championships on Grass." There was a "World Hard Court Championships" (clay), staged in Paris, also a moveable "World Covered Court Championships." When these grandiose titles were abolished soon after World War I, the U.S. felt comfortable in joining.

An early winner of the women's singles in the 1914 World Hard Court Championships in Paris was a promising French schoolgirl, only 15. Also winner of the doubles with American Elizabeth "Bunny" Ryan, she came from Picardy, and was named Suzanne Lenglen, an all-time great-to-be.

Ryan's name was also to echo reverberatingly. Even before 1914, this Californian had laid the foundation of her career as an assiduous, effective competitor. The women's and mixed doubles at Wimbledon were accepted as official championships in 1913, the World title on grass attached to them. In 1914, indefatigable Ryan partnered Agnes Morton to win the women's doubles, the first of her 19 Wimbledon titles, a record that stood until 1979 when Billie Jean King won her 20th title (Martina Navratilova would equal King's record in 2003).

The Riviera season was by then a well-established feature of the game, reflecting an exclusive atmosphere of fashion, wealth, royalty and internationalism which had become as much a part of tennis in Europe, as exemplified by Newport. Immediately prior to the war, however, it was perhaps Imperial Russia that

represented the high point of tennis in its smart social context. British men who played in St. Petersburg in the Russian Championships of 1913 recorded that the ball boys were footmen in ornate uniforms who passed the balls on silver salvers. Ryan was the last women's champion of Imperial Russia, a title she was never able to defend.

Ryan was overshadowed at this time, like all other women, by Mrs. Lambert Chambers, as Dorothea "Dolly" Douglass had become. Dolly made 13 attempts to win the Wimbledon singles between 1902 and 1920, and was beaten only six times. At the age of 24, she won for the first time, in 1903, over Ethel Thomson. Her seventh success, 1914, over Thomson (who had become Mrs. Dudley Larcombe) set Dolly apart as the precursor of great, near-invincible players. During this period, it was still possible to be on top, yet excel at other sports. Dolly was also a champion at badminton and a top field hockey player.

The Davis Cup helped boost tennis internationally. Prior to 1914, when war brought the competition to a temporary halt, there were nine entries: The U.S., British Isles, Belgium, France, Australasia, Austria, Germany, Canada, South Africa. The Australian Championships, staged first in 1905, and won by Rod Heath, would gain recognition as the third major.

A notable champion, perhaps the greatest monopolizer of any national title, Miss K. M. Nunneley held the New Zealand title for 13 successive years from 1895. Across the Tasman Sea, Australia didn't hold a women's championship until 1922 when Margaret Mutch "Mall" Molesworth won the first of her two.

The French, prior to the war, made an impact with men of high caliber, Andre Gobert and Max Decugis most notably. They won the men's doubles at Wimbledon in 1911, but it was not until 1925 that the French Championships was opened to non-citizens, standing forth as the fourth major. A German pair, Heinrich Kleinschroth and Friedrich Rahe, were runners-up for the Wimbledon title in 1913. In 1912, Kleinschroth competed in the U.S. Championships at Newport but did not survive the opening round. The German Championships was an event favored by British players and among the fashionable happenings of the season, staged in Hamburg from 1892.

Canada's first national championship was held two years earlier, in 1890, 12 years after the country's initial tournament on the turf of the Montreal Cricket Club. Like those in the U.S., the first official championships, for men, followed the founding of the Canadian Lawn Tennis Association in Toronto in 1890, with the championships for women launched two years later.

In Europe, war brought a halt to tournament tennis in 1914. Australia kept its championships going for the 1915 season, and a Brit, Gordon Lowe, was the winner, over lefty Horace Rice, 4-6, 6-1, 6-1, 6-4. Rice retaliated in the doubles final, joining with Clairie Todd to beat Lowe and the only one-handed man to grace a major final, a lefty, Bert St. John, 8-6, 6-4, 7-9, 6-3.

Although the American game was affected to a lesser degree by war, the international field dried up. In 1917, after the U.S. had become directly involved in hostilities, there was something of a break. The U.S. Championships was not played as such, but conducted under the heading of "Patriotic Tournaments," with proceeds going to wartime charities. Eventually the winners in 1917-18, Lindley Murray and Molla Bjurstedt (the future Mrs. Mallory), were granted full championship status.

In 1918, a tall, somewhat ungainly Philadelphian, William Tatem Tilden II, did well on his third attempt in the U.S. ("Patriotic") singles. Reaching the final, he was handcuffed by the potent left-handed serve of Murray, 6-3, 6-1, 7-5. Murray's aggressiveness had been on display the year before at the expense of figure skating champ Nat Niles from Boston. The juggernaut, Molla, won her sixth and seventh titles. Tilden did, however, inscribe his name earlier on the U.S. Championship rolls, accompanying Mary K. Browne to the mixed doubles title of 1913-1914, and 15-year-old Vinnie Richards—the youngest male winner of a major—to the doubles title of 1918.

But, making his first significant mark, Tilden was a late developer, 27, at his breakthrough to the singles championships of Wimbledon and the U.S. in 1920. Nevertheless, he was on his way, a principal in 1918, the first of his eight consecutive U.S. finals, six of which he would win. A seventh, in 1929, allowed him to catch up with Sears and Larned. Ultimately, Tilden's career would far surpass theirs, and perhaps that of any other American man.

The Golden Age

Bill Tilden (left) and **Rene Lacoste** were two central figures in tennis in the 1920s.

It was called "The Golden Age of Sport"—hyperbolic, probably, considering the purple language of the sports pages of the past, although there was some truth to it. Sport came on strong in the "Roaring Twenties" as never before, held high by such highly-publicized stars as Babe Ruth in baseball, Jack Dempsey in boxing, Red Grange in football, Bobby Jones in golf, Man o' War in horse racing. Tennis was right up there, too, with players whose names had a broad public impact: Big Bill Tilden, Suzanne Lenglen, Helen Wills Moody, the Gallic "Four Musketeers"—Jean Borotra, Jacques Brugnon, Henri Cochet and Rene Lacoste. World War I was over, the trenches were silent and a prosperous period, with more leisure, seemed ripe for games-playing heroes and heroines who could be colored gold.

1919 Bonjour Suzanne!

ing and doubles, with Elizabeth Ryan, in the World Hard Court (clay) Championships. She was 15, so she was not exactly an unknown when she came to Wimbledon upon the resumption of play following World War I. Playing on grass for the first time, Lenglen won the title in a match that is still regarded as one of the greatest Wimbledon women's finals.

Although the stocky Lenglen was no conventional beauty, and never married, she had a captivating allure and numerous love affairs, an appeal that was dynamite at the box office. Her magnetism and invincibility made the original Wimbledon too small, leading to the construction of the 'new' (present) complex in 1922. Her long, Gallic nose and prominent chin were complemented by a fiery disposition, a chic appearance and a dancer's movements. She was 20 and advanced to the Wimbledon challenge round past Phyllis Satterthwaite, 6-1, 6-1, in the all-comers final to face the seven-time champion, Britain's Mrs. Dorothea Douglass Chambers. Chambers had won her first Wimbledon in 1903 and was two months from her 41st birthday.

Lenglen's dress created a sensation. The British had been accustomed to seeing their women in tight-fitting corsets, blouses and layers of petticoats. When Suzanne stepped onto Centre Court in a revealing one-piece dress, with sleeves daringly just above the elbow, her hemline only just below the knee, reaction ranged from outrage on the part of many women spectators—some reportedly walked out during her matches, muttering "shocking"—to delight among the men.

But everybody was also impressed by the young Frenchwoman's grace and disciplined shotmaking as she won the title,

The year 1919 was the year of Suzanne Lenglen's arrival on the world tennis stage: She would dominate until she turned pro in 1926. A product of constant drilling by her father, Charles Lenglen, a well-to-do Frenchman, she had style as well as ability and, along with contemporary Helen Wills Moody, would come to be ranked among the greatest women players of all time.

Lenglen appeared in her first tournament at age 12. In 1914 Suzanne won the singles, 6-2, 6-1, over Germaine Gold-

10-8, 4-6, 9-7, the 44 games amounting to the longest female final until Margaret Court's 14-12, 11-9 victory over Billie Jean King topped it by two games in 1970.

Future champ Kitty McKane, an eyewitness in the full-house crowd of perhaps 8,500 that included King George V and Queen Mary, wrote: "It was a very hot afternoon, and I think Suzanne wanted to quit when she was behind, 4-1, in the 2nd set. But her father would have none of it, shaking his umbrella furiously at her, and tossing her sugar cubes soaked with brandy. After losing the second set, she seemed back in control with a 4-1 lead in the third. But Mrs. Chambers, who'd missed out on two set points in the first at 6-5, came back to win five games to 6-5 and 40-15 on her serve, on the verge of her eighth championship with two match points. Suzanne was lucky on the first. Reaching for a lob she hit it barely, on the frame, and the ball hit the net cord; dropping over. But the second she saved with a backhand down the line. She was unstoppable after that."

In the Wimbledon men's championship, another golden oldie was involved as the defender, Aussie Norman Brookes, 41, like Dolly Chambers a holdover from 1914, aimed to be the tourney's most elderly monarch, surpassing Arthur Gore, who was younger by two months when he won in 1909 (Brookes had defeated Gore in the 1907 finale, 6-4, 6-2, 6-2). However, another Aussie and a Wimbledon rookie, Gerald Patterson, got in Brookes' way. Known as "The Catapult" for his huge serve, Patterson advanced to the challenge round by beating Britain's Algernon Kingscote, 6-2, 6-1, 6-3, in the all-comers, and then Brookes, 6-3, 7-5, 6-2. Theirs was the first of 10 totally Aussie title shootouts on Centre Court.

In the 1919 resumption of Davis Cup after a four-year hiatus, Australasia (a combination of Australia and New Zealand) retained the Cup it had won in 1914, beating the British Isles, 4-1. The U.S. did not enter. Patterson was the dominant player, sandwiching singles wins over Arthur Lowe, 6-4, 6-3, 2-6, 6-3, and Kingscote, 6-4, 6-4, 8-6, around a doubles bashing with Brookes of Alfred Beamish and Kingscote, 6-0, 6-0, 6-2. This was the last of six Cups that Brookes, then 42, had a hand in winning. Kingscote, who had won the sole British point over Jim (J.O.) Anderson, redeemed himself by winning the Australian singles over Eric Pockley, 6-4, 6-0, 6-3.

The U.S. final at Forest Hills between the 1915 champion, 5-foot-8, 120-pound William "Little Bill" Johnston, and 6-foot-2, William 'Big Bill' Tilden, was billed in *The New York Times* as the battle for the title, "William the Conqueror." It was the first of six meetings between the two Bills in the final of the U.S. Championships, and the only one Johnston would win. Tilden had first played in the U.S. Championships in 1912 and lost, 6-2, 6-3, 6-4, in the opening round to fellow Philadelphian Wallace Johnson (his victim in the 1921 final). He waited four years before trying again, at age 23, and was a first-round flop again, to a teenager, American Harold Throckmorton, 4-6, 6-4, 6-2, 8-6. He finally won a couple of rounds at Forest Hills in 1917 before losing to the champion-to-be, big-serving lefty Lindley Murray, 3-6, 6-4, 6-3, 6-3. At last, at 25 in 1918, Bill was getting it together and made his way to the first of his 10 U.S. finals, losing once more to Murray, 6-3, 6-1, 7-5.

By 1919, he was already being called by some the greatest player of all time - but that designation turned out to be slightly premature. Johnston spotted a weakness in Tilden, a backhand that was totally defensive, hit invariably with underspin. Having beaten Tilden in Chicago for the U.S. Clay Court title, 6-0, 6-1, 4-6, 6-2, Little Bill kept pounding away at the flaw at Forest Hills, winning relatively easily, 6-4, 6-3, 6-3. Johnston's best win was eliminating Wimbledon champ Patterson, 6-2, 3-6, 6-4, 7-5, in the fourth round, prior to derailing 1917-18 champ Murray, ending his 15-match streak in the Championships, 5-7, 6-1, 6-2, 6-4.

Australia, which presently would play an important—at times domineering—role in the U.S. Championships had its first titlists in the persons of Brookes and Patterson, winning the doubles at Boston's Longwood Cricket Club over defenders, 16-year-old Vinnie Richards and Tilden 8-6, 6-3, 4-6, 4-6, 6-2.

For the women's championship, the Challenge Round was abolished and Mrs. Hazel Hotchkiss Wightman won the title, snapping a four-year reign by Norwegian-American Molla Bjurstedt. Marion Zinderstein eliminated Molla in the semifinals, 4-6, 6-1, 6-2, ending an 18-match streak, but was beaten 6-1, 6-2, in the all-Bostonian final by Wightman. Hazel, the champ in 1909-10-11 as a single woman, responded to a challenge from her father to be the first mother to win the title. Wightman's toughest match was the 6-3, 4-6, 6-4, third rounder over Eleanor Goss, a New Yorker who ranked No. 2 for the year behind the champion.

1919 CHAMPIONS AND LEADERS

Australian Championships
Men's Singles: Algernon Kingscote (GBR) def. Eric Pockley (AUS), 6-4, 6-0, 6-3
Men's Doubles: Pat O'Hara Wood and Ronald Thomas (AUS) def. James Anderson (AUS) and Arthur Lowe (GBR) 7-5, 6-1, 7-9, 3-6, 6-3

Wimbledon
Men's Singles: Gerald Patterson (AUS) def. Norman Brookes (AUS), 6-3, 7-5, 6-2
Women's Singles: Suzanne Lenglen (FRA) def. Dorothea Chambers (GBR) 10-8, 4-6, 9-7
Men's Doubles: Ronald Thomas (GBR) and Pat O'Hara Wood (AUS) def. Randolph Lycett (GBR) and Rodney Heath (AUS), 6-4, 6-2, 4-6, 6-2
Women's Doubles: Suzanne Lenglen (FRA) and Elizabeth Ryan (USA) def. Ethel Thomson Larcombe and Dorothea Chambers (GBR) 4-6, 7-5, 6-3
Mixed Doubles: Elizabeth Ryan (USA) and Randolph Lycett (GBR) def. Albert Prebble and Dorothea Chambers (GBR), 6-0, 6-0

U.S. Championships
Men's Singles: Bill Johnston (USA) def. Bill Tilden (USA), 6-4, 6-4, 6-3
Women's Singles: Hazel Hotchkiss Wightman (USA) def. Marion Zinderstein (USA), 6-1, 6-2
Men's Doubles: Norman Brookes and Gerald Patterson (AUS) def. Bill Tilden and Vinnie Richards (USA), 8-6, 6-3, 4-6, 4-6, 6-2
Women's Doubles: Marion Zinderstein and Eleanora Goss (USA) def. Eleanor Sears and Hazel Hotchkiss Wightman (USA), 10-8, 9-7
Mixed Doubles: Marion Zinderstein and Vinnie Richards (USA) def. Florence Ballin and Bill Tilden (USA), 6-4, 7-5

Year-End No. 1
Men: Gerald Patterson (AUS)

Davis Cup: Australasia

1920 Big Bill Tilden Makes His Mark

William Tatem Tilden II, born in 1893, the son of a Philadelphia wool merchant and prominent civic figure, came of age at 27. He won at Wimbledon and the U.S. Championships at Forest Hills, and helped the United States win the Davis Cup for the first time since 1913.

In the all-comers final at Wimbledon against Japan's sly Zenzo Shimidzu, Tilden fell behind in all three sets, 1-4, 2-4,

Bill Tilden won Wimbledon, the U.S. Championships and brought the Davis Cup back to the United States.

2-5, but rallied each time to win, 6-4, 6-4, 13-11. It became the mark of Tilden to put on a show and entertain as well as win. In his remarkable biography, *Big Bill Tilden*, Frank Deford wrote:

"Nobody realized it at the time, but it was one of Tilden's amusements, a favor to the crowd, to give lesser opponents a head start." Tilden had whipped Shimidzu, 6-1, 6-1, in a tournament prior to Wimbledon. In the Challenge Round, Tilden defeated the defending champion, Australian Gerald Patterson, 2-6, 6-3, 6-2, 6-4 to win the title. The Associated Press reported that "Tilden in the first set opened with experiments all around the court and then settled down mercilessly to feeding his opponent's backhand, and, as the game progressed, Patterson got worse and worse ... Tilden exploited his famous cut-stroke to his opponent's backhand again and again."

The British marveled at Tilden, acclaimed him the greatest of all-time. One observer rhapsodized, "His silhouette as he prepares to serve suggests an Egyptian pharaoh about to administer punishment."

However, few knew they were witnessing a new, transformed Tilden. He had spent the winter hidden away in Providence, Rhode Island, working out in secret on the private indoor court of J.D.E. Jones, fine-tuning his errant backhand. His sparring partner was J.D.E.'s son Arnold, a top-flight American player. Such an improvement-seeking hiatus would be impossible today of uninterrupted tournament play.

In the U.S. Championships, Tilden beat Bill Johnston in a dramatic five-set final, 6-1, 1-6, 7-5, 5-7, 6-3, in what was regarded as the greatest championship battle up to that time. During the match, a Navy photographic plane crashed near the West Side Tennis Club while making passes over Forest Hills and disrupted the match momentarily. The pilot and the photographer were killed. Pandemonium struck. As many spectators noisily departed, rushing toward the accident, umpire Edward Conlin queried the adversaries: "Are you able to continue?" Tilden and Johnston nodded affirmatively and the crowd settled down.

It was the first of six straight national titles for Tilden, a flamboyant and controversial figure who dominated any match, win or lose. Tilden would not lose an important match until 1926.

In men's doubles, Johnston paired with Clarence Griffin, the uncle of future American TV personality Merv Griffin, and won the men's doubles crown.

In the women's event at Wimbledon, Dorothea Douglass Chambers defeated Americans Molla Bjurstedt Mallory, 6-0, 6-3, and Elizabeth Ryan, 6-2, 6-1, on the way to a return match with Suzanne Lenglen in the Challenge Round. Lenglen beat Chambers, 6-3, 6-0 to win the title. Mallory regained the U.S. title, defeating Marion Zinderstein, 6-3, 6-1.

The bullying, bageling Bills—Tilden and Johnston—were emphatic about regaining the Davis Cup: 3-0 over France and 5-0 over Britain, both in England, and 5-0 over Cup-holding Australasia at Auckland, losing just 11 sets in 13 matches. They handled everything, each going 5-0 in singles, and 3-0 as doubles collaborators.

France was no problem: Johnston defeated Andre Gobert, 6-3, 8-6, 6-3 and Tilden bested William Laurentz, 4-6, 6-2, 6-1, 6-3, followed by the doubles involving the same guys – the Americans winning 6-2, 6-3, 6-2. Little Bill had to go five to beat Britain's Jim Parke 6-4, 6-4, 2-6, 3-6, 6-2 on opening day - a companion piece to Tilden's 4-6, 6-1, 6-3, 6-1 win over Algernon Kingscote. The Bills needed five to clinch over Parke and Kingscote by 6-4, 4-6, 3-6, 6-4, 7-5.

The wizardly Brookes remained competitive at 43, and made Tilden earn the leadoff match in the Challenge Round, 10-8, 6-4, 1-6, 6-4, but Johnston overwhelmed Patterson, 6-3, 6-1, 6-1. Brookes and Patterson got rapped together in the wrap-up doubles, 4-6, 6-4, 6-0, 6-4, and the Cup was going home.

1920 CHAMPIONS AND LEADERS

Australian Championships

Men's Singles: Pat O'Hara Wood (AUS) def. Ron Thomas (AUS), 6-3, 4-6, 6-8, 6-1, 6-3

Men's Doubles: Pat O'Hara Wood and Ron Thomas (AUS) def. Horrie Rice and Ron Taylor (AUS) 6-1, 6-0, 7-5

Wimbledon

Men's Singles: Women's Singles: Suzanne Lenglen (FRA) def. Dorothea Chambers (GBR), 6-3, 6-0

Men's Doubles: Dick Williams and Chuck Garland (USA) def. Algernon Kingscote and Jim Parke (GBR), 4-6, 6-4, 7-5, 6-2

Women's Doubles: Suzanne Lenglen (FRA) and Elizabeth Ryan (USA) def. Ethel Thomson Larcombe and Dorothea Chambers (GBR), 6-4, 6-0

Mixed Doubles: Suzanne Lenglen (FRA) and Gerald Patterson (AUS) def. Elizabeth Ryan (USA) and Randolph Lycett (GBR) 7-5, 6-3

U.S. Championships

Men's Singles: Bill Tilden (USA) def. Bill Johnston (USA) 6-1, 1-6, 7-5, 5-7, 6-3

Women's Singles: Molla Bjurstedt Mallory (USA) def. Marion Zinderstein (USA) 6-3, 6-1

Men's Doubles: Bill Johnston (USA) and Clarence Griffin (USA) def. Willis Davis and Roland Roberts (USA), 6-2, 6-2, 6-3

Women's Doubles: Marion Zinderstein and Eleanor Goss (USA) def. Eleanor Tennant and Helen Baker (USA), 13-11, 4-6, 6-3

Mixed Doubles: Hazel Hotchkiss Wightman and Wallace Johnson (USA) def. Molla Bjurstedt Mallory and Craig Biddle (USA) 6-4, 6-3

Year-End No. 1

Men: Bill Tilden

Davis Cup: United States

1920 OLYMPICS, ANTWERP, BELGIUM

Men's Singles

GOLD: Louis Raymond (RSA)
SILVER: Ichiya Kumagae (JPN)
BRONZE: Charles Winslow (RSA)

Women's Singles

GOLD: Suzanne Lenglen (FRA)
SILVER: Dorothy Holman (GBR)
BRONZE: Kitty McKane (GBR)

Men's Doubles

GOLD: Noel Turnbull (RSA) and Max Woosnam (GBR)
SILVER: Seiichiro Kashio and Ichiya Kumagae (JPN)
BRONZE: Max Decugis and Pierre Albarran (FRA)

Women's Doubles

GOLD: Kitty McKane and Winifred McNair (GBR)
SILVER: Geraldine Beamish and Dorothy Holman (GBR)
BRONZE: Suzanne Lenglen and Elisabeth d'Ayen (FRA)

Mixed Doubles:

GOLD: Suzanne Lenglen and Max Decugis (FRA)
SILVER: Kitty McKane and Max Woosnam (GBR)
BRONZE: Milada Skrbkova and Ladislav "Razny" Zemla (CZE)

1921 Lenglen's Default To Mallory Causes Stir

Bill Tilden had a flair for the dramatic in 1921, coming from two sets down to win at Wimbledon and in Davis Cup.

"She probably did more for women's tennis than any girl who ever played it. She broke down barriers and created a vogue, reforming tennis dress, substituting acrobatics and something of the art of the ballet where decorum had been the rule. In England and on the Continent, this slim, not very pretty but fascinating French maiden was the most popular performer in sport or out of it on the post-war scene. She became the rage, almost a cult. Even royalty gave her its favor and she partnered King Gustav of Sweden in mixed doubles more than once."

Lenglen was beaten by the defending champion, Molla Mallory, in the second round of the first U.S. Championships at Forest Hills, six years prior to the advent of seeds. Lenglen lost the first set 6-2, seeming weak and nervous, coughing from time to time, causing some concern to those who had seen her play. Then, when she lost the first point of the second set and double-faulted to trail, 2-6, 0-30, she started weeping. She went to the umpire's chair and, speaking French, said she was too ill to continue. As she and the disappointed Mallory walked off the court, there was a faint hissing sound from the crowd of 8,000, the largest ever to witness a women's match in the United States.

S uzanne Lenglen, who hadn't lost a match to anyone since the end of the war, came to the United States for the first time and suffered the lone defeat of her life at the top—on a default. It was one of the most stunning results in tennis, and was long talked about and cited whenever Lenglen was discussed.

The position occupied by Lenglen at the time of the great default was described by the eminent tennis writer, Al Laney:

The newspapers reported Lenglen told the umpire that she was unable to breathe and that she coughed throughout the previous night. Others recalled her saying she did not feel like playing and had been listless in a practice session. If she was suffering from menstrual cramps, that was not mentioned because it was then a taboo subject in the public prints. It was also pointed out that she had arrived in the U.S. only four days before her first

scheduled match. Her opponent, Eleanor Goss, withdrew, so she did not have a warm-up before her match with Mallory.

Lenglen incurred criticism because she appeared at Forest Hills the next day in good spirits, continuing to attend parties. Despite her signs of physical distress in the match, it was not considered acceptable to default and there arose speculation about whether Lenglen could accept defeat, something with which she'd had no experience in singles since 1914. For some time the phrase pertaining to her—"to cough and quit— was in vogue in New York. In France, there were accusations of mistreatment by the Americans and the charge that her first-round opponent had purposely defaulted to help set up Lenglen for defeat.

Mallory went on to win the U.S. Championship, her sixth title, with a 4-6, 6-4, 6-2 victory in the final over Mary K. Browne. Lenglen had breezed to her third Wimbledon title with a 6-2, 6-0 victory over American Elizabeth Ryan,

Bill Tilden retained his Wimbledon crown, coming out of a sickbed to defend against South African Brian "Babe" Norton in the Challenge Round. Tilden won 4-6, 2-6, 6-1, 6-0, 7-5. It was the third successive five-setter for 21-year-old Norton, who on the way had defeated Frank Hunter, 6-0, 6-3, 5-7, 5-7, 6-2, and, in the all-comers final, Spaniard Manuel Alonso, 5-7, 4-6, 7-5, 6-3, 6-3. In the quarters, Japan's Zenzo Shimidzu, plus considerable champagne, took their toll on staggering Brit Randolph Lycett. Too many refreshing pauses for Lycett, who felt a sip in time might save his spine. Wobbling noticeably in the last stages, he was at least able—barely —to stagger to the distant finish line, the loser, 6-3, 9-11, 3-6, 6-2, 10-8. Alonso had a struggle with Shimidzu before winning 3-6, 7-5, 3-6, 6-4, 8-6.

In the wind-up, after losing the first two sets to Norton, Tilden gave up his normal hard-hitting game, took to chops and slices, and turned the match around. This displeased observers, who booed Tilden despite the remonstrations of the umpire that he was playing quite fairly and within the rules. Norton recovered in the last set, led 5-4 with two match points, but Tilden rallied to hold serve, and prevailed by serving an ace on his own match point. F. P. Adams wrote: "He is an artist, more of an artist than nine-tenths of the artists I know. It is the beauty of the game that Tilden loves; it is the chase always, rather than the quarry."

Still not fully recovered from his illness in England, Tilden registered one of his more difficult and dramatic victories in the 5-0 defense of the Davis Cup over unexpected opposition, Japan. Mighty mites in straw hats, unorthodox-stroking but quick, 5-foot-6 Shimidzu and Ichiya Kumagae had stunned favored Australasia in the semifinal at Newport, contortedly using the same racket face for forehands and backhands. Johnston opened with a swift 6-2, 6-4, 6-1 win over Kumagae, but the clever retriever, Shimidzu, took the first two sets and was within two points of beating Tilden with a 5-3, 30-15 lead in the third. Groping on a boiling 100-degree afternoon and hobbled by a boil on his foot, Tilden somehow reeled off four games to get through the set. A physician lanced the boil during the intermission, and Bill charged back to win the match, 5-7, 4-6, 7-5, 6-2, 6-1.

At the U.S. Championships, played at Tilden's home club, the Germantown Cricket Club, for a three-year period (1921-23), Tilden, through the luck of the unseeded draw, faced his fore-most foe and 1920 finalist Johnston in the fourth round, winning 4-6, 7-5, 6-4, 6-3. He didn't lose another set and one of his victims was Shimidzu, 6-4, 6-4, 6-1. Taking his second straight title in an all-Philadelphia final, he toned down chop-and-slice maestro Wallace Johnson, 6-1, 6-3, 6-1. Johnson had stopped Aussie J.O. Anderson 6-4, 3-6, 8-6, 6-3 in the semifinals.

Rice Gemmell won an uninspiring Australian Championship over Alf Hedemann, 7-5, 6-1, 6-4.

1921 CHAMPIONS AND LEADERS

Australian Championships
Men's Singles: Rice Gemmell (AUS) def. Alf Hedemann (AUS) 7-5, 6-1, 6-4
Men's Doubles: Stanley Eaton and Rice Gemmell (AUS) def. E. Stokes and N. Brearley, 7-5, 6-3, 6-3

Wimbledon
Men's Singles: Bill Tilden (USA) def. Brian Norton (RSA) 4-6, 2-6, 6-1, 6-0, 7-5.
Women's Singles: Suzanne Lenglen (FRA) def. Elizabeth Ryan (USA) 6-2, 6-0
Men's Doubles: Randolph Lycett and Max Woosnam (GBR) def. Arthur Lowe and Frank Lowe (GBR) 6-3, 6-0, 7-5
Women's Doubles: Suzanne Lenglen (FRA) and Elizabeth Ryan (USA) def. Ethel Thomson Larcombe and Dorothea Chambers (GBR), 6-1, 6-2
Mixed Doubles: Elizabeth Ryan (USA) and Randolph Lycett (AUS) def. Phyllis Howkins and Max Woosnam (GBR), 6-3, 6-1

U.S. Championships
Men's Singles: Bill Tilden (USA) def. Wallace Johnson (USA) 6-1, 6-3, 6-1
Women's Singles: Molla Bjurstedt Mallory (USA) def. Mary K. Browne (USA), 4-6, 6-4, 6-2
Men's Doubles: Bill Tilden and Vinnie Richards (USA) def. Dick Williams and Watson Washburn (USA), 13-11, 12-10, 6-1
Women's Doubles: Mary K. Browne and Louise Riddell Williams (USA) def. Helen Gilleaudeau and Aletta Bailey Morris (USA), 6-3, 6-2.
Mixed Doubles: Mary K. Browne and Bill Johnston (USA) def. Molla Bjurstedt Mallory and Bill Tilden (USA), 3-6, 6-4, 6-3.

Year-End No. 1
Men: Bill Tilden
Women: Suzanne Lenglen

Davis Cup: United States

A New Site For Wimbledon, Lenglen Avenges

Suzanne Lenglen of France (right) and **Molla Mallory** of the USA stand on court before their women's singles final match at Wimbledon.

Having outgrown the Worple Road Grounds in the London suburb of Wimbledon it had occupied since 1877, the All England Club moved to its present site in a picturesque hollow at the foot of Church Road near Wimbledon Common, at a construction cost of 140,000 pounds. King George V and Queen Mary attended the opening on June 22 at the new Centre Court holding 9,989 seats, with room for 3,600 standees—a total of 13,589 fans, although it was frequently crammed with more (the previous arena held 8,500). Present-day crowd control laws now limit Centre Court to 13,791 seats with no standing since 1990.

The royals saw the first match at the new facility, played by two of their subjects, with Algernon Kingscote beating Leslie Godfree 6-1, 6-3, 6-0.

Portents of the future? Rain fell every day of the tournament, which concluded on the third Wednesday. Showers delayed the debut of architect Stanley Peach's magnificent dodecagon, Centre Court, by an hour on the opening day. However, with the usual stiffened upper lip of nobility, King George struck a gong thrice at 3:45 p.m. and the Big W was on its frequently wet way into the future, and Centre Court, to its destiny as perhaps the planet's most renowned playpen. The first American to tread the hallowed-to-be sod of Centre Court was a Yale alumnus studying at Oxford, Amos Wilder (younger brother of noted playwright Thornton Wilder), who lost a doubles match with Frank Kingsley of Great Britain to eventual champs J.O. Anderson and Randolph Lycett, 6-2, 2-6, 6-1, 9-7. A first-round loser who would make his name in the game much later as daddy of the tie-breaker, was an American at Cambridge, Jimmy Van Alen, who fell to L.A. Meldon of Britain, 6-3, 6-4, 5-7, 6-2.

Wimbledon abolished the Challenge Round as Bill Tilden did not choose to make the Atlantic crossing to defend his title, won by Australia's Gerald Patterson, whom Tilden had dethroned in 1920. Patterson defeated Lycett (the champagne imbiber of 1921) in the final, 6-3, 6-4, 6-2. An Aussie trail to the final was made when Anderson beat Pat O'Hara Wood in the quarters, 6-3, 6-3, 2-6, 2-6, 6-4, then lost to Patterson, 6-1, 3-6, 7-9, 6-1, 6-3.

Suzanne Lenglen avenged her controversial default to Molla Mallory at Forest Hills the year before when she trounced Mallory in the Wimbledon final, 6-2, 6-0. Lenglen's appeal was such that before her first match, a 6-1, 7-5 decision over Britain's Kitty McKane, "a line stretched more than a mile and a half from the underground station to the entrance to the All England Club," wrote Wimbledon official Duncan Macaulay. "People used to call it the 'Lenglen trail a-winding' after the famous World War I song of those days ['a long, long trail...']." Lenglen won three Wimbledon titles for the second time, teaming with Aussie Pat O'Hara Wood to win the mixed doubles, over Elizabeth Ryan and Lycett, 6-4, 6-3, and, with Ryan, the doubles over McKane and her sister, Margaret McKane Stocks, 6-0, 6-4.

After her loss to Lenglen at Wimbledon, Mallory, 38, returned to Forest Hills to win her seventh U.S. title, defeating 16-year-old Helen Wills in the final, 6-3, 6-1. It was the greatest disparity in ages for any major final.

The meeting between perennial rivals Bill Tilden and Bill Johnston in the U.S. Championships at the Germantown Cricket Club was called "a match for the Greek gods." They played for a coveted championship bowl, which each had won twice and which would be retired permanently by any three-time winner. Tilden advanced to the final by beating Wimbledon champion Gerald Patterson 4-6, 6-4, 6-3, 6-1, while Johnston defeated a promising newcomer, 19-year-old Vinnie Richards, 8-6, 6-2, 6-1. Tilden lost the first two sets to Little Bill, then came back to win, 4-6, 3-6, 6-2, 6-3, 6-4. The trophy gained by Tilden had on it the names of such previous winners as William Larned, Lindley Murray, Maurice McLoughlin, Dick Williams and Johnston.

In the Davis Cup, Australasia advanced past Spain to the Challenge Round, only to be beaten by the United States 4-1 at Forest Hills. In those days of unusual interest in Davis Cup, something of a stir was created by the loss of the doubles by Tilden and Richards to Patterson and Pat O'Hara Wood, 6-4, 6-0, 6-3. Bill and Vinnie had joined forces for the first time in 1918 to win the U.S. title. But if their reunion was disappointing, Johnston soon destroyed the Aussies' faint hopes with the decisive point, a 6-2, 6-2, 6-1 flattening of Patterson, who had been beaten by Big Bill on the first day, 7-5, 10-8, 6-0.

Patterson also fell in his own national championship to J.O. Anderson, 6-0, 3-6, 3-6, 6-3, 6-2. It was time for an Australian championship for the women, too, the inaugural won, by 27-year-old Margaret "Mall" Mutch Molesworth over Esna Boyd, 6-3, 10-8.

1922 CHAMPIONS AND LEADERS

Australian Championships

Men's Singles: James Anderson (AUS) def. Gerald Patterson (AUS) 6-0, 3-6, 3-6, 6-3,6-2

Women's Singles: Mall Molesworth (AUS) def. Esna Boyd (AUS) 6-3, 10-8

Men's Doubles: Jack Hawkes and Gerald Patterson (AUS) def. James Anderson and Norman Peach (AUS), 8-10, 6-0, 6-0, 7-5

Women's Doubles: Esna Boyd and Marjorie Mountain (AUS) def. Floris St. George and Lorna Utz (AUS), 1-6, 6-4, 7-5

Mixed Doubles: Esna Boyd and Jack Hawkes (AUS) def. Gwendolyn Chiplin and Harold Utz (AUS), 6-1, 6-1

Wimbledon

Men's Singles: Gerald Patterson (AUS) def. Randolph Lycett (AUS), 6-3, 6-4, 6-2

Women's Singles: Suzanne Lenglen (FRA) def. Molla Bjurstedt Mallory (USA), 6-2, 6-0

Men's Doubles: James Anderson (AUS) and Randolph Lycett (GBR) def. Gerald Patterson and Pat O'Hara Wood (AUS) 3-6, 7-9, 6-4, 6-3, 11-9

Women's Doubles: Suzanne Lenglen (FRA) and Elizabeth Ryan (USA) def. Kitty McKane and Margaret McKane Stocks (GBR), 6-0, 6-4

Mixed Doubles: Suzanne Lenglen (FRA) and Pat O'Hara Wood (AUS) def. Elizabeth Ryan (USA) and Randolph Lycett (GBR), 6-4, 6-3

U.S. Championships

Men's Singles: Bill Tilden (USA) def. Bill Johnston (USA) 4-6, 3-6, 6-2, 6-3, 6-4

Women's Singles; Molla Bjurstedt Mallory (USA) def. Helen Wills (USA) 6-3, 6-1

Men's Doubles: Bill Tilden and Vinnie Richards (USA) def. Gerald Patterson and Pat O'Hara Wood (AUS), 4-6, 6-1, 6-3, 6-4

Women's Doubles: Marion Zinderstein Jessup and Helen Wills (USA), def. Edith Sigourney (USA) and Molla Bjurstedt Mallory (USA), 6-4, 7-9, 6-3

Mixed Doubles: Molla Bjurstedt Mallory and Bill Tilden (USA) def. Helen Wills and Howard Kinsey (USA), 6-4, 6-3

Year-End No. 1

Men: Bill Tilden
Women: Suzanne Lenglen

Davis Cup: United States

1923 Wightman Cup Christens New Stadium at Forest Hills

American tennis players (left to right) **Helen Wills**, **Molla Mallory** and **Hazel Wightman**, founder of the Wightman Cup, with the trophy and two British players.

A new stadium was constructed at the West Side Tennis Club grounds in Forest Hills, but the men's U.S. Championships wouldn't return from Philadelphia until 1924. Built at a cost of $250,000, the concrete horseshoe that would eventually seat 14,000 opened on August 10 with the inauguration of the Wightman Cup matches.

The competition was the brainchild of Hazel Hotchkiss Wightman, a champion in pre-World War I days who would compete until she was past 70, winning the last of her 45 U.S. titles (senior doubles) at the age of 67. She had conceived the idea of a women's competition equivalent to the Davis Cup in 1920 and donated a silver vase. But the idea lay fallow until seized upon by Julian Myrick, a U.S. Lawn Tennis Association official, as a way of launching the new Forest Hills stadium.

The competition between Great Britain and the United States consisted of five singles matches and two doubles, and though Wightman hoped to make it an international tournament by bringing in France, that never came to pass. With Wightman as captain, the U.S. team of Molla Mallory, Helen Wills and Eleanor Goss scored a 7-0 sweep, starting with the baptismal match before 5,000 fans who watched Wills beat Kitty McKane, 6-2, 7-5.

Wills won the first of her seven U.S. titles, unseating Mallory, 6-2, 6-1, severing Molla's 22-match U.S. Championships streak. Mal-

lory thus had won 40 of 42 matches, beginning with her first title campaign of 1915. Suzanne Lenglen breezed through the Wimbledon field for the fifth straight year, yielding only 11 games in the 12 sets she played, defeating McKane in the final, 6-2, 6-2. She won the doubles again with Elizabeth Ryan, 6-3, 6-1, over Joan Austin and Evelyn Colyer of Great Britain.

With Bill Tilden, universally regarded as the kingpin of tennis, absent again from Wimbledon, the Other Bill—Johnston—won for the only time. In straight sets, he swept past countryman Vinnie Richards, 6-4, 6-3, 9-7, South African Brian Norton, 6-4, 6-2, 6-4, and then another Yank, Frank Hunter, in a 45-minute final, 6-0, 6-3, 6-1. Johnston's success at Wimbledon would not carry over to the U.S. Championships, where he was crushed by Tilden in the final, 6-4, 6-1, 6-4.

Pat O'Hara Wood won the Australian title, 6-1, 6-1, 6-3, over a marvelous, extraordinary athlete, one-handed Bert St. John, a lefty. A losing finalist in the 1915 doubles, St. John was also a star cricketer and soccer player for Queensland, the lone major finalist crippled by the loss of a hand. Thus, Pat put an O'Hara Wood duo in a select cast of brothers—three sets of them— who've won major singles titles. His older sibling (by a year), Dr. Arthur O'Hara Wood, won the Aussie in 1914 over Gerald Patterson, 6-4, 6-3, 5-7, 6-1, then went off to World War I - and death - when his Royal Air Force plane was shot down in France a month prior to the Armistice in 1918. Prior to the O'Hara Wood successes, Englishmen Willie (seven times) and Ernest Renshaw (once), and Laurie (five) and Reggie Doherty (four) were Wimbledon champs.

Mall Molesworth retained her Aussie title, again beating Esna Boyd, 6-1, 7-5.

In a Davis Cup field increased to 17 entries from 11, Australasia beat France to challenge the U.S. The U.S. won 4-1 at Forest Hills, although it went into the third day because speedy J.O. Anderson, called "Greyhound" by his mates, shocked Bill Johnston in the opener, 4-6, 6-2, 2-6, 7-5, 6-2. Tilden tied it briskly over lefty Jack Hawkes, 6-4, 6-2, 6-1, and he and playing captain Dick Williams surged ahead in a suspenseful win over Anderson and Hawkes, 17-15, 11-13, 2-6, 6-3, 6-2 – the 32-game first set tying the record for the longest doubles set in a Cup finale. Johnston then made up for his first-day stumble, and solidified the American hold on the Cup for a fourth successive year by blasting Hawkes, 6-0, 6-2, 6-1. Tilden then beat Anderson, 6-2, 6-3, 1-6, 7-5 in the meaningless fifth rubber.

It is difficult today to appreciate how significant the Davis Cup used to be before Open tennis. Prior to 1968, there were no prize-money tournaments, fewer inducements in a schedule that has now grown to world-wide and practically 12-month proportions. Today's players often choose to skip the high-pressure, nationalistic Cup to conserve themselves for chasing big money and computer points (even though prize money and generous guarantees have become part of the Cup deal). After World War I, an atmosphere of international good fellowship took hold and the Davis Cup acquired tremendous significance, partly because of the U.S. dominance of the competition. It was front-page news then and controversies such as Tilden's threats to quit were looked upon as almost national calamities.

1923 CHAMPIONS AND LEADERS

Australian Championships
Men's Singles: Pat O'Hara Wood (AUS) def. Bert St. John (AUS), 6-1, 6-1, 6-3
Women's Singles: Mall Molesworth (AUS) def. Esna Boyd (AUS), 6-1, 7-5
Men's Doubles: Pat O'Hara Wood and Bert St. John (AUS) def. Dudley Bullough and Horrie Rice (AUS), 6-4, 6-3, 3-6, 6-0
Women's Doubles: Esna Boyd and Sylvia Lance (AUS) def. Mall Molesworth and H. Turner (AUS), 6-1, 6-4
Mixed Doubles: Sylvia Lance and Horrie Rice (AUS) def. Mall Molesworth and Bert St. John (AUS), 2-6, 6-4, 6-4

Wimbledon
Men's Singles: Bill Johnston (USA) def. Frank Hunter (USA), 6-0, 6-3, 6-1
Women's Singles: Suzanne Lenglen (FRA) def. Kitty McKane (GBR), 6-2, 6-2
Men's Doubles: Leslie Godfree (GBR) and Randolph Lycett (GBR) def. Manuel de Gormar and Eduardo Flaquer (ESP), 6-3, 6-4, 3-6, 6-3
Women's Doubles: Suzanne Lenglen (FRA) and Elizabeth Ryan (USA) def. Joan Austin and Evelyn Colyer (GBR), 6-3, 6-1
Mixed Doubles: Elizabeth Ryan (USA) and Randolph Lycett (GBR), def. Dorothy Shepherd Barron and Leslie Godfree (GBR) 6-4, 7-5

U.S. Championships
Men's Singles: Bill Tilden (USA) def. Bill Johnston (USA), 6-4, 6-1, 6-4
Women's Singles: Helen Wills (USA) def. Molla Bjurstedt Mallory (USA), 6-2, 6-1
Men's Doubles: Bill Tilden (USA) and Brian Norton (RSA) def. Dick Williams and Watson Washburn (USA), 3-6, 6-2, 6-3, 5-7, 6-2
Women's Doubles: Kitty McKane and Phyllis Howkins Covell (GBR) def. Hazel Hotchkiss Wightman and Eleanor Goss (USA), 2-6, 6-2, 6-1
Mixed Doubles: Molla Bjurstedt Mallory and Bill Tilden (USA) def. Kitty McKane (GBR) and Jack Hawkes (AUS), 6-3, 2-6, 10-8

Year-End No. 1
Men: Bill Tilden
Women: Suzanne Lenglen

Davis Cup: United States

Wightman Cup: United States

1924 Tennis Gains A French Accent

Jean Borotra, the "Bounding Basque," ushered in an era of French dominance by winning Wimbledon.

In the latter part of the 1920s, when the French would dominate men's tennis, each of the three great Frenchmen won two Wimbledon singles championships, beginning with the 1924 all-French final at the All England Club in which 25-year-old Jean Borotra defeated 19-year-old Rene Lacoste, 6-1, 3-6, 6-1, 3-6, 6-4.

Borotra, the colorful "Bounding Basque" who wore a beret while playing, and Lacoste, the "Crocodile," were two of the Four Musketeers, along with 22-year-old Henri "The Ballboy of Lyon" Cochet and 29-year-old Jacques "Toto" Brugnon, who was essentially a doubles specialist. Wimbledon Secretary Duncan Macaulay wrote in *Behind the Scenes at Wimbledon*: "They were all very different in style and temperament, and they sometimes clashed bitterly with one another on the courts. But whenever they felt they were playing for France ... they always put France first. Thus it was the combined pressure of Lacoste and Cochet which began to rock the great Bill Tilden on his pedestal, and finally toppled him off it."

Norman Brookes, the 47-year-old Australian immortal who had first played at Wimbledon 20 years before, highlighted early play by upsetting Frank Hunter, finalist the previous year and ranked No. 5 in the world, in the third round, 3-6, 6-3, 6-4, 5-7, 6-3.

Suzanne Lenglen, a five-time winner at Wimbledon weakened by an attack of jaundice earlier in the year, was forced to drop out after winning a quarterfinal over American Elizabeth Ryan in three tough sets, 6-2, 6-8, 6-4. It was the first singles set

Lenglen lost—except the great default to Molla Mallory at Forest Hills in 1921—since 1919. Britain's Kitty McKane got a walkover from her in the semifinals and then defeated Helen Wills in the final, 4-6, 6-4, 6-4 after trailing 1-4 in the second, and facing four break points to trail 1-5. It was Helen's lone loss in 56 Wimbledon matches. Years later, asked what happened—how could unbendable Helen allow such a lead to disappear?—she was forthright: "Something happened to me that had never happened before. I lost my concentration. But I never let that happen again." Apparently not. She would win her next 50 matches at Wimbledon—the longest streak, male or female, at any major—and a record eight titles, a mark broken by Martina Navratilova's ninth in 1990.

Kitty and Helen had met only a few days earlier in the Wightman Cup at Wimbledon. McKane won, 6-2, 6-2, after beating Molla Mallory, 6-3, 6-3. The British evened the series at 1-1, winning the competition 6-1. The only U.S. point came on a doubles triumph by Wills and the Cup's namesake, 37-year-old Hazel Hotchkiss Wightman, over McKane and Evelyn Colyer, 2-6, 6-2, 6-4. Eighteen-year-old Wills won her second successive U.S. title, defeating Mallory again, 6-1, 6-3.

Tilden, increasingly at odds with the tennis establishment, sent a letter of resignation to the U.S. Lawn Tennis Association, bowing out of the Davis Cup because of a proposed ban on his writing for newspapers about tennis. That was in conflict with amateur rules. The threat of not having Tilden's gate appeal in the Davis Cup competition forced tennis administrators to cave in. Tilden plus Bill Johnston and 21-year-old singles rookie Vinnie Richards swept the Australian team of Gerald Patterson and Pat O'Hara Wood, 5-0 in Tilden's Philly neighborhood, the Germantown Cricket Club. Neither Tilden nor Richards lost a set, and the re-issue of the double-valued Bills of 1920 triumphs—Tilden and Johnston co-habiting the court—took care of the sealing point in a fifth straight Cup, 5-7, 6-3, 6-4, 6-1, over O'Hara Wood and Patterson. Tilden led off, 6-4, 6-2, 6-2, over Patterson, followed by Richards's stunning of O'Hara Wood, 6-3, 6-2, 6-4.

Underdog rooters hopeful that Little Bill would break Big Bill's spell over him had reason to believe that Johnston would crash through in the U.S. Championships. Tilden's feud with the USLTA and the increased time he was devoting to a hopeful-but-doomed-by-critics theatrical career led to charges that he was out of shape. He came to the final with a desultory five-set semifinal victory over Richards, 4-6, 6-2, 8-6, 4-6, 6-4, while Johnston routed Patterson, 6-2, 6-0, 6-0. In the final, however, Tilden crushed Johnston, 6-1, 9-7, 6-2 in a stirring display that tennis savant Al Laney later called, "Tilden at his absolute peak, and I have not since seen the like of it." Patterson said: "Tilden is the only player in the world—the rest of us are second-graders."

In Australia, the men's championship was won by J.O. Anderson over Bob Schlesinger, 6-3, 6-4, 3-6, 5-7, 6-3, the second of his three titles. Sylvia Lance was the women's champ. Runner-up Esna Boyd, who was making a bad habit of it, lost her third consecutive final, this time 6-3, 3-6, 8-6.

1924 CHAMPIONS AND LEADERS

Australian Championships

Men's Singles: James Anderson (AUS) def. Bob Schlesinger (AUS), 6-3, 6-4, 3-6, 5-7, 6-3

Women's Singles: Sylvia Lance (AUS) def. Esna Boyd (AUS), 6-3, 3-6, 6-4.

Men's Doubles: James Anderson and Norman Brookes (AUS) def. Gerald Patterson and Pat O'Hara Wood (AUS) 6-2, 6-4, 6-3

Women's Doubles: Daphne Akhurst and Sylvia Lance (AUS) def. Katherine LeMesurier and Meryl O'Hara Wood (AUS), 7-5, 6-2

Mixed Doubles: Daphne Akhurst and John Willard (AUS) def. Esna Boyd and Gar Hone (AUS), 6-3, 6-4

Wimbledon

Men's Singles: Jean Borotra (FRA) def. Rene Lacoste (FRA), 6-1, 3-6, 6-1, 3-6, 6-4

Women's Singles: Kitty McKane (GBR) def. Helen Wills (USA), 4-6, 6-4, 6-4

Men's Doubles: Frank Hunter and Vinnie Richards (USA) def. Dick Williams and Watson Washburn (USA), 6-3, 3-6, 8-10, 8-6, 6-3

Women's Doubles: Hazel Hotchkiss Wightman and Helen Wills (USA) def. Kitty McKane and Phyllis Howkins Covell (GBR), 6-4, 6-4

Mixed Doubles: Kitty McKane and Brian Gilbert (GBR) def. Dorothy Shepherd and Leslie Godfree (GBR), 6-3, 3-6, 6-3

U.S. Championships

Men's Singles: Bill Tilden (USA) def. Bill Johnston (USA), 6-1, 9-7, 6-2

Women's Singles: Helen Wills (USA) def. Molla Bjurstedt Mallory (USA) 6-1, 6-3

Men's Doubles: Howard Kinsey and Robert Kinsey (USA) def. Gerald Patterson and Pat O'Hara Wood (AUS) 7-5, 5-7, 7-9, 6-3, 6-4

Women's Doubles: Hazel Hotchkiss Wightman and Helen Wills (USA) def. Eleanor Goss and Marion Zinderstein Jessup (USA), 6-4, 6-3

Mixed Doubles: Helen Wills and Vinnie Richards (USA) def. Molla Bjurstedt Mallory and Bill Tilden (USA), 6-8, 7-5, 6-0

Year-End No. 1

Men: Bill Tilden
Women: Suzanne Lenglen

Davis Cup: United States

Wightman Cup: Great Britain

1924 OLYMPIC GAMES—PARIS, FRANCE

Men's Singles

GOLD: Vinnie Richards (USA)
SILVER: Henri Cochet (FRA)
BRONZE: Umberto Luigi de Morpurgo (ITA)

Women's Singles

GOLD: Helen Wills (USA)
SILVER: Didi Vlasto (FRA)
BRONZE: Kitty McKane (GBR)

Men's Doubles

GOLD: Frank Hunter and Vinnie Richards (USA)
SILVER: Jacques Brugnon and Henri Cochet (FRA)
BRONZE: Jean Borotra and Rene Lacoste (FRA)

Women's Doubles

GOLD: Hazel Hotchkiss Wightman and Helen Wills (USA)
SILVER: Kitty McKane and Phyllis Howkins Covell (GBR)
BRONZE: Dorothy Sheperd-Barron and Evelyn Colyer (GBR)

Mixed Doubles

GOLD: Hazel Hotchkiss Wightman and Dick Williams (USA)
SILVER: Marion Zinderstein Jessup and Vinnie Richards (USA)
BRONZE: Hendrik Timmer and Cornelia Bouman (NED)

1925 Lenglen, Lacoste A Dynamic Duo

The French dominated Wimbledon as it had never been dominated before, scoring almost a clean sweep of the championships, winning the men's singles and doubles, the mixed doubles and women's singles—and half of the women's doubles. Suzanne Lenglen, reaching the zenith of her career, lost only five games in sweeping through five opponents. She scored a 6-0, 6-0 semifinal triumph over defending champion Kitty McKane, who had won the title when Lenglen was incapacitated the previous year by jaundice, and defeated another Englishwoman, Joan Fry, in the

Rene Lacoste and **Suzanne Lenglen** won at both the French Championships and at Wimbledon.

final, 6-2, 6-0. In fact, in the three rounds prior to the final, she double-bageled in succession three of the world's leading women: Elizabeth Ryan, Winifred Ramsey Beamish and McKane. Lenglen combined with American Ryan to win the women's doubles for the sixth time over Katherine Bridge and Mary McIlquham, 6-2,

6-2, and made her third "Big W" triple crown (the others, 1920, 1922) by winning the mixed doubles with Jean Borotra over Ryan and Umberto de Morpurgo of Italy 6-3, 6-3.

The men's final was a rematch of 1924—this time reversed by 20-year-old Rene Lacoste, who scored a 6-3, 6-3, 4-6, 8-6 victory over net-rushing Borotra, who was troubled by numerous foot-fault calls. Rene was the greenest Wimbledon champ since 19-year-old Wilfred Baddeley in 1891. In the quarterfinals, Henri Cochet began to gain a Tilden-like reputation for comebacks, losing the first two sets to American John Hennessey, then sweeping the last three to win 7-9, 4-6, 6-1, 6-3, 6-0, before losing to Borotra, 5-7, 8-6, 6-4, 6-1 in their semifinal.

In the first year the French Championships was opened to players from all countries, Lacoste triumphed over Borotra, 7-5, 6-1, 6-4, while Lenglen quickly beat McKane, 6-1, 6-2.

James Anderson won his third Australian title, 11-9, 2-6, 6-2, 6-3 in the final over Gerald Patterson, who served 29 aces and 29 double faults. Daphne Akhurst, for whom the championship cup was eventually named, won the first of her five Australian titles, and Esna Boyd swallowed her fourth successive final-round loss 1-6, 8-6, 6-4.

Bill Tilden achieved the distinction of winning 57 straight games during a two-tournament stretch over the summer. The stage was set for another Big Bill-Little Bill confrontation in the U.S. final at Forest Hills. In the semifinals, Tilden beat Vinnie Richards, 6-8, 6-4, 6-4, 6-1 and Johnston sidelined Dick Williams 7-5, 6-3, 6-2. Despite an injured shoulder, which prevented him from holding barely half his service games in a long, five-set match, Tilden defeated Johnston, 4-6, 11-9, 6-3, 4-6, 6-3.

Johnston said immediately afterward: "I can't beat him; I can't beat the son of a bitch, I can't beat him." It was the last of Tilden's six straight U.S. titles and the last time he and Johnston would play for it. Tilden, like most tennis people, admired Johnston greatly, and after Johnston's premature death from tuberculosis in 1946, dedicated his memoirs to Little Bill.

The French made their first breakthrough into the Davis Cup Challenge Round and lost 5-0 at Philadelphia's Germantown Cricket Club, in what was nonetheless a difficult series for the Cup-holders. Though the Musketeers—Lacoste and Borotra in singles and doubles—were swept by Tilden and Johnston in singles and Dick Williams and Vinnie Richards in doubles, both Frenchmen extended Tilden to five sets. Borotra, leading off, came within two points of shocking Tilden and the U.S. at the outset, serving for victory at 6-5 in the fourth set (and leading 2-0 in the fifth). But Big Bill called on all his wiles to win, 4-6, 6-0, 2-6, 9-7, 6-4. Then Johnston quelled Lacoste, 6-1, 6-1, 6-8, 6-3. On the second day, the outcome was decided by Richards and playing-captain Williams, who defeated Borotra and Lacoste, 6-4, 6-4, 6-3. Later, Tilden had to save four match points to beat Lacoste, 3-6, 10-12, 8-6, 7-5, 6-2—65 games, the longest of all the master's 30 Cup singles.

Helen Wills won her third straight U.S. Championship final, defeating Kitty McKane of Great Britain, 3-6, 6-0, 6-2. Wills won both her Wightman Cup matches at Forest Hills, 6-0, 7-5, over Joan Fry and a 6-1, 1-6, 9-7, struggle over McKane. However, it was to no avail as Great Britain won the Cup for the second straight year,

4-3. Dorothea Douglass Chambers was the difference, shortly before her 47th birthday. She won her singles match over No. 5 American Eleanor Goss, 7-5, 3-6, 6-1, and, yoked to Ermyntrude Harvey, won the doubles, 10-8, 6-1, from antiques Molla Mallory, 41, and May Sutton Bundy, almost 38 and a bygone antagonist of Chambers in the Wimbledon finals of 1905-06-07. That made it 3-3, whereupon McKane and Evelyn Colyer plucked the victory, 6-0, 6-3, over Wills and 34-year-old Mary K. Browne.

1925 CHAMPIONS AND LEADERS

Australian Championships
Men's Singles: James Anderson (AUS) def. Gerald Patterson (AUS), 11-9, 2-6, 6-2, 6-3

Women's Singles: Daphne Akhurst (AUS) def. Esna Boyd (AUS), 1-6, 8-6, 6-4

Men's Doubles: Pat O'Hara Wood and Gerald Patterson (AUS) def. James Anderson and Fred Kalmus (AUS), 6-4, 8-6, 7-5

Women's Doubles: Sylvia Lance Harper and Daphne Akhurst (AUS) def. Esna Boyd and Katherine LeMesurier (AUS), 6-4, 6-3

Mixed Doubles: Daphne Akhurst and John Willard (AUS) def. Esna Boyd and Katherine LeMesurier (AUS) 6-4, 6-3

French Championships
Men's Singles: Rene Lacoste (FRA) def. Jean Borotra (FRA), 7-5, 6-1, 6-4

Women's Singles: Suzanne Lenglen (FRA) def. Kitty McKane (GBR), 6-1, 6-2

Men's Doubles: Jean Borotra and Rene Lacoste (FRA) def. Henri Cochet and Jacques Brugnon (FRA), 7-5, 4-6, 6-3, 2-6, 6-3

Women's Doubles: Suzanne Lenglen and Didi Vlasto (FRA) def. Evelyn Colyer and Kitty McKane (GBR), 6-1, 9-11, 6-2

Mixed Doubles: Suzanne Lenglen and Jacques Brugnon (FRA) def. Didi Vlasto and Henri Cochet (FRA), 6-2, 6-2

Wimbledon
Men's Singles: Rene Lacoste (FRA) def. Jean Borotra (FRA), 6-3, 6-3, 4-6, 8-6

Women's Singles: Suzanne Lenglen (FRA) def. Joan Fry (GBR), 6-3, 6-0

Men's Doubles: Jean Borotra and Rene Lacoste (FRA) def. John Hennessey and Ray Casey (USA), 6-4, 11-9, 4-6, 1-6, 6-3

Women's Doubles: Suzanne Lenglen (FRA) and Elizabeth Ryan (USA) def. Kathleen Lidderdale Bridge and Mary Hart McIlquham (GBR), 6-2, 6-2

Mixed Doubles: Suzanne Lenglen and Jean Borotra (FRA) def. Elizabeth Ryan (USA) and Umberto de Morpurgo (ITA), 6-3, 6-3.

U.S. Championships
Men's Singles: Bill Tilden (USA) def. Bill Johnston (USA), 4-16, 11-9, 6-3, 4-6, 6-3

Women's Singles: Helen Wills (USA) def. Kitty McKane (GBR) 3-6, 6-0, 6-2

Men's Doubles: Dick Williams and Vinnie Richards (USA) def. Gerald Patterson and Jack Hawkes (AUS), 6-2, 8-10, 6-4, 11-9

Women's Doubles: Mary K. Browne and Helen Wills (USA) def. May Sutton Bundy and Elizabeth Ryan (USA), 6-4, 6-3

Mixed Doubles: Kitty McKane (GBR) and Jack Hawkes (AUS), def. Ermyntrude Harvey (GBR) and Vinnie Richards (USA), 6-2, 6-4.

Year-End No. 1
Men: Bill Tilden
Women: Suzanne Lenglen

Davis Cup: United States

Wightman Cup: Great Britain

1926 Lenglen Beats Wills in Historic Cannes Showdown

Suzanne Lenglen beat Helen Wills in Cannes in a match for the ages.

Suzanne Lenglen and Helen Wills met in springtime on the French Riviera in what would be the only confrontation between the two all-time greats—and one of the most hyped sporting events ever. It was front page stuff all the way. One writer called it "the most important sporting event of modern times exclusively in the hands of the fair sex"—this almost five decades before Margaret Smith Court and Billie Jean King both met Bobby Riggs.

Wills took off early in the year for a trip to southern France to participate in invitational tournaments and what some observers regarded as a chance for a showdown with Lenglen. "This girl must be mad," Lenglen told a close friend. "Does she think she can come and beat me on my home court?"

Chaotic and dramatic was the scene as they collided in the final of the normally insignificant Carlton Club tournament at Cannes, which was a magnet for press from around the globe. Ticket scalpers abounded, getting as much as $60, then a princely sum. Carpenters barely completed auxiliary stands before the first serve. Those shut out at the gate commandeered ladders, rooftops and trees for a glimpse of the two goddesses of the game, squaring off in the limited arena crammed with about 3,000 witnesses. Lenglen won, 6-3, 8-6, in 63 minutes, though given a fright, pushed as never before or after, falling apart in tears after Wills erred on a fourth match point.

Confusion took over as Lenglen served at double-match point, 6-5, 40-15, and a spectator called "Out!" though a Wills forehand sped along the line for a winner. Thinking she'd won, Lenglen relaxed, basking in the cheers of compatriots who, prematurely, felt she'd turned back the California invader. However, the no-nonsense Wimbledonian umpire George Hillyard restored order after ascertaining that Wills' shot was good. Play resumed. Frazzled, Lenglen lost serve to 6-6. Then she turned on her greatness again, perhaps for the last time, and seized the remaining two furiously contested games, both going to deuce twice. "She's terrific," lauded Wills. "It was one of my greatest matches."

It was Wimbledon's Jubilee Year—the 50th year celebration—presided over by King George V and Queen Mary bestowing medals on champions. Among the decorated was the elder, the original lobster P. Frank Hadow, 71, whose sky balls in 1878 unseated the short-reigned inaugural champ, Spencer Gore of 1877. Also honored was Maud Watson, 61, who started the women's regal line by winning in 1884.

Marring the festivities was the unexpected demise of Lenglen's brilliant amateur career, coming to a sad end amid controversy at Wimbledon when she failed to show up on time for a women's doubles match at which the King and Queen were present. Due to a mix-up after a scheduling change, Lenglen arrived at Centre Court after the Royal Couple had departed. This drew a reprimand and she became hysterical and never quite recovered, though the officials agreed to postpone her match. Meeting hostility from the crowds and the press, Lenglen, with compatriot Didi Vlasto, were upended 3-6, 9-7, 6-2, by the eventual champs, Elizabeth Ryan and Mary K. Browne. It was Suzanne's solitary doubles defeat in 30 such matches at the Big W where her overall record was 90-3 (32-0 in singles, 29-2 in mixed). She won her first two singles matches– 6-2, 6-3 over Mary K. Browne, the 35-year-old ex-U.S. champ and her foil-to-be on the subsequent pro tour—and 6-2, 6-2 over Mrs. G.J. Dewhurst of Britain. She also won a mixed doubles match with Borotra over Miss B.C. Brown and H.I.P. Aitken, both of Britain, 6-3, 6-0, and those were her last matches as an amateur. She withdrew, never to play another amateur tournament.

Signing on as the first touring pro with American promoter Charles C. "Cash and Carry" Pyle, Suzanne went on a North American tour, winning nightly (36-0) over Browne. Unable to entice the Bills, Johnston and Tilden, to turn pro, even with big bills, Pyle settled for the next best American, Vinnie Richards, just 23. He completed the Lenglen troupe with Americans Howard Kinsey

and Harvey Snodgrass, Frenchman Paul Feret and Browne, the original cast of barnstorming pros to make their way across the land on one-night stands.

After debuting at New York's Madison Square Garden on October 9, where they drew 13,000 fans and grossed $40,000, they traveled the U.S. and into Canada by train. Lasting four months over the winter of 1926-27, the tour was a success. It was reported that Lenglen was paid a $25,000 bonus beyond her $50,000 guarantee, and that Pyle, who had no interest in tennis as such, made about $80,000 while putting pro tennis into operation, and went off to other interests. Lenglen, barred from the significant tourneys as a pro, retired from competition and did some coaching until her death in 1938. She had traveled the pro tour like an empress: private railway car, chef, maid, press agent and lover, Baldwin Baldwin, a wealthy strangely-named American.

With Lenglen out, the Wimbledon title was won by Great Britain's Kitty McKane Godfree, who beat Lili de Alvarez of Spain, 6-2, 4-6, 6-3, despite lagging 1-3 and a point from 1-4 in the third. The U.S. title, which had been the property of Helen Wills, was opened to others when she was sidelined after an appendectomy. Molla Mallory came back to the winner's circle, seizing the championship for a record eighth time in her record 10th final. Molla was 42, the oldest of all major singles champs. The sentimental favorite of the crowd, she defeated 34-year-old Elizabeth (Bunny) Ryan, 4-6, 6-4, 9-7, after trailing 4-0 in the third set and saving a match point. It was the most elderly of major title bouts.

The six-year reign of Bill Tilden ended in the U.S. Championships when he was eliminated in the quarterfinals by Henri Cochet, 6-8, 6-1, 6-3, 1-6, 8-6. This stopped Tilden's record U.S. run at 42 matches.

In many ways, Tilden came to be more popular in defeat than he had been as the kingpin of the sport. Allison Danzig wrote of the Tilden-Cochet match: "The climax of the match, the point at which the gallery broke into the wildest demonstrations, was during the final set when Tilden, trailing at 1-4, rallied to volley Cochet dizzy with one of the most sensational exhibitions he ever gave at the net and pull up to 4-all. Every winning shot of the American was greeted with roars and wild applause. Tilden, 33, then led, 15-40, on Cochet's serve, but fell back."

Bill Johnston also lost in the same round, to Jean Borotra in five sets, 3-6, 4-6, 6-3, 6-4, 6-4. Borotra advanced to make it the first all-foreigners U.S. final by eliminating Richards, 3-6, 6-4, 4-6, 8-6, 6-2. Rene Lacoste eliminated Cochet in the semifinals, patiently getting into the groove, 2-6, 4-6, 6-4, 6-4, 6-3, and then defeated volley specialist Borotra for the title, 6-4, 6-0, 6-4.

It was the first U.S. final since 1917 without Tilden, the first time since 1920 he didn't win, and the first of three years in which Forest Hills and Wimbledon would be swept by the French.

Although Lacoste was ill and unable to defend his title at the All England Club, a third straight all-French final was the Wimbledon prospect as Borotra eluded a set point in the second while squeezing past Cochet, 2-6, 7-5, 2-6, 6-3, 7-5 in one semifinal. Jacques Brugnon held five match points in the fifth set against Howard Kinsey in the other semifinal, but the American escaped, 6-4, 4-6, 6-3, 3-6, 9-7. In the final, Borotra's volleys overcame Kinsey's

defense and clever lobs with the Frenchman prevailing 8-6, 6-1, 6-3. Kinsey carried on to make a rare "cripple," losing the doubles and mixed finals as well, with Vinnie Richards to Brugnon and Cochet 7-5, 4-6, 6-3, 6-2, and Mary K. Browne, to the only wife-husband victors, Kitty and Leslie Godfree, 6-3, 6-4. It was a last splash for Howard before turning pro with the Lenglen tour.

Uncommon attention focused on a men's doubles first-rounder as the left-handed 31-year-old Duke of York (later King George VI) played alongside Louis Grieg. Perhaps it was the aura of the Jubilee that lured the ill-advised Duke. He and Grieg were soundly beaten, 6-1, 6-3, 6-2, by a couple of commoners, old crocks and ex-champs, Herbert Roper Barrett, 52, and Arthur Gore, 58. (Was the draw rigged to give His Royal Highness a sporting chance?) He looked His Royal Hackerness just the same. Embarrassed, the lone member of the royal family ever to compete thereafter abstained as an entrant.

A record seventh straight Davis Cup was taken by the U.S., a 4-1 victory over the ever-advancing French at Germantown Cricket Club in Philadelphia. Johnston's and Tilden's respective opening-day sweep of Lacoste, 6-0, 6-4, 0-6, 6-0, and Borotra, 6-2, 6-3, 6-3, plus Richards and playing-captain Dick Williams's 6-4, 6-4, 6-2 putdown of Cochet and Brugnon, made the third day meaningless. Except that Tilden, showing signs of wear, was beaten by Lacoste, 4-6, 6-4, 8-6, 8-6. It was Big Bill's first ever singles loss in Davis Cup, ending his Cup singles streak at 16, a record not broken until 1975 by 19-year-old Bjorn Borg, leading Sweden to the Cup. Borg increased the record to 33 straight.

The French title went to Cochet, 6-2, 6-4, 6-3 over Lacoste, the second all-domestic final after the tournament welcomed "aliens" in 1925. Lenglen gave Miss Browne a taste of what was coming on their professional head-to-head odyssey, 6-1, 6-0, for her second French championship—the last of her eight major singles. She tripled, as she had in 1925 with the same accomplices, winning the doubles with Julia (Didi) Vlasto over Kitty McKane Godfree and Evelyn Colyer, 6-1, 6-1, and the mixed with Brugnon over Suzanne LeBesnerais and Borotra, 6-4, 6-3, to conclude her career with 21 majors: eight singles, eight doubles, five mixed, all at Wimbledon and the French. Her collection of major triples (five) is a record, probably imperishable. Suzanne had made that agonizing cameo at the U.S. in 1921, and never felt impelled to travel to Australia.

Lefty Jack Hawkes took the Australian without much opposition from Jim Willard, 6-1, 6-3, 6-1, and so did Daphne Akhurst, her second, while the 6-1, 6-3, loser, Esna Boyd set an unenviable majors record: five final losses in a row.

Though playing without Helen Wills, the U.S. tied the Wightman Cup competition at 2-2, defeating Great Britain at Wimbledon, 4-3, winning both doubles at the climax and splitting the singles. Kitty Godfree's win over Ryan, 6-1, 5-7, 6-4, made it 3-1 for the home side. But Marion Zinderstein Jessup squeaked past Dorothy Shepherd Barron 6-1, 5-7, 6-4, and returned to the court with Eleanor Goss for a 6-4, 6-2, win over Barron and last-flinging Dorothea Douglass Chambers, 47. It was 3-3, and longer-in-the-tooth-than-most Ryan, 34, and Browne, 35, grabbed the Cup from Godfrey, 30, and Evelyn Colyer, 24, in a tense decision, 2-6, 6-2, 6-4.

Australian Championships

Men's Singles Final: Jack Hawkes (AUS) def. Jim Willard (AUS), 6-1, 6-3, 6-1

Women's Singles Final: Daphne Akhurst (AUS) def. Esna Boyd (AUS), 6-1, 6-3

Men's Doubles Final: Jack Hawkes and Gerald Patterson (AUS) def. James Anderson and Pat OHara Wood (AUS), 6-1, 6-4, 6-2

Women's Doubles Final: Meryl O'Hara Wood and Esna Boyd (AUS) def. Daphne Akhurst and Marjorie Cox (AUS), 6-3, 6-8, 8-6

Mixed Doubles Final: Esna Boyd and Jack Hawkes (AUS) def. Daphne Akhurst and Jim Willard (AUS), 6-2, 6-4

French Championships

Men's Singles Final: Henri Cochet (FRA) def. Rene Lacoste (FRA), 6-2, 6-4, 6-3

Women's Singles Final: Suzanne Lenglen (FRA) def. Mary K. Browne (USA), 6-1, 6-0

Men's Doubles Final: Vinnie Richards and Howard Kinsey (USA) def. Henri Cochet and Jacques Brugnon (FRA), 6-4, 6-1, 4-6, 6-4

Women's Doubles Final: Suzanne Lenglen and Didi Vlasto (FRA) def. Kitty McKane Godfree and Evelyn Colyer (GBR), 6-1, 6-1

Mixed Doubles Final: Suzanne Lenglen and Jacques Brugnon (FRA) def. Jean Borotra and Suzanne LeBesnerais (FRA), 6-4 6-3

Wimbledon

Men's Singles Final: Jean Borotra (FRA) def. Howard Kinsey (USA)8-6, 6-1, 6-3

Women's Singles Final: Kitty McKane Godfree (GBR) def. Lili de Alvarez (ESP), 6-2, 6-4

Men's Doubles Final: Jacques Brugnon and Henri Cochet (FRA) def. Howard Kinsey and Vinnie Richards (USA), 7-5, 4-6, 6-3, 6-2

Women's Doubles Final: Mary K. Browne and Elizabeth Ryan (USA) def. Kitty McKane Godfree and Evelyn Coyer (GBR), 6-1, 6-1

Mixed Doubles Final: Kitty McKane Godfree and Leslie Godfree (GBR) def. Mary K. Browne and Howard Kinsey (USA), 6-3, 6-4

U.S. Championships

Men's Singles Final: Rene Lacoste (FRA) def. Jean Borotra (FRA), 6-4, 6-0, 6-4

Women's Singles Final: Molla Bjurstedt Mallory (USA) def. Elizabeth Ryan (USA), 4-6, 6-4, 9-7

Men's Doubles Final: Dick Williams and Vinnie Richards (USA) def. Bill Tilden and Alfred Chapin (USA), 6-4, 6-8, 11-9, 6-3

Women's Doubles Final: Elizabeth Ryan and Eleanor Goss (USA) def. Mary K. Browne and Charlotte Hosmer Chapin (USA), 3-6, 6-4, 12-10

Mixed Doubles Final: Elizabeth Ryan (USA) and Jean Borotra (FRA) def. Hazel Hotchkiss Wightman (USA) and Rene Lacoste (FRA), 6-4, 7-5

Year-End No. 1

Men: Rene Lacoste
Women: Suzanne Lenglen

Davis Cup: United States

Wightman Cup: United States

1927 Vive la France! France Wins Davis Cup

The Four Musketeers (from L to R) **Jacques Brugnon**, **Henri Cochet**, **Rene Lacoste** and **Jean Borotra** won the Davis Cup over the United States.

One of the most astounding turnarounds in the history of tennis occurred in the semifinals of Wimbledon. Bill Tilden at 34 was no longer El Supremo, but he was a legendary figure, imposing and formidable still, seeded No. 2 (seedings had just been introduced) only to Rene Lacoste in his first appearance at Wimbledon since winning in 1921. Playing No. 4 seed Henri Cochet, Tilden won the first two sets, reached 5-1, 15-all in the third set and then lost, probably as great a collapse as any outstanding tennis figure would ever experience.

Big Bill had beaten Cochet in a straight-set semifinal at the French, 9-7, 6-3, 6-2 and he may have felt he needed to do the same this time, remembering that he'd lost the three-hour Paris final in five sets, 6-4, 4-6, 5-7, 6-3, 11-9, to Lacoste—61 games, the longest French title match (Tilden held two match points on serve, 9-8, 40-15. Rain was falling, and in three games so was he, double-faulting on match point).

So Tilden went for winners with big forehands, missing three, and Cochet was off on a 17-point binge that lifted him to 5-5, 30-0. Even though Tilden got back in it on a break to 3-2 in the fifth, the inexorable force was with Cochet, roaring to per-

haps the most remarkable of Wimbledon championships. His finishing off of Tilden, 2-6, 4-6, 7-5, 6-4, 6-3, was only the appetizer, as it turned out.

Tilden later wrote: "I have heard many interesting, curious, quite inaccurate accounts of what happened. One ingenious explanation was that King Alfonso of Spain arrived at 5-1 in the third set and I decided to let him see some of the match. Ridiculous! I didn't even know he was there. Another was that a group of Hindus hypnotized me. If they did, I didn't know it, but they certainly did a swell job. Personally, I have no satisfactory explanation. All I know is my coordination cracked wide open and I couldn't put a ball in court."

Before ambushing Tilden, Cochet had also come from a 0-2 deficit to beat Bill's doubles partner, Frank Hunter, 3-6, 3-6, 6-2, 6-2, 6-3 in the quarterfinal. But he saved the most exciting for last, overcoming Borotra, who had beaten Lacoste, 6-4, 6-3, 1-6, 1-6, 6-2, in the semifinal. Cochet made it through a minefield of six match points laid by the Bounding Basque at the climax before winning 4-6, 4-6, 6-3, 6-4, 7-5. He dodged one hazard on his own serve to 3-5, then five more with Borotra trying to serve it out in the next game. From the sixth match point (Borotra missing a volley), Cochet pounced, grabbing 15 of the remaining 18 points. He was the Lazarus of Centre Court.

Wallis Myers, the game's foremost critic, declared Cochet "was favored by the gods." Obviously. Wimbledon Secretary Duncan Macaulay wrote: "Cochet was incredibly cool in a crisis—so much that I sometimes wondered whether he really knew what the score was." Footnote: In the doubles final, Cochet and Jacques Brugnon led Tilden and Frank Hunter, two sets to love, 5-3, 40-15—two match points—on Cochet's serve for the match, only to be stiffed, 1-6, 4-6, 8-6, 6-3, 6-4.

The only people feeling worse than Cochet's singles victims were the members of the tourney committee, tormented by one of the dampest Championships. Rain fell nearly every day, pushing the finish to the third Tuesday.

The "Crocodile," Lacoste, won three great matches over Tilden this year to establish his own supremacy in the sport. He won the French, from two match points down, and U.S. Championships in extraordinary finals and also beat Tilden in a crucial Davis Cup match. In the Forest Hills final, Lacoste may have played the best tennis of his life, winning 11-9, 6-3, 11-9.

"It was a match," Allison Danzig wrote, "the like of which will not be seen again soon. On one side of the net stood [Tilden] the perfect tactician and most ruthless stroker the game

probably has ever seen, master of every shot and skilled in the necromancy of spin. On the other side was the player who has reduced defense to a mathematical science; who has done more than that, who has developed his defense to the state where it becomes an offense, subconscious in its workings but nonetheless effective in the pressure it brings to bear as the ball is sent back deeper and deeper and into more and more remote territory."

Lacoste, whose career was cut short by ill health and who became famous for conceiving the famed polo shirts bearing the crocodile emblem—thus emancipating male arms from long-sleeved white dress shirts—never played, at Forest Hills again.

America's record seven-year reign came to an end in the Davis Cup. France broke through in its third challenge with a 3-2 victory over a U.S. team that included the two men who had brought the Cup to America in 1920—Tilden and Johnston. Lacoste beat the fading Johnston, 6-3, 6-2, 6-2, then Tilden beat Cochet, 6-4, 2-6, 6-2, 8-6, and the Americans took a 2-1 lead on a trying doubles victory by Tilden and Hunter over Borotra and Brugnon, 3-6, 6-3, 6-3, 4-6, 6-0. Tilden could not come through with another victory, losing to Lacoste, 6-3, 4-6, 6-3, 6-2. The Cup got a boat ticket to France when Johnston was beaten by Cochet, 6-4, 4-6, 6-2, 6-4 in a dramatic match.

The overflow crowd of 15,000 at the Germantown Cricket Club was so carried away in loudly pulling for an American victory that, one report said, "It broke all bounds of tennis etiquette and cheered madly both Johnston's winning shots and Cochet's mistakes." Tilden and Lacoste took in the scene calmly, sitting side by side.

With Suzanne Lenglen off in professional ranks, Helen Wills (called Little Miss Poker Face because of her lack of expression on court) assumed complete dominance of the women's ranks at 22. She began a string of four Wimbledon titles with a 6-2, 6-3, victory over Spaniard Lili de Alvarez. Wills won her fifth U.S. Championship, striking down two Hall of Fame-bound teen-agers: 19-year-old Californian Helen Jacobs—soon to be her foremost rival—in a semifinal, 6-0, 6-2, and 16-year-old Betty Nuthall of Britain in the final, 6-1, 6-4. Helen had beaten the French champ, Netherlander Kea Bouman, in the quarterfinals 6-1, 6-2. Charlotte Hosmer Chapin dethroned the energetic 43-year-old defender Molla Mallory, barely, in the quarterfinal, 6-3, 1-6, 6-4.

Lacking Lenglen, the French title went to Bouman over South African Irene Bowder Peacock, 6-2, 6-4.

The United States went ahead in Wightman Cup play, 3-2, beating the British 5-2 at Forest Hills. Wills and Mallory were ruthless. Helen beat Kitty Godfree, 6-1, 6-1, and Joan Fry, 6-2, 6-0; Molla knocked off those two respectively, 6-4, 6-2, and 6-1, 11-9. The donor, Hazel Wightman, 40, won a doubles with Wills over Ermyntrude Harvey and Godfree, 6-4, 4-6, 6-3.

A new concrete horseshoe stadium seating 13,000 at Kooyong in Melbourne, in the style of Forest Hills, was opened for the Australian Championships and remained the focal point of tennis Down Under for six decades until the 1988 unveiling of Flinders Park (now Melbourne Park). The title matches were suitably grand. In high 90s heat for more than three hours, Gerald Patterson fought off Jack Hawkes, 3-6, 6-4, 3-6, 18-16, 6-3. He served

his way off the ledge of four match points at 12-13, and another at 15-16. Runner-up five straight years, Esna Boyd snapped out of reverse to beat Sylvia Lance, 5-7, 6-1, 6-2.

The first U.S. Pro Championships was played in New York—Vinnie Richards winning $1,000 of the $2,000 pot over Howard Kinsey, 11-9, 6-4, 6-3, at the public courts of the long-since-disappeared Notlek Tennis Club in Manhattan.

1927 CHAMPIONS AND LEADERS

Australian Championships
Men's Singles Final: Gerald Patterson (AUS) def., Jack Hawkes (AUS), 3-6, 6-4, 3-6, 18-16, 6-3
Women's Singles Final: Esna Boyd (AUS) def. Syliva Lance Harper (AUS), 5-7, 6-1, 6-2
Men's Doubles Final: Jack Hawkes and Gerald Patterson (AUS), def. Pat O'Hara Wood and Ian McInness (AUS), 8-6, 6-2, 6-1
Women's Doubles Final: Meryl O'Hara Wood and Louie Bickerton (AUS) def. Esna Boyd and Sylvia Lance Harper (AUS), 6-3, 6-3.
Mixed Doubles Final: Esna Boyd and Jack Hawkes (AUS) def. Youtha Anthony and Jim Willard (AUS), 6-1, 6-3

French Championships
Men's Singles Final: Rene Lacoste (FRA) def. Bill Tilden (USA) 6-4, 4-6, 5-7, 6-3, 11-9
Women's Singles: Kea Bouman (NED) def. Irene Bowder Peacock (RSA), 6-2, 6-4
Men's Doubles Final: Henri Cochet and Jacques Brugnon (FRA) def. Jean Borotra and Rene Lacoste (FRA), 2-6, 6-2, 6-0, 1-6, 6-4
Women's Doubles: Irene Bowder Peacock and Bobbie Heine (RSA) def. Peggy Saunders and Phoebe Holcroft Watson (GBR), 6-2, 6-1
Mixed Doubles Final: Marguerite Broquedis Bordes and Jean Borotra (FRA) def. Lili De Alvarez (ESP) and Bill Tilden (USA), 6-4, 2-6, 6-2

Wimbledon
Men's Singles Final: Henri Cochet (FRA) def. Jean Borotra (FRA), 4-6, 4-6, 6-3, 6-4, 7-5
Women's Singles Final: Helen Wills (USA) def. Lili de Alvarez (ESP), 6-2, 6-4
Men's Doubles Final: Frank Hunter and Bill Tilden (USA) def. Jacques Brugnon and Henri Cochet (FRA), 1-6, 4-6, 8-6, 6-3, 6-4
Women's Doubles Final: Helen Wills and Elizabeth Ryan (USA) def. Bobbie Heine and Irene Bowder Peacock (RSA), 6-3, 6-2
Mixed Doubles Final: Elizabeth Ryan and Frank Hunter (USA) def. Kitty McKane Godfree and Leslie Godfree (GBR), 8-6, 6-0

U.S. Championships
Men's Singles Final: Rene Lacoste (FRA) def. Bill Tilden (USA), 11-9, 6-3, 11-9
Women's Singles: Helen Wills (USA) def. Betty Nuthall (GBR), 6-1, 6-4
Men's Doubles Final: Bill Tilden and Frank Hunter (USA), def. Bill Johnston and Dick Williams (USA), 10-8, 6-3, 6-3
Women's Doubles Final: Kitty McKane Godfree and Ermyntrude Harvey (GBR) def. Betty Nuthall and Joan Fry (GBR), 6-1, 4-6, 6-4
Mixed Doubles Final: Eileen Bennett (GBR) and Henri Cochet (FRA) def. Hazel Hotchkiss Wightman (USA) and Rene Lacoste (FRA), 6-2, 0-6, 6-2

Year-End No. 1
Men: Rene Lacoste
Women: Helen Wills

Davis Cup: France

Wightman Cup: United States

1928 Roland Garros Debuts, Wills Takes Three

the finale with France approached—the first overseas voyage to challenge for the U.S. since 1920—other members of the American team threatened to strike. Rene Lacoste announced he would not defend his title at Forest Hills. He said: "We would rather lose the Davis Cup than retain it where there may be some excuse in the absence of Tilden."

Having built Stade Roland Garros for the Cup defense (and subsequent French Championships), and needing Tilden's presence to fill the seats, French tennis officials protested the suspension, as did the press and public. To the rescue, U.S. Ambassador Myron T. Herrick defused a potential Franco-American crisis by suggesting to U.S. State Department superiors that they lean on the U.S. Lawn Tennis Association to reinstate Tilden. The USLTA diplomatically bowed for the moment, then barring Big Bill again to keep him out of the U.S. Championships.

Then 35, Tilden went out and played what teammate George Lott called his greatest match ever. He defeated Lacoste on clay—the first time that grass hadn't been the surface for the Cup-deciding round—1-6, 6-4, 6-4, 2-6, 6-3. Afterward, Lacoste said: "Two years ago I knew at last how to beat him. Now, he beats me. I never knew how the ball would come off the court; he concealed it so well. I had to wait to see how much it was spinning— and sometimes it didn't spin at all. Is he not the greatest player of all time?"

Controversy raged much of the year between Bill Tilden and the U.S. Lawn Tennis Association over his writing newspaper articles about tennis, a violation of amateur rules. Tilden was suspended, missing the inter-zone Davis Cup win over Italy. As

That victory was not enough. Cochet beat rookie John Hennessey, 5-7, 9-7, 6-3, 6-0 and on the third day he beat Tilden, 6-4, 4-6, 6-2, 6-4, clinching after Jean Borotra and Cochet nipped Frank Hunter and Tilden, 6-4, 6-8, 7-5. 4-6, 6-2 in the doubles. A third day

was too much for Big Bill, and France won 4-1, the pick of the 33 nations that started.

French supremacy carried to the major championships where, for the first time, one country's representatives swept all four majors, a "Gallic Grand Slam." Cochet won the U.S. and French crowns, carrying his homeland title over Lacoste, 5-7, 6-3, 6-1, 6-3. But Lacoste paid Henri back for his second Wimbledon title.

Borotra turned the Australian Championship into a Vive la France fete. He won the singles, despite almost letting it get away in five sets to a local, Jack Cummings, 6-4, 6-1, 4-6, 5-7, 6-3. The semifinal hadn't been a snap either, five sets with 19-year-old future champ Jack Crawford, 4-6, 6-3, 1-6, 7-5, 6-3 (twice two points from defeat at 4-5), In fact, the Basque bounded to a triple, taking the doubles with Brugnon over Jim Willard and Gar Moon, 6-2, 4-6, 6-4, 6-4, and the mixed with Daphne Akhurst on a default from defending champions Esna Boyd and Jack Hawkes. Akhurst regained her title, 7-5, 6-2, from Boyd, the extremely experienced loser of finals. It was Akhurst's third title, and Boyd's sixth final-round disappointment, a tournament record for futility.

With Tilden and Lacoste missing from Forest Hills, Cochet won the U.S. title by beating Frank Shields in the semifinals, 6-2, 8-6, 6-4, and Frank Hunter in the final, 4-6, 6-4, 3-6, 7-5, 6-3- It was the third straight victory by a Frenchman there, and it would be the last. Except for Cochet, runner-up in the 1932 U.S. final, there would be no outstanding Frenchman to play in the United States, let alone win, after the retirements of Lacoste and Borotra, until Cedric Pioline lost the 1993 final to Pete Sampras, 6-4, 6-4, 6-3. At Wimbledon, a Lacoste-Cochet final was set up when Lacoste scored a five-set victory over Tilden, 2-6, 6-4, 2-6, 6-4, 6-3 (down a break, 2-1, in the fifth), and Cochet beat countryman Christian Boussus, 11-9, 3-6, 6-2, 6-3. Lacoste won for the second time, 6-1, 4-6, 6-4, 6-2.

Great Britain evened the Wightman Cup series again, 3-3, with a 4-3 victory. Although Helen Wills blew away Phoebe Holcroft Watson, 6-1, 6-2, and Eileen Bennett, 6-3, 6-2, Molla Mallory was past it at 44, losing to Bennett, 6-1, 6-2, and Watson, 2-6, 6-1, 6-2. In a clash of future U.S. champs, American rookie Helen Jacobs, 19, beat 17-year-old Betty Nuthall, 6-3, 6-1. But the Brits swept the doubles: Ermyntrude Harvey and Peggy Saunders over Eleanor Goss and Jacobs, 6-4, 6-1, climaxing with Bennett and Watson over Penelope Anderson and Wills, 6-2, 6-1.

Wills became the first to win three majors in one year, and convincingly: 6-1, 6-2 over Bennett at the French; 6-2, 6-3 over Spaniard Lili de Alvarez at Wimbledon; 6-2, 6-1 over Jacobs at the U.S., the second of the intriguing battles of the two Helens from Berkeley. (Wills never journeyed to Australia.) As much was made of Wills' reserved manner as her skills, W. O. McGeehan wrote in the *New York Herald Tribune*: "She is powerful, repressed and imperturbable. She plays her game with a silent, deadly earnestness, concentrated on her work. That, of course, is the way to win games, but it does not please galleries. Of course, there is no reason why an amateur athlete should try to please galleries."

Vinnie Richards, 25, succeeded C. C. Pyle as promoter (continuing as player) of professional matches, importing Karel Kozeluh, a Czech who was being acclaimed as a great player even though he had never played on the amateur circuit. In a head-to-head duel with Richards, Kozeluh proved superior on clay and hardwood, winning a majority of the matches (13-7). But he lost on grass at Forest Hills to Richards in the second U.S. Pro Championships, 8-6, 6-3, 0-6, 6-2.

1928 CHAMPIONS AND LEADERS

Australian Championships
Men's Singles Final: Jean Borotra (FRA) def. Jack Cummings (AUS), 6-4, 6-1, 4-6, 5-7, 6-2
Women's Singles Final: Daphne Akhurst (AUS) def. Esna Boyd (AUS), 7-5, 6-2
Men's Doubles Final: Jean Borotra and Jacques Brugnon (FRA) def. Jim Willard and Gar Moon (AUS), 6-2, 4-6, 6-4, 6-4
Women's Doubles Final: Daphne Akhurst and Esna Boyd (AUS) def. Dorothy Weston (GBR) and Katherine LeMesurier (AUS), 6-3, 6-1
Mixed Doubles Final: Daphne Akhurst (AUS) and Jean Borotra (FRA) def. Esna Boyd and Jack Hawkes (AUS), default

French Championships
Men's Singles Final: Henri Cochet (FRA) def. Rene Lacoste (FRA), 5-7, 6-3, 6-1, 6-3
Women's Singles Final: Helen Wills (USA) def. Eileen Bennett (GBR), 6-1, 6-2
Men's Doubles Final: Jean Borotra and Jacques Brugnon (FRA) def. Henri Cochet and Rene De Buzelet (FRA), 6-4, 3-6, 6-2, 3-6, 6-4
Women's Doubles Final: Phoebe Holcroft Watson and Eileen Bennett (GBR) def. Suzanne Deve and Sylvia Lafaurie (FRA), 6-0, 6-2
Mixed Doubles Final: Eileen Bennett (GBR) and Henri Cochet (FRA) def. Helen Wills and Frank Hunter (USA), 3-6, 6-3, 6-3

Wimbledon
Men's Singles: Rene Lacoste (FRA) def. Henri Cochet (FRA), 6-1, 4-6, 6-4, 6-2
Women's Singles: Helen Wills (USA) def. Lili de Alvarez (ESP), 6-2, 6-3
Men's Doubles Final: Jacques Brugnon and Henri Cochet (FRA) def. Gerald Patterson and Jack Hawkes (AUS), 13-11, 6-4, 6-4
Women's Doubles Final: Peggy Saunders and Phoebe Holcroft Watson (GBR) def. Eileen Bennett and Ermyntrude Harvey (GBR), 6-2, 6-3
Mixed Doubles Final: Elizabeth Ryan (USA) and Pat Spence (RSA) def. Daphne Akhurst and Jack Crawford (AUS), 7-5, 6-4

U.S. Championships
Men's Singles Final: Henri Cochet (FRA) def. Frank Hunter (USA), 4-6, 6-4, 3-6, 7-5, 6-3
Women's Singles Final: Helen Wills (USA) def. Helen Jacobs (USA), 6-2, 6-1
Men's Doubles Final: George Lott and John Hennessey (USA) def. Gerald Patterson and Jack Hawkes (AUS), 6-2, 6-1, 6-2
Women's Doubles Final: Hazel Hotchkiss Wightman and Helen Wills (USA) def. Editih Cross and Anna McCune Harper (USA), 6-2, 6-2
Mixed Doubles Final: Helen Wills (USA) and Jack Hawkes (AUS) def. Edith Cross (USA) and Gar Moon (AUS), 6-1, 6-3

Year-End No. 1
Men: Henri Cochet
Women: Helen Wills

Davis Cup: France

Wightman Cup: Great Britain

1929 Tilden Wins "Geezer's Gala" For Seventh U.S. Title

In the years the French were dominating Wimbledon and Forest Hills, Tilden was still the most dynamic figure in the sport. Rene Lacoste wrote: "He seems to exercise a strange fascination over his opponents as well as his spectators. Tilden, even when beaten, always leaves the impression on the public mind that he was superior to the victor."

The French had broken Tilden's six-year dominance at Forest Hills, and now Tilden ended the three-year French reign. He won the U.S. title for the seventh time, coming from behind in

Henri Cochet claimed France's sixth straight men's singles title at Wimbledon.

the last three matches - 7-5, 2-6, 9-7, 6-2 over American Johnny Van Ryn, from 3-5 in the third in the quarterfinals; 4-6, 6-2, 2-6, 6-4, 6-3 over the bullet-serving lefty Johnny Doeg, from a break, 1-2 in the fourth and a break, 0-1 in the fifth in the semifinals; and 3-6, 6-3, 4-6, 6-2, 6-4 over Frank Hunter for his seventh title. This was

the Geezers Gala, the 71-year-old final—Hunter, 35, and Tilden, 36, the second-oldest man to wear the U.S. crown. Bill Larned won in 1910 and 1911 at 37 and 38. Only Arthur Gore, 40, over Herbert Roper Barrett, 34, in 1908 at Wimbledon contested a major final with more mileage on the adversaries.

After Lacoste gave way to failing health (he lived to 92 nevertheless) following his French championship, Henri Cochet became the No. 1 Frenchman. He won the last all-French final at Wimbledon, beating Jean Borotra, 6-4, 6-3, 6-4, after defeating Tilden in the semifinal, 6-4, 6-1, 7-5. Great Britain's future great, Fred Perry, made his Wimbledon debut by losing in the third round to countryman John Olliff 6-4, 6-2, 2-6, 6-3.

France was extended in winning a third successive Davis Cup over the United States, 3-2 in Paris at the wire. Cochet beat Tilden, 6-3, 6-1, 6-2, then Borotra beat American newcomer George Lott, 6-1, 3-6, 6-4, 7-5. In doubles, John Van Ryn and Wilmer Allison kept it alive for the Yanks, flattening Cochet and Borotra, 6-1, 8-6, 6-4, setting up a tie with Tilden's defeat of Borotra, 4-6, 6-1, 6-4, 7-5. Cochet made the difference, defeating 22-year-old Lott, 6-1, 3-6, 6-0, 6-3.

Helen Wills, now Mrs. Frederick Moody, was never more supreme. She swept Wimbledon and Forest Hills for the third straight year and the French Championship for the second, 6-3, 6-4 over Simone Mathieu of France. In her first of four Wimbledon final-round triumphs over Helen Jacobs, she romped, 6-1, 6-2.

At the U.S. Championships, Jacobs was eliminated in the semifinals by Britain's Phoebe Watson, 6-1, 4-6, 6-4, as Watson won 12 straight points to take a 5-3 lead in the third. Molla Mallory, 45 but yet a force to be reckoned with, made the semifinal, only to be double-bageled in 21 minutes (8 minutes for the first set and 13 in the second) by Moody, whom she'd beaten for the title seven years earlier. Then Helen beat Watson, 6-4, 6-2.

South African Billie Tapscott caused an echoing wave of criticism by being the first female player to be seen at Wimbledon without stockings. Lengen could have gotten away with baring her legs – but not an unknown.

Wills led the American team to a 4-3 Wightman Cup victory on the strength of singles superiority. She beat Watson, 6-1, 6-4, and Betty Nuthall, 8-6, 8-6. Jacobs beat Nuthall, 7-5, 8-6, and Edith Cross beat Peggy Saunders Michell, 6-3, 3-6, 6-3. That was sufficient, so the doubles loss of founder Hazel Wightman, 42, and Jacobs to Dorothy Shepherd Barron and Phyllis Howkins Covell, 6-2, 6-1, was of no consequence. The U.S. led in the series, 4-3.

Colin Gregory became the third Brit to win the Australian, beating 1924 finalist Bob Schlesinger, 6-2, 6-2, 5-7, 7-5. Twenty-three years later, Yorkshireman Dr. Gregory, a physician and the team captain, would become the oldest to win a Davis Cup match at 48, when he and Tony Mottram took the doubles in a 3-2 win over Yugoslavia, a 6-4, 1-6, 9-11, 6-2, 6-2, defeat of Pallada and Laszlo. Daphne Akhurst's title was her fourth, 6-1, 5-7, 6-2 over Louie Bickerton.

In what still was a minor aspect of the sport, the third U.S. Pro Championship went to Czech Karel Kozeluh, who dethroned Vinnie Richards, 6-4, 6-4, 4-6, 4-6, 7-5, at Forest Hills.

1929 CHAMPIONS AND LEADERS

Australian Championships

Men's Singles Final: Colin Gregory (GBR) def. Bob Schlesinger (AUS), 6-2, 6-2, 5-7, 7-5

Women's Singles Final: Daphne Akhurst (AUS) def. Louie Bickerton (AUS), 6-1, 5-7, 6-2

Men's Doubles Final: Jack Crawford and Harry Hopman (AUS) def. Jack Cummings and Gar Moon (AUS), 6-1, 6-8, 4-6, 6-1, 6-3

Women's Doubles Final: Daphne Akhurst and Louie Bickerton (AUS) def. Sylvia Lance Harper and Meryl O'Hara Wood (AUS), 6-2, 3-6, 6-2

Mixed Doubles Final: Daphne Akhurst and Gar Moon (AUS) def. Marjorie Cox and Jack Crawford (AUS), 6-0, 7-5

French Championships

Men's Singles Final: Rene Lacoste (FRA) def. Jean Borotra (FRA), 6-3, 2-6, 6-0, 2-6, 8-6

Women's Singles Final: Helen Wills (USA) def. Simone Passemard Mathieu (FRA), 6-3, 6-4

Men's Doubles Final: Rene Lacoste and Jean Borotra (FRA) def. Henri Cochet and Jacques Brugnon (FRA), 6-3, 3-6, 6-3, 3-6, 8-6

Women's Doubles Final: Lili de Alvarez (ESP) and Kea Bouman (NED) def. Bobbie Heine and Alida Neave (RSA), 7-5, 6-3

Mixed Doubles Final: Eileen Bennett (GBR) and Henri Cochet (FRA) def. Helen Wills and Frank Hunter (USA), 6-3, 6-2

Wimbledon

Men's Singles Final: Henri Cochet (FRA) def. Jean Borotra (FRA), 6-4, 6-3, 6-4

Women's Singles: Helen Wills (USA) def. Helen Jacobs (USA), 6-1, 6-2

Men's Doubles Final: Wilmer Allison and John Van Ryn (USA) def. Colin Gregory and Ian Collins (GBR), 6-4, 5-7, 6-3, 10-12, 6-4

Women's Doubles Final: Peggy Saunders Michell and Phoebe Holcroft Watson (GBR) def. Phyllis Howkins Covell and Dorothy Shepherd Barron (GBR), 6-4, 8-6

Mixed Doubles Final: Helen Wills and Frank Hunter (USA) def. Joan Fry and Ian Collins (GBR), 6-1, 6-4

U.S. Championships

Men's Singles Final: Bill Tilden (USA) def. Frank Hunter (USA) 3-6, 6-3, 4-6, 6-2, 6-4

Women's Singles Final: Helen Wills Moody (USA) def. Phoebe Holcroft Watson (GBR), 6-4, 6-2

Men's Doubles Final: George Lott and Johnny Doeg (USA) def. Berkeley Bell and Lewis White (USA), 10-8, 16-14, 6-1

Women's Doubles Final: Phoebe Holcroft Watson and Peggy Michell (GBR) def. Phyllis Howkins Covell and Dorothy Shepherd Barron (GBR) 2-6, 6-3, 6-4

Mixed Doubles Final: Betty Nuthall (GBR) and George Lott (USA) def. Phyllis Howkins Covell and Bunny Austin (GBR), 6-3, 6-3

Year-End No. 1

Men: Henri Cochet
Women: Helen Wills Moody

Davis Cup: France

Wightman Cup: United States

1930 Curtain Call For The Tilden Era

Bill Tilden won his third Wimbledon title at age 37.

beat Tilden two months later on the way to winning the U.S. title.

Tilden had his most successful European tour, winning the Austrian, Italian and Dutch titles, losing to Henri Cochet in the French final, 3-6, 8-6, 6-3, 6-1. Previously closed to foreigners, the Italian went international at Milan, and Tilden routinely beat Italian Davis Cupper Umberto de Morpurgo, 6-1, 6-1, 6-2.

Ranked No. 1 in the United States for a record 10th time, Tilden wanted badly to break a tie with Bill Larned and Richard Sears by winning his eighth U.S. title. He made it to the semifinals where the heavy left arm of 21-year-old Californian Doeg fell on him like an executioner's axe, severing Big Bill from his dream. His powerful serve made Doeg, nephew of May Sutton Bundy, a former champion of Wimbledon (1905, 1907) and the U.S. Championships (1904), a formidable opponent when he had control of his ground game. Eighth seed Doeg whammed 28 aces, 12 in the final set, losing his serve only once in 29 games, to beat Tilden, 10-8, 6-3, 3-6, 12-10. He hit his serve so hard it was reported that he turned the ball into an ellipse—his "egg ball." The loss marked the first time Tilden had been beaten by a countryman in a U.S. Championship since Bill Johnston, 11 years earlier. Doeg then beat 19-year-old Frank Shields in the final, 10-8, 1-6, 6-4, 16-14. Shields, seeded 11th, had a set point at 13-14 cancelled by an ace.

Tilden's record in U.S. Championships was 71-7. He had played 78 matches, at least one every year since 1916 (plus one in 1912), except for 1928 when he was suspended. He won 210 and lost 56 sets.

Tilden, who had a long love-hate relationship with crowds that admired his gallant efforts in the face of defeat and his sportsmanship but didn't like some of his showboating, now had no great goals to achieve as an amateur. Wrote Tilden biographer Frank Deford,

Bill Tilden's magnificent career as an amateur came to an end on the last day of the year when he officially announced he was turning professional. He bowed out after one of the most glorious victories of his career. He won his third Wimbledon, becoming at 37 years, five months, the second-oldest man to take the singles title. Arthur Gore won his third singles title at 41 in 1909.

Seeded No. 2, Tilden beat an unseeded 25-year-old Texan, Wilmer Allison, 10 years and six days after winning his first Wimbledon over Gerald Patterson. Before defeating Allison, 6-3, 9-7, 6-4, Tilden survived a tough one, 0-6, 6-4, 4-6, 6-0, 7-5 over Jean Borotra, who led 3-1 in the stretch. Allison removed first-seeded Henri Cochet in the quarterfinal, 6-4, 6-4, 6-3, then sidelined No. 4 seeded countryman John Doeg, 6-3, 4-6, 8-6, 3-6, 7-5. Doeg would

"Frustrated by the reductions of age, appearing more effeminate in his gestures Tilden would die a lonely, broken figure at 60 after two convictions on morals charges. He became testier, even petty, on the court. Once, on the Riviera in a match of no consequence, the umpire, an Englishman, finally just got up and departed when Tilden kept fussing. Once, at South Orange, New Jersey, he rudely informed the tournament chairman that Big Bill Tilden was not accustomed to competing on grass that had the texture of a cow pasture, and had to be coaxed back onto the court."

Earlier in the year, Tilden played in his 11th consecutive and last Davis Cup final round, a 4-1 defeat in Paris as the French kept the Cup for a fourth year. Despite an injured ankle, he came back from a slow start in the opening match, beating Jean Borotra, 2-6, 7-5, 6-4, 7-5. But the U.S. back-up wasn't up to Bill's standard. Cochet beat George Lott, better known as a shrewd doubles player, 6-4, 6-2, 6-2, and linked with another clever doublist, 35-year-old Jacques Brugnon, to give France a 2-1 lead, 6-3, 7-5, 1-6, 6-2, over Johnny Van Ryn and Allison. Borotra applied the finishing touch to Lott, 6-3, 2-6, 6-2, 8-6. It was over as far as the result, and then for Tilden, the Cup stalwart for so long. Cochet was his bye-bye guy, defeating Tilden 4-6, 6-3, 6-1, 7-5. Bill went out with a 25-5 Cup singles record.

The year marked the first appearances in the U.S. Top 10 rankings of Sidney Wood, No. 4; Ellsworth Vines, No. 8; and Bitsy Grant, No. 10.

Queen Helen, now Mrs. Helen Wills Moody at 24, won Wimbledon for the fourth straight year without working up much of a sweat in a 6-2, 6-2 final triumph over a perennial, Elizabeth Ryan, 38. Moody and Ryan teamed to win the doubles over Edith Cross and Sarah Palfrey, both of the U.S., 6-2, 9-7. Bostonian Sarah, a future Hall of Famer, was making her Wimbledon debut at 17. Although Moody won the French for a third successive year, beating the other Helen (Jacobs), 6-2, 6-1, she skipped Forest Hills. England's 19-year-old Betty Nuthall, finalist to Helen in 1927, won the U.S. title over Anna McCune Harper of Oakland, Calif., 6-1, 6-4. The lone English entry, Betty became the first woman of her country to triumph in the ex-colony, rising from 2-4 in the second set to beat Bostonian Midge Morrill in a semifinal, 6-8, 6-4, 6-2, and winning the last four games of the final.

Daphne Akhurst won the Australian women's title for the third straight year in a battle with 1927 finalist Sylvia Lance Harper, 10-8, 2-6, 7-5, the longest of their country's female finals in games played, 38. This was Daphne's fifth title overall, the Australian record until Margaret Smith Court won 11 between 1960 and 1973. It was also the last singles title for the tragic champ, who died in childbirth three years later at 29. As Mrs. Roy Cozens, she did win the doubles, teaming with Louie Bickerton in 1931, 6-0, 6-4, over Nell Lloyd and Lorna Utz. Gar Moon defeated Harry Hopman for the men's crown, 6-3, 6-1, 6-3. But Harry, who would gain renown as the winningest Davis Cup captain (16 titles for Australia), and coming singles champ Jack Crawford won the doubles for a second straight year, this time over Jack Hawkes and Tim Fitchett, 8-6, 6-1, 2-6, 6-3.

With a 4-3 victory at Wimbledon, Britain evened the Wightman Cup rivalry at 4-4. It was no problem for Moody in singles, 6-1, 6-1 over Joan Fry and 7-5, 6-1 over Phoebe Holcroft Watson.

But Jacobs, who also beat Fry, 6-0, 6-3, was upset by Watson, 2-6, 6-2, 6-4, and rookie Palfrey lost to Phyllis Mudford, 6-0, 6-2. Doubles superiority saved the Brits: Ermyntrude Harvey and Fry over Edith Cross and Palfrey, 2-6, 6-2, 6-4; Kitty McKane Godfree and Watson over the Helens, Jacobs and Moody, 7-5, 1-6, 6-4.

Women's dress continued to be less cumbersome. Lili de Alvarez was wearing a pagoda-like trouser dress. Eileen Bennett and Betty Nuthall showed up at Wimbledon with open-backed tennis dresses, and necklines continued to drop.

At Forest Hills, Vinnie Richards regained his U.S. Pro title from Karel Kozeluh, 2-6, 10-8, 6-3, 6-4.

1930 CHAMPIONS AND LEADERS

Australian Championships
Men's Singles Final: Gar Moon (AUS) def. Harry Hopman (AUS), 6-3, 6-1, 6-3

Women's Singles Final: Daphne Akhurst (AUS) def. Sylvia Lance Harper (AUS), 10-8, 2-6, 7-5

Men's Doubles Final: Jack Crawford and Harry Hopman (AUS) def. Jack Hawkes and Tim Fitchett (AUS), 8-6, 6-1, 2-6, 6-3

Women's Doubles Final: Mall Molesworth and Emily Hood (AUS), def. Marjorie Cox and Sylvia Lance Harper (AUS), 6-3, 0-6, 7-5.

Mixed Doubles Final: Nell Hall (AUS) and Harry Hopman (AUS) def. Marjorie Cox (AUS) and Jack Crawford (AUS), 11-9, 3-6, 6-3

French Championships
Men's Singles: Henri Cochet (FRA) def. Bill Tilden (USA), 3-6, 8-6, 6-3, 6-1

Women's Singles Final: Helen Wills Moody (USA) def. Helen Jacobs (USA), 6-2, 6-1

Men's Doubles Final: Henri Cochet and Jacques Brugnon (FRA) def. Harry Hopman and Jim Willard (AUS), 6-2, 9-7, 6-3

Women's Doubles Final: Helen Wills Moody and Elizabeth Ryan (USA) def. Simone Barbier and Simone Passemard Mathieu (FRA), 6-3, 6-1

Mixed Doubles Final: Cilly Aussem (GER) and Bill Tilden (USA) def. Eileen Bennett Whittingstall (GBR) and Henri Cochet (FRA), 6-4, 6-4

Wimbledon
Men's Singles: Bill Tilden (USA) def. Wilmer Allison (USA), 6-3, 9-7, 6-4

Women's Singles Final: Helen Wills Moody (USA) def. Elizabeth Ryan (USA), 6-2, 6-2

Men's Doubles Final: Wilmer Allison and John Van Ryn (USA) def. Johnny Doeg and George Lott (USA), 6-3, 6-3, 6-2

Women's Doubles Final: Helen Wills Moody and Elizabeth Ryan (USA) def. Edith Cross and Sarah Palfrey (USA), 6-2, 9-7

Mixed Doubles Final: Elizabeth Ryan (USA) and Jack Crawford (AUS) def. Hilde Krawinkel and Daniel Prenn (GER), 6-1, 6-3

U.S. Championships
Men's Singles: Johnny Doeg (USA) def. Frank Shields (USA), 10-8, 1-6, 6-4, 16-14

Women's Singles: Betty Nuthall (GBR) def. Anna McCune Harper (USA) 6-1, 6-4

Men's Doubles: George Lott and Johnny Doeg (USA) def. John Van Ryn and Wilmer Allison (USA) 8-6, 6-3, 4-6, 13-15, 6-4

Women's Doubles: Betty Nuthall (GBR) and Sarah Palfrey (USA) def. Edith Cross and Anna McCune Harper (USA), 3-6, 6-3, 7-5

Mixed Doubles: Edith Cross and Wilmer Allison (USA) def. Marjorie Morrill and Frank Shields (USA), 6-4, 6-4

Year-End No. 1
Men: Henri Cochet
Women: Helen Wills Moody

Davis Cup: France

Wightman Cup: Great Britain

1931

The Wimbledon Final That Was Never Played

Sidney Wood, in action against Fred Perry of Britain in the Wimbledon semifinals, wins the Wimbledon final in a default.

Sidney Wood first appeared at Wimbledon as a 15-year-old wearing white knickers on the Centre Court in 1927, the youngest to play in the Championships at that time, losing to Rene Lacoste, 6-1, 6-3, 6-1. Sidney returned at 19, became the youngest player in the 20th century (until 17-year-old Boris Becker in 1985) to win and the only one ever to win an unplayed Wimbledon final. His opponent, U.S. Davis Cup teammate Frank Shields, withdrew with an ankle injury.

Wood, seeded No. 7, advanced to the final, 4-6, 6-2, 6-4, 6-2, over 22-year-old Fred Perry, a fourth round winner over a promising young German, future three-time finalist Gottfried von Cramm, 7-5, 6-2, 6-4.

Facing top-seeded Jean Borotra, who was fresh from winning the French, Shields managed to take their semifinal, 7-5, 3-6, 6-4, 6-4, twisting his ankle near the end. Frank was ordered by the U.S. Davis Cup Committee to default to teammate Wood in order to recuperate for a Cup semifinal against Britain the following weekend in Paris. There, the winner would challenge France for the Cup. "Frank wanted to play me, and it was an insult to Wimbledon and the public that he didn't," recalled Wood. "But it gives you an idea of the importance of Davis Cup then, and the USLTA's tight control of American amateurs. Can you imagine a player today abandoning a Wimbledon final to save himself for Davis Cup? But, as amateurs, we had no say.

Frank played well against the Brits, beating Fred Perry, but we lost, 3-2."

Californian Ellsworth Vines, who had been ranked No. 8 in 1930 and hadn't been picked for the Davis Cup team early in the year, came into his own at 19 by winning the U.S. Championship in September. From Pasadena, Vines was a lanky 6-foot-1, weighing only 145 pounds, and with a great cannonball serve. Analyst Julius Heldman wrote: "He had the flattest set of ground strokes ever seen and they were hit so hard, particularly on the forehand, that they could not clear the net by more than a few inches without going out."

Fred Perry scared Vines in the semifinal by winning the first two sets, but the champ served his way out (4-6, 3-6, 6-4, 6-4, 6-3) and concluded by beating George Lott for the title, 7-9, 6-3, 9-7, 7-5, despite trailing 5-3 in the third set and 5-2 in the fourth. Lott, who came from two sets down to outlast Johnny Van Ryn in the quarterfinal, 5-7, 1-6, 6-0, 7-5, 6-1, next knocked out the defender, Johnny Doeg, 7-5, 6-3, 6-0.

At Sydney, uniquely among the majors, a husband and wife took shots at the Australian singles titles. All-timer Jack Crawford

made it, the first of his four, 6-4, 6-2, 2-6, 6-1 over Harry Hopman, but Marjorie Cox Crawford couldn't bring in a spouse's double, falling to Coral Buttsworth, 1-6, 6-3, 6-4. Still, the Crawfords won the mixed, 7-5, 6-4, over Emily Hood Westacott and Aubrey Willard, to start a three-year run of success as a togetherness-plus couple.

Playing without Bill Tilden, the U.S. failed to appear in the Davis Cup Challenge Round for the first time since 1914. It appeared the Yanks would have a crack at the French for the right to win the Cup when they took a 2-1 semifinal lead over Britain in Paris on the doubles win of Johnny Van Ryn and Lott over George Hughes and Perry, 6-1, 6-3, 4-6, 6-3. Bunny Austin came through as the Brits' bright boy, getting a first day split, beating Wood, 2-6, 6-0, 8-6, 7-5. Shields, fully recovered from the Wimbledon injury, squared the windy first day by beating Perry, 10-8, 6-4, 6-2. But the Brits roared back the third day, with Perry stopping Wood, 6-3, 8-10, 6-3, 6-3, and Austin shutting down Shields in the decider, 8-6, 6-3, 7-5.

That was almost enough impetus for them to dislodge the Cup from Stade Roland Garros. But the French, triumphant for a fifth consecutive year, had triple-threat master Cochet in the 3-2 finale that went down to an excruciating fifth match. There, Cochet out-dueled Perry, 6-4, 1-6, 9-7, 6-3. Cochet also beat Austin on the first day, 3-6, 11-9, 6-2, 6-4, but Perry stopped Borotra, 4-6, 10-8, 6-0, 4-6, 6-4. Returning, Cochet sided with 36-year-old Jacques Brugnon to repel Charles Kingsley and Pat Hughes, 6-1, 5-7, 6-3, 8-6 for the go-ahead point. However, Austin squared it again, over Borotra 7-5, 6-3, 3-6, 7-5 – leaving it up to France's Cup body guard, Cochet.

When Helen Wills Moody chose not to play at Wimbledon, it appeared that Helen Jacobs could win, particularly after winning her 6-2, 6-3 quarterfinal over reigning U.S. champ Betty Nuthall. However, Jacobs fell in the semifinal to Hilde Krahwinkel, 10-8, 0-6, 6-4. In the only all-German Wimbledon women's final, five-foot Cilly Aussem defeated Krahwinkel, 6-2, 7-5.

Aussem had also won the French by beating Nuthall in the final, 8-6, 6-1. Borotra, loser of the 1925 and 1929 title matches to Rene Lacoste, finally grabbed the trophy in another intramural final, defeating Christian Boussus 2-6, 6-4, 7-5, 6-4.

Arriving at Forest Hills after missing the 1930 U.S. tourney, and deprived of a major title for the first time in five years (having passed on Wimbledon and the French), Moody rectified that in a hurry. She took her seventh (and last) U.S. title in 35 minutes over Eileen Bennett Whittingstall of Britain, 6-4, 6-1. By the end of 1931, Moody had gone four years without losing a set at the U.S. Championships.

As the U.S. and Great Britain prepared for the Wightman Cup matches, they were tied at 4-4. The U.S. won 5-2 at Forest Hills, thanks to the two Helens. Each won a pair of singles: Moody over Nuthall, 6-4, 6-2, and Phyllis Mudford, 6-1, 6-4; Jacobs over Nuthall, 8-6, 6-4, and Mudford, 6-4, 6-2. This was the start of a 21-year string of U.S. Cup victories that would not be broken until 1958.

Bill Tilden made his long-awaited debut as a professional in the midst of The Great Depression. As co-promoter of his tour with entrepreneur William O'Brien, Tilden opened against Czech Karel Kozeluh at Madison Square Garden on February 18 before a crowd of 13,000 paying $36,000. Tilden won, 6-4, 6-2, 6-4, then ran off

16 straight victories and went on to beat Kozeluh before big galleries at almost every stop (63-13) of a cross-country tour that grossed $238,000. Americans Frank Hunter, Bobby Seller and Emmett Pare played subordinate roles on the tour. Other professionals at the time were Hans Nusslein and Roman Najuch of Germany, the Irish Burke brothers—Albert and Edmund—living in France; and Major Rendell of England. At Forest Hills during the summer, the U.S. Pro Championships drew a field of 39, with Tilden trouncing Vinnie Richards, 7-5, 6-2, 6-1, in the final.

1931 CHAMPIONS AND LEADERS

Australian Championships
Men's Singles Final: Jack Crawford (AUS) def. Harry Hopman (AUS), 6-4, 6-2, 2-6, 6-1

Women's Singles Final: Coral McInnes Buttsworth (AUS) def. Marjorie Cox Crawford (AUS), 1-6, 6-3, 6-4

Men's Doubles Final: Charles Donohoe and Ray Dunlop (AUS) def. Harry Hopman and Jack Crawford (AUS), 8-6, 6-2, 5-7, 7-9, 6-4

Women's Doubles Final: Daphne Akhurst Cozens and Louie Bickerton (AUS) def. Nell Lloyd and Lorna Utz (AUS), 6-0, 6-4

Mixed Doubles: Marjorie Cox Crawford and Jack Crawford (AUS) def. Emily Hood Westacott and Aubrey Willard (AUS), 7-5, 6-4

French Championships
Men's Singles Final: Jean Borotra (FRA) def. Christian Boussus (FRA) 2-6, 6-4, 7-5, 6-4

Women's Singles Final: Cilly Aussem (GER) def. Betty Nuthall (GBR), 8-6, 6-1

Men's Doubles Final: George Lott and John Van Ryn (USA) def. Vernon Kirby and Norman Farquharson (RSA), 6-4, 6-3, 6-4

Women's Doubles Final: Eileen Bennett Whittingstall and Betty Nuthall (GBR) def. Cilly Assem (GER) and Elizabeth Ryan (USA), 9-7, 6-2

Mixed Doubles Final: Betty Nuthall (GBR) and Pat Spence (RSA) def. Dorothy Shepherd Barron and Bunny Austin (GBR), 6-3, 5-7, 6-3

Wimbledon
Men's Singles Final: Sidney Wood (USA) def. Frank Shields (USA), walkover

Women's Singles Final: Cilly Aussem (GER) def. Hilde Krahwinkel Sperling (GER), 6-2, 4-6, 7-5

Men's Doubles Final: George Lott and John Van Ryn (USA) def. Jacques Brugnon and Henri Cochet (FRA), 6-2, 10-8, 9-11, 3-6, 6-3

Women's Doubles Final: Dorothy Shepherd Barron and Phyllis Mudford (GBR) def. Doris Metaxa (FRA) and Josane Sigart (BEL), 3-6, 6-3, 6-4

Mixed Doubles Final: Anna McCune Harper and George Lott (USA) def. Joan Ridley and Ian Collins (GBR), 6-3, 1-6, 6-1

U.S. Championships
Men's Singles Final: Ellsworth Vines (USA) def. George Lott (USA), 7-9, 6-3, 9-7, 7-5

Women's Singles Final: Helen Wills Moody (USA) def. Eileen Bennett Whittingstall (GBR), 6-4, 6-1

Men's Doubles Final: Wilmer Allison and John Van Ryn (USA) def. Greg Mangin and Berkeley Bell (USA), 6-4, 8-6, 6-3

Women's Doubles Final: Betty Nuthall and Eileen Bennett Whittingstall (GBR) def. Helen Jacobs (USA) and Dorothy Round (GBR), 6-2, 6-4

Mixed Doubles Final: Betty Nuthall (GBR) and George Lott (USA) def. Anna McCune Harper and Wilmer Allison (USA), 6-3, 6-3

Year-End No. 1
Men: Henri Cochet
Women: Helen Wills Moody

Davis Cup: France

Wightman Cup: United States

1932
Vines Wins Wimbledon, U.S. Titles

Ellsworth Vines hits a backhand against Jack Crawford of Australia at Wimbledon.

Ellsworth Vines became the first man since Bill Tilden in 1921 to win both the Wimbledon and U.S. Championships. Competing in his first Wimbledon at 20, Vines was so impressive that some English reporters were calling him the greatest player of all time.

He defeated Australian Harry Hopman, 7-5, 6-2, 7-5, in the third round and sailed through Australian Jack Crawford, 6-2, 6-1, 6-3, and Britain's Bunny Austin, 6-4, 6-2, 6-0, in the last two rounds.

Vines launched 30 aces against Austin, who broke his serve only once. Ellsworth's match point was a service ace and Austin said: "I saw him swing his racket and I heard the ball hit the back canvas. The umpire called game, set and match, so I knew it was all

over, but I never saw the ball." The serve was timed at 121 miles per hour.

Crawford, the winner of the Australian Championship by beating Hopman for the second straight year, 4-6, 6-3, 3-6, 6-3, 6-1, had topped Fred Perry in the Wimbledon quarterfinal pairing of two future champs, 7-5, 8-6, 2-6, 8-6. An oddity of the tournament was top-seeded Henri Cochet losing in the second round to Brit Ian Collins, 6-2, 8-6, 0-6, 6-3, then entering and winning the All England Plate competition for also-rans eliminated in the first two rounds. He became the first ex-champion to win the Plate.

Americans, so impressed with Vines at Wimbledon, had high hopes the U.S. would regain the Davis Cup after a 3-2 semifinal win over Germany in Paris. Vines had handled the slow clay of Roland Garros handsomely, beating Daniel Prenn, 6-3, 6-3, 0-6, 6-4, after the ascending 23-year-old Baron Gottfried von Cramm won a tough battle with Frank Shields, 7-5, 5-7, 6-4, 8-6. Reliables Johnny Van Ryn and Wilmer Allison went through Prenn-von Cramm 6-3, 6-4, 6-1, setting up Vines for the clincher over von Cramm, 3-6, 6-3, 9-7, 6-3, though Elly was two points from losing the third set at 6-7, 30-all.

But then came the incident called by many "The Great Cup Robbery" in the Challenge Round. Vines showed that he was less than invincible in losing to crafty Jean Borotra in the first singles match, 6-4, 6-2, 3-6, 6-4. U.S. Captain Bernon Prentice had replaced Shields in the singles with Allison, and when Cochet fought past him, 5-7, 7-5, 7-5, 6-2, to make it 2-0, it looked as if France would win easily. However, a thrilling doubles triumph by Allison and Van Ryn over Cochet and Jacques Brugnon, 6-3, 11-13, 7-5, 4-6, 6-4, tightened the engagement, and set up one of the most controversial episodes in Davis Cup history.

First, the groundskeepers heavily watered the clay at Stade Roland Garros in the hope of slowing the court down to hamper Vines in his final match. The slow court served instead to bother Borotra in the third singles match, against Allison. But Borotra, only days from his 34th birthday and reluctant to join the team, had one last gallant Cup thrust within him. Despite losing the first two sets to Allison, he rode the roars of a jam-packed crowd of 10,000 and volleyed his way back to parity. With gestures, he called for their help, and thrice the Bounding Basque bought revival time in the fifth set by changing his flimsy espadrille-style shoes, once during a game.

Still, Allison took a 5-3 lead with serve, 40-15, then advantage—but squandered three match points, one a net cord shot by the Frenchman, the others on over-hit passers. The final blow came at a subsequent match point on Borotra's serve at 4-5. Borotra netted his first serve. The second was long, so long that a relieved Allison, who had performed so well over the three hot days—this his 14th set—hit the ball aside, making no attempt to play it. He moved to the net to shake hands.

"We were cheering," recalled Van Ryn, "thinking it was all tied up at 2-2. Wilmer had won." Or had he? "But then the umpire [Morin] announced, 'Egalite'— deuce—and we couldn't believe it. The service linesman (Gerrard le Ferrier, thereafter considering himself a notable patriot) had stolen the win. He made no call and indicated the serve was good. The umpire backed him

up." That was too much for Wilmer, and he lost the last three games, and 10 of the remaining 12 points, the final score, 1-6, 3-6, 6-4, 6-2, 7-5. "Dwight Davis, who sat next to me, was so mad that he withheld us from attending the official dinner that night," added Van Ryn. "It was an incredible rebuke to the French from such a great sportsman. I only heard him cuss once, and it was then. He said: 'I'm sorry I ever gave the goddam Cup!'" Most newspaper accounts, including the French, agreed that Borotra's second serve was clearly long.

Fans were left to debate whether Cochet, who won the first two sets and then lost the final match to Vines, 4-6, 0-6, 7-5, 8-6, 6-2, would have been able to pull through if France had needed that point. The 3-2 decision meant a sixth straight Davis Cup for France, but it would be her last until 1991.

Vines, who often wore a white cap, had a curious windmill stroke in which the racket made an almost 360-degree sweep. Starting on high as though he were going to serve, he brought the racket head back almost to the ground and swept up to the ball. He put no spin on it, however, thereby hitting a flat shot with tremendous force that made him unbeatable when he was on.

Opponents came to realize that the way to beat him was to keep the ball in play, hitting him soft stuff until he started making errors. A harbinger was the memorable U.S. semifinal at Forest Hills. Cliff Sutter, the National Intercollegiate champ from Tulane, slowed things down and won the first two sets, and twice came within two points of victory (5-6, deuce in the third set; 5-6, 30-all in the fourth). But Vines persevered in the exhausting 75-game, 2 1/2-hour struggle, 4-6, 8-10, 12-10, 10-8, 6-1. That left little time for the Cochet-Allison semifinal, and they were chased by darkness at 2-2. It meant finishing the semifinal the same day as the final, the lone such incident in the history of the U.S. Championships. Beating Allison in the 45-minute fifth set, Cochet—almost 31—was the winner, 6-1, 10-12, 4-6, 6-3, 7-5. He was given about two hours to rest for the final against Vines, who wouldn't be 21 until the end of the month. He complained, justifiably, about having to play again that day, but the U.S. Lawn Tennis Association wasn't going to turn away an overflow crowd of 15,000. Henri had a point in saying that American treatment of a foreigner was no better than that received, and bemoaned, by the Americans in the recent Davis Cup contest in Paris. He was plainly weary in a 6-4, 6-4, 6-4 defeat. Twice he was unable to move out of the way in time to avoid being hit by Vines' blinding serve. The last two aces of the match by Vines were so hard that they bounced into the stands. Cochet never returned to Forest Hills.

But Helen Wills Moody did return to Wimbledon after a one-year absence and won her fifth title, losing only 13 games in 12 sets. For the second time in the final she met Helen Jacobs, winning 6-3, 6-1. Moody also won her fourth French Championship, 7-5, 6-1 over long-striving Simone Passemard Mathieu, the native who would absorb a tournament record of six final-round defeats before finally becoming champion in 1938. Jacobs raised English eyebrows at Wimbledon when she played in what now are regarded as Bermuda shorts.

With Moody absent from Forest Hills, Jacobs raised her world ranking to No. 2 (behind Moody) by winning the U.S. title for the first time. She had lost the final in 1928 to Moody, but this time

Jacobs beat another Californian, third-seeded Carolin Babcock, 6-2, 6-2. Future Hall of Famer Alice Marble made her first appearance in the U.S. Top 10 at No. 7.

Cochet notched his fourth French title, the record until Bjorn Borg came along almost five decades later to win a fifth in 1980 before adding a sixth the following year. Cochet turned back the only ambidextrous man to occupy a major final, Italian Giorgio de Stefani, 6-0, 6-4, 4-6, 6-3. Coral McInnes Buttsworth won her second straight Australian title, beating Katherine LeMesurier, 9-7, 6-4, and also won the doubles with Marjorie Cox Crawford over LeMesurier and Dorothy Weston, both Australians, 6-2, 6-2. It was a splendid Australian Championships for the Crawfords. Gentleman Jack, as he was called, tripled by adding the men's doubles with Gar Moon over Harry Hopman and Gerald Patterson, 12-10, 6-3, 4-6, 6-4, and the mixed with wife Marjorie over the Aussie-Japanese combo of Meryl O'Hara Wood and Jiro Satoh 6-8, 8-6, 6-3. Three other married couples have won major mixed titles: Americans Clarence and Augusta Schultz Hobart, the U.S. in 1905; Brits Leslie and Kitty McKane Godfree, Wimbledon in 1926; Aussies Harry and Nell Hall Hopman, the Australian in 1936-37, 39; and the Crawfords, taking their homeland title in 1931-32-33. But only Jack Crawford had a trifecta year.

The two Helens were almost enough as the U.S. took a 6-4 lead in the Wightman Cup at Wimbledon, 4-3. Moody beat future Wimbledon champ Dorothy Round, 6-2, 6-3, and Eileen Bennett Whittingstall, 6-2, 6-4. Jacobs beat Round, 6-4, 6-3, but lost to Whittingstall, 6-4, 1-6, 6-1. That left it up to Jacobs to revive, accompanying Anne McCune Harper in a decisive doubles over Peggy Saunders Michell and Round, 6-4, 6-1.

Bill Tilden continued to command the thin professional ranks with a mixture of tennis skill and theatrical showmanship. Tilden, Vinnie Richards and Germany's Hans Nusslein were the tour's standouts. Tilden faced Nusslein about 150 times, winning 100, and was 12-1 over Richards. But it was Czech Karel Kozeluh who beat Nusslein, 6-2, 6-2, 7-5, for his second U.S. Pro title.

1932 CHAMPIONS AND LEADERS

Australian Championships
Men's Singles Final: Jack Crawford (AUS) def. Harry Hopman (AUS), 4-6, 6-3, 3-6, 6-3, 6-1
Women's Singles Final: Coral McInnes Buttsworth (AUS) def. Katherine LeMesurier (AUS), 9-7, 6-4
Men's Doubles Final: Jack Crawford and Gar Moon (AUS) def. Harry Hopman and Gerald Patterson (AUS), 12-10, 6-3, 4-6, 6-4
Women's Doubles Final: Coral McInnes Buttsworth and Marjorie Cox Crawford (AUS) def. Katherine LeMesurier and Dorothy Weston (AUS), 6-2, 6-2
Mixed Doubles Final: Marjorie Cox Crawford and Jack Crawford (AUS) def. Meryl O'Hara Wood (AUS) and Jiro Satoh (JPN), 6-8, 8-6, 6-3

French Championships
Men's Singles Final: Henri Cochet (FRA) def. Giorgio de Stefani (ITA), 6-0, 6-4, 4-6, 6-3
Women's Singles Final: Helen Wills Moody (USA) def. Simone Passemard Mathieu (FRA), 7-5, 6-1
Men's Doubles Final: Henri Cochet and Jacques Brugnon (FRA) def. Christian Boussus and Marcel Bernard (FRA), 6-4, 3-6, 7-5, 6-3
Women's Doubles Final: Helen Wills Moody and Elizabeth Ryan (USA) def. Betty Nuthall and Eileen Bennett Whittinghall (GBR), 6-1, 6-3
Mixed Doubles Final: Betty Nuthall and Fred Perry (GBR) def. Helen Wills Moody and Sidney Wood (USA), 6-4, 6-2

Wimbledon
Men's Singles Final: Ellsworth Vines (USA) def. Bunny Austin (GBR), 6-4, 6-2, 6-0
Women's Singles Final: Helen Wills Moody (USA) def. Helen Jacobs (USA), 6-3, 6-1
Men's Doubles Final: Jean Borotra and Jacques Brugnon (FRA) def. Fred Perry and Pat Hughes (GBR), 6-0, 4-6, 3-6, 7-5, 7-5
Women's Doubles Final: Doris Metaxa (FRA) and Josane Sigart (BEL) def. Helen Jacobs and Elizabeth Ryan (USA), 6-4, 6-3
Mixed Doubles Final: Elizabeth Ryan (USA) and Enrique Maier (ESP) def. Josane Sigart (BEL) and Harry Hopman (AUS), 7-5, 6-2

U.S. Championships
Men's Singles Final: Ellsworth Vines (USA) def. Henri Cochet (FRA), 6-4, 6-4, 6-4
Women's Singles Final: Helen Jacobs (USA) def. Carolin Babcock (USA), 6-2, 6-2
Men's Doubles Final: Ellsworth Vines and Keith Gledhill (USA) def. Wilmer Allison and John Van Ryn (USA) 6-4, 6-3, 6-2
Women's Doubles Final: Helen Jacobs and Sarah Palfrey (USA) def. Marjorie Morrill Painter and Alice Marble (USA), 8-6, 6-1
Mixed Doubles Final: Sarah Palfrey (USA) and Fred Perry (GBR) def. Helen Jacobs and Ellsworth Vines (USA), 6-3, 7-5

Year-End No. 1
Men: Ellsworth Vines
Women: Helen Wills Moody

Davis Cup: France

Wightman Cup: United States

1933

A Tainted Win For Jacobs, A Near Slam for Crawford

Jack Crawford (left) beats **Ellsworth Vines** (right) at Wimbledon, but falls one match shy of the first "Grand Slam".

that year, over Dorothy Round, 6-4, 6-8, 6-3. She had won seven U.S. titles and never lost to Jacobs after trouncing her 6-0, 6-0 the first time they collided. Moody beat Jacobs in two Wimbledon finals and the 1928 U.S. final. Jacobs had won the U.S. in 1932 when Moody abstained. Though Jacobs insisted there was no feud, she wanted badly to beat Moody. She turned to Lenglen, who drilled her in hitting crosscourt so that she would avoid giving Moody the backcourt dominance she liked best. The faster Jacobs was determined to play the net as often as possible. In the semifinal, Moody lost her first set in seven years at Forest Hills to Betty Nuthall, 2-6, 6-3, 6-2, while Jacobs beat future Wimbledon champ Dorothy Round, 6-4, 5-7, 6-2. With the title at stake, Jacobs took her first set ever from Moody, 8-6. Moody won the second, 6-3, tiring her opponent with drop shots. Given a respite in the intermission, Jacobs broke Moody's service twice for a 3-0 advantage. In his history of tennis, Will Grimsley wrote: "At this point Moody strode to the umpire's chair and put on her sweater. 'I am sorry, my back pains me. I cannot go on,' she said tersely. That was all she said. Wearing a long coat, her familiar eyeshade pulled low, she strode to the dressing room, declining interviews."

Although Helen Wills Moody and Suzanne Lenglen are regarded as two of the greatest women players of all time, it's ironic that both are also remembered for matches in which they defaulted and walked off the court at Forest Hills. Lenglen defaulted to Molla Mallory in 1921, and Moody quit in the middle of her U.S. final with Helen Jacobs in 1933. The two Helens—Moody, almost 28, tall, dark-haired, and coldly methodical, and Jacobs, 25, stocky and outgoing—were natural rivals. Both came from the San Francisco Bay area. Both had the same coach, William "Pop" Fuller, and the Jacobs family lived in the house where the Wills family had lived. When they met for the second time in a U.S. final (the first was 1928), Moody had long been a practically invulnerable figure. She had won her sixth Wimbledon title

It was reported that Jacobs pleaded with her to continue. Jacobs denied this, saying she merely inquired if she would like to rest. Moody said no and walked away without shaking hands. The fans were stunned. The press lambasted her. She was accused of being a poor sport, a quitter, ungracious. Later she said: "1 feel that I have spoiled the finish of the U.S. Championships and wish that I had followed the advice of my doctor and returned to California. I still feel I did right in withdrawing because I was on the verge of collapse on the court." The loss was her first since 1926.

Lining up without Moody (due to her back injury) and Alice Marble (heat exhaustion) in singles, the U.S. still won the Wightman Cup over Britain, 4-3. Jacobs and 20-year-old Sarah Palfrey were the difference at Forest Hills. Helen beat Round, 6-4, 6-2, and Peggy Scriven, 5-7, 6-2, 7-5. Sarah beat Scriven, 6-3, 6-1. A Helen-Sarah combo got the clincher over Mary Heeley and Round, 6-4, 6-2.

But, days before, the unfortunate ordeal of 19-year-old Marble in an abbreviated, three-day tourney at Easthampton, N.Y., kept her out of Cup singles and diminished her at Forest Hills (fourth round loss to Nuthall, 6-8, 6-0, 7-5, despite a 5-1 lead and three match points). At Easthampton during an oppressive 104 degree afternoon, Alice played 108 games, singles and doubles semifinals and finals, suffering sunstroke. She beat Midge Gladman Van Ryn, 6-3, 6-8, 6-1, lost the final to Nuthall, 5-7, 6-5, 6-0. She and Moody beat Mary Heeley and Nuthall, 6-4, 4-6, 6-1, lost the final to Elizabeth Ryan and Scriven, 6-2, 9-7. Hoping to play only doubles, Marble was told by USLTA official Julian Myrick that she must play both to be considered for the Wightman team. It was another instance of tight control of amateur players by their associations, and may have contributed to her physical collapse and absence from tennis for most of 1934 and 1935. "I was heartbroken," she wrote, "when a doctor told me I was too weak to play singles. I'd never been on the team and worked so hard to make it."

The man who almost won something that didn't exist—the Grand Slam—was Aussie Jack Crawford, traveling the world in unprecedented championship style. By the time he reached Forest Hills for the 1933 U.S. Championships, "Gentleman Jack," who parted his hair down the middle, had departed from Melbourne, Paris and London with three major titles in his satchel. Nobody had ever done that.

Before Don Budge was to come along and popularize the notion of the Grand Slam—the four majors within a calendar year—Crawford came within a set of achieving that sweep, missing out only at Forest Hills in a five-set loss to Fred Perry.

Wimbledon Secretary Duncan Macaulay wrote in *Behind the Scenes at Wimbledon*: "Jack Crawford was one of the most popular champions who ever appeared at Wimbledon. Although he was only 25 when he won the title, he always seemed much older. Perhaps it was the effect of his hairstyle, the sleeves of his cricket shirt buttoned at the wrist [though he was known to roll them up in moments of crisis] and, most of all, the old-fashioned square-headed racquet with which he always played. In a long match he liked to have a pot of tea, complete with milk and sugar, and reserves of hot water, by the umpire's chair, instead of the iced beverages and other revivers favored by the moderns."

English authority Max Robertson wrote in 1974 that if a poll were taken about the best men's singles final at Wimbledon, "the Crawford-Ellsworth Vines match in 1933 would probably head it; certainly it would have to be included in the top six." With 13 aces, Vines ran out 11 service games at love. Crawford played a defensive game against Vines' power, concentrating on Vines' relatively weak backhand. They split the first four sets before Crawford changed tactics, rushing the net. He took Vines' title away, breaking the last game at love, 4-6, 11-9, 6-2, 2-6, 6-4.

The crowd exulted over the first victory by a British Empire player (although Crawford was pressed in the opening round by Spaniard Enrique Maier, 7-5, 6-4, 2-6, 3-6, 6-4) since Gerald Patterson, another Australian, won in 1923. Macaulay wrote: "The cheering of the spectators went on and on, and their enthusiasm was so great there appeared to be a distinct danger that the sacred turf of the Centre Court would be invaded by the multitude."

There were two innovations at Wimbledon. Australian Vivian McGrath showed his revolutionary two-handed backhand, winning two rounds. Brit Bunny Austin, a loser in the quarterfinal to No. 7 seed Jiro Satoh of Japan, 7-5, 6-3, 2-6, 2-6, 6-2, wore shorts for the first time on the Centre Court, having pioneered them at Forest Hills in 1932. Henri Cochet put on a pair, but only for the mixed doubles, and his opponent, Norman Farquharson of South Africa, rolled up his trousers. The tragic Satoh, who committed suicide the following year, achieved the highest major finish for a Japanese male other than Zenzo Shimidzu's appearance in the 1920 all-comers final, losing to Crawford, 6-3, 6-4, 2-6, 6-4, in the semifinals.

A big disappointment was No. 6-seeded Fred Perry, who lost in the second round to Farquharson 7-5, 6-1, 3-6, 4-6, 6-4. Perry finally won his first major title at Forest Hills, when he outlasted Crawford in a grueling match, 6-3, 11-13, 4-6, 6-0, 6-1. Defending champion Vines was staggered in the fourth round, 6-3, 6-3, 6-3, by the dogged retriever 5-foot-4 Bitsy Grant in what was called a Mutt & Jeff match.

The term "Grand Slam" didn't exist when Crawford began his championship journey by winning his homeland's title for a third time in succession, over Californian Keith Gledhill, 2-6, 7-5, 6-3, 6-2, through rain interruptions on a soggy Melbourne court. An attractive 19-year-old Australian Joan Hartigan unseated champ Coral Buttsworth, 6-4, 6-3, the first of her three titles. Crawford shared the marquee with "The Freak," his 17-year-old countryman Vivian McGrath, who knocked out favorite Ellsworth Vines, 6-3, 2-6, 8-6, 7-5 in the quarterfinals. Right-hander McGrath's unconventional two-fisted backhand drives, the first both-handed stroke seen in the upper class, didn't fool Gledhill, who slow-balled the kid out, 6-4, 6-1, 6-1.

Stricken by an asthma attack in France, Crawford recovered in time to wreck Henri Cochet's quest for a fifth title, dethroning the daring half-volleyer, 8-6, 6-1, 6-3. Crawford was the first alien male to win the French. Completing the distress of the locals was the loss by Parisienne Simone Passemard Mathieu, to an unseeded 20-year-old British lefty, Peggy Scriven, 6-2, 4-6, 6-4.

Next for Crawford came Wimbledon. By the time Jack arrived—against his wishes—in New York, he was bushed, anxious to go home after almost five months on the road. Having won 13 straight tournaments, troubled by insomnia and asthma, he wanted to skip the U.S. However, the Australian Association got a $1,500 payment from the USLTA guaranteeing his presence and he had no choice. People were beginning to talk of an unprecedented "clean sweep of the Big Four titles," and *New York Times* columnist John Kieran, a bridge player, wrote: "If Crawford wins, it would be something like scoring a grand slam on the courts, doubled and vulnerable."

It looked as though he would, reaching the final losing only two sets, and leading Perry 2-1 in sets at the intermission. But Jack was through, and would win only one more game. While Perry showered and changed, returning to the court refreshed, Crawford, drained, unwisely remained at the court, sitting in wet clothes. Unknown to him, his friend Vinnie Richards had spiked his tea with bourbon as a pick-me-up. It was no help, perhaps a hindrance. But no alibis—there never were from Crawford. And Perry—"I just went mad!"—came on like a firehorse to win eight games on a gallop and his first major, 6-2, 11-13, 4-6, 6-0, 6-1. There would be no sweep or Grand Slam. Perry's roughest test had been Gledhill in the fourth round, 6-2, 4-6, 1-6, 6-3, 6-3. Not for five years would the Grand Slam topic surface again.

After Wimbledon, Perry began his move to greatness. It started in Pans with the heist of the Davis Cup. After he spearheaded Britain's first Cup-seizing triumph since 1912, the front-page headline in London's *Daily Express* read simply: FRED! The Brits ended France's six-year, 11-victory reign, 3-2, at Stade Roland Garros.

In the first day of the finale, Perry stopped Henri Cochet in five, 8-10, 6-4, 8-6, 3-6, 6-1, blotting a set point in the third. Bunny Austin whipped 19-year-old lefty Andre Merlin quickly, 6-3, 6-4, 6-0, and it was 2-0. But the 72-year-old team, Jean Borotra (34) and Jacques Brugnon (38) raced through the doubles past Pat Hughes and Harold Lee, 6-3, 8-6, 6-2, and the third-day crowd of 10,000 was agog as Cochet tied it by outlasting Austin, 5-7, 6-4, 4-6, 6-4, 6-4, coming back from a 1-3 deficit in the fourth and running the last four games of the fifth with irresistible volleying. Perry, dodging two set points in the second, overcame a spirited rookie, Merlin, in the decisive fifth match, 4-6, 8-6, 6-2, 7-5. Merlin was a stroke from a two-set lead over Perry, two set points at 5-4, but the Brit turned Fred-hot. In the decisive fourth, Perry blew a 5-1 lead, but pulled himself together one last time.

Working 13 of a possible 14 singles and six of seven doubles over the Cup run, Perry was 12-1 and 4-2. Austin, the fashion plate (Perry was the only singles player in long trousers), was 13-1 in singles.

The Brits had primed for the final with 4-1 semifinal win over the U.S. It began with Austin stunning Vines 6-1, 6-1, 6-4. Elly's magic of two years had just about run out. Perry knocked off Allison, 6-1, 7-5, 6-4. Johnny Van Ryn and George Lott, Wimbledon doubles winners in 1931, delayed the Brits for a day, 8-6, 6-4, 6-1, over Hughes and Perry, before Austin shoved aside a highly competitive Allison, 6-2, 7-9, 6-3, 6-4. The Brits had won, but in the meaningless fifth match, with Perry leading Vines, 1-6, 6-0, 4-6, 7-5, 7-6 (40-15), the American fainted and was carried from the court in defeat, an agonizing farewell to Paris.

In the quarterfinals, the Aussies started well, with Crawford beating Austin, 4-6, 6-2, 6-2, 6-3. But teenager Viv McGrath couldn't keep up with Perry, 6-2, 6-4 6-2, and with Austin in the clincher of the 3-2 decision 6-4, 7-5, 6-3. In the doubles, Hughes and Perry made the difference over Adrian Quist and Don Turnbull, 7-5, 6-4, 3-6, 6-3.

Bill Tilden's opponent on the pro tour was again Hans Nusslein of Germany. Tilden dominated, though gross receipts dropped from $86,000 to $62,000. Henri Cochet also turned pro

and was beaten by Tilden in his debut in Paris, 6-2, 6-4, 6-2. Vinnie Richards won his fourth U.S. Pro title, beating Frank Hunter, 6-3, 6-0, 6-2.

1933 CHAMPIONS AND LEADERS

Australian Championships
Men's Singles Final: Jack Crawford (AUS) def. Keith Gledhill (USA), 2-6, 7-5, 6-3, 6-2
Women's Singles Final: Joan Hartigan (AUS) def. Coral McInnes Buttsworth (AUS), 6-4, 6-3
Men's Doubles Final: Keith Gledhill and Ellsworth Vines (USA) def. Jack Crawford and Gar Moon (AUS), 6-4, 10-8, 6-2
Women's Doubles Final: Mall Molesworth and Emily Hood Westcott (AUS) def. Joan Hartigan (AUS) and Marjorie Gladman Van Ryn (USA), 6-3, 6-2
Mixed Doubles Final: Marjorie Cox Crawford and Jack Crawford (AUS) def. Marjorie Gladman Van Ryn and Ellsworth Vines (USA), 3-6, 7-5, 13-11

French Championships
Men's Singles: Jack Crawford (AUS) def. Henri Cochet (FRA), 8-6, 6-1, 6-3
Women's Singles: Margaret Scriven (GBR) def. Simone Passemard Mathieu (FRA), 6-2, 4-6, 6-4
Men's Doubles: Pat Hughes and Fred Perry (GBR) def. Adrian Quist and Viv McGrath (AUS), 6-2, 6-4, 2-6, 7-5
Women's Doubles: Simone Passemard Mathieu (FRA) and Elizabeth Ryan (USA) def. Sylvie Jung Henrotin and Colette Rosambert (FRA), 6-1, 6-3
Mixed Doubles: Margaret Scriven (GBR) and Jack Crawford (AUS) def. Betty Nuthall and Fred Perry (GBR), 6-2, 6-3

Wimbledon
Men's Singles Final: Jack Crawford (AUS) def. Ellsworth Vines (USA), 4-6, 11-9, 6-2, 2-6, 6-4
Women's Singles Final: Helen Wills Moody (USA) def. Dorothy Round (GBR), 6-4, 6-8, 6-3
Men's Doubles Final: Jean Borotra and Jacques Brugnon (FRA) def. Ryosuki Nunoi and Jiro Satoh (JPN), 4-6, 6-3, 6-3, 7-5
Women's Doubles Final: Simone Passemard Mathieu (FRA) and Elizabeth Ryan (USA) def. Freda James and Billie Yorke (GBR), 6-2, 9-11, 6-4
Mixed Doubles Final: Hilde Krahwinkel and Gottfried von Cramm (GER) def. Mary Heeley (GBR) and Norman Farquharson (RSA), 7-5, 8-6

U.S. Championships
Men's Singles Final: Fred Perry (GBR) def. Jack Crawford (AUS), 6-3, 11-13, 4-6, 6-0, 6-1,
Women's Singles Final: Helen Jacobs (USA) def. Helen Wills Moody (USA), 8-6, 3-6, 3-0, ret.
Men's Doubles Final: George Lott and Lester Stoefen (USA) def. Frank Shields and Frank Parker (USA), 11-13, 9-7, 9-7, 6-3
Women's Doubles Final: Betty Nuthall and Freda James (GBR) def. Helen Wills Moody and Elizabeth Ryan (USA), walkover
Mixed Doubles Final: Elizabeth Ryan and Ellsworth Vines (USA) def. Sarah Palfrey and George Lott (USA), 11-9, 6-1

Year-End No. 1
Men: Jack Crawford
Women: Helen Wills Moody

Davis Cup: Britain

Wightman Cup: United States

1934 Perry Nets Three Majors

Fred Perry prepares to hit a backhand at Wimbledon in 1934.

F red Perry came into his own as the best, capturing Britain's first Wimbledon title since 1909 (Arthur Gore), the year Perry was born. He also became the second man to hold three majors in one year, following up on Jack Crawford's splendid 1933. But just as Fred had dashed Crawford's bid for a "Grand Slam" at the U.S., his own was cancelled in the French quarterfinal by the forehands-only man, ambidextrous Italian racket-switcher Giorgio de Stefani. Perry's resistance was sapped by spraining his right ankle in the last set, and he fell, 6-2, 1-6, 9-7, 6-2.

Conversely, Crawford was the first to lose three major finals in one year: the Australian, French and Wimbledon (he passed on the U.S.). Perry shattered Crawford's three-year grip on the Australian in Sydney, 6-3, 7-5, 6-1, and repeated in the U.S., beating Texan Wilmer Allison, 6-4, 6-3, 1-6, 3-6, 8-6.

In between, Perry collaborated again with Bunny Austin to keep the Davis Cup in London, 4-1 over the U.S.

The Americans' only Cup comeback ever from 0-2 put the quartet of Sidney Wood, Frank Shields, George Lott and Les Stoefen into the Challenge Round, 3-2, over Australia. Incidentally, the "Miracle Man," Titanic survivor Dick Williams, was the U.S. captain. Lott and Stoefen won over Crawford and Adrian Quist,

6-4, 6-4, 2-6, 6-4, and then Wood and Shields reversed the singles results: Sidney jolted Crawford 6-3, 9-7, 4-6, 6-2 and Shields forcefully clinched over 18-year-old Viv McGrath, 6-4, 6-2, 6-4.

However, Lott and Stoefen, the Wimbledon and U.S. champs, beating Harold Lee and George Hughes, 7-5, 6-0, 4-6, 9-7, wasn't enough to divert the British tide. Austin and Perry beat up on Wood and Shields in singles. Austin beat Shields 6-4, 6-4, 6-1 in the opener, while Perry made it 2-0 with a 6-1, 4-6, 5-7, 6-0, 6-3 win over Wood. Perry then met tremendous resistance from Shields in clinching, 6-4, 4-6, 6-2, 15-13, breaking the tall American's serve in the fourth set though Shields led, 11-10, 15-0.

In his *History of Forest Hills*, Robert Minton wrote: "Perry combined speed with a wristy forehand developed from first playing table tennis, in which he became the world champion. He was an enormous crowd pleaser; handsome enough to be a movie star, and a cocky showman in a white blazer and an unlit pipe, as though he were a lord, and not the son of a Labor Party Member of Parliament. He never ruffled anyone with a display of temper, for he was phlegmatic and won his matches by outlasting his opponents. His physical condition was second to none."

Reporter Ferdinand Kuhn said of Perry's 6-3, 6-0, 7-5, Wimbledon triumph that disenfranchised Crawford: "Perry was always the complete master. He didn't make a half-dozen bad shots in the whole match. He was lithe as a panther, always holding the opponent in check and beating Crawford at his own cool, cautious game. Once he performed the amazing feat of capturing 12 games in a row." Perry said: "If I live to be 100, I'll never play so well again."

At the end, with Crawford serving at match point, he hit what looked like an ace, but he was called for a foot fault. He was so shaken by the call that he served into the net, the first time anybody could remember a Wimbledon final ending on a double fault.

Britain's joy was complete when Dorothy Round won the women's title, over Helen Jacobs—flunking on Centre Court for a third time—6-2, 5-7, 6-3. Afterward, to a tumultuous ovation, she and Perry were summoned to the Royal Box to be presented to King George V and Queen Mary. A quarter-century interval had ended. Two British players had won the singles for the first time since 1909 when Arthur Gore was complemented by Dora Boothby's victory over Agnes Morton, 6-4, 4-6, 8-6. It hasn't happened again.

The women's final had come down to a meeting between Round, beaten in the 1933 final by Helen Wills Moody, and Jacobs,

loser to Moody in the 1929 and 1932 final. Playing before the King and Queen, Dorothy was caught up in a scene much like Virginia Wade's Wimbledon Centenary victory in 1977, attended by the Royal Couple's granddaughter, Elizabeth II. Round fought off the invader in a strong third set as Wade would 43 years later.

At the French, slick-stroking German nobleman, Baron Gottfried von Cramm, almost 25, made his first big move, taking the title from Crawford, 6-4, 7-9, 3-6, 7-5, 6-3, by erasing a match point at 5-4 in the fourth with a brilliant overhead smash from the baseline. The Baron had semifinal difficulty with both de Stefani's forehands, 3-6, 6-4, 6-1, 3-6, 6-2. Jacobs was unlucky in Paris, too, as English southpaw Peggy Scriven beat her 7-5, 4-6, 6-1 for the crown.

Another repeater was Joan Hartigan at the Australian, denying a startling bid by the champ of 1922-23, the 40-year-old Mall Molesworth, 6-1, 6-4.

By now shorts and bare legs were much in evidence at Wimbledon. The Prince of Wales said: "I see no reason on earth why any woman should not wear shorts for lawn tennis. They are very comfortable and quite the most practical costume for the game; and I don't think the wearers lose anything in looks."

Elizabeth (Bunny) Ryan, 42, teamed with France's Simone Passemard Mathieu to win the women's doubles crown, 6-3, 6-3, over the American-French combo of Dorothy Andrus and Sylvia Jung Henrotin. It was Bunny's 19th Wimbledon doubles title, 20 years after her first, a record that Billie Jean King would surpass in 1979. Ryan won 12 doubles and seven mixed-doubles titles. Wimbledon official Duncan Macaulay offered this insight as to why Ryan, so strong in doubles, never won a major singles championship: "Firstly, her era coincided with that of two superlative singles champions, Suzanne Lenglen and Mrs. Moody; and secondly, Miss Ryan's only stroke on the forehead was a sizzling chop, very effective in doubles—particularly against women—but not so effective in singles as a good flat or topspin drive such as Lenglen or Moody played to perfection."

At Forest Hills, South African Vernon Kirby was the rain-tormented sensation, beating a 19-year-old future great, first-timer Don Budge in the fourth round, 4-6, 6-4, 6-4, 6-4 and then top-seeded American Frank Shields, 4-6, 6-4, 6-4, 6-3. But Perry cooled him in the semifinal, 6-2, 4-6, 6-4, 6-2, and steadied at the climax of the final to beat Wilmer Allison, 6-4, 6-3, 3-6, 1-6, 8-6, after a threatening Allison had volleyed away Fred's 5-2 lead in the fifth. Allison was strong in his semifinal over Wood, 6-3, 6-2, 6-3, after Wood eliminated 18-year-old Frank Parker, 6-4, 6-4, 7-5. Parker would wait a decade to fulfill his callow promise by winning the championship.

Sarah Palfrey Fabyan, almost 22 and playing her seventh U.S. Championships, got to her first final, but Jacobs—winning a third straight—was too tough, 6-1, 6-4. Sarah was still seven years removed from taking that last step. George Lott and Lester Stoefen, team of the year, won the U.S. doubles again, over Allison and Johnny Van Ryn, 6-4, 9-7, 3-6, 6-4, at Longwood in Boston, virtuoso George's fifth title, the 6-foot-4 Stoefen his third partner.

The pro tour needed some new blood and got it with the arrival of Ellsworth Vines. With much fanfare before a Madison Square Garden crowd of 14,637, the 23-year-old made his debut against Bill Tilden, 41. The match grossed $30,125 and Tilden won,

8-6, 6-3, 6-2. They went on a tour of 72 cities, grossing $243,000, the most ever for the pros, and Vines beat Tilden, 47 matches to 26. Vines won a match in Los Angeles, 6-0, 21-23, 7-5, 3-6, 6-2. Another memorable match between old adversaries Tilden and Henri Cochet took place at the Garden where 12,663 paid $20,000. Tilden outlasted the 32-year-old Cochet, 7-9, 6-1, 4-6, 6-3, 6-3.

1934 CHAMPIONS AND LEADERS

Australian Championships

Men's Singles Final: Fred Perry (GBR) def. Jack Crawford (AUS), 6-3, 7-5, 6-1

Women's Singles Final: Joan Hartigan (AUS) def. Mall Molesworth (AUS), 6-1, 6-4

Men's Doubles Final: Fred Perry and Pat Hughes (GBR) def. Adrian Quist and Don Turnbull (AUS), 6-8, 6-3, 6-4, 3-6, 6-3

Women's Doubles Final: Mall Molesworth and Emily Hood Westacott (AUS) def. Joan Hartigan and Ula Valkenburg (AUS), 6-8, 6-4, 6-4.

Mixed Doubles Final: Joan Hartigan and Gar Moon (AUS) def. Emily Hood Westacott and Ray Dunlop (AUS) 6-3, 6-4

French Championships

Men's Singles Final: Gottfried von Cramm (GER) def. Jack Crawford (AUS), 6-4, 7-9, 3-6, 7-5, 6-3

Women's Singles Final: Margaret Scriven (GBR) def. Helen Jacobs (USA), 7-5, 4-6, 6-1

Men's Doubles Final: Jean Borotra and Jacques Brugnon (FRA) def. Jack Crawford and Viv McGrath (AUS), 11-9, 6-3, 2-6, 4-6, 9-7

Women's Doubles Final: Simone Passemard Mathieu (FRA) and Elizabeth Ryan (USA) def. Helen Jacobs and Sarah Palfrey (USA), 3-6, 6-4, 6-2

Mixed Doubles Final: Colette Rosambert and Jean Borotra (FRA) def. Elizabeth Ryan (USA) and Adrian Quist (AUS), 6-2, 6-4

Wimbledon

Men's Singles Final: Fred Perry (GBR) def. Jack Crawford (AUS), 6-3, 6-0, 7-5

Women's Singles Final: Dorothy Round (GBR) def. Helen Jacobs (USA), 6-2, 5-7, 6-3

Men's Doubles Final: George Lott and Lester Stoefen (USA) def., Jean Borotra and Jacques Brugnon (FRA), 6-2, 6-3, 6-4

Women's Doubles Final: Simone Passemard Mathieu (FRA) and Elizabeth Ryan (USA) def. Dorothy Andrus and Sylvie Jung Henrotin (FRA), 6-3, 6-3

Mixed Doubles Final: Dorothy Round (GBR) and Ryuki Miki (FRA) def. Dorothy Shepherd Barron and Bunny Austin (GBR), 3-6, 6-4, 6-0

U.S. Championships

Men's Singles Final: Fred Perry (GBR) def. Wilmer Allison (USA), 6-4, 6-3, 3-6, 1-6, 8-6

Women's Singles Final: Helen Jacobs (USA) def. Sarah Palfrey (USA), 6-1, 6-4

Men's Doubles Final: George Lott and Lester Stoefen (USA) def. Wilmer Allison and John Van Ryn (USA), 6-4, 9-7, 3-6, 6-4

Women's Doubles Final: Helen Jacobs and Sarah Palfrey (USA) def. Carolin Babock and Dorothy Andrus (USA), 4-6, 6-3, 6-4

Mixed Doubles Final: Helen Jacobs and George Lott (USA) def. Elizabeth Ryan and Lester Stoefen (USA), 4-6, 13-11, 6-2

Year-End No. 1

Men: Fred Perry
Women: Dorothy Round

Davis Cup: Britain

Wightman Cup: United States

1935 Jacobs Loses Wimbledon Heartbreaker

Helen Wills Moody (left) wins at Wimbledon and **Helen Jacobs** (right) wins at Forest Hills in 1935.

Probably no player ever suffered as much frustration against an arch-rival as Helen Jacobs did opposite Helen Wills Moody. The only time Jacobs beat Moody, the victory was less than fully satisfying because Moody quit with back trouble in the 1933 final at Forest Hills. While Jacobs came out on the losing end every other time they played perhaps her toughest setback was the 1935 Wimbledon final.

Moody, seeking her seventh Wimbledon title, had played little the year before and was seeded only No. 4. Early in the season, she lost a set to Mary Hardwick, even lost a match to English lefty Kay Stammers in the semifinals at the pre-Wimbledon tournament at Beckenham. In a Wimbledon fourth rounder against an unknown Czech, Slenca Cepkova, she lost the first set and was within a point of trailing 4-1 before rallying to win, 3-6, 6-4, 6-2.

Slender Aussie Joan Hartigan knocked the crown from Round's head in the quarterfinals, 4-6, 6-4, 6-3, only to fall to Moody, 6-3, 6-3. Jacobs, seeded No. 3, beat 1931 runner-up Hilde Krahwinkel Sperling, 6-3, 6-0, but in the final, she fell behind 4-0 to Moody in the first set, almost tied at 4-4, then faltered and lost the set 6-3. Of the second set, British authority Max Robertson wrote: "Jacobs' length improved; her favorite forehand chop became as dangerous as a scimitar. Mrs. Moody tried to come to the net but she was never able to run up and down the court as well as she could cover it from side to side." Jacobs won the second set, 6-3.

Jacobs took a winning 4-2 lead in the third, with one powerful serve knocking the racket from Moody's hand. She then broke Moody's serve to lead 5-2, but Moody broke back to 3-5 in a game where she was facing a match point at 40-30 and Moody

flicked a desperation lob with Jacobs at the net. It looked like a simple smash, but a gusty wind caused the ball to sink so swiftly that Jacobs had to drop to her knees to hit it...into the net. That turned the match around. Jacobs went down fighting, serving two aces when trailing 5-6, but losing the match, 6-3, 3-6, 7-5. It was her fourth loss to Moody at Wimbledon, three in a final. Jacobs also lost to Moody in the 1928 U.S. final.

Fred Perry was clearly the cream of the men's sector for the second straight year, even through an injury probably caused him to lose his U.S. title, and Jack Crawford rose up to deprive him of the Australian in a base-lining rematch of the 1934 final, 2-6, 6-4, 6-4, 6-4. However, Fred would always chuckle over his triple-bageling (6-0, 6-0, 6-0) of Giorgio de Stefani in the quarterfinal: "I told Giorgio after he beat me in Paris '34 [possibly costing Fred a Grand Slam] that I wouldn't allow him a game next time, and I meant it." Illness kept Joan Hartigan from going for a third straight Aussie title, and instead two Englishwomen fought for it, Dorothy Round beating Nancy Lyle, 1-6, 6-1, 6-3.

In Paris, Perry exacted his revenge over Crawford, 6-3, 8-6, 6-3, in the semifinal, ending Jack's run of consecutive major final-round roles at eight. In the title round, Perry bounced 1934 champ Gottfried von Cramm, 6-3, 3-6, 6-1, 6-3, adding the French to his stash and becoming the first to win all four majors. His countrywoman, Peggy Scriven, didn't fare as well. After two straight titles and 14 match wins in a row on the clay, she delighted the locals by losing to Simone Passemard Mathieu in the semifinal, 8-6, 6-1. But their joy was short-lived as long-legged German-born Danish citizen Sperling followed up on her semifinal elimination of Jacobs (7-5, 6-3) to beat Mathieu for the title, 6-2, 6-1.

At Wimbledon, Perry beat Crawford, 6-2, 3-6, 6-4, 6-4, then trounced von Cramm, the first German male to make the final, 6-2, 6-4, 6-4 to win the title. Von Cramm had eliminated Don Budge in a semifinal, 4-6, 6-4, 6-4, 6-2. It was Budge, unseeded, who created the sensation of the tournament by stopping No. 3-seeded Bunny Austin in a quarterfinal 3-6, 10-8, 6-4, 7-5. During that match,

there was an interruption for Queen Mary to take her seat in the Royal Box. It was written by one British reporter the next day that Budge had waved to the Queen. The story grew that Budge even cried: "Hi, Queenie." Budge took pains in his autobiography to point out that he did not wave, that he did wipe his brow, a reflex gesture. Two years later, though, when Budge was again at Wimbledon and met the Queen, he said she told him: "You know, Mr. Budge, I did not see you a few years ago when you waved to me, but had I, I want you to know that I would have waved back."

The Wimbledon mixed final was marked by the appearance of Mr. and Mrs. Harry Hopman—she the former Nell Hall—of Australia. They had won their own title in 1930, but were beaten in the final by Perry and Dorothy Round, 7-5, 4-6, 6-2.

Budge appeared in the U.S. Davis Cup line-up for the first time and drove the team straight to the Challenge Round with five straight singles wins, the last two over Henner Henkel, 7-5, 11-9, 6-8, 6-1, and von Cramm, 0-6, 9-7, 8-6, 6-3 in a 4-1 win over Germany at Wimbledon. Wilmer Allison and Johnny Van Ryn rescued five match points in winning the electrifying and pivotal doubles over von Cramm and Kay Lund, 3-6, 6-3, 5-7, 9-7, 8-6, to set up attack-minded Allison for the clincher over Henkel, 6-1, 7-5, 11-9.

But the Americans' high spirits and hopes to seize the Cup from the Brits were splintered. Allison missed a huge opportunity in the tense opener against Austin. Serving match game at 4-5, Austin double-faulted to 15-30 as the overflowing crowd of 16,000 in Centre Court groaned. The next point proved painful for the invaders as Allison, charging, netted a routine volley that would have placed him at double match point. Reprieved, Austin ran it out, 6-2, 2-6, 4-6, 6-3, 7-5, and the 5-0 British avalanche to a third straight Cup was under way. Perry sprang on Budge, 6-0, 6-8, 6-3, 6-4, while Allison and Van Ryn couldn't find their usual Cup touch in the clutch, falling to the newly-paired Pat Hughes and Charles Tuckey, 6-2, 1-6, 6-8, 6-3, 6-3.

Thirty-year-old Allison would feel a lot better at Forest Hills in his eighth assault on the U.S. title. He had fallen short against Perry in 1934, but this time Perry fell, literally and heavily, on damp grass in the seventh game of their semifinal. It was discovered that Perry, clutching his back throughout, had damaged a kidney in losing the title he'd won the two previous years, 7-5, 6-3, 6-2. Perry got that far on an oppressive quarterfinal finish against Frank Shields, 6-4, 4-6, 8-6, 6-0, stamping out two set points in the fourth.

Second-seeded Don Budge was felled in the quarterfinal, in unlikely fashion, by tiny, pesky go-getter-of-everything, Bitsy Grant, 6-4, 6-4, 5-7, 6-3. Thereupon Sidney Wood stepped over Grant, 6-2, 4-6, 12-10, 6-2, to the final where he was a 40-minute lunch for Allison, 6-2, 6-2, 6-3. A loser in the quarterfinals in 1929, and the semifinals in 1932, the No. 1-seeded Allison wasn't going to miss. His superb groundies and furious volleying made certain. It was a suitable going-away gift. He would not be seen at Forest Hills again.

For the first time, the women were seen along with the men in the merging of singles championships, a togetherness continuing to this day. Relentless Jacobs, permitting 30 games and no sets in six starts, won her fourth in a row, equaling the 1915-18 surge of Molla Mallory. In a reprise of the 1934 final, Helen beat Sarah Palfrey Fabyan, 6-2, 6-4, a persistent semifinal victor over Kay Stammers, 9-7, 7-5.

George Lott and Les Stoefen turned pro, but Tilden, at 42, let Lott know who was in charge. Before a record American crowd of 16,000 at Madison Square Garden, the old master gave the 29-year-old rookie a 6-4, 7-5 paddling. Big Bill, though bageled twice, won his second U.S. Pro title, 0-6, 6-1, 6-4, 0-6, 6-4, over Karel Kozeluh at the Terrace Club in Brooklyn.

1935 CHAMPIONS AND LEADERS

Australian Championships
Men's Singles Final: Jack Crawford (AUS) def. Fred Perry (GBR), 2-6, 6-4, 6-4, 6-4
Women's Singles Final: Dorothy Round (GBR) def. Nancy Lyle (GBR), 1-6, 6-1, 6-3
Men's Doubles Final: Jack Crawford and Viv McGrath (AUS) def. Pat Hughes and Fred Perry (GBR), 6-4, 8-6, 6-2
Women's Doubles Final: Evelyn Dearman and Nancy Lyle (GBR) def. Louie Bickerton and Nell Hall Hopman (AUS), 6-3, 6-4
Mixed Doubles Final: Louie Bickerton (AUS) and Christian Boussus (FRA) def. G. Bond (AUS) and Vernon Kirby (RSA), 1-6, 6-3, 6-3

French Championships
Men's Singles Final: Fred Perry (GBR) def. Gottfried von Cramm (GER), 6-3, 3-6, 6-1, 6-3
Women's Singles Final: Hilde Krahwinkel Sperling (DEN) def. Simone Passemard Mathieu (FRA), 6-2, 6-1
Men's Doubles Final: Jack Crawford and Adrian Quist (AUS) def. Viv McGrath and Don Turnbull (AUS), 6-1, 6-4, 6-2
Women's Doubles Final: Margaret Scriven and Kay Stammers (GBR) def. Ida Adamoff (FRA) and Hilde Krahwinkel Sperling (GER), 6-4, 6-0
Mixed Doubles Final: Lolette Payot and Marcel Bernard (FRA) def. Martin Legeay and Sylvie Jung Henrotin (FRA), 4-6, 6-2, 6-4

Wimbledon
Men's Singles Final: Fred Perry (GBR) def. Gottfried von Cramm (GER), 6-2, 6-4, 6-4
Women's Singles Final: Helen Wills Moody (USA) def. Helen Jacobs (USA), 6-3, 3-6, 7-5
Men's Doubles Final: Jack Crawford and Adrian Quist (AUS) def. Wilmer Allison and John Van Ryn (USA), 6-3, 5-7, 6-2, 5-7, 7-5
Women's Doubles Final: Freda James and Kay Stammers (GBR) def. Simone Passemard Mathieu (FRA) and Hilde Krahwinkel Sperling (DEN) 6-1, 6-4
Mixed Doubles Final: Dorothy Round and Fred Perry (GBR) def. Nell Hall Hopman and Harry Hopman (AUS), 7-5, 4-6, 6-2

U.S. Championships
Men's Singles Final: Wilmer Allison (USA) def. Sidney Wood (USA), 6-1, 6-2, 6-3
Women's Singles Final: Helen Jacobs (USA) def. Sarah Palfrey Fabyan (USA), 6-2, 6-4
Men's Doubles Final: Wilmer Allison and John Van Ryn (USA) def. Don Budge and Gene Mako (USA), 6-4, 6-2, 3-6, 2-6, 6-1
Women's Doubles Final: Helen Jacobs and Sarah Palfrey Fabyan (USA) def. Carolin Babcock and Dorothy Andrus (USA), 6-4, 6-2
Mixed Doubles Final: Sarah Palfrey Fabyan (USA) and Enrique Maier (ESP) def. Kay Stammers (GBR) and Roderich Menzel (CZE), 6-3, 3-6, 6-4

Year-End No. 1
Men: Fred Perry
Women: Helen Wills Moody

Davis Cup: Britain

Wightman Cup: United States

1936 Perry Exits With Third Wimbledon Title

Fred Perry easily beats an injured Gottfried von Cramm at Wimbledon.

Fred Perry turned pro late in the year after dominating tennis for four years as few men have. He won three successive Wimbledon titles, three U.S., a French and an Australian, and nine out of 10 Davis Cup Challenge Round starts.

Perry was laid up for seven months after his kidney injury at Forest Hills the year before, and when he was beaten in the French by Gottfried von Cramm, 6-0, 2-6, 6-2, 2-6, 6-0—the last set

in ten minutes—there was some question whether he could retain his form. At Wimbledon, however, he quickly established that he would be formidable by sailing through early-round

opponents. He beat the diminutive nuisance, Bitsy Grant, 6-4, 6-3, 6-1, in the quarterfinal, then in what were his only difficult moments of the tournament, lost the first set to No. 5-seeded Don Budge in the semifinal, before rallying to win, 5-7, 6-4, 6-3, 6-4. He had an easy time in the final—von Cramm ruptured an Achilles tendon in the first set. He continued, limping on a bad leg, and Perry won, 6-1, 6-1, 6-0, the widest margin of victory in a Wimbledon final.

It was the first time since the pre-World War I days that somebody won three straight Wimbledons and when Bjorn Borg did it in 1978, Perry was there as a radio commentator.

This was the last Wimbledon in which the hosts fared so well, taking four of the five titles. Champions joining Perry: Pat Hughes and Charles Tuckey over compatriots Charlie Hare and Frank Wilde, 6-4, 3-6, 7-9, 6-1, 6-4; Freda James and Kay Stammers over Sarah Palfrey Fabyan and Helen Jacobs, 6-2, 6-1; Perry and Dorothy Round in mixed, over Fabyan and Budge, 7-9, 7-5, 6-4. Only women's singles was captured by an invader, Helen Jacobs, at last.

So many times the "other Helen" had come agonizingly close, but on her ninth visit to the All England Club, she went all the way in her fifth final, winning the championship 6-2, 4-6, 7-5 over Hilde Krahwinkel Sperling, the French champ. Finishing jitters appeared to get Jacobs after leading 3-1 in the second and third sets. Serving for the championship at 6-5, 40-15, she missed on two match points, and slumped to a break point. Was it a sour echo of 1935? Nope. She firmed up and took the last three points.

Kept out of the 1935 Australian by illness, Joan Hartigan was back to win her third straight, 6-4, 6-4, over a fresh face, 18-year-old Nancye Wynne, a setter of records Down Under. Nancye won the doubles with Thelma Coyne over Australians May Blick and Kath LeMesurier, 6-2, 6-4. The Nancye-Thelma partnership would ultimately account for 10 homeland titles, the last in 1952. Jack Crawford reached his sixth straight final and he lost a close one to a rising shorty, Adrian Quist 6-2, 6-3, 4-6, 3-6, 9-7.

There was a repeat final at the French and a repeat champion—Sperling, who disappointed the home folks again by beating Simone Mathieu, 6-3, 6-4.

Crawford and Quist combined for Australia to astound the U.S. in the Americans' second Davis Cup series of the year, 3-2, at Germantown Cricket Club. This, despite Don Budge's beating both Crawford 6-2, 6-3, 4-6, 1-6, 13-11 on the first day, and Quist 6-2, 6-2, 6-4, when it no longer counted. It was, however, the last hurrah for U.S. champ Wilmer Allison—a hoarse one—as one of the more illustrious Cup careers (eight years) ended in two defeats: first day to Quist, 6-3, 5-7, 6-4, 6-1, and the clincher by Crawford, 4-6, 6-3, 4-6, 6-2, 6-2. The series had turned on the doubles, a debut together that went awry for Budge and Gene Mako, a great alliance in the making. Quist slithered out of two match points at 4-5, 15-40 in the fourth, initially as Mako bungled a short and simple smash. The Aussies regrouped for a 4-6, 2-6, 6-4, 7-5, 6-4 victory in which they lost but seven points in the last five games.

Not for a dozen years had a team from Down Under ascended to the Davis Cup Challenge Round. Australia had lost to the U.S. in 1924. Now the Aussies were back again, 3-2 vic-

tors over Germany in the penultimate series at Wimbledon. Von Cramm knocked out Quist altogether on the grim, blustery first day after Crawford had beaten a flu-ridden Henner Henkel (6-2, 6-2, default). Not only did von Cramm save three match points at 7-8, 0-40 in the fifth set, he won on a 10th match point, 4-6, 6-4, 4-6, 6-4, 11-9. But it turned into a TKO because the scrappy Quist twisted an ankle and was finished for the series. From the bench came 21-year-old Viv McGrath, who sided with Crawford for a 6-4, 4-6, 6-4, 6-4 win over Henkel and von Cramm. Viv then clinched the win in singles 6-3, 5-7, 6-4, 6-4 over Henkel.

But the same good old impediments awaited the challenger: The one-two punches of Perry, the good-bye guy in the last four Cup successes, and Austin. They did their first-day stuff for 2-0—Austin scored his first significant win over Crawford, 4-6, 6-3, 6-1, 6-1, before Perry sidestepped a set point while inflating from 5-1 down in the third to beat Quist, 6-1, 4-6, 7-5, 6-2. The Aussies stormed back to take the doubles from Hughes and Tuckey, 6-4, 2-6, 7-5, 10-8, and arrived at 2-2 as Quist stung Austin, 6-4, 3-6, 7-5, 6-2. What a moment for Perry to stride onto the revered greensward for his Centre Court valedictory before 16,000 patriots. His 52nd and last Cup assignment on behalf of his country concluded a sixth campaign. He had broken a 2-2 deadlock three years before to wrest the Cup from France. Again he was in a similar cauldron with the Cup at stake. It was what he lived for, and Fred bolted from the starting gate, rushing his long-time foe and friend Crawford off the court, 6-2, 6-3, 6-3. During their four years on top, in Britain's run of 10-0, Perry and Austin had been virtually untouchable in singles with respective marks of 18-1 and 17-3.

Perry and Budge, Wimbledon antagonists, met for a final time in a major setting, the U.S. title bout. It was a classic: five gripping sets, twice interrupted by downpours, a spiky encounter in which both wore spikes, and future Grand Slammer Budge, 21, clung to two match points on his serve at 5-3 in the fifth. But he lacked the resolve to cash one against fiercely resisting Fred, who won 2-6, 6-2, 1-6, 8-6, 10-8. Point and counter-point they went as Budge, in his first major final, neared the championship again and again, two points away at 7-6 and 8-7, only to be blocked. Every point was a war, but Perry coolly won the last three games, the only man other than Bill Tilden to carry off three titles from Forest Hills. It was Fred's eight major singles, good for second place all-time then behind Tilden's 10. Budge would play six more major finals, winning them all.

Of the fifth set against Perry, Budge later wrote: "We held serve to 3-2, my favor, and then I got the break for 4-2. Promptly, I permitted Fred to break me back. My serve was a dishrag. However, tired as I was, I was able to break him back again, so I stood at 5-3, serving twice one point away for the championship of my country against the No. 1 player in the world. All I had to do was hold my serve. I could not. I was so exhausted in reaching up to hit my serve that I felt as if I were leaning on the ball. There was no life in my shots. The stretching and reaching for the serve particularly wore on me. He broke me again—our fourth loss of service in a row—held his own serve at last, and tied the set at 5-all."

Probably the greatest recovery from physical and emotional trauma to date was Alice Marble's to win the U.S. Champion-

ship in 1936. Ranked No. 3 in the U.S. for 1933, she collapsed during a match in Paris the following spring and was hospitalized. Cut down by anemia and pleurisy, Alice didn't play competitively for almost two years. But she was rehabilitated by the American summer of '36, and even though she won the Southern California title on concrete in May, the doubting U.S. Tennis Association didn't select her for the Wightman Cup team, and even refused her entries to Eastern grass-circuit tourneys. Marble had to prove herself in practice matches at Forest Hills before she was allowed to play at the height of the season. But her fitness was clear as she won two grass-court events en route to the U.S. Championships: The Longwood Bowl in Boston, over Carolyn Roberts, 6-1, 8-6, and Seabright (N.J.), over Carolin Babcock, 6-0, 6-3 in 35 minutes.

Alice Marble, in the month of her 23rd birthday, was ready to puncture the U.S. bubble of Helen Jacobs, who had won four straight and took a 28-match Forest Hills streak into the final. Neither had lost a set, Jacobs relinquishing but 14 games in five matches. But the striking advances made by the 5-foot-8 Marble, who'd become a net-seizing, serve-and-volleyer, were obvious in her surge to a 4-6, 6-3, 6-2 triumph, winning 10 of 11 games from 0-2 down in the second. "The first set was a relief," recalled Marble, who would become the dominant female until she turned pro in 1940. "I was afraid Helen would whitewash me. But I came close, and knew I could beat her."

Even without Marble, the Wightman Cup thrilled Wimbledon with the closest finish ever, right down to 5-5 in the last set of the last doubles. Sarah Palfrey Fabyan was the heroine of the 4-3 U.S. victory, bearing lefty Kay Stammers in a critical second-day singles, 6-3, 6-4, after both Stammers and Dorothy Round had stopped Jacobs, 12-10, 6-1, and 6-3, 6-3, respectively. Moreover, Sarah propped Jacobs in the decisive doubles revival, from 1-3 in the third to 1-6, 6-3, 7-5, to disappoint a crowd of 14,000. Carolin Babcock lent strong support to the U.S. cause, beating rookie Mary Hardwick, 6-4, 4-6, 6-2, and coalescing with rookie Midge Gladman Van Ryn (wife of the Davis Cupper John van Ryn) in a doubles win over Evelyn Dearman and Nancy Lyle, 6-2, 1-6, 6-3.

It was a year of struggle and money-losing tours for the pros. Promoter Bill O'Brien's gimmick was signing on two American women of little appeal. Ethel Burkhart Arnold beat Jane Sharp—they were No. 2 and No. 13 in the U.S. rankings of 1935—in the usual tour opening at Madison Square Garden. In the Wembley indoor tourney in London, often the best of the pros' infrequent tournaments, Ellsworth Vines won for the third successive year, beating Hans Nusslein, 6-4, 6-4, 6-2. The U.S. Pro, avoided by the leaders, went to Joe Whalen over Charlie Wood, 4-6, 4-6, 6-3, 6-2, 6-3,.

1936 CHAMPIONS AND LEADERS

Australian Championships
Men's Singles Final: Adrian Quist (AUS) def. Jack Crawford (AUS), 6-2, 6-3, 4-6, 3-6, 9-7
Women's Singles Final: Joan Hartigan (AUS) def. Nancye Wynne (USA), 6-4, 6-4
Men's Doubles Final: Adrian Quist and Don Turnbull (AUS) def. Jack Crawford and Viv McGrath (AUS) 6-8, 6-2 6-1, 3-6, 6-2
Women's Doubles Final: Thelma Coyne Long and Nancye Wynne (AUS) def. May Blick and Katherine LeMesurier (AUS), 6-2, 6-4
Mixed Doubles Final: Nell Hall Hopman and Harry Hopman (AUS) def. May Blick and Abe Kay (AUS), 6-2, 6-0

French Championships
Men's Singles Final: Gottfried von Cramm (GER) def. Fred Perry (GBR), 6-0, 2-6, 6-2, 2-6, 6-0
Women's Singles Final: Hilde Krahwinkel Sperling (DEN) def Simone Passemard Mathieu (FRA), 6-3, 6-4
Men's Doubles Final: Jean Borotra and Marcel Bernard (FRA) def. Charles Tuckey and Pat Hughes (GBR), 6-2, 3-6, 9-7, 6-1
Women's Doubles Final: Simone Passemard Mathieu and Billie Yorke (GBR) def. Susan Noel (FRA) and Jadwiga Jedrzejowska (POL), 2-6, 6-4, 6-4
Mixed Doubles Final: Billie Yorke (GBR) and Marcel Bernard (FRA) def. Sylvie Jung Henrotin and Martin Legeay (FRA), 7-5, 6-8, 6-3

Wimbledon
Men's Singles Final: Fred Perry (GBR) def. Gottfried von Cramm (GER), 6-1, 6-1, 6-0
Women's Singles Final: Helen Jacobs (USA) def. Hilde Krahwinkel Sperling (DEN), 6-2, 4-6, 7-5
Men's Doubles Final: Pat Hughes and Charles Tuckey (GBR) def. Charles Hare and Frank Wilde (GBR) 6-4, 3-6, 7-9, 6-1, 6-4
Women's Doubles Final: Freda James and Kay Stammers (GBR) def. Sarah Palfrey Fabyan and Helen Jacobs (USA), 6-2, 6-1
Mixed Doubles Final: Dorothy Round and Fred Perry (GBR) def. Sarah Palfrey Fabyan and Don Budge (USA), 7-9, 7-5, 6-4

U.S. Championships
Men's Singles Final: Fred Perry (GBR) def. Don Budge (USA) 2-6, 6-2, 8-6, 1-6, 10-8
Women's Singles Final: Alice Marble (USA) def. Helen Jacobs (USA), 4-6, 6-3, 6-2
Men's Doubles Final: Don Budge and Gene Mako (USA) def. Wilmer Allison and John Van Ryn (USA), 6-4, 6-2, 6-4
Women's Doubles Final: Marjorie Gladman Van Ryn and Carolin Babcock (USA) def. Helen Jacobs and Sarah Palfrey Fabyan (USA), 9-7, 2-6, 6-4
Mixed Doubles Final: Alice Marble and Gene Mako (USA) def. Sarah Palfrey Fabyan and Don Budge (USA), 6-3, 6-2

Year-End No. 1
Men: Fred Perry
Women: Helen Jacobs

Davis Cup: Britain

Wightman Cup: United States

1937 A Davis Cup Classic: Budge vs. von Cramm

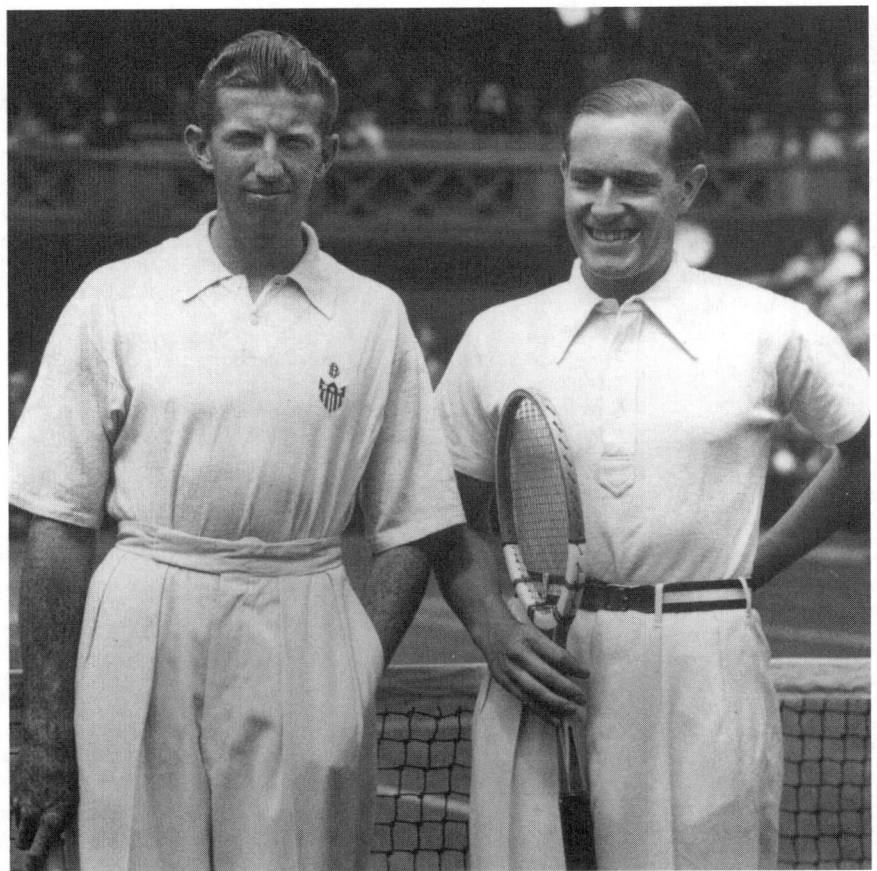

The line of dominant players, which started with Bill Tilden in the 1920s and continued through the French trio of Rene Lacoste, Henri Cochet and Jean Borotra, then Ellsworth Vines and Fred Perry, continued with the imposing red-headed figure of Don Budge. The 22-year-old American swept Wimbledon and Forest Hills and sailed through the Davis Cup, winning what many rate as the greatest Davis Cup match ever played.

Almost 29 and apparently subsiding, Jack Crawford expected to grace a seventh straight Australian final, and failed because a decidedly bizarre-stroking 18-year-old, John Bromwich, stopped him in the semifinal, 6-1, 7-9, 6-4, 8-6. Bromwich was also on his own way to the Hall of Fame, a loping left-hander who served rightie with a loosely strung racket and used a two-handed backhand on the right side. Viv McGrath, at 21, reached his zenith, barely beating Brom for the title, 6-3, 1-6, 6-0, 2-6, 6-1, the first major

final in which both competitors employed both-handed backhands. Nancye Wynne, 19, took the first of her six Aussie titles, 6-3, 5-7, 6-4, over Emily Hood Westacott.

With Franco-German tension growing, the home folks didn't much care for the second straight Teutonic double at Roland Garros, especially when Hilde Krahwinkel Sperling (German-born but a Danish citizen through marriage) beat Parisienne Simone Mathieu for a third year in a row, 6-2, 6-4. Sperling's three-peat duplicated Helen Wills' 1928-30 feat, the two of them equaled by Monica Seles' French reign, 1990-92. Although Gottfried von Cramm didn't defend in Paris, his 22-year-old Davis Cup sidekick Henner Henkel came through for the Fatherland, 6-1, 6-4, 6-3, over Bunny Austin in the final.

With Perry moving to professional ranks, it was obvious Great Britain would yield the Davis Cup to the strong challenger that emerged from the semifinal. Budge spearheaded 5-0 U.S. victories over Japan and Australia, beating Aussies Jack Crawford, 6-1, 6-3, 6-2, and John Bromwich, 6-2, 6-3, 5-7, 6-1, on Forest Hills turf. Bitsy Grant opened by out-retrieving Bromwich, 6-2, 7-5, 6-1, and Gene Mako and Budge put it out of reach, 7-5, 6-1, 8-6 over Crawford and McGrath to arrange a showdown with Germany.

Before Davis Cup play came Wimbledon. Budge was the No. 1 seed and von Cramm was No. 2. On his way to the final, Budge lost only one set, to teammate Frank Parker in the semifinal, 2-6, 6-4, 6-4, 6-1, while von Cramm was extended by Crawford, 8-6, 6-3, 12-14, 6-1. Budge then defeated von Cramm 6-3, 6-4, 6-2 to win the title. Becoming the first man ever to score a Wimbledon triple, Don added the doubles title with Mako over Pat Hughes and Charles Tuckey, 6-0, 6-4, 6-8, 6-1, and the mixed with Alice Marble over France's Mathieu and Yvon Petra, 6-4, 6-1.

On to the Davis Cup and a match that had implications beyond the tennis court. "War talk was everywhere," Budge recalled. "Hitler was doing everything he could to stir up Germany. The atmosphere was filled with tension although von Cramm was a known anti-Nazi and remained one of the finest gentlemen and most popular players on the circuit."

Two weeks after Budge won Wimbledon, he and teammates Mako, Parker and Grant were back at Centre Court to clash with Germany, and they stayed there, winning on a July Tuesday. They began stripping the Cup from Britain four days later.

Von Cramm took about an hour to beat Bitsy Grant, 6-3, 6-4, 6-2, and Budge less than that to flatten Henkel, 6-2, 6-1, 6-3 to knot the teams at 1-1. Wimbledon doubles champs Budge and Mako won the vital, nip-and-tuck doubles over Henkel and von Cramm, 4-6, 7-5, 8-6, 6-4, even though Henkel served for the second set at 5-4, the Germans had a set point against Budge at 4-5 in the third and led 4-1 in the fourth. How vital it was soon became clear: Henkel, with stronger serve and better volley, ran up big leads in all but the second set and hung on to topple Grant, 7-5, 2-6, 6-3, 6-4. That set up the decisive match—tantamount to determining the Cup itself—with that dedicated Budge fan, Queen Mary, in the Royal Box.

Just before Budge and von Cramm went onto the court, the Baron was called to the telephone. It was a long-distance call from Adolf Hitler exhorting von Cramm to win for the Fatherland. Budge recalls that "Gottfried came out pale and serious and played as if his life depended on every point." Von Cramm would be imprisoned for anti-Nazi views, and eventually sent to the Russian front as a soldier, seemingly a death sentence. Henkel was killed in that campaign. However, von Cramm performed valiantly and won an Iron Cross.

Von Cramm won the first two sets. Budge rallied, took the next two, then fell behind, 1-4. He then took desperate measures. Attacking von Cramm's serve, going to the net behind his returns, he got the matching break in the seventh game, making the score 3-4, and held service to 4-4. The score went to 5-5, then 6-6. In the 13th game, Budge achieved another break. He reached match point five times on his own serve only to see von Cramm fight back to the sanctuary of deuce. "The crowd was so quiet I am sure they could hear us breathing," Budge recalled.

"On the sixth match point, there was a prolonged rally," Will Grimsley wrote. "Von Cramm sent up a lob. Budge raced back and returned it. Von Cramm then hit a forehand crosscourt. Budge tore after the ball, got his racket on it and took a desperate swing, sprawling to the court. It was a placement—a shot that the fallen Budge didn't see. Game, set, match and the Davis Cup series: 6-8, 5-7, 6-4, 6-2, 8-6. The two-hour, 33-minute match ended at 8:45 p.m. in semi-darkness. The two players went to their dressing rooms, relaxed, dressed and returned more than an hour later to find most of the crowd still on hand, buzzing over the spectacular final."

Because von Cramm was the underdog and the British thought they might have a better chance in a final against the Germans, the crowd slightly favored von Cramm. An oddity was that the Germans were coached by Bill Tilden. It wasn't unusual for a pro in one country to coach another country's Davis Cup team, but it was uncommon for a coach to hold the post when it meant working against his own. At one point, Tilden was so animated in his rooting he infuriated American show-business celebrities Jack Benny, Paul Lukas and columnist Ed Sullivan (a future TV host), who challenged Tilden to a fight. Tilden later told Budge this was the greatest tennis match ever played.

Strictly anti-climactic was the Challenge Round. Bereft of Perry, Britain could win only the opening match, Bunny Austin's 6-3, 6-2, 7-5 decision over Parker, inserted for Grant. Rookie Charlie Hare, an attack-minded southpaw, kept 11,000 loyalists hopeful of a 2-0 lead for a long while, leading 3-1 and serving for the first set at 5-4. But Budge was unbudgeable, 15-13, 6-1, 6-2, and a 4-1 victory was in the works. Had the Brits, Frank Wilde and Charles Tuckey, cashed a set point against Mako at 9-10 in the fourth, they might have caused some panic in the go-ahead doubles, won by Gene and Don, 6-3, 7-5, 7-9, 12-10. That left it to Parker to apply the finishing touches, which he did smartly, beating Hare, 6-2, 6-4, 6-2. The Cup was headed home after 11 years abroad. As 10,000 fans applauded, who could guess that Parker 11 years later would win both his singles to help the U.S. defeat Australia in the Challenge Round, the lone man to play singles with Cup-winners before and after World War II?

The Americans returned with the trophy to a ticker-tape parade in New York, and Budge was later greeted with a parade in his hometown, Oakland, receiving a signet ring featuring the city seal flanked by diamonds.

At Forest Hills, von Cramm was pushed hard on his way to the final: four sets by Americans Don McNeill, 6-2, 6-3, 2-6, 6-4, and Hal Surface, 8-6, 7-5, 3-6, 7-5. Those were followed by three full-distance battles: 9-7, 2-6, 2-6, 6-3, 6-3 over troublemaker Grant in the quarterfinal; 0-6, 8-6, 6-8, 6-3, 6-2, in the semifinal over another feisty wind-up doll and future champ, 19-year-old Bobby Riggs, No. 6 in the U.S. rankings.

In the final, von Cramm extended Budge to five sets, yet the American said he felt none of the trauma he found at Wimbledon, which he had won in straight sets. The score this time: 6-1, 7-9, 6-1, 3-6, 6-1. The packed crowd of 14,000 (5,000 were turned away) roared all the way for Budge. He became the first tennis player to win the Sullivan Award, as the outstanding amateur athlete in the U.S.

Despite the victory by Alice Marble over Helen Jacobs at Forest Hills in 1936, Jacobs was seeded No. 1 at Wimbledon and Marble at No. 5. Alice was No. 1 and Helen No. 2 at the U.S. Championships, but seedings and marquee names meant nothing in a curious year for the women at the two biggies. There, the mischief-makers were a couple of hardly-knowns who'd been playing well in England: A chunky, unpronounceable and unrestrainedly hard-hitting Pole, Jadwiga Jedrzejowska, and a subtle mite of a Chilean, 5-footer Anita Lizana.

At Wimbledon, No. 7-seeded Dorothy Round, the champ of 1934, deflated the defender (Jacobs), 6-4, 6-2 in the quarterfinals, and Jedrzejowska brought down Marble in the semifinal, 8-6, 6-2. Jadwiga led Round in their third set, 4-2, but championship experience kept Dorothy calm in her third final, and she won it, 6-2, 2-6, 7-5.

Lizana, a quarterfinal loser at Wimbledon to Simone Mathieu, 6-3, 6-3, had led Jacobs at the same stage in 1936 (4-2, 30-0 in the third). But re-crossing the Atlantic, petite Anita accomplished an incomprehensible tour de force at the U.S. Championships: One visit only to Forest Hills, one title, no sets lost (in fact merely 28 games in six easy matches). Her quickness and maddening drop shots carried the No. 2 foreign seed well. Around Lizana others fell: No. 3-seeded ex-finalist Sarah Palfrey Fabyan in a first-round shaker to No. 13 American Dorothy Andrus of New York, 12-10, 0-6, 7-5; a too-casual defending champion Marble in the quarterfinals to eager 21-year-old Californian Dodo Bundy (daughter of 1904 champ, May Sutton), 1-6, 7-5, 6-1; Jacobs in the semifinal to Jedrzejowska, 6-4, 6-4.

Lizana cooled the blazing forehand of the Pole in winning, 6-4, 6-2, the first all-foreign U.S. final. That completed a shutout of American women at the four majors, making it their most poverty-stricken year since 1918 when Norwegian Molla Mallory won the lone major available in that war year.

But international female success for the U.S. came in Wightman Cup play— a 6-1 victory over Great Britain, the seventh straight American victory for an 11-4 edge in the series. Marble and Jacobs provided all that was needed: Alice heat Mary Hardwick, 4-6, 6-2, 6-4, and Kay Stammers, 6-3, 6-1; Helen administered similar treatment, 2-6, 6-4, 6-2, and 6-1, 4-6, 6-4, respectively.

Interest in pro tennis was revived with the debut of Fred Perry playing a cross-country tour against Ellsworth Vines, promoted by Frank Hunter, Bill Tilden's old doubles partner, and S. Howard Voshell. Perry opened at Madison Square Garden in fine fashion, defeating Vines, 7-5, 3-6, 6-3, 6-4, before a record crowd of 17,630, paying $58,120, a financial record for the tour. Perry won the first six matches, but Vines finished strongly, winning the series, 32-29. The tour grossed $412,181. Perry, with his guarantee, received the bigger slice, $91,335. Vines got $34,195.

Though Vines was regarded as the "official" pro champion, Tilden scheduled himself against Perry in the Garden later in the year. Tilden was 44, Perry was 28, and though the crowd of 15,132 cheered mightily for the old guy, he was outclassed. He lost in the Garden for the first time, 6-1, 6-3, 4-6, 6-0. Wrote Al Laney: "All they can do is beat him; they cannot ever be his equal." It was estimated Tilden had netted $500,000 (in Depression dollars) since turning pro six years earlier.

The Europeans won the significant pro tournaments: German Hans Nusslein won the French Pro Championships over Henri Cochet, 6-2, 8-6, 6-3, and Wembley over Tilden, 6-4, 3-6, 6-3, 2-6, 6-3. Czech Karel Kozeluh took his third U.S. Pro over Texan Bruce Barnes, 6-2, 6-3, 4-6, 4-6, 6-1. This was held in October at the posh Greenbrier resort, White Sulphur Springs, West Virginia, and billed, prematurely—31 years before its time—rather plaintively as the "first open championship." Prize money was offered, but no amateurs of note rushed in to test the waters, and the few unknowns who did were suspended by the U.S. Lawn Tennis Association. Vines, Tilden and Perry stayed away, too.

1937 CHAMPIONS AND LEADERS

Australian Championships
Men's Singles Final: Viv McGrath (AUS) def. John Bromwich (AUS), 6-3, 1-6, 6-0, 2-6, 6-1

Women's Singles Final: Nancye Wynne (AUS) def. Emily Hood Westacott (AUS), 6-3, 5-7, 6-4

Men's Doubles Final: Adrian Quist and Don Turnbull (AUS) def. John Bromwich and Jack Harper (AUS), 6-2, 9-7, 1-6, 6-8, 6-4

Women's Doubles Final: Thelma Coyne Long and Nancye Wynne (AUS) def. Nell Hall Hopman and Emily Hood Westacott (AUS), 6-2, 6-2

Mixed Doubles Final: Nell Hall Hopman and Harry Hopman (AUS) def. Dorothy Stevenson and Don Turnbull (AUS), 3-6, 6-3, 6-2

French Championships
Men's Singles Final: Henner Henkel (GER) def. Bunny Austin (GBR), 6-1, 6-4, 6-3

Women's Singles Final: Hilde Krahwinkel Sperling (DEN) def. Simone Passemard Mathieu (FRA), 6-2, 6-4

Men's Doubles Final: Gottfried von Cramm and Henner Henkel (GER) def. Noman Farquharson and Vernon Kirby (RSA), 6-4, 7-5, 3-6, 6-1

Women's Doubles Final: Simone Passemard Mathieu (FRA) and Billie Yorke (GBR) def. Dorothy Andrus (USA) and Sylvie Jung Henrotin (FRA), 3-6, 6-2, 6-2

Mixed Doubles Final: Simone Passemard Mathieu and Yvon Petra (FRA) def. Marie Luise Horn and Roland Journu (FRA), 7-5, 7-5

Wimbledon
Men's Singles Final: Don Budge (USA) def. Gottfried von Cramm (GER), 6-3, 6-4, 6-2

Women's Singles Final: Dorothy Round (GBR) def. Jadwiga Jedrzejowska (POL), 6-2, 2-6, 7-5

Men's Doubles Final: Don Budge and Gene Mako (USA) def Pat Hughes and Charles Tuckey (GBR), 6-0, 6-4, 6-8, 6-1

Women's Doubles Final: Simone Passemard Mathieu (FRA) and Billie Yorke (GBR) def. Phyllis Mudford King and Eisie Goldsack Pittman (GBR), 6-3, 6-3

Mixed Doubles Final: Alice Marble and Don Budge (USA) def. Simone Passemard Mathieu and Yvon Petra (FRA), 6-4, 6-1

U.S. Championships
Men's Singles Final: Don Budge (USA) def. Gottfried von Cramm (GER), 6-1, 7-9, 6-1, 3-6, 6-1

Women's Singles Final: Anita Lizana (CHI) def. Jadwiga Jedrzejowska (POL), 6-4, 6-2

Men's Doubles Final: Gottfried von Cramm and Henner Henkel (GER) def. Don Budge and Gene Mako (USA), 6-4, 7-5, 6-4

Women's Doubles Final: Sarah Palfrey Fabyan and Alice Marble (USA) def. Marjorie Gladman Van Ryn and Carolin Babcock (USA), 7-5, 6-4

Mixed Doubles Final: Sarah Palfrey Fabyan and Don Budge (USA) def. Sylvie Jung Henrotin and Yvon Petra (FRA), 6-2, 8-10, 6-0

Year-End No. 1
Men: Don Budge
Women: Anita Lizana

Davis Cup: United States

Wightman Cup: United States

1938 Budge Births The Grand Slam

Don Budge (left) clinches the Grand Slam by beating his doubles partner **Gene Mako** (right) in the final at Forest Hills.

At 23, Don Budge had one of the most successful year of any player in tennis history. He won the four major championships— Australia, France, Wimbledon and the U.S.—a feat that came to be known as the "Grand Slam" after Budge accomplished it. He also won the triple crown at Wimbledon for the second straight year and helped the U.S. retain the Davis Cup.

Budge had received his first substantial offer to go professional in 1937. He turned it down because he felt indebted to amateur tennis to the extent of helping defend the Davis Cup the U.S. had won in 1937, and for the first time since 1926."The Grand Slam then occurred to me as something of an afterthought," Budge said. He laid his plans carefully, telling only his pal and doubles partner Gene Mako, resolving not to extend himself at any time, so that he shouldn't tire along the way, as Jack Crawford had in 1933 when he won the first three major titles before losing in the final at Forest Hills.

Budge started in Australia, after losing frequently in leisurely tune-ups, and swept through the championships, beating John Bromwich, 6-4, 6-1, 6-1 in under an hour in the final at Adelaide's Memorial Drive. Baron Gottfried von Cramm was there, losing to Bromwich in the semifinal, 6-3, 7-5, 6-1, but shortly afterwards he—Budge's friend—was arrested and thrown into jail, charged with homosexuality but probably imprisoned because of his opposition to Nazi rule. Budge led an unsuccessful athletes' appeal for von Cramm's release.

In the French Championships, though suffering from diarrhea, Budge had a fairly

easy time. He was extended to five sets by a Yugoslav lefty, Franjo Kukuljevic, in the third round. Never behind, Budge said later he didn't feel threatened. Where von Cramm might have been his opponent in the final, he faced 6-foot-4 Czech Roderich Menzel, an outstanding clay-court player. Budge romped, 6-3, 6-2, 6-4, in less than an hour. He recalled the party afterward, at which virtuoso cellist Pablo Casals gave a concert in Budge's honor at Casals' apartment within view of the Eiffel Tower. Mako may have been Don's doubles partner, but he preferred that night to "be elsewhere," watching the toast of Paris, the sexy Josephine Baker dancing rather than hearing Casals fiddling.

At Wimbledon, Budge won without losing a set, yet there was a time in the tournament when he felt panic because he had been having trouble with his backhand. It was his most celebrated weapon, considered by many to have been the greatest backhand of them all. He was undercutting the stroke, and only while watching an older female member of the All England Club on a side court, hitting with topspin on her backhand, did he realize his error. He won his second successive Wimbledon by sailing past Britain's No. 2-seeded Bunny Austin in the final, 6-1, 6-0, 6-3, then completed another triple with Mako in men's doubles, 6-4, 3-6, 6-4, 8-6, over Germans Henner Henkel and Georg von Metaxa, and with Marble in the mixed, 6-1, 6-4, over Sarah Fabyan and Henkel.

Peppery Californian Bobby Riggs, a Davis Cup rookie, was starting to be noticed as a potential Budge successor. He won the U.S. Clay Court title for a third successive year, beating Gardnar Mulloy, 6-4, 5-7, 4-6, 6-1, 7-5, and was just the singles collaborator Budge needed against Australia in the Davis Cup Challenge Round. Lobbing and passing cleverly, Riggs led off with a 4-6, 6-0, 8-6, 6-1 victory over net-charging Adrian Quist to the delight of 10,000 customers at Philadelphia's Germantown Cricket Club. Budge followed up, 6-2, 6-3, 4-6, 7-5, over Bromwich, who in later years called Budge "the greatest player I've ever seen or played against." Quist and Bromwich kept it alive by beating Budge and Mako, 0-6, 6-3, 6-4, 6-2, giving Don the opportunity to close his Cup career with a clinching crushing of Quist, 8-6, 6-1, 6-2, ending with a 14-match Cup streak.

Budge had been suffering from the flu and lost his voice off and on during the year. However, he proceeded to romp through the U.S. Championship with straight-set victories over Welby Van Horn 6-0, 6-0, 6-1; Bob Kamrath 6-3, 7-5, 9-7; Charlie Hare 6-3, 6-2, 6-0; Harry Hopman 6-3, 6-1, 6-3, and No. 4-seeded Sidney Wood, 6-3, 6-3, 6-3 to reach the final against an astonishing Mako. Gene had become the second unseeded player ever to reach the U.S. final, following the 1930 example of Frank Shields. He beat the top foreign seed, Bromwich, 6-1, 7-5, 6-4, in the semifinal but Gene's best win was over No. 6 seed Frank Kovacs 6-0, 6-2, 8-6, in the third round.

To some it looked like a set-up for Budge, but he responded: "Gene was as likely to roll over and play dead for me as peace was to come in our time." Mako did win the second set, only the fifth Budge lost in the four major tournaments. Budge then had to explain that he did not intentionally throw a set to his friend (it was 6-3, 6-8, 6-2, 6-1) certainly not at Forest Hills with so much at stake:"And I had too much respect and affection for Gene to treat

him as if he were an inferior player who could be given a set for his troubles, rather like a condescending pat on the head."

Bromwich and future king Riggs, who would be ranked No. 3 and No. 4 in the world for the year, were the only ones given a chance to jam the Slam. But No. 2-seeded Bobby left early, removed in the fourth round by No. 19 American Gil Hunt, who paced himself with nolo-contendere sets to win, 6-2, 0-6, 9-7, 0-6, 6-4. Bromwich fell to Mako, who could not prevent his pal Budge from rolling to the historic Grand Slam before 12,000 witnesses.

However. Budge could be stopped—by Mother Nature. He and Mako were put on hold for a week, waiting out the unpredicted, super-destructive 1938 hurricane, devastating the American northeast. It was nameless—hurricanes weren't baptized just yet—but nonetheless notorious. "We were rooming together," says Mako. "We went out on the town, but made sure nobody had the edge in sleep."

Budge, winner of the U.S. doubles at Boston's Longwood with Mako over Aussies Bromwich and Quist, 6-3, 6-2, 6-1, and the mixed with Marble over Aussie Thelma Coyne and Bromwich, 6-1, 6-2, thus tripled. He was the first man to do so in the U.S. Championships since Bill Tilden, 1922-23. So did Marble, whose doubles accomplice was Sarah Palfrey Fabyan over Simone Mathieu and Jadwiga Jedrzejowska , 6-8, 6-4, 6-3.

An undefeated season was not to be for Budge, who took a 1937-38 winning streak home to California. The Aussies got him at last. Quist, in the semifinals of the Pacific Southwest at Los Angeles, 7-5, 6-2, 5-7, 6-3, ended the 92-match, 14-tournament string that dated from a January 1937 loss to Bitsy Grant at Tampa. Then Harry Hopman made Budge's farewell to amateurism a downer, 6-2, 5-7, 6-1, in the quarterfinals of the Pacific Coast Championships. But for two years nobody beat Don when it really mattered. His summary for 1938: Won six of eight tournaments, 43-2 in matches.

Californian Dorothy "Dodo" Bundy shared some of the hurrahs with Budge in Adelaide as the first American woman to conquer the Australian, beating Aussie Dorothy Stevenson, 6-3, 6-2. Stevenson knocked off three-time champ Joan Hartigan, 6-3, 1-6, 6-1, and future champ Nancye Wynne, 6-3, 6-3. Today, as Mrs. Dodo Bundy Cheney (competing at 92 in 2008), she has far outreached any of her contemporaries, continuing to add to her record number of U.S. senior championships.

Vive la Mathieu! At last, Simone Mathieu heartened her neighbors by winning the French title that eluded her in six other finals, including the immediately previous to Hilda Krahwinkel Sperling, who didn't enter. Mathieu beat Nelly Adamson Landry, 6-0, 6-3. A left-hander, she was the only Belgian (though holder of a French passport through marriage to Paul Landry) to reach a major final, 6-0, 6-3, until 2001 when Kim Clijsters lost to Jennifer Capriati at the French, and Justine Henin lost to Venus Williams at Wimbledon. Moreover, Simone won the doubles with Billie Yorke and mixed with compatriot Yvon Petra, an uncommon triple, a distinction she shares only with Suzanne Lenglen (1925-26) among French at the French.

Aside from Budge's heroics, Wimbledon was marked by a strong women's field, featuring the return after a two-year absence of 32-year-old Helen Wills Moody, who was seeking a

record eighth title. Though she had been extended by Kay Stammers in Wightman Cup play and had lost in the semifinals at Queen's Club, the Wimbledon tune-up, to Hilde Sperling. (Sperling then lost to Jedrzejowska, 6-3, 6-0), Moody was top seeded. Unseeded Helen Jacobs, closing in on her 30th birthday, knew her way around to uproot the No. 8 and No. 3 seeds, Peggy Scriven, 6-3, 6-0, and 1937 finalist, Jedrzejowska, 6-2, 6-3. She next beat the No. 2 seed, ex-U.S. champ Alice Marble, spoiling the final everyone wanted: The aging goddess, Moody, against the fresh phenom, Marble. Alas, the final, their fourth at Wimbledon and the last of 11 Hellenic confrontations, was a bust. Unfortunately Jacobs, playing so well, had severely strained an Achilles tendon. She came onto the court with it bandaged, struggled to 4-4, then was useless in a 6-4, 6-0, defeat.

Moody, with the 10-1 edge in the celebrated rivalry with the "other Helen," shut her major championships book at 19 singles titles, the record until Margaret Smith Court stepped ahead in 1970 on the way to 24. Steffi Graf, who also passed Moody in 1996, wound up with 22, and in 1990 Martina Navratilova pushed ahead of her at Wimbledon with a ninth title. But can anybody possibly surpass Helen's match record of 55-1 at the Big W, the last 50 uninterrupted? An irony of timing was that during the 1938 tournament Suzanne Lenglen, the woman never beaten there (27-0), died from pernicious anemia. She was 39. Moody had enough. She had played her last tournament, and did not enter Forest Hills.

All the female favorites at Forest Hills were imperiled at one time or another. Top-seeded Jacobs, four-time champ and never worse than a quarterfinalist since a 1927 debut, was bounced in the third round by a young British lefty, Margot Lumb, 7-5, 6-2. Marble, reinstating herself as champ, escaped by hairs –two match points—from Fabyan in a volley-rich roller-coaster semifinal, 5-7, 7-5, 7-5. Marble led 5-1, then trailed 0-4 and 2-5, 15-40 in the second, 1-3 in the third.

Australian Nancye Wynne, the other finalist, scraped through three consecutive three-setters: 8-6, 3-6, 6-1 over American Helen Pedersen 6-4, 5-7, 6-1 over Lumb; 5-7, 6-4, 8-6 over Bundy to become the first Aussie in the title round other than Wilberforce Eaves in 1897 and Jack Crawford in 1933. There wasn't much left, however, and for 22 minutes Marble was Hurricane Alice, winning 6-0, 6-3.

Moody bade good-bye to Wightman Cupping as well as Wimbledon, having been absent since 1932. She scored wins over Peggy Scriven, 6-0, 7-5, and the clincher, 6-2, 3-6, 6-3, over Stammers, her 18th win in 20 singles starts, as the U.S. defeated the Brits, 5-2.

Fred Perry and Ellsworth Vines joined together as co-promoters and foes on the pro tour, won by Vines, 49-35. But Perry won the U.S. Pro title, 6-3, 6-2, 6-4, over Texan Bruce Barnes on canvas at the Chicago Arena, earning $690. Hans Nusslein ruled the European roost, beating Bill Tilden in the Wembley final, 7-5, 3-6, 6-3, 3-6, 6-2, and the French Pro final, 6-0, 6-1, 6-2.

1938 CHAMPIONS AND LEADERS

Australian Championships
Men's Singles Final: Don Budge (USA) def. John Bromwich (AUS), 6-4, 6-2, 6-1

Women's Singles Final: Dorothy Bundy (USA) def. Dorothy Stevenson (AUS), 6-3, 6-2

Men's Doubles Final: John Bromwich and Adrian Quist (AUS) def. Gottfried von Cramm and Henner Henkel (GER), 7-5, 6-4, 6-0

Women's Doubles Final: Thelma Coyne Long and Nancye Wynne (AUS) def. Dorothy Bundy and Dorothy Workman (USA), 9-7, 6-4

Mixed Doubles Final: Margaret Wilson and John Bromwich (AUS) def. Nancye Wynne and Colin Long (AUS), 6-3, 6-2

French Championships
Men's Singles Final: Don Budge (USA) def. Roderich Menzel (CZE), 6-3, 6-2, 6-4

Women's Singles Final: Simone Passemard Mathieu (FRA) def. Nelly Adamson Landry (FRA), 6-0, 6-3

Men's Doubles Final: Bernard Destremau and Yvon Petra (FRA) def. Don Budge and Gene Mako (USA), 3-6, 6-3, 9-7, 6-1

Women's Doubles Final: Simone Passemard Mathieu (FRA) and Billie Yorke (GBR) def. Arlette Halff and Nelly Adamson Landry (FRA), 6-3, 6-3

Mixed Doubles Final: Simone Passemard Mathieu (FRA) and Dragutin Mitic (YUG) def. Nancy Wynne (AUS) and Christian Boussus (FRA) 2-6, 6-3, 6-4

Wimbledon
Men's Singles Final: Don Budge (USA) def. Bunny Austin (GBR), 6-1, 6-0, 6-3

Women's Singles Final: Helen Wills Moody (USA) def. Helen Jacobs (USA), 6-4, 6-0

Men's Doubles Final: Don Budge and Gene Mako (USA) def. Henner Henkel and Georg von Metaxa (GER), 6-4, 3-6, 6-3, 8-6

Women's Doubles Final: Sarah Palfrey Fabyan and Alice Marble (USA) def. Simone Passemard Mathieu (FRA) and Billie Yorke (GBR), 6-2, 6-3

Mixed Doubles Final: Alice Marble and Don Budge (USA) def. Sarah Palfrey Fabyan (USA) and Henner Henkel (GER), 6-1, 6-4

U.S. Championships
Men's Singles Final: Don Budge (USA) def. Gene Mako (USA), 6-3, 6-8, 6-2, 6-1

Women's Singles Final: Alice Marble (USA) def. Nancye Wynne (AUS), 6-0, 6-3

Men's Doubles Final: Don Budge and Gene Mako (USA) def. Adrian Quist and John Bromwich (AUS), 6-3, 6-2, 6-1

Women's Doubles Final: Sarah Palfrey Fabyan and Alice Marble (USA) def. Simone Passemard Mathieu (FRA) and Jadwiga Jedrzejowsaka (POL), 6-8, 6-4, 6-3

Mixed Doubles Final: Alice Marble and Don Budge (USA) def. Thelma Coyne Long and John Bromwich (AUS), 6-1, 6-2

Year-End No. 1
Men: Don Budge
Women: Helen Wills Moody

Davis Cup: United States

Wightman Cup: United States

1939 A Hustler Collects Big

Bobby Riggs cashed in by winning the triple crown at Wimbledon.

Grand Slammer Don Budge had gone to the pros, but as the world teetered on the brink of war, a cocky and quick little Californian—Bobby Riggs—was ready to take over. And he did just that, showing up in three of the major finals and winning two, Wimbledon and the U.S.

Another Californian, Alice Marble, outdid him by winning those two majors—and everything else she went after to craft an undefeated season: 9-for-9 in tournaments, 45-0 in matches.

Bobby Riggs' fresh attitude, his willingness to bet on anything, his entire shtick, may have clouded his greatness on court and his resourcefulness in all situations. But foes, especially the better ones, never doubted. He is the only man to play Wimbledon once and win all three titles. He claimed he won $108,000 betting on himself to make the triple.

"I started with 500 bucks," he recalled. "A London bookmaker gave me 3-to-1 odds on the singles, where I was seeded second behind Bunny Austin. I said if I win, let it ride on the doubles so he gave me 6-to-1 on that. I said let's keep going, so he gave me 12-to-1 on the mixed. I had to win the three or lose it all.

"Even though bookmaking was legal there, I was an amateur, and the USLTA would have frowned on betting on tennis. I was afraid of what the USLTA would do if they knew an amateur had all that money so I was hush-hush about it. I left the dough in a London bank, figuring I'd pick it up after I turned pro. But the war came, so it sat there gathering interest. A nice nest egg when I got out of the Navy.

I sure was praying for the British to fight off Hitler and save my money."

Alice Marble also won the singles—6-2, 6-0 over Kay Stammers after double-bageling ex-French champ Hilde Krahwinkel Sperling in the semifinals. With Sarah Palfrey Fabyan, she won the doubles. However, she had no idea how important the mixed was to Bobby. Her triple, hand in hand with a tripling man, was also unique. Stammers, seeded No. 6, had knocked off ex-champ No. 2-seeded Helen Jacobs, 6-2, 6-2, then Fabyan in the semifinals, 7-5, 2-6, 6-3.

When it got down to the last two days of singles, even Riggs must have been edgy. He had a harder time than usual beating No. 6-seeded American Elwood Cooke for the title from 1-4 down in the second, 2-6, 8-6, 3-6, 6-3, 6-2. Partner Cooke had done him a big favor by removing Austin 6-3, 6-0, 6-1 and No. 5-seeded Henner Henkel 6-3, 4-6, 6-4, 6-4. In the semifinals, Bobby beat Yugoslav Ferenc Puncec, 6-2, 6-3, 6-4.

"When I was down 2-1 in sets to Cooke, I thought about my investment," Riggs said. "I think the parlay was a big incentive to my success. We had some close calls in the doubles, but I was too near to let it get away." Probably the toughest was his and Cooke's 6-3, 3-6, 6-8, 6-2, 11-9 quarterfinal win over Brits Henry Billington and Pat Hughes. They beat two more Brits, Charlie Hare and Frank Wilde, in the final, 6-3, 3-6, 6-3, 9-7. In the mixed, Bobby and Alice lost a couple of sets, but finished strong over Brits Nina Brown and Wilde, 9-7, 6-1. Bobby, the ultimate hustler, was rich.

Alice's doubles end of her triple, with Fabyan, was a cakewalk over Jacobs and Billie Yorke, 6-1, 6-0.

No Americans journeyed to defend the Australian titles won in 1938 by Budge and Dodo Bundy. John Bromwich, who sandwiched his two titles around the war, beat his doubles partner, Adrian Quist, 6-4, 6-1, 6-3. Emily Hood Westacott beat Nell Hall Hopman, 6-1, 6-2, for the other singles, but Nell won the mixed with her spouse, Harry Hopman. Bromwich reversed the 1937 final by defeating Viv McGrath in the semifinals, 6-0, 6-3, 6-4, while Quist mastered the old master, 30-year-old Jack Crawford, 6-1, 7-5, 6-3. Bromwich and Quist grabbed the second of eight straight doubles titles, 6-4, 7-5, 6-2, over Don Turnbull and Colin Long.

Just 21, a college boy from Kenyon out of Oklahoma, Don McNeill was a scholarly surprise at the French, running 11 straight games in the final to beat Riggs for the first time, 7-5, 6-0, 6-3. United with another American, Charlie Harris, he also took the doubles, 4-6, 6-4, 6-0, 2-6, 10-8, over the last of the Musketeers, Jacques Brugnon, 44, and Jean Borotra, 40, even though Borotra had four match points on serve at 6-5. Love was blooming in the mixed, won by Cooke and Mrs. Fabyan (later Mrs. Cooke) over Simone Mathieu and Franjo Kukuljevic, 4-6, 6-1, 7-5. Mathieu, in her eighth French singles final, retained the title that she'd missed out on six times, holding off the sturdy Pole, Jadwiga Jedrzejowska, 6-3, 8-6. The two, however, blended well to win the doubles, 7-5, 7-5, over Hella Kovac and Alice Florian.

Minus Budge, the U.S. was still favored to retain the Davis Cup at Philadelphia's Merion Cricket Club. The singles line-up of holdovers from the 1937 and 1938 victories, Riggs and Frank Parker, looked solid against Australia—the first day. Riggs crushed Bromwich, his conqueror of the 1938 challenge round, 6-4, 6-0, 7-5,

coming back from 0-4 in the third, and Parker hung on to take Quist, 6-3, 2-6, 6-4, 1-6, 7-5. The 0-2 deficit wasn't the worst of it for the Aussies. Gloom thickened the next day, September 3. As part of the British Empire, they were at war against Germany.

Bromwich recalled: "We didn't know if we'd ever play tennis again. We reckoned we'd have to go into the service almost immediately." They were permitted to remain for the completion of the U.S. summer season. "But we also felt we still had a chance here. Quisty and I were sure we could win the doubles [they'd recently won the U.S. title over teammates Crawford and Hopman, 8-6, 6-1, 6-4], and that we'd play better singles on the third day. We badly wanted to be the first to win as Australia." The last Cup triumph for the Down Under guys had been in 1919 as Australasia.

But 0-2? No country had ever rebounded from 0-2 before (nor since) to win in a Cup finale. The Aussies did. Rookies Joe Hunt, 20, and Jack Kramer, 18, (the youngest American to play a challenge round), both future U.S. champs, were an untried team, and couldn't hold up against the canny Bromwich and dashing Quist, 5-7, 6-2, 7-5, 6-2, despite leading 3-0 in the third. Once they had a sniff of champagne from the Cup, the Aussies went all out to insure a swill. Riggs fought well after falling way behind, but Quist's passing shots brought him down, 6-1, 6-4, 3-6, 6-4. In the fifth and decisive rubber, Bromwich unswervingly concentrated on Frank's right side in long rallies until it collapsed entirely to the dismay of 9,000 fans. Said Bromwich, "I made up my mind to hit a thousand balls to Parker's forehand if that's what it took." Bromwich won the first seven games and the Cup, 6-0, 6-3, 6-1, the most one-sided clinching singles until 1989 when Boris Becker of Germany beat Mats Wilander of Sweden, also in 22 games, 6-2, 6-0, 6-2.

The victory atmosphere was somber, as it had been in 1914 when the Australasian side of Norman Brookes and Tony Wilding lifted the Cup from the U.S. just after the outbreak of World War I. There would again be a long hiatus in Davis Cup, six years. The sterling prize sat out the war in a lonely vault of the Bank of New South Wales at Melbourne.

The Wightman Cup went into storage, too, after a 5-2 U.S. victory sparked by Marble's two singles wins, 6-3, 6-4 over Mary Hardwick, and 3-6, 6-3, 6-4 over Stammers.

A mere footnote, but one boding immense implications, was the initial televising of tennis in the U.S. (it began in 1937 at Wimbledon). Matches at the Rye, N.Y., tournament were covered by NBC primitively, including Riggs' 1-6, 6-4, 6-4, 7-5, victory in the final over Parker. Few sets (with 4-by-3 inch screens) were in use and, according to *American Lawn Tennis* magazine: "When the entire court was shown the figures of the players were so small and far-away-looking that only general movements could be followed; the ball was seldom discernible."

At Forest Hills, Riggs ran into a bright young hope, 19-year-old Californian Welby Van Horn. As the third unseeded finalist (following Frank Shields in 1930, and Gene Mako, in 1938), 6-foot-1 Van Horn displayed sharp volleying in running over No. 3-seeded Cooke, 6-3, 8-10, 6-4, 7-5; No. 8-seeded Wayne Sabin, 4-6, 2-6, 6-4, 7-5, 6-3, and top foreigner, Australian champ Bromwich, 2-6, 4-6, 6-2, 6-4, 8-6, in the semifinal. Riggs eliminated No. 6 seed Joe Hunt

in the semifinal, 6-1, 6-2, 4-6, 6-1. Hunt had outlasted No. 4 seed McNeill, 6-4, 15-13, 8-10, 4-6, 6-2.

Van Horn opened the final with two aces, and the supportive crowd roared with approval. Riggs then took charge. The score: 6-4, 6-2, 6-4, and the U.S. had its first short-trousered champ.

Meanwhile, Marble completed one of the most powerful seasons ever enjoyed by a woman. She was threatened by Helen Jacobs, the four-time champion who reached the final by overcoming Stammers, 7-5; 6-0. Bageled in the first set, 6-0, Jacobs won the second 10-8, and took a 3-1 lead in the third before Marble prevailed, 6-0, 8-10, 6-4. Allison Danzig wrote in *The New York Times*: "Here was one of the most dramatic battles that women's tennis had produced in years, fought out for an hour-and-a-half in gusty cross-currents of wind that raised havoc with the strokes, while the gallery of 8,500 roared and screamed its encouragement at Miss Jacobs. The crescendo of the enthusiasm was reached in the final game, a furiously disputed 20-point session in which Miss Jacobs five times came within a stroke of 5-all and twice stood off match points, only to yield finally to Miss Marble's more powerful attacking weapons."

Thus, Marble completed her second U.S. triple in a row, having won the women's doubles with Sarah Palfrey Fabyan for the third straight year (7-5, 8-6 over Freda James Hammersley and Stammers), and then the mixed doubles, not with Riggs, but with the 33-year-old Australian captain Hopman over French champs Fabyan and Cooke, 9-7, 6-1. Riggs' splendid season encompassed nine titles in 13 tournaments, 54 wins in 59 starts.

When Don Budge made his pro debut in Madison Square Garden in January, he was a slight underdog to champion Ellsworth Vines. A crowd of 16,725 paid $47,120. Many of them were USLTA officials who showed their devotion to Budge for his loyalty in delaying his departure from the amateur ranks in order to defend the Davis Cup. Budge trounced Vines, 6-3, 6-4, 6-2, perhaps because Vines had played only eight matches with Fred Perry in South America that summer.

Later, Budge made a second Garden appearance against Perry, his master as an amateur, but Budge won easily, 6-1, 6-3, 6-0. On a tour played mostly in big cities, Budge asserted his superiority, beating Vines, 22-17, and Perry, 28-8. Budge collected more than $100,000, including a $75,000 guarantee, from the $204,503 gross. Vines got $23,000, then deserted tennis for a successful pro golf career. Budge, however, stayed out of the $2,000 U.S. Pro Championships, won in a brilliant three-hour struggle by Vines over Perry, 8-6, 6-8, 6-1, 20-18, at Beverly Hills. Vines took home the magnificent sum of $340.05.

1939 CHAMPIONS AND LEADERS

Australian Championships
Men's Singles Final: John Bromwich (AUS) def. Adrian Quist (AUS), 6-4, 6-1, 6-2
Women's Singles Final: Emily Hood Westacott (AUS) def. Nell Hall Hopman (AUS), 6-1, 6-2
Men's Doubles Final: John Bromwich and Adrian Quist (AUS) def. Don Turnbull and Colin Long (AUS), 6-4, 7-5, 6-2
Women's Doubles Final: Thelma Coyne Long and Nancye Wynne (AUS) def. May Hardcastle and Emily Hood Westacott (AUS), 7-5, 6-4
Mixed Doubles Final: Nell Hall Hopman and Harry Hopman (AUS) def. Margaret Wilson and John Bromwich (AUS), 6-8, 6-2, 6-3

French Championships
Men's Singles Final: Don NcNeill (USA) def. Bobby Riggs (USA), 7-5, 6-0, 6-3
Women's Singles Final: Simone Passemard Mathieu (FRA) def. Jadwiga Jedrzejowska (POL), 6-3, 8-6
Men's Doubles Final: Don McNeill and Charles Harris (USA) def. Jean Borotra and Jacques Brugnon (FRA), 4-6, 6-4, 6-0, 2-6, 10-8
Women's Doubles Final: Simone Passemard Mathieu (FRA) and Jadwiga Jedrzejowska (POL), def. Alice Florian and Hella Kovac (YUG), 7-5, 7-5
Mixed Doubles Final: Sarah Palfrey Fabyan and Elwood Cooke (USA) def. Simone Passemard Mathieu (FRA) and Franjo Kuklujevic (YUG), 4-6, 6-1, 7-5

Wimbledon
Men's Singles Final: Bobby Riggs (USA) def. Elwood Cooke (USA), 2-6, 8-6, 3-6, 6-3, 6-2
Women's Singles Final: Alice Marble (USA) def Kay Stammers (GBR), 6-2, 6-0
Men's Doubles Final: Elwood Cooke and Bobby Riggs (USA) def. Charles Hare and Frank Wilde (GBR), 6-3, 3-6, 6-3, 9-7
Women's Doubles Final: Sarah Palfrey Fabyan and Alice Marble (USA) def. Helen Jacobs (USA) and Billie Yorke (GBR), 6-1, 6-0
Mixed Doubles Final: Alice Marble and Bobby Riggs (USA) def. Nina Brown and Frank Wilde (GBR), 9-7, 6-1

U.S. Championships
Men's Singles Final: Bobby Riggs (USA) def. Welby Van Horn (USA), 6-4, 6-2, 6-4
Women's Singles Final: Alice Marble (USA) def. Helen Jacobs (USA), 6-0, 8-10, 6-4
Men's Doubles Final: Adrian Quist and John Bromwich (AUS) def. Jack Crawford and Harry Hopman (AUS), 8-6, 6-1, 6-4
Women's Doubles Final: Sarah Palfrey Fabyan and Alice Marble (USA) def. Kay Stammers and Freda James Hammersley (GBR), 7-5, 8-6
Mixed Doubles Final: Alice Marble (USA) and Harry Hopman (AUS) def. Sarah Palfrey Fabyan and Elwood Cooke (USA), 9-7, 6-1

Year-End No. 1
Men: Bobby Riggs
Women: Alice Marble

Davis Cup: Australia

Wightman Cup: United States

1940

Marble Rolls To Perfect 83-0 Mark

Alice Marble posted an incredible 83-0 record in 1940.

Bombs landed on Wimbledon during the Nazi blitzing of London, and international play virtually ceased, at least in the most important locations beyond U.S. borders. Wimbledon and the French were out of business until 1946. The curtain didn't fall as quickly on the Australian. Adrian Quist won his second title over Jack Crawford, in his seventh final, 6-3, 6-1, 6-2. Nancye Wynne, on her way to six titles, won her second at the expense of her doubles partner, Thelma Coyne, 5-7, 6-4, 6-0.

Stade Roland Garros had a shameful wartime chapter as a concentration camp, first run by a frantically insecure French government to intern political dissidents, aliens and other suspect types. Later, with the German occupation, it housed Jews who would be shipped east to their doom. Not up to Nazi standards, Roland Garros was returned to the French Federation in 1941. Regardless of an acute shortage of balls and rackets, national tournaments of sorts were held through 1945. Yvon Petra, recovered from his wounds after a stint as a POW, won the men's titles in 1943-44-45, and stayed fit for his successful shot at the first post-war Wimbledon title. In 1943, he beat a re-appeared 41-year-old Musketeer, Henri Cochet, in the final. A friend, ex-French Davis Cupper Robert Abdesselam, says that four-time champ Cochet "felt it important to play during the war, to show himself so that our dispirited youth would know that a Frenchman had been a world champion."

Philippe Chatrier, later head of the French Federation and the ITF, an exceptional administrator named to the Interna-

tional Tennis Hall of Fame, was a young player growing up during the war. He remembered a few cans of new balls—something he and his friends had never seen—arriving at Roland Garros through the Red Cross, a gift from the USLTA. "What a wonderful country America must be to do that," he thought.

Wimbledon's courts languished untended, used as a civil defense center, with the parking lots tilled and planted as victory gardens—and a home for pigs and chickens. The first bombs struck on October 11, blowing a hole in the Centre Court roof. The club would be damaged from the air three more times during the year.

But the American season went on normally, meaning Alice Marble was omnipotent for another unbeaten year. Not so normal, though, for No. 1 Bobby Riggs, who lost his U.S. Championship (and No. 1 ranking) to Don McNeill, the newly crowned king of the Intercollegiates for tiny Kenyon in Gambier, Ohio. McNeill, a 22-year-old Oklahoman, fought one of the great come-from-behind battles against Riggs in a match marked by outstanding sportsmanship. The score: 4-6, 6-8, 6-3, 6-3, 7-5.

McNeill had no fear of Riggs. He'd beaten Bobby a few weeks earlier in the U.S. Clay final, 6-1, 6-4, 7-9, 6-3, and the year before in the French final. But Bobby felt confident on the faster surface, having beaten Don in the U.S. Indoor final, 3-6, 6-1, 6-4, 2-6, 6-2. With the score 4-4 and deuce in the last set, McNeill hit a shot to Riggs' sideline that the linesman first called out. As Riggs turned his back and prepared to serve, the official reversed his call, declaring it good. Riggs did not know of the change until he heard the call, "Advantage McNeill." Allison Danzig wrote: "The defending champion, who rarely questions a decision, turned at the call and then walked back toward the linesman, asking him why he had changed his ruling. The official maintained that the ball was good. Riggs, without quibbling, accepted the costly decision and lost the next point and the game."

Then, in the opening rally of the concluding game, Riggs had to hit a ball that was falling just over the net and he gingerly endeavored to keep from touching the tape. The umpire instantly announced Riggs' foot touched the net and he lost the point. "At that critical state," Danzig wrote, "it was a bitter pill to swallow, but Riggs took it without arguing. McNeill, however, apparently did not like to win the point that way, even though the ruling was correct, and when he knocked Riggs' next service far out of court, the stadium rang with applause."

After losing the first set, McNeill rallied from 1-5 and 15-40 in the second set to tie, saved four set points, went on to take a 6-5 lead, but then dropped the set anyway, 8-6. Down two sets, he still came back, and with the crowd almost completely behind the valiant underdog, he squared the match and then pulled out the final set.

Alice Marble, about to turn 27—and pro—was supreme-plus, charging to her fourth U.S. singles title while never endangered, winning 12 sets, losing only 27 games. This put the finishing touches on her amateur career that had purred uninterruptedly victorious since a Wimbledon semifinal loss to Helen Jacobs in 1938. As in 1939, Alice won nine tournaments, and 45 matches. Moreover, she was 27-0 in doubles, 11-0 in mixed for a stupendous 83-0 record. She left intact a 22-tournament, 111-match

streak, third only to Suzanne Lenglen's 44-179 and Helen Wills Moody's 27—158.

Regal and self-assured in her jaunty white cap, the tallest of U.S. champs at 5-foot-8 until Althea Gibson (5-foot-11) came along, Alice was too strong in the final for the No. 2-seeded Jacobs, 6-2, 6-3, a tame rematch of their 1939 championship encounter. England's Mary Hardwick—after defeating No. 5-seeded Sarah Palfrey, 6-1, 6-3, and No. 3-seeded Pauline Betz, 5-7, 6-1, 6-2—harried Jacobs in the semis, 2-6, 6-1, 6-4. Marble, having won a third straight U.S. doubles with Palfrey, over Dodo Bundy and Midge Van Ryn (6-4, 6-3) and the mixed with Riggs over Bundy and Jack Kramer (9-7, 6-1), became a triple-tripler. That put her up there with Hazel Hotchkiss Wightman (1909-10-11) and Mary K. Browne (1912-13-14) in U.S. annals. Marble also tripled at Wimbledon in 1939.

Newlyweds Sarah Palfrey and Elwood Cooke, he a quarterfinal loser to McNeill, were nationally ranked Nos. 6 and 9 in singles, the second spousal pair to be together in the upper echelon, following Johnny Van Ryn (No. 9 in 1930, No. 4 in 1931) and wife Midge Gladman Van Ryn (No. 7 and 8 those years).

Although there was no pro tour, Don Budge remained king, taking his first U.S. Pro title, 6-3, 5-7, 6-4, 6-3, over Fred Perry.

1940 CHAMPIONS

Australian Championships

Men's Singles Final: Adrian Quist (AUS) def. Jack Crawford (AUS), 6-3, 6-1, 6-2

Women's Singles Final: Nancye Wynne (AUS) def. Thelma Coyne Long (AUS), 5-7, 6-4, 6-0

Men's Doubles Final: John Bromwich and Adrian Quist (AUS) def. Jack Crawford and Viv McGrath (AUS), 6-3, 7-5, 6-1

Women's Doubles Final: Thelma Coyne Long and Nancye Wynne (AUS) def. Joan Hartigan Bathurst and Emily Neimeyer (AUS), 7-5, 6-2

Mixed Doubles Final: Nancye Wynne and Colin Long (AUS) def. Nell Hall Hopman and Harry Hopman (AUS) 7-5, 2-6, 6-4

U.S. Championships

Men's Singles Final: Don McNeill (USA) def. Bobby Riggs (USA), 4-6, 6-8, 6-3, 6-3, 7-5

Women's Singles Final: Alice Marble (USA) def. Helen Jacobs (USA), 6-2, 6-3

Men's Doubles Final: Jack Kramer and Ted Schroeder (USA) def. Gardnar Mulloy and Henry Prussoff (USA), 6-4, 8-6, 9-7

Women's Doubles Final: Sarah Palfrey Fabyan and Alice Marble (USA) def. Dorothy Bundy and Marjorie Van Ryn (USA), 6-4, 6-3

Mixed Doubles Final: Alice Marble and Bobby Riggs (USA) def. Dorothy Bundy and Jack Kramer (USA), 9-7, 6-1

1941 Riggs Back On Top, Jacobs Bows Out

Frustration ended at Forest Hills for gorgeous Sarah Palfrey Cooke and gambling Bobby Riggs. Hers was longer-term. Sarah, who had divorced Marshall Fabyan and married sometimes mixed doubles partner, Elwood Cooke, arrived at the U.S. Championships for a 13th time, seeded second, having done everything but win. A 15-year-old when she first appeared in 1928, she had been seeded every year since 1933, made the final twice (1934 and 1935, losing to Helen Jacobs), the semis (1938), the quarters (1933) and flopped in the first round (1936 to Dodo Bundy, 2-6, 6-3, 6-4; 1937 to Dorothy Andrus, 12-10, 0-6, 7-5) when seeded second and third.

No woman had waited longer, but her hour at last came. Though the path was strewn with champs past and future, Sarah remained in an offensive frame of mind all the way to beating Pauline Betz, 7-5, 6-2, in the final. She was days from her 29th birthday. Only Maud Barger-Wallach, 38 in 1908, and Molla Mallory, 31 in 1915, were older first-time champs. American junior champ Louise Brough, who would rule six years down the road, was a stubborn first-round obstacle (4-6, 6-1, 6-1), as was Sarah's long-time nemesis, Jacobs (6-3, 2-6, 6-1) in the semis. Since she'd delighted her hometown, Boston, by winning the doubles with Margaret Osborne over Dodo Bundy and Betz, 3-6, 6-1, 6-4, and the mixed with Jack Kramer over Betz and Riggs, 4-6, 6-4, 6-4, at Longwood (her home club), Sarah had the triple, joining a select group of 15 U.S. women.

Jacobs' illustrious career at Forest Hills closed after 14 years, four titles, four

other finals and 63 match wins, second at the time only to Molla Mallory's 65, although both would be surpassed by Chris Evert (101), Martina Navratilova (89) and Steffi Graf (73).

Riggs, the happy-go-lucky hustler and shrewd strategist, mourned that by losing the 1940 final to Don McNeill he'd wasted a big income year (a $25,000 guaranteed offer to turn pro was withdrawn). Bobby made sure not to flunk Forest Hills this time, making it the year he checked out of amateurism as No. 1. The coup de grace was his 5-7, 6-1, 6-3, 6-3 triumph over fellow American Frank Kovacs, his most difficult adversary of the year. Riggs' hardest task was beating Stanford collegian Ted Schroeder in the semis, 6-4, 6-4, 1-6, 9-11, 7-5. Kovacs, a tall, dark and handsome (plus highly talented and entertaining) 21-year-old who sometimes let his showboating get in the way, would earn the No. 2 ranking and turn pro with Riggs. He dethroned McNeill in the semis, 6-4, 6-2, 10-8.

Riggs won six tournaments, but was beaten in the final of the U.S. Clay, 6-3, 7-5, 6-8, 4-6, 6-3, by Frank Parker, who also took six titles. Kovacs won four, including a U.S. Indoor triumph over fellow American Wayne Sabin, 6-0, 6-4, 6-2. Betz won six, among them the U.S. Clay (over Mary Arnold, 6-3, 6-1) and U.S. Indoor (over Dodo Bundy, 6-1, 10-12, 6-2). Sarah Cooke's six titles would be her last until 1945—motherhood and life as a Navy wife intervened.

Marble joined the pros and beat Britain's Mary Hardwick, 8-6, 8-6, in their debut at Madison Square Garden. Bill Tilden, 48, came out of semi-retirement to face Don Budge and lost, 6-3, 6-4. The tour was a relative bust, with Budge winning 51 of 58 matches from Tilden. Budge later wrote: "Tilden was still capable of some sustained great play that could occasionally even carry him all the way through a match. Most of the time he could, at his best, hang on for at least a set or two. Despite his age, he was no pushover. The people came out primarily for the show—to see me at my peak, and to see Tilden because they might never have the chance again. Bill could invariably manage to keep things close for a while. It was seldom, however, that he could extend me to the end."

Johnny Faunce did more than extend defending champ Budge in a shook-up U.S. Pro tourney on clay at Chicago, a show stolen by little-known teaching pros such as Faunce. He evicted top-seed Budge in the second round, 6-4, 6-1, 6-3. Keith Gledhill ousted third-seeded Tilden, 6-2, 6-3, 6-3. Another pedagogue, unexpected finalist, Dick Skeen, eliminated 1936 champ Joe Whalen, 6-2, 6-4, 6-4, and Faunce, 6-3, 8-6, 2-6, 6-3, before being beaten by Fred Perry, 6-4, 6-8, 6-2, 6-3.

1941 CHAMPIONS

U.S. Championships

Men's Singles Final: Bobby Riggs (USA) def. Frank Kovacs (USA), 5-7, 6-1, 6-3, 6-3

Women's Singles: Sarah Palfrey Cooke (USA) def. Pauline Betz (USA), 7-5, 6-2

Men's Doubles: Jack Kramer and Ted Schroeder (USA) def. Wayne Sabin and Gardnar Mulloy (USA), 9-7, 6-4, 6-2

Women's Doubles: Sarah Palfrey Cooke and Margaret Osborne (USA) def. Pauline Betz and Dorothy Bundy (USA), 3-6, 6-1, 6-4

Mixed Doubles Final: Sarah Palfrey Cooke and Jack Kramer (USA) def. Pauline Betz and Bobby Riggs (USA), 4-6, 6-4, 6-4

1942 Despite War, The Show Goes On

The United States, stunned by Pearl Harbor, was at war, with all the uncertainties that entailed. But organized sports—particularly baseball and college athletics—were given the go-ahead to continue by the White House, as morale boosters for the home front and troops overseas. The U.S. Lawn Tennis Association voted cautiously to hold the U.S. Championships at Forest Hills "as usual, unless..." By that USLTA President Holcombe Ward (an original Davis Cupper) meant: "We will gladly eliminate tennis if it interferes with winning the war. But our government doesn't want us to abandon tennis. On the contrary, the Physical Fitness Program sponsored by the government calls

Ted Schroeder won the National Intercollegiate Championships in New Orleans for Stanford University and the U.S. Championships at Forest Hills.

for expansion in sports. As long as the government releases moderate amounts of reclaimed rubber for the manufacture of balls, we'll carry on."

Still, numerous tournaments were cancelled for the duration—notably the oldest, in Newport, R.I., the Men's Invitational which began as the U.S. Championships in 1881. The tourna-

ment went unplayed from 1943 to 1945. Others, including the U.S. Championships at Forest Hills, were reduced in time and entrants. It was decided that all five U.S. titles would be bunched in New York, removing the doubles from Boston to cut down on travel, and permit servicemen on short furloughs to play. Men's matches, beginning in 1943, were best-of-three sets until the semifinals.

Players were advised to use balls longer, because there would be a shortage. Men were called up for service in the armed forces by their draft boards. The women's game was pretty much unaffected and maintained a high standard. "We got more attention at the tournaments with the top men gone," said Pauline Betz. "Transportation could be difficult, but the Eastern grass tournaments were pretty close together, and we'd pool gas rationing coupons, and share cars. We got around." In London, there were no balls to be purchased. Clubs such as Queen's rented them on a per-match basis to members to be used, re-used and overused until disintegrating.

The annual pro tour, promoted by Lex Thompson, was launched December 26, 1941, at Madison Square Garden before 8,000 customers and introduced two headstrong individualists, Bobby Riggs and Frank Kovacs, as neophytes. According to USLTA officials, Riggs and Kovacs, ranked No. 1 and No. 2, had deserted amateurism not a moment too soon. They were to be suspended for accepting too much expense money, hardly an uncommon practice. Seeming snake-bitten, the tour didn't last long. Wartime travel difficulties and injuries to Kovacs and Fred Perry closed the show April 5, in Palm Springs, the 71st stop.

On opening night of the round-robin barnstorming, Kovacs beat Don Budge, 6-4, 2-6, 6-4, and Riggs beat Perry, 6-3, 4-6, 5-4, 30-15 (default). It ended as Perry fell on his right elbow, suffering an injury that virtually finished his career. At the end, Budge had a 15-10 edge on Riggs, a rivalry they would resume on the first post-war tour, and headed the pack with a 52-18 overall record. Riggs was 36-36, Kovacs 25-26, Perry 23-30. All would soon be in military uniforms, but they did reassemble a couple of months later for the U.S. Pro at Forest Hills, where Budge trimmed Riggs, 6-2, 6-2, 6-2.

The first prominent players to enter the service were No. 4 Don McNeill (Navy), the U.S. champ of 1940. Hal Surface, No. 12 in 1940, and Frank Guernsey, National Intercollegiate champ for Rice in 1938-39, went into the Army Air Corps.

The U.S. Clay Court tourney in St. Louis was an amusing mess. Heavy rains delayed the end of the tournament and the final was defaulted in progress—then resumed against "orders" only to be lost by the supposed victor, through his good sportsmanship. Both finalists, Harris Everett of North Carolina and Seymour Greenberg of Northwestern, were expected immediately in New Orleans for the National Intercollegiate Championships. The train that would get them there on time was leaving at 6 p.m. Locked at 6-6 in the fifth set, Greenberg was ordered by his coach, Paul Bennett, to default so they could catch the train, the college event deemed more important. On the way to the dressing room, Everett, apparently the champ, said to Greenberg: "Aw, to hell with New Orleans. I don't want to win it this way. Let's go back and finish." They did. Greenberg won the next

two games and became the genuine champ, 5-7, 7-5, 7-9, 7-5, 8-6. They caught the train the next day, and were excused for their tardy arrival. Neither reached the final. It was a unique all-Stanford production as Ted Schroeder beat teammate Larry Dee, 6-2, 0-6, 6-2, 6-3.

Moreover, Ted, a 21-year-old volleying virtuoso, said so-long to civilian life on a high note. He conquered the U.S. Championships at Forest Hills on his fourth attempt, 8-6, 7-5, 3-6, 4-6, 6-2, over long-suffering Frank Parker, 26. On his 11th try, and in the quarters as far back as 1934, Parker beat a newcomer from Ecuador, Francisco "Pancho" Segura, in the semis, 6-1, 6-1, 2-6, 6-2.

It seemed only a logical progression to Schroeder, loser in the third round in 1939, then the quarters and semis. It put him in a class with McNeill, the only men to win the college and U.S. titles the same year. Ted lost a set in the third round to Jimmy Evert, 6-4, 9-11, 6-4, 6-4, a Chicagoan whose future daughter, Chris, would carry off the title 33 years later. Gar Mulloy won the first of his doubles titles in the company of Bill Talbert over Sidney Wood and Schroeder, 9-7, 7-5, 6-1. Schroeder also won the mixed with Louise Brough, over Pat Canning Todd and Argentine Alejo Russell, 3-6, 6-1, 6-4.

Nineteen-year-old Californian Louise Brough - winning the grass tests at Easthampton, N.Y. (6-3, 7-5 over Pauline Betz), Philadelphia (Margaret Osborne, 6-4, 10-8), Boston (Osborne, 6-2, 6-1) and Manchester, Mass. (Betz, 6-3, 1-6, 6-3) - came into Forest Hills as the top-seeded favorite. But swift-footed Betz, 23 and the finalist 12 months before, proved a tough cookie under pressure, launching her three-year reign by snapping back to beat Brough for the title, 4-6, 6-1, 6-4. It was tighter in the semis where Pauline quashed a match point with Margaret Osborne leading 5-3 in the third to win, 6-4, 4-6, 7-5. Only 5,148 attended the final; it seemed that many tennis fans had other things on their minds. A new pairing that would result in a record total of 20 major doubles titles, Brough and Margaret Osborne (later du Pont), took their first, over Betz and Doris Hart, 2-6, 7-5, 6-0.

But tennis did go on elsewhere, including South America and India, and Lt. McNeill, showing up in Buenos Aires as a U.S. Naval attaché, won the Argentine title over Andres Hammersley of Chile.

1942 CHAMPIONS

U.S. Championships

Men's Singles Final: Ted Schroeder (USA) def. Frank Parker (USA), 8-6, 7-5, 3-6, 4-6, 6-2

Women's Singles Final: Pauline Betz (USA) def. Louise Brough (USA), 4-6, 6-1, 6-4

Men's Doubles Final: Gardnar Mulloy and Bill Talbert (USA) def. Ted Schroeder and Sidney Wood (USA), 9-7, 7-5, 6-1

Women's Doubles Final: Louise Brough and Margaret Osborne (USA) def. Pauline Betz and Doris Hart (USA), 2-6, 7-5, 6-0

Mixed Doubles Final: Louise Brough and Ted Schroeder (USA) def. Patricia Todd (USA) and Alejo Russell (ARG), 3-6, 6-1, 6-4

1943 First–and Last–Title For Joe Hunt

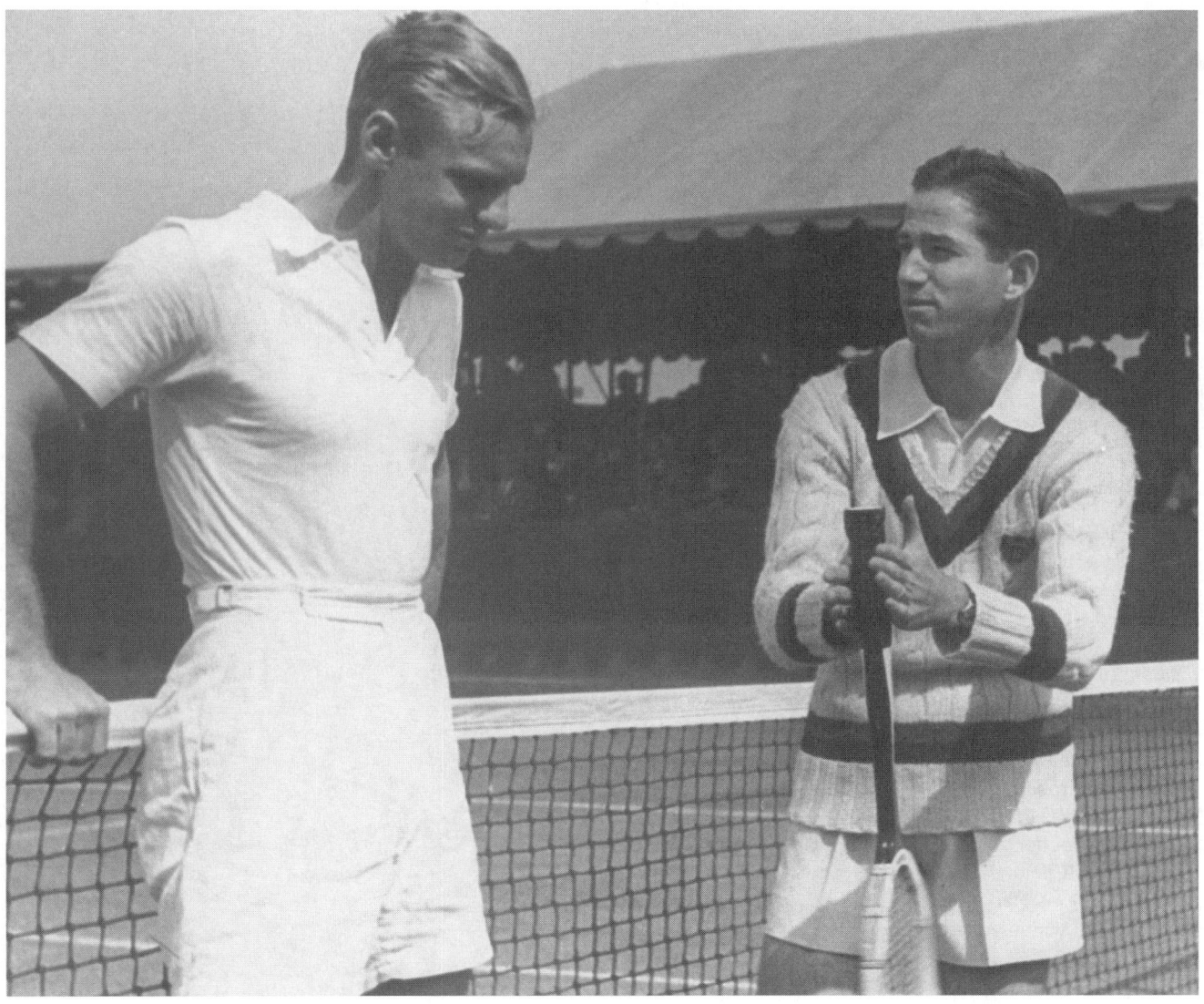

Joe Hunt (left), with **Bobby Riggs** at the 1940 U.S. Championships at Forest Hills, won the singles title at the 1943 U.S. Championships. He was tragically killed in a fighter plane crash in 1945.

Francisco "Pancho" Segura, a curious and ebullient character, arrived on the scene from Ecuador in 1941 with a big smile, little English, scrawny bowed legs and a deadly double-fisted forehand. He had the two-handed act all to himself now that Viv McGrath and John Bromwich were in the Australian army. By 1943, Pancho had the depleted tournament circuit practically to himself, too. Shipped to the University of Miami for an education, he was definitely a tennis scholar, winning a record

three straight National Intercollegiate titles through 1945. In 1943, his victim was future Wimbledon finalist and U.S. Davis Cupper Tom Brown of California-Berkeley, 6-2, 6-1, 6-3. Segura,

22, had the year's most impressive slate, winning seven of ten tournaments, 38 of 41 matches, and scorched the grass courts. He took titles at Rye, N.Y. (over Naval Lieutenant Joe Hunt 6-4, 6-1, 6-3) and Southampton, N.Y. (over Sidney Wood 6-3, 7-5, 9-7), and moved easily to the semis of the U.S. Championships, which had been compressed to six days and 32 entries, 12 of them servicemen on leave.

But two of those excused from duty for a few days were strapping blond Californians of serve-and-volley persuasion: second-seeded Coast Guard Seaman Jack Kramer, 22, and seventh-seeded Naval Lieutenant Joe Hunt, 24, a tragic figure who had won National Intercollegiate titles for Southern California in doubles (1938) and the singles (1941 over Ted Olewine of Southern California). As kids, they were Davis Cup doubles partners in the 1939 finale, losing to Aussies Adrian Quist and Bromwich. Another was Army Air Corps Corporal Frank Parker, seeded No. 1 ahead of Segura. Bill Talbert, kept out of the service by diabetes, was the lone civilian in the semis, losing to Hunt, 3-6, 6-4, 6-2, 6-4, after Hunt had bulldozed Parker, 8-6, 6-2, 6-3. Though weakened by food poisoning, Kramer hung on to beat Segura, 2-6, 6-4, 7-5, 6-3. However, Kramer was spent after three sets against Hunt, who won the final in a 6-3, 6-8, 10-8, 6-0 decision. Jack, who served for the third set at 5-4, remembers the bizarre ending: "I hit a forehand long on match point. If I'd kept that ball in court I think I would have been the champ by default." Because as the ball flew beyond him, Hunt crumpled onto the court with leg cramps, probably unable to play another point.

Hunt would not return to Forest Hills. Unable to get leave from sea duty in 1944, he was killed in a plane crash on a training mission in 1945. It happened off Daytona Beach, Fla., when the fighter plane he was piloting plunged into the Atlantic, an accident that was never explained. Playing only four tournaments in 1943, and winning one—in La Jolla, Calif.,—Joe was accorded the No. 1 ranking.

Pauline Betz, winner of seven tournaments, completed a national surface triple at Forest Hills, after taking the U.S. Indoor (over Kay Winthrop, 6-4, 6-1) and the U.S. Clay (Nancy Corbett, 6-0, 6-1). Beating Catherine Wolf, 6-0, 6-2, for the Tri-State title in Cincinnati, Pauline scored a golden bagel, winning all 24 first-set points while stroking 18 winners. Lefty Seymour Greenberg won the U.S. Clay over Talbert, 6-1, 4-6, 6-2, 6-3.

Gunning for her second title at Forest Hills, Betz earned it in a rematch struggle of the one-two seeds, beating Louise Brough, 6-3, 5-7, 6-3. Doris Hart, the 18-year-old U.S. junior champ—12 years short of winning the big one—took Betz to three sets in the quarters, 9-7, 2-6, 6-1. A first-round loser to seventh-seed Mary Arnold, 6-1, 6-1, was Gloria Thompson, who had won St. Louis earlier in the summer. She would be back years later with the son she reared to be a great champion, Jimmy Connors.

Keeping the pros alive was the Officers Club of Fort Knox, Ky. As an entertainment treat—free admission—for the post (and the town), the Army played host to the U.S. Pro, building an 11,000-seat temporary stadium with floodlights, and putting up a $2,000 purse. The stands were filled, possibly the event's largest-ever crowd, as Navy Lieutenant Bruce Barnes beat teaching pro John Nogrady, 6-1, 7-9, 7-5, 4-6, 6-3, for the title.

U.S. Championships

Men's Singles Final: Joseph R. Hunt (USA) def. Jack Kramer (USA), 6-3, 6-8, 10-8, 6-0

Women's Singles Final: Pauline Betz (USA) def. Louise Brough (USA), 6-3, 5-7, 6-3

Men's Doubles Final: Jack Kramer and Frank Parker (USA) def. David Freeman and Bill Talbert (USA), 6-2 6-4, 6-4

Women's Doubles Final: Louise Brough and Margaret Osborne (USA) def. Mary Prentiss and Patricia Todd (USA), 6-1, 6-3

Mixed Doubles Final: Margaret Osborne and Bill Talbert (USA) def. Pauline Betz (USA) and Pancho Segura (ECU), 10-6, 6-4

1944 Parker, Betz Reign Supreme

Pauline Betz won a third set women's singles title at the U.S. Championships in 1944.

Civilians Bill Talbert and Pancho Segura had things pretty much their way during the American season—until Forest Hills, another six-day event with 32 men's singles entries, 15 of them servicemen on leave. Dauntless Sergeant Frank Parker of the Army Air Corp's Muroc (Calif.) base reappeared to snatch the title he had chased for a dozen years. Seeded No. 4, Frank proved the 13th time lucky, despite playing only one preparatory tournament. The longest male chase for the title was over as the dark-haired 28-year-old, wearing dark glasses, brought down No. 3-seeded Talbert for the title, 6-4, 3-6, 6-3, 6-3, before a final-round gathering of 8,000.

Talbert wore himself down expelling top seed Segura, 3-6, 6-3, 6-0, 6-8, 6-3, while Parker won his semis over 1940 champ, Navy Lieutenant Don McNeill, 6-4, 3-6, 6-2, 6-2. In the second round, McNeill beat 46-year-old Gil Hall, who had been discharged from the Army earlier in the year, a veteran of tank warfare, 7-5, 6-4. Hall became unique that week, not only winning a round in the Championships—over Richard Bender, 0-6, 6-3, 6-4—but capturing the concurrent Senior (over-45) title, over William Nassau, Jr., 6-3, 6-2. That made Hall the only man to hold an unusual dual top-10 national ranking: No. 10 among the men and No. 1 among the seniors. He would hold the latter title through 1950.

Even the national junior champ was in the service, too. Air Cadet Bob Falkenburg, 18, of Hollywood, Calif., won the 18s title while on leave, 0-6, 6-4, 6-4, 6-2, over a future Davis Cupper, lefty Bernard 'Tut' Bartzen of San Angelo, Texas. A future Wimble-

don champ, Falkenburg won his first major at Forest Hills, the doubles with McNeill, over Segura and Talbert, 7-5, 6-4, 3-6, 6-1. He lost in the singles quarters to Talbert, 6-4, 6-4, 6-3.

A third straight U.S. title for Pauline Betz highlighted the ladies' side as she sprinted through the tournament losing but one set (6-4, 6-8, 6-4, over Virginia Wolfenden Kovacs in the quarters), and brushing aside 1943 finalist Louise Brough, 6-2, 6-3, in the semis and Margaret Osborne, 6-3, 8-6, for the crown. The second set against Osborne was troublesome, Pauline accelerating from 1-4 down and dodging a set point at 4-5.

The busiest player was Segura, again National Intercollegiate champ for Miami (over Charles Samson of Notre Dame, 6-0, 6-4, 6-0). He beat Talbert, 9-11, 6-2, 7-5, 2-6, 7-5, to win the U.S. Clay, and altogether bagged six of 10 tournaments while going 36-4 in matches. Talbert won two of nine with a 32-7 record while Parker, who won two of three tournaments and was 13-1, got the No. 1 ranking. Betz won eight tournaments and had a 44-5 match record, but didn't retain the U.S. Clay, losing in the semis 7-5, 6-3 to Dodo Bundy, the champ on a 7-5, 6-4, decision over Mary Arnold. Osborne won three of 11 tournaments and was 33-8, Brough three of 12 with a 30-9 record.

The U.S. Pro tourney became a wartime casualty, but ever-energetic Bill Tilden, 51, kept on the go by playing exhibitions for the troops at military bases all over the country, or benefits for the Red Cross and other charitable causes associated with war relief. Don Budge, in the Army Air Force, beat Coast Guardsman Jack Kramer, 7-5, 7-5, heading a mid-winter fund-raiser at New York's 7th Regiment Armory that sold $2,706,000 in war bonds. Naval couple Elwood and Sarah Palfrey Cooke, out of sight since 1941, made a cameo at the La Jolla tourney, each winning the singles titles.

The uncle Chris Evert never knew, Jack Evert, one of the four tennis-playing brothers from Chicago, was killed at 22 with the Army in France where a future champ, Art Larsen, was also fighting. Jacque Virgil Hunt, wife of the 1943 champion, Lieutenant Joe Hunt, won the Southern title over Sara Comer, 6-4, 6-2. Refused leave from Naval flight training to compete at Forest Hills, Joe and 1942 champ Ted Schroeder had to settle for a weekend near their base, the Pensacola Labor Day tourney. Playing his last competitive tennis, Joe defeated Ted in the final, 6-3, 7-5.

1944 CHAMPIONS

U.S. Championships

Men's Singles Final: Frank Parker (USA) def. Bill Talbert (USA), 6-4, 3-6, 6-3, 6-3

Women's Singles Final: Pauline Betz (USA) def. Margaret Osbourne (USA), 6-3, 8-6

Men's Doubles Final: Don McNeill and Bob Falkenburg (USA) def. Pancho Segura (ECU) and Bill Talbert (USA), 7-5, 6-4, 3-6, 6-1

Women's Doubles Final: Louise Brough and Margaret Osborne (USA) def. Pauline Betz and Doris Hart (USA), 4-6, 6-4, 6-3

Mixed Doubles Final: Margaret Osborne and Bill Talbert (USA) def. Dorothy Bundy and Donald McNeill (USA), 6-2, 6-3

1945

A Mom and Champ, Cooke Follows Hazel

Sarah Palfrey Cooke achieved her goal of winning the U.S. singles title as a mother, beating three-time defending champ **Pauline Betz** at Forest Hills.

Peace was clearly on the way, and broke out days before Forest Hills threw open its gates again for a joyful renewal of the U.S. Championships. Attendance was up—35,506, compared to 26,999 for the 1944 tourney and 23,893 for 1943. Sixteen of the male entry list enlarged to 48 were still in uniform but wouldn't be for long. Wimbledon, closed six years, invited the public in June 30 for a U.S. vs. British Empire match between allied armed forces teams. Centre Court had been too badly bombed to be available, but 5,000 witnesses, including Queen Mary, were happy to be back at Court One. Army sergeant George Lott spurred a 4-1 U.S. victory.

Out of the Navy and traveling the American circuit again were Elwood and Sarah Palfrey Cooke, to reclaim Top 10 national rankings they last held in 1941, this time No. 1 for her, the champion at Forest Hills, and No. 4 for him, a semifinal achiever, the highest finish ever for a married couple. An extreme illustration

of the manpower shortage was the leniency of tourney officials at the Tri-State in Cincinnati, where the Cookes were permitted to enter the men's doubles as a team. A singular feat, they made it to the final, losing to Bill Talbert and Hal Surface, 6-2, 6-2.

A somber note was the absence of 1943 champion Joe Hunt, the naval pilot killed Feb. 2 in the never-explained plunge of his fighter plane into the Atlantic. Hunt, 26, the highest regarded American player to die in the war, had been expected to shine in the peacetime game.

Army Air Force Sergeant Frank Parker, winner in 1944, was thought to be far out of the picture, stationed on Guam. But his commanding general, Curtis LeMay, had other ideas. He ordered Frank to fly almost 8,000 miles back to the U.S. to defend his title. Parker, 29, had been playing exhibitions with such ex-U.S. champs as Naval Seaman Bobby Riggs and Army Air Corps Lieutenant Don Budge for the troops on Pacific Islands. He was fit and ready. Top seeded, Frank cruised to his second title by winning all 13 sets he played, encountering real difficulty only at the outset of the rematch final against Bill Talbert. Frank won his semis, 6-1, 8-6, 7-5, over 1939 Wimbledon finalist Elwood Cooke, who had won the only five-set match of the tournament, in a quarterfinal over 1931 Wimbledon champ Sidney Wood, 10-12, 7-5, 6-4, 2-6, 6-0. Subsequently, Parker won the Pacific Southwest over Herbie Flam, 6-2, 6-4, and the Pan American over Ecuador's Pancho Segura, 9-7, 3-6, 6-2, 8-6, at Mexico City. His three for three and 16-0 match mark assured him of remaining No. 1.

As civilians, Talbert and Segura—Pancho winner of a third successive Intercollegiate title for the University of Miami, 6-2, 6-2, 6-3, over Frank Mehner of the U.S. Military Academy—were again dominant figures. Bill won eight of 11 tournaments, on a 48-3 record in matches. He beat Segura for the U.S. Clay title, 6-4, 4-6,

6-2, 2-6, 6-2, and took four of five grass-court tests: Southampton over Argentine Alejo Russell 6-4, 6-2, 6-4; Rye over Segura 4-6, 6-3, 6-2, 5-7, 6-0; Wilmington over Segura 0-6, 6-2, 6-2; Seabright (N.J.) over Naval Lieutenant Gardnar Mulloy 6-2, 3-6, 6-2, 6-4, losing only to Parker at Forest Hills.

In defeating No. 3-seeded Segura 7-5, 6-3, 6-4 in the semis, No. 2-seeded Talbert wrenched his left knee. Gamely, wearing flannel trousers to hide the strapping, Bill endured an epic afternoon of four matches and 96 games, cheered by 11,556 fans, as he won two titles after bowing to Parker. He held a set point against Parker's serve at 9-10 in the 76-minute first set, 22 games, the longest to that time in a singles final. But that was Talbert's last thrust in the lengthy struggle. Parker's consistency was too much and he won 14-12, 6-1, 6-2.

Returning to the court to complete the doubles final, halted by darkness the previous night at 10-10 in the third, Talbert and Mulloy finished their second title triumph together, 12-10, 8-10, 12-10, 6-2, over Army Sergeant Jack Tuero and Air Cadet Bob Falkenburg. Then it was time for mixed: A semifinal that Talbert and Margaret Osborne won over Louise Brough and Frank Shields, 6-3, 9-7. It was 6:45 p.m., time for the final. Osborne, who had won the doubles with Brough, was in the third match of her two-title 65-game afternoon. She and Talbert had to play quickly to beat darkness at 7:25, not to mention Hart and Falkenburg, 6-4, 6-4.

Sarah Cooke, a sharp volleyer who won 16 major doubles titles, always wanted to win the U.S. singles and emulate her mentor, Hazel Hotchkiss Wightman, and she did just that in 1941. Now, two weeks prior to her 33rd birthday, Sarah wanted to follow Hazel again by winning as a mother. She accomplished this as well, joining an exclusive matronly club whose fourth and fifth members member would be Margaret Smith Court in 1973, and Evonne Goolagong in 1980. (Dorothea Chambers was the first mom to win a major singles title, winning Wimbledon in 1910, 1911, 1913 and 1914 as a mother). In a sensational comeback for her last season as an amateur, after almost four years away from the game, Sarah won seven of 13 tournaments and went 43-6 in matches. Her chief rival, defending champion Pauline Betz—they were No. 1 and No. 2 in the rankings—won six of 12 and was 42-6. Sarah beat Pauline for the U.S. Clay title, 8-6, 7-5, and at Forest Hills clipped Pauline's streak of three titles and 19 matches, 3-6, 8-6, 6-4.

"She was a good friend and a thorn in my side," said Pauline, who might well have won a record six straight U.S. crowns but for Sarah, her conqueror in the 1941 and 1945 championship bouts. Sarah led 5-2 in the second and almost let it slip away. She then stormed back in the third from a service break down to 3-4, taking the last three games. They both turned pro after the season, touring against one another. The 6-3, 6-3 victory Brough and Osborne scored over Betz and Hart was their fourth straight doubles title, breaking the three straight tourney record (1918-20) of Marion Zinderstein and Eleanor Goss. Many more would follow for Louise and Margaret.

The pros regrouped to re-establish their U.S. Championships at Rip's Courts in Manhattan after a one-year wartime layoff, and the singles was won by Welby Van Horn over John Nogrady, 6-4, 6-2, 6-2. The doubles was won by the 94-year-old team of Bill Tilden, 52, and Vinnie Richards, 42, over Dick Skeen and Van Horn, 7-5, 6-4, 6-2. Bill and Vinnie had first linked in Boston in 1918 to win the U.S. Doubles.

1945 CHAMPIONS

U.S. Championships

Men's Singles Final: Frank Parker (USA) def. Bill Talbert (USA), 14-12, 6-1, 6-2

Women's Singles Final: Sarah Palfrey Cooke (USA) def. Pauline Betz (USA), 3-6, 8-6, 6-4

Men's Doubles Final: Gardnar Mulloy and Bill Talbert (USA) def. Bob Falkenburg and Jack Tuero (USA), 12-10, 8-10, 12-10, 6-2

Women's Doubles Final: Louise Brough and Margaret Osborne (USA) def. Pauline Betz and Doris Hart (USA), 6-3, 6-3

Mixed Doubles Final: Margaret Osborne and Bill Talbert (USA) def. Doris Hart and Bob Falkenburg (USA), 6-4, 6-4

A Game Divided

Jack Kramer was a dominant figure in the post-war era as a player and a promoter.

World War II was over and international tennis resumed much as before with many of the old names, but also a group of new champions such as Jack Kramer, Pancho Gonzalez and Dinny Pails, bursting from uniform. Unfortunately, despite agitation for a broader outlook, the conservative officials who operated the largely amateur game could not find it in their best self-interest to integrate pros and amateurs into "Open" tennis, emulating golf.

Thus the great divide of the 1930s remained, keeping the game fractured and probably stifling its growth. In this schizophrenic world of big-time tennis, so-called amateurs held sway in the conventional tournaments, anchored by the four majors—the Australian, French, Wimbledon and U.S.—plus the Davis Cup. On the other side, the declared professionals wandered almost anonymously, city to city, continent to continent, a gypsy band on a treadmill of one-nighters plus a few tournaments. They took their money in broad daylight, on the table, but in doing so, reaped minimal attention when compared to the "shamateurs," who were often paid generous "expenses" as gate-primers by tournaments or by their national federations, thereby maintaining their eligibility for team events such as the Davis and, later, Federation Cups.

Down Under, a dynasty was forming, with the blossoming Aussies—Frank Sedgman, Lew Hoad, Ken Rosewall, Roy Emerson, Rod Laver et al—placed on sporting goods firms' payrolls to maintain their amateur standing as long as possible. But at the same time, burgeoning air travel was making the Australian Championships—and, therefore, the prospect of the elusive Grand Slam—accessible to all, and the game more far flung than ever.

1946
Advantage U.S. As Game Revives

The year 1946 was one of reconstruction for international tennis. The French and Wimbledon Championships and the Davis Cup had last been played in 1939, the Australian Championships in 1940. The U.S. Championships had continued uninterrupted, although greatly reduced in number of entrants.

Jack Kramer, who had entered the Coast Guard as a seaman and was discharged as a lieutenant after seeing action in the Pacific, returned at the age of 24 to claim the No. 1 U.S. ranking that had been predicted for him since 1942.

It was comparatively easy re-starting championships in countries that had not been ravaged by the war. In Australia, John Bromwich re-established a linkage with the prewar era. He had been the 1939 singles champion and regained the Australian title with a five-set victory over countryman Dinny Pails, 5-7, 6-3, 7-5, 3-6, 6-2. In doubles, it was as if the war had never occurred: Adrian Quist, who had won his national doubles title with Don Turnbull in 1936 and 1937 and with Bromwich in 1938, 1939 and 1940, successfully teamed with Bromwich once again, re-establishing a monopoly that would last through 1950.

In Paris, French tennis fans crowned the first native champion since Henri Cochet in 1932: left-hander Marcel Bernard. Intending to play only doubles, the 32-year-old Bernard was put in the draw when another player dropped out, and he upset the favorite, Czech Jaroslav Drobny, 3-6, 2-6, 6-1, 6-4, 6-3. Then he teamed with countryman Yvon Petra to win the dou-

bles, 7-5, 6-3, 0-6, 1-6, 10-8, over the Latin combine of Enrique Morea of Argentina and Pancho Segura of Ecuador.

More startling was Petra's triumph in the singles at Wimbledon, the first Frenchman to win there since Cochet beat Jean Borotra in the all-French final of 1929. (Borotra was refused entry to Wimbledon in 1946 because he had been Minister of Sport in the Vichy government of France, though he was later a Nazi prisoner.)

Kramer, though seeded No. 2, was the favorite, but was done in by a nasty blister on his right hand that had caused him to default at the Queen's Club tune-up tournament the week before. Kramer gave full credit to slick shot-maker Drobny, who beat him in the fourth round, 2-6, 17-15, 6-3, 3-6, 6-3, after Kramer had lost only five games in the three previous rounds despite his ailment.

Pails, 25, was the top seed, but he got lost on the London Underground on his way to Wimbledon for his quarterfinal match and arrived late. (No chauffered cars as today.) Unsettled, he lost to the No. 5-seeded Petra in four sets, 7-5, 7-5, 6-8, 6-4. Petra, a lanky 6-foot-5 with less than polished strokes, then reached the final by beating San Franciscan Tom Brown, 4-6, 4-6, 6-3, 7-5, 8-6. Petra did not figure to have a chance in the final against Australian Geoff Brown, a player of medium build with a devastating serve and great pace on the rest of his shots, the first to show a two-fisted backhand in a Wimbledon singles final. But Brown made the curious tactical miscalculation of trying to slow-ball during the first two sets. He did win the third and fourth, but by that time was psychologically exhausted, and when he dropped his serve in the opening game of the fifth set, Petra ran out the match, 6-2, 6-4, 7-9, 5-7, 6-4. The Big W had its loftiest champ.

Kramer, playing with his damaged racket hand encased in bandages and a glove, dominated the doubles final, teaming with Tom Brown for a straight-set victory over Geoff Brown and Pails, 6-4, 6-4, 6-2.

There had been some reluctance on the part of the All England Lawn Tennis & Croquet Club to stage The Championships at all in 1946. The club had been heavily damaged by German bombs, and a gaping hole in the Centre Court competitors' stand and adjacent seats had to be cordoned off. The organizing committee did not want to have a tournament if Wimbledon's prewar standards of preeminence could not be maintained. Colonel Duncan Macaulay, who returned as the club's full-time secretary after the war, summarized the obstacles in his book *Behind the Scenes at Wimbledon*: "The groundsmen were not back from the war, the mowers wouldn't work, the rollers wouldn't roll, nothing would function. We were surrounded by bomb-shelters, improvised buildings and huts of every sort. The back part of the club was covered with broken glass as a result of flying bombs. Britain was under a tight wartime economy and nothing could be obtained without a license or a coupon. There was the difficulty of supplies of balls and rackets and the printing of tickets. Paper was very short. Soap, too, was strictly rationed. Clothes were rationed and tennis flannels and costumes were almost non-existent. And of course, food was rationed, too—and there would be hungry thousands to be fed each day. The club's ration of whiskey was one bottle a month!"

Nevertheless, with customary efficiency and industry, The Championships was staged and again established as a showcase of the tennis world. There was considerable drama on court, both because of the early upsets of the favorites and the uncertainty of form that resulted from the wartime hiatus.

One fact amply demonstrated was the superiority of American women, who put a stranglehold on their side of the game in the immediate postwar years and maintained it through the 1950s, until Australia, Latin America and Europe again began producing champions in the early 1960s.

Macaulay explained the phenomenon quite logically. "Least upset by the war of all the lawn tennis-playing nations was the United States. Whereas lawn tennis in Britain and on the Continent closed down completely during the war and only started up again with many creaks and groans, with ruined courts and grave shortages of equipment, the American lawn tennis courts and clubs remained in being and the U.S. Championships continued all through the war. It was in the sphere of women's tennis that the United States gained such a tremendous advantage during these years."

Few non-Australian women ventured Down Under in those days, so the Australian Championships remained a native affair. Nancye Wynne, the 1940 champ, had become Mrs. Bolton, and continued on top, 6-4, 6-4, over Joyce Fitch. But American women won just about every other title of consequence, setting the pattern for ensuing years.

Margaret Osborne, saving two match points, defeated Pauline Betz, 1-6, 8-6, 7-5, in the French final (Pauline had led 6-5, 40-15, in the second set. They teamed with Louise Brough and Doris Hart to rout Great Britain in the resumption of the Wightman Cup at Wimbledon. The Americans did not lose a set in romping, 7-0. None of the four had ever been to England before, but this was the strongest Wightman Cup team assembled to date, and they would all leave their mark.

Betz, an accomplished ground-stroker, lost only 20 games in six matches in winning her sole Wimbledon title, and overcame net-rusher Brough in the final, 6-2, 6-4. Betz had won the U.S. Championship in 1942-43-44, beating Brough the first two years and Osborne the third, but had been runner-up to Sarah Palfrey Cooke in 1945. In her sixth straight year as finalist, a female record, Pauline took her fourth title, 11-9, 6-3, over Hart. Winning her last 27 matches, she etched a marvelous season embellished with eight titles in a dozen tournaments.

Brough and Osborne teamed to win the first of their three French and five Wimbledon doubles titles. The two of them continued their homeland streak as the U.S. Doubles Championships returned to Boston, winning a fifth straight time, 6-1, 6-3, over Pat Canning Todd and Mary Arnold Prentiss. But the sensation was the 74-game men's doubles final, a third trophy for Bill Talbert and Gardnar Mulloy, who side-stepped seven match points in the fifth set of the longest title bout, beating Frank Guernsey and Don McNeill, 3-6, 6-4, 2-6, 6-3, 20-18. Seeming beaten several times, the victors clung tough, Mulloy serving out of five match points (6-7, 0-40, and 10-11, 15-40) and Talbert 2 (13-14, 30-40 and ad out).

Don Budge and Bobby Riggs, the best players in the world immediately before the war, were antagonists again on the pro

circuit. Riggs, who had succeeded Budge as Wimbledon and U.S. champ in 1939 and won the U.S. crown again in 1941, was signed by promoter Jack Harris when he got out of the service. In an abbreviated tour against Budge, Bobby won, 18 matches to 16, lobbing incessantly to take full advantage of Budge's ailing shoulder. He trounced Budge, 6-3, 6-1, 6-1, in the final of the U.S. Pro Championship, which went virtually unnoticed at Forest Hills.

The tournament that did draw attention at Forest Hills, naturally, was the U.S. Nationals, as America's premier tennis event was called before it became the U.S. Open in 1968. It was here that Jack Kramer finally assumed the crown and top ranking that had been more or less reserved for him, as Hannibal Coons intimated in an article in *Collier's* in August 1946:

"Six-feet-one, powerfully built and a natural athlete, Jack Kramer has been the logical heir to the American tennis throne since he was 14. Successively U.S. Boys' and Interscholastic champion, a Davis Cupper at 18, and three times U.S. doubles champion, twice with Ted Schroeder and once with Frank Parker, Kramer has for four years been shoved away from the singles title only by the whim of circumstance."

Kramer had re-established himself as a force in the game after his three-year military service by winning the singles (over Frank Parker, 8-6, 6-1, 9-7), the doubles (with Schroeder) and mixed doubles (with Helen Wills Moody Roark) without losing a set at the Southern California Championships at Los Angeles in May. His Wimbledon blisters had extended his reputation as "the hard-luck kid," but at Forest Hills there was no stopping him. Kramer had developed his aggressive, hard-hitting game on the concrete courts of the Los Angeles Tennis Club under the watchful eye of the longtime iron-handed developer of Southern California junior talent, Perry T. Jones, and his coach and onetime idol, Ellsworth Vines. Kramer always had a thunderous serve and forehand, and with the formidable backhand he developed on a South American exhibition tour in 1941 also in harness, he ravaged Tom Brown, 9-7, 6-3, 6-0. Brown had beaten defending champ Parker, 6-3, 6-4, 6-8, 3-6, 6-1.

There was one task left for Kramer in 1946: Recovery of the Davis Cup. He had been an 18-year-old rookie for the U.S. in 1939, playing only doubles with Joe Hunt in a four-set loss to Adrian Quist and John Bromwich as Australia won, 3-2. Now Kramer and his friend Schroeder, 12 days his senior, went to Melbourne's Kooyong Lawn Tennis Club in December and socked it to the Aussies, 5-0, the beginning of a four-year U.S. reign.

It was a contentious time for the Yanks. Captain Walter Pate had tough choices to make with six hungry guys available. Talbert and Mulloy thought they should play the doubles. Parker, Mulloy, Schroeder and Brown each thought he should have the other singles job with Kramer. Pate wanted to live-or-die with Schroeder all the way, a two-man lineup. When he announced his singles choices to the team, Audrey Parker, Frank's wife, was livid, saying that Pate had promised her man a singles job. The couple walked out. When Ted delivered in the opener, 3-6, 6-1, 6-2, 0-6, 6-2, over Bromwich, it was a parade that rained on 15,000 faithful jamming the concrete horseshoe. Kramer followed up by confounding Pails, 8-6, 6-2, 9-7, and the two net-swarming buddies—the U.S. champs in 1941 and 1947—wrapped it solidly,

6-2, 7-5, 6-4, over Bromwich and Quist. Thus, the Cup was liberated from its seven-year wartime internment in Melbourne.

Kramer, Schroeder et al were the first Davis Cuppers to fly to Australia, then a four-day trip in a propeller-driven aircraft, a converted flying boat that, Schroeder recalls, "was lucky to make 75 mph against headwinds. We thought we'd never get there." The Aussies were sorry they did. Prior to 1946, tennis players had gone to Australia by boat, making the journey in a leisurely month, stopping off and playing exhibitions at ports en route to stay sharp.

1946 CHAMPIONS AND LEADERS

Australian Championships
Men's Singles Final: John Bromwich (AUS) def. Dinny Pails (AUS), 5-7, 6-3, 7-5, 3-6, 6-2
Women's Singles Final: Nancye Wynne Bolton (AUS) def. Joyce Fitch (AUS), 6-4, 6-4
Men's Doubles Final: John Bromwich and Adrian Quist (AUS) def. Max Newcombe and Len Schwartz (AUS), 6-3, 6-1, 9-7
Women's Doubles Final: Joyce Fitch and Mary Bevis (AUS) def. Nancye Wynne Bolton and Thelma Coyne Long (USA), 9-7, 6-4
Mixed Doubles Final: Nancye Wynne Bolton and Colin Long (AUS) def. Joyce Fitch and John Bromwich (AUS), 6-0, 6-4

French Championships
Men's Singles Final: Marcel Bernard (FRA) def. Jaroslav Drobny (CZE), 3-6, 2-6, 6-1, 6-4, 6-3
Women's Singles Final: Margaret Osborne (USA) def. Pauline Betz (USA), 1-6, 8-6, 7-5
Men's Doubles Singles Final: Marcel Bernard and Yvon Petra (FRA) def. Enrique Morea (ARG) and Pancho Segura (ECU), 7-5, 6-3, 0-6, 1-6, 10-8
Women's Doubles Singles Final: Louise Brough and Margaret Osborne (USA) def. Pauline Betz and Doris Hart (USA), 6-4, 0-6, 6-1
Mixed Doubles Final: Pauline Betz and Budge Patty (USA) def. Dorothy Bundy and Tom Brown (USA), 7-5, 9-7

Wimbledon
Men's Singles Final: Yvon Petra (FRA) def. Geoff Brown (AUS), 6-2, 6-4, 7-9, 5-7, 6-4
Women's Singles Final: Pauline Betz (USA) def. Louise Brough (USA), 6-2, 6-4
Men's Doubles Final: Tom Brown and Jack Kramer (USA) def. Geoff Brown and Dinny Pails (AUS), 6-4, 6-4, 6-2
Women's Doubles Final: Louise Brough and Margaret Osborne (USA) def. Pauline Betz and Doris Hart (USA), 6-3, 2-6, 6-3
Mixed Doubles Final: Louise Brough and Tom Brown (USA) def. Dorothy Bundy (USA) and Geoff Brown (AUS), 6-4, 6-4

U.S. Championships
Men's Singles Final: Jack Kramer (USA) def. Tom Brown (USA), 9-7, 6-3, 6-0
Women's Singles Final: Pauline Betz (USA) def. Doris Hart (USA), 11-9, 6-3
Men's Doubles Final: Gardnar Mulloy and Bill Talbert (USA) def. Don McNeill and Frank Guernsey (USA), 3-6, 6-4, 2-6, 6-3, 20-18
Women's Doubles Final: Louise Brough and Margaret Osborne (USA) def. Pat Canning Todd and Mary Arnold Prentiss (USA), 6-1, 6-3
Mixed Doubles Final: Margaret Osborne and Bill Talbert (USA) def. Louise Brough and Robert Kimbrell (USA) 6-3, 6-4

Year-End No. 1
Men: Jack Kramer
Women: Pauline Betz

Davis Cup: United States

Wightman Cup: United States

1947 A Banner Year For Jack Kramer

Jack Kramer (left) and **Tom Brown** pose prior to the men's singles final at Wimbledon, won by Kramer in only 48 minutes 6-1, 6-3, 6-2.

The tennis world returned to normal in 1947. Of the nine countries (Germany, Italy, Japan, Bulgaria, Finland, Hungary, Romania, Thailand and Libya) that had been expelled from the International Tennis Federation at its first postwar meeting in 1946, four (Italy, Hungary, Finland, and Romania) were re-admitted, reflecting a cooling of hatreds that had been kindled by the war. This trend would continue.

If 1946 had marked Jack Kramer's emergence, 1947 verified his greatness. He dominated the amateur game, paving the way for the most significant professional contract of the era. Kramer did not play the Australian or French Championships. But he won the singles and doubles titles of Wimbledon and the U.S.

He also took both his singles as the U.S. defended the Davis Cup with a 4-1 victory over Australia at Forest Hills. Surprisingly Jack and Ted Schroeder lost the doubles to Colin Long and John Bromwich, 6-4, 2-6, 6-2, 6-4, stalling the procession until Ted clinched over a staunchly resisting Pails, 6-3, 8-6, 4-6, 9-11, 10-8. It was a near thing on damp, slick turf, Schroeder saving five set points in the second set from 0-40, 5-6, and a match point with a serve-and-volley to reach 7-7 in the decisive fifth. Losing traction and falling frequently, Ted shed his socks and shoes in the second set and became a barefoot boy with a cheeky plan to attack the net incessantly. He then resorted to spikes (which Pails declined) in the sixth game of the fifth set, and went the rest of the way on barbed feet.

Pails and Bromwich were again the finalists in the Australian Championships, but this time Pails reversed the decision of the previous year in another five-setter, 4-6, 6-4, 3-6, 7-5, 8-6, for his only major singles title. Nancye Wynne Bolton beat Nell Hall Hopman, wife of Harry, the Australian Davis Cup captain, 6-3, 6-2, for the fourth of her six Australian singles titles. She also teamed with Thelma Long for the sixth of their 10 doubles titles together, re-grasping the championships they had captured from 1936 through 1940 under their maiden names of Wynne and Coyne.

Re-admission of Hungary to the ITF permitted unseeded Joszef Asboth, an artistic clay court specialist, back into the international fixtures, and he won the French over South African Eric Sturgess, 8-6, 7-5, 6-4, a slim but accomplished player with superbly accurate ground strokes. Pat Canning Todd, a statuesque and graceful Californian who was largely overshadowed by her American contemporaries, beat Doris Hart for the French women's title, 6-3, 3-6, 6-4.

Hart, a remarkable player who had been stricken with a serious knee infection at age 11 and took up tennis to strengthen her right leg, beat Louise Brough, 2-6, 8-6, 6-4, in the semifinal at Wimbledon, but had little left for Margaret Osborne in the final and was relegated to being runner-up, 6-2, 6-4. Brough and Osborne had successfully defended their French doubles title over Hart and Todd, 7-5, 6-2, but were dethroned in the Wimbledon final by Hart and Todd, despite holding three match points, 3-6, 6-4, 7-5.

The U.S. Wightman Cup team, a powerhouse—Brough, Osborne, Hart, Todd—goose-egged the Brits again, 7-0, at Forest Hills but did concede a couple of sets in the process. No. 1 Pauline Betz had won her first three tournaments of the year, including the U.S. Indoor over Hart, 6-2, 7-5, and had a 39-match streak going when the U.S. Lawn Tennis Association sternly suspended her indefinitely for merely discussing the possibility of turning pro. So she did, to barnstorm with Sarah Palfrey Cooke, with whom she'd split 18 matches as an amateur.

With Betz banished, Brough came through at the U.S., winning the first of her six major singles titles, beating her championship doubles partner, Osborne, 8-6, 4-6, 6-1. But she was fortunate to escape Aussie Bolton in the semifinal, 4-6, 6-1, 7-5. Bolton held three match points, serving at 5-2, 40-0 in the third, but lost the

game. At 5-3 the match was blacked out by nightfall. Unluckily for Bolton, still so close to victory, the two had agreed beforehand to utilize a rule available at the time: To replay any set halted by curfew, which they did the following day. Brough, who had won the doubles with Osborne at Longwood in Boston (a 5-7, 6-3, 7-5, battle with Hart and Todd) their sixth straight, also seized the mixed with John Bromwich, 6-3, 6-1, over Gussy Moran and Pancho Segura. That packaged a U.S. triple for Louise, last accomplished by Alice Marble in 1940.

Kramer's domination of Wimbledon was so great that ex-player John Olliff, longtime tennis correspondent of London's *Daily Telegraph*, referred to him as "a presence of unutterable awe." In his book *The Romance of Wimbledon*, Olliff recalls: "It became almost boring to watch him mowing down his victims when it was so obvious that nothing short of a physical injury could possibly prevent him from winning. He was an automaton of crushing consistency."

En route to the title, Kramer lost only 37 games in seven matches. In the quarterfinal, he beat Geoff Brown, the 1946 runner-up; 6-0, 6-1, 6-3; in the semifinals, Dinny Pails, 6-1, 3-6, 6-1, 6-0, and in the final, Tom Brown, 6-1, 6-3, 6-2, in just 48 minutes. King George VI and Queen Elizabeth were in the Royal Box, and His Majesty presented the champion's trophy to Kramer, the first titlist in abbreviated costume, shorts, instead of long white flannels. It was the King's first visit to Wimbledon since, as the Duke of York, he had played in the men's doubles in 1926.

Ted Schroeder did not play Wimbledon, but Kramer teamed with Bob Falkenburg—another tall American with a big serve—to win the doubles without losing a set, the final, 8-6, 6-3, 6-3, over the Anglo-Aussie alliance of Tony Mottram and Billy Sidwell. So on to Forest Hills. Kramer, who had won the U.S. Doubles in Boston — a fourth time, the third time with Schroeder, 6-4, 7-5, 6-3, over Talbert and Sidwell — was again top-seeded in singles, considered a cinch winner. In fact, he had already signed on Sept. 3, 1947, with promoter Jack Harris to play a tour against Bobby Biggs in 1948. Riggs had beaten Don Budge on a short tour for the second consecutive year, 24 matches to 22 this time, and had edged Budge for the U.S. Pro title, 3-6, 6-3, 10-8, 4-6, 6-3. Kramer was to be the new challenger for pro king Riggs, but the deal—a no-no for an alleged amateur—had to be hushed up until after the U.S. Championships, ending Sept. 14.

Everything went according to plan until, as Kramer recalled in a *Sports Illustrated* article, "I almost blew the whole thing sky high. Here I was, signed and sealed for delivery to Riggs, and I lost the first two sets in the final to Frankie Parker. He was playing his best, but I did my best to help him. I can still remember looking up into the first row of the stadium seats and seeing the top of Jack Harris' bald head because he had it bowed forward in despair." But Kramer pulled himself together, starting the third set with two aces and the first of many winning drop shots. He purged the errors from his game and brought Harris back to life by winning the last three sets easily before a full house of 14,000, 4-6, 2-6, 6-1, 6-0, 6-3.

Allison Danzig, the venerable tennis writer of *The New York Times*, reported on the final: "Not since Sidney Wood tamed the lethal strokes of Ellsworth Vines at Seabright in 1930 with his soft-ball strategy and reduced the Californian to a state of helplessness, has so cleverly designed and executed a plan of battle been in evidence on American turf as Parker employed in this match.

"In the end, the plan failed, as the challenger's strength ebbed and the champion, extricating himself from a morass of errors, loosed the full fury of his attack to win in five sets. But the gallery would long remember the thrill and the chill of those first two sets and also the tense final chapter as the 31-year-old Parker gave his heavily favored and younger opponent the scare of his life."

Kramer exited amateurism on a 41-match streak. He had lost only once during the year, early to Bill Talbert in the Bahamas, taking eight of nine tournaments and going 48-1 in matches, including the U.S. Indoor over Bob Falkenburg, 6-1, 6-2, 6-2. Jack's match loss total after returning to civilian life in 1946: three.

1947 CHAMPIONS AND LEADERS

Australian Championships
Men's Singles Final: Dinny Pails (AUS) def. John Bromwich (AUS), 4-6, 6-4, 3-6, 7-5, 8-6
Women's Singles Final: Nancye Wynne Bolton (AUS) def. Nell Hall Hopman (AUS), 6-3, 6-2
Men's Doubles Final: John Bromwich and Adrian Quist (AUS) def. Frank Sedgman and George Worthington (AUS), 6-1, 6-3, 6-1
Women's Doubles Final: Thelma Coyne Long and Nancye Wynne Bolton (AUS) def. Mary Bevis and Joyce Fitch (AUS), 6-3, 6-3
Mixed Doubles Final: Nancye Wynne Bolton and Colin Long (AUS) def. Joyce Fitch and John Bromwich (AUS), 6-3, 6-3

French Championships
Men's Singles Final: Joszef Asboth (HUN) def. Eric Sturgess (RSA), 8-6, 7-5, 6-4
Women's Singles Final: Pat Canning Todd (USA) def. Doris Hart (USA), 6-3, 3-6, 6-4
Men's Doubles Final: Eustace Fannin and Eric Sturgess (RSA) def. Tom Brown (USA) and Bill Sidwell (AUS), 6-4, 4-6, 6-4, 6-3
Women's Doubles Final: Louise Brough and Margaret Osborne (USA) def. Doris Hart and Patricia Canning Todd (USA), 7-5, 6-2
Mixed Doubles Final: Sheila Piercey Summers and Eric Sturgess (RSA) def. Jadwiga Jedrzejowska (POL) and Christian Caralulis (ROM), 6-0, 6-0

Wimbledon
Men's Singles Final: Jack Kramer (USA) def. Tom Brown (USA), 6-1, 6-3, 6-2
Women's Singles Final: Margaret Osborne (USA) def. Doris Hart (USA), 6-2, 6-4
Men's Doubles Final: Bob Falkenburg and Jack Kramer (USA) def. Tony Mottram (GBR) and Bill Sidwell (AUS), 8-6, 6-3, 6-3
Women's Doubles Final: Doris Hart and Pat Canning Todd (USA) def. Louise Brough and Margaret Osbourne (USA), 3-6, 6-4, 7-5
Mixed Doubles Final: Louise Brough (USA) and John Bromwich (AUS) def. Nancye Wynne Bolton and Colin Long (AUS), 1-6, 6-4, 6-2

U.S. Championships
Men's Singles Final: Jack Kramer (USA) def. Frank Parker (USA), 4-6, 2-6, 6-1, 6-0, 6-3
Women's Singles Final: Louise Brough (USA) def. Margaret Osbourne duPont (USA), 8-6, 4-6, 6-1
Men's Doubles Final: Jack Kramer and Ted Schroeder (USA) def. Bill Talbert (USA) and Bill Sidwell (AUS), 6-4, 7-5, 6-3
Women's Doubles Final: Louise Brough and Margaret Osborne (USA) def. Pat Canning Todd and Doris Hart (USA), 5-7, 6-3, 7-5
Mixed Doubles Final: Louise Brough (USA) and John Bromwich (AUS) def. Gussy Moran (USA) and Pancho Segura (ECU), 6-3, 6-1

Davis Cup: United States

Wightman Cup: United States

Year-End No. 1
Men: Jack Kramer
Women: Margaret Osborne duPont

Young Pancho Wins Forest Hills

Pancho Gonzalez bursts on the scene and wins the U.S. Championships at age 20.

Perhaps the most unforgettable event of the tennis year 1948 actually took place on December 26, 1947: Jack Kramer's professional debut against Bobby Riggs at Madison Square Garden as a raging blizzard buffeted New York.

"The city lay paralyzed by the heaviest snowfall in its history," was how esteemed columnist Red Smith recalled the night in *The New York Times* 30 years later. "Yet with taxis, buses, commuter trains and private cars stalled and the subways limping, 15,114 customers found their way into the big barn at Eighth Avenue and 50th Street."

Kramer, the top amateur of 1947, had been signed to face 1946-47 pro champ Riggs on a long tour. Francisco "Pancho"

Segura of Ecuador and Australian Dinny Pails came along as the preliminary attraction—"the donkey act" in the vernacular of the tour. As was customary, the long and winding road of one-night stands began in the Garden, then the American Mecca of pro tennis.

Riggs won the opener, 6-2, 10-8, 4-6, 6-4, but Kramer gradually got accustomed to the grind of the tour and the style that playing night after night on a lightning-fast canvas court required. He learned to hit a high-kicking second serve to keep the quick and clever Riggs from scooting in behind his return, and to attack constantly, rushing the net on virtually every point and hammering away at Riggs' backhand.

"I began to really get comfortable with this new style around the time our tour reached San Francisco, when we were tied at 13 matches apiece," Kramer reminisced. "I won there, and then we flew to Denver, and Bobby got something started with the stewardess, and that gave me Denver, and then we went into Salt Lake City, where we played on a tremendously slick wood surface. Bobby couldn't handle my serve there, and all of a sudden it was 16-13. And that was it. Now he had to gamble on my serve. He had to take chances or I could get to the net, and he was dead. He was thoroughly demoralized."

By the time the tour worked its way through the hinterlands, a demoralized Riggs was "tanking" matches. Kramer won 56 of the last 63, finishing with a 69-20 record, the last amateur to overthrow the pro king. Kramer, whose cut of the opening-night receipts at the Garden had been $8,800, earned $89,000. Riggs made $50,000.

Kramer also won the U.S. Pro Championships at Forest Hills. He had a tough match against Welby Van Horn in the quarter-finals, 3-6, 16-14, 4-6, 8-6, 6-4, then beat aging but still formidable Don Budge in the semifinals, 6-4, 8-10, 3-6, 6-4, 6-0. Al Laney, who covered tennis for 50 years, many of them for the *New York Herald Tribune*, made no secret of his low regard for the pros "because for so many years they have preferred exhibitions to real tournaments," but he begrudgingly put this one on his list of all-time memorable matches. The next day, Kramer put away Riggs, 14-12, 6-2, 3-6, 6-3, becoming the undisputed ruler of the pros as he had been of the amateurs.

With Kramer out of the amateur ranks, three other Americans took major titles. Parker won the French over Czech lefty Jaroslav Drobny, 6-4, 7-5, 5-7, 8-6. Bob Falkenburg startled Wimbledon by taking the men's singles title over John Bromwich. Richard "Pancho" Gonzalez stormed to the first of his back-to-back U.S. titles, over South African Eric Sturgess.

Adrian Quist, the last pre-war champ, had regained the Australian singles title over doubles partner Bromwich, 6-4, 3-6, 6-3, 2-6, 6-3, but was able to win only one set in the Davis Cup Challenge Round as Australia fell to the United States 5-0 at Forest Hills. Parker—denied a singles berth in 1946 and 1947—and Ted Schroeder beat Quist and Billy Sidwell to sweep the four singles matches. The first day disaster for the Aussies: Parker over Sidwell, 6-4, 6-4, 6-4, Schroeder over 35-year-old Quist, 6-3, 4-6, 6-0, 6-0—gave them no chance. But clinching it was still up to the old firm, Bill Talbert, 30, and Gardnar Mulloy, 34, winners of their fourth U.S. doubles title that year over Parker and Schroeder, 1-6,

9-7, 6-3, 3-6, 9-7. Bill and Gar beat Sidwell and Colin Long, 8-6, 9-7, 2-6, 7-5, and the Cup stayed home.

Falkenburg, 23, was a 6-foot-3, skinny Californian who dawdled between points, apparently stalling to upset opponents, and threw games or whole sets to grab a breather and pace himself, sometimes actually lying down on the court. He later moved to Rio de Janeiro and played in the Davis Cup for Brazil. Seeded No. 7 at Wimbledon, Falkie beat 20-year-old Aussie Frank Sedgman in the fourth round, 6-1, 6-2, 6-4. In the quarterfinal, he won 6-4, 6-2, 3-6, 6-4 over Swede Lennart Bergelin (conqueror of top-seeded Parker in five sets, 5-7, 7-5, 9-7, 0-6, 10-8). An acrimonious conflict was his semifinal win over Mulloy, 6-4, 6-4, 8-6, who objected to Falkenburg's delays. Then he met Bromwich, 29, in the final.

Lance Tingay, in his book *100 Years of Wimbledon*, described Falkenburg's topsy-turvy 7-5, 0-6, 6-3, 3-6, 7-5, victory: "Bromwich was a much-loved player. Not only did he have a gentle personality but a persuasively gentle game. Craft and skill and guile were his all, never muscle and pace. His racket was lightweight, the grip small and could have been a girl's. With a lefty forehand, he was doubled-fisted on the right. His ability to tease pace-making opponents into defeat by the accuracy of his slow returns was entrancing to watch. Falkenburg, having won the first set, 7-5, palpably threw the second at 6-0. The tactics were legitimate but they hardly endeared him to the crowd. He took the third set, 6-2. Bromwich won the fourth, 6-3. By then the effectiveness of Falkenburg's big serve had declined. And he was missing much with his forehand volley. Bromwich controlled the fifth set decisively, so much so that he led 5-2, 40-15, on his own service. On the two match points, Falkenburg played shots that were pure gambles, screaming backhand returns of service. Bromwich had his third match point at advantage and Falkenburg repeated his performance. The Australian, who thought the last of the match point returns was going long, let it pass rather than volley the ball. When it landed as a winner Bromwich 'died' as an effective player. Falkenburg devoured the remaining games. If Bromwich was heart-broken he shared the sentiment with nearly every spectator round the court."

Falkenburg refused to discuss his highly unpopular tactics of throwing sets and stalling, seemingly unsportingly. But later it came out that he was physically infirm, feeling a frequent need to pause and rest.

He was "diagnosed as suffering from myexoedema: excessive thyroid which prevented him from conserving energy for any length of time," wrote English author Norman Cutler in his 1954 book, *Inside Tennis*.

Falkie's career was short. Bromwich, whose career was long, never won the Wimbledon singles but salvaged some 1948 consolation by taking both doubles: with 20-year-old Sedgman over Mulloy and Tom Brown, 5-7 7-5, 7-5, 9-7, and successfully defending the mixed with Louise Brough, 6-2, 3-6, 6-3, over Hart and Sedgman.

After all the Wimbledon surprises, Forest Hills in 1948 was considered a wide-open affair. Ted Schroeder, generally regarded as Kramer's heir apparent, did not play. Frank Parker was the top-seeded American, ahead of Falkenburg. Virtually ignored, seeded No. 8, was Gonzalez, 20, one of seven children of a poor Mexican-

American family from Los Angeles. His father wished he would give up tennis and get an education, but Pancho preferred to be a truant, going to movies or developing the blazing serve that was his hallmark.

Gonzalez was a lean 6-foot-3, 185-pounder whose theatricality, smoldering Latin temper, sex appeal, and combination of power and touch gave him a kind of animalistic magnetism. He upset Parker in the quarterfinals, 8-6, 2-6, 7-5, 6-3, Jaroslav Drobny in the semifinals, 8-10, 11-9, 6-0, 6-3, and the South African Sturgess in the final, 6-2, 6-3, 14-12. A friend had once described Gonzalez as "even tempered—he's always mad." The fact that his worthiness as champion was questioned because Schroeder had not played made him an even angrier young man.

U.S. women continued to rule internationally, though Nancye Bolton regained Australia, over Marie Toomey, 6-3, 6-1. A Belgian-born French citizen, Nelly Adamson Landry won in Paris, beating Shirley Fry by the bizarre score of 6-2, 0-6, 6-0 to become the only non-American to win between 1946 and 1958. The U.S. clobbered Great Britain again in the Wightman Cup, 6-1, at Wimbledon. Louise Brough won her first major singles title overseas, starting a three-year Wimbledon reign by beating Doris Hart, 6-3, 8-6. Margaret Osborne, who had become Mrs. William duPont, beat Brough in a scintillating Forest Hills final, 4-6, 6-4, 15-13, the first of her three consecutive triumphs there, and she and Brough combined for an eighth successive U.S. title, over Hart and Pat Todd, 6-4, 8-10, 6-1.

Hart and Todd had dethroned Brough-duPont at Wimbledon in 1947, but Brough-duPont turned the tables this time, 6-3, 3-6, 6-3 When Brough left Centre Court at 8:15 p.m. on the final Saturday of Wimbledon, after defending her title with Bromwich over Sedgman and Hart, 6-2, 3-6, 6-3, she was the reigning singles, doubles, and mixed champion of both the United States and Great Britain, a feat previously achieved only by Alice Marble in 1939.

1948 CHAMPIONS AND LEADERS

Australian Championships

Men's Singles Final: Adrian Quist (AUS) def. John Bromwich (AUS), 6-4, 3-6, 6-3, 2-6, 6-3

Women's Singles Final: Nancye Bolton (AUS) def. Marie Toomey (AUS) 6-3, 6-1

Men's Doubles Final: John Bromwich and Adrian Quist (AUS) def. Frank Sedgman and Colin Long (AUS), 1-6, 6-8, 9-7, 6-3, 8-6

Women's Doubles Final: Thelma Coyne Long and Nancye Wynne Bolton (AUS) def. Mary Bevis and Pat Jones (AUS), 6-3, 6-3

Mixed Doubles Final: Nancye Wynne Bolton and Colin Long (AUS), def. Thelma Coyne Long and Bill Sidwell (AUS), 7-5, 5-7, 8-6

French Championships

Men's Singles Final: Frank Parker (USA) def. Jaroslav Drobny (CZE) 6-4, 7-5, 5-7, 8-6

Women's Singles Final: Nelly Adamson Landry (FRA) def. Shirley Fry (USA), 6-2, 0-6, 6-0

Men's Doubles Final: Lennart Bergelin (SWE) and Jaroslav Drobny (CZE) def. Harry Hopman and Frank Sedgman (AUS), 8-6, 6-1, 12-10

Women's Doubles Final: Doris Hart and Pat Canning Todd (USA) def. Shirley Fry and Arnold Prentiss (USA), 6-4, 6-2

Mixed Doubles Final: Pat Canning Todd (USA) and Jaroslav Drobny (CZE) def. Doris Hart (USA) and Frank Sedgman (AUS), 6-3, 3-6, 6-3

Wimbledon

Men's Singles Final: Bob Falkenburg (USA) def. John Bromwich (AUS), 7-5, 0-6, 6-2, 3-6, 7-5

Women's Singles Final: Louise Brough (USA) def. Doris Hart (USA), 6-3, 8-6

Men's Doubles Final: John Bromwich and Frank Sedgman (AUS) def. Tom Brown and Gardnar Mulloy (USA), 5-7, 7-5, 7-5, 9-7

Women's Doubles Final: Louise Brough and Margaret Osborne duPont (USA) def. Doris Hart and Patricia Canning Todd (USA), 6-3, 3-6, 6-3

Mixed Doubles Final: Louise Brough (USA) and John Bromwich (AUS) def. Doris Hart (USA) and Frank Sedgman (AUS), 6-2, 3-6, 6-3

U.S. Championships

Men's Singles Final: Pancho Gonzalez (USA) def. Eric Sturgess (RSA), 6-2, 6-3, 14-12

Women's Singles Final: Margaret Osborne duPont (USA) def. Louise Brough (USA), 4-6, 6-4, 15-13

Men's Doubles Final: Gardnar Mulloy and Bill Talbert (USA) def. Frank Parker and Ted Schroeder (USA), 1-6, 9-7, 6-3, 3-6, 9-7

Women's Doubles Final: Louise Brough and Margaret Osborne DuPont (USA) def. Pat Canning Todd and Doris Hart (USA), 6-4, 8-10, 6-1

Mixed Doubles Final: Louise Brough and Tom Brown (USA) def. Margaret Osborne duPont and Bill Talbert (USA), 6-4, 6-4

Davis Cup: United States

Wightman Cup: United States

Year-End No. 1
Men: Frank Parker
Women: Margaret Osborne duPont

1949 Gorgeous Gussy Shocks Wimbledon

"Gorgeous" Gussy Moran hits a forehand and reveals her famed lace panties—that was the sensation at Wimbledon—and tennis—in 1949.

Ted Schroeder won the Wimbledon singles on his first and only attempt, and Richard "Pancho" Gonzalez proved that he was not the "cheese champion" some had called him. But 1949 will always be remembered as the year of Gertrude "Gorgeous Gussy" Moran and the lace-trimmed panties that shocked Wimbledon.

Couturier Teddy Tinling, a tennis insider since he umpired matches for Suzanne Lenglen on the Riviera decades earlier, had waged a one-man battle against the unflattering white jersey and skirt that pretty much constituted women's tennis attire. He had experimented with touches of color on the dresses he made for Englishwoman Joy Gannon in 1947, without objection, but ran into problems in 1948 when Mrs. Hazel Wightman, captain of the

U.S. team playing for the Cup she had donated, objected to bits of color on the Tinling frock of British No. 1 Betty Hilton. This resulted in Wimbledon officials issuing an "all-white" rule.

Tinling called Wightman the "Queen Canute of tennis, trying to hold back the fashion tide."

In 1949, unable to use color as requested by the attractive and sexy Californian Moran out of Santa Monica, Tinling put a half inch of lace trim around her panties, trying to satisfy Gussy's wish for some distinctive adornment. This was probably done innocently, but when the flamboyant Gussy posed for photographers at the pre-Wimbledon garden party at the Hurlingham Club, she caused a sensation. The first time she twirled on Centre Court a tremor went through the staid old arena. "Tennis was then suddenly treated to the spectacle of photographers lying flat on the ground trying to shoot Gussy's panties," Tinling remembered. The "coquettish" undergarment became the subject of Parliamentary debate and photo-stories on front pages around the world.

"No one in their wildest dreams could have foreseen the furor, the outcry, the sensation..." Tinling wrote. "Wimbledon interpreted the lace as an intentional device, a sinister plot by Gussy and myself for the sole purpose of guiding men's eyes to her bottom. At Wimbledon, I was told that I had put 'vulgarity and sin' into tennis, and I resigned the Master of Ceremonies job I had held there for 23 years." Fortunately, he continued designing for and dressing most post-war women champions.

The year had begun with Frank Sedgman, age 21, winning his first major title, beating John Bromwich 6-3, 6-3, 6-2 in the final of the Australian Championships. Bromwich was thus runner-up for the third straight year after winning in 1946, but again captured the doubles with Adrian Quist—it seemed almost a formality by now, their seventh straight, this at the expense of Geoff Brown and Billy Sidwell, 1-6, 7-5, 6-2, 6-3. So it was as well for Nancye Wynne Bolton and Thelma Coyne Long in the women's doubles, who won their eighth out of nine tourneys 6-0, 6-1, over Marie Toomey and Doris Hart. However, Hart ended Bolton's quest for a fifth consecutive singles title, defeating her 6-3, 6-4 in the final making Doris the first overseas champion since Californian Dodo Bundy in 1938.

Frank Parker defended his French singles title over the elegant Budge Patty, 6-3, 1-6, 6-1, 6-4, and teamed with Gonzalez to win the doubles, 6-3, 8-6, 5-7, 6-3, over South Africans Eustace Fannin and Eric Sturgess. Margaret Osborne duPont recovered the singles title she had won in Paris in 1946, dethroning Nelly Landry, 7-5, 6-2, and teamed with Louise Brough to regain the doubles title they had won in 1946 and 1947 downing Britain's Joy Gannon and Betty Hilton 7-5, 6-1..

At Wimbledon, spectators were anxious to see the man Americans called "Lucky" Schroeder. Though almost 28, he had never played the world's premier championship, but was well known worldwide for his Davis Cup exploits. "Rather stocky, he had a rolling gait which made him look as though he had just got off a horse," remembered Lance Tingay. "Except when he was actually playing he always seemed to have a pipe in his mouth, a corn cob as often as not." Britons found him an intriguing character. Schroeder, the top seed, lost the first two sets of his first-round match to the dangerous Gardnar Mulloy, whom he had

beaten in the final at Queen's Club just two days earlier, but rescued himself 3-6, 9-11, 6-1, 6-0, 7-5. In the quarterfinals, he was again down two sets to Frank Sedgman, trailed 0-3 in the fifth, and had a match point against him at 4-5. He was called for a foot fault, but coolly followed his second serve to the net and hit a winning volley off the wood. He saved another match point at 5-6, this time with a bold backhand passing shot, and finally pulled out the match, 3-6, 6-8, 6-3, 6-2, 9-7, never having led until the final minutes.

Schroeder continued to live precariously, coming back from two sets to one down against Eric Sturgess in the semifinals, 3-6, 7-5, 5-7, 6-1, 6-2. In the final, he had his fourth five-setter in seven matches, edging the popular Czech Jaroslav Drobny, 3-6, 6-0, 6-3, 4-6, 6-4, after being within a point of a 0-2 deficit in the fifth set. "Lucky" Schroeder, indeed; he was always living on the edge of the ledge.

The women's final came down to a memorable duel between the top two seeds, Louise Brough and duPont. Brough won the first set, 10-8, duPont the second, 6-1, and at 8-all in the third, the difference between them was no more than the breadth of a blade of Wimbledon's celebrated grass. Brough served out of a 0-40 predicament like a champion, and then broke for the match and successful defense of her title, 10-8.

Second-seeded Gonzalez, beaten in the fourth round by Aussie Geoff Brown, 2-6, 6-3, 6-2, 6-1, and Parker added the Wimbledon doubles to the French they had won earlier, over Mulloy and Schroeder, 6-4, 6-4, 6-2, while Brough and duPont joined forces to defend their title over Pat Todd and Moran. The score was 8-6, 7-5—close enough to prevent anyone from quipping that the champs had beaten the lace panties off Gorgeous Gussy.

The American women continued their relentless domination of the Wightman Cup, drubbing Great Britain, 7-0, at Haverford, Pa., riding the singles wins of duPont over Betty Hilton, 6-1, 6-3, and Jean Smith, 6-4, 6-2, and Hart over Smith, 6-3, 6-1, and Hilton, 6-1, 6-3.

Schroeder and Gonzalez gave the U.S. all four singles points as the U.S. men made it four straight victories over Australia in the Davis Cup Challenge Round at Forest Hills, 4-1. Schroeder was up to his usual five-set high-jinks in the opening match, beating Bill Sidwell, 6-1, 5-7, 4-6, 6-2, 6-3, but he put away Sedgman in straight sets, 6-4, 6-3, 6-3, to clinch. Gonzalez made it 2-0 over Sedgman, 8-6, 6-4, 9-7. The Americans lost only the doubles, Sidwell and Bromwich beating Bill Talbert and Mulloy, 3-6, 4-6, 10-8, 9-7, 9-7. They also won the U.S. doubles at Longwood, an all-Aussie showdown, 6-4, 6-0, 6-1, over Sedgman and George Worthington.

There was keen interest in a Schroeder-Gonzalez U.S. Championships clash at Forest Hills. Because Gonzalez had gone out early to Geoff Brown at Wimbledon, there was speculation that his 1948 U.S. victory had been a fluke. One writer flatly called him a "cheese champ"—which is one version of how Gonzalez got his nickname, "Gorgo," short for "Gorgonzola." The other that stuck over the long run was that his colleagues on the pro tour, which consumed his best years, felt he acted like the big cheese (which he did, and was). Gonzalez cared neither for "Gorgo" nor "Pancho," and those close to him used Richard.

Gonzalez was taken to five sets by lefty Art Larsen, 4-6, 6-1, 6-3, 2-6, 6-1 in the quarterfinal, and to four by Parker, who let him off the hook in the semifinal, 3-6, 9-7, 6-3, 6-2. Schroeder was pushed to the limit by Sedgman in the quarterfinal, 6-3, 0-6, 6-4, 6-8, 6-4, and Talbert in the semfinal, 2-6, 6-4, 4-6, 6-4, 6-4. Finally, the two men people wanted to see had arrived safely in the final.

The old 15,000-seat horseshoe stadium at the West Side Tennis Club was packed and tense as Schroeder and Gonzalez fought to 16-all in the first set. Gonzalez, who was 1-7 against Schroeder, fell behind 0-40, but three big serves got him up to deuce. A net-cord winner gave Schroeder another break point, and Gonzalez lost his serve on a volley that he thought was good. A linesman called it wide. Schroeder served out the set, then donned spikes on the slippery turf and quickly ran out the second set, 6-2. Gonzalez seethed.

But Pancho always had a knack of channeling his temper, and he turned the rage surging within him to his advantage. Serving and attacking furiously, he achieved one of the great Forest Hills comebacks, 16-18, 2-6, 6-1, 6-2, 6-4, serving 27 aces, 16 of them in the 73-minute first set. Kissing his racket before serving the concluding game, Gonzalez had to smack his way out of a break point, and, on match point could only watch helplessly as Ted passed him with a forehand—that fell barely wide.

Meanwhile, duPont won her second major title of the year, easily, a 6-4, 6-1 victor over Hart in the other final, after the sure-thing firm of Brough-duPont rolled to their eighth U.S. doubles in a row, over Shirley Fry and Hart, 6-4, 10-8. Margaret's pal, Louise, cost her a triple, however, in the mixed final where Brough and Eric Sturgess beat duPont and Talbert, 4-6, 6-3, 7-5.

Jack Harris had quit the promotional game after the success-ful Kramer-Riggs tour. The new promoter was Riggs, who had won the U.S. Pro title at Forest Hills over Don Budge, 9-7, 3-6, 6-3, 7-5, while Kramer sat out, awaiting a new amateur king.

That was supposed to be Schroeder, who actually had signed after winning Wimbledon but then changed his mind, deciding that his intense constitution was not suited for the nightly grind of the tour. If he had won at Forest Hills, Schroeder undoubtedly would have signed so as not to leave his old friend Kramer in the lurch. Kramer thought that in the back of his mind Schroeder wanted to lose to Gonzalez for that reason.

But in any event, Gonzalez, as two-time U.S. champ, became the only viable alternative, and Riggs signed him for the lon-gest head-to-head tour yet. Frank Parker came along to play Pancho Segura in the prelims. The tour stretched from October 1949 to May 1950, and Kramer clobbered the talented but surly and immature Gonzalez, 96 matches to 27. Both players made $72,000, but the future seemed a dead end for Gonzalez, who was only 21 years old.

1949 CHAMPIONS AND LEADERS

Australian Championships
Men's Singles Final: Frank Sedgman (AUS) def. John Bromwich (AUS), 6-3, 6-2, 6-2

Women's Singles Final: Doris Hart (USA) def. Nancye Bolton (AUS), 6-3, 6-4

Men's Doubles Final: John Bromwich and Adrian Quist (AUS) def. Geoff Brown and Bill Sidwell (AUS), 1-6, 7-5, 6-2, 6-3

Women's Doubles Final: Thelma Coyne Long and Nancye Wynne Bolton (AUS) def. Doris Hart (USA) and Marie Toomey (AUS), 6-0, 6-1

Mixed Doubles Final: Doris Hart (USA) and Frank Sedgman (AUS) def. Joyce Fitch and John Bromwich (AUS), 6-1, 5-7, 12-10

French Championships
Men's Singles Final: Frank Parker (USA) def. Budge Patty (USA), 6-3, 1-6, 6-1, 6-4

Women's Singles Final: Margaret Osborne duPont (USA) def. Nelly Adamson Landry (FRA), 7-5, 6-2

Men's Doubles Final: Pancho Gonzalez and Frank Parker (USA) def. Eustice Fannon and Eric Sturgess (RSA), 6-3, 8-6, 5-7, 6-3

Women's Doubles Final: Margaret Osborne duPont and Louise Brough (USA) def. Joy Gannon and Betty Hilton (GBR), 7-5, 6-1

Mixed Doubles Final: Sheila Piercey Summers and Eric Sturgess (RSA) def. Jean Quertier and Gerry Oakley (GBR), 6-1, 6-1

Wimbledon
Men's Singles Final: Ted Schroeder (USA) def. Jaroslav Drobny (CZE), 3-6, 6-0, 6-3, 4-6, 6-4

Women's Singles Final: Louise Brough (USA) def. Margaret Osborne DuPont (USA), 10-8, 1-6, 10-8

Men's Doubles Final: Pancho Gonzalez and Frank Parker (USA) def. Gardnar Mulloy and Ted Schroeder (USA), 6-4, 6-4, 6-2

Women's Doubles Final: Louise Brough and Margaret Osborne duPont (USA) def. Gussy Moran and Pat Canning Todd (USA), 8-6, 7-5

Mixed Doubles Final: Sheila Piercey Summers and Eric Sturgess (RSA) def. Louise Brough (USA) and John Bromwich (AUS), 9-7, 9-11, 7-5

U.S. Championships
Men's Singles Final: Pancho Gonzalez (USA) def. Ted Schroeder (USA), 16-18, 2-6, 6-1, 6-2, 6-4

Women's Singles Final: Margaret Osborne duPont (USA) def. Doris Hart (USA) 6-4, 6-1

Men's Doubles Final: John Bromwich and Bill Sidwell (AUS), def. Frank Sedgman and George Worthington (AUS), 6-4, 6-0, 6-1

Women's Doubles Final: Louise Brough and Margaret Osborne duPont (USA) def. Doris Hart and Shirley Fry (USA), 6-4, 10-8

Mixed Doubles Final: Louise Brough (USA) and Eric Strugess (RSA) def. Margaret Osborne duPont and Bill Talbert (USA), 4-6, 6-3, 7-5

Year-End No. 1
Men: Pancho Gonzalez
Women: Margaret Osborne duPont

Davis Cup: United States

Wightman Cup: United States

Gibson Breaks
Color Barrier

The year 1950 was in many ways not only the start of a new decade, but also of a new era in tennis. With Jack Kramer, Pancho Gonzalez, and Frank Parker now pros, the American stranglehold on the international game was loosened. A new crop of Yanks was coming along, led by touch artists Art Larsen and Herbie Flam, the expatriate Californian Budge Patty and the forthright Tony Trabert and Vic Seixas. But Frank Sedgman, Ken McGregor and Mervyn Rose signaled a powerful new line of Australian resistance.

Budge Patty becomes the first man since Don Budge in 1938 to win the French-Wimbledon double.

Germany and Japan were re-admitted to the International Lawn Tennis Federation, indicating that wartime wounds had healed. The Italian Championships was played for the first time since 1935, revived by the energetic promotion of Carlo della Vida, who was intent on building it into one of the international

showcases. Despite rains that threatened to flood the sunken Campo Centrale at Rome's Il Foro Italico, the tournament was a success, won by the clay court artist, Jaroslav Drobny, over Bill Talbert, 6-4, 6-3, 7-9, 6-2. Annelies Ullstein Bossi, an Austrian married to an Italian, took the women's prize over Brit Joan Curry, 6-4, 6-4. Not until Raffaella Reggi, 35 years later, did a female holder of an Italian passport win the title.

The self-exiled Czech, Drobny, who traveled on an Egyptian passport until becoming a British citizen in 1959, also won the German championship over enduring 41-year-old Baron Gottfried von Cramm, 6-3, 6-4, 6-4 in an event that had started to rebuild slowly as a Germans-only affair in 1948 and 1949. Von Cramm, the aristocratic and sporting pre-war star, had won both years. The Hamburg and Rome tournaments were destined to rise simultaneously to a stature just below the French Championships as the most important clay court events of Europe.

Sedgman, an athletic serve-and-volleyer with a crunching forehand, defeated McGregor for his second straight Australian singles title, 6-3, 6-4, 4-6, 6-1, while Adrian Quist and John Bromwich won their record eighth doubles title in a tight struggle with Drobny and Eric Sturgess, 6-3, 5-7, 4-6, 6-3, 8-6.

J. Edward "Budge" Patty, an urbane California native who lived in Paris, won the French over Drobny in a duel of enchanting shot-making, 6-1, 6-2, 3-6, 5-7, 7-5. In his semifinal, Patty needed seven match points to subdue Talbert in a furious marathon, 2-6, 6-4, 4-6, 6-4, 12-10. Drobny, who had crawled through the traps laid by Vic Seixas in the quarterfinals 7-5, 17-15 (80 minutes for that set), 5-7, 6-4, had a rough semifinal, too, 6-4, 7-5, 3-6, 12-10, over Sturgess. Patty then became the first player since Don Budge in 1938 to win the Paris-Wimbledon double, beating Frank Sedgman in the final at the All England Club, 6-1, 8-10, 6-2, 6-3, as gracefully as he had overcome Drobny on clay.

Patty was a great stylist, fluent on all his strokes and mesmerizing with the effortlessness of his forehand volley. He was also a painter and patron of the arts. "I have a way to go to catch Rembrandt, but Renoir doesn't stand a chance," he commented once, upon the opening of an exhibition of his canvases in Paris. "He gave the impression," noted journalist Lance Tingay, "of being the most sophisticated champion of all time."

Unsophisticated, flaky, eccentric, and totally original was Art "Tappy" Larsen, so nicknamed because of his habit, one of many superstitions, of tapping objects from net posts to opponents in ritualistic "good luck" sequences. Patty was known as a suave playboy who only occasionally trained; Larsen was an eager if unpolished ladies' man who never trained. But he had a great gift for the game, and magnificent touch, as he amply demonstrated in winning the U.S. title over his pal Flam in a lovely match of wits and angles, 6-3, 4-6, 5-7, 6-4, 6-3.

In doubles, Bill Talbert partnered his athletic 19-year-old Cincinnati protégé, Tony Trabert, also a star guard for the University of Cincinnati basketball team, to the French title over Drobny and Sturgess, 6-2, 1-6, 10-8, 6-2. Quist and Bromwich won their only Wimbledon title together, outlasting Geoff Brown and Billy Sidwell, 7-5, 3-6, 6-3, 3-6, 6-2. Bromwich and Sedgman won the U.S. doubles over four-time champs Talbert and Gardnar Mulloy, 7-5, 8-6, 3-6, 6-1.

Australia, with Harry Hopman returned to the captain's chair that he had occupied in victorious 1939, pried loose the four-year American grip on the Davis Cup with a 4-1 victory in the Challenge Round at Forest Hills. Sedgman walloped Tom Brown, 6-0, 8-6, 9-7, and surprise starter McGregor ambushed Ted Schroeder, 13-11, 6-3, 6-4, in the opening singles. The next day, Sedgman and 31-year-old Bromwich—a holdover from '39— sealed the Aussie triumph by beating Schroeder and Mulloy in the doubles, 4-6, 6-4, 6-2, 4-6, 6-4, and the Cup was traveling south again.

America's women extended their monotonous superiority over Great Britain with another Wightman Cup bagel, 7-0 at Wimbledon, and hoarded all the major titles in singles and doubles. Margaret Osborne duPont and doubles accomplice Louise Brough did the heavy Wightman damage. Both beat Betty Hilton (Margaret, 6-3, 6-4; Louise, 2-6, 6-2, 7-5) and Jean Walker-Smith (Margaret, 6-3, 6-2; Louise, 6-0, 6-0). They also won a doubles over Kay Tuckey and Hilton, 6-2, 6-0.

The Australian final was the first all-American affair, Brough succeeding Doris Hart as champion with a 6-4, 3-6, 6-4 victory over defender Doris. They then teamed to win the doubles, interrupting the long reign of eight-time champions Nancye Bolton and Thelma Long, 6-2, 2-6, 6-3.

Hart won her first French singles, over Pat Todd, 6-4, 4-6, 6-2. Brough and duPont were not only beaten in singles, but the three-time champs lost in the doubles final to Shirley Fry and Hart, 1-6, 7-5, 6-2, despite holding a match point in the second set. Italian Annalies Bossi felt lonely in the quarterfinal surrounded by seven Americans.

Brough won her third straight Wimbledon title, beating duPont, 6-1, 3-6, 6-1. Then they shared the same side of the court to grab a fourth doubles championship, avenging the French defeat by beating Fry and Hart, 6-4, 5-7, 6-1. Coupling with Sturgess, Louise completed a triple with the mixed prize, 11-9, 1-6, 6-4, over Todd and Geoff Brown, duplicating her 1948 acquisition. It was her fourth mixed title, with a third collaborator, in five years.

At Forest Hills, duPont took her third straight U.S. crown, dispatching Hart in the final, 6-3, 6-3, after partnering Brough to their ninth straight doubles success in Boston, 6-2, 6-3, over Fry and Hart. Margaret found an Aussie escort, McGregor, to cement a triple of her own. They won the mixed over Hart and the other Aussie Davis Cup burglar, Sedgman, 6-4, 3-6, 6-3.

An historic breakthrough was the appearance of a future champion and Hall of Famer, 23-year-old Althea Gibson, the first black to play in the U.S. Championships at Forest Hills. (Although she had been admitted to the U.S. Indoor in 1949, winning a round, and again, in 1950, to beat Midge Gladman Buck, 6-2, 4-6, 7-5, and reach the final, a 6-0, 6-2, defeat by Nancy Chaffee.) But Forest Hills was the biggie that everybody noticed, and Althea's was a leap of the color bar in tennis every bit as significant as Jackie Robinson's debut with the Brooklyn Dodgers had been three years before. To cement that reality, Gibson nearly toppled the Wimbledon champ, fourth-seeded Louise Brough, in the second round.

Starting off with a prophetic victory over Barbara Knapp, 6-2, 6-2, Gibson overcame nerves and a 1-6 opening set against Brough to seize the second, 6-3. As the sky darkened, Gibson

battled to a 7-6 lead in the decisive set. At that moment, Brough may have been reprieved: Forest Hills was struck by a thunderstorm so fierce that lightning knocked one of the brooding concrete eagles from the upper rim of the stadium. Resuming the following afternoon, Gibson may have had too much time to think about victory lying within her long reach—four points away. Brough held serve, and won the next two games to escape, 6-1, 3-6, 9-7.

"When lightning put down that eagle," Gibson laughed years later, "maybe it was an omen times was a-changing. Brough was a little too experienced for me in that situation, but my day would come." And so it did with titles in 1957 and 1958.

A new order was brought to the U.S. Pro Championships at the Cleveland Skating Club as Pancho Segura knocked off Jack Kramer in the semifinals, 6-4, 8-10, 1-6, 6-4, 6-3, while Frank Kovacs uprooted 1949 champ Bobby Riggs, 6-2, 6-3, 5-7, 7-5. Kovacs broke down with cramps in the final, a 6-4, 1-6, 8-6, 4-4 TKO for Segura. There was no amateur recruit to challenge Kramer for supremacy of the pro game, but Riggs put together a tour with Segura—the swarthy little Ecuadorian with bowed legs, a murderous two-fisted forehand and enormous competitive heart—as the challenger at $1,000 per week salary against five percent of the gate. Kramer got 25 percent. Unfortunately, the cunning "Segoo" simply could not handle Kramer's big serve on fast indoor courts, and the tour was not competitive. Riggs tried to spice it up by signing Gussy Moran to a lucrative contract—$35,000 guaranteed, against 25 percent of profits—to play Pauline Betz. Gussy got tremendous publicity as the glamour girl of the lace panties, but she was not in the same class with Betz, who was overwhelming even after Riggs suggested she try to "carry" her fashionable but outclassed opponent.

The tour was an artistic, competitive, and financial flop. Kramer was still the king, Segura went back to being a prelim boy, Moran tried to make it in showbiz, and Betz, who married noted *Washington Post* sports writer Bob Addie, became a respected teaching pro in Washington.

1950 CHAMPIONS AND LEADERS

Australian Championships
Men's Singles Final: Frank Sedgman (AUS) def. Ken McGregor (AUS), 6-3, 6-4, 4-6, 6-1

Women's Singles Final: Louise Brough (USA) def. Helen Angwin (AUS), 6-2, 6-3

Men's Doubles Final: John Bromwich and Adrian Quist (AUS) def. Eric Sturgess (RSA) and Jaroslav Drobny (CZE), 6-3, 5-7, 4-6, 6-3, 8-6

Women's Doubles Final: Louise Brough and Doris Hart (USA) def. Nancye Wynne Bolton and Thelma Coyne Long (AUS), 6-2, 2-6, 6-3

Mixed Doubles Final: Doris Hart (USA) and Frank Sedgman (AUS) def. Joyce Fitch (AUS) and Eric Sturgess (RSA), 8-6, 6-4

French Championships
Men's Singles Final: Budge Patty (USA) def. Jaroslav Drobny (CZE), 6-1, 6-2, 3-6, 5-7, 7-5

Women's Singles Final: Doris Hart (USA) def. Pat Canning Todd (USA), 6-4, 4-6, 6-2

Men's Doubles Final: Bill Talbert and Tony Trabert (USA) def. Jaroslav Drobny (CZE) and Eric Sturgess (RSA), 6-2, 1-6, 10-8, 6-2

Women's Doubles Final: Doris Hart and Shirley Fry (USA) def. Louise Brough and Margaret Osbourne duPont (USA), 1-6, 7-5, 6-2

Mixed Doubles Final: Barbara Scofield (USA) and Enrique Morea (ARG) def. Pat Canning Todd and Bill Talbert (USA), walkover

Wimbledon
Men's Singles Final: Budge Patty (USA) def. Frank Sedgman (AUS), 6-1, 8-10, 6-2, 6-3

Women's Singles Final: Louise Brough (USA) def. Margaret Osbourne duPont (USA), 6-1, 3-6, 6-1

Men's Doubles Final: John Bromwich and Adrian Quist (AUS) def. Geoff Brown and Bill Sidwell (AUS), 7-5, 3-6, 6-3, 3-6, 6-2

Women's Doubles Final: Louise Brough and Margaret Osborne duPont (USA) def. Shirley Fry and Doris Hart (USA), 6-4, 5-7, 6-1

Mixed Doubles Final: Louise Brough (USA) and Eric Sturgess (RSA) def. Pat Canning Todd (USA) and Geoff Brown (AUS), 11-9, 1-6, 6-4

U.S. Championships
Men's Singles Final: Art Larsen (USA) def. Herbie Flam (USA), 6-3, 4-6, 5-7, 6-4, 6-3

Women's Singles Final: Margaret Osborne duPont (USA) def. Doris Hart (USA), 6-3, 6-3

Men's Doubles Final: John Bromwich and Frank Sedgman (AUS) def. Bill Talbert and Gardnar Mulloy (USA), 7-5, 8-6, 3-6, 6-1

Women's Doubles Final: Louise Brough and Margaret Osborne duPont (USA) def. Doris Hart and Shirley Fry (USA), 6-2, 6-3

Mixed Doubles Final: Margaret Osborne duPont (USA) and Ken McGregor (AUS) def. Doris Hart (USA) and Frank Sedgman (AUS), 6-4, 3-6, 6-3

Year-End No. 1
Men: Budge Patty
Women: Margaret Osborne duPont

Davis Cup: Australia

Wightman Cup: United States

Sedgman and McGregor Net Doubles Grand Slam

Dick Savitt won the Wimbledon men's singles title, defeating Ken McGregor in the final.

The new era continued to take shape on the world's tennis courts in 1951. American Dick Savitt surprisingly won the Australian and Wimbledon singles titles, but Frank Sedgman and Ken McGregor helped forge the foundation of a new Australian dynasty, holding onto the Davis Cup and fashioning the only male Grand Slam of doubles. Meanwhile, American women continued their postwar supremacy, but the dominance of Louise Brough, Margaret Osborne duPont, Doris Hart and Shirley Fry was challenged by a stirring new teen-age talent: Maureen Connolly.

Savitt, 24, a rawboned and hulking competitor from Orange, N.J., and Cornell University, sported a big serve, a solid ground game, and an impressive, hard-hit backhand. He was the first American to win the Australian singles—in fact, the first non-Australian finalist since Don Budge in 1938. He deposed the champ, Sedgman, 2-6, 7-5, 1-6, 6-3, 6-4 in the semifinals and beat McGregor, 6-3, 2-6, 6-3, 6-1 for the title. Sedgman and McGregor, in closing down the supremacy of John Bromwich and Adrian Quist—Australian doubles champs eight consecutive times from 1938—kicked off their unique Grand Slam in the stubbornly fought final, 11-9, 2-6, 6-3, 4-6, 6-3.

Like Ted Schroeder two years earlier, No. 6-seeded Savitt won Wimbledon on his first attempt. He was aided by Herbie Flam's defeat of top-seeded Sedgman from two sets down in the quarterfinals, 2-6, 1-6, 6-3, 6-4, 7-5, as well as Englishman Tony Mottram's third-round upset of No.

2-seeded Jaroslav Drobny, 5-7, 6-4, 2-6, 7-5, 8-6, and defending champion Budge Patty's demise in the second round, at the hands of 17-year-old Tulane star Ham Richardson, 4-6, 6-3, 4-6, 10-8, 6-4.

Savitt also had a narrow escape from Flam, whom the BBC's extraordinary radio commentator Max Robertson called "the Paul Newman of tennis players, with hunched and self-deprecating look." Savitt trailed 1-6, 1-5 in the semifinals before salvaging the second set, 15-13, to turn the match a round. "A couple of points the other way and my whole life might have been different," Savitt mused on the occasion of Wimbledon's Centenary 'Parade of Champions' in 1977. As it happened, he lost only five games in the third and fourth sets against Flam, 1-6, 15-13, 6-3, 6-2, and then chastened McGregor in the final 6-4, 6-4, 6-4. Title No. 3 in their circumnavigating Slam was hotly contested, too, but Sedgman and McGregor successfully resisted Jaroslav Drobny and Eric Sturgess, 3-6, 6-2, 6-3, 3-6, 6-3.

Drobny, the crafty left-hander with mournful countenance, spectacles, and a wonderful repertoire of touch and spin to go with his tricky serve, defeated Eric Sturgess, 6-3, 6-3, 6-3, to win the French singles for the first time after being runner-up in 1946, 1948 and 1950. Americans in Paris were in the way of Slam-happy Sedgman and McGregor, but Gar Mulloy and Savitt couldn't derail them in the final, 6-2, 2-6, 9-7, 7-5.

Sedgman, the personification of robust Australian fitness with an unerring forehand volley, atoned for his Wimbledon failure by winning the first of back-to-back U.S. titles. He was the first Australian player to win the U.S., and the first in the final since Jack Crawford lost to Fred Perry in 1933. Sedgman got there in devastating form, ravaging defending champion Art Larsen in the semifinals, 6-1, 6-2, 6-0, in just 49 minutes, the worst beating ever inflicted on a title-holder. Wrote Allison Danzig in *The New York Times*, "The radiance of the performance turned in by the 23-year-old Sedgman has not often been equaled. With his easy, almost effortless production of stabbing strokes, he pierced the dazed champion's defenses to score at will with a regularity and dispatch that made Larsen's plight almost pitiable."

In the final against No. 7-seeded Philadelphian Vic Seixas, Sedgman was nearly as awesome, winning 6-4, 6-1, 6-1. Seixas had played superbly until then, beating McGregor, 4-6, 7-5, 7-5, 6-4; Flam, 1-6, 9-7, 2-6, 6-2, 6-3; then Savitt in the semifinal, 6-0, 3-6, 6-3, 6-2. Savitt was the top seed, but severely hobbled by an infected left leg, which had to be lanced the day before he faced Seixas.

Sedgman and McGregor's superb cohabitation of a tennis court (Ken on the right) resulted in a tale of two cities finish of their Grand Slam that should have been saluted in lights—except that it all happened in daylight. Rain delayed them after three victories at the usual U.S. doubles site, Boston's Longwood Cricket Club, and the final was re-scheduled for the following week as part of the carnival of Forest Hills. It was an entirely Aussie gala, Frank and Ken downing the would-be party-poopers, Mervyn Rose and Don Candy, 10-8, 6-4, 4-6, 7-5. Forest Hills was

solidly Sedgman since he also won the mixed with Hart over Fry and Rose, 6-3, 6-2.

In Davis Cup, Savitt had played zone matches against Japan (re-admitted to the competition, along with Germany, for the first time since the war) and Canada. But Captain Frank Shields passed him over—angering him and many supporters—for the Challenge Round in Sydney. Seixas handled lefty Mervyn Rose, 6-3, 6-4, 9-7 and Sedgman beat Ted Schroeder, 6-4, 6-3, 4-6, 6-4 to make it 1-1 on opening day, but the series hinged on the doubles. Schroeder had one of his worst days—"I wanted to cry for him, he was so bad," recalls old friend Jack Kramer—and he and 21-year-old rookie Tony Trabert were beaten by Sedgman and McGregor, 6-2, 9-7, 6-3. Schroeder did pull himself together after a nervous, sleepless night to beat Rose in a gritty performance, 6-4, 13-11, 7-5. However, Sedgman continued as "The Man of the Year" rolling over Seixas in the fifth match, 6-4, 6-2, 6-2, for a 3-2 Australian victory.

U.S. women cruised as expected in a 6-1 Wightman Cup victory over Britain at Longwood as 16-year-old Maureen "Little Mo" Connolly got her sneakers wet in international competition, and delivered in her only start, 6-1, 6-3, over Kay Tuckey. In the absence of an overseas challenge, Nancye Bolton recaptured the Australian singles title over her partner Thelma Long, 6-1, 7-5, and the two of them took the doubles for the ninth time, 6-2, 6-1, over Mary Hawton and Joyce Fitch.

But Americans again won everything else. Fry, persistent as ever from the backcourt, beat Hart in the French final, 6-3, 3-6, 6-3, but they were together to win the doubles over Barbara Schofield and Beryl Bartlett, 10-8, 6-3.

Fry got her comeuppance at Wimbledon, where Hart thrashed her, 6-1, 6-0. This was Hart's only singles title at the Big W, where she had been runner-up in 1947 and 1948. She parlayed it into a triple, taking the women's doubles with Fry (starting a three-year rule) over perennials Margaret duPont and Louise Brough, 6-3, 13-11. Her mixed doubles with Sedgman came at the expense of Aussies Bolton and Rose, 7-5, 6-2. What a man's lady. Doris had the first of her five successive mixed triumphs, two with Sedgman and three with Seixas.

After winning the U.S. doubles title at Longwood with Fry over Nancy Chaffee and Pat Todd, 6-4, 6-2, Hart was the top seed at Forest Hills. Everybody thought she was the best in the world, but Doris was given a rude jolt in the semifinals by the kid, relatively inexperienced 16-year-old Maureen Connolly out of San Diego. Blasting her flawless groundstrokes from both wings, Connolly overcame a 0-4 deficit to win the first set on a drizzly, miserable day, 6-4. Hart asked several times that the match be halted. It was, but Connolly won the second set the following afternoon, 6-4. In the final, the tenacious and mentally uncompromising No. 4-seeded Connolly beat Fry, 6-3, 1-6, 6-4, for the first of three straight championships, becoming the greenest ever U.S. champion until Tracy Austin, a younger 16 in 1979. "I later kidded Maureen that she was lucky to beat me in '51," Hart has said. "But after that she became, unquestionably, the greatest woman player who ever lived."

A distasteful Forest Hills outburst by No. 7 American Earl Cochell brought swift retribution from the U.S. Lawn Tennis Association, a demonstration of the arbitrary power national associations held over players prior to the "Open" era and the forming of player unions. Clearly Cochell was out of line in the fourth-rounder, a four-set loss, 4-6, 6-2, 6-1, 6-2, to Gar Mulloy. He acerbically questioned many line calls, erupted in bursts of temper, argued with the umpire and spectators, tried to climb the umpire's chair and grab the microphone to lecture the crowd, and blatantly threw a number of games, batting balls into the stands or playing left-handed (he was right-handed). What really did him in was his abusive verbal attack on the referee, Dr. Ellsworth Davenport, who reprimanded him.

The upshot was that the USLTA suspended Cochell for life. Some years later the sentence was lifted, but Cochell, unfairly unranked for 1951, lost perhaps his best years.

It was Little Pancho (Segura) against Big Pancho (Gonzalez) for the U.S. Pro crown, and Segura defended successfully at Forest Hills, 6-3, 6-4, 6-2.

1951 CHAMPIONS AND LEADERS

Australian Championships
Men's Singles Final: Dick Savitt (USA) def. Ken McGregor (AUS), 6-3, 2-6, 6-3, 6-1
Women's Singles Final: Nancye Bolton (USA) def. Thelma Long (AUS), 6-1, 7-5
Men's Doubles Final: Ken McGregor and Frank Sedgman (AUS) def. John Bromwich and Adrian Quist (AUS), 11-9, 2-6, 6-3, 4-6, 6-3
Women's Doubles Final: Thelma Coyne Long and Nancye Wynne Bolton (AUS) def. Joyce Fitch and Mary Bevis Hawton (AUS), 6-2, 6-1
Mixed Doubles Final: Thelma Coyne Long and George Worthington (AUS) def. Clare Proctor and Jack May (AUS), 6-4, 3-6

French Championships
Men's Singles Final: Jaroslav Drobny (CZE) def. Eric Sturgess (RSA), 6-3, 6-3, 6-3
Women's Singles Final: Shirley Fry (USA) def. Doris Hart (USA), 6-3, 3-6, 6-3
Men's Doubles Final: Ken McGregor and Frank Sedgman (AUS) def. Gardnar Mulloy and Dick Savitt (USA), 6-2, 2-6, 9-7, 7-5
Women's Doubles Final: Doris Hart and Shirley Fry (USA) def. Beryl Bartlett (RSA) and Barbara Scofield (USA), 10-8, 6-3
Mixed Doubles Final: Doris Hart (USA) and Frank Sedgman (AUS) def. Thelma Coyne Long and Merv Rose (AUS), 7-5, 6-2

Wimbledon
Men's Singles Final: Dick Savitt (USA) def. Ken McGregor (AUS), 6-4, 6-4, 6-4
Women's Singles Final: Doris Hart (USA) def. Shirley Fry (USA), 6-1, 6-0
Men's Doubles Final: Ken McGregor and Frank Sedgman (AUS) def. Jaroslav Drobny (CZE) and Eric Sturgess (RSA), 3-6, 6-2, 6-3, 3-6, 6-3
Women's Doubles Final: Shirley Fry and Doris Hart (USA) def. Louise Brough and Margaret Osborne duPont (USA), 6-3, 13-11
Mixed Doubles Final: Doris Hart (USA) and Frank Sedgman (AUS) def. Nancye Wynne Bolton and Merv Rose (AUS), 7-5, 6-2

U.S. Championships
Men's Singles Final: Frank Sedgman (AUS) def. Vic Seixas (USA), 6-4, 6-1, 6-1
Women's Singles Final: Maureen Connolly (USA) def. Shirley Fry (USA), 6-3, 1-6, 6-4
Men's Doubles Final: Ken McGregor and Frank Sedgman (AUS) def. Don Candy and Merv Rose (AUS), 10-8, 6-4, 4-6, 7-5
Women's Doubles Final: Shirley Fry and Doris Hart (USA) def. Nancy Chaffee and Pat Canning Todd (USA), 6-4, 6-2
Mixed Doubles Final: Doris Hart (USA) and Frank Sedgman (AUS) def. Shirley Fry (USA) and Merv Rose (AUS), 6-3, 6-2

Year-End No. 1
Men: Frank Sedgman
Women: Doris Hart

Davis Cup: Australia

Wightman Cup: United States

1952 Sedgman Plays Major Finals Across The Board

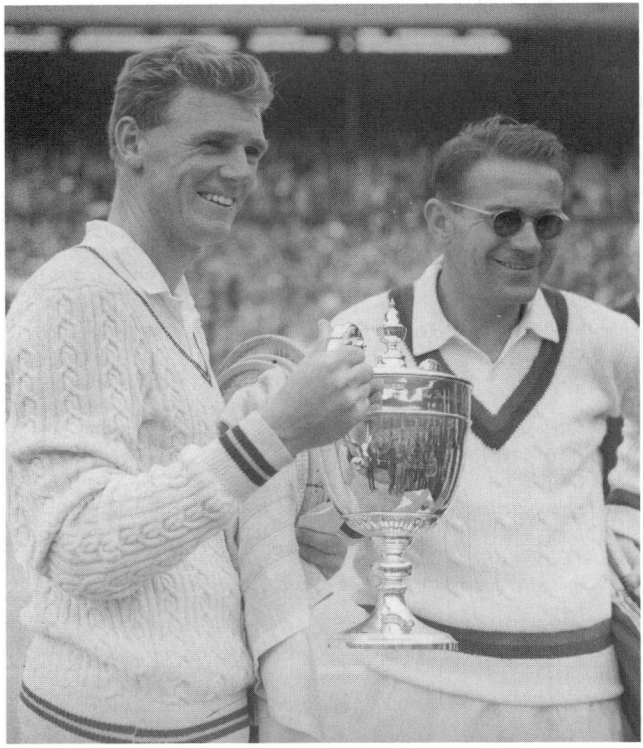

Another patch in the nearly complete postwar reconstruction of tennis was put in place in 1952 when the King's Cup, a European team competition for a trophy donated by Swedish monarch and tennis patron Gustav V in 1936, was resumed. But other than Jaroslav Drobny's second straight French title, Europe had little impact on the world tennis stage. Australian men and American women dominated the major championships.

Among the men, it was Frank Sedgman's year all the way. The aggressive, diligent Aussie was in all four of the major finals in singles and doubles, and three in mixed—incredibly 11 of the 12. He bagged eight of them—singles at Wimbledon and the U.S., all but the U.S. in doubles with Ken McGregor, and, with Doris Hart; all but Australia in the mixed (which he didn't enter). His collection amounted to a one-year record-tying haul of silver, eight major championship trophies. Don Budge had turned a similar trick in 1938.

Sedgman was on the losing end of the first two singles finals, however, beaten by his partner McGregor in the Australian, 7-5, 12-10, 2-6, 6-2, and by the ever-dangerous Drobny on the salmon-colored clay of Paris, 6-2, 6-0, 3-6, 6-3. Together, Frank and Ken, Grand Slammers of 1951, took their fifth straight doubles major, the Aussie, beating the countrymen against whom they'd completed their Slam, Don Candy and Mervyn Rose, 6-4, 7-5, 6-3. They made it six in a row with the French, a repeat over Americans Dick Savitt and Gar Mulloy, 6-3, 6-4, 6-4.

Sedgman got his revenge on "Old Drob" in the final at Wimbledon, 4-6, 6-2, 6-3, 6-2, becoming the first Aussie champ there since Jack Crawford in 1933. Two other Aussies, all-timers in the making, embarked on their first overseas tour, and ended up reaching the doubles semifinal. There would be plenty to hear in the future from Lew Hoad and Ken Rosewall, both 17 years of age.

Drobny took the first set of the final, but Sedgman seized control of the match in a swirling wind on Centre Court when he tuned in his crushing overhead smash. Sedgman, in fact, lost only two sets at Wimbledon, underscoring his superiority. His doubles bandwagon with McGregor continued to roll to a seventh straight major, too fast for Eric Sturgess and Vic Seixas, 6-3, 7-5, 6-4. Doris Hart was his companion in the mixed title, a 4-6, 6-3, 6-4, decision over an Aussie-Argentine yoking of Thelma Long and Enrique Morea. It meant a Wimbledon triple for Sedgman, joining select male company of Don Budge (1937-38) and Bobby Riggs (1939).

At the U.S. Championships, Sedgman rolled impressively to his second straight title. He crunched countryman Mervyn Rose in the semifinals, 6-3, 6-3, 6-4, and made the final against surprising 37-year-old Gardnar Mulloy look as simple as one-two-three: 6-1, 6-2, 6-3. But he and McGregor had lost out on a second Grand Slam in the U.S. final at Longwood, brought down in a stirring five sets by the Aussie-American coalition of Rose and Seixas, 3-6, 10-8, 10-8, 6-8, 8-6. Still, they had a sensational record—seven straight major titles—and Sedgman had eight since he'd won the 1950 U.S. with John Bromwich. England's Doherty brothers, Laurie and Reggie, had won five straight on two different runs: All Wimbledons, 1897-1901; and U.S. 1902, Wimbledon, 1903, U.S. 1903, Wimbledon 1904-05.

Sedgman also won the Italian, showing Drobny he could handle clay, 7-5, 6-3, 1-6, 6-4.

Adelaide was the scene of Sedgman and McGregor's farewell Davis Cup defense, and they were brutal to the U.S. tourists, Vic Seixas and Tony Trabert, 4-1, dropping only one set that counted in establishing a 3-0 lead. For starters Sedgman beat Seixas, 6-3,

6-4, 6-3, and Ken got rid of Trabert, 11-9, 6-4, 6-1. The finishing doubles went to the peerless pair, 6-3, 6-4, 1-6, 6-3, over Tony and Vic. That was three straight for Captain Harry Hopman's tribe.

American women again avoided the long journey to Australia, allowing Thelma Long to win her first singles title, 6-2, 6-3, over Helen Angwin, team with Nancye Bolton for their 10th doubles title together, 6-1, 6-1 over Allison Baker and Mary Hawton. (Long later won two more.)

But U.S. women were oppressive in the other major championships, as had become their custom. Doris Hart won her second French singles title, reversing the final-round result of a year earlier to beat Shirley Fry, 6-4, 6-4. Fry's semifinal pigeon was Hazel Reddick-Smith, 7-5, 6-4, while Hart beat Dorothy Head Knode, 6-2, 8-6.

Maureen Connolly ascended to the world No. 1 ranking at age 17, taking the Wimbledon title away from three-time champ Louise Brough, 7-5, 6-3. Two months later she broke down Hart, 6-3, 7-5, to defend her U.S. crown at Forest Hills. Hart and Fry had taken over from Margaret duPont and Louise Brough as double juggernauts, winning the French, Wimbledon and U.S. without the loss of a set in the finals. They knocked off Brough and Connolly at Wimbledon, 8-6, 6-3, and the U.S., 10-8, 6-4.

Connolly's first appearance at Wimbledon, seeded No. 2 behind Hart, was a celebrated event. "The pressures under which she played were enormous," noted Lance Tingay. "There was the basic pressure of being expected to win. There was a blaze of publicity because Miss Connolly, for reasons of her skill, her charm and achievement, was "news" in everything she did. And her guidance went sour at this her first Wimbledon challenge. Her coach—strong-willed, overly-protective, and domineering Eleanor "Teach" Tennant, who had also developed Alice Marble and imbued her with killer psychology—advised Connolly to withdraw because of a mild shoulder strain. Maureen refused and parted company with Tennant forever, removing a stifling weight from her personality."

Connolly lost sets to Susan Partridge, 6-3, 5-7, 7-5, who slowballed her, giving neither the pace nor angle on which Maureen thrived, and to Long, 5-7, 6-2, 6-0, in the quarterfinal. Partridge, who had won the Italian in an all-Brit final, 6-3, 7-5, over Betty Harrison, proved her toughest foe. Hart was beaten in a long quarterfinal, 6-8, 7-5, 6-4, by Pat Todd, leaving Connolly to mow down Fry, 6-4, 6-3, and Brough, 7-5, 6-3, in the last two rounds. Connolly's scythe-like strokes were as deadly as the British had seen or heard; in fact, in three years she never lost a singles match in Great Britain.

Great Britain suffered a Wimbledon embarrassment in the Wightman Cup, winning only one set, losing 7-0. Hart knocked the hyphens out of Jean Quertier-Rinkel, 6-3, 6-3, and Jean Walker-Smith, 7-5, 6-2. Connolly beat both of them, too, but Walker-Smith resisted strongly, 3-6, 6-1, 7-5.

Bobby Riggs had tried to sign Sedgman and McGregor to tour as pros with himself, Pancho Gonzalez and Pancho Segura in 1952, dismissing Jack Kramer by saying he had retired. Riggs struck a deal, but later Gonzalez wanted to change the agreed-upon terms, and Riggs—about to re-marry—got disgusted and left the promoting business.

There was no pro tour in 1952, but Segura startled Gonzalez in the final of the U.S. Pro, 3-6, 6-4, 3-6, 6-4, 6-0, from 3-0 down in the fourth, at Lakewood Park in Cleveland. Afterwards the victor chortled, "Here I am, 30, six years older, and I outlast him." Kramer, who had no intention of retiring, took over as player-promoter, signing Sedgman to a contract ($75,000 guarantee) that was announced right after the Davis Cup Challenge Round. McGregor also turned pro to face Segura in the prelims on the 1953 tour. Many Australian fans resented their departure.

1952 CHAMPIONS AND LEADERS

Australian Championships

Men's Singles Final: Ken McGregor (AUS) def. Frank Sedgman (AUS), 7-5, 12-10, 2-6, 6-2

Women's Singles Final: Thelma Long (AUS) def. Helen Angwin (AUS), 6-2, 6-3

Men's Doubles Final: Ken McGregor and Frank Sedgman (AUS) def. Don Candy and Merv Rose (AUS), 6-4, 7-5, 6-3

Women's Doubles Final: Thelma Coyne Long and Nancye Wynne Bolton (AUS) def. Allison Burton Baker and Mary Bevis Hawton (AUS), 6-1, 6-1

Mixed Doubles Final: Thelma Coyne Long and George Worthington (AUS) def. Gwen Thiele and Tom Warhurst (AUS), 9-7, 7-5

French Championships

Men's Singles Final: Jaroslav Drobny (CZE) def. Frank Sedgman (AUS), 6-2, 6-0, 3-6, 6-4

Women's Singles Final: Doris Hart (USA) def. Shirley Fry (USA), 6-4, 6-4

Men's Doubles Final: Ken McGregor and Frank Sedgman (AUS) def. Gardnar Mulloy and Dick Savitt (USA), 6-3, 6-4, 6-4

Women's Doubles Final: Doris Hart and Shirley Fry (USA) def. Hazel Redick-Smith and Julie Wipplinger (RSA), 7-5, 6-1

Mixed Doubles Final: Doris Hart (USA) and Frank Sedgman (AUS) def. Shirley Fry (USA) and Eric Sturgess (RSA), 6-8, 6-3, 6-3

Wimbledon

Men's Singles Final: Frank Sedgman (AUS) def. Jaroslav Drobny (CZE), 4-6, 6-2, 6-3, 6-2

Women's Singles Final: Maureen Connolly (USA) def. Louise Brough (USA), 7-5, 6-3

Men's Doubles Final: Ken McGregor and Frank Sedgman (AUS) def. Vic Seixas (USA) and Eric Sturgess (RSA), 6-3, 7-5, 6-4

Women's Doubles Final: Shirley Fry and Doris Hart (USA) def. Louise Brough and Maureen Connolly (USA), 8-6, 6-3

Mixed Doubles Final: Doris Hart (USA) and Frank Sedgman (AUS) def. Thelma Coyne Long (AUS) and Enrique Morea (ARG), 4-6, 6-3, 6-4

U.S. Championships

Men's Singles Final: Frank Sedgman (AUS) def. Gardnar Mulloy (USA), 6-1, 6-2, 6-3

Women's Singles Final: Maureen Connolly (USA) def. Doris Hart (USA), 6-3, 7-5

Men's Doubles Final: Merv Rose (AUS) and Vic Seixas (USA) def. Ken McGregor and Frank Sedgman (AUS), 3-6, 10-8, 10-8, 6-8, 8-6

Women's Doubles Final: Shirley Fry and Doris Hart (USA) def. Louise Brough and Maureen Connolly (USA), 10-8, 6-4

Mixed Doubles Final: Doris Hart (USA) and Frank Sedgman (AUS) def. Thelma Coyne Long and Lew Hoad (AUS), 6-3, 7-5

Year-End No. 1

Men: Frank Sedgman
Women: Maureen Connolly

Davis Cup: Australia

Wightman Cup: United States

1953 Invincible Connolly Wins Grand Slam

Maureen "Little Mo" Connolly stands with the Wimbledon trophy, her award for winning the third leg of her historic Grand Slam.

The year 1953 provided the tennis world with the lovely teen-age days of "Little Mo" and Ken Rosewall. The incomparable Maureen Connolly, nicknamed "Little Mo" by hometown (San Diego) sportswriter Nelson Fisher, because she was as invincible as the World War II battleship *Missouri* ("Big Mo"), steamed to only the game's second Grand Slam in singles. Following in the sneaker steps of another Californian Don Budge 15 years earlier, the 18-year-old swept the Australian, French, Wimbledon and U.S. singles championships. Overall, she won 10 of 12 tournaments and compiled a 61-2 record. This was the crowning year of an abbreviated career that was to end through injury, after just 3-1/2 awesome seasons, in 1954.

Meanwhile, Kenneth Robert Rosewall, also 18 (21 days older than his fellow Australian whiz kid Lew Hoad), took the Australian and French singles titles, the first major accomplishments of a phenomenal career matchless in its longevity. Rosewall would still be going strong a quarter of a century later, nine years after Connolly's death from cancer at age 34. Rosewall, called "Muscles" by his mates because he had none showing, was the youngest to carry his homeland, a record that yet stands.

Connolly was the first to emulate Don Budge, who took all the "Big Four" singles titles in 1938 and popularized the feat by calling it the Grand Slam. In doing so, she trampled 22 opponents, losing just one set and a total of 82 games.

"Little Mo" started in Australia, demolishing her partner, Californian Julie Samp-

son, 6-3, 6-2, before they teamed up to win the doubles over Beryl Penrose and Mary Hawton, 6-4, 6-1. Julie deprived Mo of a triple, ganging up with Aussie Rex Hartwig to beat Connolly and 19-year-old Louisianan Hamilton Richardson, 6-4, 6-3.

In the quarterfinals at Paris, Connolly lost that lone set, to Susan Partridge Chatrier, her toughest rival at Wimbledon the year before. By this time, Partridge had married France's Philippe Chatrier (future president of the French Federation and the International Tennis Federation). Susan slow-balled again, but Connolly hit her way out of trouble, blasting her groundstrokes even harder, deeper, and closer to the lines than usual, prevailing by 3-6, 6-2, 6-2. Then she drubbed two Americans, Dorothy Head Knode, 6-3, 6-3, and Doris Hart in the final, 6-2, 6-4.

Hart was also her final-round opponent at Wimbledon and the U.S. at Forest Hills. "The Wimbledon final was the finest match of the Slam: 8-6, 7-5. The two great players called it the best of their life," noted a silver anniversary tribute to Little Mo's wondrous 1953 record. In the homestretch at Forest Hills, Connolly won driving, as they say at the racetrack, 6-2, 6-3 over Althea Gibson in the quarterfinals; 6-1, 6-1 over Shirley Fry in the semifinals; and 6-2, 6-4 over Hart in the final. During the 22 matches that covered the Slam, Connolly permitted foes an average of three games a match.

In fact, Connolly lost only two matches during the year, to Hart in the final of the Italian, 4-6, 9-7, 6-3, and to Fry, 6-2, 7-5, in the Pacific Southwest at Los Angeles, a tourney Shirley won over Hart, 1-6, 6-3, 6-4. Maureen paid Shirley back in the Pacific Coast final, 9-7, 6-0.

Hart and Fry teamed for the French doubles title, a third successive year, beating Connolly and Sampson, 6-4, 6-3, and did the same at Wimbledon. Only that time Mo, not a standout doubles player because of her distaste for net play, had, with Sampson the negative distinction of not winning a single game. At the time it was the lone 6-0, 6-0 final in the history of major women's doubles. (Margaret Court and Evonne Goolagong equaled the double-bagel in winning the 1971 Australian final over Jill Emmerson and Lesley Hunt.) Just before entering the court, Maureen had received a telephone call from her fiancé (and future husband), Olympic equestrian Norman Brinker, telling her he was being sent to the Korean War zone by the U.S. Navy.

Hart and Fry also won the third of their four successive U.S. doubles titles, but it was a titanic struggle at Longwood to end the 41-match and record nine straight majors streak of Louise Brough and Margaret duPont in the final by a 6-2, 7-9, 9-7 margin. Brough and duPont, abstainers from the 1951 and 1952 championships, looked safe when they pinched Fry at 2-5 and two match points, but a skillful barrage of lobs undid the perennial champs.

Rosewall, a 5-foot-7, 145-pounder with an angelic face and neither a hair nor a footstep out of place, took the first of his four Australian singles titles, spanning 19 years, by beating left-hander Mervyn Rose, 6-0, 6-3, 6-4. Rosewall beat Vic Seixas, 6-3, 6-4, 1-6, 6-2, in the French final, the first tournament covered by a new magazine, *World Tennis*, which debuted in June 1953 and would become an influential force in the game. It was edited and published by New Yorker Gladys Heldman. The story under Gardnar Mulloy's by-line described Rosewall as "a young kid with stamina, hard-hitting ground strokes and plenty of confidence."

The Wimbledon and U.S. titles came back into American possession, property of Vic Seixas and Tony Trabert. Seixas, according to Lance Tingay's official history of Wimbledon, was "hardly the prettiest player in the world, for his strokes smacked more of expediency than fluency and polish, but he gave the impression of being prepared to go on attacking forever." In five long sets, Vic edged Hoad in the quarterfinals, 5-7, 6-4, 6-3, 1-6, 9-7, and Rose in the semifinals, 6-4, 10-12, 9-11, 6-4, 6-3. In the final, he beat unseeded Kurt Nielsen, 9-7, 6-3, 6-4. The Dane used his chopped forehand down the middle of the court to upset top seed Rosewall in the quarterfinals, 7-5, 4-6, 6-8, 6-0, 6-2, bursting whatever dream Kenny might have had of a Grand Slam.

The match of the tournament was the third-round classic in which Jaroslav Drobny defeated his good friend and constant touring companion, Budge Patty, 8-6, 16-18, 3-6, 8-6, 12-10. The Herculean epic began at 5:00 p.m. and ended at nightfall four hours, 23 minutes later, Drobny surviving three match points in the fourth set, three more in the fifth. He won the last two games after the referee's decision at 10-10 was conveyed to a groaning full-house crowd—only enough light remained to play two more games that evening. Those 93 games, played at a consistently high standard, were the most in any Wimbledon singles to that time. But Drobny had torn a muscle in his right leg, and after somehow limping through victories over Australian Rex Hartwig, 6-1, 6-1, 6-3, and Swede Sven Davidson, 7-5, 6-4, 6-0, lost to the surprising Nielsen in the semifinal, 6-4, 6-3, 6-2.

Trabert did in Rosewall, 7-5, 6-3, 6-3, and Seixas beat Hoad, 7-5, 6-4, 6-4, in the U.S. semifinals at Forest Hills. Then Trabert—serving and volleying consistently and returning superbly whether Seixas charged the net or stayed back—beat the Wimbledon champ for the title, 6-3, 6-2, 6-3, in just one hour. Trabert was less than three months out of the U.S. Navy, but he had trained hard to regain his speed and match fitness, and he leveled Seixas with a vicious onslaught from backcourt and net, off both wings—especially his topspin backhand.

Hoad and Rosewall captured the Australian, French, and Wimbledon doubles titles, each final a totally Aussie production, in order: 9-11, 6-4, 10-8, 6-4, over Mervyn Rose and Don Candy in Melbourne; 6-2, 6-1, 6-1 over Rose and Clive Wilderspin in Paris; 6-4, 7-5, 4-6, 7-5, over Rex Hartwig and Rose in London. But they missed out on emulating the 1951 Grand Slam of Frank Sedgman and Ken McGregor on the last leg, the U.S. at Longwood. The quarterfinals were their grassy quicksand, as they were upset by Americans Straight Clark and lefty Hal Burrows, 5-7, 14-12, 18-16, 9-7. Nevertheless, an Australian flavor remained. Ken and Lew's countrymen, Hartwig and Rose, took the title over popular oldies Bill Talbert, 35, and Gar Mulloy, 38, finalists together for a sixth time, 6-4, 4-6, 6-2, 6-4.

Australia, favored in the Davis Cup Challenge Round at Melbourne, with their green-but-keen kiddies Hoad and Rosewall just turned 19, nearly threw it away when the team selectors ordered Captain Harry Hopman to nominate Hartwig and Hoad,

both right-court players, as his doubles team. That, strangely, instead of either of the experienced pairs available: Rosewall-Hoad or Hartwig-Rose. The confused Aussie duo lost to Trabert and Seixas, 6-2, 6-4, 6-4.

Hoad had beaten Seixas, 6-4, 6-2, 6-3, and Trabert had stomped Rosewall, 6-3, 6-4, 6-4 the first day. But Australia won from 1-2 down, Hoad beating Trabert, 13-11, 6-3, 2-6, 3-6, 7-5 in the pivotal fourth match, one of the greatest in Davis Cup history. As a crowd of 17,500 huddled in the Kooyong stadium under newspapers to protect themselves from rain, Trabert lost his serve at love at 5-6 in the desperate final set, double faulting to 0-40 and then netting a half volley off a return to his shoe-tops. The next day, Rosewall finished the thriller by defeating Seixas, 6-2, 2-6, 6-3, 6-4. Never before, or since, have a couple of teenagers been responsible for winning the Cup.

Meanwhile Frank Sedgman, the Davis Cup hero of a year earlier, lost a pro tour to Jack Kramer, 54 matches to 41, but earned $102,000, the highest payoff to date. The tally was closer than it might have been because Kramer was bothered by an arthritic back and was as interested in promoting as playing. Pancho Gonzalez won the U.S. Pro title over Don Budge, 4-6, 6-4, 7-5, 6-2, at Lakewood Park in Cleveland. It was the first of Gonzalez' record eight triumphs in nine years in the event, shakily maintained for the handful of outcast pros.

1953 CHAMPIONS AND LEADERS

Australian Championships
Men's Singles Final: Ken Rosewall (AUS) def. Merv Rose (AUS), 6-0, 6-3, 6-4
Women's Singles Final: Maureen Connolly (USA) def. Julia Sampson (USA), 6-3, 6-2
Men's Doubles Final: Lew Hoad and Ken Rosewall (AUS) def. Don Candy and Merv Rose (AUS), 9-11, 6-4, 10-8, 6-4
Women's Doubles Final: Maureen Connolly and Julia Sampson (USA) def. Mary Bevis Hawton and Beryl Penrose (AUS), 6-4, 6-2
Mixed Doubles Final: Julia Sampson (USA) and Rex Hartwig (AUS) def. Maureen Connolly and Ham Richardson (USA), 6-4, 6-3

French Championships
Men's Singles Final: Ken Rosewall (AUS) def. Vic Seixas (USA), 6-3, 6-4, 1-6, 6-2
Women's Singles Final: Maureen Connolly (USA) def. Doris Hart (USA), 6-2, 6-4
Men's Doubles Final: Lew Hoad and Ken Rosewall (AUS) def. Merv Rose and Clive Wilderspin (AUS), 6-2, 6-1, 6-1
Women's Doubles Final: Doris Hart and Shirley Fry (USA) def. Maureen Connolly and Julia Sampson (USA), 6-4, 6-3
Mixed Doubles Final: Doris Hart and Vic Seixas (USA) def. Maureen Connolly (USA) and Merv Rose (AUS), 4-6, 6-4, 6-0

Wimbledon
Men's Singles Final: Vic Seixas (USA) def Kurt Nielsen (DEN), 9-7, 6-3, 6-4
Women's Singles Final: Maureen Connolly (USA) def. Doris Hart (USA), 8-6, 7-5
Men's Doubles Final: Lew Hoad and Ken Rosewall (AUS) def. Rex Hartwig and Merv Rose (AUS), 6-4, 7-5, 4-6, 7-5
Women's Doubles Final: Shirley Fry and Doris Hart (USA) def. Maureen Connolly and Julia Sampson (USA), 6-0, 6-0
Mixed Doubles Final: Doris Hart and Vic Seixas (USA) def. Shirley Fry (USA) and Enrique Morea (ARG), 9-7, 7-5

U.S. Championships
Men's Singles Final: Tony Trabert (USA) def. Vic Seixas (USA), 6-3, 6-2, 6-3
Women's Singles Final: Maureen Connolly (USA) def. Doris Hart (USA), 6-2, 6-4
Men's Doubles Final: Rex Hartwig and Merv Rose (AUS) def. Gardnar Mulloy and Bill Talbert (USA), 6-4, 4-6, 6-2, 6-4
Women's Doubles Final: Shirley Fry and Doris Hart (USA) def. Louise Brough and Margaret Osborne duPont (USA), 6-2, 7-9, 9-7
Mixed Doubles Final: Doris Hart and Vic Seixas (USA) def. Julia Sampson (USA) and Rex Hartwig (AUS), 6-2, 4-6, 6-4

Year-End No. 1
Men: Tony Trabert
Women: Maureen Connolly

Davis Cup: Australia

Wightman Cup: United States

1954 Triumph, Tragedy For Little Mo

Maureen Connolly (right) won the French and Wimbledon titles before a tragic accident ended her career. **Vic Seixas** (left) won the U.S. Championships and helped the U.S. re-capture the Davis Cup.

The quotation that hangs above the competitors' entrance to the Centre Court at Wimbledon, and was also adopted for a similar exalted position in the marquee at the stadium at Forest Hills, is from the poem *If* by Rudyard Kipling. It says, "If you can meet with triumph and disaster, and treat those two impostors just the same..." The words seldom seemed more appropriate than in 1954, for it was a year of continued triumph and then sudden, unmitigated disaster for Maureen Connolly.

"Little Mo" did not go to Australia to try for another Grand Slam. Experienced Thelma Long, 35, filled the gap, winning her homeland's title a second time, 6-3, 6-4, over Jenny Staley, Lew Hoad's wife-to-be.

But Maureen defended her French title without straining. Her 6-0, 6-1, semifinal win over Italian Sylvia Lazzarino took 26 minutes. In the final, she coasted, 6-4, 6-1, over Ginette Bucaille, who had beaten 1948 champ Nelly Adamson, 6-2, 6-4. Connolly also beat Brit Pat Ward, 6-3, 6-0, to take the Italian that had eluded her in 1953. At Wimbledon, Maureen defeated Louise Brough in the final, 6-2, 7-5. Lance Tingay wrote, "The whole event was accounted a trifle dull

because of the inevitability of the eventual winner. Miss Connolly, without losing a set, won 73 games and lost but 19."

Little did anyone know that this would be Little Mo's last major title. During the interval between Wimbledon and Forest Hills, she was riding her horse, Colonel Merryboy—a gift from a group of San Diegans after her 1952 Wimbledon triumph—and was struck by a truck. Most people thought she would return in 1955, but in her autobiography Maureen wrote that she knew she was finished: "My right leg was slashed to the bone. All the calf muscles were severed and the fibula broken. Eventually, I got on-court again, but I was aware that I could never play tournament tennis."

It was the shortest of great careers, but few got more done in many more years. During those 3-1/2 years when she was undisputed No. 1, the youngest of five Grand Slammers, she won nine straight majors, a tremendous accomplishment: Australian, 1953; French, 1953-54; Wimbledon, 1952-53-54; U.S. 1951-52-53, on a match record of 50-0. (Her complete record for the majors was 52-2, since she lost in the second round of the U.S. in 1949 and 1950 as a 14 and then 15-year-old.) Moreover, there were the Italian, 1954; Irish, 1952-53; the U.S. Clay, 1953-54 (6-4, 6-4, over Althea Gibson, and, then, 6-3, 6-1, over Doris Hart, her last tournament); plus 7-for-7 in Wightman Cup.

Southpaw Mervyn Rose won his only Australian singles title, over countryman Rex Hartwig, 6-2, 0-6, 6-4, 6-2. Rugged Tony Trabert—firing like the big guns that adorned the aircraft carrier on which he had served the year before—blasted fellow American, lefty Art Larsen in the French final, 6-4, 7-5, 6-1. Defending champ Ken Rosewall was plucked from the fourth round by Sven Davidson, 6-3, 3-6, 6-3, 6-3, as was his sidekick, Lew Hoad, by 40-year-old Gar Mulloy, 6-2, 2-6, 7-5, 6-4. But the year ultimately belonged to three players who savored sentimental triumphs that came when they were seemingly a shade past their prime: Jaroslav Drobny, Vic Seixas, and Doris Hart.

Drobny at 32 still had a punishing serve, though not as oppressive as it had been prior to a shoulder injury. He was seeded only No. 11 in his 11th appearance at Wimbledon, but upset No. 2-seed Lew Hoad in the quarterfinals, 6-4, 6-3, 6-3, and beat old rival Budge Patty in the semifinals, 6-2, 6-4, 4-6, 9-7. Ken Rosewall overturned top-seeded Tony Trabert in their semifinal, 3-6, 6-3,

4-6, 6-1, 6-1, but couldn't get past Drobny in the final, 13-11, 4-6, 6-2, 9-7, in two hours, 37 minutes. Drob became only the second left-handed champion, following Norman Brookes in 1907. No one could have imagined that Rosewall, in the final for the first of four times at age 19, would never win the singles title he coveted most. The galleries loved Drobny, the expansive Czech refugee in dark prescription glasses. "No better final had been seen since Crawford and Vines 21 years before," judged Lance Tingay. "The warmth of Drobny's reception as champion could not have been greater had he been a genial Englishman. In a sense he was, for he had married an Englishwoman and lives in Sussex."

The U.S. triumphs of Vic Seixas and Doris Hart at Forest Hills were just as popular with the American audience. Seixas, 31, and competing for the 13th time, finally won in his third appearance in the final. He stopped the run of Rex Hartwig, 3-6, 6-2, 6-4, 6-4. Rex had upset defending champion Tony Trabert, 6-2, 8-6, 2-6, 6-2 in the quarterfinals, and Rosewall, 6-4, 6-3, 6-4 in the semifinals. Hart, runner-up five times in 13 appearances but never champion, at last triumphed, 6-8, 6-1, 8-6 over ex-champ Louise Brough, in her fifth final. Doris vaulted three match points as Brough netted backhand returns, one at 4-5, two more at 5-6.

Seixas, according to Allison Danzig's report in *The New York Times*, "made the most of his equipment and he never lagged in carrying the attack to his opponent. His speed and quickness, the effectiveness of his service, his strong return of service and his staunch volleying all contributed to the victory. Too, he found a vulnerable point in his opponent's game and exploited it by directing his twist service to Hartwig's backhand."

Hart and Seixas built themselves U.S. triples. She started it by winning the doubles with Shirley Fry in Boston for a fourth time, again striking down nine-time champs Margaret duPont and Brough, 6-4, 6-4. He took the same route, registering a Longwood victory with Trabert over Hoad and Rosewall, 3-6, 6-4, 8-6, 6-3.

Then, after their Forest Hills singles triumphs, Doris and Vic collaborated in the mixed final, over duPont and Rosewall, 4-6, 6-1, 6-1.

Trabert and Seixas, who also beat Hoad and Rosewall for the French 6-4, 6-2, 6-2, split the majors with Hartwig and Rose. The two Aussies won their own title, over 20-year-old lefty Neale Fraser and Clive Wilderspin 6-3, 6-4, 6-2, and Wimbledon over Trabert and Seixas 6-4, 6-4, 3-6, 6-4.

Connolly showed some doubles skill in Paris, abetting her friend, Nell Hopman (wife of the Aussie Davis Cup captain Harry Hopman) to win the French over homebodies Maude Galtier and Suzanne Schmitt, 7-5, 4-6, 6-0. The mixed triumph, chaperoned by Lew Hoad, over Jacqueline Patorni of France and Hartwig, gave Little Mo a triple, 6-4, 6-3.

At Wimbledon Brough and duPont recaptured the title they had won in 1948-49-50, over Fry and Hart, 4-6, 9-7, 6-3, avoiding two match points in the second—their 16th major together.

After four straight losses to the Aussies of captain Hopman, the U.S., in captain Bill Talbert's third of six years at the helm, recovered the Davis Cup on the strokes of Trabert and Seixas, 3-2. This was a disappointment to the record tennis crowds of 25,578 jamming Sydney's White City ground, enlarged with towering auxiliary stands. Seixas, earning his spot because of his Forest Hills form, and Trabert did a flip-flop of 1953. Tony outgunned Hoad, 6-4, 2-6,

12-10, 6-3, and Seixas, previously Rosewall's pigeon, came through for a 2-0 lead, 8-6, 6-8, 6-4, 6-3. Lew, serving at set point at 10-9 in the second, saw it whisked away by Tony's desperate two-handed reflex volley. Tony and Vic finished the job the next day, beating Hoad-Rosewall, 6-2, 4-6, 6-2, 10-8, in the decisive doubles.

Jack Kramer retired as undefeated pro champion and promoted a round-robin tour involving Pancho Gonzalez, Frank Sedgman, Pancho Segura and Don Budge. Gonzalez won it, narrowly defeating Segura and Sedgman, and thus gained a previously unheard-of second life in the head-to-head pro tour.

1954 CHAMPIONSHIPS AND LEADERS

Australian Championships
Men's Singles Final: Merv Rose (AUS) def. Rex Hartwig (AUS), 6-2, 0-6, 6-4, 6-2
Women's Singles Final: Thelma Long (AUS) def. Jenny Staley (AUS), 6-3, 6-4
Men's Doubles Final: Rex Hartwig and Merv Rose (AUS) def. Neale Fraser and Clive Wilderspin (AUS), 6-3, 6-4, 6-2
Women's Doubles Final: Mary Bevis Hawton and Beryl Penrose (AUS) def. Hazel Redick-Smith and Julia Wipplinger (RSA), 6-3, 8-6
Mixed Doubles Final: Thelma Coyne Long and Rex Hartwig (AUS) def. Beryl Penrose and John Bromwich (AUS), 4-6, 6-1, 6-2

French Championships
Men's Singles Final: Tony Trabert (USA) def. Art Larsen (USA), 6-4, 7-5, 6-1
Women's Singles Final: Maureen Connolly (USA) def. Ginette Bucaille (FRA), 6-4, 6-1
Men's Doubles Final: Vic Seixas and Tony Trabert (USA) def. Lew Hoad and Ken Rosewall (AUS), 6-4, 6-2, 6-1
Women's Doubles Final: Maureen Connolly (USA) and Nell Hall Hopman (AUS) def Maude Galtier and Suzanne Schmitt (FRA), 7-5, 4-6, 6-0
Mixed Doubles Final: Maureen Connolly (USA) and Lew Hoad (AUS) def. Jacqueline Patorni (FRA) and Rex Hartwig (AUS), 6-4, 6-3

Wimbledon
Men's Singles Final: Jaroslav Drobny (CZE) def. Ken Rosewall (AUS), 13-11, 4-6, 6-2, 9-7
Women's Singles Final: Maureen Connolly (USA) def. Louise Brough (USA), 6-2, 7-5
Men's Doubles Final: Rex Hartwig and Merv Rose (USA) def. Vic Seixas and Tony Trabert (USA), 6-4, 6-4, 3-6, 6-4
Women's Doubles Final: Louise Brough and Margaret Osborne duPont (USA) def. Shirley Fry and Doris Hart (USA), 4-6, 9-7, 6-3
Mixed Doubles Final: Doris Hart and Vic Seixas (USA) def. Margaret Osborne duPont (USA) and Ken Rosewall (AUS), 5-7, 6-4, 6-3

U.S. Championships
Men's Singles Final: Vic Seixas (USA) def. Rex Hartwig (AUS), 3-6, 6-2, 6-4, 6-4
Women's Singles Final: Doris Hart (USA) def. Louise Brough (USA), 6-8, 6-1, 8-6.
Men's Doubles Final: Vic Seixas and Tony Trabert (USA) def. Lew Hoad and Ken Rosewall (AUS), 3-6, 6-4, 8-6, 6-3
Women's Doubles Final: Shirley Fry and Doris Hart (USA) def. Louise Brough and Margaret Osborne duPont (USA), 6-4, 6-4
Mixed Doubles Final: Doris Hart and Vic Seixas (USA) def. Margaret Osborne duPont (USA) and Ken Rosewall (AUS), 4-6, 6-1, 6-1

Year-End No. 1
Men: Jaroslav Drobny
Women: Maureen Connolly

Davis Cup: United States

Wightman Cup: United States

1955 An Epic Year For Trabert

Tony Trabert hits a forehand at the 1955 French Championships, where he defeated Sven Davidson in the final. Trabert went on to win Wimbledon and the U.S. Championships to complete one of the most successful seasons in the history of the sport.

At the midpoint of the postwar decade, 1955, American Tony Trabert established himself as the best player in the world, his Australian rivals snatched back the Davis Cup with a vengeance, and a couple of gallant American women who had left a considerable legacy—Louise Brough and Doris Hart—took their final bows in the world tennis arena.

Ken Rosewall beat Lew Hoad, 9-7, 6-4, 6-4, for his second Australian singles title, but Trabert—the All-American boy from Cincinnati with his ginger crew cut, freckles, and uncompromisingly aggressive game—won the French, Wimbledon and U.S. singles. He

might have had a Grand Slam, but never considered it since he lost to Rosewall in the semifinals of the Australian, 8-6, 6-3, 6-3.

In the Italian Championships, two of the most unorthodox but combative clay-court specialists of Europe—tall and gangly Fausto Gardini ('The Spider') and tiny, gentle Beppe Merlo ('The Little Bird')—met in an all-native final before a raucous Roman crowd. They had their customary epic battle—"We were always like a dog and a cat," Merlo recalls—with Gardini claiming victory, 6-1, 1-6, 3-6, 6-6, as Merlo collapsed with cramps. To make sure his opponent could not recover and win, Gardini counted off one minute while Merlo writhed in pain, then rolled down the net and raised his arms triumphantly.

There were no such histrionics in Paris, where Trabert bulled his way to the French title over Swede Sven Davidson, 2-6, 6-1, 6-4, 6-2. At Wimbledon, Trabert eliminated defending champion Jaroslav Drobny in the quarterfinals, 8-6, 6-1, 6-4, and Budge Patty in the semifinals, 8-6, 6-2, 6-2. In the final, Trabert expected to meet Rosewall, but instead came up against 1953 runner-up Kurt Nielsen, who had upset the Australian champ, this time in the semifinals, 11-9, 6-2, 2-6, 6-4. "Nielsen clearly remembered his success against the Little Master in 1953, when he hit his approach shots down the middle and came to the net, making it difficult for Rosewall to play his favorite passing shots decisively," wrote Max Robertson. "He pursued the same tactics and with the same result; for the second time he had reached the final unseeded—a record which could stand forever." Trabert denied him a more satisfying immortality, however, prevailing 6-3, 7-5, 6-1.

The only real stain on Trabert's record for the year, one of the greatest in history—he won 18 singles and 12 doubles titles—came in late August in the Davis Cup Challenge Round at Forest Hills. After Rosewall had beaten Vic Seixas, 6-3, 10-8, 4-6, 6-2, Trabert went down, 4-6, 6-3, 6-3, 8-6, to Hoad in the critical second match. Hoad played with immense power and brilliance. The next afternoon, Hoad and Rex Hartwig—two years earlier thrown together as first-time doubles partners, with disastrous results—blended beautifully to clinch the Cup with a 12-14, 6-4, 6-3, 3-6, 7-5 victory over Seixas and Trabert that had 12,000 spectators howling with delight through five scintillating sets. The Auss-

ies had their cake and put frosting on it too, running up a 5-0 final margin the next day.

Trabert had the last laugh, though, drilling Rosewall in the U.S. final at Forest Hills, 9-7, 6-3, 6-3. That set him up as the new amateur champ, the fourth man to take at least three of the four majors within a calendar year, following Jack Crawford in 1933, Fred Perry in 1934, and Grand Slammer Don Budge in 1938. Actually, promoter Jack Kramer had signed Hoad and Rosewall as well, to tour with him and Trabert playing a Davis Cup—style format, but the deal fell through. Slazenger, the racket company that Rosewall represented, gave him a bonus, and Jenny Hoad persuaded her husband to make one more grand tour as an amateur. So Trabert's indoctrination into the pros in 1956 wound up taking the more conventional form, a head-to-head tour against the champ, Pancho Gonzalez.

On the women's side, new singles champions were crowned in Australia, where Beryl Penrose defeated Thelma Long, 6-4, 6-3, and in France, where England's Angela Mortimer, a future Hall of Famer, topped American Dorothy Head Knode, 2-6, 7-5, 10-8.

At Wimbledon, 1948-49-50 champion Louise Brough, seeded No. 2, defeated demonstrative newcomer Darlene Hard in the semifinals, 6-3, 8-6, reaching the final for the seventh time. Her Californian opponent was ambidextrous (she did not use a backhand, but switched hands on the racket as necessary) Beverly Baker Fleitz, who, serving right-handed, upset top seed Doris Hart, 6-3, 6-0, in the semifinals. Beverly was the only female ambidextrous player to reach a major final, sharing the oddity with Italian Giorgio de Stefani, loser of the French to Henri Cochet in 1932.

"Louise was always prone to tighten up at important points but had a greater breadth of stroke and experience at her command, which just saw her through a keenly fought struggle," reported Max Robertson. "In the sixth game of the second set, for example, it was only after nine deuces and five advantages to Fleitz that Louise wrong-footed her near exhausted opponent with a backhand slice down the line to lead 4-2. This was the turning point and Louise went on to win for the fourth time, 7-5, 8-6."

That was Brough's last of six major singles titles on her way to the Hall of Fame. Hart, also a majestic champion, won her last of six, the U.S. at Forest Hills, site of her narrow and jubilant victory over Brough the year before. This time it was much easier as Hart drubbed Brit Patricia Ward 6-4, 6-2.

Hart also made her last appearance in the Wightman Cup as the U.S. defeated Great Britain 6-1 at the Westchester Country Club in Rye, N.Y. She had been on the U.S. team since 1946, compiling a record of 13-1 in singles and 8-1 in doubles. Mortimer handed Hart her lone defeat, 6-4, 1-6, 7-5, but she beat Shirley Bloomer, 7-5, 6-3, and other necessary points were provided by Brough (6-0, 6-2 over Mortimer and 6-2, 6-4 over Bloomer) and Knode (6-3, 6-3, over Angela Buxton). At year's end, Doris became a teaching pro.

As for doubles titles in 1955, Brough and Margaret duPont, who had reigned nine successive years between 1942 and 1950, took the U.S. title away from Fry-Hart, 6-3, 1-6, 6-3, starting a new three-year run. Seixas and Trabert won the Australian, over Hoad and Rosewall, 6-3, 6-2, 2-6, 3-6, 6-1, and the French over Italians Nicola Pietrangeli and Orlando Sirola, 6-1, 4-6, 6-2, 6-4. But Hoad and Hartwig, presaging their Davis Cup heroics, won Wimble-

don, over mates Neale Fraser and Rosewall, 7-5, 6-4, 6-3. The little-known team of Japanese Davis Cuppers Kosei Kamo and Atsushi Miyagi won the U.S. doubles, primarily because they were willing to hang around Longwood Cricket Club through Hurricane Diane as most of the favored teams fled Boston. When the three-foot deep lake that Longwood's grass courts became under the assault of fierce downpours finally receded, the tournament ended one week late. The Japanese took their country's only major, triumphing over young unseeded Americans Bill Quillian, 21, and Jerry Moss, 19, in five, 6-2, 6-3, 3-6, 1-6, 6-4.

Australian Championships

Men's Singles Final: Ken Rosewall (AUS) def. Lew Hoad (AUS), 9-7, 6-4, 6-4

Women's Singles Final: Beryl Penrose (AUS) def. Thelma Long (USA), 6-4, 6-3

Men's Doubles Final: Vic Seixas and Tony Trabert (USA) def. Lew Hoad and Ken Rosewall (AUS), 6-3, 6-2, 2-6, 3-6, 6-1

Women's Doubles Final: Mary Bevis Hawton and Beryl Penrose (AUS) def. Nell Hall Hopman and Gwen Thiele (AUS), 7-5, 6-1

Mixed Doubles Final: Thelma Coyne Long and George Worthington (AUS) def. Jenny Staley and Lew Hoad (AUS), 6-2, 6-1

French Championships

Men's Singles Final: Tony Trabert (USA) def. Sven Davidson (SWE), 2-6, 6-1, 6-4, 6-2

Women's Singles Final: Angela Mortimer (GBR) def. Dorothy Head Knode (USA), 2-6, 7-5, 10-8

Men's Doubles Final: Vic Seixas and Tony Trabert (USA) def. Nicola Pietrangeli and Orlando Sirola (ITA), 6-1, 4-6, 6-2, 6-4

Women's Doubles Final: Beverly Baker Fleitz and Darlene Hard (USA) def. Shirley Bloomer and Pat Ward (GBR), 7-5, 6-8, 13-11

Mixed Doubles Final: Doris Hart (USA) and Gordon Forbes (RSA) def. Jenny Staley (USA) and Luis Ayala (CHI), 5-7, 6-1, 6-2

Wimbledon

Men's Singles Final: Tony Trabert (USA) def. Kurt Nielsen (DEN), 6-3, 7-5, 6-1

Women's Singles Final: Louise Brough (USA) def. Beverly Baker Fleitz (USA), 7-5, 8-6

Men's Doubles Final: Rex Hartwig and Lew Hoad (AUS) def. Neale Fraser and Ken Rosewall (AUS), 7-5, 6-4, 6-3

Women's Doubles Final: Angela Mortimer and Anne Shilcock (GBR) def. Shirley Bloomer and Pat Ward (GBR), 7-5, 6-1

Mixed Doubles Final: Doris Hart and Vic Seixas (USA) def. Louise Brough (USA) and Enrique Morea (ARG), 8-6, 2-6, 6-3

U.S. Championships

Men's Singles Final: Tony Trabert (USA) def. Ken Rosewall (AUS), 9-7, 6-3, 6-3

Women's Singles Final: Doris Hart (USA) def. Pat Ward (GBR), 6-4, 6-2

Men's Doubles Final: Kosei Kamo and Atsushi Miyagi (JPN) def. Gerald Moss and Bill Quillian (USA), 6-2, 6-3, 3-6, 1-6, 6-4

Women's Doubles Final: Louise Brough and Margaret Osborne DuPont (USA) def. Doris Hart and Shirley Fry (USA), 6-3, 1-6, 6-3

Mixed Doubles Final: Doris Hart and Vic Seixas (USA) def. Shirley Fry and Gardnar Mulloy (USA), 7-5, 5-7, 6-2

Year-End No. 1

Men: Tony Trabert
Women: Louise Brough

Davis Cup: Australia

Wightman Cup: United States

1956

A Near Slam For Hoad, Gibson Wins French Title

Lew Hoad holds his men's singles trophy at Wimbledon, earned with a final-round victory over fellow Australian Ken Rosewall.

Lew Hoad holds his men's singles trophy at Wimbledon, earned with a final-round victory over fellow Australian Ken Rosewall.

In 1956, the 21-year-old former "Whiz Kids" of Australia, Lew Hoad and Ken Rosewall, had clearly grown up into the best amateur tennis players in the world. They smothered the United States in the Davis Cup Challenge Round, 5-0, for the second straight year, and played each other in three of the four major singles finals. Ultimately, on the last day of Forest Hills, it was Rosewall who prevented his slightly younger countryman from pulling off a Grand Slam.

This was the Golden Jubilee year of the U.S. Championships at Forest Hills and Rosewall captivated a crowd of 12,000. Hills with his 4-6, 6-2, 6-3, 6-3 victory in the first all-foreign final since 1933, when Britain's Fred Perry thwarted Australian Jack Crawford's bid for a Grand Slam. But there was more interest in the trailblazer, "the colored girl," as many referred to Althea Gibson out of Harlem, who powerfully drove to the final in her precinct.

Gibson had registered the first major title for a black by winning the French over Brit Angela Mortimer, 6-0, 12-10. She added the doubles with another Brit, Angela Buxton, 6-8, 8-6, 6-1, over fellow Americans Darlene Hard and Dorothy Knode. Buxton was also Althea's partner shortly thereafter in putting the first black on the Wimbledon championship roll, 6-1, 8-6, over Aussies Fay Muller and Daphne Seeney. Earlier, Althea had displayed an affinity for continental clay by winning her first important title, the Italian, over Hungarian Suzi Kormoczi, 6-3, 7-5.

The Hoad-Rosewall rivalry reached its zenith at Forest Hills where, as Allison Danzig wrote in *The New York Times*, "If there were any doubts about the little Australian measuring up to the caliber of a truly great player, they were dispelled by his play in the championship. His performance in breaking down the powerful attack and then the will to win over the favored Hoad was even more convincing, considering the breezy conditions, than his wizardry in his unforgettable quarterfinal match against Richard Savitt. Against the powerful, rangy Savitt, Rosewall's ground strokes were the chief instruments of a 6-4, 7-5, 4-6, 8-10, 6-1, victory in a crescendo of lethal driving exchanges seldom equaled on the Forest Hills turf. The final match between possibly the two most accomplished 21-year-old finalists in the tournament's history was a madcap, lightning-fast duel. The shots were taken out of the air with rapidity and radiance despite a strong wind that played tricks with the ball."

So it had been much of the year, the blond-haired, blue-eyed, muscular, and positively engaging Hoad rousing galleries around the world with his remarkable weight of shot and free-wheeling attack; the immaculate, compact and quicksilver Rosewall challenging him but constantly rebuffed, until now.

Hoad had beaten Rosewall in the finals of the Australian, 6-4, 3-6, 6-4, 7-5, and Wimbledon, 6-2, 4-6, 7-5, 6-4. He had beaten Sven Davidson in the French final, 6-4, 8-6, 6-3, and won the Italian and German titles on clay as well. Davidson fell before him in Rome, 7-5, 6-2, 6-0, and Orlando Sirola in Hamburg, 6-2, 5-7, 6-4, 8-6. But finally Rosewall got him.

Doris Hart, who had climaxed 15 appearances with back-to-back Forest Hills titles in 1954 and 1955, had, like Trabert, turned pro - she to give lessons. In her absence, her old doubles partner, Shirley Fry, took the Wimbledon and Forest Hills

singles titles for the first and only time. At Wimbledon, Shirley beat Angela Buxton, 6-3, 6-1, and at Forest Hills, her final victim was Italian and French champion, the New Yorker Gibson. Althea was beaten in her Wimbledon debut by Fry, 4-6, 6-3, 6-4, in the quarterfinal.

For Fry, 29, it was a glorious journey's end. Begun as a 14-year-old with a first-round look-in at Forest Hills in 1941, the long trip, the quest, was over at destination championship: Shirley's 6-3, 6-4 victory over Gibson completed the most drawn-out of all treks to a U.S. title. It was her 16th sortie, from youngest entrant ever (a record that stood until Kathleen Horvath, a younger 14 in 1979) to one of the oldest champs. She had beaten Althea to win the U.S. Clay, 7-5, 6-1. This time Fry maintained her mastery by attacking the net constantly in the first set, then staying back and thwarting Gibson's attack with deep, accurate ground strokes in the second.

The addition of Buxton, and the improvement of Mortimer, made the British Wightman Cup team more competitive than it had been at any time since the war, but the U.S. still prevailed, 5-2, at Wimbledon. Brough and Fry were the mainstays. Louise beat Mortimer, 3-6, 6-4, 7-5, and Buxton, 3-6, 6-3, 6-4. Shirley, beaten by Mortimer, 6-4, 6-3, won over Buxton, 6-2, 6-8. 7-5, and accompanied Brough in a doubles win over Buxton and Mortimer, 6-2, 6-2.

Brough and Margaret duPont continued their unmatched supremacy in the U.S. doubles, winning their 11th title, 6-3, 6-0, over Betty Rosenquest Pratt and Fry.

Hoad and Rosewall, masterful returner Kenny in the right court, took three of the four doubles majors: Australian over Don Candy and Mervyn Rose, 13-11, 10-8, 6-4; Wimbledon over Italians Nicola Pietrangeli and Orlando Sirola, 7-5, 6-2, 6-1; U.S. over Ham Richardson and Vic Seixas, 6-2, 6-2, 3-6, 6-4. They didn't play together at the French where Hoad, in the company of countryman and future Hall of Famer, Ashley Cooper, lost the final to the Aussie-American combine of Candy and Bob Perry, 7-5, 6-3, 6-3.

Ken and Lew thoroughly blinded and blanked the U.S., 5-0 in the Davis Cup Challenge Round at Adelaide. Hoad went through Herbie Flam with ease, 6-2, 6-3, 6-3, and Rosewall had little more trouble with Seixas, 6-1, 6-4, 4-6, 6-1, before the Aussies thumped Seixas and Texan Sammy Giammalva, 1-6, 6-1, 7-5, 6-4, to make sure the third day was merely a workout.

Pro promoter Jack Kramer wanted to sign Hoad, who had won 15 tournaments, but when he vacillated, Kramer went after Rosewall instead, regarding him as the next best attraction to oppose Pancho Gonzalez in 1957. Kramer had started training to play 1955 amateur king Tony Trabert himself in 1956, but was persuaded by Gonzalez' s wife, Henrietta, to let Pancho face Trabert on the head-to-head tour. Kramer, now badly afflicted with arthritis, was just as happy to do the promotion and let the strong and hungry Gonzalez play. Gonzalez, very likely the best player in the world even though few realized it, crushed Trabert, 74 matches to 24. Gonzalez also won the U.S. Pro Championship over Pancho Segura, 21-15, 13-21, 21-14, 22-20 (a ping-pong scoring experiment) indoors at the Cleveland Arena, and beat Frank Sedgman, 4-6, 11-9, 11-9, 9-7, in a match of remarkably high quality at Wembley.

"Wembley, a London suburb of fast-fading respectability, is a shrine of English soccer. In those days its indoor arena was also a shrine of pro tennis," wrote Rex Bellamy in *World Tennis* more than two decades later. "That night, public transport ceased long before the match did. Stranded spectators did not much mind. They were unlikely to see such a match again."

1956 CHAMPIONS AND LEADERS

Australian Championships
Men's Singles Final: Lew Hoad (AUS) def. Ken Rosewall (AUS), 6-4, 3-6, 6-4, 7-5
Women's Singles Final: Mary Carter (AUS) def. Thelma Long (AUS), 3-6, 6-2, 9-7
Men's Doubles Final: Lew Hoad and Ken Rosewall (AUS) def. Don Candy and Merv Rose (AUS), 10-8, 13-11, 6-4
Women's Doubles Final: Mary Bevis Hawton and Thelma Coyne Long (AUS) def. Mary Carter and Beryl Penrose (AUS), 6-2, 5-7, 9-7
Mixed Doubles Final: Beryl Penrose and Neale Fraser (AUS) def. Mary Bevis Hawton and Roy Emerson (AUS), 6-2, 6-4

French Championships
Men's Singles Final: Lew Hoad (AUS) def. Sven Davidson (SWE), 6-4, 8-6, 6-3
Women's Singles Final: Althea Gibson (USA) def. Angela Mortimer (GBR), 6-0, 12-10
Men's Doubles Final: Don Candy (AUS) and Robert Perry (USA) def. Ashley Cooper and Lew Hoad (AUS), 7-5, 6-3, 6-3
Women's Doubles Final: Angela Buxton (GBR) and Althea Gibson (USA) def. Darlene Hard and Dorothy Head Knode (USA), 6-8, 8-6, 6-1
Mixed Doubles Final: Thelma Coyne Long (AUS) and Luis Ayala (CHI) def. Doris Hart (USA) and Bob Howe (AUS), 4-6, 6-4, 6-1

Wimbledon
Men's Singles Final: Lew Hoad (AUS) def. Ken Rosewall (AUS), 6-2, 4-6, 7-5, 6-4
Women's Singles Final: Shirley Fry (USA) def. Angela Buxton (GBR), 6-3, 6-1
Men's Doubles Final: Lew Hoad and Ken Rosewall (AUS) def. Nicola Pietrangeli and Orlando Sirola (ITA), 7-5, 6-2, 6-1
Women's Doubles Final: Angela Buxton (GBR) and Althea Gibson (USA) def. Fay Muller and Daphne Seeney (AUS), 6-1, 8-6
Mixed Doubles Final: Shirley Fry and Vic Seixas (USA) def. Althea Gibson and Gardnar Mulloy (USA), 2-6, 6-2, 7-5

U.S. Championships
Men's Singles Final: Ken Rosewall (AUS) def. Lew Hoad (USA), 4-6, 6-2, 6-3, 6-3
Women's Singles Final: Shirley Fry (USA) def. Althea Gibson (USA), 6-3, 6-4
Men's Doubles Final: Lew Hoad and Ken Rosewall (AUS) def. Ham Richardson and Vic Seixas (USA), 6-2, 6-2, 3-6, 6-4
Women's Doubles Final: Louise Brough and Margaret Osborne duPont (USA) def. Betty Pratt and Shirley Fry (USA), 6-3, 6-0
Mixed Doubles Final: Margaret Osborne duPont (USA) and Ken Rosewall (AUS) def. Darlene Hard (USA) and Lew Hoad (AUS), 9-7, 6-1

Year-End No. 1
Men: Lew Hoad
Women: Shirley Fry

Davis Cup: Australia

Wightman Cup: United States

1957 Gibson Reigns Supreme

Althea Gibson (right) receives a kiss from **Darlene Hard**, whom she beat to become the first black woman to win the singles title at Wimbledon.

The order that had prevailed in international tennis in the early part of the 1950s was changing rapidly by 1957. A year that began with Lew Hoad and Shirley Fry on top of the world ended with Althea Gibson as the dominant woman and surprising Mal Anderson challenging Ashley Cooper for the top spot among the men.

Any designs Hoad may have on the Grand Slam—he had come within one match in 1956—were shattered quickly. The "baby bull" was upset in the semifinals of the Australian, 7-5,

3-6, 6-1, 6-4, by a promising young left-hander, Neale Fraser, son of a prominent Labor politician. Cooper, a rather mechanical but solid and determined player who, with Fraser and Anderson, represented the new products off Harry Hopman's Australian Davis

Cup assembly line, then won his first major title by beating Fraser in the final, 6-3, 9-11, 6-4, 6-2. Hoad and Fraser took the doubles over Anderson and Cooper, 6-3, 8-6, 6-4.

Shortly after the pro tour between Pancho Gonzalez and Ken Rosewall—Gonzalez would win 50-26—had begun in Australia at the New Year, Hoad had a friend contact promoter Jack Kramer and tell him that he was again interested in turning pro. Kramer was baffled, since Hoad had recently refused his entreaties. Later Kramer figured that Hoad was starting to encounter the back problems that eventually cut short his career, and decided he'd better get his payday while he still could.

Kramer signed Hoad—sending Ted Schroeder to the bank with him to make sure he cashed a $5,000 advance, which would provide proof of a contract if Hoad changed his mind again—but agreed to keep the pact secret until after Wimbledon.

Sven Davidson, the Swedish Davis Cup stalwart who was runner-up the previous two years, won the French singles over Herbie Flam, the last American man in the Paris final for 19 years, 6-3, 6-4, 6-4. Anderson and Cooper were the doubles champs, 6-3, 6-0, 6-3, over Don Candy and Merv Rose.

Hoad, whose season had been erratic, made his last amateur tournament a memorable one. At Wimbledon, he lost only one set, to fellow Aussie Rose in the quarterfinals, 6-4, 4-6, 10-8, 6-3. Then he routed Davidson, the only non-Australian in the semifinals, 6-4, 6-4, 7-5, while Cooper won a tougher semifinal in the other half over Fraser, 1-6, 14-12, 6-3, 8-6. In the final, Hoad was brilliant, humbling Cooper, 6-2, 6-1, 6-2, in a mere 57 minutes. "It was a display of genius and it is to be doubted if such dynamic shot making was sustained with such accuracy before. If Cooper felt he had played badly, he had no chance to do anything else," wrote Lance Tingay. "Hoad was superhuman. It never began to be a contested match."

Gardnar Mulloy, age 43, and Budge Patty, 10 years younger, won their only Wimbledon doubles title—an exciting and sentimental occasion—over top-seeded Fraser and Hoad, 8-10, 6-4, 6-4, 6-4.

Hoad joined the pros, Kramer carefully trying to get him ready for a serious run at Gonzalez the following year. "I used him in a couple of round-robins in the States, and then I made myself into a sparring partner and, with Rosewall and [Pancho] Segura, we took off on an around-the-world tour to get Hoad in shape for Gonzalez," Kramer recalled. "If Hoad could beat Gonzalez, that was my chance to get rid of that tiger. Gonzalez knew what I was doing, too, and he was furious. We played a brutal death march, going to Europe, then across Africa, through India and Southeast Asia, all the way to Manila. I was impressed by how strong Hoad was. He was personally as gentle as a lamb, but on the trip his body could tolerate almost anything."

With Hoad gone from the amateur ranks, the 20-year-old Cooper was the top seed and heavy favorite to win Forest Hills. However, Cooper was upset in the final by Anderson, who became the first unseeded U.S. champion. Anderson, a country boy from a remote Queensland cattle station, had lost to Cooper in five of six previous meetings, but in the month before Forest Hills, the thin, quick, dark-haired lad of 22 had become an entirely different player. Early in the year he had suffered from nervous

exhaustion and heat prostration. At Wimbledon, he broke a toe. But at Newport, R.I., on the U.S. grass court circuit, he beat U.S. No. 1 Ham Richardson, 6-1, 3-6, 6-0, 6-1, and, in the final, Welshman Mike Davies, 4-6, 6-1, 6-4, 1-6, 6-2, getting a confidence-boosting title under his belt.

At Forest Hills, he clobbered Dick Savitt, who had a cold, 6-4, 6-3, 6-1, then put on a dazzling display of piercing service returns and passing shots to crush Chilean Luis Ayala, 6-1, 6-3, 6-1. In the semifinals, he overcame Sven Davidson (conqueror of Vic Seixas at Wimbledon) from a 1-2 deficit in sets, 5-7, 6-2, 4-6, 6-3, 6-4.

In his 10-8, 7-5, 6-4 triumph over top-seeded Cooper, Anderson was so good that he inspired rhapsodic prose and superlatives from Allison Danzig in the next day's *The New York Times*: "Anderson's performance ranks with the finest displays of offensive tennis of recent years. His speed of stroke and foot, the inevitability of his volley, his hair-trigger reaction and facileness on the half-volley, the rapidity of his service and passing shots and the adroitness of his return of service, compelling Cooper to volley up, all bore the stamp of a master of the racket. It was offensive tennis all the way, sustained without a letup. The margin of safety on most shots was almost nil. The most difficult shots were taken in stride with the acme of timing, going in or swiftly moving to the side."

Less artistically satisfying, but just as dramatic, was Althea Gibson's 6-3, 6-2 victory in the women's final over Louise Brough. In 1950, when Gibson made history as the first black player admitted to the U.S. Championships, she had gained widespread attention by nearly beating Brough, then the Wimbledon champion, in the second round.

At the start of the year, Shirley Fry captured the Australian, the only one of the major singles titles she had not previously won, over Gibson, 6-3, 6-4. They teamed to win the doubles over Mary Hawton and Fay Muller, 6-2, 6-1. These were Fry's last big titles before retiring to become a housewife and teaching pro in Connecticut.

Englishwoman Shirley Bloomer's victory in the Italian (over Dorothy Head Knode, 1-6, 9-7, 6-2) was overshadowed by the first men's title of the stylish Nicola Pietrangeli over Beppe Merlo, 8-6, 6-2, 6-4. Shirley also took the French over Knode, 6-1, 6-3, and teamed with Darlene Hard for the doubles crown, 7-5, 4-6, 7-5, over Mexicans Yola Ramirez and Rosie Reyes.

But thereafter Gibson reigned supreme, clobbering Californian Hard, 6-3, 6-2, in the Wimbledon final. Althea won two singles (6-4, 4-6, 6-2, over Bloomer, and 6-4, 6-2, over Christine Truman) and a doubles as the U.S. defeated Great Britain, 6-1, in the Wightman Cup. Althea also won the Wimbledon doubles with Hard, over Aussies Hawton and Thelma Long, 6-1, 6-2, but they lost in the U.S. final, 6-2, 7-5, to Louise Brough and Margaret duPont, who took their last title. It was their third straight and 12th in all, a U.S. record, completing an overall record of winning 20 career majors.

Fifteen years earlier, Gibson had been playing paddle tennis on the streets of Harlem. She had as difficult a path to the pinnacle of tennis as anyone ever did. She had to stare down bigotry as well as formidable opponents. Some tournaments had gone out of existence rather than admit her. But finally, at age 30,

she was standing on the stadium court at Forest Hills, already the Wimbledon champion, accepting the trophy that symbolized supremacy in American women's tennis from Vice President Richard Nixon. The cup had white gladiolas and red roses in it, and "Big Al" had tears in her eyes.

There was one other important piece of silverware at stake in 1957. With Hoad and Rosewall gone, Australia was vulnerable to a U.S. raiding party invading Melbourne for the Davis Cup Challenge Round. But Anderson edged big-serving Barry MacKay, 6-3, 7-5, 3-6, 7-9, 6-3; Cooper bumped 34-year-old Vic Seixas in a similarly tortuous match, 3-6, 7-5, 6-1, 1-6, 6-3; and Anderson and Mervyn Rose—chosen even though Cooper and Fraser had won the U.S. doubles title— combined to demoralize MacKay and Seixas, 6-4, 6-4, 8-6, in the clincher. The second-largest Davis Cup crowds, 22,000 a day at Kooyong, witnessed the matches. There were no flowers in the cup, but for the third straight year Aussies drank libations of victory beer from it.

1957 CHAMPIONS AND LEADERS

Australian Championships
Men's Singles Final: Ashley Cooper (AUS) def. Neale Fraser (AUS), 6-3, 9-11, 6-4, 6-2

Women's Singles Final: Shirley Fry (USA) def. Althea Gibson (USA), 6-3, 6-4

Men's Doubles Final: Neale Fraser and Lew Hoad (AUS) def. Mal Anderson and Ashley Cooper (USA), 6-3, 8-6, 6-4

Women's Doubles Final: Althea Gibson and Shirley Fry (USA) def. Mary Bevis Hawton and Fay Muller (AUS), 6-2, 6-1

Mixed Doubles Final: Fay Muller and Mal Anderson (AUS) def. Billy Knight (GBR) and Jill Langley (AUS), 7-5, 3-6, 6-1

French Championships
Men's Singles Final: Sven Davidson (SWE) def. Herb Flam (USA), 6-3, 6-4, 6-4

Women's Singles Final: Shirley Bloomer (GBR) def. Dorothy Head Knode (USA), 6-1, 6-3

Men's Doubles Final: Mal Anderson and Ashley Cooper (AUS) def. Don Candy and Merv Rose (AUS), 6-3, 6-0, 6-3

Women's Doubles Final: Shirley Bloomer (GBR) and Darlene Hard (USA) def. Yola Ramirez and Rosie Reyes (MEX), 7-5, 4-6, 7-5

Mixed Doubles Final: Vera Puzejova and Jiri Javorsky (CZE) def. Edda Buding (GER) and Luis Ayala (CHI), 6-3, 6-4

Wimbledon
Men's Singles Final: Lew Hoad (AUS) def. Ashley Cooper (AUS), 6-2, 6-1, 6-2

Women's Singles Final: Althea Gibson (USA) def. Darlene Hard (USA), 6-3, 6-2

Men's Doubles Final: Budge Patty and Gardnar Mulloy (USA) def. Neale Fraser and Lew Hoad (AUS), 8-10, 6-4, 6-4, 6-4

Women's Doubles Final: Althea Gibson and Darlene Hard (USA) def. Mary Bevis Hawton and Thelma Coyne Long (AUS), 6-1, 6-2

Mixed Doubles Final: Darlene Hard (USA) and Merv Rose (AUS) def. Althea Gibson (USA) and Neale Fraser (AUS), 6-4, 7-5

U.S. Championships
Men's Singles Final: Mal Anderson (AUS) def. Ashley Cooper (AUS), 10-8, 7-5, 6-4

Women's Singles Final: Althea Gibson (USA) def. Louise Brough (USA), 6-3, 6-2

Men's Doubles Final: Ashley Cooper and Neale Fraser (AUS) def. Gardnar Mulloy and Budge Patty (USA), 4-6, 6-3, 9-7, 6-3

Women's Doubles Final: Louise Brough and Margaret Osborne duPont (USA) def. Althea Gibson and Darlene Hard (USA), 6-2, 7-5

Mixed Doubles Finla: Althea Gibson (USA) and Kurt Nielsen (DEN) def. Darlene Hard (USA) and Bob Howe (AUS), 6-3, 9-7

Year-End No. 1
Men: Ashley Cooper
Women: Althea Gibson

Davis Cup: Australia

Wightman Cup: United States

1958 Cooper Corrals Three Majors

In 1958, Australians Ashley Cooper, Mal Anderson and Mervyn Rose were the top men in amateur tennis, and American Althea Gibson the outstanding woman. By the end of the year, they had all turned professional, underscoring the rapidly growing distance in quality between the small band of pros who wandered around the world playing one-and two-night stands as unsanctioned outcasts and the amateurs who basked in the limelight of the traditional fixtures.

Ashley Cooper kisses the men's singles trophy at Wimbledon after defeating countryman Neale Fraser in the title match.

The previous year the issue of "open competition" between amateurs and pros was raised formally within the councils of the U.S. Lawn Tennis Association for the first time since the 1930s. A special committee report favored open tournaments. This docu-

ment was promptly tabled since the leadership of the USLTA was not nearly as progressive as the committee, but the ferment that ultimately led to the open game a decade later had started, and not only in America.

With Hoad and Rosewall touring professionally with Jack Kramer's World Tennis, Inc., Cooper took over the top amateur ranking by winning the three legs of the Grand Slam played on grass courts: the Australian, Wimbledon and the U.S.

He reversed the result of the 1957 Forest Hills final and took the Australian singles by beating Mal Anderson, 7-5, 6-3, 6-4. At Wimbledon, loaded with Aussies, No. 2-seeded Anderson injured himself in the quarterfinals, defaulting to Kurt Nielsen at 6-2, 6-3, and Cooper very nearly stumbled in the same round, probably coming within one point of defeat against Bobby Wilson, the pudgy but talented Englishman who delighted British galleries with his deft touch. Wilson had a break points for 6-5 in the fifth set, but Cooper rifled a backhand crosscourt winner within an inch of the sideline, and thereafter fortune favored the bold, 6-4, 6-2, 3-6, 4-6, 7-5. Cooper dominated Rose after losing the first set, 7-9, 6-2, 6-2, 6-3. Then in the final, he beat Neale Fraser, 3-6, 6-3, 6-3, 13-11. Cooper and Fraser were beaten in the doubles final, however, as the title went to an unseeded pair for the second straight year, the strapping Sven Davidson and Ulf Schmidt becoming the first Swedes to have their names inscribed on a Wimbledon championship trophy, 6-4, 6-4, 8-6.

At Forest Hills, Cooper and Anderson advanced to the final for the second consecutive year. Anderson beat Dick Savitt, 6-1, 3-6, 6-3, 18-16, and Swede Ulf Schmidt, 6-4, 7-5, 6-2. Cooper got there past Vic Seixas, 9-7, 6-2, 3-6, 6-2, and Fraser, 8-6, 6-1, 6-1. But in this championship rematch, Cooper prevailed in the longest final since Gonzalez-Schroeder in 1949, 6-2, 3-6, 4-6, 10-8, 8-6.

Gardnar Mulloy, reporting the match for *World Tennis*, wrote that the final set had "all the drama of a *First Night*," and suggested that Cooper merited an Oscar for his theatrics. The even-tempered Anderson served for the match at 5-4, but lost his serve at love. At 6-6, 30-15, Cooper apparently twisting an ankle, writhed in pain, hobbled to the sideline, and finally went back out to play after several minutes, to tumultuous applause. He "ran like a deer and served as well or better than he had all afternoon," opined Mulloy, a bit skeptical about the "injury." Cooper promptly held serve and then broke Anderson for the match. "Cooper is strong, tenacious, smart, and merciless," wrote Mulloy. "And don't forget his famous one-act play, *The Dying Swan*, a real tear-jerker which clinched the championship for him."

Merv Rose, with his tormenting left-handed serve, was the leading Aussie on clay, winning both the Italian and the French, saddening Romans by dethroning Nicola Pietrangeli, 5-7, 8-6, 6-4, 1-6, 6-2, and ripping the Chilean Davis Cupper Luis Ayala in the Paris final 6-3, 6-4, 6-4. The most astounding match of the tournament was Frenchman Robert Haillet's resurrection in the fourth round to beat ex-champ Budge Patty, 5-7, 7-5, 10-8, 4-6, 7-5, after Patty served at 5-0, 40-0 in the fifth, and had four match points at 5-4. Cooper and Fraser won the doubles, over South Africa's Abe Segal and Australia's Bob Howe, 3-6, 8-6, 6-3, 7-5, following up on their Australian title, but were to advance no farther toward a Grand Slam.

Australia was heavily favored to defend the Davis Cup at the end of the year, but the United States had a potent and somewhat controversial weapon: The sleek, bronze-skinned, personable Alejandro "Alex" Olmedo: 22, from Arequipa in the snowcapped Peruvian Andes. The nimble 6-foot, 160-pounder was a student at the University of Southern California (National Intercollegiate champ over Stanford's Jack Douglas, 6-3, 3-6, 6-4, 6-1) and a protégé of Perry Jones, czar of tennis in the Southern Cal section. Jones, also U.S. Davis Cup captain, lobbied successfully for Olmedo's inclusion on the U.S. team, permissible since Peru did not have a Davis Cup team. "The Chief," as he was called because of his regal Incan appearance, had lost a tough five-set semifinal to Fraser at Forest Hills, 3-6, 6-1, 8-6, 3-6, 6-3. But he had won the U.S. doubles with Ham Richardson at Longwood in their first tournament together, jolting defending champs Fraser and Cooper in the semifinal, 7-9, 7-5, 6-3, 6-4 and Americans Sammy Giammalva and Barry MacKay 3-6, 6-3, 6-4, 6-4 for the title.

In the 3-2 Davis Cup victory, Olmedo was magnificent. For openers, before a capacity crowd of 18,000 at the Milton Courts in Brisbane, Olmedo stunned Anderson, 8-6, 2-6, 9-7, 8-6. Cooper beat MacKay, 4-6, 6-3, 6-2, 6-4, to make it 1-1, but on the second day Olmedo teamed with Richardson to outlast Fraser and Anderson, 10-12, 3-6, 16-14, 6-3, 7-5—82 games, a Cup record for final-round doubles, saving two match points along the way. Olmedo then capped his bravura performance by clinching the Cup with a 6-3, 4-6, 6-4, 8-6, victory over Cooper. Olmedo was rewarded with the No. 2 U.S. ranking behind Richardson.

No. 1 among the women, in the U.S. and the world was clearly the 5-foot-11, 145-pound Gibson, who used her thunderous serve and overhead, long reach and touch on the volley, and hard, flat, deep ground strokes to defend her Wimbledon and U.S singles titles. At Wimbledon she beat a local, Angela Mortimer, in the final, 8-6, 6-2.

Mortimer had won the Australian title over Lorraine Coghlan, 6-3, 6-4. At Forest Hills, Gibson's final victim was Darlene Hard, 3-6, 6-1, 6-2. Gibson teamed with Maria Bueno to win the Wimbledon doubles over American Margaret Varne and 40-year-old Margaret duPont, 6-3, 7-5, but they were beaten in the U.S. final by Jeanne Arth and Hard, 2-6, 6-3, 6-4. This was the first of Hard's five consecutive U.S. titles. She won six in all with four partners. Bueno, the enchanting Brazilian, making her first overseas tour at age 18, had won the Italian title, over Aussie Coghlan, 3-6, 6-3, 6-3, and would be a major factor at Wimbledon and Forest Hills.

Gibson lost only four matches during the year, three in the early season (to Beverly Baker Fleitz and Janet Hopps twice), but the one that hurt was to tall Englishwoman Christine Truman in the pivotal match of the Wightman Cup. The British had a fine young team with Truman, Shirley Bloomer (runner-up to Hungarian Suzi Kormoczi, 6-4, 1-6, 6-2, in the French final), and left-hander Ann Haydon, even though Angela Mortimer didn't play. To the glee of the crowd at Wimbledon's Court No. 1, the British won the Cup for the first time since 1930, 4-3. Truman's 2-6, 6-3, 6-4 upset of Gibson paved the way, and the left-handed Haydon's scrambling 6-3, 5-7, 6-3 triumph over Mimi Arnold was the clincher.

After Forest Hills, Gibson announced her retirement "to pursue a musical career." She needed a source of income. The next year she accepted an offer to turn pro and play pre-game exhibitions at Harlem Globetrotters' basketball games against American Karol Fageros, a popular glamour girl noted for her gold lame panties, but not a player of Gibson's standard. Gibson won the tour with a 114-4 record, and said she made $100,000. But the matches, added attractions usually of one-set duration on a basketball court, seemed artificial, demeaning to such a great champion.

Lew Hoad found pro tennis even more lucrative. Even though he lost his 1958 tour against Gonzalez, 51-36, Hoad made $148,000. Gonzalez, who rallied from a 9-18 deficit after Hoad developed a stiff back in Palm Springs, Calif., made over $100,000. "That was the last tour to make any real money, though," promoter Kramer later said. It had been a doozy. In Australia at the start of the year, Hoad was awesome, winning eight of 13 matches against a stale and overweight Gonzalez. In San Francisco, on a canvas court indoors, Hoad won, 6-4, 20-18, to inaugurate the U.S. segment of the tour. The next night Gonzalez won in his hometown of Los Angeles, 3-6, 24-22, 6-1. Before a crowd of 15,237 at Madison Square Garden, Gonzalez won the only best-of-five-setter, 7-9, 6-0, 6-4, 6-4.

Then Hoad, strong as an ox and beating Gonzalez in every department—serve, overhead, volley, and ground-strokes—surged to an 18-9 lead. But the bad back got him, and he was never again the factor he had been. Gonzalez won the tour and beat Hoad in the U.S. Pro Championships at the Arena in Cleveland, 3-6, 4-6, 14-12, 6-1, 6-4. Gonzalez was the best in the world, and the next year—Cooper and Anderson coming aboard for a round robin—he proved it decisively.

1958 CHAMPIONS AND LEADERS

Australian Championships

Men's Singles Final: Ashley Cooper (AUS) def. Mal Anderson (AUS), 7-5, 6-3, 6-4

Women's Singles Final: Angela Mortimer (GBR) def. Lorraine Coghlan (AUS), 6-3, 6-4

Men's Doubles Final: Ashley Cooper and Neale Fraser (AUS) def. Roy Emerson and Bob Mark (AUS), 7-5, 6-8, 3-6, 6-3, 7-5

Women's Doubles Final: Mary Bevis Hawton and Thelma Coyne Long (AUS) def. Lorraine Coghlan (AUS) and Angela Mortimer (GBR), 7-5, 6-8, 6-2

Mixed Doubles Final: Mary Bevis Hawton and Bob Howe (AUS) def. Angela Mortimer (GBR) and Peter Newman (AUS), 9-11, 6-1, 6-2

French Championships

Men's Singles Final: Merv Rose (AUS) def. Luis Ayala (CHI), 6-3, 6-4, 6-4

Women's Singles Final: Suzi Kormoczi (HUN) def. Shirley Bloomer (GBR), 6-4, 1-6, 6-2

Men's Doubles Final: Ashley Cooper and Neale Fraser (AUS) def. Bob Howe (AUS) and Abe Segal (RSA), 3-6, 8-6, 6-3, 7-5

Women's Doubles Final: Rosie Reyes and Yola Ramirez (MEX) def. Mary Bevis Hawton and Thelma Coyne Long (AUS), 6-4, 7-5

Mixed Doubles Final: Shirley Bloomer (GBR) and Nicola Pietrangeli (ITA) def. Lorraine Coghlan and Bob Howe (AUS), 8-6, 6-2

Wimbledon

Men's Singles Final: Ashley Cooper (AUS) def. Neale Fraser (AUS) 3-6, 6-3, 6-4, 13-11

Women's Singles Final: Althea Gibson (USA) def. Angela Mortimer (GBR), 8-6, 6-2

Men's Doubles Final: Sven Davidson and Ulf Schmidt (SWE) def. Ashley Cooper and Neale Fraser (AUS), 6-4, 6-4, 8-6

Women's Doubles Final: Maria Bueno (BRA) and Althea Gibson (USA) def. Margaret Osborne duPont and Margaret Varner (USA), 6-3, 7-5

Mixed Doubles Final: Lorraine Coghlan and Bob Howe (AUS) def. Althea Gibson (USA) and Kurt Nielsen (DEN), 6-3, 11-9

U.S. Championships

Men's Singles Final: Ashley Cooper (AUS) def. Mal Anderson (AUS), 6-2, 3-6, 4-6, 10-8, 8-6

Women's Singles Final: Althea Gibson (USA) def. Darlene Hard (USA), 3-6, 6-1, 6-2

Men's Doubles Final: Alex Olmedo (PER) and Hamilton Richardson (USA) def. Sammy Giammalva and Barry MacKay (USA), 3-6, 6-3, 6-4, 6-4

Women's Doubles Final: Jeanne Arth and Darlene Hard (USA) def. Althea Gibson and Maria Bueno (BRA), 2-6, 6-3, 6-4

Mixed Doubles Final: Margaret Osborne duPont (USA) and Neale Fraser (AUS) def. Maria Bueno (BRA) and Alex Olmedo (PER), 6-4, 3-6, 9-7

Year-End No. 1

Men: Ashley Cooper
Women: Althea Gibson

Davis Cup: United States

Wightman Cup: Great Britain

1959 A Latin Beat Wafts Through Majors

The folly of the uneasy arrangement between amateur officials and pro promoter Jack Kramer during the "shamateur" days of the late 1950s and early 1960s was apparent in this passage from a 1958 *Sports Illustrated* story on Kramer by Dick Phelan:

"'I look on the amateurs as my farm system' he [Kramer] says flatly, and this has been true particularly in Australia. There, he is denounced as a public enemy because his money tempts the best Australian players to abandon their amateur status and thus their eligibility for Davis Cup play. Then when his troupe arrives in Australia, the very public that reviled him, flocks to his matches and profits mount. This leads the amateur tennis officials, whose own tournaments sometimes follow Kramer's and don't draw nearly so well, to lambaste him afresh. But they let him come back. Their share of his gate receipts helps support the Australian amateurs."

After the heady peak of the Pancho Gonzalez—Lew Hoad tour in 1958, the profits of Kramer's World Tennis, Inc., started to dwindle, despite his personal flair for promotion. Mal Anderson and Ashley Cooper joined the vanquished Hoad and the victorious Gonzalez in a round-robin tour, but the thrill was gone. They did not draw well, nor did similar tours with other personnel. If they had, it might have hastened the willingness of the ama-

teur officials to consider "Open" tennis. With Cooper, Anderson and Mervyn Rose gone, Alex Olmedo and Neale Fraser ruled the amateur roost, sharing the world stage with the fiery Latin grace of Maria Bueno.

Olmedo, still buoyed by his Herculean accomplishment in the Davis Cup Challenge Round at the end of 1958, stayed and took the 1959 Australian singles title over southpaw Fraser, 6-1, 6-2, 3-6, 6-3. Rod Laver, starting the climb to greatness, and Bob Mark took the first of their three straight Aussie doubles titles, 9-7, 6-4, 6-2, over Don Candy and Bob Howe.

Olmedo then returned to the United States and won the U.S. Indoor in New York, 7-9, 6-3, 6-4, 5-7, 12-10, withstanding 28 aces, over Dick Savitt. Olmedo did not play the Italian Championship, where Luis Ayala prevailed over Fraser, 6-3, 3-6, 6-3, 6-3, or the French, where the great Italian artist Nicola Pietrangeli beat South African Ian Vermaak in the final, 3-6, 6-3, 6-4, 6-1. Pietrangeli and Italian Davis Cup teammate Orlando Sirola won the doubles over the champions of Italy, Fraser and Roy Emerson, 6-3, 6-2, 14-12. Olmedo's 1958 Davis Cup triumph for the United States elevated him into a national hero in his native Peru, and he made a triumphant tour there along with teammate Butch Buchholz, Davis Cup Captain Perry Jones—and the Cup itself.

Olmedo added to his skyrocketing reputation by winning Wimbledon, scoring a double Aussie KO, over Emerson in the semifinal, 6-4, 6-0, 6-4, and Laver, whose talent was enormous but as yet unconsolidated, in the final, 6-4, 6-3, 6-4. Emerson took the first of his eventual record 16 major men's doubles titles, alongside Fraser, over Laver and Mark, 8-6, 6-3, 14-16, 9-7.

Wimbledon was the peak of Olmedo's year, however. Fraser beat him in the U.S. final at Forest Hills, 6-3, 5-7, 6-2, 6-4, as the Chief's serve lacked its customary zip because of a shoulder strain he had suffered in a mixed doubles match the night before. Olmedo had beaten Emerson again, 6-4, 3-6, 6-2, 6-3 in the quarterfinals, and American Ron Holmberg, 15-13, 6-4, 3-6, 6-1 in the semifinals. The hot, unseeded Holmberg had eliminated

Dick Savitt, 1-6, 6-4, 7-5, 2-6, 9-7 in the third round, Butch Buchholz, 6-3, 7-5, 8-10, 5-7, 6-3 in the quarterfinals, and Laver, 6-8, 7-5, 6-0, 6-3 in the semifinals. Fraser had few problems, beating another lefty, Texan Bernard "Tut" Bartzen in his semifinal, 6-3, 6-2, 6-2.

Australia regained the Davis Cup at Forest Hills, 3-2, Olmedo never finding the form to which he had risen the previous December. Fraser beat him again in the opening match, 8-6, 6-8, 6-4, 8-6. Barry MacKay, the hulking "Ohio Bear" out of Dayton, served mightily in beating Laver, 7-5, 6-4, 6-1, but in the doubles, Emerson and Fraser outclassed Olmedo and Butch Buchholz, 7-5, 7-5, 6-4. The Aussies had prevailed to win the U.S. doubles title over Alex and Butch by the breadth of their fingernails, 3-6, 6-3, 5-7, 6-4, 7-5, but this time the nails became claws.

Olmedo raised his game to beat Laver, 9-7, 4-6, 10-8, 12-10, to tie the series at 2-all, but Fraser clinched by beating MacKay in a match that was played over two days. They split sets before darkness forced a postponement, but after a long rain delay, Fraser, returning splendidly, won the last two sets easily for a soggy 8-6, 3-6, 6-2, 6-4, victory.

On the women's side, Mary Carter Reitano won the Australian singles, 6-2, 6-3, over South African Renee Schuurman, who teamed with her countrywoman Sandra Reynolds for the doubles crown, over the all-Aussie pair of Lorraine Coghland and Mary Carter Reitano, 7-5, 6-4. Englishwoman Christine Truman, 18, won both the Italian (over Reynolds, 6-0, 6-1) and French titles, dethroning Hungarian clay-court specialist Suzi Kormoczi in the Paris final, 6-4, 7-5, to become the youngest champ until Steffi Graf, 17, in 1987. Reynolds and Schuurman won the doubles, over Mexicans Yola Ramirez and Rosie Reyes, 2-6, 6-0, 6-1..

Thereafter the season belonged to the incomparably balletic and flamboyant Bueno. Volleying beautifully, playing with breathtaking boldness and panache, the lithe Brazilian became the first South American woman to win the Wimbledon singles title, beating Darlene Hard 6-4, 6-3 in the final. Hard did team with Jeanne Arth to add the Wimbledon doubles (over Beverly Baker Fleitz and Truman, 2-6, 6-2, 6-3) to the U.S. crown they captured the previous year. Darlene also won the mixed with Laver, 6-4, 6-3, over Bueno and Fraser.

Bueno then inspired the galleries at Forest Hills as she had at London, the top-seeded Sao Paulo Swallow flitting through the draw on the loss of one set, to Arth in the third round (4-6, 6-3, 7-5). In the final, she flew past the tall and sporting Truman, 6-1, 6-4. It was an occasion for the golden old and young. Louise Brough Clapp, 36, the champ 12 years before and holder of four Wimbledons, said farewell on her 18th appearance, winning three matches, losing to Bueno in the quarterfinals, 6-3, 6-2. Another Californian, 15-year-old Billie Jean Moffitt, took a first peek, lost to St. Louis lefty Justina Bricka, 4-6, 7-5, 6-4—but would be the champ seven years hence as Mrs. King.

Hard and Arth repeated as U.S. doubles champions at Longwood, 6-2, 6-3, over Sally Moore of the USA and Bueno, 6-2, 6-3.

The United States regained the Wightman Cup from Great Britain with a 4-3 victory at the Edgeworth Club in Sewickley, Pa. The British won the final two matches, but only after Hard's 6-3, 6-8, 6-4 victory over Angela Mortimer, and Beverly Baker Fleitz's 6-4, 6-4 conquest of Truman had given the Americans an unbeatable 4-1 lead.

Gonzalez remained the pro champion. He beat Hoad for the second straight year in the final of the U.S. Pro Championships at Cleveland, 6-4, 6-2, 6-4, after romping in the round-robin tour against Hoad, Cooper, and Anderson. Anderson took the biggie, London, at Wembley, in a tight one with Pancho Segura, 4-6, 6-4, 3-6, 6-3, 8-6.

1959 CHAMPIONS AND LEADERS

Australian Championships
Men's Singles Final: Alex Olmedo (PER) def. Neale Fraser (AUS), 6-1, 6-2, 3-6, 6-3

Women's Singles Final: Mary Carter Reitano (AUS) def. Renee Schuurman (RSA), 6-2, 6-3

Men's Doubles Final: Rod Laver and Bob Mark (AUS) def. Don Candy and Bob Howe (AUS), 9-7, 6-4, 6-2

Women's Doubles Final: Renee Schuurman and Sandra Reynolds (RSA) def. Lorraine Coghlan and Mary Carter Reitano (AUS), 7-5, 6-4

Mixed Doubles Final: Sandra Reynolds and Bob Mark (AUS) def. Renee Schuurman (RSA) and Rod Laver (AUS), 4-6, 13-11, 6-1

French Championships
Men's Singles Final: Nicola Pietrangeli (ITA) def. Ian Vermaak (RSA), 3-6, 6-3, 6-4, 6-1

Women's Singles Final: Christine Truman (GBR) def. Suzi Kormoczi (HUN), 6-4, 7-5

Men's Doubles Final: Orlando Sirola and Nicola Pietrangeli (ITA) def. Roy Emerson and Neale Fraser (AUS), 6-3, 6-2, 14-12

Women's Doubles Final: Sandra Reynolds and Renee Schuurman (RSA) def. Yola Ramirez and Rosie Reyes (MEX), 2-6, 6-0, 6-1

Mixed Doubles Final: Yola Ramirez (MEX) and Billy Knight (GBR) def. Rene Schuurman (RSA) and Rod Laver (AUS), 6-4, 6-4

Wimbledon
Men's Singles Final: Alex Olmedo (PER) def. Rod Laver (AUS) 6-4, 6-3, 6-4

Women's Singles Final: Maria Bueno (BRA) def. Darlene Hard (USA), 6-4, 6-3

Men's Doubles Final: Roy Emerson and Neale Fraser (AUS) def. Rod Laver and Bob Mark (AUS), 8-6, 6-3, 14-16, 9-7

Women's Doubles Final: Jeanne Arth and Darlene Hard (USA) def. Beverly Baker Fleitz (USA) and def. Christine Truman (GBR), 2-6, 6-2, 6-3

Mixed Doubles Final: Darlene Hard (USA) and Rod Laver (AUS) def. Maria Bueno (BRA) and Neale Fraser (AUS), 6-4, 6-3

U.S. Championships
Men's Singles Final: Neale Fraser (AUS) def. Alex Olmedo (PER), 6-3, 5-7, 6-2, 6-4

Women's Singles Final: Maria Bueno (BRA) def. Christine Truman (GBR), 6-1, 6-4

Men's Doubles Final: Neale Fraser and Roy Emerson (AUS) def. Alex Olmedo (PER) and Butch Buchholz (USA), 3-6, 6-3, 5-7, 6-4, 7-5

Women's Doubles Final: Jeanne Arth and Darlene Hard (USA) def. Maria Bueno (BRA) and Sally Moore (USA), 6-2, 6-3

Mixed Doubles Final: Margaret Osborne duPont (USA) and Neale Fraser (AUS) def. Janet Hopps (USA) and Bob Mark (AUS), 7-5, 13-15, 6-2

Year-End No. 1
Men: Neale Fraser
Women: Maria Bueno

Davis Cup: Australia

Wightman Cup: United States

1960 Maggie And "The Rocket" Win First Majors

Once again, the start of a new decade was the dawn of a new era in tennis. As 1950 had been, so 1960 was an eventful year. It began with an Australian Championships that heralded a man and woman who would be king and queen of tennis. Rod Laver skirted a match point at 4-5 in the fourth set to beat fellow Aussie left-hander Neale Fraser in an epic final, 5-7, 3-6, 6-3, 8-6, 8-6, the first of his eventual 11 major singles titles. Margaret Smith, who would later become Mrs. Barry Court, beat her countrywoman Jan Lehane, 7-5, 6-2, for the first of seven consecutive Australian

titles and 24 major singles in all—both records. It was a teen-age final that Smith, 17, and Lehane, 18, would repeat in 1961, unique to the majors until Arantxa Sanchez Vicario, 17, beat Steffi Graf, 19, to win the 1989 French.

It would have been much more of a landmark year but for five votes at the annual general meeting of the International Lawn Tennis Federation. By that slim margin, a proposal calling for sanction of between eight and 13 "Open" tournaments in which pros and amateurs would compete together failed to muster the two-thirds majority needed for passage. The proposal had the backing of the U.S., British, French and Australian associations, and the proponents of the "Open" movement were bitterly disappointed when it failed.

Another proposal put forth by the French federation calling for creation of a category of "registered" players who could capitalize on their skill by bargaining with tournaments for appearance fees higher than the expenses allowed amateurs, was tabled. The U.S. Lawn Tennis Association had voted to oppose this resolution on the basis that "registered player" was just another name for a pro.

Top-seeded Maria Bueno did not reach the semifinals of the Australian singles (cut off in the quarterfinals by Smith, 7-5, 3-6, 6-4), but she teamed with Christine Truman to win the doubles over Smith and Lorraine Coghlan Robinson, 6-2, 5-7, 6-2. That was the first leg of a doubles Grand Slam by Bueno. She went on to win the French, Wimbledon and U.S. titles with American Darlene Hard, losing only one more set along the way, to Americans Karen Hantze and Janet Hopps in the semifinals at Wimbledon, 3-6, 6-1, 6-4.

Hard won her first major singles title, the French at Paris, strugglingin the early rounds, hanging in over South African Renee Schuurman in the quarterfinals, 5-7, 6-2, 11-9, then whipping Bueno in the semifinals, 6-3, 6-2, and the quick little Mexican Yola Ramirez in the final, 6-3, 6-4. Ramirez beat South African Sandra Reynolds, 8-10, 6-3, 6-3, in their semifinal. Darlene came aboard Maria's prospective Slam, a final-round triumph over Brits Pat Ward Hales and Ann Haydon, 6-2, 7-5. One of the luckiest in the tournament's history was an Egyptian woman (a rarity in itself), Betty Abbas, who only closed out one match, yet found herself in the quarterfinals. Opening with a shaky 6-2, 2-6, 9-7, win over Italy's Lucia Bassi, Abbas trailed 1958 champ Suzy Kormoczi, 4-5, but won on a default when the Hungarian sprained an ankle, unable to continue. Her next foe was Aussie Mary Hawton, who sprained an ankle in the warm-up. That default lifted the Egyptian to the last eight where Ramirez easily beat her, 6-0, 6-4.

Leg No. 2 in Bueno's doubles Slam was her victory with Hard 6-2, 7-5, over Brits Pat Ward Hales and Ann Haydon.

At Wimbledon, where American women had been so dominant for more than a decade after the war, not one of the 10 Americans who entered reached the semifinals. This had not happened since 1925. Hard, the best U.S. hope, lost 6-1, 2-6, 6-1 in the quarterfinals to Reynolds, who reached the final but lost to Bueno, 8-6, 6-0. A year earlier, journalist Lance Tingay had pointed out that the difference between being very good or very bad was, for Bueno, a thin line based on her timing. "Mundane shots did not exist for her," he observed. "It was either caviar or starvation." For the second year in a row it was mostly caviar, and a feast for the spectators. Her Wimbledon performance was good enough to earn Bueno the No. 1 world ranking by a shade over Hard. It was also Leg III in Maria's doubles Slam, aided by Hard, over South Africans Reynolds and Schuurman, 6-4, 6-0. Maria missed out on a triple, however, because of Hard, who, accompanied by Laver, took the mixed, 13-11, 3-6, 8-6, over Bueno and Aussie Bob Howe.

Hard came up with her second singles major after returning to the homeland, the U.S. Championship at Forest Hills, beating Bueno, 6-4, 10-12, 6-4. But, after sinking Donna Floyd, 6-1, 7-5, she and Bueno, a 6-3, 9-7, winner over Christine Truman, had to wait an idle week for the final. Reminiscent of two previous U.S. Championships felled by huge blows, this too was interrupted by a hurricane, one named Donna. The final was postponed as it had been for Don Budge and Gene Mako in 1938 when a no-name hurricane lashed the northeast. At the U.S. Doubles at Longwood—itself delayed by Hurricane Diane in 1955—Hard and Bueno completed Maria's doubles Grand Slam—the first for a woman—steamrolling Brits Deidre Catt and Haydon, 6-1, 6-1.

Britain won the Wightman Cup for the second time in three years, snatching a 4-3 victory at Wimbledon by winning the final two matches. Hard had given the U.S. a 3-2 lead with a 5-7, 6-2, 6-1 triumph over Ann Haydon, but Mortimer beat Janet Hopps, 6-8, 6-4, 6-1, and Christine Truman paired with Shirley Bloomer Brasher to beat Hopps and Dorothy Head Knode, 6-4, 9-7.

Nicola Pietrangeli defended his French singles title over Luis Ayala, runner-up for the second time in three years, 3-6, 6-3, 6-4, 4-6, 6-3. The third round was an Aussie disaster, Roy Emerson losing to Italian giant Orlando Sirola, 3-6, 7-5, 8-6, 7-5, and Laver to nifty Spaniard Manolo Santana, 6-1, 4-6, 6-4, 5-7, 6-3. Then mate Neale Fraser, collapsing with leg cramps at the end, was beaten by homeboy Robert Haillet, 6-4, 6-2, 8-10, 3-6, 6-5, default. Ayala was also second best in Rome, where Barry MacKay amazingly served and volleyed on the slow clay, winning the final by a most peculiar score: 7-5, 7-5, 0-6, 0-6, 6-1. MacKay had won the U.S. Indoor in New York on wood in February, 6-2, 2-6, 10-12, 6-1, 6-4, over Dick Savitt, so within four months he took titles on just about the fastest and slowest court surfaces in the world. Emerson and Fraser combined for the French doubles title, over Spaniards Andres Gimeno and Luis Arilla, 6-2, 8-10, 7-5, 6-4, the first of Emmo's six straight, with five partners.

Fraser took over as the No. 1 man in the amateur ranks by winning Wimbledon and the U.S. Championship. As with the women, no American man got to the semifinals at Wimbledon. MacKay was beaten in the quarterfinals by Pietrangeli, 16-14, 6-2, 3-6, 6-4, and Butch Buchholz, 19, led Fraser by 6-4, 3-6, 6-4, 15-15, in the same round and had five match points in the fourth set before being seized with cramps that left him unable to continue. Fraser, 26 and playing for the seventh time, was a sporting and popular champion. His left-handed serve had a wicked kick, and he was a daring and resourceful volleyer. He beat Laver, five years his junior, in the final, 6-4, 3-6, 9-7, 7-5.

A small measure of U.S. pride was saved when the unseeded team of Dennis Ralston, 17, and agile 21-year-old Mexican Rafael Osuna won the men's doubles, the second-youngest team to win Wimbledon. They beat Brits Humphrey Truman and Gerald Oakley in the first round, 6-3, 6-4, 9-11, 5-7, 16-14, and second-seeded Laver and Bob Mark, the Australian champions, 4-6, 10-8, 15-13, 4-6, 11-9, in the semifinals. After that pulsating contest, the final was comparatively easy: 7-5, 6-3, 10-8 over Welshman Mike Davies and Englishman Bobby Wilson.

Laver foreshadowed greatness to come by ripping up the U.S. Eastern grass court circuit, winning four consecutive titles: Pennsylvania Grass over New Yorker Ron Holmberg, 9-7, 8-6, 6-3; Southampton, N.Y. over Holmberg, 12-10, 6-3, 3-6, 2-6, 6-3; Orange, N.J., over Donald Dell, 6-1, 12-10, 6-4; Newport, R.I., over Buchholz, 6-1, 6-8, 6-1, 6-2. Laver and Mark got revenge on Ralston and Osuna in the semifinals of the U.S. Doubles at Longwood, 6-2, 8-6, 6-2, but lost the final to Fraser and Emerson, 9-7, 6-2, 6-4.

At Forest Hills, Laver got to the U.S. final by beating Buchholz, who had three match points before suffering a debilitating attack of cramps—as at Wimbledon—and losing, 4-6, 5-7, 6-4, 6-2, 7-5. Fraser beat the precocious Ralston, 11-9, 6-3, 6-2, and then, after sitting around through a week of Hurricane Donna's rain and wind, slogged to the title over Laver, 6-4, 6-4, 10-8. That closed down Laver's 29-match streak on the green.

For the first time since 1936, the United States failed to reach the Challenge Round of the Davis Cup, falling to Italy, 3-2 in the inter-zone semifinals at Perth, Australia, in December. Although the Yanks were heavy favorites on grass, and held a 2-0 first day lead (Buchholz over Sirola, 6-8, 7-5, 11-9, 6-2, and MacKay—quashing eight match points—over Pietrangeli, 8-6, 3-6, 8-10, 8-6, 13-11), the Italians startlingly took over the wild affair. They won the doubles over 19-year-old Chuck McKinley and Buchholz,

3-6, 10-8, 6-4, 13-11, caught up with Pietrangeli over Buchholz, 6-1, 6-2, 6-8, 3-6, 6-4. Sirola then flattened MacKay in the deciding big guys bash, 9-7, 6-3, 8-6.

Italy's first appearance in the Challenge Round a couple of weeks later was less auspicious, a 4-1 Aussie victory that was over in three matches as Fraser and Laver swept opening day in Sydney: Neale beat Orlando Sirola, 4-6, 6-3, 6-3, 6-3, and Rod went through Pietrangeli, 8-6, 6-4, 6-3. Fraser and Emerson mopped up the two Italians, 10-8, 5-7, 6-2, 6-4.

This time the Aussies suffered no defections to the pro tour immediately after the Davis Cup, but the Americans did. Mac-Kay and Buchholz, undoubtedly thinking that open tennis was near and wanting a piece of Jack Kramer's checkbook before it arrived, signed to make a tour in 1961 with Lew Hoad, Frank Sedgman, Tony Trabert, Ashley Cooper, Alex Olmedo and the Spaniard Andres Gimeno.

Meanwhile the 1960 tour, won by Pancho Gonzalez over Olmedo, Pancho Segura and Ken Rosewall, was not a financial success. Olmedo, the Wimbledon champ a year before, beat Trabert in the U.S. Pro final, 7-5, 6-4, at Cleveland.

1960 CHAMPIONS AND LEADERS

Australian Championships
Men's Singles Final: Rod Laver (AUS) def. Neale Fraser (AUS), 5-7, 3-6, 6-3, 8-6, 8-6

Women's Singles Final: Margaret Smith (AUS) def. Jan Lehane (AUS) 7-5, 6-2

Men's Doubles Final: Rod Laver and Bob Mark (AUS) def. Roy Emerson and Neale Fraser (AUS), 1-6, 6-2, 6-4, 6-4

Women's Doubles Final: Maria Bueno and Christine Truman (AUS) def. Margaret Smith and Lorraine Coghlan Robinson (AUS), 6-2, 5-7, 6-2

Mixed Doubles Final: Jan Lehane and Trevor Fancutt (AUS), def. Mary Carter Reitano and Bob Mark (AUS), 6-2, 7-5

French Championships
Men's Singles Final: Nicola Pietrangeli (ITA) def. Luis Ayala (CHI), 3-6, 6-3, 6-4, 4-6, 6-3

Women's Singles Final: Darlene Hard (USA) def. Yola Ramirez (MEX), 6-3, 6-4

Men's Doubles Final: Roy Emerson and Neale Fraser (AUS) def. Jose-Luis Arilla and Andres Gimeno (ESP), 6-2, 8-10, 7-5, 6-4

Women's Doubles Final: Maria Bueno (BRA) and Darlene Hard (USA) def. Pat Ward Hales and Ann Haydon (GBR), 6-2, 7-5

Mixed Doubles Final: Maria Bueno (BRA) and Bob Howe (AUS) def. Ann Haydon (GBR) and Roy Emerson (AUS), 1-6, 6-1, 6-2

Wimbledon
Men's Singles Final: Neale Fraser (AUS) def. Rod Laver (AUS), 6-4, 3-6, 9-7, 7-5

Women's Singles Final: Maria Bueno (BRA) def. Sandra Reynolds (RSA), 8-6, 6-0

Men's Doubles Final: Rafael Osuna (MEX) and Dennis Ralston (USA) def. Mike Davies and Bobby Wilson (GBR), 7-5, 6-3, 10-8

Women's Doubles Final: Maria Bueno (BRA) and Darlene Hard (USA) def. Sandra Reynolds and Renee Schuurman (RSA), 6-4, 6-0

Mixed Doubles Final: Darlene Hard (USA) and Rod Laver (USA) def. Maria Bueno (BRA) and Bob Howe (AUS), 13-11, 3-6, 8-6

U.S. Championships
Men's Singles Final: Neale Fraser (AUS) def. Rod Laver (AUS), 6-4, 6-4, 9-7

Women's Singles Final: Darlene Hard (USA) def. Maria Bueno (BRA), 6-4, 10-12, 6-4

Men's Doubles Final: Neale Fraser and Roy Emerson (USA) def. Rod Laver and Bob Mark (AUS), 9-7, 6-2, 6-4

Women's Doubles Final: Maria Bueno (BRA) and Darlene Hard (USA) def. Ann Haydon and Deidre Catt (GBR), 6-1, 6-1

Mixed Doubles Final: Margaret Osborne duPont (USA) and Neale Fraser (AUS) def. Maria Bueno and Antonio Palafox (MEX), 6-3, 6-2

Year-End No. 1
Men: Neale Fraser
Women: Maria Bueno

Davis Cup: Australia

Wightman Cup: Great Britain

1961 Mortimer Carries Flag For British Women

In 1961, the amateur tennis establishment was stunned and smarting from a wholesale raid on its ranks by pro promoter Jack Kramer, who in 1960 signed to contracts several middling players: Spaniard Andres Gimeno, Welshman Mike Davies, Frenchman Robert Haillet and Dane Kurt Nielsen, as well as the young No. 1 and No. 3 ranked Americans, Barry MacKay and Butch Buchholz. Kramer tried without success to lure into his fold Australian Neale Fraser, the Wimbledon and Forest Hills champion; Italian Nicola Pietrangeli, champion of France; and Chilean Luis Ayala, runner-up at the 1960 Italian and French Championships.

When a proposal for introducing "Open" tournaments was unexpectedly stymied by just five votes at the 1960 International Lawn Tennis Federation annual meeting, there was relatively lit-

Angela Mortimer beat Christine Truman in the all-British women's final at Wimbledon.

tle official grieving among the member national associations and their officials. However, Kramer's response of taking out his wallet and waving it in front of practically every player of moderate reputation—amateur powers-that-be thought Kramer both irresponsible and reprehensible—started alarm bells sounding. Suddenly the national associations saw their tournaments, and hence their revenues, in grave danger. Kramer became Public Enemy No. 1.

But if his motive was to force the ITF into "open" competition by his mass signings, as most suspected, he failed. Amateur

officials did not like being bullied. A new "Open" proposal was rejected at the 1961 ILTF annual meeting at Stockholm. Delegates approved a resolution agreeing "to the principle of an experiment of a limited number of open tournaments," but referred the matter to a committee for another year of study to see how the experiment might be conducted. A U.S.-sponsored "home rule" resolution, which would have permitted national associations to stage open tournaments at their own discretion, was defeated. The ILTF was able to stand up to Kramer because he had been able to sign only two of the previous year's top handful of players: world No. 3, MacKay, and No. 5, Buchholz. The amateurs still had Fraser, Rod Laver, Pietrangeli, Roy Emerson and Ayala. But the battle lines had been drawn. Instead of the uneasy coexistence of the past, the amateur associations and Kramer were now at war.

Emerson, a magnificently fit and affable fellow with slick black hair that shone like patent leather and a smile that sparkled with gold fillings, served and volleyed relentlessly to defeat his fellow Queenslander Laver in the Australian final, 1-6, 6-3, 7-5, 6-4. This was the first of six Australian titles in seven years for "Emmo," the first of a men's record (at the time) 12 major singles titles in all. Laver and Bob Mark annexed the doubles crown for the third straight year, over mates Emerson and Marty Mulligan, 6-3, 7-5, 3-6, 9-11, 6-2. On the women's side, "Mighty Margaret" Smith beat Jan Lehane again in the singles final, 6-1, 6-4, and teamed with Mary Carter Reitano for the first of Smith's eight Australian doubles titles, outplaying Mary Hawton and Lehane, 6-4, 3-6, 7-5.

In Paris, the two greatest European virtuosi of the '60s met in the final. English writer Rex Bellamy was there: "Nicola Pietrangeli, the favorite to win for the third consecutive year, was beaten by the young Manuel "Manolo" Santana, the first Spaniard to win a major title. The match lasted five sets. Santana and Pietrangeli were like artists at work in a studio exposed to a vast public in the heat of the afternoon. Each in turn played his finest tennis. The flame of Pietrangeli's inspiration eventually died, his brushstrokes overlaid by Santana's flickering finesse. But long before that, these two Latins had established a close rapport with a Latin crowd enjoying a rare blend of sport and aesthetics. At the end, there was a tumult of noise. Santana, his nerves strung up to the breaking point, dropped his racket and cried. And Pietrangeli, disappointed yet instantly responsive to the Spaniard's feelings, went around the net, took Santana in his arms, and patted him on the back like a father comforting a child." The score was 4-6, 6-1, 3-6, 6-0, 6-2, but bald numbers could hardly convey the emotion of this long afternoon, especially for the toothy Santana. He got to the final by upsetting Emerson, 9-7, 6-2, 6-2, and Laver, 3-6, 6-2, 4-6, 6-4, 6-0. Pietrangeli teased the home folks before beating Gerard Pilet, 6-4, 6-8, 6-3, 6-1, and took out Swede Jan-Erik Lundquist in a semifinal, 6-4, 6-4, 6-4, A vivid contrast in style to the gliding and caressing strokes of the singles finalists was provided by Laver and Emerson, who bore in on the net for murderous volleys in winning the doubles over countrymen Bob Howe and Bob Mark, 3-6, 6-1, 6-1, 6-4.

Left-hander Ann Haydon showed the legs, heart, and brain of a clay court stalwart in beating agile volleyer Yola Ramirez, 6-2, 6-1, for the French women's title. Top seed Maria Bueno was removed in the quarterfinals, 6-3, 6-3 by ex-champ Suzi Kor-

moczi, who then fell to Haydon, 3-6, 6-1, 6-3. South Africans Renee Schuurman and Sandra Reynolds won the doubles, a default from Bueno, who was ill, and Hard.

Bueno, who had beaten Australian Lesley Turner in the Italian final, 6-4, 6-4, was bedridden in Paris with hepatitis after her loss to Kormoczi. Lacking funds to pay for hospital care, she was confined to a tiny hotel chamber for a month, with the rest of the floor quarantined, until she was able to go home to Brazil.

Bueno was thus unable to defend her Wimbledon title. Darlene Hard, her doubles partner and the U.S. champ, also withdrew and generously stayed in Paris to care for her friend. Karen Hantze was the only American to reach the women's quarterfinals. This was the 75th-anniversary Wimbledon, and through the wreckage came No. 7 seed Angela Mortimer and No. 6 seed Christine Truman, opponents in the first all-British women's final since 1914. The crowd adored Truman, 20, a smiling six-footer with a big forehand and attacking game, epitomizing all the best British sporting traits, and they moaned when she fell awkwardly on a rain-slicked court in the third set of the final. That tumble cost her the momentum she had built up against the more defensive Mortimer, 29, who, on her 11th try, didn't hesitate to lob and dropshot in a 4-6, 6-4, 7-5 victory. It had been a long time coming—since the last English champ, Dorothy Round in 1937.

Historically Angela and Christine would be overshadowed by another finalist, bouncing, bubbly Billie Jean Moffitt, 17. She and Hantze, 18, won the doubles over Aussies Smith and Lehane, 6-3, 6-4. Unseeded, they were the youngest pair ever to seize a Wimbledon crown. But BJ would go on and on, eventually the Mother Freedom of tennis, and 18 years later, snared her 10th doubles title to become the Big W's big winner of titles: 20 (six singles, 10 doubles, four mixed). Incidentally, Lehane's two-handed backhand—seeming freaky then—was the first such instrument used by a woman in a major final.

Laver, the red-haired Queenslander called "The Rocket," won the men's title for the first time, over American Chuck McKinley, 6-3, 6-1, 6-4. This was the start of an unprecedented reign: Laver would win 31 singles matches without a defeat at Wimbledon in five appearances, going to the fourth round in 1970, winning four singles titles plus a BBC-sponsored pro tournament in 1967. In the semifinals, Laver ran over Indian Ramanathan Krishnan, 6-2, 8-6, 6-2, and McKinley tamed the heavy serving of a rare Brit in the last four, Mike Sangster, 6-4, 6-4, 8-6. Top-seeded Neale Fraser had lost his title in the round of 16, banished by Englishman Bobby Wilson, 1-6, 6-0, 13-11, 9-7. But Neale captured the doubles with Emerson, over fellow Aussies Fred Stolle and Bob Hewitt, 6-4, 6-8, 6-4, 6-8, 8-6, however then returning home to tend an ailing knee.

Great Britain had both Wimbledon singles finalists and the French champion on its team, but was startlingly ambushed, 6-1, in the Wightman Cup by a "mod squad" of eager American juniors. Hantze beat Haydon, 6-1, 6-4, and Truman, 7-9, 6-1, 6-1. Moffitt beat Haydon, 6-4, 6-4, and 18-year-old St. Louis lefty Justina Bricka shocked Mortimer, 10-8, 4-6, 6-3. Hantze-Moffitt clobbered Truman-Deidre Catt, 7-5, 6-2, and the U.S. won the final doubles when Mortimer defaulted with foot cramps. Truman's singles win over Moffitt, 6-3, 6-2, was the only one the shell-shocked English could salvage from the massacre on clay at Chicago's Saddle and Cycle Club.

Texan Bernard "Tut" Bartzen won his fourth U.S. Clay Court singles since 1954, beating Donald Dell, 6-1, 2-6, 6-2, 6-0. Dell, earlier in the year had gone with doubles partner Mike Franks on a State Department tour of South Africa, the Middle East and the Soviet Union, the first Americans to play in Russia since the 1917 Revolution.

McKinley and Dennis Ralston won the rain-delayed U.S. Doubles Championship over Mexicans Rafe Osuna and Antonio Palafox, 6-3, 6-4, 2-6, 13-11. Hard teamed with Lesley Turner for her fourth successive doubles title, this over the German-Mexican combine of Edda Buding and Yola Ramirez, 6-4, 5-7, 6-0, and was supposed to play with Ralston against Margaret Smith and Bob Mark in the mixed final, at Longwood. But rain postponed the match until Forest Hills, and Ralston was unable to play because he was unfairly suspended by the U.S. Lawn Tennis Association for his behavior earlier in a Davis Cup series against Mexico.

At Forest Hills, spacy, unorthodox Californian Whitney Reed—he never trained, partied all night, but had such a wonderful touch that he earned the No. 1 U.S. ranking—upset No. 2-seeded McKinley 6-3, 9-7, 3-6, 6-3 in the third round but fell to Osuna, 6-8, 6-3, 6-3, 6-2, in a beguiling battle of touch-shot practitioners. Emerson barely got by the catlike and clever Osuna, 6-3, 6-2, 3-6, 5-7, 9-7, in a rousing semifinal, but then overwhelmed top-seeded Laver in the final, 7-5, 6-3, 6-2, to lay claim to the No. 1 ranking among the amateurs.

Darlene Hard, the only American in the women's quarterfinal, battled past Ramirez, 6-3, 6-1, Smith, 6-4, 3-6, 6-3, and Haydon in the final, 6-3, 6-4, for her second straight U.S. title.

With MacKay and Buchholz professionals, U.S. Davis Cup Captain David Freed named a 14-man squad that accented youth. The U.S. beat British West Indies and Ecuador, both 5-0. Then they slipped past Mexico, 3-2, coming from 1-2 on Cleveland clay as McKinley beat Mario Llamas 6-4, 7-5, 10-8, and lefty Bartzen settled it over Osuna, 6-3, 6-3, 7-5. India, with clever Ramanathan Krishnan winning two singles, was difficult on New Delhi grass, 3-2, But McKinley beat Jaidip Mukerjea, 6-4, 6-4, 9-7, to start and Reed came through over Mukerjea in the clincher, 6-2, 6-2, 6-3, after Dell and McKinley won the doubles over the two Indians, 5-7, 6-0, 6-3, 6-2. However, Italy again was the barrier to the Challenge Round and Australia, defeating the U.S. 4-1, in the earthen trap, Rome's Il Foro Italico. The invaders started surprisingly well as rebounding Jack Douglas, a one time Stanford quarterback, sneaked past and wore out Fausto Gardini, 4-6, 4-6, 7-5, 10-8, 6-0. Reed grabbed the first two sets from Pietrangeli—but couldn't hold on, 2-6, 6-8, 6-4, 6-4, 6-4. But the Yanks had no more ammo. Pietrangeli and hulking Orlando Sirola took the doubles, 6-4, 3-6, 6-3, 6-2, and Pietrangeli bought the Australia tickets, 9-7, 6-3, 6-2, over Douglas.

Gardini refused to go to Australia for the Challenge Round unless he was assured of a singles berth. However, he wasn't, and Nicola Pietrangeli and Orlando Sirola couldn't get even one set on the grass at Melbourne until the decisive three matches had been played: Emerson over Pietrangeli, 8-6, 6-4, 6-0; Laver, over Sirola, 6-1, 6-4, 6-3; Emerson and Fraser over the pasta pair, 6-2, 6-3, 6-4, confirming the Aussie defense of the Cup. Final score, 5-0, a third straight Cup.

Kramer's expanded traveling circus—Pancho Gonzalez, Lew Hoad, Frank Sedgman, Ken Rosewall, Tony Trabert, Ashley Cooper, Alex Olmedo, Andres Gimeno, MacKay and Buchholz as principals, plus the others—did not make enough to cover his vastly increased overhead. Gonzalez beat Sedgman, 6-3, 7-5, in Cleveland for his record eighth and last U.S. Pro title, 6-3, 7-5, and Rosewall won Wembley over Hoad, 6-3, 3-6, 6-2, 6-3. However, the pros were in trouble, and Kramer's grandstanding of the previous autumn had not ultimately helped the cause of open competition.

1961 CHAMPIONS AND LEADERS

Australian Championships
Men's Singles Final: Roy Emerson (AUS) def. Rod Laver (AUS), 1-6, 6-3, 7-5, 6-4
Women's Singles Final: Margaret Smith (AUS) def. Jan Lehane (AUS), 6-1, 6-4
Men's Doubles Final: Rod Laver and Bob Mark (AUS) def. Roy Emerson and Marty Mulligan (AUS), 6-3, 7-5, 3-6, 9-11, 6-2
Women's Doubles Final: Mary Carter Reitano and Margaret Smith (AUS) def. Mary Bevis Hawton and Jan Lehane (AUS), 6-4, 3-6, 7-5
Mixed Doubles Final: Jan Lehane and Bob Hewitt (AUS) def. Mary Carter Reitano and John Pearce (AUS), 9-7, 6-2

French Championships
Men's Singles Final: Manolo Santana (ESP) def. Nicola Pietrangeli (ITA), 4-6, 6-1, 3-6, 6-0, 6-2
Women's Singles Final: Ann Haydon (GBR) def. Yola Ramirez (MEX), 6-2, 6-1
Men's Doubles Final: Roy Emerson and Rod Laver (AUS) def. Bob Howe and Bob Mark (AUS), 3-6, 6-1, 6-1, 6-4
Women's Doubles Final: Sandra Reynolds and Renee Schuurman (RSA) def. Maria Bueno (BRA) and Darlene Hard (USA), default
Mixed Doubles Final: Darlene Hard (USA) and Rod Laver (AUS) def. Vera Puzejova and Jiri Javorsky (CZE), 6-0, 2-6, 6-3

Wimbledon
Men's Singles Final: Rod Laver (AUS) def. Chuck McKinley (USA), 6-3, 6-1, 6-4
Women's Singles Final: Angela Mortimer (GBR) def. Christine Truman (GBR), 4-6, 6-4, 7-5
Men's Doubles Final: Roy Emerson and Neale Fraser (AUS) def. Bob Hewitt and Fred Stolle (AUS), 6-4, 6-8, 6-4, 6-8, 8-6
Women's Doubles Final: Karen Hantze and Billie Jean Moffitt (USA) def. Jan Lehane and Margaret Smith (AUS), 6-3, 6-4
Mixed Doubles Final: Lesley Turner and Fred Stolle (AUS) def. Edda Buding (GER) and Bob Howe (AUS), 11-9, 6-2

U.S. Championships
Men's Singles Final: Roy Emerson (AUS) def. Rod Laver (AUS), 7-5, 6-3, 6-2
Women's Singles Final: Darlene Hard (USA) def. Ann Haydon (GBR), 6-3, 6-4
Men's Doubles Final: Chuck McKinley and Dennis Ralston (USA) def. Rafael Osuna and Antonio Palafox (MEX), 6-3, 6-4, 2-6, 13-11
Women's Doubles Final: Darlene Hard (USA) and Lesley Turner (AUS) def. Edda Buding (GER) and Yola Ramirez (MEX), 6-4, 5-7, 6-0
Mixed Doubles Final: Margaret Smith and Bob Mark (AUS) def. Darlene Hard and Dennis Ralston (USA), default (Ralston suspension)

Year-End No. 1
Men: Rod Laver
Women: Angela Mortimer

Davis Cup: Australia

Wightman Cup: United States

1962

Laver Nets Slam, Maggie Falls Short

Davis Cup Challenge Round. In all, Laver won 22 of 27 tournaments and 167 of 182 singles matches during his long and incomparably successful year.

Smith (to become better known as Margaret Court after marriage to Barry Court) was staggered in the first round of Wimbledon by the pudgy chatterbox who would grow up to be her archrival, Billie Jean Moffitt (later Billie Jean King), but otherwise won just about everything in sight. Smith's only other loss was to another young American, Carole Caldwell, but "Mighty Maggie" won 13 of 15 tournaments, including the Australian, French and U.S., and 67 of 69 singles matches.

Laver, the "Rockhampton Rocket" from that Queensland town, started his Slam at White City Stadium in Sydney, beating Roy Emerson, 8-6, 0-6, 6-4, 6-4, not that he'd had an easy time making it that far. Laver was particularly harried by Geoff Pares in the third round before prevailing, 10-8, 18-16, 7-9, 7-5. Emerson and Neale Fraser took the doubles, 4-6, 4-6, 6-1, 6-4, 11-9, over mates Fred Stolle and Bob Hewitt.

Laver lived precariously at the French in Paris, the only leg of the Slam on slow clay, going the maximum sets down the stretch. He saved a match point in beating countryman Marty Mulligan in the quarterfinals, 6-4, 3-6, 2-6, 10-8, 6-2. He also went five with Fraser in the semifinals, 3-6, 6-3, 6-2, 3-6, 7-5, and with Emerson again in the final, 3-6, 2-6, 6-3, 9-7, 6-2. Emerson and Fraser racked up another doubles title, 6-3, 6-4, 7-5, over Germans Christian Kuhnke and Wilhelm Bungert.

At Wimbledon, Laver lost only one set to Manolo Santana in a 14-16, 9-7, 6-2, 6-2, quarterfinal victory. There were no Americans in the quarters for the first time since 1922, and hardly room for anyone but Australians—six of them—as Yank Frank

The Australian grip—both hands firmly around the throat of players of any other nationality—was in vogue in 1962, the season of Rod Laver's first Grand Slam and Margaret Smith's near-Slam.

Laver duplicated Don Budge's supreme feat of 1938, sweeping the singles titles of Australia, France, Great Britain (Wimbledon) and the United States. He also won the Italian and German titles, not to mention the less prestigious Norwegian, Irish and Swiss, and led Australia to a 5-0 blitz of upstart Mexico in the

Froehling fell to Santana, 12-10, 6-3, 8-10, 6-3, in the fourth round. The semis were an all-Aussie show: Laver, Mulligan, Neale Fraser and his brother John Fraser, a physician by profession, who got an uncommonly lucky draw. Laver beat Neale Fraser, 10-8, 6-1, 7-5, and trampled Mulligan in the final, 6-2, 6-2, 6-1. With Emerson sidelined by the painful toe, defaulting to Mulligan in the quarterfinals, Aussies Bob Hewitt and Fred Stolle won the doubles over two new faces, Yugoslavs Boro Jovanovic and Nikki Pilic, 6-2, 5-7, 6-2, 6-4.

At Forest Hills, Laver lost only one set again en route to the U.S. final—to gangly Froehling in a 6-3, 13-11, 4-6, 6-3 quarterfinal victory. The athletic Emerson was back, but Laver repelled him as he had in Sydney, Rome (6-2, 1-6, 3-6, 6-3, 6-1 in the Italian final) and Paris. Laver hit four fearsome backhand returns to break serve in the first game and dominated the first two sets with his varied backhand, either bashed or chipped, a topspin forehand, and ruthless serving and net play. Emerson, always barreling forward and battling, aroused a crowd of 9,000 by winning the third set, but Laver closed out the match and the Slam, 6-2, 6-4, 5-7, 6-4, and was greeted by original Slammer Budge afterward. They had the male precinct of the ultra-exclusive club to themselves, sharing with only Maureen Connolly.

Astonishingly, there were again no Aussies in the final of the U.S. Doubles Championships at Longwood, where the "Mexican Thumping Beans," collegians Rafe Osuna and Tony Palafox, out-hustled temperamental Americans Chuck McKinley and Dennis Ralston, reversing the previous year's final result, 6-4, 10-12, 1-6, 9-7, 6-3.

Osuna and Palafox had scored a victory of much greater import over Ralston-McKinley earlier in the year, in the pivotal match of Mexico's 3-2 upset of the U.S. in the Davis Cup. Palafox beat Jack Douglas in the rarefied atmosphere of Mexico City, 6-3, 6-1, 3-6, 7-5 after McKinley had disposed of Osuna, 6-2, 7-5, 6-3, in the opener. The doubles point provided the impetus, 8-6, 10-12, 3-6, 6-3, 6-2. The next day Osuna was carried off on the shoulders of jubilant countrymen when he out-nerved Douglas, 9-7, 6-3, 6-8, 3-6, 6-1, for the clinching 3-1 point. This was the first time Mexico had defeated the U.S. in 15 tries and won the American Zone. Osuna and Palafox lugged their adoring nation all the way to the Challenge Round – defeating Yugoslavia, 4-1, Sweden, 3-2 (Osuna taking the tingling fifth match in Mexico City over Jan-Erik Lundquist, 3-6, 6-4, 6-3, 1-6, 6-3) and India, 4-1 at Madras.

Osuna had gone 5-1 in singles, Palafox 3-2 and they were 4-0 in doubles, all on clay. However, the left-handers Laver and Fraser on the swift grass of Brisbane were too steep a proposition, 5-0: Laver slamming Osuna, 6-2, 6-1, 7-5, and Fraser taking Palafox, 7-9, 6-3, 6-4, 11-9. Queensland mates Emerson and Laver settled it over the game Mexicans, 7-5, 6-2, 6-4.

For the third straight year, Margaret Smith, 19, drubbed Jan Lehane, 20, in the final of the Australian, 6-0, 6-2, where Jan, with her then-rare double-handed backhand, removed second-seeded Darlene Hard 7-5, 6-4 in the quarterfinals.

But Margaret had a much closer French final against another countrywoman, Lesley Turner. In a meeting of two future Hall of Famers, Smith had shown she could play on clay too, winning the Italian title, defeating Maria Bueno 8-6, 5-7, 6-4 in the final. In Paris, Smith prevailed over Turner 6-3, 3-6, 7-5, rescuing a match point at 3-5 in the third.

By that time, she must have been entertaining thoughts of duplicating the Grand Slam, joining Connolly, who had emulated Budge in 1953. But 18-year-old Billie Jean Moffitt, who had a premonition weeks earlier that she would draw Smith in her opening match at Wimbledon, rudely wrecked the dream, 1-6, 6-3, 7-5. It was the first time that the top-seeded female failed to survive one round. (Steffi Graf would lose to Lori McNeil in 1994, Martina Hingis to Jelena Dokic in 1999, and to Virginia Ruano Pascal in 2001.) Her victory established "Little Miss Moffitt" as a force to be reckoned with on the Centre Court that already was her favorite stage.

It was eighth-seeded Karen Hantze Susman taking the singles at age 19 without losing a set, and never in trouble. An outstanding volleyer, Susman was nudged a little in the semifinal by Ann Jones, 8-6, 6-1, and captured the title with a 6-4, 6-4 victory over unseeded Vera Sukova of Czechoslovakia. A sturdy 31-year-old baseliner, Vera, who would later give birth to two world class players, Helena Sukova and Cyril Suk, had run rampant through a patch of seeds: sixth-seeded, defending champ Angela Mortimer, 1-6, 6-4, 6-3; second-seeded Hard, 6-3, 6-3; third-seeded Maria Bueno, 6-4, 6-3. Billie Jean's singles raves came to a halt in the quarters, 6-3, 6-1, to Jones, but repeated in the doubles with Susman, getting ahead in a 5-7, 6-3, 7-5, scrap with South Africans Sandra Reynolds Price and Renee Schuurman.

Smith was back in form at Forest Hills. With her enormous reach, athleticism, weight of shot and solid arsenal from the backcourt and net alike, she beat Hard in a nerve-wracking match, 9-7, 6-4 to become the first Australian woman to win the U.S. singles. She saved a set point in the 10th game of the first, and benefited from 16 double faults by Hard, who was perplexed by numerous close line calls and burst into prolonged tears in the sixth game of the second set. Smith had beaten third-seeded Bueno in a dandy semi, 6-8, 6-3, 6-4. But where were those teen-age darlings of Wimbledon—Moffitt and Susman? Both were early victims of one of the original grunters, 17-year-old Victoria Palmer of Phoenix. Palmer beat Billie Jean, who was injured, in the first round, 6-8, 5-0, default, and eliminated second-seeded Karen in the third round, 6-2, 3-6, 6-3. She lost a semifinal to Hard, 6-2, 6-3.

Hard beat Christine Truman, 6-2, 6-2, and Haydon, 6-3, 6-8, 6-4, as the U.S. edged Britain, 4-3 in the Wightman Cup at Wimbledon. Captain Margaret Osborne duPont, 44, teamed up with Margaret Varner to show that she could still win at doubles, 6-3, 2-6, 6-2, over Liz Starkie and Deidre Catt. Susman chipped in a 6-4, 7-5, win over Truman.

While the interest generated by Laver and Smith signaled a banner year for amateur tennis, the pros struggled. Pancho Gonzalez had retired for the time being, leaving Butch Buchholz to win the U.S. Pro title over Pancho Segura, 6-4, 6-3, 6-4, in Cleveland. Ken Rosewall won at Wembley defeating Lew Hoad 6-4, 5-7, 15-13, 7-5.

Jack Kramer had also given up the ghost as promoter. "We had all the best players, but the public didn't want to see them,"

he recalled. "There was no acceptance for our players. The conservative and powerful amateur officials were secure. Among other things, they had succeeded in making me the issue. If you were for pro tennis, you were in favor of handing over all of tennis to Jack Kramer. That was their argument." That is vastly oversimplified, of course. Kramer in many ways had only himself to blame for antagonism. But name-calling aside, the pro game was in sorry shape.

Rosewall was the top dog, but he had little flair for promotion, and the top amateurs no longer were tempted to turn pro and face an uncertain, anonymous future. Under-the-table payments afforded a comfortable if not lavish lifestyle for the top "amateurs." For the second time in the post-war era, there was no pro tour in the United States. Rosewall and Hoad were contemplating retirement. Their only chance at reviving interest, they thought, was to induce Laver to join them, and they pooled resources and personally guaranteed him $125,000 to come aboard for 1963. In the end, he decided he couldn't reject such a generous offer.

1962 CHAMPIONS AND LEADERS

Australian Championships
Men's Singles Final: Rod Laver (AUS) def. Roy Emerson (AUS), 8-6, 0-6, 6-4, 6-4

Women's Singles Final: Margaret Smith (AUS) def. Jan Lehane (AUS), 6-0, 6-2

Men's Doubles Final: Roy Emerson and Neale Fraser (AUS) def. Bob Hewitt and Fred Stolle (AUS), 4-6, 4-6, 6-1, 6-4,11-9

Women's Doubles Final: Margaret Smith and Robyn Ebbern (AUS) def. Darlene Hard (USA) and Mary Carter Reitano (AUS), 6-4, 6-4

Mixed Doubles Final: Lesley Turner and Fred Stolle (AUS) def. Darlene Hard (USA) and Roger Taylor (GBR), 6-3, 9-7

French Championships
Men's Singles Final: Rod Laver (AUS) def. Roy Emerson (AUS), 3-6, 2-6, 6-3, 9-7, 6-2

Women's Singles Final: Margaret Smith (AUS) def. Lesley Turner (AUS), 6-3, 3-6, 7-5

Men's Doubles Final: Roy Emerson and Neale Fraser (AUS) def. Wilhelm Bungert and Christian Kuhnke (GER), 6-3, 6-4, 7-5

Women's Doubles Final: Sandra Reynolds Price and Renee Schuurman (RSA) def. Justina Bricka (USA) and Margaret Smith (AUS), 6-4, 6-4

Mixed Doubles Final: Renee Schuurman (RSA) and Bob Howe (AUS) def. Lesley Turner and Fred Stolle (AUS), 3-6, 6-4, 6-4

Wimbledon
Men's Singles Final: Rod Laver (AUS) def. Marty Mulligan (AUS), 6-2, 6-2, 6-1

Women's Singles Final: Karen Hantze Susman (USA) def. Vera Sukova (CZE), 6-4, 6-4

Men's Doubles Final: Bob Hewitt and Fred Stolle (AUS) def. Boro Jovanovic and Nikki Pilic (YUG), 6-2, 5-7, 6-2, 6-4

Women's Doubles Final: Billie Jean Moffitt and Karen Hantze Susman (USA) def. Sandra Reynolds Price and Renee Schuurman (RSA), 5-7, 6-3, 7-5

Mixed Doubles Final: Margaret Osborne duPont (USA) and Neale Fraser (AUS) def. Ann Haydon (GBR) and Dennis Ralston (USA), 2-6, 6-3, 13-11

U.S. Championships
Men's Singles Final: Rod Laver (AUS) def. Roy Emerson (AUS), 6-2, 6-4, 5-7, 6-4

Women's Singles Final: Margaret Smith (AUS) def. Darlene Hard (USA), 9-7, 6-4

Men's Doubles Final: Rafael Osuna and Antonio Palafox (MEX) def. Chuck McKinley and Dennis Ralston (USA), 6-4, 10-12, 1-6, 9-7, 6-3

Women's Doubles Final: Darlene Hard (USA) and Maria Bueno (BRA) def. Karen Hantze Susman and Billie Jean Moffitt (USA), 4-6, 6-3, 6-2

Mixed Doubles Final: Margaret Smith and Fred Stolle (AUS) def. Lesley Turner and Frank Froehling, III, 7-5, 6-2

Year-End No. 1
Men: Rod Laver
Women: Margaret Smith

Davis Cup: Australia

Wightman Cup: United States

1963 Emmo Revs it Up, Fed Cup Born

With Rod Laver out of the amateur ranks, another Australian—the peerlessly fit and universally popular Roy Emerson of rural Blackbutt, Queensland—set his sights on the Grand Slam that Laver had achieved in 1962. Emerson won the first two legs, but was thwarted at Wimbledon as Australian supremacy waned. By the end of the year, Latin America had scored a unique double at Forest Hills, and the United States had both recovered the Davis Cup and captured the newly-minted Federation Cup, the women's equivalent.

Politically, it was not a progressive year. With Jack Kramer retired from promoting, amateur officials worldwide felt they had won a battle against some dark specter, and the movement for "Open" competition lagged. In the United States, which had supported the principles of "self-determination" and experimentation with open tournaments, the Old Guard reasserted itself, repudiating far-sighted U.S. Lawn Tennis Association President Ed Turville, a supporter of Open tennis. The USLTA instructed its delegates to the International Lawn Tennis Federation to oppose "opens" and "home rule."

Emerson, 26, romped to the Australian title over countryman Ken Fletcher, 6-3, 6-3, 6-1, losing only one set, to Bob Hewitt in the semifinals, 8-6, 6-4, 3-6, 9-7, while Hewitt and Fred Stolle took the doubles over Fletcher and young John Newcombe, 6-2, 3-6, 6-3, 3-6, 6-3. Margaret Smith systematically disposed of two-fisted backhander Jan Lehane, 6-2, 6-2, for the fourth straight year in the women's final. Margaret, losing no singles sets for the third straight year, tripled. She won the doubles with Robyn Ebbern, over Lehane and Lesley Turner, 6-1. 6-3. Moreover, she united with Fletcher for a 7-5, 5-7, 6-4, victory over Turner and Fred Stolle. She and Fletch were on their way to a mixed Grand Slam.

Emerson won the French over the first native to reach the men's final since Marcel Bernard's victory in 1946, the suave and sporting Pierre Darmon, who in the 1970s would return to Roland Garros as tournament director. The score was 3-6, 6-1, 6-4, 6-4. Darmon had ejected 1961 champ Manolo Santana, 6-3, 4-6, 2-6, 9-7, 6-2, to the rapturous cheers of Parisians in the semifinals, where Emmo extinguished the torrid serves of Brit Mike Sangster, 8-6, 6-3, 6-4. Emerson then teamed up with Santana for the doubles title, 6-2, 6-4, 6-4, over South Africans Gordon Forbes,

who would write one of the best tennis books, *A Handful of Summers*, and a star of that book, Abe Segal.

Leading seed Smith's designs on a singles Slam were scrambled in the quarters 6-3, 8-6, by the steadiness of Czech Vera Sukova, the unseeded Wimbledon finalist of 1962, who was more at home on Parisian clay, and then lost to Ann Haydon Jones, 6-0, 6-1. The title did remain in Australian hands, however, Turner beating Jones 2-6, 6-3, 7-5 in the final. Jones teamed with Renee Schuurman for the doubles trophy, a 7-5, 6-4 decision over Smith and another Aussie, Robyn Ebbern. Smith and Fletcher did shake a leg for Leg No. 2 in pursuit of a mixed Grand Slam, 6-1, 6-2, over Turner and Stolle.

Wimbledon, which had seen five all-Australian men's singles finals in seven years, got its first U.S. male champion since Tony Trabert in 1955: 22-year-old sparkplug Chuck McKinley, a Missourian attending Trinity University in San Antonio, Texas. He was also the first since Trabert to win the title without losing a set, but it was a peculiar year. No seeded men collided.

Emerson, the favorite, ran into Germany's Wilhelm Bungert on a hot day and was beaten in the quarters, 8-6, 3-6, 6-3, 4-6, 6-3. McKinley, a small but athletic man who charged the net like a toy top gone wild, was too sure in his volleying for Bungert, 6-2, 6-4, 8-6, in the semifinals and Fred Stolle in the final, 9-7, 6-1, 6-4. The unseeded Stolle took care of second-seeded Santana in the semis, 8-6, 6-1, 7-5, en route to the first of his three straight futile sojourns into the Wimbledon final. Mexican Cuppers Rafe Osuna and Antonio Palafox became singular as doublists, the lone Latin American team ever to win, beating the French Jean-Claude Barclay and Darmon, 4-6, 6-2, 6-2, 6-2.

Margaret Smith, who had already won four Australian, two Italian, a French and a U.S. titles, became the first Australian woman to carry Wimbledon. In the final, she avenged her first round defeat by Billie Jean Moffitt the previous year, beating the unseeded Californian, 6-3, 6-4, for the title. Billie Jean clipped the wings of the graceful "Sao Paulo Swallow," Maria Bueno, in the quarters, 6-2, 7-5. Smith never strained, losing but one set, to Rene Schuurman in the quarters, 3-6, 6-0, 6-1. In the semifinal, Margaret bounced Darlene Hard, 6-3, 6-3, and BJ dampened local hopes, 6-4, 6-4, over Jones. The title was not decided until the start of the third week because of rain, and thus Smith did not get to dance the traditional champions' first foxtrot with McKinley at the Wimbledon Ball. He was perhaps relieved, since he was four inches shorter than Smith. Instead, he guided his wife around the hardwood floor. But Margaret and Ken Fletcher had rhythm, too, winning Leg No. 3 of their mixed Grand Slam, 11-9, 6-4, over Hard and Hewitt.

Established as a world championship team event for women comparable to the Davis Cup, the Federation Cup—two singles and a doubles, all at one site—was inaugurated at Queen's Club in London to celebrate the 50th anniversary of the International Lawn Tennis Federation, attracting 16 entries. The U.S. blanked the Netherlands, Italy, and Great Britain 3-0, then upset Australia, 2-1 for the Cup. Smith flattened Hard, 6-3, 6-0, in the opening match, but Billie Jean countered against Turner, 5-7, 6-0, 6-3, and allied with Darlene to take the excruciating doubles from Smith and Turner, 3-6, 13-11, 6-3. Inclement weather drove the final indoors onto swift boards.

The U.S. also beat Britain, 6-1, in the Wightman Cup on clay at the Cleveland Skating Club. Ann Jones beat Hard in the opening match, 6-1, 0-6, 8-6, but Moffitt outlasted Truman, 6-4, 19-17 (the second set a female record for length), to turn things around for teammates Hard, who beat Truman, 6-3, 6-0, and Nancy Richey, 14-12, 6-3, winner over Deidre Catt. Billie Jean also beat Jones, 6-4, 4-6, 6-3.

Richey won the first of her six consecutive U.S. Clay Court titles, 6-1, 6-1, over Victoria Palmer, and McKinley showed he could be a dirt-kicking dandy, too, stopping his partner and Davis Cup teammate, Dennis Ralston, 6-2, 6-2, 6-4 in the men's final.

For the first time, no American woman made it to the semifinals at Forest Hills. Hard, a finalist the previous three years and champion twice, was beaten by Jones in the quarters, 6-4, 6-3, where Richey was bumped out by the champ-to-be, Bueno, 6-3, 6-2. Billie Jean got off in the fourth round, pushed by 5-footer Catt, 2-6, 8-6, 7-5. Even more curious, Australia was shut out of the men's after having had both finalists in six of the previous seven years.

This was a south-of-the-border year, Mexican Rafael Osuna taking the men's singles, and Brazilian Maria Bueno recapturing the women's title she had won in 1959 with a breathtaking display of shot-making in beating Jones, 1-6, 6-2, 9-7, then Smith for the trophy, 7-5, 6-4.

Osuna, a gallery favorite because of his quickness of hand, foot, and smile, ousted Wimbledon champ McKinley in the semis, 6-4, 6-4, 10-8, and unseeded Floridian Frank Froehling III in the final, 7-5, 6-4, 6-2. Froehling, a spare spire of 6-foot-3-1/2 called "Spider-Man," had served devastatingly to upset Emerson, 6-4, 4-6, 9-7, 6-2 in the round of 16, creep past Bobby Wilson in the quarters in five 6-8, 4-6, 6-3, 6-3, 9-7, and bar another Brazilian, Ronnie Barnes, from the final, 6-3, 6-1, 6-4 in the semifinals. But Osuna cleverly neutralized Froehling's power with wonderfully conceived and executed tactics, especially lobbed service returns from 10 to 12 feet behind the baseline. Occasionally Osuna would stand in and take Froehling's serve on the rise, chipping the backhand, but more often he lobbed returns to disrupt Froehling's serve-volley rhythm and break down his suspect overhead. In fact, nimble Osuna climbed the wall of the stadium to retrieve smashes and float back perfect lobs, frustrating Froehling with his speed around the court, touch and tactical variations.

Bueno was also brilliant, especially in the second set of her victory over Smith. "With the score 1-4 and 0-30 against her, Maria set the gallery wild with the dazzling strokes that stemmed from her racket," wrote Allison Danzig in *The New York Times*. "Her service was never so strong. Her volleys and overhead smashes were the last word, and she hit blazing winners from the backhand and threw up lobs in an overwhelming assault." One more mixed doubles title for Smith and Fletcher was enough for them to fill in the last blank for a Grand Slam, 3-6, 8-6, 6-2, over Aussie Judy Tegart and lefty American Eddie Rubinoff.

At Longwood, Hard was not able to snag a sixth straight doubles title, as she and Bueno fell in the final to Smith and Robyn Ebbern, 4-6, 10-8, 6-3. McKinley and Ralston met Osuna and Palafox for the third straight year in the men's final, Chuck saving two

match points on his serve in recapturing the title, 9-7, 4-6, 5-7, 6-3, 11-9, before a record crowd of 7,000.

That was immediately after they combined to beat Osuna and Palafox, 4-1, in a Davis Cup series at Los Angeles, atoning for the 1962 defeat at Mexico City. Captained by Bob Kelleher and coached by Pancho Gonzalez, the Americans also conquered Iran, Venezuela, Britain and India—all 5-0—to return to the Challenge Round for the first time in three years, and lift the Cup from Australia at Adelaide, 3-2 on McKinley's dramatic fifth match victory over 19-year-old rookie John Newcombe in sets. It had been a long, arduous campaign, mainly on the road, taxing competitively and medically. Ralston nearly lost an eye in an accident in England, McKinley had dysentery in India, Froehling needed his abscessed backside lanced, and McKinley had back spasms.

But the squad persevered and took the Cup back from Australia, which had held it in a Melbourne bank vault 11 of the last 13 years. Only Mexico and Venezuela, at Denver, were home series. Ralston took over after McKinley lost the opener to Osuna, 6-2, 3-6, 6-2, 2-6, 6-3, beating Palafox, 6-1, 6-4, 3-6, 6-3, and providing a steady hand in helping overturn the Wimbledon champs, 6-1, 6-3, 8-6, for a 2-1 lead. Facing Osuna, his pal and Southern Cal teammate, the man with whom he had won Wimbledon three years before, Ralston was incisive and relentless, clinching, 6-1, 6-3, 7-5.

Venezuela gets a footnote only because that series unveiled 20-year-old Arthur Ashe on the superfluous third day, the first black man to represent the U.S. It was a quickie, 6-1, 6-1, 6-0, over Orlando Bracamonte. Arthur would be an important cog in the Cups won in 1968-69-70 and 1978.

Five years had passed since the last U.S. Cup heist on Australian grass, Ralston squandered three match points on serve, but pulled himself together to win the jittery opener over 19-year-old Cup novitiate Newcombe, 6-4, 6-1, 3-6, 4-6, 7-5. McKinley couldn't hold off Emerson, 6-3, 3-6, 7-5, 7-5, but the Americans had a 2-1 lead after a 6-3, 3-6, 11-9, 11-9 defeat of Emerson and Neale Fraser, 30 and bowing out. Emerson flattened Ralston to tie it again, 6-2, 6-3, 3-6, 6-2. With a sellout crowd of 7,500 at Memorial Drive roaring behind him, power-serving Newcombe built a 4-2, 30-0 third-set lead. But the iron-willed teddy bear, McKinley—"this is where I want to be, everything riding on one match"—retaliated with backhand passers and quickness to clinch the Cup, 10-12, 6-2, 9-7, 6-2.

In the pro ranks, Laver was beaten regularly by both Ken Rosewall and Lew Hoad, who had jointly staked him to a $125,000 bankroll in hopes of keeping the fading pro game alive. They succeeded, but barely. Rosewall was supreme, seizing the two biggest tourneys. He beat Lew Hoad at Wembley, 6-4, 6-2, 4-6, 6-3, and Laver in the final of the U.S. Pro Championships Forest Hills, 6-4, 6-2, 6-2. All Kenny and Rod got in New York was a warm handshake. The promoter copped a plea of bankruptcy, no prize money. That was the sad state of the pros.

1963 CHAMPIONS AND LEADERS

Australian Championships

Men's Singles Final: Roy Emerson (AUS) def. Ken Fletcher (AUS), 6-3, 6-3, 6-1

Women's Singles Final: Margaret Smith (AUS) def. Jan Lehane (AUS), 6-2, 6-2

Men's Doubles Final: Bob Hewitt and Fred Stolle (AUS) def. Ken Fletcher and John Newcombe (AUS), 6-2, 3-6, 6-3, 3-6, 6-3

Women's Doubles Final: Margaret Smith and Robyn Ebbern (AUS) def. Jan Lehane and Lesley Turner (AUS), 6-1, 6-3

Mixed Doubles Final: Margaret Smith and Ken Fletcher (AUS) def. Lesley Turner and Fred Stolle (AUS), 7-5, 5-7, 6-4

French Championships

Men's Singles Final: Roy Emerson (AUS) def. Pierre Darmon (FRA), 3-6, 6-1, 6-4, 6-4

Women's Singles Final: Lesley Turner (AUS) def. Ann Haydon Jones (GBR), 2-6, 6-3, 7-5

Men's Doubles Final: Roy Emerson (AUS) and Manolo Santana (ESP) def. Gordon Forbes and Abe Segal (RSA), 6-2, 6-4, 6-4

Women's Doubles Final: Ann Haydon Jones (GBR) and Renee Schuurman (RSA), def. Robyn Ebbern and Margaret Smith (AUS), 7-5, 6-4

Mixed Doubles Final: Margaret Smith and Ken Fletcher (AUS) def. Lesley Turner and Fred Stolle (AUS), 6-1, 6-2

Wimbledon

Men's Singles Final: Chuck McKinley (USA) def. Fred Stolle (AUS), 9-7, 6-1, 6-4

Women's Singles Final: Margaret Smith (AUS) def. Billie Jean Moffitt (USA), 6-3, 6-4

Men's Doubles Final: Rafael Osuna and Antonio Palafox (MEX) def. Jean Claude Barclay and Pierre Darmon (FRA), 4-6, 6-2, 6-2, 6-2

Women's Doubles Final: Maria Bueno (BRA) and Darlene Hard (USA) def. Robyn Ebbern and Margaret Smith (AUS), 8-6, 9-7

Mixed Doubles Final: Margaret Smith and Ken Fletcher (AUS) def. Darlene Hard (USA) and Bob Hewitt (AUS), 11-9, 6-4

U.S. Championships

Men's Singles Final: Rafael Osuna (MEX) def. Frank Froehling, III (USA), 7-5, 6-4, 6-2

Women's Singles Final: Maria Bueno (BRA) def. Margaret Smith (AUS), 7-5, 6-4

Men's Doubles Final: Chuck McKinley and Dennis Ralston (USA) def. Rafael Osuna and Antonio Palafox (MEX), 9-7, 4-6, 5-7, 6-3, 11-9

Women's Doubles Final: Robyn Ebbern and Margaret Smith (AUS) def. Darlene Hard (USA) and Maria Bueno (BRA), 4-6, 10-8, 6-3

Mixed Doubles Final: Margaret Smith and Ken Fletcher (AUS) def. Judy Tegart (AUS) and Ed Rubinoff (USA), 3-6, 8-6, 6-2

Year-End No. 1

Men: Rafael Osuna
Women: Margaret Smith

Davis Cup: United States

Federation Cup: United States

Wightman Cup: United States

1964 Emmo Beats Stolle In Three Major Finals

As if any additional evidence were necessary to prove the depth of tennis talent in Australia, the Davis Cup went back Down Under for the 11th time in 14 years even though three members of the Aussies squad fled to other countries because of an altercation with the autocratic Lawn Tennis Association of Australia.

Roy Emerson, Fred Stolle, Marty Mulligan, Bob Hewitt and Ken Fletcher were all suspended by the LTAA for the grievous

Roy Emerson (right) with **Fred Stolle** after Emerson beat his fellow Aussie in the men's singles final at Wimbledon.

offense of leaving for the overseas tournament circuit earlier than permitted. Emerson and Stolle were reinstated after reaching the final at Wimbledon—in time, of course, to go about their Davis Cup duties for the homeland.

Emerson beat Stolle in the singles final of three majors— the Australian, Wimbledon and U.S. Championships—but had his notions of a Slam punctured by Nicola Pietrangeli in the French quarterfinals. "Emmo" and Fred were the core of the raiding party that took the Cup back from the U.S. in Cleveland, the first time a Challenge Round in the United States was played beyond the New York-Philadelphia-Boston triangle, and not on grass. The battleground was clay.

The other three continued to have problems. Mulligan moved to Italy, where he married, became a successful businessman, and played in Davis Cup competition in 1968, nicknamed "Martino Mulligano" by disapproving Italian journalists. (He had been on the Australian squad but never played, so he was eligible to compete).

Hewitt married a Johannesburg model and became a mainstay of the South African Davis Cup team, continuing to develop into one of the world's best doubles players. Fletcher took up residence in Hong Kong. It is a measure of the strength of Aussie Captain Harry Hopman's production line that Australia won the Cup four years in a row, never missing this trio of talented players.

The affable Emerson—strong enough to quaff beer and sing choruses of "Waltzing Matilda" into the wee hours of the morning, then get up early to train and play magnificently athletic tennis—ruled the amateur world in 1964. He won 55 straight singles matches in one stretch, finishing the year with 19 tournament championships and a 122-6 record, including two singles victories in the Davis Cup Challenge Round. Emmo won three-quarters of a Slam, derailed only at the French by Pietrangeli, 6-1, 6-3, 6-3. But Nicola fell short of his third title, denied by Manolo Santana, winning his second title by a 6-3, 6-1, 4-6, 7-5 margin.

Emerson thumped Stolle in all three finals—the Australian, 6-3, 6-4, 6-2, Wimbledon, 6-4, 12-10, 4-6, 6-3, and the U.S., 6-4, 6-1, 6-4. Emmo also took the French doubles, practically an annual acquisition (his fifth straight), this with Fletcher, 7-5, 6-3, 3-6, 7-5. Hewitt and Stolle took the Australian, 6-4, 7-5, 3-6, 14-12, and Wimbledon doubles, 7-5, 11-9, 6-4, while Chuck McKinley and Dennis Ralston captured the U.S. title at Longwood for the third time in four years, 6-3, 6-2, 6-4 over Brits Graham Stilwell and Mike Sangster the first three-timers since Bill Talbert and Gardnar Mulloy (1942, 45-46 and 1948).

A preview of America's Davis Cup fate was offered in the most dramatic match of the U.S. Championships, a quarterfinal in which Ralston fought back from two sets down against Stolle, saved a match point at 3-5 in the fifth, and hauled himself back to 7-7 before the gripping encounter was halted by darkness. Ralston had two break points at 15-40 as Stolle served the first game of the resumption the next morning, but the lean Aussie, with the pained gait and delightful wit, held and broke Ralston from 40-15 in the next game for the match, 6-2, 6-3, 4-6, 3-6, 9-7.

It was the 25-year-old Stolle's 7-5, 6-3, 3-6, 9-11, 6-4, triumph over Ralston on a clay court at newly built and jam-packed (7,000 a day, at top dollar) Harold T. Clark Stadium in Cleveland that broke America's back in the Challenge Round. As they had only nine months before, the Americans held a 2-1 lead on Chuck and Denny's squeaky win over Roy and Fred, 6-4, 4-6,

4-6, 6-3, 6-4. (The first day split was achieved by McKinley over Stolle, 6-1, 9-7, 4-6, 6-2, and Emerson retaliating over Ralston, 6-3, 6-4, 6-2.) On a gray September Sunday, after a long rain delay, they played a majestic match for a national television audience. Ralston saved a match point, serving at 4-5 in the fifth, but Stolle blasted a forehand crosscourt passing shot by him on the next. Emerson wrapped up a 3-2 Australian victory the next afternoon, running like a greyhound and whacking piercing ground strokes and volleys to sear McKinley, 3-6, 6-2, 6-4, 6-4, sending the Davis Cup back to Melbourne.

The French, Italian and German titles, the three biggest on continental clay, all went to Europeans: Manolo Santana beat Nicola Pietrangeli, 6-3, 6-1, 4-6, 7-5, in a rematch of their more memorable meeting in the Parisian final three years earlier; Swede Jan-Erik Lundquist won in Rome over Stolle, 1-6, 7-5, 6-3, 6-1; Wilhelm Bungert took his national ride in Hamburg, defeating left-handed compatriot Christian Kuhnke, 0-6, 6-4, 7-5, 6-2.

Among the worldly women of tennis, Margaret Smith had an awesome record, losing only two matches during the year, but those were at Wimbledon and Forest Hills, where Maria Bueno won both titles, and thus took back the No. 1 world ranking that illness and Smith had stripped from her. Smith beat countrywoman Lesley Turner 6-3, 6-2, in the Australian final, a fifth straight title, having beaten up on her usual finalist foil, Jan Lehane, a fifth straight time, though this time in the semis, 6-4, 6-2.

Margaret was 2-1 against Bueno, beating the Brazilian, 5-7, 6-1, 6-2, for the French title. However, Maria's one win over Margaret was the most important—the final at Wimbledon, 6-4, 7-9, 6-3. This was a match of almost unbearable tension, a patchwork of glorious shots and awful ones, and Bueno ultimately controlled her nerves better. Smith seemed more serene beforehand, but her anxiety showed in her usually oppressive serve. She was a little cautious, and double-faulted badly on several key points. "I guess I beat myself. I felt pressure all the way," she said afterward. "It was like beating my head against a wall."

Karen Hantze Susman, the 1962 Wimbledon champion who was back for a fling after temporary retirement for childbirth, troubled Smith in the third round at Wimbledon, 11-9, 6-0, and beat her in the fourth round at Forest Hills, 4-6, 6-4, 6-4. That paved the way for Bueno, who raced through the championship without losing a set. In the final, she met surprising ninth-seeded Carole Caldwell Graebner, who had resolutely upset Susman, 6-4, 6-8, 6-3, and, Nancy Richey, 2-6, 9-7, 6-4 (Richey was the quarterfinal bouncer of Billie Jean Moffitt, 6-4, 6-4.) Carole did all this despite suffering from painful second-degree sunburns of the arms, face and hands. In the final it was not the sun's rays but Bueno who blistered her for the title, 6-1, 6-0, in just 25 minutes. Poor Carole thus shared the bleak tourney record for championship futility (winning one game) as suffered by Laura Knight (6-1, 6-0 to Ellen Hansell, 1887); Maud Barger-Wallach (6-0, 6-1 to Hazel Hotchkiss, 1909); Louise Hammond Raymond (6-0, 6-1, to Molla Bjurstedt, 1916).

Bueno thus usurped Smith's room at the top, even though her record of 82-10 and seven titles was not quite as formidable as Smith's 67-2 and 13 championships. Smith had a 39-match winning streak at one stage.

Lesley Turner blended with Judy Tegart Dalton to win the Australian doubles, 6-4, 6-4, over Robyn Ebbern and Smith and with Smith to win the French, 6-3, 6-1, over the Argentine-German combine of Norma Baylon and Helga Schultze and Wimbledon, 7-5, 6-2 over Billie Jean Moffitt and Karen Hantze Susman. But Lesley's bid for a Grand Slam, in a last shot alongside Smith, was denied in the final of the U.S. by Susman and Moffitt, 3-6, 6-2, 6-4.

With Darlene Hard, the U.S. No. 1 of the past four years, retired to a teaching pro career, the U.S. relinquished the Federation Cup to Australia, 2-1, in the final of a 24-nation assemblage in Philadelphia. Smith beat Moffitt, 6-2, 6-3, and Turner did in No. 1 American Nancy Richey, 7-5, 6-1.

In a 5-2 Wightman Cup triumph for the U.S. at London, Richey and Moffitt won both their singles; Nancy over Deidre Catt, 4-6, 6-4, 7-5, and Ann Haydon Jones, 7-5, 11-9; Billie Jean over Catt, 6-3, 4-6, 6-3, and Jones, 4-6, 6-2, 6-3. Graebner added a victory over Liz Starkie, 6-4, 1-6, 6-3.

Most of the male pros were scattered around the globe, playing the odd exhibition here and there, badly disorganized. Ken Rosewall, the pro king, was observed playing Pancho Segura in a shopping-center parking lot exhibition in Los Angeles.

One who thought this wrong was Ed Hickey of the New England Merchants National Bank in Boston, who convinced his boss to put up $10,000 in sponsorship money to revive the U.S. Pro Championships, gone bust at Forest Hills in 1963. John Bottomley, president of the Longwood Cricket Club, threw his support to the project. Jack Kramer was enlisted to contact the far-flung gypsies and put together, with the help of Butch Buchholz, a short summer tournament circuit with about $80,000 in total prize money.

A dozen pros were assembled and Rod Laver won the climactic event at Longwood over Pancho Gonzalez, 4-6, 6-3, 7-5, 6-4, in a rainstorm, a nor'easter that turned the lawn into a quagmire, but didn't diminish their skills. "The show must go on" was the battle cry of those humble pros, who demonstrated ably. "We have to play," reasoned Laver, soon headed to the airport, "because we're scheduled in Scotland tomorrow night."

It was a humble renaissance with a $2,200 first prize— "seemed like a million then," said a grateful Laver—but the 37-year-old U.S. Pro, the longest running pro tourney, somehow stayed in business and was to become a fixture at Longwood, as was Laver. He won there four more times. It may not have been strawberries-and-cream a la Wimbledon, but it was spinach green cash, and the pros were on the rocky road to a comeback.

1964 CHAMPIONS AND LEADERS

Australian Championships
Men's Singles Final: Roy Emerson (AUS) def. Fred Stolle (AUS), 6-3, 6-4, 6-2

Women's Singles Final: Margaret Smith (AUS) def. Lesley Turner (AUS), 6-3, 6-2

Men's Doubles Final: Bob Hewitt and Fred Stolle (AUS) def. Roy Emerson and Ken Fletcher (AUS), 6-4, 7-5, 3-6, 4-6, 14-12

Women's Doubles Final: Judy Tegart Dalton and Lesley Turner (AUS) def Robyn Ebbern and Margaret Smith (AUS), 6-4, 6-4

Mixed Doubles Final: Margaret Smith and Ken Fletcher (AUS) def. Jan Lehane (AUS) and Mike Sangster (GBR), 6-3, 6-2

French Championships
Men's Singles Final: Manolo Santana (ESP) def. Nicola Pietrangeli (ITA), 6-3, 6-1, 4-6, 7-5

Women's Singles Final: Margaret Smith (AUS) def. Maria Bueno (BRA), 5-7, 6-1, 6-2

Men's Doubles Final: Roy Emerson and Ken Fletcher (AUS) def. John Newcombe and Tony Roche (AUS), 7-5, 6-3, 3-6, 7-5

Women's Doubles Final: Margaret Smith and Lesley Turner (AUS) def. Norma Baylon (ARG) and Helga Schultze (GER), 6-3, 6-1

Mixed Doubles Final: Margaret Smith and Ken Fletcher (AUS) def. Lesley Turner and Fred Stolle (AUS), 6-3, 4-6, 8-6

Wimbledon
Men's Singles Final: Roy Emerson (AUS) def. Fred Stolle (AUS), 6-4, 12-10, 4-6, 6-3

Women's Singles Final: Maria Bueno (BRA) def. Margaret Smith (AUS), 6-4, 7-9 6-3

Men's Doubles Final: Bob Hewitt and Fred Stolle (AUS) def. Roy Emerson and Ken Fletcher (AUS), 7-5, 11-9, 6-4

Women's Doubles Final: Margaret Smith and Lesley Turner (AUS) def. Billie Jean Moffitt and Karen Hantze Susman (USA), 7-5, 6-2

Mixed Doubles Final: Lesley Turner and Fred Stolle (AUS) def. Margaret Smith and Ken Fletcher (AUS), 6-4, 6-4

U.S. Championships
Men's Singles Final: Roy Emerson (AUS) def. Fred Stolle (AUS), 6-4, 6-2, 6-4

Women's Singles Final: Maria Bueno (BRA) def. Carole Caldwell (USA), 6-1, 6-0

Men's Doubles Final: Chuck McKinley and Dennis Ralston (USA) def. Graham Stilwell and Mike Sangster (GBR) 6-3, 6-2, 6-4

Women's Doubles Final: Billie Jean Moffitt and Karen Hantze Susman (USA) def. Margaret Smith and Lesley Turner (AUS), 3-6, 6-2, 6-4

Mixed Doubles Final: Margaret Smith and John Newcombe (AUS) def. Judy Tegart Dalton (AUS) and Ed Rubinoff (USA), 10-8, 4-6, 6-3

Year-End No. 1
Men: Roy Emerson
Women: Margaret Smith

Davis Cup: Australia

Federation Cup: Australia

Wightman Cup: United States

Santana Wins Forest Hills But Aussies Rule Elsewhere

Manuel Santana became the first Spaniard to win the U.S. Championships and helped Spain reach the Davis Cup Challenge Round.

The gloom of a drizzly, gray September afternoon in Forest Hills was pierced by Spanish singing and dancing, and the unmistakable click of castanets filled the old concrete stadium of the West Side Tennis Club. Loud choruses of "Ole" and "Bravo, Manolo!" bounced off the clouds. The discreet charm of the bourgeoisie that so long characterized tennis audiences gave way to unabashed Latin celebration as Manolo Santana beat South African Cliff Drysdale in four absorbing sets, 6-2, 7-9, 7-5, 6-1, to become the first Spaniard to win the U.S. singles title. The balletic and crowd-pleasing Santana, age 27, provided other occasions for rejoicing in 1965, but few places came alive as Forest Hills did

when a troupe of entertainers from the Spanish Pavilion at the nearby World's Fair arrived to urge him on with an up-tempo Latin beat. Santana was arguably the No. 1 amateur in the world, winning 10 of 16 tournaments, compiling a 71-7 record, and a 25-match winning streak, longest of the season. He did not enter Wimbledon, devoting his summer instead to Davis Cup preparation and duty on clay.

Such diligence paid off. Ringleader Santana (singles wins over Frank Froehling, Denny Ralston) & Co. lit up the Barcelona sky by bumping off the U.S. 4-1. His gang was on its way to the Challenge Round at Sydney. An unknown to the Americans, awkward-looking Juan Gisbert, stayed steady from 1-4 in the second set to paralyze Ralston, 3-6, 8-6, 6-1, 6-3, at the outset. A momentous resurgence in the doubles by Santana and Luis Arilla over Ralston and Clark Graebner settled the outcome, 4-6, 3-6, 6-3, 6-4, 11-9, even though Ralston came within two points, serving for it at 5-3, deuce. A break of Graebner in the 19th game, and Arilla's hold set off a bullring-style fiesta, pillows flying from the overjoyed crowd of 5,000, littering the court where the two Spaniards were carried round and round triumphantly by strong-shouldered aficionados.

Not that Spanish music replaced "Waltzing Matilda" as the anthem of the world tennis empire. Australia won the Cup again, for the 14th time since 1950, as Roy Emerson and Fred Stolle gunned down the Spaniards 4-1 at Sydney.

Australians also captured the Federation Cup, not to mention the other three men's major singles titles, and all four of the women's. Seven for eight ain't bad. Five of those finals were all-Aussie affairs. In doubles, Aussies took six for eight, and, mixed,

four for four. Aussies grasped seventeen of the 20 premier championships. Never before had one national dominated a tennis year so thoroughly. This was the tennis version of the Holy Roman Empire, and Emerson, Stolle, Smith, Lesley Turner, John Newcombe, Tony Roche et al were holy terrors.

At the Australian Championships, Emerson, winning for a fourth time, out-slugged Stolle from two sets down 7-9, 2-6, 6-4, 7-5, 6-1. John Newcombe and lefty Tony Roche, the latest in a long line of great Aussie pairs, took their first of a record 12 major doubles titles, in a rip-roaring final over Emmo and Stolle, 3-6, 4-6, 13-11, 6-3, 6-4.

Roche, a ruggedly muscular left-hander with an unerring backhand volley, spoiled Emerson's latest vision of a Grand Slam in a French semifinals, 6-1, 6-4, 3-6, 6-0. With his chief nemesis out of the way, as well as prickly South African Cliff Drysdale whom Stolle shaded, 6-8, 6-4, 6-1, 4-6, 6-4, Fred prevailed in Paris over Roche, 3-6, 6-0, 6-2, 6-3. It was his first major title after being runner-up in an Australian, two Wimbledons, and a U.S. Championship. Emerson and Stolle took the doubles over more of their blood, Ken Fletcher and Bob Hewitt, 6-8, 6-3, 8-6, 6-2—Emerson's sixth title in a row in Paris.

Emerson powered his way through the Wimbledon draw again, a tour de force justifying his top seeding, and made Stolle the bridesmaid for the third consecutive year. This time it was easier than in 1964, 6-2, 6-4, 6-4. Dennis Ralston, seeded fourth, was the U.S. hope after out-volleying another Yank, Marty Riessen, in the quarters, 3-6, 2-6, 6-4, 6-2, 6-2, but was chilled by Emmo, 6-1, 6-2, 7-9, 6-1, in the semifinals. Newcombe and Roche won the first of their five Wimbledon doubles titles together, Fletcher and Hewitt sinking again, 7-5, 6-3, 6-4.

Only at Forest Hills, where the U.S. had experienced all-Aussie finals seven of the last nine years, did the Aussie juggernaut falter. None of the men from Down Under made the semis. The Emerson-Stolle monopoly was busted up by Charlie Pasarell, ambushing Stolle in the second round, 6-3, 6-4, 6-2, and Arthur Ashe, who was to gain the No. 2 U.S. ranking behind Dennis Ralston, delivering huge serves and fatal backhands in enough glorious clusters to topple Emerson in the quarterfinals, 13-11, 6-4, 10-12, 6-2. It was Hall of Fame-bound Ashe's initial significant win, but Santana cooled him, 2-6, 6-4, 6-2, 6-4, in the semifinals.

Another mischief-maker with his novel—so it seemed at the time, a double-fisted backhand—24-year-old Drysdale, revived to dust off the top American, Ralston, saving a match point in the quarterfinals, 2-6, 3-6, 7-5, 6-3, 8-6, and brought down 1963 champ Rafael Osuna, 6-3, 4-6, 6-4, 6-1 in the semifinals. Rafael had lamed unseeded Charlie Pasarell's trot in the quarters, 1-6, 6-3, 6-3, 7-5. Santana vs. Drysdale for the crown that no one from their countries had worn was thoughtful, much of it from the backcourt, between two intelligent and stylish men. Two-fisted backhands would become common after Chris Evert arrived six years later, but Drysdale's was the first to be seen in a U.S. final. Rain interrupted the match and made the footing slick, but it couldn't dampen Santana's flashy shot-making or the castanets saluting his 6-2, 7-9, 7-5, 6-1, triumph.

Emerson and Stolle were unbeaten in doubles on the U.S. circuit, winning six tournaments and 31 matches, a run climaxed by a 6-4, 10-12, 7-5, 6-4 triumph over Pasarell and Frank Froehling in the U.S. final at Longwood.

Emerson won seven of 22 tournaments in singles for an 85-16 record. He was 0-2 against Santana, demolished on clay in the Swedish Championship final, 6-1, 6-1, 6-4, and edged, 2-6, 6-3, 6-3, 15-13, on grass at Sydney in Davis Cup, but the final had been decided by then. A lifelong dream to play for his country in his hometown was fulfilled by Stolle as leadoff man. Reassembling his composure after falling way behind, Fred snapped Santana's 19-match Cup streak, 10-12, 3-6, 6-1, 6-4, 7-5, closing a tense struggle with his 19th ace to reward a cheering throng of 10,000 at White City. That was the blow from which the Spaniards never recovered. Emerson took care of Gisbert quickly, 6-3, 6-2, 6-2, for his 13th Cup singles win without defeat, and the rookies, Newcombe and Roche, put it away, 6-3, 4-6, 7-5, 6-2, over Arilla-Santana. Though meaningless to the result, Santana did hand Emerson his lone Cup defeat on the third day.

Australia beat the United States, 2-1, in the final of the Federation Cup at Kooyong in Melbourne. Lesley Turner beat Carole Graebner, 6-3, 2-6, 6-3, and Margaret Smith stopped Billie Jean Moffitt, 6-4, 8-6.

Smith, 23, won three of the major singles titles in one season for the second time in her still ascendant career. She beat Maria Bueno, who retired with an ankle injury while trailing, 5-7, 6-3, 5-2 in the last set of the Australian final. This was Margaret's sixth straight championship (tying Nancye Wynne Bolton's total between 1937 and 1951), covering a run of 29 successive matches in which she lost just five sets.

She beat Bueno again to win Wimbledon, 6-4, 7-5, and Moffitt to win the U.S., 8-6, 7-5. Only one match kept her from a Grand Slam, the final of the French, lost to Turner, 6-3, 6-4. Turner had clung to Bueno, winning that semifinal, 2-6, 6-4, 8-6, while Smith, averting two set points in the first, eliminated Richey, 7-5, 6-4.

After that, Smith didn't lose another all year, piling up 58 consecutive victories for a season of 103-7, including 18 titles in 25 tournaments.

Bueno, 25, won the Italian, 6-1, 1-6, 6-3, over Nancy Richey, and two other of the 11 tournaments she entered, finishing 40-8 in a year in which she was hampered by a knee injury that required surgery. She played Forest Hills against the advice of her doctor, losing to Billie Jean in the semifinals, 6-2, 6-3. Smith's procession to the title at Forest Hills was impressive: 6-0, 6-0 over lefty Justina Bricka; 6-1, 6-0 over quick and clever Francoise Durr in the quarterfinals; 6-2, 6-2 over Richey in the semifinals. But Billie Jean battled her, leading 5-3 in both sets of the final, and had two set points in the second. Even though she lost, Moffitt later said this was turning-point match in her career, adding a great deal to her self-awareness. She knew that the forehand she had gone to Australia to rebuild from scratch the previous year was coming around, complementing her backhand and volleying, and that she had the ability to rival Smith for No. 1. Billie Jean married Larry King, an attorney-to-be, shortly after Forest Hills, and she knew she was coming of age as a player. She had beaten Turner, 6-2. 6-1, to reach the Wimbledon semis where Bueno, though aching, slipped past B.J., 6-4, 5-7, 6-3. The only unseeded outsider in the last four,

6-footer Christine Truman expunged Richey, 6-4, 1-6, 7-5, before falling to Smith, 6-4, 6-0.

Billie Jean was co-ranked No. 1 in the U.S. with Nancy Richey, an unprecedented decision by the U.S. Lawn Tennis Association ranking committee. Moffitt had shone on the grass court circuit, which Richey avoided after winning the U.S. Indoor, over Carol Hanks Aucamp 6-3, 6-2 and U.S. Clay Court over Julie Heldman 5-7, 6-3, 9-7. The two did not meet. Unique were the Clay Court finals at Chicago in that each contained a Richey. Nancy's 18-year-old kid brother, Cliff, lost his to Ralston, 6-4, 4-6, 6-4, 6-3. Swede Jan-Erik Lundquist took the U.S. Indoor at Salisbury, Md., over Ralston, 4-6, 13-11, 6-4, 11-9.

Billie Jean and Nancy split their Wightman Cup singles in the 5-2 U.S. victory over Britain at Cleveland. BJ beat Liz Starkie, 6-3, 6-2, but lost to Ann Jones, 6-2, 6-4. Nancy did likewise, 6-1, 6-0, over Starkie but 6-4, 9-7, to Jones. They got help from Graebner's win over newcomer Virginia Wade, 3-6, 10-8, 6-4, and the doubles: Moffitt-Karen Susman over Jones-Wade, 6-3, 8-6, and Graebner-Richey (the U.S. champs) over Nell Truman-Starkie, 6-1, 6-0.

Richey and Carole Graebner (whose husband, Clark, ranked No. 13 among the U.S. men and would return to the Top Ten the next year) earned the top U.S. ranking in doubles after winning at Longwood, defeating the defenders Moffitt and Susman in the final, 6-4, 6-4.

Turner teamed with Smith to take the Australian and French. Moffitt captured her third title at Wimbledon with her second partner, Maria Bueno. Smith took three mixed majors, alongside Ken Fletcher at the French and Wimbledon and Stolle at the U.S.

The itinerant pros were still trying to organize. Mike Davies, Butch Buchholz and Barry MacKay were among the driving forces behind the International Professional Tennis Players' Association (IPTPA) formed in 1965, hopeful of forming some structure for the amorphous, struggling outcasts. The U.S. Pro Championships returned to Longwood, Ken Rosewall regaining the title he had won in 1963, and getting paid—albeit modestly, $3,000—this time for beating Rod Laver, 6-4, 6-3, 6-3.

Patrician scoring reformer Jimmy Van Alen of Newport, R.I., whose "Van Alen Streamlined Scoring System" (VASSS) would become the basis for "sudden death" tie-breakers in 1970, hosted a pro tournament at the famed Newport Casino, where the U.S. Championships had been played from their inauguration in 1881 until 1915. Van Alen put up $10,000 in prize money, on the condition that the pros use his radical VASSS round robin, medal-play format, in which every point counted and each was worth $5. The players were happy to play any way as long as they were paid, though Pancho Segura spoke for most of his colleagues when he disparaged the Van Alen system, saying "It seems half-VASSS to me." Laver won over Rosewall.

1965 CHAMPIONS AND LEADERS

Australian Championships

Men's Singles Final: Roy Emerson (AUS) def. Fred Stolle (AUS), 7-9, 2-6, 6-4, 7-5, 6-1

Women's Singles Final: Margaret Smith (AUS) def. Maria Bueno (BRA), 5-7, 6-3, 5-2, ret.

Men's Doubles Final: John Newcombe and Tony Roche (AUS) def. Roy Emerson and Fred Stolle (AUS), 3-6, 4-6, 13-11, 6-3, 6-4.

Women's Doubles Final: Margaret Smith and Lesley Turner (AUS) def. Robyn Ebbern (AUS) and Billie Jean Moffitt (USA), 1-6, 6-2, 6-3

Mixed Doubles Final: Robyn Ebbern and Owen Davidson (AUS) and Margaret Smith / John Newcombe (AUS) - SHARED

French Championships

Men's Singles Final: Fred Stolle (AUS) def. Tony Roche (AUS), 3-6, 6-0, 6-2, 6-3

Women's Singles Final: Lesley Turner (AUS) def. Margaret Smith (AUS), 6-3, 6-4

Men's Doubles Final: Roy Emerson and Fred Stolle (AUS) def. Ken Fletcher and Bob Hewitt (AUS), 6-8, 6-3, 8-6, 6-2

Women's Doubles Final: Margaret Smith and Lesley Turner (AUS) def. Francoise Durr and Jeanine Lieffrig (FRA), 6-3, 6-1

Mixed Doubles Final: Margaret Smith and Ken Fletcher (AUS) def. Maria Bueno (BRA) and John Newcombe (AUS), 6-4, 6-4

Wimbledon

Men's Singles Final: Roy Emerson (AUS) def. Fred Stolle (AUS), 6-2, 6-4, 6-4

Women's Singles Final: Margaret Smith (AUS) def. Maria Bueno (BRA), 6-4, 7-5

Men's Doubles Final: John Newcombe and Tony Roche (AUS) def. Ken Fletcher and Bob Hewitt (AUS), 7-5, 6-3, 6-4

Women's Doubles Final: Maria Bueno (BRA) and Billie Jean Moffitt (USA) def. Francoise Durr and Jeanine Lieffrig (FRA), 6-2, 7-5

Mixed Doubles Final: Margaret Smith and Ken Fletcher (AUS) def. Judy Tegart Dalton and Tony Roche (AUS), 12-10, 6-3

U.S. Championships

Men's Singles Final: Manolo Santana (ESP) def. Cliff Drysdale (RSA), 6-2, 7-9, 7-5, 6-1

Women's Singles Final: Margaret Smith (AUS) def. Billie Jean Moffitt (USA), 8-6, 7-5

Men's Doubles Final: Roy Emerson and Fred Stolle (AUS) def. Frank Froehling, III and Charlie Pasarell (USA), 6-4, 10-12, 7-5, 6-3

Women's Doubles Final: Carole Caldwell Graebner and Nancy Richey (USA) def. Billie Jean Moffitt and Rosie Casals (USA), 6-3, 6-4

Mixed Doubles Final: Margaret Smith and Fred Stolle (AUS) def. Judy Tegart Dalton (AUS) and Frank Froehling, III (USA), 6-2, 6-2

Year-End No. 1

Men: Roy Emerson
Women: Margaret Smith

Davis Cup: Australia

Federation Cup: Australia

Wightman Cup: United States

1966 Unseeded Stolle Wins U.S. Title As Parity Prevails

Maria Bueno wins her fourth title at the U.S. Championships and the last of her seven major singles titles.

If variety is indeed the spice of life, 1966 was a flavorful year for international tennis. There were no one-man or one-woman gangs, as the game's major titles got spread around. For the first time since 1948, no player, man or woman, captured more than one of the four major singles crowns.

Fred Stolle, thought to be past his prime at age 27, didn't win a single tournament until August, then came on like the old Australian Mafia. He won the German Championship on clay over Hungarian Istvan Gulyas, 2-6, 7-5, 6-1, 6-2, and took the U.S. title at Forest Hills unseeded, the second to do so, following the 1957 example of countryman Mal Anderson. Peeved at the lack of

respect extended to him by the tourney administration, Stolle routed pal/nemesis Roy Emerson in the semifinals, 6-4, 6-1, 6-1, with an astounding display of power and control, and withstood 21 aces served by the similarly unseeded John Newcombe to win the title, 4-6, 12-10, 6-3, 6-4. Thereafter Stolle won tournaments in California (Pacific Coast on concrete over Charlie Pasarell, 6-4, 2-6, 6-4), and Australia (on grass at Melbourne over Emerson, 6-2, 9-7, 6-3).

Fiery Fred beat both Ramanathan Krishnan, 6-3, 6-2, 6-4 and Jaidip Mukerjea, 7-5, 6-8, 6-3, 5-7, 6-3, as Australia pummeled India, 4-1, in the Davis Cup Challenge Round. (The lone Aussie loss, delaying champagne celebrations in Melbourne until the third day, was the doubles upset of Newcombe and Tony Roche, 4-6, 7-5, 6-4, 6-4 by Mukerjea and Krishnan.) Emerson clinched it by going through Krishnan, 6-0, 6-2, 10-8. (The latter's son, Ramesh Krishnan, would follow in the old man's sneaker steps to a Cup final 21 years later in Sweden, a father-son feat that is theirs alone.) That was the climax of Stolle's amateur career, as he turned pro at the end of the year.

Stolle's Davis Cup accomplice, Emerson, started the year by grabbing their national championship for the fourth consecutive time, a 6-4, 6-8, 6-2, 6-3 extinguishing of Arthur Ashe. The smooth Aussie then went right back on court, accompanied by Stolle, to complete the doubles final over Newcombe and Roche, an 87-game, three match point-saving victory, 7-9, 3-6, 8-6, 14-12, 12-10, that had stopped for darkness at 7-7 in the fourth the previous evening. That meant Emerson played 128 games within 24 hours. He and Fred went on to post the year's best doubles record, adding the Italian, South African and, over Dennis Ralston and Clark Graebner, 6-4, 6-4, 6-4, the U.S. Championship.

Emerson was perhaps never in better condition or form than at the start of Wimbledon, where he was keen to become the first man to win three successive singles titles since Fred Perry in 1934-35-36. He looked as if he would until fate and his own eagerness intervened during his quarterfinal against a compatriot, left-hander Owen Davidson. Richard Evans described what happened in *World Tennis*:

"The first set took Emerson precisely 14 minutes to win 6-1. His first service was going in, his volleys were crisp and accurate, his groundstrokes laden with power and spin. There was no danger in sight unless it lay in the greasy, rain-slicked turf and of this, surely, Emerson was aware. So it surprised many people when he raced for a Davidson drop-volley in the third game of the second set. And it horrified us all when he skidded headlong into the umpire's chair and brought the BBC microphone crashing down on top of him. He was up in a moment, flexing his left shoulder and telling Davidson that he thought he had heard something snap. In fact, he had torn the shoulder ligaments—an injury that, in a fatal second, had shattered a dream, ruined weeks of arduous preparation and deprived Wimbledon of its champion." Emmo didn't quit, but was soon thoroughly beaten, 1-6, 6-3, 6-4, 6-4.

Manolo Santana, the clay-court artist who had proved himself a man for all surfaces by winning Forest Hills on grass the previous year, inherited the throne that Emerson abdicated, and he was a popular champion. Grinning and playing extraordinary shots when behind, he beat Aussies in suspenseful struggles: Ken Fletcher, 6-2, 3-6, 8-6, 4-6, 7-5 in the quarterfinals, and then Davidson, 6-2, 4-6, 9-7, 3-6, 7-5 in the semifinals. In the final, he repelled Dennis Ralston, who had more firepower but less control, 6-4, 11-9, 6-4.

But Santana had his own problems with injuries during the season. A painful shoulder plagued him as Spain, the 1965 runner-up, went out to Brazil in an early Davis Cup round, and a bad ankle reduced his Forest Hills' defense to a limp. Nevertheless, he was able to beat Chuck McKinley, 9-7, 9-7, 8-6, in the fourth round and hang in to edge Bill Bowrey, 6-8, 6-2, 8-6, 5-7, 6-4, before losing to Newcombe, 6-3, 6-4, 6-8, 8-6, in the semifinals.

It was not Santana but Australian lefty Tony Roche who was the 1966 man of the year on clay. He won the Italian, 11-9, 6-1, 6-3 over the aging 32-year-old homeboy Nicola Pietrangeli. Roche then claimed his lone singles major, the French, beating Hungarian roadrunner Gulyas, 6-1, 6-4, 7-5, despite pain-killing injections in a troublesome ankle, which would thereafter hamper his effectiveness.

So who was the world's No. 1 amateur? Take your pick of the major victors. Stolle won four of 19 tournaments, 70 of 85 matches. Emerson won eight of 16 tournaments, including the rising South African Championship, 6-3, 2-6, 3-6, 6-4, 7-5 over Bob Hewitt and 67 of 78 matches. Santana was 52-16, winning only two of 17 tournaments, but one of those was the biggest, Wimbledon. Roche played the most ambitious schedule, winning 10 of 29 tournaments and 106 of 125 matches.

Ralston, generally considered No. 5 in the world, was No. 1 in the U.S. for the third year in a row, the first man so honored since Don Budge in 1936-37-38. He was, however, frustrated by his failure to win a major singles title. He turned pro with Stolle at the end of the year, leaving Ashe, a lieutenant in the U.S. Army, as heir apparent.

Ralston did have one particularly satisfying doubles triumph, teaming with Clark Graebner to become the first American champions of France since 1955. Their final-round victims, Romanians little known until later, were the hulking Ion Tiriac and his wet-behind-the-ears but gifted protégé, Ilie Nastase, 6-3, 6-3, 6-0. Newcombe, separated from regular partner Roche, won the Wimbledon doubles anyway, with Ken Fletcher, another all-Aussie picnic, 6-3, 6-4, 3-6, 6-3, over Bowrey and Davidson.

It was a dark year for the U.S. in the Davis Cup as Captain George MacCall's team was bushwhacked, 3-2, by unheralded Brazil at Porto Alegre. Cliff Richey was upset in singles by both Edison Mandarino, 5-7, 6-3, 7-5, 6-3, and lefty Tom Koch, 6-1, 7-5, 6-1, Koch knotting it, 2-2, after Ashe and Ralston had beaten the two Brazilians, 7-5, 6-4, 4-6, 6-2. Mandarino took Ralston in the fifth match, 4-6, 6-4, 4-6, 6-4, 6-1. This was the beginning of Latin laments for Americans, who would lose on dirt south of the border six more times over the next 17 years.

The world's most successful player was the No. 1 woman, Billie Jean King, who won her first Wimbledon singles title at age 23 and spearheaded successful team efforts in the Federation and Wightman Cups. A virus infection diminished her effectiveness later, but Billie Jean won 10 of 16 tournaments and compiled a 57-8 record.

Nancy Richey, co-ranked No. 1 with Billie Jean in 1965, slipped to No. 2 despite reaching the finals of the Australian, French and U.S. championships, winning six of 14 tournaments and posting a 55-9 record. She also won her fourth straight U.S. Clay Court title, beating lefty Stephanie DeFina, 6-2, 6-2, while her brother, Cliff, 19, topped Frank Froehling, 13-11, 6-1, 6-3, to complete a singular family double. Nancy won three of the major doubles titles; the Australian with Carole Graebner over Margaret Smith and Lesley Turner, 6-4, 7-5, and Wimbledon and the U.S. with Maria Bueno, respectively over Smith and Judy Tegart Dalton, 6-3, 4-6, 6-4, and over 17-year-old Rosie Casals and King, 6-3, 6-4.

Margaret Smith won her record seventh consecutive Australian singles title without raising her racquet, accepting a final-round default from Richey, who injured a knee while beating Kerry Melville, 6-2, 8-6, in the semifinals. That snapped the tie with Nancye Wynne Bolton, whose half-dozen Aussie titles were registered between 1937 and 1951. Margaret's third consecutive French doubles was with Tegart Dalton over compatriots Fay Toyne and Jill Blackman, 4-6, 6-1, 6-1. But she was increasingly burdened by the pressure and loneliness of big-time tennis competition. Shortly after losing her Wimbledon title in a semifinal defeat by King, she announced her retirement at age 24 to open a clothing boutique in Perth—the first of several short-lived retirements, as it turned out.

Ann Haydon Jones won her second French singles title, over Richey, 6-3, 6-1.

At Wimbledon, King, seeded fourth, was magnificently aggressive. Grass staining her knees on low volleys, she played better than anyone else, as her husband of less than a year sat nervously in the competitors' guest stand. Having dispatched

one old rival, top-seeded Smith, in the semis, 6-3, 6-3, she did in another, second-seeded Bueno, in the final, 6-3, 3-6, 6-1, then tossed her racket high in the air and squealed with glee. Bueno, three-time champ, had to battle to get past Jones, 6-3, 9-11, 7-5 in the semifinals to get into her fifth final. Billie Jean's toughest on the way was a quarterfinal over tall, powerful Annette van Zyl, 1-6, 6-2, 6-4.

King, Julie Heldman and Carole Graebner carried the U.S. to a 3-0 victory over surprise finalist, West Germany, in the Federation Cup on clay at Turin, Italy. Julie beat Helga Niessen, 4-6, 7-5, 6-1, Billie Jean beat Edda Buding, 6-3, 3-6, 6-1, and joined Carole for a mop-up, 6-4, 6-2, over Helga Schultze and Buding.

King, Richey, Mary Ann Eisel and Jane Albert were the Americans in a 4-3 Wightman Cup victory over Great Britain at Wimbledon. Richey and Eisel contributed the decisive point in doubles, over Elizabeth Starkie and Rita Bentley, 6-1, 6-2. Billie Jean won both her singles, 6-2, 6-3, over Virginia Wade, and 5-7, 6-2, 6-3, over Jones, while Richey beat Wade, 2-6, 6-2, 7-5.

Maria Bueno captured her fourth U.S. title, the last of her seven major singles crowns, by beating Richey 6-3, 6-1 with an all-court display of grace and shot-making magic that completely thwarted Nancy's back-court game. They had teamed for the U.S. doubles title at Longwood, over the new but potent partnership of King and Casals, 6-3, 6-4. But in the singles final Bueno treated Richey more like a stranger, winning in just 50 minutes. The best match of the tournament had been Bueno's 6-2, 10-12, 6-3 victory over the diminutive, 17-year-old Casals, a feast of dazzling footwork and shot making that captivated a crowd of 14,000. King was jolted in the second round by Aussie 19-year-old Kerry Melville, 6-4, 6-4, who made it to a semifinal defeat by Richey, 6-3, 6-2.

Also noteworthy in 1966 were the longest singles matches on record in top-level competition: Roger Taylor of Britain in 126 games defeated Wieslaw Gasiorek of Poland, 27-29, 31-29, 6-4, on a slick wood surface in a King's Cup match that lasted five hours and 27 minutes, and stretched until the early hours of a bitterly cold Warsaw morning. Perhaps just to show he wasn't out of interminable sets, Taylor, in the same series, was part of the third longest singles set, beating Taddeus Nowicki, 33-31, 6-1. In the female precinct, American Kathy Blake (who would, in 1978, bear the U.S. Davis Cup doubles pair, Mike and Bob Bryan), was in a record-length 62-game match. She outlasted Mexico's Elena Subirats 12-10, 6-8, 14-12 on grass at the Piping Rock Country Club on Long Island, N.Y.

Vigorous Vic Seixas, Hall of Famer-to-be, could talk about a long match, too, his 94-game victory over 22-year-old Aussie Bill Bowrey at the Pennsylvania Grass Championships, 32-34, 6-4, 10-8, took almost four hours. Vic, a month short of his 43rd birthday, lost the next day, 6-3, 6-8, 6-3, to Clark Graebner, who won the title over Stan Smith, 6-3, 6-4, 6-3. Vic ranked No. 9, his 13th time in the U.S. Top Ten, which he headed in 1951, 1954 and 1957.

The pros had decided to cast their fate to small tournament-format events rather than head-to-head tours, as in the past, but the going was still rough. The U.S. Pro at Longwood remained an encouraging beacon, lighting the future, and Rod Laver signaled his takeover from Ken Rosewall as the pro king, beating "Mus-cles," 6-4, 4-6, 6-2, 8-10, 6-3. He had also beaten Rosewall, 6-2, 6-2, 6-3, for his third straight World Pro title at Wembley, a crown that Ken wore in 1957 and 1960 through 1963. But Rosewall was Laver's master for fourth year in a row at the French Pro, 6-3, 6-2, 14-12, his seventh straight triumph (a record eight in total) in Paris.

1966 CHAMPIONS AND LEADERS

Australian Championships
Men's Singles Final: Roy Emerson (AUS) def. Arthur Ashe (USA), 6-4, 6-8, 6-2, 6-3

Women's Singles Final: Margaret Smith (AUS) def. Nancy Richey (USA), default

Men's Doubles Final: Roy Emerson and Fred Stolle (AUS) def. John Newcombe and Tony Roche (AUS), 7-9, 6-3, 6-8, 14-12, 12-10

Women's Doubles Final: Carole Caldwell Graebner and Nancy Richey (USA) def. Margaret Smith and Lesley Turner (AUS), 6-4, 7-5

Mixed Doubles Final: Judy Tegart Dalton and Tony Roche (AUS) def. Robyn Ebbern and Bill Bowrey (AUS), 6-1, 6-3

French Championships
Men's Singles (AUS): Tony Roche (AUS) def. Istvan Gulyas (HUN), 6-1, 6-4, 7-5

Women's Singles Final: Ann Haydon Jones (GBR) def. Nancy Richey (USA), 6-3, 6-1

Men's Doubles Final: Clark Graebner and Dennis Ralston (USA) def. Ilie Nastase and Ion Tiriac (ROM), 6-3, 6-3, 6-0

Women's Doubles Final: Margaret Smith and Judy Tegart Dalton (AUS) def. Jill Blackman and Fay Toyne (AUS), 4-6, 6-1, 6-1

Mixed Doubles Final: Annette Van Zyl and Frew McMillan (RSA) def. Ann Haydon Jones (GBR) and Clark Graebner (USA), 1-6, 6-3, 6-2

Wimbledon
Men's Singles Final: Manolo Santana (ESP) def. Dennis Ralston (USA), 6-4, 11-9, 6-4

Women's Singles Final: Billie Jean King (USA) def. Maria Bueno (BRA), 6-2, 3-6, 6-1

Men's Doubles Final: Ken Fletcher and John Newcombe (AUS) def. Bill Bowrey and Owen Davidson (AUS), 6-3, 6-4, 3-6, 6-3

Women's Doubles Final: Maria Bueno (BRA) and Nancy Richey (USA) def. Margaret Smith and Judy Tegart Dalton (AUS), 6-3, 4-6, 6-4

Mixed Doubles Final: Margaret Smith and Ken Fletcher (AUS) def. Billie Jean Moffitt King and Dennis Ralston (USA), 4-6, 6-3, 6-3

U.S. Championships
Men's Singles Final: Fred Stolle (AUS) def. John Newcombe (AUS), 4-6, 12-10, 6-3, 6-4

Women's Singles Final: Maria Bueno (BRA) def. Nancy Richey (USA), 6-3, 6-1

Men's Doubles Final: Roy Emerson and Fred Stolle (AUS) def. Clark Graebner and Dennis Ralston (USA), 6-4, 6-4, 6-4

Women's Doubles Final: Maria Bueno (BRA) and Nancy Richey (USA) def. Billie Jean King and Rosie Casals (USA), 6-3, 6-4

Mixed Doubles Final: Donna Floyd Fales (USA) and Owen Davidson (AUS) def. Carol Hanks Aucamp and Ed Rubinoff (USA), 6-1, 6-3

Year-End No. 1
Men: Manolo Santana
Women: Billie Jean King

Davis Cup: Australia

Federation Cup: United States

Wightman Cup: United States

1967 Newcombe, King Closing Monarchs of Amateur Era

By sweeping the singles titles at Wimbledon and Forest Hills, Australian John Newcombe and Californian Billie Jean Moffitt King reigned as the king and queen of amateur tennis in 1967, the last year of the amateur era. By the end of the year, two professional troupes—World Championship Tennis (WCT) and the National Tennis League (NTL)—had been formed, prompting Newcombe and a half dozen other leading amateur men to turn pro.

John Newcombe jumps net at Wimbledon after beating Wilhelm Bungert of Germany in the men's singles final at Wimbledon.

With the blessing of the All England Club and its forceful chairman, Herman David, pros appeared in late summer on Centre Court for an eight-man tourney sponsored and televised by

the BBC. The brilliant final of that event—Rod Laver over Ken Rosewall, 6-2, 6-2, 12-10—dwarfed the Newcombe-Bungert Wimbledon final the month before, and was but another factor in whetting the public's appetite for "Open" tennis, and taking the game to the brink of rebellion destined to change forever the old order.

The call to revolution was sounded in December by the Lawn Tennis Association of Britain, spurred by David, who had denounced "shamateurism" as "a living lie" and urged open competition for some time. When the International Lawn Tennis Federation again voted against opens once more at its mid-year annual meeting, David declared, "It seems that we have come to the end of the road constitutionally." He vowed that Wimbledon would continue to be the world's premier tournament, with a field commensurate with that reputation, even if it had to "go it alone" as a pioneer of open competition. Backing him, the LTA took an unconstitutional, revolutionary step by voting overwhelmingly at its December meeting to make British tournaments open in 1968.

The International Lawn Tennis Federation threatened to expel the British from the international organization, but its hand had been forced. A number of compromises later, open tennis became a reality in 1968, though in a much more limited and qualified way than the British had envisioned.

Early in the year, such upheaval did not seem to be in prospect. The U.S. Lawn Tennis Association hired Robert Malaga, a successful promoter of the Wightman Cup and Davis Cup in his hometown, Cleveland, as its first full-time executive secretary and signed a product-endorsement agreement with Licensing Corporation of America.

The competitive year began the same way the previous four had, with Roy Emerson winning his native Australian singles title for a record sixth time over a seven-year span.

Arthur Ashe was his victim in the final for the second straight year, this time in straight sets: 6-4, 6-1, 6-4. Otherwise the triumph was a rough slog for Emmo, getting past Tony Roche in the semis in 83 games: 6-3, 4-6, 15-13, 13-15, 6-2. Also for Ashe in beating John Newcombe in 81 games: 12-10, 20-22, 6-3, 6-2. Newcombe and Roche paired to win the doubles title—they would also win in Paris and New York for a three-major season—beating countrymen Owen Davidson and Bill Bowrey in a rousing final, 3-6, 6-3, 7-5, 6-8, 8-6.

Nancy Richey, the runner-up to Margaret Smith in 1965, took advantage of Margaret's temporary retirement to capture the women's title, a 6-1, 6-4, triumph over Lesley Turner. Nancy didn't lose a set, but Turner fought off Francoise Durr 6-1, 10-8 in the quarters and 18-year-old Rosie Casals, 4-6, 6-1, 6-4 in the semifinals. A 15-year-old newcomer who would be heard from, Evonne Goolagong, won two rounds. Turner and Judy Tegart Dalton captured the doubles over the Aussie-French combine of Lorraine Robinson-Evelyne Terras, 6-0, 6-2.

Turner stung Maria Bueno 6-3, 6-3 in the Italian final, and won the first set of the French final before losing it to Durr, whose 4-6, 6-3, 6-4, victory was the first by a French citizen since Simone Mathieu in 1939. Durr teamed with Australian Gail Sherriff to beat South African Annette Van Zyl and Rhodesian and Pat

Walkden 6-2, 6-2, for the first of five consecutive doubles titles, two with Ann Jones, and two more with Sherriff, who by then had become a French citizen as Mme. Jean Baptiste Chanfreau. (Gail would win again in 1976 as Mme. Jean Lovera, with Uruguayan Fiorella Bonicelli.)

Emerson, fit as ever, powered his way to the French men's singles title, dethroning fellow Aussie Tony Roche in the final, 6-1, 6-4, 2-6, 6-2. Roche had to fight off another lefty, Yugoslav Nikki Pilic in the semis, 3-6, 6-3, 6-4, 2-6, 6-4. Emmo lost only two other sets, and galloped past Pierre Darmon in the quarters, 6-0, 6-4, 6-4, then Hungarian Istvan Gulyas 6-3, 6-4, 6-1 in the semis. It was Emmo's 12th major singles title, the male record until Pete Sampras won his 13th at Wimbledon in 2000. Emmo had eclipsed Bill Tilden's 10 by winning the Aussie five months earlier, but nobody, including himself, noticed. Years later, when Sampras was stalking him, Emerson said, "I wasn't aware that there was a record. We didn't think about stuff like that."

Roche had earlier lost his Italian title to transplanted Aussie Marty "Martino Mulligano" Mulligan, 6-3, 0-6, 6-4, 6-1. Having cleared the troublesome hurdle of Parisian clay, Emerson set his sights again on the elusive Grand Slam, but his vision was shattered in the fourth round at Wimbledon by tall lefty Pilic, 6-4, 5-7, 6-3, 6-4. Emerson was the favorite after the startling first-round ambush of Manolo Santana by American Charlie Pasarell, 10-8, 6-3, 2-6, 8-6. It was the curtain raiser on Centre Court, the only time a defending male champion and top seed was ever beaten in the first round, until Lleyton Hewitt lost to qualifier No. 203 Ivo Karlovic, 1-6, 7-6 (7-5), 6-3, 6-4 in 2003.

That was the prelude to an upset-filled fortnight. By the quarterfinals, there were no seeded players left in the top half of the draw. The only meeting of seeds came in the quarterfinals, No. 3 Newcombe overpowering No. 6 Ken Fletcher, 6-4, 6-2, 6-4. Two unseeded semifinalists were lefties—Pilic, a 14-12, 8-10, 6-4, 6-2 quarterfinal winner over Aussie John Cooper (younger brother of 1958 champ Ashley Cooper), and rugged Yorkshireman Roger Taylor, a 6-4, 8-6, 6-4 winner over Aussie lefty Ray Ruffels. So was West German Wilhelm Bungert, who registered a 6-4, 4-6, 4-6, 6-1, 6-3 quarterfinal win over Brazilian Tom Koch, yet another southpaw. While Newcombe beat Pilic 9-7, 4-6, 6-3, 6-4 in one semi, Bungert depressed the home folks, ever yearning for a champ of their own to succeed Fred Perry (the 1934-35-36 champion), erasing Taylor, 6-4, 6-8, 2-6, 6-4, 6-4. But he had nothing left for the final and offered only halfhearted resistance as Newcombe claimed the title, 6-3, 6-1, 6-1. Bungert's five games equaled the post-war futility of Ashley Cooper's 1957 final loss to Lew Hoad, and Mulligan's to Rod Laver in 1962. In doubles, Newcombe and Roche, reunited and favored to regain the title, fell in the quarters to Englishmen Graham Stilwell and Peter Curtis, 6-4, 4-6, 6-4, 3-6, 8-6. The title went to the freshly-minted South African Davis Cup team of Frew McMillan and Bob Hewitt (the latter as an Australian had won twice with Fred Stolle, 1962, 64). They drubbed Emerson and Fletcher (Fletch the winner in 1966 with Newcombe), 6-2, 6-3, 6-4.

Cumulative attendance for the last amateur Wimbledon exceeded 300,000 for the first time, as 301,896 spectators went through the turnstiles.

Newcombe took the No.1 world ranking at age 23 by winning eight of 24 tournaments and 83 of 99 matches. A sciatic nerve condition nearly cost him the U.S. Doubles Championship, which was decided for the 46th and last time at Longwood Cricket Club, but he and Roche pulled through over Bowrey and Davidson, 6-8, 9-7, 6-3, 6-3. His lower back was still worrying "Newk" going into the U.S. singles, but he experienced no ill effects in plowing to victory at Forest Hills with the loss of but four sets.

It was Emerson who suffered, plagued first by back problems, then by torn thigh muscles in his quarterfinal loss to Clark Graebner of the United States. Graebner, one of several players swinging the new steel T-2000 rackets recently introduced by manufacturer Wilson, crunched 25 aces in his 8-6, 3-6, 19-17, 6-1 victory, and three in a row from 30-40 to end his scintillating 3-6, 3-6, 7-5, 6-4, 7-5 semifinal victory over unseeded Jan Leschly, the clever and sporting left-handed Dane. Graebner, seeking to become the first native champ since 1955, was out-slugged by Newcombe in a serve-and-volley final, 6-4, 6-4, 8-6.

Sharing attention with the winners at Forest Hills were the steel rackets used by women's champ Billie Jean King, fourth rounder Rosie Casals, Graebner and semifinalist Gene Scott, among others. Wilson's equipment innovation, adapted from a French design pioneered by clothier and ex-champion Rene Lacoste, was the harbinger of a wave of new racket designs and materials that flooded the market during the next decade. Scott, then a 29-year-old Wall Street lawyer and part-time player who would later become a Hall of Famer as a self-styled Renaissance Man of tennis who fulfilled many a Walter Mitty fantasy by working mornings in his office and taking the train to Forest Hills, where he reached the Final Four, defeating Aussie Davidson, 6-3, 8-6, 9-7, before Newcombe jolted him back to reality, 6-4, 6-3, 6-3. Scott predicted that wood rackets would soon be obsolete, but his accurate prophecy did not come to pass immediately.

Woman of the Year in 1967 was Billie Jean Moffitt King, 24, who scored triples—victories in singles, doubles and mixed doubles—at both Wimbledon and the U.S. Championships. Only Don Budge in 1938 and Alice Marble in 1939 had also achieved this feat. Billie Jean and Rosie Casals won all their singles (4-0) in carrying the U.S. to the Federation Cup on clay at Berlin: 3-0 sweeps of Rhodesia, South Africa and West Germany into the final. There it was 2-0 over Great Britain: Billie Jean over Ann Jones, 6-3, 6-4, Rosie over Virginia Wade, 9-7, 8-6.

It was the same story in the Wightman Cup, this time 6-1 over Britain at Cleveland. Billie Jean beat Wade, 6-3, 6-2, and Jones, 6-1, 6-2. Nancy Richey beat Jones, 6-2, 6-2, and took the clinching fourth point grittily over Wade, 3-6, 8-6, 6-2, despite a pulled muscle in her back that pained her through the last six games.

King compiled a 68-5 record during the ranking season and won 10 tournaments. In addition to seizing the Wimbledon and U.S. titles without losing a set, she won the U.S. Indoor, 6-1, 6-0, over left-handed Netherlander Trudy Groenman. She had the season's two longest winning streaks: 23 and 25 matches. In Johannesburg, beating Bueno for the South African title, 7-5,

5-7, 6-2, she scored another triple (Bueno had a 'cripple,' losing all three.)

BJK teamed triumphantly with Casals her partner in U.S. (4-6, 6-3, 6-4, over Mary Ann Eisel-Donna Floyd Fales) and Wimbledon (9-11, 6-4, 6-2, over Bueno-Richey) doubles championships. They beat Bueno and Judy Tegart Dalton, 4-6, 6-1, 6-3 at Jo'burg. With Owen Davidson, her mixed partner in French (6-3, 6-1, over Jones-Ion Tiriac), Wimbledon (7-5, 6-2, over Bueno-Fletcher), and U.S. (6-3, 6-2, over Casals-Stan Smith) Championships.

Thus southpaw Davidson scored a Mixed Grand Slam, having first teamed with Lesley Turner to win the Australian title, over Judy Tegart Dalton and Roche, 9-7, 6-4.

King beat Ann Jones, the tenacious British left-hander, in the Wimbledon final, 6-3, 6-4, and again in the U.S. title match, 11-9, 6-4. At Forest Hills, Jones ignored a pulled hamstring and gallantly fought off nine match points before succumbing. Injuries had influenced the women's singles from the outset, four-time champion Maria Bueno pulling out with tendinitis in the right arm and Nancy Richey with the back ailment sustained in Wightman Cup. Jane "Peaches" Bartkowicz, a sturdy 18-year-old from Hamtramck, Mich., the first female to ride a two-handed backhand so high, knocked off Casals, 4-6, 6-3, 7-5, before subsiding against Jones, 7-5, 2-6, 6-1, in the quarterfinals. Jones then beat Turner, 6-2, 6-4, and King defeated, by the same score, French champ Francoise Durr. Francoise reached a U.S. Championships high for a Frenchwoman, topping Simone Mathieu's quarterfinal finish in 1938, but was eclipsed by Mary Pierce reaching the U.S. final in 2005.

Richey earlier won her fifth consecutive U.S. Clay Court title, gunning down Casals, 6-2, 6-3, after little Rosie conquered King in the semifinal, 6-4, 6-4. Arthur Ashe, whose duties as a lieutenant in the U.S. Army kept him out of Wimbledon and Forest Hills, won the men's version for the only time, beating Marty Riessen, 6-3, 6-1, 7-5. Ashe was ranked No. 2 in the U.S. behind Charlie Pasarell, who beat him twice in three under-cover meetings: U.S. Indoor final, 13-11, 6-2, 2-6, 9-7; Richmond Indoor final, in Ashe's hometown, 6-3, 8-6. Arthur beat Charlie for the Philadelphia indoor title, 7-5, 9-7, 6-3. Pasarell won three tournaments to Ashe's five.

The U.S. outdoor season survived the longest (147 games) tournament match of all time, in the doubles of the Newport Casino Invitational in Rhode Island. Dick Leach and Dick Dell defeated Len Schloss and Tom Mozur, 3-6, 49-47, 22-20. The journey of these Americans consumed six hours and 10 minutes over two days, and undoubtedly provided impetus for the scoring reform championed by Newport's impresario, Jimmy Van Alen. Jimmy's "sudden death" tie-breaker, designed to terminate such monster matches, was finally adopted in 1970.

It was a summer of Social Security number scores that drove not only Van Alen but schedule-making tournament referees wild. Two were played on the lawn of the Meadow Club at Southampton, N.Y. Dick Knight and Mike Sprengelmeyer. Americans, traveled 107 games, Knight winning, 32-30, 3-6, 19-17, in five hours, 30 minutes. Schloss and Mozur, those long-distance

guys of Newport, won this time, 90 games, over an Aussie-American alliance of Chris Bovett and Butch Seewagen, 7-5, 48-46. It took South Africans Ray Moore and Cliff Drysdale 105 games to beat the Aussie-Brazilian lineup of Emerson and Ronnie Barnes, 29-31, 8-6, 3-6, 8-6, 6-2, during the U.S. Championships at Longwood. It stands as the U.S. record, tying with the 105-gamer only the year before in which Mexicans Joaquin Loyo-Mayo and Marcelo Lara beat the Mexican-Spanish entry, Luis Garcia, and Santana, 10-12, 24-22, 11-9, 3-6, 6-2.

For the third consecutive year under hapless captain George MacCall, the U.S. Davis Cup team was helpless on foreign soil— slow, red clay. The 1967 loss to Ecuador, 3-2, at Guayaquil was the most ignominious of all for Americans, probably the most startling upset in the long history of Davis Cup competition. Ecuador's two players, Pancho Guzman and Miguel Olvera, were barely known internationally.

Cliff Richey, the most comfortable of the Americans on clay, won the first match, beating Guzman, 6-2, 2-6, 8-6, 6-4, and the inconsequential fifth, but the middle three spelled disaster for the Yanks. Olvera, a scrawny 26-year-old who had been sidelined by tuberculosis, was a winner, 4-6, 6-4, 6-4, 6-2, over Ashe, whose Cup record (10-0) included two singles wins earlier in the year in a 4-1 win over Mexico on Mexico City clay. Ecuadorian Captain Danny Carrera was so thrilled with Olvera's win that he attempted to leap the net to embrace his charge, tripped and broke his leg. Still, the 1-1 score did not seem too worrying for the U.S. until the scrambling Olvera and his 21-year-old sidekick Guzman overcame a 0-6, 2-5, deficit and stunned Marty Riessen and Clark Graebner, 0-6, 9-7, 6-4, 4-6, 8-6, setting the stage for a raucous third day. The giddy crowd of 2,200 at the Guayaquil Tennis Club cheered wildly for their sudden heroes and unsettled the Americans with a shower of abuse. Panic gripped MacCall as the slow-balling Guzman withstood two rushes from Ashe and won the decisive match by a score as bizarre as the whole series: 0-6, 6-4, 6-2, 0-6, 6-3.

With the U.S. out, South Africa was expected to reach the Challenge Round against Australia with Bob Hewitt, Cliff Drysdale and young Ray Moore, three formidable singles players, and Hewitt-McMillan the doubles team of the year. (Their 53-1 record included victories in the Italian, Wimbledon and South African Championships, plus seven other tournaments. Newcombe-Roche won 12 of 19 tournaments, including the Australian, French and U.S.) But Hewitt broke his ankle in the quarterfinal series against India and was unavailable for the semis, in which Spain eliminated South Africa, 3-2. In Australia for the Challenge Round for the second time in three years, Spain was outclassed again on grass, this time at Brisbane. Emerson took advantage of one of Santana's rare poor matches and won the opener in a rout, 6-4, 6-1, 6-1. Newcombe swamped 18-year-old Cup rookie lefty Manuel Orantes, 6-3, 6-3, 6-2, then teamed with Roche to scald Santana and Orantes, 6-4, 6-4, 6-4, losing only 16 points in 15 service games. The 3-0 lead assured Australia's 15th Cup victory in 18 years.

Emerson, 31, blasted Orantes, 6-1, 6-1, 2-6, 6-4, ending a peerless Davis Cup career in which he was 11-1 in singles, 6-0 in doubles during nine Challenge Rounds, eight of them won by Australia. Emmo, whose overall Cup record (including zone matches) was 21-2 in singles, 13-2 in doubles, guzzled champagne triumphantly from the sterling tub on eight occasions, more than any other player, and had played the clincher five times, thrice in doubles. Newcombe's last match as an amateur was not as successful. He lost to Santana, making the final score 4-1.

Immediately after the Challenge Round, Newcombe, Roche, Emerson and Owen Davidson turned pro. Newcombe, Roche, Cliff Drysdale, Roger Taylor and Nikki Pilic signed with New Orleans promoter Dave Dixon, who, bankrolled by Texas oilman Lamar Hunt and his nephew, Al Hill, Jr., had founded World Championship Tennis, Inc. (WCT). Emerson signed with MacCall, who had corralled Rod Laver, Ken Rosewall, Pancho Gonzalez, Andres Gimeno (runner-up to Laver, 4-6, 6-4, 6-3, 7-5, in the U.S. Pro final), Fred Stolle and a few others for his National Tennis League (NTL). MacCall's acquisitions included a female troupe—King, Casals, Durr and Jones. Davidson became the pro at the All England Club and Britain's national coach.

The formation of WCT's "Handsome Eight" barnstorming troupe—seasoned pros Dennis Ralston, Pierre Barthes and Butch Buchholz complementing the five converted amateurs— had an enormous impact on the amateur tennis establishment. In one day, Dixon and his partner Bob Briner, a tennis neophyte who would later become executive director of the ATP (Association of Tennis Professionals), signed Newcombe, Roche, Pilic and Taylor, accounting for three of the 1967 Wimbledon semifinalists. Ralston had been their first-signed, and they soon added Drysdale, Buchholz and Barthes.

"We had in one fell swoop taken all the stars out of the game. If anyone was ever going to see them again at Wimbledon and Forest Hills, the ITF had to make an accommodation," Briner remembers. "Open tennis came about so fast after that, it was pitiful."

1967 CHAMPIONS AND LEADERS

Australian Championships
Men's Singles Final: Roy Emerson (AUS) def. Arthur Ashe (USA), 6-4, 6-1, 6-4

Women's Singles Final: Nancy Richey (USA) def. Lesley Turner (AUS), 6-1, 6-4

Men's Doubles Final: John Newcombe and Tony Roche (AUS) def. Bill Bowrey and Owen Davidson (AUS), 3-6, 6-3, 7-5, 6-8, 8-6

Women's Doubles Final: Lesley Turner and Judy Tegart Dalton (AUS) def. Lorraine Coghlan Robinson (AUS) and Evelyn Terras (FRA), 6-0, 6-2

Mixed Doubles Final: Lesley Turner and Owen Davidson (AUS) def. Judy Tegart Dalton and Tony Roche (AUS), 9-7, 6-4

French Championships
Men's Singles Final: Roy Emerson (AUS) def. Tony Roche (AUS), 6-1, 6-4, 2-6, 6-2

Women's Singles Final: Francoise Durr (FRA) def. Lesley Turner (AUS), 4-6, 6-3, 6-4

Men's Doubles Final: John Newcombe and Tony Roche (AUS) def. Roy Emerson and Ken Fletcher (AUS), 6-3, 9-7, 12-10

Women's Doubles Final: Francoise Durr and Gail Sherriff (FRA) def. Annette Van Zyl (RSA) and Pat Walkden (RHO), 6-2, 6-2

Mixed Doubles Final: Billie Jean King (USA) and Owen Davidson (AUS) def. Ann Haydon Jones (GBR) and Ion Tiriac (ROM), 6-3, 6-1

Wimbledon

Men's Singles Final: John Newcombe (AUS) def. Wilhelm Bungert (GER), 6-3, 6-1, 6-1

Women's Singles Final: Billie Jean King (USA) def. Ann Haydon Jones (GBR), 6-3, 6-4

Men's Doubles Final: Bob Hewitt and Frew McMillan (RSA) def. Roy Emerson and Ken Fletcher (AUS), 6-2, 6-3, 6-4

Women's Doubles Final: Rosie Casals and Billie Jean King (USA) def. Maria Bueno (BRA) and Nancy Richey (USA), 9-11, 6-4, 6-2

Mixed Doubles Final: Billie Jean King (USA) and Owen Davidson (AUS) def. Maria Bueno (BRA) and Ken Fletcher (AUS), 7-5, 6-2

U.S. Championships

Men's Singles Final: John Newcombe (AUS) def. Clark Graebner (USA), 6-4, 6-4, 8-6

Women's Singles Final: Billie Jean King (USA) def. Ann Haydon Jones (GBR), 11-9, 6-4

Men's Doubles Final: John Newcombe and Tony Roche (AUS) def. Bill Bowrey and Owen Davidson (AUS), 6-8, 9-7, 6-3, 6-3

Women's Doubles Final: Rosie Casals and Billie Jean King (USA) def. Mary Ann Eisel and Donna Floyd Fales (USA), 4-6, 6-3, 6-4

Mixed Doubles Final: Billie Jean King (USA) and Owen Davidson (AUS) def. Rosie Casals and Stan Smith (USA), 6-3, 6-2

Year-End No. 1

Men: John Newcombe
Women: Billie Jean King

Davis Cup: Australia

Federation Cup: United States

Wightman Cup: United States

The Open Era

Billie Jean King was a major agent of change in the "Open" era of tennis, pushing for equal prize money for men and women, becoming an integral part of in the founding of the Women's Tennis Association and beating Bobby Riggs in the celebrated "Battle of Sexes" match that thrust tennis into unprecedented popularity. She also won four more Wimbledon singles titles, three more US Open titles as well as an Australian and French singles title in the post-1968 era.

It took a long time, and many failed attempts, but a wave of sanity finally coursed through the boardrooms of the game in 1967. When the dust settled, the most obvious result—a tremendous surge in the popularity of the game—made everyone wonder anew why it had taken so long.

The fixing-up brought mixing-up—and a brilliant new look and outlook in the sector of the game that most needed repairing, namely highest-level tournament tennis. Since their inception, the four majors—the Australian, French, Wimbledon and U.S. Championships—and the traditional tournament circuit, had belonged solely to the amateurs. Finally, in 1968, they joined hands with their on-court superiors, the outcast minority of professionals, and "Open" tennis was born.

In the 1970s, tennis became truly the "in" sport of the great middle class, first in the United States, then abroad. In a single decade, the sport threw off and trampled its starched, white flannel past and became a favored diversion of the modern leisure class—attired in pastels and playing tiebreaker sets in public parks and clubs. They were equipped with a bewildering variety of gear, from optic yellow, heavy-duty balls to double-strung graphite rackets.

All this was inspired by the advent of the "opens." By making tennis at the top level professional, honest, and unabashedly commercial, opens ushered in an era of dramatic growth and development. For an expanding group of pros, this was boom-time, a veritable bonanza of opportunities. They enjoyed and reaped the benefits of a brave new world of televised matches and two-fisted backhands, evolution of technique and technology, full-blown tours for women and over-45s, exposure and cash undreamed of even by Wimbledon champions in the pre-Open era.

1968 Laver, Ashe Excel As Open Era Dawns

Unfortunately, the hypocrisy and confusion of the "shamateur" period was not done away with quickly and cleanly. Rather than accept the British proposal that all competitors would be referred to simply as "players," abolishing the distinction between amateur and professional, the ILTF bowed to heavy pressure from Eastern European countries and their voting allies and effected a compromise that called for four classifications:

- Amateurs, who would not accept prize money.
- Teaching professionals, who could compete with amateurs only in open events.
- "Contract professionals," who made their living playing tennis but did not accept the authority of their national associations affiliated to the ILTF, signing guaranteed contracts instead with independent promoters.
- "Registered players," who could accept prize money in open tournaments but still obeyed their national associations and retained eligibility for amateur events, including the Davis, Federation and Wightman Cups.

The prime example of this last strange and short-lived new breed was Dutchman Tom Okker, who won the Italian and South African Championships (not yet prize-money events) and was runner-up to Arthur Ashe in the first U.S. Open at Forest Hills. Okker pocketed $14,000 in first-prize money while Ashe, then a lieutenant in the U.S. Army and a member of the U.S. Davis Cup team, had to remain an amateur to maintain his Cup eligibility. The USLTA had not adopted the "registered player" concept so he received only $20 per day expenses.

The dawning of "Open" competition some 40 years after the issue was first raised made 1968 truly a watershed year for tennis. The British "revolt" of December 1967 was reinforced by far-seeing U.S. Lawn Tennis Association President Bob Kelleher and his orchestration of the association's vote in favor of open tennis at its annual meeting in February. That led to the emergency meeting of the International Lawn Tennis Federation in Paris and approval of 12 open tournaments for 1968.

Other ludicrous examples abounded. Margaret Smith Court, for instance, won and accepted nearly $10,000 in open tournaments in Britain, then came to America and played in the U.S. Amateur in Boston for expenses only, beating old rival Maria Bueno in the final, 6-2, 6-2.

But despite such anomalies of the transition period, great progress had undeniably been made toward a more honest and prosperous international game.

The first Open tournament, a month after the concept was approved at the conference table, was the $14,000 British Hard Court Championships. (In Europe, "hard court" refers to a clay surface, not concrete or similar hard surfaces as the term is used in the U.S.) Staged at the coastal resort of Bournemouth, it was the historic first chapter, and it began damply, coolly on a drizzly, raw Monday, April 22. The "Open" era lurched into being with a minor young Briton, John Clifton, winning the first point but losing his match, 6-2, 6-3, 4-6, 8-6 against Australian pro Owen Davidson—then the British national coach—on the red shale courts of the West Hants Lawn Tennis Club.

The field at Bournemouth was not as distinguished as the historic nature of the occasion warranted. The "Handsome Eight" of World Championship Tennis were off playing their own tour, leaving the professional portion of the field largely to George MacCall's National Tennis League, plus Davidson and former Chilean Davis Cupper Luis Ayala, then a coach in Puerto Rico, who paid his own way to take part. The top-line amateurs, wary of immediate confrontation with the pros, stayed away. None of the world top 10 amateurs entered, and Englishman Bobby Wilson was the only amateur seeded. On the women's side, the only four pros at the time— Billie Jean King, Rosemary Casals, Francoise Durr and Ann Haydon Jones, who had just signed contracts with MacCall—were otherwise engaged.

The male pros were expected to dominate the amateur field of Englishmen and a few second-line Australians. But many of the pros were jittery. They knew their reputations were on the line, and the most discerning realized they were ill prepared, given long absence from best-of-five-set matches and exposure to new faces and playing styles. Pancho Gonzalez particularly recognized the hazards posed by sudden emergence from a small circle of familiar opponents, with its well-established pecking order. It didn't take long for his apprehension to prove justified. In the second round, Mark Cox, a Cambridge-educated, 24-year-old English left-hander ranked only No. 3 in Britain, outlasted Gonzalez, 0-6, 6-2, 4-6, 6-3, 6-3, becoming the first amateur to topple a pro.

Gonzalez, only a month from his 40th birthday, hadn't played a five-set match in four years, but his defeat sent shock waves through the tennis world. Buoyed by his instant celebrity, Cox ousted a two-time Wimbledon champ, rookie pro Roy Emerson the next day, 6-0, 6-1, 7-5, to reach the semifinals. Obviously the pros were not invincible—a notion that would be reinforced convincingly throughout the year. But the best of their number, Rod Laver and Ken Rosewall, proved they still inhabited the top echelon. Laver canceled Cox's extravagant run in the semis, 6-4, 6-1, 6-0, and Rosewall—a man for all seasons whose longevity at

the top level of international competition is unsurpassed—beat Andres Gimeno, 6-2, 6-1, 6-3, and then Laver, 3-6, 6-2, 6-0, 6-3, in the title match that, because of rain, stretched over two days. Ken, ruling the 32-man draw, collected the initial "Open" paycheck, $2,400, while the loser settled for half.

Attracting almost 30,000 customers during a moist, chilly week at the small club, pioneering Bournemouth was deemed a grand success. The British LTA may have opened the new production out-of-town, (a New Haven pre-Broadway try-out?) so that had it bombed, Wimbledon could discreetly resume the old ways.

But there was no going back. Virginia Wade, the British No. 1 (No. 8 in the world), would be going forward as a pro, but not until later in the year. However, as wary as Cox was about abdicating amateur status at this mysterious time, she declined the female first prize ($720) for winning the title at Bournemouth over Winnie Shaw, 6-4, 6-1. Virginia and kindred cautious amateurs—"Suppose it doesn't work, and we're banned as amateurs, out in the cold?" was the common plaint—got $120 for expenses. Luis Ayala, the pro half of the first integrated heterosexual open team, with Californian Valerie Ziegenfuss as the amateur half, won all of $24 for their semifinal finish in the mixed. Since he got $96 as a second-round singles loser, Luis and Valerie came out even. But could they afford room and board? Welcome to the new land of milk and honey.

Rosewall beat Laver again in the final of the second open tournament, the French Championships, also on clay. As the first of the traditional major/Big Four tournaments to be opened, its field still lacked most of the top American men and Tom Okker, but was considerably stronger than Bournemouth had been.

The French was also memorable because it was played during the general strike and student riots of '68. Paris was a troubled, crippled city, without public transportation or essential services, but record crowds flocked to Stade Roland Garros on the western outskirts of the city—many by bicycle or on foot—because literally nothing else of a sporting nature was happening. Players, many of whom had harrowing true-life adventures getting to Paris, found accommodations within walking distance of the courts.

"Roland Garros was a port in a storm," recalled Rex Bellamy of the *Times of London.* "One thought of Drake and his bowls, Nero and his fiddle. In a strife-torn city, the soaring center court blazed with color. People even perched on the scoreboards, which was as high as they could get without a ladder. "So the fortnight's excitement was two-edged: A revolution on the courts, and a whiff of revolution in the streets ...The first major open was played in the sort of environment that nightmares are made of. But the tennis was often like a dream."

In the quarterfinals, Laver was taken to five sets by the lumbering Romanian Ion Tiriac, 4-6, 4-6, 6-3, 6-3, 6-0, one of numerous protracted struggles that kept the packed galleries gasping appreciatively. Laver then easily handled the 40-year-old Gonzalez, 6-3, 6-3, 6-1. But Pancho had enchanted spectators earlier, winning five matches in 19 sets, outlasting Emerson, nine years his junior, in the quarters, 7-5, 6-3, 3-6, 4-6, 6-4, to stand as the oldest ever semifinalist in Paris. In the final, Rosewall again asserted his clay-court mastery at Laver's expense, 6-3, 6-1, 2-6, 6-2—15 years

after he'd won the title as a callow amateur of 18. The payoff was $3,000.

The women's singles was also full of surprises. In fourth-round fun for amateurs, Gail Sherriff (later Gail Chanfreau Lovera) bounced third-seeded defending champ Francoise Durr, 6-3, 6-3, and Mexican Elena Subirats eliminated fourth-seeded Rosie Casals, 6-4, 6-3. Nancy Richey, the No. 5-seeded, clay-court specialist playing as an amateur—and soon regretting it after having to forego the $1,000 first prize—registered a 2-6, 6-3, 6-4 semifinal win over top-seeded Billie Jean King, who always preferred faster and more sure-footed surfaces. She won the title over the last of the four women pros, Ann Jones, who had been considered the world's leading dirt-kicking lady, 5-7, 6-4, 6-1.

There was more upheaval on the courts amid the giddy jubilation of a once-in-a-lifetime occasion, at the first open Wimbledon. This was a richly sentimental fortnight, as legendary champions who had been stripped of their All England Club membership upon turning pro were welcomed back to the shrine of the game and again permitted to wear its mauve-and-green colors. Even old-time champions no longer able to compete came back for the festivities surrounding the enactment of a long-held dream. The tournament began with five days of intermittent rain, which held down crowds, but even this couldn't dampen soaring spirits.

Wimbledon, offering a $63,000 pot, was also the first of the open tournaments that every player of consequence entered. The seeding list for the men's singles read like a Who's Who of the present and immediate past: Top-seeded Laver, Rosewall, Andres Gimeno, defending champion John Newcombe, Emerson, Manolo Santana, Lew Hoad, Gonzalez, Dennis Ralston, Butch Buchholz, Fred Stolle, Okker, Ashe, Cliff Drysdale, Tony Roche and Nikki Pilic.

There were numerous surprises, none more unsettling to the pros than the third-round defeat of No. 3-seeded Gimeno, the elegant Spaniard who was regarded as just a shade below Laver and Rosewall. That was committed by long-haired, unheralded, 21-year-old South African Ray (Wolfman) Moore, 4-6, 6-3, 7-5, 2-6, 6-2. Hoad, the champ 11 years before, was beaten by Bob Hewitt, 6-3, 9-11, 1-6, 6-3, 6-3, and Gonzalez by Soviet Alex Metreveli, 4-6, 6-4, 6-3, 7-5, in the same round, demonstrating again that the pros were unaccustomed to this Brave New World. Indeed, in the quarters only two old pros—Laver and Buchholz—shared the stage with two relatively recent pros (Ralston and Roche), three amateurs (Clark Graebner, Ashe and Moore) and the lone "registered player," Okker. Rosewall, second-seeded, who had won everything but Wimbledon as an amateur in the '50s, was upset in the riotous fourth round by the tricky left-handed spins of Roche, 9-7, 6-3, 6-2. It was the round in which two ex-champs were banished: Emerson by Okker, 6-3, 9-11, 7-5, 7-5, and defender Newcombe by Ashe, 6-4, 6-4, 4-6, 1-6, 6-3. Three-time finalist, Stolle, was also beaten by unseeded Graebner, 6-1, 7-5, 7-5. Graebner, in dark-horn-rimmed spectacles, resembled Clark Kent and called "Superboy," had eliminated 1966 champ Santana, 9-7, 6-2, 6-1 in the third round. He went to the semis, also defeating the upstart Moore, 6-2, 6-0, 9-7. Ashe was also there, defeating Okker 7-9, 9-7, 9-7, 6-2 in the quarterfinals–and joined Davis Cup teammate

Graebner—the last time two amateurs would occupy that echelon at Wimbledon.

For a moment or so, the prospect of an all-amateur final danced giddily in the delighted minds of anti-open protesters. But Roche, who had beaten Buchholz in the quarters, 3-6, 7-5, 6-4, 6-4, got through two rough sets, scraping by Graebner, 9-7, 8-10, 6-4, 8-6. Laver picked up speed in leveling Ashe, 7-5, 6-2, 6-4. He started his run to a third title by beating Gene Scott, 6-4, 4-6, 6-3, 6-2; Stan Smith, 6-3, 6-4, 6-4; Marty Riessen, 6-4, 3-6, 7-5, 6-3; and Cox, 9-7, 5-7, 6-2, 6-0, and into the quarters where Ralston made him go the distance, 4-6, 6-3, 6-1, 4-6, 6-2. The title was his almost immediately in a 59-minute clobbering of Roche, 6-3, 6-4, 6-2 to again command the stage he had made his in 1961 and 1962.

Having artistically made the pros' return to the premier championship of the game triumphant, Laver received $4,800, but said decisively that money had never entered his thoughts. "Wimbledon's first open tournament enabled this fine left-hander to prove his magnificent worth. Wimbledon endorsed his quality," wrote Lance Tingay of London's *Daily Telegraph*. "Equally, Laver endorsed Wimbledon's renewed status as the de facto world championship."

The cream also rose in the women's singles. Billie Jean King won her third consecutive singles title and $1,800, equaling a feat last achieved by Maureen Connolly (1952—54). She beat a surprise finalist, No. 7-seeded Judy Tegart Dalton, 9-7, 7-5. An accomplished doubles player, this affable Australian earned her day in the sun by beating second-seeded Margaret Smith Court in the quarters, 4-6, 8-6, 6-1 and third-seeded Nancy Richey in the semis, 6-3, 6-1. BJK was pushed by Jones in the semis, 4-6, 7-5, 6-2. She also repeated her doubles triumph of 1967 with Casals, over Durr and Jones, 3-6, 6-4, 7-5. However, she was unable to defend the mixed doubles title with Owen Davidson for a second consecutive "triple." Australians Ken Fletcher (then playing out of Hong Kong) and Court ended their reign in the semis, 6-4, 9-7, and went on to defeat Metreveli and Olga Morozova, the first Soviet players to reach a major final, 6-1, 14-12. Newcombe and Roche beat Rosewall and Stolle in a splendid doubles final made up entirely of Aussie pros, 3-6, 8-6, 5-7, 14-12, 6-3.

One more great "first Open" of 1968 remained: The $100,000 U.S. Open at Forest Hills, richest of the year's events, which was lavishly promoted by Madison Square Garden in the first year of an ultimately uneasy five-year contract with the USLTA.

By the end of the summer, observers were no longer startled when amateurs knocked off pros. The biggest upsets were the fourth-round knockouts of the Wimbledon men's singles finalists: A badly off-form top-seeded Laver by Drysdale, 4-6, 6-4, 3-6, 6-1, 6-1, and second-seeded Roche by the clever and rejuvenated Gonzalez, 8-6, 6-4, 6-2.

Gonzalez, a graying grandfather but still the glorious "Old Wolf," was the darling of the crowds in the stadium where he had prevailed as a hungry young rebel with a cause in 1948 and 1949. But the speedy "Flying Dutchman," Okker, was too fresh for him in the quarters. Gonzalez melted in a broiling sun, 14-16, 6-3, 10-8, 6-3.

Joining Okker in the semis were Rosewall, Ashe and Graebner. Okker was too quick for Rosewall, 8-6, 6-4, 6-8, 6-1 and Ashe

too powerful for Graebner, 4-6, 8-6, 7-5, 6-2—the match around which author John McPhee wove his brilliant tome, *Levels of the Game.*

Ashe's flashing fireworks—26 aces, a lightning backhand, and superior volleying—overcame Okker in a superb final, 14-12, 5-7, 6-3, 3-6, 6-3. It was the first five-set final since Ashley Cooper over Mal Anderson a decade earlier, and produced the first native champion since Tony Trabert in 1955. Since Arthur had won the U.S. Amateur final two weeks previously in Boston, he had a record that should stand uniquely forever: The lone amateur to win the U.S. Amateur and U.S. Open.

Ashe and Gimeno, an unlikely duo, survived two match points and beat Graebner and Charlie Pasarell, 6-4, 3-6, 4-6, 20-18, 15-13, in the semifinals of the doubles, the longest match in Forest Hills history to that point (95 games). But they had little left for the final. Stan Smith and Lutz, ascending 21-year-old Californians who had won the U.S. Amateur Doubles over South Africans Hewitt and Moore, 6-4, 6-4, 9-7, two weeks earlier, losing no sets in Boston, took the Open title, 11-9, 6-1, 7-5. They won 11 of 19 tournaments, 57 of 66 matches on the season, to claim the No. 1 U.S. doubles ranking for the first time.

King was unable to defend her title. Like Laver, she was far from peak form and struggled grittily through three sets with South African Maryna Godwin in the quarterfinals, 6-3, 3-6, 6-3, and Bueno in the semifinals, 3-6, 6-4, 6-2. Wade, a 23-year-old No. 6-seeded Englishwoman of regal bearing and recently graduated from Sussex University with a degree in math and physics, stopped Wimbledon finalist Dalton, 6-3, 6-2, and countrywoman Jones, 7-5, 6-1, on the way to beating BJK in the final, 6-4, 6-2. Wade, who had worked Bournemouth for an expense check of $120, raked in the $6,000 first prize. Court and Bueno dislodged the defending champs, King and Casals, in the women's doubles final, 4-6, 9-7, 8-6.

There was only one other open tournament in the U.S., the Pacific Southwest at Los Angeles, and form held truer on concrete as Laver beat Rosewall in the final, 4-6, 6-0, 6-0, and Casals beat Bueno for the women's title, 6-4, 6-1.

Despite Laver's Wimbledon triumph and No. 1 world ranking, Ashe, at No. 2, was the "Man of the Year" in tennis. Winner of 10 tournaments, he earned the No. 1 U.S. ranking for the first time after three straight years at No. 2. The first black male to win a major title, he triumphed at Forest Hills while commuting to his Army duties as a data processing instructor at West Point, N.Y. Ashe won 27 straight matches from the start of the Pennsylvania Grass Courts, beating Marty Riessen 6-2, 6-3, 6-3 for the title. His streak continued through the U.S. Amateur, U.S. Open and the Las Vegas Invitational, where he beat Graebner, 9-7, 6-3. It was ended in the semis of the Pacific Southwest by Rosewall, 6-3, 6-2. Also included were singles victories over Juan Gisbert, 6-2, 6-4, 6-2, and Manolo Santana, 11-13, 7-5, 6-3, 13-15, 6-4, in the 4-1 U.S. victory over Spain in the Davis Cup quarterfinal. The last, 83 games, the longest Cup singles match for an American to that time, was in a sense meaningless since the U.S. was already ahead, 3-1. Ashe also won the Inter-Service championship over Air Force Pfc. Pasarell.

As cautious about open tennis as some of the players, the USLTA closed down a 51-year-old tradition, the U.S. Doubles

Championships in Boston, and awarded the pre-Forest Hills week at Longwood as the U.S. Amateur Championships. The USLTA wanted this event to be a continuation of the national tournament that dated to 1881. In the event this two-headed newcomer called the U.S. Open turned out to be a monster, it could be laid away with a minimum of fuss, and the old structure would be in place. Of course the Open only got bigger, better and more profitable, transforming the creaky, penny-pinching USLTA into the wealthy bureaucracy it is today.

But during the transitional year of 1968, the Amateur was a significant event, a useful vehicle especially for the U.S. Davis Cup team that a young new captain, Donald Dell, was grooming to take over for the Aussie dynasty that had been riddled by Newcombe, Roche and Emerson's defection to the pros. Curiously, contract pros were ineligible for Davis Cup.

It was at the Amateur, nationally televised on PBS, that Ashe really began to make his name. Seeded No. 1, he crashed 18 aces and came through an exciting five-set final over unseeded Bob Lutz, 4-6, 6-3, 8-10, 6-0, 6-4. He had launched a singular double, completed at the U.S. Open two Sundays later. Amateur and Open champ. Arthur alone. Though a U.S. Amateur Championships exists today, it is for honest-to-goodness amateurs, people who couldn't get near Flushing Meadows without a ticket.

Ashe and Graebner were the singles players for the U.S. as it recaptured the Davis Cup for the first time since 1963. Once again it was on Adelaide turf in December, a 4-1 victory over Australia. Imbued with great esprit de corps by 29-year-old Dell, the Americans (Ashe, Graebner, Smith, Lutz and Pasarell) made winning back the Cup into "a quest." They plowed through the West Indies, Mexico, Ecuador – all bagels – Spain India and Australia, losing only 3 matches. But Spain was difficult as Santana took Graebner apart at the outset, 6-2, 6-3, 6-3. And so was India as sly Ramanathan Krishnan did the same, 7-5, 4-6, 6-2, 6-1. But Ashe was dependable with two no-nonsense singles wins in each, and the doubles went the U.S. way, Pasarell and Graebner over Spaniards Santana and Juan Gisbert, 11-13, 17-15, 7-5, 6-2, and Smith and Lutz over Premjit Lall and Krishnan, 6-2, 6-3, 6-2.

Stripped of their marquee names, the Aussies had no chance in the Challenge Round. Bill Bowrey made Graebner struggle in the opener, 8-10, 6-4, 8-6, 3-6, 6-1, but Ashe, after a slow start, drilled lefty Ray Ruffels, 6-8, 7-5, 6-3, 6-3, and the kids, Smith and Lutz, mopped up to take the Cup, 6-4, 6-4, 6-2, over Ruffels and 17-year-old John Alexander, who would help win the 1977 Cup. It was a farewell Cup final for eminent Australian captain, Harry Hopman, his 21st, of which he guided a record 16 winners.

There were a couple of other notable achievements during this landmark season.

Nancy Richey made one of the fantastic comebacks in history. Climbing from match point down (6-4, 5-1), the determined Texan won 12 straight games (39 of the final 53 points), to beat King, 4-6, 7-5, 6-0, in the semifinals of the Madison Square Garden International. That was King's last match as an amateur. Within days she and Emerson signed on with George MacCall's short-lived NTL troupe. Richey beat Dalton in one Garden final, 7-5, 7-5, and Ashe won the other over Emerson, 6-4, 6-4, 7-5.

With King and Casals unavailable in the still-amateur women's team competitions, the U.S. relinquished both the Federation and Wightman Cups. The Netherlands beat the U.S. in the Federation semifinals at Paris, and, Australia snared the Cup, 3-0 over the Dutch. At Wimbledon, the Truman sisters, Nell and Christine Janes, were socko siblings in the decisive Wightman seventh match, beating Stephanie DeFina and Kathy Harter, 6-3, 2-6, 6-3, to break a U.S. streak of seven years.

The longest match in national championship annals, in terms of playing time and games, took place at Salisbury, Maryland, the U.S. Indoor, when Englishmen Bobby Wilson and Mark Cox defeated Pasarell and Graebner, 26-24, 17-19, 30-28, in a quarterfinal: six hours, 20 minutes, 144 games. They then lost to Smith and Lutz, 13-11, 4-6, 6-3, who were then beaten for the title by Tom Koch and Okker, 6-3, 10-12, 8-6. Richey won the singles over Graebner, 6-4, 6-4, 6-4.

King and Casals cleaned up at their version of the U.S. Indoor at Winchester, Mass. Billie Jean stopped Rosie in the singles final, 6-3, 9-7, but they were on the same side in a 6-2, 6-2, prize winner over Mary Ann Eisel and Kathy Harter.

1968 CHAMPIONS AND LEADERS

Australian Championships
Men's Singles Final: Bill Bowrey (AUS) def. Juan Gisbert (ESP), 7-5, 2-6, 9-7, 6-4
Women's Singles Final: Billie Jean King (USA) def. Margaret Smith Court (AUS), 6-1, 6-2
Men's Doubles Final: Dick Crealy and Allan Stone (AUS) def. Terry Addison and Ray Keldie (AUS), 10-8, 6-4, 6-3
Women's Doubles Final: Karen Krantzcke and Kerry Melville (AUS) def. Judy Tegart Dalton and Lesley Turner (AUS), 6-4, 3-6, 6-2
Mixed Doubles Final: Billie Jean King (USA) and Dick Crealy (AUS) def. Margaret Smith Court and Allan Stone (AUS), default

French Open
Men's Singles Final: Ken Rosewall (AUS) def. Rod Laver (AUS), 6-3, 6-1, 2-6, 6-2
Women's Singles Final: Nancy Richey (USA) def. Ann Haydon Jones (GBR), 5-7, 6-4, 6-1
Men's Doubles Final: Ken Rosewall and Fred Stolle (AUS) def. Roy Emerson and Rod Laver (AUS), 6-3, 6-4, 6-3
Women's Doubles Final: Francoise Durr (FRA) and Ann Haydon Jones (GBR) def. Rosie Casals and Billie Jean King (USA), 7-5, 4-6, 6-4
Mixed Doubles Final: Francoise Durr and Jean Claude Barclay (FRA) def. Billie Jean King (USA) and Owen Davidson (AUS), 6-1, 6-4

Wimbledon
Men's Singles Final: Rod Laver (AUS) def. Tony Roche (AUS), 6-3, 6-4, 6-2
Women's Singles Final: Billie Jean King (USA) def. Judy Tegart Dalton (AUS), 9-7, 7-5
Men's Doubles Final: John Newcombe and Tony Roche (AUS) def. Ken Rosewall and Fred Stolle (AUS), 3-6, 8-6, 5-7, 14-12, 6-3
Women's Doubles Final: Rosie Casals and Billie Jean King (USA) def. Francoise Durr (FRA) and Ann Haydon Jones (GBR), 3-6, 6-4, 7-5
Mixed Doubles Final: Margaret Smith Court (AUS) and Ken Fletcher (HKG) def. Olga Morozova and Alex Metreveli (USSR), 6-1, 14-12

U.S. Championships (Amateur)
Men's Singles Final: Arthur Ashe (USA) def. Bob Lutz (USA), 4-6, 6-3, 8-10, 6-0, 6-4
Women's Singles Final: Margaret Smith Court (AUS) def. Maria Bueno (BRA), 6-2, 6-2
Men's Doubles Final: Bob Lutz and Stan Smith (USA) def. Bob Hewitt and Ray Moore (RSA), 6-4, 6-4, 9-7
Women's Doubles Final: Maria Bueno (BRA) and Margaret Smith Court (AUS) def. Virginia Wade and Joyce Barclay Williams (GBR), 6-3, 7-5
Mixed Doubles Final: Mary Ann Eisel and Peter Curtis (USA) def. Tory Ann Fretz and Robert Perry (USA), 6-4, 7-5

U.S. Open
Men's Singles Final: Arthur Ashe (USA) def. Tom Okker (NED), 14-12, 5-7, 6-3, 3-6, 6-3
Women's Singles Final: Virginia Wade (GBR) def. Billie Jean King (USA), 6-4, 6-2
Men's Doubles Final: Bob Lutz and Stan Smith (USA) def. Arthur Ashe (USA) and Andres Gimeno (ESP), 11-9, 6-1, 7-5
Women's Doubles Final: Maria Bueno (BRA) and Margaret Smith Court (AUS) def. Billie Jean King and Rosie Casals (USA), 4-6, 9-7, 8-6

Year-End No. 1
Men: Rod Laver
Women: Billie Jean King

Top Player Earnings
Men: Rod Laver $70,359

Davis Cup: United States

Federation Cup: Australia

Wightman Cup: Great Britain

1969 Laver Nets Second Slam

Rod Laver wins Wimbledon for a fourth time in 1969—the third leg of his unprecedented second "Grand Slam."

Rod Laver wins Wimbledon for a fourth time in 1969—the third leg of his unprecedented second "Grand Slam."

The second year of "Open" tennis was one of continued progress but lingering confusion on the political front—and towering on-court performances by Margaret Smith Court and most notably Rod Laver, who netted an unprecedented second Grand Slam.

There were 30 open tournaments around the world and prize money escalated to about $1.3 million. Laver was the leading money winner with $124,000, followed by Tony Roche ($75,045), Tom Okker ($65,451), Roy Emerson ($62,629) and John Newcombe ($52,610).

The Davis Cup and other international team competitions continued to be governed by reactionaries, however, and admitted only players under the jurisdiction of their national associations. This left "contract pros"—who were paid guarantees and obligated by contract to adhere to the schedule set by independent promoters—on the outs, while players who accepted prize money but remained under the aegis of their national associations were allowed to play. At the end of the year, a proposal to end this silly double standard and include the contract pros was rejected by the Davis Cup nations in a 21-19 vote.

The "registered player" concept, borne of compromise a year earlier, persisted until finally being abolished by a newly-elected and more forward-looking International Lawn Tennis Federation Committee of Management in July. Still, the public found it difficult to understand who was and who was not a pro. In the United States, those who took prize money but remained under the authority of the U.S. Lawn Tennis Association were officially called "players."

Under the leadership of Captain Donald Dell, the members of the U.S. Davis Cup team preferred to call themselves "independent pros," making it clear that they were competing for prize money. The USLTA leadership would have preferred to keep the U.S. tournament circuit amateur, paying expenses only, except for five open events given ILTF sanction (Philadelphia Indoor, Madison Square Garden, the U.S. Open, Pacific Southwest, Howard Hughes Invitational in Las Vegas). This would have kept down spiraling overhead costs, a threat to the exclusive clubs, which resisted sponsorship but did not want to lose their traditional events.

Dell and the Davis Cup team refused to play in tournaments that offered expenses and guarantees instead of prize money, however, and thus effectively forced a full prize-money circuit into being in the United States.

Dell led the way by organizing the $25,000 Washington Star International in his hometown. It was a prototype tournament in many ways, commercially sponsored and played in a public park for over-the-table prize money rather than under-the-table appearance fees. Other tournaments followed suit, and a new and successful U.S. Summer Circuit began to emerge. In all, 15 U.S. tournaments offered $440,000 in prize money, with the $137,000 U.S. Open again the world's richest event. In 1968, there had been only two prize-money open tournaments in the U.S., the $100,000 U.S. Open and the $30,000 Pacific Southwest.

A few peculiar hybrid events—half-amateur, half professional—remained. The most obviously unnecessary was the $25,000 National Singles and Doubles at Longwood Cricket Club, which welcomed amateurs and independent pros but excluded the contract pros. Stan Smith beat Bob Lutz 9-7, 6-3, 6-0, and Court

prevailed over Virginia Wade 4-6, 6-3, 6-0, for the singles titles, but the grandly named tournament was essentially meaningless, except to those cashing checks, and vanished from the scene the next year in a natural sorting-out process.

A U.S. Amateur Championships also was played on clay in Rochester, the telecast of which was interrupted by a sexist act that wouldn't even be contemplated today. Linda Tuero of Metairie, La., and Gwyneth Thomas of Cleveland, hyper-patient, unrepentant baseliners, were contesting the women's final with endless rallies, one point lasting 10-1/2 minutes and 326 strokes. It was too much for referee Ernie Oberlaender. After two hours, 20 minutes, and with no end in sight, he yanked them. He moved them to a court away from the cameras and installed the men's finalists for a match shorter in time, longer in games, won by Butch Seewagen of New York over Zan Guerry of Lookout Mountain, Tenn., 9-7, 6-8, 1-6, 6-2, 6-4.

"What else could I do," the referee was apologetic. "Two fine players, but they got locked into patballing, and neither would give. The crowd and the TV people were getting restless." Linda and Gwyneth actually seemed relieved. "I'm glad they got us off TV," said Tuero, eventually the victor, 4-6, 6-1, 6-2. "I wouldn't have watched it 10 minutes myself."

If the labels put on tournaments and players boggled the public mind, there was no doubt as to who the world's No. 1 players were: Australians Laver and Court.

Laver repeated his 1962 Grand Slam by sweeping the Australian, French, Wimbledon and U.S. titles the first year all four were open. Laver also won the South African Open over Okker, 6-3, 10-8, 6-3, and finished the season with a 106-16 record and winning 18 of 32 tournaments. He didn't lose a match from the start of Wimbledon in June until the second round of the Pacific Southwest Open in late September, when Ray Moore ended the winning streak at 31 matches, 7-5, 3-6, 6-2. During that stretch, Laver won seven tournaments, including his fourth Wimbledon (where he had not lost since the 1960 final), his second Forest Hills and his fifth U.S. Pro Championship. By the time he got to Los Angeles, Rod just wanted to get 45 minutes farther south to his adopted home of Corona Del Mar, Calif., where his wife, Mary, had just given birth to his son, Rick Rodney.

The most difficult match for Laver of the 26 that constituted the Slam came early, in the semifinals of the Australian. He beat Roche, 7-5, 22-20, 9-11, 1-6, 6-3, enduring more than four hours in the sweltering, 105-degree heat of a Brisbane afternoon. Both players got groggy in the brutal sun, even though they employed an old Aussie trick of putting wet cabbage leaves in their hats to help stay cool. It was so close that it could easily have gone either way, and a controversial line call helped Laver grasp the final set. Having survived, Laver beat Andres Gimeno in the final, 6-3, 6-4, 7-5. Rod had survived an Aussie gauntlet: Emerson in the fourth round, 6-2, 6-4, 3-6, 9-7, Stolle in the quarters, 6-4, 18-16, 6-4, and Roche. Gimeno traveled a less hazardous route, defeating Butch Buchholz 6-1, 6-2, 6-2 and Ray Ruffels 6-2, 11-9, 6-2.

At the French Open, another Aussie, Dick Crealy, took the first two sets from Laver in a second-rounder, 3-6, 7-9, 6-2, 6-2, 6-4, but the red-haired "Rocket" accelerated, stopping the increasingly dangerous Stan Smith in the fourth round, 6-4, 6-2, 6-4, Gimeno in

the quarters, 4-6, 6-4, 6-2, 6-4 and Okker in the semis, 4-6, 6-0, 6-2, 6-4. Ultimately he played one of his best clay-court matches to beat defender Ken Rosewall in the final, 6-4, 6-3, 6-4, after "Muscles" had knocked off Roche, 7-5, 6-2, 6-2.

An unheralded Indian named Premjit Lall similarly captured the first two sets in the second round at Wimbledon, but Laver awoke to dispose of him, 3-6, 4-6, 6-3, 6-0, 6-0. Stan Smith then took Laver to five sets, 6-4, 6-2, 7-9, 3-6, 6-3, in the fourth round. In the quarters, Cliff Drysdale wasn't the impediment he'd been a year before at the U.S. Open, going down, 6-4, 6-2, 6-3. To finish, Rod burst from ambushes to raise the heat and tone down Arthur Ashe in the semis, 2-6, 6-2, 9-7, 6-0, then Newcombe, who had eliminated Roche, 3-6, 6-1, 14-12, 6-4. Despite Newcombe's thoughtful game plan of using lobs and changes of pace instead of the straightforward power for which he was known, Laver prevailed, 6-4, 5-7, 6-4, 6-4.

Then, to complete the Slam, it was on to the U.S. Open. But first, the U.S. Pro at Longwood in Boston where Laver, winning for the fifth time, reprised over Newcombe, 7-5, 6-2, 4-6, 6-1. "How could he do that the week after Wimbledon?" marveled Ashe. But that was Laver in '69, virtually invincible to any physical and mental obstacles.

The climax came at Forest Hills, where Philip Morris and its tennis-minded chairman of the board, Joe Cullman, had infused heavy promotional dollars into the U.S. Open. He brought flamboyant South African promoter Owen Williams in from Johannesburg to run a jazzed-up show and foster corporate patronage. They drew record crowds until the weather turned surly. Rain inundated the already soft and uneven lawns, played havoc with the schedule and pushed the tournament days past its scheduled conclusion.

Despite the trying conditions and the imminent birth of his son on the West Coast, Laver remained intent. He was taken to five sets only by persistent Dennis Ralston, 6-4, 4-6, 4-6, 6-2, 6-3 in the fourth round. After that, Laver disposed of ever-prickly Emerson, 4-6, 8-6, 13-11, 6-4 in the quarterfinals, and defender Ashe, 8-6, 6-3, 14-12 in the semifinals. Arthur had brushed aside Rosewall, 8-6, 6-4, 6-3 in the quarterfinals. Roche, in a wowser, denied his mate Newcombe a place in the final, defeating his doubles partner 3-6, 6-4, 4-6, 6-3, 8-6 in the semifinals.

Then they waited through two days of rain as either the Grand Slam or a grand slap hovered. Laver, an old hand at the old ways with the feet, donned spikes in the second set. He became a sure-soled bog runner in climbing over Roche, 7-9, 6-1, 6-3, 6-2, on a gloomy Tuesday before a gathering of only 3,708 fans who sat through rain delays of 90 and 30 minutes. The weather certainly dampened the occasion, but it was appropriate that Roche—clearly No. 2 in the world, and regarded as Laver's heir apparent until a series of left arm injuries started to plague him the next year—provided the final hurdle. The ruggedly muscular Roche was the only player with a winning record over Laver (5-3) for the year.

Laver uncharacteristically leaped the net in the Fred Perry style of the 1930s—"I don't know why I did that!—and shed a few tears as USLTA President Alastair Martin presented him the champion's trophy and check for $16,000, saying, "You're the greatest in the world ... perhaps the greatest we've ever seen."

"I never really think of myself in those terms, but I feel honored that people see fit to say such things about me," said Laver shyly. "Tennis-wise, this year was much tougher than '62. At the time the best players—Ken Rosewall, Lew Hoad, Pancho Gonzalez—were not in the amateur ranks. I didn't find out who were the best until I turned pro and had my brains beaten out for six months at the start of 1963."

Now, in the open era, there was no question who was best.

Margaret Smith Court, who had returned to action following a brief retirement (the first of several in her long career), was almost as monopolistic as Laver. She lost only five matches the entire season, winning 19 of 24 tournaments and 98 of 103 matches. She won the Australian over Billie Jean King, 6-4, 6-1, after trailing Kerry Melville, 3-5 in the last set in the semifinal, running four games to 3-6, 6-2, 7-5. In the French, Court won the last four rounds by beating Rhodesia's Pat Pretorius Walkden, 6-4, 6-0; Melville, 9-7, 6-1; defending champ Nancy Richey, 6-3, 4-6, 7-5 and finally Ann Haydon Jones, 6-1, 4-6, 6-3—all splendid clay-court players.

Court's dream of a Grand Slam ended at Wimbledon, however, where Jones beat her in the semifinals, 10-12, 6-3, 6-2. To the unbridled joy of her British countrymen, the left-handed, 30-year-old Ann Haydon Jones (Mrs. Philip 'Pip' Jones) won her first Wimbledon title after 14 years of trying, squashing King's bid for a fourth consecutive crown, 3-6, 6-3, 6-2. Billie Jean was shaken by the noisy partisanship of the customarily proper British gallery and what she thought were some dubious line calls, but the British hailed the popular Jones as a conquering heroine.

Injury kept the top-seeded Jones out of the U.S. Open, won by second-seeded Court on a loss of no sets. In fact, she lost more than two games in a set only twice in six matches, in beating fellow Aussie Karen Krantzcke in the quarterfinals, 6-0, 9-7, and fifth-seeded defender Wade in the semifinals, 7-5, 6-0. Richey, seeded sixth—eschewing her usual baseline game for net-rushing tactics quite foreign to her—helped Margaret out. She eliminated third-seeded King in the quarters, 6-4, 8-6, but found herself passed repeatedly in the final by some of Court's finest ground-stroking, 6-2, 6-2.

But if Laver and Court clearly reigned supreme, there were other notable heroes, heroines and achievements in 1969. Phenomenally Pancho Gonzalez, at 41, mowed down in succession four Hall of Famers-to-be—Newcombe, 6-1, 6-2, Rosewall, 6-4, 1-6, 6-3, Smith, 8-6, 7-9, 6-4, and Ashe, 6-0, 6-2, 6-4—to win the $50,000 Howard Hughes Open at Las Vegas, and the $12,500 first prize, second only to the U.S. Open. Gonzalez also won the Pacific Southwest Open over Cliff Richey, 6-0, 7-5, and had a 2-0 record over Smith, who was ranked No. 1 in the U.S. for the first time. Gonzalez was the top U.S. money-winner with $46,288, and might have returned to the No. 1 spot he occupied in 1948 and 1949 if the USLTA had included contract pros in its rankings.

Gonzalez' most dramatic performance, however, came at Wimbledon, where he beat Charlie Pasarell in the opening round in the longest match in the history of the oldest and most prestigious of championships. It consumed five hours, 12 minutes and 112 games over two days. Gonzalez lost a marathon first set and virtually threw the second, complaining bitterly that it was too dark to continue play. He was whistled and hooted by the normally genteel Centre Court crowd, but won back all his detractors the next day with a gallant display. Pasarell played well, but Gonzalez was magnificent. In the fifth set, he staved off seven match points, twice serving out of 0-40 holes, and won, 22-24, 1-6, 16-14, 6-3, 11-9. Gonzalez lasted until the fourth round, when his protégé, Ashe, beat him, 7-5, 4-6, 6-3, 6-3.

Stan Smith won eight tournaments, including the U.S. Indoor over Egyptian lefty Ismail El Shafei, 6-3, 6-8, 6-4, 6-4, to replace Ashe atop the U.S. rankings. Ashe, bothered by a nagging elbow injury and numerous non-tennis distractions following his big year in 1968, won only two tournaments but had an 83-24 match record and more wins than any other American.

The United States defeated long-shot Romania, 5-0, in the Davis Cup Challenge Round on a fast asphalt court at Cleveland, painted and polished to make it even slicker, to the home team's benefit. Ashe defeated Ilie Nastase in the opening singles, 6-2, 15-13, 7-5, and Smith escaped the hulking and wily Ion Tiriac, 6-8, 6-3, 5-7, 6-4, 6-4. In the pivotal doubles, Smith and Lutz closed out the Romanians, 8-6, 6-1, 11-9. President Richard M. Nixon, a bowler and golfer who secretly despised tennis, hosted both final-round teams at a White House reception. This was a nice gesture, but the Chief Executive caused a few awkward stares when, as a memento of the occasion, he presented each player with a golf ball. Perhaps these were left over, some speculated, from the golf-happy Eisenhower administration. "I'm a Republican, but I'll never vote for him again," grumbled Richey. "Why he do this?" said a puzzled Tiriac. "No golf courses in Romania."

Tiny Romania, with the lion-hearted Tiriac and the immensely talented Nastase its only players of international standard, was proud to have gotten past Egypt, Spain, the Soviet Union, India and Great Britain. Australia failed to reach the final for the first time since 1937—beaten in its first series by Mexico, 3-2, the first opening-round loss ever for Captain Harry Hopman, and for the Aussies since falling to Italy in 1928. Rafael Osuna, Mexico's popular tennis hero, defeated Bill Bowrey in the decisive fifth match, 6-2, 3-6, 8-6, 6-3, and was hailed triumphantly by his countrymen. This was the engaging Osuna's last hurrah, however. He died tragically shortly thereafter, at age 30, when a private plane carrying him on a business trip crashed into the mountains outside of Monterrey.

In another significant development, the Davis Cup nations voted South Africa and Rhodesia out of the competition for 1970 and 1971 because demonstrations against their racial policies, and the refusal of some nations to play them made their presence in the draw disruptive.

Nancy Richey was upset in the semifinals of the U.S. Clay Court Championships by Gail Sherriff Chanfreau, 6-3, 6-4, ending her tournament record female winning streak at 33 straight matches over seven years. She was trying to become only the second player to win seven consecutive U.S. titles, matching the feat of Richard Sears in the first seven U.S. Men's Championships (1881—87). Chanfreau won that title over Linda Tuero, 6-2, 6-2. Yugoslav Zeljko Franulovic won the other over Ashe, 8-6, 6-3, 6-4.

Clark Graebner, uniting with Bill Bowrey in a 6-4, 4-6, 6-4 victory over Aussies Crealy and Allan Stone, had his fifth U.S. Clay doubles title, passing Bill Talbert's record set in 1946.

Richey, who retained the No. 1 U.S. women's ranking teamed with Julie Heldman and Jane "Peaches" Bartkowicz to regain the Federation Cup at Athens and the Wightman Cup at Cleveland. Richey was undefeated in singles (4-0) and Heldman lost only to Court as the U.S. defeated Bulgaria, Italy, Netherlands (each 3-0) and Australia, 2-1, for the world team championship. Heldman, a clever player who nicknamed herself "Junkball Julie," set the tone of the 5-2 Wightman Cup victory by upsetting Wade in the opening match, 3-6, 6-1, 8-6, and also beat Winnie Shaw, 6-3, 6-4. Richey topped Shaw, 8-6, 6-2, and Bartkowicz stopped Christine Truman Janes, 8-6, 6-0.

Ranked No. 2 nationally with eight titles in 20 tournaments and a 67-13 match record, 24-year-old Heldman also became the first American woman to win the Italian Championships since Althea Gibson in 1956, beating three outstanding clay courters—Lesley Turner Bowrey (wife of Bill), 3-6, 6-4, 6-1, Jones, 4-6, 6-4, 6-1, and Kerry Melville, 7-5, 6-3.

One of the most remarkable and crowd-pleasing victories of the year was that of Darlene Hard and Francoise Durr in the U.S. Open doubles. They were a "pickup" team; Hard, by then a 33-year-old teaching pro, had entered as a lark. Out of tournament condition, she was an embarrassment in losing the first eight games of the final, but seemed suddenly to remember the skills and instincts that had made her the world's premier doubles player, winner of five previous U.S. women's titles. As the crowd loudly cheered their revival, Hard and Durr stunned heavily favored Court and Wade, 0-6, 6-3, 6-4.

Forest Hills had begun with a match of record duration. F. D. Robbins defeated Dick Dell, younger brother of Donald, 22-20, 9-7, 6-8, 8-10, 6-4, the longest in number of singles games—100—in the history of the U.S. Championships. When the tournament ran three days over, the men's doubles finished in a disgraceful shambles, Rosewall and Fred Stolle beating Ralston and Pasarell, 2-6, 7-5, 13-11, 6-3, before a few hundred spectators on a soggy Wednesday. Pasarell-Ralston got defaults from Wimbledon champs Newcombe and Roche in the quarters and Australian Open winners Laver and Emerson in the semis, who were off to other pursuits. Newcombe-Roche were urged to leave waterlogged New York by their employers, WCT, in order to meet other commitments, a decision that rankled the ILTF in its increasingly uneasy dealings with the new pro promoters. After all, it was unseemly for the No. 1 team to walk out on a major. They had repeated at Wimbledon, over Tom Okker-Marty Riessen, 7-5, 11-9, 6-3, and won three other tournaments, including the French (over Emerson and Laver, 4-6, 6-1, 3-6, 6-4, 6-4).

1969 CHAMPIONS AND LEADERS

Australian Open
Men's Singles Final: Rod Laver (AUS) def. Andres Gimeno (ESP), 6-3, 6-4, 7-5
Women's Singles Final: Margaret Smith Court (AUS) def. Billie Jean King (USA), 6-4, 6-1
Men's Doubles Final: Roy Emerson and Rod Laver (AUS) def. Ken Rosewall and Fred Stolle (AUS), 6-4, 6-4 (shortened by mutual agreement)

Women's Doubles Final: Margaret Smith Court and Judy Tegart Dalton (AUS) def. Rosie Casals and Billie Jean King (USA), 6-4, 6-4
Mixed Doubles Final: Ann Haydon Jones (GBR) and Fred Stolle (AUS) and Margaret Smith Court and Marty Riessen (SHARED)

French Open
Men's Singles Final: Rod Laver (AUS) def. Ken Rosewall (AUS), 6-4, 6-3, 6-4
Women's Singles Final: Margaret Smith Court (AUS) def. Ann Haydon Jones (GBR), 6-1, 4-6, 6-3
Men's Doubles Final: John Newcombe and Tony Roche (AUS) def. Roy Emerson and Rod Laver (AUS), 4-6, 6-1, 3-6, 6-4, 6-4
Women's Doubles Final: Francoise Durr (FRA) and Ann Haydon Jones (GBR) def. Margaret Smith Court (AUS) and Nancy Richey (USA), 6-0, 4-6, 7-5
Mixed Doubles Final: Margaret Smith Court (AUS) and Marty Riessen (USA) def. Francoise Durr and Jean Claude Barclay (FRA), 6-3, 6-2

Wimbledon
Men's Singles Final: Rod Laver (AUS) def. John Newcombe (AUS), 6-4, 5-7, 6-4, 6-4
Women's Singles Final: Ann Haydon Jones (GBR) def. Billie Jean King (USA), 3-6, 6-3, 6-2
Men's Doubles Final: John Newcombe and Tony Roche (AUS) def. Tom Okker (NED) and Marty Riessen (USA), 7-5, 11-9, 6-3
Women's Doubles Final: Margaret Smith Court and Judy Tegart Dalton (AUS) def. Patty Hogan and Peggy Michel (USA) 9-7, 6-2
Mixed Doubles Final: Ann Haydon Jones (GBR) and Fred Stolle (AUS) def. Judy Tegart Dalton and Tony Roche (AUS), 6-3, 6-2

U.S. Championships (Amateur)
Men's Singles Final: Stan Smith (USA) def. Bob Lutz (USA), 9-7, 6-3, 6-1
Women's Singles Final: Margaret Smith Court (AUS) def. Virginia Wade (GBR), 4-6, 6-3, 6-0
Men's Doubles Final: Dick Crealy and Allan Stone (AUS) def. Bill Bowrey (AUS) and Charlie Pasarell (USA), 9-11, 6-3, 7-5
Women's Doubles Final: Virginia Wade (GBR) and Margaret Smith Court (AUS) def. Mary Ann Eisel Curtis and Valerie Ziegenfuss (USA), 6-1, 6-3
Mixed Doubles Final: Patti Hogan and Paul Sullivan (USA) def. Kristy Pigeon (USA) and Terry Addison (AUS), 6-4, 2-6, 12-10

U.S. Open
Men's Singles Final: Rod Laver (AUS) def. Tony Roche (AUS), 7-9, 6-1, 6-2, 6-2
Women's Singles Final: Margaret Smith Court (AUS) def. Nancy Richey (USA), 6-2, 6-2
Men's Doubles Final: Ken Rosewall and Fred Stolle (AUS) def. Charlie Pasarell and Dennis Ralston (USA), 2-6, 7-5, 13-11, 6-3
Women's Doubles Final: Françoise Durr (FRA) and Darlene Hard (USA) def. Margaret Smith Court (AUS) and Virginia Wade (GBR), 0-6, 6-4, 6-4
Mixed Doubles Final: Margaret Smith Court (AUS) and Marty Riessen (USA) def. Francoise Durr (FRA) and Dennis Ralston (USA) 7-5, 6-3

Year-End No. 1
Men: Rod Laver
Women: Margaret Smith Court

Top Player Earnings
Men: Rod Laver $124,000

Davis Cup: United States

Federation Cup: United States

Wightman Cup: United States

1970 Maggie Finally Claims Her Slam

As in 1950 and 1960, the beginning of a new decade also was, in many ways, the start of a new era for tennis. In 1970, the professional game for both men and women fitfully began to assume the structure that would characterize the decade of its most rapid growth.

This was the first year of the men's Grand Prix—a point system under the aegis of the International Lawn Tennis Federation, that

Margaret Court won all four majors during the 1970 calendar year, becoming the second woman to win the Grand Slam.

linked together tournaments, leading to year-end bonus awards for the top finishers in the standings and berths in a new tournament at the end of the year: The Grand Prix Masters. The brainchild of protean Jack Kramer, the Grand Prix was announced

late in 1969 and sponsored by Pepsico. Players earned points, round by round, in the Grand Prix tournaments they entered, and at season's end the top men received cash awards scaled according to their order of finish. Cliff Richey, for example, collected $25,000 for topping the standings; Arthur Ashe earned $17,000 for placing second; Ken Rosewall $15,000 for coming in third, etc. There were 19 tournaments in the Grand Prix in 1970. The "bonus pool" totaled $150,000 and another $50,000 was at stake in the six-man Masters.

The underlying intent of the Grand Prix, clearly, was to keep players from signing guaranteed contracts with the professional troupes, World Championship Tennis (WCT) and the struggling National Tennis League (NTL). WCT, which loomed as an ever more formidable rival to the ILTF and its 93-member national associations for control of the burgeoning pro game, responded by swiftly signing more players to contracts, then increasing its stable to 30 players by swallowing the NTL in May.

Mike Davies, executive director of WCT, became a member of the ILTF scheduling committee, but wariness and distrust between the maneuvering giants continued. It became increasingly difficult for traditional tournaments to count on the participation of the WCT players because of the "management fees" demanded by WCT in order to cover their guarantees to the players.

In September, at the U.S. Open, WCT took the wraps off a Grand Prix-style competition of its own, announcing a "million-dollar circuit" for 1971. The first World Championship of Tennis, for 32 players to be selected by an international press panel, would consist of 20 tournaments with uniform prize money and point standings, leading to a rich, nationally televised playoff with a $50,000 first prize.

This was considered a declaration of war by WCT against the ILTF, especially since Davies had never mentioned it to the ILTF calendar committee. The battle intensified when, shortly thereafter, WCT announced that it had signed Ashe, Charlie Pasarell and Bob Lutz to five-year contracts in a package deal. The ILTF went ahead and announced an expanded Grand Prix, worth $1.5 million, in 1971, but the battle lines had already been drawn.

The beneficiaries of the infighting, of course, were the players, who found themselves the objects of a giddy bidding war between the ILTF, which offered ever-bigger prize money tournaments but no guarantees, and WCT, with its long-term, guaranteed contracts.

Rod Laver did not retain any of the major titles he monopolized in 1969, but still became the first tennis player to crack the $200,000 barrier in winnings.

He collected $201,453, compared to the $157,037 won by Lee Trevino, top earner on the professional golf circuit. This had heretofore been unimaginable. But prize money was escalating at a rate no one had foreseen—nearly $1 million was up for grabs in U.S. tournaments alone—and three players (Laver, U.S. Open champ Rosewall and Ashe) won more than $100,000.

Growing along with the total purses, however, was the disparity in prize money for men and women. Despite Margaret Smith Court's fulfillment of a long-held ambition—a singles Grand Slam of the Australian, French, Wimbledon and U.S. titles—1970 was for the majority of women players the autumn of their dis-

content. A group of pioneers, led by the determined Gladys Heldman—a tough, shrewd businesswoman who had founded *World Tennis* magazine in 1953— decided that the women would have to split away from mixed tournaments and form their own tour if they were ever to corner a significant share of the sport's mushrooming riches and publicity. This was a bold step, but the women decided to take it in September, and from a little acorn—a $7,500 renegade tournament for nine women in Houston—there eventually grew a mighty oak, the women's pro tour in the U.S.

The political kettle was boiling, but 1970 was also a spectacularly eventful year on the court. It was made singularly exciting by the advent of the game's first major scoring innovation—tie-breakers—and towering performances by several players, notably Rosewall and Court.

"Mighty Margaret" had twice before (1962, 69) won three of the four major singles titles in a season. In 1970, at age 28, she finally corralled the Grand Slam previously achieved by only one woman—Maureen Connolly in 1953. Court compiled a 104-6 record, winning 21 of 27 tournaments, and had the season's longest winning streak, 39 matches.

But a glitch for Margaret was a small September post-Open tournament at Charlotte, N.C., where she was beaten in the semifinal by a pony-tailed adolescent whom she would presently face on major battlegrounds: 15-year-old Chris Evert, who defeated her 7-6, 7-6. The kid, an amateur in her first final among pros, then lost to Nancy Richey, 6-4, 6-1.

Court lost only three sets during the Grand Slam, none in winning her ninth Australian singles title. She defeated Kerry Melville—one of only four women to beat her during the season—in the final, 6-3, 6-1, and teamed with Judy Tegart Dalton to win the doubles by the same score over Melville and Karen Krantzcke. Rising 18-year-old Evonne Goolagong was her quarterfinal victim, 6-3, 6-1, and a rare foe she looked up to, 6-foot-2 Krantzcke, in the semifinal, 6-1, 6-3.

At the French, only rising Soviet Olga Morozova pushed Court to three sets, in the second round, 3-6, 8-6, 6-1. Everything else was straight sets: Rosie Casals, 7-5, 6-2, in the quarters, Heldman, 6-0, 6-2, in the semis, finally, 6-2, 6-4, over 6-foot German Helga Niessen, who had removed Billie Jean King, 2-6, 8-6, 6-1, in the quarters. Francoise Durr won her fourth consecutive doubles title, alongside Gail Sherriff Chanfreau, over Casals and King, 6-1, 3-6, 6-3.

At Wimbledon, the tall, languid Niessen—not considered a threat on grass courts—took the first set from Court in the quarterfinals, but did not get another game, 6-8, 6-0, 6-0. After Margaret disposed of Casals, 6-4, 6-1, and Billie Jean dumped Durr, 6-3, 7-5, their final was a masterpiece of drama and shot-making under duress. Both players were hurt. Court had a painfully strained and swollen ankle tightly strapped as she went on court. She had taken a pain-killing injection beforehand. King was hobbling on a deteriorated kneecap, which required surgery immediately after Wimbledon.

Nevertheless, BJK broke serve in the first set three times. Each time Court broke back. Their injuries partially dictated the pattern of play, but both players produced magnificent shots

under pressure. It was the longest women's final ever at Wimbledon— 46 games— Court finally winning by 14-12, 11-9, in 2-1/2 hours, well after the anesthetic effects of her injection had worn off. King saved three match points with gutsy shots worthy of the contest. "It was a bit like one of those 990-page novels that Trollope and Arnold Bennett used to write," suggested British journalist David Gray, who in 1977 would become general secretary of the International Tennis Federation. "It started a little slowly, but had so many fascinating twists of character and plot that in the end it became a matter of utter compulsion to see how it all ended."

King took her sixth doubles title, her third with Casals, 6-2, 6-3 over Durr and Virginia Wade. Rosie teamed with Ilie Nastase to win the mixed, over the Soviets, Morozova and Alex Metreveli, 6-3, 4-6, 9-7. Billie Jean was the only player who truly challenged Court, splitting their four matches during the year, but King was still recuperating from her post-Wimbledon surgery.

In her absence, Court completed the Slam at Forest Hills, losing only 13 games in mowing down Pam Austin (6-1, 6-0), Patti Hogan (6-1, 6-1), Pat Faulkner (6-0, 6-2), Helen Gourlay (6-2, 6-2) and Richey (6-1, 6-3). Casals, who had out-volleyed Wade 6-2, 6-7 (4-5) 6-2 in the semis, kept attacking furiously to win the middle set of the final. It was a game but futile effort, Court winning 6-2, 2-6, 6-1. "Her arms seemed a mile long," shrugged the diminutive "Rosebud," only 5-foot-2 to Court's 5-foot-11. Court also took the doubles, in tandem with Dalton over Casals and Wade, 6-3, 6-4, and the mixed doubles with Marty Riessen, over Dalton and Frew McMillan, 6-4, 6-4, her first U.S. and fifth major triple. Don Budge had tripled to complete his Slam, but the doubles was taken previously at Boston. Margaret did it all at one stopover, Forest Hills. She banked $7,500 for the singles and $1,000 each for the doubles.

Court won approximately $50,000 in prize money on the year, about one quarter of what Laver earned for a far less productive season. In most tournaments, the women's share of the prize money was one quarter or less that of the men's. In the Italian Open, for example, King received a mere $600 for beating Heldman 6-1, 6-3 in the final, while Nastase earned $3,500 for whipping Jan Kodes, 6-3, 1-6, 6-3, 8-6, for the other title.

Court, never a crusader or champion of causes, wanted no part of a "women's lib" movement in tennis, but King and several others resented the growing inequity in prize-money ratio between men and women. They enlisted determined activist Gladys Heldman as their negotiator and spokeswoman, and focused on the Pacific Southwest Open at Los Angeles— favoring men by an 8-to-1 ratio—as an example of their plight.

Heldman tried to get tournament chairman Jack Kramer to raise the women's purse. He would not. At a highly publicized Forest Hills press conference, a group of nine women declared they would boycott the Los Angeles tournament and play in a $7,500 event in Houston, sponsored by Virginia Slims cigarettes. The U.S. Lawn Tennis Association said it would not sanction this rebel event. The women said they would play anyway—and did. After signing token one-dollar contracts with Heldman, the Houston Nine (King, Casals, Heldman, Melville, Dalton, Richey, Kristy Pigeon, Peaches Bartkowicz and Valerie Ziegenfuss) com-

peted in an event that was unexpectedly successful, paving the way for the first Virginia Slims circuit the next year. Casals won over Dalton, 5-7, 6-1, 7-5.

Meanwhile, the major men's singles titles monopolized by Laver in 1969 went to four different players: Ashe, the runner-up in 1966 and 1967, became the fourth American to win the Australian singles, the first since Dick Savitt 19 years earlier. Laver did not defend, and Dennis Ralston eliminated Newcombe in a 94-game quarterfinal (the sixth-longest in history), 19-17, 20-18, 4-6, 6-4. Ashe then took out a worn out Ralston, who begged off in the fourth set, 6-3, 8-10, 6-3, 2-1, retired. The final was straightforward for Arthur, over towering Dick Crealy, 6-4, 9-7, 6-2, while the doubles went to Stan Smith and Lutz over locals John Alexander and Phil Dent, 8-6, 6-3, 6-4, the first Yanks to win since Vic Seixas and Tony Trabert 17 years earlier.

With Laver, Rosewall, and their fellow "contract pros" out of the French Championships because their bosses couldn't come to a financial accommodation with the French Tennis Federation for their appearance, Czech Jan Kodes, Yugoslav Zeljko Franulovic, American Richey and Frenchman Georges Goven reached the semifinals of the richest ($100,000) tournament outside America. Kodes labored against the homeboy, Goven, 2-6, 6-2, 5-7, 6-2, 6-3. Next, playing for the first Czech major title since Jaroslav Drobny (by then a defector) in 1954, Wimbledon, determined Jan won 6-2, 6-4, 6-0 over Franulovic, who had rebounded to dodge two match points and deny Richey, 6-4, 4-6, 1-6, 7-5, 7-5. Romanians Nastase and Ion Tiriac took the doubles over Ashe and Pasarell, 6-4, 6-2, 6-3.

At Wimbledon, Laver's record 31-match winning streak (dating back to 1961) in the world's most important tournament, was snapped when he came up badly off-form against English lefty Roger Taylor in the fourth round and tumbled, 4-6, 6-4, 6-2, 6-1. John Newcombe withstood five break points in the fifth set of an excruciating three-hour quarterfinal against fellow Aussie Roy Emerson. He won it, 6-1, 5-7, 3-6, 6-2, 11-9, then crushed Spaniard Andres Gimeno, 6-3, 8-6, 6-0 (the Spaniard had beaten Ashe, 7-5, 7-5, 6-2). In the final, Newk, the 1967 champ, beat back Rosewall's third shot at ruling Centre Court, 5-7, 6-3, 6-2, 3-6, 6-1. This was the first five-set final in 21 years, and the 10th all-Aussie men's final in 15 years. Rosewall had beaten left-handers Tony Roche, 10-8, 6-1, 4-6, 6-2, and Taylor, 6-3, 4-6, 6-2, 6-2, to reach the final 14 years after losing to fellow Aussie "Whiz Kid" Lew Hoad, but again failed at the last hurdle. Newcombe and Roche teamed for their third consecutive doubles triumph. As the first to achieve this since Reggie and Laurie Doherty, the English brothers in 1903-04-05, they won an all-Oz final, over Fred Stolle and Rosewall, 10-8, 6-3, 6-1.

Rosewall, two months shy of his 36th birthday, reigned at Forest Hills, where 14 years earlier he had halted Hoad's Grand Slam bid. It was a wild U.S. Open, the richest in the world with a $176,000 pot. Pastel clothing was permitted in lieu of the traditional "all white," and red flags flew every time a set reached 6-6 and went into one of the "sudden death" best-of-nine-points tie-breakers. Suddenly strange-looking 7-6 scores (seeming typographical errors) were blossoming.

Record crowds totaling 122,996 came out to see all the revolutionary happenings, but Rosewall interjected a reactionary

note. After Ralston had achieved one of his career high points, knocking off defending champ and top-seeded Laver in the fourth round, 7-6 (5-3), 7-5, 5-7, 4-6, 6-3, to lead a charge of Americans into the last quarterfinal, third seeded Rosewall took over. He blasted Stan Smith, 6-2, 6-2, 6-2, and second seeded Newcombe, 6-3, 6-4, 6-3, before relegating fourth seeded Roche to the runner-up spot for the second consecutive year, 2-6, 6-4, 7-6 (5-2), 6-3. Roche had beaten Cliff Richey, 6-2, 7-6 (5-3), 6-1, after Cliff eliminated Ralston, 7-6, 6-3, 6-4. Rosewall was the oldest champ at Forest Hills since Bill Tilden, 36, won for the seventh and last time in 1929.

The men's doubles event was notable for several reasons. Pancho Gonzalez, the oldest man in the tournament at 42, entered with a then unknown protege, Jimmy Connors, who at 18 was the youngest guy in the event, and reached the quarters. Nikki Pilic of Yugoslavia and Pierre Barthes of France slew Emerson and Laver in the final, 6-3, 7-6 (5-2), 4-6, 7-6 (5-4), to become the second European team to win the U.S. Doubles, 34 years after Germany's Gottfried von Cramm and Henner Henkel in Boston. The victors won eight of their 15 sets in tie-breakers, the scoring innovation by Jimmy Van Alen that was given its first widespread exposure in the U.S. Pro Championships and the U.S. Open.

Players were skeptical, as usual conservative—"It's like rolling dice," said Newcombe—and the best of them presented a petition to tournament director Bill Talbert demanding that the Open not be reduced to a craps shoot by tie-breakers. Talbert laughed them off, saying, "Did you ever know a player who bought a ticket?" Agreeing with Talbert, customers, schedule-makers and television producers loved them. So tie-breakers were here to stay—although the more conservative "12-point, but win-by-2" method gradually won favor over 9-point-max sudden death in professional tournaments.

Although the tie-breaker, springing from Van Alen's revolutionary pros-only tourney at the Newport (R.I.) Casino in 1965, was approved by the USLTA for 1970 use, it didn't get wide exposure until the televised U.S. Pro. In a second rounder, Drysdale led Rosewall, 6-4, 6-6. At 4-4 in the breaker it was simultaneous match point for Cliff, set point for Ken, the server. Sudden death. "How strange to play all your life and never be in a situation like this before," said Drysdale, who won the point and the decision.

Two weeks later, during the Pennsylvania Grass Championships in Philadelphia, Tom Gorman, the future U.S. Davis Cup captain, also found himself in the new "weirdness"—the closest match ever played—against Pakistani Haroon Rahim in the second round. "I'd grown up believing that if you never lost your serve in a match you couldn't lose," said Gorman. "Wrong that day. I didn't lose serve. But neither did Haroon"—the victor by one point, 6-7 (3-5), 7-6 (5-1), 7-6 (5-4). Rahim was 4-for-4 in breakers until he got the same sort of one-point treatment by Chilean Jaime Fillol, 6-3, 5-7, 7-6 (5-4). Fillol lost the final to Aussie lefty Ray Ruffels, 6-2, 7-6 (5-3), 6-3.

Laver also won the "Tennis Champions Classic," a series of head-to-head, winner-take-all challenge matches played in seven cities. He beat Rosewall for the $35,000 top prize at Madison Square Garden, 6-4, 6-3, 6-3.

Nastase underscored his emerging brilliance by winning titles on one of the world's fastest courts—the canvas of the U.S. Indoor at Salisbury, Md., where he escaped a two-set deficit and two match points in the fourth set to beat Richey, 6-8, 3-6, 6-4, 9-7, 6-0—as well as on one of the slowest, the red clay of Il Foro Italico in Rome. There, he beat Kodes for the Italian title, 6-3, 1-6, 6-3, 8-6.

Richey, a scrappy Texan with more tenacity than natural talent, earned the No. 1 U.S. ranking, thereby establishing a unique family achievement. His sister, Nancy, had been the top-ranked U.S woman in 1964-65, '68-69. Cliff won eight of 27 tournaments he played during the season, was runner-up in five more and went farther than any other American man at Forest Hills, the semifinals. His match record for the year was 93-19.

But the unlikely way he seized No. 1 from the 1969 holder, Stan Smith, seemed made in Hollywood. Colliding in the semifinals of their season finale, the Pacific Coast Championships at Berkeley, Calif., they fought their way to 6-6 in the fifth set: a sudden death tie-breaker on which the preeminent ranking hung. At three points-all Richey suffered a mini-break and faced two match points. He saved the first, to 4-4, with an overhead, then the second – match point for both – with an unbelievable diving volley. He was No. 1 by one point! Richey's 7-6, 6-7, 6-4, 4-6, 7-6 (5-4) decision earned him the No. 1 ranking, though No. 3 Ashe beat Cliff in the final, 6-4, 6-2, 6-4.

Earlier, Richey also was the unexpected hero of the lackluster 1970 Davis Cup Challenge Round. U.S. Captain Ed Turville agonized over the selection, but finally chose Richey over Smith to face upstart West Germany on a fast asphalt court in Cleveland. Richey, who felt he had been slighted by not being chosen in 1969, responded by clobbering smooth-stroking lefty Christian Kuhnke, 6-3, 6-4, 6-2, and former Wimbledon finalist Willy Bungert, 6-4, 6-4, 7-5, to spearhead a 5-0 U.S. victory. Ashe beat Bungert, 6-2, 10-8, 6-2, in the opener. Later, he erased Kuhnke, 6-8, 10-12, 9-7, 13-11, 6-4, in the meaningless fifth match, the longest singles—86 games—ever in a Davis Cup final. Smith and Lutz beat Bungert and Kuhnke, 6-3, 7-5, 6-4, becoming the only doubles team to clinch the Cup three straight years.

It was a disappointing final, concluding a tarnished Davis Cup campaign. The exclusion of contract pros, even though all major tournaments were now "Open," left the Davis Cup a second-rate event.

Australia, denied the services of perhaps its 10 best players, fell pathetically to India, 3-1. Premjit Lall beat Ray Ruffels, 6-2, 6-8, 6-3, 3-6, 14-12, and Dick Crealy, 8-6, 6-2, 6-2. Jai Mukerjea also beat Crealy, 3-6, 6-8, 6-4, 6-3, 6-2, and that was enough for Aussie Captain Harry Hopman. After 22 years and 16 Cups, the most renowned of captains bugged out, moving to the United States to become an outstanding teaching pro.

India lost on quick grass at home in Poona to the Germans, convincing the victors that they could pull a fast one—as to home court advantage—on highly favored Spain in the semifinal. Called the "Miracle in Dusseldorf," an asphalt court costing $15,000, was laid in a football stadium in 55 hours, torn up as soon as the 4-1 German upset was completed. On the clay-loving Continent, it was an alien surface to both teams, but the Spaniards

were stunned. Kuhnke, charging as a serve-and-volleyer, whipped the Spanish god, Santana, 6-4, 6-8, 12-10, 6-2, and Manolo Orantes, 6-3, 6-3, 7-5. With Bungert, he dominated a 6-4, 12-10, 6-3, doubles win over Santana and Juan Gisbert.

Future political turmoil within the Cup was also foreshadowed as South Africa was expelled for two years because the apartheid racial policy of its government was considered disruptive to the competition. Rhodesia also withdrew to avoid political problems.

Largely because contract pros were excluded from the Davis Cup, a new competition—grandly misnamed the World Cup—was organized as a charity event in Boston. It put a two man team of Australian pros, Newcombe and Stolle, against U.S. Davis Cuppers Richey, Smith, Ashe and Clark Graebner for $20,000 in prize money. The Aussies won, 5-2, even though Richey beat both of them.

West Germany's women also made a global team final and also got bageled in their title bid, 3-0 by Australia in the Federation Cup. Even though Court abstained, Australia won its fourth title at Freiburg, West Germany. Dalton and Krantzcke swept through the competition without losing a match, clinching it as Judy beat Niessen, 4-6, 6-3, 6-3, and Karen beat Helga Schultze Hoesl, 6-2, 6-3. The U.S. lost the Cup in the semifinal, 2-1 to the Germans. Doubles was the difference, Niessen and Hoesl over Mary Ann Eisel Curtis and Julie Heldman, 7-5, 4-6, 6-0, after Bartkowicz had beaten Hoesl, 6-2, 6-2, and Niessen put away Heldman, 6-0, 8-6.

King was back in the Wightman Cup, beating Wade, 8-6, 6-4, and Jones, 6-4, 6-2, and linking with Bartkowicz for the first time to win the decisive doubles, over Wade and Winnie Shaw, 7-5, 6-8, 6-2. Heldman chipped in a win over Joyce Barclay Williams, 6-3, 6-2, and the outcome was 4-3 for the U.S. at Wimbledon. Wade's singles win over Richey, 6-3, 6-2, had given the British a 3-2 lead.

The season ended with the first Grand Prix Masters tournament, a six-man round-robin in Tokyo. Richey, who topped the Grand Prix point standings, was ill and couldn't participate. Smith and Laver both had 4-1 records in the round-robin, but Smith took the $15,000 first prize because of his head-to-head win over Laver, 4-6, 6-3, 6-4.

The next year, because of the growing strain of the tug-of-war between WCT and the ILTF, Smith and Laver would not be playing in the same season-ending playoff tournament. Negotiations throughout the fall of 1970 attempted to develop an accord, and in December, the WCT and the ILTF issued a joint communique pledging that they would "work together toward the development and spectator appeal of the game throughout the world." An agreement in principle for the appearance of WCT contract pros in the 1971 French, Wimbledon, and U.S. Open Championships also was announced, but the cautious harmony turned out to be brief.

1970 CHAMPIONS AND LEADERS

Australian Open
Men's Singles Final: Arthur Ashe (USA) def. Dick Crealy (AUS), 6-4, 9-7, 6-2
Women's Singles Final: Margaret Smith Court (AUS) def. Kerry Melville (AUS), 6-1, 6-3
Men's Doubles Final: Bob Lutz and Stan Smith (USA) def. John Alexander and Phil Dent (AUS), 8-6, 6-3, 6-4
Women's Doubles Final: Margaret Smith Court and Judy Tegart Dalton (AUS) def. Karen Krantzcke (USA) and Kerry Melville (AUS), 6-3, 6-1
Mixed Doubles – Not held

French Open
Men's Singles Final: Jan Kodes (CZE) def. Zeljko Franulovic (YUG), 6-2, 6-4, 6-0
Women's Singles Final: Margaret Smith Court (AUS) def. Helga Niessen–Masthoff (GER), 6-2, 6-4
Men's Doubles Final: Ilie Nastase and Ion Tiriac (ROM) def. Arthur Ashe and Charlie Pasarell (USA), 6-2, 6-4, 6-3
Women's Doubles Final: Gail Sherriff Chanfreau and Francoise Durr (FRA) def. Rosie Casals and Billie Jean King (USA), 6-1, 3-6, 6-3
Mixed Doubles Final: Billie Jean King (USA) and Bob Hewitt (RSA) def. Francoise Durr and Jean Claude Barclay (FRA), 3-6, 6-4, 6-2

Wimbledon
Men's Singles Final: John Newcombe (AUS) def. Ken Rosewall (AUS), 5-7, 6-3, 6-3, 3-6, 6-1
Women's Singles Final: Margaret Smith Court (AUS) def. Billie Jean King (USA), 14-12, 11-9
Men's Doubles Final: John Newcombe and Tony Roche (AUS) def. Ken Rosewall and Fred Stolle (AUS), 10-8, 6-3, 6-1
Women's Doubles Final: Rosie Casals and Billie Jean King (USA) def. Francoise Durr (FRA) and Virginia Wade (GBR), 6-2, 6-3
Mixed Doubles Final: Rosie Casals (USA) and Ilie Nastase (ROM) def. Olga Morozova and Alex Metreveli (USSR), 6-3, 4-6, 9-7

U.S. Open
Men's Singles Final: Ken Rosewall (AUS) def. Tony Roche (AUS), 2-6, 6-4, 7-6 (5-2), 6-3
Women's Singles Final: Margaret Smith Court (AUS) def. Rosie Casals (USA), 6-2, 2-6, 6-1
Men's Doubles Final: Pierre Barthes (FRA) and Nikki Pilic (YUG) def. Roy Emerson and Rod Laver (AUS), 6-3, 7-6 (5-4), 4-6, 7-6 (5-2)
Women's Doubles Final: Margaret Smith Court and Judy Tegart Dalton (AUS) def. Rosie Casals (USA) and Virginia Wade (GBR), 6-3, 6-4
Mixed Doubles Final: Margaret Smith Court (AUS) and Marty Riessen (USA) def. Judy Tegart Dalton (AUS) and Frew McMillan (RSA), 6-4, 6-4

Year-End No. 1
Men: John Newcombe
Women: Margaret Smith Court

Top Player Earnings
Men: Rod Laver $201,453

Davis Cup: United States

Federation Cup: Australia

Wightman Cup: United States

Grand Prix Masters, Tokyo—Stan Smith

1971 King The Catalyst For Women's Tour

John Newcombe (left) and **Stan Smith** before their singles final at the Wimbledon, won by Newcombe in five sets. Smith won the U.S. Open later in the summer.

In 1971, both men's and women's professional tennis were split into rival camps. It was an uneasy, acrimonious year politically, but the game prospered. On court, there were many highlights: John Newcombe's second consecutive Wimbledon triumph, after he trailed U.S. Army Corporal Stan Smith, 2-1 in sets in the final; Smith's impressive triumph at Forest Hills; the first "World Championship of Tennis," in which Ken Rosewall upset Rod Laver in the final; a new women's pro tour, dominated by the indefatigable Billie Jean King; and the emergence of Evonne Goolagong, who won the French Open and Wimble-

don at age 19 and Chris Evert, who reached the semifinals of the U.S. Open at age 16.

Rosewall, who in 1970 had captured his second U.S. Championship 14 years after the first, continued to perform geriatric marvels. He dethroned Arthur Ashe in the Australian Open final,

6-1, 7-5, 6-3, regaining a title he first held in 1953. Flawless all the way, "Muscles" did not lose a set, and was pushed to only two tie-breakers, canceling ex-champ Roy Emerson in the quarters, 6-4, 6-4, 6-3, then Tom Okker, 6-2, 7-6, 6-4. Rosewall's triumph was made easier by upset third-round losses inflicted upon top-seed Laver, who lost to Mark Cox, 6-3, 4-6, 6-3, 7-6; No. 7 seed Newcombe, who lost to Marty Riessen, 6-7, 6-1, 7-6, 7-6, and No. 5 seed Tony Roche, who lost to Cliff Drysdale, 4-6, 6-4, 6-7, 7-6, 6-1. Newcombe and Roche won the third of their four Australian doubles titles over Marty Riessen and Okker, 6-2, 7-6.

Unfortunately for much of the season, the 34 men under contract to World Championship Tennis and the "independent pros" who remained under the authority of their national associations played separate tournaments. WCT's new "World Championship of Tennis" - a million-dollar series of 20 tournaments in nine countries on four continents - got off to a promising start with the Philadelphia Indoor, where Newcombe beat Laver, 7-6 (7-5), 7-6 (7-1), 6-4, for only the second time in a dozen career meetings.

Meanwhile, the independent pros were playing on an expanding indoor circuit promoted by Bill Riordan under the aegis of the U.S. Lawn Tennis Association. The highlight was the U.S. Indoor at Riordan's hometown, Salisbury, Md., where Clark Graebner came from two sets down to upend Romanian Ilie Nastase in the semifinals (2-6, 1-6, 6-4, 6-2, 6-2), then survived two match points in beating Cliff Richey for the title, 2-6, 7-6 (5-4), 1-6, 7-6 (5-4), 6-0.

The Italian Open at Rome was one of several strange hybrid events, co-promoted by WCT as part of its 20-tournament series, but also open to non-contract pros. This made for a week of exceptional matches and excitement on the red clay of Il Foro Italico. Record crowds and profits were recorded before Laver defeated Czech Jan Kodes in the final, 7-5, 6-3, 6-3.

Only a few of the WCT players entered the French Open. After five months of a grueling travel and playing schedule, Ashe, never a factor on European clay, was the only WCT top name who opted to go to Paris for two weeks of physically demanding best-of-five-set matches in very hot weather. The mass nonappearance of the "contract pros" infuriated the International Lawn Tennis Federation and was a major factor in polarizing opposition to WCT.

Meanwhile, the dour but energetically industrious Kodes won his second straight French title, beating the more gifted but less persistent Nastase, 8-6, 6-2, 2-6, 7-5, in an absorbing final. Ashe and Riessen, the top two WCT players entered, won the doubles in a unique Parisian all-American final over Smith and Tom Gorman, 6-8, 4-6, 6-3, 6-4, 11-9.

At Wimbledon, top seed Laver was ambushed in the quarterfinals by the inspired serving and volleying of Gorman, 9-7, 8-6, 6-3. The best match was an enchanting four-hour quarterfinal in which Rosewall finally out-stroked Cliff Richey, 6-8, 5-7, 6-4, 9-7, 7-5, at nightfall. The final between Newcombe and Smith had fewer breathtaking rallies and was dominated by slam-bang points accentuating the serve-volley power of both, but it also became gripping in the end. Smith seemed in control after a seven game run that took him to 1-0 in the fourth set, but this was his first major final and he got "a little tired mentally." Newcombe

was tougher and seized control, ending his 6-3, 5-7, 2-6, 6-4, 6-4 triumph with an ace. In the semis, Newk had emphatically avoided the five sets of the 1970 final by putting away Rosewall, 6-1, 6-1, 6-3, while Smith leaned on Gorman, 6-3, 8-6, 6-2.

Emerson, twice a titleist with Neale Fraser (1959 and 1961), partnered Laver to the latter's only Wimbledon doubles title over Ashe and Dennis Ralston, 4-6, 9-7, 6-8, 6-4, 6-4.

The U.S. Open—minus Laver, defending champ Rosewall, and Emerson, who opted to rest—was less than three hours old when Wimbledon champ Newcombe was rudely dismissed by Kodes, 2-6, 7-6, 7-6, 6-3. Jan, the French champ, was extremely unhappy about being unseeded even though he said tennis on grass courts was "a joke" that he found totally unfunny. This was the first time in 41 years that a top seed failed to survive his opening match.

But Kodes proved it was no fluke. He came back from two sets down against Pierre Barthes, 2-6, 5-7, 6-4, 6-4, 6-3, and from two-sets-to-one and a service break down in the fourth to beat Ashe in the rain-spattered semifinal, 7-6 (5-3), 3-6, 4-6, 6-3, 6-4. Kodes also won the first set of the final against Smith, but the 6-foot-4 Californian had learned from his near miss at Wimbledon. Unflinching on the crucial points, he erased the "bouncing Czech" 3-6, 6-3, 6-2, 7-6 (5-3).

Smith and Erik van Dillen were even at two sets apiece against Newcombe and Englishman Roger Taylor in the doubles final when darkness closed in. Rather than resume the next day, it was agreed, questionably, and with no precedent, to improvise—a sudden-death tie-breaker would decide the championship. In a cheap abbreviation unique to the men's majors, Newcombe-Taylor won it, 5-points-to-3, thus the title, 6-7, 6-3, 7-6, 4-6, with a big asterisk. It was contrary to all tennis principals.

As the tourney began, a 19-year-old Jimmy Connors, registered his initial singles victory, a rousing rebound over 35-year-old ex-Wimbledon champ Alex Olmedo, 2-6, 5-7, 6-4, 7-5, 7-5. Twenty-one years later he would rack up his last, his 98th, a U.S. male record.

It was indeed a curious year for men's tennis, climaxed by separate playoffs for the leading contract and independent pros. Laver, Okker, Rosewall, Cliff Drysdale, Ashe, Newcombe, Riessen and Bob Lutz were the "Elite Eight" men in the WCT standings. They had their playoffs in Houston (two rounds) and Dallas. Rosewall won two magnificent tie-breakers to seize the $50,000— staggering at the time—top prize at Dallas' Memorial Auditorium over Laver as 8,000 watched, 6-4, 1-6, 7-6 (7-3), 7-6 (7-4).

Smith, Nastase, Zeljko Franulovic, Kodes, Richey, Barthes and Gorman were the seven men who made the round-robin Grand Prix Masters at Paris. Smith collected the $25,000 top bonus prize from the season-long point standings, but Nastase went 6-0 in the Masters' unsatisfactory round-robin, including a 5-7, 7-6, 6-3 beating of second place Smith (4-2), who also lost to Kodes, 6-4, 3-6, 6-4. Collecting the tournament's $15,000 top prize, Nastase won the first of his four Masters championships.

At year's end, Newcombe and Smith shared Player of the Year honors, but there was no clear-cut No. 1.

The Italian was Laver's biggest title, but, at 33, he kept moving busily, winning seven of 26 tournaments, 82 of 100 matches, and was far and away the leading money winner with $292,717, which made him tennis' first career millionaire. His nine year pro winnings: $1,006,974. His most astounding string came in the second (and last) Tennis Champions Classic, a series of head-to-head, winner-take-all matches in various cities, leading to a four man playoff in Madison Square Garden. Laver incredibly swept all 13 of his matches against top opponents to win $160,000 in this one event, beating Okker in the final.

Rosewall won seven of 23 tournaments (70 of 86 matches), including the Australian and South African (over Fred Stolle, 6-4, 6-0, 6-4) Opens and his third U.S. Pro Championship, (over Drysdale, 6-4, 6-3, 6-0). He earned $138,371 and would have been unchallenged as "Old Man of the Year" except for Pancho Gonzalez. Now 43, and a grandfather, the "Old Wolf" knocked aside like tenpins kiddies Roscoe Tanner, 3-6, 6-1, 6-1, Richey, 7-5, 6-2 and Connors, 3-6, 6-3, 6-3, to win the $10,000 top prize in the Pacific Southwest Open at Los Angeles.

Newcombe captured five of 19 tournaments, 53 of 67 matches, and amassed $101,514. Smith, who missed the early season because he was in basic training with the U.S. Army, won six of 19 tournaments and compiled a 70-13 record that included beating Nastase in the opening match and Ion Tiriac in the decisive singles of the 3-2 U.S. Davis Cup Challenge Round victory over Romania. Smith earned $100,086. Nastase, who finished the season spectacularly, was the top "independent" earner with $114,000 in winnings.

Relations between the ILTF and WCT, strained at the start of the year and aggravated by the French Open, broke down completely at Wimbledon. In a bitter, turbulent press conference, fueled by misunderstanding over several WCT "points of negotiation" that were falsely interpreted by ILTF as "demands," both sides admitted that talks aimed at establishing a unified circuit for 1972 had failed miserably.

Two weeks later, at its annual meeting in the northern Italian resort town of Stresa, the ILTF voted to ban WCT's "contract pros" from all tournaments and facilities controlled by the ILTF and its 93-member national associations, effective at the start of 1972. After 3-1/2 years of "open" tournaments, the contract pros were to be made outcasts again.

In November, new ILTF president Allan Heyman announced that Commercial Union Assurance, a London-based worldwide insurance group, was taking over sponsorship of the Grand Prix from Pepsico, and expanding the financial commitment to more than $250,000. WCT, meanwhile, said that it would focus its attention on strengthening its own tournament series, which it shifted to a May windup in 1972 for maximum TV exposure in the U.S. In the first week of 1972, Rosewall would win his second consecutive Australian Open. Ironically, this little man who had won the first Open tournament in 1968 also was going to win the last of the now interrupted Open era to set a longevity record for the majors—19 years between his first and last titles, both Australian, 1953 and 1972. But more would be heard on this clash of factions.

Meanwhile, women's tennis took a dramatically vibrant upturn. A year earlier it seemed to be overshadowed by the men's game and suffering from a dearth of refreshing young talent. But the renegade Virginia Slims of Houston tournament the previous September blossomed into a new women's tour with $309,000 in prize money. King, who energetically promoted the Virginia Slims Circuit—one observer suggested that she "single-handedly talked it into prominence"—won the lioness' share of the rewards: $117,000. She became the first woman athlete to break the $100,000-in-a-year milestone.

Publisher Gladys Heldman was the behind-the-scenes driving force, arranging 14 tournaments with combined prize money of $189,100 for the first four months in 1971, while King was the on-court dynamo and chief drumbeater. Trumpeting that she had "my wheels back" after knee surgery in July 1970, Billie Jean won the first five tournaments on the new tour—at San Francisco, her native Long Beach, Milwaukee, Oklahoma City and Chattanooga. She beat Rosemary Casals in the first four final, then Ann Jones. BJK teamed with Casals to win the doubles at the first Slims tournaments.

At Philadelphia—where word came that the USLTA had lifted its suspension of the "rebel" women—Francoise Durr snapped King's singles streak of 22 matches in the semis, 6-2, 5-7, 7-6, and Casals won the tournament, 6-3, 3-6, 6-2. King, who had been ineligible as a "contract pro" for two years, then recovered the U.S. Indoor title she had held from 1966 through 1968, beating Casals again in the final at Boston, 4-6, 6-2, 6-3. Rosie, so long the whipping girl, got revenge in the tour's disappointing New York stop, 6-4, 6-4, at the shabby old 34th Street Armory. In all, King won eight of the inaugural 14 tournaments. Jones won the biggest prize ($9,000) at Las Vegas, bearing King; 7-5, 6-4.

However, an amateur intruded on the working women on the clay at St. Petersburg. Schoolgirl Evert, 16, was the most surprising winner, striking down Durr, 6-0, 7-5, Judy Alvarez, 6-0, 6-2, an ailing King, 6-7, 6-3, ret., then, Julie Heldman, 6-1, 6-2, to capture the first of her 157 pro tourney titles. She also won the Southern Championship, 6-1, 6-0, over kid sister, Jeanne Evert, 13, the country's No. 1 in the 14-and-under precinct.

The winter/spring tour—which captured a great deal of media attention, thanks to the clever and energetic promotion of Heldman and King and the emerging fascination with women's liberation—was so successful that the women's tour added five summer tournaments, starting with a $40,000 Virginia Slims International at Houston. King captured the $10,000 first prize there, beating Australian Kerry Melville in the final, 6-4, 4-6, 6-1, and went on to take the $10,000 top bonus in the first women's Grand Prix. King's total of $117,000 in prize money was the highest sum for any American, male or female.

While King & Co. were pioneering under the banner of "Women's Lob," Margaret Smith Court and Goolagong dominated the traditional early season. Court beat Jones, 6-8, 6-3, 6-2, and Goolagong walloped Virginia Wade, 6-4, 6-1 as Australia won the 1971 Federation Cup at Perth (actually played the last week in 1970), 3-0 over Great Britain in the final.

The Australian Open was played in March, three months later than usual, and Court beat Goolagong, 2-6, 7-6 (7-0) 7-5, to take her sixth consecutive major singles title (1969 U.S.; 1970 Australian, French Wimbledon and U.S.; 1971 Australian). Ameri-

can Helen Wills Moody, playing the majors irregularly and never traveling to Australia, won 16 straight between 1924 and 1933, while Maureen Connolly won nine straight from 1951 to 1954, although, like Helen, she didn't play that many in a row.

Margaret beat Evonne again, 6-3, 6-1, in the final of the South African Open (Goolagong, of aboriginal descent, was the first "non-white" of note to compete in Johannesburg). They teamed to win the doubles, over locals Brenda Kirk and Laura Roussouw, 6-4, 7-5.

Wade won the Italian Open and King the German, both over Helga Niessen Masthoff in the final: Virginia by a 6-4, 6-4 score; BJK by 6-3, 6-4. But in Paris, Court's major winning streak of 35 matches was surprisingly terminated in the fourth round of the French by Aussie-born French citizen (through marriage) Gail Sherriff Chanfreau, who, bashing her high-rolling topspin forehand, played the match of her life, 6-3, 6-4. She lost in the next round to another Aussie, Helen Gourlay, 6-4, 3-6, 6-3, who went on to beat 1968 titlist Nancy Richey Gunter in the semifinal, 6-2, 6-3. Nevertheless, the Australian flavor was maintained as carefree 19-year-old Goolagong came through the other half easily over Netherlander Marijke Schaar, 6-4, 6-1, and beat Gourlay in the final, 6-3, 7-5. Evonne was the first since Althea Gibson in 1956 to win the tournament on the first try. Surrounded by Aussies, Parisienne Durr, alongside Chanfreau, won her fifth consecutive doubles title, over Gourlay and Kerry Harris, 6-4, 6-1.

Having won the most prestigious clay-court title, third-seeded Goolagong cemented the No. 1 women's ranking for the year by winning Wimbledon in her second appearance on the grass of the All England Club. The most ethereal of tennis players, graceful, smiling, and free-spirited, she captivated the galleries in dismissing Richey in the quarters, 6-3, 6-2; second seeded Billie Jean in the semis, 6-4, 6-4; and No. 1 seeded, but nervous, Court in the final, 6-4, 6-1, winning the last six games in a rush.

Couturier Teddy Tinling made Goolagong a special dress for the final, white with a scalloped hem and lilac lining and adornments; his staff worked through the night to get it ready, and sent it to Wimbledon with a "good luck" message sewn in, and a silver horseshoe. Such was the spirit of the occasion as Evonne became the youngest champion since Karen Susman, 19, in 1962. King and Casals collaborated on their fourth Wimbledon doubles title, over Court and Goolagong, 6-3, 6-2. Court registered a rare "cripple" in her third final as she and Marty Riessen fell to Billie Jean and Owen Davidson in the mixed, 3-6, 6-2, 15-13. The last set was the longest in any major mixed final.

Despite her triumphs in Paris and London, Goolagong was kept out of the U.S. Open as her coach, Vic Edwards, adhered to his long-range plan of avoiding the U.S. circuit until 1972. Neither Court nor Jones, both of whom were pregnant, entered Forest Hills. But just when it appeared that King would have the stage to herself, Evert emerged as another appealing young rival.

Evert, a 16-year-old high-school student from Fort Lauderdale, Fla., had beaten Court on clay the previous fall and won the Virginia Slims tournament at St. Petersberg on the same surface. However, she gained national attention for the first time as the heroine of the 4-3 U.S. Wightman Cup victory over Great Britain on an ultra-slow rubberized court in Cleveland in August. Chris crunched Winnie Shaw, 6-0, 6-4, in the opener and a nervous and off-form Wade, 6-1, 6-1, in the decisive sixth match, which clinched victory for the injury-riddled U.S. team that had trailed, 2-1.

Evert then moved on to the Eastern Grass Court Championships at South Orange, N.J., and conquered an international field, winning over Gourlay, 6-4, 6-0. Her only previous tournament on grass had been the U.S. Girls 18 singles, won over Janet Newberry, 6-1, 6-3, two weeks earlier.

At Forest Hills, she immediately became the darling of U.S. Open crowds, the star of the show since three prominent men were missing. Playing every match in the old concrete stadium, she beat German Edda Buding, 6-1, 6-0, then No. 4 American Mary Ann Eisel, 4-6, 7-6 (5-1), 6-1. Mary Ann served for it at 6-5, 40-0, and had six match points, but Chrissie calmly kept belting her groundies in an astounding introduction to her country via TV. Next victims were fifth-seeded Durr, 2-6, 6-2, 6-3; and Aussie Lesley Hunt, 4-6, 6-2, 6-3, Chrissie becoming the youngest semifinalist, 16 years, 9 months, since Betty Nuthall of England, 16 years, 3-1/2 months in 1927. Eisel, Durr and Hunt all departed in tears, intimidated by the kid's cool backcourt stroking and the wildly partisan crowds cheering for "Cinderella in Sneakers."

King had too much of a fast-court arsenal for Evert in the semifinals and ended her fairy tale, and 22-match winning streak, 6-3, 6-2, before 13,647. Chrissie's initiation to the uppermost level left her with a No. 10 world ranking and the unique dual U.S. ranking of No. 1 junior and No. 3 woman.

Although she didn't win the championship, the kid really was the game's big winner, and the Chrissie Craze in America had begun on the wings of her two handed backhand—unusual, but soon the "Chrissie does it!" model.

BJK wrapped up her second Forest Hills title by beating Casals, 6-4, 7-6 (5-2), sealing the No. 1 U.S. ranking for the fifth time. Her record for the season was 112-13, including victories in 17 out of 31 tournaments.

King's persistent drive to the $100,000 landmark was slowed when she and Casals walked off the court because of a line call dispute at 6-6 in the first set of the Pacific Southwest Open final. Were they trying to embarrass promoter Jack Kramer, whose prize money stinginess the previous year had led the foremost women to boycott the tournament? It was one of the strangest episodes in U.S. tournament history—a match without a winner but two losers—and both were later fined for their "double—default." BJK finally went over the 100-grand mark at Phoenix, where she again beat Casals, 7-5, 6-1, in the final. BJK celebrated with champagne in the dressing room, and at a news conference in New York the following week, received a congratulatory phone call from President Richard Nixon.

The last Davis Cup Challenge Round was coming up, and the 71-year-old Davis Cup format was about to be scrapped. Therein the Cup-holding country was required to play only once, against the challenger, survivor of the virtually year-long tournament. Feeling that it gave the holder a big edge, choice of home location and surface, the Davis Cup nations decided that the champion would have to enter the tourney proper in 1972.

As defending U.S. captain, Ed Turville infuriated his singles ace of 1970, Cliff Richey, by sportingly deciding that the 1971

windup would be contested on clay, at Charlotte, N.C. Romania, on the backs of Nastase and Tiriac, had come through six matches to reach the ultimate round for a second time. Two years earlier in Cleveland, they had been blasted off a lickety-split asphalt court, and Turville felt it would be more entertaining and fairer to stage this one on clay. Richey felt it was treason, giving it away to the dirt-bred Romanians, and he quit the team.

Turville's contention that it would be more exciting was certainly confirmed: A 3-2 U.S. victory minus Richey. Searching for a singles replacement to accompany Smith, he came up with a surprise, 28-year-old Frank Froehling, III, who hadn't been on the team for six years. After Smith beat Nastase, 7-5, 6-3, 6-1, to give the U.S. a 1-0 lead, long-legged, spindly Froehling (called "Spider-Man" and "Boy Octopus") had his own surprise for Tiriac: The greatest Cup round comeback for an American in more than a half-century, 3-6, 1-6, 6-1, 6-3, 8-6. That was the critical point for the U.S. since Nastase and Tiriac snuffed Smith and Erik van Dillen in doubles, 7-5, 6-4, 8-6, before Smith clinched over Tiriac, 8-6, 6-3, 6-0. With little more than a forehand, and heart, Froehling dodged seven break points, three in the opening game, to take the third set and begin turning it his way. Tiriac fought back from a break down, saved a match point in the fifth set to 5-5. Darkness, at 6-6, pushed them to the next day. Froehling broke Tiriac on a second match point with a buzzing forehand, and the U.S. was on its way to a fourth straight Cup.

1971 CHAMPIONS AND LEADERS

Australian Open
Men's Singles Final: Ken Rosewall (AUS) def. Arthur Ashe (USA), 6-1, 7-5, 6-3
Women's Singles Final: Margaret Smith Court (AUS) def. Evonne Goolagong (AUS), 2-6, 7-6 (7-0), 7-5
Men's Doubles Final: John Newcombe and Tony Roche (AUS) def. Tom Okker (NED) and Marty Riessen (USA), 6-2, 7-6
Women's Doubles Final: Margaret Smith Court and Evonne Goolagong (AUS) def. Jill Emmerson and Lesley Hunt (AUS), 6-0, 6-0
Mixed Doubles: Not Played

French Open
Men's Singles Final: Jan Kodes (CZE) def. Ilie Nastase (ROM), 8-6, 6-2, 2-6, 7-5
Women's Singles Final: Evonne Goolagong (USA) def. Helen Gourlay (AUS), 6-3, 7-5
Men's Doubles Final: Arthur Ashe and Marty Riessen (USA) def. Tom Gorman and Stan Smith (USA), 6-8, 4-6, 6-3, 6-4, 11-9
Women's Doubles Final: Gail Sherriff Chanfreau and Francoise Durr (FRA) def. Helen Gourlay and Kerry Harris (AUS), 6-4, 6-1
Mixed Doubles Final: Francoise Durr and Jean Claude Barclay (FRA) def. Winnie Shaw (GBR) and Tomas Lejus (USSR), 6-2, 6-4

Wimbledon
Men's Singles Final: John Newcombe (AUS) def. Stan Smith (USA), 6-3, 5-7, 2-6, 6-4, 6-4
Women's Singles Final: Evonne Goolagong (AUS) def. Margaret Smith Court (AUS), 6-4, 6-1
Men's Doubles Final: Roy Emerson and Rod Laver (AUS) def. Arthur Ashe and Dennis Ralston (USA), 4-6, 9-7, 6-8, 6-4, 6-4
Women's Doubles Final: Rosie Casals and Billie Jean King (USA) def. Margaret Smith Court and Evonne Goolagong (AUS), 6-3, 6-2

Mixed Doubles Final: Billie Jean King (USA) and Owen Davidson (AUS) def. Margaret Smith Court (AUS) and Marty Riessen (USA), 3-6, 6-2, 15-13

U.S. Open
Men's Singles Final: Stan Smith (USA) def. Jan Kodes (CZE), 3-6, 6-3, 6-2, 7-6 (5-3)
Women's Singles Final: Billie Jean King (USA) def. Rosie Casals (USA), 6-4, 7-6 (5-2)
Men's Doubles Final: John Newcombe (USA) and Roger Taylor (GBR) def. Stan Smith and Erik van Dillen (USA), 6-7, 6-3, 7-6, 4-6, (5-3 Tie-break played by mutual consent in lieu of a fifth set)
Women's Doubles Final: Rosie Casals (USA) and Judy Tegart Dalton (AUS) def. Gail Sherriff Chanfreau (FRA) and Francoise Durr (FRA), 6-3, 6-3
Mixed Doubles Final: Billie Jean King (USA) and Owen Davidson (AUS) def. Betty Stove (NED) and Rob Maud (RSA), 6-3, 7-5

Year-End No. 1
Men: John Newcombe
Women: Billie Jean King

Top Player Earnings
Men: Rod Laver $292,717
Women: Billie Jean King $117,000

Davis Cup: United States

Federation Cup: Australia

Wightman Cup: United States

Grand Prix Masters, Paris—Ilie Nastase
WCT, Dallas—Ken Rosewall

Smith Edges Nastase At Wimbledon, Davis Cup

Stan Smith (right) raises his arms in triumph after beating **Ilie Nastase** 4-6, 6-3, 6-3, 4-6, 7-5 in the men's singles final at Wimbledon.

I n 1972, a peace agreement was reached between the International Lawn Tennis Federation and World Championship Tennis, reintegrating a men's game that had briefly and regrettably regressed into segregated "contract pro" and "independent pro" circuits. But the agreement came too late for the 32 WCT contractees to participate in the French Open or Wimbledon. Stan Smith's triumphs over Ilie Nastase in the Wimbledon final and the Davis Cup gave him the edge over the mercurial Romanian, who won the U.S. Open, for the No. 1 men's ranking. Meanwhile, Billie Jean King swept the French, Wimbledon and U.S. Open titles—she didn't enter the Australian—and again dominated the ascending Virginia Slims circuit, emphatically ruling women's tennis and giving the U.S. dual supremacy in men's and women's tennis for the first time since 1955.

Despite the unsatisfactory separate circuits for men most of the year, prize money kept spiraling, to more than $5 million worldwide. Nastase was the top earner at $176,000, with Smith, property of the U.S. Army, second at $142,300, as probably the highest paid corporal (or any rank) in the world. Four other men (WCT employees Ken Rosewall, Arthur Ashe, John Newcombe and Rod Laver) and one woman, King, collected more than $100,000.

It also was a year of outstanding matches, none finer than the three-hour, 34-minute classic between Rosewall and Laver in the final of the WCT Championships at Dallas in May. Laver was favored to grab the $50,000 plum that had eluded him the previous November, but Rosewall, an enduring marvel at age 37, again stole it. Laver revived himself from 1-4 in the final set, saved a match point with an ace, and had the match on his racket at 5-4 in the "lingering death" tie-breaker, with two serves to come. He pounded both deep to Rosewall's backhand corner, but the most splendid antique in tennis reached for vintage return winners. Laver failed to return the exhausted Rosewall's last serve and it was over, 4-6, 6-0, 6-3, 6-7 (3-7), 7-6 (7-5). This had been a duel of torrid, exquisite shot-making on a 90-degree Mother's Day afternoon, and the sell-out crowd of 9,500 at Moody Coliseum, plus a national television audience of 21 million, was enthralled. Many old hands said it might have been the greatest match of all time, and it was certainly the one that put tennis over as a TV sport in America. It was the closest finish of an important tourney until 1988, when Boris Becker won the Masters final over Ivan Lendl, also a 7-5 fifth-set tie-breaker.

In order to restructure its season for a spring windup, the most advantageous time for U.S. television, WCT counted the last 10 tournaments of 1971 and 10 between January and April 1972 in its point standings. Laver won the Philadelphia opener, rechristened the U.S. Pro Indoor, over Rosewall, 4-6, 6-2, 6-2, 6-2, and four more tournaments to top the point standings heading into the Dallas playoffs. Behind him were Rosewall, Tom Okker, Cliff Drysdale, Marty Riessen, Ashe, Bob Lutz and Newcombe.

Meanwhile, the "independent pros" were playing the U.S. Lawn Tennis Association Indoor Circuit organized by Bill Riordan. Smith played only five of 13 events, but won four in a row, starting with the U.S. Indoor over Nastase, 5-7, 6-2, 6-3, 6-4. Also prominent were rookie pro Jimmy Connors—he dropped out of UCLA after becoming the first freshman to win the National Intercollegiate singles in 1971—and "Old Wolf" Pancho Gonzalez. At 43, Pancho beat Frenchman Georges Goven from two sets down, 3-6, 4-6, 6-3, 6-4, 6-2, to win the Des Moines Indoor. He was the oldest male title winner of the Open era.

Rosewall began the New Year by beating 36-year-old fellow Aussie Mal Anderson, 7-6 (7-2), 6-3, 7-5 in the final of the Australian Open, the last ILTF tournament open to WCT pros before the ban voted the previous July went into effect. Rosewall's last Australian championship came 19 years after his first, a unique span between major singles championships, and the final was almost the all-time antique major showdown, totaling 73 years. They topped Bill Tilden, 36, beating Frank Hunter, 35, in the U.S. final of 1929, but not Englishmen Arthur Gore, 40, over Herbert Roper Barrett, 37, in the 1908 Wimbledon championship.

Another Aussie old boy, 35-year-old Roy Emerson, saved a match point and beat Lutz, 4-6, 7-6, 6-3, to give his country the pivotal point in a 6-1 World Cup victory over the U.S. at Hartford, Conn., marked by Laver's first appearance.

A contemporary of Laver and Emerson, the elegant Spaniard Andres Gimeno, nearly 35, who had left WCT to return to "independent pro" status, won his only major singles title, taking the French Open, over surprising ninth-seeded Frenchman Patrick Proisy, 4-6, 6-3, 6-1, 6-1. Gimeno became the event's oldest champ. Proisy ended top-seeded Jan Kodes' 17-match French winning streak and bid for a third successive title in the quarterfinals, 6-4, 6-2, 6-4. He then eliminated fourth-seeded Manolo Orantes in the semis, 6-3, 7-5, 6-2. Bob Hewitt and Frew McMillan captured their first French doubles title, over the Chileans Jaime Fillol and Pato Cornejo, 6-3, 8-6, 6-3, 6-1 and within a month would add the Wimbledon crown, over Smith and Erik van Dillen, 6-2, 6-2, 9-7. Orantes extended the Spanish reach to Rome, winning the Italian over Kodes, 4-6, 6-1, 7-5, 6-2.

Smith, 1971 runner-up to the now disenfranchised Newcombe (who went to court to try to break the ILTF ban and get a crack at a third straight title), was an overwhelming favorite at Wimbledon. The men's singles was dull until the final—the first ever played on Sunday, after a rain delay—when Smith and Nastase went after each other for five absorbing sets. It was Smith's serve-volley power and forthright resolve against Nastase's incomparable speed, agility and eccentric artistry. The fifth set was electrifying. Smith escaped two break points in the fifth game, which went to seven agonizing deuces, the first with a lunging volley off the wooden frame of his racket. Nastase brushed aside two match points on his serve at 4-5, saved another after having 40-0 at 5-6, then netted an easy, high backhand volley on match point No. 4. A scintillating triumph for Smith: 4-6, 6-3, 6-3, 4-6, 7-5.

It was a tournament dotted with strange-looking 9-8 set scores, signifying Wimbledon's reluctant acceptance of the tiebreaker (called "tie-break" in that circle). The conservative Brits felt the set to be a better test if, in singles, each party served at least eight games before going to the radical overtime. However, by 1979 the breaker at 6-6 was certified.

Back in America, unseeded Lutz, on a wonderful run that included wins over top-seeded Newcombe and Laver, won the U.S. Pro Championship at Longwood, over 11th-seeded Okker, 6-4, 2-6, 6-1, 6-4, ending a nine-year Australian rule to become the first American champ since Butch Buchholz in 1962.

But it was the U.S. Open that commanded the most attention. Lamar Hunt, the Texas millionaire who bankrolled WCT, and Allan Heyman, the Danish-born English lawyer who was president of the ILTF, had been meeting secretly throughout the winter and spring. Prompted by Americans Donald Dell and Jack Kramer, they were seeking a way to reunify the men's game. In April, they reached an accord to divide the season into two segments, starting in 1973. WCT would have free reign the first four months of the year, expanding to two groups of 32 players each that would play an 11-tournament series to qualify four men from each group for the May WCT Finals in Dallas. During that period, no other tournaments with more than $20,000 would be sanctioned. The last eight months of the year would belong to the ILTF for its Grand Prix and Masters.

With this agreement—later modified considerably, under pressure of an antitrust suit by Riordan, who felt he had been sold down the river—the ban of WCT players from the traditional circuit was removed in July, making Forest Hills the year's only big event open to everybody.

USTA Vice President Walter Elcock (responsible for granting the women equal prize money during his subsequent presidency) had made it clear to all parties that no players would be banned from the 1972 U.S. Open despite what the other majors had done. He knew Forest Hills would be a flop without the marquee names.

It turned out to be a wild tournament. Second-seeded Rosewall was defeated by Mark Cox in the second round, 1-6, 6-3, 7-6 (5-3), 7-6 (5-4) Eighth-seeded Kodes was also beaten in the second round by Alex "Sandy" Mayer, 6-7 (3-6), 7-6 (6-5), 6-1. The third round saw fifth-seeded Newcombe fall to Fred Stolle, 7-6 (5-1), 6-4, 5-7, 7-6 (5-3), and seventh-seeded Okker get drilled by Roscoe Tanner, 6-4, 3-6, 7-5, 6-3. Third-seeded Laver was removed by Cliff Richey in the fourth, 3-6, 7-6, 7-6, 6-3, while defending champ, first-seeded Smith left courtesy of Ashe in the quarters 7-6 (5-4), 6-4, 7-5, double faulting at match point.

Ashe, Richey and Tom Gorman all made the semifinals - three-quarter American for the first time in 21 years - but the lone foreigner, fourth-seeded Nastase, beat Ashe in the final to win the tournament. "Nasty" incurred the enmity of 14,690 spectators with temper tantrums early in the final but gradually won them over with his shot-making genius. Nasty became the first European since Manolo Santana in 1965, and the first ever from Eastern Europe to triumph on the soft grass at Forest Hills, 3-6, 6-3, 6-7 (1-5), 6-4, 6-3, even though Ashe led 4-2 in the fourth and broke serve to open the fifth. Roger Taylor, champ with Newcombe the year before, teamed up with Cliff Drysdale to whip Newcombe and Owen Davidson in the doubles final, 6-4, 7-6 (5-3), 6-3.

Smith sealed his No. 1 ranking in the fall, winning the Pacific Southwest Open over Tanner, 6-4, 6-4; Stockholm over Okker, 6-4, 6-3; and the Paris Indoor over Gimeno, 6-2, 6-2, 7-5. He also gave a towering performance in the Davis Cup final at Bucharest.

The Davis Cup nations had voted in 1971 to do away with the Challenge Round in which the defending nation sat out and awaited a challenger to plow through zonal competitions. Thus the U.S. had to follow an unprecedented road for a defending champion—five matches, all in the foes' backyards, the last four on dreaded crimson clay. The U.S. lost but one singles match in sprinting past Commonwealth Caribbean, 4-1, Mexico, 5-0 and Chile, 5-0, to the 3-2 semifinal in Spain. It was left to Smith,

the Cup stalwart for whom clinching was a specialty, to get the U.S. past Spain and into the final. Feeling more comfortable on European soil, Smith patiently beat Juan Gisbert in the deciding match, 11-9, 10-8, 6-4, ordering the tickets for the final destination. Flabbergastingly, it turned out to be Bucharest, where the Romanians were unbeaten for the campaign.

Although the draw for the new Cup format gave the U.S. choice of ground for the final against Romania, the shrewd Ion Tiriac convinced USLTA President Robert Colwell that the Romanians were being treated unfairly and should have that privilege since they'd played the 1969 and 1971 Challenge Rounds in the U.S. The U.S. team, startled and hurt that Colwell would give away the home-court edge, threatened mutiny. Dennis Ralston, ever calm, sold them on being underdogs, beating the other guys at their place.

Romania, with the brilliant Nastase and the menacing Tiriac at home on the red clay of the Progresul Sports Club, was a heavy favorite. Nastase boasted, "We cannot lose at home"—and his record of 19 straight Cup singles victories and 13 consecutive Romanian triumphs in Bucharest seemed to support his braggadocio. Turgid clay, an adoring and vocal home crowd and notoriously patriotic line judges all favored Nastase and Tiriac.

This was the first Davis Cup finale in Europe in 39 years, and perhaps the greatest international sporting occasion ever in Bucharest, where likenesses of Nastase and Tiriac were everywhere. But the pressure of great expectations worked in reverse. Smith played undoubtedly his finest match on clay, while Nastase was high-strung and erratic as the American took the critical opener, 11-9, 6-2, 6-3. Tiriac, the brooding former ice hockey international who claimed kinship with Dracula, used every ploy of gamesmanship, orchestrating the crowd and the linesmen, to come from two sets down and beat Gorman, 4-6, 2-6, 6-4, 6-3, 6-2, in the second match. The doubles, however, was a Romanian disaster.

Once one of the world's premier teams (22-4 in Cup play), Nastase and Tiriac had fallen out as friends, and their incompatibility showed as Smith and van Dillen, playing with skill and flair, humiliated the home team, 6-2, 6-0, 6-3. Tiriac summoned all his wiles and battled fiercely, as though his life depended on it, in the fourth match. Despite numerous pro-Tiriac officiating calls, Smith, knowing he had to hit winners inside the lines, was too good for Ion. He clinched the Cup, 4-6, 6-2, 6-4, 2-6, 6-0, saying he had a headache from concentrating. No Yank abroad in Davis Cup has ever done better.

It had been a wild weekend in Bucharest, made unforgettable by the fervor of the fans, the thievery of the linesmen, the machinations of Tiriac, and extraordinarily heavy security in the aftermath of the Olympic massacre at Munich. (There had been rumors of threats against two Jewish members of the U.S. squad, Harold Solomon and Brian Gottfried.) But in the end, Captain Ralston's brigade, inspired by Ralston's calm in the cauldron, could savor the finest victory ever by a U.S. team away from home,

A footnote to the Cup that year was the debut of a 15-year-old for Sweden. Bjorn Borg, a comeback winner over New Zealand's Onny Parun, 4-6, 3-6, 6-3, 6-4, 6-4, during a 4-1 victory, would lead his homeland to the Cup in 1975.

Once again there were separate playoffs for "contract pros" and "independents" at the end of the year. WCT scheduled a makeshift "winter championship" in Rome for the top eight men in a summer-fall circuit that filled the gap before a new two-group format started in 1973. Ashe won the $25,000 first prize, beating Nikki Pilic, 7-6, 6-1, Okker, 6-7 (9-11), 6-3, 6-3, and Lutz, 6-2, 3-6, 6-3, 3-6, 7-6 (7-2).

The Commercial Union Masters was played in Barcelona with the new format—two four-man round-robin groups, with the two players with the best records in each advancing to a "knock-out" semis and final. Gorman had Smith beaten, holding a match point, 7-6, 6-7, 7-5, 5-4, 40-30 in one semi. But Tom, having hurt his back, sportingly defaulted (at 2:35 a.m.) so as not to wreck the final. Nastase, a 6-2, 6-3, 6-2, semifinal victor over Connors, repeated as champion, beating Smith in a rousing final, 6-3, 6-2, 3-6, 2-6, 6-3, pocketing $15,000. But it was his only victory in five meetings on the year with the tall Californian. Gorman was given a sportsmanship bonus of $2,500 for letting the show go on in the final.

One of the most significant developments of 1972 was the formation, at the U.S. Open, of a new players' guild, ATP (Association of Tennis Professionals). Some 50 players paid $400 initial dues, and Washington attorney Donald Dell, the former U.S. Davis Cup captain and personal manager for a number of top players, enlisted Kramer as executive director. The urbane Drysdale was elected president and Dell became the Association's legal counsel. Other players' associations had come and gone in the past, but the ATP was carefully constituted and loomed as a major new force in the pro game's politics and administration.

The politics of women's tennis in 1972 began with conciliation and ended with a new rift.

Early in the year Gladys Heldman, organizer of the rebel women's pro tour the year before, was appointed by the USLTA as coordinator of women's tennis and director of the women's tour in a peace effort. Thus empowered, she expanded the winter tour to $302,000 in prize money. But by September, the honeymoon was over. Heldman resigned her USLTA post amid mutual mistrust and formed the WITF (Women's International Tennis Federation). She took the USLTA to court for alleged antitrust violations. Meanwhile, the USLTA appointed U.S. Wightman Cup Captain, Edy McGoldrick to form a women's tour in opposition to Heldman's in the winter-spring of 1973.

On the tennis court, there was no question who was boss in 1972. King did not play the Australian Open, but swept the rest of the major singles titles with the loss of only one set, to Virginia Wade in the Wimbledon quarterfinals (6-1, 3-6, 6-3). Billie Jean won 10 of 24 tournaments, compiled an 87-13 record, ran away with the women's Grand Prix top prize, and exceeded her prize money landmark of 1971, earning $119,000. Against her greatest career rivals, she was 3-2 over Margaret Smith Court (back on the circuit after the birth of her first child, Daniel) and 4-3 over Nancy Richey Gunter for the year.

Wade won the Australian, her second major, over Evonne Goolagong, 6-4, 6-4. King won her seventh major singles title, the French, over Goolagong, 6-3, 6-3, thus joining Doris Hart, Maureen Connolly, Shirley Fry and Court as the only women to have won all four major singles titles. (They would be joined by Chris Evert in 1982, Martina Navratilova in 1983, Steffi Graf in 1988 and Serena Williams in 2003). BJK also dethroned Goolagong, 6-3, 6-3, at

Wimbledon after Evonne had thrillingly won her first meeting with debutante Evert in the semis, 4-6, 6-3, 6-4. King was a semifinal winner over Rosie Casals, 6-2, 6-4.

At the U.S. Open, King beat Wade in the quarters, 6-2, 7-5; Court in the semis, 6-4, 6-4; and, for the title and $10,000, Kerry Melville, 6-3. 7-5. Aussie Kerry had ripped Evert, in the semis, 6-4, 6-2, by skidding clever slices short, low and wide to Chrissie's two-fisted backhand.

Imposing six-foot Dutchwoman Betty Stove was the woman of the year in doubles, teaming with King to win the French (over Brits Winnie Shaw and Christine Truman Janes, 6-1, 6-2) and Wimbledon (over Judy Dalton and Francoise Durr, 6-2, 4-6, 6-3). Then she took up with Durr to seize the U.S., over Court and Wade, 6-3, 1-6, 6-3, the first woman to win all three in a season since Darlene Hard and Maria Bueno in 1960.

Evert, still an amateur at age 17, was the only player with a winning record over King for the year, 3-1, including a 6-1, 6-0 victory in the final of the Virginia Slims tournament in her hometown of Fort Lauderdale. She also won the richest women's tournament, the inaugural season-ending $100,000 Virginia Slims Championship at Boca Raton, Fla., a climactic gathering of the "Little Broads," as Heldman called the Long Way Babies.

Chrissie beat King, 6-4, 6-2, and Melville, 7-5, 6-4, in the final two rounds. But Chrissie couldn't accept the $25,000 first prize. Amateurism was costly, but Colette and Jimmy Evert, her parents, wouldn't let her become a working woman until she had a high school diploma. The millions would come.

Chrissie, 47-7 on the year and winner of four tournaments, spearheaded the 5-2 U.S. Wightman Cup victory over Great Britain at Wimbledon, beating Wade, 6-4, 6-4, and Joyce Williams, 6-2, 6-3, and sharing a doubles win with Patti Hogan over Nell Truman and Shaw, 7-5, 6-4. Soon after Evert beat Court 6-3, 6-3, and Goolagong, 6-1, 6-3 for the only two U.S. victories in a 5-2 loss to Australia in the inaugural Bonne Bell Cup (U.S. vs Australia) at Cleveland. Evert also won her first adult national title—the first of four consecutive U.S. Clay Court singles at Indianapolis—by beating Court in the semis, 6-3, 7-6, and Goolagong in the final, 7-6, 6-1.

The Maureen Connolly Brinker Indoor at Dallas was the first tournament in which both Goolagong and Evert competed, but King delayed their first meeting. She fought off a 1-3, 15-40 deficit and later cramps in the final set to beat Evert in the quarters, 6-7, 6-3, 7-5, and came from behind again to beat Goolagong in the semis, 1-6, 6-4, 6-1. Exhausted, she fell easily to unseeded Gunter in the final, 7-6, 6-1.

The magical first encounter between the two radiant new princesses of women's tennis came, appropriately, in the semis at Wimbledon. It was a majestic match worthy of the occasion, Goolagong winning, 4-6, 6-3, 6-4, after trailing 0-3 in the second and 2-3 (down a break) in the third. Evert promptly won their next two meetings, however, setting the tone for their career rivalry.

The Virginia Slims circuit continued to grow, offering $525,775 in prize purses for 21 tournaments, but the appeal of Evert and Goolagong—they couldn't be enticed by Heldman to side with her in a war against the ILTF establishment—made them the cornerstones of the rival USLTA circuit in 1973.

Australian Open

Men's Singles Final: Ken Rosewall (AUS) def. Mal Anderson (AUS), 7-6 (7-2), 6-3, 7-5

Women's Singles Final: Virginia Wade (GBR) def. Evonne Goolagong (AUS), 6-4, 6-4

Men's Doubles Final: Owen Davidson and Ken Rosewall (AUS) def. Ross Case and Geoff Masters (AUS), 3-6, 7-6, 6-2

Women's Doubles Final: Kerry Harris and Helen Gourlay (AUS) def. Patricia Coleman and Karen Krantzcke (AUS), 6-0, 6-4

Mixed Doubles: Not Played

French Open

Men's Singles Final: Andres Gimeno (ESP) def. Patrick Proisy (FRA), 4-6, 6-3, 6-1, 6-1

Women's Singles Final: Billie Jean King (USA) def. Evonne Goolagong (AUS), 6-3, 6-3

Men's Doubles Final: Bob Hewitt and Frew McMillan (RSA) def. Patricio Cornejo and Jaime Fillol (CHI), 6-3, 8-6, 3-6, 6-1

Women's Doubles Final: Billie Jean King (USA) and Betty Stove (NED) def. Winnie Shaw and Christine Truman Janes (GBR), 6-1, 6-2

Mixed Doubles Final: Evonne Goolagong and Kim Warwick (AUS) def. Francois Durr and Jean Claude Barclay (FRA), 6-2, 6-4

Wimbledon

Men's Singles Final: Stan Smith (USA) def. Ilie Nastase (ROM), 4-6, 6-3, 6-3, 4-6, 7-5

Women's Singles Final: Billie Jean King (USA) def. Evonne Goolagong (AUS), 6-3, 6-3

Men's Doubles Final: Bob Hewitt and Frew McMillan (RSA) def. Stan Smith and Erik van Dillen (USA), 6-2, 6-2, 9-7

Women's Doubles Final: Billie Jean King (USA) and Betty Stove (NED) def. Judy Tegart Dalton (AUS) and Francoise Durr (FRA), 6-2, 4-6, 6-3

Mixed Doubles Final: Rosie Casals (USA) and Ilie Nastase (ROM) def. Evonne Goolagong and Kim Warwick (AUS), 6-4, 6-4

U.S. Open

Men's Singles Final: Ilie Nastase (ROM) def. Arthur Ashe (USA), 3-6, 6-3, 6-7 (1-5), 6-4, 6-3

Women's Singles Final: Billie Jean King (USA) def. Kerry Melville (AUS), 6-3, 7-5

Men's Doubles Final: Cliff Drysdale (RSA) and Roger Taylor (GBR) def. Owen Davidson and John Newcombe (AUS), 6-4, 7-6 (5-3), 6-3

Women's Doubles Final: Francoise Durr (FRA) and Betty Stove (NED) def. Margaret Smith Court (AUS) and Virginia Wade (GBR), 6-3, 1-6, 6-3

Mixed Doubles Final: Margaret Smith Court (AUS) and Marty Riessen (USA) def. Rosie Casals (USA) and Ilie Nastase (ROM), 6-3, 7-5

Year-End No. 1

Men: Stan Smith
Women: Billie Jean King

Top Player Earnings

Men: Ilie Nastase $176,000
Women: Billie Jean King $119,000

Davis Cup: United States

Federation Cup: South Africa

Wightman Cup: United States

Grand Prix Masters, Barcelona—Ilie Nastase
WCT, Dallas—Ken Rosewall
Virginia Slims Championships, Boca Raton—Chris Evert

1973   Billie Beats Bobby In Battle of the Sexes

A questionable Centennial was celebrated throughout tennis in 1973. It commemorated the then-accepted, but subsequently disproved, theory of the origin of the modern sport at a shooting party in Wales. Supposedly Major Walter Clopton Wingfield introduced the game he later patented in 1874. Perhaps that misplaced celebration was fitting, considering that 1973 was the game's most peculiar year, one that embraced unprecedented labor strife, a boycott of Wimbledon by most of the foremost guys.

The landmark match of the year did not come in any of the traditional major tournaments. There was nothing traditional at all about the celebrated "Battle of the Sexes" between 29-year-old Billie Jean King and 55-year-old Bobby Riggs, the self-proclaimed "King of Male Chauvinist Pigs," at Houston's Astrodome the night of September 20. But this spectacle—roughly equal parts tennis, carnival and sociological phenomenon—captured the fancy of America as no pure tennis match ever had. The shlockathon meant nothing and yet it meant everything: it had no bearing on the game of tennis, yet it stirred the populace. The crowd of 30,472, paying as much as $100 a seat, was the largest ever to witness a tennis match. Some 50 million more watched on prime-time television. The whole gaudy promotion was worth supposedly $3 million, and King collected a $100,000 alleged

winner-take-all purse, plus ancillary revenues, for squashing Riggs, 6-4, 6-3, 6-3. He got a big chunk of cash, too.

Riggs, the outspoken hustler who had won Wimbledon and U.S. Championships in 1939, created the bonanza by a challenge proclaiming that women's lib was a farce and that the best of the female tennis pros couldn't even beat him, "an old man with one foot in the grave." He challenged Margaret Smith Court to a winner-take-all challenge match on Mother's Day at a California resort he was plugging in Ramona. She was the ideal victim for his well-perfected "psych job" and assortment of junk shots, including lobs into the sun at high noon. Margaret choked and Riggs won, 6-2, 6-1. That set the stage for the haranguing challenge against Billie Jean, the leading voice of women's lib in sports. The whole ballyhooed extravaganza was just right for the times, and it became a national media event, front-page news in papers and magazines across the country, even the world. King exulted in her victory, not as a great competitive triumph but as "a culmination" of her years of striving to demonstrate that tennis could be big-league entertainment for the masses, and that women could play.

Tennis was clearly the "in" sport of the mid-'70s. Sales of tennis equipment, clothing and vacations were burgeoning, and though the pro game remained plagued with disputes—notably a boycott of Wimbledon by the men's Association of Tennis Professionals and an antitrust suit in women's tennis—it continued to grow quickly. Prize money in 1973 rose to nearly $6 million.

World Championship Tennis introduced the new format agreed to in its 1972 accord with the International Lawn Tennis Federation: A January-through-May series with a field of 64 players split into two groups of 32, playing parallel tours of 11, $50,000 tournaments. The top four men of each group (Stan Smith, Rod Laver, Roy Emerson and John Alexander of 'A'; Ken Rosewall, Arthur Ashe, Marty Riessen and Roger Taylor of 'B')

went to Dallas for the $100,000 final. Smith, who had won four consecutive tournaments and six of 11 to top Laver (three victories in his group), took the $50,000 top prize by beating Ashe, 6-3, 6-3, 4-6, 6-4 in the final. Ashe had ended Rosewall's bid for a third straight Dallas title in a five set semifinal, 6-4, 6-2, 5-7, 1-6, 6-2, and Smith waylaid Laver, 4-6, 6-4, 7-6, 7-5. For the first time, WCT also conducted a doubles competition, using the same format as singles. Smith and Bob Lutz won the $40,000 first prize in the playoffs at Montreal, beating Riessen and Tom Okker, 6-2, 7-6, 6-0.

Running concurrently with the WCT tour for three months was the U.S. Lawn Tennis Association Indoor Circuit of Bill Riordan. He refused to be dealt out by the WCT-International Lawn Tennis Federation deal dividing the season, and threatened restraint-of-trade proceedings if forced to limit the prize money in his tournaments. His headliners were Jimmy Connors and Ilie Nastase, both of whom he managed at the time. Connors won six of the eight events he played, including the U.S. Indoor over German Karl Meiler, 3-6, 7-6, 7-6, 6-3.

John Newcombe started the year by winning his first Australian Open title over New Zealander Onny Parun, 6-3, 6-7, 7-5, 6-1. Onny was the first Kiwi in a major final since Harry Parker, loser of the Aussie to Ernest Parker in 1913. Newcombe also shared the doubles with countryman Mal Anderson, over Phil Dent and Alexander, 6-3, 6-4. 7-6. Newcombe won the French doubles, too, with Okker, over Connors and Nastase, 6-1, 3-6, 6-3, 5-7, 6-4, but slumped badly until rededicating himself late in the year, winning the U.S. Open, and teaming with Laver to return the Davis Cup to Australia in the first year it was open to "contract pros."

On balance, the No. 1 ranking had to go to Nastase, the volatile Romanian. He was fine or fined (accumulating fines totaling $11,000) while winning 15 of 31 tournaments, 118 of 135 matches, and led the prize money list with $228,750, including a $55,000 bonus for topping the Grand Prix standings. He manhandled Manuel Orantes in the most one-sided Italian Open final, 6-1, 6-1, 6-1; swept through the French Open without losing a set (Nikki Pilic was his final victim, 6-3, 6-3, 6-0), and won the Masters for the third straight year, beating Newcombe in the round-robin, 7-5, 6-3, and personal nemesis Okker in the final, 6-3, 7-5, 4-6, 6-3, at Boston.

Defender Andres Gimeno wasn't around long in Paris, topspun from the second round by young Argentine lefty, Guillermo Vilas, 6-2, 5-7, 8-6. Tom Gorman evicted two-time champ Jan Kodes, 6-4, 7-6 (8-6), 4-6, 6-1, to reach the semis where Nastase trimmed him, 6-3, 6-4, 6-1. Adriano Panatta, beaten by Pilic in the semis, 6-4, 6-3, 6-1, had halted the surge of Swedish novitiate, Bjorn Borg, 7-6, 2-6, 7-5, 7-6. The cool kid with blond tresses and a blowout mentality, had baselined his way past the experienced Cliff Richey, 6-2, 6-3, Pierre Barthes, 3-6, 6-1, 8-6, and Dick Stockton, 6-7, 7-5, 6-2, 7-6, and would carry off a record six championships by 1981.

Nastase played indifferently at Wimbledon, where he was considered a shoo-in because of the boycott, but was beaten in the fourth round by National Intercollegiate champ Alex "Sandy" Mayer of Stanford, 6-4, 8-6, 6-8, 6-4 and at Forest Hills, where Andrew Pattison of Rhodesia ambushed him in the second round, 6-7, 2-6, 6-3, 6-4, 6-4. But his overall record was the best.

The No. 1 U.S. men's ranking was shared for the only time. Puzzled, the ranking committee could not choose between Smith, who won eight of 19 tournaments and 81 of 103 matches but lost his world-beating form after peaking in May, and Connors, who won 10 of 21 tournaments and 81 of 97 matches, sensationally capturing the U.S. Pro and South African, both over Ashe.

Connors, just 20, was the brightest of several ascending youngsters, including Borg and Brian Gottfried (winner of the $30,000 first prize at the ATP's Alan King Classic in Las Vegas, over Ashe, 6-1, 6-3). Connors was the youngest man atop the American rankings since one of his mentors, Pancho Gonzalez, ruled at 20 in 1948, and Smith was the first to be No. 1 for four times since Bill Tilden gained the top spot for the 10th time in 1929.

Brimming with confidence after his fine showing on the less-strenuous-than-WCT U.S. Indoor circuit, Connors scattered seeds all over Boston in the U.S. Pro. First he knocked off top-seeded Smith, and went on to whip Ray Moore, sixth seeded Stockton, fifth-seeded Richey, and, in the final, second-seeded Ashe 6-3, 4-6, 6-4, 3-6, 6-2.

He saved a match point in beating Smith again at the Pacific Southwest, 3-6, 6-4, 7-6 in the quarters—proceeding to win the title over Okker, 7-5, 7-6—and escaped two match points in beating out Smith, 6-0, 3-6, 7-6 (8-6) for a semifinal berth in the Grand Prix Masters. That gave him a 3-0 record against Stan for the calendar year. Smith was the only player to reach both the WCT and Masters playoffs.

The already turbulent political waters in tennis were roiled further by formation of a league called World Team Tennis, which planned to start intercity team competition using a unique, Americanized format in 1974. Dennis Murphy, who had helped found the American Basketball Association and the World Hockey Association, envisioned 16 teams with six players apiece (men and women) under contract competing in a May-through-August season.

Jack Kramer and the ATP board came out staunchly opposed to WTT, saying it would harm the long-range players' interest in a healthy worldwide tournament circuit. But even as discussions between the ILTF and ATP about team tennis were scheduled, a more immediate problem arose. When ATP member Pilic was suspended by the Yugoslav Tennis Federation for failing to participate in a Davis Cup series in New Zealand, to which he had allegedly committed himself, ATP members objected. They protested that this was precisely the sort of arbitrary disciplinary power by a national association that the ATP was meant to counteract. An ATP threat to withdraw all its 70 members from the French Open if Pilic was barred from the tournament was averted by a delaying tactic, an appeal hearing before the ILTF Emergency Committee, which reduced Pilic's suspension from three months to one month.

This did not satisfy the ATP board, which contended that only their own association should have disciplinary authority over players. Many also felt that the one month suspension, which included Wimbledon, was devised by the ILTF to demonstrate its muscle, believing the players would never support a boycott of the world's premier tournament. Thus "The Pilic Affair" became a test of the will and organization of the new association. Many ATP leaders felt that if they gave in on this first showdown, they would never be strong, whereas if they

held firm and proved to the ILTF that even Wimbledon was not sacred, the ATP's unity and power would never be doubted in the future.

After days of tortuous meetings and attempts to find compromises, including the ATP's seeking an injunction in Britain's High Court forcing the All England Club to accept Pilic's entry, ATP members voted to withdraw en masse if Pilic were barred from Wimbledon. Seventy-nine men did withdraw their entries, including 13 of the original 16 seeds. Nastase, Englishman Roger Taylor and Australian Ray Keldie were the only members who did not withdraw. (They were later fined by the ATP.)

Amid ferocious English press criticism and bitterness, the tournament was played with a second-rate men's field. The British public, taking up the press crusade that "Wimbledon is bigger than a few spoiled players," turned out in near-record numbers. They made heroes of Nastase, Taylor and such attractive newcomers as Connors and Swedish teen-ager Borg, who, in long blond locks, became the immediate heartthrob of squealing British schoolgirls.

Borg, destined to become the "Angelic Assassin" of Centre Court with five straight titles (1976-80), made his debut on that sacred sod memorable for the fact that he and Indian Premjit Lall engaged in the longest singles tie-breaker in a major championship. As it grew and grew and grew like Jack's beanstalk, to a 38th point climax, the scene was punctuated by much laughter from spectators. It was only the beginning of Wimbledon's second year of tie-breaking, and nobody had witnessed such an elongated passage. Borg, Lall and court officials, especially the traveling service line judge, shared the confusion. At last, after Lall had saved seven match points and had six set points himself, it ended at 20-18, and Borg had his first Wimbledon match win, 6-3, 6-4, 9-8 (20-18). He would go on to the quarterfinals, losing to Taylor 6-1, 6-8, 3-6, 6-3, 7-5.

Nastase, an overwhelming favorite, was beaten at the end of the first week by constantly attacking Alex "Sandy" Mayer, 6-4, 8-6, 6-8, 6-4. Sandy went on to reach the semifinals, losing to the Soviet Georgian Alex Metreveli, 6-3, 3-6, 6-3, 6-4. Kodes became the first Czech champ since expatriate Jaroslav Drobny in 1954, beating Metreveli, 6-1, 9-8 (7-5), 6-3, in a predictably uninspiring final. Left-handed Yorkshireman Taylor, conqueror of Laver in 1970, was probably the best equipped to win his semifinal, but the pressure on a homeboy to end the interminable post-Fred Perry drought was fiercer than ever. Not only did the Brits yearn for a champ of their own but they wanted Roger to upstage the boycott. Added pressure of disapproval came from his lodge brothers, whom he didn't join in the walkout. He wasn't quite up to it, falling to Kodes in five sets, 8-9, 9-7, 5-7, 6-4, 7-5. Kodes' quarterfinal was tight, too, 6-4, 3-6, 4-6, 6-3, 7-5, over tall and stylish Indian 19-year-old Vijay Amritraj, who nearly served-and-volleyed him off the lawn. Connors, beaten by Metreveli, 8-6, 6-2, 5-7, 6-4, paired with Nastase as they clowned their way through five sets to win the doubles title over Australians John Cooper (younger brother of 1958 champ Ashley) and ex-champ, 39-year-old Neale Fraser, 3-6, 6-3, 6-4, 8-9 (3-7), 6-1.

Meanwhile, with Wimbledon sacrificed for one year, the U.S. Open became the men's most important competitive test of 1973, luring record attendance of 137,488, and crowds of 15,137 and 15,241 on the last two days.

Defender Nastase, co-seeded first with Smith, squandered a second set lead and lost to Rhodesian journeyman Pattison in the second round, 6-7, 2-6, 6-3, 6-4, 6-4. Kodes, who resented being downgraded as a "cheese champion" at Wimbledon, returned serve spectacularly in going all the way to the final, avoiding a match point at nightfall to outstroke Smith, 7-5, 6-7 (4-5), 1-6, 6-1, 7-5, in the semifinals. Jan almost repeated his 1971 upset over Newcombe, this time in the final instead of the opening round, but the rugged Australian ultimately had too much firepower and won a spectacular finale, 6-4, 1-6, 4-6, 6-2, 6-3. In the doubles final, Newcombe and Owen Davidson beat countrymen Laver and Rosewall, 7-5, 2-6, 7-5, 7-5.

Even though they'd been away from Davis Cup for a long time in the wilderness of professionalism, each artifact in Captain Neale Fraser's "Antique Show"—Rosewall, 38, Anderson, 38, Laver, 35, Newcombe, 29—made solid contributions in victories over Japan, India, Czechoslovakia and the U.S. that restored the silver tub to Australia. They may have been the greatest quartet assembled for such a purpose, born again, as though they'd been dug up within a time capsule: Laver absent for 10 campaigns, Rosewall 16, Anderson 14, Newcombe five. Laver decided late in the year to be part of it. Captain Fraser challenged him, saying that his name and past glories weren't enough. He had to prove himself as the best Aussie in autumn tournaments—and the Rocket did.

Welcomed back for the semifinal series against Czechoslovakia in Melbourne, Laver won all six of his matches (four singles, beating Czechs Kodes 6-3, 7-5, 7-5, and Jiri Hrebec 5-7, 6-3, 6-4, 4-6, 6-4, who had stunned Newcombe, 6-4, 8-10, 6-4, 7-5). Again the great lefty was an integral figure in the team world championship, his fifth title tacked onto winning campaigns in 1959-60-61-62. Quite different from those sunny occasions on grass, was the 1973 final against the Cup-holding Americans in Cleveland's Public Auditorium. A hothouse showdown was completely new, although indoor Cup championship rounds have since been virtually the rule. Strangely it was poorly promoted and attended, about 10,000 showing up over three days. Clevelanders, who had always supported Davis Cup handsomely, apparently didn't like the idea of tennis-under-a-roof.

Newcombe set the mood by beating Smith in the opener, 6-1, 3-6, 6-3, 3-6, 6-4. Artistically, this might well have been the match of the year. Newcombe—an enforced absentee from Davis Cup since 1967—came back from 1-3 and a break point in the fifth set with some sublime play, featuring thoughtful baselining to go with his volleying.

Amid volleying fireworks of the second match, Laver beat Gorman, 8-10, 8-6, 6-8, 6-3, 6-1, then surprisingly teamed with Newcombe to pummel Smith and Erik van Dillen in the decisive doubles, 6-1, 6-2, 6-4. Just as Laver had one of his Grand Slams as an amateur, and one as a pro, he now had a Cup as a pro to go with those of amateur days. Within three matches and 13 sets, the U.S. record of 17 wins in a row ended (but remains the record), though five straight Cups is third behind the U.S. seven (1920–26) and the French six (1927–32).

At year's end, the ATP board remained opposed to World Team Tennis and to guaranteed contracts for players—a stance it was forced to reverse the next year, under growing pressure from members who wanted to accept guarantees. WTT named former U.S. Davis Cup captain George MacCall as its commissioner, announced that it would begin operations in May 1974, and signed such prominent players as Newcombe, Rosewall, King and Evonne Goolagong to lucrative contracts.

On the women's side, two separate tours were played in the winter and spring of 1973. The Virginia Slims Circuit of 14 events, starring King and Margaret Smith Court, was conducted under the auspices of the Women's International Tennis Federation (WITF), incorporated as an autonomous body by Gladys Heldman. The USLTA—claiming that it had been hoodwinked and double-crossed by Heldman—hastily arranged a circuit of eight tournaments featuring Chris Evert, Goolagong and Virginia Wade.

Noticed by no one but the two players themselves was a first-round match at Akron, a 7-6 (5-4), 6-3, win by Evert (the tournament victor) over a chubby Czech named Martina Navratilova. That initial meeting was merely the first step in the lustrous rivalry that was to run for 80 encounters over 16 years. Evert beat Olga Morozova, 6-3, 6-4, in the final.

In Heldman's suit against the USLTA in Federal District Court in New York, Judge Milton Pollack ruled against her, rendering the WITF short-lived. The players who signed with WITF were declared ineligible for the 1973 Commercial Union Grand Prix (won by Evert), but by June an agreement was reached between the USLTA and Philip Morris, Inc., parent company of Virginia Slims, for a single women's tour under USLTA/ILTF auspices starting in September, 1973. Part of the compromise was that Heldman would not be involved.

Out of the wreckage of the WITF, a new women players' guild, the WTA (Women's Tennis Association) was formed at Wimbledon. With King as its first president, the WTA worked closely with the USLTA's Edy McGoldrick in organizing a strong women's circuit for 1974 and beyond.

It is ironic that, because of Bobby Riggs, 1973 will be remembered as the year of Court's humiliation and King's triumph. In fact, Court was the dominant No. 1 player of the season, winning the Australian, French and U.S. Opens (her third year of taking three majors). Bagging 18 of 25 tournaments, and $204,000 in prize money, the female high, she hadn't been beaten since a loss to Jeanne Evert in Boca Raton the previous fall, a streak of 59. For the calendar year, her record was 102-6. She beat King in three of four meetings.

Court started the year by beating Goolagong in the Australian Open final for the third consecutive year, 6-4, 7-5. She then teamed with Wade to win the doubles for the eighth time in 13 years, with her sixth different partner, over two Kerry's—Harris and Melville—neither of whom could carry the other, 6-4, 6-4.

Court was down 3-5 in the second set in the French final, and two points from defeat, but recovered to beat Evert, 6-7 (5-7), 7-6 (8-6), 6-4. It was her fifth French, topping Helen Wills' title collection (1928-29-30, 32), and would remain the record for a dozen years until the same Evert won a sixth in 1985 (and a

seventh a year later). Margaret and Chris waged a battle of torrid groundstroking in the most memorable women's match of the year. Court also won her fourth French doubles title, with Wade, over Francoise Durr and Betty Stove, 6-2, 6-3.

Only Wimbledon prevented Court from recording a second Grand Slam. All eight seeds advanced to the quarters, and the only reversal of form was fourth seeded Evert's 6-1, 1-6, 6-1 defeat of top-seeded Court in the semis. This was unexpected, as much so as grass-loving Margaret beating clay maven Chrissie in Paris. King, superbly conditioned physically and mentally and operating at a high emotional pitch, beat Goolagong in the volley-happy semifinal, 6-3, 5-7, 6-3, and blasted Evert in the final, 6-0, 7-5. BJK became the first five-time singles winner since Helen Wills Moody four decades earlier. She also teamed with Rosie Casals to win the doubles over Durr and Stove, 6-1, 4-6, 7-5—B.J.'s ninth doubles title and fifth alongside Rosie. Calling on Owen Davidson for a helping left hand, B.J. fashioned her second triple at the Big W, winning a second mixed, 6-3, 6-2, over Mexican Raul Ramirez and Californian Janet Newberry.

At the U.S. Open, the icon, 1971-72 champion, King, fell off her pedestal momentarily. She quit her title defense, walking out while trailing Julie Heldman, 1-4 in the final set of a fourth round match played in exhausting heat and humidity. Heldman complained, her right under the rules, that King was taking far more than the one minute allowed at changeovers. "If you want the match that badly, you can have it," seethed King, who later said she was suffering from a virus that had sapped her strength.

Court beat Wade in two tie-breakers in the quarters and avenged her Wimbledon defeat by Evert by a 7-5, 2-6, 6-2 margin in the semis. In the final, she made Goolagong a bridesmaid again, 7-6 (5-2), 5-7, 6-2. For her victory, Margaret received $25,000, the same as Newcombe, since the women achieved prize money parity with men in a major championship for the first time. The singles triumph was her record 24th—and last—major singles title. Court teamed with Wade for Court's 18th major doubles title, this over Casals and King, 3-6, 6-3, 7-5.

King, despite being hampered by injuries in the early season, won eight of 19 tournaments and 58 of 68 matches. Including her $100,000 triumph over Riggs, she earned $197,000 for the year. In taking the No. 1 U.S. ranking for the seventh time, she equaled a feat previously achieved only by Molla Mallory (between 1915 and 1926) and Moody (between 1923 and 1931).

Evert, having turned pro on her 18th birthday, December 21, 1972, earned $151,352 in her (financial) rookie season. She virtually monopolized the USLTA winter tour, winning six of seven tournaments, beating Goolagong in the final of the last three. Evert went on to win 12 of 21 tournaments, 88 of 98 matches, including the Virginia Slims Championship at Boca Raton on clay, defeating her personal nemesis, Nancy Richey Gunter, 6-3, 6-3. Though disappointed to lose three big finals in a row at midseason—the Italian Open to Goolagong, 7-6 (8-6), 6-0, the French to Court, and Wimbledon to King—Chrissie took her first significant international title in the autumn, the South African Open over Goolagong, 6-3, 6-3. Shortly after this tournament, flashing a South African diamond, she announced her engagement to Connors, which was later called off.

Evert also led the U.S. to a 5-2 victory over a young and, except for Wade, inexperienced British team in the Wightman Cup. As the 50th anniversary of the competition, it was played at Longwood Cricket Club, only yards from the home of Cup donor Hazel Hotchkiss Wightman, who was present and active in the celebrations at age 86. Chrissie beat Wade, 6-4, 6-2, and Veronica Burton, 6-3, 6-0. Her kid sister, Jeannie, shared a doubles win with Patti Hogan over Lindsey Beaven and Lesley Charles, 6-3, 4-6, 8-6.

Court wasn't available, but Goolagong and Patti Coleman, a five footer, got the Federation Cup job done for Australia. In the final at Bad Homburg, Germany, Goolagong beat Pat Pretorius Walkden, 6-0, 6-2, and Coleman wore down Brenda Kirk, 10-8, 6-0, in a 3-0 triumph over South Africa. Goolagong's 6-4, 6-3 victory over Evert and Melville's triumph over Heldman, 2-6, 6-1, 6-4, spearheaded an Australian comeback and 6-3 victory over the U.S. in the second Bonne Bell Cup, at Sydney.

Other notable happenings during the year: Casals took the biggest check, $30,000, for winning the new Family Circle Cup at Hilton Head, S.C., over Nancy Richey Gunter, 3-6, 6-1, 7-5, the first tourney to offer a purse of $100,000 to the women. Goolagong beat Evert in the final of the Western Championships at Cincinnati, 6-2, 7-5, Chris' last defeat on clay for nearly six years. Evert won her second U.S. Clay Court title the next week over Burton, 6-4, 6-3, beginning an astounding streak on her favorite surface that would stretch to 25 tournaments and 125 matches (including the only three U.S. Opens played on clay) until her defeat by Tracy Austin in the Italian Open semifinal in May, 1979. Floridian Kathy Kuykendall turned pro at age 16, and then Californian Robin Tenney did her one better, becoming the youngest pro at the time at age 15. However, three years later, having been unsuccessful on the tour, she applied for and was granted a return to amateur status in order to play college tennis.

Previously denied a visa to South Africa because of his anti-apartheid views and statements, Ashe made an emotional pilgrimage to that country in November, becoming the only "non-white" male to win a South African title. That was the doubles with Okker over Lew Hoad and Rob Maud, 6-2, 4-6, 6-2, 6-4. Connors was too strong for him in the singles final, 6-4, 7-6, (7-3), 6-3. Evert's title made it a lovebird sweep for the couple. Goolagong had hurdled the color bar on entrants in 1971, followed in 1972 by minor players Wanaro N'Godrella, a black Frenchman from New Caledonia, and Bonnie Logan, a black American. Logan was a first-round loser, but Ashe, playing an exhibition in Soweto, and meeting with political leaders, white and black, was widely covered, making a distinct impact.

1973 CHAMPIONS AND LEADERS

Australian Open
Men's Singles Final: John Newcombe (AUS) def. Onny Parun (NZL), 6-3, 6-7, 7-5, 6-1
Women's Singles Final: Margaret Smith Court (AUS) def. Evonne Goolagong (AUS), 6-4, 7-5
Men's Doubles Final: Mal Anderson and John Newcombe (AUS) def. John Alexander and Phil Dent (AUS), 6-3, 6-4, 7-6

Women's Doubles Final: Margaret Smith Court (AUS) and Virginia Wade (GBR) def. Kerry Harris and Kerry Melville (AUS), 6-4, 6-4
Mixed Doubles: Not Played

French Open
Men's Singles Final: Ilie Nastase (ROM) def. Nikki Pilic (YUG), 6-3, 6-3, 6-0
Women's Singles Final: Margaret Smith Court (AUS) def. Chris Evert (USA), 6-7 (7-5), 7-6 (8-6), 6-4
Men's Doubles Final: John Newcombe (AUS) and Tom Okker (NED) def. Jimmy Connors (USA) and Ilie Nastase (ROM), 6-1, 3-6, 6-3, 5-7, 6-4
Women's Doubles Final: Margaret Smith Court (AUS) and Virginia Wade (GBR) def. Francoise Durr (FRA) and Betty Stove (NED), 6-2, 6-3
Mixed Doubles Final: Francoise Durr and Jean Claude Barclay (FRA) def. Betty Stove (NED) and Patrice Dominguez (FRA), 6-1, 6-4

Wimbledon
Men's Singles Final: Jan Kodes (CZE) def. Alex Metreveli (USSR), 6-1, 9-8 (7-5), 6-3
Women's Singles Final: Billie Jean King (USA) def. Chris Evert (USA), 6-0, 7-5
Men's Doubles Final: Jimmy Connors (USA) and Ilie Nastase (ROM) def. John Cooper and Neale Fraser (AUS), 3-6, 6-3, 6-4, 8-9 (7-3) 6-1
Women's Doubles Final: Rosie Casals and Billie Jean King (USA) def. Francois Durr (FRA) and Betty Stove (NED). 6-1, 4-6, 7-5
Mixed Doubles Final: Billie Jean Moffitt King (USA) and Owen Davidson (AUS) def. Janet Newberry (USA) and Raul Ramirez (MEX), 6-3, 6-2

U.S. Open
Men's Singles Final: John Newcombe (AUS) def. Jan Kodes (CZE), 6-4, 1-6, 4-6, 6-2, 6-3
Women's Singles Final: Margaret Smith Court (AUS) def. Evonne Goolagong (AUS), 3-6, 6-3, 7-5
Men's Doubles Final: Owen Davidson and John Newcombe (AUS) def. Rod Laver and Ken Rosewall (AUS), 7-5, 2-6, 7-5, 7-5
Women's Doubles Final: Margaret Smith Court (AUS) and Virginia Wade (GBR) def. Billie Jean King and Rosie Casals (USA), 3-6, 6-3, 7-5
Mixed Doubles Final: Billie Jean King (USA) and Owen Davidson (AUS) def. Margaret Smith Court (AUS) and Marty Riessen (USA), 3-6, 7-6

Year-End No. 1
Men: Ilie Nastase
Women: Margaret Smith Court

Top Player Earnings
Men: Ilie Nastase $228,750
Women: Margaret Smith Court $204,400

Wightman Cup: United States

Davis Cup: Australia

Federation Cup: Australia

Grand Prix Masters, Boston—Ilie Nastase
WCT, Dallas—Stan Smith
Virginia Slims Championships, Boca Raton—Chris Evert

1974 Connors Rides Tennis Boom

Jimmy Connors and **Chris Evert** complete the "love double" at Wimbledon as the engaged couple win the men's and women's singles titles at Wimbledon.

Two young Americans—21-year-old Jimmy Connors and 19-year-old Chris Evert, who had announced their engagement late in 1973 but called it off before getting to the altar the next fall—reigned as the king and queen of tennis in 1974. As the American game celebrated its actual centennial, two startling surveys revealed just how popular the game had become in the United States.

The respected A.C. Nielsen Company made its first survey of tennis in 1970, estimating that 10.3 million Americans played occasionally and projecting that the number would increase to 15 million by 1980. A second survey in 1973 indicated that the growth rate was much faster, and fixed the number of players at 20.2 million. A third study, released in September 1974, indicated a staggering 68 percent increase to 33.9 million Americans who said they played tennis "from time to time," and a more significant estimate that 23.4 million played at least three times a month.

Almost as surprising as the rate of the participation boom was a Louis Harris survey that indicated a substantial rise in tennis' popularity as a spectator sport. "The number [of sports fans] who say they "follow" tennis has risen from 17 to 26 percent just in the last year, by far the most dramatic change in American sports preferences," the Harris organization said. This growth was reflected in the tennis industry, as new companies rushed in to offer a dizzying variety of equipment to the burgeoning market, and in the professional game, where prize money continued to skyrocket. Four men and one woman exceeded the $200,000 prize money barrier, which had seemed unattainable just a few years earlier. Connors ($281,309) and Evert ($261,460) led the parade of six-figure earners.

Connors rampaged to the most successful season of any American man since Tony Trabert in 1955, and also became the center of a new political storm in men's tennis. Jimmy won 99 out of 103 matches during the year, 15 of 21 tournaments, includ-

ing the Australian Open, Wimbledon and the U.S. Open as well as the U.S. Indoor, the U.S. Clay Court Championships and the South African Open. He was denied a chance at the Grand Slam when the French Tennis Federation, then led by the iron-willed Philippe Chatrier, barred any player who had signed a contract to compete in the new World Team Tennis league in the United States, which Europeans viewed as a threat to their summer tournaments.

Thus Connors, who had signed to play some matches with the World Team Tennis Baltimore Banners, and Evonne Goolagong, contracted to the Pittsburgh Triangles, were kept out of the world's premier clay court championship after having won the Australian at the start of the year.

Bill Riordan, Connors' maverick manager, knew there was no way he could sue the French Federation directly, but filed a $40 million antitrust suit against Association of Tennis Professionals officers Jack Kramer and Donald Dell, who had been anti-WTT activists, and Commercial Union Assurance, sponsor of the International Lawn Tennis Federation Grand Prix, alleging a conspiracy to monopolize professional tennis and keep Connors (and other WTT players) out of the French.

Few envisioned what a world-beating year it would be for the brash left-handed Connors when he beat Australian Phil Dent, 7-6 (9-7), 6-4, 4-6, 6-3, for the Australian title. His chief rival, John Newcombe, fell in the quarters, 7-6, 6-2, 7-5, to Ross "Snake" Case, who couldn't slither past Dent, 6-4, 6-1, 2-6, 6-2. Aussies Geoff Masters and Case took the doubles at Kooyong in Melbourne, their first major title, beating countrymen Syd Ball and Bob Giltinan, 6-7, 6-3, 6-4.

Connors dominated Riordan's U.S. Lawn Tennis Association Indoor Circuit—played at the same time as an expanded, three-group WCT Tour—winning seven of the nine tournaments he played. That included the U.S. Indoor, his second of a record seven such titles, over Frew McMillan, 6-4, 7-5, 6-3.

At Wimbledon, Connors came within two points of defeat at the hands of Dent in the second round, but pulled away from 5-6, 0-30 in the fifth set to win 5-7, 6-3, 3-6, 6-3, 10-8. He beat defending champ Jan Kodes in five rugged sets in the quarterfinals, 3-6, 6-3, 6-3, 6-8, 6-3, and Dick Stockton in a four-set semifinal, 4-6, 6-2, 6-3, 6-4. Stockton had beaten No. 2 seed Ilie Nastase, 4-6, 6-2, 6-3, 9-8 (7-5) in the fourth round. Ageless Ken Rosewall made mincemeat of a couple of considerably younger ex-champs. In the quarters, he tripped his conqueror of the 1970 final, Newcombe, 6-1, 1-6, 6-0, 7-5. Next he sidestepped a match point in the tie-breaker while beating the returned champ of 1972, a 1973 boycotter, Stan Smith, 6-8, 4-6, 9-8 (8-6), 6-1, 6-3. But in the final, unlucky Rosewall's fourth, Connors made him feel twice his 39 years, dismembering "Muscles," 6-1, 6-1, 6-4.

Connors' ferocious returns of Rosewall's unintimidating serves kept the old man constantly on the defensive, the young lion always on the attack. Consequently, Connors became the youngest champion since Lew Hoad beat Rosewall at age 22 in the 1956 final. Rosewall, the sentimental choice who had been runner-up in 1954, 56, 70, remains, along with Pancho Gonzalez, Gottfried von Cramm, Fred Stolle and Ivan Lendl "the greatest players who never won Wimbledon." Meanwhile, Newcombe captured his sixth doubles title, the fifth with fellow Aussie Tony Roche, over Bob Lutz and Smith, 8-6, 6-4, 6-4.

Connors had a virus that left him doubtful for the last U.S. Open played on grass courts. He lost a great deal of weight, but turned out to be lean and mean as he barreled through the tournament without serious danger, beating Alex Metreveli in the quarters, 3-6, 6-3, 6-4, 6-1, and Roscoe Tanner, 7-6 (5-2), 7-6 (5-2), 6-4, in the semis. Crushing Rosewall again in the final, 6-1, 6-0, 6-1, Jimmy dealt the worst championship beating in U.S. as well as majors history, tying the two games that Willie Renshaw allowed John Hartley in 1881, and Fred Perry permitted Gottfried von Cramm in 1936, both at Wimbledon. Tanner had beaten both Nastase, 4-6, 6-7, 7-5, 6-4, 6-4, and Smith, 7-6 (5-2), 6-2, 3-6, 6-1. Although Newcombe had beaten Arthur Ashe in a suspenseful quarters, 4-6, 6-3, 3-6, 7-6 (5-4), 6-4, Rosewall, two months shy of his 40th birthday, trimmed him, as he had at Wimbledon, 6-7 (3-5), 6-4, 7-6 (5-1), 6-3. Connors became the youngest Forest Hills champion since, ironically, Rosewall in 1956. The doubles title also stayed in America, Smith and Lutz regaining the prize they first won in 1968, beating Chileans Jaime Fillol and Pato Cornejo, 6-3, 6-3.

Connors was the main man, but there were other outstanding performers during the year. Bjorn Borg, the ascending "Teen Angel" from Sweden, became the youngest player to win the Italian (17) and French (just turned 18) Opens and the U.S. Pro Championship. He beat Nastase in Rome, 6-3, 6-4, 6-1; Manolo Orantes in Paris, reviving, 2-6, 6-7 (1-7), 6-0, 6-1, 6-1; over Tom Okker in Boston, 7-6 (7-3), 6-1, 6-1, a tournament in which he re-inflated from 1-5 down in the fifth set to beat Kodes in an astonishing semifinal, 7-6 (7-3), 6-0, 1-6, 2-6, 7-6 (7-4). Borg won nine tournaments and was runner-up in five more, including the WCT Finals at Dallas. There, he coolly beat Ashe, 7-5, 6-4, 7-6, and Kodes, 4-6, 6-4, 6-3, 6-2, before running up against Newcombe, 30, who won this one for the older generation, 4-6, 6-3, 6-3, 6-2.

Borg was also runner-up to Connors at the U.S. Clay Courts, 5-7, 6-3, 6-4, their only meeting of the year. Bjorn had won their first meeting in the semifinal of the 1973 Stockholm Open, 6-4, 3-6, 7-6, but now Connors was off on a seven-match run in what would develop into the rivalry of the '70s in the men's game. Their lifetime head-to-head ended up 10-7 for Borg.

Newcombe was the dominant player of the WCT season, winning five of the 11 tournaments in his group (Nastase and Laver won four each in theirs). But the new format of tricolor groups (Red, Blue, Green), each playing 11 tournaments to qualify their two point leaders plus two "wild cards" for the eight man Dallas final, was not very successful. The product was too diluted, difficult to follow, and the zig-zagging global travel schedule taxed the players. WCT, which two years before had the inside track in the men's pro game, had over-expanded and suffered in prestige in the process.

Bob Hewitt and McMillan won the WCT doubles final at Montreal, sharing $40,000 for beating Newcombe and Owen Davidson in the final, 6-2, 6-7, 6-1, 6-2. A makeshift young Mexican-American doubles team of Raul Ramirez and Brian Gottfried was formed in the spring and immediately proved to be a successful partnership, winning the first of four consecutive Italian doubles titles, 6-3, 6-2, 6-3, over Nastase and Juan Gisbert.

After Wimbledon, another 22-year-old left-hander arose and edged out Connors for the $100,000 top prize in the Commercial

Union Grand Prix. Guillermo Vilas of Argentina, who had shown promise of things to come by knocking out defending champ Andres Gimeno at the French Open in 1973, ruled the U.S. summer circuit and won six of his last 15 tournaments.

The attractive and sensitive young Latin, a former law student and part-time poet, also won the Grand Prix Masters at Melbourne, which Connors boycotted. (He claimed a dental problem, but most blamed his suit against sponsor Commercial Union for his absence.) Even though Vilas did not like grass courts, unsuited to his heavy topspin game, he beat Newcombe, 6-4, 7-6, Borg, 7-5, 6-1, and Onny Parun, 7-5, 3-6, 11-9 to win his round-robin group, then Ramirez in the semifinal, 4-6, 6-3, 6-2, 7-5. Finally, he beat Nastase in a brilliant shot-fest, 7-6, 6-2, 3-6, 3-6, 6-4, to claim his biggest title to date.

At season's end, Vilas was not far behind Connors on the money list, having earned $274,327. Newcombe was third with $273,299, Borg fourth with $215,229. Laver won six tournaments, including the U.S. Pro Indoor over Ashe (his 15th consecutive victory over Arthur in 15 years), 6-1, 6-4, 3-6, 6-4, and the rich Alan King Classic in Las Vegas over Marty Riessen, 6-2, 6-2. Temporarily, he remained the all-time money winner with a career total of $1,379,454. Connors would catch him soon enough.

Meanwhile, World Team Tennis made its raucous debut in May, offering players a lucrative alternative to tournaments during the summer. Sixteen teams embarked on a schedule of 44 contests each, the format being five one-set matches (men's and women's singles and doubles plus mixed doubles with the cumulative games won in all five deciding the contest.

The Philadelphia Freedoms, with Billie Jean King as player-coach (and with a theme song, *Philadelphia Freedom*, written for her by her great admirer and friend, Elton John) defeated coach Ken Rosewall's Pittsburgh Triangles in the ballyhooed opener at Philadelphia's Spectrum, 31-25. Philadelphia had the best season record, 39-5, but lost the playoffs in two straight to the Denver Racquets, 27-21, 28-24, who promptly moved to Phoenix. No team made money, and the average loss per franchise was estimated to be $300,000. The league was cut down to 12 teams in 1975, and only one came back for the second season with the original owners.

A more traditional team competition, the Davis Cup, continued to be tarnished by political problems and cumbersome scheduling that often left countries playing matches without their best players. Such was the case with both the U.S., ambushed by Colombia, 4-1, at Bogota in January, and Australia, traveling to India undermanned and beaten by the same score. For the first time in the history of the competition, the 74-year-old Cup was decided by default. South Africa became the fifth nation to hold the sterling silver punchbowl when the Indian Government refused to let its team play the final, a protest of South Africa's apartheid racial policies.

Connors declined to play for the U.S. in either the Davis Cup or the World Cup, won by Australia at Hartford, 5-2, with Newcombe spearheading the attack, beating Ashe and Smith and teaming with Roche to beat them in doubles. Laver came aboard to beat Smith but his ownership of Ashe ended. Zero-for-15 against the "Rocket" over a 15-year stretch, Arthur splintered the jinx, 6-3, 6-3.

Evert became the youngest to gain the No. 1 U.S. female ranking since Maureen Connolly reigned supreme in 1951-52-53. Chrissie won 16 tournaments—including Wimbledon, the French, Italian and U.S. Clay Courts and was never beaten before the semifinals in compiling a 100-7 record in 23 tournaments. Her $261,460 in prize money far outdistanced Margaret Smith Court's record of the previous year. In winning her third straight U.S. Clay Court title, Chrissie savaged the 1969 champ Gail Chanfreau, 6-0, 6-0, rationing five opponents to a total of eight games.

Evert did not have things entirely her own way, even though she compiled a 55-match winning streak in mid-season. Goolagong beat her in four of six meetings, including the final of the Australian Open and the Virginia Slims Championship at Los Angeles, as well as in the semifinals of the U.S. Open. King won the Open and took two of three from Evert, including the final of the U.S. Indoor, which BJK captured for the fifth time, 6-3, 3-6, 6-2.

Goolagong played inspired tennis in celebrating the New Year with a 7-6 (7-5), 4-6, 6-0 triumph over Evert at Melbourne, winning her native title for the first time after being runner-up the previous three years. Evonne also paired with American Peggy Michel, her Pittsburgh Triangles teammate and partner in WTT, to win the doubles titles of Australia (over Kerry Harris and Kerry Melville, 7-5, 6-3) and Wimbledon (over Helen Gourlay and Karen Krantzcke, 2-6, 6-4, 6-3).

With Goolagong, King, Melville (who would marry her Boston Lobsters teammate Grover 'Raz' Reid), and most of the other leading women playing WTT during the summer, Evert had the European daytime season pretty much to herself. She beat Martina Navratilova, the promising young Czech left-hander who had played the USLTA women's circuit at age 16 in 1973, in the Italian final, 6-3, 6-3, and Soviet No. 1 Olga Morozova in the French final, 6-1, 6-2. Evert and Morozova won both doubles titles, (a walkover in Rome, a 6-4, 2-6, 6-1 decision over Chanfreau and Katja Ebbinghaus in Paris).

Evert barely survived her opening match at Wimbledon-squeezed by Lesley Hunt, 8-6, 5-7, 11-9. Their thriller was delayed for several hours by rain, breathtakingly played despite a slippery court, and suspended overnight by darkness at 9-9 in the third set. But Chris went on to complete her "Old World Triple" by crunching eighth-seeded Morozova in the final, 6-0, 6-4.

Evert did not have to play her two greatest rivals, top-seeded King and Goolagong, because they both came up flat and were stunned in the quarterfinals—Billie Jean by Morozova, 7-5, 6-2 and Goolagong by Melville, 9-7, 1-6, 6-2. Evert got to dance the champions' traditional first foxtrot at the Wimbledon Ball with her fiancé, Connors. The "lovebird double," a Connors-Evert parlay, paid bettors 33-to-1 in England's legalized gambling shops.

Evert won 10 consecutive tournaments after losing the U.S. Indoor to King, but her streak ended nerve-wrackingly at 55 matches in the semifinals at Forest Hills. Goolagong raced to a 6-0, 4-3 lead before rain suspended their match. The next day, Evert pulled level after Goolagong served for the match at 5-4 in the second set, four times reaching deuce. Evonne came within two points of victory twice more when she served at 6-5. Evert broke again, won the tie-breaker, 5-1, but couldn't contend with

Goolagong's outstanding volleying in relinquishing the excruciating final set, winning, 6-0, 6-7 (1-5), 6-3.

King avenged her bitter loss of the year before by beating Julie Heldman, 2-6, 6-3, 6-1, in the other semifinal, and toppled Goolagong, 3-6, 6-3, 7-5, in a final of enthralling shotmaking that delighted a Monday sellout crowd of 15,303. Vastly more entertaining than the massacre of the men's final, this volleying masterpiece was alive until the very end. Goolagong broke at love when King served for the match at 5-4, but BJK won eight of the last nine points to seal her fourth singles title. She also collaborated with Rosie Casals for their second U.S. doubles crown, a tight one over Francoise Durr and Betty Stove, 7-6 (5-4), 6-7 (2-5), 6-4. Bulldozers moved into the stadium at the West Side Tennis Club the next day to dig up the grass courts, which were to be replaced with synthetic clay.

Goolagong beat Evert, 7-5, 3-6, 6-4, in the final of the Virginia Slims tournament at Denver and again in the Slims playoff, where she took the richest women's prize to date, $32,000, with a 6-3, 6-4 victory over the 1972-73 champ. That evened their career rivalry at 8-8 over three years.

Melville, who had been runner-up, 6-1, 6-3, to Evert for the $30,000 top prize in the Family Circle Cup in the spring, won the South African Open, her biggest international title, over Australian 17-year-old lefty Dianne Fromholtz, 6-3, 7-5. Fromholtz registered a 6-4, 6-4 win over Court, who was making a comeback after the birth of her second child.

America's top two players, Evert and King, sat out the Federation, Wightman and Bonne Bell Cups.

Player-captain Heldman rang up a triple, beating both Goolagong, 6-3, 6-1, and Hunt, 6-4, 6-4 in leading the U.S. to a shocking 5-4 victory over Australia in the third Bell Cup, in Cleveland. Julie also blended with lefty Kris Kemmer to take a doubles over Krantzcke and Gourlay, 6-4, 3-6, 6-4. Alas, that concluded the rivalry; the competition was unfortunately, abandoned.

Great Britain, psyched by player-captain Virginia Wade's 5-7, 9-7, 6-4 victory over Heldman, sprinted to a 6-1 victory in the Wightman Cup, only their eighth in 46 meetings with the United States. Glynis Coles also beat Heldman, 6-0, 6-4, and Wade followed up with a 6-1, 6-3, decision over Janet Newberry. Wimbledon was neglected for the first time in the rivalry, this engagement staged at Deeside, Wales. Cup donor Hazel Wightman died at age 87 in December, shortly after the series.

Jeanne Evert, 17, Chrissie's younger sister, finished the year ranked No. 9 as she and Chris became the first pair of U.S. top 10 ranked sisters since the California Suttons, Ethel (No. 2) and Florence (No. 3) in 1913. Jeanne and Heldman took the U.S. to the final of the Federation Cup in Naples, Italy, before falling to Australia, 2-1. Goolagong beat Heldman, 6-1, 7-5, for her 13th straight Fed Cup singles without a loss and teamed with Janet Young for the clincher, 7-5, 8-6, over Heldman and Sharon Walsh after Jeanne beat Fromholtz, 2-6, 7-5, 6-4.

Chris Evert was elected to succeed the more activist King as president of the WTA at Wimbledon, where the women threatened to boycott in 1975 unless they received "equal parity" with the men in prize money, as Evert put it. That was about the only political story in the women's game, however, and it turned out to be no more than a mild tempest in a teapot, solved by teatime.

1974 CHAMPIONS AND LEADERS

Australian Open
Men's Singles Final: Jimmy Connors (USA) def. Phil Dent (AUS), 7-6 (9-7), 6-4, 4-6, 6-3
Women's Singles Final: Evonne Goolagong (AUS) def. Chris Evert (USA), 7-6 (7-5), 4-6, 6-0
Men's Doubles Final: Ross Case and Geoff Masters (AUS) def. Syd Ball and Bob Giltinian (AUS), 6-7, 6-3, 6-4
Women's Doubles Final: Evonne Goolagong (AUS) and Peggy Michel (USA) def. Kerry Harris and Kerry Melville (AUS), 7-5, 6-3
Mixed Doubles: Not Played

French Open
Men's Singles Final: Bjorn Borg (SWE) def. Manolo Orantes (ESP), 2-6, 6-7(1-7), 6-0, 6-1, 6-1
Women's Singles Final: Chris Evert (USA) def. Olga Morozova (USSR), 6-1, 6-2
Men's Doubles Final: Dick Crealy (AUS) and Onny Parun (NZL) def. Stan Smith and Bob Lutz (USA), 6-3, 6-2, 3-6, 5-7, 6-1
Women's Doubles Final: Chris Evert (USA) and Olga Morozova (USSR) def. Gail Sherriff Chanfreau (FRA) and Katja Ebbinghaus (GER), 6-4, 2-6, 6-1
Mixed Doubles Final: Martina Navratilova (USA) and Ivan Molina (COL) def Marcelo Lara and Rosie Reyes Darmon (MEX), 6-3, 6-3

Wimbledon
Men's Singles Final: Jimmy Connors (USA) def. Ken Rosewall (AUS), 6-1, 6-1, 6-4
Women's Singles Final: Chris Evert (USA) def. Olga Morozova (USSR), 6-0, 6-4
Men's Doubles Final: John Newcombe and Tony Roche (AUS) def. Bob Lutz and Stan Smith (USA), 8-6, 6-4, 6-4
Women's Doubles Final: Evonne Goolagong and Peggy Michel (AUS) def. Helen Gourlay (AUS) and Karen Krantzcke (USA), 2-6, 6-4, 6-3
Mixed Doubles Final: Billie Jean King (USA) and Owen Davidson (AUS) def. Lesley Charles and Mark Farrell (GBR), 6-3, 9-7

U.S. Open
Men's Singles Final: Jimmy Connors (USA) def. Ken Rosewall (AUS), 6-1, 6-0, 6-1
Women's Singles Final: Billie Jean King (USA) def. Evonne Goolagong (AUS), 3-6, 6-3, 7-5
Men's Doubles Final: Bob Lutz and Stan Smith (USA) def. Patricio Cornejo and Jaime Fillol (CHI), 6-3, 6-3
Women's Doubles Final: Rosie Casals and Billie Jean King (USA) def. Francoise Durr (FRA) and Betty Stove (NED), 7-6 (7-4), 6-7 (2-7), 6-4
Mixed Doubles Final: Pam Teeguarden (USA) and Geoff Masters (AUS) def. Chris Evert and Jimmy Connors (USA), 6-1, 7-6

Year-End No. 1
Men: Jimmy Connors
Women: Billie Jean King

Top Player Earnings
Men: Jimmy Connors $285,490
Women: Chris Evert $261,460

Davis Cup: South Africa

Federation Cup: Australia

Wightman Cup: Great Britain

Grand Prix Masters, Melbourne—Guillermo Vilas
WCT, Dallas—John Newcombe
Virginia Slims Championships, Los Angeles—Evonne Goolagong

Wimbledon Magic For Ashe

Arthur Ashe stunned the heavily favored Jimmy Connors to win the men's singles title at Wimbledon.

Jimmy Connors joined world leaders as a cover subject for *Time* magazine in 1975, as he first beat Rod Laver and then John Newcombe (avenging a loss in the Australian Open final) in ballyhooed "Heavyweight Championship of Tennis" challenge matches in Las Vegas.

These extravaganzas—the focal point of a TV sports scandal two years later because of the CBS network's misleading "winner-take-all" hype—gained high ratings and massive exposure. Connors and his clever, prizefight-style manager Bill Riordan—who were to split bitterly before the end of the year as Connors dropped the controversial antitrust suit he filed in 1974—were the kings of hype. But the ruler of men's tennis was King Arthur Ashe.

At age 32, after nearly 15 years in the big time, Ashe finally fulfilled the promise that had been acclaimed for him in 1968

and gradually abandoned. Seemingly a perennial bridesmaid, loser of 14 of his last 19 final-round matches as the year began, Ashe became the best by dedicating himself to training and positive thinking as never before.

In 29 tournaments, he got to 14 finals, winning nine of them, including the two he really set out to win: The WCT Finals in Dallas (over Bjorn Borg, 3-6, 6-4, 6-4, 6-0), and Wimbledon (over Connors in a four-set stunner). Ashe's $338,337 earnings for the year boosted his total in seven years as a pro to $1,052,202, making him the sport's third million-dollar winner.

Meanwhile, despite Billie Jean King's dramatic sixth Wimbledon singles title, a postwar record, Chris Evert was the indisputable sovereign of women's tennis. Before celebrating her 21st birthday on Dec. 21, Chrissie defended her Italian and French Open titles, won the first U.S. Open on clay by out-gritting archrival Evonne Goolagong, dethroned Goolagong to recapture the Virginia Slims throne, won 16 of 22 tournaments for the year and set an all-time single-season winnings record of $350,977. She didn't lose a match the last six months of the season after succumbing to King in the Wimbledon semifinal, and was never beaten before the quarterfinals of a tournament.

Ashe was the Man of the Year, but the season began with another self-reclamation project. Newcombe, who was slowed by injuries after winning the WCT title in May 1974, and was to miss Wimbledon and the U.S. Open with new ailments, flogged himself into shape for the Australian Open by doing miles of roadwork and charging countless times up the hill behind his attractive split-level home in the Sydney suburb of Pymble. He struggled to the final (past Geoff Masters, 1-6, 6-3, 6-7, 6-3, 10-8 in the quarterfinals, and Tony Roche, 6-4, 4-6, 6-4, 2-6, 11-9 in the semifinals). But Newk was ready for Connors, serving ferociously to win, 7-5, 3-6, 6-4, 7-5.

Already set before the loss to Newcombe was the first of Connors' challenge matches at Caesar's Palace, the Las Vegas hotel-casino. The opponent was Laver, the Grand Slammer of 1962 and 1969—a "natural" pairing since they had never played each other. Connors won, 6-4, 6-2, 3-6, 7-5, seizing what was said to be a $100,000 "winner-take-all" purse, but it was widely reported that both players took home big checks from "ancillary" revenues.

The success of the venture of CBS-TV made a second "Heavyweight Championship" inevitable, Newcombe being the logical challenger after his popular victory at Melbourne on New Year's Day. Connors won again, 6-3, 4-6, 6-2, 6-2. Connors was said to receive a $250,000 "winner-take-all" purse, but it was later revealed that the match had been structured like a championship prize fight, each player receiving a pre-agreed percentage, win or lose. Connors made $480,000; Newcombe, $280,000.

Although he won these indoor bouts amid the heavyweight hoopla on which he thrived, Connors lost in the final of the three major championships he had swept the previous year. Newcombe set the example in Australia. Ashe, considered a prohibitive underdog (10-to-1 on the day), came up with a tactical masterpiece in the Wimbledon final, 6-1, 6-1, 5-7, 6-4. Arthur's friends worried that he'd be embarrassed in the title bout as Ken Rosewall had been 12 months earlier. Their concern was unnecessary. Arthur changed speed and spin smartly, fed junk to Connors' forehand, exposing the vulnerability of that wing to paceless shots, and sliced his serves wide to Connors' backhand, exploiting the slightly limited reach of his two handed shot.

This was an extraordinary final, the only one between litigants in a lawsuit since President Ashe, along with other officers of the ATP, were named in the $40-million antitrust suit Connors and Riordan had filed against attorney Donald Dell, Jack Kramer and Grand Prix sponsor Commercial Union. There were several other suits and counterclaims associated with this one, but all were quietly settled, out of court and without payment of damages, not long after Ashe's emotion-charged and enormously popular victory.

A bright new event was the Spalding Mixed Doubles Classic in Dallas at the Moody Coliseum, scene of the WCT Championship. Betty Stove and Dick Stockton took the title over Rosie Casals and Marty Riessen, 6-7, 6-2, 6-4, 3-6, 6-3.

Ashe was not considered a serious threat at the U.S. Open after the grass courts at the West Side Tennis Club in Forest Hills were dug up immediately after the 1974 tournament, replaced with a synthetic pea-green clay called Har-Tru, which became the predominant surface of the U.S. summer circuit. Sure enough, clay specialist Eddie Dibbs—one of a group of scrappy young Americans coming up to succeed Ashe's generation— beat No. 4-seeded Arthur in the fourth round, 6-4, 6-2, 6-3.

Forest Hills, previously dominated by grass-loving Americans and Australians, suddenly became a happy hunting ground for clay-reared Europeans and South Americans. The most successful was third-seeded Manolo Orantes, the elegant left-hander from Barcelona. In the semifinal, he revived himself from two sets and 0-2 down, and from 0-5 in the fourth set, saving five match points to beat No. 2-seeded Argentine left-hander Guillermo Vilas, 4-6, 1-6, 6-2, 7-5, 6-4. That three-hour, 44-minute marathon did not end until 10:40 p.m. on Saturday, the installation of all-weather courts permitting floodlighting and night play for the first time. Orantes didn't get to bed until 3 a.m. because of a plumbing failure in his hotel room. He was assumed to be a lamb going to slaughter in the final against top-seeded Connors, who had hammered Borg in the other semifinal, 7-5, 7-5, 7-5, early the previous afternoon.

But taking his cue from Ashe's strategy at Wimbledon, Orantes slow-balled Connors and cleverly mixed up his game. He dropshotted and lobbed, chipped and passed, traded ground strokes and sometimes dashed in to take away the forecourt, snaring Connors in his butterfly net. It was 10 years since Manuel Santana had become the first Spaniard to win at Forest Hills, and again the old concrete stadium was filled with Latin chants and shouts of "Bravo!" and "Ole" as 15,669 spectators roared Orantes to an astonishing 6-4, 6-3, 6-3 victory. At the end, he fell to his knees, jubilant, his toothy face the definitive portrait of ecstasy. Why not? His last 24 hours had constituted the most remarkable feat of any player in a major championship since Wimbledon in 1927, when Frenchman Henri Cochet elevated himself from two sets and 1-5 down to beat Bill Tilden in the semifinal, then from two sets and six match points down to overhaul Jean Borotra in the final.

Connors lost his stranglehold on men's tennis, but did not have a bad year by anyone's standards except his own. He entered 19 tournaments and won nine—five of them on Riordan's USLTA Indoor circuit, including the U.S. Indoor over Vitas Gerulaitis, 5-7, 7-5, 6-1, 3-6, 6-0. Connors was runner-up in six others, including the Australian, Wimbledon, and U.S. Open, compiling an 83-10 record, earning well over a half-million dollars with all his "special" matches. But Ashe was the prize-money leader with $306,712.

In the fall, Connors also split with Riordan. He had prospered, financially and competitively, under Riordan's tutelage, but also had become the isolated man of the locker room, despised and openly cold-shouldered by his colleagues. With the divorce from his manager, Connors gradually came in from the cold, re-establishing cordial if never close relations with his fellow players. "I think Jimmy just decided that it wasn't worth going through life hated," said his contemporary, Roscoe Tanner.

Ashe, who had been one of the first to recognize that a deep freeze by his peers would be the most effective way of ending the divisive lawsuits Connors fronted for Riordan, won four of eight tournaments in his group during the WCT season, while Connors was playing the smaller Riordan-organized tour. Laver won four consecutive WCT tournaments and 23 straight matches. But Ashe earned a solid gold tennis ball, valued at $33,333 (188.7 ounces of 24 carat gold—13 pounds but wouldn't bounce), as the top point-winner on the tour. Divided into three groups (Red, Blue and Green) it consisted of 25 tournaments. Arthur won the $50,000 top prize in the eight-man WCT Finals in Dallas by beating Mark Cox, 1-6, 6-4, 6-4, 7-6, John Alexander, 3-6, 6-1, 6-3, 6-4 and 18-year-old Borg, 3-6, 6-4, 6-4, 6-0.

A man who came close to perfection, Laver was bidding farewell to Dallas, where he'd lost two of these finals, and, at 36 he went out marvelously in a mesmerizing shot-making feast of a semifinal with Borg, 7-6, 3-6, 5-7, 7-6 (7-2), 6-2.

Ashe also played a substantial number of events in the $4-million dollar Commercial Union Grand Prix, which embraced 42 tournaments in 19 countries during its May-through-December calendar, boosting the total prize money available in men's tennis to more than $8 million dollars. Ashe compiled a 16-match winning streak in the fall, winning two tournaments to qualify for the eight-man Grand Prix Masters

playoff at Stockholm. He had visions of a unique WCT-Masters double, but was upended in the semifinals of the Masters by Borg, 6-4, 3-6, 6-2, 6-2, and concluded, "I don't think anybody is strong enough, mentally and physically, to win WCT and the Masters in the same year."

Borg, the unflappable baseliner supreme, was runner-up in both—to Ashe in Dallas and to Ilie Nastase (who came back from a disqualification against Ashe in his opening round-robin match of the Masters) in Stockholm. "Teen Angel" was in the waning days of his 18th year when he beat Laver in Dallas, perhaps the year's finest match. He had turned 19 by the time he shut down Vilas, 6-2, 6-3, 6-4, for his second consecutive French Open title. Later, Borg steamrolled Vilas again, 6-3, 6-4, 6-2, to defend his U.S. Pro crown in Boston. Borg won five of 23 tournaments on the year and amassed a 78-19 record.

He carried Sweden to its first possession of the Davis Cup, winning all 12 of his singles matches against Poland, West Germany, the Soviet Union, Spain, Chile and, finally, Czechoslovakia at Stockholm. The final was essentially Borg against Jan Kodes, with their seconds, Ove Bengtson, and a combination of Jiri Hrebec and Vladimir Zednik, the fall guys.

Bjorn beat Hrebec for openers, and got the clincher over Kodes, 6-4, 6-2, 6-2, making it 3-1. Both Czechs downed Bengtson, but tall Ove's doubles prowess alongside Bjorn was essential, 6-4, 6-4, 6-4, over Kodes-Zednik. Borg's record of 16 consecutive Davis Cup singles victories over three years tied the all-time Cup record set by Bill Tilden between 1920 and 1926, and would stretch to the record, 33, by his retirement.

Vilas didn't take any of the big international titles, but won six of 23 tournaments—including Washington and Louisville during a 16-match winning streak early in the U.S. summer circuit—and reached at least the quarterfinals of 21 to seize the $100,000 top prize in the Commercial Union Grand Prix for the second straight year.

Nastase won the Masters for the fourth time in five years, coming back from his disqualification in the opening round-robin match against Ashe. Uncharacteristically furious at Nastase's behavior and stalling, Arthur (ahead, 1-6, 7-5, 4-1) lost his customary cool. He stormed off the court, disqualifying himself. Referee Horst Klosterkemper, declaring that "in my mind I was about to default Nastase" just as Ashe quit, found himself with two losers of the same match. It was ironed out the next day with Ashe announced as the winner. Nevertheless, Nastase, by defeating Orantes, 3-6, 6-4, 6-4, and Italian Adriano Panatta, 7-6, 3-6, 6-0, in his remaining round-robin matches, scraped into the semifinal. There, he beat Vilas, 6-0, 6-3, 6-4, and went on to destroy Borg's rhythm with changes of spins and pace for a 6-2, 6-2, 6-1 championship triumph. This was by far the biggest of Nastase's seven tournament victories for the year. However, he set a dubious achievement record by being defaulted three times, quitting his semifinal match at the Italian Open to ultimate champion Raul Ramirez, and "tanking" the Canadian Open final to Orantes, 7-6, 6-0, 6-1 after going bonkers over a line call in the first set tie-breaker.

For this unprofessional conduct, Nastase was fined $8,000 by the newly formed Men's International Professional Tennis Council, a tripartite body made up of three representatives each of the male players, the International Lawn Tennis Federation, and worldwide tournament directors. Nastase's lawyers appealed, and the fine was reduced, but the "Pro Council" had established itself as an important new administrative and judicial force in the men's game. It was designed to be legislative as well, and became the autonomous governing body of the Grand Prix circuit.

It was a peculiar year in men's doubles. Brian Gottfried and Ramirez were the Team of the Year. They began their reign in the U.S. Pro Indoor at Philadelphia over Stockton and Erik van Dillen, 6-3, 3-6, 7-6 and won the WCT doubles title at Mexico City over Cox and Cliff Drysdale, 7-6, 6-7, 6-2, 7-6. Gottfried-Ramirez also won a special "Challenge Match" during the WCT singles finals at Dallas over South African Davis Cuppers Bob Hewitt and Frew McMillan, 7-5, 6-3, 4-6, 2-6, 7-5. The South African pair had been rudely kicked out of Mexico shortly after their arrival for the doubles playoff—a clumsy power play by the Mexican government to protest the apartheid racial policies of South Africa.

Gottfried-Ramirez also won the French title, over John Alexander-Phil Dent, 6-4, 2-6, 6-2, 6-4 and the U.S. Pro, over Mike Estep and John Andrews, 4-6, 6-3, 7-6. But they came up flat at the end of the year, failing to win a match in the Masters as a four team doubles playoff was inaugurated alongside the singles. The doubles was a round-robin affair, which proved to be an unsatisfactory format when three teams tied with identical 2-1 records. Spanish Davis Cuppers Orantes and Juan Gisbert were declared champions on the basis of having the best percentage of games won for their three matches, even though they were beaten head-to-head, 6-0, 6-3, by the spirited new American tandem of Sherwood Stewart and Freddie McNair.

The Wimbledon doubles turned into a wildly unpredictable scramble as only one seeded team reached the quarterfinals. Alex "Sandy" Mayer and Vitas Gerulaitis, who had not blended well earlier in the year, became the first American champions in 18 years (since Budge Patty and Gar Mulloy) with a 7-5, 8-6, 6-4 victory in the final over similarly unseeded Allan Stone of Australia and Colin Dowdeswell of Rhodesia, who had never even met each other until introduced in the tea room the first day of the tournament.

Connors got his only major title of the year by teaming with Nastase to win the U.S. Open doubles over Riessen and Tom Okker, 6-4, 7-6. Connors seldom played doubles thereafter, a trend soon followed by Borg and Vilas as top players began to concentrate singularly on singles.

Connors also ended—only temporarily, as it turned out—his one man boycott of the U.S. Davis Cup team. Former French, Wimbledon and U.S. champion Tony Trabert replaced Dennis Ralston as the American captain after Raul Ramirez led a 3-2 Mexican ambush of the U.S. at Palm Springs in February 1975, ironically the same weekend that Connors was beating Laver in the first Las Vegas Challenge Match. Ramirez, the best Mexican to play the game other than Rafe Osuna, a quick, resourceful, strong volleyer, was peskier for the U.S. than Pancho Villa. He led two raiding parties within 10 months that eliminated the *norteamericanos*. The notion that Connors' presence alone assured victory in the American Zone was dispelled as Ramirez,

an inspired Davis Cup player, led Mexico to another 3-2 upset. This was in the second round of the 1976 competition, actually played December 19-21, 1975. It all came down to the No. 1 players of the two countries in the decisive fifth match, and Ramirez, was as high as the 6,000-foot altitude of Mexico City as he beat Connors, 2-6, 6-3, 6-3, 6-4, in a match suspended overnight by darkness.

The Davis Cup continued to be plagued by political turmoil. Mexico, after eliminating the U.S., refused to play South Africa. Colombia similarly defaulted, putting South Africa—winner of the Cup by default the previous year—into the American Zone final without playing a match. But administrators were momentarily relieved as South African was eliminated by Chile at Santiago, 5-0. But then Chilean No. 1 Jaime Fillol received a death threat from opponents of the military junta in his homeland, forcing massive security precautions for the semifinal in Sweden. The stadium at Bastad was kept almost empty except for thousands of police and troops. Boats patrolled the harbor, aircraft hovered overhead, and huge nets around the stadium protected the players from projectiles hurled by anti-Chile demonstrators. In this unnerving atmosphere, Borg and Birger Andersson whipped the Chileans, 4-1, to set up their Cup clinching victory over Czechoslovakia in Stockholm just before Christmas.

The ATP, in a rather clumsy effort to force a consolidation of the Davis Cup into a one or two-week showdown at one site, staged a new competition with just such a Federation Cup-style format, calling it the Nations Cup. The American team of Ashe and Tanner defeated Great Britain's Roger Taylor and Buster Mottram, 2-1, in Jamaica, but the competition was not a success. Meanwhile, Laver and 40-year-old Rosewall helped Australia to a 4-3 victory over the U.S. in the World Cup at Hartford, showing that the Aussie dynasty was not entirely dead.

World Team Tennis, despite the huge financial losses of its inaugural season and a ludicrous player draft (numerous show-biz personalities were named by teams in a publicity stunt that made a mockery of the league), surprised many by coming out for a second season. There were 12 teams, four fewer than in 1974, and only one returned with the original ownership, but the league staggered along. Pittsburgh, led by Gerulaitis and Goolagong, beat the San Francisco Bay Area's Golden Gaters in the championship series, 25-26, 28-25, 21-14.

Goolagong started the season by repeating as Australian Open champion, beating Martina Navratilova, 6-3, 6-2, in an emotional final. (Evonne's father had been killed in an auto accident, and Evonne wept on the shoulder of her coach and guardian, Vic Edwards, at the presentation ceremonies.) Goolagong also successfully defended her doubles title with WTT teammate Peggy Michel, over Margaret Smith Court and Russian Olga Morozova 7-6, 7-6.

Evert cashed the biggest check for women in "special events"—$50,000 for winning the four-woman L'Eggs World Series over King at Lakeway, Texas, 4-6, 6-3, 7-6. She also won $40,000 for adding her third triumph in the Virginia Slims Championship at Los Angeles, over Navratilova, 6-4, 6-2. Navratilova won the U.S. Indoor at Boston, beating Goolagong in the final,

6-2, 4-6, 6-4, but she lost again to Evert, 7-5, 6-4, in the final of the rich Family Circle Cup.

With most of the top women committed to World Team Tennis, Evert and Navratilova were the class of the women's field in the Italian and French Opens. They reached the singles finals of both, Evert winning Rome, 6-1, 6-0, and Paris, 2-6, 6-2, 6-1. Chris and Martina then teamed up to win both the doubles titles, Italian over Sue Barker and Glynis Coles 6-1, 6-2 and the French over Julie Anthony and Olga Morozova 6-3, 6-2.

King, always considering the Centre Court at Wimbledon her favorite stage, never performed more majestically there than in coming from 0-3 down in the third set to beat Evert in the semifinals, 2-6, 6-2, 6-3, and burying Goolagong, 6-0, 6-1, in the most lopsided women's final since 1911. BJK's sixth singles title was her 19th in all at Wimbledon, tying the career record of Elizabeth Ryan, who never won the singles but captured 12 doubles and seven mixed crowns between 1914 and 1934. King said this was her last appearance in singles because of a deteriorating knee—"I want to quit on top," she said, "and I can't get much higher than this"—but she eventually returned in 1977.

The women's doubles champions turned out to be as unlikely as the men's, Kazuko Sawamatsu of Japan and Ann Kiyomura, an American of Japanese ancestry, teaming to upset Francoise Durr and Stove in the final, 7-5, 1-6, 7-5. Court teamed with Riessen for the mixed doubles title over Stove and Allan Stone, 6-3, 2-6, 7-5. Margaret was just about at the end of her tremendous journey of 16 years up a record mountain of 62 major titles. Could anybody ever equal that haul? This mixed was the 61st, and she would close two months later with the 62nd, the U.S. doubles with Virginia Wade, 7-5, 2-6, 7-6 (7-5), over King and Rosie Casals. It was 33-year-old Court's 19th doubles, complementing 24 singles and 19 mixed.

Evert won the U.S. Open, dropping only one set. That was in the final, where her 5-7, 6-4, 6-2 victory over Goolagong relegated Evonne to the record books as the only woman to lose three consecutive U.S. singles finals.

More important than tennis was Navratilova's decision, announced at Forest Hills, to defect from her native Czechoslovakia and seek U.S. citizenship. She made the decision after the Czech Tennis Federation, chiding her for becoming "too Americanized," initially refused her a visa to compete in the U.S. Open. Navratilova felt she had to follow the lead of the great Czech player Jaroslav Drobny, who defected in 1949, if she were to develop as a tennis player and as a person, but the decision was painful. She knew her action meant that it would be years before she would see her parents and younger sister, Jana, again.

Martina's declaration of independence was issued the day that Orantes jarred Connors. The men's upset led sports pages, but Navratilova's political shocker, upstaging them, was on front page.

Navratilova (5-0 in singles) and Renata Tomanova (4-1) had led Czechoslovakia past Ireland, 3-0, Netherlands, 2-0, West Germany, 2-1, France, 3-0 and Australia, 3-0 to win the 30-nation Federation Cup at Aix-en-Provence in southern France. The Aussies made the final for the 10th time, but Navratilova ended Goolagong's 16-match unbeaten streak in Cup singles, 6-3, 6-4. Tomanova ambushed Helen Gourlay, 6-4, 6-2, and the Czechs

had their first Cup. However, Martina would now be helping the U.S. add to its Cup total.

Britain also humbled the U.S., 5-2, in the Wightman Cup for the second straight year, its first back-to-back wins since 1924-25. Evert won both her singles, over Wade, 6-3, 7-6 and Glynis Coles, 6-4, 6-1, but that's all the U.S. could get at Cleveland's Public Auditorium. Wade beat Mona Schallau, 6-2, 6-2, as did Coles, 6-3, 7-6. Sue Barker beat Janet Newberry, 6-4, 7-5, and 37-year-old Ann Jones, returning to the fray, got a big doubles win with Wade over Julie Anthony and Newberry, 6-2, 6-3.

The most spectacular comeback of the year belonged to Evert, who trailed Nancy Richey Gunter, 6-7, 0-5, 15-40—double match point in the semifinals of the U.S. Clay Court Championships in Indianapolis. After that, Chrissie didn't make a mistake in roaring back to win, 6-7, 7-5, 4-2, default. Gunter finally had to quit with cramps. Evert went on to thrash Dianne Fromholtz in the final, 6-3, 6-4, for her fourth consecutive U.S. Clay crown.

A couple of administrative happenings during 1975 are worthy of note. Over the protests of tournament chairman and director Bill Talbert, the U.S. Open adopted a so-called 12-point tie-breaker (actually best-of-12 but with a margin of two) replacing the best-of nine-point "sudden death" that had been in use since 1970. This was a victory for the ATP, whose members preferred the less nerve-wracking "lingering death." The change of the surface at Forest Hills permitted night play there for the first time, and a resultant dramatic increase in total attendance, to a record 216,683. This was also the year the U.S. Lawn Tennis Association voted to drop the "Lawn" from its name, becoming simply the USTA. It was the beginning of a fashion that would, in 1977, see the International Lawn Tennis Federation become the ITF.

1975 CHAMPIONS AND LEADERS

Australian Open
Men's Singles Final: John Newcombe (AUS) def. Jimmy Connors (USA), 7-5, 3-6, 6-4, 7-6 (9-7)
Women's Singles Final: Evonne Goolagong (AUS) def. Martina Navratilova (CZE), 6-3, 6-2
Men's Doubles Final: John Alexander and Phil Dent (AUS) def. Bob Carmichel and Allan Stone (AUS), 6-3, 7-6
Women's Doubles Final: Evonne Goolagong (AUS) and Peggy Michel (USA) def. Margaret Smith Court (AUS) and Olga Morozova (USSR), 7-6, 7-6
Mixed Doubles: Not Played

French Open
Men's Singles Final: Bjorn Borg (SWE) def. Guillermo Vilas (ARG), 6-2, 6-3, 6-4
Women's Singles Final: Chris Evert (USA) def. Martina Navratilova (CZE), 2-6, 6-2, 6-1
Men's Doubles Final: Brian Gottfried (USA) and Raul Ramirez (MEX) def. John Alexander and Phil Dent (AUS), 6-2, 2-6, 6-2, 6-4
Women's Doubles Final: Chris Evert (USA) and Martina Navratilova (CZE) def. Julie Anthony (USA) and Olga Morozova (USSR), 6-3, 6-2
Mixed Doubles Final: Fiorella Bonicelli (URU) and Thomaz Koch (BRA) def. Pam Teeguardan (USA) and Jaime Fillol (CHI), 6-4, 7-6

Wimbledon
Men's Singles Final: Arthur Ashe (USA) def. Jimmy Connors (USA), 6-1, 6-1, 5-7, 6-4
Women's Singles Final: Billie Jean King (USA) def. Evonne Goolagong (AUS), 6-0, 6-1
Men's Doubles Final: Vitas Gerulaitis and Alex Mayer (USA) def. Colin Dowdeswell (RHO) and Allan Stone (AUS), 7-5, 8-6, 6-4
Women's Doubles Final: Ann Kiyomura (USA) and Kazuko Sawamatsu (JPN), def. Francoise Durr (FRA) and Betty Stove (NED), 7-5, 1-6, 7-5
Mixed Doubles Final: Margaret Smith Court (AUS) and Marty Riessen (USA) def. Betty Stove (NED) and Allan Stone (AUS), 6-4, 7-5

U.S. Open
Men's Singles Final: Manolo Orantes (ESP) def. Jimmy Connors (USA), 6-4, 6-3, 6-3
Women's Singles Final: Chris Evert (USA) def. Evonne Goolagong (AUS), 5-7, 6-4, 6-2
Men's Doubles Final: Jimmy Connors (USA) and Ilie Nastase (ROM) def. Tom Okker (NED) and Marty Riessen (USA), 6-4, 7-6
Women's Doubles Final: Margaret Smith Court (AUS) and Virginia Wade (GBR) def. Billie Jean King and Rosie Casals (USA), 7-5, 2-6, 7-6 (7-5)
Mixed Doubles Final: Rosie Casals and Dick Stockton (USA) def. Billie Jean King (USA) and Fred Stolle (AUS), 6-3, 7-6

Year-End No. 1
Men: Jimmy Connors
Women: Chris Evert

Top Player Earnings
Men Arthur Ashe $326,750
Women Chris Evert $370,227

Davis Cup: Sweden

Federation Cup: Czechoslovakia

Wightman Cup: Great Britain

ATP World Championships, Stockholm—Ilie Nastase
WCT, Dallas—Arthur Ashe
Virginia Slims Championships, Los Angeles—Chris Evert

1976 Connors Back On Top, Renee Comes Out

the U.S. men's 35-and-over championships in 1972. In August 1975, he had sex reassignment surgery and moved west to Newport Beach, Calif., to start a new life and practice as Dr. Renee Richards.

In July 1976, Dr. Richards—a 6-foot-2 lefthander—entered and won a local women's tournament in La Jolla, Calif. A former acquaintance noticed her resemblance in playing style to Richard Raskind, verified her identity and tipped off a San Diego television sportscaster, who broke the story. Dr. Richards, who had sought a clean start in California, far from her former wife and four-year-old son in New York, decided to "go public" and put aside her brilliant career as an eye surgeon in order to play professional tennis.

"I started getting letters, poignant letters from other transsexuals who were considering suicide, whose friends and families won't see them," she explained to *Newsday* reporter Jane Gross. "I realized that this was more than just a tennis thing, my hobby. I could easily give that up. But, if I can do anything for those people, I will. I am in a position to try and make people see that such individuals should be allowed to hold up their heads. I realize this is important from a social standpoint."

Jimmy Connors returned to the pinnacle of men's tennis in 1976 and Chris Evert consolidated her stranglehold on the women's game. But the most bizarre and compelling story of the year was the emergence of pro sport's first transsexual.

Richard Raskind, a 41-year-old ophthalmologist, was a good enough player to captain the Yale University varsity in 1954, play at Wimbledon and Forest Hills, and later reach the semifinals of

The Richards case caused an extraordinary, highly publicized stir in women's tennis. The Women's Tennis Association opposed her eligibility for tournaments, and sided with the USTA in its hasty ruling that women would have to pass an Olympic-style chromosome test before being accepted for women's national championships, including the U.S. Open. Dr. Richards refused to take the test, claiming that it was an unsat-

isfactory means of determining gender, given the advances of modern medicine.

Many women felt that Dr. Richards would have an unfair competitive advantage because of her size, strength and past experience in competition against men. Others feared that her acceptance would set a bad precedent, paving the way for a younger, stronger transsexuals to dominate women's tennis in the future. Many WTA members liked Richards personally, admired her courage, but still opposed her acceptance in tournaments.

Dr. Richards, denied admission to the U.S. Open— she took her case to court, and was admitted in 1977 by court order—did play in a pre-Forest Hills tournament at South Orange, NJ. Most WTA members withdrew in protest, but the tournament attracted national television coverage and massive publicity. Richards was beaten in the semifinals by 17-year-old Lea Antonoplis, 6-7, 6-3, 6-0. Early fears that Dr. Richards would upset the competitive balance of the women's game were unfounded. Richards played several other small tournaments, two in Hawaii, winning at Kauai, at the end of the year over No. 10 American Kathy Kuykendall, 6-1, 6-4, and losing the Kona final to 1962 Wimbledon champ, 35-year-old Karen Hantze Susman, 4-6, 6-4, 6-2.

Along more conventional lines, Connors recaptured the No. 1 world ranking even though he won only one major championship, the U.S. Open, in which he edged his major rival, Bjorn Borg, in a superlative four-set final.

Connors compiled a 100-12 record, winning 13 of 23 tournaments he played. He won the only two WCT events he entered, the two big prize-money events promoted by the ATP (American Airlines Games at Palm Springs, over Roscoe Tanner, 6-4, 6-4 and the Alan King Classic at Las Vegas over evergreen 41-year-old Ken Rosewall, 6-1, 6-3) and six of the 10 Commercial Union Grand Prix events he played. He collected $303,335 in prize money plus more than double that amount in exhibitions—including $500,000 for beating up on Spaniard Manuel Orantes in another 'Heavyweight Championship of Tennis' Challenge Match at Las Vegas. (Orantes, guaranteed more than $250,000 just for showing up, did little more than that, winning three games in three pathetic sets.)

More important in deciding the global game of king-of-the-hill, Connors was 3-0 in head-to-head clashes with Borg. Connors vanquished the young Swede in the U.S. Pro Indoor final at Philadelphia, 7-6, 6-4, 6-0, the semis of the American Airlines Games, 6-1, 6-4, and the U.S. Open final, 6-4, 3-6, 7-6 (11-9), 6-4.

Otherwise, Borg had an outstanding season, winning seven of 19 tournaments and 63 of 77 matches. He continued his domination of his good friend and sometimes doubles partner, Guillermo Vilas, to win the WCT Finals in Dallas, 1-6, 6-1, 7-5, 6-1, in May, 27 days before his 20th birthday. He failed in his bid for a third consecutive French Open title, losing to eventual champ, Italian Adriano Panatta in the quarterfinals, 6-3, 6-3, 2-6, 7-6 (7-2). But Bjorn prepared diligently on grass courts and became the third youngest champion in the history of Wimbledon, the first man to sweep through the most prestigious of championships without losing a set since Chuck McKinley in 1963. Borg pulled a muscle in his abdomen in a doubles match the first week, but deadened the pain in his last four singles matches by tak-

ing pre-match cortisone injections and spraying his abdomen at changeovers with an aerosol freeze spray. Despite the injury, the No. 4 seed never served or smashed more authoritatively than in routing Brian Gottfried 6-2, 6-2, 7-5 in the fourth round, Vilas 6-3, 6-0, 6-2 in the quarterfinals; Roscoe Tanner 6-4, 9-8 (7-2), 6-4 in the semifinals; and Ilie Nastase in the final, 6-4, 6-2, 9-7.

After a seven-week layoff to recuperate—a period during which Sweden relinquished the Davis Cup—Borg extended his winning streak to 19 matches, winning a third consecutive U.S. Pro title, over Harold Solomon, 6-7 (3-7), 6-4, 6-1, 6-2) and reaching the final of the U.S. Open. That match hinged on a tingling 20-point third-set tie-breaker in which Connors escaped four set points, tilting an epic his way, 6-4, 3-6, 7-6 (11-9), 6-4. A brouhaha was avoided when umpire John Coman lost track of the score in the tie-breaker, but an anonymous ballboy straightened the ump out unnoticed by the crowd.

The year began with perhaps the most startling result ever in one of the major championships—21-year-old Australian Mark Edmondson, a burly aunknown serve-and-volleyer recently removed from employment as a janitor and odd-jobs man, won the Australian Open. Ranked No. 212 and the lowest-ranked player ever to capture a major, he beat two former champions, 42-year-old Rosewall in the semifinals, 6-1, 2-6, 6-2, 6-4, and defender John Newcombe, 6-7, 6-3, 7-6, 6-1, the final played in fierce winds and eerie weather of a gathering storm. Edmondson quickly found his level in Paris, losing in the first round of the French to Paraguayan Victor Pecci, 6-3, 6-3, 3-6, 6-3.

Panatta, the handsome and dashing Italian No. 1, won the French during a dazzling 16-match winning streak that established him as the king of European clay for the year. Panatta was superb, dispatching Borg, 6-3, 6-3, 2-6, 7-6 (7-2) in the quarterfinals, Eddie Dibbs in the semifinals, 6-3, 6-2, 6-4 and the "Human Grindstone," Solomon, 6-1, 6-4, 4-6, 7-6 (7-3), in the sweltering final. However, Adriano was nearly a dead duck from the start, facing a match point in the first round against Czech Pavel Hutka, and rescuing it with a stretching volley in the fifth set to win, 2-6, 6-2, 6-2, 0-6, 12-10.

At the Italian Open, Panatta withstood 11 match points against Aussie Kim Warwick in the first round, winning, 3-6, 6-4, 7-6, then went on to win the title before his adoring hometown fans in Rome, beating Vilas in the final, 2-6, 7-6 (7-5), 6-2, 7-6 (7-1). He got a big break in the quarterfinals when gutsy little Solomon was beating him, 2-6, 7-5, 5-4 with serve. At 0-15 Panatta lobbed—clearly long—but the line judge signaled the ball to be good in an ordinary display of patriotism. But Solly blew up, losing his temper and the match by walking away.

Arthur Ashe, 1975's No. 1, got off to the best start of his career, winning five of his first six tournaments and 29 of 30 matches. He again topped the WCT point standings, earning a $50,000 bonus, but lost his crown in the first round of the WCT Finals in Dallas, beaten by Solomon, 7-5, 3-6, 6-1, 6-3, and did little thereafter. His fade was in part attributed to inflammation of a chronic heel injury that required surgery in February of 1977.

A pinched nerve in his elbow slowed another of the 1975 heroes, Orantes, but therapy and a switch to a lighter aluminum racket revived him in the autumn.

Orantes won five of his last eight tournaments (assembling the year's longest winning streak, 23 matches), reached two other finals and resurrected himself from 1-4 down in the fourth to win a stirring Grand Prix Masters final at Houston over Poland's Wojtek Fibak, the most improved pro of the year, 5-7, 6-2, 0-6, 7-6 (7-1), 6-1.

The Masters concluded five years of Grand Prix sponsorship by the Commercial Union Assurance group, which withdrew because of flagging profits in the insurance business and was replaced by Colgate-Palmolive, which already had undertaken sponsorship of the women's grand prix setup, known as the Colgate International Series. Commercial Union's swan song was soured when Connors decided to pass up the Masters for a third consecutive year (thereby forfeiting the $60,000 he already had earned from the Grand Prix bonus pool for finishing third in the season-long standings). Borg and Nastase chose to play exhibitions in the fall instead of Grand Prix tournaments that could have qualified them for the eight man Masters.

Mexican Raul Ramirez won only four of 32 tournaments, but he was a tireless and consistent campaigner. His diligence paid off as he earned both the $150,000 prize for topping the Grand Prix singles standings and the $40,000 award for heading the doubles standings, a unique accomplishment. In all, the Grand Prix encompassed 48 tournaments (and produced 23 different winners) in 22 countries, with more than $5 million in prize purses. With the WCT (24 16-man tournaments) and U.S. Indoor circuits added in, more than $9 million was available in men's tournaments worldwide.

The riches available were demonstrated graphically when Nastase collected $180,000 in a single tournament, the WCT-run Avis Challenge Cup, a series of winner-take-all round-robin matches played throughout the winter and spring in Hawaii. Nastase beat Ashe in a five-set final on asphalt, 6-3, 1-6, 6-7, 6-3, 6-1. On the year, Nastase won five of 23 tournaments, compiled a 76-17 record, reached the final at Wimbledon and the semifinals at Forest Hills, and was the only player with a winning record over Connors (4-1), shutting off Jimmy's four-year hold on the U.S. Indoor, 6-2, 6-3, 7-6. But Connors won the U.S. Clay for a second time, 6-2, 6-4, over Fibak.

In doubles, Newcombe and Tony Roche won their fourth Australian title, over Ross Case and Geoff Masters, 7-6, 6-4. However, team-of-the-year honors were shared by Ramirez-Brian Gottfried and Sherwood Stewart-Freddie McNair, who underscored the old axiom that two ordinary singles players can blend extraordinarily in doubles. Stewart-McNair won the French Open, dethroning Gottfried-Ramirez, 7-6 (8-6), 6-3, 6-1, and came back from 1-4 in the fourth set to stun the same team in the Masters doubles final, 6-3, 5-7, 5-7, 6-4, 6-4.

A surprising German-Polish patchwork alliance, Karl Meiler and Fibak won the WCT doubles at Kansas City, hanging tough in five sets, beating Stan Smith and Bob Lutz, 6-3, 2-6, 3-6, 6-3, 6-4, for the title after deposing the defenders, Gottfried-Ramirez, in the semifinal, 6-4, 6-4, 4-6, 4-6, 6-4.

Gottfried and Ramirez won their third straight Italian title, over Newcombe and Masters, 7-6, 5-7, 6-3, 3-6, 6-3, in a bizarre long-distance, two-continent affair. Completion of the final in

Rome was delayed by darkness after the fourth set, and concluded four months later at the Woodlands, outside Houston. At the same event, Gottfried and Ramirez also won the $100,000 ATP Doubles, over Aussies Allan Stone and Phil Dent, 6-1, 6-4, 5-7, 7-6. One stop, two titles. Brian and Raul were so hot they double-bageled Case and Masters, 6-0, 6-0! They had also won Wimbledon, knocking off curiously unseeded Newcombe-Roche (five time champions) in a tense first rounder—tantamount to a final—7-9, 8-9, 9-7, 6-3, 6-4, and then, in the rousing genuine final, Masters-Case, 3-6, 6-3, 8-6, 2-6, 7-5. Tom Okker and Marty Riessen took the U.S. Open over long shot Aussies Paul Kronk and Cliff Letcher, 6-4, 6-4.

It was a quiet year politically in men's tennis, aside from the Davis Cup and storms arising from Nastase's tempestuous behavior. The rambunctious Romanian was at his worst in an ugly second round victory, 7-6 (7-5), 4-6, 7-6 (9-7) over Germany's Hans Pohmann at Forest Hills, saving two match points and winning it on a fifth. Nastase's gamesmanship and outbursts of obscene language, gestures and spitting, along with delays when Pohmann suffered cramps that should have disqualified him, caused this match to get out of control. Nastase, who kept moving to a semifinal defeat by Borg, 6-3, 6-3, 6-4, was eventually fined $1,000, which increased his aggregate disciplinary fines for a 12-month period to more than $3,000 and triggered an automatic 21-day suspension, under provisions of a new Code of Conduct enacted by the Men's International Professional Tennis Council primarily as a reaction to Nastase. (It should have been called the Nastase Code of Conduct.) The suspension was a joke, however, since it applied only to Grand Prix tournaments; Nastase played exhibition tournaments and earned more than $50,000 during the time he was supposed to be disciplined.

In the Davis Cup, Mexico, after upsetting the U.S., 3-2, in the American Zone, refused to play South Africa for the second consecutive year, and defaulted. When the Davis Cup nations refused to take action against Mexico at its annual meeting, the U.S. led a walkout of the major Cup nations, including France and Great Britain, for 1977. A compromise was worked out within two weeks, however, and these nations returned. The Soviet Union defaulted its semifinal series to Chile in protest of the military junta that had overthrown the socialist regime of Salvador Allende in Santiago in 1973. This was precisely the sort of political disruption that the U.S. was opposing, and a reconstituted Davis Cup Committee of Management threw the USSR out of the 1977 competition.

Italy, runner-up in 1960 and 1961, won the Davis Cup for the first time, beating Chile in Santiago, 4-1, in a final distinguished more by the enthusiasm and sportsmanship of the sellout crowds of 6,500 than by the quality of play. Corrado Barazzutti upset Chilean No. 1 Jaime Fillol at the start, 7-5, 4-6, 7-5, 6-1. Panatta defeated game but overmatched Patricio Cornejo, 6-3, 6-1, 6-3, then teamed with Paolo Bertolucci to down Cornejo-Fillol, 3-6, 6-2, 9-7, 6-3, for an unbeatable 3-0 lead as Captain Nicola Pietrangeli, the star of the final round 1960 and 1961 Italian teams, exulted at courtside. Though the political situation had been tense, Italian leftists having opposing the matches, Italian joy at winning was generally unrestrained.

Earlier in the year, Connors had made his first appearance for the U.S. in the World Cup. The former antagonists, Connors and Ashe, both thrashed Newcombe and Roche in singles, leading Captain Dennis Ralston's American squad to a 6-1 victory over declining Australia before sellout crowds of 10,000 in Hartford.

World Team Tennis was more stable in its third season, but even with Evert as a shining new attraction and the respected Butch Buchholz aboard as commissioner, all of the 10 franchises continued to operate in the red. The New York Sets, led by Sandy Mayer, Billie Jean King, Virginia Wade and Phil Dent, captured the league title over the Golden Gaters (San Francisco Bay Area) in the playoff final series, 31-23, 29-31, 31-13. Evert, of the Phoenix Racquets, was the female MVP, her singles winning percentage (.700) the best of any player in WTT.

Evert was unquestionably the queen of tournament tennis as well. She won 75 of 80 matches, 12 of 17 tournaments, including Wimbledon, the U.S. Open and the rich Colgate Inaugural (over Francoise Durr, 6-1, 6-2) at Palm Springs in October. That launched the new Colgate International Series, and was to serve thereafter as its climactic playoff. Its $45,000 top prize was the biggest of the year in women's tennis. It boosted Evert's season winnings to $289,165 and her career winnings to $1,026,604, making her the first woman to earn more than $1 million in prize money. Only four players—Evonne Goolagong (twice), Wade, Martina Navratilova and Dianne Fromholtz—were able to beat Evert during the year.

Goolagong (newly married to Englishman Roger Cawley) started the year by winning her third straight Australian Open title, a 6-2, 6-2 rout of Czech Renata Tomanova, and teaming with Helen Gourlay to defend the doubles titles in a schlocky final over Lesley Turner Bowrey and Tomanova, 8-games-to-1, a so-called "pro set," the distance somehow agreed on beforehand.

The lithe Australian was at her best during the January through April Virginia Slims circuit, winning 38 of 40 matches, dropping only 10 sets, and at one point running off 16 consecutive victories without loss of a set. She climaxed her record $133,675 Slims season (en route to a $195,452 year) by beating Evert, 6-3, 5-7, 6-3, in a magnificent match at the Los Angeles Sports Arena, the final of the Virginia Slims Championships. On the season, Evonne won eight of 14 tournaments, 58 of 64 matches. She reached the final of every tournament she played, was 7-0 vs. Wade, 6-0 vs. Rosie Casals, 4-0 over Navratilova and 4-0 over Sue Barker. Evonne had the second-best winning percentage in singles among WTT players, and aside from one-set WTT matches, lost to only two players, Evert five times, and King in the Federation Cup at Philadelphia. This was Evonne's most consistent season. But still, as she announced at season's end that she was taking maternity leave, she was overshadowed by Evert.

After losing the Virginia Slims final, Chrissie won her next six tournaments in a dazzling 36-match winning streak, and lost only one more match the rest of the year. Her streak began with her third consecutive triumph in the Family Circle Cup, over Australian Kerry Melville Reid, 6-2, 6-2.

At Wimbledon, where all eight seeds reached the quarters, Evert beat Olga Morozova, 6-3, 6-0, Navratilova, 4-6, 6-3, 6-4, and Goolagong, 6-3, 4-6, 8-6, in a thrilling final that ended Evonne's

25-match streak. This was Evert's first triumph ever over Goolagong on grass. Evert and Navratilova then took the doubles title over Betty Stove and King, 6-1, 3-6, 7-5.

Evert was at her domineering best on the clay at Forest Hills, winning her second consecutive U.S. Open title with the loss of only 12 games in six matches. (Helen Wills Moody, losing just eight games in six matches in 1929, is the only champion to ever have a more devastating run). Evert stomped Goolagong, 6-3, 6-0, in the most lopsided final since 1964, running the last 10 games. This extended Evert's clay-court winning streak to 21 tournaments and 101 matches, dating to August 1973.

Because of a downpour, unseeded Yugoslav Mima Jausovec could say she battled Evert in the semifinal almost seven hours—most of it sitting in the clubhouse after rain halted play at 5-2. Returning under floodlights, Chrissie finished the 69-minute playing-time victory, 6-3, 6-1. On a sentimental journey, 36-year-old Maria Bueno, champion in 1959, 63-64, 66, reached the third round before Casals dismissed her, 7-5, 6-0. A shocker was the first-round dumping of third-seeded Navratilova by No. 8 American Janet Newberry, 1-6, 6-4, 6-3, a low point in Martina's career that left her sobbing beside the court. She wouldn't lose a first-rounder again in a major until the French in 1994. But it was a tough early-going year for names – fourth-seeded Wade, lost to Mima Jausovec 6-3, 6-3; fifth-seeded Nancy Richey lost to Virginia Ruzici, 3-6, 7-6, 7-5 and seventh-seeded Kerry Reid who lost to Zenda Liess, 5-5 default, all bounced in the second round.

Delina "Linky" Boshoff and Ilana Kloss startlingly won the doubles title over Wade and Morozova, 6-1, 6-4, becoming the first South African women to win a U.S. title. King and another WTT teammate, Dent, won the mixed over Stove and Frew McMillan, 3-6, 6-2, 7-5.

King came out of her self-imposed singles retirement in the Federation Cup at Philadelphia's Spectrum in August. Colgate assumed sponsorship of this women's team competition, and infused it with prize money for the first time—$130,000 for teams representing 32 nations, $40,000 to the winners. Unfortunately, a political hassle developed when the Soviet Union reneged on a previous promise and led a four-nation walkout (1975 champion Czechoslovakia, Hungary and the Philippines joined the USSR in refusing to play) to protest the inclusion of South Africa and Rhodesia. The defaulting nations were subsequently fined by the ITF, but they had succeeded in making the draw a shambles.

Billie Jean filled in unexpectedly in singles for Evert, who withdrew with a sore wrist. Playing for the U.S. for the first time since 1967, she teamed with old doubles partner Casals in a two woman tour de force. They sprinted through four 3-0 victories to a meeting with favored Australia in the final. Reid beat Casals, 1-6, 6-3, 7-5, but King found a wellspring of her old inspiration to beat Goolagong, 7-6, 6-4, in a match of exceptionally high standard. King-Casals then toppled Reid-Goolagong, 7-5, 6-3, for the championship.

After rare back-to-back losses in 1974 and 1975, the U.S. regained the Wightman Cup with a 5-2 victory over Great Britain, indoors at London's Crystal Palace. Evert led the way, beating Wade, 6-2, 3-6, 6-3, and then Sue Barker in the decisive match, 2-6, 6-2, 6-2.

In the absence of the leading women, who were contracted to WTT, Barker won the German over Tomanova, 6-3, 6-1, and earned preeminence on European clay by taking the French, also over Tomanova, 6-2, 0-6, 6-2. Jausovec won the Italian, over Lesley Hunt, 6-1, 6-3. Evert put her U.S. Clay title on hold after four victorious years, and tall Kathy May, 20, swung into the void to beat South African Brigitte Cuypers, 6-4, 4-6, 6-2.

A major innovation in equipment was introduced in 1976. New rackets in a dizzying variety of designs and materials— wood, metal, fiberglass, alloys, composites— had been marketed over the previous decade, but the biggest stir since the introduction of Wilson's steel T-2000 in 1967 was created by the Prince racket, with its oversized head. Howard Head, founder of Head Ski and architect of that company's headlong plunge into tennis equipment, joined forces with the manufacturer of Prince ball machines to produce the revolutionary and subsequently imitated new racket, which had much the same balance as conventional rackets but twice the hitting area.

1976 CHAMPIONS AND LEADERS

Australian Open
Men's Singles Final: Mark Edmondson (AUS) def. John Newcombe (AUS), 6-7, 6-3, 7-6, 6-1
Women's Singles Final: Evonne Goolagong (AUS) def. Renata Tomanova (CZE), 6-2, 6-2
Men's Doubles Final: John Newcombe and Tony Roche (AUS) def. Ross Case and Geoff Masters (AUS), 7-6, 6-4
Women's Doubles Final: Evonne Goolagong and Helen Gourlay (AUS) def. Lesley Turner Bowrey (AUS) and Olga Morozova (USSR), 8-1 (pro set by mutual consent)
Mixed Doubles: Not Played

French Open
Men's Singles Final: Adriano Panatta (ITA) def. Harold Solomon (USA), 6-1, 6-4, 4-6, 7-6 (3)
Women's Singles Final: Sue Barker (GBR) def. Renata Tomanova (CZE) 6-2, 0-6, 6-2
Men's Doubles Final: Fred McNair and Sherwood Stewart (USA) def. Brian Gottfried (USA) and Raul Ramirez (MEX), 7-6 (8-6), 6-3, 6-1
Women's Doubles Final: Fiorella Bonicelli (URU) and Gail Sherriff Lovera (FRA) def. Kathy Harter (USA) and Helga Niessen-Masthoff (GER), 6-4, 1-6, 6-3
Mixed Doubles Final: Ilana Kloss (RSA) and Kim Warwick (AUS) def. Delina Boshoff and Colin Dowdeswell (RHO) 5-7, 7-6, 6-2

Wimbledon
Men's Singles Final: Bjorn Borg (SWE) def. Ilie Nastase (ROM), 6-4, 6-2, 9-7
Women's Singles Final: Chris Evert (USA) def. Evonne Goolagong (AUS), 6-3, 4-6, 8-6
Men's Doubles Final: Brian Gottfried (USA) and Raul Ramirez (MEX) def. Ross Case and Geoff Masters (AUS), 3-6, 6-3,8-6, 2-6, 7-5
Women's Doubles Final: Chris Evert (USA) and Martina Navratilova (CZE) def. Billie Jean King (USA) and Betty Stove (NED), 6-1, 3-6, 7-5
Mixed Doubles Final: Francoise Durr (FRA) and Tony Roche (AUS) def. Rosie Casals and Dick Stockton (USA), 6-3, 2-6, 7-5

U.S. Open
Men's Singles Final: Jimmy Connors (USA) def. Bjorn Borg (SWE), 6-4, 3-6, 7-6 (11-9), 6-4
Women's Singles Final: Chris Evert (USA) def. Evonne Goolagong (AUS), 6-3, 6-0
Men's Doubles Final: Tom Okker (NED) and Marty Riessen (USA) def. Paul Kronk and Cliff Letcher (AUS), 6-4, 6-4
Women's Doubles Final: Delina Boshoff and Ilana Kloss (RSA) def. Virginia Wade (GBR) and Olga Morozova (USSR), 6-1, 6-4
Mixed Doubles Final: Billie Jean King (USA) and Phil Dent (AUS), def. Betty Stove (NED) and Frew McMillian (RSA), 3-6, 6-2, 7-5

Year-End No. 1
Men: Jimmy Connors
Women: Chris Evert

Top Player Earnings
Men: Raul Ramirez $484,343
Women: Chris Evert $343,165

Davis Cup: Italy

Federation Cup: United States

Wightman Cup: United States

Grand Prix Masters, Houston—Manuel Orantes
WCT, Dallas—Bjorn Borg
Virginia Slims Championships, Los Angeles—Evonne Goolagong

Jimbo, Vilas, Borg Battle for No. 1

Guillermo Vilas won the French and the U.S. Opens in 1977 and had a 50-match winning streak.

Guillermo Vilas won the French and the U.S. Opens in 1977 and had a 50-match winning streak.

10 years of the Open era. Connors won the WCT Finals in Dallas and the Grand Prix Masters, and was runner-up at Wimbledon and Forest Hills. The debate as to who was No. 1 continued right through the Masters, which, because of U.S. television considerations, was moved back by new Grand Prix sponsor Colgate-Palmolive to the first week of January 1978.

There was no similar disagreement as to who was the ruler of women's tennis. Chris Evert remained the indisputable No. 1, despite Virginia Wade's coronation—after 15 years as the lady-in-waiting—as the queen of Wimbledon. The celebrations of Wimbledon's Centenary fortnight began with the All England Lawn Tennis & Croquet Club honoring 41 of the 52 living singles champions. A crowd of 14,000 packed Centre Court, and their applause swelled as the Band of the Welsh Guards played *The March of the King* from the opera "Aida," signaling a wonderfully nostalgic "Parade of Champions." The former winners strode out onto the most famous lawn in tennis to receive commemorative medals from the Duke of Kent in a brief, dignified ceremony. In a touching final gesture, medals were presented to Elizabeth "Bunny" Ryan, 85, and Jacques "Toto" Brugnon, 82, "representing all the doubles champions." Ryan, winner of 12 women's doubles and seven mixed titles between 1914 and 1934, moved slowly, on walking sticks, but cast them aside to wave to the crowd. Brugnon, winner of Wimbledon doubles titles, twice each with fellow French "Musketeers" Henri Cochet and Jean Borotra, used a cane and later held the arm of the fourth "Musketeer," Rene Lacoste. Toto died the next winter, but for this moment, he was ebullient.

The tournament was also richly memorable. Lefthander John McEnroe, 18, of Douglaston, N.Y., became the youngest male to make the semifinal in Wimbledon's 100 years, the first player ever to come through the qualifying rounds and get that far. He won eight matches in all before Connors brought him back to reality, 6-3, 6-3, 4-6, 6-4. In the other semifinal, Borg defeated the swift and flashy Vitas Gerulaitis, 6-4, 3-6, 6-3, 3-6, 8-6, in breathtaking combat between the charging Lithuanian Lion and the baseline defending Swede. The sustained quality of the shotmaking and drama made this, in the opinion of longtime observers, one of the all-time Centre Court classics.

The final also lived up to a majestic standard. Borg and Connors—destined to be remembered as the archrivals of the

By any standard, 1977 was a landmark year for tennis. Wimbledon, the oldest of tournaments, celebrated its Centenary. The U.S. Open was played at Forest Hills for the last time. And a technological innovation, the "double strung" or "spaghetti" racket, caused such a stir that it was banned from tournament play several months after gaining notoriety, leading to the definition of a racket for the first time in the official rules of the game.

Three men—Bjorn Borg, Guillermo Vilas and Jimmy Connors—waged their own version of the year's hit movie, the science-fiction classic "Star Wars." They were in a stratospheric super class, a galaxy above anyone.

Borg won Wimbledon and had the most solid record, including winning margins against both his rivals. Vilas won the French and U.S. Opens and fashioned the longest winning streak of the

'70s—battled each other from the baseline in torrid rallies seldom seen on grass. Connors seemed out of it at 0-4 in the fifth set, but roused himself for one last challenge and came back to 4-4 before a crucial double fault in the ninth game cost him his momentum, his serve and the match, 3-6, 6-2, 6-1, 5-7, 6-4.

In the women's singles, 14-year-old Californian Tracy Austin became one of the youngest players to compete at Wimbledon (Austrian Mita Klima was 13 in 1907). She defeated Ellie Vessies-Appel, 6-3, 6-3, then showed tremendous poise and groundstrokes in losing a Centre Court match to defending champion Evert, 6-1, 6-1. That match, and her first victory ever over Billie Jean King on grass—6-1, 6-2 in the quarterfinals—took an enormous emotional toll on Evert and left her curiously flat for her semifinal against Wade.

"Our Ginny," as the British affectionately called third-seeded Wade, had never prepared better for a tournament, nor felt more self-confident. She hadn't gone beyond the semifinal in 15 previous Wimbledons, but she kept the pressure on with bold approach shots and magnificent net play to beat Evert, 6-2, 4-6, 6-1. Wade was much more passive in the final against 6-foot, 170-pound Betty Stove, the first Dutch finalist at Wimbledon, who had knocked off second-seeded Martina Navratilova in the quarters, 9-8 (8-6), 3-6, 6-1. But Ginny settled down and let her erratic opponent make the mistakes. Wade won nine of the last 10 games and the match, 4-6, 6-3, 6-1. Wade, the first Englishwoman to win her national title since Ann Jones in 1969, accepted the gold championship plate from Queen Elizabeth II, who was making her first appearance at Wimbledon since 1962 in honor of the Centenary and her own Silver Jubilee celebration. British reserve gave way to an unbridled outpouring of patriotic sentiment. The Duchess of Kent waved excitedly to Wade from the Royal Box, and thousands of delighted Britons broke into a spontaneous, moving chorus of *For She's a Jolly Good Fellow*.

Stove wound up with a "cripple" as a triple loser of finals—runner-up with Navratilova in the women's doubles to unseeded Floridian JoAnne Russell and Aussie Helen Gourlay Cawley, 6-3, 6-3, and with Frew McMillan in the mixed to South Africans Bob Hewitt and Greer Stevens, 3-6, 7-5, 6-4. In the men's doubles, the first-seeded defending champions Brian Gottfried and Raul Ramirez fell to the Indian-American entry of Sashi Menon and Jim Delaney in the first round, 3-6, 7-5, 6-8, 6-2, 6-3, paving the way for an all-Australian final. Ross Case and Geoff Masters, runners-up the previous year, beat John Alexander and Phil Dent in another thriller, 6-3, 6-4, 3-6, 8-9 (4-7), 6-4.

Though Wimbledon was the highlight of the year, the most impressive achievement was the winning streak Vilas compiled the last six months of the year. Vilas started the year as runner-up to Roscoe Tanner, the hard-serving left-hander, in the Australian Open, 6-3, 6-3, 6-3. Tanner beat perpetual Ken Rosewall, 42, in the semis, 6-4, 3-6, 6-4, 6-1. Rosewall had avenged his semifinal loss of a year previous by dethroning Mark Edmondson, 6-4, 7-6, 4-6, 6-4. Vilas' semifinal victim, 6-4, 1-6, 6-3, 6-4, was Alexander, who had toppled ex-champ Arthur Ashe, 6-3, 6-4, 4-6, 7-6.

By winning the French Open in the absence of Borg and Connors, Vilas lost only one set in seven matches, and his 6-0, 6-3, 6-0 victory over Gottfried in the drizzly final was the most decisive since the tournament went international in 1925. Thus Guillermo shed his image as "The Eternal Second"—"they call me that in the Argentine press"—and removed an enormous psychological burden.

Driven by his coach-manager, the hirsute and menacing Romanian Ion Tiriac, Vilas became the fittest and most iron-willed player on the professional circuit. Over his last six months of 1977 he won 13 of 14 tournaments, 80 of 81 matches, including the U.S. Open. His 50-match, July-through-September winning streak was the longest since the advent of Open tennis, eclipsing Rod Laver's 31 straight matches of 1969. And he immediately launched another streak of 30.

The record streak ended controversially the first week in October in the final of a tournament at Aix-en-Provence, France, Vilas defaulting angrily after losing the first two sets to Ilie Nastase, who was using the "spaghetti" racket that had just been barred, effective the following week.

The crowning glory of Vilas' streak was winning the U.S. Open, played at the West Side Tennis Club in the Forest Hills section of New York's borough of Queens for the last time after 68 years as the site of the event. Clumsy last-ditch efforts by the club's officials to retain the Open could not compensate for their years of foot-dragging on making physical improvements. W. E. "Slew" Hester of Jackson, Miss., president of the USTA, decided that the neighborhood was too congested, the club management too stubbornly old-fashioned, to accommodate America's premier tournament, which was given 28 hours of television coverage by CBS-TV under a new five-year, $10-million rights contract. Hester set in motion ambitious plans for building a new USTA National Tennis Center in nearby Flushing Meadows Park, site of the 1939-40 and 1964-65 New York World's Fairs.

Vilas helped make "The last Forest Hills" memorable. He lost only 16 games in five matches up to the semifinal, in which he beat Harold Solomon, 6-2, 7-6 (7-3), 6-2. Connors removed his nemesis of the 1975 final, Manolo Orantes, 6-4, 6-2, 6-3, and then the first Italian ever to get so far, Corrado Barazzutti, 7-5, 6-3, 7-5. In the final, Vilas displayed great physical and mental stamina and a new technical weapon—a finely sliced backhand approach shot—to beat Connors in a match of brutish grace, 2-6, 6-3, 7-6 (7-4), 6-0. The sellout crowd of more than 16,000 cheered for the popular Argentine left-hander against "the ugly American." After the last point, many Latins in the crowd spilled into the court, hoisted Vilas to their shoulders and carried him around the old horseshoe stadium like a conquering hero. Connors, furious at both the outcome and the reception given the victor, left in a snit, not bothering to wait for the trophy presentation ceremonies.

Probably the only one leaving Forest Hills feeling worse than Connors was a spectator named James Reilly, suffering a bullet wound during McEnroe's 6-2, 4-6, 6-4, win over Eddie Dibbs, a third-round night match. It was a random shot from outside the stadium, never traced, and Reilly, carted away to hospital in a stretcher, was only mildly scratched in his left thigh. Dibbs and Mac left the court for a few minutes. The police were wary and nervous for a while because it was the time of the "Son of Sam" killings that terrorized New York, particularly Queens.

Vilas dominated the Grand Prix point standings, winning the $300,000 prize earmarked as the top share of the $1.5-million bonus pool put up by Colgate. On the year, Vilas won a record 17 tournaments and $800,642 in prize money—more than he had earned in five previous pro seasons. He played the most ambitious tournament schedule of any of the top men and finished with a 145-14 record, including Davis Cup matches. (With Vilas and Ricardo Cano playing singles, Argentina upset the United States, 3-2, in the American Zone final to reach the Cup semifinal for the first time.)

Cano, a minor figure, another of those virtually unknown Latins who caused norteamericano headaches on clay, startled Dick Stockton in the opener, 3-6, 6-4, 8-6, 6-4, and the U.S. couldn't catch up. Vilas ran through Brian Gottfried, 6-4, 6-0, 6-2, and Stockton, 5-7, 6-2, 6-2, 6-2, and that was it.

During his 50-match streak, which included a four-match tournament victory at an event in Rye, N.Y., not officially recognized by the ATP, Vilas won an astonishing 109 of 125 sets. Starting with the French Open, he won 53 consecutive matches on clay.

But even though *World Tennis* magazine declared him No. 1 for the year, most other authorities disagreed and bestowed that mythical honor on Borg, who, top-seeded, defaulted to Dick Stockton, 3-6, 6-4, 1-0, in the fourth round of the U.S. Open with a shoulder injury. The 21-year-old Swede had the best winning percentage for the season—.920, on a record of 81-7. He won 13 of the 20 tournaments he played. Including the Masters— played in 1978, but considered the climax of the 1977 season—Borg was 3-0 over Vilas (two victories in the spring, the third in the semis of the Masters, 6-3, 6-3), and 2-1 over Connors, who beat him in the Masters final, 6-4, 1-6, 6-4, before a crowd of 17,150 at Madison Square Garden.

Connors may have had the season-ending last laugh, but he finished No. 3 after having been the best player in the world in 1974 and 1976, and No. 2 to Arthur Ashe in 1975. Connors won eight of 21 tournaments, 70 of 81 matches. He was in four important finals, winning the WCT Finals over Stockton, 6-7, 6-1, 6-3, 6-3, and the Masters, losing to Borg at Wimbledon and to Vilas at Forest Hills. But Connors was 1-2 head-to-head against Borg and 0-2 against Vilas, including a gripping match in the round-robin portion of the Masters, won by Vilas, 6-4, 3-6, 7-5. This spellbinder kept a record tournament crowd of 18,590 riveted to their seats in the Garden until past midnight, 42 minutes into a Friday morning.

While Borg, Vilas and Connors constituted the ruling triumvirate of men's tennis, there were other noteworthy performers. Spaniard Orantes underwent surgery to repair a pinched nerve in his left elbow in the spring, but came back splendidly to bedazzle Connors, 6-1, 6-3, in the U.S. Clay Court final at Indianapolis and to topple Dibbs, 7-6 (7-3), 7-5, 6-4, in the 50th anniversary U.S. Pro Championships.

Gerulaitis became the first American since Barry MacKay in 1960 to win the Italian on slow clay, beating paisano Tonino Zugarelli, 6-2, 7-6 (7-2), 3-6, 7-6 (7-1) in three hours, 20 minutes. Later Vitas, the boulevardier, demonstrated his versatility by winning the second Australian Open of the calendar year (yes, there were two!) on grass at Melbourne, over Englishman John Lloyd, 6-3, 7-6 (7-1), 5-7, 3-6, 6-2. The tournament was moved up to mid-

December so that it could be included in the Grand Prix.

In doubles, South Africans Hewitt, 37, and Frew McMillan, 35, won 13 tournaments, even though separated for four months during the summer because McMillan played World Team Tennis. Their biggest victory came at Forest Hills, where they captured their first U.S. Open doubles title over Gottfried and Ramirez, 6-4, 6-0. Hewitt and McMillan also won the Masters over Stan Smith and Bob Lutz, 7-5, 7-6, 6-3.

Gottfried and Ramirez won the Italian Open doubles for a record fourth consecutive year, over McNair and Stewart, 7-6 (7-2), 6-7 (6-8), 7-5, and recaptured the French Open title, over a Czech-Polish blend of Jan Kodes and Wojtek Fibak, 7-6, 4-6, 6-3, 6-4. Ashe and Tony Roche won the Australian Open, Part I in January, over Americans Erik van Dillen and Charlie Pasarell, 6-4, 6-4. It reverted to an Aussie party in December's Part II, Allan Stone and lefty Ray Ruffels beating Dent and Alexander, 7-6, 7-6. Vijay Amritraj and Stockton made their only doubles victory together count, collecting $40,000 apiece for beating the makeshift pair of Italian Adriano Panatta and Gerulaitis in the WCT doubles finals at Kansas City, 7-6, 7-6, 4-6, 6-3.

The Colgate Grand Prix embraced 76 tournaments, with total prize money of approximately $9 million. Worldwide, men's tournaments offered about $12 million, excluding World Team Tennis and exhibition matches. Fifteen players made more than $200,000 in prize money, including Bob Hewitt ($234,184), whose earnings came mostly in doubles. Five players (Vilas, Borg, Ramirez, Smith, and Orantes) crossed the once unimaginable $1-million career earnings mark, increasing the number of tennis millionaires to 13 since Laver first passed the milestone in 1971.

Australia recovered the Davis Cup for the first time since 1973 and tied the U.S. for the most possessions (24). Italy, arriving in Sydney to defend, got a left-handed surprise. Roche, at 32, seemingly well past his prime, had last played for the Cup 10 years before, then only in the clinching doubles with John Newcombe over Spain. But he was Captain Neale Fraser's ace from deep in the hole for the showdown on White City grass, and justified the long-shot gamble with serve-and-volleying flair to astound Panatta, 6-3, 6-4, 6-4. Alexander took care of Barazzutti, combative though never having won a match on the green, 6-2, 8-6, 4-6, 6-2, and it looked like a romp. However Adriano Panatta and Paolo Bertolucci, jarred Alexander and Dent, 6-4, 6-4, 7-5. It was 2-1. With a goodly number of Italian immigrants in the crowd screaming for him—"Dai [come on], Adriano?'— Panatta drove Alexander to the brink of defeat in a difficult swirling wind, but J.A. shoved harder when pushed to wrap up the Cup in five, 6-4, 4-6, 2-6, 8-6, 11-9.

Rosie Casals and Stockton repeated as champions at the third (and last) Spalding Mixed Doubles Classic in Dallas, beating Stove and McMillan, 4-6, 7-6, 6-7, 6-2, 7-6. Despite good attendance and TV exposure, an appealing event was scrapped because players couldn't fit it into their singles-emphasizing schedules.

World Team Tennis completed its fourth season, with the Boston Lobsters topping the East Division, and the Phoenix Racquets the West Division. Ten teams played 44 matches each, and again all operated in the red. The New York Apples, led by King

and Sandy Mayer, won the league championship, defeating Phoenix in the final round of the playoffs, 27-22, 28-17.

Evert won three of the four richest women's tournaments, her fourth Virginia Slims Championship, played at Madison Square Garden, over Englishwoman Sue Barker, 2-6, 6-1, 6-1; her third consecutive U.S. Open, matching a feat last accomplished by Maureen Connolly, 1951– 53, and the Colgate Series Championship.

Chrissie represented the United States for the first time in the Federation Cup, which attracted 42 nations to the grass courts of Devonshire Park in Eastbourne, England, the week before Wimbledon. She didn't lose a set in singles as the United States romped past Austria, Switzerland, France, South Africa and Australia. Evert defeated Kerry Reid, 7-5, 6-3, and King disposed of Dianne Fromholtz, 6-1, 2-6, 6-2, to clinch the championship.

Evert and King were too much for Britain as the U.S claimed a 39th victory, 7-0, in the 54-year-old Wightman Cup, played on the West Coast for the first time, at the Oakland Coliseum. Chrissie opened with a 7-5, 7-6, victory over Wade, and trimmed Barker, 6-1, 6-2. King blistered Barker, 6-1, 6-4, and slipped past Wade, 6-4, 3-6, 8-6, the two of them treating a crowd of 11,317 to a glorious evening.

In all, Evert, at age 22, won 11 of 14 tournaments, 70 of 74 matches, and $453,134 in prize money. She was ranked No. 1 in the U.S. for the fourth consecutive year and No. 1 in doubles for the first time, with Casals. Evert won the U.S. Open without losing a set for the second straight year and stretched her remarkable clay-court winning streak to 23 tournaments and 113 matches, dating back to August, 1973. Even though Fromholtz surprised her in the round-robin portion of the eight-woman Colgate Series Championships, 7-6 (5-4), 6-4, Evert reached the final and claimed the richest prize in women's tennis, $75,000, by beating King, 6-2, 6-2.

Although Evert was the dominant force, and Wade the sentimental success story, there were other notable achievements in 1977. Austin, five feet tall and weighing 90 pounds, reached the quarters of the U.S. Open, beating No. 4 seed Barker, 6-1, 6-4, and Ruzici, 6-3, 7-5, before Stove sent her back to school, 6-2, 6-2. The 14-year-old took enough time off from her eighth and ninth-grade classes in Rolling Hills, Calif., to play 10 professional tournaments and wound up ranked No. 12 in the world, and No. 4 in the United States—the youngest ever to crack the Top Ten until Jennifer Capriati, a younger 14 in 1990.

Martina Navratilova, starting the season slimmed down and determined to make up for a disappointing 1976, won four of 11 tournaments on the Virginia Slims circuit, beating Evert in the final of the season opener at Washington, D.C., 6-2, 6-3.

Transsexual Renee Richards won her year-long legal struggle for acceptance in women's tournaments when a New York judge ruled that she could not be barred from the U.S. Open for failing the Olympic chromosome test. The court ruled that medical evidence proved Richards was "female," and the USTA and WTA dropped efforts to bar her. She lost in the first round of the Open singles, but reached the doubles final with Californian Betty Ann Grubb Stuart before losing to Navratilova and Stove, 6-1, 7-6. (Stove also won the mixed with Frew McMillan, over King and Gerulaitis, 6-2, 3-6, 6-3.) Thereafter, Richards—the lone entrant to

have used both men's and women's dressing rooms at the U.S. Championships—became a regular competitor on the women's circuit, though several players defaulted against her in protest. Renee lost to Wimbledon champs in her Forest Hills ventures: To Neale Fraser, 6-0, 6-1, 6-1, in 1960, and Wade, 6-1, 6-4 in 1977, both first rounders. She did win a minor tournament, Pensacola, Fla., defeating Evert in the semis (Jeanne Evert, that is), 6-1, 4-6, 6-2, and Caroline Stoll in the final, 6-2, 6-2.

King, recovered from knee surgery the previous November, worked her way back into shape and won three consecutive tournaments and 18 straight matches in autumn to reach the playoff finale of the $2-million Colgate Series, which carried a $600,000 bonus pool. She was 0-4 on the year against Evert, but 2-0 against WTT teammate Wade, 3-0 against Navratilova, 1-0 against Barker and 4-0 against Stove. King, winning six titles, finished the year with a 53-6 record, ranked No. 2 in the U.S. While the topcats were away, employed in WTT, lesser ladies were at play in Europe: Janet Newberry won the Italian, 6-3, 7-6, (7-5) over Czech Renata Tomanova. Mima Jausovec became the first Yugoslav to win the French, beating Romanian Florenta Mihai, 6-2, 6-7 (5-7), 6-1.

Kerry Reid, at 29, won the two-headed Australian Open for the first time—Part I over fellow Aussie Dianne Fromholtz, 7-5, 6-2. Part II, in December, went to Goolagong, her fourth, over Helen Gourlay Cawley, 6-3, 6-0. Formally it was Mrs. Roger Cawley defeating Mrs. Robert Cawley (the respective English and Australian husbands unrelated). That extended her Aussie streak to 20 match wins. Kept out of the January version because she was pregnant, Goolagong gave birth to her first child—daughter Kelly—in May, and launched a comeback in the fall.

Hottest political controversy of the year concerned the rise and fall of the "double strung" or "spaghetti" racket, which was actually a radical stringing technique that could be applied to any standard racket frame. There were several versions, but they all used two sets of vertical strings, supported by five or six cross strings threaded through them, and braced with fish line, adhesive tape, rope or other protuberances, including a plastic tubing called "spaghetti." While rackets thus strung generally had a very low tension—between 35 and 55 pounds—they were able to generate tremendous power because of a "trampoline effect," the ball sinking deep in the double layer of strings and being propelled out. Because the dual layer of strings also moved, they were able to "brush" the ball, artificially imitating a heavy topspin stroke. Thus, some players were able to hit the ball extremely hard from the backcourt and still keep it in play. The "spaghetti" racket was all the more maddening to play against because the ball came off it with a dull thud that made it difficult to judge.

The "double strung" racket was invented in West Germany by a former horticulturist named Werner Fischer, and it created a major scandal in club and national tournaments there as second and third-line players became champions with it. An adaptation of the racket was first used in a major tournament by Australian lefty Barry Phillips-Moore in the French Open, where he beat Chilean Davis Cupper Pato Cornejo, ranked considerably above him, 6-4, 6-4, 6-0, before losing to 15th-seeded Balazs Taroczy. A number of professional players used it in Europe dur-

ing the summer and it gained further notoriety at the U.S. Open when an obscure American player named Mike Fishbach used his homemade version to trounce Billy Martin, 6-1, 7-5, and 16th-seeded ex-champ Stan Smith, 6-0, 6-2, in the first two rounds. Alarm bells rang but Brit John Feaver quelled the fever for a while, 2-6, 6-4, 6-0.

However, a couple of weeks later, Nastase was beaten, 6-4, 2-6, 6-4, by a French player, Georges Goven, using a "spaghetti" racket in Paris and swore he would never play against it again. The following week he turned up with one himself and used it to win a tournament at Aix-en-Provence, ending Vilas' long winning streak in the best-of-five-set final. Vilas quit after two sets, down 6-1, 7-5, claiming that playing against the exaggerated spin injured his elbow.

The ITF had already acted by that time, however, putting a "temporary freeze" on use of the double-strung rackets in tournaments, effective Oct. 2. Unfortunately for Vilas, that was the day the tournament ended. The ITF based its decision on a report by the University of Brunswick in West Germany, which indicated that every hit with the racket was in fact a "double hit," in violation of the rules. The ITF made its ban permanent the following June by adopting a definition of a racket for the first time: "A racket shall consist of a frame, which may be of any material, weight, size of shape and stringing. The stringing must be uniform and smooth and may be of any material. The strings must be alternately interlaced or bonded where they cross. The distance between the main and/or cross strings shall not be less than one quarter of an inch nor more than one-half inch. If there are attachments they must be used only to prevent wear and tear and must not alter the flight of the ball. They must be uniform with a maximum protrusion of .04 of an inch."

In November, 11 days after his 43rd birthday, Rosewall won Hong Kong, 6-3, 5-7, 6-4, 6-4, over 31-year-old Tom Gorman. He was not quite as old as Pancho Gonzalez, 43, had been in winning Des Moines in 1972. It was Rosewall's 32nd (and last) singles championship of the Open era. But, of course, "Muscles," or "The Doomsday Stroking Machine," won many more during his amateur days and Kramer Pro days. The little Aussie had been a title winner for almost three decades, and he would glide into 1978 to show some kids what it was all about.

1977 CHAMPIONS AND LEADERS

Australian Open
Men's Singles Final (Jan.): Roscoe Tanner (USA) def. Guillermo Vilas (ARG), 6-3, 6-3, 6-3

Men's Singles Final (Dec): Vitas Gerulaitis (USA) def. John Lloyd (GBR), 6-3, 7-6 (1), 5-7, 3-6, 6-2

Women's Singles Final (Jan.): Kerry Melville Reid (AUS) def. Dianne Fromholtz (AUS), 7-5, 6-2

Women's Singles Final (Dec): Evonne Goolagong Cawley (AUS) def. Helen Gourlay Cawley (AUS), 6-3, 6-0

Men's Doubles Final (Jan.): Arthur Ashe (USA) and Tony Roche (AUS) def. Charlie Pasarell and Erik van Dillen (USA), 6-4, 6-4

Men's Doubles Final (Dec): Ray Ruffels and Allan Stone (AUS) def. John Alexander and Phil Dent (AUS), 7-6, 7-6

Women's Doubles Final (Jan.): Dianne Fromholtz and Helen Gourlay Cawley (AUS) def. Betsy Nagelsen (USA) and Kerry Melville Reid (AUS), 5-7, 61, 7-5

Women's Doubles Final (Dec): Evonne Goolagong Cawley and Helen Gourlay Cawley (AUS) and Mona Schallau Guerrant (USA) and Kerry Melville Reid (SHARED - RAINED OUT)

Mixed Doubles: Not Played

French Open
Men's Singles Final: Guillermo Vilas (ARG) def. Brian Gottfried (USA), 6-0, 6-3, 6-0

Women's Singles Final: Mima Jausovec (YUG) def. Florenta Mihai (ROM), 6-2, 6-7 (5), 6-1

Men's Doubles Final: Brian Gottfried (USA) and Raul Ramirez (MEX) def. Wojtek Fibak (POL) and Jan Kodes (CZE), 7-6, 4-6, 6-3, 6-4

Women's Doubles Final: Regina Marsikova (CZE) and Pam Teeguarden (USA) def. Rayni Fox (USA) and Helen Gourlay (AUS) ,5-7, 6-4, 6-2

Mixed Doubles Final: Mary Carillo and John McEnroe (USA) def. Florenta Mihai (ROM) and Ivan Molina (COL), 7-6, 6-3

Wimbledon
Men's Singles Final: Bjorn Borg (SWE) def. Jimmy Connors (USA), 3-6, 6-2, 6-1, 5-7, 6-4

Women's Singles Final: Virginia Wade (GBR) def. Betty Stove (NED), 4-6, 6-3, 6-1

Men's Doubles Final: Geoff Masters and Ross Case (AUS) def. John Aelexander and Phil Dent (AUS) 6-3, 6-4, 3-6, 8-9 (4), 6-4

Women's Doubles Final: Helen Gourlay Cawley (AUS) and JoAnne Russell (USA) def. Martina Navratilova (CZE) and Betty Stove (NED), 6-3, 6-3

Mixed Doubles Final: Greer Stevens and Bob Hewitt (RSA) def. Betty Stove (NED) and Frew McMillian (RSA), 3-6, 7-5, 6-4

U.S. Open
Men's Singles Final: Guillermo Vilas (ARG) def. Jimmy Connors (USA), 2-6, 6-3, 7-6 (9), 6-0

Women's Singles Final: Chris Evert (USA) def. Wendy Turnbull (AUS), 7-6 (3), 6-2

Men's Doubles Final: Bob Hewitt and Frew McMillan (RSA) def. Brian Gottfried and Raul Ramirez (MEX), 6-4, 6-0

Women's Doubles Final: Martina Navratilova (USA) and Betty Stove (NED) def. Renee Richards and Betty Ann Grubb Stuart (USA), 6-1, 7-6

Mixed Doubles Final: Betty Stove (NED) and Frew McMillan (RSA) def. Billie Jean King and Vitas Gerulaitis (USA), 6-2, 3-6, 6-3

Year-End No. 1
Men: Jimmy Connors
Women: Chris Evert

Top Player Earnings
Men: Guillermo Vilas $766,065
Women: Chris Evert $503,134

Davis Cup: Australia

Federation Cup: United States

Wightman Cup: United States

Grand Prix Masters, NYC—Jimmy Connors
WCT, Dallas—Jimmy Connors
Virginia Slims Championships, NYC—Chris Evert

1978 U.S. Open Gets A New Home

Bjorn Borg is congratulated by **Fred Perry** after Borg became the first man since Perry to win three straight men's singles titles at Wimbledon.

In 1978, as Wimbledon began its second century and Stade Roland Garros in Paris celebrated its 50th anniversary, the U.S. Open moved to the new U.S. Tennis Association National Tennis Center, the most important new arena for international tennis in half a century.

Bjorn Borg and Jimmy Connors continued their spirited battle for king-of-the-hill in men's tennis, Martina Navratilova and Chris Evert waged a similarly lovely little war for the No. 1 ranking among the women, and several precocious young talents blossomed—19-year-old John McEnroe starting to challenge the top men, and high-school girls Tracy Austin and Pam Shriver asserting themselves in women's tournaments.

Perhaps nothing better symbolized what happened to the once-elitist, white-flanneled sport of tennis in the 1970s than the fact that the U.S. Open, America's premier tournament, moved to a public park, in Flushing Meadow, Queens, N.Y. The USTA National Tennis Center was built, remarkably, in one year on 16 acres of city-owned land in Flushing Meadow-Corona Park, adjacent to Shea Stadium.

Relocated to Flushing by drawling, cigar-chomping USTA President W.E. "Slew" Hester, a 66-year-old wildcat oilman from Jackson, Miss., the U.S. Championships was retreating from 97 years in such patrician clubs as Newport (R.I.) Casino, Philadelphia Cricket Club and the West Side Tennis Club. Hester talked like a Southern conservative, but proved in a memorable two-year term to be perhaps the most progressive president in the history of the USTA. Many second-guessed him in September 1977 when, fed up with the reactionary board of governors of the West Side Tennis Club, he announced that the Open would be moved. Few believed the new complex Hester envisioned a couple of miles away could be completed in 12 months, and many considered the project "Hester's Folly." But Hester's perseverance and leadership, despite arthritis so severe it was difficult for him to walk, enabled the USTA to cut through bureaucratic red tape, union disputes and cost overruns and get the splendid complex built in time for the 1978 Open.

The USTA National Tennis Center was dedicated on Aug. 30, 1978. Its main arena—Louis Armstrong Stadium, site of the Singer Bowl for the 1964-65 World's Fair and named for the late jazz great who lived nearby—accommodated nearly 20,000 spectators, with barely a bad seat in the house. In addition to the steeply banked, red, white and blue stadium, the complex included a

6,000-seat grandstand, 25 additional lighted outdoor courts, and nine indoor courts, all with the same acrylic asphalt surface that approximates the hard courts most Americans play on. Under a lease agreement between the USTA and the city of New York, the facility is open to the public year-round and is available to the USTA for tournaments and special events 60 days a year, at a modest fee. The USTA, in turn, spent $10 million to renovate and enlarge a stadium that was intended for concerts but had fallen into terrible disrepair.

The result was the most significant new venue for world tennis since the modern All England Club was opened in the London suburb of Wimbledon in 1922 and Stade Roland Garros was dedicated as a civic monument in Paris for the 1928 Davis Cup Challenge Round.

Roland Garros celebrated its golden anniversary during the 1978 French Open Championships. On balance, this was a dull tournament, but on a day when 32 past champions were honored in gala center-court ceremonies, Borg asserted himself as one of the greatest by winning the most important clay court test for the third time, five days past his 20th birthday. His win came two weeks after he'd won the Italian Open in five difficult sets over Italian Adriano Panatta, 1-6, 6-3, 6-1, 4-6, 6-3, (Romans saluted Borg with showers of jeers and coins for depriving their matinee idol of victory). He repeated the arduous clay-court "double" he had first achieved in 1974 by sweeping through seven matches in Paris in 21 straight sets, dropping only 32 games. In the final, he trounced defending champion Guillermo Vilas, 6-1, 6-1, 6-3.

Borg went on to become the first man since Rod Laver in 1962 to sweep the Italian, French and Wimbledon singles—the "Old World Triple"—in one season. In dominating the grass of Wimbledon as he had the clay in Rome and Paris, Borg also equaled a more important milestone. He became the first man since Englishman Fred Perry in 1934-35-36 to win the Wimbledon singles three successive years.

Borg routed a rejuvenated Tom Okker, 6-4, 6-4, 6-4, in one semifinal while Connors blunted Vitas Gerulaitis, 9-7, 6-2, 6-1, in the other. In a one-sided final, Borg served, volleyed and smashed as never before to win 6-2, 6-2, 6-3. He also displayed a new weapon, a sliced backhand approach shot to Connors' vulnerable forehand, which stayed low on the fast grass. "The way Borg played today," marveled Perry, who hustled down from behind his microphone in the BBC radio commentary booth to congratulate the young Swede on Centre Court, "if he had fallen out of a 45th-story window of a skyscraper, he would have gone straight up."

At the midpoint of the season, it seemed that Borg, with his beefed-up serve, had begun to dominate his grand rivalry with Connors. Despite a loss in the 1977 Grand Prix Masters the first week of the New Year, Borg had won five of their last six meetings, giving up only 11 games in six sets, through Wimbledon.

But Connors immediately began to train for another showdown, vowing to "follow that son-of-a-bitch to the ends of the earth" for revenge. He worked on adding oomph to his serve—which deserted him in the Wimbledon final—and shoring up his forehand. Having won 18 straight matches going into the Wimbledon final, he didn't lose another the rest of the summer, winning Grand Prix tournaments at Washington over Eddie

Dibbs, 7-5, 7-5, Indianapolis (the U.S. Clay Court) over Jose Higueras, 7-5, 6-1, and Stowe, Vt., over Tim Gullikson, 6-2, 6-3, as he honed his game for the U.S. Open.

Connors' moment of truth at the Open came in a fourth round victory over Panatta. Panatta served for the match at 5-4 in the fifth set of this three hour 36-minute epic, came within two points of victory at 30-30, and later fended off four match points. Connors got to the fifth match point with an astounding shot—a backhand down the line on the dead run from 10 feet wide of the court, which he somehow reached and drilled one-handed around the net post for a winner, practically parting net judge Reid Johnson's hair.

Moments later, Connors had the match, 4-6, 6-4, 6-1, 1-6, 7-5, and that, he said later, gave him the impetus to steamroll through the final three rounds without losing a set: over Brian Gottfried, 6-2, 7-6 (7-0), 6-1; McEnroe, 6-2, 6-2, 7-5, and Borg, 6-4, 6-2, 6-2. Never before were Connors' skill, will and churning internal aggression better shown than in the final. He annihilated Borg, who had a blister on the thumb of his racket hand, almost as badly as Jimmy himself had been savaged at Wimbledon, ending the Swede's 39-match streak.

Connors, the first man since Bill Tilden in the 1920s to reach the singles final five consecutive years, thus became the first man since Perry in 1933-34, 36 to win three U.S. singles titles, and the first American to do so since Tilden. By quirk of history, Connors also gained the singular distinction of having won on grass (1974), clay (1976), and hard court (1978).

The U.S. Open final was the last meeting of the year between Borg and Connors. The last four months of the season belonged to McEnroe, the often-irate left-hander from Douglaston, N.Y., who was the only man other than Ken Rosewall, 19 in 1954, to have reached the semifinal at both Wimbledon and the U.S. Championships while still a teen-ager.

After losing to Connors at the Open, McEnroe broke his maiden, winning four Grand Prix singles tournaments, at Hartford over Johan Kriek, 6-2, 6-4, San Francisco over Dick Stockton, 2-6, 7-6, 6-2, Stockholm over Tim Gullikson, 6-2, 6-2, and London over Gullikson, 6-7, 6-4, 7-6, 6-2. He also won seven doubles events, led the U.S. to its first possession of the Davis Cup since 1972 with a spectacular singles debut, and won both the singles and doubles titles at the Colgate Grand Prix Masters at Madison Square Garden the second week in January 1979. His singles record over that stretch was 49-7. McEnroe collected $463,866 in the six months after he turned pro in June following his National Intercollegiate singles title as a Stanford University freshman, defeating John Sadri of North Carolina State University, 7-6, 7-6, 5-7, 7-6.

At Stockholm, on a fast tile court, he won his introductory meeting with Borg, 6-3, 6-4. His left-handed serve, sliced low and wide so that it skidded away from Borg's two-fisted backhand, was so effective that McEnroe lost only seven points in 10 service games. It was the first time that Borg, 22, had lost to a younger player.

McEnroe, still virtually unknown, made his Davis Cup debut in doubles in September. He partnered Gottfried to the decisive point in America's 3-2 victory over Chile in the American Zone Final at Santiago, 3-6, 6-3, 8-6, 6-3, over Jaime Fillol and Belus Pra-

joux. That clinched it for the U.S. after Gottfried beat Fillol, 6-4, 7-5, 6-2, and Solomon put away Hans Gildemeister, 7-5, 3-6, 6-3, 6-1.

Captain Tony Trabert used Arthur Ashe and Gerulaitis in singles in the 3-2 semifinal against Sweden in Goteborg, and neither could cope with Borg. But both beat Kjell Johansson (Vitas, 6-2, 6-1, 6-4, and Arthur, 6-2, 6-0, 7-5), sandwiched around reliables Stan Smith and Bob Lutz's tight one over Ove Bengtson and Borg, 2-6, 6-3, 3-6, 7-5, 6-3.

Following that, McEnroe had his spectacular Davis Cup singles coming-out party in the final against Great Britain at Rancho Mirage, Calif. He lost his serve only once in demoralizing John Lloyd, 6-1, 6-2, 6-2, in the opening match and Buster Mottram, 6-2, 6-2, 6-1, in the clincher of the 4-1 U.S. victory. Mottram's second match stinging of Gottfried, 4-6, 2-6, 10-8, 6-4, 6-3, cheered the Brits, 41 years after their last presence in the final. But that was a mere speed bump. Smith and Lutz handled David Lloyd and Mark Cox, 6-2, 6-2, 6-3, and left the rest to Mac.

This ended a five-year drought for the numerous gang of Captain Trabert, and gave the U.S. possession of the trophy symbolizing international team supremacy for a record 25th time. Tony used nine players during the victorious campaign, a record.

As for McEnroe's dominance, it should be noted that never before in 67 Davis Cup windups had a player lost as few as 10 games in two singles matches. Bill Tilden in 1924, Jack Kramer in 1946 and Borg in 1975 gave up 12. Mac was the only teen-ager to spearhead a U.S. Cup triumph with two singles wins, although Michael Chang, at age 18 in 1990, would win one.

McEnroe went into the season-ending Masters playoff at New York's Madison Square Garden eager for a showdown with Connors, who had beaten him in all four of their career meetings. The Masters, designed to bring together the top eight finishers in the previous year's Grand Prix standings for a $400,000 shootout, had lost much of its luster because Borg and Vilas declined invitations. They had not played the minimum 20 Grand Prix tournaments required to qualify for shares of the $2-million Grand Prix bonus pool, and so turned their backs on the showcase finale. Connors did not qualify for his bonus either, but was coaxed at the 11th hour into defending his title.

The Connors-McEnroe duel was seen as the savior of a disappointing tournament, but it also fizzled because Connors aggravated a blood blister on his foot in the first set of their meeting in the round-robin portion of the tournament, and defaulted while trailing, 7-5, 3-0. McEnroe beat Eddie Dibbs in the semifinals, 6-1, 6-4, and come-backing 35-year-old Ashe, 6-7 (5-7), 6-3, 7-5, in a scintillating final.

But even if McEnroe was, as Ashe called him, "the best player in the world the last four months of 1978," he was not in the running for Player of the Year honors based on his full-season record of 75-20. The run for the No. 1 ranking was strictly a match race between Borg and Connors. *Tennis* magazine's ranking panel voted for Connors, but *World Tennis* and the International Tennis Federation— instituting a "world champion" award—went for Borg. The "World Champion" title was a new honor to be awarded annually by the International Tennis Federation for men and women. It was intended to establish an official No. 1 player for each calendar year and eliminate the confusion caused by diverse and often contradictory sets of rankings. Borg was the unanimous choice of the selection committee of three former champions, Fred Perry, Lew Hoad and Don Budge. Their decision was based primarily on his superior record in traditional major events, although Borg also held a 3-2 edge over Connors in head-to-head meetings, including three four man "special events."

Borg's record for the entire season was 88-8, including a 9-0 singles record in spurring Sweden past Ireland, Yugoslavia, Spain and Hungary to the semifinals of the Davis Cup. He won 12 titles. Connors, who won 14, was 84-7 overall. He monopolized U.S titles, winning the U.S. Indoor over Tim Gullikson, 7-6, 6-3, plus the U.S. Clay Courts and the U.S. Open. Following the Wimbledon final, he compiled a 30-match winning streak.

Other notable achievements in 1978 included, "Broadway" Vitas, the flamboyant 23-year-old New Yorker, getting a default over injured Borg in the semifinal and capturing the $100,000 top prize in the eight-man World Championship of Tennis Finals in Dallas with an impressive 6-3, 6-2, 6-1 victory over Dibbs. Gerulaitis also collected the $100,000 top prize in WCT's 12-man, $300,000 invitational tournament at Forest Hills in July, beating Ilie Nastase in the final, 6-2, 6-0.

Vilas won eight tournaments, including the German Open over Pole Wojtek Fibak, 6-2, 6-4, 6-2, and the Australian Open, which ended Jan. 3, 1979. His 6-4, 6-4, 3-6, 6-3 triumph over unseeded Aussie John Marks was his third major singles title, to go along with his French and U.S. Open crowns of 1977. Amazing four-time champ Rosewall, accorded a seventh seed at 44, won two rounds in this his 14th (and last) Aussie. Shut out of the titles department for the first time, Rosewall nevertheless would tack up a No. 34 ranking at the end of the year, earning $52,368 in prize money. Not bad for the clever codger.

Ashe, the Wimbledon champion of 1975, started the year ranked only No. 257 because he had missed almost the entire 1977 season after surgery on a chronic heel ailment. He won three Grand Prix tournaments: San Jose over South African Bernie Mitton, 6-7, 6-1, 6-2, Columbus over Lutz, 6-3, 6-4, and Los Angeles over Gottfried, 6-2, 6-4. He also reached the Masters final and finished the season ranked No. 11.

Bob Hewitt and Frew McMillan won seven doubles titles, including their third at Wimbledon, over Peter Fleming and McEnroe, 6-1, 6-4, 6-2. Okker and Fibak also won seven titles, including the WCT Finals at Kansas City over Smith and Lutz, 6-7, 6-4, 6-0, 6-3, for which they split an $80,000 prize. Smith and Lutz captured their third U.S. Open doubles, over Sherwood Stewart and Marty Riessen, 1-6, 7-5, 6-3. McEnroe and Fleming were the hottest team the second half of the season, winning six tournaments between August and December, plus the 1978 Masters over Okker and Fibak, 6-4, 6-2, 6-4, early in January, 1979.

On the women's side, the first half of the year belonged to Navratilova, the second half to Evert. With Evert taking the first three months of the year as a vacation, Navratilova, at age 21, began to fulfill her rich promise. She dominated the Virginia Slims winter circuit—the last under the cigarette company's sponsorship—winning the first seven tournaments and the $150,000 final playoff at Oakland, Calif., over Evonne Goolagong,

7-6 (5-3), 6-3. That was Navratilova's most important victory to date, an important psychological breakthrough for the expatriate Czech left-hander.

Evert returned to competition in the spring, but Navratilova, supremely fit and confident, beat her in the final of the pre-Wimbledon grass court tournament at Eastbourne, England, coming back from 1-4 in the final set and saving a break point, 6-4, 4-6, 9-7.

They met again in the Wimbledon final, and this time Navratilova came back from 2-4 in the last set, serving magnificently and out-steadying as well as overpowering Evert to win, 2-6, 6-4, 7-5. An Evert volley that beaned her seemed to shake the cobwebs from Martina in the second set as she held serve to 4-2 through two deuces and three match points. Navratilova, whose emotions had regularly overwhelmed her abundant talent, won 12 of the last 13 points. When it was over, Navratilova looked ecstatically toward her friend and manager, Hall of Fame golfer Sandra Haynie, an important stabilizing influence in her life. Martina shed a flood of tears and was puffy-eyed when she received the championship trophy from the Duchess of Kent.

"I don't know if I should cry or scream or laugh. I feel very happy that I won, but at the same time I'm very sad that I can't share this with my family," said Navratilova, who had not seen her parents or her 15-year-old sister, Jana, since defecting to the United States during the 1975 U.S. Open. Her victory, predictably, was all but neglected in the government-controlled media of Czechoslovakia, but her parents watched it on German television by driving to a town near the German border.

Billie Jean King was again foiled in her attempt to win a record-setting 20th career Wimbledon title, losing with Navratilova in the quarters of the doubles to Mona Schallau Guerrant and Sue Barker, 6-3, 4-6, 6-4. But they did win the U.S. Open title, over Wimbledon champs Kerry Reid and Wendy Turnbull, 7-6 (9-7), 6-4. Australians Reid and Turnbull saved two match points in the tie-breaker to take the Wimbledon crown, a 4-6, 9-8 (12-10), 6-3, thriller over French Open champs, Mima Jausovec and Virginia Ruzici. Betty Stove and McMillan won the mixed at Wimbledon, 6-2, 6-2, and U.S. Open, 6-3, 7-6, both over King and Ray Ruffels. In a second-rounder at Flushing, Mareen Louie and Andy Lucchesi set a mixed doubles tie-breaker record—34 points—in beating Diane Desfor and Horace Reid, 6-2, 6-7, 7-6 (18-16).

Navratilova won her first 37 matches of the year, but the streak finally came to an end in the quarterfinals of the Virginia Slims in Dallas where she was beaten by 15-year-old Californian Austin, 6-3, 2-6, 7-6 (5-4). The tingling match before 10,000 enthralled spectators went down to the final point of a best-of-nine-point tie-breaker, simultaneous match point. The tournament produced several startling upsets and three teen-agers in the semifinals—Austin, 15-year-old Shriver of Lutherville, Md., and 18-year-old Anne Smith of Dallas. Goolagong, 26, eventually beat Austin in the final, 4-6, 6-0, 6-2. "Someday, that tournament may be looked upon as a landmark, the beginning of a new order," predicted pioneer King.

Those words appeared prophetic as Austin, Shriver and Smith all landed in the U.S. Top 10 for 1978, at Nos. 3-5-8. They appeared to be the vanguard of a wave of promising young women, a notion fortified by the victory of 13-year-old Andrea Jaeger in the 18-and-under division of the prestigious Orange Bowl junior tournament at the end of the year, beating South African Rosalyn Fairbank, 6-1, 6-3.

Austin rose to No. 6 in the world before turning 16 on Dec. 12. She beat Shriver in the finals of the U.S. Girls' 16 and 18 championships, increasing her record total of U.S. junior titles to 27. Tracy turned pro in October, won her first tournament as a professional at Stuttgart, Germany, over Stove, 6-3, 6-3, and won $70,000 within three months.

Shriver, while 0-9 against Austin in their junior careers, one-upped her at the U.S. Open, becoming the youngest finalist in the tournament's history. Seeded No. 16, Pam, the 6-foot "Great Whomping Crane," upset eighth-seeded Reid, 6-2, 6-4, an injured Lesley Hunt, 6-2, 6-0, and top-seed Navratilova, 7-6 (7-5), 7-6 (7-3), in a rain-interrupted semifinal that was arguably the greatest upset in women's major tournament history. Playing nervelessly and aggressively with her Prince (oversized head) racket, Shriver used her serve-and-volley game to extend second-seeded Evert to 7-5, 6-4 before losing an exciting final. But she was the youngest of all U.S. finalists, 16-years, two months, undercutting Maureen Connolly, 1951, by nine months.

Both Austin and Shriver, who remained an amateur, were named to the U.S. Wightman Cup team, which was upset by Great Britain, 4-3, at London's Royal Albert Hall. Evert routed Barker, 6-2, 6-1, and Virginia Wade, 6-0, 6-1, but the British preyed on the inexperience of the American teen-agers. Michele Tyler upset Shriver, 5-7, 6-3, 6-3. Wade (3-6, 7-5, 6-3) and Barker (6-3, 3-6, 6-0) each beat Austin. Wade and Barker teamed up to beat Shriver and Evert, 6-0, 5-7, 6-4, in the decisive doubles match.

Austin also joined Evert and captain King as the U.S. won the Federation Cup for the third straight year in Melbourne, Australia. The U.S. nipped Australia, 2-1, in the final - Evert and King teaming for the decisive point over Reid and Turnbull, 4-6, 6-1, 6-4. In singles, Kerry Reid defeated Austin, 6-3, 6-3; Evert defeated Wendy Turnbull 3-6, 6-1, 6-1.

Evert did not lose a tournament match after the Wimbledon final, winning her last 34 of the year, including three over Navratilova, finishing with a 56-3 record, six victories in 10 tournaments, and $443,540 in prize money. Chrissie became only the third woman to win the U.S. singles four consecutive years, the first since Helen Jacobs from 1932-35. Evert won the U.S. Open without losing a set for the third consecutive year, an astonishing feat, especially since the surface was changed from clay (on which she had not lost since August 1973) to medium-fast hard courts that were not ideally suited to her backcourt game. She finished the year with a 3-2 record against Navratilova and was voted the ITF "World Champion" by a panel of three former women champions: Ann Jones, Margaret Smith Court and Margaret Osborne duPont.

Again devalued in the female precinct by the loss of talent to WTT, the Italian went to Czech Regina Marsikova over Romanian Virginia Ruzici, 7-5, 7-5, but Virginia turned up the burner to depose Virginia Mima Jausovec at the French, 6-2, 6-2. They were the first women of their countries to win those titles.

Tallest major winner of the year was unseeded, six-footer

Chris O'Neil, who ruled her island by winning the Australian Open, defeating No. 7-seeded and No. 68-ranked Betsy Nagelsen, 6-3, 7-6 (7-4). Ranked No. 111, O'Neil was the longest shot ever to win a female major. A tepid field contested for the $35,000 pot, the champ getting help from compatriot Di Evers, who knocked out top-seeded Barker, No. 26, in the quarters, 6-2, 7-6. Nevertheless, 22-year-old serve-and-volleying O'Neil, with the lone title of her career and $6,000 to show for it, joined another record long shot achiever, countryman Mark Edmondson, No. 212 as the 1976 Australian victor.

Evert also was voted the Most Valuable Player in World Team Tennis, leading her Los Angeles Strings to their first championship of the intercity league. The Strings beat the Boston Lobsters in the playoff finale, 24-21, 30-20, 26-27, 28-25. But after five years of financial losses, WTT was shaky as the year ended. Half of the league's 10 teams announced that they were ceasing operations in the fall and, despite some optimistic noises from the commissioner's office in St. Louis, the chances of finding replacements appeared slim.

Plans for a seven-week, $1-million women's tournament circuit in Europe in the spring gave Evert, Navratilova and the other women stars of WTT a lucrative alternative. The failure of the league to sign top players for 1979 caused several influential owners to give up the ghost, and the league seemed to unravel quickly after the Boston Lobsters and the New York Apples folded.

Virginia Slims, which had pioneered the promotion of women's tennis since 1971, startlingly departed from the sponsorship scene in April when the WTA board of directors voted not to renew its contract for the winter circuit. The WTA cited "differences in philosophy on the structure of the circuit" for the divorce from the company, which had poured more than $8 million into women's pro tennis over eight years. Some players thought the termination of the contract was a grave mistake and that no comparable patron of the women's game could be found.

But in June it was announced that Avon—the huge cosmetic and costume jewelry firm that had for two years sponsored the "Futures" satellite circuit—was the new angel. Avon signed a two-year contract, with additional renewal options, to take over sponsorship of the major circuit as well as the "Futures." Avon's $2.2 million annual commitment was to fund 11 "Championship" tournaments with purses between $125,000 and $200,000, leading to a $325,000 singles and doubles championship playoff, and an expanded circuit of $25,000 "Futures" tournaments.

Despite growing pains, sometimes acute, it was obvious that professional tennis was still on the rise as the 1980s approached.

1978 CHAMPIONS AND LEADERS

Australian Open

Men's Singles Final: Guillermo Vilas (ARG) def. John Marks (AUS), 6-4, 6-4, 3-6, 6-3

Women's Singles Final: Chris O'Neil (AUS) def. Betsy Nagelsen (USA), 6-3, 7-6 (4)

Men's Doubles Final: Wojtek Fibak (POL) and Kim Warwick (AUS) def. Paul Kronk and Cliff Letcher (AUS), 7-6, 7-5

Women's Doubles Final: Betsy Nagelsen (USA) and Renata Tomanova (CZE), def. Naoko Sato (JPN) and Pam Whytcross (AUS), 7-5, 6-2

Mixed Doubles: Not Played

French Open

Men's Singles Final: Bjorn Borg (SWE) def. Guillermo Vilas (ARG), 6-1, 6-1, 6-3

Women's Singles Final: Virginia Ruzici (ROM) def. Mima Jausovec (YUG), 6-2, 6-2

Men's Doubles Final: Gene Mayer and Hank Pfister (USA) def. Jose Higueras and Manuel Orantes (ESP), 6-3, 6-2, 6-2

Women's Doubles Final: Mima Jausovec (YUG) and Virginia Ruzici (ROM) def. Lesley Turner Bowrey (AUS) and Gail Sherriff Lovera (FRA), 5-7, 6-4, 8-6

Mixed Doubles Final: Renata Tomanova and Pavel Slozil (CZE) def. Virginia Ruzici (ROM) and Patrice Dominguez (FRA), 7-6, ret.

Wimbledon

Men's Singles Final: Bjorn Borg (SWE) def. Jimmy Connors (USA), 6-2, 6-2, 6-3

Women's Singles Final: Martina Navratilova (CZE) def. Chris Evert (USA), 2-6, 6-4, 7-5

Men's Doubles Final: Bob Hewitt and Frew McMillan (RSA) def. Peter Fleming and John McEnroe (USA), 6-1, 6-4, 6-2

Women's Doubles Final: Kerry Melville Reid and Wendy Turnbull (AUS) def. Mima Jausovec (YUG) and Virginia Ruzici (ROM), 4-6, 9-8 (10), 6-3

Mixed Doubles Final: Betty Stove (NED) and Frew McMillan (RSA) def. Billie Jean King (USA) and Ray Ruffels (AUS), 6-2, 6-2

U.S. Open

Men's Singles Final: Jimmy Connors (USA) def. Bjorn Borg (SWE), 6-4, 6-2, 6-2

Women's Singles Final: Chris Evert (USA) def. Pam Shriver (USA), 7-5, 6-4

Men's Doubles Final: Bob Lutz and Stan Smith (USA) def. Marty Riessen and Sherwood Stewart (USA), 1-6, 7-5, 6-3

Women's Doubles Final: Billie Jean King (USA) and Martina Navratilova (CZE) def. Kerry Melville Reid and Wendy Turnbull (AUS), 7-6 (7), 6-4

Mixed Doubles Final: Betty Stove (NED) and Frew McMillan (RSA) def. Billie Jean King (USA) and Ray Ruffels (AUS), 6-3, 7-6

Year-End No. 1

Men: Jimmy Connors
Women: Martina Navratilova

Top Player Earnings

Men: Eddie Dibbs $575,273
Top Player Earnings: Women Chris Evert $454,486

Davis Cup: United States

Federation Cup: United States

Wightman Cup: Great Britain

Grand Prix Masters, NYC—John McEnroe
WCT, Dallas—Vitas Gerulaitis
Virginia Slims Championships, Oakland—Martina Navratilova

1979 Austin, 16, Becomes Youngest U.S. Champ

The United Nations designated 1979 as the "International Year of the Child," and, in tennis, youth was well served. This was most evident at the U.S. Open, Tracy Austin, 16, became the youngest women's singles champion in the history of America's premier championships, and John McEnroe, 20, reigned as the youngest men's champion since Pancho Gonzalez in 1948.

But while firmly establishing themselves as contenders for the No. 1 world rankings, the "kids" were not ready to ascend the throne quite yet. The positions of honor in the last year of tennis' remarkable growth decade belonged to old-timers: Martina Navratilova, 22, who won the Avon Championships climaxing the women's indoor circuit and her second consecutive Wimbledon title, and the irrepressible Bjorn Borg, 23, who captured his fourth French Open title and his fourth in a row at Wimbledon, a feat no man had accomplished since before World War I.

Still, it was an exceptional season for the young overachievers, Austin and McEnroe. In addition to her triumph in the Open, Tracy was runner-up to Navratilova in the Avon Championships and snapped Chris Evert Lloyd's six-year, 125-match clay-court

winning streak en route to victory in the Italian Open, her first big international title. McEnroe, who had started the year by winning the 1978 Grand Prix Masters, added the World Championship of Tennis title with back-to-back beatings of Jimmy Connors and Borg, and coordinated with Peter Fleming to win the Wimbledon and U.S. Open doubles. They were clearly the best doubles pair in the world.

The rapid ascendance of Austin and McEnroe symbolized a significant change in the old order that had ruled much of the latter part of the decade. Evert and Connors, who had reached the pinnacle of the game in 1974 as the "Lovebird Double," young champions engaged to wed, finally did get married - but not to each other. Evert became the bride of British Davis Cupper John Lloyd. A few weeks earlier, Connors revealed that he had already married, secretly the previous autumn in Japan to Patti McGuire, a former playmate-of-the-year (*Playboy* magazine version). The couple's first child, Brett David, was born in August.

Meanwhile, though still formidable, neither Evert Lloyd nor Connors was quite the force of before. Their marriages and apparent off-court happiness seemed to coincide with a slight but noticeable decline in their competitive fires.

Evert Lloyd said she was no longer obsessed with the ambition to be the No. 1 player in the world. She did recapture the French Open title in the absence of Navratilova and Austin, but never really resembled her dominant and awesomely consistent form of the prior five years. She failed to reach the semifinal of the Avon Championships, was runner-up to Navratilova at Wimbledon for the second straight year and succumbed to Austin one hurdle short of an unprecedented fifth consecutive U.S. Open title.

Connors, after being in the finals at Wimbledon four of the five previous years and the U.S. Open five straight times, fell in the semis of each and at the same stage in the WCT Finals and French Open as well. Moreover, Borg established indisputable superiority in their splendid, long-running rivalry, crushing Connors in straight sets in four meetings on four different surfaces: clay at Boca Raton, Fla., 6-2, 6-3; hard at Las Vegas, 6-3, 6-2; grass at Wimbledon, 6-2, 6-3, 6-2; indoors in Tokyo, 6-2, 6-2.

Connors did defend his titles in both the U.S. Pro Indoor at Philadelphia and the U.S. Indoor at Memphis. In both finals, 6-3, 6-4, 6-1, and 6-4, 5-7, 6-3, respectively, he beat Arthur Ashe, who had made an impressive comeback from heel surgery, but shockingly

suffered a mild heart attack at age 36 in August. The latter, the U.S. Indoor dating to 1898, is the only national prize to elude Arthur, won for the fifth time by Jimmy.

It was at Moody Coliseum in Dallas, at the end of the winter-spring men's indoor season, that McEnroe gave a convincing glimpse of great things ahead. Appearing in the WCT Finals for the first time, he beat Australian John Alexander, 6-4, 6-0, 6-2; Connors, 6-1, 6-4, 6-4; and, finally, Borg, 7-5, 4-6, 6-2, 7-6 (7-5). He won the $100,000 first prize with the kind of left-handed serve-and-volley attack—rich in variations of speed and spin, touch and improvisation—not seen since the salad days of Rod Laver.

Navratilova was the prevailing figure on the 12-week, $2.2-million Avon Championship Series, winning four of seven tournaments she played plus the showcase $275,000 finale at Madison Square Garden. In the climactic match, Martina clinched the $100,000 top prize by overcoming her own shaky backhand and Austin's persistent backcourt game, 6-3, 3-6, 6-2.

The most startling development of the Avon Championships, which climaxed a successful first year for the cosmetics firm as heir to Virginia Slims in sponsoring the women's indoor circuit, was the failure of Evert to get through the round-robin portion of the playoffs to the semifinal. Until 1979, Chrissie had never lost two matches in a row in her professional career. That astounding landmark of consistency was broken when Navratilova beat her in the final of an Avon tournament at Oakland, 7-5, 7-5, and young South African Greer Stevens beat her in the first round at Hollywood, Fla., 6-2, 6-3. In the playoffs at New York, Evert, her mind obviously more on her upcoming wedding than tennis, lost listlessly on successive nights to Austin, 6-3, 6-1, and Dianne Fromholtz, 6-2, 6-3.

Evert did regroup to win her last tournament before her April 17 nuptials, coming from behind to beat Fromholtz (conqueror of Navratilova), 3-6, 6-3, 6-1, for the $100,000 first prize in the four-woman Clairol Crown special event at Carlsbad, Calif.

After a two week honeymoon, Evert Lloyd teamed with Austin, Billie Jean King, and Rosie Casals to give the U.S. its fourth straight victory in the Federation Cup, on clay at Madrid. They beat Australia, 3-0: Austin over Kerry Melville Reid, 6-3, 6-0; Chrissie over Dianne Fromholtz, 2-6, 6-3, 8-6; B.J. and Rosie over Wendy Turnbull-Reid, 3-6, 6-3, 8-6.

Later in the year, an expanded U.S. squad also white-washed Great Britain, 7-0, in the Wightman Cup in Palm Beach, Fla., with a one-two punch of Evert Lloyd and Austin. Chrissie defeated Sue Barker 7-5, 6-2 and Virginia Wade 6-1, 6-1. Austin defeated Wade 6-1, 6-4, and Barker 6-4, 6-2.

This was the year the WTA embarked on a bold experiment of breaking away from joint events with the men in the leading championships of Europe and playing their own separate tournaments, except in Paris.

Attendance at the new women's-only events was generally disappointing. This was especially true in Rome, where the paid attendance was only about 5,000 for the week, despite the glorious semifinal in which Austin defeated Evert Lloyd, 6-4, 2-6, 7-6 (7-4). The three-point margin in overtime, May 12, marked the end of an illustrious dirt path that stretched almost six years. It was the first time Evert Lloyd had lost a match on a clay court since Aug. 12, 1973, when Evonne Goolagong beat her in the final

of the Western Championships at Cincinnati, a fantastic streak covering 25 tournaments and 125 matches. Only eight of those matches stretched to three sets. Evert Lloyd said she was more relieved than stunned when the streak finally ended. Austin was thrilled, and celebrated the next day by beating pudgy West German left-hander Sylvia Hanika—voted the most improved player of the year by the WTA—6-4, 1-6, 6-3 in the final.

It was a shame that the streak ended before such a sparse and seemingly uninterested audience, however. There were only about 1,500 spectators at Il Foro Italico, compared with a howling sell-out throng of more than 9,000 for the final of the men's Italian Open two weeks later. That was a glorious match, too. Vitas Gerulaitis, the insouciant New Yorker, defeated Guillermo Vilas, 6-7 (4-7), 7-6 (7-0), 6-7 (5-7), 6-4, 6-2, in an enthralling battle of wit and grit begun in the mid-afternoon sunshine and ended in the cool of the evening. In terms of playing time, this is thought to be the longest final ever in big tournament history: five hours, eight minutes. Title-holding Americans in Rome are rare. Vitas had his second in three years, and 14 years would pass before another Yank had two, Jim Courier in 1992-93.

Interest in the women's matches was also clearly secondary in the French Open at Stade Roland Garros, where the center court was enlarged to 17,000 seats as part of a major renovation targeted at producing a second "show" arena in 1980. Twelve of the tournament's 14 days were sold out, the French Open having become almost as much of an "in thing" in Paris as Wimbledon is in London. But only 10,000 spectators turned out on the final Saturday to view the women's singles final. In a terribly tedious match, Evert Lloyd ground down erring Wendy Turnbull, 6-2, 6-0. Chrissie, the champion of 1974 and 1975, lost only one set in regaining the title she had abdicated in order to play in World Team Tennis, the American intercity league which was gasping for breath at the end of 1978 and was pronounced officially dead early in 1979 (to be resurrected later).

The men's singles in Paris was expected to produce another duel between Borg and Connors. Jimmy entered the premier clay court championship for the first time since 1973, ending his personal boycott, a reaction to the tourney barring him in 1974 for his WTT affiliation. Instead, it was exciting primarily because of Victor Pecci, a 6-foot-3 Paraguayan with a diamond in his right ear, power in his serve and flamboyant groundies, who arrived ranked No. 30 in the world. Unseeded, he convincingly knocked off the sixth-third-second seeds in succession—1976 runner-up Harold Solomon, 6-1, 6-4, 6-3, 1977 champion Vilas, 6-0, 6-2, 7-5, and Connors, 7-5, 6-4, 5-7, 6-3. In the final, Pecci stirred a capacity crowd on a drizzly day by coming back from two sets and 2-5 down to push Borg before bowing, 6-3, 6-1, 6-7 (6-8), 6-4. Gene and Sandy Mayer won the men's doubles over Australians Ross Case and Phil Dent, 6-4, 6-4, 6-4, the first brothers to win a major since the U.S. champs of 1924, fellow Americans Bob and Howard Kinsey. Betty Stove and Wendy Turnbull won the women's doubles over Virginia Wade and Francoise Durr, 2-6, 7-5, 6-4.

McEnroe, who had missed Rome and Paris because of a pulled groin muscle, returned to action and won a Wimbledon tune-up tournament on grass at London's Queen's Club over Pecci, 6-7, 6-1, 6-1, and was simultaneously grilled in the British press for his surly

deportment. Dubbed "Superbrat," he dominated pre-Wimbledon publicity and was seeded No. 2 to Borg, largely because Connors did not reveal until after the draw was made whether he would play or remain at home with his expectant wife.

McEnroe, still bothered by the groin pull, was upset in the round of 16 by Tim Gullikson, 6-4, 6-2, 6-4, culminating a first week that was tumultuous for the men (10 of the 16 seeds were beaten in the first five days) and formful for the women. Most observers thought the semifinal between Borg and Connors, who had met in the previous two finals, would be the de facto title match, but Borg was in his most devastating form and annihilated his long-time arch rival, 6-2, 6-3, 6-2, in 1:46.

Left-hander Roscoe Tanner, seeded fifth, had been in the semifinal twice before, and this time came through the wreckage in the other half of the draw, past Gullikson, 6-1, 6-4, 6-7 (3-7), 6-2, and 6-foot-3 American Pat DuPre, 6-3, 7-6 (7-3), 6-3, to reach the final for the first time. Given little chance, Roscoe, the Stanford refugee with the low toss and high velocity serve, attacked at every opportunity. Playing thoughtfully and well, he pushed Borg to the limit in an absorbing final that kept 15,000 spectators and a live television audience in 28 countries spellbound for 2:29. This was the start of NBC's "Breakfast at Wimbledon" telecasts, the inaugural of live coverage in the U.S., Bud Collins and Donald Dell in the announcers' booth.

Half an hour after his 6-7 (4-7), 6-1, 3-6, 6-3, 6-4 win, which made him the first man since New Zealander Tony Wilding, 1910 – 13, to win the Wimbledon singles four years running, Borg said: "I feel much, much older than when I went on the court. Especially at the end of the match, I have never been so nervous in my whole life. I almost couldn't hold my racket."

Coupled with Navratilova's 6-4, 6-4 victory over Evert Lloyd in the women's final the previous day, Borg's victory marked the first time that both the men's and women's singles champions had successfully defended their titles since Bill Tilden and Suzanne Lenglen won in 1920 and 1921.

Navratilova was entitled to a first round bye, but chose instead to play a match in order to enjoy the champion's traditional honor of playing the opening female contest on Centre Court. She had good reason for making this decision: watching her from the competitors' guest box was her mother, whom she had not seen since defecting from Czechoslovakia during the 1975 U.S. Open. Jana Navratilova was granted a two-week tourist visa to visit her daughter in London with the personal approval of Czechoslovak Prime Minister Dr. Lubomir Strougal. "Winning here last year was the greatest moment of my career," a tearful Navratilova said after an unexpectedly tense 4-6, 6-2, 6-1 victory over qualifier Tanya Harford, "but yesterday [the airport reunion with her mother] was one of the greatest moments of my life."

Fighting a cold, Navratilova struggled into the semifinal, losing sets to Stevens, 7-6 (8-6), 6-7, 6-3 and Fromholtz, 2-6, 6-3, 6-0. But there was no stopping her in the stretch, a 7-5, 6-1, victory over Austin and then Evert Lloyd. Her stepfather, Mirek, and 16-year-old sister, Jana, who were not granted visas, watched the match live on West German television in the border town of Pilsen, as they had the year before. But this time, instead of ignoring the expatriate's victory, the government-controlled Czech media gave it prominent attention in newspapers and on television.

Navratilova had another thrill in partnering King to the women's doubles title, 5-7, 6-3, 6-2, over Turnbull and Stove. This was King's record 20th Wimbledon title, a 10th doubles to go with six singles and four mixed in the world's most prestigious tournament.

But the occasion was saddened by the death the previous day of 87-year-old Elizabeth "Bunny" Ryan, with whom King had shared the record since 1975. Miss Ryan, a native Californian who lived in London, was stricken with a heart attack while watching the women's singles final, collapsed in a ladies room at the All England Club and died on the way to a hospital. Winner of 12 doubles and seven mixed doubles titles between 1914 and 1934, but never the singles, Ryan had told friends of a premonition that this would be the year King broke her cherished record. She dreaded the moment, but, happily, never saw it. She died less than 24 hours before being erased from the record book.

Back in the United States, Connors won the U.S. Clay Court singles for the fourth time, beating Vilas in the final, 6-1, 2-6, 6-4. Evert Lloyd—returning after a three year absence—won her fifth Clay title, this over Goolagong, 6-4, 6-3, extending her personal winning streak in the tournament to 26 straight matches.

The U.S. Open was played for the second time at New York's USTA National Tennis Center in Flushing. Amid the cacophony of planes roaring overhead and spectators moving about during play, the youngsters came to the fore. McEnroe's toughest battle came in the second round against Ilie Nastase, no longer the exquisite shot-maker he'd been, but still a tempestuous personality. McEnroe won, 6-4, 4-6, 6-3, 6-2, in a stormy match that could be completed only with great difficulty after the raucous pro-Nastase crowd of 10,000—many of them heavily into their cups at a session that ran past midnight—became a negative influence.

Veteran umpire Frank Hammond, growing flustered, had already hit Nastase earlier in the match with a warning, presently a point penalty for conspicuous stalling. When Hammond justifiably awarded McEnroe a penalty game, raising his lead to 3-1 in the fourth, the customers reacted furiously, showering the court with beer cans and other refuse in protest. Nastase's refusal to play brought referee Mike Blanchard onto the court. Amid the clamor, he appealed for a restoration of order, and urged the players to resume. But the noise worsened. As Nastase refused to comply, Blanchard instructed Hammond to "put the clock on him." Hammond had no choice but to invoke correctly the fourth step in the penalty route: default.

That nearly brought the house down. Tourney director Bill Talbert, fearful of a riot, reinstated Nastase and removed Hammond from the chair, replacing him with Blanchard. With that tarnished bone thrown to the assemblage, the second-round match was completed in four more games.

McEnroe was at home on the asphalt-based courts less than 15 minutes from his front door in Douglastown, N.Y., though never a favorite with the home crowds because of his incessant pouting and grousing. He won two matches in walk-overs (default), including his quarterfinal over injured Eddie Dibbs, but stayed

sharp playing doubles. In the semis, he routed Connors, who was inhibited by back spasms, 6-3, 6-3, 7-5. He won the final with similar ease over Long Island neighbor Gerulaitis, 7-5, 6-3, 6-3.

Gerulaitis had made a magnificent comeback from two sets and a service break down in the semis to beat Tanner, 3-6, 2-6, 7-6 (7-5), 6-3, 6-3. Tanner had served magnificently in upsetting the top-seeded Borg in the quarterfinals, 6-2, 4-6, 6-2, 7-6 (7-2). Borg hated playing at night, especially against a big server like Tanner, and was thus foiled for the second straight year in his attempt to nail down the third leg of a possible French-Wimbledon-U.S.-Australian Grand Slam. Bjorn may have seen the handwriting on the net during the chilly evening. One of Roscoe's missiles had snapped the net cord, and the Swede, looking very unhappy, had to cool his sneakered heels for 15 minutes, waiting for a replacement to be installed.

In the women's singles, seven of the top eight seeds reached the quarters, but third-seeded Austin stopped second-seeded Navratilova in the semis, 7-5, 7-5, and Evert Lloyd in the final, 6-4, 6-3. At 16-years, nine months, the cool Californian became the youngest U.S. champion ever, three days younger than May Sutton in 1904 and two months younger than Maureen Connolly in 1951. Austin, who had beaten Kathy Jordan, 4-6, 6-1, 7-6 (7-5), and Andrea Jaeger, 6-2, 6-2, respectively in the first two rounds, showed a deft finishing touch in out-steadying Evert Lloyd in 1:33. Chrissie had demolished King in the semifinal in a 13-game rush, 6-1, 6-0, probably 35-year-old Billie Jean's most painful afternoon in New York.

"I thought the title might intimidate Tracy," said Evert Lloyd, who until a 4-6, 6-0, 6-2 victory over Sherry Acker in the fourth round had not lost a set in the U.S. Open since the 1975 final and took a 31-match Open streak into the final. "But Tracy was out there like it was just another tennis match."

McEnroe and Fleming won the men's doubles over Stan Smith and Bob Lutz, 6-2, 6-4. The sentimental story, however, was the reunion of Australians Roy Emerson, 42, and Fred Stolle, 40, who had last played together in the U.S. Doubles Championships when it was held in Boston. They were the champions of 1965 and 1966, and added four more victories to reach 15 in a row before Smith and Lutz toppled them in the semis, 7-5, 3-6, 7-5. Stove-Turnbull reversed the result of the Wimbledon final, beating King-Navratilova for the women's title, 7-5, 6-3, while Stevens and Bob Hewitt repeated their Wimbledon victory over Stove and Frew McMillan in the mixed final, 6-3, 7-5.

In the Davis Cup final against Italy, McEnroe and Gerulaitis asserted themselves fast: Mac over Adriano Panatta, 6-2, 6-3, 6-4, Vitas over Corrado Barazzutti, who had to quit with a leg injury, 6-3, 3-2. It was a 5-0 blitz for the U.S., a totally straight-set affair in 14 sets. McEnroe was 8-0 in singles for the campaign (plus 1-0 in doubles). Smith and Lutz, with a 6-4, 12-10, 6-2 decision over Panatta and Paolo Bertolucci, registered their fourth (1968-69-70, '79) Cup-clinching performance, a record eclipsing the 1904-05-06 wins of the British Doherty brothers, Laurie and Reggie. Smith also set an individual Cup-clinching record of six, having also won the decisive singles in 1971 and 1972. Staged at San Francisco's Civic Auditorium, it was the first final won indoors by the United States. McEnroe was nearing the end of an Open-era season record for dual labor and production: 27 titles overall,

surpassing Nastase's 23 (15 singles, eight doubles) in 1973. Mac won 10 of 22 singles tournaments on 91-13 in matches, 17 of 21 doubles on 84-5.

1979 CHAMPIONS AND LEADERS

Australian Open
Men's Singles Final: Guillermo Vilas (ARG) def. John Sadri (USA), 7-6 (4), 6-3, 6-2
Women's Singles Final: Barbara Jordan (USA) def. Sharon Walsh (USA), 6-3, 6-3
Men's Doubles Final: Peter McNamara and Paul McNamee (AUS) def. Paul Kronk and Cliff Letcher (AUS), 7-6, 6-2
Women's Doubles Final: Judy Chaloner (NZL) and Dianne Evers (AUS) def. Leanne Harrison (AUS) and Marcella Mesker (NED), 6-1, 3-6, 6-0
Mixed Doubles: Not Played

French Open
Men's Singles Final: Bjorn Borg (SWE) def. Victor Pecci (PAR), 6-3, 6-1, 6-7 (6), 6-4
Women's Singles: Chris Evert Lloyd (USA) def. Wendy Turnbull (AUS), 6-2, 6-0
Men's Doubles: Gene Mayer and Alex Mayer (USA) def. Ross Case and Phil Dent (AUS), 6-4, 6-4, 6-4
Women's Doubles: Betty Stove (NED) and Wendy Turnbull (AUS) def. Francoise Durr (FRA) and Virginia Wade (GBR), 3-6, 7-5, 6-4
Mixed Doubles Final: Wendy Turnbull (AUS) and Bob Hewitt (RSA) def. Virginia Ruzici and Ion Tiriac (ROM), 6-3, 2-6, 6-3

Wimbledon
Men's Singles Final: Bjorn Borg (SWE) def. Roscoe Tanner (USA), 6-7 (4), 6-1, 3-6, 6-3, 6-4
Women's Singles Final: Martina Navratilova (CZE) def. Chris Evert Lloyd (USA), 6-4, 6-4
Men's Doubles Final: Peter Fleming and John McEnroe (USA) def. Brian Gottfried (USA) and Raul Ramirez (MEX), 4-6, 6-4, 6-2, 6-3
Women's Doubles Final: Billie Jean King (USA) and Martina Navratilova (CZE) def. Betty Stove and Wendy Turnbull (AUS), 5-7, 6-3, 6-2
Mixed Doubles Final: Greer Stevens and Bob Hewitt (RSA) def. Betty Stove (NED) and Frew McMillan (RSA), 7-5, 76- (7)

U.S. Open
Men's Singles Final: John McEnroe (USA) def. Vitas Gerulaitis (USA), 7-5, 6-3, 6-3
Women's Singles Final: Tracy Austin (USA) def. Chris Evert Lloyd (USA), 6-4, 6-3
Men's Doubles Final: John McEnroe and Peter Fleming (USA) def. Bob Lutz and Stan Smith (USA), 6-2, 6-4
Women's Doubles Final: Betty Stove (NED) and Wendy Turnbull (AUS) def. Billie Jean King (USA) and Martina Navratilova (CZE), 7-5, 6-3
Mixed Doubles Final: Greer Stevens and Bob Hewitt (RSA) def. Betty Stove (NED) and Frew McMillan (RSA), 6-3, 7-5

Year-End No. 1
Men: Bjorn Borg
Women: Martina Navratilova

Top Player Earnings
Men: Bjom Borg $1,008,742
Women: Martina Navratilova $618,698

Davis Cup: United States

Federation Cup: United States

Wightman Cup: United States

Grand Prix Masters, NYC—Bjom Borg
WCT, Dallas—John McEnroe
Avon Championships, NYC—Martina Navratilova

1980 Borg vs. McEnroe— A Match for the Ages

Bjorn Borg fended off John McEnroe to hoist the Wimbledon trophy over his head for a fifth-consecutive year.

For such a moment is the grass maintained with tender loving care. For such a moment are the vines trimmed and the roses tended. For such a moment are the stands of the All England Lawn Tennis & Croquet Club retouched every year in a somber shade of green. The moment is everything. It is at the root of all this, beneath the ivy and the proper manners and even the hallowed lawns. Scratch deep enough at Wimbledon and a hundred matches of high drama rise from the earth. They are the foundation of the most significant tennis tournament in the world, the source of the tradition that sets the event apart from all others.

Wimbledon exists for Borg vs. McEnroe, Centre Court, July 5, 1980. The defending champion reeling. His opponent seeking to score the most memorable of upsets. And a huge crowd engrossed in great theatre.

That's Wimbledon at its best, the most marvelous of backdrops for a haunting match, perhaps the most gripping in the history of what club officials call simply The Championships. Bjorn Borg sur-

vived the loss of seven match points in the fourth set of the men's final, and, finally, the set itself. Then he survived the loss of seven break points in the deciding set before defeating John McEnroe, 1-6, 7-5, 6-3, 6-7 (16-18), 8-6, in a three hour-53 minute epic.

At the instant he fell to his knees in that signature ritual of triumph, the man was at the top of his game and at the peak of a career that challenged history for an equal. It marked his fifth consecutive Wimbledon title, following on the heels of a fifth French Open championship, all achieved at the tender age of 24. He would close out the year by winning the concluding Masters for a second successive year and stand unchallenged as the leading figure in the sport.

But even in his most satisfying season, there were intimations that Borg's grip on tennis was loosening. He had won his last 13 five-set matches when he looked across the net at McEnroe at the start of yet another life-and-death encounter in the final of the U.S. Open. This time he couldn't summon the will to outlast the covetous American on his hard home terrain.

McEnroe's 7-6 (7-4), 6-1, 6-7 (5-7), 5-7, 6-4 victory, a second consecutive U.S. title, canceled plans for a tennis migration to Australia for what would have been the concluding act of a quest for a men's Grand Slam, last achieved by Rod Laver in 1969. Without that added incentive, Borg and most of his major adversaries bypassed the Christmas season in Melbourne, leaving the Australian Open to lesser mortals. American Brian Teacher, No. 12 and seeded No. 8, won the men's title by defeating Aussie Kim Warwick, 7-5, 7-6 (7-4), 6-3. Warwick, ranked No. 22 and seeded No. 14, was a shocker, cutting off Guillermo Vilas's run of two titles and 16 matches in the semifinals, 6-7, 6-4, 6-2, 2-6, 6-4.

Eighteen-year-old Czech Hana Mandlikova, a daring volleyer, seized the first of her three majors, the Australian, with a swift start, 6-0, 7-5, over Queenslander Wendy Turnbull. A 6-4, 7-5, decision over Martina Navratilova followed her toughest match 6-1, 3-6, 6-4 over Virginia Ruzici in the quarters.

Although overshadowed by the duel of titans on the male side, Chris Evert Lloyd starred in a drama of her own making by dominating the spotlight on the women's tour. Suffering from fatigue, burnout or mid-life crisis—take your pick—she emerged from a three-month sabbatical to capture clay titles at Rome and Paris, reach the final of a Wimbledon which belonged, unexpect-

edly, to a blithe spirit from the past, Evonne Goolagong Cawley, and reclaim her U.S. Open birthright by overcoming, among others, Tracy Austin, her most recent nemesis.

Austin failed to add a major title to her collection, yet she won a dozen others—including the Avon Championships and the Colgate Series Championships—and banked more than $600,000 in prize money. Not bad for a high school student.

Also fast-rising, precocious Andrea Jaeger, 15, was in a quarterfinal at Wimbledon and a semifinal at the U.S. Open. Navratilova, suddenly caught in a time warp, had no majors to call her own. She compensated by leading all women in prize money with earnings of $749,250.

Still, it was the men who held the attention of the world, particularly in those instances when Borg and McEnroe shared a major stage. If the Swede added to his legend on the English grass, then the Yank confirmed his mettle by holding his ground on American asphalt. Their two matches formed an exquisite set of mantel pieces that bracketed the summer of 1980.

As the Wimbledon Championships got underway, Borg was in a class of his own. He had ripped with ease through a field at the French Open that featured 17 of the top 20 players in the world. The man dropped no sets and never more than the seven games he yielded to Vitas Gerulaitis in his 6-4, 6-1, 6-2, grasp of the final. With that victory, he became the only man to win the tournament three years in a row and five times in all.

"For most of us, Paris is a great tournament because of the city, the food, the Continental experience," said Victor Amaya, who won the doubles in the company of Hank Pfister, over Brian Gottfried and Raul Ramirez, 1-6, 6-4, 6-4, 6-3. "But some people don't realize this is the Borg Invitational. They think they can actually win the thing. What a joke!"

At Wimbledon, the Swede was busy establishing the Borg Invitational II. Unlike his experience in previous years, he needed no escape hatches in advancing to the final, losing only two sets along the way. Centre Court belonged to him as it did to no other. Only McEnroe, jeered at the start of the tournament for intemperate outbursts, stood between Borg and a measure of immortality. Earlier in the week, when he was questioned about his motivation after having won so easily, the Swede said he would like the final "to be 12-10 in the fifth, but only if I know I win." McEnroe came perilously close to meeting that challenge, so much so that Borg actually doubted he would win.

It was in the 34-point fourth set tie-breaker that a battle for the ages was joined. At 5-4, Borg had only to serve it out for his 35th consecutive triumph on Wimbledon grass. He promptly rolled to a 40-15 advantage, double match point. But McEnroe saved both points and then broke service. At 6-6, the combatants began a tie-breaker that lasted 22 minutes. It featured five championship points for Borg, seven set points for his opponent. Finally, on the 34th point, with the crowd exhausted from the emotion of the moment, the champion failed to execute a difficult drop volley and the match was tied at two sets apiece.

"I thought mentally he'd get down after that," McEnroe said. "It would've gotten me a little down, but it didn't seem to get to him. He's won it four times. You'd think he might let down and say forget it."

Indeed, Borg did admit to being discouraged at the start of the fifth set. "When I lost those match points, I couldn't believe it," the man conceded. "I was thinking then maybe I will end up losing the match. It is a terrible feeling."

The disappointment lasted two points into the fifth set. Borg fell behind 0-30 on his serve, then dipped deeply into his vast reserve of spirit. He won the next four points to take a 1-0 edge. From that instant, McEnroe was waging an uphill fight.

Borg would serve 25 more times in the match and win 24 points. He gained his break in the 14th game when, at 15-15, the Swede won the last three points with a return down the line, a volley McEnroe couldn't retrieve and a backhand passing shot. Then he fell to his knees in supplication, as ever, and added an impromptu collapse on the well-worn grass.

"At this rate," McEnroe said, "I don't know when he's ever going to lose here. He hits harder than when I first saw him. He volleys better."

And it was not out of the question then to consider him in the context of Tilden, Budge, Laver. Not with 10 major championships, not with the U.S. Open and a Grand Slam within his sights. "I want to be remembered as the greatest ever," Borg said.

In the afterglow of that triumph, Borg took a bride, the fair Mariana Simionescu, a Romanian player of modest accomplishment. His warm-up for the U.S. Open was jeopardized by a knee injury that caused him to retire in the midst of the Canadian Open final against an ascending star, 20-year-old Ivan Lendl of Czechoslovakia (while ahead, 6-4, 4-5). Earlier in the same tournament, McEnroe twisted an ankle and, ahead 4-3, defaulted to Erik van Dillen in the second round, then was beaten in the first round at Atlanta the following week by John Austin (Tracy's brother), 7-6, 6-4.

Despite hysterical headlines suggesting that neither man might be able to walk—let alone run—on the court at Louis Armstrong Stadium, there was no stopping the two from an appointment in the U.S. Open finale. Their journeys, however, were not without obstacles.

Borg survived a quarterfinal scare, 6-4, 4-6, 3-6, 7-5, 6-3, from Roscoe Tanner, who'd eliminated Borg in the quarterfinals the previous year, and then yielded the first two sets to unseeded Johan Kriek in the semifinal before overwhelming the expatriate South African, 4-6, 4-6, 6-1, 6-1, 6-1. Kriek became the fifth player to take the first two sets of a best-of-five match against Borg and the fifth player to fail to put away the Swede.

Meanwhile, McEnroe had some shaky moments against Lendl in the quarters before rallying for a 4-6, 6-3, 6-2, 7-5 victory. Next up was an amazing semifinal against three time champion Jimmy Connors that stretched 4:17 as the mutual vitriol flowed. Connors took a 2-1 lead in sets but McEnroe rallied to win the fourth and served for the match at 5-4 in the fifth, only to be broken. Mac finally prevailed in a tie-breaker, 6-4, 5-7, 0-6, 6-3, 7-6 (7-3). Not the ideal preparation for a final against Borg set to start less than 24 hours later.

This was the pairing everyone hoped to see, even McEnroe. "I just want to win the tournament," the defender said on the first day of the two week event, "but if I knew beforehand that I'd win, I'd rather play Borg in the final. Say 22-20 in the fifth set." When a man noted they play fifth-set tie-breakers at the

Open, Mac altered the score. "Okay," he said, "make it 7-0 in the tie-breaker."

As it developed, a decisive tie-breaker wasn't necessary. But that was about all the match lacked. Such was the pressure in what became a battle of survival that McEnroe felt like wilting after Borg squared the score at two sets apiece. "When I lost the fourth set," the 21-year-old American said, "I thought my body was going to fall off."

Neither man played with the artistry that marked the historic match at Wimbledon two months earlier. The record Open crowd of 21,072 appeared not to notice. If it wasn't a classic, it still left people breathless with excitement. McEnroe jousted with the umpires and with a linesman. He slammed a racket against his chair and at one stage he felt so strongly about his game that he handed his weapon to Jack Kramer, seated in a courtside box. Borg served with all the assurance of a waiter in an earthquake. He was reported missing in action during the second set. He kicked one ball over the net after breaking his racket on a serve and it was his best-looking shot in several games.

"I was trying my best," he said, "but I was not playing well. I had no feel for the ball."

And yet somehow the two staggered into an excruciatingly dramatic final scene, stumbling into a cliff-hanger finish. The tension was suffocating. The fatal break occurred in the seventh game of the fifth set after Borg had committed two of his nine uncharacteristic double faults. McEnroe laid claim to the title with a sharp volley at 40-15 of the 10th game, four hours, 13 minutes after the initial serve. He became the first repeat champion since Australian Neale Fraser in 1959-60 and the first Yank to win national honors in consecutive years since Pancho Gonzalez in 1948-49.

The pair met only twice more during the 1980 season, Borg triumphing, 6-3, 6-4, at the Stockholm Open in November and in three tight sets, 6-4, 6-7 (3-7), 7-6 (7-2), in the preliminary round of the Masters.

McEnroe enjoyed a superb year, leading the men in earnings ($972,369) and tournament victories (10). Despite his losses to Borg at Wimbledon and to Connors, 2-6, 7-6, 6-1, 6-2, in the WCT Finals before 16,181 at the brand new Reunion Arena in Dallas, he was a legitimate candidate for the top spot in the world when the leading players converged on Madison Square Garden for the Masters. There, he inexplicably lost all three round-robin matches, to Gene Mayer, 3-6, 7-6, 6-2, Jose-Luis Clerc, 6-3, 6-0 and Borg, 6-4, 6-7, 7-6. Bjorn beat Connors in the semis, 6-4, 6-7 (4-7), 6-3, and Lendl beat Mayer, 6-3, 6-4. The title went to Bjorn, 6-4, 6-2, 6-2, along with the $100,000 top prize and the clear designation as No. 1.

Lendl, who scored a season-high 113 victories in a grueling 142 tournament matches, had his greatest satisfaction in team competition, leading Czechoslovakia to a 4-1 victory over Italy in Prague for its first Davis Cup. Ivan was unbeaten (7-0 in singles, 3-0 in doubles), but it was Tomas Smid who sent the home team off to a bright start by bringing down favored Adriano Panatta, 3-6, 3-6, 6-3, 6-4, 6-4, before a howling crowd. Lendl followed, 4-6, 6-1, 6-1, 6-2, over Corrado Barazzutti, and he and Smid persisted to settle it over Panatta and Paolo Bertolucci, 3-6, 6-3, 3-6, 6-3, 6-4.

The Czechoslovaks took a 3-2 semifinal over Argentina at Buenos Aires with Lendl beating Vilas and Clerc. Italy struggled,

too, 3-2, over Australia at Rome. Panatta pulled them through by beating Paul McNamee, 5-7, 6-4, 6-0, 6-4 and Peter McNamara, 6-1, 7-5, 6-4 in the clincher after a crowd-wowing doubles win with Bertolucci over the Macs, 2-6, 9-7, 9-7, 2-6, 6-4. But Prague was the end of the contending line for the Panatta-backboned Italians. The 1976 victors were appearing in their fourth final in five years, but would not place so high again until 1998.

Argentine soil and solid Vilas and Clerc took the Yanks out fast in an earlier American zonal tie, 4-1 with Clerc defeating McEnroe 6-3, 6-2, 4-6, 14-12, Vilas over Brian Gottfried, 7-5, 6-4, 6-3. In the doubles, Peter Fleming and McEnroe defeated Ricardo Cano and Carlos Gattiker, 6-0, 6-1, 6-4. Vilas clinched over McEnroe, 6-2, 4-6, 6-3, 2-6, 6-4.

Comebacks marked women's play, the most remarkable being Goolagong's at Wimbledon. Her previous victory on the lawns had occurred nine years earlier as an ethereal teenager. "I just happened to win," she recalled. "I didn't think much of it at the time."

And the thought remained buried as she went on to lose her next seven appearances in a Wimbledon or U.S. final. But neither age, nor her marriage to Roger Cawley and motherhood had dimmed the luster of her strokes and the effortless grace of her movement. She rose to the occasion one last time at 28. Her career had been interrupted several times by injuries and illness but 1980 had been particularly trying. Before she returned to action in June, she hadn't hit a ball for seven weeks. Goolagong, fourth seeded, played herself into shape at Wimbledon. She was down a set to Betty Stove in the third round (winning 3-6, 6-2, 6-3), and trailed Mandlikova by a set and a break in the fourth round (6-7 (6-8), 6-3, 6-1). That experience served her well in the semifinal when she faced Austin, who had won 35 of her previous 36 matches. Despite the loss of seven consecutive games, Goolagong rebounded to nip the young American, 6-3, 0-6, 6-4. (Tracy didn't leave empty-handed. She shared the mixed-doubles title with older brother John, becoming the first sister-brother team to win a major.)

Goolagong then upset Evert Lloyd in the final, 6-1, 7-6 (7-4), the first time in the tournament's history that a singles championship was been decided by a tiebreaker. Goolagong became the third mother to claim a Wimbledon singles title since Dorothea Douglass Chambers in 1914, and compatriot Margaret Smith Court in 1973. Evert Lloyd had interrupted top-seeded Navratilova's championship progress at two titles and 19 matches in the semifinal, 4-6, 6-4, 6-2. Martina had beaten 36-year-old Billie Jean King in a quarters epic, 7-6 (8-6), 1-6, 10-8, needing nine match points to win a dramatic two-part struggle that began on a cold (48 degree) afternoon, was halted by rain after one set, and concluded the next day.

That Wimbledon defeat represented one of the few setbacks suffered by Evert Lloyd after her return to competitive tennis in time for the European clay circuit.

After being beaten by Austin in the opener of the Avon series at Cincinnati, 6-2, 6-1, and losing to Navratilova at Chicago, 6-4, 6-4, Evert Lloyd had departed the tour in Seattle for what she later called a "leave of absence." Apparently refreshed, she returned and seized her third Italian title in Rome over Ruzici, 5-7, 6-2, 6-2, and then, in the absence of Austin, Navratilova and Goolagong, won

her fourth French championship, thrashing 1978 champ Ruzici, 6-0, 6-3, in the final. Evert Lloyd increased her winning streak to 25 matches before losing at Wimbledon to Goolagong.

Chrissie stepped up the pace back in the States, winning a U.S. Clay Court title for the sixth time, defeating Andrea Jaeger, 6-4, 6-3 (tying Nancy Richey's record) and taking a second Canadian title (a championship her father, Jimmy Evert, had won in 1947), over Ruzici, 6-3, 6-1. Evert Lloyd was primed to regain her U.S. Open crown and to defeat Austin, the clone who had whipped her five consecutive times. She got her opportunity in the semifinal round.

On the eve of the match, she described herself as a nervous wreck. She told her husband, "I've never wanted a match more." It showed at the start, when she dropped the first four games and the set, 6-4. But the slimmed-down, quicker, hungrier version of the former champion emerged in magnificent fashion thereafter. Forcing Austin into 54 errors in the match, she swept into the final by winning the last two sets convincingly, 6-1, 6-1.

What she called her "most emotional victory" preceded her most satisfying moment of the year. Evert Lloyd had invited her father, her first tennis teacher, from Florida to witness the semifinal. Papa, preferring to stay far in the background and not engage his nervous system, had never seen his daughter win a major championship in person. So Evert Lloyd's 5-7, 6-1, 6-1 conquest of 18-year-old Hana Mandlikova - rock-ribbed defense beat daring offense —represented a first of sorts even as it reestablished an old pattern. The ninth-seeded Czech had upset her idol, second-seeded Navratilova in a fourth round volleying showdown, 7-6 (7-2), 6-4, and overcame 15-year-old Jaeger in a battle of prodigies, 6-1, 3-6, 7-6 (7-4), in the semifinal. Mandlikova began strongly against Evert Lloyd, but Hana didn't have the concentration or will to withstand the relentless American. After claiming her fifth Open championship, Evert Lloyd had a 53-5 match record in the tournament.

Nor did she stop there. A month later, she annexed her 100th professional tournament singles title at Deerfield Beach, Fla., over Jaeger, 6-4, 6-1.

Evert Lloyd also enjoyed remarkable success in team play. In the Federation Cup, she (5-0) and teammates won all 15 matches, including a sweep of Australia in the championship round at West Berlin where she beat Diane Fromholtz, 4-6, 6-1, 6-1, and Austin defeated Turnbull, 6-2, 6-3. Captain Chrissie concluded a remarkable campaign by leading the U.S. over Britain, 5-2, in the Wightman Cup. She won both singles, over Sue Barker, 6-1, 6-2, and Virginia Wade, in the deciding match, 7-5, 3-6, 7-5. Chrissie teamed with Rosie Casals to win her doubles match over Anne Hobbs and Glynis Coles, 6-3, 6-3. It was Evert Lloyd's 23rd overall victory in Wightman play, surpassing Louise Brough's record.

Another Brough standard, one she shared with Nancy Richey—most years in the U.S. top ten, 16—was eclipsed by King, celebrating her 17th year among the elite with a finish at No. 5. Billie Jean, who turned 37 in November, won three singles and 11 doubles titles, including the U.S. Open in partnership with Navratilova, over Pam Shriver and Stove, 7-6 (7-2), 7-5. It was B.J.'s 39th—and last—major title, second then only to Margaret Smith Court's 62. But it was Navratilova's ninth, and she was on her way

to eclipsing King, getting her 59th remarkably in 2006, the U.S. mixed with fellow American Bob Bryan.

1980 CHAMPIONS AND LEADERS

Australian Open
Men's Singles Final: Brian Teacher (USA) def. Kim Warwick (AUS), 7-5, 7-6 (4), 6-3

Women's Singles Final: Hana Mandlikova (CZE) def. Wendy Turnbull (AUS), 6-0, 7-5

Men's Doubles Final: Mark Edmondson and Kim Warwick (AUS) def. Paul McNamee and Peter McNamara (AUS), 7-5, 6-4

Women's Doubles Final: Martina Navratilova (CZE) and Betsy Nagelsen (USA) def. Ann Kiyomura and Candy Reynolds (USA), 6-4, 6-4

Mixed Doubles: Not Played

French Open
Men's Singles Final: Bjorn Borg (SWE) def. Vitas Gerulaitis (USA), 6-4, 6-1, 6-2

Women's Singles Final: Chris Evert Lloyd (USA) def. Virginia Ruzici (ROM), 6-0, 6-3

Men's Doubles Final: Victor Amaya and Hank Pfister (USA) def. Brian Gottfried (USA) and Raul Ramirez (MEX), 1-6, 6-4, 6-4, 6-3

Women's Doubles Final: Kathy Jordan and Anne Smith (USA) def. Ivana Madruga and Adriana Villagran (ARG), 6-1, 6-0

Mixed Doubles Final: Anne Smith and Billy Martin (USA) def. Renata Tomanova and Stanislav Birner (CZE), 2-6, 6-4, 8-6

Wimbledon
Men's Singles Final: Bjorn Borg (SWE) def. John McEnroe (USA), 1-6, 7-5, 6-3, 6-7 (16-18), 8-6

Women's Singles Final: Evonne Goolagong Cawley (AUS) def. Chris Evert Lloyd (USA), 6-1, 7-6 (4)

Men's Doubles Final: Peter McNamara and Paul McNamee (AUS) def. Bob Lutz and Stand Smith (USA), 7-6 (5), 6-3, 6-7 (4), 6-4

Women's Doubles Final: Kathy Jordan and Anne Smith (USA) def. Rosie Casals (USA) and Wendy Turnbull (AUS), 4-6, 7-5, 6-1

Mixed Doubles Final: Tracy Austin and John Austin (USA) def. Dianne Fromholtz and Mark Edmondson (AUS), 4-6, 7-6 (6), 6-3

U.S. Open
Men's Singles Final: John McEnroe (USA) def. Bjorn Borg (SWE), 7-6 (4), 6-1, 6-7 (5), 5-7, 6-4

Women's Singles Final: Chris Evert (USA) def. Hana Mandlikova (CZE), 5-7, 6-1, 6-1

Men's Doubles Final: Bob Lutz and Stan Smith (USA) def. Peter Fleming and John McEnroe (USA), 7-5, 3-6, 6-1, 3-6, 6-3

Women's Doubles Final: Billie Jean King (USA) and Martina Navratilova (CZE) def. Pam Shriver (USA) and Betty Stove (NED), 7-6 (2), 7-5

Mixed Doubles Final: Wendy Turnbull (AUS) and Marty Riessen (USA) def. Betty Stove (NED) and Frew McMillan (RSA), 7-5, 6-2

Year-End No. 1
Men: Bjorn Borg
Women: Chris Evert Lloyd

Top Player Earnings
Men: John McEnroe $972,369
Women: Martina Navratilova $749,250

Davis Cup: Czechoslovakia

Federation Cup: United States

Wightman Cup: United States

Grand Prix Masters, NYC–Bjorn Borg
WCT, Dallas–Jimmy Connors
Avon Championships, NYC–Tracy Austin

1981 Last Major for Borg, Mac Reaches No. 1

Wimbledon and the 100th anniversary U.S. Championships. It represented a stunning development in the wake of the Swede's victory at Paris, his sixth French Open title and his 11th major, tying Rod Laver, one behind record-holder Roy Emerson. There would be no others. At 25, the man decided to remove his headband and let down his hair after a decade of single-minded devotion.

He may have been suffering from burnout or come to the realization that he was never going to achieve a U.S. title, let alone the Grand Slam that seemed so close and yet so far. Clearly, the brash McEnroe, three years his junior, had gained sufficient composure and mental toughness to suggest he wasn't going to be easily dislodged.

At Wimbledon, the American had battled with linesmen, umpires, tournament officials and the tabloid press and still exhibited the poise to deprive Borg of a sixth successive title on his own personal lawn. Two months later, McEnroe completed his coup on the hard courts at Flushing Meadow. The defeat was the Swede's fourth in a U.S. Open final, and marked him as the most accomplished player never to claim the U.S. championship: Zero for 10 years.

In a land rich in ceremony, men's tennis staged a changing of the guard. Not only did John McEnroe topple Bjorn Borg from his Wimbledon throne in 1981, he replaced Borg as the ruler of his sport. By year's end, the former monarch relinquished all claims to the territories he once commanded.

Borg's decision to reduce his schedule was so drastic that it resulted in virtual retirement from competitive tennis following humbling four-set losses to McEnroe in the final of both the

There was no such seismographic activity in the women's ranks. Each of the four major titles was claimed by a different player. Hana Mandlikova won her second major, the French Open, Chris Evert Lloyd excelled at Wimbledon for the third time, Tracy Austin added a second U.S. Open and Martina Navratilova triumphed over a complete women's field in Australia. Chrissie's nine titles, raising her career total to 110, maintained her as world No. 1.

Yet, there wasn't much doubt that Navratilova enjoyed the finest year of the four, and not only for the quality of her tennis. She won 10 tournaments playing singles, a circuit best, and she also combined with Pam Shriver to claim 11 doubles titles, including Wimbledon. Additionally, she was granted U.S. citizenship in midsummer and then, with tears in her eyes, bathed in the sustained applause of the crowd at the USTA National Tennis Center, her National Tennis Center, following a loss to Austin in a brilliant Open final.

If Borg cried following his loss to McEnroe the following day, it was on the inside. For the first time in memory, the well-mannered Swede ignored the protocol of the trophy presentation, spoke not a word to the fans or the press assembled at Flushing Meadow and left the grounds in a huff or, as one timekeeper noted, a minute and a huff. The previous day, while blasting Jimmy Connors in a men's semifinal, he had reportedly been the subject of a telephoned death threat. But for the man who had purchased a luxurious house on Long Island for the express purpose of establishing a home-court advantage at the previously inhospitable playground, it seemed the disappointment of the moment simply overwhelmed him.

That it would be the final picture of Borg at a championship event was perhaps the crudest twist of fate in a season that had started with such promise at Paris, his 6-1, 4-6, 6-2, 3-6, 6-1 French Open triumph over Ivan Lendl. At the time, it appeared inevitable that the Swede would establish a standard of his own for men's tennis, perhaps before the year was out.

His performance in the French temporarily silenced questions about the man's future. Borg had reported to Paris following an absence from competition of nearly two months, the result of a tender right shoulder. He had played in only three tournaments since January, failing to advance past the second round in two of them, and even he was uncertain of his form.

Still, two weeks of serious practice had left him fit. "I feel strong," he said. "I can be out on the court for a long time if I have to." It wasn't necessary, at least not until the final. The man mowed down his half of the draw until he came to Lendl, who had beaten McEnroe in the quarterfinal, 6-4, 6-4, 7-5, and overcome Italian Open champ, Jose-Luis Clerc, in five sets in the semis, 3-6, 6-4, 4-6, 7-6, 6-2, halting the Argentine's 16-match winning streak. (Clerc had defeated Victor Pecci in Rome, 6-3, 6-4, 6-0. The ascendant Lendl answered back twice after Borg took the first and third sets but, in the end, he was worn down by the champion's sheer inexhaustibility.

With a fourth straight French title, six in all (and the tournament's record male winning streak, 28 matches), he turned his attention to Wimbledon. A sixth consecutive championship in the London suburb would tie him with Willie Renshaw, who competed before the turn of the century (1881– 86) when defenders were treated to a bye into the final.

But it was McEnroe who received a greater share of attention—for all the wrong reasons. During his first match win, 7-6, 7-5, 6-3, over Tom Gullikson, McEnroe launched a verbal assault on umpire Ted James ("the pits of the world") and tournament referee Fred Hoyles. The tournament committee actually considered showing him the gate before settling on $1,500 in fines.

McEnroe, labeled "Superbrat" by the tabloids, grumbled his way into the semifinal where he again dressed down Hoyles during an interminable victory, 7-6 (7-2), 6-4, 7-5, over unseeded Australian Rod Frawley that was fraught with objections and unprintables.

But the real brouhaha began in the interview room after the Yank had vented his spleen on the British tabloid press in the wake of some baiting by a gossip columnist. There followed a dialogue on the nature of journalism among emissaries from various countries and soon an Englishman, Nigel Clark, and an American, Charlie Steiner, were rolling, wrestling, on the floor. It was scored a dead heat, no tie-breaker needed, but can you imagine two ill-conditioned scribblers battling over McEnroe's honor?

Through all the tumult, Borg kept rolling. He overcame a major challenge from Connors in the semifinals, rallying from yet another two-set deficit to oust his old adversary, 0-6, 4-6, 6-3, 6-0, 6-4, in a tense match that rivaled any the two had produced for quality and tension, the last Bjorn would win there. "He had to play his best stuff to beat me," Connors said. And it was true.

But even a sharp and determined Borg wasn't enough to hold off a McEnroe who had learned to orchestrate his talents, if not his temper. Uncharacteristically, the defender started fast. Shockingly, he finished second. The American triumphed, 4-6, 7-6 (7-1), 7-6 (7-4), 6-4. The king was dead.

For all practical purposes, Borg lost his title in game 10 of the third set, where he enjoyed four set points for a 2-1 lead. First, McEnroe served out of a 15-40 hole, then overcame two Borg ads in the six deuce game. He took control of the tie-breaker with two sensational passing shots after Borg served at 3-4. In the fourth set, the one that terminated Borg's Wimbledon male-record winning streak at 41, McEnroe attacked at every opportunity and dominated with his big first serve.

"I was surprised that I served so well," McEnroe said. "I wanted to show that Bjorn's not the only one who can come from behind and win."

The denouement occurred on the Fourth of July in a country not disposed to celebrating revolutions. Attired in blue and white tennis togs and sporting a jaunty red headband—"Stick a feather in his cap and call him McEnroney," telecaster Bud Collins observed—Superbrat closed out an era with a forehand volley winner on his second championship point.

Horrified officials of the All England Club had their revenge. They declined to tender McEnroe an honorary membership, a traditional spoil of victory. Not that the man had any desire to join.

In advance of the U.S. Open, McEnroe whipped Chris Lewis in the final at Cincinnati, 6-3, 6-4. Otherwise, the American circuit had been dominated by Clerc, who added four clay-court titles to his dirt demolition of Paraguayan Victor Pecci, 6-3, 6-4, 6-0 in Rome: U.S. Pro over Chilean Hans Gildemeister; 0-6, 6-3, 6-2; Washington over countryman Guillermo Vilas, 7-5, 6-2; North Conway, N.H., over Vilas, 6-3, 6-2; U.S. Clay Court in Indianapolis over Lendl, 4-6, 6-4, 6-2. But the lean Argentine would be no factor on the Open surface.

The Flushing field was reduced to the usual suspects for the semifinals. McEnroe, who had lost opening sets to the likes of Juan Nunez and Ramesh Krishnan, lost his cool on several

occasions against Vitas Gerulaitis before breaking a racket string against the intrusive CBS courtside microphone. Relieved, he then completed a 5-7, 6-3, 6-2, 4-6, 6-3 triumph. Borg, serving as well as he ever had, wiped out Connors in their semifinal, 6-2, 7-5, 6-4. He had 14 aces plus many unreturnable serves and all of them appeared to occur on the big points.

The victory extended Borg's streak over Connors to 10 matches. Shortly before the match, the switchboard operator at the USTA National Tennis Center received a call from a man threatening Borg's life. Additional security guards ringed the stadium court as a precaution but Borg was not informed until after he had vanquished Connors.

As he had at Wimbledon, Borg jumped out in front of McEnroe in the final. But the Yank swept the last three sets to post a 4-6, 6-2, 6-4, 6-3 victory, stamping him as the first man to capture a third successive U.S. singles title since the legendary Bill Tilden strung together six during the Roaring '20s.

Borg's best chance evaporated in the third set when, leading 4-3, he was broken in stunning fashion as McEnroe unleashed four winners, including a pair of spectacular running topspin lobs, to draw even. "I felt I could do anything," the American said. He won eight of the last 11 games. Borg's future flashed before his eyes. It did not include competitive tennis, and his illustrious career was essentially terminated.

One month later, the former No. 1 player in the world said he was taking his first extended vacation from tennis until the following April. Borg also said he would participate in only seven tournaments, a number insufficient for placement in the main draw under the rules of the Men's International Professional Tennis Council. He would have to quality for every Grand Prix tournament he entered, a course he would pursue with apparent disinterest.

Suddenly, the stage was all McEnroe's. Although newly-naturalized U.S. citizen Johan Kriek out of South Africa, whom Mac had defeated in the WCT Finals in Dallas, 6-1, 6-2, 6-4, would emerge from a depleted field to take the Australian title, a 6-2, 7-6 (7-1), 6-7 (1-7), 6-4 victory over Texan Steve Denton. Despite Lendl's first-place finish in the Grand Prix standings and his subsequent triumph over Gerulaitis in the Masters final, 6-7 (5-7), 2-6, 7-6 (8-6), 6-2, 6-4, McEnroe was the unchallenged leader of the pack.

Not only did the left-hander win nine of 17 singles tournaments, he also teamed with Peter Fleming to win an equal number of doubles titles, including both the championships of Wimbledon, over Stan Smith and Bob Lutz, 6-4, 6-4, 6-4 and the U.S. Open, a default gimme from Heinz Gunthardt and Peter McNamara because Gunthardt was ill.

Additionally, he guided the U.S. to the Davis Cup, a third with him on board, winning seven of eight singles and two doubles. In the tight windup against Argentina, 3-1, at Cincinnati's Riverfront Coliseum. (In the newly remodeled Davis Cup format, a World Group was established at the top and only 16 countries would be eligible for the Cup. The other nations were to be consigned to zonal warfare below, hoping for promotion the following year.) Clerc, with his deadly, rolling topspin backhand, was primed for Cincy, even though the footing was carpet rather than

the clay of Argentina's triumph over the U.S. the year before. He whipped Roscoe Tanner, 7-5, 6-3, 8-6, after McEnroe bashed Vilas, 6-3, 6-2, 6-2. The Argentines then played the doubles of their lives against Fleming and McEnroe, constantly changing tactics in the wild and acrimonious battle—the teams came close to a fistfight at one point—and the Argentines actually moved into winning position late in the fifth set: Match game, Vilas serving at 7-6. Four points away, and with a 2-1 lead, the Argentines could envision taking the Cup home. They came no closer as McEnroe took over, cracking three winners and an awesome backhand return to capsize Vilas. Mac held brilliantly through four deuces and two break points to 8-7, and Vilas averted a match point to 9-9. But McEnroe's net-skimming backhand return tipped Clerc at match point point and the four hour-11-minute wowser ended, 6-3, 4-6, 6-4, 4-6, 11-9.

Subsequently it was up to the raging Mac to jerk Clerc. To the roars of 13,327, he fulfilled their pleas, again in a boiling fifth set, 7-5, 5-7, 6-3, 3-6, 6-3. His serves (15 aces) and volleys overcame the tall Latin's groundies. No man had swept the singles at Wimbledon, the U.S. and in the Cup final since Don Budge in 1938, the year of his Grand Slam.

Furthermore, his facility in doubles marked Mac as the most complete champion since John Newcombe was lending his mustache to a line of tennis gear. Fittingly, the representatives of two generations held an improbable meeting on the stadium court at Flushing Meadow in the U.S. doubles semifinals. Newk, 37, and partner Fred Stolle, 42, both U.S. singles titleists in their halcyon days, had a merry romp through the first four rounds of the draw, in contrast to the grim attitude of Mac and Fleming, finishing their nocturnal third-round win over Americans Tony Graham and Bruce Nichols, 3-6, 6-3, 7-6, 4-6, 6-4, at 1:45 in the morning.

Stolle and Newcombe darned near won the title, squeezing Mac and Fleming into a fifth set tie-breaker, losing by a measly four points, their third consecutive encounter of five sets. Their semifinal was tantamount to a final, which wasn't played because of Gunthardt's illness. The Americans beat the devil-may-care Aussie geezers, 6-2, 6-2, 5-7, 6-7 (2-7), 7-6 (7-3).

They won the match but not the crowd, which cheered and laughed as the old Aussies reprised a few vaudeville routines, sometimes sending one man to the other side of the net ostensibly to help their glowering foes. "We always had a fair bit of fun playing doubles in my day," Stolle said.

To Newcombe, who chose not to live his life between the white lines, the current attitude was unfortunate. "I feel sorry for them," he said. "It's a sport. It's a living, too, yes, but they take it over the fringe."

The list of fines for the year indicated just how much court conduct had deteriorated. McEnroe, Gerulaitis and Ilie Nastase all drew 21-day suspensions for exceeding $5,000 in fines. Of the three, Gerulaitis created the biggest stir. In a protest against officiating, he refused to continue playing at 5-5 in the decisive third set of the Australian Indoor final against Peter McNamara, an offense that earned him a record (at that time) $10,000 penalty.

Tim Mayotte, the husky 21-year-old out of Springfield, Mass., the National Intercollegiate champion for Stanford, made an

auspicious professional debut and was honored as Rookie of the Year. He reached the quarters at Wimbledon in only his second tournament as a pro. (In fact he was out of footwear when he arrived, borrowing a pair of Smith's size 13s for his first match.) Tim won 28 of 43 matches in 15 events and finished the year at No. 31.

The march of children into the women's ranks continued with the presence of Kathy Rinaldi at the French Open. In becoming the youngest player to compete in that tournament, the 14-year-old skipped her graduation exercises at St. Joseph's School in Stuart, Fla., and journeyed to Paris where she upset No. 8 seed Dianne Fromholtz, 6-2, 7-5, and No. 11 seed Anne Smith, 6-1, 4-6, 6-3, before bowing to Hana Mandlikova in the quarterfinals, 6-1, 6-3.

Having disposed of the latest princess, Mandlikova went after the queen. Now 19, she sent Evert Lloyd to her second defeat on clay in the last 191 matches, 7-5, 6-4, in the semifinal. Mandlikova closed out her second major title by stopping Sylvia Hanika, 6-2, 6-4. Hanika, a chunky German lefty, beat Andrea Jaeger, 4-6, 6-1, 6-4, in the other semifinal. But Jaeger, 15, carried the teen theme to the top with fellow Yank, Jimmy Arias, 16, of Buffalo. They became the youngest of all major doubles champs, taking the mixed, 7-6, 6-4, over the Dutch-American hookup of Betty Stove and Fred McNair.

Mandlikova carried her form onto the grass at Wimbledon, a tournament that lost its defending champion because Evonne Goolagong Cawley interrupted her career to give birth to a second child. That absence was offset by the return of Austin, who missed the first five months of the season with a sciatic nerve condition. In the presence of Rinaldi and Jaeger, Austin, 18, was perceived as a veteran.

Rinaldi became the youngest player to win a match at Wimbledon, a record she would lose in 1990 to Jennifer Capriati, a greener 14 by one day. Averting a third-set match point, Kathy beat South African Sue Rollinson in a two-hour 32-minute struggle, 6-3, 2-6, 9-7. But, worn down, she then lost to Swiss qualifier Claudia Pasquale, 3-6, 6-0, 6-0. Jaeger, 16, was upset by Mima Jausovec, 6-4, 7-6, and an unsteady third-seeded Austin was stunned in the quarters by an overjoyed, almost unbelieving seventh-seeded Shriver, 7-5, 6-4. "Tracy's been beating up on me since I was 11," bubbled Shriver, who was 0-9 against Austin in the juniors, 0-2 as a pro.

The semifinal matched attackers: Mandlikova (who had double-bageled Wendy Turnbull in the quarters) and Navratilova. Hana, the younger, seeded second despite her ranking of No. 5 on the computer, justified her placement with a 7-5, 4-6, 6-1 victory, winning 11 of the last 13 points in the process. Now all she had to do to claim her third consecutive major title was beat Evert Lloyd, who had moved into a flat just down the road with her husband, John. No small feat that. Evert Lloyd, who practiced hard in preparation, was peerless once the tournament began. Her 6-3, 6-1 rout of Shriver in the semis was typical of her fortnight. So was the final.

After three consecutive defeats in the championship round, Evert Lloyd took apart a nervous Mandlikova, 6-2, 6-2. "I told myself that if I played Hana at Wimbledon," she said, "I would

beat her." And so she did, with relative ease. "Boom-boom-boom... quick-quick-quick!" was the appraisal by Willem Mandlik of his daughter's 61-minute demise.

Not so quick was the 94-hour first-round doubles victory of Americans Chris Dunk and Marty Davis over Aussie brothers Michael and Charlie Fancutt, 7-6, 6-4, 1-6, 7-6, begun on the first Tuesday and played in bits and pieces (because of rain, nightfall and scheduling difficulties) to conclusion four days later, Saturday, on Court 15.

Youth was served on the summer circuit. Most notably at Indianapolis, where 16-year-old Jaeger became the youngest winner of the U.S. Clay Court championship, thrashing the seasoned Romanian, Virginia Ruzici, in the final, 6-1, 6-0. Austin demonstrated she had regained her fitness by outlasting Shriver at San Diego, 6-2, 5-7, 6-2, and then dethroning Evert Lloyd at the Canadian Open, 6-1, 6-4.

For Austin, it was ideal preparation for the U.S. Open, where she breezed through 12 effortless sets to the final. The path for the third-seeded Austin was smoothed by Jaeger's second round collapse against Andrea Leand. One of those rare birds—an amateur!—17-year-old Leand from Brooklandville, Md., was in her first pro tourney and had no ranking. She pulled off one of the largest upsets in U.S. annals over second-seeded Jaeger, 1-6, 7-5, 6-3, and pushed ahead to within two points of the quarters, losing to No. 11-seeded lefty Barbara Potter, 6-7, 7-6 (7-5), 6-3.

Form prevailed in the other half of the draw, where Evert Lloyd advanced to her eleventh consecutive Open semifinal. Her opponent was Navratilova, who had been frustrated in the tournament since that September day in 1975 when she announced her defection to the U.S. at Forest Hills. After years of complaining about the noise, the constant movement of the crowds and all the other distractions at the Open, Navratilova dispatched Evert Lloyd, 7-5, 4-6, 6-4, in a marvelous and emotional match that was interrupted by beery heckling of Navratilova and a fight broken up by security guards.

That qualified Navratilova for her first U.S. final, where she seized the initiative in the first set, 6-1. But the gritty Austin fought back to win the last two sets in tie-breakers, 7-6 (4), 7-6 (1), and claim the first major championship decided by an ultimate set breaker. Although Martina double faulted on championship point, ending the longest U.S. final (2:42), the fans' reaction to the loser's efforts thrilled Navratilova as much as anything in her career. Their warm applause interrupted her concession speech on several occasions. She cried from happiness as she turned to all four sides of the court and made a little bow, the kind expected at Wimbledon but seen so rarely in the New World.

A month after the Open, Navratilova snapped Austin's 28-match winning streak with a 6-0, 6-2 victory in the U.S. Indoor final at Minneapolis. Gene Mayer won the male version over Tanner, 6-2, 6-4, in Memphis, where Trey Waltke sabotaged top-seeded McEnroe in the first round, 6-3, 6-4. Navratilova also annexed the Avon Championships at Madison Square Garden over Jaeger, 6-3, 7-6 (7-3).

Martina won the final major event of the year, over coming Evert Lloyd, 6-7 (4-7), 6-4, 7-5, in the Australian final. That boosted Martina's singles titles in 1981 to 10 which, combined with the 11

doubles titles she shared with Shriver, enabled her to set a one-season earnings record of $865,437.

Austin rebounded to win the Toyota Series Championship that closed out the year at the Meadowlands in East Rutherford, N.J., overcoming Navratilova, 2-6, 6-4, 6-2.

Evert Lloyd ran her singles records in the Wightman Cup and Federation Cup to 20-0 and 23-0, respectively as the U.S. won all its matches in both competitions - each title won in shutouts of Britain. Tokyo hosted the Federation tourney, where Chrissie beat Sue Barker, 6-2, 6-1 and Jaeger took Virginia Wade, 6-3, 6-1, in the 3-0 final. Wade and Barker were the foils also in the 7-0 Wightman romp in Chicago - Evert Lloyd and Austin each won twice, Chrissie over Wade, 6-1, 6-3, and Barker, 6-3, 6-0; Tracy over Wade, 6-3, 6-1, and Barker, 7-5, 6-3.

1981 CHAMPIONS AND LEADERS

Australian Open
Men's Singles Final: Johan Kriek (USA) def. Steve Denton (USA), 6-2, 7-6 (1), 6-7 (1), 6-4
Women's Singles Final: Martina Navratilova (CZE) def. Chris Evert Lloyd (USA), 6-7 (4), 6-4, 7-5
Men's Doubles Final: Mark Edmondson and Kim Warwick (AUS) def. Hank Pfister and John Sadri (USA), 6-3, 6-7, 6-3
Women's Doubles Final: Kathy Jordan and Anne Smith (USA) def. Martina Navratilova (CZE) and Pam Shriver (USA), 6-2, 7-5
Mixed Doubles: Not Played

French Open
Men's Singles Final: Bjorn Borg (SWE) def. Ivan Lendl (CZE), 6-1, 4-6, 6-2, 3-6, 6-1
Women's Singles Final: Hana Mandlikova (CZE) def. Sylvia Hanika (GER), 6-2, 6-4
Men's Doubles Final: Heinz Gunthardt (SUI) and Balazs Taroczy (HUN) def. Terry Moor and Eliot Teltscher (USA), 6-2, 7-6, 6-3
Women's Doubles Final: Rosalyn Fairbank and Tayna Harford (RSA) def. Candy Reynolds and Paula Smith (USA), 6-1, 6-3
Mixed Doubles Final: Andrea Jaeger and Jimmy Arias (USA) def. Betty Stove (NED) and Fred McNair (USA), 7-6, 6-4

Wimbledon
Men's Singles Final: John McEnroe (USA) def. Bjorn Borg (SWE), 4-6, 7-6 (1), 7-6 (4), 6-4
Women's Singles Final: Chris Evert Lloyd (USA) def. Hana Mandlikova (CZE), 6-2, 6-2
Men's Doubles Final: Peter Fleming and John McEnroe (USA) def. Bob Lutz and Stan Smith (USA), 6-4, 6-4, 6-4
Women's Doubles Final: Martina Navratilova (CZE) and Pam Shriver (USA) def. Kathy Jordan and Anne Smith (USA), 6-3, 7-6 (6)
Mixed Doubles Final: Betty Stove (NED) and Frew McMillan (RSA) def. Tracy Austin and John Austin (USA), 4-6, 7-6 (2), 6-3

U.S. Open
Men's Singles Final: John McEnroe (USA) def. Bjorn Borg (SWE), 4-6, 6-2, 6-4, 6-3
Women's Singles Final: Tracy Austin (USA) def. Martina Navratilova (USA), 1-6, 7-6 (4), 7-6 (1)
Men's Doubles Final: Peter Fleming and John McEnroe (USA) def. Heinz Gunthardt (SUI) and Peter McNamara (AUS), walkover (Gunthardt ill)
Women's Doubles Final: Anne Smith and Kathy Jordan (USA) def. Rosie Casals (USA) and Wendy Turnbull (AUS), 6-3, 6-3
Mixed Doubles Final: Anne Smith (USA) and Kevin Curren (RSA) def. Joanne Russell and Steve Denton (USA), 6-4, 7-6 (4)

Year-End No. 1
Men: John McEnroe
Women: Chris Evert Lloyd

Top Player Earnings
Men: John McEnroe $991,000
Women: Martina Navratilova $865,437

Davis Cup: United States

Federation Cup: United States

Wightman Cup: United States

Grand Prix Masters, NYC—Ivan Lendl
WCT, Dallas—John McEnroe
Avon Championships, NYC—Martina Navratilova

1982

Jimbo, Chrissie Go Dancing Again

Something on the order of the Wimbledon Ball would have been appropriate. And for one reason—so Jimmy Connors, men's champion, could have the first dance with Chris Evert Lloyd, the women's champion.

What a picture that would have made. And what a fitting commentary on the state of the sport eight years after they'd reigned as the sweethearts of Centre Court. They had taken divergent paths since 1974 and yet, before the eyes of enthralled spectators and in front of a worldwide television audience, they wound up in the same spot—champions of the New World, Connors at 30 and Evert Lloyd at 27.

They grew up before our eyes. Chrissie, a beribboned semifinalist at sweet 16, did so with considerably more grace, but Connors got there nonetheless, maturing after his marriage to Patti McGuire and the birth of a son. They had first appeared in the tournament when it was staged at Forest Hills, when the surface was grass, when tennis players dressed only in white.

So Connors' 6-3, 6-2, 4-6, 6-4 victory over Ivan Lendl, which followed by a day Evert Lloyd's 6-3, 6-1 conquest of Hana Mandlikova, was, as much as anything, a triumph of the familiar. And it continued an all-American winning tradition in the

N ormally, a prim-and-proper grand finale would be out of place in such a proletarian celebration as the U.S. Open, staged in a municipally-owned complex in a public park. After all, people at the USTA National Tennis Center consider a sweater looped over the shoulders as evening wear. But on this one occasion, the tournament of the people, by the people and for the people was worthy of a formal send off.

singles since the tournament was shifted to Flushing Meadow four years earlier.

It was at the U.S. Open where Martina Navratilova's quest for a second major title ended prematurely in a quarterfinal loss to her doubles partner, Pam Shriver, 1-6, 7-6 (7-5), 6-2. Evert Lloyd made the most of that opportunity, then defeated Navratilova in the Australian final, 6-3, 2-6, 6-3, to even the score in major tour-

naments for 1982 at two apiece. But the naturalized American still reigned as the foremost figure in women's tennis, winning 29 tournaments (15 in singles), earning a record of $1,475,055 and securing the season-closing Toyota Series playoffs, climaxed by a 4-6, 6-1, 6-1 triumph over Chrissie. Her match record was a phenomenal 90-3 in singles, 70-4 in doubles.

Among the men, Connors stood alone after completing a double that appeared beyond his reach at the age of 30. The irrepressible left-hander prevailed over John McEnroe in the first Wimbledon final of the post-Borg era, then turned back Lendl at Flushing Meadow, while climbing back to the pinnacle from which he had been ousted by Borg and McEnroe.

Mats Wilander, from the first class of Swedish youngsters inspired by Borg, ascended to the French Open title at the tender unseeded age of 17 years, 10 months, becoming the youngest man to annex a major title. Borg was two months older when he won at Paris for the first time in 1974. Wilander, the first non-seed to win since Hungarian Joszef Asboth in 1947, outlasted third-seeded 1977 champion Guillermo Vilas, 1-6, 7-6 (8-6), 6-0, 6-4, in four hours, 42 minutes on a sweltering June afternoon. Quick, sturdy and untiring, Wilander had to show his mettle against seasoned seeded pros in reaching the final: 4-6, 7-5, 3-6, 6-4, 6-2, over second-seeded Lendl; 6-3, 6-3, 4-6, 6-4, over fifth Vitas Gerulaitis; 7-5, 6-2, 1-6, 7-5, over fourth Jose-Luis Clerc. Top-seeded Connors was expelled by Jose Higueras from the quarters, 6-2, 6-2, 6-2. Before the year was over, Wilander would win four of 20 tournaments, compile a match record of 60-18 and walk off with rookie honors as well as the No. 7 ranking.

In what was a replay of the 1981 Australian Open final, Johan Kriek, a native South African resettled in Florida, routed hard-serving Texan Steve Denton, 6-3, 6-3, 6-2, at Melbourne. Earlier in the year, Kriek had stripped McEnroe of yet another prize, the U.S. Indoor championship, 6-3, 3-6, 6-4. Mac wasn't nearly as upset by Kriek's other coup, replacing the feisty one himself atop the punitive standings: $11,500 to $2,060 in fines.

Lendl continued to outwork—and out-earn—everyone else on the men's tour. Balancing his schedule between the Grand Prix and the more lucrative rival circuit, World Championship Tennis, the lean Czech captured 16 of 24 tournaments he entered, won 107 of 166 matches and overpowered Yannick Noah, 6-4, 7-5, Connors, 6-3, 6-1 and McEnroe, 6-4, 6-4, 6-2, to claim a second consecutive Masters title. He also threatened Vilas' Open era record of 50 consecutive match wins before Noah terminated his match-winning streak at 44 in February at LaQuinta, Calif., 6-3, 2-6, 7-5.

For all of that, and despite a record one-season haul of $2,028,850 that almost doubled Connors' payoff of $1,173,850, Lendl was denied the No. 1 position by his failure to win a major. He didn't even bother to enter Wimbledon, claiming an allergy to grass while he worked on his golf game back in the States. Nor was he the only defector from the world's most prestigious tournament as no fewer than five of the top 10 males on the ATP computer skipped the event, including the mysterious Borg, and Vilas, whose country was at war with Great Britain over the status of the Falkland Islands.

By then, Borg had become a figure of intrigue. Deciding to play again in the spring but refusing to commit to 10 Grand Prix events, he petitioned the Men's International Professional Tennis Council for a rule change. The nine members, including three player representatives, met in Monaco in conjunction with the Monte Carlo Open, which happened to mark the Swede's debut as a qualifier.

Sir Brian Burnett, chairman of the Wimbledon championships, joined the discussions. He was eager for a compromise that would make it unnecessary for Borg to qualify at Wimbledon. The council was willing. "But," said Arthur Ashe, a council member, "Borg wasn't. For him, it was a matter of principle." Standing on principle, Borg, inactive seven months, won his three qualifying matches in April at Monte Carlo, where he made his home. But he performed strangely in the main draw. He prepared to serve from the wrong side of the court in one match. In another, he served underhanded after two double faults. And he whistled during a 6-1, 6-2 loss to Noah in the quarterfinals, after re-launching himself by beating Spaniard Fernando Luna, 6-4, 6-3, and bygone nemesis Adriano Panatta, 6-2, 3-6, 6-4.

Burnett announced the compromise proposal the following week in London. Borg would be accepted for the main draw at Wimbledon if he agreed to play in 10 Grand Prix tournaments before March 31, 1983. Borg, who had taken his principles to Tokyo for a couple of lucrative exhibition matches, declined. He would play according to the dictates of his own schedule, and he would not play qualifying matches at Wimbledon. So much for tradition.

While officials were digesting that news, Borg made a surprise appearance in the qualifying round of the glitzy Alan King-Caesars Palace Classic at Las Vegas, two weeks after Monte Carlo. He played like it was a death sentence, squeaking past Victor Amaya before his elimination at the hands of Dick Stockton, 7-6, 1-6, 6-2. In the course of the latter match, the former champion missed a lob and served with an extra ball in his left hand. Borg, observers recalled, clearly, hits his backhand with two hands on the racket. "I don't think he had his heart in the qualifying," Stockton reported.

Following that experience, Borg stated he would play only exhibitions for the remainder of the year but return to the circuit in 1983. Months later, during the Masters, he amended that decision with the announcement he was retiring from competitive tennis.

No wonder it was so much easier to follow the fortunes of the women, especially given the dominant manner in which Navratilova started the season. She was unbeaten in five tournaments on the Avon circuit before the cosmetics company withdrew as winter sponsor, to be replaced by year-round angel Virginia Slims. No sooner had her 27-match winning streak been interrupted by Sylvia Hanika in the Avon finale at Madison Square Garden, 1-6, 6-3, 6-4, then she began a 41-match run that wouldn't be stopped until defeat to Shriver at the U.S. Open in September. Her quarterfinal loss at Flushing Meadow marked the first time all year she had failed to reach a tournament final.

To her immense satisfaction, Navratilova proved as formidable on the clay as she had been on the grass by sweeping both the Family Circle Cup at Hilton Head, S.C., and the French Open. On both occasions, Andrea Jaeger had done the dirty work, eliminating perennial champion Evert Lloyd in the semis. Prior to her meeting with the Illinois high school student, Evert Lloyd not only had won six previous Family Circle Cups in a row, but all 64 sets in which she had participated. Jaeger showed her disrespect with a 6-1, 1-6, 6-2 triumph. A few weeks later, she gave herself a 17th-birthday present by stunning top-seeded Evert Lloyd, favored to win a fifth French title, 6-3, 6-1. Chrissie got to the semifinal, 6-2, 6-4, past Romanian Lucia Romanov, an identical twin. (Sometimes when Lucia and sister Maria were doubles partners, and losing, Lucia, the better of the two, would serve more often if their foes didn't catch on.)

In both tournaments, however, baseline baby Jaeger received her comeuppance from Navratilova. Martina followed a 6-4, 6-2 victory at Hilton Head with a 7-6 (8-6), 6-1 decision at Paris, saving a set point in the tie-breaker. Thus ended the run of the youngest French finalist.

Although Navratilova carried her form onto grass, winning at Eastbourne over Mandlikova, 6-4, 6-3, the major news of the pre-Wimbledon circuit was provided by Billie Jean King. After playing only a few matches in 1981, when she was buffeted by the agonizing, highly publicized palimony lawsuit filed by ex-lover Marilyn Barnett, the 38-year-old Mother Freedom of the women's tour returned with a vengeance. In the Edgbaston Cup at Birmingham, she defeated Rosalyn Fairbank, 6-2, 6-1, for her first tournament singles title in two years and her 66th as a pro. It was a most favorable omen for a Wimbledon desperately in need of an electric charge.

Wimbledon was inundated by so much rain during the first week that the vice chairman of the tournament was summoned to the interview room to discuss the weather. A subway strike only added to the gloom, flooding streets around the club with traffic. Into this dreary setting stepped a revitalized King and the old tennis shrine fairly glowed with her reflection. On the occasion of her first match, her 100th singles battle at Wimbledon, the club planned to present her with a centennial plate.

Officials didn't announce the ceremony in advance because they feared she would lose to 19-year-old Claudia Pasquale of Switzerland. They also sent her to Court 14, "out in the boondocks," according to King, because her seeding of 12th was based as much on sentiment as recent results. The gift appeared to be the British equivalent of a gold watch: Thanks for your contributions to the game and enjoy your retirement.

But the self-styled Old Lady had other plans. She hammered Pasquale, 6-3, 6-2, saved triple match point against South African Tanya Harford in a remarkable 5-7, 7-6 (7-2), 6-2, third-round triumph and then announced she was a genuine title contender by overcoming third-seeded Tracy Austin 3-6, 6-4, 6-2 in the quarterfinals, pouncing for a 3-0 lead in the third. St. Billie of the Grassblades hadn't come back to Wimbledon, her favorite haunt, just for a testimonial.

King knew what she wanted when she took a look in the mirror the previous fall. She lifted weights and she ran and she took the first steps back up the ladder, occasionally falling but getting back on her feet and climbing higher. Wimbledon was her goal and she had more than a trinket in mind when she walked onto the grounds. She wanted the Duke and Duchess of Kent and everyone else who occupied the Royal Box to empty their pockets on the table. This was a holdup. "Unless you win the whole woiks" she said, flavoring the All England Club with a dollop of Brooklynese, "it doesn't mean anything."

King's victory over Austin catapulted her into a semifinal against Evert Lloyd, one that was all anyone could have anticipated and more. They presented the tournament with a blast from the past. The younger woman prevailed, but not before King fought off four match points, and performed a medley of her greatest shots, perfected over two decades. So small was the edge in Evert Lloyd's 7-6 (7-4), 2-6, 6-3 triumph that the two women split the 30 games and King achieved one more service break.

Meanwhile, Navratilova was cruising through an upset-strewn half of the draw, without the loss of a set, beating German 19-year-old Bettina Bunge, 6-2, 6-2, in the semis. "I really can't believe I've won as easily as I have," she said. "I haven't been tested."

Her test came in the final when she found herself down a break in the third set. A finalist for the sixth consecutive year, Evert Lloyd won the last four games of the second set and broke Navratilova's service in the third game of the third set, stirring uneasy memories of the 1981 U.S. final when the latter unraveled in two tie-breakers against Austin.

"Martina kind of choked that match," Evert Lloyd said. "When she's been in a tough situation in the past, Tracy or I have come out better. But she won this match. She played well under pressure." Indeed, Navratilova needed mental strength commensurate with her physical talents to beat Evert Lloyd, 6-2, 3-6, 6-2, for her third successive major title, including the Australian Open championship she had claimed in December.

London rains clogged scheduling at tourney's end, forcing the mixed doubles champs, a Texas-South African amalgam of Anne Smith and Kevin Curren, to go four rounds the last day—113 games—winning the title over the Anglo-Aussie team of John Lloyd and Wendy Turnbull, 2-6, 6-3, 7-5.

All went well until the second week of the U.S. Open where top-seeded Navratilova was afflicted by a case of toxoplasmosis, a viral condition transmitted by her cat. She was then was victimized in the quarters by Shriver, who rallied from a 1-6, 4-5, 15-30 predicament to oust her doubles partner, 1-6, 7-6 (7-5), 6-2, shattering the top-seed's 41-match streak. The two women then hugged at the net and both left the court in tears.

Shriver failed to survive the semifinal, beaten by Mandlikova, 6-4, 2-6, 6-2, who earlier had eliminated defending champ Austin, 4-6, 6-4, 6-4, competing in only her second tournament since Wimbledon. Second-seeded Evert Lloyd received her only real challenge in the quarters from an unlikely source, a 19-year-old former gymnast from Florida, Bonnie Gadusek, dropping one set before sweeping the last 12 games for a 4-6, 6-1, 6-0 triumph.

Evert Lloyd then overwhelmed Jaeger 6-1, 6-2 in the semifinal, and dispatched Mandlikova 6-3, 6-1 to clinch her sixth Open singles title.

Evert Lloyd continued winning until Navratilova stopped her streak at 31 matches, 6-1, 6-4, in the final at Brighton, England, in late October. Five weeks later, she reversed the outcome, defeating Navratilova, 6-3, 2-6, 6-3, for her first Australian title. In that instant she became the 10th player of either sex to win all four major singles championships.

The two rivals also teamed for the first time in Federation Cup play as the U.S. stretched its unbeaten streak to 34 rounds en-route to its seventh consecutive team championship, 3-0 over Germany. Chrissie beat towering Claudia Kohde-Kilsch, 2-6, 6-1, 6-3, and Martina stopped Bunge, 6-4, 6-4, in the final at Santa Clara, Calif.

Evert Lloyd also captained the American squad to its fourth consecutive Wightman Cup victory over Great Britain, 6-1, winning both her singles and surpassing Helen Wills Moody's U.S. record for most matches entered with 32. Martina abstained, but the captain's wins over Jo Durie, 6-2, 6-2, and Sue Barker, 6-4, 6-3, plus rookie lefty Barbie Potter's decisions over Barker, 6-2, 6-2, and Durie, 5-7, 7-6, 6-2, were sufficient.

Connors' resurrection salvaged what had been a lackluster Wimbledon among the men. With so many top players absent and with the rain pelting down, the primary topic of conversation was McEnroe's relationship with the All England Club. He complimented officials for their attitude following his opening match but he was not entirely pleased, noting that he had not yet received his trophies from the previous year.

Ted Tinling, the liaison between players and the club, explained that McEnroe had not picked up the silver replicas of the President's Cup, the Challenge Cup and the Renshaw Cup on his way out the door in 1981. Nor had he attended the champion's dinner that night. Tinling said the club considered shipping the silverware to New York but found the insurance prohibitive.

So there they sat until the player's father claimed the prizes later that day. As for membership in the club, which Mac also sought, Tinling said that was another matter entirely. "I explained to Mr. McEnroe," he said, "that it's not an automatic to become a member if you win. It's an elected privilege." Eventually it would all be settled positively.

Unlike the previous year, his advance to the final was virtually free of controversy. He was warned once, for ball abuse, in a second-round victory over Eddie Edwards, 6-3, 6-3, 7-5, and drew a $500 fine for verbal abuse in his 6-3, 6-1, 6-2 semifinal thrashing of Tim Mayotte, the unseeded second year pro who improved one round on his Wimbledon debut in 1981. Mac's title defense would be against Connors, who had easily turned aside another surprise in the semifinal, 12th-seeded Mark Edmondson, 6-4, 6-3, 6-1.

It had been eight years since Connors reigned as men's singles champion. He was a whiz kid of 21 when he demolished Ken Rosewall in the '74 final. Only Big Bill Tilden (1921-30) and Evonne Goolagong (1971-80) had gone a longer time between Wimbledon titles.

Brandishing a redesigned serve and hungry for another major championship, Connors outlasted McEnroe, 3-6, 6-3, 6-7 (2-7), 7-6 (7-5), 6-4, in a match that was distinguished more by its length (a Wimbledon final record four hours, 15 minutes) than its brilliance. Despite 13 double faults, Connors grabbed his sixth major title, charging back when it seemed he must lose. McEnroe, with a 2-1 lead in sets, was merely points from victory at 3-2 in the tie-breaker with two serves to come, then 4-3—three points away—after his 17th ace, but Jimmy allowed him no closer. "I'm not a one-timer," he announced, "someone to be forgotten. I've had chances [in final] three times since then. And I was going to do anything not to let the chance slip by today."

As a special consolation prize, McEnroe was granted the honorary membership denied the previous year. He was so advised between the singles final and doubles final, which he and Peter Fleming lost to Peter McNamara and Paul McNamee of Australia, 6-4, 6-3, 6-4, relinquishing the title they'd won in 1981. "I guess I'm happy," Mac said after being welcomed to the club.

Two months later in New York, he was separated from his other major singles title. The culprit this time was Lendl, whose serves backed McEnroe almost to the wall in a 6-4, 6-4, 7-6 (8-6) semifinal victory. Connors had a better idea. After dismissing Vilas in the semis, 6-1, 3-6, 6-2, 6-3, he dared Lendl to drive the ball past him. Standing almost contemptuously just behind the baseline, he startled and demoralized the Czech with his returns in a 6-3, 6-2, 4-6, 6-4 triumph that returned the man to the top of the tennis world just when his career appeared to be in eclipse.

"When I won before," Connors said, "everybody thought I would. When I won now, everybody thought I wouldn't. And that's very satisfying." So he was joining the likes of Tilden, Fred Perry, Don Budge, Rod Laver and McEnroe as the only men twice to win Wimbledon and the U.S. in the same year.

Although failing to win a major individual title for the first time in four years, McEnroe did lead Captain Arthur Ashe's U.S. force to a second consecutive Davis Cup. The 4-1 final over France in Grenoble was notable mainly for McEnroe's 12-10, 1-6, 3-6, 6-2, 6-3 victory over Noah on a clay court built to stop him inside the former Olympic ice rink. Gene Mayer, the first two-way double-hander in a Cup final followed up over left-handed rookie Henri Leconte, 6-2, 6-2, 7-9, 6-4, and McEnroe-Fleming was the crusher of the two Frenchmen, 6-3, 6-4, 9-7. On the 50th anniversary of the "The Great Cup Robbery" (see 1932), the U.S. win must have been satisfying to American survivors Elly Vines and Johnny Van Ryn.

But even Mac's superb four-hour, 21-minute battle with Noah paled in comparison to his extraordinary 9-7, 6-2, 15-17, 3-6, 8-6 triumph over Wilander in a decisive fifth match of the U.S.-Sweden quarterfinals at St. Louis. Time of play: A male singles record of six hours 22 minutes. Mac had beaten Anders Jarryd, 10-8, 6-3, 6-3, the first day, but the strong 17-year-old Mats eroded Teltscher in five sets, 6-4, 7-5, 3-6, 3-6, 6-0, to tie it. Though Mac and Fleming were go-ahead guys over Hans Simonsson and Jarryd, 6-4, 6-3, 6-0, Jarryd responded to tie it again, beating sub Brian Gottfried, 6-2, 6-2, 6-4.

McEnroe and Teltscher started the 4-1 opening round victory over India at Carlsbad, Calif. John won a volleying faceoff with the stylish Indian Captain Vijay Amritraj, 6-4, 9-7, 7-5, and Eliot took the deft Ramesh Krishnan, 6-3, 6-3, 6-4. Fleming and McEnroe settled it over the Amritraj brothers, Anand and Vijay, 6-3, 6-1, 7-5.

In the semifinal on an indoor carpet in Perth, it was 5-0 over the Aussies in brisk, four-set order: Mac over McNamara, 6-4, 4-6, 6-2, 6-4; Mayer over Alexander, 6-4, 3-6, 6-1, 6-2; the Fleming-McEnroe express over their Wimbledon conquerors, McNamee and McNamara, 6-2, 6-2, 3-6, 8-6. For McEnroe, it was an unblemished campaign: 8-0 in singles, 4-0 in doubles.

1982 CHAMPIONS AND LEADERS

Australian Open
Men's Singles Final: Johan Kriek (USA) def. Steven Denton (USA), 6-3, 6-3, 6-2
Women's Singles Final: Chris Evert Lloyd (USA) def. Martina Navratilova (USA), 6-3, 2-6, 6-3
Men's Doubles Final: John Alexander and John Fitzgerald (AUS) def. Andy Andrews and John Sadri (USA), 6-4, 7-6
Women's Doubles Final: Martina Navratilova and Pam Shriver (USA) def. Claudia Kohde-Kilsch and Eva Pfaff (GER), 6-4, 6-2
Mixed Doubles: Not Played

French Open
Men's Singles Final: Mats Wilander (SWE) def. Guilllermo Vilas (ARG), 1-6, 7-6 (6), 6-0, 6-4
Women's Singles Final: Martina Navratilova (USA) def. Andrea Jaeger (USA), 7-6 (6), 6-1
Men's Doubles Final: Sherwood Stewart and Ferdi Taygan (USA) def. Hans Gildemeister and Belus Prajoux (CHI), 7-5, 6-3, 1-1, ret.
Women's Doubles Final: Martina Navratilova and Anne Smith (USA) def. Rosie Casals (USA) and Wendy Turnbull (AUS), 6-3, 6-4
Mixed Doubles Final: Wendy Turnbull (AUS) and John Lloyd (GBR) def. Claudia Monteiro and Cassio Motta (BRA), 6-2, 7-6

Wimbledon
Men's Singles Final: Jimmy Connors (USA) def. John McEnroe (USA), 3-6, 6-3, 6-7 (2), 7-6 (5), 6-4
Women's Singles Final: Martina Navratilova (USA) def. Chris Evert Lloyd (USA), 6-1, 3-6, 6-2
Men's Doubles Final: Peter McNamara and Paul McNamee (AUS) def. Peter Fleming and John McEnroe (USA), 6-3, 6-2
Women's Doubles Final: Martina Navratilova and Pam Shriver (USA) def. Kathy Jordan and Anne Smith (USA), 6-4, 6-1
Mixed Doubles Final: Anne Smith (USA) and Kevin Curren (RSA) def. Wendy Turnbull (AUS) and John Lloyd (GBR), 2-6, 6-3, 7-5

U.S. Open
Men's Singles Final: Jimmy Connors (USA) def. Ivan Lendl (CZE), 6-3, 6-2, 4-6, 6-4
Women's Singles Final: Chris Evert Lloyd (USA) def. Hana Mandlikova (CZE), 6-3, 6-1
Men's Doubles Final: Kevin Curren (RSA) and Steve Denton (USA) def. Victor Amaya and Hank Pfister (USA), 6-2, 6-7 (4), 5-7, 6-2, 6-4
Women's Doubles Final: Rosie Casals (USA) and Wendy Turnbull (AUS) def. Sharon Walsh and Barbara Potter (USA), 6-4, 6-4
Mixed Doubles Final: Anne Smith (USA) and Kevin Curren (RSA) def. Barbara Potter and Ferdi Taygan (USA), 6-7, 7-6, 7-6

Year-End No. 1
Men: John McEnroe
Women: Martina Navratilova

Top Player Earnings
Men: Ivan Lendl $2,028,850
Women: Martina Navratilova $1,475,055

Davis Cup: United States

Federation Cup: United States

Wightman Cup: United States

Grand Prix Masters, NYC—Ivan Lendl
WCT, Dallas—Ivan Lendl
Avon Championships, NYC—Sylvia Hanika

Martina Almost Perfect, Noah Creates French Frenzy

Yannick Noah became the first Frenchman since Marcel Bernard in 1946 to win the men's singles title at Roland Garros.

igy, Erica Kathleen Horvath of Hopewell Junction, N.Y, had been runner-up to Chris Evert Lloyd at the German Open the previous week. But nothing prepared her and the tennis world for what happened at Stade Roland Garros.

The unseeded American, a pupil of Harry Hopman, posted a stunning 6-4, 0-6, 6-3 victory. The ramifications of that upset wouldn't be felt for months. Following the defeat, Navratilova won her next 50 matches and swept the field at Wimbledon, the U.S. Open and the Australian Open championships. Not only had Horvath denied her the opportunity of achieving a Grand Slam, but spoiled what might have been the first perfect campaign in the Open era.

Navratilova's domination of the women, marred only by that single loss, and Evert Lloyd's march to a record-tying fifth French title, was the story of the year in tennis. It overshadowed a mad scramble on the men's circuit as the major championships were divided four ways for the first time in seven years. The race for No. 1 wasn't decided until the Masters in the 13th month of an exhausting season. At the end, the distinction belonged once again to John McEnroe, who boasted a second Wimbledon crown among his seven singles titles.

For breadth of accomplishment however, Mats Wilander emerged as Male Player of the Year. Not only did he win the most matches (82) and singles tournaments (nine), but he went 8-0 in Davis Cup while leading Sweden to a second-place finish to Australia. He also compiled the best record in the major tournaments. He captured the Australian title, was runner-up at the French, reached the quarterfinals at the U.S. and the third round at Wimbledon. He also finished atop the Volvo Grand Prix stand-

Considering their backgrounds, their forehand and their achievements, one would not expect to mention them in the same sentence, but on May 28, Martina Navratilova and Kathy Horvath shared a court in Paris. In retrospect, it may have been the most significant match of the year.

Even at the time, it was something special. Navratilova had won her first 36 matches of 1983 before meeting the teen-ager in the fourth round of the French Open. A former child prod-

ings, pocketing a $600,000 bonus which enabled him to finish third in prize money behind Ivan Lendl and McEnroe.

In terms of shock value and fan satisfaction, however, perhaps nothing compared to Yannick Noah's victory in Paris. By turning back defending champ Wilander in the final, the acrobatic athlete from Cameroon became the first French citizen in 37 years to hold the French title. He also became such a celebrity that he found it necessary to flee to little old New York for privacy.

On another national front, Jimmy Connors continued his mastery of the Flushing Meadow hard courts, claiming his fifth U.S. crown while denying Lendl a first major title. The angular Czech also stumbled in the Masters final. He was consoled by checks totaling $1,747,128.

Lendl's earnings exceeded even those of Navratilova. But the $1,456,030 she collected, more than triple the take of Evert Lloyd, was only one indicator of the success she enjoyed. At the very least, it was the most stellar female performance since Margaret Smith Court completed her Grand Slam in 1970. Suzanne Lenglen of France and Americans Helen Wills Moody and Alice Marble posted unbeaten seasons earlier in the century, but they didn't play in all the major championships or endure the same demanding schedule.

Consider that Navratilova won 16 of the 17 singles events she entered and added 13 doubles championships, including 11 in the company of Pam Shriver. Her greatest satisfaction occurred in New York, where she annexed her first U.S. Open title. That brought to 11 the number of players, male and female, to have won all four of the major championships.

But for the intervention of Horvath, it might have been a season unlike any other. Horvath, at 17, was almost four years removed from her greatest moment of fame. An eighth-grader, she had advanced through the qualifying rounds to reach the main draw of the 1979 U.S. Open less than a week after her 14th birthday, the youngest ever entered, and received a first-round bye before being ousted, not without a struggle, by sixth-seeded Dianne Fromholtz, 7-6, 6-2.

After two years of consistent progress, Horvath received a setback in 1982 when she was sidelined for four months by a back injury. But she worked her way up to No. 33 on the computer by the spring of 1983, winning Nashville on the satellite circuit over Czech Marcela Skuherska and reaching the semifinals of the Italian Open. Unseeded at the German Open, Horvath knocked off sixth-seeded Bonnie Gadusek, 1-6, 6-2, 6-2, 13th-seeded Andrea Leand, 6-3, 6-3, third-seeded Bettina Bunge, 6-4, 7-6, and second-seeded Andrea Jaeger, 1-6, 7-6, 7-5, en route to the final where she succumbed to Evert Lloyd, 6-4, 7-6 (7-3).

Understandably, these achievements paled alongside those of Navratilova, who stormed through four tournaments on the Virginia Slims circuit, then overpowered Evert Lloyd, 6-2, 6-0, in the championship finale at New York. Adapting quickly to clay, she won a second consecutive Family Circle Cup at Hilton Head, overcoming Tracy Austin, 5-7, 6-1, 6-0. Limited by injuries to eight tournaments, the luckless Austin appeared in only the one final.

Entering the French, Navratilova appeared unbeatable. She was backstopped by a trainer and motivator (Nancy Lieber-

man), a regular coach (Mike Estep), a strategist (Renee Richards) and even a nutritionist. The entourage was called "Team Navratilova."

Against the biggest arsenal in the game, Horvath marshaled her resolve and an attack strategy that contrasted with her earlier years as a baseline mechanic. "To be in the rankings these days," she said, "you have to be really steady from the baseline but you also have to be able to finish up the point. Against a serve-and-volleyer, when it's close, it's important to get to the net first. They're used to being there, and if you take that away from them, they get shaky."

She did exactly as planned against Navratilova, and the defending champion was as bothered as Horvath had hoped. The youngster kept hitting to Navratilova's backhand and volleying her increasingly weak returns. Evert Lloyd didn't appear any more pleased than her rival when she heard the score. "All I thought was, 'Damn, I wish I'd been the one to beat her,'" she said.

In six meetings that year, Evert Lloyd failed to do just that but she never got the chance on her best surface. She had to be satisfied with beating Helena Sukova, 6-2, 3-6, 6-3, eighth-seeded Hana Mandlikova, 4-6, 6-3, 6-2; third-seeded Jaeger, 6-3, 6-1 and Mima Jausovec, 6-1, 6-2 in the last four rounds to clinch her fifth French title, tying Court's record. Jausovec, the 1977 champion, ended Horvath's dream in the quarterfinals, 6-1, 6-1. Another dream was beginning to hatch, though unnoticed, belonging to a 13-year-old German named Steffi Graf. She won, 6-4, 6-1, over Swede Carina Karlsson and then lost, 6-0, 7-6, to South African Bev Mould, but it was enough to make her believe she'd win it all one day—and she would, six times, starting four years later.

It didn't take Navratilova long to start on a new streak. She prepared for Wimbledon by routing Wendy Turnbull in the final at Eastbourne, 6-1, 6-1, and was at her devastating best at Wimbledon, where her matches averaged 47 minutes. The field was weakened notably by Evert Lloyd's colossal dismissal in the third round. Suffering from the after-effects of flu, the three-time champion was eliminated by Kathy Jordan, 6-1, 7-6 (7-2). It marked the first time in 35 major tournaments, dating back to 1971, that she failed to reach the semifinal.

In her absence, Billie Jean King made another run as the 10th seed at age 39. For the second consecutive year, she won the warmup at Birmingham, over the 1982 National Intercollegiate champ, Stanford's Alycia Moulton, 6-0, 7-5, and then advanced to the round of four at the All England Club with a 7-5, 6-4 triumph over Jordan in the quarterfinal.

The Old Lady, however, was no match for Jaeger in the semis. The 18-year-old, not even half King's age, passed and lobbed her opponent into submission, 6-1, 6-1, to become the youngest women's finalist at Wimbledon since Maureen Connolly in 1952. She had little time or reason to savor the honor. Navratilova, who had crushed unseeded Yvonne Vermaak, a tiny South African in the other semi, 6-1, 6-1, overwhelmed third-seeded Jaeger, 6-0, 6-3, and proudly accepted the mantle of No. 1 player in the world.

Although no other female player on earth possessed her combination of strength and agility, there remained the faintest of doubts about her composure as she prepared for her final frontier, the U.S. Open. It was the mental edge to which Evert

Lloyd clung, even after she fell in the final to Navratilova at the Virginia Slims of Los Angeles, 6-1, 6-3, and the Canadian Open, 6-4, 4-6, 6-1, in consecutive weeks. The defending champ seemed to be counting upon her rival to fall apart at Flushing Meadow once again.

Certainly, no other threat materialized in the course of the tournament. Navratilova waded through the field with almost as much dispatch as she displayed at Wimbledon. She failed to drop more than four games in any of her first five matches and she continued to limit her court time to under one hour through the semifinal, where she avenged her 1982 loss to Shriver in businesslike fashion, 6-2, 6-1.

Nor did Evert Lloyd struggle unduly. Her run of straight-set victories included a 6-3, 7-6 (8-6) payback triumph over Jordan in the fourth round. In turning back Jo Durie of Great Britain, 6-4, 6-4, in the semifinal, she qualified to defend the title she had regained the previous year. If there was any stopping Navratilova, this was the time and, particularly, the place.

But Navratilova had come too far, had worked too hard to trip over her own anxieties. She took charge of the match at the outset, en-route to a decisive 6-1, 6-3 victory in 63 minutes. It was the most satisfying victory of her career in her 11th U.S. Open try after one final and four semifinals. "If I don't win another tournament in my life," she said, "I can still say I've done it all."

With the last jewel in her crown, she silenced criticism of her emotional fortitude. In the second set, Evert Lloyd had rallied briefly for her lone break and then held serve at love for a 3-2 lead. But Navratilova tightened the screws, holding her own serve and then breaking Evert Lloyd at love before running out the set. The first-time U.S. champion set a record for fewest games lost in a seven-match tournament (19 of 103).

Navratilova continued to cut a swath through the women's tour all the way to Melbourne and the Australian Open. There, in the absence of Evert Lloyd, she was almost undone in the quarters by a soggy lawn and eighth-seed Jo Durie, another net-seeker. The Englishwoman captured the first set before rain postponed the match. Navratilova rallied the following day to win, 4-6, 6-3, 6-4, taking five of the last six games.

She then turned back Shriver, 6-4, 6-3, and Jordan, 6-2, 7-6 (7-5), completing the campaign with her 50th consecutive victory in her ninth successive tournament final. Sparky 16-year-old Carling Bassett out of Toronto beat Sharon Walsh, 7-6, 6-4, to make the quarters, a high point in a major at the time for a Canadian, before losing to Shriver, 6-0, 6-1.

Remarkably, Navratilova also teamed with Shriver to retain the doubles title, defeating Turnbull and Anne Hobbs, 6-4, 6-7 (5-7), 6-2—an encore of their championships at Wimbledon, 6-2, 6-2, over Rosie Casals and Turnbull, and the U.S, 6-7 (4-7), 6-1, 6-3, over Ros Fairbank and Candy Reynolds. They had scratched from the French due to a Shriver injury, unable to pursue the Grand Slam that would be theirs in 1984.

No female doubles team had won three majors in a season since Court and Virginia Wade 10 years earlier. Their lone defeat, by King and Anne Smith at the Tournament of Champions final in April, 6-3, 1-6, 7-6 (11-9), ended a 40-match streak. So they started another that reached 31 by season's end.

Navratilova also assumed Evert Lloyd's former role as captain and chief assassin of the Wightman Cup team, leading the U.S. to a 6-1 victory over Great Britain at Williamsburg, Va. The captain and Shriver each beat Durie, and Sue Barker by virtual no-contest scores.

Neither Martina nor Chrissie was available for the Federation Cup in Zurich, however, and the U.S. was beaten in the semifinal, 3-0, by champion Czechoslovakia, taking the Cup for a second time. Candy Reynolds gave way to Helena Sukova, 6-2, 6-2, and Jaeger to Mandlikova, 7-5, 5-7, 6-3, terminating a U.S. streak of seven Cups and 37 series. The one-two punch of unbeaten Mandlikova (5-0) and Sukova (4-1) then took care of West Germany 2-1 final. It was over after Hana beat Bettina Bunge, 6-2. 3-0, ret., and Helena beat Claudia Kohde-Kilsch, 6-4, 2-6, 6-2.

Only two women other than Navratilova won more than two tournaments all year. Evert Lloyd captured six titles and, aside from her six losses to Navratilova, slipped only twice—to Jordan at Wimbledon and to Lisa Bonder, 7-5, 4-6, 6-4, in the first round at Tokyo. Hungarian Andrea Temesvari won two events besides her Italian Open title (over Bonnie Gadusek, 6-1, 6-0): The U.S. Clay Courts over Zina Garrison, 6-2, 6-2, and Hittfield, Germany, over German Eva Pfaff, 6-4, 6-2. And Horvath, the obstacle to perfection at Paris, won the minor league Ginny championship playoff at Honolulu in November over Bassett, 4-6, 6-2, 7-6.

Although the men offered no transcendent figure, they were a lot more competitive from the start of the European season to the finish of a dandy Masters in January, 1984. In a year of new faces, the youngest and freshest belonged to Jimmy Arias, who became the dirt-kicking King of Italy, waving his huge forehand as a sceptre in sweeping the country's soil: First, in Florence over native Francesco Cancellotti, 6-4, 6-3; then the Open in Rome, 6-2, 6-7 (3-7), 6-1, 6-4, over Spaniard Jose Higueras, at age 18; finally in Palermo, as a new 19-year-old, over Argentine Jose-Luis Clerc, 6-2, 2-6, 6-0. A third year pro who was in the first wave of coach Nick Bollettieri's baseline prodigies, Arias would go on to capture the U.S. Clay Courts over Ecuadorian Andres Gomez, 6-4, 2-6, 6-4, skyrocket to No. 6 on the ATP computer and, besieged by injuries, fail to win another tournament in the decade.

Emotionally, no one made a more spectacular jump than Noah, even though he was 23 and had been a steady winner on the tour for five seasons. Until this year, however, he hadn't advanced beyond the quarterfinals of a major event. But on the occasion of the 1983 French Open, he was more than a gifted entertainer. He was a champion. With a running start provided by his victory at the German Open, where he deposed Jose Higueras, 3-6, 7-5, 6-2, 6-0. Seeded No. 6, Noah tore through Paris, dropping only one set, that to No. 3-seeded Lendl in the quarters, 7-6 (7-5), 6-2, 5-7, 6-0. The fans at Roland Garros were treated to the extraordinary sight of two Frenchmen in the semis after wild card Christophe Roger-Vasselin, ranked No. 230, shocked top-seeded Connors in straight sets, 6-4, 6-4, 7-6 (7-5), the upset of the year and one of the most stunning in French history. The last time two natives had gone so far was 1946: Champion Marcel Bernard overcoming Yvon Petra, 5-7, 6-2, 6-3, 5-7, 6-2, then beating favored Czech Jaroslav Drobny for the title, 3-6, 2-6, 6-1, 6-4, 6-3.

Noah easily disposed of his countryman, 6-3, 6-0, 6-0 in the semis, and then ground down the defending champ, resourceful No. 5 seed Wilander, 6-2, 7-5, 7-6 (7-3). In the quarters, Wilander spectacularly evicted second-seeded McEnroe, 1-6, 6-2, 6-4, 6-0—winning the last 11 games and 23 straight points to 1-0, 40-0 (45 of last 57 points)! The last set of the two-hour, 12-minute match took 24 minutes.

The aftermath wasn't nearly so inspirational. Noah was idled by a 42-day suspension for failing to show up and represent France at the World Team Cup in Dusseldorf, and by a knee injury. He played in only four more tournaments, including the U.S. Open where he lost to Arias in a splendid quarterfinal, 7-6 (7-4), 4-6, 6-3, 1-6, 7-5.

But before Flushing Meadow, there was Wimbledon and a new cast of up-and-comers. These included Nduka "Duke" Odizor of Nigeria and the University of Houston. Serving 14 aces while bouncing fourth-seeded Guillermo Vilas in the opening round, 3-6, 5-7, 7-6 (9-7), 7-5, 6-2, he reached the fourth round. Hard-serving Kevin Curren of South Africa dismantled top-seeded Connors, 4-6, 7-6 (7-4), 6-2, 7-6 (8-6), in the fourth round with the help of 33 aces, and went past Tim Mayotte, 4-6, 7-6 (7-4), 6-2, 7-6 (8-6) to the semifinal. There he met Chris Lewis, a dashing Kiwi ranked No. 91, who outlasted Curren in a brilliant five-set semifinal that left the participants applauding each other, 6-7 (3-7), 6-4, 7-6 (7-4), 6-7 (3-7), 8-6.

Lewis became the first unseeded player to reach a Wimbledon final since Willy Bungert in 1967 and the first New Zealander in the championship match since the much-idolized Tony Wilding won four consecutive titles, 1910 - 1913. There, however, reality struck in the form of McEnroe's impenetrable serving and superb court sense. In three immaculate sets of serve-and-volley tennis, the American won easily, 6-2, 6-2, 6-2, in 85 minutes, to regain the honor he last held in 1981. McEnroe dropped but one set, that to Romanian Florin Segarceanu in the second round.

Californian Trey Waltke, 28, won only his first rounder (over an ex-champ, Stan Smith, 37, 6-4, 3-6, 2-6, 6-3, 2-0, ret.), but he lent a nostalgic air to proceedings in long white trousers. Such were universal male apparel for about 60 years until shorts (bravely introduced by Bunny Austin in 1932) took over after World War II. Though it was uncertain who had last appeared in trousers, Yvon Petra in 1946 was the most recent champion.

Two surprise packages at the U.S. Open were a stocky double-hander all the way, Greg Holmes, the National Intercollegiate (Utah) and Pan American Games champ, and skinny 16-year-old Aaron Krickstein from Grosse Pointe, Mich., the country's youngest junior champ. Both made the last 16. Holmes, ranked No. 450, knocked off an ex-champ, sixth-seeded Vilas, 6-2, 6-2, 6-3, in the third round. Amateur Krickstein, with no ranking, was, like Arias, a product of Nick Bollettieri's Florida finishing school of two-fisted backhands. Playing in his first major tournament, he attracted attention by waylaying a big name, 15th-seeded Vitas Gerulaitis from way behind, 3-6, 3-6, 6-4, 6-3, 6-4. Krickstein then fell to Noah, 6-3, 7-6, 6-3, who, in turn was eliminated by Aaron's stablemate, Arias, in a five-set match of very good feeling and trick shots, 7-6 (7-4), 4-6, 6-3, 1-6, 7-5. Arias, who had celebrated his 19th birthday three weeks earlier, became the youngest American in the semis

since 17-year-old Oliver Campbell in 1888. This impressed Lendl not a bit, and he sent the King of Italy home to Bradenton, Fla., 6-4, 6-4, 7-6 (7-4), after he defeated Wilander, 6-2, 7-6 (7-3), 6-1 in the quarters.

Awaiting Lendl in the final was Connors, the defending champion. To reach the championship round for a seventh time, third-seeded Connors gave a 6-2, 6-3, 6-2 brush-off to slick-volleying Bill Scanlon, who had out-nerved and out-served McEnroe in the fourth round, 7-6 (7-2), 7-6 (7-3), 4-6, 6-3. Moving on, Scanlon labored hour after hour well into the following morning, and the fifth hour, to defeat, in a fifth-set tie-breaker, the tourney's hypnotic over-achiever, No. 96 Mark Dickson, 3-6, 6-4, 4-6, 6-3, 7-6 (7-4). A Floridian dawdler, Dickson routinely bounced the ball 30-or-so times before serving. That inspired a plaintive wall message in red paint in a men's room: I SURVIVED SCANLON-DICKSON—4:14.

Because Connors, just turned 31, was playing with a bone spur on his right little toe, was suffering from diarrhea (he rushed to the men's room late in the second set) and was combating court temperatures in excess of 100 degrees, the time appeared ripe for Lendl. After splitting the first two sets, the Czech expatriate served for the third set at 5-4. The title appeared within his reach. Then, inexplicably, he double-faulted at set point. After that, he said, "I could never recover." In a mysterious meltdown, the man who hadn't lost a set until the final, never won another game. Connors whipped through the last nine games to win his fifth U.S. title, 6-3, 6-7 (2-7), 7-5, 6-0. An international statistical panel recently had ruled that some of his early achievements were of an exhibition nature and revised his total of career tournament victories to 99, so Connors re-celebrated his centennial in his favorite setting.

One of those was on the carpet at Memphis, where Jimmy broke a tie with a forgotten rival while winning the U.S. Indoor for a record sixth time. In beating Gene Mayer, 7-5, 6-0, he renewed a title he first won at Salisbury, Md., a decade before. That sent him ahead of long-departed Wylie Grant from deep in the long-trousered era, a five-time champ, too: 1903-04, 1906, 1908, 1912.

As the season waned, boy Krickstein also found his way into the record book by winning his first pro title. He was 16-years, two months, he was the youngest to take a professional tournament. It was a long-shot special, wild card Aaron, No. 489, beating No. 189, German Christopher Zipf, 7-6, 6-3, in Tel Aviv, Israel. Krickstein, at 15 earlier in the year, became the youngest to play in a pro event, Philadelphia, losing in the first round to Fritz Buehning, 6-2, 6-3.

At the Australian Open, which attracted most of the elite, although Connors bypassed, 19-year-old Wilander knocked off defending champ Kriek, 6-3, 6-4, 7-6; McEnroe, 4-6, 6-3, 6-4, 6-3, and, finally, Lendl, 6-1, 6-4, 6-4, to become the youngest champion Down Under since Ken Rosewall won at 18 in 1953. It was his ninth victory of a season in which 10 players won three or more tour events and 46 men earned at least $100,000 in prize money.

Parity was in the air, and a handful of players had a chance to claim the No. 1 ranking when the Masters got underway at Madison Square Garden. There was only one notable absentee,

1974 champion Vilas, who had been hit with a one-year suspension by the MIPTC for allegedly accepting $60,000 illicit appearance money at Rotterdam. He subsequently lost an appeal and was fined $20,000. Although the suspension was waived in January 1984, he already had been sidelined for six months.

After reversing his fortune against Wilander, 6-2, 6-4, in the semifinal, McEnroe decisively whipped Lendl, 6-3, 6-4, 6-4, for the title and the top ranking. "John deserves to be No. 1," Lendl said. "He had the most consistent year." For good measure, McEnroe and Peter Fleming, the best doubles team in the world, reprised their Wimbledon and U.S. championship performances by beating the second best team of Pavel Slozil and Tomas Smid, 6-2, 6-2. It was their sixth Masters doubles crown in as many years.

Despite McEnroe's brilliance, he couldn't cope with a dirty deal in Buenos Aires: Argentine clay, plus hometown crowd-inspired Vilas and Jose-Luis Clerc. Thus the defending champion U.S. folded Davis Cup repeat ambitions at the starting gate, 3-2. Mac and Fleming won a hotly contested doubles over the boys from the 'hood, 2-6, 10-8, 6-1, 3-6, 6-1. But by that time Vilas had beaten Gene Mayer, 6-3, 6-3, 6-4, and Clerc had nosed out Mac, 6-4, 6-0, 3-6, 4-6, 7-5. Vilas clinched through a spent McEnroe, 6-4, 6-1, 6-0.

Temporary ownership of the Cup came down to the final at Melbourne and a familiar victor, a grass-loving band of Aussies, 3-2 over Wilander-driven Sweden. Mats kicked it off well, beating the Aussie ace, Patrick Cash, 6-3, 4-6, 9-7, 6-3. It wasn't enough. The locals won the next three: John Fitzgerald over Joakim Nystrom, 6-4, 6-2, 4-6, 6-4; Mark Edmondson and Paul McNamee over Anders Jarryd-Hans Simonsson, 6-4, 6-4, 6-2; Cash over Nystrom, 6-4, 6-1, 6-1.

1983 CHAMPIONS AND LEADERS

Australian Open
Men's Singles Final: Mats Wilander (SWE) def. Ivan Lendl (CZE), 6-1, 6-4, 6-4

Women's Singles Final: Martina Navratilova (USA) def. Kathy Jordan (USA), 6-2, 7-6 (5)

Men's Doubles Final: Mark Edmondson and Paul McNamee (AUS) def. Steve Denton and Sherwood Stewart (USA), 6-3, 7-6

Women's Doubles Final: Martina Navratilova and Pam Shriver (USA) def. Anne Hobbs (GBR) and Wendy Turnbull (AUS), 6-4, 6-7, 6-2

Mixed Doubles: Not Played

French Open
Men's Singles Final: Yannick Noah (FRA) def. Mats Wilander (SWE), 6-2, 7-5, 7-6 (3)

Women's Singles Final: Chris Evert Lloyd (USA) def. Mima Jausovec (YUG), 6-1, 6-2

Men's Doubles Final: Anders Jarryd and Hans Simonsson (SWE) def. Mark Edmondson (AUS) and Sherwood Stewart (USA), 7-6 (4), 6-4, 6-2

Women's Doubles Final: Rosalyn Fairbank (RSA) and Candy Reynolds (USA) def. Kathy Jordan and Anne Smith (USA), 5-7, 7-5, 6-2

Mixed Doubles Final: Barbara Jordan and Eliot Teltscher (USA) def. Leslie Allen and Charles Strode (USA), 6-2, 6-3

Wimbledon
Men's Singles Final: John McEnroe (USA) def. Chris Lewis (NZL), 6-2, 6-2, 6-2

Women's Singles Final: Martina Navratilova (USA) def. Andrea Jaeger (USA), 6-0, 6-3

Men's Doubles Final: Peter Fleming and John McEnroe (USA) def. Tim Gullikson and Tom Gullikson (USA), 6-4, 6-3, 6-4

Women's Doubles Final: Martina Navratilova and Pam Shriver (USA) def. Rosie Casals (USA) and Wendy Turnbull (AUS), 6-2, 6-2

Mixed Doubles Final: Wendy Turnbull (AUS) and John Lloyd (GBR) def. Billie Jean King and Steve Denton (USA), 6-7 (5), 7-6 (5), 7-5

U.S. Open
Men's Singles Final: Jimmy Connors (USA) def. Ivan Lendl (CZE), 6-3, 6-7 (2), 7-5, 6-0

Women's Singles Final: Martina Navratilova (USA) def. Chris Evert Lloyd (USA), 6-1, 6-3

Men's Doubles Final: Peter Fleming and John McEnroe (USA) def. Fritz Buehning and Van Winitsky (USA), 6-3, 6-4, 6-2

Women's Doubles Final: Pam Shriver and Martina Navratilova (USA) def. Ros Fairbank (RSA) and Candy Reynolds (USA), 6-7 (4), 6-1, 6-3

Mixed Doubles Final: Elizabeth Sayers and John Fitzgerald (AUS) def. Barbara Potter and Ferdi Taygan (USA), 3-6, 6-3, 6-4

Year-End No. 1
Men: John McEnroe
Women: Martina Navratilova

Top Player Earnings
Men: Ivan Lendl $1,747,128
Women: Martina Navratilova $1,456,030

Davis Cup: Australia

Federation Cup: Czechoslovakia

Wightman Cup: United States

Grand Prix Masters, NYC—John McEnroe
WCT, Dallas—John McEnroe
Virginia Slims Championships, NYC—Martina Navratilova

1984 A Vintage Year for McEnroe

John McEnroe posted an Open era men's best 82-3 record and won titles at Wimbledon and the US Open.

But for an occasional slip, it might have been said that the only man capable of beating McEnroe this year was McEnroe himself. Certainly, he had to be credited at least with an assist when he allowed himself to be distracted while holding a two-set lead over Ivan Lendl in the final of the French Open. Lendl went on to win the match for his first major triumph.

Thereafter, McEnroe was magnificent in duplicating his 1981 feat of sweeping Wimbledon and the U.S. Open. He also counted the U.S. Pro Indoor title, the WCT Finals, the Canadian Open and the season-ending Masters among his 13 tournament victories. In addition to the loss in Paris, he suffered only two more singles defeats, to Vijay Amritraj at Cincinnati, 6-7, 6-2, 6-3, and to Henrik Sundstrom in the Davis Cup final at Goteborg, 13-11, 6-4, 6-3. McEnroe's 82-3 record produced a .965 winning percentage, highest of the Open era among men. In finishing at the top of the computer rankings for the fourth consecutive year, he enjoyed the most dominant season since Jimmy Connors won the only three major events he entered and compiled a 99-4 mark in 1974, a .961 winning percentage. Jimmy was still going strong 10 years after his big year, claiming five titles, reaching the final at Wimbledon and pushing McEnroe to five sets in a brilliant semifinal showdown at Flushing Meadow.

An 82-3 record, the best by a male in the Open era.

Rare as it may be for any athlete to be identified as a genius, it's more unlikely still to be branded a tormented genius. But John McEnroe fit the billing, never more than in 1984. En route to the greatest season of his career, he jousted with the furies and toyed with his peers.

Andres Gomez, the finest player from Ecuador since Pancho Segura, ascended to the Top 10 by winning five tournaments, including the Italian Open over Aaron Krickstein during a dust storm, 2-6, 6-1, 6-2, 6-2, and the U.S. Clay Courts over Hungarian Balazs Taroczy, 6-0, 7-6. But the biggest breakthrough occurred among the Swedes. Bjorn Borg's legacy was a nation of nine mil-

lion swarming with tennis talent. Mats Wilander and four compatriots—Sundstrom, Anders Jarryd, Joakim Nystrom, Stefan Edberg—not only seized the Davis Cup for the first time in nine years but they accounted for 14 tournament victories.

Yet, the only individual to challenge McEnroe for supremacy and attention was Martina Navratilova, who continued her mastery of the women's tour. She won three of the major tournaments and 78 of 80 singles matches, a phenomenal season by any standard but the one she established the previous year. This time, Navratilova fell two victories short of a Grand Slam when she was upset by Helena Sukova in the semifinals of the Australian Open in December. She had suffered her only other loss of the year to Hana Mandlikova 11 months earlier in Oakland. Both women once had served as ballgirls at Navratilova's matches in Czechoslovakia.

In addition to her 13 tournament victories, Martina posted the longest (74 matches) winning streak of the Open era and, at the time, the third-longest (54). She also surpassed her great rival, Chris Evert Lloyd, in head-to-head competition by winning all six meetings, with the loss of only one set.

Evert Lloyd did claim the Australian Open title by beating Sukova, thereby extending to 11 years her incredible streak of having won at least one major championship. That was her 132nd professional tournament singles victory and increased her total of matches won to 1,003, having nailed her 1,000th over Pascale Paradis of France in the third round, 6-1, 6-7 (5-7), 6-2.

Manuela Maleeva, a 17-year-old Bulgarian, made the biggest jump among the women. She vaulted from No. 31 to No. 6 in the world rankings by winning four tournaments, among them the rain-plagued Italian Open, where she stunned five-time champion Evert Lloyd 6-3, 6-3, Manuela's third victory of a strenuous last day in Perugia. She started with a 7-6, 4-6, 6-4 win over Virginia, Ruzici, followed, 6-2, 6-2, over Carling Bassett, and finished with Evert—67 games. Headed in the opposite direction were Tracy Austin, who played in only one tournament before being sidelined again with a chronic back ailment, and Andrea Jaeger, who withdrew from the tour to enter college after lackluster efforts in six events.

At the Richmond, Va., indoor tournament, a couple of women, Vicki Nelson-Dunbar, 21, of Wooster, Ohio, and Jean Hepner, 25, of Atherton, Calif., had no idea when they went on court for a first rounder that they wouldn't leave for more than six hours. They recorded the longest documented match played at the time: six hours, 31 minutes, won by Nelson-Dunbar, 6-3, 7-6 (13-11). (Fabrice Santoro later beat Arnaud Clement in 6:33 at the 2004 French.) Steadfast, stubborn baseliners, involved in interminable rallies, they devoted 1:47 to the tie-breaker alone, one point of which lasted 29 minutes and 643 strokes.

Yikes – suppose they'd played a third set!

But the year will belong forever to McEnroe and Navratilova, who never again would stand unchallenged. (Although only 25, McEnroe would not win another major in singles.) The two shared a physical characteristic, left-handedness, and a love for doubles.

McEnroe won seven doubles titles. In six of those tournaments, including Wimbledon and the Masters, he was joined by

his steady partner Peter Fleming. Together, they raised their victory total to 52 titles.

According to Fleming, "The best doubles team in the world is John McEnroe and whoever he plays with." As if to prove it, Mac took his 17-year-old brother Patrick, a top junior, to a WCT tournament in Richmond and they routed Kevin Curren and Steve Denton, the 1982 U.S. Open champions, in the final, 7-6 (7-3), 6-2.

Navratilova enjoyed even greater success in doubles, losing one of 61 matches. But with Pam Shriver, she was perfection. She and Pam completed the Open era's only undefeated season by a team: 11 titles, 53 matches. Pam's personal doubles match record was 59-2. The pair also registered the only Grand Slam by a female doubles team, equaling the 1951 feat of Aussies Frank Sedgman and Ken McGregor. Martina and Pam were 22-0 over that four-way stretch, losing two sets. By beating Sukova and German Claudia Kohde-Kilsch, 6-3, 6-4, they added the Australian title to the other three: French over Kohde-Kilsch and Mandlikova, 5-7, 6-3, 6-2; Wimbledon over countrywomen Anne Smith and Kathy Jordan, 6-3, 6-4; and U.S. over the Anglo-Aussie combine of Anne Hobbs and Wendy Turnbull, 6-2, 6-4. The Australian was their 52nd career triumph.

Despite the parallel success of the two champions, however, there was a significant distinction in their approach to the sport. Having reshuffled her entourage midway through the 1983 season, Navratilova continued to improve her conditioning under coach Mike Estep and became a disciple of Robert Haas, the nutritionist, whose *Eat to Win* diet found favor among a number of players.

That led a reporter to inquire of McEnroe, who played doubles in order to avoid tedious practice sessions and whose appetite was ruled by his taste buds, whether he had tried the Haas diet. "No," he smirked, "I prefer the Haagen-Dazs diet."

McEnroe was never better than in 1984, which he began in spectacular fashion. Following his Masters victory, he thrashed Lendl at the U.S. Pro Indoor in Philadelphia, 6-3, 3-6, 6-3, 7-6 (7-3), the Belgian Indoor in Brussels, 6-1, 6-3, the WCT Tournament of Champions at Forest Hills, 6-4, 6-2, and the World Team Cup at Dusseldorf, 6-3, 6-2. He also dismissed Tomas Smid at the Grand Prix de Madrid, 6-0, 6-4, and overwhelmed Connors, 6-1, 6-2, 6-3, at the WCT Finals in Dallas. In reaching the championship round of the French Open for the first time, he extended his winning streak to 42 matches, an Open era high for an American man.

Not that his form left him serene. Paris was a struggle from the outset. There, in addition to opponents, Mac battled the usual suspects—courtside photographers, groundskeepers, line judges—as well as the ambience of the tournament and city itself, of which he had once declared in full voice, "I hate this place."

Top-seeded McEnroe demanded court repairs during a third-round victory over Mel Purcell, 6-4, 6-4, 6-1, drilled two balls into the photographers' pit while beating Jose Higueras, 6-4, 7-6 (7-5), 3-6, 6-3, and complained so much about calls in a semifinal 7-5, 6-1, 6-2, spanking of Connors that the latter offered some free advice while approaching the net. "Shut up," the onetime bad boy yelled. "Grow up. You're a baby."

While the top seed battled his personal demons, Lendl tore through his half of the draw virtually unscathed. He dropped

only one set in reaching the final. In the semis, he blasted the steady Wilander, 6-2, 6-3, 7-5, who had eliminated defending champion Yannlck Noah, 7-6 (7-4), 2-6, 3-6, 6-3, 6-3. For the first two sets of their showdown on clay, McEnroe was completely in charge, granting only 10 points on his serve. He appeared certain to become the first American male since Tony Trabert (1954-55) to win at Roland Garros.

Given his form and past performances at Wimbledon and the U.S. Open, a Grand Slam was not out of the question. At that critical juncture of history, however, McEnroe snapped. He objected to a television cameraman's headset that was emitting a director's instructions, began grousing at photographers and became the object of hooting and whistling from the crowd.

Meanwhile, Lendl, 0-for-4 in previous major championship finals, was ready to shed his reputation for gagging in the majors. He was the stronger down the fifth set stretch to win 3-6, 2-6, 6-4, 7-5, 7-5 in four hours, eight minutes. "It feels great to finally answer some different questions," the new champion said after becoming only the 14th man in 107 years to overcome a two-set deficit in the final of a major event. An alleged choker no more, Lendl had the first of his eight majors that decorated a great career, after failing in his title bids at Roland Garros to Bjorn Borg in 1981, the U.S. in 1982 and 1983 to Connors and the Australian to Wilander in 1983.

McEnroe appeared to have learned his lessons from Paris in time for Wimbledon. Either that or the uncharacteristically benign weather left him mellow. The defending champ behaved impeccably at the All England Club and he performed brilliantly. Whether the one had anything to do with the other was pure conjecture.

He ceded only one set in the tournament—to Paul McNamee in the first round. 6-4, 6-4, 6-7 (7-9), 6-1—and was mesmerizing in dismissing Connors, 6-1, 6-1, 6-2, in the final. That followed brisk victories over Billy Scanlon, 6-3, 6-3, 6-1; John Sadri, 6-3, 6-3, 6-1 and over future champ Pat Cash, 6-3, 7-6 (7-5), 6-4. Even McEnroe, the perfectionist, allowed that the title bout, almost error-free, was "maybe the best match of my life." Connors had beaten Lendl, 6-7 (4-7), 6-3, 7-5, 6-1, to get there.

It had been 46 years since a Wimbledon championship was concluded in such decisive fashion (Don Budge over Bunny Austin, 6-1, 6-0, 6-3). Incredibly, McEnroe didn't commit the first of his two unforced errors until the 62-minute mark of Connors' 90-minute ordeal. The champion served 75 percent, with 11 aces, and never permitted Connors a break point in becoming the second American male to win Wimbledon for a third time, following the lead of Bill Tilden, and the first to hold consecutive titles since Budge in 1937 and 1938.

Although this would be the last of 15 major finals for 31-year-old Connors, he had more bullets in his gun, some of them fired at Memphis, where he extended his U.S. Indoor record to seven titles, beating Henri Leconte, 6-3, 4-6, 7-5. Only three American men had won that many U.S. prizes on a particular surface: Dick Sears, Bill Larned and Bill Tilden ruled the foremost U.S. Championship, then played on grass, seven times. Jimmy joined them with his hothouse variety. There were bullets, too, for the U.S. Open, where he fed on the energy of the crowds.

En-route to the next duel of American titans, McEnroe suffered his second loss of the year. He was defeated by Indian Vijay Amritraj, a budding film star, in the first round at Cincinnati, 6-7, 6-2, 6-3, on the day after he wrapped up his first Canadian Open championship with a straight-set conquest of Vitas Gerulaitis, 6-0, 6-3. Amritraj, who had slipped to No. 104 in the rankings, had won his first Grand Prix tournament in four years only a month earlier, overcoming Tim Mayotte on the last American grass tournament, Newport, 3-6, 6-4, 6-4.

Still, there wasn't any question but that McEnroe was poised to dethrone Connors at the U.S. Open. On the Flushing hard courts, McEnroe raced through his first five opponents, including the young Swede who had won an unofficial gold medal (demonstration class) at the Los Angeles Olympics. The 6-1, 6-0, 6-2 rout of Edberg was a barometer of how well he was playing. Meanwhile, Connors, back home on his favorite surface, also won all 15 sets in advancing to the semifinal, including a victory in a surprising quarterfinal, John (Mr. Chris Evert) Lloyd, 7-5, 6-2, 6-0.

Those who couldn't wait for the showdown of the perennial bad boys had a very long afternoon on Super Saturday at the USTA National Tennis Center. They went on last following a men's 35 match between legends John Newcombe and Stan Smith, the first men's semifinal between Lendl and brash Cash and the women's final between those rivals for the ages, Navratilova and Evert Lloyd. All four matches were carried to the ultimate set and the tennis, which began at 11 a.m., didn't conclude until 11:14 p.m.

Even McEnroe, annoyed that he didn't strike his first ball until 7:28, allowed that, "It had to be the best day (for fans) at the Open ... ever." Certainly, the day's finale qualified as the match of the tournament, if not the year.

After 37 minutes, Connors had equaled the four games he won in the Wimbledon final. Within 90 minutes, he had won a set and broken McEnroe's serve for the fourth time for a 3-1 lead in the third set. In the end, only a scant few shots separated the pair, perhaps none more important than a missed forehand by Connors on break point in the seventh game of the fifth set. Connors finished with 45 winners, to 20 for the winner. But McEnroe's 19 aces pushed him over the top in a magnificent 6-4, 4-6, 7-5, 4-6, 6-3 victory. They agreed the match was superior to their epic 1980 semifinal.

In the final, Lendl, who barely survived his semifinal over Cash, 3-6, 6-3, 6-4, 6-7(5-7), 7-6(8-6)—saving a match point in the fifth with a sensational topspin lob on the run—was no match for a McEnroe at his peak. Eighteen hours after vanquishing Connors, McEnroe routed Lendl, 6-4, 6-3, 6-1, to claim his fourth U.S. title.

The rest of the year wasn't nearly so satisfying for Mac, whose dark side re-emerged while winning the Stockholm Open over Wilander, 6-2, 3-6, 6-2. In the course of a semifinal victory over Jarryd, 1-6, 7-6, 6-2, Mac was fined $2,100 for ball abuse, abuse of an official and unsportsmanlike behavior. The total pushed him over the $7,500 limit, triggering a 21-day suspension.

During his suspension, he injured his left wrist in practice. That caused him to withdraw from the Australian Open, where

second-seeded Wilander had a clear path to his second consecutive title, bashing two-time champ Johan Kriek, 6-1, 6-0, 6-2, in the semifinal, and overcoming Kevin Curren in the final, 6-7 (5-7), 6-4, 7-6 (7-3), 6-2.

With Connors at his side, McEnroe was healed in time for the Davis Cup final in Goteborg. On paper, Captain Arthur Ashe's side was perhaps the strongest of all U.S. Cup lineups, containing the world Nos. 1 and 2 in singles and No. 1 in doubles. However, it was played not on paper but clay, a surface on which eight of 10 previous U.S. defeats over the last 20 years had occurred. Priced at $30,000, a specially-laid court made of 42 tons of crushed bricks was installed within the Scandinavium. Connors had committed himself to the full year of Cup play for the first time but, distracted by the impending birth of his second child, was as unprepared as McEnroe for the tough Swedes on clay. He hadn't competed in weeks, wasn't speaking to McEnroe, and neither had much to say to Captain Ashe.

In what was a dark first day for American tennis, weak on esprit, both Connors and McEnroe were drubbed and Connors embarrassed himself and his team by incurring a game penalty and adding a $2,000 fine for profane language. Wilander handled Connors easily, 6-1, 6-3, 6-3, but the real surprise occurred in the next match when McEnroe was upset by lanky 20-year-old Henrik Sundstrom, 13-11, 6-4, 6-3.

ITF (International Tennis Federation) management stipulated that Connors apologize for his misbehavior or the entire series would be forfeited to Sweden. Halfheartedly he did, and the show went on. One day later, Jarryd and Edberg applied the finishing strokes to the great doubles team of McEnroe and Fleming. The pair had won 14 Cup matches without defeat but weren't up to the task against the Swedes. The 18-year-old Edberg, with his kicking serve, was particularly effective in the right court in the 7-5, 5-7, 6-2, 7-5 triumph. He became the youngest winning player in a Cup title round.

Although McEnroe's 6-3, 5-7, 6-3 third-day victory over Wilander was mostly cosmetic, it did spare the U.S. the ignominy of a 5-0 shutout and helped to prepare him for the season-ending Masters. Back in New York, McEnroe defeated both Jarryd, 2-6, 6-4, 6-2, and Wilander, 6-1, 6-1, en-route to the final, where he crushed Lendl, 7-5, 6-0, 6-4. That raised Mac's earnings to $2,026,109. For good measure, he then combined with Fleming to turn back Mark Edmondson and Sherwood Stewart, 6-3, 6-1, for their seventh consecutive Masters doubles title.

In the scarcely shared opinion of the ITF, which ruled in 1982 that a player need only win four consecutive majors to claim a Grand Slam, Navratilova completed the quartet in early June at the French Open. Her reward from the ITF was a $1 million bonus. Still, few were prepared to grant her admission to the select group of those who had won the four majors in the course of a calendar year—Don Budge, 1938; Maureen Connolly, 1953; Rod Laver, 1962 and 1969; and Margaret Smith Court, 1970.

After Navratilova routed Evert Lloyd, 6-3, 6-1, in Paris, however, few doubted that this would be the year for such a feat. She hadn't lost a match since her first tournament in January. And only Mandlikova, in the semifinal, took a set off her at Stade Roland Garros, 3-6, 6-2, 6-2.

At Wimbledon, Martina was even more formidable. Her only persistent opposition in England came from the tabloid press, which outdid itself in pursuing Navratilova's relationship with her newest traveling companion, former Texas beauty queen Judy Nelson. On the court, she was tested only in the championship match when Evert Lloyd, who hadn't lost a set either, began with two service breaks for a 3-0 lead. Not to worry. Navratilova stormed back for a 7-6 (7-5), 6-2 victory, handing Evert Lloyd her sixth final defeat.

It marked the second consecutive Wimbledon in which Navratilova had failed to drop a set. Her third successive title was the first for a female since Billie Jean King's 1966 – 68 run. As a sidebar, Steffi Graf, who had peeked into the French and Australian Opens in 1983, tried her third major, Wimbledon, and, at 15, showed signs of the "Fraulein Forehand" she would become, winning three rounds before losing in the fourth round to Jo Durie, 3-6, 6-3, 9-7.

The Navratilova pattern continued at Flushing Meadow, which produced one notable sidelight. Gabriela Sabatini, a 14-year, four-month old Argentine, introduced herself to the world. A future champ, Gaby became the youngest player ever to win a U.S. Open match, 6-3, 3-6, 6-2, over American Paula Smith. Unsatisfied with one, she actually won another, over Kim Schaefer, 6-4, 6-1, before losing to Sukova, 6-4, 6-4.

Sukova reached the quarters, 4-6, 7-5, 6-4, over Lisa Bonder, where she was beaten, 6-3, 6-3, by Navratilova, whom her mother, 1962 Wimbledon finalist Vera Sukova, once had coached back in Czechoslovakia. The top-ranked player in the world marched into the final without the loss of a set, stopping Turnbull in the semis, 6-4, 6-1. Ditto her great rival, Evert Lloyd, who had beaten the Torontonian, 14th-seeded Carling Bassett, 6-2, 6-2. Carling's semifinal arrival was the utmost performance for a Canadian in a major.

When Navratilova and Evert Lloyd collided in Louis Armstrong Stadium on Sept. 8, their series stood at 30 victories apiece. Additionally, Navratilova had won 54 consecutive matches, one shy of her opponent's Open era record. With all that and an Open title at stake, Evert Lloyd played superbly, perhaps the best of any of her nine U.S. finals. Still, it was insufficient. Navratilova rallied for a 4-6, 6-4, 6-4 victory. "It's just not enough to play a good match against her anymore," Evert Lloyd lamented.

With six consecutive majors to Navratilova's credit, the Australian Open appeared a formality. She prepared herself for the grass at Kooyong by winning a doubles tournament at Brisbane with Shriver (their 78th straight match win together) and the singles at Sydney over Ann Henrickson, 6-1, 6-1. At Melbourne, she dropped only one set (to Kathy Rinaldi, 4-6, 6-0, 6-1, in the fourth round) in advancing to the semifinal and then raced through a 6-1 first set against Sukova.

But the 6-foot-2 Sukova, who, at 19, had just notched her first important singles title at Brisbane over Aussie Liz Sayers, 6-4, 6-4, broke for 4-2 in the second set and, at 5-5 in the third, achieved the deciding break. Navratilova didn't go down without a fight, saving five match points with a series of admirable forehands before her backhand return sailed over the baseline.

"It hurts but I'm sure I'll get over it," she said after the 1-6, 6-3, 7-5 defeat that terminated her streak at 74 matches and ended

the dream of a genuine Grand Slam. Sukova, the ninth seed, carried the momentum into the final but couldn't sustain it as the steady Evert Lloyd rallied for a 6-7 (4-7), 6-1, 6-3 triumph, her 16th major singles championship, marking the eleventh straight year in which she had won a major.

Earlier, Evert Lloyd, with singles wins over Hobbs and Durie, had led the U.S. to its sixth successive Wightman Cup triumph over Britain, 5-2, in London. The Americans rebounded from 1-2 as Evert Lloyd and rookie Alycia Moulton beat Virginia Wade and Amanda Brown, 6-2, 6-2, and Barbie Potter beat Hobbs, 6-1, 6-3.

In the absence of both Evert Lloyd and Navratilova, the U.S. was up-ended at Sao Paulo, Brazil, by Australia in a Federation Cup semifinal, 2-1, as Liz Sayers and Turnbull took the decisive doubles over Jordan and Smith, 7-6, 6-4. In the final, Australian Anne Minter made it a perfect five-for-five in singles, beating Sukova, 7-5, 7-5, but the Czechs snapped back to their second successive Cup as Mandlikova floored Sayers, 6-1, 6-0, and combined with Sukova, 6-2, 6-2, over Sayers-Turnbull.

1984 CHAMPIONS AND LEADERS

Australian Open
Men's Singles Final: Mats Wilander (SWE) def. Kevin Curren (RSA), 6-7 (5), 6-4, 7-6 (3), 6-2
Women's Singles Final: Chris Evert Lloyd (USA) def. Helena Sukova (CZE), 6-7 (4), 6-1, 6-3
Men's Doubles Final: Mark Edmondson (AUS) and Sherwood Stewart (USA) def. Joakim Nystrom and Mats Wilander (SWE), 6-2, 6-2, 7-5
Women's Doubles Final: Martina Navratilova and Pam Shriver (USA) def. Claudia Kohde-Kilsch (GER) and Helena Sukova (CZE), 6-3, 6-4
Mixed Doubles: Not Played

French Open
Men's Singles Final: Ivan Lendl (CZE) def. John McEnroe (USA), 3-6, 2-6, 6-4, 7-5, 7-5
Women's Singles Final: Martina Navratilova (USA) def. Chris Evert Lloyd (USA), 6-3, 6-1
Men's Doubles Final: Henri Leconte and Yannick Noah (FRA) def. Pavel Slozil and Tomas Smid (CZE), 6-4, 2-6, 3-6, 6-3, 6-2
Women's Doubles Final: Martina Navratilova and Pam Shriver (USA) def. Claudia Kohde-Kilsch (GER) and Hana Mandlikova (CZE), 5-7, 6-3, 6-2
Mixed Doubles Final: Anne Smith and Dick Stockton (USA) def. Anne Minter and Laurie Warder (AUS), 6-2, 6-4

Wimbledon
Men's Singles Final: John McEnroe (USA) def. Jimmy Connors (USA), 6-1, 6-1, 6-2
Women's Singles Final: Martina Navratilova (USA) def Chris Evert Lloyd (USA), 7-6 (5), 6-2.
Men's Doubles Final: Peter Fleming and John McEnroe (USA) def. Pat Cash and Paul McNamee (AUS), 6-2, 5-7, 6-2, 3-6, 6-3
Women's Doubles Final: Martina Navratilova and Pam Shriver (USA) def. Kathy Jordan and Anne Smith (USA), 6-3, 6-4
Mixed Doubles Final: Wendy Turnbull (AUS) and John Lloyd (GBR) def. Kathy Jordan and Steve Denton (USA), 6-3, 6-3

U.S. Open
Men's Singles Final: John McEnroe (USA) def. Ivan Lendl (CZE) 6-3, 6-4, 6-1
Women's Singles Final: Martina Navratilova (USA) def. Chris Evert Lloyd (USA), 4-6, 6-4, 6-4
Men's Doubles Final: John Fitzgerald (AUS) and Tomas Smid (CZE) def. Stefan Edberg and Anders Jarryd (SWE), 7-6, 6-3, 6-3

Women's Doubles Final: Pam Shriver and Martina Navratilova (USA) def. Anne Hobbs (GBR) and Wendy Turnbull (AUS), 6-2, 6-4
Mixed Doubles Final: Manuela Maleeva (BUL) and Tom Gullikson (USA) def. Elizabeth Sayers and John Fitzgerald (AUS), 2-6, 7-5, 6-4

Year-End No.1
Men: John McEnroe
Women: Martina Navratilova

Top Player Earnings
Men: John McEnroe $2,026,109
Women: Martina Navratilova $2,173,556

Davis Cup: Sweden

Federation Cup: Czechoslovakia

Wightman Cup: United States

Grand Prix Masters, NYC—John McEnroe
WCT, Dallas—John McEnroe
Virginia Slims Championships, NYC—Martina Navratilova

1985 Wunderkind Boris Wows Wimbledon

Boris Becker hits a volley against Kevin Curren in the Wimbledon men's singles final, where Becker, at age 17, became the tournament's youngest men's singles champion.

ment that prizes tradition above all else, Becker challenged the past and won.

Never had anyone so young claimed a men's title at The Lawn Tennis Championships. Never had an unseeded player been fitted for a singles crown. Never had a German male ascended to the throne of tennis. Becker changed all of the above in the span of three hours and 18 minutes on one sunlit, summer afternoon. The youngster, who had won only one previous event on the men's tour (three weeks earlier at Queen's Club in London, over Johan Kriek 6-2, 6-3), climaxed a breathtaking rise to prominence by wearing down eighth-seeded Kevin Curren, 6-3, 6-7 (4-7), 7-6 (7-3), 6-4, in the Wimbledon final. By the end of the season, he had made a spectacular jump in the rankings from No. 65 to No. 6 and became the symbol of change sweeping over the sport.

When Stefan Edberg of Sweden, 22 months older than Becker, dethroned countryman Mats Wilander at the Australian Open, it represented the first time two teen-aged males reigned as champions of the four major tournaments in the same year. Following Wilander's victory at the French Open and Ivan Lendl's breakthrough in the U.S. Open, this also completed a Continental sweep of the major events. Never before had European males held all four majors.

Although Lendl's presence was a familiar one and although he was a relatively old 25, he made a significant contribution to the new order by completing his long and arduous climb to the top of the ATP computer rankings. He posted the biggest triumph of his career by overwhelming John McEnroe, who hadn't

Attention, please. Or, in the native tongue of Boris Becker, Achtung! Not only did a new champion appear on the tennis scene in 1985, he also ushered in a new era.

In a year that sparkled with fresh faces, the brightest and most engaging belonged to a 17-year-old son of a West German architect, a teen-ager either too cool or too naive to know he had no business playing with grown men. At Wimbledon, a tourna-

lost in four previous U.S. finals, at Flushing Meadow, 7-6 (7-1), 6-3, 6-4. He solidified his position at the season-ending Masters in January, 1986, where he lost no sets en route to his third title in five years.

Newcomers also made an impact on the women's circuits, although none came away with major prizes. In what were portents of the future, 15-year-old Gabriela Sabatini of Argentina reached the semifinals of her first French Open and 16-year-old Steffi Graf of West Germany advanced to the final four of the U.S. Open. Additionally, Katerina Maleeva, at 16, two years younger than older sister Manuela, won two tournaments, and Floridian Mary Joe Fernandez became the most callow winner of a U.S. Open match (14 years, eight days), over Italian Laura Garrone, 3-6, 6-1, 6-3.

While Martina Navratilova remained queen of the sport, she yielded two of her dominions. Chris Evert Lloyd unseated her at the French Open and Hana Mandlikova did the honors at the U.S. Open. Navratilova even was separated from her No. 1 ranking by Evert Lloyd after 156 consecutive weeks at the top but she regained her place by the end of the season, in which she added the Australian championship to her sixth Wimbledon singles title.

The stranglehold Navratilova and Pam Shriver had on women's doubles competition also was loosened. Their monumental 26-month winning streak, comprising 109 matches and 23 tournaments, ended on Centre Court in the Wimbledon final, where they were beaten by the Aussie-American alliance of Liz Sayers Smylie and Kathy Jordan, 5-7, 6-3, 6-4. They had also won a record eight consecutive majors. Later in the summer, they also surrendered their U.S. title to the "Twin Towers," 6-foot-1 Claudia Kohde-Kilsch of West Germany and 6-foot-2 Helena Sukova of Czechoslovakia, 6-7 (5-7), 6-2, 6-3.

Coincidentally, McEnroe and Peter Fleming abdicated after the better part of a decade atop men's doubles. Mac decided to put doubles aside after three tournaments, among them Wimbledon, where they faltered before Aussies Pat Cash and John Fitzgerald, 7-6(7-4), 2-6, 6-1, 6-4, two rounds short of defending their title. Their lone victory, at Houston over Hank Pfister and Ben Testerman, 6-3, 6-2, raised their career total to 53 titles. The Wimbledon title went to the Hungarian-Swiss yoking of Balazs Taroczy and Heinz Gunthardt over Cash and Fitzgerald, 6-4, 6-3, 4-6, 6-3. A first-round win by a Danish-Swedish lineup of Michael Mortensen and Jan Gunnarsson over an Aussie-Paraguayan pairing of John Frawley and Victor Pecci concluded with the longest of tie-breakers—50 points, 6-3, 6-4, 4-6, 7-6 (26-24).

A pair of young Americans quickly filled the vacuum. Ken Flach and Robert Seguso, both 22, inherited the U.S. Davis Cup role from the perennial team, compiled a match record of 62-22 and won eight tournaments, including the U.S. Open over the French Yannick Noah and Henri Leconte, 6-7 (5-7), 7-6 (7-1), 7-6 (8-6), 6-0, and U.S. Clay Courts over the Aussie-Czech blend of Kim Warwick and Pavel Slozil 6-4, 6-4.

But the French pair, Noah and Leconte, hotly disputed the title outcome of Flushing Meadow. Did the French lose by a hair? They thought so: Flach's hair. They accused the Americans of cheating. The play in question came with Seguso serving at 4-6 in the third-set tiebreaker, set point. In a furious exchange Leconte swatted a ball that bounded off the net cord and appeared to touch Flach's abundant Afghan-houndly mane on its way out of court. The French claimed a clear touch, thus the point and set. Seguso indicated agreement by starting to change courts. But Flach said, "It could have, but I'm not sure, so I couldn't make the call. We're pros—it's up to the umpire."

Umpire Zeno Pfau said he didn't see it, so couldn't rule. The French chafed and moaned, saying their foes had violated the sporting code by not calling the point against themselves. The Americans accused the French of the professional sin of giving up after losing the set, as seemed true. It was a $65,000 question (first prize). The result stood. Noah and Leconte went home feeling they'd been clipped.

But there was no arguing that Americans Steve "Bull" Denton and Richard Matuszewski served like a couple of unshorn Samsons in a hardly-noticed first-rounder. It went to No. 482 Matuszewski, a qualifier who hummed 19 aces, 6-7 (8-10), 7-6 (7-4), 6-7 (8-10), 6-4, 6-3. But not before they'd bashed away four hours, 11 minutes, and Denton had set a U.S. record with 39 aces (not to mention 24 double faults)—a feat later surpassed by Richard Krajicek's 49 aces in a 1999 five-set quarterfinal against Yevgeny Kafelnikov. The Denton-Matuszewski match was a record, too, as the most ace-splattered match (58), a mark that would last a decade.

Nowhere were the changing times better illustrated than at Wimbledon. None of the usual suspects even made it to the last day. Second-seeded Lendl, whose bid for a second successive French title was ended in the final by Wilander, 3-6, 6-4, 6-2, 6-2, was wiped out in the round of 16 by Leconte, 3-6, 6-4, 6-3, 6-1. Curren, who became a U.S. citizen in March, demolished both top-seeded McEnroe in the quarters, 6-1, 6-2, 6-4 and third-seeded Jimmy Connors in the semis, 6-2, 6-2, 6-1.

Bellyflopping Boris, who threw himself at balls with teenage abandon, injured his left ankle in the fourth round against Tim Mayotte and wanted to quit after the fourth set. His manager, Ion Tiriac, dissuaded him. Becker probably should have been defaulted because of the overly long delay in being treated. He resumed thanks only to the sporting forbearance of Mayotte, winning, 6-3, 4-6, 6-7 (7-9), 7-6 (7-5), 6-2. It was soon obvious that this was a charmed fortnight for the husky redhead. Three of his first six matches were suspended and held over for another day, a circumstance that would unnerve even veteran players.

Not Becker. He responded to every challenge like a man, yet still reacted with the infectious enthusiasm of a boy. In taking his semi from Anders Jarryd, 2-6, 7-6 (7-3), 6-3, 6-3, he served his way out of two set points in the second set. In the final, before a capacity crowd that included assorted princes and princesses, the 6-foot-3 man-child answered Curren's serve with a bludgeon of his own— 21 aces to Kevin's 19. He also out-volleyed and out-steadied his 27-year-old opponent from the baseline.

"I should have had the advantage," Curren said. "Being older, being to the semifinals [1983], being on Centre Court. Maybe he was too young to know about all that stuff. I couldn't imagine that I'd beat both McEnroe and Connors in the same tournament—and not win it."

Or at least too young to rattle. Becker became such a sensation in the early stages of the tournament with his reckless dives—"Usually, he comes off the court with blood on him," observed Tiriac—that the bookmaking chain, Ladbrokes, installed him as a 7-4 favorite after the quarterfinals.

His popularity with the fans was not echoed in the British press, which did not let anyone forget he was a German. Even the respectable broadsheets relentlessly used war analogies in describing the player. In *The Times*, the respected Rex Bellamy duly noted that scheduled television programming in Becker's homeland was interrupted to carry his quarterfinal victory over Leconte and added, "How odd it was that Germany should have such a personal interest in a court on which, in 1940, they dropped a bomb."

It's true a bomb did land on the roof of Centre Court in October of 1940, destroying 1,200 seats. And no German was permitted to enter the tournament for four years after it was resumed in 1946. (Germans had been banned for nine years after WWI.) Ironically, Becker's shining moment occurred on July 7, the birth date of Baron Gottfried von Cramm. For more than half of the century, the Baron was regarded as one of the finest players never to have won Wimbledon.

The new generation of males wasn't as successful in the cauldron that was Flushing Meadow. Seeded eighth, Becker made 64 unforced errors in bowing to tenth-seeded Joakim Nystrom 6-3, 6-4, 4-6, 6-4 in the round of 16. In was also in the fourth round where the 11th-seeded Edberg came to grief against fourth-seeded Connors 6-4, 3-6, 6-3, 6-4. Wilander, an old man of 21, seeded third, did push top-seed McEnroe to five sets in the semifinals but couldn't put the 26-year-old codger away, falling 3-6, 6-4, 4-6, 6-3, 6-3.

Two other familiar faces turned up in the other semifinal, where second-seeded Lendl romped over Connors, 6-2, 6-3, 7-5. It had been a frustrating season for the 33-year-old campaigner. For the first time in his professional career, Connors failed to win a tournament all year. Yet, he reached the semis of the French, Wimbledon and the U.S., the latter for the twelfth successive year.

For Lendl, the victory also was the continuation of a streak. This was his fourth consecutive final at Flushing Meadow. Alas, he had lost in all three previous trips. After their Saturday night match, Connors said he didn't expect the man to play well on Sunday. "Because he never has," the gracious loser said. Certainly, there was little in the early going to indicate otherwise. Lendl was broken in his first service game and failed to get a single point off McEnroe's serve through seven games, creating a 2-5 deficit. But, at set point, the Czech who had moved into a comfortable estate in nearby Greenwich, Conn., hit a cross-court backhand winner for deuce, held service and then broke McEnroe for the first time. He eventually won a tie-breaker by a stunning 7-1 margin and raced through the next two sets 6-3, 6-4 for the most satisfying triumph of his career.

"It's the biggest tournament in the world," the first-time title-holder said dryly. "And it is the championship of the country where I enjoy living so much. I have won the Czechoslovakian Open three times, in my native country, but I don't think that is the same." It was the climax of a superb year for Lendl. He annexed the first of 11

titles by beating Mayotte at the WCT Finals in Dallas, 7-6, 6-4, 6-1. At the Tournament of Champions at Forest Hills, Lendl prevailed over Mac, 6-3, 6-3, and he also stopped the lefty at Dusseldorf at the World Team Cup, 6-7, 7-6, 6-3. A singles victory by Connors over Miloslav Mecir, 6-3, 3-6, 7-5, and a doubles triumph by Flach and Seguso over Lendl and Tomas Smid, 6-4, 7-6, lifted the U.S. to a 2-1 victory over the Czechs and the World Team Cup trophy.

Seeded No. 1 at the Australian Open, Lendl appeared to have a clear path to another major title when fourth-seeded Becker was bounced in the first round by No. 188, Dutchman Michiel Schapers, 3-6, 6-4, 7-6, 4-6, 6-3, and McEnroe was eliminated in the quarters by massive 6-foot-5 Slobodan "Bobo" Zivojinovic of Yugoslavia, 2-6, 6-3, 1-6, 6-4, 6-0. But that's when Edberg asserted himself. The teenager from Vastervik snapped Lendl's 31-match winning streak, 6-7 (3-7), 7-5, 6-1, 4-6, 9-7 in the semifinals and then overpowered defending champ Wilander, 6-4, 6-3, 6-3, in a rain-delayed final. It marked the first time two Swedes met for a major championship, but Edberg barely escaped match point in a fourth-rounder over No. 142 Wally Masur 6-7 (4), 2-6, 7-6 (4), 6-4, 6-2.

Both McEnroe and Lendl argued so incessantly about the slippery condition of the Kooyong courts and other distractions that they surpassed the fine limit, earning 21-day suspensions. Not that either was inclined to play any more in December. For the first time in a while, McEnroe didn't even have Davis Cup commitments.

He had declined to sign a so-called "behavior guideline" instigated by the U.S. team's sponsor, Louisiana Pacific, to guarantee there would be no repetition of the ruckus at Goteborg the previous year. Since Connors— the prime instigator—had no intention of returning, the U.S. squad was led by Eliot Teltscher and Aaron Krickstein, who turned 18 just in time for a second-round encounter against West Germany. That was as far as the Americans went, Germany winning 3-2 on clay at Hamburg as Becker bashed Krickstein in the decisive fifth match, 6-2, 6-2, 6-1. Boris had beaten Teltscher to lead off 6-2, 6-2, 6-3, and his lightly-regarded companion, Hansjorg Schwaier, supplied the pivotal point by beating Krickstein 2-6, 6-1, 2-6, 6-1, 8-6 for a 2-0 lead.

Becker carried the fatherland all the way to the final and nearly upset the Swedes as he defeated both Edberg 6-3, 3-6, 7-5, 8-6 and Wilander 6-3, 2-6, 6-3, 6-3 to tie it, 2-2. Not for 21 years, when Roy Emerson beat Chuck McKinley to lift the Cup from the U.S. to Australia, had the fate of the Cup hung on the fifth match. As the sellout crowd of 11,000 rocked Munich's Olympiahalle with stomping and chanting of "MEE-KILE! MEE-KILE!," hulking, 20-year-old Michael Westphal, ranked No. 51, served ace after ace (15) past 19-year-old Edberg to win the first set. But Edberg, No. 5, blunted the German's fury with his own serve-and-volley rhythms, overcame the aces (28) and silenced the home crowd, 3-6, 7-5, 6-4, 6-3, enabling Sweden to become the first European nation to retain the Cup in five decades.

Remarkably, that nation qualified four men for the season-ending Grand Prix Masters, whose field was raised to 16 under the first-time sponsorship of Nabisco. But none of the Swedes was a factor. Edberg lost in the first round to Kriek, 6-2, 4-6, 6-2, Wilander was beaten by Becker in the quarters, 6-4, 4-6, 6-3 and Jarryd, who had defeated Nystrom in a first-rounder, was stopped

by Becker in the semifinals, 6-3, 6-4. The most resounding loss of all, however, involved McEnroe who, tired and out of sorts, went down in the first round to Brad Gilbert, 5-7, 6-4, 6-1.

In the end, Lendl reverting to the form he had displayed in the U.S. Open, turned back Becker in commanding fashion, 6-2, 7-6 (7-1), 6-3, and raised his earnings to $1,971,074. At last, he was clearly the top male player in the world.

For the first time in what seemed like ages, there actually was some doubt about the identity of the leading woman. The competition wasn't settled until Navratilova beat Mandlikova, her U.S. Open conqueror, in the semifinals of the Australian Open, 6-7 (5-7), 6-1, 6-4, and then wore down French Open queen Evert Lloyd, 6-2, 4-6, 6-2 in the final at Melbourne. She concluded her season with 12 tournament victories and an 80-5 match record, slightly ahead of Evert Lloyd's 10 titles and an 81-8 mark.

Chrissie also led the U.S. to its seventh consecutive victory over Great Britain in Wightman Cup play, 7-0, at Williamsburg, Va., beating Jo Durie, 6-2, 6-3 and Annabel Croft, 6-3, 6-0. Shriver did likewise over Croft, 6-0, 6-0, and Durie, 6-4, 6-4.

By defeating Navratilova in their thrilling French final, 6-3, 6-7 (4-7), 7-5, Evert Lloyd won the tournament for an unprecedented sixth time and extended to a dozen years her standard for winning at least one of the major titles. It also marked the second time in five months she had overcome her nemesis, the first being at Key Biscayne, Fla., in late January, 6-2, 6-4 dead-locking their rivalry at 31-31.

Following that loss in Florida and one to Mandlikova in the semifinals of the U.S. Indoors, 7-6 (4), 6-0, Navratilova went to an eye doctor. She emerged with spectacles and promptly won 23 consecutive matches (and 46 sets), including the Virginia Slims Championship at Madison Square Garden, beating Sukova, 6-3, 7-5, 6-4. Evert Lloyd interrupted that string at Paris.

"I just hope Chrissie stays around a little bit longer," Navratilova said, "because, quite honestly, she's playing better tennis now than she ever did. It must be nice to know that you can still improve at 30." Defeat cost Navratilova the honor of being the first player since tripler Margaret Smith Court in 1964 to hold the three French titles simultaneously. She combined with Shriver to win the women's doubles, beating Kohde-Kilsch and Sukova 4-6, 6-2, 6-2 for their eighth straight major championship, and with Heinz Gunthardt, she won the mixed over Paula Smith and Francisco Gonzalez, 2-6, 6-3, 6-2.

Future Hall of Famer Gabriela Sabatini had created a great stir at Hilton Head, S.C., in April by beating three Top 10 players (Zina Garrison, Shriver and Manuela Maleeva), en-route to the final. She had a tall order Sunday morning. After completing a rain-delayed quarter with Shriver 5-7, 7-5, 6-4, then beating Maleeva, 6-1, 7-6, she was entitled by the rules to put off the final until Monday. But Gaby, the youngest to reach a pro final at that time (14 years, 11 months), insisted on being part of the televised title match. She competed well for a set before losing to Chrissie, 6-4, 6-0.

In Paris, Sabatini, now 15, top-spun her way into the semifinals. Her victims included Ros Fairbank, 6-0, 1-6, 7-5 and fourth-seeded Manuela Maleeva, 6-3, 1-6, 6-1. Once again, it took a woman twice her age to stop her, Evert Lloyd, 6-4, 6-1.

Sabatini's showing convinced her coach, Pato Apey, that she should enter Wimbledon, where the "Pearl of the Pampas" became the youngest player ever to be seeded (15th at 15 in a masterstroke of British symmetry). Her presence caused an immediate stir. The tabloids dubbed her "Gorgeous Gaby" and the special eligibility Commission of the International Tennis Federation called for a "gradual, carefully monitored entry" into pro tennis, restricting the number of events a player can enter before reaching 16. Sabatini won two matches, beating local Amanda Brown, 3-6, 6-3, 6-3, and American teen-ager Camille Benjamin, 6-3, 6-4, losing to Catherine Tanvier of France, 6-7 (3-7), 6-4, 6-1.

But the tournament sensation was willowy 24-year-old blonde American Anne White, who showed up— and showed very well—for a first rounder with Shriver in a crowd-attracting body stocking. Her costume satisfied the requirement for white clothing, but its clinging, unconventional nature made the authorities, uncomfortable. Having split sets at dusk, their match was postponed until the following day and No. 93-ranked White was instructed to leave the leotard at home. She returned in a skirt and top, and lost the match, 6-3, 6-7 (7-9), 6-3. "It was chilly. I wanted to be fully covered," said un-contrite White.

The most surprising of the final eight was No. 154 Molly Van Nostrand, a 20-year-old qualifier from New York who defeated fourth-seeded Manuela Maleeva, 7-5, 6-2, and was only three games from a semifinal meeting with Navratilova before faltering against Garrison, 2-6, 6-3, 6-0. Kathy Rinaldi, still only 18, made her deepest penetration in a major when she advanced to the semifinals past sixth-seeded Sukova, 6-1, 1-6, 6-1, in the quarterfinals.

Not that there was ever any doubt but that the women's competition was a two-filly race, but they played the semis anyway: Evert Lloyd over Rinaldi, 6-2, 6-0; Navratilova over Garrison, 6-4, 7-6 (7-3). In a most unusual move, the tournament committee jointly seeded Evert Lloyd and Navratilova No. 1. And their final was almost as close, with Navratilova rallying for a 4-6, 6-3, 6-2 victory.

She became only the third woman in history to win the singles titles four years in a row and the first since Helen Wills Moody in 1930. "This court," Evert decided, "is her court." It also marked Navratilova's sixth triumph in as many Wimbledon finals, equaling the feat of Suzanne Lenglen, the legendary French star of the Roaring '20s.

One of the most affecting moments of the tournament was Virginia Wade's 205th Wimbledon match, her last in the singles draw. "Our Ginny," England's last great champion, was beaten by Shriver, 6-2, 5-7, 6-2, in an enthralling third-round match—one week shy of her 40th birthday. She left to a standing ovation.

Youth once again was served at the start of the U.S. Open when Mary Joe Fernandez, who had just turned 14, beat towering Sarah Gomer, a 6-foot-3 Brit, in the first round, 6-1, 6-4, undercutting by four months the Sabatini of 1984 as the greenest to win a match there. But the teen-ager who wowed the crowds at Flushing Meadows was 11th-seeded Graf. In reaching the semifinals, she knocked off Manuela Maleeva, 6-2, 6-2, and, in the match of the tournament, Shriver, 7-6 (7-4), 6-7 (4-7), 7-6 (7-4). It marked the only major match composed entirely of tie-breakers and the

longest women's struggle (39 games) since the advent of such overtimes in 1970.

Still, it was a brilliantly-attacking Mandlikova who took home the prize. And she did it in remarkable fashion, beating two ex-champs—Evert Lloyd, 4-6, 6-2, 6-3 in the semifinals, and Navratilova, 7-6 (7-3), 1-6, 7-6 (7-2) in the final. That route hadn't been taken since 1962 when Margaret Smith (Court) won the last two matches over 1959 champ Maria Bueno and defender Darlene Hard. Graf ran out of zip against Martina in the semis, 6-2, 6-3.

The Open title was one of Hana's two great rewards in 1985. The second occurred a month later in Nagoya, Japan, where she won all five of her singles and two deciding doubles in Czecho-slovakia's third successive victory in the Federation Cup.

At the Australian Open, order was restored. Navratilova dispensed with Mandlikova, 6-7 (5-7), 6-1, 6-4, en route to another final showdown with Evert Lloyd. It was their 67th meeting and Navratilova's all-out attack won the day, 6-2, 4-6, 6-2, increasing her margin in the rivalry of the age to 35-32. "Martina and I have pushed each other to get better and better," Evert Lloyd said. And they weren't planning to stop anytime soon.

1985 CHAMPIONS AND LEADERS

Australian Open
Men's Singles Final: Stefan Edberg (SWE) def. Mats Wilander (SWE), 6-4, 6-3,6-2
Women's Singles Final: Martina Navratilova (USA) def. Chris Evert Lloyd (USA), 6-2, 4-6, 6-2
Men's Doubles Final: Paul Annacone (USA) and Christo Van Rensburg (RSA), def. Mark Edmondson and Kim Warwick (AUS), 3-6, 7-6, 6-4, 6-4
Women's Doubles Final: Martina Navratilova and Pam Shriver (USA) def. Claudia Kohde-Kilsch (GER) and Helena Sukova (CZE), 6-3, 6-4
Mixed Doubles: Not Played

French Open
Men's Singles Final: Mats Wilander (SWE) def. Ivan Lendl (CZE), 3-6, 6-4, 6-2, 6-2
Women's Singles Final: Chris Evert Lloyd (USA) def. Martina Navratilova (USA), 6-3, 6-7 (4), 7-5
Men's Doubles Final: Mark Edmondson and Kim Warwick (AUS) def. Shlomo Glickstein (ISR) and Hans Simonsson (SWE), 6-3, 6-4, 6-7, 6-3
Women's Doubles Final: Martina Navratilova and Pam Shriver (USA) def. Claudia Kohde-Kilsch (GER) and Helena Sukova (CZE), 4-6, 6-2, 6-2
Mixed Doubles Final: Martina Navratilova (USA) and Heinz Gunthardt (SUI) def. Paula Smith (USA) and Francisco Gonzalez (PAR), 2-6, 6-3, 6-2

Wimbledon
Men's Singles Final: Boris Becker (GER) def. Kevin Curren (USA), 6-3, 6-7 (4), 7-6 (3), 6-4
Women's Singles Final: Martina Navratilova (USA) def. Chris Evert Lloyd (USA), 4-6, 6-3, 6-2
Men's Doubles Final: Heinz Gunthardt (SUI) and Balazs Taroczy (HUN) def. Pat Cash and John Fitzgerald (AUS), 6-4, 6-3, 4-6, 6-3
Women's Doubles Final: Kathy Jordan (USA) and Elizabeth Sayers Smylie (AUS), def. Martina Navratilova and Pam Shriver (USA), 5-7, 6-3, 6-4
Mixed Doubles Final: Martina Navratilova (USA) and Paul McNamee (AUS) def. Elizabeth Sayers Smylie and John Fitzgerald (AUS), 7-5, 4-6, 6-2

U.S. Open
Men's Singles Final: Ivan Lendl (CZE) def. John McEnroe (USA), 7-6 (1), 6-3, 6-4
Women's Singles Final: Hana Mandlikova (CZE) def. Martina Navratilova (USA), 7-6 (3), 1-6, 7-6 (2)
Men's Doubles Final: Ken Flach and Robert Seguso (USA) def. Yannick Noah and Henri Leconte (FRA), 6-7 (5), 7-6 (1), 7-6 (6), 6-0
Women's Doubles Final: Claudia Kohde Kilsch (GER) and Helena Sukova (CZE) def. Martina Navratilova and Pam Shriver (USA), 6-7, 6-2, 6-3
Mixed Doubles Final: Martina Navratilova (USA) and Heinz Gunthardt (SUI) def. Elizabeth Sayers Smylie and John Fitzgerald (AUS), 6-3, 6-4

Year-End No. 1
Men: Ivan Lendl
Women: Martina Navratilova

Top Player Earnings
Men: Ivan Lendl $1,971,074
Women: Martina Navratilova $1,328,829

Davis Cup: Sweden

Federation Cup: Czechoslovakia

Wightman Cup: United States

Grand Prix Masters, NYC—Ivan Lendl
WCT, Dallas—Ivan Lendl
Virginia Slims Championships, NYC—Martina Navratilova

1986

A Prague Summer All Over the World

Martina Navratilova (left) chats with **Chris Evert** after Evert won her seventh women's singles title at the French Open.

They got together on a Sunday in September at a public park. Two men and two women raised Czechoslovakia met for an afternoon of tennis. Twenty years earlier, when the iron curtain and the sport both were closed, they might have been limited to a game of mixed doubles in Prague but now they gathered as professionals in New York to contest the most important singles championships in the New World. An orchestra should have played the lusty "New World Symphony" composed by the Czech Antonin Dvorak.

What an extraordinary development not only for the U.S. Open but for the sport. When Ivan Lendl and Miloslav Mecir followed Martina Navratilova and Helena Sukova onto the stadium court of the USTA National Tennis Center, they raised the profile of a nation whose history had been fragmented and difficult but whose culture was old. Theirs was an unprecedented achievement.

The presence of four finalists born in the same distant land had occurred only four times previously in the history of the major tournaments, twice at Wimbledon and twice at the French Open. Never before had it happened at the U.S. Open and never before had the delegation hailed from Czechoslovakia. Suddenly, the country of 15 million inhabitants ranked as the first nation of tennis.

That Navratilova had received her citizenship papers in the United States and that Lendl was an aspiring Connecticut Yankee, or Mecir, a Slovak, didn't diminish the impact. All had learned the game, had taken their first steps to prosperity on Czechoslovak clay. And, by virtue of their victories in the third and last major

tournament of the year in which there was no Australian Open (a schedule adjustment moved the Aussie to the front of the year from the rear), the expatriates solidified their places at the top of the women's and men's rankings.

Better yet for the land of their youth, Prague welcomed the first significant international tennis event in Eastern Europe. The Federation Cup attracted teams from 40 nations to brand new Stvanice Stadium where the Czech defenders were denied a fourth successive triumph by the U.S. It so happened that Navratilova won her singles match and paired with Pam Shriver to win the doubles in a 3-0 victory that completed an emotional homecoming for the woman who had defected 11 years earlier.

"The whole experience," she said through tears after a heartwarming reception, "was beyond my wildest dreams."

Aside from the success of its foreign imports, the U.S. endured a desultory year. Chris Evert Lloyd, who won yet another French Open, was the only American-born player to reach the final of a major event, whose number temporarily was reduced to three due to the Australian Open's calendar. She also was the only native of either gender to be ranked among the top five players in the game.

Of course, as Navratilova pointed out at Flushing Meadow, if you stress only the country of origin, "... then John McEnroe was born in Germany but he's as red-blooded American as you can get." It's true that McEnroe was born in Wiesbaden, where his father was serving as an officer of the U.S. Air Force. But then McEnroe was not relevant to the discussion, having decided to take a sabbatical for the first six months of the year and having been bounced out of the Open in the very first round by Paul Annacone.

In his absence, Jimmy Connors was the highest-ranked American male, No. 8 on the computer at year's end. However, for a second consecutive season, he failed to win a tournament. Connors didn't even survive the first round at Wimbledon and was a third-round victim at Flushing Meadow, beaten by Todd Witsken, 6-2, 6-4, 7-5. Once again, the men's tour was dominated by Europeans. Lendl won both the French Open, defeating upstart Mikael Pernfors of Sweden in the final, and the U.S. Open, as well as the Masters. He also reached the final at Wimbledon, only to be stopped one step short of his goal by defending champion Boris Becker. The latter also pressed Lendl at the Masters and rose to No. 2 in the world at the age of 18.

On the women's side, Navratilova continued her reign over Wimbledon by defeating another Czech, Hana Mandlikova. Her only major defeat of the year occurred in Paris, where Evert Lloyd prevailed in a bid for a record seventh singles championship. By the end of 1986, however, it was clear that Steffi Graf was prepared to challenge both women.

"Fraulein Forehand," as the teen-aged German was known, won eight tournaments, two more than Evert, and almost denied Navratilova the U.S. Open title. Graf held three match points, the last in a sensational third-set tie-breaker, in the semifinals, losing 6-1, 6-7 (7-3), 7-6 (10-8). "I was lucky," Navratilova said. "I was lucky and I was gutsy, too. But anyone could have won."

Two months later, Navratilova again held off Graf at the second Virginia Slims Championships at Madison Square Garden,

7-6 (7-1), 6-3, 6-2. The year-end women's championships represented one of several schedule adjustments that finally brought tennis into line with the calendar. Back in March, Martina had won the first Virginia Slims, the one that purported to be the season-ending event of the 1985 circuit, a 6-2, 6-0, 3-6, 6-1 triumph over Mandlikova. With a victory over Graf, she clinched the designation of No. 1 for 1986.

The men also managed to cram their play into a 12-month season. For the first time since 1976, the Masters was given December dates. Lendl certainly didn't appear rushed. After reaching the final for the seventh consecutive year, he blasted an eager Becker, 6-4, 6-4, 6-4, forestalling the future a while longer.

Perhaps the most far-reaching development of the year occurred at the start. In the wake of a disappointing loss to Brad Gilbert in the first round of the (1985) Masters in January, McEnroe decided to drop off the tour for at least 60 days. His long-standing relationship with actress Tatum O'Neal and impending fatherhood had become more important than his career. "My attitude is very bad, very negative," he said. "I'm not happy with my movement ... I shouldn't be playing tennis now ... I'm letting things affect me and I'm embarrassed. As a person I'll learn and grow from what is happening. I hope others do, too. They didn't seem to learn from Borg. Now, they see it happening to me."

McEnroe was 26, one year older than Bjorn Borg when the latter walked away from competitive tennis. Like Borg, McEnroe was No. 2 in the world. Unlike the Swede, the American would be back, although not with the same fire.

Meanwhile, Connors sabotaged his own season by walking out of a semifinal match against Lendl at the Lipton International Players Championship at Boca Raton, Fla. Lendl was leading, 5-2, in the fifth set when Connors began arguing a linesman's call. He insisted that umpire Jeremy Shales overrule the call and, when that failed, demanded that Shales be removed from the chair. Not satisfied, Connors walked off the court and was defaulted. Not only did he lose the match but he was suspended for 70 days, a period that carried through the French Open, where he had been a semifinalist in each of the two previous years. He was also fined a record $20,000.

With the field at Paris thinned by the abstention of the two top Yanks, Sweden was in position to take over the men's competition. Not only had a Swede won the 1985 edition and six of the previous eight tournaments, but representatives of that nation were granted four of the top eight seeds: Mats Wilander (No. 2), Stefan Edberg (No. 5), Joakim Nystrom (No. 6) and Anders Jarryd (No. 7). Yet the only Swede to make it to the quarterfinals and beyond was a total outsider, 10 months a pro, ranked No. 16 at home, No. 27 on the planet.

Mikael Pernfors, out of the village of Hollviksnas, a 22-year-old who had gone the American collegiate route, made his French Open debut a memorable one. The two-time National Intercollegiate champion (1984-85) from the University of Georgia upset four of the top 11 seeds en route to the final: No. 5 Edberg, 6-7 (5-7), 7-5, 6-3, 2-6, 6-4 in the second round; No. 11 Argentine Martin Jaite, 6-1, 3-6, 7-6 (8-6), 7-6 (7-3) in the fourth round; No. 3 Becker in the quarterfinals, 2-6, 6-4, 6-2, 6-0; and, in

the semifinals, shot-making magician, No. 8 Henri Leconte, 2-6, 7-5, 7-6 (7-4), 6-3. Defending champ and No. 2 seed Wilander was stunned, 6-2. 6-3, 6-2, in the third round by Russian Andrei Chesnokov, No. 81 in the world, who advanced to the quarterfinals.

Meanwhile, Lendl thundered through the top half of the draw with the loss of only one set. With the same championship form he had displayed in winning his first Italian Open three weeks earlier, over Spaniard Emilio Sanchez (7-5, 4-6, 6-1, 6-1), Lendl dispatched the speedy, scrappy Pernfors, 6-3, 6-2, 6-4.

Some uncertainty was injected into the women's tournament by Mary Joe Fernandez, the Florida teen-ager making her debut in Paris where she would be a finalist in 1993. Mary Joe, the youngest player ever to win a match at the U.S. Open eight months earlier, overcame two seeds: No. 14 Andrea Temesvari, 5-7, 6-2, 6-3, and No. 4 Claudia Kohde-Kilsch, 7-6 (9-7), 7-5, in advancing to the quarterfinals. There, the 14-year-old ranked No. 70, was stopped by sixth-seeded Sukova, 6-2, 6-4.

It was also in the quarters that Graf's 23-match winning streak—including titles at Hilton Head, over Evert Lloyd, 6-4, 7-5; Amelia Island, over Kohde-Kilsch, 6-4, 5-7, 7-6 (7-3); the U.S. Clay Courts, over Sabatini, 2-6, 7-6 (7-5), 6-4; and Berlin, over Navratilova, 6-2, 6-3—came to an abrupt end. After holding a match point on Mandlikova, Steffi succumbed 2-6, 7-6 (7-3), 6-1. In the semifinals, Navratilova registered a slippery 4-6, 7-6 (7-4), 6-2 win over Sukova, and Evert Lloyd bested Mandlikova, 6-1, 6-1.

Navratilova and Evert met in yet another final. The world would never see its like again. Although no one realized it at the moment, it was the last time the two would meet in the championship round of a major. Evert Lloyd, in her penultimate Big Four final, made the most of it with a commanding 2-6, 6-3, 6-3 victory, closing the second set from 0-40, four break points, showing off brilliant backhand passers. That raised her total of major singles titles to 18 and extended to 13 years her fantastic longevity record of at least one major conquest.

The cosmetic changes at the 100th edition of Wimbledon included the introduction of yellow tennis balls, the unavailability of McEnroe, who was back in the States changing diapers, and the earliest departure from a major on Connors' record in 14 years, since losing 6-1, 3-6, 6-7, 7-5, 6-4 to Tom Gorman in the first round of the 1972 U.S. Open. Connors, the two-time champion and five-time finalist, seeded No. 3, was shown the London gate in the first round by Robert Seguso, ranked No. 31 and known as a doubles specialist, 6-3, 3-6, 7-6 (7-5), 7-6 (10-8).

"You don't know what you have until you lose it," said Connors, indicating Wimbledon would miss him more than he would Wimbledon, "and that's what you're feeling toward McEnroe right now." The first-round failures also included eleventh-seeded Kevin Curren, runner-up in 1985, to No. 32 Eric Jelen, a saver of four match points, 6-4, 6-7 (4-7), 2-6, 6-4, 12-10. John Lloyd also lost, blowing a two-set lead to South African Christo Steyn, 3-6, 2-6, 6-3, 6-3, 6-1, and immediately retired.

Meanwhile Lloyd's second-seeded wife experienced unaccustomed difficulty of her own. A finalist in seven of the previous eight years, Chrissie struggled through a difficult draw, dropping sets to Pam Casale, 6-0, 5-7, 6-1, and, in the quarterfinals, to seventh-seeded Sukova, 7-6 (10-8), 4-6, 6-4. In the semis, she was elim-

inated by Mandlikova, 7-6 (7-5), 7-5—nevertheless, Chrissie's 14th final four showing.

Hana said she was much better prepared for her second Wimbledon final than her first, five years earlier against Evert Lloyd. "I slept very well," she said of her Navratilova eve. "Maybe, as it turned out, too well," she decided afterward. By contrast, Navratilova was particularly eager for the meeting after rolling unopposed through her first six matches. "I've never, ever been so excited about being in a final," she said. "I couldn't wait to go to sleep so I could get up and play."

Not since the reign of Suzanne Lenglen six decades earlier had a woman won five consecutive singles championships at Wimbledon. And history was no more prepared to stop Martina than was Mandlikova. She finished off the challenger, 7-6 (7-1), 6-3, in 72 minutes. In five years of supremacy, she had dropped only two sets.

Lendl, the top-seeded male, worked harder than any player in the tournament in his effort to secure a Wimbledon title. He struggled past Matt Anger, 6-7 (7-9), 7-6 (7-2), 6-4, 7-6 (12-10) in the fourth round, and Tim Mayotte, 6-4, 4-6, 6-4, 3-6, 9-7 in the quarterfinals, to reach the semis, where he was pushed to the limit again by rocket-serving Serb, 6-foot-6 Slobodan Zivojinovic, 6-2, 6-7 (5-7), 6-3, 6-7 (1-7), 6-4.

His opponent in the final was the defending champ, Becker, as comfortable on the grass as Lendl was wary. Seeded fourth, Becker defeated Leconte in their semi, 6-2, 6-4, 6-7 (4-7), 6-3, after marching through a bottom half of the draw that was pock-marked by upsets, most notably Mecir's dismissal of second-seeded Edberg, 6-4, 6-4, 6-4, and fifth-seeded Wilander's 4-6, 7-5, 6-4, 6-3 loss to Pat Cash, who entered the tournament as a wild card two-and-a-half weeks following an appendectomy.

One point illustrated the distinction in the opponents' approach to the grass. In the final game of the third set, Becker serving for the match, but at 15-30, Lendl hit what appeared to be a forehand winner down the line. The German knifed through the air to intercept with a backhand stop volley. Lendl pounced to deliver another hopeful passer, but the ball caught the net cord and crawled over after Becker had landed on his stomach. Without a moment's hesitation, he sprang to his feet and spontaneously chipped a backhand winner crosscourt.

He then pounded two more service winners at Lendl to formalize the 6-4, 6-3, 7-5 victory. No wonder Becker said Wimbledon "feels like my tournament." Lendl, fighting the grass and his allergies and the fans who rallied behind more graceful and flamboyant players, had never felt that.

Two weeks after Wimbledon, the top female players in the world assembled in Czechoslovakia for the most eagerly anticipated Federation Cup in the 24-year history of the event. From start to finish, it was Navratilova's show. Certainly, there was supreme irony in the idea of her leading an American team (with Evert Lloyd, Shriver and Zina Garrison) into Prague. It was shortly after contributing to Czechoslovakia's first Cup victory, in 1975, that she had sought political asylum in the U.S.

For the longest time, her success was not publicized in her native land. Her name did not appear in the Czech press, her matches were not seen on television. Yet, she was welcomed

home as a returning heroine. She set out to demonstrate to her long-lost fans what they had missed.

Navratilova played brilliantly, winning every singles and doubles match (4-0 in each) in the course of carrying an unblemished record into her anxiously awaited final-round confrontation with Mandlikova, who made news of her own by marrying a Sydney restaurant owner in Prague's town hall. The U.S. beat China, Spain, West Germany, all 3-0, and Italy, 2-1. The Czechs, Sukova and Mandlikova, were unbeaten, too, in 3-0 wins over Greece, Switzerland, Australia, and 2-1 over Argentina.

The tournament produced one freak accident when an umbrella stand fell on Graf's foot, breaking her big toe. Evert Lloyd was wearing a brace on a balky knee at the start of the event. Following a loss to Italy's Sandra Cecchini 3-6, 6-4, 6-3, she removed it, and won her last two matches, against Bettina Bunge of Germany, 6-3, 6-4 and Sukova, 7-5, 7-6 (7-5). Her win over Sukova was the first point in the final round, leaving Navratilova in position to regain the Cup for the United States. She did so by beating Mandlikova, 7-5, 6-1. Then she combined with Shriver, a pairing that won all three major doubles events contested in 1986, to defeat Mandlikova and Sukova, 6-4, 6-2. Martina was cheered loudly. Afterward, she cried tears of happiness.

The journey to her old neighborhood only intensified Navratilova's desire to win another U.S. Open which she now considered her national tournament. The biggest test she would face in New York was administered by Graf after she breezed through the first five rounds. It happened in an epic semifinal match that required two hours and 16 minutes stretched over two days. Navratilova held a 4-1 lead in the first set when rain interrupted play on Friday night and she quickly closed out the set upon its resumption on Saturday. Thereafter, however, it was a struggle, with both the second and third sets decided by tie-breakers. Graf had two match points in the 10th game of the third set and then a third at 8-7 in the tie-breaker.

"The last time I saved three match points [and won]," Navratilova said after the 6-1, 6-7 (3-7), 7-6 (10-8) victory, "I think I was 10 years old. I know I faced 15 match points once and I lost. Whenever it happened last, I know I was little."

Her great rival, Evert Lloyd, wasn't able to dig so deep against Sukova in their semifinal. The tall Czech hadn't beaten the American in 14 previous meetings but it took her only 70 minutes to dispose of the six-time Open champion, 6-2, 6-4. "Helena, Hana, Steffi, they're not intimidated by Martina or me anymore," said Evert Lloyd, who rested her ailing knee for the remainder of the season, passing up another 7-0 Wightman Cup romp by the U.S. (It was ably handled in London by the lesser lights Kathy Rinaldi and Bonnie Gadusek).

Still, Navratilova held the hammer over Sukova, once a ball-girl for Martina back in Prague. In the final that was pushed back until Sunday and staged just before the men's championship, the No. 1 player in the world scored a 6-3, 6-2 victory in 60 minutes. She was presented with her third Open trophy and a check for $210,000, as much as any player had ever won at a single tournament.

The men's competition, even as it wound to a predictable conclusion, was much less orderly. McEnroe and Connors,

responsible for seven of the eight previous singles titles, failed to last the first week. In fact, McEnroe, seeded No. 9, didn't make it past sundown on the first day, drilled by Annacone's 25 aces in four sets, 1-6, 6-1, 6-3, 6-3.

To make matters worse, the former king of Queens and partner Peter Fleming arrived six minutes late for their first doubles start and were defaulted. McEnroe's subsequent profane tirade resulted in a $1,000 fine. Weeks later, after Mac's winning three fall tournaments, his intemperate outburst at the Paris Indoor Championships led to a $3,000 fine, pushing him beyond the $7,500 limit and triggering a 42-day suspension that removed whatever slim possibility existed of his qualifying for the Masters.

Those expecting sixth-seeded Connors to ride to the rescue at Flushing Meadow were sadly disappointed. The five-time champion saved six match points but finally lost in three sets to third-year pro, No. 95-ranked Todd Witsken in the third round. It was his earliest exit from his national since 1972. No American reached the semifinals for the first time in two decades.

Fittingly, the mystery man of the Open was a Slovak. The 6-foot-3 Mecir, forever disinterested in appearance but astonishingly quick to the ball, knocked off the second-seeded Wilander, 6-7 (3-7), 6-3, 6-3, 6-4; the seventh-seeded Nystrom, 6-4, 6-2, 3-6, 6-2; and the third-seeded Becker, 4-6, 6-3, 6-4, 3-6, 6-3, in succession to arrive at the final. He had presented his credentials at Wimbledon, where he reached the quarterfinals, but at Flushing Meadow, his performance stunned observers, especially considering how much he professed to dislike New York ("too big") and how much he missed his favorite form of entertainment ("fishing").

"He is maybe the fastest player I've ever played against," Becker said. Indeed, the 22-year-old was called "Gattone" (Big Cat) by Italians. And his assortment of junkballs and deceptive strokes befuddled some of the best players in the world, especially Swedes, against whom he was 18-3. But in Lendl, he met his match. Lendl, who had dropped only one set, was not mesmerized by the sight of his former countryman. And Mecir, so fluid earlier in the tournament, seemed rooted to the ground, content merely to trade groundies with the steady Lendl. The match produced a lot of yawns in the crowd, which shrank steadily in size over the course of the 6-4, 6-2, 6-0 rout by the two-time champion.

Lendl finished the year with a match record of 74-6 and nine titles, second in the world only to Navratilova's 90-3 mark and 14 championships. In the race to the bank between the two practicing capitalists from Czechoslovakia, Lendl won by a money clip—$1,987,537 to $1,905,841.

Cash flow settled the Davis Cup account in Australia's favor for a 26th time as Patrick Cash flowed through a 6-0 singles and 3-1 doubles campaign. He capped it with a tremendous triple on turf, illuminated by a bounce-back singles victory in his hometown, Melbourne, to strip Sweden of the old silver crock, 3-2. Slow starts and brilliant finishes characterized vicious volleyer's singles wins. He beat the king of Kooyong, Edberg, Aussie Open title-holder, 13-11, 13-11, 6-4 and, after Pernfors beat Paul McNamee, 6-3, 6-1, 6-3, to deadlock the first day, Cash teamed with John Fitzgerald to upset Edberg and Jarryd, 6-3, 6-4, 4-6, 6-1. With

Australia ahead 2-1, Cash met Pernfors and quickly dropped the first two sets. Only once before with the Cup at stake had the clinching match been won from two sets down: Jean Borotra of France over American Wilmer Allison in 1932. But Cash charged relentlessly to what captain Neale Fraser called "Australia's greatest Davis Cup performance"—2-6, 4-6, 6-3, 6-4, 6-3.

Patrick was also the clincher in the 3-1 semifinal victory over the United States, beating Tim Mayotte on opening day, 4-6, 6-1, 6-2, 6-2, and Gilbert, 3-6, 6-2, 6-3, 6-4; on Brisbane sod. Gilbert also lost to McNamee, 2-6, 6-3, 3-6, 6-0, 6-1, the first day. The chief American problem was the absence of McEnroe, whose accumulated churlish behavior got him ruled off by USTA President Randy Gregson.

1986 CHAMPIONS AND LEADERS

Australian Open
Not held

French Open
Men's Singles Final: Ivan Lendl (CZE) def. Mikael Pernfors (SWE), 6-3, 6-2, 6-4

Women's Singles Final: Chris Evert Lloyd (USA) def. Martina Navratilova (USA), 2-6, 6-3, 6-3

Men's Doubles Final: John Fitzgerald (AUS) and Tomas Smid (CZE) def. Stefan Edberg and Anders Jarryd (SWE), 6-3, 4-6, 6-3, 6-7 (4), 14-12

Women's Doubles Final: Martina Navratilova (USA) and Andrea Temesvari (HUN), def. Steffi Graf (GER) and Gabriela Sabatini (ARG), 6-1, 6-2

Mixed Doubles Final: Kathy Jordan and Ken Flach (USA) def. Ros Fairbank (RSA) and Mark Edmondson (AUS), 3-6, 7-6 (3), 6-3

Wimbledon
Men's Singles Final: Boris Becker (GER) def. Ivan Lendl (CZE), 6-4, 6-3, 7-5

Women's Singles Final: Martina Navratilova (USA) def. Hana Mandlikova (CZE), 7-6 (1), 6-3

Men's Doubles Final: Joakim Nystrom and Mats Wilander (SWE) def. Gary Donnelly and Peter Fleming (USA), 7-6 (4), 6-3, 6-3

Women's Doubles Final: Martina Navratilova and Pam Shriver (USA) def. Hana Mandlikova and Wendy Turnbull (AUS), 6-1, 6-3

Mixed Doubles Final: Kathy Jordan and Ken Flach (USA) def. Martina Navratilova (USA) and Heinz Gunthardt (SUI), 6-3, 7-6 (7)

U.S. Open
Men's Singles Final: Ivan Lendl (CZE) def. Miloslav Mecir (CZE), 6-4, 6-2, 6-0

Women's Singles Final: Martina Navratilova (USA) def. Helena Sukova (CZE), 6-3, 6-2

Men's Doubles Final: Andres Gomez (ECU) and Slobodan Zivojinovic (YUG), def. Joakim Nystrom and Mats Wilander (SWE), 4-6, 6-3, 6-3, 4-6, 6-3

Women's Doubles Final: Martina Navratilova (USA) and Pam Shriver (USA) def. Hana Mandlikova (CZE) and Wendy Turnbull (AUS), 6-4, 3-6, 6-3

Mixed Doubles Final: Raffaella Reggi (ITA) and Sergio Casal (ESP) def. Martina Navratilova and Peter Fleming (USA), 6-4, 6-4

Year-End No. 1
Men: Ivan Lendl
Women: Martina Navratilova

Top Player Earnings
Men: Ivan Lendl $1,987,537
Women: Martina Navratilova $1,905,841

Davis Cup: Australia

Federation Cup: United States

Wightman Cup: United States

Grand Prix Masters, NYC—Ivan Lendl
WCT, Dallas—Anders Jarryd
Virginia Slims Championships (spring), NYC—Martina Navratilova
Virginia Slims Championships (fall), NYC—Martina Navratilova

1987 Lendl and Navratilova Continue Title Collections

In a year of mixed blessings for the most relentless campaigners on the world stage, Martina Navratilova and Ivan Lendl added to their collections of major tournament titles by two apiece. But there was a down side for both in 1987. She lost one of her most treasured possessions and he failed once again to win the prize that mattered most.

Navratilova's reign as the No. 1 female practitioner of tennis ended despite victories at Wimbledon and the U.S. Open. The queen was far from dead but, nonetheless, someone else was seated on her throne at the conclusion of the season. Her successor was Steffi Graf, who not only won her first major title in Paris but 75 of the 77 matches in which she participated.

Ivan Lendl won the French Open and the US Open but lost to **Pat Cash** in the Wimbledon final.

Fortified by triumphs at the French Open and at Flushing Meadow, Lendl continued to hold the top spot in the men's rankings. But he would have traded all his trophies and perhaps thrown in a generous share of his $2,003,656 earnings for the great honor that eluded him for a second successive year. Once more, he lost in the final at Wimbledon. His nemesis was Pat Cash, who had beaten Lendl six months earlier in the last Australian Open played on grass.

But for those two flaws, the Czech native might have joined the list of Grand Slam immortals. As it was, Lendl forged the most victories (25) in the four major tournaments by a male since Rod Laver went 26-0 in his 1969 Grand Slam. Yet he had to stand by and watch forlornly as Cash joyously celebrated the first Wimbledon championship by an Aussie in 16 years with an unprecedented climb through the stands at Centre Court. "It's a miserable feeling," the losing finalist decided.

Before the year was out, Lendl would win eight tournaments, including a third consecutive Masters, to gain a total of 70 titles. He tied John McEnroe for second place behind Jimmy Connors (105) in the all-time standings. Remarkably, neither American won an event in 1987, although the 35-year-old Connors did reach the semifinal round at both Wimbledon and the U.S. Open and rose to No. 4 on the ATP computer.

The shutout was the first in McEnroe's professional career. Not only was he afflicted by lapses in concentration and an aching back but he contributed to his demise with temper tantrums at the World Team Cup in May and at Flushing Meadow. For walking off the court in Dusseldorf, he defaulted the match to Miloslav Mecir and was fined $10,000. For a profane tirade during a third-round victory over Slobodan Zivojinovic at the U.S. Open, he received point and game penalties, fines totaling $17,500 and a two-month suspension.

It was a measure of McEnroe's season that his gamest, most impressive performance came in defeat. In a Davis Cup relegation playoff to determine which nation would be banished to the boondocks (zonal competition) the following year, he played an historic five-set match on behalf of the United States against Boris Becker, representing West Germany, in late July. Becker's 4-6, 15-13, 8-10, 6-2, 6-2 victory consumed six hours and 20 minutes, two minutes shy of the Cup singles record set by McEnroe and Mats Wilander in a 1982 quarterfinal match at St. Louis.

Tim Mayotte, whose five tournament victories topped U.S. players, accompanied McEnroe for that U.S. last stand against West Germany at the Hartford Civic Center. However, the 3-2 defeat appeared sealed when 26-year-old Tim lost the opening match in five sets to No. 68 Eric Jelen, 6-8, 6-2, 1-6, 6-3, 6-2. Mac went down and it was 0-2. Ken Flach and Robert Seguso prolonged hope, over Ricki Osterthun and Jelen, 6-3, 8-6, 14-12, as did McEnroe over Jelen, 7-5, 6-2, 6-1. But Becker loomed, a set too good for Mayotte, five sets again, 6-2, 6-3, 5-7, 4-6, 6-2.

The trouble began for the U.S. on that treacherous-for-Yanks footing, clay, in Asuncion, Paraguay, where an intimidating crowd and a revved-up Victor Pecci took a 3-2 decision over the U.S. and forced the Yanks into the relegation lottery. Jimmy Arias had a chance to clinch the win for the U.S., but, in one of the strangest matches in the Cup's history, he lost to No. 285th-ranked Hugo Chapacu 6-4, 6-1, 5-7, 3-6, 9-7 in five hours and five minutes to tie up the tie at 2-2. Chapacu was unable to convert a match point at 5-4 in the third set, but came back from a 1-5 fifth-set deficit and saved three match points to win and set up Pecci's clincher in the decisive match against Aaron Krickstein, 6-2, 8-6, 9-7.

The losses to Paraguay and West Germany relegated the U.S. from the 16-entry World Group to the American Zone for 1988,

ineligible to compete for the Cup for the first time. Germany, a first round loser to Mexico, stayed with the elite.

Wilander was the strength as the Swedes won a third Davis Cup in four years. He and Anders Jarryd handled the singles in the 5-0 final-round bogging down of upstart India on indoor clay in Goteborg. Mats beat Ramesh Krishnan, 6-4, 6-1, 6-3 and Jarryd beat Vijay Amritraj, 6-3, 6-3, 6-1. When the Flying Amritraj Brothers lost to Joakim Nystrom and Wilander, 6-2, 3-6, 6-1, 6-2, it was all over. Nevertheless, the Indians made a nice story, the peerless sportsmen from the subcontinent seeming to be players from another, earlier era. It was a splendid career closer for the Brothers—Vijay and Anand—to play a final, even though winning just one set, that together. Thirteen years before, Vijay and Anand lifted India to the same position where they were forced to default to South Africa as their government's anti-apartheid gesture. But in their 16th year of Davis Cup, they'd made it again, along with another name in their country's sporting history: Krishnan. This was Ramesh, 26-year-old son of the man—Ramanathan Krishnan—who had carried India to the Davis Cup Challenge Round in 1966. Never before, or after, had a son followed his father to the Cup finals.

American females weren't treated so badly, not with Navratilova still near the top of her form, but there was one jarring note. Chris Evert not only jettisoned her married name following a divorce from John Lloyd but also relinquished her hold on the majors. For the first time since 1974, she failed to win any of the Big Four tournaments. In fact, she wasn't even a finalist.

Furthermore, her performance at Flushing Meadow signaled the beginning of the end of an all-time career. For the first time in 16 years, since her debut at Forest Hills in the era of grass, she failed to reach the semifinals of the U.S. Open. At least her conqueror was an American, 23-year-old volleyer Lori McNeil, up from a public park in Houston, who beat Evert 3-6, 6-2, 6-4 in the quarterfinals.

By taking Evert's accustomed spot in the final four, McNeil provided a shot in the arm for minorities. Not since Arthur Ashe, in 1972, had a black advanced to a singles semifinal at the Open. Not since Althea Gibson won the tournament in 1958 had a black woman had such an impact. And McNeil did herself proud by pushing Graf to a third set before succumbing, 4-6, 6-2, 6-4.

In the end, of course, it was Navratilova's tournament. Not only did she defeat Graf for the singles title, 7-6 (7-4), 6-1, but she also won the women's doubles with Pam Shriver over Kathy Jordan and Liz Sayers-Smylie, 5-7, 6-4, 6-2, and, after a lunch break, a thrilling mixed title with Spaniard Emilio Sanchez over Betsy Nagelsen and Paul Annacone, 6-4, 6-7 (6-8), 7-6 (14-12), saving two match points. Billie Jean King had scored the last triple, at Wimbledon, in 1973. No one had tripled at the U.S. Championships since Margaret Smith Court in 1970.

Still, despite a brilliant Open, reaching the final in all four major singles and winning three majors doubles titles, it was a disappointing season for Navratilova. She won only four of the 12 singles tournaments she entered, fell short of the $1 million mark ($932,102) for the first time since 1981 and faltered in the season-ending Virginia Slims Championships at Madison Square Garden. She never got to contest Graf's claim to No. 1,

her 21-match winning streak in the event terminated in straight sets by Gabriela Sabatini in the quarterfinals of the year-end championships, 6-4, 7-5.

And yet, Martina and Pam (36-1 in doubles) might have had a Grand Slam to match their 1984 extravaganza. After winning the Australian in an eyeblink, 6-1, 6-0, over Zina Garrison and McNeil, and the French almost as fast, 6-2, 6-1 over Graf and Sabatini, they blipped at the Wimbledon quarters, losing to Soviets Larisa Savchenko and Svetlana Parkhomenko 6-2, 6-4. How much sweeter their U.S. title could have been—but three for four majors ain't bad. Nor was the fact that Martina inhabited nine of the 12 major finals altogether, winning six of them.

Graf, whose only two defeats were inflicted by Navratilova in major finals, overcame Sabatini, 4-6, 6-4, 6-0, 6-4, to win her first Slims title and confirm her place at the top of women's tennis. She also raised her earnings for the year to $1,063,785.

While Evert and Graf bypassed the resurrected Australian Open, staged for the last time on the grass at Kooyong, Navratilova journeyed Down Under and came away empty, beaten in the final by Hana Mandlikova, 7-5, 7-6 (7-2). That curtailed a 58-match winning streak dating back to the 1986 French Open and sent her into a downward spiral. Forced to contend with a persistent foot injury and a breakup with coach Mike Estep, she was beaten by Graf in the semis at the Lipton International Players Championship in Key Biscayne, Fla., 6-3, 6-2. "Today," Navratilova said, "she was the best player in the world and she will be until I play her again."

While she waited for the next meeting, Navratilova was overcome by Evert, 3-6, 6-1, 7-6 (7-4) in the final of the Virginia Slims of Houston and routed by Sabatini, 7-6 (7-2), 6-1, in the semifinals of the Italian Open in Rome, where the ladies at long last returned after being relegated to the hinterlands for six years, five at Perugia and 1986 at Taranto. Graf beat Gaby for the title, 7-5, 4-6, 6-0, but was not amused by journalists' satirical references to her nose and didn't return until 1996.

It was in Paris where Navratilova appeared to regain her form, smashing Evert, 6-2, 6-2, in the semifinal and earning another shot at Graf, who had come from 3-5 in the third set against Sabatini to reach the championship round, 6-4, 4-6, 7-5. Again, in a magnificent final, the German lass trailed 3-5 in the third. Again, Graf escaped with a 6-4, 4-6, 8-6 triumph for her first French crown. It ran her string of victories to seven tournaments, comprising 39 matches.

Navratilova had to take solace in extending her streak to nine consecutive singles final appearances in major tournaments, a record in the Open era. However, Helen Wills Moody and Maureen Connolly, who didn't travel as much, appeared in 22 and nine respectively.

Even the return to blessed English grass didn't reverse her fortunes, at least not instantly. At Eastbourne, where she had tuned her game for Wimbledon by winning each of the five preceding years, she was denied by Helena Sukova, 7-6 (7-5), 6-3, in the final. But just when it seemed that her fall was complete, Navratilova dug in her heels at the All England Club. She defeated Evert, 6-2, 5-7, 6-4, in a match worthy of the great rivalry. Yet, it was a sign of the times that the 73rd meeting of the pair occurred in the semifinal. Theirs had become a warm-up act.

In the other semi, Graf needed merely 51 minutes to bludgeon Shriver, 6-0, 6-2. "I can't believe Steffi is only 18 and is so strong," Shriver said. "The ball comes off her racket with unbelievable force."

That force finally was blunted in the final, where Navratilova needed all her athleticism and experience to win, 7-5, 6-3. Not only did it stop Graf's 45-match streak but it gave Navratilova an unprecedented sixth consecutive Wimbledon women's singles championship and her eighth overall, tying the record established by Helen Wills Moody 49 years earlier.

"How many more Wimbledons do you want?" Graf asked. Replied Navratilova: "Nine is my lucky number."

Meanwhile, Graf soared onward. Undefeated, she led West Germany against the United States in the final of the Federation Cup at Vancouver, winning all five of her singles and three doubles. Steffi's 6-2, 6-1 rout of Evert offset Shriver's 6-0, 7-6 victory over Claudia Kohde-Kilsch and the two German ladies then rallied from a 1-6, 0-4 deficit to defeat Evert and Shriver in the decisive doubles, 1-6, 7-5, 6-4. Thus their nation became the fifth to win the Cup.

Two weeks later, after Evert posted a semifinal victory over Navratilova, 6-2, 6-1, in Los Angeles, Graf dismissed her elder, 6-3, 6-4, in the final and ascended to No. 1.

So shaky was the game of the former Ice Maiden that she even lost to Shriver in the semifinal round of the Canadian Open. After nine years and 18 unsuccessful attempts, Shriver defeated Evert, 6-4, 6-1, then followed with a 6-4, 6-1 triumph over Garrison for her most significant singles title. She would finish a splendid season with four tournament victories, a match record of 67-13.

Pam also had the honor of captaining the U.S. Wightman Cup team, which beat a British squad for the ninth straight year, by the score of 5-2 at Williamsburg, Va. She beat Jo Durie, 6-1, 7-5, and Anne Hobbs, 6-4, 6-3, and got a singles win each out of Garrison, 7-5, 6-2, over Hobbs and McNeil, 6-2, 6-1, over Sara Gomer.

The most touching moment of the U.S. Open didn't occur in the final or even during Evert's quarterfinal loss to McNeil. It took place in the round of 16, where McNeil was matched against Garrison, her friend since childhood. Zina and Lori were pupils of John Wilkerson, the coach at McGregor Park's public courts. Garrison and McNeil, whose father, Charlie McNeil once played defensive back for the NFL's San Diego Chargers, were doubles partners and virtually inseparable on the tour. One month older, Garrison had enjoyed the more successful career and had won two of her first three tournaments of 1987, at Sydney over Shriver, 6-2, 6-4, and Oakland over German Sylvia Hanika, 7-5, 4-6, 6-3. But this was McNeil's moment, her tournament, and she survived two match points and defeated Garrison in a third-set tie-breaker, 7-6 (7-0), 3-6, 7-6 (8-6).

That boosted her into the quarterfinals, where her attacking game wore down Evert, 3-6, 6-2, 6-4, before an agonizing grandstand crowd. Without a clothing company to dress her or endorsements decorating her outfit, McNeil proved she belonged in such surroundings when she jumped on Graf to take the first set of their semifinal. But Graf eventually took control to win 4-6, 6-2, 6-4. In he final, Navratilova, who'd won all 12 sets, including the last two over Sukova, 6-2, 6-2, awaited the German.

The match turned in the tie-breaker when, at 3-3, Graf missed two backhands. Navratilova assumed command and closed out the challenger, 7-6 (7-4), 6-1, in one hour, 17 minutes.

As Navratilova held up the trophy, her fourth U.S. singles prize, both she and Graf were aware that the result wouldn't alter the computer ratings. After convincing victories in the world's two biggest tournaments, Navratilova said, "I'd have to think I have the edge right now." She paused. "Nothing is worse than when people say you're washed up."

She was a long way from that but still she needed to outlast Graf at the Slims Championships if she hoped to reclaim her eminence for the year. Instead, she lost to Sabatini in the quarterfinal, 6-4, 7-5. Her old rival had an even worse experience as pudgy lefty Hanika beat Evert in the opening round, 6-4, 6-4. A new generation made its mark as Graf closed out the season at Madison Square Garden with her 11th title and the designation as best in the game, putting down Sabatini in the best-of-five-set final 4-6, 6-4, 6-0, 6-4.

There would be no change at the top of the men's rankings but that didn't mean the circuit suffered from tired blood. The man who put a charge into the season was Cash, the Australian with the checkered headband, a diamond stud in his ear, a chip on his shoulder and an American temper. He regarded himself as a "yobbo," one of the boys. In his hometown of Melbourne, he became one of the finalists. Starting as the 11th seed, Cash advanced to the title match of the Australian Open by beating third-seeded Yannick Noah, 6-4, 6-2, 2-6, 6-0 in the quarterfinals, and top-seeded Lendl, 7-6, 5-7, 7-6, 6-4 in the semifinals. In the championship match, fourth-seeded Stefan Edberg prevailed, 6-3, 6-4, 3-6, 5-7, 6-3, the first of six tournament victories that would boost him into second place in the rankings. Another Aussie, Wally Masur, who upset No. 2 seed Boris Becker in the round of 16, 4-6, 7-6, 6-4, 6-7, 6-2, fell to Edberg in the semis, 6-2, 6-4, 7-6.

Edberg followed with a victory at the U.S. Indoor at Memphis where Connors, a seven-time champion, suffered a knee injury and had to default to Stefan, who led, 6-3, 2-1.

A tournament that one day would become the second-most important in the U.S. found its home on Key Biscayne, across the bay from Miami. Launched by Butch Buchholz as the Lipton International in Delray Beach, Fla., in 1985, it moved to Boca Raton the following year, then farther south, to Key Biscayne's Crandon Park, where the titles went to Mecir over Lendl, 7-5, 6-2, 7-5, and Graf over Evert, 6-1, 6-2.

At the Italian Open, Wilander, warmed up for Paris by beating McEnroe, 6-1, 6-3, and Argentine Martin Jaite, 6-3, 6-4, 6-4, in the last two rounds to win the title. In a fierce battle to avoid elimination in the first round by diminutive Argentine lefty Franco Davin, McEnroe was given relief and rest when the lights failed a couple of times for delays, each of almost a half-hour. Eventually he pulled through, 3-6, 6-2, 6-3. Faulty equipment? Or maybe it was a courtesy to a big ticket seller who had filled Il Foro Italico with 8,000 customers that night? Who can tell?

For McEnroe, his form on the clay was encouraging after a frustrating early season where he reached the finals of the U.S. Pro Indoor at Philadelphia and the WCT Finals in Dallas, only to lose to Mayotte 3-6, 6-1, 6-3, 6-1 and Mecir, 6-0, 3-6, 6-2, 6-2,

respectively. But it proved to be an illusion as he staggered in the very first round of the French Open, falling, 4-6, 6-2, 6-4, 6-2, to No. 49 Horacio de la Pena, an Argentine lefty. He flew home with a sore back, not to be seen again until the Davis Cup match with West Germany.

So depressed was the state of American men's tennis that Connors, 34, was the only Yank to reach the quarters in Paris, where he was blown away by Becker, 6-3, 6-3, 7-5. The final, between Lendl and Wilander, was an excruciatingly tiresome, four-hour, 30-minute exchange of ground strokes. The first set alone took 100 minutes. Lendl won, 7-5, 6-2, 3-6, 7-6 (7-3).

But it was Wimbledon—one of the wettest—for which Lendl hungered. This looked like it might be the year after Peter Doohan, an Aussie ranked No. 70, stunned Becker, the two-time defending champ, in the second round, 7-6 (7-4), 4-6 6-2, 6-4. In the same round, Lendl survived a five-set challenge from No. 45 Paolo Cane of Italy 3-6, 7-6 (7-5), 6-7 (2-7), 7-5, 6-1 but had smoother sailing thereafter. His semifinal defeat of Edberg, 3-6, 6-4, 7-6 (12-10), 6-4, dodging two set points in the tie-breaker, was impressive.

If Lendl's passage was relatively quiet, that was the result of some pyrotechnics in the other half of the draw, most of it caused by that old rabble-rouser, Connors. In the round of 16, the man staged one of the great rallies in the history of tennis by rising from a 1-6, 1-6, 1-4 deficit against Mikael Pernfors to win the last three sets 7-5, 6-4, 6-1. "Phenomenal," Connors decided, "right?" Right.

Then the geezer dodged the thunderbolt serves of Bobo Zivojinovic in a 7-6 (7-5), 7-5, 6-3 quarterfinal triumph. It appeared that Jimmy might really have a chance to win a third title. However, he was no match for Cash in the semifinal, losing 6-4, 6-4, 6-1.

That wasn't the only indication the 11th-seeded Aussie was ready to take the biggest step of his career. But grass was his best surface. He was fit after an injury-plagued season and he was a battler. And Cash knew how to play on grass. It was instinctive, the way he covered the net, the way he volleyed. For all his countless hours of practice, Lendl wasn't a natural. He was mechanical. And it showed as the 22-year-old Cash crushed his opponent's spirit, 7-6 (7-5), 6-2, 7-5.

There followed perhaps the most amazing victory celebration in the annals of the proper All England Club. Cash didn't wait to accept the congratulations of the Duke and Duchess of Kent. Instead, he clambered through the crowd massed at one corner of Centre Court and over the ledge to the second level of stands where were gathered his coach, psychologist, sister, father and girlfriend as well as the couple's 14-month-old son, not to mention his London pub mate.

Lendl tuned up for the green slabs of Flushing Meadow by winning at Washington, over Brad Gilbert, 6-1, 6-0, reaching the rained-out final at Stratton Mountain against McEnroe, and beating Edberg in the Canadian Open, 6-4, 7-6. Cash, seeded No. 7 in New York, continued to celebrate, which helped to explain his first-round U.S. Open loss to No. 47, Swede Peter Lundgren, 6-4, 4-6, 6-4, 6-4. (Later, a knee injury limited Cash to doubles duty as Australia was jolted in Davis Cup competition by India.)

The U.S. received a nice surprise when Michael Chang, the new U.S. junior champion and the youngest male, 15 years, six months, to compete in the U.S. Championships since Vinnie Richards in 1918, ran down everything and defeated ex-Aussie Davis Cupper, 32-year-old Paul McNamee in his first match, 6-3, 6-7, 6-4, 6-4. Nigerian Duke Odizor sent him packing, barely, in the second round, 6-1, 6-2, 6-7, 3-6, 6-4. Ken Flach, better known for his doubles prowess, penetrated to the fourth round before Wilander beat him, 6-3, 6-3, 7-6. Ken's second-round victory over Mike Cahill climaxed with the lengthiest tiebreaker to date at the Open, 32 points: 1-6, 6-4, 3-6, 6-1, 7-6 (17-15), on the strength of five match points dodged in the breaker. But it wasn't long before the American presence was reduced, once again, to McEnroe and Connors.

Mac caused a commotion not with his play but his behavior. He went ballistic, spewing curses at chair umpire Richard Ings and a courtside cameraman while beating Zivojinovic in the third round, 6-4, 5-7, 6-7 (5-7), 6-4, 6-3. Awaiting sentencing, he got to the quarterfinals, where he was overpowered in straight sets by Lendl, 6-3, 6-3, 6-4. The $17,500 fine and suspension he received ended his season.

Once again, Connors was the lone American survivor in the final four but he, too, was set down by Lendl in straight sets, 6-4, 6-2, 6-2. The final, against Wilander, delayed one day by rain, was a replay of the French. Although the quality of tennis was higher, so was the quantity. Lendl's 6-7 (7-9), 6-0, 7-6 (7-4), 6-4 victory lasted four hours, 47 minutes, a U.S. final record these two players would break in 1988. Three weeks after the Open, Lendl was shocked in the semifinals by Lundgren, 6-3, 4-6, 7-6, at San Francisco, ending a 25-match winning streak. Lundgren won the title in a totally unseeded final over double-handed-both-ways Californian Jim Pugh, 6-1, 7-5. But Lendl readied himself for the Masters, where he dropped only a set in the round-robin and pounded Wilander, 6-2, 6-3, in the final for a record fifth title, topping Ilie Nastase (1971-'72-'73, '75). Once again, Ivan was No. 1, perhaps with an asterisk that noted "except for Wimbledon."

1987 CHAMPIONS AND LEADERS

Australian Open
Men's Singles Final: Stefan Edberg (SWE) def. Pat Cash (AUS), 6-3, 6-4, 3-6, 5-7, 6-3
Women's Singles Final: Hana Mandlikova (CZE) def. Martina Navratilova (USA) 7-5, 7-6(2)
Men's Doubles Final: Stefan Edberg and Anders Jarryd (SWE), def. Peter Doohan and Laurie Warder (AUS), 6-4, 6-4, 7-6 (3)
Women's Doubles Final: Martina Navratilova and Pam Shriver (USA) def. Zina Garrison and Lori McNeil (USA), 6-1, 6-0
Mixed Doubles Final: Zina Garrison and Sherwood Stewart (USA) def. Anne Hobbs and Andrew Castle (GBR), 3-6, 7-6 (5), 6-3

French Open
Men's Singles Final: Ivan Lendl (CZE) def. Mats Wilander (SWE), 7-5, 6-2, 3-6,7-6 (3)
Women's Singles Final: Steffi Graf (GER) def. Martina Navratilova (USA), 6-4, 4-6, 8-6
Men's Doubles Final: Anders Jarryd (SWE) and Robert Seguso (USA) def. Guy Forget and Yannick Noah (FRA), 6-7, 6-7, 6-3, 6-4, 6-2
Women's Doubles Final: Martina Navratilova and Pam Shriver (USA), def. Steffi Graf (GER) and Gabriela Sabatini (ARG), 6-2, 6-1

Mixed Doubles Final: Pam Shriver (USA) and Emilio Sanchez (ESP) def. Sherwood Stewart and Lori McNeil (USA), 6-3, 7-6 (4)

Wimbledon
Men's Singles Final: Pat Cash (AUS) def. Ivan Lendl (CZE), 7-6 (5), 6-2, 7-5
Women's Singles Final: Martina Navratilova (USA) def. Steffi Graf (GER), 7-5, 6-3
Men's Doubles Final: Ken Flach and Robert Seguso (USA) def. Sergio Casal and Emilio Sanchez (ESP), 3-6, 6-7 (6), 7-6 (3), 6-1, 6-4
Women's Doubles Final: Claudia Kohde Kilsch (GER) and Helena Sukova (CZE) def. Betsy Nagelsen (USA) and Elizabeth Sayers Smylie (AUS), 7-5, 7-5
Mixed Doubles Final: Jo Durie and Jeremy Bates (GBR) def. Nicole Provis and Darren Cahill (AUS), 7-6 (10), 6-3

U.S. Open
Men's Singles Final: Ivan Lendl (CZE) def. Mats Wilander (SWE), 6-7 (7), 6-0, 7-6 (4), 6-4
Women's Singles Final: Martina Navratilova (USA) def. Steffi Graf (GER), 7-6 (4), 6-1
Men's Doubles Final: Stefan Edberg and Anders Jarryd (SWE) def. Ken Flach and Robert Seguso (USA), 7-6 (1), 6-2, 4-6, 5-7, 7-6 (2)
Women's Doubles Final: Martina Navratilova and Pam Shriver (USA) def. Kathy Jordan (USA) and Elizabeth Sayers Smylie (AUS), 5-7, 6-4, 6-2
Mixed Doubles Final: Martina Navratilova (USA) and Emilio Sanchez (ESP) def. Betsy Nagelsen and Paul Annacone (USA), 6-4, 6-7 (6), 7-6 (14-12)

Year-End No. 1
Men: Ivan Lendl
Women: Steffi Graf

Top Player Earnings
Men: Ivan Lendl $2,003,656
Women: Steffi Graf $1,063,785

Davis Cup: Sweden

Federation Cup: W. Germany

Wightman Cup: United States

Grand Prix Masters, NYC—Ivan Lendl
WCT, Dallas—Miloslav Mecir
Virginia Slims Championships, NYC—Steffi Graf

1988 Steffi Scales Peak with Golden Slam

Steffi Graf won the "Golden Slam"—all four major singles titles and Olympic gold at the Seoul Olympics.

Steffi Graf added the Grand Slam to her resume in 1988, sweeping the championships of Australia, France, Wimbledon and the United States. And Don Budge, the first person to win all four of the world's major tournaments in one season, witnessed each of her conquests. While the West German prodigy expressed mostly relief, the courtly American seemed enormously pleased with Graf's Slam-clinching, U.S. Open victory over Gabriela Sabatini.

In welcoming Graf to the most exclusive club in tennis, Budge, who'd accomplished his Grand Slam 50 years earlier, whispered into her ear during the award ceremonies at Flushing Meadow. "He said he knew it all the way," she recalled later. "He said he thinks I'm going to do it a couple more times."

Graf would not achieve a second Grand Slam (of the five persons who have claimed the four major titles within a calendar year, only Rod Laver did so twice) but that in no way diminished what she accomplished in 1988. She lost but two sets in her triumphant march, the first to Martina Navratilova in the Wimbledon final and the second to Sabatini. Budge said he expected Graf to capture the Slam after watching her in Australia. At the Wimbledon Ball, he told her, "Steffi, when you win the Grand Slam, I hope they let me present the trophy."

The U.S. Tennis Association was too conscious of tradition to allow such a radical departure, but Budge was included in the ceremony on the golden anniversary of his achievement. He held one handle of the silver jug while Gordon Jorgensen, the USTA president, held the other. They were surrounded by the Stars and Stripes, the Union Jack, the Tricolor and the Southern Cross.

Clearly, the sport's dominant player in 1988 was a teen-aged female who followed in the Grand Slam steps of Maureen Connolly (1953) and Margaret Smith Court (1970). In fact, Graf took a few steps beyond by adding the Olympic title to her collection—call it a Golden Slam.

"There's nothing quite as special as winning a gold medal for your country," she said after her September triumph on a hard court in Seoul, South Korea.

For the first time since 1924, tennis returned to the Olympics as a medal sport. The acceptance of tennis as a full-fledged medal sport marked a breakthrough—or official breakdown of amateurism—hardly noticed at the time. The ITF got permission from the IOC (International Olympic Committee) to approve the best players available for the Games if nominated by their countries. That meant out-and-out pros. It changed the complexion of the next Games in 1992 at Barcelona, where the U.S. NBA "Dream Team" took basketball gold, and numerous other declared pros took part. Tennis had led the way, for better or worse.

A slam of sorts was registered in men's competition as well. But this was national and not individual. As the result of Mats Wilander's victories at the Australian, French and U.S. championships and Stefan Edberg's ascendancy at Wimbledon, each of the major events was captured by a Swede. There hadn't been

a male sweep by citizens of one country since Laver ran the table in 1969.

In a season that would stand forth regardless of Graf's transcendent performance, Wilander also bumped Ivan Lendl from the top spot on the computer. Lendl, slipping from the No. 1 position for the first time in 156 weeks, reached only one Big Four final, at the U.S. Open. He also surrendered his Masters title, which he had held for three years, to Boris Becker.

Becker, beaten by Edberg in the Wimbledon final, won seven tournaments and also led West Germany to its first Davis Cup, dethroning Sweden, 4-1, at Goteborg.

Miloslav Mecir, the enigmatic Czech, took home the Olympic gold medal and also denied Wilander any chance of a Grand Slam by defeating the Swede in the Wimbledon quarterfinals.

It was another empty year for America's two controversial stars. Neither John McEnroe nor Jimmy Connors advanced beyond the quarters of a major and both sagged in the rankings, Mac to No. 11 and Connors to No. 7. Each won two tournaments, the first for Connors in four years.

Suddenly, however, the future appeared bright for men's tennis in the United States. Andre Agassi, an 18-year-old graduate of Nick Bollettieri's groundstroke academy who had won his first Grand Prix tournament only the previous November at Itaparica, Brazil, over Luiz Mattar, 7-6, 6-2, captured six titles, reached the semifinals at the French and U.S. Opens and shot from No. 25 to No. 3 in the world standings.

Andre also led the "back from the boonies" march of the U.S. Davis Cup team captained by Tom Gorman. It included a McEnroe cameo at Buenos Aires as the Yanks took the American zone title with road victories over Peru, 3-0, and Argentina, 4-1, returning the U.S. to the Davis Cup World Group for 1989. (The U.S. had been relegated in 1987 after losses to Paraguay and West Germany.) Rookies Agassi and Jay Berger had a rough time, but came through in Lima, Jay in five hours, 35 minutes to beat Pablo Arraya, 7-5, 6-1, 5-7, 1-6, 7-5. So did Andre, 6-8, 7-5, 6-1, 6-2, over Jaime Yzaga. Ken Flach and Robert Seguso sealed it, 6-2, 4-6, 6-4, 6-3, over Yzaga and Carlos DiLaura.

McEnroe, bothered that he had absorbed four Cup singles defeats in Argentina (two each by Guillermo Vilas and Jose-Luis Clerc in 1980 and 1983) itched for some revenge. He got it, winning the last four games of the opener and a five-set decision over Guillermo Perez-Roldan, 6-2, 5-7, 6-2, 3-6, 6-3. Agassi got Martin Jaite, 6-2, 6-2, 6-1, and Flach-Seguso punched the ticket out of the basement, 6-2, 6-3, 6-4, over Christian Miniussi and Javier Frana.

Two years younger than Agassi, Michael Chang also made great strides. By defeating Johan Kriek to win San Francisco in early October, 6-2, 6-3, he became the second-youngest winner of a men's pro tournament at 16 years, seven months (Aaron Krickstein had been 16 years, two months when he triumphed at Israel five years earlier). Chang rose 133 places in the rankings, from No. 163 to No. 30, in his first full season on the circuit.

Graf's monumental accomplishment guaranteed that U.S. women would be denied a major title for the first time since Court's Grand Slam 18 years earlier. Additionally, Navratilova hadn't been blanked in the Big Four since 1980. Still, Martina was

a solid No. 2, winning nine tournaments (two fewer than Graf) and amassing a 70-7 record. But Navratilova reached the final of only one major tournament, Wimbledon. In the first Australian Open played on hard courts in the sparkling new complex at Melbourne's Flinders Park, she was a straight set, semifinal loser to Chris Evert, 6-2, 7-5. At the French, she was stunned by 17-year-old Belarussian Natalia Zvereva in the fourth round, 6-3, 7-6 (7-5). Zina Garrison did the honors in a quarterfinal match at Flushing Meadows, 6-4, 6-7 (3-7), 7-5.

In doubles, Navratilova and Pam Shriver continued their successful amalgam, winning 28 of 30 matches and five championships, including a sixth Australian, over Wendy Turnbull and Evert, 6-0, 7-5 and a record-tying fourth French, over Claudia Kohde-Kilsch and Helena Sukova, 6-2, 7-5.

Shriver later teamed with Garrison against a Czechoslovakian team of Sukova and Jana Novotna to win an Olympic gold medal in doubles, 4-6, 6-2, 10-8. That equaled the feat of Ken Flach and Robert Seguso, who defeated Spaniards Emilio Sanchez and Sergio Casal, 6-3, 6-4, 6-7 (5-7), 6-7 (1-7), 9-7 in the gold medal match.

Graf, the 6-3, 6-3 golden victor over Sabatini, was the first Olympic women's singles champion since Helen Wills in 1924. Steffi, lost but three matches all year. Sabatini triumphed twice, beating Graf, 2-6, 6-3, 6-1, for the first time after 11 consecutive losses to win Boca Raton in March, and in a semifinal at Amelia Island one month later, 6-3, 4-6, 7-5, in a tournament won by Navratilova, 6-0, 6-2. Shriver applied the final blemish to Graf's record, 6-3, 7-6 (7-5), in the semifinals of the Virginia Slims Championship, which the 18-year-old Sabatini won for her fourth title of the season, beating Shriver 7-5, 6-2, 6-2.

Graf zipped through the Australian without the loss of a set but she was pressed in the final by Evert, playing in her 34th and last major final of her career. But for tennis, the match was an unprecedented, schizophrenic, outdoor-indoor title bout made possible by the new stadium's sliding roof. It was, according to Evert, "the weirdest [final] I ever played."

Rain suspended the match with Graf ahead, 2-1 in the first. Officials decided to close the roof and, after a 91-minute delay, the outdoor tournament resumed indoors. Graf adapted better to the change, racing to a 6-1, 5-1 lead before Evert steadied herself. She won four of the next five games and came within two points of squaring the match before the German prevailed, 6-1, 7-6 (7-3).

Navratilova won five consecutive tournaments and 29 matches in the U.S. before she was again stopped by Evert at Houston in their 77th meeting, 6-0, 6-4. But Navratilova would win their last three matches—a Wimbledon semifinal, 6-1, 4-6, 7-5, and finals in Filderstadt, Germany, 6-2, 6-3 and Chicago, 6-2. 6-2—raising her record in the enduring, 80-match rivalry to a concluded 43-37. Their global warfare, concussive but caring, began in Ohio in 1973 and ceased 15 years later in Chicago, touching down in several countries along the way.

Any semblance of competition at the French vanished when third-seeded Evert was dismissed in the third round by future champ, 16-year-old Arantxa Sanchez of Spain, 6-3, 7-6 (7-4), and second-seeded Navratilova was surprised by 13th-

seeded Zvereva in the round of 16, 6-3, 7-6 (7-5). Zvereva then upset sixth-seeded Sukova, 6-2, 6-3. Next the coltish 17-year-old from Minsk outlasted unseeded Australian Nicole Provis in two hours, six minutes, 6-3, 6-7 (3-7), 7-5 to land in her only major singles final.

Graf, who had beaten Sabatini in the semifinals, 6-3, 7-6 (7-3), was brutally efficient against her star-struck opponent. Her 6-0, 6-0, romp lasted only 32 minutes, the most exciting feature of which was an hour rain delay. There hadn't been such a one-sided major tournament championship match since 1911 when Dorothea Chambers rang up two goose eggs over Dora Boothby in an all-English Wimbledon final. Navratilova added another major, keeping the doubles with Shriver, 6-2, 7-5, over Kohde-Kilsch and Sukova.

It was Wimbledon, of course, that loomed as the biggest obstacle to a Steffi Slam. Wimbledon was the seat of Navratilova's power. "Wimbledon is the last thing she's holding onto, the last thing she dominates in women's tennis," Shriver said. The naturalized American was in position to surpass the record for most singles championships at the All England Club and she prepared in her usual fashion, winning at Eastbourne against Zvereva, 6-2, 6-2. But Navratilova was less than commanding once the tournament got underway. She struggled both in the quarterfinals and semifinals, edging Ros Fairbank, 4-6, 6-4, 7-5, and Evert, 6-1, 4-6, 7-5. Indeed, after holding out through three match points in their 78th meeting, Evert picked Graf to win.

Graf appeared jumpy in the first set, serving below her standard and committing a bundle of unforced errors. Navratilova had raced to a 7-5, 2-0 lead and appeared well on her way to another glorious moment. Then Graf broke Navratilova's second service of the second set. Remarkably, the defending champion would not hold service again in the match. Graf allowed Navratilova only one more game and the only delay in a 5-7, 6-2, 6-1 triumph was caused by rain after four games of the third set.

"I hit good volleys," Navratilova reasoned. "I hit good balls that other people wouldn't get to, and then she hits winners. I didn't succumb to pressure today. I succumbed to a better player ... I still played pretty damn well, but she was hitting winners all over the place." Steffi had stolen seemingly sure Navratilova points with her legs.

And so ended one phase of Martina's pursuit of Helen Wills Moody, who won a record 50 consecutive matches while capturing eight Wimbledon singles title. Graf snipped Martina's match streak at 47, but the loser would get that ninth title two years down the road.

Graf was only one title away from an achievement that had eluded Navratilova in her prime. She even teamed with Sabatini to win the Wimbledon doubles championship, defeating the Soviet pairing of Zvereva and Larisa Savchenko, 6-3, 1-6, 12-10. The Soviets stopped defending champs Navratilova and Shriver in the third round, 7-6, 6-2.

Fittingly, the only genuine competition Graf faced at the U.S. Open was contemporary in nature. Having failed to derail her at Wimbledon, Navratilova lost any opportunity at Flushing Meadow when she was ousted in an exciting quarterfinal by Garrison, 6-4, 6-7 (3-7), 7-5, her first win over Martina in 22

starts. Evert, recently married to former Olympic skier Andy Mill, earned a chance to thwart the Grand Slam but had to withdraw on the day of the semis with a stomach virus that left her so weak she could barely get out of bed.

That left Sabatini, Graf's doubles partner and the person responsible for the "2" in Graf's 61-2 record at that point. Sabatini defeated Garrison in their semi, 6-4, 7-5, and became the first Argentine to qualify for a major women's final. In the end, although Sabatini did extend "Fraulein Forehand" to a third set, Graf added the U.S. title to her necklace of jewels with a 6-3, 3-6, 6-1 victory.

After the victory, Graf seemed more relieved than thrilled. She didn't jump for joy or kneel in supplication. Graf merely jogged to the stands to embrace her family and she barely smiled during the award ceremony. "Now I've done it," she said. "There's no more pressure."

In doubles, Navratilova and Shriver were terminated in the semis, 4-6, 6-3, 6-3, by Gigi Fernandez and Robin White, who then defeated the U.S.-Canadian alliance of Patty Fendick and Jill Hetherington, 6-4, 6-1, in the final.

Steffi didn't have much time to savor the moment.

The Olympic tournament was scheduled to begin in a week. Naturally, Graf was seeded No. 1. Naturally, she won. In the final, she again bested Sabatini, this time by the definitive score of 6-3, 6-3. A sign of the times: Of the seven Americans representing the U.S. in tennis at Seoul, the only player not to medal was Evert, a third-round victim of Italy's Raffaella Reggi, 2-6, 6-4, 6-1. Tim Mayotte was decorated with silver as the 3-6, 6-2, 6-4, 6-2, final round loser to Czechoslovakia's Mecir.

Neither Evert nor Navratilova survived the quarters at the season-ending Slims Championships in New York. Martina lost to Sukova, 2-6, 7-5, 6-3, and Evert to Shriver, 7-5, 6-4, who then terminated Graf's 46-match winning streak with a 6-3, 7-6 (7-5) decision in the semifinals. But Sabatini upheld the new order with a 7-5, 6-2, 6-2 victory.

Garrison, the captain, and her pal, Lori McNeil, starred in a 7-0 Wightman Cup victory over a woefully weak British squad that won only one set at London. But McNeil, beaten by Catarina Lindqvist, 6-4, 7-5, and Pstty Fendick, defeated by No. 107 Maria Strandlund, 6-2, 7-6 were a second-round Federation Cup flop for the U.S., losing 2-1 to Sweden.

Sukova was the anchor for a fifth Czechoslovak triumph, 2-1 over the Soviet Union. Sukova beat Zvereva, 6-3, 6-4, and Radka Zrubakova beat Larisa Savchenko, 6-1, 7-6 (7-2). They went undefeated at the 1988 Fed Cup in five singles matches. However, the date and place of the competition—December in Melbourne—diminished the quality of the participants.

Eleven months earlier in Melbourne, the baptism of Flinders Park (named at the time for Captain Matthew Flinders of the British Navy, an explorer of those parts near the end of the 18th century. The complex was later renamed Melbourne Park) sent Australia well ahead of the rest of the tennis world, a very long jump from 61-year-old grass-carpeted Kooyong. The focal point of the complex was an asphalt-floored, $70-million techno-wonder stadium, with 15,000 seats, air-cooled private boxes and a sliding ceiling that put an end to rainouts.

It was a lively, controversial debut. Curiously, in this he-man land, a "Sheila" (woman) was selected to do the opening honors. Dianne Fromholtz Ballestrat, seeded 14th, was beaten by a totally unknown 23-year-old American qualifier, No. 304 Wendy Wood, 6-2, 4-6, 8-6. The crowd within was anxious for Wood and Ballestrat to move on so they could watch the hometown hero, fourth-seeded, 1987 runner-up Patrick Cash, beat Thomas Muster, 7-5, 6-1, 6-4. Well, not heroic to all. Cash had attracted some barbs for playing in South Africa—winning that country's Open over Brad Gilbert near the end of the 1987 season. On entering the court, he was greeted by anti-apartheid banners and shouting protesters. On the changeover after the seventh game, activists pitched two-dozen black tennis balls at Patrick.

For the second consecutive year, Cash qualified for the final by beating Lendl, 6-4, 2-6, 6-2, 4-6, 6-2, and for the second consecutive year, he lost his national championship in five sets to a Swede. In 1987, Cash slipped on the grass against Edberg. This time, on hard courts, he was beaten by Wilander, 6-3, 6-7 (3-7), 3-6, 6-1, 8-6, in what would be remembered as the year's most captivating major final, an all-around battle of extraordinary offense and defense as Wilander's retrieving and lobs finally broke down Cash's volleying. By defeating Edberg, 6-0, 6-7 (5-7), 6-3, 3-6, 6-1, and Cash back-to-back, Wilander not only eliminated the two previous finalists but became only the second man to win major titles on three different surfaces—grass, clay, now hard—matching the achievement of Jimmy Connors, who turned the trick alone at the U.S. Open.

Memphis was the launch pad for Agassi, who moved to No. 18 after winning his second career tournament, the U.S. Indoor Championship, over Swede Mikael Pernfors, 6-4, 6-4, 7-5. At 17 years, 10 months, he was the youngest player to win the second oldest of U.S. titles. He followed with victories over Jimmy Arias at the U.S. Clay Courts, 6-2, 6-2, and Slobodan Zivojinovic, 7-5, 7-6, 7-5, in the Tournament of Champions at Forest Hills. As a result, he was seeded ninth in the French Open.

There, Agassi reached the semifinals, the best American finish in three years, before he was worn down by Wilander in five sets, 4-6, 6-2, 7-5, 5-7, 6-0. But the Yank who received the best reception was, of all people, McEnroe. He had returned from a seven-month hiatus (and a plunge to No. 25 in world rankings) to defeat Edberg in the final of the Japan Open, 6-2, 6-2. In Paris, he wowed the crowd with a reasonable facsimile of his championship form and three straight-set victories, the last over Chang, 6-0, 6-3, 6-1. But McEnroe was eliminated, 6-7 (3-7), 7-6 (7-3), 6-4, 6-4, by Lendl, the defending champ, who in turn was eliminated by unseeded Swede Jonas Svensson in the quarterfinals, 7-6 (7-5), 7-5, 6-2. Henri Leconte then beat Svensson, 7-6 (7-3), 6-2, 6-3, to meet Wilander in the final. Wilander missed only two of 74 first serves and committed only nine unforced errors in a 7-5, 6-2, 6-1 rout of the local hero.

Wimbledon was an American wasteland other than in doubles, where Ken Flach and Robert Seguso earned a second consecutive title, over the Aussie-Swede linkup of John Fitzgerald and Anders Jarryd, 6-4, 2-6, 6-4, 7-6 (7-3). Agassi, no fan of grass, went home to Las Vegas after the French. McEnroe should have followed his lead. The man, seeded an unrealistic eighth, won

only one match at the All England Club, over Austrian Horst Skoff, 6-1, 7-5, 6-1, before being flattened 7-5, 7-6 (7-5), 6-3 by No. 64 Wally Masur of Australia. Connors, the fifth seed, lasted until the fourth round where he was bounced by hefty-serving German Patrik Kuhnen, 5-7, 7-6 (9-7), 7-6 (7-2), 6-7 (4-7), 6-3, over two rainy afternoons in the sodden "Graveyard" (Court 2), where the ball hardly bounced.

Connors, twice champion, winner of more singles here than any other man (81), was understandably peeved to be assigned for interment in that plot at that stage of the tournament and his career. He said he wouldn't return (but of course he did). Any dreams Wilander had of a Grand Slam ended in the quarters, where he lost to Mecir, 6-3, 6-1, 6-3. "My style is not suited to this surface," Wilander said. "If we played three of the four majors on clay, maybe I'd have a chance for the Slam."

One Swede suited for grass was Edberg. He was down two sets to none and 3-3, 0-40 in the third against the crafty Mecir in the semifinals before staging the comeback of his young career, 4-6, 2-6, 6-4, 6-3, 6-4, boosting him into the championship match against Becker. The two-time champion had eliminated Cash, 6-4, 6-3, 6-4, and Lendl, 6-4, 6-3, 6-7 (8-10), 6-4, en-route to another final. Two weeks earlier, Edberg had double-faulted away the final of the Queen's Club tournament to Becker, 6-1, 3-6, 6-3. But this time, Edberg was mentally prepared for the challenge, even after London's dismal weather interrupted play in the first set and delayed completion of the match until Monday. He served well and volleyed impeccably in scoring a 4-6, 7-6 (7-2), 6-4, 6-2 victory that fulfilled the Swede's immense promise. Edberg fell to his knees and then onto his back on match point. "I couldn't think of anything else to do," he said.

Connors bounded back into the picture by beating Andres Gomez, 6-1, 6-4, in 102-degree heat in Washington, his first tournament victory in 45 months, and rolled into the U.S. Open quarterfinals without much opposition. But there, the past was no match for the future as Agassi blasted him, 6-2, 7-6 (8-6), 6-1, securing the No. 1 U.S. ranking for the year. A round later, Agassi bowed to Lendl, 7-6 (7-4), 6-1, 3-6, 6-1.

McEnroe, seeded a lowly 16th, stumbled in the other half of the draw, falling to Mark Woodforde in the second round, 7-5, 4-6, 6-7 (5-7), 6-3, 6-1. Wilander, the second seed, defeated two more unseeded players, No. 21 Emilio Sanchez of Spain in the quarterfinals 3-6, 7-6 (7-3), 6-0, 6-4 and No. 33 Darren Cahill of Australia in the semifinals, 6-4, 6-4, 6-2, to gain a final berth. Seeking to become the first man to win four consecutive U.S. championships since the era of Bill Tilden, and closing in on Connors' record of 159 weeks at the top of the rankings, Lendl fell one set and three weeks short against his Connecticut neighbor. In the longest Open final on record (four hours, 54 minutes), Wilander won his third major title of the year and moved to the top of the ATP ladder, 6-4, 4-6, 6-3, 5-7, 6-4. "I don't think I've ever felt better," he said.

Earlier in the tournament, he had served as a spokesman for the ATP, the players' association, which announced it was assuming control of the men's tour starting in the 1990 season. Nothing that happened in the last three months of 1988 altered the final standings. Not even Becker's gutsy 5-7, 7-6 (7-5), 3-6,

6-2, 7-6 (7-5) conquest of Lendl in the Masters final that ended with a whimper, a net-cord dribbler off Boris' racket. The match equaled the closest finish—two points—of an important final: Ken Rosewall's 7-5 fifth set tie-breaker win over Rod Laver in the 1972 WCT Final.

Ironically, neither Wilander nor Edberg, the major champions of the season, could stop Becker and West Germany from wresting away the Davis Cup, 4-1, in Goteborg in the waning days of the year. No fan of clay Becker nevertheless beat Edberg, 6-3, 6-1, 6-4. But it was No. 79, lefty Charlie Steeb, who truly stunned the home folks by ducking a match point while leading of with a resurgent 8-10, 1-6, 6-2, 6-4, 8-6, triumph over Wilander. Becker and Eric Jelen banked the Cup by short-changing Edberg and Jarryd, 3-6, 2-6, 7-5, 6-3. 6-2. Wilander's No. 1 ranking (made with three majors; and three other titles on a 53-11 mark in 15 tourneys) quickly vanished, like the Cup.

1988 CHAMPIONS AND LEADERS

Australian Open
Men's Singles Final: Mats Wilander (SWE) def. Pat Cash (AUS), 6-3, 6-7 (3), 3-6, 6-1, 8-6
Women's Singles Final: Steffi Graf (GER) def. Chris Evert (USA), 6-1, 7-6 (3)
Men's Doubles Final: Rick Leach and Jim Pugh (USA) def. Jeremy Bates (GBR) and Peter Lundgren (SWE), 6-3, 6-2, 6-3
Women's Doubles Final: Martina Navratilova and Pam Shriver (USA) def. Chris Evert (USA) and Wendy Turnbull (AUS), 6-0, 7-5
Mixed Doubles Final: Jana Novotna (CZE) and Jim Pugh (USA) def. Martina Navratilova and Tim Gullikson (USA), 5-7, 6-2, 6-4

French Open
Men's Singles Final: Mats Wilander (SWE) def. Henri Leconte (FRA), 7-5, 6-2, 6-1
Women's Singles Final: Steffi Graf (GER) def. Natalia Zvereva (USSR), 6-0, 6-0
Men's Doubles Final: Andres Gomez (ECU) and Emilio Sanchez (ESP) def. John Fitzgerald (AUS) and Anders Jarryd (SWE), 6-3, 6-7 (8), 6-4, 6-3
Women's Doubles Final: Martina Navratilova and Pam Shriver (USA) def. Claudia Kohde-Kilsch (GER) and Helena Sukova (CZE), 6-2, 7-5
Mixed Doubles Final: Lori McNeil (USA) and Jorge Lozano (MEX) def. Brenda Schultz and Michael Schapers (NED), 7-5, 6-2

Wimbledon
Men's Singles Final: Stefan Edberg (SWE) def. Boris Becker (GER), 4-6, 7-6 (2), 6-4, 6-2
Women's Singles Final: Steffi Graf (GER) def. Martina Navratilova (USA), 5-7, 6-2, 6-1
Men's Doubles Final: Ken Flach and Robert Seguso (USA) def. John Fitzgerald (AUS) and Anders Jarryd (SWE), 6-4, 2-6, 6-4, 7-6 (3)
Women's Doubles Final: Steffi Graf (GER) and Gabriela Sabatini (ARG), Larisa Savchenko and Natalia Zvereva (USSR), 6-3, 1-6, 12-10
Mixed Doubles Final: Zina Garrison and Sherwood Stewart (USA) def. Gretchen Rush Magers and Kelly Jones (USA), 6-1, 7-6 (3)

U.S. Open
Men's Singles Final: Mats Wilander (SWE) def. Ivan Lendl (CZE), 6-4, 4-6, 6-3, 5-7, 6-4
Women's Singles Final: Steffi Graf (GER) def. Gabriela Sabatini (ARG), 6-3, 3-6, 6-1
Men's Doubles Final: Sergio Casal and Emilio Sanchez (ESP) def. Rick Leach and Jim Pugh (USA), walkover

Women's Doubles Final: Gigi Fernandez and Robin White (USA) def. Patty Fendick (USA) and Jill Hetherington (CAN), 6-4, 6-1
Mixed Doubles Final: Jana Novotna (CZE) and Jim Pugh (USA) def. Elizabeth Sayers Smylie (AUS) and Patrick McEnroe (USA), 7-5, 6-3

Year-End No. 1
Men: Mats Wilander
Women: Steffi Graf

Top Player Earnings
Men: Mats Wilander $1,726,731
Women: Steffi Graf $1,378,128

Davis Cup: Germany

Federation Cup: Czechoslovakia

Wightman Cup: United States

Grand Prix Masters, NYC—Boris Becker
WCT, Dallas—Boris Becker
Virginia Slims Championships, NYC—Gabriela Sabatini

1988 OLYMPIC GAMES—SEOUL, SOUTH KOREA

Men's singles:
GOLD: Miloslav Mecir (CZE)
SILVER: Tim Mayotte (USA)
BRONZE: Stefan Edberg (SWE)
Brad Gilbert (USA)

Women's singles:
GOLD: Steffi Graf (GER)
SILVER: Gabriela Sabatini (ARG)
BRONZE: Zina Garrison (USA)
Manuela Maleeva (BUL)

Men's doubles:
GOLD: Ken Flach and Robert Seguso USA)
SILVER: Sergio Casal and Emilio Sanchez (ESP)
BRONZE: Miloslav Mecir and Milan Srejber (CZE)
Stefan Edberg and Anders Jarryd (SWE)

Women's doubles:
GOLD: Zina Garrison and Pam Shriver (USA)
SILVER: Jana Novotna and Helena Sukova (CZE)
BRONZE: Elizabeth Smylie and Wendy Turnbull (AUS)
Steffi Graf and Claudia Kohde-Kilsch (GER)

1989 Evert Bids Adieu

Michael Chang became one of the most unlikely winners of a major title, winning at Roland Garros at age 17.

That individual was Ivan Lendl, the fit Czech expatriate who captured his first Australian Open title at the outset of the season, regained his No. 1 ranking and, at the advanced age of 29, held off a late charge by Boris Becker. The latter added a first U.S. Open crown to his third Wimbledon title and capped an outstanding year by leading West Germany to its second consecutive Davis Cup. However, it was Chang, the 17-year-old American, who provided the most distinctive victory on the men's tour with an improbable triumph at the French Open.

Chang was born in 1972, one year after a 16-year-old Evert made her sensational debut in the U.S. Open. At 34, Evert decided to make her final tournament appearance in the same event where she first rose to prominence. The last of her major matches was a quarterfinal loss to Zina Garrison, 7-6 (7-2), 6-1, at Flushing Meadow. She concluded her career one month later by teaming with Martina Navratilova in the U.S. drive to a Federation Cup title in Tokyo.

As she had the previous year, Steffi Graf dominated the women's tour. At 20, the German lass even surpassed her 1988 record by winning 86 of 88 matches and 14 of 16 tournaments. But the road to an unprecedented second successive Grand Slam was barricaded by 17-year-old Arantxa Sanchez Vicario, 7-6 (8-6), 3-6, 7-5, in the French final. Sanchez Vicario

At the end of a memorable decade, the world said hello to Michael Chang and goodbye to Chris Evert. If further proof were needed that a new era was at hand, it was to be found in the disposition of the major championships. Only one of the eight singles championships was awarded to a player older than 21.

became the first Spanish woman to win at Paris, as well as the youngest of any nationality, at 17 years, six months. She had a reputation as a dogged competitor on clay, had risen to No. 10 on the computer before the start of the tournament and was seeded seventh in the event.

By comparison, Chang was a nobody. Well, that's not completely true. He also demonstrated the patience to play forever, a requirement on dirt, had climbed to No. 19 in the rankings and was seeded 15th. Still, who was he to beat the likes of Lendl and Stefan Edberg? Well, he was the youngest male (17 years, three months) to win any of the four majors and he was the first U.S. man to succeed at Roland Garros in 34 years. Not since Tony Trabert defeated Sven Davidson for his second consecutive title in 1955 had an American reigned in Paris.

By the end of the season, no fewer than six Americans held places in the Top 10, topped by McEnroe's climb to No. 4. For the first time since the advent of the computer in 1973, however, the elite group did not include Connors. The 37-year-old campaigner slipped to No. 11 despite increasing to 109 his career record for tournament victories with triumphs at Toulouse (over McEnroe, 6-3, 6-3) and Tel Aviv (over Gilad Bloom, 6-1, 4-6, 6-1).

Connors won his first major tournament in 1974 (Australia), the same year Evert made her breakthrough at the French. They were more than contemporaries. Once upon a time, they were engaged to be married, but whereas Evert formally bade farewell to the crowd at Flushing Meadow, Connors, having knocked off Edberg, 6-2, 6-3, 6-1, vowed to press on.

Of course, there was a major difference in the amount of fight left in the player. The 37-year-old Connors forced 19-year-old Andre Agassi, the top-ranked American, to a fifth set before yielding in a dramatic men's quarterfinal, 6-1, 4-6, 0-6, 6-3, 6-4. He never surrendered. "The people were excited," Connors decided. "You know what? I was excited, too."

Damn right, he was planning to continue. But Evert knew she had had enough after her first season without a single tournament victory, let alone a major. She lost three consecutive finals in the spring, to Graf, 4-6, 6-2, 6-3, at Boca Raton; to Gabriela Sabatini, 6-1, 4-6, 6-2, at Key Biscayne (Lipton); and, finally—did this convince her?—to 15-year-old Monica Seles of Yugoslavia, 3-6, 6-1, 6-4, in Houston. Evert did manage to reach the semifinals at Wimbledon for the 17th time in 18 appearances and she bashed Seles, 6-0, 6-2, in her penultimate match at the U.S. Open.

Chrissie, the symbol of athletic consistency, finished on a high note, winning all five of her matches in the Federation Cup at Tokyo. Navratilova also was 5-0 as the U.S. defeated Spain 3-0—Chrissie over Conchita Martinez, 6-3, 6-2; Martina over Sanchez Vicario, 0-6, 6-3, 6-4—and won the team championship for the first time since the great rivals last pooled their talents in 1986 at Prague. Sadly, Evert and Navratilova did not oppose each other at all in 1989 and the record of their meetings remained fixed in history at 43-37 in favor of Navratilova.

Although she retained her No. 2 ranking and won eight of 15 tournaments, Navratilova was frustrated by Graf in the two most significant tournaments she entered. The Fraulein needed three sets on both occasions but nonetheless defeated Navratilova in the final at Wimbledon, 6-2, 6-7 (1-7), 6-1, and at the U.S. Open, 3-6, 7-5, 6-1. Graf also turned back Martina in the final of the Virginia Slims Championships, 6-4, 7-5, 2-6, 6-2.

Agassi, continuing to avoid Wimbledon, seemed to have the Italian Open wrapped up in four, but wasted a match point, and folded, losing to the Argentine swatter of explosive groundies,

Alberto Mancini, 6-3, 4-6, 2-6, 7-6 (7-2), 6-1. Sanchez Vicario was gaining respect, though losing the women's title to Rome's favorite, Sabatini, 6-2, 5-7, 6-4.

But Arantxa was getting primed for Paris. By the end of the year, she had scrambled from No. 18 to No. 5, one place ahead of Seles. The 15-year-old Yugoslav, operating out of her new home base in Florida, made a stunning professional debut in Washington. She had straight-set wins over Larisa Savchenko, Robin White and Manuela Maleeva, to reach the semifinals, where an ankle injury forced her to default to Garrison. Then she defeated Evert in the Houston final before pushing Graf in the French Open semifinals, 6-3, 3-6, 6-3.

Another teen-ager, Spain's Conchita Martinez, also made inroads, zooming to No. 7 on the WTA computer as a result of three tour victories. And, in a brief promo of coming attractions, 13-year-old Floridian Jennifer Capriati blitzed Clare Wood, 6-0, 6-0, in the course of another 7-0 Wightman Cup wipeout of the Brits at Williamsburg, Va. by the United States. Still an amateur, Capriati was the youngest participant ever in the event by a full two years.

Not only were the Brits shut out, but—regrettably, dismayingly—so was the 66-year-old Cup itself. It was a TKO. Britain, often an equal in the early years of a special rivalry, could no longer compete realistically. Winning only eight matches while losing the last 11 contests, the Brits had struck a dead end. It was agreed to stop the bleeding, with the hope that someday the United Kingdom would once again produce world class players.

While Graf remained atop the women's rankings, Mats Wilander began a precipitous drop from No. 1 to No. 13 at the Australian Open, one of three major titles he had claimed the previous year. The first-seeded Swede, a three-time champion in the event, stumbled in the second round against No. 51 Ramesh Krishnan of India, 6-3, 6-2, 7-6, and never regained his equilibrium. Complaining of shin splints and a loss of motivation, Wilander failed to win a single tournament and reached only one final.

The other Swede with a major title to his credit in 1988 also was shut out. But Edberg was a finalist both at Paris and Wimbledon and he actually climbed the ladder to No. 3 with a strong finish, culminating in a 4-6, 7-6 (8-6), 6-3, 6-1 victory over Becker at the year-end Masters. He, too, had his problems in Melbourne when he suffered a back injury in the course of a 6-4, 6-0, 6-2, fourth-round victory over Pat Cash and had to withdraw.

With the Australian field thinned, Lendl had a clear shot to one of the two Big Four titles that had eluded him and he made the most of the opportunity. He blasted No. 7 seed John McEnroe, 7-6, 6-2, 7-6, in a quarterfinal, overcame No. 11 seed Thomas Muster of Austria, 6-2, 6-4, 5-7, 7-5 in the semis, and then overpowered No. 9 seed Miloslav Mecir in the final, 6-2, 6-2, 6-2.

The women weren't much more competitive after Helena Sukova handed Navratilova a quarterfinal defeat, 6-2, 3-6, 9-7, and outlasted unseeded Belinda Cordwell of New Zealand, 7-6 (7-2), 4-6, 6-2, in the semis. But Sukova received a 6-4, 6-4 spanking in the final from Graf, who had crushed Sabatini in the semis, 6-3, 6-0.

A fiefdom operated by Navratilova and Pam Shriver—that was the women's doubles—was controlled for the seventh con-

secutive time, with a 3-6, 6-3, 6-2 win over a U.S.-Canadian enterprise, Patty Fendick and Jill Hetherington. However, that was the end of their illustrious line of 20 majors (seven Aussie, four French, five Wimbledon, four U.S.), launched in 1981. By the end of the year they had parted, and were on opposite sides of the net for the U.S. Open final, Martina and Hana Mandlikova defeating Pam and Mary Joe Fernandez, 5-7, 6-4, 6-4. Americans Louise Brough and Margaret Osborne duPont had held the record alone for a long time, their 20 made between 1942 and 1957. (None in Australia.)

It was at Paris that the season took an abrupt turn. After both Evert and Navratilova declined to enter—preferring to devote extra time on preparations for Wimbledon—and Sabatini was upset in the fourth round by Mary Joe Fernandez, 6-4, 6-4, a third French title for Graf appeared a mere formality. She ceded a set to Seles in the semifinal, but it was unthinkable that Steffi would lose to a 17-year-old appearing in her first major final.

Not since the 1962 Wimbledon final (Karen Hantze Susman over Vera Sukova, 6-4, 6-4) had a woman seeded as low as seventh won a major against a world-class field. But Sanchez Vicario had the spunk, the shots and the determination to stay in a grueling match against a woman primed for her sixth consecutive Big Four title. Their match consumed two hours, 58 minutes, and it was a riveting demonstration of championship tennis.

Sanchez Vicario achieved her upset with an extraordinary comeback from 3-5 in the third set, winning the last four games and 16 of the last 19 points. "This is a great day for me," she said. "This is the tournament I wanted to win all my life." She had grown up the smallest at 5-foot-5 in a tennis family. Two older brothers, Emilio and Javier, were on the men's tour and an older sister, Marisa, had played for Pepperdine University in California. She was the most competitive of the group.

"Off the court, she is sweet and charming," said her coach, Juan Nunez. "But when she gets on the court, she turns into a lion. What you saw out there was the lion."

Graf appeared pale and sad-eyed after failing to equal Navratilova's streak of six consecutive major titles. "Arantxa is a wonderful girl and she played unbelievable to win," said the German, who suffered cramps in the third set. "But I did nothing at all. It wasn't me out there. It was another person hitting those balls." It was the second and final loss of the year for Graf, following a three-set defeat by Sabatini in the Amelia Island final, 3-6, 6-3, 7-5. But, for Sanchez Vicario, it was a peerless achievement. At the end of the match, she tossed her racket into the air and collapsed on the red clay. "It is the most joyous moment of my life," she said.

No less remarkable was 15th-seeded Chang's feat. If anything, it may have been more improbable. The 5-foot-8, 135-pounder would have been unseeded if not for the absence of McEnroe and Muster (who suffered a serious knee injury when hit by a drunken driver on the eve of the Lipton final in Key Biscayne.) The son of research chemists who had emigrated from Taiwan, the 17-year-old youngster seemed too small and too inexperienced for such a Herculean task.

But he proved his stamina and his mettle in a fourth-round battle against top-ranked Lendl, whom he trailed two sets to love.

Instead of capitulating, he fought through debilitating cramps to oust the No. 1 guy, 4-6, 4-6, 6-3, 6-3, 6-3. He was in such distress late in the fourth set and early in the fifth that he stood at changeovers, munched on bananas, staggered about the court between points and even served underhanded on one occasion. Michael psyched Lendl into a double fault, ending the four-hour, 39-minute struggle by standing directly behind the service line to receive.

"I've never seen a player show such courage on a tennis court," said Trabert. Chang's coach, Jose Higueras, called it "the most incredible match I've ever seen."

But that only earned him a berth in the quarterfinals. Chang then had to grind out difficult, very long wins over Ronald Agenor of Haiti, 6-4, 2-6, 6-4 (from 1-4), 7-6 (8-6), saving a set point, in three hours, 12 minutes; and tenacious Russian Andrei Chesnokov, 6-1, 5-7, 7-6 (7-4), 7-5, in four hours, five minutes.

Awaiting in the final was Edberg, who had defeated Italian Open champ Alberto Mancini, 6-1, 6-3, 7-6 (7-5) in the quarterfinals and Boris Becker, 6-3, 6-4, 5-7, 3-6, 6-2, in the semifinals.

Realistically, the final should have been the end of the road for Chang. But the youngster stretched the imagination once more, rallying from one set down and saving 13 straight break points over one stretch. He emerged with a shocking 6-2, 3-6, 4-6, 6-4, 6-2 victory from 0-2 in the fifth. "Whatever happens from now on, good or bad," he said, "this will stay with me for the rest of my life."

Edberg, with three major titles to his credit as well as a superior serve and volley, appeared rattled by his opponent's bottomless reserve. He had 26 break points in the match and converted only six.

"He just keeps coming back," the Swede said. "I have to admire him for it. But you know these young guys. They just hit. They don't have to think." With his victory, Chang surpassed Wilander (17 years, nine months) as the youngest male winner in Paris and supplanted Becker (17 years, seven months) as the youngest male winner of a major.

"Chang is a little bit different from other young players," said Trabert. "Too many of them aren't patient and willing to play long points. I think it should be a personal point of pride to be a well-rounded player." Michael's patience had lasted through 21 hours, 18 minutes on court in burying the U.S. jinx at Roland Garros, where 532 American guys had been laid to rest in the amber soil between Trabert's and his victory.

If that event offered an unlikely duo of titlists, the next major produced a seemingly inevitable pairing. Becker and Graf had been raised in nearby towns in the southeastern corner of West Germany and had known each other since they were children. "I used to be the worst in the boys and she was the best in the girls," Becker recalled with good humor. "So, when I was maybe nine and she was eight, I would have to hit with her."

Each had grown up to be a Wimbledon champion but not in the same year. In 1989, on the grass of the All England Club, they became the Teutonic Twosome. Even the weather cooperated, in a fashion. Rain pushed back the women's final one day so that Graf and Becker might receive their awards at Centre Court on the same afternoon.

Graf, the defender, had the tougher final. Navratilova was the only foe to take a set from her, but that wasn't enough. Steffi subdued the eight-time champ to gain her own second title, 6-2, 6-7 (1-7), 6-1, finishing in championship form, firing an ace. Graf won 17 of 22 points on her serve in the final set and said she was playing so well, "I was starting to laugh ... I was so loose out there and it showed in my tennis."

Earlier in the tournament, she had toyed with the opposition, including Evert. Chrissie had made one last never-say-die charge from 2-5 in the third to topple Laura Golarsa of Italy, 6-3, 2-6, 7-5, and to earn a farewell trip to the Wimbledon semifinals, her 17th. At least, that gave Evert an opportunity to wave goodbye from Centre Court after her thrashing by Graf, 6-2, 6-1.

In contrast to Graf, Becker had a difficult semifinal. He was thankful for the 76-minute rain delay in the midst of the third set against Lendl, wherein he regained his composure to post a 7-5, 6-7 (2-7), 2-6, 6-4, 6-3 victory. Taking the first set in 22 minutes, he then overpowered Edberg, 6-0, 7-6 (7-1), 6-4, to reverse the result of the previous year's final.

It was Becker's third Wimbledon title but, after two years of disappointment, he seemed to appreciate this one more than the others. "Then it was like a fairy tale," he said of the consecutive championships he won as a teenager. This was real. And the two champions shared the first dance at the Wimbledon Ball.

The U.S. Open lacks such a formal conclusion. Otherwise, the pair could have continued their dance in New York. Graf and Becker each left Flushing Meadow with another major title. They had to work harder than at Wimbledon, and they had to share the spotlight with a departing champion. Graf was severely tested twice, by Sabatini in the semifinals, 3-6, 6-4, 6-2, and, once again, by Navratilova in the ultimate match. Navratilova appeared to have the final won on at least a couple of occasions. She was only two games from victory in the second set—confidently, prematurely waving two fingers at friends in the stands—before double-faulting away a service game. Then she had a break point for a 5-4 lead and squandered that. Seeing the opening, Graf mobilized her gifts and won, 3-6, 7-5, 6-1.

"I was close," said Navratilova, her face streaked with tears. "I was as close as you get."

Becker almost didn't make it out of the second round, where he faced two match points against vagabond Derrick Rostagno in a fourth-set tie-breaker. On the second, his running forehand ticked the net and hopped over the Californian's waiting racket. Becker took that bit of good luck and won the next two points for the set, and the arduous match that had looked lost long before, 1-6, 6-7 (1-7), 6-3, 7-6 (8-6), 6-3.

Connors' 16th trip to the quarters was unrewarded as Agassi made a surprising charge to score his own first victory in a five-set trial, 6-1, 4-6, 0-6, 6-3, 6-4. Jimmy, with the crowd straining behind him, gave them hope as Andre served for it at 5-2. Flashing the old moxie, the champ seized nine of 10 points to 5-4, 0-15 —but had nothing more to give. McEnroe, seeded fourth, didn't get that far, banished from the second round by a qualifier, No. 110 Paul Haarhuis, 6-4, 4-6, 6-3, 7-5.

"Where are you from?" a reporter asked the anonymous Dutchman. "Mars," was the smiling reply, and Mac may have

believed it. Defending champ Wilander, fifth-seeded, undoubtedly wondered about the provenance of his kid conqueror, 5-7, 6-3, 1-6, 6-1, 6-4, also in the second round. The 18-year-old's name was Pete Sampras, who in 12 months would illuminate the Meadow, and continue to do so, passing Mac and Wilander, Connors and others in the matter of majors—eventually holding the record himself at 14.

Lendl took care of Agassi in one semi, 7-6 (7-4), 6-1, 3-6, 6-1, and Becker cruised past Aaron Krickstein in the other, 6-4, 6-3, 6-4. In the final, Becker needed three hours and 51 minutes to defeat Lendl, 7-6 (7-2), 1-6, 6-3, 7-6 (7-4). Ivan was appearing in his eighth consecutive final, a Tilden-tying achievement. But after Becker got a full head of serving-and-volleying steam, neither Ivan nor the ghost of Big Bill could stop him. "He just has more power in his game than I do." Lendl said. For Becker, the victory proved he was more than splendor in the grass, that he was able to beat a world-class field somewhere other than Wimbledon. He had filled in the gaps in his game since the summer of '85, firmed his groundstrokes along with his tenacity. Now he was a worthy challenger for the honor of top-ranked men's player on the planet. "If I'm not No. 1," he said, "then I'm quite close to it."

But he couldn't close the narrow gap before year's end, despite his two majors and a 64-8 match record on winning six of 13 tournaments. Boris' magnificent year had included possibly the most remarkable win—6-7 (4-7), 6-7 (5-7), 7-6 (7-3), 6-3, 6-4, over Agassi in the Davis Cup semifinals. They had stopped at midnight, returning the next day for the fifth. From a break behind in the last set, 4-3, Boris swooped to take the last three games, and launch the 3-2 victory over the U.S. at Munich.

That made it 1-1 since Brad Gilbert had opened, 6-2, 2-6, 2-6, 6-4, 6-4, over Charlie Steeb. But lefty Steeb was back, and better for the clinching decision over Agassi, 4-6, 6-4, 6-4, 6-2, after Becker and Eric Jelen took the 2-1 lead over Ken Flach and Robert Seguso, 3-6, 7-6 (7-5), 6-4, 7-6 (7-3).

If anything, Boris was even more brutally "Beckerian" in the final (3-2 over Sweden at Stuttgart for a second straight Cup). He ripped up No. 3 Edberg and the previous year's No. 1 Wilander on a loss of 12 games: Respective 6-2, 6-2, 6-4, and 6-2, 6-0, 6-2, triumphs, probably the worst thrashings dealt such elite men in Cup history. Boris wrapped those around his and Jelen's rock-ribbed, tense victory over Jan Gunnarson and Anders Jarryd, 7-6 (8-6), 6-4, 3-6, 6-7 (4-7), 6-4.

With all his heroics, Becker was still second to Lendl, who won 10 of 17 starts on a 79-7 record with record earnings of $2,334,367. Ivan lost the Masters semifinal, 7-6, 7-5 to Edberg, who then cut down Becker the following day, 4-6, 7-6 (8-6), 6-3, 6-1.

Still, the U.S. Open was as notable for a dignified exit as for Becker's grand entrance into the circle of champions. Evert made her last stand on the stadium court in the quarterfinals against Garrison, an opponent who had lined up for her autograph 10 years earlier in Houston. In the end, Evert's nerves betrayed her. Twice she served for the first set and was broken both times, losing 7-6 (1), 6-2.

Evert departed with records for most Open victories (101) and most career singles titles (157). Her 5-0 record in the subse-

quent Federation Cup brought her lifetime record to 1,309-146, an astonishing percentage of .900.

Also fading away was the men's Grand Prix format, a victim of the ATP revolt. For the record, the last Grand Prix event in history was the Masters Doubles at the Royal Albert Hall in London on Dec. 10. McEnroe's younger brother, Patrick, teamed with Jim Grabb to beat Wimbledon champions Jarryd and John Fitzgerald in the match that brought down the curtain on two decades of play, Jack Kramer's brainchild, the Grand Prix, 7-5. 7-6 (7-4), 5-7, 6-3.

1989 CHAMPIONS AND LEADERS

Australian Open
Men's Singles Final: Ivan Lendl (CZE) def. Miloslav Mecir (CZE), 6-2, 6-2, 6-2

Women's Singles Final: Steffi Graf (GER) def. Helena Sukova (CZE), 6-4, 6-4

Men's Doubles Final: Rick Leach and Jim Pugh (USA) def. Darren Cahill and Mark Kratzmann (AUS), 6-4, 6-4, 6-4

Women's Doubles: Martina Navratilova and Pam Shriver (USA) def. Patty Fendick (USA) and Jill Hetherington (CAN), 3-6, 6-3, 6-2

Mixed Doubles Final: Jana Novotna (CZE) and Jim Pugh (USA) def. Zina Garrison and Sherwood Stewart (USA), 6-3, 6-4

French Open
Men's Singles Final: Michael Chang (USA) def. Stefan Edberg (SWE), 6-1, 3-6, 4-6, 6-4, 6-2

Women's Singles Final: Arantxa Sanchez Vicario (ESP) def. Steffi Graf (GER), 7-6 (8), 3-6, 7-5

Men's Doubles Final: Jim Grabb and Patrick McEnroe (USA) def. Mansour Bahrami (IRI) and Eric Winogradsky (FRA), 6-4, 2-6, 6-4, 7-6 (5)

Women's Doubles Final: Larisa Savchenko and Natalia Zvereva (USSR) def. Steffi Graf (GER) and Gabriela Sabatini (ARG), 6-4, 6-4

Mixed Doubles Final: Manon Bollegraf and Tom Nijssen (NED) def. Arantxa Sanchez Vicario (ESP) and Horacio de la Pena (ARG), 6-3, 6-7 (3), 6-2

Wimbledon
Men's Singles Final: Boris Becker (GER) def. Stefan Edberg (SWE), 6-0, 7-6 (1), 6-4

Women's Singles Final: Steffi Graf (GER) def. Martina Navratilova (USA), 6-2, 6-7 (1), 6-1

Men's Doubles Final: John Fitzgerald (AUS) and Anders Jarryd (SWE) def. Rick Leach and Jim Pugh (USA), 3-6, 7-6 (4), 6-4, 7-6 (4)

Women's Doubles Final: Jana Novotna and Helena Sukova (CZE) def. Larisa Savchenko and Natalia Zvereva (USSR), 6-1, 6-2

Mixed Doubles Final: Jana Novotna (CZE) and Jim Pugh (USA) def. Jenny Byrne and Mark Kratzmann (AUS), 6-4, 5-7, 6-4

U.S. Open
Men's Singles Final: Boris Becker (GER) def. Ivan Lendl (CZE), 7-6 (2), 1-6, 6-3, 7-6 (4)

Women's Singles Final: Steffi Graf (GER) def. Martina Navratilova (USA), 3-6, 7-5, 6-1

Men's Doubles Final: John McEnroe (USA) and Mark Woodforde (AUS) def. Ken Flach and Robert Seguso (USA), 6-4, 4-6, 6-3, 6-3

Women's Doubles Final: Hana Mandlikova (CZE) and Martina Navratilova (USA) def. Mary Joe Fernandez and Pam Shriver (USA), 5-7, 6-4, 6-4

Mixed Doubles: Robin White and Shelby Cannon (USA) def. Meredith McGrath and Rick Leach (USA), 3-6, 6-2, 7-5

Year-End No. 1
Men: Ivan Lendl
Women: Steffi Graf

Top Player Earnings
Men: Ivan Lendl $2,344,367
Women: Steffi Graf $1,562,905

Davis Cup: Germany

Federation Cup: United States

Wightman Cup: United States

Grand Prix Masters, NYC—Stefan Edberg
WCT, Dallas—John McEnroe
Virginia Slims Championships, NYC—Steffi Graf

1990 Martina Wins Ninth Wimbledon

For the first time in the Open era, tennis was just that. The four major singles titles for men and women were divided eight ways. The champions represented seven different nations on three continents and at least two generations.

While Martina Navratilova set a record for the ages, Monica Seles established another for the under-aged. Although the gap wasn't quite so large among their male counterparts, Andres Gomez scored a stunning triumph for the 30-and-over crowd in Paris and Pete Sampras became a U.S. Open champion 28 days after celebrating his 19th birthday. Each defeated Andre Agassi for his first major title.

This also was the year in which Stefan Edberg, the Wimbledon champion for a second time, dislodged Australian winner Ivan Lendl from No. 1. Steffi Graf continued at the top of the women's charts but, after losing the French and U.S. finals to Seles and Gabriela Sabatini, respectively, her reign was seriously threatened. John McEnroe paid for his years of sins against the tennis establishment when he was defaulted in the midst of a major, the Australian.

Astonishing, and then some, was Thomas Muster. Not only was he back in uniform—he was winning, and more impressively than ever, rising to his highest ranking, No. 7. This only months after his career seemed to have been left in a Key Biscayne parking lot where his left knee was wrecked in a collision with a drunken driver. He went at rehab as though it was a major final, and he showed up at the Italian Open, in a wheelchair, vowing he would play at Il Foro Italico in 1990. True to his word, the bellowing "Moo Man" returned to take the Italian title, beating Andrei Chesnokov, 6-1, 6-3, 6-1, after dodging three match points in the semi over Andres Gomez, 5-7, 6-4, 7-6 (7-2) He had actually returned to competition in autumn of 1989, reaching the quarters at Barcelona and semis at Vienna. Eight months after the accident, in January, he won Adelaide over Jimmy Arias, 3-6, 6-2, 7-5, and never looked back.

Perhaps the most encouraging development at the start of a new decade was the emergence of Florida teenager Jennifer Capriati, who received $5 million in endorsement contracts before striking her first pulverizing groundstrokes for pay. Making the most widely ballyhooed professional debut in tennis history, 23 days before her 14th birthday at Boca Raton, Fla., she declared perceptively, "The press is out of control!" True enough as reporters and cameras appeared from across the world to record the carnival and the child's initial pro steps, a 7-6 (7-1), 6-1, win over seasoned Mary Lou Piatek Daniels.

True, too, she demonstrated what the fuss was all about, mowing down four more experienced foes before losing a close final to Sabatini, 6-4, 7-5. She even had an odd-couple doubles win (first and last pro appearances) with 46-year-old Billie Jean

King (6-2, 6-3, over Laura Golarsa and Claudia Porwik) in a tournament that quickly became known as the Virginia Slims of Capriati. Then she became the youngest ever semifinalist at any of the majors, the French. A fourth-rounder at Wimbledon and at the U.S. Open, she plucked her first title at Puerto Rico (over Zina Garrison, 5-7, 6-4, 6-1), had a 42-11 match record and a No. 8 world ranking at season's close.

Another prosperous rookie was the men's tour, managed for the first time by the players themselves, under new executive director Hamilton Jordan, former chief of staff to U.S. President Jimmy Carter. The ATP conducted 75 tournaments on six continents, culminating in season-ending singles and doubles championships. Agassi won the former, defeating Edberg in the final at Frankfurt, 5-7, 7-6 (7-5), 7-5, 6-2, and the Franco-Swiss team of Guy Forget and Jakob Hlasek triumphed over Spaniards Sergio Casal and Emilio Sanchez in the latter, 6-4, 7-6, 5-7, 6-4, staged at Sanctuary Cove, Australia.

Less successful was the Grand Slam Cup, inaugurated by the International Tennis Federation in conjunction with officials of the four majors to combat the muscle of the ATP—the game is never peaceful—and add to the confusing silliness by presenting a second supposedly climactic championship. Entry was based on performance solely in the majors. Although the December event carried a staggering purse of $6 million, many elite pros—including German star Boris Becker—boycotted the competition in Munich because it detracted from the ATP Tour playoffs. Sampras defeated fellow American Brad Gilbert in straight sets, 6-3, 6-4, 6-2 for the $2-million first prize.

The U.S. claimed each of the major team championships. Capriati, the Federation Cup rookie, won all five of her singles matches without the loss of a set, 7-6, 6-2, over Leila Meshki in the final. But it took a Gigi Fernandez—Zina Garrison doubles operation as the clincher, 6-4, 6-3, over Larisa Savchenko and Natasha Zvereva, as the U.S. retained the Cup by defeating the Soviet Union, 2-1, in Atlanta.

Agassi and Michael Chang were the stalwarts as the host country took possession of the Davis Cup for the first time in eight years by beating Australia, 3-2. Agassi struggled to beat 6-foot-4 Tasmanian Richard Fromberg, 4-6, 6-2, 4-6, 6-2, 6-4, and Chang crushed Darren Cahill, 6-2, 7-6 (7-4), 6-0 setting up Jim Pugh and Rick Leach for the 6-4, 6-2, 3-6, 7-6 (7-2) clincher over Pat Cash and John Fitzgerald. It was a bizarre windup to the 29th Cup for the U.S., played indoors in Florida while sun baked the roof of St. Petersburg's Suncoast Dome—and on clay, so often the burial ground for U.S. teams. The dirt, specially trucked in at a cost of $50,000, was what Captain Tom Gorman ordered to bog down the best Aussie, Cash, who thus wasn't even selected in singles to oppose the American baseliners. The engagement drew American record Cup crowds, 50,962 in total—18,156 on the middle day.

Czechoslovakia was the quarterfinal problem in Prague, solved largely by lifesaving Aaron Krickstein, a last-minute stand-in for pouting Agassi. Kricker stopped towering Milan Srejber 4-6, 7-6 (7-5), 7-6 (7-5), 6-7 (4-7), 6-3. Although Petr Korda razed Brad Gilbert, 6-2, 6-3, 6-3, for 1-1, Leach and Pugh beat the two Czechs, 6-4, 6-4, 6-4, setting up Kricker to close the deal over Korda, 6-2, 6-3, 1-6, 6-3.

It was Chang, 18 and the youngest American to play for a Cup winner, who gave the critical push into the final, salvaging the 3-2 semifinal victory over Austria at damp, gloomy Vienna. Southpaw Muster, improving his clay court Cup record to 24-0 had busted both Chang, 4-6, 6-2, 6-2, 6-4, and the returned prodigal Agassi, 6-2, 6-2, 7-6 (7-2). But Agassi had Horst Skoff's number, 7-6 (7-3), 6-0, 6-1, and the Leach-Pugh combine stopped Muster-Alex Antonitsch, 7-6 (7-4), 3-6. 6-0, 7-5. That left it up to Michael, who started miserably, losing the first two sets as a crowd of 18,000 howled for his blood and urging their man "Horstie." Onward.

No American had been in such a trap since Don Budge 53 years before in the semi against Germany that would assure the end of the only Cup drought longer than this one: 10 years. With everything riding on the fifth set of the fifth match in 1937, both Budge (over Gottfried von Cramm) and now Chang revived from two sets back. Two dissimilar characters and settings: these Californians, Budge tall, stylish, big server; stubby kid Chang, the tireless baseline retriever. Budge was on the sunny lawn of neutral Wimbledon, Chang in the Sturm und Drang of the bleak enemy camp. But they had fighting hearts in common, Budge surging from 1-4 in the fifth, Chang having to sleep on it, darkness intervening after the third set. His legs and grit brought Michael through, 3-6, 6-7 (4-7), 6-4, 6-4, 6-3—and hauled the U.S. into the final.

For a topsy-turvy year, 1990 began in conventional fashion. Graf won an eighth major championship in her last nine attempts by out-stroking Mary Joe Fernandez, 6-3, 3-6, 6-4, at the Australian Open. The top men turned out in greater numbers at the Australian Open but the final ended in disappointment. Edberg played brilliantly in routing Mats Wilander in the semifinals, 6-1, 6-1, 6-2, but suffered a torn abdominal muscle in the midst of the third set of his showdown with Lendl and could not continue. Lendl was awarded a 4-6, 7-6 (7-3), 5-2, default, victory and his second consecutive Australian title.

In Melbourne, the first of the majors was spiced by the spectacle of McEnroe's banishment. After the testy one received two code violations for racket abuse and intimidation of a linesman during his fourth-round match against Mikael Pernfors, he cursed umpire Gerry Armstrong and referee Ken Farrar. Under the new three-step code of conduct introduced at the start of the season, Mac was automatically disqualified, though in the lead, 1-6, 6-4, 5-7, 4-2.

Despite his history of misbehavior, it marked the man's only default in a major. McEnroe, who had disqualified himself in 1987 by walking away from a World Team Cup final, was fined $6,500. The setback was the first of many in an erratic year that saw him, bounced in the first round at Wimbledon by No. 129 Derrick Rostagno, 7-5, 6-4, 6-4, reach the semifinals of the U.S. Open, post a lone tournament victory, Basel, and drop from No. 4 to No. 13 in the world rankings.

As it had been the previous year, Paris was the site of two startling results. Considering the form Monica Seles displayed in routing Navratilova, 6-1, 6-1 in the Italian Open final and in terminating Graf's 66-match winning streak (second longest of the modern era) in the final of the German Open, 6-4, 6-3, her triumph in the French was not a stunning upset. Still, the two-fisted teenager's 7-6 (8-6), 6-4 conquest of Graf suggested a new order in women's tennis.

Before taking on the top-ranked German, second-seeded Seles came close to defeat by Bulgarian Manuela Maleeva, 3-6, 6-1, 7-5 in the quarters. Then she eliminated Capriati, 6-2, 6-2 in a match that was a preview of the future. For Capriati, who had dropped only 20 games in her five previous matches, the 62-minute rout was an educational experience. Her opponent was sure she would be back. "I have the feeling we're going to be playing many, many more times," Seles said.

Monica's current rivalry, however, was with Graf and, suddenly, they appeared to be equals. Although the German still had that booming forehand, her sliced backhand left her vulnerable to Seles, who powers the ball from both sides with both hands. "She hits like she means it," Graf said. Additionally, Graf was bothered by allergies that plague her every spring in Paris and from press reports from back home that charged her father with impregnating a German model only slightly older than Steffi. There was a vulnerability about her that no one had sensed since she ascended to the top.

Graf rallied from a 1-4 deficit to force a tie-breaker, where she won the first five points and led, 6-2. One point from the set, however, she dropped the next six, double-faulting on her fourth and final set point. "That's when I knew I had her," Seles said. In her first major final, Monica saved two break points in the ninth game of the second set and then broke Graf in the following game for the biggest victory of her burgeoning career.

At the very least, the victory at Roland Garros made her famous for something other than her grunting on court, her cackle during press interviews and her unruly mane. "I didn't want to go into the history books 20 years from now," she said, "and have people read, 'She was a great grunter, a great giggler and had a lot of hair.'"

Among the missing from Paris were Navratilova and Lendl. Both were consumed with preparations for Wimbledon, a tournament where she would be seeking a record ninth title and he a fulfilling first. Inadvertently, Lendl's decision not to enter the French had a major impact on the results. Gomez, the man who would become king on the clay, was weighing an offer to serve as a commentator on Ecuadorian television at Paris until he learned that Lendl was bypassing the tournament to practice on grass. The Czech star had eliminated him in four previous French Opens. At 30, the 6-foot-4 left-hander seemed an unlikely semifinalist, let alone champion. But, given his first chance at a final four in a major event, fourth-seeded Andres bulldozed Muster, 7-5, 6-1, 7-5 to earn him a berth opposite the outrageous Agassi, who appeared finally to be living up to his advertising image as the hottest thing on tour.

The youngster from Las Vegas, seeded third, emerged as the favorite in the draw after the Tuesday Massacre, the unprecedented first-round removals of the first and second seeds. Edberg, the finalist of 1989, tumbled to No. 46, Sergi Bruguera (a future champ), 6-4, 6-2, 6-1, and Becker lost to a missile-serving lefty (19 aces), No. 51 Goran Ivanisevic, 5-7, 6-4, 7-5, 6-2.

Agassi also gained attention by engaging in a verbal battle with Philippe Chattier, president of the ITF and the reigning potentate of the tournament. He took one look at Agassi's hot lava (pink) and black tennis ensemble and issued a statement that the French Open would consider requiring predominantly white clothing the following year. Agassi responded by calling the man a "bozo," an insult even in a country that reveres Jerry Lewis.

But the man brought more than bicycle shorts and a matching bandana to the event. He had the talent to whip his 1989 Paris conqueror, Jim Courier, 6-7 (8-10), 6-1, 6-4, 6-0, defending champion Michael Chang, 6-2, 6-1, 4-6, 6-2, and Jonas Svensson, 6-1, 6-4, 3-6, 6-3, en route to what appeared to be a coronation. Gomez was one of the most popular players in the world among his peers but, Agassi pledged, "He's going to be in for a long afternoon because I want it bad."

Surprise. Gomez made relatively short work of the American, 10 years his junior. In the match of his career, he dismissed Agassi, 6-3, 2-6, 6-4, 6-4, claiming the first Big Four title for Ecuador. "I've been coming here for many [11] years," he said, "and I've been dreaming about this day."

At 33, Navratilova was seeking a final sunrise of her own at Wimbledon. Three years without a major victory, she trained diligently under Craig Kardon and her latest coach/motivator, Billie Jean King, for the triumph that would distance her from Helen Wills Moody, the eight-time champion of an earlier era. As it developed, she was virtually unchallenged.

Despite her problems in Paris, Graf still was favored. However, from the moment she set foot in London, the German was under siege. If it wasn't the sinus problem that caused her to fly home for treatment during a weekend break, then it was the tabloid press which had a field day with the story of her father and the suddenly notorious Nicole Meissner, whose provocative photos appeared almost daily in the sensational journals.

When they weren't harassing Graf, the arbiters of England's morals were going after the new generation of grunters, Seles in particular. *The Sun* tabloid unveiled a Grunt-o-meter, which allegedly measured the chief offender at 82 decibels—"between a pneumatic drill and a diesel train." As silly as this appeared, the new chairman of the tournament, John Curry, said he would "readily relax the all-white clothes rule if I could just get rid of the grunts."

"Gaby [Sabatini], [Anke] Huber and Jennifer [Capriati] grunt," Seles said. "But probably I'm the loudest. I don't know. I don't even realize I do it until I watch tape of myself on television. I think it's better than it was last year or in the French Open but I can't get rid of it."

Garrison saved officials the trouble of silencing the teenager. Overcoming a match point with a forehand blast, the U.S. veteran rallied to defeat Seles, 3-6, 6-3, 9-7, in the quarterfinals. Not only did it halt her opponent's winning streak at six tournaments and 36 matches but it prevented a semifinal showdown between Seles and Graf. Garrison spent years trying unsuccessfully to crack the ranks of the elite when Chris Evert and Navratilova ruled the sport. Then Graf had zoomed past, followed by Seles. The previous fall, after her loss to Navratilova at Flushing Meadow and her marriage to Willard Jackson, she said, "Since I was 16, I felt I would win Wimbledon and the U.S. Open. I still do." It didn't seem to faze her that her next opponent would be Graf, who had ended Capriati's summer vacation in the fourth round, 6-2, 6-4. Although Garrison had beaten Graf only once in

six matches—their first meeting when the German was 16—the American was confident. "I've always wanted to play her on the grass," she said.

She made the most of the opportunity in what the normally understated Dan Maskell, who had been telecasting the championships for the BBC since the dawn of time, called an "epic match." In denying Graf entry to a major final after an Open era record of 13 consecutive such appearances, Garrison overcame not only the German but her own nerves in a 6-3, 3-6, 6-4 triumph, serving out the concluding game in four points, closing with an ace.

To her credit, Graf declined to blame her third loss of the year on either physical or emotional problems, although the ever-vigilant club committee shielded her from elaboration. "I was eager, I was ready," she said. "She didn't make mistakes. She used to make much more errors, unforced errors especially, but she didn't do that today at all." Nevertheless, Graf decided, her conqueror had no chance in the final. "Zina doesn't have the game to beat Martina," she said.

Certainly, there was little in the head-to-head record that suggested a titanic struggle. Of the 28 matches between the two friends, Navratilova had won 27. Moreover, in her 6-3, 6-4 semifinal victory over Sabatini, she had demonstrated she was still near the top of her form. Garrison, who didn't have a clothing deal and was wearing Navratilova's signature line, was compensated on the eve of the championship by a six-figure contract with Reebok. Additionally, her presence in the title match stirred Althea Gibson, the only black woman to win a major to fly in from New York. But no amount of personal or financial support for her opponent was going to stop Navratilova when she was this close to an historic accomplishment. In the match and the tournament that defined her career, Navratilova was more than triumphant. She was regal in a 6-4, 6-1 victory. Martina's virtually flawless solo performance on Centre Court, where nerves can be stretched as taut as racket strings, was one to be preserved in a time capsule. "It was my match to win," Navratilova decided, "and I wasn't afraid of it."

Thus she surpassed Wills Moody, who lost only one of 56 singles matches at Wimbledon in nine tournaments from 1924 through 1933. "Little Miss Poker Face," as Wills was known, won her last Wimbledon final at the age of 32 years, 270 days, making her the oldest female champion since 1914. The 33-year-old Navratilova, 99-9 on the most famous lawns in the world, also took that distinction from Wills. Charlotte Cooper Sterry was 37 as the 1908 champ.

But Zina did get a Wimbledon championship: The mixed doubles with lefty Rick Leach over Aussies Liz Sayers Smylie and Fitzgerald, 7-5, 6-2.

Czechs Jana Novotna and Helena Sukova were moving closer to a Grand Slam when they arrived at Wimbledon. They had already taken the Australian title over Americans Patty Fendick and Mary Joe Fernandez, 7-6 (7-5), 7-6 (8-6), and the French over Soviets Savchenko and Zvereva, 6-4, 7-5. They dispatched Liz Sayers Smylie and Kathy Jordan 6-3, 6-4 to give them the third leg of the Slam. But the team to jam a Slam was that of Gigi Fernandez and Navratilova. They scissored the Novotna-Sukova

44-match winning string, 6-2, 6-4, in the final of the U.S. Open—the last of Martina's 31 majors in doubles.

Navratilova was rewarded for her decision to train harder, to bypass Paris for additional practice on the grass. Lendl was not, even after making a greater commitment, journeying to Australia during the winter for seven weeks of training under coach Tony Roche, and (after attending the birth of his first child, Marika) spending six weeks on the grass in England. After playing brilliantly in the traditional warm-up tournament at Queen's Club, blasting McEnroe, 6-2, 6-4, and Becker, 6-3, 6-2, in the last two rounds, he wilted at Wimbledon.

Seeded No. 1, Lendl used a Czech term to describe his obsession for the only major title he lacked. "Zazrany," he called it. "It means very much into it, almost stubborn." Alas, after weaving fitfully into the semifinals past no-names, he staggered out of the tournament following a crushing 6-1, 7-6 (7-2), 6-3, semifinal loss to Edberg.

Seeded No. 3, Edberg earned his third trip to the final, all against Becker, who received a 4-6, 7-6 (7-4), 6-0, 7-5, scare from 18-year-old hotshot Ivanisevic—his conqueror at the French Open—in the semifinals. Not since 1894, when homeboy Wilfred Baddeley challenged Ireland's Joshua Pimm in their fourth consecutive championship match, had the title contest been an object of such familiarity. This time they produced the longest men's final since Jimmy Connors—sidelined almost the entire 1990 season by a wrist injury that would require surgery—defeated McEnroe in 1982. However, the five-setter wasn't nearly as strained, partly because their similar serve-and-volley styles allowed for no rallies. Edberg won, 6-2, 6-2, 3-6, 3-6, 6-4.

Inspired by the victory, Edberg won his next three tournaments: Los Angeles, 7-6, 2-6, 7-6 over Chang; Cincinnati, 6-1, 6-1 over Brad Gilbert; and Long Island, 7-6, 6-3 over Ivanisevic. That run of 21 matches took him to the top of the rankings, displacing Lendl on Aug. 13.

Inexplicably, the No. 1 player in the world then lost his first-round match at the U.S. Open to No. 52, lefty Alexander Volkov of the Soviet Union, an all-time opening upset, 6-3, 7-6 (7-1), 6-2, considering Edberg's top-seeding and Wimbledon title. Lendl also was disappointed, failing to reach the final at Flushing Meadows for the first time since 1981. Explosive Pete Sampras, with 24 aces and 27 service winners, beat him in a five-set quarterfinal, 6-4, 7-6 (7-4), 3-6, 4-6, 6-2.

Much of the crowd's attention at the Open was diverted by the restoration of the McEnroe legend. Unseeded for the first time since his Open debut 13 years earlier, the former champion went back to his old coach, Tony Palafox, prepared diligently and then won over the fans by beating 10th-seeded Andrei Chesnokov, 6-3, 7-5, 6-4, seventh-seeded Emilio Sanchez, 7-6 (8-6), 3-6, 4-6, 6-4, 6-3 (canceling a set point in the tie-breaker), and David Wheaton, 6-1, 6-4, 6-4. But he couldn't cope with Sampras' power, the youngster finishing him off in the semifinals, 6-2, 6-4, 3-6, 6-3, with a 17th ace. "It's been a great run," McEnroe decided.

It was an even more remarkable tournament for 12th-seeded Sampras, the lanky and laid-back Californian who was ranked No. 81 as recently as January, and hadn't won his first pro tournament until February, the U.S. Pro Indoor in Philadelphia, over Gomez,

7-6 (7-4), 7-5, 6-2. But the best was yet to come—against Agassi. Andre, seeded No. 4, had overcome second-seeded Becker, the defending champ, 6-7 (10-12), 6-3, 6-2, 6-3 in the semifinals, setting the stage for the first all-American men's final since McEnroe-Gerulaitis in 1979. And Agassi, who had changed to "electric lime" for this tournament, was nearly undressed in the championship match. Sampras fired 13 more aces, raising his tournament total to a record 100, added 12 service winners and never was broken in demolishing his opponent, 6-4, 6-3, 6-2, in one hour, 42 minutes. "It was a good old-fashioned street mugging," Agassi said.

Sampras was the youngest male player to win America's national championship, supplanting Oliver Campbell, an older 19 one century earlier. Sampras shrugged. "I'm just a normal 19-year-old with an unusual job, doing unusual things," he said.

At 20, Sabatini had been doing unusual things for five years, since her breakthrough season of 1985, but she had reached only one major final (U.S., 1988). However, attacking boldly, she applied the finishing touch to Graf's unhappy post-Australian campaign in the majors. In the final, Gaby bounded off to 4-0, and would win 6-2, 7-6 (5), closing with a massive forehand winner. But not before a torrid back-and-forth windup as Graf nearly pulled herself off the ledge. "I had to win in two," Gaby confessed wearily.

Attacking and volleying more than ever before, she squeezed by Mary Joe Fernandez in a semi, 7-5, 5-7, 6-3, though down 4-1 in the first, while the defender, Graf, belted Arantxa Sanchez Vicario, 6-1, 6-2. Steffi went ahead of Gaby 6-5 in the second, had two set points, but the fading Argentine held on, sending them into overtime. There the German led 3-points-to-1, but the new champ took her title away by charging and seizing six of the last eight points closing with an all-or-nothing forehand blast.

Thirteen years after her childhood hero, Guillermo Vilas, ruled Forest Hills, fifth-seeded Sabatini gave Argentina another U.S. champ, the first Latin woman to embrace a major since Brazilian Maria Bueno's 1966 U.S. conquest.

Nevertheless, Steffi retained No. 1 because her pursuer, Seles, was bumped in the third round by No. 82, Italian Linda Ferrando, 1-6, 6-1, 7-6 (7-3). That was one of two huge first-week upsets. Second-seeded Navratilova was burned by Manuela Maleeva-Fragniere in the fourth round, 7-5, 3-6, 6-3.

Graf recovered to win four tournaments in the fall, including two at Sabatini's expense. (Although Gaby got revenge, 6-4, 6-4 in the semifinals of the year-end Virginia Slims Championships at Madison Square Garden.) Seles, however, served notice of future intentions in November when she became the youngest to win the year-end Slims title, defeating Sabatini in a five-set final, 6-4, 5-7, 3-6, 6-4, 6-2, in three hours, 47 minutes, wowing 17,290 witnesses. It was the first five-set women's match since flowing skirts and corsets were de rigeur and Bessie Moore beat Myrtle McAteer, 6-4, 3-6, 7-5, 2-6, 6-2, for the 1901 U.S. title.

1990 CHAMPIONS AND LEADERS

Australian Open
Men's Singles Final: Ivan Lendl (CZE) def. Stefan Edberg (SWE), 4-6, 7-6 (3), 5-2, retire

Women's Singles Final: Steffi Graf (GER) def. Mary Joe Fernandez (USA), 6-3, 6-4
Men's Doubles Final: Pieter Aldrich and Danie Visser (RSA) def. Grant Connell and Glenn Michibata (CAN), 6-4, 4-6, 6-1, 6-4
Women's Doubles Final: Jana Novotna and Helena Sukova (CZE) def. Patty Fendick and Mary Joe Fernandez (USA), 7-6 (5), 7-6 (6)
Mixed Doubles Final: Natalia Zvereva (USSR) and Jim Pugh (USA) def. Zina Garrison and Rick Leach (USA), 4-6, 6-2, 6-3

French Open
Men's Singles Final: Andres Gomez (ECU) def. Andre Agassi (USA), 6-3, 2-6, 6-4, 6-4
Women's Singles Final: Monica Seles (YUG) def. Steffi Graf (GER), 7-6 (6), 6-4
Men's Doubles Final: Sergio Casal and Emilio Sanchez (ESP) def. Goran Ivanisevic (YUG) and Petr Korda (CZE), 7-5, 6-3
Women's Doubles Final: Jana Novotna and Helena Sukova (CZE) def. Larisa Savchenko and Natalia Zvereva (USSR), 6-4, 7-5
Mixed Doubles Final: Arantxa Sanchez Vicario (ESP) and Jorge Lozano (MEX) def. Nicole Provis (AUS) and Danie Visser (RSA), 7-6 (5), 7-6 (8)

Wimbledon
Men's Singles Final: Stefan Edberg (SWE) def. Boris Becker (GER), 6-2, 6-2, 3-6, 3-6, 6-4
Women's Singles Final: Martina Navratilova (USA) def. Zina Garrison (USA), 6-4, 6-1
Men's Doubles Final: Rick Leach and Jim Pugh (USA) def. Pieter Aldrich and Danie Visser (RSA), 7-6 (5), 7-6 (4), 7-6 (5)
Women's Doubles Final: Jana Novotna and Helena Sukova (CZE), def. Kathy Jordan (USA) and Elizabeth Sayers Smylie (AUS), 6-3, 6-4
Mixed Doubles Final: Zina Garrison and Rick Leach (USA) def. Elizabeth Sayers Smylie and John Fitzgerald (AUS), 7-5, 6-2

U.S. Open
Men's Singles Final: Pete Sampras (USA) def. Andre Agassi (USA), 6-4, 6-3, 6-2
Women's Singles Final: Gabriela Sabatini (ARG) def. Steffi Graf (GER), 6-2, 7-6 (4)
Men's Doubles Final: Pieter Aldrich and Danie Visser (RSA) def. Paul Annacone and David Wheaton (USA), 6-2, 7-6 (3), 6-2
Women's Doubles Final: Gigi Fernandez and Martina Navratilova (USA) def. Jana Novotna and Helena Sukova (CZE), 6-2, 6-4
Mixed Doubles Final: Elizabeth Sayers Smylie and Todd Woodbridge (AUS) def. Natalia Zvereva (USSR) and Jim Pugh (USA), 6-4, 6-2

Year-End No. 1
Men: Stefan Edberg
Women: Steffi Graf

Top Player Earnings
Men: Pete Sampras $2,900,057
Women: Steffi Graf $1,921,853

Davis Cup: United States

Federation Cup: United States

ATP World Championships, Frankfurt—Andre Agassi
Grand Slam Cup, Munich—Pete Sampras
Virginia Slims Championships, NYC—Monica Seles

1991 Seles Slams Three Majors

Monica Seles won all three major events she played in 1991 and was a mystery absentee from Wimbledon.

It was the source of the former that the tennis establishment found distasteful, if not embarrassing. A professed admirer of pop singer Madonna and the glamour associated with movie stars, Seles gained a greater share of attention not for her victories at the Australian, French and U.S. Opens but for her mysterious withdrawal from Wimbledon without a suitable explanation. Her subsequent self-imposed exile created a rash of rumors popular in supermarket tabloids.

If her disappearance from public view revealed a fascination for Garbo, her return to tennis at an exhibition event for which she reportedly received a $300,000 appearance fee indicated she also had studied Gabor. On the day of her arrival at the Pathmark Tennis Classic in New Jersey, she posed for photographers with her dog tucked under her arm. Zsa Zsa would have been proud, darling.

In Seles' absence, Graf did manage to regain self-respect by claiming a third Wimbledon title. But the top ranking she had held for an unprecedented 186 weeks slipped away on March 10. The German did regain the No. 1 position for two brief periods during the summer but Seles zoomed back in front after her victory over Martina Navratilova at Flushing Meadow and opened a comfortable margin by winning three late-season tournaments and the Slims Championships, where Graf was upset by Jana Novotna in the quarterfinals.

Her talent was undeniable. After she won the three major events she chose to enter, her credentials were impeccable. By the end of the year, only Monica Seles' judgment was considered suspect.

In her third season as a professional, Seles dislodged Steffi Graf as the No. 1 woman in the world and won more money ($2,457,758) than any previous practitioner of tennis, male or female. Not until she had wrapped a ribbon around 1991 by earning a second consecutive Virginia Slims Championship did she turn 18. The teenager pursued and embraced both fame and fortune.

Graf, in fact, failed to reach the final of any major outside of Wimbledon, and at that, she barely held off Gabriela Sabatini for second place. Although Navratilova fell to No. 4 and endured a drawn-out palimony suit brought by former companion Judy Nelson, she surpassed Chris Evert's record of 1,309 tour-match victories and equaled her standard of 157 career singles titles

by defeating Seles at Oakland, 6-3, 3-6, 6-3 in November. She also advanced to the final of the Slims in New York before falling to the transplanted Yugoslav.

As was the case the previous year, no man won more than one major. Boris Becker won the Australian Open for the first time but was a losing finalist at Wimbledon for the second consecutive year, bowing to countryman Michael Stich in the first all-German title match at the world's most prestigious tournament. Jim Courier became the third young American in three years to win a major event when he defeated Andre Agassi at the French but he was overwhelmed by Stefan Edberg in the final of the U.S. Open.

The last of the major tournaments was energized by the spectacular comeback of Jimmy Connors. After losing all three of his matches the previous year, he underwent surgery on his left wrist, enjoying rebirth in 1991 when he celebrated his 39th birthday at Flushing Meadow with a sentimental journey to the semifinals. Over the course of a season in which he also earned standing ovations in Paris and London, Connors rose from No. 936 on the ATP computer to No. 48, a gain of 888 positions.

Courier, a Floridian who turned 21 in mid-August, had the most significant jump of all. With his first major title, the baseline basher in the baseball cap vaulted from No. 25 to No. 3 in the rankings, the highest achievement by an American since John McEnroe in 1985. Mac fell from No. 13 to 28, his lowest finish as a pro, despite gaining his 77th career title. It occurred in Chicago at the expense of his younger brother, 24-year-old Patrick, who rose to No. 36 after he reached the Australian Open semifinals and achieved his first singles tournament final.

Edberg, who spent much of the year dueling Becker for the top spot, took command at the U.S. Open and became only the fifth player in the Open era to finish No. 1 for consecutive seasons, joining Connors, Bjorn Borg, McEnroe and Ivan Lendl. He won six of eight finals, compiled a tour-best 76-17 match record and earned a men's record $2,363,575. Tendinitis in the knee, however, caused the Swede to withdraw from the year-end ATP Championships in Frankfurt. Pete Sampras, whose hangover from his remarkable 1990 success lasted until August, added the season-ending title to three other tour victories in the second half of the season. But Pete finished the year on a down note when he lost both his singles matches in an emotional Davis Cup final won by France in Lyon.

In a bizarre sideshow, Bjorn Borg attempted a comeback in Monte Carlo - 10 years after his last major event. He played with a wooden racket, and lost in the opening round to Spain's Jordi Arrese, 6-2, 6-3. After saying he would make an appearance at the French Open, he decided not to ask for a wild card into the main draw and did not appear again for a year.

Seles, born six months before Borg won his first major tournament, emerged as the youngest world champion in history. She began her climb to the top at the Australian Open, where she dropped only 12 games in the first five rounds. She qualified for the final, canceling a third-set match point while struggling past Mary Joe Fernandez, 6-3, 0-6, 9-7, and, in the final beat Jana Novotna, 5-7, 6-3, 6-1. Novotna, seeded No. 10, had upset eighth-seeded Zina Garrison, 7-6 (7-1), 6-4, first-seeded Graf, 5-7,

6-4, 8-6, and sixth-seeded Arantxa Sanchez Vicario, 6-2, 6-4, to reach her first major final. For Graf, it was the first time in 17 Big Four appearances she failed to advance to the semifinals.

Graf's 1,310-day reign as No. 1 ended with her loss to Sabatini, 6-4, 7-6 (8-6) in the final at Boca Raton. She did have the satisfaction of defeating Seles, 6-4, 6-3, in the final of the U.S. Hard Court Championships in San Antonio three weeks later and in Hamburg, 7-5, 6-7 (4-7), 6-3 weeks after that.

But Seles entered the French Open as the top-ranked player and emerged as the clear leader. Both Graf and Sabatini had the opportunity to move to the top of the ladder with a victory in Paris. But Seles (loser of the Italian Open finale to Sabatini, 6-3, 6-2) defeated Gaby in the semifinals, 6-4, 6-1, shortly after Graf (with 44 errors) was humbled by Sanchez Vicario, 6-0, 6-2. The two games were the fewest won by Graf in a complete match since turning pro in October 1982, at the age of 13.

"That hasn't happened in a long, long time," Graf said. "And I hope it's going to be a long, long time until it happens again. I can't remember the last time I played that bad."

Seles, who had dropped only one set in the tournament, defeated Sanchez Vicario in routine fashion, 6-3, 6-4, for her second consecutive French title.

It was somewhere between Paris and London, at least in terms of the WTA schedule, that the season took a strange twist. With the public considering the possibility of a second female Grand Slam in three years, Wimbledon officials were startled to receive a message that Seles had withdrawn from the event "due to an injury caused by a minor accident." There was no additional explanation, no contact with the player herself and the tournament was due to start in three days. Her whereabouts became the hottest topic in tennis.

Was she undergoing treatment for a knee injury in Vail, Colorado? Or was she having her legs checked in New York? Or was she in hiding at entrepreneur Donald Trump's vast estate in Florida? Maybe it wasn't an injury at all, some tabloids speculated, coming to the conclusion that she was pregnant. Another report had her skipping the grass-court event to preserve her ranking and a $1-million bonus from the company that manufactured her racket. About the only possibility overlooked was that she had been spirited away by a UFO. Meanwhile, she could not be reached by reporters or agents or the WTA, which levied a $6,000 fine for a late withdrawal.

While she was away, Jennifer Capriati had the time of her life at Wimbledon. The 15-year-old not only became the youngest semifinalist in tournament history but she did so at the expense of Navratilova. Capriati stunned the most successful singles champion in the annals of the All England Club in the quarterfinals, 6-4, 7-5. It was Navratilova's earliest exit from Wimbledon in 14 years and ended a record streak of nine consecutive finals. Capriati scored her first triumph over a player ranked in the top four and qualified for the semifinals against Sabatini, where Sabatini won, 6-4, 6-4. Meanwhile, Graf whipped Garrison, 6-1, 6-3, and Mary Joe Fernandez, 6-2, 6-4, en route to the final. The championship match was a terrific, though lost, opportunity for Sabatini, and Graf pulled out a 6-4, 3-6, 8-6 victory, the first extended women's final at Wimbledon since 1976. Steffi double

faulted away the ninth game of the third set, allowing Gaby to serve for it at 5-4—and again at 6-5, 30-15, two points from the prize. But the Argentine, who had been attacking, hung back, and Graf made the most of it.

The Seles media circus was called to order weeks later at Mahwah, New Jersey, where Monica made her first public appearance since her withdrawal from Wimbledon. Sixteen microphones and 13 television cameras were in place as she met the press. The truth, she said, was that she had skipped the most prestigious tournament because of shin splints and the beginning of a stress fracture [left leg]. "People were looking for more exciting answers," she said. "It's so simple, but they were expecting me to say, 'Yes, I'm pregnant.' or, 'Yes, it's the Yonex contract.' or, 'Yes, it's some other reason.' I mean, why would I miss Wimbledon? It's the biggest tournament."

The site of her return certainly didn't mollify WTA officials. She chose an exhibition tournament, offering a huge guarantee, over an official tour event the following week in nearby Westchester County, N.Y. For that offense, she was fined $20,000, a penalty paid by the local promoter, John Korff. He also paid the $2,500 fine assessed to Capriati, who defeated Seles in the final of the 16-woman event.

From there, Capriati flew to Nottingham, England, where the U.S. team qualified for the final of the Federation Cup. Despite her singles victory over Conchita Martinez, 4-6, 7-6 (7-3), 6-1, the Americans lost to Spain, 2-1, as Sanchez Vicario defeated Mary Joe Fernandez, 6-3, 6-4, and the team of Garrison and Gigi Fernandez was thwarted by the two Spaniards in the doubles, 3-6, 6-1, 6-1.

Returning to the tour at the end of July, Seles was upset by Capriati, 4-6, 6-1, 7-6 (7-2), at San Diego in a match that boasted a pairing of the two youngest finalists in the Open era. Two weeks later, Seles beat Kimiko Date, a rising Japanese player, 6-3, 6-1, to win Los Angeles. Twice in August, however, Graf supplanted Seles at the top of the rankings and the German entered the U.S. Open in the familiar role of No. 1.

It was not to last at this Open, which became the Garden of the Golden Oldies, notable because of 39-year-old semifinalist Connors and 34-year-old finalist Navratilova. Never had two players in one tournament given so much joy to the geriatric set. Playing her classic serve-and-volley stuff, the oldest woman in the place had an adventurous excursion, beating Manuela Maleeva Fragniere, 7-6 (7-5), 1-6, 6-2; Sanchez Vicario, 6-7 (6-8), 7-6 (7-5), 6-2; and Graf, 7-6 (7-2), 6-7 (6-8), 6-4, to advance to her eighth U.S. final—and a date with Seles. There was nothing subtle about the other semi, a slugfest of nakedly ferocious, thundering groundies that absorbed the crowd for almost two hours. Mysterious Monica won by the skin of the last four points, stopping Capriati, 6-3, 3-6, 7-6 (7-4).

On the following afternoon, Seles demolished Navratilova, 7-6 (7-1), 6-1, passing her elder at will from either end of the baseline. Navratilova won only 34 points on 76 approaches to the net and committed 26 unforced errors to the champion's five. Seles thus won her third major title of the season in as many attempts. She did not win many new fans, especially after publicly thanking the controversial real estate mogul Donald Trump in post-match ceremonies.

The victory restored her to No. 1, which she held for the remainder of the year. Seles said she didn't regret the decision to withdraw from Wimbledon. "I can't erase it," she said. "But if I were to play Wimbledon, I don't think I could have played the Open [because of the time for recuperation]... there will always be that little emptiness."

Seles finished the season in style, defeating Navratilova, 6-4, 3-6, 7-5, 6-0, at Madison Square Garden in the final of the Slims Championships. Navratilova teamed with her old partner, Pam Shriver, to win the doubles title for the first time in three years, their 10th in this event, over Novotna and Gigi Fernandez, 4-6, 7-5, 6-4.

The men's tour offered surprises as early as the first major tournament, where one of the semifinalists advised the press, "It's just like you all expected—Edberg, Lendl, Becker and McEnroe." Except that the speaker was Patrick McEnroe and it was the doubles specialist who had advanced to the final four, rather than older brother John. The latter hadn't even made the trip to Australia following his disqualification the previous year.

In his semifinal, unseeded McEnroe, who had defeated 12th-seeded American Jay Berger, 6-1, 7-5, 7-5; Aussie lefty Mark Woodforde, 6-2, 6-4, 6-1; and Italian Cristiano Caratti, 7-6 (7-2), 6-3, 4-6, 4-6, 6-2; battled Becker for four sets before the German prevailed, 6-7 (2-7), 6-4, 6-1, 6-4. Lendl had a tougher time getting to the final, weathering two match points in beating Edberg in five sets, 6-4, 5-7, 3-6, 7-6 (7-3), 6-4. But Lendl couldn't keep the crown, bowing to Becker, 1-6, 6-4, 6-4, 6-4.

Paris belonged to the Americans. For the first time since 1954 (Tony Trabert over Art Larsen) a pair of Yanks made the final. But long before Courier and Agassi walked into Roland Garros to contest the championship, Connors stole the show. A wild-card entry in the only major championship he never won, the 38-year-old Connors eliminated Todd Witsken, 6-3, 6-3, 7-5, and outlasted No. 28 Haitian Ronald Agenor, 6-4, 6-2, 3-6, 0-6, 6-4, in three hours, 39 minutes. That was his concluding victory in Paris, the 40th, but not quite the conclusion. His last match was majestic, another crowd-tugging drainer of 3:32. Jimmy won the last point—but ex-champ Michael Chang got the win, 4-6, 7-5, 6-2, 4-6, 0-15, retire. After belting a backhand return winner for the first point of the fifth—"I was ahead, wasn't I?"—Connors surrendered to a man half his age, giving in to a gimpy back and exhaustion.

"I'm sorry," he said to umpire Bruno Rebeuh. "I did all I could. I just can't play anymore. Believe me, if I could ... I would."

Certainly, that's what the public believed. The fans accorded him—"JEEM-BO!"—and several standing ovations. "To be honest, I felt awful," Connors said after getting an ice massage and an intravenous solution. "I've been run ragged and my back's stiff. But, boy, was it fun. To get a stadium rocking like that is a kick you can't believe."

Agassi, wearing a purple, gray and white outfit that was subdued in comparison to the hot pink ensemble of 1990, advanced to his second consecutive French final by blasting Becker in the semis, 7-5, 6-3, 3-6, 6-1. Courier, four months younger than Agassi, had a more hazardous trip to his first major title match, struggling with powerful Swede Magnus Larsson, 6-3, 4-6, 4-6, 7-5, 6-2, ousting Todd Martin, 6-2, 6-3, 6-3, then top-seeded Edberg, 6-4, 2-6, 6-3, 6-4, in the quarterfinals before beating Stich, 6-2, 6-7, (8-10), 6-2, 6-4.

It marked only the fourth all-American men's final in Paris. Both players had trained at the Nick Bollettieri Tennis Academy, but Courier left when he decided Agassi was receiving most of the coach's attention. Agassi had taken a faster track to the spotlight, but it was Courier who was the more poised in the end, ignoring a couple of rain delays and strong winds and swirling dust in a 3-6, 6-4, 2-6, 6-1, 6-4 victory.

It was Courier's fourth career triumph in as many finals and the $451,660 he pocketed exceeded his total prize money from 1990. He closed with an ace, then flopped backward onto the clay. "There have been lots of happy moments in my life and there will be lots more," the champion said, "but at the moment, this is the happiest."

Agassi received greater attention just for showing up at Wimbledon than he did for any of his 1991 results. He hadn't made an appearance at the All England Club since a first-round loss in 1987 to Henri Leconte, 6-2, 6-1, 6-2, in under an hour. He said he wasn't ready for the grass and it wasn't clear if officials were ready for a peacock.

And then fifth-seeded Agassi removed the white warmup suit in which he practiced, teasing photographers and spectators alike, to reveal all-white attire without a stripe of color. His only concession to the '90s and his image was the pair of lycra tights that peeked from beneath his white denim shorts. More significantly, after a five-set opening round escape from Canadian Grant Connell, 4-6, 6-1, 6-7 (6-8), 7-5, 6-3, he played reasonably well on the lawns, making the quarterfinals, where he was shot down in five sets, 6-2, 0-6, 3-6, 7-6 (7-3), 6-2, by David Wheaton, a 22-year-old American with a big serve.

Unseeded Wheaton, who would cap his season with the $2-million first-place check for beating Chang, 7-5, 6-2, 6-4, at the Grand Slam Cup in December, was the only outsider in the semifinals of a tournament that, in an unprecedented move, opened the gates on the middle Sunday in order to clear a backlog of matches postponed by massive amounts of rain. Tickets were hastily printed after the announcement on Friday and all seats were unreserved, causing a mad dash from the turnstiles. So enthusiastic and unfamiliar with tradition were the fans at Centre Court that they even performed a wave. To the disappointment of that throng, Connors was beaten by tall Californian Derrick Rostagno, 7-6 (7-2), 6-1, 6-4.

Order was restored in time for the final between stick-figure-thin Stich and Becker, who had turned back Wheaton in straight sets, 6-4, 7-6 (7-4), 7-5. Stich, 6-foot-4, had uprooted defender Edberg, 4-6, 7-6 (7-5), 7-6 (7-5), 7-6 (7-2), Edberg not losing serve the entire match. Stich, the tie-breaker maven, prevented a fourth straight Becker-Edberg title bout. Strikingly, on this most tie-breakerish day at the Big W, the man who concocted the set-terminating method in 1965 died at Newport, R.I. Jimmy Van Alen was 88. "If he hadn't lived," Edberg said afterwards, not disrespectfully, "Michael and I might still be out there playing."

By winning his match after Edberg lost, Becker climbed to No. 1 in the rankings for the second time in the season. But the added stature did not intimidate Stich. Eleven months younger than Becker, the relatively anonymous German had only one tournament title to his name, Memphis in 1990. He broke his

more celebrated compatriot in the first game, slugged 16 aces (for a tournament total of 97) and overwhelmed the three-time champion, 6-4, 7-6 (7-4), 6-4. He would be remembered as the man who beat No. 1 twice in the same tournament.

"It's an incredible feeling," Stich said. To which Becker nodded in agreement. "I know the feeling," the loser said. "He was a nobody, but today he is a star."

Becker held onto the top spot in the rankings until the U.S. Open, where he was upset in the third round by No. 45 Paul Haarhuis, 6-3, 6-4, 6-2. Edberg, who had never reached the final at Flushing Meadow, the major he liked least, made the most of the opportunity. He had straight-set wins, 7-6 (7-2), 7-5, 6-3, over Chang; 6-3, 6-2, 6-3 over Javier Sanchez; and 6-3, 6-3, 6-4 over Lendl to advance to the final against Courier. (Chang had beaten John McEnroe, 6-4, 4-6, 7-6 (7-1), 2-6, 6-3, in four hours, 30 minutes, a third rounder ending at 1:30 a.m.)

Courier, who had terminated the 361-day US Open reign of Sampras in the quarters, 6-2, 7-6 (7-4), 7-6 (7-5), wasn't off his game against Edberg. But Jim was off the court in 122 minutes because Stefan was in such an oppressive, overpowering serve-and-volleying state, winning, 6-2, 6-4, 6-0. Edberg would often refer to this as "the best match I ever played."

But the star of the tournament was Connors, the wild card with a No. 174 ranking. He owned the crowds in winning five matches, against Patrick McEnroe, Michiel Schapers, 10th-seeded Karel Novacek, Aaron Krickstein and Haarhuis. Connors was almost out of it in a first-round match under the lights against McEnroe, trailing by two sets and 0-3, but by 1:35 a.m., after four hours, 18 minutes, he had it, 4-6, 6-7 (4-7), 6-4, 6-2, 6-4. Schapers was easy, 6-3, 6-2, 6-3, and so was Novacek, 6-1, 6-4, 6-3.

Next it was "Happy Birthday to me!" Connors turned 39 the day he played Krickstein—a 7-5, 7-6 (7-4), 6-2 first-round stunner of fourth-seeded Agassi—and had the crowd singing Happy Birthday after his melodramatic, four-hour, 41-minute victory, 3-6, 7-6 (10-8), 1-6, 6-3, 7-6 (7-4).

This despite Kricker holding two set points in the second, holding to 5-2 in the fifth through eight deuces and three break points, and twice two points from triumph at 5-3. But Jimmy threw everything he knew into the magnificent conclusion—lobs, sneak volleys, line drives and capital H—Heart.

Then came Haarhuis. Some of the 20,000 customers for the nocturnal quarterfinal had paid scalpers $500 to get in, and felt they got off cheaply. Jimmy won 4-6, 7-6 (7-3), 6-4, 6-2, but the Dutchman served for a two-set lead at 5-4. A delicious backhand return took Jimmy to break point, followed by the point of the tournament: intercepting four overhead smashes with his legs and lobs, he nailed it with a roaring backhand passer. The multitude shrieked lovingly and wanted to hug him, the second oldest semifinalist in U.S. history, behind Ken Rosewall, whom he drubbed in the 1974 final on grass at Forest Hills. He was also the only wild card to advance that far. But Connors ran out of miracles against Courier, losing 6-3, 6-3, 6-2, in a match that was coldly efficient and brutally quick.

Courier also reached the final of the year-end ATP World Championship, losing to Sampras, 3-6, 7-6 (7-5), 6-3, 6-4. In the doubles event, which reopened South Africa to the men's tour,

John Fitzgerald and Anders Jarryd culminated an outstanding year in which they claimed three majors: the French, over Americans Rick Leach-Jim Pugh, 6-0, 7-6 (7-2); Wimbledon, over the Argentine-Mexican pair, Javier Frana-Leonardo Lavalle, 6-3, 6-4, 6-7 (7-9), 6-1; U.S. Open, over Americans Scott Davis-David Pate, 6-3, 3-6, 6-3, 6-3. The Aussie-Swedish combo beat Ken Flach and Robert Seguso at Johannesburg, 6-4, 6-4, 2-6, 6-4.

Still, the historic highlight of the season occurred at Lyon when the Captain Yannick Noah-inspired French team of "Two Musketeers," Guy Forget and Leconte—the only pair of lefties to win the Cup—scored a 3-1 victory over the U.S. to return the Davis Cup to France for the first time since 1932.

Forget, who enjoyed his finest year as a pro with six singles titles and his first Top 10 ranking (No. 7) defeated Sampras in the clinching match, 7-6 (8-6), 3-6, 6-3, 6-4, avoiding a set point in the breaker with one of his 17 aces, brushing off 10 of 11 break points. When he pumped four aces while serving out the third set through three deuces and four break points, the Cup was virtually guaranteed. That came after Guy combined with Henri to upset Flach and Seguso in doubles, 6-1, 6-4, 4-6, 6-2. Leconte, No. 159 and thought to be finished after back surgery four months earlier, also defeated the 20-year-old Sampras, 6-4, 7-5, 6-4, after Agassi had posted a 1-0 U.S. lead by beating Forget, 6-7 (7-9), 6-2, 6-1, 6-2.

Victory was followed by an hour-long celebration by French players and 8,000 jubilant witnesses who had filled and rocked the smoky Palais des Sports for three days. Noah, who had successfully sold "our dream for France" to his latter-day Musketeers was hoisted with them on jubilant shoulders as a conga line snaked around the court. Everybody was tearfully singing *La Marseillaise*. One of the celebrants, sharing champagne from the Cup, said he "couldn't wait much longer" for this reprise. He was 93-year-old Jean Borotra, an original of the "Four Musketeers," who pried the Cup from the U.S. in 1927 and kept it six years.

Germany in Kansas City was the 3-2 U.S. steppingstone on indoor clay to the final. Agassi and Courier gave the home side a 2-0 start, Andre over Stich, 6-3, 6-1, 6-4, Jim over Charlie Steeb, 4-6, 6-1, 6-3, 6-4. However, Eric Jelen and Stich produced a speed bump, 7-6 (7-3), 6-4, 6-4, over rookies David Pate and Scott Davis. When Stich beat Courier, 6-4, 7-5, 6-4, it was up to Agassi to save the day: 6-2, 6-2, 6-3, over Steeb.

1991 CHAMPIONS AND LEADERS

Australian Open
Men's Singles Final: Boris Becker (GER) def. Ivan Lendl (CZE), 1-6, 6-4, 6-4, 6-4
Women's Singles Final: Monica Seles (YUG) def. Jana Novotna (CZE), 5-7, 6-3, 6-1
Men's Doubles Final: Scott Davis and David Pate (USA) def. Patrick McEnroe and David Wheaton (USA), 6-7 (4), 7-6 (8), 6-3, 7-5
Women's Doubles Final: Patty Fendick and Mary Joe Fernandez (USA) def. Gigi Fernandez (USA) and Jana Novotna (CZE), 7-6 (4), 6-1
Mixed Doubles Final: Jo Durie and Jeremy Bates (GBR) def. Robin White and Scott Davis (USA), 2-6, 6-4, 6-4

French Open
Men's Singles Final: Jim Courier (USA) def. Andre Agassi (USA), 3-6, 6-4, 2-6, 6-1, 6-4

Women's Singles Final: Monica Seles (YUG) def. Arantxa Sanchez Vicario (ESP), 6-3, 6-4
Men's Doubles Final: John Fitzgerald (AUS) and Anders Jarryd (SWE) def. Rick Leach and Jim Pugh (USA), 6-0, 7-6 (2)
Women's Doubles Final: Gigi Fernandez (USA) and Jana Novotna (CZE) def. Larisa Savchenko and Natalia Zvereva (USSR), 6-4, 6-0
Mixed Doubles Final: Helena Sukova and Cyril Suk (CZE) def. Caroline Vis and Paul Haarhuis (NED), 3-6, 6-4, 6-1

Wimbledon
Men's Singles Final: Michael Stich (GER) def. Boris Becker (GER), 6-4, 7-6 (4), 6-4
Women's Singles Final: Steffi Graf (GER) def. Gabriela Sabatini (ARG), 6-4, 3-6, 8-6
Men's Doubles Final: John Fitzgerald (AUS) and Anders Jarryd (SWE) def. Javier Frana (ARG) and Leonardo Lavalle (MEX), 6-3, 6-4, 6-7 (1), 6-1
Women's Doubles Final: Larisa Savchenko and Natalia Zvereva (USSR) def. Gigi Fernandez (USA) and Jana Novotna (CZE), 6-4, 3-6, 6-4
Mixed Doubles Final: Elizabeth Sayers Smylie and John Fitzgerald (AUS) def. Natalia Zvereva (USSR) and Jim Pugh (USA), 7-6 (2), 6-2

U.S. Open
Men's Singles Final: Stefan Edberg (SWE) def. Jim Courier (USA), 6-2, 6-4, 6-0
Women's Singles Final: Monica Seles (YUG) def. Martina Navratilova (USA), 7-6 (1), 6-1
Men's Doubles Final: John Fitzgerald (AUS) and Anders Jarryd (SWE) def. Scott Davis and David Pate (USA), 6-3, 3-6, 6-3, 6-3
Women's Doubles Final: Pam Shriver (USA) and Natalia Zvereva (USSR) def. Jana Novotna (CZE) and Larisa Savchenko (USSR), 6-4, 4-6, 7-6 (5)
Mixed Doubles Final: Manon Bollegraf and Tom Nijssen (NED) def. Arantxa Sanchez Vicario and Emilio Sanchez (ESP), 6-2, 7-6 (2)

Year-End No. 1
Men: Stefan Edberg
Women: Monica Seles

Top Player Earnings
Men: David Wheaton $2,479,239
Women: Monica Seles $2,457,758

Davis Cup: France

Federation Cup: Spain

ATP World Championships, Frankfurt—Pete Sampras
Grand Slam Cup, Munich—David Wheaton
Virginia Slims Championships, NYC—Monica Seles

1992 Courier Delivers

In a year in which the U.S. regained the summit of men's tennis, Americans accounted for all but one of the major singles titles. Ironically, the championship that eluded them was the one they prized most, the U.S. Open. Stefan Edberg, the Swede who discovered New York can be a nice place to visit, triumphed at Flushing Meadows for the second consecutive year.

Elsewhere, however, the U.S. reigned supreme. Jim Courier added a second French title to the Australian crown he won five months earlier and finished the season as the No. 1 player in the world, the first Yank to claim that honor since John McEnroe in 1984. Andre Agassi finally annexed his first major at Wimbledon, of all places. And Pete Sampras, a beaten finalist at the U.S. Open, compiled the best match record, 70-18, while gaining No. 3 in the final rankings.

Then, in a classic melding of generations, Courier, Agassi and Sampras combined with McEnroe to reclaim the Davis Cup for

Jim Courier celebrates his victory over Petr Korda in the final of the French Open.

the United States, beating Switzerland in the final. Courier was a loser on opening day to six-foot-seven Olympic champ Marc Rosset, 6-3, 6-7 (9-11), 3-6, 6-4, 6-4, aced 27 times. But Jim won the clinching singles, 6-3, 3-6, 6-3, 6-4 over Jakob Hlasek, in an uproarious 3-1 U.S. triumph in Ft. Worth, Texas., a former cow town where hundreds of cowbells, wielded by a good-natured contingent of 1,500 Swiss supporters, clanged incessantly among the crowds of 12,000. Switzerland, never before a factor in the Cup, rode Nos. 35 and 36 Rosset and Hlasek to the small country's first final, upsetting defending champs France 3-2 in the quarterfinals.

The pivotal match came in the doubles, where McEnroe paired with Sampras against Hlasek and Rosset. The Swiss gave the Yanks a scare before the Americans settled down to win, 6-7 (5-7), 6-7 (7-9), 7-5, 6-1, 6-2 to put the U.S. up 2-1, setting the stage for Courier's heroics. Had Rosset held serve to 6-6 in the third, the Swiss might have captured it for a 2-1 lead. But the going and coming alignment—Daddy & Disciple?—delivered forehand returns to start it the other way. It was the first such doubles comeback in a final since 1958, Ham Richardson and Alex Olmedo for the victorious U.S. over Australians Mal Anderson and Neale Fraser. Agassi (7-0 for the Cup campaign) launched the win over Hlasek, 6-1, 6-2, 6-2.

After his French final flop of 1991, Sampras was feeling better to slurp from the Cup, also allied with McEnroe in a tough semifinal clincher over Sweden's Stefan Edberg and Anders Jarryd, 6-1, 6-7 (2-7), 4-6, 6-3, 6-3. Courier and Agassi got the start-up 2-0 lead, respectively over Nicklas Kulti, 4-6, 7-6 (7-1), 6-3, 7-5, and Edberg, 5-7, 6-3, 7-6 (7-1), 6-3.

The male American influence was apparent throughout the entire tour as players from the States accounted for 24 of the 82 singles titles, triple the total of runners-up Spain and Germany. Five U.S. citizens ranked among the Top 10 men, including No. 8 Ivan Lendl, who ended a 14-month drought by winning the Seiko Championships in Tokyo, three months after receiving his naturalization papers. In all, 43 individuals from 18 countries captured at least one tournament and no player won more than five.

Of the three who shared that distinction—Courier and Sampras were the other two—Boris Becker finished the year on the highest note. The German, shut out of a major final for only the

second time in eight years, won the year-end ATP World Championship by defeating Courier, 6-4, 6-3, 7-5, in Frankfurt on his 25th birthday. It marked his third victory in the final eight weeks of the season and raised his ranking to No. 5.

A somber note was Arthur Ashe's revelation in April that he had contracted AIDS through a blood transfusion while undergoing surgery in 1988. Characteristically, he asked not for sympathy, but continued a heavy schedule of obligations in charitable work and TV commentary. He also became active in the fight against AIDS, raising funds for education, research and treatment.

Competition among the women was more one-sided. For the second successive year, Monica Seles captured the Australian, French and U.S. Open titles, won the Virginia Slims Championship, finished atop the WTA rankings and established a record for tennis earnings ($2,622,352). But, in 1992, she was not denied a Grand Slam by an error of omission. This time she entered Wimbledon and took her case to the final, where she was overwhelmed by Steffi Graf. The German, whose eight victories included a four-tournament winning streak in the fall, demolished Seles, 6-2, 6-1, equaling Martina Navratilova's 6-0, 6-3 conquest of Andrea Jaeger in 1983 as the second most lopsided Wimbledon of the Open era. Graf's singles title was her fourth in five years at Wimbledon and her 11th in a major event.

Although Navratilova slipped to No. 5 and failed to reach a Big Four final, she won Chicago, saving two match points, over Jana Novotna, 7-6 (7-4), 4-6, 7-5, to break the record for most tournament victories she had shared with Chris Evert at 157. Martina concluded the season with three more titles for a total of 161: the U.S. Hard Courts over Nathalie Tauziat, 6-2, 6-1; Los Angeles over Seles, 6-4, 6-2 and the last achieved in Filderstadt, Germany, 7-6 (7-1), 6-3, over Gabriela Sabatini, on her 36th birthday. And the grande dame did reach the last round of the Virginia Slims Championship in New York, where she was drubbed by Seles, 7-5, 6-3, 6-1.

Two months earlier, in a gimmick-ridden send-up of the Battle of the Sexes waged by Billie Jean King and Bobby Riggs 19 years earlier, Navratilova had unraveled in a match against Jimmy Connors at Caesars Palace. She double-faulted on set point in the first set and lost, 7-5, 6-2, despite getting two serves to her opponent's one and hitting into a court four feet wider. Each player received $500,000 in appearance money and Connors earned an extra $500,000 for his tame victory. He had won his first-round match over Jaime Oncins, 6-1, 6-2, 6-3 at the U.S. Open on his 40th birthday, but was dispatched by Lendl, 3-6, 6-3, 6-2, 6-0 in his Open swan song.

Of greater consequence, 16-year-old Jennifer Capriati picked up a gold medal in the Olympic Games at Barcelona. She did so in dream-like fashion, defeating the defending champion, Graf, in the final. Capriati's 3-6, 6-3, 6-4, victory, the first of her career over Steffi, lifted her out of the doldrums in a season in which she reportedly balked at the heavy schedule arranged by her father and appeared to lose her zest for tennis.

Three months later, in the semifinals at Philadelphia, Graf crushed the American teenager, 6-0, 6-1, en route to her fourth consecutive tournament victory, over Arantxa Sanchez Vicario, 6-3, 3-6, 6-1. The German, upset by Lori McNeil, 7-6 (7-1), 6-4 in the

first round of the Slims showdown, hadn't lost prior to the quarterfinals since 1985.

She finished the season ranked No. 2 behind Seles.

Graf was not on hand when Seles took her first major step of the year toward continued domination of women's tennis. She was recuperating from—no kidding—German measles during the Australian Open, where Seles was not taxed. The champion won her second Aussie, 6-2, 6-3, over Mary Joe Fernandez, who had upset Sabatini in the semifinals, 6-1, 6-4

In contrast, the French Open provided some of the finest moments and tightest matches of the year. Merely to qualify for an epic final against Graf, Seles twice had to rally from third-set deficits. The first of her comebacks occurred in the fourth round when she trailed No. 150 Akiko Kijimuta of Japan, 1-4 in the third, before running off five consecutive games for a 6-1, 3-6, 6-4 victory. Then, in the semifinals, she was down 2-4 in the third against the eminently more formidable Sabatini before putting her away, 6-3, 4-6, 6-4.

When it was over, the loser was dumbfounded. "She seemed tired and then suddenly she started hitting the ball very hard," Sabatini said. "I don't know where she got the power."

Graf also passed a critical test in the semifinals by overcoming Sanchez Vicario, 6-2, 6-2, who had demolished the German, 6-0, 6-2 in similar circumstances a year earlier. The result was a final for which the Paris fans were clamoring: Graf-Seles, the first match between the two in more than a year. It disappointed no one save the loser and her family. And even Graf conceded it was a remarkable experience after saving five championship points in Seles' sharpshooting 6-2, 3-6, 10-8 victory that consumed two hours and 43 minutes. "It definitely was a special match, no doubt about it," Graf said.

On the following day, second-seeded Courier joined Seles, a fellow Florida resident, halfway to a Grand Slam. In the Australian Open final, he avenged the blowout by Edberg in the 1991 U.S. Open four months earlier by beating the Swede, 6-3, 3-6, 6-4, 6-2. He celebrated the victory, which enabled him to leapfrog top-seeded Edberg to No. 1 in the rankings, by jumping into the nearby polluted Yarra River, so fit that not even the multitude of germs could get him.

Courier displayed a destructive forehand and competitive verve to ascend to No. 1—the first of five changes at the top in 1992—to end nearly a seven-year drought for Americans since McEnroe was toppled from No. 1 in mid-1985. At 21 years, five months, Courier was the third-youngest male to hold the No. 1 spot, after McEnroe (21 and 15 days) and Bjorn Borg (21 and two months). Yet, his elevation apparently failed to impress Agassi, with whom he had split matches in the two previous French Opens.

Once more, the pairings in Paris pitted the longtime rivals, this time in the semifinals. Agassi carried the pre-match buildup by claiming that Courier's game was built on hard work and mental strength because "I don't think he has a lot of natural ability to fall back on." Courier saved his talk for after the match, which he won most convincingly, 6-3, 6-2, 6-2.

"I've been reading about how I don't have much talent," Courier said. "There are many different talents besides hitting a ten-

nis ball. Having guts on the court is a talent; having desire is a talent; having courage to go for a shot when you are love-40 down is a talent. I may not hit the ball as cleanly as anybody out there, but I have got a few talents that are just as good as anybody else's."

Courier's triumph over Agassi pushed his winning streak to 22 matches, which he extended in the final by blasting seventh-seeded Czech, Petr Korda, 7-5, 6-2, 6-1. Unlike the women's final, the men offered little drama. Courier finished off his nervous opponent in one hour, 59 minutes. The normally free-swinging lefty Korda, who had never previously advanced beyond the third round of a major event, had 49 unforced errors and nine double faults.

"I think I played big feet today," he said. "I tell you I was very nervous. My hand is still tight. I couldn't play my game. My body didn't work too much today."

Wimbledon, of course, represented a huge hurdle for Seles and Courier. Hard-hitting baseliners are not at home on grass. Neither had advanced beyond the quarterfinals in previous appearances. Courier's quest and a 25-match streak came to an abrupt end in the third round when he stumbled against an obscure Russian, the No. 193-ranked Andrei Olhovskiy, 6-4, 4-6, 6-4, 6-4. That defeat opened the door for McEnroe, a first-round washout to Nicklas Kulti at the French, who had gained impetus in what he said would be his last Wimbledon. In an engaging four-hour, nine-minute clash of aging ex-champs in the second round, No. 30 Mac beat No. 191 Patrick Cash, 6-7 (3-7), 6-4, 6-7 (1-7), 6-3, 6-2. Another old-boy champ saying goodbye, Connors, did it fast in his 20th Big W, a first-round loss to a Mexican lefty, No. 86 Luis Herrera, 6-2, 1-6, 7-5, 6-3. But Jimmy left behind the male wins record, 84 of 102 matches.

After beating David Wheaton, 6-3, 6-4, 6-4 in the third round, and Olhovskiy, 7-5, 6-3, 7-6, (12-10) in the fourth round, McEnroe reached his eighth semifinal, over ninth-seeded Guy Forget, 6-2, 7-6 (11-9), 6-3, wriggling his way out of six set points in the breaker. He had become the talk of London, and a crowd favorite at the tournament where so often he had played the boor.

Awaiting him was another surprise. In the midst of a sour season, Agassi had managed to overcome his fear of grass to win five matches, most notably over three-time Wimbledon champ Becker, 4-6, 6-2, 6-2, 4-6, 6-3, in the quarters. The meeting of the old rebel and the young anarchist was a stunning development, enriched by their growing friendship. After being thrust together on the Davis Cup team, McEnroe and Agassi became occasional dinner companions, frequently practiced against each other, and were doubles sidekicks at the French, winning three matches in reaching the quarterfinals.

Indeed, Agassi asked McEnroe for his advice on coping with the Wimbledon grass and the flattered former champion readily agreed. "We hit it off well," McEnroe said. "He's young, he's really inquisitive and he's very, very smart. He asks good questions."

Agassi learned his lessons well. The only help he needed from McEnroe on, fittingly, the Fourth of July, was a reminder to bow to the Duke and Duchess of Kent as he was departing the court after his commanding victory. The shaggy-haired American required only one hour, 51 minutes to cut down McEnroe,

6-4, 6-2, 6-3. Agassi, returning brilliantly, converted all seven break points he held, lost his serve only twice and was in control from the very first game, which McEnroe double-faulted away. McEnroe departed Wimbledon as he greeted it in 1977, a semifinalist, compiling a 59-11 record for 14 visits.

On the other side of the draw the "Incendiary I," Goran Ivanisevic, was a skinny 6-foot-4 Croatian conflagration, the most prolific firer of aces the place had known. Seeded eighth, he had 17 aces in beating German Lars Koslowski, 6-2, 6-2, 6-3; 34 over Mark Woodforde, 6-4, 6-4, 6-7 (4-7), 6-3; 22 over Rosset, 7-6 (7-4), 6-4, 6-4; 27 over Lendl, 6-7 (7-9), 6-1, 6-4, 1-0, ret.; 33 over Edberg, 6-7 (10-12), 7-5, 6-1, 3-6, 6-3; and 36 in a semifinal win over Sampras, 6-7 (4-7), 7-6 (7-5), 6-4, 6-2, a battle of 20-year-old prodigies.

Ironically, maturity may have been Agassi's greatest advantage in the final. He failed to wither when confronted by Ivanisevic's serve, producing 37 more aces for a stunning tournament record total of 206. Andre failed to lose serve until the second game of the fourth set and appeared much calmer than the easily-distracted Goran. The 22-year-old Yank persevered 6-7 (8-10), 6-4, 6-4, 1-6, 6-4 for his first major title, sneaking in for a volley to save a critical break point in the fifth.

At the moment of triumph, Andre, whose past displays had seemed as calculated as his television commercials ("Image is everything"), fell to his knees, sprawled face-first on the turf and appeared genuinely moved. "I've realized my dream of winning a Grand Slam tournament," he said. "To do it here is more than I could ever ask for."

Nor did McEnroe leave the All England Club empty-handed. Fitter and sharper than he had been in years, working with new coach Larry Stefanki, he teamed with Stich, the grass court whiz of 1991, to claim the men's doubles prize. Following the singles championship, unseeded Mac and Michael began a two-day defeating of fourth-seeded Americans Jim Grabb and Richey Reneberg. The match consumed a final-round record five hours and one minute, and was decided by a 36-game fifth set, Wimbledon's longest ultimate set. Stopped by darkness at 9:21 p.m., the fifth set was completed on the third Monday. Resuming at 13-13, it took 10 more games and 34 minutes to complete the result, 5-7, 7-6 (7-5), 3-6, 7-6 (7-5), 19-17. It was the last of McEnroe's 17 major titles, the 10th in doubles.

Seles was a lot more successful than Courier in her assault on the grass but she also endured greater frustration. The complaints about her grunting actually grew in volume and opponents joined in the controversy fueled by the tabloid press. Nathalie Tauziat of France raised the issue before her straight-set dismissal in the quarterfinals, 6-1, 6-3, and Navratilova did her one better, reporting Seles to umpire Fran McDowell, who called her to the chair for an admonition in the midst of the ladies' semifinal. Seles still prevailed, 6-2, 6-7 (3-7), 6-4.

"It just gets loud and louder," Navratilova said. "You cannot hear the ball being hit... I know she is not doing it on purpose, but she can stop it on purpose."

That's exactly what Seles did in the final. She barely uttered a peep against Graf. Was she psyched out? Whether that was a cause or an effect of her listless performance was a matter for conjecture. The German woman was crisp and dominating from

the outset, winning 6-2, 6-1. Although the match lasted 5-1/2 hours, rain delays meant only 58 minutes were devoted to tennis.

"I didn't want to think about it," the loser said of her sudden silence. "I just thought hopefully I can start [not grunting] somewhere, so I started here." Monica was stopped after winning five major singles titles and 41 matches in a row. Because she failed to participate in the 1991 Federation Cup, Seles was not eligible for the Olympics. Neither were Navratilova and Sabatini. But Graf, who had helped Germany defeat Spain, 2-1 in the 1992 Federation Cup final (she beat Sanchez Vicario, 6-4, 6-2, and Anke Huber beat Conchita Martinez, 6-3, 6-7 (1-7), 6-1), arrived for Barcelona clay in pursuit of a second consecutive gold medal. She was one match away from a repeat of Seoul when beaten by Capriati in the final, 6-3, 3-6, 6-4. Capriati bubbled with delight on the medal stand. "I had chills the whole time," the youngster said. "Right now this means more to me than any of the Grand Slams."

The men's competition in intense heat on turgid courts produced bigger surprises. Five of the first six seeds—Courier, Edberg, Sampras, Becker and Chang—were gone by the end of the third round: top-seed Courier, swept away by the man of destiny, the Swiss, Rosset, 6-4, 6-2, 6-1; second Edberg by Russian Andrei Chesnokov, 6-0, 6-4, 6-4; third Sampras by Russian Andrei Cherkasov, 6-7 (7-9), 1-6, 7-5, 6-0, 6-3; fifth Becker by Fabrice Santoro of France, 6-1, 3-6, 6-1, 6-3; sixth Chang by Brazilian Jaime Oncins, 6-2, 3-6, 6-3, 6-3. Rosset, who didn't let the dirt hurt his serving, drove the Spanish crowds to anguish by beating homeboys Emilio Sanchez, 6-4, 7-6 (7-2) 3-6, 7-6 (11-9) in the quarterfinals and, for the gold Jordi Arrese, the 16th seed, in a five-hour, three-minute gold medal match, 7-6 (7-2), 6-3, 3-6, 4-6, 8-6, speckled with No. 44 Marc's 38 aces. Ivanisevic, playing for his newly-independent Croatia, won four five-setters in a row, before losing to Rosset in the semifinals and sharing bronze with Cherkasov.

Becker and Stich combined to win the men's doubles for a unified German team over South Africa's Wayne Ferreira and Piet Norval, 7-6 (7-5), 4-6, 7-6 (7-5), 6-3. Ferreira-Norval were their nation's first medalists since 1960 in Rome. The unrelated Fernandez women, Gigi and Mary Joe, captured the gold medal in doubles for the U.S., beating hometown-ers Sanchez Vicario and Conchita Martinez, 7-5, 2-6, 6-2.

In retrospect, Gigi Fernandez may have enjoyed the best season of any American woman. In addition to her Olympic honor, she teamed with Belarussian Natalia Zvereva of Minsk to win three doubles majors: the U.S., 7-6 (7-4), 6-1 over Jana Novotna and Larisa Savchenko Neiland; Wimbledon 6-4, 6-1, over Novotna-Neiland; the French, 6-3, 6-2, over Sanchez Vicario-Martinez. They had no Grand Slam opportunity since each had another partner at the Australian. They would become one of the finest teams in history, amassing 14 majors through 1997.

At Flushing Meadow, Navratilova suffered a shocking second-round defeat administered by No. 17 Magdalena, the third of the three Maleeva sisters on the circuit. One year after she became the oldest woman's major finalist in the Open era, she was ousted by a 17-year-old precisely half her age, 6-4, 0-6, 6-3. It marked her earliest exit from the Open since 1976 when she departed in tears following a first-round knockout by Janet Newberry at Forest Hills. Maggie got to the quarters where she

fell to the oldest of the Maleeva trio, Manuela Fragniere, 6-2, 5-3, retired.

Shocking, too, was Olympic champ Capriati's third-round departure courtesy of petite Cambodian-born Canadian citizen, No. 36 Patricia Hy, 7-5, 6-4. Hy then beat former finalist, 13th-seeded Sukova, 6-1, 7-5, to stand out as the lone Cambodian to go so far, and the second Canadian (Carling Bassett made the semis in 1984). That was far enough. Seles beat her, 6-1, 6-2. In other quarters, Graf lost to Sanchez Vicario, 7-6 (7-5), 6-3, and Sabatini lost to Mary Joe Fernandez, 6-2, 1-6, 6-4, clearing the last major obstacles from Seles' path. She cakewalked to the title without the loss of a set, turning back Fernandez in a semifinal, 6-3, 6-2 and Sanchez Vicario in the final, 6-3, 6-3.

The men had much greater difficulty settling their differences. They played from here to "Infiniti," which happened to be the corporate sponsor of the men's singles. Although all four top seeds reached the semis, it was not without a struggle. Seldom, if ever, had a champion labored longer for his silver and gold than Edberg. Of the 21 five-set matches recorded, he played three—in a row—over Richard Krajicek, 6-4, 6-7 (6-8), 6-3, 3-6, 6-4, down a break in the fifth; over Lendl, 6-3, 6-3, 3-6, 5-7, 7-6 (7-3) again down a break in the fifth; and Chang. The five hour, 26 minute epic against Chang, 6-7 (3-7), 7-5, 7-6 (7-3), 5-7, 6-4, was the longest match of either's life, and the longest of all major matches at the time, outdoing the 5:12 two-day Wimbledon siege that Pancho Gonzalez won over Charlie Pasarell in 1969. Stefan's last four steps to his second title took 19 sets, one under the maximum, a journey such as taken by only one other U.S. champ, Bob Wrenn in 1896. There was no breathing room until Stefan won the final, 6-3, 4-6, 7-6 (7-5), 6-2 over Sampras in a steadfast performance of only two hours, 52 minutes.

Sampras had gunned down top-seeded Courier, 6-1, 3-6, 6-2, 6-2, in the semis, and then went down himself, racing to the bathroom with stomach problems. Had Pete beaten Edberg, Americans would have possessed all four major championships for the first time since Don Budge did it single-handedly in 1938. Their last triple was accomplished by Connors (Australian, Wimbledon, U.S.) in 1974. It was in this final that a deeply disappointed Sampras developed his hatred of losing, and made up his mind to be more than a one-major champ (13 more majors would be his before he said, Enough).

Edberg lost his place at the top of the computer in the fall and failed a final opportunity at the ATP World Championships when he was eliminated in preliminary round-robin play with losses to Sampras, 6-3, 3-6, 7-5, and Becker, 6-4, 6-0. Nevertheless, Edberg finished the season as the leader in official earnings, with $2,341,804.

Of course, Stich almost equaled that total in one December weekend. Although he plummeted from the Top 10, the German managed to regain his singles form in time for the Grand Slam Cup in Munich, where he won the first-place prize of $2 million by defeating Chang in the final, 6-2, 6-3, 6-2. Semifinalist Ivanisevic belted 25 aces while losing to Chang, 6-7 (3-7), 6-2, 6-4, 3-6, 6-3, ending the year with a record 1,017.

The men's season was notable for two other developments. Lendl posted his 1,000th tour victory, second only to Connors,

by beating Brett Stevens of New Zealand 7-5, 7-5 at the Sydney Indoor Championships in October, and Borg, 36, failed to capture a set in eight matches of a murky comeback attempt. The legend did, however, win his first tournament of any kind since 1981 when he handled Roscoe Tanner, 6-4, 6-1, at the Advanta Champions Tour event in Chicago for players 35 and older.

The "Woodies," the Australian duo of Todd Woodbridge and Mark Woodforde, won eight doubles titles, including their own national title, over Americans Kelly Jones and Rick Leach 6-4, 6-3, 6-4, plus the ATP World Championship in Johannesburg, over the Aussie-Swedish hookup of John Fitzgerald and Anders Jarryd, 6-2, 7-6, 5-7, 3-6, 6-3.

Among the women, Navratilova pledged to continue playing a full schedule through 1993 but she ended the 12-year doubles partnership with Pam Shriver in order to concentrate on singles. After 79 titles, 20 majors—all four in 1984 for a Grand Slam—plus 10 trips to the winner's circle at the Virginia Slims Championship, they went their separate ways following the season-ending event at Madison Square Garden. The defending champions lost a semifinal to the Spanish-Czech yoking of Sanchez Vicario and Helena Sukova, 6-4, 7-5, the eventual champs in a 7-6, 6-1, victory over Novotna and Neiland.

1992 CHAMPIONS AND LEADERS

Australian Open
Men's Singles Final: Jim Courier (USA) def. Stefan Edberg (SWE), 6-3, 3-6, 6-4, 6-2
Women's Singles Final: Monica Seles (YUG) def. Mary Joe Fernandez (USA), 6-2, 6-3
Men's Doubles Final: Todd Woodbridge and Mark Woodforde (AUS) def. Kelly Jones and Rick Leach (USA), 6-4, 6-3, 6-4
Women's Doubles Final: Arantxa Sanchez Vicario (ESP) and Helena Sukova (CZE) def. Mary Joe Fernandez and Zina Garrison (USA), 6-4, 7-6 (3)
Mixed Doubles Final: Nicole Provis and Mark Woodforde (AUS) def. Arantxa Sanchez Vicario (ESP) and Todd Woodbridge (AUS), 6-3, 4-6, 11-9

French Open
Men's Singles Final: Jim Courier (USA) def. Petr Korda (CZE), 7-5, 6-2, 6-1
Women's Singles Final: Monica Seles (YUG) def. Steffi Graf (GER), 6-2, 3-6, 10-8
Men's Doubles Final: Jakob Hlasek and Marc Rosset (SUI) def. David Adams (RSA) and Andrei Olhovskiy (CIS), 7-6 (4), 6-7 (3), 7-5
Women's Doubles Final: Gigi Fernandez (USA) and Natalia Zvereva (CIS), def. Arantxa Sanchez Vicario and Conchita Martinez (ESP), 6-3, 6-2
Mixed Doubles Final: Arantxa Sanchez Vicario (ESP) and Mark Woodforde (AUS) def. Lori McNeil and Bryan Shelton (USA), 6-2, 6-3

Wimbledon
Men's Singles Final: Andre Agassi (USA) def. Goran Ivanisevic (CRO), 6-7 (8), 6-4, 6-4, 1-6, 6-4
Women's Singles Final: Steffi Graf (GER) def. Monica Seles (YUG), 6-2, 6-1
Men's Doubles Final: John McEnroe (USA and Michael Stich (GER) def. Richey Reneberg and Jim Grabb (USA) 5-7, 7-6 (5), 3-6, 7-6 (5), 19-17
Women's Doubles Final: Gigi Fernandez (USA) and Natalia Zvereva (CIS) def. Jana Novotna and Larisa Savchenko Neiland (CIS), 6-4, 6-1

Mixed Doubles Final: Larisa Savchenko Neiland (CIS) and Cyril Suk (CZE) def. Miriam Oremans and Jacco Eltingh (NED), 7-6 (2), 6-2

U.S. Open
Men's Singles Final: Stefan Edberg (SWE) def. Pete Sampras (USA), 3-6, 6-4, 7-6 (5), 6-2
Women's Singles Final: Monica Seles (YUG) def. Arantxa Sanchez Vicario (ESP), 6-3, 6-3
Men's Doubles Final: Jim Grabb and Richey Reneberg (USA) def. Kelly Jones and Rick Leach (USA), 3-6, 7-6 (2), 6-3, 6-3
Women's Doubles Final: Gigi Fernandez (USA) and Natalia Zvereva (CIS) def. Jana Novotna (CZE) and Larisa Savchenko Neiland (CIS), 7-6 (4), 6-1
Mixed Doubles Final: Nicole Provis and Mark Woodforde (AUS) def. Helena Sukova (CZE) and Tom Nijssen (NED), 4-6, 6-3, 6-3
* (CIS) – Commonwealth of Independent States (formerly the Soviet Union)

Year-End No. 1
Men: Jim Courier
Women: Monica Seles

Top Player Earnings
Men: Michael Stich $2,777,411
Women: Monica Seles $2,622,352

Davis Cup: United States

Federation Cup: Germany

ATP World Championships, Frankfurt–Boris Becker
Grand Slam Cup, Munich–Michael Stich
Virginia Slims Championships, NYC–Monica Seles

1992 OLYMPIC GAMES—BARCELONA, SPAIN

Men's singles:
GOLD: Marc Rosset (SUI)
SILVER: Jordi Arrese (ESP)
BRONZE: Goran Ivanisevic (CRO)
Andrei Cherkasov (CIS)

Women's singles:
GOLD: Jennifer Capriati (USA)
SILVER: Steffi Graf (GER)
BRONZE: Mary Joe Fernandez (USA)
Arantxa Sanchez Vicario (ESP)

Men's doubles:
GOLD: Boris Becker and Michael Stich (GER)
SILVER: Wayne Ferreira and Piet Norval (RSA)
BRONZE: Goran Ivanisevic and Goran Prpic (CRO)
Javier Frana and Christian Carlos Miniussi (ARG)

Women's doubles:
GOLD: Gigi Fernandez and Mary Joe Fernandez (USA)
SILVER: Conchita Martinez and Arantxa Sanchez Vicario (ESP)
BRONZE: Natalia Zvereva and Leila Meskhi (CIS)
Rachel McQuillan and Nicole Provis (AUS)

1993 Attack on Seles Mars Year

It seemed like just another April afternoon in Hamburg, Germany. Monica Seles found herself engaged in a Citizen Cup quarterfinal on the slow red clay against Bulgarian Magdalena Maleeva. The 19-year-old left-hander was sitting at a changeover, holding a 6-4, 4-3 lead, hoping to use this tournament to propel her toward a fourth consecutive French Open championship beginning the following month.

But then, suddenly, a possibly deranged German named Guenther Parche emerged from the stands and stabbed Seles in the back with a nine-inch boning knife. The world No. 1 was carried off the court and rushed to the hospital. The physical harm from this tragic moment was not terribly damaging, but the psychological scars would stay with her for some time to come. She wouldn't return to competition until nearly 28 months later.

The Seles Saga was without question the most significant story of 1993, transcending the sport, reminding everyone that even in the relatively tranquil world of tennis, random acts of violence could take place. The game triumphed on a number of other levels, with a surging Pete Sampras and a stalwart Steffi Graf setting the pace, establishing themselves as the top-ranked players for the year.

Sampras captured the two most prestigious titles, collecting his first major crown in nearly three years when he won Wimbledon, then concluding a remarkable summer with a second U.S. Open triumph. Graf secured three of the four biggest crowns, sweeping her third French Open, her fifth Wimbledon, and her third U.S. Open. Beyond that, the 22-year-old American and the 24-year-old German were prolific winners across the board on the men's and women's tours. Sampras was victorious in eight of 23 tournaments, finishing with an impressive 85-16 (.841) match record, posting a 19-match winning streak in the spring. Graf won 10 of 15 tournaments and 76 of 82 matches for an astounding .927 winning percentage. Only once in her last nine tournament appearances was Graf beaten, suffering one other loss in Federation Cup.

Graf garnered the season-ending Virginia Slims Championship at New York's Madison Square Garden while Sampras got to the final of the ATP Tour Championships in Frankfurt. But neither Sampras nor Graf came through in the first of the season's premier events. Jim Courier, the No. 1 ranked player in the world for 1992, successfully defended in the Australian Open final, defeating Stefan Edberg, 6-2, 6-1, 2-6, 7-5, a rematch of the previous year. Courier's crackling backhand returns off Edberg's renowned kick serve were too much for the stylish Swede. Edberg had eliminated Sampras, 7-6 (7-5), 6-3, 7-6 (7-3) in one semi, while Courier beat Michael Stich in the other, 7-6 (7-4), 6-4, 6-2. Ex-champs Boris Becker, seeded fourth, and eighth-seeded Ivan Lendl both made immediate exits, courtesy of low-ranked Swedes, Boris to qualifier Anders Jarryd, 3-6, 7-5, 3-6, 6-3, 6-2, Ivan to Christian Bergstrom, 6-4, 6-4, 2-6, 6-4.

When Seles collided with Graf at Melbourne, it marked the third time in the last four major events that the two superstars had battled in the final. Seles had somehow held back her chief adversary, 6-2, 3-6, 10-8, in the French Open in 1992 but then had been battered, 6-2, 6-1, in the Wimbledon final a month later. Now they had another bruising skirmish under a broiling sun. Although Seles prevailed, 4-6, 6-3, 6-2, to extend her winning streak to three titles and 21 matches in a row in Melbourne, the

match was much closer than the score reflects. They produced one glorious rally after another, driving their groundstrokes with astonishing pace and precision, exploring every inch of the court, pushing each other to the hilt. It took a top-of-the-line Seles to get through this arduous struggle against an almost defiant Graf. On this occasion, the superior shotmaker beat the better athlete.

When all of the leading players assembled again at the world's premier clay court championship, Courier narrowly failed in his spirited bid to become the first American man ever to capture the French three years in a row. The 22-year-old Floridian played with immense pride and professionalism on a day when his primary weapon—the inside-out forehand—was often betraying him, and in the end the ungainly but wily and unwavering Spaniard Sergi Bruguera was too solid in a 6-4, 2-6, 6-2, 3-6, 6-3 victory. It was Bruguera's first major title and the first major for a Spanish man since Manolo Orantes won at Forest Hills in 1975.

Bruguera, 22, had ousted Sampras in the quarterfinals, 6-3, 4-6, 6-1, 6-4 before dismissing the gifted Andrei Medvedev, 6-0, 6-4, 6-2, in a semifinal. A man who had owned Roland Garros for three titles (1984, 86-87), seventh-seeded Lendl was taken out in the opening round of his 52nd major by a French qualifier, No. 297 Stephane Huet, 3-6, 7-5, 6-0, 7-6 (7-2).

Graf, meanwhile, was far from the upper level of her game on her worst surface. She was bothered by a nagging foot injury and may have suffered in a strange way from the absence of Seles. But Steffi beat in succession Jennifer Capriati, 6-3, 7-5, and countrywoman Anke Huber, 6-1, 6-1, to be severely challenged in the final by fifth-seeded Mary Joe Fernandez, the popular American whom she had beaten in the final of the 1990 Australian Open. That had been a relatively uneventful straight-set skirmish with the issue seldom, if ever, in doubt.

This one was a suspenseful showdown from beginning to end. The 21-year-old from Miami, who was 0-10 against Graf, worked her way to a 4-3, 30-15 lead in the third with serve—but Steffi wouldn't budge, 4-6, 6-2, 6-4, winning Roland Garros for the first time since 1988.

In the quarters, Mary Joe staged one of the most extraordinary bounce-backs ever to eliminate Gabriela Sabatini, 1-6, 7-6 (7-4), 10-8. In less than an hour she was ready to be counted out, behind, 6-1, 5-1, 40-30, match point. Gaby lost that point on a double fault, but it seemed insignificant. She was so far ahead. But her breezing became a reverse hurricane of three hours, 34 minutes as Mary Joe ducked three more match points at 5-3, and a fifth in the next game, turning the set her way. She resisted again as Sabatini served for the win at 7-6 in the third, and closed with a blistering backhand for the decisive service break. Prior to that, Sabatini blocked four match points herself. Elated by her survival, Mary Joe beat ex-champ Sanchez Vicario, 6-2, 6-2, in the semis.

During Capriati's fourth-round win over Mary Pierce, 6-4, 7-6 (7-5), Mary's troublesome father, Jim Pierce, was removed from the stands by security guards, who said he was acting "violently," shoving other spectators and shouting at the players. Tournament management withdrew his credentials. It was the start of his being banned from the circuit, eventuating in Mary obtaining a restraining order against him.

Sampras had taken over the No. 1 ranking back in April, but, at Wimbledon, he was still searching for his first major prize since the 1990 U.S. Open. A shoulder injury nearly kept him out of the tournament, but, ultimately, Sampras was ready to make his move. In an All-American final held appropriately on July 4th, Sampras stopped a tenacious Courier, 7-6 (7-3), 7-6 (8-6), 3-6, 6-3. Sampras lost his serve only once in four sets. He was clearly the better grass-court player, but was also fortunate. The conclusion was not easy for Sampras. When he served for the match and reached 40-15, he crouched over in obvious pain with abdominal cramps. Courier saved the first match point, but Sampras sealed his title on the second.

"I was more nervous for this match than for any match I have ever played. I wanted that Wimbledon title, and I couldn't sleep the night before," Sampras said.

In the quarterfinals, he had ousted the seventh-seeded defending champion Andre Agassi in a captivating Centre Court skirmish witnessed by Agassi's renowned friend Barbra Streisand, who caused a considerable commotion when she walked into the celebrated cathedral of the sport. Feeding the Las Vegas glitz kid a barrage of soft sliced backhands and moderately paced forehands, robbing Agassi completely of his rhythm, Sampras stormed to a two-sets-to-love lead. Agassi, however, blasted his way into the contest with some spectacular returns and stellar passing shots. It took stupendous serving and a cool head to pull Sampras through. Serving for the match at 5-4 in the fifth, he delivered three consecutive aces for 40-0 to firmly settle the issue, 6-2, 6-2, 3-6, 3-6, 6-4.

Coming off that emotionally draining victory, Sampras had to deal with three-time former titlist, fourth-seeded Boris Becker in a semifinal. But Sampras didn't lose his serve in a convincing 7-6 (7-5), 6-4, 6-4 win. Third-seeded Courier's semifinal victim was the two-time champ, second-seeded Edberg, 4-6, 6-4, 6-2, 6-4. Surprising himself on the green, Jim got the attention of his mother in the stands, pointed to himself and mouthed, "Who, me?" For the first time since seedings were instituted in 1927, seeds No. 1 through No. 4 made the final four.

The women's final featured Jana Novotna at the peak of her powers right up until the absolute crunch of her contest against the top-seeded Graf. After losing the first set, the 24-year-old Czech demonstrated unequalled completeness in the women's game. She attacked persistently and intelligently to win 10 of the next 12 games, building a 4-1, 40-30 third-set lead. It seemed certain that the eighth-seeded Novotna was going to secure her first major title. But then she double-faulted and fell apart, and Graf came back for a 7-6 (8-6), 1-6, 6-4 victory that was surely a fortunate escape as Novotna flagrantly choked.

"The worst part for Novotna is not so much that she lost the final but that she gave it away, and that will be very hard to live with," said Ann Jones, the 1969 Wimbledon champion who called the match for BBC.

It was a lost opportunity of spectacular proportions for Novotna. She had performed with poise defeating Sabatini in the quarters, 6-4, 6-3, and Martina Navratilova, 6-4, 6-4, in the semis. For the 16th time in 21 Wimbledon appearances, Navratilova had reached the semifinal round, but she seemed ill at ease and out of sorts throughout her loss.

When the last major championship of the season, the U.S. Open, took place at Flushing Meadow, the No. 1 world ranking was on the line. It seemed likely that Courier and Sampras would meet in the final to settle the issue. Courier had appeared in the last three major finals, while Sampras had clearly picked up steam with his Wimbledon success. But that scenario was spoiled when Courier gave a desultory performance on a dark afternoon against the standout, yet erratic, Frenchman Cedric Pioline. Seeded No. 15, Pioline had never beaten Courier. Only three weeks earlier in Indianapolis, Courier dispatched Pioline, 6-3, 6-4, on the way to winning that title over Becker, 7-5, 6-3. But here in the round of 16, Courier lost his intensity and couldn't find his range off the ground. He went down somewhat tamely, 7-5, 6-7 (4-7), 6-4, 6-4, only moments before rain arrived in the stadium. In every conceivable way, Courier had lost his timing.

Not so Sampras. He was stable and confident despite a wave of upsets surrounding him all through the tournament. In the final, Sampras overwhelmed Pioline, 6-4, 6-4, 6-3, for his second Open crown. He was a class above the 24-year-old Frenchman, serving too severely, returning with more authority and consistency.

Courier, the top seed, was not the only leading player who did not deliver. Joining him in the land of upsets were third-seeded Edberg, the two-time defending champion, who fell in the second-round to Karel Novacek, 7-6 (7-3), 6-4, 4-6, 6-4 and No. 4 Becker, taken apart by Sweden's Magnus Larsson, in the fourth round, 6-2, 6-3, 3-6, 7-5.

The semifinals included three players of lowly station: Unseeded Wally Masur and 14th and 15th seeds Aleksandr Volkov of Russia and Pioline. You had to search back to 1967 at Forest Hills to uncover a more common U.S. Championship crowd. Masur staged one of the most incredible comebacks in the fourth round— fighting off a match-point, a two-set deficit and 0-5 fifth-set dearth to beat fellow Aussie Jaime Morgan 3-6, 4-6, 6-3, 6-4, 7-5. Diminished to 13th seed, Lendl, once a final round fixture at Flushing, completed his worst season in the majors, one win at Wimbledon. Back pains contributed to his first-round U.S. loss, to Aussie Neil Borwick: 4-6, 6-4, 3-1, retire.

The women had some surprises of their own, but nothing to compare with the men. Graf won her third Open and her first since 1989, a 6-3, 6-3 triumph over 13th seed Helena Sukova, the 28-year-old Czech who had lost the 1986 final to Navratilova. Graf was too quick, confident and relaxed. She exploited her topspin backhand passing shot with inordinate success. It was hardly a contest. Sukova had come from behind to startle her doubles partner, Sanchez Vicario in the semifinals, 6-7 (3-7), 7-5, 6-2, toppling the second seed with her shrewd, attacking game plan. Sukova also knocked out the third-seeded Navratilova in the round of 16 with first rate serving-and-volleying, 7-5, 6-4. That match, ultimately Navratilova's final U.S. Open singles match, called to mind Sukova's upset of Martina in the 1984 Australian Open, preventing Martina from crafting a Grand Slam that year and also ending her Open era record 74-match winning streak. Graf, meanwhile had trouble getting past Sabatini in the quarters, 6-2, 5-7, 6-1, and Manuela Maleeva Fragniere in the semis, 4-6, 6-1, 6-0.

Despite the absence of Becker, Germany captured the

Davis Cup with a 4-1 victory over Australia in Dusseldorf. The 1991 Wimbledon champion, Stich, led the charge with victories over Jason Stoltenberg, 6-7 (2-7), 6-3, 6-1, 4-6, 6-3 (from 0-2 in the fifth), and the icer over Richard Fromberg, 6-4, 6-2, 6-2. A superior accomplishment probably was the least expected, Stich joining Patrik Kuhnen to jar the world's foremost pair, Mark Woodforde and Todd Woodbridge, 7-6 (7-4), 4-6, 6-3, 7-6 (7-4), for a 2-1 lead after Richard Fromberg beat Marc Goellner, 3-6, 5-7, 7-6 (10-8), 6-2, 9-7, rescuing five match points.

Disappointingly, the U.S. had bowed out in the opening round, 4-1 to Australia on grass in Melbourne. This setback came shortly after the U.S. regained the Cup against Switzerland at the close of 1992 with a team of Agassi, Courier, Sampras and John McEnroe. None of those cared to make the trip Down Under, and the hosts virtually wrapped it up the first day before slight gatherings at Kooyong, a crowded bastion during the Aussies' glory days. Wally Masur stopped Brad Gilbert, 6-3, 6-7 (6-8), 6-4, 6-2, and Mark Woodforde took David Wheaton, 3-6, 7-6 (7-1), 6-4, 6-4, returning on the second day with Todd Woodbridge for the finisher over Jim Grabb and Richey Reneberg, 7-6 (7-5), 6-2, 3-6, 6-7 (3-7), 6-4.

But Agassi reappeared as the U.S. avoided a free-fall to the nether regions (as in 1987) in the September relegation match, a 5-0 win over the Bahamas at Charlotte, N.C., the last of Captain Tom Gorman's U.S. record 16 victories. MaliVai Washington followed Arthur Ashe as the second black to play for the U.S., beating Mark Knowles, 6-7 (5-7), 6-4, 4-6, default, injury, after Agassi ran through Roger Smith, 6-2, 6-2, 6-3. Another new face, Patrick McEnroe, appeared for the clincher (with Reneberg, 6-7 (5-7), 7-5, 6-4, 6-2, over Knowles-Smith), and would captain a victorious U.S. team 14 years later.

Spain's accomplished duo of Sanchez Vicario and Conchita Martinez took apart the Australians in the Fed Cup final at Frankfurt, winning, 3-0. Conchita beat Michelle Jaggard-Lai, 6-0, 6-2, and Arantxa beat Nicole Provis, 6-2, 6-3. But Provis produced an astonishing upset in the opening round, a 2-1 win over Germany. Nicole—a semifinalist at the French Open back in 1988—startled Graf, 6-4, 1-6, 6-1, in the female upset of the year. Liz Smylie and Rennae Stubbs won the decisive doubles over Huber and Barbara Rittner, 7-5, 4-6, 6-3.

Meanwhile, the Germans Graf and Stich came through to claim the singles crowns at the season-ending events in New York and Frankfurt, respectively. Graf got off to a good start and repelled a challenge from Sanchez Vicario in the Virginia Slims final, prevailing 6-1, 6-4, 3-6, 6-1. Stich had his most impressive win of the year when he overturned Sampras in the final of the ATP Tour Championships. Serving seven consecutive aces over two service games in the fourth set, Stich surprised the American, 7-6 (7-3), 2-6, 7-6 (9-7), 6-2, to conclude a terrific late-season surge and move past Courier to No. 2 in the year-end rankings.

All in all, it was a captivating year. In 88 ATP Tour events, 45 different champions surfaced. Americans accounted for 27 of those titles, with no other nation coming close to that total. On another statistical note, Sampras' superiority as a server was reflected emphatically in his tour-leading numbers. He served no fewer than 1,011 aces in 94 charted matches, more than 200

beyond the total of anyone else. He held serve 90 percent of the time and won 82 percent of his first serve points.

Meanwhile, the exuberant combination of Gigi Fernandez and Natasha Zvereva came within two matches of a Grand Slam in doubles, a feat realized only by Navratilova and Pam Shriver in 1984. Fernandez-Zvereva took the Australian over the Aussie-American lineup of Liz Sayers Smylie and Shriver, 6-4, 6-3, and both the French, 6-3, 7-5, and Wimbledon, 6-4, 6-7 (9-11), 6-4 over the Latvian-Czech combo, Larisa Savchenko Neiland and Novotna. They climbed all the way to the penultimate round of the U.S. Open only to have their Slam bid halted by Sukova and Sanchez Vicario, 1-6, 6-3, 6-4. Arantxa and Helena took that title, 6-4, 6-2, over the Argentine-South Africa splicing of Ines Gorrochategui and Amanda Coetzer.

The men's doubles majors were divided four ways. The most extraordinary result occurred at the French where the frequently comedic American brothers, unseeded Murphy and ambidextrous Luke Jensen, settled down to beat also unseeded Germans Marc Goellner and David Prinosil, 6-4, 6-7 (4-7), 6-4. They were the second fraternal victors, following Americans Gene and Sandy Mayer in 1978. Ken Flach, winner of three majors with Robert Seguso, had a new accomplice, lefty Rick Leach, a blending of U.S. Davis Cuppers in taking the homeland title over Czechs Martin Damm and Karel Novacek, 6-7 (3-7), 6-4, 6-2. The Aussie "Woodies," Woodforde and Woodbridge, started their run of success (six titles) at Wimbledon defeating a North American combo, American Pat Galbraith and Canadian Grant Connell, 7-5, 6-3, 7-6 (7-4). But the Australian title went to South African Danie Visser with homeboy Laurie Warder over the Aussie-Swedish pair of John Fitzgerald and Anders Jarryd, 6-4, 6-3, 6-4.

Bjorn Borg's brief, fruitless comebacks were over. He played three more tourneys, and the closest he came to winning a match was his definite farewell to the big league in a town he was visiting for the first time, Moscow. A match point was yanked away by Aleksandr Volkov, who beat him, 4-6, 6-3, 7-6 (9-7), in the Kremlin Cup's first round.

Ultimately, beyond all of the positive developments in 1993, looking past the traumatic experience of Seles, the tennis world mourned the loss of one of its most remarkable leaders. On February 6, Arthur Ashe died of AIDS complications at 49. A singularly revered statesman and spokesman, unofficial worldwide ambassador for the sport, always a voice of reason and integrity, Ashe left behind a shining legacy. The winner of the first U.S. Open in 1968, Australian Open titlist two years later, and a dignified Davis Cup player and captain for his country, Ashe had enjoyed the crowning moment of his career in 1975 when he toppled the mighty Jimmy Connors, 6-1, 6-1, 5-7, 6-4, with a strategic masterpiece in the Wimbledon final.

1993 CHAMPIONS AND LEADERS

Australian Open
Men's Singles Final: Jim Courier (USA) def. Stefan Edberg (SWE), 6-2, 6-1, 2-6, 7-5
Women's Singles Final: Monica Seles (YUG) def. Steff Graf (GER), 4-6, 6-3, 6-2

Men's Doubles Final: Danie Visser (RSA) and Laurie Warder (AUS) def. John Fitzgerald (AUS) and Anders Jarryd (SWE), 6-4, 6-3, 6-4
Women's Doubles Final: Gigi Fernandez (USA) and Natalia Zvereva (BLR) def. Pam Shriver (USA) and Elizabeth Sayers Smylie (AUS), 6-4, 6-3
Mixed Doubles Final: Arantxa Sanchez Vicario (ESP) and Todd Woodbridge (AUS) def. Zina Garrison and Rick Leach (USA), 7-5, 6-4

French Open
Men's Singles Final: Sergi Bruguera (ESP) def. Jim Courier (USA), 6-4, 2-6, 6-2, 3-6, 6-3
Women's Singles Final: Steffi Graf (GER) def. Mary Joe Fernandez (USA), 4-6, 6-2, 6-4
Men's Doubles Final: Luke Jensen and Murphy Jensen (USA) def. Marc Goellner and David Prinosil (GER), 6-4, 6-7 (4), 6-4
Women's Doubles: Gigi Fernandez (USA) and Natalia Zvereva (BLR) def. Larisa Savchenko Neiland (LAT) and Jana Novotna (CZE), 6-3, 7-5
Mixed Doubles Final: Eugenia Maniokova and Andrei Olhovskiy (RUS) def. Elna Reinach and Danie Visser (RSA), 6-2, 4-6, 6-4

Wimbledon
Men's Singles Final: Pete Sampras (USA) def. Jim Courier (USA), 7-6 (3), 7-6 (6), 3-6, 6-3
Women's Singles Final: Steffi Graf (GER) def. Jana Novotna (CZE), 7-6 (6), 1-6, 6-4
Men's Doubles Final: Todd Woodbridge and Mark Woodforde (AUS) def. Grant Connell (CAN) and Patrick Galbraith (USA), 7-5, 6-3, 7-6 (4)
Women's Doubles Final: Gigi Fernandez (USA) and Natalia Zvereva (BLR) def. Jana Novotna (CZE) and Larisa Savchenko Neiland (LAT), 6-4, 6-7 (4), 6-4
Mixed Doubles Final: Martina Navratilova (USA) and Mark Woodforde (AUS) def. Manon Bollegraf and Tom Nijssen (NED), 6-3, 6-4

U.S. Open
Men's Singles Final: Pete Sampras (USA) def. Cedric Pioline (FRA), 6-4, 6-4, 6-3
Women's Singles Final: Steffi Graf (GER) def. Helena Sukova (CZE), 6-3, 6-3
Men's Doubles Final: Ken Flach and Rick Leach (USA) def. Martin Damm and Karel Novacek (CZE), 6-7 (3), 6-4, 6-2
Women's Doubles Final: Arantxa Sanchez Vicario (ESP) and Helena Sukova (CZE) def. Amanda Coetzer (RSA) and Ines Gorrochategui (ARG), 6-4, 6-2
Mixed Doubles Final: Helena Sukova (CZE) and Todd Woodbridge (AUS) def. Martina Navratilova (USA) and Mark Woodforde (AUS), 6-3, 7-6 (6)

Year-End No. 1
Men: Pete Sampras
Women: Steffi Graf

Top Player Earnings
Men: Pete Sampras $4,579,325
Women: Steffi Graf $2,821,337

Davis Cup: Germany

Federation Cup: Spain

ATP World Championships, Frankfurt—Michael Stich
Grand Slam Cup, Munich—Petr Korda
Virginia Slims Championships, NYC—Steffi Graf

A French-U.S. Double For Arantxa

Arantxa Sanchez Vicario won at both the French Open and the US Open in 1994.

As the curtain closed on 1994, two of the greatest players in the history of the game retired simultaneously, taking unparalleled accomplishments with them and leaving with few regrets. Martina Navratilova had planned her departure from singles events nearly a year earlier and realized this would be her final campaign. Ivan Lendl had no intention of quitting, but a nagging back injury forced him to step permanently away from the sport he had dominated with pride and professionalism.

Lendl had little to show for his last year on the ATP Tour. He finished with a mediocre 28-18 match record, reaching only one final in Sydney, losing that to Pete Sampras, 7-6 (5), 6-4 sinking

to No. 54 in the year-end rankings. In his last match as a professional, he walked off the court in the second round at the U.S. Open, his back causing him too much pain to continue. As Lendl left the stadium that afternoon, trailing Bernd Karbacher, 6-4, 7-6 (7-5), 1-0, default, no one had a clue he wouldn't return. Defeating Aussie Neil Borwick in the first round, 7-5, 6-2, 6-3, Ivan registered the last of his 1,070 professional singles wins.

But he was 34, his best days clearly behind him. When the year came to an end, he acknowledged that he would no longer compete.

He had amassed a career prize-money total of $21,624,417. He had been ranked No. 1 in the world a record 270 weeks in all, including 157 weeks in a row during one stretch, on top at year's end four times (1985, '86, '87, '89). From 1981 through 1992 he was never out of the first five. He had appeared in a Tilden-tying record eight consecutive U.S. finals (1982-89), winning the tournament three times during that span. He had captured three French Opens, two Australian Opens and had twice been a Wimbledon finalist. Altogether, he won 94 singles titles, second to Jimmy Connors' 109 for the Open era.

Navratilova lived along the same lines of achievement, but was more of a force in what she said would be her final year. Three months before she turned 38, she reached her 12th Wimbledon singles final, only to fall narrowly short of a 10th title. Nevertheless, she concluded the year at No. 8 in the world, celebrating her 20th consecutive season among the Top 10. Remarkably, 1994 was the only time in that span that Navratilova failed to finish a year in the Top Five.

She was nine times the Wimbledon singles champion, collecting four U.S. Open titles, three Australian, and two French. She won an Open era record 167 singles titles, was ranked No. 1 in the world for a total of 332 weeks, concluding seven seasons on top of the charts. And in one nearly impeccable stretch, she enjoyed five years on the edge of invincibility, winning 44 of 50 tournaments from 1982 through 1986, taking 254 of 260 matches, and setting a modern record with her 74-match winning streak in 1984. Her career match record was 1,438-212 (.872). Both she and Lendl were headed for the International Tennis Hall of Fame.

And yet, while the departures of Lendl and Navratilova were significant (despite the fact that Martina would continue to play

top-flight doubles and mixed doubles, as well as seven singles events from 2002 to 2006) there were other prominent stories.

In the women's game, the effervescent Arantxa Sanchez Vicario came of age at 23. Heading into the 1994 campaign, she had secured only one of the major championships, at Roland Garros five years earlier. In 1994, the cunning baseliner was the only woman to win two majors, capturing a second French Open crown and sealing a first U.S. Open championship.

Although Steffi Graf would remain at No. 1 at year's end, most experts accorded the less talented but incomparably tenacious Spaniard the top ranking, including the ITF. The game's venerable governing body named Sanchez Vicario as their official "World Champion" for 1994 over Graf, an assessment based on Sanchez Vicario's greater accumulation of Virginia Slims points.

But both the ITF and keen analysts among the media based their belief in Sanchez Vicario's preeminence primarily on her outstanding showing in the majors. Meanwhile, Steffi did seize a fourth consecutive major singles title at the start of the season, gaining a fourth Australian Open championship. But it became a year of unexpected diversity after that, with Sanchez Vicario posting her two big triumphs and her countrywoman Conchita Martinez breaking through at Wimbledon for her only major success.

As was the case with the women, three different men took the top prizes. Pete Sampras won the Australian Open for the first time and won Wimbledon again. Sergi Bruguera held on stubbornly to his French Open title. And then a resurgent Andre Agassi captured the championship of his country, at long last the boss at the U.S. Open.

The season started with the favorites flowing Down Under. Sampras had missed two of the previous three Australian Opens with injuries, and was appearing in Melbourne for only the fourth time. But the deeply driven American proceeded to register a third major championship in a row, becoming the first man since Rod Laver in the Australian's Grand Slam campaign of 1969 to pull off this hat trick of sorts. Sampras stopped his countryman and golfing buddy Todd Martin in the final, overcoming a cautious start to win comfortably, 7-6 (7-4), 6-4, 6-4.

Graf was close to letter perfect in her 6-0, 6-2 dismantling of Sanchez Vicario in the women's final, driving her formidable forehand with depth and accuracy and serving with overwhelming power and precision. Both the top-seeded German and the second seed from Spain were clear-cut semifinal victors, Graf upending 10th seed Kimiko Date of Japan, 6-3, 6-3, and Sanchez Vicario dismissing Gabriela Sabatini, 6-1, 6-2. Date's final four appearance was the best major finish for a Japanese woman.

When the best players came to Roland Garros for the French Open, there were many pieces of intrigue spread out across the clay court capital of the world. But above and beyond anyone else, it was Mary Pierce's tournament. The 19-year-old citizen of France, born in Montreal and raised in Florida, blitzed through the draw with ease, hitting her lethal groundstrokes with a velocity seldom, if ever, seen in the women's game. On her way to a first appearance in a major final, Pierce conceded a mere ten games in six matches. The 12th seed was picking everyone apart meticulously. Even the great Graf couldn't contain her. In a dazzling display in the penultimate round, Pierce toppled the top

seed, 6-2, 6-2. In eight service games, Graf was broken a staggering six times, seldom looking so helpless. It was arguably the single most potent performance by a woman all year long, reminiscent in some ways of the absent champ, Monica Seles.

Pierce's remarkable run was suitably noticed by her rivals. As Lindsay Davenport said, "Even Monica couldn't destroy Steffi Graf the way Mary did. It's amazing what Mary has done, great for our game. This is just what we needed, not another Steffi French Open."

But then reality set in for the final. Facing 1989 champion Sanchez Vicario (a semis winner over Martinez, 6-3, 6-1), Pierce was forced to sit around all afternoon, waiting for the rain to stop. They finally started at 6:22 p.m., but had to stop when it rained again with Sanchez Vicario serving at 1-2 and a break point down in the first set. When they returned at noon the next day, the pendulum swung decidedly. Pierce self destructed and the Spaniard won, 6-4, 6-4.

As for the men, Sampras saw his 25-match winning streak in majors end at the hands of Courier in the quarterfinals, 6-4, 5-7, 6-4, 6-4. The week before Roland Garros, Sampras' career-high 29 match-winning streak had come to an end in the World Team Cup against Michael Stich, 3-6, 7-6 (9-7), 6-2. Despite winning the Italian Open over Boris Becker, 6-1, 6-2, 6-2, Pete didn't seem to believe it was his time to rule on the Parisian clay. Courier, close to the top of his game, defeated Sampras for only the third time in 13 meetings to date.

But for the second year in a row, Courier couldn't cope with an imperturbable Bruguera. With the wind blowing fiercely, the defending champion used the adverse conditions to his advantage, while Courier sprayed his groundstrokes dismally out of court. Bruguera won, 6-3, 5-7, 6-3, 6-3, and then handled his unorthodox countryman, Alberto Berasategui, using the same face of the racket for backhand and forehand, 6-3, 7-5, 2-6, 6-1, to keep his French crown.

At Wimbledon, Sampras reaffirmed his status as the best player in the world, losing only a single set in seven matches, setting the record straight with his troublesome adversary Goran Ivanisevic. In 1992, Ivanisevic had stopped Sampras in a four-set semifinal, but this time the American prevailed, 7-6 (7-2), 7-6 (7-5), 6-0, in the final.

Ivanisevic had demoralized Sampras in their 1992 meeting when he released 36 aces over four sets. The towering left-handed Croat came at Sampras with full force again in this battle, banging 16 aces in the first set alone, but Sampras came through in the two tie-breakers and then glided through the third as his opponent surrendered.

The women's Wimbledon was turned upside down on a dark and rainy Tuesday afternoon. Graf was a firm favorite to win her fourth crown in a row, a sixth overall. But she drew the dangerous Lori McNeil in the first round and didn't survive. The 30-year-old from Houston—a U.S. Open semifinalist to Graf seven years earlier and a first-rate grass court player—produced one of the most significant upsets in the history of the tournament, holding her nerve admirably through two rain delays, to win 7-5, 7-6 (7-5).

Never before in the history of the world's most prestigious tournament had the women's No. 1 seed and defending cham-

pion fallen in the first round. And not since the 1984 U.S. Open had Graf made a first-round exit from a major. Graf's startling departure opened up windows everywhere in that half of the draw, and ultimately third-seeded Martinez exploited the opportunity. She crafted an unprecedented run of four consecutive three-set wins to take the title, halting Navratilova in the final with a flock of backhand passers, 6-4, 3-6, 6-3. En route to the championship match, Martinez beat Kristine Radford in the third round, 3-6, 6-3, 6-4; Lindsay Davenport, 6-2, 6-7 (4-7), 6-3 in the quarterfinals; and McNeil, 3-6, 6-2, 10-8 in a dramatic semifinal. Lori had come within two points of winning as Conchita served at 5-6, 30-all.

The 1:59 Martinez-Navratilova showdown on a sweltering afternoon was easily the most compelling female major final of the year. It was Martina's 22nd and, at the time thought to be her last appearance at the All England Club as a singles competitor. When it was over, she took some blades of Centre Court grass with her, and then paid proper tribute to the magnificent counter-attacking of her rival. "No one has ever passed me better off the backhand than Conchita did today," she asserted. Navratilova, a semifinal victor over No. 99 Gigi Fernandez, 6-4, 7-6 (8-6), did make one more Wimbledon singles cameo in 2004, beating Catalina Castano, 6-0, 6-1, losing in the second round to Gisela Dulko, 3-6, 6-3, 6-3.

Through the end of Wimbledon, Sampras had won eight of his 12 tournaments and was thoroughly dominating the game. But over the summer he hardly competed as tendinitis flared up in his ankle after a Davis Cup loss to Richard Krajicek in Rotterdam. Sampras didn't play a single hard-court tournament on the way to the Open.

That set the stage for an unpredictable tournament. Picked off in the first round were No. 2-seeded Ivanisevic by No. 68, hulking German, Markus Zoecke, 6-2, 7-5, 3-6, 7-5, and No. 7-seeded ex-champ Becker by No. 48 Richey Reneberg, 6-1, 6-4, 4-6, 1-6, 7-6 (7-5). In the fourth round, Sampras, the top-seeded defending champ, came in cold and lost gamely on blistered feet during a scorching afternoon to Peruvian Jaime Yzaga, 3-6, 6-3, 4-6, 7-6 (7-4), 7-5. His defeat made many men believe in their chances, but it was an unseeded American who sensed better than anyone else what was entirely possible.

The 1992 Wimbledon champion, Agassi, was ranked a deceptively low No. 20 in the world because he had started his season in March after wrist surgery the previous December. But, like the last unseeded U.S. victor, Fred Stolle, way back in 1966, Andre had too outstanding a dossier to be considered an upstart. In a record run, Andre knocked out five seeds on his way to the Open crown that eluded him in the 1990 final.

It began with No. 12 seed Wayne Ferreira, 7-5, 6-1, 7-5, continued with No. 6 seed Michael Chang, 6-1, 6-7 (3-7) 6-3, 3-6, 6-1, and included No. 13 Thomas Muster, 7-6 (7-5), 6-3, 6-0, and No. 9 Todd Martin, 6-3, 4-6, 6-2, 6-3, setting up a final with Stich, the No. 4 seed. Stich was appearing in his first major final since his stunning run through Wimbledon three years earlier. But on the Flushing hard courts he couldn't stay with Agassi. Stich's first serve and agility around the net were more than neutralized by Agassi's incomparable return of serve and passing shots in the American's 6-1, 7-6 (7-5), 7-5 triumph.

Cheered on by his actress companion, Brooke Shields, Agassi didn't lose serve, allowing Stich 13 points in 14 service games. Agassi won 69 of 89 points on serve, not because he was hurting Stich severely with his serve, but because he dominated the baseline exchanges. Agassi was utterly in control of the rallies.

The women's final was a stirring clash between Graf and Sanchez Vicario. The two leading players had won one major apiece in 1994. Furthermore, Sanchez Vicario had already stopped Graf twice during the year, in finals at Hamburg, saving two match points, 4-6, 7-6 (7-3), 7-6 (8-6), and saving four more at the Canadian Open, 7-5, 1-6, 7-6 (7-4). Now they were at it again on a hard court and Sanchez Vicario won again, 1-6, 7-6 (7-3), 6-4, in a rousing match that lasted two hours, seven minutes.

Graf raced through a 22-minute first set and, in the second, had a break point for 5-4, and might have served for the title if she hadn't missed a backhand return. But Steffi looked apprehensive—a trainer had come on court to treat her painful back after the ninth game—and Arantxa was accelerating. Even though Graf saved three set points to 5-5, and had a 3-2 lead in the tie-breaker with two serves to come, the bouncy Spaniard closed in a five-point rush. The duo kept breaking each other in the tumultuous third, cheered by 21,045 witnesses. But, holding to 4-3, Steffi couldn't resist the scrambling Arantxa, who hung on to take the rest of the games.

Although the German remained safely ahead of Sanchez Vicario in the race for No. 1, this enormously important match convinced the cognoscenti that Sanchez Vicario was now the best player in the world.

In autumn, the long-awaited professional debut of 14-year-old Venus Williams captivated the public. Having been away from even junior tournaments for three years, the tall and talented black girl made her first professional appearance as a wild card in Oakland. She upended Shaun Stafford, 1988 National Intercollegiate champ for Florida, in her first-rounder, 6-3, 6-4, and then bolted to a stunning 6-2, 3-1 lead against Sanchez Vicario. The Spaniard needed all of her renowned guile and match-playing experience to pull through, 2-6, 6-3, 6-0. But Williams had demonstrated that she would be a serious force in the years ahead.

Arantxa won the tournament over Navratilova, 1-6, 7-6 (7-5), 7-6 (7-3), the end of the singles finals line for Martina, her 239th final.

A month earlier, another celebrated coming-out party for a 14-year-old occurred in Zurich. Swiss Martina Hingis (three months younger than Venus and named after Martina Navratilova) was a more familiar figure than Venus, having won international junior titles from age 12. Also a wild card entry in her pro debut, she beat ex-American Intercollegiate champ Patty Fendick 6-4, 6-3 before losing to second-seeded Pierce, 6-4, 6-0 in the second round.

At the end of the season, it was time for Sampras to step forward again and underline his greatness. Having been hobbled by injuries too often in the second half of the year, he won the ATP Tour World Championship in Frankfurt to remain No. 1 for the second straight year.

After overcoming a surging Agassi in a hotly contested semifinal, 4-6, 7-6 (7-5), 6-3, Sampras reversed a loss to Becker in the round robin by besting the German, 4-6, 6-3, 7-5, 6-4. Sampras had

won his 10th tournament of the year, a feat last realized by Lendl in 1989.

That same November week at New York's Madison Square Garden, Sabatini came out of a long slump to capture the Virginia Slims Championship. She crushed Davenport, 6-3, 6-2, 6-4, in the final for her first tournament win since the 1992 Italian Open. The 24-year-old "Divine Argentine" had opened the week with an emotional 6-4, 6-2 victory over Navratilova in Martina's singles finale. It was "Martina Navratilova Night" in the Garden as a banner bearing her name was hoisted to the rafters.

Meanwhile, there was one more big-money event left for the men, the Grand Slam Cup in Munich, and Sweden's Magnus Larsson took it. The multi-faceted 24-year-old ousted Agassi 6-3, 1-6, 6-0 in the quarterfinals, Martin 6-4, 6-4, 6-1 in a best-of-five-set semifials and, in the final, singed Sampras, 7-6 (8-6), 4-6, 7-6 (7-5), 6-4.

Larsson, an intimidating 6-foot-5 blond basher, collected $1,500,000, but he would be prouder of his role in helping to bring Sweden its fifth Davis Cup, defeating Russia, in the final in Moscow. The Russians were first-time finalists, having astonishingly sabotaged Germany in Hamburg, 4-1. With tennis addict President Boris Yeltsin in the crowds of 14,000 at Moscow's cavernous Olympic Stadium, the home side, led by the brilliant 20-year-old Yevgeny Kafelnikov—who rose from No. 103 to No. 11 within a year—had a wonderful chance. But the Swedes were more composed in the crunch, winning the first three matches in a 4-1 decision. In singles, Stefan Edberg, ducking a match point, led off over lefty Aleksandr Volkov, 6-4, 6-2, 6-7 (2-7), 0-6, 8-6 and Larsson beat Kafelnikov, 6-0, 6-2, 3-6, 2-6, 6-3, setting up a Cup-clinching doubles win for Jan Apell and Jonas Bjorkman over Kafelnikov and Andrei Olhovskiy, 6-7 (4-7), 6-2, 6-3, 1-6, 8-6 .

Sweden had defeated the U.S. in a semifinal at Goteborg after rookie Captain Tom Gullikson called on a worn-out Sampras. Clearly not fit, Sampras barely got through the first day, defeating Larsson, 6-7 (3-7), 6-4, 6-2, 7-6 (7-3). Todd Martin stopped Edberg, 6-2, 2-6, 6-4, 6-3, so the U.S. led 2-1 when Apell and Bjorkman, the ATP world doubles champs, and 4-0 in Cup play, kept it alive with a 6-4, 6-4, 3-6, 6-2 win over rookies Jared Palmer and Jonathan Stark. However, Sampras had to quit with a calf injury after losing the first set, 6-3, to Edberg. Sweden then clinched the victory, 3-2, on Larsson's 5-7, 6-2, 6-2, 6-4, decision over Martin.

Spain, in the lively persons of Sanchez Vicario and Martinez, ruled the women's world again, beating the U.S. 3-0 in the Federation Cup finale at Frankfurt. Neither singles starter came close in the worst of all American beatings (14 games): Davenport lost to Arantxa, 6-2, 6-1, and Mary Joe Fernandez to Conchita, 6-2, 6-2 as the Spaniards, enjoying Frankfurt clay, seized their third Cup. As icing, Arantxa and Conchita beat the two Fernandez's, 6-3, 6-4.

1994 CHAMPIONS AND LEADERS

Australian Open
Men's Singles Final: Pete Sampras (USA) def. Todd Martin (USA), 7-6 (4), 6-4, 6-4
Women's Singles Final: Steffi Graf (GER) def. Arantxa Sanchez Vicario (ESP), 6-0, 6-2

Men's Doubles Final: Jacco Eltingh and Paul Haarhuis (NED) def. Byron Black (ZIM) and Jonathan Stark (USA), 6-7 (3), 6-3, 6-4, 6-3
Women's Doubles Final: Gigi Fernandez (USA) and Natalia Zvereva (BLR) def. Patty Fendick and Meredith McGrath (USA), 6-3, 4-6, 6-4
Mixed Doubles Final: Larisa Savchenko Neiland (LAT) and Andrei Olhovskiy (RUS) def. Helena Sukova (CZE) and Todd Woodbridge (AUS), 7-5, 6-7 (3), 6-4

French Open
Men's Singles Final: Sergi Bruguera (ESP) def. Alberto Berasategui (ESP), 6-3, 7-5, 2-6, 6-1
Women's Singles Final: Arantxa Sanchez Vicario (ESP) def. Mary Pierce (FRA), 6-4, 6-4
Men's Doubles: Byron Black (ZIM) and Jonathan Stark (USA) def. Jan Apell and Jonas Bjorkman (SWE), 6-4, 7-6 (5)
Women's Doubles Final: Gigi Fernandez (USA) and Natalia Zvereva (BLR) def. Lindsay Davenport and Lisa Raymond (USA), 6-2, 6-2
Mixed Doubles Final: Kristie Boogert and Menno Oosting (NED) def. Larisa Savchenko Neiland (LAT) and Andrei Olhovskiy (RUS), 7-5, 3-6, 7-5

Wimbledon
Men's Singles Final: Pete Sampras (USA) def. Goran Ivanisevic (CRO), 7-6 (2), 7-6 (5), 6-0
Women's Singles Final: Conchita Martinez (ESP) def. Martina Navratilova (USA), 6-4, 3-6, 6-3
Men's Doubles Final: Todd Woodbridge and Mark Woodforde (AUS) def. Grant Connell (CAN) and Patrick Galbraith (USA), 7-6 (3), 6-3, 6-1
Women's Doubles Final: Gigi Fernandez (USA) and Natalia Zvereva (BLR) def. Jana Novotna (CZE) and Arantxa Sanchez Vicario (ESP), 6-4, 6-1
Mixed Doubles Final: Helena Sukova (CZE) and Todd Woodbridge (AUS) def. Lori McNeil and T.J. Middleton (USA), 3-6, 7-5, 6-3

U.S. Open
Men's Singles Final: Andre Agassi (USA) def. Michael Stich (GER), 6-1, 7-6 (5), 7-5
Women's Singles Final: Arantxa Sanchez Vicario (ESP) def. Steffi Graf (GER), 1-6, 7-6 (3), 6-4
Men's Doubles Final: Jacco Eltingh and Paul Haarhuis (NED) def. Todd Woodbridge and Mark Woodforde (AUS), 6-3, 7-6 (1)
Women's Doubles Final: Arantxa Sanchez Vicario (ESP) and Jana Novotna (CZE) def. Katerina Maleeva (BUL) and Robin White (USA), 6-3, 6-3
Mixed Doubles Final: Elna Reinach (RSA) and Patrick Galbraith (USA) def. Jana Novotna (CZE) and Todd Woodbridge (USA), 6-2, 6-4

Year-End No. 1
Men: Pete Sampras
Women: Steffi Graf

Top Player Earnings
Men: Pete Sampras $4,857,812
Women: Arantxa Sanchez Vicario $2,943,665

Davis Cup: Sweden

Federation Cup: Spain

ATP World Championships, Frankfurt—Pete Sampras
Grand Slam Cup, Munich—Magnus Larrson
Virginia Slims Championships, New York—Gabriela Sabatini

1995

Simply The Best
Sampras vs. Agassi

Andre Agassi shared the same goals and knew that more often than not they would need to go through each other to get what they wanted. That meant competing on a very lofty level, which the two Americans emphatically did over and over again.

In the end, it was Sampras who demonstrated beyond a doubt that he was the better big-match player despite losing three of his five skirmishes with his countryman. Agassi had come out of the blocks in style at the Australian Open, overcoming the defending champion Sampras in a hard-fought, four-set final. Sampras then retaliated at Indian Wells, Calif. Agassi struck back at The Lipton at Key Biscayne, Fla., and then he subdued Sampras again to take the Canadian Open.

By the time the two best players in the world reached the final of the U.S. Open in September, they were not deceiving themselves in the least. They knew precisely what was at stake, fully recognized the magnitude of the moment. With Sampras having won Wimbledon two months earlier and Agassi boasting a record of decidedly more consistency, this was the closest tennis could come to a heavyweight championship of the world. And when it was over, only Sampras was still standing, a four-set winner over his worthiest rival, and now the holder of the two most prestigious prizes in tennis.

All year long, they went at it in a genuine battle for supremacy. They met in the first major final of the season and again in the last. Their contrasting playing styles and personalities gave the game a spark that had been missing. To be sure, this was a rivalry between two great players devoid of animosity toward each other. But the fact remained that both Pete Sampras and

And yet, the year provided drama on other levels. At Wimbledon, the volatile left-handed American Jeff Tarango confronted Germany's Alex Mronz in a third-round match on an outside court. Mronz had won the first set in a tie-breaker, then fell behind early in the second. Umpire Bruno Rebeuh overruled on a service call which was questioned by Tarango. The crowd

came down on Tarango, with some of the fans yelling at him, prompting Tarango to respond: "Shut up!"

Rebeuh gave Tarango a code violation for an "audible obscenity," a very questionable decision in light of Tarango's relatively tame comment. Tarango was losing control now, and called Rebeuh "corrupt." The umpire then assessed a point penalty against Tarango, which cost Tarango a game. Tarango asked for a supervisor, who stuck by Rebeuh's decisions. Tarango then walked off the court. As if that was not extraordinary theater in itself, Tarango's wife, Benedicte, went after Rebeuh, catching up to the umpire near the referee's office and slapping him a couple of times, according to an eyewitness.

On to the interview room, where Tarango disgraced himself even more with a rambling press conference, elaborating on his ludicrous charge of "corruption" against Rebeuh. He was fined $5,000 for walking off the court, $10,000 for his insulting remarks about Rebeuh, and another $500 for his "shut up" stance against the courtside crowd.

But the largely self-inflicted damage was not done. He was suspended from ATP Tour events for two weeks later in the year, and fined $20,000, a figure upheld by the ATP. Furthermore, Tarango was banned from Wimbledon the following year for his actions. The fines were later reduced on appeal, and, in fairness to the player, umpire Rebeuh should have recused himself since there was animosity between them.

Beyond the Tarango happening and the Sampras-Agassi rivalry, the game welcomed back a superstar, a player of inimitable shotmaking skills, a champion who realized that the time had come to put the past behind her and get on with her future. Monica Seles did just that, did it as only she can, and made a remarkable return to tennis.

Still trying to sort out that horrific moment in April, 1993, when she had been stabbed in Hamburg, she had taken a long time to recover emotionally. Now she was ready at last, and the 21-year-old made a spectacular return in Toronto. She had been gone almost 28 months but there was scant evidence of that as she resumed her winning ways immediately.

Cracking groundstrokes with her customary authority, moving opponents around at will, competing with unabashed joy, she rolled through the field at the Canadian Open, dropping only 14 games in five matches, routing Gabriela Sabatini, 6-1, 6-1, in the semifinals, crushing Amanda Coetzer in a lopsided final, 6-0, 6-1. She was nearly as impressive at the U.S. Open and, despite losing a rousing final to Steffi Graf, she remained on top of her game. But tendinitis in her knee and an ankle injury kept her out of action for the rest of the year.

It was a year which began with Mary Pierce delivering on the promise she had made the previous year as runner-up at the French Open. Having trained with dedication in the month leading up to the Australian Open, she was rewarded with her first major title. In seven nearly flawless matches, she did not drop a set; not once was she pushed beyond 6-4. She cut down a cluster of players who had given her serious problems in the past. Seeded No. 4, she halted Germany's Anke Huber, 6-2, 6-4, in the round of 16, Natasha Zvereva, 6-1, 6-4, in the quarters, second seed Conchita Martinez, 6-3, 6-1, in the semifinals, and then avenged her Roland Garros defeat by Arantxa Sanchez Vicario, toppling the top seed, 6-3, 6-2, in the final.

Mary had come a long way in a few years, enduring the pain of an abusive father, Jim Pierce, who was banned from all tournaments for his unruly behavior. But while she paid tribute to her then coach Nick Bollettieri for her breakthrough triumph in Melbourne, she also gave her father the credit she felt he deserved for the work ethic he instilled for Mary in the early years. As Pierce said after her Australian Open success, "I used to train all day long until the sun went down. My father pushed me very hard. In eight years, I probably did the equivalent of 15 years work. But I don't regret it. I have the discipline now, and I am a perfectionist."

Andre Agassi could have spoken almost identical words after the Australian, his second straight major title. He, too, had a father, Mike Agassi, who pushed him to the hilt, and now he was reaping the rewards of his tennis upbringing, not to mention his years of hard work at the Bollettieri boot camp, and strong strategic guidance alongside the brainy Brad Gilbert. Agassi beat Sampras, 4-6, 6-1, 7-6 (8-6), 6-4, in a remarkable final which was settled in the third-set tie-break. As Gilbert would say later, "I felt whoever won that tie-breaker would take control of the match"—which Andre did with splendid returns from two set points down.

For Agassi, playing in his first Australian Open, it was a landmark achievement. For Sampras, it was a stressful time. His coach and close friend Tim Gullikson had collapsed early in the tournament during a practice session, was sent to the hospital for tests, and had to fly home for treatment of a brain tumor before Sampras met Jim Courier in the quarterfinals.

Sampras bested Courier from two-sets-to-love down, 6-7 (4-7), 6-7 (3-7), 6-3, 6-4, 6-3, in a classic, but not before a fan yelled out early in the final set, "Do it for your coach." That jarred the normally imperturbable Sampras, who broke down in tears at a changeover and continued to cry when he went to the opposite side of the court to serve the next game. But he somehow kept serving aces through his tears and got the job done. Before Courier, he had erased a two-set lead of Magnus Larsson, 4-6, 6-7 (4-7), 7-5, 6-4, 6-4. After Courier, he came from a set down to stop Michael Chang and reach the final, 6-7 (6-8), 6-3, 6-4, 6-4.

By the time the French Open had begun, Sampras himself was more vulnerable on the court than he had been for a long while. He had suffered a crisis of confidence on the European clay-court circuit, losing in the first round at the Italian to Fabrice Santoro, 6-4, 6-3. Pete's title passed on to Thomas Muster, who beat Sergi Bruguera, 3-6, 7-6 (7-5), 6-2, 6-3. Pete's feet of clay were on display at the French in a first-round loss spread over two days to an obscure Austrian, persistent No. 24 Gilbert Schaller, 7-6 (7-3), 4-6, 6-7 (4-7), 6-4.

Agassi, who had moved past Sampras to No. 1 on the weekly ATP computer in April, was a bigger threat to win on the slow red dirt of Roland Garros. He stormed into the quarterfinals without the loss of a set but then was ushered out of the tournament abruptly by the Russian Yevgeny Kafelnikov, 6-4, 6-3, 7-5. But Kafelnikov was no match for the relentlessly consistent left-handed Austrian, Muster, 6-4, 6-0, 6-4, who moved into his first major final with full conviction. Muster's self-assurance was more than justi-

fiable. He would win 65 of 67 matches on clay over the season, and secured no fewer than 11 titles on that surface. Six years after his magnificent championship of 1989, 23-year-old Chang, seeded No. 6, was back in the title bout, having brought down two-time champ, Bruguera, 6-4, 7-6 (7-5), 7-6 (7-0). Perpetual motion Michael rang up a 5-2 lead that melted as Muster muscled his way through nine straight games, taking over for a 7-5, 6-2, 6-4, triumph.

Graf missed the Australian Open due to a calf injury and coming into Roland Garros, she was skeptical about her chances as perennial problems with her back persisted. But Graf came to play, played to win, and emerged with an immensely satisfying 16th major title. In securing a fourth French Open crown, Graf renewed her rivalry with Sanchez Vicario. Arantxa, the defending champion, looked likely to hold on to her title when she split the first two sets of the final with Steffi, but Graf produced perhaps the best set of clay-court tennis in her career to prevail, 7-5, 4-6, 6-0. In the final set, a devastating Graf, won 24 of 30 points. She had a hard semifinal, snapping Conchita Martinez's 24-match winning streak, 6-3, 6-7 (5-7), 6-3.

"There were some very difficult weeks for me before I came to this tournament," reflected Graf. "I never really thought I could get to the final. I only had eight or nine days of practice before the tournament and I had been sick. I wasn't sure if that would be enough to get me through."

It was the year of the miracle comeback. In the third round, American Chanda Rubin, in the deepest of pits—0-5, 0-40 in the third set, somehow leaped nine match points to beat No. 5-seeded Czech Jana Novotna, 7-6 (10-8), 4-6, 8-6!

At Wimbledon, Sampras took another substantial step up the historical ladder of the sport, becoming the first American man ever to win the world's most prestigious tournament three years in a row. A morale-boosting tournament triumph at Queen's Club in London over missile-serving German Marc Goellner, 6-7 (4), 6-2, 13-11 in the semifinals and Guy Forget 7-6 (7-3), 7-6 (8-6) in the final—only the second tournament win for Sampras all year—gave the concussive American just the lift he needed. Sampras was given a demanding test by Goran Ivanisevic in his semifinal, 7-6 (9-7), 4-6, 6-3, 4-6, 6-3 as the Croatian left-hander, seeded fourth, served 38 aces. But Sampras' greater stability pulled him through in a five-set victory. In a battle of Wimbledon heroes for the title, Sampras was too good for the three-time champ Boris Becker. In four sets, he was impervious on serve, didn't even face a single break point. Thus, in three Wimbledon finals encompassing eleven sets and a trio of different opponents—Sampras had lost only one service game!

Becker gave himself a considerable boost by taking the first set, in a 7-5 tie-breaker, but was soundly beaten, 6-7 (5-7), 6-2, 6-4, 6-2, as Sampras broke him five times over the next three sets. "In the 1980s," said a sporting Becker after his loss, "Centre Court was my court. But now it belongs to Pete Sampras."

Nevertheless, Becker had brought back those glory days of the '80s in a rousing semifinal comeback over Agassi, the top seed. Agassi was almost beyond belief at the outset, sprinkling the Centre Court with brilliant service returns and passing shots, making the game look impossibly easy in building a 6-2, 4-1, two-

service-break lead. But then Becker found his form. When the burly German got back on even terms by seizing the second set, 7-1, in the tie-breaker, Agassi's despondency was almost tangible and Becker completed a 2-6, 7-6 (7-1), 6-4, 7-6 (7-1) triumph.

The men surely had a very good Wimbledon, but in many ways the women upstaged them at the end. Graf and Sanchez Vicario contested a final which will be placed up there among the five best Open era title matches. It had already been a bruising and alluring battle when the two towering competitors reached 5-5 in the third. But the 11th game of the final set took the match into another category altogether. They fought ferociously for 20 minutes, through 13 deuces and 32 points. Sanchez Vicario had eight game points before Graf, with lusty forehands, set up her sixth break point and cashed it. Ultimately, Arantxa lost a third straight major tournament final, 4-6, 6-1, 7-5. Perhaps it was the single greatest game in the history of women's tennis at Wimbledon.

As a footnote Martina Navratilova continued to romp on Wimbledon sod. She and Jonathan Stark grabbed the mixed title over Gigi Fernandez and Czech Cyril Suk, 6-4, 6-4. It was the 38-year-old southpaw's 56th major.

As the players moved into the heart of summer, no one sizzled more than Agassi. Along the way to Flushing Meadow, Agassi played too well for his own good, capturing four tournament titles in a row: Washington over Stefan Edberg, 6-4, 2-6, 7-5; the Canadian Open over Sampras, 3-6, 6-2, 6-3; Cincinnati over Chang, 7-5, 6-2 and New Haven over Richard Krajicek, 3-6, 7-6 (7-2), 6-3. Andre won 20 matches in a row and he thrived in the oppressive heat to become the clear favorite to win the U.S. Open. But second-seeded Sampras was not unduly worried. The pivotal showdown of the year, the final that everyone had been hoping for, was settled to a very large extent by the final point of the opening set. Agassi was serving down a set point—4-5, advantage out—when the two players produced a rally they did not replicate for the rest of their careers. Driving each other from corner to corner, they went for their shots boldly but not recklessly. Finally, Sampras concluded the suspenseful 21-stroke sequence with a perfectly controlled, high-trajectory topspin backhand crosscourt into an empty space. Sampras had the set and it carried him swiftly through the second set. Although Agassi came from a break down to take the third, he could not hold Sampras back in the fourth and Sampras closed out the account, 6-4, 6-3, 4-6, 7-5. In the semifinals, it was Andre getting back at Becker, 7-6 (7-4), 7-6 (7-2), 4-6, 6-4, and Pete, breaking in the last games of the first, third and fourth sets, handling Courier, 6-4, 5-7, 6-4, 7-5.

"That final was the biggest match of the year for me," he commented, "and one of the biggest in my career. Everything kind of built up to that match the whole year. When I woke up in the morning I thought if I lost, how crushed I would have felt, how great it would be to win. I realized how important it all was to me."

The women, meanwhile, were celebrating a similar conclusion to their Open. Not since January of 1993— Seles over Graf at the Australian Open—had Monica and Steffi met head-to-head. This was a particularly emotional reunion for the two superstars, both vividly recalling that an allegedly deranged Guenther

Parche, allegedly a fan of Graf's, had interrupted Seles' career for more than two years with a knife stroke.

The two great champions were ready for this confrontation, plainly delighted to be bringing out the best in each other. The first set was as good as it gets, featuring one remarkable baseline rally after another. Graf lost only six points in six service games on her way to a first-set tie-breaker which Seles led, 6-5, serving at set point. Monica was convinced she had served an ace on the center line at this critical point, but it was called fault, a fraction of an inch wide.

Seles was rattled. Then Graf rifled a forehand return winner off a second serve. Steffi took that sequence, 8-points-to-6, but let her guard down, and Seles struck all of her targets in a 6-0 second set. Graf was down, 0-30, in the first game of the third and break point in the third game, but held on both times. It was her match now as her serve regained velocity and accuracy, and her conviction came back. Seles seemed weary, and her forehand return deteriorated. And so for the seventh time in 11 career meetings—the fourth time in seven at major events—Graf had won, 7-6 (8-6), 0-6, 6-3. But Seles had unmistakably triumphed by even returning to that elite level of the game.

Nobody else is welcome (well, almost)—that was the directive from the doubles teams of Gigi Fernandez-Zvereva and Novotna-Sanchez Vicario. They were adversaries in three of the four major finals. Australia and Wimbledon went to Arantxa and Jana, 6-3, 6-7 (3-7), 6-4, and 5-7, 7-5, 6-4. France went to Gigi and Natasha, 6-7 (6-8), 6-4, 7-5—as did the U.S., but over Rennae Stubbs and Brenda Schultz-McCarthy, 7-5, 6-3. The Aussie-Dutch pair the quarterfinal conquerors of Arantxa and Jana.

Aussies Mark Woodforde and Todd Woodbridge captured the two biggest of the biggies: Wimbledon for a third straight time, over Americans Rick Leach and Scott Melville, 7-5, 7-6 (10-8), 7-6 (7-5) and the U.S. over an American-Aussie connection of Alex O'Brien and Sandon Stolle (son of Hall of Famer Fred Stolle), 6-3, 6-3.

In November, the men's and women's season-ending championships needlessly competed against each other again. In Frankfurt, Becker was at his best in a 7-6 (7-3), 6-0, 7-6 (7-5) final-round win over Chang. Chang had ousted Sampras, 6-4, 6-4, in the semifinals, but Sampras was aware by then that the No. 1 computer ranking for the year already belonged to him. Becker won a close three-set skirmish with Sweden's Thomas Enqvist in his semifinal, 6-4, 6-7 (5-7), 7-5.

Meanwhile, at Madison Square Garden in New York the same week, Graf managed to conduct one last piece of productive business. She survived an entertaining and fast-paced five sets with countrywoman Anke Huber, 6-1, 4-6, 6-1, 4-6, 6-3 to win the WTA Tour Championship. With this triumph, she concluded what she acknowledged was her most satisfying year. She waged a more selective campaign, playing fewer matches than any of her other big years, but won the three most important tournaments and four of the top five events. Furthermore, Graf won 47 of 49 matches, won 32 matches in a row and, in one stretch, six consecutive tournaments. It was indeed a very good year.

Sampras, whose Davis Cup singles experiences hadn't been positive, turned that part of his life around by winning all six

starts—the last two spectacular—as the U.S. took the Cup in a Cold War-revisited drama over Russia, 3-2, at Moscow. Pete illuminated his greatness within Olympic Stadium, on a clay court that had been trucked in especially to thwart him, by belting his way to the rarest of triples: Having a hand in all the points in a 3-2 (or 3-1) Cup round victory. He is only the tenth member of that club, launched by Henri Cochet of France against Great Britain in 1931.

But it all may have come down to one stroke, the last one Pete hit in his opening salvo, a 3-6, 6-4, 6-3, 6-7 (5-7), 6-4, squeaker over ceaseless retriever Andrei Chesnokov. Sampras was dehydrated and cramping as he and Chesnokov neared the climax. At 5-4, 40-15 in the fifth set, Sampras missed a volley, blowing a first match point. Then came a desperate all-court exchange. Pete going to the net, being pushed back. Stroke after stroke. Pete approached again on a net-skinning forehand, the 22nd stroke, and Chesnokov ran feverishly, overtaking the ball—but couldn't flick it within the court. As he raised his arms in victory, Sampras abruptly collapsed. He was lugged to the dressing room by teammates and team staff to be revitalized.

"If my ball is good I don't think Pete can hit another shot... I win," said Chesnokov. Sampras tended to agree. "I don't know if I could have gone on."

Sampras was back the next day to play doubles. After Kafelnikov beat Courier to make it 1-1, Pete and Todd Martin (returning superbly from the left court) were dynamite in demoralizing Kafelnikov and Andrei Olhovskiy, 7-5, 6-4, 6-3. Pete then turned in a bravura Cup-embracing performance that quickly dampened and muted the crowd of 16,000, beating Kafelnikov, 6-2, 6-4, 7-6 (7-4).

Chesnokov had been the hero of Russia's 3-2 semifinal jolting of Germany, scoring the decisive point in a totally unbelievable four-hour, 18-minute triumph over Michael Stich, 6-4, 1-6, 1-6, 6-3, 14-12, in which he blocked nine match points against Stich's serve. The Russians had set a speed trap for Germany's Becker and Stich by importing clay from Sweden at a cost of $70,000. The expenditure was repeated, the seating enlarged to 16,000, for the American visitors, but there was no dirty trick permitted that time. To further slow the Germans, the hosts had watered the court down to a morass. For that bit of liquid refreshing of the home-court advantage, the Russian federation was fined $25,000 by the International Tennis Federation.

France was the first U.S. victim in the Davis Cup chase, 4-1, indoors at St. Petersburg, Fla. Martin lost to Cedric Pioline, 7-5, 6-2, 6-4, but was charged up to take the clincher from Guy Forget, 6-3, 7-6 (7-3), 7-6 (7-5) after Courier beat Forget, 6-1, 6-2, 6-2, and the Palmer-Reneberg unit beat Olivier Delaitre and Forget, 6-4, 3-6, 6-3, 6-4. Italy was easy, 5-0, on clay at Palermo, as Agassi and Sampras came aboard.

Martin was the decider again at Las Vegas in a 4-1 semifinal decision over Sweden, subbing for Agassi, who was injured while beating 30-year-old re-tread Mats Wilander the first day, 7-6 (7-5), 6-2, 6-2. Pete beat Thomas Enqvist, 6-3, 6-4, 3-6, 6-3, and it was 2-0. But doubles went Sweden's way, 29-year-old Edberg and Bjorkman over Martin and Stark, 6-3, 6-4, 6-4. So Martin came in for Andre and took Enqvist, 7-5, 7-5, 7-6 (7-2), to book the tickets to Moscow.

Davis Cup-like alterations came to the Federation Cup, the name of which was pointlessly shaved to Fed Cup. A World Group was formed for eight countries to compete for the Cup itself in a Davis Cup-style best-of-five match series, either home or away, over a period of seven months. This replaced the best-of-three match format used since 1963, with all entrants gathering in one location for a week of competition.

The results didn't change in 1995. Those sensational senoritas, Sanchez Vicario and Martinez, won a third straight Cup for Spain, 3-2, over the U.S. in Valencia. Martinez (6-0 for the season) had led off over Chanda Rubin, 7-5, 7-6 (7-3), and clinched the next day in the third match, over Mary Joe Fernandez, 6-3, 6-4. Sanchez Vicario took the second point over Fernandez, 6-3, 6-2, and the Spaniards had won 13 straight series.

1995 CHAMPIONS AND LEADERS

Australian Open
Men's Singles Final: Andre Agassi (USA) def. Pete Sampras (USA), 4-6, 6-1, 7-6 (8-6), 6-4

Women's Singles Final: Mary Pierce (FRA) def. Arantxa Sanchez Vicario (ESP), 6-3, 6-2

Men's Doubles Final: Jared Palmer and Richey Reneberg (USA) def. Mark Knowles (BAH) and Daniel Nestor (CAN), 6-3, 3-6, 6-3, 6-2

Women's Doubles Final: Jana Novotna (CZE) and Arantxa Sanchez Vicario (ESP) def. Gigi Fernandez (USA) and Natalia Zvereva (BLR), 6-3, 6-7 (3), 6-4

Mixed Doubles Final: Natalia Zvereva (BLR) and Rick Leach (USA) def. Gigi Fernandez (USA) and Cyril Suk (CZE), 7-6 (4), 5-7 (3), 6-4

French Open
Men's Singles Final: Thomas Muster (AUT) def. Michael Chang (USA), 7-5, 6-2, 6-4

Women's Singles Final: Steffi Graf (GER) def. Arantxa Sanchez Vicario (ESP), 7-5, 4-6, 6-0

Men's Doubles Final: Jacco Eltingh and Paul Haarhuis (NED) def. Nicklas Kulti and Magnus Larsson (SWE), 6-7 (3), 6-4, 6-1

Women's Doubles Final: Gigi Fernandez (USA) and Natalia Zvereva (BLR) def. Jana Novotna (CZE) and Arantxa Sanchez Vicario (ESP), 6-7 (6), 6-4, 7-5

Mixed Doubles Final: Larisa Savchenko Neiland (LAT) and Mark Woodforde (AUS) def. Jill Hetherington (CAN) and John-Laffnie de Jager (RSA), 7-6 (8), 7-6 (4)

Wimbledon
Men's Singles Final: Pete Sampras (USA) def. Boris Becker (GER), 6-7(5), 6-2, 6-4, 6-2

Women's Singles Final: Steffi Graf (GER) def. Arantxa Sanchez Vicario (ESP), 4-6, 6-1, 7-5

Men's Doubles Final: Todd Woodbridge and Mark Woodforde (AUS) def. Rick Leach and Scott Melville (USA), 7-5, 7-6 (8), 7-6 (5)

Women's Doubles Final: Jana Novotna (CZE) and Arantxa Sanchez Vicario (ESP) def. Gigi Fernandez (USA) and Natalia Zvereva (BLR), 5-7, 7-5, 6-4

Mixed Doubles Final: Martina Navratilova and Jonathan Stark (USA) def. Gigi Fernandez (USA) and Cyril Suk (CZE), 6-4, 6-4

U.S. Open
Men's Singles Final: Pete Sampras (USA) def. Andre Agassi (USA), 6-4, 6-3, 4-6, 7-5

Women's Singles Final: Steffi Graf (GER) def. Monica Seles (USA), 7-6 (6), 0-6, 6-3

Men's Doubles Final: Todd Woodbridge and Mark Woodforde (AUS) def. Alex O'Brien (USA) and Sandon Stolle (AUS), 6-3, 6-3

Women's Doubles Final: Gigi Fernandez (USA) and Natalia Zvereva (BLR) def. Brenda Schultz-McCarthy (NED) and Rennae Stubbs (AUS), 7-5, 6-3

Mixed Doubles Final: Meredith McGrath and Matt Lucena (USA) def. Gigi Fernandez (USA) and Cyril Suk (CZE), 6-4, 6-4

Year-End No. 1
Men: Pete Sampras
Women: Steffi Graf & Monica Seles

Top Player Earnings
Men: Pete Sampras $5,415,066
Women: Steffi Graf $2,538,620

Davis Cup: United States

Fed Cup: Spain

ATP World Championships, Frankfurt—Boris Becker
Grand Slam Cup, Munich—Goran Ivanisevic
Corel Championships, NYC—Steffi Graf

1996 A Wimbledon Surprise, Agassi Wins Olympic Gold

greensward as the Championships' singular streaker, she was perhaps Britain's most notable unclothed athlete since the jockey Godiva.

To the astonishment of Dutchman Richard Krajicek and American MaliVai Washington, a striking Melissa ran past the players and continuously flashed her small white apron, and body, at a stunned Duke and Duchess of Kent in the Royal Box. Moments later, a pair of policemen arrested her and took her to the station, where she was identified as a part-time Wimbledon waitress.

After that, the final proved anticlimactic. Washington lost in straight sets. Asked what role the streaker had played in his performance, the American replied: "I saw these things wobbling around and, jeez, she smiled at me. I was flustered. Three sets later, I was gone: If she'd come back, I might have had more luck." While that was a rare time of irreverence for a sport sometimes lacking lighter moments, this was a year of serious business for the best players.

Boris Becker knew precisely what he wanted to achieve when he commenced his campaign Down Under at Melbourne. Now 28, he was coming off an enviable 1995 and searching for his first major singles title in five years. He realized that goal

Many a performer has felt naked on Centre Court, stripped bare and defenseless by an overpowering opponent. Tony Roche, after losing the 1968 Wimbledon final in under an hour to Rod Laver, lamented, "I just wanted to dig a hole and disappear."

But 23-year-old Englishwoman Melissa Johnson took it a few steps further in a distinctive Centre Court debut. She was a winner, judging from public reaction to her truly letting it all hang out as no champion before. In a final-day dash across the

when he took apart tenacious Michael Chang in the final of the year's first major. Becker sparred successfully with Chang from the baseline, served him off the court and attacked whenever that avenue was available. With his 6-2, 6-4, 2-6, 6-2 triumph over fifth seed Chang, the fourth seed gathered a sixth major crown over an 11-year span.

For the most part, the tournament was devoid of drama. Before Chang had eliminated Andre Agassi, 6-1, 6-4, 7-6 (7-1) in

a semifinal, Agassi had bounced another ex-champ, Jim Courier, 6-7 (7-9), 2-6, 6-3, 6-4, 6-2. Otherwise, the only surprise was delivered by 19-year-old Australian Mark Philippoussis, a 6-foot-4, 202-pounder, who beat world No. 1 Pete Sampras in the third round, 6-4, 7-6 (11-9), 7-6 (7-3), unbroken with 29 aces.

With Steffi Graf coming off foot surgery and unable to appear in Melbourne for the second year in a row, Monica Seles was the class of the field. But she was battling a variety of injuries and hurt her shoulder prior to a semifinal showdown with the talented and athletic Chanda Rubin, a 19-year-old black American with an explosive all-court game. Rubin was coming off a 6-4, 2-6, 16-14 quarterfinal upset of third-seeded Arantxa Sanchez Vicario, prevailing in three hours, 33 minutes, a tournament record for women. Against Seles, Chanda got within sight of an upset before losing 6-7 (1-7), 6-1, 7-5.

But there was no luck involved in the hard-hitting final, a 6-4, 6-1 victory by Seles over German Anke Huber, who was debuting in a major final. Unbeaten in Australia (32-0), Monica had her fourth Open title and her ninth major crown. In the semifinals, Huber had beaten tireless South African Amanda Coetzer, 4-6, 6-4, 6-2, whose quarterfinal prey, 7-5, 4-6, 6-1, was 15-year-old Swiss Martina Hingis, making her first impression in a major. Hingis would win it the next three years.

Seles, arriving in Paris for the French Open, had made a questionable professional judgment by moving on from Melbourne to Tokyo the week after the Australian Open, losing, 1-6, 7-6 (7-5), 6-4 in the quarters to steadily improving Croat, Iva Majoli, who won the tournament over Sanchez Vicario, 6-4, 6-1. Having won in Sydney the week before Melbourne over Lindsay Davenport, 4-6, 7-6 (9-7), 6-3 Seles, going to Tokyo was setting herself up for a fourth consecutive week of competition. That must have exacerbated her shoulder injury, and she didn't return to tournament play until the week before Roland Garros, where she won one match in Madrid before she pulled out to protect her shoulder.

Seles arrived at the French Open still not fully recuperated from her shoulder woes. She struggled through to the quarterfinals and was halted by Jana Novotna, 7-6 (9-7), 6-3. Monica's 25-match winning streak in the world's most prestigious clay court event came to an end. With Seles gone, and Novotna losing in the semifinals to her doubles partner Sanchez Vicario, 6-3, 7-5, it was time for another Graf—Sanchez Vicario final, Steffi having beaten Conchita Martinez, 6-3, 6-1 in the semifinals. This one was even better than the 1995 Wimbledon title match.

It lasted three hours and four minutes—a female French Open final round record—and it was hard and brilliantly fought from beginning to end. Graf took the first set and seemed headed for a straight-set win when she got to 4-1 in the second-set tiebreaker. But then the Spaniard snapped a forehand winner to make it 4-2 and Graf sank into a nervous patch. Four straight unforced errors and a double fault later, she had lost the tiebreaker, 7-points-to-4, and she found herself in a third set she could hardly have relished.

Graf fell behind 2-4 in the third, and Sanchez Vicario twice reached break point for 5-2. Graf held on. But the unwavering Sanchez Vicario served for the match twice at 5-4 and 7-6, only to be denied again. In those two memorable games, Graf did not make a single unforced error. In the end, Graf came through, 6-3, 6-7 (4-7), 10-8. It was a final so stupendous that only Chris Evert's 6-3, 6-7 (4-7), 7-5 triumph over Martina Navratilova in the 1985 final and Seles' 6-2, 3-6, 10-8 title win over Graf in 1992 might be rated above it.

The heart of the men's event at Roland Garros took place long before the final, and the one who took over the spotlight was none other than Sampras. On his way to a first French Open semifinal—he had been in the quarterfinals 1992 through 1994—the world No. 1 survived three bruising five-set skirmishes. He beat 1993-94 titlist Sergi Bruguera, 6-3, 6-4, 6-7 (2-7), 2-6, 6-3 in a gruelling second-round contest and then subdued 29-ace serving Todd Martin in the third round, 3-6, 6-4, 7-5, 4-6, 6-2. In the quarterfinals, Sampras dropped the first two sets to Courier, but fought back to win his third five-set confrontation of the tournament, 6-7 (4-7), 4-6, 6-4, 6-4, 6-4.

But even with two days off to rest, Pete had passed his physical and emotional limits. His coach, Tim Gullikson, was lost to brain cancer three-and-a-half weeks before, and a mourning Sampras hadn't prepared for Roland Garros as he would have wanted. He had played his way through to the penultimate round with Gullikson at the center of his mind, wanting to win this one for a friend he had cherished and a coach he knew had turned him into a true champion. But with the thermometer soaring to 93 degrees, Sampras wilted in the heat and surrendered to Yevgeny Kafelnikov, 7-6 (7-4), 6-0, 6-2, conceding that "the balloon had burst."

Defending champion Thomas Muster had seemed a safe bet to retain his title. He had won 16 of his last 20 tournaments, 97 of his last 100 matches on clay when he took the court against 1991 Wimbledon champion Michael Stich in the round of 16. But a rejuvenated Stich jarred Muster, 4-6, 6-4, 6-1, 7-6 (7-1). Having endured ankle surgery three months before, Stich had come to Paris hoping only to get a few matches in before Wimbledon. He had considered bypassing the event but was persuaded by his coach Sven Groenveld to play. Dismaying the French patrons, Stich next knocked off Cedric Pioline, 6-4, 4-6, 6-3, 6-2, and, following a straight-set semifinal win over Switzerland's Marc Rosset, 6-3, 6-4, 6-2, Stich found himself in his third major final.

But Kafelnikov stopped Stich 7-6 (7-4), 7-5, 7-6 (7-4), even though Stich led 5-2 in the second, 3-1 in the third. Kafelnikov, the lone Russian to rule a major, doubled his good fortune by taking the doubles title with Czech Daniel Vacek, over the French-Swiss joint venture, Guy Forget and Jakob Hlasek, 6-2, 6-3. The Russian was the first to win both men's titles in Paris since Ken Rosewall (with Fred Stolle) in 1968.

It was not a vintage Wimbledon. The weather during the second week was miserable, rain constantly causing delays during big matches, and the atmosphere dampened for everyone. Nevertheless, the towering Krajicek produced the brightest brand of tennis of his career and thoroughly deserved his major title. The 6-foot-5, 24-year-old Netherlander became the only man from his nation to win one in singles. He was ranked No. 13 but overlooked by the Wimbledon seeding committee. When the seventh-seeded Muster withdrew with an injury, Krajicek was placed in the draw as the next in line, and, after the fact, considered the unorthodox

17th seed by the All England Club (but by nobody else). This was way after the world press had correctly anointed Krajicek as the only unseeded winner other than Becker in 1985.

He had a terrific run. He upset 1991 titlist Stich, 6-4, 7-6 (7-5), 6-4, in the round of 16 then brought down the mighty Sampras in the quarters, 7-5, 7-6 (7-3), 6-4. Sampras had won 25 straight matches at Wimbledon but he could not break his unwavering opponent or cope with Krajicek's razor-sharp backhand. Krajicek then ousted unseeded Jason Stoltenberg, 7-5, 6-2, 6-1, after the Australian upset No. 4 seed Goran Ivanisevic, 6-3, 7-6 (7-3), 6-7 (3-7), 7-6 (7-3), in the quarterfinals.

On the opposite half of the draw, Washington upset No. 9 seeded Thomas Enqvist, 6-4, 7-6 (7-5), 6-3, in the second round, saved two match points in a five-set quarterfinal win over Germany's Alex Radulescu, 6-7 (5-7), 7-6 (7-1), 5-7, 7-6 (7-3), 6-4, and then stunned countryman and close friend Martin to win their semifinal, 5-7, 6-4, 6-7 (5-7), 6-3, 10-8, rising from 1-5 in the last set.

Washington, the first black male in the final since Arthur Ashe in 1975, was overwhelmed by Krajicek, 6-3, 6-4, 6-3, in the final, as the Dutchman launched 14 aces to raise his tournament-high total to 147. Washington lost serve in the second game, and never caught up. Even a 68-minute stoppage for rain after one game of the third set couldn't dampen Krajicek's thrust. He lost serve just once, but by then was ahead 4-1 in the third.

The women couldn't reproduce their dazzling moments of a year before. Graf was just too good, too sharp and concentrated, this time around in a rematch of the 1995 final. She moved rapidly to a 6-3, 4-0 lead. Sanchez Vicario was typically combative in fighting her way back to 5-5, taking advantage of two damaging double faults from Graf, serving for the match at 5-4. Had it gone into a third set, Graf could well have been vulnerable, but she raised her game markedly in the next two games, conceding only one more point to close out a 6-3, 7-5 victory for her seventh singles title on Centre Court.

Graf, the great champion, may have been given a break by the referee, who halted her semifinal with surging Kimiko Date after two sets at 8:56 P.M. Date, hot winner of the second set (the only set Steffi lost), wanted to continue, said the visibility was fine. They returned the next day, the Japanese cooled off and loser of the best-of-one-set conclusion, 6-2, 2-6, 6-3.

Agassi crashed from his dismal slump by winning the prize he had proclaimed was utmost on his 1996 wish list: The Olympic gold medal on the hard courts of Atlanta's Stone Mountain complex. He did it after numerous escapes—2-6, 6-4, 6-2 over Italian Andrea Gaudenzi in the third round and 7-5, 4-6, 7-5 over South African Wayne Ferreira in the quarterfinals, to name two—before he got the gold by assaulting the Spaniard Bruguera, 6-2, 6-3, 6-1.

Even more impressively, another American won in women's singles. Californian Lindsay Davenport was seeded only ninth but she toppled fifth seed Huber, 6-13-6, 6-3, fourth seed Majoli, 7-5, 6-3, seventh seed, good friend and teammate Mary Joe Fernandez, 6-2, 7-6 (8-6), and third seed Sanchez Vicario, 7-6 (8-6), 6-2, to win gold.

Despite his proud achievement, Agassi was fortunate not to have been thrown out of the Olympics for untoward behavior

that included incredibly abusive language directed at complaisant umpires. But he wasn't so lucky a couple of weeks later at encountering ATP officials at Indianapolis who wouldn't stand for that sort of treatment, and disqualified him. Andre was the first prominent player since John McEnroe, at the Australian of 1990, to be ejected. While winning easily against Canadian Daniel Nestor in the second round, he was tossed out after a warning for ball abuse and then a four-letter-word tirade against umpire Dana Loconto. Supervisor Mark Darby, told by Loconto precisely what Agassi had said, showed the gumption to evict one of the game's greatest drawing cards.

Controversy surrounded the U.S. Open before a single ball was struck. The USTA has almost always used the current ATP computer rankings to determine seedings for the last major championship of the season. But this time around, tourney officials chose to make a number of significant departures from the rankings in their projection. They moved Chang past Muster to second in the seedings (reversing their rankings), elevated Agassi from his No. 8 ranking to sixth in the seedings to take into account his recent record, and made a few other suspect changes as well without telling the ATP beforehand.

Kafelnikov, the French Open champion, was furious. He had talked about possibly pulling out of the Open the week before because of an injury. Then he became petulant about the seedings and withdrew. The Russian claimed that his pride had been wounded irreparably by being seeded seventh instead of where he stood in the rankings at No. 4. On top of all of this, the USTA did have to remake the draw after breaking procedure the first time around—and untraditionally in secret—although they defiantly stuck by their seedings.

In the end, order was restored as the unquestioned world No. 1 Sampras secured his only major crown of the season, seventh over the last four years, and eighth altogether, tying him with Jimmy Connors, Ken Rosewall, Ivan Lendl and Fred Perry in the all-time chase, not too far behind Roy Emerson (12), Rod Laver and Bjorn Borg (11) and Bill Tilden (10), although nobody was talking about breaking the record then, and Emerson was unaware that he held it.

Sampras was blazing at the start of his final with Chang, revealing the full range of his fluid talent, breaking down his adversary from the baseline, applying pressure when he needed to, serving with striking assurance. Before Chang knew what had hit him, he was down two sets to love. Sampras fought off a set point, serving at 5-6 in the third and then calmly and confidently completed his mission, 6-1, 6-4, 7-6 (7-3), for a fourth Open crown and an eighth major title.

The seedings had held up well. In the semifinals, the top-seeded Sampras had defeated fourth-seed Ivanisevic, 6-3, 6-4, 6-7 (9-11), 6-3 after letting a 6-3, triple-match-point lead slip from his grasp in the tie-breaker. Sampras broke the big left-hander at 3-4 in the fourth, and went unbroken in four sets. Chang obliterated Agassi, 6-3, 6-2, 6-2, cracking 16 aces and not losing his serve. It was his third win in five 1996 meetings with Agassi, his second in a major event.

But none of those matches could compare to Sampras' monumental struggle with 22-year-old Spaniard Alex Corretja in the

quarterfinals. In a four-hour, nine-minute confrontation, Sampras trailed two sets to one, struck back to win the fourth. But burdened by extreme dehydration, he vomited near the back of the court at 1-1 in the fifth-set tie-breaker, and was given a code violation warning for taking too much time between points.

As the tie-breaker progressed, it was increasingly apparent that Sampras was in agony. At 6-5, Sampras had a match point but missed a running forehand. He then went down match point at 6-7 and somehow came up with a stunning forehand stretch volley into an open court. Exhausted now, wanting the ordeal to be over, Sampras sent the stadium crowd into a complete frenzy when he hooked an audacious 90 m.p.h. second-serve ace wide to Corretja's forehand in the right court. "How could he do that?" sighed Corretja later. Pete said, "I don't know where it came from, but I knew I didn't want to hit another ball. I don't know if I could have." He didn't have to. Until then No. 31 Corretja had played the match of his life, giving away nothing, in fact outplaying Sampras—even out-acing him with 25. But Pete's second-ball ace seemed to unnerve Alex. The only way the Spaniard could lose was to not put the ball into play—a double fault. As Alex's second serve landed beyond the service line, Sampras was the winner, 7-6 (7-5), 5-7, 5-7, 6-4, 7-6 (9-7). It was the match of the '90s at Flushing Meadow, and easily among the five best in the Open era. Pete lost his lunch but not the title.

For the second year in a row, Graf completed a sweep of the three majors she entered when she repeated her 1995 final-round triumph over Seles, 7-5, 6-4, but this was more thorough. Fraulein Forehand's blasts kept the less fit Seles running from corner to corner, and in vain. Graf, 27, banged 10 aces, lost serve but once, was too unrelentingly skillful in securing her 21st major title and her fifth U.S. title. She had broken from the pack in Paris, leaving Chris Evert and Martina Navratilova behind with 18 majors apiece. At Wimbledon, she cruised past Helen Wills Moody's 19, and now Margaret Smith Court's mighty record 24—once seeming Everest—appeared within reach.

But she nearly tripped in the semis over the latest Martina, child Hingis, 15. Cunning Martina II was having a good time, playing and winning more (19 hours, 44 minutes, 12 victories) than anyone else in reaching the semis of singles, doubles and mixed, the first such accomplishment since Martina I tripled in 1987. Her doubles title at Wimbledon (in the company of 31-year-old Helena Sukova, 5-7, 7-5, 6-1, over Larisa Neiland and Meredith McGrath), made Hingis, 15 years, 10 months, the youngest by three days to win a major female title, undercutting Lottie Dod, the 1887 Wimbledon singles champ. After eliminating third-seeded 1994 champ Sanchez Vicario, 6-1, 3-6, 6-4, and seventh-seeded Novotna, 7-6 (7-1), 6-4, she had her sights on Graf. Only Steffi's stonewalling of five set points in the first set rescued her, 7-5, 6-3. Steffi socked three winners, benefited from two errors on those set points.

Captain Billie Jean King's U.S. team, with a rookie, Seles, on board, pried the Fed Cup away from Spain (a.k.a. Sanchez Vicario and Martinez), 5-0 at Atlantic City. Monica beat Conchita, 6-2, 6-4, and Arantxa, 3-6, 6-3, 6-1, and Davenport downed Sanchez Vicario, 7-5, 6-1, and that was enough.

But Mary Joe Fernandez, with a triple, was the life-saver at the sticky start, 3-2 over Austria at Salzburg. Her wins over Judith Wiesner, 6-3, 7-6 (7-5), and Barbara Paulus, 6-3, 7-6 (7-4), backboned the victory that went down to the last match: Gigi Fernandez and Mary Joe over Wiesner and Petra Schwarz, 6-0, 6-4. Then a lineup of Seles and Davenport overpowered Japan, 5-0, at Nagoya, both beating up Date, the home ace: Lindsay, 6-2, 6-1; Monica, 6-0, 6-2.

Befitting the year's No. 1's, Sampras and Graf won the climactic playoffs, the ATP World Championship at Hanover, Germany, and WTA (Chase Championships) at New York's Madison Square Garden respectively, though each was pushed to the five-set limit. Beaten by Becker in the round-robin phase, Sampras rebounded to tip Boris in a gripping four-hour final, 3-6, 7-6 (7-5), 7-6 (7-4), 6-7 (11-13), 6-4, breaking serve only once. Muting a Boris chorus of 15,000 German fans, Pete had his third ATP and eighth title for the year (a career 44th), during which he won 65 of 76 matches, and $3,702,919.

Graf seemed in trouble as 16-year-old Hingis, the youngest finalist since Andrea Jaeger, 15, in 1981, led her 5-1 in the fourth set. But leg cramps seized the kid, and Steffi came through in the year-ender for a fifth time, 6-3, 4-6, 0-6, 6-4, 6-0, her seventh title of a season in which she won 54 of 58 matches and a female record $2,665,706.

As in 1993, indifference at the top scuttled U.S. hopes of keeping the Davis Cup. Sampras, Agassi and Courier declined invitations to go for another Cup, saying the team event interrupted their schedules. Martin, the only holdover from Moscow '95 willing to show for a quarterfinal in Prague, was admirable in the 3-2 defeat to the Czech Republic, securing both points. Todd beat Petr Korda, 6-2, 6-4, 7-5, and Daniel Vacek, 7-6 (7-1), 6-3, 6-1. But in the decisive fifth encounter, Washington, who had lost a tense struggle to Vacek (4-6, 6-3, 6-4, 5-7, 6-4), couldn't hold off Korda, 7-6 (7-1), 6-3, 6-1. Korda-Vacek got the go-ahead point from the Patricks, Galbraith and McEnroe, 6-2, 6-3, 6-3.

But perhaps it was poetic that the year of the passing of 92-year-old Rene Lacoste, the last of France's magnificent Four Musketeers, was capped by an unexpected, nerve-jingling French triumph, 3-2, in the Davis Cup final at Malmo, Sweden. It featured the longest (nine hours, 12 minutes), and possibly the wildest last day in Cup annals. Full-house crowds of 5,600, prepared to hail the farewell appearances of No. 14 Stefan Edberg, were saddened instead by his injury, a twisted right ankle, in losing the opener to No. 21 Pioline, 6-3, 6-4, 6-3. Further grief was theirs two days later as No. 31 Arnaud Boetsch battled uphill to win the closest of all Cup finale fifth matches, the decider, over Edberg's stand-in, No. 64 Nicklas Kulti, 7-6 (7-2), 2-6, 4-6, 7-6 (7-5), 10-8. Boetsch revived from triple-Cup point down, 6-7, 0-40, in four hours, 47 minutes. Swede Thomas Enqvist, No. 9, came from way back, too, to tie it, 2-2, by beating Pioline from 2-5 in the fifth, 3-6, 6-7 (8-10), 6-4, 6-4, 9-7, in four hours, 25 minutes. But it turned out that wasn't enough to keep the Cup from the French whose Guillaume Raoux and Guy Forget won the vital doubles over Jonas Bjorkman and Kulti, 6-3, 1-6, 6-3, 6-3.

They must have sensed it was their year after a resurrection from 0-2 in the semifinal at Nantes to beat Italy, 3-2, with Boetsch rehearsing for the decisive victory in the fifth match, beating Andrea Gaudenzi, 6-4, 6-2, 7-6 (8). The U-turn began in doubles,

Forget and Raoux blocking Gaudenzi and Diego Nargiso, 6-3, 6-4, 6-2. Pioline tied it over Renzo Furlan, 6-3, 2-6, 6-2, 6-4.

Crowed inspirational captain Yannick Noah, who had led France's 1991 victory over the U.S., "Davis Cup's not about rankings, reputations or schedules. It's about team, and who will give up things for others, for the team."

1996 CHAMPIONS AND LEADERS

Australian Open
Men's Singles Final: Boris Becker (GER) def. Michael Chang (USA), 6-2, 6-4, 2-6, 6-2

Women's Singles Final: Monica Seles (USA) def. Anke Huber (GER), 6-4, 6-1

Men's Doubles Final: Stefan Edberg (SWE) and Petr Korda (CZE) def. Alex O'Brien (USA) and Sebastien Lareau (CAN), 7-5, 7-5, 4-6, 6-1

Women's Doubles Final: Chanda Rubin (USA) Arantxa Sanchez Vicario (ESP) def. Lindsay Davenport and Mary Joe Fernandez (USA), 7-5, 2-6, 6-4

Mixed Doubles Final: Larisa Savchenko Neiland (LAT) def. Mark Woodforde (AUS) def. Nicole Arendt and Luke Jensen (USA), 4-6, 7-5, 6-0

French Open
Men's Singles Final: Yevgeny Kafelnikov (RUS) def. Michael Stich (GER), 7-6 (4), 7-5, 7-6 (4)

Women's Singles Final: Steffi Graf (GER) def. Arantxa Sanchez Vicario (ESP), 6-3, 6-7 (4), 10-8

Men's Doubles Final: Yevgeny Kafelnikov (RUS) and Daniel Vacek (CZE) def. Guy Forget (FRA) and Jakob Hlasek (SUI), 6-2, 6-3

Women's Doubles Final: Lindsay Davenport and Mary Joe Fernandez (USA) def. Gigi Fernandez (USA) and Natalia Zvereva (BLR), 6-2, 6-1

Mixed Doubles Final: Patricia Tarabini and Javier Frana (ARG) def. Nicole Arendt and Luke Jensen (USA), 6-2, 6-2

Wimbledon
Men's Singles Final: Richard Krajicek (NED) def. MaliVai Washington (USA), 6-3, 6-4, 6-3

Women's Singles Final: Steffi Graf (GER) def. Arantxa Sanchez Vicario (ESP), 6-3, 7-5

Men's Doubles Final: Todd Woodbridge and Mark Woodforde (AUS) def. Byron Black (ZIM) and Grant Connell (CAN), 4-6, 6-1, 6-3, 6-2

Women's Doubles Final: Martina Hingis (SUI) and Helena Sukova (CZE) def. Meredith McGrath (USA) and Larisa Savchenko Neiland (LAT), 5-7, 7-5, 6-1

Mixed Doubles Final: Helena Sukova and Cyril Suk (CZE) def. Larisa Savchenko Neiland (LAT) and Mark Woodforde (AUS), 1-6, 6-3, 6-2

U.S. Open
Men's Singles Final: Pete Sampras (USA) def. Michael Chang (USA), 6-1, 6-4, 7-6 (3)

Women's Singles Final: Steffi Graf (GER) def. Monica Seles (USA), 7-5, 6-4

Men's Doubles Final: Todd Woodbridge and Mark Woodforde (AUS) def. Paul Haarhuis and Jacco Eltingh (NED), 4-6, 7-6 (5), 7-6 (2)

Women's Doubles Final: Natalia Zvereva (BLR) and Gigi Fernandez (USA) def. Jana Novotna (CZE) and Arantxa Sanchez Vicario (ESP), 1-6, 6-1, 6-4

Mixed Doubles Final: Lisa Raymond and Patrick Galbraith (USA) def. Manon Bollegraf (NED) and Rick Leach (USA), 7-6 (6), 7-6 (4)

Year-End No. 1
Men: Pete Sampras
Women: Steffi Graf

Top Player Earnings
Men: Boris Becker $4,313,007
Women: Steffi Graf $2,664,178

Davis Cup: France

Fed Cup: United States

ATP World Championships, Hanover—Pete Sampras
Grand Slam Cup, Munich—Boris Becker
Chase Championships, NYC—Steffi Graf

1996 OLYMPICS—ATLANTA, UNITED STATES

Men's singles:
GOLD: Andre Agassi (USA)
SILVER: Sergi Bruguera (ESP)
BRONZE: Leander Paes (IND)

Women's singles:
GOLD: Lindsay Davenport (USA)
SILVER: Arantxa Sanchez Vicario (ESP)
BRONZE: Jana Novotna (CZE)

Men's doubles:
GOLD: Todd Woodbridge and Mark Woodforde (AUS)
SILVER: Tim Henman and Neil Broad (GBR)
BRONZE: Marc-Kevin Goellner and David Prinosil (GER)

Women's doubles:
GOLD: Mary Joe Fernandez and Gigi Fernandez (USA)
SILVER: Jana Novotna and Helena Sukova (CZE)
BRONZE: Conchita Martinez and Arantxa Sanchez Vicario (ESP)

1997 16-Year-Old Hingis Takes Three Majors

No one in professional tennis achieved more during this memorable season than Switzerland's stylish and precocious Martina Hingis. Before she turned 17 at the end of September, she had appeared in all four major championship tournament finals.

Displaying a strategic acumen far exceeding her years, Hingis won three of those four majors. Across the year, she was victorious in 75 of 80 matches, capturing 12 of 17 tournaments, garnering $3,400,196 to set the prize-money pace among the women. She dominated the game with brain rather than brawn, ruling from the baseline with superb timing, exemplary ball control, and a deceptive two-handed backhand down the line. After big hitters Steffi Graf and Monica Seles had controlled the female game for a decade, Hingis brought a refreshingly different style and personality to top-level tennis.

The season began in earnest for Hingis and everyone else Down Under in Melbourne. Martina became the youngest player of the 20th Century (at 16 years, three months, 26 days) to secure a major championship, obliterating 1995 winner Mary Pierce 6-2, 6-2 to claim the Australian Open crown, refusing to concede a set in the entire tournament. No Swiss player had ever captured a major singles championship. Lottie Dod had been two months shy of her 16th birthday when she became the youngest ever to take a major, winning Wimbledon in 1887.

Fourth-seed Hingis lost no sets, unseeded Pierce only two, but they got a gift from Amanda Coetzer, who beat top-seed Steffi Graf, 6-2, 7-5, in the fourth round.

Pete Sampras came through in resolute fashion to capture the men's Australian Open title, upending Spain's startling Carlos Moya, who had toppled defending champion Boris Becker, 5-7, 7-6 (7-4), 3-6, 6-1, 6-4, at the start, and Michael Chang, 7-5, 6-2, 6-4, in the semifinals to reach his first major final. Top-seeded Sampras had trailed the imposing Dominik Hrbaty of Slovakia 2-4, 15-40 in the fifth set on a stifling afternoon in the round of 16, but swept four games in a row to seal the 6-7 (4-7), 6-3, 6-4, 3-6, 6-4, victory. He was pressed in another five-set confrontation by Spain's Albert Costa in the quarters, 6-3, 6-7 (5-7), 6-1, 3-6, 6-2, but, then, in straight-set encounters, accounted for both Thomas Muster, 6-1, 7-6 (7-3), 6-3, and Moya, 6-2, 6-3, 6-3.

At the next major championship in Paris, the flamboyant Brazilian Gustavo Kuerten, ranked No. 66, made a spectacular unseeded run to come away with his first major title. The 20-year-old exploited his magnificent one-handed top-spin backhand and disposed of no fewer than three former champions in the ruling on the slow red clay of Roland Garros. He knocked out 1995 champion Muster in a five-set, third-round showdown, 6-7 (3-7), 6-1, 6-3, 3-6, 6-4 - after falling behind 3-0 in the final set - prevailed again in five arduous sets against defending champion Yevgeny Kafelnikov in the quarterfinals, 6-2, 5-7, 2-6, 6-0, 6-4, and crushed 1993-94 victor Sergi Bruguera of Spain 6-3, 6-4, 6-2 in the final. Kuerten came into Roland Garros a stranger, and left with a rapidly rising reputation.

Hingis had hurt her knee in a horse-riding accident less than two months before the French Open. Still struggling to find

the top of her game, she managed to make it to the final, but could not contain Iva Majoli, a 19-year-old Croatian with good court sense and stinging ground strokes off both sides. Majoli established herself as the first player from her nation to take one of the majors, upending Hingis in 78 solid minutes, prevailing 6-4, 6-2 without facing a single break point in the match. Martina's 37-match winning streak was over; she was beaten for the first time all year. Hingis had overcome three-time former champion Monica Seles 6-7 (2-7), 7-5, 6-4 in a stirring semifinal, while long-shot ninth-seed Majoli edged Coetzer, 6-3, 4-6, 7-5. Again tiny Coetzer did the champ a favor, eliminating Graf in the quarters, 6-1, 6-4.

At Wimbledon, Hingis got back on the winning track. Her victim in the final was Jana Novotna, a superb grass-court player who was in a class by herself at the net, boasting the best volley off either side in women's tennis. Novotna, the No. 4 seed, attacked skillfully in a devastatingly efficient opening set, but Hingis found her range with impeccable passing shots in a 2-6, 6-3, 6-3 victory. Majoli fell in the quarterfinals 7-6 (7-1), 6-4 to non-seed Anna Kournikova, who then lost to Hingis, 6-3, 6-2. Novotna took her semifinal over Arantxa Sanchez Vicario, 6-4, 6-2. Graf, injured, did not defend the title.

Sampras, meanwhile, was celebrating one of the great serving fortnights of his career. In sweeping to his fourth Wimbledon tournament win in five years, he held serve in 116 of 118 games. He was hard pressed to defeat the left-handed Petr Korda in a five-set, two-day, round-of-16 collision, 6-4, 6-3, 6-7 (8-10), 6-7 (1-7), 6-4, but that was his only genuine scare. Korda never broke the American but counter-attacked tenaciously. Sampras halted three-time former champion Becker in a four-set quarterfinal, 6-1, 6-7 (5-7), 6-1, 6-4. Becker told Sampras at the net after the match that it was his last Wimbledon. (He would take one more run on the grass again in 1999).

After defeating surprise semifinalist and doubles specialist Todd Woodbridge of Australia 6-2, 6-1, 7-6 (7-3), Pete went on to rout an apprehensive Cedric Pioline 6-4, 6-2, 6-4 in the final, repeating his straight-set triumph over the gifted Frenchman in the 1993 U.S. Open final. Pioline had stopped Michael Stich of Germany in a scintillating five-set semifinal clash, 6-7 (2-7), 6-2, 6-1, 5-7, 6-4. Stich, 28, said that 1997 would be his final year of tennis. But after the loss, on Centre Court: "Basically, I made up my mind after the match, that that was going to be my last match," said Stich, the Wimbledon champion in 1991. "And I just said (to Pioline), `Thanks for making it so exciting.' "

When the leading players assembled at Flushing Meadow for the last major of the season, they moved into a brand new 23,000-seat Arthur Ashe Stadium, named after the dignified man who had won the first U.S. Open in 1968. The new theater was not to the liking of most longtime fans, who felt it was marred by two levels of luxury suites and was an impersonal stage that was too large for tennis. Hingis and Sampras were the firm favorites. In the end, she came through to claim the most prestigious hard-court crown, but he did not. Hingis found herself facing 17-year-old rookie Venus Williams in the final, the first black since Althea Gibson at Forest Hills in 1958 to reach a U.S. women's title-round match.

Williams, the second unseeded finalist in the championships of her country following Darlene Hard in 1958, was understandably jittery on the big occasion and went down rather tamely 6-0, 6-4. But the 17-year-old acquitted herself well in the second set, rallying from 1-3 down to reach 4-4, 30-0 before delivering a costly double fault. At No. 66 in the world, she was the lowest-ranked woman to reach a major final since Barbara Jordan, No. 68, won the Australian Open in 1979.

However, Venus's semifinal triumph over 11th seed Romanian Irina Spirlea, 7-6 (7-5), 4-6, 7-6 (9-7), brought down the house in 2:42. Spirlea, with an impressive display of forehand winners, had knocked off second-seed Monica Seles, 1-6, 6-2, 6-2, in the quarters, and had two match points in the closing tie-breaker— only to see them erased by Venus's two-fisted backhands. Hingis, losing no sets as in Australia, beat Lindsay Davenport in the semis, 6-2, 6-4. Injured Graf was unable to defend the championship.

Hingis joined a very exclusive club with her triumph, becoming only the seventh woman in history to record three major triumphs in a season, joining Maureen Connolly, Margaret Smith Court, Billie Jean King, Martina Navratilova, Graf and Seles.

Top-seeded Sampras was ousted in a suspenseful, round of 16, Labor Day meeting with Korda. As was the case at Wimbledon, they went the full five sets again. Sampras was up a break in the fifth, serving at 3-1. But a ferociously determined Korda, two points from defeat at 5-6 in the fifth, struck back boldly to win 6-7 (4-7), 7-5, 7-6 (7-2), 3-6, 7-6 (7-2). Curiously, Korda retired, losing, 7-6 (7-3), 6-2, 1-0, in his quarterfinal against Sweden's Jonas Bjorkman, claiming he was hindered by a cold. In the end, a red-hot Patrick Rafter burst into his own and was a worthy champion.

The 24-year-old Australian serve-and-volleyer had won only one tournament over the course of his career, and had lost in five finals across the season. But his heavy kick serve worked wonders on the surface, and he lifted both his game and confidence to unprecedented levels. In the final, the No. 13-seed Rafter defeated unseeded Greg Rusedski of Great Britain, 6-3, 6-2, 4-6, 7-5, outplaying the big-serving left-hander in every facet of the game, most notably returning serve with more conviction. Speaking of the five finals he had lost leading up to the Open, Rafter said, "I learned a lot from those experiences about how to handle myself in this final." Rafter had peaked propitiously for his semifinal appointment with second seed Chang, taking apart the dispirited American, 6-3, 6-3, 6-4, with an unwavering demonstration of aggression.

Stunned Chang was crestfallen when it was over, knowing he would have no better opening to secure a second major title. "All I can say," he lamented, "is that all of these losses hurt. I just hope that my perseverance will pay off one day. When you have these opportunities and don't win, it's frustrating."

Another American who had the misfortune to meet the formidable Rafter was 1994 champion Agassi, who was suffering through a miserable season. Having married actress Brooke Shields in the spring, Agassi did not play any of the other major tournaments. Looking overweight and overanxious, Agassi lost to the hard-charging Rafter in a four-set, round-of-16 collision under the lights, 6-3, 7-6 (7-4), 4-6, 6-3. He finished the year with a 12-12 match record, and his ranking plunged to No. 141 in the world.

At the end of the season, he forced himself to play in two minor-league Challenger events—in his hometown of Las Vegas and in Burbank, Calif., to help resurrect his game—and his career.

Climaxing the year, Sampras won the season-ending ATP Tour World Championships, the Masters, in Hannover with a straight-set demolition of an outclassed Kafelnikov, 6-3, 6-2, 6-2, while Novotna took the Chase Championships at New York's Madison Square Garden over Pierce, 7-6 (7-5), 6-2, 6-3.

Of larger significance was this: Sweden won the Davis Cup for the sixth time in 11 final-round appearances, ousting the United States 5-0 at Goteborg. Jonas Bjorkman and Magnus Larsson led the way, Jonas beating Chang, 7-5, 1-6, 6-3, 6-3, Magnus ahead of Sampras when a leg injury made it a TKO, 3-6, 7-6 (7-1), 2-1. A 6-4, 6-4, 6-4, victory of Nicklas Kulti and Bjorkman over Todd Martin and Jonathan Stark, settled it fast.

In the Fed Cup final at Hertogenbosch, Netherlands, France toppled the homeside 4-1 with Sandrine Testud taking the decisive match 0-6, 6-3, 6-3 over Miriam Oremans. Making a major contribution to the French cause was none other than the ubiquitous Yannick Noah, who had led France into the Davis Cup Final as a player in 1982. He then won the French Open in 1983. He was the Davis Cup captain when France was victorious in 1991 and 1996. And then he led the women to this team triumph, completing a unique range of achievements.

Meanwhile, one of the game's great doubles players decided to retire from tennis. Gigi Fernandez captured her last two major titles during the year, taking the French Open and Wimbledon alongside her longtime partner Natalia Zvereva - Paris over Mary Joe Fernandez and Lisa Raymond, 6-2, 6-3 and London over Manon Bollegraf and Nicole Arendt, 7-6 (7-4), 6-4. Gigi, 33, left the stage with 17 major tournament prizes in her possession, and the knowledge that she was walking away when she was close to the peak of her powers.

1997 CHAMPIONS AND LEADERS

Australian Open
Men's Singles Final: Pete Sampras (USA) def. Carlos Moya (ESP), 6-2, 6-2, 6-3
Women's Singles Final: Martina Hingis (SUI) def. Mary Pierce (FRA), 6-2, 6-2
Men's Doubles Final: Todd Woodbridge and Mark Woodforde (AUS) def. Sebastien Lareau (CAN) and Alex O'Brien (USA), 4-6, 7-5, 7-5, 6-3
Women's Doubles Final: Martina Hingis (SUI) and Natasha Zvereva (BLR) def. Lindsay Davenport and Lisa Raymond (USA), 6-2, 6-2
Mixed Doubles Final: Manon Bollegraf (NED) and Rick Leach (USA) def. Larisa Savchenko Neiland (LAT) and John-Laffnie de Jager (RSA), 6-3, 6-7 (5-7), 7-5

French Open
Men's Singles Final: Gustavo Kuerten (BRA) def. Sergi Bruguera (ESP), 6-3, 6-4, 6-2
Women's Singles Final: Iva Majoli (CRO) def. Martina Hingis (SUI), 6-4, 6-2
Men's Doubles Final: Yevgeny Kafelnikov (RUS) and Daniel Vacek (CZE) def. Mark Woodforde and Todd Woodbridge (AUS), 7-6 (12), 4-6, 6-3

Women's Doubles Final: Gigi Fernandez (USA) and Natasha Zvereva (BLR) def. Mary Joe Fernandez and Lisa Raymond (USA), 6-2, 6-3
Mixed Doubles Final: Rika Hiraki (JPN) and Mahesh Bhupathi (IND) def. Lisa Raymond and Patrick Galbraith (USA), 6-4, 6-1

Wimbledon
Men's Singles Final: Pete Sampras (USA) def. Cedric Pioline (FRA), 6-4, 6-2, 6-4
Women's Singles Final: Martina Hingis (USA) def. Jana Novotna (CZE), 2-6, 6-3, 6-2
Men's Doubles Final: Todd Woodbridge and Mark Woodforde (AUS) def. Jacco Eltingh and Paul Haarhuis (NED), 7-6 (4), 7-6 (7), 5-7, 6-3
Women's Doubles Final: Gigi Fernandez (USA) and Natasha Zvereva (BLR) def. Nicole Arendt (USA) and Manon Bollegraf (NED), 7-6 (4), 6-4
Mixed Doubles Final: Helena Sukova and Cyril Suk (CZE) def. Larisa Savchenko Neiland (LAT) and Andrei Olhovskiy (RUS), 4-6, 6-3, 6-4

U.S. Open
Men's Singles Final: Patrick Rafter (AUS) def. Greg Rusedski (GBR), 6-3, 6-2, 4-6, 7-5
Women's Singles Final: Martina Hingis (SUI) def. Venus Williams (USA), 6-0, 6-4
Men's Doubles Final: Yevgeny Kafelnikov (RUS) and Daniel Vacek (CZE) def. Jonas Bjorkman and Nicklas Kulti (SWE), 7-6 (8), 6-3
Women's Doubles Final: Jana Novotna (CZE) and Lindsay Davenport (USA) def. Gigi Fernandez (USA) and Natasha Zvereva (BLR), 6-3, 6-4
Mixed Doubles Final: Manon Bollegraf (NED) and Rick Leach (USA) def. Mercedes Paz and Pablo Albano (ARG), 3-6, 7-5, 7-6 (3)

Year-End No. 1
Men: Pete Sampras
Women: Martina Hingis

Top Player Earnings
Men: Pete Sampras $6,498,311
Women: Martina Hingis $3,400,196

Davis Cup: Sweden

Fed Cup: France

ATP World Championships, Hanover–Pete Sampras
Grand Slam Cup, Munich–Pete Sampras
Chase Championships, NYC–Jana Novotna

1998

Sampras Earns Year-End No. 1 For Sixth Time

Lindsay Davenport proved her Olympic gold from 1996 was no fluke, beating Martina Hingis to win the US Open.

career biography. So exhausting was his effort to finish as the year No. 1 that Sampras would skip the first major of 1999—the Australian Open—to catch his breath.

Otherwise, the tennis season was highlighted by its parity—in both the men's and women's game—as eight different players claimed the eight men's and women's majors during the season—the first time since 1990 this has occurred and only the second time in the Open era.

Among the women, Martina Hingis defended her Australian Open title, and the bubbly Barcelona Bumblebee, Arantxa Sanchez Vicario, ruled at Roland Garros for the third time. New to the majors club were Jana Novotna, who finally broke through to win at Wimbledon, and Lindsay Davenport, the gold medalist from the 1996 Olympics, who proved that was no fluke by winning the U.S. Open.

With the men, the left-handed Petr Korda was the surprise winner at the Australian Open, while Spain's Carlos Moya

Pete Sampras' relentless run at the records of tennis was in a full sprint in 1998 as the 27-year-old had the record for most men's major singles titles in his sights. Pete's victories the previous year in Australia and at Wimbledon gave him 10 majors—two shy of Roy Emerson's record of 12 that Pete had designs on.

Sampras was only able to secure one major in 1998—not surprisingly at Wimbledon, where he picked up his fifth title in six years—and placed him alongside his idol Rod Laver as well as Bjorn Borg on the all-time list of major titles with 11.

Almost equally impressive was Sampras and his efforts to finish the year ranked No. 1 for a sixth straight year—breaking the record of five he shared with Jimmy Connors (1974—78), and pulling him abreast of Big Bill Tilden (1920—25). Sampras played the last six weeks of the indoor tournament season in Europe in order to stake claim to another bullet point under his

took the top honor at Roland Garros. Sampras again ruled at Wimbledon, while Patrick Rafter repeated at the U.S. Open.

At the Australian Open, Korda finally showed that he was worthy of a leading role in a major championship as opposed to being a minor character, with an occasionally dramatic appearance. He turned 30 during the fortnight in Melbourne, but his state of mind was considerably younger. In the quarterfinals, Korda, seeded No. 6, came back from a two-set crater to upset No. 4 Jonas Bjorkman 3-6, 5-7, 6-3, 6-4, 6-2. In a round where he would usually run into a buzz saw named Sampras or Agassi, Korda faced Slovak Karol Kucera in the semifinals—Kucera having removed Sampras from the picture in a rocking 6-4, 6-2, 6-7 (5-7), 6-3, quarterfinal upset. Korda's experiences—and losses—in the later rounds of major events served him well against the first time major semifinalist Kucera, Korda advancing 6-1, 6-4, 1-6, 6-2. Awaiting the final was the No. 9

seed Chile's Marcelo Rios, a fellow left-hander with flair similar to Korda's. Rios had quietly come through a comfortable draw—not playing a seeded player until Korda in the final, beating Nicolas Escude, 6-1, 6-3, 6-2, in the semis.

Alberto Berasategui, the Spaniard who reached the 1994 French final, proved to be a draw wrecker for Down Under-ites, taking out homeboy, second-seed Rafter in the third round, 6-7 (2-7), 7-6 (9-7), 6-2, 7-6 (7-4), and then re-emerging, shaky Andre Agassi in the fourth round, 3-6, 3-6, 6-2, 6-3, 6-3. Rios ended Alberto's run, 6-7 (6), 6-4, 6-4, 6-0, in the quarters.

Nerves got the best of the frosty and surly Chilean as Korda rolled to the title in a 6-2, 6-2, 6-2 decision. His trademark "scissors kick" dance was an exclamation point to this victory.

While the men's draw was filled with upsets and startling turnarounds, the top-seeded Swiss Miss—Hingis—refused to abdicate her women's crown, ousting eighth seed Conchita Martinez of Spain 6-3, 6-3 in the final. Martinez, looking to win her first major since her triumph at Wimbledon four years earlier, had accounted for second seed Davenport in a come-from-behind, three-set semifinal, 4-6, 6-3, 6-3. But the 25-year-old—one of the craftiest match players in the business—was out of her element against a highly-charged Hingis, who captured her fourth major in fine fashion. Martina had a bit of a semis struggle, 6-1, 2-6, 6-1, over Anke Huber of Germany.

A cavalcade of spirited clay-court players arrived at Roland Garros in search of the world's premier clay-court title. But, in the end, it was more like a Spanish Invasion as the capable Moya and the indefatigable Sanchez Vicario swept the singles championships. Moya capped a remarkable event by halting countryman Alex Corretja 6-3, 7-5, 6-3 in the final. His more penetrating forehand and wider range of talent carried him to victory in his second major final. When it was over, Corretja came around to Moya's side of the net and embraced his conqueror.

The women's event came down to the fourth seed Sanchez Vicario against sixth seed Monica Seles in a bruising battle of champions. Seles was seeking a fourth Roland Garros triumph, and was the sentimental favorite. Her father and coach Karolj had died less than two weeks before the start of the tournament. Monica contemplated skipping the event, but chose to participate after weighing every angle of the issue in her mind.

She came agonizingly close to taking the tournament. Against Sanchez Vicario, Monica led 5-3, 30-30 in the opening set but faltered at that critical moment and eventually lost the set in a tie-breaker. Seles stormed through the second set, but lost steam in the third. Sanchez Vicario, beaten in 14 of 16 previous head-to-head collisions with Monica, came out on top in this encounter, 7-6 (7-5), 0-6, 6-2, to collect a fourth major championship win. In a poignant post-match ceremony, Sanchez Vicario said sportingly, "I'd like to congratulate Monica for getting to the final. I'm sorry I had to beat you. I have so much respect for you. All the players are sorry that your father passed away."

In the semifinals, Seles was breathtakingly impressive in routing Hingis. Taking full advantage of her sizzling, left-handed, two-fisted strokes off both wings, Seles set the tactical agenda throughout and came away deservedly with a 6-3, 6-2 victory, her first in six career clashes against the Swiss stylist. Sanchez

Vicario took her place in the final with a 6-3, 7-6 (7-5) mastering of the No. 2 seed Davenport, who looked out of her element on the slow red clay. The towering Californian held serve only twice in ten service games as her Spanish adversary defended from the backcourt with supreme skill.

To Wimbledon, where Sampras put on one of the most determined stands of his illustrious career. He had won only two of his ten tournaments heading into The Big W. Confronted by the ever-daunting Goran Ivanisevic in the final, Sampras was stretched into his first ever five-set final at a major. In the second set tie-breaker, the 26-year-old American was twice a point away from trailing two sets to love. The top seed missed his first serve in both cases, but Ivanisevic drove backhand returns into the net. Sampras climbed out of that dark corner, and prevailed in the bright sunshine on Centre Court 6-7 (2-7), 7-6 (11-9), 6-4, 3-6, 6-2. From 2-2 in the final set, Sampras collected 16 of the last 19 points to secure his fifth singles championship at Wimbledon, and his 10th major title. A despondent Ivanisevic was beaten for the third time in a Wimbledon final, and it was his second defeat against Sampras in a confrontation for the title. "This is the worst moment of my life," said Ivanisevic. "It hurts the most because this time I had the chance."

Ivanisevic had ousted 1996 champion Richard Krajicek 6-4, 6-3, 5-7, 6-7 (5-7), 15-13 in a tumultuous semifinal. The big left-hander reached double match point at 5-4 in the fourth set, serving an apparent ace. Both players thought the match was over, but a let had been called. Somehow, Krajicek managed to break serve. He took that set in a tiebreak and went up a break in the fifth before faltering. Ivanisevic survived the suspenseful 28-game fifth. Later that afternoon, Sampras beat British No. 1 Tim Henman 6-3, 4-6, 7-5, 6-3 in a spirited skirmish.

Novotna cast aside all her demons in winning Wimbledon on her 13th attempt. She had wasted a 4-1, two-service-break lead in the final set against Steffi Graf in the final five years earlier, had faded after a blazing beginning against Hingis the previous year. Now, in her third final, with everyone wondering how well her nerves would hold up, Novotna stood firmly to the challenge. She was fortunate to be facing Nathalie Tauziat, the No. 16 seed from France and the first woman from her nation to reach the final on Centre Court since Suzanne Lenglen in 1925. Tauziat, 30, had never been beyond the quarterfinals of a major event before.

Third seed Novotna was the decidedly better grass-court player, winning 6-4, 7-6 (7-2). Novotna trailed 2-0, 40-15 in the first set before taking matters into her own hands. She served for the match at 5-4 in the second set but her normally impeccable forehand volley let her down in that game. Nevertheless, Novotna quickly regained the ascendancy in the tie-breaker, and confidently closed it out. "This is a definite dream come true for me," said a jubilant Novotna. "It's really important to always believe in yourself and to have a dream. This is what I have been waiting and working for."

Novotna's best match by far was her 6-4, 6-4 semifinal victory over the top-seeded and defending champion Hingis. Martina held a 6-2 career head-to-head edge over Novotna, sweeping the previous four battles they had fought. But the key to the verdict this time was the opening set. Hingis led 3-0, 0-40 but dropped

six of the next seven games. The momentum had unmistakably swung, and the top seed could not recover. Meanwhile, in the most stunning development of the tournament, seven-time champion Graf bowed 6-4, 7-5 in the third round to Natalia Zvereva, who then beat Seles, 7-6 (7-4), 6-2, on her way to the semifinals, losing there to Tauziat, 1-6, 7-6 (7-1), 6-3. Graf had not suffered a loss against Zvereva in 17 previous meetings, including Graf's famous 6-0, 6-0 decision in the final of the 1988 French Open.

At Flushing Meadow, Rafter was hard pressed to survive the opening round, withstanding a barrage of brilliant groundstrokes from the freewheeling and inventive Hicham Arazi, the clever left-hander from Morocco. Arazi's shotmaking was magnificent for two sets against the all-out aggression from his Australian adversary, but Rafter staged a stupendous comeback. Boosted by a vocal contingent of Aussie fans enjoying the night session in Ashe Stadium, Rafter rallied valiantly for a 4-6, 4-6, 6-3, 6-3, 6-1 first-round victory. A champion who didn't make it out of the first round was fourth-seed Petr Korda, winner in Australia, but given the immediate heave-ho by No. 155, German Bernd Karbacher, 2-6, 6-3, 6-2, 6-1.

From that juncture on, Rafter was near the top of his game. In the semifinals, however, he was fortunate to escape again, this time at the hands of the top-seeded Sampras.

Pete built a two-sets-to-one lead over the defending champion, but was hobbled over the last two sets by a strained left quadruple muscle near the hip. His mobility significantly impaired, Sampras could not stay with the crisp and confident Rafter, who prevailed 6-7 (8-10), 6-4, 2-6, 6-4, 6-3. Sampras would not get his chance to tie Rafter's countrymen, Emerson, at 12 in the majors title race and would have to wait.

In the final, matters were much easier for the athletic third-seed, and he crushed countryman Mark Philippoussis, 6-3, 3-6, 6-2, 6-0. In four sets, Rafter made merely five unforced errors. Philippoussis, unseeded but long overdue to be in a big final, had upended fifth-seed Moya in the semis, 6-1, 6-4, 5-7, 6-4.

Sampras avenged his Australian loss to Kucera with an emphatic, 6-3, 7-5, 6-4, quarterfinal victory on a chilly evening. Kucera had overcome eighth-seeded Agassi in a two-day, five-set match clouded by controversy. Ninth-seed Kucera had irritated the 1994 champion by frequently letting his high service tosses drop to the ground, waiting until he got the toss precisely where he wanted it before starting the point.

Agassi, exasperated by the constant delays, chose a cheap way to retaliate, imitating his opponent. He deliberately kept letting his own service tosses drop to the ground. Kucera had a commanding two-sets-to-love lead but Agassi took the third and went up a break in the fourth before rain stopped play. The next day, Agassi won the fourth, and led 2-0, 15-40 in the fifth before Kucera revived for a 6-3, 6-3, 6-7 (5-7), 1-6, 6-3 victory.

Davenport had played superb tennis all summer, winning three consecutive events at Stanford, Calif., over Venus Williams, 6-4, 5-7, 6-4; San Diego, over Mary Pierce, 6-3, 6-1; Los Angeles, over Hingis, 4-6, 6-4, 6-3. Although she lost to Graf in the semifinals at New Haven, 6-3, 7-6 (8-6), Davenport came to New York in the best possible frame of mind. On a balmy afternoon in the final at Flushing Meadows, Davenport struck down the defending champion Hingis, 6-3, 7-5.

Davenport overpowered Hingis from the outset, driving her forehand with surprisingly good ball control and depth, blasting her almost impeccable two-handed backhand into the corners with uncanny regularity. The barrage of big strokes Davenport was sending her way overwhelmed Hingis, but Martina made her move in the second set. At 5-4, she served for equality. Had she held there, she might well have won in three sets. But Davenport swept 12 of the next 15 points to close the account in style. In her first final round test at a major event, Davenport passed with flying colors.

Both the third-seeded Novotna and No. 5 Venus Williams made it to the semifinals. Williams stopped No. 4 seed Sanchez Vicario 2-6, 6-1, 6-1 in the quarterfinals, but lost to Lindsay, 6-4, 6-4. Novotna accounted for No. 11 Patty Schnyder, 6-2, 6-3, before losing to Hingis, 3-6, 6-1, 6-4. Schnyder, a left-hander with a deceptive inside-out top-spin forehand, had ousted the five-time champion Graf in the round of 16, 6-3, 6-4. It would be Graf's final match at the U.S. Open.

Although Hingis beat Novotna in singles, she was delighted at Jana's assistance in doubles. Their 6-3, 6-3, decision over Davenport and Zvereva meant a rare Grand Slam for Martina, the fourth woman to be thus involved. Her circumnavigation of the quintessential quadrangle began in Melbourne where she and another teen-ager, Croat Mirjana Lucic took the Australian over Davenport-Zvereva, 6-4, 2-6, 6-3. She was with Novotna the rest of the way: French over Davenport-Zverereva, 6-1, 7-6 (7-4); Wimbledon over Davenport-Zvereva, 6-3, 3-6, 8-6. (Would those results make it a Grand Slump for Davenport and Zvereva?)

Martina's Slamming predecessors were Brazilian Maria Bueno in 1960, also with two partners (Christine Truman, then Darlene Hard for the last three), and Martina Navratilova and Pam Shriver in 1984. Winning the doubles title with Czech Cyril Suk, Aussie Sandon Stolle followed the 1965-1966 example of Hall of Fame dad Fred, a unique majors capturing by father and son.

Following the U.S. Open, Sampras took a month-and-a-half European trip to stave off Rios and Rafter for the year-end No. 1, which was his for a record sixth straight year, tying Bill Tilden of the pre-computer era (1920-25). During Jimmy Connors's five straight years on top (1974—78), he won five singles majors, none in 1975 and 1977. Bill Tilden won eight during his six year reign at No. 1. Sampras had taken 10 major singles titles from 1993-98, winning at least one major in each of those seasons.

In any event, he had to work down to the wire, six successive tournaments, to reach his goal. Sampras lost in the first round of Basel, Switzerland (to Wayne Ferreira, 4-6, 7-6 (7-3), 6-3)—won Vienna, (defeating Kucera, 6-3, 7-6 (7-3), 6-1); lost in the quarterfinals of Lyon, France (to Tommy Haas in a walk-over with a back injury); lost in the semifinals of Stuttgart (to Richard Krajicek, 6-7 (2-7), 6-4, 7-6 (7-5)); lost in the final of Paris (to Greg Rusedski, 6-4, 7-6 (7-4), 6-3); lost in the first round of Stockholm (to Jason Stoltenberg, 7-6 (7-5), 4-6, 6-4).

It was not until Rios pulled out on the eve of the year-end ATP World Finals, the Masters, in Hannover, Germany, that Sampras finally clinched the year-end top spot. He won only four of 22 tournaments during the year, but his overall consistency was superior to nearest rivals Rios and Rafter.

In Hannover, Pete easily won all three of his round-robin matches, but lost an excruciatingly close semifinal contest to

Corretja. The Spaniard saved three match points to take out the Pistol 4-6, 6-3, 7-6 (7-3). Corretja, meanwhile, made another astonishing recovery in the final, overcoming countryman Moya 3-6, 3-6, 7-5, 6-3, 7-5 to capture the most prestigious prize of his career.

At Madison Square Garden in New York, Hingis stopped Davenport in the best-of-five set Chase Championships final 7-5, 6-4, 4-6, 6-2, to garner a fifth singles title for the year. The victory gave Hingis a 7-6 lead in her career series with Lindsay. But Davenport—the winner of six tournaments and the pivotal U.S. Open collision with Hingis—took the No. 1 world ranking from Hingis despite her end-of-season setback.

Italy hosted the Davis Cup final for the first time as Sweden journeyed to Milan to take on and beat the upstart Italians, 4-1. The opening match of the tie provided all the excitement of the series as Andrea Gaudenzi battled Magnus Norman valiantly for nearly five hours, before his shoulder gave out, forcing him to quit the match at 6-6 in the fifth set, after coming back from 0-4 down. Score, for Norman: 6-7, 7-6, 4-6, 6-3, 6-6, retire. Magnus Gustafsson allowed only five games to Davide Sanguinetti in the second match, 6-1, 6-4, 6-0, and Bjorkman and Nicklas Kulti clinched the Davis Cup in doubles for a second straight year, taking out Diego Nargiso and Sanguinetti, 7-6, 6-1, 6-3.

The United States, missing both Sampras and Agassi, fell meekly to the Italians 4-1 in an uninspiring environment in Milwaukee. Gaudenzi's gimpy shoulder held together long enough for an in-and-out win over Jan-Michael Gambill, 6-2, 0-6, 7-6 (7-0), 7-6 (7-4), and Sanguinetti handled Todd Martin, 7-6 (7-0), 6-3, 7-6 (10-8). The doubles finished the hosts, Nargiso and Gaudenzi beating Justin Gimelstob and Martin, 6-4, 7-6 (7-3), 5-7, 2-6, 6-3.

The big surprise for the Italians was the court. They expected a fast indoor surface, but the U.S. Tennis Association goofed, and a slow court suited the startled European guests just fine.

Sampras was a Davis Cup no-show all year, while Agassi played in the first round win over Russia, won 3-2 on Jim Courier's fifth-match recovery over Marat Safin, 0-6, 6-4, 4-6, 6-1, 6-4. Andre also helped in the 4-1 quarterfinal victory over Belgium, but begged off the U.S. team in the semis in a dispute with the USTA over how much influence players should have in the running of the team.

In the Fed Cup final at Geneva, Spain narrowly moved past Switzerland 3-2. Hingis won both of her singles—defeating Sanchez Vicario, 7-6 (7-5), 6-3, and Conchita Martinez, 6-4, 6-4—but Martinez managed to stop a determined Schnyder 6-3, 2-6, 9-7 on the last day in a hard fought, three hour, 18-minute tussle. The two nations were locked at 2-2, but Sanchez Vicario and Martinez crushed a depleted Schnyder and Hingis 6-0, 6-2 to finish the task.

Two Americans, Davenport and Sampras, finished the season deservedly on top of the world. But no one dominated the game in either women's or men's precincts, and in many ways the game was better for that.

1998 CHAMPIONS AND LEADERS

Australian Open
Men's Singles Final: Petr Korda (CZE) def. Marcelo Rios (CHI), 6-2, 6-2, 6-2

Women's Singles Final: Martina Hingis (SUI) def. Conchita Martinez (ESP), 6-3, 6-3

Men's Doubles Final: Jonas Bjorkman (SWE) and Jacco Eltingh (NED) def. Todd Woodbridge and Mark Woodforde (AUS), 6-2, 5-7, 2-6, 6-4, 6-3

Women's Doubles Final: Martina Hingis (SUI) and Mirjana Lucic (CRO) def. Lindsay Davenport (USA) and Natasha Zvereva (BLR), 6-4, 2-6, 6-3

Mixed Doubles Final: Venus Williams and Justin Gimelstob (USA) def. Helena Sukova and Cyril Suk (CZE), 6-2, 6-1

French Open
Men's Singles Final: Carlos Moya (ESP) def. Alex Corretja (ESP), 6-3, 7-5, 6-3

Women's Singles Final: Arantxa Sanchez Vicario (ESP) def. Monica Seles (USA), 7-6 (5), 0-6, 6-2

Men's Doubles Final: Jacco Eltingh and Paul Haarhuis (NED) def. Mark Knowles (BAH) and Daniel Nestor (CAN), 6-3, 3-6, 6-3

Women's Doubles Final: Martina Hingis (SUI) and Jana Novotna (CZE) def. Lindsay Davenport and Natasha Zvereva (BLR), 6-1, 7-6 (4)

Mixed Doubles Final: Venus Williams and Justin Gimelstob (USA) def. Serena Williams (USA) and Luis Lobo (ARG), 6-4, 6-4

Wimbledon
Men's Singles Final: Pete Sampras (USA) def. Goran Ivanisevic (CRO), 6-7 (2), 7-6 (9), 6-4, 3-6, 6-2

Women's Singles Final: Jana Novotna (CZE) def. Nathalie Tauziat (FRA), 6-4, 7-6 (2)

Men's Doubles Final: Jacco Eltingh and Paul Haarhuis (NED) def. Todd Woodbridge and Mark Woodforde (AUS), 2-6, 6-4, 7-6 (3), 5-7, 10-8

Women's Doubles Final: Martina Hingis (SUI) and Jana Novotna (CZE) def. Lindsay Davenport (USA) and Natasha Zvereva (BLR), 6-3, 3-6, 8-6

Mixed Doubles Final: Serena Williams (USA) and Max Mirnyi (BLR) def. Mirjana Lucic (CRO) and Mahesh Bhupathi (IND), 6-4, 6-4

U.S. Open
Men's Singles Final: Patrick Rafter (AUS) def. Mark Philippoussis (AUS), 6-3, 3-6, 6-2, 6-0

Women's Singles Final: Lindsay Davenport (USA) def. Martina Hingis (SUI) 6-3, 7-5

Men's Doubles Final: Sandon Stolle (AUS) and Cyril Suk (CZE) def. Mark Knowles (BAH) and Daniel Nestor (CAN), 4-6, 7-6, 6-2

Women's Doubles Final: Martina Hingis (SUI) and Jana Novotna (CZE) def. Lindsay Davenport (USA) and Natasha Zvereva (BLR), 6-3, 6-3

Mixed Doubles Final: Serena Williams (USA) and Max Mirnyi (BLR) def. Lisa Raymond and Patrick Galbraith (USA), 6-2, 6-2

Year-End No. 1
Men: Pete Sampras
Women: Lindsay Davenport

Top Player Earnings
Men: Pete Sampras $3,931,497
Women: Martina Hingis $3,175,631

Davis Cup: Sweden

Fed Cup: Spain

ATP World Championships, Hanover—Alex Corretja
Grand Slam Cup, Munich—Marcelo Rios
Chase Championships, NYC—Martina Hingis
Grand Slam Cup, Munich—Venus Williams

1999

Agassi, Graf Headliners On and Off The Court

Eighteen-months after being ranked No. 141 in the world and on the edge of quitting the game, **Andre Agassi** won the French Open to complete a "Career Grand Slam."

Graf won her 22nd and last major, the French Open—the site of her first major tournament title in 1987—in bizarre fashion over No. 1 Martina Hingis, with almost 15,000 witnesses chanting "STEF-FI! STEF-FI!" to urge her on to victory. Graf then reached the final at Wimbledon, only to be stopped by American Lindsay Davenport. Steffi, alone as the only champ to win each of the majors at least four times, said she had nothing else to play for in tennis and walked off into the sunset.

Off the court, Agassi and Graf became unlikely lovebirds. The two eventually married, and began raising a family.

Agassi also reached the final at Wimbledon, where he lost to chief rival Pete Sampras. Pete collected his 12th career major title, tying him with Roy Emerson for the most ever by a male player. Sampras did beat Agassi four out of five times they played during the year and if he hadn't herniated a disc and pulled out of the U.S. Open, he may have finished the year as the world No. 1 for a seventh straight year. Incidentally, like Agassi, Sam-

Andre Agassi and Steffi Graf were the stories of men's and women's tennis, respectively in 1999—both on and off the court. Agassi completed his incredible comeback from the desolation of a ranking of No. 141 in the latter stages of the 1997 season (and more than just whispers that he should give it up and retire) and won two majors—the U.S. and French Opens. His win in Paris completed his "Career Grand Slam" en route to recapturing the No. 1 ranking. At the end of the year, he would still be at that ranking—the first time he finished a year in the top spot. Andre became the fifth to hold all four majors, following Fred Perry, Don Budge, Rod Laver, Roy Emerson—Laver the most recent in 1962.

pras also began the courtship of his wife, actress Bridgette Wilson, during the year, having a friend set him up with the actress after seeing her in a movie during his recuperation time from his back injury.

The women had another compelling campaign, highlighted by Graf's win in France. Hingis won the first major of the year in Australia and Davenport broke through to win her second major at Wimbledon. Serena Williams stepped into the spotlight in New York with a surprising run to the title at the U.S. Open.

It all began in earnest, of course, at the Australian Open. Russian Yevgeny Kafelnikov—often his own worst enemy in big set-

tings—came away with a second major crown. The 24-year-old was solid and unusually stable over the fortnight Down Under, toppling an apprehensive, unseeded No. 21 Thomas Enqvist of Sweden, 4-6, 6-0, 6-3 7-6 (7-1), in the final. The 10th-seed Kafelnikov took full advantage of an excellent draw, and was forced to confront only one other seeded player, beating No. 15 seed Todd Martin, the 1994 finalist, 6-2, 7-6 (7-1), 6-2, in the quarters. But Romanian Andrei Pavel took him to five sets in the fourth round, 6-3, 7-6 (7-5), 6-7 (5-7), 3-6, 6-4.

Though Enqvist had the country against him, he managed to repel huge-serving Aussie Mark Philippoussis, 6-2, 6-4, 6-7 (3-7), 4-6, 6-2, in the fourth round, and the widely-admired U.S. Open champ Patrick Rafter, 6-4, 4-6, 6-4, 6-4, in the third. A lethargic fifth seed Agassi went out also in the fourth, to compatriot Vinnie Spadea, 6-1, 7-5, 6-7 (3-7), 6-3, who then fell in the quarters to German Tommy Haas, 7-6 (7-5), 7-5, 6-3. In the semis, it was Kafelnikov over Haas, 6-3, 6-4, 7-5, and Enqvist over Ecuadorian Nico Lapentti, 6-3, 7-5, 6-1. With Sampras absent, resting after his exhausting campaign at the end of 1998, Kafelnikov said, "Pete not playing kind of opened up the draw for everybody. A lot of guys thought they could win, even myself."

The champ, second-seed Hingis, was at the top of her game once more in Melbourne, winning the title for the third year in a row, dropping only one set along the way. In the final, she was too poised and polished for the sporadically brilliant upstart Amelie Mauresmo of France. Hingis rolled to a 6-2, 6-3 triumph and was rewarded with a fifth major championship. The unseeded Mauresmo's versatile shotmaking and her all court prowess was evident all through the contest, but she could not break down her opponent's defenses. Hingis gave almost nothing away while Mauresmo drifted into difficulty frequently with bad shot selection.

Nevertheless, Mauresmo produced a mammoth upset in the semifinals when she ousted top-seeded Davenport 4-6, 7-5, 7-5 after the American took a 4-2, final-set lead. Davenport had been in enviable form during a 6-4, 6-0 rout of fifth-seed Venus Williams in the quarters, but did not press her advantage against Mauresmo and paid a substantial price for her lack of conviction. In the quarterfinals, Monica Seles registered her final win against Steffi Graf 7-5, 6-1, before losing to Hingis 6-2, 6-4.

At the French Open, Agassi came out of one crisis after another. In the second round, he was two points away from a four-set defeat against Frenchman Arnaud Clement, recovering for a 6-2, 4-6, 2-6, 7-5, 6-0 win as the Frenchman faded in the final set with cramps. In the round of 16, Agassi was on the ropes against the defending champion Carlos Moya, with Moya up a set and two breaks in the second, serving at 4-1. The 29-year-old American worked his way out of that bind, forcing the issue with the Spaniard to gut out a 4-6, 7-5, 7-5, 6-1 victory. In the semis, the No. 13 seeded Agassi (the only seed to make the Final Four) edged Slovakia's Dominik Hrbaty, 6-4, 7-6 (8-6), 3-6, 6-4. The gritty Slovak, ranked No. 31, had bounced top-seed Kafelnikov in the second round, 6-4, 6-1, 6-4, and No. 9 seed Marcelo Rios in the quarters, 7-6 (7-4), 6-2, 6-7 (6-8), 6-3.

In the final, Agassi was obliterated for two sets by an inspired Andrei Medvedev, the unseeded Ukrainian ranked No. 100, who had once resided in the top five. Medvedev had been brilliant in the wind, but a rain delay late in the second set was just what Agassi needed to restore himself.

Slowly but surely, Agassi found his range off the ground, and the high-strung Medvedev lost his nerve. Agassi surged back methodically for a 1-6, 2-6, 6-4, 6-3, 6-4 triumph. When it was over, he wept as he turned to greet his coach Brad Gilbert and trainer Gil Reyes in the stands. Then he accepted the trophy from none other than Rod Laver.

Andre called his improbable Roland Garros triumph "sheer destiny." Medvedev's run to the final was highlighted by a second-round win over second-seeded and "still-unlucky-in-Paris," Sampras, 7-5, 1-6, 6-4, 6-3, and a quarterfinal win over 1997 French champion, eighth-seeded Gustavo Kuerten, 7-5, 6-4, 6-4.

The women provided similar drama on the red clay as a highly-charged Graf won her first major title in three years and her 22nd overall by battling back mightily to down the top-seeded Hingis 4-6, 7-5, 6-2. Hingis came agonizingly close to winning the only major she had not yet mastered. But her first big mistake occurred when she led 2-0 in the second set. On the first point of the third game, her forehand return was called long. She looked for help from umpire Anne Lasserre, who got out of the chair and conferred with the linesman that the call was correct. Hingis should have ended her protest right then and there, but a dangerous lapse in judgment cost her dearly. She walked around to Graf's side of the net to check the mark herself, a blatant violation of the rules. Referee Georgina Clark was called out to the court and Hingis was assessed a point penalty following her earlier warning for racket abuse.

The Roland Garros crowd of 16,761 came down hard on the teen-ager, and turned up the volume of their support for the veteran Graf. But Hingis regrouped. She served for the match at 5-4 in the second set and reached 15-0, standing three points away from a decisive, straight-set victory. But she drove a routine two-handed backhand beyond the baseline for 15-15. Graf broke her at 30 for 5-5, then swept eight of the next nine points to reach one set all.

By the time Graf reached 3-0 in the third set, she had run off six games in a row, and had collected 24 of 29 points in that span. Although Hingis managed to break back for 2-3 in the third and even had a point for 3-3, she was not the same player she had been for nearly two sets. Graf prevailed, seizing a sixth French Open crown. The German told the crowd at the post-match ceremony, "I feel French. I've played all over the world, but I've never had a crowd like this one—ever." Later, Graf added, "This is the biggest win I've ever had for sure. I've had a lot of unexpected ones. But this is by far the most unexpected. I really came into the tournament without belief. This has been incredible."

Hingis left the court in tears and had to be prodded by her mother, Melanie Molitor, to return to the court for the trophy presentation ceremony. En route to the final, Hingis beat Arantxa Sanchez Vicario 6-3, 6-2 in the semifinals. Graf beat Seles 6-7 (2), 6-3, 6-4 in their 15th and final confrontation (Graf winning the series 10-5).

Little did Graf know then that the 1999 French would be her last major championship victory. She would reach the final of Wimbledon the following month, over the battling bodies of

sixth-seed Venus Williams, 6-2, 3-6, 6-4, and surprising No. 134, unseeded 17-year-old Croat Mirjana Lucic, 6-7 (3-7), 6-4, 6-3.

It took a top-of-the-line Davenport to stop her 6-4, 7-5 in the final. Davenport broke the seven-time champion once in each set. Graf squandered three game points in a tense opening game before surrendering her serve. That was enough to carry the Californian through the first set. Then, at 5-5 in the second after a rain delay, she caught Steffi off guard again, breaking at that critical juncture, then serving out the match with brio.

In six previous appearances at the All England Club, Davenport had never advanced beyond the quarterfinals, but she won this time around without the loss of a set in seven matches, unseating the 1998 champ Jana Novotna, 6-3, 6-4, in the quarters.

Hingis was seen as a brief blip, victim at the starting gate in an all-time upset. Top-seeded Martina was KO'd, 6-2, 6-0, by a qualifier, No. 129 Jelena Dokic, a 16-year-old Aussie. Dokic would reach the quarters where another teen-age qualifier, American Alexandra Stevenson, 18, caught up with her, 6-3, 1-6, 6-3, before Davenport silenced the No. 86 upstart, 6-1, 6-1.

Furthermore Davenport never lost her serve against the imposing Graf, and conceded only five points on her delivery in her last four service games. The third seed gave perhaps the greatest performance of her career. She struck the ball with admirable pace, depth, and precision, and played the big points better than her revered rival, who waved goodbye to the Centre Court audience for the final time as a competitor. In her 14 visits to Wimbledon, Steffi had won the world's premier tournament seven times, reaching two additional finals. Moreover, she had triumphed in 22 of 53 career major events, an astonishing success rate of .415. Moreover, she had been beaten only nine times in 31 major finals, and had captured 107 tournament titles altogether in her 17 seasons on the tour, a figure surpassed in the Open era only by Navratilova (167) and Evert (154). Despite saying she would not play the French Open and Wimbledon again, Steffi said she would play out the rest of the year. However, days after retiring with a hamstring injury in her first round match in early August in San Diego against Amy Frazier, Graf announced her immediate retirement, saying, "I have done everything I wanted to do in tennis….I feel I have nothing left to accomplish. The weeks following Wimbledon weren't easy for me. I'm not having fun anymore. After Wimbledon, for the first time in my career, I didn't feel like going to a tournament."

Graf, however, did make an appearance at the U.S. Open, sitting in the upper bowl seating section, out of the view of the public, watching her then secret boyfriend and future husband Agassi win the U.S. Open final.

At Wimbledon, the future "Mr. Steffi Graf" stormed into the men's final on Centre Court with a scintillating, straight-set victory over Rafter 7-5, 7-6 (5), 6-2. On the other half of the draw, Sampras avoided a potential pitfall when his quarterfinal foe, Philippoussis, broke down, injuring a knee while leading 6-4, 1-2 and was forced to default. Sampras then ended the British hopes for a homegrown champion, defeating Tim Henman 3-6, 6-4, 6-3, 6-4 in the semifinal for the second straight year.

And so the stage was set for the two prodigious Americans to meet for the fourth time in a major final. Sampras held a 2-1

edge in major finals heading into this contest. Based on recent form and Agassi's renewed passion and intensity, many insiders believed he would rule on the grass courts at the shrine of the sport for the second time after a seven-year gap.

But too many astute observers overlooked Sampras' propensity to raise his game ineffably for the matches that mattered most to him. The Centre Court was undeniably his home abroad, and he performed in that theater as he did nowhere else. Serving commandingly, backing up his delivery with first volleys of the highest order, returning with unrelenting aggression, he played perhaps the masterpiece match of his career, taking apart his greatest rival 6-3, 6-4, 7-5, to win Wimbledon for the sixth time in seven years. He had captured the crown three years in a row for the second time. He had surely earned the label, "Man of the Century" at Wimbledon - and Sampras had secured a 12th major tournament singles title, locking him in a tie with Roy Emerson for the men's record.

The key to the outcome was the seventh game of the match. Sampras served at 3-3, 0-40. Agassi stung him three straight times with brilliant, scorching returns. But calmly and purposefully, Sampras served his way stupendously out of that corner, and never looked back. Before Agassi realized what had hit him, Sampras had run out that first set and built a 2-0 second-set lead, sweeping five games in a row. He had soared to another level, and there was no way Agassi could possibly rise with him. Sampras summed it up well: "It was the best tennis I think I've ever played on that court. I think when Andre and I are both playing well, it's the best tennis, maybe ever. He's made me a better player over the years."

Former finalist Jim Courier, in his final Wimbledon, played three epic five-setters in a run to the round of 16. He beat Carlos Moya 6-3, 3-6, 7-6 (7-1), 3-6, 6-2 in the second round and Sjeng Schalken of the Netherlands 7-6 (7-2), 3-6, 3-6, 7-5, 13-11 in 4:24 in the third round. Henman ended Jim's run in the fourth round, 4-6, 7-5, 7-5, 6-7 (5-7), 9-7.

Boris Becker said goodbye to Wimbledon—for a second time—reaching the fourth round. Becker, who told Pete Sampras after losing to him in the 1997 quarterfinals that he had just played his last Wimbledon match, decided Wimbledon was an addiction and he needed one more dose. In the first round, he nearly made a hero of No. 298-ranked Miles Maclagan of Britain, who led the three-time champion two sets to love and held three match points before losing, 5-7, 6-7 (7-9), 6-4, 7-5, 6-2. Becker then dispatched 15th-seeded countryman Nicolas Kiefer 6-4, 6-2, 6-4, then future Wimbledon champion Lleyton Hewitt in the third round, 6-1, 6-4, 7-6 (7-5). Rafter then ended Becker's career in the fourth round 6-3, 6-2, 6-3.

Post Wimbledon, Sampras beat Agassi two more times over the summer, 7-6 (7-3), 7-6 (13-11), in the final of Los Angeles and, 7-6 (9-7), 6-4, in the semifinals of Cincinnati. Pete's win in Cincy, defeating Rafter in the final, 7-6 (9-7), 6-3, was his fourth tournament title in a row. A hip injury in a quarterfinal match with Vince Spadea in Indianapolis forced him to default after splitting sets, ending his 24-match winning streak. His status as the heavy favorite to win the U.S. Open, however, was not altered. But in a practice session at the USTA National Tennis Center the day before

the tournament began, Sampras herniated a disc in his back and withdrew from the tournament.

Suddenly, irrevocably, Agassi became the man to beat in Flushing. The 1994 U.S. Open champion had a comfortable journey to the final, losing only two sets—to Justin Gimelstob, 6-1, 4-6, 6-3, 6-4, in the third round and Yevgeny Kafelnikov, 1-6, 6-3, 6-3, 6-3 in the semifinals. But he was given a stern test that afternoon by 6-foot-6 Todd Martin, who was playing the hard court tennis of his life. Martin narrowly escaped a first-round fifth-set tie-breaker over Stephane Huet of France 6-4, 6-3, 6-7 (2-7), 6-7 (5-7), 7-6 (7-3) and, in a fourth-round night match against Greg Rusedski, staged one of the most memorable comebacks in the recent history of the tournament. Rusedski served for the match at 5-4 in the third set and led 4-1 in the fifth-set, but Martin got him, 5-7, 0-6, 7-6 (7-3), 6-4, 6-4. Amid chants of "Let's Go Todd!" from the evening crowd at Arthur Ashe Stadium, Martin won 20 of the last 21 points of the match to advance into the next day (and the quarterfinals), in a match that concluded at 12:50 a.m.

After beating Czech Slava Dosedel, 6-3, 5-7, 6-4, 6-4, in the quarterfinals and Cedric Pioline in the semifinals, 6-4, 6-1, 6-2, Martin advanced into his second career major final. Against Agassi, Martin knew he had to strike relatively quickly in the rallies against the great groundstroker from Las Vegas and serve with authority.

Todd lost his serve only once in the first three sets, and played two magnificent tie-breakers to build a two-sets-to-one lead. With Agassi serving at 4-3 in the fourth, Martin had two break points. Had he converted, he might well have gone on to victory. As it was, Agassi did not acquiesce. He held on, and wore down his debilitated rival 6-4, 6-7 (5-7), 6-7 (2-7), 6-4, 6-2. This three-hour, 23-minute skirmish was the first five-set final at the Open since 1988, when Mats Wilander prevented Ivan Lendl from winning a fourth straight title. In his third consecutive major final, Agassi was too good when it counted. He said, "I don't remember any five setter that I've ever played where I did not lose my serve. I really had to make every point incredibly important. I felt like I was hanging by a thread for most of the match. Todd was really executing in a way that was giving me a lot of problems."

Two-time defending champion Patrick Rafter, seeded fourth, became the first defender ever to lose his opener in the 119-year history of the U.S. Championships, falling to Pioline 4-6, 4-6, 6-3, 7-5, 1-0, retire, the Australian's aching shoulder forcing him to surrender.

In the quarterfinals, Kafelnikov and Richard Krajicek engaged in an Open classic, Kafelnikov winning 7-6 (7-0), 7-6 (7-4), 3-6, 1-6, 7-6 (7-5). Krajicek fired the tournament's Open era record 49 aces—in vain, as was Ed Kauder who lost to Ham Richardson despite his 59 aces in 1955.

On the women's side, the words of Richard Williams—sire of Venus and Serena—that kid sister is the more talented of the two began to ring true. Seventh-seed Serena, 17, became the first Williams to win a major singles title, and the first black since Althea Gibson at Forest Hills in 1958 to take a major female championship. Her run to the title was not a cake walk. In the third round, she was on the brink of defeat against 16-year-old Belgian Kim Clijsters, a future Open champion, with Clijsters leading 5-3 in

the final set before Serena won 16 of the last 17 points to close, 4-6, 6-2, 7-5. In the round of 16, Serena rallied from a set down to top Conchita Martinez, 4-6, 6-2, 6-2. Facing Monica Seles in the quarters, Serena dropped the first set again before recording a 4-6, 6-3, 6-2 victory. Next on her agenda was defending champion Davenport. Serena took that one 6-4, 1-6, 6-4.

Serena had played 16 sets, but she was ready for the final against top-seeded Hingis, winner of a bruising battle over Big Sister Venus 6-1, 4-6, 6-3 the day before that shut off a prospective all-Williams final. Hingis took too much out of herself in that strenuous showdown, and Serena was just hitting her stride. Williams led 3-6, 3-5, 15-40, double match point against an overwhelmed Hingis, but Martina refused to walk away. She took three games in a row and was two points away from parity at one set all. Hingis led 6-5, 30-0 but Serena rekindled her energy and enthusiasm and came away with a 6-3, 7-6 (7-4), victory in her first major final. As Serena finished off Hingis, big sister Venus watched from the stands, wearing a bittersweet expression. She had been expected to win a big championship before Serena, but the following afternoon the two sisters joined forces to capture the doubles title over Chanda Rubin and Sandrine Testud, 4-6, 6-1, 6-4.

At the men's year-end ATP Tour World Championships in Hannover, Sampras put together another superb performance to overcome Agassi 6-1, 7-5, 6-4 in the final. Agassi had beaten Sampras in the round robin 6-2, 6-2 during the week, but his top rival came through when the chips were down. Entering Hannover, he had played only one match all fall after missing the U.S. Open, aggravating his back at the indoor event in Paris during a first-round win over Francisco Clavet, 4-6, 6-3, 7-6 and withdrew. But, in Hannover, Sampras sparkled again.

Meanwhile, in New York, Hingis was beaten 6-4, 6-2 by an inspired Davenport in the final of the year-end Chase Championships. But Hingis, who won seven singles titles and reached the final in 13 of her 20 events, finished the season at No. 1 in the world for the second time.

At the Fed Cup final at Stanford, Calif., perhaps the finest U.S. team in history assembled for a 4-1 triumph over Russia. Venus Williams and Davenport took on the singles assignments while Serena Williams joined her sister for the doubles. U.S. captain Billie Jean King rejoiced in riches of talent surrounding her. Despite her Flushing Meadows brilliance, Serena Williams was not chosen for singles. No matter. Venus won over Elena Likhovtseva 6-3, 6-4 and then Davenport downed Elena Dementieva 6-4, 6-0. Davenport then beat Likhovtseva, 6-4, 6-4 in the clincher and Venus lost to Dementieva, 1-6, 6-3, 7-6 (7-5). The Williams sisters finished if off, beating Elena Makarova and Dementieva, 6-2, 6-1.

Davis Cup was a celebration of the 100th year of the competition. Appropriately enough, the United States and Britain—the two teams that kicked off the competition back in 1900—drew each other in the Centenary year.

The U.S. team that faced Britain in Birmingham, England was without its top two players, Pete Sampras and Andre Agassi. Sampras still could not be convinced to return to the competition due to scheduling problems and Agassi was still in dispute with the USTA, gasoline thrown onto that fire when the USTA fired its team physician, Agassi's friend, Dr. George Fareed.

Captain Tom Gullikson fielded a team led by Todd Martin and Jim Courier, set to face top tenners Tim Henman and Greg Rusedski. The U.S. were underdogs, but in predictable Davis Cup fashion, the unpredictable happened—the U.S. took a 2-0 lead on day one—Courier over Henman 7-6 (7-2), 2-6, 7-6 (7-3), 6-7 (10-12), 7-5 and Martin blitzing Rusedski 6-4, 6-4, 6-2. In the doubles, Martin and Alex O'Brien were unable to close out a shutout, losing to Henman and Rusedski 3-6, 7-5, 6-3, 6-7 (5-7), 6-3. On the final day, Martin lost to Henman 4-6, 7-5, 6-3, 7-6 (7-4), setting up the heart-stopping decider between Courier and Rusedski. Courier, the cool man for a fifth match, delivered with a last serve-cracking backhand return, 6-4, 6-7 (3-7), 6-3, 1-6, 8-6.

That thrust the U.S. into a sweltering quarterfinal series with Australia, staged poetically enough, at Boston's Longwood Cricket Club, host of the Davis Cup inauguration in 1900. Sampras, inspired by the U.S. effort against Britain, returned to the U.S. team, but, strangely, the Wimbledon champ declined to play singles. That possibly cost the U.S. the Cup. It may have been out of respect to Courier and Martin, who got the job done versus the Brits.

Speedy 18-year-old rookie Lleyton Hewitt got the Aussies, captained by John Newcombe, off to an early start, upsetting Martin 6-4, 6-7 (1-7), 6-3, 6-0, before Rafter took out Courier 7-6 (7-5), 6-4, 6-4. Sampras paired with O'Brien in the doubles, keeping the U.S. alive, beating Mark Woodforde and Sandon Stolle 6-4, 6-3, 3-6, 4-6, 6-3.

Martin, game as ever but still feeling the affects of the 100-plus degree temperatures from his Friday match, needed an IV just before the fourth match with Rafter. U.S. Captain Gullikson unsuccessfully attempted to replace him with Sampras, against Davis Cup rules at the time, except for injury or illness (ITF officials did not believe Martin's condition was serious, feeling the U.S. wanted Sampras in the lineup, an obvious advantage.) Martin, in his weakened condition, nevertheless bravely went for broke and attempted winners at every opportunity. Incredibly, he connected on most shots and took a two-set lead, only to return to earth and run out of gas, losing 4-6, 5-7, 6-3, 6-2, 6-4, clinching the win for the Aussies. Newk's team went on to beat Russia 4-1 in the semifinals and France 3-2 in the final in Nice. Mark Philippoussis, absent from the quarterfinal and semifinal matches due to injury, was the hero, winning his opening-day singles over Sebastien Grosjean in straight sets, and clinching the tie with a 6-3, 5-7, 6-1, 6-2 over Pioline. Australia seized the Cup for the 27th time, prevailing as the world champion team nation for the first time since 1973.

1999 CHAMPIONS AND LEADERS

Australian Open

Men's Singles Final: Yevgeny Kafelnikov (RUS) def. Thomas Enqvist (SWE), 4-6, 6-0, 6-3, 7-6 (1)
Women's Singles Final: Martina Hingis (SUI) def. Amelie Mauresmo (FRA), 6-2, 6-3
Men's Doubles Final: Patrick Rafter (AUS) and Jonas Bjorkman (SWE) def. Leander Paes and Mahesh Bhupathi (IND), 6-3, 4-6, 6-4, 6-7 (10), 6-4
Women's Doubles Final: Martina Hingis (SUI) and Anna Kournikova (RUS) def. Lindsay Davenport (USA) and Natasha Zvereva (BLR), 7-5, 6-3
Mixed Doubles Final: Mariaan de Swardt and David Adams (RSA) def. Serena Williams (USA) and Max Mirnyi (BLR), 6-4, 4-6, 7-6 (5)

French Open

Men's Singles Final: Andre Agassi (USA) def. Andrei Medvedev (UKR), 1-6, 2-6, 6-4, 6-3, 6-4
Women's Singles Final: Steffi Graf (GER) def. Martina Hingis (SUI), 4-6, 7-5, 6-2
Men's Doubles Final: Mahesh Bhupathi and Leander Paes (IND) def. Goran Ivanisevic (CRO) and Jeff Tarango (USA), 6-2, 7-5
Women's Doubles Final: Venus Williams and Serena Williams (USA) def. Martina Hingis (SUI) and Anna Kournikova (RUS), 6-3, 6-7 (2), 8-6
Mixed Doubles Final: Katarina Srebotnik (SLO) and Piet Norval (RSA) def. Larisa Savchenko Neiland (LAT) and Rick Leach (USA), 6-3, 3-6, 6-3

Wimbledon

Men's Singles Final: Pete Sampras (USA) def. Andre Agassi (USA), 6-3, 6-4, 7-5
Women's Singles Final: Lindsay Davenport (USA) def. Steffi Graf (GER), 6-4, 7-5
Men's Doubles Final: Mahesh Bhupathi and Leander Paes (IND) def. Paul Haarhuis (NED) and Jared Palmer (USA), 6-7 (10), 6-3, 6-4, 7-6 (4)
Women's Doubles Final: Lindsay Davenport and Corina Morariu (USA) def. Mariaan de Swardt (RSA) and Elena Tatarkova (UKR), 6-4, 6-4
Mixed Doubles Final: Lisa Raymond (USA) and Leander Paes (IND) def. Anna Kournikova (RUS) and Jonas Bjorkman (SWE), 6-4, 3-6, 6-3

U.S. Open

Men's Singles Final: Andre Agassi (USA) def. Todd Martin (USA), 6-4, 6-7 (5), 6-7 (2), 6-3, 6-2
Women's Singles Final: Serena Williams (USA) def. Martina Hingis (SUI), 6-3, 7-6 (4)
Men's Doubles Final: Sebastien Lareau (CAN) and Alex O'Brien (USA) def. Leander Paes and Mahesh Bhupathi (IND), 7-6 (7), 6-4
Women's Doubles Final: Serena Williams and Venus Williams (USA) def. Chanda Rubin (USA) and Sandrine Testud (FRA), 4-6, 6-1, 6-4
Mixed Doubles Final: Ai Sugiyama (JPN) and Mahesh Bhupathi (IND) def. Kimberly Po and Don Johnson (USA), 6-4, 6-4

Year-End No. 1

Men: Andre Agassi
Women: Martina Hingis

Top Player Earnings

Men: Andre Agassi $4,269,265
Women Martina Hingis $3,291,780

Davis Cup: Australia

Fed Cup: United States

ATP World Championships, Hanover—Pete Sampras
Grand Slam Cup, Munich—Greg Rusedski
Chase Championships, NYC—Lindsay Davenport
Grand Slam Cup, Munich—Serena Williams

Sampras Wins Record 13th Major, Venus Is Golden

Venus Williams enjoyed a golden year in 2000, winning her first two major singles titles at Wimbledon and the US Open while also winning singles and doubles gold at the Sydney Olympics.

When a compelling season came to an end, this much was certain: Brazil's enormously popular Gustavo Kuerten and the strikingly improved Venus Williams were the two players who achieved the most. Kuerten captured the French Open for the second time, and closed his campaign magnificently with a triumph at the elite Tennis Masters Cup in Lisbon, dramatically moving past Russian Marat Safin to finish No. 1 in the world.

Venus went to work with more passion and purpose than ever before, sweeping the Wimbledon and U.S. Open titles. Despite securing six singles championships including the gold medal at the Olympic Games, Venus was ranked only No. 3 in the

world behind Martina Hingis and Lindsay Davenport. But, given the fact that she had won the two biggest tournaments in tennis, Williams was considered the best player in the world by the vast majority of authorities.

To be sure, it was a year when the prestigious prizes were divided among a cluster of leading players. Andre Agassi took the Australian Open for the second time. Safin peaked propitiously at the U.S. Open to collect his first major championship. Most notably, Pete Sampras made history of the highest order, winning Wimbledon to set a record with 13 major singles championships. And two big, powerful hitters, Davenport and Mary Pierce, made their presence known by coming through impressively at majors.

Hingis had been hoping to seal a fourth singles title in a row in Melbourne at the Australian Open, but an inspired Davenport denied her that opportunity. Raising her record to 3-0 in major finals, Davenport blasted her familiar rival off the court 6-1, 7-5. The American led 5-1 in the second set before the plucky Hingis pressed hard with pride to draw level at 5-5. Undismayed, Davenport took two games in a row for the win. Lindsay didn't lose a set, and Martina lost only the two in the final. Jennifer Capriati, making an unseeded, but impressive, stand—she had played only three matches in Melbourne since a 1993 quarterfinal—made it to the semis where Davenport stopped her, 6-2, 7-6 (7-4).

The pivotal men's match in formful Melbourne was Agassi's semifinal with Sampras. Agassi approached that riveting contest with an 11-17 record against his most revered rival; he came away with an exhilarating 6-4, 3-6, 6-7 (0-7), 7-6 (7-5), 6-2 triumph. Sampras was two points away from a four-set win when he led 5-4 on serve in the fourth set tie-breaker, but Agassi turned the corner and never looked back, prevailing despite 37 aces from a determined Sampras.

In the final, top-seed Agassi banished defending champion, second-seeded Yevgeny Kafelnikov 3-6, 6-3, 6-2, 6-4 with another dazzling display. It was the sixth major tournament victory for Agassi in his storied career, but he did not take another title of any kind for the rest of the year.

Kuerten stepped up commandingly in the next major, ruling on the slow red clay of Roland Garros. Seeded fifth, the Brazil-

ian overcame Sweden's industrious third-seeded Magnus Norman 6-2, 6-3, 3-6 7-6 (8-6), but not before the Swede had saved 10 match points in the latter stages of the hectic championship battle. Kuerten had hung on tenaciously to defeat 1996 champion Kafelnikov, 6-3, 3-6, 4-6, 6-4, 6-2, from 2-4 in the fourth in a quarterfinal before taking apart the markedly improved Juan Carlos Ferrero of Spain, 7-5, 4-6, 2-6, 6-4, 6-3, in the semis. Agassi's crown was knocked of early, by the Slovak, Karol Kucera, in the second round, 2-6, 7-5, 6-1, 6-0.

Pierce had finally found the top of her game after a string of disappointing seasons. A finalist at the French Open in 1994 and the winner of the Australian Open in 1995, she had not lived up to those high standards in the ensuing years. But now, at 25, she had reached a new level of maturity. She became the first French passport holding woman since Francoise Durr in 1967 to prevail at Roland Garros.

Seeded sixth, Pierce fought back gamely to remove three-time titlist Monica Seles 4-6, 6-3, 6-4 in the quarterfinals. In the semis, she downed top-seeded Hingis 6-4, 5-7, 6-2 in a suspenseful struggle. After those uplifting victories, the final was almost anti-climactic for Pierce. She beat Spain's resourceful Conchita Martinez 6-2, 7-5 to claim her second career major in exemplary fashion. Pierce served at 4-5 in the second set, but ran out the match capably from there.

On the grass at the All England Club, Venus Williams was unbeatable. Not since Althea Gibson 42 years earlier had a black woman won Wimbledon. Venus came through a difficult draw, holding back a trio of accomplished adversaries: top-seed Hingis, 6-3, 3-6, 6-4; her sister, Serena, 6-2, 7-6 (7-3) and Davenport, 6-3, 7-6 (7-3). The best of those battles was against Hingis. Venus took the first set comfortably, then went up a break at 3-2 in the second. Thereafter, Hingis asserted herself. She broke twice to take the second set. By the time the players were locked at 2-2 in the third, there had been eight consecutive service breaks. Hingis, however, had spent too much of her energy, and Venus picked up her velocity and placement on serve to close out the historic triumph.

The Venus-Serena semifinal confrontation was only the third ever meeting between sisters at Wimbledon, and the first of the Open era. Many among the cognoscenti looked for Serena to beat her older sibling for only the second time in five career head-to-head clashes. She had marched into this battle having lost only 13 games in five matches. She had lost her serve only once in ten sets. She had been breathtakingly effective in all facets of her game. But Big Sister dominated the day. Serena had a 4-2, second-set lead with three break points at her disposal. Venus hung on tenaciously. In the tie-breaker, Serena moved ahead 3-1 but never won another point. A despondent Serena was in tears as she congratulated her sister at the net. Venus put her arm around Serena to console her. But their father and coach, Richard Williams, was not at courtside. He chose to wander through the town of Wimbledon while his daughters competed, claiming it was too painful for him to watch.

When it was over, Serena astutely summed up the match: "I didn't think I played that well today. I missed a lot of shots, especially on my forehand side. Venus brought out her best game

against me and I guess I wasn't all that ready. It was my goal to do better in this tournament, but that's okay. I'm only 18. Venus is 20. I have a lot of years ahead of me."

In the final, Venus Williams knocked out the defending champion Davenport in a lackluster showdown. Venus served for the match at 5-4 in the second set, but two double faults and an unprovoked backhand error cost her that game. Nevertheless, she controlled the tie-breaker, racing to a 5-1 advantage and moved persuasively to the victory.

Venus admitted, "We were both feeling the pressure. I know I was rushing too much on my serve." Davenport was largely in accord, saying, "There were a few points that I'd love to take back, a few things I wish I could have done better. But a lot of that was caused by Venus. She was hitting the ball a lot deeper that I was."

In the men's Centre Court final, Sampras concluded an emotional fortnight with a joyous moment in the twilight. Finishing his 6-7 (10-12), 7-6 (7-5), 6-4, 6-2 final-round triumph over Patrick Rafter at 8:57 p.m. after rain had twice delayed play earlier in the day, the 28-year-old American climbed up into the stands to embrace his mother, Georgia, and father, Sam, who had flown over from California for the title match. They had never seen him win a major title. Also in the stands was Bridgette Wilson, Pete's fiance. (They would marry on September 30). As he said later, "Having my parents and future wife there was about as good as it is going to get for me as an athlete."

From the second round on, Sampras played with tendinitis in his left foot and ankle. He managed to win a rugged four set meeting with the dangerous Karol Kucera, 7-6 (11-9), 3-6, 6-3, 6-4, in the second round but would not practice in between matches. He took injections before each match to combat the pain, and willed his way on. He had a favorable draw, not meeting a seed until he took on the attack-minded 12th-seed Rafter, who had beaten second-seeded Agassi in a brilliantly played five-set semifinal, 7-5, 4-6, 7-5, 4-6, 6-3. But driven by deep pride and a sense of history, Sampras staged a spectacular revival against his worthy Australian rival.

Rafter served with a 4-1 lead in the second set tiebreak, standing three points away from a commanding two-sets-to-love lead. Bingo! Sampras swept six of the next seven points to get back on level terms at one set all, and refused to look back. Serving with increasing authority, Finding the range on his backhand returns, hardly missing a volley, his second serve deadly, Sampras soared over the last two sets.

He didn't lose serve even once in this showdown—the fifth time in seven victorious Wimbledon finals that he had accomplished that remarkable feat. Sampras had not been broken in his last 17 sets of the tournament, holding his delivery an incredible 85 times in a row. He had broken the record he shared with Australia's Roy Emerson, capturing a 13th career major crown, leading many knowledgeable observers to the conclusion that he was the greatest player of all time.

On to New York, for the U.S. Open. Although Marat Safin had made significant strides over the course of the season—winning Barcelona, over Juan Carlos Ferrero, 6-3, 6-3, 6-4 and Mallorca, 6-4, 6-3 over Mikael Tilstrom on clay in the spring, taking the Cana-

dian Open in Toronto on summertime hard courts over Harel Levy, 6-2, 6-3—no one was really prepared for the devastatingly potent tennis he would produce on the mean green slabs at Flushing Meadow. In the final, he stunned Sampras 6-4, 6-3, 6-3, in 98 minutes, competing with immense poise in his first major final. It was one of the most comprehensive defeats ever suffered by his illustrious opponent, who was beaten for only the third time in 16 major finals.

Not once did Sampras break Safin's explosive serve and the 20-year-old Russian broke Sampras four times. Pete had lost his delivery the same number of times against his previous six opponents. He simply came up against a madly inspired man who did not fully understand what he was doing. "He reminded me of when I was 19 and won here for the first time," Sampras said of Safin. "He passed and returned my serve as well as anyone I've seen."

Safin had started off the year with a dismal 5-11 match record, but he was in full flight at the last major the season. He was pushed into arduous five-set showdowns with both the 35-year-old Italian Gianluca Pozzi, 6-3, 3-6, 6-3, 3-6, 6-4, in the second round, and the fleet-footed Frenchman Sebastien Grosjean, in the third, 6-4, 7-6 (7-3), 1-6, 3-6, 7-6 (7-5). That one was gulper. With Grosjean serving at 4-5 in the decisive tie-breaker, a downpour chased them from the court for one hour, 45 minutes. Grosjean won the point when they returned, but Safin got the mini-break on a forehand return, and forced an error on the last point. The Russian held his ground when it counted.

Sampras, too, was hard pressed to make it to the final. In the quarters, he confronted Richard Krajicek, the 6-foot-5 Dutchman who had beaten him in four of their last five clashes, including a straight-set Wimbledon quarterfinal in 1996. Krajicek came at Sampras in full serve-and-volley throttle, taking the first set and moving to 6-2, quadruple set point in the second set tiebreak. In a dazzling sequence, Sampras took six points in a row to reach one set all, a flash of lightning such as he exhibited to derange Rafter at Wimbledon He was brimming with conviction thereafter, winning this exhilarating collision 4-6, 7-6 (8-6), 6-4, 6-2. He then defeated Lleyton Hewitt, 7-6 (9-7), 6-4, 7-6 (7-5) in a semifinal where Safin sidelined Todd Martin, 6-3, 7-6 (7-4), 7-6 (7-1).

Venus Williams demonstrated her grace under pressure in winning the championship of her country for the first time, taking her second straight major in the process. Facing a first-rate Hingis in the semifinals, Venus trailed 3-5, 15-30 in the third set. With an opportunity to reach double match point, Hingis played a cautious overhead down the middle. Venus replied boldly, driving her two-handed backhand down the line for a winner. She had escaped from a precarious position, and proceeded to win four games in a row to come through 4-6, 6-3, 7-5.

In the final against Davenport, Venus was in jeopardy again as the Californian served for a 5-1 first set lead. Venus collected five games in a row to take that set, and the match, 6-4, 7-5. This was a bit of family revenge since Davenport had made Serena the ex-champ, 6-2, 7-6 (7-5), in the quarters. Lindsay was pushed in the second round, 4-6, 6-2, 6-2, by a Belgian 17-year-old who would be champion five years later: Kim Clijsters. Hingis got into the semis by beating Monica Seles, 6-0, 7-5.

Only a few weeks after the Open, Venus Williams and Kafelnikov came away with gold medals at the Olympic Games on the hard courts at Sydney. Venus jolted Russian Elena Dementieva 6-2, 6-4. Dual golds for the Williams family were the order of the day as Serena joined Venus to win the doubles over Netherlands' Kristie Boogert and Miriam Oremans, 6-1, 6-1. Venus was the first player since Helen Wills in 1924 to sweep the singles and doubles. Kafelnikov was surprisingly resilient in a five-set triumph over Germany's Tommy Haas in the men's final, safely coming through that contest 7-6 (7-4), 3-6, 6-2, 4-6, 6-3.

Safin seemed certain to finish the year at No. 1 in the world when he won his seventh tournament of the season—indoors at Paris over Mark Philippoussis, 3-6, 7-6 (9-7), 6-4, 3-6, 7-6 (10-8). However, Kuerten somehow surpassed him at the last hurdle. The flamboyant Brazilian—nourishing on the slow hard court surface indoors—ousted Sampras in the semifinals, 6-7 (5-7), 6-3 6-4 and Agassi in the final, 6-4, 6-4, 6-4, to take the Tennis Masters Cup title in Lisbon. Had he not lost to Agassi, 6-3, 6-3, Safin would have been the year's top player. But Kuerten was magnificent in crushing Agassi with a relentless barrage of sharply angled topspin backhands doing most of the damage. He was the first South American man ever to finish at No. 1 on the official ATP computer since the inception of the rankings in 1973.

Despite not taking any of the four majors, Hingis finished No. 1 among the women for the third time in four years. Her unfailing consistency kept her at the top. The Swiss backcourt stylist won nine tournaments including the year-end Chase Championships in New York, where she came from behind to flatten Seles, 6-7 (5-7), 6-4, 6-4, raising her record against Monica to 12-2. But, of course, nearly everyone considered Venus Williams the best player since she won the two biggest tournaments.

Spain established itself as the tenth country to win the Davis Cup. In Barcelona, they struck down the Australians 3-1 on red clay. In the series-clinching triumph, Juan Carlos Ferrero was regal in stopping Hewitt 6-2, 7-6 (7-5), 4-6 6-4, while another Juan Carlos (the king) and Queen Sofia cheered him on. Spain, beaten in the 1965 and 1967 finals, was too tough for the Australians on the turgid surface in front of their vociferous home fans.

Hewitt got the Aussies an opening day split, beating Albert Costa, 3-6, 6-1, 2-6, 6-4, 6-4, before Ferrero broke down Rafter, 6-7 (4-7) 7-6 (7-2), 6-2, 3-1, ret. (injured shoulder). Alex Corretja and Juan Balcells grabbed the doubles over Mark Woodforde and Sandon Stolle, 6-4, 6-4, 6-4, leaving the rest to Juan Carlos.

In the United States, a one-year captaincy for John McEnroe didn't quite work out. The U.S. won two fifth-match indoor thrillers - 3-2 defeats of Zimbabwe in Harare and Czech Republic at Los Angeles. Agassi beat both Black brothers, Wayne, 7-5, 6-3, 7-5, and Byron, 6-2, 6-3, 7-6 (7-4), during the initial U.S. venture into Africa. But it took a clutch performance by rookie Chris Woodruff, 6-3, 6-7 (2-7), 6-2, 6-4, over Wayne to settle it.

Against the Czechs, the U.S. was again behind 2-1 on the third day, having started badly as Jiri Novak confused Sampras 7-6 (7-1), 6-3, 6-2. However, Agassi was good for a pair of wins, 6-3, 6-3, 6-3, over Slava Dosedel, and 6-3, 6-3, 6-1, over Novak, giving

Pete the opportunity to end it over Dosedel, 6-4, 6-4, 7-6 (7-2).

The bitter end came in the dirt at Santander, Spain—5-0. McEnroe couldn't convince Pete and Andre to travel. Only the clinching doubles was close: Martin and Woodruff losing to Corretja and Balcells, 7-6 (8-6), 2-6, 6-3, 6-7 (5-7), 6-3. John McEnroe resigned, to be replaced by his younger brother, Patrick McEnroe.

The U.S ladies took care of Spain, though, retaining the Fed Cup, 5-0, with Davenport and Seles leading the way at Las Vegas. Davenport took apart Conchita Martinez, 6-1, 6-2, to give the U.S. an insurmountable 3-0 lead. She also beat Arantxa Sanchez Vicario, 6-2, 1-6, 6-3. Seles beat Martinez, 6-2, 6-3. It wasn't a bad year for U.S. women, winning three of the four majors, the Fed Cup and both Olympic golds.

Meanwhile, Jim Courier retired from tennis early in the year at 29. The redheaded, industrious, enterprising American won back-to-back French Open titles in 1991-92, and took the Australian Open in 1992-93. Courier reached the finals of the U.S. Open in 1991 and Wimbledon two years later. He played on two victorious U.S. Davis Cup teams (1992 and 1995). Ranked No. 1 in the world in 1992, he was also in the Top 10 in 1991, 1993 and 1995.

2000 CHAMPIONS AND LEADERS

Australian Open
Men's Singles Final: Andre Agassi (USA) def. Yevgeny Kafelnikov (RUS), 3-6, 6-3, 6-2, 6-4
Women's Singles Final: Lindsay Davenport (USA) def. Martina Hingis (SUI), 6-1, 7-5
Men's Doubles Final: Rick Leach (USA) and Ellis Ferreira (RSA) def. Andrew Kratzmann (AUS) and Wayne Black (ZIM), 6-4, 3-6, 6-3, 3-6, 18-16
Women's Doubles Final: Lisa Raymond (USA) and Rennae Stubbs (AUS) def. Martina Hingis (SUI) and Mary Pierce (FRA), 6-4, 5-7, 6-4
Mixed Doubles Final: Rennae Stubbs (AUS) and Jared Palmer (USA) def. Arantxa Sanchez Vicario (ESP) and Todd Woodbridge (AUS), 7-5, 7-6 (3)

French Open
Men's Singles Final: Gustavo Kuerten (BRA) def. Magnus Norman (SWE), 6-2, 6-3, 2-6, 7-6 (6)
Women's Singles Final: Mary Pierce (FRA) def. Conchita Martinez (ESP), 6-2, 7-5
Men's Doubles Final: Mark Woodforde and Todd Woodbridge (AUS) def. Paul Haarhuis (NED) and Sandon Stolle (AUS), 7-6, 6-4
Women's Doubles Final: Martina Hingis (SUI) and Mary Pierce (FRA) def. Virginia Ruano Pascual (ESP) and Paola Suarez (ARG), 6-2, 6-4
Mixed Doubles Final: Mariaan de Swardt and David Adams (RSA) def. Rennae Stubbs and Todd Woodbridge (AUS), 6-3, 3-6, 6-3

Wimbledon
Men's Singles Final: Pete Sampras (USA) def. Patrick Rafter (AUS), 6-7 (10), 7-6 (5), 6-4, 6-2
Women's Singles Final: Venus Williams (USA) def. Lindsay Davenport (USA), 6-3, 7-6 (3)
Men's Doubles Final: Todd Woodbridge and Mark Woodforde (AUS) def. Paul Haarhuis (NED) and Sandon Stolle (AUS) 6-3, 6-4, 6-1
Women's Doubles Final: Venus Williams and Serena Williams (USA) def. Ai Sugiyama (JPN) and Julie Halard Decugis (FRA), 6-3, 6-2
Mixed Doubles Final: Kimberly Po and Donald Johnson (USA) def. Kim

Clijsters (BEL) and Lleyton Hewitt (AUS), 6-4, 7-6 (3)

U.S. Open
Men's Singles Final: Marat Safin (RUS) def. Pete Sampras (USA), 6-4, 6-3, 6-3
Women's Singles Final: Venus Williams (USA) def. Lindsay Davenport (USA), 6-4, 7-5
Men's Doubles Final: Lleyton Hewitt (AUS) and Max Mirnyi (BLR) def. Rick Leach (USA) and Ellis Ferreira (RSA), 6-4, 5-7, 7-6
Women's Doubles Final: Julie Halard-Decugis (FRA) and Ai Sugiyama (JPN) def. Cara Black (ZIM) and Elena Likhovtseva (RUS), 6-0, 1-6, 6-1
Mixed Doubles Final: Arantxa Sanchez Vicario (ESP) and Jared Palmer (USA) def. Anna Kournikova (RUS) and Max Mirnyi (BLR), 6-4, 6-3

Year-End No. 1
Men: Gustavo Kuerten
Women: Martina Hingis

Top Player Earnings
Men: Gustavo Kuerten $4,701,610
Women: Martina Hingis $3,457,049

Davis Cup: Spain

Fed Cup: United States

Tennis Masters Cup, Lisbon—Gustavo Kuerten
Chase Championships, New York—Martina Hingis

2000 OLYMPICS—SYDNEY, AUSTRALIA

Men's singles:
GOLD: Yevgeny Kafelnikov (RUS)
SILVER: Tommy Haas (GER)
BRONZE: Arnaud Di Pasquale (FRA)

Women's singles:
GOLD: Venus Williams (USA)
SILVER: Elena Dementieva (RUS)
BRONZE: Monica Seles (USA)

Men's doubles:
GOLD: Daniel Nestor and Sebastien Lareau (CAN)
SILVER: Todd Woodbridge and Mark Woodforde (AUS)
BRONZE: Alex Corretja and Albert Costa (ESP)

Women's doubles
GOLD: Venus Williams and Serena Williams (USA)
SILVER: Kristie Boogert and Miriam Oremans (AUS)
BRONZE: Dominique Van Roost and Els Callens (BEL)

2001

Capriati Is Comeback Kid

Jennifer Capriati celebrates her win over Kim Clijsters in the French Open women's singles final.

She was indisputably "Tennis Player of the Year." Roaring back into view in one of the most extraordinary revivals in the modern world of sports, she reached the top of her profession, won two major championships, and re-captured the hearts of tennis fans across the globe with her unwavering spirit. Astonishingly resurgent, Jennifer Capriati overshadowed almost everyone else with her exploits.

Capriati had endured some tumultuous times on her way to the summit. When she turned pro in 1990 shortly before her 14th birthday, she was expected to move swiftly to the top of her sport. She built an impressive record in her first four years as a pro, finishing each of those seasons among the Top 10 in the world,

reaching the semifinals of Wimbledon in 1990 and the U.S. Open in 1991, winning the gold medal at the Olympic Games in 1992. Then she fell upon hard times from late 1993 until she returned to the Top 25 in the world in 1996. In that span, she was arrested for drug possession after an earlier shoplifting charge. She had a few more difficult seasons before rising to No. 23 in the world in 1999, then No. 14 in 2000.

So, to be sure, she had planted some promising seeds as she headed into 2001. But not even Capriati herself could have anticipated such a dramatic reversal of fortunes. It all began at the Australian Open in Melbourne. Henrieta Nagyova, a 22-year-old Slovakian, pushed her to 4-6, 6-2, 7-5, in the opening round. In the quarterfinals, Capriati cut down Monica Seles, 5-7, 6-4, 6-3, after trailing 4-2 in the second. In the semis, Capriati accounted for defending champion Lindsay Davenport, 6-3, 6-4. Last, but not least, she upstaged Martina Hingis 6-4, 6-3 to win her first major title. Hingis had won all five of her career meetings with Capriati until then, but had to get through the barbed wire of the Williams duo, beating Serena, 6-2, 3-6, 8-6 in the quarterfinals, and Venus, 6-1, 6-1 in the semifinals.

When it was over, a beaming No. 12 seeded Capriati said, "Dreams do come true. If you keep believing in yourself, anything can happen. I'm no longer going to doubt myself in anything." With good reason.

She had taken only one set in her five losses to Hingis. She was appearing in her first major final while Hingis was in her 11th. But Capriati's flat, penetrating groundstrokes were too much for Martina, who was rushed out of points time and again by the American's pace and precision. Hingis rallied from 1-5 to 4-5 in the first set, but Capriati held for the set, and took over from there.

Operating skillfully from the backcourt in the stifling heat Down Under, Andre Agassi crushed Frenchman Arnaud Clement, the energetic counter-puncher who had knocked him out of the U.S. Open in the second round in 2000. This time around, Agassi was in vintage form, coasting to a 6-4, 6-2, 6-2 final-round triumph for his seventh major title.

The real test for the bald-headed American was his semifinal with Patrick Rafter. The first three sets of that encounter were played at an astounding level as the Australian came forward

relentlessly, forcing Agassi to keep coming up with impeccable passing shots. The home fans cheered unabashedly for their man as Rafter moved ahead two sets to one, but he was a spent force. Agassi easily resumed his command to win 7-5, 2-6, 6-7 (5-7), 6-2, 6-3. Clement had gotten there by flushing 1999 champ Yevgeny Kafelnikov, 6-4, 5-7, 7-6 (7-3), 7-6 (7-3), and, in a squeaker, compatriot Sebastien Grosjean, 5-7, 2-6, 7-6 (7-4), 7-5, 6-2.

At Roland Garros, Gustavo Kuerten was the man to beat once more. The Brazilian took the French Open title for the second year in a row and the third time in all, picking apart Spain's Alex Corretja as burdensome winds and light rain gave way to sunshine and calmer conditions. Kuerten stopped Corretja 6-7 (3-7), 7-5, 6-2, 6-0. The 24-year-old cast aside his inhibitions across the last two sets and played with verve and imagination.

Kuerten had nearly suffered a mammoth upset the previous Sunday afternoon against American qualifier, No. 135 Michael Russell, rescuing himself from two-sets-to-love and match point down at 5-3 in the third. Guga's forehand, a 25th stroke, nicked the baseline on the match point, and he escaped the fourth rounder, 3-6, 4-6, 7-6 (7-3), 6-3, 6-1. He went on to dismantle 1996 champ Kafelnikov, 6-1, 3-6, 7-6 (7-3), 6-4, and Spain's Juan Carlos Ferrero, 6-4, 6-4, 6-3.

Agassi, seeded third, was ushered out of the tournament in the quarterfinals by Grosjean 1-6, 6-1, 6-1, 6-3. After the American had raced through the first set, former President Clinton entered the stadium to watch the rest of the match. He was greeted with a rousing round of applause from the crowd. Thereafter, Agassi went sharply into decline, losing his authority and the match. Later, he unconvincingly claimed he was not aware that Clinton had been present.

An 18-year-old American rookie, Andy Roddick made a fire-powering impression in the second round, banging the tourney record 37 aces while overcoming ex-champ Michael Chang, 5-7, 6-3, 6-4, 6-7 (5-7), 7-5, in 3:46.

Capriati remained on the ascendancy at Roland Garros, winning a gripping final-round confrontation from Kim Clijsters 1-6, 6-4, 12-10, her second straight major crown.

It was one of the hardest fought and most tightly contested women's major finals of modern times. Both Belgian kids—the Brussels Sprouts—were in the semis. Kim, 18, struck back boldly from a set and 4-2 down to defeat 19-year-old Justine Henin 2-6, 7-5, 6-3.

Against Capriati, she exploited her often-brilliant, inside-out forehand and forced the Floridian back on her heels. Clijsters controlled the opening set, then lost a relatively tight second set. The third set hung in the balance until the end. Four times, Capriati was two points away from losing, and yet she kept creating chances for herself as well. After serving to save the match at 4-5 and 5-6 in the third, Capriati tried to serve it out at 7-6. An obstinate Clijsters would not go away. When Capriati took eight points in a row to lead 10-9, she seemed certain to finish the job.

Clijsters broke back again for 10-10, but that was her limit. Capriati closed the account with some timely attacking, and won the longest third-set ever in a Roland Garros women's final. "I'm just really happy I pulled it out," she said. "It was such a tough match. I was just fighting to the end because I wanted to win so much." Clijsters, gracious in defeat, said, "I can't really blame myself that I lost. One of us had to lose, and eventually it had to be me today. She's playing with so much confidence."

That confidence nearly carried Capriati through Wimbledon. Two matches away from a third straight major crown, hoping to become the first woman since Graf in 1988 to make a Grand Slam, she started superbly against Justine Henin in the semifinals. In 21 minutes, she rolled through the first set. But Henin's exquisite, one-handed topspin backhand was a weapon not to be denied, and Justine began exploiting the sharp angles off that side, taking Capriati off the court on her two-handed side. The complexion of the match changed irrevocably. Henin succeeded 2-6, 6-4, 6-2.

"Everybody was making such a big deal out of the Grand Slam," said Capriati, who had downed Serena in the quarters, 6-7 (4-7), 7-5, 6-3, for her 18th straight majors match win. "But I'm pretty happy with how the year has gone. Justine was a different player in the last two sets from the beginning. She was going for it—all or nothing—and she was on."

Henin was hard pressed to play at the top of her game in the final against Sister Venus, a 6-2, 6-7 (1-7), 6-1, winner over Davenport in the semifinals. Venus's big serving and aggression off the ground and on the drive volley propelled her through the first set, but Henin took three games in a row from 3-3 in the second, losing only one point in two service games, breaking Venus in between.

But Venus kept attacking at the right times, winning 18 of her 24 net approaches. She picked up her serving, and swept to a 6-1, 3-6, 6-0 victory—her second championship season in a row on Centre Court. Venus did not gloat; rather, she saluted Henin. "She's really very good. In my first [major] final, I didn't win a set [against Hingis at the 1997 U.S. Open]. Justine is a great player and I want to congratulate her."

Strangely, top-seed Hingis was bumped in the first round for the second time in three years—a record for elite incompetence. This time, a Spaniard, No. 83 Virginia Ruano Pascual, did the dirty deed, 6-4, 6-2.

Ranked No. 125, Goran Ivanisevic arrived at Wimbledon like a beggar with a tin cup, and departed as the king. He asked for a wild card and got it, based on his three final round appearances (1992, 94, 98). Having failed in qualifying at the Australian Open, Goran seemed to have no hope. No wild card or anyone so far down the scale had ever won a Wimbledon title.

Nevertheless, there was the spindly 6-foot-4 Croat, the Incendiary I, in his seventh match, gracing the uproarious final on Peasants' Monday—and winning!

For the men's final—held a day late due to inclement weather—tickets were on a first-come-first-served basis, and Centre was crowded with ordinary folk, mostly young Aussies and Croats, ready to light up the gray day by screaming for their guy, either Goran or the favorite, third-seeded Patrick Rafter. Up and down, round and round it went suspensefully for a minute longer than three hours. Serve-and-volley points were short but exciting. They stayed as close as the hairs in Goran's beard, until a ripping forehand broke Rafter to 7-8, and Goran served it out

through three deuces, 6-3, 3-6, 6-3, 2-6, 9-7 to capture his first major title at age 29. But left-hander Goran somehow rekindled his old serving prowess, breaking his own 1992 tournament record of 206 aces by serving 212 against a sterling cast of opponents including Carlos Moya, Andy Roddick, Greg Rusedski, Marat Safin, Tim Henman, and Rafter—27 against Rafter, 41 against Roddick. When he served at 6-7, 15-30 in the fifth set against Rafter, he was two points away from losing. But he held on for 7-7 and assertively took the last two games to hand Rafter a second straight agonizing final-round defeat on the Centre Court. It was not one of the best-played Wimbledon finals, but it was surely one of the most excrutiating and emotional.

Rafter won the highest caliber contest of the fortnight, narrowly escaping defeat against second-seeded Agassi. Agassi served for the match at 5-4 in the fifth set and reached 30-15, but Rafter attacked at the propitious moments in that critical game and broke back. He defeated the 31-year-old American 2-6, 6-3, 3-6, 6-2, 8-6. For the second year in a row, he had bested Agassi in the penultimate round of game's biggest tournament.

That battle ended on Friday afternoon. Ivanisevic followed against the homeboy, Britain's darling Tim Henman. Henman built a two-sets-to-one lead and they were on serve in the fourth when rain intruded. They returned Saturday, and Ivanisevic regrouped to capture the fourth set. But more rain forced another postponement until Sunday, with Ivanisevic completing a three-day ordeal with a 7-5 6-7 (6-8), 0-6, 7-6 (7-5), 6-3 victory.

Henman had seemed an answer to homeland prayers because Pete Sampras, his semifinal conqueror in 1998-99, was nowhere to be seen. Pete's 31-match Wimbledon streak had been scissored dramatically by a 19-year-old Swiss named Roger Federer in the fourth round, 7-6 (9-7), 5-7, 6-4, 6-7 (2-7), 7-5. Sampras, the champion for seven of the previous eight years, had two break points at 4-4 in the final set but did not convert.

But then, Federer (who would be heard from, and then some), was beaten by Henman, 7-5, 7-6 (8-6), 2-6, 7-6 (8-6), and life looked beautiful for Tim—until showers and Goran rained on his parade.

At the U.S. Open, Sampras was striving to become the first man ever to capture at least one major title for nine consecutive years, and he came remarkably close to realizing that goal. In an unprecedented run, he stopped the three men who had controlled the tournament since he had won his fourth and most recent title in 1996. In the round of 16, Sampras took down 1997-98 champion Rafter, 6-3, 6-2, 6-7 (5-7), 6-4, to set up a quarter-final appointment with 1994 and 1999 victor Agassi, who had beaten Pete in their last three head-to-head battles.

But in one of the finest matches in the history of the game, Sampras halted Agassi 6-7 (7-9), 7-6 (7-2), 7-6 (7-2), 7-6 (7-5). Neither man broke serve in four scintillating sets under the lights. Agassi had made a mere 19 unforced errors, and still lost. Before the start of the last tie-breaker, the crowd gave both players a well-deserved standing ovation. Finally, Sampras cut down Safin, avenging his loss to the Russian in the 2000 final with an emphatic 6-4, 7-6 (7-5), 6-3 semifinal triumph.

By the time Sampras arrived in the final, he had held serve no fewer than 87 straight times since the second round. He

seemed ready to run another victory lap. But waiting for him on the last day was none other than No. 4 seed Lleyton Hewitt, the Australian with the small frame but large heart. He played surpassingly to defeat Sampras on a windswept afternoon, claiming his first major title with a 7-6 (7-4), 6-1, 6-1 win.

The consistency of Hewitt's service returning was extraordinary. He broke Sampras six times, and produced dazzling passing shots as well. He was much fresher and more highly charged than his 30-year-old adversary. Despite his heroics, Sampras had fallen short. "I'm sure as times goes by," he lamented, "I'll reflect and feel good about what I did here. But only one name gets on the trophy and it's not mine. That's the harsh reality of it."

Scrappy Hewitt had come through Roddick, slimly, in a quarterfinal, 6-7 (5-7), 6-3, 6-4, 3-6, 6-4, but, mangling Yevgeny Kafelnikov, 6-1, 6-2, 6-1, he posted the worst semis blowout since 1951, champ Frank Sedgman over defender Art Larsen, 6-1, 6-2, 6-0.

As for the women, Venus Williams was every bit as convincing in defending her Open title as she had been in ruling again at Wimbledon. In a Saturday night, prime-time final under the lights, she held the upper hand throughout in a 6-2, 6-4 triumph over her sister Serena, her fourth win in five matches against her younger sibling. From 1-2 in the first set, Venus won seven games in a row. Serena found her timing off in this big-hitting battle and led 4-3 on serve in the second. Venus took over from there to win the last three games. She committed 17 fewer unforced errors than Serena, and that made all the difference.

Venus had overcome Capriati 6-4, 6-1 in an uneven semifinal while Serena had peaked in a 6-3, 6-2 drubbing of top-seeded Hingis. Venus, seeded No. 4, looked every inch the best player in the world, and the No. 10-seeded Serena made it unmistakably clear that she belonged much closer to the top of her profession.

At the close of the season in Munich, Serena took the year-end Sanex Championships, a much more alluring event when it was played in New York. Davenport, out for two-and-a-half months earlier in the season with a knee injury, hurt it again in a hard fought semifinal victory over Clijsters, 1-6, 6-3, 7-6 (7-3), then was forced to default the final to Serena. Despite her loss to Venus at the U.S. Open, Serena finished her season with a flourish.

Meanwhile, the men's Tennis Masters Cup moved to Sydney, where Hewitt firmly established himself as the best player in the world. In the round-robin portion of that event, he stopped Grosjean, 3-6, 6-2, 6-3; Rafter, 6-2, 6-4; and Agassi, 6-3, 6-4. He knocked off Ferrero in the semifinals, 6-4, 6-3, then toppled Grosjean again in the final, 6-3, 6-3, 6-4 to end his season in style.

At 20 years, 10 months, Lleyton became the youngest ever year-end No. 1 male, two months younger than American Ellsworth Vines in 1932, the winner of Wimbledon and the U.S. that year. He also was the youngest No. 1 since the inception of the ATP computer rankings in 1973, the first Aussie at No. 1 since John Newcombe in 1971.

There were 142 nations contending for the Davis Cup, but the sole survivor was France, a surprising 3-2 winner over Australia in the final on grass in Melbourne. Hewitt fell on opening day to the excellent attacking play of Nicolas Escude, 4-6, 6-3, 3-6, 6-3, 6-4, but Rafter, who went into sabbatical and eventually announced his retirement in early 2003, took care of Grosjean, 6-3, 7-6 (8-6), 7-5.

Then Australian captain John Fitzgerald elected to play Rafter and Hewitt in the doubles, and they lost to Cedric Pioline and Fabrice Santoro, 2-6, 6-3, 7-6 (7-5), 6-1. Hewitt got Australia even at 2-2 by erasing Grosjean, 6-3, 6-2, 6-3. However, Rafter, unfit with a sore shoulder, was replaced for the decisive fifth by slippery-serving left-hander Wayne Arthurs. The 30-year-old, ranked No. 64, was caught in Escude's volleying heat, 7-6 (7-3), 6-7 (5-7), 6-3, 6-3, and the Cup went to Paris.

In another sign of their growing stature in the women's game, Clijsters and Henin captured a first Fed Cup title for Belgium in a 2-1 bagel-decorated defeat of Russia at Madrid. Clijsters crushed Elena Dementieva, 6-0, 6-4, and Henin toppled Nadia Petrova, 6-0, 6-3. While the Williams sisters, Capriati, Davenport and Seles gave the U.S. a presence in the upper echelons that no other country could come close to matching, the fact remained: Belgium was surging on the talent and tenacity of Clijsters and Henin.

2001 CHAMPIONS AND LEADERS

Australian Open

Men's Singles Final: Andre Agassi (USA) def. Arnaud Clement (FRA), 6-4, 6-2, 6-2
Women's Singles Final: Jennifer Capriati (USA) def. Martina Hingis (SUI), 6-4, 6-3
Men's Doubles Final: Jonas Bjorkman (SWE) and Todd Woodbridge (AUS) def. Byron Black (ZIM) and David Prinosil (GER), 6-1, 5-7, 6-4, 6-4
Women's Doubles Final: Serena Williams and Venus Williams (USA) def. Lindsay Davenport and Corina Morariu (USA), 6-2, 2-6, 6-4
Mixed Doubles Final: Corina Morariu (USA) and Ellis Ferreira (RSA) def. Barbara Schett (AUT) and Joshua Eagle (AUS), 6-1, 6-3

French Open

Men's Singles Final: Gustavo Kuerten (BRA) def. Alex Corretja (ESP), 6-7 (3), 7-5, 6-2, 6-0
Women's Singles Final: Jennifer Capriati (USA) def. Kim Clijsters (BEL), 1-6, 6-4, 12-10
Men's Doubles Final: Mahesh Bhupathi and Leander Paes (IND) def. Petr Pala and Pavel Vizner (CZE), 7-6, 6-3
Women's Doubles Final: Virginia Ruano Pascual (ESP) and Paola Suarez (ARG) def. Jelena Dokic (AUS) and Conchita Martinez (ESP), 6-2, 6-1
Mixed Doubles Final: Virginia Ruano Pascual and Tomas Carbonell (ESP) def. Paola Suarez (ARG) and Jaime Oncins (BRA), 7-5, 6-3

Wimbledon

Men's Singles Final: Goran Ivanisevic (CRO) def. Patrick Rafter (AUS), 6-3, 3-6, 6-3, 2-6, 9-7
Women's Singles Final: Venus Williams (USA) def. Justine Henin (BEL), 6-1, 3-6, 6-0
Men's Doubles Final: Donald Johnson and Jared Palmer (USA) def. Jiri Novak and David Rikl (CZE), 6-4, 4-6, 6-3,
Women's Doubles Final: Lisa Raymond (USA) and Rennae Stubbs (AUS) def. Kim Clijsters (BEL) and Ai Sugiyama (JPN), 6-4, 6-3
Mixed Doubles Final: Daniela Hantuchova (SVK) and Leos Friedl (CZE) def. Liezel Huber (RSA) and Mike Bryan (USA), 4-6, 6-3, 6-2

U.S. Open

Men's Singles Final: Lleyton Hewitt (AUS) def. Pete Sampras (USA), 7-6 (4), 6-1, 6-1
Women's Singles Final: Venus Williams (USA) def. Serena Williams (USA), 6-2, 6-4
Men's Doubles Final: Wayne Black and Kevin Ullyett (ZIM) def. Donald Johnson and Jared Palmer (USA), 7-6, 2-6, 6-3
Women's Doubles Final: Rennae Stubbs (AUS) and Lisa Raymond (USA) def. Kimberly Po-Messerli and Nathalie Tauziat (FRA), 6-2, 5-7, 7-5
Mixed Doubles Final: Rennae Stubbs and Todd Woodbridge (AUS) def. Lisa Raymond (USA) and Leander Paes (IND), 6-4, 5-7, 7-6 (9)

Year-End No. 1

Men: Lleyton Hewitt
Women: Lindsay Davenport

Top Player Earnings

Men: Gustavo Kuerten $4,091,004
Women: Venus Williams $2,662,610

Davis Cup: France

Fed Cup: Belgium

Tennis Masters Cup, Sydney—Lleyton Hewitt
Sanex Championships, Munich—Serena Williams

In many ways, it was a landmark season in the world of tennis. Serena Williams celebrated more than anyone else, winning eight of 13 tournaments, capturing 56 of 61 matches, securing three of the four major titles. Lleyton Hewitt stood on top of the world for the second straight year, winning Wimbledon for the first time and taking his second straight Tennis Masters Cup title. Veterans Albert Costa of Spain and Thomas Johansson of Sweden came away with their first major titles, and Jennifer Capriati triumphed at the Australian Open for her third major crown.

But perhaps the biggest story of the year was the re-emergence of Pete Sampras, who broke an agonizing 33-tournament

Pete Sampras holds up the US Open trophy after beating an on-looking **Andre Agassi** in the final at Flushing Meadow. The title was a career-closing performance for Sampras and his record 14th major championship.

losing streak by winning the U.S. Open for the fifth time, recording a 14th major triumph in the process. Pete, at 31, became the oldest men's U.S. Open champion since 35-year-old Ken Rosewall took the top honor at Forest Hills in 1970. Moreover, Sampras was the oldest man to rule at any major since Arthur Ashe (five days shy of his 32nd birthday) won Wimbledon in 1975.

To be sure, the soft-spoken yet deeply-driven American was the "Comeback Player of the Year." In winning at Flushing Meadow for the first time in six years, Sampras emphatically answered the many media critics who insisted he no longer could play at that level. As usual, he spoke eloquently with his racket.

Clearly, no one thought that Johansson would place his name on the winner's trophy Down Under. In 24 previous appearances at the majors, the 26-year-old Swede had never been beyond the quarterfinals. He had finished two years (including 2001) among the top 20 in the world, but did not seem to have the tools to compete at the top of his trade. But the No. 16 seed took full advantage of an excellent draw, and then had the good fortune to meet the enigmatic Marat Safin in the final.

Safin had played his best brand of big-tournament tennis since his breakthrough victory at the U.S. Open 16 months earlier. He won a high-quality 6-2, 6-4, 6-7 (5-7), 7-6 (12-10) skirmish from Sampras in the round of 16, and battled back gamely from two sets to one down to topple Tommy Haas, 6-7 (5-7), 7-6 (7-4), 3-6, 6-0, 6-2 in the semifinals. Seemingly poised to pick off another major, he took the first set from Johansson but slowly came apart at the seams thereafter. Johansson's forehand return was his best feature, and he served progressively better after the opening set. In the end, the Swede prevailed 3-6, 6-4, 6-4, 7-6 (7-4). While Johansson competed with unwavering intensity, Safin surely did not display the fighting attitude he needed for such an important occasion, also his 22nd birthday, seemingly more devoted to blondes than backhands.

Astoundingly, both top seeds disappeared in the first round: No. 1 Hewitt to No. 39, Spaniard Alberto Martin, 1-6, 6-4, 6-4, 7-6 (7-4), and No. 2 Guga Kuerten to No. 49, Frenchman Julien Boutter, 3-6, 4-6, 7-5, 6-3, 6-3.

Capriati, meanwhile, fought as ferociously as any player could in overcoming three-time champ Martina Hingis in a gripping final. With temperatures on court measured at 107 degrees fahrenheit, the 25-year-old American had her back to the wall from the outset. She lost the first set, then trailed 4-0 in the second. Hingis, closing in on her first major championship since the 1999 Australian Open, was exploiting her extraordinary ball control off both sides, moving Capriati craftily around the court, luring Jennifer into mistakes. But Martina had lost the art of closing a deal of this magnitude. She started playing not to lose rather than trying to control her own destiny.

Capriati would not fold. She rallied from 0-4 to 3-4, only to lose her serve again. Hingis served for the match at 5-3 and had a match point. Capriati clipped the line with a backhand crosscourt for a winner. Hingis double faulted at break point down to make it 5-4. Capriati got back to 5-5, but the American double faulted at 5-6, 30-30 to give Martina a second match point; Capriati took it right away by forcing a forehand error from Hingis. The Swiss Miss made it to match point for the third time, but Capriati's forehand approach volley provoked a forehand long from Hingis.

On they went to the tie-breaker. Hingis saved a set point at 5-6, then reached 7-6 and her fourth match point. She drove a two-hander crosscourt; the shot landed inches long. Capriati took the tie-breaker 9-7. Both players left the court for bathroom breaks in the middle of the second set. They were granted a ten-minute break before the start of the third. Hingis led 2-1 but, thoroughly debilitated, she never won another game.

Capriati, the victor, 4-6, 7-6 (9-7), 6-2, became the first woman to come back from match point down in a major final since Margaret Smith [Court] stopped Lesley Turner [Bowrey] in the French Championships final of 1962. "It was really hard to breathe out there," said Capriati "The air was so thick and hot. But the whole time, even though I was coming from behind, I never thought of myself as being defeated."

Jenny's four match points saved were a women's majors record, surpassing the three that Blanche Bingley Hillyard of England squelched while beating Helena Rice, 4-6, 8-6, 6-4, in the 1889 Wimbledon final.

In the quarterfinals, Monica Seles went for her first win in seven meetings with Venus Williams, and got it. As the eighth-seed, she beat the second-seeded Venus 6-7 (4-7), 6-2, 6-3. But Monica could not sustain her sparkling form after a strong start against Hingis, bowing 4-6, 6-1, 6-4 in that semifinal. Capriati accounted for No. 4 seed Kim Clijsters 7-5, 3-6, 6-1 in the other semifinal.

When the next major took place at Roland Garros, third-seeded Serena crushed 2000 champion Mary Pierce 6-1, 6-1 in the quarters, and then won a pulsating encounter with Capriati in the semifinals. Capriati took the first set and led 6-5 on serve in the second, but Serena's immense poise under pressure lifted her to a 3-6, 7-6 (7-2), 6-2 victory. Capriati was aided by Jelena Dokic's 14 double faults in her, 6-4, 4-6, 6-1, quarterfinal win.

In the final, Serena struck down big sister Venus 7-5, 6-3. Venus served for the first set at 5-3 but began that crucial game with a double fault. She proceeded to drop seven games in a row. Serena had more margin for error in the hard-hitting backcourt exchanges, and her second serve was decidedly better than that of Venus, who lost her serve eight out of 11 times in the match. The bottom line was that Serena was now the better player, and the best in the world. Speaking of the arduous three years she had endured since winning her first major at the U.S. Open of 1999, Serena said, "It was kind of discouraging. I didn't want to be a one hit wonder. I had to get there again. Serena Williams has, in my mind, always been the best tennis player. It was just maybe a lack of results. But in my mind I've always felt that I've been No. 1."

Albert Costa of Spain, seeded No. 20, claimed the men's crown at Roland Garros with a series of fine wins. By a 6-4, 7-5, 6-4, score he evicted the three-time champion Gustavo Kuerten, still rusty after a long layoff for hip surgery, in the fourth round, followed by a 7-5, 3-6, 6-7 (3-7), 6-4, 6-0 decision—from 2-4 in the fourth set—over Guillermo Canas in the quarterfinals. (Canas had removed top-seed Hewitt, 6-7 (1-7), 7-6 (15-13), 6-4, 6-3 in the fourth round.) Next, Costa halted countryman Alex Corretja in a semifinal, 6-3, 6-4, 3-6, 6-3, and stunned No. 11 Juan Carlos Ferrero on a bleak afternoon 6-1, 6-0, 4-6, 6-3. Compadre Ferrero, a nervous wreck for two sets, then made a much better match of it. He had beaten fourth-seed Andre Agassi, 6-3, 5-7, 7-5, 6-3, in the quarters and clipped second-seed Safin, 6-3, 6-2, 6-4 in the semis. But he put himself in too deep a hole against Costa, who had not won a tournament since 1999.

No major was more tumultuous than Wimbledon. On the third day, three of the big favorites fell in startling second-round upsets. Seven-time champion Sampras, seeded No. 6, was exiled to infamous Court 2 (better known as the Graveyard of Champions), there to be beaten by a lucky loser, No. 145 George Bastl of Switzerland, in five humiliating sets, 6-3, 6-2, 4-6, 3-6, 6-4. (A match that ultimately was the Wimbledon swan song for Sampras). Safin, the second- seed, went down like Gulliver, 6-2, 6-4, 3-6, 7-6 (7-1) before Belgium's 5-foot-4, No.84-ranked Olivier Rochus. Then third-seeded Agassi was eliminated, 6-4, 7-6 (7-5), 6-2, by the rapidly rising No. 67 Paradorn Srichaphan of Thailand. Srichaphan put on a shot-making clinic, releasing one blazing winner after another as an astounded Agassi found himself hopelessly out of sync on the Centre Court.

In the end, top-seeded Hewitt restored order. He picked apart Argentina's David Nalbandian, 6-1, 6-3, 6-2 to win his second major title. Nalbandian, the No. 28 seed, was thoroughly outclassed in his first major final, but could console himself: he was the first man from his nation ever to reach the final at the All England Club. Along the way, Hewitt had only one dangerous match. Facing the stylish Dutchman Sjeng Schalken in the fourth round, Hewitt, the groundstroking maven squandered a two-sets-to-love lead before coming through 6-2, 6-2, 6-7 (5-7) 1-6, 7-5.

Considered a heretic by the old boy Aussies who used to own Wimbledon, Hewitt hung at the baseline and didn't play one serve-and-volley point. ("I thought about it—but didn't.") But they were proud of him, their first champ since Patrick Cash in 1987.

Serena and Venus Williams always seemed certain to reach the women's final. Serena had moved past her sister to No. 1 in the world, with Venus remaining stationed at No. 2. They had thus fulfilled the prophecy of their father/coach Richard, who had said many years before that his daughters would become the two best players in the world. The siblings marched into the final after never being unduly troubled along the way. Venus, trying to become the first woman since Steffi Graf (1991-93) to win Wimbledon three years running, routed sixth-seed Justine Henin 6-3, 6-2 in the semifinals. Serena handled Frenchwoman Amelie Mauresmo with awesome ease, winning 6-2, 6-1 in the other semifinal. Mauresmo had given an exquisite display against Capriati in the quarterfinals, sprinkling the court with spectacular winners off her flowing topspin backhand, attacking cleverly, volleying crisply. Her 6-3, 6-2 upset of the third-seed was encouraging to her band of supporters, but Serena shut her down with unrelenting power and panache.

The final was the best match yet between the two sisters, but once more Serena was superior in every facet of the game, most notably with her second serve and forehand groundstrokes. The most telling statistic was this: Serena was on target with 67 percent of her first serves, winning 73 percent of those points. Venus finished at 70 percent, but won only 63 percent of those points. Serena also had a 10 percent edge in second-serve points won. Serena made Venus go for higher-percentage first serves, and Venus compromised too much on the speed of her delivery. Her average first serve for the tournament was 109 mph; against Serena, that figure fell to 100 mph.

Nevertheless, Venus battled fiercely. Serena served for the first set at 5-4, and reached 30-0 in that tenth game. Venus came out of that corner with some excellent retrieving and returning, broke back for 5-5, and got into a tiebreaker. Serving at 3-4, Venus produced an ill-conceived drop shot off the forehand when she had a short ball she should have punished. Serena easily passed Venus off the backhand to lead 5-3. Serving at 6-4, Serena aced Venus wide to the forehand. Umpire Jane Harvey called a let, but neither player heard her. They proceeded to take their seats at the changeover, and Harvey inexplicably did not interject. Set to Serena.

Venus made another bid to sink her teeth into the match in the second set, breaking back for 3-4. Venus reached 30-30 in her quest to make it back to 4-4, but released a costly double fault. Serena promptly broke her sister, then held at love to close out the 7-6 (7-4), 6-3 victory.

Said Serena, "In the beginning of this year, I said, 'I don't care what happens this year, but I want to win Wimbledon.' It was an extra bonus for me to win the French. I couldn't believe I won that. But I really wanted Wimbledon to be a part of history."

A classy Venus said, "To be honest, I think I played well. I played high-percentage tennis. She was just pressing me and hitting a lot of forceful shots. Serena was just tremendous today, but it wasn't like there was a lot between us."

As summer ended and the best in the business came to New York in search of the last major of the year, Sampras played his finest tennis since 1999.

Despite a difficult hard-court season leading up to Flushing Meadows—he won only three of six matches in the three events he played—Sampras, seeded No. 17, was determined to peak at his country's championships where he had been a finalist the previous two years. He made good on that goal, and then some. In the third round, he beat 1997 finalist Greg Rusedski, 7-6 (7-4), 4-6, 7-6 (7-3), 3-6, 6-4, a match contested over two nights as rain badly disrupted the Open program. Rusedski was not a gracious loser. He said bitterly, "I lost the match. He didn't win it...I'd be surprised if he wins his next match against [Tommy] Haas. To be honest with you, I'd be very surprised. He's a step-and-a-half slow coming to the net. You can get the ball down. He's a great player from the past. You're used to seeing Pete Sampras, 13-time Grand Slam champion. He's not the same player."

Sampras was jovial in his response to Rusedski, but witty as well. "Against him," he retorted, "I don't really need to be a step-and-a-half quicker."

But Sampras responded with alacrity on the court. He took a hard fought contest from the third-seeded Haas, 7-5, 6-4, 6-7 (5-7), 7-5 and then gave a scintillating account of his all-court talent in a 6-3, 6-2, 6-4 quarterfinal rout of Andy Roddick. It was a signature performance. Sampras had lost to the 20-year-old in their only two previous meetings, but this time around he was not to be denied, winning in 90 nearly immaculate minutes. He then easily dismissed the unflappable Schalken 7-6 (8-6), 7-6 (7-4), 6-2 in the semifinals.

Agassi, meanwhile, was also at the top of his game. He delighted the capacity semifinal crowd on Saturday by beating top-seed Hewitt, ending a three-match losing string to the

pugnacious Aussie. But Hewitt was Sampras's ally, keeping Andre hustling long and hard for three hours in the late afternoon decision, 6-4, 7-6 (7-5), 6-7 (1-7), 6-2. It was hot and taxing.

The dream final between the two icons, Pete and Andre, materialized.

Sampras was primed for the occasion. He was devastatingly potent over the first two sets, dishing out 12 aces alone in the opening set. From 3-3 in the opening set, he won eight of the next ten games. Agassi fought back valiantly to capture the third set. Sampras served at 5-6 to reach a tie-breaker and had five game points, but a surging Agassi came up with some trademark scorching returns to get the break as Sampras struggled in vain, serving into the wind.

In the fourth set, Sampras served into the wind again in a crucial game at 1-2. It went to seven deuces with Sampras surviving two break points, one of them with a miraculous backhand drop half-volley that caught a dumbfounded Agassi in his tracks. At 3-4, Sampras was break point down again, but he kicked his serve high to the Agassi two-hander to elicit a netted return. He held on with an ace, broke Agassi in the following game, and then served out the match with characteristic brio. At 5-4, 30-0, with the wind at his back, Sampras came up with a clutch, second serve ace down the T. It was his 33rd of the match, a personal record for a major final. Two points later, he dispatched a backhand volley into the clear to complete a 6-3, 6-4, 5-7, 6-4 triumph.

He had beaten Agassi for the fourth time at the U.S Open without a loss (the third time in a final), and extended his career edge over his chief rival to 20-14. Sampras now stood at 14-4 in major finals, while Agassi was 7-6.

With his fifth Open prize in hand—placing him in a tie for the Open era record with Jimmy Connors—Sampras climbed into the stands to embrace his wife Bridgette. He was so gratified to be back on top at an elite event that he was unable to decide whether to continue, or quit on the pinnacle.

Retirement won out in his thoughts. Although he would return in five years for brief appearances in exhibitions, World Team Tennis and senior events, and looked very good, his big league days were over.

It's almost unheard of to walk away after winning a major. Shirley Fry did after the Australian, 1957, Helen Wills Moody after Wimbledon in 1938. Now, Pete.

Serena and Venus, seeded No. 1 and No. 2, took their expected places for the women's final, their third consecutive championship match at a major. The top-seeded Serena had overcome Lindsay Davenport 6-3, 7-5 in the semifinals, recouping from 2-5 down in the second set, saving three set points in the tenth game with typical gusto. Venus had survived two serious skirmishes on her half of the draw. Seeking to become the first woman since Chris Evert (1975-78) to win three or more Opens in a row, Venus struggled inordinately to reach peak form. She won three tournaments in a row over the summer, but at Flushing Meadow, Venus lost her edge.

In the round of 16 against No. 14 seed Chanda Rubin, Venus was break point down at 1-4 in the final set before registering a 6-2, 4-6, 7-5 victory. In the semis, Venus was extended and reg-

istered a 6-3, 5-7, 6-4 win over Mauresmo, who was fresh from her third straight win over Capriati in the quarters 4-6, 7-6 (7-5), 6-3 after Capriati served for the match. Mauresmo worried Venus all through their gripping confrontation. In the last game of the match, Williams was down 0-40 but she pulled out of that predicament with a series of scorching deliveries.

Against Serena, Venus was error-plagued off the forehand from the outset, and her serve let her down again. Serena broke Venus five times, lost her own delivery only twice, and rolled to victory. Venus led 4-4, 30-0 in the first set but lost six of the next seven games as Serena prevailed 6-4, 6-3. Venus committed 17 more unforced errors than her tidier-hitting sister, and that was the essential difference. Serena, victorious for the fourth time in a major, was now tied with Venus in that category, and had a rare triple: titles at the French, Wimbledon and U.S. Championships.

Also rare, incidentally, was the Grand Slop completed by fetching Anna Kournikova, ranked No. 37. She lost in the first round of every major during the year, finishing up (or down) in a 6-3, 6-0, defeat by No. 75-ranked Indonesian Angelique Widjaja in the first round in Flushing Meadow. French qualifier Marion Bartoli beat Arantxa Sanchez Vicario 6-3, 6-1, the first time a former women's champ lost in the first round since Billie Jean King fell to Susan Mascarin in 1982.

Agassi battled on after the Open in search of the No. 1 world ranking, hoping to end a year at the top of the charts for the second time in his career. But when he lost two round-robin matches in a row at the Tennis Masters Cup in Shanghai to Jiri Novak, 7-5, 6-1, and Ferrero, 7-5, 2-6, 7-6 (8-6), his chance was gone. With Agassi out of the running for No. 1, Hewitt could have let go of some of his ambition. He refused. The feisty "Little Big Man" closed out his second straight Tennis Masters Cup with a pair of phenomenal victories. In the semifinals, he beat Roger Federer 7-5, 5-7, 7-5. The next day, he overcame Ferrero after trailing 1-3 in the fifth set, winning, 7-5, 7-5, 2-6, 2-6, 6-4. He reminded everyone why he deserved his status as the best in the world.

Serena Williams suffered only her fifth defeat of the year in the final of the women's year-end championships in Los Angeles. A resolute Kim Clijsters jarred the world No. 1, 7-5, 6-3, to win the biggest title of her career.

In the Fed Cup final at Gran Canaria, Spain, the Slovak Republic toppled Spain 3-1. The six-foot siren Daniela Hantuchova— one of the most improved players in the women's game over the course of the season—won the decisive match over Conchita Martinez in three hours, 21 minutes 6-7 (8-10), 7-5, 6-4. She also beat Magui Serna, 6-2, 6-1, and got help from Janette Husarova's 6-0, 6-2 defeat of Hall of Famer-to-be Sanchez Vicario, who soon announced her retirement. Said Daniela, "Even when I lost the first set, I was really happy with the way I was fighting. I would not give up. I am very proud."

Sanchez Vicario had been out there on the pro tour for 16 productive years, winning four major singles titles, rising to No. 1 in the world in 1995. She also set Fed Cup records for most matches played (100), most series (58) and most appearances in the final (10). She would have a brief return to competitive play in 2004 in doubles in order to qualify and eventually compete in her fifth Olympic Games.

Russian Mikhail Youzhny was just beginning what might become a remarkable career. The 20-year-old found himself in a demanding position at the Davis Cup final indoors on clay in Paris. His nation had never won the Davis Cup. When the Russians lost the 1995 final to the U.S. in Moscow, he was a ballboy. Youzhny was asked to play the fifth and decisive match against France when Yevgeny Kafelnikov begged off. He was down two sets to love against another 20-year-old, Paul-Henri Mathieu. Former Russian President Boris Yeltsin was cheering him on from the stands, but to no avail—for a while.

Down a break at 2-1 in the third, Youzhny broke back and won the set, but fell behind again 4-2 in the fourth. In the end, Youzhny, propelled by his marvelously fluent and effective one-handed topspin backhand, came out improbably on top, 3-6, 2-6, 6-3, 7-5, 6-4. No one had ever come from two sets to love down in the fifth and decisive match of a Davis Cup final.

2002 CHAMPIONS AND LEADERS

Australian Open
Men's Singles Final: Thomas Johansson (SWE) def. Marat Safin (RUS), 3-6, 6-4, 6-4, 7-6 (4)
Women's Singles Final: Jennifer Capriati (USA) def. Martina Hingis (SUI), 4-6, 7-6 (7), 6-2
Men's Doubles Final: Mark Knowles (BAH) and Daniel Nestor (CAN) def. Michael Llodra and Fabrice Santoro (FRA), 7-6 (4), 6-3
Women's Doubles Final: Martina Hingis (SUI) and Anna Kournikova (RUS) def. Arantxa Sanchez Vicario (ESP) and Daniela Hantuchova (SVK), 6-2, 6-7 (4), 6-1
Mixed Doubles Final: Daniela Hantuchova (SVK) and Kevin Ullyett (ZIM) def. Paola Suarez and Gaston Etlis (ARG), 6-3, 6-2

French Open
Men's Singles Final: Albert Costa (ESP) def. Juan Carlos Ferrero (ESP), 6-1, 6-0, 4-6, 6-3
Women's Singles Final: Serena Williams (USA) def. Venus Williams (USA), 7-5, 6-3
Men's Doubles Final: Paul Haarhuis (NED) and Yevgeny Kafelnikov (RUS) def. Mark Knowles (BAH) and Daniel Nestor (CAN), 7-5, 6-4
Women's Doubles Final: Virginia Ruano Pascual (ESP) and Paola Suarez (ARG) def. Lisa Raymond (USA) and Rennae Stubbs (AUS), 6-4, 6-2
Mixed Doubles Final: Cara Black and Wayne Black (ZIM) def. Elena Bovina (RUS) and Mark Knowles (BAH), 6-3, 6-3

Wimbledon
Men's Singles Final: Lleyton Hewitt (AUS) def. David Nalbandian (ARG), 6-1, 6-3, 6-2
Women's Singles Final: Serena Williams (USA) def. Venus Williams (USA), 7-6 (4), 6-3
Men's Doubles Final: Todd Woodbridge (AUS) and Jonas Bjorkman (SWE) def. Mark Knowles (BAH) and Daniel Nestor (CAN), 6-1, 6-2, 6-7 (7), 7-5
Women's Doubles Final: Venus Williams and Serena Williams (USA) def. Virgina Ruano Pascual (ESP) and Paola Suarez (ARG), 6-4, 6-3
Mixed Doubles Final: Elena Likhovtseva (RUS) and Mahesh Bhupathi (IND) def. Daniela Hantuchova (SVK) and Kevin Ullyett (ZIM), 6-2, 1-6, 6-1

U.S. Open
Men's Singles Final: Pete Sampras (USA) def. Andre Agassi (USA), 6-3, 6-4, 5-7, 6-4
Women's Singles Final: Serena Williams (USA) def. Venus Williams (USA), 6-4, 6-3
Men's Doubles Final: Max Mirnyi (BLR) and Mahesh Bhupathi (IND) def. Jiri Novak and Radek Stepanek (CZE), 6-3, 3-6, 6-4
Women's Doubles Final: Paola Suarez (ARG) and Virginia Ruano Pascual (ESP) def. Elena Dementieva (RUS) and Janette Husarova (SVK), 6-2, 6-1
Mixed Doubles Final: Lisa Raymond and Mike Bryan (USA) def. Katarina Srebotnik (SLO) and Bob Bryan (USA), 7-6 (9), 7-6 (1)

Year-End No. 1
Men: Lleyton Hewitt
Women: Serena Williams

Top Player Earnings
Men: Lleyton Hewitt $4,619,386
Women: Serena Williams $3,935,668

Davis Cup: Russia

Fed Cup: Slovak Republic

Tennis Masters Cup, Shanghai—Lleyton Hewitt
Home Depot Championships, Los Angeles—Kim Clijsters

2003   Roddick Takes The Torch, A Serena Slam Is Conceived

Andre Agassi showed no signs of joining Sampras on retirement golf courses, winning the first major of the year in Australia, reclaiming the No. 1 ranking for 12 weeks, and winning four of his first five events, before slowing for the rest of year, ending with a runner-up showing at the Tennis Masters Cup.

Women's tennis would be a battle between the Williams sisters—Venus and Serena—and those Serena dubbed "the Belgian sisters"—Justine Henin-Hardenne and Kim Cljisters. The Williams sisters would play against each other in two major finals, Australian and Wimbledon, while the Belgians would compete against one another in the other two finals, French and U.S. Opens. Henin-Hardenne would end the year as No. 1—with her two major titles and two semifinals. She won 75 matches, eight titles and $3,667,430— all three categories second fiddle to year-end No. 2 Clijsters with 90 match wins, nine titles and over four million in prize money.

It took Sampras about five months into the 2003 season to finally decide to hang up his racket for good. Sampras withdrew from one event after another in the first half of the season, waiting for his motivation to return to the courts. When his competitive juices that normally rushed into his veins before his annual visit to the All England Club did not percolate, he knew it was time to retire. While many anticipated the announcement would come at any day after he was a no-show at Wimbledon, it wasn't until the opening day of the U.S. Open where Sampras made it official and the USTA sent him off with riveting ceremony on the opening night of the tournament.

Sampras's biggest rival and contemporary, Agassi, however, continued his assault on majors, winning the Australian Open, blasting unseeded Rainer Schuettler of Germany in the final 6-2, 6-2, 6-1. Agassi steamrolled through the final three rounds of the tournament losing only 19 games combined, over Sebastien Grosjean, 6-3, 6-2, 6-2, in the quarterfinals, Wayne Ferreira, 6-2, 6-2 6-3, in the semifinals and Schuettler. The title was Agassi's fourth at the Australian Open (an Open era men's record) and his eighth and final major.

The highlight of the tournament was the 83-game, five-hour epic quarterfinal match won by Roddick over lanky Younes El Aynaoui of Morocco, 4-6, 7-6 (7-5), 4-6, 6-4, 21-19. The match was 10 games shorter than the Australian record set by Dennis Ralston in defeating John Newcombe, 19-17, 20-18, 4-6, 6-3, in 1970.

A passing of the torch occurred in men's tennis throughout the 2003 season. The most prolific champion in the men's game, Pete Sampras waited until the fourth and final major championship of the year to officially announce the end of his playing career. Andy Roddick used the same tournament where Pete made his retirement official to win his baptismal major title and assume the crown of top dog in the U.S.

By year's end, Andy would take over as world No. 1 as well. Roddick also reached the semifinals of Australia, Wimbledon and the year-end Tennis Masters Cup and punched out a 27-1 summer hard court run. The man who would ultimately become the biggest threat to Pete's hard-earned records, Roger Federer, also broke through to win his first of many major titles at Wimbledon and capped the year by taking the Tennis Masters Cup. Federer led the men's tour in tournament victories (seven), matches won (78) and prize money ($4,000,680), but curiously finished the year ranked No. 2 in the ATP rankings behind Roddick.

The 40-game fifth set, however, played for two-and-a-half hours, was the longest fifth-set in Aussie history.

El Aynaoui had upset top-seed Lleyton Hewitt 6-7 (7-9), 7-6 (7-4), 7-6 (7-5), 6-4 in the fourth round, while Roddick came from a two-sets-to-love deficit for the first time, disappointing Mikhail Youzhny 6-7 (4-7), 3-6, 7-5, 6-3, 6-2. After his marathon with El Aynaoui, an aching Roddick had nothing left against Schuettler in the semifinals, falling, 7-5, 2-6, 6-3, 6-3.

The Spanish Armanda continued its domination of the French Open as four men (Tommy Robredo, Carlos Moya, Alberto Costa, and Juan Carlos Ferrero) all reached the quarterfinals. Robredo, named Tommy by his parents, fans of The Who's famous rock opera by the same name, knocked off top-seed Lleyton Hewitt in the third round from a two-set deficit 4-6, 1-6, 6-3, 6-2, 6-3 and three-time champion Gustavo Kuerten in the quarters, 6-4, 1-6, 7-6 (7-2), 6-4.

Defending champion, ninth-seeded Albert Costa was stubborn in relinquishing his title, winning his first three matches in five sets. In the first round, he narrowly escaped being the first defending champ to lose in the first round at Roland Garros, defeating Argentine "lucky loser" Sergio Roitman 6-7 (3-7), 2-6, 7-5, 6-2, 6-2 (he trailed 4-1 in the third set and faced a break point to go down 5-1.) He beat Czech Radek Stepanek, 6-3, 5-7, 6-4, 3-6, 6-4 in the second round and Ecuador's Nicolas Lapentti 4-6, 4-6, 6-3, 6-4, 6-4 in the third round. After a routine, fourth-round 6-2, 7-5, 7-5 win over Frenchman Arnaud Clement, Costa pulled his third two-sets-to-love comeback of the tournament against Robredo, beating Tommy 2-6, 3-6, 6-4, 7-5, 6-2. But he had nothing left in the semifinals against Ferrero, who avenged his title loss from a year before, 6-3, 7-6 (7-5), 6-4. In six matches, Costa spent 21 hours and 15 minutes on court.

One of the more unlikely finalists in the majors' history was Ferrero's foe in the final, No. 46 Martin Verkerk of Netherlands, who entered Roland Garrros having never won a singles match previously at a major. The 6-foot-6 Verkerk advanced with wins over Luis Horna of Peru (the first-round conqueror of Federer), who blew four match points in losing, 4-6, 6-4, 4-6, 7-5, 6-2. Then, with big serving, Verkerk rapped rap-singing Vinnie Spadea, 5-7, 6-4, 6-2, 7-5, Schuettler, 6-3, 6-3, 7-5, 1998 champion Moya, 6-3, 6-4, 5-7, 4-6, 8-6, and, most astoundingly, in the semifinals, seventh-seeded Argentine Guillermo Coria, 7-6 (7-4), 6-4, 7-6 (7-0). (Coria had beaten second-seed Agassi 4-6, 6-3, 6-2, 6-4 in the quarters) and Poof! The dragon's magic was gone, and the engaging Verkerk went down meekly, 6-1, 6-3, 6-2, Ferrero winning his first major title.

A giant pulled a gigantic upset for the ages in opening Centre Court on day one of Wimbledon as 6-foot-10 Ivo Karlovic, a Croatian qualifier ranked No. 203, made an undreamed of debut. He didn't know the way to Centre Court, but once there victimized none other than the top-seeded defending champion Lleyton Hewitt, 1-6, 7-6 (7-5), 6-3, 6-4. Such treatment of such an eminence had never before occurred. But after an understandably nervous beginning, the 24-year-old Karlovic attacked, overwhelming Hewitt with heavy serving and nifty volleying. The historic Ivo, who failed to qualify in three previous Wimbledons, lost in the third round to Max Mirnyi, 7-6 (7-5), 3-6, 6-3, 7-6 (7-4).

Eight different nations were represented in the men's quarterfinals—Jonas Bjorkman (Sweden), Roddick (U.S.), Federer (Switzerland), Sjeng Schalken (Netherlands), Tim Henman (Britain), Sebastien Grosjean (France), Alexander Popp (Germany), Mark Philippoussis (Australia). Roddick (over Bjorkman 6-4, 6-2, 6-4), Federer (over Schalken 6-3, 6-4, 6-4), Grosjean (over Henman 7-6 (10-8), 3-6, 6-3, 6-4) and Philippoussis (over Popp 4-6, 4-6, 6-3, 6-3, 8-6) advanced into the final four. Second-seed Agassi had almost as much trouble with El Aynaoui as Roddick in Australia, prevailing in the third round, 5-7, 6-4, 7-6 (7-4), 7-6 (7-4). But, pelted by 46 aces, Andre was dropped by No. 48 Philippoussis, 6-3, 2-6, 6-7 (4-7), 6-3, 6-4.

Roddick, having won the title at Queen's over Sebastien Grosjean, 6-3, 6-3, and tapped by many as the tournament favorite, could not convert a routine forehand on set point in the first-set tie-breaker against Federer in the semifinals, and went down 7-6 (8-6), 6-3, 6-3. Philippoussis, a U.S. Open finalist in 1998, also advanced to the final by almost the same score against Grosjean, 7-6 (7-3), 6-3, 6-3.

After numerous majors disappointments since his upset of Sampras in the Wimbledon fourth round of 2001, Federer would not be denied in his first final, defeating Philippoussis 7-6 (7-5), 6-2, 7-6 (7-3) to become the first Swiss man to win a major singles title.

While playing the tournament at Gstaad the week after Wimbledon, Federer received an unusual congratulatory prize from admirers: a cow named Juliette. He would never starve for lack of milk or cheese.

Roddick took the hard court season by the horns, winning titles in Indianapolis, 7-6 (7-2), over Paradorn Srichaphan, the Canadian Open, 6-1, 6-3, over David Nalbandian and Cincinnati, 4-6, 7-6 (7-3), 7-6 (7-4) over Mardy Fish—losing only in the semifinals of Washington, D.C., to Tim Henman, 1-6, 6-3, 7-6 (7-1).

At the U.S. Open, after the opening night ceremony that closed the books on the career of Sampras, Roddick officially took the mantle of American tennis for the next generation as he plowed through the draw to claim his first major title. Roddick lost only one set in reaching the semifinals, that in a contentious second rounder over Ivan Ljubicic, 6-3, 6-7 (4-7), 6-3, 7-6 (10-8). But Andy had to duck a match point with a service winner in the third-set tie-breaker to escape Argentine David Nalbandian, 6-7 (4-7), 3-6, 7-6 (9-7), 6-1, 6-3 to advance into the final. Nalbandian, the Wimbledon finalist in 2002, hotly contested the call on Roddick's service winner, insisting it was a fault. He was the fourth round stopper of Federer, 3-6, 7-6 (7-1), 6-4, 6-3.

Ferrero, showing an aptitude for other than clay, took out Hewitt, 4-6, 6-3, 7-6 (7-5), 6-1, then top-seeded Agassi, 6-4, 6-3, 3-6, 6-4 in the other semifinal becoming the first Spainard to reach the Open final since champion Manolo Orantes in 1975. Roddick was too strong for Ferrero, even playing serve-and-volley on second balls, blitzed the French champion, 6-3, 7-6 (7-2), 6-3, in the final. Ferrero's consolation was taking the No. 1 ranking from Agassi, temporarily.

Leaving Shanghai, the Masters moved to the intimate, friendly West Side Tennis Club of Houston. There, Federer acquired his first such title, beating Agassi, 6-3, 6-0, 6-4. Roddick made the final four on two victories in the round robin phase: over Moya, 6-2, 3-6, 6-3, and Coria, 6-3, 6-7 (3-7), 6-3. Though losing his semifinal

to Federer, 7-6 (7-2), 6-2, he went home with the year's No. 1 ranking in his possession.

Serena, the youngest of the Sisters Sledgehammer, was perhaps at the pinnacle of her career in Australia, completing her so-called "Serena Slam" (not a Grand Slam), joining Steffi Graf, Martina Navratilova, Maureen Connolly and Margaret Court as the only players to hold all four majors at one time. Serena became one of nine women to win all four majors in her career, with Billie Jean King, Chris Evert, Shirley Fry and Doris Hart also being added to the list.

For the fourth straight major, Sister Venus again was the fall girl in the final—also a first for any two players—this time, 7-6 (4), 3-6, 6-4—the closest of their 11 professional encounters that gave Serena the lead, 6-5.

The sisters were not satisfied with dominating the singles draw as they won the doubles titles as well—their sixth major—defeating Paola Suarez and Virginia Ruano Pascual, 4-6, 6-4, 6-3, in the final.

Serena had two hiccups en route to the final, edging tiny left-hander Emilie Loit 3-6, 7-6 (5), 7-5 in the first round and coming back from 1-5 in the third set, saving two match points (at 2-5) in defeating Kim Clijsters of Belgium 4-6, 6-3, 7-5. Venus did not lose a set en route to the final, including a 6-3, 6-3 win over fifth-seeded Justine Henin-Hardenne in the semis. Henin-Hardenne defeated Russian pin-up Anna Kournikova 6-0, 6-1 in the second round in what was Kournikova's last major singles match, and former Aussie champ Lindsay Davenport 7-5, 5-7, 9-7 in the fourth round.

However, third-seed Jennifer Capriati made news negatively. She became the first defending Australian champion to go off the road in the first round, bowing to No. 90, Marlene Weingartner of Germany 2-6, 7-6 (6), 6-4.

Serena went from Australia to titles at the Paris Indoor (over Amelie Mauresmo, 6-3, 6-2), and Key Biscayne (over Capriati, 4-6, 6-4, 6-1, before having her 21-match winning streak snapped by Henin-Hardenne, 6-3, 6-4, in the Charleston final.

Henin-Hardenne would end Serena's majors streaks at four titles and 33 match wins, defeating her 6-2, 4-6, 7-5 in a controversial semifinal at Roland Garros. Played before a raucously pro-Henin-Hardenne crowd, the match produced an incident in the third set that would prove contentious and acrimonious between the two rivals for years to come. With Serena serving at 4-2, 30-0, in the final set, Henin-Hardenne raised her hand indicating she wasn't ready to return serve. Serena served into the net, then protested, to no avail, to the chair umpire and tournament referee that she should be given a first serve. Justine said nothing of her gesture. Williams then lost the next four points to drop her service-break advantage and eventually the match.

Said the fourth-seeded Henin-Hardenne, "I wasn't ready to play the point. The chair umpire is there to deal with these kind of situations. I just tried to stay focused on myself and tried to forget all the other things…It's her point of view but that's mine now and I feel comfortable with it….I didn't have any discussion with the chair umpire. He didn't ask me anything. I was just trying to focus on playing the returns. She saw me and she served. It was her decision to serve. I just tried to stay focused on the second

serve. One point in the match doesn't change the outcome."

Two days later, Henin-Hardenne became the first Belgian to win a major title, defeating countrywomen Clijsters, 6-0, 6-4, in the final. Clijsters, seeded No. 2 , lost only one set en-route to the final: a first set bagel to Maggie Maleeva of Bulgaria in a 0-6, 6-2, 6-1 fourth rounder. In the semifinals, she beat Nadia Petrova of Russia, 7-5, 6-1. Nadia beat two ex-champs - Monica Seles 6-4, 6-0 in the first round, and Capriati in the fourth round 6-3, 4-6, 6-3. Another Russian, Vera Zvonareva, beat third-seeded Venus in the fourth round 2-6, 6-2, 6-4.

Williams world was restored to order at Wimbledon as Serena defeated Venus 4-6, 6-4, 6-2 in the final. The Williams's dismissed Belgium in the semifinals, Serena avenging her loss to Justine, 6-2, 6-2; Venus over Kim, 4-6, 6-3, 6-1. A 16-year-old Russian wildcard, Maria Sharapova, made her debut at the All England Club, reaching the fourth round, losing to countrywoman Svetlana Kuznetsova 6-1, 2-6, 7-5. Serena tore her left knee quad in the final, requiring surgery in August, prematurely ending her season with a 38-3 record. With Serena absent, Clijsters ended her 57-week reign as world No. 1 on August 11.

Rain-plagued—it took Francesca Schiavone four days, seven times on and off the court in a third rounder to beat Ai Sugiyama, 6-7 (5-7), 7-5, 6-2—the U.S. Open also became "Williams-less" when Venus withdrew, too, injured. Minus the Sisters—the Axis of Anxiety to the rest of their colleagues—the Brussels Sprouts, Kim and Justine, took center stage as the top-two seeded players. The semifinals became a USA vs. Belgium affair. Clijsters blasted through Lindsay Davenport, 6-2, 6-3, but Justine and Capriati fought 27 minutes past midnight in one of the event's greatest matches, the Belgian scrambling out of constant danger to win, 4-6, 7-5, 7-6 (7-4).

Despite leg cramps on a cool, damp evening, and the foe, husky Capriati, two points from victory on 11 occasions (serving for the match at 5-3 in the third), scrawny Henin-Hardenne persisted in the three-hour-and-three-minute feat of furious shot-making. Justine showed wider variety, her volleying often saving her. They laid their hearts on the line. At 5-6, after breaking back twice, the Paperweight Tiger of 120 pounds was two points from losing again. Getting out of that pit, she seized the first three points of the tie-breaker, and was ahead to stay. Following the match, she received IV-treatment for dehydration, then later in the day was back in Flushing to hurdle a set point while keeping the championship out of Kim's grasp, 7-5, 6-1.

Kim, however, ended the year by winning the WTA Tour Championships in Los Angeles, defeating Mauresmo 6-2, 6-0 in a field missing Serena and Venus due to injury. Henin-Hardenne lost to Mauresmo 7-5, 3-6, 6-3 in one semifinal, Capriati falling to Kim 4-6, 6-3, 6-0 in the other. Clijsters and Japan's Sugiyama reached the doubles final, falling to Virgina Ruano Pascual and Paola Suarez 6-4, 3-6, 6-3.

Forty-six-year-old Martina Navratilova was the headliner in doubles play for the year, pairing with Leander Paes of India to win the mixed doubles titles at the Australian Open and Wimbledon—making her the oldest major tournament champion (46 years, eight months, a record she would break at age 49 with her U.S. Open mixed title in 2006). In Australia, she and Paes defeated Aussie Todd Woodbridge and Greek Eleni Daniilidou, 6-4, 7-5, the

last of the 12 major events to complete a perfect resume. Only Margaret Smith Court also has all 12. At Wimbledon, she and Leander beat the Russian-Israeli coupling of Anastassia Rodionova and Andy Ram, 6-3, 6-3, giving Navratilova her 20th Wimbledon title, tying Billie Jean King's record. Martina had abetted Billie Jean's reaching 20 by partnering her in the 1979 doubles championship.

At the French, identical twins, Bob and Mike Bryan, became the first Americans to win the men's doubles final since another pair of brothers—the Jensens, Luke and Murphy in 1993—beating Paul Haarhuis and Yevgeny Kafelnikov 7-6, 6-3. Mike Bryan added the mixed in Paris with compatriot Lisa Raymond, over Elena Likhovtseva and Mahesh Bhupathi 6-3, 6-4.

At Wimbledon, Todd Woodbridge, six-time champion with Mark Woodforde, won this time with Jonas Bjorkman, beating Mahesh Bhupathi and Max Mirnyi, 3-6, 6-3, 7-6 (4), 6-3 in the final. Woodbridge and Bjorkman made it two in a row, beating the Bryans at the U.S., 5-7, 6-0, 7-5. (Bob took the mixed title in New York, however, with Slovenia's Katarina Srebotnik over the Russian-Canadian coalition, Lina Krasnoroutskaya and Daniel Nestor, 5-7, 7-5, 7-6 (7-5).)

The Bryans, however, finished as the year-end No. 1 team, rousingly winning the Masters at Houston over the French reps, Michael Llodra and Fabrice Santoro, 6-7 (6-8), 6-3, 3-6, 7-6 (7-3), 6-4.

Virginia Ruano Pascual of Spain and Paola Saurez of Argentina reached all four major doubles finals, but carried off just one title, the U.S., over Svetlana Kuznetsova and Navratilova, 6-2, 6-3.

Despite his inconsistencies, Philippoussis ended the year on a high, grabbing the Davis Cup-deciding point for Australia in a 3-1 win over Spain in the final on a specially installed grass court at Rod Laver Arena. Philippoussis clinched a second Cup title for his country in four years, beating Ferrero, 7-5, 6-3, 1-6, 2-6, 6-0, despite tearing a pectoral muscle in the second set. Hewitt beat Ferrero in the opening rubber, 3-6, 6-3, 3-6, 7-6 (7-0), 6-2, while Philippoussis bowed to Moya, 6-4, 6-4, 4-6, 7-6 (7-4). Woodbridge and lefty Wayne Arthurs dominated Alex Corretja and Feliciano Lopez 6-3, 6-1, 6-3, to give Philippoussis the opportunity to become the hometown hero.

In the semifinals against Federer and Switzerland—also at the Rod Laver Arena—Hewitt provided the drama, coming from 0-2 down to beat the Wimbledon champ, 5-7, 2-6, 7-6 (7-4), 7-5, 6-1, and certify the 3-2 win.

The U.S. was out early, zapped in Zagreb by Ivan Ljubicic in the 4-1 defeat by Croatia. Ljubicic, blasting aces and winners on the lightning-fast indoor court, beat Mardy Fish, 7-5, 6-3, 6-4, and clinched over James Blake, 6-3, 6-7 (5-7), 6-4, 6-3, after pairing with a revived Goran Ivanisevic for the wild doubles point over Blake-Fish, 3-6, 4-6, 7-6 (7-4), 6-4, 6-4.

France won the Fed Cup in Moscow, 4-1 over the U.S. entry weakened by injuries to the absent Sisters Williams. Meghann Shaughnessy and Lisa Raymond were strong enough to beat Belgium (minus Henin-Hardenne and Clijsters) in the semis. However, Mauresmo did the heavy-lifting for her side, beating Raymond, 6-4, 6-3, and Shaughnessy in the decider, 6-2, 6-1. Mary Pierce fought off Shaughnessy, 6-3, 3-6, 8-6.

Australian Open

Men's Singles Final: Andre Agassi (USA) def. Rainer Schuettler (GER), 6-2, 6-2, 6-1

Women's Singles Final: Serena Williams (USA) def. Venus Willams (USA), 7-6 (7-4), 3-6, 6-4

Men's Doubles Final: Michael Llodra and Fabrice Santoro (FRA) def. Mark Knowles (BAH) and Daniel Nestor (CAN), 6-4, 3-6, 6-3

Women's Doubles Final: Serena Williams and Venus Williams (USA) def. Virginia Ruano Pascal (ESP) and Paola Suarez (ARG), 4-6, 6-4, 6-3

Mixed Doubles Final: Martina Navratilova (USA) and Leander Paes (IND) def. Todd Woodbridge (AUS) and Eleni Daniilidou (GRE), 6-4, 7-5

French Open

Men's Singles Final: Juan Carlos Ferrero (ESP) def. Martin Verkerk (NED), 6-1, 6-3, 6-2

Women's Singles Final: Justine Henin-Hardenne (BEL) def. Kim Clijsters (BEL), 6-0, 6-4

Men's Doubles Final: Bob Bryan and Mike Bryan (USA) def. Paul Haarhuis (NED) and Yevgeny Kafelnikov (RUS), 7-6 (3), 6-3

Women's Doubles Final: Kim Clijsters (BEL) and Ai Sugiyama (JPN) def. Virginia Ruano Pascual (ESP) and Paola Suarez (ARG), 6-7 (7-5), 6-2, 9-7

Mixed Doubles: Lisa Raymond and Mike Bryan (USA) def. Elena Likhovtseva (RUS) and Mahesh Bhupathi (IND), 6-3, 6-4

Wimbledon

Men's Singles Final: Roger Federer (USA) def. Mark Philippoussis (AUS), 7-6 (7-5), 6-2, 7-6 (7-3)

Women's Singles Final: Serena Williams (USA) def. Venus Williams (USA), 4-6, 6-4, 6-2

Men's Doubles Final: Jonas Bjorkman (SWE) and Todd Woodbridge (AUS) def. Mahesh Bhupathi (IND) and Max Mirnyi (BLR), 3-6, 6-3, 7-6 (7-4), 6-3

Women's Doubles Final: Kim Clijsters (BEL) and Ai Sugiyama (JPN) def. Virginia Ruano Pascual (ESP) and Paola Suarez (ARG), 6-4, 6-4

Mixed Doubles Final: Martina Navratilova (USA) and Leander Paes (IND) def. Andy Ram (ISR) and Anastassia Rodionova (RUS), 6-3, 6-3

U.S. Open

Men's Singles Final: Andy Roddick (USA) def. Juan Carlos Ferrero (ESP), 6-3, 7-6 (7-2), 6-3

Women's Singles Final: Justine Henin-Hardenne (BEL) def. Kim Clijsters (BEL), 7-5, 6-1

Men's Doubles Final: Jonas Bjorkman (SWE) and Todd Woodbridge (AUS) def. Bob Bryan and Mike Bryan (USA), 5-7, 6-0, 7-5

Women's Doubles Final: Virginia Ruano Pascual (ESP) and Paola Suarez (ARG) def. Martina Navratilova (USA) and Svetlana Kuznetsova (RUS), 6-2, 6-3

Mixed Doubles Final: Katarina Srebotnik (SLO) and Bob Bryan (USA) def. Lina Krasnoroutskaya (RUS) and Daniel Nestor (CAN), 5-7, 7-5, 7-6 (7-5)

Year-End No. 1

Men: Andy Roddick

Women: Justine Henin-Hardenne

Top Player Earnings

Men: Roger Federer $4,000,680

Women: Kim Clijsters $4,466, 345

Davis Cup: Australia

Fed Cup: France

Tennis Masters Cup, Houston—Roger Federer

WTA Tour Championships, Los Angeles—Kim Clijsters

2004 King Roger Ascends The Throne

The Coronation of King Roger I came only 33 days into the 2004 season when the merciless Swiss maestro traveled to the distant land of Australia to conqueror the tennis world and claimed his second major championship at the Australian Open.

One day after his final-round triumph Down Under over Russia's Marat Safin, Feb. 2, Roger Federer assumed the throne as the main man of men's tennis atop the ATP singles rankings. His reign would make him the longest-serving monarch in men's tennis—over 200 weeks entering the 2008 tennis season, shattering

Roger Federer celebrates his victory over Andy Roddick in the men's singles final at Wimbledon—the Swiss maestro's second of three major singles title victories in 2004.

the record of 160 weeks set by Jimmy Connors in the 1970s for consecutive weeks as the No. 1 player.

Federer enjoyed the view from the top and went on to claim two more major titles for the year—defending his Wimbledon crown and claiming a first title at the U.S. Open in New York—to

conclude one of the most successful seasons in the history of the sport. As the first since Mats Wilander in 1988 to take three majors in a year, he joined the other illustrious triplers: Jack Crawford, 1933; Fred Perry, 1934; Don Budge, 1938 (Grand Slam); Lew Hoad, 1956; Tony Trabert, 1955; Ashley Cooper, 1958; Rod Laver, 1962 and 1969 (Grand Slams); Roy Emerson, 1964; Jimmy Connors, 1974. But Federer stands alone, tripling again in 2006-2007.

Roger broke the bank in 2004—earning $6,498,311. He won all 11 singles finals, the first to win at least 10 titles since Thomas Muster's 12 in 1995. Mr. No. 1 was successful 92.5 percent of the time (75-6 in matches). He also established an Open era record by winning 13 straight finals (going back to 2003), surpassing the mark held by Hall-of-Famers Borg and McEnroe, who won 12 straight He went 18-0 against foes in the Top 10, beating every one of them.

His only important hiccups came in a third-round loss to former champ Gustavo Kuerten at the French, and a surprising second-round loss to Czech Tomas Berdych at the Olympic Games in Athens, 4-6, 7-5, 7-5.

The dominating force in women's tennis was not an individual, but a country—Russia. Never before represented by a major female champion, Russia had three different natives in the majors winners circle at tournaments during the year, missing out only to Justine Henin-Hardenne at the Australian where Anastasia Myskina was a quarterfinalist. But Myskina became the first Russian woman to win a major singles title in France, while Siberian-born, American-raised starlet Maria Sharapova arrived on the scene suddenly at Wimbledon and St. Petersburg native Svetlana Kuznetsova was an even more unlikely winner at the US Open.

At the season's first major, Federer picked up where he left off at the end of the 2003 season when he barreled through the field at the Tennis Masters Cup. Federer lost only two sets en route to being the far up man Down Under—one to the great Aussie hope No. 15-seed Lleyton Hewitt 4-6, 6-3, 6-0, 6-4 in the fourth round, the other to eighth-seed David Nalbandian of Argentina 7-5, 6-4, 5-7, 6-3, in the quarterfinals.

Federer's rout of Spain's Juan Carlos Ferrero, 6-4, 6-1, 6-4, in the semifinals clinched the No. 1 ranking for the Swiss man—combined with the defeat of the man he evicted, Andy Roddick. Andy was shocked by Marat Safin 2-6, 6-3, 7-5, 6-7 (0-7), 6-4 in the quarterfinals. The moody Russian, ranked No. 86 after missing much of the 2003 season with a wrist injury, was not content at dumping Roddick. In the semifinals, he banished fourth-seeded defending champion Andre Agassi 7-6 (10-8), 7-6 (10-8), 5-7, 1-6, 6-3. Safin couldn't scale three mountains in a row, and after a hard-fought first set, surrendered the final to the new No. 1, 7-6 (7-3), 6-4, 6-2.

Belgium's two greatest ambassadors, Justine Henin-Hardenne and Kim Clijsters, seeded one-two, made it an all-homeland final the third time in the last four majors—each reaching her first Australian Open final without losing a set. Like the French and U.S. finals the year before, Henin-Hardenne proved stronger, winning 6-3, 4-6, 6-3. Fabiola Zuluaga of Colombia was the first singles major semifinalist from her country, benefiting from Amelie Mauresmo's quarterfinal default (injured back), but losing to

Henin-Hardenne 6-2, 6-2. Patty Schnyder, the crafty lefty, was also an unexpected visitor in the final four, falling to Clijsters 6-2, 7-6 (7-2). Venus Williams, the third-seed, lost to countrywomen Lisa Raymond 6-4, 7-6 (7-5) in the third round. Serena Williams was absent, (injured knee) and Lindsay Davenport was a 7-5, 6-3 loser to Henin-Hardenne in the quarters.

In doubles, the French team of Michael Llodra and Fabrice Santoro took out the American twins Bob and Mike Bryan 7-6 (7-4), 6-3. The Spanish-Argentine combo of Virginia Ruano Pascual and Paola Saurez won their fifth major, beating Russian's Svetlana Kuznetsova and Elena Likhovtseva 6-4, 6-3.

Ageless Martina Navratiova, 47, failed to win her 10th major mixed title - falling with Indian partner Leander Paes to the Russian-Serbian combo of Elena Bovina and Nenad Zimonjic 6-1, 7-6 (7-3).

On came the hard-working Russian ladies, making Roland Garros their private salt mine, digging up the title for sixth-seed Anastasia Myskina and the runner-up prize for No. 9 seed Elena Dementieva, a couple of 22-year-old Muscovites, who played for pizzas as kids. In a listless first-ever all-Russian final, it was Myskina who won, 6-1, 6-2, as Dementieva contributed 10 double faults and 33 unforced errors.

It was tougher earlier. Myskina escaped a match point in a fourth-rounder against another Russian, Kuznetsova, in a 1-6, 6-4, 8-6 win, and followed with wins over ex-No. 1's, Venus, 6-3, 6-4, and Jennifer Capriati, 6-2, 6-2, surprisingly flat after beating second-seed Serena, 6-3, 2-6, 6-3 to reach the semifinal. Dementieva beat Lindsay Davenport, 6-1, 6-3 in the fourth round, home-grown hope Amelie Mauresmo, 6-4, 6-3 in the quarterfinals and 14th seed, Argentine doubles specialist Suarez, 6-0, 7-5 in the semifinals.

Shockingly, the favorite, Henin-Hardenne was booted from the second round by Italy's Tatiana Garbin 7-5, 6-4—the earliest exit ever for a No. 1 women's seed at Roland Garros. Also making noise in the draw was the shrieker 17-year-old Maria Sharapova, a quarterfinal loser to Suarez, 6-1, 6-3.

Argentina loomed large among the men with four quarterfinalists: Guillermo Coria, David Nalbandian, Gaston Gaudio and Juan Ignacio Chela - with Chela being the odd man out in the semifinals. Coria and Gaudio survived to the play the first all-Argentine major final—with one of them to be the second countryman to carry the French title, joining 1977 champ Guillermo Vilas. They performed one of the strangest of showdowns.

Unseeded Gaudio, ranked No. 44, was gripped by nerves and lost the first set in 24 minutes to the third-seed Coria, then regarded as the best clay court player in the world. At the 60-minute mark, Coria was up two-sets-to-love, 6-0, 6-3. The French crowd attempted to rally Gaudio by chanting his name and doing the wave around Court Central. Suddenly, Coria began to unravel—just two games from victory at 4-3 in the third—and lost the third set. Early in the fourth set, Coria was treated for cramping legs and meekly surrendered the set 1-6. The fifth-set featured five service breaks, Coria taking a 4-2 lead, but in his faltering physical and mental condition, was unable to hang onto his lead. He held his first match point at 6-5, ad-in, but missed a backhand after a

long rally. A point later, he had championship match point No. 2, but missed a forehand after another long rally. Gaudio soon broke Coria for 6-6, held for 7-6 then broke for the incredible 0-6, 3-6, 6-4, 6-1, 8-6 victory.

Gaudio was the first unseeded champion since Brazilian Gustavo Kuerten in 1997, and there was Vilas to present the trophy to his successor after 27 years. Gaudio was also the first man to save a match point in a French final since 1934 when Germany's Gottfried von Cramm bested Jack Crawford of Australia.

Britain's Tim Henman served and volleyed his way to an unlikely semifinal showing, there stopped by Coria, 3-6, 6-4, 6-0, 7-5, while three-time champ Kuerten defeated an uncertain top-seed Federer 6-3, 6-3, 6-3 in the third round, en-route to the quarterfinals, the last good showing for the injury-plagued Guga. Defending champ Juan Carlos Ferrero—returning to professional tennis after a bout of mononucleosis—was lethargic in a 6-4, 6-2, 6-3, second-round loss to young Russian Igor Andreev.

The green grass of Wimbledon provided Federer with relief, restoring the look of No. 1 to his person after stumbling on Parisian clay. He lost only one set during a return trip to the final, that to ex-champ Hewitt in the quarters, 6-1, 6-7 (1-7), 6-0, 6-4. Roddick, his semifinal victim the previous year, would also get a set, which would make the final interesting as the American served huge and attacked. Still, it was Roger who came out the 4-6, 7-5, 7-6 (7-3), 6-4 victor - and his cow, Juliette, undoubtedly moo-ed joyfully.

Croatia's Mario Ancic—a first-round winner over Federer at Wimbledon, 2002—was a semifinalist, bumped by Roddick, 6-4, 4-6, 7-5, 7-5, but not before ending the Wimbledon revery of Henman, and England, 7-6 (7-5), 6-4, 6-2 in the quarterfinals. Frenchman Sebastien Grosjean reached his second straight Wimbledon semifinal, losing to Federer 6-2, 6-3, 7-6 (7-6). Goran Ivanisevic, the celebrated 2001 champion, finally made a return trip to Wimbledon after missing two years due to injury, and bid adieu to his career on Centre Court, losing to seventh-seed Hewitt 6-2, 6-3, 6-4 in the third round.

From whatever galaxy, the shrieking, stunning "Siberian Siren," aka Maria Sharapova, fell on the Big W as a glamorous fighter, its longest-shot champion on only her second try. Seeded No. 13, ranked No. 15, Maria, a 6-foot, 17-year-old remained calm while she pounded flat groundies to come from behind and break down her last three foes—Ai Sugiyama, 5-7, 7-5, 6-1; Davenport, 2-6, 7-6 (7-5), 6-1, and the deposed champ, top-seed Serena, 6-1, 6-4, from 1-4 down in the second set in the final. Maria became the tourney's third youngest champ, behind Lottie Dod, 15 in 1887, and Martina Hingis, 16 in 1997.

Serena dismantled Capriati 6-1, 6-1 in the quarters and overcame the talented though jittery Mauresmo 6-7 (4-7), 7-5, 6-4 in the semis. Venus, however, had departed in the second round—beaten by unseeded Croat Karolina Sprem 7-6 (7-5), 7-6 (8-6) in most peculiar circumstances on Centre Court. With Sprem serving at 1-2 in the second-set tie-breaker, chair umpire Ted Watts loses track of the score. After Williams hits a second-serve return-of-serve winner for a 3-1 lead, Watts calls the score 3-2, seemingly mistaking Sprem's missed first serve and subsequent non-cha-

lant backhand into an open court as an actual played point. Sprem was given an extra point, which ultimately helped her close out Williams in an 8-6 tie-breaker win.

Todd Woodbridge made history in men's doubles, pairing with Sweden's Jonas Bjorkman to win his record ninth Wimbledon title, defeating Julian Knowle of Austria and Nenad Zimonjic of Serbia, 6-1, 6-4, 4-6, 6-4. Woodbridge won six of his titles as the other half of "The Woodies," his partnership with fellow Aussie Mark Woodforde. The English Doherty brothers, Reggie and Laurie won eight together between 1897 and 1904.

Cara Black, the youngest of three tennis playing Blacks, was raised with older brothers, Byron and Wayne, on a grass court at their father's avocado farm in Zimbabwe. She claimed two Wimbledon titles, winning the doubles with Australian Rennae Stubbs, 6-3, 7-6 (7-5), over Sugiyama and South African Liezel Huber. She then teamed with brother Wayne to win the mixed title, defeating Aussies Woodbridge and Alicia Molik 3-6, 7-6 (10-8), 6-4.

Could anything he wanted possibly have eluded Federer? Yes. Olympic gold.

A semifinalist to German silver medalist Tommy Haas at Sydney in 2000, 6-3, 6-2, and loser of the bronze playoff against Arnaud Di Pasquale of France, 7-6 (7-5), 6-7 (7-9), 6-3, Roger did at least meet and begin his romance with Swiss Olympic tennis teammate, Mirka Vavrinec.

By the 2004 Games in Athens, he was No. 1. Gold was in the air, but astoundingly, not for Roger, beaten in the second round by Czech Tomas Berdych, 4-6, 7-5, 7-5.

Two golds went to Chilean Nicolas Massu, singles victor over Mardy Fish of the U.S., 6-3, 3-6, 2-6, 6-3, 6-4, and, alongside Fernando Gonzalez in the doubles victory over Germany's Rainer Schuettler and Nicolas Kiefer 6-2, 4-6, 3-6, 7-6 (9-7), 6-4. These were Chile's only Olympic medals of any sort, and made Nicolas and Fernando national heroes, honored by their president.

In the semis, Gonzalez, who had beaten second-seed Roddick, 6-4, 6-4, lost to Fish, 3-6, 6-3, 6-4, while the No. 10 seed Massu took care of American Taylor Dent, 7-6 (7-5), 6-1. Gonzalez, with his fierce forehand, took the bronze playoff from Dent, 6-2, 4-6, 16-14.

In another long-runner, Mario Ancic and Ivan Ljubicic of Croatia outlasted India's Leander Paes and Mahesh Bhupathi 7-6 (7-5), 4-6, 16-14, for the doubles bronze.

Unlike Federer, the other No. 1, Henin-Hardenne, went all the way to gold, finishing with Myskina, 7-5, 5-7, 8-6 in the semifinals (coming back from 1-5 down in the third), and Mauresmo, 6-3, 6-3 in the final. Myskina lost the bronze playoff to Aussie Molik, 6-3, 6-4. Defending singles and doubles champ Venus failed to lift new hardware, crashing in the third round to Pierce 6-4, 6-4. Allied to Chanda Rubin and not sister Serena, absent, injured, she lost in the first round to eventual gold medalists, Chinese Ting Li and Tiantian Sun, 7-5, 1-6, 6-3. Scoring China's first Olympic gold in tennis, Li and Sun beat Spain's Conchita Martinez and Ruano Pascual, 6-3, 6-3, in the final

At age 47 years, 10 months, Martina Navratilova was not the oldest member of the U.S. Olympic contingent in Athens (she was trumped by a 52-year old female shooter, a 50-year-

old female archer and a 49-year-old female equestrian), but she was the oldest player to compete in the tennis competition in the modern era of the Games. She and partner Lisa Raymond came up one round shy of the medal round, losing to the Japanese pair of Sugiyama and Shinobu Asagoe 6-4, 4-6, 6-4 in the quarterfinals.

At the U.S. Open, it was Hewitt with hot hands. He skipped the Olympic Games, and won the two titles played alongside the Greek festivities—Washington, D.C., 6-3, 6-4, over Gilles Muller of Luxembourg and Long Island, 6-3, 6-1, over Luis Horna of Peru. Seeded No. 4, the 2001 champion did not surrender a set in his six matches driving to the final, but there Federer's theme was "Roll Out the Bagel," and he collared Hewitt with a pair, 6-0, 7-6 (7-4), 6-0. It was merely the third double-bageling in a major final, following Dick Sears's 6-0, 1-6, 6-0, 6-2, job on Howard Taylor at the U.S., 1884, and Vilas's 6-0, 6-3, 6-0, put down of Brian Gottfried at the French, 1977.

Federer's run to his first Open title was highlighted by an extremely difficult quarterfinal clash with Agassi. The two titans played three sets at night, Federer leading 6-3, 2-6, 7-5, before rains suspended play until the following day. Gale force winds—as part of a weather front left over from Hurricane Frances—played havoc with both players, Federer making fewer mistakes in the final two sets to edge Agassi 6-2, 2-6, 7-5, 3-6, 6-3. Henman equaled his French Final Four finish in Flushing, losing in the penultimate round to Federer 6-3, 6-4, 6-4.

But the biggest remaining man, 6-foot-6 Swede Joachim Johansson, No. 28, served up the biggest startler, knocking out No. 2 seed and defending champion Roddick 6-4, 6-4, 3-6, 2-6, 6-4, in the quarterfinals, before falling to Hewitt, 6-4, 7-5, 6-3.

Hewitt's first round victim, Wayne Ferreira, established a record for consecutive major tournaments played—56 straight dating back to 1991. Ferreira's third-round showing at Wimbledon pushed him past Stefan Edberg's previous record of 54.

A Russia-U.S. shootout, the women's semifinals went East. Davenport couldn't hang on against Kuznetsova, the 19-year-old from St. Petersburg, 1-6, 6-2, 6-4. Even though Capriati (a 2-6, 6-4, 6-4, winner over Serena in the quarters), served for victory at 6-5 in the third, Dementieva denied her and clipped her, 6-0, 2-6, 7-6 (7-5). As in France, the all-Russian final was nyet for drama, Kuznetsova taking honors, 6-3, 7-5.

Top-seeded Henin-Hardenne, the defender, went the way of Roddick, expelled by yet another Russian, powerful Nadia Petrova, 6-3, 6-2, in the fourth round. Russians had no mercy on Russians. French champ Myskina was kicked out by 17-year-old Anna Chakvetadze, 7-6 (7-3), 6-3, in the second round.

Although Venus hammered a 125 mph serve while beating Chanda Rubin, 7-6 (7-4), 6-3, Davenport took her in the quarters, 7-5, 6-4. Mary Pierce, helped by 14 double faults, downed Sharapova in the third round, but lost to Kuznetsova, 7-6 (7-5), 6-2 in the fourth. Thus eight holders of major titles—Serena, Venus, Capriati, Davenport, Myskina, Sharapova, Pierce, Henin-Hardenne—were shoved aside to make room for Kuznetsova.

In doubles, Ruano Pascual and Suarez claimed their third major of the year, beating Kuznetsova and Likhovtseva 6-4, 7-5. The Bahamas-Canada combination, Mark Knowles and Daniel Nestor, took the men's, beating Indian Paes and Czech David Rikl 6-3, 6-3. The mixed went to Russian Vera Zvonareva and the lefty American twin Bob Bryan, 6-3, 6-4 over Aussies Woodbridge and Alicia Molik.

After an absence of seven years, the U.S. returned to a Davis Cup final. But chances were slim. The engagement was on alien, Spanish clay in Seville where the Yanks were barbered, 3-2, and the world was becoming aware of 18-year-old Rafael Nadal. Benefiting from three home victories over Austria (5-0), Sweden (4-1) and Belarus (5-0), the Americans not only faced dirt-kicking experts in Carlos Moya and Nadal, but were surrounded by record, partisan crowds of 27,200 at Estadio Olympico, a football ground with a temporary roof. Attendance, second in tennis only to Billie Jean King-Bobby Riggs in 1973 (30,472), eclipsed the 25,578 at Sydney for the U.S.-Australia Cup finale in 1954.

Young lefty Nadal was a surprise pick of captain Jordi Arrese over 2003 French Open champ Juan Carlos Ferrero. But after Fish, the Olympic silver medalist, was filleted by Moya, 6-4, 6-2, 6-3, rookie Rafael, running down everything, eroded Roddick, 6-7 (6-8), 6-2, 7-6 (8-6), 6-2, and the visitors were gone. The Bryans were life support for a day, 6-0, 6-3, 6-2, over Ferrero and Tommy Robredo—until Moya resoundingly brought down Roddick, 6-2, 7-6 (7-1), 7-6 (7-5), and Spain had a second Cup victory.

In this year of Russian women, the Fed Cup was theirs, too. Appropriately, the final was in Moscow, a 3-2 victory over defender France that went down to the wire, the fifth match, Myskina and Zvonareva beating Emilie Loit and Marion Bartoli 7-6 (7-5), 7-5. Myskina, the French Open champion, was the heroine for her country again, winning three points, also beating both Tatiana Golovin, 6-4, 7-6 (7-5), and Natalie Dechy, 6-3, 6-4.

The Tennis Masters Cup returned to Houston and Federer had a perfect record in the round robin, winning a record-length tie-breaker over Safin in the semifinals, 6-3, 7-6 (20-18)—the thirty-eight point tie-breaker equaling the record set by Bjorn Borg and Premjit Lall at Wimbledon in 1973. Federer then won the final in a breeze - 6-3, 6-2 over Hewitt. The Bryan twins repeated in doubles, beating Zimbabweans Kevin Ullyett and Wayne Black, 4-6, 7-5, 6-4, 6-2.

As she had at Wimbledon, Sharapova rebounded to overcome Serena in the final of the year-end WTA Championships, 4-6, 7-6 (7-2), 6-4. Doubles was shared by a Russian, Petrova, and American Meghann Shaughnessy, a 7-5, 6-2, decision over the Zimbabwe-Australian coalition of Cara Black and Rennae Stubbs in the final.

Australian Open

Men's Singles Final: Roger Federer (SUI) def. Marat Safin (RUS), 7-6 (7-3), 6-4, 6-2

Women's Singles Final: Justine Henin-Hardenne (BEL) def. Kim Clijsters (BEL), 6-3, 4-6, 6-3

Men's Doubles Final: Michael Llodra and Fabrice Santoro (FRA) def. Bob Bryan and Mike Bryan (USA), 7-6 (7-4), 6-3

Women's Doubles: Virginia Ruano Pascual (ESP) and Paola Suarez (ARG) def. Svetlana Kuznetsova and Elena Likhovtseva (RUS), 6-4, 6-3

Mixed Doubles Final: Elena Bovina (RUS) and Nenad Zimonjic (SRB) def. Martina Navratilova (USA) and Leander Paes (IND), 6-1, 7-6 (7-3)

French Open

Men's Singles Final: Gaston Gaudio (ARG) def. Guillermo Coria (ARG), 0-6, 3-6, 6-4, 6-1, 8-6

Women's Singles Final: Anastasia Myskina (RUS) def. Elena Dementieva (RUS), 6-1, 6-2

Men's Doubles Final: Xavier Malisse and Olivier Rochus (BEL) def. Michael Llodra and Fabrice Santoro (FRA), 7-5, 7-5

Women's Doubles Final: Virginia Ruano Pascual (ESP) and Paola Suarez (ARG) def. Svetlana Kuznetsova and Elena Likhovtseva (RUS), 6-0, 6-3

Mixed Doubles Final: Tatiana Golovin and Richard Gasquet (FRA) def. Cara Black and Wayne Black (ZIM), 6-3, 6-4

Wimbledon

Men's Singles Final: Roger Federer (SUI) def. Andy Roddick (USA), 4-6, 7-5, 7-6 (7-3), 6-3

Women's Singles Final: Maria Sharapova (RUS) def. Serena Williams (USA), 6-1, 6-4

Men's Doubles Final: Todd Woodbridge (AUS) and Jonas Bjorkman (SWE) def. Julian Knowle (AUT) and Nenad Zimonjic (SRB), 6-1, 6-4, 4-6, 6-4

Women's Doubles Final: Cara Black (ZIM) and Rennae Stubbs (AUS) def Liezel Huber (RSA) and Ai Sugiyama (JPN), 6-3, 7-6 (5)

Mixed Doubles Final: Cara Black and Wayne Black (ZIM) def. Todd Woodbridge and Alicia Molik (AUS), 3-6, 7-6 (10-8), 6-4

U.S. Open

Men's Singles Final: Roger Federer (SUI) def. Lleyton Hewitt (AUS), 6-0, 7-6 (3), 6-0

Women's Singles Final: Svetlana Kuznetsova (RUS) def. Elena Dementieva (RUS), 6-3, 7-5

Men's Doubles Final: Mark Knowles (BAH) and Daniel Nestor (CAN) def. Leander Paes (IND) and David Rikl (CZE), 6-3, 6-3

Women's Doubles Final: Virginia Ruano Pascual (ESP) and Paola Suarez (ARG) def. Svetlana Kuznetsova and Elena Likhovtseva (RUS), 6-4, 7-5

Mixed Doubles Final: Vera Zvonareva (RUS) and Bob Bryan (USA) def. Alicia Molik and Todd Woodbridge (AUS), 6-3, 6-4

Year-End No. 1

Men: Roger Federer

Women: Lindsay Davenport

Top Player Earnings

Men: Roger Federer $6,357,547

Women: Maria Sharapova $2,506, 263

Davis Cup: Spain

Fed Cup: Russia

Tennis Masters Cup, Houston—Roger Federer

WTA Tour Championships, Los Angeles—Maria Sharapova

2004 OLYMPIC GAMES—ATHENS, GREECE

Men's Singles

GOLD: Nicolas Massu (CHI)

SILVER: Mardy Fish (USA)

BRONZE: Fernando Gonazalez (CHI)

Women's Singles

GOLD: Justine Henin-Hardenne (BEL)

SILVER: Amelie Mauresmo (FRA)

BRONZE: Alicia Molik (AUS)

Men's Doubles

GOLD: Nicolas Massu and Fernando Gonzalez (CHI)

SILVER: Rainer Schuettler and Nicolas Kiefer (GER)

BRONZE: Ivan Ljubicic and Mario Ancic (CRO)

Women's Doubles

GOLD: Li Ting and Sun Tian Tian (CHN)

SILVER: Conchita Martinez and Virginia Ruano Pascual (ESP)

BRONZE: Paola Suarez and Patricia Tarabini (ARG)

2005 Vamos Rafa

"Vamos, Rafa!"

That was the cry heard increasingly throughout the world as the big, fast and vivacious 19-year-old Spaniard Rafael Nadal came into view. Not just "promising," which would be enough for most at that age—but as a major champion.

It's thrilling as tennis evolves to watch a kid burst onto the scene and make an historic mark. Think of Billie Jean King at the 1961 Wimbledon doubles, Chris Evert at the 1971 U.S. Open, Evonne Goolagong at 1971 Wimbledon, Jimmy Connors at the 1973 U.S. Pro, Bjorn Borg at the 1974 French, Tracy Austin at the 1977 U.S. Open, Martina Navratilova at 1978 Wimbledon, Boris Becker at 1985 Wimbledon, Steffi Graf at the 1986 U.S. Open,

Rafael Nadal burst to the top of the tennis scene and won the French Open in his first attempt and two days after his 19th birthday.

Arantxa Sanchez Vicario and Michael Chang at the 1989 French, the Sisters Williams at the U.S. Open—Venus in 1997, Serena in 1999—Martina Hingis at the 1997 Australian.

And Mats Wilander, 17, at the 1982 French, winning it on the first visit. It was Nadal who made such a move in 2005, champion as a novitiate. Only he and the Swede, Mats, won at Roland Garros in their first attempt. In fact, Rafa, as 2008 dawned, remained

undefeated in Paris, overpowering Argentine Mariano Puerta in 2005, then none other than Roger Federer in 2006-08.

After a round of 16 showing at the Australian Open, losing to eventual finalist Lleyton Hewitt in a titanic struggle 7-5, 3-6, 1-6, 7-6 (7-3), 6-2, Nadal took clay titles at Costa Do Sauipe, Brazil, 6-0, 6-7 (2-7), 6-1, over Spain's Alberto Martin, and Acapulco, Mexico, 6-1, 6-0, over another Spaniard Albert Montanes, and made an impressive hard-court gallop to the final of Key Biscayne, simmering down against Federer in the final, 2-6, 6-7 (4-7), 7-6 (7-5), 6-3, 6-1.

Back to the comfort of clay, Rafa hiccuped in a quarterfinal loss to Russia's Igor Andreev in Valencia, 7-5, 6-2, but would not lose another match on the dirt for another 25 months. He won Monte Carlo, beating Guillermo Coria, 6-3, 6-1, 0-6, 7-5, then Barcelona, taking out Juan Carlos Ferrero, 6-1, 7-6 (7-4), 6-3, and then in Rome in an epic Italian final over Coria, 6-4, 3-6, 6-3, 4-6, 7-6 (8-6). The excellently fought five hour and 14 minute job was the longest ever final at Il Foro Italico, and the match of the year, as Nadal rose from 0-3 in the fifth, watched Coria blunt three match points in the tie-breaker before missing a backhand. Called "El Mago" (magician) by his admirers, Coria made himself disappear with the concluding error.

At the French, Nadal surrendered sets to Sebastien Grosjean (6-4, 3-6, 6-0, 6-3 in the round of 16), and to Federer (6-3, 4-6, 6-4, 6-3 in the semifinals) before hanging on to take out the difficult unseeded upstart, No. 37 Puerta, 6-7 (6-8), 6-3, 6-1, 7-5, in the rare all-lefty final. Nadal was the seventh Spaniard to win the men's prize at Roland Garros and one of five teen-age champs. In December, it was announced that Puerta failed a drug test after the French final—testing positive for the stimulant etilefrine. Puerta was forced to return his prize money, was stripped of his points and suspended eight years (later shortened to two years on appeal).

Had drugs helped his endurance? Some thought so, considering his long battles in the quarters and semis: over Argentine Willy Canas, 6-2, 3-6, 1-6, 6-3, 6-4, and over Russian Nikolay Davydenko, 6-3, 5-7, 2-6, 6-4, 6-4, but a three-person panel concluded that Puerta mistakenly ingested the drug while drinking out of his wife's wine glass.

Nadal finished the year with 11 titles—tied with Federer for tops for the year - a 70-15 won-loss record, but was a solid No. 2 behind Federer, who won Wimbledon for a third straight year and the U.S. Open for a second time.

Down Under in January at the Australian Open, Federer seemed poised to win at Melbourne Park for a second straight year, rolling into the semifinals without the loss of a set, including a 6-3, 6-4, 6-4 quarterfinal bashing of Andre Agassi. Russian Marat Safin, Federer's final round victim 12 months earlier, put up stiff resistance in the semifinals, even though Federer was on the verge of victory, leading two sets to one and holding match point in the fourth-set tie-breaker. Then, as Rene Stauffer in *The Roger Federer Story, Quest for Perfection*, describes: "Federer held a match point at 6-5 and rushed the net, only to see Safin counter with a superb lob over his head. In his confident manner, Federer attempted an aggressive and risky between-the-legs retrieval of the lob, only to have his trick shot land in the net. Two points later, Safin won the fourth set tie-break to even the match at two sets apiece."

Eighty-minutes later, Safin registered the upset of the year, 7-5, 4-6, 7-5, 7-6 (8-6), 9-7. Roger may have been a bit casual with his wicket shot, figuring another match point would appear. It didn't. That loss might have cost him the Grand Slam, although Nadal and Paris blocked him, too.

Hewitt thrilled the hometown fans, making a spirited run to the final, including wins over James Blake, 4-6, 7-6 (10-8), 6-0, 6-3 in the second round, Nadal, 7-5, 3-6, 1-6, 7-6 (7-3), 6-2 in the fourth round, eighth seed David Nalbandian, 6-3, 6-2, 6-1, 6-3, 10-8 in the quarters and second-seed Andy Roddick, 3-6, 7-6 (7-3), 7-6 (7-4), 6-1 in the semis.

Like Pat Cash in 1987 and 1988, Hewitt nearly became the first homegrown champ since Mark Edmondson in 1976, but Safin's rugged brilliance was too much for the scrappy Hewitt 1-6, 6-3, 6-4, 6-4. Hewitt, so exhausted at his run to the final, was on his knees hours after the final, proposing to girlfriend, Australian TV actress and future wife Bec Cartwright.

In the fourth round, Joachim "Pim Pim" Johansson of Sweden set a tourney serving record, belting 51 aces past Andre Agassi—not a minor feat considering Agassi's return prowess—in the fourth round. Pim Pim's total eclipsed the previous record, 45, by Jonathan Stark in 1997. But aces aren't everything. Stark lost to Lionel Roux, as did Johansson to Agassi, the four-time Australian champ, 6-7 (4-7), 7-6 (7-5), 7-6 (7-3), 6-4.

After being blanked at the majors in 2004, the Sisters Williams were back with their championship attitudes and ramming strokes. Serena got the family back in the major title business for the first time in 18 months, beating top-seed Lindsay Davenport 2-6, 6-3, 6-0 in the Australian final. Seeded seventh, Serena banked her seventh major—her second at Melbourne Park. Davenport, with a second-set lead, faltered for an instant—and was gone.

Serena was on the brink against Maria Sharapova, too, facing two match points, staring them down to win a titanic struggle, 2-6, 7-5, 8-6 in the semifinals. That was a payback for the 2004 Wimbledon final. Davenport took out Nathalie Dechy of France 2-6, 7-6 (9-7), 6-4 in the other semifinal. Alicia Molik, showing the confidence she gained from earning Olympic singles bronze in Athens, had perhaps her biggest win in the fourth round, upsetting Venus Williams 7-5, 7-6 (7-3), before falling to Davenport in the quarters, 6-4, 4-6, 9-7.

Davenport was a precarious top-seed at the French, having had little success—a 1998 semifinal—on the crimson earth. In reaching the quarters, a 6-3, 6-2, loss to French citizen Mary Pierce, Lindsay at least fared far better than 2004 victor Anastasia Myskina. Gone from champ to chump right away, Myskina, the first defender ever to depart in the opening round, was hastened homeward by Spaniard Maria Sanchez Lorenzo, 6-4, 4-6, 6-0.

Recovered from a serious virus and seeded only No. 10, Justine Henin-Hardenne had it rough until the final where she stomped Pierce, 6-1, 6-1. Leading off, it took three sets to dispense of ex-Wimbledon champ Conchita Martinez 6-0, 4-6, 6-4 in the first round, three more over Anabel Medina Garrigues 4-6, 6-2, 6-3 in the third round, fending off two match points at 3-5 in the third while beating U.S. Open champ Svetlana Kuznetsova 7-6 (8-6), 4-6, 7-5 in the fourth round. Still there were second-seed Sharapova, 6-4, 6-2 in the quarterfinals, and seventh-seed Nadia

Petrova, 6-2, 6-3 in the semifinals. Justine's blazing backhand and moxie brought her through it all. But the usual Paris shakes got to third-seeded native Amelie Mauresmo, losing to a 17-year-old Serb, No. 31 Ana Ivanovic, 6-4, 3-6, 6-4, in the third round. Same round another stalwart, Venus, had teen-ager blues, too, losing to 16-year-old Bulgarian, No. 98 Sesil Karatancheva, 6-3, 1-6, 6-1.

Crossing the Channel to London were three Wimbledon champions who would progress to the final, two of them— Venus Williams and Roger Federer—to register third titles, the other, Lindsay Davenport, to miss out by one point.

For the Sisters Sledgehammer it would be a high/low Big W. Venus, avoiding that championship point in the third set, became the aged tournament's longest-shot queen, seeded No. 14, one seed slot lower than Maria Sharapova 12 months earlier (Venus since broke her own record, winning the title in 2007 as the No. 31 seed). However Serena, the champ of 2002-03, seeded No. 4, became one of the all-time victims, interred in the infamous Court 2 (the "Graveyard") in the third round. Wielding a racket as shovel was a fellow American, No. 83 Jill Craybas, who defeated the younger sister 6-3, 7-6 (7-4).

A one-time U.S. Open champ, Andy Roddick, felt the increasing sting of Federer's shotmaking for the second time in a Wimbledon final. "Just too good," said Andy, beaten, 6-2, 7-6 (7-2), 6-4. Nicolas Kiefer took a set—it was like robbing Ft. Knox—from Federer, 6-2, 6-7 (5-7), 6-1, 7-5, in the fourth round, but that was all anybody got. Second-seed Roddick had a trio of tussles, coming along fine over Daniele Bracciali, 7-5, 6-3, 6-7 (3-7), 4-6, 6-3, in the second round, Sebastien Grosjean, 3-6, 6-2, 6-1, 3-6, 6-3, in the quarters, Tom Johansson, 6-7 (6-8), 6-2, 7-6 (12-10), 7-6 (7-5) in the semis.

Other than Serena, the women were formful, eight seeds in the quarters, five of those seeded to get there, whereupon Venus sat down Pierce, 6-0, 7-6 (12-10), Sharapova, 7-6 (7-2), 6-1 (the woman who lifted the title from Little Sister a year before), and, for the crown, Davenport, 4-6, 7-6 (7-4), 9-7. Lindsay had beaten Kuznetsova, 7-6 (7-1), 6-3, and held her nerve in a tight one against Mauresmo, 6-7 (5-7), 7-6 (7-4), 6-4 in the semifinals.

Davenport, the champ of 1999, finalist to Venus in 2000, went at Big Sister with roaring groundies and double determination. It was mutual as they slugged away at each other on Centre Court for two hours, 46 minutes, the women's tournament record for time in a final. Lindsay served for it at 6-5 in the second. Venus wouldn't let her have it. The match point surfaced, at 4-5 in the third, a flame put out by Venus's massive backhand during a furious rally. Too good a shot to moan about it, and Lindsay didn't.

Victor Venus practically lifted off into orbit, giddily excited and pleased with a title no one outside the Williams family thought feasible. Up and down she leaped, almost unable to stop. Ding-dong - the four-year title drought was broken. More female bang for the bucks had never been seen in this arena. Two ladies in white were red-hot blasters. Witnesses, would treasure what they'd watched during a chill, glum afternoon. Their go-for-broke shot-making illuminated the gray sky.

Carrying the planetary No. 1 rating and the 1999 title, Lindsay came so close to winning that she had a fingernail on the championship platter, could feel and taste the prize. Not for 70 years had any woman found a way past a match point to seize the title.

Venus did it, joining the illustrious eight-time champ, Helen Wills Moody, who wriggled out of one to beat arch-rival Helen Jacobs in 1935, a Californian showdown. Little Sister Serena had done it a couple of times in winning majors (the Australian of 2003 and 2005) but not in a final.

Removing two champions, defender Sharapova and Davenport, a rare accomplishment, Venus closed the gap in the longest current rivalry to 14-13, Lindsay. She says she never lost faith in herself and "my destiny—to win big titles. I wasn't supposed to win this, but…"

Historic—who they?—oddities were South African Wesley Moodie, 26, and Aussie Stephen Huss, 19. They didn't know each other, had never played doubles together—yet, as lowly qualifiers they won six matches to become the Wimbledon most unlikely men's champions. It had never been done before. All they had to do in the final was beat the planetary No. 1 pair, Mike and Bob Bryan—which they did, 7-6 (7-4), 6-3, 6-7 (2-7), 6-3. It was no more of an upset than the Berlin Wall falling.

At age 35, Andre Agassi was running out of time. His gimpy back wrecked the French for him (a first round loss to No. 90 Jarkko Nieminen, 7-5, 4-6, 6-7 (6-8), 6-1, 6-0), and kept him out of Wimbledon. But he had one helluva U.S. Open left in him—his tournament even though Federer beat him in the title bout, 6-3, 2-6, 7-6 (7-1), 6-1.

His back, with cortisone shots, was better. He won Los Angeles, over 6-4, 7-5, his 60th (and last) career singles title, and lost the Canadian Open final to Nadal, 6-3, 4-6, 6-2. Seeded No. 7 at Flushing, Andre played a clutch tie-breaker to beat Tomas Berdych, 3-6, 6-1, 6-4, 7-6(7-2), was pushed to five by the dangerous X-Man from Belgium, Xavier Malisse, 6-3, 6-4, 6-7 (5-7), 4-6, 6-2, to set-up a quarterfinal with fellow American James Blake.

This was as dramatic as it gets. Blake, trying to restore his game, recovering from a broken neck (struck his head on a net post in Rome), shingles with attendant vision problems, and, worst, the death of his father, was in gear at the Open. He had jolted second-seed Nadal, rushed him, 6-4, 4-6, 6-3, 6-1, and No. 19 Tommy Robredo from set point down in the second, 4-6, 7-5, 6-2, 6-3. Now he jumped Agassi for a two-set lead and a service break.

What those two did to each other spectacularly brings back a bygone refrain: "It's 3 o'clock in the morning—we've danced the whole night through…"

OK, so it was only 1:09 a.m. when the quick-stepping dance of Agassi and Blake ended with a bang—but not a whimper. Then they hugged like two prizefighters who've Sunday-punched each other through 15 arduous rounds and knew they had created a masterpiece. And through their night and morning of a sporting gavotte, they slugged with clubs, not gloves, taking who-knows-how-many millions of witnesses along with them on an enthralling, sometimes heart-stopping, journey.

Just when it seemed that Blake was to be this Open's child of destiny—two points from the knockout, his club poised to deliver the final blows—Andre, an old hand at the destiny shtick, intervened to throw the fateful punches himself.

The last of those, a forehand, brutalized Blake's last serve, standing forth as an exclamation point punctuating Andre's out-

of-nowhere triumph, 3-6, 3-6, 6-3, 6-3, 7-6 (8-6), in two hours, 51 minutes.

Farther behind than the U.S. deficit, Andre tap-danced out of the negativity of losing the first two sets, service breaks in the third and fifth sets and Blake leaning on him at 5-4 in the final-set tie-breaker. Forehand winner for Andre, error for James: match point. James ignores it with a winning forehand, 6-6. But there the old guy changes pace, a feathery drop shot that not even zephyr James can touch: 6-7. James misses the first serve— a death warrant. Andre shuffles to his left and nails an unplayable inside-out forehand return. The match of the year is over, the tournament goes on.

Andre has to work five again to leap Robby Ginepri 6-4, 5-7, 6-3, 4-6, 6-3 to reach the final where he gave Federer a deserved fright. En route to the final, Roger toyed with the opposition, although Kiefer (as at Wimbledon) got a set, 6-4, 6-7 (3-7), 6-4, 6-4 in the fourth round, and so did Hewitt in the semis, 6-3, 7-6 (7-0), 4-6, 6-3.

There are times when one guy goes home with the cup and the serious cash when, nevertheless, you can put a W beside the other guy's name.

This is what happened in the final. Sure, Roger, the Basel Dazzle, showed 23,352 gawkers why he is every bit the virtuoso on strings as Yo-Yo Ma. Highjacking the U.S. title for the second year in a row, Roger shipped the silver chalice with his name on it and $1.1 million in gold back to Switzerland.

It was enough to set cowbells ringing across his small homeland, the kind of ominous chimes he induces within the skulls of his opponents.

Yes, he rang Andre Agassi's bells for two hours and 20 minutes, and came off with a 6-3, 2-6, 7-6 (7-1), 6-1 win, his tenth title of the year. But you could score the afternoon as a W for Andre, too, for his was a triumphant performance of resistance, of stonewalling for a long time that Richard Nixon would have envied.

Andre Kirk Agassi, a 5-to-1 short-ender with London bookmakers, was gracing his 20th Open. He had busied himself by winning three consecutive five-set battles and running marathons on the unforgiving asphalt, the last merely 24 hours before confronting Federer.

What Andre did in stalking the champion, hindering, laying traps and leading him 4-2 in the third set—hanging on into the tie-breaker – brought to mind the legend of the little Dutch boy plugging a hole in the dike with a finger. Boldly Andre fired harmful groundies, dueled crosscourt in fierce forehand and backhand exchanges and won numerous of them. He even charged and volleyed, and was at his most stubborn in escaping break points—14 of 18.

But Andre didn't have enough fingers to control all the leaks that began to spring. Nobody does. When the tie-breaker arrived, Federer, the virtuoso on strings was playing the ominous "Danse Macabre" for Andre who had held him off a long contentious time. Federer began to spurt aces and winners all over the place, and the dike gave way.

"I had fun, the crowd was great, but the first thing is assessing a loss…the other guy was better. He plays the game in a very special way I haven't seen before. Pete [Sampras] was great. No question. But there was a place to get to with Pete, you knew what you had to do. If you do it, it could be on your terms. There's no such place like that with Roger."

From an American standpoint, Andy Roddick was as down as Agassi, Ginepri and Blake were up. Seeded No. 4, the 2003 champ Andy couldn't get out of the first round, unable to solve the left-handed serve of No. 68-ranked Gilles Muller out of Luxembourg, 7-6 (7-4), 7-6 (10-8), 7-6 (7-1).

It was time for Kim Clijsters to make her breakthrough, after four finals and three semifinals in the majors, and never has a tennis breakthrough paid so well. After getting to the quarters without losing a set, then charging through third sets past Venus, 4-6, 7-5, 6-1, and Sharapova, 6-2, 6-7 (4-7), 6-3, Kim was ready for a record jackpot: $ 2.2 million. Having won the "prelims"—the U.S. Open Series – she had the opportunity of doubling the $1.1 million first prize by winning the main event, the final. Clijsters had little trouble with Mary Pierce in the final, winning 6-3, 6-1 to earn a sweet couple of million. That's a lot of Belgian chocolates.

Pierce had won a French intramural, beating Mauresmo, 6-4, 6-1, in the quarterfinals, but was the center of a storm of protest in her semifinal over 2004 finalist Elena Dementieva. After losing the first set to the Russian, Pierce took a 12-minute, double-injury timeout to have her right quad and back treated. Dementieva cried foul and gamesmanship after losing 3-6, 6-2, 6-2. Said Dementieva, "By taking a 12-minute timeout, I don't think it was a fair play, but she could do it by the rules. And she did it. If that's the only way she can beat me."

But for Clijsters, the championship was the day she got out of jail, lost her ball and chain, tossed into the trash the hairshirt with the scarlet letter "C" on it. Liberation day, at last winning a major singles title and shedding the mental shackles that are attached by fans and the press to athletes whom they tag with "Can't win the big one!"

For all those people, usually thoughtless and unfair, the victory removed the "C" (for Choker) from her persona. Particularly in her small neighborhood called Belgium.

The grim history was Kim's zero for four in major finals: French, 2001, 03, U.S., 2003, Australian, 2004. Moreover, at the 2003 Aussie, Kim let the champ-to-be Serena Williams off the hook in the semis by squandering two match points on her own serve. If that wasn't King Kong on her back, it was at least an orangutan. But in this semifinal something very good happened to help the ever-sunny Clijsters's reputation among her skeptical countryfolk. She not only beat No. 1 Sharapova, but blew five match points while doing so.

Belgian correspondents shook their heads. The derisive nickname they had given Kim, despite all her success—"Poulidor"— was cycling through their minds. Raymon Poulidor was a French bicycle racer in the 1960s and 70s who made a habit of finishing second or third in the Tour de France and other significant European pedaling events.

"Yes, we have called her the 'Poulidor of Tennis,' says Serge Fayat, a Belgian journalist. "Never quite makes it. But finally she finished first. Everybody is happy for her."

Dwight Davis would have relished the outcome of the Davis Cup: a tiny country with two significant players beating the U.S., 3-2, in Carson, Calif., and going on to hug the Cup itself. That would be Croatia, powered by Ivan Ljubicic and Mario Ancic,

defeating another small country, Slovak Republic, 3-2, going right down to a fifth match finish.

That honor went to 6-foot-5 inch, 21-year-old Ancic, on the road, yet, beating 26-year-old Michal Mertinak, 7-6 (7-1), 6-3, 6-4, in Bratislava. The loser, No. 166, was a sub.

"It's an unforgettable match and an unforgettable day," Ancic, No. 22, said. "I am not sure people realize how big it is to be at the top of the pyramid." Croatia became the 12th different nation to win the title in the competition's 105-year history.

Croatia's Nikki Pilic became the first captain to win the trophy for different nations, having led Germany to the Cup in 1988-89, 93.

No. 9 Ljubicic, 26, who won seven of eight singles and four of four doubles with Ancic, led off over Karol Kucera, 6-3, 6-4, 6-3.

Nothing like this had happened since the Cup's earliest days, when, in 1907, lightly-populated Australasia (Australia and New Zealand) won a first Cup. It underlined donor Davis's theme that, under the format, small countries could compete with much larger ones. Croatia and Slovakia didn't even exist as such at the Cup's debut in 1900, Croatia splitting off from Yugoslavia in 1991.

Agassi reporting for his last Davis Cup duty, the opening round in March, was disappointingly off his timing, losing to Ljubicic, 6-3, 7-6 (7-0), 6-3. Roddick got the split over Ancic, 4-6, 6-2, 6-1, 6-4. But the Bryan twins crashed to Ancic and Ljubicic, 3-6, 7-6 (10-8), 6-4, 6-4, their first Cup defeat, Ivan then hanging tough with big backhands in the exciting clincher over Roddick, 4-6, 6-3, 7-6 (13-11), 6-7 (7-9), 6-2. Captain Patrick McEnroe had a better team than his 2003 first round losers to Croatia, and a court of hand-picked paving, but...it was in the stars for the Croats.

In the final, Slovak Dominik Hrbaty, No. 19, was bold and invincible in singles, nine sets: over Ancic, 7-6 (7-4), 6-3, 6-7 (4-7), 6-4, and Ljubicic, 4-6, 6-3, 6-4, 3-6, 6-4 to tie it, 2-2. It wasn't enough. The go-ahead doubles had gone to the Croats over Hrbaty-Mertinak, 7-6 (7-5), 6-3, 7-6 (7-5), and Ancic was ready for the moment of his tennis life.

Russia won the Fed Cup for the second time, beating France 3-2 at Roland Garros—Dementieva and Dinara Safina (Marat's younger sister) beating Mauresmo and Pierce 6-4, 1-6, 6-3 in the fifth and decisive doubles.

Federer got a shock from an old nemesis, Argentine David Nalbandian, at the Tennis Masters Cup in Shanghai. Winner the previous two years, and holder of the first two sets in the final, as well as the balls to serve for the title at 6-5 in the fifth set, Roger nevertheless was caught and passed, 6-7 (4-7), 6-7 (11-13), 6-2, 6-1, 7-6 (7-3). Only twice in his career had he waffled with a two-set lead, the other time a Davis Cup series against Hewitt at Melbourne in 5-7, 2-6, 7-6(7-4), 7-5, 6-1.

The French pair of Michael Llodra and Fabrice Santoro snared the doubles title in Shanghai, narrowly over Leander Paes and Nenad Zimonjic, 6-7 (6-8), 6-3, 7-6 (7-4).

A Gallic frolic settled the WTA Championship, in Los Angeles. It went to Mauresmo, her most imposing title to date, over Pierce, 5-7, 7-6 (7-3), 6-4 in the final. Lisa Raymond and Samantha Stosur, an American-Aussie alliance, won the doubles prize over Cara Black and Rennae Stubbs, a Zimbabwe-Aussie connection, 6-7 (5-7), 7-5, 6-4.

2005 CHAMPIONS AND LEADERS

Australian Open
Men's Singles Final: Marat Safin (RUS) def. Lleyton Hewitt (AUS), 1-6, 6-3, 6-4, 6-4
Women's Singles Final: Serena Williams (USA) def. Lindsay Davenport (USA), 2-6, 6-3, 6-0
Men's Doubles Final: Wayne Black and Kevin Ullyett (ZIM) def. Bob Bryan and Mike Bryan (USA), 6-4, 6-4
Women's Doubles Final: Svetlana Kuznetsova (RUS) and Alicia Molik (AUS) def. Lindsay Davenport and Corina Morariu (USA), 6-3, 6-4
Mixed Doubles Final: Samantha Stosur and Scott Draper (AUS) def. Liezel Huber (RSA) and Kevin Ullyett (ZIM), 6-2, 2-6, 10-6 (Match Tie-Break)

French Open
Men's Singles Final: Rafael Nadal (ESP) def. Mariano Puerta (ARG), 6-7 (6-8), 6-3, 6-1, 7-5
Women's Singles Final: Justine Henin-Hardenne (BEL) def. Mary Pierce (FRA), 6-1, 6-1
Men's Doubles Final: Jonas Bjorkman (SWE) and Max Mirnyi (BLR) def. Bob Bryan and Mike Bryan (USA), 2-6, 6-1, 6-4
Women's Doubles Final: Virginia Ruano Pascal (ESP) and Paola Suarez (ARG) def. Cara Black (ZIM) and Liezel Huber (RSA), 4-6, 6-3, 6-3
Mixed Doubles Final: Daniela Hantuchova (SVK) and Fabrice Santoro (FRA) def. Martina Navratilova (USA) and Leander Paes (IND), 3-6, 6-3, 6-2

Wimbledon
Men's Singles Final: Roger Federer (SUI) def. Andy Roddick (USA), 6-2, 7-6 (7-2), 6-4
Women's Singles Final: Venus Williams (USA) def. Lindsay Davenport (USA), 4-6, 7-6 (7-4), 9-7
Men's Doubles Final: Stephen Huss and Wesley Moodie (RSA) def. Bob Bryan and Mike Bryan (USA), 7-6 (7-4), 6-3, 6-7 (7-2), 6-3
Women's Doubles Final: Cara Black (ZIM) and Liezel Huber (RSA) def. Svetlana Kuznetsova (RUS) and Amelie Mauresmo (FRA), 6-2, 6-1
Mixed Doubles Final: Mary Pierce (FRA) and Mahesh Bhupathi (IND) def. Tatiana Perebiynis (UKR) and Paul Hanley (AUS), 6-4, 6-2

U.S. Open
Men's Singles Final: Roger Federer (SUI) def. Andre Agassi (USA) 6-3, 2-6, 7-6 (7-1), 6-1
Women's Singles Final: Kim Clijsters (BEL) def. Mary Pierce (FRA), 6-3, 6-1
Men's Doubles Final: Bob Bryan and Mike Bryan (USA) def. Jonas Bjorkman (SWE) and Max Mirnyi (BLR), 6-1, 6-4
Women's Doubles Final: Lisa Raymond (USA) and Samantha Stosur (AUS) def. Elena Dementieva (RUS) and Flavia Pennatta (ITA), 6-2, 5-7, 6-3
Mixed Doubles Final: Daniela Hantuchova (SVK) and Mahesh Bhupathi (IND) def. Katarina Srebotnik (SLO) and Nenad Zimonjic (SRB), 6-4, 6-2

Year-End No. 1
Men: Roger Federer
Women: Lindsay Davenport

Top Player Earnings
Men: Roger Federer $6,137,018
Women: Kim Clijsters $3,983,654

Davis Cup: Croatia

Fed Cup: Russia

Tennis Masters Cup, Shanghai—David Nalbandian
WTA Championships, Los Angeles—Amelie Mauresmo

2006 Allez Amelie

Mother Freedom: it is now the USTA Billie Jean King National Tennis Center.

In Paris, the Lord of the Swings—Roger Federer—was not smiling. The combination of the naughty crimson earth and big bad Rafa Nadal trapped him again. But the smile returned at Wimbledon and the U.S. Open as he finished with another major triple. And he closed down the year mightily, winning all five Masters matches, flattening James Blake in the title round, 6-0, 6-3, 6-4.

Unlike Roger, Justine Henin-Hardenne was smiling in Paris. Like him, she accomplished the seldom-done act of making all four major finals—but she won only the French.

In Italy, they were smiling about something that usually draws little attention: women's tennis. The signorinas were world team champs, winning the Fed Cup over Belgium, 3-2, as Francesca Schiavone and Roberta Vinci took the deciding doubles.

The biggest smile in Melbourne belonged to thrice-champ Martina Hingis, back in business after a three-year injuries time-out, showing she could still play, making the quarterfinals.

In Moscow, the smiler was Dmitry Tursunov, happy to live in the U.S., but just as happy to play for Russia and beat Andy Roddick in a hyper-extended match that virtually guaranteed the Davis Cup for his native land.

Somewhere Suzanne Lenglen was smiling. Eighty-one years after the last of her six Wimbledon championships, another French woman, Amelie Mauresmo, was in the winner's circle.

At Flushing Meadow, Billie Jean was smiling. The U.S. Tennis Association named its multi-court playpen for her, the game's

Was she REALLY gone? At the U.S. Open, fans of herself (49-year-old Martina Navratilova) and doubles didn't know whether to smile or cry as they witnessed her announced fare-

well, resulting in a 59th major title. With Bob Bryan, 28, at her side, she won the mixed over a couple from her homeland, Czechs Kveta Peschke and Martin Damm, 6-2, 6-3. She was lucky to age so well. We were lucky to watch, and would never see such artistry at doubles again.

In her seventh year in the Top 10, heartened by her WTA Championship that closed out 2005, Mauresmo rewarded herself with something else new: two major titles, the Australian and Wimbledon. France's last winner of a pair was the great Lenglen in 1925, the French and Wimbledon. Some might say that Amelie's Australian was tainted by foes' misfortunes: Michaella Krajicek, ill after one set; Kim Clijsters injured in a third set semis tumble; Henin-Hardenne quitting with stomach pains (the Belgian Bellyache?), trailing 6-1, 2-0, in the title bout. Justine had beaten top-seed Lindsay Davenport, 2-6, 6-2, 6-3, and fourth Maria Sharapova, 4-6, 6-1, 6-4, to get there. Clijsters had stopped Hingis, 6-3, 2-6, 6-4.

There were no gimme's for Mauresmo at Wimbledon. Nine battling sets she needed for the last three matches, all against former major champs: Anastasia Myskina, 6-1, 3-6, 6-3 in the quarters; Maria Sharapova, 6-3, 3-6, 6-2 in the semis; Henin-Hardenne, 2-6, 6-3, 6-4 in the final. Defending champ, Venus, had been expelled by young Serb, Jelena "Jelly" Jankovic, 7-6 (10-8), 4-6, 6-4, in the third round.

Though brilliant, she had been French toast too many times, burned by critics who complained that in the clutch her nerves went as haywire as the wild horses roaming France's Camargue.

But now, Amelie Mauresmo was the toast of the town, all of France and anywhere else the game of tennis is played. On Centre Court, she stood as tall and sturdy as the Eiffel Tower, playing the closing game of her life.

Closing is everything, as Boston Red Sox ace reliever Jonathan Papelbom would tell you, and it's the same principle in tennis. Stick the ball where the other guy can't hurt you.

Good prescription for success, and Amelie followed it. This one was sweet because it was so tight, because it was Wimbledon. When it came to that last game at 5-4, and Justine clawing at the door, Amelie performed her closing act with severity. She had to because Justine, the French Open champ and holder of four other majors, was just two swats away from catching her.

As the multitude of 13,798 yelled for both, and a tricky wind swirled through the sunny arena, Mauresmo, ever a splendid athlete, never an alibier despite failings, stood confidently at the baseline to serve for the championship.

"My heart was going…" she makes an unintelligible noise like a drum roll. "But my nerves were OK. I don't want anybody to talk about my nerves anymore, no?"

Hers held up better than Justine's in an unevenly played match where there were more shanks than you'll find in a butcher shop. But that concluding game will stay with Amelie and us for a while. It was a spectacular gift that she, a complete shotmaker, gave herself a day after her 27th birthday.

For openers, she hooked an ace on Justine's forehand sideline, 15-0. And duplicated it for 30-15 after the Belgian socked a forehand passer. Justine wasn't through, stabbing at a forehand return that fell on the baseline, 30-all. Amelie was going to charge,

no matter what, coming through with a marvelous backhand volley: 40-30, match point. It was the last thrust of an extraordinary matinee of serve-and-volleying by both of them (a relief from the predominant baseline grinding). Amelie then stayed back, waiting for Justine to miss, which she did much too often. Her midcourt forehand went weakly into the net, and Amelie went strongly, ecstatically on a victory trot.

"This is it!" she told herself. "It's over! I'm coming off this court a winner!" All of the hideous collapses can be forgotten now. "I've won the most prestigious tournament, and I've learned to deal with my nerves and get past it."

Little noticed with big deeds, China's first majors, were the doublists Zi Yan, 21, and Jie Zheng, 23, who won the Australian over Samantha Stosur and Lisa Raymond, 2-6, 7-6 (9-7), 6-3, and Wimbledon over Virginia Ruano Pascual and Paola Suarez, 6-3, 3-6, 6-2.

The French—too close to home?—remained a stumbling block for top-seed Mauresmo, beaten in the fourth round by 17-year-old Czech Nicole Vaidisova, 6-7 (5-7), 6-1, 6-2. Nicole then cut down Venus, 6-7 (5-7), 6-1, 6-3. The show, however, belonged to fifth-seeded Henin-Hardenne on the clay she loved, where she was guarding her title and had also won in 2003. She didn't lose a set, wasn't even caught up in a tie-breaker, as she sent off three major champions: Anastasia Myskina, 6-1, 6-4; Kim Clijsters, 6-3, 6-2; and in the final Svetlana Kuznetsova, 6-4, 6-4.

Mauresmo and Henin-Hardenne arrived at the U.S. Open seeded one-two, but the fortnight's fireball was was tall, blonde and heavy-hitting Sharapova, who knocked off both of them as though they didn't belong on the same court. She was overpoweringly ready to add the U.S. to her Wimbledon of two years before, and had grown two inches to 6-feet-2. Ranked No. 91, oft-injured Serena represented the Williams clan on a wild card, until Mauresmo dropped her in the fourth round, 6-4, 0-6, 6-2.

Justine and Amelie were doing fine until their paths crossed Maria's. The Belgian beat Davenport, 6-4, 6-4 in the quarters and Jankovic, 4-6, 6-4, 6-0 in the semis. The French tourist got to her semifinal by chasing off Marat Safin's kid sister, Dinara Safina, 6-2, 6-3. But that was the end. Sharapova wrapped a double-bagel around Mauresmo's brief hope, 6-0, 4-6, 6-0, and then battered Henin-Hardenne, 6-4, 6-4.

Justine, however, had the season's last laugh, beating Sharapova, 6-2, 7-6 (7-5), and Mauresmo, 6-4, 6-3, to win the WTA Championship in Madrid, and install herself as No. 1.

You don't see many tennis exceptionals from Cyprus. There's only one, Greek-blooded Marcos Baghdatis, a bearded, good-humored 20-year-old who turned the Australian Open into a feel-good festival. Accompanied by a joyful Greek chorus—his cheering section of young Melbournian admirers—unseeded Baghdatis seemed to dance his way to the final, a Zorba in sneakers. Once there, he even threatened Roger Federer by grabbing the first set. Not until then was order restored at Rod Laver Arena: Roger, 5-7, 7-5, 6-0, 6-2, for his second Aussie title. But if the full-house crowd of 15,000 was awed by the way he took over, Roger himself was awed to tears to receive the trophy from Rod Laver.

The Baghdatis surge began in the fourth round when he ambushed second-seed Andy Roddick, 6-4, 1-6, 6-3, 6-4. The theme

seemed: Look out for Greek choruses. One of them might be singing your dirge. This one was, with Roddick in mind. Perched up high on sort of an Olympian slope within, Laver Arena, the chorus of 50 blue-shirted youths sang, chanted, flapped blue-and-white Greek flags, even danced in place, loudly and constantly praising and encouraging their hero, who was battling on the green asphalt plain below.

If Cassandra, the ancient psychic who warned the Trojans about that damned horse, had been in the house, she would have cautioned: "Beware of a Greek bearing double-barreled backhands!"

Marcos, No. 54, is undoubtedly No. 1 with whatever gods still hang out with Zeus.

On he went on a trail through seeds: needing five sets to highjack No. 7 Ivan Ljubicic, 6-4, 6-2, 4-6, 3-6, 6-3, and No. 4 David Nalbandian, a rousing comeback, 3-6, 5-7, 6-3, 6-4, 6-4. Entering the tournament, he had never played five sets, but this was his third (he beat No. 17 Radek Stepanek in the second round, 6-4, 6-3, 3-6, 0-6, 7-5).

Federer was moving along as expected, but having probably his toughest test in the quarters where a couple more points for the solid baseliner, Russian Nikolay Davydenko, might have produced an upset, 6-4, 3-6, 7-6 (9-7), 7-6 (7-5). He also lost his usual one set set to Nicolas Kiefer in the semis, 6-3, 5-7, 6-0, 6-2.

Roger reveled in American winter sunshine, winning Indian Wells over James Blake, 7-5, 6-3, 6-0, and Key Biscayne over Ljubicic in tantalizing (for the loser) tie-breakers, 7-6 (7-5), 7-6 (7-4), 7-6 (8-6). "Not a beautiful way to win," sighed Ljubicic. He watched helplessly the match point shot, a ball that slithered along the net cord, and dropped dead on his side.

But back on native European clay life wasn't so pleasant for Federer, discourtesy of Nadal. Rafa got him in the Monte Carlo final, 6-2, 6-7 (2-7), 6-3, 7-6 (7-5). And even worse in Rome because Roger had two fifth-set match points, bungling routine forehands, as the Spaniard retained his Italian title, a nail-biting 6-7 (0-7), 7-6 (7-5), 6-3, 2-6, 7-6 (7-5), decision. (Hingis did better at the Italian, winning her last meaningful title, 6-2, 7-5, over Dinara Safina.)

And the worst yet for Roger, the French final that would shut down Roger's dreams of a Grand Slam, 1-6, 6-1, 6-4, 7-6 (7-4). After a strong start, Federer became cautious, and there was no beating Rafa from the baseline.

A relatively new and quite promising face showed in the quarters, 19-year-old Serb Novak Djokovic. Injured in the third set, he was losing, 6-4, 6-4, to Nadal, who had beaten Hewitt, 6-2, 5-7, 6-4, 6-2. Third-seed Nalbandian, after beating Davydenko, 6-3, 6-3, 2-6, 6-4, appeared to have Federer's semifinal number. Hazy at first, Roger said, "I was panicking, couldn't play…" But he came out of the haze to win, 3-6, 6-4, 5-2, ret. capitalizing on the Argentine's injury, and had his final-round appointment with a daymare named Nadal. In the first round, a 6-2, 7-5, 6-1 victory, Nadal beat difficult winds, a Swede, Robin Soderling, and the Open era record for consecutive wins on clay. This one was Rafa's 54th in a row, topping the 53 of another Spanish-speaking lefty, Guillermo Vilas of Argentina, set in 1977. Nadal's last dirty defeat was by Russian Igor Andreev, April 2, 2005, at Valencia.

Like his cow, Juliette, Federer sought some soothing grass—and found it on Centre Court, where he would triumph for a fourth consecutive year. He strode onto Centre looking as stylish as some of his long-ago championship predecessors such as Bill Tilden, Fred Perry, Don Budge in white blazer and trousers. Of course he removed them to blaze through the draw without the loss of a set—until the final where Rafa loomed once again, to be beaten this time (though winning a set), 6-0, 7-6 (7-5), 6-7 (2-7), 6-3.

Though Nadal was thought to be a dirtkicker at sea on grass, undeserving of second-seeding, he was determined to contradict that notion. Only in the second round, two points from defeat by American qualifier, No. 237 Robert Kendrick, did he look out of it—but won, 6-7 (4-7), 3-6, 7-6 (7-2), 7-5, 6-4. In the semis, he ripped through Marcos Baghdatis, 6-1, 7-5, 6-3, after the great Greek of Melbourne, had crunched the 2002 champ, Hewitt, 6-1, 5-7, 7-6 (7-5), 6-2. From an American standpoint nothing was happening after the third round: Roddick went out to 19-year-old Scot, Andy Murray (hope for Britain?), 7-6 (7-4), 6-4, 6-4; James Blake got one game after leading Max Mirnyi two-sets-to-one 6-4, 3-6, 4-6, 6-1, 6-0.

Nerves clenched bageled Nadal as the final began, but he soon was competing well, losing whatever European antipathy he might have had for grass. He was the man terminating Andre Agassi's 11-tournament Wimbledon career, 7-6 (7-5), 6-2, 6-4, in the third round.

Like a genie, Jimmy Connors appeared as the new mentor for coach-du-jour Roddick, who had totaled five match wins in the three previous majors. It was a good fit as ninth-seed Andy bolted all the way to Federer and the U.S. Open title round that was his the year before Roger took over in 2004. Improving his backhand and volleying, Andy got by some rough spots: lefty Fernando Verdasco, 6-7 (5-7), 6-3, 6-4, 6-7 (4-7), 6-2, in the third round; 2001 champ Hewitt, 6-3, 7-5, 6-4, in the quarters; fluent-stroking Russian Mikhail Youzhny, 6-7 (5-7), 6-0, 7-6 (7-3), 6-3 in the semifinals.

Federer, cool and smooth on his way to Roddick, lost one set, to Blake in a furious quarter, 7-6 (9-7), 6-0, 6-7 (9-11), 6-4, then plunked Davydenko 6-1, 7-5, 6-4 in the semifinals. Roddick lived up to his mentor's stonewalling ways of the old days, holding back Federer for almost three sets—then overrun, 6-2, 4-6, 7-5, 6-1.

But the matches of the tournament were long past: the hail and farewell of Agassi in his uninterrupted journey of 21 U.S. Opens. Stars in the early morning skies, tears in his eyes, the fading yet luminous star of so many dramas on the asphalt stage abruptly realized that—even though past his geezerly bedtime—it was not yet time to take his final bow.

How did he do it? With his aching back throbbing, Andre shuffled past clever Romanian, Andrei Pavel, 6-7 (4-7), 7-6 (10-8), 7-6 (8-6), 6-2, from 0-4 down in the third, only his 16th match of an injury-sprinkled season. The people plaintively wanted an encore from Father Timeless. And they got it big-time—five pained but wondrous sets –the goodbye-guy stroking a masterpiece, subduing eighth-seed Marcos Baghdatis, 6-4, 6-4, 3-6, 5-7, 7-5, losing his serve in the first game of the fifth, as everybody needed diapers.

It was a win to die for, and shortly Andre's career would perish. Andre's father urged him not to play the third rounder, but he said, "I didn't come here to quit." Hurting, he did remarkably well against a German named Becker. Not the old rival, Boris, but a qualifier ranked No. 112, Benjamin Becker, the 2004 NCAA champ for Baylor. Banging 27 aces, he sent Andre home, en-route to the Hall of Fame, 7-5, 6-7 (4-7), 6-4, 7-5.

"The scoreboard said I lost today, but what the scoreboard doesn't say is what it is I have found. And over the last 21 years, I have found loyalty. You have pulled for me on the court and also in life. I've found inspiration. You have willed me to succeed sometimes even in my lowest moments. And I've found generosity. You have given me your shoulders to stand on to reach for my dreams, dreams I could never have reached without you. Over the last 21 years, I have found you and I will take you and the memory of you with me for the rest of my life. Thank you."

What a way to go.

The longest way to go on the year-long pursuit of the Davis Cup was taken by winner Tursunov and loser Roddick: 72 games over four hours, 48 minutes, giving the home team an insurmountable 3-1 lead in the semifinal series. Terrain within Moscow's Olympic Stadium was important—clay for the Yanks, who won their most recent Cup there in 1995, and a quick carpet for Argentina, slimly defeated for the Cup, 3-2 by Marat Safin's fifth match bagging of Jose Acasuso, 6-3, 3-6, 6-3, 7-6 (7-5).

Safin launched the 3-2 victory over the U.S., outslugging Roddick, 6-4, 6-3, 7-6 (7-5). Youzhny followed with a flock of handsome backhands, 7-5, 1-6, 6-1, 7-5, over James Blake. A pause was effected by the Bryan twins, 6-3, 6-4, 6-2, over Tursunov and Youzhny. But despite Andy's determined rebound from two sets down, and serving for the match at 6-5 in the fifth, he couldn't harness Tursunov, 6-3, 6-4, 5-7, 3-6, 17-15. Chances abounded for both in a nerve-wracker. Andy sidestepped two match points to 12-12, but the Russian resident of Folsom, Calif., fired three of his 32 aces to 16-15. Then he delighted 15,000 onlookers with a doorslamming backhand passer.

Nalbandian was a final round thorn in the Russians, beating Safin, 6-4, 6-4, 6-4, and Davydenko, 6-2, 6-2, 4-6, 6-4. But he couldn't do much in the doubles with Agustin Calleri, losers to Safin-Tursunov, 6-2, 6-3, 6-4. Davydenko's leadoff win over Juan Ignacio Chela, 6-1, 6-2, 5-7, 6-4, got the other Russian point. Capt. Shamil Tarpischev and Russia had their second Cup.

With No. 1 Justine Henin-Hardenne in the lineup, Belgium figured to win the equivalent Fed Cup over Italy that, nevertheless, went down to the fifth match, a doubles match, in Charleroi, Belgium. Justine was a first day winner over Flavia Pennetta, 6-4, 7-5, and on the second day over Francesca Schiavone, 6-4, 7-5, to give Belgium a 2-1 lead. But Mara Santangelo knotted it by beating Kirsten Flipkens, 6-7 (3-7), 6-3, 6-0. Justine had strained a knee, but kept going until she and Kirsten trailed Schiavone and Vinci, 3-6, 6-2, 2-0. Then she surrendered. Italy won the Cup, its first, by default. But a Cup is a Cup, and Captain Corrado Barazzutti was smiling.

2006 CHAMPIONS AND LEADERS

Australian Open
Men's Singles Final: Roger Federer (SUI) def. Marcos Baghdatis (CYP), 5-7, 7-5, 6-0, 6-2

Women's Singles Final: Amelie Mauresmo (FRA) def. Justine Henin Hardenne (BEL), 6-1, 2-0, ret.

Men's Doubles Final: Bob Bryan and Mike Bryan (USA) def. Martin Damm (CZE) and Leander Paes (IND), 4-6, 6-3, 6-4

Women's Doubles Final: Zi Yan and Jie Zheng (CHN) def. Samantha Stosur (AUS) and Lisa Raymond (USA), 2-6, 7-6 (9-7), 6-3

Mixed Doubles Final: Martina Hingis (SUI) and Mahesh Bhupathi (IND) def. Elena Likhovtseva (RUS) and Daniel Nestor (CAN), 6-3, 6-3

French Open
Men's Singles Final: Rafael Nadal (ESP) def. Roger Federer (SUI), 1-6, 6-1, 6-4, 7-6 (7-4)

Women's Singles Final: Justine Henin-Hardenne (BEL) def. Svetlana Kuznetsova (RUS), 6-4, 6-4

Men's Doubles Final: Jonas Bjorkman (SWE) and Max Mirnyi (BLR) def. Bob Bryan and Mike Bryan (USA), 6-7 (7-5), 6-4, 7-5

Women's Doubles Final: Lisa Raymond (USA) and Samantha Stosur (AUS) def. Daniela Hantuchova (SVK) and Ai Sugiyama (JPN), 6-3, 6-2

Mixed Doubles Final: Katarina Srebotnik (SLO) and Nenad Zimonjic (SRB) def. Elena Likhovtseva (RUS) and Daniel Nestor (CAN), 6-3, 6-4

Wimbledon
Men's Singles Final: Roger Federer (SUI) def. Rafael Nadal (ESP), 6-0, 7-6 (7-5), 6-7 (7-2), 6-3

Women's Singles Final: Amelie Mauresmo (FRA) def. Justin Henin-Hardenne (BEL), 2-6, 6-3, 6-4

Men's Doubles Final: Bob Bryan and Mike Bryan (USA) def. Fabrice Santoro (FRA) and Nenad Zimonjic (SRB), 6-3, 4-6, 6-4, 6-2

Women's Doubles Final: Zi Yan and Jie Zheng (CHN) def. Virginia Ruano Pascual (ESP) and Paola Saurez (ARG), 6-3, 3-6, 6-2

Mixed Doubles Final: Vera Zvonareva (RUS) and Andy Ram (ISR) def. Venus Williams (USA) and Bob Bryan (USA), 6-3, 6-2

U.S. Open
Men's Singles Final: Roger Federer (SUI) def. Andy Roddick (USA), 6-2, 4-6, 7-5, 6-1

Women's Singles Final: Maria Sharapova (RUS) def. Justine Henin Hardenne (BEL), 6-4, 6-4

Men's Doubles Final: Martin Damm (CZE) and Leander Paes (IND) def. Jonas Bjorkman (SWE) and Max Mirnyi (BLR), 6-7 (7-5), 6-4, 6-3

Women's Doubles Final: Nathalie Dechy (FRA) and Vera Zvonareva (RUS) def. Dinara Safina (RUS) and Katarina Srebotnik (SLO), 7-6 (5), 7-5

Mixed Doubles Final: Martina Navratilova and Bob Bryan (USA) def. Kveta Peschke and Martin Damm (CZE), 6-2, 6-3

Year-End No. 1
Men: Roger Federer
Women: Justine Henin-Hardenne

Top Player Earnings
Men: Roger Federer $8,343,885
Women: Justine Henin-Hardenne $4,204, 810

Davis Cup: Russia

Fed Cup: Italy

Tennis Masters Cup, Shanghai—Roger Federer
Sony Ericsson WTA Championships, Madrid—Justine Henin-Hardenne

2007 U.S. Ends Davis Cup Drought

Drought-busters, who guzzled victory champagne from the aged crock were Andy Roddick, James Blake and the double-dippers Bob and Mike Bryan, plus their captain through good times and bad, Pat Mac.

"Maybe yes. Maybe no" had been the reaction of prominent Americans when U.S. captains recruited teams. But it was ever "yes" when this McEnroe took over the captaincy from his older brother, John, in 2001. "Our goal has always been the Cup, whatever it took," said Roddick.

It wasn't a promising start for the younger McEnroe: defeat at Switzerland in the first round in 2001, engineered by a little known youngster named Federer, who would reap tall headlines a few months later by snipping Pete Sampras's 31-match Wimbledon streak.

Pat's gang were up and down: a no-chance final on Spanish soil in 2004; semis at France in 2002, and at Russia in 2006 (both on clay); first round fumbles against Croatia in 2003 and 2005.

But this was the year, they felt, to end a Saharan dry spell that preceded them—12 years, a U.S. futility record, since the last Cup, Sampras-produced, in Moscow in 1995.

So it was, with reversals of the 2006 defeat in Moscow. Roddick avenged in 17-15 in the fifth loss from the previous year and got back at Dmitry Tursunov, 6-4,

The seven-year itch of Patrick McEnroe and his loyal band of Davis Cup seekers was at long last scratched positively. Sure, it was raining—the location was Portland, Oregon, after all—but this parade was an inside job, swiping the coveted punchbowl from Russia within Memorial Coliseum as sellout crowds of 12,000 raved at the overdue success.

6-4, 6-2, and Blake at Mikhail Youzhny, 6-3, 7-6 (7-4), 6-7 (3-7), 7-6 (7-3). Unchanged were the fraternal fireballs, the Bryans, pulling their out-with-the-drought act at the expense of Nikolay Davydenko and Igor Andreev, 7-6 (7-4), 6-4, 6-2.

The 3-0 lead meant that it was over, and the after the dry spell came the deluge, Americans enveloped in a shower of stream-

ers from the ceiling. Unbroken, troubled by only one break point, the Bryans improved their Cup mark to 13-1, winners of the last eight. In a familial finish, Mike served Cup point that was punctuated by Bob's overhead smash. The 107-year-old prize—called "Dwight's pot" by Harvard buddies of donor Dwight Davis—would return to the land of its origin.

The original 1900 triumphant U.S. team (Player-Captain Davis, Holcombe Ward, Mal Whitman) was an entirely-Harvard side. For the first time since the U.S. win in 1926 (including Harvard Man Dick Williams, a doubles victor), a Harvardian was aboard again: Blake played two years for the Crimson in 1998 and 1999. Andy was 6-0 for the campaign, while James was 5-2, losing to Swede Tom Johansson in the semifinals 6-4, 6-2, 3-6, 6-3 in Goteborg.

Russia traveled probably the most precariously bumpy road to a Cup final: three 3-2 decisions, each decided in the fifth match—Igor Andreev over Chilean Nicolas Massu, 6-2, 6-1, 6-7 (1-7), 6-4 in the first round; Marat Safin over France's Paul-Henri Mathieu, 7-6 (7-3), 6-3, 6-2 in the quarterfinals; Andreev over German Philipp Kohlschreiber, 6-3, 3-6, 6-0, 6-3 in the semifinals.

The Americans may have been fortunate that Safin declined to play the final, but they came through a difficult opener on Czech, clay at Ostrava, 4-1, Roddick winning two, beating Tomas Berdych to decide it, 4-6, 6-3, 6-2, 7-6 (7-4). Blake lost to Berdych on the first day, 6-1, 2-6, 7-5, 7-5, but the Bryans took out Lukas Dlouhy and Pavel Vizner 6-4, 6-4, 6-4 in the mid-point doubles.

Spain, minus an injured Rafael Nadal, fell meekly 4-1 to Roddick and the boys in the quarterfinals on a lighting fast indoor court in Winston-Salem. Roddick and Blake didn't lose a set on day one against Fernando Verdasco and Tommy Robredo respectively, while the Bryans surrendered only one set in beating Verdasco and Feliciano Lopez to clinch it on day two.

The American curse in Goteborg, Sweden was exorcised in the semifinals—Roddick winning against both Joachim Johansson and Jonas Bjorkman in straight sets—to give the U.S. a 4-1 win and end a three-match skid for American Davis Cup teams in the Swedish city.

Absence of a Davis Cup title, alas, is one of the very few chinks in Roger Federer's armor, although he may fit it into his schedule one day. Nevertheless, frustrated again in the dust and dirt of Paris for a third successive year by his Iberian Inhibitor, Rafa Nadal, the Sweet Swinger of Switzerland had another Alpine season, towering above everybody else like the Matterhorn.

Inhabiting No. 1 for the fourth straight year, he broke Jimmy Connors' Open era record of 160 weeks in the top spot on Feb. 26—and did not surrender it for the rest of the year. He won eight singles titles (increasing his career total to 53) on a 66-9 match mark. And he closed business by winning the Tennis Masters Cup for a fourth time, beating Spaniard David Ferrer, 6-2, 6-3, 6-2, in Shanghai. The doubles went to Bahamian Mark Knowles and Canadian Danny Nestor over Austrian Julian Knowle and Swede Simon Aspelin, 6-2, 6-3.

But more importantly, though Paris denied Roger a Grand Slam, he won three majors in a calendar year for a record third time (2004, 2006-2007), seizing the Australian, Wimbledon and U.S. majors. Of the other nine triplers (Jack Crawford, Fred Perry,

Don Budge, Rod Laver, Tony Trabert, Lew Hoad, Roy Emerson, Jimmy Connors, Mats Wilander), only Laver has done it twice—as Grand Slams.

Extending her stay at No. 1 for a second year, Justine Henin was wisely dropping things and becoming a new, more relaxed person as she doubled, winning the French and U.S. championships.

She dropped the hyphen, and the husband that went with it (Yves Hardenne), and, joyfully, the estrangement from her father and family. Her game became the most varied among the women, thoughtful, featuring more volleying. Like Federer, she concluded a No. 1 year looking the part, beating Maria Sharapova for the WTA Championship, 5-7, 7-5, 6-3, in Madrid.

Of course Nadal, undefeated at Roland Garros, won the French, defeating Federer, 6-3, 4-6, 6-3, 6-4, in three hours, seven minutes, and the Italian, 6-2, 6-2, over Fernando Gonzalez, both titles for the third time. But Federer was heartened at pre-Roland Garros event in Hamburg, beating Nadal, 2-6, 6-2, 6-0, to sever his Open era record clay court streak at 81.

At the Australian Open, Federer pitched a shutout, pocketing his third title Down Under, losing no sets, stretched only in two tie-breakers—6-3, 6-3, 7-6 (7-5) by Youzhny in the third round, 7-6 (7-2), 6-4, 6-4 by Chilean Fernando Gonzalez, the surprise finalist who had out-clevered No. 2 Nadal in the quarterfinals, 6-2, 6-4, 6-3.

Seeded No. 10, Gonzo tamed his typical thunder, used slice and off-speed stuff, too, beating No. 19-seeded ex-No. 1 Lleyton Hewitt, 6-2, 6-2, 5-7, 6-4 in the third round, fifth-seeded Blake 7-5, 6-4, 7-6 (7-4) in the fourth round and No. 12-seeded Tommy Haas, 6-1, 6-3, 6-1 in the semifinals. It worked for a set against Federer, who had wrecked Roddick in the semis, 6-4, 6-0, 6-2.

But the story was in the female precinct belonging to Little Sister Serena. Sure the name was Serena Williams, but in the pecking order of the tennis universe she was an overlooked No. 81, and hadn't done anything for two years.

So she came to Australia to do something—to turn the Down Under championship upside down, and walk away, doing a little soft shoe, after her last blast, to become an improbable wearer of the crown that had been hers in 2003 and 2005.

Shall we call this the Great Masquerade? Impersonating No. 81 for a while, two rounds, Serena began to show her true—almost forgotten—colors in the third round, moving the extra poundage incredibly, astonishingly—insisting that being astonished was for onlookers. Not her.

Melbourne bookies had Sister Serena at the back of the pack of known names, 17-to-1, when the Australian began, and she should have been out of there in the third round when fifth-seed Russian Nadia Petrova served for victory, three points away, but lost 1-6, 7-5, 6-3. Also in the quarterfinals as Israeli Shahar Peer served for it, two points distant but lost 3-6, 6-2, 8-6.

But this was Sister Serena, a big lady with a bigger competitive heart, and she didn't come to Melbourne Park to look like No. 81, even though she'd been evicted in the third round here by Daniela Hantuchova a year ago. It was a year better forgotten, of injuries, indifference and abysmal performances in only four tournaments.

She came to win seven matches, each from women ranked ahead of her, five of them seeded (Also No. 11 Jelena Jankovic, 6-3, 6-2 in the fourth round, and in the semis, No. 10 Nicole Vaidisova, 7-6 (7-5), 6-4)—and to look like No. 1 again.

To do that in the final, with rain on the closed roof, and ice water in her veins, Serena had to defeat No. 1 Maria Sharapova, who had lost one set and chased Kim Clijsters, 6-4, 6-2 in the semis. Defeat? That's too mild a word for what Serena did. The closest Maria came was standing at the net with Serena and the umpire for the pre-match coin toss.

Then Serena embarked on her personal 63-minute demolition derby: 6-1, 6-2, the worst final round thrashing since Steffi Graf over Arantxa Sanchez Vicario in 1994, 6-0, 6-2. It was hot rodding through the park from the moment Serena bopped a backhand winner for the first of her 61 points (Maria had 35) until she duplicated that stroke for match point.

A strange thing happened to Federer on his American winter sojourn: he lost in successive tournaments—and to the same guy, the quick, scrappy Argentine Willie Canas. Reinstated after a drug suspension, Willie suspended belief by beating Roger at Indian Wells, 7-5, 6-2, and Key Biscayne 7-6 (7-2), 2-6, 7-6 (7-5). Nadal won the title in California over the bright Serbian newcomer Novak Djokovic, 6-2, 7-5. But it was turned around in Florida, Djokovic beating Nadal, 6-3, 6-4, on the way to a final round caning of Canas, 6-3, 6-2, 6-4.

On the same route, Daniela Hantuchova beat Svetlana Kuznetsova, 6-3, 6-4, in the desert, and Serena pulled another of her patented escapes beside the Atlantic. Gripped by two championship points with Henin serving (6-0, 5-4, 40-15), Serena, counterpunched to a 0-6, 7-5, 6-3 win in Key Biscayne.

At Roland Garros, one had to ask whether guys not named Federer or Nadal were wasting their time?

Rafa became the champ once again (a third straight title), losing just one set, that in the final against Federer, preventing the Basel Dazzle from completing a career Grand Slam and a run of four majors in a row.

The 2007 French Open was a wasteland for nine American men, none of whom won a match. Tommy Robredo sneaked a set from Federer in the quarterfinals, 7-5, 1-6, 6-1, 6-2, and Nikolay Davydenko made him pay attention in the semis, 7-5, 7-6 (7-5), 7-6 (9-7). Nadal didn't like playing boyhood idol, fellow Mallorcan, Carlos Moya, the 1998 champ, but got it over as quickly as possible, 6-4, 6-3, 6-0 in the quarterfinals. He then beat Djokovic in the semifinals, 6-3, 6-3, 6-3.

Losing no sets and forcing no tie-breakers, Henin was ferocious in scooping up her fourth French title, slapping down Serena, 6-4, 6-3 in the quarterfinals, and the rising Serbian kids, Jelly Jankovic, 6-2, 6-2 in the semifinals, and a terribly jittery 19-year-old Ana Ivanovic, 6-1, 6-2 in the final. (Jankovic had arrived as the Italian victor, 7-5, 6-1, over Svetlana Kuznetsova.) After spilling third-seed Kuznetsova, 6-0, 3-6, 6-1, and second Sharapova, 6-2, 6-1, Ivanovic found her major final debut (and Henin) too much for her. Henin's feat of winning three straight years was last accomplished by Monica Seles, 1990—92. Helen Wills Moody did it, 1928—30, as well as Hilde Sperling, 1935—37.

If Nadal is the Duke of Dirt, he may soon become a Grandee of Grass, judging from the way he came close to beating Federer in their tremendous Wimbledon final, 7-6 (9-7), 4-6, 7-6 (7-3), 2-6, 6-2.

And a day earlier there was Venus, hanging out tough. Serena had her major for the year, Australia, so shouldn't Venus have one, too—her fourth at the Big W?

With one last blast, a 124 mph serve, Venus reclaimed the space that she occupied in 2000-01, and 2005, defeating upstart Marion Bartoli 6-4, 6-1 in the women's final. Little Sister Serena, the occupant in 2002-03, watched approvingly from a courtside box among 13,800 risking sunstroke while Bartoli, a nice French kid, was felled by Venus-stroke, having burned top-seeded Henin in the semis.

Bartoli's remarks after being flattened in 90 minutes told the story; "Venus play some unbelievable tennis. She reached some balls like I never see one person reach, and she would hit it harder back to me. She serve 120 miles on first serve, sometimes hurting my wrist so bad because the ball was coming so fast to me. So I really try the best, but it's not possible to beat her."

With her quirky game of hanging onto the racket with both hands for both forehands and backhands, and hopping about between points, Bartoli, in white cap and overflowing black hair, enjoyed her most serious payday ($700,000, half of Venus's). But she took away more than that. Marion, seeded No. 19, had made some history by beating No. 1 Henin 1-6, 7-5, 6-1 in the semis. It was the most prominent upset here in 13 years, since No. 22 Lori McNeil knocked off the defending champ, No. 1 Steffi Graf. But that was in the first round. No lesser light had ever stopped No. 1 at the gate to the final.

A joint effort, Marion and No. 31 Venus put together the least likely, lowest-ranked championship bout in Wimbledon annals. Sure, that was something of an illusion because Venus has been star quality since she won her first professional match as a 14-year-old in 1994 at Oakland. It was apparent at the U.S. Open of 1997, cruising to the final ranked No. 66 before losing to No. 1 Martina Hingis.

The Williams Era had begun, and the Sisters were to delight in fooling the doubters. Serena, written off, won the Australian Open this year, and said, "Nobody has more doubters than us, but that makes us work harder."

Like a ghost of championships past, the pale visage of Bjorn Borg floated above the tennis pasture that used to be his. Actually he was seated among the swells of Wimbledon's Royal Box, behind a baseline in Centre Court, waiting to be caught.

As tennis royalty goes, Borg stands out as the primo of those who have ruled Wimbledon. Women pursued him, other fans adored him, too, as the goldilocked Swede rang up five consecutive championships between 1976 and 1980, and sparked a tennis epidemic.

But, as sunshine highlighted his silver hair, he was chased again. Not by voluptuaries and well-wishers, but by a guy from Switzerland, the Basel Dazzle, Roger Federer—and Bjorn was overtaken. His streak was matched by Federer, as well as his stash of major titles: 11. Federer could have beaten him in a foot race, too, but of course Borg is 51.

However, Federer very nearly lost out to Borg and another person hounding him: Rafa Nadal. Borg said he showed up to congratulate Federer, and seemed pleased to share his tremendous run of victories.

Federer's shot at Borg almost perished in the frantic fifth set of perhaps the finest final here since Borg edged John McEnroe in 1980.

Fortunately for Federer, the muscular lefty can't produce the extra-high spinning bounce on grass that nullified Roger's backhand on clay. Had the Spaniard grabbed one of four break points—15-40 in both the third and fifth games of the fifth set—he would have been on his way to severing Roger's strings of match wins at Wimbledon (34), and overall on grass (54).

It didn't happen because the greatness genie within Federer asserted itself. Within six minutes, the three and three-quarter hours battle flip-flopped and went to the champion.

He has been No. 1 for four years because he remains cool and thoughtful in the rough, and cranks that deceptively deadly serve. It's no faster than Venus's—in the 120s – but seeks the lines and corners like homing pigeons. It was good for 24 aces and 19 service winners, the backbone of his winning the two crucial tie-breakers.

"Maybe the difference was his serve," conceded Rafa. His own sizzling passing shots, the onerous inside-out forehands and even his improved volleying would have discouraged anyone else—but in the crunch it was the Lone Roger riding to his own rescue.

At 1-1 and 2-2 in the fifth set, Rafa opened up break point holes at 15-40. Federer saved the first with a big serve, and was lucky on the second as Nadal missed a forehand drive along the sideline – a fraction wide. Two games later, same thing, 15-40. Federer says, "I got out of the first…when the second comes around I'm thinking, 'Oh my God!' I don't know if I can do it.'"

Nadal blew a second serve return, then Roger rammed a service winner. Gone were the breakers that could have lifted Nadal to 4-1.

"I served well, played smart," Roger said. "I was so happy when I came out of that because I knew he'd probably missed his chance."

Suddenly, Federer was the monster. Having eluded the spiky break points, he railroaded the remaining three games, scoring the decisive break himself (to 4-2) on a dizziying point in which he hit three lines, closing with a forehand winner.

"At 5-2 I was getting emotional, starting to cry. I had to calm down to get it done."

From beginning to end, they were two men alone on their own green planet, shotmaking geniuses way above the crowd of their colleagues. Tennis can't be performed with more imagination, style, brilliance and maneuvering. Federer's rifling groundies, contrasted with Nadal's mastery of spin. They were thieves in short pants, constantly, amazingly wowing the full-house congregation of 13,800 by stealing points from each other on the run, catching up with balls and belting them for winners.

None of Federer's 10 previous major finals had gone the five-set distance. His last Wimbledonian fifth-set encounter was won,

as a 19–year-old in 2001 over Pete Sampras. That prevented Pete from equaling Borg's five straight titles.

"It was a huge occasion for me," Roger said. "Huge pressure from Bjorn Borg watching. John McEnroe and Jimmy Connors, too, and Boris Becker. Then in the end to lift the trophy." As customary he kissed it. Not very romantic, but a good photo.

On the way to the U.S. Open a couple of towering young Americans made footnotes with their rampaging serves. Sam Querrey, 6-foot-6, banged 10 aces in a row (34 in all) while overturning James Blake at Indianapolis, 7-6 (6-8), 6-7 (4-7), 7-6 (7-4). But Dmitry Tursunov won the title over Canadian Frank Dancevic, 6-4, 7-5. Rookie John Isner, the tallest American pro ever at 6-10, accepted a wild card at Washington, and proceeded to live on the edge in an unprecedented run of five straight third-set tie-breaker wins before a losing final to Roddick, 6-4, 7-6 (7-4). Long John served 144 aces for the week!

Henin began her North American supremacy by taking the Canadian Open in Toronto over Jankovic, 7-6 (7-3), 7-5. In the male version in Montreal, Djokovic sensationally underlined his prospects for Flushing with a Nos. 3-2-1 dash through the elite to the title: Roddick, 7-6 (7-4), 6-4, in the quarters, Nadal, 7-5, 6-3, and Federer, 7-6 (7-2), 2-6, 7-6 (7-2), even though Roger had six set points on serve in the first.

Henin stormed into New York and left the opposition flatter than Belgian waffles, in a tour de force performance that startlingly included both Williams ladies as victims. Nobody had done that before in a U.S. Open. Tight-fisted Justine gave up no sets, but was enmeshed in tie-breakers by the Sisters, beating Serena in the quarters, 7-6 (7-3), 6-1, and Venus in the semis, 7-6 (7-2), 6-4, before roughing up 2004 champ Kuznetsova, 6-1, 6-3 in the final. The most absorbing match was the quarterfinal of the swifties, Venus over Jankovic, 4-6, 6-1, 7-6 (7-4).

Federer, winning major No. 12, wasn't much more charitable than Henin, who won major No. 7. He lost two sets: to serving cyclone, Long John Isner, 6-7 (4-7), 6-2, 6-4, 6-2 in the third round, and deft Spanish lefty Feliciano Lopez, 3-6, 6-3, 7-6 (7-5), 7-5 in the round of 16. But he was ready to give nothing, demolishing a combative Roddick in the quarters, 7-6 (7-5), 7-6 (7-4), 6-2.

Nadal has never sparkled at Flushing, and he was out-ground-stroked this time in the fourth round by No. 15-seeded compatriot David Ferrer, 6-7 (3-7), 6-4, 7-6 (7-4), 6-2. A bigger surprise in the third round was an anonymous 19-year-old lanky Latvian, No. 88 Ernests Gulbis, bumping No. 8 seed Tommy Robredo, 6-1, 6-3, 6-2. Perhaps the match of the tournament was a rip-roaring second rounder, No. 3-seeded Djokovic escaping the clutches of Radek Stepanek, 6-7 (4-7), 7-6 (7-5), 5-7, 7-5, 7-6 (7-2).

Soon enough, Djokovic beat Moya, 6-4, 7-6 (9-7), 6-1, and Ferrer, 6-2, 6-3, 7-5, and was in the final with the man he'd defeated in Toronto.

In the final, Federer, in his all-black Nike outfit, saved seven set points over the course of a 7-6 (7-4), 7-6 (7-2), 6-4 final in two hours and 26 minutes.

But it was suspenseful. And hopeful for a while. They were getting ready to dance in the streets of Belgrade when the carefree Novak came close to winning the unwinnable contest.

Djokovic held five set points on his own serve at 6-5 in the first set: 40-0, then two advantages. On Federer's serve at 5-6 in the second set, he held two more.

Djokovic was the 27th U.S. Open victim in a row that Federer interred in the Meadow's asphalt – the last to foil him at his devilish game and get away alive was an Argentine named David Nalbandian in 2003. Federer was the first man to win four straight U.S. titles since Bill Tilden in 1923.

For the year, Federer was the $10 million man—earning a record $10,130,620 in prize money.

2007 CHAMPIONS AND LEADERS

Australian Open

Men's Singles Final: Roger Federer (SUI) def. Fernando Gonzalez (CHI), 7-6 (7-2), 6-4, 6-4

Women's Singles Final: Serena Williams (USA) def. Maria Sharapova (RUS), 6-1, 6-2

Men's Doubles Final: Bob Bryan and Mike Bryan (USA) def. Jonas Bjorkman (SWE) and Max Mirnyi (BLR), 7-5, 7-5

Women's Doubles Final: Cara Black (ZIM) and Liezel Huber (RSA) def. ChanYung-Jan and Chuang Chia-Jung (TPE) 6-4, 6-7 (7-4), 6-1

Mixed Doubles Final: Daniel Nestor (CAN) and Elena Likhovtseva (RUS) def. Max Mirnyi and Victoria Azarenka (BLR), 6-4, 6-4

French Open

Men's Singles Final: Rafael Nadal (ESP) def. Roger Federer (SUI), 6-3, 4-6, 6-3, 6-4

Women's Singles Final: Justine Henin (BEL) def. Ana Ivanovic (SRB), 6-1, 6-2

Men's Doubles Final: Mark Knowles (BAH) and Daniel Nestor (CAN) def. Lukas Dlouhy and Pavel Vizner (CZE), 2-6, 6-3, 6-4

Women's Doubles Final: Alicia Molik (AUS) and Mara Santangelo (ITA) def. Katarina Srebotnik (SLO) and Ai Sugiyama (JPN), 7-6 (7-5), 6-4

Mixed Doubles Final: Nathalie Dechy (FRA) and Andy Ram (ISR) def. Nenad Zimonjic (SRB) and Katarina Srebotnik (SLO), 7-5, 6-3

Wimbledon

Men's Singles Final: Roger Federer (SUI) def. Rafael Nadal (ESP), 7-6 (9-7), 4-6, 7-6 (7-3), 2-6, 6-2.

Women's Singles Final: Venus Williams (USA) def. Marion Bartoli (FRA), 6-4, 6-1

Men's Doubles Final: Arnaud Clement and Michael Llodra (FRA) def. Bob Bryan and Mike Bryan (USA), 6-7 (7-5), 6-3, 6-4, 6-4

Women's Doubles Final: Cara Black (ZIM) and Liezel Huber (RSA) def. Katarina Srebotnik (SLO) and Ai Sugiyama (JPN), 3-6, 6-3, 6-2

Mixed Doubles Final: Jaime Murray (GBR) and Jelena Jankovic (SRB) def. Jonas Bjorkman (SWE) and Alicia Molik (AUS), 6-4, 3-6, 6-1

U.S. Open

Men's Singles Final: Roger Federer (SUI) def. Novak Djokovic (SRB), 7-6 (7-4), 7-6 (7-2), 6-4

Women's Singles Final: Justine Henin (BEL) def. Svetlana Kuznetsova (RUS), 6-1, 6-3

Men's Doubles Final: Simon Aspelin (SWE) and Julian Knowle (AUT) def. Lukas Dlouhy and Paul Vizner (CZE), 7-5, 6-4

Women's Doubles Final: Nathalie Dechy (FRA) and Dinara Safina (RUS) def. ChanYung-Jan and Chuang Chia-Jung (TPE), 6-4, 6-2

Mixed Doubles Final: Victoria Azarenka and Max Mirnyi (BLR) def. Meghann Shaughnessy (USA) and Leander Paes (IND), 6-4, 7-6 (10-8)

Year-End No. 1

Men: Roger Federer
Women: Justine Henin

Top Player Earnings

Men: Roger Federer: $10,130,620
Women: Justine Henin $5,367,086

Davis Cup: United States

Fed Cup: Russia

Tennis Masters Cup, Shanghai—Roger Federer
Sony Ericsson WTA Championships, Madrid—Justine Henin

The Major Championships

SECTION II

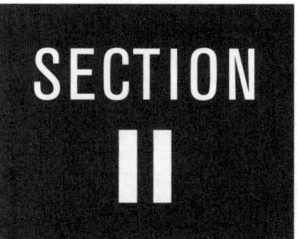

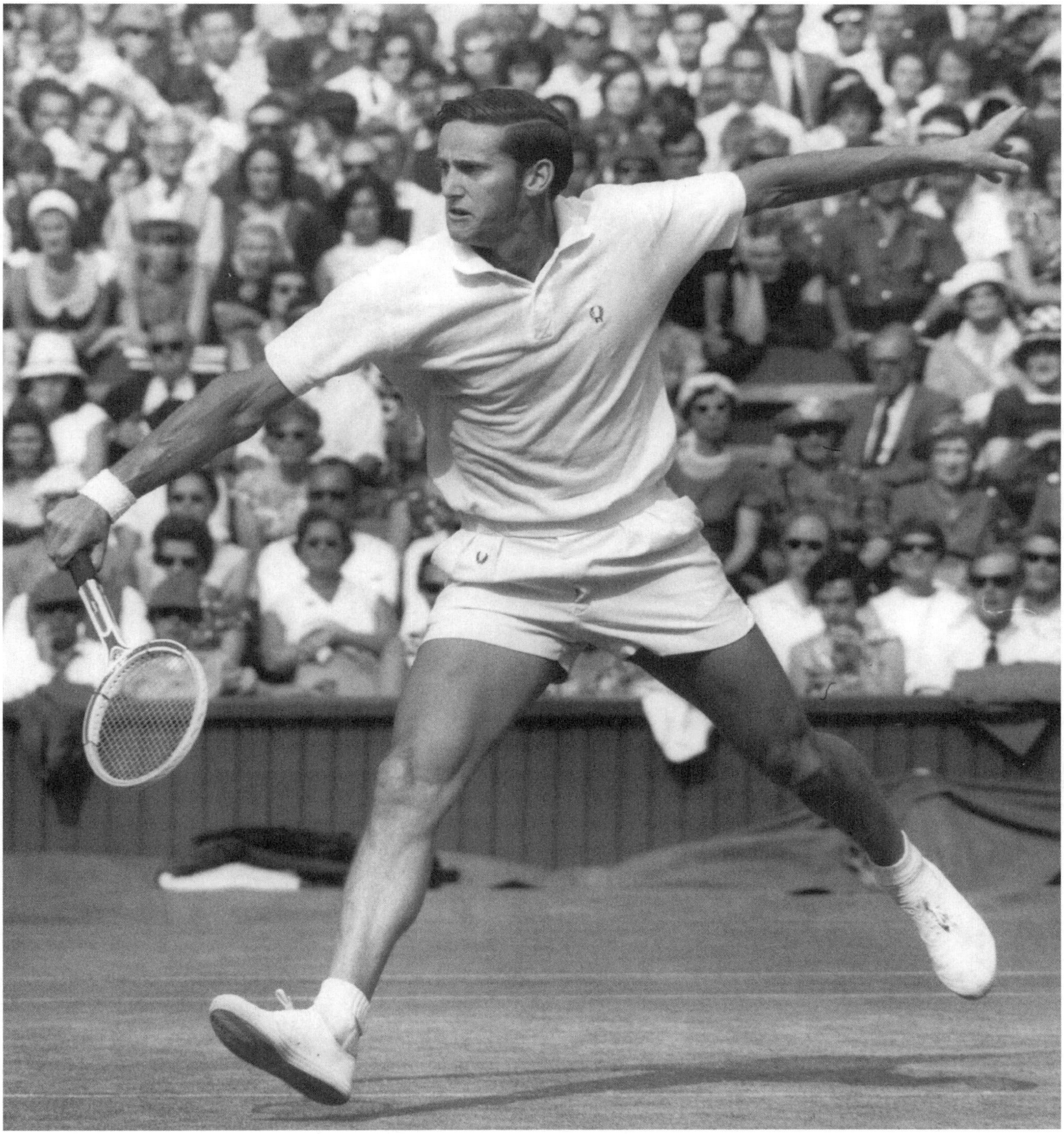

No man won more major championships than **Roy Emerson**, who collected 28 during his career, including 12 major singles titles.

The Majors and The Grand Slam

Rod Laver (left) beat **Ken Rosewall** in the final of the French Championships in 1969— the second leg of his second Grand Slam. Laver won 11 major singles titles during his career, while Rosewall won eight major singles titles.

Jack Crawford, the stylish Australian of the 1930s, had no idea when he departed his homeland by steamship in the spring of 1933 that he would, unknowingly, be the instigator of a concept eventually known as the Grand Slam. He had won the Australian title for the third successive year, defeating Californian Keith Gledhill, 2-6, 7-5, 6-3, 6-2, and was headed for Europe.

In Paris, Jack became the first non-Frenchman to seize the championship of France, dethroning Henri Cochet of France, 8-6, 6-1, 6-3. Then, crossing the Channel to London, he lifted the Wimbledon title from another Californian, Ellsworth Vines, in a splendid final, 4-6, 11-9, 6-2, 2-6, 6-4.

Nobody had won those three majors in a row, but Jack had enough. He'd been through a grueling campaign, was bothered by asthma and insomnia, and wanted to go home. However, as an amateur he was controlled by his country's tennis administration, the LTAA (Lawn Tennis Association of Australia), insisting that he play the U.S. Champi-

onships at Forest Hills because a fee due the Association for his appearance was involved.

The prospect of his winning that one, too, intrigued a *New York Times* columnist, John Kieran. If he did, wrote Kieran, it would be something like a "grand slam" in bridge. But Crawford didn't, although he battled gamely to the final. Drained physically and emotionally, he led Brit Fred Perry two-sets-to-one but could win only one more game, falling, 6-3, 11-13, 4-6, 6-0, 6-1.

No Grand Slam, which Jack hadn't set out to accomplish, anyway. But the idea had sprouted, and it made an impression on a kid in California, 18-year-old Don Budge. Having become No. 1 and retrieved the Davis Cup for the U.S. in 1937, Budge determined that 1938 would be his last as an amateur. He wanted a goal, something extra, and quietly set out (telling no one but his buddy, doubles partner Gene Mako) to conquer the Big Four, as they were known—the only countries to win the Davis Cup.

With little difficulty, losing three sets in 24 matches (one to Mako in the U.S. final), Budge posted the initial Grand Slam. It was duly noted by Allison Danzig, tennis correspondent for the *New York Times*. But it took a long time catching on. However, nurtured as a pro by Mr. Grand Slam, Budge, who dined out on it, the Slam became a popular term in tennis. Also a misused one, as proprietors of the four majors carelessly called their events Grand Slams, confusing the public. Although there is no written rule, a Grand Slam has come to be accepted as winning all four within a calendar year. Each tournament is a major, not a Slam.

Budge had the territory all to himself for 15 years until American teenager Maureen Connolly performed the first female Grand Slam in 1953, concluding over countrywoman Doris Hart, 6-2, 6-4 in the U.S. final.

Then came the double Slammer, Aussie Rod Laver, in 1962. Sweeping the four in his final amateur year, 1962, winding up with Roy Emerson 6-2, 6-4, 5-7, 6-4, Laver understood that several of the best players—Pancho Gonzalez, Ken Rosewall, Lew Hoad to name three—were barred from the quest as pros. But when "Open" tennis arrived in 1968, and Australia accepted the concept in 1969, for the first time a Grand Slam was available to all players, and Laver made it plain that he was going after it. He welcomed the opportunity denied him for six years, and set out to be the true king of the hill.

On a rainy afternoon at Forest Hills, shortly after his 31st birthday, Rod beat another Aussie country boy, Tony Roche, 7-9, 6-1, 6-2, 6-2, to take the last leg, the U.S., on the Quintessential Quadrangle.

Aussie Margaret Court, 27, got her Grand Slam the following year, finishing it off over Rosie Casals, 6-2, 2-6, 6-1 at Forest Hills.

Eighteen years passed before the next Slammer—so far the most recent—appeared in the person of 19-year-old German Steffi Graf. It was a different Slam. Previously it had been three-quarters grass plus clay at the French, and in familiar places. Steffi started hers at a brand new Australian complex in Melbourne (Flinders Park, later re-named Melbourne Park) on a hard court, defeating Chris Evert, 6-1, 7-6 (7-3). She wrapped it up at Flushing Meadow in New York, 6-3, 3-6, 6-1, over Gabriela Sabatini, also on a hard court. Grass remained only at Wimbledon; the Slam was half pavement.

As you can see, the Grand Slam is a very exclusive club. But there are a few other Slammers who navigated the treacherous route in doubles. Three teams made it: Aussies Frank Sedgman and Ken McGregor in men's doubles in 1951; Margaret Court and Ken Fletcher of Australia in mixed in 1963; Americans Martina Navratilova and Pam Shriver in 1984 in women's doubles.

Maria Bueno of Brazil made it in women's doubles with two partners in 1960 as did Owen Davidson of Australia in mixed, 1967, and Switzerland's Martina Hingis in women's doubles in 1998. Unique was Americans Venus and Serena Williams' so-called "Family Slam" in mixed in 1998. Winning all four finals, they split the titles, two for Venus and fellow American Justin Gimelstob, the Australian and French; two for Serena and Max Mirnyi of Belarus, Wimbledon and the U.S.

The Grand Slams

The complete record of all Grand Slams follows:

Singles

DON BUDGE, 1938

Australian Championships at Memorial Drive, Adelaide

First Round – def. Les Hancock (AUS), 6-2, 6-3, 6-4

Second Round – def. Harold Whillans (AUS), 6-1, 6-0, 6-1

Quarterfinals – def. Len Schwartz (AUS), 6-4, 6-3, 10-8

Semifinals – def. Adrian Quist (AUS), 5-7, 6-4, 6-1, 6-2

Final – def. John Bromwich (AUS), 6-4, 6-2, 6-1

French Championships at Roland Garros, Paris

First Round – def. Antoine Gentien (FRA), 6-1, 6-2, 6-4

Second Round – def. Ghaus Mohammed (IND/GBR), 6-1, 6-1, 5-7, 6-0

Third Round – def. Franjo Kukuljevic (YUG), 6-2, 8-6, 2-6, 1-6, 6-1

Quarterfinals – def. Bernard Destremau (FRA), 6-4, 6-3, 6-4

Semifinals – def. Josip Pallada (YUG), 6-2, 6-3, 6-3

Final – def. Roderich Menzel (CZE), 6-3, 6-2, 6-4

The Championships at Wimbledon

First Round – def. Kenneth Gandar Dower (GBR), 6-2, 6-3, 6-3

Second Round – def. Henry Billington (GBR), 7-5, 6-1, 6-1

Third Round – def. George Lyttleton Rogers (IRL), 6-0, 7-5, 6-1

Fourth Round – def. Ronald Shayes (GBR), 6-3, 6-4, 6-1

Quarterfinals – def. Franz Cejnar (CZE), 6-3, 6-0, 7-5

Semifinals – def. Ferenc Puncec (YUG), 6-2, 6-4, 6-0

Final – def. Henry "Bunny" Austin (GBR), 6-1, 6-0, 6-3

U.S. Championships at Forest Hills, New York

First Round – def. Welby Van Horn (USA), 6-0, 6-0, 6-1

Second Round – def. Bob Kamrath (USA), 6-3, 7-5, 9-7

Third Round – def. Charles Hare (GBR), 6-3, 6-4, 6-0

Quarterfinals – def. Harry Hopman (AUS), 6-3, 6-1, 6-3

Semifinals – def. Sidney Wood (USA), 6-3, 6-3, 6-3

Final – def. Gene Mako (USA), 6-3, 6-8, 6-2, 6-1

MAUREEN CONNOLLY, 1953

Australian Championships at Kooyong, Melbourne

First Round – def. Carmen Borelli (AUS), 6-0, 6-1

Second Round – def. Alison Burton Baker (AUS), 6-1, 6-0

Quarterfinals – def. Pam Southcombe (AUS), 6-0, 6-1

Semifinals – def. Mary Bevis Hawton (AUS), 6-2, 6-1

Final – def. Julie Sampson (USA), 6-3, 6-2

French Championships at Roland Garros, Paris

First Round – def. Christiane Mercelis (BEL), 6-1, 6-3

Second Round – def. Raymonde Verber Jones (FRA), 6-3, 6-1

Quarterfinals – def. Susan Partridge Chatrier (FRA), 3-6, 6-2, 6-2

Semifinals – def. Dorothy Head Knode (USA), 6-3, 6-3

Final – def. Doris Hart (USA), 6-2, 6-4

The Championships at Wimbledon

First Round – def. Dora Killian (RSA), 6-0, 6-0

Second Round – def Jean Petchell (GBR), 6-1, 6-1

Third Round – def. Anne Shilcock (GBR), 6-0, 6-1

Quarterfinals – def. Erika Vollmer (GER), 6-3, 6-0

Semifinals – def. Shirley Fry (USA), 6-1, 6-1

Final – def. Doris Hart (USA), 8-6, 7-5

U.S. Championships at Forest Hills, New York

First Round – def. Jean Fallot (FRA), 6-1, 6-0

Second Round – def. Pat Stewart (USA), 6-3, 6-1

Third Round – def. Jeanne Arth (USA), 6-1, 6-3

Quarterfinals – def. Althea Gibson (USA), 6-2, 6-3

Semifinals – def. Shirley Fry (USA), 6-1, 6-1

Final – def. Doris Hart (USA), 6-2, 6-4

ROD LAVER, 1962

Australian Championships at White City, Sydney

First Round – def. Fred Sherriff (AUS), 8-6, 6-2, 6-4

Second Round – def. Geoff Pares (AUS), 10-8, 18-16, 7-9, 7-5

Quarterfinals – def. Owen Davidson (AUS), 6-4, 9-7, 6-4

Semifinals – def. Bob Hewitt (AUS), 6-1, 4-6, 6-4, 7-5

Final – def. Roy Emerson (AUS), 8-6, 0-6, 6-4, 6-4

French Champions at Roland Garros, Paris

First Round – def. Michele Pirro (ITA), 6-4, 6-0, 6-2

Second Round – def. Tony Pickard (GBR), 6-2, 9-7, 4-6, 6-1

Third Round – def. Sergio Jacobini (ITA), 4-6, 6-3, 7-5, 6-1

Quarterfinals – def. Marty Mulligan (AUS), 6-4, 3-6, 2-6, 10-8, 6-2

Semifinals – def. Neale Fraser (AUS), 3-6, 6-3, 6-2, 7-5

Final – def. Roy Emerson (AUS), 3-6, 2-6, 6-3, 9-7, 6-2

The Championships at Wimbledon

First Round – def. Naresh Kumar (IND), 7-5, 6-1, 6-2

Second Round – def. Tony Pickard (GBR), 6-1, 6-2, 6-2

Third Round – def. Whitney Reed (USA), 6-4, 6-1, 6-4

Fourth Round – def. Pierre Darmon (FRA), 6-3, 6-2, 13-11

Quarterfinals – def. Manolo Santana (ESP), 14-16, 9-7, 6-2, 6-2

Semifinals – def. Neale Fraser (AUS), 10-8, 6-1, 7-5

Final – def. Marty Mulligan (AUS), 6-2, 6-2, 6-1

U.S. Championships at Forest Hills, New York

First Round – def. Eleazar Davidman (ISR), 6-3, 6-2, 6-3

Second Round – def. Eduardo Zuleta (ECU), 6-3, 6-3, 6-1

Third Round – def. Bodo Nitsche (GER), 9-7, 6-1, 6-1

Fourth Round – def. Antonio Palafox (MEX), 6-1, 6-2, 6-2

Quarterfinals – def. Frank Froehling (USA), 6-3, 13-11, 4-6, 6-3

Semifinals – def. Rafael Osuna (MEX), 6-1, 6-3, 6-4

Final – def. Roy Emerson (AUS), 6-2, 6-4, 5-7, 6-4

ROD LAVER, 1969

Australian Open at Milton Courts, Brisbane
First Round – def. Massimo di Domenico (ITA), 6-2, 6-2, 6-3
Second Round – def. Roy Emerson (AUS), 6-2, 6-3, 3-6, 9-7
Quarterfinals – def. Fred Stolle (AUS), 6-4, 18-16, 6-2
Semifinals – def. Tony Roche (AUS), 7-5, 22-20, 9-11, 1-6, 6-3
Final – def. Andres Gimeno (ESP), 6-3, 6-4, 7-5

French Open at Roland Garros, Paris
First Round – def. Koji Watanabe (JPN), 6-1, 6-1, 6-1
Second Round – def. Dick Crealy (AUS), 3-6, 7-9, 6-2, 6-2, 6-4
Third Round – def. Pietro Marzano (ITA), 6-1, 6-0, 8-6
Fourth Round – def. Stan Smith (USA), 6-4, 6-2, 6-4
Quarterfinals – def. Andres Gimeno (ESP), 3-6, 6-3, 6-4, 6-3
Semifinals – def. Tom Okker (NED), 4-6, 6-0, 6-2, 6-4
Final – def. Ken Rosewall (USA), 6-4, 6-3, 6-4

The Championships at Wimbledon
First Round – def. Nicola Pietrangeli (ITA), 6-1, 6-2, 6-2
Second Round – def. Premjit Lall (IND), 3-6, 4-6, 6-3, 6-0, 6-0
Third Round – def. Jan Leschly (DEN), 6-3, 6-3, 6-3
Fourth Round – def. Stan Smith (USA), 6-4, 6-2, 7-9, 3-6, 6-3
Quarterfinals – def. Cliff Drysdale (RSA), 6-4, 6-2, 6-3
Semifinals – def. Arthur Ashe (USA), 2-6, 6-2, 9-7, 6-0
Final – def. John Newcombe (AUS), 6-4, 5-7, 6-4, 6-4

U.S. Open at Forest Hills, New York
First Round – def. Luis Garcia (MEX), 6-2, 6-4, 6-2
Second Round – def. Jaime Pinto-Bravo (CHI), 6-4, 7-5, 6-2
Third Round – def. Jaime Fillol (CHI), 8-6, 6-1, 6-2
Fourth Round – def. Dennis Ralston (USA), 6-4, 4-6, 4-6, 6-2, 6-3
Quarterfinals – def. Roy Emerson (AUS), 4-6, 8-6, 13-11, 6-4
Semifinals – def. Arthur Ashe (USA), 8-6, 6-3, 14-12
Final – def. Tony Roche (AUS), 7-9, 6-1, 6-2, 6-2

MARGARET SMITH COURT, 1970

Australian Open at White City, Sydney
First Round – def. Robyn Ebbern Langsford (AUS), 6-0, 6-0
Second Round – def. Kerry Wilkinson (AUS), 6-0, 6-1
Quarterfinals – def. Evonne Goolagong (AUS), 6-3, 6-1
Semifinals – def. Karen Krantzke (AUS), 6-1, 6-3
Final – def. Kerry Melville (AUS), 6-3, 6-1

French Open at Roland Garros, Paris
First Round – def. Marijke Jansen Schaar (NED), 6-1, 6-1
Second Round – def. Olga Morozova (USSR), 3-6, 8-6, 6-1
Third Round – def. Lesley Hunt (AUS), 6-2, 6-1
Quarterfinals – def. Rosie Casals (USA), 7-5, 6-2
Semifinals – def. Julie Heldman (USA), 6-0, 6-2
Final – def. Helga Masthof Niessen (GER), 6-2, 6-4

The Championships at Wimbledon
First Round – def. Sue Alexander (AUS), 6-0, 6-1
Second Round – def. Maria Guzman (ECU), 6-0, 6-1
Third Round – def. Vlasta Vopickova (CZE), 6-3, 6-3
Quarterfinals – def. Helga Masthof Niessen (GER), 6-8, 6-0, 6-0
Semifinals – def. Rosie Casals (USA), 6-4, 6-1
Final – def. Billie Jean King (USA), 14-12, 11-9

U.S. Open at Forest Hills, New York
First Round – def. Pam Austin (USA), 6-1, 6-0
Second Round – def. Patti Hogan (USA), 6-1, 6-1
Third Round – def. Pat Faulkner (AUS), 6-0, 6-2
Quarterfinals – def. Helen Gourlay (AUS), 6-2, 6-2
Semifinals – def. Nancy Richey (USA), 6-1, 6-3
Final – def. Rosie Casals (USA), 6-2, 2-6, 6-1

STEFFI GRAF, 1988

Australian Open at Flinders Park, Melbourne
First Round – def. Amy Jonsson (NOR), 6-3, 6-1
Second Round – def. Janine Thompson (AUS), 6-0, 6-1
Third Round – def. Cammy MacGregor (USA), 6-1, 6-2
Fourth Round – def. Catarina Lindqvist (SWE), 6-0, 7-5
Quarterfinals – def. Hana Mandlikova (CZE), 6-2, 6-2
Semifinals – def. Claudia Kohde Kilsch (GER), 6-2, 6-3
Final – def. Chris Evert (USA), 6-1, 7-6 (7-3)

French Open at Roland Garros, Paris
First Round – def. Natalie Guerree (FRA), 6-0, 6-4
Second Round – def. Ronni Reis (USA), 6-1, 6-0
Third Round – def. Susan Sloane (USA), 6-0, 6-1
Fourth Round – def. Nathalie Tauziat (FRA), 6-1, 6-3
Quarterfinals – def. Bettina Fulco (ARG), 6-0, 6-1
Semifinals – def. Gabriela Sabatini (ARG), 6-3, 7-6 (7-3)
Final – def. Natalia Zvereva (USSR), 6-0, 6-0

The Championships at Wimbledon
First Round – def. Hu Na (USA), 6-0, 6-0
Second Round – def. Katrine Quentrec (FRA), 6-2, 6-0
Third Round – def. Terry Phelps (USA), 6-3, 6-1
Fourth Round – def. Mary Joe Fernandez (USA), 6-2, 6-2
Quarterfinals – def. Pascale Paradis (FRA), 6-3, 6-1
Semifinals – def. Pam Shriver (USA), 6-1, 6-2
Final – def. Martina Navratilova (USA), 5-7, 6-2, 6-1

U.S Open at Flushing Meadow, New York
First Round – def. Elizabeth Minter (AUS), 6-1, 6-1
Second Round – def. Manon Bollegraf (NED), 6-1, 6-0
Third Round – def. Nathalie Herreman (FRA), 6-0, 6-1
Fourth Round – def. Patty Fendick (USA), 6-4, 6-2
Quarterfinals – def. Katerina Maleeva (BUL), 6-3, 6-0
Semifinals – def. Chris Evert (USA), default (illness)
Final – def. Gabriela Sabatini (ARG), 6-3, 3-6, 6-1

Doubles

FRANK SEDGMAN-KEN MCGREGOR, 1951

Australian at White City, Sydney d. Don Rocavert-Jim Gilchrist, 6-1, 6-3, 13-11; John Mehaffey-Clive Wilderspin, 6-4, 6-4, 6-3; Merv Rose-Don Candy, 8-6, 6-4, 6-3; Adrian Quist-John Bromwich, 11-9, 2-6, 6-3, 4-6, 6-3

French at Roland Garros, Paris d. Antoine Gentien-Pierre Grandquillot, 6-0, 6-0, 6-0; Umberto "Biddy" Bergamo-Beppe Merlo, 6-2, 7-5, 6-1; Robert Abdesselam-Paul Remy, 6-2, 6-2, 4-6, 6-3; Merv Rose-Ham Richardson, 6-3, 7-5, 6-2; Gardnar Mulloy-Dick Savitt, 6-2, 2-6, 9-7, 7-5

The Championships at Wimbledon d. Vladimir Petrovic-Petko Milojkovic, 6-1, 6-1, 6-3; Raymundo Deyro-Gene Garrett, 6-4, 6-4, 6-3; Bernard Destremau-Torsten Johansson, 3-6, 6-3, 6-2, 9-7; Gianni Cucelli-Marcello del Bello, 6-4, 7-5, 16-14; Budge Patty-Ham Richardson, 6-4, 6-2, 6-3; Eric Sturgess-Jaroslav Drobny, 3-6, 6-2, 6-3, 3-6, 6-3

United States at Longwood Cricket Club, Boston d. Harrison Rowbotham-Sumner Rodman, 6-2, 6-3, 6-3; Dave Mesker-Ed Wesely, 6-1, 6-1, 6-1; Earl Cochell-Ham Richardson, default; Budge Patty-Tony Trabert, 6-3, 6-1, 6-4; Don Candy-Merv Rose, 10-8, 4-6, 6-4, 7-5 (final-round match played at Forest Hills, moved from Boston due to heavy rains)

MARTINA NAVRATILOVA-PAM SHRIVER, 1984

French at Roland Garros, Paris d. Heather Crowe-Kim Steinmetz, 6-2, 6-1; Carling Bassett-Andrea Temesvari, 6-4, 6-2; Sandy Collins-Alycia Moulton, 6-2, 6-4; Brenda Remilton-Naoko Sato, 6-2, 6-2; Kathleen Horvath-Virginia Ruzici, 6-0, 7-6; Claudia Kohde Kilsch-Hana Mandlikova, 5-7, 6-3, 6-2

The Championships at Wimbledon d. Pam Casale-Lucia Romanov, 6-1, 6-1; Peanut Louie-Heather Ludloff, 6-4, 6-1; Lisa Bonder-Susan Mascarin, 6-0, 6-0; Claudia Kohde Kilsch-Hana Mandlikova, 6-7 (1-7), 6-4, 6-2; Jo Durie-Ann Kiyomura Hayashi, 6-3, 6-3; Kathy Jordan-Anne Smith, 6-3, 6-4

United States at Flushing Meadow, New York d. Jennifer Mundel-Felicia Raschiatore, 6-2, 6-1; Leslie Allen-Kim Shaefer, 6-1, 7-6 (7-4); Catherine Tanvier-Tina Scheuer-Larsen, 6-3, 6-3; Rosalyn Fairbank-Candy Reynolds, 6-3, 6-4; Betsy Nagelsen-Anne White, 6-4, 7-5; Anne Hobbs-Wendy Turnbull, 6-2, 6-4

Australian at Kooyong Stadium, Melbourne d. Rosalyn Fairbank-Candy Reynolds, 7-6, 6-4; Jennifer Mundel-Yvonne Vermaak, 6-2, 6-1; Carling Bassett-Zina Garrison, 6-2, 6-0; Chris Evert Lloyd-Wendy Turnbull, 6-4, 6-3; Claudia Kohde Kilsch-Helena Sukova, 6-3, 6-4

MARIA BUENO (WITH TWO PARTNERS), 1960

Australian at Milton Courts, Brisbane: with Christine Truman d. Val Craig-Hortense Saywell, 6-2, 6-1; Betty Holstein-Sandra Shipton, 6-3, 6-4; Fay Muller-Mary Bevis Hawton, 6-4, 11-9; Margaret Smith-Lorraine Coghlan Robinson, 6-3, 5-7, 6-2

French at Roland Garros, Paris with Darlene Hard d. Jacqueline Kermina-Pierette Seghers, 6-2, 6-2; Jacqueline Rees Lewis-Jacqueline Morales, 6-2, 6-0; Josette Billaz-Suzanne Le Besnerais, 6-4, 6-4; Mary Bevis Hawton-Jan Lehane, 6-3, 7-5; Pat Ward Hales-Ann Haydon, 6-2, 7-5

The Championships at Wimbledon with Darlene Hard d. Myrtle Cheadle-Gem Hoahing, 6-1, 6-2; Pat Hird-Caroline Yates Bell, 6-2, 7-5; Edda Buding-Vera Puzejova, 6-2, 6-3; Karen Hantze-Janet Hopps, 3-6, 6-1, 6-4; Renee Schuurman-Sandra Reynolds, 6-4, 6-0

United States at Longwood Cricket Club, Boston with Darlene Hard d. Lorraine Carder-Polly Knowlton, 6-0, 6-2; Linda Vail-Marilyn Montgomery, 6-1, 7-5; Carol Loop-Carole Wright, 6-2, 6-4; Mary Bevis Hawton-Jan Lehane, 8-6, 6-4; Ann Haydon-Deidre Catt, 6-1, 6-1

MARTINA HINGIS (WITH TWO PARTNERS), 1998

Australian at Melbourne Park, Melbourne with Mirjana Lucic d. Saeki Miho-Yoshida Yuka, 6-2, 6-3; Larisa Savchenko Neiland-Anna Kournikova, 7-5, 6-2; Svetlana Krivencheva-Elena Tatarkova, 6-1, 6-3; Manon Bollegraf-Arantxa Sanchez Vicario, 6-1, 6-1; Lisa Raymond-Rennae Stubbs, 4-6, 6-4, 6-1; Lindsay Davenport-Natalia Zvereva, 6-4, 2-6, 6-3

French at Roland Garros, Paris, with Jana Novotna d. Ann Wunderlich-Rika Hiraki, 6-1, 6-0; Shi-Ting Wang-Janet Lee, 6-0, 6-2; Kristine Kunce-Corina Morariu, 6-0, 6-1; Conchita Martinez-Patricia Tarabini, 6-3, 6-2; Arantxa Sanchez Vicario-Helena Sukova, 7-5, 7-6 (7-2); Lindsay Davenport-Natalia Zvereva, 6-1, 7-6 (7-4)

The Championships at Wimbledon, with Jana Novotna d. Surina de Beer-Lindsay Lee-Waters, 6-1, 6-1; Tina Krizan-Katarina Srebotnik, 4-6, 6-1, 6-2; Naoko Kijimuta-Nana Miyagi, 6-3, 6-4; Julie Halard-Decugis-Els Callens, 6-1, 6-4; Lisa Raymond-Rennae Stubbs, 6-3, 6-2; Lindsay Davenport-Natalia Zvereva, 6-3, 3-6, 8-6

United States at Flushing Meadow, with Jana Novotna d. Elena Wagner-Pavlina Nola, 6-4, 6-2; Karina Habsudova-Tamarine Tanasugarn, 7-6 (7-0), 6-0; Rachel McQuillan-Julie Halard-Decugis, 6-1, 6-0; Barbara Schett-Patty Schnyder, 6-3, 6-4; Lisa Raymond-Rennae Stubbs, 6-2, 6-2; Lindsay Davenport-Natalia Zvereva, 6-3, 6-3

Mixed Doubles

MARGARET SMITH COURT-KEN FLETCHER, 1963

Australian at Memorial Drive, Adelaide d. Faye Toyne-Bill Bowrey, 6-2, 6-2; Jill Blackman-Roger Taylor, 6-3, 6-3; Liz Starkie-Mark Cox, 7-5, 6-4; Lesley Turner-Fred Stolle, 7-5, 5-7, 6-4

French at Roland Garros, Paris d. Claudine Rouire-Michel Lagard, 6-2, 6-1; Marie Dusapt-Ion Tiriac, 6-0, 6-2; Mary Habicht-Peter Strobl, 6-3, 6-0; Margaret Hunt-Cliff Drysdale, 7-5, 4-6, 6-1; Judy Tegart-Ed Rubinoff, 6-3, 6-1; Lesley Turner-Fred Stolle, 6-1, 6-2

The Championships at Wimbledon d. Judy Tegart-Ed Rubinoff, 6-2, 6-2; Judy Alvarez-John Fraser, 6-2, 9-7; Yola Ramirez Ochoa-Alfonso Ochoa, 6-4, 6-4; Renee Schuurman-Wilhelm Bungert, 6-2, 6-1; Ann Jones-Dennis Ralston, 6-1, 7-5; Darlene Hard-Bob Hewitt, 11-9, 6-4

United States at Forest Hills, New York d. Heidi Schildnecht-Peter Scholl, 6-2, 6-3; Jill Rook Mills-Alan Mills, 6-4, 3-6, 6-1; Robyn Ebbern-Owen Davidson, 6-2, 6-2; Billie Jean Moffitt-Donald Dell, 5-7, 8-6, 6-4; Judy Tegart-Ed Rubinoff, 3-6, 8-6, 6-2

OWEN DAVIDSON (WITH TWO PARTNERS), 1967

Australian at Memorial Drive, Adelaide with Lesley Turner d. Margaret Foster-Brenton Higgins, 6-1, 7-5; Margaret Starr-Paul McPherson, 6-2, 6-4; Jan Lehane O'Neill-Ray Ruffels, 7-5, 6-4; Judy Tegart-Tony Roche, 9-7, 6-4

French at Roland Garros, Paris with Billie Jean King d. Maria Zuleta-Eduardo Zuleta, 6-2, 6-4; Pat Walkden-Colin Stubs, 6-2, 2-6, 6-3; Trudy Groenman-Tom Okker, 6-1, 6-2; Christine Truman-Bob Howe, 6-2, 6-4; Ann Haydon Jones-Ion Tiriac, 6-3, 6-1

The Championships at Wimbledon with Billie Jean King d. Betty Stove-Bob Howe, 6-1, 6-1; Ingrid Lofdahl-Patricio Cornejo, 6-4, 6-1; Mr. and Mrs. John Cottrill, 6-4, 6-1; Annette van Zyl-Frew McMillan, 6-3, 3-6, 6-1; Maria Bueno-Ken Fletcher, 7-5, 6-2

United States at Longwood Cricket Club, Boston, with Billie Jean King d. Joyce Barclay Williams-George Seewagen, Jr., 6-4, 6-4; Donna Floyd Fales-Paul Sullivan, 6-2, 6-2; Mary Ann Eisel-Peter Curtis, 6-4, 6-3; Kristy Pigeon-Terry Addison, 6-4, 6-4; Rosie Casals-Stan Smith, 6-3, 6-2

Triplers

Since the French Championships became open to non-French players in 1925, 116 individuals and teams have won three of the four major titles in the same calendar year. Here is a complete list of those to complete a Three-Quarter Slam.

MEN'S SINGLES

Jack Crawford	1933	(Australian, French, Wimbledon)
Fred Perry	1934	(Australian, Wimbledon, U.S.)
TonyTrabert	1955	(French, Wimbledon, U.S.)
Lew Hoad	1956	(Australian, French, Wimbledon)
Ashley Cooper	1958	(Australian, Wimbledon, U.S.)
Roy Emerson	1964	(Australian, Wimbledon, U.S.)
Jimmy Connors	1974	(Australian, Wimbledon, U.S.)
Mats Wilander	1988	(Australian, French, U.S.)
Roger Federer	2004	(Australian, Wimbledon, U.S.)
Roger Federer	2006	(Australian, Wimbledon, U.S.)
Roger Federer	2007	(Australian, Wimbledon, U.S)

WOMEN'S SINGLES

Helen Wills Moody	1928	(French, Wimbledon, U.S.)
Helen Wills Moody	1929	(French, Wimbledon, U.S.)
Margaret Smith	1962	(Australian, French, U.S.)
Margaret Smith	1965	(Australian, Wimbledon, U.S.)
Margaret Smith Court	1969	(Australian, French, U.S.)
Billie Jean King	1972	(French, Wimbledon, U.S.)
Margaret Smith Court	1973	(Australian, French, U.S.)
Martina Navratilova	1983	(Australian, Wimbledon, U.S.)
Martina Navratilova	1984	(French, Wimbledon, U.S.)
Steffi Graf	1989	(Australian, Wimbledon, U.S.)
Monica Seles	1991	(Australian, French, U.S.)
Monica Seles	1992	(Australian, French, U.S.)
Steffi Graf	1993	(French, Wimbledon, U.S.)
Steffi Graf	1995	(French, Wimbledon, U.S.)
Steffi Graf	1996	(French, Wimbledon, U.S.)
Martina Hingis	1997	(Australian, Wimbledon, U.S.)
Serena Williams	2002	(French, Wimbledon, U.S.)

MEN'S DOUBLES – TEAM

Ken McGregor/ Frank Sedgman	1952	(Australian, French, Wimbledon)
Lew Hoad / Ken Rosewall	1953	(Australian, French, Wimbledon)
Lew Hoad / Ken Rosewall	1956	(Australian, Wimbledon, U.S.)
John Newcombe /Tony Roche	1967	(Australian, French, U.S.)
John Fitzgerald/Anders Jarryd	1991	(French, Wimbledon, U.S.)

MEN'S DOUBLES – INDIVIDUAL

Jacques Brugnon	1928	(Australian, French, Wimbledon)
John Van Ryn	1931	(French, Wimbledon, U.S.)
Jack Crawford	1935	(Australian, French, Wimbledon)
John Bromwich	1950	(Australian, Wimbledon, U.S.)
Frank Sedgman	1952	(Australian, French, Wimbledon)
Ken McGregor	1952	(Australian, French, Wimbledon)
Ken Rosewall	1953	(Australian, French, Wimbledon)
Lew Hoad	1953	(Australian, French, Wimbledon)
Ken Rosewall	1956	(Australian, Wimbledon, U.S.)
Lew Hoad	1956	(Australian, Wimbledon, U.S.)
John Newcombe	1967	(Australian, French, U.S.)
Tony Roche	1967	(Australian, French, U.S.)
John Newcombe	1973	(Australian, French, U.S.)
Anders Jarryd	1987	(Australian, French, U.S.)
Anders Jarryd	1991	(French, Wimbledon, U.S.)
John Fitzgerald	1991	(French, Wimbledon, U.S.)
Jacco Eltingh	1998	(Australian, French, Wimbledon)

WOMEN'S DOUBLES – TEAM

Louise Brough/Margaret Osborne duPont	1946	(French, Wimbledon, U.S.)
Louise Brough/Margaret Osborne duPont	1949	(French, Wimbledon, U.S.)
Doris Hart / Shirley Fry	1951	(French, Wimbledon, U.S.)
Doris Hart / Shirley Fry	1952	(French, Wimbledon, U.S.)
Doris Hart / Shirley Fry	1953	(French, Wimbledon, U.S.)
Darlene Hard / Maria Bueno	1960	(French, Wimbledon, U.S.)
Margaret Smith Court / Virginia Wade	1973	(Australian, French, U.S.)
Martina Navratilova/ Pam Shriver	1983	(Australian, Wimbledon, U.S.)
Martina Navratilova/ Pam Shriver	1987	(Australian, French, U.S.)
Jana Novotna / Helena Sukova	1990	(Australian, French, Wimbledon)
Gigi Fernandez / Natalia Zvereva	1992	(French, Wimbledon, U.S.)
Gigi Fernandez / Natalia Zvereva	1993	(Australian, French, Wimbledon)
Gigi Fernandez / Natalia Zvereva	1994	(Australian, French, Wimbledon)
Martina Hingis / Jana Novotna	1998	(French, Wimbledon, U.S.)
Virginia Ruano Pascual / Paola Suarez	2004	(Australian, French, U.S)

WOMEN'S DOUBLES – INDIVIDUAL

Louise Brough	1946	(French, Wimbledon, U.S.)
Margaret Osborne duPont	1946	(French, Wimbledon, U.S.)
Louise Brough	1949	(French, Wimbledon, U.S.)
Margaret Osborne duPont	1949	(French, Wimbledon, U.S.)
Louise Brough	1950	(Australian, Wimbledon, U.S.)
Doris Hart	1951	(French, Wimbledon, U.S.)
Shirley Fry	1951	(French, Wimbledon, U.S.)
Doris Hart	1952	(French, Wimbledon, U.S.)
Shirley Fry	1952	(French, Wimbledon, U.S.)
Doris Hart	1953	(French, Wimbledon, U.S.)
Shirley Fry	1953	(French, Wimbledon, U.S.)
Darlene Hard	1960	(French, Wimbledon, U.S.)
Lesley Turner	1964	(Australian, French, Wimbledon)
Nancy Richey	1966	(Australian, Wimbledon, U.S.)
Betty Stove	1972	(French, Wimbledon, U.S.)
Margaret Smith Court	1973	(Australian, French, U.S.)
Virginia Wade	1973	(Australian, French, U.S.)
Martina Navratilova	1982	(Australian, French, Wimbledon)
Martina Navratilova	1983	(Australian, Wimbledon, U.S.)
Pam Shriver	1983	(Australian, Wimbledon, U.S.)
Martina Navratilova	1986	(French, Wimbledon, U.S.)
Martina Navratilova	1987	(Australian, French, U.S.)
Pam Shriver	1987	(Australian, French, U.S.)
Helena Sukova	1990	(Australian, French, Wimbledon)
Jana Novotna	1990	(Australian, French, Wimbledon)
Gigi Fernandez	1992	(French, Wimbledon, U.S.)
Natalia Zvereva	1992	(French, Wimbledon, U.S.)
Gigi Fernandez	1993	(Australian, French, Wimbledon)
Natalia Zvereva	1993	(Australian, French, Wimbledon)
Gigi Fernandez	1994	(Australian, French, Wimbledon)
Natalia Zvereva	1994	(Australian, French, Wimbledon)
Natalia Zvereva	1997	(Australian, French, Wimbledon)
Jana Novotna	1998	(French, Wimbledon, U.S.)

MIXED DOUBLES – TEAM

Doris Hart / Frank Sedgman	1951	(French, Wimbledon, U.S.)
Doris Hart / Frank Sedgman	1952	(French, Wimbledon, U.S.)
Doris Hart / Vic Seixas	1953	(French, Wimbledon, U.S.)
Billie Jean King / Owen Davidson	1967	(French, Wimbledon, U.S.)

MIXED DOUBLES – MEN INDIVIDUAL

Eric Sturgess	1949	(French, Wimbledon, U.S.)
Frank Sedgman	1951	(French, Wimbledon, U.S.)
Frank Sedgman	1952	(French, Wimbledon, U.S.)
Vic Seixas	1953	(French, Wimbledon, U.S.)
Bob Hewitt	1979	(French, Wimbledon, U.S.)
Mark Woodforde	1992	(Australian, French, U.S.)

MIXED DOUBLES – WOMEN INDIVIDUAL

Doris Hart	1951	(French, Wimbledon, U.S.)
Doris Hart	1952	(French, Wimbledon, U.S.)
Doris Hart	1953	(French, Wimbledon, U.S.)
Doris Hart	1955	(French, Wimbledon, U.S.)
Margaret Smith Court	1964	(Australian, French, U.S.)
Margaret Smith Court	1965	(French, Wimbledon, U.S.)
Billie Jean King	1967	(French, Wimbledon, U.S.)
Martina Navratilova	1985	(French, Wimbledon, U.S.)

All-Time Major Champions – Men

Through 2009

Name	TOTAL Wins	S	D	M	Australia S	D	M	French S	D	M	Wimbledon S	D	M	U.S. S	D	M
Roy Emerson (AUS)	28	12	16		6	3		2	6		2	3		2	4	
John Newcombe (AUS)	25	7	17	1	2	5			3		3	6		2	3	1
Frank Sedgman(AUS)	22	5	9	8	2	2	2		2	2	1	3	2	2	2	2
Todd Woodbridge (AUS)	21		16	5		3	1		1			9	1		3	3
Bill Tilden (USA)	21	10	6	5						1	3	1		7	5	4
Rod Laver (AUS)	20	11	6	3	3	4		2	1	1	4	1	2	2		
John Bromwich (AUS)	19	2	13	4	2	8	1				2	2		3	1	
Neale Fraser (AUS)	19	3	11	5		3	1		3		1	2	1	2	3	3
Fred Stolle (AUS)	18	2	10	6		3	1	1	2			2	3	1	3	2
Jean Borotra (FRA)	18	4	9	5	1	1	1	1	5	2	2	3	1			1
Ken Rosewall (AUS)	18	8	9	1	4	3		2	2			2		2	2	1
Mark Woodforde (AUS)	18		12	6		2	2		1	2		6	1		3	1
Adrian Quist (AUS)	17	3	14		3	10			1			2			1	
Jack Crawford (AUS)	17	6	6	5	4	4	3	1	1	1	1	1	1			
John McEnroe (USA)	17	7	9	1						1	3	5		4	4	
Laurie Doherty (GBR)	16	6	10								5	8		1	2	
Tony Roche (AUS)	16	1	13	2		5	1	1	2			5	1		1	
Roger Federer (SUI)	15	15			3			1			6			5		
Bob Hewitt (RSA)	15		9	6		2	1		1	2		5	2		1	1
Henri Cochet (FRA)	15	7	5	3				4	3	2	2	2		1		1
Vic Seixas (USA)	15	2	5	8		1			2	1	1		4	1	2	3
Don Budge (USA)	14	6	4	4	1			1			2	2	2	2	2	2
Fred Perry (GBR)	14	8	2	4	1	1		1	1	1	3		2	3		1
Pete Sampras (USA)	14	14			2						7			5		
Reggie Doherty (GBR)	14		4	10							4	8			2	
Bob Bryan (USA)	13	0	7	6	0	3	0	0	1	2	0	1	1	0	2	3
Dick Sears (USA)	13		7	6										7	6	
Lew Hoad (AUS)	13	4	8	1	1	3		1	1	1	2	3		1		
George Lott (USA)	12		8	4					1			2	1		5	3
Jacques Brugnon (FRA)	12		10	2		1			5	2		4				
Ken Fletcher (AUS)	12		2	10			2		1	3		1	4			1
Owen Davidson (AUS)	12		2	10		1	1			1			4		1	4
Willie Renshaw (GBR)	12		7	5							7	5				
Bjorn Borg (SWE)	11	11						6			5					
Tony Wilding (NZL)	11	6	5		2	1					4	4				
Frew McMillan (RSA)	10		5	5					1	1		3	2		1	2
Gerald Patterson (AUS)	10	3	6	1	1	5					2		1	1		
Jack Kramer (USA)	10	3	6	1							1	2		2	4	1
Jimmy Connors (USA)	10	8	2		1						2	1		5	1	
Rene Lacoste (FRA)	10	7	3					3	2		2	1		2		
Tony Trabert (USA)	10	5	5			1		2	3		1			2	1	
Mike Bryan (USA)	9	0	7	2	0	3			1	1	0	1	0	0	2	1
Bill Talbert (USA)	9		5	4					1						4	4
Jack Hawkes (AUS)	9	1	3	5	1	3	3									2
John Fitzgerald (AUS)	9		7	2		1			2			2	1		2	1
Ken McGregor (AUS)	9	1	7	1	1	2			2			2			1	1
Rick Leach (USA)	9		5	4		3	2					1	1		1	1
Stefan Edberg (SWE)	9	6	3		2	2						2		2	1	
Vinnie Richards (USA)	9		7	2					1			1			5	2
Jonas Bjorkman (SWE)	9		9			3			2			3			1	

All-Time Major Champions – Women

Through 2009

Name	TOTAL Wins	S	D	M	Australia S	D	M	French S	D	M	Wimbledon S	D	M	U.S. S	D	M
Margaret Smith Court (AUS)	62	24	19	19	11	8	2	5	4	4	3	2	5	5	5	8
Martina Navratilova (USA)	59	18	31	10	3	8	1	2	7	2	9	7	4	4	9	3
Billie Jean King (USA)	39	12	16	11	1			1	1	3	6	10	4	4	5	4
Margaret Osborne duPont (USA)	37	6	21	10				2	3		1	5	1	3	13	9
Doris Hart (USA)	35	6	14	15	1	1	2	2	5	2	1	4	5	2	4	5
Louise Brough (USA)	35	6	21	8	1	1			3		4	5	4	1	12	4
Helen Wills Moody (USA)	31	19	9	3				4	2		8	3	1	7	4	2
Elizabeth Ryan (USA)	26		17	9					4			12	7		1	2
Steffi Graf (GER)	23	22	1		4			6			7	1		5		
Serena Williams (USA)	22	11	9	2	4	3		1	1		3	4	1	3	1	1
Pam Shriver (USA)	22		21	1		7			4	1		5			5	
Chris Evert (USA)	21	18	3		2			7	2		3	1		6		
Darlene Hard (USA)	21	3	13	5				1	3	2		4	3	2	6	
Suzanne Lenglen (FRA)	21	8	8	5				2	2	2	6	6	3			
Nancye Bolton (AUS)	20	6	10	4	6	10	4									
Natalia Zvereva (BLR)	20		18	2		3	2		6			5			4	
Maria Bueno (BRA)	19	7	11	1		1			1	1	3	5		4	4	
Thelma Long (AUS)	19	2	12	5	2	12	4			1						
Venus Williams (USA)	18	7	9	2		4	1		1	1	5	4		2	1	
Alice Marble (USA)	18	5	6	7							1	2	3	4	4	4
Sarah Palfrey Cooke (USA)	18	2	11	5						1		2		2	9	4
Gigi Fernandez (USA)	17		17			2			6			4			5	
Hazel Hotchkiss Wightman (USA)	17	4	7	6								1		4	6	6
Jana Novotna (CZE)	17	1	12	4		2	2		3		1	4	1		3	1
Shirley Fry (USA)	17	4	12	1	1	1		1	4		1	3	1	1	4	
Martina Hingis (SUI)	15	5	9	1	3	4	1		2		1	2		1	1	
Arantxa Sanchez Vicario (ESP)	14	4	6	4		3	1	3		2		1		1	2	1
Daphne Akhurst (AUS)	14	5	5	4	5	5	4									
Helena Sukova (CZE)	14		9	5		2			1	1		4	3		2	1
Evonne Goolagong (AUS)	13	7	5	1	4	4		1		1	2	1				
Juliette Atkinson (USA)	13	3	7	3										3	7	3
Lesley Turner (AUS)	13	2	7	4		3	2	2	2			1	2		1	
Mary K. Browne (USA)	13	3	6	4								1		3	5	4
Molla Mallory (USA)	13	8	2	3										8	2	3
Simone Passemard Mathieu (FRA)	13	2	9	2				2	6	2		3				
Francoise Durr (FRA)	12	1	7	4				1	5	3			1		2	
Maureen Connolly (USA)	12	9	2	1	1	1		2	1	1	3			3		
Rosie Casals (USA)	12		9	3								5	2		4	1
Althea Gibson (USA)	11	5	5	1		1		1	1		2	3		2		1
Annie Smith (USA)	10		5	5		1			2	2		1	1		1	2
Betty Stove (NED)	10		6	4					2			1	2		3	2
Lisa Raymond (USA)	9		5	4		1			1	1		1	1		2	2
Betty Nuthall (GBR)	9	1	4	4					1	2				1	3	2
Helen Jacobs (USA)	9	5	3	1							1			4	3	1
Judy Dalton (AUS)	9		8	1		4	1		1			1			2	
Monica Seles (USA)	9	9			4			3						2		
Wendy Turnbull (AUS)	9		4	5					1	2		1	2		2	1

All-Time Major Champions – Records

Through 2009

Men's Singles – Titles

	TOTAL		Aus.	Fre.	Wim.	U.S
Roger Federer	15	(2003-2009)	3	1	6	5
Pete Sampras	14	(1990-2002)	2		7	5
Roy Emerson	12	(1961-1967)	6	2	2	2
Bjorn Borg	11	(1974-1981)			6	5
Rod Laver	11	(1960-1969)	3	2	4	2
Bill Tilden	10	(1920-1930)			3	7
Andre Agassi	8	(1992-2003)	4	1	1	2
Fred Perry	8	(1933-1936)	1	1	3	3
Ivan Lendl	8	(1984-1990)	2	3		3
Jimmy Connors	8	(1974-1983)	1		2	5
Ken Rosewall	8	(1953-1972)	4	2		2
Bill Larned	7	(1901-1911)				7
Dick Sears	7	(1881-1887)				7
Henri Cochet	7	(1926-1932)		4	2	1
John McEnroe	7	(1979-1984)			3	4
John Newcombe	7	(1967-1975)	2		3	2
Mats Wilander	7	(1982-1988)	3	3		1
Rene Lacoste	7	(1925-1929)		3	2	2
Willie Renshaw	7	(1881-1889)			7	
Rafael Nadal	6	(2005-2009)	1	4	1	
Boris Becker	6	(1985-1996)	2		3	1
Don Budge	6	(1937-1938)	1	1	2	2
Jack Crawford	6	(1931-1935)	4	1	1	
Laurie Doherty	6	(1902-1906)			5	1
Stefan Edberg	6	(1985-1992)	2		2	2
Tony Wilding	6	(1906-1913)	2		4	
Frank Sedgman	5	(1949-1952)	2		1	2
Tony Trabert	5	(1953-1955)		2	1	2
Ashley Cooper	4	(1957-1958)	2		1	1
Frank Parker	4	(1944-1949)		2		2
Guillermo Vilas	4	(1977-1979)	2	1		1
Jean Borotra	4	(1924-1931)	1	1	2	
Jim Courier	4	(1991-1993)	2	2		
Lew Hoad	4	(1956-1957)	1	1	2	
Manolo Santana	4	(1961-1966)		2	1	1
Reggie Doherty	4	(1897-1900)			4	
Robert Wrenn	4	(1893-1897)				4

Men's Singles – Final Appearances

	TOTAL		Aus.	Fre.	Wim.	U.S
Roger Federer	20	(2003-2009)	4	4	7	5
Ivan Lendl	19	(1981-1991)	4	5	2	8
Pete Sampras	18	(1990-2002)	3		7	8
Rod Laver	17	(1960-1969)	4	3	6	4
Bjorn Borg	16	(1974-1981)		6	6	4
Ken Rosewall	16	(1953-1974)	5	3	4	4
Bill Tilden	15	(1918-1930)	2		3	10
Jimmy Connors	15	(1974-1984)	2		6	7
Roy Emerson	15	(1961-1967)	7	3	2	3
Andre Agassi	13	(1990-2002)	3	3	2	5
Jack Crawford	12	(1931-1940)	7	2	2	1
John McEnroe	11	(1979-1985)		1	5	5
Mats Wilander	11	(1982-1988)	4	5		2
Stefan Edberg	11	(1985-1993)	5	1	3	2
Boris Becker	10	(1985-1996)	2		7	1
Fred Perry	10	(1933-1936)	2	2	3	3
Henri Cochet	10	(1926-1933)		5	3	2
Jean Borotra	10	(1924-1931)	1	3	5	1
John Newcombe	10	(1967-1976)	3		4	3
Rene Lacoste	10	(1925-1929)		5	3	2
Bill Johnston	9	(1915-1925)			1	8
Rafael Nadal	8	(2005-2009)	1	4	3	
Arthur Gore	8	(1899-1912)			8	
Bill Larned	8	(1901-1911)				8
Frank Sedgman	8	(1949-1952)	3	1	2	2
Fred Stolle	8	(1963-1966)	2	1	3	2
Guillermo Vilas	8	(1975-1982)	3	4		1
Jaroslav Drobny	8	(1946-1954)		5	3	
John Bromwich	8	(1937-1949)	7		1	
Willie Renshaw	8	(1881-1890)			8	

Men's Singles – Final Losses

	TOTAL		Aus.	Fre.	Wim.	U.S
Ivan Lendl	11	(1981-1991)	2	2	2	5
Ken Rosewall	8	(1953-1974)	1	1	4	2
Jimmy Connors	7	(1974-1984)	1		4	2
Andre Agassi	7	(1990-2003)		2	1	4
Bill Johnston	6	(1915-1925)				6
Fred Stolle	6	(1963-1966)	2		3	1
Jack Crawford	6	(1933-1940)	3	1	1	1
Jean Borotra	6	(1924-1931)		2	3	1
John Bromwich	6	(1937-1949)	5	1		
Rod Laver	6	(1960-1969)	1	1	2	2
Roger Federer	5	(2003-2009)	1	3	1	
Arthur Gore	5	(1899-1912)			5	
Bill Tilden	5	(1918-1930)			2	3
Bjorn Borg	5	(1974-1981)			1	4
Gottfried von Cramm	5	(1935-1937)		1	3	1
Herbert Lawford	5	(1880-1888)			5	
Jaroslav Drobny	5	(1946-1954)		3	2	
Stefan Edberg	5	(1985-1993)	3	1	1	
Tony Roche	5	(1965-1970)		2	1	2
Andy Roddick	4	(2003-2009)			3	1
Arthur Ashe	4	(1966-1972)	3			1

	TOTAL		Aus.	Fre.	Wim.	U.S
Boris Becker	4	(1985-1996)			4	
Ernest Renshaw	4	(1882-1889)			4	
Gerald Patterson	4	(1914-1925)	3		1	
Guillermo Vilas	4	(1975-1982)	1	3		
John McEnroe	4	(1979-1985)		1	2	1
Mats Wilander	4	(1982-1988)	1	2		1
Maurice McLoughlin	4	(1911-1915)			1	3
Neale Fraser	4	(1957-1960)	3		1	
Pete Sampras	4	(1990-2002)	1			3

Men's Singles – Semifinal Appearances

(1925-2007)

	TOTAL		Aus.	Fre.	Wim.	U.S
Jimmy Connors	31	(1974-1991)	2	4	11	14
Ivan Lendl	28	(1981-1991)	7	5	7	9
Ken Rosewall	25	(1953-1977)	8	3	6	8
Pete Sampras	23	(1990-2002)	5	1	8	9
Andre Agassi	26	(1988-2005)	6	5	5	10
Jack Crawford	19	(1928-1940)	11	3	4	1
John McEnroe	19	(1977-1992)	1	2	8	8
Roy Emerson	19	(1959-1967)	8	4	3	4
Stefan Edberg	19	(1985-1994)	8	1	6	4
Boris Becker	18	(1985-1996)	2	3	9	4
Rod Laver	18	(1959-1969)	4	4	6	4
Roger Federer	23	(2003-2009)	6	5	7	5
Bjorn Borg	17	(1974-1981)		6	6	5
Henri Cochet	16	(1926-1933)		7	6	3
John Newcombe	16	(1965-1976)	6		4	6
Neale Fraser	16	(1956-1962)	6	2	4	4
Jaroslav Drobny	14	(1946-1954)		6	6	2
Jean Borotra	14	(1925-1931)	1	6	6	1
John Bromwich	14	(1937-1954)	9		2	3
Mats Wilander	14	(1982-1990)	5	6		3
Arthur Ashe	13	(1965-1978)	5		3	5
Fred Perry	13	(1931-1936)	2	2	4	5
Tony Roche	13	(1965-1975)	4	4	3	2
Guillermo Vilas	12	(1975-1982)	4	4		4
Bill Tilden	11	(1925-1930)		3	4	4
Fred Stolle	11	(1961-1966)	5	1	3	2
Jim Courier	11	(1991-1995)	3	4	1	3
Andy Roddick	10	(2003-2009)	4		4	2
Eric Sturgess	10	(1947-1952)	1	6	2	1
Frank Parker	10	(1936-1949)		2	1	7
Frank Sedgman	10	(1949-1952)	4	2	2	2
Merv Rose	10	(1952-1958)	4	2	3	1
Rene Lacoste	10	(1925-1929)		5	3	2
Vic Seixas	10	(1950-1956)	1	1	3	5

Women's Singles – Titles

	TOTAL		Aus.	Fre.	Wim.	U.S
Margaret Smith Court	24	(1960-1973)	11	5	3	5
Steffi Graf	22	(1987-1999)	4	6	7	5
Helen Wills Moody	19	(1923-1938)		4	8	7
Chris Evert	18	(1974-1986)	2	7	3	6
Martina Navratilova	18	(1978-1990)	3	2	9	4
Billie Jean King	12	(1966-1975)	1	1	6	4
Serena Williams	11	(1999-2009)	4	1	3	3
Maureen Connolly	9	(1951-1954)	1	2	3	3
Monica Seles	9	(1990-1996)	4	3		2
Molla Mallory	8	(1915-1926)				8
Suzanne Lenglen	8	(1919-1926)		2	6	
Venus Williams	7	(2000-2009)			5	2
Justine Henin	7	(2003-2007)	1	4	0	2
Dorothea Douglass Chambers	7	(1903-1914)			7	
Evonne Goolagong	7	(1971-1980)	4	1	2	
Maria Bueno	7	(1959-1966)			3	4
Blanche Bingley Hillyard	6	(1886-1900)			6	
Doris Hart	6	(1949-1955)	1	2	1	2
Louise Brough	6	(1947-1955)	1		4	1
Margaret Osborne duPont	6	(1946-1950)		2	1	3
Nancye Bolton	6	(1937-1951)	6			
Alice Marble	5	(1936-1940)			1	4
Althea Gibson	5	(1956-1958)		1	2	2
Charlotte Cooper Sterry	5	(1895-1908)			5	
Daphe Akhurst	5	(1925-1930)	5			
Helen Jacobs	5	(1932-1936)			1	4
Lottie Dod	5	(1887-1893)			5	
Martina Hingis	5	(1997-1999)	3		1	1
Pauline Betz	5	(1942-1946)			1	4
Serena Williams	5	(1999-2002)	1	1	1	2
Arantxa Sanchez Vicario	4	(1989-1998)		3		1
Bessie Moore	4	(1896-1905)				4
Hana Mandilkova	4	(1980-1987)	2	1		1
Hazel Hotchkiss Wightman	4	(1909-1919)				4
Shirley Fry	4	(1951-1957)	1	1	1	1

Women's Singles – Final Appearances

	TOTAL		Aus.	Fre.	Wim.	U.S
Chris Evert	34	(1973-1988)	6	9	10	9
Martina Navratilova	32	(1975-1994)	6	6	12	8
Steffi Graf	31	(1987-1999)	5	9	9	8
Margaret Smith Court	29	(1960-1973)	12	6	5	6
Helen Wills Moody	22	(1923-1938)		4	9	9
Billie Jean King	18	(1963-1975)	2	1	9	6
Doris Hart	18	(1946-1955)	2	5	4	7
Evonne Goolagong	18	(1971-1980)	7	2	5	4
Helen Jacobs	16	(1928-1940)		2	6	8
Venus Williams	14	(1997-2009)	1	1	8	4
Louise Brough	14	(1942-1957)	1		7	6
Serena Williams	13	(1999-2009)	4	1	5	4
Blanche Bingley Hillyard	13	(1885-1901)			13	
Monica Seles	13	(1990-1998)	4	4	1	4
Arantxa Sanchez Vicario	12	(1989-1998)	2	6	2	2
Maria Bueno	12	(1959-1966)	1	1	5	5
Martina Hingis	12	(1997-2002)	6	2	1	3
Justine Henin	11	(2001-2007)	2	4	2	3
Charlotte Cooper Sterry	11	(1895-1912)			11	
Dorothea Douglass Chambers	11	(1903-1920)			11	

	TOTAL		Aus.	Fre.	Wim.	U.S
Molla Mallory	11	(1915-1926)			1	10
Margaret Osborne duPont	10	(1944-1950)		2	3	5
Ann Haydon	9	(1961-1969)		5	2	2
Maureen Connolly	9	(1951-1954)	1	2	3	3
Nancye Bolton	9	(1936-1951)	8			1
Hana Mandilkova	8	(1980-1987)	2	1	2	3
Pauline Betz	8	(1942-1946)		1	1	6
Shirley Fry	8	(1948-1957)	1	3	2	2
Simone Passemard Mathieu	8	(1929-1939)		8		
Suzanne Lenglen	8	(1919-1926)		2	6	

Women's Singles – Final Losses

	TOTAL		Aus.	Fre.	Wim.	U.S
Chris Evert	16	(1973-1988)	4	2	7	3
Martina Navratilova	14	(1975-1994)	3	4	3	4
Doris Hart	12	(1946-1953)	1	3	3	5
Evonne Goolagong	11	(1971-1976)	3	1	3	4
Helen Jacobs	11	(1928-1940)		2	5	4
Steffi Graf	9	(1987-1999)	1	3	2	3
Arantxa Sanchez Vicario	8	(1991-1996)	2	3	2	1
Louise Brough	8	(1942-1957)			3	5
Venus Williams	7	(1997-2009)	1	1	3	2
Blanche Bingley Hillyard	7	(1885-1901)			7	
Martina Hingis	7	(1997-2002)	3	2		2
Ann Haydon	6	(1961-1969)		3	1	2
Billie Jean King	6	(1963-1970)	1		3	2
Charlotte Cooper Sterry	6	(1897-1912)			6	
Esna Boyd	6	(1922-1928)	6			
Simone Passemard Mathieu	6	(1929-1937)		6		
Margaret Smith Court	5	(1963-1971)	1	1	2	1
Maria Bueno	5	(1960-1966)	1	1	2	1
Kim Clijsters	4	(2001-2004)	1	2		1
Darlene Hard	4	(1957-1962)			2	2
Dorothea Douglass Chamber	4	(1905-1920)			4	
Hana Mandilkova	4	(1980-1986)			2	2
Helena Sukova	4	(1984-1993)	2			2
Jan Lehane	4	(1960-1963)	4			
Lesley Turner	4	(1962-1967)	2	2		
Margaret Osborne duPont	4	(1944-1950)			2	2
Monica Seles	4	(1992-1998)		1	1	2
Nancy Richey	4	(1966-1969)	1	1		2
Shirley Fry	4	(1948-1952)		2	1	1
Thelma Long	4	(1940-1956)	4			

Women's Singles – Semifinal Appearances

(1925–2007)

	TOTAL		Aus.	Fre.	Wim.	U.S
Chris Evert	52	(1971-1989)	6	12	17	17
Martina Navratilova	44	(1975-1994)	9	6	17	12
Steffi Graf	37	(1985-1999)	5	11	10	11
Margaret Smith Court	36	(1960-1975)	12	7	9	8
Billie Jean King	26	(1963-1983)	3	2	14	7
Doris Hart	26	(1943-1955)	2	6	7	11

	TOTAL		Aus.	Fre.	Wim.	U.S
Louise Brough	25	(1942-1957)	1	3	10	11
Helen Jacobs	24	(1927-1941)		4	8	12
Arantxa Sanchez Vicario	22	(1989-2000)	5	10	3	4
Evonne Goolagong	22	(1971-1980)	7	3	8	4
Ann Haydon	21	(1957-1969)	1	7	8	5
Maria Bueno	20	(1958-1968)	1	5	6	8
Martina Hingis	19	(1996-2002)	6	5	2	6
Lindsay Davenport	18	(1997-2005)	5	1	5	7
Venus Williams	18	(1997-2009)	2	1	8	7
Gabriela Sabatini	18	(1985-1995)	4	5	4	5
Helen Wills Moody	18	(1925-1938)		4	8	6
Monica Seles	18	(1989-2002)	6	7	1	4
Serena Williams	16	(1999-2009)	4	2	6	4
Justine Henin	16	(2001-2007)	3	5	5	3
Margaret Osborne duPont	16	(1941-1951)		4	5	7
Simone Passemard Mathieu	15	(1929-1939)		9	6	
Hana Mandilkova	14	(1980-1987)	3	5	3	3
Shirley Fry	14	(1948-1957)	1	4	4	5
Jennifer Capriati	13	(1990-2004)	3	4	2	4
Kerry Melville	13	(1966-1977)	8	1	1	3
Lindsay Davenport	13	(1997-2002)	4	1	3	5
Nancy Richey	13	(1964-1971)	2	5	1	5
Nancye Bolton	13	(1936-1951)	11			2
Conchita Martinez	12	(1993-2000)	3	4	3	2
Darlene Hard	12	(1954-1963)		1	4	7
Lesley Turner	12	(1962-1969)	4	6	1	1
Hilde Krahwinkel Sperling	11	(1931-1939)		5	6	
Thelma Long	11	(1936-1956)	11			
Jennifer Capriati	10	(1990-2002)	3	3	2	2

Men's Doubles – Titles – Individual

	TOTAL		Aus.	Fre.	Wim.	U.S
John Newcombe	17	(1965-1976)	5	3	6	3
Todd Woodbridge	16	(1997-2004)	3	1	9	3
Roy Emerson	16	(1959-1971)	3	6	3	4
Adrian Quist	14	(1935-1950)	10	1	2	1
John Bromwich	13	(1938-1950)	8		2	3
Tony Roche	13	(1965-1977)	5	2	5	1
Mark Woodforde	12	(1989-2000)	2	1	6	3
Neale Fraser	11	(1957-1962)	3	3	2	3
Fred Stolle	10	(1962-1969)	3	2	2	3
Jacques Brugnon	10	(1926-1934)	1	5	4	
Laurie Doherty	10	(1897-1905)			8	2
Reggie Doherty	10	(1897-1905)			8	2
Jonas Bjorkman	9	(1998-2006)	3	2	3	1
Bob Hewitt	9	(1962-1978)	2	1	5	1
Frank Sedgman	9	(1948-1952)	2	2	3	2
Jean Borotra	9	(1925-1936)	1	5	3	
John McEnroe	9	(1979-1992)			5	4
Ken Rosewall	9	(1953-1972)	3	2	2	2
Anders Jarryd	8	(1983-1991)	1	3	2	2
George Lott	8	(1928-1934)		1	2	5
Lew Hoad	8	(1953-1957)	3	1	3	1

	TOTAL		Aus.	Fre.	Wim.	U.S
Bob Bryan	7	(2003-2009)	3	1	1	2
Mike Bryan	7	(2003-2009)	3	1	1	2
John Fitzgerald	7	(1982-1991)	1	2	2	2
Ken McGregor	7	(1951-1952)	2	2	2	1
Peter Fleming	7	(1979-1984)			4	3
Vinnie Richards	7	(1918-1926)		1	1	5

Men's Doubles – Final Appearances – Individual

	TOTAL		Aus.	Fre.	Wim.	U.S
Roy Emerson	28	(1958-1971)	8	10	5	5
John Newcombe	21	(1963-1976)	7	4	6	4
Todd Woodbridge	20	(1997-2004)	4	2	10	4
Adrian Quist	18	(1933-1951)	12	2	2	2
Neale Fraser	18	(1954-1973)	5	4	6	3
Jacques Brugnon	17	(1925-1939)	1	9	7	
Ken Rosewall	17	(1953-1973)	5	3	5	4
Todd Woodbridge	17	(1992-2002)	4	2	8	3
Fred Stolle	16	(1961-1970)	6	2	5	3
John Bromwich	16	(1937-1951)	10		2	4
Mark Woodforde	16	(1989-2000)	3	2	7	4
Bob Bryan	15	(2003-2009)	5	3	4	3
Mike Bryan	15	(2003-2009)	5	3	4	3
Jonas Bjorkman	15	(1998-2008)	4	3	4	4
Tony Roche	15	(1964-1977)	6	3	5	1
Frank Sedgman	14	(1947-1952)	4	3	3	4
Gardnar Mulloy	14	(1940-1957)		2	3	9
Gerald Patterson	14	(1914-1932)	7		2	5
Anders Jarryd	13	(1983-1993)	2	5	3	3
Bob Hewitt	13	(1961-1978)	3	2	7	1
Lew Hoad	13	(1953-1957)	4	3	4	2
Reggie Doherty	13	(1896-1906)			11	2
Stan Smith	13	(1968-1981)	1	2	4	6

Men's Doubles – Final Losses – Individual

	TOTAL		Aus.	Fre.	Wim.	U.S
Roy Emerson	17	(1958-1970)	5	4	2	1
Gardnar Mulloy	9	(1940-1957)		2	2	5
Bob Bryan	8	(2003-2009)	2	2	3	1
Mike Bryan	8	(2003-2009)	2	2	3	1
Gerald Patterson	8	(1922-1932)	2		2	4
Ken Rosewall	8	(1954-1973)	2	1	3	2
Stan Smith	8	(1971-1981)		2	4	2
Mark Knowles	7	(1995-2009)	3	2	1	1
Jacques Brugnon	7	(1925-1939)		4	3	
Ken Fletcher	7	(1963-1967)	2	2	3	
Merv Rose	7	(1951-1957)	3	2	1	1
Neale Fraser	7	(1954-1973)	2	1	4	
Rich Leach	7	(1988-2000)	1	1	2	3
Daniel Nestor	6	(1995-2003)	2	2	1	1
Don Candy	6	(1951-1959)	4	1		1
Fred Stolle	6	(1961-1970)	3		3	
Henri Cochet	6	(1925-1931)		4	2	

	TOTAL		Aus.	Fre.	Wim.	U.S
Jack Crawford	6	(1931-1940)	4	1		1
Pat O'Hara Wood	6	(1922-1927)	3		1	2
Phil Dent	6	(1970-1979)	3	2	1	
Rod Laver	6	(1959-1973)		2	1	3

Men's Doubles – Titles – Team

	TOTAL		Aus.	Fre.	Wim.	U.S
John Newcombe / Tony Roche	12	(1965-1976)	4	2	5	1
Todd Woodbridge / Mark Woodforde	11	(1992-2000)	2	1	6	2
Adrian Quist / John Bromwich	10	(1938-1950)	8		1	1
Reggie Doherty / Laurie Doherty	10	(1897-1905)			8	2
Bob Bryan / Mike Bryan	7	(2003-2009)	3	1	1	2
John McEnroe / Peter Fleming	7	(1979-1984)			4	3
Ken McGregor / Frank Sedgman	7	(1951-1952)	2	2	2	1
Lew Hoad / Ken Rosewall	6	(1953-1956)	2	1	2	1
Jonas Bjorkman / Todd Woodbridge	5	(2001-2004)	1		3	1
Bob Hewitt / Frew McMillan	5	(1967-1978)		1	3	1
Bob Lutz / Stan Smith	5	(1968-1980)	1			4
Henri Cochet / Jacques Brugnon	5	(1926-1932)		3	2	
Jacco Eltingh / Paul Haarhuis	5	(1994-1998)	1	2	1	1
Jean Borotra / Jacques Brugnon	5	(1928-1934)	1	2	2	
Richard Sears / James Dwight	5	(1882-1887)				5
Willie Renshaw / Ernest Renshaw	5	(1884-1889)			5	
Bill Talbert / Gardnar Mulloy	4	(1942-1948)				4
Bob Hewitt / Fred Stolle	4	(1962-1964)	2		2	
Don Budge / Mako Gene	4	(1936-1938)			2	2
Fred Alexander / Harold Hackett	4	(1907-1910)				4
John Fitzgerald / Anders Jarryd	4	(1989-1991)		1	2	1
Roy Emerson / Fred Stolle	4	(1965-1966)	1	1		2
Vic Seixas / Tony Trabert	4	(1954-1955)	1	2		1
Wilfred Baddeley / Herbert Baddeley	4	(1891-1896)			4	
Wilmer Allison / John Van Ryn	4	(1929-1935)			2	2

Men's Doubles – Final Appearances – Team

	TOTAL		Aus.	Fre.	Wim.	U.S
Bob Bryan / Mike Bryan	15	(2003-2009)	5	3	4	3
Todd Woodbridge / Mark Woodforde	15	(1992-2000)	3	2	7	3
John Newcombe / Tony Roche	14	(1964-1976)	5	3	5	1
Adrian Quist / John Bromwich	12	(1938-1951)	9		1	2
Reggie Doherty / Laurie Doherty	12	(1897-1906)			10	2
Bob Lutz / Stan Smith	10	(1968-1981)	1	1	3	5
Henri Cochet / Jacques Brugnon	10	(1925-1932)		6	4	
John McEnroe / Peter Fleming	10	(1978-1984)			6	4
Mark Knowles / Daniel Nestor	9	(1995-2007)	3	3	1	2
Lew Hoad / Ken Rosewall	9	(1953-1956)	3	2	2	2
Neale Fraser / Roy Emerson	9	(1959-1962)	2	3	2	2
Ken McGregor / Frank Sedgman	8	(1951-1952)	2	2	2	2
Wilmer Allison / John Van Ryn	8	(1929-1936)			3	5
Brian Gottfried / Raul Ramirez	7	(1975-1980)		4	2	1
Don Budge / Mako Gene	7	(1935-1938)		1	2	4
Fred Alexander / Harold Hackett	7	(1905-1911)				7
Jacco Eltingh / Paul Haarhuis	7	(1994-1998)	1	2	2	2
Jean Borotra / Jacques Brugnon	7	(1928-1939)	1	3	3	
John Fitzgerald / Anders Jarryd	7	(1988-1993)	1	2	3	1

Men's Doubles – Final Losses – Team

	TOTAL		Aus.	Fre.	Wim.	U.S
Bob Bryan / Mike Bryan	8	(2003-2009)	2	2	3	1
Mark Knowles / Daniel Nestor	6	(1995-2007)	2	2	1	1
Bob Lutz / Stan Smith	5	(1974-1981)		1	3	1
Don Candy / Merv Rose	5	(1951-1957)	3	1		1
Henri Cochet / Jacques Brugnon	5	(1925-1931)		3	2	
John Alexander / Phil Dent	5	(1970-1977)	3	1	1	
Brian Gottfried / Raul Ramirez	4	(1976-1980)		2	1	1
Gerald Patterson / Pat O'Hara Wood	4	(1922-1924)	1		1	2
Roy Emerson / Ken Fletcher	4	(1964-1967)	1	1	2	
Todd Woodbridge / Mark Woodforde	4	(1994-1998)	1	1	1	1
Wilmer Allison / John Van Ryn	4	(1932-1936)			1	3
Bill Bowrey / Owen Davidson	3	(1966-1967)	1		1	1
Dick Williams / Watson Washburn	3	(1921-1924)			1	2
Don Budge / Mako Gene	3	(1935-1938)		1		2
Dwight / Holcombe Ward	3	(1898-1902)			1	2
Eric Sturgess / Jaroslav Drobny	3	(1950-1951)	1	1	1	
Fred Alexander / Harold Hackett	3	(1905-1911)				3
Geoff Masters / Ross Case	3	(1972-1976)	2		1	
Gerald Patterson / Jack Hawkes	3	(1925-1928)			1	2
Jack Crawford / Viv McGrath	3	(1934-1940)	2	1		
John Fitzgerald / Anders Jarryd	3	(1988-1993)	1	1	1	
John McEnroe / Peter Fleming	3	(1978-1982)			2	1
Ken Rosewall / Fred Stolle	3	(1968-1970)	1		2	
Lew Hoad / Ken Rosewall	3	(1954-1955)	1	1		1
Paul Kronk / Cliff Letcher	3	(1976-1979)	2			1
Rick Leach / Jim Pugh	3	(1988-1991)		1	1	1
Roy Emerson / Rod Laver	3	(1968-1970)	2			1
Sidney H. Smith / Frank Riseley	3	(1903-1905)			3	
Tom Okker / Marty Riessen	3	(1969-1975)	1		1	1
Jonas Bjorkman / Todd Woodbridge	3	(2005-2007)	1			2

Women's Doubles – Titles – Individual

	TOTAL		Aus.	Fre.	Wim.	U.S
Martina Navratilova	31	(1975-1990)	8	7	7	9
Loiuse Brough	21	(1942-1957)	1	3	5	12
Margaret Osborne duPont	21	(1941-1957)		3	5	13
Pam Shiver	21	(1981-1991)	7	4	5	5
Margaret Smith Court	19	(1961-1975)	8	4	2	5
Natalia Zvereva	18	(1989-1997)	3	6	5	4
Elizabeth Ryan	17	(1914-1934)		4	12	1
Gigi Fernandez	17	(1988-1997)	2	6	4	5
Billie Jean King	16	(1961-1980)		1	10	5
Doris Hart	14	(1947-1954)	1	5	4	4
Darlene Hard	13	(1955-1969)		3	4	6
Jana Novotna	12	(1989-1998)	2	3	4	3
Shirley Fry	12	(1950-1957)	1	4	3	4
Thelma Long	12	(1936-1958)	12			
Maria Bueno	11	(1958-1968)	1	1	5	4
Sarah Palfrey Fabyan	11	(1930-1941)			2	9
Virginia Ruano Pascual	10	(2001-2009)	1	6		3
Nancye Bolton	10	(1936-1952)	10			
Venus Williams	9	(1997-2009)	3	1	4	1
Serena Williams	9	(1997-2009)	3	1	4	1
Helen Wills Moody	9	(1922-1932)		2	3	4
Helena Sukova	9	(1985-1996)	2	1	4	2
Martina Hingis	9	(1996-2002)	4	2	2	1
Rosie Casals	9	(1967-1982)			5	4
Simone Passernard Mathieu	9	(1933-1939)		6	3	
Judy Dalton	8	(1964-1971)	4	1	1	2
Suzanne Lenglen	8	(1919-1926)		2	6	
Paola Suarez	8	(2001-2005)	1	4		3

Women's Doubles – Final Appearances – Individual

	TOTAL		Aus.	Fre.	Wim.	U.S
Martina Navratilova	36	(1975-2003)	9	7	9	12
Margaret Smith Court	33	(1960-1975)	12	7	6	8
Natalia Zvereva	31	(1988-1999)	6	10	9	6
Doris Hart	30	(1942-1955)	2	7	8	13
Billie Jean King	29	(1961-1980)	2	3	12	12
Loiuse Brough	28	(1942-1957)	1	4	8	15
Margaret Osborne duPont	27	(1941-1958)		4	8	15
Pam Shiver	27	(1980-1993)	9	4	6	8
Gigi Fernandez	23	(1988-1997)	4	7	6	6
Jana Novotna	23	(1989-1998)	3	5	8	7
Elizabeth Ryan	21	(1914-1934)		5	13	3
Rosie Casals	21	(1966-1983)	1	3	7	10
Shirley Fry	19	(1948-1957)	1	5	5	8
Darlene Hard	18	(1955-1969)	1	5	4	8
Francoise Durr	18	(1965-1979)		8	6	4
Virginia Ruano Pascual	16	(2001-2009)	2	8	3	3
Maria Bueno	16	(1958-1968)	1	2	6	7
Thelma Long	16	(1936-1958)	14	1	1	
Sarah Palfrey Fabyan	15	(1930-1941)		1	4	10
Wendy Turnbull	15	(1978-1988)	2	2	5	6
Betty Stove	14	(1972-1980)		3	6	5
Wendy Turnbull	14	(1984-1996)	4	3	4	3
Mary Bevis Hawton	14	(1946-1961)	12	1	1	
Paola Suarez	14	(2001-2006)	2	6	3	3

Women's Doubles – Final Losses – Individual

	TOTAL		Aus.	Fre.	Wim.	U.S
Doris Hart	16	(1942-1955)	1	2	4	9
Margaret Smith Court	14	(1960-1975)	4	3	4	3
Billie Jean King	13	(1962-1979)	2	2	2	7
Natalia Zvereva	13	(1988-1999)	3	4	4	2
Rosie Casals	12	(1966-1983)	1	3	3	6
Francoise Durr	11	(1965-1979)		3	6	2
Jana Novotna	11	(1990-1996)	1	2	4	4
Wendy Turnbull	11	(1978-1988)	2	1	4	4
Larisa Savchenko Neiland	10	(1988-1996)		3	5	2
Lindsay Davenport	10	(1994-2005)	6	2	1	1
Mary Bevis Hawton	9	(1947-1961)	7	1	1	
Betty Stove	8	(1973-1980)		1	5	2

	TOTAL		Aus.	Fre.	Wim.	U.S
Lisa Raymond	7	(1994-2008)	2	3	1	1
Louise Brough	7	(1947-1954)		1	3	3
Pat Todd	7	(1946-1951)		1	2	4
Pauline Betz	7	(1941-1946)		1	1	5
Shirley Fry	7	(1948-1956)		1	2	4
Claudia Kohde Kilsch	6	(1982-1988)	3	3		
Gigi Fernandez	6	(1991-1997)	2	1	2	1
Helen Jacobs	6	(1931-1939)		1	3	2
Kathy Jordan	6	(1981-1990)		1	4	1
Lesley Turner	6	(1963-1978)	4	1		1
Margaret Osborne duPont	6	(1947-1958)		1	3	2
Pam Shriver	6	(1980-1993)	2		1	3
Virginia Wade	6	(1969-1979)		1	1	4
Virgina Ruano Pascual	6	(2001-2006)	1	2	3	
Paola Suarez	6	(2001-2006)	1	2	3	

Women's Doubles – Titles – Team

	TOTAL		Aus.	Fre.	Wim.	U.S
Louise Brough / Margaret Osborne duPont	20	(1942-1957)		3	5	12
Martina Navratilova / Pam Shiver	20	(1981-1989)	7	4	5	4
Gigi Fernandez / Natalia Zvereva	14	(1992-1997)	2	5	4	3
Doris Hart / Shirley Fry	11	(1950-1954)		4	3	4
Nancye Bolton / Thelma Long	10	(1936-1952)	10			
Venus Williams / Serena Williams	9	(1999-2009)	3	1	4	1
Virginia Ruano Pascual / Paola Suarez	8	(2001-2005)	1	4		3
Billie Jean King / Rosie Casals	7	(1967-1974)			5	2
Sarah Palfrey / Alice Marble	6	(1937-1940)			2	4
Suzanne Lenglen / Elizabeth Ryan	6	(1919-1925)		6		
Darlene Hard / Maria Bueno	5	(1960-1963)		1	2	2
Margaret Smith Court / Judy Dalton	5	(1966-1970)	2	1	1	1
Anne Smith / Kathy Jordan	4	(1980-1981)	1	1	1	1
Helen Wills / Elizabeth Ryan	4	(1927-1932)		2	2	
Jana Novotna / Helena Sukova	4	(1989-1990)	1	1	2	
Margaret Smith Court / Lesley Turner	4	(1964-1965)	1	2	1	
Margaret Smith Court / Virginia Wade	4	(1973-1975)	1	1		2
Renee Schuurman / Sandra Reynolds	4	(1959-1962)	1	3		
Simone Passemard Mathieu / Billie Yorke	4	(1936-1938)		3	1	
Simone Passemard Mathieu /Elizabeth Ryan	4	(1933-1934)		2	2	

Women's Doubles – Final Appearances – Team

	TOTAL		Aus.	Fre.	Wim.	U.S
Louise Brough / Margaret Osborne duPont	25	(1942-1957)		4	7	14
Martina Navratilova / Pam Shiver	23	(1981-1989)	8	4	6	5
Gigi Fernandez / Natalia Zvereva	18	(1992-1997)	3	6	5	4
Doris Hart / Shirley Fry	16	(1949-1955)		4	5	7
Virginia Ruano Pascual / Paola Suarez	14	(2001-2006)	2	6	3	3
Billie Jean King / Rosie Casals	14	(1966-1975)	1	2	5	6
Nancye Bolton / Thelma Long	12	(1936-1952)	12			
Venus Williams / Serena Williams	9	(1999-2009)	3	1	4	1
Anne Smith / Kathy Jordan	8	(1980-1984)	1	2	4	1
Darlene Hard / Maria Bueno	7	(1960-1963)		2	2	3
Arantxa Sanchez Vicario / Jana Novotna	6	(1994-1996)	1	1	2	2

	TOTAL		Aus.	Fre.	Wim.	U.S
Billie Jean King / Karen Hantze Susman	6	(1961-1965)			3	3
Claudia Kohde Kilsch / Helena Sukova	6	(1984-1988)	2	2	1	1
Doris Hart / Pat Canning Todd	6	(1947-1948)		2	2	2
Helen Jacobs / Sarah Palfrey	6	(1932-1936)		1	1	4
Larisa Savchenko Neiland / Natalia Zvereva	6	(1988-1991)		3	3	
Margaret Court Smith / Judy Dalton	6	(1966-1970)	2	1	2	1
Margaret Smith Court / Lesley Turner	6	(1964-1966)	2	2	1	1
Margaret Smith Court / Robyn Ebbern	6	(1962-1964)	3	1	1	1
Margaret Smith Court / Virginia Wade	6	(1969-1975)	1	1		4
Pauline Betz / Doris Hart	6	(1942-1946)		1	1	4
Renee Schuurman / Sandra Reynolds	6	(1959-1962)	1	3	2	
Sarah Palfrey / Alice Marble	6	(1937-1940)			2	4
Suzanne Lenglen / Elizabeth Ryan	6	(1919-1925)		6		

Women's Doubles – Final Losses – Team

	TOTAL		Aus.	Fre.	Wim.	U.S
Billie Jean King / Rosie Casals	7	(1966-1975)	1	2		4
Virginia Ruano Pascual / Paola Suarez	6	(2001-2006)	1	2	3	
Pauline Betz / Doris Hart	6	(1942-1946)		1	1	4
Doris Hart / Shirley Fry	6	(1949-1955)			2	3
Jana Novotna / Larisa Savchenko Neiland	5	(1991-1993)		1	2	2
Lindsay Daveport / Natalie Zvereva	5	(1998-1999)	2	1	1	1
Louise Brough / Margaret Osborne duPont	5	(1947-1954)		1	2	2
Anne Smith / Kathy Jordan	4	(1981-1984)		1	3	
Claudia Kohde Kilsch / Helena Sukova	4	(1984-1988)	2	2		
Doris Hart / Pat Canning Todd	4	(1947-1948)		1	1	2
Francoise Durr / Betty Stove	4	(1973-1975)		1	2	1
Gigi Fernandez / Natalia Zvereva	4	(1995-1997)	1	1	1	1
Larisa Savchenko Neiland / Natalia Zvereva	4	(1988-1991)		2	2	
Rosie Casals / Wendy Turnbull	4	(1980-1983)		1	2	1
Arantxa Sanchez Vicario / Jana Novotna	3	(1994-1996)		1	1	1
Billie Jean King / Karen Hantze Susman	3	(1962-1965)			1	2
Evelyn Colyer / Kitty Godfree	3	(1925-1926)		2	1	
Helen Jacobs / Sarah Palfrey	3	(1934-1936)		1	1	1
Margaret Smith Court / Robyn Ebbern	3	(1963-1964)	1	1	1	
Martina Navratilova / Pam Shriver	4	(1981-1985)	1		1	1
Steffi Graf / Gabriela Sabatini	3	(1986-1989)		3		

Mixed Doubles – Titles – Men

	TOTAL		Aus.	Fre.	Wim.	U.S
Ken Fletcher	10	(1963-1968)	8	7	7	9
Owen Davidson	10	(1966-1974)	1	1	4	4
Frank Sedgman	8	(1949-1952)	2	2	2	2
Vic Seixas	8	(1953-1956)		1	4	3
Mahesh Bhupathi	7	(1997-2009)	2	1	2	2
Bob Bryan	6	(2003-2009)		2	1	3
Bob Hewitt	6	(1961-1979)	1	2	2	1
Fred Stolle	6	(1961-1969)	1		3	2
Mark Woodforde	6	(1992-1996)	2	2	1	1
Marty Riessen	6	(1969-1980)		1	1	4

Mixed Doubles – Final Appearances – Men

	TOTAL		Aus.	Fre.	Wim.	U.S
Todd Woodbridge	14	(1990-2004)	6	1	2	5
Ken Fletcher	12	(1963-1968)	2	3	6	1
Mahesh Bhupathi	11	(1994-2009)	3	3	3	2
Bill Tilden	11	(1913-1930)		2		9
Frank Sedgman	11	(1948-1952)	2	3	3	3
Fred Stolle	11	(1961-1975)	2	3	3	3
Frew McMillan	11	(1966-1981)		1	4	6
John Bromwich	11	(1938-1954)	6		3	2
Owen Davidson	11	(1966-1974)	1	2	4	4
Todd Woodbridge	11	(1990-2001)	5	1	1	4

Mixed Doubles – Final Losses – Men

	TOTAL		Aus.	Fre.	Wim.	U.S
Todd Woodbridge	9	(1992-2004)	5	1	1	2
John Bromwich	7	(1938-1954)	5		1	1
Bill Tilden	6	(1916-1927)		1		5
Frew McMillan	6	(1970-1980)			2	4

Mixed Doubles – Titles – Women

	TOTAL		Aus.	Fre.	Wim.	U.S
Margaret Court Smith	19	(1961-1975)	2	4	5	8
Doris Hart	15	(1949-1955)	2	3	5	5
Billie Jean King	11	(1967-1976)	1	2	4	4
Martina Navratilova	10	(1974-2006)	1	2	4	3
Margaret Osborne duPont	10	(1943-1962)			1	9
Elizabeth Ryan	9	(1919-1933)			7	2
Louise Brough	8	(1942-1950)			4	4

Mixed Doubles – Final Appearances – Women

	TOTAL		Aus.	Fre.	Wim.	U.S
Margaret Smith Court	23	(1961-1975)	3	4	7	9
Doris Hart	19	(1945-1955)	2	4	6	7
Billie Jean King	18	(1966-1983)	1	3	7	7
Martina Navratilova	17	(1974-2006)	4	3	5	5
Elizabeth Ryan	14	(1919-1934)		1	10	3
Margaret Osborne duPont	14	(1943-1962)			2	12
Betty Stove	13	(1971-1981)		2	5	6

Mixed Doubles – Final Losses – Women

	TOTAL		Aus.	Fre.	Wim.	U.S
Martina Navratilova	7	(1974-2006)	3	1	1	2
Betty Stove	7	(1971-1981)		2	3	4
Billie Jean King	7	(1966-1983)		1	3	3
Judy Dalton	7	(1963-1970)	1		2	4
Darlene Hard	6	(1956-1963)	1	1	1	3
Maria Bueno	6	(1958-1967)		1	3	2

Mixed Doubles – Titles – Team

	TOTAL		Aus.	Fre.	Wim.	U.S
Margaret Smith Court / Ken Fletcher	10	(1963-1968)	2	3	4	1
Billie Jean King / Owen Davidson	8	(1967-1974)		1	4	3
Doris Hart / Frank Sedgman	8	(1949-1952)	2	2	2	2
Doris Hart / Vic Seixas	7	(1953-1975)		1	3	3
Margaret Smith Court / Marty Riessen	5	(1969-1975)		1	1	3
Betty Stove / Frew McMillan	4	(1977-1981)			2	2
Jana Novotna / Jim Pugh	4	(1988-1989)	2		1	1
Margaret Osborne duPont / Bill Talbert	4	(1943-1946)				4
Margaret Osborne duPont / Neale Fraser	4	(1958-1962)			1	3
Nancye Bolton / Colin Long	4	(1940-1948)	4			
Neil Hall Hopman / Harry Hopman	4	(1930-1939)	4			

Mixed Doubles – Final Appearances – Team

	TOTAL		Aus.	Fre.	Wim.	U.S
Doris Hart / Frank Sedgman	11	(1948-1952)	2	3	3	3
Margaret Smith Court / Ken Fletcher	11	(1963-1968)	2	3	5	1
Betty Stove / Frew McMillian	9	(1976-1981)			4	5
Billie Jean King / Owen Davidson	9	(1967-1974)		2	4	3
Doris Hart / Vic Seixas	7	(1953-1955)		1	3	3
Lesley Turner / Fred Stolle	7	(1961-1964)	2	3	2	
Margaret Smith Court / Marty Riessen	7	(1969-1975)		1	2	4
Elizabeth Sayer Smylie / John Fitzgerald	6	(1983-1991)			3	3
Francoise Durr / Jean Claude Barclay	6	(1968-1973)		6		
Margaret Osborne duPont / Billie Talbert	6	(1943-1949)				6
Nancye Bolton / Colin Long	6	(1930-1940)	5		1	
Neil Hall Hopman / Harry Hopman	6	(1930-1940)	5		1	

Mixed Doubles – Final Losses – Team

	TOTAL		Aus.	Fre.	Wim.	U.S
Betty Stove / Frew McMillian	5	(1976-1981)			2	3
Elizabeth Sayer Smylie / John Fitzgerald	4	(1984-1990)			2	2
Lesley Turner / Fred Stolle	4	(1962-1964)	1	3		

Australian Championships

Serena Williams won her third women's singles title at the Australian Open in 2007.

Tennis had been played Down Under for 25 years before a national championship was organized in 1905 in Melbourne at the Warehousemen's Ground—this four years after six British Colonies had come together as the Commonwealth of Australia. It was men only at first, as was the case with the U.S. and Wimbledon championships. The tournament was called the Australasian Championships, a cooperative venture with neighboring New Zealand, a country that also shared a Davis Cup team with the Aussies, notably in the person of Kiwi Tony Wilding. Wilding and Aussie Norman Brookes won four Cups for Australasia: 1907-08-09, 14. New Zealand dropped from the alliance after 1922, and in 1927, this event became the Australian Championships.

Strikingly, the first champ in 1905, and 64 years later the first champ of the "Open" era were Rodneys: Rodney Heath, the initial victor over Arthur Curtis, 4-6, 6-3, 6-4, 6-4 in a field of 17; Rodney Laver, 6-3, 6-4, 7-5, over Spaniard Andres Gimeno in a field of 48 at Brisbane in 1969. In 1908, American Fred Alexander was the first foreigner to win the singles and doubles titles–3-6, 3-6, 6-0, 6-2, 6-3 over homeboy Alf Dunlop then joined Dunlop to complete a personal sweep.

Not until 1922 did women enter the picture when 27-year-old Mall Molesworth beat 20-year-old Esna Boyd, 6-3, 10-8, in the final in Sydney. They played alongside the men, except for three separate tournaments, 1980–82. Dorothy Round, in 1935 at Melbourne, was the first female outsider as champion, beating Nancy Lyle in an all-English final, 1-6, 6-1, 6-3. Dorothy Bundy (now a Hall of Famer as Mrs. "Dodo" Cheney), was the first American woman to win, defeating Dorothy Stevenson, 6-3, 6-2, in 1938 at Adelaide. That year, another Yank, Don Budge, launched the original Grand Slam with a 6-4, 6-2, 6-1, victory over John Bromwich.

The courts for the tournament were grass until 1988. Then, a rubberized hard court surface called Rebound Ace complemented the new national tennis complex called Flinders Park (the name changed to Melbourne Park in 1998). Because that pavement became sticky on very hot summer days, it was replaced in 2008 by hard courts called plexicushion, colored blue rather than the customary green.

Though Melbourne has been the site of the tournament since 1972, it moved about often in earlier days among five Australian cities: Brisbane (1907, 15, 23, 56, 60, 64, 69); Sydney (1908, 19, 22, 25, 28, 31, 34, 37, 40, 47, 51, 54, 58, 62, 66, 70-71); Perth (1909, 13, 21); Adelaide (1910, 20, 26, 29, 32, 36, 38, 46, 49, 52, 55, 59, 63, 67); Melbourne (1911, 14, 24, 27, 30, 33, 35, 39, 48, 50, 53, 57, 61, 65, 68); and two in New Zealand: Christchurch (1906); Hastings (1912). Melbourne was the most successful host after the Kooyong Lawn Tennis Club erected a 12,000 seat concrete horseshoe in 1927. Stadia at White City, Sydney (1922), Memorial Drive, Adelaide (1920), and Milton Courts, Brisbane, were other prominent locations.

Australia, lagging behind the other three majors in prestige, interest, prize money and player fields, needed a lift and got a tremendous one in 1988 with the christening of the attractive new playpen, Flinders/Melbourne Park. Modernity took over. Suddenly the Australian was the style-setter with a retract-able roof for the principal stadium (named Rod Laver Arena in 1992), seating 14,820. In 2000, another such arena was added, the Vodafone Arena seating 11,000 and also with a retractable roof. The Aussies were ahead of the game with no bothersome rain-outs, nor TV networks stalled with nothing live to show. Strangely (obtusely?), Wimbledon and the U.S. weren't respective copycats when the new Court 1 and Ashe Stadium were opened, respectively, in 1997.

Abandoned, as a big-time stop on the tour as Forest Hills had been in 1978, famed Kooyong (using temporary stands to pack in 17,500 for the 1953 Davis Cup final) settled into a comfortable private club existence. An attendance record (140,000) was set for Kooyong's farewell to the Open, 1987. That was quickly surpassed at Melbourne Park. In 2008, the event drew a record 605,735 fans.

Two championships were held in 1977 when the tournament moved from January to December dates, and no event was held in 1986 to readjust to the traditional January date. The tie-breaker was adopted in 1971, not in force for ultimate sets, the fifth for men, third for women.

Showing some reluctance in joining the "Open" era, the Australian was the last of the three majors to take the plunge, remaining amateur in 1968, then integrating with $25,000 in prize money the following year. That figure accelerated to $18,813,400 in 2008, prize money equally paid the women since 2001. Laver got $5,000 as the 1969 champ, Margaret Smith Court $1,500, a pittance compared with $1,217,930 in 2008 with singles winners Novak Djokovic and Maria Sharapova winning just shy of $1.2 million. The event's championship cups honor the memory of two bygone champs, both Australian, Daphne Akhurst for the women and Norman Brookes for the men. Alas for the citizenry, no homebody has clung to that silver since Chris O'Neil in 1978 and Mark Edmondson in 1976.

Australian Championships — Tournament Results

Legend: F: Final; S: Semifinal; Q: Quarterfinal; Set: S1, S2, S3, S4, S5

Men's Singles

Rd	Winner	Defeated	S1	S2	S3	S4	S5
1905 (MELBOURNE)							
F	Rodney Heath (AUS)	Arthur Curtis (AUS)	4-6	6-3	6-4	6-4	
S	Rodney Heath (AUS)	Randolph Lycett (GBR)	6-3	9-11	6-3	6-1	
S	Arthur Curtis (AUS)	Alf Dunlop (AUS)	4-6	11-9	6-3	6-4	
Q	Rodney Heath (AUS)	Herbert Turner (AUS)	6-2	6-1	6-2		
Q	Randolph Lycett (GBR)	Gordon Wright (AUS)	(walkover)				
Q	Arthur Curtis (AUS)	Eric Pockley (AUS)	3-6	7-5	6-3	6-4	
Q	Alf Dunlop (AUS)	Reggie Fraser (AUS)	6-4	6-3	6-2		
1906 (CHRISTCHURCH, N.Z.)							
F	Anthony Wilding (NZL)	Francis Fisher (AUS)	6-0	6-4	6-4		
S	Anthony Wilding (NZL)	Harry Parker (AUS)	6-4	7-5	3-6	6-0	
S	Francis Fisher (AUS)	T.R. Quill (AUS)	6-4	3-6	6-2	6-3	
Q	Anthony Wilding (NZL)	Charles Cecil Cox (AUS)	6-2	6-2	6-1		
Q	Harry Parker (AUS)	R. D. Harman (AUS)	6-1	6-2	6-0		
Q	Francis Fisher (AUS)	Rodney Heath (AUS)	2-6	7-5	6-1	5-7	6-2
Q	T.R. Quill (AUS)	William Goss (AUS)	(walkover)				
1907 (BRISBANE)							
F	Horrie Rice (AUS)	Harry Parker (AUS)	6-3	6-4	6-4		
S	Horrie Rice (AUS)	Bill Gregg (AUS)	6-0	6-2	3-6	6-4	
S	Harry Parker (AUS)	Eric Pockley (AUS)	8-6	6-0	2-6	6-3	
Q	Horrie Rice (AUS)	Macauley Turner (AUS)	4-6	6-1	6-0	6-3	
Q	Bill Gregg (AUS)	Mr. Turton (AUS)	6-2	2-6	6-2	2-6	7-5
Q	Harry Parker (AUS)	William Rudder (AUS)	6-1	6-1	6-3		
Q	Eric Pockley (AUS)	George Wright (AUS)	8-6	6-2	7-5		
1908 (SYDNEY)							
F	Fred Alexander (USA)	Alfred Dunlop (AUS)	3-6	3-6	6-0	6-2	6-3
S	Fred Alexander (USA)	Harry Parker (AUS)	6-3	8-6	1-6	6-0	
S	Alfred Dunlop (AUS)	Eric Pockley (AUS)	6-2	6-3	6-2		
Q	Fred Alexander (USA)	Harry Gibbes (AUS)	6-2	6-1	6-1		
Q	Harry Parker (AUS)	Mr. Cupples (AUS)	6-1	6-3	6-2		
Q	Alfred Dunlop (AUS)	Stanley Doust (AUS)	6-3	6-4	4-6	8-6	
Q	Eric Pockley (AUS)	Percy Colquhoum (AUS)	7-5	1-6	7-5	7-5	
1909 (PERTH)							
F	Anthony Wilding (NZL)	Ernest Parker (AUS)	6-1	7-5	6-2		
S	Anthony Wilding (NZL)	Ronald Kelsey (AUS)	6-0	6-0	6-1		
S	Ernest Parker (AUS)	G.M. O'Dea (AUS)	6-1	6-2	6-0		
Q	Anthony Wilding (NZL)	R. Eagle (AUS)	6-0	6-1	6-0		
Q	Ronald Kelsey (AUS)	Ivan Gibbs (AUS)	6-4	6-4	2-1	(retired)	
Q	Ernest Parker (AUS)	Ian Gaze (AUS)	6-1	6-0	6-0		
Q	G.M. O'Dea (AUS)	Tom Crooks (AUS)	3-6	6-3	6-4	6-3	
1910 (ADELAIDE)							
F	Rodney Heath (AUS)	Horrie Rice (AUS)	6-4	6-3	6-2		
S	Rodney Heath (AUS)	R. Reid (AUS)	6-0	6-3	7-5		
S	Horrie Rice (AUS)	R. Bowen (AUS)	6-3	6-1	6-3	7-5	
Q	Rodney Heath (AUS)	Harry Parker (AUS)	6-2	6-4	9-7		
Q	R. Reid (AUS)	Robert Paxton (AUS)	6-0	6-3	6-1		
Q	Horrie Rice (AUS)	Ashley Campbell (AUS)	6-2	6-2	4-6	6-2	
Q	R. Bowen (AUS)	Harold Hunt (AUS	11-9	6-4	6-3		
1911 (MELBOURNE)							
F	Norman Brookes (AUS)	Horrie Rice (AUS)	6-1	6-2	6-3		
S	Norman Brookes (AUS)	Ron Rolland (AUS)	7-5	6-3	6-1		
S	Horrie Rice (AUS)	Arthur O'Hara Wood (AUS)	7-5	6-3	2-6	6-1	
Q	Norman Brookes (AUS)	Rodney Heath (AUS)	4-6	6-4	6-2	6-3	
Q	Ron Rolland (AUS)	F. Down (AUS)	6-3	6-4	6-3		
Q	Horrie Rice (AUS)	Ron Thomas (AUS)	6-1	6-4	6-3		
Q	Arthur O'Hara Wood (AUS)	S. England (AUS)	6-1	6-2	6-3		
1912 (HASTINGS, N.Z.)							
F	Jim Parke (IRL)	Alfred Beamish (GBR)	3-6	6-3	1-6	6-1	7-5
S	Jim Parke (IRL)	R. Swanston (AUS)	6-2	6-2	6-3		
S	Alfred Beamish (GBR)	H. Brown (AUS)	6-1	6-1	6-2		
Q	Jim Parke (IRL)	Geoff Ollivier (AUS)	6-4	6-1	8-6		
Q	R. Swanston (AUS)	W. Pearce (AUS)	6-2	6-1	6-2		
Q	Alfred Beamish (GBR)	Charles Dixon (AUS)	4-6	3-6	6-2	7-5	6-1
Q	H. Brown (AUS)	R. Harman (AUS)	6-4	6-1	6-3		
1913 (PERTH)							
F	Ernest Parker (AUS)	Harry Parker (AUS)	2-6	6-1	6-3	6-2	
S	Ernest Parker (AUS)	Geoff Thomas (AUS)	6-2	6-2	6-3		
S	Harry Parker (NZL)	Ron Taylor (AUS)	6-2	4-6	2-6	6-0	6-1
Q	Ernest Parker (AUS)	Edward Stokes (AUS)	6-4	6-3	6-2		
Q	Geoff Thomas (AUS)	Mr. Kent (AUS)	3-6	6-3	6-4	6-0	
Q	Harry Parker ((NZL)	Alf Hedemann (AUS)	2-6	6-3	6-1	6-3	
Q	Ron Taylor (AUS)	Arnold Leschen (AUS)	6-4	6-1	6-1		
1914 (MELBOURNE)							
F	Arthur O'Hara Wood (AUS)	Gerald Patterson (AUS)	6-4	6-3	5-7	6-1	
S	Arthur O'Hara Wood (AUS)	Rupert Wertheim (AUS)	6-3	6-0	3-6	6-4	
S	Gerald Patterson (AUS)	Rodney Heath (AUS)	6-3	6-2	6-4		
Q	Arthur O'Hara Wood (AUS)	Clarence Buckley (AUS)	6-4	6-2	6-3		
Q	Rupert Wertheim (AUS)	Ron Taylor (AUS)	6-3	6-4	3-6	6-3	
Q	Gerald Patterson (AUS)	L. Rainey (AUS)	6-3	6-4	6-2		
Q	Rodney Heath (AUS)	Ron Thomas (AUS)	6-1	3-6	6-2	6-3	

1915 (BRISBANE)

Rd	Winner	Defeated	S1	S2	S3	S4	S5
F	Gordon Lowe (GBR)	Horrie Rice (AUS)	4-6	6-1	6-1	6-4	
S	Gordon Lowe (GBR)	Bert St. John (AUS)	3-6	6-3	7-5	7-5	
S	Horrie Rice (AUS)	Clarrie Todd (AUS)	4-6	2-6	8-6	6-1	7-5
Q	Gordon Lowe (GBR)	R. Highett (AUS)	6-3	6-2	6-3		
Q	Bert St. John (AUS)	R. Goodman (AUS)	6-3	6-3	6-2		
Q	Clarie Todd (AUS)	W. Smith (AUS)	6-2	6-3	6-2		
Q	Horrie Rice (AUS)	F. Lendrum (AUS)	6-3	6-2	6-3		

1916-18 NOT HELD—WW I

1919 (SYDNEY)

Rd	Winner	Defeated	S1	S2	S3	S4	S5
F	Algernon Kingscote (GBR)	Eric Pockley (AUS)	6-4	6-0	6-3		
S	Algernon Kingscote (GBR)	James Anderson (AUS)	3-6	7-5	6-4	6-3	
S	Eric Pockley (AUS)	Arthur Lowe (GBR)	6-4	6-3	6-1		
Q	Algernon Kingscote (GBR)	Alfred Beamish (GBR)	(walkover)				
Q	James Anderson (AUS)	Henry Marsh (AUS)	6-1	6-8	6-4	6-3	
Q	Arthur Lowe (GBR)	Pat O'Hara Wood (AUS)	6-3	6-2	6-2		
Q	Eric Pockley (AUS)	L. Darby (AUS)	6-3	6-4	6-0		

1920 (ADELAIDE)

Rd	Winner	Defeated	S1	S2	S3	S4	S5
F	Pat O'Hara Wood (AUS)	Ron Thomas (AUS)	6-3	4-6	6-8	6-1	6-3
S	Pat O'Hara Wood (AUS)	Ron Taylor (AUS)	6-3	6-1	7-5		
S	Ron Thomas (AUS)	Horrie Rice (AUS)	6-4	4-6	6-1	5-7	6-2
Q	Pat O'Hara Wood (AUS)	B. Utz (AUS)	6-1	6-1	6-2		
Q	Ron Taylor (AUS)	A. Scott (AUS)	3-6	3-6	6-2	6-2	6-3
Q	Horrie Rice (AUS)	C. Gurner (AUS)	6-2	6-2	6-2		
Q	Ron Thomas (AUS)	G. O'Dea (AUS)	6-0	6-2	6-4		

1921 (PERTH)

Rd	Winner	Defeated	S1	S2	S3	S4	S5
F	Rice Gemmell (AUS)	Alf Hedemann (AUS)	7-5	6-1	6-4		
S	Rice Gemmell (AUS)	Roy Treolar (AUS)	6-2	6-1	6-3		
S	Alf Hedemann (AUS)	Mr. McDougall (AUS)	6-4	3-6	6-1	6-2	
Q	Rice Gemmell (AUS)	E. Barker (AUS)	6-0	6-3	6-0		
Q	Roy Treolar (AUS)	Mr. Henville (AUS)	6-3	6-2	6-2		
Q	Mr. McDougall (AUS)	W. Hayman (AUS)	2-6	12-10	6-2	6-0	
Q	Alf Hedemann (AUS)	N. Brearley (AUS)	6-2	6-1	6-3		

1922 (SYDNEY)

Rd	Winner	Defeated	S1	S2	S3	S4	S5
F	James Anderson (AUS)	Gerald Patterson (AUS)	6-0	3-6	3-6	6-3	6-2
S	James Anderson (AUS)	Norman Peach (AUS)	1-6	6-2	6-2	6-4	
S	Gerald Patterson (AUS)	Jack Hawkes (AUS)	8-6	4-6	7-5	3-6	10-8
Q	James Anderson (AUS)	W. Dive (AUS)	7-5	6-4	6-3		
Q	Norman Peach (AUS)	Jack Clemenger (AUS)	6-1	6-1	9-7		
Q	Jack Hawkes (AUS)	A. Huthnance (AUS)	(walkover)				
Q	Gerald Patterson (AUS)	E. Jones (AUS)	6-4	5-7	6-1	10-8	

1923 (BRISBANE)

Rd	Winner	Defeated	S1	S2	S3	S4	S5
F	Pat O'Hara Wood (AUS)	Bert St. John (AUS)	6-1	6-1	6-3		
S	Pat O'Hara Wood (AUS)	E. Jordan (AUS)	6-1	6-1	6-1		
S	Bert St. John (AUS)	Horrie Rice (AUS)	9-7	3-6	7-5	6-3	
Q	Pat O'Hara Wood (AUS)	Mr. Cory (AUS)	6-0	6-4	6-1		
Q	E. Jordan (AUS)	L. Oxenham (AUS)	5-7	3-6	6-3	6-4	7-5
Q	Horrie Rice (AUS)	C. Ferguson (AUS)	6-2	6-2	6-2		
Q	Bert St. John (AUS)	Dudley Bullough (AUS)	6-4	6-2	6-2		

1924 (MELBOURNE)

Rd	Winner	Defeated	S1	S2	S3	S4	S5
F	James Anderson (AUS)	Bob Schlesinger (AUS)	6-3	6-4	3-6	5-7	6-3
S	James Anderson (AUS)	Gar Hone (AUS)	6-2	6-3	6-2		
S	Bob Schlesinger (AUS)	Fred Kalmus (AUS)	7-5	8-6	6-0		
Q	James Anderson (AUS)	Cecil Stuart (AUS)	8-6	6-1	6-2		
Q	Gar Hone (AUS)	G. Dickinson (AUS)	7-5	6-0	6-4		
Q	Fred Kalmus (AUS)	Rupert Wertheim (AUS)	5-7	5-7	6-1	6-1	8-6
Q	Bob Schlesinger (AUS)	Ian McInness (AUS)	5-7	6-3	6-3	9-7	

1925 (SYDNEY)

Rd	Winner	Defeated	S1	S2	S3	S4	S5
F	James Anderson (AUS)	Gerald Patterson (AUS)	11-9	2-6	6-2	6-3	
S	James Anderson (AUS)	Pat O'Hara Wood (AUS)	6-2	6-3	6-3		
S	Gerald Patterson (AUS)	Bob Schlesinger (AUS)	6-4	6-4	4-6	6-4	
Q	James Anderson (AUS)	Gar Hone (AUS)	6-2	6-0	8-6		
Q	Pat O'Hara Wood (AUS)	Fred Kalmus (AUS)	6-3	6-2	6-3		
Q	Bob Schlesinger (AUS)	Norman Peach (AUS)	6-3	6-2	6-2		
Q	Gerald Patterson (AUS)	Aubrey Willard (AUS)	6-0	6-2	9-7		

1926 (ADELAIDE)

Rd	Winner	Defeated	S1	S2	S3	S4	S5
F	Jack Hawkes (AUS)	Jim Willard (AUS)	6-1	6-3	6-1		
S	Jack Hawkes (AUS)	James Anderson (AUS)	6-8	7-5	6-3	6-4	
S	Jim Willard (AUS)	Bob Schlesinger (AUS)	3-6	6-3	6-0	6-4	
Q	Jack Hawkes (AUS)	Gar Hone (AUS)	4-6	6-0	6-2	6-2	
Q	James Anderson (AUS)	Pat O'Hara Wood (AUS)	6-3	6-2	3-6	6-2	
Q	Bob Schlesinger (AUS)	Norman Peach (AUS)	6-4	6-1	5-7	6-3	
Q	Jim Willard (AUS)	Ernest Rowe (AUS)	6-3	6-1	0-6	6-1	

1927 (MELBOURNE)

Rd	Winner	Defeated	S1	S2	S3	S4	S5
F	Gerald Patterson (AUS)	Jack Hawkes (AUS)	3-6	6-4	3-6	18-16	6-3
S	Jack Hawkes (AUS)	Gar Moon (AUS)	6-3	6-3	9-7		
S	Gerald Patterson (AUS)	Jim Willard (AUS)	6-0	4-6	6-2	6-1	
Q	Gerald Patterson (AUS)	Bob Schlesinger (AUS)	6-2	6-3	2-6	6-2	
Q	Gar Moon (AUS)	Jack Crawford (AUS)	2-6	9-11	8-6	6-3	8-6
Q	Jim Willard (AUS)	Gordon Lum (CHN)	6-2	6-0	6-4		
Q	Jack Hawkes (AUS)	Alan Coldham (AUS)	6-4	6-0	6-1		

1928 (SYDNEY)

Rd	Winner	Defeated	S1	S2	S3	S4	S5
F	Jean Borotra (FRA)	Jack Cummings (AUS)	6-4	6-1	4-6	5-7	6-3
S	Jean Borotra (FRA)	Jack Crawford (AUS)	4-6	6-3	1-6	7-5	6-4
S	Jack Cummings (AUS)	Bob Schlesinger (AUS)	6-1	2-6	6-4	8-6	
Q	Jean Borotra (FRA)	Harry Hopman (AUS)	6-4	6-4	6-3		
Q	Jack Crawford (AUS)	Jack Hawkes (AUS)	6-2	8-6	6-3		
Q	Jack Cummings (AUS)	Fred Kalmus (AUS)	4-6	2-6	6-3	8-6	6-1
Q	Bob Schlesinger (AUS)	Gerald Patterson (AUS)	6-4	7-9	6-4	(retired)	

1929 (ADELAIDE)

Rd	Winner	Defeated	S1	S2	S3	S4	S5
F	Colin Gregory (GBR)	Bob Schlesinger (AUS)	6-2	6-2	5-7	7-5	
S	Colin Gregory (GBR)	Gar Moon (AUS)	6-1	7-5	6-2		
S	Bob Schlesinger (AUS)	Harry Hopman (AUS)	6-2	6-1	0-6	6-2	
Q	Colin Gregory (GBR)	Ernest Rowe (AUS)	6-4	6-2	6-4		
Q	Gar Moon (AUS)	Bunny Austin (GBR)	2-6	5-7	6-1	6-2	6-4
Q	Harry Hopman (AUS)	Pat O'Hara Wood (AUS)	6-2	11-9	7-5		
Q	Bob Schlesinger (AUS)	Jack Crawford (AUS)	6-2	6-3	2-6	6-4	

1930 (MELBOURNE)

Rd	Winner	Defeated	S1	S2	S3	S4	S5
F	Gar Moon (AUS)	Harry Hopman (AUS)	6-3	6-1	6-3		
S	Gar Moon (AUS)	Jack Crawford (AUS) (AUS)	7-5	6-4	4-6	6-3	
S	Harry Hopman (AUS)	Jim Willard (AUS)	6-4	6-2	6-0		
Q	Gar Moon (AUS)	Jack Cummings (AUS)	6-4	6-2	6-2		
Q	Jack Crawford (AUS)	Cliff Sproule (AUS)	6-3	6-2	6-1		
Q	Jim Willard (AUS)	Bob Schlesinger (AUS)	2-6	6-1	10-8	6-2	
Q	Harry Hopman (AUS)	Jack Clemenger (AUS)	4-6	6-2	3-6	7-5	6-3

1931 (SYDNEY)

Rd	Winner	Defeated	S1	S2	S3	S4	S5
F	Jack Crawford (AUS)	Harry Hopman (AUS)	9-4	6-2	2-6	6-1	
S	Jack Crawford (AUS)	Don Turnbull (AUS)	6-2	6-2	12-10		
S	Harry Hopman (AUS)	Jack Cummings (AUS)	8-2	6-2	6-4		
Q	Jack Crawford (AUS)	Cliff Sproule (AUS)	6-0	3-6	6-0	6-3	
Q	Don Turnbull (AUS)	Gar Moon (AUS)	9-7	2-6	6-3	4-6	6-2
Q	Jack Cummings (AUS)	Harry Hassett (AUS)	6-2	6-2	6-4		
Q	Harry Hopman (AUS)	Aubrey Willard (AUS)	5-7	6-3	6-4	6-4	

1932 (ADELAIDE)

Rd	Winner	Defeated	S1	S2	S3	S4	S5
F	Jack Crawford (AUS)	Harry Hopman (AUS)	4-6	6-3	3-6	6-3	6-1
S	Jack Crawford (AUS)	Cliff Sproule (AUS)	6-4	2-6	6-2	6-1	
S	Harry Hopman (AUS)	Jiro Satoh (JPN)	0-6	6-2	6-3	4-6	6-4
Q	Jack Crawford (AUS)	Ryosuki Nunoi (JPN)	3-6	7-5	6-4	6-1	
Q	Cliff Sproule (AUS)	Jim Willard (AUS)	6-4	6-2	8-6		
Q	Jiro Satoh (JPN)	Viv McGrath (AUS)	6-3	6-3	6-2		
Q	Harry Hopman (AUS)	Aubrey Willard (AUS)	12-10	6-3	8-6		

1933 (MELBOURNE)

Rd	Winner	Defeated	S1	S2	S3	S4	S5
F	Jack Crawford (AUS)	Keith Gledhill (USA)	2-6	7-5	6-3	6-2	
S	Keith Gledhill (USA)	Viv McGrath (AUS)	6-4	6-1	6-1		
S	Jack Crawford (AUS)	Wilmer Allison (USA)	6-3	3-6	3-6	6-0	6-3
Q	Viv McGrath (AUS)	Ellsworth Vines (USA)	6-3	2-6	8-6	7-5	
Q	Keith Gledhill (USA)	Harry Hopman (AUS)	3-6	2-6	8-6	6-20	6-3
Q	Jack Crawford (AUS)	Don Turnbull (AUS)	6-1	6-3	6-2		
Q	Wilmer Allison (USA)	Adrian Quist (AUS)	1-6	3-6	9-7	6-2	6-2

1934 (SYDNEY)

Rd	Winner	Defeated	S1	S2	S3	S4	S5
F	Fred Perry (GBR)	Jack Crawford (AUS)	6-3	7-5	6-1		
S	Jack Crawford (AUS)	Adrian Quist (AUS)	6-4	6-2	6-2		
S	Fred Perry (GBR)	Viv McGrath (AUS)	2-6	5-7	6-4	6-4	6-1
Q	Jack Crawford (AUS)	Harold G.N. Lee (GBR)	6-2	7-5	3-6	6-2	
Q	Adrian Quist (AUS)	Gar Moon (AUS)	6-3	6-3	6-1		
Q	Fred Perry (GBR)	Harry Hopman (AUS)	6-3	6-4	6-3		
Q	Viv McGrath (AUS)	Don Turnbull (AUS)	6-4	6-3	6-3		

1935 (MELBOURNE)

Rd	Winner	Defeated	S1	S2	S3	S4	S5
F	Jack Crawford (AUS)	Fred Perry (GBR)	2-6	6-4	6-4	6-4	
S	Fred Perry (GBR)	Viv McGrath (AUS)	6-2	6-3	6-1		
S	Jack Crawford (AUS)	Adrian Quist (AUS)	6-1	1-6	6-2	3-6	6-3
Q	Fred Perry (GBR)	Giorgio de Stefani (ITA)	6-0	6-0	6-0		
Q	Viv McGrath (AUS)	Don Turnbull (AUS)	9-7	5-7	6-4	2-6	6-3
Q	Jack Crawford (AUS)	Gar Moon (AUS)	6-0	10-8	6-2		
Q	Adrian Quist (AUS)	Roderich Menzel (CZE)	6-1	6-3	8-10	1-6	6-1

1936 (ADELAIDE)

Rd	Winner	Defeated	S1	S2	S3	S4	S5
F	Adrian Quist (AUS)	Jack Crawford (AUS)	6-2	6-3	4-6	3-6	-97
S	Adrian Quist (AUS)	Harry Hopman (AUS)	4-6	6-2	10-8	6-3	
S	Jack Crawford (AUS)	Abe Kay (AUS)	6-2	9-7	6-2		
Q	Adrian Quist (AUS)	John Bromwich (AUS)	6-1	6-4	6-1		
Q	Harry Hopman (AUS)	Viv McGrath (AUS)	6-3	0-6	6-3	7-5	
Q	Abe Kay (AUS)	Don Turnbull (AUS)	6-3	6-4	3-6	7-5	
Q	Jack Crawford (AUS)	Gar Moon (AUS)	6-2	6-3	9-7		

1937 (SYDNEY)

Rd	Winner	Defeated	S1	S2	S3	S4	S5
F	Viv McGrath (AUS)	John Bromwich (AUS)	6-3	1-6	6-0	2-6	6-1
S	John Bromwich (AUS)	Jack Crawford (AUS)	6-1	7-9	6-4	8-6	
S	Viv McGrath (AUS)	Harry Hopman (AUS)	6-4	6-1	7-5		
Q	Jack Crawford (AUS)	Leonard Schwartz (AUS)	6-3	2-6	3-6	6-2	6-3
Q	John Bromwich (AUS)	Don Turnbull (AUS)	6-2	6-2	6-0		
Q	Viv McGrath (AUS)	Abe Kay (AUS)	6-2	6-2	8-6		
Q	Harry Hopman (AUS)	Adrian Quist (AUS)	11-9	3-6	7-5	6-3	

1938 (ADELAIDE)

Rd	Winner	Defeated	S1	S2	S3	S4	S5
F	Don Budge (USA)	John Bromwich (AUS)	6-4	6-2	6-1		
S	John Bromwich (AUS)	Gottfried von Cramm (GER)	6-3	7-5	6-1		
S	Don Budge (USA)	Adrian Quist (AUS)	6-4	6-2	8-6		
Q	Gottfried von Cramm (GER)	Viv McGrath (AUS)	6-2	3-6	4-6	7-5	6-0
Q	John Bromwich (AUS)	Gene Mako (USA)	6-4	7-5	6-2		
Q	Don Budge (USA)	Leonard Schwartz (AUS)	6-4	6-3	10-8		
Q	Adrian Quist (AUS)	George Holland (AUS)	5-7	6-4	6-1	6-2	

1939 (MELBOURNE)

Rd	Winner	Defeated	S1	S2	S3	S4	S5
F	John Bromwich (AUS)	Adrian Quist (AUS)	6-4	6-1	6-2		
S	John Bromwich (AUS)	Viv McGrath (AUS)	6-0	6-3	6-4		
S	Adrian Quist (AUS)	Jack Crawford (AUS)	6-1	7-5	6-3		
Q	John Bromwich (AUS)	Don Turnbull (AUS)	7-5	6-1	6-0		
Q	Viv McGrath (AUS)	Harry Hopman (AUS)	6-1	4-6	6-4	6-3	
Q	Jack Crawford (AUS)	Jim Gilchrist (AUS)	4-6	6-4	2-6	6-3	6-4
Q	Adrian Quist (AUS)	Lionel Brodie (AUS)	6-3	6-2	6-8	6-3	

1940 (SYDNEY)

Rd	Winner	Defeated	S1	S2	S3	S4	S5
F	Adrian Quist (AUS)	Jack Crawford (AUS)	6-3	6-1	6-2		
S	Jack Crawford (AUS)	John Bromwich (AUS)	6-4	6-1	9-7		
S	Adrian Quist (AUS)	Viv McGrath (AUS)	6-4	10-8	6-3		
Q	John Bromwich (AUS)	Dinny Pails (AUS)	7-5	6-0	6-0		
Q	Jack Crawford (AUS)	Max Newcombe (AUS)	6-3	6-0	7-5		
Q	Adrian Quist (AUS)	Bill Sidwell (AUS)	6-3	11-13	6-3	6-2	
Q	Viv McGrath (AUS)	Harry Hopman (AUS)	6-8	6-1	7-5	6-2	

1941-45 NOT HELD —WW II

1946 (ADELAIDE)

Rd	Winner	Defeated	S1	S2	S3	S4	S5
F	John Bromwich (AUS)	Dinny Pails (AUS)	5-7	6-3	7-5	3-6	6-2
S	John Bromwich (AUS)	Geoff Brown (AUS)	6-3	6-2	6-1		
S	Dinny Pails (AUS)	Adrian Quist (AUS)	6-2	6-4	6-2		
Q	John Bromwich (AUS)	Jack Harper (AUS)	6-1	6-2	6-1		
Q	Geoff Brown (AUS)	Harry Hopman (AUS)	4-6	6-4	6-3	6-2	
Q	Adrian Quist (AUS)	Max Bonner (AUS)	6-0	8-6	3-6	6-2	
Q	Dinny Pails (AUS)	Lionel Brodie (AUS)	6-2	6-2	6-0		

1947 (SYDNEY)

Rd	Winner	Defeated	S1	S2	S3	S4	S5
F	Dinny Pails (AUS)	John Bromwich (AUS)	4-6	6-4	3-6	7-5	8-6
S	Dinny Pails (AUS)	Tom Brown (USA)	6-2	6-4	6-1		
S	John Bromwich (AUS)	Gardnar Mulloy (USA)	6-2	6-4	1-6	6-4	
Q	Dinny Pails (AUS)	Bill Sidwell (AUS)	6-3	10-8	6-3		
Q	Tom Brown (USA)	Adrian Quist (AUS)	8-6	6-4	5-7	6-2	
Q	John Bromwich (AUS)	Colin Long (AUS)	6-2	7-5	4-6	6-0	
Q	Gardnar Mulloy (USA)	Lionel Brodie (AUS)	6-2	6-8	6-2	5-7	6-1

1948 (MELBOURNE)

Rd	Winner	Defeated	S1	S2	S3	S4	S5
F	Adrian Quist (AUS)	John Bromwich (AUS)	6-4	3-6	6-3	2-6	6-3
S	John Bromwich (AUS)	Geoff Brown (AUS)	3-6	2-6	6-4	6-4	7-5
S	Adrian Quist (AUS)	Bill Sidwell (AUS)	6-1	6-2	1-6	6-3	
Q	John Bromwich (AUS)	Frank Sedgman (AUS)	6-2	6-4	6-4		
Q	Geoff Brown (AUS)	Eddie Moylan (USA)	7-5	6-2	2-6	7-5	
Q	Bill Sidwell (AUS)	Colin Long (AUS)	6-2	5-7	6-2	6-0	
Q	Adrian Quist (AUS)	Robert McCarthy (AUS)	6-3	6-2	6-3		

1949 (ADELAIDE)

Rd	Winner	Defeated	S1	S2	S3	S4	S5
F	Frank Sedgman (AUS)	John Bromwich (AUS)	6-3	6-2	6-2		
S	Frank Sedgman (AUS)	Bill Sidwell (AUS)	6-3	6-3	6-2		
S	John Bromwich (AUS)	Geoff Brown (AUS)	1-6	6-3	6-3	6-3	
Q	Bill Sidwell (AUS)	Tom Warhurst (AUS)	6-3	6-1	4-6	6-4	
Q	Frank Sedgman (AUS)	Adrian Quist (AUS)	6-2	4-6	6-4	6-4	
Q	Geoff Brown (AUS)	George Worthington (USA)	6-1	6-3	4-6	6-1	
Q	John Bromwich (AUS)	Colin Long (AUS)	6-4	6-4	1-6	6-2	

1950 (ADELAIDE)

Rd	Winner	Defeated	S1	S2	S3	S4	S5
F	Frank Sedgman (AUS)	Ken McGregor (AUS)	6-3	6-4	4-6	6-1	
S	Ken McGregor (AUS)	Bill Sidwell (AUS)	7-5	9-7	6-3		
S	Frank Sedgman (AUS)	Eric Sturgess (RSA)	6-2	6-3	6-8	4-6	6-4
Q	Ken McGregor (AUS)	George Worthington (AUS)	6-3	8-6	6-1		
Q	Bill Sidwell (AUS)	Colin Long (AUS)	7-5	7-5	7-5		
Q	Frank Sedgman (AUS)	John Bromwich (AUS)	5-7	6-3	6-4	6-1	
Q	Eric Sturgess (RSA)	Merv Rose (AUS)	7-5	6-4	6-1		

1951 (SYDNEY)

Rd	Winner	Defeated	S1	S2	S3	S4	S5
F	Richard Savitt (USA)	Ken McGregor (AUS)	6-3	2-6	6-3	6-1	
S	Richard Savitt (USA)	Frank Sedgman (AUS)	2-6	7-5	1-6	6-3	6-4
S	Ken McGregor (AUS)	Art Larsen (USA)	6-2	6-2	5-7	6-1	
Q	Frank Sedgman (AUS)	George Worthington (USA)	6-2	7-5	6-0		
Q	Richard Savitt (USA)	John Bromwich (AUS)	6-4	6-3	6-1		
Q	Art Larsen (USA)	Merv Rose (AUS)	6-2	3-6	5-7	6-4	6-2
Q	Ken McGregor (AUS)	Adrian Quist (AUS)	8-6	6-2	7-5		

1952 (ADELAIDE)

Rd	Winner	Defeated	S1	S2	S3	S4	S5
F	Ken McGregor (AUS)	Frank Sedgman (AUS)	7-5	12-10	2-6	6-2	
S	Ken McGregor (AUS)	Dick Savitt (USA)	6-4	6-4	3-6	6-4	
S	Frank Sedgman (AUS)	Merv Rose (AUS)	6-2	6-4	6-2		
Q	Dick Savitt (USA)	Ian Ayre (AUS)	6-1	6-4	5-7	4-6	6-4
Q	Ken McGregor (AUS)	Geoff Brown (AUS)	6-4	6-2	12-10		
Q	Merv Rose (AUS)	Ken Rosewall (AUS)	6-4	6-4	5-7	2-6	6-2
Q	Frank Sedgman (AUS)	Don Candy (AUS)	7-5	6-1	6-4		

1953 (MELBOURNE)

Rd	Winner	Defeated	S1	S2	S3	S4	S5
F	Ken Rosewall (AUS)	Merv Rose (AUS)	6-0	6-3	6-4		
S	Merv Rose (AUS)	Ian Ayre (AUS)	4-6	4-6	6-1	6-4	6-4
S	Ken Rosewall (AUS)	Vic Seixas (USA)	6-3	2-6	7-5	6-4	
Q	Merv Rose (AUS)	Hamilton Richardson (USA)	8-10	6-4	1-6	8-6	
Q	Ian Ayre (AUS)	Clive Wilderspin (AUS)	6-4	11-9	1-6	8-6	
Q	Vic Seixas (USA)	Geoff Brown (AUS)	6-4	6-4	7-5		
Q	Ken Rosewall (AUS)	Straight Clark (USA)	6-4	6-4	6-2		

1954 (SYDNEY)

Rd	Winner	Defeated	S1	S2	S3	S4	S5
F	Merv Rose (AUS)	Rex Hartwig (AUS)	6-2	0-6	6-4	6-2	
S	Merv Rose (AUS)	Ken Rosewall (AUS)	6-3	6-3	3-6	1-6	7-5
S	Rex Hartwig (AUS)	John Bromwich (AUS)	8-6	6-4	9-7		
Q	Ken Rosewall (AUS)	Hamilton Richardson (USA)	6-3	6-4	9-7		
Q	Merv Rose (AUS)	Vic Seixas (USA)	8-6	9-7	9-11	6-4	
Q	John Bromwich (AUS)	George Worthington (AUS)	3-6	6-3	2-6	6-3	6-1
Q	Rex Hartwig (AUS)	Ashley Cooper (AUS)	6-8	6-3	6-4		

1955 (ADELAIDE)

Rd	Winner	Defeated	S1	S2	S3	S4	S5
F	Ken Rosewall (AUS)	Lew Hoad (AUS)	9-7	6-4	6-2		
S	Ken Rosewall (AUS)	Tony Trabert (USA)	8-6	6-3	6-3		
S	Lew Hoad (AUS)	Rex Hartwig (AUS)	6-1	6-4	6-4		
Q	Ken Rosewall (AUS)	Ashley Cooper (AUS)	6-4	6-2	6-0		
Q	Tony Trabert (USA)	Merv Rose (AUS)	7-5	4-6	6-3	6-1	
Q	Lew Hoad (AUS)	Vic Seixas (USA)	4-6	6-3	6-4	8-6	
Q	Rex Hartwig (AUS)	Lennart Bergelin (SWE)	4-6	6-2	4-6	6-4	6-3

1956 (BRISBANE)

Rd	Winner	Defeated	S1	S2	S3	S4	S5
F	Lew Hoad (AUS)	Ken Rosewall (AUS)	6-4	3-6	6-4	7-5	
S	Lew Hoad (AUS)	Neale Fraser (AUS)	6-3	6-2	6-0		
S	Ken Rosewall (AUS)	Herbie Flam (USA)	6-4	6-0	6-2		
Q	Lew Hoad (AUS)	Merv Rose (AUS)	3-6	6-1	6-8	6-2	9-7
Q	Neale Fraser (AUS)	Gilbert Shea (AUS)	6-2	6-4	6-3		
Q	Herbie Flam (USA)	Ashley Cooper (AUS)	6-8	6-3	6-2	6-3	
Q	Ken Rosewall (AUS)	Mal Anderson (AUS)	6-4	6-3	5-7	8-6	

Rd	Winner	Defeated	S1	S2	S3	S4	S5

1957 (MELBOURNE)

Rd	Winner	Defeated	S1	S2	S3	S4	S5
F	Ashley Cooper (AUS)	Neale Fraser (AUS)	6-3	9-11	6-4	6-2	
S	Neale Fraser (AUS)	Lew Hoad (AUS)	7-5	3-6	6-1	6-4	
S	Ashley Cooper (AUS)	Mal Anderson (AUS)	6-4	9-7	6-4		
Q	Lew Hoad (AUS)	Mike Green (USA)	4-6	3-6	6-2	6-3	6-3
Q	Neale Fraser (AUS)	Graham Lovett (AUS)	6-0	6-1	6-0		
Q	Mal Anderson (AUS)	Nicola Pietrangeli (ITA)	9-7	9-7	6-2		
Q	Ashley Cooper (AUS)	Warren Woodcock (AUS)	6-2	3-6	6-1	6-4	

1958 (SYDNEY)

Rd	Winner	Defeated	S1	S2	S3	S4	S5
F	Ashley Cooper (AUS)	Mal Anderson (AUS)	7-5	6-3	6-4		
S	Ashley Cooper (AUS)	Neale Fraser (AUS)	6-3	3-6	10-8	6-3	
S	Mal Anderson (AUS)	Merv Rose (AUS)	6-2	5-7	6-4	19-17	
Q	Ashley Cooper (AUS)	Mike Green (USA)	6-1	6-2	4-6	5-7	6-2
Q	Neale Fraser (AUS)	Roy Emerson (AUS)	4-6	6-1	6-4	6-3	
Q	Merv Rose (AUS)	Bob Howe (AUS)	3-6	4-6	6-1	8-6	6-0
Q	Mal Anderson (AUS)	Trevor Fancutt (RSA)	6-3	6-4	5-7	12-10	

1959 (ADELAIDE)

Rd	Winner	Defeated	S1	S2	S3	S4	S5
F	Alex Olmedo (PER)	Neale Fraser (AUS)	6-1	6-2	3-6	6-3	
S	Neale Fraser (AUS)	Bob Mark (AUS)	6-4	6-4	6-3		
S	Alex Olmedo (PER)	Barry MacKay (USA)	3-6	8-6	6-1	3-6	6-3
Q	Neale Fraser (AUS)	Don Candy (AUS)	6-2	6-4	4-6	6-4	
Q	Bob Mark (AUS)	Andres Gimeno (ESP)	6-4	3-6	7-5	6-4	
Q	Alex Olmedo (PER)	Ulf Schmidt (SWE)	6-4	9-7	3-6	3-6	7-5
Q	Barry MacKay (USA)	Roy Emerson (AUS)	4-6	10-8	6-3	8-6	

1960 (BRISBANE)

Rd	Winner	Defeated	S1	S2	S3	S4	S5
F	Rod Laver (AUS)	Neale Fraser (AUS)	5-7	3-6	6-3	8-6	8-6
S	Neale Fraser (AUS)	Bob Hewitt (AUS)	8-6	6-4	11-9		
S	Rod Laver (AUS)	Roy Emerson (AUS)	4-6	6-1	9-7	3-6	7-5
Q	Neale Fraser (AUS)	John Pearce (AUS)	4-6	7-5	6-3	6-8	6-2
Q	Bob Hewitt (AUS)	Bob Mark (AUS)	12-10	6-2	6-1		
Q	Rod Laver (AUS)	Ken Fletcher (AUS)	6-3	8-6	4-6	6-4	
Q	Roy Emerson (AUS)	Marty Mulligan (AUS)	6-4	6-1			(retired)

1961 (MELBOURNE)

Rd	Winner	Defeated	S1	S2	S3	S4	S5
F	Roy Emerson (AUS)	Rod Laver (AUS)	1-6	6-3	7-5	6-4	
S	Rod Laver (AUS)	Barry Phillips-Moore (AUS)	6-2	6-2	6-4		
S	Roy Emerson (AUS)	Fred Stolle (AUS)	8-6	6-2	-7-5		
Q	Rod Laver (AUS)	Ken Fletcher (AUS)	6-2	2-4			(retired)
Q	Barry Phillips-Moore (AUS)	Christian Kuhnke (GER)	5-7	6-3	6-2	6-3	
Q	Fred Stolle (AUS)	Mike Sangster (GBR)	6-3	6-4	6-3		
Q	Roy Emerson (AUS)	John Pearce (AUS)	6-1	6-2	6-3		

1962 (SYDNEY)

Rd	Winner	Defeated	S1	S2	S3	S4	S5
F	Rod Laver (AUS)	Roy Emerson (AUS)	8-6	0-6	6-4	6-4	
S	Rod Laver (AUS)	Bob Hewitt (AUS)	6-1	4-6	6-4	7-5	
S	Roy Emerson (AUS)	Neale Fraser (AUS)	6-4	6-3	6-1		
Q	Rod Laver (AUS)	Owen Davidson (AUS)	6-4	9-7	6-4		
Q	Bob Hewitt (AUS)	Wilhelm Bungert (GER)	8-6	6-2	4-6	4-6	
Q	Neale Fraser (AUS)	Fred Stolle (AUS)	6-2	4-6	6-2	6-3	
Q	Roy Emerson (AUS)	John Newcombe (AUS)	7-9	6-1	6-2	6-2	

1963 (ADELAIDE)

Rd	Winner	Defeated	S1	S2	S3	S4	S5
F	Roy Emerson (AUS)	Ken Fletcher (AUS)	6-3	6-3	6-1		
S	Roy Emerson (AUS)	Bob Hewitt (AUS)	8-6	6-4	3-6	9-7	
S	Ken Fletcher (AUS)	Fred Stolle (AUS)	6-3	6-4	7-5		
Q	Roy Emerson (AUS)	John Fraser (AUS)	6-1	7-5	6-2		
Q	Bob Hewitt (AUS)	John Newcombe (AUS)	6-3	6-4	5-7	6-4	
Q	Fred Stolle (AUS)	Owen Davidson (AUS)	5-7	6-4	6-2	6-2	
Q	Ken Fletcher (AUS)	Bob Howe (AUS)	6-4	9-7	6-2		

1964 (BRISBANE)

Rd	Winner	Defeated	S1	S2	S3	S4	S5
F	Roy Emerson (AUS)	Fred Stolle (AUS)	6-3	6-4	6-2		
S	Roy Emerson (AUS)	Marty Mulligan (AUS)	6-2	9-7	6-4		
S	Fred Stolle (AUS)	Ken Fletcher (AUS)	6-4	3-6	6-3	3-6	6-3
Q	Roy Emerson (AUS)	Tony Roche (AUS)	7-5	6-2	6-2		
Q	Marty Mulligan (AUS)	John Newcombe (AUS)	3-6	6-4	6-3	6-8	8-6
Q	Ken Fletcher (AUS)	Mike Sangster (GBR)	17-15	4-6	6-0	6-1	
Q	Fred Stolle (AUS)	Owen Davidson (AUS)	1-6	7-5	6-3	6-2	

1965 (MELBOURNE)

Rd	Winner	Defeated	S1	S2	S3	S4	S5
F	Roy Emerson (AUS)	Fred Stolle (AUS)	7-9	2-6	6-4	7-5	6-1
S	Roy Emerson (AUS)	John Newcombe (AUS)	7-5	6-4	6-1		
S	Fred Stolle (AUS)	Tony Roche (AUS)	6-4	8-6	9-7		
Q	Roy Emerson (AUS)	Juan Gisbert (ESP)	6-3	6-3	6-1		
Q	John Newcombe (AUS)	Bill Bowrey (AUS)	6-2	4-6	2-6	6-3	6-4
Q	Tony Roche (AUS)	Pierre Darmon (FRA)	6-8	6-2	6-3	6-0	
Q	Fred Stolle (AUS)	Owen Davidson (AUS)	3-6	6-0	6-3	6-3	

1966 (SYDNEY)

Rd	Winner	Defeated	S1	S2	S3	S4	S5
F	Roy Emerson (AUS)	Arthur Ashe (USA)	6-4	6-8	6-2	6-3	
S	Roy Emerson (AUS)	John Newcombe (AUS)	4-6	6-2	6-1	6-2	
S	Arthur Ashe (USA)	Fred Stolle (AUS)	6-4	6-2	6-1	6-2	
Q	Roy Emerson (AUS)	Bill Bowrey (AUS)	9-7	4-6	4-6	7-5	9-7
Q	John Newcombe (AUS)	Clark Graebner (USA)	2-6	6-1	6-3	7-5	
Q	Fred Stolle (AUS)	Lew Gerrard (NZL)	6-2	7-5	7-5		
Q	Arthur Ashe (USA)	Tony Roche (AUS)	14-12	6-4	6-3		

1967 (ADELAIDE)

Rd	Winner	Defeated	S1	S2	S3	S4	S5
F	Roy Emerson (AUS)	Arthur Ashe (USA)	6-4	6-1	6-4		
S	Roy Emerson (AUS)	Tony Roche (AUS)	6-3	4-6	15-13	13-15	6-2
S	Arthur Ashe (USA)	John Newcombe (AUS)	12-10	20-22	6-3	6-2	
Q	Roy Emerson (AUS)	Bill Bowrey (AUS)	4-6	6-4	11-9	16-14	
Q	Tony Roche (AUS)	Cliff Richey (USA)	10-8	7-5	4-6	5-7	6-1
Q	John Newcombe (AUS)	Mark Cox (GBR)	6-3	7-5	6-4		
Q	Arthur Ashe (USA)	Owen Davidson (AUS)	6-1	6-3	6-2		

1968 (MELBOURNE)

Rd	Winner	Defeated	S1	S2	S3	S4	S5
F	Bill Bowrey (AUS)	Juan Gisbert (ESP)	7-5	2-6	9-7	6-4	
S	Bill Bowrey (AUS)	Barry Phillips-Moore (AUS)	10-8	6-4	7-5		
S	Juan Gisbert (ESP)	Ray Ruffels (AUS)	10-8	3-6	6-2	6-2	
Q	Bill Bowrey (AUS)	Michael Belkin (CAN)	16-14	6-3	6-3		
Q	Barry Phillips-Moore (AUS)	Manolo Orantes (ESP)	6-1	4-6	6-3	4-6	6-1
Q	Juan Gisbert (ESP)	Dick Crealy (AUS)	6-4	10-12	7-5	7-5	
Q	Ray Ruffels (AUS)	Phil Dent (AUS)	1-6	6-2	6-1	3-6	6-0

Rd	Winner	Defeated	S1	S2	S3	S4	S5

1969 (BRISBANE)

Rd	Winner	Defeated	S1	S2	S3	S4	S5
F	Rod Laver (AUS)	Andres Gimeno (ESP)	6-3	6-4	7-5		
S	Rod Laver (AUS)	Tony Roche (AUS)	7-5	22-20	9-11	1-6	6-3
S	Andres Gimeno (ESP)	Ray Ruffels (AUS)	6-2	11-9	6-2		
Q	Rod Laver (AUS)	Fred Stolle (AUS)	6-4	18-16	6-4		
Q	Tony Roche (AUS)	John Newcombe (AUS)	10-8	4-6	6-8	7-5	6-3
Q	Ray Ruffels (AUS)	Bill Bowrey (AUS)	9-11	2-6	6-0	6-3	6-4
Q	Andres Gimeno (ESP)	Butch Buchholz (USA)	6-1	6-2	6-2		

1970 (SYDNEY)

Rd	Winner	Defeated	S1	S2	S3	S4	S5
F	Arthur Ashe (USA)	Dick Crealy (AUS)	6-4	9-7	6-2		
S	Dick Crealy (AUS)	Roger Taylor (GBR)	6-2	9-11	8-6	3-6	8-6
S	Arthur Ashe (USA)	Dennis Ralston (USA)	6-3	8-10	6-3	2-1(retired)	
Q	Roger Taylor (GBR)	Tony Roche (AUS)	9-7	7-5	7-5		
Q	Dick Crealy (AUS)	Tom Okker (NED)	6-1	3-6	4-6	7-5	6-3
Q	Arthur Ashe (USA)	Ray Ruffels (AUS)	6-8	6-3	6-4	6-2	
Q	Dennis Ralston (USA)	John Newcombe (AUS)	19-17	20-18	4-6	6-3	

1971 (SYDNEY)

Rd	Winner	Defeated	S1	S2	S3	S4	S5
F	Ken Rosewall (AUS)	Arthur Ashe (USA)	6-1	7-5	6-3		
S	Arthur Ashe (USA)	Bob Lutz (USA)	6-4	6-4	7-6		
S	Ken Rosewall (AUS)	Tom Okker (NED)	6-2	7-6	6-4		
Q	Bob Lutz (USA)	Mark Cox (GBR)	6-2	6-1	6-2		
Q	Arthur Ashe (USA)	Cliff Drysdale (RSA)	7-6	7-6	2-6	6-2	
Q	Tom Okker (NED)	Marty Riessen (USA)	6-3	6-3	6-3		
Q	Ken Rosewall (AUS)	Roy Emerson (AUS)	6-4	6-4	6-3		

1972 (MELBOURNE)

Rd	Winner	Defeated	S1	S2	S3	S4	S5
F	Ken Rosewall (AUS)	Mal Anderson (AUS)	7-6(2)	6-3	7-5		
S	Mal Anderson (AUS)	Alex Metreveli (USSR)	6-2	7-6	7-6		
S	Ken Rosewall (AUS)	Allan Stone (AUS)	2-6	6-3	6-4	3-6	9-7
Q	Mal Anderson (AUS)	John Newcombe (AUS)	2-6	6-3	6-4	3-6	9-7
Q	Alex Metreveli (USSR)	John Cooper (AUS)	6-7	6-2	6-3	6-4	
Q	Allan Stone (AUS)	Barry Phillips-Moore (AUS)	5-7	7-6	7-6	6-3	
Q	Ken Rosewall (AUS)	Dick Crealy (AUS)	6-3	-6-1	6-3		

1973 (MELBOURNE)

Rd	Winner	Defeated	S1	S2	S3	S4	S5
F	John Newcombe (AUS)	Onny Parun (NZL)	6-3	6-7	7-5	6-1	
S	Onny Parun (NZL)	Karl Meiler (GER)	2-6	6-3	7-5	6-1	
S	John Newcombe (AUS)	Patrick Proisy (FRA)	7-6	6-4	6-3		
Q	Karl Meiler (GER)	Wanaro N'Godrella (FRA)	7-6	6-7	6-3	7-6	
Q	Onny Parun (NZL)	Alex Metreveli (USSR)	6-4	3-6	6-3	6-7	6-3
Q	Patrick Proisy (FRA)	John Cooper (AUS)	6-4	3-6	6-1	7-6	
Q	John Newcombe (AUS)	Bob Carmichel (AUS)	6-4	7-5	6-3		

1974 (MELBOURNE)

Rd	Winner	Defeated	S1	S2	S3	S4	S5
F	Jimmy Connors (USA)	Phil Dent (AUS)	7-6(7)	6-4	4-6	6-3	
S	Phil Dent (AUS)	Ross Case (AUS)	6-4	6-1	2-6	6-2	
S	Jimmy Connors (USA)	John Alexander (AUS)	7-6	6-4	6-4		
Q	Ross Case (AUS)	John Newcombe (AUS)	7-6	6-2	7-5		
Q	Phil Dent (AUS)	Colin Dibley (AUS)	6-4	6-4	6-4		
Q	John Alexander (AUS)	Bob Giltinan (AUS)	6-1	5-7	6-1	6-2	
Q	Jimmy Connors (USA)	Vladimir Zednik (CZE)	3-6	7-5	6-3	6-4	

1975 (MELBOURNE)

Rd	Winner	Defeated	S1	S2	S3	S4	S5
F	John Newcombe (AUS)	Jimmy Connors (USA)	7-5	3-6	6-4	7-6(7)	
S	John Newcombe (AUS)	Tony Roche (AUS)	6-4	4-6	6-4	2-6	11-9
S	Jimmy Connors (USA)	Dick Crealy (AUS)	6-4	6-3	6-4		
Q	John Newcombe (AUS)	Geoff Masters (AUS)	1-6	6-3	6-7	6-3	10-8
Q	Tony Roche (AUS)	Alex Metreveli (USSR)	7-6	3-6	6-4	6-3	
Q	Jimmy Connors (USA)	Kim Warwick (AUS)	6-3	6-1	6-2		
Q	Dick Crealy (AUS)	John Alexander (AUS)	6-3	4-6	6-3	7-6	

1976 (MELBOURNE)

Rd	Winner	Defeated	S1	S2	S3	S4	S5
F	Mark Edmondson (AUS)	John Newcombe (AUS)	6-7	6-3	7-6	6-1	
S	Mark Edmondson (AUS)	Ken Rosewall (AUS)	6-1	2-6	6-2	6-4	
S	John Newcombe (AUS)	Ray Ruffels (AUS)	6-4	6-4	7-6		
Q	Ken Rosewall (AUS)	Brad Drewett (AUS)	6-4	3-6	6-2	6-2	
Q	Mark Edmondson (AUS)	Dick Crealy (AUS)	7-5	7-6	6-2		
Q	Ray Ruffels (AUS)	Tony Roche (AUS)	7-6	2-6	6-7	7-6	6-4
Q	John Newcombe (AUS)	Ross Case (AUS)	6-4	6-4	6-1		

1977 (JAN.) (MELBOURNE)

Rd	Winner	Defeated	S1	S2	S3	S4	S5
F	Roscoe Tanner (USA)	Guillermo Vilas (ARG)	6-3	6-3	6-3		
S	Guillermo Vilas (ARG)	John Alexander (AUS)	6-4	1-6	6-3	6-4	
S	Roscoe Tanner (USA)	Ken Rosewall (AUS)	6-4	3-6	6-4	6-1	
Q	Guillermo Vilas (ARG)	Ross Case (AUS)	6-4	7-5	1-6	6-3	
Q	John Alexander (AUS)	Arthur Ashe (USA)	6-3	6-4	4-6	7-6	
Q	Ken Rosewall (AUS)	Mark Edmondson (AUS)	6-4	7-6	4-6	6-4	
Q	Roscoe Tanner (USA)	Phil Dent (AUS)	6-3	6-4	6-2		

1977 (DEC.) (MELBOURNE)

Rd	Winner	Defeated	S1	S2	S3	S4	S5
F	Vitas Gerulaitis (USA)	John Lloyd (GBR)	6-3	7-6(1)	5-7	3-6	6-2
S	Vitas Gerulaitis (USA)	John Alexander (AUS)	6-1	6-2	6-4		
S	John Lloyd (GBR)	Bob Giltinan (AUS)	6-4	6-2	6-0		
Q	Vitas Gerulaitis (USA)	Ray Ruffels (AUS)	6-7	6-4	6-4	6-2	
Q	John Alexander (AUS)	Ken Rosewall (AUS)	7-6	7-6	4-6	6-1	
Q	John Lloyd (GBR)	John Newcombe (AUS)	3-6	6-3	7-5	7-5	
Q	Bob Giltinan (AUS)	Robin Drysdale (GBR)	6-4	6-4	3-6	7-6	

1978 (MELBOURNE)

Rd	Winner	Defeated	S1	S2	S3	S4	S5
F	Guillermo Vilas (ARG)	John Marks (AUS)	6-4	6-4	3-6	6-3	
S	Guillermo Vilas (ARG)	Hank Pfister (USA)	6-2	6-0	6-4		
S	John Marks (AUS)	Arthur Ashe (USA)	6-4	6-2	2-6	1-6	9-7
Q	Guillermo Vilas (ARG)	Tony Roche (AUS)	3-6	6-1	3-6	6-3	6-2
Q	Hank Pfister (USA)	Paul Kronk (AUS)	7-5	6-3	6-3		
Q	Arthur Ashe (USA)	Peter Feigl (AUT)	4-6	6-2	4-6	6-3	6-2
Q	John Marks (AUS)	John Alexander (AUS)	6-4	6-4	7-5		

1979 (MELBOURNE)

Rd	Winner	Defeated	S1	S2	S3	S4	S5
F	Guillermo Vilas (ARG)	John Sadri (USA)	7-6(4)	6-3	6-2		
S	Guillermo Vilas (ARG)	Victor Amaya (USA)	7-5	3-6	7-6	7-6	
S	John Sadri (USA)	Colin Dibley (AUS)	6-4	7-6	6-7	6-4	
Q	Guillermo Vilas (ARG)	Phil Dent (AUS)	6-2	3-6	7-6	4-6	6-4
Q	Victor Amaya (USA)	Peter Rennert (USA)	7-6	6-4	6-4		
Q	John Sadri (USA)	Rod Frawley (AUS)	7-6	6-3	7-6	4-6	6-2
Q	Colin Dibley (AUS)	Mark Edmondson (AUS)	3-6	6-4	3-6	7-6	6-4

THE MAJOR CHAMPIONSHIPS

Rd	Winner	Defeated	S1	S2	S3	S4	S5		Rd	Winner	Defeated	S1	S2	S3	S4	S5

1980 (MELBOURNE)

Rd	Winner	Defeated	S1	S2	S3	S4	S5
F	Brian Teacher (USA)	Kim Warwick (AUS)	7-5	7-6(4)	6-3		
S	Kim Warwick (AUS)	Guillermo Vilas (ARG)	6-7	6-4	6-2	2-6	6-4
S	Brian Teacher (USA)	Peter McNamara (AUS)	6-7	7-5	6-3	6-4	
Q	Guillermo Vilas (ARG)	John Sadri (USA)	7-5	6-4	2-6	4-6	6-3
Q	Kim Warwick (AUS)	Bill Scanlon (USA)	6-4	6-2	4-6	6-1	
Q	Brian Teacher (USA)	Paul McNamee (AUS)	6-4	4-6	6-0	7-6	
Q	Peter McNamara (AUS)	Peter Rennert (USA)	7-6	5-7	6-2	6-7	6-3

1981 (MELBOURNE)

Rd	Winner	Defeated	S1	S2	S3	S4	S5
F	Johan Kriek (RSA)	Steve Denton (USA)	6-2	7-6(1)	6-7(1)	6-4	
S	Steve Denton (USA)	Hank Pfister (USA)	7-6	6-7	61	3-6	6-3
S	Johan Kriek (RSA)	Mark Edmondson (AUS)	6-0	7-6	7-5		
Q	Hank Pfister (USA)	Kim Warwick (AUS)	6-1	4-6	6-4	6-3	
Q	Steve Denton (USA)	Shlomo Glickstein (ISR)	6-4	3-6	7-6	6-0	
Q	Johan Kriek (RSA)	Tim Mayotte (USA)	7-6	6-3	7-5		
Q	Mark Edmondson (AUS)	Peter McNamara (AUS)					

1982 (MELBOURNE)

Rd	Winner	Defeated	S1	S2	S3	S4	S5
F	Johan Kriek (RSA)	Steve Denton (USA)	6-3	6-3	6-2		
S	Johan Kriek (RSA)	Paul McNamee (AUS)	7-6	7-6	4-6	3-6	7-5
S	Steve Denton (USA)	Hank Pfister (USA)	6-4	4-6	6-3	3'6	7-6
Q	Johan Kriek (USA)	Drew Gitlin (USA)	6-0	6-4	6-1		
Q	Paul McNamee (AUS)	Pat Cash (AUS)	6-4	6-7	6-3	6-4	
Q	Hank Pfister (USA)	Brian Teacher (USA)	6-1	6-3	6-7	1-6	7-6
Q	Steve Denton (USA)	Sammy Giammalva (USA)	4-6	6-3	6-3	2-6	6-3

1983 (MELBOURNE)

Rd	Winner	Defeated	S1	S2	S3	S4	S5
F	Mats Wilander (SWE)	Ivan Lendl (CZE)	6-1	6-4	6-4		
S	Ivan Lendl (CZE)	Tim Mayotte (USA)	6-1	7-6	6-3		
S	Mats Wilander (SWE)	John McEnroe (USA)	4-6	6-3	6-4	6-3	
Q	Ivan Lendl (CZE)	Tomas Smid (CZE)	7-6	2-6	6-1	6-2	
Q	Tim Mayotte (USA)	Eliot Teltscher (USA)	6-4	6-2	3-6	7-6	
Q	Mats Wilander (SWE)	Johan Kriek (USA)	6-3	6-4	7-6		
Q	John McEnroe (USA)	Wally Masur (AUS)	6-2	6-1	6-2		

1984 (MELBOURNE)

Rd	Winner	Defeated	S1	S2	S3	S4	S5
F	Mats Wilander (SWE)	Kevin Curren(RSA)	6-7(5)	6-4	7-6(3)	6-2	
S	Kevin Curren (RSA)	Ben Testerman (USA)	2-6	4-6	6-3	6-4	6-4
S	Mats Wilander (SWE)	Johan Kriek (USA)	6-1	6-0	6-2		
Q	Kevin Curren (RSA)	Scott Davis (USA)	7-5	6-2	6-3		
Q	Ben Testerman (USA)	Boris Becker (GER)	6-4	6-3	6-4		
Q	Johan Kriek (RSA)	Pat Cash (AUS)	7-5	6-1	7-6		
Q	Mats Wilander (SWE)	Stefan Edberg (SWE)	7-5	6-3	1-6	6-4	

1985 (MELBOURNE)

Rd	Winner	Defeated	S1	S2	S3	S4	S5
F	Stefan Edberg (SWE)	Mats Wilander (SWE)	6-4	6-3	6-3		
S	Stefan Edberg (SWE)	Ivan Lendl (CZE)	6-7(3)	7-5	6-1	4-6	9-7
S	Mats Wilander (SWE)	Slobodan Zivojinovic (YUG)	7-5	6-1	6-3		
Q	Ivan Lendl (CZE)	John Lloyd (GBR)	7-6(5)	6-2	6-1		
Q	Stefan Edberg (SWE)	Michiel Schapers (NED)	6-0	7-5	6-4		
Q	Mats Wilander (SWE)	Johan Kriek (USA)	6-3	7-5	6-2		
Q	Slobodan Zivojinovic (YUG)	John McEnroe (USA)	2-6	6-3	1-6	6-4	6-0

1987 (MELBOURNE)

Rd	Winner	Defeated	S1	S2	S3	S4	S5
F	Stefan Edberg (SWE)	Pat Cash (AUS)	6-3	6-4	3-6	5-7	6-3
S	Pat Cash (AUS)	Ivan Lendl (CZE)	7-6	5-7	7-6	6-4	
S	Stefan Edberg (SWE)	Wally Masur (AUS)	6-2	6-4	7-6		
Q	Ivan Lendl (CZE)	Anders Jarryd (SWE)	7-6	6-1	6-3		
Q	Pat Cash (AUS)	Yannick Noah (FRA)	6-4	6-2	2-6	6-0	
Q	Stefan Edberg (SWE)	Miloslav Mecir (CZE)	6-1	6-4	6-4		
Q	Wally Masur (AUS)	Kelly Evernden (NZL)	6-3	7-5	6-4		

1988 (MELBOURNE)

Rd	Winner	Defeated	S1	S2	S3	S4	S5
F	Mats Wilander (SWE)	Pat Cash (AUS)	6-3	6-7(3)	3-6	6-1	8-6
S	Pat Cash (AUS)	Ivan Lendl (CZE)	6-4	2-6	6-2	4-6	6-2
S	Mats Wilander (SWE)	Stefan Edberg (SWE)	6-0	6-7(5)	6-3	3-6	6-1
Q	Ivan Lendl (CZE)	Todd Witsken (USA)	6-2	6-1	7-6(4)		
Q	Pat Cash (AUS)	Michiel Schapers (NED)	6-1	6-4	6-2		
Q	Mats Wilander (SWE)	Anders Jarryd (SWE)	7-6	6-2	6-3		
Q	Stefan Edberg (SWE)	Andrei Chesnokov (RUS)	4-6	7-6(5)	6-4	6-4	

1989 (MELBOURNE)

Rd	Winner	Defeated	S1	S2	S3	S4	S5
F	Ivan Lendl (CZE)	Miloslav Mecir (CZE)	6-2	6-2	6-2		
S	Miloslav Mecir (CZE)	Jan Gunnarsson (SWE)	7-5	6-2	6-2		
S	Ivan Lendl (CZE)	Thomas Muster (AUT)	6-2	6-4	5-7	7-5	
Q	Miloslav Mecir (CZE)	Goran Ivanisevic (YUG)	7-5	6-0	6-3		
Q	Jan Gunnarsson (SWE)	Jonas Svensson (SWE)	6-0	6-3	4-6	6-4	
Q	Thomas Muster (AUT)	Stefan Edberg (SWE)	(walkover)				
Q	Ivan Lendl (CZE)	John McEnroe (USA)	7-6(0)	6-2	7-6(2)		

1990 (MELBOURNE)

Rd	Winner	Defeated	S1	S2	S3	S4	S5
F	Ivan Lendl (CZE)	Stefan Edberg (SWE)	4-6	7-6(3)	5-2	(ret. inj.)	
S	Ivan Lendl (CZE)	Yannick Noah (FRA)	6-4	6-1	6-2		
S	Stefan Edberg (SWE)	Mats Wilander (SWE)	6-1	6-1	6-2		
Q	Ivan Lendl (CZE)	Andrei Cherkasov (RUS)	6-3	6-2	6-3		
Q	Yannick Noah (FRA)	Mikael Pernfors (SWE)	6-3	7-5	6-2		
Q	Stefan Edberg (SWE)	David Wheaton (USA)	7-5	7-5	3-6	6-2	
Q	Yannick Noah (FRA)	Boris Becker (GER)	6-4	6-4	6-2		

1991 (MELBOURNE)

Rd	Winner	Defeated	S1	S2	S3	S4	S5
F	Boris Becker (GER)	Ivan Lendl (CZE)	1-6	6-4	6-4	6-4	
S	Ivan Lendl (CZE)	Stefan Edberg (SWE)	6-4	5-7	3-6	7-6(3)	6-4
S	Boris Becker (GER)	Patrick McEnroe (USA)	6-7(2)	6-4	6-1	6-4	
Q	Stefan Edberg (SWE)	Jaime Yzaga (PER)	6-2	6-3	6-2		
Q	Ivan Lendl (CZE)	Goran Prpic (YUG)	6-0	7-6(1)	7-6(2)		
Q	Patrick McEnroe (USA)	Cristiano Caratti (ITA)	7-6(2)	6-3	4-6	4-6	6-2
Q	Boris Becker (GER)	Guy Forget (FRA)	6-2	7-6(2)	6-3		

1992 (MELBOURNE)

Rd	Winner	Defeated	S1	S2	S3	S4	S5
F	Jim Courier (USA)	Stefan Edberg (SWE)	6-3	3-6	6-4	6-2	
S	Stefan Edberg (SWE)	Wayne Ferreira (RSA)	7-6(2)	6-1	6-2		
S	Jim Courier (USA)	Richard Krajicek (NED)	(walkover)				
Q	Stefan Edberg (SWE)	Ivan Lendl (CZE)	4-6	7-5	6-1	6-7(5)	6-1
Q	Wayne Ferreira (RSA)	John McEnroe (USA)	6-4	6-4	6-4		
Q	Richard Krajicek (NED)	Michael Stich (GER)	5-7	7-6(2)	6-7(1)	6-4	6-4
Q	Jim Courier (USA)	Amos Mansdorf (ISR)	6-3	6-2	6-2		

1993 (MELBOURNE)

Rd	Winner	Defeated	S1	S2	S3	S4	S5
F	Jim Courier (USA)	Stefan Edberg (SWE)	6-2	6-1	2-6	7-5	
S	Jim Courier (USA)	Michael Stich (GER)	7-6(4)	6-4	6-2		
S	Stefan Edberg (SWE)	Pete Sampras (USA)	7-6(5)	6-3	7-6(3)		
Q	Jim Courier (USA)	Petr Korda (CZE)	6-1	6-0	6-4		
Q	Michael Stich (GER)	Guy Forget (FRA)	6-4	6-4	6-4		
Q	Pete Sampras (USA)	Brett Steven (NZL)	6-3	6-2	6-3		
Q	Stefan Edberg (SWE)	Christian Bergstorm (SWE)	6-4	6-4	6-1		

1994 (MELBOURNE)

Rd	Winner	Defeated	S1	S2	S3	S4	S5
F	Pete Sampras (USA)	Todd Martin (USA)	7-6(4)	6-4	6-4		
S	Pete Sampras (USA)	Jim Courier (USA)	6-3	6-4	6-4		
S	Todd Martin (USA)	Stefan Edberg (SWE)	3-6	7-6(7)	7-6(7)	7-6(7)	
Q	Pete Sampras (USA)	Magnus Gustafsson (SWE)	7-6(4)	2-6	6-3	7-6(4)	
Q	Jim Courier (USA)	Goran Ivanisevic (CRO)	7-6(7)	6-4	6-2		
Q	Stefan Edberg (SWE)	Thomas Muster (AUT)	6-2	6-3	6-4		
Q	Todd Martin (USA)	MaliVai Washington (USA)	6-2	7-6(4)	7-6(5)		

1995 (MELBOURNE)

Rd	Winner	Defeated	S1	S2	S3	S4	S5
F	Andre Agassi (USA)	Pete Sampras (USA)	4-6	6-1	7-6(5)	6-4	
S	Pete Sampras (USA)	Michael Chang (USA)	6-7(6)	6-3	6-4	6-4	
S	Andre Agassi (USA)	Aaron Krickstein (USA)	6-4	6-4	3-0	(retired)	
Q	Pete Sampras (USA)	Jim Courier (USA)	6-7(4)	6-7(3)	6-3	6-4	6-3
Q	Michael Chang (USA)	Andrei Medvedev (UKR)	7-6(7)	7-5	6-3		
Q	Aaron Krickstein (USA)	Jacco Eltingh (NED)	7-6(3)	6-4	5-7	6-4	
Q	Andre Agassi (USA)	Yevgeny Kafelnikov (RUS)	6-2	7-5	6-0		

1996 (MELBOURNE)

Rd	Winner	Defeated	S1	S2	S3	S4	S5
F	Boris Becker (GER)	Michael Chang (USA)	6-2	6-4	2-6	6-2	
S	Boris Becker (GER)	Mark Woodforde (AUS)	6-4	6-2	6-0		
S	Michael Chang (USA)	Andre Agassi (USA)	6-1	6-4	7-6(1)		
Q	Mark Woodforde (AUS)	Thomas Enqvist (SWE)	6-4	6-4	6-4		
Q	Boris Becker (GER)	Yevgeny Kafelnikov (RUS)	6-4	7-6(9)	6-1		
Q	Michael Chang (USA)	Mikael Tillstrom (SWE)	6-0	6-2	6-4		
Q	Andre Agassi (USA)	Jim Courier (USA)	6-7(7)	2-6	6-3	6-4	6-2

1997 (MELBOURNE)

Rd	Winner	Defeated	S1	S2	S3	S4	S5
F	Pete Sampras (USA)	Carlos Moya (ESP)	6-2	6-3	6-3		
S	Pete Sampras (USA)	Thomas Muster (AUT)	6-1	7-6(3)	6-3		
S	Carlos Moya (ESP)	Michael Chang (USA)	7-5	6-2	6-4		
Q	Pete Sampras (USA)	Albert Costa (ESP)	6-3	6-7(5)	6-1	3-6	6-2
Q	Thomas Muster (AUT)	Goran Ivanisevic (CRO)	6-4	6-2	6-3		
Q	Carlos Moya (ESP)	Felix Mantilla (ESP)	7-5	6-2	6-7(5)	6-2	
Q	Michael Chang (USA)	Marcelo Rios (CHI)	7-5	6-1	6-4		

1998 (MELBOURNE)

Rd	Winner	Defeated	S1	S2	S3	S4	S5
F	Petr Korda (CZE)	Marcelo Rios (CHI)	6-2	6-2	6-2		
S	Petr Korda (CZE)	Karol Kucera (SVK)	6-1	6-4	1-6	6-2	
S	Marcelo Rios (CHI)	Nicolas Escude (FRA)	6-1	6-3	6-2		
Q	Karol Kucera (SVK)	Pete Sampras (USA)	6-4	6-2	6-7(5)	6-3	
Q	Petr Korda (CZE)	Jonas Bjorkman (SWE)	3-6	5-7	6-3	6-4	6-2
Q	Nicolas Escude (FRA)	Nicolas Kiefer (GER)	4-6	3-6	6-4	6-1	6-2
Q	Marcelo Rios (CHI)	Alberto Berasategui (ESP)	6-7(6)	6-4	6-4	6-0	

1999 (MELBOURNE)

Rd	Winner	Defeated	S1	S2	S3	S4	S5
F	Yevgeny Kafelnikov (RUS)	Thomas Enqvist (SWE)	4-6	6-0	6-3	7-6(1)	
S	Yevgeny Kafelnikov (RUS)	Tommy Haas (GER)	6-3	6-4	7-5		
S	Thomas Enqvist (SWE)	Nicolas Lapentti (ECU)	6-3	7-5	6-1		
Q	Yevgeny Kafelnikov (RUS)	Todd Martin (USA)	6-2	7-6(1)	6-2		
Q	Tommy Haas (GER)	Vincent Spadea (USA)	7-6(5)	7-5	6-3		
Q	Thomas Enqvist (SWE)	Marc Rosset (SUI)	6-3	6-4	6-4		
Q	Nicolas Lapentti (ECU)	Karol Kucera (SVK)	7-6(4)	6-7(6)	6-2	0-6	8-6

2000 (MELBOURNE)

Rd	Winner	Defeated	S1	S2	S3	S4	S5
F	Andre Agassi (USA)	Yevgeny Kafelnikov (RUS)	3-6	6-3	6-2	6-4	
S	Andre Agassi (USA)	Pete Sampras (USA)	6-4	3-6	6-7(0)	7-6(5)	6-1
S	Yevgeny Kafelnikov (RUS)	Magnus Norman (SWE)	6-1	6-2	6-4		
Q	Andre Agassi (USA)	Hicham Arazi (MAR)	6-4	6-4	6-2		
Q	Pete Sampras (USA)	Chris Woodruff (USA)	7-5	6-3	6-3		
Q	Magnus Norman (SWE)	Nicolas Kiefer (GER)	3-6	6-3	6-1	7-6(4)	
Q	Yevgeny Kafelnikov (RUS)	Younes El Aynaoui (MAR)	6-0	6-3	7-6(4)		

2001 (MELBOURNE)

Rd	Winner	Defeated	S1	S2	S3	S4	S5
F	Andre Agassi (USA)	Arnaud Clement (FRA)	6-4	6-2	6-2		
S	Arnaud Clement (FRA)	Sebastian Grosjean (FRA)	5-7	2-6	7-6(4)	7-5	6-2
S	Andre Agassi (USA)	Patrick Rafter (AUS)	7-5	2-6	6-7(5)	6-2	6-3
Q	Arnaud Clement (FRA)	Yevgeny Kafelnikov (RUS)	6-4	5-7	7-6(3)	7-6(3)	
Q	Sebastian Grosjean (FRA)	Carlos Moya (ESP)	6-1	6-4	6-2		
Q	Andre Agassi (USA)	Todd Martin (USA)	7-5	6-3	6-4		
Q	Patrick Rafter (AUS)	Dominik Hrbaty (SVK)	6-2	6-7(4)	7-5	6-0	

2002 (MELBOURNE)

Rd	Winner	Defeated	S1	S2	S3	S4	S5
F	Thomas Johansson (SWE)	Marat Safin (RUS)	3-6	6-4	6-4	7-6(4)	
S	Marat Safin (RUS)	Tommy Haas (GER)	6-7(5)	7-6(4)	3-6	6-0	6-2
S	Thomas Johansson (SWE)	Jiri Novak (CZE)	7-6(5)	0-6	4-6	6-3	6-4
Q	Tommy Haas (GER)	Marcelo Rios (CHI)	7-6(2)	6-4	6-7(2)	7-6(5)	
Q	Marat Safin (RUS)	Wayne Ferreira (RSA)	5-2			(retired)	
Q	Jiri Novak (CZE)	Stefan Koubek (AUT)	6-2	6-3	6-2		
Q	Thomas Johansson (SWE)	Jonas Bjorkman (SWE)	6-0	2-6	6-3	6-4	

2003 (MELBOURNE)

Rd	Winner	Defeated	S1	S2	S3	S4	S5
F	Andre Agassi (USA)	Rainer Schuettler (GER)	6-2	6-2	6-1		
S	Rainer Schuettler (GER)	Andy Roddick (USA)	7-5	2-6	6-3	6-3	
S	Andre Agassi (USA)	Wayne Ferreira (RSA)	6-2	6-2	6-3		
Q	Andy Roddick (USA)	Younes El Aynaoui (MAR)	4-6	7-6(5)	4-6	6-4	21-19
Q	Rainer Schuettler (GER)	David Nalbandian (ARG)	6-3	5-7	6-1	6-0	
Q	Wayne Ferreira (RSA)	Juan Carlos Ferrero (ESP)	7-6(4)	7-6(5)	6-1		
Q	Andre Agassi (USA)	Sebastian Grosjean (FRA)	6-3	6-2	6-2		

2004 (MELBOURNE)

Rd	Winner	Defeated	S1	S2	S3	S4	S5
F	Roger Federer (SUI)	Marat Safin (RUS)	7-6(3)	6-4	6-2		
S	Marat Safin (RUS)	Andre Agassi (USA)	7-6(8)	7-6(8)	5-7	1-6	6-3
S	Roger Federer (SUI)	Juan Carlos Ferrero (ESP)	6-4	6-1	6-4		
Q	Marat Safin (RUS)	Andy Roddick (USA)	2-6	6-3	7-5	6-7(0)	6-4
Q	Andre Agassi (USA)	Sebastien Grosjean (FRA)	6-2	2-0	(retired)		
Q	Juan Carlos Ferrero (ESP)	Hicham Arazi (MAR)	6-1	7-6(6)	7-6(5)		
Q	Roger Federer (SUI)	David Nalbandian (ARG)	7-5	6-4	5-7	6-3	

Rd	Winner	Defeated	S1	S2	S3	S4	S5

2005 (MELBOURNE)

Rd	Winner	Defeated	S1	S2	S3	S4	S5
F	Marat Safin (RUS)	Lleyton Hewitt (AUS)	1-6	6-3	6-4	6-4	
S	Marat Safin (RUS)	Roger Federer (SUI)	5-7	6-4	5-7	7-6(6)	9-7
S	Lleyton Hewitt (AUS)	Andy Roddick (USA)	3-6	7-6(3)	7-6(4)	6-1	
Q	Roger Federer (SUI)	Andre Agassi (USA)	6-3	6-4	6-4		
Q	Marat Safin (RUS)	Dominik Hrbaty (SVK)	6-2	6-4	6-2		
Q	Lleyton Hewitt (AUS)	David Nalbandian (ARG)	6-3	6-2	1-6	3-6	10-8
Q	Andy Roddick (USA)	Nikolay Davydenko (RUS)	6-3	7-5	4-1	(retired)	

2006 (MELBOURNE)

Rd	Winner	Defeated	S1	S2	S3	S4	S5
F	Roger Federer (SUI)	Marcos Baghdatis (CYP)	5-7	7-5	6-0	6-2	
S	Roger Federer (SUI)	Nicolas Kiefer (GER)	6-3	5-7	6-0	6-2	
S	Marcos Baghdatis (CYP)	David Nalbandian (ARG)	3-6	5-7	6-3	6-4	6-4
Q	Roger Federer (SUI)	Nikolay Davydenko (RUS)	6-4	3-6	7-6(7)	7-6(5)	
Q	Nicolas Kiefer (GER)	Sebastien Grosjean (FRA)	6-3	0-6	6-4	6-7(1)	8-6
Q	David Nalbandian (ARG)	Fabrice Santoro (FRA)	7-5	6-0	6-0		
Q	Marcos Baghdatis (CYP)	Ivan Ljubicic (CRO)	6-4	6-2	4-6	3-6	6-3

2007 (MELBOURNE)

Rd	Winner	Defeated	S1	S2	S3	S4	S5
F	Roger Federer (SUI)	Fernando Gonzalez (CHI)	7-6(2)	6-4	6-4		
S	Roger Federer (SUI)	Andy Roddick (USA)	6-4	6-0	6-2		
S	Fernando Gonzalez (CHI)	Tommy Haas (GER)	6-1	6-3	6-1		
Q	Roger Federer (SUI)	Tommy Robredo (ESP)	6-3	7-6(2)	7-5		
Q	Andy Roddick (USA)	Mardy Fish (USA)	6-2	6-2	6-2		
Q	Tommy Haas (GER)	Nikolay Davydenko (RUS)	6-3	2-6	1-6	6-1	7-5
Q	Fernando Gonzalez (CHI)	Rafael Nadal (ESP)	6-2	6-4	6-3		

2008 (MELBOURNE)

Rd	Winner	Defeated	S1	S2	S3	S4	S5
F	Novak Djokovic (SRB)	Jo-Wilfried Tsonga (FRA)	4-6	6-4	6-3	7-6(2)	
S	Novak Djokovic (SRB)	Roger Federer (SUI)	7-5	6-3	7-6(5)		
S	Jo-Wilfried Tsonga (FRA)	Rafael Nadal (ESP)	6-2	6-3	6-2		
Q	Roger Federer (SUI)	James Blake (USA)	7-5	7-6(5)	6-4		
Q	Novak Djokovic (SRB)	David Ferrer (ESP)	6-0	6-3	7-5		
Q	Jo-Wilfried Tsonga (FRA)	Mikhail Youzhny (RUS)	7-5	6-0	7-6(6)		
Q	Rafael Nadal (ESP)	Jarkko Nieminen (FIN)	7-5	6-3	6-1		

2009 (MELBOURNE)

Rd	Winner	Defeated	S1	S2	S3	S4	S5
F	Rafael Nadal (ESP)	Roger Federer (SUI)	7-5	3-6	7-6(3)	3-6	6-2
S	Rafael Nadal (ESP)	Fernando Verdasco (ESP)	6-7(4)	6-4	7-6(2)	6-7(1)	6-4
S	Roger Federer (SUI)	Andy Roddick (USA)	6-2	7-5	7-5		
Q	Rafael Nadal (ESP)	Gilles Simon (FRA)	6-2	7-5	7-5		
Q	Fernando Verdasco (ESP)	Jo-Wilfried Tsonga (FRA)	7-6(2)	3-6	6-3	6-2	
Q	Andy Roddick (USA)	Novak Djokovic (SRB)	6-7(3)	6-4	6-2	2-1	ret.
Q	Roger Federer (SUI)	Juan Martin Del Potro (ARG)	6-3	6-0	6-0		

Women's Singles

Rd	Winner	Defeated	S1	S2	S3

1922 (SYDNEY)

Rd	Winner	Defeated	S1	S2	S3
F	Mall Molesworth (AUS)	Esna Boyd (AUS)	6-3	10-8	
S	Mall Molesworth (AUS)	Gwendoline Chiplin Utz (AUS)	6-2	6-3	
S	Esna Boyd (AUS)	Sylvia Lance (AUS)	6-4	10-8	
Q	Mall Molesworth (AUS)	Marjorie Mountain (AUS)	6-4	6-4	
Q	Gwendoline Chiplin Utz (AUS)	S. Carr (AUS)	(walkover)		
Q	Sylvia Lance (AUS)	Mary Elliott (AUS)	6-1	6-2	
Q	Esna Boyd (AUS)	Jessie Watson (AUS)	6-3	6-2	

1923 (BRISBANE)

Rd	Winner	Defeated	S1	S2	S3
F	Mall Molesworth (AUS)	Esna Boyd (AUS)	6-1	7-5	
S	Mall Molesworth (AUS)	Sylvia Lance (AUS)	3-6	6-4	8-6
S	Esna Boyd (AUS)	Ms Haymen (AUS)	6-2	6-2	
Q	Mall Molesworth (AUS)	A. Bell (AUS)	6-2	6-1	
Q	Sylvia Lance (AUS)	Rose Roe (AUS)	6-0	6-4	
Q	Ms Haymen (AUS)	Jessie Watson (AUS)	7-5	8-6	
Q	Esna Boyd (AUS)	Ms Mitchell (AUS)	6-1	6-3	

1924 (MELBOURNE)

Rd	Winner	Defeated	S1	S2	S3
F	Sylvia Lance (AUS)	Esna Boyd (AUS)	6-3	3-6	6-4
S	Sylvia Lance (AUS)	Katherine Le Mesurier (AUS)	6-2	6-2	
S	Esna Boyd (AUS)	Daphne Akhurst (AUS)	6-1	6-4	
Q	Sylvia Lance (AUS)	Ms Todd (AUS)	1-6	6-4	6-1
Q	Katherine Le Mesurier (AUS)	Mall Molesworth (AUS)	7-9	6-3	8-6
Q	Daphne Akhurst (AUS)	Ms Mather (AUS)	6-1	6-4	
Q	Esna Boyd (AUS)	Ms Simpson (AUS)	6-1	6-1	

1925 (SYDNEY)

Rd	Winner	Defeated	S1	S2	S3
F	Daphne Akhurst (AUS)	Esna Boyd (AUS)	1-6	8-6	6-4
S	Daphne Akhurst (AUS)	M. Richardson (AUS)	6-1	6-1	
S	Esna Boyd (AUS)	Sylvia Lance Harper (AUS)	6-2	6-3	
Q	Daphne Akhurst (AUS)	Jessie Watson (AUS)	6-1	6-4	
Q	M. Richardson (AUS)	Patricia Meaney (AUS)	6-4	1-6	6-2
Q	Sylvia Lance Harper (AUS)	Ms Knoblanche (AUS)	6-1	6-1	
Q	Esna Boyd (AUS)	Marjorie Cox (AUS)	4-6	6-0	9-7

1926 (ADELAIDE)

Rd	Winner	Defeated	S1	S2	S3
F	Daphne Akhurst (AUS)	Esna Boyd (AUS)	6-1	6-3	
S	Daphne Akhurst (AUS)	Marjorie Cox (AUS)	6-1	6-3	
S	Esna Boyd (AUS)	Sylvia Lance Harper (AUS)	6-4	3-6	6-3
Q	Daphne Akhurst (AUS)	Kathrine Le Mesurier (AUS)	7-5	6-2	
Q	Marjorie Cox (AUS)	M. Richardson (AUS)	6-2	6-2	
Q	Sylvia Lance Harper (AUS)	H. Turner (AUS)	6-1	6-4	
Q	Esna Boyd (AUS)	Meryl O'Hara Wood (AUS)	6-1	7-5	

1927 (MELBOURNE)

Rd	Winner	Defeated	S1	S2	S3
F	Esna Boyd (AUS)	Sylvia Lance Harper (AUS)	5-7	6-1	6-2
S	Esna Boyd (AUS)	Louie Bickerton (AUS)	6-3	6-1	
S	Sylvia Lance Harper (AUS)	H. Turner (AUS)	6-2	6-0	
Q	Esna Boyd (AUS)	Dorothy Bellamy (AUS)	6-2	6-3	
Q	Louie Bickerton (AUS)	Kathrine Le Mesurier (AUS)	6-4	4-6	6-2
Q	H. Turner (AUS)	Dorothy Weston (AUS)	6-4	6-0	
Q	Sylvia Lance Harper (AUS)	Marjorie Cox (AUS)	1-6	6-3	6-3

1928 (SYDNEY)

Rd	Winner	Defeated	S1	S2	S3
F	Daphne Akhurst (AUS)	Esna Boyd (AUS)	7-5	6-2	
S	Daphne Akhurst (AUS)	Meryl O'Hara Wood (AUS)	6-2	7-5	
S	Esna Boyd (AUS)	Louie Bickerton (AUS)	6-2	6-3	
Q	Daphne Akhurst (AUS)	Dorothy Weston (AUS)	6-1	6-2	
Q	Meryl O'Hara Wood (AUS)	Kathrine Lemesurier (AUS)	1-6	6-4	6-2
Q	Louie Bickerton (AUS)	Patricia Meaney (AUS)	4-6	6-1	6-1
Q	Esna Boyd (AUS)	Mall Molesworth (AUS)	7-5	6-2	

1929 (ADELAIDE)

Rd	Winner	Defeated	S1	S2	S3
F	Daphne Akhurst (AUS)	Louie Bickerton (AUS)	6-1	5-7	6-2
S	Daphne Akhurst (AUS)	Sylvia Lance Harper (AUS)	6-3	6-1	
S	Louie Bickerton (AUS)	Marjorie Cox (AUS)	6-1	6-3	
Q	Daphne Akhurst (AUS)	Meryl O'Hara Wood (AUS)	6-4	6-3	
Q	Sylvia Lance Harper (AUS)	Mall Molesworth (AUS)	6-1	6-4	
Q	Marjorie Cox (AUS)	Emily Hood (AUS)	6-0	6-1	
Q	Loule Bickerton (AUS)	Kathrine Le Mesurier (AUS)	6-0	8-6	

1930 (MELBOURNE)

Rd	Winner	Defeated	S1	S2	S3
F	Daphne Akhurst (AUS)	Sylvia Lance Harper (AUS)	10-8	2-6	7-5
S	Daphne Akhurst (AUS)	Birdie Bond (AUS)	6-0	6-2	
S	Sylvia Lance Harper (AUS)	Louie Bickerton (AUS)	6-3	8-6	
Q	Daphne Akhurst (AUS)	Youtha Anthony (AUS)	6-1	3-6	6-4
Q	Birdie Bond (AUS)	Marjorie Cox (AUS)	7-5	6-4	
Q	Louie Bickerton (AUS)	A. Price (AUS)	6-4	7-5	
Q	Sylvia Lance Harper (AUS)	Frances Hoddle-Wrigley (AUS)	6-4	3-6	6-2

1931 (SYDNEY)

Rd	Winner	Defeated	S1	S2	S3
F	Coral McInnes Buttsworth (AUS)	Marjorie Cox Crawford (AUS)	1-6	6-3	6-4
S	Coral McInnes Buttsworth (AUS)	Sylvia Lance Harper (AUS)	0-6	6-4	(retired)
S	Marjorie Cox Crawford (AUS)	Kathrine Le Mesurier (AUS)	3-6	6-2	7-5
Q	Coral McInnes Buttsworth (AUS)	Frances Hoddle-Wrigley (AUS)	6-1	6-2	
Q	Sylvia Lance Harper (AUS)	Patricia Meaney (AUS)	6-1	6-2	
Q	Kathrine Le Mesurier (AUS)	Loule Bickerton (AUS)	6-1	6-3	
Q	Marjorie Cox Crawford (AUS)	Joan Hartigan (AUS)	6-4	4-6	6-4

1932 (ADELAIDE)

Rd	Winner	Defeated	S1	S2	S3
F	Coral McInnes Buttsworth (AUS)	Kathrine Le Mesurier (AUS)	9-7	6-4	
S	Coral McInnes Buttsworth (AUS)	Dorothy Weston (AUS)	6-1	6-1	
S	Kathrine Le Mesurier (AUS)	Emily Hood Westacott (AUS)	10-8	7-5	
Q	Coral McInnes Buttsworth (AUS)	Meryl O'Hara Wood (AUS)	6-1	6-3	
Q	Dorothy Weston (AUS)	J. Wilson (AUS)	6-1	6-0	
Q	Emily Hood Westacott (AUS)	Frances Hoddle-Wrigley (AUS)	6-4	7-5	
Q	Kathrine Le Mesurier (AUS)	Marjorie Cox Crawford (AUS)	6-2	6-4	

1933 (MELBOURNE)

Rd	Winner	Defeated	S1	S2	S3
F	Joan Hartigan (AUS)	Coral McInnes Buttsworth (AUS)	6-4	6-3	
S	Joan Hartigan (AUS)	Frances Hoddle-Wrigley (AUS)	4-6	6-0	6-4
S	Coral McInnes Buttsworth (AUS)	Emily Hood Westacott (AUS)	9-7	3-6	6-3
Q	Joan Hartigan (AUS)	Mall Molesworth (AUS)	4-6	8-6	9-7
Q	Frances Hoddle-Wrigley (AUS)	Birdie Bond (AUS)	3-6	8-6	6-4
Q	Emily Hood Westacott (AUS)	Nancy Lewis (AUS)	6-3	6-4	
Q	Coral McInnes Buttsworth (AUS)	Nell Hall (AUS)	6-4	6-2	

1934 (SYDNEY)

Rd	Winner	Defeated	S1	S2	S3
F	Joan Hartigan (AUS)	Mall Molesworth (AUS)	6-1	6-4	
S	Joan Hartigan (AUS)	Louie Bickerton (AUS)	6-1	6-3	
S	Mall Molesworth (AUS)	Kathrine Le Mesurier (AUS)	7-5	6-4	
Q	Joan Hartigan (AUS)	Ula Valkenburg (AUS)	6-1	6-4	
Q	Louie Bickerton (AUS)	Kathrine Le Mesurier (AUS)	6-3	6-1	
Q	Kathrine Le Mesurier (AUS)	Emily Hood Westacott (AUS)	2-6	10-8	6-3
Q	Mall Molesworth (AUS)	Nell Hall (AUS)	6-4	6-1	

1935 (MELBOURNE)

Rd	Winner	Defeated	S1	S2	S3
F	Dorothy Round (GBR)	Nancy Lyle (GBR)	1-6	6-1	6-3
S	Dorothy Round (GBR)	Emily Hood Westacott (AUS)	6-4	6-2	
S	Nancy Lyle (GBR)	Nell Hall Hopman (AUS)	6-1	7-5	
Q	Dorothy Round (GBR)	May Blick (AUS)	6-4	6-0	
Q	Emily Hood Westacott (AUS)	Evelyn Dearman (GBR)	9-7	7-5	
Q	Nell Hall Hopman (AUS)	Joan Walters (AUS)	4-6	6-1	6-3
Q	Nancy Lyle (GBR)	Louie Bickerton (AUS)	6-2	8-6	

1936 (ADELAIDE)

Rd	Winner	Defeated	S1	S2	S3
F	Joan Hartigan (AUS)	Nancye Wynne (AUS)	6-4	6-4	
S	Joan Hartigan (AUS)	May Blick (AUS)	7-5	6-3	
S	Nancye Wynne (AUS)	Thelma Coyne Long (AUS)	1-6	7-5	7-5
Q	Joan Hartigan (AUS)	Gwen Griffiths (AUS)	6-1	6-4	
Q	May Blick (AUS)	Joan Walters (AUS)	5-7	6-1	6-1
Q	Thelma Coyne Long (AUS)	May Hardcastle (AUS)	6-2	8-6	
Q	Nancye Wynne (AUS)	Nell Hall Hopman (AUS)	3-6	6-3	6-4

1937 (SYDNEY)

Rd	Winner	Defeated	S1	S2	S3
F	Nancye Wynne (AUS)	Emily Hood Westacott (AUS)	6-3	5-7	6-4
S	Nancye Wynne (AUS)	Thelma Coyne Long (AUS)	7-5	4-6	6-4
S	Emily Hood Westacott (AUS)	Dorothy Stevenson (AUS)	3-6	8-6	9-7
Q	Nancye Wynne (AUS)	Sadie Berryman (AUS)	6-0	6-1	
Q	Thelma Coyne Long (AUS)	Vera Selwyn (AUS)	6-1	6-1	
Q	Dorothy Stevenson (AUS)	Joan Hartigan (AUS)	4-6	6-3	6-4
Q	Emily Hood Westacott (AUS)	Margeret Wilson (AUS)	7-5	8-6	

1938 (ADELAIDE)

Rd	Winner	Defeated	S1	S2	S3
F	Dorothy Bundy (USA)	Dorothy Stevenson (AUS)	6-3	6-2	
S	Dorothy Bundy (USA)	Nell Hall Hopman (AUS)	6-2	6-3	
S	Dorothy Stevenson (AUS)	Nancye Wynne (AUS)	6-3	6-3	
Q	Dorothy Bundy (USA)	Mary Hardcastle (AUS)	6-3	6-4	
Q	Nell Hall Hopman (AUS)	Thelma Coyne Long (AUS)	6-4	6-2	
Q	Nancye Wynne (AUS)	Dorothy Workman (AUS)	6-4	6-3	
Q	Dorothy Stevenson (AUS)	Joan Hartigan (AUS)	6-3	1-6	6-1

Rd	Winner	Defeated	S1	S2	S3

1939 (MELBOURNE)

Rd	Winner	Defeated	S1	S2	S3
F	Emily Hood Westacott (AUS)	Nell Hall Hopman (AUS)	6-1	6-2	
S	Emily Hood Westacott (AUS)	Joan Hartigan (AUS)	6-2	6-3	
S	Nell Hall Hopman (AUS)	Thelma Coyne Long (AUS)	6-3	6-4	
Q	Emily Hood Westacott (AUS)	Connie Coate (AUS)	6-4	6-2	
Q	Joan Hartigan (AUS)	Sadie Berryman (AUS)	6-1	6-4	
Q	Thelma Coyne Long (AUS)	May Blick (AUS)	1-6	6-4	6-1
Q	Nell Hall Hopman (AUS)	Mary Hardcastle (AUS)	6-3	6-3	

1940 (SYDNEY)

Rd	Winner	Defeated	S1	S2	S3
F	Nancye Wynne (AUS)	Thelma Coyne Long (AUS)	5-7	6-4	6-0
S	Nancye Wynne (AUS)	Joan Hartigan (AUS)	6-0	1-6	6-1
S	Thelma Coyne Long (AUS)	Nell Hall Hopman (AUS)	6-4	2-6	6-3
Q	Nancye Wynne (AUS)	Gwen O'Halloran (AUS)	6-0	6-3	
Q	Joan Hartigan (AUS)	Mary Hardcastle (AUS)	6-2	6-3	
Q	Nell Hall Hopman (AUS)	Alison Hattersley (AUS)	6-3	6-4	
Q	Thelma Coyne Long (AUS)	Connie Coate (AUS)	6-1	6-3	

1941-45 NOT HELD —WWII

1946 (ADELAIDE)

Rd	Winner	Defeated	S1	S2	S3
F	Nancye Wynne Bolton (AUS)	Joyce Fitch (AUS)	6-4	6-4	
S	Joyce Fitch (AUS)	Marie Toomey (AUS)	7-5	6-4	
S	Nancye Wynne Bolton (AUS)	Connie Coate Wilson (AUS)	6-2	6-1	
Q	Marie Toomey (AUS)	Nell Hall Hopman (AUS)	6-2	4-6	6-3
Q	Joyce Fitch (AUS)	Thelma Coyne Long (AUS)	6-2	6-4	
Q	Nancye Wynne Bolton (AUS)	Dulcie Whittaker (AUS)	6-2	6-2	
Q	Connie Coate Wilson (AUS)	Joan Hartigan (AUS)	6-2	8-6	

1947 (SYDNEY)

Rd	Winner	Defeated	S1	S2	S3
F	Nancye Wynne Bolton (AUS)	Nell Hall Hopman (AUS)	6-3	6-2	
S	Nancye Wynne Bolton (AUS)	Pat Jones (AUS)	6-2	6-1	
S	Nell Hall Hopman (AUS)	Thelma Coyne Long (AUS)	6-4	6-1	
Q	Nancye Wynne Bolton (AUS)	Mary Bevis (AUS)	6-3	6-1	
Q	Pat Jones (AUS)	Marie Toomey (AUS)	7-5	2-6	7-5
Q	Thelma Coyne Long (AUS)	Connie Coate Wilson (AUS)	6-2	6-4	
Q	Nell Hall Hopman (AUS)	Joyce Fitch (AUS)	6-2	2-6	6-0

1948 (MELBOURNE)

Rd	Winner	Defeated	S1	S2	S3
F	Nancye Wynne Bolton (AUS)	Marie Toomey (AUS)	6-3	6-1	
S	Nancye Wynne Bolton (AUS)	Mary Bevis (AUS)	6-3	6-4	
S	Marie Toomey (AUS)	Esme Ashford (AUS)	4-6	7-5	6-4
Q	Nancye Wynne Bolton (AUS)	Joan Tuckfield (AUS)	6-2	6-0	
Q	Mary Bevis (AUS)	Nell Hall Hopman (AUS)	7-5	6-4	
Q	Marie Toomey (AUS)	Dorothy Jenkins (AUS)	8-6	6-3	
Q	Esme Ashford (AUS)	Clare Proctor (AUS)	6-1	6-0	

1949 (ADELAIDE)

Rd	Winner	Defeated	S1	S2	S3
F	Doris Hart (USA)	Nancye Wynne Bolton (AUS)	6-3	6-4	
S	Doris Hart (USA)	Allison Burton Baker (AUS)	6-3	6-1	
S	Nancye Wynne Bolton (AUS)	Thelma Coyne Long (AUS)	6-4	6-2	
Q	Doris Hart (USA)	Dukie Whittaker (AUS)	3-6	6-3	6-2
Q	Allison Burton Baker (AUS)	Marie Toomey (AUS)	6-3	1-6	6-3
Q	Thelma Coyne Long (AUS)	Sadie Berryman Newcombe (AUS)	6-0	6-3	
Q	Nancye Wynne Bolton (AUS)	Mary Bevis Hawton (AUS)	6-1	6-1	

1950 (ADELAIDE)

Rd	Winner	Defeated	S1	S2	S3
F	Louise Brough (USA)	Doris Hart (USA)	6-4	3-6	6-4
S	Louise Brough (USA)	Joyce Fitch (AUS)	6-4	6-4	
S	Doris Hart (USA)	Nancye Wynne Bolton (AUS)	6-2	6-3	
Q	Louise Brough (USA)	Sadie Berryman Newcombe (AUS)	6-2	6-2	
Q	Joyce Fitch (AUS)	Thelma Coyne Long (AUS)	7-5	0-6	6-4
Q	Nancye Wynne Bolton (AUS)	Mary Bevis Hawton (AUS)	6-0	6-2	
Q	Doris Hart (USA)	Nell Hall Hopman (AUS)	6-0	6-1	

1951 (SYDNEY)

Rd	Winner	Defeated	S1	S2	S3
F	Nancye Wynne Bolton (AUS)	Thelma Coyne Long (AUS)	6-1	7-5	
S	Nancye Wynne Bolton (AUS)	Esme Ashford (AUS)	6-1	6-0	
S	Thelma Coyne Long (AUS)	Joyce Fitch (AUS)	6-8	6-4	6-2
Q	Nancye Wynne Bolton (AUS)	Beryln Penrose (AUS)	8-6	6-2	
Q	Esme Ashford (AUS)	Mary Bevis Hawton (AUS)	6-1	4-6	6-3
Q	Thelma Coyne Long (AUS)	Nell Hall Hopman (AUS)	6-2	6-1	
Q	Joyce Fitch (AUS)	Clare Proctor (AUS)	4-6	6-1	6-3

1952 (ADELAIDE)

Rd	Winner	Defeated	S1	S2	S3
F	Thelma Coyne Long (AUS)	Helen Angwin (AUS)	6-2	6-3	
S	Helen Angwin (AUS)	Nancye Wynne Bolton (AUS)	4-6	6-4	6-4
S	Thelma Coyne Long (AUS)	Mary Bevis Hawton (AUS)	6-0	7-5	
Q	Nancye Wynne Bolton (AUS)	Alison Burton Baker (AUS)	6-1	6-1	
Q	Helen Angwin (AUS)	Beryln Penrose (AUS)	2-6	6-1	6-2
Q	Mary Bevis Hawton (AUS)	Mary Schultz (AUS)	6-1	6-3	
Q	Thelma Coyne Long (AUS)	Ann Theile (AUS)	6-0	4-6	6-2

1953 (MELBOURNE)

Rd	Winner	Defeated	S1	S2	S3
F	Maureen Connolly (USA)	Julia Sampson (USA)	6-3	6-2	
S	Maureen Connolly (USA)	Mary Bevis Hawton (AUS)	6-2	6-1	
S	Julia Sampson (USA)	Dorn Fogarty (AUS)	3-6	6-3	6-4
Q	Mary Bevis Hawton (AUS)	Fay Muller (AUS)	6-1	6-2	
Q	Maureen Connolly (USA)	Pam Southcombe (AUS)	6-0	6-1	
Q	Julia Sampson (USA)	Ann Theile (AUS)	6-2	6-2	
Q	Dorn Fogarty (AUS)	Jenny Staley (AUS)	6-4	5-7	6-2

1954 (SYDNEY)

Rd	Winner	Defeated	S1	S2	S3
F	Thelma Coyne Long (AUS)	Jenny Staley (AUS)	6-3	6-4	
S	Thelma Coyne Long (AUS)	Mary Carter (AUS)	6-2	6-3	
S	Jenny Staley (AUS)	Mary Bevis Hawton (AUS)	6-1	6-1	
Q	Thelma Coyne Long (AUS)	Nell Hall Hopman (AUS)	6-0	6-0	
Q	Mary Carter (AUS)	Loris Nichols (AUS)	7-5	6-4	
Q	Jenny Staley (AUS)	Hazel Redick-Smith (RSA)	10-8	5-7	6-3
Q	Mary Bevis Hawton (AUS)	Barbara Warby (AUS)	6-4	6-3	

1955 (ADELAIDE)

Rd	Winner	Defeated	S1	S2	S3
F	Beryl Penrose (AUS)	Thelma Coyne Long (AUS)	6-4	6-3	
S	Thelma Coyne Long (AUS)	Mary Carter (AUS)	6-2	6-1	
S	Beryln Penrose (AUS)	Jenny Staley (AUS)	6-4	8-6	
Q	Thelma Coyne Long (AUS)	Norma Ellis (AUS)	6-0	6-3	
Q	Mary Carter (AUS)	Fay Muller (AUS)	4-6	6-2	6-3
Q	Jenny Staley (AUS)	Nell Hall Hopman (AUS)	6-3	6-0	
Q	Beryln Penrose (AUS)	Mary Bevis Hawton (AUS)	6-1	1-6	8-6

1956 (BRISBANE)

	Winner	Defeated	S1	S2	S3
F	Mary Carter (AUS)	Thelma Coyne Long (AUS)	3-6	6-2	9-7
S	Thelma Coyne Long (AUS)	Mary Bevis Hawton (AUS)	0-6	6-3	9-7
S	Mary Carter (AUS)	Daphne Seeney (AUS)	6-3	7-5	
Q	Mary Bevis Hawton (AUS)	Lorraine Coghlan (AUS)	0-6	6-0	6-3
Q	Thelma Coyne Long (AUS)	Fay Muller (AUS)	7-5	6-1	
Q	Daphne Seeney (AUS)	Beryln Penrose (AUS)	6-2	6-1	
Q	Mary Carter (AUS)	Loris Nichols Southam (AUS)	6-1	7-5	

1957 (MELBOURNE)

	Winner	Defeated	S1	S2	S3
F	Shirley Fry (USA)	Althea Gibson (USA)	6-3	6-4	
S	Shirley Fry (USA)	Beryln Penrose (AUS)	6-3	6-4	
S	Althea Gibson (USA)	Lorraine Coghlan (AUS)	7-5	9-7	
Q	Shirley Fry (USA)	Mary Bevis Hawton (AUS)	6-1	9-7	
Q	Beryln Penrose (AUS)	Jenny Staley (AUS)	7-5	6-2	
Q	Lorraine Coghlan (AUS)	Mary Carter (AUS)	8-10	6-4	6-1
Q	Althea Gibson (USA)	Loris Nichols Southam (AUS)	6-1	6-3	

1958 (SYDNEY)

	Winner	Defeated	S1	S2	S3
F	Angela Mortimer (GBR)	Lorraine Coghlan (AUS)	6-3	6-4	
S	Lorraine Coghlan (AUS)	Mary Carter (AUS)	6-1	6-1	
S	Angela Mortimer (GBR)	Betty Holstein (AUS)	6-2	6-1	
Q	Lorraine Coghlan (AUS)	Margaret Rayson (AUS)	6-3	6-1	
Q	Mary Carter (AUS)	Bertha Jones(AUS)	8-6	6-1	
Q	Betty Holstein (AUS)	Mary Bevis Hawton (AUS)	7-5	6-8	6-4
Q	Angela Mortimer (GBR)	Fay Muller (AUS)		6-1	6-2

1959 (ADELAIDE)

	Winner	Defeated	S1	S2	S3
F	Mary Carter Reitano (AUS)	Renee Schuurman (RSA)	6-2	6-3	
S	Renee Schuurman (RSA)	Mary Bevis Hawton (AUS)	6-3	6-0	
S	Mary Carter Reitano (AUS)	Jan Lehane (AUS)	6-3	6-0	
Q	Renee Schuurman (RSA)	Lesley Turner (AUS)	6-2	6-0	
Q	Mary Bevis Hawton (AUS)	Lorraine Coghlan (AUS)	6-4	4-6	6-0
Q	Mary Carter Reitano (AUS)	Beverly Rae (AUS)	8-6	6-4	
Q	Jan Lehane (AUS)	Sandra Reynolds (RSA)	6-3	6-4	

1960 (BRISBANE)

	Winner	Defeated	S1	S2	S3
F	Margaret Smith (AUS)	Jan Lehane (AUS)	7-5	6-2	
S	Jan Lehane (AUS)	Christine Truman (GBR)	7-5	3-6	7-5
S	Margaret Smith (AUS)	Mary Carter Reitano (AUS)	7-5	2-6	6-2
Q	Christine Truman (GBR)	Fay Muller (AUS)	6-0	6-0	
Q	Jan Lehane (AUS)	L. Coghlan Robinson (AUS)	6-1	6-1	
Q	Margaret Smith (AUS)	Mary Bevis Hawton (AUS)	6-2	8-6	
Q	Mary Carter Reitano (AUS)	Maria Bueno (BRA)	7-5	3-6	6-4

1961 (MELBOURNE)

	Winner	Defeated	S1	S2	S3
F	Margaret Smith (AUS)	Jan Lehane (AUS)	6-1	6-4	
S	Margaret Smith (AUS)	Robyn Ebbern (AUS)	6-2	6-0	
S	Jan Lehane (AUS)	Mary Carter Reitano (AUS)	6-2	4-6	6-1
Q	Margaret Smith (AUS)	Kaye Dening (AUS)	6-4	6-3	
Q	Robyn Ebbern (AUS)	Val Wicks (AUS)	6-4	6-2	
Q	Mary Carter Reitano (AUS)	Mary Carter Reitano (AUS)	6-4	6-2	
Q	Jan Lehane (AUS)	L. Coghlan Robinson (AUS)	6-2	6-2	

1962 (SYDNEY)

	Winner	Defeated	S1	S2	S3
F	Margaret Smith (AUS)	Jan Lehane (AUS)	6-0	6-2	
S	Margaret Smith (AUS)	Yola Ramirez (MEX)	6-2	6-1	
S	Jan Lehane (AUS)	Mary Carter Reitano (AUS)	6-2	2-6	6-4
Q	Margaret Smith (AUS)	Judy Tegart (AUS)	6-2	7-5	
Q	Yola Ramirez (MEX)	Norma Marsh (AUS)	5-7	6-0	6-2
Q	Mary Carter Reitano (AUS)	Lesley Turner (AUS)	6-1	1-6	6-2
Q	Jan Lehane (AUS)	Darlene Hard (USA)	7-5	6-4	

1963 (ADELAIDE)

	Winner	Defeated	S1	S2	S3
F	Margaret Smith (AUS)	Jan Lehane (AUS)	6-2	6-2	
S	Jan Lehane (AUS)	Lesley Turner (AUS)	5-7	6-3	6-2
S	Margaret Smith (AUS)	Robyn Ebbern (AUS)	6-1	6-3	
Q	Lesley Turner (AUS)	Elisabeth Starkie (GBR)	6-2	1-6	6-2
Q	Jan Lehane (AUS)	Madonna Schacht (AUS)	6-1	6-4	
Q	Robyn Ebbern (AUS)	Kaye Dening (AUS)	6-2	6-4	
Q	Margaret Smith (AUS)	Rita Lauder (AUS)	6-1	6-3	

1964 (BRISBANE)

	Winner	Defeated	S1	S2	S3
F	Margaret Smith (AUS)	Lesley Turner (AUS)	6-3	6-2	
S	Lesley Turner (AUS)	Robyn Ebbern (AUS)	6-3	6-1	
S	Margaret Smith (AUS)	Jan Lehane (AUS)	6-4	6-2	
Q	Lesley Turner (AUS)	Jill Blackman (AUS)	6-1	6-3	
Q	Robyn Ebbern (AUS)	Judy Tegart (AUS)	6-2	6-4	
Q	Jan Lehane (AUS)	Helen Gourlay (AUS)	6-2	6-0	
Q	Margaret Smith (AUS)	Madonna Schacht (AUS)	4-6	6-1	6-1

1965 (MELBOURNE)

	Winner	Defeated	S1	S2	S3
F	Margaret Smith (AUS)	Maria Bueno (BRA)	5-7	6-3 5-2(retired)	
S	Maria Bueno (BRA)	Annette Van Zyl (RSA)	6-2	6-3	
S	Margaret Smith (AUS)	Billie Jean Moffitt (USA)	6-1	8-6	
Q	Annette Van Zyl (RSA)	Lesley Turner (AUS)	6-3	6-4	
Q	Maria Bueno (BRA)	Judy Tegart (AUS)	6-2	6-2	
Q	Billie Jean Moffitt (USA)	Kerry Melville (AUS)	6-1	6-2	
Q	Margaret Smith (AUS)	Francoise Durr (FRA)	6-3	6-3	

1966 (MELBOURNE)

	Winner	Defeated	S1	S2	S3
F	Margaret Smith (AUS)	Nancy Richey (USA)	(walkover)		
S	Margaret Smith (AUS)	Carole Graebner (USA)	6-2	6-4	
S	Nancy Richey (USA)	Kerry Melville (AUS)	6-2	8-6	
Q	Margaret Smith (AUS)	Madonna Schacht (AUS)	6-1	6-3	
Q	Carole Graebner (USA)	Judy Tegart (AUS)	6-3	6-3	
Q	Kerry Melville (AUS)	Joan Gibson (AUS)	6-2	3-6	6-4
Q	Nancy Richey (USA)	Helen Amos (AUS)	6-2	6-3	

1967 (MELBOURNE)

	Winner	Defeated	S1	S2	S3
F	Nancy Richey (USA)	Lesley Turner (AUS)	6-1	6-4	
S	Lesley Turner (AUS)	Rosie Casals (USA)	4-6	6-1	6-4
S	Nancy Richey (USA)	Kerry Melville (AUS)	6-4	6-1	
Q	Lesley Turner (AUS)	Francoise Durr (FRA)	6-1	10-8	
Q	Rosie Casals (USA)	Gail Sheriff (AUS)	6-3	6-3	
Q	Kerry Melville (AUS)	Judy Tegart (AUS)	6-1	4-6	10-8
Q	Nancy Richey (USA)	L. Coghlan Robinson (AUS)	6-3	1-0	(retired)

1968 (MELBOURNE)

Rd	Winner	Defeated	S1	S2	S3
F	Billie Jean King (USA)	Margaret Smith Court (AUS)	6-1	6-2	
S	Margaret Smith Court (AUS)	Lesley Turner (AUS)	6-2	6-3	
S	Billie Jean King (USA)	Judy Tegart (AUS)	4-6	6-1	6-1
Q	Lesley Turner (AUS)	Kathy Harter (USA)	3-6	6-2	6-2
Q	Margaret Smith Court (AUS)	Rosie Casals (USA)	6-0	6-2	
Q	Judy Tegart (AUS)	Karen Krantzcke (AUS)	4-6	10-8	6-3
Q	Billie Jean King (USA)	Astrid Suurbeck (NED)	6-1	6-2	

1969 (BRISBANE)

Rd	Winner	Defeated	S1	S2	S3
F	Margaret Smith Court (AUS)	Billie Jean King (USA)	6-4	6-1	
S	Billie Jean King (USA)	Ann Haydon Jones (GBR)	4-6	6-2	6-3
S	Margaret Smith Court (AUS)	Kerry Melville (AUS)	3-6	6-2	7-5
Q	Billie Jean King (USA)	Karen Krantzcke (AUS)	11-9	7-5	
Q	Ann Haydon Jones (GBR)	Lesley Hunt (AUS)	6-3	6-1	
Q	Kerry Melville (AUS)	Helen Gourlay (AUS)	6-3	4-6	6-4
Q	Margaret Smith Court (AUS)	Rosie Casals (USA)	6-4	6-1	

1970 (SYDNEY)

Rd	Winner	Defeated	S1	S2	S3
F	Margaret Smith Court (AUS)	Kerry Melville (AUS)	6-1	6-3	
S	Kerry Melville (AUS)	Winnie Shaw (GBR)	8-6	6-3	
S	Margaret Smith Court (AUS)	Karen Krantzcke (AUS)	6-1	6-2	
Q	Margaret Smith Court (AUS)	Evonne Goolagong (AUS)	6-3	6-1	
Q	Karen Krantzcke (AUS)	Judy Tegart Dalton (AUS)	8-6	11-9	
Q	Kerry Melville (AUS)	Christina Sandberg (SWE)	6-0	6-2	
Q	Winnie Shaw (GBR)	Lesley Hunt (AUS)	6-4	6-3	

1971 (SYDNEY)

Rd	Winner	Defeated	S1	S2	S3
F	Margaret Smith Court (AUS)	Evonne Goolagong (AUS)	2-6	7-6(0)	7-5
S	Evonne Goolagong (AUS)	Winnie Shaw (GBR)	7-6	6-1	
S	Margaret Smith Court (AUS)	Lesley Hunt (AUS)	6-0	6-3	
Q	Margaret Smith Court (AUS)	Helen Gourlay Cawley (AUS)	6-0	6-4	
Q	Lesley Hunt (AUS)	Jan Lehane O'Neill (AUS)	6-4	6-4	
Q	Winnie Shaw (GBR)	Norma Marsh (AUS)	6-0	7-6	
Q	Evonne Goolagong (AUS)	Sharon Walsh (USA)	6-3	6-4	

1972 (MELBOURNE)

Rd	Winner	Defeated	S1	S2	S3
F	Virginia Wade (GBR)	Evonne Goolagong (AUS)	6-4	6-4	
S	Virginia Wade (GBR)	Kerry Harris (AUS)	7-6	2-6	6-0
S	Evonne Goolagong (AUS)	Helen Gourlay (AUS)	6-2	7-6	
Q	Evonne Goolagong (AUS)	Barbara Hawcroft (AUS)	6-1	3-6	6-1
Q	Helen Gourlay (AUS)	Olga Morozova (USSR)	6-2	6-1	
Q	Kerry Harris (AUS)	Gail Sherriff Chanfreau (FRA)	6-3	7-6	
Q	Virginia Wade (GBR)	Patricia Coleman (AUS)	6-2	6-2	

1973 (MELBOURNE)

Rd	Winner	Defeated	S1	S2	S3
F	Margaret Smith Court (AUS)	Evonne Goolagong (AUS)	6-4	7-5	
S	Evonne Goolagong (AUS)	Kazuko Sawamatsu (JPN)	6-4	6-3	
S	Margaret Smith Court (AUS)	Kerry Melville (AUS)	6-1	6-0	
Q	Margaret Smith Court (AUS)	Karen Krantzcke (AUS)	6-4	6-3	
Q	Kerry Melville (AUS)	Dianne Fromholtz (AUS)	6-1	6-3	
Q	Kazuko Sawamatsu (JPN)	Virginia Wade (GBR)	0-6	6-1	6-4
Q	Evonne Goolagong (AUS)	Kerry Harris (AUS)	6-4	6-3	

1974 (MELBOURNE)

Rd	Winner	Defeated	S1	S2	S3
F	Evonne Goolagong (AUS)	Chris Evert (USA)	7-6(5)	4-6	6-0
S	Evonne Goolagong (AUS)	Kerry Melville (AUS)	7-6	5-7	6-1
S	Chris Evert (USA)	Julie Heldman (USA)	6-2	6-3	
Q	Chris Evert (USA)	Janet Newberry (USA)	6-2	6-4	
Q	Julie Heldman (USA)	Lesley Hunt (AUS)	7-5	6-7	6-2
Q	Kerry Melville (AUS)	Judy Tegart Dalton (AUS)	6-3	6-4	
Q	Evonne Goolagong (AUS)	Karen Krantzcke (AUS)	4-6	6-3	6-2

1975 (MELBOURNE)

Rd	Winner	Defeated	S1	S2	S3
F	Evonne Goolagong (AUS)	Martina Navratilova (CZE)	6-3	6-2	
S	Martina Navratilova (CZE)	Natasha Chmyreva (USSR)	6-4	6-4	
S	Evonne Goolagong (AUS)	Sue Barker (GBR)	6-2	6-4	
Q	Martina Navratilova (CZE)	Margaret Smith Court (AUS)	6-4	6-3	
Q	Natasha Chmyreva (USSR)	Christine Matison (AUS)	3-6	6-2	7-5
Q	Evonne Goolagong (AUS)	Kazuko Sawamatsu (JPN)	6-3	7-5	
Q	Sue Barker (GBR)	Olga Morozova (USSR)	6-2	7-6	

1976 (MELBOURNE)

Rd	Winner	Defeated	S1	S2	S3
F	Evonne Goolagong Cawley (AUS)	Renata Tomanova (CZE)	6-2	6-2	
S	Evonne Goolagong Cawley (AUS)	Helen Gourlay (AUS)	6-3	6-3	
S	Renata Tomanova (CZE)	Elizabeth Ekblom (SWE)	6-3	6-2	
Q	Evonne Goolagong Cawley (AUS)	Lesley Turner Bowrey (AUS)	6-1	7-6	
Q	Helen Gourlay (AUS)	Heidi Eisterlehner (GER)	6-3	6-7	6-2
Q	Renata Tomanova (CZE)	Helga Masthoff (GER)	4-6	7-5	6-1
Q	Elizabeth Ekblom (SWE)	Christine Matison (AUS)	4-6	6-3	6-1

1977 (JAN.) (MELBOURNE)

Rd	Winner	Defeated	S1	S2	S3
F	Kerry Melville Reid (AUS)	Dianne Fromholtz (AUS)	7-5	6-2	
S	Kerry Melville Reid (AUS)	Helen Gourlay (AUS)	6-2	1-6	6-3
S	Dianne Fromholtz (AUS)	Karen Krantzcke (AUS)	7-6(7)	6-4	
Q	Dianne Fromholtz (AUS)	Jan Wilson (AUS)	6-3	4-6	6-1
Q	Karen Krantzcke (AUS)	Naoko Sato (JPN)	6-3	4-6	6-0
Q	Helen Gourlay (AUS)	Mary Sawyer (AUS)	6-1	6-4	
Q	Kerry Melville Reid (AUS)	Katja Ebbinghaus (GER)	6-0	6-4	

1977 (DEC.) (MELBOURNE)

Rd	Winner	Defeated	S1	S2	S3
F	Evonne Goolagong Cawley (AUS)	Helen Gourlay Cawley (AUS)	6-3	6-0	
S	Helen Gourlay Cawley (AUS)	Sue Barker (GBR)	7-5	6-4	
S	Evonne Goolagong Cawley (AUS)	Kerry Melville Reid (AUS)	6-1	6-3	
Q	Evonne Goolagong Cawley (AUS)	Judy Tegart Dalton (AUS)	6-3	6-1	
Q	Kerry Melville Reid (AUS)	Kathy Harter (USA)	6-1	7-5	
Q	Helen Gourlay Cawley (AUS)	Mona Schallau Guerrant (USA)	3-6	6-1	6-4
Q	Sue Barker (GBR)	Rayni Fox (USA)	6-3	6-0	

1978 (MELBOURNE)

Rd	Winner	Defeated	S1	S2	S3
F	Chris O'Neil (AUS)	Betsy Nagelsen (USA)	6-3	7-6(4)	
S	Chris O'Neil (AUS)	Diane Evers (AUS)	6-0	6-3	
S	Betsy Nagelsen (USA)	Christine Matison (AUS)	7-5	6-4	
Q	Diane Evers (AUS)	Sue Barker (GBR)	6-2	7-6	
Q	Chris O'Neil (AUS)	Dorte Ekner (DEN)	7-5	6-1	
Q	Christine Matison (AUS)	Mary Sawyer (AUS)	6-4	6-3	
Q	Betsy Nagelsen (USA)	Renata Tomanova (CZE)	6-4	6-4	

1979 (MELBOURNE)

Rd	Winner	Defeated	S1	S2	S3
F	Barbara Jordan (USA)	Sharon Walsh (USA)	6-3	6-3	
S	Sharon Walsh (USA)	Mary Sawyer (AUS)	7-6	6-3	
S	Barbara Jordan (USA)	Renata Tomanova (CZE)	5-7	6-3	6-3
Q	Mary Sawyer (AUS)	Janet Newberry (USA)	7-6	6-3	
Q	Sharon Walsh (USA)	Michele Gurdal (BEL)	6-0	6-3	
Q	Renata Tomanova (CZE)	Cynthia Doerner (AUS)	6-2	6-1	
Q	Barbara Jordan (USA)	Hana Mandlikova (CZE)	6-2	6-2	

1980 (MELBOURNE)

Rd	Winner	Defeated	S1	S2	S3
F	Hana Mandlikova (CZE)	Wendy Turnbull (AUS)	6-0	7-5	
S	Wendy Turnbull (AUS)	Martina Navratilova (CZE)	6-4	7-5	
S	Hana Mandlikova (CZE)	Mima Jausovec (YUG)	6-4	6-1	
Q	Martina Navratilova (CZE)	Greer Stevens (RSA)	4-6	6-1	7-6
Q	Wendy Turnbull (AUS)	Pam Shriver (USA)	3-6	6-3	6-2
Q	Hana Mandlikova (CZE)	Virginia Ruzici (ROU)	6-1	3-6	6-4
Q	Mima Jausovec (YUG)	Candy Reynolds (USA)	4-6	6-3	6-3

1981 (MELBOURNE)

Rd	Winner	Defeated	S1	S2	S3
F	Martina Navratilova (USA)	Chris Evert Lloyd (USA)	6-7(4)	6-4	7-5
S	Chris Evert Lloyd (USA)	Wendy Turnbull (AUS)	6-4	7-6(1)	
S	Martina Navratilova (USA)	Pam Shriver (USA)	6-3	7-5	
Q	Chris Evert Lloyd (USA)	Hana Mandlikova (CZE)	6-4	7-5	
Q	Wendy Turnbull (AUS)	Andrea Jaeger (USA)	6-3	7-6(10)	
Q	Martina Navratilova (USA)	Evonne Goolagong (AUS)	6-3	6-1	
Q	Pam Shriver (USA)	Tracy Austin (USA)	7-5	7-6(4)	

1982 (MELBOURNE)

Rd	Winner	Defeated	S1	S2	S3
F	Chris Evert Lloyd (USA)	Martina Navratilova (USA)	6-3	2-6	6-3
S	Martina Navratilova (USA)	Pam Shriver (USA)	6-3	6-4	
S	Chris Evert Lloyd (USA)	Andrea Jaeger (USA)	6-1	6-0	
Q	Martina Navratilova (USA)	Anne Smith (USA)	6-2	6-1	
Q	Pam Shriver (USA)	Wendy Turnbull (AUS)	6-7	6-3	6-3
Q	Andrea Jaeger (USA)	Eva Pfaff (GER)	7-5	6-2	
Q	Chris Evert Lloyd (USA)	Billie Jean King (USA)	6-2	6-2	

1983 (MELBOURNE)

Rd	Winner	Defeated	S1	S2	S3
F	Martina Navratilova (USA)	Kathy Jordan (USA)	6-2	7-6(5)	
S	Martina Navratilova (USA)	Pam Shriver (USA)	6-4	6-3	
S	Kathy Jordan (USA)	Zina Garrison (USA)	7-6	6-1	
Q	Martina Navratilova (USA)	Jo Durie (GBR)	4-6	6-3	6-4
Q	Pam Shriver (USA)	Carling Bassett (CAN)	6-0	6-1	
Q	Zina Garrison (USA)	Wendy Turnbull (AUS)	6-2	7-6	
Q	Kathy Jordan (USA)	Sylvia Hanika (GER)	7-6	7-5	

1984 (MELBOURNE)

Rd	Winner	Defeated	S1	S2	S3
F	Chris Evert Lloyd (USA)	Helena Sukova (CZE)	6-7(4)	6-1	6-2
S	Helena Sukova (CZE)	Martina Navratilova (USA)	6-1	7-6(8)	
S	Chris Evert Lloyd (USA)	Wendy Turnbull (AUS)	6-7(5)	6-1	6-4
Q	Martina Navratilova (USA)	Barbara Potter (USA)	6-3	6-3	
Q	Helena Sukova (CZE)	Pam Shriver (USA)	6-4	6-0	
Q	Wendy Turnbull (AUS)	Sharon Walsh (USA)	2-6	6-3	6-3
Q	Chris Evert Lloyd (USA)	Sophie Amiach (FRA)	6-2	6-2	

1985 (MELBOURNE)

Rd	Winner	Defeated	S1	S2	S3
F	Martina Navratilova (USA)	Chris Evert Lloyd (USA)	6-2	4-6	6-2
S	Chris Evert Lloyd (USA)	Claudia Kohde Kilsch (GER)	6-1	7-6(8)	
S	Martina Navratilova (USA)	Hana Mandlikova (CZE)	6-7(5)	6-1	6-4
Q	Chris Evert Lloyd (USA)	Manuela Maleeva (BUL)	6-3	6-3	
Q	Claudia Kohde Kilsch (GER)	Catarina Lindqvist (SWE)	6-4	6-0	
Q	Hana Mandlikova (CZE)	Zina Garrison (USA)	2-6	6-3	6-3
Q	Martina Navratilova (USA)	Helena Sukova (CZE)	6-2	6-2	

1986 (MELBOURNE)

Rd	Winner	Defeated	S1	S2	S3
F	Hana Mandlikova (CZE)	Martina Navratilova (USA)	7-5	7-6(2)	
S	Hana Mandlikova (CZE)	Claudia Kohde Kilsch (GER)	6-1	0-6	6-3
S	Martina Navratilova (USA)	Catarina Lindqvist (SWE)	6-3	6-2	
Q	Claudia Kohde Kilsch (GER)	Liz Sayers Smylie (AUS)	7-6	4-6	6-2
Q	Hana Mandlikova (CZE)	Lori McNeil (USA)	6-0	6-0	
Q	Catarina Lindqvist (SWE)	Pam Shriver (USA)	6-3	6-1	
Q	Martina Navratilova (USA)	Zina Garrison (USA)	6-0	6-3	

1988 (MELBOURNE)

Rd	Winner	Defeated	S1	S2	S3
F	Steffi Graf (GER)	Chris Evert (USA)	6-1	7-6(3)	
S	Chris Evert (USA)	Martina Navratilova (USA)	6-2	7-5	
S	Steffi Graf (GER)	Claudia Kohde Klisch (GER)	6-2	6-3	
Q	Chris Evert (USA)	Claudia Porwik (GER)	6-3	6-1	
Q	Martina Navratilova (USA)	Helena Sukova (CZE)	6-4	7-6(3)	
Q	Steffi Graf (GER)	Hana Mandlikova (CZE)	6-2	6-2	
Q	Claudia Kohde Klisch (GER)	Anne Minter (AUS)	6-2	6-4	

1989 (MELBOURNE)

Rd	Winner	Defeated	S1	S2	S3
F	Steffi Graf (GER)	Helena Sukova (CZE)	6-4	6-4	
S	Helena Sukova (CZE)	Belinda Cordwell (AUS)	7-6(2)	4-6	6-2
S	Steffi Graf (GER)	Gabriela Sabatini (ARG)	6-3	6-0	
Q	Belinda Cordwell (AUS)	Catarina Lindqvist (SWE)	6-2	2-6	6-1
Q	Helena Sukova (CZE)	Martina Navratilova (USA)	6-2	3-6	9-7
Q	Gabriela Sabatini (ARG)	Zina Garrison Jackson (USA)	6-4	2-6	6-4
Q	Steffi Graf (GER)	Claudia Kohde Kilsch (GER)	6-2	6-3	

1990 (MELBOURNE)

Rd	Winner	Defeated	S1	S2	S3
F	Steffi Graf (GER)	Mary Joe Fernandez (USA)	6-3	6-4	
S	Steffi Graf (GER)	Helena Sukova (CZE)	6-3	3-6	6-4
S	Mary Joe Fernandez (USA)	Claudia Porwik (GER)	6-2	6-1	
Q	Steffi Graf (GER)	Patty Fendick (USA)	6-3	7-5	
Q	Helena Sukova (CZE)	Katerina Maleeva (BUL)	6-4	6-3	
Q	Mary Joe Fernandez (USA)	Zina Garrison (USA)	1-6	6-2	8-6
Q	Claudia Porwik (GER)	Angelica Gavaldon (MEX)	6-4	6-3	

1991 (MELBOURNE)

Rd	Winner	Defeated	S1	S2	S3
F	Monica Seles (YUG)	Jana Novotna (CZE)	5-7	6-3	6-1
S	Jana Novotna (CZE)	Arantxa Sanchez Vicario(ESP)	6-2	6-4	
S	Monica Seles (YUG)	Mary Joe Fernandez (USA)	6-3	0-6	9-7
Q	Jana Novotna (CZE)	Steffi Graf (GER)	5-7	6-4	8-6
Q	Arantxa Sanchez Vicario(ESP)	Gabriela Sabatini (ARG)	6-1	6-3	
Q	Mary Joe Fernandez (USA)	Katerina Maleeva (BUL)	6-3	6-2	
Q	Monica Seles (YUG)	Anke Huber (GER)	6-3	6-1	

Rd	Winner	Defeated	S1	S2	S3

1992 (MELBOURNE)

Rd	Winner	Defeated	S1	S2	S3
F	**Monica Seles (YUG)**	**Mary Joe Fernandez (USA)**	6-2	6-3	
S	Monica Seles (YUG)	Arantxa Sanchez Vicario(ESP)	6-2	6-2	
S	Mary Joe Fernandez (USA)	Gabriela Sabatini (ARG)	6-1	6-4	
Q	Monica Seles (YUG)	Anke Huber (GER)	7-5	6-3	
Q	Arantxa Sanchez Vicario(ESP)	Manuela Maleeva Fragniere (SUI)	(walkover)		
Q	Gabriela Sabatini (ARG)	Jennifer Capriati (USA)	6-4	7-6(1)	
Q	Mary Joe Fernandez (USA)	Amy Frazier (USA)	6-4	7-6(6)	

1993 (MELBOURNE)

Rd	Winner	Defeated	S1	S2	S3
F	**Monica Seles (YUG)**	**Steffi Graf (GER)**	4-6	6-3	6-2
S	Monica Seles (YUG)	Gabriela Sabatini (ARG)	6-1	6-2	
S	Steffi Graf (GER)	Arantxa Sanchez Vicario(ESP)	7-5	6-4	
Q	Monica Seles (YUG)	Julie Halard (FRA)	6-2	6-7(7)	6-0
Q	Gabriela Sabatini (ARG)	Mary Pierce (FRA)	4-6	7-6(7)	6-0
Q	Arantxa Sanchez Vicario(ESP)	Mary Joe Fernandez (USA)	7-5	6-4	
Q	Steffi Graf (GER)	Jennifer Capriati (USA)	7-5	6-2	

1994 (MELBOURNE)

Rd	Winner	Defeated	S1	S2	S3
F	**Steffi Graf (GER)**	**Arantxa Sanchez Vicario(ESP)**	6-0	6-2	
S	Steffi Graf (GER)	Kimiko Date (JPN)	6-3	6-3	
S	Arantxa Sanchez Vicario(ESP)	Gabriela Sabatini (ARG)	6-1	6-2	
Q	Steffi Graf (GER)	Lindsay Davenport (USA)	6-3	6-2	
Q	Kimiko Date (JPN)	Conchita Martinez (ESP)	6-2	4-6	6-3
Q	Gabriela Sabatini (ARG)	Jana Novotna (CZE)	6-3	6-4	
Q	Arantxa Sanchez Vicario(ESP)	M. Maleeva-Fragniere (SUI)	7-6(3)	6-4	

1995 (MELBOURNE)

Rd	Winner	Defeated	S1	S2	S3
F	**Mary Pierce (FRA)**	**Arantxa Sanchez Vicario(ESP)**	6-3	6-2	
S	Arantxa Sanchez Vicario(ESP)	M. Werdel Witmeyer (USA)	6-4	6-1	
S	Mary Pierce (FRA)	Conchita Martinez (ESP)	6-3	6-1	
Q	Arantxa Sanchez Vicario(ESP)	Naoko Sawamatsu (JPN)	6-1	6-3	
Q	M. Werdel Witmeyer (USA)	Angelica Gavaldon (MEX)	6-1	6-2	
Q	Mary Pierce (FRA)	Natasha Zvereva (BLR)	6-1	6-4	
Q	Conchita Martinez (ESP)	Lindsay Davenport (USA)	6-3	4-6	6-3

1996 (MELBOURNE)

Rd	Winner	Defeated	S1	S2	S3
F	**Monica Seles (USA)**	**Anke Huber (GER)**	6-4	6-1	
S	Monica Seles (USA)	Chanda Rubin (USA)	6-7(2)	6-1	7-5
S	Anke Huber (GER)	Amanda Coetzer (RSA)	4-6	6-4	6-2
Q	Monica Seles (USA)	Iva Majoli (CRO)	6-1	6-2	
Q	Chanda Rubin (USA)	Arantxa Sanchez Vicario (ESP)	6-4	2-6	16-14
Q	Amanda Coetzer (RSA)	Martina Hingis (SUI)	7-5	4-6	6-1
Q	Anke Huber (GER)	Conchita Martinez (ESP)	4-6	6-2	6-1

1997 (MELBOURNE)

Rd	Winner	Defeated	S1	S2	S3
F	**Martina Hingis (SUI)**	**Mary Pierce (FRA)**	6-2	6-2	
S	Mary Pierce (FRA)	Amanda Coetzer (RSA)	7-5	6-1	
S	Martina Hingis (SUI)	Mary Joe Fernandez (USA)	6-1	6-3	
Q	Amanda Coetzer (RSA)	Kimberly Po (USA)	6-4	6-1	
Q	Mary Joe Fernandez (USA)	Sabine Appelmans (BEL)	1-6	6-4	6-4
Q	Martina Hingis (SUI)	Irina Spirlea (ROM)	7-5	6-2	
Q	Mary Pierce (FRA)	Dominique Van Roost (BEL)	7-5	4-0	(retired)

1998 (MELBOURNE)

Rd	Winner	Defeated	S1	S2	S3
F	**Martina Hingis (SUI)**	**Conchita Martinez (ESP)**	6-3	6-3	
S	Martina Hingis (SUI)	Anke Huber (GER)	6-1	2-6	6-1
S	Conchita Martinez (ESP)	Lindsay Davenport (USA)	4-6	6-3	6-3
Q	Martina Hingis (SUI)	Mary Pierce (FRA)	6-2	6-3	
Q	Anke Huber (GER)	Arantxa Sanchez Vicario (ESP)	7-6(7)	7-5	
Q	Conchita Martinez (ESP)	Sandrine Testud (FRA)	6-3	6-2	
Q	Lindsay Davenport (USA)	Venus Williams (USA)	1-6	7-5	6-3

1999 (MELBOURNE)

Rd	Winner	Defeated	S1	S2	S3
F	**Martina Hingis (SUI)**	**Amelie Mauresmo (FRA)**	6-2	6-3	
S	Amelie Mauresmo (FRA)	Lindsay Davenport (USA)	4-6	7-5	7-5
S	Martina Hingis (SUI)	Monica Seles (USA)	6-2	6-4	
Q	Lindsay Davenport (USA)	Venus Williams (USA)	6-4	6-0	
Q	Amelie Mauresmo (FRA)	Dominique Van Roost (BEL)	6-3	7-6(3)	
Q	Monica Seles (USA)	Steffi Graf (GER)	7-5	6-1	
Q	Martina Hingis (SUI)	Mary Pierce (FRA)	6-3	6-4	

2000 (MELBOURNE)

Rd	Winner	Defeated	S1	S2	S3
F	**Lindsay Davenport (USA)**	**Martina Hingis (SUI)**	6-1	7-5	
S	Martina Hingis (SUI)	Conchita Martinez (ESP)	6-3	6-2	
S	Lindsay Davenport (USA)	Jennifer Capriati (USA)	6-2	7-6(4)	
Q	Martina Hingis (SUI)	Arantxa Sanchez Vicario (ESP)	6-1	6-1	
Q	Conchita Martinez (ESP)	Elena Likhovtseva (RUS)	6-3	4-6	9-7
Q	Jennifer Capriati (USA)	Ai Sugiyama (JPN)	6-0	6-2	
Q	Lindsay Davenport (USA)	Julie Halard-Decugis (FRA)	6-1	6-2	

2001 (MELBOURNE)

Rd	Winner	Defeated	S1	S2	S3
F	**Jennifer Capriati (USA)**	**Martina Hingis (SUI)**	6-4	6-3	
S	Martina Hingis (SUI)	Venus Williams (USA)	6-1	6-1	
S	Jennifer Capriati (USA)	Lindsay Davenport (USA)	6-3	6-4	
Q	Martina Hingis (SUI)	Serena Williams (USA)	6-2	3-6	8-6
Q	Venus Williams (USA)	Amanda Coetzer (RSA)	2-6	6-1	8-6
Q	Jennifer Capriati (USA)	Monica Seles (USA)	5-7	6-4	6-3
Q	Lindsay Davenport (USA)	Anna Kournikova (RUS)	6-4	6-2	

2002 (MELBOURNE)

Rd	Winner	Defeated	S1	S2	S3
F	**Jennifer Capriati (USA)**	**Martina Hingis (SUI)**	4-6	7-6(7)	6-2
S	Jennifer Capriati (USA)	Kim Clijsters (BEL)	7-5	3-6	6-1
S	Martina Hingis (SUI)	Monica Seles (USA)	4-6	6-1	6-4
Q	Jennifer Capriati (USA)	Amelie Mauresmo (FRA)	6-2	6-2	
Q	Kim Clijsters (BEL)	Justine Henin (BEL)	6-2	6-3	
Q	Martina Hingis (SUI)	Arantxa Sanchez Vicario (ESP)	6-2	6-3	
Q	Monica Seles (USA)	Venus Williams (USA)	6-7(4)	6-2	6-3

2003 (MELBOURNE)

Rd	Winner	Defeated	S1	S2	S3
F	**Serena Williams (USA)**	**Venus Williams (USA)**	7-6(4)	3-6	6-4
S	Serena Williams (USA)	Kim Clijsters (BEL)	4-6	6-3	7-5
S	Venus Williams (USA)	Justine Henin-Hardenne (BEL)	6-3	6-3	
Q	Serena Williams (USA)	Meghann Shaughnessy (USA)	6-2	6-2	
Q	Kim Clijsters (BEL)	Anastasia Myskina (RUS)	6-2	6-4	
Q	Justine Henin-Hardenne (BEL)	Virginia Ruano Pascual (ESP)	6-2	6-2	
Q	Venus Williams (USA)	Daniela Hantuchova (SVK)	6-4	6-3	

Rd	Winner	Defeated	S1	S2	S3

2004 (MELBOURNE)

Rd	Winner	Defeated	S1	S2	S3
F	Justine Henin-Hardenne (BEL)	Kim Clijsters (BEL)	6-3	4-6	6-3
S	Justine Henin-Hardenne (BEL)	Fabiola Zuluaga (COL)	6-2	6-2	
S	Kim Clijsters (BEL)	Patty Schnyder (SUI)	6-2	7-6(9)	
Q	Justine Henin-Hardenne (BEL)	Lindsay Davenport (USA)	7-5	6-3	
Q	Fabiola Zuluaga (COL)	Amelie Mauresmo (FRA)	(walkover)		
Q	Patty Schnyder (SUI)	Lisa Raymond (USA)	7-6(2)	6-3	
Q	Kim Clijsters (BEL)	Anastasia Myskina (RUS)	6-2	7-6(9)	

2005 (MELBOURNE)

Rd	Winner	Defeated	S1	S2	S3
F	Serena Williams (USA)	Lindsay Davenport (USA)	2-6	6-3	6-0
S	Lindsay Davenport (USA)	Nathalie Dechy (FRA)	2-6	7-6(5)	6-4
S	Serena Williams (USA)	Maria Sharapova (RUS)	2-6	7-5	8-6
Q	Lindsay Davenport (USA)	Alicia Molik (AUS)	6-4	4-6	9-7
Q	Nathalie Dechy (FRA)	Patty Schnyder (SUI)	5-7	6-1	7-5
Q	Maria Sharapova (RUS)	Svetlana Kuznetsova (RUS)	4-6	6-2	6-2
Q	Serena Williams (USA)	Amelie Mauresmo (FRA)	6-2	6-2	

2006 (MELBOURNE)

Rd	Winner	Defeated	S1	S2	S3
F	Amelie Mauresmo (FRA)	Justine Henin-Hardenne (BEL)	6-1	2-0 (retired)	
S	Justine Henin-Hardenne (BEL)	Maria Sharapova (RUS)	4-6	6-1	6-4
S	Amelie Mauresmo (FRA)	Kim Clijsters (BEL)	5-7	6-2	3-2(retired)
Q	Justine Henin-Hardenne (BEL)	Lindsay Davenport (USA)	2-6	6-2	6-3
Q	Maria Sharapova (RUS)	Nadia Petrova (RUS)	7-6(6)	6-4	
Q	Amelie Mauresmo (FRA)	Patty Schnyder (SUI)	6-3	6-0	
Q	Kim Clijsters (BEL)	Martina Hingis (SUI)	6-3	2-6	6-4

2007 (MELBOURNE)

Rd	Winner	Defeated	S1	S2	S3
F	Serena Williams (USA)	Maria Sharapova (RUS)	6-1	6-2	
S	Maria Sharapova (RUS)	Kim Clijsters (BEL)	6-4	6-2	
S	Serena Williams (USA)	Nicole Vaidisova (CZE)	7-6(5)	6-4	
Q	Maria Sharapova (RUS)	Anna Chakvetadze (RUS)	7-6(5)	7-5	
Q	Kim Clijsters (BEL)	Martina Hingis (SUI)	3-6	6-4	6-3
Q	Serena Williams (USA)	Shahar Peer (ISR)	3-6	6-2	8-6
Q	Nicole Vaidisova (CZE)	Lucie Safarova (CZE)	6-1	6-4	

2008 (MELBOURNE)

Rd	Winner	Defeated	S1	S2	S3
F	Maria Sharapova (RUS)	Ana Ivanovic (SRB)	7-5	6-3	
S	Maria Sharapova (RUS)	Jelena Jankovic (SRB)	6-3	6-1	
S	Ana Ivanovic (SRB)	Daniela Hantuchova (SVK)	0-6	6-3	6-4
Q	Maria Sharapova (RUS)	Justine Henin (BEL)	6-4	6-0	
Q	Jelena Jankovic (SRB)	Serena Williams (USA)	6-3	6-4	
Q	Ana Ivanovic (SRB)	Venus Williams (USA)	7-6 (3)	6-4	
Q	Daniela Huntuchova (SVK)	Agnieszka Radwanska (POL)	6-2	6-2	

2009 (MELBOURNE)

Rd	Winner	Defeated	S1	S2	S3
F	Venus Williams (USA)	Dinara Safina (RUS)	6-0	6-3	
S	Dinara Safina (RUS)	Vera Zvonareva (RUS)	6-3	7-6 (4)	
S	Serena Williams (USA)	Elena Dementieva (RUS)	6-3	6-4	
Q	Vera Zvonareva (RUS)	Marion Bartoli (FRA)	6-3	6-0	
Q	Dinara Safina (RUS)	Jelena Dokic (AUS)	6-4	4-6	6-4
Q	Elena Dementieva (RUS)	Carla Sanchez Navarro (ESP)	6-2	6-2	
Q	Serena Williams (USA)	Svetlana Kuznetsova (RUS)	5-7	7-5	6-1

Men's Doubles

Year	Winner	Defeated	S1	S2	S3	S4	S5
1905	Randolph Lycett (GBR) Tom Tachell (AUS)	Edgar T. Barnard (AUS) Basil Spence (AUS)	11-9	8-6	1-6	4-6	6-1
1906	Rodney Heath (AUS) Tony Wilding (NZL)	Harry Parker (AUS) Charles Cecil Cox (AUS)	6-2	6-4	6-2		
1907	Bill Gregg (AUS) Harry Parker (NZL)	Horrie Rice (AUS) George Wright (AUS)	6-2	3-6	6-2	6-2	
1908	Fred Alexander (USA) Alfred Dunlop (AUS)	Granville G. Sharp (AUS) Tony Wildlng (NZL)	6-3	6-2	6-1		
1909	J. P. Keane (AUS) Ernest Parker (AUS)	Tom Crooks (AUS) Tony Wildlng (NZL)	1-6	6-1	6-1	9-7	
1910	Ashley Campbell (AUS) Horrie Rice (AUS)	Rodney Heath (AUS) James O'Day (AUS)	6-3	6-3	6-2		
1911	Rodney Heath (AUS) Randolph Lycett (GBR)	John Addison (AUS) Norman Brookes (AUS)	6-2	7-5	6-0		
1912	Jim Parke (IRL) Charles Dixon (GBR)	Alfred Beamish (GBR) Gordon Lowe (GBR)	6-4	6-4	6-2		
1913	Alf Hedemann (AUS) Ernest Parker (NZL)	Harry Parker (NZL) Ron Taylor (AUS)	8-6	4-6	6-4	6-4	
1914	Ashley Campbell (AUS) Gerald Patterson (AUS)	Rodney Heath (AUS) Arthur O'Hara Wood (AUS)	7-5	3-6	6-3	6-3	
1915	Horrie Rice (AUS) Clarrie Todd (AUS)	Gordon Lowe (GBR) Bert St. John (AUS)	8-6	6-4	7-9	6-3	
1916-18	Not held—WWI						
1919	Pat O'Hara Wood (AUS) Ron Thomas (AUS)	James Anderson (AUS) Arthur Lowe (GBR)	7-5	6-1	7-9	3-6	6-3
1920	Pat O'Hara Wood (AUS) Ron Thomas (AUS)	Horrie Rice (AUS) Ron Taylor (AUS)	6-1	6-0	7-5		
1921	Sidney H. Eaton (AUS) Rice Gemmell (AUS)	N. Brearley (AUS) Edward Stokes (AUS)	7-5	6-3	6-3		
1922	Jack Hawkes (AUS) Gerald Patterson (AUS)	James Anderson (AUS) Norman Peach (AUS)	8-10	6-0	6-0	7-5	
1923	Pat O'Hara Wood (AUS) Bert St. John (AUS)	Dudley Bullough (AUS) Horrie Rice (AUS)	6-4	6-3	3-6	6-0	
1924	James Anderson (AUS) Norman Brookes (AUS)	Gerald Patterson (AUS) Pat O'Hara Wood (AUS)	6-2	6-4	6-3		
1925	Pat O'Hara Wood (AUS) Gerald Patterson (AUS)	James Anderson (AUS) Fred Kalmus (AUS)	6-4	8-6	7-5		
1926	Jack Hawkes (AUS) Gerald Patterson (AUS)	James Anderson (AUS) Pat O'Hara Wood (AUS)	6-1	6-4	6-2		
1927	Jack Hawkes (AUS) Gerald Patterson (AUS)	Pat O'Hara Wood (AUS) Ian McInness (AUS)	8-6	6-2	6-1		
1928	Jean Borotra (FRA) Jacques Brugnon (FRA)	Jim Willard (AUS) Gar Moon (AUS)	6-2	4-6	6-4	6-4	
1929	Jack Crawford (AUS) Harry Hopman (AUS)	Jack Cummings (AUS) Gar Moon (AUS)	6-1	6-8	4-6	6-1	6-3
1930	Jack Crawford (AUS) Harry Hopman (AUS)	Jack Hawkes (AUS) Tim Fitchett (AUS)	8-6	6-1	2-6	6-3	
1931	Charles Donohoe (AUS) Ray Dunlop (AUS)	Jack Crawford (AUS) Harry Hopman (AUS)	8-6	6-2	5-7	7-9	6-4
1932	Jack Crawford (AUS) Gar Moon (AUS)	Harry Hopman (AUS) Gerald Patterson (AUS)	12-10	6-3	4-6	6-4	

Year	Winner	Defeated	S1	S2	S3	S4	S5
1933	Keith Gledhill (USA) Ellsworth Vines (USA)	Jack Crawford (AUS) Gar Moon (AUS)	6-4	10-8	6-2		
1934	Fred Perry (GBR) Pat Hughes (GBR)	Adrian Quist (AUS) Don Turnbull (AUS)	6-8	6-3	6-4	3-6	6-3
1935	Jack Crawford (AUS) Viv McGrath (AUS)	Pat Hughes (GBR) Fred Perry (GBR)	6-4	8-6	6-2		
1936	Adrian Quist (AUS) Don Turnbull (AUS)	Jack Crawford (AUS) Viv McGrath (AUS)	6-8	6-2	6-1	3-6	6-2
1937	Adrian Quist (AUS) Don Turnbull (AUS)	John Bromwich (AUS) Jack Harper (AUS)	6-2	9-7	1-6	6-8	6-4
1938	John Bromwich (AUS) Adrian Quist (AUS)	Gottfried von Cramm (GER) Henner Henkel (GER)	7-5	6-4	6-0		
1939	John Bromwich (AUS) Adrian Quist (AUS)	Don Turnbull (AUS) Colin Long (AUS)	6-4	7-5	6-2		
1940	John Bromwich (AUS) Adrian Quist (AUS)	Jack Crawford (AUS) Viv McGrath (AUS)	6-3	7-5	6-1		
1941-45	Not held—WW II						
1946	John Bromwich (AUS) Adrian Quist (AUS)	Max Newcombe (AUS) Len Schwartz (AUS)	6-3	6-1	9-7		
1947	John Bromwich (AUS) Adrian Quist (AUS)	Frank Sedgman (AUS) George Worthington (AUS)	6-1	6-3	6-1		
1948	John Bromwich (AUS) Adrian Quist (AUS)	Frank Sedgman (AUS) Colin Long (AUS)	1-6	6-8	9-7	6-3	8-6
1949	John Bromwich (AUS) Adrian Quist (AUS)	Geoff Brown (AUS) Bill Sidwell (AUS)	1-6	7-5	6-2	6-3	
1950	John Bromwich (AUS) Adrian Quist (AUS)	Eric Sturgess (RSA) Jaroslav Drobny (GBR)	6-3	5-7	4-6	6-3	8-6
1951	Ken McGregor (AUS) Frank Sedgman (AUS)	John Bromwich (AUS) Adrian Quist (AUS)	11-9	2-6	6-3	4-6	6-3
1952	Ken McGregor (AUS) Frank Sedgman (AUS)	Don Candy (AUS) Merv Rose (AUS)	6-4	7-5	6-3		
1953	Lew Hoad (AUS) Ken Rosewell (AUS)	Don Candy (AUS) Merv Rose (AUS)	9-11	6-4	10-8	6-4	
1954	Rex Hartwig (AUS) Merv Rose (AUS)	Neale Fraser (AUS) Clive Wilderspin (AUS)	6-3	6-4	6-2		
1955	Vic Seixas (USA) Tony Trabert (USA)	Lew Hoad (AUS) Ken Rosewall (AUS)	6-3	6-2	2-6	3-6	6-1
1956	Lew Hoad (AUS) Ken Rosewell (AUS)	Don Candy (AUS) Merv Rose (AUS)	10-8	13-11	6-4		
1957	Neale Fraser (AUS) Lew Hoad (AUS)	Mal Anderson (AUS) Ashley Cooper (AUS)	6-3	8-6	6-4		
1958	Ashley Cooper (AUS) Neale Fraser (AUS)	Roy Emerson (AUS) Bob Mark (AUS)	7-5	6-8	3-6	6-3	7-5
1959	Rod Laver (AUS) Bob Mark (AUS)	Don Candy (AUS) Bob Howe (AUS)	9-7	6-4	6-2		
1960	Rod Laver (AUS) Bob Mark (AUS)	Roy Emerson (AUS) Neale Fraser (AUS)	1-6	6-2	6-4	6-4	
1961	Rod Laver (AUS) Bob Mark (AUS)	Roy Emerson (AUS) Marty Mulligan (AUS)	6-3	7-5	3-6	9-11	6-2
1962	Roy Emerson (AUS) Marty Mulligan (AUS)	Bob Hewitt (AUS) Fred Stolle (AUS)	4-6	4-6	6-1	6-4	11-9
1963	Bob Hewitt (AUS) Fred Stolle (AUS)	Ken Fletcher (AUS) John Newcombe (AUS)	6-2	3-6	6-3	3-6	6-3
1964	Bob Hewitt (AUS) Fred Stolle (AUS)	Roy Emerson (AUS) Ken Fletcher (AUS)	6-4	7-5	3-6	4-6	14-12
1965	John Newcombe (AUS) Tony Roche (AUS)	Roy Emerson (AUS) Fred Stolle (AUS)	3-6	4-6	13-11	6-3	6-4
1966	Roy Emerson (AUS) Fred Stolle (AUS)	John Newcombe (AUS) Tony Roche (AUS)	7-9	6-3	6-8	14-12	12-10
1967	John Newcombe (AUS) Tony Roche (AUS)	Bill Bowrey (AUS) Owen Davidson (AUS)	3-6	6-3	7-5	6-8	8-6
1968	Dick Crealy (AUS) Allan Stone (AUS)	Terry Addison (AUS) Ray Keldie (AUS)	10-8	6-4	6-3		
1969	Roy Emerson (AUS) Rod Laver (AUS)	Ken Rosewall (AUS) Fred Stolle (AUS)	6-4	6-4 (shortened by agreement)			
1970	Bob Lutz (AUS) Stan Smith (AUS)	John Alexander (AUS) Phil Dent (AUS)	8-6	6-3	6-4		
1971	John Newcombe (AUS) Tony Roche (AUS)	Tom Okker (NED) Marty Riessen (USA)	6-2	7-6			
1972	Owen Davidson (AUS) Ken Rosewall (AUS)	Ross Case (AUS) Geoff Masters (AUS)	3-6	7-6	6-2		
1973	Mal Anderson (AUS) Ken Rosewall (AUS)	John Alexander (AUS) Phil Dent (AUS)	6-3	6-4	7-6		
1974	Ross Case (AUS) Geoff Masters (AUS)	Syd Ball (AUS) Bob Giltinan (AUS)	6-7	6-3	6-4		
1975	John Alexander (AUS) Phil Dent (AUS)	Bob Carmichael (AUS) Allan Stone (AUS)	6-3	7-6			
1976	John Newcombe (AUS) Tony Roche (AUS)	Ross Case (AUS) Geoff Masters (AUS)	7-6	6-4			
1977 (Jan.)	Arthur Ashe (USA) Tony Roche (AUS)	Charlie Pasarell (USA) Erik van Dillen (USA)	6-4	6-4			
1977 (Dec.)	Ray Ruffels (AUS) Allan Stone (AUS)	John Alexander (AUS) Phil Dent (AUS)	7-6	7-6			
1978	Wojtek Fibak (POL) Kim Warwick (AUS)	Paul Kronk (AUS) Cliff Letcher (AUS)	7-6	7-5			
1979	Peter McNamara (AUS) Paul McNamee (AUS)	Paul Kronk (AUS) Cliff Letcher (AUS)	7-6	6-2			
1980	Mark Edmondson (AUS) Kim Warwick (AUS)	Peter McNamara (AUS) Paul McNamee (AUS)	7-5	6-4			
1981	Mark Edmondson (AUS) Kim Warwick (AUS)	Hank Pfister (USA) John Sadri (USA)	6-3	6-7	6-3		
1982	John Alexander (AUS) John Fitzgerald (AUS)	Andy Andrews (USA) John Sadri (USA)	6-4	7-6			
1983	Mark Edmondson (AUS) Paul McNamee (AUS)	Steve Denton (USA) Sherwood Stewart (USA)	6-3	7-6			
1984	Mark Edmondson (AUS) Sherwood Stewart (USA)	Joakim Nystrom (SWE) Mats Wilander (SWE)	6-2	6-2	7-5		
1985	Paul Annacone (USA) Christo van Rensburg (RSA)	Mark Edmondson (AUS) Kim Warwick (AUS)	3-6	7-6	6-4	6-4	
1986	Not held due to change in dates						
1987	Stefan Edberg (SWE) Anders Jarryd (SWE)	Peter Doohan (AUS) Laurie Warder (AUS)	6-4	6-4	7-6(3)		
1988	Rick Leach (USA) Jim Pugh (USA)	Jeremy Bates (GBR) Peter Lundgren (SWE)	6-3	6-2	6-3		
1989	Rick Leach (USA) Jim Pugh (USA)	Darren Cahill (AUS) Mark Kratzmann (AUS)	6-4	6-4	6-4		

Year	Winner	Defeated	S1	S2	S3	S4	S5
1990	Pieter Aldrich (RSA) Danie Visser (RSA)	Grant Connell (CAN) Glenn Michibata (CAN)	6-4	4-6	6-1	6-4	
1991	Scott Davis (USA) David Pate (USA)	Patrick McEnroe (USA) David Wheaton (USA)	6-7(4)	7-6(8)	6-3	7-5	
1992	Todd Woodbridge (USA) Mark Woodforde (USA)	Kelly Jones (USA) Rick Leach (USA)	6-4	6-3	6-4		
1993	Danie Visser (RSA) Laurie Warder (AUS)	John Fitzgerald (AUS) Anders Jarryd (SWE)	6-4	6-3	6-4		
1994	Jacco Eltingh (NED) Paul Haarhuis (NED)	Byron Black (ZIM) Jonathan Stark (USA)	6-7(3)	6-3	6-4	6-3	
1995	Jared Palmer (USA) Richey Reneberg (USA)	Mark Knowles (BAH) Daniel Nestor (CAN)	6-3	3-6	6-3	6-2	
1996	Stefan Edberg (SWE) Petr Korda (CZE)	Alex O'Brien (USA) Sebastian Lareau (CAN)	7-5	7-5	4-6	6-1	
1997	Todd Woodbridge (AUS) Mark Woodforde (AUS)	Alex O'Brien (USA) Sebastian Lareau (CAN)	4-6	7-5	7-5	6-3	
1998	Jonas Bjorkman (SWE) Jacco Eltingh (NED)	Todd Woodbridge (AUS) Mark Woodforde (AUS)	6-2	5-7	2-6	6-4	6-3
1999	Patrick Rafter (AUS) Jonas Bjorkman (SWE)	Leander Paes (IND) Mahesh Bhupathi (IND)	6-3	4-6	6-4	6-7(10)	6-4
2000	Rick Leach (USA) Ellis Ferreira (RSA)	Andrew Kratzmann (AUS) Wayne Black (ZIM)	6-4	3-6	6-3	3-6	18-16
2001	Jonas Bjorkman (SWE) Todd Woodbridge (AUS)	Byron Black (ZIM) David Prinosil (GER)	6-1	5-7	6-4	6-4	
2002	Daniel Nestor (CAN) Mark Knowles (BAH)	Michael Llodra (FRA) Fabrice Santoro (FRA)	7-6(4)	6-3			
2003	Michael Llodra (FRA) Fabrice Santoro (FRA)	Daniel Nestor (CAN) Mark Knowles (BAH)	6-4	3-6	6-3		
2004	Michael Llodra (FRA) Fabrice Santoro (FRA)	Bob Bryan (USA) Mike Bryan (USA)	7-6(4)	6-3			
2005	Wayne Black (ZIM) Kevin Ullyett (ZIM)	Bob Bryan (USA) Mike Bryan (USA)	6-4	6-4			
2006	Bob Bryan (USA) Mike Bryan (USA)	Martin Damm (CZE) Leander Paes (IND)	4-6	6-3	6-4		
2007	Bob Bryan (USA) Mike Bryan (USA)	Jonas Bjorkman (SWE) Max Mirnyi (BLR)	7-5	7-5			
2008	Andy Ram (ISR) Jonathan Erlich (ISR)	Arnaud Clement (FRA) Michael Llodra (FRA)	7 5	7-6(4)			
2009	Bob Bryan (USA) Mike Bryan (USA)	Mahesh Bhupathi (IND) Mark Knowles (BAH)	2-6	7-5	6-0		

Women's Doubles

Year	Winner	Defeated	S1	S2	S3
1922	Esna Boyd (AUS) Marjorie Mountain (AUS)	Floris St. George (AUS) Gwendolyn Chiplin Utz (AUS)	1-6	6-4	7-5
1923	Esna Boyd (AUS) Sylvia Lance (AUS)	Mall Molesworth (AUS) Mrs. H.M. Turner (AUS)	6-1	6-4	
1924	Daphne Akhurst (AUS) Sylvia Lance Harper (AUS)	Kathrine Le Mesurier (AUS) Meryl O'Hara Wood (AUS)	7-5	6-2	

Year	Winner	Defeated	S1	S2	S3
1925	Sylvia Lance Harper (AUS) Daphne Akhurst (AUS)	Esna Boyd (AUS) Kathrine Le Mesurier (AUS)	6-4	6-3	
1926	Meryl O'Hara Wood (AUS) Esna Boyd (AUS)	Daphne Akhurst (AUS) Marjorie Cox (AUS)	6-3	6-8	8-6
1927	Meryl O'Hara Wood (AUS) Louie Bickerton (AUS)	Esna Boyd (AUS) Sylvia Lance Harper (AUS)	6-3	6-3	
1928	Daphne Akhurst (AUS) Esna Boyd (AUS)	Kathrine Le Mesurier (AUS) Dorothy Weston (AUS)	6-3	6-1	
1929	Daphne Akhurst (AUS) Louie Bickerton (AUS)	Sylvia Lance Harper (AUS) Meryl O'Hara Wood (AUS)	6-2	3-6	6-2
1930	Mall Molesworth (AUS) Emily Hood (AUS)	Marjorie Cox (AUS) Sylvia Lance Harper (AUS)	6-3	0-6	7-5
1931	D. Akhurst Cozens (AUS) Louie Bickerton (AUS)	Nell Lloyd (AUS) Gwendolyn Chiplin (AUS)	6-0	6-4	
1932	C. McInnes Buttsworth (AUS) Marjorie Cox Crawford (AUS)	Kathrine Le Mesurier (AUS) Dorothy Weston (AUS)	6-2	6-2	
1933	Mall Molesworth (AUS) Emily Hood Westacott (AUS)	Joan Hartigan (AUS) Marjorie Gladman Van Ryn (USA)	6-3	6-2	
1934	Mall Molesworth (AUS) Emily Hood Westacott (AUS)	Joan Hartigan (AUS) Ula Valkenburg (AUS)	6-8	6-4	6-4
1935	Evelyn Dearman (GBR) Nancy Lyle (GBR)	Louie Bickerton (AUS) Nell Hall Hopman (AUS)	6-3	6-4	
1936	Thelma Coyne Long (AUS) Nancye Wynne (AUS)	May Blick (AUS) Katherine Le Mesurier (AUS)	6-2	6-4	
1937	Thelma Coyne Long (AUS) Nancye Wynne (AUS)	Nell Hall Hopman (AUS) Emily Hood Westacott (AUS)	6-2	6-2	
1938	Thelma Coyne Long (AUS) Nancye Wynne (AUS)	Dorothy Bundy (USA) Dorothy Workman (AUS)	9-7	6-4	
1939	Thelma Coyne Long (AUS) Nancye Wynne (AUS)	May Hardcastle (AUS) Emily Hood Westacott (AUS)	7-5	6-4	
1940	Thelma Coyne Long (AUS) Nancye Wynne (AUS)	Joan Nartigan (AUS) Emily Niemeyer (AUS)	7-5	6-2	
1941-45	Not Held—WW II				
1946	Joyce Fitch (AUS) Mary Bevis (AUS)	Nancye Wynne Bolton (AUS) Thelma Coyne Long (AUS)	9-7	6-4	
1947	Thelma Coyne Long (AUS) Nancye Wynne Bolton (AUS)	Mary Bevis (AUS) Joyce Fitch (AUS)	6-3	6-3	
1948	Thelma Coyne Long (AUS) Nancye Wynne Bolton (AUS)	Mary Bevis (AUS) Pat Jones (AUS)	6-3	6-3	
1949	Thelma Coyne Long (AUS) Nancye Wynne Bolton (AUS)	Doris Hart (USA) Marie Toomey (AUS)	6-0	6-1	
1950	Louise Brough (USA) Doris Hart (USA)	Nancye Wynne Bolton (AUS) Thelma Coyne Long (AUS)	6-2	2-6	6-3
1951	Thelma Coyne Long (AUS) Nancye Wynne Bolton (AUS)	Joyce Fitch (AUS) Mary Bevis Hawton (AUS)	6-2	6-1	
1952	Thelma Coyne Long (AUS) Nancye Wynne Bolton (AUS)	Alison Burton Baker (AUS) Mary Bevis Hawton (AUS)	6-1	6-1	
1953	Maureen Connolly (USA) Julia Sampson (USA)	Mary Bevis Hawton (AUS) Beryl Penrose (AUS)	6-4	6-2	
1954	Mary Bevis Hawton (AUS) Beryl Penrose (AUS)	Hazel Redick-Smith (RSA) Julia Wipplinger (AUS)	6-3	8-6	
1955	Mary Bevis Hawton (AUS) Beryl Penrose (AUS)	Nell Hall Hopman (AUS) Gwen Thiele (AUS)	7-5	6-1	

Year	Winner	Defeated	S1	S2	S3
1956	Mary Bevis Hawton (AUS) Thelma Coyne Long (AUS)	Mary Carter (AUS) Beryl Penrose (AUS)	6-2	5-7	9-7
1957	Althea Gibson (USA) Shirley Fry (USA)	Mary Bevis Hawton (AUS) Fay Muller (AUS)	6-2	6-1	
1958	Mary Bevis Hawton (AUS) Thelma Coyne Long (AUS)	Lorraine Coghlan (AUS) Angela Mortimer (GBR)	7-5	6-8	6-2
1959	Renee Schuurman (RSA) Sandra Reynolds (RSA)	Lorraine Coghlan (AUS) Mary Carter Reitano (AUS)	7-5	6-4	
1960	Maria Bueno (BRA) Christine Truman (GBR)	L. Coghlan Robinson (AUS) Margaret Smith (AUS)	6-2	5-7	6-2
1961	Mary Carter Reitano (AUS) Margaret Smith (AUS)	Mary Bevis Hawton (AUS) Jan Lehane (AUS)	6-4	3-6	7-5
1962	Margaret Smith (AUS) Robyn Ebbern (AUS)	Darlene Hard (AUS) Mary Carter Reitano (AUS)	6-4	6-4	
1963	Margaret Smith (AUS) Robyn Ebbern (AUS)	Jan Lehane (AUS) Lesley Turner (AUS)	6-1	6-3	
1964	Judy Tegart Dalton (AUS) Lesley Turner (AUS)	Robyn Ebbern (AUS) Margaret Smith (AUS)	6-4	6-4	
1965	Margaret Smith (AUS) Lesley Turner (AUS)	Robyn Ebbern (AUS) Bilie Jean Moffitt (USA)	1-6	6-2	6-3
1966	C. Caldwell Graebner (USA) Nancy Richey (USA)	Margaret Smith (AUS) Lesley Turner (AUS)	6-4	7-5	
1967	Lesley Turner (AUS) Judy Tegart Dalton (AUS)	L. Coghlan Robinson (AUS) Evelyn Terras (AUS)	6-0	6-2	
1968	Karen Krantzcke (AUS) Kerry Melville (AUS)	Judy Tegart Dalton (AUS) Lesley Turner (AUS)	6-4	3-6	6-2
1969	Margaret Smith Court (AUS) Judy Tegart Dalton (AUS)	Rosie Casals (USA) Billie Jean King (USA)	6-4	6-4	
1970	Margaret Smith Court (AUS) Judy Tegart Dalton (AUS)	Karen Krantzcke (AUS) Kerry Melville (AUS)	6-3	6-1	
1971	Margaret Smith Court (AUS) Evonne Goolagong (AUS)	Jill Emmerson (AUS) Lesley Hunt (AUS)	6-0	6-0	
1972	Kerry Harris (AUS) Helen Gourlay (AUS)	Patricia Coleman (AUS) Karen Krantzcke (AUS)	6-0	6-4	
1973	Margaret Smith Court (AUS) Virginia Wade (GBR)	Kerry Harris (AUS) Kerry Melville (AUS)	6-4	6-4	
1974	Evonne Goolagong (AUS) Peggy Michel (USA)	Kerry Harris (AUS) Kerry Melville (AUS)	7-5	6-3	
1975	Evonne Goolagong (AUS) Peggy Michel (USA)	Margaret Smith Court (AUS) Olga Morozova (USSR)	7-6	7-6	
1976	Evonne Goolagong (AUS) Helen Gourley (AUS)	Lesley Turner Bowrey (AUS) Renata Tomanova (CZE)	8-1	(1 pro set by mutual agrement)	
1977 (Jan.)	Dianne Fromholtz (AUS) Helen Gourlay Crawley (AUS)	Betsy Nagelsen (USA) Kerry Melville Reid (AUS)	5-7	6-1	7-5
1977 (Dec.)	E. Goolagong Cawley (AUS) Helen Gourlay Cawley (AUS)	Mona Schallau Guerrant (USA) Kerry Melville Reid (AUS)	(Shared title due to rained-out final)		
1978	Betsy Nagelsen (USA) Renata Tomanova (CZE)	Naoko Sato (JPN) Pam Whytcross (AUS)	7-5	6-2	
1979	Judy Chaloner (NZL) Dianne Evers (AUS)	Leanne Harrison (AUS) Marcella Mesker (NED)	6-1	3-6	6-0
1980	Martina Navratilova (CZE) Betsy Nagelsen (USA)	Ann Kiyomura (USA) Candy Reynolds (USA)	6-4	6-4	
1981	Kathy Jordan (USA) Anne Smith (USA)	Martina Navratilova (USA) Pam Shriver (USA)	6-2	7-5	
1982	Martina Navratilova (USA) Pam Shriver (USA)	Claudia Kohde Kilsch (GER) Eva Pfaff (GER)	6-4	6-2	
1983	Martina Navratilova (USA) Pam Shriver (USA)	Anne Hobbs (GBR) Wendy Turnbull (AUS)	6-4	6-7	6-2
1984	Martina Navratilova (USA) Pam Shriver (USA)	Claudia Kohde-Kilsch (GER) Helena Sukova (CZE)	6-3	6-4	
1985	Martina Navratilova (USA) Pam Shriver (USA)	Claudia Kohde Kilsch (GER) Helena Sukova (CZE)	6-3	6-4	
1986	Not held due to change in dates				
1987	Martina Navratilova (USA) Pam Shriver (USA)	Zina Garrison (USA) Lori McNeil (USA)	6-1	6-0	
1988	Martina Navratilova (USA) Pam Shriver (USA)	Chris Evert (USA) Wendy Turnbull (AUS)	6-0	7-5	
1989	Martina Navratilova (USA) Pam Shriver (USA)	Patty Fendick (USA) Jill Hetherington (CAN)	3-6	6-3	6-2
1990	Jana Novotna (CZE) Helena Sukova (CZE)	Patty Fendick (USA) Mary Joe Fernandez (USA)	7-6(5)	7-6(6)	
1991	Patty Fendick (USA) Mary Joe Fernandez (USA)	Gigi Fernandez (USA) Jana Novotna (CZE)	7-6(4)	6-1	
1992	A. Sanchez Vicario (ESP) Helena Sukova (CZE)	Mary Joe Fernandez (USA) Zina Garrison (USA)	6-4	7-6(3)	
1993	Gigi Fernandez (USA) Natalia Zvereva (BLR)	Pam Shriver (USA) Elizabeth Sayers Smylie (AUS)	6-4	6-3	
1994	Gigi Fernandez (USA) Natalia Zvereva (BLR)	Patty Fendick (USA) Meredith McGrath (USA)	6-3	4-6	6-4
1995	Jana Novotna (CZE) A. Sanchez Vicario (ESP)	Gigi Fernandez (USA) Natalia Zvereva (BLR)	6-3	6-7(3)	6-4
1996	Chanda Rubin (USA) A. Sanchez Vicario (ESP)	Lindsay Davenport (USA) Mary Joe Fernandez (USA)	7-5	2-6	6-4
1997	Martina Hingis (SUI) Natalia Zvereva (BLR)	Lindsay Davenport (USA) Lisa Raymond (USA)	6-2	6-2	
1998	Martina Hingis (SUI) Mirjana Lucic (CRO)	Lindsay Davenport (USA) Natalia Zvereva (BLR)	6-4	2-6	6-3
1999	Martina Hingis (SUI) Anna Kournikova (RUS)	Lindsay Davenport (USA) Natalia Zvereva (BLR)	7-5	6-3	
2000	Lisa Raymond (USA) Rennae Stubbs (AUS)	Martina Hingis (SUI) Mary Pierce (FRA)	6-4	5-7	6-4
2001	Serena Williams (USA) Venus Williams (USA)	Lindsay Davenport (USA) Corina Morariu (USA)	6-2	2-6	6-4
2002	Martina Hingis (SUI) Anna Kournikova (RUS)	Arantxa Sanchez Vicario (ESP) Daniela Hantuchova (SVK)	6-2	6-7(4)	6-1
2003	Serena Williams (USA) Venus Williams (USA)	Virginia Ruano Pascual (ESP) Paola Suarez (ARG)	4-6	6-4	6-3
2004	Virginia Ruano Pascual (ESP) Paola Suarez (ARG)	Svetlana Kuznetsova (RUS) Elena Likhovtseva (RUS)	6-4	6-3	
2005	Svetlana Kuznetsova (RUS) Alicia Molik (AUS)	Lindsay Davenport (USA) Corina Morariu (USA)	6-3	6-4	
2006	Zi Yan (CHN) Jie Zheng (CHN)	Lisa Raymond (USA) Samantha Stosur (AUS)	2-6	7-6(7)	6-3
2007	Cara Black (ZIM) Liezel Huber (RSA)	Yung-Jan Chan (TPE) Chia-Jung Chuang (TPE)	6-4	6-7(4)	6-1
2008	Alona Bondarenko (UKR) Kateryna Bondarenko (UKR)	Victoria Azarenka (BLR) Shahar Peer (ISR)	2 6	6 1	6 4
2009	Serena Williams (USA) Venus Williams (USA)	Daniela Hantuchova (SVK) Ai Sugiyama (JPN)	6-3	6-3	

Mixed Doubles

Year	Winner	Defeated	S1	S2	S3
1922	Esna Boyd (AUS) Jack Hawkes (AUS)	Gwendolyn Chiplin Utz (AUS) Harold Utz (AIUS)	6-1	6-1	
1923	Sylvia Lance (AUS) Horrie Rice (AUS)	Mall Molesworth (AUS) Bert St. John (AUS)	2-6	6-4	6-4
1924	Daphne Akhurst (AUS) John Willard (AUS)	Sylvia Lance Harper (AUS) Bob Schlesinger (AUS)	6-3	6-4	
1925	Daphne Akhurst (AUS) John Willard (AUS)	Sylvia Lance Harper (AUS) Bob Schlesinger (AUS)	6-4	6-4	
1926	Esna Boyd (AUS) Jack Hawkes (AUS)	Daphne Akhurst (AUS) Jim Willard (AUS)	6-2	6-4	
1927	Esna Boyd (AUS) Jack Hawkes (AUS)	Youtha Anthony (AUS) Jim Willard (AUS)	6-1	6-3	
1928	Daphne Akhurst (AUS) Jean Borotra (FRA)	Esna Boyd (AUS) Jack Crawford (AUS)	default		
1929	Daphne Akhurst (AUS) Gar Moon (AUS)	Marjorie Cox (AUS) Jack Crawford (AUS)	6-0	7-5	
1930	Nell Hall (AUS) Harry Hopman (AUS)	Marjorie Cox (AUS) Jack Crawford (AUS)	11-9	3-6	6-3
1931	Marjorie Cox Crawford (AUS) Jack Crawford (AUS)	Emily Hood Westacott (AUS) Aubrey Willard (AUS)	7-5	6-4	
1932	Marjorie Cox Crawford (AUS) Jack Crawford (AUS)	Meryl O'Hara Wood (AUS) Jiro Satoh (JPN)	6-8	8-6	6-3
1933	Marjorie Cox Crawford (AUS) Jack Crawford (AUS)	M. Gladman Van Ryn (USA) Ellsworth Vines (USA)	3-6	7-5	13-11
1934	Joan Hartigan (AUS) Gar Moon (AUS)	Emily Hood Westacott (AUS) Ray Dunlop (AUS)	6-3	6-4	
1935	Louie Bickerton (AUS) Christian Boussus (FRA)	Birdie Bond (AUS) Vernon Kirby (RSA)	1-6	6-3	6-3
1936	Nell Hall Hopman (AUS) Harry Hopman (AUS)	May Blick (AUS) Abe Kay (AUS)	6-2	6-0	
1937	Nell Hall Hopman (AUS) Harry Hopman (AUS)	Dorothy Stevenson (AUS) Don Turnbull (AUS)	3-6	6-3	6-2
1938	Margaret Wilson (AUS) John Bromwich (AUS)	Nancye Wynne (AUS) Colin Long (AUS)	6-3	6-2	
1939	Nell Hall Hopman (AUS) Harry Hopman (AUS)	Margaret Wilson (AUS) John Bromwich (AUS)	6-8	6-2	6-3
1940	Nancye Wynne (AUS) Colin Long (AUS)	Nell Hall Hopman (AUS) Harry Hopman (AUS)	7-5	2-6	6-4

1941-45 Not held—WW II

Year	Winner	Defeated	S1	S2	S3
1946	Nancye Wynne Bolton (AUS) Colin Long (AUS)	Joyce Fitch (AUS) John Bromwich (AUS)	6-0	6-4	
1947	Nancye Wynne Bolton (AUS) Colin Long (AUS)	Joyce Fitch (AUS) John Bromwich (AUS)	6-3	6-3	
1948	Nancye Wynne Bolton (AUS) Colin Long (AUS)	Thelma Coyne Long (AUS) Bill Sidwell (AUS)	7-5	4-6	8-6
1949	Doris Hart (USA) Frank Sedgman (AUS)	Joyce Fitch (AUS) John Bromwich (AUS)	6-1	5-7	12-10
1950	Doris Hart (USA) Frank Sedgman (AUS)	Joyce Fitch (AUS) Eric Sturgess (RSA)	8-6	6-4	
1951	Thelma Coyne Long (AUS) George Worthington (AUS)	Clare Proctor (AUS) Jack May (AUS)	6-4	3-6	

Year	Winner	Defeated	S1	S2	S3
1952	Thelma Coyne Long (AUS) George Worthington (AUS)	Gwen Thiele (AUS) Tom Warhurst (AUS)	9-7	7-5	
1953	Julia Sampson (USA) Rex Hartwig (AUS)	Maureen Connolly (USA) Hamilton Richardson (USA)	6-4	6-3	
1954	Thelma Coyne Long (AUS) Rex Hartwig (AUS)	Beryl Penrose (AUS) John Bromwich (AUS)	4-6	6-1	6-2
1955	Thelma Coyne Long (AUS) George Worthington (AUS)	Jenny Staley (AUS) Lew Hoad (AUS)	6-2	6-1	
1956	Beryl Penrose (AUS) Neale Fraser (AUS)	Mary Bevis Hawton (AUS) Roy Emerson (AUS)	6-2	6-4	
1957	Fay Muller (AUS) Mal Anderson (AUS)	J. Langley (AUS) Billy Knight (GBR)	7-5	3-6	6-1
1958	Mary Bevis Hawton (AUS) Bob Mark (AUS)	Angela Mortimer (GBR) Peter Newman (AUS)	9-11	6-1	6-2
1959	Mary Bevis Hawton (AUS) Bob Mark (AUS)	Renee Schuurman (RSA) Rod Laver (AUS)	4-6	13-11	6-1
1960	Jan Lehane (AUS) Trevor Fancutt (RSA)	Mary Carter Reitano (AUS) Bob Mark (AUS)	6-2	7-5	
1961	Jan Lehane (AUS) Bob Hewitt (AUS)	Mary Carter Reitano (AUS) John Pearce (AUS)	9-7	6-2	
1962	Lesley Turner (AUS) Fred Stolle (AUS)	Darlene Hard (USA) Roger Taylor (GBR)	6-3	9-7	
1963	Margaret Smith (AUS) Ken Fletcher (AUS)	Lesley Turner (AUS) Fred Stolle (AUS)	7-5	5-7	6-4
1964	Margaret Smith (AUS) Ken Fletcher (AUS)	Jan Lehane (AUS) Mike Sangster (GBR)	6-3	6-2	
1965	Margaret Smith (AUS) John Newcombe (AUS)	Robyn Ebbern (AUS) Owen Davidson (AUS)	(Shared title, final not played)		
1966	Judy Tegart (AUS) Tony Roche (AUS)	Robyn Ebbern (AUS) Bill Bowrey (AUS)	6-1	6-3	
1967	Lesley Turner (AUS) Owen Davidson (AUS)	Judy Tegart (AUS) Tony Roche (AUS)	9-7	6-4	
1968	Billie Jean King (USA) Dick Crealy (AUS)	Margaret Smith Court (AUS) Allan Stone (AUS)	(walkover)		
1969	Margaret Smith Court (AUS) Marty Riessen (USA)	Ann Haydon Jones (GBR) Fred Stolle (AUS)	(Shared title, final not played)		

1970-86 Not held

Year	Winner	Defeated	S1	S2	S3
1987	Zina Garrison (USA) Sherwood Stewart (USA)	Anne Hobbs (GBR) Andrew Castle (GBR)	3-6	7-6(5)	6-3
1988	Jana Novotna (CZE) Jim Pugh (USA)	Martina Navratilova (USA) Tim Gullikson (USA)	5-7	6-2	6-4
1989	Jana Novotna (CZE) Jim Pugh (USA)	Zina Garrison (USA) Sherwood Stewart (USA)	6-3	6-4	
1990	Natalia Zvereva (BLR) Jim Pugh (USA)	Zina Garrison (USA) Rick Leach (USA)	4-6	6-2	6-3
1991	Jo Durie (GBR) Jeremy Bates (GBR)	Robin White (USA) Scott Davis (USA)	2-6	6-4	6-4
1992	Nicole Provis (AUS) Mark Woodforde (AUS)	Arantxa Sanchez Vicario (ESP) Todd Woodbridge (AUS)	6-3	4-6	11-9
1993	Arantxa Sanchez Vicario (ESP) Todd Woodbridge (AUS)	Zina Garrison Jackson (USA) Rick Leach (USA)	7-5	6-4	
1994	L. Savchenko Neiland (LAT) Andrei Olhovskiy (RUS)	Helena Sukova (CZE) Todd Woodbridge (AUS)	7-5	6-7(0)	6-2

Year	Winner	Defeated	S1	S2	S3
1995	Natalia Zvereva (BLR) Rick Leach (USA)	Gigi Fernandez (USA) Cyril Suk (CZE)	7-6(4)	6-7(3)	6-4
1996	L. Savchenko Neiland (LAT) Mark Woodforde (AUS)	Nicole Arendt (USA) Luke Jensen (USA)	4-6	7-5	6-0
1997	Manon Bollegraf (NED) Rick Leach (USA)	L. Savchenko Neiland (LAT) John-Laffnie de Jager (RSA)	6-3	6-7(5)	7-5
1998	Venus Williams (USA) Justin Gimelstob (USA)	Helena Sukova (CZE) Cyril Suk (CZE)	6-2	6-1	
1999	Mariaan de Swardt (RSA) David Adams (RSA)	Serena Williams (USA) Max Mirnyi (BEL)	6-4	4-6	7-6(5)
2000	Rennae Stubbs (AUS) Jared Palmer (USA)	Arantxa Sanchez Vicario (ESP) Todd Woodbridge (AUS)	7-5	7-6(3)	
2001	Corina Morariu (USA) Ellis Ferreira (RSA)	Barbara Schett (AUT) Joshua Eagle (AUS)	6-1	6-3	
2002	Daniela Hantuchova (SVK) Kevin Ullyett (ZIM)	Paola Suarez (ARG) Gaston Etlis (ARG)	6-3	6-2	

Year	Winner	Defeated	S1	S2	S3
2003	Martina Navratilova (USA) Leander Paes (IND)	Eleni Daniilidou (GRE) Todd Woodbridge (USA)	6-4	7-5	
2004	Elena Bovina (RUS) Nenad Zimonjic (SRB)	Martina Navratilova (USA) Leander Paes (IND)	6-1	7-6(3)	
2005	Samantha Stosur (AUS) Scott Draper (AUS)	Liezel Huber (RSA) Kevin Ullyett (ZIM	6-2	2-6	[10-6]
2006	Martina Hingis (SUI) Mahesh Bhupathi (IND)	Elena Likhovtseva (RUS) Daniel Nestor (CAN)	6-3	6-3	
2007	Elena Likhovtseva (RUS) Daniel Nestor (CAN)	Viktoria Azarenka (BLR) Max Mirnyi (BLR)	6-4	6-4	
2008	Tiantian Sun (CHN) Nenad Zimonjic (SRB)	Sania Mirza (IND) Mahesh Bhupathi (IND)	7-6(4)	6-3	
2009	Sania Mirza (IND) Mahesh Bhupathi (IND)	Nathalie Dechy (FRA) Andy Ram (ISR)	6-3	6-1	

Australian Championships – Records

MOST TITLES

Men

13	Adrian Quist	(1936-1950)	3 singles, 10 doubles, 0 mixed
11	Jack Crawford	(1929-1935)	4 singles, 4 doubles, 3 mixed
	John Bromwich	(1938-1950)	2 singles, 8 doubles, 1 mixed
9	Roy Emerson	(1961-1969)	6 singles, 3 doubles, 0 mixed
7	Jack Hawkes	(1922-1927)	1 singles, 3 doubles, 3 mixed
	John Newcombe	(1965-1976)	2 singles, 5 doubles, 0 mixed
	Ken Rosewall	(1953-1972)	4 singles, 3 doubles, 0 mixed
	Rod Laver	(1959-1969)	3 singles, 4 doubles, 0 mixed
6	Frank Sedgman	(1949-1952)	2 singles, 2 doubles, 2 mixed
	Gerald Patterson	(1914-1927)	1 singles, 5 doubles, 0 mixed
	Harry Hopman	(1929-1939)	0 singles, 2 doubles, 4 mixed
	Pat O'Hara Wood	(1919-1925)	2 singles, 4 doubles, 0 mixed
	Tony Roche	(1965-1977)	0 singles, 5 doubles, 1 mixed
5	Jim Pugh	(1988-1990)	0 singles, 2 doubles, 3 mixed
	Mark Edmondson	(1976-1984)	1 singles, 4 doubles, 0 mixed
	Rick Leach	(1988-2000)	0 singles, 3 doubles, 2 mixed
4	Bob Mark	(1959-1961)	0 singles, 3 doubles, 1 mixed
	Colin Long	(1940-1948)	0 singles, 0 doubles, 4 mixed
	Fred Stolle	(1962-1969)	0 singles, 3 doubles, 1 mixed
	Gar Moon	(1929-1934)	1 singles, 1 doubles, 2 mixed
	Horrie Rice	(1907-1923)	1 singles, 2 doubles, 1 mixed
	James Anderson	(1922-1925)	3 singles, 1 doubles, 1 mixed
	Lew Hoad	(1953-1957)	1 singles, 3 doubles, 0 mixed
	Mark Woodforde	(1992-1997)	0 singles, 2 doubles, 2 mixed
	Neale Fraser	(1956-1962)	0 singles, 3 doubles, 1 mixed
	Rodney Heath	(1905-1911)	2 singles, 2 doubles, 0 mixed
	Stefan Edberg	(1985-1996)	2 singles, 2 doubles, 0 mixed
	Todd Woodbridge	(1992-2001)	0 singles, 3 doubles, 1 mixed
	Andre Agassi	(1995-2003)	4 singles, 0 doubles, 0 mixed

Women

21	Margaret Smith Court	(1960-1973)	11 singles, 8 doubles, 2 mixed
20	Nancye Bolton	(1936-1952)	6 singles, 10 doubles, 4 mixed
18	Thelma Long	(1936-1958)	2 singles, 12 doubles, 4 mixed
14	Daphne Akhurst	(1924-1931)	5 singles, 5 doubles, 4 mixed
12	Martina Navratilova	(1980-2003)	3 singles, 8 doubles, 1 mixed
8	Esna Boyd	(1922-1928)	3 singles, 4 doubles, 1 mixed
	Evonne Goolagong	(1971-1977)	4 singles, 4 doubles, 0 mixed
	Martina Hingis	(1997-2006)	3 singles, 4 doubles, 1 mixed
7	Serena Willams	(2002-2007)	4 singles, 3 doubles, 0 mixed
	Pam Shriver	(1982-1989)	0 singles, 7 doubles, 0 mixed
6	Mary Bevis Hawton	(1946-1958)	0 singles, 5 doubles, 1 mixed
5	Judy Dalton	(1964-1970)	0 singles, 4 doubles, 1 mixed
	Lesley Turner	(1962-1967)	0 singles, 3 doubles, 2 mixed
	Mall Molesworth	(1922-1934)	2 singles, 2 doubles, 0 mixed
	Natalia Zvereva	(1990-1997)	0 singles, 3 doubles, 2 mixed
4	Arantxa Sanchez Vicario	(1992-1996)	0 singles, 3 doubles, 1 mixed
	Beryl Penrose	(1954-1956)	1 singles, 2 doubles, 1 mixed
	Doris Hart	(1949-1950)	1 singles, 1 doubles, 2 mixed.
	Emily Hood Westacott	(1930-1939)	1 singles, 3 doubles, 0 mixed
	Jana Novotna	(1988-1995)	0 singles, 2 doubles, 2 mixed
	Joan Hartigan	(1933-1936)	3 singles, 0 doubles, 1 mixed
	Louie Bickerton	(1927-1935)	0 singles, 3 doubles, 1 mixed
	Marjorie Cox	(1931-1933)	0 singles, 1 doubles, 3 mixed
	Monica Seles	(1991-1996)	4 singles, 0 doubles, 0 mixed
	Nell Hall Hopman	(1930-1939)	0 singles, 0 doubles, 4 mixed
	Steffi Graf	(1988-1994)	4 singles, 0 doubles, 0 mixed
	Sylvia Lance	(1923-1924)	1 singles, 2 doubles, 1 mixed

MOST SINGLES TITLES

Men

6	Roy Emerson	(1961, 1963-1967)
4	Andre Agassi	(1995, 2000-2001, 2003)
	Jack Crawford	(1931-1933, 1935)
	Ken Rosewall	(1953, 1955, 1971-1972)
3	Roger Federer	(2004, 2006-2007)
	Adrian Quist	(1936, 1940, 1948)
	James Anderson	(1922, 1924-1925)
	Mats Wilander	(1983-1984, 1988)
	Rod Laver	(1960, 1962, 1969)

Women

11	Margaret Smith Court	(1960-1966, 1969-1971, 1973)
6	Nancye Bolton	(1937, 1940, 1946-1948, 1951)
5	Daphne Akhurst	(1925-1926, 1928-1930)
4	Serena Williams	(2003, 2005, 2007, 2009)
	Evonne Goolagong	(1974-1977)
	Monica Seles	(1991-1993, 1996)
	Steffi Graf	(1988-1990, 1994)

MOST SINGLES FINAL APPEARANCES

Men

7	Jack Crawford	(1931-1936, 1940)
	John Bromwich	(1937-1939, 1946-1949)
	Roy Emerson	(1961-1967)
5	Ken Rosewall	(1953, 1955-1956, 1971-1972)
	Stefan Edberg	(1985, 1987, 1990, 1992-1993)

Women

12	Margaret Smith Court	(1960-1966, 1968-1971, 1973)
8	Nancye Bolton	(1936-1937, 1940, 1946-1949, 1951)
7	Esna Boyd	(1922-1928)
	Evonne Goolagong	(1971-1977)

MOST SINGLES FINAL LOSSES

Men

5	John Bromwich	(1937-1938, 1947-1949)
3	Arthur Ashe	(1966-1967, 1971)
	Gerald Patterson	(1914, 1922, 1925)
	Harry Hopman	(1930-1932)
	Horrie Rice	(1910-1911, 1915)
	Jack Crawford	(1934, 1936, 1940)
	Neale Fraser	(1957, 1959-1960)
	Stefan Edberg	(1990, 1992-1993)

Women

6	Esna Boyd	(1922-1926, 1928)
4	Chris Evert	(1974, 1981, 1985, 1988)
	Jan Lehane	(1960-1963)
	Thelma Long	(1940, 1951, 1955-1956)
3	Evonne Goolagong	(1971-1973)
	Martina Hingis	(2000-2002)
	Martina Navratilova	(1975, 1982, 1987)

BIGGEST GAP BETWEEN FIRST AND LAST SINGLES TITLE

Men

19 years—Ken Rosewall 1953- 72

Women

14 years—Nancye Wynne Bolton 1937-51

13 years— Margaret Smith Court 1960-73

TOURNAMENTS PLAYED

Men

20 Jack Crawford   (1927-40, 46-48)

Women

14 Margaret Smith Court   (1959-1975)

MOST SINGLES MATCHES PLAYED

Men

67 Stefan Edberg   (1983-1996)

Women

65 Margaret Smith Court   (1959-1975)

MOST SINGLES MATCHES WON

Men

56 Stefan Edberg   (1983-1996)

Women

60 Margaret Smith Court   (1959-1975)

MOST SINGLES MATCHES WON CONSECUTIVELY

Men

27 Roy Emerson   (1963-1969)

Women

38 Margaret Smith Court   (1960-1968)

SINGLES MATCH WINNING PERCENTAGE

Men

.870	Roger Federer	(47 wins, 7 losses through 2009)
.836	Stefan Edberg	(56 wins, 11 losses) (1983-1996)

Women

.952   Margaret Smith Court   (60 wins, 3 losses) (1959-1975)

TRIPLES

(Winner of all three events in one year)

Men

1926	Jack Hawkes	(MD-Gerald Patterson; MXD-Esna Boyd)
1928	Jean Borotra	(MD-Jacques Brugnon; MXD-Daphne Akhurst)
1932	Jack Crawford	(MD-Gar Moon; MXD-Marjorie Cox Crawford)

Women

1925	Daphne Akhurst	(WD-Sylvia Lance Harper; MXD-John Willard)
1928	Daphne Akhurst	(WD-Esna Boyd; MXD-Jean Borotra)
1929	Daphne Akhurst	(WD-Louie Bickerton; MXD-Gar Moon)
1940	Nancye Bolton	(WD-Thelma Coyne Long; MXD-Colin Long)
1947	Nancye Bolton	(WD-Thelma Coyne Long; MXD-Colin Long)
1948	Nancye Bolton	(WD-Thelma Coyne Long; MXD-Colin Long)
1952	Thelma Long	(WD-Nancy Bolton; MXD-George Worthington)
1963	Margaret Smith Court	
		(WD with Robyn Ebbern; M-Ken Fletcher)

MOST DOUBLES TITLES – TEAM

Men

8	Adrian Quist / John Bromwich	(1938-1950)
4	John Newcombe / Tony Roche	(1965-1976)
3	Gerald Patterson / Jack Hawkes	(1922-1927)
	Rod Laver / Bob Mark	(1959-1961)

Women

10	Nancye Bolton / Thelma Long	(1936-1952)
7	Martina Navratilova / Pam Shriver	(1982-1989)
3	Venus Williams / Serena Williams	(2001-2009)
	Mall Molesworth / Emily Westacott	(1930-1934)

MOST DOUBLES TITLES – INDIVIDUAL

Men

10	Adrian Quist	(1936-1950)
8	John Bromwich	(1938-1950)
5	Gerald Patterson	(1914-1927)
	John Newcombe	(1965-1976)
	Tony Roche	(1965-1977)

Women

12	Thelma Long	(1936-1958)
10	Nancye Bolton	(1936-1952)
8	Margaret Smith Court	(1961 -1973)
	Martina Navratilova	(1980-1989)

MOST DOUBLES FINAL APPEARANCES – TEAM

Men

9	Adrian Quist / John Bromwich	(1938-1951)
5	John Newcombe / Tony Roche	(1965-1976)
4	John Alexander / Phil Dent	(1970-1977)

Women

12	Nancye Bolton / Thelma Long	(1936-1952)
8	Martina Navratilova / Pam Shriver	(1981 -1989)
3	Gigi Fernandez / Natalia Zvereva	(1993-1995)
	Joyce Fitch / Mary Bevis Hawton	(1946-1951)
	Judy Dalton / Lesley Turner	(1964-1968)
	Mall Molesworth / Emily Westacott	(1930-1934)
	Margaret Smith Court / Robyn Ebbern	(1962-1964)
	Mary Bevis Hawton / Beryl Penrose	(1953-1955)

MOST DOUBLES FINAL APPEARANCES – INDIVIDUAL

Men

12	Adrian Quist	(1934-1951)
10	John Bromwich	(1937-1951)

| 8 | Jack Crawford | (1929-1940) |
| | Roy Emerson | (1958-1969) |

Women

14	Thelma Long	(1936-1958)
12	Margaret Smith Court	(1960-1975)
	Mary Bevis Hawton	(1946-1961)
	Nancye Bolton	(1936-1952)

MOST DOUBLES FINAL LOSSES – TEAM

Men

3	Don Candy / Merv Rose	(1952-1956)
	John Alexander / Phil Dent	(1970-1977)
2	Alex O'Brien / Sebastien Lareau	(1996-1997)
	Daniel Nestor / Mark Knowles	(1995-2003)
	Geoff Masters / Ross Case	(1972-1976)
	Jack Crawford / Viv McGrath	(1936-1940)
	Paul Kronk / Cliff Letcher	(1978-1979)

Women

	Claudia Kohde Kilsch / Helena Sukova	(1984-1985)
	Joyce Fitch / Mary Bevis Hawton	(1947-1951)
	Kathrine LeMesurier / Dorothy Weston	(1928-1932)
	Kerry Harris / Kerry Melville	(1973-1974)
	Lindsay Davenport / Natalia Zvereva	(1998-1999)
	Nancye Bolton / Thelma Long	(1946-1950)

MOST DOUBLES FINAL LOSSES – INDIVIDUAL

Men

5	Roy Emerson	(1958-1965)
4	Don Candy	(1952-1959)
	Jack Crawford	(1931 -1940)
	James Anderson	(1919-1926)

Women

7	Mary Bevis Hawton	(1947-1961)
5	Lindsay Davenport	(1996-2001)
4	Kathrine LeMesurier	(1924-1932)
	Kerry Melville	(1970-1977)
	Lesley Turner	(1963-1976)
	Lorraine Coghian	(1958-1967)
	Margaret Smith Court	(1960-1975)

MOST MIXED DOUBLES TITLES – TEAM

4	Nancye Bolton / Colin Long	(1940-1948)
	Nell Hall / Harry Hopman	(1930-1939)
3	Esna Boyd / Jack Hawkes	(1922-1927)
	Marjorie Cox / Jack Crawford	(1931 -1933)
	Thelma Coyne Long / George Worthington	(1951 -1955)

MOST MIXED DOUBLES TITLES

Men

4	Colin Long	(1940-1948)
	Harry Hopman	(1930-1939)
3	George Worthington	(1951-1955)
	Jack Crawford	(1931 -1933)
	Jack Hawkes	(1922-1927)
	Jim Pugh	(1988-1990)

Women

4	Daphne Akhurst	(1924-1929)
	Nancye Bolton	(1940-1948)
	Nell Hall Hopman	(1930-1939)
	Thelma Long	(1951-1955)

MOST MIXED DOUBLES FINAL APPEARANCES – TEAM

5	Marjorie Cox / Jack Crawford	(1929-1933)
	Nancye Bolton / Colin Long	(1938-1948)
	Nell Hall / Harry Hopman	(1930-1940)
4	Esna Boyd / Jack Hawkes	(1922-1928)

MOST MIXED DOUBLES FINAL APPEARANCES

Men

6	John Bromwich	(1938-1954)
5	Colin Long	(1938-1948)
	Harry Hopman	(1930-1940)
	Jack Crawford	(1929-1933)
	Todd Woodbridge	(1992-2003)

Women

5	Daphne Akhurst	(1924-1929)
	Esna Boyd	(1922-1928)
	Marjorie Cox	(1929-1933)
	Nancye Bolton	(1938-1948)
	Nell Hall Hopman	(1930-1940)
	Thelma Long	(1948-1955)

MOST MIXED DOUBLES FINAL LOSSES – TEAM

3	Joyce Fitch / John Bromwich	(1946-1949)
2	Arantxa Sanchez Vicario / Todd Woodbridge	(1992-2000)
	Marjorie Cox / Jack Crawford	(1929-1930)
	Zina Garrison / Rick Leach	(1990-1993)

OLDEST SINGLES CHAMPION

Men

Ken Rosewall—37 years, 2 months (1972)

Women

Thelma Long—35 years, 7 months (1954)

YOUNGEST SINGLES CHAMPION

Men

Ken Rosewall—18 years, 2 months (1953)

Women

Martina Hingis—16 years, 4 months (1997)

OLDEST DOUBLES CHAMPION

Men

Norman Brookes—46 years, 2 months (1924)

OLDEST MIXED DOUBLES CHAMPION

Men

Horace "Horrie" Rice—52 years (1923)
Sherwood Stewart USA—40 years, 7 months (1987)

Women

Martina Navratilova—46 years, 3 months (2003)

Women

Thelma Long—37 years, 7 months (1956)

YOUNGEST DOUBLES CHAMPION

Men

Lew Hoad—18 years, 2 months (born Nov 23, 1934) (1953)
Ken Rosewall—18 years, 2 months (born Nov 2, 1934) (1953)

Women

Mirjana Lucic—15 years, 10 months (1998)

YOUNGEST MIXED DOUBLES CHAMPION

Men

Tony Roche—20 years, 8 months (1966)

Women

Venus Williams—17 years, 7 months (1998)

LONGEST MATCHES – TOTAL GAMES

Men's Singles

93 games   Dennis Ralston d. John Newcombe, 19-17, 20-18, 4-6, 6-3, quarters, 1970

Men's Doubles

94 games   Max Senior / Paul Avery d. Warren Jacques / Cedric Mason, 4-6, 18-16, 7-9, 17-15, 2-0, retired, 1st rd., 1968

Women's Singles:

48 games   Chanda Rubin d. Arantxa Sanchez Vicario, 6-4, 2-6, 16-14, quarters, 1996

Women's Doubles

42 games   Linda Gates / Alycia Moulton d. Katerina Maleeva / Manuela Maleeva, 4-6, 6-2, 13-11, 2nd rd., 1985

42 games   Lise Gregory / Manon Bollegraf, d. Elise Burgin / Roslyn Fairbank Nideffer, 5-7, 6-4, 11-9, 3rd rd., 1991

Mixed Doubles

47 games   Jo-Anne Faull / Jason Stoltenberg d. Paula Smith / Mike Bauer, 7-6(7-5), 4-6, 13-11, 1st rd., 1988

MOST NUMBER OF GAMES SINGLES FINAL

Men

1927   Gerald Patterson d. Jack Hawkes, 3-6, 6-4, 3-6, 18-16, 6-3, Melbourne, 71 games

Women

1930   Daphne Akhurst d. Sylvia Harper, 10-8, 2-6, 7-5, Melbourne, 38 games

1981   Martina Navratilova d. Chris Evert, 6-7 (4-7), 6-4, 7-5, Melbourne, 35 games

LEAST NUMBER OF GAMES SINGLES FINAL

Men

1923   Pat O'Hara Wood d. Bert St. John, 6-1, 6-1, 6-3, Brisbane, 23 games

1926   Jack Hawkes d. Jim Willard, 6-1, 6-3, 6-1, Adelaide, 23 games

2003   Andre Agassi d. Rainer Schuettler, 6-2, 6-2 6-1, Melbourn,e 23 games

Women

1962   Margaret Smith d. Jan Lehane, 6-0, 6-2, Sydney, 14 games

1994   Steffi Graf d. Arantxa Sanchez Vicario, 6-0, 6-2, Melbourne, 14 games

LONGEST MATCHES – PLAYING TIME

Men's Singles

5 hours, 14 minutes   Rafael Nadal d. Fernando Verdasco 6-7 (5), 6-4, 7-6 (2), 6-7 (1), 6-4, SF, 2009

5 hours, 11 minutes   Boris Becker d. Omar Camporese, 7-6 (7-4), 7-6 (7-5), 0-6, 4-6, 14-12, 3rd rd., 1991

4 hours, 59 minutes   Andy Roddick d. Younes El Aynaoui, 4-6, 7-6 (7-5), 4-6, 6-4, 21-19, QF, 2003. The fifth set took 2:23, Roddick saved MP in 10th game of the fifth with inside-out forehand

4 hours, 59 minutes   Pete Sampras def. Tim Mayotte, 7-6, 6-7, 4-6, 7-5, 12-10, 1st rd, 1990

Men's Doubles

5 hours, 29 minutes   Pieter Aldrich / Danie Visser, d. Scott Davis-Bob Van't Hof, 6-4, 4-6, 7-6 (7-4), 4-6, 23-21 (last set took 2 hours, 53 minutes), QF, 1990

Women's Singles

3 hours, 33 minutes   Chanda Rubin d. Arantxa Sanchez Vicario, 6-4, 2-6, 16-14, QF, 1996

LATEST FINISH

2008   Lleyton Hewitt d. Marcos Baghdatis 4-6, 7-5, 7-5, 6-7 (4-7), 6-3, Began at 11:49 PM Saturday, ended 4:34 AM Sunday

2007   Andreas Seppi d. Bobby Reynolds, 6-1, 6-7 (4-7), 6-7(5-7), 7-6 (7-3), 6-3, 1st rd. 3:49. Began Tuesday ended 3:44 AM Wednesday

LONGEST TIE-BREAKERS

Men's Singles

20-18   first set, Andy Roddick d. Jo-Wilfried Tsonga, 6-7 (18-20), 7-6 (2), 6-2, 6-3, 1st rd., 2007

17-15   third set, Omar Camporese d. Lars Wahlgren, 6-4, 6-2, 7-6(17-15), 3rd rd., 1992

Women's Singles

15-13   first set, Silke Meier d. Jane Taylor, 7-6 (15-13), 2-6, 6-2, 1st rd., 1995

EARLIEST LOSS OF A NO. 1 SEED

Men

2002   No. 1 seed Lleyton Hewitt lost to Alberto Martin 1-6, 6-1, 6-4, 7-6 (4), 1st rd.

Women

1979   Mary Sawyer d. 1st seed Virginia Ruzici, 0-6, 6-2, 6-4, 1st rd.

EARLIEST LOSS OF A DEFENDING CHAMPION

Men

1997   Carlos Moya (No. 24) d. 6th seed defending champ Boris Becker, 5-7, 7-6 (7-4), 3-6, 6-1, 6-4, 1st rd.

Women

2003   No. 3 seed Jennifer Capriati lost to Marlene Weingartner, 1st rd 2-6, 7-6(6), 6-4

OTHER BIG UPSETS

Men

1926	Gar Moon d. Gerald Patterson (former champion, 2nd seed) 6-8, 5-7, 7-5, 6-4, 6-3 1st rd.
1933	Viv McGrath d. 1st seed Ellsworth Vines (world No. 1), 6-2, 2-6, 8-6, 7-5, QF
1950	Ken McGregor d. 1st seed Jaroslav Drobny, 11-9, 6-1, 6-3, 2nd rd.
1970	Mark Cox d. 1st seed Rod Laver, 6-3, 4-6, 6-3, 7-6, 3rd rd.
1976	Mark Edmondson (No. 212) d. 5th seed Phil Dent, 6-0, 6-4, 4-6, 6-3, 2nd rd.; 1st seed Ken Rosewall, 6-1, 2-6, 6-2, 6-4, SF; 2nd seed John Newcombe, 6-7. 6-3, 7-6, 6-1, F
1978	John Marks (No. 177) d. 3rd seed Arthur Ashe, 6-4, 6-2, 2-6, 1-6, 9-7, SF (saved 2 MP, 5th)
1980	14th seed Kim Warwick d. 1st seed defending champ Guillermo Vilas, 6-7, 6-4, 6-2, 2-6, 6-4, SF
1985	Slobodan Zivojinovic (No. 66) d. 2nd seed John McEnroe, 2-6, 6-3, 1-6, 6-4, 6-0, QF
1989	Ramesh Krishnan (No. 40) d. 1st seed defending champ Mats Wilander, 6-3, 6-2, 7-6, 2nd rd.
1993	Christian Bergstrom (No. 62) d. 8th seed Ivan Lendl, 6-4, 6-4, 2-6, 6-4, 1st rd, also qualifier Anders Jarryd (No. 151) d. 4th seed Boris Becker 3-6, 7-5, 3-6, 6-3, 6-2, 1st rd.
1994	MaliVai Washington (No. 26) d. 2nd seed Michael Stich, 7-6 (7-4), 6-3, 3-6, 6-2, 1st rd.
1996	Mark Philippoussis (No. 40) d. 1st seed, Pete Sampras, 6-4, 7-6 (11-9), 7-6 (7-3), 3rd rd.
1998	Karol Kucera (No. 20) d. 1st seed Pete Sampras, 6-4, 6-2, 6-7 (5-7), 6-3, QF. Also Alberto Berasategui (No. 25) d. 2nd seed Patrick Rafter, 6-7 (2-7), 7-6 (9-7), 6-2, 7-6 (7-4), 3rd rd.; (No. 87) Andre Agassi, 3-6, 3-6, 6-2, 6-3, 6-3, 4th rd.
2002	Julien Boutter (No. 49) d. 2nd seed Gustavo Kuerten, 3-6, 4-6, 7-5, 6-3, 6-3, 1st rd. Also qualifier Alex Kim (No. 234) d. 4th seed Yevgeny Kafelnikov, 6-3, 7-5, 6-3, 2nd rd.
2003	Younes El Aynaoui (No. 22) d. 1st seed Lleyton Hewitt, 6-7(4), 7-6 (4), 7-6 (5), 6-4 in 4th rd.
2006	Marcos Baghdatis (No. 54) d. 2nd seed Andy Roddick 6-4, 1-6, 6-3, 6-4 in 4th round, 7th seed Ivan Ljubicic, 6-4, 6-2, 4-6, 3-6, 6-3 in QF and 4th seed David Nalbandian 3-6, 5-7, 6-3, 6-4, 6-4 in SF
2008	Jo-Wilfried Tsonga (No. 38) d. 2nd seed Rafael Nadal 6-2, 6-3, 6-2 in SF

Women

1924	Katherine LeMesurier d. defending champ Margaret "Mall" Mutch Molesworth, 7-9, 3-6, 8-6, QF
1966	Joan Gibson d. 2nd seed Lesley Turner, 8-6, 6-1, 3rd rd.
1976	Elisabeth Ekblom d. 2nd seed Kerry Melville Reid, 6-4, 6-3, 1st rd.
1980	Mima Jausovec (No. 20) d. 2nd seed Evonne Goolagong, 6-2, 4-6, 6-4, 2nd rd.
1988	Wendy Wood (qualifier ranked No. 306) d. 14th seed Dianne Fromholtz Balestrat, 6-2, 4-6, 8-6, 1st rd. (saved 1 MP, 3rd, at 4-5, first stadium match at new Flinders Park)

1997	12th seed Amanda Coetzer d. 1st seed Steffi Graf, 6-2, 7-5, 4th rd. Also Dominique Monami Van Roost (No. 43) d. 2nd seed Arantxa Sanchez Vicario, 1-6, 6-4, 8-6, 4th rd. Also Sabine Appelmans (No. 18) d. 3rd seed Conchita Martinez, 2-6, 7-5, 6-1, 4th rd. (all same day)
2003	Qualifier and No. 113-ranked Klara Koukalova d. No. 6 seed Monica Seles 6-7 (6), 7-5, 6-3 in 2nd rd.
2004	No. 25 seed Lisa Raymond d. No. 3 Venus Williams 6-4, 7-6 (5) in 3rd rd, 6-4, 7-6 (7-5)
2006	No. 94 Tszvetana Pironkova (playing in her first ever major tournament) d. 10th seed Venus Williams in 1st rd 2-6, 6-0, 9-7
2007	No. 70 Lucie Safarova d. No. 2 seed and defending champion Amelie Mauresmo 6-4, 6-3 in 4th rd.

BEST COMEBACKS

Men

1960	3rd seed Rod Laver d. 1st seed Neale Fraser, 5-7, 3-6, 6-3, 8-6, 8-6, F (saved 1 MP, 4th, at 4-5); d. 2nd seed Roy Emerson, 4-6, 6-1, 9-7, 3-6, 7-5 (won last 4 games from 3-5)
1985	5th seed Stefan Edberg d. Wally Masur (No. 142), 6-7 (4-7), 2-6, 7-6 (7-4), 6-4, 6-2, QF (saved 2 MP, 3rd, at 4-5)
1988	5th seed Yannick Noah d. Roger Smith (No. 147), 6-7, 5-7, 6-4, 6-2, 16-14, 1st rd. (saved 2 MP, 5th, at 7-8, 30-40 and ad-out)
1995	Pete Sampras d. Jim Courier 6-7 (4-7), 6-7 (3-7), 6-3, 6-4, 6-3 in QF (Sampras trailed 2-4 in the 4th set)
2001	15th seed Arnaud Clement d. 16th seed Sebastian Grosjean, 5-7, 2-6, 7-6 (7-4), 7-5, 6-2, SF (saved 2 MP)
2008	Vince Spadea d. No. 30 seed Radek Stepanek, 2-6, 2-6, 7-5, 6-2, 6-3 in 1st rd (trailed 2-4 in 3rd set); also James Blake d. Sebastien Grosjean 4-6, 2-6, 6-0, 7-6 (7-5), 6-2, 3rd rd. Blake trailing two service breaks 1-4 in the fourth set and 0-3, 1-4, and 3-5 in fourth-set tie-break

Women

1933	Joan Hartigan d. Margaret "Mall" Mutch Molesworth, 4-6, 8-6, 9-7, QF; also d. Frances Hoddle-Wrigley, 4-6, 6-0, 6-4, SF
1979	Mary Sawyer d. 1st seed Virginia Ruzici, 0-6, 6-2, 6-4, 1st rd.
1997	Dominique Monami Van Roost (No. 43) d. 2nd seed Arantxa Sanchez Vicario, 1-6, 6-4, 8-6, 4th rd.
1999	Amelie Mauresmo (No. 29) d. Corina Morariu, 6-7 (2-7), 7-6 (8-6), 6-2 (saved 2 MP, 2nd, at 5-2)
2008	Jelena Jankovic (seed No. 3) d. Tamira Paszek 2-6, 6-2, 12-10 in 3:09 (saved 3 MP, 3rd set, down 1-4 in 3rd set, Paszek served for the match 5 times)

MATCH POINTS SAVED BY SINGLES CHAMPION

Men

1927	F, Gerald Patterson d. Jack Hawkes, 3-6, 6-4, 3-6, 18-16, 6-3 (saved 7 MP, 4th, 4 at 13-12, 1 at 16-15)
1947	F, 2nd seed Dinny Pails d. 1st seed John Bromwich, 4-6, 6-4, 3-6, 7-5, 8-6 (saved 1 MP)
1960	F, 3rd seed Rod Laver d. 1st seed Neale Fraser, 5-7, 3-6, 6-3, 8-6, 8-6 (saved 1 MP, 4th, at 4-5)
1975	SF, 2nd seed John Newcombe d. 3rd seed Tony Roche, 6-4, 4-6, 6-4, 2-6, 11 -9 (saved 3 MP, 5th)

1982	SF, 1st seed Johan Kriek d. 16th seed Paul McNamee, 7-6, 7-6, 4-6, 3-6, 7-5 (saved 1 MP, 5th)

1982   SF, 1st seed Johan Kriek d. 16th seed Paul McNamee, 7-6, 7-6, 4-6, 3-6, 7-5 (saved 1 MP, 5th)

1985   QF, 5th seed Stefan Edberg d. Wally Masur (No. 142), 6-7 (4-7), 2-6, 7-6 (7-4), 6-4, 6-2 (saved 2 MP 3rd, at 4-5)

2005   SF, Marat Safin d. 1st seed Roger Federer 5-7, 6-4, 5-7, 7-6 (6), 9-7 (saved match point at 5-6 in fourth-set tie-break, Federer missing a between-the-legs retrieval of a lob) but Safin needed 7 match points to close it out

Women

1923   SF, Margaret "Mall" Mutch Molesworth d. Sylvia Lance, 3-6, 6-4, 8-6 (saved 1 MP, 3rd)

1956   F, 2nd seed Mary Carter d. 5th seed Thelma Coyne Long, 3-6, 6-2, 9-7 (saved 1 MP, 3rd)

1991   SF, 2nd seed Monica Seles d. 3rd seed Mary Joe Fernandez, 6-3, 0-6, 9-7 (saved 1 MP, 3rd)

2002   F, 1st seed Jennifer Capriati d. 3rd seed Martina Hingis 4-6, 7-6 (7-4), 6-2 (saved 4 MP, 2nd,1 at 5-3, 40-30, 2 at 5-6, 30-40 and ad-out, 1 at 6-7 in tie-breaker)

2003   SF, 1st seed Serena Williams d. 4th seed Kim Clijsters, 4-6, 6-3, 7-5 (saved 2 MP, 3rd, at 5-2, 40-30 and ad-in)

2005   SF, 7th seed Serena Williams d. Maria Sharapova, 2-6, 7-5, 8-6 (saved 3 MP)

UNSEEDED CHAMPIONS OPEN ERA

Men

1976   Mark Edmonson

Women

1978   Chris O'Neil

FARTHEST ADVANCEMENT OF A QUALIFIER

Men

Bob Giltinan   December 1977 Semifinals

Women

Christine Matison   1978 Semifinals

FARTHEST ADVANCEMENT OF A LUCKY LOSER

Men

Glenn Layendecker   1991 Third Round

Women

Sandra Kleinova   1997 Third Round

FARTHEST ADVANCEMENT OF A WILD CARD

Men

Tomas Smid   1983 Quarterfinals

Women

Martina Hingis   2006 Quarterfinals
Jelena Dokic   2009 Quarterfinals

ACES

Men

51   Joachim Johansson lost to Andre Agassi, 6-7 (4-7), 7-6 (7-5), 7-6 (7-3), 6-4, 2005 4th rd. (Agassi had 16 aces)

45   Jonathan Stark lost to Lionel Roux 1-6, 4-6, 7-6 (7-4), 6-2, 13-11, 1997 1st rd.

45   Chris Guccione lost to Olivier Rochus 3-6, 7-5, 7-5, 6-7 (4), 9-7, 2007 1st rd.

42   Andy Roddick lost to Philip Kohlschreiber, 6-4, 3-6, 7-6 (9), 6-7 (3), 8-6, 2008 3rd rd.

40   Bryan Shelton d. Paolo Cane 7-6 (3), 4-6, 6-3, 6-4, 1991 1st rd.

39   Roger Federer d.Janko Tipsarevic, 6-7 (5-7) 7-6 (7-1), 5-7, 6-1, 10-8. 4 hours, 27 minutes, 2008 3rd rd.

38   Joachim Johansson d. Feliciano Lopez, 2005, 6-3, 3-6, 5-7, 7-6 (7-2),13-11, 4th rd.

37   Pete Sampras lost to Andre Agassi, F, 2000, 3-6, 6-3, 6-2, 6-4

37   Arthur Ashe d. John Newcombe, SF, 1967, 12-10, 20-22, 6-3, 6-2

36   Pete Sampras over Wayne Black, 2000, 6-7 (9-11), 3-6, 6-3, 7-5, 6-3, 3rd rd.

34   Feliciano Lopez lost to Joachim Johansson, 2005, 6-3, 3-6, 5-7, 7-6 (7-2),13-11, 4th rd.

34   Jacco Eltingh d. Patrick McEnroe, 1995, 6-4, 6-4, 6-7(7-9), 5-7, 6-4, 4th rd.

33   Pete Sampras over Escude, 2002, 7-6 (7-5), 5-7, 6-4, 6-7 (6-8), 6-3, 3rd rd.

31   Andy Roddick lost to Lleyton Hewitt (14), SF, 2005, 3-6, 7-6 (7-3), 7-6 (7-4), 6-1

31   Ivo Karlovic, lost to Nikolay Davydenko, 7-5, 4-6, 3-6, 7-5, 6-3, 1st rd, 2006

29   Philippoussis over Galo Blanco, 2002, 6-3, 6-4, 7-5, 1st rd.

29   Gerald Patterson over Jack Hawkes, 1927 F, 3-6, 6-4, 3-6, 18-16, 6-3

7 aces in one game, Marzio Martelli lost to Agassi, 1998, 11 deuces, 2d game 2d set, 3-6, 7-6 (7-3), 6-2, 6-2

7 straight aces, Andy Roddick, 2005, in loss to Lleyton Hewitt, SF, 3-6, 7-6 (7-3), 7-6 (7-4), 6-4, aces 9 thru 15: 3 to end 1st set, 4 to win 2d game, 2nd set

Women

15   Serena Williams d. Victoria Azarenka, 6-3, 6-4; 3rd round, 2008, (Had a total of 40 for the tournament)

14   Lindsay Davenport d. Alicia Molik, 6-4, 4-6, 9-7 QF, 2005

TOTAL ACES MATCH

72   Total aces one match, Joachim Johansson (38) d. Feliciano Lopez (34), 6-3, 3-6, 5- 7, 7-6 (7-2), 13-11 in 3:58, 2005. Johansson's 38th ace came on MP

TOTAL ACES TOURNAMENT

126 Joachim Johansson, 2005, four rounds

DOUBLE FAULTS

Men

29   Gerald Pattterson d. Jack Hawkes 1927 F, 3-6, 6-4, 3-6, 18-16, 6-3

23   Guillermo Coria lost to Sebastien Grosjean, 6-2, 6-2, 3-6, 6-4, 2nd rd. 2006

Women

31   Anna Kournikova d. Miho Saeki 1-6, 6-4, 10-8 in 3rd rd 1999

23   Anna Kournikova d. Jill Craybas, 7-6 (7-1), 7-5, 1st rd. 1999

17   Jennifer Capriati d. Evie Dominikovic, 5-7, 6-3, 8-6, 1st rd. 1999

French Championships

Ivan Lendl (left) won his first major title—and his first of three French singles titles—with a dramatic final-round win over **John McEnroe** in 1984, coming from two-sets-to-love down to beat the American 3-6, 2-6, 6-4, 7-5, 7-5.

Crimson clay has made the French Championship distinctive, the lone major contested on the footing beloved by dirt-kicking Europeans and Latin Americans. For 46 years (1928–74), Stade Roland Garros in Paris was an earthen oasis amid grass in the Australian, Wimbledon and U.S. Championships. Wimbledon retains its lawns, the Aussies and Yanks have paved their hard, unforgiving rectangles, but clay stays the French way.

Although dating back to 1891 (men) and 1897 (women), the French Championships welcomed only citizens and permanent residents. Not until 1925 was that restriction lifted, the rest of the world invited in, and the French would become the fourth of the major international championships, making a Grand Slam possible. Even so, the concept didn't seem feasible until 1933 when an Aussie, Jack Crawford, having carried his homeland, became the first alien male to subdue Paris (8-6, 6-1, 6-3 over homeboy Henri

Cochet). He went on to win Wimbledon but his bid for a Slam was jammed by Fred Perry in the U.S. final. Don Budge showed up in 1938 and was the first American guy to conquer the clay (6-3, 6-2, 6-4 over Czech Roderich Menzel), and was halfway to his pocketing of the initial Slam.

The most successful players in the French-only days were Cecilia Masson with six titles (1897–1900, 02-03) and Max Decugis with eight titles (1903-04, 07-09, 12-14).

But leading foreigners did come to town for an international tournament entitled Championnats du Monde sur Terre Battue—terre battue the French term for clay—that ran in 1912-13-14, 21, 23 in Paris (1922 in Brussels). After that, the label World Championships on Clay was dropped, but not before a small, dark-haired girl of 15 won it in 1914, and again in 1921 at 23. She was the unbeatable Suzanne Lenglen, who put France on the tennis map.

The 1924 Olympic Games in Paris gave the French another taste of internationalism, and the mood was "very insistent," in the words of one writer, for the establishment of a French Championships (Championnats Internationaux de France) embracing players from wherever, joining the uppermost category.

Thus France was in the exclusive four-member club, with four all-timers facing off for the introductory titles - Musketeers Rene (The Crocodile) Lacoste and Jean (Bounding Basque) Borotra, Lacoste winning, 7-5, 6-1, 6-4; La Lenglen beating the only non-native, Brit Kitty McKane, 6-1, 6-2. First outlanders to enter the winners circle were Americans Vinnie Richards and Howard Kinsey in 1926 in men's doubles, beating the other half of the illustrious Four Musketeers, Henri (Ball Boy of Lyon) Cochet and Jacques (Toto) Brugnon, 6-4, 6-1, 4-6, 6-4. First among visitors to seize a singles title was Kea Bouman of the Netherlands, 6-2, 6-4, over South African Irene Bowder Peacock in 1927.

In 1925 and 1927, the tournament was played at Stade Francais in St. Cloud, and in 1926, it was held at the Racing Club of Paris, neither venue holding more than 5,000. But the Musketeers' lifting the Davis Cup from the U.S. in 1927 made a larger venue necessary for the 1928 Cup defense, as well as the Championships. Rising near the Bois de Boulogne was Stade Roland Garros, named for a heroic French aviator who died in World War I, and a Court Central seating 10,000. On the crushed brick surface, seldom adored by Americans, the French crushed Bill Tilden and the U.S., 4-1.

World War II shut down the tournament as it did Wimbledon and the Australian and brought about a sad, grisly chapter in Roland Garros history. When the war began, the French government used it as a detention center for so-called dissidents and "other undesirables," a number of them Jews who were at risk to be sent to the death camps when the Nazi invaders occupied Paris. One of the better known inmates, author Arthur

Koestler ("Darkness at Noon"), wrote that, "We called ourselves cave dwellers, sleeping on wet straw beneath the stands which leaked." Fortunately, he survived. In 1941, the Germans released the grounds to the French Federation, and the Championships resumed, obviously limited to locals and not included in official records. They resumed in 1946, with, appropriately, a native victor, unseeded Marcel Bernard over favored Czech Jaroslav Drobny, 3-6, 2-6, 6-1, 6-4, 6-3, an all-lefty finale. That French success didn't recur for 37 years, until 1983 when Yannick Noah dethroned Swede Mats Wilander, 6-2, 7-5, 7-6 (7-3), to be handed the Coupe Mousquetaires. Female victory rates the Coupe Lenglen, won in the post-Lenglen time by citizens Simone Mathieu in 1938-1939 and Francoise Durr in 1967. After another long wait, 33 years, the Franco-American Mary Pierce cheered a Parisian crowd by beating Spaniard Conchina Martinez, 6-2, 7-5, in 2000.

First major to say "bienvenue" to the pros and "Opens," the French offered a $25,000 pot in 1968. Ken Rosewall won $3,000 in an all-Aussie final over Rod Laver, 6-3, 6-1, 2-6, 6-2, but runner-up for the other title, left-handed Brit Ann Jones, got the first prize women's check of $1,000, even though she lost to Texan Nancy Richey, 5-7, 6-4, 6-1. Nancy, fearful of giving up her amateur status in that uncertain new year of prize money, is alone in the majors as a title-winning amateur woman in the post-'68 era.

Cash earnings have has gone up considerably since: $1.4 million apiece to 2007 singles champs, Belgian Justine Henin and Spaniard Rafael Nadal, out of a $20.33 million kitty. The French was the second-to-last of the major championships to offer equal prize money to both men and women—offering equal prize money for both tournament champions in 2006 and awarding equal prize money across the board beginning in 2007. The French has wandered on the calendar, but the dates have stood firmly (last week in May-first week in June) for decades.

As interest has increased from 1960s doldrums, attendance and profits have gone up considerably, the scene improved. Court Central was enlarged, now holding 15,171 (named for Hall of Famer Philippe Chatrier, the driving force for modernization as French Tennis Federation president). A second stadium, the Court Suzanne Lenglen, holding 10,018, was added in 1995. A fan favorite, Court 1 (the intimate "bull ring") accommodates 3,790.

In 2007, play began on the first of three Sundays, making the French, a daytime event, a 15-day show, the longest of the majors. A one-day attendance record, 35,750 on the grounds, was set on the first Saturday, 2007. The French tried night tennis in 1969, but wisely discarded the floodlights after that. Darkness doesn't intrude until about 9:30 PM. The French Championships were the last major to accept the tie-breaker, 1973, but never for the ultimate sets, fifth for men, third for women.

French Championships – Tournament Results

Legend: F: Final; S: Semifinal; Q: Quarterfinal; Set: S1, S2, S3, S4, S5

Men's Singles

Rd	Winner	Defeated	S1	S2	S3	S4	S5
1925							
F	**Rene Lacoste (FRA)**	**Jean Borotra (FRA)**	**7-5**	**6-1**	**6-4**		
S	Jean Borotra (FRA)	Jean Washer (BEL)	6-2	6-1	6-3		
S	Rene Lacoste (FRA)	Sydney Jacob (GBR)	6-2	6-1	4-6	7-5	
Q	Jean Washer (BEL)	Henri Cochet (FRA)	8-6	8-6	6-4		
Q	Jean Borotra (FRA)	Paul Feret (FRA)	1-6	6-3	6-3	6-2	
Q	Rene Lacoste (FRA)	Equardo Flaquer (ESP)	6-4	7-5	6-2		
Q	Sydney Jacob (GBR)	Andre Gobert FRA)	2-6	2-6	6-4	7-5 (retired)	
1926							
F	**Henri Cochet (FRA)**	**Rene Lacoste (FRA)**	**6-2**	**6-4**	**6-3**		
S	Rene Lacoste (FRA)	Jean Borotra (FRA)	8-6	3-6	6-2	6-1	
S	Henri Cochet (FRA)	Vinnie Richards (USA)	6-1	6-4	6-4		
Q	Rene Lacoste (FRA)	Nicholai Misu (ROU)	14-12	6-1	6-1		
Q	Jean Borotra (FRA)	Howard Kinsey (USA)	2-6	6-4	6-1	3-6	7-5
Q	Henri Cochet (FRA)	Jean Washer (BEL)	6-4	3-6	7-5	6-4	
Q	Vinnie Richards (USA)	Bela von Kehrling (HUN)	6-1	6-3	6-3		
1927							
F	**Rene Lacoste (FRA)**	**Bill Tilden (USA)**	**6-4**	**4-6**	**5-7**	**6-3**	**11-9**
S	Bill Tilden (USA)	Henri Cochet (FRA)	9-7	6-3	6-2		
S	Rene Lacoste (FRA)	Pat Spence (RSA)	6-1	6-3	6-2		
Q	Henri Cochet (FRA)	Otto Froitzheim (GER)	6-1	6-1	6-4		
Q	Bill Tilden (USA)	Louis Raymond (RSA)	5-7	6-2	8-6	6-3	
Q	Pat Spence (RSA)	Antoine Gentien (FRA)	6-2	3-6	6-4	6-3	
Q	Rene Lacoste (FRA)	Jacques Brugnon (FRA)	6-4	6-4	5-7	6-3	
1928							
F	**Henri Cochet (FRA)**	**Rene Lacoste (FRA)**	**5-7**	**6-3**	**6-1**	**6-3**	
S	Henri Cochet (FRA)	Jean Borotra (FRA)	6-3	2-6	7-5	6-4	
S	Rene Lacoste (FRA)	Jack Hawkes (AUS)	6-2	6-4	6-1		
Q	Henri Cochet (FRA)	Ronaldo Boyd (ARG)	7-5	6-4	6-2		
Q	Jean Borotra (FRA)	Christian Boussus (FRA)	6-1	3-6	7-5	6-3	
Q	Jack Hawkes (AUS)	Jacques Brugnon (FRA)	4-6	3-6	6-3	6-3	6-4
Q	Rene Lacoste (FRA)	Jack Crawford (AUS)	6-0	6-1	7-5		
1929							
F	**Rene Lacoste (FRA)**	**Jean Borotra (FRA)**	**6-3**	**2-6**	**6-0**	**2-6**	**8-6**
S	Rene Lacoste (FRA)	Bill Tilden (USA)	6-1	6-0	5-7	6-3	
S	Jean Borotra (FRA)	Henri Cochet (FRA)	6-3	5-7	7-5	6-4	
Q	Rene Lacoste (FRA)	Bela von Kehrling (HUN)	8-6	1-6	6-0	6-3	
Q	Bill Tilden (USA)	Umberto de Morpurgo (ITA)	9-11	3-6	6-1	6-2	8-6
Q	Jean Borotra (FRA)	Frank Hunter (USA)	6-8	10-8	4-6	3-6	6-1
Q	Henri Cochet (FRA)	Jacques Brugnon (FRA)	7-5	4-6	6-4	7-5	
1930							
F	**Henri Cochet (FRA)**	**Bill Tilden (USA)**	**3-6**	**8-6**	**6-3**	**6-1**	
S	Bill Tilden (USA)	Jean Borotra (FRA)	2-6	6-2	6-4	4-6	6-3
S	Henri Cochet (FRA)	Umberto de Morpurgo (ITA)	7-5	6-1	6-2		
Q	Bill Tilden (USA)	Geo. Lyttleton Rogers (IRL)	6-1	6-1	7-5		
Q	Jean Borotra (FRA)	Colin Gregory (GBR)	6-4	6-4	6-3		
Q	Umberto de Morpurgo (ITA)	Gar Moon (AUS)	6-2	6-2	4-6	2-6	6-3
Q	Henri Cochet (FRA)	Harry Hopman (AUS)	6-1	2-6	6-3	6-3	
1931							
F	**Jean Borotra (FRA)**	**Christian Boussus (FRA)**	**2-6**	**6-4**	**7-5**	**6-4**	
S	Christian Boussus (FRA)	Patrick Hughes (GBR)	6-1	4-6	6-2	6-3	
S	Jean Borotra (FRA)	Jiro Satoh (JPN)	10-8	2-6	5-7	6-1	6-2
Q	Patrick Hughes (GBR)	George Lott (USA)	3-6	4-6	6-2	6-2	6-4
Q	Christian Boussus (FRA)	Giorgio de Stefani (ITA)	6-4	6-3	3-6	2-6	9-7
Q	Jiro Satoh (JPN)	John Van Ryn (USA)	8-6	1-6	2-6	6-4	6-3
Q	Jean Borotra (FRA)	Benny Berthet (FRA)	6-2	6-3	6-1		
1932							
F	**Henri Cochet (FRA)**	**Giorgio de Stefani (ITA)**	**6-0**	**6-4**	**4-6**	**6-3**	
S	Giorgio de Stefani (ITA)	Roderich Menzel (CZE)	6-3	2-6	7-5	6-4	
S	Henri Cochet (FRA)	Marcel Bernard (FRA)	6-1	6-0	6-4		
Q	Roderich Menzel (CZE)	Fred Perry (GBR)	2-6	6-1	1-6	6-3	7-5
Q	Giorgio de Stefani (ITA)	Harold G.N. Lee (GBR)	6-3	9-7	6-2		
Q	Marcel Bernard (FRA)	Geo. Lyttleton Rogers (IRL)	6-4	6-8	6-4	3-6	6-2
Q	Henri Cochet (FRA)	Greg Mangin (USA)	6-3	7-5	5-7	6-3	
1933							
F	**Jack Crawford (AUS)**	**Henri Cochet (FRA)**	**8-6**	**6-1**	**6-3**		
S	Jack Crawford (AUS)	Jiro Satoh (JPN)	6-0	6-2	6-2		
S	Henri Cochet (FRA)	Harold G.N. Lee (GBR)	9-11	6-3	6-3	6-3	
Q	Jack Crawford (AUS)	Christian Boussus (FRA)	6-3	6-3	6-4		
Q	Jiro Satoh (JPN)	Fred Perry (GBR)	1-6	7-5	6-4	2-6	6-2
Q	Harold G.N. Lee (GBR)	Marcel Bernard (FRA)	10-8	6-4	5-7	6-0	
Q	Henri Cochet (FRA)	Roderich Menzel (CZE)	7-5	6-4	6-1		
1934							
F	**Gottfried von Cramm (GER)**	**Jack Crawford (AUS)**	**6-4**	**7-9**	**3-6**	**7-5**	**6-3**
S	Jack Crawford (AUS)	Christian Boussus (FRA)	6-3	2-6	7-5	6-4	
S	Gottfried von Cramm (GER)	Giorgio de Stefani (ITA)	3-6	6-4	6-1	3-6	6-2
Q	Jack Crawford (AUS)	Patrick Hughes (GBR)	4-6	6-4	6-2	6-3	
Q	Christian Boussus (FRA)	Bunny Austin (GBR)	5-7	6-2	6-2	2-6	6-1
Q	Gottfried von Cramm (GER)	Roderich Menzel (CZE)	6-2	6-3	3-6	3-6	6-3
Q	Giorgio de Stefani (ITA)	Fred Perry (GBR)	6-2	1-6	9-7	6-2	

Rd	Winner	Defeated	S1	S2	S3	S4	S5

1935

Rd	Winner	Defeated	S1	S2	S3	S4	S5
F	Fred Perry (GBR)	Gottfried von Cramm (GER)	6-3	3-6	6-1	6-3	
S	Fred Perry (GBR)	Jack Crawford (AUS)	6-3	8-6	6-3		
S	Gottfried von Cramm (GER)	Bunny Austin (GBR)	6-2	5-7	6-1	5-7	6-0
Q	Fred Perry (GBR)	Christian Boussus (FRA)	6-1	6-0	6-1		
Q	Jack Crawford (AUS)	Marcel Bernard (FRA)	6-3	6-1	6-1		
Q	Bunny Austin (GBR)	Roderich Menzel (CZE)	1-6	10-8	2-6	6-4	6-2
Q	Gottfried von Cramm (GER)	Viv MacGrath (AUS)	6-2	6-4	3-6	6-3	

1936

Rd	Winner	Defeated	S1	S2	S3	S4	S5
F	Gottfried von Cramm (GER)	Fred Perry (GBR)	6-0	2-6	6-2	2-6	6-0
S	Gottfried von Cramm (GER)	Marcel Bernard (FRA)	7-5	6-1	6-1		
S	Fred Perry (GBR)	Christian Boussus (FRA)	6-4	7-5	5-7	6-2	
Q	Gottfried von Cramm (GER)	Bernard Destremau (FRA)	6-3	6-1	6-4		
Q	Marcel Bernard (FRA)	Bunny Austin (GBR)	4-6	1-0		(retired)	
Q	Christian Boussus (FRA)	Andre Merlin (FRA)	1-6	6-3	7-5	1-6	6-1
Q	Fred Perry (GBR)	Boris Maneff (SUI)	9-7	6-3	4-6	6-3	

1937

Rd	Winner	Defeated	S1	S2	S3	S4	S5
F	Henner Henkel (GER)	Bunny Austin (GBR)	6-1	6-4	6-3		
S	Henner Henkel (GER)	Bernard Destremau (FRA)	6-1	6-4	6-3		
S	Bunny Austin (GBR)	Christian Boussus (FRA)	7-5	6-2	1-6	6-3	
Q	Bernard Destremau (FRA)	Charles Hare (GBR)	11-9	4-6	7-9	7-5	7-5
Q	Henner Henkel (GER)	Patrick Hughes (GBR)	6-3	6-4	6-2		
Q	Christian Boussus (FRA)	Franz Cejner (CZE)	6-2	6-2	6-1		
Q	Bunny Austin (GBR)	Yvon Petra (FRA)	6-4	6-2	6-1		

1938

Rd	Winner	Defeated	S1	S2	S3	S4	S5
F	Don Budge (USA)	Roderich Menzel (CZE)	6-3	6-2	6-4		
S	Roderich Menzel (CZE)	Franjo Puncec (YUG)	6-4	6-4	6-4		
S	Don Budge (USA)	Josip Pallada (YUG)	6-2	6-3	6-3		
Q	Franjo Puncec (YUG)	Franz Cejnar (CZE)	3-6	6-3	6-2	6-3	
Q	Roderich Menzel (CZE)	Dragutin Mitic (YUG)	6-0	6-0	6-1		
Q	Josip Pallada (YUG)	Christian Boussus (FRA)	6-1	3-6	4-6	6-1	6-2
Q	Don Budge (USA)	Bernard Destremau (FRA)	6-4	6-3	6-4		

1939

Rd	Winner	Defeated	S1	S2	S3	S4	S5
F	Don NcNeil (USA)	Bobby Riggs (USA)	7-5	6-0	6-3		
S	Don NcNeil (USA)	Elwood Cooke (USA)	6-2	7-5	7-9	6-2	
S	Bobby Riggs (USA)	Otto Szigeti (HUN)	6-3	6-0	6-4		
Q	Don NcNeil (USA)	Franjo Puncec (YUG)	6-4	1-6	6-3	6-1	
Q	Elwood Cooke (USA)	Henry Bilington (GBR)	6-4	6-4	6-1		
Q	Otto Szigeti (HUN)	Christian Boussus (FRA)	7-5	1-6	2-6	7-5	6-4
Q	Bobby Riggs (USA)	Hank Tloczyinski (POL)	6-2	2-6	8-6	7-5	

1940-45 NOT HELD—WW II

1946

Rd	Winner	Defeated	S1	S2	S3	S4	S5
F	Marcel Bernard (FRA)	Jaroslav Drobny (CZE)	3-6	2-6	6-1	6-4	6-3
S	Jaroslav Drobny (CZE)	Tom Brown (USA)	7-5	3-6	6-4	5-7	6-2
S	Marcel Bernard (FRA)	Yvon Petra (FRA)	5-7	6-2	6-3	5-7	6-2
Q	Tom Brown (USA)	Pierre Pellizza (FRA)	6-2	6-2	6-3		
Q	Jaroslav Drobny (CZE)	Dragutin Mitic (YUG)	6-2	7-5	6-8	8-6	
Q	Marcel Bernard (FRA)	Budge Patty (USA)	2-6	6-2	6-1	4-6	7-5
Q	Yvon Petra (FRA)	Ferdinand Vrba (CZE)	2-6	6-0	6-4	6-2	

1947

Rd	Winner	Defeated	S1	S2	S3	S4	S5
F	Joszef Asboth (HUN)	Eric Sturgess (RSA)	8-6	7-5	6-4		
S	Joszef Asboth (HUN)	Tom Brown (USA)	6-2	6-2	6-1		
S	Eric Sturgess (RSA)	Marcel Bernard (FRA)	3-6	2-6	6-3	8-6	6-3
Q	Joszef Asboth (HUN)	Yvon Petra (FRA)	4-6	6-3	6-2	6-1	
Q	Tom Brown (USA)	Pierre Pellizza (FRA)	7-5	6-1	6-2		
Q	Eric Sturgess (RSA)	Adam Stolpa (HUN)	6-4	6-3	6-2		
Q	Marcel Bernard (FRA)	Gianni Cucelli (ITA)	6-4	6-2	0-6	3-6	6-4

1948

Rd	Winner	Defeated	S1	S2	S3	S4	S5
F	Frank Parker (USA)	Jaroslav Drobny (CZE)	6-4	7-5	5-7	8-6	
S	Jaroslav Drobny (CZE)	Budge Patty (USA)	2-6	6-3	4-6	6-4	6-3
S	Frank Parker (USA)	Eric Sturgess (RSA)	6-2	6-2	6-1		
Q	Budge Patty (USA)	Marcello Del Bello (ITA)	7-5	9-7	1-0	(retired)	
Q	Jaroslav Drobny (CZE)	Lennart Bergelin (SWE)	6-2	6-1	6-4		
Q	Eric Sturgess (RSA)	Marcel Bernard (FRA)	6-3	6-2	9-7		
Q	Frank Parker (USA)	Gianni Cucelli (ITA)	6-1	6-2	6-1		

1949

Rd	Winner	Defeated	S1	S2	S3	S4	S5
F	Frank Parker (USA)	Budge Patty (USA)	6-3	1-6	6-1	6-4	
S	Budge Patty (USA)	Pancho Gonzalez (USA)	6-4	6-3	3-6	6-3	
S	Frank Parker (USA)	Eric Sturgess (RSA)	6-2	6-1	6-4		
Q	Pancho Gonazalez (USA)	Marcel Bernard (FRA)	6-1	7-5	5-7	6-1	
Q	Budge Patty (USA)	Gianni Cucelli (ITA)	7-5	10-12	6-3	8-6	
Q	Eric Sturgess (RSA)	Robert Abdesselam (FRA)	6-1	6-4	6-2		
Q	Frank Parker (USA)	Dragutin Mitic (YUG)	6-0	6-2	6-4		

1950

Rd	Winner	Defeated	S1	S2	S3	S4	S5
F	Budge Patty (USA)	Jaroslav Drobny (CZE)	6-1	6-2	3-6	5-7	7-5
S	Budge Patty (USA)	Tony Trabert (USA)	2-6	6-4	6-4	12-10	
S	Jaroslav Drobny (CZE)	Eric Sturgess (RSA)	6-4	7-5	3-6	12-10	
Q	Budge Patty (USA)	Irving Dorfman (USA)	0-6	6-1	3-6	6-1	11-9
Q	Tony Trabert (USA)	John Bromwich (AUS)	6-2	6-2	6-3		
Q	Eric Sturgess (RSA)	Art Larsen (USA)	4-6	6-3	6-2	6-4	
Q	Jaroslav Drobny (CZE)	Vic Seixas (USA)	7-5	17-15	5-7	6-4	

1951

Rd	Winner	Defeated	S1	S2	S3	S4	S5
F	Jaroslav Drobny (CZE)	Eric Sturgess (RSA)	6-3	6-3	6-3		
S	Jaroslav Drobny (CZE)	Frank Sedgman (AUS)	6-0	6-3	6-1		
S	Eric Sturgess (RSA)	Ken McGregor (AUS)	10-8	7-9	8-6	5-7	9-7
Q	Frank Sedgman (AUS)	Straight Clark (USA)	6-4	6-4	6-3		
Q	Jaroslav Drobny (CZE)	Dick Savitt (USA)	1-6	6-8	6-4	8-6	6-3
Q	Eric Sturgess (RSA)	Merv Rose (AUS)	11-9	4-6	6-3	6-3	
Q	Ken McGregor (AUS)	Lennart Bergelin (SWE)	9-7	9-7	6-1		

1952

Rd	Winner	Defeated	S1	S2	S3	S4	S5
F	Jaroslav Drobny (CZE)	Frank Sedgman (AUS)	6-2	6-0	3-6	6-4	
S	Frank Sedgman (AUS)	Eric Sturgess (RSA)	7-5	6-2	8-6		
S	Jaroslav Drobny (CZE)	Ken McGregor (AUS)	6-3	6-0	4-6	6-3	
Q	Frank Sedgman (AUS)	Budge Patty (USA)	6-4	6-2	6-2		
Q	Eric Sturgess (RSA)	Dick Savitt (USA)	6-2	6-8	4-6	8-6	6-3
Q	Ken McGregor (AUS)	Felicisimo Ampon (PHI)	6-1	6-1	6-2		
Q	Jaroslav Drobny (CZE)	Gardnar Mulloy (USA)	6-1	6-2	6-2		

1953

Rd	Winner	Defeated	S1	S2	S3	S4	S5
F	Ken Rosewall (AUS)	Vic Seixas (USA)	6-3	6-4	1-6	6-2	
S	Ken Rosewall (AUS)	Enrique Morea (ARG)	2-6	6-2	6-4	0-6	6-2
S	Vic Seixas (USA)	Jaroslav Drobny (CZE)	6-3	6-2	3-6	6-3	
Q	Enrique Morea (ARG)	Gardnar Mulloy (USA)	6-8	6-3	8-6	6-3	
Q	Ken Rosewall (AUS)	Felicisimo Ampon (PHI)	6-2	6-1	6-1		
Q	Vic Seixas (USA)	Lew Hoad (AUS)	6-3	6-3	6-4		
Q	Jaroslav Drobny (CZE)	Fausto Gardini (ITA)	6-3	6-1	1-6	6-4	

1954

Rd	Winner	Defeated	S1	S2	S3	S4	S5
F	Tony Trabert (USA)	Art Larsen (USA)	6-4	7-5	6-1		
S	Tony Trabert (USA)	Budge Patty (USA)	6-1	7-5	6-4		
S	Art Larsen (USA)	Enrique Morea (ARG)	6-4	6-3	6-4		
Q	Tony Trabert (USA)	Merv Rose (AUS)	7-5	4-6	6-4	6-2	
Q	Budge Patty (USA)	Sven Davidson (SWE)	6-4	6-0	6-4		
Q	Art Larsen (USA)	Vic Seixas (USA)	6-4	1-6	8-6	6-1	
Q	Enrique Morea (ARG)	Gardnar Mulloy (USA)	6-3	6-4	6-1		

1955

Rd	Winner	Defeated	S1	S2	S3	S4	S5
F	Tony Trabert (USA)	Sven Davidson (SWE)	2-6	6-1	6-4	6-2	
S	Sven Davidson (SWE)	Beppe Merlo (ITA)	6-3	6-3	6-2		
S	Tony Trabert (USA)	Ham Richardson (USA)	6-1	2-2		(retired)	
Q	Beppo Merlo (ITA)	Vic Seixas (USA)	12-10	6-3	6-3		
Q	Sven Davidson (SWE)	Budge Patty (USA)	7-5	10-8	6-0		
Q	Ham Richardson (USA)	Herbie Flam (USA)	6-3	4-6	6-1	6-3	
Q	Tony Trabert (USA)	Merv Rose (AUS)	6-2	3-6	6-3	6-0	

1956

Rd	Winner	Defeated	S1	S2	S3	S4	S5
F	Lew Hoad (AUS)	Sven Davidson (SWE)	6-4	8-6	6-3		
S	Sven Davidson (SWE)	Ashley Cooper (AUS)	6-2	9-7	5-7	6-3	
S	Lew Hoad (AUS)	Beppe Merlo (ITA)	6-4	7-5	6-4		
Q	Ashley Cooper (AUS)	Jacques Brichant (BEL)	6-4	8-6	2-6	6-3	
Q	Sven Davidson (SWE)	Herbie Flam (USA)	6-2	6-4	7-5		
Q	Beppe Merlo (ITA)	Paul Remy (FRA)	4-6	6-2	2-6	6-4	10-8
Q	Lew Hoad (AUS)	Nicola Pietrangeli (ITA)	6-1	6-3	6-0		

1957

Rd	Winner	Defeated	S1	S2	S3	S4	S5
F	Sven Davidson (SWE)	Herbie Flam (USA)	6-3	6-4	6-4		
S	Sven Davidson (SWE)	Ashley Cooper (AUS)	6-4	2-6	2-6	6-2	6-3
S	Herbie Flam (USA)	Merv Rose (AUS)	4-6	6-4	4-6	6-2	7-5
Q	Ashley Cooper (AUS)	Neale Fraser (AUS)	0-6	8-6	7-5	4-6	6-3
Q	Sven Davidson (SWE)	Jackie Brichant (BEL)	6-2	6-2	4-6	6-2	
Q	Merv Rose (AUS)	Robert Haillet (FRA)			(walkover)		
Q	Herbie Flam (USA)	Philippe Washer (BEL)	5-7	6-4	6-3	4-6	6-4

1958

Rd	Winner	Defeated	S1	S2	S3	S4	S5
F	Merv Rose (AUS)	Luis Ayala (CHI)	6-3	6-4	6-4		
S	Merv Rose (AUS)	Jackie Brichant (BEL)	10-8	6-1	6-3		
S	Luis Ayala (CHI)	Ashley Cooper (AUS)	9-11	4-6	6-4	6-2	7-5
Q	Jackie Brichant (BEL)	Neale Fraser (AUS)	5-7	5-7	7-5	6-0	6-3
Q	Merv Rose (AUS)	Pierre Damon (FRA)	6-4	8-10	6-3	6-1	
Q	Luis Ayala (CHI)	Robert Haillet (FRA)	6-0	7-5	6-4		
Q	Ashley Cooper (AUS)	Beppe Merlo (ITA)	7-9	6-2	7-9	6-3	6-2

1959

Rd	Winner	Defeated	S1	S2	S3	S4	S5
F	Nicola Pietrangeli (ITA)	Ian Vermaak (RSA)	3-6	6-3	6-4	6-1	
S	Nicola Pietrangeli (ITA)	Neale Fraser (AUS)	7-5	6-3	7-5		
S	Ian Vermaak (RSA)	Luis Ayala (CHI)	6-2	6-1	6-4		
Q	Neale Fraser (AUS)	Marty Mulligan (AUS)	6-4	8-6	6-1		
Q	Nicola Pietrangeli (ITA)	Billy Knight (GBR)	6-1	6-2	6-1		
Q	Ian Vermaak (RSA)	Jacques Brichant (BEL)	4-6	2-6	6-4	6-3	6-4
Q	Luis Ayala (CHI)	Roy Emerson (AUS)	1-6	6-4	6-4	6-3	

1960

Rd	Winner	Defeated	S1	S2	S3	S4	S5
F	Nicola Pietrangeli (ITA)	Luis Ayala (CHI)	3-6	6-3	6-4	4-6	6-3
S	Nicola Pietrangeli (ITA)	Robert Haillet (FRA)	6-4	7-5	7-5		
S	Luis Ayala (CHI)	Orlando Sirola (ITA)	6-4	6-0	6-2		
Q	Robert Haillet (FRA)	Neale Fraser (AUS)	6-4	6-2	8-10	3-6	6-5
							(default)
Q	Nicola Pietrangeli (ITA)	Andres Gimeno (ESP)	6-3	6-1	3-6	6-2	
Q	Luis Ayala (CHI)	Manolo Santana (ESP)	6-1	7-5	6-2		
Q	Orlando Sirola (ITA)	Barry MacKay (USA)	6-3	15-13	6-4		

1961

Rd	Winner	Defeated	S1	S2	S3	S4	S5
F	Manolo Santana (ESP)	Nicola Pietrangeli (ITA)	4-6	6-1	3-6	6-0	6-2
S	Manolo Santana (ESP)	Rod Laver (AUS)	3-6	6-2	4-6	6-4	6-0
S	Nicola Pietrangeli (ITA)	Jan-Erik Lundquist (SWE)	6-4	6-4	6-4		
Q	Rod Laver (AUS)	Ronald Holmberg (USA)	6-4	6-0	3-6	6-3	
Q	Manolo Santana (ESP)	Roy Emerson (AUS)	9-7	6-2	6-2		
Q	Jan-Erik Lundquist (SWE)	Carlos Fernandes (BRA)	6-4	6-4	6-3		
Q	Nicola Pietrangeli (ITA)	Gerard Pilet (FRA)	6-3	6-8	6-3	6-1	

1962

Rd	Winner	Defeated	S1	S2	S3	S4	S5
F	Rod Laver (AUS)	Roy Emerson (AUS)	3-6	2-6	6-3	9-7	6-2
S	Roy Emerson (AUS)	Manolo Santana (ESP)	6-4	3-6	6-1	2-6	6-3
S	Rod Laver (AUS)	Neale Fraser (AUS)	3-6	6-3	6-2	3-6	7-5
Q	Roy Emerson (AUS)	Ramanathan Krishnan (IND)	4-6	6-1	3-6	6-2	6-0
Q	Manolo Santana (ESP)	Pierre Darmon (FRA)	6-4	6-2	6-3		
Q	Neale Fraser (AUS)	Nicola Pietrangeli (ITA)	4-6	6-3	11-9	6-1	
Q	Rod Laver (AUS)	Marty Mulligan (AUS)	6-4	3-6	2-6	10-8	6-2

1963

Rd	Winner	Defeated	S1	S2	S3	S4	S5
F	Roy Emerson (AUS)	Pierre Darmon (FRA)	3-6	6-1	6-4	6-4	
S	Pierre Darmon (FRA)	Manolo Santana (ESP)	6-3	4-6	2-6	9-7	6-2
S	Roy Emerson (AUS)	Mike Sangster (GBR)	8-6	6-3	6-4		
Q	Manolo Santana (ESP)	Jean Claude Barclay (FRA)	1-6	6-2	6-0	2-6	6-3
Q	Pierre Darmon (FRA)	Bobby Wilson (GBR)	6-3	6-4	6-3		
Q	Mike Sangster (GBR)	Ken Fletcher (AUS)	8-6	6-3	6-8	6-3	
Q	Roy Emerson (AUS)	Nicola Pietrangeli (ITA)	6-8	4-6	6-1	6-3	6-4

1964

Rd	Winner	Defeated	S1	S2	S3	S4	S5
F	Manolo Santana (ESP)	Nicola Pietrangeli (ITA)	6-3	6-1	4-6	7-5	
S	Manolo Santana (ESP)	Pierre Darmon (FRA)	8-6	6-4	3-6	2-6	6-4
S	Nicola Pietrangeli (ITA)	Jan-Erik Lundquist (SWE)	4-6	6-3	6-4	6-4	
Q	Pierre Darmon (FRA)	Eugene Scott (USA)	6-3	6-2	6-0		
Q	Manolo Santana (ESP)	Ronnie Barnes (BRA)	6-4	6-3	6-3		
Q	Jan-Erik Lundquist (SWE)	Cliff Drysdale (RSA)	6-4	6-4	3-6	6-1	
Q	Nicola Pietrangeli (ITA)	Roy Emerson (AUS)	6-1	6-3	6-3		

1965

Rd	Winner	Defeated	S1	S2	S3	S4	S5
F	Fred Stolle (AUS)	Tony Roche (AUS)	3-6	6-0	6-2	6-3	
S	Tony Roche (AUS)	Roy Emerson (AUS)	6-1	6-4	3-6	6-0	
S	Fred Stolle (AUS)	Cliff Drysdale (RSA)	6-8	6-4	6-1	4-6	6-4
Q	Roy Emerson (AUS)	Pierre Barthes (FRA)	6-4	6-4	6-4		
Q	Tony Roche (AUS)	Ingo Buding (GER)	6-4	4-6	7-5	0-6	6-3
Q	Fred Stolle (AUS)	John Newcombe (AUS)	6-1	7-5	11-9		
Q	Cliff Drysdale (RSA)	Thomas Lejus (USSR)	(walkover)				

1966

Rd	Winner	Defeated	S1	S2	S3	S4	S5
F	Tony Roche (AUS)	Istvan Gulyas (HUN)	6-1	6-4	7-5		
S	Tony Roche (AUS)	Francois Jauffret (FRA)	6-3	6-4	6-4		
S	Istvan Gulyas (HUN)	Cliff Drysdale (RSA)	6-4	2-6	7-9	6-2	6-3
Q	Francois Jauffret (FRA)	Roy Emerson (AUS)	1-6	6-3	6-4	4-6	6-4
Q	Tony Roche (AUS)	Alex Metreveli (USSR)	5-7	6-3	6-1	7-5	
Q	Istvan Gulyas (HUN)	Ken Fletcher (AUS)	7-5	6-2	6-3		
Q	Cliff Drysdale (RSA)	Fred Stolle (AUS)	1-6	6-4	6-2	11-9	

1967

Rd	Winner	Defeated	S1	S2	S3	S4	S5
F	Roy Emerson (AUS)	Tony Roche (AUS)	6-1	6-4	2-6	6-2	
S	Tony Roche (AUS)	Nikki Pilic (YUG)	3-6	6-3	6-4	2-6	6-4
S	Roy Emerson (AUS)	Istvan Gulyas (HUN)	6-3	6-4	6-2		
Q	Tony Roche (AUS)	Cliff Drysdale (RSA)	2-6	2-6	6-3	6-2	6-4
Q	Nikki Pilic (YUG)	Tom Okker (NED)	6-3	11-9	6-2		
Q	Istvan Gulyas (HUN)	Owen Davidson (AUS)	5-7	6-3	6-3	6-0	
Q	Roy Emerson (AUS)	Pierre Darmon (FRA)	6-0	6-4	6-4		

1968

Rd	Winner	Defeated	S1	S2	S3	S4	S5
F	Ken Rosewall (AUS)	Rod Laver (AUS)	6-3	6-1	2-6	6-2	
S	Rod Laver (AUS)	Pancho Gonzalez (USA)	6-3	6-3	6-1		
S	Ken Rosewall (AUS)	Andres Gimeno (ESP)	3-6	6-3	7-5	3-6	6-3
Q	Rod Laver (AUS)	Ion Triac (ROU)	4-6	4-6	6-3	6-3	6-0
Q	Pancho Gonzalez (USA)	Roy Emerson (AUS)	7-5	6-3	3-6	4-6	6-4
Q	Andres Gimeno (ESP)	Boro Jovanovic (YUG)	6-4	6-0	6-2		
Q	Ken Rosewall (AUS)	Thomaz Koch (BRA)	8-6	6-2	3-6	6-3	

1969

Rd	Winner	Defeated	S1	S2	S3	S4	S5
F	Rod Laver (AUS)	Ken Rosewall (AUS)	6-4	6-3	6-4		
S	Rod Laver (AUS)	Tom Okker (NED)	4-6	6-0	6-2	6-4	
S	Ken Rosewall (AUS)	Tony Roche (AUS)	7-5	6-2	6-2		
Q	Rod Laver (AUS)	Andres Gimeno (ESP)	3-6	6-2	6-4	6-4	
Q	Tom Okker (NED)	John Newcombe (AUS)	5-7	6-2	4-6	6-2	6-2
Q	Andres Gimeno (ESP)	Zeljko Franulovic (YUG)	4-6	7-5	6-0	4-6	6-1
Q	Ken Rosewall (AUS)	Fred Stolle (AUS)	12-10	4-6	7-5	6-2	

1970

Rd	Winner	Defeated	S1	S2	S3	S4	S5
F	Jan Kodes (CZE)	Zeljko Franulovic (YUG)	6-2	6-4	6-0		
S	Zeljko Franulovic (YUG)	Cliff Richey (USA)	6-4	4-6	1-6	7-5	7-5
S	Jan Kodes (CZE)	Georges Goven (FRA)	2-6	6-2	5-7	6-2	6-3
Q	Cliff Richey (USA)	Ilie Nastase (ROU)	7-5	9-7	4-6	6-3	
Q	Zeljko Franulovic (YUG)	Arthur Ashe (USA)	6-3	3-6	10-8	4-6	6-3
Q	Georges Goven (FRA)	Francois Jauffret (FRA)	8-6	6-8	6-2	6-1	
Q	Jan Kodes (CZE)	Marty Mulligan (ITA)	6-1	6-3	7-5		

1971

Rd	Winner	Defeated	S1	S2	S3	S4	S5
F	Jan Kodes (CZE)	Ilie Nastase (ROU)	8-6	6-2	2-6	7-5	
S	Jan Kodes (CZE)	Zeljko Franulovic (YUG)	6-4	6-2	7-5		
S	Ilie Nastase (ROU)	Frank Froehling III (USA)	6-0	2-6	6-4	6-3	
Q	Jan Kodes (CZE)	Patrick Proisy (FRA)	6-4	8-6	1-6	6-1	
Q	Zeljko Franulovic (YUG)	Istvan Gulyas (HUN)	6-3	6-2	4-6	6-2	
Q	Ilie Nastase (ROU)	Stan Smith (USA)	6-1	6-3	3-6	6-4	
Q	Frank Froehling III (USA)	Arthur Ashe (USA)	6-4	4-6	6-3	3-6	8-6

1972

Rd	Winner	Defeated	S1	S2	S3	S4	S5
F	Andres Gimeno (ESP)	Patrick Proisy (FRA)	4-6	6-3	6-1	6-1	
S	Patrick Proisy (FRA)	Manolo Orantes (ESP)	6-3	7-5	6-2		
S	Andres Gimeno (ESP)	Alex Metreveli (USSR)	4-6	6-3	6-1	2-6	6-3
Q	Patrick Proisy (FRA)	Jan Kodes (CZE)	6-4	6-2	6-4		
Q	Manuel Orantes (ESP)	Harold Solomon (USA)	'6-4	5-7	6-3	6-2	
Q	Andres Gimeno (ESP)	Stan Smith (USA)	6-1	7-9	6-0	7-5	
Q	Alex Metreveli (USSR)	Adriano Panatta (ITA)	8-6	7-9	6-3	6-3	

1973

Rd	Winner	Defeated	S1	S2	S3	S4	S5
F	Ilie Nastase (ROU)	Nikki Pilic (YUG)	6-3	6-3	6-0		
S	Nikki Pilic (YUG)	Adriano Panatta (ITA)	6-4	6-3	6-2		
S	Ilie Nastase (ROU)	Tom Gorman (USA)	6-3	6-4	6-1		
Q	Adriano Panatta (ITA)	Tom Okker (NED)	6-3	5-7	6-3	6-4	
Q	Nikki Pilic (YUG)	Paolo Bertolucci (ITA)	6-3	6-4	3-6	6-4	
Q	Tom Gorman (USA)	Jan Kodes (CZE)	6-4	7-6(6)	4-6	6-1	
Q	Ilie Nastase (ROU)	Roger Taylor (USA)	6-0	6-2	7-6(6)		

1974

Rd	Winner	Defeated	S1	S2	S3	S4	S5
F	Bjorn Borg (SWE)	Manolo Orantes (ESP)	2-6	6-7(1)	6-0	6-1	6-1
S	Bjorn Borg (SWE)	Harold Solomon (USA)	6-4	2-6	6-2	6-1	
S	Manolo Orantes (ESP)	Francois Jauffret (FRA)	6-2	6-4	6-4		
Q	Harold Solomon (USA)	Ilie Nasase (ROU)	6-4	6-4	0-6	3-6	6-4
Q	Bjorn Borg (SWE)	Raul Ramirez (MEX)	6-2	5-7	4-6	6-2	6-3
Q	Manolo Orantes (ESP)	Patricio Cornejo (CHI)	6-3	6-3	6-1		
Q	Francois Jauffret (FRA)	Hans Jurgen Pohmann (GER)	7-6	6-3	6-2		

1975

Rd	Winner	Defeated	S1	S2	S3	S4	S5
F	Bjorn Borg (SWE)	Guillermo Vilas (ARG)	6-2	6-3	6-4		
S	Bjorn Borg (SWE)	Adriano Panatta (ITA)	6-4	1-6	7-5	6-4	
S	Guillermo Vilas (ARG)	Eddie Dibbs (USA)	6-1	6-4	1-6	6-1	
Q	Bjorn Borg (SWE)	Harold Solomon (USA)	6-1	7-5	6-4		
Q	Adriano Panatta (ITA)	John Andrews (USA)	6-4	5-7	7-6	6-2	
Q	Guillermo Vilas (ARG)	Onny Parun (NZL)	6-2	6-2	7-6		
Q	Eddie Dibbs (USA)	Raul Ramirez (MEX)	4-6	7-6	6-1	5-7	6-4

1976

Rd	Winner	Defeated	S1	S2	S3	S4	S5
F	Adriano Panatta (ITA)	Harold Solomon (USA)	6-1	6-4	4-6	7-6(3)	
S	Adriano Panatta (ITA)	Eddie Dibbs (USA)	6-3	6-2	6-4		
S	Harold Solomon (USA)	Raul Ramirez (MEX)	6-7(5)	6-0	4-6	6-4	6-4
Q	Adriano Panatta (ITA)	Bjorn Borg (SWE)	6-3	6-3	2-6	7-6(2)	
Q	Eddie Dibbs (USA)	Manolo Orantes (ESP)	6-3	3-6	6-3	6-3	
Q	Raul Ramirez (MEX)	Balazs Taroczy (HUN)	4-6	7-6(7)	2-6	6-1	7-5
Q	Harold Solomon (USA)	Guillermo Vilas (ARG)	6-1	0-6	4-6	6-4	6-4

1977

Rd	Winner	Defeated	S1	S2	S3	S4	S5
F	Guillermo Vilas (ARG)	Brian Gottfried (USA)	6-0	6-3	6-0		
S	Brian Gottfried (USA)	Phil Dent (AUS)	7-5	6-3	7-5		
S	Guillermo Vilas (ARG)	Raul Ramirez (MEX)	6-2	6-0	6-3		
Q	Brian Gottfried (USA)	Ilie Nastase (ROU)	4-6	3-6	6-2	6-2	6-3
Q	Phil Dent (AUS)	Jose Higueras (ESP)	6-1	6-3	3-6	6-7	6-3
Q	Guillermo Vilas (ARG)	Wojtek Fibak (POL)	6-4	6-0	6-4		
Q	Raul Ramirez (MEX)	Adriano Panatta (ITA)	7-6(6)	6-3	7-5		

1978

Rd	Winner	Defeated	S1	S2	S3	S4	S5
F	Bjorn Borg (SWE)	Guillermo Vilas (ARG)	6-1	6-1	6-3		
S	Bjorn Borg (SWE)	Corrado Barazzutti (ITA)	6-0	6-1	6-0		
S	Guillermo Vilas (ARG)	Dick Stockton (USA)	6-3	6-3	6-2		
Q	Bjorn Borg (SWE)	Raul Ramirez (MEX)	6-3	6-3	6-0		
Q	Corrado Barazzutti (ITA)	Eddie Dibbs (USA)	6-2	7-6(7)	6-1		
Q	Dick Stockton (USA)	Manolo Orantes (ESP)	7-5	6-1	6-3		
Q	Guillermo Vilas (ARG)	Hans Gildemeister (CHI)	6-4	2-6	6-1	3-6	6-3

1979

Rd	Winner	Defeated	S1	S2	S3	S4	S5
F	Bjorn Borg (SWE)	Victor Pecci (PAR)	6-3	6-1	6-7(6)	6-4	
S	Bjorn Borg (SWE)	Vitas Gerulaitis (USA)	6-2	6-1	6-0		
S	Victor Pecci (PAR)	Jimmy Connors (USA)	7-5	6-4	5-7	6-3	
Q	Bjorn Borg (SWE)	Hans Gildemeister (CHI)	6-4	6-1	7-5		
Q	Vitas Gerulaitis (USA)	Jose Higueras (ESP)	6-1	3-6	6-4	6-4	
Q	Victor Pecci (PAR)	Guillermo Vilas (ARG)	6-0	6-2	7-5		
Q	Jimmy Connors (USA)	Eddie Dibbs (USA)	6-2	2-6	6-4	6-2	

1980

Rd	Winner	Defeated	S1	S2	S3	S4	S5
F	Bjorn Borg (SWE)	Vitas Gerulaitis (USA)	6-4	6-1	6-2		
S	Bjorn Borg (SWE)	Harold Solomon (USA)	6-2	6-2	6-0		
S	Vitas Gerulaitis (USA)	Jimmy Connors (USA)	6-1	3-6	6-7(3)	6-2	6-4
Q	Bjorn Borg (SWE)	Corrado Barazzutti (ITA)	6-0	6-3	6-3		
Q	Harold Solomon (USA)	Guillermo Vilas (ARG)	1-6	6-4	7-6	7-5	
Q	Jimmy Connors (USA)	Hans Gildemeister (CHI)	6-4	6-0	6-0		
Q	Vitas Gerulaitis (USA)	Wojtek Fibak (POL)	6-3	5-7	6-4	3-6	6-3

1981

Rd	Winner	Defeated	S1	S2	S3	S4	S5
F	Bjorn Borg (SWE)	Ivan Lendl (CZE)	6-1	4-6	6-2	3-6	6-1
S	Bjorn Borg (SWE)	Victor Pecci (PAR)	6-4	6-4	7-5		
S	Ivan Lendl (CZE)	Jose-Luis Clerc (ARG)	3-6	6-4	4-6	7-6	6-2
Q	Bjorn Borg (SWE)	Balazs Taroczy (HUN)	6-3	6-3	6-2		
Q	Victor Pecci (PAR)	Yannick Noah (FRA)	3-6	6-4	6-4	6-4	
Q	Ivan Lendl (CZE)	John McEnroe (USA)	6-4	6-4	7-5		
Q	Jose-Luis Clerc (ARG)	Jimmy Connors (USA)	4-6	6-2	4-6	7-5	6-0

1982

Rd	Winner	Defeated	S1	S2	S3	S4	S5
F	Mats Wilander (SWE)	Guillermo Vilas (ARG)	1-6	7-6(6)	6-0	6-4	
S	Guillermo Vilas (ARG)	Jose Higueras (ESP)	6-1	6-3	7-6(3)		
S	Mats Wilander (SWE)	Jose-Luis Clerc (ARG)	7-5	6-2	1-6	7-5	
Q	Jose Higueras (ESP)	Jimmy Connors (USA)	6-2	6-2	6-2		
Q	Guillermo Vilas (ARG)	Yannick Noah (FRA)	7-6	6-3	6-4		
Q	Jose-Luis Clerc (ARG)	Peter McNamara (AUS)	6-2	6-2	6-2		
Q	Mats Wilander (SWE)	Vitas Gerulaitis (USA)	6-3	6-3	4-6	6-4	

1983

Rd	Winner	Defeated	S1	S2	S3	S4	S5
F	Yannick Noah (FRA)	Mats Wilander (SWE)	6-2	7-5	7-6(3)		
S	Yannick Noah (FRA)	Chris. Roger-Vasselin (FRA)	6-3	6-0	6-0		
S	Mats Wilander (SWE)	Jose Higueras (ESP)	7-5	6-7(4)	6-3	6-0	
Q	Chris. Roger-Vasselin (FRA)	Jimmy Connors (USA)	6-4	6-4	7-6(5)		
Q	Yannick Noah (FRA)	Ivan Lendl (CZE)	7-6(5)	6-2	5-7	6-0	
Q	Jose Higueras (ESP)	Guillermo Vilas (ARG)	6-2	6-7(1)	6-1	4-6	6-1
Q	Mats Wilander (SWE)	John McEnroe (USA)	1-6	6-2	6-4	6-0	

1984

Rd	Winner	Defeated	S1	S2	S3	S4	S5
F	Ivan Lendl (CZE)	John McEnroe (USA)	3-6	2-6	6-4	7-5	7-5
S	John McEnroe (USA)	Jimmy Connors (USA)	7-5	6-1	6-2		
S	Ivan Lendl (CZE)	Mats Wilander (SWE)	6-3	6-3	7-5		
Q	John McEnroe (USA)	Jimmy Arias (USA)	6-3	6-4	6-4		
Q	Jimmy Connors (USA)	Henrik Sundstrom (SWE)	7-6(4)	6-1	6-4		
Q	Mats Wilander (SWE)	Yannick Noah (FRA)	7-6(4)	2-6	3-6	6-3	6-3
Q	Ivan Lendl (CZE)	Andres Gomez (ECU)	6-3	6-7	6-4	6-3	

1985

Rd	Winner	Defeated	S1	S2	S3	S4	S5
F	Mats Wilander (SWE)	Ivan Lendl (CZE)	3-6	6-4	6-2	6-2	
S	Mats Wilander (SWE)	John McEnroe (USA)	6-1	7-5	7-5		
S	Ivan Lendl (CZE)	Jimmy Connors (USA)	6-2	6-3	6-1		
Q	John McEnroe (USA)	Joakim Nystrom (SWE)	6-7(1)	6-2	6-2	3-6	7-5
Q	Mats Wilander (SWE)	Henri Leconte (FRA)	6-4	7-6(5)	6-7(4)	7-5	
Q	Jimmy Connors (USA)	Stefan Edberg (SWE)	6-4	6-3	7-6(2)		
Q	Ivan Lendl (CZE)	Martin Jaite (ARG)	6-4	6-2	6-4		

1986

Rd	Winner	Defeated	S1	S2	S3	S4	S5
F	Ivan Lendl (CZE)	Mikael Pernfors (SWE)	6-3	6-2	6-4		
S	Ivan Lendl (CZE)	Johan Kriek (USA)	6-2	6-1	6-0		
S	Mikael Pernfors (SWE)	Henri Leconte (FRA)	2-6	7-5	7-6(4)	6-3	
Q	Ivan Lendl (CZE)	Andres Gomez (ECU)	6-7(4)	7-6(3)	6-0	6-0	
Q	Johan Kriek (USA)	Guillermo Vilas (ARG)	3-6	7-6(6)	7-6(5)	7-6	
Q	Mikael Pernfors (SWE)	Boris Becker (GER)	2-6	6-4	6-2	6-0	
Q	Henri Leconte (FRA)	Andrei Chesnokov (USSR)	6-3	6-4	6-3		

1987

Rd	Winner	Defeated	S1	S2	S3	S4	S5
F	Ivan Lendl (CZE)	Mats Wilander (SWE)	7-5	6-2	3-6	7-6(3)	
S	Ivan Lendl (CZE)	Miloslav Mecir (CZE)	6-3	6-3	7-6(4)		
S	Mats Wilander (SWE)	Boris Becker (GER)	6-4	6-1	6-2		
Q	Ivan Lendl (CZE)	Andres Gomez (ECU)	5-7	6-4	6-1	6-1	
Q	Miloslav Mecir (CZE)	Karel Novacek (CZE)	7-6(4)	6-1	6-2		
Q	Mats Wilander (SWE)	Yannick Noah (FRA)	6-4	6-3	6-2		
Q	Boris Becker (GER)	Jimmy Connors (USA)	6-3	6-3	7-5		

1988

Rd	Winner	Defeated	S1	S2	S3	S4	S5
F	Mats Wilander (SWE)	Henri Leconte (FRA)	7-5	6-2	6-1		
S	Henri Leconte (FRA)	Jonas Svensson (SWE)	7-6(3)	6-2	6-3		
S	Mats Wilander (SWE)	Andre Agassi (USA)	4-6	6-2	7-5	5-7	6-0
Q	Jonas Svensson (SWE)	Ivan Lendl (CZE)	7-6(5)	7-5	6-2		
Q	Henri Leconte (FRA)	Andrei Chesnokov (RUS)	6-3	6-2	7-6(4)		
Q	Mats Wilander (SWE)	Emilio Sanchez (ESP)	6-7(5)	7-6(3)	6-3	6-4	
Q	Andre Agassi (USA)	Guillermo Perez-Roldan (ARG)	6-2	6-2	6-4		

1989

Rd	Winner	Defeated	S1	S2	S3	S4	S5
F	Michael Chang (USA)	Stefan Edberg (SWE)	6-1	3-6	4-6	6-4	6-2
S	Michael Chang (USA)	Andrei Chesnokov (USSR)	6-1	5-7	7-6(4)	7-5	
S	Stefan Edberg (SWE)	Boris Becker (GER)	6-3	6-4	5-7	3-6	6-2
Q	Michael Chang (USA)	Ronald Agenor (HAI)	6-4	2-6	6-4	7-6	
Q	Andrei Chesnokov (USSR)	Mats Wilander (SWE)	6-4	6-0	7-5		
Q	Stefan Edberg (SWE)	Alberto Mancini (ARG)	6-1	6-3	7-6(5)		
Q	Boris Becker (GER)	Jay Berger (USA)	6-3	6-4	6-1		

1990

Rd	Winner	Defeated	S1	S2	S3	S4	S5
F	Andres Gomez (ECU)	Andre Agassi (USA)	6-3	2-6	6-4	6-4	
S	Andre Agassi (USA)	Jonas Svensson (SWE)	6-1	6-4	3-6	6-3	
S	Andres Gomez (ECU)	Thomas Muster (AUT)	7-5	6-1	7-5		
Q	Jonas Svensson (SWE)	Henri Leconte (FRA)	3-6	7-5	6-3	6-4	
Q	Andre Agassi (USA)	Michael Chang (USA)	6-2	6-1	4-6	6-2	
Q	Andres Gomez (ECU)	Thierry Champion (FRA)	6-3	6-3	6-4		
Q	Thomas Muster (AUT)	Goran Ivanisevic (YUG)	6-2	4-6	6-4	6-3	

1991

Rd	Winner	Defeated	S1	S2	S3	S4	S5
F	Jim Courier (USA)	Andre Agassi (USA)	3-6	6-4	2-6	6-1	6-4
S	Jim Courier (USA)	Michael Stich (GER)	6-2	6-7(8)	6-2	6-4	
S	Andre Agassi (USA)	Boris Becker (GER)	7-5	6-3	3-6	6-1	
Q	Jim Courier (USA)	Stefan Edberg (SWE)	6-4	2-6	6-3	6-4	
Q	Michael Stich (GER)	Franco Davin (ARG)	6-4	6-4	6-4		
Q	Andre Agassi (USA)	Jakob Hlasek (SUI)	6-3	6-1	6-1		
Q	Boris Becker (GER)	Michael Chang (USA)	6-4	6-4	6-2		

1992

Rd	Winner	Defeated	S1	S2	S3	S4	S5
F	Jim Courier (USA)	Petr Korda (CZE)	7-5	6-2	6-1		
S	Jim Courier (USA)	Andre Agassi (USA)	6-3	6-2	6-2		
S	Petr Korda (CZE)	Henri Leconte (FRA)	6-2	7-6(4)	6-3		
Q	Jim Courier (USA)	Goran Ivanisevic (CRO)	6-2	6-1	2-6	7-5	
Q	Andre Agassi (USA)	Pete Sampras (USA)	7-6(6)	6-2	6-1		
Q	Henri Leconte (FRA)	Nicklas Kulti (SWE)	6-7(8)	3-6	6-3	6-3	6-3
Q	Petr Korda (CZE)	Andrei Cherkasov (RUS)	6-4	6-7(3)	6-2	6-4	

1993

Rd	Winner	Defeated	S1	S2	S3	S4	S5
F	Sergi Bruguera (ESP)	Jim Courier (USA)	6-4	2-6	6-2	3-6	6-3
S	Sergi Bruguera (ESP)	Andrei Medvedev (UKR)	6-0	6-4	6-2		
S	Jim Courier (USA)	Richard Krajicek (NED)	6-1	6-7(2)	7-5	6-2	
Q	Sergi Bruguera (ESP)	Pete Sampras (USA)	6-3	4-6	6-1	6-4	
Q	Andrei Medvedev (UKR)	Stefan Edberg (SWE)	6-0	6-7(3)	7-5	6-4	
Q	Richard Krajicek (NED)	Karel Novacek (CZE)	3-6	6-3	3-6	6-3	6-4
Q	Jim Courier (USA)	Goran Prpic (CRO)	6-1	4-6	6-0	7-5	

1994

Rd	Winner	Defeated	S1	S2	S3	S4	S5
F	Sergi Bruguera (ESP)	Alberto Berasategui (ESP)	6-3	7-5	2-6	6-1	
S	Sergi Bruguera (ESP)	Jim Courier (USA)	6-3	5-7	6-3	6-3	
S	Alberto Berasategui (ESP)	Magnus Larsson (SWE)	6-3	6-4	6-1		
Q	Jim Courier (USA)	Pete Sampras (USA)	6-4	5-7	6-4	6-4	
Q	Sergi Bruguera (ESP)	Andrei Medvedev (UKR)	6-3	6-2	7-5		
Q	Alberto Berasategui (ESP)	Goran Ivanisevic (CRO)	6-4	6-3	6-3		
Q	Magnus Larsson (SWE)	Hendrik Dreekmann (GER)	3-6	6-7(1)	7-6(3)	6-0	6-1

1995

Rd	Winner	Defeated	S1	S2	S3	S4	S5
F	Thomas Muster (AUT)	Michael Chang (USA)	7-5	6-2	6-4		
S	Thomas Muster (AUT)	Yevgeny Kafelnikov (RUS)	6-4	6-0	6-4		
S	Michael Chang (USA)	Sergi Bruguera (ESP)	6-4	7-6(5)	7-6(0)		
Q	Yevgeny Kafelnikov (RUS)	Andre Agassi (USA)	6-4	6-3	7-5		
Q	Thomas Muster (AUT)	Albert Costa (ESP)	6-2	3-6	6-7(6)	7-5	6-2
Q	Michael Chang (USA)	Adrian Voinea (ROU)	7-5	6-0	6-1		
Q	Sergi Bruguera (ESP)	Renzo Furlan (ITA)	6-2	7-5	6-2		

1996

Rd	Winner	Defeated	S1	S2	S3	S4	S5
F	Yevgeny Kafelnikov (RUS)	Michael Stich (GER)	7-6(4)	7-5	7-6(4)		
S	Yevgeny Kafelnikov (RUS)	Pete Sampras (USA)	7-6(4)	6-0	6-2		
S	Michael Stich (GER)	Marc Rosset (SUI)	6-3	6-4	6-2		
Q	Pete Sampras (USA)	Jim Courier (USA)	6-7(4)	4-6	6-4	6-4	6-4
Q	Yevgeny Kafelnikov (RUS)	Richard Krajicek (NED)	6-3	6-4	6-7(4)	6-2	
Q	Marc Rosset (SUI)	Bernd Karbacher (GER)	4-6	4-6	6-3	7-5	6-0
Q	Michael Stich (GER)	Cedric Pioline (FRA)	4-6	6-4	6-3	6-2	

1997

Rd	Winner	Defeated	S1	S2	S3	S4	S5
F	Gustavo Kuerten (BRA)	Sergi Bruguera (ESP)	6-3	6-4	6-2		
S	Sergi Bruguera (ESP)	Patrick Rafter (AUS)	6-7(6)	6-1	7-5	7-6(1)	
S	Gustavo Kuerten (BRA)	Filip De Wulf (BEL)	6-1	3-6	6-1	7-6(4)	
Q	Filip De Wulf (BEL)	Magnus Norman (SWE)	6-2	6-7(2)	6-4	6-3	
Q	Gustavo Kuerten (BRA)	Yevgeny Kafelnikov (RUS)	6-2	5-7	2-6	6-0	6-4
Q	Patrick Rafter (AUS)	Galo Blanco (ESP)	6-3	7-6(3)	6-3		
Q	Sergi Bruguera (ESP)	Hicham Arazi (MAR)	4-6	6-3	6-2	6-2	

1998

Rd	Winner	Defeated	S1	S2	S3	S4	S5
F	Carlos Moya (ESP)	Alex Corretja (ESP)	6-3	7-5	6-3		
S	Carlos Moya (ESP)	Felix Mantilla (ESP)	5-7	6-2	6-4	6-2	
S	Alex Corretja (ESP)	Cedric Pioline (FRA)	6-3	6-4	6-2		
Q	Felix Mantilla (ESP)	Thomas Muster (AUT)	6-4	6-2	4-6	6-3	
Q	Carlos Moya (ESP)	Marcelo Rios (CHI)	6-1	2-6	6-2	6-4	
Q	Alex Corretja (ESP)	Filip De Wulf (BEL)	7-5	6-4	6-3		
Q	Cedric Pioline (FRA)	Hicham Arazi (MAR)	3-6	6-2	7-6(6)	4-6	6-3

1999

Rd	Winner	Defeated	S1	S2	S3	S4	S5
F	Andre Agassi (USA)	Andrei Medvedev (UKR)	1-6	2-6	6-4	6-3	6-4
S	Andre Agassi (USA)	Dominik Hrbaty (SVK)	6-4	7-6(6)	3-6	6-4	
S	Andrei Medvedev (UKR)	Fernando Meligeni (BRA)	7-5	3-6	6-4	7-6(6)	
Q	Dominik Hrbaty (SVK)	Marcelo Rios (CHI)	7-6(4)	6-2	6-7(6)	6-3	
Q	Andre Agassi (USA)	Marcelo Filippini (URU)	6-2	6-2	6-0		
Q	Fernando Meligeni (BRA)	Alex Corretja (ESP)	6-2	6-2	6-0		
Q	Andrei Medvedev (UKR)	Gustavo Kuerten (BRA)	7-5	6-4	6-4		

2000

Rd	Winner	Defeated	S1	S2	S3	S4	S5
F	Gustavo Kuerten (BRA)	Magnus Norman (SWE)	6-2	6-3	2-6	7-6(6)	
S	Magnus Norman (SWE)	Franco Squillari (ARG)	6-1	6-4	6-3		
S	Gustavo Kuerten (BRA)	Juan Carlos Ferrero (ESP)	7-5	4-6	2-6	6-4	6-3
Q	Franco Squillari (ARG)	Albert Costa (ESP)	6-4	6-4	2-6	6-4	
Q	Magnus Norman (SWE)	Marat Safin (RUS)	6-4	6-3	4-6	7-5	
Q	Gustavo Kuerten (BRA)	Yevgeny Kafelnikov (RUS)	6-3	3-6	4-6	6-4	6-2
Q	Juan Carlos Ferrero (ESP)	Alex Corretja (ESP)	6-4	6-4	6-2		

2001

Rd	Winner	Defeated	S1	S2	S3	S4	S5
F	Gustavo Kuerten (BRA)	Alex Corretja (ESP)	6-7(3)	7-5	6-2	6-0	
S	Gustavo Kuerten (BRA)	Juan Carlos Ferrero (ESP)	6-4	6-4	6-3		
S	Alex Corretja (ESP)	Sebastien Grosjean (FRA)	7-6(2)	6-4	6-4		
Q	Gustavo Kuerten (BRA)	Yevgeny Kafelnikov (RUS)	6-1	3-6	7-6(3)	6-4	
Q	Juan Carlos Ferrero (ESP)	Lleyton Hewitt (AUS)	6-4	6-2	6-1		
Q	Sebastien Grosjean	Andre Agassi (USA)	1-6	6-1	6-1	6-3	
Q	Alex Corretja (ESP)	Roger Federer (SUI)	7-5	6-1	7-5		

2002

Rd	Winner	Defeated	S1	S2	S3	S4	S5
F	Albert Costa (ESP)	Juan Carlos Ferrero (ESP)	6-1	6-0	4-6	6-3	
S	Albert Costa (ESP)	Alex Corretja (ESP)	6-3	6-4	3-6	6-3	
S	Juan Carlos Ferrero (ESP)	Marat Safin (RUS)	6-3	6-2	6-4		
Q	Albert Costa (ESP)	Guillermo Canas (ARG)	7-5	3-6	6-7(3)	6-4	6-0
Q	Alex Corretja (ESP)	Andrei Pavel (ROU)	7-6(5)	7-5	7-5		
Q	Juan Carlos Ferrero (ESP)	Andre Agassi (USA)	6-3	5-7	7-5	6-3	
Q	Marat Safin (RUS)	Sebastien Grosjean (FRA)	6-3	6-2	6-2		

2003

Rd	Winner	Defeated	S1	S2	S3	S4	S5
F	Juan Carlos Ferrero (ESP)	Martin Verkerk (NED)	6-1	6-3	6-2		
S	Juan Carlos Ferrero (ESP)	Albert Costa (ESP)	6-3	7-6(5)	6-4		
S	Martin Verkerk (NED)	Guillermo Coria (ARG)	7-6(4)	6-4	7-6(0)		
Q	Albert Costa (ESP)	Tommy Robredo (ESP)	2-6	3-6	6-4	7-5	6-2
Q	Juan Carlos Ferrero (ESP)	Fernando Gonzalez (CHI)	6-1	3-6	6-1	5-7	6-4
Q	Martin Verkerk (NED)	Carlos Moya (ESP)	6-3	6-4	5-7	4-6	8-6
Q	Guillermo Coria (ARG)	Andre Agassi (USA)	4-6	6-3	6-2	6-4	

2004

Rd	Winner	Defeated	S1	S2	S3	S4	S5
F	Gaston Gaudio (ARG)	Guillermo Coria (ARG)	0-6	3-6	6-4	6-1	8-6
S	Gaston Gaudio (ARG)	David Nalbandian (ARG)	6-3	7-6(5)	6-0		
S	Guillermo Coria (ARG)	Tim Henman (GBR)	3-6	6-4	6-0	7-5	
Q	David Nalbandian (ARG)	Gustavo Kuerten (BRA)	6-2	3-6	6-4	7-6(6)	
Q	Gaston Gaudio (ARG)	Lleyton Hewitt (AUS)	6-3	6-2	6-2		
Q	Guillermo Coria (ARG)	Carlos Moya (ESP)	7-5	7-6(3)	6-3		
Q	Tim Henman (GBR)	Juan Ignacio Chela (ARG)	6-2	6-4	6-4		

2005

Rd	Winner	Defeated	S1	S2	S3	S4	S5
F	Rafael Nadal (ESP)	Mariano Puerta (ARG)	6-7(6)	6-3	6-1	7-5	
S	Rafael Nadal (ESP)	Roger Federer (SUI)	6-3	4-6	6-4	6-3	
S	Mariano Puerta (ARG)	Nikolay Davydenko (RUS)	6-3	5-7	2-6	6-4	6-4
Q	Roger Federer (SUI)	Victor Hanescu (ROU)	6-2	7-6(3)	6-3		
Q	Rafael Nadal (ESP)	David Ferrer (ESP)	7-5	6-2	6-0		
Q	Nikolay Davydenko (RUS)	Tommy Robredo (ESP)	3-6	6-1	6-2	4-6	6-4
Q	Mariano Puerta (ARG)	Guillermo Canas (ARG)	6-2	3-6	1-6	6-3	6-4

2006

Rd	Winner	Defeated	S1	S2	S3	S4	S5
F	Rafael Nadal (ESP)	Roger Federer (SUI)	1-6	6-1	6-4	7-6(4)	
S	Roger Federer (SUI)	David Nalbandian (ARG)	3-6	6-4	5-2	(Retired)	
S	Rafael Nadal (ESP)	Ivan Ljubicic (CRO)	6-4	6-2	7-6(7)		
Q	Roger Federer (SUI)	Mario Ancic (CRO)	6-4	6-3	6-4		
Q	David Nalbandian (ARG)	Nikolay Davydenko (RUS)	6-3	6-3	2-6	6-4	
Q	Ivan Ljubicic (CRO)	Julien Benneteau (FRA)	6-2	6-2	6-3		
Q	Rafael Nadal (ESP)	Novak Djokovic (SRB)	6-4	6-4	0-0	(Retired)	

2007

Rd	Winner	Defeated	S1	S2	S3	S4	S5
F	Rafael Nadal (ESP)	Roger Federer (SUI)	6-3	4-6	6-3	6-4	
S	Roger Federer (SUI)	Nikolay Davydenko (RUS)	7-5	7-6(5)	7-6(7)		
S	Rafael Nadal (ESP)	Novak Djokovic (SRB)	7-5	6-4	6-2		
Q	Roger Federer (SUI)	Tommy Robredo (ESP)	7-5	1-6	6-1	6-2	
Q	Nikolay Davydenko (RUS)	Guillermo Canas (ARG)	7-5	6-4	6-4		
Q	Novak Djokovic (SRB)	Igor Andreev (RUS)	6-3	6-3	6-3		
Q	Rafael Nadal (ESP)	Carlos Moya (ESP)	6-4	6-3	6-0		

2008

Rd	Winner	Defeated	S1	S2	S3	S4	S5
F	Rafael Nadal (ESP)	Roger Federer (SUI)	6-1	6-3	6-0		
S	Roger Federer (SUI)	Gael Monfils (FRA)	6-2	5-7	6-3	7-5	
S	Rafael Nadal (ESP)	Novak Djokovic (SRB)	6-4	6-2	7-6 (3)		
Q	Roger Federer (SUI)	Fernando Gonzalez (CHI)	2-6	6-2	6-3	6-4	
Q	Gael Monfils (FRA)	David Ferrer (ESP)	6-3	3-6	6-3	6-1	
Q	Novak Djokovic (SRB)	Ernests Gulbis (LAT)	7-5	7-6(3)	7-5		
Q	Rafael Nadal (ESP)	Nicolas Almagro (ESP)	6-1	6-1	6-1		

2009

Rd	Winner	Defeated	S1	S2	S3	S4	S5
F	Roger Federer (SUI)	Robin Soderling (SWE)	6-1	7-6 (1)	6-4		
S	Robin Soderling (SWE)	Fernando Gonzalez (CHI)	6-3	7-5	5-7	4-6	6-4
S	Roger Federer (SUI)	Juan Martin Del Potro (ARG)	3-6	6-7(2)	2-6	6-1	6-4
Q	Robin Soderling (SWE)	Nikolay Davydenko (RUS)	6-1	6-3	6-1		
Q	Fernando Gonzalez (CHI)	Andy Murray (GBR)	6-3	3-6	6-0	6-4	
Q	Juan Martin Del Potro (ARG)	Tommy Robredo (ESP)	6-3	6-4	6-2		
Q	Roger Federer (SUI)	Gael Monfils (FRA)	7-6(6)	6-2	6-4		

Women's Singles

Rd	Winner	Defeated	S1	S2	S3

1925

Rd	Winner	Defeated	S1	S2	S3
F	Suzanne Lenglen (FRA)	Kitty McKane (GBR)	6-1	6-2	
S	Suzanne Lenglen (FRA)	Helen Contostavlos (GRE)	6-2	6-0	
S	Kitty McKane (GBR)	Didi Vlasto (FRA)	6-2	6-2	
Q	Suzanne Lenglen (FRA)	Evelyn Colyer (GBR)	6-0	6-2	
Q	Helen Contostavlos (GRE)	Simone Passemard Mathieu (FRA)	7-5	6-3	
Q	Kitty McKane (GBR)	Marguerite Billout (FRA)	6-0	10-8	
Q	Didi Vlasto (FRA)	N. Descleres (FRA)	6-1	6-2	

1926

Rd	Winner	Defeated	S1	S2	S3
F	Suzanne Lenglen (FRA)	Mary Kendall Browne (USA)	6-1	6-0	
S	Suzanne Lenglen (FRA)	Joan Fry (GBR)	6-2	6-1	
S	Mary Kendall Browne (USA)	Kea Bouman (NED)	8-6	6-2	
Q	Suzanne Lenglen (FRA)	Simone Passemard Mathieu (FRA)	6-0	6-0	
Q	Joan Fry (GBR)	Elizabeth Ryan (USA)	7-5	3-6	11-9
Q	Mary Kendall Browne (USA)	Kitty McKane Godfree (GBR)	7-5	6-0	
Q	Kea Bouman (NED)	S. Lecaron (FRA)	6-2	7-9	8-6

Rd	Winner	Defeated	S1	S2	S3

1927

Rd	Winner	Defeated	S1	S2	S3
F	Kea Bouman (NED)	Irene Bowder Peacock (RSA)	6-2	6-4	
S	Kea Bouman (NED)	Bobbie Heine (RSA)	5-7	6-1	6-3
S	Irene Bowder Peacock (RSA)	Eileen Bennett (GBR)	5-7	6-4	9-7
Q	Bobbie Heine (RSA)	Lili de Alvarez (ESP)	3-6	7-5	7-5
Q	Kea Bouman (NED)	Billie Tapscott (RSA)	6-2	6-0	
Q	Irene Bowder Peacock (RSA)	Cilly Aussem (GER)	4-6	6-2	6-4
Q	Eileen Bennett (GBR)	Marguerite Billout (FRA)	4-6	6-2	6-2

1928

Rd	Winner	Defeated	S1	S2	S3
F	Helen Wills (USA)	Eileen Bennett (GBR)	6-1	6-2	
S	Helen Wills (USA)	Cristobel Hardie (GBR)	6-1	6-1	
S	Eileen Bennett (GBR)	Kea Bouman (NED)	6-2	8-6	
Q	Helen Wills (USA)	Rollin Couquerque (NED)	6-2	6-0	
Q	Cristobel Hardie (GBR)	Daphne Akhurst (AUS)	10-8	6-2	
Q	Kea Bouman (NED)	J. Vaussard (FRA)	6-0	6-0	
Q	Eileen Bennett (GBR)	Penelope Anderson (USA)	6-3	7-9	7-5

1929

Rd	Winner	Defeated	S1	S2	S3
F	Helen Wills (USA)	Simone Passemard Mathieu (FRA)	6-3	6-4	
S	Simone Passemard Mathieu (FRA)	Cilly Aussem (GER)	8-6	2-6	6-2
S	Helen Wills (USA)	Eileen Bennett (GBR)	6-2	7-5	
Q	Cilly Aussem (GER)	Bobbie Heine (RSA)	5-7	6-3	6-4
Q	Simone Passemard Mathieu (FRA)	Phoebe Holcroft Watson (USA)	4-6	6-3	6-1
Q	Eileen Bennett (GBR)	Alida Neave (RSA)	7-5	6-1	
Q	Helen Wills (USA)	Sylvia Henrotin (FRA)	6-4	6-1	

1930

Rd	Winner	Defeated	S1	S2	S3
F	Helen Wills Moody (USA)	Helen Jacobs (USA)	6-2	6-1	
S	Helen Jacobs (USA)	Lili de Alvarez (ESP)	6-1	6-0	
S	Helen Wills Moody (USA)	Cilly Aussem (GER)	6-2	6-1	
Q	Helen Jacobs (USA)	Phoebe Holcroft Watson (USA)	5-7	6-3	6-1
Q	Lili de Alvarez (ESP)	Simone Passemard Mathieu (FRA)	6-3	7-5	
Q	Cilly Aussem (GER)	Elizabeth Ryan (USA)	4-6	6-1	6-0
Q	Helen Wills Moody (USA)	Irmgard Rost (GER)	6-0	6-1	

1931

Rd	Winner	Defeated	S1	S2	S3
F	Cilly Aussem (GER)	Betty Nuthall (GBR)	8-6	6-1	
S	Betty Nuthall (GBR)	Hilde Krahwinkel (GER)	6-1	6-2	
S	Cilly Aussem (GER)	Lili de Alvarez (ESP)	6-0	7-5	
Q	Hilde Krahwinkel (GER)	Simone Passemard Mathieu (FRA)	6-4	6-3	
Q	Betty Nuthall (GBR)	Helen Jacobs (USA)	6-3	6-2	
Q	Lili de Alvarez (ESP)	Elizabeth Ryan (USA)	5-7	6-3	6-4
Q	Cilly Aussem (GER)	Lucia Valerio (ITA)	8-6	6-2	

1932

Rd	Winner	Defeated	S1	S2	S3
F	Helen Wills Moody (USA)	Simone Passemard Mathieu (FRA)	7-5	6-1	
S	Simone Passemard Mathieu (FRA)	Betty Nuthall (GBR)	6-2	6-4	
S	Helen Wills Moody (USA)	Hilde Krahwinkel (GER)	6-3	10-8	
Q	Betty Nuthall (GBR)	Cilly Aussem (GER)	5-7	6-4 (retired)	
Q	Simone Passemard Mathieu (FRA)	Helen Jacobs (USA)	6-4	6-4	
Q	Hilde Krahwinkel (GER)	Eileen Bennett Whittingstall (GBR)	6-3	6-3	
Q	Helen Wills Moody (USA)	Lolette Payot (SUI)	6-2	7-5	

1933

Rd	Winner	Defeated	S1	S2	S3
F	Margaret Scriven (GBR)	Simone Passemard Mathieu (FRA)	6-2	4-6	6-4
S	Simone Passemard Mathieu (FRA)	Helen Jacobs (USA)	8-6	6-3	
S	Margaret Scriven (GBR)	Betty Nuthall (GBR)	6-2	4-6	6-3
Q	Helen Jacobs (USA)	Jacqueline Goldschmidt (FRA)	1-6	6-1	6-3
Q	Simone Passemard Mathieu (FRA)	Eileen Bennett Whittingstall (GBR)	6-2	6-0	
Q	Margaret Scriven (GBR)	Mary Heeley (GBR)	6-2	6-4	
Q	Betty Nuthall (GBR)	Dorothy Burke (USA)	6-3	6-1	

1934

Rd	Winner	Defeated	S1	S2	S3
F	Margaret Scriven (GBR)	Helen Jacobs (USA)	7-5	4-6	6-1
S	Margaret Scriven (GBR)	Cilly Aussem (GER)	7-5	6-3	
S	Helen Jacobs (USA)	Simone Passemard Mathieu (FRA)	6-2	6-2	
Q	Margaret Scriven (GBR)	Nancy Lyle (GBR)	6-1	6-1	
Q	Cilly Aussem (GER)	Kay Stammers (GBR)	6-4	6-2	
Q	Simone Passemard Mathieu (FRA)	Lucia Valerio (ITA)	6-3	6-2	
Q	Helen Jacobs (USA)	Lolette Payot (SUI)	6-3	1-6	8-6

1935

Rd	Winner	Defeated	S1	S2	S3
F	Hilde Krahwinkel Sperling (DEN)	Simone Passemard Mathieu (FRA)	6-2	6-1	
S	Hilde Krahwinkel Sperling (DEN)	Helen Jacobs (USA)	7-5	6-3	
S	Simone Passemard Mathieu (FRA)	Margaret Scriven (GBR)	8-6	6-1	
Q	Helen Jacobs (USA)	Sylvie Jung Henrotin (FRA)	6-4	6-2	
Q	Hilde Krahwinkel Sperling (DEN)	Simone Iribarne (FRA)	6-2	6-2	
Q	Simone Passemard Mathieu (FRA)	Lolette Payot (SUI)	7-5	6-4	
Q	Margaret Scriven (GBR)	Rollin Couquerque (NED)	6-0	6-3	

1936

Rd	Winner	Defeated	S1	S2	S3
F	Hilde Krahwinkel Sperling (DEN)	Simone Passemard Mathieu (FRA)	6-3	6-4	
S	Simone Passemard Mathieu (FRA)	Marie Luise Horn (GER)	6-4	6-4	
S	Hilde Krahwinkel Sperling (DEN)	Lili de Alvarez (ESP)	6-2	6-1	
Q	Simone Passemard Mathieu (FRA)	Nelly Adamson (FRA)	6-0	6-2	
Q	Marie Luise Horn (GER)	Simone Goronitchenko (FRA)	6-1	6-4	
Q	Lili de Alvarez (ESP)	Simone Iribarne (FRA)	6-4	6-2	
Q	Hilde Krahwinkel Sperling (DEN)	Sylvie Jung Henrotin (FRA)	6-3	6-0	

1937

Rd	Winner	Defeated	S1	S2	S3
F	Hilde Krahwinkel Sperling (DEN)	Simone Passemard Mathieu (FRA)	6-2	6-4	
S	Simone Passemard Mathieu (FRA)	Jadwiga Jedrzejowska (POL)	7-5	7-5	
S	Hilde Krahwinkel Sperling (DEN)	Lili de Alvarez (ESP)	6-1	6-1	
Q	Simone Passemard Mathieu (FRA)	Marie Luise Horn (GER)	11-9	7-5	
Q	Jadwiga Jedrzejowska (POL)	Helen Jacobs (USA)	6-3	6-4	
Q	Lili de Alvarez (ESP)	Margaret Scriven (GBR)	6-2	1-6	6-2
Q	Hilde Krahwinkel Sperling (DEN)	Sylvie Jung Henrotin (FRA)	6-4	6-1	

1938

Rd	Winner	Defeated	S1	S2	S3
F	Simone Passemard Mathieu (FRA)	Nelly Adamson Landry (FRA)	6-0	6-3	
S	Nelly Adamson Landry (FRA)	Rollin Couquerque (NED)	6-2	6-4	
S	Simone Passemard Mathieu (FRA)	Arlette Halff (FRA)	6-1	6-1	
Q	Rollin Couquerque (NED)	Jacqueline Goldschmidt (FRA)	6-2	6-1	
Q	Nelly Adamson Landry (FRA)	Sylvie Jung Henrotin (FRA)	6-2	6-2	
Q	Arlette Halff (FRA)	Suzanne Pannetier (FRA)	2-6	6-4	6-3
Q	Simone Passemard Mathieu (FRA)	Dorothy Stevenson (AUS)	6-4	6-0	

1939

Rd	Winner	Defeated	S1	S2	S3
F	Simone Passemard Mathieu (FRA)	Jadwiga Jedrzejowska (POL)	6-3	8-6	
S	Jadwiga Jedrzejowska (POL)	M. Lebailly (FRA)	6-3	2-6	6-3
S	Simone Passemard Mathieu (FRA)	Suzanne Pannetier (FRA)	6-2	6-2	
Q	M. Lebailly (FRA)	Sarah Palfrey Fabyan (USA)	6-1	6-1	
Q	Jadwiga Jedrzejowska (POL)	Arlette Halff (FRA)	4-6	6-2	6-4
Q	Suzanne Pannetier (FRA)	Mary Hardwick (GBR)	7-5	6-4	
Q	Simone Passemard Mathieu (FRA)	Alice Weiwers (LUX)	6-3	6-3	

1940-45 NOT HELD—WW II

1946

Rd	Winner	Defeated	S1	S2	S3
F	Margaret Osborne (USA)	Pauline Betz (USA)	1-6	8-6	7-5
S	Margaret Osborne (USA)	Louise Brough (USA)	7-5	6-3	
S	Pauline Betz (USA)	Dorothy Bundy (USA)	6-3	6-4	
Q	Margaret Osborne (USA)	Alice Weiwers (LUX)	6-3	6-2	
Q	Louise Brough (USA)	Doris Hart (USA)	6-4	4-6	6-4
Q	Dorothy Bundy (USA)	Nelly Adamson Landry (FRA)	6-4	5-7	6-4
Q	Pauline Betz (USA)	Betty Hilton (GBR)	6-4	6-0	

1947

Rd	Winner	Defeated	S1	S2	S3
F	Pat Canning Todd (USA)	Doris Hart (USA)	6-3	3-6	6-4
S	Doris Hart (USA)	Louise Brough (USA)	6-2	7-5	
S	Pat Canning Todd (USA)	Margaret Osborne (USA)	2-6	6-3	6-4
Q	Doris Hart (USA)	Magda Rurac (ROU)	6-3	6-4	
Q	Louise Brough (USA)	Sheila Piercey (RSA)	6-1	6-0	
Q	Pat Canning Todd (USA)	Lucia Manfredi (ITA)	6-1	6-4	
Q	Margaret Osborne (USA)	Zsuzsi Kormoczy (HUN)	6-0	6-3	

1948

Rd	Winner	Defeated	S1	S2	S3
F	Nelly Adamson Landry (FRA)	Shirley Fry (USA)	6-2	0-6	6-0
S	Nelly Adamson Landry (FRA)	Pat Canning Todd (USA)		(walkover)	
S	Shirley Fry (USA)	Doris Hart (USA)	6-3	4-6	11-9
Q	Pat Canning Todd (USA)	Annelies Bossi (ITA)		(walkover)	
Q	Nelly Adamson Landry (FRA)	Mary Arnold Prentiss (USA)	6-4	6-3	
Q	Shirley Fry (USA)	Maria Weiss (ARG)	6-3	7-5	
Q	Doris Hart (USA)	Helen Pedersen Rihbany (USA)	6-3	6-3	

1949

Rd	Winner	Defeated	S1	S2	S3
F	Margaret Osborne duPont (USA)	Nelly Adamson Landry (FRA)	7-5	6-2	
S	Nelly Adamson Landry (FRA)	Annelies Bossi (ITA)	6-3	6-0	
S	Margaret Osborne duPont (USA)	Sheila Piercey Summers (RSA)	6-3	6-3	
Q	Annelies Bossi (ITA)	Joan Curry (GBR)	6-3	4-6	6-3
Q	Nelly Adamson Landry (FRA)	Helen Pedersen Rihbany (USA)	7-9	6-3	6-3
Q	Sheila Piercey Summers (RSA)	Anne-Marie Simon Seghers (FRA)	6-3	6-1	
Q	Margaret Osborne duPont (USA)	Jean Quertier (GBR)	6-4	6-2	

1950

Rd	Winner	Defeated	S1	S2	S3
F	Doris Hart (USA)	Pat Canning Todd (USA)	6-4	4-6	6-2
S	Doris Hart (USA)	Louise Brough (USA)	6-2	6-3	
S	Pat Canning Todd (USA)	Barbara Scofield (USA)	6-2	6-3	
Q	Louise Brough (USA)	Betty Rosenquest (USA)	6-2	6-2	
Q	Doris Hart (USA)	Annelies Bossi (ITA)	6-4	6-2	
Q	Pat Canning Todd (USA)	Shirley Fry (USA)	6-3	6-3	
Q	Barbara Scofield (USA)	Margaret Osborne duPont (USA)	3-6	6-0	6-2

1951

Rd	Winner	Defeated	S1	S2	S3
F	Shirley Fry (USA)	Doris Hart (USA)	6-3	3-6	6-3
S	Shirley Fry (USA)	Margaret Osborne duPont (USA)	6-2	9-7	
S	Doris Hart (USA)	Jean Walker Smith (GBR)	6-2	6-1	
Q	Margaret Osborne duPont (USA)	Nelly Adamson (FRA)	8-6	1-6	6-1
Q	Shirley Fry (USA)	Thelma Coyne Long (AUS)	12-10	6-1	
Q	Jean Walker Smith (GBR)	Beverly Baker (USA)	3-6	6-4	6-1
Q	Doris Hart (USA)	Arlette de Cazalet (FRA)	6-0	6-4	

1952

Rd	Winner	Defeated	S1	S2	S3
F	Doris Hart (USA)	Shirley Fry (USA)	6-4	6-4	
S	Doris Hart (USA)	Dorothy Head (USA)	6-2	8-6	
S	Shirley Fry (USA)	Hazel Redick-Smith (RSA)	7-5	6-4	
Q	Doris Hart (USA)	Julia Wipplinger (RSA)	8-6	6-4	
Q	Dorothy Head (USA)	Joy Gannon Mottram (GBR)	6-3	4-6	7-5
Q	Hazel Redick-Smith (RSA)	Maria Weiss (ARG)	6-3	6-1	
Q	Shirley Fry (USA)	Joan Curry (GBR)	4-6	6-0	6-3

1953

Rd	Winner	Defeated	S1	S2	S3
F	Maureen Connolly (USA)	Doris Hart (USA)	6-2	6-4	
S	Doris Hart (USA)	Shirley Fry (USA)	8-6	6-4	
S	Maureen Connolly (USA)	Dorothy Head (USA)	6-3	6-3	
Q	Doris Hart (USA)	Jean Rinkel-Quertier (GBR)	6-3	6-3	
Q	Shirley Fry (USA)	Nelly Adamson (FRA)	6-1	4-6	6-0
Q	Dorothy Head (USA)	Ginette Bucaille (FRA)	6-3	6-0	
Q	Maureen Connolly (USA)	Susan Partridge Chatrier (FRA)	3-6	6-2	6-2

1954

Rd	Winner	Defeated	S1	S2	S3
F	Maureen Connolly (USA)	Ginette Bucaille (FRA)	6-4	6-1	
S	Ginette Bucaille (FRA)	Nelly Adamson (FRA)	6-2	6-4	
S	Maureen Connolly (USA)	Silvana Lazzarino (ITA)	6-0	6-1	
Q	Nelly Adamson (FRA)	Dorothy Levine (USA)	6-1	6-2	
Q	Ginette Bucaille (FRA)	Josette Amouretti (FRA)	6-1	6-1	
Q	Silvana Lazzarino (ITA)	Anne-Marie Simon Seghers (FRA)	6-3	6-3	
Q	Maureen Connolly (USA)	Angela Buxton (GBR)	6-1	6-0	

1955

Rd	Winner	Defeated	S1	S2	S3
F	Angela Mortimer (GBR)	Dorothy Head Knode (USA)	2-6	7-5	10-8
S	Angela Mortimer (GBR)	Heather Brewer (BER)	6-1	6-1	
S	Dorothy Head Knode (USA)	Beverly Baker Fleitz (USA)	6-2	6-3	
Q	Angela Mortimer (GBR)	Erika Vollmer (GER)	6-3	6-4	
Q	Heather Brewer (BER)	Beryl Penrose (AUS)	7-5	6-8	6-3
Q	Dorothy Head Knode (USA)	Shirley Bloomer (GBR)	6-3	6-3	
Q	Beverly Baker Fleitz (USA)	Ginette Bucaille (FRA)	6-1	6-1	

1956

Rd	Winner	Defeated	S1	S2	S3
F	Althea Gibson (USA)	Angela Mortimer (GBR)	6-0	12-10	
S	Althea Gibson (USA)	Angela Buxton (GBR)	2-6	6-0	6-4
S	Angela Mortimer (GBR)	Zsuzsi Kormoczy (HUN)	6-4	6-3	
Q	Angela Buxton (GBR)	Edda Buding (GER)	8-6	6-2	
Q	Althea Gibson (USA)	Shirley Bloomer (GBR)	6-2	6-1	
Q	Zsuzsi Kormoczy (HUN)	Ilse Buding (GER)	6-1	6-1	
Q	Angela Mortimer (GBR)	Jenny Hoad (AUS)	6-0	4-6	7-5

1957

Rd	Winner	Defeated	S1	S2	S3
F	Shirley Bloomer (GBR)	Dorothy Head Knode (USA)	6-1	6-3	
S	Dorothy Head Knode (USA)	Ann Haydon (GBR)	6-4	10-8	
S	Shirley Bloomer (GBR)	Vera Puzejova (CZE)	6-4	2-6	6-4
Q	Dorothy Head Knode (USA)	Heather Brewer (BER)	6-1	9-7	
Q	Ann Haydon (GBR)	Christine Mercelis (BEL)	6-2	6-1	
Q	Vera Puzejova (CZE)	Darlene Hard (USA)	6-3	5-7	8-6
Q	Shirley Bloomer (GBR)	Zsuzsi Kormoczy (HUN)	6-1	6-1	

1958

Rd	Winner	Defeated	S1	S2	S3
F	Zsuzsi Kormoczy (HUN)	Shirley Bloomer (GBR)	6-4	1-6	6-2
S	Zsuzsi Kormoczy (HUN)	Heather Brewer Segal (RSA)	6-1	6-0	
S	Shirley Bloomer (GBR)	Maria Bueno (BRA)	2-6	6-1	6-2
Q	Heather Brewer Segal (RSA)	Christine Truman (GBR)	6-2	6-1	
Q	Zsuzsi Kormoczy (HUN)	Ann Haydon (GBR)	6-3	6-4	
Q	Maria Bueno (BRA)	Dorothy Head Knode (USA)	6-2	8-6	
Q	Shirley Bloomer (GBR)	Rosie Reyes (MEX)	5-7	6-4	6-2

1959

Rd	Winner	Defeated	S1	S2	S3
F	Christine Truman (GBR)	Zsuzsi Kormoczy (HUN)	6-4	7-5	
S	Christine Truman (GBR)	Sandra Reynolds (RSA)	4-6	8-6	6-2
S	Zsuzsi Kormoczy (HUN)	Rosie Reyes (MEX)	6-3	6-0	
Q	Christine Truman (GBR)	Paule Courteix (FRA)	6-1	8-6	
Q	Sandra Reynolds (RSA)	Maria Bueno (BRA)	2-6	6-4	6-2
Q	Rosie Reyes (MEX)	Mary Carter Reitano (AUS)	4-6	6-1	6-4
Q	Zsuzsi Kormoczy (HUN)	Vera Puzejova (CZE)	6-3	6-4	

1960

Rd	Winner	Defeated	S1	S2	S3
F	Darlene Hard (USA)	Yola Ramirez (MEX)	6-3	6-4	
S	Darlene Hard (USA)	Maria Bueno (BRA)	6-3	6-2	
S	Yola Ramirez (MEX)	Sandra Reynolds (RSA)	8-10	6-3	6-3
Q	Maria Bueno (BRA)	Jan Lehane (AUS)	6-1	2-6	6-3
Q	Darlene Hard (USA)	Renee Schuurman (RSA)	5-7	6-2	11-9
Q	Sandra Reynolds (RSA)	Vera Puzejova (CZE)	7-5	6-2	
Q	Yola Ramirez (MEX)	Betsy Abbas (EGY)	6-0	6-4	

1961

Rd	Winner	Defeated	S1	S2	S3
F	Ann Haydon (GBR)	Yola Ramirez (MEX)	6-2	6-1	
S	Ann Haydon (GBR)	Zsuzsi Kormoczy (HUN)	3-6	6-1	6-3
S	Yola Ramirez (MEX)	Edda Buding (GER)	6-4	4-6	6-3
Q	Zsuzsi Kormoczy (HUN)	Maria Bueno (BRA)	6-3	6-3	
Q	Ann Haydon (GBR)	Margaret Smith (AUS)	7-5	12-10	
Q	Yola Ramirez (MEX)	Christine Truman (GBR)	10-8	7-5	
Q	Edda Buding (GER)	Pilar Baril (ESP)	3-6	6-4	6-2

1962

Rd	Winner	Defeated	S1	S2	S3
F	Margaret Smith (AUS)	Lesley Turner (AUS)	6-3	3-6	7-5
S	Margaret Smith (AUS)	Renee Schuurman (RSA)	8-6	6-3	
S	Lesley Turner (AUS)	Ann Haydon (GBR)	6-4	5-7	6-3
Q	Margaret Smith (AUS)	Edda Buding (GER)	6-2	6-4	
Q	Renee Schuurman (RSA)	Donna Floyd (USA)	6-3	6-1	
Q	Lesley Turner (AUS)	Sandra Reynolds Price (RSA)	8-6	6-3	
Q	Ann Haydon (GBR)	Jan Lehane (AUS)	6-4	6-1	

1963

Rd	Winner	Defeated	S1	S2	S3
F	Lesley Turner (AUS)	Ann Haydon Jones (GBR)	2-6	6-3	7-5
S	Lesley Turner (AUS)	Christine Truman (GBR)	11-9	6-2	
S	Ann Haydon Jones (GBR)	Vera Puzejova Sukova (CZE)	6-0	6-1	
Q	Lesley Turner (AUS)	Jill Blackman (AUS)	6-4	6-4	
Q	Christine Truman (GBR)	Robyn Ebbern (AUS)	6-0	6-2	
Q	Ann Haydon Jones (GBR)	Jan Lehane (AUS)	6-0	6-0	
Q	Vera Puzejova Sukova (CZE)	Margaret Smith (AUS)	6-3	8-6	

1964

Rd	Winner	Defeated	S1	S2	S3
F	Margaret Smith (AUS)	Maria Bueno (BRA)	5-7	6-1	6-2
S	Maria Bueno (BRA)	Lesley Turner (AUS)	3-6	6-2	6-0
S	Margaret Smith (AUS)	Helga Schultze (GER)	6-3	4-6	6-2
Q	Maria Bueno (BRA)	Karen Hantze Susman (USA)	6-4	6-0	
Q	Lesley Turner (AUS)	Christine Truman (GBR)	6-1	6-3	
Q	Helga Schultze (GER)	Jan Lehane (AUS)	6-2	6-3	
Q	Margaret Smith (AUS)	Vera Puzejova Sukova (CZE)	6-1	6-1	

1965

Rd	Winner	Defeated	S1	S2	S3
F	Lesley Turner (AUS)	Margaret Smith (AUS)	6-3	6-4	
S	Lesley Turner (AUS)	Maria Bueno (BRA)	2-6	6-4	8-6
S	Margaret Smith (AUS)	Nancy Richey (USA)	7-5	6-4	
Q	Maria Bueno (BRA)	Annette Van Zyl (RSA)	6-4	6-3	
Q	Lesley Turner (AUS)	Ann Haydon Jones (GBR)		(default)	
Q	Nancy Richey (USA)	Francoise Durr (FRA)	8-6	9-7	
Q	Margaret Smith (AUS)	Norma Baylon (ARG)	6-3	6-1	

1966

Rd	Winner	Defeated	S1	S2	S3
F	Ann Haydon Jones (GBR)	Nancy Richey (USA)	6-3	6-1	
S	Ann Haydon Jones (GBR)	Maria Bueno (BRA)	4-6	8-6	6-3
S	Nancy Richey (USA)	Margaret Smith (AUS)	6-1	6-3	
Q	Maria Bueno (BRA)	Francoise Durr (FRA)	3-6	6-4	6-4
Q	Ann Haydon Jones (GBR)	Helga Schultze (GER)	6-4	6-4	
Q	Nancy Richey (USA)	Annette Van Zyl (RSA)	3-6	6-3	6-2
Q	Margaret Smith (AUS)	Julie Heldman (USA)	6-2	6-2	

1967

Rd	Winner	Defeated	S1	S2	S3
F	Francoise Durr (FRA)	Lesley Turner (AUS)	4-6	6-3	6-4
S	Francoise Durr (FRA)	Kerry Melville (AUS)	8-6	6-3	
S	Lesley Turner (AUS)	Annette Van Zyl (RSA)	6-1	6-4	
Q	Kerry Melville (AUS)	Ann Haydon Jones (GBR)	0-6	6-4	8-6
Q	Francoise Durr (FRA)	Maria Bueno (BRA)	5-7	6-1	6-4
Q	Lesley Turner (AUS)	Helga Schultze (GER)	7-5	6-2	
Q	Annette Van Zyl (RSA)	Billie Jean King (USA)	6-2	5-7	6-4

Rd	Winner	Defeated	S1	S2	S3

1968

Rd	Winner	Defeated	S1	S2	S3
F	Nancy Richey (USA)	Ann Haydon Jones (GBR)	5-7	6-4	6-1
S	Nancy Richey (USA)	Billie Jean King (USA)	2-6	6-3	6-4
S	Ann Haydon Jones (GBR)	Annette Van Zyl Du Plooy (RSA)	7-5	6-3	
Q	Ann Haydon Jones (GBR)	Vlasta Vopickova (CZE)	6-2	6-1	
Q	Annette Van Zyl Du Plooy (RSA)	Gail Sherriff Chanfreau (AUS)	8-6	6-3	
Q	Nancy Richey (USA)	Elena Subirats (MEX)	6-1	6-0	
Q	Billie Jean King (USA)	Maria Bueno (BRA)	6-4	6-4	

1969

Rd	Winner	Defeated	S1	S2	S3
F	Margaret Smith Court (AUS)	Ann Haydon Jones (GBR)	6-1	4-6	6-3
S	Margaret Smith Court (AUS)	Nancy Richey (USA)	6-3	4-6	7-5
S	Ann Haydon Jones (GBR)	Lesley Turner Bowrey (AUS)	6-1	6-2	
Q	Margaret Smith Court (AUS)	Kerry Melville (AUS)	9-7	6-1	
Q	Nancy Richey (USA)	Julie Heldman (USA)	6-3	9-7	
Q	Ann Haydon Jones (GBR)	Rosie Casals (USA)	6-2	6-0	
Q	Lesley Turner Bowrey (AUS)	Billie Jean King (USA)	6-3	6-3	

1970

Rd	Winner	Defeated	S1	S2	S3
F	Margaret Smith Court (AUS)	Helga Niessen-Masthoff (GER)	6-2	6-4	
S	Margaret Smith Court (AUS)	Julie Heldman (USA)	6-0	6-2	
S	Helga Niessen-Masthoff (GER)	Karen Krantzcke (AUS)	6-3	6-1	
Q	Margaret Smith Court (AUS)	Rosie Casals (USA)	7-5	6-2	
Q	Julie Heldman (USA)	Vlasta Vopickova (CZE)	6-1	6-3	
Q	Karen Krantzcke (AUS)	Virginia Wade (GBR)	6-2	1-6	6-3
Q	Helga Niessen-Masthoff (GER)	Bille Jean King (USA)	2-6	8-6	6-1

1971

Rd	Winner	Defeated	S1	S2	S3
F	Evonne Goolagoong (AUS)	Helen Gourlay (AUS)	6-3	7-5	
S	Helen Gourlay (AUS)	Nancy Richey Gunter (USA)	6-2	6-3	
S	Evonne Goolagoong (AUS)	Marijke Schaar (NED)	6-4	6-1	
Q	Helen Gourlay (AUS)	Gail Sherriff Chanfreau (FRA)	6-4	3-6	6-3
Q	Nancy Richey Gunter (USA)	Lesley Turner Bowrey (AUS)	6-2	6-4	
Q	Evonne Goolagoong (AUS)	Francoise Durr (FRA)	6-3	6-0	
Q	Marijke Schaar (NED)	Linda Tuero (USA)	6-2	6-3	

1972

Rd	Winner	Defeated	S1	S2	S3
F	Billie Jean King (USA)	Evonne Goolagong (AUS)	6-3	6-3	
S	Billie Jean King (USA)	Helga Niessen-Masthoff (GER)	6-4	6-4	
S	Evonne Goolagong (AUS)	Francoise Durr (FRA)	9-7	6-4	
Q	Helga Niessen-Masthoff (GER)	Katja Ebbinghaus (GER)	6-3	8-6	
Q	Billie Jean King (USA)	Virginia Wade (GBR)	6-1	6-3	
Q	Francoise Durr (FRA)	Olga Morozova (USSR)	4-6	6-3	6-2
Q	Evonne Goolagong (AUS)	Corinne Molesworth (GBR)	6-2	6-2	

1973

Rd	Winner	Defeated	S1	S2	S3
F	Margaret Smith Court (AUS)	Chris Evert (USA)	6-7(5)	7-6(6)	6-4
S	Margaret Smith Court (AUS)	Evonne Goolagong (AUS)	6-3	7-6	
S	Chris Evert (USA)	Francoise Durr (FRA)	6-1	6-0	
Q	Margaret Smith Court (AUS)	Katja Ebbinghaus (GER)	6-2	6-3	
Q	Evonne Goolagong (AUS)	Martina Navratilova (CZE)	7-6(3)	6-4	
Q	Francoise Durr (FRA)	Odile De Roubin (FRA)	6-0	1-6	6-1
Q	Chris Evert (USA)	Helga Niessen-Masthoff (GER)	6-3	6-3	

1974

Rd	Winner	Defeated	S1	S2	S3
F	Chris Evert (USA)	Olga Morozova (USSR)	6-1	6-2	
S	Olga Morozova (USSR)	Raquel Giscafre (ARG)	6-3	6-2	
S	Chris Evert (USA)	Helga Niessen-Masthoff (GER)	7-5	6-4	
Q	Raquel Giscafre (ARG)	Katja Ebbinghaus (GER)	7-5	6-7	6-3
Q	Olga Morozova (USSR)	Marie Pinterova (HUN)	6-3	6-2	
Q	Helga Niessen-Masthoff (GER)	Martina Navratilova (CZE)	7-6	6-3	
Q	Chris Evert (USA)	Julie Heldman (USA)	6-0	7-5	

1975

Rd	Winner	Defeated	S1	S2	S3
F	Chris Evert (USA)	Martina Navratilova (CZE)	2-6	6-2	6-1
S	Chris Evert (USA)	Olga Morozova (USSR)	6-4	6-0	
S	Martina Navratilova (CZE)	Janet Newberry (USA)	6-2	6-3	
Q	Chris Evert (USA)	Kazuko Sawamatsu (JPN)	6-2	6-2	
Q	Olga Morozova (USSR)	Raquel Giscafre (ARG)	7-5	6-7	6-0
Q	Janet Newberry (USA)	Eva Szabo (HUN)	6-1	6-2	
Q	Martina Navratilova (CZE)	Donna Ganz (USA)	6-1	6-1	

1976

Rd	Winner	Defeated	S1	S2	S3
F	Sue Barker (GBR)	Renata Tomanova (CZE)	6-2	0-6	6-2
S	Renata Tomanova (CZE)	Florenta Mihai (ROU)	7-5	7-6	
S	Sue Barker (GBR)	Virginia Ruzici (ROU)	6-3	1-6	6-2
Q	Renata Tomanova (CZE)	Helga Niessen-Masthoff (GER)	6-2	6-4	
Q	Florenta Mihai (ROU)	Kathy Kuykendall (USA)	6-2	0-6	6-1
Q	Virginia Ruzici (ROU)	Miroslava Holubova (CZE)	6-1	6-3	
Q	Sue Barker (GBR)	Regina Marsikova (CZE)	4-6	6-2	8-6

1977

Rd	Winner	Defeated	S1	S2	S3
F	Mima Jausovec (YUG)	Florenta Mihai (ROU)	6-2	6-7(5)	6-1
S	Florenta Mihai (ROU)	Janet Newberry (USA)	7-6	6-3	
S	Mima Jausovec (YUG)	Regina Marsikova (CZE)	6-1	3-6	6-3
Q	Janet Newberry (USA)	Kathy May (USA)	6-4	5-7	6-2
Q	Florenta Mihai (ROU)	Linky Boshoff (RSA)	6-3	4-6	7-5
Q	Regina Marsikova (CZE)	Renata Tomanova (CZE)	7-6	6-7	6-3
Q	Mima Jausovec (YUG)	Pam Teeguarden (USA)	7-5	6-4	

1978

Rd	Winner	Defeated	S1	S2	S3
F	Virginia Ruzici (ROU)	Mima Jausovec (YUG)	6-2	6-2	
S	Virginia Ruzici (ROU)	Brigitte Simon (FRA)	6-3	6-0	
S	Mima Jausovec (YUG)	Regina Marsikova (CZE)	6-3	6-4	
Q	Brigitte Simon (FRA)	Miroslava Bendlova (CZE)	6-3	6-3	
Q	Virginia Ruzici (ROU)	Florella Bonicelli (URU)	6-7	6-4	8-6
Q	Regina Marsikova (CZE)	Helga Niessen-Masthoff (GER)	6-3	6-3	
Q	Mima Jausovec (YUG)	Kathy May (USA)	6-4	6-2	

1979

Rd	Winner	Defeated	S1	S2	S3
F	Chris Evert Lloyd (USA)	Wendy Turnbull (AUS)	6-2	6-0	
S	Chris Evert Lloyd (USA)	Dianne Fromholtz Balestra (AUS)	6-1	6-3	
S	Wendy Turnbull (AUS)	Regina Marsikova (CZE)	6-4	6-3	
Q	Chris Evert Lloyd (USA)	Ruta Gerulaitis (USA)	6-0	6-4	
Q	Dianne Fromholtz Balestrat (AUS)	Virginia Ruzici (ROU)	6-0	6-4	
Q	Wendy Turnbull (AUS)	Hana Mandlikova (CZE)	6-3	6-3	
Q	Regina Marsikova (CZE)	Renata Tomanova (CZE)	6-1	6-1	

1980

Rd	Winner	Defeated	S1	S2	S3
F	Chris Evert Lloyd (USA)	Virginia Ruzici (ROU)	6-0	6-3	
S	Virginia Ruzici (ROU)	Dianne Fromholtz Balestra (AUS)	7-6	6-1	
S	Chris Evert Lloyd (USA)	Hana Mandlikova (CZE)	6-7	6-2	6-2
Q	Virginia Ruzici (ROU)	Wendy Turnbull (AUS)	6-2	6-0	
Q	Dianne Fromholtz Balestra (AUS)	Billie Jean King (USA)	6-1	6-4	
Q	Hana Mandlikova (CZE)	Ivanna Madruga (ARG)	6-2	6-3	
Q	Chris Evert Lloyd (USA)	Kathy Jordan (USA)	6-2	6-0	

1981

Rd	Winner	Defeated	S1	S2	S3
F	Hana Mandlikova (CZE)	Sylvia Hanika (GER)	6-2	6-4	
S	Sylvia Hanika (GER)	Andrea Jaeger (USA)	4-6	6-1	6-4
S	Hana Mandlikova (CZE)	Chris Evert Lloyd (USA)	7-5	6-4	
Q	Sylvia Hanika (GER)	Martina Navratilova (CZE)	6-2	6-4	
Q	Andrea Jaeger (USA)	Mima Jausovec (YUG)	4-6	6-2	6-0
Q	Hana Mandlikova (CZE)	Kathy Rinaldi (USA)	6-1	6-3	
Q	Chris Evert Lloyd (USA)	Virginia Ruzici (ROU)	6-4	6-4	

1982

Rd	Winner	Defeated	S1	S2	S3
F	Martina Navratilova (USA)	Andrea Jaeger (USA)	7-6(6)	6-1	
S	Andrea Jaeger (USA)	Chris Evert Lloyd (USA)	6-3	6-1	
S	Martina Navratilova (USA)	Hana Mandlikova (CZE)	6-0	6-2	
Q	Hana Mandlikova (CZE)	Tracy Austin (USA)	7-6	6-7	6-2
Q	Martina Navratilova (USA)	Zina Garrison (USA)	6-3	6-2	
Q	Andrea Jaeger (USA)	Virginia Ruzici (ROU)	6-1	6-0	
Q	Chris Evert Lloyd (USA)	Lucia Romanov (ROU)	6-2	6-4	

1983

Rd	Winner	Defeated	S1	S2	S3
F	Chris Evert Lloyd (USA)	Mima Jausovec (YUG)	6-1	6-2	
S	Mima Jausovec (YUG)	Jo Durie (GBR)	3-6	7-5	6-2
S	Chris Evert Lloyd (USA)	Andrea Jaeger (USA)	6-3	6-1	
Q	Andrea Jaeger (USA)	Gretchen Rush (USA)	6-2	6-2	
Q	Chris Evert Lloyd (USA)	Hana Mandlikova (CZE)	4-6	6-3	6-2
Q	Mima Jausovec (YUG)	Kathy Horvath (USA)	6-1	6-1	
Q	Jo Durie (GBR)	Tracy Austin (USA)	6-1	4-6	6-0

1984

Rd	Winner	Defeated	S1	S2	S3
F	Martina Navratilova (USA)	Chris Evert Lloyd (USA)	6-3	6-1	
S	Chris Evert Lloyd (USA)	Camille Benjamin (USA)	6-0	6-0	
S	Martina Navratilova (USA)	Hana Mandlikova (CZE)	3-6	6-2	6-2
Q	Hana Mandlikova (CZE)	Melissa Brown (USA)	6-1	6-4	
Q	Martina Navratilova (USA)	Kathy Horvath (USA)	6-4	6-2	
Q	Chris Evert Lloyd (USA)	Carling Bassett (CAN)	4-6	6-1	6-0
Q	Camille Benjamin (USA)	Lisa Bonder (USA)	7-6(3)	5-7	6-3

1985

Rd	Winner	Defeated	S1	S2	S3
F	Chris Evert Lloyd (USA)	Martina Navratilova (USA)	6-3	6-7(4)	7-5
S	Martina Navratilova (USA)	Claudia Kohde Kilsch (GER)	6-4	6-4	
S	Chris Evert Lloyd (USA)	Gabriela Sabatini (ARG)	6-4	6-1	
Q	Martina Navratilova (USA)	Sandra Cecchini (ITA)	6-2	6-2	
Q	Claudia Kohde Kilsch (GER)	Hana Mandlikova (CZE)	6-4	6-4	
Q	Gabriela Sabatini (ARG)	Manuela Maleeva (BUL)	6-3	1-6	6-1
Q	Chris Evert Lloyd (USA)	Terry Phelps (USA)	6-4	6-0	

1986

Rd	Winner	Defeated	S1	S2	S3
F	Chris Evert Lloyd (USA)	Martina Navratilova (USA)	2-6	6-3	6-3
S	Chris Evert Lloyd (USA)	Hana Mandlikova (CZE)	6-1	6-1	
S	Martina Navratilova (USA)	Helena Sukova (CZE)	4-6	7-6(4)	6-2
Q	Helena Sukova (CZE)	Mary Joe Fernandez (USA)	6-2	6-4	
Q	Martina Navratilova (USA)	Kathy Rinaldi (USA)	7-5	6-4	
Q	Hana Mandlikova (CZE)	Steffi Graf (GER)	2-6	7-6(3)	6-1
Q	Chris Evert Lloyd (USA)	Carling Bassett (CAN)	5-7	6-2	6-1

1987

Rd	Winner	Defeated	S1	S2	S3
F	Steffi Graf (GER)	Martina Navratilova (USA)	6-4	4-6	8-6
S	Martina Navratilova (USA)	Chris Evert (USA)	6-2	6-2	
S	Steffi Graf (GER)	Gabriela Sabatini (ARG)	6-4	4-6	7-5
Q	Martina Navratilova (USA)	Claudia Kohde Kilsch (GER)	6-1	6-2	
Q	Chris Evert (USA)	Raffaella Reggi (ITA)	6-2	6-2	
Q	Gabriela Sabatini (ARG)	Arantxa Sanchez Vicario (ESP)	6-4	6-0	
Q	Steffi Graf (GER)	Manuela Maleeva (BUL)	6-4	6-1	

1988

Rd	Winner	Defeated	S1	S2	S3
F	Steffi Graf (GER)	Natalia Zvereva (BLR)	6-0	6-0	
S	Steffi Graf (GER)	Gabriela Sabatini (ARG)	6-3	7-6(3)	
S	Natalia Zvereva (BLR)	Nicole Provis (AUS)	6-3	6-7(3)	7-5
Q	Steffi Graf (GER)	Bettina Fulco (ARG)	6-0	6-1	
Q	Gabriela Sabatini (ARG)	Helen Kelesi (CAN)	4-6	6-1	6-3
Q	Nicole Provis (AUS)	Arantxa Sanchez Vicario (ESP)	7-5	3-6	6-4
Q	Natalia Zvereva (BLR)	Helena Sukova (CZE)	6-2	6-3	

1989

Rd	Winner	Defeated	S1	S2	S3
F	Arantxa Sanchez Vicario (ESP)	Steffi Graf (GER)	7-6(6)	3-6	7-5
S	Steffi Graf (GER)	Monica Seles (YUG)	6-3	3-6	6-3
S	Arantxa Sanchez Vicario (ESP)	Mary Joe Fernandez (USA)	6-2	6-2	
Q	Steffi Graf (GER)	Conchita Martinez (ESP)	6-0	6-4	
Q	Monica Seles (YUG)	Manuela Maleeva (BUL)	6-3	7-5	
Q	Arantxa Sanchez Vicario (ESP)	Jana Novotna (CZE)	6-2	6-2	
Q	Mary Joe Fernandez (USA)	Helen Kelesi (CAN)	6-2	7-5	

1990

Rd	Winner	Defeated	S1	S2	S3
F	Monica Seles (YUG)	Steffi Graf (GER)	7-6(6)	6-4	
S	Steffi Graf (GER)	Jana Novotna (CZE)	6-1	6-2	
S	Monica Seles (YUG)	Jennifer Capriati (USA)	6-2	6-2	
Q	Steffi Graf (GER)	Conchita Martinez (ESP)	6-1	6-3	
Q	Jana Novotna (CZE)	Katerina Maleeva (BUL)	4-6	6-2	6-4
Q	Jennifer Capriati (USA)	Mary Joe Fernandez (USA)	6-2	6-4	
Q	Monica Seles (YUG)	Manuela Maleeva-Fragniere (BUL)	3-6	6-1	7-5

1991

Rd	Winner	Defeated	S1	S2	S3
F	Monica Seles (YUG)	Arantxa Sanchez Vicario (ESP)	6-3	6-4	
S	Monica Seles (YUG)	Gabriela Sabatini (ARG)	7-5	6-1	
S	Arantxa Sanchez Vicario (ESP)	Steffi Graf (GER)	6-0	6-2	
Q	Monica Seles (YUG)	Conchita Martinez (ESP)	6-0	7-5	
Q	Gabriela Sabatini (ARG)	Jana Novotna (CZE)	5-7	7-6(10)	6-0
Q	Arantxa Sanchez Vicario (ESP)	Mary Joe Fernandez (USA)	6-3	6-2	
Q	Steffi Graf (GER)	Nathalie Tauziat (FRA)	6-3	6-2	

1992

Rd	Winner	Defeated	S1	S2	S3
F	Monica Seles (YUG)	Steffi Graf (GER)	6-2	3-6	10-8
S	Monica Seles (YUG)	Gabriela Sabatini (ARG)	6-3	4-6	6-4
S	Steffi Graf (GER)	Arantxa Sanchez Vicario (ESP)	0-6	6-2	6-2
Q	Monica Seles (YUG)	Jennifer Capriati (USA)	6-2	6-2	
Q	Gabriela Sabatini (ARG)	Conchita Martinez (ESP)	3-6	6-3	6-2
Q	Arantxa Sanchez Vicario (ESP)	Manon Bollegraf (NED)	6-2	6-3	
Q	Steffi Graf (GER)	Natasha Zvereva (BLR)	6-3	6-7(4)	6-3

1993

Rd	Winner	Defeated	S1	S2	S3
F	Steffi Graf (GER)	Mary Joe Fernandez (USA)	4-6	6-2	6-4
S	Steffi Graf (GER)	Anke Huber (GER)	6-1	6-1	
S	Mary Joe Fernandez (USA)	Arantxa Sanchez Vicario (ESP)	6-2	6-2	
Q	Steffi Graf (GER)	Jennifer Capriati (USA)	6-3	7-5	
Q	Anke Huber (GER)	Conchita Martinez (ESP)	6-7(2)	6-4	6-4
Q	Mary Joe Fernandez (USA)	Gabriela Sabatini (ARG)	1-6	7-6(4)	10-8
Q	Arantxa Sanchez Vicario (ESP)	Jana Novotna (CZE)	6-2	7-5	

1994

Rd	Winner	Defeated	S1	S2	S3
F	Arantxa Sanchez Vicario (ESP)	Mary Pierce (FRA)	6-4	6-4	
S	Mary Pierce (FRA)	Steffi Graf (GER)	6-2	6-2	
S	Arantxa Sanchez Vicario (ESP)	Conchita Martinez (ESP)	6-3	6-1	
Q	Steffi Graf (GER)	Ines Gorrochategui (ARG)	6-4	6-1	
Q	Mary Pierce (FRA)	Petra Ritter (AUT)	6-0	6-2	
Q	Conchita Martinez (ESP)	Sabine Hack (GER)	2-6	6-0	6-0
Q	Arantxa Sanchez Vicario (ESP)	Julie Halard (FRA)	6-1	7-6(6)	

1995

Rd	Winner	Defeated	S1	S2	S3
F	Steffi Graf (GER)	Arantxa Sanchez Vicario (ESP)	7-5	4-6	6-0
S	Arantxa Sanchez Vicario (ESP)	Kimiko Date (JPN)	7-5	6-3	
S	Steffi Graf (GER)	Conchita Martinez (ESP)	6-3	6-7(5)	6-3
Q	Arantxa Sanchez Vicario (ESP)	Chanda Rubin (USA)	6-3	6-1	
Q	Kimiko Date (JPN)	Iva Majoli (CRO)	7-5	6-1	
Q	Conchita Martinez (ESP)	Virginia Ruano Pascual (ESP)	6-0	6-4	
Q	Steffi Graf (GER)	Gabriela Sabatini (ARG)	6-1	6-0	

1996

Rd	Winner	Defeated	S1	S2	S3
F	Steffi Graf (GER)	Arantxa Sanchez Vicario (ESP)	6-3	6-7(4)	10-8
S	Steffi Graf (GER)	Conchita Martinez (ESP)	6-3	6-1	
S	Arantxa Sanchez Vicario (ESP)	Jana Novotna (CZE)	6-3	7-5	
Q	Steffi Graf (GER)	Iva Majoli (CRO)	6-3	6-1	
Q	Conchita Martinez (ESP)	Lindsay Davenport (USA)	6-1	6-3	
Q	Arantxa Sanchez Vicario (ESP)	Karina Habsudova (SVK)	6-2	6-7(4)	10-8
Q	Java Novotna (CZE)	Monica Seles (USA)	7-6(7)	6-3	

1997

Rd	Winner	Defeated	S1	S2	S3
F	Iva Majoli (CRO)	Martina Hingis (SUI)	6-4	6-2	
S	Martina Hingis (SUI)	Monica Seles (USA)	6-7(2)	7-5	6-4
S	Iva Majoli (CRO)	Amanda Coetzer (RSA)	6-3	4-6	7-5
Q	Martina Hingis (SUI)	Arantxa Sanchez Vicario (ESP)	6-2	6-2	
Q	Monica Seles (USA)	Mary Joe Fernandez (USA)	3-6	6-2	7-5
Q	Iva Majoli (CRO)	Ruxandra Dragomir (ROU)	6-3	5-7	6-2
Q	Amanda Coetzer (RSA)	Steffi Graf (GER)	6-1	6-4	

1998

Rd	Winner	Defeated	S1	S2	S3
F	Arantxa Sanchez Vicario (ESP)	Monica Seles (USA)	7-6(5)	0-6	6-2
S	Arantxa Sanchez Vicario (ESP)	Lindsay Davenport (USA)	6-3	7-6(5)	
S	Monica Seles (USA)	Martina Hingis (SUI)	6-3	6-2	
Q	Martina Hingis (SUI)	Venus Williams (USA)	6-3	6-4	
Q	Monica Seles (USA)	Jana Novotna (CZE)	4-6	6-3	6-3
Q	Arantxa Sanchez Vicario (ESP)	Patty Schnyder (SUI)	6-2	6-7(5)	6-0
Q	Lindsay Davenport (USA)	Iva Majoli (CRO)	6-1	5-7	6-3

1999

Rd	Winner	Defeated	S1	S2	S3
F	Steffi Graf (GER)	Martina Hingis (SUI)	4-6	7-5	6-2
S	Steffi Graf (GER)	Monica Seles (USA)	6-7(2)	6-3	6-4
S	Martina Hingis (SUI)	Arantxa Sanchez Vicario (ESP)	6-3	6-2	
Q	Martina Hingis (SUI)	Barbara Schwartz (AUT)	6-2	6-2	
Q	Arantxa Sanchez Vicario (ESP)	Sylvia Plischke (AUT)	6-2	6-4	
Q	Monica Seles (USA)	Conchita Martinez (ESP)	6-1	6-4	
Q	Steffi Graf (GER)	Lindsay Davenport (USA)	6-1	6-7(5)	6-3

2000

Rd	Winner	Defeated	S1	S2	S3
F	Mary Pierce (FRA)	Conchita Martinez (ESP)	6-2	7-5	
S	Mary Pierce (FRA)	Martina Hingis (SUI)	6-4	5-7	6-2
S	Conchita Martinez (ESP)	Arantxa Sanchez Vicario (ESP)	6-1	6-2	
Q	Martina Hingis (SUI)	Chandra Rubin (USA)	6-1	6-3	
Q	Mary Pierce (FRA)	Monica Seles (USA)	4-6	6-3	6-4
Q	Arantxa Sanchez Vicario (ESP)	Venus Williams (USA)	6-0	1-6	6-2
Q	Conchita Martinez (ESP)	Marta Marrero (ESP)	7-6(5)	6-1	

2001

Rd	Winner	Defeated	S1	S2	S3
F	Jennifer Capriati (USA)	Kim Clijsters (BEL)	1-6	6-4	12-10
S	Jennifer Capriati (USA)	Martina Hingis (SUI)	6-4	6-3	
S	Kim Clijsters (BEL)	Justine Henin (BEL)	2-6	7-5	6-3
Q	Martina Hingis (SUI)	Francesca Schiavone (ITA)	6-1	6-4	
Q	Jennifer Capriati (USA)	Serena Williams (USA)	6-2	5-7	6-2
Q	Kim Cljsters (BEL)	Petra Mandula (HUN)	6-1	6-3	
Q	Justine Henin (BEL)	Lina Krasnoroutskaya (RUS)	6-1	6-2	

2002

Rd	Winner	Defeated	S1	S2	S3
F	Serena Williams (USA)	Venus Williams (USA)	7-5	6-3	
S	Serena Williams (USA)	Jennifer Capriati (USA)	3-6	7-6(2)	6-2
S	Venus Williams (USA)	Clarisa Fernandez (ARG)	6-1	6-4	
Q	Jennifer Capriati (USA)	Jelena Dokic (YUG)	6-4	4-6	6-1
Q	Serena Williams (USA)	Mary Pierce (FRA)	6-1	6-1	
Q	Clarisa Fernandez (ARG)	Paola Suarez (ARG)	2-6	7-6(5)	6-1
Q	Venus Williams (USA)	Monica Seles (USA)	6-4	6-3	

2003

Rd	Winner	Defeated	S1	S2	S3
F	Justine Henin-Hardenne (BEL)	Kim Clijsters (BEL)	6-4	6-0	
S	Justine Henin-Hardenne (BEL)	Serena Williams (USA)	6-2	4-6	7-5
S	Kim Clijsters (BEL)	Nadia Petrova (RUS)	7-5	6-1	
Q	Serena Williams (USA)	Amelie Mauresmo (FRA)	6-1	6-2	
Q	Justine Henin-Hardenne (BEL)	Chanda Rubin (USA)	6-3	6-2	
Q	Nadia Petrova (RUS)	Vera Zvonareva (RUS)	6-1	4-6	6-3
Q	Kim Clijsters (BEL)	Conchita Martinez (ESP)	6-2	6-1	

Rd	Winner	Defeated	S1	S2	S3

2004

F	Anastasia Myskina (RUS)	Elene Dementieva (RUS)	6-1	6-2	
S	Elena Dementieva (RUS)	Paola Suarez (ARG)	6-0	7-5	
S	Anastasia Myskina (RUS)	Jennifer Capriati (USA)	6-2	6-2	
Q	Paola Suarez (ARG)	Maria Sharapova (RUS)	6-1	6-3	
Q	Elena Dementieva (RUS)	Amelie Mauresmo (FRA)	6-4	6-3	
Q	Anastasia Myskina (RUS)	Venus Williams (USA)	6-3	6-4	
Q	Jennifer Capriati (USA)	Serena Williams (USA)	6-3	2-6	6-3

2005

F	Justine Henin-Hardenne (BEL)	Mary Pierce (FRA)	6-1	6-1	
S	Justine Henin-Hardenne (BEL)	Nadia Petrova (RUS)	6-2	6-3	
S	Mary Pierce (FRA)	Elena Likhovtseva (RUS)	6-1	6-1	
Q	Nadia Petrova (RUS)	Ana Ivanovic (SRB)	6-2	6-2	
Q	Justine Henin-Hardenne (BEL)	Maria Sharapova (RUS)	6-4	6-2	
Q	Mary Pierce (FRA)	Lindsay Davenport (USA)	6-3	6-2	
Q	Elena Likhovtseva (RUS)	Sesil Karatancheva (BUL)	2-6	6-4	6-4

2006

F	Justine Henin-Hardenne (BEL)	Svetlana Kuznetsova (RUS)	6-4	6-4	
S	Svetlana Kuznetsova (RUS)	Nicole Vaidisova (CZE)	5-7	7-6(5)	6-2
S	Justine Henin-Hardenne (BEL)	Kim Clijsters (BEL)	6-3	6-2	
Q	Nicole Vaidisova (CZE)	Venus Williams (USA)	6-7(5)	6-1	6-3
Q	Svetlana Kuznetsova (RUS)	Dinara Safina (RUS)	7-6(5)	6-0	
Q	Justine Henin-Hardenne (BEL)	Anna-Lena Groenefeld (GER)	7-5	6-2	
Q	Kim Clijsters (BEL)	Martina Hingis (SUI)	7-6(5)	6-1	

2007

F	Justine Henin (BEL)	Ana Ivanovic (SRB)	6-1	6-2	
S	Justine Henin (BEL)	Jelena Jankovic (SRB)	6-2	6-2	
S	Ana Ivanovic (SRB)	Maria Sharapova (RUS)	6-2	6-1	
Q	Justine Henin (BEL)	Serena Williams (USA)	6-4	6-3	
Q	Jelena Jankovic (SRB)	Nicole Vaidisova (CZE)	6-3	7-5	
Q	Ana Ivanovic (SRB)	Svetlana Kuznetsova (RUS)	6-0	3-6	6-1
Q	Maria Sharapova (RUS)	Anna Chakvetadze (RUS)	6-3	6-4	

2008

F	Ana Ivanovic (SRB)	Dinara Safina (RUS)	6-4	6-3	
S	Dinara Safina (RUS)	Svetlana Kuznetsova (RUS)	6-3	6-2	
S	Ana Ivanovic (SRB)	Jelena Jankovic (SRB)	6-4	3-6	6-4
Q	Dinara Safina (RUS)	Elena Dementieva (RUS)	4-6	7-6(5)	6-0
Q	Svetlana Kuznetsova (RUS)	Kaia Kanepi (EST)	7-5	6-2	
Q	Jelena Jankovic (SRB)	Carla Suarez Navarro (ESP)	6-3	6-2	
Q	Ana Ivanovic (SRB)	Patty Schnyder (SUI)	6-3	6-2	

2009

F	Svetlana Kuznetsova (RUS)	Dinara Safina (RUS)	6-4	6-2	
S	Dinara Safina (RUS)	Dominika Cibulkova (SVK)	6-3	6-3	
S	Svetlana Kuznetsova (RUS)	Samantha Stosur (AUS)	6-4	6-7(5)	6-3
Q	Dinara Safina (RUS)	Azarenka (BLR)	1-6	6-4	6-2
Q	Dominika Cibulkova (SVK)	Maria Sharapova (RUS)	6-0	6-2	
Q	Samantha Stosur (AUS)	Sorana Cirstea (ROU)	6-1	6-3	
Q	Svetlana Kuznetsova (RUS)	Serena Williams (USA)	7-6(3)	5-7	7-5

Men's Doubles

Year	Winner	Defeated	S1	S2	S3	S4	S5
1925	Jean Borotra (FRA) Rene Lacoste (FRA)	Henri Cochet (FRA) Jacques Brugnon (FRA)	7-5	4-6	6-3	2-6	6-3
1926	Vinnie Richards (USA) Howard Kinsey (USA)	Henri Cochet (FRA) Jacques Brugnon (FRA)	6-4	6-1	4-6	6-4	
1927	Henri Cochet (FRA) Jacques Brugnon (FRA)	Jean Borotra (FRA) Rene Lacoste (FRA)	2-6	6-2	6-0	1-6	6-4
1928	Jean Borotra (FRA) Jacques Brugnon (FRA)	Henri Cochet (FRA) Rene de. Buzelet (FRA)	6-4	3-6	6-2	3-6	6-4
1929	Rene Lacoste (FRA) Jean Borotra (FRA)	Henri Cochet (FRA) Jacques Brugnon (FRA)	6-3	3-6	6-3	3-6	8-6
1930	Henri Cochet (FRA) Jacques Brugnon (FRA)	Harry Hopman (AUS) Jim Willard (AUS)	6-3	9-7	6-3		
1931	George Lott John Van Ryn (USA)	Vernon Kirby (RSA) Norman Farquharson (RSA)	6-4	6-3	6-4		
1932	Henri Cochet (FRA) Jacques Brugnon (FRA)	Christian Boussus (FRA) Marcel Bernard (FRA)	6-4	3-6	7-5	6-3	
1933	Pat Hughes (GBR) Fred Perry (GBR)	Adrian Quist (AUS) Viv McGrath (AUS)	6-2	6-4	2-6	7-5	
1934	Jean Borotra (FRA) Jacques Brugnon (FRA)	Jack Crawford (AUS) Viv McGrath (AUS)	11-9	6-3	2-6	4-6	9-7
1935	Jack Crawford (AUS) Adrian Quist (AUS)	Viv McGrath (AUS) Don Turnbull (AUS)	6-1	6-4	6-2		
1936	Jean Borotra (FRA) Marcel Bernard (FRA)	Charles Tuckey (GBR) Pat Hughes (GBR)	6-2	3-6	9-7	6-1	
1937	Gottfried von Cramm (GER) Henner Henkel (GER)	Norman Farquharson (RSA) Vernon Kirby (RSA)	6-4	7-5	3-6	6-1	
1938	Bernard Destremau (FRA) Yvon Petra (FRA)	Don Budge (USA) Gene Mako (USA)	3-6	6-3	9-7	6-1	
1939	Don McNeill (USA) Charles Harris (USA)	Jean Borotra (FRA) Jacques Brugnon (FRA)	4-6	6-4	6-0	2-6	10-8
1940-45 Not held —WW II							
1946	Marcel Bernard (FRA) Yvon Petra (FRA)	Enrique Morea (ARG) Pancho Segura (ECU)	7-5	6-3	0-6	1-6	10-8
1947	Eustace Fannin (RSA) Eric Sturgess (RSA)	Tom Brown (USA) Billy Sidwell (AUS)	6-4	4-6	6-4	6-3	
1948	Lennart Bergelin (SWE) Jaroslav Drobny (GBR)	Harry Hopman (AUS) Frank Sedgman (AUS)	8-6	6-1	12-10		
1949	Pancho Gonzalez (USA) Frank Parker (USA)	Eustace Fannin (RSA) Eric Sturgess (RSA)	6-3	8-6	5-7	6-3	
1950	Bill Talbert (USA) Tony Trabert (USA)	Jaroslav Drobny (GBR) Eric Sturgess (RSA)	6-2	1-6	10-8	6-2	
1951	Ken McGregor (AUS) Frank Sedgman (AUS)	Gardnar Mulloy (USA) Dick Savitt (USA)	6-2	2-6	9-7	7-5	
1952	Ken McGregor (AUS) Frank Sedgman (AUS)	Gardnar Mulloy (USA) Dick Savitt (USA)	6-3	6-4	6-4		
1953	Lew Hoad (AUS) Ken Rosewall (AUS)	Mervyn Rose (AUS) Clive Wilderspin (AUS)	6-2	6-1	6-1		
1954	Vic Seixas (USA) Tony Trabert (USA)	Lew Hoad (AUS) Ken Rosewall (AUS)	6-4	6-2	6-1		
1955	Vic Seixas (USA) Tony Trabert (USA)	Nicola Pietrangeli (ITA) Orlando Sirola (ITA)	6-1	4-6	6-2	6-4	

Year	Winner	Defeated	S1	S2	S3	S4	S5
1956	Don Candy (AUS) Robert Perry (USA)	Ashley Cooper (AUS) Lew Hoad (AUS)	7-5	6-3	6-3		
1957	Mal Anderson (AUS) Ashley Cooper (AUS)	Don Candy (AUS) Mervyn Rose (AUS)	6-3	6-0	6-3		
1958	Ashley Cooper (AUS) Neale Fraser (AUS)	Bob Howe (AUS) Abe Segal (RSA)	3-6	8-6	6-3	7-5	
1959	Orlando Sirola (ITA) Nicola Pietrangeli (ITA)	Roy Emerson (AUS) Neale Fraser (AUS)	6-3	6-2	14-12		
1960	Roy Emerson (AUS) Neale Fraser (AUS)	Jose-Luis Arilla (ESP) Andres Gimeno (ESP)	6-2	8-10	7-5	6-4	
1961	Roy Emerson (AUS) Rod Laver (AUS)	Bob Howe (AUS) Bob Mark (AUS)	3-6	6-1	6-1	6-4	
1962	Roy Emerson (AUS) Neale Fraser (AUS)	Wilhelm Bungert (GER) Christian Kuhnke (GER)	6-3	6-4	7-5		
1963	Roy Emerson (AUS) Manuel Santana (ESP)	Gordon Forbes (RSA) Abe Segal (RSA)	6-2	6-4	6-4		
1964	Roy Emerson (AUS) Ken Fletcher (AUS)	John Newcombe (AUS) Tony Roche (AUS)	7-5	6-3	3-6	7-5	
1965	Roy Emerson (AUS) Fred Stolle (AUS)	Ken Fletcher (AUS) Bob Hewitt (AUS)	6-8	6-3	8-6	6-2	
1966	Clark Graebner (USA) Dennis Ralston (USA)	Ilie Nastase (ROU) Ion Tiriac (ROU)	6-3	6-3	6-0		
1967	John Newcombe (AUS) Tony Roche (AUS)	Roy Emerson (AUS) Ken Fletcher (AUS)	6-3	9-7	12-10		
1968	Ken Rosewall (AUS) Fred Stolle (AUS)	Roy Emerson (AUS) Rod Laver (AUS)	6-3	6-4	6-3		
1969	John Newcombe (AUS) Tony Roche (AUS)	Roy Emerson (AUS) Rod Laver (AUS)	4-6	6-1	3-6	6-4	6-4
1970	Ilie Nastase (ROU) Ion Tiriac (ROU)	Arthur Ashe (USA) Charles Pasarell (USA)	6-2	6-4	6-3		
1971	Arthur Ashe (USA) Marty Riessen (USA)	Tom Gorman (USA) Stan Smith (USA)	6-8	4-6	6-3	6-4	11-9
1972	Bob Hewitt (RSA) Frew McMillan (RSA)	Patricio Cornejo (CHI) Jaime Fillol (CHI)	6-3	8-6	3-6	6-1	
1973	John Newcombe (AUS) Tom Okker (NED)	Jimmy Connors (USA) Ilie Nastase (ROU)	6-1	3-6	6-3	5-7	6-4
1974	Dick Crealy (AUS) Onny Parun (AUS)	Stan Smith (USA) Bob Lutz (USA)	6-3	6-2	3-6	5-7	6-1
1975	Brian Gottfried (USA) Raul Ramirez (MEX)	John Alexander (AUS) Phil Dent (AUS)	6-2	2-6	6-2	6-4	
1976	Fred McNair (USA) Sherwood Stewart (USA)	Brian Gottfried (USA) Raul Ramirez (MEX)	7-6(6)	6-3	6-1		
1977	Brian Gottfried (USA) Raul Ramirez (MEX)	Wojtek Fibak (POL) Jan Kodes (CZE)	7-6	4-6	6-3	6-4	
1978	Gene Mayer (USA) Hank Pfister (USA)	Jose Higueras (ESP) Manuel Orantes (ESP)	6-3	6-2	6-2		
1979	Gene Mayer (USA) Alex Mayer (USA)	Ross Case (AUS) Phil Dent (AUS)	6-4	'6-4	6-4		
1980	Victor Amaya (USA) Hank Pfister (USA)	Brian Gottfried (USA) Raul Ramirez (MEX)	1-6	6-4	6-4	6-3	
1981	Heinz Gunthardt (SUI) Balazs Taroczy (HUN)	Terry Moor (USA) Eliot Teltscher (USA)	6-2	7-6	6-3		
1982	Sherwood Stewart (USA) Ferdi Taygan (USA)	Hans Gildemeister (CHI) Belus Prajoux (CHI)	7-5	6-3	1-1	(retired)	

Year	Winner	Defeated	S1	S2	S3	S4	S5
1983	Anders Jarryd (SWE) Hans Simonsson (SWE)	Mark Edmondson (AUS) Sherwood Stewart (USA)	7-6(4)	6-4	6-2		
1984	Henri Leconte (FRA) Yannick Noah (FRA)	Pavel Slozil (CZE) Tomas Smid (CZE)	6-4	2-6	3-6	6-3	6-2
1985	Mark Edmondson (AUS) Kim Warwick (AUS)	Shlomo Glickstein (ISR) Hans Simonsson (SWE)	6-3	6-4	6-7	6-3	
1986	John Fitzgerald (AUS) Tomas Smid (CZE)	Stefan Edberg (SWE) Anders Jarryd (SWE)	6-3	4-6	6-3	6-7(4)	14-12
1987	Anders Jarryd (SWE) Robert Seguso (USA)	Guy Forget (FRA) Yannick Noah (FRA)	6-7	6-7	6-3	6-4	6-2
1988	Andres Gomez (ECU) Emilo Sanchez (ESP)	John Fitzgerald (AUS) Anders Jarryd (SWE)	6-3	6-7(8)	6-4	6-3	
1989	Jim Grabb (USA) Patrick McEnroe (USA)	Mansour Bahrami (IRI) Eric Winogradsky (FRA)	6-4	2-6	6-4	7-6(5)	
1990	Sergio Casal (ESP) Emilo Sanchez (ESP)	Goran Ivanisevic (YUG) Petr Korda (CZE)	7-5	6-3			
1991	John Fitzgerald (AUS) Anders Jarryd (SWE)	Rick Leach (USA) Jim Pugh (USA)	6-0	7-6(2)			
1992	Jakob Hlasek (SUI) Marc Rosset (SUI)	David Adams (RSA) Andrei Olhovskiy (RUS)	7-6(4)	6-7(3)	7-5		
1993	Luke Jensen (USA) Murphy Jensen (USA)	Marc Goellner (GER) David Prinosil (GER)	6-4	6-7(4)	6-4		
1994	Byron Black (ZIM) Jonathan Stark (USA)	Jan Apell (SWE) Jonas Bjorkman (SWE)	6-4	7-6(5)			
1995	Jacco Eltingh (NED) Paul Haarhuis (NED)	Nicklas Kulti (SWE) Magnus Larsson (SWE)	6-7(3)	6-4	6-1		
1996	Yevgeny Kafelnikov (RUS) Daniel Vacek (CZE)	Guy Forget (FRA) Jakob Hlasek (SUI)	6-2	6-3			
1997	Yevgeny Kafelnikov (RUS) Daniel Vacek (CZE)	Mark Woodforde (AUS) Todd Woodbridge (AUS)	7-6(12)	4-6	6-3		
1998	Jacco Eltingh (NED) Paul Haarhuis (NED)	Daniel Nestor (CAN) Mark Knowles (BAH)	6-3	3-6	6-3		
1999	Mahesh Bhupathi (IND) Leander Paes (IND)	Goran Ivanisevic (CRO) Jeff Tarango (USA)	6-2	7-5			
2000	Mark Woodforde (AUS) Todd Woodbridge (AUS)	Paul Haarhuis (NED) Sandon Stolle (AUS)	7-6	6-4			
2001	Mahesh Bhupathi (IND) Leander Paes (IND)	Petr Pala (CZE) Pavel Vizner (CZE)	7-6	6-3			
2002	Paul Haarhuis (NED) Yevgeny Kafelnikov (RUS)	Mark Knowles (BAH) Daniel Nestor (CAN)	7-5	6-4			
2003	Bob Bryan (USA) Mike Bryan (USA)	Paul Haarhuis (NED) Yevgeny Kafelnikov (RUS)	7-6(3)	6-3			
2004	Xavier Malisse (BEL) Olivier Rochus (BEL)	Michael Llodra (FRA) Fabrice Santoro (FRA)	7-5	7-5			
2005	Jonas Bjorkman (SWE) Max Mirnyi (BLR)	Bob Bryan (USA) Mike Bryan (USA)	2-6	6-1	6-4		
2006	Jonas Bjorkman (SWE) Max Mirnyi (BLR)	Bob Bryan (USA) Mike Bryan (USA)	6-7(5)	6-4	7-5		
2007	Mark Knowles (BAH) Daniel Nestor (CAN)	Lukas Dlouhy (CZE) Pavel Vizner (CZE)	2-6	6-3	6-4		
2008	Luis Horna (PER) Pablo Cuevas (URU)	Daniel Nestor (CAN) Nenad Zimonjic (SRB)	6-2	6-3			
2009	Lukas Dlouhy (CZE) Leander Paes (IND)	Wesley Moodie (RSA) Dick Norman (BEL)	3-6	6-3	6-2		

Women's Doubles

Year	Winner	Defeated	S1	S2	S3
1925	Suzanne Lenglen (FRA) Didi Vlasto (FRA)	Evelyn Colyer (GBR) Kitty McKane (GBR)	6-1	9-11	6-2
1926	Suzanne Lenglen (FRA) Didi Vlasto (FRA)	Evelyn Colyer (GBR) Kitty Mckane Godfree (GBR)	6-1	6-1	
1927	Irene Bowder Peacock (RSA) Bobbie Heine (AUS)	Peggy Saunders (GBR) Phoebe Holcroft Watson (GBR)	6-2	6-1	
1928	Phoebe Holcroft Watson (GBR) Eileen Bennett (GBR)	Suzanne Deve (FRA) Sylvia Lafaurie (FRA)	6-0	6-2	
1929	Lili de Alvarez (ESP) Kea Bouman (NED)	Bobbie Heine (RSA) Alida Neave (RSA)	7-5	6-3	
1930	Helen Wills Moody (USA) Elizabeth Ryan (USA)	Simone Barbier (FRA) Simone Passemard Mathieu (FRA)	6-3	6-1	
1931	Eileen Bennett Whittingstall (GBR) Betty Nuthall (GBR)	Cilly Aussem (GER) Elizabeth Ryan (USA)	9-7	6-2	
1932	Helen Wills Moody (USA) Elizabeth Ryan (USA)	Betty Nuthall (GBR) Eileen Bennett Whittingstall (GBR)	6-1	6-3	
1933	Simone Passemard Mathieu (FRA) Elizabeth Ryan (USA)	Sylvie Jung Henrotin (FRA) Colette Rosambert (FRA)	6-1	6-3	
1934	Simone Passemard Mathieu (FRA) Elizabeth Ryan (USA)	Helen Jacobs (USA) Sarah Palfrey (USA)	3-6	6-4	6-2
1935	Margaret Scriven (GBR) Kay Stammers (GBR)	Ida Adamoff (GER) Hilde Krahwinkel Sperling (GER)	6-4	6-0	
1936	Simone Passemard Mathieu (FRA) Billie Yorke (GBR)	Susan Noel (GBR) Jadwiga Jedrzejowska (POL)	2-6	6-4	6-4
1937	Simone Passemard Mathieu (FRA) Billie Yorke (GBR)	Dorothy Andrus (USA) Sylvie Jung Henrotin (FRA)	3-6	6-2	6-2
1938	Simone Passemard Mathieu (FRA) Billie Yorke (GBR)	Arlette Halff (FRA) Nelly Adamson Landry (FRA)	6-3	6-3	
1939	Simone Passemard Mathieu (FRA) Jadwiga Jedrzejowska (POL)	Alice Florian (YUG) Hella Kovac (YUG)	7-5	7-5	
1940-45	Not held—WW II				
1946	Louise Brough (USA) Margaret Osborne (USA)	Pauline Betz (USA) Doris Hart (USA)	6-4	0-6	6-1
1947	Louise Brough (USA) Margaret Osborne (USA)	Doris Hart (USA) Pat Canning Todd (USA)	7-5	6-2	
1948	Doris Hart (USA) Pat Canning Todd (USA)	Shirley Fry (USA) Mary Arnold Prentiss (USA)	6-4	6-2	
1949	Margaret Osborne duPont (USA) Louise Brough (USA)	Joy Gannon (GBR) Betty Hilton (GBR)	7-5	6-1	
1950	Doris Hart (USA) Shirley Fry (USA)	Louise Brough (USA) Margaret Osborne duPont (USA)	1-6	7-5	6-2
1951	Doris Hart (USA) Shirley Fry (USA)	Beryl Bartlett (RSA) Barbara Scofield (USA)	10-8	6-3	
1952	Doris Hart (USA) Shirley Fry (USA)	Hazel Redick-Smith (RSA) Julie Wipplinger (RSA)	7-5	6-1	
1953	Doris Hart (USA) Shirley Fry (USA)	Maureen Connolly (USA) Julia Sampson (USA)	6-4	6-3	
1954	Maureen Connolly (USA) Nell Hall Hopman (AUS)	Maude Galtier (FRA) Suzanne Schmitt (FRA)	7-5	4-6	6-0
1955	Beverly Baker Fleitz (USA) Darlene Hard (USA)	Shirley Bloomer (GBR) Pat Ward (GBR)	7-5	6-8	13-11
1956	Angela Buxton (GBR) Althea Gibson (USA)	Darlene Hard (USA) Dorothy Head Knode (USA)	6-8	8-6	6-1
1957	Shirley Bloomer (GBR) Darlene Hard (USA)	Yola Ramirez (MEX) Rosie Reyes (MEX)	7-5	4-6	7-5
1958	Rosie Reyes (MEX) Yola Ramirez (MEX)	Mary Bevis Hawton (AUS) Thelma Coyne Long (AUS)	6-4	7-5	
1959	Sandra Reynolds Price (RSA) Renee Schuurman (RSA)	Yola Ramirez (MEX) Rosie Reyes (MEX)	2-6	6-0	6-1
1960	Maria Bueno (BRA) Darlene Hard (USA)	Pat Ward Hales (GBR) Ann Haydon (GBR)	6-2	7-5	
1961	Sandra Reynolds (RSA) Renee Schuurman (RSA)	Maria Bueno (BRA) Darlene Hard (USA)	(walkover)		
1962	Sandra Reynolds Price (RSA) Renee Schuurman (RSA)	Justina Bricka (USA) Margaret Smith (AUS)	6-4	6-4	
1963	Ann Haydon Jones (GBR) Renee Schuurman (RSA)	Robyn Ebbern (AUS) Margaret Smith (AUS)	7-5	6-4	
1964	Margaret Smith (AUS) Lesley Turner (AUS)	Norma Baylon (ARG) Helga Schultze (GER)	6-3	6-1	
1965	Margaret Smith (AUS) Lesley Turner (AUS)	Francoise Durr (FRA) Janine Lieffrig (RSA)	6-3	6-1	
1966	Margaret Smith (AUS) Judy Tegart (AUS)	Jill Blackman (AUS) Fay Toyne (AUS)	4-6	6-1	6-1
1967	Francoise Durr (FRA) Gail Sherriff (FRA)	Annette Van Zyl (RSA) Pat Walkden (RSA)	6-2	6-2	
1968	Francoise Durr (FRA) Ann Haydon Jones (GBR)	Rosie Casals (USA) Bille Jean King (USA)	7-5	4-6	6-4
1969	Francoise Durr (FRA) Ann Haydon Jones (GBR)	Margaret Smith (AUS) Nancy Richey (AUS)	6-0	4-6	7-5
1970	Gail Sherriff Chanfreau (FRA) Francoise Durr (FRA)	Rosie Casals (USA) Bille Jean King (USA)	6-1	3-6	6-3
1971	Gail Sherriff Chanfreau (FRA) Francoise Durr (FRA)	Helen Gourlay (AUS) Kerry Harris (AUS)	6-4	6-1	
1972	Billie Jean King (USA) Betty Stove (NED)	Winnie Shaw (GBR) Christine Truman Janes (GBR)	6-1	6-2	
1973	Margaret Smith Court (AUS) Virginia Wade (GBR)	Francoise Durr (FRA) Betty Stove (NED)	6-2	6-3	
1974	Chris Evert (USA) Olga Morozova (USSR)	Gail Sherriff Chanfreau (FRA) Katja Ebbinghaus (GER)	6-4	2-6	6-1
1975	Chris Evert (USA) Martina Navratilova (CZE)	Julie Anthony (USA) Olga Morozova (USSR)	6-3	6-2	
1976	Florella Bonicelli (URU) Gail Sherriff Chanfreau (FRA)	Kathy Harter (USA) Helga Niessen-Masthoff (GER)	6-4	1-6	6-3
1977	Regina Marsikova (CZE) Pam Teeguarden (USA)	Rayni Fox (USA) Helen Gourlay (AUS)	5-7	6-4	6-2
1978	Mima Jausovec (YUG) Virginia Ruzici (ROU)	Lesley Turner Bowrey (AUS) Gail Sherriff Lovera (FRA)	5-7	6-4	8-6
1979	Betty Stove (NED) Wendy Turnbull (AUS)	Francoise Durr (FRA) Virginia Wade (GBR)	3-6	7-5	6-4
1980	Kathy Jordan (USA) Anne Smith (USA)	Ivanna Madruga (ARG) Adriana Villagran (ARG)	6-1	6-0	
1981	Rosalyn Fairbank (RSA) Tayna Harford (RSA)	Candy Reynolds (USA) Paula Smith (USA)	6-1	6-3	
1982	Martina Navratilova (USA) Anne Smith (USA)	Rosie Casals (USA) Wendy Turnbull (AUS)	6-3	6-4	

Year	Winner	Defeated	S1	S2	S3
1983 Rosalyn Fairbank (RSA) Candy Reynolds (USA)	Kathy Jordan (USA) Anne Smith (USA)	5-7	7-5	6-2
1984 Martina Navratilova (USA) Pam Teeguarden (USA)	Claudia Kohde Kilsch (GER) Hana Mandlikova (CZE)	5-7	6-3	6-2
1985 Martina Navratilova (USA) Pam Shriver (USA)	Claudia Kohde Kilsch (GER) Helena Sukova (CZE)	4-6	6-2	6-2
1986 Martina Navratilova (USA) Andrea Temesvari (HUN)	Steffi Graf (GER) Gabriela Sabatini (ARG)	6-1	6-2	
1987 Martina Navratilova (USA) Pam Shriver (USA)	Steffi Graf (GER) Gabriela Sabatini (ARG)	6-2	6-1	
1988 Martina Navratilova (USA) Pam Shriver (USA)	Claudia Kohde Kilsch (GER) Helena Sukova (CZE)	6-2	7-5	
1989 Larisa Savchenko (USSR) Natalia Zvereva (USSR)	Steffi Graf (GER) Gabriela Sabatini (ARG)	6-4	6-4	
1990 Jana Novotna (CZE) Helena Sukova (CZE)	Larisa Savchenko (USSR) Natalia Zvereva (USSR)	6-4	7-5	
1991 Gigi Fernandez (USA) Jana Novotna (CZE)	Larisa Savchenko (USSR) Natalia Zvereva (USSR)	6-4	6-0	
1992 Gigi Fernandez (USA) Natalia Zvereva (CIS)	Conchita Martiez (ESP) Arantxa Sanchez Vicario (ESP)	6-3	6-2	
1993 Gigi Fernandez (USA) Natalia Zvereva (BLR)	Larisa Savchenko Neiland (LAT) Jana Novotna (CZE)	6-3	7-5	
1994 Gigi Fernandez (USA) Natalia Zvereva (BLR)	Lindsay Davenport (USA) Lisa Raymond (USA)	6-2	6-2	
1995 Gigi Fernandez (USA) Natalia Zvereva (BLR)	Jana Novotna (CZE) Arantxa Sanchez Vicario (ESP)	6-7(6)	6-4	7-5
1996 Lindsay Davenport (USA) Mary Joe Fernandez (USA)	Gigi Fernandez (USA) Natalia Zvereva (BLR)	6-2	6-1	
1997 Gigi Fernandez (USA) Natalia Zvereva (BLR)	Mary Joe Fernandez (USA) Lisa Raymond (USA)	6-2	6-3	
1998 Martina Hingis (SUI) Jana Novatna (CZE)	Lindsay Davenport (USA) Natalia Zvereva (BLR)	6-1	7-6(4)	
1999 Venus Williams (USA) Serena Williams (USA)	Martina Hingis (SUI) Anna Kournikova (RUS)	6-3	6-7(2)	8-6
2000 Martina Hingis (SUI) Mary Pierce (FRA)	Virginia Ruano Pascual (ESP) Paola Suarez (ARG)	6-2	6-4	
2001 Virginia Ruano Pascual (ESP) Paola Suarez (ARG)	Jelena Dokic (YUG) Conchita Martinez (ESP)	6-2	6-1	
2002 Virginia Ruano Pascual (ESP) Paola Suarez (ARG)	Lisa Raymond (USA) Rennae Stubbs (AUS)	6-4	6-2	
2003 Kim Clijsters (BEL) Ai Sugiyama (JPN)	Virginia Ruano Pascual (ESP) Paola Suarez (ARG)	6-7(5)	6-2	9-7
2004 Virginia Ruano Pascual (ESP) Paola Suarez (ARG)	Svetlana Kuznetsova (RUS) Elena Likhovtseva (RUS)	6-0	6-3	
2005 Virginia Ruano Pascual (ESP) Paola Suarez (ARG)	Cara Black (ZIM) Liezel Huber (RSA)	4-6	6-3	6-3
2006 Lisa Raymond (USA) Samantha Stosur (AUS)	Daniela Hantuchova (SVK) Ai Sugiyama (JPN)	6-3	6-2	
2007 Alicia Molik (AUS) Mara Santangelo (ITA)	Katarina Srebotnik (SLO) Ai Sugiyama (JPN)	7-6(5)	6-4	
2008 Virginia Ruano Pascual (ESP) Anabel Medina Garrigues (ESP)	Casey Dellacqua (AUS) Francesca Schiavone (ITA)	2-6	7-5	6-4
2009 Anabel Garrigues (ESP) Virginia Ruano Pascual (ESP)	Victoria Azarenka (BLR) Elena Vesnina (RUS)	6-1	6-1	

Mixed Doubles

Year	Winner	Defeated	S1	S2	S3
1925 Suzanne Lenglen (FRA) Jacques Brugnon (FRA)	Didi Vlasto (FRA) Henri Cochet (FRA)	6-2	6-2	
1926 Suzanne Lenglen (FRA) Jacques Brugnon (FRA)	Suzanne LeBesnerais (FRA) Jean Borotra (FRA)	6-4	6-3	
1927 Marg. Broquedis Bordes (FRA) Jean Borotra (FRA)	Lili de Alvarez (ESP) Bill Tilden (USA)	6-4	2-6	6-2
1928 Eileen Bennett (GBR) Henri Cochet (FRA)	Helen Wills (USA) Frank Hunter (USA)	3-6	6-3	6-3
1929 Eileen Bennett (GBR) Henri Cochet (FRA)	Helen Wills (USA) Frank Hunter (USA)	6-3	6-2	
1930 Cilly Aussem (GER) Bill Tilden (USA)	Eileen Bennett Whittingstall (GBR) Henri Cochet (FRA)	6-4	6-4	
1931 Betty Nuthall (GBR) Pat Spence (RSA)	Dorothy Shepherd Barron (GBR) Bunny Austin (GBR)	6-3	5-7	6-3
1932 Betty Nuthall (GBR) Fred Perry (GBR)	Helen Wills Moody (USA) Sidney Wood (USA)	6-4	6-2	
1933 Margaret Scriven (GBR) Jack Crawford (AUS)	Betty Nuthall (GBR) Fred Perry (GBR)	6-2	6-3	
1934 Colette Rosambert (FRA) Jean Borotra (FRA)	Elizabeth Ryan (USA) Adrian Quist (AUS)	6-2	6-4	
1935 Lolette Payot (FRA) Marcel Bernard (FRA)	Sylvie Jung Henrotin (FRA) Martin Legeay (FRA)	4-6	6-2	6-4
1936 Billie Yorke (GBR) Marcel Bernard (FRA)	Sylvie Jung Henrotin (FRA) Martin Legeay (FRA)	7-5	6-8	6-3
1937 Simone Passemard Mathieu (FRA) Yvon Petra (FRA)	Marie Luise Horn (GER) Roland Jarnu (FRA)	7-5	7-5	
1938 Simone Passemard Mathieu (FRA) Dragutin Mitic (YUG)	Nancye Wynne (AUS) Christian Boussus (FRA)	2-6	6-3	6-4
1939 Sarah Palfrey Cooke (USA) Elwood Cooke (USA)	Simone Passemard Mathieu (FRA) Franjo Kukuljevic (YUG)	4-6	6-1	7-5
1940-45 Not held—WWII				
1946 Pauline Betz (USA) Budge Patty (USA)	Dorothy Bundy (USA) Tom Brown (USA)	7-5	9-7	
1947 Sheila Piercey Summers (RSA) Eric Sturgess (RSA)	Jadwiga Jedrzejowska (POL) Christian Caralulis (ROU)	6-0	6-0	
1948 Pat Canning Todd (USA) Jaroslav Drobny (CZE)	Doris Hart (USA) Frank Sedgman (AUS)	6-3	3-6	6-3
1949 Sheila Piercey Summers (RSA) Eric Sturgess (RSA)	Jean Quertier (GBR) Gerry Oakley (GBR)	6-1	6-1	
1950 Barbara Scofield (USA Enrique Morea (ARG)	Pat Canning Todd (USA) Bill Talbert (USA)	(walkover)		
1951 Doris Hart (USA) Frank Sedgman (AUS)	Thelma Coyne Long (AUS) Merv Rose (AUS)	7-5	6-2	
1952 Doris Hart (USA) Frank Sedgman (AUS)	Shirley Fry (USA) Eric Sturgess (RSA)	6-8	6-3	6-3
1953 Doris Hart (USA) Vic Seixas (USA)	Maureen Connolly (USA) Merv Rose (AUS)	4-6	6-4	6-0
1954 Maureen Connolly (USA) Lew Hoad (AUS)	Jacqueline Patorni (AUS) Rex Hartwig (AUS)	6-4	6-3	
1955 Darleen Hard (USA) Gordon Forbes (RSA)	Jenny Staley (AUS) Luis Ayala (CHI)	5-7	6-1	6-2

Year	Winner	Defeated	S1	S2	S3
1956	Thelma Coyne Long (AUS) Luis Ayala (CHI)	Doris Hart (USA) Bob Howe (AUS)	4-6	6-4	6-1
1957	Vera Puzejova (CZE) Jiri Javorsky (CZE)	Edda Buding (GER) Luis Ayala (CHI)	6-3	6-4	
1958	Shirley Bloomer (GBR) Nicola Pietrangeli (ITA)	Lorraine Coghlan (AUS) Bob Howe (AUS)	8-6	6-2	
1959	Yola Ramirez (MEX) Billy Knight (GBR)	Renee Schuurman (RSA) Rod Laver (AUS)	6-4	6-4	
1960	Maria Bueno (BRA) Bob Howe (AUS)	Ann Haydon (GBR) Roy Emerson (AUS)	1-6	6-1	6-2
1961	Darlene Hard (USA) Rod Laver (AUS)	Vera Puzejova (CZE) Jiri Javorsky (CZE)	6-0	2-6	6-3
1962	Renee Schuurman (RSA) Bob Howe (AUS)	Lesley Turner (AUS) Fred Stolle (AUS)	3-6	6-4	6-4
1963	Margaret Smith (AUS) Ken Fletcher (AUS)	Lesley Turner (AUS) Fred Stolle (AUS)	6-1	6-2	
1964	Margaret Smith (AUS) Ken Fletcher (AUS)	Lesley Turner (AUS) Fred Stolle (AUS)	6-3	4-6	8-6
1965	Margaret Smith (AUS) Ken Fletcher (AUS)	Maria Bueno (BRA) John Newcombe (AUS)	6-4	6-4	
1966	Annette Van Zyl (RSA) Frew McMillan (RSA)	Ann Haydon Jones (GBR) Clark Graebner (USA)	1-6	6-3	6-2
1967	Bille Jean King (USA) Owen Davidson (AUS)	Ann Haydon Jones (GBR) Ion Tiriac (ROU)	6-3	6-1	
1968	Francoise Durr (FRA) Jean Claude Barclay (FRA)	Billie Jean King (USA) Owen Davidson (AUS)	6-1	6-4	
1969	Margaret Smith Court (AUS) Marty Riessen (USA)	Francoise Durr (FRA) Jean Claude Barclay (FRA)	6-3	6-2	
1970	Billie Jean King (USA) Bob Hewitt (RSA)	Francoise Durr (FRA) Jean Claude Barclay (FRA)	3-6	6-4	6-2
1971	Francoise Durr (FRA) Jean Claude Barclay (FRA)	Winnie Shaw (GBR) Tomas Lejus (USSR)	6-2	6-4	
1972	Evonne Goolagong (AUS) Kim Warwick (AUS)	Francoise Durr (FRA) Jean Claude Barclay (FRA)	6-2	6-4	
1973	Francoise Durr (FRA) Jean Claude Barclay (FRA)	Betty Stove (NED) Patrice Dominguez (FRA)	6-1	6-4	
1974	Martina Novratilova (CZE) Ivan Molina (COL)	Rosie Reyes Darmon (MEX) Marcelo Lara (MEX)	6-3	6-3	
1975	Fiorella Bonicelli (URU) Thomaz Koch (BRA)	Pam Teeguarden (USA) Jaime Fillol (CHI)	6-4	7-6	
1976	Ilana Kloss (RSA) Kim Warwick (AUS)	Delina Boshoff (RSA) Colin Dowdeswell (GBR)	5-7	7-6	6-2
1977	Mary Carillo (USA) John McEnroe (USA)	Florento Mihai (ROU) Ivan Molina (COL)	7-6	6-3	
1978	Renata Tomanova (CZE) Pavel Slozil (CZE)	Virginia Ruzici (ROU) Patrice Dominguez (FRA)	7-6	(retired)	
1979	Wendy Turnbull (AUS) Bob Hewitt (RSA)	Virginia Ruzici (ROU) Ion Tiriac (ROU)	6-3	2-6	6-3
1980	Anne Smith (USA) Billy Martin (USA)	Renata Tomanova (CZE) Stanislav Birner (CZE)	2-6	6-4	8-6
1981	Andrea Jaeger (USA) Jimmy Arias (USA)	Betty Stove (NED) Fred McNair (USA)	7-6	6-4	
1982	Wendy Turnbull (AUS) John Lloyd (GBR)	Claudia Monteiro (BRA) Cassio Motta (BRA)	6-2	7-6	
1983	Barbara Jordan (USA) Eliot Teltscher (USA)	Leslie Allen (USA) Charles Strode (USA)	6-2	6-3	
1984	Anne Smith (USA) Dick Stockton (USA)	Anne Minter (AUS) Laurie Warder (AUS)	6-2	6-4	
1985	Martina Navratilova (USA) Heinz Gunthardt (SUI)	Paula Smith (USA) Francisco Gonzalez (PAR)	2-6	6-3	6-2
1986	Kathy Jordan (USA) Ken Flach (USA)	Rosalyn Fairbank (RSA) Mark Edmondson (AUS)	3-6	7-6(3)	6-3
1987	Pam Shriver (USA) Emilio Sanchez (ESP)	Lori McNeil (USA) Sherwood Stewart (USA)	6-3	7-6(4)	
1988	Lori McNeil (USA) Jorge Lozano (MEX)	Brenda Schultz (NED) Michiel Schapers (NED)	7-5	6-2	
1989	Manon Bollegraf (NED) Tom Nijssen (NED)	Arantxa Sanchez Vicario (ESP) Horacio de la Pena (ARG)	6-3	6-7(3)	6-2
1990	Arantxa Sanchez Vicario (ESP) Jorge Lozano (MEX)	Nicole Provis (AUS) Danie Visser (RSA)	7-6(5)	7-6(8)	
1991	Helena Sukova (CZE) Cyril Suk (CZE)	Caroline Vis (NED) Paul Haarhuis (NED)	3-6	6-4	6-1
1992	Arantxa Sanchez Vicario (ESP) Todd Woodbridge (AUS)	Lori McNeil (USA) Bryan Shelton (USA)	6-2	6-3	
1993	Eugenia Maniokova (RUS) Andrei Olhovskiy (RUS)	Elna Reinach (RSA) Danie Visser (RSA)	6-2	4-6	6-4
1994	Kristie Boogert (NED) Menno Oosting (NED)	Larisa Savchenko Neiland (LAT) Andrei Olhovskiy (RUS)	7-5	3-6	7-5
1995	Larisa Savchenko Neiland (LAT) Mark Woodforde (AUS)	Jill Hetherington (CAN) John-Laffnie de Jager (RSA)	7-6(8)	7-6(4)	
1996	Patricia Tarabini (ARG) Javier Frana (ARG)	Nicole Arendt (USA) Luke Jensen (USA)	6-2	6-2	
1997	Rika Hiraki (JPN) Mahesh Bhupathi (IND)	Lisa Raymond (USA) Patrick Galbraith (USA)	6-4	6-1	
1998	Venus Williams (USA) Justin Gimelstob (USA)	Serena Williams (USA) Luis Lobo (ARG)	6-4	6-4	
1999	Katarina Srebotnik (SLO) Piet Norval (RSA)	Larisa Savchenko Neiland (LAT) Rick Leach (USA)	6-3	3-6	6-3
2000	Mariaan de Swardt (RSA) David Adams (RSA)	Rennae Stubbs (AUS) Todd Woodbridge (AUS)	6-3	3-6	6-3
2001	Virginia Ruano Pascual (ESP) Tomas Carbonell (ESP)	Paola Suarez (ARG) Jaime Oncins (BRA)	7-5	6-3	
2002	Cara Black (ZIM) Wayne Black (ZIM)	Elena Bovina (RUS) Mark Knowles (BAH)	6-3	6-3	
2003	Lisa Raymond (USA) Mike Bryan (USA)	Elena Likhovtseva (RUS) Mahesh Bhupathi (IND)	6-3	6-4	
2004	Tatiana Golovin (FRA) Richard Gasquet (FRA)	Cara Black (ZIM) Wayne Black (ZIM)	6-3	6-4	
2005	Daniela Hantuchova (SVK) Fabrice Santoro (FRA)	Martina Navratilova (USA) Leander Paes (IND)	3-6	6-3	6-2
2006	Katarina Srebotnik (SLO) Nenad Zimonjic (SRB)	Elena Likhovtseva (RUS) Daniel Nestor (CAN)	6-3	6-4	
2007	Nathalie Dechy (FRA) Andy Ram (ISR)	Katarina Srebotnik (SLO) Nenad Zimonjic (SRB)	7-5	6-3	
2008	Bob Bryan (USA) Victoria Azarenka (BLR)	Nenad Zimonjic (SRB) Katarina Srebotnik (SLO)	6-2	7-6 (4)	
2009	Liezel Huber (USA) Bob Bryan (USA)	Vania King (USA) Marcelo Melo (BRA)	5-7	7-5	(10-7)

French Championships – Records

MOST TITLES

Men

9	Henri Cochet	(1926-1932)	4 singles, 3 doubles, 2 mixed
8	Jean Borotra	(1925-1936)	1singles, 5 doubles, 2 mixed
	Roy Emerson	(1960-1967)	2 singles, 6 doubles, 0 mixed
7	Jacques Brugnon	(1925-1934)	0 singles, 5 doubles, 2 mixed
6	Bjorn Borg	(1974-1981)	6 singles, 0 doubles, 0 mixed
5	Marcel Bernard	(1935-1946)	1 singes. 2 doubles, 2 mixed
	René Lacoste	(1925-1929)	3 singles. 2 doubles, 0 mixed
	Tony Trabert	(1950-1955)	2 singles, 3 doubles, 0 mixed

Women

13	Margaret Smith Court	(1962-1973)	5 singles, 4 doubles, 4 mixed
11	Martina Navratilova	(1974-88)	2 singles, 7 doubles, 2 mixed
10	Doris Hart	(1948-1955)	2 singles, 5 doubles, 3 mixed
	Simone Passemard Mathieu		
		(1933-1939)	2 singles, 6 doubles, 2 mixed
9	Chris Evert	(1974-1986)	7 singles, 2 doubles, 0 mixed
	Francoise Durr	(1967-1973)	1 singles, 5 doubles, 3 mixed

MOST SINGLES TITLES

Men

6	Bjorn Borg	(1974, 1975, 1978-1981)
4	Henri Cochet	(1926, 1928, 1930, 1932)
	Rafael Nadal	(2005-2008)
3	Gustavo Kuerten	(1997, 2000-2001)
	Ivan Lendl	(1984, 1986-1987)
	Rene Lacoste	(1925, 1927, 1929)
	Mats Wilander	(1982, 1985, 1988)

Women

7	Chris Evert	(1974-1975, 1979-1980, 1983, 1985-1986)
6	Steffi Graf	(1987-1988, 1993, 1995-1996,1999)
5	Margaret Smith Court	(1962, 1964, 1969-1970,1973)
4	Helen Wills Moody	(1928-1930, 1932)
3	Arantxa Sanchez Vicario	(1989, 1994, 1998)
	Hilde Krahwinkel Sperling	(1935-1937)
	Monica Seles	(1990-1992)

MOST SINGLES FINAL APPEARANCES

Men

6	Bjorn Borg	(1974-1975, 1978-1981)
5	Rene Lacoste	(1925-1927, 1928-1929)
	Mats Wilander	(1982-1983, 1985, 1987-1988)
	Ivan Lendl	(1981, 1984-1987)
	Henri Cochet	(1926, 1928, 1930, 1932-1933)
	Jaroslav Drobny	(1946, 1948, 1950-1952)
4	Nicola Pietrangeli	(1959-1961, 1964)
	Guillermo Vilas	(1975, 1977-78, 1982)
	Rafael Nadal	(2005-2008)

MOST TITLES (continued)

Women

9	Chris Evert	(1973-1975, 1979-1980, 1983-1986)
	Steffi Graf	(1987-1990, 1992, 1993, 1995-1996, 1999)
8	Simone Passemard Mathieu	(1929, 1932, 1933, 1935-1939)
6	Arantxa Sanchez Vicario	(1989, 1991, 1994-1996, 1998)
	Margaret Smith Court	(1962, 1964-1965 1969-1970, 1973)
	Martina Navratilova	(1975, 1983-1987)
5	Ann Haydon	(1961, 1963, 1966, 1968-69)
	Doris Hart	(1947, 1950-1953)

MOST SINGLES FINAL LOSSES

Men

3	Jaroslav Drobny	(1946, 1948, 1950)
	Guillermo Vilas	(1975, 1978,1982)
	Roger Federer	(2006, 2007, 2008)
2	Alex Corretja	(1998, 2001)
	Andre Agassi	(1990-1991)
	Bill Tilden	(1927, 1930)
	Eric Sturgess	(1947, 1951)
	Ivan Lendl	(1925, 1929)
	Luis Ayala	(1958, 1960)
	Mats Wilander	(1983, 1987)
	Nicola Pietrangeli	(1961, 1964)
	Tony Roche	(1965, 1967)
	Rene Lacoste	(1926, 1928)
	Sven Davidson	(1955, 1956)

Women

6	Simone Passemard Mathieu	(1929-1937)
4	Martina Navratilova	(1975, 1985-1987)
3	Ann Haydon	(1963, 1966, 1969)
	Arantxa Sanchez Vicario	(1991, 1995,1996)
	Doris Hart	(1947, 1951,1953)
	Steffi Graf	(1989, 1990, 1992)

GREATEST NUMBER OF YEARS BETWEEN FIRST AND LAST SINGLES TITLES

Men

15	Ken Rosewall	(1953-first title, 1968-last title)

Women

12	Chris Evert	(1974-first title, 1986-last title)
	Steffi Graf	(1987-first title, 1999-last title)

MOST SINGLES MATCHES PLAYED – CAREER

Men

73	Guillermo Vilas	(1972-1989)
67	Nicola Pietrangeli	(1956-1973)
67	Andre Agassi	(1987-2005)
65	Ivan Lendl	(1978-1994)

Women

94	Steffi Graf	(1983-1999)
85	Arantxa Sanchez Vicario	(1987-2002)
80	Conchita Martinez	(1988-2005)
78	Chris Evert	(1973-1988)
62	Monica Seles	(1989-2003)
62	Martina Navratilova	(1973-2004)

MOST SINGLES MATCHES WON – CAREER

Men

56	Guillermo Vilas	(1972-1989)
53	Ivan Lendl	(1978-1994)
51	Andre Agassi	(1987-2005)

Women

84	Steffi Graf	(1983-1999)
72	Arantxa Sanchez Vicario	(1987-2002)
72	Chris Evert	(1973-1988)

MOST SINGLES MATCHES WON CONSECUTIVELY

Men

31	Rafael Nadal	(2005-2009)
28	Bjorn Borg	(1978-81)
20	Jim Courier	(1991-03)

Women

29	Chris Evert	(1974-75, 1979-81)
25	Monica Seles	(1990-92, 1996)

MOST SETS WON SUCCESSIVELY

Men

41	Bjorn Borg	(1979-1981)

Women

40	Helen Wills	(1926, 1928-1930, 1932)

BEST SINGLES MATCH WINNING PERCENTAGE

Men

.968	Rafael Nadal	2005-2009 (31-1)
.961	Bjorn Borg	1973-76 (49-2)

Women

1.000	Helen Wills Moody	1926-32 (20-0)
.923	Chris Evert	1973-88 (72-6)

TRIPLES

(Winner of all three events in one year)

Men

* Never been accomplished

Women

1925	Suzanne Lenglen	(WD-Didi Vlasto; MXD-Jacques Brugnon)
1926	Suzanne Lenglen	(WD-Didi Vlasto; MXD-Jacques Brugnon)
1938	Simone Passemard Mathieu	
		(WD-Billie Yorke; MXD-Dragutin Mitic)
1952	Doris Hart	(WD-Shirley Fry; MXD-Frank Sedgmen)
1954	Maureen Connolly	(WD-Nell Hall Hopman; MXD-Lew Hoad)
1964	Margaret Smith	(WD-Lesley Turner, MXD-Ken Fletcher)

MOST DOUBLES TITLES – TEAM

Men

3	Henri Cochet / Jacques Brugnon	(1927-1932)
2	Brian Gottfried / Raul Ramirez	(1975-1977)
	Leander Paes / Mahesh Bhupathi	(1999-2001)
	Vic Seixas / Tony Trabert	(1954-1955)
	Jean Borotra / Jacques Brugnon	(1928-1934)
	Yevgeny Kafelnikov / Daniel Vacek	(1996-1997)
	Jean Borotra / Rene Lacoste	(1925-1929)
	Ken McGregor / Frank Sedgman	(1951-1952)
	Neale Fraser / Roy Emerson	(19601962)
	Jacco Eltingh / Paul Haarhuis	(1995-1996)
	John Newcombe / Tony Roche	(1967-1969)

Women

5	Gigi Fernandez / Natalia Zvereva	(1992-1997)
4	Doris Hart / Shirley Fry	(1950-1953)
	Martina Navratilova / Pam Shriver	(1984-1988)
3	Renee Schuurman / Sandra Reynolds	(1959-1962)
	Louise Brough / Margaret Osborne duPont	(1946-1949)
	Simone Passemard Mathieu / Billie Yorke	(1936-1938)

MOST DOUBLES TITLES – INDIVIDUAL

Men

6	Roy Emerson	(1960-1965)
5	Jacques Brugnon	(1927-1934)
	Jean Borotra	(1925-1936)
3	Paul Haarhuis	(1995-2002)
	John Newcombe	(1967-1973)
	Neale Fraser	(1958-1962)
	Henri Cochet	(1927-1933)
	Tony Trabert	(1950-1955)
	Yevgeny Kafelnikov	(1996-2002)
	Anders Jarryd	(1983-1991)

Women

7	Martina Navratilova	(1975-1988)
6	Simone Passemard Mathieu	(1933-1939)
	Natalia Zvereva	(1989-1997)
	Gigi Fernandez	(1991-1997)
5	Doris Hart	(1948-1953)
	Francoise Durr	(1967-1971)
	Virginia Ruano-Pascual	(2001-2008)

MOST FINAL-ROUND DOUBLES APPEARANCES – TEAM

Men

6	Henri Cochet / Jacques Brugnon	(1925-1932)
4	Brian Gottfried / Raul Ramirez	(1975-1980)
3	Neale Fraser / Roy Emerson	(1959-1962)
	Jean Borotra / Jacques Brugnon	(1928-1939)
	John Newcombe / Tony Roche	(1964-1969)
	Jean Borotra / Rene Lacoste	(1925-1929)
	Roy Emerson / Rod Laver	(1961-1969)

Women

6	Gigi Fernandez / Natalia Zvereva	(1992-1997)
4	Martina Navratilova / Pam Shriver	(1984-1988)
	Doris Hart / Shirley Fry	(1950-1953)
	Louise Brough / Margaret Osborne duPont	(1946-1950)

MOST FINAL-ROUND DOUBLES APPEARANCES – INDIVIDUAL

Men

10	Roy Emerson	(1959-1969)
9	Jacques Brugnon	(1925-1939)
7	Jean Borotra	(1925-1939)
	Henri Cochet	(1925-1932)
5	Anders Jarryd	(1983-1991)

Women

10	Natalia Zvereva	(1989-1998)
8	Francoise Durr	(1965-1979)
7	Martina Navratilova	(1975-1988)
	Doris Hart	(1946-1953)
	Gigi Fernandez	(1991-1997)
	Margaret Smith Court	(1962-1973)
	Simone Passemard Mathieu	(1930-1939)
	Virginia Ruano Pascual	(2000-2008)

MOST FINAL LOSSES DOUBLES – INDIVIDUAL

Men

4	Henri Cochet	(1925-1929)
	Roy Emerson	(1959-1969)
	Jacques Brugnon	(1925-1939)

Women

4	Natalia Zvereva	(1990-1998)
3	Francoise Durr	(1966-1979)
	Gabriela Sabatini	(1986-1989)
	Margaret Smith Court	(1962-1969)
	Lisa Raymond	(1994-2002)
	Rosie Casals	(1968-1982)
	Claudia Kohde Kilsch	(1984-1986)
	Steffi Graf	(1986-1989)

MOST MIXED DOUBLES TITLES

Team

3	Francoise Durr / Jean Claude Barclay	(1968-1973)
	Margaret Smith Court / Ken Fletcher	(1963-1965)
2	Suzanne Lenglen / Jacques Brugnon	(1925-1926)
	Doris Hart / Frank Sedgman	(1951-1952)
	Sheila Piercey Summers / Eric Sturgess	(1947-1949)
	Eileen Bennett / Henri Cochet	(1928-1929)

Men

3	Jean Claude Barclay	(1968-1973)
	Ken Fletcher	(1963-1965)

Women

4	Margaret Smith Court	(1963-1969)
3	Doris Hart	(1951-1953)
	Francoise Durr	(1968-1973)

MOST MIXED DOUBLES FINAL APPEARANCES

Team

6	Francoise Durr / Jean Claude Barclay	(1968-1973)
3	Margaret Smith Court / Ken Fletcher	(1963-1965)
	Doris Hart / Frank Sedgman	(1948-1952)
	Lesley Turner / Fred Stolle	(1962-1964)

Men

6	Jean Claude Barclay	(1968-1973)
4	Henri Cochet	(1925-1930)
	Bob Howe	(1956-1962)

Women

6	Doris Hart	(1968-1973)
	Francoise Durr	(1968-1973)
4	Margaret Smith Court	(1963-1969)

YOUNGEST SINGLES CHAMPION

Men

Michael Chang—17 years, 3 months (1989)
Mats Wilander—17 years, 9 months (1982)
Bjorn Borg—18 years, two weeks (1974)
Ken Rosewall—18 years, 7 months (1953)
Rafael Nadal—19 years, 2 days (2005)

Women

Monica Seles—16 years, 6 months (1990)
Arantxa Sanchez—17 years, 5 months (1989)
Steffi Graf—17 years, 11 months (1987)

OLDEST SINGLES CHAMPION

Men

Andres Gimeno—34 years, 10 months (1972)
Ken Rosewall—33 years, 7 months (1968)
Frank Parker—33 years, 4 months (1949)

Women

Suzi Kormoczy—33 years (1958)
Nelly Adamson-Landry—31 years, 6 months (1948)
Chris Evert—31 years, 5 months (1986)

OLDEST DOUBLES CHAMPION

Men

Jacques Brugnon—39 years (1934)

Women

Nelly Adamson Landry—42 years, 3 months (1934)

YOUNGEST DOUBLES CHAMPION

Men

Lew Hoad—18 years, 7 months (1953)

Women

Martina Hingis—17 years, 4 months (1998)

OLDEST MIXED DOUBLES CHAMPION

Men

Bob Hewitt —39 years, 5 months (1979)

Women

Thelma Long Coyne—38 years (1956)

YOUNGEST MIXED DOUBLES CHAMPION

Men

Jimmy Arias —16 years, 8 months (1981)

Women

Andrea Jaeger —15 years, 11 months (1981)

LONGEST MATCHES – TOTAL GAMES

Men's Singles

83 games   Bob Mark d. Anton Jansco – 13-15, 6-3, 6-8, 8-6, 10-8, 1st rd., 1957

76 games   Eric Sturgess d. Ken McGregor, 10-8, 7-9, 8-6, 5-7, 9-7, semis, 1951

Since the introduction of the tie-breaker (1973)

71 games   Fabrice Santoro d. Arnaud Clement, 6-4, 6-3, 6-7 (5), 3-6, 16-14, 1st rd, 2004 (6 hrs, 33 min)

71 games   Ronald Agenor d. David Prinosil, 6-7 (4-7), 6-7 (2-7), 6-3, 6-4, 14-12, 2nd rd., 1994

Women's Singles

56 games   Kerry Melville Reid d. Pam Teeguarden, 9-7, 4-6, 16-14, 3rd rd., 1972

Since the introduction of the tie-breaker

46 games   Linda Wild d. Laura Gildemeister 7-6 (9-7), 6-7 (7-9), 11-9, 2nd rd., 1991

Men's Doubles

81 games   Gordon Forbes / Russell Seymour d. Merv Rose / George Worthington, 11-13, 6-1, 7-5, 4- 6, 15-13, 2nd rd.,1952

Women's Doubles

50 games   Beverly Baker Fleitz / Darlene Hard d. Shirley Bloomer Brasher / Pat Ward Hales, 7-5, 6-8, 13-11, final, 1955

Mixed Doubles

48 games   Rosie Reyes Darmon / Bob Howe d. Marina Tshuvirina / Teimuraz Kakulia, 5-7, 10-8, 10-8, 1st rd., 1972

48 games   Lucia Bassi / Francisco Contreras d. Edda Buding / Ingo Buding, 10-12, 9-7, 6-4, 2nd rd., 1960

LONGEST MATCHES – PLAYING TIME

Men's Singles

6 hours, 33 minutes   Fabrice Santoro d. Arnaud Clement, 6-4, 6-3, 6-7 (5), 3-6, 16-14, 1st rd, over two days, 2004 (all-time record in tennis)

5 hours, 31 minutes   Alex Corretja d. Hernan Gumy, 6-1, 5-7, 6-7 (4-7), 7-5, 9-7, QF, in one day, 1998

Women's Singles

4 hours, 7 minutes   Virginia Buisson d. Noelle van Lottum, 6-7 (3-7), 7-5, 6-2, 1st rd., 1996

3 hours, 55 minutes   Kerry Melville d. Pam Teeguarden, 9-7, 4-6, 16-14 1972, 3rd rd.

3 hours, 34 minutes   Mary Joe Fernandez d. Gabriela Sabatini 1-6, 7-6 (4), 10-8, QF, 1993

3 hours, 20 minutes   Karin Kschwendt d. Angelique Olivier 5-7, 6-4, 9-7, 1R, 1994

3 hours, 14 minutes   Justin Henin-Hardenne d. Svetlana Kuznetsova 7-6 (6), 4-6, 7-5, 4R, 2005 3 hours, 3 minutes Steffi Graf d. Arantxa Sanchez Vicario 6-3, 6-7 (4-7), 10-8, F, 1996

LONGEST SINGLES FINALS

Men—In games

1929   61 games – Rene Lacoste d. Bill Tilden 6-4, 4-6, 5-7, 6-3, 11-9

Since the introduction of the tie-breaker (1973)

1984   51 games – Ivan Lendl d. John McEnroe 3-6, 2-6, 6-4, 7-5, 7-5

Men—In Time

1982   4 hours, 42 minutes - Mats Wilander d. Guillermo Vilas 1-6, 7-6, 6-0, 6-4

Women—In Games

1996   40 games – Steffi Graf d. Arantxa Sanchez Vicario 6-3, 6-7, 10-8

1955   38 games – Angela Mortimer d. Dorothy Head Knode, 2-6, 7-5, 10-8

Women—In Time

1996   3 hours, 3 minutes – Steffi Graf d. Arantxa Sanchez Vicario, 6-3, 6-7 (4-7), 10-8

SHORTEST MEN'S SINGLES FINAL (GAMES)

1977   Guillermo Vilas d. Brian Gottfried, 6-0, 6-3, 6-0

SHORTEST WOMENS SINGLES FINAL (PLAYING TIME AND GAMES)

1988   Steffi Graf d. Natasha Zvereva, 6-0, 6-0, 32 minutes

LONGEST TIE-BREAKERS

Men's Singles

16-14   second set - Wayne Arthurs d. Andy Roddick, 4-6, 7-6 (16-14), 4-6, 7-5, 6-3, 1st rd., 2002

Women's Singles

16-14   first set - Nathalie Dechy d. Stephanie Foretz 6-7(14-16), 7-6(7-1), 6-1, 1st rd., 1999

EARLIEST ELIMINATION OF NO. 1 SEED

Men

1990   Sergi Bruguera (No. 46) d. 1st seed Stefan Edberg, 6-4, 6-2, 6-1, 1st rd.

Women

2004   Tatiana Garbin (No. 86) d. 1st seed and defending champion Justin Henin-Hardenne, 7-5, 6-4 in 2nd rd.

EARLIEST ELIMINATION OF DEFENDING CHAMPION

Men

1998   Gustavo Kuerten lost in the 2nd rd to qualifier Marat Safin, 3-6, 7-6 (5), 3-6, 6-1, 6-4

2000   Andre Agassi lost in the 2nd rd to Karol Kucera, 2-6, 7-5, 6-1, 6-0

2004   Juan Carlos Ferrero lost in the 2nd rd to Igor Andreev, 6-4, 6-2, 6-3

Women

2005   Maria Sanchez Lorenzo (No. 109) d. 5th seed and defending champion Anastasia Myskina, 6-4, 4-6, 6-0 in 1st rd.

OTHER BIG UPSETS

Men

1946   Marcel Bernard d. Jaroslav Drobny, 3-6,2-6,6-1, 6-4, 6-3, F, 1st unseeded champ

1979   Victor Pecci (No. 30) d. 6th seed Harold Solomon, 6-1, 6-4, 6-3, 4th rd.; d. 3rd seed Guillermo Vilas, 6-0, 6-2, 7-5, QF; d. 2nd seed Jimmy Connors, 7-5, 6-4, 5-7, 6-3, SF

1982   Mats Wilander (No. 30) d. 2nd seeded Ivan Lendl, 4-6, 7-5, 3-6, 6-4, 6-2, QF; d. 3rd seed Guillermo Vilas, 1-6, 7-6 (8-6), 6-0, 6-4, F, 2nd unseeded champ, following Bernard, 1946. Also 14th seed Jose Higueras d. 1st seed Jimmy Connors, 6-2, 6-2, 6-2, QF

1983   Wild card Christophe Roger-Vasselin (No. 230) d. 1st seed Jimmy Connors, 6-4, 6-4, 7-6 (7-5), QF

1989   15th seed Michael Chang d. 1st seed 3-time champ Ivan Lendl, 4-6, 4-6, 6-3, 6-3, 6-3, 4th rd., ending Lendl's 28-match win streak; d. 3rd seed Stefan Edberg, 6-1, 3-6, 4-6, 6-4, 6-2 in the F

1990   Sergi Bruguera (No. 46) d. 1st seed Stefan Edberg, 6-4, 6-2, 6-1, 1st rd. and Goran Ivanisevic (No. 51) d. 2nd seed Boris Becker, 5-7, 6-4, 7-5, 6-2, 1st round (same day, only time 1-2 seeds defeated 1st rd.)

1992   Jaime Oncins (72) d. Ivan Lendl (10), 3-6, 3-6, 6-3, 6-2, 8-6, 2nd rd.

1993   Wild card Stephane Huet (No. 297) d. 7th seed Ivan Lendl, 3-6, 7-5, 6-0, 7-6 (7-2), 1st rd., Huet's 1st match in a major

1996   Chris Woodruff (No. 72) d. 3rd seed Andre Agassi, 4-6, 6-4, 6-7 (7-9), 6-3, 6-2, 2nd rd.

1997   Gustavo Kuerten (No. 66), 3rd unseeded champ, d. three ex-champs: 5th seed Thomas Muster, 6-7 (3-7), 6-1, 6-3, 3-6, 6-4, 3rd rd.; 3rd seed Yevgeny Kafelnikov, 6-2, 5-7, 2-6, 6-0, 6-4, QF; 16th seed Sergi Bruguera, 6-3, 6-4, 6-2, F

1998   Qualifier Marat Safin (No. 118) d. Andre Agassi (No. 20), 5-7, 7-5, 6-2, 3-6, 6-2, 1st rd.; d. 8th seed defending champ Gustavo Kuerten, 3-6, 7-6 (7-5), 3-6, 6-1, 6-4, 2nd rd. Also qualifier Mariano Zabaleta (No. 213) d. 2nd seed Petr Korda, 6-0, 6-2, 3-6, 4-6, 6-3, 1st rd.

2002   15th seed Guillermo Canas d. 1st seed Lleyton Hewitt, 6-7 (1-7), 7-6(15-13), 6-4, 6-3, 4th rd., 4:13

2003   Martin Verkerk (ranked No. 46 and having never won a match in a major before the event) beats No. 4 Carlos Moya 6-3, 6-4, 5-7,4-6, 8-6 in QF and No. 7 seed Guillermo Coria 7-6 (4), 6-4, 7-6 (0) in SF, losing to No. 3 Juan Carlos Ferrero 6-1, 6-3, 6-2 in F

2004   Gaston Gaudio (ranked No. 44) becomes fourth unseeded champion, d. No. 8 David Nalbandian 6-3, 7-6 (5), 6-0 in SF and No. 3 Guillermo Coria in F, 0-6, 3-6, 6-4, 6-1, 8-6 (saved 2 MP)

     * Astoundingly inept and unfortunate on the clay of Roland Garros, Pete Sampras (24-13 in Paris), has suffered more defeats considered upsets than any other player, unable to win two matches only once since a SF finish in 1996: 1997 -1st seed, beaten by No. 65 Magnus Norman, 6-2, 6-4, 2-6, 6-4, 3rd rd.; 1998 - 1st seed, beaten by No. 98 Ramon Delgado, 7-6 (8-6) 6-3, 6-4, 2nd rd.; 1999 - 2nd seed, beaten by No. 100 Andrei Medvedev, 7-5, 1-6, 6-4, 6-3, 2nd rd.; 2000 - 2nd seed, beaten by No. 17 Mark Philippoussis, 4-6, 7-5, 7-6 (7-4), 4-6, 8-6, 1st rd.; 2001 - 5th seed, beaten by No. 76 Galo Blanco, 7-6 (7-4), 6-3, 6-2, 2nd rd.; 2002 - 12th seed, beaten by No. 69 Andreas Gaudenzi, 3-6, 6-4, 6-2, 7-6 (7-3), 1st rd.

Women

1971   Gail Sherriff Chanfreau d. 1st seed defending champ Margaret Smith Court, 6-3, 6-4, 3rd rd.

1972   Nathalie Fuchs d. 2nd seed Virginia Wade, 7-5, 6-4, 2nd rd.

1981   4th seed Hana Mandlikova d. 1st seed defending champ Chris Evert, 7-5, 6-4, SF, ends Evert's 29-match win streak

1983   Kathy Horvath (No. 33) d. 1st seed defending champ Martina Navratilova, 6-4, 0-6, 6-3, 4th rd. (Navratilova's only defeat of year, ending her 39-match win streak)

1988   13th seed Natasha Zvereva d. 2nd seed Martina Navratilova, 6-3, 6-7 (3-7), 7-5, SF. Also Arantxa Sanchez (No. 22) d. 3rd seed 7-time champ Chris Evert, 6-3, 7-6 (7-4). (Evert's 78th, last match in Paris)

1989   7th seed Arantxa Sanchez Vicario d. 1st seed defending champ Steffi Graf, 7-6 (8-6), 3-6, 7-5, F

1990   Mercedes Paz (No, 71) d. 3rd-seed defending champ Arantxa Sanchez Vicario, 7-5, 3-6, 6-1, 2nd rd.

1994   12th seed Mary Pierce d. 1st seed defending champ Steffi Graf, 6-2, 6-2, QF

1997   Nicole Arendt (No. 87) d. 4th seed Jana Novotna, 3-6, 6-4, 6-4, 3rd rd. (Arendt came in 1-3 in matches for year)

1999   Qualifier Barbara Schwartz (No. 124) d. 5th seed Venus Williams, 2-6, 7-6 (9-7), 6-3, 4th rd. (saved 3 MP, 2nd, at 5-6, 0-40)

2002   Qualifier Anika Kapros (No. 179) d. 5th seed Justine Henin, 4-6, 6-1, 6-0, 1st rd. Also Clarisa Fernanandez (No. 87) d. 4th seed Kim Clijsters, 6-4, 6-0, 3rd rd.

2009   No. 23 seed Robin Soderling of Sweden hands three-time defending champion, No. 1 seed Rafael Nadal of Spain 6-2, 6-7(2-7), 6-4, 7-6 (7-2) in the 2009 Fourth Round, Nadal's first loss at Roland Garros after winning his first 31 French Open matches.

MATCH POINTS SAVED BY CHAMPION

Men

1927   F, Rene Lacoste d. Bill Tilden, 6-4, 4-6, 5-7, 6-3, 11-9 (saved 2 MP, 5th, at 9-8, 40-15)

1934   F, Gottfried von Cramm, d. Jack Crawford 6-4, 7-9, 3-6, 7-5, 6-3 (saved 1 MP, 4th) at 5-4 with overhead smash from baseline)

1962   4th rd., Rod Laver d. Marty Mulligan, 6-4, 2-6, 3-6, 10-8, 6-2 (saved 1 MP, 4th, at 4-5, 30-40 with serve-and-volley, 2nd serve)

1976   1st rd, 5th seed Adriano Panatta d. Pavel Hutka, 2-6, 6-2, 6-2, 0-6, 12-10 (saved 1 MP, 5th, with lunging volley)

2001   4th rd., 1st seed Gustavo Kuerten d. qualifier Michael Russell (No. 135), 3-6, 4-6, 7-6 (7-3), 6-3, 6-1 (saved 1 MP, 3rd, at 5-3, ad-in, with forehand winner on 25th stroke; Russell 2 pts away 5 times—as Kuerten holds to 3-5 from 15-30, 30-all; 2 deuces in 9th game, 30-all in 12th game, goes on to win 3rd title)

2004   F, Gaston Gaudio (No. 44) d. No. 3 Guillermo Coria, 0-6, 3-6, 6-4, 6-1, 8-6 (saved 2 MP at 5-6 in 5th set, MP (1) 1st ad: backhand wide; MP (2) 2d ad: forehand wide) in F in 3:31

Women

1946   F, 2nd seed Margaret Osborne duPont d. 1st seed Pauline Betz,1-6, 8-6. 7-5 (saved 2 MP, 2nd, at 5-6)

| 1962 | F, Margaret Smith (Court) d. Lesley Turner (Bowrey), 6-3, 3-6, 7-5 (saved 1 MP, 3rd, at 3-5) |

| 2004 | 4R, Anastasia Myskina d. Svetlana Kuznetsova 1-6, 6-4, 8-6 (One MP saved at 5-6 3rd set) |

| 2005 | 4R, Justine Henin-Hardenne d. Svetlana Kuznetsova 7-6 (6), 4-6, 7-5 (saved two MPs at 3-5, ad out in 3rd set) in 3:14 |

OTHER COMEBACKS
Men

| 1930 | Jean Borotra d. Yoshiro Ohta, 5-7, 3-6, 6-4, 6-1, 9-7. 4th rd, (saved 4 MP, Ohta led 4-3 3rd, 4-1 5th, 2 MP vs Borotra's serve at 5-6, 2 more at 6-7, 15-40; Borotra cramps, delays 2 min, then breaks serve and wins on 3rd MP) |

| 1946 | Marcel Bernard d. Jaroslav Drobny F, from two sets down, 3-6, 2-6, 6-1, 6-4, 6-3 |

| 1958 | Robert Haillet d. Budge Patty, 5-7, 7-5, 10-8, 4-6, 7-5, 4th rd. (saved 4 MP, Patty serving, led 5-0, 40-0, 5th set, had fourth match point at 5-4, 40-30) |

| 1962 | Rod Laver d. Roy Emerson F, from two sets down, 3-6, 2-6, 6-3, 9-7, 6-2 |

| 1974 | No. 3 seed, Bjorn Borg d. Manolo Orantes F, from two sets down, 2-6, 6-7 (1-7), 6-0, 6-1, 6-1 |

| 1984 | 2nd seed Ivan Lendl d. 1st seed John McEnroe, 3-6, 2-6, 6-4, 7-5, 7-5, F (down 0-2, 3rd, 2 breaks, 4th, 2-1 and 3-2. Time 4:08, ended McEnroe's 42 match win streak) |

| 1986 | 8th seed Henri Leconte d. Cassio Motta, 1-6, 3-6, 7-6 (12-10), 6-0, 6-0, 3rd rd. (saved 2 MP in tie-breaker). Also 12th seed Guillermo Vilas d. Guy Forget, 6-2, 3-6, 4-6, 6-1, 8-6, 4th rd. (saved 1 MP, 5th, at 4-5, Time 4:15) |

| 1990 | Milan Srejber d. David Wheaton, 3-6, 5-7, 6-3, 7-6 (7-4), 6-3, (saved 2 MP in 4th set, 1st rd. Held serve to 6-6 in 4th through 2 match points, 2 deuces) |

| 1991 | Aaron Krickstein (No. 49) d. Eduardo Masso (No. 109), 6-7 (3-7), 6-4, 2-6, 6-4, 7-5, 1st rd. (saved 2 MP, 5th, at 4-5). Also, 2nd seed Boris Becker d. Todd Woodbridge (No. 40), 5-7, 1-6, 6-4, 6-4, 6-4, 2nd rd. (from 2-4, 4th, held serve to 5-4, 4th, 5 deuces, 2 break points; Time 4:29). Also 6th seed Pete Sampras d. Thomas Muster (No. 64), 4-6, 4-6, 6-4, 6-1, 6-4, 1st rd. (served match game from 0-40; lost 2nd rd. to No. 76 Thierry Champion, 6-3, 6-1, 6-1) |

| 1994 | Magnus Larsson (No. 46) d. Hendrik Dreekmann (No. 89), 3-6, 6-7 (1-7), 7-6 (7-3), 6-0, 6-1, QF (saved 6 MP, 3rd: 2 at 4-5, 4 at 5-6, 3:03).Also, Ronald Agenor (No. 31) d. David Prinosil (No. 119), 6-7 (4-7), 6-7 (2-7), 6-3. 6-4, 14-12, 2nd rd (Time 5:02, 2 days; Agenor served for victory 5 times, won on 4th MP) |

| 1999 | Andre Agassi d. Andrei Medvedev from two sets down, 1-6, 2-6, 6-4, 6-3, 6-4 in F |

| 2002 | Alex Coretja saved 4 MPs vs Arnaud Clement, 5th set 3rd rd, 6-1, 6-2, 4-6, 5-7, 8-6 (holds serve to 5-5 from 0-40 and ad out; at 30-40 Clement doesn't put away gimme forehand volley, the point continues and Corretja wins it) |

| 2003 | Albert Costa, defending champion, wins four five-set matches—three from two-sets-down to reach SF; d. Sergio Roitman 6-7(3), 2-6, 7-5, 6-2, 6-2 in 1st rd; d. Radek Stepanek 6-3, 5-7, 6-4, 3-6, 6-4 in 2nd rd; d. Nicolas Lapentti 4-6, 4-6, 6-3, 6-4, 6-4 in 3rd rd; d. Tommy Robredo 2-6, 3-6, 6-4, 7-5, 6-2 in QF. Lost to Ferrero 6-3, 7-6 (5), 6-4 in SF |

| 2004 | Vince Spadea d. Florent Serra, 7-5, 1-6, 4-6, 7-6 (9-7), 9-7, saving 9 MP and coming back from 1-5 in 5th set in the 1st rd. |

| 2004 | Marat Safin d. Potito Starace, 6-7 (4-7), 6-4, 3-6, 7-5, 7-5, saving 2 MP in 3rd rd. in 4:25. Starace served for match at 5-4 in 4th set, when Safin called an injury timeout to treat blisters. (Safin also saved 1MP in the 5th set previous round in 6-4, 2-6, 6-2, 6-7 (4),11-9 win over Felix Mantilla in 2nd rd.) |

Women

| 1926 | Simone Passemard Mathieu d. Marion Zinderstein Jessup, 2-6, 9-7, 6-0, 2nd rd. (saved 8 MP, 2nd set) |

| 1991 | 3rd seed Gabriela Sabatini d. 6th seed Jana Novotna, 5-7, 7-6 (12-10), 6-0, QF (from 2-5, 2nd, saved 2 MP in tie-breaker) |

| 1993 | 5th seed Mary Joe Fernandez d. 3rd seed Gabriela Sabatini, 1-6, 7-6 (7-4), 10-8, QF, trailing 1-6, 1-5, 30-40, saved 5 MP: 1 to 2-5, 3 at 5-3, 40-15 and ad-in, Sabatini served again for victory at 7-6, 3rd, fought off 4 MP herself in the 3rd set. Time 3:34) |

| 1993 | 1st seed Steffi Graf d. Mary Joe Fernandez, 4-6, 6-2, 6-4, F. (Mary Joe led 2-0 in the 3rd with 2 break points, also broke to lead 4-3, and led 30-15 before losing game and the next two to lose match) |

| 1994 | Qualifier Karin Kschwendt (No. 143) d. wild card Angelique Olivier (No. 242), 5-7, 6-4, 9-7, 1st rd. (saved 6 MP from 0-5 down in 3rd: 1 at 0-5, 4 at 2-5 from 0-40, 1 at 5-3; won last 9 points, Time 3:20) |

| 1995 | Chanda Rubin (No. 53) d. 5th seed Jana Novotna, 7-6 (10-8), 4-6, 8-6, 3rd rd. (from 0-5, 0-40 in 3rd, saved 9 MP: 5 to 1-5, 1 to 5-2, 3 to 5-5; also saved 2 SP in tie-breaker) |

| 1996 | Wild card Virginia Buisson (No. 198) d. wild card Noelle van Lottum (No. 161), 6-7 (3-7), 7-5, 6-2, 1st rd. (saved 3 MP, 2nd, at 2-5, 0-40, 4:07, longest French women's match) |

| 1997 | Lisa Raymond d. Maggie Maleeva, 4-6, 7-5, 6-3 (saved 3 MP, 2nd, at 5-4) |

| 1999 | 6th seed Steffi Graf d. 1st seed Martina Hingis, 4-6, 7-5, 6-2, F (Hingis served for match, 2nd, 3 points from victory at 5-4, 15-0, 15-15) |

| 2004 | Lisa Raymond d. Lubomira Kurhajcova (No. 59), 0-6, 7-5, 6-3, saved 2 MPs from 0-6, 0-5, 30-30, 1st rd. |

FARTHEST ADVANCEMENT OF A QUALIFIER
Men
| Filip DeWulf | 1997 Semifinals |

Women
Katja Ebbinghaus	1972 Quarterfinals
Corinne Molesworth	1972 Quarterfinals
Helga Masthoff	1978 Quarterfinals
Miroslava Bendlova	1978 Quarterfinals
Barbara Schwartz	1999 Quarterfinals
Marta Marrero	2000 Quarterfinals
Petra Mandula	2001 Quarterfinals
Carla Suarez Navarro	2008 Quarterfinals

FARTHEST ADVANCEMENT OF A WILD CARD
Men
| Henri Leconte | 1992 Semifinals |

Women
| Mary Pierce | 2002 Quarterfinals |

FARTHEST ADVANCEMENT OF A LUCKY LOSER

Men

Fernando Verdasco	2003 Third Round
Laurence Tieleman	1999 Third Round

Women

Maria Jose Gaidano	1993 Fourth Round

UNSEEDED CHAMPIONS

Men

Marcel Bernard	1946
Mats Wilander	1982
Gustavo Kuerten	1997
Gaston Gaudio	2004

Women

Margaret Scriven	1933

UNSEEDED RUNNER-UPS

Men

Ian Vermaak	1959
Istvan Gulyas	1966
Niki Pilic	1973
Victor Pecci	1979
Mikael Pernfors	1986
Alberto Berasategui	1994
Andrei Medvedev	1999
Martin Verkerk	2003
Mariano Puerta	2005

Women

Nelly Adamson-Landry	1938
Ginette Bucaille	1954
Helen Gourlay	1971
Renata Tomanova	1976
Florenta Mihai	1977
Mima Jausovec	1983

MOST ACES – TOURNAMENT

99 Pete Sampras (1996)

MOST ACES – MATCH

Men

55 Ivo Karlovic lost to Lleyton Hewitt 6-7 (1), 6-7 (4), 7-6 (4), 6-4, 6-3 2009, 1st rd.

37 Andy Roddick d. Michael Chang 5-7, 6-3, 6-4, 6-7 (5-7), 7-5. 2001 2nd rd. (3 hours, 46 minutes)

31 Ivo Karlovic lost to Dominik Hrbaty, 4-6, 6-4, 6-7 (2-7), 7-5, 6-2. 2006 2nd rd

29   Mark Philippoussis d. Nicklas Kulti, 6-2, 4-6, 3-6, 6-4, 6-4, 1997 1st rd.

29 Todd Martin lost to Pete Sampras, 3-6, 6-4, 7-5, 4-6, 6-2, 1996 3rd rd.

29 Jim Courier lost to Sampras, 6-7(4-7), 4-6, 6-4, 6-4, 6-4, 1996 QF

Women

16 Brenda Schultz-McCarthy lost to Mary Joe Fernandez, 1993, 2-6, 7-5, 6-3

MOST DOUBLE FAULTS – MATCH

Men

22 Vince Spadea lost to Sebastien Grosjean, 6-2, 7-6 (7-5), 6-7(5-7), 6-4, 2002 3rd rd.

Women

18 Elena Dementieva d. Mervana Jugic-Salkic, 7-6 (7-4), 1-6, 6-4, 2004 first round

17 Elena Dementieva d. Akiko Morigami, 6-3, 4-6, 6-3, 2005 third round

17 Maria Sharapova d. Eygeniya Rodina 6-1, 3-6, 8-6, 2008 first round

MOST DOUBLE FAULTS – TOURNAMENT

64 Elena Dementieva, 2004

Wimbledon CHAPTER 8

Pete Sampras (left) won seven Wimbledon men's singles titles, with his 2000 triumph over **Patrick Rafter** (right) earning the American a 13th major singles title, breaking the all-time record of 12 major singles titles set by Roy Emerson.

This is the Grand-daddy, first-born of all tournaments in the game of lawn tennis as we know it. It was 130-years-old in 2007, having hopefully entered the sporting world in 1877 and became the cynosure of the game. Considered the championships of Great Britain, the tournament is officially entitled The Lawn Tennis Championships. But one word—Wimbledon—is quite sufficient, proclaiming the majesty of it all, referring to location, the suburb of that name in southwest London.

Since the beginning, it has been conducted on the grounds of the All England Lawn Tennis and Croquet Club (1868), first at the Worple Road site, then to its present setting on Church Road in 1922. Last week in June-first week in July have been the dates for more than a century.

The first Centre Court seated about 4,000, grounds capacity 7,500. The present Centre, seating 9,989 in its 1922 debut, has held as many as 16,000, standing liberally permitted. But current law, eliminating standing, limits it to 13,802 seats. A new No. 1 Court (1997) seats 11,429. Intimate Court No. 2—the so-called "Graveyard of Champions"—held 1,900, losing its shape in a 2009 re-modeling.

Record one-day attendance on the grounds was 42,457, the first Wednesday of 2002. The tourney record for the fortnight (13 daytime sessions; no play on the middle Sunday) was 476,711 in 2001. (Overall, the record is 490,081 in 2001 when inclement weather made a 14th day necessary.) Estimates of the peak years at Worple Road range between 60,000 and 70,000. Rain, seemingly a constant antagonist, was at its worst in 1922, daily downpours pushing the conclusion to the third Wednesday. A retractable roof for Centre is to be in use by 2009.

Tennis was first played at the Club in 1875 and pretty much took over from the croquet-eers in 1882. A gathering of 200, paying about 20 cents apiece, witnessed two locals, among 22 entrants, jousting for the inaugural title, won by 27-year-old Spencer Gore, 6-1, 6-2, 6-4, over William Marshall, 28. Only 30 of the spectators were seated. Seven years later, in an intramural English clash, Maud Watson, 19, beat her 26-year-old sister, Lillian Watson, 6-8, 6-3, 6-3, and the women had their initial champ. Thirteen had entered.

The surface has always been God's own sod: grass. The challenge round system was in force for men's singles (1878 through 1921), women's singles (1885 through 1921) and men's doubles (1885 through 1921). It meant that the defending champion played only one match the following year, waiting for a challenger to emerge from the all-comers tournament. When the champion chose not to defend, the winner of the all-comers was the new champ.

In 1972, two years after the U.S. introduced the tie-breaker, Wimbledon accepted the novelty, but cautiously at 8-8 in games, not 6-6, and not the American "sudden death" style. But in 1979, Wimbledon conformed with the rest of the world at 6-6, and continued with the "lingering" ITF version, best-of-12-points, but a margin of two points required. However, the tie-breaker is not applied to ultimate sets, the fifth for men, third for women. Deuce sets, eliminating 6-5 set scores, were adopted in 1884, as were byes later than the first round.

Wimbledon had lobbied for "Open" tournaments, and welcomed pros and amateurs together in 1968, allotting $63,000 as prize money. Rod Laver got $4,800 as first prize, Billie Jean King $1,800. As the last major to offer equal prize money for men and women, the tournament in 2007 paid champs Roger Federer and Venus Williams $1.4 million apiece from of a pot of over $22.5 million. They also got to keep smaller replicas of the trophies: for men, the Challenge Cup engraved "The All England Lawn Tennis Club Single Handed Championship of the World" along with names of the champions; for women, the Rosewater Dish, engraved with names of the champions.

Unluckily for the natives, none has embraced these baubles since Virginia Wade in 1977 and Fred Perry in 1936.

Wimbledon – Tournament Results

Legend: Ch: Challenge Round; F: Final; S: Semifinal; Q: Quarterfinal; Set: S1, S2, S3, S4, S5

Men's Singles

Rd	Winner	Defeated	S1	S2	S3	S4	S5
1877							
F	Spencer Gore (GBR)	William Marshall (GBR)	6-1	6-2	6-4		
S	Spencer Gore (GBR)	C.G. Heathcote (GBR)	6-2	6-5	6-2		
S	William Marshall (GBR)		(bye)				
Q	Spencer Gore (GBR)	F.N. Langham (GBR)	6-3	6-2	5-6	6-1	
Q	C.G. Heathcote (GBR)	Julian Marshall (GBR)	6-3	6-3	6-5		
Q	William Marshall (GBR)	L. Robert Erskine (GBR)	6-5	5-6	6-4	6-1	
1878							
Ch	Frank Hadow (GBR)	Spencer Gore (GBR)	7-5	6-1	9-7		
F	Frank Hadow (GBR)	L. Robert Erskine (GBR)	6-4	6-4	6-4		
S	L. Robert Erskine (GBR)	Herbert Lawford (GBR)	6-3	6-1	6-3		
S	Frank Hadow (GBR)		(bye)				
Q	L. Robert Erskine (GBR)	C.G. Hamilton (GBR)	6-4	3-6	6-1	3-6	6-5
Q	Herbert Lawford (GBR)		(bye)				
Q	Frank Hadow (GBR)	Arthur T. Myers (GBR)	6-0	6-4	6-3		
1879							
Ch	John Hartley (GBR)	Frank Hadow (GBR)	(walkover)				
F	John Hartley (GBR)	Vere "St. Leger" Goold (IRL)	6-2	6-4	6-2		
S	John Hartley (GBR)	C.F. Parr (GBR)	2-6	6-0	6-1	6-1	
S	Vere "St. Leger" Goold (IRL)		(bye)				
Q	John Hartley (GBR)	C.G. Heathcote (GBR)	6-4	6-3	6-3		
Q	C.F. Parr (GBR)	C.D. Barry (GBR)	6-2	6-5	6-4		
Q	Vere "St. Leger" Goold (IRL)	G.E. Tabor (GBR)	6-2	6-5	5-6	6-3	
1880							
Ch	John Hartley (GBR)	Herbert Lawford (GBR)	6-3	6-2	2-6	6-3	
F	Herbert Lawford (GBR)	Otway E. Woodhouse (GBR)	6-5	6-4	6-0		
S	Otway E. Woodhouse (GBR)	Geo. A. Montgomerie (GBR)	6-4	2-6	6-3	5-6	6-1
S	Herbert Lawford (GBR)	G.M. Butterworth (GBR)	6-2	6-3	6-3		
Q	Otway E. Woodhouse (GBR)	Ernest Renshaw (GBR)	6-3	6-3	3-6	6-0	
Q	Geo. A. Montgomerie (GBR)	H.C. Jenkins (GBR)	6-3	5-6	6-2	2-6	6-3
Q	Herbert Lawford (GBR)	W.H. 'd'Esterre' (GBR)	6-0	6-3	6-1		
Q	G.M. Butterworth (GBR)	R.R. Farrer (GBR)	1-6	6-1	6-4	6-5	
1881							
Ch	Willie Renshaw (GBR)	John Hartley (GBR)	6-0	6-1	6-1		
F	Willie Renshaw (GBR)	Richard T. Richardson (GBR)	6-4	6-2	6-3		
S	Willie Renshaw (GBR)	Herbert Lawford (GBR)	1-6	6-3	6-2	5-6	6-3
S	Richard T. Richardson (GBR)		(bye)				
Q	Willie Renshaw (GBR)	Otway E. Woodhouse (GBR)	4-6	6-4	6-0	6-3	
Q	Herbert Lawford (GBR)	G.S. Murray-Hill (GBR)	6-1	6-1	6-0		
Q	Richard T. Richardson (GBR)	W.H. Darby (GBR)	6-0	6-4	6-1		
1882							
Ch	Willie Renshaw (GBR)	Ernest Renshaw (GBR)	6-1	2-6	4-6	6-2	6-2
F	Ernest Renshaw (GBR)	Richard T. Richardson (GBR)	6-5	6-3	2-6	6-3	
S	Ernest Renshaw (GBR)	Herbert Lawford (GBR)	6-4	4-6	6-2	3-6	6-0
S	Richard T. Richardson (GBR)	Frank R. Benson (GBR)	6-1	6-2	6-1		
Q	Ernest Renshaw (GBR)	Humphrey Berkeley (GBR)	6-5	6-1	6-4		
Q	Herbert Lawford (GBR)	Herbert Wilberforce (GBR)	6-2	6-5	6-5		
Q	Richard T. Richardson (GBR)	Otway E. Woodhouse (GBR)	6-1	6-0	6-2		
Q	Frank R. Benson (GBR)		(bye)				
1883							
Ch	Willie Renshaw (GBR)	Ernest Renshaw (GBR)	2-6	6-3	6-3	4-6	6-3
F	Ernest Renshaw (GBR)	Donald Stewart (GBR)	0-6	6-3	6-0	6-2	
S	Donald Stewart (GBR)	William C. Taylor (GBR)	6-0	6-1	6-3		
S	Ernest Renshaw (GBR)		(bye)				
Q	Donald Stewart (GBR)	Herbert Wilberforce (GBR)	6-5	3-6	5-6	6-5	6-4
Q	William C. Taylor (GBR)	M. Constable (GBR)	6-3	6-5	5-6	4-6	6-3
Q	Ernest Renshaw (GBR)	Charles W. Grinstead (GBR)	6-4	6-3	6-3		
1884							
Ch	Willie Renshaw (GBR)	Herbert Lawford (GBR)	6-0	6-4	9-7		
F	Herbert Lawford (GBR)	Charles W. Grinstead (GBR)	7-5	2-6	6-2	9-7	
S	Charles W. Grinstead	Ernest Renshaw (GBR)	2-6	6-4	6-2	6-3	
S	Herbert Lawford (GBR)	Herbert Chipp (GBR)	7-5	6-4	6-4		
Q	Ernest Renshaw (GBR)	Wilfred Milne (GBR)	6-3	6-3	7-5		
Q	Charles W. Grinstead (GBR)	Ernest Browne de Sylly (GBR)	5-7	4-6	7-5	6-4	6-1
Q	Herbert Chipp (GBR)	William C. Taylor (GBR)	10-8	6-1	6-4		
Q	Herbert Lawford (GBR)		(bye)				
1885							
Ch	Willie Renshaw (GBR)	Herbert Lawford (GBR)	7-5	6-2	4-6	7-5	
F	Herbert Lawford (GBR)	Ernest Renshaw (GBR)	5-7	6-1	0-6	6-2	6-4
S	Ernest Renshaw (GBR)	Ernest Browne de Sylly (GBR)	6-4	8-6	2-6	5-7	6-4
S	Herbert Lawford (GBR)	James Dwight (USA)	6-2	6-2	6-3		
Q	Ernest Renshaw (GBR)	Herbert Chipp (GBR)	6-4	6-4	7-5		
Q	Ernest Browne de Sylly (GBR)	M.G. McNamara (GBR)	6-1	7-5	6-2		
Q	James Dwight (USA)	Arthur Stanley (GBR)	6-3	6-3	6-4		
Q	Herbert Lawford (GBR)	Patrick Bowes Lyon (GBR)	6-2	7-5	6-3		

Rd	Winner	Defeated	S1	S2	S3	S4	S5

1886

Rd	Winner	Defeated	S1	S2	S3	S4	S5
Ch	Willie Renshaw (GBR)	Herbert Lawford (GBR)	6-0	5-7	6-3	6-4	
F	Herbert Lawford (GBR)	Ernest Lewis (GBR)	6-2	6-3	2-6	4-6	6-4
S	Herbert Lawford (GBR)	T.R. Garvey (GBR)	6-3	6-2	6-0		
S	Ernest Lewis (GBR)	Herbert Wilberforce (GBR)	3-6	6-2	1-6	6-1	6-3
Q	Herbert Lawford (GBR)	Willoby Hamilton (GBR)	8-6	6-1	8-6		
Q	T.R. Garvey (GBR)	William C. Taylor (GBR)	8-6	6-4	2-6	6-3	
Q	Ernest Lewis (GBR)	Ernest Renshaw (GBR)	4-6	5-7	6-4	6-1	6-0
Q	Herbert Wilberforce (GBR)	C.H.A. Ross (GBR)	3-6	2-6	6-4	6-2	6-4

1887

Rd	Winner	Defeated	S1	S2	S3	S4	S5
Ch	Herbert Lawford (GBR)	Willie Renshaw (GBR)	(walkover)				
F	Herbert Lawford (GBR)	Ernest Renshaw (GBR)	1-6	6-3	3-6	6-4	6-4
S	Herbert Lawford (GBR)	Harry Grove (GBR)	4-6	6-3	7-5	7-5	
S	Ernest Renshaw (GBR)	Charles Lacy Sweet (GBR)	(walkover)				
Q	Harry Grove (GBR)	Patrick Bowes Lyon (GBR)	6-3	6-2	10-8		
Q	Herbert Lawford (GBR)	Oswald Milne (GBR)	7-5	6-0	6-3		
Q	Ernest Renshaw (GBR)	Ernest Lewis (GBR)	7-5	6-2	6-4		
Q	Charles Lacy Sweet (GBR)	Wilfred Milne (GBR)	6-3	6-1	6-3		

1888

Rd	Winner	Defeated	S1	S2	S3	S4	S5
Ch	Ernest Renshaw (GBR)	Herbert Lawford (GBR)	6-3	7-5	6-0		
F	Ernest Renshaw (GBR)	Ernest Lewis (GBR)	7-9	6-1	8-6	6-4	
S	Ernest Renshaw (GBR)	Willoby Hamilton (GBR)	7-5	7-5	5-7	6-3	
S	Ernest Lewis (GBR)	William C. Taylor (GBR)	9-7	6-4	6-4		
Q	Ernest Renshaw (GBR)	Herbert Wilberforce (GBR)	4-6	6-3	7-5	4-6	6-0
Q	Willoby Hamilton (GBR)	Willie Renshaw (GBR)	5-7	7-5	6-4	6-2	
Q	Ernest Lewis (GBR)	Harry S. Scrivener (GBR)	7-5	6-3	6-1		
Q	William C. Taylor (GBR)	F.L. Rawson (GBR)	6-4	6-0	4-6	4-6	6-1

1889

Rd	Winner	Defeated	S1	S2	S3	S4	S5
Ch	Willie Renshaw (GBR)	Ernest Renshaw (GBR)	6-4	6-1	3-6	6-0	
F	Willie Renshaw (GBR)	Harry Barlow (GBR)	3-6	5-7	8-6	10-8	8-6
S	Harry Barlow (GBR)	Willoby Hamilton (GBR)	3-6	6-3	2-6	6-3	6-3
S	Willie Renshaw (GBR)	Herbert Lawford (GBR)	7-5	5-7	6-3	6-2	
Q	Willoby Hamilton (GBR)	Ernest Lewis (GBR)	4-6	7-5	6-3	5-7	6-4
Q	Harry Barlow (GBR)	George Hillyard (GBR)	7-5	6-2	6-4		
Q	Willie Renshaw (GBR)	Manliffe Goodbody (IRL)	7-5	6-4	6-4		
Q	Herbert Lawford (GBR)	A.G. Ziffo (GBR)	6-2	6-2	6-0		

1890

Rd	Winner	Defeated	S1	S2	S3	S4	S5
Ch	Willoby Hamilton (GBR)	Willie Renshaw (GBR)	6-8	6-2	3-6	6-1	6-1
F	Willoby Hamilton (GBR)	Harry Barlow (GBR)	2-6	6-4	6-4	4-6	7-5
S	Willoby Hamilton (GBR)	Joshua Pim (IRL)	0-6	6-4	6-4	6-2	
S	Harry Barlow (GBR)	Ernest Lewis (GBR)	7-5	6-4	4-6	7-5	
Q	Joshua Pim (IRL)	Harry S. Scrivener (GBR)	6-3	12-10	6-0		
Q	Willoby Hamilton (GBR)	Wilfred Baddeley (GBR)	6-3	6-0	6-1		
Q	Ernest Lewis (GBR)	Dean Miller (GBR)	6-3	6-1	6-1		
Q	Harry Barlow (GBR)	C. Grainger Chaytor (GBR)	8-10	6-4	2-6	6-1	6-1

1891

Rd	Winner	Defeated	S1	S2	S3	S4	S5
Ch	Wilfred Baddeley (GBR)	Willoby Hamilton (GBR)	(walkover)				
F	Wilfred Baddeley (GBR)	Joshua Pim (IRL)	6-4	1-6	7-5	6-0	
S	Wilfred Baddeley (GBR)	Ernest Renshaw (GBR)	6-0	6-1	6-1		
S	Joshua Pim (IRL)	Harold Mahony (GBR)	6-4	6-0	6-2		
Q	Ernest Renshaw (GBR)	Harry Grove (GBR)	6-3	7-5	6-2		
Q	Wilfred Baddeley (GBR)	Edward J. Avory (GBR)	6-0	6-1	4-6	6-2	
Q	Harold Mahony (GBR)	H.A.B. Chapman (GBR)	6-2	6-0	6-1		
Q	Joshua Pim (IRL)	Harry Barlow (GBR)	5-7	0-6	6-2	6-3	7-5

1892

Rd	Winner	Defeated	S1	S2	S3	S4	S5
Ch	Wilfred Baddeley (GBR)	Joshua Pim (IRL)	4-6	6-3	6-3	6-2	
F	Joshua Pim (IRL)	Ernest Lewis (GBR)	2-6	5-7	9-7	6-3	6-2
S	Ernest Lewis (GBR)	H.A.B. Chapman (GBR)	2-6	6-3	6-1	6-2	
S	Joshua Pim (IRL)	Harold Mahony (GBR)	6-1	12-10	2-6	6-2	
Q	Ernest Pim (GBR)	Wilberforce Eaves (AUS)	7-5	6-2	6-2		
Q	H.A.B. Chapman (GBR)	Reginald Gamble (GBR)	6-4	6-0	6-1		
Q	Harold Mahony (GBR)	Arthur Gore (GBR)	4-6	6-2	6-3	6-4	
Q	Joshua Pim (IRL)	Harry Barlow (GBR)	3-6	9-7	6-2	7-5	

1893

Rd	Winner	Defeated	S1	S2	S3	S4	S5
Ch	Joshua Pim (IRL)	Wilfred Baddeley (GBR)	3-6	6-1	6-3	6-2	
F	Joshua Pim (IRL)	Harold Mahony (GBR)	9-7	6-3	6-0		
S	Joshua Pim (IRL)	Harry Barlow (GBR)	9-7	6-2	6-3		
S	Harold Mahony (GBR)	Archdale Palmer (GBR)	3-6	6-3	6-3	6-1	
Q	Harry Barlow (GBR)	Arthur W. Hallward (GBR)	7-9	6-2	10-8	6-8	6-1
Q	Joshua Pim (IRL)	Manliffe Goodbody (IRL)	8-6	6-3	3-6	6-1	
Q	Harold Mahony (GBR)	Wilberforce Eaves (AUS)	10-8	11-9	6-0		
Q	Archdale Palmer (GBR)	Neville Durlacher (GBR)	6-3	6-4	7-5		

1894

Rd	Winner	Defeated	S1	S2	S3	S4	S5
Ch	Joshua Pim (IRL)	Wilfred Baddeley (GBR)	10-8	6-2	8-6		
F	Wilfred Baddeley (GBR)	Ernest Lewis (GBR)	6-0	6-1	6-0		
S	Wilfred Baddeley (GBR)	Tom Chaytor (GBR)	(walkover)				
S	Ernest Lewis (GBR)	Herbert Baddeley (GBR)	2-6	7-5	6-3	1-6	7-5
Q	Wilfred Baddeley (GBR)	John F. Talmage (GBR)	6-2	6-1	6-3		
Q	Tom Chaytor (GBR)	Ernest G. Meers (GBR)	1-6	6-1	6-8	8-6	6-4
Q	Ernest Lewis (GBR)	Geo. Mieville Simond (GBR)	6-2	6-3	6-2		
Q	Herbert Baddeley (GBR)	Harry Barlow (GBR)	0-6	6-3	4-6	6-1	6-1

1895

Rd	Winner	Defeated	S1	S2	S3	S4	S5
Ch	Wilfred Baddeley (GBR)	Joshua Pim (IRL)	(walkover)				
F	Wilfred Baddeley (GBR)	Wilberforce Eaves (AUS)	4-6	2-6	8-6	6-2	6-3
S	Wilfred Baddeley (GBR)	Herbert Baddeley (GBR)	(walkover)				
S	Wilberforce Eaves (AUS)	Ernest G. Meers (GBR)	6-3	7-9	9-11	6-4	6-1
Q	Wilfred Baddeley (GBR)	Harry Barlow (GBR)	6-1	6-4	8-6		
Q	Herbert Baddeley (GBR)	Reggie Doherty (GBR)	6-4	6-2	6-4		
Q	Ernest G. Meers (GBR)	J. M. Flavelle (GBR)	6-1	6-2	6-1		
Q	Wilberforce Eaves (AUS)	Geo. Mieville Simond (GBR)	6-4	6-2	7-5		

1896

Rd	Winner	Defeated	S1	S2	S3	S4	S5
Ch	Harold Mahony (GBR)	Wilfred Baddeley (GBR)	6-2	6-8	5-7	8-6	6-3
F	Harold Mahony (GBR)	Wilberforce Eaves (AUS)	6-2	6-2	11-9		
S	Harold Mahony (GBR)	Harold Nisbet (GBR)	6-4	2-6	8-6	4-6	6-3
S	Wilberforce Eaves (AUS)	Herbert Baddeley (GBR)	6-4	6-3	6-4		
Q	Harold Mahony (GBR)	Frank Riseley (GBR)	7-5	5-7	7-5	6-3	
Q	Harold Nisbet (GBR)	Geo. Mieville Simond (GBR)	2-6	6-4	6-4	1-6	6-3
Q	Wilberforce Eaves (AUS)	Clem Cazalet (GBR)	7-5	6-3	6-0		
Q	Herbert Baddeley (GBR)	Bill Larned (USA)	3-6	3-6	6-4	6-4	6-3

1897

Rd	Winner	Defeated	S1	S2	S3	S4	S5
Ch	Reggie Doherty (GBR)	Harold Mahony (GBR)	6-4	6-4	6-3		
F	Reggie Doherty (GBR)	Wilberforce Eaves (AUS)	6-3	7-5	2-0	(retired)	
S	Wilberforce Eaves (AUS)	Sidney H. Smith (GBR)	6-2	5-7	1-6	6-2	6-1
S	Reggie Doherty (GBR)	Wilfred Baddeley (GBR)	6-3	6-0	6-3		
Q	Sidney H. Smith (GBR)	George Hillyard (GBR)	3-6	6-4	6-2	6-4	
Q	Wilberforce Eaves (AUS)	T. George P. Greville (GBR)	6-1	6-2	8-10	6-0	
Q	Wilfred Baddeley (GBR)	Laurie Doherty (GBR)	6-4	6-2	6-2		
Q	Reggie Doherty (GBR)	Frank Riseley (GBR)	(walkover)				

1898

Rd	Winner	Defeated	S1	S2	S3	S4	S5
Ch	Reggie Doherty (GBR)	Laurie Doherty (GBR)	6-3	6-3	2-6	5-7	6-1
F	Laurie Doherty (GBR)	Harold Mahony (GBR)	6-1	6-2	4-6	2-6	14-12
S	Laurie Doherty (GBR)	Clarence Hobart (USA)	6-1	6-4	6-3		
S	Harold Mahony (GBR)	Arthur Gore (GBR)	6-2	3-6	4-6	6-2	6-4
Q	Clarence Hobart (USA)	Josiah Ritchie (GBR)	6-2	3-6	6-3	6-2	
Q	Laurie Doherty (GBR)	J. M. Flavelle (GBR)	6-2	6-3	3-6	6-0	
Q	Arthur Gore (GBR)	Sidney H. Smith (GBR)	4-6	6-0	4-6	6-3	7-5
Q	Harold Mahony (GBR)	Geo. Mieville Simond (GBR)	6-2	6-4	6-4		

1899

Rd	Winner	Defeated	S1	S2	S3	S4	S5
Ch	Reggie Doherty (GBR)	Arthur Gore (GBR)	1-6	4-6	6-3	6-3	6-3
F	Arthur Gore (GBR)	Sidney H. Smith (GBR)	3-6	6-1	6-2	6-4	
S	Arthur Gore (GBR)	Harold Mahony (GBR)	6-3	4-6	3-6	7-5	6-1
S	Sidney H. Smith (GBR)	Herbert Roper Barrett (GBR)	2-6	11-9	4-6	8-6	8-6
Q	Arthur Gore (GBR)	P.G. Pearson (GBR)	6-3	6-2	9-7		
Q	Harold Mahony (GBR)	T. George P. Greville (GBR)	6-3	9-7	2-6	10-8	
Q	Sidney H. Smith (GBR)	Harold Mahony (GBR)	6-3	7-5	6-4		
Q	Herbert Roper Barrett (GBR)	Clarence Hobart (USA)	8-6	7-5	6-4		

1900

Rd	Winner	Defeated	S1	S2	S3	S4	S5
Ch	Reggie Doherty (GBR)	Sidney H. Smith (GBR)	6-8	6-3	6-1	6-2	
F	Sidney H. Smith (GBR)	Arthur Gore (GBR)	6-4	4-6	6-2	6-1	
S	Arthur Gore (GBR)	Laurie Doherty (GBR)	4-6	8-6	8-6	6-1	
S	Sidney H. Smith (GBR)	Harold Nisbet (GBR)	6-0	6-1	6-1		
Q	Arthur Gore (GBR)	Frederick J.G. Plaskitt (GBR)	6-3	6-2	6-0		
Q	Laurie Doherty (GBR)	Robert McNair (GBR)	6-1	6-2	6-4		
Q	Sidney H. Smith (GBR)	Herbert Roper Barrett (GBR)	6-1	4-6	7-5	6-2	
Q	Harold Nisbet (GBR)	Fred W. Payn (GBR)	6-2	6-8	6-4	3-6	6-2

1901

Rd	Winner	Defeated	S1	S2	S3	S4	S5
Ch	Arthur Gore (GBR)	Reggie Doherty (GBR)	4-6	7-5	6-4	6-4	
F	Arthur Gore (GBR)	Charles Dixon (GBR)	6-4	6-0	6-3		
S	Charles Dixon (GBR)	Harold Mahony (GBR)	6-3	6-4	11-9		
S	Arthur Gore (GBR)	Herbert Roper Barrett (GBR)	8-6	6-1	7-5		
Q	Harold Mahony (GBR)	Robert McNair (GBR)	6-4	6-3	3-6	6-3	
Q	Charles Dixon (GBR)	Geo. Mieville Simond (GBR)	6-4	7-5	1-6	6-3	
Q	Herbert Roper Barrett (GBR)	Sidney H. Smith (GBR)	7-5	6-4	8-6		
Q	Arthur Gore (GBR)	George Hillyard (GBR)	6-1	2-6	4-6	8-6	6-2

1902

Rd	Winner	Defeated	S1	S2	S3	S4	S5
Ch	Laurie Doherty (GBR)	Arthur Gore (GBR)	6-4	6-3	3-6	6-0	
F	Laurie Doherty (GBR)	Josiah Ritchie (GBR)	8-6	6-3	7-5		
S	Josiah Ritchie (GBR)	Sidney H. Smith (GBR)	6-4	4-6	6-4	6-4	
S	Laurie Doherty (GBR)	Harold Mahony (GBR)	4-6	4-6	8-6	2-0	(retired)
Q	Josiah Ritchie (GBR)	Alfred Ernest Crawley (GBR)	6-2	6-1	2-6	6-3	
Q	Sidney H. Smith (GBR)	Herbert Roper Barrett (GBR)	6-3	6-4	6-3		
Q	Laurie Doherty (GBR)	T. George P. Greville (GBR)	6-1	4-6	6-3	7-5	
Q	Harold Mahony (GBR)	Fred W. Payn (GBR)	6-2	6-2	6-4		

1903

Rd	Winner	Defeated	S1	S2	S3	S4	S5
Ch	Laurie Doherty (GBR)	Frank Riseley (GBR)	7-5	6-3	6-0		
F	Frank Riseley (GBR)	Josiah Ritchie (GBR)	1-6	6-3	8-6	13-11	
S	Frank Riseley (GBR)	Sidney H. Smith (GBR)	7-5	6-3	7-9	1-6	9-7
S	Josiah Ritchie (GBR)	George Caridia (GBR)	6-1	6-0	4-6	6-1	
Q	Frank Riseley (GBR)	George Hillyard (GBR)	6-1	6-4	6-4		
Q	Sidney H. Smith (GBR)	Henry Pollard (GBR)	6-2	6-3	6-1		
Q	George Caridia (GBR)	E.S. Salmon (GBR)	6-3	6-4	6-2		
Q	Josiah Ritchie (GBR)	Ernest S. Wills (GBR)	6-1	6-2	'6-2		

1904

Rd	Winner	Defeated	S1	S2	S3	S4	S5
Ch	Laurie Doherty (GBR)	Frank Riseley (GBR)	6-1	7-5	8-6		
F	Frank Riseley (GBR)	Josiah Ritchie (GBR)	6-0	6-1	6-2		
S	Frank Riseley (GBR)	Sidney H. Smith (GBR)	7-5	5-7	8-6	5-7	(retired)
S	Josiah Ritchie (GBR)	Paul de Borman (BEL)	6-3	6-1	6-1		
Q	Frank Riseley (GBR)	Arthur Gore (GBR)	3-6	6-1	3-6	6-4	6-3
Q	Sidney H. Smith (GBR)	George Caridia (GBR)	7-5	8-6	6-3		
Q	Josiah Ritchie (GBR)	W. Lemaire de Warzee (BEL)	6-1	8-6	6-4		
Q	Paul de Borman (BEL)	Robert McNair (GBR)	6-0	6-4	6-4		

1905

Rd	Winner	Defeated	S1	S2	S3	S4	S5
Ch	Laurie Doherty (GBR)	Norman Brookes (AUS)	8-6	6-2	6-4		
F	Norman Brookes (AUS)	Sidney H. Smith (GBR)	1-6	6-4	6-1	1-6	7-5
S	Norman Brookes (AUS)	Arthur Gore (GBR)	6-3	9-7	6-2		
S	Sidney H. Smith (GBR)	Josiah Ritchie (GBR)	6-0	3-6	6-4	4-6	6-1
Q	Arthur Gore (GBR)	Tony Wilding (NZL)	8-6	6-2	6-2		
Q	Norman Brookes (AUS)	Frank Riseley (GBR)	6-3	6-2	6-4		
Q	Sidney H. Smith (GBR)	Bill Larned (USA)	6-2	6-4	6-4		
Q	Josiah Ritchie (GBR)	Arthur K. Cronin (GBR)	6-0	6-2	6-0		

1906

Rd	Winner	Defeated	S1	S2	S3	S4	S5
Ch	Laurie Doherty (GBR)	Frank Riseley (GBR)	6-4	4-6	6-2	6-3	
F	Frank Riseley (GBR)	Arthur Gore (GBR)	6-3	6-3	6-4		
S	Arthur Gore (GBR)	Tony Wilding (NZL)	9-7	6-1	8-6		
S	Frank Riseley (GBR)	Sidney H. Smith (GBR)	8-6	2-6	6-2	6-4	
Q	Tony Wilding (NZL)	Josiah Ritchie (GBR)	6-4	6-1	4-6	3-6	6-2
Q	Arthur Gore (GBR)	Alfred Ernest Crawley (GBR)	6-0	6-1	8-6		
Q	Frank Riseley (GBR)	Ray Little (USA)	6-3	6-1	6-4		
Q	Sidney H. Smith (GBR)	Clem Cazalet (GBR)	6-2	4-6	7-5		(retired)

1907

Rd	Winner	Defeated	S1	S2	S3	S4	S5
Ch	Norman Brookes (AUS)	Laurie Doherty (GBR)	(walkover)				
F	Norman Brookes (AUS)	Arthur Gore (GBR)	6-4	6-2	6-2		
S	Arthur Gore (GBR)	Wilberforce Eaves (AUS)	9-7	7-5	6-2		
S	Norman Brookes (AUS)	Josiah Ritchie (GBR)	6-0	6-1	6-4		
Q	Arthur Gore (GBR)	A.R. Sawyer (GBR)	6-0	6-3	6-0		
Q	Wilberforce Eaves (AUS)	Leonard H. Escombe (GBR)	6-0	4-6	6-3	1-6	6-3
Q	Norman Brookes (AUS)	Sidney H. Adams (GBR)	6-1	6-3	6-3		
Q	Josiah Ritchie (GBR)	Oscar Kreuzer (GER)	6-4	6-1	6-2		

1908

Rd	Winner	Defeated	S1	S2	S3	S4	S5
Ch	Arthur Gore (GBR)	Norman Brookes (AUS)	(walkover)				
F	Arthur Gore (GBR)	Herbert Roper Barrett (GBR)	6-3	6-2	4-6	3-6	6-4
S	Arthur Gore (GBR)	Robert B. Powell (CAN)	10-8	6-4	6-2		
S	Herbert Roper Barrett (GBR)	Josiah Ritchie (GBR)	6-3	6-1	3-6	6-1	
Q	Robert B. Powell (CAN)	W. Lemaire de Warzee (BEL)	6-4	8-6	6-4		
Q	Arthur Gore (GBR)	Charles Dixon (GBR)	10-8	6-3	3-6	6-0	
Q	Josiah Ritchie (GBR)	Alfred Ernest Crawley (GBR)	6-1	6-3	6-2		
Q	Herbert Roper Barrett (GBR)	Tony Wilding (NZL)	2-6	6-4	6-4	6-0	

1909

Rd	Winner	Defeated	S1	S2	S3	S4	S5
Ch	Arthur Gore (GBR)	Josiah Ritchie (GBR)	6-8	1-6	6-2	6-2	6-2
F	Josiah Ritchie (GBR)	Herbert Roper Barrett (GBR)	6-2	6-3	4-6	6-4	
S	Josiah Ritchie (GBR)	Theo. Mavrogordato (GBR)	3-6	6-3	6-3	6-2	
S	Herbert Roper Barrett (GBR)	Friedrich Rahe (GER)	6-4	6-2	6-8	7-5	
Q	Theo. Mavrogordato (GBR)	George Caridia (GBR)	6-1	9-7	2-6	4-6	6-4
Q	Josiah Ritchie (GBR)	Charles Dixon (GBR)	8-10	6-1	6-1	6-4	
Q	Herbert Roper Barrett (GBR)	Leonard H. Escombe (GBR)	4-6	7-5	11-9		(retired)
Q	Friedrich Rahe (GER)	Gordon Lowe (GBR)	12-10	6-0	6-4		

1910

Rd	Winner	Defeated	S1	S2	S3	S4	S5
Ch	Tony Wilding (NZL)	Arthur Gore (GBR)	6-4	7-5	4-6	6-2	
F	Tony Wilding (NZL)	Beals Wright (USA)	4-6	4-6	6-3	6-2	6-3
S	Tony Wilding (NZL)	Jim Parke (IRL)	7-5	6-1	6-2		
S	Beals Wright (USA)	Arthur Lowe (GBR)	6-3	3-6	6-4	6-4	
Q	Jim Parke (IRL)	Alfred Beamish (GBR)	8-6	5-7	6-4	6-3	
Q	Tony Wilding (NZL)	Otto Froitzheim (GER)	6-1	6-1	6-2		
Q	Arthur Lowe (GBR)	Stanley Doust (AUS)	6-3	6-3	2-6	6-4	
Q	Beals Wright (USA)	Robert B. Powell (CAN)	6-3	6-1	6-1		

1911

Rd	Winner	Defeated	S1	S2	S3	S4	S5
Ch	Tony Wilding (NZL)	Herbert Roper Barrett (GBR)	6-4	4-6	2-6	6-2	(ret'd)
F	Herbert Roper Barrett (GBR)	Charles Dixon (GBR)	5-7	4-6	6-4	6-3	6-1
S	Charles Dixon (GBR)	Max Decugis (FRA)	6-2	5-7	6-2	6-3	
S	Herbert Roper Barrett (GBR)	Gordon Lowe (GBR)	6-2	6-3	6-2		
Q	Max Decugis (FRA)	Rodney Heath (AUS)	10-8	6-4	7-5		
Q	Charles Dixon (GBR)	George A. Thomas (GBR)	6-4	5-7	8-6	6-3	
Q	Herbert Roper Barrett (GBR)	Alfred Beamish (GBR)	6-1	1-6	6-4	6-3	
Q	Gordon Lowe (GBR)	Friedrich Rahe (GER)	5-7	6-3	6-2	9-7	

1912

Rd	Winner	Defeated	S1	S2	S3	S4	S5
Ch	Tony Wilding (NZL)	Arthur Gore (GBR)	6-4	6-4	4-6	6-4	
F	Arthur Gore (GBR)	Andre Gobert (FRA)	9-7	2-6	7-5	6-1	
S	Andre Gobert (FRA)	Max Decugis (FRA)	6-3	6-3	1-6	4-6	6-4
S	Arthur Gore (GBR)	Alfred Beamish (GBR)	6-2	0-6	11-9	6-4	
Q	Andre Gobert (FRA)	Friedrich Rahe (GER)	6-1	6-2	7-5		
Q	Max Decugis (FRA)	Herbert Roper Barrett (GBR)	6-3	7-5	4-6	6-4	
Q	Alfred Beamish (GBR)	James Zimmerman (GBR)	6-4	6-3	6-1		
Q	Arthur Gore (GBR)	Robert B. Powell (CAN)	6-3	6-2	4-6	6-2	

1913

Rd	Winner	Defeated	S1	S2	S3	S4	S5
Ch	Tony Wilding (NZL)	Maurice McLoughlin (USA)	8-6	6-3	10-8		
F	Maurice McLoughllin	Stanley Doust (AUS)	6-3	6-4	7-5		
S	Maurice McLoughlin (USA)	Jim Parke (IRL)	6-4	7-5	6-4		
S	Stanley Doust (AUS)	Oscar Kreuzer (GER)	6-3	6-2	6-3		
Q	Maurice McLoughlin (USA)	W.A. Ingram (GBR)	6-1	6-2	6-4		
Q	Jim Parke (IRL)	R. Douglas Watson (GBR)	6-4	6-1	6-4		
Q	Oscar Kreuzer (GER)	Kenneth Powell (GBR)	6-4	6-1	5-7	6-0	
Q	Stanley Doust (AUS)	Hope Crisp (GBR)	7-5	6-3	3-6	11-9	

1914

Rd	Winner	Defeated	S1	S2	S3	S4	S5
Ch	Norman Brookes (AUS)	Tony Wilding (NZL)	6-4	6-4	7-5		
F	Norman Brookes (AUS)	Otto Froitzheim (GER)	6-2	6-1	5-7	4-6	8-6
S	Otto Froitzheim (GER)	Theo. Mavrogordato (GBR)	6-3	6-2	7-5		
S	Norman Brookes (AUS)	Alfred Beamish (GBR)	6-0	6-3	6-2		
Q	Otto Froitzheim (GER)	Jim Parke (IRL)	5-7	6-2	9-7	6-2	
Q	Theo. Mavrogordato (GBR)	Maurice Germot (FRA)	6-3	2-6	6-4	6-1	
Q	Alfred Beamish (GBR)	Percival Davson (GBR)	6-4	6-2	6-1		
Q	Norman Brookes (AUS)	Arthur Gore (GBR)	7-5	6-1	6-2		

1915–18 NOT HELD—WW I

1919

Rd	Winner	Defeated	S1	S2	S3	S4	S5
Ch	Gerald Patterson (AUS)	Norman Brookes (AUS)	6-3	7-5	6-2		
F	Gerald Patterson (AUS)	Algie Kingscote (GBR)	6-2	6-1	6-3		
S	Gerald Patterson (AUS)	Josiah Ritchie (GBR)	6-1	7-5	1-6	6-3	
S	Algie Kingscote (GBR)	Chuck Garland (USA)	6-1	6-4	2-6	5-7	6-4
Q	Josiah Ritchie (GBR)	Charles Dixon (GBR)	4-6	6-4	6-3	6-3	
Q	Gerald Patterson (AUS)	Andre Gobert (FRA)	10-8	6-3	6-2		
Q	Algie Kingscote (GBR)	Pat O'Hara Wood (AUS)	6-4	3-6	6-3	1-6	6-4
Q	Chuck Garland (USA)	Ronald Thomas (AUS)	6-4	6-0	6-1		

1920

Rd	Winner	Defeated	S1	S2	S3	S4	S5
Ch	Bill Tilden (USA)	Gerald Patterson (AUS)	2-6	6-3	6-2	6-4	
F	Bill Tilden (USA)	Zenzo Shimizu (JPN)	6-4	6-4	13-11		
S	Zenzo Shimizu (JPN)	Theo. Mavrogordato (GBR)	3-6	6-4	6-0	6-2	
S	Bill Tilden (USA)	Chuck Garland (USA)	6-4	8-6	6-2		
Q	Theo. Mavrogordato (GBR)	Dick Williams (USA)	6-3	4-6	9-7	7-5	
Q	Zenzo Shimizu (JPN)	Neville Wilford (GBR)	6-0	6-1	6-2		
Q	Bill Tilden (USA)	Randolph Lycett (GBR)	7-5	4-6	6-4	7-5	
Q	Chuck Garland (USA)	Cecil Blackbeard (RSA)	4-6	6-1	6-3	6-1	

1921

Rd	Winner	Defeated	S1	S2	S3	S4	S5
Ch	Bill Tilden (USA)	Brian Norton (RSA)	4-6	2-6	6-1	6-0	7-5
F	Brian Norton (GBR)	Manuel Alonso (ESP)	5-7	4-6	7-5	6-3	6-3
S	Manuel Alonso (ESP)	Zenzo Shimizu (JPN)	3-6	7-5	3-6	6-4	8-6
S	Brian Norton (RSA)	Frank Hunter (USA)	6-0	6-3	5-7	5-7	6-2
Q	Zenzo Shimizu (JPN)	Randolph Lycett (GBR)	6-3	9-11	3-6	6-2	10-8
Q	Manuel Alonso (ESP)	Algie Kingscote (GBR)	6-1	6-3	2-6	6-2	
Q	Frank Hunter (USA)	Cecil Campbell (GBR)	6-2	7-5	3-6	6-4	
Q	Brian Norton (RSA)	Henry Mayes (CAN)	4-6	6-2	6-2	6-2	

1922

Rd	Winner	Defeated	S1	S2	S3	S4	S5
F	Gerald Patterson (AUS)	Randolph Lycett (GBR)	6-3	6-4	6-2		
S	Randolph Lycett (GBR)	Brian Gilbert (GBR)	8-6	9-7	6-3		
S	Gerald Patterson (AUS)	James Anderson (AUS)	3-6	7-9	6-1	6-3	
Q	Randolph Lycett (GBR)	Percival Davson (GBR)	2-6	6-1	6-4	8-6	
Q	Brian Gilbert (GBR)	Theo. Mavrogordato (GBR)	6-4	3-6	6-3	3-6	6-2
Q	James Anderson (AUS)	Pat O'Hara Wood (AUS)	6-3	6-3	2-6	2-6	6-4
Q	Gerald Patterson (AUS)	Cecil Campbell (GBR)	7-9	6-3	6-2	6-1	

1923

Rd	Winner	Defeated	S1	S2	S3	S4	S5
F	Bill Johnston (USA)	Frank Hunter (USA)	6-0	6-3	6-1		
S	Frank Hunter (USA)	Gordon Lowe (GBR)	6-3	7-5	6-4		
S	Bill Johnston (USA)	Brian Norton (RSA)	6-4	6-2	6-4		
Q	Gordon Lowe (GBR)	D.M. Evans (GBR)	6-2	8-6	7-5		
Q	Frank Hunter (USA)	Manuel de Gomar (ESP)	3-6	4-6	6-1	6-3	6-2
Q	Bill Johnston (USA)	Cecil Campbell (GBR)	6-1	5-7	6-2	6-2	
Q	Brian Norton (RSA)	Max Woosnam (GBR)	7-5	6-3	6-2		

1924

Rd	Winner	Defeated	S1	S2	S3	S4	S5
F	Jean Borotra (FRA)	Rene Lacoste (FRA)	6-1	3-6	6-1	3-6	6-4
S	Jean Borotra (FRA)	Louis Raymond (RSA)	6-2	6-4	7-5		
S	Rene Lacoste (FRA)	Dick Williams (USA)	6-1	3-6	6-2	6-3	
Q	Jean Borotra (FRA)	Vinnie Richards (USA)	6-4	4-6	6-0	6-3	
Q	Louis Raymond (RSA)	Watson Washburn (USA)	6-0	7-5	17-15		
Q	Rene Lacoste (FRA)	Jean Washer (BEL)	6-1	5-7	6-4	6-2	
Q	Dick Williams (USA)	Algie Kingscote (GBR)	5-7	6-4	6-3	6-4	

1925

Rd	Winner	Defeated	S1	S2	S3	S4	S5
F	Rene Lacoste (FRA)	Jean Borotra (FRA)	6-3	6-3	4-6	8-6	
S	Rene Lacoste (FRA)	James Anderson (AUS)	6-4	7-5	6-1		
S	Jean Borotra (FRA)	Henri Cochet (FRA)	5-7	8-6	6-4	6-1	
Q	James Anderson (AUS)	Hector Fisher (SUI)	6-1	6-1	6-4		
Q	Rene Lacoste (FRA)	Sydney Jacob (GBR)	6-3	6-8	6-0	6-4	
Q	Henri Cochet (FRA)	John Hennessey (USA)	7-9	4-6	6-1	6-3	6-0
Q	Jean Borotra (FRA)	Lewis Barclay (GBR)	6-3	5-7	6-3	6-3	

1926

Rd	Winner	Defeated	S1	S2	S3	S4	S5
F	Jean Borotra (FRA)	Howard Kinsey (USA)	8-6	6-1	6-3		
S	Howard Kinsey (USA)	Jacques Brugnon (FRA)	6-4	4-6	6-3	3-6	9-7
S	Jean Borotra (FRA)	Henri Cochet (FRA)	2-6	7-5	2-6	6-3	7-5
Q	Jacques Brugnon (FRA)	Charles Kingsley (GBR)	6-2	4-6	6-2	4-6	6-4
Q	Howard Kinsey (USA)	Pat Spence (RSA)	6-3	6-3	3-6	6-3	
Q	Henri Cochet (FRA)	Colin Gregory (GBR)	3-6	6-4	6-2	4-6	6-3
Q	Jean Borotra (FRA)	Jan Kozeluh (CZE)	6-4	4-6	9-7	6-1	

1927

Rd	Winner	Defeated	S1	S2	S3	S4	S5
F	Henri Cochet (FRA)	Jean Borotra (FRA)	4-6	4-6	6-3	6-4	7-5
S	Henri Cochet (FRA)	Bill Tilden (USA)	2-6	4-6	7-5	6-4	6-3
S	Jean Borotra (FRA)	Rene Lacoste (FRA)	6-4	6-3	1-6	1-6	6-2
Q	Bill Tilden (USA)	Jacques Brugnon (FRA)	6-3	6-1	3-6	7-5	
Q	Henri Cochet (FRA)	Frank Hunter (USA)	3-6	3-6	6-2	6-2	6-3
Q	Rene Lacoste (FRA)	Jan Kozeluh (CZE)	6-4	6-3	6-4		
Q	Jean Borotra (FRA)	Henk Timmer (NED)	6-1	3-6	6-3	6-0	

1928

Rd	Winner	Defeated	S1	S2	S3	S4	S5
F	Rene Lacoste (FRA)	Henri Cochet (FRA)	6-1	4-6	6-4	6-2	
S	Henri Cochet (FRA)	Christian Boussus (FRA)	11-9	3-6	6-2	6-3	
S	Rene Lacoste (FRA)	Bill Tilden (USA)	2-6	6-4	2-6	6-4	6-3
Q	Henri Cochet (FRA)	John Hennessey (USA)	6-4	6-1	5-7	6-3	
Q	Christian Boussus (FRA)	Jacques Brugnon (FRA)	12-10	10-8	6-2		
Q	Rene Lacoste (FRA)	Umberto de Morpurgo (ITA)	6-2	6-3	6-4		
Q	Bill Tilden (USA)	Jean Borotra (FRA)	8-6	3-6	6-3	6-2	

1929

Rd	Winner	Defeated	S1	S2	S3	S4	S5
F	Henri Cochet (FRA)	Jean Borotra (FRA)	6-4	6-3	6-4		
S	Henri Cochet (FRA)	Bill Tilden (USA)	6-4	6-1	7-5		
S	Jean Borotra (FRA)	Bunny Austin (GBR)	6-1	10-8	5-7	6-1	
Q	Henri Cochet (FRA)	Henk Timmer (NED)	6-4	7-5	6-2		
Q	Bill Tilden (USA)	Paul Landry (FRA)	6-4	2-6	6-3	7-5	
Q	Jean Borotra (FRA)	George Lott (USA)	6-3	6-3	6-4		
Q	Bunny Austin (GBR)	Bela von Kehrling (HUN)	6-2	8-6	6-3		

1930

Rd	Winner	Defeated	S1	S2	S3	S4	S5
F	Bill Tilden (USA)	Wilmer Allison (USA)	6-3	9-7	6-4		
S	Wilmer Allison (USA)	Johnny Doeg (USA)	6-3	4-6	8-6	3-6	7-5
S	Bill Tilden (USA)	Jean Borotra (FRA)	0-6	6-4	4-6	6-0	7-5
Q	Wilmer Allison (USA)	Henri Cochet (FRA)	6-4	6-4	6-3		
Q	Johnny Doeg (USA)	Gregory Mangin (USA)	6-3	1-6	6-3	6-4	
Q	Bill Tilden (USA)	Colin Gregory (GBR)	6-1	6-2	6-3		
Q	Jean Borotra (FRA)	George Lott (USA)	2-6	6-3	6-3	6-4	

1931

Rd	Winner	Defeated	S1	S2	S3	S4	S5
F	Sidney Wood (USA)	Francis Shields (USA)	(walkover)				
S	Sidney Wood (USA)	Fred Perry (GBR)	4-6	6-2	6-4	6-2	
S	Francis Shields (USA)	Jean Borotra (FRA)	7-5	3-6	6-4	6-4	
Q	Sidney Wood (USA)	Pat Hughes (GBR)	4-6	6-4	6-3	6-1	
Q	Fred Perry (GBR)	John Van Ryn (USA)	6-4	8-6	7-5		
Q	Jean Borotra (FRA)	Jiro Satoh (JPN)	6-2	6-3	4-6	6-4	
Q	Francis Shields (USA)	Bunny Austin (GBR)	6-3	2-6	5-7	7-5	6-1

1932

Rd	Winner	Defeated	S1	S2	S3	S4	S5
F	Ellsworth Vines (USA)	Bunny Austin (GBR)	6-4	6-2	6-0		
S	Ellsworth Vines (USA)	Jack Crawford (AUS)	6-2	6-1	6-3		
S	Bunny Austin (GBR)	Jiro Satoh (JPN)	7-5	6-2	6-1		
Q	Ellsworth Vines (USA)	Enrique Maier (ESP)	6-2	6-3	6-2		
Q	Jack Crawford (AUS)	Fred Perry (GBR)	7-5	8-6	2-6	8-6	
Q	Bunny Austin (GBR)	Francis Shields (USA)	6-1	9-7	5-7	6-1	
Q	Jiro Satoh (JPN)	Sidney Wood (USA)	7-5	7-5	2-6	6-4	

1933

Rd	Winner	Defeated	S1	S2	S3	S4	S5
F	Jack Crawford (AUS)	Ellsworth Vines (USA)	4-6	11-9	6-2	2-6	6-4
S	Ellsworth Vines (USA)	Henri Cochet (FRA)	6-2	8-6	3-6	6-1	
S	Jack Crawford (AUS)	Jiro Satoh (JPN)	6-3	6-4	2-6	6-4	
Q	Ellsworth Vines (USA)	Roderich Menzel (CZE)	6-2	6-4	3-6	6-3	
Q	Henri Cochet (FRA)	Lester Stoefen (USA)	3-6	6-4	6-3	6-1	
Q	Jiro Satoh (JPN)	Bunny Austin (GBR)	7-5	6-3	2-6	2-6	6-2
Q	Jack Crawford (AUS)	Pat Hughes (GBR)	6-1	6-1	7-5		

1934

Rd	Winner	Defeated	S1	S2	S3	S4	S5
F	Fred Perry (GBR)	Jack Crawford (AUS)	6-3	6-0	7-5		
S	Jack Crawford (AUS)	Francis Shields (USA)	2-6	4-6	6-4	6-3	6-4
S	Fred Perry (GBR)	Sidney Wood (USA)	6-3	3-6	7-5	5-7	6-3
Q	Jack Crawford (AUS)	Lester Stoefen (USA)	7-5	2-6	7-5	6-0	
Q	Francis Shields (USA)	Bunny Austin (GBR)	4-6	2-6	7-5	6-3	7-5
Q	Fred Perry (GBR)	George Lott (USA)	6-4	2-6	7-5	10-8	
Q	Sidney Wood (USA)	Vernon Kirby (RSA)	6-1	6-4	3-6	6-0	

1935

Rd	Winner	Defeated	S1	S2	S3	S4	S5
F	Fred Perry (GBR)	Gottfried von Cramm (GER)	6-2	6-4	6-4		
S	Fred Perry (GBR)	Jack Crawford (AUS)	6-2	3-6	6-4	6-4	
S	Gottfried von Cramm (GER)	Don Budge (USA)	4-6	6-4	6-3	6-2	
Q	Fred Perry (GBR)	Roderich Menzel (CZE)	9-7	6-1	6-1		
Q	Jack Crawford (AUS)	Sidney Wood (USA)	6-4	6-3	6-8	5-7	6-1
Q	Don Budge (USA)	Bunny Austin (GBR)	3-6	10-8	6-4	7-5	
Q	Gottfried von Cramm (GER)	Viv McGrath (AUS)	6-4	6-2	4-6	6-1	

1936

Rd	Winner	Defeated	S1	S2	S3	S4	S5
F	Fred Perry (GBR)	Gottfried von Cramm (GER)	6-1	6-1	6-0		
S	Fred Perry (GBR)	Don Budge (USA)	5-7	6-4	6-3	6-4	
S	Gottfried von Cramm (GER)	Bunny Austin (GBR)	8-6	6-3	2-6	6-3	
Q	Fred Perry (GBR)	Bryan Grant Jr. (USA)	6-4	6-3	6-1		
Q	Don Budge (USA)	Adrian Quist (AUS)	6-2	6-4	6-4		
Q	Bunny Austin (GBR)	Wilmer Allison (USA)	6-1	6-4	7-5		
Q	Gottfried von Cramm (GER)	Jack Crawford (AUS)	6-1	7-5	6-4		

1937

Rd	Winner	Defeated	S1	S2	S3	S4	S5
F	Don Budge (USA)	Gottfried von Cramm (GER)	6-3	6-4	6-2		
S	Gottfried von Cramm (GER)	Bunny Austin (GBR)	8-6	6-3	12-14	6-1	
S	Don Budge (USA)	Frank Parker (USA)	2-6	6-4	6-4	6-1	
Q	Gottfried von Cramm (GER)	Jack Crawford (AUS)	6-3	8-6	3-6	2-6	6-2
Q	Bunny Austin (GBR)	Bryan Grant Jr. (USA)	6-1	7-5	6-4		
Q	Frank Parker (USA)	Henner Henkel (GER)	6-3	7-5	4-6	4-6	6-2
Q	Don Budge (USA)	Viv McGrath (AUS)	6-3	6-1	6-4		

1938

Rd	Winner	Defeated	S1	S2	S3	S4	S5
F	Don Budge (USA)	Bunny Austin (GBR)	6-1	6-0	6-3		
S	Bunny Austin (GBR)	Henner Henkel (GER)	6-2	6-4	6-0		
S	Don Budge (USA)	Franjo Puncec (YUG)	6-2	6-1	6-4		
Q	Bunny Austin (GBR)	Max S. Ellmer (SUI)	6-2	6-1	6-2		
Q	Henner Henkel (GER)	Ladislav Hecht (CZE)	7-5	6-1	6-2		
Q	Franjo Puncec (YUG)	Donald MacPhail (GBR)	6-2	6-1	6-1		
Q	Don Budge (USA)	Franz Cejnar (CZE)	6-3	6-0	7-5		

1939

Rd	Winner	Defeated	S1	S2	S3	S4	S5
F	Bobby Riggs (USA)	Elwood Cooke (USA)	2-6	8-6	3-6	6-3	6-2
S	Elwood Cooke (USA)	Henner Henkel (GER)	6-3	4-6	6-4	6-4	
S	Bobby Riggs (USA)	Franjo Puncec (YUG)	6-2	6-3	6-4		
Q	Elwood Cooke (USA)	Bunny Austin (GBR)	6-3	6-0	6-1		
Q	Henner Henkel (GER)	Franjo Kukuljevic (YUG)	6-1	6-3	6-2		
Q	Franjo Puncec (YUG)	M. Eugene Smith (USA)	6-0	6-2	6-2		
Q	Bobby Riggs (USA)	Ghaus Mohammed (IND)	6-2	6-2	6-2		

1940–1945 NOT HELD—WW II

1946

Rd	Winner	Defeated	S1	S2	S3	S4	S5
F	Yvon Petra (FRA)	Geoff Brown (AUS)	6-2	6-4	7-9	5-7	6-4
S	Yvon Petra (FRA)	Tom Brown Jr. (USA)	4-6	4-6	6-3	7-5	8-6
S	Geoff Brown (AUS)	Jaroslav Drobny (CZE)	6-4	7-5	6-2		
Q	Yvon Petra (FRA)	Dinny Pails (AUS)	7-5	7-5	6-8	6-4	
Q	Tom Brown Jr. (USA)	Franjo Puncec (YUG)	6-2	8-6	6-4		
Q	Geoff Brown (AUS)	Lennart Bergelin (SWE)	13-11	11-9	6-4		
Q	Jaroslav Drobny (CZE)	Pierre Pellizza (FRA)	6-4	6-4	6-4		

1947

Rd	Winner	Defeated	S1	S2	S3	S4	S5
F	Jack Kramer (USA)	Tom Brown Jr. (USA)	6-1	6-3	6-2		
S	Tom Brown Jr. (USA)	Budge Patty (USA)	6-3	6-3	6-3		
S	Jack Kramer (USA)	Dinny Pails (AUS)	6-1	3-6	6-1	6-0	
Q	Budge Patty (USA)	Jaroslav Drobny (CZE)	3-6	6-4	7-9	6-2	6-3
Q	Tom Brown Jr. (USA)	Yvon Petra (FRA)	7-5	6-2	6-4		
Q	Dinny Pails (AUS)	Bob Falkenburg (USA)	4-6	4-6	6-3	6-0	6-2
Q	Jack Kramer (USA)	Geoff Brown (AUS)	6-0	6-1	6-3		

1948

Rd	Winner	Defeated	S1	S2	S3	S4	S5
F	Bob Falkenburg (USA)	John Bromwich (AUS)	7-5	0-6	6-2	3-6	7-5
S	Bob Falkenburg (USA)	Gardnar Mulloy (USA)	6-4	6-4	8-6		
S	John Bromwich (AUS)	Jozsef Asboth (HUN)	6-3	14-12	6-2		
Q	Gardnar Mulloy (USA)	Tony Mottram (GBR)	6-2	1-6	7-5	6-1	
Q	Bob Falkenburg (USA)	Lennart Bergelin (SWE)	6-4	6-2	3-6	6-4	
Q	John Bromwich (AUS)	Budge Patty (USA)	6-4	7-5	6-1		
Q	Jozsef Asboth (HUN)	Tom Brown Jr. (USA)	4-6	6-3	4-6	6-1	6-1

1949

Rd	Winner	Defeated	S1	S2	S3	S4	S5
F	Ted Schroeder (USA)	Jaroslav Drobny (EGY)	3-6	6-0	6-3	4-6	6-4
S	Jaroslav Drobny (EGY)	John Bromwich (AUS)	6-1	6-3	6-2		
S	Ted Schroeder (USA)	Eric Sturgess (RSA)	3-6	7-5	5-7	6-1	6-2
Q	Jaroslav Drobny (EGY)	Geoff Brown (AUS)	2-6	7-5	1-6	6-2	6-4
Q	John Bromwich (AUS)	Bob Falkenburg (USA)	3-6	9-11	6-0	6-0	6-4
Q	Eric Sturgess (RSA)	Frank Parker (USA)	3-6	6-4	3-6	6-1	6-3
Q	Ted Schroeder (USA)	Frank Sedgman (AUS)	3-6	6-8	6-3	6-2	9-7

1950

Rd	Winner	Defeated	S1	S2	S3	S4	S5
F	Budge Patty (USA)	Frank Sedgman (AUS)	6-1	8-10	6-2	6-3	
S	Frank Sedgman (AUS)	Jaroslav Drobny (EGY)	3-6	3-6	6-3	7-5	6-2
S	Budge Patty (USA)	Vic Seixas (USA)	6-3	5-7	6-2	7-5	
Q	Frank Sedgman (AUS)	Art Larsen (USA)	8-10	5-7	7-5	6-3	7-5
Q	Jaroslav Drobny (EGY)	Gardnar Mulloy (USA)	6-3	6-4	6-4		
Q	Vic Seixas (USA)	Eric Sturgess (RSA)	9-7	6-8	3-6	6-2	7-5
Q	Budge Patty (USA)	Bill Talbert (USA)	3-6	6-4	6-2	6-3	

1951

Rd	Winner	Defeated	S1	S2	S3	S4	S5
F	Dick Savitt (USA)	Ken McGregor (AUS)	6-4	6-4	6-4		
S	Dick Savitt (USA)	Herbie Flam (USA)	1-6	15-13	6-3	6-2	
S	Ken McGregor (AUS)	Eric Sturgess (RSA)	6-4	3-6	6-3	7-5	
Q	Herbie Flam (USA)	Frank Sedgman (AUS)	2-6	1-6	6-3	6-4	7-5
Q	Dick Savitt (USA)	Art Larsen (USA)	6-1	6-4	6-4		
Q	Ken McGregor (AUS)	Armando Vieira (BRA)	6-2	6-0	6-3		
Q	Eric Sturgess (RSA)	Lennart Bergelin (SWE)	6-0	4-6	5-7	6-2	6-4

1952

Rd	Winner	Defeated	S1	S2	S3	S4	S5
F	Frank Sedgman (AUS)	Jaroslav Drobny (EGY)	4-6	6-2	6-3	6-2	
S	Frank Sedgman (AUS)	Merv Rose (AUS)	6-4	6-4	7-5		
S	Jaroslav Drobny (EGY)	Herbie Flam (USA)	6-2	6-4	0-6	8-10	6-4
Q	Frank Sedgman (AUS)	Eric Sturgess (RSA)	7-5	6-1	6-0		
Q	Merv Rose (AUS)	Dick Savitt (USA)	6-4	3-6	6-4	4-6	6-2
Q	Herbie Flam (USA)	Vic Seixas (USA)	6-4	3-6	6-3	7-5	
Q	Jaroslav Drobny (EGY)	Ken McGregor (AUS)	6-0	3-6	2-6	7-5	7-5

1953

Rd	Winner	Defeated	S1	S2	S3	S4	S5
F	Vic Seixas (USA)	Kurt Nielsen (DEN)	9-7	6-3	6-4		
S	Vic Seixas (USA)	Merv Rose (AUS)	6-4	10-12	9-11	6-4	6-3
S	Kurt Nielsen (DEN)	Jaroslav Drobny (EGY)	6-4	6-3	6-2		
Q	Vic Seixas (USA)	Lew Hoad (AUS)	5-7	6-4	6-3	1-6	9-7
Q	Merv Rose (AUS)	Art Larsen (USA)	6-3	6-3	16-14		
Q	Jaroslav Drobny (EGY)	Sven Davidson (SWE)	7-5	6-4	6-0		
Q	Kurt Nielsen (DEN)	Ken Rosewall (AUS)	7-5	4-6	6-8	6-0	6-2

1954

Rd	Winner	Defeated	S1	S2	S3	S4	S5
F	Jaroslav Drobny (EGY)	Ken Rosewall (AUS)	13-11	4-6	6-2	9-7	
S	Jaroslav Drobny (EGY)	Budge Patty (USA)	6-2	6-4	4-6	9-7	
S	Ken Rosewall (AUS)	Tony Trabert (USA)	3-6	6-3	4-6	6-1	6-1
Q	Jaroslav Drobny (EGY)	Lew Hoad (AUS)	6-4	6-3	6-3		
Q	Budge Patty (USA)	Vic Seixas (USA)	7-5	4-6	6-3	6-2	
Q	Ken Rosewall (AUS)	Rex Hartwig (AUS)	6-3	3-6	3-6	6-3	6-1
Q	Tony Trabert (USA)	Merv Rose (AUS)	6-2	6-2	7-5		

1955

Rd	Winner	Defeated	S1	S2	S3	S4	S5
F	Tony Trabert (USA)	Kurt Nielsen (DEN)	6-3	7-5	6-1		
S	Kurt Nielsen (DEN)	Ken Rosewall (AUS)	11-9	6-2	2-6	6-4	
S	Tony Trabert (USA)	Budge Patty (USA)	8-6	6-2	6-2		
Q	Ken Rosewall (AUS)	Sven Davidson (SWE)	6-4	6-1	6-2		
Q	Kurt Nielsen (DEN)	Nicola Pietrangeli (ITA)	1-6	6-3	5-7	6-2	7-5
Q	Budge Patty (USA)	Lew Hoad (AUS)	6-4	6-4	6-4		
Q	Tony Trabert (USA)	Jaroslav Drobny (GBR)	8-6	6-1	6-4		

1956

Rd	Winner	Defeated	S1	S2	S3	S4	S5
F	Lew Hoad (AUS)	Ken Rosewall (AUS)	6-2	4-6	7-5	6-4	
S	Lew Hoad (AUS)	Hamilton Richardson (USA)	3-6	6-4	6-2	6-4	
S	Ken Rosewall (AUS)	Vic Seixas (USA)	6-3	3-6	6-8	6-3	7-5
Q	Lew Hoad (AUS)	Mal Anderson (AUS)	4-6	6-1	6-1	13-11	
Q	Hamilton Richardson (USA)	Neale Fraser (AUS)	6-3	9-11	7-5	6-4	
Q	Vic Seixas (USA)	Allen Morris (USA)	13-11	6-0	6-3		
Q	Ken Rosewall (AUS)	Ulf Schmidt (SWE)	6-1	6-3	6-2		

1957

Rd	Winner	Defeated	S1	S2	S3	S4	S5
F	Lew Hoad (AUS)	Ashley Cooper (AUS)	6-2	6-1	6-2		
S	Ashley Cooper (AUS)	Neale Fraser (AUS)	1-6	14-12	6-3	8-6	
S	Lew Hoad (AUS)	Sven Davidson (SWE)	6-4	6-4	7-5		
Q	Ashley Cooper (AUS)	Herbie Flam (USA)	6-3	7-5	6-1		
Q	Neale Fraser (AUS)	Ulf Schmidt (SWE)	1-6	6-4	6-8	6-4	6-4
Q	Sven Davidson (SWE)	Vic Seixas (USA)	5-7	6-4	6-4	6-4	
Q	Lew Hoad (AUS)	Merv Rose (AUS)	6-4	4-6	10-8	6-3	

1958

Rd	Winner	Defeated	S1	S2	S3	S4	S5
F	Ashley Cooper (AUS)	Neale Fraser (AUS)	3-6	6-3	6-4	13-11	
S	Neale Fraser (AUS)	Kurt Nielsen (DEN)	6-4	6-4	17-19	6-4	
S	Ashley Cooper (AUS)	Merv Rose (AUS)	7-9	6-2	6-2	6-3	
Q	Kurt Nielsen (DEN)	Mal Anderson (AUS)	6-2	6-3			(retired)
Q	Neale Fraser (AUS)	Sven Davidson (SWE)	6-4	6-8	6-2	3-6	8-6
Q	Merv Rose (AUS)	Barry MacKay (USA)	6-2	6-4	6-4		
Q	Ashley Cooper (AUS)	Bobby Wilson (GBR)	6-4	6-2	3-6	4-6	7-5

1959

Rd	Winner	Defeated	S1	S2	S3	S4	S5
F	Alejandro Olmedo (PER)	Rod Laver (AUS)	6-4	6-3	6-4		
S	Rod Laver (AUS)	Barry MacKay (USA)	11-13	11-9	10-8	7-9	6-3
S	Alejandro Olmedo (PER)	Roy Emerson (AUS)	6-4	6-0	6-4		
Q	Barry MacKay (USA)	Neale Fraser (AUS)	5-7	10-8	0-6	6-3	6-1
Q	Rod Laver (AUS)	Jean-Claude Molinari (FRA)	6-3	6-3	6-0		
Q	Roy Emerson (AUS)	Bobby Wilson (GBR)	6-3	6-4	6-2		
Q	Alejandro Olmedo (PER)	Luis Ayala (CHI)	7-5	3-6	6-3	6-3	

1960

Rd	Winner	Defeated	S1	S2	S3	S4	S5
F	Neale Fraser (AUS)	Rod Laver (AUS)	6-4	3-6	9-7	7-5	
S	Rod Laver (AUS)	Nicola Pietrangeli (ITA)	4-6	6-3	8-10	6-2	6-4
S	Neale Fraser (AUS)	Ramanathan Krishnan (IND)	6-3	6-2	6-2		
Q	Nicola Pietrangeli (ITA)	Barry MacKay (USA)	16-14	6-2	3-6	6-4	
Q	Rod Laver (AUS)	Roy Emerson (AUS)	6-4	5-7	6-4	6-4	
Q	Ramanathan Krishnan (IND)	Luis Ayala (CHI)	7-5	10-8	6-2		
Q	Neale Fraser (AUS)	Butch Buchholz (USA)	4-6	6-3	4-6	15-15	(ret'd)

1961

Rd	Winner	Defeated	S1	S2	S3	S4	S5
F	Rod Laver (AUS)	Chuck McKinley (USA)	6-3	6-1	6-4		
S	Rod Laver (AUS)	Ramanathan Krishnan (IND)	6-2	8-6	6-2		
S	Chuck McKinley (USA)	Mike Sangster (GBR)	6-4	6-4	8-6		
Q	Rod Laver (AUS)	Luis Ayala (CHI)	6-1	6-3	6-2		
Q	Ramanathan Krishnan (IND)	Roy Emerson (AUS)	6-1	6-4	6-4		
Q	Chuck McKinley (USA)	Iyo Pimentel (VEN)	6-2	6-2	6-4		
Q	Mike Sangster (GBR)	Bobby Wilson (GBR)	6-4	6-4	4-6	6-4	

1962

Rd	Winner	Defeated	S1	S2	S3	S4	S5
F	Rod Laver (AUS)	Marty Mulligan (AUS)	6-2	6-2	6-1		
S	Rod Laver (AUS)	Neale Fraser (AUS)	10-8	6-1	7-5		
S	Marty Mulligan (AUS)	John Fraser (AUS)	6-3	6-2	6-2		
Q	Rod Laver (AUS)	Manolo Santana (ESP)	14-16	9-7	6-2	6-2	
Q	Neale Fraser (AUS)	Rafael Osuna (MEX)	6-3	6-1	4-6	4-6	6-2
Q	John Fraser (AUS)	Ken Fletcher (AUS)	1-6	7-9	6-4	6-1	6-2
Q	Marty Mulligan (AUS)	Bob Hewitt (AUS)	6-8	6-4	6-3	6-4	

1963

Rd	Winner	Defeated	S1	S2	S3	S4	S5
F	Chuck McKinley (USA)	Fred Stolle (AUS)	9-7	6-1	6-4		
S	Chuck McKinley (USA)	Wilhelm Bungert (GER)	6-2	6-4	8-6		
S	Fred Stolle (AUS)	Manolo Santana (ESP)	8-6	6-1	7-5		
Q	Wilhelm Bungert (GER)	Roy Emerson (AUS)	8-6	3-6	6-3	4-6	6-3
Q	Chuck McKinley (USA)	Bobby Wilson (GBR)	8-6	6-4	6-2		
Q	Fred Stolle (AUS)	Frank Froehling III (USA)	9-7	7-5	6-4		
Q	Manolo Santana (ESP)	Christian Kuhnke (GER)	6-3	6-4	6-4		

1964

Rd	Winner	Defeated	S1	S2	S3	S4	S5
F	Roy Emerson (AUS)	Fred Stolle (AUS)	6-4	12-10	4-6	6-3	
S	Roy Emerson (AUS)	Wilhelm Bungert (GER)	6-3	15-13	6-0		
S	Fred Stolle (AUS)	Chuck McKinley (USA)	4-6	10-8	9-7	6-4	
Q	Roy Emerson (AUS)	Bob Hewitt (AUS)	6-1	6-4	6-4		
Q	Wilhelm Bungert (GER)	Rafael Osuna (MEX)	6-4	6-2	6-3		
Q	Fred Stolle (AUS)	Christian Kuhnke (GER)	6-3	7-5	6-3		
Q	Chuck McKinley (USA)	Abe Segal (RSA)	6-3	6-3	4-6	6-4	

1965

Rd	Winner	Defeated	S1	S2	S3	S4	S5
F	Roy Emerson (AUS)	Fred Stolle (AUS)	6-2	6-4	6-4		
S	Roy Emerson (AUS)	Dennis Ralston (USA)	6-1	6-2	7-9	6-1	
S	Fred Stolle (AUS)	Cliff Drysdale (RSA)	6-3	6-4	7-5		
Q	Roy Emerson (AUS)	Keith Diepraam (RSA)	4-6	6-3	6-1	6-1	
Q	Dennis Ralston (USA)	Marty Riessen (USA)	3-6	2-6	6-4	6-2	6-2
Q	Cliff Drysdale (RSA)	Allen Fox (USA)	4-6	6-2	7-5	7-5	
Q	Fred Stolle (AUS)	Rafael Osuna (MEX)	11-13	6-3	6-1	6-2	

1966

Rd	Winner	Defeated	S1	S2	S3	S4	S5
F	Manolo Santana (ESP)	Dennis Ralston (USA)	6-4	11-9	6-4		
S	Manolo Santana (ESP)	Owen Davidson (AUS)	6-2	4-6	9-7	3-6	7-5
S	Dennis Ralston (USA)	Cliff Drysdale (RSA)	6-8	8-6	3-6	7-5	6-3
Q	Owen Davidson (AUS)	Roy Emerson (AUS)	1-6	6-3	6-4	6-4	
Q	Manolo Santana (ESP)	Ken Fletcher (AUS)	6-2	3-6	8-6	4-6	7-5
Q	Dennis Ralston (USA)	Bob Hewitt (RSA)	7-5	6-2	11-9		
Q	Cliff Drysdale (RSA)	Tony Roche (AUS)	9-7	6-2	6-2		

1967

Rd	Winner	Defeated	S1	S2	S3	S4	S5
F	John Newcombe (AUS)	Wilhelm Bungert (GER)	6-3	6-1	6-1		
S	Wilhelm Bungert (GER)	Roger Taylor (GBR)	6-4	6-8	2-6	6-4	6-4
S	John Newcombe (AUS)	Niki Pilic (YUG)	9-7	4-6	6-3	6-4	
Q	Wilhelm Bungert (GER)	Tomaz Koch (BRA)	6-4	4-6	4-6	6-1	6-3
Q	Roger Taylor (GBR)	Ray Ruffels (AUS)	6-4	8-6	6-4		
Q	John Newcombe (AUS)	Ken Fletcher (AUS)	6-4	6-2	6-4		
Q	Niki Pilic (YUG)	John Cooper (AUS)	14-12	8-10	6-4	6-2	

1968

Rd	Winner	Defeated	S1	S2	S3	S4	S5
F	Rod Laver (AUS)	Tony Roche (AUS)	6-3	6-4	6-2		
S	Rod Laver (AUS)	Arthur Ashe (USA)	7-5	6-2	6-4		
S	Tony Roche (AUS)	Clark Graebner (USA)	9-7	8-10	6-4	8-6	
Q	Rod Laver (AUS)	Dennis Ralston (USA)	4-6	6-4	6-1	4-6	6-2
Q	Arthur Ashe (USA)	Tom Okker (NED)	7-9	9-7	9-7	6-2	
Q	Clark Graebner (USA)	Raymond Moore (RSA)	6-2	6-0	9-7		
Q	Tony Roche (AUS)	Butch Buchholz (USA)	3-6	7-5	6-4	6-4	

1969

Rd	Winner	Defeated	S1	S2	S3	S4	S5
F	Rod Laver (AUS)	John Newcombe (AUS)	6-4	5-7	6-4	6-4	
S	Rod Laver (AUS)	Arthur Ashe (USA)	2-6	6-2	9-7	6-0	
S	John Newcombe (AUS)	Tony Roche (AUS)	3-6	6-1	14-12	6-4	
Q	Rod Laver (AUS)	Cliff Drysdale (RSA)	6-4	6-2	6-3		
Q	Arthur Ashe (USA)	Bob Lutz (USA)	6-4	6-2	4-6	7-5	
Q	John Newcombe (AUS)	Tom Okker (NED)	8-6	3-6	6-1	7-5	
Q	Tony Roche (AUS)	Clark Graebner (USA)	4-6	4-6	6-3	6-4	11-9

1970

Rd	Winner	Defeated	S1	S2	S3	S4	S5
F	John Newcombe (AUS)	Ken Rosewall (AUS)	5-7	6-3	6-3	3-6	6-1
S	Ken Rosewall (AUS)	Roger Taylor (GBR)	6-3	4-6	6-3	6-3	
S	John Newcombe (AUS)	Andres Gimeno (ESP)	6-3	8-6	6-0		
Q	Roger Taylor (GBR)	Clark Graebner (USA)	6-3	11-9	12-10		
Q	Ken Rosewall (AUS)	Tony Roche (AUS)	10-8	6-1	4-6	6-2	
Q	Andres Gimeno (ESP)	Bob Carmichael (AUS)	6-1	6-2	6-4		
Q	John Newcombe (AUS)	Roy Emerson (AUS)	6-1	5-7	3-6	6-2	11-9

1971

Rd	Winner	Defeated	S1	S2	S3	S4	S5
F	John Newcombe (AUS)	Stan Smith (USA)	6-3	5-7	2-6	6-4	6-4
S	Stan Smith (USA)	Tom Gorman (USA)	6-3	8-6	6-2		
S	John Newcombe (AUS)	Ken Rosewall (AUS)	6-1	6-1	6-3		
Q	Tom Gorman (USA)	Rod Laver (AUS)	9-7	8-6	6-3		
Q	Stan Smith (USA)	Onny Parun (NZL)	8-6	6-3	6-4		
Q	Ken Rosewall (AUS)	Cliff Richey (USA)	6-8	5-7	6-4	9-7	7-5
Q	John Newcombe (AUS)	Colin Dibley (AUS)	6-1	6-2	6-3		

1972

Rd	Winner	Defeated	S1	S2	S3	S4	S5
F	Stan Smith (USA)	Ilie Nastase (ROU)	4-6	6-3	6-3	4-6	7-5
S	Stan Smith (USA)	Jan Kodes (CZE)	3-6	6-4	6-1	7-5	
S	Ilie Nastase (ROU)	Manolo Orantes (ESP)	6-3	6-4	6-4		
Q	Stan Smith (USA)	Alex Metreveli (USSR)	6-2	8-6	6-2		
Q	Jan Kodes (CZE)	Onny Parun (AUS)	6-2	6-3	6-4		
Q	Manolo Orantes (ESP)	Colin Dibley (AUS)	6-2	6-0	6-2		
Q	Ilie Nastase (ROU)	Jimmy Connors (USA)	6-4	6-4	6-1		

1973

Rd	Winner	Defeated	S1	S2	S3	S4	S5
F	Jan Kodes (CZE)	Alex Metreveli (USSR)	6-1	9-8(5)	6-3		
S	Alex Metreveli (USSR)	Alex Mayer (USA)	6-3	3-6	6-3	6-4	
S	Jan Kodes (CZE)	Roger Taylor (GBR)	8-9	9-7	5-7	6-4	7-5
Q	Alex Mayer (USA)	Jurgen Fassbender (GER)	3-6	4-6	6-3	6-4	6-4
Q	Alex Metreveli (USSR)	Jimmy Connors (USA)	8-6	6-2	5-7	6-4	
Q	Roger Taylor (GBR)	Bjorn Borg (SWE)	6-1	6-8	3-6	6-3	7-5
Q	Jan Kodes (CZE)	Vijay Amritraj (IND)	6-4	3-6	4-6	6-3	7-5

1974

Rd	Winner	Defeated	S1	S2	S3	S4	S5
F	Jimmy Connors (USA)	Ken Rosewall (AUS)	6-1	6-1	6-4		
S	Ken Rosewall (AUS)	Stan Smith (USA)	6-8	4-6	9-8(6)	6-1	6-3
S	Jimmy Connors (USA)	Dick Stockton (USA)	4-6	6-2	6-3	6-4	
Q	Ken Rosewall (AUS)	John Newcombe (AUS)	6-1	1-6	6-0	7-5	
Q	Stan Smith (USA)	Ismail El Shafei (EGY)	9-8(2)	7-5	6-8	7-5	
Q	Jimmy Connors (USA)	Jan Kodes (CZE)	3-6	6-3	6-3	6-8	6-3
Q	Dick Stockton (USA)	Alex Metreveli (USSR)	6-4	7-5	6-1		

1975

Rd	Winner	Defeated	S1	S2	S3	S4	S5
F	Arthur Ashe (USA)	Jimmy Connors (USA)	6-1	6-1	5-7	6-4	
S	Jimmy Connors (USA)	Roscoe Tanner (USA)	6-4	6-1	6-4		
S	Arthur Ashe (USA)	Tony Roche (AUS)	5-7	6-4	7-5	8-9(4)	6-4
Q	Jimmy Connors (USA)	Raul Ramirez (MEX)	6-4	8-6	6-2		
Q	Roscoe Tanner (USA)	Guillermo Vilas (ARG)	6-4	5-7	6-8	6-2	6-2
Q	Arthur Ashe (USA)	Bjorn Borg (SWE)	2-6	6-4	8-6	6-1	
Q	Tony Roche (AUS)	Tom Okker (NED)	2-6	9-8(11)	2-6	6-4	6-2

1976

Rd	Winner	Defeated	S1	S2	S3	S4	S5
F	Bjorn Borg (SWE)	Ilie Nastase (ROU)	6-4	6-2	9-7		
S	Ilie Nastase (ROU)	Raul Ramirez (MEX)	6-2	9-7	6-3		
S	Bjorn Borg (SWE)	Roscoe Tanner (USA)	6-4	9-8(2)	6-4		
Q	Raul Ramirez (MEX)	Vitas Gerulaitis (USA)	4-6	6-4	6-2	6-4	
Q	Ilie Nastase (ROU)	Charles Pasarell (USA)	6-4	6-2	6-3		
Q	Bjorn Borg (SWE)	Guillermo Vilas (ARG)	6-3	6-0	6-2		
Q	Raul Ramirez (MEX)	Jimmy Connors (USA)	6-4	6-2	8-6		

1977

Rd	Winner	Defeated	S1	S2	S3	S4	S5
F	Bjorn Borg (SWE)	Jimmy Connors (USA)	3-6	6-2	6-1	5-7	6-4
S	Jimmy Connors (USA)	John McEnroe (USA)	6-3	6-3	4-6	6-4	
S	Bjorn Borg (SWE)	Vitas Gerulaitis (USA)	6-4	3-6	6-3	3-6	8-6
Q	Jimmy Connors (USA)	Byron Bertram (RSA)	6-4	3-6	6-4	6-2	
Q	John McEnroe (USA)	Phil Dent (AUS)	6-4	8-9(7)	4-6	6-3	6-4
Q	Bjorn Borg (SWE)	Ilie Nastase (ROU)	6-0	8-6	6-3		
Q	Vitas Gerulaitis (USA)	Billy Martin (USA)	6-2	8-9	6-2	6-2	

1978

Rd	Winner	Defeated	S1	S2	S3	S4	S5
F	Bjorn Borg (SWE)	Jimmy Connors (USA)	6-2	6-2	6-3		
S	Bjorn Borg (SWE)	Tom Okker (NED)	6-4	6-4	6-4		
S	Jimmy Connors (USA)	Vitas Gerulaitis (USA)	9-7	6-2	6-1		
Q	Bjorn Borg (SWE)	Alex Mayer (USA)	7-5	6-4	6-3		
Q	Tom Okker (NED)	Ilie Nastase (ROU)	7-5	6-1	2-6	6-3	
Q	Vitas Gerulaitis (USA)	Brian Gottfried (USA)	7-5	4-6	9-7	6-2	
Q	Jimmy Connors (USA)	Raul Ramirez (MEX)	6-4	6-4	6-2		

1979

Rd	Winner	Defeated	S1	S2	S3	S4	S5
F	Bjorn Borg (SWE)	Roscoe Tanner (USA)	6-7(4)	6-1	3-6	6-3	6-4
S	Bjorn Borg (SWE)	Jimmy Connors (USA)	6-2	6-3	6-2		
S	Roscoe Tanner (USA)	Pat Dupre (USA)	6-3	7-6(3)	6-3		
Q	Bjorn Borg (SWE)	Tom Okker (NED)	6-2	6-1	6-3		
Q	Jimmy Connors (USA)	Bill Scanlon (USA)	6-3	4-6	7-6(1)	6-4	
Q	Pat Dupre (USA)	Adriano Panatta (ITA)	3-6	6-4	6-7(3)	6-4	6-3
Q	Roscoe Tanner (USA)	Tim Gullikson (USA)	6-1	6-4	6-7(3)	6-2	

1980

Rd	Winner	Defeated	S1	S2	S3	S4	S5
F	Bjorn Borg (SWE)	John McEnroe (USA)	1-6	7-5	6-3	6-7(16)	8-6
S	Bjorn Borg (SWE)	Brian Gottfried (USA)	6-2	4-6	6-2	6-0	
S	John McEnroe (USA)	Jimmy Connors (USA)	6-3	3-6	6-3	6-4	
Q	Bjorn Borg (SWE)	Gene Mayer (USA)	7-5	6-3	7-5		
Q	Brian Gottfried (USA)	Wojtek Fibak (POL)	6-4	7-6	6-2		
Q	Jimmy Connors (USA)	Roscoe Tanner (USA)	1-6	6-2	4-6	6-2	6-2
Q	John McEnroe (USA)	Peter Fleming (USA)	6-3	6-2	6-2		

1981

Rd	Winner	Defeated	S1	S2	S3	S4	S5
F	John McEnroe (USA)	Bjorn Borg (SWE)	4-6	7-6(1)	7-6(4)	6-4	
S	Bjorn Borg (SWE)	Jimmy Connors (USA)	0-6	4-6	6-3	6-0	6-4
S	John McEnroe (USA)	Rod Frawley (AUS)	7-6(2)	6-4	7-5		
Q	Bjorn Borg (SWE)	Peter McNamara (AUS)	7-6(2)	6-2	6-3		
Q	Jimmy Connors (USA)	Vijay Amritraj (IND)	2-6	5-7	6-4	6-3	6-2
Q	Rod Frawley (AUS)	Tim Mayotte (USA)	4-6	7-6(5)	7-6(4)	6-3	
Q	John McEnroe (USA)	Johan Kriek (RSA)	6-1	7-5	6-1		

1982

Rd	Winner	Defeated	S1	S2	S3	S4	S5
F	Jimmy Connors (USA)	John McEnroe (USA)	3-6	6-3	6-7(2)	7-6(5)	6-4
S	John McEnroe (USA)	Tim Mayotte (USA)	6-3	6-1	6-2		
S	Jimmy Connors (USA)	Mark Edmondson (AUS)	6-4	6-3	6-1		
Q	John McEnroe (USA)	Johan Kriek (RSA)	4-6	6-2	7-5	6-3	
Q	Tim Mayotte (USA)	Brian Teacher (AUS)	6-7	7-6	7-5	3-6	6-1
Q	Mark Edmondson (AUS)	Vitas Gerulaitis (USA)	7-6	3-6	6-4	6-3	
Q	Jimmy Connors (USA)	Gene Mayer (USA)	6-1	6-2	7-6		

1983

Rd	Winner	Defeated	S1	S2	S3	S4	S5
F	John McEnroe (USA)	Chris Lewis (AUS)	6-2	6-2	6-2		
S	Chris Lewis (AUS)	Kevin Curren (RSA)	6-7(3)	6-4	7-6(4)	6-7(3)	8-6
S	John McEnroe (USA)	Ivan Lendl (CZE)	7-6(5)	6-4	6-4		
Q	Kevin Curren (RSA)	Tim Mayotte (USA)	4-6	7-6(4)	6-2	7-6(6)	
Q	Chris Lewis (AUS)	Mel Purcell (USA)	6-7	6-0	6-4	7-6	
Q	Ivan Lendl (CZE)	Roscoe Tanner (USA)	7-5	7-6(3)	6-3		
Q	John McEnroe (USA)	Alex Mayer (USA)	6-3	7-5	6-0		

1984

Rd	Winner	Defeated	S1	S2	S3	S4	S5
F	John McEnroe (USA)	Jimmy Connors (USA)	6-1	6-1	6-2		
S	John McEnroe (USA)	Pat Cash (AUS)	6-3	7-6(5)	6-4		
S	Jimmy Connors (USA)	Ivan Lendl (CZE)	6-7(4)	6-3	7-5	6-1	
Q	John McEnroe (USA)	John Sadri (USA)	6-3	6-3	6-1		
Q	Pat Cash (AUS)	Andres Gomez (ECU)	6-4	6-4	6-7	7-6	
Q	Jimmy Connors (USA)	Paul Annacone (USA)	6-2	6-4	6-2		
Q	Ivan Lendl (CZE)	Tomas Smid (CZE)	6-1	7-6	6-3		

1985

Rd	Winner	Defeated	S1	S2	S3	S4	S5
F	Boris Becker (GER)	Kevin Curren (USA)	6-3	6-7(4)	7-6(3)	6-4	
S	Kevin Curren (USA)	Jimmy Connors (USA)	6-2	6-2	6-1		
S	Boris Becker (GER)	Anders Jarryd (SWE)	2-6	7-6(3)	6-3	6-3	
Q	Kevin Curren (USA)	John McEnroe (USA)	6-2	6-2	6-4		
Q	Jimmy Connors (USA)	Ricardo Acuna (CHI)	6-1	7-6(3)	6-2		
Q	Anders Jarryd (SWE)	Heinz Gunthardt (SUI)	6-4	6-3	6-2		
Q	Boris Becker (GER)	Henri Leconte (FRA)	7-6(7)	3-6	6-3	6-4	

1986

Rd	Winner	Defeated	S1	S2	S3	S4	S5
F	Boris Becker (GER)	Ivan Lendl (CZE)	6-4	6-3	7-5		
S	Ivan Lendl (CZE)	Slobodan Zivojinovic (YUG)	6-2	6-7(5)	6-3	6-7(1)	6-4
S	Boris Becker (GER)	Henri Leconte (FRA)	6-2	6-4	6-7(4)	6-3	
Q	Ivan Lendl (CZE)	Tim Mayotte (USA)	6-4	4-6	6-4	3-6	9-7
Q	Slobodan Zivojinovic (YUG)	Ramesh Krishnan (IND)	6-2	7-6(4)	4-6	6-3	
Q	Boris Becker (GER)	Miloslav Mecir (CZE)	6-4	6-2	7-6(5)		
Q	Henri Leconte (FRA)	Pat Cash (AUS)	4-6	7-6(7)	7-6(5)	6-3	

1987

Rd	Winner	Defeated	S1	S2	S3	S4	S5
F	Pat Cash (AUS)	Ivan Lendl (CZE)	7-6(5)	6-2	7-5		
S	Pat Cash (AUS)	Jimmy Connors (USA)	6-4	6-4	6-1		
S	Ivan Lendl (CZE)	Stefan Edberg (SWE)	3-6	6-4	7-6(8)	6-4	
Q	Jimmy Connors (USA)	Slobodan Zivojinovic (YUG)	7-6(5)	7-5	6-3		
Q	Pat Cash (AUS)	Mats Wilander (SWE)	6-3	7-5	6-4		
Q	Stefan Edberg (SWE)	Andres Jarryd (SWE)	4-6	6-4	6-1	6-3	
Q	Ivan Lendl (CZE)	Henri Leconte (FRA)	7-6(5)	6-3	7-6(6)		

1988

Rd	Winner	Defeated	S1	S2	S3	S4	S5
F	Stefan Edberg (SWE)	Boris Becker (GER)	4-6	7-6(2)	6-4	6-2	
S	Boris Becker (GER)	Ivan Lendl (CZE)	6-4	6-3	6-7(8)	6-4	
S	Stefan Edberg (SWE)	Miloslav Mecir (CZE)	4-6	2-6	6-4	6-3	6-4
Q	Ivan Lendl (CZE)	Tim Mayotte (USA)	7-6(2)	7-6(1)	6-3		
Q	Boris Becker (GER)	Pat Cash (AUS)	6-4	6-3	6-4		
Q	Stefan Edberg (SWE)	Patrik Kuhnen (GER)	6-3	4-6	6-1	7-6(2)	
Q	Miloslav Mecir (CZE)	Mats Wilander (SWE)	6-3	6-1	6-3		

1989

Rd	Winner	Defeated	S1	S2	S3	S4	S5
F	Boris Becker (GER)	Stefan Edberg (SWE)	6-0	7-6(1)	6-4		
S	Boris Becker (GER)	Ivan Lendl (CZE)	7-5	6-7(2)	2-6	6-4	6-3
S	Stefan Edberg (SWE)	John McEnroe (USA)	7-5	7-6(2)	7-6(5)		
Q	Ivan Lendl (CZE)	Dan Goldie (USA)	7-6(8)	7-6(4)	6-0		
Q	Boris Becker (GER)	Paul Chamberlin (USA)	6-1	6-2	6-0		
Q	John McEnroe (USA)	Mats Wilander (SWE)	7-6(6)	3-6	6-3	6-4	
Q	Stefan Edberg (SWE)	Tim Mayotte (USA)	7-6(2)	7-6(12)	6-3		

1990

Rd	Winner	Defeated	S1	S2	S3	S4	S5
F	Stefan Edberg (SWE)	Boris Becker (GER)	6-2	6-2	3-6	3-6	6-4
S	Stefan Edberg (SWE)	Ivan Lendl (CZE)	6-1	7-6(2)	6-3		
S	Boris Becker (GER)	Goran Ivanisevic (YUG)	4-6	7-6(4)	6-0	7-6(5)	
Q	Ivan Lendl (CZE)	Brad Pearce (USA)	6-4	6-4	5-7	6-4	
Q	Stefan Edberg (SWE)	Christian Bergstrom (SWE)	6-3	6-2	6-4		
Q	Goran Ivanisevic (YUG)	Kevin Curren (USA)	4-6	6-4	6-4	6-7(8)	6-3
Q	Boris Becker (GER)	Brad Gilbert (USA)	6-4	6-4	6-1		

1991

Rd	Winner	Defeated	S1	S2	S3	S4	S5
F	Michael Stich (GER)	Boris Becker (GER)	6-4	7-6(4)	6-4		
S	Michael Stich (GER)	Stefan Edberg (SWE)	4-6	7-6(5)	7-6(5)	7-6(2)	
S	Boris Becker (GER)	David Wheaton (USA)	6-4	7-6(4)	7-5		
Q	Stefan Edberg (SWE)	Thierry Champion (FRA)	6-3	6-2	7-5		
Q	Michael Stich (GER)	Jim Courier (USA)	6-3	7-6(2)	6-2		
Q	David Wheaton (USA)	Andre Agassi (USA)	6-2	0-6	3-6	7-6(3)	6-2
Q	Boris Becker (GER)	Guy Forget (FRA)	6-7(5)	7-6(3)	6-2	7-6(7)	

1992

Rd	Winner	Defeated	S1	S2	S3	S4	S5
F	Andre Agassi (USA)	Goran Ivanisevic (CRO)	6-7(8)	6-4	6-4	1-6	6-4
S	Andre Agassi (USA)	John McEnroe (USA)	6-4	6-2	6-3		
S	Goran Ivanisevic (CRO)	Pete Sampras (USA)	6-7(4)	7-6(5)	6-4	6-2	
Q	John McEnroe (USA)	Guy Forget (FRA)	6-2	7-6(9)	6-3		
Q	Andre Agassi (USA)	Boris Becker (GER)	4-6	6-2	6-2	4-6	6-3
Q	Pete Sampras (USA)	Michael Stich (GER)	6-3	6-2	6-4		
Q	Goran Ivanisevic (CRO)	Stefan Edberg (SWE)	6-7(8)	7-5	6-1	3-6	6-3

1993

Rd	Winner	Defeated	S1	S2	S3	S4	S5
F	Pete Sampras (USA)	Jim Courier (USA)	7-6(3)	7-6(6)	3-6	6-3	
S	Pete Sampras (USA)	Boris Becker (GER)	7-6(5)	6-4	6-4		
S	Jim Courier (USA)	Stefan Edberg (SWE)	4-6	6-4	6-2	6-4	
Q	Pete Sampras (USA)	Andre Agassi (USA)	6-2	6-2	3-6	3-6	6-4
Q	Boris Becker (GER)	Michael Stich (GER)	7-5	6-7(5)	6-7(5)	6-2	6-4
Q	Jim Courier (USA)	Todd Martin (USA)	6-2	7-6(5)	6-3		
Q	Stefan Edberg (SWE)	Cedric Pioline (FRA)	7-5	7-5	6-3		

1994

Rd	Winner	Defeated	S1	S2	S3	S4	S5
F	Pete Sampras (USA)	Goran Ivanisevic (CRO)	7-6(2)	7-6(5)	6-0		
S	Pete Sampras (USA)	Todd Martin (USA)	6-4	6-4	3-6	6-3	
S	Goran Ivanisevic (CRO)	Boris Becker (GER)	6-2	7-6(6)	6-4		
Q	Pete Sampras (USA)	Michael Chang (USA)	6-4	6-1	6-3		
Q	Todd Martin (USA)	Wayne Ferreira (RSA)	6-3	6-2	3-6	5-7	7-5
Q	Goran Ivanisevic (CRO)	Guy Forget (FRA)	7-6(3)	7-6(3)	6-4		
Q	Boris Becker (GER)	Christian Bergstrom (SWE)	7-6(5)	6-4	6-3		

1995

Rd	Winner	Defeated	S1	S2	S3	S4	S5
F	Pete Sampras (USA)	Boris Becker (GER)	6-7(5)	6-2	6-4	6-2	
S	Boris Becker (GER)	Andre Agassi (USA)	2-6	7-6(1)	6-4	7-6(1)	
S	Pete Sampras (USA)	Goran Ivanisevic (CRO)	7-6(7)	4-6	6-3	4-6	6-3
Q	Andre Agassi (USA)	Jacco Eltingh (NED)	6-2	6-3	6-4		
Q	Boris Becker (GER)	Cedric Pioline (FRA)	6-3	6-1	6-7(6)	6-7(10)	9-7
Q	Goran Ivanisevic (CRO)	Yevgeny Kafelnikov (RUS)	7-5	7-6(11)	6-3		
Q	Pete Sampras (USA)	Shuzo Matsuoka (JPN)	6-7(5)	6-3	6-4	6-2	

1996

Rd	Winner	Defeated	S1	S2	S3	S4	S5
F	Richard Krajicek (NED)	MaliVai Washington (USA)	6-3	6-4	6-3		
S	Richard Krajicek (NED)	Jason Stoltenberg (AUS)	7-5	6-2	6-1		
S	MaliVai Washington (USA)	Todd Martin (USA)	5-7	6-4	6-7(6)	6-3	10-8
Q	Richard Krajicek (NED)	Pete Sampras (USA)	7-5	7-6(3)	6-4		
Q	Jason Stoltenberg (AUS)	Goran Ivanisevic (CRO)	6-3	7-6(3)	6-7(3)	7-6(3)	
Q	Todd Martin (USA)	Tim Henman (GBR)	7-6(5)	7-6(2)	6-4		
Q	MaliVai Washington (USA)	Alex Radulescu (GER)	6-7(5)	7-6(1)	5-7	7-6(3)	6-4

1997

Rd	Winner	Defeated	S1	S2	S3	S4	S5
F	Pete Sampras (USA)	Cedric Pioline (FRA)	6-4	6-2	6-4		
S	Pete Sampras (USA)	Todd Woodbridge (AUS)	6-2	6-1	7-6(3)		
S	Cedric Pioline (FRA)	Michael Stich (GER)	6-7(2)	6-2	6-1	5-7	6-4
Q	Pete Sampras (USA)	Boris Becker (GER)	6-1	6-7(5)	6-1	6-4	
Q	Todd Woodbridge (AUS)	Nicolas Kiefer (GER)	7-6(7)	2-6	6-0	6-4	
Q	Michael Stich (GER)	Tim Henman (GBR)	6-3	6-2	6-4		
Q	Cedric Pioline (FRA)	Greg Rusedski (GBR)	6-4	4-6	6-4	6-3	

1998

Rd	Winner	Defeated	S1	S2	S3	S4	S5
F	Pete Sampras (USA)	Goran Ivanisevic (CRO)	6-7(2)	7-6(9)	6-4	3-6	6-2
S	Pete Sampras (USA)	Tim Henman (GBR)	6-3	4-6	7-5	6-3	
S	Goran Ivanisevic (CRO)	Richard Krajicek (NED)	6-3	6-4	5-7	6-7(5)	15-13
Q	Pete Sampras (USA)	Mark Philippoussis (AUS)	7-6(5)	6-4	6-4		
Q	Tim Henman (GBR)	Petr Korda (CZE)	6-3	6-4	6-2		
Q	Goran Ivanisevic (CRO)	Jan Siemerink (NED)	7-6(10)	7-6(5)	7-6(6)		
Q	Richard Krajicek (NED)	Davide Sanguinetti (ITA)	6-2	6-3	6-4		

1999

Rd	Winner	Defeated	S1	S2	S3	S4	S5
F	Pete Sampras (USA)	Andre Agassi (USA)	6-3	6-4	7-5		
S	Pete Sampras (USA)	Tim Henman (GBR)	3-6	6-4	6-3	6-4	
S	Andre Agassi (USA)	Patrick Rafter (AUS)	7-5	7-6(5)	6-2		
Q	Pete Sampras (USA)	Mark Philippoussis (AUS)	4-6	2-1			(retired)
Q	Tim Henman (GBR)	Cedric Pioline (FRA)	6-4	6-2	4-6	6-3	
Q	Andre Agassi (USA)	Gustavo Kuerten (BRA)	6-3	6-4	6-4		
Q	Patrick Rafter (AUS)	Todd Martin (USA)	6-3	6-7(5)	7-6(5)	7-6(3)	

2000

Rd	Winner	Defeated	S1	S2	S3	S4	S5
F	Pete Sampras (USA)	Patrick Rafter (AUS)	6-7(10)	7-6(5)	6-4	6-2	
S	Pete Sampras (USA)	Vladimir Voltchkov (BLR)	7-6(4)	6-2	6-4		
S	Patrick Rafter (AUS)	Andre Agassi (USA)	7-5	4-6	7-5	4-6	6-3
Q	Pete Sampras (USA)	Jan-Michael Gambill (USA)	6-4	6-7(4)	6-4	6-4	
Q	Vladimir Voltchkov (BLR)	Byron Black (ZIM)	7-6(2)	7-6(2)	6-4		
Q	Patrick Rafter (AUS)	Alexander Popp (GER)	6-3	6-2	7-6(1)		
Q	Andre Agassi (USA)	Mark Philippoussis (AUS)	7-6(4)	6-3	6-4		

2001

Rd	Winner	Defeated	S1	S2	S3	S4	S5
F	Goran Ivanisevic (CRO)	Patrick Rafter (AUS)	6-3	3-6	6-3	2-6	9-7
S	Goran Ivanisevic (CRO)	Tim Henman (GBR)	7-5	6-7(6)	0-6	7-6(5)	6-3
S	Patrick Rafter (AUS)	Andre Agassi (USA)	2-6	6-3	3-6	6-2	8-6
Q	Tim Henman (GBR)	Roger Federer (SUI)	7-5	7-6(6)	2-6	7-6(6)	
Q	Goran Ivanisevic (CRO)	Marat Safin (RUS)	7-6(2)	7-5	3-6	7-6(3)	
Q	Patrick Rafter (AUS)	Thomas Enqvist (SWE)	6-1	6-3	7-6(5)		
Q	Andre Agassi (USA)	Nicolas Escude (FRA)	6-7(3)	6-3	6-4	6-2	

2002

Rd	Winner	Defeated	S1	S2	S3	S4	S5
F	Lleyton Hewitt (AUS)	David Nalbandian (ARG)	6-1	6-3	6-2		
S	Lleyton Hewitt (AUS)	Tim Henman (GBR)	7-5	6-1	7-5		
S	David Nalbandian (ARG)	Xavier Malisse (BEL)	7-6(2)	6-4	1-6	2-6	6-2
Q	Lleyton Hewitt (AUS)	Sjeng Schalken (NED)	6-2	6-2	6-7(5)	1-6	7-5
Q	Tim Henman (GBR)	Andre Sa (BRA)	6-3	5-7	6-4	6-3	
Q	Xavier Malisse (BEL)	Richard Krajicek (NED)	6-1	4-6	6-2	3-6	9-7
Q	David Nalbandian (ARG)	Nicolas Lapentti (ECU)	6-4	6-4	4-6	4-6	6-4

2003

Rd	Winner	Defeated	S1	S2	S3	S4	S5
F	Roger Federer (SUI)	Mark Philippoussis (AUS)	7-6(5)	6-2	7-6(3)		
S	Roger Federer (SUI)	Andy Roddick (USA)	7-6(6)	6-3	6-3		
S	Mark Philippoussis (AUS)	Sebastien Grosjean (FRA)	7-6(3)	6-3	6-3		
Q	Andy Roddick (USA)	Jonas Bjorkman (SWE)	6-4	6-2	6-4		
Q	Roger Federer (SUI)	Sjeng Schalken (NED)	6-3	6-4	6-4		
Q	Sebastien Grosjean (FRA)	Tim Henman (GBR)	7-6(8)	6-3	3-6	6-4	
Q	Mark Philippoussis (AUS)	Alexander Popp (GER)	4-6	4-6	6-3	6-3	8-6

2004

Rd	Winner	Defeated	S1	S2	S3	S4	S5
F	Roger Federer (SUI)	Andy Roddick (USA)	4-6	7-5	7-6(3)	6-4	
S	Roger Federer (SUI)	Sebastien Grosjean (FRA)	6-2	6-3	7-6(6)		
S	Andy Roddick (USA)	Mario Ancic (CRO)	6-4	4-6	7-5	7-5	
Q	Roger Federer (SUI)	Lleyton Hewitt (AUS)	6-1	6-7(1)	6-0	6-4	
Q	Sebastien Grosjean (FRA)	Florian Mayer (GER)	7-5	6-4	6-2		
Q	Mario Ancic (CRO)	Tim Henman (GBR)	7-6(5)	6-4	6-2		
Q	Andy Roddick (USA)	Sjeng Schalken (NED)	7-6(4)	7-6(9)	6-3		

2005

Rd	Winner	Defeated	S1	S2	S3	S4	S5
F	Roger Federer (SUI)	Andy Roddick (USA)	6-2	7-6(2)	6-4		
S	Roger Federer (SUI)	Lleyton Hewitt (AUS)	6-3	6-4	7-6(1)		
S	Andy Roddick (USA)	Thomas Johansson (SWE)	6-7(6)	6-2	7-6(10)	7-6(5)	
Q	Roger Federer (SUI)	Fernando Gonzalez (CHI)	7-5	6-2	7-6(2)		
Q	Lleyton Hewitt (AUS)	Feliciano Lopez (ESP)	7-5	6-4	7-6(2)		
Q	Thomas Johansson (SWE)	David Nalbandian (ARG)	7-6(5)	6-2	6-2		
Q	Andy Roddick (USA)	Sebastien Grosjean (FRA)	6-3	2-6	1-6	6-3	6-3

2006

Rd	Winner	Defeated	S1	S2	S3	S4	S5
F	Roger Federer (SUI)	Rafael Nadal (ESP)	6-0	7-6(5)	6-7(2)	6-3	
S	Roger Federer (SUI)	Jonas Bjorkman (SWE)	6-2	6-0	6-2		
S	Rafael Nadal (ESP)	Marcos Baghdatis (CYP)	6-1	7-5	6-3		
Q	Roger Federer (SUI)	Mario Ancic (CRO)	6-4	6-4	6-4		
Q	Jonas Bjorkman (SWE)	Radek Stepanek (CZE)	7-6(3)	4-6	6-7(5)	7-6(7)	6-4
Q	Marcos Baghdatis (CYP)	Lleyton Hewitt (AUS)	6-1	5-7	7-6(5)	6-2	
Q	Rafael Nadal (ESP)	Jarkko Nieminen (FIN)	6-3	6-4	6-4		

2007

Rd	Winner	Defeated	S1	S2	S3	S4	S5
F	Roger Federer (SUI)	Rafael Nadal (ESP)	7-6(7)	4-6	7-6(3)	2-6	6-2
S	Roger Federer (SUI)	Richard Gasquet (FRA)	7-5	6-3	6-4		
S	Rafael Nadal (ESP)	Novak Djokovic (SRB)	3-6	6-1	4-1	(Retired)	
Q	Roger Federer (SUI)	Juan Carlos Ferrero (ESP)	7-6(2)	3-6	6-1	6-3	
Q	Richard Gasquet (FRA)	Andy Roddick (USA)	4-6	4-6	7-6(2)	7-6(3)	8-6
Q	Novak Djokovic (SRB)	Marcos Baghdatis (CYP)	7-6(4)	7-6(9)	6-7(3)	4-6	7-5
Q	Rafael Nadal (ESP)	Tomas Berdych (CZE)	7-6(1)	6-4	6-2		

2008

Rd	Winner	Defeated	S1	S2	S3	S4	S5
F	Rafael Nadal (ESP)	Roger Federer (SUI)	6-4	6-4	6-7(5)	6-7(8)	9-7
S	Roger Federer (SUI)	Marat Safin (RUS)	6-3	7-6(3)	6-4		
S	Rafael Nadal (ESP)	Rainer Schuettler (GER)	6-1	7-6(3)	6-4		
Q	Roger Federer (SUI)	Mario Ancic (CRO)	6-1	7-5	6-4		
Q	Marat Safin (RUS)	Feliciano Lopez (ESP)	3-6	7-5	7-6(1)	6-3	
Q	Rainer Schuettler (GER)	Arnaud Clement (FRA)	6-3	5-7	7-6(6)	6-7(7)	8-6
Q	Rafael Nadal (ESP)	Andy Murray (GBR)	6-3	6-2	6-4		

2009

Rd	Winner	Defeated	S1	S2	S3	S4	S5
F	Roger Federer (SUI)	Andy Roddick (USA)	5-7	7-6(6)	7-6(5)	3-6	16-14
S	Andy Roddick (USA)	Andy Murray (GBR)	6-4	4-6	7-6(7)	7-6(5)	
S	Roger Federer (SUI)	Tommy Haas (GER)	7-6(5)	7-5	6-3		
Q	Andy Roddick (USA)	Lleyton Hewitt (AUS)	6-3	6-7(10)	7-6(1)	4-6	6-4
Q	Andy Murray (GBR)	Juan Carlos Ferrero (ESP)	7-5	6-3	6-2		
Q	Tommy Haas (GER)	Novak Djokovic (SRB)	7-5	7-6(6)	4-6	6-3	
Q	Roger Federer (SUI)	Ivo Karlovic (CRO)	6-3	7-5	7-6(3)		

Women's Singles

1884

Rd	Winner	Defeated	S1	S2	S3
F	Maud Watson (GBR)	Lillian Watson (GBR)	6-8	6-3	6-3
S	Maud Watson (GBR)	Blanche Bingley (GBR)	3-6	6-4	6-2
S	Lillian Watson (GBR)	M. Leslie (GBR)	7-5	5-7	6-3
Q	Maud Watson (GBR)	B.E. Williams (GBR)	7-5	6-0	
Q	Blanche Bingley (GBR)	F.M Winckworth (GBR)	6-0	6-8	6-3
Q	Lillian Watson (GBR)	Mrs G. J. Cooper (GBR)	7-5	5-7	6-3
Q	M. Leslie (GBR)		(bye)		

1885

Rd	Winner	Defeated	S1	S2	S3
F	Maud Watson (GBR)	Blanche Bingley (GBR)	6-1	7-5	
S	Blanche Bingley (GBR)	E. Gurney (GBR)	6-1	6-2	
S	Maud Watson (GBR)	E.F. Hudson (GBR)	6-0	6-1	
Q	Blanche Bingley (GBR)	Mrs. Dransfield (GBR)	(walkover)		
Q	E. Gurney (GBR)	J. Meilke (GBR)	7-5	6-4	
Q	E.F. Hudson (GBR)	Miss Bryan (GBR)	6-3	6-0	
Q	Maud Watson (GBR)	May Langrishe (GBR)	6-0	6-0	

1886

Rd	Winner	Defeated	S1	S2	S3
Ch	Blanche Bingley (GBR)	Maud Watson (GBR)	6-3	6-3	
F	Blanche Bingley (GBR)	A. Tabor (GBR)	6-2	6-0	
S	A. Tabor (GBR)	Edith Maud Shackle (GBR)	6-4	7-5	
S	Blanche Bingley (GBR)	Lillian Watson (GBR)	6-3	8-6	
Q	Edith Maud Shackle (GBR)	J. Mackenzie (GBR)	6-3	6-4	
Q	A. Tabor (GBR)	F.M. Pearson (GBR)	6-1	6-2	
Q	Blanche Bingley (GBR)	J. Shackle (GBR)	6-2	6-1	
Q	Lillian Watson (GBR)	A.M. Chambers (GBR)	6-3	6-3	

1887

Rd	Winner	Defeated	S1	S2	S3
Ch	Charlotte Dod (GBR)	Blanche Bingley Hillyard (GBR)	6-2	6-0	
F	Charlotte Dod (GBR)	Edith Mary Cole (GBR)	6-2	6-3	
S	Charlotte Dod (GBR)	B. James (GBR)	6-1	6-1	
S	Edith Mary Cole (GBR)	J. Shackle (GBR)	6-4	6-1	
Q	Charlotte Dod (GBR)		(bye)		
Q	B. James (GBR)	Edith Maud Shackle (GBR)	8-6	6-2	
Q	Edith Mary Cole (GBR)		(bye)		
Q	J. Shackle (GBR)		(bye)		

1888

Rd	Winner	Defeated	S1	S2	S3
Ch	Charlotte Dod (GBR)	Blanche Bingley Hillyard (GBR)	6-3	6-3	
F	Blanche Bingley Hillyard (GBR)	Miss Howes (GBR)	6-1	6-2	
S	Miss Howes (GBR)	Miss D. Patterson (GBR)	6-4	6-2	
S	Blanche Bingley Hillyard (GBR)	Miss Phillimore (GBR)	(walkover)		
Q	Miss Howes (GBR)		(bye)		
Q	Miss D. Patterson (GBR)	B.E. Williams (GBR)	6-0	6-3	
Q	Blanche Bingley Hillyard (GBR)	Miss Canning (GBR)	6-2	6-2	
Q	Miss Phillimore (GBR)		(bye)		

1889

Rd	Winner	Defeated	S1	S2	S3
Ch	Blanche Bingley Hillyard (GBR)	Charlotte Dod (GBR)	(walkover)		
F	Blanche Bingley Hillyard (GBR)	Helena Rice (IRL)	4-6	8-6	6-4
S	Helena Rice (IRL)	M. Jacks (GBR)	6-2	6-0	
S	Blanche Bingley Hillyard (GBR)	Bertha Steedman (GBR)	8-6	6-1	
Q	Helena Rice (IRL)		(bye)		
Q	M. Jacks (GBR)	Mary Steedman (GBR)	6-4	6-2	
Q	Blanche Bingley Hillyard (GBR)	Annie Elizabeth Rice (GBR)	6-3	6-0	
Q	Bertha Steedman (GBR)		(bye)		

1890

Rd	Winner	Defeated	S1	S2	S3
Ch	Helena Rice (IRL)	Blanche Bingley Hillyard (GBR)	(walkover)		
F	Helena Rice (IRL)	M. Jacks (GBR)	6-4	6-1	
S	M. Jacks (GBR)	Edith Mary Cole (GBR)	6-4	7-5	
S	Helena Rice (IRL)	Mary Steedman (GBR)	7-5	6-2	

1891

Rd	Winner	Defeated	S1	S2	S3
Ch	Charlotte Dod (GBR)	Helena Rice (IRL)	(walkover)		
F	Charlotte Dod (GBR)	Blanche Bingley Hillyard (GBR)	6-2	6-1	
S	Charlotte Dod (GBR)	Bertha Steedman (GBR)	6-3	6-1	
S	Blanche Bingley Hillyard (GBR)	May Langrishe (GBR)	6-4	6-1	
Q	Charlotte Dod (GBR)	Mrs. Parsons (GBR)	6-0	6-0	
Q	Bertha Steedman (GBR)	Helen Jackson (GBR)	6-2	6-2	
Q	May Langrishe (GBR)	M. Jacks (GBR)	11-9	6-3	
Q	Blanche Bingley Hillyard (GBR)	P. Legh (GBR)	6-3	6-2	

1892

Rd	Winner	Defeated	S1	S2	S3
Ch	Charlotte Dod (GBR)	Blanche Bingley Hillyard (GBR)	6-1	6-1	
F	Blanche Bingley Hillyard (GBR)	Edith Maud Shackle (GBR)	6-1	6-4	
S	Edith Maud Shackle (GBR)	Bertha Steedman (GBR)	6-4	6-3	
S	Blanche Bingley Hillyard (GBR)	Mrs. C. Martin (GBR)	1-6	6-3	9-7
Q	Bertha Steedman (GBR)	Miss Barefoot (GBR)	6-0	6-1	
Q	Edith Maud Shackle (GBR)	Helen Jackson (GBR)	6-3	6-4	
Q	Blanche Bingley Hillyard (GBR)	Mrs. G.A. Draffen (GBR)	6-2	6-2	
Q	Mrs. C. Martin (GBR)		(bye)		

1893

Rd	Winner	Defeated	S1	S2	S3
Ch	Charlotte Dod (GBR)	Blanche Bingley Hillyard (GBR)	6-8	6-1	6-4
F	Blanche Bingley Hillyard (GBR)	Edith Maud Shackle (GBR)	6-3	6-2	
S	Edith Maud Shackle (GBR)	Edith Austin (GBR)	6-0	6-2	
S	Blanche Bingley Hillyard (GBR)	Charlotte Cooper (GBR)	6-3	6-1	
Q	Edith Austin (GBR)	S. Robins (GBR)	6-2	6-1	
Q	Edith Maud Shackle (GBR)	P. Legh (GBR)	10-8	6-1	
Q	Charlotte Cooper (GBR)	Henrietta Horncastle (GBR)	6-4	6-1	
Q	Blanche Bingley Hillyard (GBR)		(bye)		

1894

Rd	Winner	Defeated	S1	S2	S3
Ch	Blanche Bingley Hillyard (GBR)	Charlotte Dod (GBR)	(walkover)		
F	Blanche Bingley Hillyard (GBR)	Edith Austin (GBR)	6-1	6-1	
S	Blanche Bingley Hillyard (GBR)	Miss Bryan (GBR)	6-1	6-1	
S	Edith Austin (GBR)	S. Robins (GBR)	6-1	6-1	
Q	Blanche Bingley Hillyard (GBR)	Chatterton Clarke (GBR)	6-1	6-0	
Q	Miss Bryan (GBR)	Mrs. G.A. Draffen (GBR)	6-3	7-5	
Q	Edith Austin (GBR)	Charlotte Dod (GBR)	6-1	3-6	6-3
Q	S. Robins (GBR)	Mrs. Edwardes (GBR)	6-2	6-1	

1895

Rd	Winner	Defeated	S1	S2	S3
Ch	Charlotte Cooper (GBR)	Blanche Bingley Hillyard (GBR)	(walkover)		
F	Charlotte Cooper (GBR)	Helen Jackson (GBR)	7-5	8-6	
S	Helen Jackson (GBR)	Alice Simpson Pickering (GBR)	6-4	3-6	8-6
S	Charlotte Cooper (GBR)	Mrs. G.A. Draffen (GBR)	6-2	6-8	6-1
Q	Alice Simpson Pickering (GBR)	Edith Maud Shackle (GBR)	3-6	6-3	6-3
Q	Helen Jackson (GBR)	Miss Bernard (GBR)	6-0	6-2	
Q	Charlotte Cooper (GBR)	L.H. Patterson (GBR)	6-3	9-11	6-2
Q	Mrs. G.A. Draffen (GBR)	Henrietta Horncastle (GBR)	6-2	6-0	

1896

Rd	Winner	Defeated	S1	S2	S3
Ch	Charlotte Cooper (GBR)	Alice Simpson Pickering (GBR)	6-2	6-3	
F	Alice Simpson Pickering (GBR)	Edith Austin (GBR)	4-6	6-3	6-3
S	Edith Austin (GBR)	Henrietta Horncastle (GBR)	(walkover)		
S	Alice Simpson Pickering (GBR)	Mrs. G.A. Draffen (GBR)	6-3	7-5	
Q	Henrietta Horncastle (GBR)		(bye)		
Q	Edith Austin (GBR)	L.H. Patterson (GBR)	6-4	6-1	
Q	Alice Simpson Pickering (GBR)	Miss 'Hungerford' (GBR)	6-1	6-0	
Q	Mrs. G.A. Draffen (GBR)		(bye)		

1897

Rd	Winner	Defeated	S1	S2	S3
Ch	Blanche Bingley Hillyard (GBR)	Charlotte Cooper (GBR)	5-7	7-5	6-2
F	Blanche Bingley Hillyard (GBR)	Alice Simpson Pickering (GBR)	6-2	7-5	
S	Blanche Bingley Hillyard (GBR)	Henrietta Horncastle (GBR)	(walkover)		
S	Alice Simpson Pickering (GBR)	Ruth Dyes (GBR)	6-4	4-6	6-1
Q	Blanche Bingley Hillyard (GBR)	Edith Austin (GBR)	6-0	6-1	
Q	Henrietta Horncastle (GBR)	E.M. Thyme (GBR)	12-106-4		
Q	Ruth Dyes (GBR)	E.J. Bromfield (GBR)	6-0	6-3	
Q	Alice Simpson Pickering (GBR)		(bye)		

1898

Rd	Winner	Defeated	S1	S2	S3
Ch	Charlotte Cooper (GBR)	Blanche Bingley Hillyard (GBR)	(walkover)		
F	Charlotte Cooper (GBR)	Louisa Martin (GBR)	6-4	6-4	
S	Louisa Martin (GBR)	P. Legh (GBR)	(walkover)		
S	Charlotte Cooper (GBR)	Edith Austin (GBR)	6-4	6-1	
Q	P. Legh (GBR)	C. Morgan (GBR)	6-0	6-1	
Q	Louisa Martin (GBR)	E.R. Morgan (GBR)	6-2	6-0	
Q	Edith Austin (GBR)	Ruth Dyes (GBR)	4-6	6-3	6-4
Q	Charlotte Cooper (GBR)	Bertha Steedman (GBR)	4-6	6-3	6-4

1899

Rd	Winner	Defeated	S1	S2	S3
Ch	Blanche Bingley Hillyard (GBR)	Charlotte Cooper (GBR)	6-2	6-3	
F	Blanche Bingley Hillyard (GBR)	Ruth Durlacher (GBR)	7-5	6-8	6-1
S	Ruth Durlacher (GBR)	Bertha Steedman (GBR)	6-4	6-2	
S	Blanche Bingley Hillyard (GBR)	Beryl Tulloch (GBR)	6-3	3-6	6-2
Q	Ruth Durlacher (GBR)	Muriel Robb (GBR)	6-1	5-7	6-3
Q	Bertha Steedman (GBR)	H.A. Kirby (GBR)	4-6	6-2	6-2
Q	Blanche Bingley Hillyard (GBR)	Edith Austin (GBR)	8-6	6-4	
Q	Beryl Tulloch (GBR)	E.J. Bromfield (GBR)	3-6	6-2	6-1

1900

Rd	Winner	Defeated	S1	S2	S3
Ch	Blanche Bingley Hillyard (GBR)	Charlotte Cooper (GBR)	4-6	6-4	6-4
F	Charlotte Cooper (GBR)	Louisa Martin (GBR)	8-6	5-7	6-1
S	Charlotte Cooper (GBR)	Edith Greville (GBR)	6-1	6-2	
S	Louisa Martin (GBR)	Ellen Evered (GBR)	6-0	6-2	
Q	Charlotte Cooper (GBR)	Muriel Robb (GBR)	6-3	9-7	
Q	Edith Greville (GBR)	Beryl Tulloch (GBR)	7-5	6-0	
Q	Ellen Evered (GBR)	Marion Jones (USA)	7-5	6-2	
Q	Louisa Martin (GBR)	Dorothea Douglass (GBR)	6-4	6-3	

1901

Rd	Winner	Defeated	S1	S2	S3
Ch	Charlotte Cooper Sterry (GBR)	Blanche Bingley Hillyard (GBR)	6-2	6-2	
F	Charlotte Cooper Sterry (GBR)	Louisa Martin (GBR)	6-3	6-4	
S	Louisa Martin (GBR)	Agnes Morton (GBR)	7-5	6-2	
S	Charlotte Cooper Sterry (GBR)	Miss Adams (GBR)	6-1	6-1	
Q	Louisa Martin (GBR)	Edith Greville (GBR)	4-6	6-3	6-4
Q	Agnes Morton (GBR)	Alice Simpson Pickering (GBR)	6-3	7-5	
Q	Charlotte Cooper Sterry (GBR)	Muriel Robb (GBR)	6-0	6-0	
Q	Miss Adams (GBR)	Miss Hughes D'Eath (GBR)	6-1	6-0	

1902

Rd	Winner	Defeated	S1	S2	S3
Ch	Muriel Robb (GBR)	Charlotte Cooper Sterry (GBR)	7-5	6-1	
F	Muriel Robb (GBR)	Agnes Morton (GBR)	7-5	6-4	
S	Muriel Robb (GBR)	Dorothea Douglass (GBR)	6-4	2-6	9-7
S	Agnes Morton (GBR)	Edith Greville (GBR)	7-5	6-4	
Q	Muriel Robb (GBR)	Hilda Lane (GBR)	6-1	7-5	
Q	Dorothea Douglass (GBR)	Ruth Durlacher (GBR)	6-2	10-8	
Q	Agnes Morton (GBR)	Winifred Longhurst (GBR)	6-3	6-4	
Q	Edith Greville (GBR)	Bertha Steedman (GBR)	6-1	3-6	6-2

1903

Rd	Winner	Defeated	S1	S2	S3
Ch	Dorothea Douglass (GBR)	Muriel Robb (GBR)	(walkover)		
F	Dorothea Douglass (GBR)	Ethel Thomson (GBR)	4-6	6-4	6-2
S	Dorothea Douglass (GBR)	Towpie Lowther (GBR)	6-4	6-2	
S	Ethel Thomson (GBR)	Angela Greene (GBR)	6-3	6-1	
Q	Towpie Lowther (GBR)	Agnes Morton (GBR)	6-1	6-0	
Q	Dorothea Douglass (GBR)	Getrude Houselander (GBR)	6-2	6-0	
Q	Ethel Thomson (GBR)	Constance M. Wilson (GBR)	6-4	8-6	
Q	Angela Greene (GBR)	E.J. Bromfield (GBR)	6-0	4-6	6-3

1904

Rd	Winner	Defeated	S1	S2	S3
Ch	Dorothea Douglass (GBR)	Charlotte Cooper Sterry (GBR)	6-0	6-3	
F	Charlotte Cooper Sterry (GBR)	Agnes Morton (GBR)	6-3	6-3	
S	Charlotte Cooper Sterry (GBR)	Angela Greene (GBR)	6-2	6-1	
S	Agnes Morton (GBR)	Constance M. Wilson (GBR)	3-6	6-4	8-6
Q	Charlotte Cooper Sterry (GBR)	Edith Greville (GBR)	8-6	9-7	
Q	Angela Greene (GBR)	Ruth Winch (GBR)	6-4	6-4	
Q	Agnes Morton (GBR)	Winifred Longhurst (GBR)	6-1	6-4	
Q	Constance M. Wilson (GBR)	E.L. Bosworth (GBR)	6-3	6-4	

1905

Rd	Winner	Defeated	S1	S2	S3
Ch	May Sutton (USA)	Dorothea Douglass (GBR)	6-3	6-4	
F	May Sutton (USA)	Constance M. Wilson (GBR)	6-3	8-6	
S	May Sutton (USA)	Agnes Morton (GBR)	6-4	6-0	
S	Constance M. Wilson (GBR)	Blanche Bingley Hillyard (GBR)	7-5	9-11	6-2
Q	Agnes Morton (GBR)	Mrs. H.I. Harper (GBR)	6-2	6-4	
Q	May Sutton (USA)	Ethel Thomson (GBR)	8-6	6-1	
Q	Blanche Bingley Hillyard (GBR)	Dora Boothby (GBR)	6-3	6-2	
Q	Constance M. Wilson (GBR)	B.M. Holder (GBR)	6-2	6-0	

1906

Rd	Winner	Defeated	S1	S2	S3
Ch	Dorothea Douglass (GBR)	May Sutton (USA)	6-3	9-7	
F	Dorothea Douglass (GBR)	Charlotte Cooper Sterry (GBR)	6-2	6-2	
S	Dorothea Douglass (GBR)	Beryl Tulloch (GBR)	6-2	6-2	
S	Charlotte Cooper Sterry (GBR)	Towpie Lowther (GBR)	4-6	8-6	6-4
Q	Dorothea Douglass (GBR)	Winifred Longhurst (GBR)	6-4	6-3	
Q	Beryl Tulloch (GBR)	Blanche Bingley Hillyard (GBR)	6-3	6-1	
Q	Charlotte Cooper Sterry (GBR)	Violet Pickney (GBR)	6-4	6-2	
Q	Towpie Lowther (GBR)	Gladys Eastlake Smith (GBR)	6-3	6-3	

1907

Rd	Winner	Defeated	S1	S2	S3
Ch	May Sutton (USA)	D. Douglass Chambers (GBR)	6-1	6-4	
F	May Sutton (USA)	Constance M. Wilson (GBR)	6-4	6-2	
S	May Sutton (USA)	E.L. Bosworth (GBR)	6-2	6-2	
S	Constance M. Wilson (GBR)	Blanche Bingley Hillyard (GBR)	6-3	6-2	
Q	E.L. Bosworth (GBR)	M.E. Brown (GBR)	6-1	6-2	
Q	May Sutton (USA)	Constance Meyer (GBR)	6-0	6-3	
Q	Constance M. Wilson (GBR)	Angela Greene (GBR)	6-2	9-7	
Q	Blanche Bingley Hillyard (GBR)	Edith G. Johnson (GBR)	6-2	6-3	

1908

Rd	Winner	Defeated	S1	S2	S3
Ch	Charlotte Cooper Sterry (GBR)	May Sutton (USA)	(walkover)		
F	Charlotte Cooper Sterry (GBR)	Agnes Morton (GBR)	6-4	6-4	
S	Charlotte Cooper Sterry (GBR)	Dora Boothby (GBR)	6-2	6-4	
S	Agnes Morton (GBR)	Gladys Lamplough (GBR)	6-3	6-4	
Q	Dora Boothby (GBR)	Violet Pickney (GBR)	6-1	6-4	
Q	Charlotte Cooper Sterry (GBR)	Dorothea Douglass Chambers (GBR)	6-3	7-5	
Q	Agnes Morton (GBR)	Beryl Tulloch (GBR)	7-5	6-1	
Q	Gladys Lamplough (GBR)	Agnes Daniell Tuckey (GBR)	6-3	6-1	

1909

Rd	Winner	Defeated	S1	S2	S3
Ch	Dora Boothby (GBR)	Charlotte Cooper Sterry (GBR)	(walkover)		
F	Dora Boothby (GBR)	Agnes Morton (GBR)	6-4	4-6	8-6
S	Agnes Morton (GBR)	Aurea Edgington (GBR)	6-0	6-2	
S	Dora Boothby (GBR)	Maud Garfitt (GBR)	6-2	6-1	
Q	Aurea Edgington (GBR)	Madeline O'Neill (GBR)	7-5	6-4	
Q	Agnes Morton (GBR)	Edith G. Johnson (GBR)	6-0	6-3	
Q	Maud Garfitt (GBR)	Mabel Parton (GBR)	6-3	6-4	
Q	Dora Boothby (GBR)	Francis Helen Aitchison (GBR)	6-4	3-0 (retired)	

1910

Rd	Winner	Defeated	S1	S2	S3
Ch	Dorothea Douglass Chambers (GBR)	Dora Boothby (GBR)	6-2	6-2	
F	Dorothea Douglass Chambers (GBR)	Edith G. Johnson (GBR)	6-4	6-2	
S	Edith G. Johnson (GBR)	Gladys Lamplough (GBR)	1-6	6-0	6-3
S	Dorothea Douglass Chambers (GBR)	Winifred Slocock McNair (GBR)	6-1	6-0	
Q	Gladys Lamplough (GBR)	Sophie Castenschiold (GBR)	7-9	6-4	6-3
Q	Edith G. Johnson (GBR)	Mabel Parton (GBR)	7-5	6-4	
Q	Dorothea Douglass Chambers (GBR)	Francis Helen Aitchison (GBR)	6-2	6-1	
Q	Winifred Slocock McNair (GBR)	Aurea Edgington (GBR)	2-6	6-3	6-3

1911

Rd	Winner	Defeated	S1	S2	S3
Ch	Dorothea Douglass Chambers (GBR)	Dora Boothby (GBR)	6-0	6-0	
F	Dora Boothby (GBR)	Edith Hannam (GBR)	6-2	7-5	
S	Edith Hannam (GBR)	Francis Helen Aitchison (GBR)	6-3	6-8	7-5
S	Dora Boothby (GBR)	Mabel Parton (GBR)	6-3	6-4	
Q	Edith Hannam (GBR)	Mildred Coles (GBR)	6-4	4-6	7-5
Q	Francis Helen Aitchison (GBR)	Marie Hazel (GBR)	6-0	6-3	
Q	Dora Boothby (GBR)	Aurea Edgington (GBR)	6-2	6-4	
Q	Mabel Parton (GBR)	Dorothy Holman (GBR)	6-0	8-6	

1912

Rd	Winner	Defeated	S1	S2	S3
Ch	Ethel Thomson Larcombe (GBR)	D. Douglass Chambers (GBR)	(walkover)		
F	Ethel Thomson Larcombe (GBR)	Charlotte Cooper Sterry (GBR)	6-3	6-1	
S	Charlotte Cooper Sterry (GBR)	Dorothy Holman (GBR)	6-3	4-6	7-5
S	Ethel Thomson Larcombe (GBR)	Blanche Bingley Hillyard (GBR)	6-1	6-0	
Q	Charlotte Cooper Sterry (GBR)	Winifred Longhurst (GBR)	6-1	6-3	
Q	Dorothy Holman (GBR)	Agnes Morton (GBR)	7-5	6-2	
Q	Ethel Thomson Larcombe (GBR)	Winifred Slocock McNair (GBR)	6-2	5-7	6-0
Q	Blanche Bingley Hillyard (GBR)	Elizabeth Ryan (USA)	3-6	8-6	6-3

1913

Rd	Winner	Defeated	S1	S2	S3
Ch	Dorothea Douglass Chambers (GBR)	Ethel Thomson Larcombe (GBR)	(walkover)		
F	Dorothea Douglass Chambers (GBR)	Winifred Slocock McNair (GBR)	6-0	6-4	
S	Winifred Slocock McNair (GBR)	Dorothy Holman (GBR)	2-6	6-2	7-5
S	Dorothea Douglass Chambers (GBR)	Francis Helen Aitchison (GBR)	6-2	6-3	
Q	Winifred Slocock McNair (GBR)	Charlotte Cooper Sterry (GBR)	0-6	6-4	9-7
Q	Dorothy Holman (GBR)	Phyllis Satterthwaite (GBR)	6-4	6-1	
Q	Dorothea Douglass Chambers (GBR)	Mildred Coles (GBR)	6-1	6-0	
Q	Francis Helen Aitchison (GBR)	Madeline O'Neill (GBR)	6-2	6-0	

1914

Rd	Winner	Defeated	S1	S2	S3
Ch	Dorothea Douglass Chambers (GBR)	Ethel Thomson Larcombe (GBR)	7-5	6-4	
F	Ethel Thomson Larcombe (GBR)	Elizabeth Ryan (USA)	6-3	6-2	
S	Ethel Thomson Larcombe (GBR)	Aurea Edgington (GBR)	6-4	6-3	
S	Elizabeth Ryan (USA)	Francis Helen Aitchison (GBR)	6-4	6-3	
Q	Aurea Edgington (GBR)	Doris Covell Craddock (GBR)	6-1	6-3	
Q	Ethel Thomson Larcombe (GBR)	Agnes Daniell Tuckey (GBR)	(walkover)		
Q	Francis Helen Aitchison (GBR)	B. Leader (GBR)	6-2	6-0	
Q	Elizabeth Ryan (USA)	Betty Crundall Punnett (GBR)	6-0	6-3	

1915–1918 NOT HELD—WW I

1919

Rd	Winner	Defeated	S1	S2	S3
Ch	Suzanne Lenglen (FRA)	Dorothea Douglass Chambers (GBR)	10-8	4-6	9-7
F	Suzanne Lenglen (FRA)	Phyllis Satterthwaite (GBR)	6-1	6-1	
S	Phyllis Satterthwaite (GBR)	Geraldine Ramsey Beamish (GBR)	6-4	10-8	
S	Suzanne Lenglen (FRA)	Elizabeth Ryan (USA)	6-4	7-5	
Q	Geraldine Ramsey Beamish (GBR)	Aurea Edgington (GBR)	6-8	6-3	6-2
Q	Phyllis Satterthwaite (GBR)	Ruth Winch (GBR)	6-3	6-4	
Q	Suzanne Lenglen (FRA)	Kitty McKane (GBR)	6-0	6-1	
Q	Elizabeth Ryan (USA)	Mabel Parton (GBR)	6-2	6-3	

1920

Rd	Winner	Defeated	S1	S2	S3
Ch	Suzanne Lenglen (FRA)	Dorothea Douglass Chambers (GBR)	6-3	6-0	
F	Dorothea Douglass Chambers (GBR)	Elizabeth Ryan (USA)	6-2	6-1	
S	Elizabeth Ryan (USA)	Mabel Parton (GBR)	6-4	6-2	
S	Dorothea Douglass Chambers (GBR)	Molla Bjurstedt Mallory (USA)	6-0	6-3	
Q	Elizabeth Ryan (USA)	Violet Pickney (GBR)	(walkover)		
Q	Mabel Parton (GBR)	Phyllis Satterthwaite (GBR)	6-4	6-4	
Q	Molla Bjurstedt Mallory (USA)	Helen Leisk (GBR)	6-3	6-1	
Q	Dorothea Douglass Chambers (GBR)	Winifred Slocock McNair (GBR)	3-6	6-0	6-2

1921

Rd	Winner	Defeated	S1	S2	S3
Ch	Suzanne Lenglen (FRA)	Elizabeth Ryan (USA)	6-2	6-0	
F	Elizabeth Ryan (USA)	Phyllis Satterthwaite (GBR)	6-1	6-0	
S	Phyllis Satterthwaite (GBR)	Mabel Clayton (GBR)	8-6	6-2	
S	Elizabeth Ryan (USA)	Irene Bowder Peacock (RSA)	8-6	6-4	
Q	Mabel Clayton (GBR)	Dorothy Shepherd (GBR)	6-3	6-2	
Q	Phyllis Satterthwaite (GBR)	Phyllis Howkins (GBR)	6-1	6-8	6-1
Q	Elizabeth Ryan (USA)	Winifred Slocock McNair (GBR)	7-5	2-6	6-4
Q	Irene Bowder Peacock (RSA)	Molla Bjurstedt Mallory (USA)	0-6	6-4	6-4

1922

Rd	Winner	Defeated	S1	S2	S3
F	Suzanne Lenglen (FRA)	Molla Bjurstedt Mallory (USA)	6-2	6-0	
S	Suzanne Lenglen (FRA)	Irene Bowder Peacock (RSA)	6-4	6-1	
S	Molla Bjurstedt Mallory (USA)	Geraldine Ramsey Beamish (GBR)	6-2	6-2	
Q	Suzanne Lenglen (FRA)	Elizabeth Ryan (USA)	6-1	8-6	
Q	Irene Bowder Peacock (RSA)	Peggy Dransfield (GBR)	6-2	6-2	
Q	Geraldine Ramsey Beamish (GBR)	Mrs I.F.L. Elliot (GBR)	'8-6	6-1	
Q	Molla Bjurstedt Mallory (USA)	Aurea Edgington (GBR)	6-2	6-4	

1923

Rd	Winner	Defeated	S1	S2	S3
F	Suzanne Lenglen (FRA)	Kitty McKane (GBR)	6-2	6-2	
S	Suzanne Lenglen (FRA)	Geraldine Ramsey Beamish (GBR)	6-0	6-0	
S	Kitty McKane (GBR)	Elizabeth Ryan (USA)	1-6	6-2	6-4
Q	Suzanne Lenglen (FRA)	Marie Hazel (GBR)	6-2	6-1	
Q	Geraldine Ramsey Beamish (GBR)	Molla Bjurstedt Mallory (USA)	4-6	7-5	6-4
Q	Kitty McKane (GBR)	Eleanor Goss (USA)	6-2	6-2	
Q	Elizabeth Ryan (USA)	Eleanor Florence Rose (GBR)	6-0	6-0	

1924

Rd	Winner	Defeated	S1	S2	S3
F	Kitty McKane (GBR)	Helen Wills (USA)	4-6	6-4	6-4
S	Helen Wills (USA)	Phyllis Satterthwaite (GBR)	6-2	6-1	
S	Kitty McKane (GBR)	Suzanne Lenglen (FRA)	(walkover)		
Q	Phyllis Satterthwaite (GBR)	Dorothy Shepherd Barron (GBR)	6-4	10-8	
Q	Helen Wills (USA)	Mrs. J.S. Colegate (GBR)	6-1	6-0	
Q	Kitty McKane (GBR)	Marion Zinderstein Jessup (USA)	6-1	6-3	
Q	Suzanne Lenglen (FRA)	Elizabeth Ryan (USA)	6-2	6-8	6-4

1925

Rd	Winner	Defeated	S1	S2	S3
F	Suzanne Lenglen (FRA)	Joan Fry (GBR)	6-2	6-0	
S	Suzanne Lenglen (FRA)	Kitty McKane (GBR)	6-0	6-0	
S	Joan Fry (GBR)	Marguerite Billout (FRA)	6-2	4-6	6-3
Q	Kitty McKane (GBR)	Esna Boyd (AUS)	6-1	6-1	
Q	Suzanne Lenglen (FRA)	Geraldine Ramsey Beamish (GBR)	6-0	6-0	
Q	Joan Fry (GBR)	Daphne Akhurst (AUS)	2-6	6-4	6-3
Q	Marguerite Billout (FRA)	Mary Hart McIlquham (GBR)	6-3	6-3	

1926

Rd	Winner	Defeated	S1	S2	S3
F	Kitty McKane Godfree (GBR)	Lili de Alvarez (ESP)	6-2	4-6	6-3
S	Lili de Alvarez (ESP)	Molla Bjurstedt Mallory (USA)	6-2	6-2	
S	Kitty McKane Godfree (GBR)	Didi Vlasto (FRA)	6-4	6-0	
Q	Lili de Alvarez (ESP)	Claire Beckingham (GBR)	6-2	6-2	
Q	Molla Bjurstedt Mallory (USA)	Kea Bouman (NED)	3-6	7-5	6-3
Q	Didi Vlasto (FRA)	Helen Contostavlos (GRE)	6-3	6-3	
Q	Kitty McKane Godfree (GBR)	C. Tyrrell (GBR)	6-2	6-0	

1927

Rd	Winner	Defeated	S1	S2	S3
F	Helen Wills (USA)	Lili de Alvarez (ESP)	6-2	6-4	
S	Lili de Alvarez (ESP)	Elizabeth Ryan (USA)	2-6	6-0	6-4
S	Helen Wills (USA)	Joan Fry (GBR)	6-3	6-1	
Q	Elizabeth Ryan (USA)	Kitty McKane Godfree (GBR)	3-6	6-4	6-4
Q	Lili de Alvarez (ESP)	Phoebe Holcroft Watson (GBR)	6-3	3-6	8-6
Q	Helen Wills (USA)	Irene Bowder Peacock (RSA)	6-3	6-1	
Q	Joan Fry (GBR)	Betty Nuthall (GBR)	1-6	6-3	6-4

1928

Rd	Winner	Defeated	S1	S2	S3
F	Helen Wills (USA)	Lili de Alvarez (ESP)	6-2	6-3	
S	Helen Wills (USA)	Elizabeth Ryan (USA)	6-1	6-1	
S	Lili de Alvarez (ESP)	Daphne Akhurst (AUS)	6-3	6-0	
Q	Helen Wills (USA)	Phoebe Holcroft Watson (GBR)	6-3	6-0	
Q	Elizabeth Ryan (USA)	Helene Nicolopoulos (GRE)	6-1	4-6	6-2
Q	Lili de Alvarez (ESP)	Cilly Aussem (GER)	7-5	6-2	
Q	Daphne Akhurst (AUS)	Eileen Bennett (GBR)	2-6	6-3	6-2

1929

Rd	Winner	Defeated	S1	S2	S3
F	Helen Wills (USA)	Helen Jacobs (USA)	6-1	6-2	
S	Helen Wills (USA)	Elsie Goldsack (GBR)	6-2	6-4	
S	Helen Jacobs (USA)	Joan Ridley (GBR)	6-2	6-2	
Q	Helen Wills (USA)	Bobbie Heine (RSA)	6-2	6-4	
Q	Elsie Goldsack (GBR)	Billie Tapscott (RSA)	6-3	6-3	
Q	Helen Jacobs (USA)	Mary Hart McIlquham (GBR)	6-1	6-0	
Q	Joan Ridley (GBR)	May Sutton Bundy (USA)	6-3	6-2	

1930

Rd	Winner	Defeated	S1	S2	S3
F	Helen Wills Moody (USA)	Elizabeth Ryan (USA)	6-2	6-2	
S	Helen Wills Moody (USA)	Simone Passemard Mathieu (FRA)	6-3	6-2	
S	Elizabeth Ryan (USA)	Cilly Aussem (GER)	6-3	0-6	4-4 (retired)
Q	Helen Wills Moody (USA)	Phyllis Mudford (GBR)	6-1	6-2	
Q	Simone Passemard Mathieu (FRA)	Joan Ridley (GBR)	6-2	6-1	
Q	Elizabeth Ryan (USA)	Betty Nuthall (GBR)	6-2	2-6	6-0
Q	Cilly Aussem (GER)	Helen Jacobs (USA)	6-2	6-1	

1931

Rd	Winner	Defeated	S1	S2	S3
F	Cilly Aussem (GER)	Hilde Krahwinkel (GER)	6-2	7-5	
S	Cilly Aussem (GER)	Simone Passemard Mathieu (FRA)	6-0	2-6	6-3
S	Hilde Krahwinkel (GER)	Helen Jacobs (USA)	10-8	0-6	6-4
Q	Cilly Aussem (GER)	Lolette Payot (SUI)	2-6	6-2	6-1
Q	Simone Passemard Mathieu (FRA)	Margaret Scriven (GBR)	1-6	6-2	7-5
Q	Helen Jacobs (USA)	Betty Nuthall (GBR)	6-2	6-3	
Q	Hilde Krahwinkel (GER)	Dorothy Round (GBR)	7-5	6-3	

1932

Rd	Winner	Defeated	S1	S2	S3
F	Helen Wills Moody (USA)	Helen Jacobs (USA)	6-3	6-1	
S	Helen Wills Moody (USA)	Mary Heeley (GBR)	6-2	6-0	
S	Helen Jacobs (USA)	Simone Passemard Mathieu (FRA)	7-5	6-1	
Q	Helen Wills Moody (USA)	Dorothy Round (GBR)	6-0	6-1	
Q	Mary Heeley (GBR)	Eileen Bennett Whittingstall (GBR)	6-4	6-0	
Q	Helen Jacobs (USA)	Hilde Krahwinkel (GER)	6-2	6-4	
Q	Simone Passemard Mathieu (FRA)	Betty Nuthall (GBR)	6-0	6-3	

1933

Rd	Winner	Defeated	S1	S2	S3
F	Helen Wills Moody (USA)	Dorothy Round (GBR)	6-4	6-8	6-3
S	Dorothy Round (GBR)	Helen Jacobs (USA)	4-6	6-4	6-2
S	Helen Wills Moody (USA)	Hilde Krahwinkel (GER)	6-4	6-3	
Q	Dorothy Round (GBR)	Lucia Valerio (ITA)	6-3	6-2	
Q	Helen Jacobs (USA)	Simone Passemard Mathieu (FRA)	6-1	1-6	6-2
Q	Hilde Krahwinkel (GER)	Margaret Scriven (GBR)	6-4	3-6	6-1
Q	Helen Wills Moody (USA)	Lolette Payot (SUI)	6-4	6-1	

1934

Rd	Winner	Defeated	S1	S2	S3
F	Dorothy Round (GBR)	Helen Jacobs (USA)	6-2	5-7	6-3
S	Dorothy Round (GBR)	Simone Passemard Mathieu (FRA)	6-4	5-7	6-2
S	Helen Jacobs (USA)	Joan Hartigan (AUS)	6-2	6-2	
Q	Dorothy Round (GBR)	Lolette Payot (SUI)	6-4	6-2	
Q	Simone Passemard Mathieu (FRA)	Sarah Palfrey (USA)	6-3	6-8	6-2
Q	Helen Jacobs (USA)	Cilly Aussem (GER)	6-0	6-2	
Q	Joan Hartigan (AUS)	Margaret Scriven (GBR)	3-6	6-3	6-1

1935

Rd	Winner	Defeated	S1	S2	S3
F	Helen Wills Moody (USA)	Helen Jacobs (USA)	6-3	3-6	7-5
S	Helen Wills Moody (USA)	Joan Hartigan (AUS)	6-3	6-3	
S	Helen Jacobs (USA)	Hilde Krahwinkel Sperling (GER)	6-3	6-0	
Q	Joan Hartigan (AUS)	Dorothy Round (GBR)	4-6	6-4	6-3
Q	Helen Wills Moody (USA)	Simone Passemard Mathieu (FRA)	6-3	6-0	
Q	Helen Jacobs (USA)	Jadwiga Jedrzejowska (POL)	6-1	9-7	
Q	Hilde Krahwinkel Sperling (GER)	Kay Stammers (GBR)	7-5	7-5	

1936

Rd	Winner	Defeated	S1	S2	S3
F	Helen Jacobs (USA)	Hilde Krahwinkel Sperling (DEN)	6-2	4-6	7-5
S	Helen Jacobs (USA)	Jadwiga Jedrzejowska (POL)	6-4	6-2	
S	Hilde Krahwinkel Sperling (DEN)	Simone Passemard Mathieu (FRA)	6-3	6-2	
Q	Helen Jacobs (USA)	Anita Lizana (CHI)	6-2	1-6	6-4
Q	Jadwiga Jedrzejowska (POL)	Kay Stammers (GBR)	6-2	6-3	
Q	Simone Passemard Mathieu (FRA)	Marie Luise Horn (GER)	7-5	6-3	
Q	Hilde Krahwinkel Sperling (DEN)	Dorothy Round (GBR)	6-3	8-6	

1937

Rd	Winner	Defeated	S1	S2	S3
F	Dorothy Round (GBR)	Jadwiga Jedrzejowska (POL)	6-2	2-6	7-5
S	Jadwiga Jedrzejowska (POL)	Alice Marble (USA)	8-6	6-2	
S	Dorothy Round (GBR)	Simone Passemard Mathieu (FRA)	6-4	6-0	
Q	Alice Marble (USA)	Hilde Krahwinkel Sperling (DEN)	7-5	2-6	6-3
Q	Jadwiga Jedrzejowska (POL)	Margaret Scriven (GBR)	6-1	6-2	
Q	Simone Passemard Mathieu (FRA)	Anita Lizana (CHI)	6-3	6-3	
Q	Dorothy Round (GBR)	Helen Jacobs (USA)	6-4	6-2	

1938

Rd	Winner	Defeated	S1	S2	S3
F	Helen Wills Moody (USA)	Helen Jacobs (USA)	6-4	6-0	
S	Helen Jacobs (USA)	Alice Marble (USA)	6-4	6-4	
S	Helen Wills Moody (USA)	Hilde Krahwinkel Sperling (DEN)	12-10	6-4	
Q	Alice Marble (USA)	Simone Passemard Mathieu (FRA)	6-2	6-3	
Q	Helen Jacobs (USA)	Jadwiga Jedrzejowska (POL)	6-2	6-3	
Q	Hilde Krahwinkel Sperling (DEN)	Sarah Palfrey Fabyan (USA)	4-6	6-4	6-4
Q	Helen Wills Moody (USA)	Kay Stammers (GBR)	6-2	6-1	

1939

Rd	Winner	Defeated	S1	S2	S3
F	Alice Marble (USA)	Kay Stammers (GBR)	6-2	6-0	
S	Kay Stammers (GBR)	Sarah Palfrey Fabyan (USA)	7-5	2-6	6-3
S	Alice Marble (USA)	Hilde Krahwinkel Sperling (DEN)	6-0	6-0	
Q	Kay Stammers (GBR)	Helen Jacobs (USA)	6-2	6-2	
Q	Sarah Palfrey Fabyan (USA)	Simone Passemard Mathieu (FRA)	6-4	6-2	
Q	Hilde Krahwinkel Sperling (DEN)	Mary Hardwick (GBR)	6-4	6-0	
Q	Alice Marble (USA)	Jadwiga Jedrzejowska (POL)	6-1	6-4	

1940–1945 NOT HELD—WW II

1946

Rd	Winner	Defeated	S1	S2	S3
F	Pauline Betz (USA)	Louise Brough (USA)	6-2	6-4	
S	Pauline Betz (USA)	Dorothy Bundy (USA)	6-2	6-3	
S	Louise Brough (USA)	Margaret Osborne (USA)	8-6	7-5	
Q	Pauline Betz (USA)	Joan Curry (GBR)	6-0	6-3	
Q	Dorothy Bundy (USA)	Kay Stammers Menzies (GBR)	4-6	6-1	6-3
Q	Louise Brough (USA)	Jean Bostock (GBR)	6-1	6-2	
Q	Margaret Osborne (USA)	Doris Hart (USA)	5-7	6-4	6-4

1947

Rd	Winner	Defeated	S1	S2	S3
F	Margaret Osborne (USA)	Doris Hart (USA)	6-2	6-4	
S	Doris Hart (USA)	Louise Brough (USA)	2-6	8-6	6-4
S	Margaret Osborne (USA)	Sheila Piercey Summers (RSA)	6-1	6-2	
Q	Louise Brough (USA)	Nancye Wynne Bolton (AUS)	6-2	6-3	
Q	Doris Hart (USA)	Jean Bostock (GBR)	4-6	6-1	6-2
Q	Sheila Piercey Summers (RSA)	Pat Canning Todd (USA)	7-5	6-4	
Q	Margaret Osborne (USA)	Kay Stammers Menzies (GBR)	6-2	6-4	

1948

Rd	Winner	Defeated	S1	S2	S3
F	Louise Brough (USA)	Doris Hart (USA)	6-3	8-6	
S	Doris Hart (USA)	Margaret Osborne duPont (USA)	6-4	2-6	6-3
S	Louise Brough (USA)	Pat Canning Todd (USA)	6-3	7-5	
Q	Margaret Osborne duPont (USA)	Jean Bostock (GBR)	7-5	6-3	
Q	Doris Hart (USA)	Nelly Adamson Landry (FRA)	6-0	6-2	
Q	Pat Canning Todd (USA)	Jean Quertier (GBR)	6-2	6-4	
Q	Louise Brough (USA)	Shirley Fry (USA)	3-1	(retired)	

1949

Rd	Winner	Defeated	S1	S2	S3
F	Louise Brough (USA)	Margaret Osborne duPont (USA)	10-8	1-6	10-8
S	Louise Brough (USA)	Pat Canning Todd (USA)	6-3	6-0	
S	Margaret Osborne duPont (USA)	Helen Pedersen Rihbany (USA)	6-2	6-2	
Q	Louise Brough (USA)	Molly Lincoln Blair (GBR)	6-2	6-3	
Q	Pat Canning Todd (USA)	Jean Walker Smith (GBR)	3-6	6-4	6-3
Q	Helen Pedersen Rihbany (USA)	Peggy Dawson-Scott (GBR)	7-5	7-5	
Q	Margaret Osborne duPont (USA)	Betty Hilton (GBR)	6-1	6-3	

1950

Rd	Winner	Defeated	S1	S2	S3
F	Louise Brough (USA)	Margaret Osborne duPont (USA)	6-1	3-6	6-1
S	Louise Brough (USA)	Doris Hart (USA)	6-4	6-3	
S	Margaret Osborne duPont (USA)	Pat Canning Todd (USA)	8-6	4-6	8-6
Q	Louise Brough (USA)	Shirley Fry (USA)	2-6	6-3	6-0
Q	Doris Hart (USA)	Barbara Scofield (USA)	6-1	6-1	
Q	Pat Canning Todd (USA)	Betty Harrison (GBR)	6-2	6-2	
Q	Margaret Osborne duPont (USA)	Gussy Moran (USA)	6-4	6-4	

1951

Rd	Winner	Defeated	S1	S2	S3
F	Doris Hart (USA)	Shirley Fry (USA)	6-1	6-0	
S	Doris Hart (USA)	Beverly Baker (USA)	6-3	6-1	
S	Shirley Fry (USA)	Louise Brough (USA)	6-4	6-2	
Q	Beverly Baker (USA)	Margaret Osborne duPont (USA)	6-1	4-6	6-3
Q	Doris Hart (USA)	Nancy Chaffee (USA)	6-3	6-3	
Q	Shirley Fry (USA)	Jean Walker Smith (GBR)	8-6	6-4	
Q	Louise Brough (USA)	Kay Tuckey (GBR)	5-7	6-1	6-3

1952

Rd	Winner	Defeated	S1	S2	S3
F	Maureen Connolly (USA)	Louise Brough (USA)	7-5	6-3	
S	Maureen Connolly (USA)	Shirley Fry (USA)	6-4	6-3	
S	Louise Brough (USA)	Pat Canning Todd (USA)	6-3	3-6	6-1
Q	Maureen Connolly (USA)	Thelma Coyne Long (AUS)	5-7	2-6	6-0
Q	Shirley Fry (USA)	Jean Walker Smith (GBR)	6-3	6-3	
Q	Louise Brough (USA)	Jean Quertier-Rinkel (GBR)	6-1	9-7	
Q	Pat Canning Todd (USA)	Doris Hart (USA)	6-8	7-5	6-4

1953

Rd	Winner	Defeated	S1	S2	S3
F	Maureen Connolly (USA)	Doris Hart (USA)	8-6	7-5	
S	Doris Hart (USA)	Dorothy Head Knode (USA)	6-2	6-2	
S	Maureen Connolly (USA)	Shirley Fry (USA)	6-1	6-1	
Q	Doris Hart (USA)	Zsuzsi Kormoczi (HUN)	7-5	7-5	
Q	Dorothy Head Knode (USA)	Angela Mortimer (GBR)	6-4	6-3	
Q	Shirley Fry (USA)	Julia Sampson (USA)	6-4	6-2	
Q	Maureen Connolly (USA)	Erika Vollmer (GER)	6-3	6-0	

1954

Rd	Winner	Defeated	S1	S2	S3
F	Maureen Connolly (USA)	Louise Brough (USA)	6-2	7-5	
S	Louise Brough (USA)	Doris Hart (USA)	2-6	6-3	6-3
S	Maureen Connolly (USA)	Betty Rosenquest Pratt (USA)	6-1	6-1	
Q	Doris Hart (USA)	Helen Fletcher (GBR)	6-1	6-3	
Q	Louise Brough (USA)	Angela Mortimer (GBR)	6-1	6-3	
Q	Betty Rosenquest Pratt (USA)	Shirley Fry (USA)	6-4	9-11	6-3
Q	Maureen Connolly (USA)	Margaret Osborne duPont (USA)	6-1	6-1	

1955

Rd	Winner	Defeated	S1	S2	S3
F	Louise Brough (USA)	Beverly Beverly Fleitz (USA)	7-5	8-6	
S	Beverly Beverly Fleitz (USA)	Doris Hart (USA)	6-3	6-0	
S	Louise Brough (USA)	Darlene Hard (USA)	6-3	8-6	
Q	Doris Hart (USA)	Dorothy Head Knode (USA)	6-4	6-3	
Q	Beverly Beverly Fleitz (USA)	Angela Buxton (GBR)	6-2	6-2	
Q	Darlene Hard (USA)	Zsuzsi Kormoczi (HUN)	6-2	6-3	
Q	Louise Brough (USA)	Beryl Penrose (AUS)	6-2	6-0	

1956

Rd	Winner	Defeated	S1	S2	S3
F	Shirley Fry (USA)	Angela Buxton (GBR)	6-3	6-1	
S	Angela Buxton (GBR)	Pat Ward (GBR)	6-1	6-4	
S	Shirley Fry (USA)	Louise Brough (USA)	6-4	4-6	6-3
Q	Angela Buxton (GBR)	Beverly Beverly Fleitz (USA)	(walkover)		
Q	Pat Ward (GBR)	Angela Mortimer (GBR)	6-3	6-0	
Q	Shirley Fry (USA)	Althea Gibson (USA)	4-6	6-3	6-4
Q	Louise Brough (USA)	Shirley Bloomer (GBR)	5-7	6-1	6-3

1957

Rd	Winner	Defeated	S1	S2	S3
F	Althea Gibson (USA)	Darlene Hard (USA)	6-3	6-2	
S	Darlene Hard (USA)	Dorothy Head Knode (USA)	6-2	6-3	
S	Althea Gibson (USA)	Christine Truman (GBR)	6-1	6-1	
Q	Darlene Hard (USA)	Louise Brough (USA)	6-2	6-2	
Q	Dorothy Head Knode (USA)	Rosie Reyes (MEX)	6-4	6-0	
Q	Christine Truman (GBR)	Betty Rosenquest Pratt (USA)	9-7	5-7	6-4
Q	Althea Gibson (USA)	Sandra Reynolds (RSA)	6-3	6-4	

1958

Rd	Winner	Defeated	S1	S2	S3
F	Althea Gibson (USA)	Angela Mortimer (GBR)	8-6	6-2	
S	Angela Mortimer (GBR)	Zsuzsi Kormoczi (HUN)	6-0	6-1	
S	Althea Gibson (USA)	Ann Haydon (GBR)	6-2	6-0	
Q	Zsuzsi Kormoczi (HUN)	Mimi Arnold (USA)	6-1	5-7	8-6
Q	Angela Mortimer (GBR)	Margaret Osborne duPont (USA)	4-6	6-3	10-8
Q	Ann Haydon (GBR)	Maria Bueno (BRA)	6-3	7-5	
Q	Althea Gibson (USA)	Shirley Bloomer (GBR)	6-3	6-8	6-2

1959

Rd	Winner	Defeated	S1	S2	S3
F	Maria Bueno (BRA)	Darlene Hard (USA)	6-4	6-3	
S	Darlene Hard (USA)	Sandra Reynolds (RSA)	6-4	6-4	
S	Maria Bueno (BRA)	Sally Moore (USA)	6-2	6-4	
Q	Sandra Reynolds (RSA)	Angela Mortimer (GBR)	7-5	8-6	
Q	Darlene Hard (USA)	Ann Haydon (GBR)	1-6	6-4	7-5
Q	Maria Bueno (BRA)	Edda Buding (GER)	6-3	6-3	
Q	Sally Moore (USA)	Yola Ramirez (MEX)	6-3	6-2	

1960

Rd	Winner	Defeated	S1	S2	S3
F	Maria Bueno (BRA)	Sandra Reynolds (RSA)	8-6	6-0	
S	Maria Bueno (BRA)	Christine Truman (GBR)	6-0	5-7	6-1
S	Sandra Reynolds (RSA)	Ann Haydon (GBR)	6-3	2-6	6-4
Q	Maria Bueno (BRA)	Angela Mortimer (GBR)	6-1	6-1	
Q	Christine Truman (GBR)	Karen Hantze (USA)	4-6	6-4	6-4
Q	Ann Haydon (GBR)	Renee Schuurman (RSA)	7-5	1-6	6-2
Q	Sandra Reynolds (RSA)	Darlene Hard (USA)	6-1	2-6	6-1

1961

Rd	Winner	Defeated	S1	S2	S3
F	Angela Mortimer (GBR)	Christine Truman (GBR)	4-6	6-4	7-5
S	Christine Truman (GBR)	Renee Schuurman (RSA)	6-4	6-4	
S	Angela Mortimer (GBR)	Sandra Reynolds (RSA)	11-9	6-3	
Q	Christine Truman (GBR)	Margaret Smith (AUS)	3-6	6-3	9-7
Q	Renee Schuurman (RSA)	Karen Hantze (USA)	6-4	2-6	7-5
Q	Angela Mortimer (GBR)	Vera Puzejova Sukova (CZE)	6-3	6-4	
Q	Sandra Reynolds (RSA)	Yola Ramirez (MEX)	4-6	6-3	6-0

1962

Rd	Winner	Defeated	S1	S2	S3
F	Karen Hantze Susman (USA)	Vera Puzejova Sukova (CZE)	6-4	6-4	
S	Karen Hantze Susman (USA)	Ann Haydon (GBR)	8-6	6-1	
S	Vera Puzejova Sukova (CZE)	Maria Bueno (BRA)	6-4	6-3	
Q	Ann Haydon (GBR)	Billie Jean Moffitt (USA)	6-3	6-1	
Q	Karen Hantze Susman (USA)	Renee Schuurman (RSA)	6-4	6-4	
Q	Maria Bueno (BRA)	Lesley Turner (AUS)	2-6	6-4	6-2
Q	Vera Puzejova Sukova (CZE)	Darlene Hard (USA)	6-4	6-3	

1963

Rd	Winner	Defeated	S1	S2	S3
F	Maria Bueno (BRA)	Billie Jean Moffitt (USA)	6-3	6-4	
S	Margaret Smith (AUS)	Darlene Hard (USA)	6-3	6-3	
S	Billie Jean Moffitt (USA)	Ann Haydon Jones (GBR)	6-4	6-4	
Q	Margaret Smith (AUS)	Renee Schuurman (RSA)	3-6	6-0	6-1
Q	Darlene Hard (USA)	Jan Lehane (AUS)	6-1	1-2 (retired)	
Q	Ann Haydon Jones (GBR)	Donna Floyd Fales (USA)	6-4	6-1	
Q	Billie Jean Moffitt (USA)	Maria Bueno (BRA)	6-2	7-5	

1964

Rd	Winner	Defeated	S1	S2	S3
F	Maria Bueno (BRA)	Margaret Smith (AUS)	6-4	7-9	6-3
S	Margaret Smith (AUS)	Billie Jean Moffitt (USA)	6-3	6-4	
S	Maria Bueno (BRA)	Lesley Turner (AUS)	3-6	6-4	6-4
Q	Margaret Smith (AUS)	Norman Baylon (ARG)	6-0	2-0 (retired)	
Q	Billie Jean Moffitt (USA)	Ann Haydon Jones (GBR)	6-3	6-3	
Q	Lesley Turner (AUS)	Nancy Richey (USA)	6-3	6-4	
Q	Maria Bueno (BRA)	Robyn Ebbern (AUS)	6-4	6-1	

1965

Rd	Winner	Defeated	S1	S2	S3
F	Margaret Smith (AUS)	Maria Bueno (BRA)	6-4	7-5	
S	Maria Bueno (BRA)	Billie Jean Moffitt (USA)	6-4	5-7	6-3
S	Margaret Smith (AUS)	Christine Truman (GBR)	6-4	6-0	
Q	Maria Bueno (BRA)	Jane Albert (USA)	6-2	6-2	
Q	Billie Jean Moffitt (USA)	Lesley Turner (AUS)	6-2	6-1	
Q	Christine Truman (GBR)	Nancy Richey (USA)	6-4	1-6	7-5
Q	Margaret Smith (AUS)	Justina Bricka (USA)	6-3	6-0	

1966

Rd	Winner	Defeated	S1	S2	S3
F	Billie Jean King (USA)	Maria Bueno (BRA)	6-3	3-6	6-1
S	Billie Jean King (USA)	Margaret Smith (AUS)	6-3	6-3	
S	Maria Bueno (BRA)	Ann Haydon Jones (GBR)	6-3	9-11	7-5
Q	Margaret Smith (AUS)	Trudy Groenman (NED)	6-0	6-4	
Q	Billie Jean King (USA)	Annette Van Zyl (RSA)	1-6	6-2	6-4
Q	Ann Haydon Jones (GBR)	Nancy Richey (USA)	4-6	6-1	6-1
Q	Maria Bueno (BRA)	Francoise Durr (FRA)	6-4	6-3	

1967

Rd	Winner	Defeated	S1	S2	S3
F	Billie Jean King (USA)	Ann Haydon Jones (GBR)	6-3	6-4	
S	Billie Jean King (USA)	Kathy Harter (USA)	6-0	6-3	
S	Ann Haydon Jones (GBR)	Rosie Casals (USA)	2-6	6-3	7-5
Q	Billie Jean King (USA)	Virginia Wade (GBR)	7-5	6-2	
Q	Kathy Harter (USA)	Lesley Turner (AUS)	7-5	1-6	6-2
Q	Ann Haydon Jones (GBR)	Mary Ann Eisel (USA)	6-2	4-6	7-5
Q	Rosie Casals (USA)	Judy Tegart (AUS)	7-5	6-4	

1968

Rd	Winner	Defeated	S1	S2	S3
F	Billie Jean King (USA)	Judy Tegart (AUS)	9-7	7-5	
S	Judy Tegart (AUS)	Nancy Richey (USA)	6-3	6-1	
S	Billie Jean King (USA)	Ann Haydon Jones (GBR)	4-6	7-5	6-2
Q	Judy Tegart (AUS)	Margaret Smith Court (AUS)	4-6	8-6	6-1
Q	Nancy Richey (USA)	Maria Bueno (BRA)	6-4	6-2	
Q	Ann Haydon Jones (GBR)	Francoise Durr (FRA)	6-2	6-2	
Q	Billie Jean King (USA)	Lesley Turner Bowrey (AUS)	6-3	6-4	

1969

Rd	Winner	Defeated	S1	S2	S3
F	Ann Haydon Jones (GBR)	Billie Jean King (USA)	3-6	6-3	6-2
S	Ann Haydon Jones (GBR)	Margaret Smith Court (AUS)	10-12	6-3	6-2
S	Billie Jean King (USA)	Rosie Casals (USA)	6-1	6-0	
Q	Rosie Casals (USA)	Lesley Turner Bowrey (AUS)	3-6	9-7	7-5
Q	Billie Jean King (USA)	Judy Tegart (AUS)	4-6	7-5	8-6
Q	Ann Haydon Jones (GBR)	Nancy Richey (USA)	6-2	7-5	
Q	Margaret Smith Court (AUS)	Julie Heldman (USA)	4-6	6-3	6-3

1970

Rd	Winner	Defeated	S1	S2	S3
F	Margaret Smith Court (AUS)	Billie Jean King (USA)	14-12	11-9	
S	Billie Jean King (USA)	Francoise Durr (FRA)	6-3	7-5	
S	Margaret Smith Court (AUS)	Rosie Casals (USA)	6-4	6-1	
Q	Francoise Durr (FRA)	Cecilia Martinez (USA)	6-0	6-4	
Q	Billie Jean King (USA)	Karen Krantzcke (USA)	3-6	6-3	6-2
Q	Rosie Casals (USA)	Winnie Shaw (GBR)	6-2	6-0	
Q	Margaret Smith Court (AUS)	Helga Niessen Masthoff (GER)	6-8	6-0	6-0

Rd	Winner	Defeated	S1	S2	S3

1971

Rd	Winner	Defeated	S1	S2	S3
F	**Evonne Goolagong (AUS)**	**Margaret Smith Court (AUS)**	**6-4**	**6-1**	
S	Evonne Goolagong (AUS)	Billie Jean King (USA)	6-4	6-4	
S	Margaret Smith Court (AUS)	Judy Tegart Dalton (AUS)	4-6	6-1	6-0
Q	Margaret Smith Court (AUS)	Winnie Shaw (GBR)	6-2	6-1	
Q	Judy Tegart Dalton (AUS)	Kerry Melville (AUS)	6-2	3-6	6-3
Q	Evonne Goolagong (AUS)	Nancy Richey Gunter (USA)	6-3	6-2	
Q	Billie Jean King (USA)	Francoise Durr (FRA)	2-6	6-2	6-2

1972

Rd	Winner	Defeated	S1	S2	S3
F	**Billie Jean King (USA)**	**Evonne Goolagong (AUS)**	**6-3**	**6-3**	
S	Billie Jean King (USA)	Rosie Casals (USA)	6-2	6-4	
S	Evonne Goolagong (AUS)	Chris Evert (USA)	4-6	6-3	6-4
Q	Chris Evert (USA)	Patti Hogan (USA)	6-2	4-6	6-1
Q	Evonne Goolagong (AUS)	Francoise Durr (FRA)	8-6	7-5	
Q	Rosie Casals (USA)	Nancy Richey Gunter (USA)	3-6	6-4	6-0
Q	Billie Jean King (USA)	Virginia Wade (GBR)	6-1	3-6	6-3

1973

Rd	Winner	Defeated	S1	S2	S3
F	**Billie Jean King (USA)**	**Chris Evert (USA)**	**6-0**	**7-5**	
S	Chris Evert (USA)	Margaret Smith Court (AUS)	6-1	1-6	6-1
S	Billie Jean King (USA)	Evonne Goolagong (AUS)	6-3	5-7	6-3
Q	Margaret Smith Court (AUS)	Olga Morozova (USSR)	4-6	6-4	6-1
Q	Chris Evert (USA)	Rosie Casals (USA)	6-2	4-6	6-2
Q	Evonne Goolagong (AUS)	Virginia Wade (GBR)	6-3	6-3	
Q	Billie Jean King (USA)	Kerry Melville (AUS)	9-8(5)	8-6	

1974

Rd	Winner	Defeated	S1	S2	S3
F	**Chris Evert (USA)**	**Olga Morozova (USSR)**	**6-0**	**6-4**	
S	Olga Morozova (USSR)	Virginia Wade (GBR)	1-6	7-5	6-4
S	Chris Evert (USA)	Kerry Melville (AUS)	6-2	6-3	
Q	Olga Morozova (USSR)	Billie Jean King (USA)	7-5	6-2	
Q	Virginia Wade (GBR)	Linky Boshoff (RSA)	6-3	6-2	
Q	Kerry Melville (AUS)	Evonne Goolagong (AUS)	9-7	1-6	6-2
Q	Chris Evert (USA)	Helga Niessen Masthoff (GER)	6-4	6-2	

1975

Rd	Winner	Defeated	S1	S2	S3
F	**Billie Jean King (USA)**	**Evonne Goolagong Cawley (AUS)**	**6-0**	**6-1**	
S	Evonne Goolagong (AUS)	Margaret Smith Court (AUS)	6-4	6-4	
S	Billie Jean King (USA)	Chris Evert (USA)	2-6	6-2	6-3
Q	Chris Evert (USA)	Betty Stove (NED)	5-7	7-5	6-0
Q	Billie Jean King (USA)	Olga Morozova (USSR)	6-3	6-3	
Q	Evonne Goolagong (AUS)	Virginia Wade (GBR)	5-7	6-3	9-7
Q	Margaret Smith Court (AUS)	Martina Navratilova (CZE)	6-3	6-4	

1976

Rd	Winner	Defeated	S1	S2	S3
F	**Chris Evert (USA)**	**Evonne Goolagong Cawley (AUS)**	**6-3**	**4-6**	**8-6**
S	Evonne Goolagong Cawley (AUS)	Virginia Wade (GBR)	6-1	6-2	
S	Chris Evert (USA)	Martina Navratilova (CZE)	6-3	4-6	6-4
Q	Chris Evert (USA)	Olga Morozova (USSR)	6-3	6-0	
Q	Martina Navratilova (CZE)	Sue Barker (GBR)	6-3	3-6	7-5
Q	Virginia Wade (GBR)	Kerry Melville Reid (AUS)	6-4	6-2	
Q	Evonne Goolagong Cawley (AUS)	Rosie Casals (USA)	7-5	6-3	

1977

Rd	Winner	Defeated	S1	S2	S3
F	**Virginia Wade (GBR)**	**Betty Stove (NED)**	**4-6**	**6-3**	**6-1**
S	Betty Stove (NED)	Sue Barker (GBR)	6-4	2-6	6-4
S	Virginia Wade (GBR)	Chris Evert (USA)	6-2	4-6	6-1
Q	Chris Evert (USA)	Billie Jean King (USA)	6-1	6-2	
Q	Virginia Wade (GBR)	Rosie Casals (USA)	7-5	6-2	
Q	Sue Barker (GBR)	Kerry Melville Reid (AUS)	6-3	6-4	
Q	Betty Stove (NED)	Martina Navratilova (CZE)	9-8(6)	3-6	6-1

1978

Rd	Winner	Defeated	S1	S2	S3
F	**Martina Navratilova (CZE)**	**Chris Evert Lloyd (USA)**	**2-6**	**6-4**	**7-5**
S	Martina Navratilova (CZE)	Evonne Goolagong Cawley (AUS)	2-6	6-4	6-4
S	Chris Evert (USA)	Virginia Wade (GBR)	8-6	6-2	
Q	Chris Evert (USA)	Billie Jean King (USA)	6-3	3-6	6-2
Q	Virginia Wade (GBR)	Mima Jausovec (YUG)	6-0	6-4	
Q	Evonne Goolagong Cawley (AUS)	Virginia Ruzici (ROU)	7-5	6-3	
Q	Martina Navratilova (CZE)	Marise Kruger (RSA)	6-2	6-4	

1979

Rd	Winner	Defeated	S1	S2	S3
F	**Martina Navratilova (CZE)**	**Chris Evert Lloyd (USA)**	**6-4**	**6-4**	
S	Chris Evert Lloyd (USA)	Evonne Goolagong Cawley (AUS)	6-3	6-2	
S	Martina Navratilova (CZE)	Tracy Austin (USA)	7-5	6-1	
Q	Tracy Austin (USA)	Billie Jean King (USA)	6-4	6-7(5)	6-2
Q	Evonne Goolagong Cawley (AUS)	Virginia Wade (GBR)	6-4	6-0	
Q	Chris Evert Lloyd (USA)	Wendy Turnbull (AUS)	6-3	6-4	
Q	Martina Navratilova (CZE)	Dianne Fromholtz (AUS)	2-6	6-3	6-0

1980

Rd	Winner	Defeated	S1	S2	S3
F	**Evonne Goolagong Cawley (AUS)**	**Chris Evert Lloyd (USA)**	**6-1**	**7-6(4)**	
S	Evonne Goolagong Cawley (AUS)	Tracy Austin (USA)	6-3	0-6	6-4
S	Chris Evert Lloyd (USA)	Martina Navratilova (CZE)	4-6	6-4	6-2
Q	Martina Navratilova (CZE)	Billie Jean King (USA)	7-6(6)	1-6	10-8
Q	Evonne Goolagong Cawley (AUS)	Wendy Turnbull (AUS)	6-3	6-2	
Q	Chris Evert Lloyd (USA)	Andrea Jaeger (USA)	6-1	6-1	
Q	Tracy Austin (USA)	Greer Stevens (RSA)	6-3	6-3	

1981

Rd	Winner	Defeated	S1	S2	S3
F	**Chris Evert Lloyd (USA)**	**Hana Mandlikova (CZE)**	**6-2**	**6-2**	
S	Hana Mandlikova (CZE)	Martina Navratilova (USA)	7-5	4-6	6-1
S	Chris Evert Lloyd (USA)	Pam Shriver (USA)	6-3	6-1	
Q	Chris Evert Lloyd (USA)	Mima Jausovec (YUG)	6-2	6-2	
Q	Pam Shriver (USA)	Tracy Austin (USA)	7-5	6-4	
Q	Martina Navratilova (USA)	Virginia Ruzici (ROU)	6-2	6-3	
Q	Hana Mandlikova (CZE)	Wendy Turnbull (AUS)	6-0	6-0	

1982

Rd	Winner	Defeated	S1	S2	S3
F	**Martina Navratilova (USA)**	**Chris Evert Lloyd (USA)**	**6-1**	**3-6**	**6-2**
S	Chris Evert Lloyd (USA)	Billie Jean King (USA)	7-6(4)	2-6	6-3
S	Martina Navratilova (USA)	Bettina Bunge (GER)	6-2	6-2	
Q	Martina Navratilova (USA)	JoAnne Russell (USA)	6-3	6-4	
Q	Bettina Bunge (GER)	Anne Smith (USA)	6-3	2-6	6-0
Q	Billie Jean King (USA)	Tracy Austin (USA)	3-6	6-4	6-2
Q	Chris Evert Lloyd (USA)	Barbara Potter (USA)	6-2	6-1	

1983

Rd	Winner	Defeated	S1	S2	S3
F	Martina Navratilova (USA)	Andrea Jaeger (USA)	6-0	6-3	
S	Andrea Jaeger (USA)	Billie Jean King (USA)	6-1	6-1	
S	Martina Navratilova (USA)	Yvonne Vermaak (RSA)	6-1	6-1	
Q	Martina Navratilova (USA)	Jennifer Mundel (RSA)	6-3	6-1	
Q	Yvonne Vermaak (RSA)	Virginia Wade (GBR)	6-3	2-6	6-2
Q	Andrea Jaeger (USA)	Barbara Potter (USA)	6-4	6-1	
Q	Billie Jean King (USA)	Kathy Jordan (USA)	7-5	6-4	

1984

Rd	Winner	Defeated	S1	S2	S3
F	Martina Navratilova (USA)	Chris Evert Lloyd (USA)	7-6(5)	6-2	
S	Chris Evert Lloyd (USA)	Hana Mandlikova (CZE)	6-1	6-2	
S	Martina Navratilova (USA)	Kathy Jordan (USA)	6-3	6-4	
Q	Martina Navratilova (USA)	Manuela Maleeva (BUL)	6-3	6-2	
Q	Kathy Jordan (USA)	Pam Shriver (USA)	2-6	6-3	6-4
Q	Hana Mandlikova (CZE)	Jo Durie (GBR)	6-1	6-4	
Q	Chris Evert Lloyd (USA)	Carina Karlsson (SWE)	6-2	6-2	

1985

Rd	Winner	Defeated	S1	S2	S3
F	Martina Navratilova (USA)	Chris Evert Lloyd (USA)	4-6	6-3	6-2
S	Martina Navratilova (USA)	Zina Garrison (USA)	6-4	7-6(3)	
S	Chris Evert Lloyd (USA)	Kathy Rinaldi (USA)	6-2	6-0	
Q	Chris Evert Lloyd (USA)	Barbara Potter (USA)	6-2	6-1	
Q	Kathy Rinaldi (USA)	Helena Sukova (CZE)	6-1	1-6	6-1
Q	Zina Garrison (USA)	Molly Van Nostrand (USA)	2-6	6-3	6-0
Q	Martina Navratilova (USA)	Pam Shriver (USA)	7-5(5)	6-3	

1986

Rd	Winner	Defeated	S1	S2	S3
F	Martina Navratilova (USA)	Hana Mandlikova (CZE)	7-6(1)	6-3	
S	Hana Mandlikova (CZE)	Chris Evert Lloyd (USA)	7-6(5)	7-5	
S	Martina Navratilova (USA)	Gabriela Sabatini (ARG)	6-2	6-2	
Q	Martina Navratilova (USA)	Bettina Bunge (GER)	6-1	6-3	
Q	Gabriela Sabatini (ARG)	Catarina Lindqvist (SWE)	6-2	6-3	
Q	Hana Mandlikova (CZE)	Lori McNeil (USA)	6-7(4)	6-0	6-2
Q	Chris Evert Lloyd (USA)	Helena Sukova (CZE)	7-6(8)	4-6	6-4

1987

Rd	Winner	Defeated	S1	S2	S3
F	Martina Navratilova (USA)	Steffi Graf (GER)	7-5	6-3	
S	Martina Navratilova (USA)	Chris Evert (USA)	6-2	5-7	6-4
S	Steffi Graf (GER)	Pam Shriver (USA)	6-0	6-2	
Q	Martina Navratilova (USA)	Dianne Fromholtz Balestrat (AUS)	6-2	6-1	
Q	Chris Evert (USA)	Claudia Kohde Kilsch (GER)	6-1	6-3	
Q	Pam Shriver (USA)	Helena Sukova (CZE)	4-6	7-6(1)	10-8
Q	Steffi Graf (GER)	Gabriela Sabatini (ARG)	4-6	6-1	6-1

1988

Rd	Winner	Defeated	S1	S2	S3
F	Steffi Graf (GER)	Martina Navratilova (USA)	5-7	6-2	6-1
S	Steffi Graf (GER)	Pam Shriver (USA)	6-1	6-2	
S	Martina Navratilova (USA)	Chris Evert (USA)	6-1	4-6	7-5
Q	Steffi Graf (GER)	Pascale Paradis (FRA)	6-3	6-1	
Q	Pam Shriver (USA)	Zina Garrison (USA)	6-4	6-4	
Q	Chris Evert (USA)	Helena Sukova (CZE)	6-3	7-6(4)	
Q	Martina Navratilova (USA)	Rosalyn Fairbank (RSA)	4-6	6-4	7-5

1989

Rd	Winner	Defeated	S1	S2	S3
F	Steffi Graf (GER)	Martina Navratilova (USA)	6-2	6-7(1)	6-1
S	Steffi Graf (GER)	Chris Evert (USA)	6-2	6-1	
S	Martina Navratilova (USA)	Catarina Lindqvist (SWE)	7-6(5)	6-2	
Q	Steffi Graf (GER)	Arantxa Sanchez Vicario (ESP)	7-5	6-1	
Q	Chris Evert (USA)	Laura Golarsa (ITA)	6-3	2-6	7-5
Q	Catarina Lindqvist (SWE)	Rosalyn Fairbank (RSA)	7-5	7-5	
Q	Martina Navratilova (USA)	Gretchen Rush Magers (USA)	6-1	6-2	

1990

Rd	Winner	Defeated	S1	S2	S3
F	Martina Navratilova (USA)	Zina Garrison (USA)	6-4	6-1	
S	Zina Garrison (USA)	Steffi Graf (GER)	6-3	3-6	6-4
S	Martina Navratilova (USA)	Gabriela Sabatini (ARG)	6-3	6-4	
Q	Steffi Graf (GER)	Jana Novotna (CZE)	7-5	6-2	
Q	Zina Garrison (USA)	Monica Seles (YUG)	3-6	6-3	9-7
Q	Gabriela Sabatini (ARG)	Natalia Zvereva (BLR)	6-2	2-6	8-6
Q	Martina Navratilova (USA)	Katerina Maleeva (BUL)	6-1	6-1	

1991

Rd	Winner	Defeated	S1	S2	S3
F	Steffi Graf (GER)	Gabriela Sabatini (ARG)	6-4	3-6	8-6
S	Steffi Graf (GER)	Mary Joe Fernandez (USA)	6-2	6-4	
S	Gabriela Sabatini (ARG)	Jennifer Capriati (USA)	6-4	6-4	
Q	Steffi Graf (GER)	Zina Garrison (USA)	6-1	6-3	
Q	Mary Joe Fernandez (USA)	Arantxa Sanchez Vicario (ESP)	6-2	7-5	
Q	Jennifer Capriati (USA)	Martina Navratilova (USA)	6-4	7-5	
Q	Gabriela Sabatini (ARG)	Laura Gildemeister (PER)	6-2	6-1	

1992

Rd	Winner	Defeated	S1	S2	S3
F	Steffi Graf (GER)	Monica Seles (YUG)	6-2	6-1	
S	Monica Seles (YUG)	Martina Navratilova (USA)	6-2	6-7(3)	6-4
S	Steffi Graf (GER)	Gabriela Sabatini (ARG)	6-3	6-3	
Q	Monica Seles (YUG)	Nathalie Tauziat (FRA)	6-1	6-3	
Q	Martina Navratilova (USA)	Katerina Maleeva (BUL)	6-3	7-6(2)	
Q	Gabriela Sabatini (ARG)	Jennifer Capriati (USA)	6-1	3-6	6-3
Q	Steffi Graf (GER)	Natasha Zvereva (BLR)	6-3	6-1	

1993

Rd	Winner	Defeated	S1	S2	S3
F	Steffi Graf (GER)	Jana Novotna (CZE)	7-6(6)	1-6	6-4
S	Steffi Graf (GER)	Conchita Martinez (ESP)	7-6(0)	6-3	
S	Jana Novotna (CZE)	Martina Navratilova (USA)	6-4	6-4	
Q	Steffi Graf (GER)	Jennifer Capriati (USA)	7-6(3)	6-1	
Q	Conchita Martinez (ESP)	Helena Sukova (CZE)	6-1	6-4	
Q	Jana Novotna (CZE)	Gabriela Sabatini (ARG)	6-4	6-3	
Q	Martina Navratilova (USA)	Natasha Zvereva (BLR)	6-3	6-1	

1994

Rd	Winner	Defeated	S1	S2	S3
F	Conchita Martinez (ESP)	Martina Navratilova (USA)	6-4	3-6	6-3
S	Conchita Martinez (ESP)	Lori McNeil (USA)	3-6	6-2	10-8
S	Martina Navratilova (USA)	Gigi Fernandez (USA)	6-4	7-6(6)	
Q	Lori McNeil (USA)	Larisa Savchenko Neiland (LAT)	6-3	6-4	
Q	Conchita Martinez (ESP)	Lindsay Davenport (USA)	6-2	6-7(4)	6-3
Q	Martina Navratilova (USA)	Jana Novotna (CZE)	5-7	6-0	6-1
Q	Gigi Fernandez (USA)	Zina Garrison Jackson (USA)	6-4	6-4	

1995

Rd	Winner	Defeated	S1	S2	S3
F	Steffi Graf (GER)	Arantxa Sanchez Vicario (ESP)	4-6	6-1	7-5
S	Steffi Graf (GER)	Jana Novotna (CZE)	5-7	6-4	6-2
S	Arantxa Sanchez Vicario (ESP)	Conchita Martinez (ESP)	6-3	6-7(5)	6-1
Q	Steffi Graf (GER)	Mary Joe Fernandez (USA)	6-3	6-0	
Q	Jana Novotna (CZE)	Kimiko Date (JPN)	6-2	6-3	
Q	Conchita Martinez (ESP)	Gabriela Sabatini (ARG)	7-5	7-6(5)	
Q	Arantxa Sanchez Vicario (ESP)	Brenda Schultz-McCarthy (NED)	6-4	7-6(4)	

1996

Rd	Winner	Defeated	S1	S2	S3
F	Steffi Graf (GER)	Arantxa Sanchez Vicario (ESP)	6-3	7-5	
S	Steffi Graf (GER)	Kimiko Date (JPN)	6-2	2-6	6-3
S	Arantxa Sanchez Vicario (ESP)	Meredith McGrath (USA)	6-2	6-1	
Q	Steffi Graf (GER)	Jana Novotna (CZE)	6-3	6-2	
Q	Kimiko Date (JPN)	Mary Pierce (FRA)	3-6	6-3	6-1
Q	Arantxa Sanchez Vicario (ESP)	Judith Wiesner (AUT)	6-4	6-0	
Q	Meredith McGrath (USA)	Mary Joe Fernandez (USA)	6-3	6-1	

1997

Rd	Winner	Defeated	S1	S2	S3
F	Martina Hingis (SUI)	Jana Novotna (CZE)	2-6	6-3	6-3
S	Martina Hingis (SUI)	Anna Kournikova (RUS)	6-3	6-2	
S	Jana Novotna (CZE)	Arantxa Sanchez Vicario (ESP)	6-4	6-2	
Q	Martina Hingis (SUI)	Denisa Chladkova (CZE)	6-3	6-2	
Q	Anna Kournikova (RUS)	Iva Majoli (CRO)	7-6(1)	6-4	
Q	Jana Novotna (CZE)	Yayuk Basuki (INA)	6-3	6-3	
Q	Arantxa Sanchez Vicario (ESP)	Nathalie Tauziat (FRA)	6-2	7-5	

1998

Rd	Winner	Defeated	S1	S2	S3
F	Jana Novotna (CZE)	Nathalie Tauziat (FRA)	6-4	7-6(2)	
S	Jana Novotna (CZE)	Martina Hingis (SUI)	6-4	6-4	
S	Nathalie Tauziat (FRA)	Natasha Zvereva (BLR)	1-6	7-6(1)	6-3
Q	Martina Hingis (SUI)	Arantxa Sanchez Vicario (ESP)	6-3	3-6	6-3
Q	Jana Novotna (CZE)	Venus Williams (USA)	7-5	7-6(2)	
Q	Natasha Zvereva (BLR)	Monica Seles (USA)	7-6(4)	6-2	
Q	Nathalie Tauziat (FRA)	Lindsay Davenport (USA)	6-3	6-3	

1999

Rd	Winner	Defeated	S1	S2	S3
F	Lindsay Davenport (USA)	Steffi Graf (GER)	6-4	7-5	
S	Lindsay Davenport (USA)	Alexandra Stevenson (USA)	6-1	6-1	
S	Steffi Graf (GER)	Mirjana Lucic (CRO)	6-7(3)	6-4	6-3
Q	Alexandra Stevenson (USA)	Jelena Dokic (AUS)	6-3	1-6	6-3
Q	Lindsay Davenport (USA)	Jana Novotna (CZE)	6-3	6-4	
Q	Mirjana Lucic (CRO)	Nathalie Tauziat (FRA)	4-6	6-4	7-5
Q	Steffi Graf (GER)	Venus Williams (USA)	6-2	3-6	6-4

2000

Rd	Winner	Defeated	S1	S2	S3
F	Venus Williams (USA)	Lindsay Davenport (USA)	6-3	7-6(3)	
S	Venus Williams (USA)	Serena Williams (USA)	6-2	7-6(3)	
S	Lindsay Davenport (USA)	Jelena Dokic (AUS)	6-4	6-2	
Q	Venus Williams (USA)	Martina Hingis (SUI)	6-3	4-6	6-4
Q	Serena Williams (USA)	Lisa Raymond (USA)	6-2	6-0	
Q	Jelena Dokic (AUS)	Magui Serna (ESP)	6-3	6-2	
Q	Lindsay Davenport (USA)	Monica Seles (USA)	6-7(4)	6-4	6-0

2001

Rd	Winner	Defeated	S1	S2	S3
F	Venus Williams (USA)	Justine Henin (BEL)	6-1	3-6	6-0
S	Justine Henin (BEL)	Jennifer Capriati (USA)	2-6	6-4	6-2
S	Venus Williams (USA)	Lindsay Davenport (USA)	6-2	6-7(1)	6-1
Q	Justine Henin (BEL)	Conchita Martinez (ESP)	6-1	6-0	
Q	Jennifer Capriati (USA)	Serena Williams (USA)	6-7(4)	7-5	6-3
Q	Lindsay Davenport (USA)	Kim Clijsters (BEL)	6-1	6-2	
Q	Venus Williams (USA)	Nathalie Tauziat (FRA)	7-5	7-1	

2002

Rd	Winner	Defeated	S1	S2	S3
F	Serena Williams (USA)	Venus Williams (USA)	7-6(4)	6-3	
S	Venus Williams (USA)	Justine Henin (BEL)	6-3	6-2	
S	Serena Williams (USA)	Amelie Mauresmo (FRA)	6-2	6-1	
Q	Venus Williams (USA)	Elena Likhovtseva (RUS)	6-2	6-0	
Q	Justine Henin (BEL)	Monica Seles (USA)	7-5	7-6(4)	
Q	Amelie Mauresmo (FRA)	Jennifer Capriati (USA)	6-3	6-2	
Q	Serena Williams (USA)	Daniela Hantuchova (SVK)	6-3	6-2	

2003

Rd	Winner	Defeated	S1	S2	S3
F	Serena Williams (USA)	Venus Williams (USA)	4-6	6-4	6-2
S	Serena Williams (USA)	Justine Henin-Hardenne (BEL)	6-3	6-2	
S	Venus Williams (USA)	Kim Clijsters (BEL)	4-6	6-3	6-1
Q	Serena Williams (USA)	Jennifer Capriati (USA)	2-6	6-2	6-3
Q	Justine Henin-Hardenne (BEL)	Svetlana Kuznetsova (RUS)	6-2	6-2	
Q	Venus Williams (USA)	Lindsay Davenport (USA)	6-2	2-6	6-1
Q	Kim Clijsters (BEL)	Silvia Farina Elia (ITA)	5-7	6-0	6-1

2004

Rd	Winner	Defeated	S1	S2	S3
F	Maria Sharapova (RUS)	Serena Williams (USA)	6-1	6-4	
S	Serena Williams (USA)	Amelie Mauresmo (FRA)	6-7(4)	7-5	6-4
S	Maria Sharapova (RUS)	Lindsay Davenport (USA)	2-6	7-6(5)	6-1
Q	Serena Williams (USA)	Jennifer Capriati (USA)	6-1	6-1	
Q	Amelie Mauresmo (FRA)	Paola Suarez (ARG)	6-0	5-7	6-1
Q	Lindsay Davenport (USA)	Karolina Sprem (CRO)	6-2	6-2	
Q	Maria Sharapova (RUS)	Ai Sugiyama (JPN)	5-7	7-5	6-1

2005

Rd	Winner	Defeated	S1	S2	S3
F	Venus Williams (USA)	Lindsay Davenport (USA)	4-6	7-6(4)	9-7
S	Lindsay Davenport (USA)	Amelie Mauresmo (FRA)	6-7(5)	7-6(4)	6-4
S	Venus Williams (USA)	Maria Sharapova (RUS)	7-6(2)	6-1	
Q	Lindsay Davenport (USA)	Svetlana Kuznetsova (RUS)	7-6(1)	6-3	
Q	Amelie Mauresmo (FRA)	Anastasia Myskina (RUS)	6-3	6-4	
Q	Venus Williams (USA)	Mary Pierce (FRA)	6-0	7-6(10)	
Q	Maria Sharapova (RUS)	Nadia Petrova (RUS)	7-6(6)	6-3	

2006

Rd	Winner	Defeated	S1	S2	S3
F	Amelie Mauresmo (FRA)	Justine Henin-Hardenne (BEL)	2-6	6-3	6-4
S	Amelie Mauresmo (FRA)	Maria Sharapova (RUS)	6-3	3-6	6-2
S	Justine Henin-Hardenne (BEL)	Kim Clijsters (BEL)	6-4	7-6(4)	
Q	Amelie Mauresmo (FRA)	Anastasia Myskina (RUS)	6-1	3-6	6-3
Q	Maria Sharapova (RUS)	Elena Dementieva (RUS)	6-1	6-4	
Q	Justine Henin-Hardenne (BEL)	Severine Bremond (FRA)	6-4	6-4	
Q	Kim Clijsters (BEL)	Na Li (CHN)	6-4	7-5	

Rd	Winner	Defeated	S1	S2	S3
2007					
F	**Venus Williams (USA)**	**Marion Bartoli (FRA)**	**6-4**	**6-1**	
S	Marion Bartoli (FRA)	Justine Henin (BEL)	1-6	7-5	6-1
S	Venus Williams (USA)	Ana Ivanovic (SRB)	6-2	6-4	
Q	Justine Henin (BEL)	Serena Williams (USA)	6-4	3-6	6-3
Q	Marion Bartoli (FRA)	Michaella Krajicek (NED)	3-6	6-3	6-2
Q	Ana Ivanovic (SRB)	Nicole Vaidisova (CZE)	4-6	6-2	7-5
Q	Venus Williams (USA)	Svetlana Kuznetsova (RUS)	6-3	6-4	
2008					
F	**Venus Williams (USA)**	**Serena Williams (USA)**	**7-5**	**6-4**	
S	Serena Williams (USA)	Jie Zheng (CHN)	6-2	7-6 (5)	
S	Venus Williams (USA)	Elena Dementieva (RUS)	6-1	7-6 (3)	
Q	Jie Zheng (CHN)	Nicole Vaidisova (CZE)	6-2	5-7	6-1
Q	Serena Williams (USA)	Agnieszka Radwanska (POL)	6-4	6-0	
Q	Elena Dementieva (RUS)	Nadia Petrova (RUS)	6-1	6-7 (6)	6-3
Q	Venus Williams (USA)	Tamarine Tanasugarn (THA)	6-4	6-3	
2009					
F	**Serena Williams (USA)**	**Venus Williams (USA)**	**7-6 (3)**	**6-2**	
S	Venus Williams (USA)	Dinara Safina (RUS)	6-1	6-0	
S	Serena Williams (USA)	Elena Dementieva (RUS)	6-7 (4)	7-5	8-6
Q	Dinara Safina (RUS)	Sabine Lisicki (GER)	6-7 (5)	6-4	6-1
Q	Venus Williams (USA)	Agnieszka Radwanska (POL)	6-1	6-2	
Q	Elena Dementieva (RUS)	Francesca Schiavone (ITA)	6-2	6-2	
Q	Serena Williams (USA)	Victoria Azarenka (BLR)	6-2	6-3	

Men's Doubles

Year	Winner	Defeated	S1	S2	S3	S4	S5
1884	Willie Renshaw (GBR) Ernest Renshaw (GBR)	Ernest Lewis (GBR) Edward Williams (GBR)	6-3	6-1	1-6	6-4	
1885	Willie Renshaw (GBR) Ernest Renshaw (GBR)	Claude Farrar (GBR) Arthur Stanley (GBR)	6-3	6-3	10-8 (challenge round instituted)		
1886	Willie Renshaw (GBR) Ernest Renshaw (GBR)	Claude Farrar (GBR) Arthur Stanley (GBR)	6-3	6-3	4-6	7-5	
1887	Herbert Wilberforce (GBR) Patrick Bowes Lyon (GBR)	James Crisp (GBR) Barratt Smith (GBR)	7-5	6-3	6-2		
1888	Willie Renshaw (GBR) Ernest Renshaw (GBR)	Herbert Wilberforce (GBR) Patrick Bowes Lyon (GBR)	2-6	1-6	6-3	6-4	6-3
1889	Willie Renshaw (GBR) Ernest Renshaw (GBR)	Ernest Lewis (GBR) George Hillyard (GBR)	6-4	6-4	3-6	0-6	6-1
1890	Joshua Pim (IRL) Frank Stoker (GBR)	Ernest Lewis (GBR) George Hillyard (GBR)	6-0	7-5	6-4		
1891	Wilfred Baddeley (GBR) Herbert Baddeley (GBR)	Joshua Pim (IRL) Frank Stoker (GBR)	6-1	6-3	1-6	6-2	
1892	Ernest Lewis (GBR) Harry Barlow (GBR)	Wilfred Baddeley (GBR) Herbert Baddeley (GBR)	4-6	6-2	8-6	6-4	
1893	Joshua Pim (IRL) Frank Stoker (GBR)	Ernest Lewis (GBR) Harry Barlow (GBR)	4-6	6-3	6-1	2-6	6-0

Year	Winner	Defeated	S1	S2	S3	S4	S5
1894	Wilfred Baddeley (GBR) Herbert Baddeley (GBR)	Harry Barlow (GBR) Charles Martin (USA)	5-7	7-5	4-6	6-3	8-6
1895	Wilfred Baddeley (GBR) Herbert Baddeley (GBR)	Ernest Lewis (GBR) Wilberforce Eaves (AUS)	8-6	5-7	6-4	6-3	
1896	Wilfred Baddeley (GBR) Herbert Baddeley (GBR)	Reggie Doherty (GBR) Harold Nisbet (GBR)	1-6	3-6	6-4	6-2	6-1
1897	Reggie Doherty (GBR) Laurie Doherty (GBR)	Wilfred Baddeley (GBR) Herbert Baddeley (GBR)	6-4	4-6	8-6	6-4	
1898	Reggie Doherty (GBR) Laurie Doherty (GBR)	Harold Nisbet (GBR) Clarence Hobart (USA)	6-4	6-4	6-2		
1899	Reggie Doherty (GBR) Laurie Doherty (GBR)	Harold Nisbet (GBR) Clarence Hobart (USA)	7-5	6-0	6-2		
1900	Reggie Doherty (GBR) Laurie Doherty (GBR)	Herbert Roper Barrett (GBR) Harold Nisbet (GBR)	9-7	7-5	4-6	3-6	6-3
1901	Reggie Doherty (GBR) Laurie Doherty (GBR)	Dwight Davis (USA) Holcombe Ward (USA)	4-6	6-2	6-3	9-7	
1902	Sidney H. Smith (GBR) Frank Riseley (GBR)	Reggie Doherty (GBR) Laurie Doherty (GBR)	4-6	8-6	6-3	4-6	11-9
1903	Reggie Doherty (GBR) Laurie Doherty (GBR)	Sidney J. Smith (GBR) Frank Riseley (GBR)	6-4	6-4	6-4		
1904	Reggie Doherty (GBR) Laurie Doherty (GBR)	Sidney J. Smith (GBR) Frank Riseley (GBR)	6-1	6-2	6-4		
1905	Reggie Doherty (GBR) Laurie Doherty (GBR)	Sidney J. Smith (GBR) Frank Riseley (GBR)	6-2	6-4	6-8	6-3	
1906	Sidney H. Smith (GBR) Frank Riseley (GBR)	Reggie Doherty (GBR) Laurie Doherty (GBR)	6-8	6-4	5-7	6-3	6-3
1907	Norman Brookes (AUS) Tony Wilding (NZL)	Beals Wright (USA) Karl Behr (USA)	6-4	6-4	6-2		
1908	Tony Wilding (NZL) Josiah Ritchie (GBR)	Arthur Gore (GBR) Herbert Roper Barrett (GBR)	6-1	6-2	1-6	1-6	9-7
1909	Arthur Gore (GBR) Herbert Roper Barrett (GBR)	Stanley Doust (AUS) Harry Parker (NZL)	6-2	6-1	6-4		
1910	Tony Wilding (NZL) Josiah Ritchie (GBR)	Arthur Gore (GBR) Herbert Roper Barrett (GBR)	6-1	6-1	6-2		
1911	Andre Gobert (FRA) Max Decugis (FRA)	Tony Wilding (NZL) Josiah Ritchie (GBR)	9-7	5-7	6-3	2-6	6-2
1912	Herbert Roper Barrett (GBR) Charles Dixon (GBR)	Andre Gobert (FRA) Max Decugis (FRA)	3-6	6-3	6-4	7-5	
1913	Herbert Roper Barrett (GBR) Charles Dixon (GBR)	Friedrich Rahe (GER) Heinrich Kleinschroth (GER)	6-2	6-4	4-6	6-2	
1914	Norman Brookes (AUS) Tony Wilding (NZL)	Herbert Roper Barrett (GBR) Charles Dixon (GBR)	6-1	6-1	5-7	8-6	
1915–18 Not held—WW II							
1919	Ronald Thomas (AUS) Pat O'Hara Wood (AUS)	Randolph Lycett (GBR) Rodney Heath (AUS)	6-4	6-2	4-6	6-2	
1920	Dick Williams (USA) Chuck Garland (USA)	Algie Kingscote (GBR) Jim Parke (IRL)	4-6	6-4	7-5	6-2	
1921	Randolph Lycett (GBR) Max Woosnam (GBR)	Arthur Lowe (GBR) Frank Lowe (GBR)	6-3	6-0	7-5		
1922	James Anderson (AUS) Randolph Lycett (GBR)	Gerald Patterson (AUS) Pat O'Hara Wood (AUS)	3-6	7-9	6-4	6-3	11-9
1923	Leslie Godfree (GBR) Randolph Lycett (GBR)	Manuel de Gomar (ESP) Eduardo Flaquar (ESP)	6-3	6-4	3-6	6-3	

Year	Winner	Defeated	S1	S2	S3	S4	S5
1924	Frank Hunter (USA) Vinnie Richards (USA)	Dick Williams (USA) Watson Washburn (USA)	6-3	3-6	8-10	8-6	6-3
1925	Jean Borotra (FRA) Rene Lacoste (FRA)	John Hennessey (USA) Ray Casey (USA)	6-4	11-9	4-6	1-6	6-3
1926	Jacques Brugnon (FRA) Henri Cochet (FRA)	Howard Kinsey (USA) Vinnie Richards (USA)	7-5	4-6	6-3	6-2	
1927	Frank Hunter (USA) Bill Tilden (USA)	Jacques Brugnon (FRA) Henri Cochet (FRA)	1-6	4-6	8-6	6-3	6-4
1928	Jacques Brugnon (FRA) Henri Cochet (FRA)	Gerald Patterson (AUS) Jack Hawkes (AUS)	13-11	6-4	6-4		
1929	Wilmer Allison (USA) John Van Ryn (USA)	Colin Gregory (GBR) Ian Collins (GBR)	6-4	5-7	6-3	10-12	6-4
1930	Wilmer Allison (USA) John Van Ryn (USA)	Johnny Doeg (USA) George Lott (USA)	6-3	6-3	6-2		
1931	George Lott (USA) John Van Ryn (USA)	Jacques Brugnon (FRA) Henri Cochet (FRA)	6-2	10-8	9-11	3-6	6-3
1932	Jean Borotra (FRA) Jacques Brugnon (FRA)	Fred Perry (GBR) Pat Hughes (GBR)	6-0	4-6	3-6	7-5	7-5
1933	Jean Borotra (FRA) Jacques Brugnon (FRA)	Ryosuki Nunoi (JPN) Jiro Satoh (JPN)	4-6	6-3	6-3	7-5	
1934	George Lott (USA) Lester Stoefen (USA)	Jean Borotra (FRA) Jacques Brugnon (FRA)	6-2	6-3	6-4		
1935	Jack Crawford (AUS) Adrian Quist (AUS)	Wilmer Allison (USA) John Van Ryn (USA)	6-3	5-7	6-2	5-7	7-5
1936	Pat Hughes (GBR) Charles Tuckey (GBR)	Charles Hare (GBR) Frank Wilde (GBR)	6-4	3-6	7-9	6-1	6-4
1937	Don Budge (USA) Gene Mako (USA)	Pat Hughes (GBR) Charles Tuckey (GBR)	6-0	6-4	6-8	6-1	
1938	Don Budge (USA) Gene Mako (USA)	Henner Henkel (GER) Georg von Metaxa (GER)	6-4	3-6	6-3	8-6	
1939	Elwood Cooke (USA) Bobby Riggs (USA)	Charles Hare (GBR) Frank Wilde (GBR)	6-3	3-6	6-3	9-7	
1940–1945 Not held—WW II							
1946	Tom Brown Jr. (USA) Jack Kramer (USA)	Geoff Brown (AUS) Dinny Pails (AUS)	6-4	6-4	6-2		
1947	Bob Falkenburg (USA) Jack Kramer (USA)	Tony Mottram (GBR) Bill Sidwell (AUS)	8-6	6-3	6-3		
1948	John Bromwich (AUS) Frank Sedgman (AUS)	Tom Brown Jr. (USA) Gardnar Mulloy (USA)	5-7	7-5	7-5	9-7	
1949	Pancho Gonzalez (USA) Frank Parker (USA)	Gardnar Mulloy (USA) Ted Schroeder (USA)	6-4	6-4	6-2		
1950	John Bromwich (AUS) Adrian Quist (AUS)	Geoff Brown (AUS) Bill Sidwell (AUS)	7-5	3-6	6-3	3-6	6-2
1951	Ken McGregor (AUS) Frank Sedgman (AUS)	Jaroslav Drobny (EGY) Eric Sturgess (RSA)	3-6	6-2	6-3	3-6	6-3
1952	Ken McGregor (AUS) Frank Sedgman (AUS)	Vic Seixas (USA) Eric Sturgess (RSA)	6-3	7-5	6-4		
1953	Lew Hoad (AUS) Ken Rosewall (AUS)	Rex Hartwig (AUS) Merv Rose (AUS)	6-4	7-5	4-6	7-5	
1954	Rex Hartwig (AUS) Merv Rose (AUS)	Vic Seixas (USA) Tony Trabert (USA)	6-4	6-4	3-6	6-4	
1955	Rex Hartwig (AUS) Lew Hoad (AUS)	Neale Fraser (AUS) Ken Rosewall (AUS)	7-5	6-4	6-3		

Year	Winner	Defeated	S1	S2	S3	S4	S5
1956	Lew Hoad (AUS) Ken Rosewall (AUS)	Nicola Pietrangeli (ITA) Orlando Sirola (ITA)	7-5	6-2	6-1		
1957	Budge Patty (USA) Gardnar Mulloy (USA)	Neale Fraser (AUS) Lew Hoad (AUS)	8-10	6-4	6-4	6-4	
1958	Sven Davidson (SWE) Ulf Schmidt (SWE)	Ashley Cooper (AUS) Neale Fraser (AUS)	6-4	6-4	8-6		
1959	Roy Emerson (AUS) Neale Fraser (AUS)	Rod Laver (AUS) Bob Mark (AUS)	8-6	6-3	14-16	9-7	
1960	Rafael Osuna (MEX) Dennis Ralston (USA)	Mike Davies (GBR) Bobby Wilson (GBR)	7-5	6-3	10-8		
1961	Roy Emerson (AUS) Neale Fraser (AUS)	Bob Hewitt (AUS) Fred Stolle (AUS)	6-4	6-8	6-4	6-8	8-6
1962	Bob Hewitt (AUS) Fred Stolle (AUS)	Boro Jovanovic (YUG) Niki Pilic (YUG)	6-2	5-7	6-2	6-4	
1963	Rafael Osuna (MEX) Antonio Palafox (MEX)	Jean Claude Barclay (FRA) Pierre Darmon (FRA)	4-6	6-2	6-2	6-2	
1964	Bob Hewitt (AUS) Fred Stolle (AUS)	Roy Emerson (AUS) Ken Fletcher (AUS)	7-5	11-9	6-4		
1965	John Newcombe (AUS) Tony Roche (AUS)	Ken Fletcher (AUS) Bob Hewitt (AUS)	7-5	6-3	6-4		
1966	Ken Fletcher (AUS) John Newcombe (AUS)	Bill Bowrey (AUS) Owen Davidson (AUS)	6-3	6-4	3-6	6-3	
1967	Bob Hewitt (RSA) Frew McMillan (RSA)	Roy Emerson (AUS) Ken Fletcher (AUS)	6-2	6-3	6-4		
1968	John Newcombe (AUS) Tony Roche (AUS)	Ken Rosewall (AUS) Fred Stolle (AUS)	3-6	8-6	5-7	14-12	6-3
1969	John Newcombe (AUS) Tony Roche (AUS)	Tom Okker (NED) Marty Riessen (USA)	7-5	11-9	6-3		
1970	John Newcombe (AUS) Tony Roche (AUS)	Ken Rosewall (AUS) Fred Stolle (AUS)	10-8	6-3	6-1		
1971	Roy Emerson (AUS) Rod Laver (AUS)	Arthur Ashe (USA) Dennis Ralston (USA)	4-6	9-7	6-8	6-4	6-4
1972	Bob Hewitt (RSA) Frew McMillan (RSA)	Stan Smith (USA) Erik van Dillen (USA)	6-2	6-2	9-7		
1973	Jimmy Connors (USA) Ilie Nastase (ROU)	John Cooper (AUS) Neale Fraser (AUS)	3-6	6-3	6-4	8-9(3)	6-1
1974	John Newcombe (AUS) Tony Roche (AUS)	Bob Lutz (USA) Stan Smith (USA)	8-6	6-4	6-4		
1975	Vitas Gerulaitis (USA) Alex Mayer (USA)	Colin Dowdeswell (RHO) Allan Stone (AUS)	7-5	8-6	6-4		
1976	Brian Gottfried (USA) Raul Ramirez (MEX)	Ross Case (AUS) Geoff Masters (AUS)	3-6	6-3	8-6	2-6	7-5
1977	Geoff Masters (AUS) Ross Case (AUS)	John Alexander (AUS) Phil Dent (AUS)	6-3	6-4	3-6	8-9(4)	6-4
1978	Bob Hewitt (RSA) Frew McMillan (RSA)	Peter Fleming (USA) John McEnroe (USA)	6-1	6-4	6-2		
1979	Peter Fleming (USA) John McEnroe (USA)	Brian Gottfried (USA) Raul Ramirez (MEX)	4-6	6-4	6-2	6-2	
1980	Peter McNamara (AUS) Paul McNamee (AUS)	Bob Lutz (USA) Stan Smith (USA)	7-6(5)	6-3	6-7(4)	6-4	
1981	Peter Fleming (USA) John McEnroe (USA)	Bob Lutz (USA) Stan Smith (USA)	6-4	6-4	6-4		
1982	Peter McNamara (AUS) Paul McNamee (AUS)	Peter Fleming (USA) John McEnroe (USA)	6-3	6-2			

Year	Winner	Defeated	S1	S2	S3	S4	S5
1983	Peter Fleming (USA) John McEnroe (USA)	Tim Gullikson (USA) Tom Gullikson (USA)	6-4	6-3	6-4		
1984	Peter Fleming (USA) John McEnroe (USA)	Pat Cash (AUS) Paul McNamee (AUS)	6-2	5-7	6-2	3-6	6-3
1985	Heinz Gunthardt (SUI) Balazs Taroczy (HUN)	Pat Cash (AUS) John Fitzgerald (AUS)	6-4	6-3	4-6	6-3	
1986	Joakim Nystrom (SWE) Mats Wilander (SWE)	Gary Donnelly (USA) Peter Fleming (USA)	7-6(4)	6-3	6-3		
1987	Ken Flach (USA) Robert Seguso (USA)	Sergio Casal (ESP) Emilo Sanchez (ESP)	3-6	6-7(6)	7-6(3)	6-1	6-4
1988	Ken Flach (USA) Robert Seguso (USA)	John Fitzgerald (AUS) Anders Jarryd (SWE)	6-4	2-6	6-4	7-6(3)	
1989	John Fitzgerald (AUS) Anders Jarryd (SWE)	Rick Leach (USA) Jim Pugh (USA)	3-6	7-6(4)	6-4	7-6(4)	
1990	Rick Leach (USA) Jim Pugh (USA)	Pieter Aldrich (RSA) Danie Visser (RSA)	7-6(5)	7-6(4)	7-6(5)		
1991	John Fitzgerald (AUS) Anders Jarryd (SWE)	Javier Frana (ARG) Leonardo Lavalle (MEX)	6-3	6-4	6-7(7)	6-1	
1992	John McEnroe (USA) Michael Stich (GER)	Jim Grabb (USA) Richey Reneberg (USA)	5-7	7-6(5)	3-6	7-6(5)	19-17
1993	Todd Woodbridge (AUS) Mark Woodforde (AUS)	Grant Connell (CAN) Patrick Galbraith (USA)	7-5	6-3	7-6(4)		
1994	Todd Woodbridge (AUS) Mark Woodforde (AUS)	Grant Connell (CAN) Patrick Galbraith (USA)	7-6(3)	6-3	6-1		
1995	Todd Woodbridge (AUS) Mark Woodforde (AUS)	Rick Leach (USA) Scott Melville (USA)	7-5	7-6(8)	7-6(5)		
1996	Todd Woodbridge (AUS) Mark Woodforde (AUS)	Byron Black (ZIM) Grant Connell (CAN)	4-6	6-1	6-3	6-2	
1997	Todd Woodbridge (AUS) Mark Woodforde (AUS)	Jacco Eltingh (NED) Paul Haarhuis (NED)	7-6(4)	7-6(7)	5-7	6-3	
1998	Jacco Eltingh (NED) Paul Haarhuis (NED)	Todd Woodbridge (AUS) Mark Woodforde (AUS)	2-6	6-4	7-6(3)	5-7	10-8
1999	Mahesh Bhupathi (IND) Leander Paes (IND)	Paul Haarhuis (NED) Jared Palmer (USA)	6-7(10)	6-3	6-4	7-6(4)	
2000	Todd Woodbridge (AUS) Mark Woodforde (AUS)	Paul Haarhuis (NED) Sandon Stolle (AUS)	6-3	6-4	6-1		
2001	Donald Johnson (USA) Jared Palmer (USA)	Jiri Novak (CZE) David Rikl (CZE)	6-4	4-6	6-3	7-6(6)	
2002	Todd Woodbridge (AUS) Jonas Bjorkman (SWE)	Daniel Nestor (CAN) Mark Knowles (BAH)	6-1	6-2	6-7(7)	7-5	
2003	Jonas Bjorkman (SWE) Tood Woodbridge (AUS)	Mahesh Bhupathi (IND) Max Mirnyi (BLR)	3-6	6-3	7-6(4)	6-3	
2004	Jonas Bjorkman (SWE) Tood Woodbridge (AUS)	Julian Knowle (AUT) Nenad Zimonjic (SRB)	6-1	6-4	4-6	6-4	
2005	Stephen Huss (AUS) Wesley Moodie (RSA)	Bob Bryan (USA) Mike Bryan (USA)	7-6(4)	6-3	6-7(2)	6-3	
2006	Bob Bryan (USA) Mike Bryan (USA)	Fabrice Santoro (FRA) Nenad Zimonjic (SRB)	6-3	4-6	6-4	6-2	
2007	Arnaud Clement (FRA) Michael Llodra (FRA)	Bob Bryan (USA) Mike Bryan (USA)	6-7(5)	6-3	6-4	6-4	
2008	Daniel Nestor (CAN) Nenad Zimonjic (SRB)	Kevin Ullyett (ZIM) Jonas Bjorkman (SWE)	7-6(12)	6-7(3)	6-3	6-3	
2009	Daniel Nestor (CAN) Nenad Zimonjic (SRB)	Bob Bryan (USA) Mike Bryan (USA)	7-6(7)	6-7(3)	7-6(3)	6-3	

Women's Doubles

Year	Winner	Defeated	S1	S2	S3
1913	Winifred Slocock McNair (GBR) Dora Boothby (GBR)	Charlotte Cooper Sterry (GBR) Dorothea Douglass Chambers (GBR)	4-6	2-4 (retired)	
1914	Agnes Morton (GBR) Elizabeth Ryan (USA)	Edith Boucher Hannam (GBR) Ethel Thomson Larcombe (GBR)	6-1	6-3	
1915–18 Not held—WW II					
1919	Suzanne Lenglen (FRA) Elizabeth Ryan (USA)	Ethel Thomson Larcombe (GBR) Dorothea Douglass Chambers (GBR)	4-6	7-5	6-3
1920	Suzanne Lenglen (FRA) Elizabeth Ryan (USA)	Ethel Thomson Larcombe (GBR) Dorothea Douglass Chambers (GBR)	6-4	6-0	
1921	Suzanne Lenglen (FRA) Elizabeth Ryan (USA)	Geraldine Ramsey Beamish (GBR) Irene Bowder Peacock (RSA)	6-1	6-2	
1922	Suzanne Lenglen (FRA) Elizabeth Ryan (USA)	Kitty McKane (GBR) Margaret McKane Stocks (GBR)	6-0	6-4	
1923	Suzanne Lenglen (FRA) Elizabeth Ryan (USA)	Joan Austin (GBR) Evelyn Colyer (GBR)	6-3	6-1	
1924	Hazel Hotchkiss Wightman (USA) Helen Wills (USA)	Phyllis Howkins Covell (GBR) Kitty McKane (GBR)	6-4	6-4	
1925	Suzanne Lenglen (FRA) Elizabeth Ryan (USA)	Kathleen Lidderdale Bridge (GBR) Mary Hart McIlquham (GBR)	6-2	6-2	
1926	Mary K. Browne (USA) Elizabeth Ryan (USA)	Kitty McKane Godfree (GBR) Evelyn Colyer (GBR)	6-1	6-1	
1927	Helen Wills (USA) Elizabeth Ryan (USA)	Bobbie Heine (RSA) Irene Bowder Peacock (RSA)	6-3	6-2	
1928	Peggy Saunders (GBR) Phoebe Holcroft Watson (GBR)	Eileen Bennett (GBR) Ermyntrude Harvey (GBR)	6-2	6-3	
1929	Peggy Sauders Michell (GBR) Phoebe Holcroft Watson (GBR)	Phyllis Howkins Covell (GBR) Dorothy Shepherd Barron (GBR)	6-4	8-6	
1930	Helen Wills Moody (USA) Elizabeth Ryan (USA)	Edith Cross (USA) Sarah Palfrey (USA)	6-2	9-7	
1931	Dorothy Shepherd Barron (GBR) Phyllis Mudford (GBR)	Doris Metaxa (FRA) Josane Sigart (BEL)	3-6	6-3	6-4
1932	Doris Metaxa (FRA) Josane Sigart (BEL)	Helen Jacobs (USA) Elizabeth Ryan (USA)	6-4	6-3	
1933	Simone Passemard Mathieu (FRA) Elizabeth Ryan (USA)	Freda James (GBR) Billie Yorke (GBR)	6-2	9-11	6-4
1934	Simone Passemard Mathieu (FRA) Elizabeth Ryan (USA)	Dorothy Andrus (USA) Sylvie Jung Henrotin (FRA)	6-3	6-3	
1935	Freda James (GBR) Kay Stammers (GBR)	Simone Passemard Mathieu (FRA) Hilde Krahwinkel Sperling (DEN)	6-1	6-4	
1936	Freda James (GBR) Kay Stammers (GBR)	Sarah Palfrey Fabyan (USA) Helen Jacobs (USA)	6-2	6-1	
1937	Simone Passemard Mathieu (FRA) Billie Yorke (GBR)	Phyllis Mudford King (GBR) Elsie Goldsack Pittman (GBR)	6-3	6-3	
1938	Sarah Palfrey Fabyan (USA) Alice Marble (USA)	Simone Passemard Mathieu (FRA) Billie Yorke (GBR)	6-2	6-3	
1939	Sarah Palfrey Fabyan (USA) Alice Marble (USA)	Helen Jacobs (USA) Billie Yorke (GBR)	6-1	6-0	
1940–45 Not held—WW II					
1946	Louise Brough (USA) Margaret Osborne (USA)	Pauline Betz (USA) Doris Hart (USA)	6-3	2-6	6-3

Year	Winner	Defeated	S1	S2	S3
1947	Doris Hart (USA) Pat Canning Todd (USA)	Louise Brough (USA) Margaret Osborne (USA)	3-6	6-4	7-5
1948	Louise Brough (USA) Margaret Osborne duPont (USA)	Doris Hart (USA) Pat Canning Todd (USA)	6-3	3-6	6-3
1949	Louise Brough (USA) Margaret Osborne duPont (USA)	Gussy Moran (USA) Pat Canning Todd (USA)	8-6	7-5	
1950	Louise Brough (USA) Margaret Osborne duPont (USA)	Shirley Fry (USA) Doris Hart (USA)	6-4	5-7	6-1
1951	Shirley Fry (USA) Doris Hart (USA)	Louise Brough (USA) Margaret Osborne duPont (USA)	6-3	13-11	
1952	Shirley Fry (USA) Doris Hart (USA)	Louise Brough (USA) Maureen Connolly (USA)	8-6	6-3	
1953	Shirley Fry (USA) Doris Hart (USA)	Maureen Connolly (USA) Julia Sampson (USA)	6-0	6-0	
1954	Louise Brough (USA) Margaret Osborne duPont (USA)	Shirley Fry (USA) Doris Hart (USA)	4-6	9-7	6-3
1955	Angela Mortimer (GBR) Anne Shilcock (GBR)	Shirley Fry (USA) Pat Ward (GBR)	7-5	6-1	
1956	Angela Buxton (GBR) Althea Gibson (USA)	Fay Muller (AUS) Daphne Seeney (AUS)	6-1	8-6	
1957	Althea Gibson (USA) Darlene Hard (USA)	Mary Bevis Hawton (AUS) Thelma Coyne Long (AUS)	6-1	6-2	
1958	Maria Bueno (BRA) Althea Gibson (USA)	Margaret Osborne duPont (USA) Margaret Varner (USA)	6-3	7-5	
1959	Jeanne Arth (USA) Darlene Hard (USA)	Beverly Beverly Fleitz (USA) Christine Truman (GBR)	2-6	6-2	6-3
1960	Maria Bueno (BRA) Darlene Hard (USA)	Sandra Reynolds (RSA) Renee Schuurman (RSA)	6-4	6-0	
1961	Karen Hantze (USA) Billie Jean Moffitt (USA)	Jan Lehane (AUS) Margaret Smith (AUS)	6-3	6-4	
1962	Billie Jean Moffitt (USA) Karen Hantze Susman (USA)	Sandra Reynolds Price (RSA) Renee Schuurman (RSA)	5-7	6-3	7-5
1963	Maria Bueno (BRA) Darlene Hard (USA)	Robyn Ebbern (AUS) Margaret Smith (AUS)	8-6	9-7	
1964	Margaret Smith (AUS) Lesley Turner (AUS)	Billie Jean Moffitt (USA) Karen Hantze Susman (USA)	7-5	6-2	
1965	Maria Bueno (BRA) Billie Jean Moffitt (USA)	Francoise Durr (FRA) Jeanine Lieffrig (FRA)	6-2	7-5	
1966	Maria Bueno (BRA) Nancy Richey (USA)	Margaret Smith (AUS) Judy Tegart (AUS)	6-3	4-6	6-4
1967	Rosie Casals (USA) Billie Jean King (USA)	Maria Bueno (BRA) Nancy Richey (USA)	9-11	6-4	6-2
1968	Rosie Casals (USA) Billie Jean King (USA)	Francoise Durr (FRA) Ann Haydon Jones (GBR)	3-6	6-4	7-5
1969	Margaret Smith Court (AUS) Judy Tegart (AUS)	Patti Hogan (USA) Peggy Michel (USA)	9-7	6-2	
1970	Rosie Casals (USA) Billie Jean King (USA)	Francoise Durr (FRA) Virginia Wade (GBR)	6-2	6-3	
1971	Rosie Casals (USA) Billie Jean King (USA)	Margaret Smith Court (AUS) Evonne Goolagong (AUS)	6-3	6-2	
1972	Billie Jean King (USA) Betty Stove (NED)	Judy Tegart Dalton (AUS) Francoise Durr (FRA)	6-2	4-6	6-3
1973	Rosie Casals (USA) Billie Jean King (USA)	Francoise Durr (FRA) Betty Stove (NED)	6-1	4-6	7-5
1974	Evonne Goolagong (AUS) Peggy Michel (USA)	Helen Gourlay (AUS) Karen Krantzcke (AUS)	2-6	6-4	6-3
1975	Ann Kiyomura (USA) Kazuko Sawamatsu (JPN)	Francoise Durr (FRA) Betty Stove (NED)	7-5	1-6	7-5
1976	Chris Evert (USA) Martina Navratilova (CZE)	Billie Jean King (USA) Betty Stove (NED)	6-1	3-6	7-5
1977	Helen Gourlay Cawley (AUS) JoAnne Russell (USA)	Martina Navratilova (CZE) Betty Stove (NED)	6-3	6-3	
1978	Kerry Melville Reid (AUS) Wendy Turnbull (AUS)	Mima Jausovec (YUG) Virginia Ruzici (ROU)	4-6	9-8(10)	6-3
1979	Billie Jean King (USA) Martina Navratilova (CZE)	Betty Stove (NED) Wendy Turnbull (AUS)	5-7	6-3	6-2
1980	Kathy Jordan (USA) Anne Smith (USA)	Rosie Casals (USA) Wendy Turnbull (AUS)	4-6	7-5	6-1
1981	Martina Navratilova (USA) Pam Shriver (USA)	Kathy Jordan (USA) Anne Smith (USA)	6-3	7-6(6)	
1982	Martina Navratilova (USA) Pam Shriver (USA)	Kathy Jordan (USA) Anne Smith (USA)	6-4	6-1	
1983	Martina Navratilova (USA) Pam Shriver (USA)	Rosie Casals (USA) Wendy Turnbull (AUS)	6-2	6-2	
1984	Martina Navratilova (USA) Pam Shriver (USA)	Kathy Jordan (USA) Anne Smith (USA)	6-3	6-4	
1985	Kathy Jordan (USA) Elizabeth Sayers Smylie (AUS)	Martina Navratilova (USA) Pam Shriver (USA)	5-7	6-3	6-4
1986	Martina Navratilova (USA) Pam Shriver (USA)	Hana Mandlikova (CZE) Wendy Turnbull (AUS)	6-1	6-3	
1987	Claudia Kohde Kilsch (GER) Helena Sukova (CZE)	Betsy Nagelsen (AUS) Elizabeth Sayers Smylie (AUS)	7-5	7-5	
1988	Steffi Graf (GER) Gabriela Sabatini (ARG)	Larisa Savchenko (LAT) Natalia Zvereva (USSR)	6-3	1-6	12-10
1989	Jana Novotna (CZE) Helena Sukova (CZE)	Larisa Savchenko (LAT) Natalia Zvereva (USSR)	6-1	6-2	
1990	Jana Novotna (CZE) Helena Sukova (CZE)	Kathy Jordan (USA) Elizabeth Sayers Smylie (AUS)	6-3	6-4	
1991	Larisa Savchenko (LAT) Natalia Zvereva (USSR)	Gigi Fernandez (USA) Jana Novotna (CZE)	6-4	3-6	6-4
1992	Gigi Fernandez (USA) Natalia Zvereva (CIS)	Jana Novotna (CZE) Larisa Savchenko Neiland (LAT)	6-4	6-1	
1993	Gigi Fernandez (USA) Natalia Zvereva (BLR)	Jana Novotna (CZE) Larisa Savchenko Neiland (LAT)	6-4	67(4)	6-4
1994	Gigi Fernandez (USA) Natalia Zvereva (BLR)	Jana Novotna (CZE) Arantxa Sanchez Vicario (ESP)	6-4	6-1	
1995	Jana Novotna (CZE) Arantxa Sanchez Vicario (ESP)	Gigi Fernandez (USA) Natasha Zvereva (BLR)	5-7	7-5	6-4
1996	Martina Hingis (SUI) Helena Sukova (CZE)	Meredith McGrath (USA) Larisa Savchenko Neiland (LAT)	5-7	7-5	6-1
1997	Gigi Fernandez (USA) Natasha Zvereva (BLR)	Nicole Arendt (USA) Manon Bollegraf (NED)	7-6(4)	6-4	
1998	Martina Hingis (SUI) Jana Novotna (CZE)	Lindsay Davenport (USA) Natasha Zvereva (BLR)	6-3	3-6	8-6
1999	Lindsay Davenport (USA) Corina Morariu (USA)	Mariaan de Swardt (RSA) Elena Tatarkova (UKR)	6-4	6-4	
2000	Venus Williams (USA) Serena Williams (USA)	Ai Sugiyama (JPN) Julie Halard-Decugis (FRA)	6-3	6-2	

Year	Winner	Defeated	S1	S2	S3
2001	Lisa Raymond (USA) Rennae Stubbs (AUS)	Kim Clijsters (BEL) Ai Sugiyama (JPN)	6-4	6-3	
2002	Venus Williams (USA) Serena Williams (USA)	Virginia Ruano Pascual (ESP) Paola Suarez (ARG)	6-2	7-5	
2003	Kim Clijsters (BEL) Ai Sugiyama (JPN)	Virginia Ruano Pascual (ESP) Paola Suarez (ARG)	6-4	6-4	
2004	Cara Black (ZIM) Rennae Stubbs (AUS)	Liezel Huber (RSA) Ai Sugiyama (JPN)	6-3	7-6(5)	
2005	Cara Black (ZIM) Liezel Huber (RSA)	Svetlana Kuznetsova (RUS) Amelie Mauresmo (FRA)	6-2	6-1	
2006	Zi Yan (CHN) Jie Zheng (CHN)	Virginia Ruano Pascual (ESP) Paola Suarez (ARG)	6-3	3-6	6-2
2007	Cara Black (ZIM) Liezel Huber (RSA)	Katarina Srebotnik (SLO) Ai Sugiyama (JPN)	3-6	6-3	6-2
2008	Serena Williams (USA) Venus Williams (USA)	Samantha Stosur (AUS) Lisa Raymond (USA)	6-2	6-2	
2009	Serena Williams (USA) Venus Williams (USA)	Samantha Stosur (AUS) Rennae Stubbs (AUS)	7-6(4)	6-4	

Mixed Doubles

Rd	Winner	Defeated	S1	S2	S3
1913	Agnes Daniell Tuckey (GBR) Hope Crisp (GBR)	Ethel Thomson Larcombe (GBR) Jim Parke (IRL)	3-6	5-3 (retired)	
1914	Ethel Thomson Larcombe (GBR) Jim Parke (IRL)	Marguerite Broquedis (FRA) Tony Wilding (NZL)	4-6	6-4	6-2
1915–18 Not held—WW II					
1919	Elizabeth Ryan (USA) Randolph Lycett (GBR)	Dorothea Douglass Chambers (GBR) Albert Prebble (GBR)	6-0	6-0	
1920	Suzanne Lenglen (FRA) Gerald Patterson (AUS)	Elizabeth Ryan (USA) Randolph Lycett (GBR)	7-5	6-3	
1921	Elizabeth Ryan (USA) Randolph Lycett (GBR)	Phyllis Howkins (GBR) Max Woosnam (GBR)	6-3	6-1	
1922	Suzanne Lenglen (FRA) Pat O'Hara Wood (AUS)	Elizabeth Ryan (USA) Randolph Lycett (GBR)	6-4	6-3	
1923	Elizabeth Ryan (USA) Randolph Lycett (GBR)	Dorothy Shepherd Barron (GBR) Lewis Deane (IND)	6-4	7-5	
1924	Kitty McKane (GBR) Brian Gilbert (GBR)	Dorothy Shepherd Barron (GBR) Leslie Godfree (GBR)	6-3	3-6	6-3
1925	Suzanne Lenglen (FRA) Jean Borotra (FRA)	Elizabeth Ryan (USA) Umberto de Morpurgo (ITA)	6-3	6-3	
1926	Kitty McKane Godfree (GBR) Leslie Godfree (GBR)	Mary K. Browne (USA) Howard Kinsey (USA)	6-3	6-4	
1927	Elizabeth Ryan (USA) Frank Hunter (USA)	Kitty McKane Godfree (GBR) Leslie Godfree (GBR)	8-6	6-0	
1928	Elizabeth Ryan (USA) Pat Spence (RSA)	Daphne Akhurst (AUS) Jack Crawford (AUS)	7-5	6-4	

Year	Winner	Defeated	S1	S2	S3
1929	Helen Wills (USA) Frank Hunter (USA)	Joan Fry (GBR) Ian Collins (GBR)	6-1	6-4	
1930	Elizabeth Ryan (USA) Jack Crawford (AUS)	Hilde Krahwinkel (GER) Daniel Prenn (GER)	6-1	6-3	
1931	Anna McCune Harper (USA) George Lott (USA)	Joan Ridley (GBR) Ian Collins (GBR)	6-3	1-6	6-1
1932	Elizabeth Ryan (USA) Enrique Maier (ESP)	Josane Sigart (BEL) Harry Hopman (AUS)	7-5	6-2	
1933	Hilde Krahwinkel (GER) Gottfried von Cramm (GER)	Mary Heeley (GBR) Norman Farquharson (GBR)	7-5	8-6	
1934	Dorothy Round (GBR) Ryuki Miki (JPN)	Dorothy Shepherd Barron (GBR) Bunny Austin (GBR)	3-6	6-4	6-0
1935	Dorothy Round (GBR) Fred Perry (GBR)	Nell Hall Hopman (AUS) Harry Hopman (AUS)	7-5	4-6	6-2
1936	Dorothy Round (GBR) Fred Perry (GBR)	Sarah Palfrey Fabyan (USA) Don Budge (USA)	7-9	7-5	6-4
1937	Alice Marble (USA) Don Budge (USA)	Simone Passemard Mathieu (FRA) Yvon Petra (FRA)	6-4	6-1	
1938	Alice Marble (USA) Don Budge (USA)	Sarah Palfrey Fabyan (USA) Henner Henkel (GER)	6-1	6-4	
1939	Alice Marble (USA) Bobby Riggs (USA)	Nina Brown (GBR) Frank Wilde (GBR)	9-7	6-1	
1940–1945 Not held—WW II					
1946	Louise Brough (USA) Tom Brown Jr. (USA)	Dorothy Bundy (USA) Geoff Brown (AUS)	6-4	6-4	
1947	Louise Brough (USA) John Bromwich (AUS)	Nancye Wynne Bolton (AUS) Colin Long (AUS)	1-6	6-4	6-2
1948	Louise Brough (USA) John Bromwich (AUS)	Doris Hart (USA) Frank Sedgman (AUS)	6-2	3-6	6-3
1949	Sheila Piercey Summers (RSA) Eric Sturgess (RSA)	Louise Brough (USA) John Bromwich (AUS)	9-7	9-11	7-5
1950	Louise Brough (USA) Eric Sturgess (RSA)	Pat Canning Todd (USA) Geoff Brown (AUS)	11-9	1-6	6-4
1951	Doris Hart (USA) Frank Sedgman (AUS)	Nancye Wynne Bolton (AUS) Merv Rose (AUS)	7-5	6-2	
1952	Doris Hart (USA) Frank Sedgman (AUS)	Thelma Coyne Long (AUS) Enrique Morea (ARG)	4-6	6-3	6-4
1953	Doris Hart (USA) Vic Seixas (USA)	Shirley Fry (USA) Enrique Morea (ARG)	9-7	7-5	
1954	Doris Hart (USA) Vic Seixas (USA)	Margaret Osborne duPont (USA) Ken Rosewall (AUS)	5-7	6-4	6-3
1955	Doris Hart (USA) Vic Seixas (USA)	Louise Brough (USA) Enrique Morea (ARG)	8-6	2-6	6-3
1956	Shirley Fry (USA) Vic Seixas (USA)	Althea Gibson (USA) Gardnar Mulloy (USA)	2-6	6-2	7-5
1957	Darlene Hard (USA) Merv Rose (AUS)	Althea Gibson (USA) Gardnar Mulloy (USA)	6-4	7-5	
1958	Lorraine Coghlan (AUS) Bob Howe (AUS)	Althea Gibson (USA) Kurt Nielsen (DEN)	6-3	13-11	
1959	Darlene Hard (USA) Rod Laver (AUS)	Maria Bueno (BRA) Neale Fraser (AUS)	6-4	6-3	

Year	Winner	Defeated	S1	S2	S3
1960	Darlene Hard (USA) Rod Laver (AUS)	Maria Bueno (BRA) Bob Howe (AUS)	13-11	3-6	8-6
1961	Lesley Turner (AUS) Fred Stolle (AUS)	Edda Buding (GER) Bob Howe (AUS)	11-9	6-2	
1962	Margaret Osborne duPont (USA) Neale Fraser (AUS)	Ann Haydon (GBR) Dennis Ralston (USA)	2-6	6-3	13-11
1963	Margaret Smith (AUS) Ken Fletcher (AUS)	Darlene Hard (USA) Bob Hewitt (AUS)	11-9	6-4	
1964	Lesley Turner (AUS) Fred Stolle (AUS)	Margaret Smith (AUS) Ken Fletcher (AUS)	6-4	6-4	
1965	Margaret Smith (AUS) Ken Fletcher (AUS)	Judy Tegart (AUS) Tony Roche (AUS)	12-10	6-3	
1966	Margaret Smith (AUS) Ken Fletcher (AUS)	Billie Jean Moffitt King (USA) Dennis Ralston (USA)	4-6	6-3	6-3
1967	Billie Jean Moffitt King (USA) Owen Davidson (AUS)	Maria Bueno (BRA) Ken Fletcher (AUS)	7-5	6-2	
1968	Margaret Smith Court (AUS) Ken Fletcher (AUS)	Olga Morozova (USSR) Alex Metreveli (USSR)	6-1	14-12	
1969	Ann Haydon Jones (GBR) Fred Stolle (AUS)	Judy Tegart (AUS) Tony Roche (AUS)	6-3	6-2	
1970	Rosie Casals (USA) Ilie Nastase (ROU)	Olga Morozova (USSR) Alex Metreveli (USSR)	6-3	4-6	9-7
1971	Billie Jean Moffitt King (USA) Owen Davidson (AUS)	Margaret Smith Court (AUS) Marty Riessen (USA)	3-6	6-2	15-13
1972	Rosie Casals (USA) Ilie Nastase (ROU)	Evonne Goolagong (AUS) Kim Warwick (AUS)	6-4	6-4	
1973	Billie Jean Moffitt King (USA) Owen Davidson (AUS)	Janet Newberry (USA) Raul Ramirez (MEX)	6-3	6-2	
1974	Billie Jean Moffitt King (USA) Owen Davidson (AUS)	Lesley Charles (GBR) Mark Farrell (GBR)	6-3	9-7	
1975	Margaret Smith Court (AUS) Marty Riessen (USA)	Betty Stove (NED) Allan Stone (AUS)	6-4	7-5	
1976	Francoise Durr (FRA) Tony Roche (AUS)	Rosie Casals (USA) Dick Stockton (USA)	6-3	2-6	7-5
1977	Greer Stevens (RSA) Bob Hewitt (RSA)	Betty Stove (NED) Frew McMillan (RSA)	3-6	7-5	6-4
1978	Betty Stove (NED) Frew McMillan (RSA)	Billie Jean King (USA) Ray Ruffels (AUS)	6-2	6-2	
1979	Greer Stevens (RSA) Bob Hewitt (RSA)	Betty Stove (NED) Frew McMillan (RSA)	7-5	7-6(7)	
1980	Tracy Austin (USA) John Austin (USA)	Dianne Fromholtz (AUS) Mark Edmondson (AUS)	4-6	7-6(6)	6-3
1981	Betty Stove (NED) Frew McMillan (RSA)	Tracy Austin (USA) John Austin (USA)	4-6	7-6(2)	6-3
1982	Anne Smith (USA) Kevin Curren (RSA)	Wendy Turnbull (AUS) John Lloyd (GBR)	2-6	6-3	7-5
1983	Wendy Turnbull (AUS) John Lloyd (GBR)	Billie Jean King (USA) Steve Denton (USA)	67(5)	7-6(5)	7-5
1984	Wendy Turnbull (AUS) John Lloyd (GBR)	Kathy Jordan (USA) Steve Denton (USA)	6-3	6-3	
1985	Martina Navratilova (USA) Paul McNamee (AUS)	Elizabeth Sayers Smylie (AUS) John Fitzgerald (AUS)	7-5	4-6	6-2
1986	Kathy Jordan (USA) Ken Flach (USA)	Martina Navratilova (USA) Heinz Gunthardt (SUI)	6-3	7-6(7)	
1987	Jo Durie (GBR) Jeremy Bates (GBR)	Nicole Provis (AUS) Darren Cahill (AUS)	76(10)	6-3	
1988	Zina Garrison (USA) Sherwood Stewart (USA)	Gretchen Rush Magers (USA) Kelly Jones USA)	6-1	7-6(3)	
1989	Jana Novotna (CZE) Jim Pugh (USA)	Jenny Byrne (AUS) Mark Kratzmann (AUS)	6-4	5-7	6-4
1990	Zina Garrison (USA) Rick Leach (USA)	Elizabeth Sayers Smylie (AUS) John Fitzgerald (AUS)	7-5	6-2	
1991	Elizabeth Sayers Smylie (AUS) John Fitzgerald (AUS)	Natalia Zvereva (BLR) Jim Pugh (USA)	7-6(4)	6-2	
1992	Larisa Savchenko Neiland (LAT) Cyril Suk (CZE)	Miriam Oremans (NED) Jacco Eltingh (NED)	7-6(2)	6-2	
1993	Martina Navratilova (USA) Mark Woodforde (AUS)	Manon Bollegraf (NED) Tom Nijssen (NED)	6-3	6-4	
1994	Helena Sukova (CZE) Todd Woodbridge (AUS)	Lori McNeil (USA) T.J. Middleton (USA)	3-6	7-5	6-3
1995	Martina Navratilova (USA) Jonathan Stark (USA)	Gigi Fernandez (USA) Cyril Suk (CZE)	6-4	6-4	
1996	Helena Sukova (CZE) Cyril Suk (CZE)	Larisa Savchenko Neiland (LAT) Mark Woodforde (AUS)	1-6	6-3	6-2
1997	Helena Sukova (CZE) Cyril Suk (CZE)	Larisa Savchenko Neiland (LAT) Andrei Olhovskiy (RUS)	4-6	6-3	6-4
1998	Serena Williams (USA) Max Mirnyi (BLR)	Mirjana Lucic (CRO) Mahesh Bhupathi (IND)	6-4	6-4	
1999	Lisa Raymond (USA) Leander Paes (IND)	Anna Kournikova (RUS) Jonas Bjorkman (SWE)	6-4	3-6	6-3
2000	Kimberly Po (USA) Donald Johnson (USA)	Kim Clijsters (BEL) Lleyton Hewitt (AUS)	6-4	7-6(3)	
2001	Daniela Hantuchova (SVK) Leos Friedl (CZE)	Liezel Huber (RSA) Mike Bryan (USA)	4-6	6-3	6-2
2002	Elena Likhovtseva (RUS) Mahesh Bhupathi (IND)	Daniela Hantuchova (SVK) Kevin Ullyett (ZIM)	6-2	1-6	6-1
2003	Martina Navratilova (USA) Leander Paes (IND)	Anastasia Rodionova (RUS) Andy Ram (ISR)	6-3	6-3	
2004	Cara Black (ZIM) Wayne Black (ZIM)	Alicia Molik (AUS) Todd Woodbridge (AUS)	3-6	7-6(8)	6-4
2005	Mary Pierce (FRA) Mahesh Bhupathi (IND)	Tatiana Perebiynis (UKR) Paul Hanley (AUS)	6-4	6-2	
2006	Vera Zvonareva (RUS) Andy Ram (ISR)	Venus Williams (USA) Bob Bryan (USA)	6-3	6-2	
2007	Jelena Jankovic (SRB) Jamie Murray (GBR)	Alicia Molik (AUS) Jonas Bjorkman (SWE)	6-4	3-6	6-1
2008	Bob Bryan (USA) Samantha Stosur (AUS)	Mike Bryan (USA) Katarina Srebotnik (SRB)	7-5	6-4	
2009	Mark Knowles (BAH) Anna-Lena Groenefeld (GER)	Leander Paes (IND) Cara Black (ZIM)	7-5	6-3	

Wimbledon – Records

MOST TITLES

Men

13	Laurie Doherty	(1897-1906)	5 singles, 8 doubles
12	Reggie Doherty	(1897-1905)	4 singles. 8 doubles
	Willie Renshaw	(1881-1889)	7 singles, 5 doubles
10	Todd Woodbridge	(1993-2004)	9 doubles, 1 mixed
7	Pete Sampras	(1993-2000)	7 singles
	Rod Laver	(1959-1971)	4 singles, 1 doubles, 2 mixed
	Wilfred Baddeley	(1891-1896)	3 singles, 4 doubles
	Mark Woodforde	(1993-2000)	6 doubles, 1 mixed
6	Roger Federer	(2003-2009)	6 singles
	Don Budge	(1937-1938)	2 singles. 2 doubles, 2 mixed
	Ernest Renshaw	(1884-1889)	1 singles, 5 doubles
	Frank Sedgman	(1948.1952)	1 singles, 3 doubles. 2 mixed
	Jean Borotra	(1924-1933)	2 singles, 3 doubles, 1 mixed

Women

20	Billie Jean King	(1961-1979)	6 singles, 10 doubles, 4 mixed
	Martina Navratilova	(1976-2003)	9 singles, 7 doubles, 4 mixed
19	Elizabeth Ryan	(1914-1934)	0 singles, 12 doubles, 7 mixed
15	Suzanne Lenglen	(1919-1925)	6 singles, 6 doubles, 3 mixed
13	Louise Brough	(1946-1955)	4 singles, 5 doubles, 4 mixed
12	Helen Wills Moody	(1924-1938)	8 singles, 3 doubles, 1 mixed
10	Doris Hart	(1947-1955)	1 singles, 4 doubles, 5 mixed
	Margaret Smith Court	(1963-1975)	3 singles, 2 doubles, 5 mixed
9	Venus Williams	(2000-2009)	5 singles, 4 doubles
8	Serena Williams	(1998-2009)	3 singles, 4 doubles, 1 mixed
	Maria Bueno	(1958-1966)	3 singles, 5 doubles, 0 mixed
	Steffi Graf	(1988-1996)	7 singles, 1 doubles, 0 mixed

MOST SINGLES TITLES

Challenge Round and Non-Challenge Round Era

Men

7	Willie Renshaw	(1881-1886, 1889)
	Pete Sampras	(1993-1995, 1997-2000)
6	Roger Federer	(2003-2007, 2009)
5	Bjorn Borg	(1976-1980)
	Laurie Doherty	(1902-1906)
4	Rod Laver	(1961-1962, 1968-1969)
	Tony Wilding	(1910-1913)
	Reggie Doherty	(1897-1900)
3	Wilfred Baddeley	(1891-1892, 1895)
	Arthur Gore	(1901-1908-1909)
	Bill Tilden	(1920-1921,1930)
	Boris Becker	(1985-1986, 1989)
	Fred Perry	(1934-1936)
	John Newcombe	(1967, 1970-1971)
	John McEnroe	(1981, 1983-1984)

Women

9	Martina Navratilova	(1978-1979; 1982-1987, 1990)
8	Helen Wills Moody	(1927-1930, 1932-1933, 1935, 1938)

7	Dorothea Douglass Chambers	(1903-1904, 1906, 1910-1911, 1913-1914)
	Steffi Graf	(1988-1989, 1991-1993, 1995-1996)
6	Blanche Bingley Hillyard	(1886, 1889, 1894, 1897, 1899-1900)
	Suzanne Lenglen	(1919-1923, 1925)
	Billie Jean King	(1966-1968, 1972-1973, 1975)
5	Venus Williams	(2000-2001, 2005, 2007, 2008)
	Lottie Dod	(1887-1888, 1891-1893)
	Charlotte Cooper Sterry	(1895-1896, 1898, 1901, 1908)
4	Louise Brough	(1948-1950, 1955)
3	Serena Williams	(2002-2003, 2009)
	Chris Evert	(1974, 1976, 1981)
	Margaret Court	(1963, 1965, 1970)
	Maria Bueno	(1959-1960, 1964)

MOST SINGLES TITLES

(1922 to 2009 – Post Challenge Round Era)

Men

7	Pete Sampras	(1993-1995, 1997-2000)
6	Roger Federer	(2003-2007, 2009)
5	Bjorn Borg	(1976-1980)
4	Rod Laver	(1961-1962, 1968-1969)
3	John Newcombe	(1967, 1970-1971)
	Fred Perry	(1934-1936)
	John McEnroe	(1981, 1983-1984)
	Boris Becker	(1985-1986, 1989)

Women

9	Martina Navratilova	(1978-1979, 1982-1987, 1990)
8	Helen Wills Moody	(1927-1930, 1932-1933, 1935, 1938)
7	Steffi Graf	(1988-1989, 1991-1993, 1995-1996)
6	Billie Jean King	(1966-1968, 1972-1973, 1975)
	Suzanne Lenglen	(1922-1923 1925)
5	Venus Williams	(2000-2001, 2005, 2007-2008)
4	Louise Brough	(1948-1950, 1955)
3	Serena Williams	(2002-2003, 2009)
	Margaret Smith Court	(1963, 1965, 1970)
	Chris Evert	(1974, 1976, 1981)
	Maureen Connolly	(1952-1954)
	Maria Bueno	(1959, 1960, 1964)

MOST SINGLES FINAL APPEARANCES

Men

9	Willie Renshaw	(1881-1887, 1889-1890) Challenge Round—1878-1921
7	Roger Federer	(2003-2009)
	Arthur Gore	(1899, 1901-1902, 1908-1910,1912) Challenge Round—1878-1921
	Boris Becker	(1985-1986, 1988-1991, 1995)
	Pete Sampras	(1993-1995, 1997-2000)

6	Jimmy Connors	(1974-1975, 1977-1978, 1982, 1984)
	Bjorn Borg	1976-1981
	Rod Laver	(1959-1962, 1968-1969)
5	Jean Borotra	(1924-1927, 1929)
	John McEnroe	(1980-1984)
4	Goran Ivanisevic	(1992, 1994, 1998, 2001)
	Ken Rosewall	(1954, 1956, 1970, 1974)
	John Newcombe	(1967, 1969-1971)

Women

12	Martina Navratilova	(1978-1979, 1982-1990, 1994)
12	Blanche Bingley Hilliard	(1886-89, 1892-1895, 1897, 1899-1901) Challenge Round (1884-1921)
11	Dorothea Douglass Chambers	(1903-07, 10-1911,1913-1914, 1919-1920) Challenge Round (1884-1921)
10	Chris Evert	(1973-1974, 1976, 1978-1982, 1984-1985)
	Charlotte Cooper Sterry	(1895-1902, 1904, 1908) Challenge Round (1884-1921)
9	Helen Wills Moody	(1924, 1927-1930, 1932-1933, 1935, 1938)
	Steffi Graf	(1987-1989, 1991-1993, 1995-1996, 1999)
	Billie Jean King	(1963, 1966-1970, 1972-1973, 1975)
8	Venus Williams	(2000-2003, 2005, 2007-2009)
7	Louise Brough	(1946, 1948-1950, 1952, 1954-1955)
6	Helen Jacobs	(1929, 1932, 1934-1936, 1938)
5	Serena Williams	2002-2004, 2008-2009
	Maria Bueno	(1959-1960, 1964-1966)
	Evonne Goolagong	(1971-1972, 1975-1976,1980)
	Margaret Smith Court	(1963-1965, 1970-1971)

MOST LOSSES IN SINGLES FINAL (SINCE 1922)

Men

4	Boris Becker	(1988, 1990-1991, 1995)
	Jimmy Connors	(1975, 1977-1978, 1984)
	Ken Rosewall	(1954, 1956, 1970, 1974)
3	Andy Roddick	(2004-2005, 2009)
	Jean Borotra	(1925, 1927, 1929)
	Fred Stolle	(1963-1965)
	Goran Ivanisevic	(1992, 1994, 1998)
	Gottfried von Cramm	(1935-1937)

Women

7	Chris Evert	(1973-1985)
5	Helen Jacobs	(1929-1938)
3	Louise Brough	(1946-1954)
	Evonne Goolagong	(1972-1976)
	Doris Hart	(1947-1953)
	Lili de Alvarez	(1926-1928)
	Billie Jean King	(1963-1970)
	Martina Navratilova	(1988-1994)

MOST TOURNAMENTS PLAYED

Men's Singles

30	Arthur Gore	(1888-1922)

Women's Singles

20	Blanche Bingley Hilyard	(1884-1913)
	Virginia Wade	(1962-1985)

MOST MATCHES PLAYED

Men Overall

223	Jean Borotra	(1922-39, 1948-64)
	Singles W 55, L 10	
	Doubles W 59, L 31	
	Mixed W 40, L 28	

Women Overall

326	Martina Navratilova	(1973-1996, 2000-2006)
	Singles W 120, L 14	
	Doubles W 100, L 21	
	Mixed W 56, L 15	

MOST MATCHES PLAYED

Men's Singles

102	Jimmy Connors	(1972-1996, 1991-1992)

Women's Singles

134	Martina Navratilova	(1973-1996, 2000-2006)

MOST MATCHES WON

Men's Singles

84	Jimmy Connors	(1972-1989, 1991-1992)

Women's Singles

120	Martina Navratilova	(1973-1996, 2000-2006)

MATCHES WON CONSECUTIVELY

Men's Singles

41	Bjorn Borg	(1976-81)

Women's Singles

50	Helen Wills Moody	(1927-1930, 1932, 1933, 1935, 1938)

MATCH WINNING PERCENTAGE

Men's Singles

.927	Bjorn Borg	(51-4) (1973-81)

Women's Singles

1.000	Suzanne Lenglen	(28-0) (1919-1925)
.982	Helen Wills Moody	(55-1) (1924-1938)

TRIPLERS

(Winner of all three events in one year)

Men

1937	Don Budge	(with MD-Gene Mako; MXD-Alice Marble)
1938	Don Budge	(with MD-Gene Mako; MXD-Alice Marble)
1939	Bobby Riggs	(with MD-Elwood Cooke; MXD-Alice Marble)
1952	Frank Sedgman	(with MD-Ken McGregor; MXD-Doris Hart)

Women

1920	Suzanne Lenglen	(with WD-Elizabeth Ryan; MXD-Gerald Patterson)
1922	Suzanne Lenglen	(with WD-Elizabeth Ryan; MXD-Pat O'Hara Wood)
1925	Suzanne Lenglen	(with WD-Elizabeth Ryan; MXD-Jean Borotra)

1939	Alice Marble	(with WD-Sarah Palfrey Fabyan MXD-Bobby Riggs)
1948	Louise Brough	(with WD-Margaret Osborne duPont; MXD-John Bromwich)
1950	Louise Brough	(with WD-Margaret Osborne duPont; MXD-Eric Sturgess)
1951	Doris Hart	(with WD-Shirley Fry; MXD-Frank Sedgman)
1967	Billie Jean King	(with WD-Rosie Casals; MXD-Owen Davidson)
1973	Billie Jean King	(with WD-Rosie Casals; MXD-Owen Davidson)

MOST DOUBLES TITLES – TEAM

Men

8	Reggie Doherty / Laurie Doherty	(1897-1905)
6	Todd Woodbridge / Mark Woodforde	(1993-2000)
5	Willie Renshaw / Ernest Renshaw	(1884-1889)
	John Newcombe / Tony Roche	(1965-1974)
4	Wilfred Baddeley / Herbert Baddeley	(1891-1896)
	John McEnroe / Peter Fleming	(1979-1984)
3	Bob Hewitt / Frew McMillan	(1967-1978)
	Todd Woodbridge / Jonas Bjorkman	(2001-2004)

Women

6	Suzanne Lenglen / Elizabeth Ryan	(1919-1925)
5	Billie Jean King / Rosie Casals	(1967-1973)
	Martina Navratilova / Pam Shriver	(1981-1986)
	Louise Brough / Margaret Osborne duPont	(1946-1954)
4	Venus Williams / Serena Williams	(2000, 2002, 2008, 2009)
	Gigi Fernandez / Natalia Zvereva	(1992-1997)
3	Doris Hart / Shirley Fry	(1951-1953)

MOST DOUBLES TITLES – INDIVIDUAL

Men

9	Todd Woodbridge	(1993-2004)
8	Laurie Doherty	(1897-1905)
	Reggie Doherty	(1897-1905)
6	John Newcombe	(1965-1974)
	Mark Woodforde	(1993-2000)
5	Bob Hewitt	(1962-1978)
	Ernest Renshaw	1884-1889)
	John McEnroe	(1979-1992)
	Tony Roche	(1965-1974)
	Willie Renshaw	(1884-1889)

Women

12	Elizabeth Ryan	(1914-1934)
10	Billie Jean King	(1961-1979)
7	Martina Navratilova	(1976-1986)
6	Suzanne Lenglen	(1919-1925)
5	Margaret Osborne duPont	(1946-1954)
	Louise Brough	(1946-1954)
	Maria Bueno	(1958-1964)
	Natalia Zvereva	(1991-1997)
	Pam Shriver	(1981-1986)
	Rosie Casals	(1967-1973)

MOST DOUBLES FINAL APPEARANCES – INDIVIDUAL

Men

11	Reggie Doherty	(1896-1906)
10	Laurie Doherty	(1897-1906)
	Todd Woodbridge	(1993-2004)
7	Herbert Roper Barrett	(1900-1914)
	Mark Woodforde	(1993-2000)
	Jacques Brugnon	(1926-1934)
	Peter Fleming	(1978-1986)
	Bob Hewitt	(1961-1978)
	John McEnroe	(1978-1992)

Women

13	Elizabeth Ryan	(1914-1934)
12	Billie Jean King	(1961-1979)
9	Natalia Zvereva	(1988-1998)
	Martina Navratilova	(1976-1986)
8	Jana Novotna	(1989-1998)
	Louise Brough	(1946-1954)
	Margaret Osborne duPont	(1946-1958)
	Doris Hart	(1946-1954)

MOST DOUBLES FINAL APPEARANCES – TEAM

Men

10	Reggie Doherty / Laurie Doherty	(1887-1906)
7	Todd Woodbridge / Mark Woodforde	(1993-2000)
6	Wilfred Baddeley / Herbert Baddeley	(1891-1897)
	John McEnroe / Peter Fleming	(1978-1984)
5	Willie Renshaw / Ernest Renshaw	(1884-1889)
	John Newcombe / Tony Roche	(1965-1974)
	Sidney H. Smith / Frank Riseley	(1902-1906)
4	Bob Bryan / Mike Bryan	(2005-2009)
	Henri Cochet / Jacques Brugnon	(1926-1931)

Women

7	Louise Brough / Margaret Osborne duPont	(1946-1954)
5	Suzanne Lenglen / Elizabeth Ryan	(1919-1925)
	Martina Navratilova / Pam Shriver	(1981-1986)
5	Billie Jean King / Rosie Casals	(1967-1973)
	Doris Hart / Shirley Fry	(1950-1954)
	Gigi Fernandez / Natalia Zvereva	(1992-1997)
4	Venus Williams / Serena Williams	(2000, 2002, 2008, 2009)
	Anne Smith / Kathy Jordan	(1980-1984)

MOST DOUBLES FINAL LOSSES – TEAM

Men

3	Bob Bryan / Mike Bryan	(2005-2009)
	Bob Lutz / Stan Smith	(1974-1981)
	Sidney H. Smith / Frank Riseley	(1903-1905)

Women

| 3 | Anne Smith / Kathy Jordan | (1981-1984) |
| | Virgina Ruano Pascual / Paola Suarez | (2002-2006) |

MOST DOUBLES FINAL LOSSES – INDIVIDUAL

Men

| 5 | Ernest Lewis | (1884-1895) |

Women

| 6 | Francoise Durr | (1965-1975) |

MOST MIXED DOUBLES TITLES – TEAM

4	Margaret Smith Court / Ken Fletcher	(1963 -1968)
	Billie Jean King / Owen Davidson	(1967-1974)
3	Elizabeth Ryan / Randolph Lycett	(1919-1923)
	Doris Hart / Vic Seixas	(1953-1955)

MOST MIXED DOUBLES TITLES

Men

4	Owen Davidson	(1967-1974)
	Ken Fletcher	(1963-1968)
	Vic Seixas	(1953-56)
3	Fred Stolle	(1961-1969)
	Randolph Lycett	(1919-1923)
	Cyril Suk	(1992-1997)

Women

7	Elizabeth Ryan	(1919-1932)
5	Margaret Smith Court	(1963-1975)
	Doris Hart	(1951-1955)
4	Billie Jean King	(1967-1974)
	Louise Brough	(1946-1950)

MOST MIXED DOUBLES FINAL APPEARANCES

Men

6	Ken Fletcher	(1963-1968)
5	Randolph Lycett	(1919-1923)
4	Frew McMillan	(1977-1981)

Women

10	Elizabeth Ryan	(1919-1932)
7	Margaret Smith Court	(1963-1975)
	Billie Jean King	(1966-1983)

MOST MIXED DOUBLES FINAL APPEARANCES–TEAM

5	Elizabeth Ryan / Randolph Lycett	(1919-1923)
	Margaret Smith Court / Ken Fletcher	(1963-1968)
4	Betty Stove / Frew McMillan	(1977-1981)
	Billie Jean King / Owen Davidson	(1967-1974)

MOST MIXED DOUBLES FINAL LOSSES–TEAM

2	Olga Morozova / Alex Metreveli	(1968-1970)
	Judy Tegart Dalton / Tony Roche	1965-1969)
	Elizabeth Ryan / Randolph Lycett	(1920-1922)
	Elizabeth Sayers Smylie / John Fitzgerald	(1985-1990)
	Betty Stove / Frew McMillan	(1977-1979)

MOST MIXED DOUBLES FINAL LOSSES

Men

3	Enrique Morea	(1952-1955)

Women

3	Elizabeth Ryan	(1920-1925)
	Althea Gibson	(1956-1958)
	Betty Stove	(1975-1979)
	Billie Jean King	(1965-1983)
	Maria Bueno	(1959-1967)
	Dorothy Shephard Barron	(1923-1934)

YOUNGEST SINGLES CHAMPION

Men

Boris Becker—17 years, 227 days (1985)

Women

Charlotte "Lottie" Dod—15 years, 285 days (1887)

OLDEST SINGLES CHAMPION

Men

Arthur Gore—41 years, 182 days (1909)

Women

Charlotte Cooper Sterry—37 years, 282 days (1908)

YOUNGEST COMPETITOR

Men's Singles

Sidney Wood—15 years, 231 days (1927)

Men's Doubles

Sidney Wood—15 years, 234 days (1927)

Women's Singles

Jennifer Capriati—14 years, 90 days (1990)

Kathy Rinaldi—14 years, 91 days (1981)

Women's Doubles

Jennifer Capriati—14 years 92 days (1990)

OLDEST COMPETITOR

Men's Singles

Joshiah Ritchie—55 years, 247 days in 1926

Men's Doubles

Jean Borotra—65 years, 317 days in 1964

Women's Singles

Madeline O'Neill—54 years, 304 days in 1922

Women's Doubles

Mrs. C. O. Tuckey—54 years, 352 days in 1932

Mixed Doubles

Jean Borotra—64 years, 320 days in 1963

Maddeline O'Neill—55 years, 304 days in 1923

OLDEST DOUBLES CHAMPION

Men

Gardnar Mulloy—43 years, 226 days (1957)

Women

Elizabeth Ryan—42 years, 152 days (1934)

YOUNGEST DOUBLES CHAMPION

Men

Dennis Ralston—17 years, 341 days (1960)

Women

Martina Hingis—15 years, 282 days (1996)

OLDEST MIXED DOUBLES CHAMPION

Men

Sherwood Stewart—42 years. 28 days (1988)

Women

Martina Navratilova—46 years, 261 days (2003)

YOUNGEST MIXED DOUBLES CHAMPION

Men

Rod Laver—20 years, 328 days (1959)

Women

Serena Williams—16 years. 282 days (1998)

LONGEST MATCHES, TOTAL GAMES

Men's Singles

112 games   Richard "Pancho" Gonzalez d. Charlie Pasarell 22-24, 1-6, 16-14, 6-3, 11-9. 1969 1st rd., (5 hours, 12 minutes)

Men's Doubles

102 games   Marcelo Melo / Andre Sa d. Paul Hanley / Kevin Ullyett 5-7, 7-6 (4), 4-6, 7-6 (7), 28-26, 2007 3rd rd, (5 hours, 58 minutes)

98 games   Nikki Pilic/ Gene Scott d. Cliff Richey / Torben Ulrich 19-21, 12-10, 6-4. 4-6, 9-7, 1st rd., 1966

Women's Singles

58 games   Chanda Rubin d. Patricia Hy-Boulais, 7-6(7-4), 6-7(5-7). 17-15. 2nd rd., 1996 (3 hours, 45 minutes)

Women's Doubles

50 games   Martina Hingis / Arantxa Sanchez Vicario d. Chanda Rubin / Brenda Schultz-McCarthy, 7-6(14-12). 6-7 (6-8), 13-11, 3rd, 1997 (3 hours, 9 minutes)

Mixed Doubles

77 games   Brenda Schultz (McCarthy) / Michiel Schapers d. Andrea Temesvarl / Tom Nijssen, 6-3, 5-7, 29-27, 1991 1st rd., (4 hours 14 minutes)

LONGEST MATCHES, TIME

Men's Singles

5 hours, 28 minutes	Greg Holmes d. Todd Witsken, 5-7, 6-4, 7-6 (7-5), 4-6, 14-12, 2nd rd., 1989 (played over 3 days)
5 hours, 12 minutes	Richard "Pancho" Gonzalez d. Charlie Pasarell, 22-24,1-6, 16-14, 6-3, 11-9 1969, 1R (played over 2 days)
	Rainer Schuettler d. Arnaud Clement, 6-3, 5-7, 7-6 (6), 6-7 (7), 8-6, 2008, QF (played over 2 days)
5 hours, 5 minutes	Mark Philippoussis d. Sjeng Schalken 4-6, 6-3, 6-7 (7-9), 7-6 (7-4), 20-18, 2000 3rd rd., (1 day)
4 hours, 56 minutes	Stefano Galvanic d. Alex Waske, 4-6, 7-6 (7-2), 6-4, 3-6, 16-14, 1st rd, 2006

Men's Doubles

6 hours, 9 minutes	Mark Knowles / Daniel Nestor d. Simon Aspelin / Todd Perry 5-7, 6-3, 6-7 (5-7), 6-3, 23-21 QF 2006 (played over two days), 5th set lasted 3:13
5 hours, 58 minutes	Marcelo Melo / Andre Sa d. Paul Hanley / Kevin Ullyett 5-7, 7-6 (7-4), 4-6, 7-6 (9-7), 28-26, longest fifth set, 3rd rd, 2007 (played over five days)
5 hours, 5 minutes	Heinz Gunthardt / Balazs Taroczy d. Paul Annacone / Christo van Rensburg, 6-4, 2-6, 6-4, 24-22, QF 1985

Women's Singles

3 hours, 45 minutes	Chanda Rubin d. Patricia Hy-Boulais 7-6(7-4), 6-7(6-7), 17-15, 2nd rd. 1996

Women's Doubles

3 hours, 9 minutes	Martina Hingis / Arantxa Sanchez Vicario d. Chanda Rubin / Brenda Schultz-MoCarthy, 7-6(14-12). 6-7 (6-8), 13-11, 3rd, 1997

Mixed Doubles

4 hours, 14 minutes	Michael Schapers / Brenda Schultz d. Tom Nijssen / Andrea Temesvari, 6-3, 5-7, 29-27, 1st Rd. 1991, played in one day

LONGEST TIE-BREAKERS

Men's singles

38 points   Bjom Borg d. Premjit Lall, 6-3, 6-4, 9-8 (20-18), 1st rd., 1973

Men's Doubles

50 points   Jan Gunnarson / Michael Mortensen d. John Frawley / Victor Pecci, 6-3, 6-4, 3-6, 7-6 (26-24), 1st rd. 1985

Women's singles

28 points   Virginia Wade, d. Jo Durie, 3-6, 7-6(15-13), 6-2. 1st rd., 1982

Women's Doubles

26 points   Martina Hingis / Arantxa Sanchez Vicario d. Chanda Rubin / Brenda Schultz-McCarthy, 7-6 (14-12), 6-7 (6-8), 13-11, 3rd rd., 1997

Mixed Doubles

32 points   Leos Friedl / Anke Huber d. Martin Damm / Barbara Rittner, 7-6 (17-15), 6-0, 2nd round, 2003

LONGEST SHOT CHAMPIONS

Men Singles

2001   Goran Ivanisevic, wildcard ranked No. 125 d. No. 3 Patrick Rafter, 6-3, 3-6, 6-3, 2-6, 9-7

1996   Richard Krajicek, unseeded/No. 17, d. MaliVai Washington, unseeded (only unseeded final) 6-3, 6-4, 6-3

1985   Boris Becker, unseeded, d. No. 8 Kevin Curren, 6-3, 6-7 (4-7), 7-6 (7-3), 6-4

Women's Singles

(No unseeded player has ever won)

2007   Venus Williams (No. 31, seeded 23), d. Marion Bartoli (Seeded No. 18), 6-4, 6-1 (Longshot based on her 31 ranking, otherwise, a three time champion would never be a longshot)

2004   Maria Sharapova (Seeded No. 13) d. defending champion and No. 1 seed Serena Williams, 6-1, 6-4

EARLIEST LOSS OF A NO. 1 SEED

Men

1967   Charlie Pasarell d. 1st seed defending champ Manuel Santana, 10-8, 6-3, 2-6, 8-6 in first round

2003   Qualifier Ivo Karlovic, ranked No. 203, d. defending champion and No. 1 seed Lleyton Hewitt 1-6, 7-6 (5), 6-3, 6-4 in only second time a defending men's singles champion lost in the first round

Women

1962   Unseeded Billie Jean Moffitt (King) d. 1st seed Margaret Court, 1-6, 6-3, 7-5, 2nd rd. (1st defeat for 1st seed in 1st match)

1994   Lorl McNeil (No. 22) d. 1st seed defending champ Steffi Graf, 7-5, 7-6(7-5), 1st rd. (only 1st rd defeat of a No. 1 seeded defending champion)

1999   Jelena Dokic (Q) def. No. 1 seed Martina Hingis, 6-2, 6-0 in 1st rd.

2001   Virginia Ruano Pascual (No. 83) d. 1st seed Martina Hingis, 6-4, 6-2, 1st rd.

EARLIEST LOSS OF A DEFENDING CHAMPION
Men

1967   Charlie Pasarell d. 1st seed defending champ Manuel Santana, 10-8, 6-3, 2-6, 8-6 in first round

2003   Qualifier Ivo Karlovic ranked No. 203, d. defending champion and No. 1 seed Lleyton Hewitt 1-6, 7- 6 (7-5), 6-3, 6-4 in only second time a defending men's singles champion lost in the first round

Women

1994   Lori McNeil (No. 22) d. 1st seed defending champ Steffi Graf, 7-5, 7-6(7-5), 1st rd. (only 1st rd defeat of a No. 1 seeded defending champion)

OTHER BIG UPSETS
Men

1932   Non-seed Ian Collins d. 1st seed Henri Cochet, 6-2, 8-6, 0-6. 6-3, 2nd rd.

1946   Non-seed Jaroslav Drobny d. 2nd seed Jack Kramer 2-6, 17-15, 6.3, 3-6, 6-3, 4th rd.

1970   16th seed Roger Taylor d. 1st seed defending champ Rod Laver, 4-6, 6-4, 6-2. 6-1, 4th rd. ends Laver's 31-match streak at Wimbledon

1971   Non-seed Tom Gorman d. 1st seed Rod Laver, 9-7, 8-6, 6-3 4th rd.

1973   Non-seed Alex Mayer d. 1st seed Ilie Nastase 6-4, 8-6, 6-8, 6-4, 4th rd. (Court Two)

1975   No. 6 seed Arthur Ashe d. 1st seed defending champ Jimmy Connors, 6-1, 6-1. 5-7, 6-4. F

1979   15th seed Tim Gullikson d. 2nd seed John McEnroe, 6-4, 6-2. 6-4, 4th rd. (Court Two)

1983   12th seed Kevin Curren d. 1st seed defending champ Jimmy Connors, 6-3, 6-7 (6-8). 6-3, 7-6 (7-4), 4th rd. (Court Two)

1985   Non-seed Boris Becker d. 7th seed Joakim Nystrom, 3-6, 7-6 (7-5), 6-1, 4-6, 9-7, 3rd rd.; 16th seed Tim Mayotte, 6-3, 4-6, 6-7 (7-9), 7-6(7-5), 6-2, 4th rd.; 5th seed Anders Jarryd, 2-6, 7-6 (7-3), 6-3, 6-3, SF: No. 8 seed Kevin Curren, 6-3, 6-7 (4-7), 7-6(7-3), 6-4, F. Curren d. 1st seed John McEnroe, 6-2, 6-2. 6-4, QF; 3rd seed Jimmy Connors, 6-2, 6-2. 6-1, SF. Also, qualifier Ricardo Acuna (No. 133) d. No. 6 Pat Cash (6), 7-6(7-4), 6-3, 3-6, 6-7(7-9), 6-4, 2nd rd. (Court Two)

1987   Peter Doohan (No. 70) d. 1st seed defending champ Boris Becker, 7-6 (7-4), 2-6, 6-2, 6-4, 2nd rd.

1990   Derrick Rostagno (No. 129) d. 4th seed John McEnroe 7-5. 6-4, 6-4, 1st rd.

1992   Qualifier Andrei Olhovskiy (No. 193) d. 1st seed Jim Courier, 6-4, 4-6, 6-4, 6-4, 3rd rd.

1994   Qualifier Bryan Shelton d. 2nd seed Michael Stich, 6-3, 7-5, 1-6, 6-7 (7-9), 6-2. 1st rd. (Court Two)

1995   Lucky loser Dick Norman (No. 178) d. 13th seed Stefan Edberg, 6-3, 6-4, 6-4 2nd rd.

1996   Unseeded Richard Krajicek d. 1st seed defending champ Pete Sampras, 7-5, 7-6(7-3), 6-4, OF, ends Sampras' 25-match Wimbledon streak. Also, qualifier Doug Flach (No. 281) d. 3rd seed Andre Agassi, 2-6, 7-6 (7-1), 6-4, 7-6 (8-6), 1st rd. (Court Two)

1997   Nicolas Kiefer (No. 98) d. No. 3 Yevgeny Kafelnikov, 6-2, 7-5, 2-6, 6-1, (Court Two)

1998   Francisco Clavet (No. 36) d. No. 2 seed Marcelo Rios, 6-3, 3-6, 7-5, 3-6, 6-3, 1st rd. (Court Two)

1999   Lorenzo Manta (No. 196) d. No. 5 seed Richard Krajicek, 6-3, 7-6(7-5), 4-6, 4-6, 6-4, 3rd rd. (Court Two)

2000   Qualifier Olivier Rochus (No. 179) d. 3rd seed Magnus Norman, 6-4, 2-6, 6-4, 6-7 (4), 6-1, 2nd rd. Also, Alexander Popp (No. 114) d. No. 4 Gustavo Kuerten, 7-6 (8-6), 6-2, 6-1, 4th rd., (Court Two)

2001   15th seed Roger Federer d. 1st seed defending champion Pete Sampras 7-6(7), 5-7, 6-4, 6-7(2), 7-5 4th rd. ends Sampras' 31-match Wimbledon streak. Also, wild card Goran Ivanisevic (ranked No. 125) d. 4th seeded Marat Safin 7-6 (2), 7-5, 3-6, 7-6 (3) in the QF, 6th seed Tim Henman 7-5, 6-7 (6), 0-6, 7-6 (5), 6-3 in the SF, 3rd seed Patrick Rafter 6-3, 3-6, 6-3, 2-6, 9-7 in the F

2002   Lucky loser George Bastl (No. 145) d. 6th seed Pete Sampras, 6-3, 6-2, 4-6, 3-6, 6-4 in 2nd rd. (Court Two) Also, Olivier Rochus (No. 84), d. 2nd seed Marat Safin 6-2, 6-4, 3-6, 7-6(1) in the 2nd rd. Also Paradorn Srichaphan (No. 67) d. 3rd seed Andre Agassi 6-4, 7-6 (5), 6-2 in 2nd rd. (all same day)

Women

1921   Non-seed Betty Nuthall d. 6th seed MoIla Mallory, 2-6, 6-2, 6-0, 3rd rd.

1928   Non-seed Helene Contostavlos Nicolopoulo d. 5th seed Kea Bouman, 12-10, 8-6, 3rd rd.

1929   Non-seed Mary Hart McIlquham d. 2nd seed Lili de Alvarez, 1928 finalist, 6-4, 4-6, 6-2, 4th rd.

1959   Non-seed Yola Ramirez d. 1st seed Christine Truman, 6-3, 6-2, QF

1962   Non-seed Vera Puzejova Sukova d. 6th seed defending champ Angela Mortimer, 1-6, 6-4, 6-3, 4th rd.: 2nd seed Darlene Hard, 6-4, 6-3, QF; 3rd seed Maria Bueno, 6-4, 6-3, SF

1974   8th seed Olga Morozova d. 1st seed defending champ Billie Jean King, 7-5, 6-2, QF

1983   Non-seed Kathy Jordan d. 2nd seed Chris Evert, 6-1, 7-6 (7-2), 3rd rd. (only time Evert failed to make SF at Wimbledon)

1985   Non-seed Liz Sayers Smylie d. 3rd seed Hana Mandlikova, 6-1, 7-6(7-5), 3rd rd. Also qualifier Molly Van Nostrand (No. 154) d. 4th seed Manuela Maleeva, 7-5, 6-2 in 4th rd.

1986   Anne Hobbs (No. 51) d. No. 9 seed Zina Garrison, 6-4, 0-6, 6-4, (Court Two), 2nd rd.

1990   5th seed Zina Garrison d. 3rd seed Monica Seles. 3-6, 6-3, 9-7 in the QF; 1st seed and defending champ Steffi Graf, 6-3, 3-6, 6-4 in the SF

1991   9th seed Jennifer Capriati, d. 3rd seed and defending champ Martina Navratilova, 6-4, 7-5, QF

1996   Katarina Studenikova (No. 59) d. 2nd seed Monica Seles, 7-5, 5-7, 6-4, 2nd rd.

1997   Anna Kournikova (No. 43) d. 4th seed Iva Majoli, 7-6 (7-1), 6-4, QF. Also, Denise Chladkova (No. 89) d. 5th seed Lindsay Davenport, 7-5, 6-2, 2nd rd.

1998   Non-seed Natasha Zvereva (No. 22) d. 4th seed Steffi Graf, 6-4, 7-5, 3rd rd.; and 6th seed Monica Seles, 7-6 (7-4), 6-2 in the QF. Also, wild card Samantha Smith (No. 94) d. Conchita Martinez (No. 7), 2-6, 6-3, 7-5, (Court Two), 3rd rd.

1999   Mirjana Lucic (No. 134) d. 8th seed Nathalie Tauziat. 4-6. 6-4, 7-5, in QF. Also, Jelena Dokic (No.129) d. No. 1 Martina Hingis, 6-2, 6-0, 1st rd and No. 9 Mary Pierce, 6-4, 6-3, (Court Two) QF

2001   Lilia Osterloh (No. 51) d. No. 13 seed Arantxa Sanchez Vicario, 7-6 (7-4), 7-5, (Court Two), 2nd rd.

2004   No. 13 seed Maria Sharapova d. Serena Williams (Seeded No. 1, defending champion), F, 6-1, 6-4. Also, Karolina Sprem (No. 30) d. No. 3 seed Venus Williams 7-6 (5), 7-6 (6) in 2nd rd. Also, No. 31 seed Amy Frazier d. No. 2 seed Anastasia Myskina 4-6, 6-4, 6-4 in 3rd rd

2005   No. 85-ranked Jill Craybas d. No. 3 seed Serena Williams 6-3, 7-6 (4) in 3rd rd. (Court Two), Also, No. 76 Eleni Daniilidou d. No. 7 seed Justine Henin Hardenne 7-6 (6), 2-6, 7-5 in 1st rd, ending 24-match winning streak

2007   No. 18 seed Marion Bartoli d. No. 1 seed Justine Henin 1-6, 7-5, 6-1 in SF. Also, Laura Granville (No. 77) d. Martina Hingis (Seed No. 9), 6-4, 6-2, (Court Two), 3rd rd.

MATCH POINT SAVED BY SINGLES CHAMPION

Men

1895   F, Wilfred Baddeley d. Wilberforce Eaves, 4-6, 2-6, 8-6, 6-2, 6-3 (Saved 1 MP in the 3rd at 5-6, his lob was 6" long)

1889   F, All-comers, Willie Renshaw d. Harry Barlow, 3-6, 5-7, 8-6, 10-8, 8-6 (Saved 6 MP in the 4th set, 2 at 2-5, 2 at 3-5 and 2 at 6-7, had trailed 0-5 in fifth)

1901   QF, Arthur Gore d. George Hillyard 6-1, 2-6, 4-6, 8-6, 6-2. (Saved 2 MP in the 4th, at 4-5, net cord on MP)

1921   F, Bill Tilden d. Brian "Babe" Norton, 4-6, 2-6, 6-1, 6-0, 7-5. (Saved 2 MP in the 5th, at 4-5)

1927   F, 4th seed Henri Cochet d. 3rd seed Jean Borotra, 4-6, 4-6, 6-3, 6-4, 7-5. (Saved 6 MP in the 5th, 1 at 2-3, 5 at 5-3)

1948   F, 7th seed Bob Falkenburg d. 2nd seed John Bromwich, 7-5, 0-6, 6-2, 3-6, 7-5. (Saved 3 MP in the 5th at 3-5)

1949   QF, 1st seed Ted Schroeder d. 8th seeded Frank Sedgman, 3-6, 6-8, 6-3, 6-2, 9-7 (Saved 2 MP in the 5th, 1 at 4-5, 1 at 5-6)

1960   QF, 1st seed Neale Fraser d. 8th seed Butch Buchholz 4-6, 6-3, 4-6, 15-15, retired, cramps. (Saved 5 MP in the 4th, 1 at 4-5, 2 at 5-6, 2 at 13-14)

Women

1889   F, Blanche Bingley Hillyard d. Helena Rice, 4-6, 8-6, 6-4. (Saved 3 MP, 2nd, at 3-5)

1919   F, Suzanne Lenglen d. Dorothea Douglass Chambers, 10-8, 4-6, 9-7. (Saved 2 MP in the 3rd at 5-6)

1935   F, 4th seed Helen Wills Moody d. 3rd seed Helen Jacobs, 6-3, 3-6, 7-5. (Saved 1 MP in the 3rd, at 3-5)

2005   Venus Williams (Seeded No. 14) d. Lindsay Davenport (Seeded No. 1), 4-6, 7-6 (7-4), 9-7. 2 hours 46 minutes, longest women's final, MP at 4-5 in the third set

2009   Serena Williams d. Elena Dementieva 6-7 (4), 7-5, 8-6, in 2:49, longest women's semifinal at Wimbledon, MP at 4-5, 30-40 in the third set

OTHER GREAT COMEBACKS

Men

1927   All-time champion come-backer: 4th seed Henri Cochet d. non-seed U.S. No. 2 Frank Hunter, 3-6, 2-6, 6-2, 6-2, 6-3 in the QF; 2nd seed Bill Tilden, 3-6, 4-6, 7-5, 6-4, 6-3 in the SF (won 17 straight points from 1-5, 15-all to 5-5, 30-0 in the 3rd set. Was also down a break down, 3-2 in the 5th); 3rd seed defending champ Jean Borotra, 4-6, 4-6, 6-3, 6-4, 7-5, F (saved 6 MP in the 5th, 1 at 2-5, 5 at 5-3)

1953   4th seed Jaroslav Drobny d. non-seed Budge Patty, 8-6, 16-18, 3-6, 8-6, 12-10, 3rd rd., 4:20 (saved 6 MP, 3 in 4th set, 3 in 5th set)

1969   Richard "Pancho" Gonzalez d. Charlie Pasarell, 22-24, 1-6, 16-14, 6-3, 11-9, 1st rd. (saved 7 MP in the 5th, twice serving out of 0-40 to 4-4 and 6-6, won last 11 points)

1974   9th seed Ken Rosewall d. 4th seed Stan Smith, 6-8, 4-6, 9-8 (8-6), 6-1, 6-3, SF (saved 1 MP, 5-6 in tie-breaker. Smith served for the match at 5-4 in 3rd set)

1986   Eric Jelen d. Kevin Curren, 6-4, 6-7 (4-7), 2-6, 6-4, 14-12, (saved 4 MP in 5th set, 1st rd.

1987   7th seed Jimmy Connors d. Mikael Pernfors, 1-6, 1-6, 7-5, 6-4, 6-2, 4th rd. (from 1-4, 3rd, 0-2, 4th)

1988   3rd seed Stefan Edberg d. 9th seed Miloslav Mecir, 4-6, 2-6, 6-4, 6-3, 6-4 (from 3-3, 0-40 in the 3rd, 3-3, 4 break points, 4 deuces in the fourth and from 3-1 down in the 5th). Also qualifier Ricardo Acuna d. David Pate, 3-6, 5-7, 7-6, 7-6 (7-1), 6-4 (saved 4 MP in the 4th in 2R) and Ivan Lendl saved 1 MP in defeating Mark Woodforde, 7-5, 6-7 (6-8), 6-7 (4-7), 7-5, 10-8 in 4R

1996   Non-seed MaliVai Washington (No. 20) d. Alex Radulescu (No. 91), 6-7 (5-7), 7-6 (7-1), 5-7, 7-6 (7-3), 6-4, QF (saved 2 MP, serving at 5-6, 15-40, 4th); also d. 13th seed Todd Martin, 5-7, 6-4, 6-7 (6-8), 6-3, 10-8 (from 2-0 and 5-1 down in the 5th set, 2 points from defeat 4 times: 5-4, 30-15 and 30-all. 6-7, 15-30 and 30-all)

1999   Jim Courier d. Sjeng Schalken 7-6 (2), 3-6, 3-6, 7-5, 13-11, 3d rd. (Saved 2 MP, 1st in 4th set, at 4-5 with forehand inside out winner)

1999   Tim Henman d. Jim Courier, 4-6, 7-5, 5-7, 7-6 (5), 9-7, 4th rd, (Saved 3 MP in 5th set)

1999	Boris Becker d. Miles MacLagan, 5-7, 6-7 (7), 6-4, 7-5, 6-2, (saved 3 MP 4th set, 1st rd.)
2000	2nd seed Andre Agassi d. Todd Martin, 6-4, 2-6, 7-6 (7-3), 2-6, 10-8, 2nd rd. (from 2-5 down: 5th, saved 2 MP at 4-5)
2007	Richard Gasquet d. Andy Roddick 4-6, 4-6, 7-6 (2), 7-6 (3), 8-6 in QF

Women

1924	Kitty McKane d. Helen Wills, 4-6, 6-4, 6-4, F (from 1-4 and 4 break points, 2nd, 3-3, 3rd)
1966	Helga Schultz d. Jeanine Lieffrrig, 4-6, 11-9, 12-10, 1st rd. (saved 11 MP)
1975	3rd seed Billie Jean King d. 1st seed Chris Evert, 2-6, 6-2, 6-3, SF (from 0-3 and 2 break points in 3rd set)
1977	Maria Bueno d. Janet Newberry, 1-6, 8-6, 8-6, 2nd rd. (saved 1 MP at 6-5, 3rd)
1978	14th seed Sue Barker d. Pam Shriver, 2-6, 8-6, 7-5, 3rd rd. (from 0-3. 3-5 3rd; saved 3 MP, 3rd, 1 at 5-3, 2 at 5-4)
1980	5th seed Billie Jean King d. Pam Shriver, 5-7, 7-6 (7-5), 10-8, 4th rd. (saved 1 MP, 2d, at 5-4; behind 4-2, 3rd)
1982	12th seed Billie Jean King d. Tanya Harford, 5-7, 7-6 (7-5), 6-3, 3rd rd. (saved 3 MP in the 2nd at 4-5, 0-40): Also, JoAnne Russell (No. 32) d. 8th seed Mima Jausovec, 6-7 (2-7), 6-3, 7-5 (saved 2 MP in 3rd). Also Virginia Wade d. Jo Durie, 3-6, 7-6 (15-13), 6-2, 1st rd. (saved 4 MP in tie-break)
1983	Virginia Wade d. Eva Pfaff, 3-6, 7-6 (7-5), 7-5, 4th rd. (saved MP at 4-5 in the 3rd)
1987	5th seed Pam Shriver d. 16th seed Sylvia Hanika, 6-7(4-7), 7-5, 10-8 in 4th rd (saved 2 MP in the 3rd at 5-6) Also, Shriver d. 4th seed Helena Sukova 4-6, 7-6 (1), 10-8 in QF (save 1 MP in 3rd at 6-7)
1990	5th seed Zina Garrison d. 3rd seed Monica Seles, 3-6, 6-3. 9-7 in QF (saved MP at 6-7, 3rd, with forehand winner)
1995	Chanda Rubln d. Patricia Hy-Boulais 7-5 (7-4). 6-7(5-7), 17-15. 2nd rd. (broke Hy-Boulais when she served for the match at 10-9, 13-12, 15-14. Time. 3:45)
1998	16th seed Nathalie Tauziat d. Natasha Zvereva (No. 22), 1-6, 7-6 (7-1), 6-3, SF (3 points from defeat, 2nd, at 5-6, 15-15)
2006	Qualifier Severine Bremond d. Gisela Dulko 7-6 (6), 5-7, 7-5 (saved 5 MP) in 3rd rd. Also, in 4th rd d. No. 18 seed Ai Sugiyama 7-6 (11), 6-3, saving 9 set points in first set.
2007	Martina Hingis d. Naomi Cavady 6-7 (1-7), 7-5, 6-0 in 1st rd (saved two match points at 5-4 in second set, before winning last nine games)
2007	Ana Ivanovic d. Nicole Vaidisova 4-6, 6-2, 7-5 in the QF (saved 3 MP at 5-3 in 3rd set)

MATCH POINTS SAVED BY DOUBLES CHAMPIONS

Men

1927	F, Frank T. Hunter / Bill Tilden d. Jacques Brugnon / Henri Cochet, 1-6, 4-6, 8-6, 6-3, 6-4. (Saved 2 MPs in 3rd set at 4-5)
1935	F, Jack Crawford / Adrian Quist d. Wilmer Allison / Johnny Van Ryn, 6-3, 5-7, 6-2, 5-7, 7-5. (Saved 1 MP at 4-5 in 5th set)

1986	QF, Joakim Nystrom / Mats Wilander, d. Ken Flach / Robert Seguso, 3-6, 4-6, 7-6 (8-6), 6-4, 11-9. (Saved 6 MPs, 4 in 3rd set, 3 at 4-5, 1 in the tie breaker and 2 in 5th set at 4-5)
1989	1st round, John Fitzgerald / Anders Jarryd d. Matt Anger / Marty Davis, 6-7 (3-7), 6-4, 6-4, 4-6, 18-16. (Saved 1 MP in 5th set at 10-11)
1992	F, John McEnroe / Michael Stich d. Jim Grabb / Richey Reneberg, 5-7, 7-6 (7-5), 3-6, 7-6 (7-5), 19-17. (Saved 2 MPs in the 5th set at 6-7)
2001	QF, Don Johnson / Jared Palmer d. Juan Balcells / Sjeng Schalken, 3-6, 6-7 (5-7), 7-6 (7-5), 7-6 (8-6), 6-4. (Saved 4 MPs in 4th set at 4-5)

Women

1926	2nd rd., Mary K. Browne / Elizabeth Ryan d. Suzanne Lenglen / Didi Vlasto, 3-6, 9-7, 6-2. (Saved 3 MPs in 2nd set at 6-7)
1932	1st rd., Doris Metaxa / Josane Sigart d. G.M. Heeley / Freda James, 2-6, 6-4, 7-5. (Saved 3 MPs in 3rd set at 2-5)
1947	F, Doris Hart / Pat Canning Todd d. Louise Brough / Margaret Osborne (duPont), 3-6, 6-4, 7-5. (Saved 3 MPs in 3rd set at 3-5)
1954	F, Louise Brough / Margaret Osborne duPont d. Shirley Fry / Doris Hart, 4-6, 9-7, 6-3. (Saved 2 MPs in 2nd set at 3-5)
1978	F, Kerry Melville Reid / Wendy Turnbull d. Mima Jausovec / Virginia Ruzici, 4-6, 9-8 (12-10), 6-3. (Saved 2 MPs in 2nd set tiebreaker)
1988	F., Steffi Graf / Gabriela Sabatini d. Larisa Savchenko / Natasha Zvereva, 6-3, 1-6, 12-10. (Saved 2 MPs in 3rd set at 4-5)
1992	SF, Gigi Fernandez / Natasha Zvereva d. Arantxa Sanchez-Vicario / Helena Sukova 6-1, 6-7 (2-7), 7-5. (Saved 1 MP at 4-5 in the 3rd set)

MATCH POINTS SAVED BY MIXED DOUBLES CHAMPIONS TEAM

1960	F, Rod Laver / Darlene Hard d. Bob Howe / Maria Bueno 13-11, 3-6, 8-6. (Saved 3 MPs in the 3rd set at 4-5)
1976	F, Tony Roche / Francoise Durr d. Dick Stockton and Rosie Casals, 6-3, 2-6, 7-5. (Saved 1 MP in 3rd set at 4-5)
1980	F., John Austin / Tracy Austin d. Mark Edmonson / Dianne Fromholtz, 4-6, 7-6 (8-6), 6-3. (Saved 3 MPs in 2nd set, one at 4-5, two in the tie-breaker)
1985	SF., Paul McNamee / Martina Navratilova d. Scott Davis / Betsy Nagelson 6-7 (4-7), 7-5, 23-21. (Saved 2 MPs, one in 2nd set at 4-5, one in 3rd set at 6-7)
1989	QF, Jim Pugh / Jana Novotna d. David Wheaton / Mary Joe Fernandez, 2-6, 6-4, 9-7. (Saved 1 MP in 3rd set at 6-7)
1991	SF, John Fitzgerald / Liz Smylie d. Christo Van Rensburg / Elna Reinach, 7-5, 3-6, 7-5. (Saved I MP in 3rd set at 4-5)
1996	2nd rd., Cyril Suk / Helena Sukova d. Peter Tramacchi / Rennae Stubbs, 5-7, 7-6 (7-3), 6-2. (Saved 1 MP in 2nd set, at 4-5)
2004	3rd rd., Wayne Black / Cara Black d. Leander Paes / Martina Navratilova 7-6 (9-7), 6-7 (5-7), 13-11. (Saved 2 MPs, 3rd set at 4-5)

2004   F., Wayne Black / Cara Black d. Todd Woodbridge / Alicia Molik, 3-6, 7-6 (10-8), 6-4. (Saved 6 MPs in 2nd set tiebreaker)

MOST YEARS SEEDED

Men

Jimmy Connors	17

Women

Martina Navratilova	20

MOST YEARS SEEDED NO. 1

Men

Pete Sampras	8

Women

Margaret Smith Court	8
Martina Navratilova	
Steffi Graf	

UNSEEDED CHAMPIONS

Men

1985	Boris Becker
1996	Richard Krajicek
2001	Goran Ivanisevic

Women

None

UNSEEDED FINALISTS

Men

1930	Wilmer Allison
1953	Kurt Nielsen
1955	Kurt Neilsen
1959	Rod Laver
1962	Marty Mulligan
1963	Fred Stolle
1967	Willy Bungert
1983	Chris Lewis
1985	Boris Becker
1996	Richard Krajicek
1996	MaliVai Washington
1997	Cedric Pioline
2001	Goran Ivanisevic
2003	Mark Philippoussis

Women

1938	Helen Jacobs
1958	Angela Mortimer
1962	Vera Sukova
1963	Billie Jean Moffitt

FARTHEST ADVANCEMENT OF A QUALIFIER

Men

John McEnroe	1978 semifinals
Vladimir Voltchov	2000 semifinals

Women

Alexandra Stevenson	1999 semifinals

FARTHEST ADVANCEMENT OF A LUCKY LOSER

Men

Bernie Mitton	1973 fourth round
Jaidip Mukerjea	1973 fourth round
John McCurdy	1983 fourth round
Dick Norman	1995 fourth round

Women

Francoise Lemal	1955 Third Round
Erika Launert	1959 Third Round
Tine Zwann	1974 Third Round

FARTHEST ADVANCEMENT OF A WILD CARD

Men

Goran Ivanisevic	2001 champion

Women

Zina Garrison	1982 Fourth Round
Anne Smith	1985 Fourth Round
Samantha Smith	1998 Fourth Round
Maria Sharapova	2003 Fourth Round
Zheng Jie	2008 Semifinals

ACES

Men

54	Gary Muller d. Peter Lundgren, 1993 qualifying tournament, 1993
51	Ivo Karlovic lost to Daniele Bracciali 6-7 (4-7), 7-6 (10-8), 3-6, 7-6 (7-5), 12-10, 1st rd. (Bracciali had 31; overall record 82, both players), 2005
50	Roger Federer d. Andy Roddick 5-7, 7-6 (6), 7-6 (5), 3-6, 16-14, F, 2009
46	Ivo Karlovic, def Jo-Wilfried Tsonga, 7-6 (7-5), 6-7 (5-7), 7-5, 7-6 (7-5), 2009 3rd rd.
46	Goran Ivanisevic lost to Magnus Norman (25 aces), 6-3, 2-6, 7-6 (7-4), 4-6, 14-12, 3rd rd., 1997
46	Mark Phílippoussis d. Andre Agassi, 6-3, 2-6, 6-7 (4-7), 6-3, 6-4, QF, 2003
44	Mark Philippoussis d. Sjeng Schalken (34 aces), 4-6, 6-3, 6-7 (7-9), 7-6 (7-4), 20-18, 4th rd., 2000
44	Goran Ivanisevic d. Daniel Vacek, (12 aces), 6-7 (6-8), 7-6 (7-4), 6-3, 6-4, 4th rd., 1998
43	Andy Roddick d. Lleyton Hewitt 6-3, 6-7 (10), 7-6 (1), 4-6, 6-4, 2008 QF
43	Alex Waske lost to Stefano Galvani, 4-6, 7-6 (7-2), 6-4, 3-6, 16-14, 1st rd, 2006, 14th DF on MP 53 total aces, 25 DF
43	Goran Ivanisevic d. Richard Krajicek (28 aces), 6-3, 6-4, 5-7, 6-7 (5-7), 15-13, SF, 1998
43	Steve Warner, 16 DF, d. Matt Anger (14 A, 9 DF), 7-5, 1-6, 7-6 (7-2), 28-26, qualifying tournament, 1989, in 5:16
42	John Feaver lost to John Newcombe, 6-3, 3-6, 8-9, 6-4, 6-4, 3rd. rd., 1976
41	Marc Goellner d. Jordi Burillo (23 aces), 4-6, 5-7, 6-3, 6-1, 6-2, 1st rd., 1998

41   Goran Ivanisevic d. Andy Roddick, (had 20 aces), 7-6 (7-5), 7-5, 3-6, 6-3, 3rd rd. 2001

40   Marc Goellner (also had 34 DF) d. David Prinosil, 6-4, 6-7 (7-9), 4-6, 6-3, 13-11, 1st rd., 1995

Women

20   Serena Williams d. Elena Dementieva 6-7 (4), 7-5, 8-6, SF, 2009

19   Meghann Shaughnessy d. Nuria Llagostera Vives 6-4, 4-6, 10-8, 2nd rd, 2004

18   Samantha Stosur d. Kristina Brandi, 4-6, 6-2, 6-2, 1st rd., 2007

18   Julie Coin (lost to Dominika Cibulkova 6-4, 3-6, 6-3, 1st rd, 2009)

17   Brenda Schultz-McCarthy d. Radka Bobkova, 6-7(4-7), 7-6(7-3), 6-1, 1st rd., 1995

ACES FOR TOURNAMENT

Men

212   Goran Ivanisevic   2001

206   Goran Ivanisevic   1992

SERVICE SPEED

Men

146 mph Andy Roddick   2004

Women

128 mph Venus Williams   2008

DOUBLE FAULTS

Men

34 Marc Goellner (also had 40 aces) d. David Prinosil 6-4, 6-7 (7-9), 4-6, 6-3, 13-11, 1st rd. 1995

26 Marc Rosset lost to Michael Joyce, 6-0, 6-7 (8-10), 7-5, 6-2, 1st rd., 1995

Women

17 Elena Dementieva d. Sabine Klaschka 2-6, 6-3, 8-6, 2d rd., 2005

U.S. Championships CHAPTER 9

Jimmy Connors is one player who is synonymous with the U.S. Championships—winning five men's singles titles and being the only player to win the title on three different surfaces (grass, clay and hard). In 1991, at the age of 39, he had a celebrated and passionate run to the semifinals.

Four years after the All England Club (Wimbledon) introduced tournament tennis in 1877, the United States got into the game with a national championship at a Rhode Island site, the newly constructed Newport Casino. It was a men-only affair at that inaugural United States Championships, the U.S. Tennis Association-owned event that would evolve in 1968 to what we now know as the U.S. Open (for men and women).

Dick Sears, a 19-year-old Bostonian studying at Harvard, made his way to Newport in 1881 and won the first title, a 6-0, 6-3, 6-2 decision over an Englishman summering in Newport, William Glyn. Twenty-four others showed up, and the tournament was profitable, netting $4.32. Financially it became more rewarding, earning about $130 million in 2007.

That initial triumph was the start of a unique run of seven singles titles for Sears, who also won the doubles six straight times from 1882, five with his mentor, Bostonian Dr. James Dwight, the Father of American tennis.

As years passed, a variety of locations played host to the Championships, which were often called the Nationals. The longest-running site—1915 through 1977—was the West Side Tennis Club of New York, located in the Forest Hills neighborhood of Queens. Wherever, the surface was always an Elysian Field, grass—until 1975 when clay was installed for the Open's last three years at Forest Hills.

In 1978, the Open moved a few miles to Flushing Meadow, though remaining in Queens, at a new ground, the USTA National Tennis Center featuring hard courts of asphalt composition. It was re-named the USTA Billie Jean King National Tennis Center in 2006.

After a 34-year stand at the Newport Casino, the men's U.S. Championships, reflecting increased, broader interest in the game, shifted to New York and Forest Hills. (Never-

theless, the Casino, the world's elder among active tennis venues, continued to present an annual men's tourney, a stopover on the Eastern grass circuit through 1967. In 1965, professional tennis came to the Casino, and remains to this day in a July week on the ATP tournament calendar). The Casino is also home of the International Tennis Hall of Fame, founded in 1954, proposed by long-time habitue Jimmy Van Alen

In 1887, six years after the first men's championship, the women's U.S. Championships (singles and doubles) was launched at the Philadelphia Cricket Club, and remained there through 1920, along with mixed doubles, begun in 1892. A 17-year-old Philadelphian, Ellen Hansell, was the original champ, defeating Laura Knight, 6-1, 6-0.

In 1921, the women's singles and doubles moved to Forest Hills, but as an event prior to and separate from the men's championship, while the mixed doubles moved to Boston's Longwood Cricket Club, to be played concurrently with the men's doubles.

The doubles tournament has a wandering history. The men's variety was played along with singles at Newport between 1881 and 1886. From 1887 through 1914, sectional doubles tournaments, East and West, sometimes North and South as well, were staged at a variety of locations with the winners playing off for the title at Newport. In 1915, with the singles moving to Forest Hills, the doubles final for sectional winners went along, too. But in 1917, the men's doubles championship, a newly minted tournament standing on its own, as the U.S. (or National) Doubles, settled in at Longwood through 1967 with two exceptions: 1934 at Philadelphia's Germantown Cricket Club; 1942 through 1945 at Forest Hills during World War II.

The men's singles parted briefly with Forest Hills for three years (1921—23, at Germantown), then returned to benefit from the freshly-built concrete horseshoe stadium.

At last, integration of the men's and women's singles championships took place in 1935 at Forest Hills, the women's doubles sent to Longwood as part of the U.S. Doubles. Wartime travel restrictions prompted bunching the five championships at one site, Forest Hills, 1942—45. In 1946, men's and women's doubles returned to Longwood but the mixed remained at Forest Hills until a 1967 placement at Longwood.

Of the majors, only the U.S. operated during World Wars I and II. Although the 1917-18 tournaments were considered "Patriotic" events, raising money for war relief, they were later recognized as official U.S. Championships.

"Open" tennis dawned in 1968, uniting amateurs and pros, and took American form at Forest Hills as the first U.S. Open, offering a prize money pot of $100,000. The Championships, an amateur event closed to professionals since 1881 inception, was relocated at Longwood. Men's and women's singles and doubles and mixed were played under the banner of the U.S. Amateur in 1968-69. (Some negative officials, fearing that the Open would be a costly flop, saw to it that the USTA maintained the continuity of the Championships as an amateur event in case the "Open" concept was abandoned.) That obviously didn't happen. But for two years, 1968 and 1969, the USTA confusingly listed two Championships (Curiously, prize money was paid at the 1969 "Amateur".)

Lieut. Arthur Ashe of the U.S. Army, an amateur, won both the U.S. Amateur and U.S. Open in 1968, a feat that appears very unlikely to happen again. He beat Davis Cup teammate Bob Lutz at Longwood, 4-6, 6-3, 8-10, 6-0, 6-4, and Netherlander Tom Okker at Forest Hills, 14-12, 5-7, 6-3, 3-6, 6-3. But Okker, a pro, was awarded first prize, $14,000. Aussie Margaret Court beat Brazilian Maria Bueno, 6-2, 6-2, for the Amateur title. Brit Virginia Wade took Billie Jean King, 6-4, 6-4, and $6,000 first prize at the Open.

Since 1973, equal prize money has been paid men and women, the U.S. the first major to do so. Aussies Margaret Court and John Newcombe collected $25,000 apiece as champs. Escalating prize money reached $19.6 million in 2007. The champs, Swiss Roger Federer and Belgian Justine Henin, got $1.4 million each.

In singles, the challenge round system was in force in the early days: from 1884 through 1911 for men, 1888 through 1919 for women. This meant that the defending champion played only one match, waiting for a challenger to emerge from an all-comers tournament. If the defender chose not to play in the year following his/her victory, the winner of the all-comers final became champion.

In 1970, the USTA approved use of a tie-breaker to conclude sets that reached 6-6 in games—a first for a major. All sets are created equal in the U.S., but the other three majors, while presently adopting the tie-breaker, play out the ultimate sets (fifth for men, third for women) as deuce sets requiring settlement by a two-game margin. From 1970 through 1974, the U.S. used a "sudden death," best-of-nine-points breaker. Thereafter, the U.S. joined the rest of the world in the ITF breaker, best-of-12-points, but with a margin of at least two points, thus "lingering death."

Night play began in 1975 when floodlights illuminated the Forest Hills stadium, and continued at the Meadow with several courts lighted.

The original championship venues, the Casino and Philadelphia Cricket held about 3000. Temporary stands at the West Side Tennis Club at Forest Hills accommodated about 10,000 from 1915 to 1922. The club's concrete horseshoe stadium, ready in 1923, seated 15,000, although a record 16,253, crowded in for the Jimmy Connors over Bjorn Borg final of 1976. With 21,000-seat Louis Armstrong Stadium (named for the jazz trumpeter who lived in the neighborhood) available in Flushing, attendance soared. Even more so when 23,737-seat Arthur Ashe Stadium (the world's largest tennis pen) was added to the complex in 1997. In 2007, attendance records were set: 61,083 for combined day/night session record on Saturday, Sept. 1; and the tournament (26 sessions), 715,587.

Over the years, U.S. Championships of lesser importance have been determined on clay, hard and indoor courts at various locations for men and women. Only the men's Clay Court has been held annually from its establishment at Omaha, Nebraska, in 1910, and was most recently played at Houston in 2009. The women joined the men in 1912 at Pittsburgh, and the event moved about the country, the female tourney discontinued after 1986. The Indoor Championships, begun at New York's Seventh Regiment Armory in 1898 for men and 1907 for women, were discontinued after 1988 and 1987, respectively.

Seeding, to separate leading players, began at the U.S. men's championships of 1922, and was introduced at Wimbledon in 1924.

U.S. Championships — Tournament Results

Legend: Ch: Challenge Round; **F:** Final; **S:** Semifinal; **Q:** Quarterfinal; **Set:** S1, S2, S3, S4, S5

Men's Singles

Rd	Winner	Defeated	S1	S2	S3	S4	S5
1881							
F	Richard Sears (USA)	William Glyn (GBR)	6-0	6-3	6-2		
S	Richard Sears (USA)	Edward Gray (USA)	6-3	6-0			
S	William Glyn (GBR)	Robert Gould Shaw (USA)	6-2	6-2			
Q	Richard Sears (USA)	Crawford Nightingale (USA)	6-3	6-5			
Q	Edward Gray (USA)		(bye)				
Q	William Glyn (GBR)	William Gammell, Jr. (USA)	6-4	4-6	6-4		
Q	Robert Gould Shaw (USA)	Mr. Kessler (USA)	6-1	6-2			
1882							
F	Richard Sears (USA)	Clarence Clark (USA)	6-1	6-4	6-0		
S	Richard Sears (USA)		(bye)				
S	Clarence Clark (USA)	Edward Gray (USA)	6-2	6-2			
Q	Richard Sears (USA)	James Rankine (USA)	6-0	6-4			
Q	Clarence Clark (USA)	James Dwight (USA)	(default)				
Q	Edward Gray (USA)		(bye)				
1883							
F	Richard Sears (USA)	James Dwight (USA)	6-2	6-0	9-7		
S	Richard Sears (USA)	Foxhall Keane (USA)	6-0	6-0			
S	James Dwight (USA)	Richard Conover (USA)	6-4	6-3			
Q	Richard Sears (USA)	H. Willing Hare Powell (USA)	6-2	6-0			
Q	Foxhall Keane (USA)	G. Mathewson Smith (USA)	6-3	6-4			
Q	James Dwight (USA)	Godfrey Brinley (USA)	6-2	6-3			
Q	Richard Conover (USA)		(bye)				
1884							
Ch	Richard Sears (USA)	Howard Taylor (USA)	6-0	1-6	6-0	6-2	
F	Howard Taylor (USA)	William V.S. Thorne (USA)	6-4	4-6	6-1	6-4	
S	Howard Taylor (USA)	Percy Knapp (USA)	6-2	2-6	6-1		
S	William V.S. Thorne (USA)	Clarence Clark (USA)	2-6	6-2	6-3		
Q	Percy Knapp (USA)	Livingston Beeckman (USA)	6-1	6-2			
Q	Howard Taylor (USA)	Alex. Van Rensselaer (USA)	6-4	6-1			
Q	William V.S. Thorne (USA)	George Richards (USA)			(default)		
Q	Clarence Clark (USA)	A.C. Galt (USA)	6-2	6-2			
1885							
Ch	Richard Sears (USA)	Godfrey Brinley (USA)	6-3	4-6	6-0	6-3	
F	Godfrey Brinley (USA)	Percy Knapp (USA)	6-3	6-3	3-6	6-4	
S	Percy Knapp (USA)	Joseph Clark (USA)	6-4	6-3			
S	Godfrey Brinley (USA)	Walter Berry (USA)	3-6	9-7	6-1		
Q	Joseph Clark (USA)	Alex Moffat (USA)	7-6	1-6	6-3		
Q	Percy Knapp (USA)	Howard Taylor (USA)	4-6	10-8	6-2		
Q	Godfrey Brinley (USA)	Charles Belmont Davis (USA)	6-2	6-1			
Q	Walter Berry (USA)	Foxhall Keane (USA)	6-2	6-1			
1886							
Ch	Richard Sears (USA)	Livingston Beeckman (USA)	4-6	6-1	6-3	6-4	
F	Livingston Beeckman (USA)	Howard Taylor (USA)	2-6	6-3	6-4	6-2	
S	Howard Taylor (USA)	Joseph Clark (USA)	6-5	6-2	6-3		
S	Livingston Beeckman (USA)	Charles Chase (USA)	6-4	6-0	6-2		
Q	Joseph Clark (USA)	Henry Slocum (USA)	1-6	6-5	6-5	6-2	
Q	Howard Taylor (USA)	Quincy A. Shaw (USA)	6-3	6-5	6-5		
Q	Livingston Beeckman (USA)	Fred Mansfield (USA)	6-4	3-6	6-0	6-3	
Q	Charles Chase (USA)	Morgan G. Post (USA)	6-0	6-2	6-4		
1887							
Ch	Richard Sears (USA)	Henry Slocum (USA)	6-1	6-3	6-2		
F	Henry Slocum (USA)	Howard Taylor (USA)	12-10	7-5	6-4		
S	Henry Slocum (USA)	Joseph Clark (USA)	6-8	6-4	6-3	6-2	
S	Howard Taylor (USA)	William L. Thatcher (USA)	6-3	6-1	6-1		
Q	Joseph Clark (USA)	Fred Mansfield (USA)	3-6	6-2	6-8	6-1	6-4
Q	Henry Slocum (USA)	George Fearing (USA)	6-1	7-5	6-2		
Q	Howard Taylor (USA)	Philip Sears (USA)	6-1	1-6	6-3	6-1	
Q	William L. Tatcher (USA)	Godfrey Brinley (USA)	6-4	8-6	3-6	6-4	
1888							
Ch	Henry Slocum (USA)	Richard Sears (USA)	(default)				
F	Henry Slocum (USA)	Howard Taylor (USA)	6-4	6-1	6-0		
S	Henry Slocum (USA)	Oliver Campbell (USA)	6-2	6-3	6-4		
S	Howard Taylor (USA)	Philip Sears (USA)	5-7	6-4	6-2	6-2	
Q	Henry Slocum (USA)	James Dwight (USA)	4-6	6-3	6-0	6-2	
Q	Oliver Campbell (USA)	A. Empie Wright (USA)	4-6	6-3	1-6	8-6	6-2
Q	Philip Sears (USA)	John Ryerson (USA)	8-6	6-0	6-4		
Q	Howard Taylor (USA)	Arhur L. Williston (USA)	6-2	6-3	7-5		
1889							
Ch	Henry Slocum (USA)	Quincy A. Shaw (USA)	6-3	6-1	4-6	6-2	
F	Quincy A. Shaw (USA)	Oliver Campbell (USA)	1-6	6-4	6-3	6-4	
S	Quincy A. Shaw (USA)	Percy Knapp (USA)	4-6	6-1	6-4	6-4	
S	Oliver Campbell (USA)	Ernest G. Meers (USA)	5-7	6-1	5-7	6-4	6-2
Q	Quincy A. Shaw (USA)	Charles Chase (USA)	6-4	6-4	4-6	6-3	
Q	Percy Knapp (USA)	Dean Miller (USA)	6-4	6-3	6-2		
Q	Ernest G. Meers (USA)	Fred Mansfield (USA)	6-1	6-2	6-2		
Q	Oliver Campbell (USA)	Joseph Clark (USA)	10-12	7-5	6-3	6-3	

1890

Rd	Winner	Defeated	S1	S2	S3	S4	S5
Ch	Oliver Campbell (USA)	Henry Slocum (USA)	6-2	4-6	6-3	6-1	
F	Oliver Campbell (USA)	Percy Knapp (USA)	8-6	0-6	6-2	6-3	
S	Percy Knapp (USA)	Clarence Hobart (USA)	10-8	7-5	6-2		
S	Oliver Campbell (USA)	Bob Huntington (USA)	3-6	6-2	5-7	6-2	6-1
Q	Clarence Hobart (USA)	Valentine Hall (USA)	6-4	6-3	5-7	3-6	6-3
Q	Percy Knapp (USA)	Charles Chase (USA)	6-2	6-8	6-3	6-3	
Q	Oliver Campbell (USA)	John Ryerson (USA)	6-1	7-5	6-3		
Q	Bob Huntington (USA)	George W. Lee (USA)	5-7	6-1	6-1	6-1	

1891

Rd	Winner	Defeated	S1	S2	S3	S4	S5
Ch	Oliver Campbell (USA)	Clarence Hobart (USA)	2-6	7-5	7-9	6-1	6-2
F	Clarence Hobart (USA)	Fred Hovey (USA)	6-4	3-6	6-4	6-8	6-0
S	Clarence Hobart (USA)	Valentine Hall (USA)	6-2	6-4	6-2		
S	Fred Hovey (USA)	Marmaduke Smith (USA)	6-4	6-2	3-6	1-6	6-4
Q	Clarence Hobart (USA)	Edward Hall (USA)	3-6	6-4	11-9	6-4	
Q	Valentine Hall (USA)	Charles Lee (USA)	6-4	6-4	0-6	6-0	
Q	Fred Hovey (USA)	Allison W. Post (USA)	4-6	6-4	6-3	6-0	2-6
Q	Marmaduke Smith (USA)	Joseph Clark (USA)	6-1	6-0	6-4		

1892

Rd	Winner	Defeated	S1	S2	S3	S4	S5
Ch	Oliver Campbell (USA)	Fred Hovey (USA)	7-5	3-6	6-3	7-5	
F	Fred Hovey (USA)	Bill Larned (USA)	6-0	6-2	7-5		
S	Fred Hovey (USA)	Robert Wrenn (USA)	6-4	7-5	6-3		
S	Bill Larned (USA)	Edward Hall (USA)	2-6	6-0	6-4	1-6	8-6
Q	Robert Wrenn (USA)	Mantle Fielding (USA)	6-1	4-6	9-7	6-0	
Q	Fred Hovey (USA)	Richard Stevens (USA)	6-1	6-4	6-0		
Q	Edward Hall (USA)	Samuel Chase (USA)	1-6	6-3	4-6	6-2	6-3
Q	Bill Larned (USA)	Valentine Hall (USA)	6-4	6-3	7-5		

1893

Rd	Winner	Defeated	S1	S2	S3	S4	S5
Ch	Robert Wrenn (USA)	Oliver Campbell (USA)	(default)				
F	Robert Wrenn (USA)	Fred Hovey (USA)	6-4	3-6	6-4	6-4	
S	Robert Wrenn (USA)	Samuel Chase (USA)	8-6	6-1	6-2		
S	Fred Hovey (USA)	Clarence Hobart (USA)	7-5	6-0	6-3		
Q	Robert Wrenn (USA)	Richard Stevens (USA)	6-1	6-2	2-6	6-2	
Q	Samuel Chase (USA)	Duncan Candler (USA)	6-3	6-4	6-2		
Q	Clarence Hobart (USA)	Bill Larned (USA)	6-3	6-4	3-6	5-7	6-2
Q	Fred Hovey (USA)	Valentine Hall (USA)	6-2	5-7	8-6	6-2	

1894

Rd	Winner	Defeated	S1	S2	S3	S4	S5
Ch	Robert Wrenn (USA)	Manliffe Goodbody (IRL)	6-8	6-1	6-4	6-4	
F	Manliffe Goodbody (IRL)	Bill Larned (USA)	4-6	6-1	3-6	7-5	6-2
S	Manliffe Goodbody (IRL)	J.B. Read (USA)	3-6	6-0	6-0	6-1	
S	Bill Larned (USA)	Malcolm Chace (USA)	6-4	6-2	8-6		
Q	J.B. Read (USA)	Samuel G. Thomson (USA)	6-3	6-1	6-2		
Q	Manliffe Goodbody (IRL)	Clarence Hobart (USA)	6-2	6-2	2-6	3-6	8-6
Q	Bill Larned (USA)	Richard Stevens (USA)	6-2	4-6	6-3	8-6	
Q	Malcolm Chace (USA)	Charles E. Sands (USA)	7-5	6-2	7-5		

1895

Rd	Winner	Defeated	S1	S2	S3	S4	S5
Ch	Fred Hovey (USA)	Robert Wrenn (USA)	6-3	6-2	6-4		
F	Fred Hovey (USA)	Bill Larned (USA)	6-1	9-7	6-4		
S	Fred Hovey (USA)	Carr Neel (USA)	6-4	6-4	6-4		
S	Bill Larned (USA)	John Howland (USA)	7-5	8-6	6-1		
Q	Fred Hovey (USA)	Charles Hinckley (USA)	6-1	6-2	7-5		
Q	Carr Neel (USA)	Malcolm Chace (USA)	6-4	6-1	6-4		
Q	John Howland (USA)	Clarence Budlong (USA)	6-3	2-6	6-4	6-3	
Q	Bill Larned (USA)	Arthur Foote (USA)	6-3	6-4	3-6	6-1	

1896

Rd	Winner	Defeated	S1	S2	S3	S4	S5
Ch	Robert Wrenn (USA)	Fred Hovey (USA)	7-5	3-6	6-0	1-6	6-1
F	Robert Wrenn (USA)	Bill Larned (USA)	4-6	3-6	6-4	6-4	6-3
S	Robert Wrenn (USA)	Carr Neel (USA)	2-6	14-12	4-6	6-4	6-1
S	Bill Larned (USA)	Edwin Fischer (USA)	6-1	6-2	6-1		
Q	Carr Neel (USA)	Richard Stevens (USA)	6-4	6-0	7-9	9-7	
Q	Robert Wrenn (USA)	George Wrenn (USA)	2-6	9-7	7-5	9-7	
Q	Bill Larned (USA)	Malcolm Whitman (USA)	6-4	6-1	6-2		
Q	Edwin Fischer (USA)	George Sheldon (USA)	6-4	7-5	2-6	8-6	

1897

Rd	Winner	Defeated	S1	S2	S3	S4	S5
Ch	Robert Wrenn (USA)	Wilberforce Eaves (AUS)	4-6	8-6	6-3	2-6	6-2
F	Wilberforce Eaves (AUS)	Harold Nisbet (GBR)	7-5	6-3	6-2		
S	Harold Nisbet (GBR)	Bill Larned (USA)	3-6	2-6	9-7	6-4	6-4
S	Wilberforce Eaves (AUS)	Leo Ware (USA)	6-0	6-2	6-4		
Q	Harold Nisbet (GBR)	Malcolm Whitman (USA)	8-6	4-6	6-4	3-6	7-5
Q	Bill Larned (USA)	Edwin Fischer (USA)	6-4	6-1	6-3		
Q	Wilberforce Eaves (AUS)	Parmly Paret (USA)	6-4	6-1	3-6	6-3	
Q	Leo Ware (USA)	Holcombe Ward (USA)	6-3	6-4	6-4		

1898

Rd	Winner	Defeated	S1	S2	S3	S4	S5
Ch	Malcolm Whitman (USA)	Robert Wrenn (USA)	(default)				
F	Malcolm Whitman (USA)	Dwight Davis (USA)	3-6	6-2	6-2	6-1	
S	Dwight Davis (USA)	William Bond (USA)	6-1	11-13	6-4	6-3	
S	Malcolm Whitman (USA)	Leo Ware (USA)	6-2	6-0	6-2		
Q	William Bond (USA)	Holcombe Ward (USA)	6-3	6-3	6-4		
Q	Dwight Davis (USA)	Richard Stevens (USA)	8-6	6-4	7-5		
Q	Leo Ware (USA)	George W. Lee (USA)	6-2	6-3	6-4		
Q	Malcolm Whitman (USA)	Clarence Budlong (USA)	11-9	4-6	4-6	6-2	8-6

1899

Rd	Winner	Defeated	S1	S2	S3	S4	S5
Ch	Malcolm Whitman (USA)	Parmly Paret (USA)	6-1	6-2	3-6	7-5	
F	Parmly Paret (USA)	Dwight Davis (USA)	7-5	8-10	6-3	2-6	6-4
S	Parmly Paret (USA)	Leo Ware (USA)	7-5	6-2	6-4		
S	Dwight Davis (USA)	Kreigh Collins (USA)	6-4	6-1	8-6		
Q	Leo Ware (USA)	Holcombe Ward (USA)	3-6	6-4	9-11	6-2	6-4
Q	Parmly Paret (USA)	Bob Huntington (USA)	3-6	6-3	4-6	6-4	6-0
Q	Dwight Davis (USA)	William Bond (USA)	6-4	6-4	1-6	6-4	
Q	Kreigh Collins (USA)	George Wrenn (USA)	8-6	4-6	4-6	6-4	6-3

1900

Rd	Winner	Defeated	S1	S2	S3	S4	S5
Ch	Malcolm Whitman (USA)	Bill Larned (USA)	6-4	1-6	6-2	6-2	
F	Bill Larned (USA)	George Wrenn (USA)	6-3	6-2	6-2		
S	Bill Larned (USA)	Beals Wright (USA)	11-9	8-6	1-6	6-3	
S	George Wrenn (USA)	Arthur Gore (GBR)	9-7	1-6	0-6	6-2	6-2
Q	Beals Wright (USA)	Dwight Davis (USA)	4-6	4-6	8-6	6-3	6-2
Q	Bill Larned (USA)	Malcolm Chace (USA)	6-1	6-1	4-6	6-0	
Q	Arthur Gore (GBR)	Enest D. Black (GBR)	6-0	7-5	6-0		
Q	George Wrenn (USA)	Robert Wrenn (USA)	6-4	6-1	6-4		

1901

Rd	Winner	Defeated	S1	S2	S3	S4	S5
Ch	Bill Larned (USA)	Malcolm Whitman (USA)	(default)				
F	Bill Larned (USA)	Beals Wright (USA)	6-2	6-8	6-4	6-4	
S	Bill Larned (USA)	Leo Ware (USA)	6-3	6-2	6-2		
S	Beals Wright (USA)	Ray Little (USA)	7-5	2-6	6-1	6-2	
Q	Leo Ware (USA)	Edgar Leonard (USA)	6-2	6-2	6-1		
Q	Bill Larned (USA)	Edward Larned (USA)	(default)				
Q	Ray Little (USA)	Bill Clothier (USA)	6-3	10-8	1-6	6-1	
Q	Beals Wright (USA)	Clarence Hobart (USA)	6-3	8-5	6-4		

1902

Rd	Winner	Defeated	S1	S2	S3	S4	S5
Ch	Bill Larned (USA)	Reggie Doherty (GBR)	4-6	6-2	6-4	8-6	
F	Reggie Doherty (GBR)	Malcolm Whitman (USA)	6-1	3-6	6-3	6-0	
S	Malcolm Whitman (USA)	Bob Huntington (USA)	10-8	4-6	6-1	6-2	
S	Reggie Doherty (GBR)	Laurie Doherty (GBR)	(default)				
Q	Bob Huntington (USA)	Ray Little (USA)	8-6	6-2	6-2		
Q	Malcolm Whitman (USA)	Kreigh Collins (USA)	6-0	6-1	6-4		
Q	Laurie Doherty (GBR)	Leo Ware (USA)	6-3	6-2	6-2		
Q	Reggie Doherty (GBR)	L.H. Waldner (USA)	(default)				

1903

Rd	Winner	Defeated	S1	S2	S3	S4	S5
Ch	Laurie Doherty (GBR)	Bill Larned (USA)	6-0	6-3	10-8		
F	Laurie Doherty (GBR)	Bill Clothier (USA)	6-3	6-2	6-3		
S	Laurie Doherty (GBR)	Richard Carleton (USA)	6-2	6-0	6-0		
S	Bill Clothier (USA)	Edward Larned (USA)	6-3	6-1	6-2		
Q	Richard Carleton (USA)	R.C. Seaver (USA)	6-3	6-2	6-1		
Q	Laurie Doherty (GBR)	Reggie Doherty (GBR)	(default)				
Q	Edward Larned (USA)	Bob Huntington (USA)	6-0	4-6	6-0	6-3	
Q	Bill Clothier (USA)	Harry Allen (USA)	6-3	6-1	6-2		

1904

Rd	Winner	Defeated	S1	S2	S3	S4	S5
Ch	Holcombe Ward (USA)	Laurie Doherty (GBR)	(default)				
F	Holcombe Ward (USA)	Bill Clothier (USA)	10-8	6-4	9-7		
S	Bill Clothier (USA)	Bill Larned (USA)	6-4	3-6	2-6	6-2	6-3
S	Holcombe Ward (USA)	Edgar Leonard (USA)	6-3	6-4	6-4		
Q	Bill Larned (USA)	Beals Wright (USA)	6-1	6-0	6-3		
Q	Bill Clothier (USA)	Alphonzo Bell (USA)	6-3	7-5	6-3		
Q	Holcombe Ward (USA)	Fred Alexander (USA)	6-4	9-7	7-5		
Q	Edgar Leonard (USA)	Nathaniel Niles (USA)	6-0	6-1	6-1		

1905

Rd	Winner	Defeated	S1	S2	S3	S4	S5
Ch	Beals Wright (USA)	Holcombe Ward (USA)	6-2	6-1	11-9		
F	Beals Wright (USA)	Clarence Hobart (USA)	6-4	6-1	6-3		
S	Clarence Hobart (USA)	Kreigh Collins (USA)	4-6	6-4	7-9	6-4	6-4
S	Beals Wright (USA)	Bill Larned (USA)	4-6	6-3	6-2	6-2	
Q	Kreigh Collins (USA)	Jed Jones (USA)	7-5	5-7	6-3	6-1	
Q	Clarence Hobart (USA)	Richard Stevens (USA)	2-6	6-4	6-2	6-4	
Q	Beals Wright (USA)	Bill Clothier (USA)	9-7	6-2	6-2		
Q	Bill Larned (USA)	Karl Behr (USA)	6-2	6-1	6-1		

1906

Rd	Winner	Defeated	S1	S2	S3	S4	S5
Ch	Bill Clothier (USA)	Beals Wright (USA)	6-3	6-0	6-4		
F	Bill Clothier (USA)	Karl Behr (USA)	6-2	6-4	6-2		
S	Bill Clothier (USA)	Jed Jones (USA)	6-3	6-3	6-3		
S	Karl Behr (USA)	Ray Little (USA)	2-6	6-2	6-8	11-9	6-4
Q	Jed Jones (USA)	Edgar Leonard (USA)	6-2	6-3	6-1		
Q	Bill Clothier (USA)	Fred Alexander (USA)	8-6	6-2	4-6	1-6	7-5
Q	Karl Behr (USA)	Bob LeRoy (USA)	1-6	6-4	6-3	6-3	
Q	Ray Little (USA)	Harold Hackett (USA)	6-2	2-1		(default)	

1907

Rd	Winner	Defeated	S1	S2	S3	S4	S5
Ch	Bill Larned (USA)	Bill Clothier (USA)	(default)				
F	Bill Larned (USA)	Bob LeRoy (USA)	6-2	6-2	6-4		
S	Bill Larned (USA)	Clarence Hobart (USA)	6-2	6-2	6-1		
S	Bob LeRoy (USA)	Henry J. Mollenhauer (USA)	4-6	6-4	1-6	8-6	6-0
Q	Bill Larned (USA)	H.LaVerne Westfall (USA)	6-4	6-1	6-0		
Q	Clarence Hobart (USA)	Wallace Johnson (USA)	6-4	6-3	5-7	5-7	6-2
Q	Henry J. Mollenhauer (USA)	Leroy Russ (USA)	6-4	11-9	5-7	6-4	
Q	Bob LeRoy (USA)	Richard Palmer (USA)	6-0	6-2	6-2		

1908

Rd	Winner	Defeated	S1	S2	S3	S4	S5
Ch	Bill Larned (USA)	Beals Wright (USA)	6-1	6-2	8-6		
F	Beals Wright (USA)	Fred Alexander (USA)	6-3	6-3	6-3		
S	Fred Alexander (USA)	Bill Clothier (USA)	7-5	7-5	6-3		
S	Beals Wright (USA)	Nat Emerson (USA)	6-2	6-4	5-7	6-3	
Q	Fred Alexander (USA)	Frank Sulloway (USA)	6-1	6-3	6-1		
Q	Bill Clothier (USA)	Gus Touchard (USA)	6-1	8-6	6-0		
Q	Nat Emerson (USA)	Jed Jones (USA)	6-8	10-8	6-1	2-6	9-7
Q	Beals Wright (USA)	Henry Torrance, Jr. (USA)	6-3	6-1	6-3		

1909

Rd	Winner	Defeated	S1	S2	S3	S4	S5
Ch	Bill Larned (USA)	Bill Clothier (USA)	6-1	6-2	5-7	1-6	6-1
F	Bill Clothier (USA)	Maurice McLoughlin (USA)	7-5	6-4	9-11	6-3	
S	Maurice McLoughlin (USA)	Tom Bundy (USA)	6-3	6-3	6-8	7-5	
S	Bill Clothier (USA)	Gus Touchard (USA)	6-3	4-6	7-5	6-2	
Q	Bill Clothier (USA)	Edward H. Whitney (USA)	6-1	7-5	6-4		
Q	Tom Bundy (USA)	William B. Cragin Jr. (USA)	6-1	7-5	6-2		
Q	Maurice McLoughlin (USA)	Richard Palmer (USA)	7-5	6-4	6-2		
Q	Gus Touchard (USA)	Fred C. Inman (USA)	6-4	4-6	4-6	8-6	6-2

1910

Rd	Winner	Defeated	S1	S2	S3	S4	S5
Ch	Bill Larned (USA)	Tom Bundy (USA)	6-1	5-7	6-2	6-8	6-1
F	Tom Bundy (USA)	Beals Wright (USA)	6-8	6-3	6-2	10-8	
S	Beals Wright (USA)	Edward H. Whitney (USA)	4-6	7-5	4-6	6-2	7-5
S	Tom Bundy (USA)	Fred Colston (USA)	6-8	6-1	6-3	6-3	
Q	Edward H. Whitney (USA)	Charles S. Cutting (USA)	6-2	6-3	7-5		
Q	Beals Wright (USA)	Maurice McLoughlin (USA)	6-3	6-3	6-2		
Q	Fred Colston (USA)	Dean Mathey (USA)	6-4	8-6	6-4		
Q	Tom Bundy (USA)	William B. Cragin Jr. (USA)	4-6	6-4	6-3	6-2	

1911

Rd	Winner	Defeated	S1	S2	S3	S4	S5
Ch	Bill Larned (USA)	Maurice McLoughlin (USA)	6-4	6-4	6-2		
F	Maurice McLoughlin (USA)	Beals Wright (USA)	6-4	4-6	7-5	6-3	
S	Maurice McLoughlin (USA)	Gus Touchard (USA)	6-2	6-4	6-3		
S	Beals Wright (USA)	Tom Bundy (USA)	6-4	6-3	6-1		
Q	Gus Touchard (USA)	Carlton Gardner (USA)	6-3	6-4	7-5		
Q	Maurice McLoughlin (USA)	Watson Washburn (USA)	6-1	6-2	6-4		
Q	Beals Wright (USA)	Nathaniel Niles (USA)	6-8	1-6	6-3	10-8	7-5
Q	Tom Bundy (USA)	Jed Jones (USA)	6-3	8-6	6-3		

1912

Rd	Winner	Defeated	S1	S2	S3	S4	S5
F	Maurice McLoughlin (USA)	Wallace Johnson (USA)	3-6	2-6	6-2	6-4	6-2
S	Maurice McLoughlin (USA)	Bill Clothier (USA)	8-6	6-2	3-6	6-4	
S	Wallace Johnson (USA)	Karl Behr (USA)	4-6	6-0	6-3	6-2	
Q	Maurice McLoughlin (USA)	Dick Williams (USA)	6-4	5-7	6-4	3-6	6-3
Q	Bill Clothier (USA)	Ray Little (USA)	7-5	6-0	6-1		
Q	Karl Behr (USA)	George Church (USA)	6-2	6-2	6-0		
Q	Wallace Johnson (USA)	Watson Washburn (USA)	8-6	6-2	3-6	6-3	

1913

Rd	Winner	Defeated	S1	S2	S3	S4	S5
F	Maurice McLoughlin (USA)	Dick Williams (USA)	6-4	5-7	6-3	6-1	
S	Dick Williams (USA)	Nathaniel Niles (USA)	6-4	7-5	3-6	6-1	
S	Maurice McLoughlin (USA)	Wallace Johnson (USA)	6-0	7-5	6-1		
Q	Nathaniel Niles (USA)	Leonard Beekman (USA)	6-0	9-7	6-2		
Q	Dick Williams (USA)	Watson Washburn (USA)	6-1	7-5	6-3		
Q	Wallace Johnson (USA)	John Strachan (USA)	2-6	6-2	6-2	6-4	
Q	Maurice McLoughlin (USA)	Bill Clothier (USA)	6-3	7-5	6-4		

1914

Rd	Winner	Defeated	S1	S2	S3	S4	S5
F	Dick Williams (USA)	Maurice McLoughlin (USA)	6-3	8-6	10-8		
S	Dick Williams (USA)	Elia Fottrell (USA)	6-4	6-3	6-2		
S	Maurice McLoughlin (USA)	Bill Clothier (USA)	6-4	6-4	6-3		
Q	Elia Fottrell (USA)	Gus Touchard (USA)	6-1	6-1	6-2		
Q	Dick Williams (USA)	Karl Behr (USA)	6-1	6-2	7-5		
Q	Bill Clothier (USA)	Watson Washburn (USA)	6-2	9-7	6-1		
Q	Maurice McLoughlin (USA)	Clarence Griffin (USA)	6-1	6-4	3-6	8-6	

1915

Rd	Winner	Defeated	S1	S2	S3	S4	S5
F	Bill Johnston (USA)	Maurice McLoughlin (USA)	1-6	6-0	7-5	10-8	
S	Bill Johnston (USA)	Dick Williams (USA)	5-7	6-4	5-7	6-2	6-2
S	Maurice McLoughlin (USA)	Theodore Pell (USA)	6-2	6-0	7-5		
Q	Bill Johnston (USA)	Clarence Griffin (USA)	6-2	6-1	6-8	5-7	6-1
Q	Dick Williams (USA)	William Rand III (USA)	8-6	7-5	6-1		
Q	Maurice McLoughlin (USA)	Frank Hunter (USA)	6-2	6-4	6-0		
Q	Theodore Pell (USA)	Irving Wright (USA)	6-3	6-1	6-1		

1916

Rd	Winner	Defeated	S1	S2	S3	S4	S5
F	Dick Williams (USA)	Bill Johnston (USA)	4-6	6-4	0-6	6-2	6-4
S	Dick Williams (USA)	Clarence Griffin (USA)	6-3	6-3	6-3		
S	Bill Johnston (USA)	Lindley Murray (USA)	6-2	6-3	6-1		
Q	Clarence Griffin (USA)	Wallace Johnson (USA)	6-4	6-2	6-2		
Q	Dick Williams (USA)	Douglas Watters (USA)	3-6	6-1	6-1	6-2	
Q	Bill Johnston (USA)	Watson Washburn (USA)	6-2	6-2	7-5		
Q	Lindley Murray (USA)	George Church (USA)	3-6	4-6	6-2	6-4	6-4

1917

Rd	Winner	Defeated	S1	S2	S3	S4	S5
F	Lindley Murray (USA)	Nathaniel Niles (USA)	5-7	8-6	6-3	6-3	
S	Lindley Murray (USA)	John Strachan (USA)	4-6	6-3	6-3	6-1	
S	Nathaniel Niles (USA)	Dick Williams (USA)	6-2	4-6	6-4	6-3	
Q	Lindley Murray (USA)	Craig Biddle (USA)	4-6	6-1	6-4	4-6	6-2
Q	John Strachan (USA)	Chuck Garland (USA)	6-1	2-6	6-2	6-3	
Q	Nathaniel Niles (USA)	Clarence Griffin (USA)	6-1	6-3	6-0		
Q	Dick Williams (USA)	Harold Throckmorton (USA)	4-6	6-3	7-5		

1918

Rd	Winner	Defeated	S1	S2	S3	S4	S5
F	Lindley Murray (USA)	Bill Tilden (USA)	6-3	6-1	7-5		
S	Lindley Murray (USA)	S. Howard Voshell (USA)	6-4	6-3	8-6		
S	Bill Tilden (USA)	Ichiya Kumagae (JPN)	6-2	6-2	6-0		
Q	S. Howard Voshell (USA)	Craig Biddle (USA)	6-2	6-3	9-7		
Q	Lindley Murray (USA)	Nathaniel Niles (USA)	7-5	6-4	2-6	7-5	
Q	Ichiya Kumagae (JPN)	Lyle Mahan (USA)	4-6	6-3	6-0	6-1	
Q	Bill Tilden (USA)	Walter Merrill Hall (USA)	3-6	6-1	5-7	7-5	6-1

1919

Rd	Winner	Defeated	S1	S2	S3	S4	S5
F	Bill Johnston (USA)	Bill Tilden (USA)	6-4	6-4	6-3		
S	Bill Johnston (USA)	Wallace Johnson (USA)	2-6	6-1	6-3	6-3	
S	Bill Tilden (USA)	Dick Williams (USA)	6-1	7-5	6-3		
Q	Bill Johnston (USA)	Lindley Murray (USA)	5-7	6-1	6-2	6-4	
Q	Wallace Johnson (USA)	Walter Merrill Hall (USA)	6-4	6-0	6-2		
Q	Bill Tilden (USA)	Norman Brookes (AUS)	1-6	6-4	7-5	6-3	
Q	Dick Williams (USA)	Maurice McLoughlin (USA)	6-0	6-3	6-2		

1920

Rd	Winner	Defeated	S1	S2	S3	S4	S5
F	Bill Tilden (USA)	Bill Johnston (USA)	6-1	1-6	7-5	5-7	6-3
S	Bill Johnston (USA)	G.Colket Caner (USA)	6-3	4-6	8-6	6-4	
S	Bill Tilden (USA)	Wallace Johnson (USA)	14-12	6-4	6-4		
Q	G.Colket Caner (USA)	Irving Wright (USA)	6-3	6-4	6-2		
Q	Bill Johnston (USA)	Watson Washburn (USA)	6-4	6-4	7-5		
Q	Wallace Johnson (USA)	Clarence Griffin (USA)	6-1	6-3	2-6	6-4	
Q	Bill Tilden (USA)	Walter Wesbrook (USA)	6-3	8-6	6-1		

1921

Rd	Winner	Defeated	S1	S2	S3	S4	S5
F	Bill Tilden (USA)	Wallace Johnson (USA)	6-1	6-3	6-1		
S	Wallace Johnson (USA)	James Anderson (AUS)	6-4	3-6	8-6	6-3	
S	Bill Tilden (USA)	Willis Davis (USA)	10-8	6-2	6-1		
Q	Wallace Johnson (USA)	Craig Biddle (USA)	6-0	6-3	6-4		
Q	James Anderson (AUS)	Frank Hunter (USA)	6-1	6-3	6-4		
Q	Bill Tilden (USA)	Gordon Lowe (GBR)	6-4	6-3	6-4		
Q	Willis Davis (USA)	Robert Kinsey (USA)	6-3	4-6	6-4	1-6	6-4

1922

Rd	Winner	Defeated	S1	S2	S3	S4	S5
F	**Bill Tilden (USA)**	**Bill Johnston (USA)**	4-6	3-6	6-2	6-3	6-4
S	Bill Johnston (USA)	Vinnie Richards (USA)	8-6	6-2	6-1		
S	Bill Tilden (USA)	Gerald Patterson (AUS)	4-6	6-4	6-3	6-1	
Q	Bill Johnston (USA)	Manuel Alonso (ESP)	6-0	6-2	7-5		
Q	Vinnie Richards (USA)	James Anderson (AUS)	6-4	6-2	7-5		
Q	Bill Tilden (USA)	Zenzo Shimizu (JPN)	6-2	6-3	6-1		
Q	Gerald Patterson (AUS)	Dick Williams (USA)	6-3	6-3	6-4		

1923

Rd	Winner	Defeated	S1	S2	S3	S4	S5
F	**Bill Tilden (USA)**	**Bill Johnston (USA)**	6-4	6-1	6-4		
S	Bill Tilden (USA)	Brian Norton (RSA)	6-3	7-5	6-2		
S	Bill Johnston (USA)	Frank Hunter (USA)	6-4	6-2	7-5		
Q	Bill Tilden (USA)	Manuel Alonso (ESP)	6-0	6-0	6-2		
Q	Brian Norton (RSA)	Dick Williams (USA)	1-6	6-3	6-4	3-6	6-4
Q	Bill Johnston (USA)	Frank T. Anderson (USA)	8-6	6-1	7-5		
Q	Frank Hunter (USA)	Robert Kinsey (USA)	6-2	6-4	8-6		

1924

Rd	Winner	Defeated	S1	S2	S3	S4	S5
F	**Bill Tilden (USA)**	**Bill Johnston (USA)**	6-1	9-7	6-2		
S	Bill Tilden (USA)	Vinnie Richards (USA)	4-6	6-2	8-6	4-6	6-4
S	Bill Johnston (USA)	Gerald Patterson (AUS)	6-2	6-0	6-0		
Q	Bill Tilden (USA)	Howard Kinsey (USA)	6-3	6-4	3-6	6-2	
Q	Vinnie Richards (USA)	Wallace Johnson (USA)	6-1	6-4	11-9		
Q	Bill Johnston (USA)	Rene Lacoste (FRA)	6-3	6-3	6-3		
Q	Vinnie Richards (USA)	George Lott (USA)	6-1	6-4	6-3		

1925

Rd	Winner	Defeated	S1	S2	S3	S4	S5
F	**Bill Tilden (USA)**	**Bill Johnston (USA)**	4-6	11-9	6-3	4-6	6-3
S	Bill Johnston (USA)	Dick Williams (USA)	7-5	6-3	6-2		
S	Bill Tilden (USA)	Vinnie Richards (USA)	6-8	6-4	6-4	6-1	
Q	Bill Johnston (USA)	Manuel Alonso (ESP)	6-3	6-8	6-1	6-2	
Q	Dick Williams (USA)	Howard Kinsey (USA)	7-5	6-4	6-3		
Q	Bill Tilden (USA)	Wallace Johnson (USA)	6-4	6-0	6-4		
Q	Vinnie Richards (USA)	Rene Lacoste (FRA)	6-4	6-4	6-3		

1926

Rd	Winner	Defeated	S1	S2	S3	S4	S5
F	**Rene Lacoste (FRA)**	**Jean Borotra (FRA)**	6-4	6-0	6-4		
S	Rene Lacoste (FRA)	Henri Cochet (FRA)	2-6	4-6	6-4	6-4	6-3
S	Jean Borotra (FRA)	Vinnie Richards (USA)	3-6	6-4	4-6	8-6	6-2
Q	Henri Cochet (FRA)	Bill Tilden (USA)	6-8	6-1	6-3	1-6	8-6
Q	Rene Lacoste (FRA)	Dick Williams (USA)	6-0	6-3	8-6		
Q	Vinnie Richards (USA)	Jacques Brugnon (FRA)	6-2	6-1	6-2		
Q	Jean Borotra (FRA)	Bill Johnston (USA)	3-6	4-6	6-3	6-4	6-4

1927

Rd	Winner	Defeated	S1	S2	S3	S4	S5
F	**Rene Lacoste (FRA)**	**Bill Tilden (USA)**	11-9	6-3	11-9		
S	Bill Tilden (USA)	Frank Hunter (USA)	14-12	6-1	4-6	9-7	
S	Rene Lacoste (FRA)	Bill Johnston (USA)	6-2	2-6	6-4	6-4	
Q	Bill Tilden (USA)	Jean Borotra (FRA)	6-1	3-6	10-8	6-1	
Q	Frank Hunter (USA)	John Hennessey (USA)	4-6	5-7	6-0	6-3	6-4
Q	Bill Johnston (USA)	Jacques Brugnon (FRA)	3-6	6-2	6-4	6-4	
Q	Rene Lacoste (FRA)	Manuel Alonso (ESP)	6-8	6-4	6-1	6-2	

1928

Rd	Winner	Defeated	S1	S2	S3	S4	S5
F	**Henri Cochet (FRA)**	**Frank Hunter (USA)**	4-6	6-4	3-6	7-5	6-3
S	Frank Hunter (USA)	George Lott (USA)	6-8	6-4	6-3	6-4	
S	Henri Cochet (FRA)	Francis Shields (USA)	6-2	8-6	6-4		
Q	George Lott (USA)	Johnny Doeg (USA)	6-2	6-2	7-5		
Q	Frank Hunter (USA)	Jack Crawford (AUS)	7-5	3-6	6-3	6-4	
Q	Francis Shields (USA)	Jacques Brugnon (FRA)	7-5	6-1	6-0		
Q	Henri Cochet (FRA)	Gregory Mangin (USA)	4-6	6-3	6-1	6-2	

1929

Rd	Winner	Defeated	S1	S2	S3	S4	S5
F	**Bill Tilden (USA)**	**Frank Hunter (USA)**	3-6	6-3	4-6	6-2	6-4
S	Bill Tilden (USA)	Johnny Doeg (USA)	4-6	6-2	2-6	6-4	6-3
S	Frank Hunter (USA)	Fritz Mercur (USA)	6-4	6-8	6-4	6-3	
Q	Bill Tilden (USA)	John Van Ryn (USA)	7-5	2-6	9-7	6-2	
Q	Johnny Doeg (USA)	Bunny Austin (GBR)	6-4	6-4	6-3		
Q	Fritz Mercur (USA)	Wilmer Allison (USA)	8-6	10-8	6-4		
Q	Frank Hunter (USA)	Dick Williams (USA)	6-0	6-3	6-4		

1930

Rd	Winner	Defeated	S1	S2	S3	S4	S5
F	**Johnny Doeg (USA)**	**Francis Shields (USA)**	10-8	1-6	6-4	16-14	
S	Francis Shields (USA)	Sidney Wood (USA)	6-2	6-3	4-6	6-3	
S	Johnny Doeg (USA)	Bill Tilden (USA)	10-8	6-3	3-6	12-10	
Q	Francis Shields (USA)	Gregory Mangin (USA)	3-6	6-8	6-2	6-1	6-1
Q	Sidney Wood (USA)	Clifford Sutter (USA)	6-4	6-3	2-6	7-5	
Q	Bill Tilden (USA)	John Van Ryn (USA)	4-6	6-2	6-4	6-4	
Q	Johnny Doeg (USA)	Frank Hunter (USA)	11-13	6-4	3-6	6-2	6-4

1931

Rd	Winner	Defeated	S1	S2	S3	S4	S5
F	**Ellsworth Vines (USA)**	**George Lott (USA)**	7-9	6-3	9-7	7-5	
S	Ellsworth Vines (USA)	George Lott (USA)	4-6	3-6	6-4	6-4	6-3
S	George Lott (USA)	Fred Perry (GBR)	7-5	6-3	6-0		
Q	Ellsworth Vines (USA)	Johnny Doeg (USA)	6-1	6-4	8-6		
Q	Fred Perry (GBR)	Berkeley Bell (USA)	6-2	6-3	6-4		
Q	Johnny Doeg (USA)	Frank Bowden (USA)	6-2	11-9	4-6	8-6	
Q	George Lott (USA)	John Van Ryn (USA)	5-7	1-6	6-0	7-5	6-1

1932

Rd	Winner	Defeated	S1	S2	S3	S4	S5
F	**Ellsworth Vines (USA)**	**Henri Cochet (FRA)**	6-4	6-4	6-4		
S	Ellsworth Vines (USA)	Clifford Sutter (USA)	4-6	8-10	12-10	10-8	6-1
S	Henri Cochet (FRA)	Wilmer Allison (USA)	6-1	10-12	4-6	6-3	7-5
Q	Ellsworth Vines (USA)	Lester Stoefen (USA)	6-3	7-5	6-4		
Q	Clifford Sutter (USA)	George Lott (USA)	10-8	6-0	6-0		
Q	Wilmer Allison (USA)	Sidney Wood (USA)	5-7	6-3	6-2	6-4	
Q	Henri Cochet (FRA)	Francis Shields (USA)	4-6	6-3	6-4	6-0	

1933

Rd	Winner	Defeated	S1	S2	S3	S4	S5
F	**Fred Perry (GBR)**	**Jack Crawford (AUS)**	6-3	11-13	4-6	6-0	6-1
S	Fred Perry (GBR)	Lester Stoefen (USA)	6-3	6-2	6-2		
S	Jack Crawford (AUS)	Francis Shields (USA)	7-5	6-4	6-3		
Q	Lester Stoefen (USA)	Bryan Grant Jr. (USA)	8-6	6-4	3-6	7-5	
Q	Fred Perry (GBR)	Adrian Quist (AUS)	6-4	6-4	6-0		
Q	Francis Shields (USA)	Gregory Mangin (USA)	6-4	6-4	4-6	6-3	
Q	Jack Crawford (AUS)	Clifford Sutter (USA)	6-3	6-4	6-4		

1934

Rd	Winner	Defeated	S1	S2	S3	S4	S5
F	Fred Perry (GBR)	Wilmer Allison (USA)	6-4	6-3	3-6	1-6	8-6
S	Fred Perry (GBR)	Vernon Kirby (RSA)	6-2	2-6	6-4	6-2	
S	Wilmer Allison (USA)	Sidney Wood (USA)	8-6	6-2	6-3		
Q	Vernon Kirby (RSA)	Francis Shields (USA)	4-6	6-4	6-4	6-3	
Q	Fred Perry (GBR)	Clifford Sutter (USA)	6-3	6-0	6-2		
Q	Wilmer Allison (USA)	Lester Stoefen (USA)	8-6	4-6	11-9	6-8	6-3
Q	Sidney Wood (USA)	Frank Parker (USA)	6-4	6-4	7-5		

1935

Rd	Winner	Defeated	S1	S2	S3	S4	S5
F	Wilmer Allison (USA)	Sidney Wood (USA)	6-2	6-2	6-3		
S	Sidney Wood (USA)	Bryan Grant Jr. (USA)	6-2	4-6	12-10	6-2	
S	Wilmer Allison (USA)	Fred Perry (GBR)	7-5	6-3	6-3		
Q	Bryan Grant Jr. (USA)	Don Budge (USA)	6-4	6-4	5-7	6-3	
Q	Sidney Wood (USA)	Gregory Mangin (USA)	3-6	6-1	6-1	6-2	
Q	Wilmer Allison (USA)	Enrique Maier (ESP)	6-2	6-4	6-4		
Q	Fred Perry (GBR)	Francis Shields (USA)	6-4	4-6	8-6	6-0	

1936

Rd	Winner	Defeated	S1	S2	S3	S4	S5
F	Fred Perry (GBR)	Don Budge (USA)	2-6	6-2	8-6	1-6	10-8
S	Fred Perry (GBR)	Bryan Grant Jr. (USA)	6-4	3-6	7-5	6-2	
S	Don Budge (USA)	Frank Parker (USA)	6-4	6-3	6-3		
Q	Bryan Grant Jr. (USA)	John Van Ryn (USA)	3-6	8-6	6-0	6-3	
Q	Fred Perry (GBR)	Henry Culley (USA)	6-3	6-2	6-1		
Q	Don Budge (USA)	John McDiarmid (USA)	6-4	6-3	6-2		
Q	Frank Parker (USA)	Gregory Mangin (USA)	10-12	6-0	4-6	6-1	6-3

1937

Rd	Winner	Defeated	S1	S2	S3	S4	S5
F	Don Budge (USA)	Gottfried von Cramm (GER)	6-1	7-9	6-1	3-6	6-1
S	Don Budge (USA)	Frank Parker (USA)	6-2	6-1	6-3		
S	Gottfried von Cramm (GER)	Bobby Riggs (USA)	0-6	8-6	6-8	6-3	6-2
Q	Don Budge (USA)	Joseph R. Hunt (USA)	6-1	6-2	6-4		
Q	Frank Parker (USA)	John Van Ryn (USA)	6-2	12-10	6-2		
Q	Bobby Riggs (USA)	Charles Hare (GBR)	4-6	1-6	6-3	6-0	7-5
Q	Gottfried von Cramm (GER)	Bryan Grant Jr. (USA)	9-7	2-6	2-6	6-3	6-3

1938

Rd	Winner	Defeated	S1	S2	S3	S4	S5
F	Don Budge (USA)	Gene Mako (USA)	6-3	6-8	6-2	6-1	
S	Don Budge (USA)	Sidney Wood (USA)	6-3	6-3	6-3		
S	Gene Mako (USA)	John Bromwich (AUS)	6-3	7-5	6-4		
Q	Don Budge (USA)	Harry Hopman (AUS)	6-3	6-1	6-3		
Q	Sidney Wood (USA)	Bryan Grant Jr. (USA)	6-2	6-3	6-2		
Q	Gene Mako (USA)	Gilbert A. Hunt Jr. (USA)	7-5	1-6	8-6	6-0	
Q	John Bromwich (AUS)	Joseph R. Hunt (USA)	6-1	9-11	6-3	6-4	

1939

Rd	Winner	Defeated	S1	S2	S3	S4	S5
F	Bobby Riggs (USA)	Welby Van Horn (USA)	6-4	6-2	6-4		
S	Bobby Riggs (USA)	Joseph R. Hunt (USA)	6-1	6-2	4-6	6-1	
S	Welby Van Horn (USA)	John Bromwich (AUS)	2-6	4-6	6-2	6-4	8-6
Q	Bobby Riggs (USA)	Harry Hopman (AUS)	6-1	10-8	6-3		
Q	Joseph R. Hunt (USA)	Don McNeill (USA)	15-13	8-10	4-6	6-2	
Q	John Bromwich (AUS)	Gilbert A. Hunt Jr. (USA)	6-3	6-4	6-1		
Q	Welby Van Horn (USA)	Wayne Sabin (USA)	4-6	2-6	6-4	7-5	6-3

1940

Rd	Winner	Defeated	S1	S2	S3	S4	S5
F	Don McNeill (USA)	Bobby Riggs (USA)	4-6	6-8	6-3	6-3	7-5
S	Don McNeill (USA)	Jack Kramer (USA)	6-1	5-7	6-4	6-3	
S	Bobby Riggs (USA)	Joseph R. Hunt (USA)	4-6	6-3	5-7	6-3	6-4
Q	Don McNeill (USA)	Elwood Cooke (USA)	9-7	6-8	6-4	6-3	
Q	Jack Kramer (USA)	Frank Parker (USA)	1-6	6-1	3-6	6-3	6-1
Q	Bobby Riggs (USA)	Ted Schroeder (USA)	6-1	5-7	6-3	6-4	
Q	Joseph R. Hunt (USA)	Frank Kovacs (USA)	6-4	6-1	6-4		

1941

Rd	Winner	Defeated	S1	S2	S3	S4	S5
F	Bobby Riggs (USA)	Frank Kovacs (USA)	5-7	6-1	6-3	6-3	
S	Frank Kovacs (USA)	Don McNeill (USA)	6-4	6-2	10-8		
S	Bobby Riggs (USA)	Ted Schroeder (USA)	6-4	6-4	1-6	9-11	7-5
Q	Frank Kovacs (USA)	Jack Kramer (USA)	6-4	7-5	7-5		
Q	Don McNeill (USA)	Wayne Sabin (USA)	6-3	7-5	3-6	6-3	
Q	Bobby Riggs (USA)	Frank Parker (USA)	6-4	6-3	4-6	6-2	
Q	Ted Schroeder (USA)	Bryan Grant Jr. (USA)	6-8	6-1	6-2	6-3	

1942

Rd	Winner	Defeated	S1	S2	S3	S4	S5
F	Ted Schroeder (USA)	Frank Parker (USA)	8-6	7-5	3-6	4-6	6-2
S	Frank Parker (USA)	Pancho Segura (ECU)	6-1	6-1	2-6	6-2	
S	Ted Schroeder (USA)	Gardnar Mulloy (USA)	9-7	6-3	6-4		
Q	Frank Parker (USA)	Seymour Greenburg (USA)	6-0	6-0	6-4		
Q	Pancho Segura (ECU)	Bill Talbert (USA)	6-4	3-6	6-2	6-4	
Q	Ted Schroeder (USA)	Alejo Russell (ARG)	6-3	6-8	6-3	7-5	
Q	Gardnar Mulloy (USA)	George Richards (USA)	6-2	8-6	7-5		

1943

Rd	Winner	Defeated	S1	S2	S3	S4	S5
F	Joseph R. Hunt (USA)	Jack Kramer (USA)	6-3	6-8	10-8	6-2	
S	Jack Kramer (USA)	Pancho Segura (ECU)	2-6	6-4	7-5	6-3	
S	Joseph R. Hunt (USA)	Bill Talbert (USA)	3-6	6-4	6-2	6-4	
Q	Pancho Segura (ECU)	Seymour Greenburg (USA)	6-2	6-4	6-1		
Q	Jack Kramer (USA)	Jack Tuero (USA)	6-1	6-2	6-4		
Q	Joseph R. Hunt (USA)	Frank Parker (USA)	8-6	6-2	6-3		
Q	Bill Talbert (USA)	Elwood Cooke (USA)	6-1	4-6	8-6	6-4	

1944

Rd	Winner	Defeated	S1	S2	S3	S4	S5
F	Frank Parker (USA)	Bill Talbert (USA)	6-4	3-6	6-3	6-3	
S	Bill Talbert (USA)	Pancho Segura (ECU)	3-6	6-3	6-0	6-8	6-3
S	Frank Parker (USA)	Don McNeill (USA)	6-4	3-6	6-2	6-2	
Q	Pancho Segura (ECU)	Alexander H. Carver (USA)	6-0	6-3	6-4		
Q	Bill Talbert (USA)	Bob Falkenburg (USA)	6-4	6-4	6-3		
Q	Don McNeill (USA)	Seymour Greenburg (USA)	6-3	4-6	3-6	6-1	8-6
Q	Frank Parker (USA)	Charles Oliver (USA)	6-2	6-4	6-1		

1945

Rd	Winner	Defeated	S1	S2	S3	S4	S5
F	Frank Parker (USA)	Bill Talbert (USA)	14-12	6-1	6-2		
S	Frank Parker (USA)	Elwood Cooke (USA)	6-4	8-6	7-5		
S	Bill Talbert (USA)	Pancho Segura (ECU)	7-5	6-3	6-4		
Q	Frank Parker (USA)	Seymour Greenburg (USA)	6-2	6-3	6-2		
Q	Elwood Cooke (USA)	Sidney Wood (USA)	10-12	7-5	6-4	2-6	6-0
Q	Bill Talbert (USA)	Alejo Russell (ARG)	6-1	6-2	9-7		
Q	Pancho Segura (ECU)	Bob Falkenburg (BRA)	6-2	4-6	6-1	6-1	

Rd	Winner	Defeated	S1	S2	S3	S4	S5

1946

Rd	Winner	Defeated	S1	S2	S3	S4	S5
F	Jack Kramer (USA)	Tom Brown Jr. (USA)	9-7	6-3	6-0		
S	Jack Kramer (USA)	Bob Falkenburg (USA)	6-0	6-4	6-4		
S	Tom Brown Jr. (USA)	Gardnar Mulloy (USA)	6-4	6-2	6-4		
Q	Jack Kramer (USA)	Don McNeill (USA)	6-3	6-2	1-6	6-2	
Q	Bob Falkenburg (USA)	Bill Talbert (USA)	3-6	6-1	2-6	6-2	7-5
Q	Tom Brown Jr. (USA)	Frank Parker (USA)	6-3	6-4	6-8	3-6	6-1
Q	Gardnar Mulloy (USA)	Pancho Segura (ECU)	4-6	6-4	12-10	6-3	

1947

Rd	Winner	Defeated	S1	S2	S3	S4	S5
F	Jack Kramer (USA)	Frank Parker (USA)	4-6	2-6	6-1	6-0	6-3
S	Jack Kramer (USA)	Jaroslav Drobny (CZE)	3-6	6-3	6-0	6-1	
S	Frank Parker (USA)	John Bromwich (AUS)	6-3	4-6	6-3	6-8	8-6
Q	Jack Kramer (USA)	Bob Falkenburg (BRA)	6-2	7-5	6-1		
Q	Jaroslav Drobny (CZE)	Tom Brown Jr. (USA)	7-5	6-3	6-4		
Q	Frank Parker (USA)	Pancho Segura (ECU)	6-3	11-9	6-4		
Q	John Bromwich (AUS)	Gardnar Mulloy (USA)	7-5	6-1	6-1		

1948

Rd	Winner	Defeated	S1	S2	S3	S4	S5
F	Pancho Gonzalez (USA)	Eric Sturgess (USA)	6-2	6-3	14-12		
S	Pancho Gonzalez (USA)	Jaroslav Drobny (CZE)	8-10	11-9	6-0	6-3	
S	Eric Sturgess (USA)	Herbie Flam (USA)	9-7	6-3	6-2		
Q	Pancho Gonzalez (USA)	Frank Parker (USA)	8-6	2-6	7-5	6-3	
Q	Jaroslav Drobny (CZE)	Bob Falkenburg (USA)	8-6	6-1	6-3		
Q	Eric Sturgess (USA)	Earl Cochell (USA)	6-2	8-6	3-6	5-7	6-3
Q	Herbie Flam (USA)	Harry Likas Jr. (USA)	2-6	6-4	6-1	6-0	

1949

Rd	Winner	Defeated	S1	S2	S3	S4	S5
F	Pancho Gonzalez (USA)	Ted Schroeder (USA)	16-18	2-6	6-1	6-2	6-4
S	Pancho Gonzalez (USA)	Frank Parker (USA)	3-6	9-7	6-3	6-2	
S	Ted Schroeder (USA)	Bill Talbert (USA)	2-6	6-4	4-6	6-4	6-4
Q	Pancho Gonzalez (USA)	Art Larsen (USA)	4-6	6-1	6-3	2-6	6-1
Q	Frank Parker (USA)	Galdnar Mulloy (USA)	6-4	6-2	6-4		
Q	Ted Schroeder (USA)	Frank Sedgman (AUS)	6-3	0-6	6-4	6-8	6-4
Q	Bill Talbert (USA)	Jaroslav Drobny (CZE)	6-4	6-2	6-2		

1950

Rd	Winner	Defeated	S1	S2	S3	S4	S5
F	Art Larsen (USA)	Herbie Flam (USA)	6-3	4-6	5-7	6-4	6-3
S	Herbie Flam (USA)	Gardnar Mulloy (USA)	2-6	6-2	9-11	6-1	6-3
S	Art Larsen (USA)	Dick Savitt (USA)	6-2	10-8	7-9	6-2	
Q	Herbie Flam (USA)	Bill Talbert (USA)	9-7	6-4	6-3		
Q	Gardnar Mulloy (USA)	Earl Cochell (USA)	6-3	7-5	6-2		
Q	Dick Savitt (USA)	Sidney Schwartz (USA)	8-6	6-2	2-6	6-3	
Q	Art Larsen (USA)	Tom Brown Jr. (USA)	6-3	2-6	6-1	6-4	

1951

Rd	Winner	Defeated	S1	S2	S3	S4	S5
F	Frank Sedgman (AUS)	Vic Seixas (USA)	6-4	6-1	6-1		
S	Vic Seixas (USA)	Dick Savitt (USA)	6-0	3-6	6-3	6-2	
S	Frank Sedgman (AUS)	Art Larsen (USA)	6-1	6-2	6-0		
Q	Dick Savitt (USA)	Budge Patty (USA)	6-3	1-6	4-6	6-1	6-4
Q	Vic Seixas (USA)	Herbie Flam (USA)	1-6	9-7	2-6	6-2	6-3
Q	Art Larsen (USA)	Gardnar Mulloy (USA)	6-8	6-1	6-2	6-4	
Q	Frank Sedgman (AUS)	Tony Trabert (USA)	3-6	6-2	7-5	3-6	6-3

1952

Rd	Winner	Defeated	S1	S2	S3	S4	S5
F	Frank Sedgman (AUS)	Gardnar Mulloy (USA)	6-1	6-2	6-3		
S	Gardnar Mulloy (USA)	Hamilton Richardson (USA)	10-8	6-0	8-6		
S	Frank Sedgman (AUS)	Merv Rose (AUS)	6-3	6-3	6-4		
Q	Gardnar Mulloy (USA)	Ken Rosewall (AUS)	6-4	3-6	4-6	7-5	7-5
Q	Hamilton Richardson (USA)	Straight Clark (USA)	6-8	11-9	5-7	8-6	6-4
Q	Merv Rose (AUS)	Dick Savitt (USA)	6-3	8-6	8-6		
Q	Frank Sedgman (AUS)	Lew Hoad (AUS)	6-2	6-1	6-3		

1953

Rd	Winner	Defeated	S1	S2	S3	S4	S5
F	Tony Trabert (USA)	Vic Seixas (USA)	6-3	6-2	6-3		
S	Tony Trabert (USA)	Ken Rosewall (AUS)	7-5	6-3	6-3		
S	Vic Seixas (USA)	Lew Hoad (AUS)	7-5	6-4	6-4		
Q	Tony Trabert (USA)	Budge Patty (USA)	6-4	6-4	6-2		
Q	Ken Rosewall (AUS)	Sven Davidson (SWE)	6-0	8-10	2-6	6-0	11-9
Q	Vic Seixas (USA)	Kurt Nielsen (DEN)	6-3	7-9	8-6	6-4	
Q	Lew Hoad (AUS)	Gardnar Mulloy (USA)	6-4	6-2	11-9		

1954

Rd	Winner	Defeated	S1	S2	S3	S4	S5
F	Vic Seixas (USA)	Rex Hartwig (AUS)	3-6	6-2	6-4	6-4	
S	Rex Hartwig (AUS)	Ken Rosewall (AUS)	6-4	6-3	6-4		
S	Vic Seixas (USA)	Hamilton Richardson (USA)	6-3	12-14	8-6	6-2	
Q	Rex Hartwig (AUS)	Tony Trabert (USA)	6-2	8-6	2-6	6-2	
Q	Ken Rosewall (AUS)	Art Larsen (USA)	9-7	4-6	4-6	6-3	6-4
Q	Vic Seixas (USA)	Tom Brown Jr. (USA)	6-4	6-2	6-2		
Q	Hamilton Richardson (USA)	Lew Hoad (AUS)	6-4	7-5	11-13	4-6	6-3

1955

Rd	Winner	Defeated	S1	S2	S3	S4	S5
F	Tony Trabert (USA)	Ken Rosewall (AUS)	9-7	6-3	6-3		
S	Ken Rosewall (AUS)	Vic Seixas (USA)	6-4	6-4	7-5		
S	Tony Trabert (USA)	Lew Hoad (AUS)	6-4	6-2	6-1		
Q	Vic Seixas (USA)	Bernard Bartzen (USA)	6-3	6-1	13-11		
Q	Ken Rosewall (AUS)	Hamilton Richardson (USA)	6-4	9-7	2-6	6-3	
Q	Tony Trabert (USA)	Herbie Flam (USA)	6-2	6-3	6-4		
Q	Lew Hoad (AUS)	Sammy Giammalva (USA)	6-3	6-2	5-7	6-3	

1956

Rd	Winner	Defeated	S1	S2	S3	S4	S5
F	Ken Rosewall (AUS)	Lew Hoad (AUS)	4-6	6-2	6-3	6-3	
S	Ken Rosewall (AUS)	Vic Seixas (USA)	10-8	6-0	6-3		
S	Lew Hoad (AUS)	Neale Fraser (AUS)	15-13	6-2	6-4		
Q	Ken Rosewall (AUS)	Dick Savitt (USA)	6-4	7-5	4-6	8-10	6-1
Q	Vic Seixas (USA)	Ashley Cooper (AUS)	9-7	3-6	9-7	10-12	6-4
Q	Lew Hoad (AUS)	Roy Emerson (AUS)	8-6	6-3	7-5		
Q	Neale Fraser (AUS)	Hamilton Richardson (USA)	3-6	6-3	6-2	6-4	

1957

Rd	Winner	Defeated	S1	S2	S3	S4	S5
F	Mal Anderson (AUS)	Ashley Cooper (AUS)	10-8	7-5	6-4		
S	Ashley Cooper (AUS)	Herbie Flam (USA)	6-1	7-5	6-4		
S	Mal Anderson (AUS)	Sven Davidson (SWE)	5-7	6-2	4-6	6-3	6-4
Q	Ashley Cooper (AUS)	Budge Patty (USA)	6-2	6-3	6-1		
Q	Herbie Flam (USA)	Vic Seixas (USA)	6-4	3-6	6-4	4-6	6-1
Q	Mal Anderson (AUS)	Luis Ayala (CHI)	6-1	6-3	6-1		
Q	Sven Davidson (SWE)	Cliff Mayne (USA)	3-6	6-3	7-5	6-4	

1958

Rd	Winner	Defeated	S1	S2	S3	S4	S5
F	Ashley Cooper (AUS)	Mal Anderson (AUS)	6-2	3-6	4-6	10-8	8-6
S	Ashley Cooper (AUS)	Neale Fraser (AUS)	8-6	8-6	6-1		
S	Mal Anderson (AUS)	Ulf Schmidt (SWE)	6-4	7-5	6-2		
Q	Ashley Cooper (AUS)	Vic Seixas (USA)	9-7	6-2	3-6	6-2	
Q	Neale Fraser (AUS)	Alex Olmedo (PER)	3-6	6-1	8-6	3-6	6-3
Q	Mal Anderson (AUS)	Dick Savitt (USA)	18-16	6-1	3-6	6-3	
Q	Ulf Schmidt (SWE)	Herbie Flam (USA)	7-5	8-6	8-6		

1959

Rd	Winner	Defeated	S1	S2	S3	S4	S5
F	Neale Fraser (AUS)	Alex Olmedo (PER)	6-3	5-7	6-2	6-4	
S	Neale Fraser (AUS)	Bernard Bartzen (USA)	6-3	6-2	6-2		
S	Alex Olmedo (PER)	Ronald Holmberg (USA)	15-13	6-4	3-6	6-1	
Q	Neale Fraser (AUS)	Luis Ayala (CHI)	6-3	6-4	6-4		
Q	Bernard Bartzen (USA)	Barry MacKay (USA)	6-3	6-4	6-4		
Q	Alex Olmedo (PER)	Roy Emerson (AUS)	6-4	3-6	6-2	6-3	
Q	Ronald Holmberg (USA)	Rod Laver (AUS)	6-8	7-5	6-0	6-3	

1960

Rd	Winner	Defeated	S1	S2	S3	S4	S5
F	Neale Fraser (AUS)	Rod Laver (AUS)	6-4	6-4	9-7		
S	Rod Laver (AUS)	Earl Buchholtz Jr. (USA)	4-6	5-7	6-4	6-2	7-5
S	Neale Fraser (AUS)	Dennis Ralston (USA)	11-9	6-3	6-2		
Q	Rod Laver (AUS)	Bobby Wilson (GBR)	9-7	6-1	6-3		
Q	Earl Buchholtz Jr. (USA)	Hamilton Richardson (USA)	3-6	6-3	6-4	6-4	
Q	Neale Fraser (AUS)	Chuck McKinley (USA)	6-2	6-4	6-2		
Q	Dennis Ralston (USA)	Bob Mark (AUS)	1-6	6-3	6-3	6-2	

1961

Rd	Winner	Defeated	S1	S2	S3	S4	S5
F	Roy Emerson (AUS)	Rod Laver (AUS)	7-5	6-3	6-2		
S	Rod Laver (AUS)	Mike Sangster (GBR)	13-11	7-5	6-4		
S	Roy Emerson (AUS)	Rafael Osuna (MEX)	6-3	6-2	3-6	5-7	9-7
Q	Rod Laver (AUS)	Donald Dell (USA)	6-4	7-9	6-3	6-4	
Q	Mike Sangster (GBR)	Jon Douglas (USA)	6-4	7-5	6-1		
Q	Rafael Osuna (MEX)	Whitney Reed (USA)	6-8	6-3	6-3	6-2	
Q	Roy Emerson (AUS)	Ron Holmberg (USA)	6-4	6-2	7-5		

1962

Rd	Winner	Defeated	S1	S2	S3	S4	S5
F	Rod Laver (AUS)	Roy Emerson (AUS)	6-2	6-4	5-7	6-4	
S	Rod Laver (AUS)	Rafael Osuna (MEX)	6-1	6-3	6-4		
S	Roy Emerson (AUS)	Chuck McKinley (USA)	4-6	6-4	6-3	6-2	
Q	Rod Laver (AUS)	Frank Froehling III (USA)	6-3	13-11	4-6	6-3	
Q	Rafael Osuna (MEX)	Gordon Forbes (RSA)	6-4	6-4	7-5		
Q	Roy Emerson (AUS)	Andy Lloyd (USA)	6-1	6-1	6-3		
Q	Chuck McKinley (USA)	Hamilton Richardson (USA)	6-2	6-2	6-8	6-4	

1963

Rd	Winner	Defeated	S1	S2	S3	S4	S5
F	Rafael Osuna (MEX)	Frank Froehling III (USA)	7-5	6-4	6-2		
S	Rafael Osuna (MEX)	Chuck McKinley (USA)	6-4	6-4	10-8		
S	Frank Froehling III (USA)	Ronald Barnes (BRA)	6-3	6-1	6-4		
Q	Chuck McKinley (USA)	Tomaz Koch (BRA)	6-4	4-6	4-6	8-6	6-4
Q	Rafael Osuna (MEX)	Marty Riessen (USA)	3-6	9-7	9-7	6-3	
Q	Ronald Barnes (BRA)	Dennis Ralston (USA)	6-4	7-5	7-5		
Q	Frank Froehling III (USA)	Bobby Wilson (GBR)	6-8	4-6	6-4	6-3	9-7

1964

Rd	Winner	Defeated	S1	S2	S3	S4	S5
F	Roy Emerson (AUS)	Fred Stolle (AUS)	6-4	6-1	6-4		
S	Roy Emerson (AUS)	Chuck McKinley (USA)	7-5	11-9	6-4		
S	Fred Stolle (AUS)	Rafael Osuna (MEX)	6-3	8-6	6-3		
Q	Roy Emerson (AUS)	Tony Roche (AUS)	13-11	8-6	6-2		
Q	Chuck McKinley (USA)	Roger Taylor (GBR)	13-11	9-7	6-1		
Q	Rafael Osuna (MEX)	Mike Sangster (GBR)	3-6	9-7	12-10	6-3	
Q	Fred Stolle (AUS)	Dennis Ralston (USA)	6-2	6-3	4-6	3-6	9-7

1965

Rd	Winner	Defeated	S1	S2	S3	S4	S5
F	Manolo Santana (ESP)	Cliff Drysdale (RSA)	6-2	7-9	7-5	6-1	
S	Manolo Santana (ESP)	Arthur Ashe (USA)	2-6	6-4	6-2	6-4	
S	Cliff Drysdale (RSA)	Rafael Osuna (MEX)	6-3	4-6	6-4	6-1	
Q	Arthur Ashe (USA)	Roy Emerson (AUS)	13-11	6-4	10-12	6-2	
Q	Manolo Santana (ESP)	Antonio Palafox (MEX)	6-3	9-7	6-1		
Q	Cliff Drysdale (RSA)	Dennis Ralston (USA)	2-6	3-6	7-5	6-3	8-6
Q	Rafael Osuna (MEX)	Charlie Pasarell (USA)	1-6	6-3	6-3	7-5	

1966

Rd	Winner	Defeated	S1	S2	S3	S4	S5
F	Fred Stolle (AUS)	John Newcombe (AUS)	4-6	12-10	6-3	6-4	
S	John Newcombe (AUS)	Manolo Santana (ESP)	6-3	6-4	6-8	8-6	
S	Fred Stolle (AUS)	Roy Emerson (AUS)	6-4	6-1	6-1		
Q	Manolo Santana (ESP)	Bill Bowrey (AUS)	6-8	6-2	8-6	5-7	6-4
Q	John Newcombe (AUS)	Mark Cox (GBR)	3-6	6-1	3-6	6-2	6-1
Q	Fred Stolle (AUS)	Clark Graebner (USA)	6-3	6-4	6-2		
Q	Roy Emerson (AUS)	Owen Davidson (AUS)	10-12	6-4	6-3	6-2	

1967

Rd	Winner	Defeated	S1	S2	S3	S4	S5
F	John Newcombe (AUS)	Clark Graebner (USA)	6-4	6-4	8-6		
S	John Newcombe (AUS)	Eugene Scott (USA)	6-4	6-3	6-3		
S	Clark Graebner (USA)	Jan Leschly (DEN)	3-6	3-6	7-5	6-4	7-5
Q	John Newcombe (AUS)	Bob Hewitt (RSA)	4-6	6-0	7-5	6-3	
Q	Eugene Scott (USA)	Owen Davidson (AUS)	6-3	8-6	9-7		
Q	Jan Leschly (DEN)	Ronald Barnes (BRA)	7-9	6-4	2-6	6-3	8-6
Q	Clark Graebner (USA)	Roy Emerson (AUS)	8-6	3-6	19-17	6-1	

1968

Rd	Winner	Defeated	S1	S2	S3	S4	S5
F	Arthur Ashe (USA)	Tom Okker (NED)	14-12	5-7	6-3	3-6	6-3
S	Arthur Ashe (USA)	Clark Graebner (USA)	4-6	8-6	7-5	6-2	
S	Tom Okker (NED)	Ken Rosewall (AUS)	8-6	6-4	6-8	6-1	
Q	Arthur Ashe (USA)	Cliff Drysdale (RSA)	8-10	6-3	9-7	6-4	
Q	Clark Graebner (USA)	John Newcombe (AUS)	5-7	11-9	6-1	6-4	
Q	Ken Rosewall (AUS)	Dennis Ralston (USA)	6-2	6-2	6-3		
Q	Tom Okker (NED)	Pancho Gonzalez (USA)	14-16	6-3	10-8	6-3	

1968—AMATEUR

Rd	Winner	Defeated	S1	S2	S3	S4	S5
F	Arthur Ashe (USA)	Bob Lutz (USA)	4-6	6-3	8-10	6-0	6-4
S	Arthur Ashe (USA)	Jim McManus (USA)	6-4	6-2	14-16	6-3	
S	Bob Lutz (USA)	Clark Graebner (USA)	6-4	7-5	6-4		
Q	Arthur Ashe (USA)	Allan Stone (AUS)	3-6	7-5	9-7	6-3	
Q	Jim McManus (USA)	Patricio Cornejo (CHI)	6-2	6-3	6-2		
Q	Bob Lutz (USA)	Bob Hewitt (RSA)	9-7	1-6	6-3	6-2	
Q	Clark Graebner (USA)	Joaquin Loyo-Mayo (MEX)	6-1	6-4	6-3		

1969

Rd	Winner	Defeated	S1	S2	S3	S4	S5
F	Rod Laver (AUS)	Tony Roche (AUS)	7-9	6-1	6-2	6-2	
S	Rod Laver (AUS)	Arthur Ashe (USA)	8-6	6-3	14-12		
S	Tony Roche (AUS)	John Newcombe (AUS)	3-6	6-4	4-6	6-3	8-6
Q	Rod Laver (AUS)	Roy Emerson (AUS)	4-6	8-6	13-11	6-4	
Q	Arthur Ashe (USA)	Ken Rosewall (AUS)	8-6	6-3	6-4		
Q	Tony Roche (AUS)	Butch Buchholz (USA)	6-1	9-7	5-7	6-0	
Q	John Newcombe (AUS)	Fred Stolle (AUS)	7-9	3-6	6-1	6-4	13-11

1969–AMATEUR

Rd	Winner	Defeated	S1	S2	S3	S4	S5
F	Stan Smith (USA)	Bob Lutz (USA)	9-7	6-3	6-1		
S	Bob Lutz (USA)	Arthur Ashe (USA)	6-4	4-6	10-8	6-8	6-4
S	Stan Smith (USA)	Charlie Pasarell (USA)	4-6	2-6	6-2	8-6	15-13
Q	Arthur Ashe (USA)	Allan Stone (AUS)	3-6	6-3	6-8	8-6	6-4
Q	Bob Lutz (USA)	Roy Barth (USA)	6-3	3-6	10-8	6-2	
Q	Charlie Pasarell (USA)	Clark Graebner (USA)	8-6	3-6	3-6	6-2	6-4
Q	Stan Smith (USA)	Ray Ruffels (AUS)	3-6	6-3	6-2	3-6	12-10

1970

Rd	Winner	Defeated	S1	S2	S3	S4	S5
F	Ken Rosewall (AUS)	Tony Roche (AUS)	2-6	6-4	7-6(2)	6-3	
S	Tony Roche (AUS)	Cliff Richey (USA)	6-2	7-6(3)	6-1		
S	Ken Rosewall (AUS)	John Newcombe (AUS)	6-3	6-4	6-3		
Q	Cliff Richey (USA)	Dennis Ralston (USA)	7-6	6-3	6-4		
Q	Tony Roche (AUS)	Brian Fairlie (NZL)	6-3	7-5	7-6		
Q	Ken Rosewall (AUS)	Stan Smith (USA)	6-2	6-2	6-2		
Q	John Newcombe (AUS)	Arthur Ashe (USA)	6-1	7-6(4)	5-7	7-6(2)	

1971

Rd	Winner	Defeated	S1	S2	S3	S4	S5
F	Stan Smith (USA)	Jan Kodes (CZE)	3-6	6-3	6-2	7-6(3)	
S	Jan Kodes (CZE)	Arthur Ashe (USA)	7-6(3)	3-6	4-6	6-3	6-4
S	Stan Smith (USA)	Tom Okker (NED)	7-6(4)	6-3	3-6	2-6	6-3
Q	Jan Kodes (CZE)	Frank Froehling III (USA)	6-0	7-6	6-3		
Q	Arthur Ashe (USA)	Manolo Orantes (ESP)	6-1	6-2	7-6		
Q	Tom Okker (NED)	Clark Graebner (USA)	6-2	6-3	6-4		
Q	Stan Smith (USA)	Marty Riessen (USA)	7-6(4)	6-2	7-6(1)		

1972

Rd	Winner	Defeated	S1	S2	S3	S4	S5
F	Ilie Nastase (ROU)	Arthur Ashe (USA)	3-6	6-3	6-7(1)	6-4	6-3
S	Arthur Ashe (USA)	Cliff Richey (USA)	6-1	6-4	7-6(4)		
S	Ilie Nastase (ROU)	Tom Gorman (USA)	4-6	7-6(4)	6-2	6-1	
Q	Arthur Ashe (USA)	Stan Smith (USA)	7-6	6-4	7-5		
Q	Cliff Richey (USA)	Frew McMillan (RSA)	3-6	6-1	6-4	6-2	
Q	Ilie Nastase (ROU)	Fred Stolle (AUS)	6-4	3-6	6-3	6-2	
Q	Tom Gorman (USA)	Roscoe Tanner (USA)	7-6	5-7	7-6	5-7	6-4

1973

Rd	Winner	Defeated	S1	S2	S3	S4	S5
F	John Newcombe (AUS)	Jan Kodes (CZE)	6-4	1-6	4-6	6-2	6-3
S	Jan Kodes (CZE)	Stan Smith (USA)	7-5	6-7(4)	1-6	6-1	7-5
S	John Newcombe (AUS)	Ken Rosewall (AUS)	6-4	7-6(3)	6-3		
Q	Stan Smith (USA)	Onny Parun (NZL)	6-3	6-3	6-2		
Q	Jan Kodes (CZE)	Nikki Pilic (YUG)	6-2	4-6	6-1	3-6	7-5
Q	Ken Rosewall (AUS)	Vijay Amritraj (IND)	6-4	6-3	6-3		
Q	John Newcombe (AUS)	Jimmy Connors (USA)	6-4	7-6(4)	7-6(4)		

1974

Rd	Winner	Defeated	S1	S2	S3	S4	S5
F	Jimmy Connors (USA)	Ken Rosewall (AUS)	6-1	6-0	6-1		
S	Jimmy Connors (USA)	Roscoe Tanner (USA)	7-6(2)	7-6(2)	6-4		
S	Ken Rosewall (AUS)	John Newcombe (AUS)	6-7(3)	6-4	7-6(1)	6-3	
Q	Jimmy Connors (USA)	Alex Metreveli (USSR)	3-6	6-1	6-4	6-1	
Q	Roscoe Tanner (USA)	Stan Smith (USA)	7-6(2)	6-2	3-6	6-1	
Q	Ken Rosewall (AUS)	Vijay Amritraj (IND)	2-6	6-3	6-3	6-2	
Q	John Newcombe (AUS)	Arthur Ashe (USA)	4-6	6-3	3-6	7-6(0)	6-4

1975

Rd	Winner	Defeated	S1	S2	S3	S4	S5
F	Manolo Orantes (ESP)	Jimmy Connors (USA)	6-4	6-3	6-3		
S	Jimmy Connors (USA)	Bjorn Borg (SWE)	7-5	7-5	7-5		
S	Manolo Orantes (ESP)	Guillermo Vilas (ARG)	4-6	1-6	6-2	7-5	6-4
Q	Jimmy Connors (USA)	Andrew Pattison (RHO)	6-2	6-1	6-2		
Q	Bjorn Borg (SWE)	Eddie Dibbs (USA)	6-4	7-6	4-6	7-6	
Q	Manolo Orantes (ESP)	Ilie Nastase (ROU)	6-2	6-4	3-6	7-3	
Q	Guillermo Vilas (ARG)	Jaime Fillol (CHI)	6-4	6-0	6-1		

1976

Rd	Winner	Defeated	S1	S2	S3	S4	S5
F	Jimmy Connors (USA)	Bjorn Borg (SWE)	6-4	3-6	7-6(9)	6-4	
S	Jimmy Connors (USA)	Guillermo Vilas (ARG)	6-4	6-2	6-1		
S	Bjorn Borg (SWE)	Ilie Nastase (ROU)	6-3	6-3	6-4		
Q	Jimmy Connors (USA)	Jan Kodes (CZE)	7-5	6-3	6-1		
Q	Guillermo Vilas (ARG)	Eddie Dibbs (USA)	6-1	2-6	7-6(5)	7-6(2)	
Q	Bjorn Borg (SWE)	Manolo Orantes (ESP)	4-6	6-0	6-2	5-7	6-4
Q	Ilie Nastase (ROU)	Dick Stockton (USA)	4-6	6-4	6-2	6-3	

1977

Rd	Winner	Defeated	S1	S2	S3	S4	S5
F	Guillermo Vilas (ARG)	Jimmy Connors (USA)	2-6	6-3	7-6(4)	6-0	
S	Guillermo Vilas (ARG)	Harold Solomon (USA)	6-2	7-6	6-2		
S	Jimmy Connors (USA)	Corrado Barazzutti (ITA)	7-5	6-3	7-5		
Q	Harold Solomon (USA)	Dick Stockton (USA)	6-4	6-4	6-2		
Q	Guillermo Vilas (ARG)	Raymond Moore (RSA)	6-1	6-1	6-0		
Q	Corrado Barazzutti (ITA)	Brian Gottfried (USA)	6-2	6-1	6-2		
Q	Jimmy Connors (USA)	Manolo Orantes (ESP)	6-2	6-4	6-3		

1978

Rd	Winner	Defeated	S1	S2	S3	S4	S5
F	Jimmy Connors (USA)	Bjorn Borg (SWE)	6-4	6-2	6-2		
S	Bjorn Borg (SWE)	Vitas Gerulaitis (USA)	6-3	6-2	7-6(3)		
S	Jimmy Connors (USA)	John McEnroe (USA)	6-2	6-2	7-5		
Q	Bjorn Borg (SWE)	Raul Ramirez (MEX)	6-7	6-4	6-4	6-0	
Q	Vitas Gerulaitis (USA)	Johan Kriek (RSA)	6-2	6-1	6-2		
Q	John McEnroe (USA)	Butch Walts (USA)	6-1	6-2	7-6(4)		
Q	Jimmy Connors (USA)	Brian Gottfried (USA)	6-2	7-6(0)	6-1		

1979

Rd	Winner	Defeated	S1	S2	S3	S4	S5
F	John McEnroe (USA)	Vitas Gerulaitis (USA)	7-5	6-3	6-3		
S	Vitas Gerulaitis (USA)	Roscoe Tanner (USA)	3-6	2-6	7-6(5)	6-3	6-3
S	John McEnroe (USA)	Jimmy Connors (USA)	6-3	6-3	7-5		
Q	Roscoe Tanner (USA)	Bjorn Borg (SWE)	6-2	4-6	6-2	7-6(2)	
Q	Vitas Gerulaitis (USA)	Johan Kriek (RSA)	5-7	6-3	6-4	6-3	
Q	John McEnroe (USA)	Eddie Dibbs (USA)	2-1				(retired)
Q	Jimmy Connors (USA)	Pat du Pre (USA)	6-2	6-1	6-1		

Rd	Winner	Defeated	S1	S2	S3	S4	S5

1980

Rd	Winner	Defeated	S1	S2	S3	S4	S5
F	John McEnroe (USA)	Bjorn Borg (SWE)	7-6(4)	6-1	6-7(5)	5-7	6-4
S	Bjorn Borg (SWE)	Johan Kriek (RSA)	4-6	4-6	6-1	6-1	6-1
S	John McEnroe (USA)	Jimmy Connors (USA)	6-4	5-7	0-6	6-3	7-6(3)
Q	Bjorn Borg (SWE)	Roscoe Tanner (USA)	6-4	3-6	4-6	7-5	6-3
Q	Johan Kriek (RSA)	Wojtek Fibak (POL)	4-6	6-2	3-6	6-1	7-6
Q	Jimmy Connors (USA)	Eliot Teltscher (USA)	6-1	3-6	6-3	6-0	
Q	John McEnroe (USA)	Ivan Lendl (CZE)	4-6	6-3	6-2	7-5	

1981

Rd	Winner	Defeated	S1	S2	S3	S4	S5
F	John McEnroe (USA)	Bjorn Borg (SWE)	4-6	6-2	6-4	6-3	
S	Bjorn Borg (SWE)	Vitas Gerulaitis (USA)	5-7	6-3	6-2	4-6	6-3
S	John McEnroe (USA)	Jimmy Connors (USA)	6-2	7-5	6-4		
Q	Bjorn Borg (SWE)	Ramesh Krishnan (IND)	6-7	7-6	6-4	6-2	
Q	Vitas Gerulaitis (USA)	Bruce Manson (USA)	6-4	6-2	4-6	6-1	
Q	Jimmy Connors (USA)	Eliot Teltscher (USA)	6-3	6-1	6-2		
Q	John McEnroe (USA)	Roscoe Tanner (USA)	7-6(4)	6-3	6-7(4)	7-6(7)	

1982

Rd	Winner	Defeated	S1	S2	S3	S4	S5
F	Jimmy Connors (USA)	Ivan Lendl (CZE)	6-3	6-2	4-6	6-4	
S	Ivan Lendl (CZE)	John McEnroe (USA)	6-4	6-4	7-6(6)		
S	Jimmy Connors (USA)	Guillermo Vilas (ARG)	6-1	3-6	6-2	6-3	
Q	John McEnroe (USA)	Gene Mayer (USA)	4-6	7-6(4)	6-3	4-6	6-1
Q	Ivan Lendl (CZE)	Kim Warwick (AUS)	6-4	6-3	6-1		
Q	Guillermo Vilas (ARG)	Tom Gullikson (USA)	6-2	6-1	6-3		
Q	Jimmy Connors (USA)	Rodney Harmon (USA)	6-1	6-3	6-4		

1983

Rd	Winner	Defeated	S1	S2	S3	S4	S5
F	Jimmy Connors (USA)	Ivan Lendl (CZE)	6-3	6-7(2)	7-5	6-0	
S	Jimmy Connors (USA)	Bill Scanlon (USA)	6-2	6-3	6-2		
S	Ivan Lendl (CZE)	Jimmy Arias (USA)	6-2	7-6(3)	6-1		
Q	Bill Scanlon (USA)	Mark Dickson (USA)	3-6	6-4	4-6	6-3	7-6(4)
Q	Jimmy Connors (USA)	Eliot Teltscher (USA)	7-6(0)	6-2	6-2		
Q	Jimmy Arias (USA)	Yannick Noah (FRA)	7-6(4)	4-6	6-3	1-6	7-5
Q	Ivan Lendl (CZE)	Mats Wilander (SWE)	6-4	6-4	7-6(4)		

1984

Rd	Winner	Defeated	S1	S2	S3	S4	S5
F	John McEnroe (USA)	Ivan Lendl (CZE)	6-3	6-4	6-1		
S	John McEnroe (USA)	Jimmy Connors (USA)	6-4	4-6	7-5	4-6	6-3
S	Ivan Lendl (CZE)	Pat Cash (AUS)	3-6	6-3	6-4	6-7(5)	7-6(4)
Q	John McEnroe (USA)	Gene Mayer (USA)	7-5	6-3	6-4		
Q	Jimmy Connors (USA)	John Lloyd (GBR)	7-5	6-2	6-0		
Q	Pat Cash (AUS)	Mats Wilander (SWE)	7-6	6-4	2-6	6-3	
Q	Ivan Lendl (CZE)	Andres Gomez (ECU)	6-4	6-4	6-1		

1985

Rd	Winner	Defeated	S1	S2	S3	S4	S5
F	Ivan Lendl (CZE)	John McEnroe (USA)	7-6(4)	6-3	6-4		
S	John McEnroe (USA)	Mats Wilander (SWE)	3-6	6-4	4-6	6-3	6-3
S	Ivan Lendl (CZE)	Jimmy Connors (USA)	6-2	6-3	7-5		
Q	John McEnroe (USA)	Joakim Nystrom (SWE)	6-1	6-0	7-5		
Q	Mats Wilander (SWE)	Anders Jarryd (SWE)	2-6	6-2	5-0	(retired)	
Q	Jimmy Connors (USA)	Heinz Gunthardt (SUI)	6-2	6-2	6-4		
Q	Ivan Lendl (CZE)	Yannick Noah (FRA)	6-2	6-2	6-4		

1986

Rd	Winner	Defeated	S1	S2	S3	S4	S5
F	Ivan Lendl (CZE)	Miloslav Mecir (CZE)	6-4	6-2	6-0		
S	Ivan Lendl (CZE)	Stefan Edberg (SWE)	7-6(6)	6-2	6-3		
S	Miloslav Mecir (CZE)	Boris Becker (GER)	4-6	6-3	6-4	3-6	6-3
Q	Ivan Lendl (CZE)	Henri Leconte (FRA)	7-6	6-1	1-6	6-1	
Q	Stefan Edberg (SWE)	Tim Wilkison (USA)	6-3	6-3	6-3		
Q	Boris Becker (GER)	Milan Srejber (CZE)	6-3	6-2	6-1		
Q	Miloslav Mecir (CZE)	Joakim Nystrom (SWE)	6-4	6-2	3-6	6-2	

1987

Rd	Winner	Defeated	S1	S2	S3	S4	S5
F	Ivan Lendl (CZE)	Mats Wilander (SWE)	6-7(7)	6-0	7-6(4)	6-4	
S	Ivan Lendl (CZE)	Jimmy Connors (USA)	6-4	6-2	6-2		
S	Mats Wilander (SWE)	Stefan Edberg (SWE)	6-4	3-6	6-3	6-4	
Q	Ivan Lendl (CZE)	John McEnroe (USA)	6-3	6-3	6-4		
Q	Jimmy Connors (USA)	Brad Gilbert (USA)	4-6	6-3	6-4	6-0	
Q	Mats Wilander (SWE)	Miloslav Mecir (CZE)	6-3	6-7	6-4	7-6	
Q	Stefan Edberg (SWE)	Ramesh Krishnan (IND)	6-2	6-2	6-2		

1988

Rd	Winner	Defeated	S1	S2	S3	S4	S5
F	Mats Wilander (SWE)	Ivan Lendl (CZE)	6-4	4-6	6-3	5-7	6-4
S	Ivan Lendl (CZE)	Andre Agassi (USA)	4-6	6-2	6-3	6-4	
S	Mats Wilander (SWE)	Darren Cahill (AUS)	6-4	6-4	6-2		
Q	Ivan Lendl (CZE)	Derrick Rostagno (USA)	6-2	6-2	6-0		
Q	Andre Agassi (USA)	Jimmy Connors (USA)	6-2	7-6(6)	6-1		
Q	Darren Cahill (AUS)	Aaron Krickstein (USA)	6-2	5-7	7-6(2)	5-7	6-3
Q	Mats Wilander (SWE)	Emilio Sanchez (ESP)	3-6	7-6(3)	6-0	6-4	

1989

Rd	Winner	Defeated	S1	S2	S3	S4	S5
F	Boris Becker (GER)	Ivan Lendl (CZE)	7-6(2)	1-6	6-3	7-6(4)	
S	Ivan Lendl (CZE)	Andre Agassi (USA)	7-6(4)	6-1	3-6	6-1	
S	Boris Becker (GER)	Aaron Krickstein (USA)	6-4	6-3	6-4		
Q	Ivan Lendl (CZE)	Tim Mayotte (USA)	6-4	6-0	6-1		
Q	Andre Agassi (USA)	Jimmy Connors (USA)	6-1	4-6	0-6	6-3	6-4
Q	Aaron Krickstein (USA)	Jay Berger (USA)	3-6	6-4	6-2	1-0	(retired)
Q	Boris Becker (GER)	Yannick Noah (FRA)	6-3	6-3	6-2		

1990

Rd	Winner	Defeated	S1	S2	S3	S4	S5
F	Pete Sampras (USA)	Andre Agassi (USA)	6-4	6-3	6-2		
S	Pete Sampras (USA)	John McEnroe (USA)	6-2	6-4	3-6	6-3	
S	Andre Agassi (USA)	Boris Becker (GER)	6-7(10)	6-3	6-2	6-3	
Q	John McEnroe (USA)	David Wheaton (USA)	6-1	6-4	6-4		
Q	Pete Sampras (USA)	Ivan Lendl (CZE)	6-4	7-6(4)	3-6	4-6	6-2
Q	Andre Agassi (USA)	Andrei Cherkasov (USSR)	6-2	6-2	6-3		
Q	Boris Becker (GER)	Aaron Krickstein (USA)	3-6	6-3	6-2	6-3	

1991

Rd	Winner	Defeated	S1	S2	S3	S4	S5
F	Stefan Edberg (SWE)	Jim Courier (USA)	6-2	6-4	6-0		
S	Jim Courier (USA)	Jimmy Connors (USA)	6-3	6-3	6-2		
S	Stefan Edberg (SWE)	Ivan Lendl (CZE)	6-3	6-3	6-4		
Q	Jimmy Connors (USA)	Paul Haarhuis (NED)	4-6	7-6(3)	6-4	6-2	
Q	Jim Courier (USA)	Pete Sampras (USA)	6-2	7-6(4)	7-6(5)		
Q	Ivan Lendl (CZE)	Michael Stich (GER)	6-3	3-6	4-6	7-6(5)	6-1
Q	Stefan Edberg (SWE)	Javier Sanchez (ESP)	6-3	6-2	6-3		

Rd	Winner	Defeated	S1	S2	S3	S4	S5

1992

Rd	Winner	Defeated	S1	S2	S3	S4	S5
F	Stefan Edberg (SWE)	Pete Sampras (USA)	3-6	6-4	7-6(5)	6-2	
S	Pete Sampras (USA)	Jim Courier (USA)	6-1	3-6	6-2	6-2	
S	Stefan Edberg (SWE)	Michael Chang (USA)	6-7(3)	7-5	7-6(3)	5-7	6-4
Q	Jim Courier (USA)	Andre Agassi (USA)	6-3	6-7(6)	6-1	6-4	
Q	Pete Sampras (USA)	Alexander Volkov (RUS)	6-4	6-1	6-0		
Q	Michael Chang (USA)	Wayne Ferreira (RSA)	7-5	2-6	6-3	6-7(4)	6-1
Q	Stefan Edberg (SWE)	Ivan Lendl (USA)	6-3	6-3	3-6	5-7	7-6(3)

1993

Rd	Winner	Defeated	S1	S2	S3	S4	S5
F	Pete Sampras (USA)	Cedric Pioline (FRA)	6-4	6-4	6-3		
S	Cedric Pioline (FRA)	Wally Masur (AUS)	6-1	6-7(3)	7-6(2)	6-1	
S	Pete Sampras (USA)	Alexander Volkov (RUS)	6-4	6-3	6-2		
Q	Cedric Pioline (FRA)	Andrei Medvedev (UKR)	6-3	6-1	3-6	6-2	
Q	Wally Masur (AUS)	Magnus Larsson (SWE)	6-2	7-5	7-5		
Q	Alexander Volkov (RUS)	Thomas Muster (AUT)	7-6(6)	6-3	3-6	2-6	7-5
Q	Pete Sampras (USA)	Michael Chang (USA)	6-7(0)	7-6(2)	6-1	6-1	

1994

Rd	Winner	Defeated	S1	S2	S3	S4	S5
F	Andre Agassi (USA)	Michael Stich (GER)	6-1	7-6(5)	7-5		
S	Michael Stich (GER)	Karel Novacek (CZE)	7-5	6-3	7-6(4)		
S	Andre Agassi (USA)	Todd Martin (USA)	6-3	4-6	6-2	6-3	
Q	Karel Novacek (CZE)	Jaime Yzaga (PER)	6-2	6-7(7)	6-1	5-7	6-3
Q	Michael Stich (GER)	Jonas Bjorkman (SWE)	6-4	6-4	6-7(7)	6-4	
Q	Andre Agassi (USA)	Thomas Muster (AUT)	7-6(5)	6-3	6-0		
Q	Todd Martin (USA)	Bernd Karbacher (GER)	6-4	7-6(5)	4-6	6-4	

1995

Rd	Winner	Defeated	S1	S2	S3	S4	S5
F	Pete Sampras (USA)	Andre Agassi (USA)	6-4	6-3	4-6	7-5	
S	Andre Agassi (USA)	Boris Becker (GER)	7-6(4)	7-6(2)	4-6	6-4	
S	Pete Sampras (USA)	Jim Courier (USA)	7-5	4-6	6-4	7-5	
Q	Andre Agassi (USA)	Petr Korda (CZE)	6-4	6-2	1-6	7-5	
Q	Boris Becker (GER)	Patrick McEnroe (USA)	6-4	7-6(2)	6-7(3)	7-6(6)	
Q	Jim Courier (USA)	Michael Chang (USA)	7-6(5)	7-6(3)	7-5		
Q	Pete Sampras (USA)	Byron Black (ZIM)	7-6(3)	6-4	6-0		

1996

Rd	Winner	Defeated	S1	S2	S3	S4	S5
F	Pete Sampras (USA)	Michael Chang (USA)	6-1	6-4	7-6(3)		
S	Pete Sampras (USA)	Goran Ivanisevic (CRO)	6-3	6-4	6-7(9)	6-3	
S	Michael Chang (USA)	Andre Agassi (USA)	6-3	6-2	6-2		
Q	Pete Sampras (USA)	Alex Corretja (ESP)	7-6(5)	5-7	5-7	6-4	7-6(7)
Q	Goran Ivanisevic (CRO)	Stefan Edberg (SWE)	6-3	6-4	7-6(9)		
Q	Andre Agassi (USA)	Thomas Muster (AUT)	6-2	7-5	4-6	6-2	
Q	Michael Chang (USA)	Javier Sanchez (ESP)	7-5	6-3	6-7(2)	6-3	

1997

Rd	Winner	Defeated	S1	S2	S3	S4	S5
F	Patrick Rafter (AUS)	Greg Rusedski (GBR)	6-3	6-2	4-6	7-5	
S	Greg Rusedski (GBR)	Jonas Bjorkman (SWE)	6-1	3-6	3-6	6-3	7-5
S	Patrick Rafter (AUS)	Michael Chang (USA)	6-3	6-3	6-4		
Q	Jonas Bjorkman (SWE)	Petr Korda (CZE)	7-6(3)	6-2	1-0	(retired)	
Q	Greg Rusedski (GBR)	Richard Krajicek (NED)	7-5	7-6(5)	7-6(6)		
Q	Patrick Rafter (AUS)	Magnus Larsson (SWE)	7-6(4)	6-4	6-2		
Q	Michael Chang (USA)	Marcelo Rios (CHI)	7-5	6-2	4-6	4-6	6-3

1998

Rd	Winner	Defeated	S1	S2	S3	S4	S5
F	Patrick Rafter (AUS)	Mark Philippoussis (AUS)	6-3	3-6	6-2	6-0	
S	Patrick Rafter (AUS)	Pete Sampras (USA)	6-7(8)	6-4	2-6	6-4	6-3
S	Mark Philippoussis (AUS)	Carlos Moya (ESP)	6-1	6-4	5-7	6-4	
Q	Pete Sampras (USA)	Karol Kucera (SVK)	6-3	7-5	6-4		
Q	Patrick Rafter (AUS)	Jonas Bjorkman (SWE)	6-2	6-3	7-5		
Q	Mark Philippoussis (AUS)	Thomas Johansson (SWE)	4-6	6-3	6-7(3)	6-3	7-6(10)
Q	Carlos Moya (ESP)	Magnus Larsson (SWE)	6-4	6-3	6-3		

1999

Rd	Winner	Defeated	S1	S2	S3	S4	S5
F	Andre Agassi (USA)	Todd Martin (USA)	6-4	6-7(5)	6-7(2)	6-3	6-2
S	Todd Martin (USA)	Cedric Pioline (FRA)	6-4	6-1	6-2		
S	Andre Agassi (USA)	Yevgeny Kafelnikov (RUS)	1-6	6-3	6-3	6-3	
Q	Todd Martin (USA)	Slava Dosedel (CZE)	6-3	5-7	6-4	6-4	
Q	Cedric Pioline (FRA)	Gustavo Kuerten (BRA)	4-6	7-6(6)	7-6(14)	7-6(8)	
Q	Yevgeny Kafelnikov (RUS)	Richard Krajicek (NED)	7-6(0)	7-6(4)	3-6	1-6	7-6(5)
Q	Andre Agassi (USA)	Nicolas Escude (FRA)	7-6(3)	6-3	6-4		

2000

Rd	Winner	Defeated	S1	S2	S3	S4	S5
F	Marat Safin (RUS)	Pete Sampras (USA)	6-4	6-3	6-3		
S	Pete Sampras (USA)	Lleyton Hewitt (AUS)	7-6(7)	6-4	7-6(5)		
S	Marat Safin (RUS)	Todd Martin (USA)	6-3	7-6(4)	7-6(1)		
Q	Lleyton Hewitt (AUS)	Arnaud Clement (FRA)	6-2	6-4	6-3		
Q	Pete Sampras (USA)	Richard Krajicek (NED)	4-6	7-6(6)	6-4	6-2	
Q	Marat Safin (RUS)	Nicolas Kiefer (GER)	7-5	4-6	7-6(5)	6-3	
Q	Todd Martin (USA)	Thomas Johansson (SWE)	6-4	6-4	3-6	7-5	

2001

Rd	Winner	Defeated	S1	S2	S3	S4	S5
F	Lleyton Hewitt (AUS)	Pete Sampras (USA)	7-6(4)	6-1	6-1		
S	Lleyton Hewitt (AUS)	Yevgeny Kafelnikov (RUS)	6-1	6-2	6-1		
S	Pete Sampras (USA)	Marat Safin (RUS)	6-3	7-6(5)	6-3		
Q	Yevgeny Kafelnikov (RUS)	Gustavo Kuerten (BRA)	6-4	6-0	6-3		
Q	Lleyton Hewitt (AUS)	Andy Roddick (USA)	6-7(5)	6-3	6-4	3-6	6-4
Q	Marat Safin (RUS)	Mariano Zabaleta (ARG)	6-4	6-4	6-2		
Q	Pete Sampras (USA)	Andre Agassi (USA)	6-7(7)	7-6(2)	7-6(2)	7-6(5)	

2002

Rd	Winner	Defeated	S1	S2	S3	S4	S5
F	Pete Sampras (USA)	Andre Agassi (USA)	6-3	6-4	5-7	6-4	
S	Andre Agassi (USA)	Lleyton Hewitt (AUS)	6-4	7-6(5)	6-7(1)	6-2	
S	Pete Sampras (USA)	Sjeng Schalken (NED)	7-6(6)	7-6(4)	6-2		
Q	Lleyton Hewitt (AUS)	Younes El Aynaoui (MAR)	6-1	7-6(6)	4-6	6-2	
Q	Andre Agassi (USA)	Max Mirnyi (BLR)	6-7(5)	6-3	7-5	6-3	
Q	Pete Sampras (USA)	Andy Roddick (USA)	6-3	6-2	6-4		
Q	Sjeng Schalken (NED)	Fernando Gonzalez (CHI)	6-7(5)	6-3	6-3	6-7(5)	7-6(2)

2003

Rd	Winner	Defeated	S1	S2	S3	S4	S5
F	Andy Roddick (USA)	Juan Carlos Ferrero (ESP)	6-3	7-6(2)	6-3		
S	Juan Carlos Ferrero (ESP)	Andre Agassi (USA)	6-4	6-3	3-6	6-4	
S	Andy Roddick (USA)	David Nalbandian (ARG)	6-7(4)	3-6	7-6(7)	6-1	6-3
Q	Andre Agassi (USA)	Guillermo Coria (ARG)	6-4	6-3	7-5		
Q	Juan Carlos Ferrero (ESP)	Lleyton Hewitt (ARG)	4-6	6-3	7-6(5)	6-1	
Q	Andy Roddick (USA)	Sjeng Schalken (NED)	6-4	6-2	6-3		
Q	David Nalbandian (ARG)	Younes El Aynaoui (MAR)	7-6(2)	6-2	3-6	7-5	

Rd	Winner	Defeated	S1	S2	S3	S4	S5

2004

Rd	Winner	Defeated	S1	S2	S3	S4	S5
F	**Roger Federer (SUI)**	**Lleyton Hewitt (AUS)**	**6-0**	**7-6(3)**	**6-0**		
S	Roger Federer (SUI)	Tim Henman (GBR)	6-3	6-4	6-4		
S	Lleyton Hewitt (AUS)	Joachim Johansson (SWE)	6-4	7-5	6-3		
Q	Roger Federer (SUI)	Andre Agassi (USA)	6-3	2-6	7-5	3-6	6-3
Q	Tim Henman (GBR)	Dominik Hrbaty (SVK)	6-1	7-5	5-7	6-2	
Q	Lleyton Hewitt (AUS)	Tommy Haas (GER)	6-2	6-2	6-2		
Q	Joachim Johansson (SWE)	Andy Roddick (USA)	6-4	6-4	3-6	2-6	6-4

2005

Rd	Winner	Defeated	S1	S2	S3	S4	S5
F	**Roger Federer (SUI)**	**Andre Agassi (USA)**	**6-3**	**2-6**	**7-6(1)**	**6-1**	
S	Roger Federer (SUI)	Lleyton Hewitt (AUS)	6-3	7-6(0)	4-6	6-3	
S	Andre Agassi (USA)	Robby Ginepri (USA)	6-4	5-7	6-3	4-6	6-3
Q	Roger Federer (SUI)	David Nalbandian (ARG)	6-2	6-4	6-1		
Q	Lleyton Hewitt (AUS)	Jarkko Nieminen (FIN)	2-6	6-1	3-6	6-3	6-1
Q	Robby Ginepri (USA)	Guillermo Coria (ARG)	4-6	6-1	7-5	3-6	7-5
Q	Andre Agassi (USA)	James Blake (USA)	3-6	3-6	6-3	6-3	7-6(6)

2006

Rd	Winner	Defeated	S1	S2	S3	S4	S5
F	**Roger Federer (SUI)**	**Andy Roddick (USA)**	**6-2**	**4-6**	**7-5**	**6-1**	
S	Roger Federer (SUI)	Nikolay Davydenko (RUS)	6-1	7-5	6-4		
S	Andy Roddick (USA)	Mikhail Youzhny (RUS)	6-7(5)	6-0	7-6(3)	6-3	
Q	Roger Federer (SUI)	James Blake (USA)	7-6(7)	6-0	6-7(9)	6-4	
Q	Nikolay Davydenko (RUS)	Tommy Haas (GER)	4-6	6-7(3)	6-3	6-4	6-4
Q	Andy Roddick (USA)	Lleyton Hewitt (AUS)	6-3	7-5	6-4		
Q	Mikhail Youzhny (RUS)	Rafael Nadal (ESP)	6-3	5-7	7-6(5)	6-1	

2007

Rd	Winner	Defeated	S1	S2	S3	S4	S5
F	**Roger Federer (SUI)**	**Novak Djokovic (SRB)**	**7-6(4)**	**7-6(2)**	**6-4**		
S	Roger Federer (SUI)	Nikolay Davydenko (RUS)	7-5	6-1	7-5		
S	Novak Djokovic (SRB)	David Ferrer (ESP)	6-4	6-4	6-3		
Q	Roger Federer (SUI)	Andy Roddick (USA)	7-6(5)	7-6(4)	6-2		
Q	Nikolay Davydenko (RUS)	Tommy Haas (GER)	6-3	6-3	6-4		
Q	Novak Djokovic (SRB)	Carlos Moya (ESP)	6-4	7-6(7)	6-1		
Q	David Ferrer (ESP)	Juan Ignacio Chela (ARG)	6-2	6-3	7-5		

2008

Rd	Winner	Defeated	S1	S2	S3	S4	S5
F	**Roger Federer (SUI)**	**Andy Murray (GBR)**	**6-2**	**7-5**	**6-2**		
S	Andy Murray (GBR)	Rafael Nadal (ESP)	6-2	7-6 (5)	4-6	6-4	
S	Roger Federer (SUI)	Novak Djokovic (SRB)	6-3	5-7	7-5	6-2	
Q	Rafael Nadal (ESP)	Mardy Fish (USA)	3-6	6-1	6-4	6-2	
Q	Andy Murray (GBR)	Juan Martin Del Potro (ARG)	7-6 (1)	7-6 (2)	4-6	7-5	
Q	Novak Djokovic (SRB)	Andy Roddick (USA)	6-2	6-3	3-6	7-6 (5)	
Q	Roger Federer (SUI)	Gilles Muller (LUX)	7-6 (5)	6-4	7-6 (5)		

Women's Singles

Rd	Winner	Defeated	S1	S2	S3	S4	S5

1887

Rd	Winner	Defeated	S1	S2	S3	S4	S5
F	**Ellen Hansell (USA)**	**Laura Knight (USA)**	**6-1**	**6-0**			
S	Ellen Hansell (USA)	Helen Day Harris (USA)	2-6	6-4	6-4		
S	Laura Knight (USA)	Alice Janney (USA)	6-0	6-1			
Q	Ellen Hansell (USA)	Jessie Harding (USA)	6-1	6-0			
Q	Helen Day Harris (USA)	Louise Alderdice (USA)	6-3	6-5			
Q	Laura Knight (USA)	Ruth Cott (USA)	6-0	6-3			
Q	Alice Janney (USA)	(bye)					

1888

Rd	Winner	Defeated	S1	S2	S3	S4	S5
Ch	**Bertha Townsend (USA)**	**Ellen Hansell (USA)**	**6-3**	**6-5**			
F	Bertha Townsend (USA)	Marion Wright (USA)	6-2	6-2			
S	Marion Wright (USA)	(bye)					
S	Bertha Townsend (USA)	Adeline Robinson (USA)	1-6	6-5	6-3		
Q	Marion Wright (USA)	Violet Ward (USA)	6-0	6-5			
Q	Bertha Townsend (USA)	(bye)					
Q	Adeline Robinson (USA)	Ellen Roosevelt (USA)	6-4	3-6	6-3		

1889

Rd	Winner	Defeated	S1	S2	S3	S4	S5
Ch	**Bertha Townsend (USA)**	**Lida Voorhees (USA)**	**7-5**	**6-2**			
F	Lida Voorhees (USA)	Helen Day Harris (USA)	6-5	2-6	6-3		
S	Lida Voorhees (USA)	Grace Roosevelt (USA)	6-1	4-6	6-5		
S	Helen Day Harris (USA)	D.F. Butterfield (USA)	6-1	6-3			
Q	Grace Roosevelt (USA)	Marion Wright (USA)	(default)				
Q	Lida Voorhees (USA)	Laura Knight (USA)	6-1	6-2			
Q	Helen Day Harris (USA)	Rebecca H. Lycett (USA)	6-1	6-1			
Q	D.F. Butterfield (USA)	Anna C. Smith (USA)	6-3	6-1			

1890

Rd	Winner	Defeated	S1	S2	S3	S4	S5
Ch	**Ellen Roosevelt (USA)**	**Bertha Townsend (USA)**	**6-2**	**6-2**			
F	Ellen Roosevelt (USA)	Lida Voorhees (USA)	6-3	6-1			
S	Ellen Roosevelt (USA)	Mabel Cahill (IRL)	2-6	6-5	3-2	(retired)	
S	Lida Voorhees (USA)	Margarette Ballard (USA)	6-4	3-6	6-5		
Q	Ellen Roosevelt (USA)	D.F. Butterfield (USA)	6-0	6-0			
Q	Mabel Cahill (IRL)	Rebecca H. Lycett (USA)	6-1	6-1			
Q	Lida Voorhees (USA)	F.K. Gregory (USA)	6-1	3-6	6-1		
Q	Margarette Ballard (USA)	S. Day (USA)	6-2	6-1			

1891

Rd	Winner	Defeated	S1	S2	S3	S4	S5
Ch	**Mabel Cahill (IRL)**	**Ellen Roosevelt (USA)**	**6-4**	**6-1**	**4-6**	**6-3**	
F	Mabel Cahill (IRL)	Grace Roosevelt (USA)	6-3	7-5			
S	Mabel Cahill (IRL)	Lida Voorhees (USA)	6-1	6-0			
S	Grace Roosevelt (USA)	Adelaide Clarkson (USA)	6-1	6-1			
Q	Mabel Cahill (IRL)	Annabella Wistar (USA)	6-5	6-4			
Q	Lida Voorhees (USA)	Amy Williams (USA)	4-6	6-3	6-3		
Q	Adelaide Clarkson (USA)	Emma Leavitt Morgan (USA)	6-2	6-5			
Q	Grace Roosevelt (USA)	Helen Day Harris (USA)	3-6	6-3	6-4		

1892

Rd	Winner	Defeated	S1	S2	S3	S4	S5
Ch	Mabel Cahill (IRL)	Elisabeth Moore (USA)	5-7	6-3	6-4	4-6	6-2
F	Elisabeth Moore (USA)	Helen Day Harris (USA)	5-7	6-1	6-1		
S	Elisabeth Moore (USA)	Annabella Wistar (USA)	(default)				
S	Helen Day Harris (USA)	Augusta Schultz (USA)	6-2	8-6			
Q	Elisabeth Moore (USA)	Elisabeth Slevin (USA)	6-0	6-0			
Q	Annabella Wistar (USA)	Harriet Butler (USA)	6-4	2-6	8-6		
Q	Helen Day Harris (USA)	Hattie Beaumont (USA)	6-2	4-6	6-2		
Q	Augusta Schultz (USA)	Josephine White (USA)	6-1	6-1			

1893

Rd	Winner	Defeated	S1	S2	S3	S4	S5
Ch	Aline Terry (USA)	Mabel Cahill (IRL)	(default)				
F	Aline Terry (USA)	Augusta Schultz (USA)	6-1	6-3			
S	Augusta Schultz (USA)	Miss Underhill (USA)	6-2	3-6	6-0		
S	Aline Terry (USA)	Elisabeth Moore (USA)	6-3	4-6	6-4		
Q	Miss Underhill (USA)	Miss Bent (USA)	4-6	6-4	9-7		
Q	Augusta Schultz (USA)	Annabella Wistar (USA)	6-3	6-1			
Q	Elisabeth Moore (USA)	Helen Hellwig (USA)	7-5	1-6	6-4		
Q	AlineTerry (USA)	Hattie Beaumont (USA)	6-2	6-0			

1894

Rd	Winner	Defeated	S1	S2	S3	S4	S5
Ch	Helen Hellwig (USA)	Aline Terry (USA)	7-5	3-6	6-0	3-6	6-3
F	Helen Hellwig (USA)	B. Townsend Toulmin (USA)	6-2	7-5	6-4		
S	Helen Hellwig (USA)	Ethel Bankson (USA)	6-2	6-1			
S	B. Townsend Toulmin (USA)	Juliette Atkinson (USA)	4-6	6-5	6-4		
Q	Ethel Bankson (USA)	Hattie Beaumont (USA)	6-1	6-0			
Q	Helen Hellwig (USA)	Amy Williams (USA)	6-2	6-2			
Q	B. Townsend Toulmin (USA)	Mrs Clement Beecroft (USA)	6-1	6-0			
Q	Juliette Atkinson (USA)	Elizabeth Slevin (USA)	6-1	6-1			

1895

Rd	Winner	Defeated	S1	S2	S3	S4	S5
Ch	Juliette Atkinson (USA)	Helen Hellwig (USA)	6-4	6-2	6-1		
F	Juliette Atkinson (USA)	Elisabeth Moore (USA)	6-3	7-5	3-6	6-0	
S	Elisabeth Moore (USA)	B. Townsend Toulmin (USA)	6-4	6-4			
S	Juliette Atkinson (USA)	Kathleen Atkinson (USA)	6-1	6-4			
Q	Elisabeth Moore (USA)	Grace Booth (USA)	6-0	6-2			
Q	B. Townsend Toulmin (USA)	Elizabeth Taylor (USA)	6-0	6-2			
Q	Kathleen Atkinson (USA)	Mary Warren (USA)	6-3	6-2			
Q	Juliette Atkinson (USA)	Amy Williams (USA)	6-0	6-4			

1896

Rd	Winner	Defeated	S1	S2	S3	S4	S5
Ch	Elisabeth Moore (USA)	Juliette Atkinson (USA)	6-4	4-6	6-2	6-2	
F	Elisabeth Moore (USA)	Annabella Wistar (USA)	6-3	7-5	6-0		
S	Elisabeth Moore (USA)	Gertrude Kimball (USA)	6-3	6-1			
S	Annabella Wistar (USA)	Edith Rotch (USA)	6-4	6-2			
Q	Elisabeth Moore (USA)	Amy Williams (USA)	6-4	6-5			
Q	Gertrude Kimball (USA)	Kathleen Atkinson (USA)	6-5	6-1			
Q	Annabella Wistar (USA)	Grace Booth (USA)	6-2	6-1			
Q	Edith Rotch (USA)	Helen Booth (USA)	6-3	6-2			

1897

Rd	Winner	Defeated	S1	S2	S3	S4	S5
Ch	Juliette Atkinson (USA)	Elisabeth Moore (USA)	6-3	6-3	4-6	3-6	6-3
F	Juliette Atkinson (USA)	Edith Kenderline (USA)	6-2	6-4	6-0		
S	Juliette Atkinson (USA)	Kathleen Atkinson (USA)	6-1	6-3			
S	Edith Kenderline (USA)	Carrie Neely (USA)	7-5	2-6	6-1		
Q	Juliette Atkinson (USA)	Maud Banks (USA)	6-1	4-6	6-1		
Q	Kathleen Atkinson (USA)	Hattie Beaumont (USA)	6-4	6-0			
Q	Edith Kenderline (USA)	Ellen Ketcham (USA)	6-2	4-6	8-6		
Q	Carrie Neely (USA)	Mrs Frank Edwards (USA)	6-2	6-1			

1898

Rd	Winner	Defeated	S1	S2	S3	S4	S5
Ch	Juliette Atkinson (USA)	Marion Jones (USA)	6-3	5-7	6-4	2-6	7-5
F	Marion Jones (USA)	Helen Crump (USA)	6-4	7-5	6-4		
S	Marion Jones (USA)	Carrie Neely (USA)	6-0	6-0			
S	Helen Crump (USA)	Marie Wimer (USA)	6-3	2-6	10-8		
Q	Marion Jones (USA)	Kathleen Atkinson (USA)	6-4	6-3			
Q	Carrie Neely (USA)	Helen Chapman (USA)	6-3	6-2			
Q	Helen Crump (USA)	Maud Banks (USA)	6-1	6-3			
Q	Marie Wimer (USA)	Elizabeth Rastall (USA)	6-1	6-0			

1899

Rd	Winner	Defeated	S1	S2	S3	S4	S5
Ch	Marion Jones (USA)	Juliette Atkinson (USA)	(default)				
F	Marion Jones (USA)	Maud Banks (USA)	6-1	6-1	7-5		
S	Maud Banks (USA)	Carrie Neely (USA)	6-3	4-6	6-1		
S	Marion Jones (USA)	Jane Craven (USA)	6-1	6-0			
Q	Maud Banks (USA)	Myrtle McAteer (USA)	3-6	7-5	7-5		
Q	Carrie Neely (USA)	Georgina Jones (USA)	6-0	6-2			
Q	Marion Jones (USA)	Hallie Champlin (USA)	6-1	6-2			
Q	Jane Craven (USA)	Edith Parker (USA)	7-5	3-6	6-1		

1900

Rd	Winner	Defeated	S1	S2	S3	S4	S5
Ch	Myrtle McAteer (USA)	Marion Jones (USA)	(default)				
F	Myrtle McAteer (USA)	Edith Parker (USA)	6-2	6-0	6-0		
S	Edith Parker (USA)	Dorothea Morris (USA)	6-0	6-2			
S	Myrtle McAteer (USA)	Maud Banks (USA)	6-4	7-5			
Q	Dorothea Morris (USA)	Huldah J. Steel (USA)	6-2	4-6	7-5		
Q	Edith Parker (USA)	Hallie Champlin (USA)	8-6	6-2			
Q	Myrtle McAteer (USA)	Marie Wimer (USA)	6-3	6-3			
Q	Maud Banks (USA)	Margaret Hunnewell (USA)	6-3	3-6	6-3		

1901

Rd	Winner	Defeated	S1	S2	S3	S4	S5
Ch	Elisabeth Moore (USA)	Myrtle McAteer (USA)	6-4	3-6	7-5	2-6	6-2
F	Elisabeth Moore (USA)	Marion Jones (USA)	4-6	1-6	9-7	9-7	6-3
S	Elisabeth Moore (USA)	Juliette Atkinson (USA)	6-2	9-7			
S	Marion Jones (USA)	Emma Warren (USA)	6-1	6-2			
Q	Juliette Atkinson (USA)	Helen Huey (USA)	6-2	6-4			
Q	Elisabeth Moore (USA)	Carrie Neely (USA)	6-1	7-5			
Q	Marion Jones (USA)	Helen Dillingham (USA)	(default)				
Q	Emma Warren (USA)	Georgina Jones (USA)	7-5	6-4			

Rd	Winner	Defeated	S1	S2	S3

USLTA ADOPTS 3-SET FORMAT

Rd	Winner	Defeated	S1	S2	S3

1902

Rd	Winner	Defeated	S1	S2	S3
Ch	Marion Jones (USA)	Elisabeth Moore (USA)	6-1	1-0 (default)	
F	Marion Jones (USA)	Carrie Neely (USA)	8-6	6-4	
S	Carrie Neely (USA)	Juliette Atkinson (USA)	8-6	3-6	6-2
S	Marion Jones (USA)	Helen Chapman (USA)	6-1	6-0	
Q	Carrie Neely (USA)	Nona Closterman (USA)	6-2	6-0	
Q	Juliette Atkinson (USA)	Clara T. Chase (USA)	6-1	6-3	
Q	Marion Jones (USA)	Marie Wimer (USA)	6-4	6-0	
Q	Helen Chapman (USA)	Mrs M.R. Fielding (USA)	6-4	3-6	7-5

1903

Rd	Winner	Defeated	S1	S2	S3
Ch	Elisabeth Moore (USA)	Marion Jones (USA)	7-5	8-6	
F	Elisabeth Moore (USA)	Carrie Neely (USA)	6-2	6-4	
S	Elisabeth Moore (USA)	Marjorie Oberteuffer (USA)	6-0	6-0	
S	Carrie Neely (USA)	Helen Chapman (USA)	6-0	6-1	
Q	Elisabeth Moore (USA)	Miriam Hall (USA)	6-1	6-3	
Q	Marjorie Oberteuffer (USA)	Gertrude Fetterman (USA)	6-2	6-3	
Q	Helen Chapman (USA)	Corrine Mock (USA)	6-1	8-6	
Q	Carrie Neely (USA)	Clara T. Chase (USA)	6-0	6-1	

1904

Rd	Winner	Defeated	S1	S2	S3
Ch	May Sutton (USA)	Elisabeth Moore (USA)	6-1	6-2	
F	May Sutton (USA)	Helen Homans (USA)	6-1	6-1	
S	Helen Homans (USA)	Miriam Hall (USA)	6-4	6-3	
S	May Sutton (USA)	Sarah Coffin (USA)	6-1	6-0	
Q	Helen Homans (USA)	Carrie Neely (USA)	7-5	11-9	
Q	Miriam Hall (USA)	Marie Wimer (USA)	6-3	6-2	
Q	Sarah Coffin (USA)	Clara T. Chase (USA)	6-3	6-2	
Q	May Sutton (USA)	Frances Stotesbury (USA)	6-1	6-0	

1905

Rd	Winner	Defeated	S1	S2	S3
Ch	Elisabeth Moore (USA)	May Sutton (USA)	(default)		
F	Elisabeth Moore (USA)	Helen Homans (USA)	6-4	5-7	6-1
S	Elisabeth Moore (USA)	Margaret LeRoy (USA)	6-1	6-3	
S	Helen Homans (USA)	Mary Coates (USA)	6-1	6-0	
Q	Margaret LeRoy (USA)	Clara T. Chase (USA)	6-3	6-8	6-1
Q	Elisabeth Moore (USA)	Carrie Neely (USA)	4-6	6-1	6-2
Q	Mary Coates (USA)	Evelyn V. Howell (USA)	6-2	7-5	
Q	Helen Homans (USA)	Mrs. C. Wainwright (USA)	(default)		

1906

Rd	Winner	Defeated	S1	S2	S3
Ch	Helen Homans (USA)	Elisabeth Moore (USA)	(default)		
F	Helen Homans (USA)	Maud Barger Wallach (USA)	6-4	6-3	
S	Helen Homans (USA)	Edith Rotch (USA)	6-2	6-3	
S	Maud Barger Wallach (USA)	Bertha Townsend Toulmin (USA)	6-2	6-3	
Q	Edith Rotch (USA)	Clover Boldt (USA)	6-1	4-6	6-0
Q	Helen Homans (USA)	Rachel Harlan (USA)	4-6	6-4	6-4
Q	Bertha Townsend Toulmin (USA)	Gertrude Fetterman (USA)	6-1	6-2	
Q	Maud Barger Wallach (USA)	Annetta G. McCall (USA)	6-1	6-0	

1907

Rd	Winner	Defeated	S1	S2	S3
Ch	Evelyn Sears (USA)	Helen Homans (USA)	default		
F	Evelyn Sears (USA)	Carrie Neely (USA)	6-3	6-2	
S	Evelyn Sears (USA)	Mrs George L. Chapman (USA)	6-2	6-1	
S	Carrie Neely (USA)	Helen Pouch (USA)	8-6	7-5	
Q	Evelyn Sears (USA)	Elizabeth G. Ostheimer (USA)	6-1	6-1	
Q	Mrs George L. Chapman (USA)	Phyllis Green (USA)	6-2	6-0	
Q	Helen Pouch (USA)	Emily Scott (USA)	6-4	6-2	
Q	Carrie Neely (USA)	Rachel Harlan (USA)	2-6	6-4	6-3

1908

Rd	Winner	Defeated	S1	S2	S3
Ch	Maud Barger Wallach (USA)	Evelyn Sears (USA)	6-3	1-6	6-3
F	Maud Barger Wallach (USA)	Marie Wagner (USA)	4-6	6-1	6-3
S	Maud Barger Wallach (USA)	Edith Rotch (USA)	6-2	6-4	
S	Marie Wagner (USA)	M. Johnson (USA)	7-5	6-2	
Q	Edith Rotch (USA)	Helen Pouch (USA)	2-6	7-5	6-1
Q	Maud Barger Wallach (USA)	Matilda Borda (USA)	6-3	6-2	
Q	M. Johnson (USA)	Eleanor Cohen (USA)	8-6	6-2	
Q	Marie Wagner (USA)	Carrie Neely (USA)	6-4	4-6	7-5

1909

Rd	Winner	Defeated	S1	S2	S3
Ch	Hazel Hotchkiss (USA)	Maud Barger Wallach (USA)	6-0	6-1	
F	Hazel Hotchkiss (USA)	Louise Hammond (USA)	6-8	6-1	6-4
S	Hazel Hotchkiss (USA)	Edith Rotch (USA)	6-2	7-5	
S	Louise Hammond (USA)	Lois Moyes (USA)	6-0	6-2	
Q	Hazel Hotchkiss (USA)	Emily Scott (USA)	6-3	6-0	
Q	Edith Rotch (USA)	Alice Day (USA)	6-1	6-0	
Q	Louise Hammond (USA)	Gwendolyn Rees (USA)	6-4	6-1	
Q	Lois Moyes (USA)	Margaret Roberts (USA)	6-1	8-6	

1910

Rd	Winner	Defeated	S1	S2	S3
Ch	Hazel Hotchkiss (USA)	Louise Hammond (USA)	6-4	6-2	
F	Louise Hammond (USA)	Adelaide Browning (USA)	6-2	6-4	
S	Louise Hammond (USA)	Edith Rotch (USA)	7-5	6-2	
S	Adelaide Browning (USA)	Edna Wildey (USA)	6-1	6-4	
Q	Louise Hammond (USA)	Carrie Neely (USA)	6-1	8-6	
Q	Edith Rotch (USA)	Constance Evans Sullivan (USA)	6-2	6-4	
Q	Edna Wildey (USA)	Lois Moyes (USA)	6-3	6-4	
Q	Adelaide Browning (USA)	Dorothy Green (USA)	3-6	6-3	6-2

1911

Rd	Winner	Defeated	S1	S2	S3
Ch	Hazel Hotchkiss (USA)	Florence Sutton (USA)	8-10	6-1	9-7
F	Florence Sutton (USA)	Eleonora Sears (USA)	6-2	6-1	
S	Eleonora Sears (USA)	Mrs. G. Warren (USA)	6-1	6-3	
S	Florence Sutton (USA)	Adelaide Browning (USA)	6-3	6-2	
Q	Eleonora Sears (USA)	Mrs. Wallinston Hardy (USA)	6-2	6-2	
Q	Mrs. G. Warren (USA)	Edith Handy (USA)	3-6	6-2	6-3
Q	Florence Sutton (USA)	Edna Wildey (USA)	6-1	6-3	
Q	Adelaide Browning (USA)	Marie Wagner (USA)	6-3	3-6	6-2

1912

Rd	Winner	Defeated	S1	S2	S3
Ch	Mary K. Browne (USA)	Hazel Hotchkiss (USA)	(default)		
S	Mary K. Browne (USA)	Adelaide Browning (USA)	6-4	3-6	9-7
S	Eleonora Sears (USA)	Mary Merrick (USA)	5-7	6-0	6-2
Q	Adelaide Browning (USA)	Mrs. Frederick Schmitz (USA)	6-1	10-8	
Q	Mary K. Browne (USA)	Marion Fenno (USA)	6-0	6-4	
Q	Eleonora Sears (USA)	Helen D. Alexander (USA)	6-2	6-2	
Q	Mary Merrick (USA)	Effie Wheeler (USA)	(default)		

1913

Rd	Winner	Defeated	S1	S2	S3
Ch	Mary K. Browne (USA)	Dorothy Green (USA)	6-2	7-5	
F	Dorothy Green (USA)	Edna Wildey (USA)	6-3	6-4	
S	Edna Wildey (USA)	Mrs. H.J.D. Paul (USA)	6-1	6-2	
S	Dorothy Green (USA)	Louise Riddell Williams (USA)	7-5	6-3	
Q	Edna Wildey (USA)	Marion Cresswell (USA)	6-0	6-2	
Q	Mrs. H.J.D. Paul (USA)	Flora Brown Harvey (USA)	2-6	6-3	7-5
Q	Dorothy Green (USA)	Mrs. Robert Herold (USA)	6-4	6-2	
Q	Louise Riddell Williams (USA)	Helen D. Alexander (USA)	6-0	4-6	6-2

1914

Rd	Winner	Defeated	S1	S2	S3
Ch	Mary K. Browne (USA)	Marie Wagner (USA)	6-2	1-6	6-1
F	Marie Wagner (USA)	Clare Cassel (USA)	6-1	7-5	
S	Marie Wagner (USA)	Louise Hammond Raymond (USA)	6-4	6-4	
S	Clare Cassel (USA)	Isabel Pendleton (USA)	6-2	6-1	
Q	Marie Wagner (USA)	Carrie Neely (USA)	6-2	6-3	
Q	Louise Hammond Raymond (USA)	Constance Evans Sullivan (USA)	4-6	6-2	6-1
Q	Isabel Pendleton (USA)	Margarette Myers (USA)	6-2	6-1	
Q	Clare Cassel (USA)	Ann W. Sheafe (USA)	4-6	6-4	6-1

1915

Rd	Winner	Defeated	S1	S2	S3
Ch	Molla Bjurstedt (NOR)	Mary K. Browne (USA)	default		
F	Molla Bjurstedt (NOR)	Hazel Hotchkiss Wightman (USA)	4-6	6-2	6-0
S	Molla Bjurstedt (NOR)	Martha Guthrie (USA)	3-6	6-2	6-2
S	Hazel Hotchkiss Wightman (USA)	Eliza M. Fox (USA)	6-1	6-4	
Q	Molla Bjurstedt (NOR)	Ann W. Sheafe (USA)	10-8	6-2	
Q	Martha Guthrie (USA)	Marion Vanderhoef (USA)	7-5	6-0	
Q	Eliza M. Fox (USA)	Alice Cunningham (USA)	6-2	6-1	
Q	Hazel Hotchkiss Wightman (USA)	Eleonora Sears (USA)	6-3	5-7	6-2

1916

Rd	Winner	Defeated	S1	S2	S3
Ch	Molla Bjurstedt (NOR)	Louise Hammond Raymond (USA)	6-0	6-1	
F	Louise Hammond Raymond (USA)	Eleonora Sears (USA)	6-3	6-4	
S	Louise Hammond Raymond (USA)	Evelyn Sears (USA)	6-2	6-1	
S	Eleonora Sears (USA)	Susanne White (USA)	6-2	6-3	
Q	Evelyn Sears (USA)	Alice Patterson (USA)	6-3	6-2	
Q	Louise Hammond Raymond (USA)	Maud Barger Wallach (USA)	6-1	6-3	
Q	Eleonora Sears (USA)	Phyllis Walsh (USA)	6-3	6-3	
Q	Susanne White (USA)	Mrs J.R. Hall (USA)	4-6	8-6	7-5

1917

Rd	Winner	Defeated	S1	S2	S3
F	Molla Bjurstedt (NOR)	Marion Vanderhoef (USA)	4-6	6-0	6-2
S	Marion Vanderhoef (USA)	Eleonora Sears (USA)	8-6	6-3	
S	Molla Bjurstedt (NOR)	Flora Brown Harvey (USA)	4-6	6-0	6-0
Q	Marion Vanderhoef (USA)	Susanne White (USA)	3-6	6-2	6-2
Q	Eleonora Sears (USA)	Mrs Knud Dahl (USA)	6-2	6-4	
Q	Molla Bjurstedt (NOR)	Phyllis Walsh (USA)	6-4	6-1	
Q	Flora Brown Harvey (USA)	Teresa Wood (USA)	1-6	6-4	7-5

1918

Rd	Winner	Defeated	S1	S2	S3
Ch	Molla Bjurstedt (NOR)	Eleanor Goss (USA)	6-4	6-3	
F	Eleanor Goss (USA)	Helene Pollak (USA)	6-2	7-5	
S	Helene Pollak (USA)	Clare Cassel (USA)	6-3	6-0	
S	Eleanor Goss (USA)	Helen Ledoux (USA)	6-3	6-4	
Q	Helene Pollak (USA)	Dorothy Walker (USA)	6-1	6-0	
Q	Clare Cassel (USA)	Eleonora Sears (USA)	6-2	6-4	
Q	Helen Ledoux (USA)	Barbara F. Hooker (USA)	6-4	6-1	
Q	Eleanor Goss (USA)	Emily Stokes Weaver (USA)	6-2	6-4	

1919

Rd	Winner	Defeated	S1	S2	S3
F	Hazel Hotchkiss Wightman (USA)	Marion Zinderstein (USA)	6-1	6-2	
S	Hazel Hotchkiss Wightman (USA)	Flora Brown Harvey (USA)	6-2	6-2	
S	Marion Zinderstein (USA)	Molla Bjurstedt (NOR)	4-6	6-1	6-2
Q	Hazel Hotchkiss Wightman (USA)	Anne B. Townsend (USA)	6-0	6-1	
Q	Flora Brown Harvey (USA)	Leslie Bancroft (USA)	6-2	4-6	6-4
Q	Molla Bjurstedt (NOR)	Marie Wagner (USA)	6-2	6-8	6-4
Q	Marion Zinderstein (USA)	Clare Cassel (USA)	6-3	6-1	

1920

Rd	Winner	Defeated	S1	S2	S3
F	Molla Bjurstedt Mallory (USA)	Marion Zinderstein (USA)	6-3	6-1	
S	Molla Bjurstedt Mallory (USA)	Helene Pollak (USA)	6-2	6-3	
S	Marion Zinderstein (USA)	Eleanor Goss (USA)	6-3	6-4	
Q	Helene Pollak (USA)	Edith Sigourney (USA)	6-3	8-6	
Q	Molla Bjurstedt Mallory (USA)	Eleanor Tennant (USA)	6-2	2-6	6-3
Q	Eleanor Goss (USA)	Martha Niles (USA)	6-4	6-2	
Q	Marion Zinderstein (USA)	Leslie Bancroft (USA)	6-4	6-2	

1921

Rd	Winner	Defeated	S1	S2	S3
F	Molla Bjurstedt Mallory (USA)	Mary K. Browne (USA)	4-6	6-4	6-2
S	Mary K. Browne (USA)	Patricia Butlin Hitchins (USA)	6-3	6-0	
S	Molla Bjurstedt Mallory (USA)	May Sutton Bundy (USA)	8-6	6-2	
Q	Patricia Butlin Hitchins (USA)	Adelaide Browning (USA)	8-6	6-2	
Q	Mary K. Browne (USA)	Ann Sheafe Cole (USA)	6-1	6-2	
Q	Molla Bjurstedt Mallory (USA)	Helene Pollak Falk (USA)	6-2	6-1	
Q	May Sutton Bundy (USA)	Jelen Gilleaudeau (USA)	6-1	6-2	

1922

Rd	Winner	Defeated	S1	S2	S3
F	Molla Bjurstedt Mallory (USA)	Helen Wills (USA)	6-3	6-1	
S	Helen Wills (USA)	May Sutton Bundy (USA)	6-4	6-3	
S	Molla Bjurstedt Mallory (USA)	Leslie Bancroft (USA)	6-0	6-4	
Q	May Sutton Bundy (USA)	Martha Bayard (USA)	12-10	4-6	6-0
Q	Helen Wills (USA)	Marion Zinderstein Jessup (USA)	2-6	6-4	6-2
Q	Molla Bjurstedt Mallory (USA)	Edith Sigourney (USA)	6-0	6-1	
Q	Leslie Bancroft (USA)	Clare Cassel (USA)	8-6	6-3	

1923

Rd	Winner	Defeated	S1	S2	S3
F	Helen Wills (USA)	Molla Bjurstedt Mallory (USA)	6-2	6-1	
S	Helen Wills (USA)	Eleanor Goss (USA)	6-4	6-0	
S	Molla Bjurstedt Mallory (USA)	Mabel Clayton (USA)	6-4	6-2	
Q	Helen Wills (USA)	Kitty McKane (GBR)	2-6	6-2	7-5
Q	Eleanor Goss (USA)	Phyllis Howkins Covell (GBR)	6-1	2-6	8-6
Q	Molla Bjurstedt Mallory (USA)	Helen Hooker (USA)	6-3	6-1	
Q	Mabel Clayton (USA)	Leslie Bancroft (USA)	6-1	6-2	

1924

Rd	Winner	Defeated	S1	S2	S3
F	Helen Wills (USA)	Molla Bjurstedt Mallory (USA)	6-1	6-3	
S	Molla Bjurstedt Mallory (USA)	Eleanor Goss (USA)	6-3	6-4	
S	Helen Wills (USA)	Mary K. Browne (USA)	6-4	4-6	6-3
Q	Molla Bjurstedt Mallory (USA)	Edna Hauselt Roeser (USA)	6-1	6-0	
Q	Eleanor Goss (USA)	Martha Bayard (USA)	8-6	6-4	
Q	Helen Wills (USA)	Marion Zinderstein Jessup (USA)	6-3	6-3	
Q	Mary K. Browne (USA)	Mayme MacDonald (USA)	6-2	5-7	6-4

1925

Rd	Winner	Defeated	S1	S2	S3
F	Helen Wills (USA)	Kitty McKane (GBR)	3-6	6-0	6-2
S	Kitty McKane (GBR)	Molla Bjurstedt Mallory (USA)	4-6	7-5	8-6
S	Helen Wills (USA)	Eleanor Goss (USA)	3-6	6-0	6-2
Q	Kitty McKane (GBR)	Elizabeth Ryan (USA)	3-6	7-5	6-2
Q	Molla Bjurstedt Mallory (USA)	Penelope Anderson (USA)	6-2	6-1	
Q	Helen Wills (USA)	Joan Fry (GBR)	4-6	6-0	6-3
Q	Eleanor Goss (USA)	Dorothea Douglass Chambers (GBR)	6-2	11-9	

1926

Rd	Winner	Defeated	S1	S2	S3
F	Molla Bjurstedt Mallory (USA)	Elizabeth Ryan (USA)	4-6	6-4	9-7
S	Elizabeth Ryan (USA)	Mary K. Browne (USA)	6-1	6-3	
S	Molla Bjurstedt Mallory (USA)	Martha Bayard (USA)	6-3	6-3	
Q	Elizabeth Ryan (USA)	Eleanor Goss (USA)	3-6	6-0	
Q	Mary K. Browne (USA)	Penelope Anderson (USA)	7-5	6-1	
Q	Martha Bayard (USA)	Margaret Blake (USA)	6-4	6-2	
Q	Molla Bjurstedt Mallory (USA)	Charlotte Hosmer Chapin (USA)	7-5	6-0	

1927

Rd	Winner	Defeated	S1	S2	S3
F	Helen Wills (USA)	Betty Nuthall (GBR)	6-1	6-4	
S	Helen Wills (USA)	Helen Jacobs (USA)	6-0	6-2	
S	Betty Nuthall (GBR)	Charlotte Hosmer Chapin (USA)	6-1	4-6	6-3
Q	Helen Wills (USA)	Kea Bouman (NED)	6-1	6-2	
Q	Helen Jacobs (USA)	Edna Hauselt Roeser (USA)	6-8	8-6	6-2
Q	Charlotte Hosmer Chapin (USA)	Molla Bjurstedt Mallory (USA)	6-3	1-6	6-4
Q	Betty Nuthall (GBR)	Eleanor Goss (USA)	4-6	7-5	6-2

1928

Rd	Winner	Defeated	S1	S2	S3
F	Helen Wills (USA)	Helen Jacobs (USA)	6-2	6-1	
S	Helen Wills (USA)	Edith Cross (USA)	6-0	6-1	
S	Helen Jacobs (USA)	Molla Bjurstedt Mallory (USA)	6-2	7-5	
Q	Helen Wills (USA)	Charlotte Hosmer Chapin (USA)	6-2	6-4	
Q	Edith Cross (USA)	Hazel Hotchkiss Wightman (USA)	6-3	6-4	
Q	Molla Bjurstedt Mallory (USA)	Marjorie Morrill (USA)	6-2	3-6	6-3
Q	Helen Jacobs (USA)	Penelope Anderson (USA)	6-4	6-1	

1929

Rd	Winner	Defeated	S1	S2	S3
F	Helen Wills Moody (USA)	Phoebe Holcroft Watson (GBR)	6-4	6-2	
S	Helen Wills Moody (USA)	Molla Bjurstedt Mallory (USA)	6-0	6-0	
S	Phoebe Holcroft Watson (GBR)	Helen Jacobs (USA)	6-1	3-6	6-4
Q	Helen Wills Moody (USA)	Peggy Michell (GBR)	6-0	6-1	
Q	Molla Bjurstedt Mallory (USA)	Betty Nuthall (GBR)	6-3	6-3	
Q	Helen Jacobs (USA)	Mary Greef (USA)	6-2	6-2	
Q	Phoebe Holcroft Watson (GBR)	Edith Cross (USA)	2-6	6-1	6-3

1930

Rd	Winner	Defeated	S1	S2	S3
F	Betty Nuthall (GBR)	Anna McCune Harper (USA)	6-1	6-4	
S	Betty Nuthall (GBR)	Marjorie Morrill (USA)	6-8	6-4	6-2
S	Anna McCune Harper (USA)	Maud Rosenbaum Levi (USA)	6-2	6-3	
Q	Marjorie Morrill (USA)	Ethel Burkhardt (USA)	4-6	6-3	6-2
Q	Betty Nuthall (GBR)	Dorothy Weisel (USA)	6-1	6-1	
Q	Anna McCune Harper (USA)	Mary Greef (USA)	3-6	6-1	6-4
Q	Maud Rosenbaum Levi (USA)	Penelope Anderson (USA)	4-6	6-4	7-5

1931

Rd	Winner	Defeated	S1	S2	S3
F	Helen Wills Moody (USA)	Eileen Bennett Whittingstall (GBR)	6-4	6-1	
S	Helen Wills Moody (USA)	Phyllis Mudford (GBR)	6-2	6-4	
S	Eileen Bennett Whittingstall (GBR)	Betty Nuthall (GBR)	6-2	3-6	6-4
Q	Helen Wills Moody (USA)	Dorothy Weisel (USA)	6-1	6-2	
Q	Phyllis Mudford (GBR)	Anna McCune Harper (USA)	4-6	6-3	6-2
Q	Eileen Bennett Whittingstall (GBR)	Helen Jacobs (USA)	3-6	6-3	8-6
Q	Betty Nuthall (GBR)	Dorothy Shepherd Barron (GBR)	6-2	6-1	

1932

Rd	Winner	Defeated	S1	S2	S3
F	Helen Jacobs (USA)	Carolin Babcock (USA)	6-2	6-2	
S	Helen Jacobs (USA)	Elsie Goldsack Pittman (USA)	6-2	6-3	
S	Carolin Babcock (USA)	Joan Ridley (USA)	4-6	7-5	6-3
Q	Helen Jacobs (USA)	Marjorie Gladman Van Ryn (USA)	3-6	6-3	6-1
Q	Elsie Goldsack Pittman (USA)	Mary Greef (USA)	6-3	6-2	
Q	Carolin Babcock (USA)	Anna McCune Harper (USA)	6-3	7-5	
Q	Joan Ridley (USA)	Marjorie Morrill Painter (USA)	3-6	8-6	6-4

1933

Rd	Winner	Defeated	S1	S2	S3
F	Helen Jacobs (USA)	Helen Wills Moody (USA)	8-6	3-6	3-0
					(default)
S	Helen Wills Moody (USA)	Betty Nuthall (GBR)	2-6	6-3	6-2
S	Helen Jacobs (USA)	Dorothy Round (GBR)	6-4	5-7	6-2
Q	Helen Wills Moody (USA)	Mary Heeley (GBR)	6-0	6-2	
Q	Betty Nuthall (GBR)	Alice Marble (USA)	6-8	6-0	6-2
Q	Helen Jacobs (USA)	Josephine Cruickshank (USA)	11-9	6-4	
Q	Dorothy Round (GBR)	Sarah Palfrey (USA)	6-4	9-7	

1934

Rd	Winner	Defeated	S1	S2	S3
F	Helen Jacobs (USA)	Sarah Palfrey (USA)	6-1	6-4	
S	Sarah Palfrey (USA)	Dorothy Andrus (USA)	6-3	6-4	
S	Helen Jacobs (USA)	Carolin Babcock (USA)	7-5	6-0	
Q	Sarah Palfrey (USA)	Freda James (GBR)	6-3	3-6	6-1
Q	Dorothy Andrus (USA)	Maud Rosenbaum Levi (USA)	6-1	6-4	
Q	Helen Jacobs (USA)	Elizabeth Ryan (USA)	6-0	6-1	
Q	Carolin Babcock (USA)	Kay Stammers (GBR)	6-3	2-6	6-4

1935

Rd	Winner	Defeated	S1	S2	S3
F	Helen Jacobs (USA)	Sarah Palfrey Fabyan (USA)	6-2	6-4	
S	Helen Jacobs (USA)	Phyllis Mudford King (GBR)	6-4	6-3	
S	Sarah Palfrey Fabyan (USA)	Kay Stammers (GBR)	9-7	7-5	
Q	Helen Jacobs (USA)	Nancy Lyle (GBR)	6-0	6-4	
Q	Phyllis Mudford King (GBR)	Marjorie Gladman Van Ryn (USA)	6-2	6-0	
Q	Sarah Palfrey Fabyan (USA)	Freda James (GBR)	7-5	5-7	6-4
Q	Kay Stammers (GBR)	Eunice Earle Dean (USA)	5-7	6-3	6-2

1936

Rd	Winner	Defeated	S1	S2	S3
F	Alice Marble (USA)	Helen Jacobs (USA)	4-6	6-3	6-2
S	Helen Jacobs (USA)	Kay Stammers (GBR)	6-4	6-3	
S	Alice Marble (USA)	Helen Pedersen (USA)	6-1	6-1	
Q	Helen Jacobs (USA)	Gussie Raegener (USA)	6-1	6-0	
Q	Kay Stammers (GBR)	Marjorie Gladman Van Ryn (USA)	7-5	3-6	6-4
Q	Helen Pedersen (USA)	Dorothy Bundy (USA)	6-3	3-6	6-4
Q	Alice Marble (USA)	Gracyn Wheeler (USA)	6-2	11-9	

1937

Rd	Winner	Defeated	S1	S2	S3
F	Anita Lizana (CHI)	Jadwiga Jedrzejowska (POL)	6-4	6-2	
S	Jadwiga Jedrzejowska (POL)	Helen Jacobs (USA)	6-4	6-4	
S	Anita Lizana (CHI)	Dorothy Bundy (USA)	6-2	6-3	
Q	Helen Jacobs (USA)	Kay Stammers (GBR)	7-5	6-3	
Q	Jadwiga Jedrzejowska (POL)	Mary Hartwick (GBR)	6-4	6-2	
Q	Dorothy Bundy (USA)	Alice Marble (USA)	1-6	7-5	6-1
Q	Anita Lizana (CHI)	Marjorie Gladman Van Ryn (USA)	6-1	6-1	

1938

Rd	Winner	Defeated	S1	S2	S3
F	Alice Marble (USA)	Nancye Wynne (AUS)	6-0	6-3	
S	Nancye Wynne (AUS)	Dorothy Bundy (USA)	5-7	6-4	8-6
S	Alice Marble (USA)	Sarah Palfrey Fabyan (USA)	5-7	7-5	7-5
Q	Nancye Wynne (AUS)	Margot Lumb (GBR)	6-4	5-7	6-1
Q	Dorothy Bundy (USA)	Simone Passemard Mathieu (FRA)	6-3	3-6	6-0
Q	Alice Marble (USA)	Kay Stammers (GBR)	6-8	6-3	6-0
Q	Sarah Palfrey Fabyan (USA)	Jadwiga Jedrzejowska (POL)	6-1	6-4	

1939

Rd	Winner	Defeated	S1	S2	S3
F	Alice Marble (USA)	Helen Jacobs (USA)	6-0	8-10	6-4
S	Helen Jacobs (USA)	Kay Stammers (GBR)	7-5	6-0	
S	Alice Marble (USA)	Virginia Wolfenden (USA)	6-0	6-1	
Q	Helen Jacobs (USA)	Valerie Scott (GBR)	2-6	6-2	6-3
Q	Kay Stammers (GBR)	Sarah Palfrey Fabyan (USA)	1-6	6-3	6-3
Q	Alice Marble (USA)	Mary Hardwick (GBR)	6-3	6-8	6-2
Q	Virginia Wolfenden (USA)	Dorothy Bundy (USA)	2-6	6-1	6-1

1940

Rd	Winner	Defeated	S1	S2	S3
F	Alice Marble (USA)	Helen Jacobs (USA)	6-2	6-3	
S	Helen Jacobs (USA)	Mary Hardwick (GBR)	2-6	6-1	6-4
S	Alice Marble (USA)	Valerie Scott (GBR)	6-3	6-3	
Q	Helen Jacobs (USA)	Virginia Wolfenden (USA)	3-6	6-4	6-1
Q	Mary Hardwick (GBR)	Pauline Betz (USA)	5-7	6-1	6-2
Q	Alice Marble (USA)	Helen Bernhard (USA)	6-3	6-3	
Q	Valerie Scott (GBR)	Dorothy Bundy (USA)	3-6	6-4	6-3

1941

Rd	Winner	Defeated	S1	S2	S3
F	Sarah Palfrey Cooke (USA)	Pauline Betz (USA)	7-5	6-2	
S	Sarah Palfrey Cooke (USA)	Helen Jacobs (USA)	6-3	2-6	6-1
S	Pauline Betz (USA)	Margaret Osborne (USA)	6-4	6-3	
Q	Sarah Palfrey Cooke (USA)	Hope Knowles (USA)	6-4	7-5	
Q	Helen Jacobs (USA)	Dorothy Bundy (USA)	6-3	11-9	
Q	Pauline Betz (USA)	Barbara Krase (USA)	6-2	6-2	
Q	Margaret Osborne (USA)	Helen Bernhard (USA)	6-3	6-1	

1942

Rd	Winner	Defeated	S1	S2	S3
F	Pauline Betz (USA)	Louise Brough (USA)	4-6	6-1	6-4
S	Pauline Betz (USA)	Margaret Osborne (USA)	6-4	4-6	7-5
S	Louise Brough (USA)	Helen Bernhard (USA)	5-7	6-4	6-2
Q	Pauline Betz (USA)	Shirley Fry (USA)	6-2	6-0	
Q	Margaret Osborne (USA)	Doris Hart (USA)	7-5	6-0	
Q	Louise Brough (USA)	Mary Arnold (USA)	3-6	6-4	6-3
Q	Helen Bernhard (USA)	Helen Pedersen Rihbany (USA)	6-0	6-4	

1943

Rd	Winner	Defeated	S1	S2	S3
F	Pauline Betz (USA)	Louise Brough (USA)	6-3	5-7	6-3
S	Pauline Betz (USA)	Doris Hart (USA)	9-7	2-6	6-1
S	Louise Brough (USA)	Dorothy Bundy (USA)	6-4	7-5	
Q	Pauline Betz (USA)	Dorothy Head (USA)	6-0	6-1	
Q	Doris Hart (USA)	Sarah Palfrey Cooke (USA)	6-1	6-3	
Q	Louise Brough (USA)	Mary Arnold (USA)	3-6	6-3	7-5
Q	Dorothy Bundy (USA)	Margaret Osborne (USA)	6-3	3-6	7-5

1944

Rd	Winner	Defeated	S1	S2	S3
F	Pauline Betz (USA)	Margaret Osborne (USA)	6-3	8-6	
S	Pauline Betz (USA)	Louise Brough (USA)	6-2	6-3	
S	Margaret Osborne (USA)	Dorothy Bundy (USA)	4-6	6-4	6-0
Q	Pauline Betz (USA)	Virginia Kovacs (USA)	6-4	6-8	6-4
Q	Louise Brough (USA)	Mary Arnold (USA)	3-6	6-3	8-6
Q	Margaret Osborne (USA)	Shirley Fry (USA)	6-3	6-1	
Q	Dorothy Bundy (USA)	Doris Hart (USA)	5-7	8-6	6-4

1945

Rd	Winner	Defeated	S1	S2	S3
F	Sarah Palfrey Cooke (USA)	Pauline Betz (USA)	3-6	8-6	6-4
S	Sarah Palfrey Cooke (USA)	Louise Brough (USA)	6-3	6-4	
S	Pauline Betz (USA)	Doris Hart (USA)	6-3	6-2	
Q	Sarah Palfrey Cooke (USA)	Dorothy Bundy (USA)	6-3	6-4	
Q	Louise Brough (USA)	Pat Todd (USA)	6-2	6-4	
Q	Pauline Betz (USA)	Mary Arnold (USA)	0-6	6-4	6-4
Q	Doris Hart (USA)	Magaret Osborne (USA)	6-2	6-3	

1946

Rd	Winner	Defeated	S1	S2	S3
F	Pauline Betz (USA)	Doris Hart (USA)	11-9	6-3	
S	Pauline Betz (USA)	Pat Canning Todd (USA)	6-2	6-3	
S	Doris Hart (USA)	Mary Arnold Prentiss (USA)	6-3	6-3	
Q	Pauline Betz (USA)	Gussy Moran (USA)	6-1	3-6	6-2
Q	Pat Canning Todd (USA)	Louise Brough (USA)	6-2	6-2	
Q	Doris Hart (USA)	Margaret Osborne (USA)	6-4	5-7	7-5
Q	Mary Arnold Prentiss (USA)	Dorothy Head (USA)	6-2	6-1	

1947

Rd	Winner	Defeated	S1	S2	S3
F	**Louise Brough (USA)**	**Margaret Osborne duPont (USA)**	**8-6**	**4-6**	**6-1**
S	Louise Brough (USA)	Nancye Wynne Bolton (AUS)	4-6	6-4	7-5
S	Margaret Osborne duPont (USA)	Doris Hart (USA)	7-5	7-5	
Q	Louise Brough (USA)	Dorothy Head (USA)	6-8	6-2	6-0
Q	Nancye Wynne Bolton (AUS)	Pat Canning Todd (USA)	6-4	6-1	
Q	Margaret Osborne duPont (USA)	Magda Rurac (ROU)	6-4	6-4	
Q	Doris Hart (USA)	Barbara Krase (USA)	8-6	6-2	

1948

Rd	Winner	Defeated	S1	S2	S3
F	**Margaret Osborne duPont (USA)**	**Louise Brough (USA)**	**4-6**	**6-4**	**15-13**
S	Margaret Osborne duPont (USA)	Gussy Moran (USA)	10-8	6-4	
S	Louise Brough (USA)	Pat Canning Todd (USA)	6-3	6-3	
Q	Gussy Moran (USA)	Doris Hart (USA)	6-4	6-4	
Q	Margaret Osborne duPont (USA)	Beverly Baker (USA)	1-6	6-2	6-0
Q	Louise Brough (USA)	Virginia Kovacs (USA)	6-3	6-2	
Q	Pat Todd (USA)	Madge Vosters (USA)	6-3	6-1	

1949

Rd	Winner	Defeated	S1	S2	S3
F	**Margaret Osborne duPont (USA)**	**Doris Hart (USA)**	**6-4**	**6-1**	
S	Doris Hart (USA)	Louise Brough (USA)	7-5	6-1	
S	Margaret Osborne duPont (USA)	Betty Hilton (GBR)	6-2	6-3	
Q	Louise Brough (USA)	Beverly Baker (USA)	6-1	2-6	6-2
Q	Doris Hart (USA)	Barbara Scofield (USA)	6-2	6-0	
Q	Margaret Osborne duPont (USA)	Pat Canning Todd (USA)	6-3	10-8	
Q	Betty Hilton (GBR)	Helen Pastall Perez (USA)	6-4	4-6	6-3

1950

Rd	Winner	Defeated	S1	S2	S3
F	**Margaret Osborne duPont (USA)**	**Doris Hart (USA)**	**6-3**	**6-3**	
S	Margaret Osborne duPont (USA)	Nancy Chaffee (USA)	6-1	1-6	6-0
S	Doris Hart (USA)	Beverly Baker (USA)	6-4	6-1	
Q	Margaret Osborne duPont (USA)	Pat Canning Todd (USA)	6-3	6-4	
Q	Nancy Chaffee (USA)	Barbara Scofield (USA)	6-2	6-2	
Q	Doris Hart (USA)	Shirley Fry (USA)	6-4	6-4	
Q	Beverly Baker (USA)	Betty Rosenquest (USA)	6-2	9-7	

1951

Rd	Winner	Defeated	S1	S2	S3
F	**Maureen Connolly (USA)**	**Shirley Fry (USA)**	**6-3**	**1-6**	**6-4**
S	Shirley Fry (USA)	Jean Walker Smith (GBR)	2-6	6-2	6-1
S	Maureen Connolly (USA)	Doris Hart (USA)	6-4	6-4	
Q	Shirley Fry (USA)	Kay Tuckey (GBR)	9-7	3-6	6-2
Q	Jean Walker Smith (GBR)	Magda Rurac (ROU)	6-2	6-3	
Q	Doris Hart (USA)	Nancy Chaffee (USA)	6-2	6-4	
Q	Maureen Connolly (USA)	Jean Quertier (GBR)	6-3	6-3	

1952

Rd	Winner	Defeated	S1	S2	S3
F	**Maureen Connolly (USA)**	**Doris Hart (USA)**	**6-3**	**7-5**	
S	Doris Hart (USA)	Louise Brough (USA)	9-7	8-6	
S	Maureen Connolly (USA)	Shirley Fry (USA)	4-6	6-4	6-1
Q	Doris Hart (USA)	Angela Mortimer (GBR)	6-3	6-2	
Q	Louise Brough (USA)	Thelma Coyne Long (AUS)	6-4	6-2	
Q	Maureen Connolly (USA)	Nancy Chaffee Kiner (USA)	6-3	6-0	
Q	Shirley Fry (USA)	Baba Lewis (USA)	6-3	6-0	

1953

Rd	Winner	Defeated	S1	S2	S3
F	**Maureen Connolly (USA)**	**Doris Hart (USA)**	**6-2**	**6-4**	
S	Maureen Connolly (USA)	Shirley Fry (USA)	6-1	6-1	
S	Doris Hart (USA)	Louise Brough (USA)	6-2	6-4	
Q	Maureen Connolly (USA)	Althea Gibson (USA)	6-2	6-3	
Q	Shirley Fry (USA)	Margaret Osborne duPont (USA)	8-6	7-5	
Q	Doris Hart (USA)	Jean Quertier-Rinkel (GBR)	6-1	6-0	
Q	Louise Brough (USA)	Helen Pastall Perez (USA)	8-6	6-3	

1954

Rd	Winner	Defeated	S1	S2	S3
F	**Doris Hart (USA)**	**Louise Brough (USA)**	**6-8**	**6-1**	**8-6**
S	Louise Brough (USA)	Darlene Hard (USA)	6-2	6-3	
S	Doris Hart (USA)	Shirley Fry (USA)	6-2	6-0	
Q	Louise Brough (USA)	Betty Rosenquest Pratt (USA)	6-2	6-3	
Q	Darlene Hard (USA)	Dennis Bradshaw (USA)	6-3	5-7	6-2
Q	Doris Hart (USA)	Lois Felix (USA)	6-1	6-1	
Q	Shirley Fry (USA)	Beverly Baker Fleitz (USA)	(default)		

1955

Rd	Winner	Defeated	S1	S2	S3
F	**Doris Hart (USA)**	**Pat Ward (GBR)**	**6-4**	**6-2**	
S	Doris Hart (USA)	Dorothy Head Knode (USA)	6-1	6-1	
S	Pat Ward (GBR)	Barbara Breit (USA)	6-1	6-2	
Q	Doris Hart (USA)	Nancy Chaffee Kiner (USA)	6-4	6-4	
Q	Dorothy Head Knode (USA)	Shirley Fry (USA)	9-7	8-6	
Q	Pat Ward (GBR)	Belmar Gunderson (USA)	9-7	6-0	
Q	Barbara Breit (USA)	Beverly Baker Fleitz (USA)	8-6	4-6	6-0

1956

Rd	Winner	Defeated	S1	S2	S3
F	**Shirley Fry (USA)**	**Althea Gibson (USA)**	**6-3**	**6-4**	
S	Shirley Fry (USA)	Shirley Bloomer (GBR)	6-4	6-4	
S	Althea Gibson (USA)	Betty Rosenquest Pratt (USA)	6-1	10-8	
Q	Shirley Fry (USA)	Margaret Osborne duPont (USA)	6-2	4-6	6-2
Q	Shirley Bloomer (GBR)	Louise Brough (USA)	6-3	6-3	
Q	Althea Gibson (USA)	Darlene Hard (USA)	9-7	6-1	
Q	Betty Rosenquest Pratt (USA)	Dorothy Head Knode (USA)	4-6	6-0	6-2

1957

Rd	Winner	Defeated	S1	S2	S3
F	**Althea Gibson (USA)**	**Louise Brough (USA)**	**6-3**	**6-2**	
S	Althea Gibson (USA)	Dorothy Head Knode (USA)	6-2	6-2	
S	Louise Brough (USA)	Darlene Hard (USA)	6-2	6-4	
Q	Althea Gibson (USA)	Mary Bevis Hawton (AUS)	6-2	6-2	
Q	Dorothy Head Knode (USA)	Lois Felix (USA)	6-2	6-1	
Q	Louise Brough (USA)	Ann Haydon (GBR)	7-5	6-1	
Q	Darlene Hard (USA)	Shirley Bloomer (GBR)	6-0	6-1	

1958

Rd	Winner	Defeated	S1	S2	S3
F	**Althea Gibson (USA)**	**Darlene Hard (USA)**	**3-6**	**6-1**	**6-2**
S	Althea Gibson (USA)	Beverly Baker Fleitz (USA)	6-4	6-2	
S	Darlene Hard (USA)	Jeanne Arth (USA)	7-5	6-2	
Q	Althea Gibson (USA)	Christine Truman (GBR)	11-9	6-1	
Q	Beverly Baker Fleitz (USA)	Maria Bueno (BRA)	6-1	6-2	
Q	Jeanne Arth (USA)	Dorothy Head Knode (USA)	6-3	6-2	
Q	Darlene Hard (USA)	Sally Moore (USA)	6-4	6-3	

1959

Rd	Winner	Defeated	S1	S2	S3
F	Maria Bueno (BRA)	Christine Truman (GBR)	6-1	6-4	
S	Christine Truman (GBR)	Ann Haydon (GBR)	6-2	6-3	
S	Maria Bueno (BRA)	Darlene Hard (USA)	6-2	6-4	
Q	Ann Haydon (GBR)	Sandra Reynolds (RSA)	6-3	6-2	
Q	Christine Truman (GBR)	Dorothy Head Knode (USA)	6-1	6-2	
Q	Maria Bueno (BRA)	Louise Brough Clapp (USA)	6-3	6-2	
Q	Darlene Hard (USA)	Karen Hantze (USA)	5-7	9-7	6-3

1960

Rd	Winner	Defeated	S1	S2	S3
F	Darlene Hard (USA)	Maria Bueno (BRA)	6-4	10-12	6-4
S	Maria Bueno (BRA)	Christine Truman (GBR)	6-3	9-7	
S	Darlene Hard (USA)	Donna Floyd (USA)	6-1	7-5	
Q	Maria Bueno (BRA)	Nancy Richey (USA)	6-2	6-4	
Q	Christine Truman (GBR)	Bernice Vukovich (RSA)	6-3	6-3	
Q	Donna Floyd (USA)	Ann Haydon (GBR)	3-6	6-2	9-7
Q	Darlene Hard (USA)	Jan Lehane (AUS)	6-2	6-1	

1961

Rd	Winner	Defeated	S1	S2	S3
F	Darlene Hard (USA)	Ann Haydon (GBR)	6-3	6-4	
S	Darlene Hard (USA)	Margaret Smith (AUS)	6-4	4-6	6-3
S	Ann Haydon (GBR)	Angela Mortimer (GBR)	6-4	6-2	
Q	Darlene Hard (USA)	Yola Ramirez (MEX)	6-3	6-1	
Q	Margaret Smith (AUS)	Christine Truman (GBR)	8-10	6-4	6-3
Q	Angela Mortimer (GBR)	Lesley Turner (AUS)	6-3	6-4	
Q	Ann Haydon (GBR)	Jan Lehane (AUS)	6-4	5-7	6-2

1962

Rd	Winner	Defeated	S1	S2	S3
F	Margaret Smith (AUS)	Darlene Hard (USA)	9-7	6-4	
S	Margaret Smith (AUS)	Maria Bueno (BRA)	6-8	6-3	6-4
S	Darlene Hard (USA)	Victoria Palmer (USA)	6-2	6-3	
Q	Margaret Smith (AUS)	Sandra Reynolds Price (RSA)	6-3	6-3	
Q	Maria Bueno (BRA)	Donna Floyd (USA)	6-1	6-3	
Q	Victoria Palmer (USA)	Gwyneth Thomas (USA)	6-4	2-6	6-2
Q	Darlene Hard (USA)	Vera Puzejova Sukova (CZE)	6-2	6-1	

1963

Rd	Winner	Defeated	S1	S2	S3
F	Maria Bueno (BRA)	Margaret Smith (AUS)	7-5	6-4	
S	Margaret Smith (AUS)	Deidre Catt (GBR)	6-2	6-0	
S	Maria Bueno (BRA)	Ann Haydon Jones (GBR)	1-6	6-2	9-7
Q	Margaret Smith (AUS)	Christine Truman (GBR)	3-6	6-2	6-2
Q	Deidre Catt (GBR)	Yola Ramirez Ochoa (MEX)	(default)		
Q	Maria Bueno (BRA)	Nancy Richey (USA)	6-3	6-2	
Q	Ann Haydon Jones (GBR)	Darlene Hard (USA)	6-4	6-3	

1964

Rd	Winner	Defeated	S1	S2	S3
F	Maria Bueno (BRA)	Carole Caldwell Graebner (USA)	6-1	6-0	
S	Carole Caldwell Graebner (USA)	Nancy Richey (USA)	2-6	9-7	6-4
S	Maria Bueno (BRA)	Carol Hanks (USA)	6-4	6-2	
Q	Carole Caldwell Graebner (USA)	Karen Hantze Susman (USA)	6-4	6-8	6-3
Q	Nancy Richey (USA)	Billie Jean Moffitt (USA)	6-4	6-4	
Q	Carol Hanks (USA)	Ann Haydon Jones (GBR)	7-5	2-6	8-6
Q	Maria Bueno (BRA)	Robyn Ebbern (AUS)	6-4	6-1	

1965

Rd	Winner	Defeated	S1	S2	S3
F	Margaret Smith (AUS)	Billie Jean Moffitt (USA)	8-6	7-5	
S	Margaret Smith (AUS)	Nancy Richey (USA)	6-2	6-2	
S	Billie Jean Moffitt (USA)	Maria Bueno (BRA)	6-2	6-3	
Q	Margaret Smith (AUS)	Francoise Durr (FRA)	6-1	6-0	
Q	Nancy Richey (USA)	Norma Baylon (ARG)	6-4	7-5	
Q	Billie Jean Moffitt (USA)	Ann Haydon Jones (GBR)	16-14	6-2	
Q	Maria Bueno (BRA)	Carole Caldwell Graebner (USA)	8-6	1-6	9-7

1966

Rd	Winner	Defeated	S1	S2	S3
F	Maria Bueno (BRA)	Nancy Richey (USA)	6-3	6-1	
S	Maria Bueno (BRA)	Rosie Casals (USA)	6-2	10-12	6-3
S	Nancy Richey (USA)	Kerry Melville (AUS)	6-3	6-2	
Q	Maria Bueno (BRA)	Norma Baylon (ARG)	6-0	6-1	
Q	Rosie Casals (USA)	Francoise Durr (FRA)	6-4	6-4	
Q	Nancy Richey (USA)	Virginia Wade (GBR)	6-3	6-1	
Q	Kerry Melville (AUS)	Madonna Schacht (AUS)	6-1	6-2	

1967

Rd	Winner	Defeated	S1	S2	S3
F	Billie Jean King (USA)	Ann Haydon Jones (GBR)	11-9	6-4	
S	Billie Jean King (USA)	Francoise Durr (FRA)	6-2	6-4	
S	Ann Haydon Jones (GBR)	Lesley Turner (AUS)	6-2	6-4	
Q	Billie Jean King (USA)	Annette Van Zyl (RSA)	6-1	6-4	
Q	Francoise Durr (FRA)	Valerie Ziegenfuss (USA)	6-0	6-3	
Q	Lesley Turner (AUS)	Rita Bentley (GBR)	6-1	6-2	
Q	Ann Haydon Jones (GBR)	Peaches Bartkowicz (USA)	7-5	2-6	6-1

1968

Rd	Winner	Defeated	S1	S2	S3
F	Virginia Wade (GBR)	Billie Jean King (USA)	6-4	6-2	
S	Virginia Wade (GBR)	Ann Haydon Jones (GBR)	7-5	6-1	
S	Billie Jean King (USA)	Maria Bueno (BRA)	3-6	6-4	6-2
Q	Virginia Wade (GBR)	Judy Tegart Dalton (AUS)	6-3	6-2	
Q	Ann Haydon Jones (GBR)	Peaches Bartkowicz (USA)	10-8	6-3	
Q	Maria Bueno (BRA)	Margaret Smith Court (AUS)	7-5	2-6	6-3
Q	Billie Jean King (USA)	Maryna Godwin (USA)	6-3	3-6	6-3

1968—AMATEUR

Rd	Winner	Defeated	S1	S2	S3
F	Margaret Smith Court (AUS)	Maria Bueno (BRA)	6-2	6-2	
S	Maria Bueno (BRA)	Virginia Wade (GBR)	4-6	7-5	6-2
S	Margaret Smith Court (AUS)	Cecilia Martinez (USA)	6-3	6-4	
Q	Maria Bueno (BRA)	Mary Ann Eisel (USA)	9-7	6-2	
Q	Virginia Wade (GBR)	Kathy Harter (USA)	6-3	6-3	
Q	Cecilia Martinez (USA)	Linda Tuero (USA)	6-2	8-6	
Q	Margaret Smith Court (AUS)	Victoria Rogers (USA)	6-1	6-2	

1969

Rd	Winner	Defeated	S1	S2	S3
F	Margaret Smith Court (AUS)	Nancy Richey (USA)	6-2	6-2	
S	Nancy Richey (USA)	Rosie Casals (USA)	7-5	6-3	
S	Margaret Smith Court (AUS)	Virginia Wade (GBR)	7-5	6-0	
Q	Rosie Casals (USA)	Peaches Bartkowicz (USA)	6-2	6-2	
Q	Nancy Richey (USA)	Billie Jean King (USA)	6-4	8-6	
Q	Virginia Wade (GBR)	Julie Heldman (USA)	6-4	6-3	
Q	Margaret Smith Court (AUS)	Karen Krantzcke (AUS)	6-0	9-7	

1969–AMATEUR

Rd	Winner	Defeated	S1	S2	S3
F	Margaret Smith Court (AUS)	Virginia Wade (GBR)	4-6	6-3	6-0
S	Virginia Wade (GBR)	Mary Ann Eisel Curtis (USA)	10-8	6-8	6-3
S	Margaret Smith Court (AUS)	Kerry Melville (AUS)	6-2	6-2	
Q	Mary Ann Eisel Curtis (USA)	Karen Krantzcke (AUS)	3-6	6-3	6-4
Q	Virginia Wade (GBR)	Betty Ann Grubb (USA)	6-0	6-2	
Q	Kerry Melville (AUS)	Christine Truman Janes (GBR)	8-6	7-5	
Q	Margaret Smith Court (AUS)	Gail Williams (GBR)	6-1	6-1	

1970

Rd	Winner	Defeated	S1	S2	S3
F	Margaret Smith Court (AUS)	Rosie Casals (USA)	6-2	2-6	6-1
S	Rosie Casals (USA)	Virginia Wade (GBR)	6-2	6-7(4)	6-2
S	Margaret Smith Court (AUS)	Nancy Richey (USA)	6-1	6-3	
Q	Virginia Wade (GBR)	Francoise Durr (FRA)	5-7	6-4	6-0
Q	Rosie Casals (USA)	Kerry Melville (AUS)	6-4	4-6	6-4
Q	Margaret Smith Court (AUS)	Helen Gourlay Cawley (AUS)	6-2	6-2	
Q	Nancy Richey (USA)	Lesley Hunt (AUS)	6-4	6-4	

1971

Rd	Winner	Defeated	S1	S2	S3
F	Billie Jean King (USA)	Rosie Casals (USA)	6-4	7-6(2)	
S	Rosie Casals (USA)	Kerry Melville (AUS)	6-4	6-3	
S	Billie Jean King (USA)	Chris Evert (USA)	6-3	6-2	
Q	Chris Evert (USA)	Lesley Hunt (AUS)	4-6	6-2	6-3
Q	Billie Jean King (USA)	Laura DuPont (USA)	6-3	7-5	
Q	Kerry Melville (AUS)	Judy Tegart Dalton (AUS)	6-3	7-5	
Q	Rosie Casals (USA)	Joyce Williams (GBR)	6-4	2-6	6-4

1972

Rd	Winner	Defeated	S1	S2	S3
F	Billie Jean King (USA)	Kerry Melville (AUS)	6-3	7-5	
S	Billie Jean King (USA)	Margaret Smith Court (AUS)	6-4	6-4	
S	Kerry Melville (AUS)	Chris Evert (USA)	6-4	6-2	
Q	Billie Jean King (USA)	Virginia Wade (GBR)	6-2	7-5	
Q	Margaret Smith Court (AUS)	Rosie Casals (USA)	6-4	4-6	6-4
Q	Chris Evert (USA)	Olga Morozova (USSR)	3-6	6-3	7-6(1)
Q	Kerry Melville (AUS)	Pam Teeguarden (USA)	6-0	6-2	

1973

Rd	Winner	Defeated	S1	S2	S3
F	Margaret Smith Court (AUS)	Evonne Goolagong (AUS)	7-6(2)	5-7	6-2
S	Evonne Goolagong (AUS)	Helga Niessen Masthoff (GER)	6-1	4-6	6-4
S	Margaret Smith Court (AUS)	Chris Evert (USA)	7-5	2-6	6-2
Q	Helga Niessen Masthoff (GER)	Julie Heldman (USA)	6-3	6-3	
Q	Evonne Goolagong (AUS)	Kerry Melville (AUS)	6-3	7-5	
Q	Chris Evert (USA)	Rosie Casals (USA)	6-1	7-5	
Q	Margaret Smith Court (AUS)	Virginia Wade (GBR)	7-6	7-6(2)	

1974

Rd	Winner	Defeated	S1	S2	S3
F	Billie Jean King (USA)	Evonne Goolagong (AUS)	3-6	6-3	7-5
S	Evonne Goolagong (AUS)	Chris Evert (USA)	6-0	6-7(3)	6-3
S	Billie Jean King (USA)	Julie Heldman (USA)	2-6	6-3	6-1
Q	Julie Heldman (USA)	Nancy Richey Gunter (USA)	7-5	7-6	
Q	Billie Jean King (USA)	Rosie Casals (USA)	6-1	7-6	
Q	Evonne Goolagong (AUS)	Kerry Melville (AUS)	6-4	7-5	
Q	Chris Evert (USA)	Lesley Hunt (AUS)	7-6(4)	6-3	

1975

Rd	Winner	Defeated	S1	S2	S3
F	Chris Evert (USA)	Evonne Goolagong (AUS)	5-7	6-4	6-2
S	Evonne Goolagong (AUS)	Virginia Wade (GBR)	7-5	6-1	
S	Chris Evert (USA)	Martina Navratilova (CZE)	6-4	6-4	
Q	Evonne Goolagong (AUS)	Kazuko Sawamatsu (JPN)	7-6	7-5	
Q	Virginia Wade (GBR)	Katja Ebbinghaus (GER)	6-3	6-0	
Q	Martina Navratilova (CZE)	Margaret Smith Court (AUS)	6-2	6-4	
Q	Chris Evert (USA)	Kerry Melville Reid (AUS)	6-2	6-1	

1976

Rd	Winner	Defeated	S1	S2	S3
F	Chris Evert (USA)	Evonne Goolagong (AUS)	6-3	6-0	
S	Evonne Goolagong (AUS)	Dianne Fromholtz (AUS)	7-6(5)	6-0	
S	Chris Evert (USA)	Mima Jausovec (YUG)	6-3	6-1	
Q	Mima Jausovec (YUG)	Virginia Ruzici (ROU)	6-2	6-1	
Q	Chris Evert (USA)	Natasha Chmyreva (USSR)	6-1	6-2	
Q	Evonne Goolagong (AUS)	Rosie Casals (USA)	6-1	6-2	
Q	Dianne Fromholtz (AUS)	Zenda Liess (USA)	6-1	6-3	

1977

Rd	Winner	Defeated	S1	S2	S3
F	Chris Evert (USA)	Wendy Turnbull (AUS)	7-6(3)	6-2	
S	Wendy Turnbull (AUS)	Martina Navratilova (CZE)	2-6	7-5	6-4
S	Chris Evert (USA)	Betty Stove (NED)	6-3	7-5	
Q	Betty Stove (NED)	Tracy Austin (USA)	6-2	6-2	
Q	Martina Navratilova (CZE)	Mima Jausovec (YUG)	6-4	6-1	
Q	Wendy Turnbull (AUS)	Virginia Wade (GBR)	6-2	6-1	
Q	Chris Evert (USA)	Billie Jean King (USA)	6-2	6-0	

1978

Rd	Winner	Defeated	S1	S2	S3
F	Chris Evert (USA)	Pam Shriver (USA)	7-5	6-4	
S	Chris Evert (USA)	Wendy Turnbull (AUS)	6-3	6-0	
S	Pam Shriver (USA)	Martina Navratilova (CZE)	7-6(5)	7-6(3)	
Q	Wendy Turnbull (AUS)	Kathy May (USA)	3-6	7-6	6-3
Q	Chris Evert (USA)	Tracy Austin (USA)	7-5	6-1	
Q	Pam Shriver (USA)	Lesley Hunt (AUS)	6-2	6-0	
Q	Martina Navratilova (CZE)	Virginia Ruzici (ROU)	6-3	6-2	

1979

Rd	Winner	Defeated	S1	S2	S3
F	Tracy Austin (USA)	Chris Evert Lloyd (USA)	6-4	6-3	
S	Tracy Austin (USA)	Martina Navratilova (CZE)	7-5	7-5	
S	Chris Evert Lloyd (USA)	Billie Jean King (USA)	6-1	6-0	
Q	Billie Jean King (USA)	Virginia Wade (GBR)	6-3	7-6	
Q	Chris Evert Lloyd (USA)	Evonne Goolagong (AUS)	7-5	6-2	
Q	Tracy Austin (USA)	Sylvia Hanika (GER)	6-1	6-1	
Q	Martina Navratilova (CZE)	Kerry Melville Reid (AUS)	6-4	6-1	

1980

Rd	Winner	Defeated	S1	S2	S3
F	Chris Evert Lloyd (USA)	Hana Mandlikova (CZE)	5-7	6-1	6-1
S	Hana Mandlikova (CZE)	Andrea Jaeger (USA)	6-1	3-6	7-6
S	Chris Evert Lloyd (USA)	Tracy Austin (USA)	4-6	6-1	6-1
Q	Hana Mandlikova (CZE)	Barbara Hallquist (USA)	6-2	6-2	
Q	Andrea Jaeger (USA)	Ivanna Madruga (ARG)	6-1	6-3	
Q	Chris Evert Lloyd (USA)	Mima Jausovec (YUG)	7-6	6-2	
Q	Tracy Austin (USA)	Pam Shriver (USA)	6-2	6-3	

1981

Rd	Winner	Defeated	S1	S2	S3
F	Tracy Austin (USA)	Martina Navratilova (USA)	1-6	7-6(4)	7-6(1)
S	Tracy Austin (USA)	Barbara Potter (USA)	6-1	6-3	
S	Martina Navratilova (USA)	Chris Evert Lloyd (USA)	7-5	4-6	6-4
Q	Tracy Austin (USA)	Sylvia Hanika (GER)	6-4	6-3	
Q	Barbara Potter (USA)	Barbara Gerken (USA)	7-5	7-5	
Q	Martina Navratilova (USA)	Anne Smith (AUS)	7-5	6-4	
Q	Chris Evert Lloyd (USA)	Hana Mandlikova (CZE)	6-1	6-3	

1982

Rd	Winner	Defeated	S1	S2	S3
F	Chris Evert Lloyd (USA)	Hana Mandlikova (CZE)	6-3	6-1	
S	Hana Mandlikova (CZE)	Pam Shriver (USA)	6-4	2-6	6-2
S	Chris Evert Lloyd (USA)	Andrea Jaeger (USA)	6-1	6-2	
Q	Pam Shriver (USA)	Martina Navratilova (USA)	1-6	7-6(5)	6-2
Q	Hana Mandlikova (CZE)	Tracy Austin (USA)	4-6	6-4	6-4
Q	Andrea Jaeger (USA)	Gretchen Rush (USA)	3-6	6-1	6-0
Q	Chris Evert Lloyd (USA)	Bonnie Gadusek (USA)	4-6	6-1	6-0

1983

Rd	Winner	Defeated	S1	S2	S3
F	Martina Navratilova (USA)	Chris Evert Lloyd (USA)	6-1	6-3	
S	Chris Evert Lloyd (USA)	Jo Durie (GBR)	6-4	6-4	
S	Martina Navratilova (USA)	Pam Shriver (USA)	6-2	6-1	
Q	Pam Shriver (USA)	Andrea Jaeger (USA)	7-6	6-3	
Q	Chris Evert Lloyd (USA)	Hana Mandlikova (CZE)	6-4	6-3	
Q	Jo Durie (GBR)	Ivanna Madruga-Osses (ARG)	6-2	6-2	
Q	Martina Navratilova (USA)	Sylvia Hanika (GER)	6-0	6-3	

1984

Rd	Winner	Defeated	S1	S2	S3
F	Martina Navratilova (USA)	Chris Evert Lloyd (USA)	4-6	6-4	6-4
S	Chris Evert Lloyd (USA)	Carling Bassett (CAN)	6-2	6-2	
S	Martina Navratilova (USA)	Wendy Turnbull (AUS)	6-4	6-1	
Q	Chris Evert Lloyd (USA)	Sylvia Hanika (GER)	6-2	6-3	
Q	Carling Bassett (CAN)	Hana Mandlikova (CZE)	6-4	6-3	
Q	Wendy Turnbull (AUS)	Pam Shriver (USA)	2-6	6-3	6-3
Q	Martina Navratilova (USA)	Helena Sukova (CZE)	6-3	6-3	

1985

Rd	Winner	Defeated	S1	S2	S3
F	Hana Mandlikova (CZE)	Martina Navratilova (USA)	7-6(3)	1-6	7-6(2)
S	Hana Mandlikova (CZE)	Chris Evert Lloyd (USA)	4-6	6-2	6-3
S	Martina Navratilova (USA)	Steffi Graf (GER)	6-2	6-3	
Q	Hana Mandlikova (CZE)	Helena Sukova (CZE)	7-6	7-5	
Q	Chris Evert Lloyd (USA)	Claudia Kohde Kilsch (GER)	6-3	6-3	
Q	Martina Navratilova (USA)	Zina Garrison (USA)	6-2	6-3	
Q	Steffi Graf (GER)	Pam Shriver (USA)	7-6(4)	6-7(4)	7-6(4)

1986

Rd	Winner	Defeated	S1	S2	S3
F	Martina Navratilova (USA)	Helena Sukova (CZE)	6-3	6-2	
S	Helena Sukova (CZE)	Chris Evert Lloyd (USA)	6-2	6-4	
S	Martina Navratilova (USA)	Steffi Graf (GER)	6-1	6-7(3)	7-6(8)
Q	Chris Evert Lloyd (USA)	Manuela Maleeva (BUL)	6-2	6-4	
Q	Helena Sukova (CZE)	Wendy Turnbull (AUS)	6-4	6-0	
Q	Steffi Graf (GER)	Bonnie Gadusek (USA)	6-3	6-1	
Q	Martina Navratilova (USA)	Pam Shriver (USA)	6-2	6-4	

1987

Rd	Winner	Defeated	S1	S2	S3
F	Martina Navratilova (USA)	Steffi Graf (GER)	7-6(4)	6-1	
S	Martina Navratilova (USA)	Helena Sukova (CZE)	6-2	6-2	
S	Steffi Graf (GER)	Lori McNeil (USA)	4-6	6-2	6-4
Q	Martina Navratilova (USA)	Gabriela Sabatini (ARG)	7-5	6-3	
Q	Helena Sukova (CZE)	Claudia Kohde Kilsch (GER)	6-1	6-3	
Q	Lori McNeil (USA)	Chris Evert (USA)	3-6	6-2	6-4
Q	Steffi Graf (GER)	Pam Shriver (USA)	6-4	6-3	

1988

Rd	Winner	Defeated	S1	S2	S3
F	Steffi Graf (GER)	Gabriela Sabatini (ARG)	6-3	3-6	6-1
S	Steffi Graf (GER)	Chris Evert (USA)	(walkover)		
S	Gabriela Sabatini (ARG)	Zina Garrison (USA)	6-4	7-5	
Q	Steffi Graf (GER)	Katerina Maleeva (BUL)	6-3	6-0	
Q	Chris Evert (USA)	Manuela Maleeva (BUL)	3-6	6-4	6-2
Q	Gabriela Sabatini (ARG)	Larisa Savchenko (USSR)	4-6	6-4	6-1
Q	Zina Garrison (USA)	Martina Navratilova (USA)	6-4	6-7(3)	7-5

1989

Rd	Winner	Defeated	S1	S2	S3
F	Steffi Graf (GER)	Martina Navratilova (USA)	3-6	7-5	6-1
S	Steffi Graf (GER)	Gabriela Sabatini (ARG)	3-6	6-4	6-2
S	Martina Navratilova (USA)	Zina Garrison (USA)	7-6(4)	6-2	
Q	Steffi Graf (GER)	Helena Sukova (CZE)	6-1	6-1	
Q	Gabriela Sabatini (ARG)	Arantxa Sanchez Vicario (ESP)	3-6	6-4	6-1
Q	Zina Garrison (USA)	Chris Evert (USA)	7-6(1)	6-2	
Q	Martina Navratilova (USA)	Manuela Maleeva (BUL)	6-0	6-0	

1990

Rd	Winner	Defeated	S1	S2	S3
F	Gabriela Sabatini (ARG)	Steffi Graf (GER)	6-2	7-6(4)	
S	Steffi Graf (GER)	Arantxa Sanchez Vicario (ESP)	6-1	6-2	
S	Gabriela Sabatini (ARG)	Mary Joe Fernandez (USA)	7-5	5-7	6-3
Q	Steffi Graf (GER)	Jana Novotna (CZE)	6-3	6-1	
Q	Arantxa Sanchez Vicario (ESP)	Zina Garrison (USA)	6-2	6-2	
Q	Gabriela Sabatini (ARG)	Leila Meskhi (USSR)	7-6(5)	6-4	
Q	Mary Joe Fernandez (USA)	Manuela Maleeva-Fragniere (SUI)	6-2	2-6	6-1

1991

Rd	Winner	Defeated	S1	S2	S3
F	Monica Seles (YUG)	Martina Navratilova (USA)	7-6(1)	6-1	
S	Martina Navratilova (USA)	Steffi Graf (GER)	7-6(2)	6-7(6)	6-4
S	Monica Seles (YUG)	Jennifer Capriati (USA)	6-3	3-6	7-6(3)
Q	Steffi Graf (GER)	Conchita Martinez (ESP)	6-1	6-3	
Q	Martina Navratilova (USA)	Arantxa Sanchez Vicario (ESP)	6-7(6)	7-6(5)	6-2
Q	Jennifer Capriati (USA)	Gabriela Sabatini (ARG)	6-3	7-6(1)	
Q	Monica Seles (YUG)	Gigi Fernandez (USA)	6-1	6-2	

1992

Rd	Winner	Defeated	S1	S2	S3
F	Monica Seles (YUG)	Arantxa Sanchez Vicario (ESP)	6-3	6-3	
S	Monica Seles (YUG)	Mary Joe Fernandez (USA)	6-3	6-2	
S	Arantxa Sanchez Vicario (ESP)	Manuela Maleeva-Fragniere (SUI)	6-2	6-1	
Q	Monica Seles (YUG)	Patricia Hy (CAN)	6-1	6-2	
Q	Mary Joe Fernandez (USA)	Gabriela Sabatini (ARG)	6-2	1-6	6-4
Q	Manuela Maleeva-Fragniere (SUI)	Magdalena Maleeva (BUL)	6-2	5-3 (retired)	
Q	Arantxa Sanchez Vicario (ESP)	Steffi Graf (GER)	7-6(5)	6-3	

Rd	Winner	Defeated	S1	S2	S3

1993

Rd	Winner	Defeated	S1	S2	S3
F	**Steffi Graf (GER)**	**Helena Sukova (CZE)**	6-3	6-3	
S	Steffi Graf (GER)	Manuela Maleeva-Fragniere (SUI)	4-6	6-1	6-0
S	Helena Sukova (CZE)	Arantxa Sanchez Vicario (ESP)	6-7(7)	7-5	6-2
Q	Steffi Graf (GER)	Gabriela Sabatini (ARG)	6-2	5-7	6-1
Q	Manuela Maleeva-Fragniere (SUI)	Kimiko Date (JPN)	7-5	7-5	
Q	Helena Sukova (CZE)	Katerina Maleeva (BUL)	6-4	6-7(3)	6-3
Q	Arantxa Sanchez Vicario (ESP)	Natasha Zvereva (BLR)	3-0	(retired)	

1994

Rd	Winner	Defeated	S1	S2	S3
F	**Arantxa Sanchez Vicario (ESP)**	**Steffi Graf (GER)**	1-6	7-6(3)	6-4
S	Steffi Graf (GER)	Jana Novotna (CZE)	6-3	7-5	
S	Arantxa Sanchez Vicario (ESP)	Gabriela Sabatini (ARG)	6-1	7-6(6)	
Q	Steffi Graf (GER)	Amanda Coetzer (RSA)	6-0	6-2	
Q	Jana Novotna (CZE)	Mary Pierce (FRA)	6-4	6-0	
Q	Gabriela Sabatini (ARG)	Gigi Fernandez (USA)	6-2	7-5	
Q	Arantxa Sanchez Vicario (ESP)	Kimiko Date (JPN)	6-3	6-0	

1995

Rd	Winner	Defeated	S1	S2	S3
F	**Steffi Graf (GER)**	**Monica Seles (USA)**	7-6(6)	0-6	6-3
S	Steffi Graf (GER)	Gabriela Sabatini (ARG)	6-4	7-6(5)	
S	Monica Seles (USA)	Conchita Martinez (ESP)	6-2	6-2	
Q	Steffi Graf (GER)	Amy Frazier (USA)	6-2	6-3	
Q	Gabriela Sabatini (ARG)	Mary Joe Fernandez (USA)	6-1	6-3	
Q	Conchita Martinez (ESP)	Brenda Schultz McCarthy (NED)	3-6	7-6(3)	6-2
Q	Monica Seles (USA)	Jana Novotna (CZE)	7-6(5)	6-2	

1996

Rd	Winner	Defeated	S1	S2	S3
F	**Steffi Graf (GER)**	**Monica Seles (USA)**	7-5	6-4	
S	Steffi Graf (GER)	Martina Hingis (SUI)	7-5	6-3	
S	Monica Seles (USA)	Conchita Martinez (ESP)	6-4	6-3	
Q	Steffi Graf (GER)	Judith Wiesner (AUT)	7-5	6-3	
Q	Martina Hingis (SUI)	Jana Novotna (CZE)	7-6(1)	6-4	
Q	Conchita Martinez (ESP)	Linda Wild (USA)	7-6(6)	6-0	
Q	Monica Seles (USA)	Amanda Coetzer (RSA)	6-0	6-3	

1997

Rd	Winner	Defeated	S1	S2	S3
F	**Martina Hingis (SUI)**	**Venus Williams (USA)**	6-0	6-4	
S	Martina Hingis (SUI)	Lindsay Davenport (USA)	6-2	6-4	
S	Venus Williams (USA)	Irina Spirlea (ROU)	7-6(5)	4-6	7-6(7)
Q	Martina Hingis (SUI)	Arantxa Sanchez Vicario (ESP)	6-3	6-2	
Q	Lindsay Davenport (USA)	Jana Novotna (CZE)	6-2	4-6	7-6(5)
Q	Venus Williams (USA)	Sandrine Testud (FRA)	7-5	7-5	
Q	Irina Spirlea (ROU)	Monica Seles (USA)	6-7(5)	7-6(8)	6-3

1998

Rd	Winner	Defeated	S1	S2	S3
F	**Lindsay Davenport (USA)**	**Martina Hingis (SUI)**	6-3	7-5	
S	Martina Hingis (SUI)	Jana Novotna (CZE)	3-6	6-1	6-4
S	Lindsay Davenport (USA)	Venus Williams (USA)	6-4	6-4	
Q	Martina Hingis (SUI)	Monica Seles (USA)	6-4	6-4	
Q	Jana Novotna (CZE)	Patty Schnyder (SUI)	6-2	6-3	
Q	Venus Williams (USA)	Arantxa Sanchez Vicario (ESP)	2-6	6-1	6-1
Q	Lindsay Davenport (USA)	Amanda Coetzer (RSA)	6-0	6-4	

1999

Rd	Winner	Defeated	S1	S2	S3
F	**Serena Williams (USA)**	**Martina Hingis (SUI)**	6-3	7-6(4)	
S	Martina Hingis (SUI)	Venus Williams (USA)	6-1	4-6	6-3
S	Serena Williams (USA)	Lindsay Davenport (USA)	6-4	1-6	6-4
Q	Martina Hingis (SUI)	Anke Huber (GER)	6-2	6-0	
Q	Venus Williams (USA)	Barbara Schett (AUT)	6-4	6-3	
Q	Serena Williams (USA)	Monica Seles (USA)	4-6	6-3	6-2
Q	Lindsay Davenport (USA)	Mary Pierce (FRA)	6-2	6-3	7-5

2000

Rd	Winner	Defeated	S1	S2	S3
F	**Venus Williams (USA)**	**Lindsay Davenport (USA)**	6-4	7-5	
S	Venus Williams (USA)	Martina Hingis (SUI)	4-6	6-3	7-5
S	Lindsay Davenport (USA)	Elena Dementieva (RUS)	6-2	7-6(5)	
Q	Martina Hingis (SUI)	Monica Seles (USA)	6-0	7-5	
Q	Venus Williams (USA)	Nathalie Tauziat (FRA)	6-4	1-6	6-1
Q	Elena Dementieva (RUS)	Anke Huber (GER)	6-1	3-6	6-3
Q	Lindsay Davenport (USA)	Serena Williams (USA)	6-4	6-2	

2001

Rd	Winner	Defeated	S1	S2	S3
F	**Venus Williams (USA)**	**Serena Williams (USA)**	6-2	6-4	
S	Serena Williams (USA)	Martina Hingis (SUI)	6-3	6-2	
S	Venus Williams (USA)	Jennifer Capriati (USA)	6-4	6-2	
Q	Martina Hingis (SUI)	Daja Bedanova (CZE)	6-2	6-0	
Q	Serena Williams (USA)	Lindsay Davenport (USA)	6-3	6-7(7)	7-5
Q	Venus Williams (USA)	Kim Clijsters (BEL)	6-3	6-1	
Q	Jennifer Capriati (USA)	Amelie Mauresmo (FRA)	6-3	6-4	

2002

Rd	Winner	Defeated	S1	S2	S3
F	**Serena Williams (USA)**	**Venus Williams (USA)**	6-4	6-3	
S	Serena Williams (USA)	Lindsay Davenport (USA)	6-3	7-5	
S	Venus Williams (USA)	Amelie Mauresmo (FRA)	6-3	5-7	6-4
Q	Serena Williams (USA)	Daniela Hantuchova (SVK)	6-2	6-2	
Q	Lindsay Davenport (USA)	Elena Bovina (RUS)	3-6	6-0	6-2
Q	Amelie Mauresmo (FRA)	Jennifer Capriati (USA)	4-6	7-6(5)	6-3
Q	Venus Williams (USA)	Monica Seles (USA)	6-2	6-3	

2003

Rd	Winner	Defeated	S1	S2	S3
F	**Justin Henin-Hardenne (BEL)**	**Kim Clijsters (BEL)**	7-5	6-1	
S	Kim Clijsters (BEL)	Lindsay Davenport (USA)	6-2	6-3	
S	Justin Henin-Hardenne (BEL)	Jennifer Capriati (USA)	4-6	7-5	7-6(4)
Q	Kim Clijsters (BEL)	Amelie Mauresmo (FRA)	6-1	6-4	
Q	Lindsay Davenport (USA)	Paola Suarez (ARG)	6-4	6-0	
Q	Jennifer Capriati (USA)	Francesca Schiavone (ITA)	6-1	6-3	
Q	Justin Henin-Hardenne (BEL)	Anastasia Myskina (RUS)	6-2	6-3	

2004

Rd	Winner	Defeated	S1	S2	S3
F	**Svetlana Kuznetsova (RUS)**	**Elena Dementieva (RUS)**	6-3	7-5	
S	Svetlana Kuznetsova (RUS)	Lindsay Davenport (USA)	1-6	6-2	6-4
S	Elena Dementieva (RUS)	Jennifer Capriati (USA)	6-0	2-6	7-6(5)
Q	Svetlana Kuznetsova (RUS)	Nadia Petrova (RUS)	7-6(4)	6-3	
Q	Lindsay Davenport (USA)	Shinobu Asagoe (JPN)	6-1	6-1	
Q	Jennifer Capriati (USA)	Serena Williams (USA)	2-6	6-4	6-4
Q	Elena Dementieva (RUS)	Amelie Mauresmo (FRA)	4-6	6-4	7-6(1)

2005

Rd	Winner	Defeated	S1	S2	S3
F	**Kim Clijsters (BEL)**	**Mary Pierce (FRA)**	**6-3**	**6-1**	
S	Kim Clijsters (BEL)	Maria Sharapova (RUS)	6-2	6-7(4)	6-3
S	Mary Pierce (FRA)	Elena Dementieva (RUS)	3-6	6-2	6-2
Q	Maria Sharapova (RUS)	Nadia Petrova (RUS)	7-5	4-6	6-4
Q	Kim Clijsters (BEL)	Venus Williams (USA)	4-6	7-5	6-1
Q	Mary Pierce (FRA)	Amelie Mauresmo (FRA)	6-4	6-1	
Q	Elena Dementieva (RUS)	Lindsay Davenport (USA)	6-1	3-6	7-6(6)

2006

Rd	Winner	Defeated	S1	S2	S3
F	**Maria Sharapova (RUS)**	**Justin Henin-Hardenne (BEL)**	**6-4**	**6-4**	
S	Maria Sharapova (RUS)	Amelie Mauresmo (FRA)	6-0	4-6	6-0
S	Justine Henin-Hardenne (BEL)	Jelena Jankovic (SRB)	4-6	6-4	6-0
Q	Amelie Mauresmo (FRA)	Dinara Safina (RUS)	6-2	6-3	
Q	Maria Sharapova (RUS)	Tatiana Golovin (FRA)	7-6(4)	7-6(0)	
Q	Jelena Jankovic (SRB)	Elena Dementieva (RUS)	6-2	6-1	
Q	Justine Henin-Hardenne (BEL)	Lindsay Davenport (USA)	6-4	6-4	

2007

Rd	Winner	Defeated	S1	S2	S3
F	**Justine Henin (BEL)**	**Svetlana Kuznetsova (RUS)**	**6-1**	**6-3**	
S	Justine Henin (BEL)	Venus Williams (USA)	7-6(2)	6-4	
S	Svetlana Kuznetsova (RUS)	Anna Chakvetadze (RUS)	3-6	6-1	6-1
Q	Justine Henin (BEL)	Serena Williams (USA)	7-6(3)	6-1	
Q	Venus Williams (USA)	Jelena Jankovic (SRB)	4-6	6-1	7-6(4)
Q	Svetlana Kuznetsova (RUS)	Agnes Szavay (HUN)	6-1	6-4	
Q	Anna Chakvetadze (RUS)	Shahar Peer (ISR)	6-4	6-1	

2008

Rd	Winner	Defeated	S1	S2	S3
F	**Serena Williams (USA)**	**Jelena Jankovic (SRB)**	**6-4**	**7-5**	
S	Serena Williams (USA)	Dinara Safina (RUS)	6-3	6-2	
S	Jelena Jankovic (SRB)	Elena Dementieva (RUS)	6-4	6-4	
Q	Dinara Safina (RUS)	Flavia Pennetta (ITA)	6-2	6-3	
Q	Serena Williams (USA)	Venus Williams (USA)	7-6(6)	7-6(7)	
Q	Elena Dementieva (RUS)	Patty Schnyder (SUI)	6-2	6-3	
Q	Jelena Jankovic (SRB)	Sybille Bammer (AUT)	6-1	6-4	

Men's Doubles

Year	Winner	Defeated	S1	S2	S3	S4	S5
1881	Clarence Clark (USA) Fred Taylor (USA)	Alex. Van Rensselaer (USA) Arthur Newbold (USA)	6-5	6-4	6-5		
1882	Richard Sears (USA) James Dwight (USA)	Crawford Nightingale (USA) George Smith (USA)	6-2	6-4	6-4		
1883	Richard Sears (USA) James Dwight (USA)	Alex. Van Rensselaer (USA) Arthur Newbold (USA)	6-0	6-2	6-2		
1884	Richard Sears (USA) James Dwight (USA)	Alex. Van Rensselaer (USA) Walter Berry (USA)	6-4	6-1	8-10	6-4	
1885	Richard Sears (USA) Joseph Clark (USA)	Henry Slocum (USA) Percy Knapp (USA)	6-3	6-0	6-2		

Year	Winner	Defeated	S1	S2	S3	S4	S5
1886	Richard Sears (USA) James Dwight (USA)	Howard Taylor (USA) Godfrey Brinley (USA)	7-5	5-7	7-5	6-4	
1887	Richard Sears (USA) James Dwight (USA)	Howard Taylor (USA) Henry Slocum (USA)	6-4	3-6	2-6	6-3	6-3
1888	Oliver Campbell (USA) Valentine Hall (USA)	Clarence Hobart (USA) Edward MacMullen (USA)	6-4	6-2	6-4		
1889	Henry Slocum (USA) Howard Taylor (USA)	Valentine Hall (USA) Oliver Campbell (USA)	14-12	10-8	6-4		
1890	Valentine Hall (USA) Oliver Campbell (USA)	John Carver (USA) John Ryerson (USA)	6-3	4-6	6-2	2-6	6-3
1891	Oliver Campbell (USA) Bob Huntington (USA)	Valentine Hall (USA) Clarence Hobart (USA)	6-3	6-4	8-6		
1892	Oliver Campbell (USA) Bob Huntington (USA)	Valentine Hall (USA) Edward Hall (USA)	6-4	6-2	4-6	6-3	
1893	Clarence Hobart (USA) Fred Hovey (USA)	Oliver Campbell (USA) Bob Huntington (USA)	6-4	6-4	4-6	6-2	
1894	Clarence Hobart (USA) Fred Hovey (USA)	Carr Neel (USA) Sam Neel (USA)	6-3	8-6	6-1		
1895	Malcolm Chace (USA) Robert Wrenn (USA)	Clarence Hobart (USA) Fred Hovey (USA)	7-5	6-1	8-6		
1896	Carr Neel (USA) Sam Neel (USA)	Robert Wrenn (USA) Malcolm Chace (USA)	6-3	1-6	6-1	3-6	6-1
1897	Leo Ware (USA) George Sheldon (USA)	Harold Mahony (GBR) Harold Nisbet (GBR)	11-13	6-2	9-7	1-6	6-1
1898	Leo Ware (USA) George Sheldon (USA)	Holcombe Ward (USA) Dwight Davis (USA)	1-6	7-5	6-4	4-6	7-5
1899	Holcombe Ward (USA) Dwight Davis (USA)	Leo Ware (USA) George Sheldon (USA)	6-4	6-4	6-3		
1900	Holcombe Ward (USA) Dwight Davis (USA)	Fred Alexander (USA) Ray Little (USA)	6-4	9-7	12-10		
1901	Holcombe Ward (USA) Dwight Davis (USA)	Leo Ware (USA) Beals Wright (USA)	6-3	9-7	6-1		
1902	Reggie Doherty (GBR) Laurie Doherty (GBR)	Holcombe Ward (USA) Dwight Davis (USA)	11-9	12-10	6-4		
1903	Reggie Doherty (GBR) Laurie Doherty (GBR)	Kreigh Collins (USA) Harry Wainder (USA)	7-5	6-3	6-3		
1904	Holcombe Ward (USA) Beals Wright (USA)	Kreigh Collins (USA) Ray Little (USA)	1-6	6-2	3-6	6-4	6-1
1905	Holcombe Ward (USA) Beals Wright (USA)	Fred Alexander (USA) Harold Hackett (USA)	6-2	6-1	6-3		
1906	Holcombe Ward (USA) Beals Wright (USA)	Fred Alexander (USA) Harold Hackett (USA)	6-3	3-6	6-3	6-3	
1907	Fred Alexander (USA) Harold Hackett (USA)	Nat Thornton (USA) Wylie Grant (USA)	6-2	6-1	6-1		
1908	Fred Alexander (USA) Harold Hackett (USA)	Ray Little (USA) Beals Wright (USA)	6-1	7-5	6-2		
1909	Fred Alexander (USA) Harold Hackett (USA)	Maurice McLoughlin (USA) George Janes (USA)	6-4	6-4	6-0		
1910	Fred Alexander (USA) Harold Hackett (USA)	Tom Bundy (USA) Trowridge Hendrick (USA)	6-1	8-6	6-3		
1911	Ray Little (USA) Gus Touchard (USA)	Fred Alexander (USA) Harold Hackett (USA)	7-5	13-15	6-2	6-4	
1912	Maurice McLoughlin (USA) Tom Bundy (USA)	Ray Little (USA) Gus Touchard (USA)	3-6	6-2	6-1	7-5	

Year	Winner	Defeated	S1	S2	S3	S4	S5
1913	Maurice McLoughlin (USA) / Tom Bundy (USA)	John Strachan (USA) / Clarence Griffin (USA)	6-4	7-5	6-1		
1914	Maurice McLoughlin (USA) / Tom Bundy (USA)	George Church (USA) / Dean Mathey (USA)	6-4	6-2	6-4		
1915	Bill Johnston (USA) / Clarence Griffin (USA)	Maurice McLoughlin (USA) / Tom Bundy (USA)	2-6	6-3	6-4	3-6	6-3
1916	Fred Alexander (USA) / Harold Throckmorton (USA)	Maurice McLoughlin (USA) / Ward Dawson (USA)	6-4	6-3	5-7	6-3	
1917	Fred Alexander (USA) / Harold Throckmorton (USA)	Harry Johnson (USA) / Irving Wright (USA)	11-9	6-4	6-4		
1918	Bill Tilden (USA) / Vinnie Richards (USA)	Fred Alexander (USA) / Beals Wright (USA)	6-3	6-4	3-6	2-6	6-2
1919	Norman Brookes (AUS) / Gerald Patterson (AUS)	Bill Tilden (USA) / Vinnie Richards (USA)	8-6	6-3	4-6	4-6	6-2
1920	Bill Johnston (USA) / Clarence Griffin (USA)	Willis Davis (USA) / Roland Roberts (USA)	6-2	6-2	6-3		
1921	Bill Tilden (USA) / Vinnie Richards (USA)	Dick Williams (USA) / Watson Washburn (USA)	13-11	12-10	6-1		
1922	Bill Tilden (USA) / Vinnie Richards (USA)	Gerald Patterson (AUS) / Pat O'Hara Wood (AUS)	4-6	6-1	6-3	6-4	
1923	Bill Tilden (USA) / Brian Norton (RSA)	Dick Williams (USA) / Watson Washburn (USA)	3-6	6-2	6-3	5-7	6-2
1924	Howard Kinsey (USA) / Robert Kinsey (USA)	Gerald Patterson (AUS) / Pat O'Hara Wood (AUS)	7-5	5-7	7-9	6-3	6-4
1925	Dick Williams (USA) / Vinnie Richards (USA)	Gerald Patterson (AUS) / Jack Hawkes (AUS)	6-2	8-10	6-4	11-9	
1926	Dick Williams (USA) / Vinnie Richards (USA)	Bill Tilden (USA) / Al Chapin (USA)	6-4	6-8	11-9	6-3	
1927	Bill Tilden (USA) / Frank Hunter (USA)	Bill Johnson (USA) / Dick Williams (USA)	10-8	6-3	6-3		
1928	George Lott (USA) / John Hennessey (USA)	Gerald Patterson (AUS) / Jack Hawkes (AUS)	6-2	6-1	6-2		
1929	George Lott (USA) / Johnny Doeg (USA)	Berkeley Bell (USA) / Lewis White (USA)	10-8	16-14	6-1		
1930	George Lott (USA) / Johnny Doeg (USA)	John Van Ryn (USA) / Wilmer Allison (USA)	8-6	6-3	4-6	13-15	6-4
1931	Wilmer Allison (USA) / John Van Ryn (USA)	Greg Mangin (USA) / Berkeley Bell (USA)	6-4	8-6	6-3		
1932	Ellsworth Vines (USA) / Keith Gledhill (USA)	Wilmer Allison (USA) / John Van Ryn (USA)	6-4	6-3	6-2		
1933	George Lott (USA) / Lester Stoefen (USA)	Frank Shields (USA) / Frank Parker (USA)	11-13	9-7	9-7	6-3	
1934	George Lott (USA) / Lester Stoefen (USA)	Wilmer Allison (USA) / John Van Ryn (USA)	6-4	9-7	3-6	6-4	
1935	Wilmer Allison (USA) / John Van Ryn (USA)	Don Budge (USA) / Gene Mako (USA)	6-4	6-2	3-6	2-6	6-1
1936	Don Budge (USA) / Gene Mako (USA)	Wilmer Allison (USA) / John Van Ryn (USA)	6-4	6-2	6-4		
1937	Gottfried von Cramm (GER) / Henner Henkel (GER)	Don Budge (USA) / Gene Mako (USA)	6-4	7-5	6-4		
1938	Don Budge (USA) / Gene Mako (USA)	Adrian Quist (AUS) / John Bromwich (AUS)	6-3	6-2	6-1		
1939	Adrian Quist (AUS) / John Bromwich (AUS)	Jack Crawford (AUS) / Harry Hopman (AUS)	8-6	6-1	6-4		
1940	Jack Kramer (USA) / Ted Schroeder (USA)	Gardnar Mulloy (USA) / Henry Prusoff (USA)	6-4	8-6	9-7		
1941	Jack Kramer (USA) / Ted Schroeder (USA)	Wayne Sabin (USA) / Gardnar Mulloy (USA)	9-7	6-4	6-2		
1942	Gardnar Mulloy (USA) / Bill Talbert (USA)	Ted Schroeder (USA) / Sidney Wood (USA)	9-7	7-5	6-1		
1943	Jack Kramer (USA) / Frank Parker (USA)	Bill Talbert (USA) / David Freeman (USA)	6-2	6-4	6-4		
1944	Don McNeill (USA) / Bob Falkenburg (USA)	Bill Talbert (USA) / Pancho Segura (ECU)	7-5	6-4	3-6	6-1	
1945	Gardnar Mulloy (USA) / Bill Talbert (USA)	Bob Falkenburg (USA) / Jack Tuero (USA)	12-10	8-10	12-10	6-2	
1946	Gardnar Mulloy / Bill Talbert (USA)	Don McNeill (USA) / Frank Guernsey (USA)	3-6	6-4	2-6	6-3	20-18
1947	Jack Kramer (USA) / Ted Schroeder (USA)	Bill Talbert (USA) / Bill Sidwell (AUS)	6-4	7-5	6-3		
1948	Gardnar Mulloy (USA) / Bill Talbert (USA)	Frank Parker (USA) / Ted Schroeder (USA)	1-6	9-7	6-3	3-6	9-7
1949	John Bromwich (AUS) / Bill Sidwell (AUS)	Frank Sedgman (AUS) / George Worthington (AUS)	6-4	6-0	6-1		
1950	John Bromwich (AUS) / Frank Sedgman (AUS)	Bill Talbert (USA) / Gardnar Mulloy (USA)	7-5	8-6	3-6	6-1	
1951	Ken McGregor (AUS) / Frank Sedgman (AUS)	Don Candy (AUS) / Merv Rose (AUS)	10-8	6-4	4-6	7-5	
1952	Merv Rose (AUS) / Vic Seixas (USA)	Ken McGregor (AUS) / Frank Sedgman (AUS)	3-6	10-8	10-8	6-8	8-6
1953	Rex Hartwig (AUS) / Merv Rose (AUS)	Gardnar Mulloy (USA) / Bill Talbert (USA)	6-4	4-6	6-2	6-4	
1954	Vic Seixas (USA) / Tony Trabert (USA)	Lew Hoad (AUS) / Ken Rosewall (USA)	3-6	6-4	8-6	6-3	
1955	Kosei Kamo (JPN) / Atsushi Miyagi (JPN)	Gerald Moss (USA) / Bill Quillian (USA)	6-2	6-3	3-6	1-6	6-4
1956	Lew Hoad (AUS) / Ken Rosewall (AUS)	Hamilton Richardson (USA) / Vic Seixas (USA)	6-2	6-2	3-6	6-4	
1957	Ashley Cooper (AUS) / Neale Fraser (AUS)	Gardnar Mulloy (USA) / Budge Patty (USA)	4-6	6-3	9-7	6-3	
1958	Alex Olmedo (PER) / Hamilton Richardson (USA)	Sammy Giammalva (USA) / Barry MacKay (USA)	3-6	6-3	6-4	6-4	
1959	Neale Fraser (AUS) / Roy Emerson (AUS)	Alex Olmedo (PER) / Butch Buchholz (USA)	3-6	6-3	5-7	6-4	7-5
1960	Neale Fraser (AUS) / Roy Emerson (AUS)	Rod Laver (AUS) / Bob Mark (AUS)	9-7	6-2	6-4		
1961	Chuck McKinley (USA) / Dennis Ralston (USA)	Rafael Osuna (MEX) / Antonio Palafox (MEX)	6-3	6-4	2-6	13-11	
1962	Rafael Osuna (MEX) / Antonio Palafox (MEX)	Chuck McKinley (USA) / Dennis Ralston (USA)	6-4	10-12	1-6	9-7	6-3
1963	Chuck McKinley (USA) / Dennis Ralston (USA)	Rafael Osuna (MEX) / Antonio Palafox (MEX)	9-7	4-6	5-7	6-3	11-9
1964	Chuck McKinley (USA) / Dennis Ralston (USA)	Graham Stilwell (GBR) / Mike Sangster (GBR)	6-3	6-2	6-4		
1965	Roy Emerson (AUS) / Fred Stolle (AUS)	Frank Froehling III (USA) / Charlie Pasarell (USA)	6-4	10-12	7-5	6-3	
1966	Roy Emerson (AUS) / Fred Stolle (AUS)	Clark Graebner (USA) / Dennis Ralston (USA)	6-4	6-4	6-4		

Year	Winner	Defeated	S1	S2	S3	S4	S5
1967	John Newcombe (AUS) Tony Roche (AUS)	Bill Bowrey (AUS) Owen Davidson (AUS)	6-8	9-7	6-3	6-3	
1968*	Bob Lutz (USA) Stan Smith (USA)	Bob Hewitt (RSA) Raymond Moore (RSA)	6-4	6-4	9-7		
1968	Bob Lutz (USA) Stan Smith (USA)	Arthur Ashe (USA) Andres Gimeno (ESP)	11-9	6-1	7-5		
1969*	Dick Crealy (AUS) Allan Stone (AUS)	Bill Bowrey (AUS) Charlie Pasarell (USA)	9-11	6-3	7-5		
1969	Ken Rosewall (AUS) Fred Stolle (AUS)	Charlie Pasarell (USA) Dennis Ralston (USA)	2-6	7-5	13-11	6-3	
1970	Pierre Barthes (FRA) Nikki Pilic (YUG)	Roy Emerson (AUS) Rod Laver (AUS)	6-3	7-6(4)	4-6	7-6(2)	
1971 **	John Newcombe (AUS) Roger Taylor (GBR)	Stan Smith (USA) Erik van Dillen (USA)	6-7	6-3	7-6(4)	4-6	5-3
1972	Cliff Drysdale (RSA) Roger Taylor (GBR)	Owen Davidson (AUS) John Newcombe (AUS)	6-4	7-6(3)	6-3		
1973	Owen Davidson (AUS) John Newcombe (AUS)	Rod Laver (AUS) Ken Rosewall (USA)	7-5	2-6	7-5	7-5	
1974	Bob Lutz (USA) Stan Smith (USA)	Patricio Cornejo (CHI) Jaime Fillol (CHI)	6-3	6-3			
1975	Jimmy Connors (USA) Ilie Nastase (ROU)	Tom Okker (NED) Marty Riessen (USA)	6-4	7-6			
1976	Tom Okker (NED) Marty Riessen (USA)	Paul Kronk (AUS) Cliff Letcher (AUS)	6-4	6-4			
1977	Bob Hewitt (RSA) Frew McMillan (RSA)	Brian Gottfried (USA) Raul Ramirez (MEX)	6-4	6-0			
1978	Bob Lutz (USA) Stan Smith (USA)	Marty Riessen (USA) Sherwood Stewart (USA)	1-6	7-5	6-3		
1979	John McEnroe (USA) Peter Fleming (USA)	Bob Lutz (USA) Stan Smith (USA)	6-2	6-4			
1980	Bob Lutz (USA) Stan Smith (USA)	Peter Fleming (USA) John McEnroe (USA)	7-5	3-6	6-1	3-6	6-3
1981	Peter Fleming (USA) John McEnroe (USA)	Heinz Gunthardt (SUI) Peter McNamara (AUS)			(walkover)		
1982	Kevin Curren (RSA) Steve Denton (USA)	Victor Amaya (USA) Hank Pfister (USA)	6-2	6-7(4)	5-7	6-2	6-4
1983	Peter Fleming (USA) John McEnroe (USA)	Fritz Buehning (USA) Van Winitsky (USA)	6-3	6-4	6-2		
1984	John Fitzgerald (AUS) Tomas Smid (CZE)	Stefan Edberg (SWE) Anders Jarryd (SWE)	7-6	6-3	6-3		
1985	Ken Flach (USA) Robert Seguso (USA)	Henri Leconte (FRA) Yannick Noah (FRA)	6-7(5)	7-6(1)	7-6(6)	6-0	
1986	Andres Gomez (ECU) Slobodan Zivojinovic (YUG)	Joakim Nystrom (SWE) Mats Wilander (SWE)	4-6	6-3	6-3	4-6	6-3
1987	Stefan Edberg (SWE) Anders Jarryd (SWE)	Ken Flach (USA) Robert Seguso (USA)	7-6(1)	6-2	4-6	5-7	7-6(2)
1988	Sergio Casal (ESP) Emilio Sanchez (ESP)	Rick Leach (USA) Jim Pugh (USA)			(walkover)		
1989	John McEnroe (USA) Mark Woodforde (AUS)	Ken Flach (USA) Robert Seguso (USA)	6-4	4-6	6-3	6-3	
1990	Pieter Aldrich (RSA) Danie Visser (RSA)	Paul Annacone (USA) David Wheaton (USA)	6-2	7-6(3)	6-2		
1991	John Fitzgerald (AUS) Anders Jarryd (SWE)	Scott Davis (USA) David Pate (USA)	6-3	3-6	6-3	6-3	

Year	Winner	Defeated	S1	S2	S3	S4	S5
1992	Jim Grabb (USA) Richey Reneberg (USA)	Kelly Jones (USA) Rick Leach (USA)	3-6	7-6(2)	6-3	6-3	
1993	Ken Flach (USA) Rick Leach (USA)	Martin Damm (CZE) Karel Novacek (CZE)	6-7(3)	6-4	6-2		
1994	Jacco Eltingh (NED) Paul Haarhuis (NED)	Todd Woodbridge (AUS) Mark Woodforde (AUS)	6-3	7-6(1)			
1995	Todd Woodbridge (AUS) Mark Woodforde (AUS)	Alex O'Brien (USA) Sandon Stolle (AUS)	6-3	6-3			
1996	Todd Woodbridge (AUS) Mark Woodforde (AUS)	Paul Haarhuis (NED) Jacco Eltingh (NED)	4-6	7-6(5)	7-6(5)		
1997	Yevgeny Kafelnikov (RUS) Daniel Vacek (CZE)	Jonas Bjorkman (SWE) Nicklas Kulti (SWE)	7-6(8)	6-3			
1998	Sandon Stolle (AUS) Cyril Suk (CZE)	Mark Knowles (BAH) Daniel Nestor (CAN)	4-6	7-6	6-2		
1999	Sebastien Lareau (CAN) Alex O'Brien (USA)	Mahesh Bhupathi (IND) Leander Paes (IND)	7-6(7)	6-4			
2000	Lleyton Hewitt (AUS) Max Mirnyi (BLR)	Rick Leach (USA) Ellis Ferreira (RSA)	6-4	5-7	7-6		
2001	Wayne Black (ZIM) Kevin Ullyett (ZIM)	Donald Johnson (USA) Jared Palmer (USA)	7-6	2-6	6-3		
2002	Max Mirnyi (BLR) Mahesh Bhupathi (IND)	Jiri Novak (CZE) Radek Stepanek (CZE)	6-3	3-6	6-4		
2003	Jonas Bjorkman (SWE) Todd Woodbridge (AUS)	Bob Bryan (USA) Mike Bryan (USA)	5-7	6-0	7-5		
2004	Mark Knowles (BAH) Daniel Nestor (CAN)	Leander Paes (IND) David Rikl (CZE)	6-3	6-3			
2005	Bob Bryan (USA) Mike Bryan (USA)	Jonas Bjorkman (SWE) Max Mirnyi (BLR)	6-1	6-4			
2006	Martin Damm (CZE) Leander Paes (IND)	Jonas Bjorkman (SWE) Max Mirnyi (BLR)	6-7(5)	6-4	6-3		
2007	Simon Aspelin (SWE) Julian Knowle (AUT)	Lukas Dlouhy (CZE) Pavel Vizner (CZE)	7-5	6-4			
2008	Bob Bryan (USA) Mike Bryan (USA)	Leander Paes (IND) Lukas Dlouhy (CZE)	7-6(5)	7-6(10)			

Women's Doubles

Year	Winner	Defeated	S1	S2	S3	S4	S5
1889	Margarette Ballard (USA) Bertha Townsend (USA)	Marion Wright (USA) Laura Knight (USA)	6-0	6-2			
1890	Grace Roosevelt (USA) Ellen Roosevelt (USA)	Bertha Townsend (USA) Margarette Ballard (USA)	6-1	6-2			
1891	Mabel Cahill (IRL) Emma Leavitt Morgan (USA)	Grace Roosevelt (USA) Ellen Roosevelt (USA)	2-6	8-6	6-4		
1892	Mabel Cahill (IRL) Adeline McKinlay (USA)	Helen Day Harris (USA) Amy Williams (USA)	6-1	6-3			
1893	Aline Terry (USA) Harriet Butler (USA)	Augusta Schultz (USA) Ms Stone (USA)	6-4	6-3			
1894	Helen Hellwig (USA) Juliette Atkinson (USA)	Annabella Wistar (USA) Amy Williams (USA)	6-4	8-6	6-2		

Denotes amateur tournament. In 1968 and 1969, the USTA conducted both Amateur and Open Championships. Thereafter, there was only the Open as principal championships.

** At nightfall, a tie-breaker agree upon as a 5th set*

Year	Winner	Defeated	S1	S2	S3
1895	Helen Hellwig (USA) Juliette Atkinson (USA)	Elisabeth Moore (USA) Amy Williams (USA)	6-2	6-2	12-10
1896	Elisabeth Moore (USA) Juliette Atkinson (USA)	Annabella Wistar (USA) Amy Williams (USA)	6-3	9-7	
1897	Juliette Atkinson (USA) Kathleen Atkinson (USA)	Mrs. Frank Edwards (USA) Elizabeth Rastall (USA)	6-2	6-1	6-1
1898	Juliette Atkinson (USA) Kathleen Atkinson (USA)	Marie Wimer (USA) Carrie Neely (USA)	6-1 2-6	4-6 6-1	6-2
1899	Jane Craven (USA) Myrtle McAteer (USA)	Maud Banks (USA) Elizabeth Rastall (USA)	6-1	6-1	7-5
1900	Edith Parker (USA) Hallie Champlin (USA)	Marie Wimer (USA) Myrtle McAteer (USA)	9-7	6-2	6-2
1901	Juliette Atkinson (USA) Myrtle McAteer (USA)	Marion Jones (USA) Elisabeth Moore (USA)	default		

USLTA adopts 3-set format

Year	Winner	Defeated	S1	S2	S3
1902	Juliette Atkinson (USA) Marion Jones (USA)	Maud Banks (USA) Nona Closterman (USA)	6-2	7-5	
1903	Elisabeth Moore (USA) Carrie Neely (USA)	Miriam Hall (USA) Marion Jones (USA)	4-6	6-1	6-1
1904	May Sutton (USA) Miriam Hall (USA)	Elisabeth Moore (USA) Carrie Neely (USA)	3-6	6-3	6-3
1905	Helen Homans (USA) Carrie Neely (USA)	Marjorie Oberteuffer (USA) Virginia Maule (USA)	6-0	6-1	
1906	Ann Burdette Coe (USA) Ethel Bliss Platt (USA)	Helen Homans (USA) Clover Boldt (USA)	6-4	6-4	
1907	Marie Wimer (USA) Carrie Neely (USA)	Edna Wildey (USA) Natalie Wildey (USA)	6-1	2-6	6-4
1908	Evelyn Sears (USA) Margaret Curtis (USA)	Carrie Neely (USA) Marion Steever (USA)	6-3	5-7	9-7
1909	Hazel Hotchkiss (USA) Edith Rotch (USA)	Dorothy Green (USA) Lois Moyes (USA)	6-1	6-1	
1910	Hazel Hotchkiss (USA) Edith Rotch (USA)	Adelaide Browning (USA) Edna Wildey (USA)	6-4	6-4	
1911	Hazel Hotchkiss (USA) Eleonora Sears (USA)	Dorothy Green (USA) Florence Sutton (USA)	6-4	4-6	6-2
1912	Dorothy Green (USA) Mary K. Browne (USA)	Maud Barger Wallach (USA) Mrs Frederick Schmitz (USA)	6-2	5-7	6-0
1913	Mary K. Browne (USA) Louise Riddell Williams (USA)	Dorothy Green (USA) Edna Wildey (USA)	12-10	2-6	6-3
1914	Mary K. Browne (USA) Louise Riddell Williams (USA)	Louise Hammond Raymond (USA) Edna Wildey (USA)	8-6	6-2	
1915	Hazel Hotchkiss Wightman (USA) Eleonora Sears (USA)	Helen Homans McLean (USA) Mrs George L. Chapman (USA)	10-8	6-2	
1916	Molla Bjurstedt (NOR) Eleonora Sears (USA)	Louise Hammond Raymond (USA) Edna Wildey (USA)	4-6	6-2	10-8
1917	Molla Bjurstedt (NOR) Eleonora Sears (USA)	Phyllis Walsh (USA) Grace Moore LeRoy (USA)	6-2	6-4	
1918	Marion Zinderstein (USA) Eleanor Goss (USA)	Molla Bjurstedt (NOR) Mrs Johan Rogge (USA)	7-5	8-6	
1919	Marion Zinderstein (USA) Eleanor Goss (USA)	Eleonora Sears (USA) Hazel Hotchkiss Wightman (USA)	10-8	9-7	

Year	Winner	Defeated	S1	S2	S3
1920	Marion Zinderstein (USA) Eleanor Goss (USA)	Eleanor Tennant (USA) Helen Baker (USA)	13-11	4-6	6-3
1921	Mary K. Browne (USA) Louise Riddell Williams (USA)	Helen Gilleaudeau (USA) Aletta Bailey Morris (USA)	6-3	6-2	
1922	Marion Zinderstein Jessup (USA) Helen Wills (USA)	Edith Sigourney (USA) Molla Bjurstedt Mallory (USA)	6-4	7-9	6-3
1923	Kitty McKane (GBR) Phyllis Howkins Covell (GBR)	Hazel Hotchkiss Wightman (USA) Eleanor Goss (USA)	2-6	6-2	6-1
1924	Hazel Hotchkiss Wightman (USA) Helen Wills (USA)	Eleanor Goss (USA) Marion Zinderstein Jessup (USA)	6-4	6-3	
1925	Mary K. Browne (USA) Helen Wills (USA)	May Sutton Bundy (USA) Elizabeth Ryan (USA)	6-4	6-3	
1926	Elizabeth Ryan (USA) Eleanor Goss (USA)	Mary K. Browne (USA) Charlotte Hosmer Chapin (USA)	3-6	6-4	12-10
1927	Kitty McKane Godfree (GBR) Ermyntrude Harvey (GBR)	Betty Nuthall (GBR) Joan Fry (GBR)	6-1	4-6	6-4
1928	Hazel Hotchkiss Wightman (USA) Helen Wills (USA)	Edith Cross (USA) Anna McCune Harper (USA)	6-2	6-2	
1929	Phoebe Holcroft Watson (GBR) Peggy Michell (GBR)	Phyllis Howkins Covell (GBR) Dorothy Shepherd Barron (GBR)	2-6	6-3	6-4
1930	Betty Nuthall (GBR) Sarah Palfrey (USA)	Edith Cross (USA) Anna McCune Harper (USA)	3-6	6-3	7-5
1931	Betty Nuthall (GBR) Eileen Bennett Whittingstall (GBR)	Helen Jacobs (USA) Dorothy Round (GBR)	6-2	6-4	
1932	Helen Jacobs (USA) Sarah Palfrey (USA)	Marjorie Morrill Painter (USA) Alice Marble (USA)	8-6	6-1	
1933	Betty Nuthall (GBR) Freda James (GBR)	Helen Wills Moody (USA) Elizabeth Ryan (USA)	(default)		
1934	Helen Jacobs (USA) Sarah Palfrey (USA)	Carolin Babcock (USA) Dorothy Andrus (USA)	4-6	6-3	6-4
1935	Helen Jacobs (USA) Sarah Palfrey Fabyan (USA)	Carolin Babcock (USA) Dorothy Andrus (USA)	6-4	6-2	
1936	Marjorie Gladman Van Ryn (USA) Carolin Babcock (USA)	Helen Jacobs (USA) Sarah Palfrey Fabyan (USA)	9-7	2-6	6-4
1937	Sarah Palfrey Fabyan (USA) Alice Marble (USA)	Marjorie Gladman Van Ryn (USA) Carolin Babcock (USA)	7-5	6-4	
1938	Sarah Palfrey Fabyan (USA) Alice Marble (USA)	Simone Passemard Mathieu (FRA) Jadwiga Jadrzejowska (POL)	6-8	6-4	6-3
1939	Sarah Palfrey Fabyan (USA) Alice Marble (USA)	Kay Stammers (GBR) Freda James Hammersley (GBR)	7-5	8-6	
1940	Sarah Palfrey Fabyan (USA) Alice Marble (USA)	Dorothy Bundy (USA) Marjorie Gladman Van Ryn (USA)	6-4	6-3	
1941	Sarah Palfrey Fabyan Cooke (USA) Margaret Osborne (USA)	Dorothy Bundy (USA) Pauline Betz (USA)	3-6	6-1	6-4
1942	Louise Brough (USA) Margaret Osborne (USA)	Pauline Betz (USA) Doris Hart (USA)	2-6	7-5	6-0
1943	Louise Brough (USA) Margaret Osborne (USA)	Pauline Betz (USA) Doris Hart (USA)	6-4	6-3	
1944	Louise Brough (USA) Margaret Osborne (USA)	Pauline Betz (USA) Doris Hart (USA)	4-6	6-4	6-3
1945	Louise Brough (USA) Margaret Osborne (USA)	Pauline Betz (USA) Doris Hart (USA)	6-3	6-3	
1946	Louise Brough (USA) Margaret Osborne (USA)	Pat Canning Todd (USA) Mary Arnold Prentiss (USA)	6-1	6-3	

Year	Winner	Defeated	S1	S2	S3
1947	Louise Brough (USA) Margaret Osborne (USA)	Pat Canning Todd (USA) Doris Hart (USA)	5-7	6-3	7-5
1948	Louise Brough (USA) Margaret Osborne duPont (USA)	Pat Canning Todd (USA) Doris Hart (USA)	6-4	8-10	6-1
1949	Louise Brough (USA) Margaret Osborne duPont (USA)	Doris Hart (USA) Shirley Fry (USA)	6-4	10-8	
1950	Louise Brough (USA) Margaret Osborne duPont (USA)	Doris Hart (USA) Shirley Fry (USA)	6-2	6-3	
1951	Doris Hart (USA) Shirley Fry (USA)	Nancy Chaffee (USA) Pat Canning Todd (USA)	6-4	6-2	
1952	Doris Hart (USA) Shirley Fry (USA)	Louise Brough (USA) Maureen Connolly (USA)	10-8	6-4	
1953	Doris Hart (USA) Shirley Fry (USA)	Louise Brough (USA) Margaret Osborne duPont (USA)	6-2	7-9	9-7
1954	Doris Hart (USA) Shirley Fry (USA)	Louise Brough (USA) Margaret Osborne duPont (USA)	6-4	6-4	
1955	Louise Brough (USA) Margaret Osborne duPont (USA)	Doris Hart (USA) Shirley Fry (USA)	6-3	1-6	6-3
1956	Louise Brough (USA) Margaret Osborne duPont (USA)	Betty Rosenquest Pratt (USA) Shirley Fry (USA)	6-3	6-0	
1957	Louise Brough (USA) Margaret Osborne duPont (USA)	Althea Gibson (USA) Darlene Hard (USA)	6-2	7-5	
1958	Jeanne Arth (USA) Darlene Hard (USA)	Althea Gibson (USA) Maria Bueno (BRA)	2-6	6-3	6-4
1959	Jeanne Arth (USA) Darlene Hard (USA)	Maria Bueno (BRA) Sally Moore (USA)	6-2	6-3	
1960	Maria Bueno (BRA) Darlene Hard (USA)	Ann Haydon (GBR) Deidre Catt (GBR)	6-1	6-1	
1961	Darlene Hard (USA) Lesley Turner (AUS)	Edda Buding (GER) Yola Ramirez (MEX)	6-4	5-7	6-0
1962	Darlene Hard (USA) Maria Bueno (BRA)	Karen Hantze Susman (USA) Billie Jean Moffitt (USA)	4-6	6-3	6-2
1963	Robyn Ebbern (AUS) Margaret Smith (AUS)	Darlene Hard (USA) Maria Bueno (BRA)	4-6	10-8	6-3
1964	Billie Jean Moffitt (USA) Karen Hantze Susman (USA)	Margaret Smith (AUS) Lesley Turner (AUS)	3-6	6-2	6-4
1965	Carole Caldwell Graebner (USA) Nancy Richey (USA)	Billie Jean Moffitt (USA) Karen Hantze Susman (USA)	6-4	6-4	
1966	Maria Bueno (BRA) Nancy Richey (USA)	Billie Jean King (USA) Rosie Casals (USA)	6-3	6-4	
1967	Rosie Casals (USA) Billie Jean King (USA)	Mary Ann Eisel (USA) Donna Floyd Fales (USA)	4-6	6-3	6-4
1968*	Maria Bueno (BRA) Margaret Smith Court (AUS)	Virginia Wade (GBR) Joyce Barclay Williams (GBR)	6-3	7-5	
1968	Maria Bueno (BRA) Margaret Smith Court (AUS)	Billie Jean King (USA) Rosie Casals (USA)	4-6	9-7	8-6
1969*	Virginia Wade (GBR) Margaret Smith Court (AUS)	Mary Ann Eisel Curtis (USA) Valerie Ziegenfuss (USA)	6-1	6-3	
1969	Francoise Durr (FRA) Darlene Hard (USA)	Margaret Smith Court (AUS) Virginia Wade (GBR)	0-6	6-4	6-4
1970	Margaret Smith Court (AUS) Judy Tegart Dalton (AUS)	Rosie Casals (USA) Virginia Wade (GBR)	6-3	6-4	
1971	Rosie Casals (USA) Judy Tegart Dalton (AUS)	Gail Sherriff Chanfreau (FRA) Francoise Durr (FRA)	6-3	6-3	
1972	Francoise Durr (FRA) Betty Stove (NED)	Margaret Smith Court (AUS) Virginia Wade (GBR)	6-3	1-6	6-3
1973	Margaret Smith Court (AUS) Virginia Wade (GBR)	Billie Jean King (USA) Rosie Casals (USA)	3-6	6-3	7-5
1974	Rosie Casals (USA) Billie Jean King (USA)	Francoise Durr (FRA) Betty Stove (NED)	7-6(4)	6-7(2)	6-4
1975	Margaret Smith Court (AUS) Virginia Wade (GBR)	Billie Jean King (USA) Rosie Casals (USA)	7-5	2-6	7-6(5)
1976	Delina Boshoff (RSA) Ilana Kloss (RSA)	Olga Morozova (USSR) Virginia Wade (GBR)	6-1	6-4	
1977	Martina Navratilova (CZE) Betty Stove (NED)	Renee Richards (USA) Betty Ann Grubb Stuart (USA)	6-1	7-6	
1978	Billie Jean King (USA) Martina Navratilova (CZE)	Kerry Melville Reid (AUS) Wendy Turnbull (AUS)	7-6(7)	6-4	
1979	Betty Stove (NED) Wendy Turnbull (AUS)	Billie Jean King (USA) Martina Navratilova (CZE)	7-5	6-3	
1980	Billie Jean King (USA) Martina Navratilova (CZE)	Pam Shriver (USA) Betty Stove (NED)	7-6(2)	7-5	
1981	Anne Smith (USA) Kathy Jordan (USA)	Rosie Casals (USA) Wendy Turnbull (AUS)	6-3	6-3	
1982	Rosie Casals (USA) Wendy Turnbull (AUS)	Sharon Walsh (USA) Barbara Potter (USA)	6-4	6-4	
1983	Pam Shriver (USA) Martina Navratilova (USA)	Rosalyn Fairbank (RSA) Candy Reynolds (USA)	6-7(4)	6-1	6-3
1984	Pam Shriver (USA) Martina Navratilova (USA)	Anne Hobbs (GBR) Wendy Turnbull (AUS)	6-2	6-4	
1985	Claudia Kohde Kilsch (GER) Helena Sukova (CZE)	Martina Navratilova (USA) Pam Shriver (USA)	6-7	6-2	6-3
1986	Martina Navratilova (USA) Pam Shriver (USA)	Hana Mandlikova (CZE) Wendy Turnbull (AUS)	6-4	3-6	6-3
1987	Martina Navratilova (USA) Pam Shriver (USA)	Kathy Jordan (USA) Elizabeth Sayers Smylie (AUS)	5-7	6-4	6-2
1988	Gigi Fernandez (USA) Robin White (USA)	Patty Fendick (USA) Jill Hetherington (CAN)	6-4	6-1	
1989	Hana Mandlikova Martina Navratilova (USA)	Mary Joe Fernandez (USA) Pam Shriver (USA)	5-7	6-4	6-4
1990	Gigi Fernandez (USA) Martina Navratilova (USA)	Jana Novotna (CZE) Helena Sukova (CZE)	6-2	6-4	
1991	Pam Shriver (USA) Natalia Zvereva (USSR)	Jana Novotna (CZE) Larisa Savchenko (USSR)	6-4	4-6	7-6(5)
1992	Gigi Fernandez (USA) Natalia Zvereva (BLR)	Jana Novotna (CZE) Larisa Savchenko Neiland (LAT)	7-6(4)	6-1	
1993	Arantxa Sanchez Vicario (ESP) Helena Sukova (CZE)	Amanda Coetzer (RSA) Ines Gorrochategui (ARG)	6-4	6-2	
1994	Arantxa Sanchez Vicario (ESP) Jana Novotna (CZE)	Katerina Maleeva (BUL) Robin White (USA)	6-3	6-3	
1995	Gigi Fernandez (USA) Natalia Zvereva (BLR)	Brenda Schultz McCarthy (NED) Rennae Stubbs (AUS)	7-5	6-3	
1996	Gigi Fernandez (USA) Natalia Zvereva (BLR)	Jana Novotna (CZE) Arantxa Sanchez Vicario (ESP)	1-6	6-1	6-4
1997	Jana Novotna (CZE) Lindsay Davenport (USA)	Gigi Fernandez (USA) Natalia Zvereva (BLR)	6-3	6-4	
1998	Martina Hingis (SUI) Jana Novotna (CZE)	Lindsay Davenport (USA) Natalia Zvereva (BLR)	6-3	6-3	

Denotes amateur tournament. In 1968 and 1969, the USTA conducted both Amateur and Open Championships. Thereafter, there was only the Open as principal championships.

Year	Winner	Defeated			
1999	Serena Williams (USA) / Venus Williams (USA)	Chanda Rubin (USA) / Sandrine Testud (FRA)	4-6	6-1	6-4
2000	Julie Halard-Decugis (FRA) / Ai Sugiyama (JPN)	Cara Black (ZIM) / Elena Likhovtseva (RUS)	6-0	1-6	6-1
2001	Rennae Stubbs (AUS) / Lisa Raymond (USA)	Kimberly Po-Messerli (USA) / Nathalie Tauziat (FRA)	6-2	5-7	7-5
2002	Virginia Ruano Pascual (ESP) / Paola Suarez (ARG)	Elena Dementieva (RUS) / Janette Husarova (SVK)	6-2	6-1	
2003	Virginia Ruano Pascual (ESP) / Paola Suarez (ARG)	Svetlana Kuznetsova (RUS) / Martina Navratilova (USA)	6-2	6-3	
2004	Virginia Ruano Pascual (ESP) / Paola Suarez (ARG)	Svetlana Kuznetsova (RUS) / Elena Likhovtseva (RUS)	6-4	7-5	
2005	Lisa Raymond (USA) / Samantha Stosur (AUS)	Elena Dementieva (RUS) / Flavia Pennetta (ITA)	6-2	5-7	6-3
2006	Nathalie Dechy (FRA) / Vera Zvonareva (RUS)	Dinara Safina (RUS) / Katarina Srebotnik (SLO)	7-6(5)	7-5	
2007	Nathalie Dechy (FRA) / Dinara Safina (RUS)	Yung-Jan Chan (TPE) / Chia-Jung Chuang (TPE)	6-4	6-2	
2008	Cara Black (ZIM) / Liezel Huber (USA)	Samantha Stosur (AUS) / Lisa Raymond (USA)	6-3	7-6(6)	

Mixed Doubles

Year	Winner	Defeated	S1	S2	S3	S4	S5
1892	Mabel Cahill (IRL) / Clarence Hobart (USA)	Elisabeth Moore (USA) / Rod Beach (USA)	5-7	6-1	6-4		
1893	Ellen Roosevelt (USA) / Clarence Hobart (USA)	Ethel Bankson (USA) / Robert Willson Jr. (USA)	6-1	4-6	10-8	6-1	
1894	Juliette Atkinson (USA) / Edwin Fischer (USA)	Mrs. McFadden (USA) / Gustav Remack Jr. (USA)	6-3	6-2	6-1		
1895	Juliette Atkinson (USA) / Edwin Fischer (USA)	Amy Williams (USA) / Mantle Fielding (USA)	4-6	8-6	6-2		
1896	Juliette Atkinson (USA) / Edwin Fischer (USA)	Amy Williams (USA) / Mantle Fielding (USA)	6-2	6-3	6-3		
1897	Laura Henson (USA) / D. L. Magruder (USA)	Maud Banks (USA) / B. L. C. Griffiths (USA)	6-4	6-3	7-5		
1898	Carrie Neely (USA) / Edwin Fischer (USA)	Helen Chapman (USA) / J. A. Hill (USA)	6-2	6-4	8-6		
1899	Elizabeth Rastall (USA) / Albert Hoskins (USA)	Jennie Craven (USA) / James Gardner (USA)	6-4	6-0	(default)		
1900	Margaret Hunnewell (USA) / Alfred Codman (USA)	T. Shaw (USA) / George Atkinson (USA)	11-9	6-3	6-1		
1901	Marion Jones (USA) / Ray Little (USA)	Myrtle Rastall (USA) / Clyde Stevens (USA)	6-4	6-4	7-5		

USLTA adopts 3-set format

Year	Winner	Defeated	S1	S2	S3	S4	S5
1902	Elisabeth Moore (USA) / Wylie Grant (USA)	Elizabeth Rastall (USA) / Albert Hoskins (USA)	6-2	6-1			
1903	Helen Chapman (USA) / Harry Allen (USA)	Carrie Neely (USA) / W. H. Rowland (USA)	6-4	7-5			

Year	Winner	Defeated	S1	S2	S3
1904	Elisabeth Moore (USA) / Wylie Grant (USA)	May Sutton (USA) / Trevanion Dallas (USA)	6-2	6-1	
1905	Augusta Schultz Hobart (USA) / Clarence Hobart (USA)	Elisabeth Moore (USA) / Edward Dewhurst (USA)	6-2	6-4	
1906	Sarah Coffin (USA) / Edward Dewhurst (USA)	Margaret Johnson (USA) / Wallace Johnson (USA)	6-3	7-5	
1907	May Sayers (USA) / Wallace Johnson (USA)	Natalie Wildey (USA) / Herbert Morris Tilden (USA)	6-1	7-5	
1908	Edith Rotch (USA) / Nathaniel Niles (USA)	Louise Hammond (USA) / Ray Little (USA)	6-4	4-6	6-4
1909	Hazel Hotchkiss (USA) / Wallace Johnson (USA)	Louise Hammond (USA) / Ray Little (USA)	6-2	6-0	
1910	Hazel Hotchkiss (USA) / Joseph Carpenter Jr. (USA)	Edna Wildey (USA) / Herbert Morris Tilden (USA)	6-2	6-2	
1911	Hazel Hotchkiss (USA) / Wallace Johnson (USA)	Edna Wildey (USA) / Herbert Morris Tilden (USA)	6-4	6-4	
1912	Mary K. Browne (USA) / Dick Williams (USA)	Eleonora Sears (USA) / Bill Clothier (USA)	6-4	2-6	11-9
1913	Mary K. Browne (USA) / Bill Tilden (USA)	Dorothy Green (USA) / C. S. Rogers (USA)	7-5	7-5	
1914	Mary K. Browne (USA) / Bill Tilden (USA)	Margarette Myers (USA) / J. R. Rowland (USA)	6-1	6-4	
1915	Hazel Hotchkiss Wightman (USA) / Harry Johnson (USA)	Molla Bjurstedt (NOR) / Irving Wright (USA)	6-0	6-1	
1916	Eleonora Sears (USA) / Willis Davis (USA)	Florence Ballin (USA) / Bill Tilden (USA)	6-4	7-5	
1917	Molla Bjurstedt (NOR) / Irving Wright (USA)	Florence Ballin (USA) / Bill Tilden (USA)	10-12	6-1	6-3
1918	Hazel Hotchkiss Wightman (USA) / Irving Wright (USA)	Molla Bjurstedt (NOR) / Fred Alexander (USA)	6-2	6-4	
1919	Marion Zinderstein (USA) / Vinnie Richards (USA)	Florence Ballin (USA) / Bill Tilden (USA)	2-6	11-9	6-2
1920	Hazel Hotchkiss Wightman (USA) / Wallace Johnson (USA)	Molla Bjurstedt Mallory (USA) / Craig Biddle (USA)	6-4	6-3	
1921	Mary K. Browne (USA) / Bill Johnston (USA)	Molla Bjurstedt Mallory (USA) / Bill Tilden (USA)	3-6	6-4	6-3
1922	Molla Bjurstedt Mallory (USA) / Bill Tilden (USA)	Helen Wills (USA) / Howard Kinsey (USA)	6-4	6-3	
1923	Molla Bjurstedt Mallory (USA) / Bill Tilden (USA)	Kitty McKane (GBR) / Jack Hawkes (AUS)	6-3	2-6	10-8
1924	Helen Wills (USA) / Vinnie Richards (USA)	Molla Bjurstedt Mallory (USA) / Bill Tilden (USA)	6-8	7-5	6-0
1925	Kitty McKane (GBR) / Jack Hawkes (AUS)	Ermyntrude Harvey (GBR) / Vinnie Richards (USA)	6-2	6-4	
1926	Elizabeth Ryan (USA) / Jean Borotra (FRA)	Hazel Hotchkiss Wightman (USA) / Rene Lacoste (FRA)	6-4	7-5	
1927	Eileen Bennett (GBR) / Henri Cochet (FRA)	Hazel Hotchkiss Wightman (USA) / Rene Lacoste (FRA)	6-2	0-6	6-2
1928	Helen Wills (USA) / Jack Hawkes (AUS)	Edith Cross (USA) / Gar Moon (AUS)	6-1	6-3	
1929	Betty Nuthall (GBR) / George Lott (USA)	Phyllis Howkins Covell (GBR) / Bunny Austin (GBR)	6-3	6-3	
1930	Edith Cross (USA) / Wilmer Allison (USA)	Marjorie Morrill (USA) / Frank Shields (USA)	6-4	6-4	

Year	Winner	Defeated	S1	S2	S3
1931	Betty Nuthall (GBR) George Lott (USA)	Anna McCune Harper (USA) Wilmer Allison (USA)	6-3	6-3	
1932	Sarah Palfrey (USA) Fred Perry (GBR)	Helen Jacobs (USA) Ellsworth Vines (USA)	6-3	7-5	
1933	Elizabeth Ryan (USA) Ellsworth Vines (USA)	Sarah Palfrey (USA) George Lott (USA)	11-9	6-1	
1934	Helen Jacobs (USA) George Lott (USA)	Elizabeth Ryan (USA) Lester Stoefen (USA)	4-6	13-11	6-2
1935	Sarah Palfrey Fabyan (USA) Enrique Maier (ESP)	Kay Stammers (GBR) Roderich Menzel (CZE)	6-3	3-6	6-4
1936	Alice Marble (USA) Gene Mako (USA)	Sarah Palfrey Fabyan (USA) Don Budge (USA)	6-3	6-2	
1937	Sarah Palfrey Fabyan (USA) Don Budge (USA)	Sylvie Jung Henrotin (FRA) Yvon Petra (FRA)	6-2	8-10	6-0
1938	Alice Marble (USA) Don Budge (USA)	Thelma Coyne Long (AUS) John Bromwich (AUS)	6-1	6-2	
1939	Alice Marble (USA) Harry Hopman (AUS)	Sarah Palfrey Fabyan (USA) Elwood Cooke (USA)	9-7	6-1	
1940	Alice Marble (USA) Bobby Riggs (USA)	Dorothy Bundy (USA) Jack Kramer (USA)	9-7	6-1	
1941	Sarah Palfrey Fabyan Cooke (USA) Jack Kramer (USA)	Pauline Betz (USA) Bobby Riggs (USA)	4-6	6-4	6-4
1942	Louise Brough (USA) Ted Schroeder (USA)	Pat Canning Todd (USA) Alejo Russell (ARG)	3-6	6-1	6-4
1943	Margaret Osborne (USA) Bill Talbert (USA)	Pauline Betz (USA) Pancho Segura (ECU)	10-8	6-4	
1944	Margaret Osborne (USA) Bill Talbert (USA)	Dorothy Bundy (USA) Don McNeill (USA)	6-2	6-3	
1945	Margaret Osborne (USA) Bill Talbert (USA)	Doris Hart (USA) Bob Falkenburg (USA)	6-4	6-4	
1946	Margaret Osborne (USA) Bill Talbert (USA)	Louise Brough (USA) Robert Kimbrell (USA)	6-3	6-4	
1947	Louise Brough (USA) John Bromwich (AUS)	Gussy Moran (USA) Pancho Segura (ECU)	6-3	6-1	
1948	Louise Brough (USA) Tom Brown (USA)	Margaret Osborne duPont (USA) Bill Talbert (USA)	6-4	6-4	
1949	Louise Brough (USA) Eric Sturgess (RSA)	Margaret Osborne duPont (USA) Bill Talbert (USA)	4-6	6-3	7-5
1950	Margaret Osborne duPont (USA) Ken McGregor (AUS)	Doris Hart (USA) Frank Sedgman (AUS)	6-4	3-6	6-3
1951	Doris Hart (USA) Frank Sedgman (AUS)	Shirley Fry (USA) Merv Rose (AUS)	6-3	6-2	
1952	Doris Hart (USA) Frank Sedgman (AUS)	Thelma Coyne Long (AUS) Lew Hoad (AUS)	6-3	7-5	
1953	Doris Hart (USA) Vic Seixas (USA)	Julia Sampson (USA) Rex Hartwig (AUS)	6-2	4-6	6-4
1954	Doris Hart (USA) Vic Seixas (USA)	Margaret Osborne duPont (USA) Ken Rosewall (AUS)	4-6	6-1	6-4
1955	Doris Hart (USA) Vic Seixas (USA)	Shirley Fry (USA) Gardnar Mulloy (USA)	7-5	5-7	6-2
1956	Margaret Osborne duPont (USA) Ken Rosewall (AUS)	Darlene Hard (USA) Lew Hoad (AUS)	9-7	6-1	
1957	Althea Gibson (USA) Kurt Nielsen (DEN)	Darlene Hard (USA) Bob Howe (AUS)	6-3	9-7	
1958	Margaret Osborne duPont (USA) Neale Fraser (AUS)	Maria Bueno (BRA) Alex Olmedo (PER)	6-4	3-6	9-7
1959	Margaret Osborne duPont (USA) Neale Fraser (AUS)	Janet Hopps (USA) Bob Mark (AUS)	7-5	13-15	6-2
1960	Margaret Osborne duPont (USA) Neale Fraser (AUS)	Maria Bueno (BRA) Antonio Palafox (MEX)	6-3	6-2	
1961	Margaret Smith (AUS) Bob Mark (AUS)	Darlene Hard (USA) Dennis Ralston (USA)	(default—Ralston under suspension)		
1962	Margaret Smith (AUS) Fred Stolle (AUS)	Lesley Turner (AUS) Frank Froehling III (USA)	7-5	6-2	
1963	Margaret Smith (AUS) Ken Fletcher (AUS)	Judy Tegart (AUS) Ed Rubinoff (USA)	3-6	8-6	6-2
1964	Margaret Smith (AUS) John Newcombe (AUS)	Judy Tegart (AUS) Ed Rubinoff (USA)	10-8	4-6	6-3
1965	Margaret Smith (AUS) Fred Stolle (AUS)	Judy Tegart (AUS) Frank Froehling III (USA)	6-2	6-2	
1966	Donna Floyd Fales (USA) Owen Davidson (AUS)	Carol Hanks Aucamp (USA) Ed Rubinoff (USA)	6-1	6-3	
1967	Billie Jean King (USA) Owen Davidson (AUS)	Rosie Casals (USA) Stan Smith (USA)	6-3	6-2	
1968	Mary Ann Eisel (USA) Peter Curtis (USA)	Tory Ann Fretz (USA) Robert Perry (USA)	6-4	7-5	
1969	Margaret Smith Court (AUS) Marty Riessen (USA)	Francoise Durr (FRA) Dennis Ralston (USA)	7-5	6-3	
1970	Margaret Smith Court (AUS) Marty Riessen (USA)	Judy Tegart Dalton (AUS) Frew McMillan (RSA)	6-4	6-4	
1971	Billie Jean King (USA) Owen Davidson (AUS)	Betty Stove (NED) Rob Maud (RSA)	6-3	7-5	
1972	Margaret Smith Court (AUS) Marty Riessen (USA)	Rosie Casals (USA) Ilie Nastase (ROU)	6-3	7-5	
1973	Billie Jean King (USA) Owen Davidson (AUS)	Margaret Smith Court (AUS) Marty Riessen (USA)	6-3	3-6	7-6
1974	Pam Teeguarden (USA) Geoff Masters (AUS)	Chris Evert (USA) Jimmy Connors (USA)	6-1	7-6	
1975	Rosie Casals (USA) Dick Stockton (USA)	Billie Jean King (USA) Fred Stolle (AUS)	6-3	7-6	
1976	Billie Jean King (USA) Phil Dent (AUS)	Betty Stove (NED) Frew McMillan (RSA)	3-6	6-2	7-5
1977	Betty Stove (NED) Frew McMillan (RSA)	Billie Jean King (USA) Vitas Gerulaitis (USA)	6-2	3-6	6-3
1978	Betty Stove (NED) Frew McMillan (RSA)	Billie Jean King (USA) Ray Ruffels (AUS)	6-3	7-6	
1979	Greer Stevens (RSA) Bob Hewitt (RSA)	Betty Stove (NED) Frew McMillan (RSA)	6-3	7-5	
1980	Wendy Turnbull (AUS) Marty Riessen (USA)	Betty Stove (NED) Frew McMillan (RSA)	7-5	6-2	
1981	Anne Smith (USA) Kevin Curren (RSA)	JoAnne Russell (USA) Steve Denton (USA)	6-4	7-6(4)	
1982	Anne Smith (USA) Kevin Curren (RSA)	Barbara Potter (USA) Ferdi Taygan (USA)	6-7	7-6(4)	7-6(5)
1983	Elizabeth Sayers (AUS) John Fitzgerald (AUS)	Barbara Potter (USA) Ferdi Taygan (USA)	3-6	6-3	6-4
1984	Manuela Maleeva (BUL) Tom Gullikson (USA)	Elizabeth Sayers (AUS) John Fitzgerald (AUS)	2-6	7-5	6-4

Year	Winner	Defeated	S1	S2	S3
1985	Martina Navratilova (USA) Heinz Gunthardt (SUI)	Elizabeth Sayers Smylie (AUS) John Fitzgerald (AUS)	6-3	6-4	
1986	Raffaella Reggi (ITA) Sergio Casal (ESP)	Martina Navratilova (USA) Peter Fleming (USA)	6-4	6-4	
1987	Martina Navratilova (USA) Emilio Sanchez (ESP)	Betsy Nagelsen (USA) Paul Annacone (USA)	6-4	6-7(6)	7-6(12)
1988	Jana Novotna (CZE) Jim Pugh (USA)	Elizabeth Sayers Smylie (AUS) Patrick McEnroe (USA)	7-5	6-3	
1989	Robin White (USA) Shelby Cannon (USA)	Meredith McGrath (USA) Rick Leach (USA)	3-6	6-2	7-5
1990	Elilzabeth Sayers Smylie (AUS) Todd Woodbridge (AUS)	Natalia Zvereva (USSR) Jim Pugh (USA)	6-4	6-2	
1991	Manon Bollegraf (NED) Tom Nijssen (NED)	Arantxa Sanchez Vicario (ESP) Emilio Sanchez (ESP)	6-2	7-6(2)	
1992	Nicole Provis (AUS) Mark Woodforde (AUS)	Helena Sukova (CZE) Tom Nijssen (NED)	4-6	6-3	6-3
1993	Helena Sukova (CZE) Todd Woodbridge (AUS)	Martina Navratilova (USA) Mark Woodforde (AUS)	6-3	7-6(6)	
1994	Elna Reinach (RSA) Patrick Galbraith (USA)	Jana Novotna (CZE) Todd Woodbridge (AUS)	6-2	6-4	
1995	Meredith McGrath (USA) Matt Lucena (USA)	Gigi Fernandez (USA) Cyril Suk (CZE)	6-4	6-4	
1996	Lisa Raymond (USA) Patrick Galbraith (USA)	Manon Bollegraf (NED) Rick Leach (USA)	7-6(6)	7-6(4)	

Year	Winner	Defeated	S1	S2	S3
1997	Manon Bollegraf (NED) Rick Leach (USA)	Mercedes Paz (ARG) Pablo Albano (ARG)	3-6	7-5	7-6(3)
1998	Serena Williams (USA) Max Mirnyi (BLR)	Lisa Raymond (USA) Patrick Galbraith (USA)	6-2	6-2	
1999	Ai Sugiyama (JPN) Mahesh Bhupathi (IND)	Kimberly Po (USA) Donald Johnson (USA)	6-4	6-4	
2000	Arantxa Sanchez Vicario (ESP) Jared Palmer (USA)	Anna Kournikova (RUS) Max Mirnyi (BLR)	6-4	6-3	
2001	Rennae Stubbs (AUS) Todd Woodbridge (AUS)	Lisa Raymond (USA) Leander Paes (IND)	6-4	5-7	[11-9*]
2002	Lisa Raymond (USA) Mike Bryan (USA)	Katarina Srebotnik (SLO) Bob Bryan (USA)	7-6(9)	7-6(1)	
2003	Katarina Srebotnik (SLO) Bob Bryan (USA)	Lina Krasnoroutskaya (RUS) Daniel Nestor (CAN)	5-7	7-5	[10-5]
2004	Vera Zvonareva (RUS) Bob Bryan (USA)	Alicia Molik (AUS) Todd Woodbridge (AUS)	6-3	6-4	
2005	Daniela Hantuchova (SVK) Mahesh Bhupathi (IND)	Katarina Srebotnik (SLO) Nenad Zimonjic (SRB)	6-4	6-2	
2006	Martina Navratilova (USA) Bob Bryan (USA)	Kveta Peschke (CZE) Martin Damm (CZE)	6-2	6-3	
2007	Viktoria Azarenka (BLR) Max Mirnyi (BLR)	Meghann Shaughnessy (USA) Leander Paes (IND)	6-4	7-6(6)	
2008	Cara Black (ZIM) Leander Paes (IND)	Liezel Huber (USA) Jaime Murray (GBR)	7-6 (6)	6-4	

Hereinafter a "super tie-breaker" (first to 10 but with a margin of two) replaces a third-set in mixed doubles.

U.S. Championships – Records

MOST TITLES

Men

16	Bill Tilden	(1913-1929)	7 singles, 5 doubles, 4 mixed
13	Dick Sears	(1881-1887)	7 singles, 6 doubles, 0 mixed
8	Bill Talbert	(1942-1948)	0 singles, 4 doubles, 4 mixed
	George Lott	(1928-1934)	0 singles, 5 doubles, 3 mixed
	John McEnroe	(1979-1989)	4 singles, 4 doubles, 0 mixed
	Neale Fraser	(1957-1960)	2 singles, 3 doubles, 3 mixed
7	Bill Larned	(1901-1911)	7 singles, 0 doubles, 0 mixed
	Holcombe Ward	(1899-1906)	1 singles, 6 doubles, 0 mixed
	Jack Kramer	(1940-1947)	2 singles, 4 doubles, 1 mixed
	Vinnie Richards	(1918-1926)	0 singles, 5 doubles, 2 mixed
6	Bill Johnston	(1915-1921)	2 singles, 3 doubles, 1 mixed
	Clarence Hobart	(1890-1905)	0 singles, 3 doubles, 3 mixed
	Don Budge	(1936-1938)	2 singles, 2 doubles, 2 mixed
	Frank Sedgman	(1950-1952)	2 singles, 2 doubles, 2 mixed
	Fred Stolle	(1962-1969)	1 singles, 3 doubles, 2 mixed
	Jimmy Connors	(1974-1983)	5 singles, 1 doubles, 0 mixed
	John Newcombe	(1964-1973)	2 singles, 3 doubles, 1 mixed
	Oliver Campbell	(1888-1892)	3 singles, 3 doubles, 0 mixed
	Roy Emerson	(1959-1966)	2 singles, 4 doubles, 0 mixed
	Vic Seixas	(1952-1955)	1 singles, 2 doubles, 3 mixed
5	Roger Federer	(2004-2008)	5 singles
	Dick Williams	(1912-1926)	2 singles, 2 doubles, 1 mixed
	Fred Alexander	(1907-1917)	0 singles, 5 doubles, 0 mixed
	James Dwight	(1882-1887)	0 singles, 5 doubles, 0 mixed
	Ken Rosewall	(1956-1970)	2 singles, 2 doubles, 1 mixed
	Marty Riessen	(1969-1980)	0 singles, 1 doubles, 4 mixed
	Maurice McLoughlin	(1912-1914)	2 singles, 3 doubles, 0 mixed
	Owen Davidson	(1966-1973)	0 singles, 1 doubles, 4 mixed
	Pete Sampras	(1990-2002)	5 singles, 0 doubles, 0 mixed
	Robert Wrenn	(1893-1897)	4 singles, 1 doubles, 0 mixed
	Stan Smith	(1968-1980)	1 singles, 4 doubles, 0 mixed
	Ted Schroeder	(1940-1947)	1 singles, 3 doubles, 1 mixed
	Todd Woodbridge	(1990-2001)	0 singles, 2 doubles, 3 mixed

Women

25	Margaret Osborne duPont		
		(1941-1960)	3 singles, 13 doubles, 9 mixed
18	Margaret Smith Court	(1951-1975)	5 singles, 5 doubles, 8 mixed
17	Louise Brough	(1942-1957)	1 singles, 12 doubles, 4 mixed
16	Hazel Hotchkiss Wightman		
		(1909-1928)	4 singles, 6 doubles. 6 mixed
	Martina Navratilova	(1977-2006)	4 singles, 9 doubles, 3 mixed
15	Sarah Palfrey Fabyan	(1930-1945)	2 singles, 9 doubles, 4 mixed
13	Billie Jean King	(1964-1980)	4 singles, 5 doubles, 4 mixed
	Helen Wills Moody	(1922-1931)	7 singles, 4 doubles, 2 mixed
	Juliette Atkinson	(1894-1902)	3 singles, 7 doubles. 3 mixed
	Molla Bjurstedt Mallory	(1915-1926)	8 singles, 2 doubles, 3 mixed
12	Alice Marble	(1936-1940)	4 singles, 4 doubles, 4 mixed
	Mary K. Browne	(1912-1925)	3 singles, 5 doubles, 4 mixed
11	Doris Hart	(1951-1955)	2 singles, 4 doubles, 5 mixed

8	Elisabeth Moore	(1896-1905)	4 singles, 2 doubles, 2 mixed
	Darlene Hard	(1958-1969)	2 singles, 6 doubles., 0 mixed
	Helen Jacobs	(1932-1935)	4 singles, 3 doubles, 1 mixed
	Maria Bueno	(1959-1968)	4 singles, 4 doubles, 0 mixed
6	Betty Nuthall	(1929-1933)	1 singles, 3 doubles, 2 mixed
	Chris Evert	(1975-1982)	6 singles, 0 doubles, 0 mixed
5	Betty Stove	(1972-1979)	0 singles, 3 doubles, 2 mixed
	Elenora Sears	(1911-1917)	0 singles, 4 doubles, 1 mixed
	Gigi Fernandez	(1985-1996)	0 singles, 5 doubles, 0 mixed
	Mabel Cahill	(1891-1892)	2 singles, 2 doubles, 1-mixed
	Marion Jessup	(1918-1922)	0 singles, 4 doubles, 1 mixed
	Pam Shriver	(1983-1991)	0 singles, 5 doubles, 0 mixed
	Rosie Casals	(1957-1982)	0 singles, 4 doubles, 1 mixed
	Shirley Fry	(1951-1956)	1 singles, 4 doubles, 0 mixed
	Steffi Graf	(1988-1996)	5 singles, 0 doubles, 0 mixed

MOST SINGLES TITLES

Men

7	Bill Tilden	(1920-1925, 1929)
	Bill Larned	(1901-1902, 1907-1911)
	Richard Sears	(1881-1887)
5	Roger Federer	(2004-2008)
	Jimmy Connors	(1974, 1976, 1978, 1982-1983)
	Pete Sampras	(1990, 1993, 1995-1996, 2002)
4	John McEnroe	(1979-1981, 1984)
	Robert Wrenn	(1893-1894, 1896-1897)

Women

8	Molla Bjurstedt Mallory	(1915-1918, 1920-1922, 1926)
7	Helen Wills	(1923-1925, 1927-1929, 1931)
6	Chris Evert	(1975-1978, 1980, 1982)
5	Margaret Smith Court	(1962, 1965, 1969-1970, 1973)
	Steffi Graf	(1988-1989, 1993, 1995-1996)
4	Martina Navratilova	(1983-1984, 1986-1987)
	Billie Jean King	(1967, 1971-1972, 1974)
	Maria Bueno	(1959, 1963-1964, 1966)
	Pauline Betz	(1942-1944, 1946)
	Alice Marble	(1936, 1938-1940)
	Helen Jacobs	(1932-1935)
	Hazel Hotchkiss Wightman	(1909-1911, 1919)
	Elisabeth Moore	(1896, 1901, 1903, 1905)

MOST CHALLENGE ROUND APPEARANCES

Men (1884-1911)

9	Bill Lamed	(7-2) (1900-03, 07-11)
5	Robert Wrenn	(4-1) (1893-97)
4	Richard Sears	(4-0) (1884-87)

Women (1887-1918)

8	Elisabeth Moore	(4-4) (1892, 96-97, 1901-06)
4	Marion Jones	(2-2) (1898-99, 1902-03)

MOST CHALLENGE ROUND VICTORIES

Men (1884-1911)

7	Bill Larned	(1901-02, 07-11)
4	Robert Wrenn	(1893-94, 96-97)
4	Richard Sears	(1884-87)

Women (1887-1918)

4	Elisabeth Moore	(1896, 1901, 03, 05)
3	Juliette Atkinson	(1895, 1896-1897)
3	Hazel Hotchkiss	(1909-1911)

MOST CHALLENGE ROUND LOSSES

Men (1884-1911)

2	Henry Slocum	(1887, 90)
	Fred Hovey	(1892, 96)
2	Bill Larned	(1900, 03)
2	Beals Wright	(1905,1908)

Women (1887-1918)

4	Elisabeth Moore	(1892, 97, 1902, 04)
2	Louise Hammond Raymond	(1910, 16)

MOST SINGLES TITLES – NON-CHALLENGE ROUND

Men (1912-2008)

7	Bill Tilden	(1920-1925, 1929)
5	Roger Federer	(2004-2008)
	Pete Sampras	(1990, 1993, 1995-1996, 2002)
	Jimmy Connors	(1974, 1976, 1978, 1982-1983)
4	John McEnroe	(1979-1981, 1984)
3	Ivan Lendl	(1985-1987)
	Fred Perry	(1933-1934, 1936)

Women (1919-2007)

7	Helen Wills Moody	(1923-1925, 1927-1929, 1931)
6	Chris Evert	(1975-1978, 1980, 1982)
5	Steffi Graf	(1988-1989, 1993, 1995-1996)
	Margaret Smith Court	(1962, 1965, 1969-1970, 1973)
4	Martina Navratilova	(1983-1984, 1986-1987)
	Billie Jean King	(1967, 1971-1972, 1974)
	Helen Jacobs	(1932-1935)
	Alice Marble	(1936, 1938-1940)
	Maria Bueno	(1959, 1963-1964, 1966)
	Molla Bjurstedt Mallory	(1920-1922, 1926)
	Pauline Betz	(1942-1944, 1946)

MOST SINGLES FINAL APPEARANCES

Men (1912-2007)

10	Bill Tilden	(1918-1925, 1927, 1929)
8	Pete Sampras	(1990, 1992-1993, 1995-1996, 2000-2002)
	Ivan Lendl	(1982-1989)
	Bill Johnston	(1915-1916, 1919-1920, 1922-1925)
7	Jimmy Connors	(1974-1978, 1982-1983)
6	Andre Agassi	(1990, 1994-1995, 1999, 2002, 2005)
	John McEnroe	(1979, 1981, 1984-1985)

Women (1919-2007)

9	Chris Evert	(1975-1980, 1982-1984)
	Helen Wills Moody	(1922-1925, 1927-1929, 1931, 1933)
8	Steffi Graf	(1987-1990, 1993-1996)
	Helen Jacobs	(1928, 1932-1936, 1939-1940)
	Martina Navratilova	(1981, 1983-1987, 1989, 1991)
7	Doris Hart	(1946, 1949-1950, 1952-1955)
6	Billie Jean King	(1965, 1967-1968, 1971-1972, 1974)
	Molla Bjurstedt Mallory	(1920-1924, 1926)
	Margaret Smith Court	(1962-1963, 1965, 1969-1970, 1973)
	Louise Brough	(1942-1943, 1947-1948, 1954, 1957)
	Pauline Betz	(1941-1946)

MOST SINGLES FINAL ROUND LOSSES

Men (1912-2007)

6	Bill Johnston	(1916, 1920, 1922-1925)
5	Ivan Lendl	(1982-1984, 1988-1989)
4	Bjorn Borg	(1976, 1978, 1980-1981)
	Andre Agassi	(1990, 1995, 2002, 2005)
3	Pete Sampras	(1992, 2000-2001)
	Bill Tilden	(1918-1919, 1927)

Women (1919-2007)

5	Doris Hart	(1946, 1949-1950, 1952-1953)
	Louise Brough	(1942-1943, 1948, 1954, 1957)
4	Martina Navratilova	(1981,1985, 1989, 1991)
	Helen Jacobs	(1928, 1936, 1939-1940)
	Evonne Goolagong	(1973-1976)
3	Steffi Graf	(1987, 1990, 1994)
	Chris Evert	(1979, 1983-1984)

MOST SEMIFINAL APPEARANCES

Men

14	Jimmy Connors	(1974-1991)
11	Bill Tilden	(1918-1930)
10	Andre Agassi	(1988-2005)
9	Pete Sampras	(1990-2002)
	Ivan Lendl	(1982-1991)
	Bill Johnston	(1915-1927)
8	John McEnroe	(1978-1990)
	Ken Rosewall	(1953-1974)

Women

17	Chris Evert	(1971-1988)
12	Helen Jacobs	(1927-1941)
	Martina Navratilova	(1975-1991)
11	Doris Hart	(1943-1955)
	Louise Brough	(1942-1957)
	Steffi Graf	(1985-1996)
9	Helen Wills Moody	(1922-1933)
	Molla Mallory	(1920-1929)

GREATEST NUMBER OF YEARS BETWEEN FIRST AND LAST SINGLES TITLES

Men

14	Ken Rosewall	(1956-first title, 1970-last title)

Women

11	Molla Bjurstedt Mallory	(1915-first title, 1926-last title)

MOST SINGLES TOURNAMENTS PLAYED – CAREER

Men

28	Vic Seixas	(1940-42, 1944, 1946-1969)
26	Sidney B. Wood	(1927-1928, 1930-1949, 1951-1954, 1956)
23	Nathaniel Niles	(1904-1926)
	Watson Washburn	(1910-1917, 1920-1924, 1926-1930, 1933-1937)
	Frank Shields	(1926-1935, 1938-1941, 1945, 1947-1954)
	Wallace Johnson	(1904-1916, 1919-1928)
22	Jimmy Connors	(1970-1989, 1991-1992)

Women

21	Martina Navratilova	(1973-1993)
20	Virginia Wade	(1964-1970, 1972-1984)
	Marjorie Gladman Van Ryn Buck	(1927-1937, 1942-1943, 1945, 1947-1952, 1955)

MOST SINGLES TOURNAMENTS PLAYED – SUCCESSIVE

Men

24	Vic Seixas	(1946-1969)
23	Nathaniel Niles	(1904-1926)
21	Andre Agassi	(1986-2006)
20	Jimmy Connors	(1970-1989)
19	Eugene Scott	(1957-1975)

Women

21	Martina Navratilova	(1973-1993)
19	Chris Evert	(1971-1989)
18	Pam Teeguarden	(1967-1984)

MOST SINGLES MATCHES PLAYED – CAREER

Men

115	Jimmy Connors	(1970-1992)
102	Vic Seixas	(1940-1969)
98	Andre Agassi	(1986-2006)
89	Richard Norris Williams	(1912-1935)
86	Ivan Lendl	(1979-1994)
78	Bill Tilden	(1916-1930)

Women

113	Chris Evert	(1971-1989)
106	Martina Navratilova	(1973-1993)
82	Steffi Graf	(1984-1998)
75	Lindsay Davenport	(1991–)
73	Helen Jacobs	(1927-1941)
	Louise Brough	(1941-1957)
	Doris Hart	(1940-1955)

MOST SINGLES MATCHES WON – CAREER

Men

98	Jimmy Connors	(1970-1992)
79	Andre Agassi	(1986-2006)
75	Vic Seixas	(1940-1969)
73	Ivan Lendl	(1979-1994)
71	Bill Tilden	(1916-1930)
	Pete Sampras	(1988-2002)
69	Richard Norris Williams	(1912-1935)
65	John McEnroe	(1977-1992)

Women

101	Chris Evert	(1971-1989)
89	Martina Navratilova	(1973-1993)
73	Steffi Graf	(1984-1998)
65	Molla B. Mallory	(1915-1929)
63	Helen Jacobs	(1927-1941)
60	Lindsay Davenport	(1991–)
58	Billie Jean King	(1960-1979)

MOST SINGLES MATCHES WON – SUCCESSIVE

Men

42	Bill Tilden	(1920-1926)
34	Roger Federer	(2004-2008*)
27	Ivan Lendl	(1985-1988)
26	John McEnroe	(1979-1982)

Through 2009 tournament

Women

46	Helen Wills	(1927-1933)
31	Chris Evert	(1975-1979)
28	Helen Jacobs	(1932-1936)
20	Margaret Osbourne duPont	(1948-50, 1953)
	Martina Navratilova	(1983-1985)
	Venus Williams	(2000-2002)
19	Steffi Graf	(1988-1990)

MOST SETS WON – SUCCESSIVE

Men

28	Frank Sedgman	(1951-1952)
27	Tony Trabert	(1953-1954)

Women

54	Helen Wills	(1927-1933)
46	Chris Evert	(1975-1979)

TRIPLERS

(Winners Of All Three Titles In The Same Year)

Men

1922	Bill Tilden	(MD-Vinnie Richards; MXD-Molla Bjurstedt Mallory)
1923	Bill Tilden	(MD-Brian Norton; MXD-Molla Bjurstedt Mallory)
1938	Don Budge	(MD-Gene Mako; MXD-Alice Marble)
1951	Frank Sedgman	(MD-Ken McGregor; MXD-Doris Hart)
1954	Vic Seixas	(MD-Tony Trabert; MXD-Doris Hart)
1956	Ken Rosewall	(MD-Lew Hoad; MXD-Margaret Osborne duPont)
1959	Neale Fraser	(MD-Roy Emerson; MXD-Margaret Osborne duPont)
1960	Neale Fraser	(MD-Roy Emerson; MXD-Margaret Osborne duPont)

Women

1892	Mabel Cahill	(WD-Adeline McKinlay; MXD-Clarence Hobart)
1895	Juliette Atkinson	(WD-Helen Hellwig; MXD-Edwin Fisher)
1909	Hazel Hotchkiss Wightman	(WD-Edith Rotch; MXD-Wallace Johnson)

1910	Hazel Hotchkiss Wightman	
	(WD-Edith Rotch; MXD-Joseph Carpenter)	
1911	Hazel Hotchkiss Wightman	
	(WD-Eleanora Sears; MXD-Wallace Johnson)	
1912	Mary K. Browne	(WD-Dorothy Green; MXD-Dick Williams)
1913	Mary K. Browne	(WD-Louise Riddell Wiilliams; MXD-Bill Tilden)
1914	Mary K. Browne	(WD-Louise Riddell Wiilliams; MXD-Bill Tilden)
1917	Molla Bjurstedt	(WD-Eleanora Sears; MXD-Irving Wright)
1924	Helen Wills Moody	(WD-Hazel Hotchkiss Wightman; MXD-Vinnie Richards)
1928	Helen Wills Moody	(WD-Hazel Hotchkiss Wightman; MXD-Jack Hawkes)
1934	Helen Jacobs	(WD-Sarah Palfrey Fabyan; MXD-George Lott)
1938	Alice Marble	(WD-Sarah Palfrey Fabyan; MXD-Don Budge)
1939	Alice Marble	(WD-Sarah Palfrey Fabyan; MXD-Harry Hopman)
1940	Alice Marble	(WD-Sarah Palfrey Fabyan; MXD-Bobby Riggs)
1941	Sarah Palfrey Fabyan	(WD-Margaret Osborne duPont; MXD-Jack Kramer)
1947	Louise Brough	(WD-Margaret Osborne duPont; MXD-John Bromwich)
1950	Margaret Osborne duPont	
	(WD-Louise Brough; MXD-Ken McGregor)	
1954	Doris Hart	(WD-Shirley Fry; MXD-Vic Seixas)
1967	Billie Jean King	(WD-Rosie Casals; MXD-Owen Davidson)
1970	Margaret Smith Court	
	(WD-Judy Tegart; MXD-Marty Riessen)	
1987	Martina Navratilova (WD-Pam Shriver; MXD-Emilio Sanchez)	

MOST DOUBLES TITLES – TEAM

Men's

5	Richard Sears /James Dwight	(1882-84, 1986-87)
4	Bob Lutz / Stan Smith	(1968, 1974, 1978, 1980)
	Fred Alexander / Harold Hackett	(1907-10)
	Bill Talbert / Gardnar Mulloy	(1942, 1945-46, 1948)

Women's

12	Louise Brough / Margaret Osborne duPont	(1942-50, 1955-57)
4	Sarah Palfrey / Alice Marble	(1937-40)
	Martina Navratilova / Pam Shriver	(1983-84, 1986-87)
	Doris Hart / Shirley Fry	(1951-54)

MOST DOUBLES TITLES

Men

6	Richard Sears	(1882-87)
	Holcombe Ward	(1899-1901, 1904-06)
5	James Dwight	(1882-84, 1986-87)
	George Lott	(1928-30, 1933-34)
	Vinnie Richards	(1918, 1921-22, 1925-26)
	Bill Tilden	(1918, 1921-23, 1927)
	Fred Alexander	(1907-10, 1917)

Women

13	Margaret Osborne duPont	(1941-50, 1955-57)
12	Louise Brough	(1942-1950, 1955-57)
9	Martina Navratilova	(1977-78, 1980, 1983-84, 1986-87, 1989-90)
	Sarah Palfrey Fabyan Cooke	(1930, 1932, 1934-5, 1937-41-1941)
7	Juliette Atkinson	(1894-98, 1901-02)

MOST DOUBLES FINAL APPEARANCES – TEAM

Men

7	Fred Alexander / Harold Hackett	(1905-1911)
6	Bill Talbert / Gardnar Mulloy	(1942-1953)
5	Wilmer Allison /John Van Ryn	(1931-1936)
	Richard Sears/ James Dwight	(1882-1887)
	Dwight Davis / Holcombe Ward	(1898-1902)
	Bob Lutz / Stan Smith	(1968-1980)

Women

14	Louise Brough / Margaret Osborne duPont	(1942-1957)
7	Doris Hart / Shirley Fry	(1949-1955)
6	Billie Jean King / Rosie Casals	(1966-1975)
5	Martina Navratilova / Pam Shriver	(1983-1987)
4	Helen Jacobs / Sarah Palfrey	(1932-1936)
	Margaret Smith Court / Virginia Wade	(1969-1975)
	Sarah Palfrey Fabyan Cooke / Alice Marble	(1937-1940)
	Gigi Fernandez / Natalia Zvereva	(1992-1997)
	Eleanor Goss / Marion Zinderstein	(1918-1924)
	Pauline Betz / Doris Hart	(1942-1945)

MOST DOUBLES FINAL APPERANCES – INDIVIDUAL

Men

10	Fred Alexander	(1900-1918)
9	Bill Talbert	(1942-1953)
	Gardnar Mulloy	(1940-1957)
8	Holcombe Ward	(1898-1906)
7	Harold Hackett	(1905-1911)
	Bill Tilden	(1918-1927)

Women

15	Louise Brough	(1942-1957)
	Margaret Osborne duPont	(1941-1957)
13	Doris Hart	(1942-1955)
12	Billie Jean King	(1962-1980)
11	Martina Navratilova	(1977-1990)
10	Rosie Casals	(1966-1982)
	Sarah Palfrey Fabyan Cooke	(1930-1941)

MOST DOUBLES FINAL LOSSES – TEAM

Men

| 3 | Wilmer Allison / John Van Ryn | (1932-1936) |
| | Fred Alexander / Harold Hackett | (1905-1911) |

Women

4	Billie Jean King / Rosie Casals	(1966-1975)
	Pauline Betz / Doris Hart	(1942-1945)
3	Doris Hart / Shirley Fry	(1949-1955)

MOST DOUBLES FINAL LOSSES – INDIVIDUAL

Men

5	Gardnar Mulloy	(1940-1957)
	Fred Alexander	(1900-1918)
	Bill Talbert	(1943-1953)
4	Wilmer Allison	(1930-1936)
	Ray Little	(1900-1912)
	John Van Ryn	(1930-1936)
	Gerald Patterson	(1922-1928)

Women

9	Doris Hart	(1942-1955)
7	Billie Jean King	(1962-1979)
6	Rosie Casals	(1966-1981)
5	Pauline Betz	(1941-1945)
	Edna Wildey	(1907-1916)

MOST MIXED DOUBLES TITLES – TEAM

4	Margaret Osborne duPont / Bill Talbert	(1943-1946)
3	Margaret Smith Court / Marty Riessen	(1969-1972)
	Hazel Hotchkiss Wightman / Wallace Johnson	(1909-1920)
	Margaret Osborne duPont / Neale Fraser	(1958-1960)
	Juliette Atkinson / Edwin Fischer	(1894-1896)
	Doris Hart / Vic Seixas	(1953-1955)
	Billie Jean King / Owen Davidson	(1967-1973)

MOST MIXED DOUBLES TITLES

Men

4	Marty Riessen	(1969-1980)
	Wallace Johnson	(1907-1920)
	Owen Davidson	(1966-1973)
	Bill Talbert	(1943-1946)
	Bill Tilden	(1913-1923)
	Edwin Fischer	(1894-1898)

Women

9	Margaret Osborne duPont	(1943-1960)
8	Margaret Smith Court	(1961-1972)
6	Hazel Hotchkiss Wightman	(1909-1920)
6	Doris Hart	(1951-1955)

MOST MIXED DOUBLES FINAL APPEARANCES – TEAM

6	Margaret Osborne duPont / Bill Talbert	(1943-1960)
5	Betty Stove / Frew McMillan	(1976-1980)
4	Molla Mallory / Bill Tilden	(1921-1924)
	Margaret Smith Court/ Marty Riessen	(1969-1973)

MOST MIXED DOUBLES FINAL APPEARANCES

Men

9	Bill Tilden	(1913-1924)
6	Bill Talbert	(1943-1949)
	Frew McMillian	(1970-1980)
5	Wallace Johnson	(1906-1920)
	Marty Riessen	(1969-1980)

Women

12	Margaret Osborne duPont	(1943-1960)
9	Margaret Smith Court	(1961-1973)
8	Molla Mallory	(1915-1924)
	Hazel Hotchkiss Wightman	(1909-1927)

YOUNGEST SINGLES CHAMPION

Men

Pete Sampras—19 years, 28 days (1990)
Oliver S. Campbell—19 years, 6 months, 9 days (1890)
Richard D. Sears—19 years, 10 months, 8 days (1881)

Women

Tracy Austin—16 years, 8 months, 28 days (1979)
Martina Hingis—16 years, 11 months, 8 days (1997)
Maureen Connolly—16 years, 11 months, 19 days (1951)

OLDEST SINGLES CHAMPION

Men All-Time

Bill Larned—38 years, 8 months, 3 days (1911)

Men Open Era (1968)

Ken Rosewall—35 years, 10 months, 11 days (1970)

Women All-Time

Molla Bjurstedt Mallory—42 years, five months (1926)

Women Open Era (1968)

Margaret Court AUS—31 years, one month, 23 days (1973)

OLDEST DOUBLES CHAMPION

Men

Bob Hewitt—37 years, 243 days (1977) with Frew McMillan

Women

Hazel Hotchkiss Wightman—41 years, 257 days (1928) with Helen Wills

YOUNGEST DOUBLES CHAMPION

Men

Vinnie Richards—15 years, 4 months (1918) with Bill Tilden

Women

May Sutton—17 years, 11 months (1904) with Miriam Hall

OLDEST MIXED DOUBLES CHAMPION

Men

Bob Hewitt—39 years, 8 months (1979) with Greer Stevens

Women

Martina Navratilova—49 years, 10 months, nine days (2006) with Bob Bryan
Margaret Osborne DuPont—42 years, 5 months (1960) with Neale Fraser

YOUNGEST MIXED DOUBLES CHAMPION

Men

Vinnie Richards—18 years, 3 months (1919) with Marion Zinderstein

Women

Serena Williams—16 years, 11 months, 14 days (1998) with Max Mirnyi
Manuela Maleeva—17 years, 7 months (1984) with Tom Gullikson

YOUNGEST PLAYER TO PLAY A MATCH

Men

Tommy Ho—(1988) 15 years, 2 months, 14 days old when he lost in the first round to Johan Kriek

Women

Kathy Horvath—(1979) was five days past her 14th birthday when she lost in the first round to Dianne Fromholtz, 7-6, 6-2 after playing qualifying tournament

YOUNGEST PLAYER TO WIN A MATCH

Men

Vinnie Richards—(1918) was 15 years, 5 months, 8 days old when he defeated Frank Anderson in the second round after advancing in a walkover in the first round, 6-1 6-3, 6-3

Michael Chang—(1987) was 15 years, 6 months and 10 days when he defeated Paul McNamee in the first round, 6-3, 6-7, 6-4, 6-4

Women

Mary Joe Fernandez—(1985) was 14 years and 8 days when she defeated Sara Gomer in the first round, 6-1, 6-4

LONGEST MATCHES, TOTAL GAMES

Men's Singles

100 games F.D. Robbins d Dick Dell 22-20, 9-7, 6-8, 8-10, 6-4, 1st rd., 1969

Men's Doubles

105 games Marcelo Lara / Joaquin Loyo-Mayo d. Luis Garcia / Manuel Santana 10-12, 24-22, 11-9, 3-6, 6-2, 3rd rd. 1966

105 games Cliff Drysdale / Ray Moore d. Ronnie Barnes / Roy Emerson 29-31, 8-6, 3-6, 8-6. 6-2, quarterfinals, 1967

Women's Singles

51 games Juliette Atkinson d. Marion Jones, 6-3, 5-7, 6-4, 2-6, 7-5, Challenge round, F, 1898, best three out of five sets

48 games Margaret duPont d. Louise Brough, 4-6, 6-4, 15-13, F, 1948, best two out of three sets

Women's Doubles

48 games Mrs. George L. Chapman / Marion Chapman (mother daughter) d. Dorothy Green Briggs / Corinne Stanton Henry, 10-8, 6-8, 9-7, 1st rd, 1922

Mixed Doubles

71 games Margaret Osborne duPont / Bill Talbert d. Gussy Moran / Bob Falkenburg, 27-25, 5-7, 6-1

LONGEST MATCH, PLAYING TIME

Men's Singles

5 hours, 26 minutes   Stefan Edberg d. Michael Chang 6-7(3-7). 7-5, 6-7, (7-3), 5-7, 6-4, semifinals, 1992

Women's Singles

3 hours, 3 minutes   Justine Henin-Hardenne d. Jennifer Capriati 4-6, 7-5, 7-6 (7-4), semis, 2003

SHORTEST MATCH

22 minutes   Molla Bjurstedt d. Louise Hammond Raymond 6-0, 6-1, 1916 women's singles final

LONGEST TIE-BREAKERS

Men's Singles

20-18   third set, Goran Ivanisevic d. Daniel Nestor. 6-4. 7-6(7-5), 7-6 (20-18), 1st rd., 1993

Women's Singles

13-11   second set, Hana Mandlikova d. Nathalie Herreman, 6-3, 6-7 (11-13), 6-2, 2nd rd., 1987

FEWEST GAMES FINAL

Men

20 Jimmy Connors d. Ken Rosewall, 1974, 6-1, 6-0, 6-1

Women

13 Ellen Hansell d. Laura Knight, 1887, 6-1, 6-0

   Hazel Hotchkiss d. Maud Barger-Wallach, 1909, 6-0, 6-1

   Molla Bjurstedt d. Louise Hammond Raymond, 1916, 6-0, 6-1

   Maria Bueno d. Carole Graebner, 1964, 6-1, 6-0

EARLY ELIMINATION OF THE NO. 1 SEED

Men

1928   Non-seed U.S. No. 12 George King d. 1st seed John Hennessey, 7-5, 6-4, 6-4, 1st rd.

1930   Jean Borotra (No. 1 foreign seed) lost to Berkeley Bell 3-6, 6-2, 12-10, 7-5 in 1st rd.

1945   Andres Hammersley (No. 1 foreign seed) lost to James Livingstone, 6-3, 1-6, 6-3 in 1st rd.

1971   No. 1 seed John Newcombe lost to Jan Kodes 2-6, 7-6, 7-6, 6-3 in 1st rd.

1990   Alexander Volkov (No. 52) d. 1st seed Stefan Edberg (Wimbledon champion). 6-3, 7-6 (7-1). 6-2, 1st rd.

2000   Arnaud Clement (No. 37) d. 1st seed Andre Agassi, 2nd rd., 6-3, 6-2, 6-4

Women

1966   No. 1 Billie Jean King lost to Kerry Melville 6-4, 6-4 in the 2nd rd.

1973   No. 1 seed and defending champion Billie Jean King lost in the third round to Julie Heldman 3-6, 6-4, 4-1, ret. (fatigue)

2008   Jule Coin (No. 188, Q) de. Ana Ivanovic (No. 1), 6-3, 4-6, 6-3, 2nd round

EARLY ELIMINATION OF THE DEFENDING CHAMPION

Men

1973   Unranked Andy Pattison d. 2nd seed defending champ Ilie Nastase, 6-7, 2-6, 6-3, 6-3, 6-4, 2nd rd.

1989   Pete Sampras d. defending champion Mats Wilander 5-7, 6-3, 1-6, 6-1, 6-4 in 2nd rd.

1993   Two-time defending champion Stefan Edberg lost to Karel Novacek 7-6, 6-4, 4-6, 6-4 in 2nd rd.

1999   Cedric Pioline (No. 26) d. two-time defending champion Patrick Rafter, 4-6, 4-6, 6-3, 7-5, 1-0, retired (right shoulder injury) in 1st rd.

2000   Arnaud Clement (No. 37) d. 1st seed defending champ Andre Agassi, 6-3, 6-2, 6-4 in 2nd rd.

Women

1973 No. 1 seed and defending champion Billie Jean King lost in the third round to Julie Heldman 3-6, 6-4, 4-1, ret. (fatigue)

2005 Defending champion Svetlana Kuznetsova (ranked No. 97) lost in the first round to Ekaterina Bychkova 6-3, 6-2

2007 No. 30 seed Agnieszka Radwanska d. No. 2 and defending champion Maria Sharapova 6-4, 1-6, 6-2, 3rd rd.

OTHER BIG UPSETS

Men

1933 Non-seed U.S. No. 13 Bitsy Grant d. 1st seed defending champ Ellsworth Vines, 6-2, 6-3. 6-3, 4th rd.

1939 Unranked Welby Van Horn d. 3rd foreign seed John Bromwich, 2-6, 4-6, 6-2, 6-4, 8-6, SF

1957 Non-seed Mal Anderson d. 2nd seed Dick Savitt, 6-4, 6-3, 6-1; 4th rd; 3rd seed Sven Davidson, 5-7, 6-2, 4-6, 6-3. 6-4, SF: and 1st seed Ashley Cooper, 10-8, 7-5, 6-4, to win title

1968 16th seed Cliff Drysdale d. 1st seed Rod Laver, 4-6, 6-4, 3-6, 6-1, 6-1, 4th rd.

1970 Dennis Ralston (No. 19) d. 1st seed defending champ Rod Laver, 7-6 (5-3). 7-5, 5-7, 4-6, 6-3, 4th rd.

1983 16th seed Bill Scanlon d. 1st seed John McEnroe, 7-6(7-2), 7-6 (7-3), 4-6, 6-3, 4th rd.

1986 Todd Witsken (No. 95) d. 6th seed Jimmy Connors, 6-2, 6-4, 7-5, 3rd rd.; Paul Annacone (No. 43) d. 9th seed John McEnroe, 1-6. 6-1, 6-3, 6-3, 1st rd.

1989 Qualifier Paul Haarhuis (No. 116) d. 4th seed John McEnroe, 6-4, 4-6, 6-3, 7-5, 2nd rd.

1991 Paul Haarhuis (No. 45) d. 1st seed Boris Becker, 6-2, 6-3, 6-4, 3rd rd.

1994 Jaime Yzaga (No. 23) d. 1st seed defending champ Pete Sampras, 3-6, 6-3, 4-6, 7-6, (7-4), 7-5, 4th rd.

1997 15th seed Petr Korda d. 1st seed defending champ Pete Sampras, 6-7 (4-7), 7-5, 7-6 (7-2), 3-6, 7-6 (7-3)

1998 Qualifier Bernd Karbacher (No. 155) d. 4th seed Petr Korda, 2-6, 6-3. 6-2, 6-1, 1st rd.

2000 Wayne Arthurs (No. 102) d. 2nd seed Gustavo Kuerten, 4-6, 6-3, 7-6 (7-4), 7-6 (7-1) (combined with No. 1 seed Andre Agassi's loss to Arnaud Clement, it resulted in the first Open Era 3rd rd. without the No. 1 or No. 2 seeds)

2005 Gilles Muller (ranked No. 68) d. 4th-seeded Andy Roddick 7-6 (7-4), 7-6 (10-8), 7-6 (7-1) in 1st rd.

2006 Feliciano Lopez (ranked No. 77) d. 3rd-seeded Ivan Ljubicic 6-3, 6-3, 6-3 in 1st rd.

Women

1971 Chris Evert (unranked amateur) d. U.S. No. 3 Mary Ann Eisel, 4-6, 7-6 (5-1), 6-1, 2nd rd, saved 6 MP

1978 16th seeded Pam Shriver d. No.1 seed Martina Navratilova (Wimbledon champion), 7-6(7-5), 7-6(7-3), SF

1979 Qualifier Julie Harrington (No. 109) d. 14th seed Pam Shriver (1978 finalist), 6-2. 6-1, 1st rd.

1981 Andrea Leand (unranked amateur, 1st US Open) d. 2nd seed Andrea Jaeger, 1-6, 7-5, 6-3, 2nd rd.

1982 Susan Mascarin (unranked amateur) d. 12th seed Billie Jean King, 6-3, 6-2, 1st rd.

1988 Qualifer Kim Steinmetz (No. 183) d. Eighth seed Natalia Zvereva, 4-6, 6-3, 6-4. 1st rd.

1992 Maggie Maleeva (No. 17) d. 3rd seed Martina Navratilova (1991 finalist), 6-4, 0-6, 6-3, 2nd rd.

1994 Mana Endo (No. 44) d. 6th seed Lindsay Davenport, 6-3, 7-8 (7-1), 4th rd.

1997 Venus Williams (No. 66) d. 11th seed Irina Spirlea, 7-6 (7-5), 4-6, 7-6 (9-7). SF. (saved 2 MP)

2001 Daja Bedanova (No. 37) d. 7th seeded Monica Seles, 7-5, 4-6, 6-3, 4th rd.

2004 Nadia Petrova, seed 14th, d. top-seed Justine Henin-Hardenne 6-3, 6-2 in 4th rd.

MATCH POINTS SAVED BY SINGLES CHAMPION

Men

1908 QF, Bill Clothier d. Fred Alexander, 8-6, 6-2, 4-6, 1-6, 7-5, saved 3 MP at 2-5, 0-40 in 5th set

1936 F, Fred Perry d. Don Budge, 2-6, 6-2, 8-6, 1-6, 10-8, saved 2 MP at 4-5 5th set

1975 SF, Manolo Orantes d. Guillermo Vilas 4-6, 1-6, 6-2, 7-5, 6-4, saved 5 MP, 3 at 0-5 in the 4th; 2 at 5-1, 40-15. Trailed 0-2 in third and 0-5 in fourth set Won last two games after Vilas caught him at 4-4 from 2-4 in the 5th

1989 2R, Boris Becker d. Derrick Rostagno 1-6, 6-7 (1-7), 6-3, 7-6 (8-6), 6-3, saved 2 MP at 4-6 in 4th set TB

1996 QF, Pete Sampras d. Alex Corretja, 7-6 (7-5), 5-7, 5-7, 6-4, 7-6 (9-7) saved 1 MP at 6-7 in 5th set TB

2003 SF, Andy Roddick d. David Nalbandian 6-7 (4-7), 3-6, 7-6 (9-7), 6-1, 6-3 in SF (saved match point at 6-5 in 3rd set tie-break)

Women

1901 F, Elizabeth Moore d. Myrtle McAteer, 6-4, 3-6, 7-5, 2-6, 6-2 saved 1 MP in 3rd set

1911 F, Hazel Hotchkiss (Wightman) d. Florence Sutton 8-10, 6-1, 9-7, saved 1 MP Sutton serving at 6-5, 40-30 in 3rd set with overhead smash of deep lob

1926 Molla Mallory d. Bunny Ryan, 4-6, 6-4, 9-7, saved 1 MP in 3rd set, Ryan had led 4-0

1938 SF, Alice Marble d. Sarah Palfrey Fabyan, 5-7, 7-5, 7-5 saved, 2 MP at 2-5 in 3rd set

1942 SF, Pauline Betz d. Margaret Osborne duPont, saved 1 MP at 5-3 in the 3rd set, 6-4, 4-6, 7-5

1947 SF, Louise Brough d. Nancye Wynne Bolton, 4-6, 6-4, 7-5, saved 3 MP at 2-5, 0-40 in 3rd set

1948 F, Margaret Osbourne duPont d. Louise Brough, 4-6, 6-4, 15-13, saved 1 MP at 5-6 in 3rd set

1954 F, Doris Hart d. Louise Brough, 6-8, 6-1, 8-6, saved 3 MP in 3rd set

1986 SF, Martina Navratilova d. Steffi Graf 6-1, 6-7 (3-7), 7-6 (10-8), saved three MP, 2 at 4-5, ads out in 3rd set and 1 in 3rd set TB at 8-7

OTHER GREAT COMEBACKS

Men

1932 1st seed defending champ Ellsworth Vines d. U.S. No. 6 Cliff Sutter. 4-6, 8-10, 12-10, 10-8, 6-1, 4th rd. (twice 2 points from defeat, 3rd, 5-6, deuce, 4th, 5-6, 30-all)

1939 Unranked Welby Van Horn d. 3rd foreign seed John Bromwich, 2-6, 4-6, 6-2. 6-4, 8-6, SF

1946 Amado Sanchez d. Charles Sampson, 5-7, 3-6, 9-7, 9-7, 7-5, 1st rd. Saved 2 MP at 1 6-5, 3rd set and 1 at 4-5, 5th set after trailing 1-4

1960 Rod Laver d. Butch Buchholz. 4-6, 5-7, 6-4, 6-2, 7-5, SF. Saved 3 MP

1976 Ilie Nastase (2 MP saved) d. Hans Pohmann, 7-6, 4-6, 7-6 (best-of-three sets) in 2nd rd.

1979 Vitas Gerulaitis d. Roscoe Tanner, 3-6, 2-6, 7-6 (7-5), 6-3, 6-3. SF, down a break in 3rd set and 2 points from defeat

1981 Stan Smith (Saved 5 MPs) d. John Sadri, 5-7, 6-7, 7-5, 6-4, 7-6, 1st rd.

1984 Ivan Lendl (Saved 1 MP) d. Patrick Cash 3-6, 6-3, 6-4, 6-7, 7-6, SF

1987 Ken Flach USA (Saved 5 MPs) d Darren Cahill AUS 1-6, 6-4, 3-6, 6-1, 7-6 2R

1991 Wild card Jimmy Connors (No. 174) d. Aaron Krickstein 3-6, 7-6(10-8), 1-6, 6-3, 7-6 (7-4), 4th rd on Connors 39th birthday (saved 2 SP, 2nd, in tie-breaker. Came back from 2-5 in fifth set, twice 2 points from defeat, deuce, 5-3). In 1st rd, Connors d. Patrick McEnroe 4-6, 6-7 (4), 6-4, 6-2, 6-4, trailing two-sets-to-love and 3-0, 40-0 in third set, winning in 4 hours and 18 minutes at 1:35 am. In QF, d. Paul Haarhuis 4-6, 7-6 (3), 6-4, 6-2 after Haarhuis served for two-sets-to-love lead at 5-4 in second set, Connors breaking serve after retrieving four over-head smashes from Haarhuis

1993 Wally Masur d. Jamie Morgan, 3-6. 4-6, 6-3, 6-4, 7-5, 4th rd. from 0-5, 5th set. Saved 1 MP at 5-1, won 25 of last 28 points from there

1998 3rd seed defending champ Patrick Rafter d. Hicham Arazi (No. 44). 1st rd. continued to win second straight title, 4-6, 4-6, 6-3, 6-3, 6-1. Down 15-40 on serve at 3-3 in third set. Also, Carlos Moya d. Michael Chang, 3-6, 1-6, 7-6 (7-5), 6-4, 6-3. Saved 3 MP at 4-5, 3rd set 2R

1999 Todd Martin d. Greg Rusedskl, 5-7, 0-6, 7-6 (7-3), 6-4, 6-4, 4th rd. Rusedski served for match, 5-4, 3rd set, led 4-1 in 5th set, whereupon Martin won 18 straight points to 5-4, 30-0, 20 of last 21 points

2000 Todd Martin d. Carlos Moya 6-7 (3-7), 6-7 (7-9), 6-1, 7-6 (6), 6-2, 4th rd. in 4:17 in match that ended at 1:22 am. Moya held a MP at 6-5 in 4th set TB

2007 10th seed Tommy Haas d. 6th seed James Blake 4-6, 6-4, 3-6, 6-0, 7-6 (4) in 4th rd, Haas saved 3 MP serving at 4-5 in 5th

Women

1926 Molla Bjurstedt Mallory d. Elizabeth Ryan, 4-6, 6-4, 9-7, F, From 0-4, 3rd set, saved 1 MP at 6-7

1933 Betty Nuthall d. Alice Marble, 8-10, 6-0, 7-5, QF, Saved 3 MP from 5-1, 40-15, ad-in down

1971 Chris Evert d. Mary Ann Eisel, 4-6, 7-6 (5-1), 6-1, 2nd rd, Saved 6 MP, Eisel serving at 6-5, 40-0 and 3 ads-in

1983 Barbie Bramblett d. Kathy Holton, 2-6, 7-6 (7-3). 6-3, in US Open qualifying tournament, Saved 16 MP, from 0-5, 0-40 down in the 2nd set

1995 Mary Joe Fernandez d. Alexandra Fusai, 6-3, 4-6, 7-6 (12-10). Saved 6 MP
2 at 5-6, 15-40, 4 in tie-breaker

2003 Justine Henin-Hardenne d. Jennifer Capriati, 4-6, 7-5, 7-6(4) in SF in 3:03 (Capriati served for the match in both in the second and third sets and was two points from winning the match 11 times)

FARTHEST ADVANCEMENT OF A QUALIFIER

Men
Nicolas Escude	1999 Quarterfinals

Women
Barbara Gerken	1981 Quarterfinals

FARTHEST ADVANCEMENT OF A WILD CARD

Men
Jimmy Connors	1991 Semifinals

Women
Martina Hingis	2002 fourth round
Serena Williams	2006 fourth round

FARTHEST ADVANCEMENT OF A LUCKY LOSER

Men
Fernando Verdasco	2003 Third Round
Laurence Tieleman	1999 Third Round

Women
Maria Jose Gaidano	1993 Fourth Round

UNSEEDED CHAMPIONS

Men
1957	Mal Anderson
1966	Fred Stolle
1994	Andre Agassi

Women
none

UNSEEDED FINALISTS

Men
1930	Francis X. Shields
1938	Gene Mako
1939	Welby Van Horn
1957	Mal Anderson
1963	Frank Froehling
1966	Fred Stolle, John Newcombe
1971	Jan Kodes
1994	Andre Agassi
1997	Greg Rusedski
1998	Mark Philippoussis

Women
1958	Darlene Hard
1997	Venus Williams

FASTEST SERVES

Men

Andy Roddick   152 mph (2004)

Women

Venus Williams   125 mph (2004)

MOST ACES

Pete Sampras   144 aces, seven matches (includes 33 in F win over Agassi) (2002)

Women

Serena Williams   45 aces, five matches (2000)

MOST ACES IN A MATCH

Men

59   Ed Kauder lost to Ham Richardson, 1st rd., 6-2, 3-6, 9-11, 10-8, 6-0, 1955

49   Richard Krajicek lost to Yevgeny Kafelnikov, QF, 7-6 (7-0), 7-6 (7-4), 3-6, 1-6, 7-6 (7-5), 1999

39   Steve Denton lost to Richard Matuszewski, 6-7 (8-10), 7-6 (7-4), 6-7 (8-10), 6-4, 6-3, 1st rd., 1985

38   Wayne Arthurs d. No. 13 seed Alex Corretja, 6-3, 6-4, 1-6, 4-6, 7-6(8-6), 1999

Women

17   Brenda Schultz McCarthy d. Audra Keller, 7-6(8-6), 2-6, 7-6(7-3), 1st rd., 1995

15   Serena Williams d. Monica Seles, 4-6, 6-3, 6-2, QF, 1999

MOST DOUBLE FAULTS IN A MATCH

Men

24   Steve Denton lost to Richard Matuszewski, 6-7(8-10), 7-6(7-4), 6-7(8-10), 6-4, 6-3, 1st rd., 1985

23   Jaime Oncins lost to Michael Chang, 3-6, 6-1, 6-0, 7-6 (8-6), 1st rd., 1996

19   Tim Mayotte lost to Thierry Champion, 7-5, 3-6, 6-3, 7-5, 1st. rd., 1990

19   Goran Ivanisevic d. Cristiano Caratti, 6-1, 4-6, 6-2, 2-6, 6-4, 3rd rd., 1999 (Goran also had 15 aces in the match)

18   Tim Mayotte lost to Mark Woodforde, 7-6, 7-6, 3-6, 2-6, 7-6 (7-5), 3rd rd., 1987 (Mayotte also had 17 aces)

Women

19   Elena Dementieva d. Anna Chakvetadze, 6-1, 4-6, 7-6 (7-5), 3d rd, 2005

19   Allison Bradshaw d. Catalina Castano, 6-7 (3-7), 7-6 (7-5), 6-3 1st rd., 2001

16   Darlene Hard lost to Margaret Court 9-7, 6-4, F, 1962

16   Brenda Schultz-McCarthy d. Kimiko Date, 7-5, 3-6, 6-2, 4th rd., 1995

MOST YEARS SEEDED

Men

18 Jimmy Connors

17 Frank Parker

Women

19 Martina Navratilova

18 Chris Evert

International Play

SECTION III

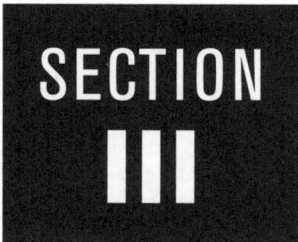

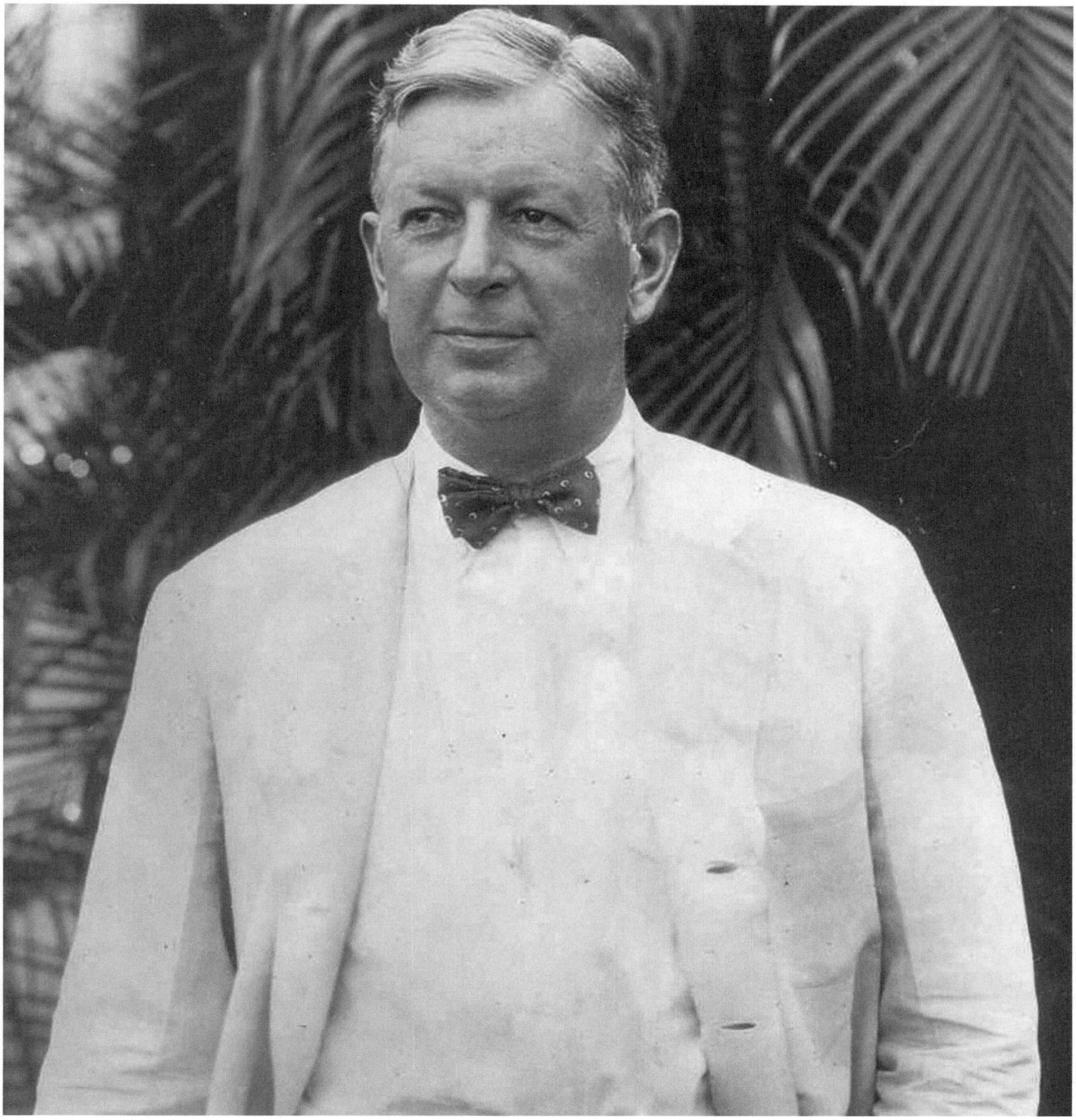

Dwight Davis was an integral part of international team play in tennis, starting the International Lawn Tennis Challenge Trophy event in 1900. The competition eventually became known as The Davis Cup.

Davis Cup

United States has been the most successful nation in the history of the Davis Cup—winning their 32nd championship in 2007 with a 4-1 win over Russia—Capt. **Patrick McEnroe** (left), **Mike Bryan**, **Bob Bryan**, **James Blake** and **Andy Roddick**.

If you peer into the sterling silver bowl, you will see this engraving: International Lawn Tennis Challenge Trophy.

That was the official name when one of the greatest sporting prizes materialized in 1900. Somewhat long, perhaps, but soon the treasure was known as the Davis Cup, the focus of annual world-wide team competition. Simply Davis Cup (easier on headline writers among others) because it was the vision of the donor, a 20-year-old Harvard student, Dwight Filley Davis. Young Davis, who came from a prosperous St. Louis family and loved tennis, felt that international friendships and understanding could be kindled through the game. He was right, although the beginning was modest: British Isles against the United States. Two countries. Today, more than 120 countries are involved.

That would gratify Davis, an unassuming man, who eventually accepted that the Cup would be referred to in his name. Friends at his club, Longwood Cricket Club in Boston, good naturedly called it "Dwight's Pot."

Davis commissioned the Cup from Boston jeweler Shreve, Crump and Lowe. It was designed by Rowland Rhodes and crafted by William Morton and Warren Peckman at the William B. Durgin Company in Concord, N.H. The price was about $1,000 but it would cost almost $200,000 to duplicate today, according to Shreve. Since the names of players of both final-round teams are engraved on the trophy (first on the bowl, then on an accompanying tray, now on silver tablets attached to three subsequently added circular bases). Longwood's grass was the scene of the 1900 inaugural. A member, Dr. James Dwight, president of the USTA at the time and considered the "Father of American Tennis," interested the British in challenging through his connections in London. He drew up the rules and oversaw the initial best-of-five match series, won 3-0 by the U.S. hosts.

It was a time when college men of the Northeast dominated the American game. Davis, as the U.S. captain and ranked No. 2 nationally, enlisted schoolmates Malcolm Whitman, No. 1, and Holcombe Ward, No. 9, to complete the home side. On the first day, playing on side by side courts, Whitman beat future Wimbledon champ Arthur Gore, 6-1, 6-3, 6-2, and Davis beat Ernest Black, 4-6, 6-2, 6-4, 6-4. Ward and Davis, the U.S. champions in doubles, settled Cup possession for that year, 6-4, 6-4, 6-4, over Herbert Roper Barrett and Black.

For the first three years of the competition, 1900, 1902 and 1903, the same two countries entered, but in 1904, Belgium and France signed on. (The U.S. dropped out). Belgium beat France for the right to challenge Britain, the 1903 winner over the United States. Australia entered in 1905 and would become the most prolific winner other than the United States. They played under the banner of Australasia until 1923, because of a partnership with New Zealand, which entered separately in 1924.

With the expansion of the competition, it became necessary to divide the world into zones for preliminary tournaments to determine one challenger to the champion nation. The champion was required to only play the title match—the Challenge Round—the following year against the winner of the preliminary tournament. By 1923, when 17 nations entered, it was necessary to divide the world into two zones—American and European. In 1955, an Eastern zone was added. In 1966, the European Zone was split into sections A and B. In 1967, the American Zone was split was split into North and South sections. That system was changed in 1972, when the Challenge Round format was abandoned and all nations were required to play in the eliminations in their respective zones - American (North and South), European (A and B Sections) and Eastern. That year the Cup-defending United States reached the final against Romania in Bucharest and won 3-2.

In 1981, the World Group of 16 countries was instituted. Only those 16 are eligible annually to compete for the Cup itself. Remaining countries engage in zonal competition with the possibility of being promoted to the World Group the following year.

A total of 139 nations have appeared in the competition, but only 12 have won the Cup: U.S. (32 times), Australia (28), Britain (9), France (8), Sweden (7), Germany (3), Spain (3), Russia (2), Czechoslovakia (1), South Africa (1), Italy (1), Croatia (1). Nine nations besides the 12 winners have qualified for the Challenge Round and/or Final: Romania (3 times), India (2), Argentina (3), Belgium (1), Japan (1), Chile (1), Switzerland (1), Mexico (1), Slovak Republic (1).

The competition was confined to amateurs until 1969 when certain professionals—those with ties to their national federations—became eligible. In 1973, it became a truly open event with all players welcome and Australia won with possibly the strongest team ever, a group of pros who had been away from Davis Cup for years—Rod Laver, Ken Rosewall, John Newcombe and Mal Anderson.

The format for a series (or tie) is four singles and one doubles—a best-of-five-series—over three days. A team may be composed of no more than four players. Two players are nominated for singles and the No. 1 computer-ranked player of each country faces the No. 2 player on the first day, with the opponents reversed on the third day. A draw determines who plays the first match on the first day, with the final day reversed. The No. 1s face off in the fourth match and the No. 2s play the final match. Nations visit one another for ties, the home team having the choice of location and court surface.

Through 2008, the competition has been held 97 times, interrupted only by two world wars and a hiatus in 1901 and 1910. Prize money was injected in 1981 (individual sums never made public, however) and amounts now to more than $9 million spread among participating nations. BNP Paribas is the title sponsor.

Longest Cup-winning streaks: U.S. seven years, 1920–26; France six years, 1927-32; U.S. five years, 1968–72; Britain four years, 1933–36; Australia four years, 1950–53, and 1959–62, and 1964–67. The record for most consecutive ties won, U.S., 17 between 1968 and the 1973 final.

Agitation for a sensible season-shortening, TV-attracting playoff among the remaining four nations is ever present, but the proprietor, the ITF, sees no reason the change. Whatever, that kid Davis sure gave us a magnificent gift.

Davis Cup Champions

Challenge Rounds

1900

United States d. British Isles 3-0 (Boston) Surface–Grass

Malcolm Whitman (USA) d. Arthur Gore (GBR) 6-1, 6-3, 6-2

Dwight Davis (USA) d. Ernest Black (GBR) 4-6, 6-2, 6-4, 6-4

Holcombe Ward-Dwight Davis (USA) d. Ernest Black-Herbert Roper Barrett (GBR) 6-4, 6-4, 6-4

Malcolm Whitman (USA) vs Ernest Black (GBR) (not played)

Dwight Davis (USA) vs Arthur Gore (GBR) 9-7, 9-9 (unfinished)

1901 not held

1902

United States d. British Isles 3-2 (Brooklyn, N.Y) Surface–Grass

Reggie Doherty (GBR) d. Bill Larned (USA) 2-6, 3-6, 6-3, 6-4, 6-4

Malcolm Whitman (USA) d. Joshua Pim (GBR) 6-1, 6-1, 1-6, 6-0

Bill Larned (USA) d. Joshua Pim (GBR) 6-3, 6-2, 6-3

Malcolm Whitman (USA) d. Reggie Doherty (GBR) 6-1, 7-5, 6-4

Reggie Doherty-Laurie Doherty (GBR) d. Holcombe Ward-Dwight Davis (USA) 3-6, 10-8, 6-3, 6-4

1903

British Isles d. United States 4-1 (Boston) Surface–Grass

Laurie Doherty (GBR) d. Robert Wrenn (USA) 6-0, 6-3, 6-4

Bill Larned (USA) d. Reggie Doherty (GBR) (walkover, injury)

Reggie Doherty-Laurie Doherty (GBR) d. Robert Wrenn-George Wrenn (USA) 7-5, 9-7, 2-6, 6-3

Laurie Doherty (GBR) d. Bill Larned (USA) 6-3, 6-8, 6-0, 2-6, 7-5

Reggie Doherty (GBR) d. Robert Wrenn (USA) 6-4, 3-6, 6-3, 6-8, 6-4

1904

British Isles d. Belgium 5-0 (Wimbledon) Surface–Grass

Laurie Doherty (GBR) d. Paul de Borman (BEL) 6-4, 6-1, 6-1

Frank Riseley (GBR) d. Willie Lemaire de Warzee (BEL) 6-1, 6-4, 6-2

Reggie Doherty-Laurie Doherty (GBR) d. Paul de Borman-Willie Lemaire de Warzee (BEL) 6-0, 6-1, 6-3

Laurie Doherty (GBR) d. Willie Lemarie de Warzee (BEL) (walkover)

Frank Riseley (GBR) d. Paul de Borman (BEL) 4-6, 6-2, 8-6, 7-5

1905

British Isles d. United States 5-0 (Wimbledon) Surface–Grass

Laurie Doherty (GBR) d. Holcombe Ward (USA) 7-9, 4-6, 6-1, 6-2, 6-0

Sidney Smith (GBR) d. Bill Larned (USA) 6-4, 6-4, 5-7, 6-4

Reggie Doherty-Laurie Doherty (GBR) d. Holcombe Ward-Beals Wright (USA) 8-10, 6-2, 6-2, 4-6, 8-6

Sidney Smith (GBR) d. Bill Clothier (USA) 4-6, 6-1, 6-4, 6-3

Laurie Doherty (GBR) d. Bill Larned (USA) 6-4, 2-6, 6-8, 6-4, 6-2

1906

British Isles d. United States 5-0 (Wimbledon) Surface–Grass

Sidney Smith (GBR) d. Raymond Little (USA) 6-4, 6-4, 6-1

Laurie Doherty (GBR) d. Holcombe Ward (USA) 6-2, 8-6, 6-3

Reggie Doherty-Laurie Doherty (GBR) d. Holcombe Ward-Raymond Little (USA) 3-6, 11-9, 9-7, 6-1

Sidney Smith (GBR) d. Holcombe Ward (USA) 6-1, 6-0, 6-4

Laurie Doherty (GBR) d. Raymond Little (USA) 3-6, 6-3, 6-8, 6-1, 6-3

1907

Australasia d. British Isles 3-2 (Wimbledon) Surface–Grass

Norman Brookes (AUS) d. Arthur Gore (GBR) 7-5, 6-1, 7-5

Tony Wilding (AUS) d. Herbert Roper Barrett (GBR) 1-6, 6-4, 6-3, 7-5

Arthur Gore-Herbert Roper Barrett (GBR) d. Norman Brookes-Tony Wilding (AUS) 3-6, 4-6, 7-5, 6-2, 13-11

Norman Brookes (AUS) d. Herbert Roper Barrett (GBR) 6-2, 6-0, 6-3

Arthur Gore (GBR) d. Tony Wilding (AUS) 3-6, 6-3, 7-5, 6-2

1908

Australasia d. United States 3-2 (Melbourne) Surface–Grass

Norman Brookes (AUS) d. Fred Alexander (AUS) 5-7, 9-7, 6-2, 4-6, 6-3

Beals Wright (USA) d. Tony Wilding (AUS) 3-6, 7-5, 6-3, 6-1

Norman Brookes-Tony Wilding (AUS) d. Beals Wright-Fred Alexander (USA) 6-4, 6-2, 5-7, 1-6, 6-4

Beals Wright (USA) d. Norman Brookes (AUS) 0-6, 3-6, 7-5, 6-2, 12-10

Tony Wilding (AUS) d. Fred Alexander (USA) 6-3, 6-4, 6-1

1909

Australasia d. United States 5-0 (Sydney) Surface–Grass

Norman Brookes (AUS) d. Maurice McLoughlin (USA) 6-2, 6-2, 6-4

Tony Wilding (AUS) d. Melville Long (USA) 6-2, 7-5, 6-1

Norman Brookes-Tony Wilding (AUS) d. Maurice McLoughlin-Melville Long (USA) 12-10, 9-7, 6-3

Norman Brookes (AUS) d. Melville Long (USA) 6-4, 7-5, 8-6

Tony Wilding (AUS) d. Maurice McLoughlin (USA) 3-6, 8-6, 6-2, 6-3

1910 No competition

1911

Australasia d. United States 5-0 (Christchurch, New Zealand) Surface–Grass

Norman Brookes (AUS) d. Beals Wright (USA) 6-4, 2-6, 6-3, 6-3

Rod Heath (AUS) d. Bill Larned (USA) 2-6, 6-1, 7-5, 6-2

Norman Brookes-Alfred Dunlop (AUS) d. Beals Wright-Maurice McLoughlin (USA) 6-4, 5-7, 7-5, 6-2

Norman Brookes (AUS) d. Maurice McLoughlin (USA) 6-4, 3-6, 4-6, 6-3, 6-4

Rod Heath (AUS) d. Beals Wright (USA) (walkover)

1912

British Isles d. Australasia 3-2 (Melbourne) Surface—Grass

James Parke (GBR) d. Norman Brookes (AUS) 8-6, 6-3, 5-7, 6-2

Charles Dixon (GBR) d. Rod Heath (AUS) 5-7, 6-4, 6-4, 6-4

Norman Brookes-Alfred Dunlop (AUS) d. Cecil Parke-Alfred Beamish (GBR) 6-4, 6-1, 7-5

James Parke (GBR) d. Rod Heath (AUS) 6-2, 6-4, 6-4

Norman Brookes (AUS) d. Charles Dixon (GBR) 6-2, 6-4, 6-4

1913

United States d. British Isles 3-2 (Wimbledon) Surface—Grass

James Parke (GBR) d. Maurice McLoughlin (USA) 8-10, 7-5, 6-4, 1-6, 7-5

Dick Williams (USA) d. Charles Dixon (GBR) 8-6, 3-6, 6-2, 1-6, 7-5

Harold Hackett-Maurice McLoughlin (USA) d. Herbert Roper Barrett-Charles Dixon (GBR) 5-7, 6-1, 2-6, 7-5, 6-4

Maurice McLoughlin (USA) d. Charles Dixon (GBR) 8-6, 6-3, 6-2

James Parke (GBR) d. Dick Williams (USA) 6-2, 5-7, 5-7, 6-4, 6-2

1914

Australasia d. United States 3-2 (Forest Hills) Surface—Grass

Tony Wilding (AUS) d. Dick Williams (USA) 7-5, 6-2, 6-3

Maurice McLoughlin (USA) d. Norman Brookes (AUS) 17-15, 6-3, 6-3

Norman Brookes-Tony Wilding (AUS) d. Maurice McLoughlin-Tom Bundy (USA) 6-3, 8-6, 9-7

Norman Brookes (AUS) d. Dick Williams (USA) 6-1, 6-2, 8-10, 6-3

Maurice McLoughlin (USA) d. Tony Wilding (AUS) 6-2, 6-3, 2-6, 6-2

1915—18 Not held, World War I

1919

Australasia d. British Isles 4-1 (Sydney) Surface—Grass

Gerald Patterson (AUS) d. Arthur Lowe (GBR) 6-4, 6-3, 2-6, 6-3

Algernon Kingscote (GBR) d. Jim Anderson (AUS) 7-5, 6-2, 6-4

Norman Brookes-Gerald Patterson (AUS) d. Algernon Kingscote-Alfred Beamish (GBR) 6-0, 6-0, 6-2

Gerald Patterson (AUS) d. Algernon Kingscote (GBR) 6-4, 6-4, 8-6

Jim Anderson (AUS) d. Arthur Lowe (GBR) 6-4, 5-7, 6-3, 4-6, 12-10

1920

United States d. Australasia 5-0 (Auckland) Surface—Grass

Bill Tilden (USA) d. Norman Brookes (AUS) 10-8, 6-4, 1-6, 6-4

Bill Johnston (USA) d. Gerald Patterson (AUS) 6-3, 6-1, 6-1

Bill Tilden-Bill Johnston (USA) d. Norman Brookes-Gerald Patterson (AUS) 4-6, 6-4, 6-0, 6-4

Bill Tilden (USA) d. Gerald Patterson (AUS) 5-7, 6-2, 6-3, 6-3

Bill Johnston (USA) d. Norman Brookes (AUS) 5-7, 7-5, 6-3, 6-3

1921

United States d. Japan 5-0 (Forest Hills) Surface—Grass

Bill Johnston (USA) d. Ichiya Kumagae (JPN) 6-2, 6-4, 6-2

Bill Tilden (USA) d. Zenzo Shimidzu (JPN) 5-7, 4-6, 7-5, 6-2, 6-1

Dick Williams-Watson Washburn (USA) d. Zenzo Shimidzu-Ichiya Kumagae (JPN) 6-2, 7-5, 4-6, 7-5

Bill Tilden (USA) d. Ichiya Kumagae (JPN) 9-7, 6-4, 6-1

Bill Johnston (USA) d. Zenzo Shimidzu (JPN) 6-3, 5-7, 6-2, 6-4

1922

United States d. Australasia 4-1 (Forest Hills) Surface—Grass

Bill Tilden (USA) d. Gerald Patterson (AUS) 7-5, 10-8, 6-0

Bill Johnston (USA) d. Jim Anderson (AUS) 6-1, 6-2, 6-3

Gerald Patterson-Pat O' Hara Wood (AUS) d. Bill Tilden-Vincent Richards (USA) 6-3, 6-0, 6-4

Bill Johnston (USA) d. Gerald Patterson (AUS) 6-2, 6-2, 6-1

Bill Tilden (USA) d. Jim Anderson (AUS) 6-4, 5-7, 3-6, 6-4, 6-2

1923

United States d. Australasia 4-1 (Forest Hills) Surface—Grass

Jim Anderson (AUS) d. Bill Johnston (USA) 4-6, 6-2, 2-6, 7-5, 6-2

Bill Tilden (USA) d. John Hawkes (AUS) 6-4, 6-2, 6-1

Bill Tilden-Dick Williams (AUS) d. Jim Anderson-John Hawkes (AUS) 17-15, 11-13, 2-6, 6-3, 6-2

Bill Johnston (USA) d. John Hawkes (AUS) 6-0, 6-2, 6-1

Bill Tilden (USA) d. Jim Anderson (AUS) 6-2, 6-3, 1-6, 7-5

1924

United States d. Australia 5-0 (Philadelphia) Surface—Grass

Bill Tilden (USA) d. Gerald Patterson (AUS) 6-4, 6-2, 6-2

Vincent Richards (USA) d. Pat O' Hara Wood (AUS) 6-3, 6-2, 6-4

Bill Tilden-Bill Johnston (USA) d. Gerald Patterson-Pat O' Hara Wood (AUS) 5-7, 6-3, 6-4, 6-1

Bill Tilden (USA) d. Pat O' Hara Wood (AUS) 6-2, 6-1, 6-1

Vincent Richards (USA) d. Gerald Patterson (AUS) 6-3, 7-5, 6-4

1925

United States d. France 5-0 (Philadelphia) Surface—Grass

Bill Tilden (USA) d. Jean Borotra (FRA) 4-6, 6-0, 2-6, 9-7, 6-4

Bill Johnston (USA) d. Rene Lacoste (FRA) 6-1, 6-1, 6-8, 6-3

Vincent Richards-Dick Williams (USA) d. Rene Lacoste-Jean Borotra (FRA) 6-4, 6-4, 6-3

Bill Tilden (USA) d. Rene Lacoste (FRA) 6-1, 6-4, 6-0

Bill Johnston (USA) d. Jean Borotra (FRA) 6-1, 6-4, 6-0

1926

United States d. France 4-1 (Philadelphia) Surface—Grass

Bill Johnston (USA) d. Rene Lacoste (FRA) 6-0, 6-4, 0-6, 6-0

Bill Tilden (USA) d. Jean Borotra (FRA) 6-2, 6-3, 6-3

Dick Williams-Vincent Richards (USA) d. Henri Cochet-Jacques Brugnon (FRA) 6-4, 6-4, 6-2

Bill Johnston (USA) d. Jean Borotra (FRA) 8-6, 6-4, 9-7

Rene Lacoste (FRA) d. Bill Tilden (USA) 4-6, 6-4, 8-6, 8-6

1927

France d. United States 3-2 (Philadelphia) Surface—Grass

Rene Lacoste (FRA) d. Bill Johnston (USA) 6-3, 6-2, 6-2

Bill Tilden (USA) d. Henri Cochet (FRA) 6-4, 2-6, 6-2, 8-6

Bill Tilden-Frank Hunter (USA) d. Jean Borotra-Jacques Brugnon (FRA) 3-6, 6-3, 6-3, 4-6, 6-0

Rene Lacoste (FRA) d. Bill Tilden (USA) 6-3, 4-6, 6-3, 6-2

Henri Cochet (FRA) d. Bill Johnston (USA) 6-4, 4-6, 6-2, 6-4

1928

France d. United States 4-1 (Paris) Surface–Clay

Bill Tilden (USA) d. Rene Lacoste (FRA) 1-6, 6-4, 6-4, 2-6, 6-3

Henri Cochet (FRA) d. John Hennessey (USA) 5-7, 9-7, 6-3, 6-0

Henri Cochet-Jean Borotra (FRA) d. Bill Tilden-Frank Hunter (USA) 6-4, 6-8, 7-5, 4-6, 6-2

Henri Cochet (FRA) d. Bill Tilden (USA) 9-7, 8-6, 6-4

Rene Lacoste (FRA) d. John Hennessey (USA) 4-6, 6-1, 7-5, 6-3

1929

France d. United States 3-2 (Paris) Surface–Clay

Jean Borotra (FRA) d. George Lott (USA) 6-1, 3-6, 6-4, 7-5

Henri Cochet (FRA) d. Bill Tilden (FRA) 6-3, 6-1, 6-2

John Van Ryn-Wilmer Allison (USA) d. Henri Cochet-Jean Borotra (FRA) 6-1, 8-6, 6-4

Bill Tilden (USA) d. Jean Borotra (FRA) 4-6, 6-1, 6-4, 7-5

Henri Cochet (FRA) d. George Lott (USA) 6-1, 3-6, 6-0, 6-3

1930

France d. United States 4-1 (Paris) Surface–Clay

Bill Tilden (USA) d. Jean Borotra (FRA) 2-6, 7-5, 6-4, 7-5

Henri Cochet (FRA) d. George Lott (USA) 6-4, 6-2, 6-2

Henri Cochet-Jacques Brugnon (FRA) d. Wilmer Allison-John Van Ryn (USA) 6-3, 7-5, 1-6, 6-2

Jean Borotra (FRA) d. George Lott (USA) 5-7, 6-3, 2-6, 6-2, 8-6

Henri Cochet (FRA) d. Bill Tilden (USA) 4-6, 6-3, 6-1, 7-5

1931

France d. Great Britain 3-2 (Paris) Surface–Clay

Henri Cochet (FRA) d. Bunny Austin (GBR) 3-6, 11-9, 6-2, 6-4

Fred Perry (GBR) d. Jean Borotra (FRA) 4-6, 10-8, 6-0, 4-6, 6-4

Henri Cochet-Jacques Brugnon (FRA) d. Pat Hughes-Charles Kingsley (GBR) 6-1, 5-7, 6-3, 8-6

Bunny Austin (GBR) d. Jean Borotra (FRA) 7-5, 6-3, 3-6, 7-5

Henri Cochet (FRA) d. Fred Perry (GBR) 6-4, 1-6, 9-7, 6-3

1932

France d. United States 3-2 (Paris) Surface–Clay

Jean Borotra (FRA) d. Elisworth Vines (USA) 6-4, 6-2, 3-6, 6-4

Henri Cochet (FRA) d. Wilmer Allison (USA) 5-7, 7-5, 7-5, 6-2

Wilmer Allison-John Van Ryn (USA) d. Henri Cochet-Jacques Brugnon (FRA) 6-3, 11-13, 7-5, 4-6, 6-4

Jean Borotra (FRA) d. Wilmer Allison (USA) 1-6, 3-6, 6-4, 6-2, 7-5

Elisworth Vines (USA) d. Henri Cochet (FRA) 4-6, 0-6, 7-5, 8-6, 6-2

1933

Great Britain d. France 3-2 (Paris) Surface–Clay

Bunny Austin (GBR) d. Andre Merlin (FRA) 6-3, 6-4, 6-0

Fred Perry (GBR) d. Henri Cochet (FRA) 8-10, 6-4, 8-6, 3-6, 6-1

Jean Borotra-Jacques Brugnon (FRA) d. Pat Hughes-Harold Lee (GBR) 6-3, 8-6, 6-2

Henri Cochet (FRA) d. Bunny Austin (GBR) 5-7, 6-4, 4-6, 6-4, 6-4

Fred Perry (GBR) d. Andre Merlin (FRA) 4-6, 8-6, 6-2, 7-5

1934

Great Britain d. United States 4-1 (Wimbledon) Surface–Grass

Bunny Austin (GBR) d. Frank Shields (USA) 6-4, 6-4, 6-1

Fred Perry (GBR) d. Sidney Wood (USA) 6-1, 4-6, 5-7, 6-0, 6-3

George Lott-Lester Stoefen (USA) d. Pat Hughes-Harold Lee (GBR) 7-5, 6-0, 4-6, 9-7

Fred Perry (GBR) d. Frank Shields (USA) 6-4, 4-6, 6-2, 15-13

Bunny Austin (GBR) d. Sidney Wood (USA) 6-4, 6-0, 6-8, 6-3

1935

Great Britain d. United States 5-0 (Wimbledon) Surface–Grass

Bunny Austin (GBR) d. Wilmer Allison (USA) 6-2, 2-6, 4-6, 6-3, 7-5

Fred Perry (GBR) d. Don Budge (USA) 6-0, 6-8, 6-3, 6-4

Pat Hughes-Charles Tuckey (GBR) d. Wilmer Allison-John Van Ryn (USA) 6-2, 1-6, 6-8, 6-3, 6-3

Bunny Austin (GBR) d. Don Budge (USA) 6-2, 6-4, 6-8, 7-5

Fred Perry (GBR) d. Wilmer Allison (USA) 4-6, 6-4, 7-5, 6-3

1936

Great Britain d. Australia 3-2 (Wimbledon) Surface–Grass

Bunny Austin (GBR) d. Jack Crawford (USA) 4-6, 6-3, 6-1, 6-1

Fred Perry (GBR) d. Adrian Quist (AUS) 6-1, 4-6, 7-5, 6-2

Jack Crawford-Adrian Quist (AUS) d. Pat Hughes-Charles Tuckey (GBR) 6-4, 2-6, 7-5, 10-8

Adrian Quist (AUS) d. Bunny Austin (GBR) 6-4, 3-6, 7-5, 6-2

Fred Perry (GBR) d. Jack Crawford (AUS) 6-2, 6-2, 6-3

1937

United States d. Great Britain 4-1 (Wimbledon) Surface–Grass

Bunny Austin (GBR) d. Frank Parker (USA) 6-3, 6-2, 7-5

Don Budge (USA) d. Charlie Hare (GBR) 15-13, 6-1, 6-2

Don Budge-Gene Mako (USA) d. Charles Tuckey-Frank Wilde (GBR) 6-3, 7-5, 7-9, 12-10

Frank Parker (USA) d. Charlie Hare (GBR) 6-2, 6-4, 6-2

Don Budge (USA) d. Bunny Austin (GBR) 8-6, 3-6, 6-4, 6-3

1938

United States d. Australia 3-2 (Philadelphia) Surface–Grass

Bobby Riggs (USA) d. Adrian Quist (AUS) 4-6, 6-0, 8-6, 6-1

Don Budge (USA) d. John Bromwich (AUS) 6-2, 6-3, 4-6, 7-5

Adrian Quist-John Bromwich (AUS) d. Don Budge-Gene Mako (USA) 0-6, 6-3, 6-4, 6-2

Don Budge (USA) d. Adrian Quist (AUS) 8-6, 6-1, 6-2

John Bromwich (AUS) d. Bobby Riggs (USA) 6-4, 4-6, 6-0, 6-2

1939

Australia d. United States 3-2 (Haverford, Pa.) Surface–Grass

Bobby Riggs (USA) d. John Bromwich (AUS) 6-4, 6-0, 7-5

Frank Parker (USA) d. Adrian Quist (AUS) 6-3, 2-6, 6-4, 1-6, 7-5

Adrian Quist-John Bromwich (AUS) d. Jack Kramer-Joe Hunt (USA) 5-7, 6-2, 7-5, 6-2

Adrian Quist (AUS) d. Bobby Riggs (USA) 6-1, 6-4, 3-6, 3-6, 6-4

John Bromwich (AUS) d. Frank Parker (USA) 6-0, 6-3, 6-1

1940-45 Not held, World War II

1946

United States d. Australia 5-0 (Melbourne) Surface–Grass

Ted Schroeder (USA) d. John Bromwich (AUS) 3-6, 6-1, 6-2, 0-6, 6-3

Jack Kramer (USA) d. Dinny Pails (AUS) 8-6, 6-2, 9-7

Jack Kramer-Ted Schroeder (USA) d. John Bromwich-Adrian Quist (AUS) 6-2, 7-5, 6-4

Gardnar Mulloy (USA) d. Dinny Pails (AUS) 6-3, 6-3, 6-4

Jack Kramer (USA) d. John Bromwich (AUS) 8-6, 6-4, 6-4

1947

United States d. Australia 4-1 (Forest Hills) Surface–Grass

Jack Kramer (USA) d. Dinny Pails (AUS) 6-2, 6-1, 6-2

Ted Schroeder (USA) d. John Bromwich (AUS) 6-4, 5-7, 6-3, 6-4

John Bromwich-Colin Long (AUS) d. Jack Kramer-Ted Schroeder (USA)
6-4, 2-6, 6-2, 6-4

Ted Schroeder (USA) d. Dinny Pails (AUS) 6-3, 8-6, 4-6, 9-11, 10-8

Jack Kramer (USA) d. John Bromwich (AUS) 6-3, 6-2, 6-2

1948

United States d. Australia 5-0 (Forest Hills) Surface–Grass

Frank Parker (USA) d. Bill Sidwell (AUS) 6-4, 6-4, 6-4

Ted Schroeder (USA) d. Adrian Quist (AUS) 6-3, 4-6, 6-0, 6-0

Bill Talbert-Gardnar Mulloy (USA) d. Bill Sidwell-Colin Long (AUS) 8-6, 9-7, 2-6, 7-5

Ted Schroeder (USA) d. Bill Sidwell (AUS) 6-2, 6-1, 6-1

Frank Parker (USA) d. Adrian Quist (AUS) 6-2, 6-2, 6-3

1949

United States d. Australia 4-1 (Forest Hills) Surface–Grass

Ted Schroeder (USA) d. Bill Sidwell (AUS) 6-1, 5-7, 4-6, 6-2, 6-3

Pancho Gonzalez (USA) d. Frank Sedgman (AUS) 8-6, 6-4, 9-7

Bill Sidwell-John Bromwich (AUS) d. Bill Talbert-Gardnar Mulloy (USA)
3-6, 4-6, 10-8, 9-7, 9-7

Ted Schroeder (USA) d. Frank Sedgman (AUS) 6-4, 6-3, 6-3

Pancho Gonzalez (USA) d. Bill Sidwell (AUS) 6-1, 6-3, 6-3

1950

Australia d. United States 4-1 (Forest Hills) Surface–Grass

Frank Sedgman (AUS) d. Tom Brown (USA) 6-0, 8-6, 9-7

Ken McGregor (AUS) d. Ted Schroeder (USA) 13-11, 6-3, 6-4

Frank Sedgman-John Bromwich (AUS) d. Ted Schroeder-Gardnar Mulloy (USA)
4-6, 6-4, 6-2, 4-6, 6-4

Frank Sedgman (AUS) d. Ted Schroeder (USA) 6-2, 6-2, 6-2

Tom Brown (USA) d. Ken McGregor (AUS) 9-11, 8-10, 11-9, 6-1, 6-4

1951

Australia d. United States 3-2 (Sydney) Surface–Grass

Vic Seixas (USA) d. Mervyn Rose (AUS) 6-3, 6-4, 9-7

Frank Sedgman (AUS) d. Ted Schroeder (USA) 6-4, 6-3, 4-6, 6-4

Ken McGregor-Frank Sedgman (AUS) d. Ted Schroeder-Tony Trabert (USA)
6-2, 9-7, 6-3

Ted Schroeder (USA) d. Mervyn Rose (AUS) 6-4, 13-11, 7-5

Frank Sedgman (AUS) d. Vic Seixas (USA) 6-4, 6-2, 6-2

1952

Australia d. United States 4-1 (Adelaide) Surface–Grass

Frank Sedgman (AUS) d. Vic Seixas (USA) 6-3, 6-4, 6-3

Ken McGregor (AUS) d. Tony Trabert (USA) 11-9, 6-4, 6-1

Ken McGregor-Frank Sedgman (AUS) d. Vic Seixas-Tony Trabert (USA)
6-3, 6-4, 1-6, 6-3

Frank Sedgman (AUS) d. Tony Trabert (USA) 7-5, 6-4, 10-8

Vic Seixas (USA) d. Ken McGregor (AUS) 6-3, 8-6, 6-8, 6-3

1953

Australia d. United States 3-2 (Melbourne) Surface–Grass

Lew Hoad (AUS) d. Vic Seixas (USA) 6-4, 6-2, 6-3

Tony Trabert (USA) d. Ken Rosewall (AUS) 6-3, 6-4, 6-4

Vic Seixas-Tony Trabert (USA) d. Rex Hartwig-Lew Hoad (AUS) 6-2, 6-4, 6-4

Lew Hoad (AUS) d. Tony Trabert (USA) 13-11, 6-3, 2-6, 3-6, 7-5

Ken Rosewall (AUS) d. Vic Seixas (USA) 6-2, 2-6, 6-3, 6-4

1954

United States d. Australia 3-2 (Sydney) Surface–Grass

Tony Trabert (USA) d. Lew Hoad (AUS) 6-4, 2-6, 12-10, 6-3

Vic Seixas (USA) d. Ken Rosewall (AUS) 8-6, 6-8, 6-4, 6-3

Vic Seixas-Tony Trabert (USA) d. Lew Hoad-Ken Rosewall (AUS) 6-2, 4-6, 6-2, 10-8

Ken Rosewall (AUS) d. Tony Trabert (USA) 9-7, 7-5, 6-3

Rex Hartwig (AUS) d. Vic Seixas (USA) 4-6, 6-3, 6-2, 6-3

1955

Australia d. United States 5-0 (Forest Hills) Surface–Grass

Ken Rosewall (AUS) d. Vic Seixas (USA) 6-3, 10-8, 4-6, 6-2

Lew Hoad (AUS) d. Tony Trabert (USA) 4-6, 6-3, 6-3, 8-6

Lew Hoad-Rex Hartwig (AUS) d. Tony Trabert-Vic Seixas (USA) 12-14, 6-4, 6-3, 3-6, 7-5

Lew Hoad (AUS) d. Vic Seixas (USA) 7-9, 6-1, 6-4, 6-4

Ken Rosewall (AUS) d. Ham Richardson (USA) 6-4, 3-6, 6-1, 6-4

1956

Australia d. United States 5-0 (Adelaide) Surface–Grass

Lew Hoad (AUS) d. Herbie Flam (USA) 6-2, 6-3, 6-3

Ken Rosewall (AUS) d. Vic Seixas (USA) 6-1, 6-4, 4-6, 6-1

Lew Hoad-Ken Rosewall (AUS) d. Sammy Giammalva-Vic Seixas (USA) 1-6, 6-1, 7-5, 6-4

Ken Rosewall (AUS) d. Sammy Giammalva (USA) 4-6, 6-1, 8-6, 7-5

Lew Hoad (AUS) d. Vic Seixas (USA) 6-2, 7-5, 6-3

1957

Australia d. United States 3-2 (Melbourne) Surface–Grass

Mal Anderson (AUS) d. Barry MacKay (USA) 6-3, 7-5, 3-6, 7-9, 6-3

Ashley Cooper (AUS) d. Vic Seixas (USA) 3-6, 7-5, 6-1, 1-6, 6-3

Mal Anderson-Mervyn Rose (USA) d. Barry MacKay-Vic Seixas (USA) 6-4, 6-4, 8-6

Vic Seixas (USA) d. Mal Anderson (AUS) 6-3, 4-6, 6-3, 0-6, 13-11

Barry MacKay (USA) d. Ashley Cooper (AUS) 6-4, 1-6, 4-6, 6-4, 6-3

1958

Australia d. United States 3-2 (Brisbane) Surface–Grass

Alex Olmedo (USA) d. Mal Anderson (AUS) 8-6, 2-6, 9-7, 8-6

Ashley Cooper (AUS) d. Barry MacKay (USA) 4-6, 6-3, 6-2, 6-4

Alex Olmedo-Ham Richardson (USA) d. Mal Anderson-Neale Fraser (AUS) 10-12, 3-6, 16-14, 6-3, 7-5

Alex Olmedo (USA) d. Ashley Cooper (AUS) 6-3, 4-6, 6-4, 8-6

Mal Anderson (AUS) d. Barry MacKay (USA) 7-5, 13-11, 11-9

1959

Australia d. United States 3-2 (Forest Hills) Surface–Grass

Neale Fraser (AUS) d. Alex Olmedo (USA) 8-6, 6-8, 6-4, 8-6

Barry MacKay (USA) d. Rod Laver (AUS) 7-5, 6-4, 6-1

Neale Fraser-Roy Emerson (AUS) d. Alex Olmedo-Butch Buchholz (USA) 7-5, 7-5, 6-4

Alex Olmedo (USA) d. Rod Laver (AUS) 9-7, 4-6, 10-8, 12-10

Neale Fraser (AUS) d. Barry MacKay (USA) 8-6, 3-6, 6-2, 6-4

1960

Australia d. Italy 4-1 (Sydney) Surface–Grass

Neale Fraser (AUS) d. Orlando Sirola (ITA) 4-6, 6-3, 6-3, 6-3

Rod Laver (AUS) d. Nicola Pietrangeli (ITA) 8-6, 6-4, 6-3

Neale Fraser-Roy Emerson (AUS) d. Nicola Pietrangeli-Orlando Sirola (ITA) 10-8, 5-7, 6-2, 6-4

Rod Laver (AUS) d. Orlando Sirola (ITA) 9-7, 6-2, 6-3

Nicola Pietrangeli (ITA) d. Neale Fraser (AUS) 11-9, 6-3, 1-6, 6-2

1961

Australia d. Italy 5-0 (Melbourne) Surface–Grass

Roy Emerson (AUS) d. Nicola Pietrangeli (ITA) 8-6, 6-4, 6-0

Rod Laver (AUS) d. Orlando Sirola (ITA) 6-1, 6-4, 6-3

Neale Fraser-Roy Emerson (AUS) d. Nicola Pietrangeli-Orlando Sirola (ITA) 6-2, 6-3, 6-4

Rod Laver (AUS) d. Nicola Pietrangeli (ITA) 6-3, 3-6, 4-6, 6-3, 8-6

Roy Emerson (AUS) d. Orlando Sirola (ITA) 6-3, 6-3, 4-6, 6-2

1962

Australia d. Mexico 5-0 (Brisbane) Surface–Grass

Rod Laver (AUS) d. Rafael Osuna (MEX) 6-2, 6-1, 7-5

Neale Fraser (AUS) d. Tony Palafox (MEX) 7-9, 6-3, 6-4, 11-9

Roy Emerson-Rod Laver (AUS) d. Rafael Osuna-Tony Palafox (MEX) 7-5, 6-2, 6-4

Neale Fraser (AUS) d. Rafael Osuna (MEX) 3-6, 11-9, 6-1, 3-6, 6-4

Rod Laver (AUS) d. Tony Palafox (MEX) 6-1, 4-6, 6-4, 8-6

1963

United States d. Australia 3-2 (Adelaide) Surface–Grass

Dennis Ralston (USA) d. John Newcombe (AUS) 6-4, 6-1, 3-6, 4-6, 7-5

Roy Emerson (AUS) d. Chuck McKinley (USA) 6-3, 3-6, 7-5, 7-5

Chuck McKinley-Dennis Ralston (USA) d. Roy Emerson-Neale Fraser (AUS) 6-3, 4-6, 11-9, 11-9

Roy Emerson (AUS) d. Dennis Ralston (USA) 6-2, 6-3, 3-6, 6-2

Chuck McKinley (USA) d. John Newcombe (AUS) 10-12, 6-2, 9-7, 6-2

1964

Australia d. United States 3-2 (Cleveland) Surface–Clay

Chuck McKinley (USA) d. Fred Stolle (AUS) 6-1, 9-7, 4-6, 6-2

Roy Emerson (AUS) d. Dennis Ralston (USA) 6-3, 6-1, 6-2

Chuck McKinley-Dennis Ralston (USA) d. Roy Emerson-Fred Stolle (AUS) 6-4, 4-6, 4-6, 6-3, 6-4

Fred Stolle (AUS) d. Dennis Ralston (USA) 7-5, 6-3, 3-6, 9-11, 6-4

Roy Emerson (AUS) d. Chuck McKinley (USA) 3-6, 6-2, 6-4, 6-4

1965

Australia d. Spain 4-1 (Sydney) Surface–Grass

Fred Stolle (AUS) d. Manuel Santana (ESP) 10-12, 3-6, 6-1, 6-4, 7-5

Roy Emerson (AUS) d. Juan Gisbert (ESP) 6-3, 6-2, 6-2

John Newcombe-Tony Roche (AUS) d. Jose Luis Arilla-Manuel Santana (ESP) 6-4, 4-6, 7-5, 6-2

Manuel Santana (ESP) d. Roy Emerson (AUS) 2-6, 6-3, 6-4, 15-13

Fred Stolle (AUS) d. Juan Gisbert (ESP) 6-2, 6-4, 8-6

1966

Australia d. India 4-1 (Melbourne) Surface–Grass

Fred Stolle (AUS) d. Ramanathan Krishnan (IND) 6-3, 6-2, 6-4

Roy Emerson (AUS) d. Jaidip Mukerjea (IND) 7-5, 6-4, 6-2

Ramanathan Krishnan-Jaidip Mukerjea (IND) d. John Newcombe-Tony Roche (AUS) 4-6, 7-5, 6-4, 6-4

Roy Emerson (AUS) d. Ramanathan Krishnan (IND) 6-0, 6-2, 10-8

Fred Stolle (AUS) d. Jaidip Mukerjea (IND) 7-5, 6-8, 6-3, 5-7, 6-3

1967

Australia d. Spain 4-1 (Brisbane) Surface–Grass

Roy Emerson (AUS) d. Manuel Santana (ESP) 6-4, 6-1, 6-1

John Newcombe (AUS) d. Manuel Orantes (ESP) 6-3, 6-3, 6-2

John Newcombe-Tony Roche (AUS) d. Manuel Santana-Manuel Orantes (ESP) 6-4, 6-4, 6-4

Manuel Santana (ESP) d. John Newcombe (AUS) 7-5, 6-4, 6-2

Roy Emerson (AUS) d. Manuel Orantes (ESP) 6-1, 6-1, 2-6, 6-4

1968

United States d. Australia 4-1 (Adelaide) Surface–Grass

Clark Graebner (USA) d. Bill Bowrey (AUS) 8-10, 6-4, 8-6, 3-6, 6-1

Arthur Ashe (USA) d. Ray Ruffels (AUS) 6-8, 7-5, 6-3, 6-3

Bob Lutz-Stan Smith (USA) d. John Alexander-Ray Ruffels (AUS) 6-4, 6-4, 6-2

Clark Graebner (USA) d. Ray Ruffels (AUS) 3-6, 8-6, 2-6, 6-3, 6-1

Bill Bowrey (AUS) d. Arthur Ashe (USA) 2-6, 6-3, 11-9, 8-6

1969

United States d. Romania 5-0 (Cleveland) Surface–Hard

Arthur Ashe (USA) d. Ilie Nastase (ROM) 6-2, 15-13, 7-5

Stan Smith (USA) d. Ion Tiriac (ROM) 6-8, 6-3, 5-7, 6-4, 6-4

Bob-Lutz-Stan Smith (USA) d. Ilie Nastase-Ion Tiriac (ROM) 8-6, 6-1, 11-9

Stan Smith (USA) d. Ilie Nastase (ROM) 4-6, 4-6, 6-4, 6-1, 11-9

Arthur Ashe (USA) d. Ion Tiriac (ROM) 6-3, 8-6, 3-6, 4-0 (default)

1970

United States d. West Germany 5-0 (Cleveland) Surface–Hard

Arthur Ashe (USA) d. Wilhelm Bungert (GER) 6-2, 10-8, 6-2

Cliff Richey (USA) d. Christian Kuhnke (GER) 6-3, 6-4, 6-2

Bob-Lutz-Stan Smith (USA) d. Christian Kuhnke-Wilhelm Bungert (GER) 6-3, 7-5, 6-4

Cliff Richey (USA) d. Wilhelm Bungert (GER) 6-4, 6-4, 7-5

Arthur Ashe (USA) d. Christian Kuhnke (GER) 6-8, 10-12, 9-7, 13-11, 6-4

1971

United States d. Romania 3-2 (Charlotte, N.C) Surface–Clay

Stan Smith (USA) d. Ilie Nastase (ROM) 7-5, 6-3-, 6-1

Frank Froehling (USA) d. Ion Tiriac (ROM) 3-6, 1-6, 6-1, 6-3, 8-6

Ilie Nastase-Ion Tiriac (ROM) d. Stan Smith-Erik Van Dillen (USA) 7-5, 6-4, 8-6

Stan Smith (USA) d. Ion Tiriac (ROM) 8-6, 6-3, 6-0

Ilie Nastase (ROM) d. Frank Froehling (USA) 6-3, 6-1, 4-6, 6-4

Final Rounds

1972

United States d. Romania 3-2 (Bucharest) Surface–Clay

Stan Smith (USA) d. Ilie Nastase (ROM) 11-9, 6-2, 6-3

Ion Tiriac (ROM) d. Tom Gorman (USA) 4-6, 2-6, 6-4, 6-3, 6-2

Stan Smith-Erik van Dillen (USA) d. Ilie Nastase-Ion Tiriac (ROM) 6-2, 6-0, 6-3

Stan Smith (USA) d. Ion Tiriac (ROM) 4-6, 6-2, 6-4, 2-6, 6-0

Ilie Nastase (ROM) d. Tom Gorman (USA) 6-1, 6-2, 5-7, 10-8

1973 (First Davis Cup open to all pros and amateurs)
Australia d. United States 5-0 (Cleveland) Surface–Indoor Carpet

John Newcombe (AUS) d. Stan Smith (USA) 6-1, 3-6, 6-3, 3-6, 6-4

Rod Laver (AUS) d. Tom Gorman (USA) 8-10, 8-6, 6-8, 6-3, 6-1

John Newcombe-Rod Laver (AUS) d. Erik van Dillen-Stan Smith (USA) 6-1, 6-2, 6-4

John Newcombe (AUS) d. Tom Gorman (USA) 6-2, 6-1, 6-3

Rod Laver (AUS) d. Stan Smith (USA) 6-3, 6-4, 3-6, 6-2

1974

South Africa d. India (default- Indian government ordered team not to play, a protest against the South African government's policy of apartheid. The South African team was Bob Hewitt, Frew McMillan, Ray Moore and Rob Maud. The Indian team was Vijay Amritraj, Anand Amritraj, Jasjit Singh and Sashi Menon.)

1975

Sweden d. Czechoslovakia 3-2 (Stockholm) Surface–Indoor Carpet

Bjorn Borg (SWE) d. Jiri Hrebec (CZE) 6-1, 6-3, 6-0

Jan Kodes (CZE) d. Ove Bengtson (SWE) 4-6, 6-2, 7-5, 6-4

Bjorn Borg-Ove Bengtson (SWE) d. Jan Kodes-Vladimir Zednik (CZE) 6-4, 6-4, 6-4

Bjorn Borg (SWE) d. Jan Kodes (CZE) 6-4, 6-2, 6-2

Jim Hrebec (CZE) d. Ove Bengston (SWE) 1-6, 6-3, 6-1, 6-4

1976

Italy d. Chile 4-1 (Santiago) Surface–Clay

Corrado Barazzutti (ITA) d. Jaime Fillol (CHI) 7-5, 4-6, 7-5, 6-1

Adriano Panatta (ITA) d. Patricio Cornejo (CHI) 6-3, 6-1, 6-3

Adriano Panatta- Paolo Bertolucci (ITA) d. Patricio Cornejo-Jaime Fillol (CHI) 3-6, 6-2, 9-7, 6-3

Adriano Panatta (ITA) d. Jaime Fillol (CHI) 8-6, 6-4, 3-6, 10-8

Belus Prajoux (CHI) d. Antonio Zugarelli (ITA) 6-4, 6-4, 6-2

1977

Australia d. Italy 3-1 (Sydney) Surface–Grass

Tony Roche (AUS) d. Adriano Panatta (ITA) 6-3, 6-4, 6-4

John Alexander (AUS) d. Corrado Barazzutti (ITA) 6-4, 8-6, 4-6, 6-2

Adriano Panatta- Paolo Bertolucci (ITA) d. John Alexander-Phil Dent (AUS) 6-4, 6-4, 7-5

John Alexander (AUS) d. Adriano Panatta (ITA) 6-4, 4-6, 2-6, 8-6, 11-9

Tony Roche (AUS) d. Corrado Barazzutti (ITA) 12-12 (unfinished)

1978

United States d. Great Britain 4-1 (Rancho Mirage, Cal) Surface–Hard

John McEnroe (USA) d. John Lloyd (GBR) 6-1, 6-2, 6-2

Buster Mottram (GBR) d. Brian Gottfried (USA) 4-6, 2-6, 10-8, 6-4, 6-3

Stan Smith-Bob Lutz (USA) d. David Lloyd-Mark Cox (GBR) 6-2, 6-2, 6-3

John McEnroe (USA) d. Buster Mottram (GBR) 6-2, 6-2, 6-1

Brian Gottfried (USA) d. John Lloyd (GBR) 6-1, 6-2, 6-4

1979

United States d. Italy 5-0 (San Francisco) Surface–Indoor Carpet

Vitas Gerulaitis (USA) d. Corrado Barazzutti (ITA) 6-3, 3-2 (default, injury)

John McEnroe (USA) d. Adriano Panatta (ITA) 6-2, 6-3, 6-4

Stan Smith-Bob Lutz (USA) d. Paolo Bertolucci-Adriano Panatta (ITA) 6-4, 12-10, 6-2

John McEnroe (USA) d. Antonio Zugarelli (ITA) 6-4, 6-3, 6-1

Vitas Gerulaitis (USA) d. Adriano Panatta (ITA) 6-1, 6-3, 6-3

1980

Czechoslovakia d. Italy 4-1 (Prague) Surface–Indoor Carpet

Tomas Smid (CZE) d. Adriano Panatta (ITA) 3-6, 3-6, 6-3, 6-4, 6-4

Ivan Lendl (CZE) d. Corrado Barazzutti (ITA) 4-6, 6-1, 6-1, 6-2

Ivan Lendl-Tomas Smid (CZE) d. Paolo Bertolucci-Adriano Panatta (ITA) 3-6, 6-3, 3-6, 6-3, 6-4

Corrado Barazzutti (ITA) d. Tomas Smid (CZE) 3-6, 6-3, 6-2

Ivan Lendl (CZE) d. Gianni Ocleppo (ITA) 6-3, 6-3

World Group: Final Round

1981

United States d. Argentina 3-1 (Cincinnati) Surface–Indoor Carpet

John McEnroe (USA) d. Guillermo Vilas (ARG) 6-3, 6-2, 6-2

Jose-Luis Clerc (ARG) d. Roscoe Tanner (USA) 7-5, 6-3, 8-6

Peter Fleming-John McEnroe (USA) d. Jose-Luis Clerc-Guillermo Vilas (ARG) 6-3, 4-6, 6-4, 4-6, 11-9

John McEnroe (USA) d. Jose-Luis Clerc (ARG) 7-5, 5-7, 6-3, 3-6, 6-3

Roscoe Tanner (USA) led Guillermo Vilas (ARG) (suspended at 11-10, first set)

SF: United States 5, Australia 0

SF: Argentina 5, Great Britain 0

QF: Argentina 3, Romania 2

QF: Great Britain 4, New Zealand 1

QF: Australia 3, Sweden 1

QF: United States 4, Czechoslovakia 1

1982

United States d. France 4-1 (Grenoble) Surface–Indoor Clay

John McEnroe (USA) d. Yannick Noah (FRA) 12-10, 1-6, 3-6, 6-2, 6-3

Gene Mayer (USA) d. Henri Leconte (FRA) 6-2, 6-2, 7-9, 6-4

Peter Fleming-John McEnroe (USA) d. Henri Leconte-Yannick Noah (FRA) 6-3, 6-4, 9-7

Yannick Noah (FRA) d. Gene Mayer (USA) 6-1, 6-0

John McEnroe (USA) d. Henri Leconte (FRA) 6-2, 6-3

SF: United States 5, Australia 0

SF: France 3, New Zealand 2

QF: United States 3, Sweden 2

QF: Australia 4, Chile 1

QF: New Zealand 3, Italy 2

QF: France 3, Czechoslovakia 2

1983

Australia d. Sweden 3-2 (Melbourne) Surface–Grass

Mats Wilander (SWE) d. Pat Cash (AUS) 6-3, 4-6, 9-7, 6-3

John Fitzgerald (AUS) d. Joakim Nystrom (SWE) 6-4, 6-2, 4-6, 6-4

Mark Edmondson-Paul McNamee (AUS) d. Anders Jarryd-Hans Simonsson (SWE) 6-4, 6-4, 6-2

Pat Cash (AUS) d. Joakim Nystrom (AUS) 6-4, 6-1, 6-1

Mats Wilander (AUS) d. John Fitzgerald (AUS) 6-8, 6-0, 6-1

SF: Australia 4, France 1

SF: Sweden 4, Argentina 1

QF: France 3, Paraguay 2

QF: Sweden 3, New Zealand 2

QF: Argentina 5, Italy 0

1984

Sweden d. United States 4-1 (Goteborg, Sweden) Surface–Indoor Clay

Mats Wilander (SWE) d. Jimmy Connors (USA) 6-1, 6-3, 6-3

Henrik Sundstrom (SWE) d. John McEnroe (USA) 13-11, 6-4, 6-3

Stefan Edberg-Anders Jarryd (SWE) d. Peter Fleming-John McEnroe (USA) 7-5, 5-7, 6-2, 7-5

John McEnroe (USA) d. Mats Wilander (SWE) 6-3, 5-7, 6-3

Henrik Sundstrom (SWE) d. Jimmy Arias (USA) 3-6, 8-6, 6-3

SF: United States 4, Australia 1

SF: Sweden 5, Czechoslovakia 0

QF: Australia 5, Italy 0

QF: United States 5, Argentina 0

QF: Czechoslovakia 3, France 2

QF: Sweden 4, Paraguay 1

1985

Sweden d. West Germany 3-2 (Munich) Surface–Indoor Carpet

Mats Wilander (SWE) d. Michael Westphal (GER) 6-3, 6-4, 10-8

Boris Becker (GER) d. Stefan Edberg (SWE) 6-3, 3-6, 7-5. 8-6

Joakim Nystrom-Mats Wilander (SWE) d. Boris Becker-Andreas Maurer (GER) 6-4, 6-2, 6-1

Boris Becker (GER) d. Mats Wilander (SWE) 6-3, 2-6, 6-3, 6-3

Stefan Edberg (SWE) d. Michael Westphal (GER) 3-6, 7-5, 6-4, 6-3

SF: Germany F.R. 5, Czechoslovakia 0

SF: Sweden 5, Australia 0

QF: Germany F.R 3 United States 2

QF: Czechoslovakia 5, Ecuador 0

QF: Australia 3, Paraguay 2

QF: Sweden 4, India 1

1986

Australia d. Sweden 3-2 (Melbourne) Surface–Grass

Pat Cash (AUS) d. Stefan Edberg (SWE) 13-11, 13-11, 6-4

Mikael Pernfors (SWE) d. Paul McNamee (AUS) 6-3, 6-1, 6-3

Pat Cash-John Fitzgerald (AUS) d. Stefan Edberg-Anders Jarryd (SWE) 6-3, 6-4, 4-6, 6-1

Pat Cash (AUS) d. Mikael Pernfors (SWE) 2-6, 4-6, 6-3, 6-4, 6-3

Stefan Edberg (SWE) d. Paul McNamee (AUS) 10-8, 6-4

SF: Australia 3, United States 1

SF: Sweden 4, Czechoslovakia 1

QF: United States 4, Mexico 1

QF: Australia 4, Great Britain 1

QF: Czechoslovakia 5, Yugoslavia 0

QF: Sweden 5, Italy 0

1987

Sweden d. India 5-0 (Goteborg, Sweden) Surface–Indoor Clay

Mats Wilander (SWE) d. Ramesh Krishnan (IND) 6-4, 6-1, 6-3

Anders Jarryd (SWE) d. Vijay Amritraj (IND) 6-3, 6-3, 6-1

Joakim Nystrom-Mats Wilander (SWE) d. Anand Amritraj-Vijay Amritraj (IND) 6-3, 3-6, 6-1, 6-2

Anders Jarryd (SWE) d. Ramesh Krishnan (IND) 6-4, 6-3

Mats Wilander (SWE) d. Vijay Amritraj (IND) 6-2, 6-0

SF: Sweden 3, Spain 2

SF: India 3, Australia 2

QF: Sweden 4, France 1

QF: Spain 3, Paraguay 2

QF: India 4, Israel 0

QF: Australia 4, Mexico 1

1988

West Germany d. Sweden 4-1 (Goteborg, Sweden) Surface–Indoor Clay

Carl-Uwe Steeb (GER) d. Mats Wilander (SWE) 8-10, 1-6, 6-2, 6-4, 8-6

Boris Becker (GER) d. Stefan Edberg (SWE) 6-3, 6-1, 6-4

Boris Becker-Eric Jelen (GER) d. Stefan Edberg-Anders Jarryd (SWE) 3-6, 2-6, 7-5, 6-3, 6-2

Stefan Edberg (SWE) d. Carl-Uwe Steeb (GER) 6-4, 8-6

Patrick Kuhnen (GER) d. Kent Carlsson (SWE) (walkover)

SF: Sweden 4, France 1

SF: Germany F.R. 5, Yugoslavia 0

QF: Sweden 3, Czechoslovakia 2

QF: France 5, Australia 0

QF: Germany F.R 5, Denmark 0

QF: Yugoslavia 5, Italy 0

1989 (* First use of tie-breaker in Davis Cup)

West Germany d Sweden 3-2 (Stuttgart, Germany) Surface–Indoor Carpet

Mats Wilander (SWE) d. Carl-Uwe Steeb (GER) 5-7, 7-6 (7-0), 6-7 (4-7), 6-2, 6-3

Boris Becker (GER) d. Stefan Edberg (SWE) 6-2, 6-2, 6-4

Boris Becker-Eric Jelen (GER) d. Jan Gunnarson-Anders Jarryd (SWE) 7-6 (8-6), 6-4, 3-6, 6-7 (4-7), 6-4

Boris Becker (GER) d. Mats Wilander (SWE) 6-2, 6-0, 6-2

Stefan Edberg (SWE) d. Carl-Uwe Steeb (GER) 6-2, 6-4

SF: Sweden 4, Yugoslavia 1

SF: Germany F.R. 3, United States 2

QF: Sweden 3, Austria 2

QF: Yugoslavia 4, Spain 1

QF: United States 5, France 0

QF: Germany F.R 3, Czechoslovakia 2

1990

United States d. Australia 3-2 (St, Petersburg, Fla.) Surface–Indoor Clay

Andre Agassi (USA) d. Richard Fromberg (AUS) 4-6, 6-2, 4-6, 6-2, 6-4

Michael Chang (USA) d. Darren Cahill (AUS) 6-2, 7-6 (7-4), 6-0

Rick Leach-Jim Pugh (USA) d. Pat Cash-John Fitzgerald (AUS) 6-4, 6-2, 3-6, 7-6 (7-2)

Darren Cahill (AUS) d. Andre Agassi (USA) 6-4, 4-6 (retired)

Richard Fromberg (AUS) d. Michael Chang (USA) 7-5, 2-6, 6-3

SF: Australia 5, Argentina 0

SF: United States 3, Austria 2

QF: Argentina 3, Germany 2

QF: Australia 3, New Zealand 2

QF: United States 4, Czechoslovakia 1

QF: Austria 5, Italy 0

1991

France d. United States 3-1 (Lyon) Surface–Indoor Carpet

Andre Agassi (USA) d. Guy Forget (FRA) 6-7 (7-9), 6-2, 6-1, 6-2

Henri Leconte (FRA) d. Pete Sampras (USA) 6-4, 7-5, 6-4

Guy Forget-Henri Leconte (FRA) d. Ken Flach-Robert Seguso (USA) 6-1, 6-4, 4-6, 6-2

Guy Forget (FRA) d. Pete Sampras (USA) 7-6 (8-6), 3-6, 6-3, 6-4

Henri Leconte v Andre Agassi (not played)

SF: United States 3, Germany 2

SF: France 5, Yugoslavia 0

QF: United States 4, Spain 1

QF: Germany 5, Argentina 0

QF: Yugoslavia 4, Czechoslovakia 1

QF: France 3, Australia 2

1992

United States d. Switzerland 3-1 (Fort Worth, Tex.) Surface–Indoor Hard

Andre Agassi (USA) d. Jakob Hlasek (SUI) 6-1, 6-2, 6-2

Marc Rosset (SUI) d. Jim Courier (USA) 6-3, 6-7 (9-11), 3-6, 6-4, 6-4

John McEnroe-Pete Sampras (USA) d. Jakob Hlasek-Marc Rosset (SUI) 6-7 (5-7), 6-7 (7-9), 7-5, 6-1, 6-2

Jim Courier (USA) d. Jakob Hlasek (SUI) 6-3, 3-6, 6-3, 6-4

Andre Agassi v. Marc Rosset (not played)

SF: Switzerland 5, Brazil 0

SF: United States 4, Sweden 1

QF: Switzerland 3, France 2

QF: Brazil 3, Italy 1

QF: Sweden 5, Australia 0

QF: United States 3, Czechoslovakia 2

1993

Germany d. Australia 4-1 (Dusseldorf) Surface–Indoor Clay

Michael Stich (GER) d. Jason Stoltenberg (AUS) 6-7 (2-7), 6-3, 6-1, 4-6, 6-3

Richard Fromberg (AUS) d. Marc Goellner (GER) 3-6, 5-7, 7-6 (10-8), 6-2, 9-7

Michael Stich-Patrick Kuhnen (GER) d. Todd Woodbridge-Mark Woodforde (AUS) 7-6 (7-4), 4-6, 6-3, 7-6 (7-4)

Michael Stich (GER) d. Richard Fromberg (AUS) 6-4, 6-2, 6-2

Marc Goellner (GER) d. Jason Stoltenberg (AUS) 6-1, 6-7 (2-7), 7-6 (7-3)

SF: Australia 5, India 0

SF: Germany 5, Sweden 1

QF: Australia 3, Italy 2

QF: India 3, France 2

QF: Sweden 4, Netherlands 1

QF: Germany 4, Czech Republic 1

1994

Sweden d. Russia 4-1 (Moscow) Surface–Indoor Carpet

Stefan Edberg (SWE) d. Alexander Volkov (RUS) 6-4, 6-2, 6-7 (2-7), 0-6, 8-6

Magnus Larsson (SWE) d. Yevgeny Kafelnikov (RUS) 6-0, 6-2, 3-6, 2-6, 6-3

Jan Apell-Jonas Bjorkman (SWE) d. Yevgeny Kafelnikov-Andrei Olhovskiy (RUS) 6-7 (4-7), 6-2, 6-3, 1-6, 8-6

Yevgeny Kafelnikov (RUS) d. Stefan Edberg (SWE) 4-6, 6-4, 6-0

Magnus Larsson (SWE) d. Alexander Volkov (RUS) 7-6 (7-4), 6-4

SF: Sweden 3, United States 2

SF: Russia 4, Germany 1

QF: United States 3, Netherlands 2

QF: Sweden 3, France 2

QF: Russia 3, Czech Republic 2

QF: Germany 3, Spain 2

1995

United States d. Russia 3-2 (Moscow) Surface–Indoor Clay

Pete Sampras (USA) d. Andrei Chesnokov (RUS) 3-6, 6-4, 6-3, 6-7 (5-7), 6-4

Yevgeny Kafelnikov (RUS) d. Jim Courier (USA) 7-6 (7-1), 7-5, 6-3

Pete Sampras-Todd Martin (USA) d. Yevgeny Kafelnikov-Andrei Olhovskiy (RUS) 7-5, 6-4, 6-3

Pete Sampras (USA) d. Yevgeny Kafelnikov (RUS) 6-2, 6-4, 7-6 (7-4)

Andrei Chesnokov (RUS) d. Jim Courier (USA) 6-7 (1-7), 7-5, 6-0

SF: United States 4, Sweden 1

SF: Russia 3, Germany 2

QF: United States 5, Italy 0

QF: Sweden 5, Austria 0

QF: Russia 4, South Africa 1

QF: Germany 4, Netherlands 1

1996

France d. Sweden 3-2 (Malmo, Sweden) Surface–Indoor Carpet

Cedric Pioline (FRA) d. Stefan Edberg (SWE) 6-3, 6-4, 6-3

Thomas Enqvist (SWE) d. Arnaud Boetsch (FRA) 6-4, 6-3, 7-6 (7-2)

Guy Forget-Guillaume Raoux (FRA) d. Jonas Bjorkman-Nicklas Kulti (SWE) 6-3, 1-6, 6-3, 6-3

Thomas Enqvist (SWE) d. Cedric Pioline (FRA) 3-6, 6-7 (8-10), 6-4, 6-4, 9-7

Arnaud Boetsch (FRA) d. Nicklas Kulti (SWE) 7-6 (7-2), 2-6, 4-6, 7-6 (7-5), 10-8

SF: France 3, Italy 2

SF: Sweden 4, Czech Republic 1

QF: Italy 4, South Africa 1

QF: France 5, Germany 0

QF: Sweden 5, India 0

QF: Czech Republic 3, United States 2

1997

Sweden d. United States 5-0 (Goteborg, Sweden) Surface–Indoor Carpet

Jonas Bjorkman (SWE) d. Michael Chang (USA) 7-5, 1-6, 6-3, 6-3

Magnus Larsson (SWE) d. Pete Sampras (USA) 3-6, 7-6 (7-1), 2-1, retired

Jonas Bjorkman-Nicklas Kulti (SWE) d. Todd Martin-Jonathan Stark (USA) 6-4, 6-4, 6-4

Jonas Bjorkman (SWE) d. Jonathan Stark (USA) 6-1, 6-1

Magnus Larsson (SWE) d. Michael Chang (USA) 7-6 (7-4), 6-7 (6-8), 6-4

SF: United States 4, Australia 1

SF: Sweden 4, Italy 1

QF: United States 4, Netherlands 1

QF: Australia 5, Czech Republic 0

QF: Italy 4, Spain 1

QF: Sweden 3, South Africa 2

1998

Sweden d. Italy 4-1 (Milan) Surface–Indoor Clay

Magnus Norman (SWE) d. Andrea Gaudenzi (ITA) 6-7, 7-6, 4-6, 6-3, 6-6, retired

Magnus Gustafsson (SWE) d. Davide Sanguinetti (ITA) 6-1, 6-4, 6-0

Jonas Bjorkman-Nicklas Kulti (SWE) d. Davide Sanguinetti-Diego Nargiso (ITA) 7-6 (7-1), 6-1, 6-3

Magnus Gustafsson (SWE) d. Gianluca Pozzi (ITA) 6-4, 6-2

Diego Nargiso (ITA) d. Magnus Norman (SWE) 6-2, 6-3

SF: Sweden 4, Spain 1

SF: Italy 4, United States 1

QF: Sweden 3, Germany 2

QF: Spain 4, Switzerland 1

QF: Italy 5, Zimbabwe 0

QF: United States 4, Belgium 1

1999

Australia d. France 3-2 (Nice) Surface–Indoor Clay

Mark Philippoussis (AUS) Sebastien Grosjean (FRA) 6-4, 6-2, 6-4

Cedric Pioline (FRA) d. Lleyton Hewitt (AUS) 7-6 (9-7), 7-6 (8-6), 7-5

Mark Woodforde-Todd Woodbridge (AUS) d. Olivier Delaitre-Fabrice Santoro (FRA) 2-6, 7-5, 6-2, 6-2

Mark Philippoussis (AUS) d. Cedric Pioline (FRA) 6-3, 5-7, 6-1, 6-2

Sebastien Grosjean (FRA) d. Lleyton Hewitt (AUS) 6-4, 6-3

SF: Australia 4, Russia 1

SF: France 4, Belgium 1

QF: Russia 3, Slovakia 2

QF: Australia 4, United States 1

QF: France 3, Brazil 2

QF: Belgium 3, Switzerland 2

2000

Spain d. Australia 3-1 (Barcelona) Surface–Indoor Clay

Lleyton Hewitt (AUS) d. Albert Costa (ESP) 3-6, 6-1, 2-6, 6-4, 6-4

Juan Carlos Ferrero (ESP) d. Patrick Rafter (AUS) 6-7 (4-7), 7-6 (7-2), 6-2, 3-1, retired

Juan Balcells-Alex Corretja (ESP) d. Mark Woodforde-Sandon Stolle (AUS) 6-4, 6-4, 6-4

Juan Carlos Ferrero (ESP) d. Lleyton Hewitt (AUS) 6-2, 7-6 (7-5), 4-6, 6-4

Albert Costa vs. Patrick Rafter, canceled

SF: Spain 5, United States 0

SF: Australia 5, Brazil 0

QF: United States 3, Czech Republic 2

QF: Spain 4, Russia 1

QF: Brazil 3, Slovakia 2

QF: Australia 3, Germany 2

2001

France d. Australia 3-2 (Melbourne) Surface–Grass

Nicolas Escude (FRA) d. Lleyton Hewitt (AUS) 4-6, 6-3, 3-6, 6-3, 6-4

Patrick Rafter (AUS) d. Sebastien Grosjean (FRA) 6-3, 7-6 (7-6), 7-5

Cedric Pioline-Fabrice Santoro (FRA) d. Lleyton Hewitt-Patrick Rafter (AUS) 2-6, 6-3, 7-6 (7-5), 6-1

Lleyton Hewitt (AUS) d. Sebastien Grosjean (FRA) 6-3, 6-2, 6-3

Nicolas Escude (FRA) d. Wayne Arthurs (AUS) 7-6 (7-3), 6-7 (5-7), 6-3, 6-3

SF: Australia 4, Sweden 1

SF: France 3, Netherlands 2

QF: Australia 3, Brazil 1

QF: Sweden 4, Russia 1

QF: France 3, Switzerland 2

QF: Netherlands 4, Germany 1

2002

Russia d. France 3-2 (Paris) Surface–Indoor Clay

Marat Safin (RUS) d. Paul-Henri Mathieu (FRA) 6-4, 3-6, 6-1, 6-4

Sebastien Grosjean (FRA) d. Yevgeny Kafelnikov (RUS) 7-6 (3), 6-3, 6-0

Fabrice Santoro-Nicolas Escude (FRA) d. Yevgeny Kafelnikov-Marat Safin (RUS) 6-3, 3-6, 5-7, 6-3, 6-4

Marat Safin (RUS) d. Sebastien Grosjean (FRA) 6-3, 6-2, 7-6 (11)

Mikhail Youzhny (RUS) d. Paul-Henri Mathieu (FRA) 3-6, 2-6, 6-3, 7-5, 6-4

SF: France 3, United States 2

SF: Russia 3, Argentina 2

QF: France 3, Czech Republic 2
QF: United States 3, Spain 1
QF: Russia 4, Sweden 1
QF: Argentina 3, Croatia 2

2003

Australia d. Spain 3-1 (Melbourne) Surface—Grass

Lleyton Hewitt (AUS) d. Juan Carlos Ferrero (ESP) 3-6, 6-3, 3-6, 7-6 (0), 6-2

Carlos Moya (ESP) d. Mark Philippoussis (AUS) 6-4, 6-4, 4-6, 7-6 (4)

Wayne Arthurs-Todd Woodbridge (AUS) d. Alex Corretja-Feliciano Lopez (ESP) 6-3, 6-1, 6-3

Mark Philippoussis (AUS) d. Juan Carlos Ferrero (ESP) 7-5, 6-3, 1-6, 2-6, 6-0

Lleyton Hewitt vs. Carlos Moya, not played

SF: Australia 3, Switzerland 2
SF: Spain 3, Argentina 2
QF: Switzerland 3, France 2
QF: Australia 5, Sweden 0
QF: Spain 5, Croatia 0
QF: Argentina 5, Russia 0

2004

Spain d. United States 3-2 (Seville) Surface—Clay

Carlos Moya (ESP) d. Mardy Fish (USA) 6-4, 6-2, 6-3

Rafael Nadal (ESP) d. Andy Roddick (USA) 6-7 (6), 6-2, 7-6 (6), 6-2

Bob Bryan-Mike Bryan (USA) d. Juan Carlos Ferrero-Tommy Robredo (ESP) 6-0, 6-3, 6-2

Carlos Moya (ESP) d. Andy Roddick (AUS) 6-2, 7-6 (1), 7-6 (5)

Mardy Fish (USA) d. Tommy Robredo (ESP) 7-6 (8), 6-2

SF: United States 4, Belarus 1
SF: Spain 4, France 1
QF: United States 4, Sweden 1
QF: Belarus 5, Argentina 0
QF: France 3, Switzerland 2
QF: Spain 4, Netherlands 1

2005

Croatia d. Slovak Republic 3-2 (Bratislava) Surface—Indoor Carpet

Ivan Ljubicic (CRO) d. Karol Kucera (SVK) 6-3, 6-4, 6-3

Dominik Hrbaty (SVK) d. Mario Ancic (CRO) 7-6 (4), 6-3, 6-7 (4), 6-4

Mario Ancic-Ivan Ljubicic (CRO) d. Dominik Hrbaty-Michal Mertinak (SVK) 7-6 (5), 6-3, 7-6 (5)

Dominik Hrbaty (SVK) d. Ivan Ljubicic (CRO) 4-6, 6-3, 6-4, 3-6, 6-4

Mario Ancic (CRO) d. Michal Mertinak (SVK) 7-6 (1), 6-3, 6-4

SF: Slovak Republic 4, Argentina 1
SF: Croatia 3, Russia 2
QF: Slovak Republic 4, Netherlands 1
QF: Argentina 4, Australia 1
QF: Russia 3, France 2
QF: Croatia 4, Romania 1

2006

Russia d. Argentina 3-2 (Moscow) Surface—Indoor Carpet

Nikolay Davydenko (RUS) d. Juan Ignacio Chela (ARG) 6-1, 6-2, 5-7, 6-4

David Nalbandian (ARG) d. Marat Safin (RUS) 6-4, 6-4, 6-4

Marat Safin-Dmitry Tursunov (RUS) d. Agustin Calleri-David Nalbandian (ARG) 6-2, 6-3, 6-4

David Nalbandian (ARG) d. Nikolay Davydenko (RUS) 6-2, 6-2, 4-6, 6-4

Marat Safin (RUS) d. Jose Acasuso (ARG) 6-3, 3-6, 6-3, 7-6 (5)

SF: Argentina 5, Australia 0
SF: Russia 3, United States 2
QF: Argentina 3, Croatia 2
QF: Australia 5, Belarus 0
QF: Russia 4, France 1
QF: United States 3, Chile 2

2007

United States d. Russia 4-1 (Portland) Surface—Indoor Carpet

Andy Roddick (USA) d. Dmitry Tursunov (RUS) 6-4, 6-4, 6-2

James Blake (USA) d. Mikhail Youzhny (RUS) 6-3, 7-6 (4), 6-7 (3), 7-6 (3)

Bob Bryan-Mike Bryan (USA) d. Igor Andreev-Nikolay Davydenko (RUS) 7-6 (4), 6-4, 6-2

Igor Andreev (RUS) d. Bob Bryan (USA) 6-3, 7-6 (4)

James Blake (USA) d. Dmitry Tursunov (RUS) 1-6, 6-3, 7-5

SF: Russia 3, Germany 2
SF: United States 4, Sweden 1
QF: Russia 3, France 2
QF: Germany 3, Belgium 2
QF: United States 4, Spain 1
QF: Sweden 4, Argentina 1

2008

Spain def. Argentina 3-1 (Mar del Plata, Arg.) - Indoor Hard

David Nalbandian (ARG) d. David Ferrer (ESP) 6-3, 6-2, 6-3

Feliciano Lopez (ESP) d. Juan Martin de Potro (ARG) 4-6, 7-6 (2), 7-6 (4), 6-3

Feliciano Lopez and Fernando Verdasco (ESP) d. Agustin Calleri and David Nalbandian (ARG) 5-7, 7-5, 7-6 (3), 6-3

Fernando Verdasco (ESP) d. Jose Acasuso (ARG) 6-3, 6-7 (3), 4-6, 6-3, 6-1

David Nalbandian (ARG) vs. Feliciano Lopez (ESP) not placed

SF: Argentina 3, Russia 2
SF: Spain 4, United States 1
QF: Argentina 4, Sweden 1
QF :Russia 3, Czech Republic 2
QF: Spain 4, Germany
QF: United States 4, France 1

Davis Cup Records

Entering 2009 Competition

Nation

MOST TITLES

	Wins	Years
USA	32	1900, 1902, 1913, 1920-26, 1937-38, 1946-49, 1954, 1958, 1963, 1968-72, 1978-79, 1981-82, 1990, 1992, 1995, 2007
Australia	28	1907-09, 1911, 1914, 1919, 1939, 1950-53, 1955-57, 1959-62, 1964-67, 1973, 1977, 1983, 1986, 1999, 2003
France	9	1927-32, 1991, 1996, 2001
Great Britain	9	1903-06, 1912, 1933-36
Sweden	7	1975, 1984-85, 1987, 1994, 1997, 1998
Spain	3	2000, 2004, 2008
Germany	3	1988-89, 1993
Russia	2	2002, 2006
Czechoslovakia	1	1980
Italy	1	1976
South Africa	1	1974
Croatia	1	2005

MOST TIES WON

	W-L	Yrs. Played	First Yr
USA	208-63	95	1900
Australia	173-62	90	1905
Italy	151-78	79	1922
France	148-81	90	1904
Sweden	143-69	76	1925
Great Britain	137-90	98	1900
Germany	135-71	74	1913
Czech Republic	110-74	76	1921
Spain	111-70	74	1921
India	107-70	73	1921
Serbia/ Yugoslavia	94-76	75	1927
Japan	95-76	75	1921
Denmark	85-83	81	1921
Belgium	83-85	87	1904
Brazil	80-61	61	1932
Russia (USSR)	78-41	45	1962

MOST FINAL APPEARANCES

	Total	W-L
USA	61	32-29
Australia	47	28-19
Great Britain	17	9- 8
France	15	9-6
Sweden	12	7-5
Italy	7	1-6
Germany	5	3-2
Spain	6	3-3
Russia	5	2-3
India	3	0-3
Romania	3	0-3
Argentina	3	0-3
Czechoslovakia	2	1-1
South Africa	1	1-0
Croatia	1	1-0
Chile	1	0 -1
Slovak Republic	1	0-1
Belgium	1	0-1
Japan	1	0-1
Mexico	1	0-1
Switzerland	1	0-1

Individual

MOST SERIES PLAYED

	Total	W-L
Vicini, Domenico (SMR)	70	52-53
Pietrangeli, Nicola (ITA)	66	120-44
Abdul-A'al, Esam (BRN)	60	77-29
Al Megayel, Badar (KSA)	58	59-45
Khalfan, Sultan (QAT)	56	46-47
Lewis, Vernon (LCA)	53	39-37
Nastase, Ilie (ROM)	52	109-37
Bahrouzyan, Omar (UAE)	51	56-30
Murashka, Rolandas (LTU)	49	56-32
Shehab, Abdul-Rahman (BRN)	48	34-39
Al Nabhani, Khalid (OMA)	47	48-35
Cooper, Allan (KEN)	47	31-44
Kedryuk, Alexey (KAZ)	47	62-30
Santana, Manuel (ESP)	46	92-28
Sirola, Orlando (ITA)	46	57-33
Al Khulaifi, Nasser-Ghanim (QAT)	45	24-47
Paes, Leander (IND)	45	84-31

MOST MATCHES PLAYED

	Total	Series
Pietrangeli, Nicola (ITA)	164	66
Nastase, Ilie (ROM)	146	52
Santana, Manuel (ESP)	120	46
Brichant, Jacques (BEL)	120	42
Tiriac, Ion (ROM)	119	43
Koch, Tomas (BRA)	118	44
Paes, Leander (IND)	115	45
Mandarino, Jose-Edison (BRA)	109	43
Krishnan, Ramanathan (IND)	107	43
Vicini, Domenico (SMR)	106	70
Abdul-A'al, Esam (BRN)	106	60

Metreveli, Alex (RUS)	105	38
Al Megayel, Badar (KSA)	104	58
Bungert, Wilhelm (GER)	103	43
Schmidt, Ulf (SWE)	102	38
Washer, Philippe (BEL)	102	39
Von Cramm, Gottfried (GER)	101	37
Panatta, Adriano (ITA)	100	38
Taroczy, Balazs (HUN)	95	33
Kodes, Jan (TCH)	95	39

MOST WINS – OVERALL

	Total	Ties
Pietrangeli, Nicola (ITA)	120-44	66
Nastase, Ilie (ROM)	109-37	52
Santana, Manuel (ESP)	92-28	46
Von Cramm, Gottfried (GER)	82-19	37
Paes, Leander (IND)	84-31	45
Metreveli, Alex (RUS)	80-25	38
Abdul-A'al, Esam (BRN)	77-29	60
Taroczy, Balazs (HUN)	76-19	33
Koch, Tomas (BRA)	74-44	44
Brichant, Jacques (BEL)	71-49	42
Tiriac, Ion (ROM)	70-39	43
Krishnan, Ramanathan (IND)	69-28	43
Mandarino, Jose-Edison (BRA)	68-41	43
Bungert, Wilhelm (GER)	67-36	43
Schmidt, Ulf (SWE)	66-36	38
Washer, Philippe (BEL)	66-36	39

MOST WINS – SINGLES

	W-L	Ties
Pietrangeli, Nicola (ITA)	78-32	66
Nastase, Ilie (ROM)	74-22	52
Santana, Manuel (ESP)	69-17	46
Von Cramm, Gottfried (GER)	58-10	37
Metreveli, Alex (RUS)	56-14	38
Abdul-A'al, Esam (BRN)	52-14	60
Bungert, Wilhelm (GER)	52-27	43
Brichant, Jacques (BEL)	52-27	42
Taroczy, Balazs (HUN)	50-12	33
Krishnan, Ramanathan (IND)	50-19	43
Paes, Leander, (IND)	48 -22	45
Lundquist, Jan-Erik (SWE)	47-16	35
Menzel, Roderich (GER)	47- 13	35
Koch, Tomas (BRA)	46-32	44
Washer, Philippe (BEL)	46-18	39
Vilas, Guillermo (ARG)	45-10	29

MOST WINS – DOUBLES

	W-L	Ties
Pietrangeli, Nicola (ITA)	42-12	66
Nastase, IIie (ROM)	35-15	52
Sirola, Orlando (ITA)	35-8	46
Paes, Leander (IND)	36-9	45
Tiriac, Ion (ROM)	30-11	43
Koch, Tomas (BRA)	38-12	44

Mandarino, Jose-Edison (BRA)	27-10	43
Panatta, Adriano (ITA)	27-10	38
Taroczy, Balazs (HUN)	26-7	33
Al Nabhani, Khalid (OMA)	26-15	47
Woodbridge, Todd (AUS)	25-7	32
Wilson, Bobby (GBR)	25-8	34
Abdul-A'al, Esam (BRN)	25-15	60

MOST WINS – DOUBLES TEAM

	W-L	Ties	Yrs
Pietrangeli, Nicola / Sirola, Orlando (ITA)	34-8	42	9
Nastase, Ilie / Tiriac, Ion (ROM)	27-7	34	10
Koch, Tomas / Mandarino, Jose-Edison (BRA)	23-9	32	10
Bertolucci, Paolo / Panatta, Adriano (ITA)	22-8	30	11
Paes, Leander / Mahesh Bhupathi (IND)	23-2	25	12
Cucelli, Giovanni / Del Bello, Marcello (ITA)	19-5	24	7
Mirnyi, Max / Voltchkov, Vladimir (BLR)	19-7	26	15
Likhachev, Sergei / Metreveli, Alex (RUS)	18-7	25	7
Szoke, Peter / Taroczy, Balazs (HUN)	17-2	19	8
Al Nabhani, Khalid / Al Nabhani Mohammed (OMA)	17-5	22	7
Amritraj, Anand / Amritraj, Vijay (IND)	17-9	26	15

MOST APPEARANCES – FINAL

	Finals	W-L
Tilden, Bill (USA)	11	21-7
Emerson, Roy (AUS)	9	15-3
Borotra, Jean (FRA)	9	7-2
Brookes, Norman (AUS)	8	15-7
Cochet, Henri (FRA)	8	14-6
Johnston, William (USA)	8	13-3
Smith, Stan (USA)	8	12-4
Edberg, Stefan (SWE)	7	6-8
Seixas, Vic (USA)	7	6-1
McEnroe, John (USA)	6	12-2
Wilander, Mats (SWE)	6	9-4
Schroeder, Ted (USA)	6	9-6
Fraser, Neale (AUS)	6	8-3
Austin, Bunny (GBR)	6	8-4
Bromwich, John (AUS)	6	7-7
Williams, Dick (USA)	6	5-3
Brugnon, Jacques (FRA)	6	3-3
Jarryd, Anders (SWE)	6	3-4
Doherty, Laurence (GBR)	5	12-0
Laver, Rod (AUS)	5	10-2
Perry, Fred (GBR)	5	9-1
Doherty, Reggie (GBR)	5	7-1
Newcombe, John (AUS)	5	6-4
Lutz, Bob (USA)	5	5-0
Quist, Adrian (AUS)	5	5-7
Trabert, Tony (USA)	5	4-8
Hughes, Patrick (GBR)	5	1-4

YOUNGEST PLAYERS

	Age	Year
Mohammed Akhtar Hossain (BAN)	13 yrs, 326 days	2003

Kenny Banzer (LIE)	14 yrs, 5 days	2000
Hadi Badri (UAE)	14 yrs, 42 days	1995
Ronald Semanda (UGA)	14 yrs, 53 days	2003
Franklyn Emmanuel (SRI)	14 yrs, 54 days	2002
Omar Bahrouzyan (UAE)	14 yrs, 63 days	1996
Sree Roy (BAN)	14 yrs, 99 days	2002

OLDEST PLAYERS

	Age	Year
Yaka-Garonfin Koptigan (TOG)	59 yrs, 147 days	2001
James McArdle (IRL)	59 yrs, 138 days	1979
Ramiro Benavides (BOL)	56 yrs, 64 days	2003
Ferenc Zentai (HUN)	50 yrs, 133 days	1985
Claude Butlin (MEX)	50 yrs, 105 days	1927
Rene Ruzic (MON)	50 yrs, 87 days	1969
Torben Ulrich (DEN)	48 yrs, 349 days	1978
Jean Borotra (FRA)	48 yrs, 306 days	1947

Miscellaneous Records

MOST CUP-WINNING YEARS
8   Roy Emerson, Australia 1959-67

MOST YEARS PLAYED
21   Torben Ulrich, Denmark 1948-68, 1978

MOST CONSECUTIVE SINGLES WINS
33   Bjorn Borg, Sweden   1973-79

BEST RECORD IN CHALLENGE ROUND AND/OR FINALS
7-0 in singles, 5-0 in doubles, Laurie Doherty, Britain, 1902-06

LONGEST RUN OF WINS (TIES)
17   USA   (May 1968 to November 1973)

LONGEST RUN OF WINS (RUBBERS)
28   Australia   (July 1955 to December 1957)

MOST COMEBACKS FROM 0-2 DOWN
5   Sweden

MOST TIES PLAYED IN A YEAR
8   Spain   1965

EVER PRESENT
Great Britain has contested every Davis Cup competition

YOUNGEST PLAYER IN A DAVIS CUP FINAL
17 years, 177 days—John Alexander (AUS) 1968 Davis Cup Final - USA d. Australia 4-1

OLDEST PLAYER IN A DAVIS CUP FINAL
43 years, 48 days—Norman Brookes (AUS) 1920 Davis Cup Final — USA d. Australia 5-0

MOST CUPS WON AS CAPTAIN
16, Harry Hopman, Australia, 1938-67

YOUNGEST CAPTAIN
19 years, 9 days—Maurice McLoughlin (USA) 1909 Davis Cup Final - Australasia d. USA 5-0

OLDEST CAPTAIN
71 years, 107 days—Perry Jones (USA) 1959 Davis Cup Final - Australia d. USA 3-2

MOST DECISIVE VICTORY IN A TIE
Sri Lanka d. Syria 5-0, 1991 Asia/Oceania Group II, for the loss of six games

MOST NUMBER OF GAMES IN A RUBBER
All-time
Singles: 100—Harry Fritz (CAN) d. Jorge Andrew (VEN) 16-14, 11-9, 9-11, 4-6, 11-9, 1982 American Zone Semifinal
Doubles: 122—Stan Smith / Erik van Dillen (USA) d. Patricio Cornejo / Jaime Fillol (CHI) 7-9, 37-39, 8-6, 6-1, 6-3, 1973 American Zone Final

World Group (since 1981)
Singles: 85—Michael Westphal (GER) d. Tomas Smid (TCH) 6-8, 1-6, 7-5, 11-9, 17-15, 1985 Semifinal
Doubles: 77 (3 times)—Paul Annacone / Ken Flach (USA) d. Pat Cash / John Fitzgerald (AUS) 8-10, 1-6, 7-5, 13-11, 9-7, 1986 Semifinal. Sergio Casal / Emilio Sanchez (ESP) d. Francisco Gonzalez / Victor Pecci (PAR) 6-2, 16-18, 6-3, 14-12, 1987 Quarterfinal Lucas Arnold-Ker / David Nalbandian (ARG) d. Yevgeny Kafelnikov / Marat Safin (RUS) 6-4, 6-4, 5-7, 3-6, 19-17, 2002 Semifinal

Since tiebreak introduced (1989)
Singles: 82—Richard Ashby (BAR) d. Jose Medrano (BOL) 4-6, 7-6, 6-3, 5-7, 20-18, 1991 Americas Group II first round
Doubles: 78 —Carlos Di Laura / Jose Luis Noriega (PER) d. Mauro Menezes / Fernando Roese (BRA) 7-5, 6-7, 7-6, 5-7, 15-13, 1991 Americas Zone Group I first round

Longest- known rubbers in elapsed time
Singles: 6 hours, 22 minutes - John McEnroe (USA) d. Mats Wilander (SWE) 9-7, 6-2, 15-17, 3-6, 8-6, 1982 World Group Quarterfinal
Doubles: 6 hours, 20 minutes - Lucas Arnold / David Nalbandian (ARG) d. Yevgeny Kafelnikov / Marat Safin (RUS) 6-4, 6-4, 5-7, 3-6, 19-17, 2002 World Group Semifinal. (This is also the longest recorded men's doubles match of all time)

MOST NUMBER OF GAMES IN A SET
Singles: 46—Dale Power (CAN) d. Alvaro Betancur (COL) 6-4, 22-24, 2-6, 6-3, 7-5, 1976 American Zone preliminary round.
Doubles: 76—Stan Smith / Erik van Dillen (USA) d. Patricio Cornejo / Jaime Fillol (CHI) 7-9, 37-39, 8-6, 6-1 6-3, 1973 American Zone Final

World Group (since 1981)
Singles: 40—Carlos Kirmayr (BRA) d. Uli Pinner (GER) 6-2, 11-13, 21-19, 6-3, 1981 World Group relegation round
Doubles: 40—Stefan Edberg / Anders Jarryd (SWE) d. Anand Amritraj / Vijay Amritraj (IND) 21-19, 2-6, 6-3 6-4, 1985 World Group Quarterfinal

Longest Final Set

Singles: 20-18 (twice)—Richard Ashby (BAR) d. Jose Medrano (BOL), 1991 Americas Group II first round, 4-6, 7-6(4), 6-3, 5-7, 20-18
Nuno Marques (POR) d. Nenad Zimonjic (YUG), 1998 Europe/Africa second round, 3-6, 6-0, 2-6, 6-3, 20-18
Doubles: 23-21—Carlos Alberto Fernandes / Armando Vieira (BRA) d. Arie Avidan-Weiss / Eleazar Davidman (ISR), 1957 American Zone semifinal, 1-6, 4-6, 6-4,6-2, 23-21

World Group (since 1981)

Singles: 17-15 (twice)—Michael Westphal (GER) d. Tomas Smid (CZE), 1985 Semifinal, 6-8, 1-6, 7-5, 11-9, 17-5, and Dmitry Tursunov d. Andy Roddick, 2006 Semifinal, 6-3, 6-4, 5-7, 3-6,17-5
Doubles: 19-17—Lucas Arnold / David Nalbandian (ARG) d. Yevgeny Kafelnikov / Marat Safin (RUS), 2002 World Group Semifinal, 6-4, 6-4, 5-7, 3-6, 19-17

LONGEST TIE-BREAKER

19-17   Young-Jun Kim (KOR) d. Aqeel Khan (PAK), 2003 Asia/Oceania Group I relegation play-off, 7-6 (17), 4-6, 6-3, 7-6

World Group (since 1981):

15-13   Patrick Rafter (AUS) d. David Rikl (CZE), 1997 first round, 7-6 (13), 0-6, 6-2

MOST ACES SERVED IN A DAVIS CUP RUBBER

47   Ivo Karlovic (CRO) def. James Blake (USA) 2009 Davis Cup Quarterfinal 6-7 (5), 4-6, 6-3, 7-6 (3), 7-5

MOST ACES SERVED IN A DAVIS CUP MATCH

47   Gustavo Kuerten (BRA) def. Daniel Nestor (CAN), 2003 World Group Play-off, 6-7(7), 7-6(0), 6-3, 6-7(7), 7-5

BIGGEST UPSETS

1921   Ichiya Kumagae, Japan, d. Jack Hawkes, Australia, 3-6, 2-6, 8-6, 6-2, 6-3, Newport, R.I. Gave Japan 2-0 lead in 4-1 upset

1932   Jean Borotra, France, d. Ellsworth Vines, U.S., 6-4, 6-2, 3-6, 6-4, challenge round, Paris. Defeat of No. 1, Wimbledon, U.S. champ, gave France 1-0 lead in 3-2, victory

1939   Adrian Quist, Australia, d. Bobby Riggs, U.S., 6-1, 6-4, 3-6, 3-6, 6-4, challenge round, Philadelphia. Defeat of No. 1, Wimbledon, U.S. champ, tied score 2-2 in all-time comeback from 0-2 to 3-2 Aussie victory

1950   Ken McGregor, Australia, d. Ted Schroeder, U.S, 13-11, 6-3, 6-4, challenge round, New York. Gave Aussies 2-0 lead in 4-1 upset

1953   Lew Hoad, Australia, d. Tony Trabert, 13-11, 6-3, 2-6, 3-6, 7-5, final, Melbourne. Defeat of U.S. champ tied score 2-2 in 3-2 Aussie victory

1967   Pancho Guzman, Ecuador, d. Arthur Ashe, U.S., 0-6, 6-4, 7-5, 0-6, 6-3, Guayaquil. Gave Ecuador decisive 3-1 lead in 3-2 victory, sealing biggest upset in U.S. history

1974   Jairo Velasco, Columbia, d. Harold Solomon, U.S., 6-1, 3-6, 4-6, 6-3, 7-5, Bogota. Gave Columbia 1-0 lead in 4-1 upset

1984   Henrik Sundstrom (No. 7) Sweden, d. John McEnroe (No. 1), 13-11, 6-4, 6-3, final, Goteborg. Gave Sweden 2-0 lead in 4-1 upset

1987   Hugo Chapacu (No. 282), Paraguay, d. Jimmy Arias (No. 54) U.S., 6-4, 6-1, 5-7, 3-6, 9-7, from 1-5 saving 3 match points in 5th. Tied score 2-2 in 3-2 upset

1991   Henri Leconte (No. 159), France d. Pete Sampras (No. 6), U.S., 6-4, 7-5, 6-4, final, Lyon. Tied score 1-1 in 3-1 French victory

1992   Daniel Nestor (No. 238), Canada, d. Stefan Edberg (No. 1), Sweden, 4-6, 6-3, 1-6, 6-3, 6-4. Gave Canada 2-0 lead in 3-2 defeat. Nestor lost clincher to Magnus Gustasfon, 6-4, 2-6, 3-6, 7-5, 6-4

2001   Nicolas Escude (No. 27) France, d. Lleyton Hewitt (No. 1), Australia, 4-6, 6-3, 3-6, 6-3, 6-4, final, Melbourne. Gave France 1-0 lead in 3-2 upset. Escude also won clincher over Wayne Arthurs, 7-6 (7-3), 6-7 (5-7), 6-3, 6-3

BEST COMEBACKS

1930   Wilmer Allison d. Giorgio deStefani, Italy, 4-6, 7-9, 6-4, 8-6, 10-8, from 2-4, 4th, 1-5, 5th, saving 18 match points, Gave U.S. 1-0 lead in 4-1 victory

1932   Jean Borotra, France, d. Wilmer Allison, U.S., 1-6, 3-6, 6-4, 6-2, 7-5, challenge round, Paris (saved 3MP, 5th, 5-3, 40-15, and 4-5, 30-40). Made score 3-1, clinching 3-2 French victory

1960   Barry MacKay U.S. d. Nicola Pietrangeli, Italy, 8-6, 3-6, 8-10, 8-6, 13-11, from 5-3 down, 5th, saving 8 match points. Gave U.S. 2-0 lead in 3-2 defeat by Italy

1965   Fred Stolle, Australia, d. Manolo Santana, Spain, 10-12, 3-6, 6-1, 6-4, 7-5, final, Sydney. Gave Aussies 1-0 lead in 4-1 victory

1971   Frank Froehling, U.S., d. Ion Tiriac, Romania, 3-6, 1-6, 6-1, 6-3, 8-6, final, Charlotte. N.C. Saved 7 vital break points in 5th, missed on 2 MP, but came back strong next day after match suspended at 6-6, 5th. Gave U.S. 2-0 lead in 4-1 victory

1986   Pat Cash, Australia, d. Mikael Pernfors, Sweden, 2-6, 4-6, 6-3, 6-4, 6-3, final, Melbourne. Clinching match, making score 3-1 in 3-2 victory

1987   Hugo Chapacu (No. 282), Paraguay, d. Jimmy Arias (No. 54) U.S., 6-4, 6-1, 5-7, 3-6, 9-7, from 1-5 saving 3 match points in 5th. Tied score 2-2 in 3-2 upset

1994   Stefan Edberg, Sweden, d. Alexander Volkov, 6-4, 6-2, 6-7, 0-6, 9-7, final Moscow. (Saved 1 MP, 5th, 5-4, ad-in; trailed 3-5). Gave Sweden 1-0 lead in 4-1 victory

1995   Andrei Chesnokov, Russia, d. Michael Stich, Germany, 6-4, 1-6, 1-6, 6-3, 14-12. Stich serving at 7-6, 5th, held 9 match points. Clinched 3-2 Russian semifinal victory

1996   Arnaud Boetsch, France, d. Nicklas Kulti, Sweden, 7-6 (7-2), 2-6, 4-6, 7-6 (7-5), 10-8, final, Malmo, Sweden. Clinched Cup, 3-2 (Saved 3 Cup points, 5th, 6-7, 0-40, won 4 of last 5 games)

2002   Mikhail Youzhny, Russia, d. Paul-Henri Mathieu, France, 3-6, 2-6, 6-3, 7-5, 6-4, final, Paris. Clinched Cup, 3-2; 2 points from defeat, 5th at 4-5, deuce

Federation/Fed Cup

CHAPTER 11

The United States has won the Fed Cup title more than any other nation. In 1999, it fielded perhaps the greatest Fed Cup team in the event's history in its 4-1 final-round victory over Russia—**Venus Williams** (left) **Monica Seles**, **Serena Williams** and **Lindsay Davenport**.

It was a splendid idea with a lame name—twice. That's the Federation/Fed Cup, the world team competition for women—a la the Davis Cup that has been running in a variety of formats since 1963. It was best-of-three matches until 1996, then best-of-five (like Davis Cup, except curiously playing the doubles last, usually meaningless).

The International Tennis Federation, the proprietor, named the Cup unimaginatively for itself. Plenty of excellent names such as Suzanne Lenglen, Helen Wills, Alice Marble were available. In 1995, a name change was advised, and—eek!—it was shortened to Fed. Wonder how much that consultation cost. King or Court Cup (for Billie Jean King or Margaret Court), stars of the event, would have been just fine.

The idea for a female team competition, complementing the Davis Cup, sprang from "Lady Tennis," American Hazel Hotchkiss Wightman, an all-time champion, who provided a Cup. But in the 1920s, there wasn't enough broad interest. Thus the Wightman Cup became a prize for a U.S.-Great Britain rivalry, launched in 1923 at Forest Hills and lasting through 1989 when the Brits ran out of talent.

Australian Nell Hopman (wife of her country's Davis Cup captain, Harry Hopman) and Englishwoman Mary Hardwick Hare, a former Wightman player, successfully lobbied the ITF on behalf of the widening women's game for a world-wide team tournament, realized in the Fed Cup. Sixteen countries entered at the 1963 start, the U.S. defeating Australia, 2-1 at Queen's Club, London, the final indoors because of rain. More than 75 entered in 2007, Russia the 4-0 victor over Italy.

Court, leading Australia to four Cups, had a 20-0 singles record. King played for six Cup winners, posting a 26-3 singles record; 26-1 in doubles. Arantxa Sanchez Vicario and Conchita Martinez carried Spain to 10 finals, winning five Cups. Arantxa tops the chart, playing 100 matches: 50-22 singles, 22-6 doubles. Conchita was right behind her, 47-18 and 21-5—and they were 18-3 together in doubles. Martina Navratilova is the only Cup winner for two different countries: Czechoslovakia in 1975 (prior to her defection that year), and the U.S. in 1982, 86, 89, and was perfect, 20-0 singles, 16-0 doubles. What about her name on the Cup?

The U.S. leads with 17 Cups, well ahead of Australia's seven.

Fed Cup Champions

1963
United States d. Australia 2-1 (London) Surface—Grass

Margaret Smith (AUS) d. Darlene Hard (USA) 6-3, 6-0

Billie Jean Moffitt (USA) d. Lesley Turner (AUS) 5-7, 6-0, 6-3

Darlene Hard- Billie Jean Moffitt (USA) d. Margaret Smith-Lesley Turner (AUS) 3-6, 13-11, 6-3

1964
Australia d. United States 2-1 (Philadelphia) Surface—Grass

Margaret Smith (AUS) d. Billie Jean Moffitt (USA) 6-2, 6-3

Lesley Turner (AUS) d. Nancy Richey (USA) 7-5, 6-1

Billie Jean Moffitt-Karen Susman (USA) d. Margaret Smith-Lesley Turner (AUS) 4-6, 7-5, 6-1

1965
Australia d. United States 2-1 (Melbourne) Surface—Grass

Lesley Turner (AUS) d. Carole Caldwell Graebner (USA) 6-3, 2-6, 6-3

Margaret Smith (AUS) d. Billie Jean Moffitt (USA) 6-4, 8-6

Billie Jean Moffitt-Carole Caldwell Graebner (USA) d. Margaret Smith-Judy Tegart (AUS) 7-5, 4-6, 6-4

1966
United States d. West Germany 3-0 (Turin) Surface—Clay

Julie Heldman (USA) d. Helga Niessen (GER) 4-6, 7-5, 6-1

Billie Jean King (USA) d. Edda Buding (GER) 6-3, 3-6, 6-1

Carole Caldwell Graebner-Billie Jean King (USA) d. Helga Schultze-Edda Budding (GER) 6-4, 6-2

1967
United States d. Great Britain 2-0 (Berlin) Surface—Clay

Rosie Casals (USA) d. Virginia Wade (GBR) 9-7, 8-6

Billie Jean King (USA) d. Ann Haydon Jones (GBR) 6-3, 6-4

Doubles match called at set-all

1968
Australia d. Netherlands 3-0 (Paris) Surface—Clay

Kerry Melville (AUS) d. Marijke Jansen (NED) 4-6, 7-5, 6-3

Margaret Smith Court (AUS) d. Astrid Suurbeek (NED) 6-1, 6-3

Margaret Smith Court-Kerry Melville (AUS) d. Astrid Suurbeek-Lidy Venneboer (NED) 6-3, 6-8, 7-5

1969
United States d. Australia 2-1 (Athens) Surface—Clay

Nancy Richey (USA) d. Kerry Melville (AUS) 6-4, 6-3

Margaret Smith Court (AUS) d. Julie Heldman (USA) 6-1, 8-6

Peaches Bartkowicz-Nancy Richey (USA) d. Margaret Smith Court-Judy Tegart (AUS) 6-4, 6-4

1970
Australia d. Germany 3-0 (Freiburg, West Germany) Surface—Clay

Karen Krantzcke (AUS) d. Helga Schultze Hoesl (GER) 6-2, 6-3

Judy Tegart Dalton (AUS) d. Helga Niessen (GER) 4-6, 6-3, 6-3

Karen Krantzcke-Judy Dalton (AUS) d. Helga Hoesl-Helga Niessen (GER) 6-2, 7-5

1971
Australia d. Great Britain 3-0 (Perth) Surface—Grass

Margaret Smith Court (AUS) d. Ann Haydon Jones (GBR) 6-8, 6-3, 6-2

Evonne Goolagong (AUS) d. Virginia Wade (GBR) 6-4, 6-1

Margaret Smith Court-Lesley Hunt (AUS) d. Virginia Wade-Winnie Shaw (GBR) 6-4, 6-4

1972
South Africa d. Great Britain 2-1 (Johannesburg) Surface—Hard

Virginia Wade (GBR) d. Pat Walkden Pretorius (RSA) 6-3, 6-2

Brenda Kirk (RSA) d. Winnie Shaw (GBR) 4-6, 7-5, 6-0

Brenda Kirk-Pat Pretorius (RSA) d. Winnie Shaw-Virginia Wade (GBR) 6-1, 7-5

1973
Australia d. South Africa 3-0 (Bad Homburg, West Germany) Surface—Clay

Evonne Goolagong (AUS) d. Pat Walkden Pretorius (RSA) 6-0, 6-2

Patti Coleman (AUS) d. Brenda Kirk (RSA) 10-8, 6-0

Evonne Goolagong-Janet Young (AUS) d. Brenda Kirk-Pat Pretorius (RSA) 6-1, 6-2

1974
Australia d. United States 2-1 (Naples, Italy) Surface—Clay

Evonne Goolagong (AUS) d. Julie Heldman (USA) 6-1, 7-5

Jeanne Evert (USA) d. Dianne Fromholtz (AUS) 2-6, 7-5, 6-4

Evonne Goolagong-Janet Young (AUS) d. Julie Heldman-Sharon Walsh (USA) 7-5, 8-6

1975
Czechoslovakia d. Australia 3-0 (Aix-en-Provence, France) Surface—Clay

Martina Navratilova (CZE) d. Evonne Goolagong (AUS) 6-3, 6-4

Renata Tomanova (CZE) d. Helen Gourlay (AUS) 6-4, 6-2

Martina Navratilova-Renata Tomanova (CZE) d. Dianne Fromholtz-Helen Gourlay (AUS) 6-3, 6-1

1976
United States d. Australia 2-1 (Philadelphia) Surface—Indoor Carpet

Kerry Melville Reid (AUS) d. Rosie Casals (USA) 1-6, 6-3, 7-5

Billie Jean King (USA) d. Evonne Goolagong (USA) 7-6 (7-4), 6-4

Billie Jean King-Rosie Casals (USA) d. Evonne Goolagong-Kerry Melville Reid (AUS) 7-5, 6-3

1977
United States d. Australia 2-1 (Eastbourne, England) Surface—Grass

Billie Jean King (USA) d. Dianne Fromholtz (AUS) 6-1, 2-6, 6-2

Chris Evert (USA) d. Kerry Melville Reid (AUS) 7-5, 6-3

Kerry Melville Reid-Wendy Turnbull (AUS) d. Chris Evert-Rosie Casals (USA) 6-3, 6-3

1978

United States d. Australia 2-1 (Melbourne) Surface—Grass

Kerry Melville Reid (AUS) d. Tracy Austin (USA) 6-3, 6-3

Chris Evert (USA) d. Wendy Turnbull (AUS) 3-6, 6-1, 6-1

Chris Evert-Billie Jean King (USA) d. Wendy Turnbull-Kerry Melville Reid (AUS) 4-6, 6-1, 6-4

1979

United States d. Australia 3-0 (Madrid) Surface—Clay

Tracy Austin (USA) d. Kerry Melville Reid (AUS) 6-3, 6-0

Chris Evert Lloyd (USA) d. Dianne Fromholtz (AUS) 2-6, 6-3, 8-6

Billie Jean King-Rosie Casals (USA) d. Wendy Turnbull-Kerry Melville Reid (AUS) 3-6, 6-3, 8-6

1980

United States d. Australia 3-0 (Berlin) Surface—Clay

Chris Evert Lloyd (USA) d. Dianne Fromholtz (AUS) 4-6, 6-1, 6-1

Tracy Austin (USA) d. Wendy Turnbull (AUS) 6-2, 6-3

Rosie Casals-Kathy Jordan (USA) d. Dianne Fromholtz-Susan Leo (AUS) 2-6, 6-4, 6-4

1981

United States d. Great Britain 3-0 (Tokyo) Surface—Clay

Chris Evert Lloyd (USA) d. Sue Barker (GBR) 6-2, 6-1

Andrea Jaeger (USA) d. Virginia Wade (GBR) 6-3, 6-1

Kathy Jordan-Rosie Casals (USA) d. Sue Barker-Virginia Wade (GBR) 6-4, 7-5

1982

United States d. West Germany 3-0 (Santa Clara, Calif.) Surface—Hard

Chris Evert Lloyd (USA) d. Claudia Kohde-Kilsch (GER) 2-6, 6-1, 6-3

Martina Navratilova (USA) d. Bettina Bunge (GER) 6-4, 6-4

Martina Navratilova-Chris Evert Lloyd (USA) d. Claudia Kohde-Kilsch-Bettina Bunge (GER) 3-6, 6-1, 6-2

1983

Czechoslovakia d. West Germany 2-1 (Zurich, Switzerland) Surface—Clay

Helena Sukova (CZE) d. Claudia Kohde-Kilsch (GER) 6-4, 2-6, 6-2

Hana Mandlikova (CZE) d. Bettina Bunge (GER) 6-2, 3-0 ret.

Claudia Kohde-Kilsch-Eva Pfaff (GER) d. Iva Budarova-Marcela Skuherska (CZE) 3-6, 6-2, 6-1

1984

Czechoslovakia d. Australia 2-1 (Sao Paulo, Brazil) Surface—Clay

Anne Minter (AUS) d. Helena Sukova (CZE) 7-5, 7-5

Hana Mandlikova (CZE) d. Elizabeth Sayers (AUS) 6-1, 6-0

Hana Mandlikova-Helena Sukova (CZE) d. Elizabeth Sayers-Wendy Turnbull (AUS) 6-2, 6-2

1985

Czechoslovakia d. United States 2-1 (Nagoya, Japan) Surface—Hard

Hana Mandlikova (CZE) d. Kathy Jordan (USA) 7-5, 6-1

Helena Sukova (CZE) d. Elise Burgin (USA) 6-3, 6-7, 6-4

Elise Burgin-Sharon Walsh (USA) d. Regina Marsikova-Andrea Holikova (CZE) 6-2, 6-3

1986

United States d. Czechoslovakia 3-0 (Prague, Czechoslovakia) Surface—Clay

Chris Evert Lloyd (USA) d. Helena Sukova (CZE) 7-5, 7-6 (7-5)

Martina Navratilova (USA) d. Hana Mandlikova (CZE) 7-5, 6-1

Martina Navratilova-Pam Shriver (USA) d. Hana Mandlikova-Helena Sukova (CZE) 6-4, 6-2

1987

West Germany d. United States 2-1 (West Vancouver, British Columbia Canada) Surface—Hard

Pam Shriver (USA) d. Claudia Kohde-Kilsch (GER) 6-0, 7-6, (7-5)

Steffi Graf (GER) d. Chris Evert (USA) 6-2, 6-1

Steffi Graf-Claudia Kohde-Kilsch (GER) d. Chris Evert-Pam Shriver (USA) 1-6, 7-5, 6-4

1988

Czechoslovakia d. U.S.S.R. 2-1 (Melbourne) Surface—Hard

Radka Zrubakova (CZE) d. Larisa Savchenko (USSR) 6-1, 7-6, (7-2)

Helena Sukova (CZE) d. Natalia Zvereva (USSR) 6-3, 6-4

Larisa Savchenko-Natalia Zvereva (USSR) d. Jana Novotna-Jana Pospisilova (CZE) 7-6, (7-5), 7-5

1989

United States d. Spain 3-0 (Tokyo) Surface—Hard

Chris Evert (USA) d. Conchita Martinez (ESP) 6-3, 6-2

Martina Navratilova (USA) d. Arantxa Sanchez Vicario (ESP) 0-6, 6-3, 6-4

Zina Garrison-Pam Shriver (USA) d. Conchita Martinez-Arantxa Sanchez Vicario (ESP) 7-5, 6-1

1990

United States d. U.S.S.R. 2-1 (Atlanta) Surface—Hard

Jennifer Capriati (USA) d. Leila Meskhi (USSR) 7-6 (13-11), 6-2

Natalia Zvereva (USSR) d. Zina Garrison (USA) 6-3, 7-5

Zina Garrison-Gigi Fernandez (USA) d. Natalia Zvereva-Larisa Savchenko (USSR) 6-4, 6-3

1991

Spain d. United States 2-1 (Nottingham, England) Surface—Hard

Jennifer Capriati (USA) d. Conchita Martinez (ESP) 4-6, 7-6 (7-3), 6-1

Arantxa Sanchez Vicario (ESP) d. Mary Joe Fernandez (USA) 6-3, 6-4

Conchita Martinez-Arantxa Sanchez Vicario (ESP) d. Gigi Fernandez-Zina Garrison (USA) 3-6, 6-1, 6-1

1992

Germany d. Spain 2-1 (Frankfurt) Surface—Clay

Steffi Graf (GER) d. Arantxa Sanchez Vicario (ESP) 6-4, 6-2

Anke Huber (GER) d. Conchita Martinez (ESP) 6-3, 6-7, (1-7), 6-1

Arantxa Sanchez Vicario-Conchita Martinez (ESP) Anke Huber-Barbara Rittner (GER) 6-1, 6-2

1993

Spain d. Australia 3-0 (Frankfurt) Surface—Clay

Conchita Martinez (ESP) d. Michelle Jaggard-Lai (AUS) 6-0, 6-2

Arantxa Sanchez Vicario (ESP) d. Nicole Provis (AUS) 6-2, 6-3

Conchita Martinez-Arantxa Sanchez Vicario (ESP) d. Liz Sayers Smylie-Rennae Stubbs (AUS) 3-6, 6-1, 6-3

1994

Spain d. United States 3-0 (Frankfurt) Surface–Clay

Conchita Martinez (ESP) d. Mary Joe Fernandez (USA) 6-2, 6-2

Arantxa Sanchez Vicario (ESP) d. Lindsay Davenport (USA) 6-2, 6-1

Conchita Martinez-Arantxa Sanchez Vicario (ESP) d. Gigi Fernandez-Mary Joe Fernandez (USA) 6-3, 6-4

1995 (Format changed to best of five-match series and home and away draw)

Spain d. United States 3-2 (Valencia, Spain) Surface–Clay

Conchita Martinez (ESP) d. Chanda Rubin (USA) 7-5, 7-6 (7-3)

Arantxa Sanchez Vicario (ESP) d. Mary Joe Fernandez (USA) 6-3, 6-2

Conchita Martinez (ESP) d. Mary Joe Fernandez (USA) 6-3, 6-4

Chanda Rubin (USA) d. Arantxa Sanchez Vicario (ESP) 1-6, 6-4, 6-4

Lindsay Davenport-Gigi Fernandez (USA) d. Virginia Ruano Pascual-Maria Antonia Sanchez Lorenzo (ESP) 6-3, 7-6 (7-3)

1996

United States d. Spain 5-0 (Atlantic City) Surface–Indoor Carpet

Monica Seles (USA) d. Conchita Martinez (ESP) 6-2, 6-4

Lindsay Davenport (USA) d. Arantxa Sanchez Vicario (ESP) 7-5, 6-1

Monica Seles (USA) d. Arantxa Sanchez Vicario (ESP) 3-6, 6-3, 6-1

Lindsay Davenport (USA) d. Gala Leon Garica (ESP) 7-5, 6-2

Mary Joe Fernandez-Lindsay Davenport (USA) d. Gala Leon Garcia-Virginia Ruano Pascual (ESP) 6-1, 6-4

1997

France d. Netherlands 4-1 (s-Hertongenbosch, Netherlands) Surface–Indoor Carpet

Sandrine Testud (FRA) d. Brenda Schultz-McCarthy (NED) 6-4, 4-6, 6-3

Mary Pierce (FRA) d. Miriam Oremans (NED) 6-4, 6-1

Brenda Schultz-McCarthy (NED) d. Mary Pierce (FRA) 4-6, 6-3, 6-4

Sandrine Testud (FRA) d. Miriam Oremans (NED) 0-6, 6-3, 6-3

Alexandra Fusai-Nathalie Tauziat (FRA) d. Manon Bollegraf-Caroline Vis (NED) 6-3, 6-4

1998

Spain d. Switzerland 3-2 (Geneva) Surface–Hard

Arantxa Sanchez Vicario (ESP) d. Patty Schnyder (SUI) 6-2, 3-6, 6-2

Martina Hingis (SUI) d. Conchita Martinez (ESP) 6-4, 6-4

Martina Hingis (SUI) d. Arantxa Sanchez Vicario (ESP) 7-6 (7-5), 6-3

Conchita Martinez (ESP) d. Patty Schnyder (SUI) 6-3, 2-6, 9-7

Conchita Martinez-Arantxa Sanchez Vicario (ESP) d. Martina Hingis-Patty Schnyder (SUI) 6-0, 6-2

1999

United States d. Russia 4-1 (Stanford, Calif.) Surface–Hard

Venus Williams (USA) d. Elena Likhovtseva (RUS) 6-3, 6-4

Lindsay Davenport (USA) d. Elena Dementieva (RUS) 6-4, 6-0

Lindsay Davenport (USA) d. Elena Likhovtseva (RUS) 6-4, 6-4

Elena Dementieva (RUS) d. Venus Williams (USA) 1-6, 6-3, 7-6 (5)

Serena Williams-Venus Williams (USA) d. Elena Dementieva-Elena Makarova (RUS) 6-2, 6-1

2000

United States d. Spain 5-0 (Las Vegas) Surface–Indoor Carpet

Monica Seles (USA) d. Conchita Martinez (ESP) 6-2, 6-3

Lindsay Davenport (USA) d. Arantxa Sanchez Vicario (ESP) 6-2, 1-6, 6-3

Lindsay Davenport (USA) d. Conchita Martinez (ESP) 6-1, 6-2

Jennifer Capriati (USA) d. Arantxa Sanchez Vicario (ESP) 6-1, 1-0, retired

Jennifer Capriati-Lisa Raymond (USA) d. Virginia Ruano-Pascual-Magui Serna (ESP) 4-6, 6-4, 6-2

2001 (format changed for one year to best-of-three)

Belgium d. Russia 2-1 (Madrid, Spain) Surface–Clay

Justine Henin (BEL) d. Nadia Petrova (RUS) 6-0, 6-3

Kim Clijsters (BEL) d. Elena Dementieva (RUS) 6-0, 6-4

Nadia Petrova-Elena Likhovtseva (RUS) d. Els Callens-Laurence Courtois (BEL) 7-5, 7-6 (7-2)

2002

Slovak Republic d. Spain 3-1 (Maspalomas, Canary Islands) Surface–Hard

Conchita Martinez (ESP) d. Jannette Husarova (SVK) 6-4, 7-6 (8-6)

Daniela Hantuchova (SVK) d. Magui Serna (ESP) 6-2, 6-1

Daniela Hantuchova (SVK) d. Conchita Martinez (ESP) 6-7 (8-10), 7-5, 6-4

Jannette Husarova (SVK) d. Arantxa Sanchez Vicario (ESP) 6-0, 6-2

Virginia Ruano Pascual-Magui Serna vs Jannette Husarova-Daniela Hantuchova, canceled

2003

France d. United States 4-1 (Moscow, Russia) Surface– Indoor Carpet

Amelie Mauresmo (FRA) d. Lisa Raymond (USA) 6-4, 6-3

Mary Pierce (FRA) d. Meghann Shaughnessy (USA) 6-3, 3-6, 8-6

Amelie Mauresmo (FRA) d. Meghann Shaughnessy (USA) 6-2, 6-1

Emilie Loit (FRA) d. Alexandra Stevenson (USA) 6-4, 6-2

Martina Navratilova-Lisa Raymond (USA) d. Stephanie Cohen-Aloro-Emilie Loit (FRA) 6-4, 6-0

2004

Russia d. France 3-2 (Moscow, Russia) Surface– Indoor Carpet

Nathalie Dechy (FRA) d. Svetlana Kuznetsova (RUS) 3-6, 7-6, 8-6

Anastasia Myskina (RUS) d. Tatiana Golovin (FRA) 6-4, 7-6

Anastasia Myskina (RUS) d. Nathalie Dechy (FRA) 6-3, 6-4

Tatiana Golovin (FRA) d. Svetlana Kuznetsova (RUS) 6-4, 6-1

Anastasia Myskina-Vera Zvonareva (RUS) d. Marion Bartoli-Emilie Loit (FRA) 7-6, 7-5

2005

Russia d. France 3-2 (Paris, France) Surface–Clay

Elena Dementieva (RUS) d. Mary Pierce (FRA) 7-6, 2-6, 6-1

Amelie Mauresmo (FRA) d. Anastasia Myskina (RUS) 6-4, 6-2

Elena Dementieva (RUS) d. Amelie Mauresmo (FRA) 6-4, 4-6, 6-2

Mary Pierce (FRA) d. Anastasia Myskina (RUS) 4-6, 6-4, 6-2

Elena Dementieva-Dinara Safina (RUS) d. Amelie Mauresmo-Mary Pierce (FRA) 6-4, 1-6, 6-3

2006

Italy d. Belgium 3-2 (Charleroi, Belgium) Surface—Hard

Francesca Schiavone (ITA) d. Kirsten Flipkens (BEL) 6-1, 6-3

Justin Henin-Hardenne (BEL) d. Flavia Pennetta (ITA) 6-4, 7-5

Justin Henin-Hardenne (BEL) d. Francesca Schiavone (ITA) 6-4, 7-5

Mara Santangelo (ITA) d. Kirsten Flipkens (BEL) 6-7, 6-3, 6-0

Francesca Schiavone-Roberta Vinci (ITA) d. Kirsten Flipkens-
    Justin Henin-Hardenne (BEL) 3-6, 6-2, 2-0 retired Henin, injury

2007

Russia d. Italy 4-0 (Moscow, Russia) Surface—Carpet

Anna Chakvetadze (RUS) d. Francesca Schiavone (ITA) 6-4, 4-6, 6-4

Svetlana Kuznetsova (RUS) d. Mara Santangelo (ITA) 6-1, 6-2

Svetlana Kuznetsova (RUS) d. Francesca Schiavone (ITA) 4-6, 7-6, 7-5

Elena Vesnina (RUS) d. Mara Santangelo (ITA) 6-3, 6-4

Nadia Petrova-Elena Vesnina vs Mara Santangelo-Roberto Vinci, not played

2008

Russia d. Spain 4-0 (Madrid, Spain) Clay

Vera Zvonareva (RUS) d. Anabel Medina Garrigues (ESP) 6-3, 6-4

Svetlana Kuznetsova (RUS) d. Carla Suarez Navarro (ESP) 6-3, 6-1

Svetlana Kuznetsova (RUS) d. Anabel Medina Garrigues (ESP) 5-7, 6-3, 6-4

Vera Zvonareva (RUS) vs. Carla Suarez Navarro (ESP) not played

Ekaterina Makerova and Elena Vesnina (RUS) d.Carla Suarez Navarro and
Nuria Llagostera Vives 6-2, 6-1

Fed Cup Records

Entering 2009 Competition

Nation

MOST TITLES

	Total	Years
USA	17	1963, 1966-67, 1969, 1976-82, 1986, 1989-90, 1996, 1999, 2000
Australia	7	1964-65, 1968, 1970-71, 1973-74
Russia	6	2004-2005, 2007, 2008
Czechoslavakia	5	1975, 1983-85, 1988
Spain	5	1991, 1993, 1994, 1995, 1998
Germany	2	1982, 1992
France	2	1997, 2003
Belgium	1	2001
Italy	1	2006
South Africa	1	1972
Slovak Republic	1	2002

MOST SERIES WON

	Total	Yrs played
USA	38-28	46
Australia	118-44	47
Great Britain	107-61	47
Netherlands	90-61	46
Czech Republic	85-34	39
Germany	85-34	45
France	81-50	47
Russia	81-33	33
Canada	81-60	46
Korea, Rep.	80-59	35
Indonesia	73-58	39
Japan	70-54	42
Spain	70-44	38

MOST FINAL APPEARANCES

	Total	Record
USA	26	17-9
Australia	17	7-10
Spain	11	4-7
Russia	8	4-4
Czechoslavakia	6	5-1
Germany	6	2-4
France	4	2-2
Great Britain	4	0-4
South Africa	2	1-1
Netherlands	2	0-2
Belgium	2	1-1
Italy	2	1-1
Slovak Republic	1	1-0
Switzerland	1	0-1

Individual

MOST SERIES PLAYED

	Total	W-L
Smashnova, Anna (ISR)	61	43-30
Sanchez Vicario, Arantxa (ESP)	58	72-28
Wade, Virginia (GBR)	57	66-33
Savchenko-Neiland, Larisa (USSR-LAT)	57	67-22
Obziler, Tzipi (ISR)	61	51-39
Basuki, Yayuk (INA)	55	58-28
Schaerer, Larissa (PAR)	55	64-32
Sukova, Helena (CZE)	54	57-16
Zvereva, Natalia (BLR)	54	59-21
Martinez, Conchita (ESP)	53	68-23

MOST MATCHES PLAYED

	Total	Series
Sanchez Vicario, Arantxa (ESP)	100	58
Wade, Virginia (GBR)	99	57
Schaerer, Larissa (PAR)	96	55
Savchenko-Neiland, Larisa (USSR-LAT)	89	57
Martinez, Conchita (ESP)	91	53
Basuki, Yayuk (INA)	86	55
Prakusya, Wynne (INA)	82	45
Zvereva, Natalia (BLR)	80	54

MOST WINS, OVERALL

	Total	Series
Sanchez Vicario, Arantxa (ESP)	72-28	58
Martinez, Conchita (ESP)	68-23	53
Wade, Virginia (GBR)	66-33	57
Savchenko-Neiland, Larisa (USSR-LAT)	65-22	55
Schaerer, Larissa (PAR)	64-32	55
Prakusya, Wynne (INA)	61-21	45
Zvereva, Natalia (BLR)	59-21	54
Basuki, Yayuk (INA)	58-28	55
Evert, Chris (USA)	57-4	42
Sukova, Helena (CZE)	57-16	54
King, Billie Jean (USA)	52-4	36
Wang, Shi-Ting (TPE)	51-25	49
Cabezas, Paula (CHI)	49-21	39
Mandlikova, Hana (CZE)	49-12	45

MOST WINS – SINGLES

	W-L	Ties
Sanchez Vicario, Arantxa (ESP)	50-22	58
Martinez, Conchita (ESP)	47-18	53
Sukova, Helena (CZE)	45-11	54
Evert, Chris (USA)	40-2	42
Schaerer, Larissa (PAR)	39-17	55
Smashnova, Anna (ISR)	38-24	61
Kremer, Anne (LUX)	38-17	54
Wade, Virginia (GBR)	36-20	57
Zvereva, Natalia (BLR)	35 -16	54
Mandlikova, Hana (CZE)	34-6	45

MOST WINS – DOUBLES

	W-L	Ties
Savchenko-Neiland, Larisa (USSR-LAT)	38-7	57
Prakusya, Wynne (INA)	38-7	45
Wade, Virginia (GBR)	30-13	57
Basuki, Yayuk (INA)	29-7	55
Turnbull, Wendy (AUS)	29-8	45
Obziler, Tzipi (ISR)	28-23	61
King, Billie Jean (USA)	26-1	36
Casals, Rosie (USA)	26-1	29
Schaerer, Larissa (PAR)	25-15	55
Krizan, Tina (SLO)	25-19	46

MOST WINS – DOUBLES TEAM

	W-L	Ties	Yrs
Martinez, Conchita / Sanchez Vicario, Arantxa (ESP)			
	18-3	21	10
Anggarkusuma, Suzanna / Basuki, Yayuk (INA)	16-0	18	3
Cabezas, Paula / Castro, Barbara (CHI)	15-5	20	5
Barker, Sue / Wade, Virginia (GBR)	13-3	16	7
Neiland, Larisa / Zvereva, Natalia (RUS)	12-1	13	4
Durie, Jo / Hobbs, Anne (GBR)	12-2	14	6
Cordova, Yamile / Montesino, Yoany (CUB)	12-5	15	6
Kim, Ii-Soon / Lee, Jeong-Myung (KOR)	12-5	17	5
Reid, Kerry / Turnbull, Wendy (AUS)	11-4	15	3

MOST APPEARANCES – FINAL

	Total	W-L
Martinez, Conchita (ESP)	10	11-9
Sanchez Vicario, Arantxa (ESP)	10	10-10
King, Billie Jean (USA)	9	12-2
Evert, Chris (USA)	9	10-3
Court, Margaret (AUS)	6	8-4
Casals, Rosie (USA)	6	5-2
Reid, Kerry (AUS)	6	5-6
Davenport, Lindsay (USA)	5	7-1
Goolagong, Evonne (AUS)	5	5-3
Sukova, Helena (CZE)	5	4-3
Turnbull, Wendy (AUS)	5	1-5
Balestrat, Dianne (AUS)	5	0-6
Navratilova, Martina (USA/CZE)	5	8-0

Miscellaneous Records

MOST CUP-WINNING YEARS

7	Billie Jean Moffitt King (USA)	1963, 1966-67, 1976-79

MOST CONSECUTIVE SERIES WON

38	USA	1976-1983

MOST CONSECUTIVE SINGLES WON

29	Chris Evert (USA)	1997-82, 86

MOST CUPS WON AS CAPTAIN

4	Shamil Tarpischev (RUS)	2004-2005, 2007-2008
	Vicki Berner (USA)	1977-80
	Miguel Margets (ESP)	1993-95, 1998
	Billie Jean King (USA)	1976, 1996, 1999-2000

LONGEST SINGLES MATCH

54 games Victoria Baldovinos (ESP) d. Judith Connor (NZL) 6-4, 11-13, 11-9, 1974

Nathalie Tauziat (FRA) d. Naoko Sawamatsu (JPN) 7-5, 4-6, 17-15, 1997

LONGEST DOUBLES MATCH

51 games Margaret Smith Court-Kerry Melville Reid (AUS) d. Winnie Shaw-Virginia Wade (GBR) 9-7, 3-6, 14-12, 1968

Olympic Games CHAPTER 12

Justine Henin-Hardenne of Belgium (center) won the gold medal in women's singles at the 2004 Olympic Games in Athens, Greece. **Amelie Mauresmo** of France (left) won the silver medal, while **Alicia Molik** of Australia (right) won the bronze medal

In 1896, when the Olympic Games of ancient Greece was revived, tennis was on the menu at Athens, and stayed there through the 1924 Games in Paris. A dispute between the ITF (International Tennis Federation) and the IOC (International Olympic Committee) knocked tennis out until 1988 in Seoul, Korea. The ITF didn't like the shabby way the IOC had been managing the tennis tournament, and the IOC questioned the amateur standing of tennis players. Much ado, but amusingly when tennis returned the pros were accepted, paving the way for professional athletes in the other sports.

Progressive ITF President Philippe Chatrier of France worked hard with chief aide David Gray (both members of the Hall of Fame) to restore their sport to the Games. Juan Antonio Samaranch, the IOC poobah, agreed that a sport should be represented by its best athletes, and permitted entrance of tennis pros, a breakthrough.

As usual, showing a lack of imagination, the ITF runs just another conventional tournament, overlooking the opportunity to innovate by adding a team competition (World Team Tennis rules), uniquely involving men and women.

German Steffi Graf's feat of 1988—the "Golden Slam"—will be very difficult to beat. Defeating Argentina's Gabriela Sabatini 6-3, 6-3 in the final, she added the gold medal to her Grand Slam.

Something of an accident was the winning of the first gold medals in 1896. John Pius Boland, an Oxford student, had stopped by Athens as a spectator, but somebody suggested he enter. Representing Britain and his native Ireland, Boland took some fun away from the hosts by beating Greece's Dionysius Kasdaglis in the singles, 7-5, 6-4, 6-1, and united with a German, Fritz Traun, to repel the locals Demetrios Petrokokkinos and Kasdaglis in the doubles, 6-2, 6-4.

Indoor and outdoor tournaments were held at London in 1908 and Stockholm in 1912. Britain's Arthur Gore, a Wimbledon champ and original Davis Cupper, won two golds inside in London, singles, and with another Davis Cup original, Herbert Roper Barrett, the doubles.

Charlotte Cooper (Sterry) of Britain, also a Wimbledon champ, was the first woman to wear gold, defeating Helene Prevost of France, 6-1, 6-4, at Paris in 1900. Charlotte also took the mixed with fellow Brit Reggie Doherty during a busy time for the Doherty brothers—three golds. Laurie won the singles, and, with Reggie, the doubles, Reggie also won a bronze in singles.

In a U.S. sweep, 1924 in Paris, Vinnie Richards hauled in two golds and a silver, winning the singles, the doubles with Frank Hunter, and as runner-up in the mixed to the oldies, Hazel Wightman, 37, and Dick Williams, 33. Helen Wills, 18, won the singles, then the doubles with Wightman.

After an intermission of 64 years, tennis was in again—Graf and Miloslav Mecir of Czechoslovakia winning in Seoul. Graf was upset by 15-year-old Jennifer Capriati of the United States, 3-6, 6-3,

6-4, for gold in Barcelona in 1992. Homeboy Jordi Arrese came from the back of the pack—he was the No. 16 seed—to earn silver, but 6-foot-6 Swiss Marc Rosset had a golden touch with 38 aces to outlast him in the longest final (56 games), 7-6 (7-2), 6-4, 4-6, 3-6, 8-6.

Mike Agassi, former Olympic boxer for Iran, was on hand in Atlanta in 1996 to cheer for the singles gold medal winner, his son Andre, a 6-2, 6-3, 6-1 victor over Spain's Sergi Bruguera.

Russia got into the act in Sydney in 2000 as Yevgeny Kafelnikov took the gold and Elena Dementieva the silver. But her task was hopeless, opposite the commanding Venus Williams, 6-2, 6-4. Venus and little sister Serena romped to the doubles gold, a sibling success like the Dohertys a century before.

Mary Joe Fernandez became an Olympic standout for the United States in the post-1924 era, winning golds in doubles with Gigi Fernandez in 1992 and 1996 and earning a bronze in 1992 in singles.

Two newcomers were heard from in 2004: Chile and Belgium—in the persons of Nicolas Massu and Justine Henin-Hardenne, singles gold medalists as the Olympics returned to Greece.

At the 2008 Olympic Games, Roger Federer fulfilled a career goal by winning a gold medal, but it unexpectedly came in doubles alongside Stan Wawrinka after an upset loss to American James Blake in the singles quarterfinals. Rafael Nadal of Spain won men's singles gold, defeating Fernando Gonzalez of Chile in the final, while Elena Dementieva topped the all-Russian medal stand in women's singles - Dinara Safina earning silver and Vera Zvonareva winning bronze. The Williams sisters won their second Olympic gold in women's doubles (to go with doubles gold from Sydney in 2000).

Olympic Results

1896 – Athens, Greece

MEDALISTS

Men's Singles
Gold John Boland (GBR)
Silver Demis Kastaglis (GRE)
Bronze Momcsillo Topavicza (HUN)

Men's Doubles
Gold John Boland (GBR) and Fritz Traun (GER)
Silver Demis Kasdaglis and Demetrious Petrokokkinos (GRE)
Bronze Edwin Hack (AUS) and George Robertson (GBR)

RESULTS

Men's Singles Gold Medal Match John Boland (GBR) def. Demis Kastaglis (GRE), 7-5, 6-4, 6-1

Men's Doubles Gold Medal Match John Boland (GBR) and Fritz Traun (GER) d. Demis Kasdaglis and Demetrios Petrokokkinos (GRE), 6-2, 6-4

1900 – Paris, France

MEDALISTS

Men's Singles
Gold Laurie Doherty (GBR)
Silver Harold Mahony (GBR)
Bronze Reggie Doherty (GBR)
Arthur Norris (GBR)

Men's Doubles
Gold Reggie Doherty and Laurie Doherty (GBR)
Silver Spalding de Garmendia (USA) and Max Decugis (FRA)
Bronze Georges de la Chapelle and Andre Prevost (FRA)
Harold Mahony and Arthur Norris (GBR)

Women's Singles
Gold Charlotte Cooper (GBR)
Silver Helene Prevost (FRA)
Bronze Marion Jones (USA)
Hedwig Rosenbaum (BOH)

Mixed Doubles
Gold Charlotte Cooper and Reggie Doherty (GBR)
Silver Helene Prevost (FRA) and Harold Mahony (GBR)
Bronze Hedwig Rosenbaum (BOH) and Archibald Walden (GBR)
Laurie Doherty (GBR) and Marion Jones (USA)

RESULTS

Men's Singles Gold Medal Match Laurie Doherty (GBR) def. Harold Mahony (GBR), 6-4, 6-2, 6-3

Men's Doubles Gold Medal Match Reggie Doherty-Laurie Doherty (GBR) def. Spalding de Garmendia (USA) and Max Decugis (FRA), 6-3, 6-3, 7-5

Women's Singles Gold Medal Match Charlotte Cooper (GBR) def. Helene Prevost (FRA), 6-3, 6-3, 7-5

Mixed Doubles Gold Medal Match Charlotte Cooper and Reggie Doherty (GBR) def. Helene Prevost (FRA) and Harold Mahony (GBR), 6-2, 6-4

1904 – St. Louis, Missouri, United States

MEDALISTS

Men's Singles
Gold Beals Wright (USA)
Silver Robert LeRoy (USA)
Bronze Alphonso Bell (USA)
Edgar Leonard (USA)

Men's Doubles
Gold Edgar Leonard and Beals Wright (USA)
Silver Alphonso Bell and Robert LeRoy (USA)
Bronze Joseph Wear and Allen West (USA)
Clarence Gamble and Arthur Wear (USA)

RESULTS

Men's Singles Gold Medal Match Beals Wright (USA) def. Robert LeRoy (USA) 6-4, 6-4

Men's Doubles Gold Medal Match Edgar Leonard and Beals Wright (USA) def. Alphonso Bell and Robert LeRoy (USA), 6-4, 6-4, 6-2

1908 – London, England (Outdoor)

MEDALISTS

Men's Singles
Gold Josiah Ritchie (GBR)
Silver Otto Froitzheim (GER)
Bronze Wilberforce Eaves (GBR)

Men's Doubles
Gold George Hillyard and Reggie Doherty (GBR)
Silver Josiah Richie and James Parke (GBR)
Bronze Charles Cazalet and Charles Dixon (GBR)

Women's Singles
Gold Dorothea Chambers (GBR)
Silver Dora Boothby (GBR)
Bronze Joan Winch (GBR)

RESULTS

Men's Singles Gold Medal Match Josiah Ritchie (GBR) def. Otto Froitzheim (GER), 7-5, 6-3, 6-4

Men's Singles Bronze Medal Match Wilberforce Eaves (GBR) def. Ivie John Richardson (RSA), 6-2, 6-2, 6-3

Men's Doubles Gold Medal Match George Hillyard and Reggie Doherty (GBR) def. Josiah Richie and James Parke (GBR) 9-7, 7-5, 9-7.

Women's Singles Gold Medal Match Dorothea Chambers (GBR) def. Dora Boothby (GBR), 6-1, 7-5

1908 – London, England (Indoor)

MEDALISTS

Men's Singles
Gold Arthur Gore (GBR)
Silver George Caridia (GBR)
Bronze Josiah Ritchie (GBR)

Men's Doubles

Gold	Arthur Gore and Herbert Roper Barrett (GBR)
Silver	George Simond and George Caridia (GBR)
Bronze	Wollmar Bostrom and Gunnar Setterwall (SWE)

Women's Singles

Gold	Gwendoline Smith (GBR)
Silver	Angela Greene (GBR)
Bronze	Martha Adlerstraille (SWE)

RESULTS

Men's Singles Gold Medal Match Arthur Gore (GBR) def. George Caridia (GBR), 6-3, 7-5, 6-4

Men's Doubles Gold Medal Match Arthur Gore and Herbert Roper Barrett (GBR) def. George Simond and George Caridia (GBR), 6-2, 2-6, 6-3, 6-3

Women's Singles Gold Medal Match Gwendoline Smith (GBR) def. Angela Greene (GBR), 6-2, 4-6, 6-0

1912 – Stockholm, Sweden (Outdoor)

MEDALISTS

Men's Singles

Gold	Charles Winslow (RSA)
Silver	Harold Kitson (RSA)
Bronze	Oskar Kreuzer (GER)

Men's Doubles

Gold	Charles Winslow and Harold Kitson (RSA)
Silver	Felix Pipes and Arthur Zborzil (AUT)
Bronze	Albert Canet and Eduard Meny De Maramgue (FRA)

Women's Singles

Gold	Marguerite Broquedis (FRA)
Silver	Dora Koring (GER)
Bronze	Molla Bjurstedt (NOR)

Mixed Doubles

Gold	Heinrich Schomburgk and Dora Koring (GER)
Silver	Gunnar Setterwall and Sigrid Fick (SWE)
Bronze	Albert Canet and Marguerite Broquedis (FRA)

RESULTS

Men's Singles Gold Medal Match Charles Winslow (RSA) def. Harold Kitson (RSA), 7-5, 4-6, 10-8, 8-6

Men's Singles Bronze Medal Match Oskar Kreuzer (GER) def. Ladislav Zemla (BOH), 6-2, 3-6, 6-3, 6-1

Men's Doubles Gold Medal Match Charles Winslow and Harold Kitson (RSA) def. Felix Pipes and Arthur Zborzil (AUT), 4-6, 6-1, 6-2, 6-2

Women's Singles Gold Medal Match Marguerite Broquedis (FRA) def. Dora Koring (GER), 4-6, 6-3, 6-4

Mixed Doubles Gold Medal Match Dora Koring and Heinrich Schomburgk (GER) def. Sigrid Fick and Gunnar Setterwall (SWE), 6-4, 6-0

1912 – Stockholm, Sweden (Indoor)

MEDALISTS

Men's Singles

Gold	Andre Gobert (FRA)
Silver	Charles Dixon (GBR)
Bronze	Anthony Wilding (NZL)

Men's Doubles

Gold	Andre Gobert and Maurice Germot (FRA)
Silver	Gunnar Setterwall and Carl Kempe (SWE)
Bronze	Arthur Beamish and Charles Dixon (GBR)

Women's Singles

Gold	Edith Hannam (GBR)
Silver	Thora Gerda Sophy Castenschiold (DEN)
Bronze	Mabel Parton (GBR)

Mixed Doubles

Gold	Charles Dixon and Edith Hannam (GBR)
Silver	Herbert Roper Barrett and Helen Aitchison (GBR)
Bronze	Gunnar Setterwall and Sigrid Fick (SWE)

RESULTS

Men's Singles Gold Medal Match Andre Gobert (FRA) def. Charles Dixon (GBR), 8-6, 6-4, 6-4

Men's Singles Bronze Medal Match Anthony Wilding (NZL) def. Gordon Lowe (GBR), 4-6, 6-2, 7-5, 6-0

Men's Doubles Gold Medal Match Andre Gobert and Maurice Germot (FRA) def. Gunnar Setterwall and Carl Kempe (SWE), 6-4, 12-14, 6-2, 6-4

Women's Singles Gold Medal Match Edith Hannam (GBR) def. Thora Gerda Sophy Castenschiold (DEN), 6-4, 6-3

Mixed Doubles Gold Medal Match Edith Hannam and Charles Dixon (GBR) def. Helen Aitchison and Herbert Roper Barrett (GBR), 6-4, 3-6, 6-2

1920 – Antwerp, Belgium

MEDALISTS

Men's Singles

Gold	Louis Raymond (RSA)
Silver	Ichiya Kumagae (JPN)
Bronze	Charles Winslow (RSA)

Men's Doubles

Gold	Noel Turnbull (RSA) and Max Woosnam (GBR)
Silver	Seiichiro Kashio and Ichiya Kumagae (JPN)
Bronze	Pierre Albarran and Max Decugis (FRA)

Women's Singles

Gold	Suzanne Lenglen (FRA)
Silver	Dorothy Holman (GBR)
Bronze	Kitty McKane (GBR)

Women's Doubles

Gold	Kitty McKane and Winifred McNair (GBR)
Silver	Geraldine Beamish and Dorothy Holman (GBR)
Bronze	Elizabeth D'Ayen and Suzanne Lenglen (FRA)

Mixed Doubles

Gold	Suzanne Lenglen and Max Decugis (FRA)
Silver	Kitty McKane and Max Woosnam (GBR)
Bronze	Milade Skrbkova and Razny Zemie (CZE)

RESULTS

Men's Singles Gold Medal Match Louis Raymond (RSA) def. Ichiya Kumagae (JPN), 5-7, 6-4, 7-5, 6-4

Men's Doubles Gold Medal Match Noel Turnbull (RSA) and Max Woosnam (GBR), def. Seiichiro Kashio and Ichiya Kumagae (JPN), 6-2, 7-5, 7-5

Women's Singles Gold Medal Match Suzanne Lenglen (FRA) def. Dorothy Holman (GBR), 6-3, 6-0

Women's Doubles Gold Medal Match Kitty McKane and Winifred McNair (GBR) def. Geraldine Beamish and Dorothy Holman (GBR), 8-6, 6-4

Mixed Doubles Gold Medal Match Suzanne Lenglen and Max Decugis (FRA) def. Kitty McKane and Max Woosnam (GBR), 6-4, 6-2

1924 – Paris, France

MEDALISTS

Men's Singles

Gold	Vincent Richards (USA)
Silver	Henri Cochet (FRA)
Bronze	Umberto Luigi de Morpurgo (ITA)

Men's Doubles

Gold	Vincent Richards and Frank Hunter (USA)
Silver	Jacques Brugnon and Henri Cochet (FRA)
Bronze	Jean Borotra and Rene Lacoste (FRA)

Women's Singles

Gold	Helen Wills (USA)
Silver	Didi Vlastro (FRA)
Bronze	Kitty McKane (GBR)

Women's Doubles

Gold	Helen Wills and Hazel Hotchkiss Wightman (USA)
Silver	Kitty McKane and Dorothy Covell (GBR)
Bronze	Evelyn Colyer and Dorothy Shepherd Barron (GBR)

Mixed Doubles

Gold	Hazel Hotchkiss Wightman and Dick Williams (USA)
Silver	Marion Jessup and Vincent Richards (USA)
Bronze	Hendrik Timmer and Cornelia Bouman (NED)

RESULTS

Men's Singles Gold Medal Match Vincent Richards (USA) def. Henri Cochet (FRA), 6-4, 6-4, 4-6, 5-7, 6-2

Men's Singles Bronze Medal Match Umberto Luigi de Morpurgo (ITA) def. Jean Borotra (FRA), 1-6, 6-1, 8-6, 4-6, 7-5

Men's Doubles Gold Medal Match Vincent Richards and Frank Hunter (USA) def. Jacques Brugnon and Henri Cochet (FRA), 4-6, 6-2, 6-3, 2-6, 6-3

Women's Singles Gold Medal Match Helen Wills (USA) def. Didi Vlastro (FRA), 6-2, 6-2

Women's Doubles Gold Medal Match Helen Wills and Hazel Hotchkiss Wightman (USA) def. Kitty McKane and Dorothy Covell (GBR), 7-5, 8-6

Mixed Doubles Gold Medal Match Hazel Hotchkiss Wightman and R. Norris Williams (USA) def. Marion Jessup and Vincent Richards (USA), 6-2, 6-3

1988 – Seoul, South Korea

MEDALISTS

Men's Singles

Gold	Miloslav Mecir (CZE)
Silver	Tim Mayotte (USA)
Bronze	Stefan Edberg (SWE) Brad Gilbert (USA)

Men's Doubles

Gold	Ken Flach and Robert Seguso (USA)
Silver	Sergio Casal and Emilio Sanchez (ESP)
Bronze	Stefan Edberg and Anders Jarryd (SWE) Miloslav Mecir and Milan Srejber (CZE)

Women's Singles

Gold	Steffi Graf (GER)
Silver	Gabriela Sabatini (ARG)
Bronze	Zina Garrison (USA) Manuela Maleeva (BUL)

Women's Doubles

Gold	Zina Garrison and Pam Shriver (USA)
Silver	Jana Novotna and Helena Sukova (CZE)
Bronze	Liz Smylie and Wendy Turnbull (AUS) Steffi Graf and Claudia Kohde Kilsch (GER)

RESULTS

Men's Singles Gold Medal Match Miloslav Mecir (CZE) def. Tim Mayotte (USA), 3-6, 6-2, 6-4, 6-2

Men's Doubles Gold Medal Match Ken Flach and Robert Seguso (USA) def. Sergio Casal and Emilio Sanchez (ESP), 6-3, 6-4, 6-7 (5-7), 6-7 (1-7), 9-7

Women's Singles Gold Medal Match Steffi Graf (GER) def. Gabriela Sabatini (ARG), 6-3, 6-3

Women's Doubles Gold Medal Match Zina Garrison and Pam Shriver (USA) def. Jana Novotna and Helena Sukova (CZE), 4-6, 6-2, 10-8

1992 – Barcelona, Spain

MEDALISTS

Men's Singles

Gold	Marc Rosset (SUI)
Silver	Jordi Arrese (ESP)
Bronze	Goran Ivanisevic (CRO) Andrei Cherkasov (CIS)

Men's Doubles

Gold	Boris Becker and Michael Stich (GER)
Silver	Wayne Ferreira and Piet Norval (RSA)
Bronze	Goran Ivanisevic and Goran Prpic (CRO) Javier Frana and Christian Miniussi (ARG)

Women's Singles

Gold	Jennifer Capriati (USA)
Silver	Steffi Graf (GER)
Bronze	Arantxa Sanchez Vicario (ESP) Mary Joe Fernandez (USA)

Women's Doubles

Gold	Mary Joe Fernandez and Gigi Fernandez (USA)
Silver	Conchita Martinez and Arantxa Sanchez Vicario (ESP)
Bronze	Natasha Zvereva and Leila Meshki (CIS) Rachael McQuillan and Nicole Provis (AUS)

RESULTS

Men's Singles Gold Medal Match Marc Rosset (SUI) def. Jordi Arrese (ESP), 7-6 (7-2), 6-4, 3-6, 4-6, 8-6

Men's Doubles Gold Medal Match Boris Becker and Michael Stich (GER) def. Wayne Ferreira and Piet Norval (RSA), 7-6 (7-5), 4-6, 7-6 (7-5), 6-3

Women's Singles Gold Medal Match Jennifer Capriati (USA) def. Steffi Graf (GER), 3-6, 6-3, 6-4

Women's Doubles Gold Medal Match Mary Joe Fernandez and Gigi Fernandez (USA) def. Conchita Martinez and Arantxa Sanchez Vicario (ESP), 7-5, 2-6, 6-2

1996 – Atlanta, Georgia, United States

MEDALISTS

Men's Singles

Gold	Andre Agassi (USA)
Silver	Sergi Bruguera (ESP)
Bronze	Leander Paes (IND)

Men's Doubles

Gold	Mark Woodforde and Todd Woodbridge (AUS)
Silver	Tim Henman and Neil Broad (GBR)
Bronze	Marc-Kevin Goellner and David Prinosil (GER)

Women's Singles

Gold	Lindsay Davenport (USA)
Silver	Arantxa Sanchez Vicario (ESP)
Bronze	Jana Novotna (CZE)

Women's Doubles

Gold	Mary Joe Fernandez and Gigi Fernandez (USA)
Silver	Jana Novotna and Helena Sukova (CZE)
Bronze	Arantxa Sanchez Vicario and Conchita Martinez (ESP)

RESULTS

Men's Singles Gold Medal Match Andre Agassi (USA) def. Sergi Bruguera (ESP), 6-2, 6-3, 6-1

Men's Singles Bronze Medal Match Leander Paes (IND) def. Fernando Meligeni (BRA), 3-6, 6-2, 6-4

Men's Doubles Gold Medal Match Mark Woodforde and Todd Woodbridge (AUS) def. Tim Henman and Neil Broad (GBR) 6-4, 6-4, 6-2

Men's Doubles Bronze Medal Match Marc-Kevin Goellner and David Prinosil (GER) def. Paul Haarhuis and Jacco Eltingh (NED), 6-2, 7-5

Women's Singles Gold Medal Match Lindsay Davenport (USA) def. Arantxa Sanchez Vicario (ESP), 7-6 (6), 6-2

Women's Singles Bronze Medal Match Jana Novotna (CZE) def. Mary Joe Fernandez (USA), 7-6 (8), 6-4

Women's Doubles Gold Medal Match Mary Joe Fernandez and Gigi Fernandez (USA) def. Jana Novona and Helena Sukova (CZE), 7-6 (6), 6-4

Women's Doubles Bronze Medal Match Conchita Martinez and Arantxa Sanchez Vicario (ESP) def. Manon Bollegraf and Brenda Schultz-McCarthy (NED), 6-1, 6-3

2000 – Sydney, Australia

MEDALISTS

Men's Singles

Gold	Yevgeny Kafelnikov (RUS)
Silver	Tommy Haas (GER)
Bronze	Arnaud DiPasquale (FRA)

Men's Doubles

Gold	Sebastien Lareau and Daniel Nestor (CAN)
Silver	Mark Woodforde and Todd Woodbridge (AUS)
Bronze	Alex Corretja and Albert Costa (ESP)

Women's Singles

Gold	Venus Williams (USA)
Silver	Elena Dementieva (RUS)
Bronze	Monica Seles (USA)

Women's Doubles

Gold	Venus Williams and Serena Williams (USA)
Silver	Miriam Oremans and Kristie Boogert (NED)
Bronze	Els Callens and Dominique Van Roost (BEL)

RESULTS

Men's Singles Gold Medal Match Yevgeny Kafelnikov (RUS) def. Tommy Haas (GER), 7-6 (4), 3-6, 6-2, 4-6, 6-3

Men's Singles Bronze Medal Match Arnaud DiPasquale (FRA) def. Roger Federer (SUI), 7-6 (5), 6-7 (7), 6-3

Men's Doubles Gold Medal Match Daniel Nestor and Sebastien Lareau (CAN) def. Mark Woodforde and Todd Woodbridge (AUS) 5-7, 6-3, 6-4, 7-6 (2)

Men's Doubles Bronze Medal Match Alex Corretja and Albert Costa (ESP), def. David Adams and John-Laffnie de Jager (RSA), 2-6, 6-4, 6-3

Women's Singles Gold Medal Match Venus Williams (USA) def. Elena Dementieva (RUS), 6-2, 6-4

Women's Singles Bronze Medal Match Monica Seles (USA) def. Jelena Dokic (AUS), 6-1, 6-4

Women's Doubles Gold Medal Match Venus Williams and Serena Williams (USA) def. Miriam Oremans and Kristie Boogert (NED) 6-1, 6-1

Women's Doubles Bronze Medal Match Els Callens and Dominique van Roost (BEL) def. Natalia Zvereva and Olga Barabanschikova (BLR), 4-6, 6-4, 6-1

2004 – Athens, Greece

MEDALISTS

Men's Singles

Gold	Nicolas Massu (CHI)
Silver	Mardy Fish (USA)
Bronze	Fernando Gonzalez (CHI)

Men's Doubles

Gold	Nicolas Massu and Fernando Gonzalez (CHI)
Silver	Nicolas Kiefer and Rainer Schuettler (GER)
Bronze	Ivan Ljubicic and Mario Ancic (CRO)

Women's Singles

Gold	Justine Henin-Hardenne (BEL)
Silver	Amelie Mauresmo (FRA)
Bronze	Alicia Molik (AUS)

Women's Doubles

Gold	Li Ting and Sun Tiantian (CHN)
Silver	Virginia Ruano Pascual and Conchita Martinez (ESP)
Bronze	Paola Suarez and Patricia Tarabini (ARG)

RESULTS

Men's Singles Gold Medal Match Nicolas Massu (CHI) def. Mardy Fish (USA) 6-3, 3-6, 2-6, 6-3, 6-4

Men's Singles Bronze Medal Match Fernando Gonzalez (CHI) def. Taylor Dent (USA), 6-4, 2-6, 16-14

Men's Doubles Gold Medal Match Nicolas Massu and Fernando Gonzalez (CHI) def. Nicolas Kiefer and Rainer Schuettler (GER), 6-2, 4-6, 3-6, 7-6 (7), 6-4

Men's Doubles Bronze Medal Match Ivan Ljubicic and Mario Ancic (CRO) def. Leander Paes and Mahesh Bhupathi (IND), 7-6 (5), 4-6, 16-14

Women's Singles Gold Medal Match Justine Henin-Hardenne (BEL) def. Amelie Mauresmo (FRA), 6-3, 6-3

Women's Singles Bronze Medal Match Alicia Molik (AUS) def. Anastasia Myskina (RUS), 6-3, 6-4

Women's Doubles Gold Medal Match Li Ting and Sun Tiantian (CHN) def. Virginia Ruano Pascual and Conchita Martinez (ESP), 6-3, 6-3

Women's Doubles Bronze Medal Match Paola Suarez and Patricia Tarabini (ARG) def. Ai Sugiyama and Shinobu Asagoe (JPN), 6-3, 6-3

2008 - Beijing, China

MEDALISTS

Men's Singles

Gold	Rafael Nadal (ESP)
Silver	Fernando Gonzalez (CHI)
Bronze	Novak Djokovic (SRB)

Men's Doubles

Gold	Roger Federer and Stan Wawrinka (SUI)
Silver	Thomas Johansson and Simon Aspelin (SWE)
Bronze	Bob Bryan and Mike Bryan (USA)

Women's Singles

Gold	Elena Dementieva (RUS)
Silver	Dinara Safina (RUS)
Bronze	Vera Zvonareva (RUS)

Women's Doubles

Gold	Venus Williams and Serena Williams (USA)
Silver	Anabel Medina Garrigues and Virginia Ruano Pascual (ESP)
Bronze	Yan Zi and Zheng Jie (CHN)

RESULTS

Men's Singles Gold Medal Match Rafael Nadal (ESP) def. Fernando Gonzalez (CHI) 6-3, 7-6 (2), 6-3

Men's Singles Bronze Medal Match Novak Djokovic (SRB) def. James Blake (USA)6-3, 7-6 (4)

Men's Doubles Gold Medal Match Roger Federer and Stan Wawrinka (SUI) def. Thomas Johansson and Simon Aspelin (SWE) 6-3, 6-4, 6-7 (4), 6-3

Men's Doubles Bronze Medal Match Bob Bryan and Mike Bryan (USA) def. Arnaud Clement and Michael Llodra (FRA) 3-6, 6-3, 6-4

Women's Singles Gold Medal Match Elena Dementieva (RUS) def. Dinara Safina (RUS) 3-6, 6-3, 7-5

Women's Singles Bronze Medal Match Vera Zvonareva (RUS) def. Na Li (CHN) 6-0, 7-5

Women's Doubles Gold Medal Match Venus Williams and Serena Williams (USA) def. Anabel Medina Garrigues and Virgina Ruano Pascual (ESP) 6-2, 6-0

Women's Doubles Bronze Medal Match Yan Zi and Zheng Jie (CHN) def. Alona Bondarenko and Kateryna Bondarenko (UKR) 6-2, 6-2

Olympics Records

Through 2008 Olympics

MOST OLYMPIC TOURNAMENTS PLAYED

Women

5   Arantxa Sanchez Vicario (ESP) 1988, 1992, 1996, 2000, 2004

Men

5	Mark Knowles (BAH)	1992, 1996, 2000, 2004, 2008
5	Leander Paes (IND)	1992, 1996, 2000, 2004, 2008
4	Max Decugis (FRA)	1900, 1908,1912, 1920
4	Mark Knowles (BAH)	1992,1996, 2000, 2004
4	Andrei Pavel (ROM)	1992, 1996, 2000, 2004
4	Leander Paes (IND)	1992, 1996, 2000, 2004

MOST MEDALS

Women

5	Kitty McKane (GBR)	1 gold, 2 silver, 2 bronze
4	Arantxa Sanchez Vicario (ESP)	2 silver, 2 bronze
3	Venus Williams (USA)	3 gold
	Mary Joe Fernandez (USA)	2 gold, 1 bronze
	Suzanne Lenglen (FRA)	2 gold, 1 bronze
	Conchita Martinez (ESP)	2 silver, 1 bronze
	Steffi Graf (GER)	1 gold, 1 silver, 1 bronze
	Jana Novotna (CZE)	2 silver, 1 bronze

Men

4	Reggie Doherty (GBR)	3 gold, 1 bronze
	Charles Dixon (GBR)	1 gold, 1 silver, 2 bronze
3	Fernando Gonzalez (CHI)	1 gold, 1 silver, 1 bronze
	Vincent Richards (USA)	2 gold, 1 silver
	Laurie Doherty (GBR)	2 gold, 1 bronze
	Harold Mahony (GBR)	2 silver, 1 bronze
	Charles Winslow (RSA)	2 gold, 1 bronze

MOST NUMBER OF GAMES IN A MATCH

76   George Lowe (GBR) d. A. Zerlendis (GRE) (Men's Singles) 14-12, 8-10, 5-7, 6-4, 6-4 - 1920 Antwerp

73   Reggie Doherty and George Hillyard (GBR) d. Charles Cazalet and Charles Dixon (GBR) (Men's Doubles) 5-7, 2-6, 6-4, 17-15, 64 - 1908 London Outdoor

65   Felix Pipes and Arthur Zborzil (AUT) d. Albert Canet and E. Meny De Marangue (FRA) (Men's Doubles) 7-5, 2-6, 3-6, 10-8 10-8 - 1912 Stockholm Outdoor

63*   Carling Bassett-Seguso and Jill Hetherington (CAN) d. Mercedes Paz and Gabriela Sabatini (ARG) (Women's Doubles) 7-6, 5-7, 20-18 - 1988 Seoul

62   George Caridia and G. Simond (GBR) d. Wilberforce Eaves and George Hillyard (GBR) (Men's Doubles) 2-6, 7-9, 6-4, 10-8, 6-4 - 1908 London Indoor

61**   Ken Flach and Robert Seguso (USA) d. Sergio Casal and Emilio Sanchez (ESP) (Men's Doubles) 6-3, 6-4, 6-7, 6-7, 9-7 - 1988 Seoul

60   Jan Kozeluh (CZE) d. S. Okamoto (JPN) (Men's Singles) 4-6, 7-5, 10-8, 4-6, 6-4 - 1924 Paris

60   J. Condon and I. Richardson (RSA) d. Watson Washburn and Richard Williams (USA) (Men's Doubles) 4-6, 11-9, 4-6, 6-4, 6-4 - 1924 Paris

60***   Goran Ivanisevic (CRO) d. Fabrice Santoro (FRA) (Men's Singles) 6-7, 6-7, 6-4, 6-4, 8-6 - 1992 Barcelona

59   Simon Aspelin and Thomas Johansson (SWE) d. Arnaud Clement and Michael Llodra (FRA) 7-6 (6), 4-6, 19-17 in 2008 semifinals

*   *Also, most number of games in a match in the tie-breaker era (post 1988) and in a best-of-three set Olympic match*

**   *Also, most number of games in a match in the tie-breaker era (post 1988)*

***   *Also, most number of games in a singles match in the tie-breaker era (post 1988)*

MOST NUMBER OF GAMES IN A GOLD MEDAL MATCH

61   Ken Flach and Robert Seguso (USA) d. Sergio Casal and Emilio Sanchez (ESP) (Men's Doubles) 6-3, 6-3, 6-7, 6-7, 9-7 - 1988 Seoul

56   Marc Rosset (SUI) d. Jordi Arrese (ESP) (Men's Singles) 7-6, 6-4, 3-6, 4-6, 8-6 - 1992 Barcelona

54   M. Germot and Andre Gobert (FRA) d. Carl Kempe and Gunner Setterwall (SWE) (Men's Doubles) 4-6, 14-12, 6-2, 6-4 - 1912 Stockholm Indoor

54   Charles Winslow (RSA) d. Harold Kitson (RSA) (Men's Singles) 7-5, 4-6, 10-8, 8-6 - 1912 Stockholm Outdoor

50   Nicolas Massu and Fernandez Gonzalez (CHI) def Nicolas Kiefer and Rainer Schuettler (GER), 6-2, 4-6, 3-6, 7-6, 6-4

50   Vincent Richards (USA) d. Henri Cochet (FRA) (Men's Singles) 6-4, 6-4, 5-7, 4-6, 6-2 - 1924 Paris

49   Yevgeny Kafelnikov (RUS) d. Tommy Haas (GER) (Men's Singles) 7-6(4), 3-6, 6-2, 4-6, 6-3 - 2000 Sydney

LEAST NUMBER OF GAMES IN A GOLD MEDAL MATCH

14   Serena Williams and Venus Williams (USA) d. Kristie Boogert and Miriam Oremans (NED) (Women's Doubles) 6-1, 6-1 - 2000 Sydney

14   Venus Williams and Serena Williams (USA) d. Anabel Medina Garrigues and Virgina Ruano Pascual (ESP) (Women's Doubles) 6-2, 6-0 - 2008 Beijing

15   Suzanne Lenglen (FRA) d. Dorothy Holman (GBR) (Women's Singles) 6-3, 6-0 - 1920 Antwerp

16   John Boland (IRL) d. D. Kasdaglis (GRE) (Men's Singles) 6-3, 6-1 - 1896 Athens

16   Heinrich Schomburgk and Dora Koring (GER) d. Gunner Setterwall and Sigrid Fick (SWE) (Mixed Doubles) 6-4, 6-0 - 1912 Stockholm Outdoor

16   Helen Wills (USA) d. Didi Vlasto (FRA) (Women's Singles) 6-2, 6-2 - 1924 Paris

WHITE-WASH MATCHES

Women's Singles

Suzanne Lenglen (FRA) d. M. Storms (BEL) 6-0, 6-0 - 1920 Antwerp R32

Suzanne Lenglen (FRA) d. Winifred McNair (GBR) 6-0, 6-0 – 1920 Antwerp R16

Suzanne Lenglen (FRA) d. L. Stromberg-Von Essen (SWE) 6-0, 6-0 – 1920 Antwerp QF

Venus Williams (USA) d. Maja Matevzic (SLO), 6-0, 6-0 – 2004 Athens, R32

Women's Doubles

Conchita Martinez and Arantxa Sanchez-Vicario (ESP) d. Dally Randriantefy and Natacha Randriantefy (MAD) 6-0, 6-0 1992 Barcelona R32

Gigi Fernandez and Mary Joe Fernandez (USA) d. Nicole Muns-Jagerman and Brenda Schultz (NED) 6-0, 6-0 1992 Barcelona R32

Jelena Dokic and Rennae Stubbs (AUS) d. Minasha Malhotra and Nirupama Vaidyanathan (IND) 6-0, 6-0 2000 Sydney F32

YOUNGEST MEDALIST

Men

17 years, 290 days—Max Decugis (FRA), 1900 Paris, Doubles Silver

18 years, 101 days—Demetrious Petrokokkinos (GRE), 1896 Athens, Doubles Silver

19 years, 207 days—Robert Le Roy (USA), 1904 St. Louis, Singles Silver; Doubles Bronze

20 years, 13 days—Fritz Traun (GER), 1896 Athens, Doubles Gold

20 years, 230 days—Arnaud Di Pasquale (FRA), 2000 Sydney, Singles Bronze

Women

16 years, 132 days—Jennifer Capriati (USA), 1992 Barcelona, Singles Gold

18 years, 139 days—Gabriela Sabatini (ARG), 1988 Seoul, Singles Silver

18 years, 287 days—Helen Wills (USA), 1924 Paris, Singles Gold, Doubles Gold

18 years, 349 days—Elena Dementieva (RUS), 2000 Sydney, Singles Silver

19 years, 2 days—Serena Williams (USA), 2000 Sydney, Doubles Gold

19 years, 79 days—Marguerite Broquedis (FRA), 1912 Stockholm (O), Singles Gold; Mixed Bronze

19 years, 109 days—Steffi Graf (GER), 1988 Seoul, Singles Gold; Doubles Bronze

OLDEST MEDALIST

Men

44 years, 159 days—George Hillyard (GBR), 1908 London (O), Doubles Gold

41 years, 111 days—George Simond (GBR), 1908 London (I), Doubles Silver

40 years, 217 days—Wilberforce Eaves (GBR), 1908 London (O), Singles Bronze

40 years, 132 days—Arthur Gore (GBR), 1908 London (I), Singles Gold; Doubles Gold

39 years, 191 days—Spalding De Garmendia (USA), 1900 Paris, Doubles Silver

Women

43 years, 13 days—Winifred McNair (GBR), 1920 Antwerp, Doubles Gold

39 years, 331 days—Martha Adlerstraille (SWE), 1908 London (I), Singles Bronze

37 years, 213 days—Hazel Wightman (USA), 1924 Paris, Doubles Gold; Mixed Gold

37 years, 36 days—Dorothy Holman (GBR), 1920 Antwerp, Singles Silver; Doubles Silver

35 years, 308 days—Wendy Turnbull (AUS), 1988 Seoul, Doubles Bronze

YOUNGEST GOLD MEDALIST

Men

20 years, 13 days—Fritz Traun (GER), 1896 Athens, Doubles Gold

21 years, 123 days—Vincent Richards (USA), 1924 Paris, Singles Gold, Doubles Gold

21 years, 224 days—Andre Gobert (FRA), 1912 Stockholm (I), Singles Gold, Doubles Gold

21 years, 275 days—Marc Rosset (SUI), 1992 Barcelona, Singles Gold

23 years, 75 days—Edgar Leonard (USA), 1904 St. Louis, Doubles Gold

Women

16 years, 132 days—Jennifer Capriati (USA), 1992 Barcelona, Singles Gold

18 years, 287 days—Helen Wills (USA), 1924 Paris, Singles Gold, Doubles Gold

19 years, 2 days—Serena Williams (USA), 2000 Sydney, Doubles Gold

OLDEST GOLD MEDALIST

Men

44 years, 159 days—George Hillyard (GBR), 1908 London (O), Doubles Gold

40 years, 132 days—Arthur Gore (GBR), 1908 London (I), Singles Gold, Doubles Gold

39 years, 93 days—Charles Dixon (GBR), 1912 Stockholm (I), Mixed Gold

38 years, 17 days—Harold Kitson (RSA), 1912 Stockholm (O), Doubles Gold

37 years, 333 days—Max Decugis (FRA), 1920 Antwerp, Mixed Gold

Women

43 years, 13 days—Winifred McNair (GBR), 1920 Antwerp Doubles Gold

37 years, 213 days—Hazel Wightman (USA), 1924 Paris Doubles Gold; Mixed Gold

33 years, 171 days—Edith Hannam (GBR), 1912 Stockholm (I) Singles Gold; Mixed Gold

32 years, 163 days—Gigi Fernandez (USA), 1996 Atlanta, Doubles Gold

BIGGEST UPSETS

2004	No. 74 Thomas Berdych (CZE) d. No. 1 Roger Federer (SUI) 4-6, 7-5, 7-5 in the 2nd rd
2000	No. 35 Fabrice Santoro (FRA) d. No. 1 Marat Safin (RUS) 1-6, 6-1, 6-4 in the 1st rd
1996	No. 104 Marcos Ondruska (RSA) d. No. 2 seed Goran Ivanisevic (CRO) 6-2, 6-4 in 1st rd
1996	No. 9 Lindsay Davenport (USA) d. No. 2 Arantxa Sanchez Vicario (ESP) 7-6 (8), 6-2 in F
1996	No. 8 Jana Novotna (CZE) d. No. 1 Monica Seles (USA) 7-5, 3-6, 8-6
1992	No. 44 Marc Rosset (SUI) d. No. 1 Jim Courier (USA) 6-4, 6-2, 6-1 in 3rd rd
1992	No. 13 Andrei Cherkasov (CIS) d. No. 3 Pete Sampras (USA) 6-7 (7), 1-6, 7-5, 6-0, 6-3 in 3rd rd

1992   No. 47 Andrei Chesnokov (CIS) d. No. 2 Stefan Edberg (SWE) 6-0, 6-4, 6-4 in 1st rd

1992   No. 2 Jennifer Capriati (USA) d. No. 1 Steffi Graf (GER) 3-6, 6-3, 6-4 in F

1988   No. 361 Kim Soo (KOR) d. No. 4 seed and No. 12 ranked Henri Leconte (FRA) 4-6, 7-5, 6-3, 3-6, 7-5 in 2nd rd

1988   Rafaella Reggi (ITA) , ranked No. 22, d. No. 2 seed Chris Evert (USA) 2-6, 6-4, 6-1 in 3rd rd

CLOSE ENCOUNTERS

1992   Mary Joe Fernandez (USA) d. Patricia Hy (CAN) 6-2, 1-6, 12-10 in 2nd rd

1996   Todd Woodbridge and Mark Woodforde (AUS) d. Paul Haarhuis and Jacco Eltingh (NED) 6-2, 5-7, 18-16 in SF

1996   Arantxa Sanchez Vicario (ESP) d. Kimiko Date (JPN) 4-6, 6-3, 10-8 in QF

1996   Neil Broad and Tim Henman (GBR) d. Marc Goellner and David Prinosil (GER), 4-6, 6-3, 10-8 in SF

2004   Ivan Ljubicic and Mario Ancic (CRO) d. Leander Paes and Mahesh Bhupathi (IND) 7-6(5), 4-6, 16-14 in bronze medal match

2004   Fernando Gonzalez (CHI) d. Taylor Dent (USA) 6-4, 2-6, 16-14 in 3:25 in bronze medal match, saving 2 MP

2004   Fernando Gonzalez and Nicolas Massu (CHI) d. Rainer Schuettler and Nicolas Kiefer (GER) 6-2,4-6, 3-6, 7- 6(7), 6-4 in 3:42 ending at 2:39 am local time, Gonzalez and Massu saving four MP to give Chile its first ever Olympic gold in any sport

2004   Justine Henin Hardenne (BEL) d. Anastasia Myskina (RUS) 7-5, 5-7, 8-6, coming back from 1-5 in 3rd set. Henin-Hardenne served for the match in 2nd set

1988   Carling Bassett-Seguso and Jill Hetherington (CAN) d. Mercedes Paz and Gabriela Sabatini (ARG) 7-6 (8), 5-7, 20-18 in the 1st rd

1988   Zina Garrison and Pam Shriver (USA) d. Jana Novotna and Helena Sukova (CZE) 4-6, 6-2, 10-8 in F

1988   Ken Flach and Robert Seguso (USA) d. Sergio Casal and Emilio Sanczhez (ESP) 6-2, 6-4, 6-7 (5), 6-7 (1), 9-7 in F

Wightman Cup

Hazel Hotchkiss Wightman (left) founded the annual international women's team competition between the United States and Britain. Her 1938 U.S. team—(left to right) **Sarah Fabyan, Dorothy Bundy, Helen Wills Moody, Alice Marble** and **Helen Jacobs**—defeated Britain 5-2 at Wimbledon.

Hoping to stimulate international interest in women's tennis as the Davis Cup did in men's, Hazel Hotchkiss Wightman, an all-time champion from Boston, donated a sterling vase to the U.S. Lawn Tennis Association as a prize for such a team competition. It was decided to invite Great Britain to challenge for the prize in 1923 to open the new Forest Hills Stadium at the West Side Tennis Club in New York. With Mrs. Wightman as player-captain, the U.S. won the inaugural, 7-0. The rivalry was rewarding to both countries and initially developed into a close competition, an annual best of seven-match series between the two with the prize soon known as the Wightman Cup. The matches were played in even years in Britain and in odd years in the United States.

Interrupted only by World War II, the series was soon dominated by the United States, which mounted a 51-10 record through 1989, when both nations mutually agreed to suspend the competition due to the British team no longer being competitive.

Wightman Cup Champions

1923

United States def. Great Britain 7-0 (Forest Hills)

Helen Wills (USA) def. Kathleen McKane (GBR) 6-2, 7-5

Molla Mallory (USA) def. Mrs. R.C. Clayton (GBR) 6-1, 8-6

Eleanor Goss (USA) def. Geraldine Beamish (GBR) 6-2, 7-5

Helen Wills (USA) def. R.C. Clayton (GBR) 6-2, 6-3

Molla Mallory (USA) def. Kathleen McKane (GBR) 6-2, 6-3

Hazel Hotchkiss Wightman and Eleanor Goss (USA) def. Kathleen McKane and Phyllis Covell (GBR) 10-8, 5-7, 6-4

Molla Mallory and Helen Wills (USA) def. Geraldine Beamish and R.C. Clayton (GBR) 6-2, 6-2

1924

Great Britain def. United States 6-1 (Wimbledon)

Phyliss Covell (GBR) def. Helen Wills (USA) 6-2, 6-4

Kathleen McKane (GBR) def. Molla Mallory (USA) 6-3, 6-3

Kathleen McKane (GBR) def. Wills (USA) 6-2, 6-2

Covell (GBR) def. Mallory (USA) 6-2, 5-7, 6-3

Geraldine Beamish (GBR) def. Eleanor Goss (USA) 6-1, 8-10, 6-3

Covell-Dorothy Shephard –Barron (GBR) def. Marion Jessup and Goss (USA) 6-2, 6-2

Hazel Hotchkiss Wightman—Wills (USA) def. McKane and Evelyn Colyer (GBR) 6-0, 6-3

1925

Great Britain def. United States 4-3 (Forest Hills)

Kathleen McKane (GBR) def. Molla Mallory (USA) 6-4, 5-7, 6-0

Helen Wills (USA) def. Joan C. Fry (GBR) 6-0, 7-5

Dorothea Chambers (GBR) def. Eleanor Goss (USA) 7-5, 3-6, 6-1

Wills (USA) def. McKane (GBR) 6-1, 1-6, 9-7

Molla Mallory (USA) def. Joan Fry (GBR) 6-3, 6-0

Chambers-Ermyntrude Harvey (GBR) def. Mallory and May Sutton Bundy (USA) 10-8, 6-1

McKane-Evelyn Colyer (GBR) def. Wills and Mary K. Browne (USA) 6-0, 6-3

1926

United States def. Great Britain 4-3 (London)

Elizabeth Ryan (USA) def. Joan C. Fry (GBR) 6-1, 6-3

Kathleen McKane Godfree (GBR) def. Mary K. Browne (USA) 6-4, 6-2

Fry (GBR) def. Browne (USA) 3-6, 6-0, 6-4

Kitty McKane Godfree (GBR) def. Elizabeth Ryan (USA) 6-1, 5-7, 6-4

Marion Zinderstein Jessup (USA) def. Dorothy Shepherd Barron (GBR) 6-1, 5-7, 6-4

Marion Zinderstein Jessup—Eleanor Goss (USA) def. Dorothea Douglass Chambers-Dorothy Shepherd Barron (GBR) 6-4, 6-2

Mary K. Browne—Elizabeth Ryan (USA) def. Kitty McKane Godfree-Evelyn Colyer (GBR) 2-6, 6-2, 6-4

1927

United States def. Great Britain 5-2 (Forest Hills)

Helen Wills (USA) def Joan Fry (GBR) 6-2, 6-0

Molla Bjurstedt Mallory (USA) def. Kitty McKane Godfree (GBR) 6-4, 6-2

Betty Nuthall (GBR) def. Helen Jacobs (GBR) 6-3, 2-6, 6-1

Helen Wills (USA) def. Kitty McKane Godfree (GBR) 6-1, 6-1

Molla Bjurstedt Mallory (USA) def. Joan Fry (GBR) 6-2, 11-9

Gwendolyn Sterry-Betty Hill (GBR) def. Eleanor Goss-Charlotte Hosmer Chapin (USA) 5-7, 7-5, 7-5

Helen Wills-Hazel Hotchkiss Wightman (USA) def. Kitty McKane Godfree-Ermyntrude Harvey 6-4, 4-6, 6-3

1928

Great Britain def. United States 4-3 (Wimbledon)

Helen Wills (USA) def. Phoebe Holcroft Watson (GBR) 6-1, 6-2

Ellen Bennett (GBR) def. Molla Bjurstedt Mallory (USA) 6-1, 6--3

Helen Wills (USA) def. Eileen Bennett (GBR) 6-3, 6-2

Phoebe Holcroft Watson (GBR) def. Molla Bjurstedt Mallory (USA) 2-6, 6-1, 6-2

Helen Jacobs (USA) def. Betty Nuthall (GBR) 6-3, 6-1

Ermyntrude Harvey-Peggy Saunders (GBR) def. Eleanor Goss-Helen Jacobs (USA) 6-4, 6-1

Eileen Bennett-Phoebe Holcroft Watson (GBR) def. Helen Wills-Penelope Anderson (USA) 6-2, 6-1

1929

United States def. Great Britain 4-3 (Forest Hills)

Helen Jacobs (USA) def. Betty Nuthall (GBR) 7-5, 8-6

Phoebe Holcroft Watson (GBR) def. Helen Jacobs (USA) 6-3, 6-2

Edith Cross (USA) d. Peggy Michell (GBR) 6-3, 3-6, 6-3

Helen Wills (USA) d. Peggy Nuthall (GBR) 8-6, 8-6

Phoebe Watson-Peggy Michell (GBR) d. Helen Wills-Edith Cross (USA) 6-4, 6-1

Phyllis Howkins Covell-Dorothy Shepherd Barron (GBR) d. Helen Jacobs-Hazel Hotchkiss Wightman (USA) 6-2, 6-1

1930

Great Britain def. United States 4-3 (Wimbledon)

Helen Wills Moody (USA) def. Joan Fry (GBR) 6-1, 6-1

Phoebe Holcroft Watson (GBR) def. Helen Jacobs (USA) 2-6, 6-2, 6-4

Helen Wills Moody (USA) def. Phoebe Watson (GBR) 7-5, 6-1

Helen Jacobs (USA) def. Joan Fry (GBR) 6-0, 6-3

Phyllis Mudford (GBR) def. Sarah Palfrey (USA) 6-0, 6-2

Joan Fry-Ermyntrude Harvey (GBR) def. Sarah Palfrey-Edith Cross (USA) 2-6, 6-2, 6-4

Phoebe Holcroft Watson-Kitty McKane Godfree (GBR) def. Helen Jacobs-Helen Wills Moody (USA) 7-5, 1-6, 6-4

1931

United States def. Great Britain 5-2 (Forest Hills)

Helen Wills Moody (USA) def. Betty Nuthall (GBR) 8-6, 6-4

Anna M. Harper (USA) def. Dorothy E. Round (GBR) 6-3, 4-6, 9-7

Helen Jacobs (USA) def. Phyl Mudford (GBR) 6-4, 6-2

Helen Wills Moody (USA) def. Mudford (GBR) 6-1, 6-4

Jacobs (USA) def. Nuthall (GBR) 8-6, 6-4

Phyl Mudford-Dorothy Shepherd-Barron (GBR) def. Sarah Palfrey-Hazel H. Wightman (USA) 64, 10-8

Nuthall-Eileen B. Whittingstall (GBR) def. Moody-Harper (USA) 8-6, 5-7, 6-3

1932

United States def. Great Britain 4-3 (Wimbledon)

Helen Jacobs (USA) def. Dorothy E. Round (GBR) 6-4, 6-3

Helen Wills Moody (USA) def. Eileen B. Whittingstall (GBR) 6-2, 6-4

Moody (USA) def. Round (GBR) 6-2, 6-3

Whittingstall (GBR) def. Jacobs (USA) 6-4, 2-6, 6-1

Phyllis M. King (GBR) def. Anna M. Harper (USA) 3-6, 6-3, 6-1

Harper-Jacobs (USA) def. Peggy S. Michell-Round (GBR) 6-4, 6-1

Whittingstall-Betty Nuthall (GBR) def. Moody-Sarah Palfrey (USA) 6-3, 1-6, 10-8

1933

United States def. Great Britain 4-3 (Forest Hills)

Helen Jacobs (USA) def. Dorothy E. Round (GBR) 6-4, 6-2

Sarah Palfrey (USA) def. Margaret Scriven (GBR) 6-3, 6-1

Betty Nuthall (GBR) def. Carolin Babcock (GBR) 1-6, 6-1, 6-3

Round (GBR) def. Palfrey (USA) 6-4, 10-8

Jacobs (USA) def. Scriven (GBR) 5-7, 6-2, 7-5

Jacobs-Palfrey (USA) def. Round-Mary Heeley (GBR) 6-4, 6-2

Nuthall-Freda James (GBR) def. Alice Marble-Marjorie Gladman Van Ryn (GBR) 7-5, 6-2

1934

United States def. Great Britain 5-2 (Wimbledon)

Sarah Palfrey (USA) def. Dorothy E. Round (GBR) 6-3, 3-6, 8-6

Helen Jacobs (USA) def. Margaret Scriven (GBR) 6-1, 6-1

Jacobs (US) def. Round (GBR) 6-4, 6-4

Palfrey (USA) def. Scriven (GBR) 4-6, 6-2, 8-6

Betty Nuthall (GBR) def. Caroline Babcock (USA) 5-7, 6-3, 6-4

Nancy Lyle-Evelyn Dearman (GBR) def. Caroline Babcock-Josephine Cruickshank (USA) 7-5, 7-5

Jacobs-Palfrey (USA) def. Kathleen McKane Godfree-Nuthall (GBR) 5-7, 6-3, 6-2

1935

United States def. Great Britain 4-3 (Forest Hills)

Kay Stammers (GBR) def. Helen Jacobs (USA) 5-7, 6-1, 9-7

Dorothy E. Round (GBR) def. Ethel B. Arnold (GBR) 6-0, 6-3

Sarah Palfrey Fabyan (USA) def. Phyllis Mudford King (GBR) 6-0, 6-3

Jacobs (USA) def. Round (GBR) 6-3, 6-2

Arnold (USA) def. Stammers (GBR) 6-2, 1-6, 6-3

Jacobs-Palfrey Fabyan (USA) def. Stammers-Freda James (GBR) 6-3, 6-2

Nancy Lyle-Evelyn Dearman (GBR) def. Dorothy Andrus-Carolin Babcock (USA) 3-6, 6-4, 6-1

1936

United States def. Great Britain 4-3 (Wimbledon)

Kay Stammers (GBR) def. Helen Jacobs (USA) 12-10, 6-1

Dorothy E. Round (GBR) def. Sarah Fabyan (USA) 6-3, 6-4

Palfrey Fabyan (USA) def. Stammers (GBR) 6-3, 6-4

Round (GBR) def. Jacobs (USA) 6-3, 6-3

Carolin Babcock (USA) def. Mary Hardwick (GBR) 6-4, 4-6, 6-2

Babcock-Marjorie Gladman Van Ryn (USA) def. Evelyn Dearman-Nancy Lyle (GBR) 6-2, 1-6, 6-3

Jacobs Fabyan (USA) def. Stammers-Freda James (GBR) 1-6, 6-3, 7-5

1937

United States def. Great Britain 6-1 (Forest Hills)

Alice Marble (USA) def. Mary Hardwick (GBR) 4-6, 6-2, 6-4

Helen Jacobs (USA) def. Kay Stammers (GBR) 6-1, 4-6, 6-4

Jacobs (USA) def. Hardwick (GBR) 2-6, 6-4, 6-2

Marble (USA) def. Stammers (GBR) 6-3, 6-1

Sarah Palfrey Fabyan (USA) def. Margot Lumb (GBR) 6-3, 6-1

Sarah Marble-Palfrey Fabyan (USA) def. Evelyn Dearman-Joan Ingram (GBR) 6-3, 6-2

Stammers-Freda James (GBR) def. Marjorie Gladman Van Ryn-Dorothy M. Bundy (USA) 6-3, 10-8

1938

United States def. Great Britain 5-2 (Wimbledon)

Kay Stammers (GBR) def. Alice Marble (USA) 3-6, 7-5, 6-3

Helen Wills Moody (USA) def. Margaret Scriven (GBR) 6-0, 7-5

Sarah Palfrey Fabyan (USA) def. Margot Lumb (GBR) 5-7, 6-2, 6-3

Marble (USA) def. Scriven (GBR) 6-3, 3-6, 6-0

Moody (USA) def. Stammers (GBR) 6-2, 3-6, 6-3

Marble Fabyan (USA) def. Lumb-Freda James (GBR) 6-4, 6-2

Evelyn M. Dearman-Joan Ingram (GBR) def. Moody-Dorothy M. Bundy (USA) 6-2, 7-5

1939

United States def Great Britain 5-2 (Forest Hills)

Alice Marble (USA) def. Mary Hardwick (GBR) 6-3, 6-4

Kay Stammers (GBR) def. Helen Jacobs (USA) 6-2, 1-6, 6-3

Valerie Scott (GBR) def. Sarah Palfrey Fabyan (USA) 6-3, 6-4

Marble (USA) def. Stammers (GBR) 3-6, 6-3, 6-4

Jacobs (USA) def. Hardwick (GBR) 6-2, 6-2

Dorothy M. Bundy-Mary Arnold (USA) def. Betty Nuthall-Nina Brown (GBR) 6-3, 6-1

Marble-Palfrey Fabyan (USA) def. Stammers-Freda James Hammersley (GBR) 7-5, 6-2

1940–1945 No Competition Due To War

1946

United States def. Great Britain 7-0 (Wimbledon)

Pauline Betz (USA) def. Jean Bostock (GBR) 6-2, 6-4

Margaret Osborne (USA) def. Bostock (GBR) 6-1, 6-4

Osborne (USA) def. Kay Stammers Menzies (GBR) 6-3, 6-2

Louise Brough (USA) def. Joan Curry (GBR) 8-6, 6-3

Betz (USA) def. Menzies (GBR) 6-4, 6-4

Osborne-Brough (USA) def. Bostock-Mary Halford (GBR) 6-2, 6-1

Betz-Doris Hart (USA) def. Betty Passingham-Molly Lincoln (GBR) 6-1, 6-3

1947

United States def. Great Britain 7-0 (Forest Hills)

Margaret Osborne (USA) def. Bostock (GBR) 6-4, 2-6, 6-2

Louise Brough (USA) def. Kay Stammers Menzies (GBR) 6-4, 6-2

Doris Hart (USA) def. Betty Hilton (GBR) 4-6, 6-3, 7-5

Brough (USA) def. Bostock (GBR) 6-4, 6-4

Osborne (USA) def. Menzies (GBR) 7-5, 6-2

Hart-Patricia Todd (USA) def. Joy Gannon-Jean Quertier (GBR) 6-1, 6-2

Osborne-Brough (USA) def. Bostock-Betty Hilton (GBR) 6-1, 6-4

1948

United Stated def. Great Britain 6-1 (Wimbledon)

Margaret Osbourne duPont (USA) def. Jean Bostock (GBR) 6-4, 8-6

Louise Brough (USA) def. Betty Hilton (GBR) 6-1, 6-1

duPont (USA) def. Hilton (GBR) 6-3, 6-4

Brough (USA) def. Bostock (GBR) 6-2, 4-6, 7-5

Doris Hart (USA) def. Joy Gannon (GBR) 6-1, 6-4

Brough duPont (USA) def. Kay Stammers Menzies-Hilton (GBR) 6-2, 6-2

Bostock-Molly L. Blair (GBR) def. Hart-Patricia C. Todd (USA) 6-3, 6-4

1949

United States def. Great Britain 7-0 (Haverford, Pa)

Doris Hart (USA) def. Jean Walker-Smith (GBR) 6-3, 6-1

Margaret Osbourne duPont (USA) def. Betty Hilton (GBR) 6-1, 6-3

Hart (USA) def. Hilton (GBR) 6-1, 6-3

duPont (US) def. Walker-Smith 64 62

Beverly Baker (USA) def. Jean Quertier (GBR) 6-4, 7-5

Hart-Shirley Fry (USA) def. Jean Quertier-Molly L. Blair (GBR) 6-1, 6-2

Gertrude Moran-Patricia C. Todd (USA) def. Hilton-Kay Tuckey (GBR) 6-4, 8-6

1950

United States def. Great Britain 7-0 (Wimbledon)

Margaret Osbourne duPont (USA) def. Betty Hilton (GBR) 6-3, 6-4

Doris Hart (USA) def. Joan Curry (GBR) 6-2, 6-4

Louise Brough (USA) def. Hilton (GBR) 2-6, 7-5

duPont (USA) def. Jean Walker-Smith (GBR) 6-3, 6-2

Louise Brough (USA) def. Walker-Smith (GBR) 6-0, 6-0

Patricia C. Todd-Hart (US) def. G. Walker-Smith-Jean Quertier (GBR) 6-2, 6-3

Brough duPont (USA) def. Hilton-Kay Tuckey (GBR) 6-2, 6-0

1951

United States def. Great Britain 6-1 (Chestnut Hill, Mass)

Doris Hart (USA) def. Jean Quertier (GBR) 6-4, 6-4

Shirley Fry (US) def. Jean Walker-Smith (GBR) 6-1, 6-4

Maureen Connolly (USA) def. Kay Tuckey (GBR) 6-1, 6-3

Hart (US) def. Walker-Smith (GBR) 6-4, 2-6, 7-5

Quertier (GBR) def. Fry (USA) 6-3, 8-6

Patricia C. Todd-Nancy Chaffee (USA) def. Pat Ward-Joy Mottram (GBR) 7-5, 6-3

Fry-Hart (USA) def. Quertier-Tuckey (GBR) 6-3, 6-3

1952

United States def. Great Britain 7-0 (Wimbledon)

Doris Hart (USA) def. Jean Quertier Rinkel (GBR) 6-3, 6-3

Maureen Connolly (USA) def. Jean Walker-Smith (GBR) 3-6, 6-1, 7-5

Hart (USA) def .Walker-Smith (GBR) 7-5, 6-2,

Connolly (USA) def. Rinkel (GBR) 9-7, 6-2

Shirley Fry (USA) def. Susan Partridge (GBR) 6-0, 8-6

Fry-Hart (USA) def. Helen Fletcher-Quertier Rinkel (GBR) 8-6, 6-4

Louise Brough-Connolly (USA) def. Joy G. Mottram-Pat Ward (GBR) 6-0, 6-3

1953

United States def. Great Britain 7-0 (Rye, N.Y.)

Maureen Connolly (USA) def. Angela Mortimer (GBR) 6-1, 6-1

Doris Hart (USA) def. Helen Fletcher (GBR) 6-4, 7-5

Shirley Fry (USA) def. Jean Quertier Rinkel (GBR) 6-2, 6-4

Connolly (USA) def. Fletcher (GBR) 6-1, 6-1

Hart (US) def. Mortimer (GBR) 6-1, 6-1

Connolly-Louise Brough (USA) def. Anne Mortimer-Shilcock (GBR) 6-2, 6-3;

Hart-Fry (USA) def. Quertier Rinkel-Fletcher (GBR) 6-2, 6-1

1954

United States def. Great Britain 6-0 (Wimbledon)

Maureen Connolly (USA) def. Helen Fletcher (GBR) 6-1, 6-3

Doris Hart (USA) def. Anne Shilcock (GBR) 6-4, 6-1

Hart (US) def. Fletcher (GBR) 6-1, 6-8, 6-2

Brough (USA) def. Angela Buxton (GBR) 8-6, 6-2

Connolly (USA) def. Shilcock (GBR) 6-2, 6-2

Brough-Margaret Osbourne duPont (USA) def. Buxton-Pat Hird (GBR) 2-6, 6-4, 7-5;

Fletcher-Shilcock (GBR) vs. Shirley Fry-Hart (USA) unplayed

1955

United States def. Great Britain 6-1 (Rye, N.Y)

Angela Mortimer (GBR) def. Doris Hart (USA) 6-4, 1-6, 7-5

Louise Brough (USA) def. Shirley Bloomer (GBR) 6-2, 6-4

Brough (USA) def. Mortimer (GBR) 6-0, 6-2

Dorothy H. Knode (USA) def. Angela Buxton (GBR) 6-3, 6-3

Hart (USA) def. Bloomer (GBR) 7-5, 6-3

Brough-Margaret Osbourne duPont (USA) def. Bloomer-Patricia Ward (GBR) 6-3, 6-3

Hart-Shirley Fry (USA) def. Mortimer-Buxton (GBR) 3-6, 6-2, 7-5

1956

United States def. Great Britain 5-2 (Wimbledon)

Louise Brough (USA) def. Angela Mortimer (GBR) 3-6, 6-4, 7-5

Shirley Fry (USA) def. Angela Buxton (GBR) 6-2, 6-8, 7-5

Brough (USA) def. Buxton (GBR) 3-6, 6-3, 6-3

Shirley Bloomer (GBR) def. Dorothy H. Knode (USA) 6-4 6-4

Mortimer (GBR) def. Fry (USA) 6-4, 6-3

Knode-Beverly Baker Fleitz (USA) def. Bloomer-Pat Ward (GBR) 6-1, 6-4

Brough-Fry (USA) def. Buxton-Mortimer (GBR) 6-2, 6-2

1957

United States def. Great Britain 6-1 (Sewickley, Pa.)

Althea Gibson (USA) def. Shirley Bloomer (GBR) 6-4, 4-6, 6-2

Dorothy Head Knode (USA) def. Christine Truman (GBR) 6-2, 11-9

Ann Haydon (GBR) def. Darlene Hard (USA) 6-3, 3-6, 6-4

Dorothy Head Knode (USA) def. Shirley Bloomer (GBR) 5-7, 6-1, 6-2

Althea Gibson (USA) def. Christine Truman (GBR) 6-4, 6-2

Althea Gibson-Darlene Hard (USA) def. Shirley Bloomer-Sheila Armstrong (GBR) 6-3, 6-4

Louise Brough-Margaret Osborne DuPont (USA) def. Anne Shilcock-Ann Haydon (GBR) 6-4, 6-1

1958

Great Britain def. United States 4-3 (Wimbledon)

Althea Gibson (USA) def. Shirley Bloomer (GBR) 6-3, 6-4

Christine Truman (GBR) def. Dorothy Head Knode (USA) 6-4, 6-4

Dorothy Head Knode (USA) def. Shirley Bloomer (GBR) 6-4, 6-2

Christine Truman (GBR) def. Althea Gibson (USA) 2-6, 6-3, 6-4

Ann Haydon (GBR) def. Mimi Arnold (USA) 6-3, 5-7, 6-3

Christine Truman-Shirley Bloomer (GBR) def. Karol Fageros-Dorothy Knode (USA) 6-2, 6-3

Althea Gibson-Janet Hopps (USA) def. Anne Shilcock-Pat Ward (GBR) 6-4, 3-6, 6-3

1959

United States def. Great Britain 4-3 Edgeworth Club (Sewickley, Pa.)

Beverly Baker Fleitz (USA) def. Angela Mortimer (GBR) 6-2, 6-1

Christine Truman (GBR) def. Darlene Hard (USA) 6-4. 2-6, 6-3

Darlene Hard (USA) def. Angela Mortimer (GBR) 6-3, 6-8, 6-4

Beverly Baker Fleitz (USA) def. Christine Truman (GBR) 6-4, 6-4

Ann Haydon (GBR) def. Sally Moore (USA) 6-1, 6-1

Darlene Hard-Jeanne Arth (USA) def. Shirley Bloomer Brasher-Christine Truman (GBR) 9-7, 9-7

Ann Haydon-Angela Mortimer (GBR) def. Janet Hopps-Sally Moore 6-2, 6-4

1960

Great Britain def. United States 4-3 (Wimbledon)

Ann Haydon (GBR) def. Karen Hantze (USA) 2-6, 11-9, 6-1

Darlene Hard (USA) def. Christine Truman (GBR) 4-6, 6-3, 6-4

Darlene Hard (USA) def. Ann Haydon (GBR) 5-7, 6-2, 6-1

Christine Truman (GBR) def. Karen Hantze (USA) 7-5, 6-3

Angela Mortimer (GBR) def. Janet Hopps (USA) 6-8, 6-4, 6-1

Karen Hantze-Darlene Hard (USA) def. Ann Haydon-Angela Mortimer (GBR) 6-0, 6-0

Christine Truman-Shirley Bloome Brasher (GBR) def. Janet Hopps-Dorothy Head Knode (USA) 6-4, 9-7

1961

United States def. Great Britain 6-1 (Chicago, Ill.)

Karen Hantze (USA) def. Christine Truman (GBR) 7-9, 6-1, 6-1

Billie Jean Moffitt (USA) def. Ann Haydon (GBR) 6-4, 6-4

Karen Hantze (USA) def. Ann Haydon (GBR) 6-1, 6-4

Christine Truman (GBR) def. Billie Jean Moffitt (USA) 6-3, 6-2

Justina Bricka (USA) def. Angela Mortimer (GBR) 10-8, 4-6, 6-3

Karen Hantze-Billie Jean Moffitt (USA) def. Christine Truman-Deidre Catt (GBR) 7-5, 6-2

Margaret Osborne duPont-Margaret Varner (USA) def. Angela Mortimer-Ann Haydon (GBR) default

1962

United States def. Great Britain 4-3 (Wimbledon)

Darlene Hard (USA) def. Christine Truman (GBR) 6-2, 6-2

Ann Haydon (GBR) def. Karen Hantze Susman (USA) 10-8, 7-5

Deidre Catt (GBR) def. Nancy Richey (USA) 6-1, 7-5

Darlene Hard (USA) def. Ann Haydon 6-3, 6-8, 6-4

Karen Susman (USA) def. Christine Truman (GBR) 6-4, 7-5

Margaret Osborne DuPont-Margaret Varner (USA) def. Deidre Catt-Elizabeth Starkie (GBR) 6-3, 2-6, 6-2

Christine Truman-Ann Haydon (GBR) def. Darlene Hard-Billie Jean Moffitt (USA) 6-4, 6-3

1963

United States def. Great Britain 6-1 (Cleveland, Ohio)

Ann Haydon Jones (GBR) def. Darlene Hard (USA) 6-1, 0-6, 8-6

Billie Jean Moffitt (USA) def. Christine Truman (GBR) 6-4, 19-17

Nancy Richey (USA) def. Deidre Catt (GBR) 14-12, 6-3

Darlene Hard (USA) def. Christine Truman (GBR) 6-3, 6-0

Billie Jean Moffitt (USA) def. Ann Jones (GBR) 6-4, 4-6, 6-3

Darlene Hard-Billie Jean Moffitt (USA) def. Christine Truman-Ann Jones (GBR) 4-6, 7-5, 6-2

Nancy Richey-Donna Floyd Fales (USA) def. Deidre Catt-Elizabeth Starkie 6-4, 6-8, 6-2

1964

United States def. Great Britain 5-2 (Wimbledon)

Nancy Richey (USA) def. Deidre Catt (GBR) 4-6, 6-4, 7-5

Billie Jean Moffitt (USA) def. Ann Haydon Jones (GBR) 4-6, 6-2, 6-3

Carole Caldwell (USA) def. Elizabeth Starkie (GBR) 6-4, 1-6, 6-3

Nancy Richey (USA) def. Ann Jones (GBR) 7-5, 11-9

Billie Jean Moffitt (USA) def. Deidre Catt (GBR) 6-3, 4-6, 6-3

Deidre Catt-Ann Jones (GBR) def. Carole Caldwell-Billie Jean Moffitt (USA) 6-3, 4-6, 6-0

Angela Mortimer-Elizabeth Starkie (GBR) def. Nancy Richey-Donna Floyd Fales (USA) 2-6 6-3, 6-4

1965

United States def. Great Britain 5-2 (Cleveland, Ohio)

Ann Haydon Jones (GBR) def. Billie Jean Moffitt (USA) 6-2, 6-4

Nancy Richey (USA) def. Elizabeth Starkie (GBR) 6-1, 6-0

Carole Graebner (USA) def. Virginia Wade (GBR) 3-6, 10-8, 6-4

Billie Jean Moffitt (USA) def. Elizabeth Starkie (GBR) 6-3, 6-2

Ann Haydon Jones (GBR) def. Nancy Richey (USA) 6-4, 9-7

Carol Graebner-Nancy Richey (USA) def. Neil Truman-Elizabeth Starkie (GBR) 6-1, 6-0

Billie Jean Moffitt-Karen Hantze Susman (USA) def. Ann Jones-Virginia Wade (GBR) 6-3, 8-6

1966

United States def. Great Britain 4-3 (Wimbledon)

Ann Haydon Jones (GBR) def. Nancy Richey (USA) 2-6, 6-4, 6-3

Billie Jean King (USA) def. Virginia Wade (GBR) 6-2, 6-3

Winnie Shaw (GBR) def. Mary Ann Eisel (USA) 6-3, 6-3

Nancy Richey (USA) def. Virginia Wade (GBR) 2-6, 6-2, 7-5

Billie Jean King (USA) def. Ann Jones (GBR) 5-7, 6-2, 6-3

Ann Jones-Virginia Wade (GBR) def. Billie Jean King-Jane Albert (USA) 7-5, 6-2

Nancy Richey-Mary Ann Eisel (USA) def. Rita Bentley-Elizabeth Starkie (GBR) 6-1, 6-2

1967

United States def. Great Britain 6-1 (Cleveland, Ohio)

Billie Jean King (USA) def. Virginia Wade (GBR) 6-3, 6-2

Nancy Richey (USA) def. Ann Haydon Jones (GBR) 6-2, 6-2

Christine Truman (GBR) def. Rosemary Casals (USA) 3-6, 7-5, 6-1

Richey (USA) def. Wade (GBR) 3-6, 8-6, 6-2

King (USA) def. Jones (GBR) 6-1, 6-2

Casals-King (USA) def. Jones-Wade (GBR) 10-8, 6-4

Mary Ann Eisel-Carole C. Graebner (USA) def. Winnie Shaw-Joyce Williams (GBR) 8-6, 12-10

1968

Great Britain def. United States 4-3 (Wimbledon)

Nancy Richey (USA) def. Christine Truman Janes (GBR) 6-1, 8-6

Virginia Wade (GBR) def. Mary Ann Eisel (USA) 6-0, 6-1

Jane Bartkowicz (USA) def. Winnie Shaw (GBR) 7-5, 3-6, 6-4

Eisel (USA) def. Janes (GBR) 6-4, 6-3

Wade (GBR) def. Richey (USA) 6-4, 2-6, 6-3

Wade-Shaw (GBR) def. Richey-Eisel (USA) 5-7, 6-4, 6-3

Nell Janes (GBR) def. Stephanie DeFina-Kathy Harter (USA) 6-3, 2-6, 6-3

1969

United States def. Great Britain 5-2 (Cleveland, Ohio)

Julie M. Heldman (USA) def. Virginia Wade (GBR) 3-6, 6-1, 8-6

Nancy Richey (USA) def. Winnie Shaw (GBR) 8-6, 6-2

Jane Bartkowicz (USA) def. Christine Truman Janes (GBR) 8-6, 6-0

Christine Truman Janes-Nell Truman (GBR) def. Mary Ann E. Curtis-Valerie Ziegenfuss (USA) 6-1, 3-6, 6-4

Wade (GBR) def. Richey (USA) 6-3, 2-6, 6-4

Heldman (USA) def. Shaw (GBR) 6-3, 6-4

Heldman-Bartkowicz (USA) def. Shaw-Wade (GBR) 6-4, 6-2

1970

United States def. Great Britain 4-3 (Wimbledon)

Billie Jean King (USA) def. Virginia Wade (GBR) 8-6, 6-4

Ann Haydon Jones (GBR) def. Nancy Richey (USA) 6-3, 6-3

Julie M. Heldman (USA) def. Joyce Williams (GBR) 6-3, 6-2

Wade (GBR) def. Richey (USA) 6-3, 6-2

King (USA) def. Jones (GBR) 6-4, 6-2

Haydon Jones-Williams (GBR) def. Mary Ann E. Curtis-Heldman (USA) 6-3, 6-2

King-Jane Bartkowicz (USA) def. Wade-Winnie Shaw (GBR) 7-5, 6-8, 6-2

1971

United States def. Great Britain 4-3 (Cleveland)

Chris Evert (USA) def. Winnie Shaw (GBR) 6-0, 6-4

Virginia Wade (GBR) def. Julie Heldman (USA) 7-5, 7-5

Joyce Williams (GBR) def. Kristy Pigeon (USA) 7-5, 3-6, 6-4

Mary Ann E. Curtis-Valerie Ziegenfuss (USA) def. Christine Truman Janes-Nell Truman (GBR) 6-1, 6-4

Ziegentuss (US) d. Shaw (GBR) 6-4, 4-6, 6-3

Evert (USA) def. Wade (GBR) 6-1, 6-1

Wade-Williams (GBR) def. Carole C. Graebner-Evert (USA) 10-8, 4-6, 6-1

1972

United States def. Great Britain 5-2 (Wimbledon)

Joyce Williams (GBR) def. Wendy Overton (USA) 6-3, 3-6, 6-3

Chris Evert (USA) def. Virginia Wade (GBR) 6-4, 6-4

Chris Evert-Patti Hogan (USA) def. Winnie Shaw-Nell Truman (GBR) 7-5, 6-4

Hogan (USA) def. Corinne Molesworth (GBR) 6-8, 6-4, 6-2

Evert (USA) def. Williams (GBR) 6-2, 6-3

Wade (GBR) def. Overton (USA) 8-6, 7-5

Valerie Ziegenfuss-Overton (USA) def. Wade-Williams (GBR) 6-3, 6-3

1973

United States def. Great Britain 5-2 (Chestnut Hill, Mass.)

Chris Evert (USA) def. Virginia Wade (GBR) 6-4, 6-2

Patti Hogan (USA) def. Veronica Burton (GBR) 6-4, 6-3

Linda Tuero (USA) def. Glynis Coles (GBR) 7-5, 6-2

Wade-Coles (GBR) def. Chris Evert-Marita Redondo (USA) 6-3, 6-4

Chris Evert (USA) def. Burton (GBR) 6-3, 6-0

Wade (GBR) def. Hogan (USA) 6-2, 6-2

Hogan-Jeanne Evert (USA) def. Lindsey Beaven-Lesley Charles (GBR) 6-3, 4-6, 8-6

1974

Great Britain def. United States 6-1 (Queensferry, Northern Wales, Great Britain)

Virginia Wade (GBR) def. Julie Heldman (USA) 5-7, 9-7, 6-4

Glynis Coles (GBR) def. Janet Newberry (USA) 4-6, 6-1, 6-3

Sue Barker (GBR) def. Jeanne Evert (USA) 4-6, 6-4, 6-1

Lesley Charles-Barker (GBR) def. Newberry-Betsy Nagelsen (USA) 4-6, 6-2, 6-1

Coles (GB) def. Heldman (USA) 6-0, 6-4

Wade (GB) def. Newberry (USA) 6-1, 6-3

Heldman-Mona Schallau Guerrant (USA) def. Wade-Coles (GBR) 7-5, 6-4

1975

Great Britain def. United States 5-2 (Cleveland, Ohio)

Virginia Wade (GBR) def. Mona Schallau (USA) 6-2, 6-2

Chris Evert (USA) def. Glynis Coles (GBR) 6-4, 6-1

Sue Barker (GBR) def. Janet Newberry (USA) 6-4, 7-5

Anne Wade-Haydon Jones (GBR) def. Newberry-Julie Anthony (USA) 6-2, 6-3

Chris Evert (USA) def. Wade (GBR) 6-3, 7-5

Coles (GBR) def. Mona Schallau Guerrant (USA) 6-3, 7-6

Coles-Barker (GBR) def. Evert-Schallau (USA), 7-5, 6-4

1976

United States def. Great Britain 5-2 (London)

Chris Evert (USA) def. Virginia Wade (GBR) 6-2, 3-6, 6-3

Sue Barker (GBR) def. Rosemary Casals (USA) 1-6, 6-3, 6-2

Terry Holladay (USA) def. Glynis Coles (GBR) 3-6, 6-1, 6-4

Evert-Casals (USA) def. Wade-Barker (GBR) 6-0, 5-7, 6-1

Wade (GBR) def. Casals (USA) 3-6, 9-7 ret.

Evert (USA) def. Barker (GBR) 2-6, 6-2, 6-2

Ann Kiyomura-Mona Schallau Guerrant (USA) def. Sue Mappin-Lesley Charles (GBR) 6-2, 6-2

1977

United States def. Great Britain 7-0 (Oakland, Calif.)

Chris Evert (USA) def. Virginia Wade (GBR) 7-5, 7-6

Billie Jean King (USA) def. Sue Barker (GBR), 6-1, 6-4

Rosie Casals (USA) def. Michelle Tyler (GBR) 6-2, 3-6, 6-4

King-JoAnne Russell (USA) def. Lesley Charles-Sue Mappin (GBR) 6-0, 6-1

King (USA) def. Wade (GBR) 6-4, 3-6, 8-6

Evert (USA) def. Barker (GBR) 6-1, 6-2

Evert-Casals (USA) def. Wade-Barker (GBR) 6-2, 6-4

1978

Great Britain def. United States 4-3 (London)

Chris Evert (USA) def. Sue Barker (GBR) 6-2, 6-1

Michelle Tyler (GBR) def. Pam Shriver (USA) 5-7, 6-3, 6-3

Virginia Wade (GBR) def. Tracy Austin (USA) 3-6, 7-5, 6-3

Billie Jean King-Austin (USA) def. Anne Hobbs-Sue Mappin (GBR) 6-2, 4-6, 6-2

Evert (USA) def. Wade (GBR) 6-0, 6-1

Barker (GBR) def. Austin (USA) 6-3, 3-6, 6-1

Barker-Wade (GBR) def. Evert-Shriver (USA) 6-0, 5-7, 6-4

1979

United States def. Great Britain 7-0 (West Palm Beach, Fla.)

Chris Evert Lloyd (USA) def. Sue Barker (GBR) 7-5, 6-2

Kathy Jordan (USA) def. Anne Hobbs (GBR) 6-4, 6-7, 6-2

Tracy Austin (USA) def. Virginia Wade (GBR) 6-1, 6-4

Austin-Ann Kiyomura (USA) def. Jo Durie-Debbie Jevans (USA) 6-3, 6-1

Austin (USA) def. Barker (GBR) 6-4, 6-2

Evert Lloyd (USA) def. Wade (GBR) 6-1, 6-1

Evert Lloyd-Rosie Casals (USA) def. Wade-Barker (GBR) 6-0, 6-1

1980

United States def. Great Britain 5-2 (London)

Chris Evert Lloyd (USA) def. Sue Barker (GBR) 6-1, 6-2

Anne Hobbs (GBR) def. Kathy Jordan (USA) 4-6, 6-4, 6-1

Andrea Jaeger (USA) def. Virginia Wade (GBR) 3-6, 6-3, 6-2

Rosie Casals-Evert Lloyd (USA) def. Glynis Coles-Hobbs (GBR) 6-3, 6-3

Evert Lloyd (USA) def. Wade (GBR) 7-5, 3-6, 7-5

Barker (GBR) def. Jaeger (USA) 5-7, 6-3, 6-3

Jordan-Anne Smith (USA) def. Barker-Wade (GBR) 6-4, 7-5

1981

United States def. Great Britain 7-0 (Chicago, Ill.)

Tracy Austin (USA) def. Sue Barker (GBR) 7-5, 6-3

Andrea Jaeger (USA) def. Anne Hobbs (GBR) 6-0, 6-0

Chris Evert Lloyd (USA) def. Virginia Wade (GBR) 6-1, 6-3

Jaeger–Shriver (USA) def. Hobbs-Jo Durie (GBR) 6-1, 6-3

Austin (USA) def. Wade (GBR) 6-3, 6-1

Evert Lloyd (USA) def. Barker (GBR) 6-3, 6-0

Rosie Casals-Evert Lloyd (USA) def. Glynis Coles-Wade 6-3, 6-3

1982

United States def. Great Britain 6-1 (London)

Barbara Potter (USA) def. Sue Barker (GBR) 6-2, 6-2

Anne Smith (USA) def. Virginia Wade (GBR) 3-6, 7-5, 6-3

Chris Evert Lloyd (USA) def. Jo Durie (GBR) 6-2, 6-2

Durie-Anne Hobbs (GBR) def. Rosie Casals-Smith (USA) 6-3, 2-6, 6-2

Potter (USA) def. Durie (GBR) 5-7, 7-6, 6-2

Evert Lloyd (USA) def. Barker (GBR) 6-4, 6-3

Potter-Sharon Walsh (USA) def. Barker-Wade (GBR) 2-6, 6-4, 6-4

1983

United States def. Great Britain 6-1 (Williamsburg, Va.)

Martina Navratilova (USA) def. Sue Barker (GBR) 6-2, 6-0

Kathy Rinaldi (USA) def. Virginia Wade (GBR) 6-2, 6-2

Pam Shriver (US) def. Jo Durie (GBR) 6-3, 6-2

Barker-Wade (GBR) def. Candy Reynolds-Paula Smith (USA) 7-5, 3-6 6-1

Shriver (USA) def. Barker (GBR) 6-0, 6-1

Navratilova (USA) def. Jo Durie (GBR) 6-3, 6-3

Navratilova-Shriver (USA) def. Annabel Croft-Durie (GBR) 6-2, 6-1

1984

United States def Great Britain 5-2 (London)

Chris Evert Lloyd (USA) def. Anne Hobbs (GBR) 6-2, 6-2

Annabel Croft (GBR) def. Alycia Moulton (USA) 6-1, 5-7, 6-4

Jo Durie (GBR) def. Barbara Potter (USA) 6-3, 7-6

Evert Lloyd-Moulton (USA) def. Amanda Brown-Virginia Wade (GBR) 6-2, 6-2

Potter (USA) def. Anne Hobbs (GBR) 6-1, 6-3

Evert Lloyd (USA) def. Durie (GBR) 7-6, 6-1

Potter-Sharon Walsh (USA) def. Durie-Hobbs (GBR) 7-6, 4-6, 9-7

1985

United States def. Great Britain 7-0 (Williamsburg, Va.)

Chris Evert Lloyd (USA) def. Jo Durie (GBR) 6-2, 6-3

Kathy Rinaldi (USA) def. Anne Hobbs (GBR) 7-5, 7-5

Pam Shriver (USA) def. Annabel Croft (GBR) 6-0, 6-0

Betsy Nagelsen-Anne White (USA) def. Croft-Wade (GBR) 6-4, 6-1

Pam Shriver (USA) def. Jo Durie (GBR) 6-4, 6-4

Evert Lloyd (USA) def. Annabel Croft (GBR) 6-3, 6-0

Evert Lloyd-Shriver (USA) def. Jo Durie-Anne Hobbs (GBR) 6-3, 6-7, 6-2

1986

United States def. Great Britain 7-0 (London)

Kathy Rinaldi (USA) def. Sara Gomer (GBR) 6-3, 7-6

Stephanie Rehe (USA) def. Annabel Croft (GBR) 6-3, 6-1

Bonnie Gadusek (USA) def. Jo Durie (GBR) 6-2, 6-4

Rinaldi and Gadusek (USA) def. Croft and Gomer (GBR) 6-3, 5-7, 6-3

Gadusek (USA) def. Anne Hobbs (GBR) 2-6, 6-4, 6-4

Rinaldi (USA) def. Durie (GBR) 6-4, 6-2

Elise Burgin and Anne White (USA) def. Durie and Hobbs (GBR) 7-6, 6-3

1987

United States def. Great Britain 5-2 (Williamsburg, Va.)

Zina Garrison (USA) def. Anne Hobbs (GBR) 7-5, 6-2

Lori McNeil (USA) def. Sara Gomer (GBR) 6-2, 6-1

Pam Shriver (USA) def. Jo Durie (GBR) 6-1, 7-5

Gigi Fernandez-Robin White (USA) def. Gomer and Clare Wood (GBR) 6-4, 6-1

Pam Shriver (USA) def. Anne Hobbs (GBR) 6-4, 6-3

Jo Durie (GBR) def. Zina Garrison (USA) 7-6, 6-3

Jo Durie-Anne Hobbs def. Zina Garrison-Lori McNeil (USA) 0-6, 6-4, 7-5

1988

United States def. Great Britain 7-0 (London)

Zina Garrison (USA) def. Jo Durie (GBR) 6-2, 6-4

Patty Fendick (USA) def. Monique Javer (GBR) 6-2, 6-1

Lori McNeil (USA) def. Sara Gomer (GBR) 6-7, 6-4, 6-4

Lori McNeil and Betsy Nagelsen (USA) def. Sara Gomer and Julie Salmon (GBR) 6-3, 6-2

Zina Garrison (USA) def. Clare Wood (GBR) 6-3, 6-2

Lori McNeil (USA) def. Jo Durie (GBR) 6-1, 6-2

Gigi Fernandez and Lori McNeil (USA) def. Jo Durie and Clare Wood (GBR) 6-1, 6-3

1989

United States def. Great Britain 7-0 (Williamsburg, Va.)

Lori McNeil (USA) def. Jo Durie (GBR) 7-5, 6-1

Jennifer Capriati (USA) def. Clare Wood (GBR) 6-0, 6-0

Mary Joe Fernandez (USA) def. Sara Gomer (GBR) 6-1, 6-2

Mary Joe Fernandez and Betsy Nagelsen (USA) def. Sara Gomer and Clare Wood (GBR) 6-2, 7-6

Lori McNeil (USA) def. Sara Gomer (GBR) 6-4, 6-2

Mary Joe Fernandez (USA) def. Jo Durie (GBR) 6-1, 7-5

Patty Fendick and Lori McNeil (USA) def. Jo Durie and Anne Hobbs (GBR) 6-3, 6-3

Biographies

SECTION IV

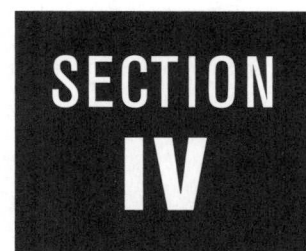

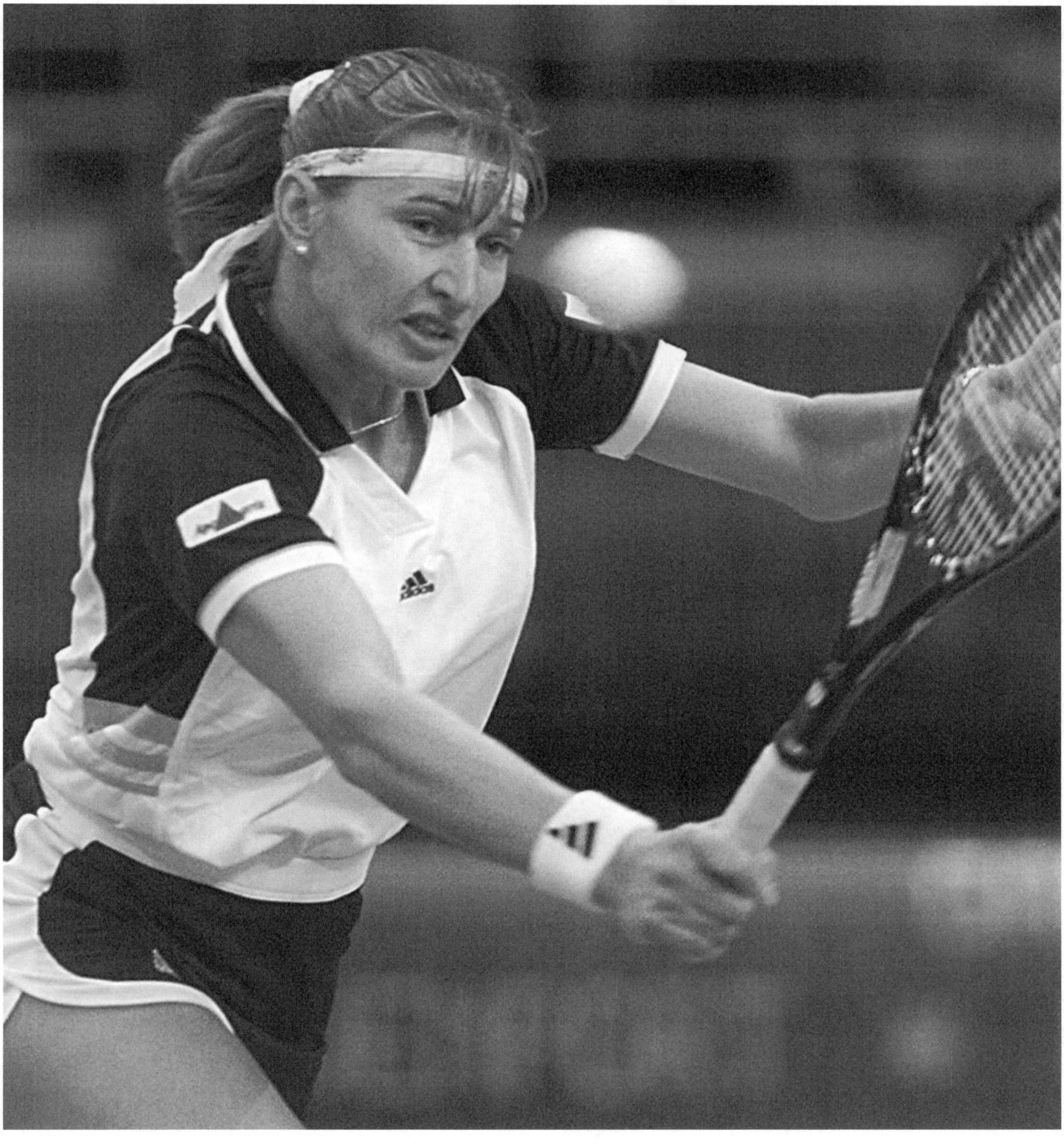

Steffi Graf was the headliner of the Class of 2004 in the International Tennis Hall of Fame.

International Tennis Hall Of Fame

The International Tennis Hall of Fame is located at The Casino in Newport, R.I., site of the first U.S. Championships in 1881.

The storehouse of memories.

That's the way I feel about 194 Bellevue Avenue in Newport, Rhode Island. My own first memory of the place goes back to a July afternoon in 1954. Driving from Ohio via New York to introduce myself to Boston, I decided to make a long-yearned-for pilgrimage. Detouring toward the ocean, I hoped for at least a glimpse of The Casino, as it's named, the aged playpen where it really all began in this country for the game called tennis.

As a rube from Ohio, I didn't know quite what to expect. I was aware that the inaugural U.S. Championships had been staged there long ago on grass (a mysterious surface to me, raised on ball-blackening asphalt), and Newport was "high society" territory. But I didn't know that the U.S. Tennis Association had just given The Casino status as the game's Valhalla. Nor could I have envisioned such a thing as the Hall of Fame's golden anniversary celebration up the road in the unimaginably distant year 2004.

Timidly pushing open one of the large green doors at the wooden-shingled entryway on Bellevue, I cautiously entered the mosaic-floored foyer. It was a private club and I didn't want to be seen as an intruder. So, remaining in the shadows, I edged toward the portal opening onto the courts until—POW!—I was hit in the eyeballs by an almost pastoral scene. In a setting of emerald green, men and women in white were at joyful play.

Enthralled, I wanted to come back. I wanted to play on those courts. Fortunately, I did (losing, of course, in the first round of the U.S. Amateur Grass Court Championships in 1976). Often I have returned to the elder among the world's tennis parlors, to absorb the atmosphere so pleasing and curative to a tennis degenerate. Sucking up the sea breeze, I walk where great champions have roamed and been enshrined, commune with their ghosts, explore the International Tennis Hall of Fame's museum, examine the artifacts and displays in the treasure trove of memories.

In 1965, having become entitled to a press pass as an ink-stained wretch—we were still using typewriters—in the employ of the *Boston Globe*, I became acquainted with the quixotically delightful Jimmy Van Alen. Tilting against the windmills of traditional scoring, he was in charge at The Casino, his beloved boyhood haunt. [It was never a gambling den, as the name might suggest, but a place of pleasure in one Italian useage.]

Jimmy had enough money, time and moxie to lobby the establishment to death and transfiguration, until the poobahs of the USTA finally accepted his baby (a bastard, some said)—the tie-breaker.

Not for some years did I learn that Van Alen, the cherubic-faced "Newport Bolshevik," had been radicalized (a few weeks after my initial peek) by the 1954 title bout of the Casino Invitational. After the U.S. Championships had outgrown The Casino and skipped to New York's Forest Hills in 1915, the men kept coming to Newport for the Invitational, an important stopover on the Eastern grass circuit. A summertime chlorophyll-green path, it was for decades the spine of American tennis, limited to so-called amateurs, until the sunrise of "Opens" in 1968. That progressive development pretty much killed grass, except at The Casino where the Jimmy Van Alen Cup is annually up for grabs, and God's own sod prevails at the Campbell's Hall of Fame Championships, an ATP Tour staple the week after Wimbledon.

Anyway, a little more than a half-century ago, the Nos. 6-5 Americans Ham Richardson and Straight Clark labored four hours to reach a decision for Richardson, 6-3, 9-7, 12-14, 6-8, 10-8. (An extremely long match in that day, considering the absence of chairs for contestants to sit on. No 90-second breaks; the bygone commandment of "continuous play" was in force.)

Van Alen thought it was worse than reading "War and Peace," and he went to war against deuce sets, issuing a piece of his mind. "No match should take that long or that many games. It's urological torture for players, fans, court officials."

Cocktail hours were spoiled as Richardson and Clark dragged on into early evening. "You see," Jimmy would recall, "the match everybody really wanted to see was the doubles final with the great Aussies. [involving three future Famers, Lew Hoad-Ken Rosewall, the losers, and Neale Fraser, plus Rex Hartwig.] Finally we had to put them on an outside court as the singles went on and on and..."

"There has to be a better way," pouted Van Alen, inspired to seek deuce-be-damned reform, and eventually finding it. Fortunately for the game. Suggestions from the Invitational's referee, Mike Blanchard, and historian Frank Phelps were helpful. But it was Jimmy's extravagant persistence that eventually carried the day, with an influential assist from another Famer, Bill Talbert, then director of the U.S. Open. Talbert, seeing the entertainment and scheduling value in eliminating those freight train-long sets and matches, put in enough good words so that, startlingly, the USTA gave tie-breaking a chance during the summer of 1970.

Enter "Sudden Death," the Van Alen version (best-of-9-points), and the rest of the world shortly inhaled the intoxicating fumes of change from his Casino laboratory. " Sudden Death," lasting five years in the U.S., was too far left elsewhere, however. Univer-

Jimmy Van Alen was the founder of the International Tennis Hall of Fame.

sally-adopted "Lingering Death," as Van Alen disdainfully called it (best-of-12 but, requiring a margin of two), clung to his bete noire, the deuce principal. Whichever, 1970 marked the official beginning of the perky Bolshevik's revolution, the overtime at 6-6 making tennis more TV-friendly. I call the breaker simply, a "Jimmy." Remarkably, he jimmied his way into the Ft. Knox-like stronghold of unwavering tradition.

The tie-breaker (baptized by himself; not as tie-break), was merely one item in his tinkering that he called VASSS: Van Alen Streamlined Scoring System. Included are no-ad (1-2-3-4 instead of 15, 30, 40, game; a sudden finish at 3-3), medal play round-robins, 31-point sets. All useful, but a hard sell in this glacially moving game—except that the ATP and WTA pros now use no-ad in doubles (first to 4 points wins a game).

Refused permission by the USTA to install the system for the Casino Invitational, the Bolshevik, anxious for a public viewing, decided to hire the "outcasts" in 1965. They, the handful of out-and-out pros, several of them all-time greats, were hustling for a living on the fringe, barred from the consequential tourneys prior to 1968.

His bringing them back to the cradle of American tennis, a scene of their amateur days, horrified some of the game's old guard. ["old goats," Famer Bob Kelleher tagged them when he was the USTA president in 1967-68, hurdling conservative factions to usher in opens.]

One of the pros, Butch Buchholz, was amazed and amused. "Some people said the grass here would turn brown if a pro set foot on it. But here we are. It still looks pretty green."

Pancho Gonzalez hadn't been there for 16 years. Rod Laver, Hoad and Rosewall, Pancho Segura, Mal Anderson (all future Famers) were gone for long stretches, too. It never occurred to them that they'd reappear in the sanctum.

They didn't understand VASSS, but Jimmy directed them during a highly spirited, compelling and successful week. And, after all, the $10,000 prize money he underwrote was such a bonanza for them at that time they would have played barefoot on steaming coals. Famer Allison Danzig, covering for the *The New York Times*, wrote that they were "wonderplayers" whose likes hadn't been seen at The Casino for many years.

As green as the grass was the tie-breaker in its debut. Spectators and players, equally puzzled, tried to follow the umpire's calls. It was a faulty example and would be adjusted. But Rosewall, winner of the tournament—though not realizing it at the moment of victory—lost the first tiebreaker to Mike Davies, 5-points-to-3. They don't remember it.

The name Candy has a significant ring at The Casino. One, Capt. Henry "Sugar" Candy, a British soldier has been practically forgotten, not seen in Newport since 1879. But the other, Candace "Candy" Van Alen, wife of the impresario and innovator, cut a wider, more elegant swath as one of the town's grande dames until her death in 2002.

Each had a connection with an idea that made all the difference in the legend of the game's bastion. Bellevue Avenue is the cord tieing the notions together. Up the street from The Casino, toward the Hotel Viking, sits a yellow frame building, a men's club called the Reading Room, where bookish blue-bloods pored over the literature on the labels identifying booze of various shades. They may even have read *The New York Herald*, the outspoken, sometimes outrageous, newspaper owned by one of their fellow moneybags who fitted both those adjectives: James Gordon Bennett, Jr.

An imposing mustachioed chap, and man about numerous sports, 38-year-old Bennett, helping to plant the seed of polo in the U.S., had imported a star, Capt. Candy, to play on his team. Hospitably, he recommended Candy for guest privileges among Reading Roomers.

Bennett, you may recall, sent the intrepid reporter Henry M. Stanley to Africa to search for and find the renowned missionary, Dr. David Livingston, thus scooping the world for his Herald. "Dr. Livingston, I presume," was the memorable greeting from Stanley on discovering his quarry in 1871 in what is now Ujiji, Uganda. Livingston wasn't lost at all, but he was annoyed by the whole affair. However, Stanley knew you never louse up a good story with the facts.

Although Bennett had a different assignment in mind for Candy, and a much shorter journey, the polo-playing cavalryman became part of a good story, too. The facts may be a little shaky, but they have come down through the years since 1879, and Bennett gets the blame for a dastardly act (in the eyes of the Reading Roomers) committed by Candy.

One dull summer afternoon, JGB, feeling puckish or peckish, either dared Candy to acquaint his (perhaps literate?) pony with great books by riding the steed up the porch steps and into the club—or bet Candy he wouldn't do it. Doesn't matter which. The captain did it, charging with the esprit of his country's Light Brigade, Bennett, a witness, probably had a big laugh as fellow members spluttered and raged. They revoked Candy's privileges, but the instigator was too powerful to be thrown out. They needn't have worried about that. He was leaving them. Peeved that they couldn't take a joke and had unduly castigated his pal, the famously irascible Bennett had an idea that—unintentionally—would benefit tenniskind.

Revenge? He got it, and then some, savoring the loud last guffaws. Reacting in rich playboy fashion, JGB built a bigger, better club, The Casino, in 1880. Purchasing land within sight of the Reading Room for $60,000, commissioning an all-star architect, Stanford White, Bennett spent $64,000 for the timber and brick masterpiece with turf courts included. It's unlikely that he imagined his playroom becoming a focal point in a game that was merely six-years-old, or that it would become even more prominent in the 21st century, at age 128, as the pantheon of the fuzzy ball.

Although The Casino was, in Bennett's mind, a hall of his own fame, well after his and Capt. Candy's departures from this earth, the latter day "Candy" (Mrs. Van Alen) arrived. With these words she sent the place in an even loftier direction: "Why doesn't tennis have a Hall of Fame, Jimmy?"

On a visit to Cooperstown, N.Y., with her husband, Candy had been taken by the Baseball Hall of Fame. Jimmy responded, "Good idea. What better place than The Casino? Our national Championships began there. The tradition is rich." Later he would say, "This is a living Hall. None like it because the game it salutes continues in that place."

He ran with the idea to the USTA, and gained, with his usual unbending determination, approval in 1954 for a U.S. Hall of Fame. The Hall went International in 1975, inducting the debonair Englishman Fred Perry, the first to hold all four major championships: Australian, 1934; French, 1935; U.S., 1933-34, 36; Wimbledon, 1934-35-36. Jocular Fred said the ceremony was "like attending your own embalming."

The Hall's original initiates in 1955 had already been embalmed: earliest U.S. champs Dick Sears, Henry Slocum, Oliver Campbell, Bob Wrenn, Malcolm Whitman, Joseph Clark as well as the "Father of American Tennis," Dr. James Dwight.

Somewhat livelier were the Class of 1956. Two of the six were able to appear: William Clothier, U.S. champ of 1906, and May Sutton Bundy, first American to win Wimbledon, 1905, 07.

There's a nice tie-in with the Class of '04, a unique parent-child connection. Dorothy Bundy "Dodo" Cheney, (daughter of May Bundy) was tapped along with Steffi Graf (aka Mrs. Andre Agassi) and Stefan Edberg. Steffi and Stefan are retired after illustrious careers containing 22 and six singles majors respectively. "Dodo," then 87, who won the Australian Championship in 1938, first American woman to do that, might retire someday if she finds time in a tournament career of seven-or-so decades and (at this writing) close to 400 U.S. senior titles.

I am hardly the first Bostonian to make the Newport pilgrimage. "Doc" Dwight, 29, and his protege, 19-year-old, Harvard kid Dick Sears, were the trailblazers to The Casino in 1881 as Americans tried something new and novel in gamesplaying. Recognized as the game's American patriarch, a Harvard-trained physician too wise to let medicine interfere with his tennis, Dwight won five U.S. doubles titles alongside Sears, but was more giving as a guiding hand in the founding of the seminal Championships, as well as Davis Cup and the USTA itself.

Sears wove an unequalled string of seven singles titles through 1887, making his mark as a vibrant volleyer. Those two and their achievements were the originals in making The Casino a destination for pilgrimages, and I am a grateful, happy pilgrim, pleased to attend the annual canonization of the game's saints every July, and mingle with the ghosts of champions past.

—*Bud Collins, 2008*

Hall of Fame

The Hall of Fame is a destination for the game's greats who are selected by an international panel of journalists, administrators and champions. While players form the majority of inductees, those who have made outstanding contributions to the game are also eligible. Players are not considered until they are five years beyond serious competition.

Russ Adams
United States (1930—)
Hall of Fame—2007—Photographer

A small town boy with worldly ambitions. It's the story of Russ Adams, born July 30, 1930, whose lenses have focused on targets across the globe, and unerring eye has preserved tennis masterpieces.

High times have marked the artistic career of Russell Harrison Adams out of Spencer, Mass., a stretch of more than a half-century that continues as he makes his living with cameras. First there was a Baby Brownie, clicking away in a 14-year-old's hands. Freelancing for *The Worcester* (Mass.) *Telegram*, he developed the films in a dark room his mother built in the kitchen. Now it's the high-tech digital stuff that graces publications across the planet, deftly embraced by the first photographer to be anointed for the Hall.

Elevation has been his lifetime theme. No doubt the highest he got was about 70,000 feet as a Cold Warrior in the early 1950s. Serving in the U.S. Air Force's Strategic Air Command, he was based at Ft. Worth, though his office was well above ground in a B-36, snapping and snooping on the Soviet Union. Of that he will say only, "They knew we were there, but we were too high for them to get us. I guess I knew Moscow and St. Petersburg [then Leningrad] and some of their missile bases better than the people who lived and worked there."

After his discharge, he returned to work as a copy boy for the eventually-deceased *Boston Herald-Traveler*. Soon he was on the photographic staff, principally sports, winning prizes for catching such Boston icons as Ted Williams, Bill Russell, Bob Cousy and Bobby Orr at their labors.

But tennis? Tennis, at which the good-natured Adams has made an inimitable international reputation, shooting on every continent but Antarctica, where the penguins presumably prefer swimming.

"I'd never seen tennis played before the sports editor sent me to Longwood Cricket Club to cover a tournament," he says. "Didn't even know how to keep score." Luckily, the game's Grande Dame, Hall of Famer Hazel Wightman, was running the tournament. "She took me in hand, showed me what to look for, introduced me to players."

He caught on quickly, though not imagining that tennis would become his mainstay.

Paris wasn't new the first of many times Russ did the French Open. "*The Herald* had sent me there to shoot fashion shows, and to Rome, Florence and Milan, too." There he was, at the height of haute couture, a long way from locker rooms. "Givenchy, Dior and Coco Chanel liked my work, and were kind and helpful to me."

A more startling change was his sideline as a high-steel photographer, moving nimbly on the beams and girders of unfinished skyscrapers way above Boston. "Never bothered me," he says. "One bad day, though, we were caught in a hail storm up high up on the Hancock Tower."

What to do? Call for a helicopter? A parachute?

"Just sat there and waited it out until the icy ladders thawed. About two hours."

His specialty was topping-off ceremonies—snapping the placing of a small Christmas tree and U.S. flag at the very top of the spiny construction.

Leaving the newspaper business, he was "off on my own, and all went well. Another of my businesses is setting up cameras in banks to identify crooks. We've caught some bank robbers."

But apprehending tennis players, such as the incomparable Aussie, Rod Laver, in their acts, has given him greater satisfaction. He's had more than 300 covers on magazines around the world, seen and captured countless wonderful matches.

If one of zillions of shots stands forth, it's the picture of Laver hurdling the net on completing his second Grand Slam by winning the U.S. Open of 1969.

Of dozens of photographers present at Forest Hills, only Adams froze Laver's leap. It was unique. Laver, no hotdog, never did it before or later, and has no idea what instinct launched him.

Russ says, "Like everybody else, I was preparing for Rod to shake hands with the loser, Tony Roche. But suddenly up he went, and"—with reflexes as sharp as Laver's—"I got him."

One of Russ's high times, all right, even though only three feet.

George Adee
United States (1874–1948)
Hall of Fame—1964—Administrator

George Townsend Adee made his sporting name as an All-American quarterback at Yale in 1894. He was elevated to the Hall of Fame in 1964 for his contributions to tennis on the administrative side. He was president of the USTA four years, 1916-19, and was also a member of the USTA Davis Cup and Amateur Rules committees. A New Yorker, he was an enthusiastic tennis player, good enough to appear six times in the U.S. Championships singles between 1903 and 1909. He served in the U.S. Army in the Spanish-American War and World War I. Born Jan. 4, 1874, in Stonington, Conn., he died July 31, 1948, in New York.

Fred Alexander
United States (1880–1969)
Hall of Fame—1961

As the first foreigner to win the Australian title, Frederick Beasley Alexander beat Alf Dunlop, 3-6, 3-6, 6-0, 6-2, 6-3, in 1908, then joined with native Dunlop to take the doubles, too, over Tony Wild-

ing and Granville Sharp, 6-3, 6-2, 6-1. In 1908, Fred also made the U.S. all-comers singles final, losing to Wright 6-3, 6-3, 6-1.

That year, he and Beals Wright were the U.S. Davis Cup team in an unsuccessful attempt to pry the Cup away from Australasia (Norman Brookes and Wilding), 3-2 in Melbourne. He lost a tough opener to Brookes, 5-7, 9-7, 6-2, 4-6, 6-3, and the decisive fifth match to Wilding, 6-3, 6-4, 6-1. Right-handed, a New Yorker and Princeton man, he won the U.S. Intercollegiate singles (1901) and doubles (1900).

He ranked six years in the U.S. Top 10: No. 7, 1904; No. 5, 1905; No. 4, 1906; No. 3, 1908, 18 (at age 38); No. 8, 1914. He was Harold Hackett's partner in a standout doubles team, U.S. finalists a record seven straight times, beginning in 1905, winning in 1907-08-09-10. In 1917, at 37, he won a fifth U.S. title, shepherding 19-year-old Harold Throckmorton to the doubles championship, over Harry Johnson-Irving Wright, 11-9, 6-4, 6-4. Lean and lanky, a smooth stroker, he was born in New York Aug. 14, 1880, and died in Beverly Hills, Calif, March 3, 1969.

MAJOR TITLES (7)—Australian singles, 1908; Australian doubles, 1908; U.S. doubles, 1907-08-09-10, 17. **OTHER U.S. TITLES** (8)—Indoor doubles, 1906-07-08, with Harold Hackett; 1911-12, with Theodore Pell; 1917, with William Rosenbaum; Intercollegiate singles, 1901; Intercollegiate doubles, 1900, with Raymond Little. **DAVIS CUP**—1908, 0-2 singles, 1-1 doubles. **SINGLES RECORD IN THE MAJORS**—Australian (4-0), US. (27-12).

Wilmer Allison
United States (1904–1977)
Hall of Fame—1963

Although the firm of Allison & Van Ryn was synonymous with doubles excellence, Texan Wilmer Lawson Allison, who played the left court, had several singles triumphs at the top of the game. Foremost, he won the U.S. Championship in 1935 when, at age 30, he shot through not only 23-year-old ex-Wimbledon champ Sidney Wood, 6-2, 6-2, 6-3, in one of the most lopsided finals, but beating 1933-34 and 1936 champ Fred Perry in the semis, 7-5, 6-3, 6-3. That ended a Forest Hills streak of 18 matches for England's Perry, and eased some of Allison's pain of losing the 1934 final to Fred, 6-4, 6-3, 3-6, 1-6, 8-6.

As a Davis Cupper, primarily in doubles, he and Johnny Van Ryn—U.S. champs in 1931 and 1935, and Wimbledon champs in 1929 and 1930—won 14 of 16 Cup doubles between 1929 and 1936, the best record by a U.S. team until Peter Fleming and John McEntoe's 14-1. Their 24 Cup series (tied with Stan Smith and Vic Seixas) are second only to McEnroe's 30 in U.S. annals. They beat the topnotch French teams in Cup finales in Paris (Jean Borotra-Henri Cochet, 6-1, 8-6, 6-4, in 1929, Cochet-Jacques Brugnon, 6-3, 11-13, 7-5, 4-6, 6-4, in 1932) but could do no more than prolong successful French defenses.

A 5-foot-11, 155-pound right-hander, Allison experienced two extraordinary Cup singles matches in Paris in 1931 and 1932. Opening the 4-1 semifinal victory over Italy in 1930, he made an all-time comeback to beat ambidextrous Giorgio de Stefani 4-6, 7-9, 6-4, 8-6, 10-8. Allison squandered four set points of his own in the second, but the most exciting was to come: from 2-5 down

in the fourth he saved two match points, and in the last set, from 1-5 down, 16 more!

The following year, with France ahead, 2-1, and the Cup at stake, he lost a controversial match to Borotra, 1-6, 3-6, 6-4, 6-2, 7-5, after the Frenchman saved four match points in the fifth set. On the fourth, at 4-5 advantage out, Borotra apparently double faulted by a considerable margin. But the local service line judge made no call, and it was a point against Allison, who was on his way to the net to shake hands.

Objective Al Laney wrote for the consumption of U.S. readers: "The U.S. has won the Cup, but the trophy remains in France. A line judge, Gerard de Ferrier, kept Allison from his just victory." Ellsworth Vines beat Cochet in the fifth match, 4-6, 0-6, 7-5, 8-6, 6-2, to make the score 3-2, France. But nobody can know how that match would have gone had it been decisive. Ferrier thought he'd done a patriotic deed.

Allison played 44 singles and doubles Cup matches, third for the U.S. behind McEnroe (69) and Seixas (55), and won 32. A U.S. semifinalist in 1932 as well, Allison did not defend his title, withdrawing from the scene after losing a 1936 Wimbledon quarterfinal to Brit Bunny Austin 6-1, 6-4, 7-5. He'd lost the 1930 final to Bill Tilden, 6-3, 9-7, 6-4, Big Bill's last major title. No. 1 American in 1934-35, he was also a resident in the U.S. Top 10 eight straight years: No. 5 in 1928; No. 7 in 1929; No. 3 in 1930; No. 9 in 1931; No. 2 in 1932-33. Wilmer was in the world top 10 five times: No. 6, 1930; No. 4, 1932, 1935; No. 5, 1934; No. 7, 1936. Born Dec. 8, 1904, in San Antonio, he won the U.S. Intercollegiate title for alma mater, Texas, in 1927. He was five times in the world's Top 10: No. 6, 1930; No. 4, 1932, 35; No. 5, 1934; No. 7, 1936.

A colonel in the U.S. Army Air Corps during World War II, he entered the Hall of Fame in 1963, and died April 20, 1977, in Austin, Texas.

MAJOR TITLES (6)—U.S. singles, 1935; Wimbledon doubles, 1929-1930; U.S. doubles,. 1931, 35; U.S. mixed, 1930. **OTHER U.S. TITLE**—Intercollegiate singles. 1927. **DAVIS CUP**—1928-29-30-31-32-33, 1935-36, 18-10 singles, 14-2 doubles. **SINGLES RECORD IN THE MAJORS**—Wimbledon (16-5), U.S. (27-8).

Manuel Alonso
Spain (1895--1984)
Hall of Fame—1977

As the first Spanish male of international stature, Manolo Alonso de Areyzaga made his country's best showing at Wimbledon and the U.S. Championships before Manolo Santana won those titles in 1966 and 1965, respectively. He beat Japanese Zenzo Shimidzu in a terrific battle, 3-6, 7-5, 3-6, 6-4, 8-6, to reach the Wimbledon all-comers final of 1921, where he lost to South Africa's Babe Norton in another tense struggle, 5-7, 4-6, 7-5, 6-3, 6-3. A U.S. resident for several years during the 1920s, he made the quarterfinals of the U.S. Championships in 1922-23, 25, 27, and was three years in the U.S. Top 10: No. 4 in 1925 and 1927; No. 2 in 1926. world's Top 10 three years: No. 8 in 1925 and 1926; No. 5 in 1927.

A dark-haired 5-foot-9, 145-pound right-hander, he played Davis Cup for Spain six years. A brother, Jose-Maria, also played

Davis Cup for Spain, 1924-25; 0-1 singles, 2-1 doubles. Manuel was born Nov. 12, 1895, in San Sebastian, died Oct. 11, 1984, in Madrid.

DAVIS CUP—1921-22, 24-25, 31, 36; 11-7 singles, 3-4 doubles. **SINGLES RECORD IN THE MAJORS**—Wimbledon (8-3), US (20-10),

Mal Anderson
Australia (1935—)
Hall of Fame—2000

They called him "Country" and "Cowboy." He came from a remote, vast territory of cattle, kangaroos, kookaburras—and home-made tennis courts made of ant bed. Knock over a few crimson ant hills, something like fireplugs, spread the grit in a rectangle, roll and line, and—presto: You've got the kind of court that rural Queensland lads like Malcolm James Anderson grew up on.

Mal Anderson, 22, was as unknown to Americans as his home turf, a cattle station [ranch] at Burnside, when he showed up at Forest Hills for the third time in 1957 and became the first unseeded guy to win the U.S. title, beating a fellow Aussie and future Davis Cup teammate, No. 1 seed Ashley Cooper, 10-8, 7-5, 6-4. He was the forerunner of the four Queenslanders emerging from what's sometimes called never-never land (so far from anything) who conquered the U.S., followed by Roy Emerson (1961, 64), Rod Laver (1962, 69), Patrick Rafter (1997-98). In a two-part career, he played on the international circuit until age 38.

Lean as a rail at 6-foot-1, dark hair slicked back, he was attack-all-the-way, quick and sure of volley, fast around the court, a worthy successor to compatriots Frank Sedgman (1951-52) and Ken Rosewall (1956). Prior to winning the U.S. title in 1957, his season had not gone well: heat prostration, later a broken toe at Wimbledon. But a win over Brit Mike Davies in the Newport final, 4-6, 6-1, 6-4, 1-6, 6-2, the second title of his career, got him in fine fettle for the drive across the Forest Hills greensward. He beat the 1-2-3 seeds—No. 2 Dick Savitt, 6-4, 6-3, 6-1, best Chilean Luis Ayala, 6-1, 6-3, 6-1 and in his most demanding, No. 3 seed Swede Sven Davidson, 5-7, 6-2, 4-6, 6-3, 6-4, crashing the final, to face the No. 1 seed. There, his slick backhand, quickness and anticipation zapped Cooper, who had lost the Wimbedon final to fellow Aussie Lew Hoad. His was a unique U.S. achievement—from first round loser in 1956, to American Mike Green, 6-3, 6-4, 6-2, to champ 12 months later—until Swede Stefan Edberg pulled it off in 1991.

Anderson's menacing 1957 form continued through victories at home, Adelaide and Melbourne, and the successful post-Christmas Davis Cup defense, 3-2, over the U.S. at Melbourne. Hoad and Rosewall had fled to the pros, and the pressure was on leadoff man, Mal. Few have made a more solid final-round debut: He cut down huge serving Barry MacKay, 6-3, 7-5, 3-6, 7-9, 6-3. On the second day (after Cooper had beaten Vic Seixas), he accompanied Mervyn Rose for the coup de grace: 6-4, 6-4, 8-6, over MacKay and Seixas.

Although he won six tournaments in 1958, repeating at Newport, this time over Cooper, 6-4, 7-5, 7-5, Anderson couldn't win the Australian championship (beaten in the final by Cooper, 7-5, 6-3, 6-4) or retain the U.S. title. He came close, losing, 6-2, 3-6, 4-6, 10-8, 8-6, to Cooper.

The Davis Cup was a disappointment, too, a 3-2 loss to the U.S., especially since the final was in Queensland, the Milton Grounds at Brisbane. Peruvian Alex Olmedo, a U.S. resident, outgunned Anderson in a tight one, 8-6, 2-6, 9-7, 8-6, and would beat Cooper in the third-day clincher. Heart-cracking was the doubles, Anderson and Cup rookie Neale Fraser overtaken, despite two match points, by Olmedo and Ham Richardson, 10-12, 3-6, 16-14, 6-3, 7-5—longest Cup final doubles, 82 games.

Those defeats reduced his value to pro promoter Jack Kramer, but Mal signed for a $22,000 guarantee over two years, and exceeded it. As a rookie in 1959, Mal won the most important of the pro championships, Wembley in London, beating Ecuador's Pancho Segura in five, 4-6, 6-4, 3-6, 6-3, 8-6. He barnstormed for a while, retired, then reappeared in 1969, at 34, attaching Part II to his resume with the advent of the Open era, adding the last five of his 21 career singles titles. Fourteen years after first gracing the Australian final, he made it again in 1972, losing to Rosewall, 7-6 (7-2), 6-3, 7-5. A year later, at 38, he took the Aussie doubles in the company of John Newcombe over Phil Dent and John Alexander, 3-6, 7-6, 6-2. He played Davis Cup for two more years, winning 10 singles, and was a contributing member of possibly the greatest of all Davis Cup teams, Capt. Neale Fraser's winning Antique Show: Rod Laver, 35, Ken Rosewall, 39, Newcombe, 29, and Anderson. Born March 5, 1935, at home in Burnside (18 miles from the nearest pub at Theodore), he grew up on a 6,000-acre property with 1,000 head of cattle. Mal spent a lot of time on horseback doing the work of a ringer (cowboy). "Fell off a few times, too," he laughs. He was sent to school in Rockhampton and was tutored at tennis by Charlie Hollis, Laver's coach. Entering the International Hall in 2000, he was named to the Australian Tennis Hall of Fame in 2001.

MAJOR TITLES (4)—U.S. singles, 1957; Australian doubles, 1973; French doubles, 1957; Australian mixed, 1957. **DAVIS CUP**—1957-58, 73, 11-3 singles, 2-3 doubles. **SINGLES RECORD IN THE MAJORS**—Australian (16-8), French (1-1), Wimbledon (13-5), U.S. (16-4).

Arthur Ashe
United States (1943–1993)
Hall of Fame—1985

A singular figure in the game's history as the first black male to win a major singles titles—the first three in fact—Arthur Robert Ashe, Jr., also set a record in 1968 that is most unlikely to be equalled: he won both the U.S. Amateur and Open championships, the first time such a double was possible. No one has come remotely close since.

That first season of the Open era was a whirlwind year for him, then 1st Lieutenant Ashe of the U.S. Army. In order to maintain Davis Cup eligibility and gain time away from duty for important tournaments, Ashe was required to maintain his amateur status. Determining that the traditional (and previously amateur) U.S. Singles Championships at Forest Hills would become the inaugural U.S. Open in 1968, the USTA designated Longwood Cricket Club grass in Boston as the site for a U.S. Amateur tournament. Seeded No. 1 in Boston, Ashe came through to the title by surging past teammate Bob Lutz in the exciting final, 4-6, 6-3, 8-10, 6-0, 6-4.

However, with pros introduced to Forest Hills, Ashe was a lightly regarded No. 5 seed. Nevertheless, at 25, he came of age as an internationalist. Unflappable over the New York fortnight, he served-and-volleyed splendidly. In the final, he clocked 26 aces, returned with precision, and held his cool in a five-set championship victory over pro Tom Okker, 14-12, 5-7, 6-3, 3-6, 6-3.

An amateur would never do so well again. As the last remaining pro, Okker got the $14,000 first prize while Ashe was happy to settle for $20 daily expenses for his historic triumph, the first major for a black since Althea Gibson's Forest Hills triumph a decade before. Ashe's victory also boosted American morale by ending the U.S. male championship drought that dated back 13 years to Tony Trabert's 1955 title.

That year Ashe was also a Davis Cup drought-buster, spearheading the U.S. drive to the sterling tub last won five years before. He won 11 straight singles (the most in one campaign for an American) in the drive to retrieve the Cup from Australia in Adelaide. In the finale, he started slowly but beat lefty Ray Ruffels on opening day, 6-8, 7-5, 6-3, 6-3, for a 2-0 lead. After the Cup was clinched by Lutz and Stan Smith in doubles, he finally gave way, losing to Bill Bowrey in a meaningless third-day match. The season closed with Ashe the winner of 10 of 22 tournaments on a 72-10 match record.

He would win both his singles in 1969 as the U.S. successfully defended the Cup, 5-0, against Romania. He beat Ilie Nastase on the first day, 6-2, 15-13, 7-5. Next came West Germany, 5-0, also at Cleveland in 1970, and his first-day win over Willy Bungert, 6-2, 10-8, 6-2. His third-day defeat of Christian Kuhnke, 6-8, 10-12, 9-7, 13-11, 6-4, was the longest match (86 games) in a Cup-deciding round. Eight years later, he reappeared for a vital cameo that led to another Cup for the U.S. His singles victory over Kjell Johansson, 6-2, 6-0, 7-5, was the clincher over Sweden, 3-2, in the semifinal at Goteborg.

Ashe put in 10 years of Davis Cup, topped for the U.S. only by John McEnroe's 12 and Bill Tilden and Stan Smith's 11 each, and won 27 singles matches. He returned in 1981 as captain for five years, piloting the victors of 1981 and 1982.

He was born July 10, 1943 in Richmond, Va., and grew up there. He was 6'1, 160 lbs and right-handed. Since racial segregation was the law at that time, he could not play in the usual junior tournaments. With the aid of the concerned Lynchburg, Va., physician, Dr. Walter Johnson (who had also befriended and helped Althea Gibson), Ashe finished high school in St. Louis where he could get the necessary tennis competition.

In 1961, after Dr. Johnson's lobbying got him into the previously segregated U.S. Interscholastic tourney, Ashe won it for Sumner High. Four years later, leading man of his alma mater's varsity (University of California at Los Angeles), he won the 1965 U.S. Intercollegiate singles over Mike Belkin of the Univ. of Miami, 6-4, 6-1, 6-1, and took the doubles with Ian Crookenden.

Although Ashe was a man of strong character, poised and able to overcome racial blocks, it took him a while to harness his power, groove his groundstrokes and become a thoughtful player, comfortable on all surfaces. He won 35 amateur singles tournaments, including the U.S. Hard Court in 1963 over Allen Fox, 6-3, 12-10, and the U.S. Clay Court in 1967 over Marty Riessen,

4-6, 6-3, 6-1, 7-5. As one whose career overflowed the amateur and Open eras, he followed the 1968 breakthrough with 11 sterling years as a professional that netted 33 singles titles including the 1970 Australian over Aussie Dick Crealy, 6-4, 9-7, 6-2, and the gloriously unexpected Wimbledon title in 1975.

Days before his 32nd birthday, seeded No. 6, he was a longer shot than he had been seven years earlier at Forest Hills. Defending champ Jimmy Connors, seemingly inviolable, was a 10-to-1 favorite in the final, but Ashe was too slick and cerebral in one of the momentous upsets, 6-1, 6-1, 5-7, 6-4. Changing pace and spin cleverly, startling Connors with a sliced serve wide to the two-fisted backhand, Arthur out-foxed the man a decade his junior.

This was the centerpiece of Ashe's preeminent year, a heavy-duty season when he won nine of 29 tourneys on a 108-23 match record and wound up No. 1 in the U.S., No. 4 in the world. He reached No. 2 in the world in 1976. Improving with age, he unfortunately was grounded prematurely, and permanently, by a heart attack in July, 1979. In 1992, he revealed that he'd contracted AIDS through a 1988 blood transfusion.

Besides 1975, he spent nine other years in the world's Top 10: No. 10 in 1965 and 1978; No. 7 in 1966; No. 9 in 1967, 1970 and 1973; No. 2 in 1968; No. 8 in 1969; No. 6 in 1971; No. 5 in 1972.

In the U.S. rankings, he was No. 1 in 1968 and 1975 and in the Top 10 10 other years: No. 6 in 1963; No. 3 in 1964 and 1976; No. 2 in 1965-66-67, 69, 71, 73; No. 4 in 1970; No. 5 in 1974.

He was one of the founders of the ATP in 1972, served as president and had been a reasoned, intelligent spokesman for the game, serving on numerous corporate boards and received several honorary degrees.

A long-time protester of apartheid in South Africa, he was, after several refusals, granted a visa to visit that country in 1973, and became the first black to win a title there, the doubles (with Okker) in the South African Open, over Lew Hoad and Rob Maud, 6-2, 4-6, 6-2, 6-4, after losing singles final to Connors, 6-4, 7-6, 6-3. "You have shown our black youth that they can compete with whites and win," poet Don Mattera lauded him.

He was gratified to return again after the dismantling of apartheid and meet with president Nelson Mandela (who identified himself as "an Ashe fan"). Ashe lent himself, his name and his money to various enlightened causes. He was arrested not long before his death in a protest against what he regarded as cruel U.S. policies toward Haitian refugees. His principal cause was fostering, furthering education for needy kids, and he was the guiding light in the Safe Passage Foundation for that purpose. He was also a warrior in the fight against AIDS. A tennis player who went well beyond the game, Arthur upheld the qualities that distinguished him as a champion: he showed that it was possible to compete ferociously while maintaining personal honor and sportsmanship. Having entered the Hall of Fame in 1985, he died Feb. 6, 1993, leaving his wife, Jeanne, and six-year-old daughter, Camera. He was posthumously awarded the Presidential Medal of Freedom by President Clinton.

During his career, he won 35 amateur singles, 33 pro singles (634-202 in matches), 18 pro doubles titles (323-176) and $1,584,909 in prize money.

MAJOR TITLES (5)—U.S. singles, 1968; Australian singles, 1970; Wimbledon singles, 1975; Australian doubles, 1977; French doubles, 1971. OTHER U.S. TITLES (8)—Amateur singles, 1968; Clay Court singles, 1967; Hard Court singles, 1963. Intercollegiate singles. 1965; Indoor doubles, 1967 with Charles Pasarell; 1970 with Stan Smith; Clay Court doubles, 1970. with Clark Graebner; Intercollegiate doubles, 1965, with Ian Crookenden. DAVIS CUP (As player)—1963, 1965-66-67-68-69-70, 75, 77, 78, 27-5 singles, 1-1 doubles. As captain—1981-82-83-84-85, record 13-3, won 1981-82 Cups.

Juliette Atkinson
United States (1873–1944)
Hall of Fame—1974

Juliette Paxton Atkinson, a right-handed 5-footer who lived in Brooklyn, N.Y., was prominent in singles for four years at the U.S. Championships, a finalist four straight years, 1895-98, winning the title thrice: 1895 over Helen Hellwig, 6-4, 6-1, 6-2; 1897 over Bessie Moore, 6-3, 6-3, 4-6, 3-6, 6-3, and 1898 over Marion Jones. She did not defend in 1899, defaulting the challenge round to Californian Jones, who gave her a terrific struggle for the 1898 title, 6-3, 5-7, 6-4, 2-6, 7-5—one of the longest matches in terms of games (51) ever played by women. But Juliette did continue to compete through 1902.

She won the U.S. doubles seven times with five different partners between 1894 and 1902. She had five in a row with three partners (1894—98), the last two with her younger sister, Kathleen. Other than the Roosevelts, Ellen and Grace in 1900, they were the only sisters to win the title until Venus and Serena Williams in 1999. They were the first sisters to face one another in the U.S. Championships, twice the semis, until the Williams' final of 2001. Juliette beat Kathleen in both, 1895, 6-1, 6-4, and 1897, 6-1, 6-3. She was born April 15, 1873, in Rahway, N.J., died Jan. 12, 1944, in Lawrenceville, Ill., and entered the Hall of Fame in 1974.

MAJOR TITLES (13)—U.S. singles, 1895, 97-98; U.S. doubles, 1894-95-96-97-98, 1901-02. U.S. mixed, 1894, 1895, 1896. SINGLES RECORD IN THE MAJORS— U.S. (14-4).

Bunny Austin
Great Britain (1906–2000)
Hall of Fame—1997

Short on fabric, long on Davis Cup exploits, the genial English gentleman Henry Wilfred "Bunny" Austin was amused that baring his knees "may have made me more famous than helping win the Cup for Britain." Liberating male legs by bravely introducing shorts to the upper level of the game would seem his finest contribution to many. But Bunny was a marvelous player—a world's Top 10 inhabitant 11 consecutive years: No. 2 in 1931 and 1938, without whom the Brits would never have relished their four years of greatest Davis Cup glory: 1933—36. Otherwise, No. 7 in 1928; No. 9 in 1929, 1932; No. 10 in 1930; No. 4 in 1933-34, 37; No. 5 in 1935-36.

"Fred Perry, of course, was the point man with his three Wimbledon championships (1934-35-36), the derby thoroughbred. And I was known as the old cab horse," Austin laughed. But a very reliable one when the business at hand was Davis Cup. He played three years beyond Fred, playing more series (24 to

20) and winning more singles (36 to 34). He was all the more remarkable in that he soldiered on through periods of a recurring mysterious, weakening illness that wasn't diagnosed until his playing career was over. "It was called Gilbert's Syndrome, a periodic liver misfunction that was discovered, and treated, when I was in the U.S. Army during World War II," Austin said shortly before his death in 2000.

A 21-year Cup drought ended for Britain, an original in the competition, during a hot July, 1933, weekend in Paris. Bunny, 26, led off by beating Henri Merlin, 6-3, 6-4, 6-0, and Perry, 24, finished it over Merlin as French rule of six years collapsed beneath the Anglo assault, 3-2. "That had been my goal since I joined the team in '29," Austin said. "It was a time of great celebration when we arrived home. It was a long campaign [seven series in all], and there was nothing like playing for your country. Especially in our three successful defenses at Wimbledon." Bunny went 13-1 during the Cup-seizing season, losing only when he tired in five sets against Henri Cochet, 5-7, 6-4, 4-6, 6-4, 6-4, on the third day.

"I think I played best in our 1934 defense against the U.S. (4-1) when I beat Frank Shields the first day [6-4, 6-4, 6-1] and Sidney Wood [6-4, 6-0, 6-8, 6-3] on the third day." The next year, 5-0 over the U.S., he rallied as leadoff man to beat Wilmer Allison, 6-2, 2-6, 4-6, 6-3, 7-5, then the rising Don Budge, 6-2, 6-4, 6-8, 7-5.

In the 1936 defense against Australia (a 3-2 win), he led off beating 1933 Wimbledon champ Jack Crawford, 4-6, 6-3, 6-1, 6-1, but lost to Adrian Quist, 6-4, 2-6, 7-5, 6-2, Perry settling it. But that was the last Cup for Britain. Perry's defection to the pros left the home side in need. Bunny made a bold, hopeful beginning against the conquering Americans, beating Frank Parker, 6-3, 6-2, 7-5, but Budge came on too strongly, beating Bunny, 8-6, 4-6, 6-4, 6-3, as the U.S. carried off the prize, 4-1.

Bunny said he had a dream of playing Wimbledon when he was four. That dream materialized in 1928, and he proceeded to the fourth round. He was one of the most consistent of Wimbledon players, never worse than the round of 16 over 13 years, a semifinalist in 1929, 36-37, and a quarterfinalist five other times, 1931-33-34-35, 39. His worst major was a third-round finish at the U.S. in 1928.

Twice he reached the Wimbledon final, but was overwhelmed by a couple of No. 1's—Ellsworth Vines in 1932, 6-4, 6-2, 6-0, and Budge in 1938, 6-1, 6-0, 6-3. He was also a losing finalist at the French in 1937, beaten by German Henner Henkel, No. 3 that year, 6-1, 6-4, 6-3.

Stylish in everything he did, Bunny, a slim, handsome 5 foot-10, a graduate of Repton School and Cambridge University, was a tennis court vision with fluid, classic strokes. "He seemed to have stepped out of a tennis textbook," said Perry. He had long harbored the desire to play in shorts, not as a rebel but a practical man. "I wore them as a schoolboy soccer player, and knew the value in running. There was an awful lot of weight in flannels between the knees and shoes, so I decided to cut it out. I had a pair made for the U.S. Championships in '32 at Forest Hills. When I left the hotel with a polo coat covering my tennis kit a kindly bellman, seeing my shins and thinking to save me from embarrassment said, 'Haven't you forgotten something, Mr. Austin? Your trousers?' The American officials didn't like it, but surprisingly,

when I wore them at Wimbledon in '33 nothing was said." However, acceptance was slow, and no male champ was crowned naked-kneed at the Big W until Jack Kramer in 1947. Bunny was also a racket innovator, unveiling a split-shaft open-throat model in 1936, a common look today, but in wood then. His older sister, Joan Austin, Wimbledon doubles finalist in 1923, was sartorially daring, too, earlier, the first to appear minus stockings on Centre Court in 1931. They were the leggy bare pair.

Born Aug. 20, 1906, he died on his 94th birthday in Coulsdon, England, pleased that he had been on Centre Court for a last time amid an assemblage of tennis notables the previous month.

DAVIS CUP—1929-30-31-32-33-34-35-36-37; 36-12 in singles, Cup winners, 1933—36. **SINGLES RECORD IN THE MAJORS**—French (12-4), Wimbledon (56-13), U.S. (9-3).

Tracy Austin
United States (1962—)
Hall of Fame—1992

One of the game's prodigies, Tracy Ann Austin was meteoric, an iron-willed girl whose blaze was glorious though fleeting. A variety of injuries cut short what had promised to be one of the great careers. At 14, her junior career was practically a memory.

She had won the U.S. 12s title at 10 in 1972, and added 21 more age-group titles. Arriving at Forest Hills in 1977, an unseeded amateur, she was already the youngest winner of a pro tournament, Portland (Ore.), beating Stacy Margolin, 6-7, 6-3, 4-1 ret., earlier in the year. Sensationally, she made her way to the last eight of the U.S. Open by beating No. 4-seeded 1976 French champ Sue Barker of Great Britain, 6-1, 6-4, and Virginia Ruzici of Romania, who would win the French in 1978, 6-3, 7-5. Wimbledon finalist Betty Stove of the Netherlands stopped her there, 6-2, 6-2, but the 5-foot, 90-pound Tracy, in ponytail and pinafore, was the youngest of all major quarterfinalists, until Jennifer Capriati, a younger 14, was a French semifinalist in 1990.

Her performance earned no dollars, but she did get a congratulatory phone call from First Hacker, President Jimmy Carter.

Two years later in 1979, at 16 years, 9 months, Tracy not only dethroned four-time champ Chris Evert, 6-4, 6-3, at Flushing Meadows but undercut Maureen Connolly (1951) as the youngest U.S. champ by a couple of months. Earlier that year, she severed Evert's 125-match clay-court winning streak in the semis of the Italian, 6-4, 2-6, 7-6 (7-4), then won the title, her first important prize, over lefty Sylvia Hanika, 6-4, 1-6, 6-3.

She won the U.S. again in 1981 in a thrilling tie-breaker finish over Martina Navratilova, 1-6, 7-6 (7-4), 7-6 (7-1). That year, she won seven other tourneys and had a 58-7 match record, and in 1980, 12 titles on 68-7. Having made her Wimbledon debut in 1977 (a third-round loss to Evert, 6-1, 6-0), she was a semifinalist in 1979 and 1980, losing to the champs, Navratilova, 6-4, 6-7 (5-7), 6-2, and Evonne Goolagong, 6-3, 0-6, 6-4.

But maladies of her back began to impair her effectiveness and sideline her for long stretches. San Diego in 1982, defeating Kathy Rinaldi, 7-6 (7-5), 6-3 in the final, was the last of Austin's 30 pro titles. By 1983, before her 21st birthday, she was virtually

finished. She tried comebacks, as recently as 1994, in two tournaments, the Australian and French Opens, but that was it. In Melbourne, however, she became a post-induction Hall of Famer to win a major singles match, beating Elna Reinach of South Africa, 6-1, 7-5, then losing to Sabine Hack of Germany, 6-1, 5-7, 6-2. In Paris, ranked No. 78, she lost to Czech Marketa Kochta 6-0, 6-1, and called it quits A near-fatal auto accident in 1989 was another discouraging factor. A resolute 5-foot-4 right-handed groundstroker of 120 lbs., she had immense patience and fortitude, and deadly passing shots. Few errors marred her performances.

Evert, who reclaimed her U.S. title in the 1980 final, beating Tracy, 4-6, 6-1, 6-1 in the semis, recalls, "Tracy's mental strength was scary. She had no weaknesses, she was obsessive about winning." By 1977, Austin was No. 4 in the U.S. rankings, the greenest to stand so high until Capriati's No. 3 in 1990. She continued in that elite group through 1983, No. 1 in 1980, and: No. 3 in 1978-79; No. 2 in 1981; No. 4 in 1982; No. 5 in 1983.

Six straight years, from 1978 at No. 6, she was in the world's Top 10: No. 2 in 1980-81; No. 3 in 1979; No. 4 in 1982; No. 9 in 1983. Briefly in 1980, she was No. 1 on the WTA computer, breaking the Evert-Navratilova stranglehold of nearly six years. She had tremendous battles with those two. At the close of 1981, she won the Toyota Championship at East Rutherford, N.J., beating Chris (6-1, 6-2) and Martina (2-6, 6-4, 6-2) in succession, the first of only three to accomplish that back-to-back double, preceding Hana Mandlikova and Steffi Graf. She made the semifinals Wimbledon in 1979-80; and the U.S. Open in 1980; she reached the quarterfinals of the Australian in 1981; at the French in 1982-83; at Wimbledon in 1978, 82; and the U.S. Open in 1977-78, 82.

She played Federation Cup in 1978-79-80 with three Cup winners; Wightman Cup in 1978-79, 81 with two Cup winners, 1979, 81. Tracy was born into a tennis family Dec. 12, 1962, in Palos Verdes, Calif., and grew up in Rolling Hills. Her older sister and brothers—Pam, Jeff and John—played the pro circuit (see Also Served), and she and John won the Wimbledon mixed in 1980, the only brother-sister pairing to do so until Helena Sukova-Cyril Suk in 1996-97. She entered the Hall of Fame in 1992, married Scott Holt in 1994, has three sons, and works frequently as a TV tennis commentator.

She turned pro, October, 23, 1978 and won 30 singles (335-90 matches), four doubles pro titles, $2,902,380 prize money.

MAJOR TITLES (3)—US. singles, 1979, 81; Wimbledon mixed, 1980, **FEDERATION CUP**—1978-79,80, 13-1 singles. **WIGHTMAN CUP**—1978-79, 81, 4-2 singles, 2-0 doubles. **SINGLES RECORD IN THE MAJORS**—Australian (3-2), French (7-3), Wimbledon (21-6). U.S. (31-4)

Larry Baker
United States (1890–1980)
Hall of Fame—1975—Administrator

Lawrence Adams Baker, very active in USTA affairs, was an officer beginning in 1932, and president three years, 1948-50. He was a founder of the National Tennis Foundation, and captained the U.S. Davis Cup ream for its 1953 win over Canada at Montreal. He also sponsored the Baker Cup, a U.S. vs. Canada event for

seniors. Baker was born June 20, 1890, in Lowdensville, S.C, lived in East Hampton, N.Y., and died there Oct. 15, 1980. He entered the Hall of Fame in 1975.

Boris Becker
Germany (1968—)
Hall of Fame—2003

A red-headed phenomenon, Boris Becker illuminated 1985 and 1986 with his Wimbledon triumphs at the improbable ages of 17 and 18.

The records came tumbling down in 1985 when the unseeded German teen-ager whammed 21 aces, beating No. 8 seed American Kevin Curren, 6-3, 6-7 (4-7), 7-6 (7-3), 6-4, in the final. Ranked No. 20, he was the first German champ, the first non-seed to win and the youngest male ever to win a major at 17 years, 7 months. (Michael Chang, at 17 years, 3 months, lowered that four years later in winning the French.) Richard Krajicek in 1996 and Goran Ivanisevic in 2001 followed his unseeded route.

A big man (6-foot-3, 180 lbs) playing a big, carefree game of booming serves, heavy forehands, penetrating volleys and diving saves, he was an immediate crowd favorite. Despite his youth, he showed sensitivity rejecting an early, obvious nickname, "Boom Boom," considering it "too warlike."

For Germany, never better than a 1970 finalist in the quest for the Davis Cup, Becker was an instant hero. Almost alone, he carried his country to the 1985 final in Munich and beat both Stefan Edberg, 6-3, 3-6, 7-5, 8-6, and Mats Wilander, 6-3, 2-6, 6-3, 6-3, in the 3-2 loss to Sweden. Three years later, he lifted the Fatherland to the long longed for Cup in a 4-1 victory over the Swedes in Goteborg. Boris pummeled his final round conqueror at Wimbledon, Edberg, 6-3, 6-1, 6-4, then paired with Eric Jelen for the exciting clinching doubles win over Edberg and Anders Jarryd, 3-6, 2-6, 7-5, 6-3, 6-2.

In 1989, he won both his singles, flattening Swedes Edberg, 6-2, 6-2, 6-4, and Wilander, 6-2, 6-0, 6-2, and took the doubles again with Jelen over Jarryd and Jan Gunnarson, 7-6 (8-6), 6-4, 3-6, 6-7 (4-7), 6-4, at Stuttgart as Germany kept the Cup, 3-2.

By the close of the 1992 season, he had won 21 straight Cup singles, and had lost only two of 34 starts, both to Sergio Casal of Spain. He didn't play in 1993-94, but in 1995, he extended the streak to 22, second longest in Cup history (to Bjorn Borg's 33), before losing to the Netherlander Paul Haarhuis, 4-6, 6-2, 6-4, 7-6 (7-4).

Becker beat Ivan Lendl, 6-4, 6-3, 7-5, in 1986 for his second Wimbledon title, and Edberg just as swiftly in 1989 for a third, 6-0, 7-6 (7-1), 6-4, developing the feeling that Centre Court was his special haunt. He and Edberg also contested the 1988 and 1990 finals, Edberg winning both times, 4-6, 7-6 (7-2), 6-4, 6-2; and 6-2, 6-2, 3-6, 3-6, 6-4, respectively. They were the first men in almost a century, since Britain's Wilfred Baddeley and Ireland's Joshua Pim to split four finals, 1891—94, to monopolize the final for at least three successive years. In the only all-German male final on Centre Court, Michael Stich upset him in 1991, 6-4, 7-6 (7-4), 6-4. He and Stich collaborated the following year for Olympic gold, defeating South Africans Wayne Ferreira and Piet Norval, 7-6 (7-5) 4-6, 7-6 (7-5), 6-3, one of Boris's 15 doubles titles.

It took him four years to work his way back to a seventh Wimbledon final. To get there required one of his more brilliant Centre Court performances, beating top seed Andre Agassi from a set and 1-4 (two breaks) down, 2-6, 7-6 (7-1), 6-4, 7-6 (7-1). But he couldn't solve Pete Sampras' serve in the title match, losing 6-7 (5-7), 6-2, 6-4, 6-2. Becker's Wimbledon farewell, a fourth-round loss to Aussie Patrick Rafter in 1999, 6-3, 6-2, 6-3, completed his match record therein at 71-12.

By 1996, it seemed that his days of winning majors were past. He was 28, had a wife, Barbara, and a young son. But he arrived in Melbourne fit and eager, (inspired by Barbara's plea, "I never saw you win a big one") and captured his sixth, the Australian, with a blistering attack on Chang, 6-2, 6-4, 2-6, 6-2.

He started out as an unlikely pauper, an 18-to-1 shot on the path strewn with close calls to that first Wimbledon title. He might not have gotten past the fourth round if not for the good nature of Tim Mayotte, who waited patiently while Becker, trailing in the match, received treatment for a twisted ankle. Becker wanted to quit, but his manager, Ion Tiriac, talked him out of it, and Mayotte sportingly permitted Boris more than a usual break to recover. Becker won, 6-3, 4-6, 6-7 (7-9), 7-6 (7-5), 6-2. A round earlier Swede Joakim Nystrom had served for the match twice in the fifth, but fell, 3-6, 7-6 (7-5), 6-1, 4-6, 9-7. Henri Leconte almost had a two-set lead in the quarters, 7-6 (9-7), 3-6, 6-3, 6-4, and another Swede, Jarryd, won the first set and held a set point in the second of the semis, a 2-6, 7-6 (7-3), 6-3, 6-3 Becker win. It didn't matter. Rain interruptions were disregarded—Boris wore a halo.

Boris Franz Becker, a right-hander, was born Nov. 22, 1967, in the small town of Leiman, Germany, and grew up there, not far from Bruhl, where the other German wunderkind, Steffi Graf, was raised. The two sometimes practiced together. A promising junior, he dropped out of high school to become a pro. An atypical European, he prefered faster surfaces to his native clay. His best finishes at the French were semifinals in 1987, 89, 91, and the quarters in 1986. He also made the semis at Wimbledon in 1994; U.S., 1986, 95; quarters Australian 1984, 90; Wimbledon, 1993, 97. Of his 49 singles titles (in 77 finals), ranking ninth in the Open era, none was on dirt.

At the conclusion of 1988, he squashed Czech Ivan Lendl's bid for a sixth Masters title by the narrowest possible of final-round margins—two points—on a net-cord dribbler that won the fifth-set tie-breaker, 7-5. He also won in 1992 over Jim Courier 6-4, 6-3, 7-5 and in 1995 over Chang 7-6 (7-3), 6-0, 7-6 (7-5), but lost four finals, 1985-86, 89, 96.

His marvelous 1989 season, during which he won six of 13 tournaments on a 64-8 match record, included his fourth major, the U.S. Open in a 7-6 (7-2), 1-6, 6-3, 7-6 (7-4) victory over No. 1 ranked Lendl.

His fifth major (the third over Lendl) was the Australian at the outset of 1991, 1-6, 6-4, 6-4, 6-4, giving him the No. 1 ranking momentarily. During his 16 years as a pro he was in the Top 10 11 years, thrice No. 2, 1986, 89, 90, otherwise: No. 6 in 1985, 96; No. 3 in 1987, 91, 94; No. 4 in 1988, 95; No. 5 in 1992.

Career: won 49 singles (713-214 matches), 15 doubles pro titles (254-136), $25,080,956 prize money, third behind Sampras, Agassi. Selected for International Tennis Hall of Fame, 2003.

MAJOR TITLES (6)—Australian singles, 1991, 96; Wimbledon singles. 1985-86, 89; U.S, singles, 1989. **DAVIS CUP**—1985-86-87-88-89, 91-92, 95, 38-3 singles, 16-9 doubles, (winning Cups 1988-89). **SINGLES RECORD IN THE MAJORS**—Australian (29-9), French (26-9), Wimbledon (71-12). U.S. (37-10).

Karl Behr
United States (1885–1949)
Hall of Fame—1969

A Yale man, Karl Howell Behr won the U.S. Intercollegiate doubles in 1904, and played on the 1907 U.S. Davis Cup team. Behr, a 5-foot-9, 155 lbs survivor of the *Titanic* sinking in 1912, forever considered himself a lucky man. So he was, recruited to row an undermanned lifeboat. But he didn't have much good fortune in his lone Cup assignment, with Beals Wright, against Australasia, a 3-2 defeat at Wimbledon in 1907. He lost a toughie to Tony Wilding the first day, 1-6, 6-3, 3-6, 7-5, 6-3, dropping the last four games, and the clincher to Norman Brookes, 4-6, 6-4, 6-1, 6-2. But he and Wright did prolong it to the third day with a stirring doubles victory over Wimbledon champs Brookes-Wilding, 3-6, 12-10, 4-6, 6-2, 6-3. Brookes and Wilding proceeded to take the Cup from Britain, 3-2. Playing Wimbledon that year, Behr made one of the better American showings of that early time, reaching the fourth round where he gave the champ, Brookes, a stiff fight, 6-4, 6-2, 2-6, 3-6, 6-1.

He ranked in the U.S. Top 10 seven times between 1906 and 1915: No. 5 in 1906; No. 3 in 1907, and 1914 (when he beat future champ Lindley Murray, 3-6, 6-2, 7-5, 3-6, 8-6, to reach U.S. quarters). There, he lost to champion-to-be, Dick Williams, 6-2, 6-2, 7-5, a moving battle of *Titanic* alumni). Also, No. 8 in 1909; No. 9 in 1911; No. 7 in 1912; No. 4 in 1915. Coming into 1906, ranked No. 11, Behr jolted an all-time champ, No. 2 Bill Larned, in the second round, 6-4, 6-4, 7-5, and fought past No. 9 Raymond Little, 2-6, 6-2, 6-8, 11-9, 6-4, to the final of the all-comers, where Bill Clothier, en route to the championship, stopped him, 6-2, 6-4, 6-2. He was a semifinalist in 1912, losing to Wallace Johnson, 4-6, 6-0, 6-3, 6-2.

Behr, a right-hander, was born May 30, 1885, in Brooklyn, N.Y., and died Oct. 15, 1949, in New York. He entered the Hall of Fame in 1969.

U.S. TITLE—Intercollegiate doubles, 1904, with George Bodman. **DAVIS CUP**—1907, 0-2 singles, 1-0 doubles. **SINGLES RECORD IN THE MAJORS**—Wimbledon (3-1), U.S. (31-13).

Pauline Betz
United States (1919—)
Hall of Fame—1965

Pauline May Betz Addie may have been the finest of the immediate post-World War II women, even though her career was cut short in her prime by a controversial USTA ruling. She won her fourth U.S. title in 1946 over Doris Hart, 11-9, 6-3. However, in 1947 she was declared a professional for merely exploring the possibilities of making a pro tour. (Sounds absurd today.)

There was no pro tennis as such for women at the time, but she did make two tours of one-night stands against Sarah Palfrey Cooke in 1947, and Gussy Moran in 1951, dominating both opponents. Then she became a teaching professional and married sportswriter Bob Addie.

Born Aug. 6, 1919, in Dayton, Ohio, Pauline grew up a lean blonde in Los Angeles, and became noted for her extreme speed and mobility. Although she could get to the net quickly and volley with sureness, she preferred to run down balls and pass the net-rushers, particularly with a penetrating backhand.

World War II deprived her of the chance for much international play, but she won Wimbledon the only time she entered, in 1946, without losing a set. Her closest match, not close at all, was the 6-2, 6-4 final over Louise Brough. In 1946, in Betz's only Wightman Cup series against Britain, she helped the U.S. win by taking both her singles matches, over Jean Bostock, 6-2, 6-4, and Kay Stammers Menzies, 6-4, 6-4, and her doubles. In her lone shot at the French, she lost the 1946 final to Osborne, despite holding two match points, 1-6, 8-6, 7-5.

Betz, world's No. 1 in 1946, first entered the U.S. Top 10, at No. 8 in 1939, and stayed in that select group for seven more years, standing at No. 1 in 1942-43-44, 46, the years she won the U.S. Championship in singles at Forest Hills. Also ranked No. 2 in 1941, 45; and No. 3 in 1940.

She closed out her amateur career in 1946 by winning eight of 12 tournaments, and her last 27 matches. That was the fourth of her most productive campaigns that netted seven titles in 1943, eight in 1944, six in 1945. In 1943, she emphasized her superbly rounded game by making a U.S. triple, with Indoor and Clay Court singles preceding Forest Hills success. Beating Catherine Wolf, 6-0, 6-2, to win the Tri-State in 1943, Pauline reaped an almost unheard of "golden set" relinquishing no points in the first set.

Top-seeded Louise Brough was the 4-6, 6-1, 6-4 victim in her first triumph at Forest Hills, but the semi was tougher, 6-4, 4-6, 7-5, over Margaret Osborne (duPont), from match point down at 3-5. She beat Brough again in 1943, 6-3, 5-7, 6-3, and Osborne in 1944, 6-3, 8-6. Two other years, 1941 and 1945, she was runner-up to Sarah Palfrey Cooke, 7-5, 6-2, and 3-6, 8-6, 6-4. She set a U.S. record of six straight finals, tied by Chris Evert, 1975—80. Pauline was 33-4, playing Forest Hills eight times. Betz captured 19 U.S. titles on various surfaces: Clay Court singles, 1941, over Mary Arnold, 6-3, 6-1; 1943, over Nancy Corbett, 6-0, 6-1; Indoor singles, 1939, over Helen Bernhard, 7-5, 4-6, 6-1; 1941, over Dorothy Bundy, 6-1, 10-12, 6-2; 1943, over Kay Winthrop, 6-4, 6-1; 1947, over Doris Hart. Twice she scored triples at the Indoors, winning singles, doubles and mixed in 1941 and 1943, a feat equaled only by Billie Jean King in 1966 and 1968. In 1943, her partner was 66-year-old Hazel Wightman, an historic coupling of Hall of Famers.

Tennis historian Jerome Scheuer called her "the fastest woman on foot ever to play the game." She was selected for the International Tennis Hall of Fame in 1965.

MAJOR TITLES (6)—Wimbledon singles, 1946, U.S. singles, 1942-43-44, 46; French mixed, 1946. **OTHER U.S. TITLES** (15)—Indoor singles, 1939, 41, 43, 47; Indoor doubles, 1941, with Dorothy Bundy; 1943, with Hazel Hotchkiss Wightman; Indoor mixed, 1939, with Wayne Sabin; 1940 with Bobby Riggs; 1941, 43, with Al Stitt; Clay Court singles, 1941, 43; Clay Court doubles, 1943, with Nancy Corbett; 1944-45, with

Doris Hart. **WIGHTMAN CUP**—1946, 2-0 singles, 1-0 doubles. **SINGLES RECORD IN THE MAJORS**—French (4-1), Wimbledon (6-0), US (33-4).

Bjorn Borg
Sweden (1956—)
Hall of Fame—1987

Before he was 21, Bjorn Rune Borg had registered feats that would set him apart as one of the games greats—and before he was 26, the headbanded, golden-locked Swede was through. No male career of the modern era has been so brief and bright.

Tennis is filled with instances of precocious achievements and championships, but none is quite as impressive as those of the seemingly emotionless Borg. Just before his 18th birthday, he was the youngest winner of the Italian Championship, over Ilie Nastase, 6-3, 6-4, 6-2. Two weeks later, breaking down Manolo Orantes 2-6, 6-7 (1-7), 6-0, 6-1, 6-1, he was the youngest winner of the French Championship (a record lowered by Swede Mats Wilander, 17, in 1982, and subsequently by American Michael Chang, a younger 17 in 1989). Eighteen months later, at 19, he climaxed a Davis Cup record winning streak of 19 singles by lifting Sweden to the 1975 Cup for the first time in a 3-2 final-round victory over Czechoslovakia. His Cup singles streak of 33 was intact at his retirement, still a record.

Although Lew Hoad and Ken Rosewall were a few months younger in 1953 when they won the Davis Cup for Australia, both were beaten during the final round. But Borg won both his singles in straight sets, over Jiri Hrebec. 6-1, 6-3, 6-0, and the clincher over Jan Kodes, 6-4, 6-2, 6-2, after teaming with Ove Bengtson for the doubles win. Borg's Davis Cup debut at 16 in 1972, as one of the youngest ever in that competition, was phenomenal: A five-set win over seasoned pro Onny Parun of New Zealand. Borg was also the youngest winner of the oldest professional championship, the U.S. Pro, whose singles he took in 1974 at 18 over Tom Okker, 7-6 (7-3), 6-1, 6-1 (and, subsequently, 1975 and 1976). Aaron Krickstein, 16, lowered that record in 1984.

A player of great strength and endurance, 5'11, 160lbs., he had a distinctive and unorthodox style and appearance, bowlegged, yet very fast. His muscular shoulders and well-developed torso gave him the strength to lash at the ball with heavy topspin on both forehand and backhand. A right-hander, he used a two-handed backhand, adapted from the slap shot in hockey, a game he favored as a child. By the time he was 13, he was beating the best of Sweden's under-18 players and Davis Cup captain Lennart Bergelin cautioned against anyone trying to change Borg's rough-looking, jerky strokes. They were effective. Through 1977, he had never lost to a player younger than himself.

Born June 6, 1956, in Sodertalje, Sweden, where he grew up, Bjorn was fascinated by a tennis racket his father had won as a prize in a ping-pong tournament. His father gave him the racket and that was the start.

Borg preferred to battle from the baseline, trading groundstrokes tirelessly in long rallies, retrieving and waiting patiently to outlast his opponent. Volleying, with his western grip forehand and two-fisted backhand, was troublesome, and his serve was not impressive at first. He didn't do much on grass until 1976,

when he was determined to win Wimbledon, and did so after devoting himself to two weeks of solid practice on serve-and-volley tactics. He won the most important tournament without loss of a set, beating favored Ilie Nastase in the final, 6-4, 6-2, 9-7. Borg was the youngest champion of the modern era at 20 years, one month, (until Boris Becker, 17, won in 1985). Borg repeated in 1977, although the tournament was more demanding. His thrilling five-set victories over Americans Vitas Gerulaitis in the semifinals, 6-4, 3-6, 6-3, 3-6, 8-6, and Jimmy Connors, 2-6, 6-2, 6-1, 5-7, 6-4 in the final were considered two of the best ever played at Wimbledon. By that time, Borg had more confidence and proficiency in his volleying. He repeated over Connors in 1978, overpoweringly, 6-2, 6-2, 6-3, becoming the first to win three successive years since Fred Perry (1934-36). He made it four in a row, escaping bullet-serving American Roscoe Tanner, 6-7 (4-7) 6-1, 3-6, 6-3, 6-4 in the 1979 final, becoming the first since Tony Wilding (1910-13) to win four straight years.

Bjorn's fifth straight in 1980 climaxed with an all-time great final, a 1-6, 7-5, 6-3, 6-7 (16-18), 8-6 triumph over John McEnroe. During one of the most electrifying passages in tennis history, the 34-point tie-breaker, Borg was stymied on five match points and saved six set points before giving way. But his famous resolve brought him through in the brilliantly fought fifth.

Borg was now flirting with the ancient Wimbledon record of six straight titles. That was the much less demanding feat of Willie Renshaw (1881-86), who, in the era of the challenge round format, needed to play only one match to win each of his last five titles. Thus his match winning streak was 13.

While winning 1980, Borg also surpassed Aussie Rod Laver's Wimbledon male match winning-streak record of 31. By reaching the 1981 final, Bjorn built that to his own record 41 (Helen Wills Moody won 50 straight between 1927 and 1938). There, he was finally dethroned by McEnroe, 4-6, 7-6 (7-1), 7-6 (7-4), 6-4.

When he won his male record sixth French title in 1981, with another record, a 28th straight match win, beating Ivan Lendl 6-1, 4-6, 6-2, 3-6, 6-1, it seemed that Borg, then 25, would surely eclipse Aussie Roy Emerson's male record of 12 major singles titles (subsequently passed by Pete Sampras' 14). Borg had 11. But he would not win another, remaining tied with Laver.

His left-handed nemesis, McEnroe, followed up on that Wimbledon drama by beating Borg in another tense five sets for the 1980 U.S. Open title, 7-6 (7-4), 6-1, 6-7 (5-7), 5-7, 6-4. A year later, Mac repeated, 4-6, 6-2, 6-4, 6-3, to take over the No. 1 ranking that the Swede had held in 1979 and 1980. That defeat, effectively ended Borg's career. He played only one event in both 1982 and 1983—the Monte Carlo Open—and retired, having won 62 singles (of 88 finals) titles, including the Masters of 1979, over Gerulaitis, 6-2, 6-2, and 1980, over Lendl, 6-4, 6-2, 6-2. He was inducted into the Hall of Fame in 1987.

Nevertheless, he did try comebacks in 1991, 1992 and 1993, all unsuccessful. The balletic footwork and marvelous anticipation couldn't be coaxed to return with him, even though others had stayed afloat and earning at 35. He lost eight first-rounders in 1992, three in 1993. Bjorn's parting shot, in Moscow's Kremlin Cup, was as close as he got, holding a match point in a farewell tie-breaker while losing to Russia's Aleksandr Volkov 4-6, 6-3, 7-6

(9-7). Thereafter, he confined himself to senior events, renewing his rivalry with Connors, against whom he had been 10-7. He was 7-7 lifetime against McEnroe.

The U.S. Open was his particular jinx, zero for 10 tries, losing four finals: 1976 and 1978 to Connors—on clay in 1976, 6-4, 3-6, 7-6 (11-9), 6-4, then the Flushing debut on hard court in 1978, 6-4, 6-2, 6-2. Thrice (1978-79-80) he was halfway to a Grand Slam after victories at the French and Wimbledon only to falter at the three-quarter pole, Flushing Meadows. His career singles win-loss record was 606-123 (.831).

During his career, he won 62 singles (587-124 matches), four doubles (87-82), pro titles, $ 3,655,751 in prize money.

MAJOR TITLES (11)—French singles 1974-75, 1978-79-80-81; Wimbledon singles 1976-77-78-79-80. **DAVIS CUP**—1972-73-74-75, 1978-79-80; 37-3 Singles, 8-8 doubles. **SINGLES RECORD IN THE MAJORS**—Australian (1-1), French (49-2), Wimbledon (51-4), U.S. (40-10).

Nancye Wynne Bolton
Australia (1916–2001)
Hall of Fame—2006

High-spirited, tall-and-sturdy, a big hitter, Nancye Hazel Meredith Wynne Bolton was the queen of Australian tennis until the all-time winner of championships, Margaret Smith Court, came along a decade later.

Nevertheless, a Hall of Famer, fellow Aussie John Bromwich, said, "I've seen them all, and I believe Nancye was our best, even though the war cut into prime years. And she didn't have many opportunities to travel." World War II cut deeper than a tennis hiatus. Her husband, Sgt George Bolton, Royal Australian Air Force, was killed in action in 1942, never seeing their daughter, Pam.

Her long amateur career was sandwiched around the war as she piled up 20 major titles (all Australian) over a span of 16 years, eight before the tourney was shut down for the duration, 12 after peace was restored. Margaret Court eclipsed her title total by one, 21.

Born June 10, 1916 in Melbourne, she attained the first of her 25 Aussie finals in 1936. She was 19, losing to countrywoman Joan Hartigan, 6-4, 6-4. But she bounced back a year later to win the first of six singles titles, 6-3, 5-7, 6-4, over another Aussie Emily Hood Westacott. Defeating her comrade in doubles dominance, Thelma Coyne Long for the 1940 singles title, 5-7, 6-4, 6-0, Nancye had to wait to feed a streak that lay dormant for six years. Eventually it would extend through four championships, and 21 matches, 1946-47-48 until the 1949 final where she fell to another Hall of Famer, Doris Hart, 6-3, 6-4.

Nancye, in the left court, and Thelma won the doubles 10 times between 1936 and 1952, second in the majors to the 12 U.S. titles of Americans Louise Brough and Margaret Osborne duPont. They ran five straight from 1936 to a final round loss in 1946 to Australians Joyce Fitch and Mary Bevis.

Historian Max Robertson wrote of her, "A player of exceptional grace fluency and power, though with a small margin of error. Her example raised both the standards and status of the women's game in Australia."

As the only Aussie woman in the world Top 10 on either side of the war (No. 10 in 1938; No. 4 in 1947-48-49), she was the first to ascend to a major final outside of the homeland, losing the U.S. in 1938 to Alice Marble, 6-0, 6-3, in 22 minutes. She did better reappearing in 1947, holding three match points in semifinal against champ Brough (on serve, 5-2, 40-0, third set), but was beaten, 4-6, 6-4, 7-5, finished the following day from 3-5.

She also made Australian semifinals in 1938, 50, 52 and the quarterfinals in 1939 and the Wimbledon quarterfinals in 1947. She died Nov. 9, 2001 in Melbourne, and was taken into the Hall, 2007.

MAJOR TITLES (20)—Australian singles, 1937, 40, 46-47-48, 51; Australian doubles—1936-37-38-39-40, 47-48-49, 51-52; Australian mixed doubles—1940, 46-47-48. **SINGLES RECORD IN THE MAJORS**—Australian (41-5), Wimbledon (3-1), U.S. (7-2).

Jean Borotra
France (1898–1994)
Hall of Fame—1976

In many ways, Jean Robert Borotra fit the image of the cosmopolitan Frenchman: A spectacular, debonair personality, a gallant kissing ladies' fingertips, a host of elegant parties aboard the *Ile de France* or at his fashionable residence in Paris.

Borotra, a right-hander, 6-foot-1, 160 lbs, was spectacular, too, on the tennis court in the 1920s and early '30s. He won Wimbledon in 1924 over Rene Lacoste, 6-1, 3-6, 6-1, 3-6, 6-4, and 1926 over American Howard Kinsey, 8-6, 6-1, 6-3, and was runner-up in 1925 and 1927. He won the championship of France in 1931 over compatriot Christian Boussus, 2-6, 6-4, 7-5, 6-4, having lost the 1925 and 1929 finals to Lacoste, who also beat him in the 1926 U.S. final.

In 1928, he was a Gallic sweeper Down Under, the first alien to register a triple at the Australian, singles over Australia's Jack Cummings, 6-4, 6-1, 4-6, 5-7, 6-3, the doubles with teammate Jacques Brugnon, and the mixed with Aussie Daphne Akhurst. He was a demon in international play, one of the Four Musketeers who in 1927 broke the U.S. grip on the Davis Cup and brought it to France for the first time.

Born on Aug. 13, 1898, at Arbonne, Basque Pyrenees country near Biarritz, France, he first attracted wide attention when he played in the 1921 Paris indoor championship. Standing out with a dramatic, aggressive style—and with the blue beret he always wore—Borotra became known as the "Bounding Basque." His energy on the court was limitless, marked by headlong assaults and dashes for the net, both on his serve and return, then racing back to retrieve lobs. No player could start faster or dash so madly. His serve was not a cannonball, but it was not to be trifled with. His backhand return of serve and backhand volley were vividly individual, thrusts for the kill. He was something of a con man, softening foes with praise while demeaning himself.

Borotra was named to France's Davis Cup team in 1922, and in 1923 he assembled with Lacoste, Henri Cochet, and Brugnon, a great doubles player, to form the Four Musketeers. Not only did the French win their first Cup in 1927, but they also held it for five years thereafter. Over that six year period of finals, Borotra was 4-4 singles, 1-2 doubles.

In the 1932 challenge round at the four-year-old Stade Roland Garros, Borotra reached heights of inspiration against the U.S. He startled No. 1 Ellsworth Vines, winner of Wimbledon and the U.S. that year, 6-4, 6-2, 3-6, 6-4. On the final day, Borotra lost the first two sets to Wilmer Allison, and with the Texan holding a fourth match point in the fifth set, Borotra's second serve appeared to be out. Allison ran forward for the handshake, thinking he had won, but the line judge insisted the serve was good and play resumed. Borotra pulled out the emotional victory, with 10,000 countrymen backing him, 1-6, 3-6, 6-4, 6-2, 7-5, and France retained the Cup, 3-2.

With his dazzling performances, Borotra was popular everywhere. This included the Seventh Regiment Armory in New York, where he was in his element on the fast board courts and four times won the U.S. Indoor Championship, 1925, 27, 29, 31, and doubles in 1925, 27, 31. He was not rated quite the player that Cochet and Lacoste were, but Borotra's celebrity endured and the legs that ran like fury kept him active in tennis into his 70s as a competitor in the senior division at Wimbledon, having played his last Davis Cup match at 48 in 1947. Before progressing into the seniors, Borotra set the Wimbledon record for most matches played, 223—50-10 singles, 50-39 doubles, 40-28 mixed. He was among the champions honored at the 1977 Wimbledon Centenary, a year after he was enshrined with the three other Musketeers in the Hall of Fame.

He was ranked in the world's Top 10 nine straight years from 1924: No. 2 in 1926; also No. 6 in 1924-25; No. 4 in 1927; No. 5 in 1928; No. 3 in 1929-30, 32; No. 7 in 1931. He made French semis in 1926, 30 and Wimbledon in 1930-31. Jean died July 17, 1994, at Arbonne, age 95, delighted that he'd seen his Cup descendants regain the prize at U.S. expense in 1991.

MAJOR TITLES (18)—Australian singles, 1928; French singles, 1931; Wimbledon singles, 1924, 26; Australian doubles, 1928; French doubles 1925, 28-29, 34, 36; Wimbledon doubles 1925, 1932-33; Australian mixed 1928; French mixed 1927, 34: Wimbledon mixed, 1925; US. mixed, 1926. **DAVIS CUP**—1922-23-24-25-26-27-28-29-30-31-32-33-34-35-36-37, 47; 19-12 singles, 17-6 doubles. **SINGLES RECORD IN THE MAJOR**S—Australian (5-0), French (30-6), Wimbledon (55-10), U.S. (13-6).

John Bromwich
Australia (1918–1999)
Hall of Fame—1984

Elected to the Hall of Fame in 1984 as one-half of the great Australian doubles team of Bromwich and Quist, John Edward Bromwich missed winning Wimbledon by the narrowest of margins. In the 1948 final, Bob Falkenburg escaped him at three match-point junctures, from 3-5, 15-40, then advantage out, in the fifth set. Bob escaped to win the match 7-5, 0-6, 6-2, 3-6, 7-5.

But Bromwich did win two major singles—the Australian in 1939, over Adrian Quist, 6-4, 6-1, 6-3, and 1946, over another fellow Aussie Dinny Pails, 5-7, 6-3, 7-5, 3-6, 6-2. He was also a three-time U.S. semifinalist, 1938-39, 47. He lost the last one to the only other U.S. semifinalist playing before and after World War II, Frank Parker, 6-3, 4-6, 6-3, 6-8, 8-6. He lost five Aussie finals: 1937 to Viv McGrath; 1938 to Don Budge, the first stop on the

Yank's Grand Slam (6-4, 6-2, 6-1); 1940 and 48 to Quist; 1947 to Pails; and 1949 to Frank Sedgman. He also made the semis of the Australian in 1940 and 54; the French in 1950 and Wimbledon in 1949.

A loping, big-jawed man, 5-foot-10, 152 lbs, with an unruly shock of blond hair, Bromwich was one of the most curious stylists in the game's history. A natural left-hander, he nevertheless served right-handed, stroked with two hands on his right side and one, the left, on his left side. Using an extremely loosely-strung racket, he had superb touch and chipped his returns maddeningly on his foes' shoetops. "People called my racket an onion bag," he laughed, "and complained they couldn't hear me hit the ball. But at least they didn't see me serve with both hands, which I did as a young player, sort of like chopping wood."

He was an attacker, his volleys well placed, and his competitive fire ever burning high.

World War II interrupted the strong partnership of himself—the right court player—and Quist, but they won their native Australian title eight straight times, 1938-1950 a team record for majors, and a 35-match streak. They gave up the title only after a tremendous struggle, 11-9, 2-6, 6-3, 4-6, 6-3, in the 1951 final against youngsters Frank Sedgman, 23, and Ken McGregor, 22. Bromwich was 33, Quist 38. The two of them scored a singular triumph as the Australian Davis Cup team in 1939, rebounding from 0-2 down to 3-2 possession over Cup-holding U.S. in Philadelphia. They began turning it around with a 5-7, 6-2, 7-5, 6-2 doubles victory over Joe Hunt and Jack Kramer, and Bromwich clinched in the decisive fifth match, 6-0, 6-3, 6-1, over Parker after Quist beat Bobby Riggs, 6-1, 6-4, 3-6, 3-6, 6-4.

Ted Schroeder recalled, "Jack and Joe were up a set and a break, but after that Brom played the most phenomenal two-and-a-half sets of doubles I've ever seen." Bromwich was described by journalist friend Jim Russell as "so tight-fisted with a point he made Scrooge seem a philanthropist," and Schroeder seconds it: "You had to win the point from Brom; he never gave one away."

Bromwich smiled at that cordially, and remembered, "in '39 our tennis association was too poor to send us to the French and Wimbledon. But there was no doubt we'd get to the U.S. to challenge for the Cup. We were sure we'd win because we'd only lost 3-2 the year before, and their great Don Budge had turned pro. Three weeks by boat to California, then train to Philadelphia. War had been declared just before the matches began so everything was up in the air. We were surprised to be down 0-2, and didn't have much confidence, even after the doubles. But Quisty was back again at his best to beat [Wimbedon champ] Riggs, and it was up to me. Our coach, Fred Perry, told me if I hit one ball to Frankie's forehand to hit 5,000. That's all I did. They tell me the first point lasted two minutes, the first game 13, and his forehand came apart. Very satisfying because we wanted to be the first to win the Cup as Australia after the Australasia years.

"But more thrilling to me was to come back 11 years later, to Forest Hills, and be part of our next winner, at 31. The Yanks had been thrashing us after the war [1946—49], and I wasn't surprised when Hop [captain Harry Hopman] went with the youngsters, Sedgman and McGregor, in the singles. I thought he'd play

them all the way, but he said he wanted my experience with Sedg in the doubles, and we took the Cup by beating Schroeder and Gar Mulloy [4-6, 6-4, 6-2, 4-6, 6-4]. A nice way for me to go out"— winning his 20th of 21 Cup doubles. Ranked in the world's Top 10 on both sides of the war, he, Quist and Parker were the only ones of such longevity. Brom made the list: No. 3 in 1938; No. 2 in 1939; No. 6 in 1946; No. 4 in 1947-48, coming back splendidly after army service in which he was wounded and contracted malaria in the New Guinea campaign.

Born Nov. 14, 1918, in Kogarah, New South Wales, he lived at Point Lonsdale, outside of Melbourne, with his wife Zenda until his death in Geelong, Oct. 21, 1999.

MAJOR TITLES (19)—Australian singles, 1939, 1946; Australian doubles, 1938-39-40-46-47-48-49-50; Wimbledon doubles, 1948, 50; U.S. doubles, 1939, 49-50; Australian mixed, 1938; Wimbledon mixed, 1947-48; U.S. mixed, 1947. **DAVIS CUP**—1937-38-39, 46-47, 49-50, 19-11 singles, 20-1 doubles. **SINGLES RECORD IN THE MAJORS**-Australian (39-9), French (4-1), Wimbledon (19-3). U.S. (16-5). **MAJOR TITLES WITH QUIST** (10)-Australian doubles, 1938-39-40, 46-47-48-49-50; Wimbledon doubles, 1950; U.S. doubles, 1939. DAVIS CUP –1938-39, 1946, 9-1 doubles.

Norman Brookes
Australia (1877–1968)
Hall of Fame—1977

They called him the Wizard. A figure of heroic stature, Sir Norman Everard Brookes was renowned both as a player—for many years Australia's best—and as an administrator. He was 5-foot-11, 150 pounds, had a sallow complexion and pale blue eyes, austere in bearing, rather taciturn, a man of strength and character to command respect and win honors.

And win honors he did. Born Nov. 14, 1877, in Melbourne, Australia, he became the first male from overseas to win the championship at Wimbledon, rousting the defender, Arthur Gore of Britain, 6-4, 6-2, 6-2 in the 1907 final having lost the 1905 final to Laurie Doherty. He won Wimbledon again in 1914, ending team-mate Tony Wilding's four year run, 6-4, 6-4, 7-5, and was runner-up in 1919 after returning from World War I. Long ranked as the best of left-handed players, the first to win Wimbledon, he was a member of nine Australasian Davis Cup teams between 1905 and 1920 and played in eight challenge rounds.

World rankings were instituted after his best days, but he was in the Top 10 four times, No. 2 in 1913-14; No. 5 in 1919; and No. 6 in 1920, the last at 43.

He was an exponent of the serve-and-volley game, the "big game" that was supposed to have originated after World War II. Brookes played that type of role in 1914, but he had more than a serve and volley. He had ground strokes adequate to hold his own from the back of the court. Because his serve was so big an asset—flat, slice, twist, even reverse twist—and he volleyed so much, his methods were characterized as unorthodox when he was in his prime. He often used the same side of the racket for forehand and backhand.

In 1907, Brookes' decisive 6-2, 6-0, 6-3 win over Herbert Roper Barrett settled Australasia's 3-2 victory at Wimbledon to break Britain's four-year hold on the Davis Cup and take the prize Down Under for the first time. It stayed there until a British reprisal in 1912, Brookes going 5-1 in singles and 3-0 in doubles as his side beat the U.S. three times. Even though he, at age 36, lost the memorable first-day match to 24-year-old Maurice McLoughlin, 17-15, 6-3, 6-3, in 1914, the Aussies spirited the Cup away, 3-2, as he clinched, 6-1, 6-2, 8-10, 6-3, over Dick Williams. Five years later, at age 41, he won the doubles with Gerald Patterson as the Aussies beat Britain, 4-1, the oldest to play with a Cup winner. A year after that, his Cup swan song, he gave Big Bill Tilden a furious battle, 10-8, 6-4, 1-6, 6-4, as the Americans retrieved the sterling bowl at Auckland

Returning to Wimbledon in 1914, his first appearance since winning seven years before, Brookes again demonstrated his all-around strength in a severe all-comers final test (6-2, 6-1, 5-7, 4-6, 8-6, over German Otto Froitzheim) preparatory to wresting the title from his close friend Wilding with a display of faultless ground strokes. (Brookes' durability was demonstrated again in 1924 at Wimbledon when, at 46, he ousted No. 5 Frank Hunter, finalist in 1923 and 17 years his junior, 3-6, 6-3, 6-4, 5-7, 6-3, in the third round.)

But five war years passed, and in his next go at Wimbledon, as the defending champ, he couldn't hold off compatriot Gerald Patterson in the challenge round, 6-3, 7-5, 6-2. However, that summer the two of them went to America to win the U.S. doubles title over Tilden and Vinnie Richards—the first of many Aussies to cart off American titles. He gave incoming champ Tilden—who called him "the greatest tennis brain"—a fright in the singles quarters, 1-6, 6-4, 7-5, 6-3. Brookes, who had won his first major, in 1907 at Wimbledon, took his last in 1924, the Aussie doubles with James Anderson. He was in his 47th year, almost the elder of all major champions, just behind 52-year-old Horrie Rice, a winner of the Australian mixed the year before.

The honors didn't stop for the man who seemed to command them. In 1926, he was named president of the Lawn Tennis Association of Australia, a post he held until 1955. He was decorated with the French Legion of Honor for his services in World War I as a captain in the British Army and, in 1939, he was knighted.

He died Sept. 28, 1968, in Melbourne and entered the Hall of Fame in 1977, becoming Sir Norman.

MAJOR TITLES (7)—Australian singles, 1911; Wimbledon singles, 1907, 1914; Australian doubles, 1924; Wimbledon doubles, 1907, 1914: U.S doubles, 1919. **DAVIS CUP**—1905, 1907-08-09, 11-12, 14, 19-20, 18-7 singles, 10-4 doubles. **SINGLES RECORD IN THE MAJORS**—Australian (5-1), Wimbledon (25-2), U.S. (4-2).

Louise Brough
United States (1923—)
Hall of Fame—1967

One of the great volleyers in history was Althea Louise Brough, whose handywork at the net earned her 13 titles at Wimbledon alone, in singles, doubles and mixed, including a rare triple—championships in singles, doubles and mixed in 1950. Of the foremost U.S. females only Chris Evert (19 times) and Billie Jean King (18) lasted longer in the U.S. Top 10. Brough was there 16 times between 1941 and 1957, No. 1 In 1947. She made the

world's Top 10 12 times between 1946 and 1957, including No. 1 in 1955, five times No. 2 and four times No. 3.

Brough was born March 11, 1923, in Oklahoma City, Okla., but grew up in Southern California, where she came to prominence as a junior, winning the U.S. 18-and-under title in 1940-41. "I had to attack; I didn't feel very comfortable on defense," she said.

Wimbledon was not held during World War II, but when the tournament reopened in 1946 Brough was ready to play a dominant role for a decade and is recalled as one of the most overwhelming players to compete there. In the first postwar visit, she appeared in every final and just missed out on a triple, losing the singles to Pauline Betz, 6-2, 6-4. But the right-handed Brough won the doubles with Margaret Osborne duPont and the mixed with Tom Brown. During the Brough decade, a Wimbledon final without her was unusual. Between 1946 and 1955, she won her way into 21 of the 30 finals, taking the singles in 1948 over Doris Hart, 6-3, 8-6; 1949 over doubles partner duPont, in a wowser, 10-8, 1-6, 10-8; 1950 over duPont, 6-1, 3-6, 6-1; and 1955 over Beverly Baker Fleitz, 7-5, 8-6. She also won the doubles five times between 1946 and 1954 with duPont, and the mixed four times, in 1946 with Tom Brown, in 1947 and 1948 with John Bromwich and in 1950 with Eric Sturgess. A bright ornament of 11 winning Wightman Cup teams, she was unbeaten: 12-0 in singles, 10-0 in doubles.

Although she won the singles title at the U.S. Championships at Forest Hills only in 1947, over duPont, 8-6, 4-6, 6-1, she was a finalist on five other occasions. Doubles was the stage for her utmost success in the U.S., allied with duPont in possibly the finest female team ever, certainly the most victorious in major events. They won 20 Big Four titles together (12 U.S., five Wimbledon, three French), a record total equaled by Martina Navratilova and Pam Shriver in 1989. Included in their record dozen U.S. titles was the longest championship run in any of the major events—nine straight doubles between 1942 and 1950. Brough and duPont did not enter the U.S. doubles in 1951 and 1952, but they returned to increase their record match winning streak to 41 before narrowly losing the 1953 final to Doris Hart and Shirley Fry, 6-2, 7-9, 9-7. As a team in the U.S. doubles, they won 12 of 14 times entered and 58 of 60 matches, losing but five sets.

Altogether, Brough won 35 of the major titles in singles, doubles and mixed doubles to rank fifth on the all-time list behind Margaret Court (62), Martina Navratilova (59), Billie Jean King (39) and Margaret duPont (37). Brough won the Australian singles in 1950 over Doris Hart, 6-4, 3-6, 6-4. Her various U.S. titles amounted to 18, and she was inducted into the Hall of Fame in 1967.

A willowy blonde, 5-foot-71/2, she was quiet but the killer in the left court when at play alongside duPont. Despite their close friendship and partnership, they were keen rivals in singles and Brough's most difficult Wimbledon triumphs were the three-set wins over duPont in 1949 and 1950. After retiring from the amateur circuit, she married Dr. A. T. Clapp, and later occasionally played in senior (over 40) tournaments, winning the U.S. Hard Court Doubles in that category in 1971 and 1975 with Barbara Green Weigandt.

MAJOR TITLES (35)—Australian singles, 1950; Wimbledon singles, 1948, 1949, 1950, 1955; U.S. singles, 1947; Australian doubles, 1950; French doubles, 1946, 1947, 1949: Wimbledon doubles, 1946 1948, 1949, 1950, 1954; U.S. doubles, 1942, 1943, 1944,
1945, 1946, 1947, 1948, 1949, 1950, 1955, 1956, 1957; Wimbledon mixed, 1946, 1947, 1948, 1950; U.S. mixed, 1942, 1947, 1948, 1949. **OTHER U.S. TITLES**—Hard Court doubles, 1948, with duPont. **WIGHTMAN CUP**—1946 1947, 1948, 1949, 1950, 1952, 1953, 1954, 1955, 1956, 1957, 12-0 singles, 10-0 doubles. **SINGLES RECORD IN THE MAJORS**—Australian (5-0), French (10-4), Wimbledon (56-7), U.S. (57-17).

Mary K. Browne
United States (1891–1971)
Hall of Fame—1957

As the first American female professional, Mary Kendall Browne left a splendid amateur record behind in 1926 to join promoter C. C. Pyle's original troupe of touring pros. (France's great Suzanne Lenglen was the centerpiece. Others: Vinnie Richards, Howard Kinsey, Harvey Snodgrass and Paul Feret.) During the winter of 1926-27, well past her prime at age 35, she played one-night stands across North America as "the opponent" against the invincible Lenglen, losing all 38 matches.

A 5-foot-2 right-hander and staunch volleyer, Browne was born June 3, 1891, in Ventura County, Calif., and came East to dominate the U.S. Championships at Philadelphia, scoring triple triples—singles, doubles, mixed titles—in 1912, 1913 and 1914. Only Hazel Hotchkiss Wightman, the previous three years, and Alice Marble (1938, 1939 and 1940) swept the field so thoroughly.

She was unique for an American woman in transferring her talent to golf, spectacularly in 1924. Shortly after making the U.S. semis at Forest Hills, losing to Helen Wills in three sets, she entered the U.S. Women's Golf Championships and beat the legendary Glenna Collett Vare to reach the final. There, she lost the title to Dorothy Campbell Hurd.

In one of the most demanding days in tennis annals, Mary played 82 games while winning the 1912 singles, doubles and mixed finals all in the same afternoon, much of it in a downpour. "The rain was coming down in torrents, and still we went on," she later recalled, "Our rackets mushy and our clothes soaked." She beat Eleo Sears, 6-4, 6-2, in the all-corners singles final to become champion since Wightman didn't defend the title. With Dorothy Green, she won the doubles, 6-2, 5-7, 6-0, over Maud Barger Wallach and Mrs. Frederick Schmitz. With Dick Williams, she won the soggy mixed, 6-4, 2-6, 11-9, over Evelyn Sears and Bill Clothier. She retained the singles over Dorothy Green in 1913, 6-2, 7-5, and Marie Wagner in 1914, 6-2, 1-6, 6-1.

Mary ranked No. 1 in the U.S. in 1913 and 1914, the first two years of the Top 10, returning to the select group at No. 2 in 1921 and 1924, and No. 6 in 1925. In 1926, she had a world ranking of No. 6, the USTA declining to give her a high ranking that she'd earned because she turned pro. She was later married to Kenneth Smith. Browne, who remained a fine golfer in her 70s, capable of shooting close to her age, died Aug. 19, 1971, in Laguna Hills, Calif.

MAJOR TITLES (13)—U.S. singles, 1912, 1913. 1914; Wimbledon doubles, 1926; U.S. doubles, 1912, 1913, 1914, 1921, 1925: U.S. mixed, 1912, 1913, 1914, 1921. **OTHER U.S. TITLES** (3)—Indoor doubles, 1926 with Elizabeth Ryan; Clay Court singles. 1914; Clay Court doubles, 1914 with Louise Riddell Williams. **WIGHTMAN CUP**—1925, 1926, 0-2 singles, 1-1 doubles. **SINGLES RECORD IN THE MAJORS**—French (4-1), Wimbledon (0-.1), U.S. (22-4).

Jacques Brugnon

France (1895–1978)
Hall of Fame—1976

Jacques "Toto" Brugnon was the elder of France's celebrated Four Musketeers who won the Davis Cup in 1927 from the U.S., and kept it six years. He preceded the other three—Jean Borotra, Henri Cochet, René Lacoste—as an internationalist, playing first on the Cup team in 1921. A master at doubles, he won Wimbledon four times, 1926 and 1928 with Cochet and 1932 and 1933 with Borotra, and appeared in three other finals. He won the French five times, three with Cochet, two with Borotra, and the Australian with Borotra, plus two French mixed for a dozen major titles.

Although doubles expertise overshadowed his singles, the small (5-foot-6, 139 pounds), neatly mustachioed and courtly, Toto had many fine moments alone. He was ranked world Nos. 10 and 9 in 1926 and 1927, golden years for the French: They were 40 percent of the Top 10, his fellow Musketeers occupying places in the first four, Lacoste at No. 1. In his greatest singles moment, his clever volleying took him to the Wimbledon semis of 1926 and five times a match point away from joining Borotra in the championship round. American Bob Kinsey got away from him, though, 6-4, 4-6, 6-3, 3-6, 9-7, slipping from 4-5, 15-40, and 5-6, 15-40 and ad out in the last set. Wallis Myers, the connoisseur, wrote: "Brugnon is a player of rare stroke variety and delicacy of touch." He was a quarterfinalist in 1927, and stands fourth among all male Wimbledonians in wins with 129: 37-19 in singles, 69-16 in doubles, 23-16 in mixed.

His Davis Cup career ran 11 years, and he had a hand in four of the Cup triumphs as a right-handed left-court player. For a time, he was a teaching professional in California. He was born May 11, 1895, in Paris, and died there March 20, 1978.

MAJOR TITLES (12)—Australian doubles, 1928; French doubles, 1927-28, 30, 32, 34; Wimbledon doubles, 1926, 28, 32-33; French mixed, 1925-26. DAVIS CUP—1921, 23-24-25-26-27, 30-31-32-33-34, 4-2 singles, 22-9 doubles. SINGLES RECORD IN THE MAJORS—Australian (1-1), French (21-13), Wimbledon (37-19), U.S. (12-11).

Butch Buchholz

United States (1940—)
Hall of Fame—2005—Contributor

If anybody in tennis has done it all (and done it superbly), he is Earl Henry "Butch" Buchholz, Jr. It was a natural that, on a July afternoon in 2005, he should arrive in a yard where he has played to be tapped for membership in the Hall of Fame.

It was the Bill Talbert Court at the Newport Casino, a rectangle named for his former mentor. Talbert, the late Hall of Famer, Butch's Davis Cup captain, could have told you that the skinny 6-foot-2 kid he called "Junior" was headed for the game's Pantheon.

A righthander, born Sept. 16, 1940, St. Louis, Missouri, Butch was a teen-age hotshot, winning the junior titles of Australia, France, Wimbledon and the United States. As a 20-year-old, he was ranked in a pair of Top 10s: No. 5 in the world, No. 3 in the U.S. However, tennis at that time was strictly divided between amateur and pro precincts, silly as it seems now. The amateurs had the conventional circuit lined with the majors and Davis Cup; the small band of pros, regarded as outcasts, were the best players, usually better paid.

As an amateur, he also held two other U.S. Top 10 rankings side (U.S. No. 6-9, 1959-58), played Davis Cup (3-1 singles, 3-2 doubles). He nearly won Wimbledon in 1960, losing in the quarterfinals to champ Neale Fraser, despite five match points. Then, he decided to try the pros. Seven years of barnstorming showed a less cushy side. He won the U.S. Pro in 1962, beating Pancho Segura of Ecuador 6-4, 6-3, 6-4 in the final. Butch played Newport as an amateur, later in Jimmy Van Alen's revolutionary pro tourney in 1965 that introduced the tie-breaker. He was one of the "Handsome Eight," Lamar Hunt's World Championship Trennis (WCT) troupe that hastened the coming of "Open" tennis by converting five top amateurs to professionalism in 1967.

Playing days over, Butch, the son of a respected St. Louis teaching pro, Earl, Sr., turned to other areas, but with the game's interests ever close to his heart, his vision as sharp as his volley. He was learning the game inside out as a thoughtful, good-humored administrator, heading World Team Tennis as commissioner, 1976-78, and the ATP as executive director, 1981-82. He did some TV commentary, but was driven by his dream of creating (along with brother Clifford Buchholz) a great tournament for the U.S.

It came true, a fan's seaside delight, launched as the Lipton in 1985 at Delray Beach, Florida, now the Sony Ericsson Open. Enmeshed in numerous crises in early days, the dauntless Brothers Buchholz have overcame all, and settled happily at Crandon Park, Key Biscayne, in a 13,800-seat stadium, their extravaganza one of the globe's finer events.

Active in charitable projects in the Miami area, he has been pleased by the work of his son, Trey Buchholz, heading First Serve, a nation-wide tennis and educational program for kids.

In 1965, when Van Alen invited the pros to play at the Casino, the cradle of the American game, Buchholz remarked, "A lot of the old guard thought the hallowed grass would turn brown if a pro set foot on it." Instead it turned greener, especially when "Butch" was taken into the Hall 40 years later.

During his outcast pro days prior to 1968 and Open tennis, he won 11 tournaments. He had a short stay in the opens, reaching the quarters at Wimbledon in 1968, and the quarters of the US Open in 1969.

U.S. TITLE (1)—Pro singles, 1962; DAVIS CUP—1959, 1960, Singles 3-1; Doubles 3-2 SINGLES RECORD IN THE MAJORS—Australian (2-2), French (1-1), Wimbledon (13-6), U.S. (11-4).

Don Budge

United States (1915–2000)
Hall of Fame—1964

In sheer achievement, John Donald Budge accomplished what nobody before 1938 had been able to do: he won the Grand Slam of tennis, capturing the championships of Australia, France, Wimbledon and the United States within that year. People were suddenly speaking of Budge in the same breath with the already immortal Bill Tilden.

Born June 13, 1915, in Oakland, Calif., Budge had been less interested in tennis than in baseball, basketball and football while growing up in the city, where his Scottish-born father, a former soccer player, had settled.

When the 6-foot-1, 160 pound right-hander turned to tennis, his strapping size enabled him to play a game of maximum power. His serve was battering, his backhand considered perhaps the finest the game has known, his net play emphatic, his overhead drastic. Quick and rhythmic, he was truly a complete player and, what is more, was temperamentally suited for the game. Affable and easygoing, he could not be shaken from the objective of winning with the utmost application of hitting power.

The redhead was a favorite wherever he played, and he moved quickly up the tennis ladder. At the age of 19, he was far enough advanced to be named to the Davis Cup team. The next year, 1936, he lost at Wimbledon and the U.S. to Fred Perry, the world's No. 1 amateur, but beat Perry in the Pacific Southwest tournament.

In 1937, Perry turned pro and Budge became the world No. 1. He won at Wimbledon and Forest Hills, both over German Baron Gottfried von Cramm, 6-3, 6-4, 6-2, and 6-1, 7-9, 6-1, 3-6, 6-1, and led the U.S. to its first Davis Cup in 11 years, 4-1 over Britain. The most brilliant act therein was his famous revival in the fifth set of the fifth match against Germany in the person of the stylish von Cramm to win the inter-zone final at neutral Wimbledon. He had already beaten Henner Henkel, 6-2, 6-1, 6-3, and won the doubles with Gene Mako over Henkel-von Cramm. So, with the score knotted, 2-2, up came the decisive test, another of his classic jousts with von Cramm. Not only was Budge far back, by two sets, but he had to rise from 1-4 down in the fifth to win on a sixth match point—a desperate running forehand—6-8, 5-7, 6-4, 6-2, 8-6, and tip the series to the U.S., 3-2.

After that, the challenge round against Britain, also at Wimbledon, was relatively easy, though Don had to beat lefty Charlie Hare in a rugged first set, and take him, 15-13, 6-1, 6-2, to offset Frank Parker's leadoff loss to Bunny Austin. Budge and Mako won the doubles, and Don beat Austin on the third day, his 11th successive singles win on his seeming home turf. Culminating a fantastic year, Budge received the Sullivan Award as America's top amateur athlete, the first tennis player to be so honored.

The high regard in which Budge was held by fellow players, spectators and officials was reflected by the loyalty he demonstrated in 1937. He was a big attraction for pro tennis but decided against leaving the amateur ranks for another year. The United States had the Davis Cup and he decided that, in return for all tennis had done for him, he must help in the defense of the Cup for at least another year.

So he turned down the professional offers, aware that poor fortunes in 1938 could hurt, if not end, his earning power as a pro. But 1938 would be his most glorious year. He defeated John Bromwich, 6-4, 6-2, 6-1, in the Australian final, losing only one set in the entire tournament. In the French he beat Roderich Menzel of Czechoslovakia in the final, 6-3, 6-2, 6-4, and yielded three sets in the tournament. At Wimbledon, he did not lose a single set, beating Bunny Austin of Britain, 6-1, 6-0, 6-3, for the title, and

at Forest Hills he gave up but one set—to pal Gene Mako in the final—in winning the U.S. crown, 6-3, 6-8, 6-2, 6-1.

At Wimbledon he registered a double triple, winning singles, doubles, mixed in 1937-38, and tripled in the U.S., 1938.

Budge had won the Grand Slam and was the toast of the tennis world. After helping the U.S. retain the Davis Cup over Australia, beating Adrian Quist, 8-6, 6-1, 6-2, and Bromwich, 6-2, 6-3, 4-6, 7-5, and after four years in the world's Top 10 (No. 1 in 1937-38) and five years in the U.S. Top 10, he left the amateur ranks. He did so with the blessing of the USTA president, Holcombe Ward, and the Davis Cup captain, Walter L. Pate, who wished him well in his pro career.

He made his professional debut at Madison Square Garden in New York early in 1939 and, before a crowd of 16,725, defeated Ellsworth Vines, 6-3, 6-4, 6-2. On tour, Budge defeated Vines, 21 matches to 18, Perry, 18-11, and 47-year-old Tilden, 51-7.

Before entering the Army Air Force in 1942, Budge won two U.S. Pro titles at Forest Hills, 1940 over Perry, 6-3, 5-7, 6-4, 6-3, and 1942 over Bobby Riggs, 6-2, 6-2, 6-2. A shoulder injury suffered in military training reduced his post-war effectiveness, and he lost the pro tour hegemony to challenger Riggs in a close journey of one-nighters, 24-22. Still, he battled to the U.S. Pro finals of 1946-47, 49, 53, losing the first three to Riggs and the last to 25-year-old Pancho Gonzalez, 13 years his junior, and left little doubt as to his greatness. "I consider him," said Tilden, "the finest player 365 days a year who ever lived."

Having set out to construct the then-unnamed "Grand Slam," Don was followed to the rare heights by only four emulators—Maureen Connolly (1953), Rod Laver (1962, 69), Margaret Court (1970) and Steffi Graf (1988). He died Jan. 26, 2000 at Poughkeepsie, N.Y.

MAJOR TITLES (14)—Australian singles 1938; French singles, 1938: Wimbledon singles, 1937-38; U.S. singles. 1937-38; Wimbledon doubles, 1937-38; U.S. doubles, 1936, 38; Wimbledon mixed, 1937-1938; U.S. mixed, 1937-38 **OTHER U.S. TITLES** (9)—Clay Court doubles, 1934, with Gene Mako; Pro singles, 1940, 42; Pro doubles, 1940-41, with Fred Perry; 1942, 47, with Bobby Riggs; 1949, with Frank Kovacs; 1953, with Pancho Gonzalez. **DAVIS CUP**–1935-36-37-38, 19-2 singles, 6-2 doubles. **SINGLES RECORD IN THE MAJORS**—Australian (5-0), French (6-0), Wimbledon (24-2), U.S. (23-3).

Maria Bueno
Brazil (1939—)
Hall of Fame—1964

Maria Esther Andion Bueno came swirling out of Brazil as a teen-ager to quickly establish herself as one of the most graceful and proficient, a delight to watch and dangerous to deal with since she had such a broad repertoire of shots, and the skill and grace to deliver them.

As the "Sao Paulo Swallow," she was slim, 5-foot-7 and quick, swooping to the net to conquer with piercing volleys. Maria was a blend of power and touch, a woman of superb movement and rhythms. Stylishly gowned by the tennis couturier Ted Tinling, she was the frilly treasure of Wimbledon's Centre Court, where she was at her best and won eight titles—three in singles (1959, 1960 and 1964), and five in doubles.

Grass was her favorite surface, suiting her attacking nature. Born Oct. 11, 1939, in São Paulo, she was clearly the best female player to come from Latin America, and was ranked in the world's Top 10 from 1958 to 1968: No. 1 in 1959 and 1960, plus No. 2 four times. In her regal choreography, the versatile right-hander was one of a triumvirate of women—including Frenchwoman Suzanne Lenglen and Australian Evonne Goolagong—whose fluidity and artistry set them apart.

She was agreeable, but reserved, a private person who underwent a number of physical career-harming agonies without complaint. Her best days were as an amateur. By the time Open tennis and prize money dawned in 1968, she was hobbled by a variety of arm and leg injuries. After a long retirement, she felt sufficiently well to try the pro tour in 1975, and returned to Wimbledon for a spiritual triumph in 1976 after a hiatus of seven years. There were glimpses of the wondrous Maria as she won three rounds, before losing, 2-6, 6-2, 6-1 to Sue Barker, and most spectators were gratified to see her again. "In her day she was so marvelous to watch," said Billie Jean King, an old rival and doubles accomplice, after defeating Maria at Wimbledon in 1977. "But it was painful to play her today. I wanted to remember her as she was." Bueno seemed undismayed to be a loser. "I have always loved tennis, and still enjoy playing. I've had my glory," she said. She crashed through to a first major singles triumph by defeating another aggressor, American Darlene Hard, 6-4, 6-3, in the 1959 Wimbledon final. Two months later, in a rare teenage final at Forest Hills, Maria, 18, beat the British 6-footer Christine Truman, 19, for the U.S. title, 6-1, 6-4. That was her first of four U.S. singles prizes. She winged to the heights in the finals of 1963 and 1964, taking a shot-making feast from Margaret Smith (Court), 7-5, 6-4, to wow the gallery, and the following year stunning the spectators by destroying Carole Caldwell, 6-1, 6-0. At Wimbledon in 1964, she and Margaret staged another rouser of volleying violence for the title that went to Maria, 6-4, 7-9, 6-3. She won her last major singles, the 1966 U.S. title, over Nancy Richey, 6-3, 6-1, but was beaten in her last important final, the U.S. Amateur of 1968, by Margaret, 6-2, 6-2.

At 18, in the company of Althea Gibson, Maria won her first Wimbledon prize, the doubles of 1958. In all, she won 18 major titles in singles, doubles and mixed. She and Hard were one of the best teams, taking the Wimbledon title twice (1960, 1963) and the U.S. twice (1960, 1962). Maria's skill at doubles was such that she won her 12 majors with six partners, and in 1960 scored one of three doubles Grand Slams, with two partners: Christine Truman in the Australian, Hard in the French, Wimbledon and U.S. She won the Japan Open in 1974, 3-6, 6-4, 6-3 over Germany's Katja Ebbinghaus, her lone pro title in singles, to complement 62 as an amateur, making her an unusual champ who won titles in three decades.

MAJOR TITLES (18)—Wimbledon singles, 1959-60, 64; U.S. singles, 1959, 63-64, 66; Australian doubles, 1960; French doubles, 1960; Wimbledon doubles, 1958, 60, 63, 65; U.S. doubles, 1960, 62, 66, 68; French mixed, 1960. **FEDERATION CUP**—1965, 1-0 singles, 0-1 doubles. **SINGLES RECORD IN THE MAJORS**—Australian (6-2), French (33-10), Wimbledon (50-9), U.S. (48-7).

May Sutton Bundy
United States (1886–1975)
Hall of Fame—1956

Although May Godfray Sutton was a U.S. citizen—the first outsider from beyond the British Isles and first American to win Wimbledon—she had a distinct English connection. Born in Plymouth on Sept. 25, 1886, daughter of a British Naval captain, Adolphus Sutton, she moved with the family at age six to a ranch outside of Pasadena, Calif. Her father built a concrete tennis court, the starting point for herself and three of her four sisters to become outstanding players. Capt. Sutton was one of the greatest tennis sires: May won Wimbledon, 1905 and 1907; grandchildren Dorothy Bundy (Cheney, daughter of May) won the Australian in 1938; John Doeg (son of Violet) won the U.S. in 1930; great grandson Brian Cheney had a U.S. national ranking and played the U.S. and Wimbledon. The saying in Southern California was, "It takes a Sutton to beat a Sutton" because four of them—May, Violet, Florence, Ethel—dominated that section for almost a generation through 1915.

May, a husky 5-foot-4½, highly competitive right-hander with a powerful topspin forehand, was the best known of them with her U.S. title in 1904, 6-1, 6-2, over defender Bessie Moore, and her two Wimbledon titles over Dorothea Douglass. Head-to-head three straight years, May took the crown from the Englishwoman, 6-3, 6-4, lost it, 6-3, 9-7, and again subdued Dorothea (now Mrs. Lambert Chambers) 6-1, 6-4. She shocked English crowds at first by rolling up her sleeves to bare her elbows, and wearing a shorter skirt than most, flashing ankles.

In 1912, she married Tom Bundy, a top player who won three U.S. doubles titles (1912, 1913, 1914) with Maurice McLoughlin. Their daughter, Australian champ Dorothy "Dodo" Cheney, ranked as high as No. 6 in the world in 1946. Now in her 80s, she continues to win a record number of U.S. senior titles. May had her best days before U.S. rankings for women were established in 1913. But her groundstrokes were formidable enough when she made a comeback in 1921 to earn her the No. 4 ranking at age 35. That made her the third of the sisters to rank in the U.S. Top 10, a record. Ethel was No. 2 in 1913; Florence Nos. 3, 2, 4 in 1913-14-15, respectively. Moreover, May played Wightman Cup for the U.S. four years later and ranked No. 5 in 1928 at 42. She entered the Hall of Fame in 1956, and died Oct. 4, 1975, in Santa Monica, Calif.

MAJOR TITLES (4)—Wimbledon singles, 1905, 1907; U.S. singles, 1904; U.S. doubles, 1904. **OTHER U.S. TITLES** (2)—Clay Court singles, 1912: Clay Court mixed, 1912, with Fred Harris. **WIGHTMAN CUP**—1925, 0-1 doubles. **SINGLES RECORD IN THE MAJORS**—Wimbledon (14-1), U.S. (10-2).

Mabel Cahill
Ireland (1863–Unknown)
Hall of Fame—1976

Little is known of Mabel Esmonde Cahill except that, as an Irish citizen, she was the first foreigner to win one of the major championships. That was the U.S. singles of 1891 when she got even with Ellen Roosevelt, who had defeated her in the all-comers final of 1890 and gone on to win the title. In 1891, Cahill, a right-hander, decimated the Roosevelts, beating Ellen's sister,

Grace, in the all-comers final, 6-3, 7-5, and then Ellen in the challenge round, 6-4, 6-1, 4-6, 6-3. She retained the title by defeating Bessie Moore in the 1892 challenge round, 5-7, 6-3, 6-4, 4-6, 6-2. That year, she also won the mixed doubles with Clarence Hobart.

She declined to return to Philadelphia for the 1893 Championships, defaulting her title to Aline Perry in the challenge round. During her residence in the U.S., she belonged to the New York Tennis Club. She was born April 2, 1863, in Ballyragget, County Kilkenny, Ireland. No details of her death, believed to have occurred in Ireland in 1904 or 1905, have been found.

MAJOR TITLES (5)—U.S. singles. 1891, 1892; U.S. doubles, 1891, 1892; U.S. mixed, 1892. SINGLES RECORD IN THE MAJORS—U.S. (6-1).

Oliver Campbell
United States (1871–1953)
Hall of Fame—1955

For a century Oliver Samuel Campbell had the distinction of being the youngest to win the U.S. singles title. He did it as a 19-year-old Columbia student in 1890. (Pete Sampras, a younger 19, became the youngest when he won the title in 1990.)

Four years earlier, Campbell, at 15 years, five months, had lost in the opening round at Newport to the man he would dethrone four years later, Henry Slocum. Oliver was the youngest male entry until 1918 when Vinnie Richards undercut him by a month.

After his first exposure to Newport, Campbell determined to transform himself from a baseliner into a net-storming volleyer. "I ran to the net behind every service until the day I retired," he later recalled. It paid off in a U.S. doubles title (his first of three) in the company of Valentine Hall in 1888, with whom he'd won the Intercollegiate doubles that year for Columbia.

Campbell, a 5-foot-11 right-hander, lost to Slocum again in the 1888 semis, and to lefty Quincy Shaw in the 1889 all-comers final. In 1890, he outbattled Bob Huntington, 3-6, 6-2, 5-7, 6-2, 6-1, in the semis, and Percy Knapp, 8-6, 0-6, 6-2, 6-3, in the all-comers final. Stronger physically, he kept rushing the net and at last beat Slocum, deposing the champ, 6-2, 4-6, 6-3, 6-1.

Campbell endured another struggle in the challenge round of 1891, 2-6, 7-5, 7-9, 6-1, 6-2, over Clarence Hobart. He made it three straight, 7-5, 3-6, 6-3, 7-5, over Fred Hovey in 1892, and retired, leaving the 1893 title to Bob Wrenn by default. In 1888, he made the U.S. Top 10 for the first of five straight years, No. 1 in 1890-91-92. He was born Feb. 25, 1871, in New York, and died July 11, 1953, in Campellton, Canada.

MAJOR TITLES (6)—U.S. singles, 1890-91-92; U.S. doubles, 1888, 91-92. OTHER U.S. TITLES (2)—Intercollegiate doubles, 1888, with Valentine Hall, 1889, with Alfred Wright. SINGLES RECORD IN THE MAJORS —U.S. (16-3)

Rosie Casals
United States (1940—)
Hall of Fame—1996

Citizen Kane, who wasn't much fun, had his mysterious "Rosebud." There was, however, no mystery about the Rosebud of tennis, Citizen Casals. She just wanted to be the best ever. Inch-for-inch she was—and the fun flowed in all directions from this diminutive dynamo who took such joy from playing, and passed it along to grateful witnesses.

Tiny package, explosive contents—tennis was no waiting game at the baseline for 62-inch Rosemary "Rosie/Rosebud" Casals. She went for the jugular fast, a serve-and-volleying dervish whose incredible arsenal of strokes and tankful of competitive verve were necessities merely to stay alive among the sisterhood that established female professional tennis during the 1970s.

"I'm out there with 'The Arm'" (5-foot-11 Aussie Margaret Court) recalls San Franciscan Casals, "with those arms and legs that stretch forever, and I had to make my shots count right away."

They counted and counted and counted during a 15-year career in the stratosphere, 12 times in the world's Top 10 (1966-77), No. 3 in 1970. So much so that she was elevated to the Hall in 1996.

Billie Jean King and protégé Rosie Casals were names that went together like wine and roses. No finer female combo illuminated doubles. But all the while their influence as pioneering pros ran deeper than the five Wimbledon and two U.S. titles together. Although Rosie, the riveting volleyer, is the smallest modern in the tennis valhalla, she and Billie Jean were giants in launching the long march of the "Long Way Babies" as the Virginia Slims circuit began to take shape in 1970.

With another Hall of Famer, Gladys Heldman, publisher of *World Tennis* magazine, as behind-the-scenes organizer and encourager, B.J. and Rosie were the ringleaders on court, close friends, doubles partners, frequent final-round foes, super saleswomen for the emerging tour. They were perfect role players, feisty but good-humored kids off the public courts who believed women had a destiny in professional sport. A born (Sept. 16, 1948) and bred San Franciscan, right-handed Rosie started at Golden Gate Park.

"Those early Slims days were an exciting time, and a little scary, too, although I laugh looking back at 1970," Rosie says. "Even though Open tennis came in in 1968, the men got most of the money and publicity. The tournaments were still like the amateur days, men and women together. We knew we had to break away, go on our own. That first Slims tournament, '70 in Houston, the USTA didn't like our rebel ways and threatened to suspend us Americans if we played. They did, and for a while we wondered if that was the end of tennis for us. Of course it wasn't."

A full Slims tour commenced in 1971 and King and Casals "played our little bahoolas off"—Billie Jean's words. That year, Rosie played a record 32 tournaments in singles, 31 in doubles, amounting to 205 matches while Billie Jean was in the same neighborhood with 36-21-210. More than 200 matches in a season? Steffi Graf played as many as 117 only once. It was, indeed, different times. "We had to play much more than they do today because the money was slight." Rosie offers her soulful gamine's smile, and shrugs when you mention her unapproachable record of playing 685 singles and doubles tournaments. "If you won both the singles and doubles, it was worth only a couple of thousand bucks. You couldn't afford to default with an injury.

And we were paying all our own expenses, not getting free hotel and per diem like the stars now. But I'm glad for them. We were trying to pave the way.

"I got $3,750 when I lost the 1970 U.S. Open final to Court, the last victim in her Grand Slam. Not even close to what a first-round loser got in 2007 [$17,500]. But it didn't matter. We thought we were rich, and there was a great feeling of family, of being together to make the tour work, provide the future for the game."

A distant relative of the cello virtuoso, Pablo Casals, the Rosebud improvised brilliant cadenzas on her strings. For sheer shot-making sorcery, plus merrymaking on one side of the net, the amalgam of Casals and Ilie Nastase, winning the Wimbledon mixed in 1970 and 1972, may never be equalled. "I had to take care of him, mother him a little when he went crazy," she says.

Doubles was her shtick, 56 of her titles were with King. But Rosie was a singles contender at all the majors, and beat King and clay maven Nancy Richey in succession to win the first big bucks tourney, the $100,000 Family Circle Cup, worth $30,000 to her, in 1973. She won 11 singles, 112 pro doubles titles, the latter second only to Martina Navratilova's 177, collecting the last as a 41-year-old, "for old times' sake," in Oakland in 1988 alongside Martina. She won career prize money of $1,364,955. Casals was a quarterfinalist or better in all the majors–Australian semi-final in 1967; French quarterfinal in 1969 and 1970: She also reached the Wimbledon semifinal in 1967, 1969, 1970, 1972 and her lone major singles finals appearances—the U.S. Open in 1970 and 1971.

Dashing dressmaker, Hall of Famer Ted Tinling, adored her, gowning Rosie in spangles, sequins, a variety of color combinations. At Wimbledon in 1972, they caused a stir when his purple-squiggled dress—with Casals in it—was evicted. "It was predominantly white, complying with the rules," she says, "but the purple designs upset the referee. He ordered me off the court to change. I loved to get their goat and enjoyed the whole scene.

"It became a famous dress and beat me to the Hall of Fame to be displayed some time ago." But Citizen Casals has caught up with her notorious frock, and a Rosebud now blooms in Newport.

MAJOR TITLES (12) (all doubles)—Wimbledon, 1967. 1968, 1970, 1971, 1973; U.S. 1967, 1971, 1974, 1982; Wimbledon mixed 1970. 1972; U.S. mixed, 1975. OTHER U.S. TITLES (8)—Hard Court singles, 1965. Indoor doubles, 1966, 1968, 1975 with Billie Jean King, 1976 with Francoise Durr; Hard Court doubles, 1966, with King; Clay Court doubles, 1970, with Gail Chanfreau; Hard Court mixed, 1966, with Ian Crookenden. FEDERATION CUP—1967, 1976 1977 1978, 1979, 1980, 1981, helped US, win all seven Cups, 8-1 singles, 27-1 doubles. WIGHTMAN CUP –1967, 1976, 1977, 1978, 1979, 1980, 1981, helped U.S. win all seven Cups, 1-3 singles, 6-1 doubles. SINGLES RECORD IN THE MAJORS—Australian (9-5). French (10-7), Wimbledon (48-18), U.S. (47-21).

Malcolm Chace
United States (1875–1955)
Hall of Fame—1961

A Rhode Islander born in Valley Falls on March 12, 1875, beanpole Malcolm Greene Chace, 6-foot-1, 150 pounds, made his first mark in the game by winning the U.S. Interscholastic title in 1892 for University Grammar in Providence. In 1893 (for Brown) and 1894 and 1895 (for Yale), he became the only, three-straight winner of both the U.S. Intercollegiate singles and doubles titles, the only man to win both for two different colleges. He was a semifinalist at the U.S. Championships in 1894, losing to Bill Lamed and won the doubles title in 1895 with Robert Wrenn over Clarence Hobart and Fred Hovey, 7-5, 6-1, 8-6. Right-handed, he ranked in the U.S. Top 10 four times, beginning in 1892, No. 3 in 1895. He died July 16, 1955 in Yarmouth, Mass.

MAJOR TITLE (1)—U.S. doubles, 1895. OTHER U.S. TITLES (6)—Intercollegiate singles, 1893, 1894, 1895; Intercollegiart doubles, 1895, with Clarence Budlong, 1894, 1895, with Arthur Foote. SINGLES RECORD IN THE MAJORS—U.S. (16-9)

Dorothea Chambers
Great Britain (1878–1960)
Hall of Fame—1981

What a clash of eras and customs it was in the Wimbledon final of 1919 when the sturdily conformed, long-skirted 40-year-old matron, Dorothea Katherine Douglass "Dolly" Chambers, seven times champion between 1903 and 1914, faced the slim new kid half her age, audacious, skimpily dressed (for the time) Suzanne Lenglen. They battled through the longest final up to that time, 44 games, Chambers narrowly missing two match points in the third set of the 10-8, 4-6, 9-7 decision, the first of six titles for Lenglen, who never lost in singles at Wimbledon.

With King George V, Queen Mary and the Princess Royal in the Royal Box, one of the finest matches to be played at Wimbledon, by men or women, was enacted. Against the all-court game of Lenglen, the right-handed Chambers delighted the gallery with superb resistance. She drove with such power and length from both forehand and backhand, passed so accurately, put up lobs so irretrievable, and had so much touch on her drop shot that her young opponent was showing signs of physical distress and found herself in danger of losing.

After two sets, the match was even and Lenglen was sipping brandy to ease her peril. In the third set, trailing, 4-1, Chambers put on a remarkable comeback and seemed to have the victory in hand at 6-5, 40-15, on her serve at double match point. But, just as remarkably, Lenglen rallied and pulled out the match, 10-8, 4-6, 9-7. Both players were so exhausted that when asked to come to the Royal Box, they said they were physically unable to do so. It had been an epic struggle between the past and the future in tennis.

Despite the interruption of World War I, Chambers was in 11 Wimbledon singles finals—third behind Blanche Hillyard's 13 and Martina Navratilova's 12—the last in 1920 when she lost again to Lenglen, and, at 41, was the oldest female finalist. Continuing to play the Big W through 1927, she played 115 matches overall there: 32-8 in singles, 29-11 in doubles, 24-11 in mixed. Dolly won two of her Wimbledons after the birth of her first child, two more after the birth of her second, the first of six women who won majors after childbirth.

As Britain's Wightman Cup captain in 1925, at 46, she helped her side win, 4-3, at Forest Hills by beating 30-year-old Eleanor

Goss, 7-5, 3-6, 6-1. She also captained the team in 1926. She was born Sept. 3, 1878, in Ealing, England and died in 1960.

MAJOR TITLES (7)—Wimbledon singles, 1903, 1904, 1906, 1910, 1911, 1913, 1914. WIGHTMAN CUP—1925, 1926; 1-0 singles, 0-1 doubles. SINGLES RECORD IN THE MAJORS—Wimbledon (32-8), U.S. (3-1).

Philippe Chatrier
France (1926–2000)
Hall of Fame—1992—Administrator

As player, journalist and administrator, Philippe Chatrier, a Parisian, made a tremendous impact on the game, and was instrumental in its growth and success, particularly during the Open era. He was a good enough player to win the French junior titles in singles and doubles in 1945, play internationally for France, and later captained the Davis Cup team.

Serving dual roles as president of the French Federation of Tennis (1972-92) and the ITF (1977-91) he was largely responsible for the renaissance of the French Open, placing it on par with the other three majors and overseeing the splendid updating of Stade Roland Garros. He fought valiantly against over-commercialization of the game, and led a campaign to restore tennis to the Olympic Games, a goal realized in 1988 after a 64-year interval.

Championing the Grand Slam concept, he worked hard to ally the four major championships in staying at the pinnacle. He was also a member of the International Olympic Committee. An intelligent chronicler of the game, he was a Paris newspaperman, and founded one of the leading magazines of the sport, *Tennis de France*. The central court at Roland Garros is named for him. He was born Feb. 2, 1926, in Paris, and died there June 23, 2000.

Michael Chang
United States (1972—)
Hall of Fame—2008

Michael Chang was cramping so badly that he couldn't risk sitting down on the changeovers. What did it matter that hot 1989 afternoon in Stade Roland Garros? Michael, a California teen-ager, was far behind No. 1 Ivan Lendl in the fourth round of the French Open, and his chances looked empty. Nevertheless, 17-years, 95 days-old, Michael was filled with hope and grit, and kept running and retrieving to pull himself back into the match from two sets back—and actually take it away from Lendl, the three-time champ, 4-6, 4-6, 6-3, 6-3, 6-3, in 4:39.

That was the start of an electrifying, unlikely dash to the title that had last been held by an American man, Tony Trabert, 34 years before, and made little Michael the youngest of all male possessors of a major singles. Despite his lack of clay court experience, Chang followed up on Lendl by out-dueling guys brought up on it: Ronald Agenor of Haiti, Andrei Chesnokov of the USSR and finally, dodging a gang of break points, defeating No. 3 Stefan Edberg, 6-1, 3-6, 4-6, 6-4, 6-2 in the final.

Those were the early steps to the 2008 posting in the Hall of Fame for 5-foot-9, 160 pound Michael. Perpetual motion personified, making few mistakes, he would be a finalist in three more majors (1995 French to Thomas Muster; 1996 Australian to Boris Becker, and 1996 U.S., to Pete Sampras), play a vital role in the American Davis Cup triumph of 1990 and bank 33 more titles, runnerup in 21 others.

During two chilly, damp afternoons in Vienna, with horn-blowing crowds of 18,000 cheering against him, Michael scored one of the greatest U.S. Davis Cup victories. Deadlocked 2-2 with Austria in the Cup semifinal, Chang found himself trapped, two sets behind Horst Skoff. He hung on to win a set before darkness intervened. Returning the following day, his serve, like his legs, revived, Michael won, 3-6, 6-7 (4-7), 6-4, 6-4, 6-3. He and Don Budge (who turned the trick in 1937 against Gottfried von Cramm of Germany) are the only U.S. Cuppers to win a decisive fifth match from two sets down.

In the final, ending a U.S. Cup slump of eight years, Chang beat Darren Cahill, 6-2, 7-6 (7-4), 6-0, the first day, for a 2-0 lead over Australia, soon defeated. He was the youngest on an American Cup winner. His record in Davis Cup; played six ties; four years, 8-4 singles.

This diminutive dynamo, a speedy right-hander with both-handed backhand, was born Feb. 22, 1972, in Hoboken, N.J. of Chinese-American parentage, raised in Southern California. He was coached by older brother, Carl Chang, a University of California-Berkeley varsity player.

Edberg caught up with him in 1992, Chang losing a record-length U.S. Open match in 5:26 (a semifinal), the second longest major singles, 6-7 (3-7), 7-5, 7-6 (7-3), 5-7, 6-4. In a 17-year professional career, he made the world's Top 10 seven years—No. 5 in 1989, 95; No. 6 in 1992, 94; No. 8 in 1993; No. 2 in 1996; No. 3 in 1997.

Prior to his 2003 retirement, he made the semis of the Australian two other times—1995 and 97; two other U.S. semifinals—1992 and 97 and the quarters of Wimbledon in 1994. He won 34 singles titles (662-312 matches) and $19,145,632 in prize money.

MAJOR TITLES (1)—French Open 1989. DAVIS CUP—1989, 1990, 1996, 1997; 8-4 singles. SINGLES RECORD IN THE MAJORS—Australian (21-10), French (38-15), Wimbledon (18-14), U.S. (43-17).

Dorothy May (Dodo) Bundy Cheney
USA (1916—)
Hall of Fame—2004

What did she want to be when she grew up?

A tennis champion.

And after she grew up?

A tennis champion, singles and doubles.

Then, when she retired?

An un-retired, perpetual tennis champion.

Of course "Dodo" Cheney didn't camp out on a tennis court for nine-plus decades. It just seemed that way as she kept and keeps on adding laurels to her status as the world's undisputed tennis champ. As a woman who has won tournament titles for more than 80 years, and sees no reason to quit, she did find room for marriage and a family, making friends wherever she went. From kids tourneys to representing the United States in winning the Wightman Cup over Britain in 1939 and 1946, and capturing

a major international singles title, the Australian Championship in 1938, she has moved onward, ever onward, plucking the foremost prizes in whatever competition.

A righthander, born Sept. 1, 1916 in Los Angeles, California, she grew up in Santa Monica, now campaigns in the U.S. senior age groups, from age 40 to…up and up…and….

Some consider these tournaments the realm of the super mature, and lively "Dodo" is undoubtedly its queen, the mother superior. No prize money involved. God knows how many millions she would be stashing away if she were 21 again, the age at which she took a three week boat trip Down Under with the original Grand Slammer, Don Budge, to show Aussies how Californians played tennis. You get something over a million bucks to win the Australian today. Cheney got a bouquet, a trophy, room, board and a steamer ticket. But that was enough. She was in it for the competition, the fun and sociability—and still is. As the first American woman to win the Australian title, she beat Australia's Dorothy Stevenson, 6-3, 6-2, then joined another American, Dorothy Workman, in losing the doubles final to Aussie's Thelma Coyne and Nancye Wynne, 9-7, 6-4.

It's hard to know how much sterling silver she has accumulated, but she's been on a gold rush since winning her first U.S. title, the Indoor Doubles in 1941 with Pauline Betz. That earned "Dodo" her initial gold ball, the reward handed out by the U.S. Tennis Association for each national title. As of December, 2007, she had a Gibraltarian pile of them: close to 400!

At 30, in 1946, she ranked No. 6 in the world. She was in the U.S. Top 10 10 times: No. 3 in 1937-38, '41; No. 4 in 1940, '44; No. 5 in 1943; No. 6 in 1939, '46; No. 8 in 1946; No. 9 in 1945. In the U.S. Championships, she made the semis in 1937-38, 43-44; and the quarters in1936, 39-40-41, 45.

Hers is a great tennis bloodline. She and mom, May Sutton Bundy (U.S. champ, 1904, Wimbledon champ, 1905, 07), are unique as the only parent-child combo in the Hall of Fame, entering 1956 and 2004, respectively. Dad, Tom Bundy, was a Davis Cupper, won the U.S. doubles, 1912-13-14 with Hall of Famer Maurice McLoughlin.

MAJOR TITLE (1)—Australian singles, 1938. **SINGLES RECORD IN THE MAJORS**— Australian (4-0), French (3-1), Wimbledon (8-2), U.S. (29-11)

Clarence Clark
United States (1859–1937)
Hall of Fame—1983

A member of a distinguished Philadelphia family, Clarence Monroe Clark had the distinction of winning the first U.S. doubles title at Newport in 1881. He and Fred Taylor beat Alexander van Rensselaer and Arthur Newbold, 6-5, 6-4, 6-5. Earlier they eliminated the favorites, Dick Sears and James Dwight. The next year at Newport he made it to the singles final, losing to Sears, the original champ, 6-1, 6-4, 6-0. His brother, Joe Clark (named to the Hall of Fame in 1955), won the first Intercollegiate title for Harvard in 1883.

Joe and Clarence tested foreign waters for Americans, journeying to England in 1883, playing and losing two doubles

matches against the dominant Renshaw twins, Willie and Ernest. Clarence was the first secretary of the newly formed USTA in 1881 and was, along with Dwight and Eugenius Outerbridge, a guiding light in the organization's establishment. He was born Aug. 27, 1859, in Germantown, Pa., and died there June 29, 1937.

MAJOR TITLE (1)—U.S. doubles, 1881. **SINGLES RECORD IN THE MAJORS**— U.S. (7-2).

Joe Clark
United States (1861–1956)
Hall of Fame—1955

Two years after the first U.S. Championships at Newport, the Intercollegiate Championships was established in 1883 and won by Joseph Sill Clark of Harvard in both singles and doubles. Clark, a senior, was the Harvard champ that year, feeling justifiably proud of himself because he won the title over classmate Dick Sears, who happened to be the U.S. champion.

The first Intercollegiates, which Sears did not enter, was played on the grounds of a mental hospital in Hartford, and Clark recalled that some of the patients served as ball boys. Clark, a right-hander, was a Philadelphian, brother of Clarence Clark, who won the first U.S. doubles title with Fred Taylor. Together he and his brother were a formidable doubles team. They played in England in 1883 after beating the reigning U.S. champs, Sears and James Dwight, in matches in Boston and New York. They represented the U.S. against the foremost English pair, the Renshaw brothers, Ernest and Willie, in a series for the so-called world championship. The Renshaws won the two matches played, losing one set in the first.

In 1885, Joe Clark joined Sears to win the U.S. doubles, 6-3, 6-0, 6-2, over Henry Slocum and Percy Knapp. Joe was a singles semifinalist in 1885, 1886 and 1887, and brother Clarence lost the 1882 final to Sears. Joe ranked in the U.S. Top 10 five straight years from 1885, No. 4 in 1888. He was born Nov. 30, 1861, in Germantown, Pa., entered the Hall of Fame in 1955, and died April 14, 1956. He was president of the USTA, 1889—91.

MAJOR TITLE (1)—U.S. doubles, 1885. **OTHER U.S. TITLES** (2) Intercollegiate singles, 1883; Intercollegiate doubles, 1883, with Howard Taylor. **SINGLES RECORD IN THE MAJORS**—U.S. (18-11).

Giovanni Emilio Clerici
Italy (1930—)
Hall of Fame—2006—Journalist

As an Italian boy of nine, summering in Alassio, beside the Mediterranean, Giovanni Clerici—the renaissance man from the renaissance land—was fascinated by tennis at a small local club, and learned the game on those courts of crimson clay. Fascination evolved to passionate love as he dreamed of a place called Wimbledon and imagined himself playing there as well as in Paris and Rome, and throughout Europe.

It happened. Seventy years have passed since his seduction by this game, and yet he continues to pursue it across the planet

as a journalist of rare understanding and literary flair, a broadcaster of discerning, witty voice. Readers of Italian newspapers since 1951 (*La Repubblica* of Rome over the last two decades) have delighted in his reports as have televiewers for more than 30 years.

Giovanni Emilio Clerici was born July 24, 1930, at Como, and has lived there since. His seven journalistic predecessors in the Hall (four Americans, three English) wrote or broadcast in the English language. Clerici, the lively European newcomer, is the first to diversify, writing in his native Italian as well as French and English, broadcasting in Italian and French.

His writing has ranged far beyond newspapers, magazines—and tennis. A scholar of tennis history, he has delved into the game's origins as deeply as the 14th century. From his meticulous research came the masterwork "500 Years of Tennis," (4th edition, 2006), blending cultural moves with the sport from the Renaissance onward. He calls this massive tome "The Brick," published in English, Italian, French, Spanish, German and Japanese.

Consumed by the history, he is ever willing to devote his expertise to projects such as the French tennis museum at Roland Garros, and the forthcoming Italian tennis museum at Milan. He is planning an institute to exhibit his magnificent collection of tennis paintings and sculpture, some of which have been displayed at Wimbledon.

Giovanni's fresh approach to the game, often treating it humorously, has set him apart in his profession, and made itself felt in an extraordinary literary output. To his credit are two tennis instructional books, guiding many onto the court. A marvelous contribution brought to life the great, though mysterious, French star of the 1920s, Suzanne Lenglen, in his definitive biography, "Divina."

That led to a 2000 drama about Lenglen on the Roman stage. No surprise to those who knew him as the honored author of Italy's Best Play of 1987, "Ottaviano e Cleopatra." His vast reach with intellect, pen and typing fingers has amounted to eight successful novels (two with tennis themes), four plays and a recent volume of poetry, "Posthumous in Life."

If he has departed from tennis from time to time, finding a variety of outlets for his unusual way with words, Giovanni has never strayed too far from his first love, and the addictive touch of putting racket to ball.

A youth falling for tennis in 1939, he was prevented by World War II from competing as a junior outside of Italy. That was a time of some danger for him, a teen-ager helping to smuggle guns to Italian partisans, guerillas harrassing the Nazis occupying Como.

How could Giovanni have imagined then that he would become a player of international caliber and title-winning deeds, a trusted literary and vocal guardian of the game—and that the road from Alassio would lead across every continent to Newport?

Bill Clothier
United States (1881–1962)
Hall of Fame—1956

Another Harvard man to win the Intercollegiate championship (1902) in the early days, William Jackson Clothier was the U.S. champ four years later, ranking No. 1 in the United States.

Clothier, a right-handed net rusher, said that "he never played better" than in the 1906 Championships, gaining confidence from his quarterfinal victory over Fred Alexander, 8-6, 6-2, 4-6, 1-6, 7-5, in which he came from triple match point down (2-5, 0-40) to race through the last five games. He took the title from Beals Wright in the challenge round, 6-3, 6-0, 6-4.

He lost the U.S. final to Holcombe Ward in 1904 and, in a five-set battle, to Bill Larned in 1909. Clothier held a U.S. Top 10 ranking for 11 years between 1901 and 1914. In 1905, he beat two French champions, Max Decugis, 6-3, 6-4, 6-4, and Maurice Germot, 6-3, 5-7, 6-1, 6-3, in the first U.S. Davis Cup engagement abroad, a 5-0 victory over France at Queen's Club in London. Although he wasn't chosen for the next series against Australasia or the final against Britain, Clothier, a powerful, aggressive 6-foot-2, 170-pounder, caught the attention of scribe Wallis Myers in a good Wimbledon showing. It was a fourth-round loss to future champ Tony Wilding, 5-7, 3-6, 8-6, 7-5, 10-8, in 3 1/2 hours on Centre Court. Bill led 5-2, 40-15 with two match points in the third. "Both men were such splendid specimens of youth and vigor, such hard hitters, such gallant fighters," Myers wrote. He and his son, William Clothier II, won U.S. Father and Son doubles titles in 1935 and 1936.

He was born in Philadelphia on Sept. 27. 1881 and died there Sept. 4, 1962.

MAJOR TITLE (1)—U.S. singles, 1906. **OTHER U.S. TITLES** (2)—Intercollegiate singles, 1902; Intercollegiate doubles, 1902, with Edward Leonard. **DAVIS CUP**—1905, 09, 4-1 singles. **SINGLES RECORD IN THE MAJORS**—Wimbledon (2-1); U.S. (57-18)

Henri Cochet
France (1901–1987)
Hall of Fame—1976

It could be said that Henri Jean Cochet had as pronounced a gift for playing tennis as anyone who attained world supremacy. A racket in his hand became a wand of magic, doing the impossible, most often in a position on the court considered untenable, and doing it with nonchalant ease and fluency. He took the ball early, volleys and half-volleys rippling off the strings. His overheads invariably scored, though his serve seemingly was innocuous.

He developed his skills early in Lyon, France, where he was born Dec. 14, 1901, and his father was secretary of the tennis club. Henri worked at the club as a ball boy and practiced with his friends and sister when nobody was using the courts. In 1921, he went to Paris where he and Jean Borotra, both unknowns, reached the final of the indoor championship, Cochet the winner.

The next year, he and Borotra played on the Davis Cup team, and in 1923 they joined with Rene Lacoste and Jacques Brugnon in the origin of the Four Musketeers. Cochet won 10 successive Davis Cup challenge round matches from the time the Musketeers wrested the Cup from the U.S. in 1927.

A sensitivity of touch and timing, resulting in moderately hit strokes of genius, accounted for the success the little Frenchman (5-foot-6, 145 pounds) had in turning back the forceful hitters of the 1920s and early 30s. Following a stunning victory over Bill Tilden, 6-8, 6-1, 6-3, 1-6, 8-6, in the quarterfinals of the 1926 U.S. Championships, ending Tilden's six-year, 42-match streak, and a

Cup-snatching triumph over Bill Johnston in the 1927 challenge round, 6-4, 4-6, 6-2, 6-4, the right-handed Cochet established himself in 1928 as the world's foremost player. Winner of the U.S., over Frank Hunter, 4-6, 6-4, 3-6, 7-5, 6-3, and French, over Lacoste, 5-7, 6-3, 6-1, 6-3, that year, and runner-up at Wimbledon to Lacoste, he became more of a national hero than ever as he scored three victories in the Cup defense, 4-1 over the U.S.

With Lacoste's retirement from international play in 1929, Cochet was France's indispensable man. He led his country to Cup-holding victories over the United States in the challenge round in 1929, 1930 and 1932, and the British in 1931.

The "Ballboy of Lyon," as he was called, was champion of France four times after it was opened to non-French citizens in 1925), and won two Wimbledons (1927, 1929) and one U.S. (1928). Probably justifiably, he felt unfairly treated in trying for a second U.S. in 1932. Darkness shut down his semifinal win over Wilmer Allison at 2-2 in sets. He had to complete that victory, 7-5, the following day, and then, after two hours rest, face the final in which the weary Frenchman was no match for a fresh Ellsworth Vines, 6-4, 6-4, 6-4.

In his last three matches in winning the Wimbledon title in 1927, he was a singular Henri Houdini. No one has concluded a major in such spectacular escapes, and all at the expense of three future Hall of Famers. Down two sets, the No. 4-seeded Cochet beat Frank Hunter in the quarters, 3-6, 3-6, 6-2, 6-2, 6-4. Trailing the great No. 2 seed Tilden, three points from defeat at 1-5, 15-all in the third, he reeled off 17 straight points, also survived a service break to 3-2 in the fifth and won the last four games to seize their semi, 3-6, 4-6, 7-5, 6-4, 6-3. For an encore magnifique in the final, he lagged again and had to repel six match points to beat No. 3 seed Borotra, 4-6, 4-6, 6-3, 6-4, 7-5: hurdling a match point at 2-5, and five more with Borotra serving at 5-3!

He ranked No. 1 from 1928 through 1931. After France lost the Davis Cup to Great Britain in 1933, Cochet turned professional. He did not have much of a career as a pro, however, and after the war, in 1945, one of the most naturally gifted tennis players in history received reinstatement as an amateur, a role in which he had once ruled the tennis world. He continued playing well. Elected to the Hall of Fame in 1976, he died April 1, 1987, in St. Germain-en-Laye, France.

MAJOR TITLES (15)—French singles, 1926 1928, 1930, 1932: Wimbledon singles, 1927 1929; U.S. singles, 1928; French doubles, 1927, 1930, 1932; Wimbledon doubles, 1926, 1928; French mixed, 1928, 1929: U.S. mixed, 1927. **DAVIS CUP**—1922, 1923, 1924, 1926, 1927, 1928, 1929, 1930. 1931, 1932, 1933, 34-8 singles, 10-6 doubles. **SINGLES RECORD IN THE MAJORS**—French (38-4), Wimbledon (43-8), US (15-3).

Bud Collins
United States (1929—)
Hall of Fame—1994—Journalist

Ubiquitous Arthur Worth "Bud" Collins, Jr. is the most visible and versatile U.S. tennis journalist. An estimable writer, broadcaster, editor, he is a man about the game whose wit, understanding and flamboyance make him more recognizable than many star players. His memory and knowledge of tennis, its history and characters, is encyclopedic.

From printed page to broadcast booth, he is identified with the sport he has done much to popularize, yet to protect for the purists. "He is to tennis what pasta is to Italy," was a line in a *Sports Illustrated* profile. Born June 17, 1929, in Lima, Ohio, he grew up in Berea (outside of Cleveland) about 50 yards from the dirt tennis courts of Baldwin-Wallace College, from which he graduated in 1951, and where his father had been head coach of football, basketball, baseball and track, as well as athletic director.

He moved east after U.S. Army service in 1954 to attend Boston University graduate school, then joined the *Boston Herald* as a sportswriter. In 1963, the year he shifted to the *Boston Globe*, Collins first did television commentary (covering the U.S. Doubles at Longwood Cricket Club) for Boston's PBS outlet, WGBH, a station that for the next 20 years, with Greg Harney as producer, would pioneer American coverage of the sport.

He worked the U.S. Open for CBS (1968-72), signed on with NBC in 1972 (thereafter closely identified with that network's presentation of Wimbledon and the French) until 2007 when he was signed by ESPN and Tennis Channel, becoming the point man for all the dualists—print-television journalists—to follow. At the *Globe* his columns on sport, travel, and a variety of other subjects, including coverage of the Vietnam War, are a continuing delight. His prose and commentary style are as multi-hued as Joseph's Amazing Technicolor Dream Coat. Seldom one to take himself or sports too seriously, he brightens reports with nicknames as colorful as his rainbow neckties and trousers, occasionally with flights of fancy. However, he can be absolutely authentic, a meticulous curator of the game's annals, passionate keeper of the flame.

He also writes for magazines and newspapers across the world such as *The Observer* in London, *The Age* in Melbourne and his website: BudCollinsTennis.com. His books include *The Education of a Tennis Player* (with Rod Laver, 1971), and *Evonne—On the Move* (with Evonne Goolagong, 1974), a memoir, *My Life with the Pros* (1989) and five editions of *Bud Collins' Tennis Encyclopedia*. Among his many awards, in 1999, he was tapped for the Associated Press' Red Smith Award, the top honor in U.S. sports journalism, and named to the National Sportswriters and Sportscasters Hall of Fame in 2002.

Although he refers to himself—and everyone else who plays below the level of the pros—as a "hacker," Collins is an accomplished now-and-again player, known for his touch, tactical cunning and preference for playing barefoot on grass courts. He won the U.S. Indoor mixed doubles (with Top Tenner Janet Hopps) in 1961, and was a finalist in the French senior doubles (with Jack Crawford) in 1975. Engaging and irrepressible, he has even coached tennis, the Brandeis University varsity, 1959-63, whose "name" player was future hippie icon Abbie Hoffman.

—*Barry Steven Lorge*

Maureen Connolly
United States (1934–1969)
Hall of Fame—1968

A too-brief flash on the tennis scene was that of Maureen Catherine Connolly, but it was incandescent. She may have been

the finest of all female players as the first woman to win the Grand Slam.

Nicknamed "Little Mo" for her big-gunning, unerring groundstrokes (an allusion to "Big Mo," the U.S. battleship *Missouri*), she was devastating from the baseline, and seldom needed to go to the net. A small and compact right-hander (5-foot-4, 120 lbs), she won her nine major singles championships as a teenager: three successive Wimbledons, 1952-54, and U.S. titles at Forest Hills, 1951–53, plus two French titles 1953-54 and an Australian in 1953. At 16 years, 11 months, she was the youngest U.S. champ ever until Tracy Austin won in 1979 at 16 years, nine months. In addition, Connolly won three other American titles and held the No. 1 U.S. ranking in 1951-53. She was undisputed world No. 1 from 1952 to 1954. Connolly was born Sept. 17, 1934, in San Diego, Calif., and grew up there. She was a pupil of Eleanor "Teach" Tennant, an instructor who had guided a previous world champ, Alice Marble. Connolly first came East in 1949 to win the U.S. junior title and repeated in 1950. She entered Forest Hills both years; losing in the second round. But she would soon have the world under her right thumb while still technically a junior, not yet 19, an obstreperous intruder overthrowing the established order of older women. Her third time around at the U.S. biggie, seeded No. 4, she ran six games from 1-4 down in the first set while beating top-seeded, 26-year-old Doris Hart, 6-4, 6-4, in a semi halted by rain after the first game of the second, and resumed the following day. A day after that completion, Maureen was given a harder time by No. 2-seeded 24-year-old Shirley Fry, but her long-range shelling was decisive, 6-3, 1-6, 6-4.

A cheerful and sporting competitor, she crushed the opposition, never losing an important match, only occasionally losing a set. She helped the U.S. beat Britain in the Wightman Cup matches of 1951-54, winning all seven of her singles.

Fifteen years after Don Budge scored the first Grand Slam, Connolly traveled the same route in 1953. Winning all the major singles championships (Australian, French, Wimbledon, U.S.) within a calendar year, she achieved the first female Slam. She lost only one set in doing so. Following the Aussie triumph over doubles partner and fellow Californian, Julie Sampson, 6-3, 6-2, Maureen had to get past Hart thrice: 6-2, 6-4 at the French, 8-6, 7-5 at Wimbledon, 6-2, 6-4 in the home stretch. That season, she won 10 of 12 tournaments on a 61-2 match record. By winning the three French titles in 1954—singles, doubles with Aussie Nell Hopman, her mentor after splitting from Tennant, and mixed with Lew Hoad—she became the fourth of five players to triple in Paris.

Nobody has measured up to her perfect record in the majors after early U.S. defeats in 1949-50. She sailed through nine successive majors (three U.S., three Wimbledons, two French, one Australian), unbeaten in 50 matches. The closest to that were four other greats who won six straight: Budge, 1937-38; Margaret Court, 1969-70, Martina Navratilova, 1983-84; Steffi Graf 1995-96. Helen Wills Moody, who played irregularly, won 15 straight majors between 1924 and 1933.

In 1954, her playing career was ended with heartbreaking suddenness, aborted by an unusual traffic accident, not long after she won her last title, the U.S. Clay singles. While riding her horse, Col. Merryboy, a gift from San Diego admirers, she was struck by a truck, severely injuring a leg. "I knew immediately I'd never play again," she said. By then, she was Mrs. Norman Brinker, wife of a U.S. Olympic equestrian. She recovered sufficiently to give tennis instruction, and helped a number of players with their games. But at 34, she died June 21, 1969, of cancer in Dallas.

She was inducted into the Hall of Fame in 1968 and is memorialized by the Maureen Connolly Brinker Cup, an international team competition between the U.S. and Britain for girls under 21.

"Whenever a great player comes along you have to ask, 'could she have beaten Maureen?'" That was the standard of Lance Tingay, the Hall of Fame tennis correspondent of the *Daily Telegraph* of London. "In every case the answer is, I think not."

MAJOR TITLES (12)—Australian singles, 1953; French singles, 1953, 1954; Wimbledon singles, 1952, 1953. 1954; U.S. singles, 1951, 1952, 1953; Australian doubles, 1953; French doubles, 1954; French mixed, 1954. **OTHER U.S. TITLES** (3)—Clay Court singles, 1953-54; Clay Court doubles, 1954, with Doris Hart. **WIGHTMAN CUP**—1951-52-53-54, 7-0 singles, 2-0 doubles. **SINGLES RECORD IN THE MAJORS**—Australian (5-0). French (10-0), Wimbledon (18-0), U.S. (19-2).

Jimmy Connors
United States (1952—)
Hall of Fame—1998

A marvel of longevity and self-motivation, he is (as onetime agent Bill Riordan boasted) "the one and only James Scott Connors."

Fiery of temperament and shotmaking, this lefty with a two-fisted backhand pounded foes for more than two professional decades in rip-roaring baseline style, a rag doll throwing himself into his groundies with utter gusto. Often controversial, he fought verbally with opponents, officials and the crowd.

Considered a feisty wiseguy in his earlier days, he eventually became a respected elder. The championships, honors and prize money piled up, but not as high as his zeal as he continued to compete forcefully against much younger men into his 41st year and through the 1992 season when he roused galleries in Paris, London and New York and compiled a 17-15 match record, ending the season with a remarkable No. 83 ranking.

Turning pro in 1972, Jimmy won his first title that year at Jacksonville, Fla., and continued at a prodigious pace, arriving at his 109th—a male pro record—in 1989 by winning in Tel Aviv, Israel. He attained 54 other finals and played more tournaments (901) and won more matches (1,337-285, an .824 average), than any other male pro, and, in fact, never announced his retirement. He also won 19 doubles titles, two of them majors: Wimbledon in 1973, and the U.S. Open in 1975, both with Ilie Nastase. Having lost a cameo first-rounder in Atlanta in 1996, he held an ATP ranking until age 44, having been No. 1 five straight years, 1974-78, an Open era record until surpassed by Sampras' six, 1993-98.

His specialty has been the U.S. Open (five titles), where he was singular in winning on all three surfaces: grass (1974) and clay (1976) at Forest Hills, and hard (1978, 1982, 1983) at Flushing Meadow. His 98 Open singles match wins are a men's record.

He also won Wimbledon twice (1974 and 1982) and the Australian (1974) for a total of eight singles majors.

Perhaps 1991 was the most extraordinary year of his progression toward a Hall of Fame berth in 1998. His career seemed over. Troubled by a deteriorated left wrist, he had played (and lost) only three matches in 1990, dropping to No. 936 in the rankings. However, surgery restored him, and he came back smoking, playing 14 tournaments and climaxing with a phenomenal semifinal finish (his 14th) at the U.S. Open.

His first and second-round victories as a Wimbledon wild card raised his tournament male record to 84 match wins. Wild-carded again at Flushing, because of a No. 174 ranking, Jimmy exploded by beating Patrick McEnroe from two sets down as well as Michael Schapers and No. 10 seed Karel Novacek in straight sets. Then he celebrated his 39th birthday in a tumultuous victory over Aaron Krickstein, soaring from 2-5 in the fifth set to win in a stirring tie-breaker, 3-6, 7-5 (10-8), 1-6, 6-3, 7-6 (7-4). Then he beat Paul Haarhuis from a set and a break down, 4-6, 7-6 (7-3), 6-4, 6-2, but was outgunned at last by Jim Courier 6-3, 6-3, 6-2. He was the oldest semifinalist since 39-year-old Rosewall lost the title match to none other than James himself 17 years before. Although Stefan Edberg won the title, it was Connors' Open in the public eye.

Ever a sensational celebrator of his own birthday (he won 10 of 11 matches on that day at the U.S. Open), Jimmy took the cake—literally, delivered on court—in 1992 on his 40th by beating Jaime Oncins of Brazil 6-1, 6-2, 6-3, notching a tournament-record 98th match win.

He was raised to be a tennis player by his mother, a teaching pro named Gloria Thompson Connors, and "Two Mom," grandmother Bertha Thompson. Connors grew up in Belleville, Ill., across the Mississippi from St. Louis. Although he was always smaller than his contemporaries on his way up the ladder, he made up for that through determination and grit. He played in his first U.S. Championship, the U.S. boys' 11-and-under of 1961, when he was only eight. He was born Sept. 2, 1952, in East St. Louis, Ill., and claimed to have begun playing when he was two. "My mother rolled balls to me, and I swung at them. I held the racket with both hands because that was the only way I could lift it."

Connors, who grew to 5-foot-10, 155 pounds, became known as a maverick when he refused to join the ATP (Association of Tennis Pros) in 1972, the then-new union embracing most male professionals, and avoided the mainstream of pro tennis to play in and dominate a series of smaller tournaments organized by Bill Riordan, his manager, a clever promoter.

In 1974, he and Riordan began bringing lawsuits, eventually amounting to $10 million, against the ATP and its president, Arthur Ashe, for allegedly restricting his freedom in the game. It stemmed from Connors' banning from the French Open in 1974 after he had signed a contract to play WTT (World Team Tennis) for Baltimore. Connors had sought to enter the French, the only major championship he did not win that year. But because the ATP and the French administration opposed WTT—it conflicted with their tournaments—the entries of WTT players were refused. The 1975 Wimbledon final, then, was unique, a duel between opponents in a lawsuit. Ashe won, and shortly thereafter Connors dropped the suits, and parted with Riordan.

Deprived unfairly by the French of a chance for a second leg on what might have been a Grand Slam, Connors nevertheless enjoyed in 1974 one of the finest seasons ever, the best by an American since Tony Trabert's 1955. Connors lost only four matches in 20 tournaments, while winning 99.

Among the 14 tournaments he won—a record for American male pros—were the Australian, Wimbledon, South African, U.S. at Forest Hills, U.S. Clay Court and U.S. Indoor. He was clearly No. 1, a status he enjoyed from July of 1974, for 159 straight weeks. He was there a total of 263 weeks, second only to Ivan Lendl's 269.

Although he trailed his foremost rivals head-to-head—Bjorn Borg, 7-10; John McEnroe, 13-20; Lendl, 13-22—he had great moments at their expense. He saved four set points to win a thrilling and vital 11-9 third-set tie-breaker while beating Borg in the 1976 U.S. final at Forest Hills, 6-4, 3-6, 7-6 (11-9), 6-4, and stunned the Swede (his conqueror at Wimbledon) to take the inaugural Flushing Meadows final in 1978, 6-4, 6-2, 6-2. Three points from defeat in the fourth-set tie-breaker, he startled McEnroe to win Wimbledon in five sets in 1982, 3-6, 6-3, 6-7 (2-7), 7-6 (7-5), 6-4, bridging a gap of eight years between titles there. Jimmy's incredible serve returning jolted Lendl in the 1982 and 1983 U.S. Open finals, 6-3, 6-2, 4-6, 6-4, and 6-3, 6-7 (2-7), 7-5, 6-0.

By winning the U.S. Indoor singles three straight years (1973-75) he tied a record set by Gus Touchard (1913-15). He made this his most successful tourney, adding wins in 1978-79, 83-84 for a record total of seven. At the U.S. Clay Court in 1974, 76, 78-79, his four titles were the most since Frank Parker's five between 1933 and 1947.

Connors seemed to delight in keeping the public off-balance. He annoyed numerous tennis fans in the U.S. with his sometimes vulgar on-court behavior, and his refusal to play Davis Cup (except briefly during the 1976, 81, 84 seasons). He was booed at Wimbledon—a rare show of disapproval there—for snubbing the Parade of Champions on the first day of the Centenary in 1977.

After irritating sponsors and tennis officials by shunning the climactic Masters for three years, Connors entered and won the 1977 event over Borg, 6-4, 1-6, 6-4 having qualified by finishing among the top eight in the worldwide Grand Prix series.

His two crushing final-round victories over Ken Rosewall in 1974 (6-1, 6-1, 6-4 at Wimbledon, and 6-1, 6-0, 6-1, at Forest Hills) made Connors seem invincible. His manager, Riordan, proclaimed Jimmy "heavyweight champion of tennis," and arranged a series of challenges over three years at Las Vegas and Puerto Rico in which Connors retained his "title" by defeating Rod Laver, John Newcombe, Manolo Orantes and Nastase. Connors grossed over a million dollars from television rights for those four exhibitions.

Beginning in 1974, Connors played in five successive U.S. finals, the first man to do so since Bill Tilden, who was in eight between 1918 and 1925. He was the first since Fred Perry (1933-34, 36) to win the U.S. title three years. Connors was jolted in the finals by Spanish-speaking lefties, Orantes in 1975, 6-4, 6-3, 6-3, and Guillermo Vilas, 2-6, 6-3, 7-6 (7-4), 6-0, in 1977, striking the last ball, an error, in championship play in Forest Hills Stadium.

Jimmy went to college one year at the University of California at Los Angeles, where he won the National Intercollegiate Singles in 1971 and attained All-American status.

It was in 1973 that he made his first big splash by winning the U.S. Pro Singles, his first significant title, at 20, toppling Ashe, the favorite, in a five-set final, 6-3, 4-6, 6-4, 3-6. 6-2. Ashe said, "I've played them all, and I never saw anybody hit the ball so hard for so long as Jimmy did." That year Connors was ranked co-No. 1 in the U.S. with Stan Smith, but was No. 1 alone seven other years (1974, 76-77-78, 82, 86-87), and in the U.S. Top 10 a record 20 times. During his 21-year pro career, he was in the world's Top 10 a record 16 times, 11 other than his No. 1's: No. 3 in 1973, 80-81, 83; No. 2 in 1979, 82, 84; No. 4 in 1985, 87; No. 8 in 1986; No. 7 in 1988. His prize money amounted to $8,641,040. Jimmy, married with two children, lived on profitably for several years as the mainstay of an over-35 senior tour. Although it had various sponsors, it was generally known as the "Connors Circuit."

MAJOR TITLES (10)—Australian singles, 1974; Wimbledon singles, 1974, 1982; U.S. singles, 1974, 1976, 1978, 1982, 1983; Wimbledon doubles, 1973; U.S. doubles, 1975. OTHER U.S. TITLES (15)—Indoor singles, 1973, 1974, 1975, 1976, 1979, 1983, 1984; Clay Court singles, 1974, 1976, 1978, 1979; Indoor doubles, 1974, with Frew McMillan; 1975, with Ilie Nastase; Clay Court doubles, 1974, with Nastase; Pro singles, 1973. DAVIS, CUP—1976, 1981, 1984, 10-3 singles. SINGLES RECORD IN THE MAJORS—Australian (10-1), French (40-13), Wimbledon (84-18), U.S. (98-17).

Sarah Palfrey Cooke
United States (1912–1996)
Hall of Fame—1963

If any player may be said to have been the sweetheart of tennis, as Mary Pickford was of the movies, her name was Sarah Palfrey. Twice U.S. champion, Sarah Hammond Palfrey Fabyan Cooke Danzig was twice a runner-up for the title to Helen Jacobs, nine times U.S. doubles champion, and twice doubles champion at Wimbledon. She was an international attraction on both sides of the Atlantic and west to the Pacific.

Born Sept. 18, 1912, in Sharon, Mass., she was a carefully-reared girl of upper-register Boston and a protege of Hazel Hotchkiss Wightman. The galleries loved her radiant smile and her unfailing graciousness in triumph and defeat alike, and they marveled at the cleverness and dispatch she used in the volleying position and at the execution of her sweeping backhand. She was one of the most accomplished performers around the net, thanks in part to the instruction of Wightman, a pioneer in introducing the volley as a major component of the women's game. A slip of a girl (5-foot-4, 116 lbs), Sarah was remarkable in the way she stood up to the more powerful hitters.

Sarah was so prized as a doubles partner in the 1930s and 1940s that she had the pick of the best. Seven times in Wightman Cup she teamed with Jacobs, three times with Alice Marble and once with Helen Wills Moody. But prestige comes from superiority in singles play, and in this the artful right-hander ranked no fewer than 13 times in the U.S. Top 10. She was No. 1, No. 2 or No. 3 seven times. She was in the world's Top 10 six times between 1933 and 1939, No. 4 in 1934.

A 14-year-old Sarah made her Forest Hills debut in 1927 (doubles and mixed), but not until her thirteenth campaign in 1941 did she win the singles, over Pauline Betz, 7-5, 6-2. She joyfully recalled her initial trip abroad, so different from the casual jet-jaunting of today: "It was 1930, and I was 17. My mother and a sister went with me aboard the liner *Scythia*. We dressed for dinner and danced away every night."

Unable to defend her 1941 U.S. singles title because of pregnancy and wartime family commitments to her husband, naval officer Elwood Cooke (1939 Wimbledon finalist to Bobby Riggs), Sarah made an extraordinary comeback to the Forest Hills scene in 1945 to win again, over Betz, 3-6, 8-6, 6-4, this time as a mother on the verge of her 33rd birthday. She mirrored her idol Wightman in this, too, becoming only the second to win the U.S. after bearing a child, the third of six to do so after winning a major.

"She was a thorn for me," says four-time champ Pauline Betz Addie, recalling that but for Sarah, she might well have run a record six straight championships. Pauline was in six successive finals. "That 1945 final was the best I played, but still Sarah beat me with her volleying." She won the last three games from a service break down.

An oddity was Sarah's appearance on a male championship honor roll. Because of the wartime man-power crisis, she and husband Elwood were permitted to enter the men's doubles of the Tri-State Championships in Cincinnati. They went to the 1945 final, losing to Hal Surface and Hall of Famer Bill Talbert. But they did win the U.S. Clay Court mixed together that year, the only married couple to win a U.S. title, 7-5, 4-6, 6-3, over Betz and Talbert.

A brood of tennis prodigies were the five Palfrey sisters, each of whom won at least one U.S. junior title, but Sarah was the one to achieve international renown. After her playing career, she was a successful business executive (as Mrs. Jerry Danzig in New York), and wrote on tennis in books and magazines.

Along with Alice Marble, she lobbied the USTA to remove the color bar and allow future Hall of Farner Althea Gibson to play at the upper level amid whites in 1950. "They were calmly persuasive, had clout as ex-champs, and got Althea into the U.S. Championships in 1950," said Gladys Heldman, founder of the women's pro tour. She was voted into the Hall of Fame in 1963, and died Feb. 27, 1996, in New York.

MAJOR TITLES (18)—U.S. singles, 1941, 1945; Wimbledon doubles, 1938, 1939; U.S. doubles, 1930, 1932, 1934, 1935, 1937, 1938, 1939, 1940, 1941; French mixed, 1939; U.S. mixed, 1932, 1935, 1937, 1941. OTHER U.S. TITLES (10)—Clay Court singles, 1945; Indoor singles, 1940; Indoor doubles, 1928, 1929, 1930, 1931, 1933, with Hazel Hotchkiss Wightman; Indoor mixed, 1931, with Larry Rice; 1933, with G. Holmes Perkins; Clay Court mixed, 1945, with husband Elwood Cooke. WIGHTMAN CUP—1930, 1931, 1932, 1933, 1934, 1935, 1936, 1937, 1938, 1939, 7-4 singles, 7-2 doubles. SINGLES RECORD IN THE MAJORS—French (2-2), Wimbledon (16-6), U.S. (41-14)

Ashley Cooper
Australia (1936—)
Hall of Fame—1991

Among the seemingly endless platoon of Aussies who were to dominate the world after Frank Sedgman showed them how,

handsome, dark-haired Ashley John Cooper was the third of their number to win Wimbledon (1958) and the fourth to capture the U.S. (also in 1958). Because he turned pro shortly after those successes, the right-handed Ashley's career in the public eye was brief though very productive. His last two amateur years, 1957 and 1958, could compare well to anyone's: six finals and four championships out of eight major starts, and two semis at the French, the only ones he didn't win.

An athletic 5-foot-10, he was of an attacking mindset, like the others of his tribe, a thorough, smooth, if not spectacular, stroker in attaining his goals at the net. He also won the Australian championship in 1958, one of only 10 men to grab three majors in one year. But whatever hopes he had for a Grand Slam were dashed in Paris by Chile's Luis Ayala, 9-11, 4-6, 6-4, 6-2, 7-5. Still, he had one of the finest years with a 25-1 match record in the majors.

Cooper, who had lost the 1957 Wimbledon final to Lew Hoad, was upset in the U.S. final by unseeded Mal Anderson, but they got together three months later to successfully defend the Davis Cup against the U.S., 3-2. Despite an ankle injury incurred during their final at Forest Hills in 1958, Cooper regrouped and came from behind to beat Anderson, 6-2, 3-6, 4-6, 10-8, 8-6. Cooper spent three years, 1956-58, in the world's Top 10, No. 1 the last two years. He was born Sept. 15, 1936, in Melbourne, and entered the Hall of Fame in 1991.

MAJOR TITLES (8)—Australian singles, 1957, 1958; Wimbledon singles, 1958; U.S. singles. 1958; Australian doubles, 1958; French doubles, 1957-58; U.S. doubles, 1957. **DAVIS CUP**—1957-58, 2-2 singles. **SINGLES RECORD IN THE MAJORS**—Australian (16-3), French (13-3), Wimbledon (19-4), U.S. (20-4)

Jim Courier
United States (1970—)
Hall of Fame—2005

He had his own deadly dance—the Backside Boogie.

That was Jim Courier, shuffling swiftly to his left to strike with a dynamite inside-out forehand. It's a fairly standard tactic now, but it was Courier who first made it pay off in substantial dividends: four major championships, and in 1992 the No. 1 world ranking. He finished in the ATP top 10 for three other years: Nos. 2, 3 and 8 in 1991, 93, 95. And also was in the U.S. top 10 eight times between 1991 and 1998, No. 1 in 1991-92.

Born Aug. 17, 1970, Sanford, Florida, as James Spencer Courier, he grew up in Dade City, Florida. Turned pro in 1988 while a hopeful at Nick Bollettieri's tennis boot camp, and the next year began his romance with French earth by jolting camp-mate, No. 5 seed Andre Agassi, 7-6 (9-7), 4-6, 6-3, 6-2, in the fourth round at Roland Garros.

The French returned his love, especially when he beat Agassi again for the 1991 title, 3-6, 6-4, 2-6, 6-1, 6-4, amid rain and a dust storm, then delivered his acceptance speech in French, unique for an American in Paris. "Beeg Jeem!" they called him, admiringly, awed by his solid frame (6-1, 182 lbs) and slugging both-handed backhand along with the racing forehand. He won again the following year, 7-5, 6-2, 6-1, over Czech Petr Korda, but couldn't make a fifth set service break hold up against Spain's Sergi Bru-

guera in the 1993 final, 6-4, 2-6, 6-2, 3-6, 6-3. Still, he was the lone American guy to make three straight French finals, alone, too, among Americans in holding the French (clay) and Australian (hard) titles at the same time, 1992. Jim beat Stefan Edberg 6-3, 3-6, 6-4, 6-2, in Melbourne, and dittoed in 1993, 6-2, 6-2, 2-6, 7-5, over the Swede for his fourth major.

Edberg got him in the 1991 U.S. title bout, 6-2, 6-4, 6-0, but Jim countered in a 1993 Wimbledon semi, 4-6, 6-4, 6-2, 6-4, then lost to Pete Sampras, 7-6 (7-3), 7-6 (8-6), 3-6, 6-3. It all meant that Courier appeared in every major final, a rarity that he shares with only two countrymen, Don Budge and Agassi. In winning the Italian twice—1992 over Carlos Costa of Spain, 7-6 (7-3), 6-0, 6-4; 1993 over Goran Ivanisevic of Croatia, 6-1, 6-2, 6-2—he is the only American man to win a pair in Rome and Paris.

A formidable competitor, he was a mainstay of seven U.S. Davis Cup teams, 1991-92, 94-95, 97-98-99, Cup winners in 1992 and 1995, 16-10 in singles. He was the Cup-clincher against Switzerland in '92, beating Jakob Hlasek, 6-3, 3-6, 6-3, 6-4. Thrice he won the decisive fifth match, a U.S. record: over Netherlander Jacco Eltingh in 1994, 6-3, 6-4, 4-6, 6-1; Russian Marat Safin in 1998, 0-6, 6-4, 4-6, 6-1, 6-4; Brit Greg Rusedski in 1999, 6-4, 6-7 (3-7), 6-3, 1-6, 8-6. The last, an excruciating screamer at Birmingham, England, enabled the U.S. and Australia to butt heads in a quarterfinal celebrating the 100th year of Davis Cup at its origin, Boston's Longwood Cricket Club. The U.S. was 13-1 with Jim in the lineup. The "1" was Australia in 1999—his Cup finale.

Retiring in 2000, he had won 23 singles (a finalist in nine others), 13 doubles pro titles, $14,033,132 in prize money, had a 25-match winning streak in 1992. His W-L in singles 506-237, doubles 124-97. In 2004, he founded his own sports and entertainment company, InsideOut Sports & Entertainment, and in 2005, brought champions (over 30) seniors tennis back to the United States starting the Outback Champions Series circuit, which grew global.

MAJOR TITLES (4)—Australian singles, 1992-93; French singles, 1991-92. **DAVIS CUP**—1991-92, 94-95, 97-98-99, 16-10 singles, 1-0 doubles. **SINGLES RECORD IN THE MAJORS**—Australian (35-7), French (40-9), Wimbledon (19-11), U.S. (24-10).

Jack Crawford
Australia (1908–1991)
Hall of Fame—1979

Few players so completely won the gallery as did John Herbert Crawford, called by one commentator the "most popular Wimbledon winner in history."

Indeed, Crawford, a right-hander, was an exemplary sportsman, as well as a handsome figure on the court (6-foot-1, 168 lbs) in his long, white flannels and long-sleeved shirt. And he moved easily, gracefully, over the turf with his flat-topped racket, a model of early vintage. He was in the world's Top 10 six times, 1932- 37, No. 1 in 1933.

Crawford, born March 22, 1908, in Albury, Australia, was a masterful player from the back of the court, driving the ball with length and pinpoint control with seemingly little strain. He played the classical game of solid, fluent strokes, and he played it

so well that he came within one set of completing a Grand Slam five years before Don Budge accomplished the feat of winning the four major championships in one calendar year.

Crawford's bid came in 1933, a year he won 16 tournaments, starting with a victory over American Keith Gledhill, 2-6, 7-5, 6-3, 6-2, in the Australian final. Next, Crawford won the French Championship, beating native Henri Cochet for the title, 8-6, 6-1, 6-3. At Wimbledon came a legendary final against Ellsworth Vines that Crawford won, 4-6, 11-9, 6-2, 2-6, 6-4.

Crawford, a 5-to-1 short-ender with London bookies, twice held from 0-40 in the critical second set, and came to the wire breaking Vines at love with four winners, abruptly surging to the net in the last two games. Al Laney wrote: "For superlative play on both sides, the blending of stroke and strategy, the unrelenting speed of serve and considered counterstroke, I cannot remember another to place above it."

So a reluctant, fatigued Crawford moved on to Forest Hills and the U.S. Championships with an opportunity to complete the ultimate sweep. After defeating Frank Shields 6-3, 6-4. 2-6, 6-4, in the semis, Crawford faced Fred Perry as the last obstacle in his path. Crawford lost the first set, but then won the next two and was one set away from a Slam. But his strength faded, owing in part to the asthma and insomnia he had at the time. Perry went on to victory in the next two sets, dashing Crawford's hopes, 6-3, 11-13, 4-6, 6-0, 6-1.

Still, the gallery loved this man—"Gentleman Jack" they called him—from Down Under. He won the championship of his country four times, and he did it all his way, seemingly never hurried, his every move appearing effortless, his serve belonging in a picture book. Jack Crawford was one of the greats of his time while playing tennis in the style of a gentleman of the old school.

Like most Aussies he got immense pleasure from Davis Cup, selected first in 1928, and was proud of being a member of the victorious 1939 team although he didn't play. In 1936, Jack led the team to a 3-2 upset of the U.S. in Philadelphia as he beat Wilmer Allison in the decider, 4-6, 6-3, 4-6, 6-2, 6-2. A victory over Germany, with him winning both singles, put the first Down Under entry as Australia (no longer Australasia) into the Cup round since 1924. But Britain resisted, 3-2, as Jack was beaten by long-time rival Perry in the fifth match, 6-2, 6-3, 6-3.

When he beat Perry to win the 1935 Australian, 2-6, 6-4, 6-4, 6-4, Jack was taking part in his 10th straight major final (he didn't enter the U.S. in 1934), extraordinary consistency. (Swiss Roger Federer was involved in 10 in a row, a streak that caught Crawford but was ended by his semis loss to Novak Djokovic at the Australian of 2008.) Bill Tilden was in 10 straight (1918—26), but his forays included only U.S. and Wimbledon. Crawford's seventh Aussie singles final, a record later tied by Roy Emerson, was lost in 1940 to Adrian Quist, but, at 32, he did knock off defending champ John Bromwich in the semis.

He took delight in winning three straight Aussie mixed titles with his wife, Marjorie Cox Crawford, 1931-33. They were a unique wedded couple in appearing in major finals, the Australian, simultaneously in 1931, he winning, over Harry Hopman, 6-4, 6-2, 2-6, 6-1, she losing to Coral Buttsworth, 1-6, 6-3, 6-4.

He entered the Hall of Fame in 1979, and died Sept. 10, 1991, in Sydney.

MAJOR TITLES (17)—Australian singles, 1931, 1932, 1933, 1935; French singles, 1933; Wimbledon singles, 1933; Australian doubles, 1929, 1930, 1932, 1935; French doubles, 1935; Wimbledon doubles, 1935; Australian mixed 1931, 1932, 1933; French mixed, 1933; Wimbledon mixed, 1930. DAVIS CUP—1928, 1930, 1932, 1933, 1934, 1935, 1936, 1937, 23-16 singles, 13-5 doubles. SINGLES RECORD IN THE MAJORS—Australian (52-15), French (19-4), Wimbledon (36-8), U.S. (10-4).

Joe Cullman
United States (1912–2004)
Hall of Fame—1990—Contributor

A lifelong love of the game led Joseph Frederick Cullman III to become a working angel in tennis, a moonlighter away from his principal position as chairman and CEO of the Philip Morris Co. As such, he benefitted tennis extraordinarily in several ways. He was chairman of the U.S. Open at Forest Hills in 1969 and 1970, formative years, and was instrumental in getting the original Open in 1968 televised.

In 1970, at the behest of another Hall of Fame member, Gladys Heldman, he came to the financial and spiritual rescue of the women, up to then second-class citizens of tournament tennis. With the backing of one of his products, Virginia Slims, a separate women's professional circuit was born. It continues as the WTA Tour.

He was president and chairman of the International Tennis Hall of Fame from 1982-88, a period during which the Hall's home, the revered and historic Newport Casino, made a recovery from years of decline, and became a sound and viable institution. A Yale alumnus, he built a tennis complex, the Cullman Center, for his alma mater. Joe was a New Yorker, born there April 9, 1912, and entered the Hall of Fame in 1990. He died April 30, 2004 in New York City.

Allison Danzig
United States (1898–1987)
Hall of Fame—1968—Journalist

The familiar and authoritative identification that topped *New York Times* stories for 45 years—By Allison Danzig—was reassuring to readers until his retirement in 1967. Before that he was a sportswriter for the *Brooklyn Eagle*, developing an incisive, perceptive style that made him the widest regarded literary voice of the game in the U.S. Al Danzig, the first journalist to enter the Hall of Fame (1968), was a thoroughgoing gentleman respected throughout the game and his profession. He covered the game from its first great impact during the Tilden, Wills and Lenglen days of the 1920s to the dawn of the Open era, and also was a nationally known chronicler of college football, rowing and the Olympic Games.

He was one of the few who could write knowledgeably about court tennis, ancestor of lawn tennis. Born in Waco, Texas, on Feb. 27, 1898, he graduated from Cornell, where he played football despite a diminutive stature, and served in the U.S. Army during World War I.

He was amused to tell about "my criminal past." At age 9, he was arrested by a sheriff in Waco who caught him peeking at a minor league baseball game through a hole in the fence, presumably cheating management of an admission. "I never saw my father, a peaceful man, so angry when he came to get me released. He told that sheriff a few things that scorched his ears. Of course later in life I had a press card, and walked right in to games."

Al became a New Yorker following college, but kept Texas in his speech, and in the kitchen. This soft-spoken man was celebrated for his torrid chili. Always immaculately turned out—coat and tie whatever the summer temperature on the Eastern grass circuit—he was generous in helping young reporters and had the respect of generations of players. He wrote books on tennis, football, the Olympics and court tennis. Danzig died Jan. 27, 1987, in Ridgewood, N.J.

In 1963, he was the first recipient of the Danzig Award, established in his name by the Longwood Cricket Club in Boston to honor leading tennis writers, and has been presented periodically.

Herman David
Great Britain (1905–1974)
Hall of Fame—1998—Administrator

History will view Herman David as the man who, through sheer force of will and belief, initiated Open tennis.

As chairman of the Diamond Development Company, Herman was acknowledged as a world expert on industrial diamonds. Exposing fakes was second nature to him. Born in Birmingham, England, June 26, 1905, Herman had already played county tennis for Warwickshire before going up to New College, Oxford to read history. Having earned his blue, he was selected for Davis Cup duty in Britain's first round tie versus Poland in 1932 and won both his singles.

After serving with the RAF as an operations controller during World War II, Herman had captained British Davis Cup teams in the 1950s and knew, as everyone close to the game did, that the unworkable amateur rules were being openly flouted by leading players in every country.

When he became chairman of the All England Club in 1959, it was inevitable that Herman would work fearlessly to expose the flaws in the game he loved. At an extraordinary General Meeting of the club that year, the members had carried a motion that called upon the LTA (Lawn Tennis Association of Britain) to stage an "Open" Championship in 1960. At that stage, Britain's governing body were not yet ready to take precipitate action that might have resulted in expulsion from the International Tennis Federation.

The narrow failure of a motion to adopt Open tennis at the ITF's annual meeting in 1961 persuaded David that he would have to work behind the scenes. By 1967, he was satisfied that the climate was right. The eight-man professional tournament staged on Wimbledon's Centre Court one month after that year's Championships was a shot across the bow of the ITF. When Rod Laver beat Ken Rosewall in a superb final that was broadcast by BBC2 to launch color television in Britain, the world realized what they had been missing.

This was the first time that professionals had been allowed to compete in this traditional amateur stronghold. It sent shock waves around the world.

At the All England Club's annual meeting in December of 1967, David proposed that the following year's Championships should be open to all players, amateurs and professionals. "Amateur tennis has become a living lie," he said, a phrase which accurately reflected the feelings of the members who carried the motion unanimously. By now, opinions at the LTA had altered. At their general meeting a few days later the LTA endorsed the club's stand and gave approval for an open Wimbledon in 1968.

At last, Herman David's dream had been realized. Tennis had finally become an honest sport. He died Feb. 25, 1974, at his home in Wimbledon, and was elevated to the Hall in 1998.

—*John Barrett*

Sven Davidson
Sweden (1928–2008)
Hall of Fame—2007

Before Borg, there was Davidson.

Sven Viktor Davidson, to be precise, who was, during the month of Bjorn Borg's birth, flirting in Paris with the possibility of giving Sweden its initial major tennis championship, the prize that Borg eventually would make his private property: the French.

Davidson didn't quite make it in 1956. He ran into an Australian whirlwind, Lew Hoad, in the final, 6-3, 6-4, 6-4. In the semifinal, Sven stopped another Aussie Ashley Cooper, 6-4, 2-6, 2-6, 6-2, 6-3. (All three would be tapped for the Hall of Fame, Davidson in 2007.)

This defeat was doubly disappointing to the slender, good humored 6-foot-2, 175 pound Swede because he had also lost the 1955 final, and to yet another future lodge brother, Tony Trabert, 2-6, 6-1, 6-4, 6-2. That was after bringing down the 1950 champ, Budge Patty in the quarters, 7-5, 10-8, 6-0, and Beppe Merlo, 12-10, 6-3, 6-3.

But, days from his 29th birthday in 1957, Sven broke the Paris combination at last, 6-3, 6-4, 6-4, over the persistent baseliner Herbie Flam, and had the title at Stade Roland Garros most coveted by Europeans. Not for another 17 years, until 18-year-old Borg won the first of his six, did another Swede hug the trophy. Davidson had to battle through 12 sets to attain the final: 6-3, 6-4, 7-5, over the homeboy, Paul Remy, 6-2, 6-2, 4-6, 6-2, over Belgium's Davis Cup stalwart Jackie Brichant, and another full-distance squirmer with Aussie Cooper, 6-4, 2-6, 2-6, 6-2, 6-3.

A congratulatory telegram arrived from King Gustav VI of Sweden. A friend, Baron Gottfried von Cramm (winner of the title two decades previously, a Hall of Famer in 1977), had a jeroboam of champagne and a mountain of caviar awaiting for victorious tasting in a suite at the Ritz that he shared with then-wife Barbara Hutton, one of the world's wealthiest residents. "No prize money, but not too bad," recalls Davidson.

"You do everything well but serving," von Cramm said, advising, "Practice serving."

"That's too boring," said Sven.

That was the last time Sven saw Paris, as a player. He did not defend. But he wasn't quite through. There was Wimbledon in 1958, a chance to show that Swedes could win on grass, too. That he did, in the men's doubles alongside countryman Ulf Schmidt. As the the only Swedes to take the doubles (until Mats Wilander and Joakim Nystrom in 1986), they were fond of volleying, not grassophobes—Ulf had made the 1956-57 quarterfinals, Sven the semis in1957 and the quarters in 1955 and 1958. Unseeded, they marched through six matches on the loss of two sets, breaking up an Australian monopoly (seven of the eight previous titles) by downing the top-seeded Down Under mates Ashley Cooper and Neale Fraser, 6-4, 6-4, 8-6. The King sent another "Hurrah!" telegram. English Princess Marina presented the trophies, and they bowed.

A righthander born July 13, 1928, in Boras, a small Swedish manufacturing town, he literally grew up on a tennis court. His father was a groundsman at the local club, and his older brother Kurt, 10, insisted that five year-old Sven play with him because nobody else would. Years later, 1958, they won the Swedish national doubles (limited to citizens). "Sven was never so tired. He had to cover the whole court," laughs his American wife, Mary. What else would a big brother expect from a Wimbledon champ?

Davidson finally turned pro in 1975 to have some fun touring with comradely rivals, on promoter Al Bunis's Grand Champions tour.

He was one of Sweden's foremost Davis Cuppers, playing 12 years from 1950, posting a record of 39-14 singles and 23-9 doubles. Teams he played on reached the final four thrice, 1950-51, 54, and were 61-10.

Besides his two major titles, he made U.S. semifinals in 1957 and won 46 other amateur singles championships in 18 different countries. Give him a plane ticket and he'd be there—including the French Indoor in 1957; the Swedish title in 1951; the British Hard Courts in 1955; the Canadian title in 1957; the U.S. Indoor in 1954 over Dane Kurt Nielsen 3-6, 6-1, 6-1, 6-4.

MAJOR TITLES (2)—French singles 1957, Wimbledon doubles, 1958. **Davis Cup**—1950-1960, 39-14 in singles, 23-9 in doubles.

Dwight Davis
United States (1879–1945)
Hall of Fame—1956

A left-handed, big-serving Harvardian who won the Intercollegiate title in 1899, 6-foot, 190-pound Dwight Filley Davis ranked in the U.S. Top 10 four times between 1898 and 1901, No. 2 in 1899 and 1900. But he is best known for launching in 1900 the great worldwide team competition that bears his name: The Davis Cup. He intended for it to be called the International Lawn Tennis Challenge Trophy when he purchased the silver bowl at the Boston jeweler, Shreve, Crump & Low. His fellow members at Longwood Cricket Club, where the inaugural was staged in 1900, jocularly referred to it as "Dwight's pot." Soon, just-plain-Davis Cup was the accepted name.

The original U.S. team was a Harvard production, Davis as playing-captain. He and schoolmates Malcolm Whitman and Holcombe Ward shared a 3-0 victory over the British Isles in 1900, the founder in two of the three: beating Ernest Black, 4-6, 6-2, 6-4, 6-4, on opening day, and clinching alongside Ward over Herbert Roper Barrett and Black, 6-4, 6-4, 6-4.

Davis went on to a distinguished career as a philanthropist, member of President Coolidge's cabinet as Secretary of War, and also served his country as governor-general of the Philippines. He was born in St. Louis July 5, 1879, where a tennis center is named for him, and died Nov. 28, 1945, in Washington, D.C. He was inducted into the Hall of Fame in 1956.

MAJOR TITLES (3)—U.S. doubles 1899, 1900, 1901, **OTHER U.S. TITLES** (2)—Intercollegiate singles, 1899; Intercollegiate doubles, 1899, with Holcombe Ward. **DAVIS CUP**—1900, 1902, 1-0 singles, 1-1 doubles. **SINGLES RECORD IN THE MAJORS**—U.S. (16-7).

Donald Lundy Dell
United States (1938–)
Hall of Fame—2009—Contributor

Donald Dell made his mark in tennis in many different avenues—as a player, as an undefeated Davis Cup captain for the United States, as a founder of ATP as a TV commentator and as seminal tennis agent. He was born in Savannah, Ga., on June 17, 1938. He was a right-handed player (6 ft 2, 170 lbs.) and was a Top 10 American player in 1960-1962 (No. 9, 1960; No. 5, 1961; No. 7, 1962) and played on the U.S. Davis Cup team in 1961 and 1963. He won seven amateur singles titles and his best showing in a major came in reaching the quarterfinals of the U.S. Championships in 1961. He was elevated to position of U.S. Davis Cup captain in 1968 where he steered his group of players, led by Stan Smith and Arthur Ashe, to the title, ending Australia's xx-year hold on the sterling silver trophy. He captained the U.S. to the title again a year later in 1969 before standing down with a perfect xx-xx record as U.S. skipper. Dell was one of the first professional sports agents, having represented players such as Arthur Ashe, Stan Smith, Jimmy Connors, Ivan Lendl, Andy Roddick among others. After graduating from Yale in 1960 and Virginia Law School in 1963, he founded the management firm ProServ at the dawn of the Open era of professional tennis in 1970. He also served as a television commentator for PBS, NBC and others since 1971.

Lottie Dod
Great Britain (1871–1960)
Hall of Fame—1983

Tall and athletic, Charlotte "Lottie" Dod became the youngest of major champions at 15 years, 10 months by winning Wimbledon in 1887, knocking off the defending champion, Blanche Bingley, 6-2, 6-0, in the challenge round. She played four other years, and never lost. In nine matches, she dropped one set though her championship foe, each time, now Mrs. Blanche Bingley Hillyard, did give her a tough match, 6-8, 6-1, 6-4, in the 1893 final. She also won three Irish titles: singles and mixed in 1887, doubles in 1892.

She served underhand but may have had an edge in attire, permitted as a schoolgirl to wear a shorter, unemcumbering skirt. Lottie was exceptional at ice skating, archery (an Olympic silver medalist in 1908), field hockey and golf. She represented Britain in international hockey in 1889 and 1890, and won the British Ladies Golf Championship in 1904 at Troon, defeating May Hezlet in the final, 1-up. Although no one has come close to taking her title as youngest singles champ, 15-year-old Martina Hingis became the youngest trophy holder, winning the 1996 doubles with Helena Sukova three days younger than Lottie.

Born Sept. 24, 1871, in Lower Bebington, England, she died June 27, 1960, in Sway, England and entered the Hall of Fame in 1983.

MAJOR TITLES (5)—Wimbledon singles 1887, 1888, 1891, 1892, 1893. **SINGLES RECORD IN THE MAJORS**—Wimbledon (9-0)

Johnny Doeg
United States (1908–1978)
Hall of Fame—1962

As the fourth left-handed U.S. champ (following Bob Wrenn, Beals Wright, Lindley Murray), John Thomas Godfray Hope Doeg hit the title jackpot in 1930 as the No. 6 seed. As a collateral exploit, he exploded 28 aces in the semis to thwart top-seeded Bill Tilden's fervent bid for a record eighth title, 10-8, 6-3, 3-6, 12-10. That was Big Bill's Forest Hills farewell. But there was more to Doeg's championship than that. His was a strenuous serve-and-volleying rush to the prize, a determination to keep pressure on foes with incessant in-your-face forays to the net. Quite different from his baselining Aunt May (Sutton), who'd won the women's title 26 years before.

But at 6-foot-1, 170 lbs, 21-year-old blond Doeg could keep the pounding going. He lost seven sets in six matches, two to Harvard football All-American Barry Wood at the outset, and two more in the quarters to Frank Hunter, 11-13, 6-4, 3-6, 6-2, 6-4. He got past the last-hurrahing 37-year-old Tilden, the Wimbledon champ (Doeg had lost there in the semis to Wilmer Allison), and was fiercely opposed by the No. 11 seed, 19-year-old Frank Shields. Refusing to bend in the record-length closing set of a major singles final, Doeg won, 10-8, 1-6, 6-4, 16-14. An ace cancelled Shields' set point at 13-14. The title won him the No. 1 U.S. ranking, No. 4 in the world, up from No. 7 in 1929. His brilliant serving, speed and spin, made him a feared foe for five years as he ranked in the U.S. Top 10 between 1927 and 1931.

Doeg and George Lott were Wimbledon doubles finalists in 1930 and won the U.S. titles of 1929 and 1930. He was the U.S. junior champ in 1926, the first of eight males to make the transition from the 18s to the adult championship. Johnny was born in Guayamas, Sonora, Mexico on Dec. 7, 1908, and grew up in California. He was a son of a Southern California champ, the former Violet Sutton.

He entered the Hall of Fame in 1962 and died April 27, 1978, in Redding, Calif.

MAJOR TITLES (3)—U.S. singles, 1930; U.S. doubles. 1929, 1930. **DAVIS CUP**—1930, 1-0 singles. **SINGLES RECORD IN THE MAJORS**—Wimbledon (5-1), U.S. (19-5).

Laurie Doherty
Great Britain (1875–1919)
Hall of Fame—1980

Laurie, or "Little Do," born Hugh Laurence Doherty, was the shorter, at 5-foot-10, younger, and probably better, of the Cambridge (Trinity College)-educated Doherty brothers who illuminated the tennis skies in their native England and at Wimbledon at the turn of the century. Although Laurie lost the 1898 Wimbledon final to Reggie, 6-3, 6-3, 2-6, 5-7, 6-1, he won the title five straight times, beginning in 1902 by evicting defender Arthur Gore, 6-4, 6-3, 3-6, 6-0, and losing only one set in the next four, to Frank Riseley, 6-4, 4-6, 6-2, 6-3, in 1906, beating the eminent Aussie Norman Brookes, 8-6, 6-2, 6-4, in 1905.

The brothers carried Britain to its first four Davis Cups, beginning in 1903, by taking it from the U.S., 4-1, in Boston after falling short, 3-2, the previous year in Brooklyn. He never lost a Cup match, winning seven singles and five doubles.

The Dohertys, who parted their dark wavy hair in the middle, also devised the more aggressive doubles formation of parting the pair, with the receiver's partner at the net, to be joined by the receiver.

As the first serious foreign contenders for the U.S. singles crown, the brothers failed in 1902 at Newport. Laurie sportingly defaulted to Reggie rather than face him in the semis, whereupon Reggie beat Malcolm Whitman in the all-corners final, 6-1, 3-6, 6-3, 6-0, but lost the challenge round to the defender, Bill Larned, 4-6, 6-2, 6-4, 8-6.

But in 1903, after Reggie returned the default courtesy to his brother in the quarters, Laurie became the initial alien male champ of the U.S., beating Bill Clothier in the all-comers, 6-3, 6-2, 6-3, and unseating Lamed, 6-0, 6-3, 10-8. The Brothers D. took the U.S. doubles both years, 1902-03, and had been gold medalists in the 1900 Olympics, winning the doubles, and Laurie taking the singles as well. Laurie was born in London, Oct. 8, 1875, and died Aug. 21, 1919, in Broadstairs, England. He accompanied his brother into the Hall of Fame in 1980.

MAJOR TITLES (16)—Wimbledon singles, 1902, 1903, 1904. 1905, 1906; U.S. singles, 1903; Wimbledon doubles, 1892, 1898, 1899, 1900, 1901, 1903, 1904, 1905; U.S. doubles, 1902, 1903. **DAVIS CUP**—1902, 1903, 1904, 1905, 1906, 7-0 singles, 5-0 doubles. **SINGLES RECORD IN THE MAJORS**—Wimbledon (21-6). U.S. (12-0).

Reggie Doherty
Great Britain (1872–1910)
Hall of Fame—1980

The appealing and dominant Doherty brothers, Reggie and Laurie, Cambridge (Trinity College) men, enhanced the popularity of tennis and Wimbledon in their homeland, England, at the turn of the century, and were the backbone of Britain's first four Davis Cup triumphs, 1903-06. Reginald Frank Doherty, the older and known as "Big Do," at 6-foot-1, only 140 pounds, was frequently ill with digestive problems, and wasn't considered as good as Laurie, but did win four straight Wimbledons (1897-1900), starting by beating Harold Mahony, 6-4, 6-4, 6-3, and defeated his sibling in the 1898 final, 6-3, 6-3, 2-6, 5-7, 6-1. In the

Doherty days, they were in 10 consecutive finals, 1897-1906, winning nine, the only interruption in 1901 when Arthur Gore beat Reggie, 4-6, 7-5, 6-4, 6-4.

Contesting a record 10 straight doubles finals together (1897-1906), they won a record eight, losing only in 1896 to the Baddeley brothers, Herbert and Wilfred, and in 1902 and 1906 to Syd Smith and Frank Riseley. Reggie, who played the left court with his brother, was in a record 11 straight doubles finals, losing with Harold Nesbit in 1897. The brothers won all five Davis Cup doubles together, clinching the 1904, 1905 and 1906 Cups. Reggie was born Oct. 14, 1872, in London and died there Dec. 29, 1910. They entered the Hall of Fame together in 1980.

MAJOR TITLES (14)—Wimbledon singles; 1897, 1898, 1899, 1900; U.S. doubles, 1902, 1903; Wimbledon doubles, 1897, 1898, 1899, 1900, 1901, 1903, 1904, 1905. **DAVIS CUP**—1902, 1903, 1904, 1905, 1906; 2-1 singles, 5-0 doubles. **SINGLES RECORD IN THE MAJORS**—Wimbledon (9-5), U.S. (7-1).

Jaroslav Drobny
Czechoslovakia / Egypt / Great Britain (1921–2001)
Hall of Fame—1983

Nobody at Wimbledon paid any attention to a 16-year-old left-hander from Czechoslovakia who lost a lively first-rounder to an Argentine, Alejo Russell, 10-8, 6-4, 7-9, 6-3. His country was in the news, threatened by the Nazi dictator, Adolf Hitler. It was 1938, war was imminent. Jaroslav Drobny would get one more crack at the Big W winning a couple of rounds in 1939, briefly noticed because he played two strong sets against top-seeded Bunny Austin before defaulting with an arm injury. Then he vanished into the cloud of World War II in his conquered homeland, wondering if he would ever play a big tournament again.

"We were just trying to stay alive. The torch of freedom with the Allies gave us hope," he said. Luckily he avoided deportation to Germany as a forced laborer, and was able to play hockey throughout the war, his best sport then. "Food was short, but we got along."

But he did take up tennis seriously again, seven years later, fashioning a magnificent 15-year amateur career that contained, despite so much time lost to the war, an amazing 133 singles titles—from Algeria to Knokke-le-Zoute—and membership in the world's Top 10 for 10 successive years from 1946, No. 1 in 1954, No. 2 in 1952, No. 3 in 1946, 51. In 1946, Drobny returned to Wimbledon for the post-war re-opening. Rusty from little play during the war, expecting nothing from himself, he beat the world's best, Jack Kramer, 2-6, 17-15, 6-3, 3-6, 6-3, in the fourth round, got to the semis and was hailed as a national hero at home, suddenly a name in the game in which he would become an all-timer.

At the time, he was a remarkable two-sport world class athlete: hockey in winter, tennis the rest of the time. So good was Drob as a forward on the ice that he played a leading role in Czechoslovakia's winning the world amateur championship in 1947 (he scored three goals in the final game against the U.S.), and gaining silver at the 1948 Olympics. By 1949, though, tennis had become his life. It was the year Drobny made the decision to leave his homeland that had become a police-state Communist

satellite in 1948, defecting with Davis Cup teammate Vladimir Cernik during a Swiss tournament at Gstaad. Twice the two of them had carried their country to the Cup semis, losses to Australia in 1947 and 1948. Drob won one of the exceptional matches in the latter, beating (fellow Hall of Famer-to-be) Adrian Quist on grass in Boston from match point down, 6-8, 3-6, 18-16, 6-3, 7-5.

A hockey injury gravely affected his eyesight, and he wore prescription dark glasses on court for the remainder of a long tennis career that included 17 Wimbledons, where his deft touch and agreeable nature made him a great favorite.

Drobny was born Oct. 12, 1921, in Prague and resided there until 1949, son of the groundskeeper at Prague's premier tennis complex on the island of Stvanice. "It was fortunate for me," he said, "because we lived at the club and I grew up in the game, ballboying, watching good players, starting out myself at age five. And we flooded the courts in winter to play hockey." During the war, he won the championship of the Nazi-occupied protectorate of Bohemia and Moravia, 1940-44, then the Czechoslovak title five straight times, 1945-49 before defecting. He solidified his 1946 Wimbledon reputation by reaching the final of the first postwar French (played after Wimbledon that year), losing to unseeded Marcel Bernard of France in five sets.

Paris was a happy hunting ground for portly Drob, a clever court manager and user of a full arsenal of varied speeds, spins, angles, lobs and drop shots. Good stuff on continental clay, but his fast and sliced serve and penetrating volleys made him a menace on fast courts as well. Five times he graced the French final losing to Americans, 1948 to Frank Parker, 1950 to Budge Patty, before crashing the winner's circle resoundingly. He beat Eric Sturgess, 6-3, 6-3, 6-3, in 1951 and, in 1952, disarmed the world No. 1, Frank Sedgman, 6-2, 6-0, 3-6, 6-4. Rome, too, was his territory as he won the Italian over Bill Talbert in 1950, Gianni Cucelli in 1951 and Lew Hoad, 6-2, 6-1, 6-2, in 1953, losing the 1952 final to Sedgman.

His fortune in the U.S. wasn't as good, although it took the champs to beat him: Kramer in 1947, Pancho Gonzalez in 1948 (both semis), and Art Larsen in the 1950 third round.

In 1949, with a stunning 6-1, 6-3, 6-2, jolting of John Bromwich, he attained the Wimbledon final. But that was the year of the five-set fireworks of Ted Schroeder, who won, 3-6, 6-0, 6-3, 4-6, 6-4. His most renowned match was a third rounder that grew to epic proportions in 1953. For four hours, 20 minutes into nightfall, he and Patty waged an engrossing war during which Drob circumvented six match points to win in 93 games, 8-6, 16-18, 3-6, 8-6, 12-10, the longest of Wimbledon singles before the 112 games, 5:12 saga of Charlie Pasarell and Gonzalez in 1969.

Though Drob, 32, was written off by 1954, 11 was his lucky number. Seeded No. 11 on his 11th try at Wimbledon, he came through, beating Patty in a semi, and outmaneuvering a 19-year-old Aussie named Ken Rosewall for the title he most wanted, 13-11, 4-6, 6-2, 9-7, in two hours, 37 minutes, the longest final at that time. Drob was the Big W's remotest-chance success then, although non-seeds Boris Becker (1985), Richard Krajicek (1996), Goran Ivanisevic (2001), No. 11 seed Pat Cash (1987) and No. 12 seed Andre Agassi (1992) were to join his long-shot club. He was dethroned by the next champ, Tony Trabert, in the 1955 quarters.

Traveling on Egyptian papers then, he became a British citizen in 1959, and lived in London with his wife, the former Rita Anderson, one-time English player. Drobny was tapped for the Hall of Fame in 1983, and died Sept. 13, 2001, in London.

MAJOR TITLES (5)—French Singles, 1951-1952; Wimbledon singles, 1954; French doubles, 1948; French mixed, 1948. **DAVIS CUP**—1946, 1947, 1948, 1949, 24-4 singles, 13-2 doubles. **SINGLES RECORD IN THE MAJORS**—Australian (0-1), French (47-13), Wimbledon (50-16), U.S. (15-5).

Francoise Durr
France (1942—)
Hall of Fame—2003

What a terrific Christmas gift to French tennis and the game as a whole in the pioneering days for the female pros. That was the birth of "Frankie" Durr. The December 25 arrival of Francoise Germaine Durr occurred in 1942 at Algiers, Algeria, the product of French parentage.

In her early days on the circuit, she may have inspired a few giggles among colleagues and fans as she confounded them with a strange, very personal style of curious grips and odd swipes. But it soon became clear that, as the "Psychedelic Strokeswoman," she was no easy mark as it may have appeared. She was a winner, pushing the ball here and there with soft shots, but very quick, accurate, smart, combative. Right-handed with a seemingly anemic serve, she was a champion of deception as well as major occasions. "She drove us crazy with her unorthodoxy," says Rosie Casals.

Her dossier includes a dozen major titles, headed by the French singles of 1967, setting her forth as probably the finest of her country since the glowing Suzanne Lenglen won it in 1925-26, certainly since Simone Mathieu won in 1939. Frankie beat 1965 champ Lesley Turner of Australia, 4-6, 6-3, 6-4. She got by the great Maria Bueno 5-7, 6-1, 6-4, in the quarters and Kerry Melville, 8-6, 6-3, in the semis. Her best efforts after that were the semis in 1972-73.

But in doubles, as a smart, piercing volleyer, she won seven women's majors and four mixed. In women's doubles, she won the French, 1967, with Gail Sherriff over Annette Van Zyl and Pat Walkden, 6-2, 6-2; 1968 with Jones over Rosie Casals-Billie Jean King 7-5, 4-6, 6-4; 1969 with Jones over Margaret Smith Court-Nancy Richey 6-0, 4-6, 7-5; 1970 with Gail Sherriff Chanfreau over Casals-King, 6-1, 3-6, 6-3; 1971, with Chanfreau over Helen Gourlay-Kerry Harris, 6-4, 6-1. U.S., 1969 with Darlene Hard over Virginia Wade-Court, 0-6, 6-4, 6-4; 1972 with Betty Stove over Wade-Court, 6-3, 1-6, 6-3. (Her record of five straight French was tied by Martina Navratilova, 1984-88.) In mixed, she won the French, 1968, with Jean Claude Barclay over King-Owen Davidson, 6-1, 6-4; 1971, with Barclay, over Winnie Shaw and Tomas Lejus, 6-2, 6-4; 1973 with Barclay over Stove and Patrice Dominguez, 6-1, 6-4; Wimbledon, 1976, with Tony Roche over Casals-Dick Stockton, 6-3, 2-6, 7-5.

In 1968, along with Billie Jean King, Rosie Casals and Ann Jones, Frankie signed on with the National Tennis League as the first female touring troupe—the questing quartet, whose quest was to establish pro tennis for women. It was a rocky journey, largely one-night stands, with little money, but they persevered and were influential in making the public conscious of the game as the "Long Way Babies" of the Virginia Slims tour began to flower.

Durr remembers, "Nobody knew who we were in the early days. But we did everything we could to promote the tournaments. We'd be on street corners trying to give tickets away, and sometimes even that didn't work. But we never gave up."

Over a 19-year career, she won 26 singles and 42 doubles pro titles, ranked in the Top 10 nine times: No. 3 in 1967; No. 6 in 1971; No. 8 in 1966; No. 9 in 1972, 75; No.10 in 1965, 70, 74, 76.

MAJOR TITLES (12)—French singles, 1967; French doubles, 1967, 1968, 1969, 1970, 1971, U.S. doubles, 1969, 1972, French mixed, 1968, 1971, 1973; Wimbledon mixed 1976. **FED CUP**—1963, 1964, 1965, 1966, 1967, 1970, 1972, 1977, 1978, 1979; 16-8 singles, 15-9 doubles. **SINGLES RECORD IN THE MAJORS**—Australian (6-3), French (35-14), Wimbledon (35-17), U.S. (28-16).

James Dwight
United States (1852–1917)
Hall of Fame—1955

Hailed deservedly as the "Father of American Tennis," Dr. James Dwight, a Bostonian and graduate of Harvard and Harvard Medical, may have introduced the game to the U.S., playing with his cousin, Fred Sears, at Nahant, Mass., in 1874. It arrived from England at several locations that year. He did organize and win the initial tournament, a sociable competition at Nahant, at 1876.

More importantly he was a driving force behind the organization of the USTA (then the U.S. National Lawn Tennis Association) in 1881, and its first National Championship that year at the Newport Casino, as well as the first Davis Cup series (1900) between the U.S. and the British Isles at his Boston club, Longwood Cricket Club.

As a player, right-handed and short (about 5-foot-5), he was more adept at doubles, sharing five U.S. titles with his protege, Dick Sears, who defeated him in the 1883 singles final. He was No. 2 in 1885 and 1886, the first years of U.S. rankings, and No. 3 in 1888. He, Sears and A.L. Rives were the American pioneers at Wimbledon in 1884, Dwight the only one to win a round. He beat F.J. Ridgeway, 6-2, 6-1, 6-1, the first U.S. victory, a small one at the Big W. Doc fought gamely against ambidextrous Herbert Chipp, who had removed Rives, but fell to nothing but forehands, 6-1, 2-6, 6-3, 2-6, 7-5. Though Dwight and Sears reached the doubles semis, the U.S. champs were no match for the dynamic, ruling Renshaw twins, Willie and Ernest, 6-0, 6-1, 6-2. Dwight returned the following year, making greater strides, to the semis where future champ Herbert Lawford topspun him out, 6-2, 6-2, 6-3.

Shepherding the USTA through its formative years, he was president 21 years, 1882-84 and 1894-1911. He entered the Hall of Fame in 1955. Born in Paris on July 14, 1852, he died July 13, 1917 in Mattapoisett, Mass. His son, Dr. Richard Dwight, a retired physician, continued to compete, in super-senior events for the over-85s until his death.

Stefan Edberg
Sweden (1966—)
Hall of Fame—2004

A stylistic misfit among the Swedish legion that rose in Bjorn Borg's sneakersteps and image, Stefan Edberg has ever been an extraordinarily graceful attacker. A serve-and-volleyer, he has done superbly with only one hand propelling his backhand.

Clay, on which he was reared, hasn't been his favorite surface, although he nearly beat Michael Chang in a five-set French final in 1989.

A splendid junior career led to great expectations, which he fulfilled with six major singles titles—two each, Australian (1985, 87), Wimbledon (1988, 90), U.S. (1991-92). In 1983, he became the lone achiever of a junior Grand Slam, winning the Australian, French, Wimbledon and U.S. 18-and-under singles titles.

Making his Davis Cup bow in 1984, at 18, he was the youngest to play for a Cup winner (until Chang, a slightly younger 18 in 1990), Edberg performed a consequential one-day role in Sweden's startling upending of the U.S. in the final at Goteborg. He and Anders Jarryd clinched the 4-1 victory by stunning Peter Fleming and John McEnroe, unbeaten in 14 previous Cup starts, 7-5, 5-7, 6-2, 7-5. In successfully defending the Cup the following year in Munich, a 3-2 victory over Germany, Edberg won it at the wire, a thrilling, rebounding fifth-match decision over Michael Westphal, 3-6, 7-5, 6-4, 6-3. Though he didn't play in the 1987 final, he had an earlier hand in winning that Cup.

A brilliant end-of-the-line backhand seized victory from Aleksandr Volkov at match point down in the fifth set as the 1994 Cup final began in Moscow. Turning that upside down for a 6-4, 6-2, 6-7 (2-7), 0-6, 8-6 win, Stefan set the tone in a 4-1 triumph, Sweden's fifth Cup. Having slipped below the standard he set for himself, he announced that the 1996 season would be his valedictory. Stefan had a good year, beating Chang at the French, playing all four to stretch his participation record to 54 straight major championship appearances at the U.S. Open, where he knocked off Wimbledon champ Richard Krajicek and made the quarters (a 25th time at that stage).

Edberg, a slim 6-foot-2 blond right hander, was born in the seaside town of Vastervik, Sweden on Jan. 19, 1966, and was reared there. He moved to London with his Swedish wife, Annette. He had a hammering serve, as well as a difficult kicker and a raking backhand, and he is one of the finest of all volleyers. His groundstrokes improved continuously throughout his career. Outwardly unemotional he dispelled doubts about his competitiveness by winning Wimbledon in 1988. He charged from two sets down to beat Miloslav Mecir in the semis, 4-6, 2-6, 6-4, 6-3, 6-4, and a set down to overcome favored Boris Becker, 4-6, 7-6 (7-2), 6-4, 6-2, for the title.

His rivalry with Becker was a highlight of the '80s and '90s. At the close his career, Becker was in the lead, 25-10.

Beating the 1983-84 champ, countryman Mats Wilander, in the final, 6-4, 6-4, 6-3, Stefan took the Australian in 1985, his first major. He repeated two years later, the last man to win it on grass, 6-3, 6-4, 3-6, 5-7, 6-3 over homeboy Pat Cash.

Flushing Meadows was almost the mystery to him that it had been for Borg (no titles in 10 tries). But on his ninth try, Edberg came through for the U.S. crown in one of the most devastating final round performances, 6-2, 6-4, 6-0, over Jim Courier, holding serve throughout. Edberg, a first-round loser the year before (to Volkov) was the second in the tournament's history to spring from such ignominy to the title (Mal Anderson of Australia did so in 1957.) Edberg refused to relinquish the title, beating Pete Sampras in the 1992 final. In the semis, he overcame Chang, 6-7 (3-7), 7-5, 7-6 (7-3), 5-7, 6-4, the longest-lasting match ever at the U.S. Open—five hours, 26 minutes. Edberg's last major final (his 10th) was the Australian of 1993, when he lost to Courier. During 14 professional seasons, he was in the world's Top 10 10 times, including No. 1 in 1990 and '91, also: No. 5 in 1985-86, 88, 93; No. 2 in 1987, 92; No. 3 in 1989; No. 7 in 1994.

Edberg represented Sweden in the 1988 and 1992 Olympics, winning a bronze in singles and doubles (with Jarryd) in the former.

Fittingly, he closed his career in Sweden in the 1996 Davis Cup final against France, to the cheering of countrymen at Malmo. However, he went out in defeat, slowed by ankle injury while losing to Cedric Pioline and couldn't play the third day of the 3-2 loss. Stefan's career achievements: Won 41 singles, 18 doubles pro titles and $20,630,941 prize money. He had an 806-270 (.749), singles average, and entered the Hall of Fame in 2004.

MAJOR TITLES (8)—Australian singless, 1985, 1987; Wimbledon singles, 1988, 1990; U.S. singles, 1991, 1992, Australian doubles, 1987; U.S. doubles, 1987. DAVIS CUP—1984, 1985, 1986, 1987, 1988, 1989, 1990, 1991, 1992, 1993, 1994, 1995, 1996, 34-14 singles, 12-8 doubles. SINGLES RECORD IN THE MAJORS—Australian (56-11), French (30-13), Wimbledon (49-12), US. (39-11).

Roy Emerson
Australia (1936—)
Hall of Fame—1982

In the grand days of Australian domination of the tennis world, nobody played as large a role as the country boy out of tiny Blackbutt in Queensland, Roy Stanley Emerson.

Emerson, a slim, quick, athletic farm kid who strengthened his wrists for tennis by milking innumerable cows on his father's property, played on eight winning Davis Cup teams between 1959 and 1967, a record. He won 28 of the major singles and doubles championships, a lofty male record. His dozen singles were six Australian (1961, 63-64-65-66-67), two each French, (1963, 67), Wimbledon (1964-65), U.S. (1961, 64). That was a record, created over seven years that he held for 33 years, without knowing it until writers noticed that he was being stalked by Pete Sampras. Sampras broke it with a thirteenth, at Wimbledon in 2000, and was congratulated by Emerson, who had eclipsed Bill Tilden's standard of 10 (set between 1920 and 1930), unaware, at winning his last Australian in 1967, that he was the new record holder. "Nobody paid attention to that sort of thing then, or kept track," he laughs. "We just played."

His accomplishments as a right-court doubles player who could make anybody look good amounted to 16 Big Four titles (6 French, 4 U.S., 3 each Wimbledon, Australian) with five different partners, the last in 1971 at Wimbledon with his old Queensland pal, Rod Laver.

His best-known alliance was with Aussie left-hander Neale Fraser, with whom he won Wimbledon in 1959 and 1961, the U.S. title in 1959-60 and the doubles of the Davis Cup triumphs of 1959-60-61.

Known as "Emmo" to his wide circle of friends, he was a rollicking, gregarious 6-foot right-hander with patent leather black hair and a golden smile (enhanced by dental fillings) who could lead the partying and singing without jeopardizing his high standards of play. Fitness was his hallmark. He trained hard and was always ready for strenuous matches and tournaments.

Although primarily a serve-and-volleyer, he could adapt to the rigors of slow courts. He won the French singles in 1963 over Pierre Darmon, 3-6, 6-1, 6-4, 6-4, and 1967, by lifting the crown from the head of teammate Tony Roche, 6-1, 6-4, 2-6, 6-2. He also led the 3-2 Davis Cup victory over the U.S. on clay in Cleveland in 1964. That year he was unbeaten in eight Davis Cup singles as the Aussies regained the Cup. Emmo had a singles winning streak of 55 matches, during that summer and autumn, third longest in male history. Establishing himself as the world's No. 1, he won 17 tournaments and 109 of 115 matches. The only prize to elude him in that majestic year of triumphs in three of the majors was a Grand Slam.

Fate may have intervened to cost him a third straight Wimbledon in 1966 when he was heavily favored. Winning a fourth rounder against Owen Davidson, he skidded chasing a short ball, crashed into the umpire's stand, damaging a shoulder, and was unable to do much but finish the match. His Australian hegemony began in 1961 when he beat Laver for the title, 1-6, 6-3, 7-5, 6-4. Laver took it back the following year as part of his Grand Slam, but after that, for five years, it was all Emmo for an Aussie male record six singles titles. The toughest title win was reversing himself from two sets down to overcome Fred Stolle in the 1965 final, 7-9, 2-6, 6-4, 7-5, 6-1. He beat Arthur Ashe in the last two, 6-4, 6-8, 6-2, 6-3 in 1966, and 6-4, 6-1, 6-1 in 1967. His Wimbledon wins were both over Stolle, 6-4, 12-10, 4-6, 6-3 in 1964, and, 6-2, 6-2, 6-4 in 1965. He beat Stolle again in the U.S. final of 1964, 6-4, 6-2, 6-4.

Ever high spirited and capable of firing up his teammates, Emerson also took part in two Australian victories in the World Cup, a since-disbanded annual competition against the U.S. He exemplified the Aussie code of sportsmanship and competitiveness, stating it as, "You should never complain about an injury. We believe that if you play, then you aren't injured, and that's that."

Emerson was born Nov. 3, 1936, in Blackbutt, a crossroads where people make a living in cattle and timber (the blackbutt is a variety of eucalyptus). His family moved to Brisbane, where he could get better competition and coaching, when his tennis talent became evident.

After resisting several offers, he turned pro in 1968 just before Open tennis began, and was still competing in 1978 as player-coach of the Boston Lobsters in World Team Tennis, directing them to the semifinals of the league playoffs. Of all Australia's Davis Cup luminaries under Capt. Harry Hopman, Emerson made the best record, vital in winning eight Cups, high for any participant, playing the decisive match in either singles or doubles six times. He won 21 of 23 singles, but never lost when it counted, and 13 of 15 doubles.

Beginning in 1959, he was in the world's Top 10 nine straight times, No. 1 in 1964-65. Also: No. 7 in 1959; No. 6 in 1960; No. 2 in 1961-62, '67; No. 3 in 1964, 66.

Emerson was elevated to the Hall of Fame in 1982 after a career that bridged the amateur and Open eras and was credited with three pro titles in singles and 30 in doubles, and $400,000 in prize money. Overall, amateur and pro, he was one of the few centurions with 103 singles titles. Other than his 12 majors, he had 88 amateur singles titles. His son, Antony, was All-American in tennis at the University of Southern California and played the pro tour briefly. They won the U.S. Hard Court Father and Son title in 1978.

MAJOR TITLES (28)—Australian singles, 1961, 1963, 1964, 1965, 1966, 1967; French singles, 1963, 1967; Wimbledon singles 1964-65; U.S. singles, 1961, 1964; Australian doubles, 1962, 1966, 1969; French doubles, 1960, 1961, 1962, 1963, 1964, 1965; Wimbledon doubles, 1959. 1961, 1971; U.S. doubles, 1959, 1960, 1965, 1966. **DAVIS CUP**–1959, 1960, 1961, 1962, 1963, 1964, 1965, 1966, 1967, 21-2 singles, 13-2 doubles. **SINGLES RECORD IN THE MAJORS**—Australian (47-8), French (43-10), Wimbledon (60-14), U.S. (59-14).

Pierre Etchebaster
France (1893–1980)
Hall of Fame—1978—Court Tennis

A Basque maestro of the racket in the complex game of court tennis (aka real tennis and royal tennis), the short, trim, elegant Pierre Etchebaster, a professional, was probably the greatest to roam the arcane concrete cubicle. Migrating to New York from his French homeland, he became the resident paragon at the Racquet & Tennis Club on Park Avenue, as player and instructor. Traveling to London to challenge for the world title in 1927, he lost to the champion G. F. Covey, 7-sets-to-5 at Prince's Club.

However, a year later on the same court, he dethroned Covey, 7-5. Thereafter, he repelled seven challenges himself, the first at Prince's, the remainder on his home paving, Racquet & Tennis.

He retired as unbeaten champion in 1954 at age 60. A right-hander, he was born Dec. 8, 1893, in St. Jean de Luz, France, and died there March 24, 1980. He entered the Hall Fame in 1978.

Chris Evert
United States (1954—)
Hall of Fame—1995

In 1970, at a small, insignificant tournament in North Carolina, 15-year-old Christine Marie Evert gave notice to the world that a dynamo was on the way up. Chrissie defeated Margaret Court, 7-6, 7-6, a woman who had recently completed her singles Grand Slam and was No. 1 in the world.

A year later in the U.S. Open at Forest Hills, Evert reconfirmed by marching resolutely to the semifinals, at 16 years, eight months,

20 days, the youngest at that time to reach that stage. Before losing to Billie Jean King, 6-3, 6-2, the eventual champion, schoolgirl Evert bowled over a succession of seasoned pros, mostly in come-from-behind thrillers that raised tears on the defeated older players and cheers in the Forest Hills stadium that Chrissie filled day after day. They went down in a row: Edna Buding of Germany, Mary Ann Eisel of the United States, No. 5 seed Françoise Durr of France and Lesley Hunt of Australia. Against Eisel, the No. 4 American, Evert wowed the first national TV audience to behold her by stonewalling when Eisel served for the match at 6-5, 40-0. Undaunted, the kid made six match points melt with bold shotmaking to win, 4-6, 7-6 (5-1), 6-1.

Although essentially a slow-court baseline specialist, raised on clay in Fort Lauderdale, Fla., where she was born Dec. 21, 1954, right-handed Evert showed that booming groundstrokes could succeed on the fast Forest Hills, Wimbledon and Australian grass. She was the "Little Ice Maiden," a pony-tailed kid, deadpan, with metronomic strokes that seldom missed. Her two-handed backhand, a powerful drive, stimulated a generation of newcomers to copy her, even though her father, teaching pro Jimmy Evert, advised against it. "I didn't teach the two-hander to her," said her father, who had won the Canadian singles in 1947. "She started that way because she was too small and weak to swing the backhand with one hand. I hoped she'd change—but how can I argue with this success?"

It was such a success that by the time she completed a 20-year career in 1989 she had won $8,896,195 in prize money and 154 pro singles titles on a 1,309-146 won-lost record. That's an .8996 winning average, highest in pro history.

Evert also was runner-up for 72 singles titles, which meant she made it to 76 percent of the finals of 303 tournaments entered.

After turning pro in 1973, she was the first to reach $1 million in career prize money, in 1976.

Her major singles titles numbered 18—six behind Margaret Court, three behind Steffi Graf, one behind Helen Wills Moody, tied with Martina Navratilova. Chris won at least one major singles for 13 consecutive years, a record. She started in Paris in 1974, beating Olga Morozova of the USSR, 6-1, 6-2, for the title, and ended in 1986 at the French where she was the all-time champ with seven championships on a 72-6 match record. Her other singles majors: Australian, 1982, 84; Wimbledon, 1974, 76, 81; U.S., 1975-76-77-78, 80, 82. Her last final, age 34, was the Australian, 1988, a stiffly resisting 6-1, 7-6 (7-3) defeat by 18-year-old Steffi Graf, launching the German's Grand Slam. Chris almost tied a longevity record of Helen Wills Moody, 16 years between major final appearances (1922-38). Her span was 15, but she was playing year after year while Moody was sporadic. While still an amateur, she won the first pro tournament she entered, St. Petersburg, Fla., in 1971.

By winning the U.S. title a fourth consecutive time in 1978 she was the first to do so since Helen Jacobs' run of 1932-35. Between 1973 and 1979 she won 125 consecutive matches on clay, including 24 tournaments. The streak came to an end in the semifinals of the Italian Open in Rome when she lost, 6-4, 2-6, 7-6 (7-4), to Tracy Austin. She won the U.S. Clay Court title six times between 1972 and 1980, tying Nancy Richey's record, 1963-68.

Her introduction to Evonne Goolagong was the 1972 Wimbledon semifinal, an exciting three-set struggle won by Goolagong, 4-6, 6-3, 6-4, the defending champion. That was the start of one of the two most compelling female rivalries of the Open era, one in which Evert held a 21-12 edge. The other, perhaps the most renowned in the game's history, was Chris' friendly feud with Martina Navratilova. From 1973 through 1988 it stretched 80 matches. Evert won the first meeting in Akron, Ohio, 7-6 (5-4), 6-3, and took a big early lead, but Navratilova overtook her, and came out ahead, 43-37, winning nine of 13 of their major final engagements.

During the Open era, the Virginia Slims circuit and its championship became prominent in women's tennis. Evert won the first of her four Slims championships in 1972 at 17. In choosing to preserve her amateur status until her 18th birthday that year, she disdained more than $50,000 in prize money, including the $25,000 Slims award for beating Kerry Reid, 7-5, 6-4.

Once she entered tennis for a living, she was a thorough exemplary professional in her relations with colleagues, press and public, and perennially a hard but sporting competitor. Fairly soon, she lost her status as the darling little girl. Her style was based on flawless barrages from the backcourt, and her constant winning seemed monotonous to many. Nevertheless, she was a smart player, able to maneuver a foe cleverly, scoring decisively with a well-disguised drop shot. She was also a better volleyer than given credit for, after overcoming an early distaste for the net. "I realize that a lot of fans think my game is boring, and they want to see me lose, or at least for somebody to give me a good fight all the time. But this is the game I played to win," she said. "Losing hurts me. I was always determined to be the best."

A lithe 5-foot-6, 125 pounds, she was in the world's Top 10 for 19 years, including five times No. 1 (1975-76-77, 80-81) and seven times No. 2 (1978-79, 82-83-84-85-86). A paragon of consistency, she entered 57 of the major tourneys, won 18, and was at least a semifinalist 53 times.

As one of five tennis-playing Evert children, she was clearly the star, but her sister, Jeanne, three years younger, was also a pro.

In 1974, Jeanne ranked No. 9 in the U.S. and they were the first sisters to be ranked in the U.S. Top 10 since Florence (No. 3) and Ethel Sutton (No. 2) in 1913. Chris and Jeanne were teammates on the victorious U.S. Wightman Cup team of 1973.

Her final-round surges past Goolagong for a first U.S. Open crown in 1975, 5-7, 6-4, 6-2, and to the Wimbledon title of 1976, 6-3, 4-6, 8-6, are well remembered. But her most satisfying victories were probably the last majors, the French final upsets of Navratilova in 1985, 6-3, 6-7 (4-7), 7-5. and, at age 33, in 1986, 2-6, 6-3, 6-3.

Her farewell to Flushing Meadow was the defeat by Zina Garrison, leaving her with a record 101 match wins in that event. She closed her career by winning all five singles matches as the U.S. won the Federation Cup in 1989. It was her ninth year and eighth Cup-winning team. She was undefeated in Wightman Cup singles (26-0), helping the U.S. win 11 Cups in the 13 years she played, captaining the team 1980-82, 85-86.

Evert was the first player to win more than 1,000 singles matches as well as 150 tournaments, the only one other than Court and King to win more than 100 matches in a season, which she did during a mammoth 1974 when she won 16 of 24 tournaments on a 103-7 record. Her 55-match winning streak in 1974 (ended at the U.S. Open by Goolagong) was an Open-era record until eclipsed by Navratilova's 74 in 1984. She also had streaks of 34 wins in a row in 1978, and 31 in 1979. Chris was on the 1988 Olympic team, but didn't medal, beaten by Italian Rafaella Reggi.

Three seasons of World Team Tennis included 1976-77 with Phoenix and 1978 with champion Los Angeles. Her eight-year marriage to English player John Lloyd ended in divorce. She then married ex-Olympic skier Andy Mill, with whom she has three sons, and was divorced again in 2006. In 2008, she married champion golfer, Aussie Greg Norman.

MAJOR TITLES (21)—Australian singles, 1982, 1984; French singles, 1974, 1975, 1979, 1980, 1983, 1985, 1986; Wimbledon singles, 1974, 1976, 1981; U.S. singles, 1975, 1976, 1977, 1978, 1980, 1982; French doubles, 1974, 1975; Wimbledon doubles, 1976. OTHER U.S. TITLES (6)—Clay Court singles, 1972-73-74-75, 79-80. FEDERATION CUP—1977-78-79-80-81-82, 86, 40-2 singles, 17-2 doubles. WIGHTMAN CUP: 1971-72-73, 75-76-77-78-79-80-81-82, 84-85, 26-0 singles, 8-4 doubles SINGLES RECORD IN THE MAJORS—Australian (30-4), French (72-6), Wimbledon (96-15), U.S. (101-12).

Bob Falkenburg
United States/Brazil (1926—)
Hall of Fame—1974

A gangling, dark-haired 6-foot-3 right-hander, Robert Falkenburg came from a tennis family. He and brother Tom won the U.S. Interscholastic title for Los Angeles Fairfax High in 1942, the same year Bob won the singles. Both played in the U.S. Championships at Forest Hills, as did sister Jinx. But Bob, seeded No. 7, made the family's name with a sensational Wimbledon triumph in 1948, eluding three match points while defeating No. 2 seed John Bromwich, 7-5, 0-6, 6-2, 3-6, 7-5. Bromwich served at 5-3, 40-15 and advantage. Falkenburg responded boldly with backhand passing returns. The last appeared futile. Brom made no attempt to play it, and the crowd gasped as the ball unexpectedly landed just inside the baseline.

He and Jack Kramer won the doubles the year before, and in 1944, at 18, he won the U.S. doubles with Don McNeill, one of few teenagers to hold that title.

A slam-bang, big-serving net-charger, he attended the University of Southern California, winning the U.S. Intercollegiate title in 1946. He was an early success, his career short. He won the U.S. junior title in 1942 and 1943, the second year while in the U.S. Army Air Force. He was one of the youngest to make his entry into the U.S. Top 10, 17 in 1943 at No. 7. He was there four more times through 1948, No. 5 the last year. He was No. 7 in the world rankings that year.

A semifinalist at the U.S. Championships in 1946 and a quarterfinalist in 1947, he lost both times to the champ, Kramer. He was also a quarterfinalist in 1948.

Bromwich had his revenge as Falkenburg defended the Wimbledon title in 1949, taking their quarterfinal, 3-6, 9-11, 6-0, 6-0, 6-4. Falkenburg did not endear himself to customers by his practice of tanking sets and sprawling on the court to rest.

Marrying a Brazilian and becoming a resident, Bob played Davis Cup for Brazil. He was born Jan. 29, 1926, in Brooklyn, N.Y., and entered the Hall of Fame in 1974.

Neale Fraser
Australia (1933—)
Hall of Fame—1984

A serve-bombing lefty whose onerous delivery was flat, sliced and kicked, Neale Fraser backed it up with tough volleying and was a marvelous competitor. Solidly built and athletic at 6-foot-1, he was especially overpowering on fast surfaces. Although he won Wimbledon in 1960 over Rod Laver, 6-4, 3-6, 9-7, 7-5, and the U.S. title in 1959 over Alex Olmedo, 6-3, 5-7, 6-2, 6-4 and 1960 over Laver, 6-4, 6-4, 9-7, Fraser found team play—doubles and Davis Cup—nearest his heart. As one of eight men to win all four majors in doubles, Fraser took three each Australian, French and U.S. and two Wimbledon with three different partners: Ashley Cooper, Lew Hoad, Roy Emerson.

His most difficult match of the 1960 Wimbledon championship was won literally over the dead-weary body of Butch Buchholz. But before the frustrated American keeled over with cramps in their quarterfinal, Fraser had to dodge five match points in the 30-game fourth set. It ended with winner Fraser on the short end in games, 4-6, 6-3, 4-6, 15-15.

His most successful alliance was with Emerson for eight majors. Losing only one singles, he was a mainstay for four Cup-winning Australia sides, starting in 1959 at Forest Hills. Then he won both his singles, and, with Emerson, the doubles in heisting the punchbowl from the U.S., 3-2. On opening day, he beat Wimbledon champ Olmedo, 8-6, 6-8, 6-4, 8-6. In the decisive fifth match, he beat Barry MacKay, 8-6, 3-6, 6-2, 6-4, a tense duel interrupted by rain and carried over to the following day. The doubles with Emerson was pivotal, 7-5, 7-5, 6-4, over Buchholz and Olmedo.

His love for Davis Cup showed when he succeeded legendary Harry Hopman as non-playing captain in 1970, and held the job for a record 23 years, piloting four winners: 1973, 1977, 1983 and 1986, and a record 49 series victories, losing the 1990 final to the U.S. He was No. 1 in the world in 1959 and 1960 and in the Top 10 every year between 1956 and 1962.

A sensational liaison with an older woman, Margaret Osborne duPont, reaped three U.S. mixed doubles, 1958-59-60, she age 42 for the last. Although he retired in 1963, he played a cameo at Wimbledon 10 years later as doubles finalist (to Jimmy Connors and Ilie Nastase) with John Cooper, younger brother of Ashley Cooper, with whom he'd won the U.S. doubles in 1957. A brother, Dr. John Fraser, a physician, was also a fine doubles player, a Wimbledon semifinalist with Rod Laver, as was Neale with Emerson in 1962. Neale was born Oct. 3, 1933, in Melbourne, where he lives, and entered the Hall of Fame in 1984.

MAJOR TITLES (19)—Wimbledon singles, 1960; U.S. singles 1959, 1960; Australian doubles, 1957, 1958, 1962; French doubles 1958, 1960, 1962; Wimbledon doubles. 1959, 1961; U.S. doubles, 1957, 1959, 1960; Australian mixed, 1956; Wimbledon mixed, 1962; U.S. Mixed, 1958-59-60. **DAVIS CUP**—1958, 1959, 1960, 1961, 1962, 1963, 11-1 singles, 7-2 doubles **SINGLES RECORD IN THE MAJORS**—Australian (25-10), French (18-5), Wimbledon (38-13), U.S. (32-5).

Shirley Fry
United States (1927—)
Hall of Fame—1970

One of the elite 13 men and women to win each of the major championships in singles, Shirley June Fry Irvin is also one of only five to win them all in doubles as well. The French was the first to fall to her in 1951, over her good friend and doubles partner, Doris Hart, 6-3, 3-6, 6-3; the Australian was the last, in 1957, over Althea Gibson, 6-3, 6-4. Walking out as a champ (it seldom happens), she retired to become Mrs. Karl Irvin, and moved to Hartford, Conn., to raise a family and teach the game.

In 1956, she won Wimbledon over Angela Buxton, 6-3, 6-1 and—on the 16th and last try—the U.S., beating Shirley Bloomer in the semis, and Gibson, 6-3, 6-4, for the title. A right-hander, born on June 30, 1927, and raised in Akron, Ohio, she was in 1941 the youngest ever to play in the U.S. Championships until slightly younger 14-year-olds, Kathy Horvath (1979) and Mary Joe Fernandez (1985). In a less nervous era in America, her parents sent her to tournaments alone on buses.

As a 15-year-old in 1942, she became, unseeded, the Championships youngest quarterfinalist. She lost the 1951 final by a 6-3, 1-6, 6-4 margin to Maureen Connolly—whom hardly anybody beat—but came through five years later, outsteadying Gibson. She had a solid groundstroking game, but showed her volleying skills in doubles alongside Hart. They were the only team to win four straight French titles (1950-53). They also won three straight Wimbledons (1951-53) and four straight U.S. titles (1951- 54).

In their hard-fought 6-2, 7-9, 9-7 final-round victory over Louise Brough and Margaret Osborne DuPont in the 1953 U.S. doubles final, Shirley and Doris terminated the Brough-duPont record streak of nine straight titles (1942-1950) and 41 matches. Their own streak, until losing the 1955 final to Brough-duPont, was 20 matches.

Shirley, 5-foot-5, 125 pounds, ranked in the U.S. Top 10 13 straight years (1944-56), No. 1 in 1956, and made the world's Top 10 nine times between 1946 and 1956, No. 1 the last year. She played Wightman Cup for the U.S. six times, never on a loser, winning 10 of her 12 matches. She entered the Hall of Fame in 1970.

MAJOR TITLES (17)—Australian singles, 1957; French singles, 1951; Wimbledon singles, 1956; U.S. singles, 1956; Australian doubles, 1957; French doubles, 1950, 1951, 1952, 1953; Wimbledon doubles, 1951, 1952, 1953: U.S. doubles, 1951, 1952, 1953, 1954; Wimbledon mixed, 1957. **OTHER U.S. TITLES** (4)—Clay Court singles, 1956; Clay Court doubles, 1946, with Mary Arnold Prentiss; 1950, with Doris Hart; 1956 with Dorothy Head Knode. **WIGHTMAN CUP**—1949, 1951, 1952, 1953, 1955, 1956, 4-2 singles, 6-0 doubles (won all 6 Cups). **SINGLES RECORD IN THE MAJORS**—Australian (5-0), French (23-4), Wimbledon (34-7), U.S. (38-14).

Chuck Garland
United States (1898–1971)
Hall of Fame—1969

A Yale man who won the U.S. Intercollegiate doubles in 1919, Charles Stedman Garland joined a Harvardian, Dick Williams, the following year to beat Algernon Kingscote and James Parke, 4-6, 6-4, 7-5, 6-2, and become the first Americans to win the doubles at Wimbledon. He also made the Wimbledon singles semifinals in 1919 and 1920.

Ranked three times in the U.S. Top 10, 1918, 1919 and 1920 (No. 8 each time), he was selected for the Hall of Fame in 1969 as much for his service to the USTA as a committeeman. One of his duties was captaining the Davis Cup-losing 1927 U.S. Cup team. Garland, a 5-foot-7-1/2 right-hander, was born Oct. 29, 1898, in Pittsburgh. He later lived in Baltimore and died there Jan. 28, 1971.

MAJOR TITLE (1) Wimbledon doubles, 1920. **OTHER U.S. TITLES** (4)—Intercollegiate singles, 1919; Intercollegiate doubles, 1919, with Ken Hawke; Clay Court doubles 1917, 1918, with Sam Hardy. **SINGLES RECORD IN THE MAJORS**—Wimbledon (12-3), U.S. (10-7).

Althea Gibson
United States (1927–2003)
Hall of Fame—1971

No player overcame more obstacles to become a champion than Althea Gibson, the first black to win at Wimbledon, Forest Hills and the French.

Her entry in the U.S. Championships of 1950 at Forest Hills was historic: The first appearance of a black American in that event. It took seven more years for Gibson to work her way to the championship there, in 1957. Tennis was pretty much a segregated sport in the U.S. until the American Tennis Association, the governing body for black tournaments, prevailed on the U.S. Tennis Association to permit the ATA female champion, Gibson, to enter Forest Hills. Two years earlier, in 1948, Dr. Reginald Weir, a New York physician, was the first black permitted in a USTA championship, playing in the U.S. Indoor event in New York.

Three years after Jackie Robinson had integrated major league baseball, playing for the Brooklyn Dodgers, Althea's first appearance at Forest Hills was not only a notable occasion, it was nearly a moment of staggering triumph. Making her historic debut in a 6-2, 6-2, win over Barbara Knapp, she encountered in the second round No. 3 seed Louise Brough, the reigning Wimbledon champion, and came within one game of winning. Recovering from nerves, Althea led, 1-6, 6-3, 7-6, when providence intervened: A thunderstorm struck Forest Hills, curtailing the match until the following day, when Brough reaffirmed her eminence by winning three straight games.

During the violent storm, a bolt of lightning had toppled one of the concrete guardian eagles from the upper reaches of the stadium. "It may have been an omen that times were changing," Althea recalled.

Born Aug. 25, 1927, in Silver, S.C., Gibson, a right-hander, grew up in Harlem. Her family was poor, but she was fortunate in coming to the attention of Dr. Walter Johnson, a Lynchburg, Va., physi-

cian who was active in the black tennis community. He became her patron, as he would later be for Arthur Ashe. Through Dr. Johnson, Gibson received better instruction and competition, and contacts were set up with the USTA to inject her into the recognized tennis scene. Ex-champs Alice Marble and Sarah Palfrey Cooke were leading voices favoring Althea's inclusion, Marble writing a strong it's-about-time editorial in influential *American Lawn Tennis Magazine*.

Tall (5-foot-11), strong, and extremely athletic, she would have come to prominence earlier but for segregation. She was 23 when she first played at Forest Hills, 30 when she won her first of two successive U.S. Championships, in 1957, finally beating Brough, 6-3, 6-2. She repeated in 1958 over Darlene Hard, 3-6, 6-1, 6-2. In her first U.S. final, 1956, she was beaten by Shirley Fry, 6-3, 6-2. During the two years she won Wimbledon, 1957 over Hard, 6-3, 6-2, and 1958 over Brit Angela Mortimer, 8-6, 6-2, she was the world No. 1. Althea was never completely at ease in amateur tennis for she realized that, despite her success, she was still unwelcome at some clubs where important tournaments were played. A mark of general acceptance, however, was her 1957 selection to represent the U.S. on the Wightman Cup team against Britain. She played two years, posting a 3-1 record in singles and 2-2 in doubles.

Gibson was a big hitter with an awesome serve. She liked to attack, but developed consistency at the baseline eventually and made her major breakthrough by winning the French of 1956, overcoming the turgid clay of Roland Garros and the steady Englishwoman, Mortimer, 6-0, 12-10. That year, she also tamed the clay of Il Foro Italico, winning the Italian over the stubborn Hungarian, Suzy Kormoczi, 6-3, 7-5. She showed that she could handle herself on any footing, and was on her way at No. 2.

Crossing the Channel, she allied herself with Englishwoman, Angela Buxton, to win the Wimbledon doubles over Aussies Fay Muller and Daphne Seeney, 6-1, 8-6, and the Big W had its pioneering black champ.

In all, Gibson won 11 major titles in singles and doubles. After six years of trying at Forest Hills, she seemed ready to win in 1956, reaching the heavily publicized final, but appeared overanxious and lost to the more controlled and experienced Shirley Fry, the Wimbledon champ in her second U.S. title match. A year later, Gibson was solidly in charge, beating Darlene Hard 6-3, 6-2 to take Wimbledon, and would at last rule her own country at Brough's expense.

After winning the U.S. a second time in 1958, Althea turned pro. She played a series of head-to-head matches in 1960 against Floridian Karol Fageros, who had been ranked No. 8 in the U.S. Their tour was played in conjunction with the Harlem Globetrotters, the matches staged on basketball courts prior to Trotter games. Gibson won 114 of 118 matches. She said she earned over $100,000 in one year as her share of the gate. But there was no professional game in tennis for women then, and she aimed at the pro golf tour for a few years. She showed an aptitude for that game, but was too late in starting.

Althea tried to play a few pro tennis events after Open tennis began in 1968, but by then she was too old. She was married briefly, to W. A. Darben, and worked as a tennis teaching pro after ceasing competition, but sadly ended her days ill and reclusive,

dying Sept. 28, 2003, at East Orange, N.J. She had been inducted into the Hall of Fame in 1971.

MAJOR TITLES (11)—French singles, 1956; Wimbledon singles, 1957, 1958; U.S. singles, 1957, 1958; Australian doubles, 1957; French doubles, 1956; Wimbledon doubles, 1956-57-58; U.S. mixed, 1957. **OTHER U.S. TITLES** (2)—Clay Court singles, 1957; Clay Court doubles, with Darlene Hard, 1957. **WIGHTMAN CUP**—1957-58, 3-1 singles, 2-0 doubles. **SINGLES RECORDS IN THE MAJORS**—Australian (4-1), French (6-0), Wimbledon (17-2), U.S. (27-7.)

Andres Gimeno
Spain (1937–)
Hall of Fame—2009

Andres Gimeno holds the distinction of being the old male winner of the French Open at the age of 34 years, 10 months in 1972. Seeded No. 6, Gimeno beat No. 3 seed Stan Smith in the quarterfinals, No. 10 seed Alex Metreveli in the semifinals and No. 9 seed Patrick Proisy of France 4-6, 6-3, 6-1, 6-1 in the final. The Spanish right-hander also reached the final of the Australian Open on grass in 1969, losing to Rod Laver 6-3, 6-4, 7-5, becoming the first of four final-round victims of Laver's historic second Grand Slam. Gimeno also won the German singles title in 1971, defeating Peter Szoke of Hungary 6-3, 6-2, 6-2, plus the doubles with John Alexander of Australia. His best years were as a touring pro, from 1960, prior to Open era. He was graceful and slender standing 6 foot 1, and weighing just under 200 pounds during his peak years. He had solid groundstrokes, a good serve and a competent volley. He was born Aug. 3, 1937 in Barcelona. He won seven singles titles, four doubles titles as a pro, but also tallied 10 amateur singles titles. He also made the semifinals of the French Open in 1968 and Wimbledon in 1970. He was also a quarterfinalist at the Australian in 1959 and at the French in 1969. As a Davis Cupper, he represented Spain in 1958-60, 1972-73, posting an 18-5 singles record and a 5-5 doubles record.

MAJOR TITLES: (1)—French singles, 1972. **DAVIS CUP**—1958-60, 1972-1973, 18-5 in singles, 5-5 in doubles.

Kitty Godfree
Great Britain (1896–1992)
Hall of Fame—1978

Kathleen McKane Godfree, a sturdy, good-natured competitor, may have been the best female player Britain has produced. In winning Wimbledon for the first time in 1924, she charged back from 1-4 in the second set to hand Helen Wills her lone defeat in nine visits to the Big W, 4-6, 6-4, 6-4. She also beat Wills in the British Wightman Cup victory that year at Wimbledon. Who else could boast of royal-flushing "Little Miss Poker Face" twice in a season?

Kitty won Wimbledon again two years later over Lili de Alvarez, 6-2, 4-6, 6-3. Thus Kitty and Dorothy Round (1934, 37) were the only Brits to win twice since World War I. She was one of a select group to play more than 100 matches (146) at Wimbledon,

19th on the list: 38-11 in singles, 33-12 in doubles, 40-12 in mixed between 1919 and 1934.

In 1923, Kitty reached her third Wimbledon final but lost to Suzanne Lenglen, 6-2, 6-2. In the U.S. Championships that year, Kitty offered a dangerous quarterfinal challenge to Wills, coming from 2-5 to 5-all in the third set before losing, 2-6, 6-2, 7-5. In 1925, she pushed Wills in the final of the U.S. Championships, losing, 3-6, 6-0, 6-2, after eliminating frequent champs Molla Mallory and Elizabeth Ryan.

She was a member of the British team that played the United States in the Wightman Cup inaugural, 1923 in the new Forest Hills stadium. She lost to Wills and Mallory. But the following year, in the first of these international team competitions held in Britain, Kitty beat Mallory, 6-3, 6-3 as well as Wills, 6-2, 6-2, and the home team won by a surprising margin of 6-1. Then in 1925, the British won again, 4-3, with Kitty defeating Mallory and losing to Wills. In 1926, she beat both Mary K. Browne and Ryan, but the British lost, 4-3, at Wimbledon despite Kitty's heroics.

Speedy, smart and a fighter with an all-around game, she was her country's most successful Olympian, gathering five medals in the 1920 and 1924 Games. In 1920, she won a gold in the doubles with Winifred McNair, a silver in mixed with Max Woosnam and a bronze in singles. Four years later, a silver in doubles with Phyllis Covell and a bronze in singles. Active throughout her long life, she was a 92-year-old spectator at the 1988 Games in Seoul, and approved the entry of professionals, saying, "It's a sign of the times if you want the best in the Olympics."

Kitty and her husband, Leslie Godfree, were the only married couple to win the Wimbledon mixed, in 1926, beating Americans about to turn pro, Mary K. Browne and Howard Kinsey, 6-3, 6-4. In 1922, she and Margaret McKane Stocks were the only sisters to contest a Wimbledon doubles final (until the Williams Sisters, Venus and Serena in 2000), losing to Lenglen and Ryan, 6-0, 6-4. She was in the world's Top 10 in 1925, 1926 and 1927—No. 2 in 1926.

Kitty was among the champions of the past who received Centenary medallions on Wimbledon's Centre Court in 1977 and was inducted into the Hall of Fame in 1978. Born May 7, 1896, in London, she died there at the age of 96 on June 19, 1992.

MAJOR TITLES (7)—Wimbledon singles, 1924, 1926; U.S. doubles, 1923, 1927; U.S. mixed, 1925; Wimbledon mixed 1924, 1926. **WIGHTMAN CUP**--1923, 1924, 1925, 1926, 1927, 1930, 1934; 5-5 singles, 2-5 doubles. **SINGLES RECORD IN THE MAJORS**—French (6-2), Wimbledon (38-11), U.S. (7-2).

Pancho Gonzalez
United States (1928–1995)
Hall of Fame—1968

Very much his own man, a loner and an acerbic competitor, Richard "Pancho" Alonzo Gonzalez was probably as good as anyone who ever played the game, if not better. Most of his great tennis was played beyond wide public attention, on the nearly secret pro tour amid a small band of gypsies of whom he was the ticket-selling mainstay.

His rages against opponents, officials, photographers, newsmen and even spectators were frequently spectacular—but they only served to intensify his own play, and didn't disturb his concentration, as fits of temper do most others. Pancho got mad and played better. "We hoped he wouldn't get upset; it just made him tougher," said Rod Laver. "Later when he got older, he would get into arguments to stall for time and rest, and we had to be careful that it didn't put us off our games."

Gonzalez, a right-hander, born May 9, 1928, in Los Angeles, was always out of the tennis mainstream, a fact that seemed to goad him to play harder. Because he came from a Chicano family, he was never acceptable in the supposedly proper upper circles of his city's tennis establishment. And because he was a truant, he wasn't permitted to play in Southern California junior tournaments. Once he got out of the Navy in 1946 there was no preventing him from mixing in the game, and beating everyone. He had a marvelously pure and effortless serving action that delivered thunderbolts, and he grew up as an attacker on fast West Coast concrete.

Although not regarded as anything more than promising on his second trip East in 1948, he was at age 20 ready to win the big one, the U.S. Championship at Forest Hills. Ranked 17th nationally at the time, and seeded No. 8, he served and volleyed his way to the final, where he beat South African Eric Sturgess with ease, 6-2, 6-3, 14-12. The following year, Gonzalez met the favorite, a Southern California antagonist, top-seeded Ted Schroeder. It was one of the most gripping finals. Schroeder won the first two sets as expected, but they were demanding and exhausting, 18-16, 6-2, and after that Gonzalez rolled up the next three, 6-1, 6-2, 6-4, for the title. In 1949, Pancho also helped the U.S. hold the Davis Cup against Australia, then went for the money, turning pro to tour against the monarch, Jack Kramer. Gonzalez was too green for Kramer, losing, 96-27, and he faded from view for several agonizing years.

When Kramer retired, Gonzalez won a tour over Don Budge, Pancho Segura and Frank Sedgman in 1954 to determine Jack's successor. He stood forth himself as Emperor Pancho, proud and imperious, for a long while, through the challenges of Tony Trabert, Ken Rosewall, Lew Hoad, Ashley Cooper, Mal Anderson, Alex Olmedo and Segura. For a decade, Gonzalez and pro tennis were synonymous. A promoter couldn't hope to attract crowds unless Pancho was on the bill. During his reign Pancho won the U.S. Pro singles a record eight times of 11 finals between 1951 and 1964, and Wembley in London, considered the world pro championship, four times of five finals between 1950 and 1956.

By the time Rosewall and Laver were reaching their zeniths during the mid-and-late-1960s, the aging Gonzalez hung on as a dangerous foe, still capable of defeating all. In 1964, his last serious bid for his ninth U.S. Pro title, he lost the final to Laver in four hard sets on grass in a rainstorm. Yet there was still much more glory ahead. In 1968, at 40, he beat the defending champion, 31-year-old Roy Emerson, 7-5, 6-3, 3-6, 4-6, 6-4, to attain the semis of the first major Open, the French, to be beaten by Laver. Three months later, at the initial U.S. Open, he toppled No. 2 seed Tony Roche (the 23-year-old Wimbledon finalist) to make the quarters, where he was defeated by Tom Okker, 14-16, 6-3, 10-8, 6-3. A year later, this grandfather (literally) electrified Wimbledon by overcoming Charlie Pasarell in the tournament's longest match, 112 games, a

first-rounder that consumed five hours, 12 minutes, a major tourney record that stood for 20 years until 1989 , eclipsed by 16 minutes at Wimbledon as Greg Holmes beat Todd Witsken in 5:28.

The marathon with Pasarell began one afternoon and concluded on the next after darkness intervened. In winning, 22-24, 1-6, 16-14, 6-3, 11-9, Gonzalez served out of seven match points in the fifth set.

Later that year, he beat John Newcombe, Rosewall, Stan Smith and Arthur Ashe in succession to win $12,500, the second-highest prize of the year, and the title in a rich tournament at Las Vegas. Early in 1970, in the opener of a series of $10,000 winner-take-all challenge matches leading to a grand final, he toppled Laver. The Aussie, just off his second Grand Slam year (and the eventual winner of this tournament), was clearly No. 1 in the world, but Pancho warmed a crowd of 14,761 at New York's Madison Square Garden with a 7-5, 3-6, 2-6, 6-3, 6-2 victory.

Three months before his 44th birthday, in 1972, he was the oldest to record a tournament title in the Open era, winning Des Moines (Iowa) over 24-year-old French Davis Cupper Georges Goven, 3-6, 4-6, 6-3, 6-4, 6-2. That year, he was No. 9 in the U.S., the oldest to rank so high, and equaled Vic Seixas' Top 10 longevity span of 24 years. As for the world's Top 10, he is alone in that he was a member in 1948-49 and again in 1968-69, ranking No. 1 in 1949 and No. 6 in 1969.

In 1968, though still active, he was named to the Hall of Fame, and he was a consistent winner on the Grand Masters tour for over-45 champs beginning in 1973. Although his high-speed serve, so effortlessly delivered, was a trademark, Gonzalez, a 6-foot-2, 180-pounder, was a splendid athlete and tactician who excelled at defense, too. "My legs, retrieving, lobs and change-of-pace service returns meant as much or more to me than my power," he said. "But people overlooked that because of the reputation of my serve." He won $911,078 between 1950 and 1972, and crossed the million mark as a Grand Master. Altogether as an amateur and a pro, he won 74 singles titles. He was married six times, the last to a good player, Rita Agassi, sister of another all-timer, Andre Agassi, by whom he had a son. Not a bad tennis bloodline for the young man, Skylar Gonzalez. Gonzalez died on July 3, 1995, of cancer in Las Vegas, where he had been a teaching pro for some time.

MAJOR TITLES (4)—U.S. singles, 1948-49; French doubles,1949; Wimbledon doubles, 1949. **OTHER U.S. TITLES** (17)—Indoor singles, 1949; Clay Court singles, 1948-1949; Indoor mixed, 1949, with Gussy Moran; Pro singles. 1953, 1954 1955, 1956 1957, 1958, 1959, 1961; Pro doubles, 1953, with Don Budge; 1954, 1958, with Pancho Segura; 1957, with Ken Rosewall; 1969, with Rod Laver. **DAVIS CUP**—1949, 2-0 singles. **SINGLES RECORD IN THE MAJORS**—Australian (2-1), French (9-2), Wimbledon (10-5), U.S. (23-7).

Evonne Goolagong
Australia (1951—)
Hall of Fame—1988

The most improbable of a long line of exceptional champions from Down Under, Evonne Fay Goolagong Cawley is the only native Australian, an Aborigine, to become a tennis internationalist. Born July 31, 1951, in Griffith, New South Wales, she grew up to a lissome 5-foot-6, in near poverty. As one of eight children of an itinerant sheep-shearer, Ken Goolagong, and his wife, Melinda, she spent her formative years in the small country town of Barellan in wheat and sheep territory west of Sydney. Her father, long-armed and limber, knew nothing of tennis. It's unlikely that she would have left Barellan if a kindly resident, Bill Kurtzman, hadn't seen her peering through the fence at the local courts and encouraged her to play.

She was a natural, a free-flowing right-hander blessed with speed, lightning reflexes and a carefree temperament. Tipped off to this by two of his assistants, Vic Edwards, proprietor of a tennis school in Sydney, journeyed upcountry to take a look. He immediately spotted the talent that would eventually result in two Wimbledon, one French and four Australian championships and a 1988 posting to the Hall of Fame.

Edwards convinced her parents to allow Evonne to move to Sydney and live in his household, where he could coach her. This she did in 1967 at 13, becoming one of the family and an early doubles partner of Edwards' daughter, Patricia. Her rise was swift. On her second world tour, in 1971, Goolagong, just before turning 20, beat countrywoman Helen Gourlay to win the French Open, 6-3, 7-5. A month later, in her last act as a teen-ager, seeded No. 3, she stunned the defending champion, her girlhood idol, Margaret Court, in the Wimbledon final, 6-4, 6-1.

Called "Sunshine Supergirl" in London, she captivated crowds wherever she played with her graceful movement and gracious manner. Three more times she got to the final, losing to Billie Jean King in 1972 and 1975, and Chris Evert in 1976. However, a unique success was to be hers: Victory again at the Big W at the end of a nine-year gap, in 1980, her last tournament triumph. Evonne, seeded No. 4, made a spirited run through 1977 runner-up Betty Stove, No. 9 seed Hana Mandlikova, No. 6 seed Wendy Turnbull, No. 2 seed U.S. champ Tracy Austin, and in the final, No. 3 seed Evert, 6-1, 7-6 (7-1).

By then she had married Englishman Roger Cawley and had the first of their two children. Thus she was the first mother to win Wimbledon since local Dorothea Douglass Chambers 66 years before. At Wimbledon, Evonne was 49-9 in singles, 21-7 in doubles and 19-8 in mixed.

Her exciting rivalry with Evert—the volleyer against the baseliner—began at the top, the 1972 Wimbledon semis, won by Evonne. Overall, Evert led 21-12, but in the majors her edge was only 5-4, Chris winning three of their five finals. Goolagong took their initial championship encounter, the 1974 Australian, 7-6 (7-5), 4-6, 6-0. She beat Martina Navratilova to repeat in the Australian in 1975, 6-3, 6-2.

Although she won the U.S. Indoor in 1973 over Virginia Wade, she couldn't quite make it at the Open, the only woman to lose the final four successive years, 1973-76, at Forest Hills, falling to Court, King, then twice to Evert.

For a decade, Evonne, refreshing as a zephyr, illuminated the world's Top 10: No. 2 in 1971 and 1974. She won the season-climaxing Virginia Slims title in 1974 and 1976, both over Evert, 6-3, 6-4, and 6-3, 5-7, 6-3. She retired after the 1983 season, with pro career totals of 68 singles (704-165 matches) and 11 doubles titles (18-16), and $1,399,431 prize money.

A seven-year mainstay of Australia's Federation Cup team, she led the way to Cups in 1971, 73-74, and finals in 1975-76. She has held government posts in Aboriginal affairs, and was named to the Australian Tennis Hall of Fame in 1994.

MAJOR TITLES (13)—Australian singles, 1974-75-76-77; French singles. 1971; Wimbledon singles, 1971, 80; Australian doubles, 1971, 1974-75-76; Wimbledon doubles, 1974; French mixed, 1972. **FEDERATION CUP**—1971-72-73-74-75-76 82; 21-3 singles, 11-2 doubles. **SINGLES RECORD IN THE MAJORS**—Australian (39-9), French (16-3), Wimbledon (49-9), U.S. (26-6).

Arthur Gore
Great Britain (1868–1928)
Hall of Fame—2006

Extremely enduring and endearing, Arthur William Wentworth Charles Gore was as familiar to Wimbledon patrons as the grass, and seemingly as evergreen. He was around for 35 of his 60 years, until, at age 59, he decided that was enough. He and his 53-year-old pal and teammate, Herbert Roper Barrett, had lost a doubles first rounder to F.T. Stowe and E.U. Williams, 3-6, 6-4, 6-4, 12-10. Gore died the following year, 1928.

Roper Barrett and Gore (unrelated to the first Wimbledon champ, Spencer Gore) were original Davis Cuppers, losing to the U.S., 3-0, at Boston in 1900. Captaining the British team, Gore was beaten in the inaugural match by Malcolm Whitman, 6-1, 6-3, 6-2. His second match, against Cup donor Dwight Davis was unfinished, halted by rain in the second set.

Although Gore was 32, the best was yet to come at the Big W: four titles, three of them singles. In 1902, he cut in on the Doherty brothers' championship monopoly with a 4-6, 7-5, 6-4, 6-4, victory over Reggie, who had won the previous four in a row. Laurie stepped up to beat Gore in the 1903 challenge round, 6-4, 6-3, 3-6, 6-0, starting his own run of five. Aussie lefty Norman Brookes won his first title in 1907 over Gore, 6-4, 6-4, 6-2, but Arthur rebounded boldly to win the next two in five-set battles: 6-3, 6-2, 4-6, 3-6, 6-4, over the ever-present Roper Barrett, and 6-8, 1-6, 6-2, 6-2, 6-2, over 38-year-old Josiah Ritchie.

At 41 years, seven months, patient right-hander Gore was the oldest of all men who won singles majors. Icing on the cake was his also grabbing the 1909 doubles with Roper Barrett, 6-2, 6-1, 6-4, over Aussies Harry Parker and Stanley Doust. Despite losing his title to rising New Zealander Tony Wilding, 6-4, 7-5, 4-6, 6-2, Gore wasn't through competing. He came right back at the champ, Wilding, two years later, 1912, a 44-year-old making it close, 6-4, 6-4, 4-6, 6-4.

Fourteen years later at age 58, he and 52-year-old Roper Barrett made headlines with a first round win because one of their 6-1, 6-3, 6-2, victims was the Duke of York (future English King George VI). Louis Grieg accompanied the nervous left-handed Duke in Wimbledon's lone competitive appearance of royalty. (Do you think that draw was rigged?) Gore played 155 Wimbledon men's matches, seventh place in that stat, winning 64 singles (second to Jimmy Connors's 84), 33 doubles, two mixed. He learned the game in 1878 on the sand courts of Dinard, France, and won his first title there, a kids' tourney, at 12, but was a late-

blooming adult. Not until his fourth Wimbledon did he even win a match. On his fourteenth try, he became the champ. Born on Jan. 2, 1868 in Lyndhurst, England, he, died on Dec. 1, 1928 in London, and entered the Hall, 2006.

MAJOR TITLES (4)— Wimbledon singles, 1901, 1908-09; Wimbledon doubles, 1909 **SINGLES RECORD IN THE MAJORS**: Wimbledon (64-26)

Steffi Graf
Germany (1969—)
Hall of Fame—2004

It was a grand moment for 16-year-old Stephanie Maria Graf. Her first pro tournament victory victimized an all-timer, Chris Evert, 6-4, 7-5, in the nationally-televised final of the 1986 Family Circle Cup at Hilton Head, S.C.

A trim blonde, 5-foot-9, 132 lbs., she was precocious and powerfully athletic, out of the small German town of Bruhl, and she would attain heights unimaginable before 1988. That year, she registered the sixth Grand Slam (third female) and topped it off with a gold medal at Seoul as tennis returned to the Olympics after a 64-year absence. It was a quintessential quintuple for "Fraulein Forehand," a right-handed proprietor of that feared weapon.

Before it was over in August of 1999, her majestic career was stocked with 22 major singles titles (seven Wimbledon, six French, five U.S., four Australian), starting with a 1987 French triumph over Martina Navratilova, 6-4, 4-6, 8-6. Although she didn't quite reach Margaret Court's record stash of 24 singles, Steffi is the only player, male of female, to win each of the majors more than four times. Finishing with tennis, she took up with Andre Agassi for a championship marriage Oct. 22, 2001 (14 majors ahead of him), and gave birth to their son, Jaden Gil, October 26, 2001, and daughter, Jaz, October 3, 2003.

Born June 14, 1969, in Bruhl, Germany, she became one of the fastest of all female players, a nimble retriever who prefered the baseline but volleyed ably. She ran and played speedily, hardly pausing, impatient to win the next point.

Steffi had her sights on being the greatest ever anywhere, and she may well have been. Despite a variety of injuries and family crises, she continued to pile up major triumphs, passing Martina Navratilova and Chris Evert (18 singles each) and even Helen Wills Moody (19). Moreover, she had her 22nd, a wild 4-6, 7-5, 6-2, put-down of 18-year-old Martina Hingis, in the 1999 French final, days from her 30th birthday. Court finished collecting at age 31, Moody at 32, Navratilova at 33, Evert at 31. Altogether, Steffi, a pro from age 13, won 107 singles titles (902-115 matches), 11 doubles titles (173-115) and $21,895,277 prize money.

After she'd dispossessed Evert (the eight-time champ) at Hilton Head in 1986, Steffi began to roll up titles at an incredible pace: 11 in 1987 and 1988, 14 in 1989, 10 in 1990. On the day before her 18th birthday, she grabbed her first major, the 1987 French. But it was in Berlin three years later that she stumbled while strongly bidding for Navratilova's Open-era record (74) for consecutive match victories. Steffi was stopped at 66 in the final by Monica Seles, 6-4, 6-3. She also had streaks of 46, 45 and 44.

As a pro, she won matches at an .887 clip (Evert was .899, Navratilova. 878). By mid-1987, she deposed Navratilova at No. 1, and hung on to the top spot for four years (a record 186 weeks) until displaced in 1991 by Seles. She took over the penthouse again in 1993, traded it on and off with Sanchez Vicario in 1995, shared it with the returned Seles until having it all alone again at the close of 1996. She was No. 3 when she quit, shortly after losing her last (31st) major final, Wimbledon, to Lindsay Davenport, 6-4, 7-5.

Steel-willed and industrious, she displayed full-speed-ahead-damn-the-slings-and-arrows character in the face of daunting physical injuries and emotional trials. Probably no great champion has played hurt so often. She was kept from the Australian in 1995 by a calf injury, and in 1996 by foot surgery. Might she have had two more majors otherwise? Back and knee problems were constant, the left knee sidelining her during the 1996 Olympics. When would-be assassin Guenther Parche removed Seles from the picture (and the No. 1 spot) with his knife in 1993, Steffi bore the anguish when Parche said he did it to restore her to the top.

Peter Graf, who raised her specifically for tennis, turning her pro in October 1982 to support the family, has been a prized target of the tabloids for his waywardness. The father's most serious scandal was his arrest and imprisonment in 1995 on the charge of income tax evasion of millions of dollars in managing her fortune. He was convicted and sentenced to a jail term in January of 1997. Nevertheless, she remained loyal to him, and steadfast in her pursuit of victory, though cutting down her schedule to 11 tournaments in 1995 and 1996.

Graf said she missed the challenge of Seles, who beat her for the Australian title in 1993, shortly before the assault by Parche. She welcomed Monica's return to the U.S. Open of 1995. In a highly-charged final, Steffi won, 7-6 (8-6), 0-6, 6-3, and one year later won the rematch even more impressively with quickness and battering forehands, 7-5, 6-4.

But the gems of those two years were Wimbledon '95 and the French '96 because of what it took to throttle the passionate Spanish opposition of Arantxa Sanchez Vicario in the finals. Perhaps the greatest single game ever was the 11th of their third set on Centre Court: A spellbinding 20-minute passage of 32 points—13 deuces—until Steffi punched through Arantxa's serve to 6-5, and won, 4-6, 6-1, 7-5. Twice the "Barcelona Bumblebee" served for victory at Roland Garros, at 5-4 and 7-6 in the third. Again, Steffi just wouldn't let her have it, 6-3, 6-7 (4-7), 10-8, in 3:03.

Centre Court was Steffi's rumpus room as much as Martina's. Steffi ran off with the 1988 and 1989 finals at Martina's expense, thus halting Navratilova's run of six straight years on top and 47 consecutive match wins, three short of Moody's Wimbledon record.

In the 1993 Wimbledon final, Steffi kept her poise when it appeared she would lose to shaky Czech Jana Novotna, taking the last five games and her fifth title, 7-6 (8-6), 1-6, 6-4.

On the other side of the coin the following year, Steffi added to Wimbledon history through defeat, the only top-seeded woman to fall in the first round—to American Lori McNeil, 7-5, 7-6 (7-5). It was her lone failure to attain at least the quarters in 45 majors since making the semis of the U.S. in 1985 (31 of which she was in the final, and, of course, won 22).

Her Grand Slam year in 1988 amounted to 11 singles titles in 14 tournaments on a 73-3 match record. In navigating the Australian, French, Wimbledon and U.S. finals, she beat Evert 6-1, 7-6 (7-3), Natalia Zvereva of the USSR 6-0, 6-0, Navratilova 5-7, 6-2, 6-1, and Gabriela Sabatini of Argentina 6-3, 3-6, 6-1, in that order. Then she beat Sabatini, 6-3, 6-3, for the 1988 Olympic crown, but relinquished it to Jennifer Capriati in the final in 1992 at Barcelona.

Almost as impressive was 1989 with 14 wins in 16 tournaments on a 86-2 match record, and 1993, winning 10 of 15 tournaments on 76-6. Four times she won the season-closing (nee Virginia Slims) Championship at Madison Square Garden, 1987, 89, 93, 95. Her swath of reaching 20 consecutive finals through the German Open of 1994 was second in that consistency to Navratilova's 23, 1983-84.

She led Germany to the 1987 and 1992 Federation Cups in which her singles record was 19-2. The ITF named her World Champion seven times, 1987-88-89-90, 93, 95-96. After losing her first pro match to Tracy Austin (the only one she played in 1982), she became a winner (21-15) in 1983, registering at No. 98 on the computer. She was the world's No. 1 eight times (1987-88-89-90, 93-94-95-96), No. 2 twice (1991-92) and among the Top 10 three other times.

MAJOR TITLES (23)—Australian singles, 1988, 1989, 1990, 1994; French singles, 1987, 1988, 1993, 1995, 1996, 1999; Wimbledon singles, 1988, 1989, 1991, 1992, 1993, 1995, 1996; U.S. singles, 1988, 1989, 1993, 1999, 1996; Wimbledon doubles, 1988. **FEDERATION CUP**—1986, 1987, 1989, 1991, 1992, 1993, 1996, 19-2 singles, 8-1 doubles. **SINGLES RECORD IN THE MAJORS**—Australian (47-6), French (87-10). Wimbledon (75-8), U.S. (73-10).

Bitsy Grant
United States (1910–1986)
Hall of Fame—1972

A scrappy little guy, 5 foot 4, 120 lbs, Bryan Morel "Bitsy" Grant was the smallest American man to attain championship stature. A right-handed retriever supreme, he was able to beat such heavy-hitting greats as Don Budge and Ellsworth Vines, even on grass. Between 1930 and 1941 he ranked nine times in the U.S. Top 10, No. 3 in 1935 and 1936. In 1936 and 1937, he was in the world's Top 10, Nos. 8 and 6, respectively.

Reared on the clay of his native Georgia, he won the U.S. title on that surface thrice (1930, 1934-35) but he had his moments on the grass at Forest Hills, reaching the U.S. semis in 1935 by beating No. 2-seeded Budge, 6-4, 6-4, 5-7, 6-3, and in 1936, losing to eventual champion, Fred Perry, 6-4, 3-6, 7-5, 6-2. He was a quarterfinalist in 1937, losing to Gottfried von Cramm, 9-7, 2-6, 2-6, 6-3, 6-3, and reached the same round a year later.

He played Davis Cup in 1935, 1936 and 1937, helping the U.S. regain the prize in 1937 after an 11-year slump. In the second round 5-0 decision over Australia at Forest Hills, Bitsy was nifty on the lawn, beating two future Hall of Famers, John Bromwich, 6-2, 7-5, 6-1, and Jack Crawford, 6-0, 6-2, 7-5. But in the semis, he couldn't overcome Germans von Cramm (6-3, 6-4, 6-2) and Henner Henkel (7-5, 2-6, 6-3, 6-4) on Wimbledon turf, leaving the decisive fifth match to Budge's unfailing touch.

He continued to compete as a senior, winning 19 U.S. singles titles on the four surfaces: Grass Court-45s (1956, 1957), 55s (1965, 1966, 1967, 1968); Indoor-55s (1966); Clay Court-45s (1959, 1960, 1961, 1963), 55s (1965, 1966, 1967, 1968, 1969), 65s (1976 and 1977); Hard Court-65s (1976).

He was born in Atlanta, Dec. 25, 1910, and died there June 5, 1986. Named for him, the Bitsy Grant Tennis Center in his hometown is one of the finest public court complexes.

U.S. TITLES (4)—Clay Court singles, 1930, 1934, 1935; Clay Court doubles, 1932, with George Lott. **DAVIS CUP**—1935, 1936, 1937, (8-2 singles.) **SINGLES RECORD IN THE MAJORS**—Wimbledon (8-2), U.S. (35-15)

David Gray
Great Britain (1927–1983)
Hall of Fame—1985—Journalist

David Gray was such a fine chronicler of the game for two decades with an exceptional English newspaper, *The Guardian*, that many regretted his departure from journalism in 1976 to become an official of the ITF (International Tennis Federation). A well-educated and witty man, he showed his grasp of tennis, its figures, matches, history and politics in his literate daily reports from across the world. But he served the game well, even without a byline, as the ITF's diplomatic general secretary from 1976 until his untimely death of cancer in 1983. He was also secretary of the Men's International Professional Tennis Council.

As a journalist he strongly advocated the abolition of phony amateurism and the adoption of Open tennis in 1968. Gray was influential in reorganizing the Davis Cup, returning tennis to the Olympics in 1988 and broadening the game's base, especially by encouraging its development on the African continent. Among the large and competitive British press contingent, he was a standout, and he brought to the game's administration a keen overall view and perception.

A graduate of Birmingham University, he worked his way up to the *Guardian* through the *Wolverhampton Express and Star*, the *Northern Daily Telegraph* and the *News Chronicle*. He could, and did, write anything and everything well, a political reporter and theater critic before getting the tennis assignment.

Another Hall of Famer, Lance Tingay of London's *Daily Telegraph*, wrote of him: "David's political experiences gave him a ready taste for the personal intrigues and machinations that form the eternal backdrop to our ballet of forehands and backhands out front."

A collection of his writings, *Shades of Gray,* was published in 1988 by Willow Books (William Collins & Sons).

He was born Dec. 31, 1927, in Kingswinford, England, and died Sept 6, 1983, in London.

Clarence Griffin
United States (1888–1973)
Hall of Fame—1970

Clarence James "Peck" Griffin ranked in the U.S. Top 10 three times (1915, 1916, 1920), No. 6 the last two, but made his mark in doubles alongside fellow Californian Bill Johnston. They won the U.S. title thrice, 1915, 1916 and 1920. In 1915, they knocked off U.S. Davis Cuppers Tom Bundy and Maurice "Comet" McLoughlin, the defenders, 2-6, 6-3, 6-4, 3-6, 6-3. He was also in the 1913 final with John Strachan. He and Strachan won the U.S. Clay Court title that year, and in 1914, Griffin reached his singles apogee in a comeback beating of Elia Fotrell, 3-6, 6-8, 8-6, 6-0, 6-2, for the Clay Court singles crown. That was the all-comers final.

Defender Strachan, unable to be in Cincinnati, defaulted the challenge round to Griffin. He was a 5-foot-7 right-hander, born Jan. 19, 1888, in San Francisco, and died March 28, 1973, in Santa Barbara Calif. He entered the Hall of Fame in 1970. His nephew was the well-known entertainer Merv Griffin.

MAJOR TITLES (3)—U.S. doubles, 1915, 1916, 1920. **OTHER U.S. TITLES** (2)—Clay Court singles, 1914; Clay Court doubles, 1913, with John Strachan. **SINGLES RECORD IN THE MAJORS**—U.S. (18-9)

King Gustav V
Sweden (1858–1950)
Hall of Fame—1980—Patron

A grand patron of the game and an enthusiastic player into his 90s, King Gustav V of Sweden learned to play during a visit to Britain in 1878, and founded his country's first tennis club on his return home. In 1936, he founded the King's Cup. Eventually disbanded during the Open era, it was a men's indoor team competition for European countries. He became king, (full name Oscar Gustav Adolf Bernadotte), on Dec. 8, 1907, ruled for 43 years and was often seen playing friendly events on the Riviera.

Entered under the pseudonym, Mr. G., looking like an aged Mr. Chips in spectacles, white mustache, flannels and straw hat, he frequently took part in handicap tourneys, partnered by famous players such as Suzanne Lenglen. During World War II, this widely respected ruler interceded to obtain better treatment for the Nazi-imprisoned Davis Cup stars, Jean Borotra of France and Gottfried von Cramm of Germany, and may have saved their lives.

Gustav was born June 16, 1858, in Drottningholm, Sweden and died Oct. 29, 1950.

Harold Hackett
United States (1878–1937)
Hall of Fame—1961

A New Yorker, Harold Humphrey Hackett was best known as the partner of Fred Alexander in one of the most successful doubles teams. The 5-foot 9 Hackett was the softer, more deceptive stroker of the two. Beginning in 1905, they were U.S. finalists a record seven successive years, winning in 1907, 1908, 1909 and 1910, losing no sets in the finals. A Yale man, right-handed, he was born July 12, 1878, in Hingham, Mass. He and Alexander won the U.S. Indoor doubles thrice (1906-08), and he completed a sweep of the surface titles available then by taking the Clay Court doubles in 1912 with Walter Hall.

The following year in 1913, Hackett was player-captain of the U.S. Davis Cup team that broke a decade drought by seizing the

Cup in a 3-2 beating of Britain at Wimbledon. He and Maurice McLoughlin won the vital go-ahead point over Herbert Roper Barrett and Charles Dixon, 5-7, 6-1, 2-6, 7-5, 6-4, and McLoughlin got the clincher. He was ranked in the U.S. Top 10 twice, 1902 and 1906, No. 7 in 1906 when he was a U.S. quarterfinalist. He was inducted into the Hall of Fame in 1961, died in New York, Nov. 20, 1937.

MAJOR TITLES (4)—U.S. doubles, 1907, 1908, 1909, 1910. **OTHER U.S. TITLES** (5)—Indoor doubles, 1906 1907, 1908, 1909, with Fred Alexander; Clay Court doubles, 1912, with Walter Hall. **DAVIS CUP**—1908, 1909, 1913, 5-1 doubles. **SINGLES RECORD IN THE MAJORS**—U.S. (3-2).

Ellen Hansell
United States (1869–1937)
Hall of Fame—1965

The original U.S. female champion, Ellen Forde Hansell Allerdice was a Philadelphian who won the title in 1887, in her hometown, not long before her 18th birthday. She beat Laura Knight, 6-1, 6-0, at the Philadelphia Cricket Club, but lost the title the following year to Bertha Townsend, 6-3, 6-5, and wasn't a factor again. A right-hander, she served sidearm, as, she said, did most of the women in that inaugural.

Forty-four years later, she recalled that she had been an anemic child, who showed some "enthusiasm and aptitude" for tennis. Her mother was advised by the family doctor to take Ellen out of school and put her on a court daily to build herself up. She remembered her mother making her tennis dresses of red plaid gingham: "A red felt hat topped the tight-collared and be-corseted body. I also wore a blazer of red and blue stripes ... we did now and then grip our overdraped, voluminous skirts with our left hand to give us a bit more limb freedom when dashing to make a swift, snappy stroke, every bit as well placed as today, but lacking the force and great physical strength of the modern girl. Is it possible for you to envision the gallery? A loving, but openly prejudiced crowd standing within two feet of the court lines, calling out hurrahs of applause plus groans of disappointment, and some suggestive criticism, such as: Run to the net! Place it to her left! Don't dare lose this game!"

She was born Sept. 18, 1869, in Philadelphia, and died, Mrs. Taylor Allderdice, May 11, 1937, in Pittsburgh. Induction into the Hall of Fame came in 1965.

MAJOR TITLE (1)—U.S. singles. 1887. **SINGLES RECORD IN THE MAJORS**—U.S. (3-1).

Darlene Hard
United States (1936—)
Hall of Fame—1973

An all-out attacking Californian with a splendid serve, volley and overhead Darlene Ruth Hard nevertheless won the 1960 French singles on slow clay over Mexico's Yola Ramirez, 6-3, 6-4 as well as U.S. titles on grass at Forest Hills: 1960, dethroning Brazil's Maria Bueno, 6-4, 10-12, 6-4, and 1961, over Brit Ann Haydon (Jones), 6-3, 6-4. Twice a Wimbledon finalist, she lost in 1957 to Althea Gibson, 6-3, 6-2, and

1959 to Bueno, 6-4, 6-3. A stocky blonde right-hander, 5-foot-5, 140 lbs, she was born Jan. 6, 1936, in Los Angeles and attended Pomona, for whom she won the U.S. Intercollegiate title in 1958.

She played with considerable zest, inspiring a variety of doubles partners, winning the U.S. title five straight years (1958-62) and again in 1969 with four different accomplices, the French twice with different partners and four Wimbledons with three different partners. The 1969 win with Françoise Durr—a last-minute, one-time amalgamation—may have been her most sensational in that Darlene, no longer competing, looked so out of place in the final. But after a disastrous start, losing the first eight games, she recalled the old moves as they beat Margaret Court and Virginia Wade, 0-6, 6-3, 6-4.

Between 1954 and 1963, she ranked in the U.S. Top 10 10 times, No. 1 four straight years (1960—63), and in the world's Top 10 nine times, No. 2 in 1960 and 1961. She was a standout Wightman and Federation Cup player.

As the grande dame of the original U.S. Fed Cup team, squiring 19-year-olds Billie Jean Moffitt (King) and Carole Caldwell (Graebner), Darlene, 27, led the way to 1963 victory. A blend of all-time doubles champs, present and future, she and B.J. won the Cup decider over Aussies Smith (Court) and Lesley Turner (Bowrey), 3-6, 13-11, 6-3, on a fast, slick, wooden court inside Queen's Club, London. She totaled 21 major titles in singles, doubles and mixed (3-13-5).

MAJOR TITLES (21)—French singles, 1960; U.S. singles, 1960, 1961; French doubles, 1955, 1957, 1960; Wimbledon doubles, 1957, 1959, 1960, 1963; US. Doubles, 1958, 1959, 1960, 1961, 1962, 1969; French mixed, 1955, 1961; Wimbledon mixed, 1957, 1959, 1960. **OTHER U.S. TITLES** (7)—Clay Court doubles, 1957, with Althea Gibson; 1960, with Billie Jean Moffitt (King); 1962, with Sue Behlmar; 1963, with Maria Bueno; Hard Court singles, 1963; Hard Court doubles, 1963, with Paulette Verzin; Intercollegiate singles, 1958. **FEDERATION CUP**—1963, 3-1 singles, 3-0 doubles. **WIGHTMAN CUP**—1957, 1959, 1960, 1962, 1963, 6-3 singles, 4-1 doubles. **SINGLES RECORD IN THE MAJORS**—French (14-4), Wimbledon (29-7), U.S. (43-9).

Doris Hart
United States (1925—)
Hall of Fame—1969

As a child, Doris Jane Hart was certainly not a candidate for sports immortality. She was stricken by a serious knee infection later erroneously publicized as polio, and faced the prospect of being crippled for life. She began to play tennis at age six as therapy, and recovered so successfully that, despite bowed legs, she became one of the all-time champions.

"One of the first newspaper stories on me described me as having recovered from polio," she once said. "It was a good story that just caught on. But it wasn't so."

Her total of 35 major championships in singles, doubles and mixed ties her with Louise Brough, behind only Margaret Court (62), Martina Navratilova (59), Billie Jean King (39) and Margaret duPont (37). Hart and Court are the only players in history, male or female, to win all 12 of the major titles at least once, and she is one of 13 to win all four singles within her career.

For 14 successive years between 1942 and 1955, she was ranked in the U.S. Top 10, standing at No. 1 in 1954-55.

Possibly her finest tournament was Wimbledon of 1951, when she scored a triple—championships in singles, doubles, and mixed—and lost only one set, that in the mixed. After handing her good friend and partner, Shirley Fry, one of the worst beatings in the tournament's history (6-1, 6-0), Doris united with Shirley for the doubles title, over rivals Brough and duPont, 6-3, 13-11, then annexed the mixed with Aussie Frank Sedgman, over Aussies Nancye Wynne Bolton and Merv Rose, 7-5, 6-2. Doris won the mixed the following year with Sedgman, and the next three years with Vic Seixas, a Wimbledon record of five straight years.

After being a singles runner-up at Forest Hills for the U.S. Championship four times, Hart finally was rewarded on her 15th try at the title. She beat Brough in a thriller, 6-8, 6-1, 8-6, in the 1954 title match, averting three match points. She retained that title, 6-4, 6-2, over Englishwoman Pat Ward, then retired to become a teaching pro.

Born June 20, 1925, in St. Louis, Hart, a right-hander, grew up in Coral Gables, Fla. She was an intelligent and solid all-round player whose strokes were crisp and stylish. She moved very well, despite the early handicap of her legs, and had an excellent disposition. She was effective at the net, or in the backcourt, as attested by her championships in the French singles of 1950, over Pat Canning Todd, 6-4, 4-6, 6-2 and 1952, 6-4, 6-4, over defender Fry, who had beaten her in the 1951 final, 6-3, 3-6, 6-3. Doris also won the U.S. Clay Court singles in 1950 over Fry, 6-1, 6-3.

During her first of two ventures to Australia, 1949, a rare American there that year, she started seizing major singles, the first of six, snipping the three-year string of Nancye Bolton, 6-3, 6-4, and won the mixed with Sedgman over Joyce Fitch and John Bromwich, 6-1, 5-7, 12-10. She lost her title to Brough the following year, 6-4, 3-6, 6-4.

She and Fry were one of the outstanding couplings in history, with 11 majors, standing behind the record 20 of Brough-duPont and Martina Navratilova-Pam Shriver, and the 14 of Gigi Fernandez and Natalia Zvereva. They won the French a record four straight times from 1950, losing only one set in all the finals, that while deposing long-time antagonists Brough and duPont in 1950, 1-6, 7-5, 6-2. (Fernandez and Zvereva tied the four-straight record as 1992-95 champs.) Hart and Fry also won three Wimbledons in a row, beginning in 1951. In the 1953 U.S. final, they ended the record streak of Brough and duPont at nine championships and 41 matches in a furious 6-2, 7-9, 9-7 struggle. In turn, their own streak of four championships and 20 matches was stopped in the 1955 final by Brough and duPont, 6-3.1-6, 6-3.

During a decade of U.S. supremacy over Britain (1946-55) in the Wightman Cup, Doris won all 14 of her singles and eight of nine doubles. She captained the winning U.S. team in 1970.

Her U.S. championships on various surfaces amounted to 22 singles and doubles. Beginning in 1946, she was in the world's Top 10 for 10 successive years, No. 1 in 1951, otherwise: No. 4 in 1946; No. 3 in 1947-48-49-50; No. 2 in 1952-53-54-55.

MAJOR TITLES (35)—Australian singles, 1949; French singles 1950, 1952; Wimbledon singles, 1951; U.S. singles, 1954, 1955; Australian doubles, 1950; French doubles, 1948, 1950, 1951, 1952, 1953; Wimbledon doubles, 1947, 1951, 1952. 1953; U.S. doubles, 1951, 1952, 1953, 1954; Australian mixed, 1949, 1950; French mixed, 1951, 1952, 1953; Wimbledon mixed 1951, 1952, 1953, 1954, 1955; U.S. mixed 1951, 1952,

1953, 1954 1955. **OTHER U.S. TITLES** (11)—Clay Court singles, 1950; Hard Court singles, 1949; Indoor doubles, 1947, 1948, with Barbara Schofield Davidson; Hard Court Mixed, 1949, with Eric Sturgess (RSA); Clay Court doubles, 1944, 1945, with Pauline Betz; 1950, with Shirley Fry; 1954, with Maureen Connolly; Indoor mixed 1947, 1948, with Bill Talbert. **WIGHTMAN CUP**—1946, 1947, 1948, 1949, 1950, 1951, 1952, 1953, 1954 1955, 14-0 singles, 8-1 doubles **SINGLES RECORD IN THE MAJORS**—Australian (8-1), French (28-5), Wimbledon (43-8), U.S. (57-13).

Gladys Heldman
United States (1922–2003)
Hall of Fame—1979—Journalist

For more than two decades, brilliant Gladys Medalie Heldman was the game's anchor, first as founder-owner- publisher-editor-chief-writer of *World Tennis* magazine (launched in 1953), later as the instigator and house-mother of a separate professional circuit for women, begun in 1970. Under her guidance, *WT* became the international literary voice of tennis. A slim, petite dynamo who often seemed shy, she came to tennis through marriage to a first-flight player, left-handed Julius Heldman, who was the U.S. junior champ in 1936, and U.S. Senior Indoor champ in 1964. They met as students at Stanford. She, a previously non-athletic New Yorker, quickly absorbed his enthusiasm for the game, becoming a maven. Their two daughters, Trixie and Julie, held national junior rankings, and Julie went on to win the Italian Open in 1969, and rank No. 5 in the world that year and in 1974. In 1970, Gladys and her magazine became the allies of disgruntled female players—Billie Jean King and Rosie Casals foremost—who felt, justifiably, that they were being demeaned, financially and attitudinally, by the game's male establishment. They believed it was necessary to break away from the traditional dual-sex tournament format and go it alone.

Heldman encouraged them, and urged a friend, Joe Cullman, head of Philip Morris, to provide an initial bankroll. Joined by the "Houston Nine" (King, Casals, daughter Julie, Peaches Bartkowicz, Kerry Melville, Valerie Ziegenfuss, Nancy Richey, Kristy Pigeon, Judy Tegart Dalton), Heldman staged the first Virginia Slims tournament in that city late in 1970.

Its success prompted Virginia Slims cigarettes to underwrite a 1971 tour, and the stunning progress of the "Long Way Babies" commenced. Though Billie Jean King was out front, preaching and playing, Gladys was the brainy ringleader.

Heldman, who became a better-than-average player herself—sold the magazine and withdrew from tennis politics in the mid-1970s. She and her husband moved to Santa Fe, New Mexico, Gladys presiding over a tennis salon at their handsome indoor court, and was involved in a number of local charities. Born May 13, 1922, in New York, she entered the Hall of Fame in 1979, and died June 22, 2003 in Santa Fe, taking her own life.

Slew Hester
United States (1912-1993)
Hall of Fame—1981—Administrator

A fine athlete, a football player at Millsaps College in his native Mississippi, William Ewing "Slew" Hester won numerous

tennis trophies. Among them were U.S. senior doubles titles such as the Grass Court 45s with Alex Wellford in 1957. But, as one of the most thoughtful and forceful USTA presidents, burly Slew made an indelible mark on the game by determining to expand the scope and potential of the U.S. Open by moving the event from Forest Hills after the 1977 Championships.

He took the Open a few miles away to Flushing Meadows and the swiftly-constructed, Hester-inspired-and-overseen USTA National Tennis Center in time for the 1978 Open. Nobody believed that could be accomplished in a year, but Slew was a bold operator who got things done. There the event annually set tennis attendance records. A gregarious cigar-smoking oilman from Jackson, Hester earned a bronze star while serving in the U.S. Army in World War II.

He was a USTA officer from 1969-77, then became president for a two-year term. Born May 8, 1912, in Hazlehurst, Miss., he was inducted into the Hall of Fame in 1981, and died Feb. 8, 1993, in Jackson, Miss.

Bob Hewitt
Australia/South Africa (1940—)
Hall of Fame—1992

Tapped for the Hall of Fame in 1992 in harness with his South African partner, Frew McMillan, Robert Anthony John Hewitt was the right-court player in the alignment of Hewitt and McMillan. They combined for five major championships and were one of the shrewdest, strongest of all teams, men whose prowess spanned the amateur and Open eras. In 1974, they were central to South Africa's winning the Davis Cup, the fifth member of the exclusive club, and first newcomer since France in 1927.

Hewitt was a born and bred Aussie, beginning life on January 12, 1940, in Dubbo, New South Wales. He became one of a tribe that terrorized the tennis world, and first came to attention winning the Wimbledon doubles in 1962 and 1964 with compatriot Fred Stolle. But love broke up that potent alliance. Hewitt fell for a South African lass named Delaille, and moved to Johannesburg to wed. Since he hadn't played Davis Cup for Australia, he was eligible, as a resident, to compete for South Africa.

In 1966, he and McMillan were put together as teammates, and they stayed together for much of the next 15 years to win Wimbledon thrice (1967, 1972, 1978), the French (1972), the U.S. (1977) plus 60 other titles. Hewitt, bald, bearded and sometimes volatile on court, was a blocky 6-footer with surprisingly delicate touch, an accurate and seldom-failing returner.

He was the better singles player, taking seven pro titles in singles (170-142 matches), along with 65 in pro doubles (502-126), the latter total placing him seventh on the all-time pro winners' list. It is believed that he has a record total of 163 doubles titles when including his amateur numbers. He was a Wimbledon quarterfinalist in 1964 and 1966, won the U.S. Clay Court singles over Jimmy Connors, 7-6, 6-1, 6-2, and three other singles tourneys in 1972 and was ranked No. 6 in the world in 1967. Hewitt had six major mixed titles, too, one of five to win all four. He won three (Wimbledon, 1977-79, U.S., 1979) with South Africa's Greer Stevens. His career prize money amounted to $613,837.

MAJOR TITLES (15)—Australian doubles, 1963, 1964; French doubles, 1972; Wimbledon doubles. 1962, 1964, 1967, 1972, 1978; U.S. doubles, 1977; Australian mixed, 1961; French mixed, 1970, 1979; Wimbledon mixed, 1977, 1979; U.S. Mixed, 1979. **DAVIS CUP**—1967, 1968, 1969, 1974, 1978, 22-3 singles, 16-1 doubles. **SINGLES RECORD IN THE MAJORS**—Australian (12-7), French (21-14), Wimbledon (34-19), U.S. (13-9). **MAJOR TITLES WITH MCMILLAN** (5)—French doubles, 1972; Wimbledon doubles, 1967, 1972, 1978; U.S. doubles, 1977. **DAVIS CUP WITH MC MILLAN**—1967, 1968, 1969, 1974, 1978, 16-1 doubles.

Lew Hoad
Australia (1934–1994)
Hall of Fame—1980

During his quarter-century career as a professional, Pancho Gonzalez faced a vast array of first-rate players, and the one he considered the most devastating was Lewis Alan Hoad. "When Lew's game was at its peak nobody could touch him," said Gonzalez, who cited Hoad as his toughest foe during his years on the pro tours, mainly head-to-head, one-nighters.

Hoad, who turned pro in 1957, after winning his second successive Wimbledon singles, was one rookie who seemed able to dethrone Gonzalez as the pro king. They were just about even when Hoad's troublesome back gave way during the winter of 1958. Gonzalez won the tour, 51-36, but felt threatened all the way, and trailed at one point, 18-9 as Lew won six straight. It was Pancho's closest brush with defeat after taking over leadership in 1954.

Hoad, a strapping 5-foot-8, 175-pounder with a gorilla chest and iron wrists, may have been the strongest man to play tennis in the world class. He blistered the ball and became impatient with rallying, preferring to hit for winners. It was a flamboyant style, and made for some bad errors when he wasn't in tune. But when his power was focused along with his concentration, Hoad came on like a tidal wave. He was strong enough to use topspin as an offensive drive. He was assault-minded, but had enough control to win the French title on slow clay in 1956, over Swede Sven Davidson, 6-4, 8-6, 6-3.

Born Nov. 23, 1934, 21 days after Ken Rosewall, in the same city, Sydney, the right-handed Hoad was bracketed with Rosewall throughout his amateur days. Although entirely different in stature, style, and personality, the two were called Australia's tennis twins, the prodigies who drew attention as teen-agers and were rivals and teammates through 1956. Hoad was stronger, but less patient and consistent, more easygoing. His back problems cut his career short in the mid-1960s while Rosewall, whose style was less taxing, kept on going into the next decade.

His countrymen fondly remember Hoad's Davis Cup triumph of 1953 over Tony Trabert on a rainy Melbourne afternoon. At 19, he and Rosewall had been selected to defend the Cup. The U.S. led, 2-1, in the finale and seemed about to clinch the Cup when the more experienced Trabert, already the U.S. champion, caught up at two sets all. Hoad hung on to win, however, 13-11, 6-3, 3-6, 2-6, 7-5, and Rosewall beat Vic Seixas the following day to save the Cup, 3-2.

Although they lost it to the Americans the next year, Hoad and Rosewall were awesome in 1955, retaking the prize from the

Yanks, 5-0. Hoad beat Wimbledon champ Trabert the first day, 4-6, 6-3, 6-3, 8-6, and got the clincher with Rex Hartwig over Trabert and Seixas. The twins defended the Cup from the U.S. for the last time together in 1956, 5-0, winning everything. Lew wiped out Herbie Flam, 6-2, 6-3, 6-3, on opening day and united with Kenny a last time to decide it, over Sammy Giammalva and Seixas, 1-6, 6-1, 7-5, 6-4.

Their first major titles were bagged in 1953, when Lew and Ken were allied to win the Australian, French, and Wimbledon doubles. They missed out on a Grand Slam on the last leg, the U.S. at Longwood in Boston, in a quarterfinal upset by unseeded Americans Straight Clark and Hal Burrows, 5-7, 14-12, 18-16, 9-7. But, taking 19 of 20 matches, he (in the left court) and Ken were the only male team other than countrymen Frank Sedgman and Ken McGregor (1951-52) and John Newcombe and Tony Roche (1967) to win three of the four in one year. Lew won 13 major titles in singles and doubles, and in 1956 appeared on his way to winning all four (Australian, French, Wimbledon and U.S.) singles within one calendar year, thus achieving a rare Grand Slam. However, after Hoad was three quarters of the way there, having beaten Rosewall for the Australian, 6-4, 3-6, 6-4, 7-5, and Wimbledon, 6-2, 4-6, 7-5, 6-4—Kenny lurked at Forest Hills to jam the Slam with a 4-6, 6-2, 6-2, 6-3, triumph. In his last significant tournament appearance in 1973, Lew reached the final of the South African doubles with Rob Maud, losing to Arthur Ashe and Tom Okker.

Despite losing out on a Grand Slam, his 1956 season was a luminous hard-working campaign that netted 32 titles: 15 victories in 26 singles tourneys on a 95-11 match record, 17 victories in 23 doubles starts on 79-5. He had planned to turn pro after that but decided to go for the Slam again. That dream was drilled almost immediately in the semis of the Australian by Neale Fraser. Though Lew resolutely and smashingly did repeat at Wimbledon on the loss of one set, blasting Ashley Cooper, 6-2, 6-1, 6-2, in the final—his 42nd singles title—he felt it was time to cash in. He accepted an offer from promoter Jack Kramer and began preparing for Gonzalez. For five straight years, he was in the world's Top 10, No. 1 in 1956.

Hoad (five attempts) and Bjorn Borg (10) are probably the two greatest players not to win the U.S. Championship. Lew married another player, countrywoman Jenny Staley (finalist in the 1954 Australian singles). He died July 3, 1994, in Fuengirola, Spain, where he and Jenny operated a tennis resort.

MAJOR TITLES (13)—Australian singles, 1956; French singles, 1956; Wimbledon singles, 1956-57; Australian doubles, 1953, 56-57; French doubles, 1953; Wimbledon doubles, 1953, 1955-56; U.S. doubles, 1956; French mixed, 1954. DAVIS CUP—1953-54-55-56, 1956; 10-2 singles, 7-2 doubles. SINGLES RECORD IN THE MAJORS—Australian (15-5), French (17-5), Wimbledon (32-7), U.S. (21-5).

Harry Hopman
Australia (1906–1985)
Hall of Fame—1978

A fine player, particularly in doubles, at which he won seven major titles, Henry Christian Hopman made his name as the most successful of all Davis Cup captains, steering Australia to 16 Cups between 1939 and 1967. His was the era of perhaps the greatest Cup players of all, the Hall of Fame Aussies from Frank Sedgman through Lew Hoad, Ken Rosewall, Ashley Cooper, Mervyn Rose, Rex Hartwig, Mal Anderson, Neale Fraser, Roy Emerson, Rod Laver, John Newcombe, Fred Stolle, Tony Roche.

Emphasizing super fitness, he drove and inspired them, and built pride in their underpopulated country's beating up on the rest of the world. The first of his 22 teams, 1938, reached the challenge round final, losing to the U.S. But he was back with the same pair, Adrian Quist and John Bromwich, to win a singular victory over the U.S. in 1939, from 0-2 down after the first day in Philadelphia.

Hop concentrated on his job as a newspaperman following World War II. But after the Aussies lost the Cup to the U.S. in 1946, and three more finales through 1949, there was a clamor for him to return to the captain's chair. With two youngsters, Sedgman and Ken McGregor, he won the Cup in New York in 1950, and the Down Under-takers were in business for a glorious near-quarter-century His teams compiled a 38-6 record.

As a player, a trim 5-foot-7, 133 pounds, he won the Australian doubles with Jack Crawford in 1929 and 1930 and four mixed titles with his first wife, the former Nell Hall, a record for married couples. In singles, his high point was the U.S. Championships of 1938 when he beat No. 5-seeded Elwood Cooke, 6-2, 4-6, 6-4, 10-8, and future U.S. and French champ Don McNeill, 6-4, 6-3, 7-5, to reach the quarters, where he was an historic footnote in Don Budge's original Grand Slam, 6-3, 6-1, 6-3.

Following his last Davis Cup series as captain, a loss to Mexico at Mexico City in 1969, he emigrated to the U.S. to become a highly-successful teaching pro, counseling such champions-to-be as Vitas Gerulaitis and John McEnroe at the Port Washington (N.Y.) Tennis Academy He later opened his own Hopman Tennis Academy with his wife, Lucy, at Largo, Fla. Hop was born Aug. 12, 1906, in Sydney and died Dec. 27, 1985, in Largo, Fla.

MAJOR TITLES (7)—Australian doubles, 1929, 1930; Australian mixed, 1930, 36-37, 39; U.S. mixed, 1939. DAVIS CUP (As player)—1928, 1930, 1932, 4-5 singles, 4-3 doubles. (As captain)—1938-39, 50-51-52-53-54-55-56-57-58-59-60-61-62-63-64-65-66-67-68-69; record 38-6, 16 Cups. SINGLES RECORD IN THE MAJORS—Australian (34-16), French (8-6), Wimbledon (15-9), U.S. (9-6)

Fred Hovey
United States (1868–1945)
Hall of Fame—1974

Frederick Howard Hovey, a Bostonian and Harvardian, won the U.S. Intercollegiate singles in 1890 and 1891 as well as the doubles with Bob Wrenn the second year. Four years later, he, a 5-foot-8, 170-pound right-hander, beat lefty Wrenn, 6-3, 6-2, 6-4, to end the Chicagoan's two-year reign as the U.S. Champion. Wrenn returned the favor the next year, 1896, 7-5, 3-6, 6-0, 1-6, 6-1, in the challenge round.

Between 1890 and 1896, he was in the U.S. Top 10 seven times, No. 1 in 1895. In 1893, he and Clarence Hobart, twice U.S. champs in doubles (1893-94), won the championship of the World Colum-

bian Exposition at Chicago. He was born Oct. 7, 1868, in Newton Centre, Mass., and died Oct. 18, 1945, in Miami Beach, Fla.

MAJOR TITLES (3)—U.S. singles, 1895; U.S. doubles, 1893-94 **OTHER U.S. TITLES** (3)—Intercollegiate singles, 1890-91, Intercollegiate doubles. 1891, with Robert Wrenn. **SINGLES RECORD IN THE MAJORS**—U.S. (25-5).

Joe Hunt
United States (1919–1945)
Hall of Fame—1966

Nobody knows for certain what went wrong when Lt. Joe Hunt sent his Navy fighter plane into its last dive. Pilot error? Mechanical failure? There were rumors of both, but the Atlantic swallowed forever all evidence of the Grumman Hellcat—along with the 1943 U.S. champion.

Fifteen days short of his 26th birthday, Joseph Raphael Hunt of the U.S. Navy was a victim of World War II, killed Feb. 2, 1945, during a routine training mission off Daytona Beach, Fla. The accident, with his training nearly complete, was never explained. Thus Hunt was the shortest-lived of Hall of Famers, ranked No. 1 for his U.S. title-winning performance, but unable the following year, 1944, to get leave from duty to defend the title.

A sturdy, handsome blond Los Angeleno, 6-feet, 165 lbs, he came from a wealthy tennis family. His father, Reuben, won the Southern championship in 1906, and his older sister Marianne in 1934, and brother Charles in 1945, ranked No. 20 nationally. His wife, Jacque Virgil, had been the No. 1 Southern California junior and played Forest Hills in 1943, too.

"He was a strong guy, big serve and volley, and took to grass, coming from the Southern California concrete," says fellow Hall of Famer Pancho Segura. "Everybody thought he'd be the big man, along with Jack Kramer, after the war."

Joe was alone in his progression to the top, the only man to win the U.S. junior 15s and 18s, the Intercollegiate singles (for the Naval Academy) and then the U.S. Championship. In a bizarre finish to his title triumph over Southern California buddy and rival, Kramer (6-3, 6-8, 10-8, 6-0), Hunt, on leave from the Atlantic fleet, won the title, so to speak, lying down. He collapsed to the turf with leg cramps as Kramer's last shot flew out of court, and might not have been able to play another point. The humid 90-degree afternoon got to him in the unique all-military final. Seaman Kramer was also on leave, from the Coast Guard. It was the last important tennis tournament for Joe, who had to report back to his destroyer. However, a year later, at Pensacola, Fla., he did win a local Labor Day event over a fellow flight trainee, 1942 U.S. champ Ted Schroeder.

In 1938, at Southern Cal (doubles) and 1941 at the Naval Academy (singles), Hunt was the only player other than Malcolm Chace (Brown and Yale, 1893, 1894, 1895), to win U.S. Intercollegiate titles for two different schools. Husky and athletic, Hunt also played football at Navy. He, 20, and Kramer, 18, were involved in the 1939 Davis Cup loss, 3-2, to Australia. As the second youngest Cup pair for the U.S., they were the first domino to fall, 5-7, 6-2, 7-5, 6-2, as Aussies John Bromwich and Adrian Quist began an historic comeback from 0-2 to victory.

One of the youngest to make the U.S. Top 10 at 17 in 1936, he was a Forest Hills quarterfinalist in 1937 and 1938, semifinalist in 1939 and 1940, losing both times to Bobby Riggs. Born Feb. 17, 1919 in San Francisco, he was inducted into the Hall of Fame in 1966.

MAJOR TITLE (1)—U.S. singles, 1943. **OTHER U.S. TITLES** (3)—Intercollegiate singles, 1941; Clay Court doubles, 1938, with Lew Wetherell; Intercollegiate doubles, 1938, with Wetherell. **DAVIS CUP**—1939, 0-1 doubles. **SINGLES RECORD IN THE MAJORS**—U.S. (21-4).

Lamar Hunt
United States (1932–2006)
Hall of Fame—1993—Administrator

A man about Halls of Fame, Texan Lamar Hunt entered the tennis valhalla in 1993, having been inducted previously into the Professional Football Hall of Fame and the Soccer Hall of Fame.

Although he played football—"I sat on the bench"— at Southern Methodist, Hunt, scion of a prominent Dallas oil industry family, made his mark in American and international sport with his organizational and promotional strengths.

He was a leading founder of the American Football League, which eventually merged with the NFL. And with his daughter, Hunt has been credited with the naming of the Super Bowl. He was owner of the Kansas City Chiefs and for a time owned the Dallas Tornados in the North American Soccer League.

It was as a partner in the establishment of World Championship Tennis (WCT)—and later its guiding light—that he was a strong global influence in transforming and professionalizing the tournament game. In 1967, a New Orleans friend, Dave Dixon, enlisted Hunt's aid in forming WCT. Headquartered in Dallas, WCT hastened the dawn of Open tennis with the signing of the elite of the amateurs.

WCT developed a circuit and season of its own, leading the way to increased paydays for the pros that forced the rest of the tennis world to catch up. The seemingly unreal $50,000 first prizes offered for the playoffs champion—first awarded in 1971 and won by Ken Rosewall—awakened the world to pro tennis.

Unfortunately (and ungratefully), the ATP (Association of Tennis Professionals), in reorganizing the men's tour in 1990, froze WCT out, and Hunt's organization ceased operations after 23 years of raising standards within the professional game. Hunt was born Aug. 2, 1932, in Eldorado, Ark. He died Dec. 13, 2006.

Frank Hunter
United States (1894–1981)
Hall of Fame—1961

As one of the earlier touring pros, Francis Townsend Hunter joined the nomad ranks in 1931 after a distinguished amateur career, having been a hockey star at Cornell. A right-handed New Yorker, he was born there June 28, 1894. He played extremely well for his country, taking a 1924 Olympic gold medal in doubles

alongside Vinnie Richards, and helping build a 2-1 lead in the losing Davis Cup 1927 finale, yoked to Bill Tilden in a five-set win over France's Jacques Brugnon and Jean Borotra.

He came close, as finalist, to the U.S. title twice in succession: 1928, lost to Henri Cochet, 4-6, 6-4, 3-6, 7-5, 6-3; and 1929 to teammate Tilden, 3-6, 6-3, 4-6, 6-2, 6-4. He also lost the 1923 Wimbledon final to another teammate, Bill Johnston, 6-0, 6-3, 6-1. And he was one of those unlucky three Wimbledon victims in a row who built futile two-set leads over 1927 Wimbledon champ Cochet only to lose. Preceding Tilden and Jean Borotra, Hunter lost in the quarterfinals, 3-6, 3-6, 6-3, 6-2, 6-3. But he won the Wimbledon doubles twice, 1924 with Olympic sidekick, Vinnie Richards, and 1927 with Tilden. Frank and Vinnie were golden at the 1924 Paris Olympics, taking the doubles from the hosts, Jacques Brugnon and Cochet, 4-6, 6-2, 6-3, 2-6, 6-3.

Hunter's greatest singles success was under cover at New York's Seventh Regiment Armory, winning the U.S. Indoor titles of 1922 over Frank Anderson, 6-4, 1-6, 7-5, 6-2, and 1930 over Julius Seligson, 6-3, 6-2, 6-3. He lost the finals of 1923 and 1924 to Richards, and 1929 to Borotra, and won the doubles in 1923 and 1924 with Richards, and 1929 with Tilden.

A favorite of the ladies, he won three straight Wimbledon mixed—1927-28 with Bunny Ryan, and 1929 with Helen Wills. Hunter, a fine volleyer, stressed power in forehand and serve, putting his 5-11, 180-pound frame into those strokes. He ranked in the U.S. Top 10 five times between 1922 and 1929, No. 2 in 1927-28-29, and in the world's Top 10, 1923, 1927, 1928 and 1929, No. 4 in 1928. He was named to the Hall of Fame in 1961 and died Dec. 2, 1981, in Palm Beach, Fla.

MAJOR TITLES (6)—U.S. doubles, 1927; Wimbledon doubles, 1924, 27; Wimbledon mixed 1927-28-29. **OTHER U.S. TITLES** (5)—Indoor singles. 1922, 30; Indoor doubles, 1923-24, with Vinnie Richards; 1929, with Bill Tilden. **DAVIS CUP**—1927-28-29, 3-1 singles, 1-1 doubles. **SINGLES RECORD IN THE MAJORS**—French (7-3), Wimbledon (18-6), U.S. (38-13).

Helen Jacobs
United States (1908–1997)
Hall of Fame—1962

Helen Hull Jacobs had the misfortune to be a contemporary of Helen Wills Moody. Four times in the battle of Helens in the final round at Wimbledon, Jacobs lost. She also lost to her archrival at Forest Hills in the 1928 U.S. final.

On top of all those defeats by Helen the First, Jacobs was beaten in the 1934 Wimbledon final by Dorothy Round of Britain, and three times she was turned back in a U.S. final by Alice Marble (1936, 1939, 1940).

Particularly bitter for her to take was a defeat in the 1935 Wimbledon final. Moody that season was struggling, and in the final round, Jacobs led at match point, 5-3 in the final set. Victory seemed at hand when Wills threw up a lob that barely got to the net, and Jacobs waited to smash it for the final point. However, a wind current caught the ball and Jacobs, off balance, hit it into the net. Moody rallied and went on to her seventh Wimbledon title, 6-3, 3-6, 7-5. At the time, Jacobs had none.

In spite of so much adversity, Jacobs, a 5-foot-6, 145-pound right-hander, born Aug. 6, 1908, in Globe, Ariz., was as stout of heart as any champion. A U.S. finalist eight times over a stretch of a dozen years (1928-40), Jacobs won four straight, 1932-35, beginning, 6-2, 6-2, over Carolin Babcock, turning into a 28-match winning streak until dropping a hard-fought 1936 final, 4-6, 6-3, 6-2, to her Forest Hills nemesis, Alice Marble. Only Helen Wills (46) and Chris Evert (31) had longer U.S. streaks, but she and Evert were the only victors four straight years.

In 1932 at Forest Hills, she caused a sartorial furor, introducing shorts to the female tournament. At last in 1936, she took the victor's silver at Wimbledon, beating Hilda Krahwinkel Sperling 6-2, 4-6, 7-5. Twice she made it to the French final, but fell to the other Helen in 1930 and lefty Peggy Scriven in 1934.

Jacobs' unflagging courage and her iron will to win were her biggest assets. She had little of the power that Moody applied, and Jacobs' forehand stroke was so unsatisfactory that she foresook it for a slice, not too effective either to stand off a full-blooded drive or to repel a volleyer. Her backhand, while not severe, was steadfast, reliable against any amount of pressure, and she won heavily with it.

It was at the net where she was most effective. She was not as conclusive with her volley or her smash as Marble, but she was a determined, skilled foe at close quarters, and her fighting traits counted most, whatever her position on the court. Even when afflicted with injuries, she refused to be discouraged. Her admirable qualities, including sportsmanship and great self-reliance, had a strong appeal for tennis galleries.

A feud was built up in publications between the two Helens that Jacobs said never existed. Moody was pictured as resenting Jacobs following in her footsteps. Both played at the Berkeley (Calif.) Tennis Club, had the same coach, William "Pop" Fuller, won national junior championships two years in a row and attended the University of California. The Jacobs family lived in the Wills' former home. The two Helens did not see each other except in connection with tennis.

Jacobs, after eight losses to Moody, finally got the victory she was after in the 1933 U.S. Championships, although even then it was not a complete one. She won the first set against Moody, 8-6, and lost the second, 6-3. When the score went to 3-0 in Jacobs' favor in the third set, Moody walked to the umpire's stand, informed the official that because of pain in her back she was unable to continue, and conceded the match. Jacobs had dealt Moody her first big defeat since 1926—snapping a 111-match chain of wins. It would be Jacobs' lone win in an 11-match rivalry.

Jacobs filled out her U.S. streak by beating Sarah Palfrey, 6-1, 6-4, and 6-2, 6-4, in the 1934-35 finals.

She was ranked in the world's Top 10 12 straight times from 1928, including No. 1 in 1936, and served in the Navy in World War II.

She was elected to the Hall of Fame in 1962 and died June 2, 1997 at East Hampton, N.Y.

MAJOR TITLES (10)—Wimbledon singles. 1936; U.S. singles, 1932, 1933, 1934, 1935; U.S. doubles, 1932, 1933, 1934, 1935; U.S. mixed, 1934. **WIGHTMAN CUP**—1927-28-

29-30-31-32-33-34-35-36-37, 39, 14-7 singles, 5-4 doubles. **SINGLES RECORD IN THE MAJORS**—French (21-7), Wimbledon (55-11), U.S. (64-11).

Robert Walter Johnson
United States (1899–)
Hall of Fame—2009—Contributor

As the imposing patron of Althea Gibson and Arthur Ashe, Dr. Robert Walter "Whirlwind" Johnson of Lynchburg, Va., (a physician), was a strong influence in breaking color line in American tennis. He guided the early phases of the careers of Gibson, the two-time U.S. and Wimbledon champion, and other black players, overseeing Gibson's entry into U.S. Tennis Association events in 1950, thus ending tennis segregation. Johnson was born on April 16, 1899 in Norfolk, Va. He graduated from Lincoln (Pa.) University (named Negro All-American football as a running back and was dubbed "Whirlwind") and Meharry (Tenn.) Medical School. Johnson developed a passion for tennis as intern at Prairie View (Tex.) Hospital. He later won six American Tennis Association mixed doubles titles with Gibson. He was selected for the Virginia Sports Hall of Fame in 1972. He died June 28, 1971 in Lynchburg. Former *USA Today* tennis writer Doug Smith wrote a biography on Johnson called *Whirlwind: The Godfather of Black Tennis* in 2004.

Bill Johnston
United States (1894–1946)
Hall of Fame—1958

William M. Johnston's name is inevitably associated with Bill Tilden's. Tilden was "Big Bill" (6-foot-2) and Johnston "Little Bill" (5-foot-8-1/2), and they were the twin terrors who turned back the Australasians, French and Japanese in the Davis Cup challenge round from 1920 through 1926, a seven-year span of invincibility unequaled in those international team matches.

Big Bill and Little Bill were teammates and they were also rivals. It was Johnston's bad luck that his career was contemporaneous with the player many regard as the greatest ever. Otherwise Johnston might have won the U.S. Championships most of the years it fell to Tilden, from 1920 to 1925. As it was, Little Bill won it twice, in 1915 and in 1919, defeating Maurice McLoughlin the first time, 0-6, 6-1, 7-5, 10-8, and Tilden in the 1919 final, 6-4, 6-4, 6-3. Johnston was runner-up six times, and in five of those years it was Tilden who beat him in the final. He got his Wimbledon title in 1923 when Tilden was absent, beating Frank Hunter, 6-0, 6-3, 6-1.

Until the French began to catch up to Big Bill and Little Bill in 1926, Johnston had been winning his Davis Cup matches with the loss of few sets. In seven challenge rounds, he won 11 of 14 matches in singles. He lost only once until 1927, when his age and his health began to tell. He ranked in the world's Top 10 eight straight years from 1919 and in the U.S. Top 10 12 times between 1913 and 1926, No. 1 in 1915 and in 1919.

The topspin forehand drive he hammered with the western grip was one of the most famous and effective shots in tennis history. No other player executed it as well as he did, taking the ball shoulder high and leaping off the ground on his follow-

through. He was also one of the best volleyers the game has known, despite meeting the ball near the service line, where he stationed himself because of his shortness. He used the same face of the racket for backhand and forehand.

A right-hander, Johnston was born Nov. 2, 1894, in San Francisco and developed many of his skills on public parks courts. His whole game was aggressive and he played to win on the merit of his strokes rather than on the opponent's errors. Though he did not have a big serve, he was secure with his overhead and angled his smash effectively. He had as much fight as anyone who was ever champion, and many times when he came off the court, dripping with perspiration after a prolonged struggle, he was five to eight pounds below his usual weight of 125.

Such was the case in his U.S. final with Tilden in 1922 at the Germantown Cricket Club in Philadelphia in which Johnston won the first two sets and led by 3-0 in the fourth. It seemed that every spectator in the stands was cheering for Johnston, the favorite of galleries virtually every time he went on the court. Both he and Tilden had two legs on the challenge trophy, and Little Bill had his heart set on retiring it for his permanent keeping in this match. It was a crushing disappointment when he lost in five sets, 4-6, 3-6, 6-2, 6-3, 6-4.

Following the 1927 season, when he lost the Cup-removal match to France's Henri Cochet, 6-4, 4-6, 6-2, 6-4, Johnston retired from competition. His health had not been robust from the time he served in the Navy in World War I. He died May 1, 1946, and 12 years later was enshrined in the Hall of Fame. Little Bill had made a big name in tennis.

MAJOR TITLES (7)—Wimbledon singles, 1923; U.S. singles, 1915, 1919; U.S. doubles. 1915-16, 20; U.S. mixed, 1921. **OTHER U.S. TITLES** (3)—Clay Court singles, 1919-20; Clay Court doubles, 1919, with Sam Hardy. **DAVIS CUP**—1920-21-22-23-24-25-26-27, 14-3 singles, 4-0 doubles. **SINGLES RECORD IN THE MAJORS**—Wimbledon (8-1), U.S. (59-11).

Ann Haydon Jones
Great Britain (1930—)
Hall of Fame—1985

The first left-handed woman to win Wimbledon, Adrianne Shirley Haydon Jones had to cool a rampaging Billie Jean King to do it in the 1969 final, 3-6, 6-3, 6-2. King had won three straight times and 24 straight matches. Before that, Ann had shown her all-around value and steadiness by winning the French in 1961 over Yola Ramirez of Mexico, 6-2, 6-1, and 1966 over Nancy Richey, 6-3, 6-1. She could attack or stay back, and had a compact service motion with little windup. In 1967, despite a leg injury that hobbled her, she pushed King hard (11-9, 6-4) in the U.S. final, gamely extricating herself from nine set points before losing the first, and two match points at the end.

A buxom blonde, 5-foot-7, 135 lbs, Ann was always a stalwart in playing for her country in Federation and Wightman Cups. In 1975, at 37, after she'd stopped touring, she set aside motherhood for a weekend to play a small but important doubles role in Britain's 5-2 Wightman triumph at Cleveland's Public Auditorium. She and Virginia Wade beat Julie Anthony and Janet Newberry,

6-2, 3-6, 7-6. Deciding to go for dollars, she, King, Francoise Durr and Rosie Casals became the first professional female touring troupe, signing with George MacCall, promoter of the National Tennis League, in 1968.

Jones was born Oct. 7, 1938, in Birmingham, England, to parents who were outstanding table tennis players. She followed in their paddling steps as a five-time finalist for various world championship titles. But she was to make her name in tennis after winning the British junior championships of 1954 and 1955, moving on to place in the world's Top 10 every year between 1957 and 1970 (except except for 1964), No. 2 in 1967 and 1969.

Her Wimbledon triumph was a gem of persistence—Ann won on her 14th try. Seeded No. 4, she beat the No. 5, No. 2 and No. 1 seeds in the stretch to do so: Richey, 6-2, 7-5; Margaret Court 10-12, 6-3, 6-2; and King. Jones played 157 matches at Wimbledon: 57-13 in singles, 33-15 in doubles, 29-10 in mixed. She married Philip "Pip" Jones in 1962 and entered the Hall of Fame in 1985.

MAJOR TITLES (7)—French singles, 1961, 66; Wimbledon singles, 1969; French doubles, 1963, 68-69; Wimbledon mixed, 1969. FEDERATION CUP—1963-64-65-66-67, 71, 11-8 singles, 13-7 doubles. WIGHTMAN CUP—1957-58-59-60-61-62-63-64-65-66-67, 70, 75, 10-11 singles, 6-5 doubles. SINGLES RECORD IN THE MAJORS—Australian (3-2), French (46-9), Wimbledon (57-13), U.S. (36-10).

Marion Jones
United States (1879–1965)
Hall of Fame—2006

A freakishly lost point cost 18-year-old Californian Marion Jones the U.S. championship in her 1898 debut. Undiscouraged, she would return to win the title twice, breaking the Eastern monopoly, the first from the far West to succeed in making the cross-country journey from Southern California to be crowned in Philadelphia.

A diminutive righthander, 5-foot-2, she was one of the shortest champs, but long on speed, accuracy, concentration and endurance even though she had been a sickly child. She was hardy by then, and had to be because the women played best-of-five set finals. In the fifth set of the 1898 final, holding a championship point against reigning Juliette Atkinson, she lost it when Juliette's shot hit a stray ball lying on Marion's court. Reprieved, Atkinson collected herself and went on to victory, 6-3, 5-7, 6-4, 2-6, 7-5. That was the challenge round. Jones had defeated Helen Crump in the all-comers final, 6-3, 2-6, 10-8.

Delayed by a year, Jones returned to seize the 1899 title, 6-1, 6-1, 7-5, over Maud Banks. Atkinson did not defend, nor did Jones in 1900. Marion couldn't quite hang on in the all-comers of 1901, losing to Elisabeth "Bessie" Moore, 4-6, 1-6, 9-7, 9-7, 6-3, again missing out on a match point. But she was back 12 months later to win the all-comers, 8-6, 6-4, over Carrie Neely. Then she scored a challenge round TKO, 6-2, 1-0, default—settling the 1902 title—overcoming Bessie Moore, who fainted after one game of the second set.

Bessie had her revenge in the 1903 challenge round, beating Marion, 7-5, 8-6. Maybe Marion needed more sets to get into it, but the best-of-five days were over. By that time, approaching her 24th birthday, she may have felt her playing days were over, too. She had been precocious, winning the first of her five straight Southern California titles (1894–98) as a 14-year-old. She was married shortly after the 1903 Championships to David Farquar, and had three children.

She had been a pioneer, the first of 30 Californians (16 women) to snare the U.S. singles title, and the first American woman to play abroad, making the 1900 quarterfinals at Wimbledon, losing to England's Mrs. G.E. Evered, 7-5, 6-2. That year in Paris she and younger sister, Georgina, were the first American women to play Olympic tennis. Marion lost in the semis to the gold medalist Charlotte Cooper of Britain, but gained two bronze medals, singles and, with Brit Laurie Doherty, mixed doubles. Georgina also played in the U.S. of 1899 and 1901, winning no matches

Neither had any concern about traveling expenses. Their father, John Percival Jones, made a fortune in silver mining in Nevada, was a U.S. senator, 1873–1903. Born Nov. 2, 1879, Gold Hill, Nevada, she died March 14, 1965, West Hollywood, Calif., and entered the Hall in 2006.

MAJOR TITLES (4)—U.S. singles, 1899, 1902; U.S. doubles, 1902; U.S. mixed, 1901. SINGLES RECORD IN THE MAJORS—Wimbledon (1-1), U.S. (17-3)

Perry T. Jones
United States (1890–1970)
Hall of Fame—1970—Administrator

A powerful figure in making Southern California a tennis vineyard of champions, Perry Thomas Jones oversaw the game from his office at the Los Angeles Tennis Club for well over a quarter-century. As president of the Southern California Association and director of the Pacific Southwest Championships, he was active in the game from bottom to top, singling out promising juniors for attention and travel and making his tournament one of the best in the U.S.

In short, Perry T., or Mr. Jones, as he was called, stood imposingly as Mr. Tennis of the West Coast, an exceptional fund-raiser whose judgment and help forwarded the careers of numerous stars, including Jack Kramer, Billie Jean King and Dennis Ralston.

The last was Alex Olmedo, the Peruvian student at the University of Southern California. Maneuvering controversially, Jones got him, the only non-citizen to play for the U.S., approved for the Davis Cup team in 1958, citing the fact that Peru had no team. Jones, the captain that year, was understandably eager to have Los Angeles resident Olmedo aboard. Olmedo led the U.S. to the Cup over Australia. Jones also captained the losing 1959 team. He was born June 22, 1890, in Etiwanda, Calif., and died September 16, 1970 in Los Angeles.

Bob Kelleher
United States (1913—)
Hall of Fame—2000—Administrator

No one has had a longer or more distinguished career in tennis than Robert Joseph Kelleher, a federal judge in Los Ange-

les, who marked his 95th birthday March 5, 2008. New York born, raised near the West Side Tennis Club, Forest Hills, he was a junior member and, for several years, during the U.S. Championships, was a ball boy there. Bob recalls working Bill Tilden's farewell to the Championships he had ruled for so long, a semifinal loss in 1930 to the champ, Johnny Doeg, 10-8, 6-3, 3- 6, 12-10, and that the great figure was "haughty and grumpy, stalling to buy time. I remember Doeg (21, Tilden's junior by 16 years] yelling, 'Come on Bill—let's play tennis!'"

That has always been Kelleher's outlook, getting on with things intelligently, in sport, law and life—with firmness, understanding and a well-tuned sense of humor, but ever moving ahead. His nature guided him well as he shepherded an historically recalcitrant U.S. Tennis Association into the uncharted land of "Opens" in 1968. The game was lucky that he was USTA president at the time, willing to buck the "old goats," as he called them, longtime officials who sought to maintain the status-quo of phony amateurism, preferring to keep the game cloistered in small private clubs.

Although the USTA has been blessed with few progressive presidents, Kelleher was one of a handful, the right man at the right time to plant the seeds that would blossom. (Fellow Hall of Famer Slew Hester, who thought big, in lifting the U.S. Open to Flushing Meadows from Forest Hills in 1978, was another.)

Like his co-revolutionary, Herman David, Wimbledon chairman (also a Hall of Famer), Kelleher "refused to be associated with a crooked enterprise," the tarnished system of under-the-table payments to so-called amateurs. He wanted to "start anew, with everything in the open." That's what he orchestrated in the U.S. as David did in Britain, respectful but independent of one another. With the two leading powers supporting Open tennis, the ITF, largely anti-Open, had no choice but to follow.

A lifelong love of tennis has spurred his urge to preserve and promote the game as player, administrator and fan. He was a fine player on the Williams College varsity, graduating in 1935. Finishing Harvard Law in 1938, he moved to Los Angeles to open a highly-regarded law practice before entering the U.S. Navy in World War II (1943-45) for duty as an officer in the Pacific. He was appointed to the federal bench in 1970.

He won the U.S. Hard Court 45s doubles with Elbert Lewis in 1958, 60, 62. His wife, Gracyn Wheeler Kelleher (1918-80), made the U.S. Top 10 five times between 1935 and 1940, No. 4 in 1936.

For two years, 1962-63, he captained the U.S. Davis Cup team, confidently and calmly leading an arduous campaign of six series, covering four continents, to the grand prize at Adelaide in 1963. Cracking an Australian stranglehold of four years, Chuck McKinley and Dennis Ralston were his workhorses.

Billie Jean King
United States (1943—)
Hall of Fame—1987

The fireman's daughter, Billie Jean Moffitt King, began blazing through the tennis world in 1960 when she first appeared in the U.S. women's rankings at No. 4. She was 17. For more than four decades she has continued as a glowing force in the game—the all-time Wimbledon champion, frequently the foremost player, a crusader in building the female professional game (enhancing the game as a whole), remaining relevant to sport today, an inspiration to millions. The Flushing Meadows home of the U.S. Open was named the USTA / Billie Jean King National Tennis Center in 2006.

Born Nov. 22, 1943, in Long Beach, Calif:, Billie Jean, a 5-foot-4 1/2, 130-pound right-hander, was named for her father, Bill Moffitt, a Long Beach fireman and an enthusiastic athlete, though not a tennis player. Her brother, Randy Moffitt, became a pitcher for the San Francisco Giants. She developed on the public courts of Long Beach and first gained international recognition in 1961 by joining 18-year-old Karen Hantze for a surprising triumph in the Wimbledon women's doubles over Aussies Margaret Smith (Court) and Jan Lehane, 6-3, 6-4. Unseeded, they were the youngest team to win it. That was the first of 20 Wimbledon championships, making King the record winner at the most prestigious tourney, sharing it since 2003 when her friend Martina Navratilova caught up. Centre Court was her magic garden from the first time she saw it in 1961.

In 1979, she got the 20th at her 19th Wimbledon, the doubles, in the company of Navratilova (over Betty Stove and Wendy Turnbull, 5-7, 6-3, 6-2). She won her last major, the U.S. doubles, in 1980, beside Martina, over Pam Shriver and Stove.

Elizabeth Ryan's 19 Wimbledon titles (between 1914 and 1934) were all in doubles and mixed doubles. King won six singles, 10 doubles, and four mixed between 1961 and 1979, and in 1979 lengthened another Wimbledon record by appearing in her 27th final, the doubles. Ryan was in 24 finals. Of all the men and women to compete at Wimbledon only Navratilova played more matches (279) than King's 265, of which B.J. was 95-15 in singles, 74-12 in doubles, 55-14 in mixed. She won 12 singles titles at major championships (one Australian, one French, six Wimbledon and four U.S.)

In her initial singles major final, Wimbledon in 1966, she beat three-time champ Maria Bueno of Brazil, 6-3, 3-6, 6-1, She followed up by beating Ann Jones of Britain in 1967, 6-3, 6-4 and Judy Tegart (Dalton) of Australia, 9-7, 7-5, in the first "Open" Wimbledon in 1968. In 1967, she took her first U.S. singles over Jones, but the most rousing of the four was 1974, a pyrotechnical performance from two assault-minded dolls, over Evonne Goolagong of Australia, 3-6, 6-3, 7-5. Probably her most memorable Wimbledon match was a loss, the record 46-game 1970 final to Court 14-12, 11-9. Neither let up in attacking, even though both were playing hurt.

Billie Jean's has been a career of firsts. In 1968, she was the first woman of the Open era to sign a pro contract to tour in a female tournament group, with Rosie Casals, Francoise Durr and Jones, the women's auxiliary of the NTL (National Tennis League), which also included six men. (A few women before King had turned pro to make head-to-head barnstorming tours, notably Suzanne Lenglen in 1926.)

In 1971, B.J. was the first woman athlete over the 100-grand hurdle, winning $117,000. During that memorable season, she played 31 tournaments in singles, winning 17, and 26 in doubles, winning a record 21. She had a match mark of 112-13 in singles, a record number of wins, and 80-5 in doubles. Overall, it added up

to 38 titles on 192 match wins, both records. Imagine how many millions such a campaign would be worth today.

In 1973, Billie Jean engaged in the widely ballyhooed "Battle of the Sexes," defeating 55-year-old ex-Wimbledon champ Bobby Riggs, 6-4, 6-3, 6-3, a nationally-televised lallapalooza that captured the nation's fancy and drew a record tennis crowd, 30,472, to Houston's Astrodome.

In 1974, she became the first woman to coach a professional team containing men when she served as player-coach of the Philadelphia Freedoms of World Team Tennis, a league she and her husband, Larry King, helped establish. As a tribute to her, Elton John composed and recorded *Philadelphia Freedom*. Traded to the New York Apples, she led that team to WTT titles in 1976-77 as a player.

Ten years after Riggs, BJK was to establish a geriatric mark herself, winning Birmingham (England) over Alycia Moulton, 6-0, 7-5. At 39 years, five months, she was the oldest woman to take a pro singles title.

An aggressive, emotional player, Billie Jean specialized in serve-and-volley tactics, aided by quickness and a highly competitive nature. She overcame several knee operations to continue as a winner into her 40th year. As a big-match player, she was unsurpassed, excelling in team situations when she represented the U.S. In nine years on the Federation Cup team, she helped the U.S. gain the final each time, and take seven Cups by winning 51 of her 55 singles and doubles. In the Wightman Cup against Britain, she played on only one losing side in 10 years, winning 21 of her 26 singles and doubles.

Outspoken on behalf of women's rights, in and out of sports—tennis in particular—she was possibly the most influential figure in popularizing professional tennis in the United States. She worked tirelessly to promote the Virginia Slims tour during the early 1970s when the women realized they must separate from the men to achieve recognition and significant prize money on their own. With the financial backing of Virginia Slims, the organizational acumen of Gladys Heldman and the salesmanship and winning verve of King, the women pros built an extremely profitable circuit.

Only two women, Margaret Smith Court (62) and Navratilova (59) won more majors than King's 39 in singles, doubles and mixed. In regard to U.S. titles on all surfaces (grass, clay, hard court, indoor), King is second at 31 behind Hazel Hotchkiss Wightman's 34. But Billie Jean is the only woman to win on all four, equalling Tony Trabert, and Art Larsen, the only men to do so. King and Casals were the only doubles team to win U.S. titles on all four surfaces. She won seven of her major doubles with Casals, her most frequent and successful partner.

Between 1963 and 1980, Billie Jean was in the world's Top 10 18 times, including five times as No. 1 (1966-67-68, 71, 74) and four times as No. 2 (1970, 73, 75, 77). She held her last world ranking, No. 13, at age 40 in 1983.

She greatly aided Owen Davidson of Australia in making his mixed doubles Grand Slam in 1967 with two partners. King and Davidson won the French, Wimbledon and U.S. after he took the Australian with Lesley Turner. She scored three major triples, winning the singles, doubles and mixed at Wimbledon in 1967

and 1973, and at the U.S. in 1967, and won the longest singles set played by a woman (36 games) in a 1963 Wightman Cup win over Christine Truman, 6-4, 19-17.

Billie Jean's major swan song occurred at 39 in 1983 at Wimbledon, a semifinal finish (her fourteenth), losing to 18-year-old Andrea Jaeger, 6-1, 6-1. Seven years later she played a cameo role in the Boca Raton, Fla., tourney, winning a doubles match with 13-year-old pro rookie Jennifer Capriari.

In a career encompassing the amateur and Open eras, she won 67 pro and 37 amateur career singles titles, 101 pro doubles. She reached 38 other pro singles finals and had 677-149 singles W-L record as a pro. Her prize money: $1,966,487.

Divorce ended her marriage. A founder and ex-president of the WTA, she remains active in World Team Tennis as an officer, formerly commissioner. She returned to her USTA roots in 1995 as captain of the Federation Cup team, having been player-captain in 1965 (a loss) and 1976 (a win). She guided the U.S. team to three Cups (1996, 1999, and 2000). As U.S. women's Olympic coach, she mentored Lindsay Davenport, Gigi Fernandez and Mary Joe Fernandez to gold medals in 1996, as well as Venus and Serena Williams to golds, and Monica Seles to a bronze in 2000.

MAJOR TITLES (39)—Australian singles, 1968; French singles, 1972; Wimbledon singles, 1966, 1967, 1968, 1972, 1973, 1975; U.S. singles, 1967, 1971, 1972, 1974; French doubles, 1972; Wimbledon doubles, 1961, 1962, 1965, 1967, 1968, 1970, 1971, 1972, 1973, 1979; U.S. Doubles, 1964, 1967, 1974, 1977, 1980; Australian mixed, 1968; French mixed, 1967, 1970; Wimbledon mixed, 1967, 1971, 1973, 1974; US. Mixed, 1967, 1971, 1973, 1976. **OTHER U.S. TITLES** (18)—Indoor singles, 1966, 1967, 1968, 1971, 1974; Clay Court singles, 1971; Hard Court singles, 1966; Indoor doubles, 1966, 1968, 1971, 1975, with Casals; 1979, with Navratilova; 1983. with Sharon Walsh; Clay Court doubles, 1960, with Darlene Hard; 1971, with Dalton; Hard Court doubles, 1966 with Casals; Indoor mixed, 1966, 1967, with Paul Sullivan (USA) **FEDERATION CUP**—1963-64-65-66-67,76-77-78-79,25-4 singles, 27-0 doubles: **WIGHTMAN CUP**—1961-62-63-64-65-66-67, 70, 77-78, 14-2 singles, 7-3 doubles **SINGLES RECORD IN THE MAJORS**—Australian (17-4), French (21-6), Wimbledon (95-15), U.S. (58-14).

Jan Kodes
Czechoslovakia (1945—)
Hall of Fame—1990

Determination marked the grim-faced Jan Kodes, who clawed and battled to many a victory, though seemingly exhausted. As a sportsman, he was even more a hero to many of his countrymen for his refusal to leave the repressed country as Jaroslav Drobny, Martina Navratilova and Ivan Lendl had done. Thus they shared more fully in his major triumphs: Wimbledon of 1973 and the French of 1970 and 1971.

A compact, muscular 5-foot-9 right-hander, Kodes was a standout and dogged groundstroker. He volleyed well, too, but was disdainful of grass even though he signalled his ability there in 1971 by knocking top-seeded John Newcombe out of the U.S. Open in the first round, 2-6, 7-6 (5-1), 7-6 (5-1), 6-3. Nothing like that had happened since 1930 when Berkeley Bell grounded top foreign-seed Jean Borotra in the opening round.

Pushing upward and onward, all the while moaning about "this joke tennis, this grass," Jan, beaten in the first round at Wimble-

don, next escaped Pierre Barthes, 2-6, 5-7, 6-4, 6-4, 6-4, who served at 4-3, 40-30 in the fifth. In the semis, he startled third-seeded Arthur Ashe, 7-6 (5-3), 3-6, 4-6, 6-3, 6-4, to become an unseeded U.S. finalist. He didn't break in tie-breakers (four-for-four) until the last one finished his astonishing journey: Stan Smith beat him in the final, 3-6, 6-3, 6-2, 7-6 (5-3). Two years later, he was the Wimbledon champ in the infamous "strike year," defeating Alex Metreveli of the USSR, 6-1, 9-8 (7-5), 6-3, and fought Newcombe in a brilliant five-set U.S. final, losing, 6-4, 1-6, 4-6, 6-2, 6-3.

Kodes, the No. 7 seed, easily beat Zeljko Franulovic, 6-2, 6-4, 6-0, to win the French in 1970, countered the artistry of Ilie Nastase, 8-6, 6-2, 2-6, 7-5, the following year, but fell to Patrick Proisy, 6-4, 6-2, 6-4, in the 1972 quarters, ending a 17-match run at Roland Garros.

As a devoted Davis Cupper, he played 15 years and 39 series for Czechoslovakia beginning in 1966, and was among the top 20 players in matches played (95) and won (60): 39-20 in singles, 21-15 in doubles. He led the team to the 1975 Cup round, a 3-2 defeat by Sweden at Stockholm, and played a cameo doubles role along the way in 1980 as he realized a dream—the Cup for Czechoslovakia, Lendl-powered.

Besides his three majors he won nine pro titles in singles, 17 in doubles, and accumulated $693,197 in career prize money. Jan was in the world's Top 10 in 1971 and 1973, No. 5 in the former. Born March 1, 1945, in Prague, he has served as his country's national coach and Davis Cup captain, and entered the Hall of Fame in 1990.

MAJOR TITLES (3)—French singles, 1970-1971; Wimbledon singles, 1973. DAVIS CUP—1966-67-68-69-70-71-72-73-74-75-76-77-78-79-80, 39-19 singles, 21-15 doubles. SINGLES RECORD IN THE MAJORS—French (43-13), Wimbledon (19-14). U.S. (27-9).

Karel Kozeluh
Czechoslovakia (1896–1950)
Hall of Fame—2006

As the best known of a distinguished Czech tennis family—six boys, one girl, all good players, one, Jan, a Davis Cupper—Karel Kozeluh was the greatest achiever, winning professional titles on both sides of the Atlantic. Born the son of a baker on March 7, 1896, in Prague, Karel, a righthander, was one of those exceptional pros of the pre-"Open" era who would have been outstanding among the amateurs roving the conventional circuit.

As the king of the pros between 1925 and 1930, Kozeluh showed his quality in battles against Big Bill Tilden, who had been the world's dominant player as an amateur and continued as the boss when he turned pro in 1931. Tilden won the 33-match tour that year against Kozeluh, 27-6. But he made Tilden work, and, like another Hall of Famer, German pro Hans Nusslein, had nowhere near the tournament experience of Big Bill. Tilden said that Kozeluh had one of the three finest backhands he'd faced. (The other two, Rene Lacoste and Nusslein. Bill had not opposed Don Budge.)

Extremely self-assured, slender, about 5-foot-8, 145 pounds., Kozeluh excelled at baseline driving, changing pace and hitting

with accuracy. He liked to "draw my opponent to the net since I have unbounded confidence in my passing shots. Can I not half-volley with the best?"

"Clearly he was a man who didn't lack faith in himself," wrote historian Paul Metzler. "Kozeluh was a baseline master and could hit the ball from any part of his court to any part of his opponent's. He commanded every stroke in the game. Tilden credited him with being even steadier than [Rene] Lacoste, and having an even greater backhand."

A Continental stylist who used no change of grip for any stroke, he had one most unusual characteristic. He made practically no use of his left arm, leaving it hanging by his side as he made his strokes; in lifting the racket for his backswing he used only his playing arm.

An expert even as a kid, he left home at 14 for a teaching job at a Munich club. Tennis won out in a three-way mental struggle. As a national level standout in soccer and hockey, he was tempted to concentrate on one of those sports, but his heart was on the court.

Vinnie Richards, who in 1926 had joined the original pro troupe promoted by C.C. Pyle, along with the nova, Suzanne Lenglen, became a promoter himself. He was hot for Kozeluh whom he characterized as seamy-faced cadaverous-looking, resembling a cigar store Indian, and signed him up for a U.S. tour in 1928. Kozeluh liked the results (13-7 over Richards) but—as a beer drinker—not the U.S., then in the grip of Prohibition. But he developed great fondness for the U.S., holding numerous teaching and coaching positions in the States. Brother Jan, playing Davis Cup for Czechoslovakia for seven years, 1924-30, was 17-10 singles and 12-7 doubles.

Karel won the the Bristol Cup at Beaulieu, France, seven straight times, 1926–32, a pro tourney considered foremost in Europe at the time. A seven-time finalist in the top American event, the U.S. Pro, he won it in 1929, 1932 and 1937, the last at age 41.

He won 11 prominent singles titles—Bristol Cup, 1926-27-28 (opponents unknown); 1929, defeating Albert Burke of Ireland, 6-3, 6-1, 6-0; 1930, defeating Roman Najuch of Germany, 6-3, 6-4, 6-4; 1931, defeating Burke, 6-3, 6-1, 5-7, 6-4; 1932, defeating Martin Plaa of France; the U.S. Pro, 1929, defeating Richards, 6-4, 6-4, 4-6, 4-6, 7-5 (saved three match points); 1932, defeating Hans Nusslein of Germany, 6-2, 6-2, 7-5; 1937, defeating Bruce Barnes of the U.S. 6-2, 6-3, 4-6, 4-6, 6-1; French Pro, 1930, defeating A. Burke, 6-1, 6-2, 6-1. He also lost four prominent finals—U.S. Pro, 1928, to Richards, 8-6, 6-3, 0-6, 6-2; 1930, to Richards, 2-6, 10-8, 6-3, 6-4; 1934, to Nusslein, 6-4, 6-2, 1-6, 7-5; 1935, to Tilden, 0-6, 6-1, 6-4, 0-6, 6-4

He was killed in an auto crash in 1950 at Klanovice, near Prague, and entered the Hall in 2006.

Jack Kramer
United States (1921—)
Hall of Fame—1968

The impact of John Albert "Jake" Kramer on tennis has been fourfold: as great player, exceptional promoter, thoughtful innovator and astute television commentator.

Kramer, born Aug. 1, 1921, in Las Vegas, Nev., grew up in the Los Angeles area. He achieved international notice in 1939 as a teenager when he was selected to play doubles, alongside Joe Hunt, for the U.S. in the Davis Cup finale against Australia. At 18, Kramer was the youngest to play in the Cup title round, although John Alexander of Australia lowered the record to 17 by playing in 1968.

Kramer and Hunt were the golden boys out of Southern California, their careers intertwined. Joe beat Jake, at Forest Hills in 1939, where they were both losing semifinalists the following year. Both were to go to sea during World War II, Jake in the Coast Guard, Joe in the Navy, and to receive leaves to play again in the U.S. Championships of 1943, where they collided in the final. Hunt won, barely, sprawling on the court with cramps as Kramer's last shot flew long. Kramer, who'd had a bout with food poisoning, laughed later, "If I could've kept that ball in play I might have been a champ on a default." Hunt was killed 17 months afterwards in a military plane crash.

Because of the war, Jake had to wait three years to return to Forest Hills. He then rose to prominence as a splendid champion, so dominant that he was voted fifth on a list of all-time greats selected by a panel of expert tennis journalists in 1969. The powerful right-hander was the leading practitioner of the "big game," rushing to the net constantly behind his serve, and frequently attacking on return of serve. His serve took opponents off the court, setting them up for the volley, as did his crushing forehand.

A blistered racket hand probably decided his gruelling fourth-round defeat by cunning lefty Jaroslav Drobny, and prevented Jake from winning the first post-war Wimbledon. But he came back awesomely in 1947, the first to win in shorts, making short work of everybody. Whipping doubles partner Tom Brown in 48 minutes, 6-1, 6-.3, 6-2, he lost merely 37 games in seven matches, the most lopsided run to the championship.

Brown had been his 1946 U.S. final-round victim, 9-7, 6-3, 6-0, another one-sided excursion for Jake, a crew-cut blond whose goal was to reclaim the Davis Cup that he and Hunt failed to clinch in 1939. In December, he and good buddy Ted Schroeder—the U.S. doubles champs of 1940—were members of a highly-talented team that captain Walter Pate took to Australia for the challenge round. Every man—those two plus Brown, Frank Parker, Gardnar Mulloy, Bill Talbert—thought he should play. Pate picked Ted and Jake to do it all, controversial until the pals paralyzed the favored Aussies on opening day. Schroeder overcame John Bromwich, 3-6, 6-1, 6-2, 0-6, 6-3 and Kramer nailed Dinny Pails, 8-6, 6-2, 9-7. Together, they grabbed the Cup by flattening the team that had beaten Hunt and Kramer in '39: Bromwich and Adrian Quist, 6-2, 7-5, 6-4.

The following summer, Jake and Ted repelled the Australian challenge for the Cup at Forest Hills. Then Kramer closed out his amateur career memorably by overhauling Parker in the U.S. final. He lost the first two sets, and was in danger of losing out on a lucrative professional contract as well as his championship. Counterpunching, he won, 4-6, 2-6, 6-1, 6-0, 6-3, and set off in pursuit of Bobby Riggs, the reigning pro champ. Kramer, who had lost only two matches in 1946, dropped but one (to Talbert) in 1947, winning eight of nine tournaments on 48-1, closing his amateur life with a 41-match rush, and 18 singles titles.

Kramer knocked Riggs off the summit by winning their odyssey of one-nighters throughout the U.S., which was the test of professional supremacy of that day. Their opener was a phenomenon: New York was buried by a blizzard that brought the city to a stop, yet 15,114 customers made it on foot to the old Madison Square Garden on Dec. 27, 1947, to watch Riggs win. But Bobby couldn't keep it up. Kramer won the tour, 69-20, and stayed in action while Riggs took over as the promoter and signed Pancho Gonzalez to challenge Kramer. Nobody was up to Kramer then. He bruised the rookie Gonzalez 96-27 on the longest of the tours. Kramer made $85,000 against Riggs as his percentage, and $72,000 against Gonzalez.

In 1952, Kramer assumed the position of promoter himself, the boss of pro tennis, a role he would hold for over a decade, well past his playing days. Kramer's last tour as a principal was against the first man he recruited, Frank Sedgman, the Aussie who was tops among amateurs. Kramer won, 54-41. An arthritic back led to his retirement as a player, but he kept the tour going, resurrecting one of his victims, Gonzalez, who became the strongman.

One of the shrewdest operators in tennis, Kramer was looked to for advice when the Open era began in 1968. He devised the Grand Prix for the men's game, a series of tournaments leading to a Masters Championship for the top eight finishers, and a bonus pool to be shared by more than a score of the leading players. The Grand Prix, incorporating the most attractive tournaments around the world, functioned from 1970 until 1990, when the ATP Tour took over the structure. In 1972, he was instrumental in forming the ATP (Association of Tennis Pros), the male players' union, and was its first executive director. His role as leader of the ATP's principled boycott of Wimbledon in 1973 made him unpopular in Britain for a time. Nevertheless, it was a landmark act, assuring the players the right to control their own destiny after being in thrall to national associations until then. Later, he served on the Men's International Professional Tennis Council, the worldwide governing board.

For more than 20 years, Kramer served as a perceptive analyst on tennis telecasts in many countries, notably for the British Broadcasting Corporation at Wimbledon and for all the American networks at Forest Hills, and at other events, second to none. He ranked in the U.S. Top 10 five times between 1940 and 1947, No. 1 in the U.S. and the world in 1946 and 1947. Kramer won the U.S. Pro title in 1948 over the defender, Riggs, 14-12, 6-2, 3-6, 7-5, and the world pro title in 1949 over Riggs, 6-4, 6-2, 6-3.

Kramer, winner of 13 U.S. singles and doubles titles, was named to the Hall of Fame in 1968. His son, Bob Kramer, continues the family's tennis interests as director of the Los Angeles ATP tourney.

MAJOR TITLES (10)—Wimbledon singles 1947: U.S. singles, 1946, 1947; Wimbledon doubles, 1946, 1947: U.S. doubles, 1940, 1941, 1943, 1947; U.S. mixed, 1941. **OTHER U.S. TITLES** (6)—Indoor singles, 1947; Pro singles. 1948; Pro doubles, 1948, 1955, with Pancho Segura; Indoor doubles, 1947, with Bob Falkenburg; Clay Court doubles, 1941, with Ted Schroeder. **DAVIS CUP**—1939, 1946-47, 6-0 singles, 1-2 doubles. **SINGLES RECORD IN THE MAJORS**—Wimbledon (10-1), U.S. (24-5)

Rene Lacoste

France (1904–1996)
Hall of Fame—1976

He was not particularly athletic in build or in his movements, and as a reserved and rather shy youth, he seemed to be more fitted for the world of education, law or medicine than for athletic achievement. But Jean René Lacoste, known as "The Crocodile", would win Wimbledon and the U.S. twice, the French thrice and become a member of the Four Musketeers, the scourges of the tennis world in the 1920s. He was in the world's Top 10 six straight years from 1924 and No. 1 in 1926-27.

Lacoste was a self-made champion, a player who won world renown through sheer hard work and devoted application rather than through the benefit of natural talent. Born in Paris, July 2, 1904, he did not go onto a court until he was 15 years old, while on a trip with his father to England. His development after that was slow.

His father, a wealthy manufacturer of automobiles, agreed to his son's devoting himself to tennis, but with the understanding that he must set himself the task of becoming a world champion and achieve his goal within five years or drop it.

In his determination to excel, Lacoste trained faithfully and read and observed everything, even keeping a notebook on the strengths and weaknesses of his contemporaries. He became a master of the backcourt game, choosing to maintain a length of inexorable pressure to exact the error or the opening for the finishing shot, and repelling the volleyer with passing shots and lobs.

In recognition of his growing success, he was selected in 1923 as the fourth Musketeer to blend with Jean Borotra, Jacques Brugnon and Henri Cochet in the alliance that would bring France the Davis Cup. The following year, he was in his first major final, Wimbledon, only to lose to Borotra. But in 1925, he came back to win the Big W, a four-set rematch, 6-3, 6-3, 4-6, 8-6, and took it for a second time in 1928 over Cochet, 6-1, 4-6, 6-4, 6-2. Also in 1925, Lacoste won the French, over Borotra, whom he also beat in a memorable rainy 1929 final.

As the French drew closer to the Cup, losing the challenge round to the U.S., 4-1, in 1926, Lacoste made the breakthrough for team morale, beating Big Bill Tilden, 4-6, 6-4, 8-6, 8-6, Big Bill's first Cup loss after 16 wins. The year 1927 was momentous, enclosing three Lacoste victories over Tilden: in the French final, 6-4, 4-6, 5-7, 6-3, 11-9 (saving two match points); in the Davis Cup Challenge Round-squaring triumph, 6-4, 4-6, 6-3, 6-2 (helping the French win the Cup); and in the final of the U.S. Championships. Perhaps the U.S. final was the most stirring, where the efficiency of his backcourt game thwarted the great one. The 34-year-old Tilden attacked for close to two hours and volleyed far more than was his custom, but despite efforts that brought him to the point of exhaustion, he could not win a set. The sphinx-like Lacoste, 22, kept the ball going back the full length of the court with the inevitability of fate and hardly an inexcusable error. The score of the fabulous match was 11-9, 6-3, 11-9, enabling Lacoste to retain the U.S. title he had won the previous year against Borotra, 6-4, 6-0, 6-4.

In 1928, Lacoste lost the opener in the Davis Cup to Tilden, 1-6, 6-4, 6-4, 2-6, 6-3—the lone U.S. point—and it marked the French-

man's last appearance in international team matches, owing to his health. After winning the French title in 1929, over Borotra, 6-3, 2-6, 6-0, 2-6, 8-6, he withdrew from competition, having more than fulfilled the goal he once never seemed suited for—that of a tennis champion.

He captained the victorious French Davis Cup teams of 1931-32. Ever seeking to improve playing conditions, he designed the first shirts specifically for tennis, the short-sleeved cotton polo so common now, and put his familiar trademark, a crocodile, on the breast, starting the flood of apparel logos. Lacoste also developed the split-shaft steel racket that appeared in 1967 as the Wilson T2000, used for years by Jimmy Connors.

His wife, Simone Thion de la Chaume, was a French amateur golf champion, and his daughter, Catherine Lacoste, won the U.S. Open golf title in 1967. He died Oct. 12, 1996, in St. Jean-de-Luz, France.

MAJOR TITLES (10)—French singles, 1925, 1927, 1929; U.S. singles, 1926, 1927; Wimbledon singles, 1925, 1928; French doubles, 1925, 1929; Wimbledon doubles, 1925. **DAVIS CUP**—1923-24-25-26-27-28, 32-8 singles, 8-3 doubles. **SINGLES RECORD IN THE MAJORS**—French (29-3), Wimbledon (28-5), U.S. (19-3).

Al Laney

United States (1895–1988)
Hall of Fame—1979—Journalist

A fine writer who made his name covering sports, Albert Gillis Laney was usually associated with tennis and golf, but he covered everything on the menu, from big league baseball to football to championship fights, with his usual understanding of what was at foot, and a keen reportorial touch. Laconic, mustachioed, usually beneath a gray fedora, he settled in Paris for a time after World War I, worked for James Joyce as secretary, and joined the staff of the renowned *Paris Herald* (now the *International Herald Tribune*).

He had an eye for compelling features, and his coverage of the epic 1926 showdown of Suzanne Lenglen and Helen Wills at Cannes graces several anthologies. He spanned the generations, having observed another epic, the Maurice McLoughlin-Norman Brookes Davis Cup duel at Forest Hills in 1914, and worked as a reporter until his last newspaper, the *New York Herald Tribune*, folded in 1966.

His *Courting the Game*, a tennis memoir remains one of the splendid tennis books. Laney was born Jan. 1895, in Pensacola, Fla., retained a Southern lilt in his speech, and died Jan. 31, 1988, in Spring Valley, N.Y. He entered the Hall of Fame in 1979.

Bill Larned

United States (1872–1926)
Hall of Fame—1956

One of the "Big Three" of the U.S. men's championships, William Augustus Larned won seven times, as did Dick Sears before him and Bill Tilden after. Like Tilden, he was a late achiever, 28 years old in 1900 when, after failing in the final before Malcolm Whitman, 6-4, 1-6, 6-2, 6-2, he won the title in 1901 for a first time,

over Beals Wright, 6-2, 6-8, 6-4, 6-4. His last, ending a five-year run, in 1911, made him the oldest male singles champ, 38, victorious over Maurice McLoughlin, 6-4, 6-4, 6-2.

He began playing the Championships in 1891 and in 19 years, through 1911, fell short of the semis only twice, making a 61-12 match record. He was ranked in the U.S. Top 10 19 times, starting with No. 6 in 1892, and probably would have been there 20 straight years if he hadn't missed the 1898 season serving with the Rough Riders in the Spanish-American War. Nineteen years with the elite was the record for eight decades, until topped by Jimmy Connors in 1991.

Bill, a strong-armed 5-foot-11, 170-pounder, was No. 1 eight times, tied by Connors, topped by Tilden's 10. Three of those years, his younger brother, Edward Larned, was also in the Top 10, No. 6 in 1903. Bill was a member of five Davis Cup teams, in 1902 a Cup winner. He was a powerful groundstroker with an oppressive top-spinning right-handed forehand.

Bill was born Dec. 30, 1872, in Summit, N.J., and attended Cornell, for whom he won the Intercollegiate title in 1892. He committed suicide on Dec. 16, 1926, in New York, inducted into the Hall of Fame in 1956.

MAJOR TITLES (7)—U.S. Singles, 1901, 1902, 1907-08-09-10-11. **OTHER U.S. TITLES** (1)—Intercollegiate singles, 1892. **DAVIS CUP**—1902-03, 05, 08-09, 11, 9-5 singles. **SINGLES RECORD IN THE MAJORS**—Wimbledon (5-2), U.S. (61-12).

Art Larsen
United States (1925—)
Hall of Fame—1969

A sleek left-hander with superb touch, Arthur David "Tappy" Larsen in 1950 was the first southpaw champion of the U.S. Championships in the post-World War II era, the first since Johnny Doeg two decades before. He battled fellow Californian Herbie Flam in a long-shot final—they were seeded No. 5 and No. 2, respectively—to win at Forest Hills, 6-3, 4-6, 5-7, 6-4, 6-3.

A European combat veteran of the U.S. Army in World War II, with three battle stars, the 5-foot-10, 150-pound Larsen was delayed in his start in big-time tennis, making the U.S. Top 10 the first of eight successive times, No. 6 in 1949 at age 24. He was No. 1 in 1950, and ranked in the world's Top 10 thrice in 1950, 1951 and 1954—No. 3 the first year.

In 1952, adding the U.S. Clay Court title over Dick Savitt, 4-6, 6-4, 6-2, 6-4, and U.S. Hard Court, over Flam, 7-5, 8-6, 7-5, then, in 1953, the U.S. Indoor over Kurt Nielsen, 5-7, 6-4, 6-3, 6-3 to his Forest Hills prize, Larsen became the first man to take the championships on all four surfaces. Only he and Tony Trabert have done so. Losing the French final to Trabert in 1954, 6-4, 7-5, 6-1, he was only the ninth of 15 American men to attain that final. He made the semis of the U.S. Championships in 1951, the quarterfinals in 1949 and 1954 and the quarterfinals at Wimbledon in 1950 and 1953.

Larsen was born April 17, 1925, in Hayward, Calif., and entered the Hall of Fame in 1969.

MAJOR TITLE (1)—U.S. singles, 1950. **OTHER U.S. TITLES** (8)—Indoor singles, 1953; Clay Court singles, 1952; Hard Court singles, 1950, 1952; Indoor doubles, 1953, with

Kurt Nielsen; Clay Court doubles, 1950, with Flam; 1952 with Grant Golden; Hard Court doubles, 1952, with Tom Brown. **DAVIS CUP** —1951-52, 4-0 singles. **SINGLES RECORD IN THE MAJORS**—French (16-4), Wimbledon (20-7), U.S. (31-8).

Rod Laver
Australia (1938—)
Hall of Fame—1981

Rod Laver was so scrawny and sickly as a child in the Australian bush that no one could guess he would become a left-handed whirlwind who would conquer the tennis world and be known as possibly the greatest player ever.

A little more than a month before Don Budge completed the first Grand Slam, Rodney George "Rocket" Laver was born Aug. 9, 1938, at Rockhampton, Queensland, Australia. Despite lack of size and early infirmities, Laver grew strong and tough on his father's cattle property and emulated Budge by making the second male Grand Slam in 1962 as an amateur—then became the only double Grand Slammer seven years later by taking the major singles (Australian, French, Wimbledon, U.S.) as a pro.

Few champions have been as devastating and dominant as Laver was as amateur and pro during the 1960s. An incessant attacker, he was nevertheless a complete player who glowed in the backcourt and at the net. Laver's 5-foot-8-1/2, 145-pound body seemed to dangle from a massive left arm that belonged to King Kong, an arm with which he bludgeoned the ball and was able to impart ferocious topspin. Although others had used topspin, Laver may have inspired a wave of heavy-hitting topspin practitioners of the 1970s such as Bjorn Borg and Guillermo Vilas. The stroke became basic after Laver.

As a teenager, he was sarcastically nicknamed "Rocket" by Australian Davis Cup Captain Harry Hopman. "He was anything but a Rocket," Hopman recalled. "But Rod was willing to work harder than the rest, and it was soon apparent to me that he had more talent than any other of our fine Australian players."

His initial international triumph came during his first trip abroad in 1956, when he won the U.S. Junior Championship at 17. Four years later, he was ready to take his place among the world's best when he won the Australian singles, snapping back to beat another lefty, Neale Fraser, 5-7, 3-6, 6-3, 8-6, 8-6, and, with Bob Mark, the doubles for a second time. He was runner-up to Alex Olmedo for the Wimbledon championship, but would win the title four times in all. The Australian victories were the first of Laver's 20 major titles in singles, doubles and mixed—placing him fifth among all-time male winners behind Roy Emerson (28), John Newcombe (25), Frank Sedgman (22) and Bill Tilden (21). Jean Borotra also won 20. Rod's 11 major singles titles (equaled by Bjorn Borg) were second to Emerson's long-standing record of 12, later eclipsed by Pete Sampras and Roger Federer.

The losing Wimbledon finals of 1959-60 to Olmedo, then Fraser were but a prelude to an incredible run of success in that tournament. He was a finalist six straight times he entered, winning in 1961 over Chuck McKinley, 6-3, 6-1, 6-4, and 1962, over Marty Mulligan, 6-2, 6-2, 6-1. After a five-year absence as an outcast professional, he returned to the fanfare of "Opens" to win again in 1968, over Tony Roche, 6-3, 6-4, 6-2, and in 1969, over New-

combe, 6-4, 5-7, 6-4, 6-4. While winning Wimbledon in four straight appearances (the only man since World War I to win four prior to Borg) and proceeding to the fourth round in 1970, Laver set a male tournament record of 31 consecutive match wins, ended by his loss to Roger Taylor (passed in 1980 by Borg, who lengthened the record to 41).

The year 1969 was Laver's finest, the redhead swooping like a Firebird, perhaps the best experienced by any player, as he won an Open-era record 17 singles tournaments (tied by Guillermo Vitas in 1977) of 32 played on a 106-16 match record. In 1962, he won 19 of 34 on 134-15. Unlike his Grand Slam year of 1962 as an amateur, he was playing in tournaments that were open to all, amateur and pro, and this Slam was all the more impressive.

After his second year running as the No. 1 amateur in 1962, and helping Australia win a fourth successive Davis Cup, Laver turned pro, his appearance saving the sagging professional game, a stimulus to keeping it breathing until "Opens" arrived in 1968. It was a disconnected life of one-nighters, but Pancho Gonzalez was no longer supreme. Kenny Rosewall was at the top and gave Laver numerous beatings as their long, illustrious rivalry began. Rosewall beat Laver to win the U.S. Pro singles in 1963, 6-4, 6-2, 6-2, but the next year Laver defeated Rosewall, then eight-time champ Gonzalez, 4-6, 6-3, 7-5, 6-4, to win the first of his five crowns, four of them in a row beginning in 1966. He had a streak of 19 wins in the U.S. Pro until losing the 1970 final to Roche.

When Open tennis dawned in 1968, Laver was ready to resume where he'd left off at the traditional tournaments, whipping Roche in less than an hour to take the first "open" Wimbledon.

In 1971, Laver won $292,717 in tournament prize money (a season record that stood until Arthur Ashe won $338,337 in 1975), enabling him to become the first tennis player to make a million dollars on the court. Until the last days of 1978, when he was playing few tournaments, Laver was still the all-time leading money-winner with $1,564,213. Jimmy Connors then surpassed him, along with numerous others.

In 1973, all professionals were at last permitted to play Davis Cup, and Laver, 35, honed himself for one last effort, after 11 years away. He was brilliant, teaming with Newcombe to end a five-year U.S. reign, 5-0. Laver beat Tom Gorman, 8-10, 8-6, 6-8, 6-3, 6-1, on the first day and paired with Newcombe for a crushing doubles victory over Stan Smith and Erik van Dillen, 6-1, 6-2, 6-4 that clinched the Cup, Laver's fifth. Of all the marvelous Aussie Davis Cup performers, he was the only one never to play in a losing series, 11 of them in all, compiling 16-4 and 4-0 marks in singles and doubles, respectively.

He was also a factor in winning three World Cups (1972, 74-75) for Australia in the since-disbanded team competition against the U.S. In 1976, as his tournament career was winding down, Laver signed with San Diego in World Team Tennis and was named the league's Rookie of the Year at age 38.

During a 23-year career that spanned the amateur and Open eras, he won 47 pro titles in singles and was runner-up 21 times. Overall, amateur and pro, he was the all-time leader with 199 singles titles, and was elevated to the International Tennis Hall of Fame in 1981, and the Australian Tennis Hall of Fame in

1993. In 2001, the principal stadium of Melbourne Park, scene of the Australian Open, was named Rod Laver Arena. Despite spending five of his prime years in the neglected wilderness of the pros, he was among the world's Top 10 12 times, 1959-1962, and 1968-75 (the last at age 37). He was No. 1 four times, 1961-62, 68-69.

Suffering a massive stroke that might have killed him in 1998, he rehabilitated with the same drive that made him a champion.

MAJOR TITLES (20)—Australian singles, 1960, 1962, 1969; French singles 1962, 1969; Wimbledon singles, 1961, 1962, 1968, 1969; U.S. singles, 1962, 1969; Australian doubles, 1959, 1960, 1961, 1969; French doubles, 1961; Wimbledon doubles, 1971; French mixed, 1961; Wimbledon mixed. 1959, 1960. **DAVIS CUP**—1959, 1960, 1961, 1962, 1973, 16-4 in singles, 4-0 in doubles. **SINGLES RECORD IN THE MAJORS**—Australian (21-6), French (25-6), Wimbledon (50-7), U.S. (44-10).

Herbert Lawford
Great Britain (1851–1925)
Hall of Fame—2006

The patient pioneer—that was Herbert Lawford, an Englishman with a distinctive style and appearance. He was a Wimbledon early bird, showing up for the second Championship in 1878, and winning a couple of matches, which (with a walkover and a bye) got him into the semifinal. But he was also late, in a sense, already 27.

However, he was determined to stick with it year after year until, on his 10th start (Wimbledon's 10th anniversary, 1887) Herbert Fortescue Lawford at last became champion, usurping the title from fellow Brit Ernie Renshaw in the challenge round, 1-6, 6-3, 3-6, 6-4, 6-4. That felt pretty good because Herbert had been floored in the previous year's final, 6-0, 5-7, 6-3, 6-4, by Willie Renshaw, Ernie's twin brother. Only two other guys had to wait outside the champs' circle longer: Arthur Gore of Great Britain, winning on the 13th try in 1901, and Czech Jaroslav Drobny on the 11th in 1954.

He was playing better than ever, making the most of a brutally fast forehand loaded with topspin. In fact, Lawford was the father of topspin, utilizing a western grip. Probably somebody else would have devised it, but he was the first. (Rafa Nadal and other such practitioners of the stroke ought to mention Lawford in their prayers.) Topspin was driving just about everybody crazy—everybody but the Renshaws.

They did not quake like their colleagues when Lawford arrived in his small black cap, white knickers and long black sox. While Willie Renshaw was ringing up his record six consecutive Wimbledon titles (1881-86), Lawford was thrice a final round victim, brother Ernie twice. And when Lawford won his lone first prize, it was snatched away by Ernie 12 months later.

Life would have been much sweeter for topspinning Herbert if the Renshaws had chosen to focus on some other activity, and not kept his head spinning. He might have won five championships. As it stands, though, he is the Big W's champion runner-up, five times coming in second—1880 to John Hartley, 6-0, 6-2, 2-6, 6-3; 1884, to Willie Renshaw, 6-0, 6-4, 9-7; 1885, to Willie Renshaw,

7-5, 6-2, 4-6, 7-5; 1886, to Willie Renshaw, 6-0, 5-7, 6-3, 6-4; 1888, to Ernie Renshaw, 1-6, 6-3, 3-6, 6-4, 6-4.

In his farewell to Centre Court at age 38 in 1889, he lost in the semifinal to—you guessed it—Willie.

Lawford was the first British Covered Court champ in 1885, won the 1880 and 1883 Prince's Club title (important at the time), and three Irish Championships, 1884-86.

Born May 15, 1851, Bayswater, Middlesex, England, he was educated at Repton School and Edinburgh University. He died on April 20, 1925, at Dess, Scotland, and was tapped for the Hall in 2006.

MAJOR TITLES (1)—Wimbledon, 1887. **SINGLES RECORD IN THE MAJORS**—Wimbledon (33-10)

Ivan Lendl
Czechoslovakia/United States (1960—)
Hall of Fame—2001

Although he'd been a prodigious winner for four years, it was not until the French final of 1984 that Ivan Lendl began to really stake his claim to greatness. Then, from two sets down to the year's leading player, John McEnroe, Lendl battled back to win in five sets, 3-6, 2-6, 6-4, 7-5, 7-5, seizing the first of his eight major singles (of 17 finals). He won two other French (1986-87), two Australian (1989-90), and three U.S. (1985-86-87).

Until 1984, at 24, his competitive zeal in big finals had been questioned, particularly after his U.S. Open finals losses to Jimmy Connors of 1982-83. But Lendl dispelled all that, and won in 1985 over McEnroe, 7-6 (7-1), 6-3, 6-4; in 1986 over Miroslav Mecir, 6-4, 6-2, 6-0, and 1987 over Mats Wilander, 6-7 (7-9), 6-0, 7-6 (7-4), 6-4. Ivan's two other French titles were banged out in 1986 and 1987 over Swedes Mikael Pernfors, 6-3, 6-2, 6-4, and Wilander, 7-5, 6-2, 3-6, 7-6 (7-3). In Australia, after falling in the 1983 final to Wilander, he bounced back to win in 1989 over Mecir, 6-2, 6-2, 6-2, and 1990 over Edberg, 4-6, 7-6 (7-3), 5-2, injury default.

His 1985 U.S. Open conquest of McEnroe hoisted him past the New Yorker to No. 1 in the world, a position he held until losing the Open in 1988, 6-4, 4-6, 6-3, 5-7, 6-4, to Wilander—156 straight weeks, three short of Jimmy Connors's then Open era record. He returned to No. 1 for 1989 and spent a record total 269 weeks at the peak during 13 seasons in the Top 10 between 1980 and 1992.

Lendl's time at Flushing Meadows was spectacular: appearing in eight successive finals (from 1982), he equalled the record of Big Bill Tilden (1918-25). His loss of the 1988 final to Wilander halted a 27-match winning streak in the U.S. championship, second only to Tilden's string of 42 between 1920 and the quarters of 1926.

Born March 7, 1960, at Ostrava, Czechoslovakia, and reared there, he has an excellent tennis bloodline. His mother, Olga Lendlova, was a Top 10 player in their homeland, ranking as high as No. 2. His father, Jiri Lendl, also was a fine player, ranking as high as No. 15, and who, in 1990, became president of the Czechoslovak Tennis Federation.

Unlike countrywoman Martina Navratilova, he did not announce his defection, but left no doubt when he settled in the U.S. in 1984, and declined to play further Davis Cup after 1985. In 1992, he became a U.S. citizen.

In 1980, Lendl, unbeaten in seven singles and three doubles, led Czechoslovakia to its lone Davis Cup. Before an uproarious final round crowd in Prague, he anchored the 4-1 triumph over Italy, winning both his singles matches. On the first day, he beat Corrado Barazzutti, 4-6, 6-1, 6-1, 6-2, and, with Tom Smid, clinched with a stirring doubles decision over Adriano Panatta and Paolo Bertolucci, 3-6, 6-3, 3-6, 6-3, 6-4.

A 6-foot-2, 175-pound, right-handed paragon of hard work and fitness, he amassed stunning numbers campaigning tirelessly between 1980 and 1983, when he won 36 of 101 tournaments. He played 32 in 1980, winning three on a 113-29 match record, and won 15 of 23 in 1982 on 107-9. He won 11 of 17 in 1985 on 84-7. His last big production year was 1989: 10 of 17 on 79-7. His 92nd pro singles title in 1992 left him second only to Connors' 109 in the Open era. In 1982, he put together the third-longest winning streak of the Open era, 44 straight matches, six shy of Guillermo Vilas' 1977 record, halted by Yannick Noah in the final at La Quinta, Calif. A basher from the baseline, relying on strength and heavy topspin, Lendl wasn't particularly stylish but got the job done with an intimidating will and appetite for victory. His anticipation and speed afoot were often overlooked.

Ivan's pursuit of the one prize beyond him, Wimbledon, was Jobian. He played 14 times at the Big W but, strain and try as he did to become a serve-and-volleyer, and as close as he came—final-round losses to Boris Becker in 1986 and Pat Cash in 1987—grass was his no-no. That may be unfair to say about a man who batted .774 there, was also thrice a semifinalist, but he joined Ken Rosewall and Pancho Gonzalez as the greatest never to win the Big W.

An aching back didn't help as the No. 7 seed, he lost his last attempt, in 1993, to Arnaud Boetsch in the second round. The damaged back caused him to default in the third set of his second rounder against Bernd Karbacher at the 1994 U.S. Open. He would not play again, and announced his retirement shortly after that at age 34, ranked No. 30. His last title, Tokyo (indoor) in 1993, was a 6-4, 6-4 win over Todd Martin, and his last final, Sydney 1994, was a loss to Pete Sampras.

Lendl's was a hefty pro career of 17 years: 94 singles and six doubles titles, and a 1,279-274 singles W-L record (.805), topped only by Connors. He was the all-time prize money champ with $21,262,417 when he quit.

MAJOR TITLES (8)—Australian singles, 1989, 1990; French singles, 1984, 86-87; U.S. singles, 1985, 1986 1987. **OTHER U.S. TITLES** (4)—Clay Court singles, 1985; Pro singles, 1992, 1993, 1994. **DAVIS CUP**—1978. 1979 1980. 1981, 1982, 1983, 1984 1985, 18-11 singles, 4-4 doubles. **SINGLES RECORD IN THE MAJORS**—Australian (48-10), French (53-12), Wimbledon 48-14, U.S. (73-13).

Suzanne Lenglen
France (1899–1938)
Hall of Fame—1978

In the days of ground-length tennis dresses, Suzanne Rachel Flore Lenglen played at Wimbledon with her dress cut just above the calf. She wept openly during matches, pouted and sipped

brandy between sets. Some called her shocking and indecent, but she was merely ahead of her time, and she brought France the greatest global sports renown it had ever known.

Right-hander Lenglen was No. 1 in 1925-26, the first years of world rankings. She won Wimbledon every year but one from 1919 through 1925, the exception being 1924, when illness led to her withdrawal after the fourth round. Her 1919 title match, at the age of 20, with 40-year-old Dorothea Douglass Chambers is one of the hallmarks of tennis history.

Chambers, the seven-time champion, was swathed in stays, petticoats, high-necked shirtwaist, and a long skirt that swept the court. The young Lenglen was in her revealing dress that shocked the British at the sight of calves and forearms. After the second set, Lenglen took some comfort from her brandy and won, 10-8, 4-6, 9-7, in a dramatic confrontation, rescuing two match points.

After her victory, Lenglen became easily the greatest drawing card tennis had known, and she was one of those who made it a major box-office attraction. Along with a magnetic personality, grace and style, she was the best woman player the world had seen.

She had first attained prominence as a wonderchild at 15, winning a 1914 tournament called the World Hard Court [clay] Championships in Paris over Germaine Golding, 6-2, 6-1. However, World War I broke out shortly after that, and she had to wait five years to get to Wimbledon, which re-opened in 1919 ready for La Belle Suzanne's takeover of the world stage.

She was golden at the 1920 Olympics, taking the singles over Brit Dorothy Holman, 6-3, 6-0, and the mixed with Max Decugis over Brits Kitty McKane (Godfree) and Max Woosnam, 6-4, 6-2. But she didn't play the 1924 Games in Paris.

Lenglen, born May 24, 1899 in Paris, played an all-court game such as few had excelled at. She moved with rare grace, unencumbered by the tight layers of garments others wore. She had extraordinary accuracy with her classical, rhythmic groundstrokes. For hours daily, her father, Charles Lenglen, had her direct the ball at a handkerchief he moved from spot to spot. Her control was so unfailing that she thought it shameful to hit the ball into the net or beyond the lines. In addition, she had so keen a sense of anticipation that she invariably was in the right position to meet her opponent's shot.

Her 1926 match against Helen Wills in a tournament at Cannes, France, caused a sensation, and world-wide attention and coverage. Tickets brought unheard-of wealth to scalpers, and the roofs and windows of apartments and hotels overlooking the court were crowded with fans. Lenglen was on the verge of collapse during the tense match, but was saved by smelling salts and brandy and defeated the 20-year-old Wills, 6-3, 8-6.

Lenglen's career was not free of setbacks, however. In the 1921 U.S. Championships, having lost the first set badly to Molla Mallory, Lenglen walked weeping and coughing to the umpire and said she could not continue, defaulting the match. She made up for it the next year at Wimbledon by defeating Mallory, 6-2, 6-0, in the final and did not lose another match for the remainder of her amateur career.

At Wimbledon in 1926, Lenglen had a terrifying ordeal. She kept Queen Mary waiting in the Royal Box for her appearance when, owing to a misunderstanding or a failure of communications, Lenglen did not have the correct information about the time she was to be on court. The ghastly error was too much. She fainted and Wimbledon saw her no more as a competitor. She withdrew from the tournament, and that year turned professional, going on tour of the U.S. with a troupe of newly-declared pros under the management of American promoter C.C. Pyle, winning all 38 matches against ex-U.S. champ, 35-year-old Mary K. Browne. It marked the beginning of professional tennis as a playing career.

Suzanne's career numbers were staggering. According to the research of Wimbledon librarian Alan Little, in his biography, *Suzanne Lenglen: Tennis Idol of the Twenties*, she won 250 championships: 83 singles (7 without the loss of a game), 74 doubles, 93 mixed. Losing one singles match in eight years—that to Mallory at the U.S. of 1921—she was unbeaten in 1919 and 1920, 1922-23-24-25-26. Sandwiching the Mallory defeat were winning streaks of 116 matches before, and 182 after to the close of her amateur days. At Wimbledon, her greatest showplace, she won 90 of 92 matches—32-0 singles, 31-1 doubles, 27-1 mixed.

She never married, despite many romances, the most serious with Baldwin Baldwin, an American millionaire who accompanied her on the professional tour.

At the age of 39, Lenglen died of pernicious anemia, July 4, 1938, in Paris. She was elected to the Hall of Fame in 1978. There was speculation that her health had been undermined by her long hours of practice as a young girl. But she had brought the glamour of the stage and the ballet to the court, and queues formed at tennis clubs where before there had been indifference. She had emancipated the female player from layers of starched clothing and set the short-hair style as well. She had brought tennis into a new era.

MAJOR TITLES (21)—French singles, 1925, 1926; Wimbledon singles, 1919, 1920, 1921, 1922, 1923, 1925; French doubles, 1925, 1926; Wimbledon doubles, 1919, 1920, 1921, 1922, 1923, 1925; French mixed, 1925, 1926; Wimbledon mixed, 1920, 1922, 1925. **SINGLES RECORD IN THE MAJORS**—French (10-0), Wimbledon (32-0), US, (0-1).

George Lott
United States (1906–1991)
Hall of Fame—1964

A good baseball player at the University of Chicago, George Martin Lott, Jr., made his name in tennis, principally in doubles, where, a slick tactician and volleyer, he could make any partner look good. He won the U.S. title five times with three different accomplices: John Hennessey in 1928; Johnny Doeg in 1929 and 1930; Les Stoefen in 1933 and 1934. He joined the touring pros in 1934.

George was a U.S. Davis Cup stalwart between 1928 and 1934, going undefeated in 11 doubles matches. He ranked in the U.S. Top 10 nine times between 1924 and 1934, No. 2 in 1931 when he lost the U.S. final at Forest Hills to Ellsworth Vines, keeping it close with his clever use of spin, 7-9, 6-3, 9-7, 7-5. George, a right-hander, came from way back to disappoint Johnny Van Ryn—hi

Wimbledon-winning comrade that year—in the quarters, 5-7, 0-6, 6-1, 7-5, 6-1, then unseated the defender, lefty Doeg, 7-5, 6-3, 6-0. He also won the Wimbledon doubles with Stoefen in 1934.

A 160-pound 6-footer, George beat demon dirt-kicker Bitsy Grant in a five-set struggle for the 1932 U.S. Clay Court title, 3-6, 6-2, 3-6, 6-3, 6-3, and had his ultimate clay opportunities in Paris as a singles starter for the U.S. in the Davis Cup finales of 1929 and 1930. The Frenchmen were just too tough at home. Henri Cochet beat him in the decisive fifth match in 1929, 6-1, 3-6, 6-0, 6-3, and Jean Borotra scored the painful clincher in 1930, 5-7, 6-3, 2-6, 6-2, 8-6.

He was born Oct. 16, 1906, in Springfield Ill., and died Dec. 2, 1991, in Chicago, where he was still active as varsity tennis coach of Loyola University. He was inducted into the Hall of Fame in 1964.

MAJOR TITLES (12)—French doubles, 1931; Wimbledon doubles, 1931, 1934; U.S. doubles, 1928, 1929, 1930, 1933, 1934; Wimbledon mixed, 1931; U.S. mixed, 1929, 1931, 1934. **OTHER U.S. TITLES** (6)—Clay Court singles, 1932; Indoor doubles, 1932, with Van Ryn; 1934, with Les Stoefen; Clay Court doubles, 1932, with Bitsy Grant; Pro doubles, 1935, with Stoefen; 1937, with Vinnie Richards. **DAVIS CUP**—1928, 1929, 1930, 1931, 1933, 1934, 7-4 singles, 11-0 doubles. **SINGLES RECORD IN THE MAJORS**—French (4-1), Wimbledon (16-5), U.S. (24-10)

Gene Mako
Hungary/United States (1916—)
Hall of Fame—1973

Though brief, the career of Hungarian-born Constantine Gene Mako was one of the most remarkable in that he achieved his foremost results after sustaining a devastating and painful right shoulder injury that would have finished most men as competitors. As a teen-ager, he had one of the most powerful serves, but he injured himself by overdoing it. This was compounded by a 1936 tumble in London that finished the job of wrecking his right (playing) shoulder, and kept him out of Wimbledon that year.

"I continued only because my friend and doubles partner, Don Budge, asked me to do so," Mako says. "I told him I'd be serving like a little old lady and would have to shovel the ball around, but it was okay with him."

Despite the sometimes puny appearance of his strokes, 6-foot, 170-pound Mako, in the right court alongside Budge, was a canny playmaker, a man who knew the angles and where to put the ball, and competed fiercely as they became one of the greatest teams. They won Wimbledon in 1937 and 1938, and were in four successive U.S. finals from 1935, triumphing in 1936 and 1938.

Gene was a formidable singles player as well. But doubles was his forte. He performed on four Davis Cup teams, Cup winners in 1937 and 1938, seizing the go-ahead point with Budge in the 1937 lifting of the Cup from Britain, 4-1, to end an 11-year U.S. dry spell. They beat Charles Tuckey and Frank Wilde, 6-3, 7-5, 7-9, 12-10. Just as vital was their go-ahead win in the previous round, a 3-2 thriller over Germany—a 4-6, 7-5, 8-6, 6-4 squeeze past Henner Henkel and Gottfried von Cramm.

They were in three successive U.S. doubles finals, bringing down the champs Wilmer Allison and Johnny Van Ryn in 1936, 6-4, 6-2, 6-4, and Aussies John Bromwich and Adrian Quist in 1938,

6-3, 6-2, 6-1, but stumbling in 1937, 6-4, 7-5, 6-4, to von Cramm and Henkel. At Wimbledon, they had two very good years, 1937-38, beating Brits Pat Hughes and Charles Tuckey, 6-0, 6-4, 6-8, 6-1; and von Cramm and Georg von Metaxa, 6-4, 3-6, 6-3, 8-6.

Mako was in the U.S. Top 10 in 1937 and 1938, No. 3 the second year, and No. 9 in the world's Top 10 of 1938. That year he was the last obstacle between Budge and the original Grand Slam in the U.S. final at Forest Hills. Unseeded Mako dashed to his only major singles final on victories over No. 6 seed Frank Kovacs, 6-0, 6-2, 8-6, and the No. 3 and No. 1 foreign seeds, Franjo Puncec of Yugoslavia, 6-2, 6-4, 9-7, and John Bromwich of Australia, 6-3, 7-5, 6-4.

He and Budge had to wait out the monstrous 1938 hurricane that soaked the courts for almost a week. Then, though Gene resisted Budge well, holding off the inevitable for four sets, he was the last piece in Don's Grand Slam plot, 6-3, 6-8, 6-2, 6-1. Mako had one of the four sets Budge lost during the Slam. He, alone, had been told at the beginning of the year that Don was planning to shoot the Grand Slam moon. Budge knew he could trust Gene not to breathe a word of it, and add to the pressure.

Gene had a brief fling at pro tennis while serving in the Navy during World War II, winning the U.S. Pro doubles in 1943 with Bruce Barnes. Upon discharge, he made another sort of sporting name on the West Coast as a semi-pro basketball player. Born in Budapest on Jan. 24, 1916, he moved with his family to Buenos Aires, then to Los Angeles when he was seven. There he remained, winning the Intercollegiate singles and doubles for Southern California in 1934. He became a gregarious art dealer and entered the Hall of Fame in 1973.

MAJOR TITLES (5)—Wimbledon doubles, 1937, 1938; U.S. doubles, 1936, 1938; U.S. Mixed, 1936. **OTHER U.S. TITLES** (6)—Clay Court doubles, 1933, with Jack Tidball; 1934, with Budge; 1939, with Frank Parker; Pro doubles, 1943, with Bruce Barnes; Intercollegiate singles, 1934; Intercollegiate doubles, 1934 with Philip Castlen. **DAVIS CUP**—1935, 1936, 1937, 1938, 0-1 singles, 6-2 doubles. **SINGLES RECORD IN THE MAJORS**—Australian (2-1), French (0-1), Wimbledon (7-2), U.S. (18-8).

Molla Mallory
Norway/United States (1884–1959)
Hall of Fame—1958

Anna Margarethe Molla Bjurstedt Mallory had less in the way of stroke equipment than most players who have become tennis champions. But the sturdy, Norwegian-born woman, the daughter of an army officer, had the heart and pride of a gladiator, could run with limitless endurance, and was a fierce competitor. She won the U.S. Championship a record eight times and she administered the only post-World War I defeat that Suzanne Lenglen suffered as an amateur.

It was her match with Lenglen in the second round of the U.S. Championship at Forest Hills in 1921 that won Mallory her greatest celebrity. She won the first set, 6-2, playing with a fury that took her opponent by surprise, running down balls interminably to wear out the French girl in long rallies, and hitting her mighty topspin forehand down the line for blazing winners. Lenglen, the Wimbledon queen, out of breath from running, cough-

ing and weeping, walked to the umpire's stand after two points of the second set and informed the official that she was ill and could not continue. This was as sensational a reversal as ever recorded on the courts.

Mallory, a right-hander, whose game was developed in Oslo, Norway, where she was born March 6, 1884, came to the United States as Molla Bjurstedt in 1915. She won the U.S. Championships of 1915, 1916, 1917, 1918, 1920, 1921, 1922—and in 1926 at age 42—as the elder among all major singles champions.

She was a player of the old school, believing that a woman could not sustain a volleying attack in a long match, and she put her reliance on her baseline game. That game amounted to a forehand attack and an omnivorous defense that wore down her opponents. She took the ball on the rise and drove it from corner to corner to keep her foe constantly on the run and destroy her control. The quick return made her passing shots all the more effective.

In her first U.S. Championships final—1915, against Hazel Hotchkiss Wightman, who had won the title three times—Mallory yielded only the first set, after which Wightman began to tire and could not get to the volleying position, and won, 4-6, 6-2, 6-0.

Eleanor Goss in the 1918 final, 6-4, 6-3, and Marion Zinderstein in the 1920 final, 6-3. 6-1, were strong volleyers, like Wightman, but neither could win a set against the Norwegian native, who had won 18 straight U.S. matches until losing to Zinderstein in the 1919 semis, 4-6, 6-1, 6-2.

Mallory yielded her title to 17-year-old Helen Wills in 1923, 6-2, 6-1, after defeating her in the 1922 final, 6-3, 6-1, and lost to her again in 1924, 6-1, 6-3. In 1926, Mallory hit one of the heights of her career when she came back from 0-4 in the third set of the final against Elizabeth Ryan and saved a match point in winning her eighth championship, 4-6, 6-4, 9-7. Never had a gallery at Forest Hills in the years of her triumphs cheered her on as it did in this remarkable rally.

Mallory reached the final at Wimbledon in 1922 and lost to Lenglen, 6-2, 6-0. Mallory was twice a semifinalist at Wimbledon, and she played on the winning Wightman Cup teams in 1923, 26-27.

Although she had won an Olympic bronze in singles for Norway in 1912 at Stockholm, and was the champion of her homeland, Molla was relatively unknown when she arrived in New York as Miss Bjurstedt to begin work as a masseuse in 1915. She entered the U.S. Indoor Championships that year, unheralded, and beat defending champ Marie Wagner, the first of five singles titles (1915-16, 18, 21-22) on the boards. Having thus made something of a name, she went outdoors to enlarge on it on Philadelphia turf by beginning her record collection of eight U.S. titles, winning, the fifth as Mrs. Franklin Mallory in 1920. In 15 U.S. Championships, her worst finish was a quarterfinal in 1927 at age 43! She bade farewell to Forest Hills as a 45-year-old semifinalist in 1929, double-bageled by Wills.

She was in the world's Top 10 in 1925, 1926 and 1927, Nos. 5, 4, 4, and the U.S. Top 10 12 years between 1915 and 1928 (no ranking roll in 1917)—No. 1 seven years, 1915-16, 18, 20-21-22, 26, 29. She entered the Hall of Fame in 1958 and died Nov. 22, 1959, in Stockholm.

MAJOR TITLES (13)—U.S. singles, 1915-16-17-18, 20-21-22, 26; U.S. doubles, 1916-17; U.S. mixed 1917, 22-23. **OTHER U.S. TITLES** (11)—Indoor singles, 1915-16, 18, 21-22; Indoor doubles, 1916, with Marie Wagner; Indoor mixed 1921-22, with Bill Tilden; Clay Court singles, 1915-16; Clay Court mixed, 1916, with George Church. **WIGHTMAN CUP**—1923-24-25, 27-28, 5-5 singles, 1-1 doubles. **SINGLES RECORD IN THE MAJORS**—French (1-1), Wimbledon (19-9), U.S. (67-7).

Hana Mandlikova
Czechoslovakia (1962—)
Hall of Fame—1994

Just possibly there are more appealing places to flop on your back than a grimy, steaming strip of asphalt in New York. But you won't convince Hana Mandlikova. It was her place in the furtive sun, and the bumpy landing she made, after whirling to bat a last spectacular volley, was a splendidly happy one. Hana gazed at the smoggy sky, and it seemed heaven as a deluge of applause and cheers from 21,169 captivated witnesses burst on her. The pavement of Flushing Meadow "didn't feel too bad. It felt nice," laughs Mandlikova, who arose from the floor as champion.

That was 1985. Seldom has the U.S. Open been illuminated by such a display of shotmaking fireworks. Hana's victim was Martina Navratilova at her zenith, 7-6 (7-3), 1-6, 7-6 (7-2). Like Martina, whom she'd admired while growing up in Prague (where she was born Feb. 19, 1962), Hana was a magnificent athlete who felt the only thing better than attacking was attacking more.

As the star of the 40th Hall of Fame class in 1994, Hana is the fifth Czech, following Jaroslav Drobny and Jan Kodes, preceding Navratilova and Karel Kozeluh. Her relatively early retirement at 28 concluded a professional career that commenced in 1978 and closed in 1990 after she had accumulated 27 singles, 15 pro doubles titles and $3,340,959 in prize money. In singles, Hana was 567-195 in matches (.783); at doubles 253-104. She left ranked No. 14, having graced the world's Top 10 seven times: No. 4 in 1980, 86; No. 5 in 1981, 87; No. 7 in 1982; No. 7 in 1984; No. 3 in 1985. Her time was emblazoned by the irresistible crescendos of winning four majors—two Australian, 1980 over Aussie Wendy Turnbull, 6-0, 7-5; 1987 over Navratilova; a French in 1981 over Germany's Sylvia Hanika 6-2, 6-4, and her crown jewel U.S. Open. She had four other shots, finals of Wimbledon in 1981 and 1986 and the U.S. in 1980 and 1982.

Her speed and jock genes came from her papa. Willem Mandlik, an Olympic 100-meter finalist for Czechoslovakia in 1956 and 1960, uttered a profound one-sentence summary of his nervous kid's one-sided defeat by Evert, 6-2, 6-2, in the 1981 Wimbledon final: "Boom-boom-boom ... miss-miss-miss ... quick-quick-quick!"

Leggy and limber, a 5-foot-8 right-hander coltish in her movement, she was as high-strung as a thoroughbred, living for flamboyant cavalry charges: "Too impatient to stay on the baseline, on clay—even though I was raised on it—or anything," Hana smiles. "Jan Kodes was my first hero. I grew up watching him. I was a ballgirl for Martina [Navratilova] when I was 12, and she was a motivation for me. We played the same way—and I wanted to be good enough to beat her some day."

And she did, spoiling several big occasions for Martina. Even though she was 7-30 in their rivalry, Hana won four of 10 major meetings, beating her elder at Wimbledon, twice at the U.S., once at the Australian. The last, the 1987 final, 7-5, 7-6 (7-2), ended Navratilova's 58-match winning streak. Three years earlier, winning Oakland, Hana snipped another of Martina's strings at 54. They got together to win the U.S. doubles in 1989. "Nice memories," she says, balancing them with the terror, the "terrible memory of the Soviet tanks coming into Prague, 1968. I was six, but I understood. It was not nice to see my country invaded. But the political conditions proved a motivation for me and others to improve, to be so good we could get out to travel abroad."

Billie Jean King says, "Hana could reach highs beyond any of us—inexplicable lows, too. She had incredibly broad shotmaking ability, but trouble sustaining her best. Maybe because she couldn't resist going for the most spectacular shots." She came at foes in a red-bandana'd rush like Geronimo in sneakers. So it was that September afternoon of '85 when she knocked off Chris Evert and Navratilova in succession for the U.S. title, a singular twin-killing of those two all-timers, first time in a major, although Steffi Graf did it at Wimbledon. Like her father, Hana represented her country proudly, backboning three successive Czechoslovak Federation Cup triumphs, 1983—85.

MAJOR TITLES (5)—Australian singles, 1980, 87; French singles, 1981; U.S. singles, 1985; U.S. doubles, 1989. **FEDERATION CUP**—1978-79-80-81-82-83-84-85-86-87, 34-6 singles, 15-6 doubles. **SINGLES RECORD IN THE MAJORS**—Australian (29-8), French (39-11), Wimbledon (34-11), U.S. (41-10).

Alice Marble
United States (1913–1990)
Hall of Fame—1964

One of the most attractive players to grace the courts, Alice Marble was deceptive. Her blonde loveliness and trim athletic figure belied the fact that she played tennis in the late 1930s in a masculine manner that more closely approximated the game of Don Budge or Ellsworth Vines than it did the game of any woman.

There had been women before her who could volley and hit overheads—Suzanne Lenglen and Helen Wills Moody among them. But none played the "big game," the game of the big serve-and-volley as it was to be called years later, as their standard method of attack the way Marble did regularly. No woman had a stronger serve. Her first serve was as severe as any, and she delivered the taxing American twist serve as few women had been able to do. She followed it to the net for emphatic volleys or the strongest kind of overhead smash.

A right-hander pressing the attack without a letup, she could win from the back of the court as well as at the net. Her groundstrokes, made with a short backswing and taking the ball on the rise, were not overpowering, and her forehand was not always steadfast against the many fine backcourt players of her day, in part because of her daring in playing for winners. But in the aggressive all-court game she played, with her speed and agility, and skill in the use of the drop shot, all served to carry her to

four U.S. titles and to the 1939 Wimbledon Championship. World War II brought about French, Wimbledon and Australian tournament suspension or she might have added appreciably to her major conquests.

Her dominance is evidenced by her record of invincibility in 1939 and 1940. She did not lose a match of consequence either year. In winning her fourth U.S. title in 1940, over Helen Jacobs, 6-2, 6-3, she did not yield a set. She was voted by sportswriters the Woman Athlete of the Year in 1939 and 1940. She made the world's Top 10 in 1933, 1936, 1937, 1938 and 1939—No. 1 the last year; the U.S. Top 10 those years, plus 1932 and 1940, No. 1 from 1936-40.

Second-seeded at Wimbledon in 1938, but jolted in the semis by unseeded Helen Jacobs, Alice then embarked invulnerably on one of the greatest passages in the game's history. She won the remaining 18 tournaments and 111 matches of her amateur tenure, posting nine tourney titles and 45-0 match marks in 1939 and 1940. The streak was second only among Americans to Helen Wills Moody's 27 titles, 158-match procession to the 1933 U.S. final. (France's Suzanne Lenglen had a streak of 182, 1921 to the close of her career in 1926.) Thus, for Alice's last three years of amateurism, she won 23 of 24 tournaments, 120 of 122 matches.

Born Sept. 28, 1913, on a farm in Plumas County, Calif., she was a product of the public courts of San Francisco's Golden Gate Park, a natural athlete who worked out with the minor league baseball players of the local Seals (including Joe DiMaggio) when she was their 13-year-old mascot. Marble made perhaps the most remarkable recovery from illness and obscurity in the game's annals to become the very best of her time.

Her soaring career—in 1933 she was No. 10 in the world and a U.S. quarterfinalist—seemed over by her 20th birthday, and she vanished from the scene for almost two years. In a weekend tourney at Easthampton, N.Y., that year she had to play singles and doubles semifinals and finals on the last day (108 games!) in 100-degree heat. The result was sunstroke, keeping her from Wightman Cup singles, weakening her for the remainder of the season. The following spring, during team matches in Paris, Alice collapsed and was hospitalized. Cut down by anemia and pleurisy, frustrated and depressed by a misdiagnosis of tuberculosis and the medical judgment that she must forget tennis, she didn't recover her health fully until 1936.

She began to play again in 1935 in California, and changed to the eastern grip. When in 1936 Marble returned to the East, officials of the USTA were fearful that she might jeopardize her health permanently if she resumed serious competition. But she was determined, and with the help of her coach, Eleanor Tennant, she undertook to re-establish herself and get back to the top.

Then, startlingly, she won the first of her four U.S. titles, deposing Helen Jacobs, 4-6, 6-3, 6-2.

Encouraged by halting Jacobs' four-championship run, and becoming her country's No. 1, she was on her way to the pinnacle. In 1937, she lost in the quarterfinals to Dodo Bundy (Cheney), but again was ranked No. 1. Marble hung on to the top spot in 1938-39-40. She won the U.S. crown all three years: 1938 over Aussie Nancye Wynne Bolton, 6-0, 6-3; 1939 over Jacobs, 6-0, 8-10,

6-4. She tripled at Wimbledon in 1939, winning all three titles, helping Bobby Riggs finish his lucrative triple in the mixed, 9-7, 6-1, over Brits Nina Brown and Frank Wilde. (Hope Bobby took her to dinner.) In four Wightman Cup-winning years, she lost but one match—each in singles and doubles.

An aging Bill Tilden, 48, and Don Budge, 25, at the top of his game, headlined the 1941 pro tour that opened at Madison Square Garden, along with Alice Marble and Mary Hardwick of Great Britain. Budge won, 51-7, and Marble was 72-3 in the head-to-head series of matches.

In her 1991 autobiography, *Courting Danger*, Alice wrote that she decided to turn pro at the end of 1940 because, "What's left for me? I'm champion ... and may as well make the most of it." She got a $75,000 guarantee from L.B. Icely, the president of Wilson, who bankrolled the tour. This, she said, despite a $100,000 offer from the wealthy tennis fan Will duPont (who later married Margaret Osborne), to deter her from turning pro because he enjoyed watching her on the Eastern grass circuit. During World War II, she played exhibitions at military installations across the U.S., and revealed in her book, that she was "sent as a government agent to Switzerland in 1945 to spy on Nazis before the war ended." Who knows?

She entered the Hall of Fame in 1964, and died Dec. 13, 1990, in Palm Springs, Calif.

MAJOR TITLES (18)—Wimbledon singles, 1939; U.S. singles, 1936, 1938, 1939, 1940; Wimbledon doubles, 1938, 1939; U.S. doubles, 1937, 1938, 1939, 1940; Wimbledon mixed, 1937, 1938, 1939; U.S. mixed, 1936, 1937, 1938, 1940. **OTHER U.S. TITLES** (2)—Clay Court singles, 1940; Clay Court doubles, 1940, with Mary Arnold. **WIGHTMAN CUP**—1933, 1937, 1938, 1939, 5-1 singles, 3-1 doubles. **SINGLES RECORD IN THE MAJORS**—Wimbledon (14-2), U.S. (31-4).

Alastair Martin
United States (1915—)
Hall of Fame—1973—Contributor

A mild yet determined man, Alastair Bradley Martin qualified for 1973 induction to the Hall of Fame on two counts: He was a progressive vice president and president of the USTA during the critical transition period between the amateur and Open eras. And he was one of the finest of all court tennis players, U.S. amateur champion in singles eight times, doubles 10 times. He also challenged the great pro Pierre Etchebaster (a fellow Hall of Fame member) for Etchebaster's world title, vainly in 1950 and 1952.

Alastair was a good enough lawn tennis player to have competed in the U.S. Championships at Forest Hills several times before and after World War II. As vice president of the USTA in 1967 and 1968, he worked closely with president Bob Kelleher, advocating, with the British, the revolutionary adoption of Open tennis.

He was USTA president in the trying days of 1969-70 as the game became professionalized, and the amateur associations maintained their standing. He founded the Eastern Tennis Patrons in 1951 and served as president of the National Tennis Foundation. A New Yorker, he was born there March 11, 1915.

Bill Martin
United States (1906–1998)
Hall of Fame—1982—Contributor

A distinguished figure in finance and government when Chairman of the Federal Reserve Board for 20 years (1951-70), William McChesney Martin was long devoted to the game, working behind the scenes to improve its condition in such positions as president of the National Tennis Foundation and the International Tennis Hall of Fame.

In 1992, he was elected honorary chairrman of the Hall, and worked diligently to make sure that its home, the historic Newport Casino, imperiled by age and apathy, was preserved and put into fine condition, regaining its former glory, evident today.

Martin married into an honored tennis family, wedding Cynthia Davis, daughter of Dwight Davis, donor of the Cup bearing his name. Like the Davises, he was raised in St. Louis, born there Dec. 17, 1906. He entered the Hall of Fame in 1982 and resided and died in Washington, D.C. July 27, 1998.

Dan Maskell
Great Britain (1908–1992)
Hall of Fame—1996—Journalist

To his legion of admirers Dan Maskell was the voice of Wimbledon from his first broadcast for BBC-TV in 1951 to his last in 1991. Dan's mellow and mellifluous tones, always thoughtful, always reverent, never wasteful, would illuminate the matches he covered with masterly understatement. Dan's reflections—perhaps a subtle change of tactics or a revealing grimace that told a story—added to the enjoyment of his viewers without being intrusive. "Oh, I say!" was a trademark, a meaningful exclamation that told much in three words.

Before his television career began, Dan spent two years with BBC Radio at Wimbledon, working as the summarizer with Max Rolbertson. He didn't miss a single day of play at Wimbledon from 1929 to 1991, and had seen every final since 1924.

Maskell was born April 11, 1908, in the London neighborhood of Fulham, just a pitch-and-putt from Queen's Club. He was the seventh of eight children, the fourth boy. As he grew up, Dan was captivated by rhe glamor of the famous club with its affluent members, many of them prominent in the worlds of entertainment, politics and sport.

First as a ballboy, then as a coach—never having a chance to play as an amateur—Dan was on the Queen's staff from 1923 to 1929 when he moved to the All England Lawn Tennis and Croquet Club at Wimbledon to become their first-ever teaching professional. For 16 years, Maskell, an excellent player, was the professional champion of Britain.

In 1933, Dan was surprised to be selected to accompany the British Davis Cup team to Paris for the semifinal against the U.S. This was unprecedented in those amateur days. Professionals never aided teams, which seems curious today when most leading players have personal coaches. Victories over the U.S. and then Cup-holding France began a four-year British reign, with Maskell a fundamental part of that success.

It was partly this team experience that prepared Dan to make an important contribution to his country during World War II. As the Royal Air Force's first rehabilitation officer, he revealed qualities of devotion and innovation that were recognized by the Crown with the award of an OBE (Order of the British Empire) in 1945.

Following the war, Dan resumed his duties at the All England Club for nine years. In 1955, he ended his coaching duties there to become the Lawn Tennis Association's training manager. He was in charge of the training of coaches and promoting the game nationwide. He also coached Prince Charles and Princess Anne. In 1982, he received his second award from the Crown, a CBE (Commander of the British Empire) for services to tennis, including broadcasting, and also an honorary MA degree from Loughborough University, where he was based during the war. He died Dec. 10, 1992, at 82.

—John Barrett

Simone Passemard Mathieu
France (1908—1980)
Hall of Fame—2006

If at first you don't succeed…

There was great rejoicing among French followers of sport on that summer day of 1938 when 30-year-old Simone Passemard Mathieu, trying again for the 13th year, did succeed in keeping the championship of La Belle France at home.

Not since the incomparable Suzanne Lenglen won in 1925-26 had a French woman taken the title. Admittedly, it was a French win either way in '38 since Mathieu's, 6-0, 6-3, victim, left-handed Nelly Adamson Landry, born of Belgian parentage, held a passport through marriage to Paul Landry, a French player.

But Mathieu's story of high frustration rang more bells. Six times she had crashed the final—and then crashed: 1929 to Helen Wills Moody, 6-3, 6-4; 1932 to Moody, 7-5, 6-1; 1933 to Peggy Scriven, 6-2, 4-6, 6-4; 1935 to Hilde Krahwinkel Sperling, 6-2, 6-1; 1936 to Sperling, 6-3, 6-4; 1937 to Sperling, 6-2, 6-4.

In 1939, shortly before both finalists' countries were enveloped by World War II, Simone hung onto her title in a 6-3, 8-6, beating of the jaunty Jadwiga Jedrzejowska of Poland, with whom she won the doubles. That was the end of tennis heroics for her, the best French female between Lenglen and 1967 champ Francoise Durr. More serious matters awaited, working for the Free French in London after escaping France where the collaborationist Vichy government had sentenced her to death.

She had spent happier times in London, her Wimbledon performances among the best of the pre-war decade: six semifinals, four quarterfinals, a consistent groundstroker with strong topspin backhand. "Very, very steady," says Midge Morrill Whiting, No. 2 in the U.S. in 1930, who played the French in 1929. Simone also made two French semifinals (1929, 34), four quarterfinals (1925-26, 30-31), and one U.S. quarterfinal (1938).

A righthander, born Jan. 11, 1908 in Neuilly-sur-Seine, France, she married Rene Mathieu in 1925 and died Jan. 7, 1980, in Paris.

Besides the 1938-39 singles Simone won nine other major titles, all doubles. She lost five major doubles finals. Simone's Parisian triple in 1938, winning singles, doubles, mixed, put her

in a select group with three other women who did that: Lenglen, 1925-26; Maureen Connolly, 1954; Margaret Smith Court, 1964.

MAJOR TITLES (12)—French singles, 1938, 1939; French doubles, 1933, 1934, 1936, 1937, 1938, 1939; French mixed, 1937, 1938; Wimbledon doubles, 1937; Wimbledon mixed, 1938; **SINGLES RECORDS IN THE MAJORS**—French (45-12), Wimbledon (46-13), U.S. (3-1).

Mark McCormack
United States (1930-2003)
Hall of Fame—2008—Contributor

By founding IMG (International Management Group) as a young man of 29, Mark Hume McCormack would revolutionize sports agentry and marketing on a world-wide level, much of it to the benefit and growth of tennis.

McCormack, a lawyer and an exceptional golfer who qualified for the U.S. Open and British Amateur, first turned his attention to that sport. Tremendously imaginative, a business genius, he sensed new opportunity on the links. It was in the forms of three men who would become all-time greats: Arnold Palmer, Jack Nicklaus and Gary Player. Through their play and his management they became wealthy and kindled increasing interest in golf.

When tennis became "open" in 1968, blending amateurs with the previously outlawed professionals, McCormack was quick to act, realizing that this game should attain far broader popularity, and that he could be a positive force in its rise.

Immediately, he signed on to represent the world's foremost player, Australian Rod Laver, also to represent the All England Lawn Tennis & Croquet Club (aka Wimbledon), a relationship that continues to this day.

Laver was the first of a long line of tennis players to select McCormack's IMG as their agent. Among them other Hall of Famers Chris Evert, Martina Navratilova, Bjorn Borg, Jim Courier, Pete Sampras.

Mark's thoughts and ideas flowed in all directions in sport, and beyond. IMG became the world's largest independent producer of TV sports programming. His system has spread and promoted economic advances for players, tournaments, tennis institutions and the game's industry as a whole. In 1992, the *Times of London* named him one of "A Thousand People Who Most Influenced The 20th Century."

Born Nov. 6, 1930, in Chicago, he grew up there, graduated from William and Mary College ('51) and Yale Law School ('54), and served a year in the U.S. Army in 1956. He was inducted into William and Mary's Athletic Hall of Fame for golfing prowess in 1958.

IMG acquired the Nick Bollettieri Sports Academy in 1987, continuing Nick's successful tennis "boot camp" that trains outstanding players from across the globe.

As an author, he somehow found time to write *Things They Don't Teach You at Harvard Business School,* a best seller in 1984 published in 82 countries.

Mark's second marriage was to a standout American tennis player, Betsy Nagelsen in 1986, eight years after she was the final-

ist at the Australian Open. A 2008 inductee to the International Tennis Hall of Fame, he died May 16, 2003, in New York.

John McEnroe
United States (1959—)
Hall of Fame—1999

Right from the start, in his 1977 introduction to pro tennis, John Patrick McEnroe, Jr., was a hit.

An 18-year-old amateur (he would not turn pro until winning the National Intercollegiate singles as a Stanford freshman in 1978), McEnroe made his first splash in Paris, a boy edging into man's territory. He won his first of 17 major titles there, the French mixed with childhood pal, Mary Carillo over the Romanian-Colombian combine of Florenta Mihai and Ivan Molina, 7-6, 6-3.

Soon after, electrifying Wimbledon, he went through the qualifying tourney and all the way to the semis, losing to Jimmy Connors, 6-3, 6-3, 4-6, 6-4. It was the first time a qualifier had traveled so far in a major. Immediately, Mac was a player to reckon with.

Born on Feb. 16, 1959 in Wiesbaden, Germany, where his father was stationed with the U.S. Air Force, he grew up in the Long Island suburb of Douglaston, N.Y. A 5-foot-11, 170-pound left-hander, McEnroe stands as perhaps the most skilled and controversial of all players. Brilliant in doubles and singles, he was distinguished by shotmaking artistry, competitive fire and a volatile temper. The last led to heavy fines, suspensions and, at the 1990 Australian Open, an extraordinary fourth-round disqualification for showering abusive language on court officials.

A magnificent volleyer with a feathery touch, he was an attacker whose fast court style netted four U.S. Open and three Wimbledon singles. He had the baselining strength to do well on clay at the French. He might have won that at his zenith, but in the 1984 final, he led Ivan Lendl, 2-0 in sets, only to he distracted by temperamental outbursts, and was beaten, 3-6, 2-6, 6-4, 7-5, 7-5.

He revived American interest in the Davis Cup that had been shunned by Connors and other leading countrymen, saying, "My mother made me promise her I'd always play for my country if I was asked." Right from the start, as a 19-year-old rookie in 1978, he gave Capt. Tony Trabert's team a lift, and the U.S. the Cup that had belonged to other countries since 1973. In the championship round against Britain at Rancho Mirage, Calif., he evinced none of the jitters so common to many other greats in the nationalistic setting. Mac was a miser, rationing John Lloyd (6-1, 6-2, 6-2) and Buster Mottram (6-2, 6-2, 6-1) to 10 games.

Nobody had been stingier in a final. He was the most callow American to do so well in the Cup round, although Lew Hoad, a younger 19 by eight months for victorious Australia, also took both his singles in 1953, and American Michael Chang, 18, won one singles in the victorious 1990 final. Aussie Lleyton Hewitt, was also 18, splitting his singles in the triumphant 1999 final.

McEnroe continued as a mainstay in helping the U.S. win four more Cups (1979, 81-82, 92), and set numerous U.S. records: years played (12), series (30), singles wins (41), singles and doubles wins altogether (59). A workhorse, he played both singles and doubles in 13 series, and he and Peter Fleming won 14 of 15 Cup doubles together.

An epic performance was his Davis Cup record time 6-hour-22 minute, five-set victory 9-7, 6-2, 15-17, 3-6, 8-6 over Mats Wilander in St. Louis, clinching a 1982 quarterfinal, a 3-2 win over Sweden. He and German Boris Becker nearly topped that, using 6 hours, 21 minutes for Boris' 1987 4-6, 15-13, 8-10, 6-2, 6-3 Cup relegation victory at Hartford. Another thriller was Mac's five-set win over Jose-Luis Clerc of Argentina, 6-3, 4-6, 6-4, 4-6, 11-9, to send the Cup to the U.S. in the 1981 final at Cincinnati.

After his playing career, McEnroe was named the U.S. Davis Cup captain in 1999 and served one year, 2000, quitting after three series (3-2 wins over Zimbabwe and the Czech Republic, a 5-0 loss to Spain), and was replaced by his younger brother, Patrick McEnroe.

At 20, John won his first U.S. title, over fellow New Yorker Vitas Gerulaitis, 7-5, 6-3, 6-3, the youngest winner since Pancho Gonzalez, also 20, 31 years before. He repeated in dramatic battles with Bjorn Borg in 1980, 7-6 (7-4), 6-1, 6-7 (5-7), 5-7, 6-4, and 1981, 4-6, 6-2, 6-4, 6-3. Borg retired shortly thereafter. McEnroe won for the last time in 1984, over Ivan Lendl, 6-3, 6-4, 6-1. But he was defeated in the Flushing Meadow rematch 12 months later, 7-6 (7-1), 6-3, 6-4, relinquishing to Lendl the world No. 1 ranking McEnroe had held for four years.

His most celebrated result may have been a loss, the 1980 Wimbledon final called by many the greatest of all. Beaten, 1-6, 7-5, 6-3, 6-7 (16-18), 8-6, McEnroe nervelessly staved off five match points during the monumental fourth-set tie-breaker to fight Borg to the fifth-set wire. A year later, he cut down Borg on Centre Court, 4-6, 7-6 (7-1), 7-6 (7-4), 6-4, ending Bjorn's incredible five-year, 41-match Wimbledon run.

McEnroe won again in 1983, a quickie with unseeded New Zealander Chris Lewis, and in 1984, reaching the pinnacle of his virtuosity, a virtually flawless wipeout of Connors, 6-1, 6-2, 6-2. There were many ups and downs at Wimbledon, where McEnroe came close to being tossed out prior to his initial championship in 1981, following a second-round flareup while beating Tom Gullikson. It was the infamous scene of labeling the umpire, Ted James, "pits of the world," and calling the referee every name but Fred Hoyles (which was his name). He went out in grand manner in 1992. Unseeded at No. 30, the 33-year-old Mac wound up where he'd begun 15 years before: the semis, unseeded, on a stirring 6-2, 7-6 (11-9), 6-3, knockout of No. 9-seeded Guy Forget. He'd already beaten 16th-seeded David Wheaton in three, and won a rousing 4-hour-9-minute battle of champions over Aussie Pat Cash, 6-7 (3-7), 6-4, 6-7 (1-7), 6-3, 6-2. But champ-to-be Andre Agassi was too much for him in the goodbye singles, 6-4, 6-2, 6-3.

Yet there was more, and Mac's fading presence would be stretched triumphantly over two days and Wimbledon's longest closing act on the third Monday: his fifth doubles title, this time without old collaborator Peter Fleming, but with a stranger who did just fine, Michael Stich. Two points from defeat in the fourth-set tie-breaker, tied at darkness, 13-13, the German-American combine came through over Americans Richey Renberg and Jim Grabb, 5-7, 7-6 (7-5), 3-6, 7-6 (7-5), 19-17, a record-length final of 5:01. Eight years had passed since his last title. "It was a great

atmosphere [Court 1 was packed with 6,500 Mac fans] a great way to go out," Mac said.

Three intense rivalries stand out during his career. He had the edge on Connors (31-20), but not Lendl (15-21), and was even with Borg (7-7). Except for the French Open lapse against Lendl, he was unbeatable in 1984, winning 13 of 15 singles tournaments on an 82-3 record. Other big seasons were 1979 (10 titles on a 94-12 record), 1980 (10 titles on 88-18). In 1979, he set an Open era record with 27 overall tournament victories, 17 in doubles, winning a record total of 177 matches. He won the season-climaxing Masters singles thrice, 1978, '83-'84, and is the all-time overall Open era leader with 155 tournament victories: a 77-78 singles-doubles split. Registering the last doubles, 2006 in San Jose, he was in the company of Swede Jonas Bjorkman, over Paul Goldstein-Jim Thomas—thus a champ in four decades. He is third in singles titles behind Connors's 109 and Lendl's 92, tied for second in doubles with Tom Okker's 78—both behind Todd Woodbridge with 83. His career singles W-L record is 849-184.

Ten years a member of the world's Top 10, he was four times No. 1 (1981-84). Brother, Patrick McEnroe, younger by seven years (born July 1, 1966), followed him as a standout pro, winning the French doubles (with Grabb) in 1989, ranking as high as No. 28 in 1995. In 1991, they met in the Chicago final, the second such clash of brothers (Emilio Sanchez defeated Javier Sanchez in the 1987 Madrid final). John won, 3-6, 6-2, 6-4. John's prize money for 15 years as a pro was $12,539,827. He has three children by ex-wife Tatum O'Neal, two by wife Patty Smyth, and transitioned from his professional career into a popular TV tennis commentator.

MAJOR TITLES (17)—Wimbledon singles, 1981, 1983, 1984; U.S. singles, 1979, 1980, 1981, 1984; Wimbledon doubles, 1979, 1981, 1983, 1984, 1992; U.S. doubles, 1979, 1981, 1983, 1984: French mixed, 1977. **OTHER U.S. TITLES** (4)—Indoor singles, 1980: Hard Court singles, 1989: Indoor doubles, 1980, with Brian Gottfried; Clay Court doubles, 1979, with Gene Mayer. **DAVIS CUP**—1978, 1979. 1980, 1981, 1982, 1983, 1984, 1987, 1988, 1989, 1991, 1992, 41-8 singles, 18-2 doubles. **SINGLES RECORD IN THE MAJORS**—Australian (18-5). French (25-10), Wimbledon (59-11), U.S. (65-12).

Ken McGregor
Australia (1929-2007)
Hall of Fame—1999

"It was a surprise to me, the Yanks—and everybody else," smiled Kenneth Bruce McGregor, recounting the 1950 weekend when Australia began taking over the tennis world. He was the unexpected, relatively inexperienced taker, selected for a singles role by Capt. Harry Hopman in an effort to halt a U.S. Davis Cup landslide in the challenge round final on the lawn of Forest Hills in New York.

The Americans had heisted the Cup from Australia, 5-0, at Melbourne in 1946, as McGregor, a 17-year-old more interested in football [Australian rules], listened at home in Adelaide to the sad tidings on the radio. U.S. victories over challenging Australia in 1947-48-49 compounded the distress Down Under, and the Yanks were favored again.

"It was assumed that John Bromwich would get the other singles job with my doubles partner, Frank Sedgman," Ken said. "But Hopman picked me, and used Brom with Frank in the doubles."

That arrangement worked splendidly in a 4-1 triumph. McGregor, a late blossomer with only three previous Cup singles in routine preliminary rounds that year on his resume, could feel his country on his back, wondering about Hop's judgement. But he responded handsomely, beating an Aussie nemesis, Ted Schroeder, in the second match, 13-11, 6-3, 6-4. Schroeder had been 7-0 since 1946 against the Aussies. "The first set was tense, but after that I was very confident. Sedg took some of the pressure away by beating Tom Brown [6-0, 8-6, 9-7] in the first match." Sedgman and Bromwich clinched in the doubles over Schroeder and Gar Mulloy, 4-6, 6-4, 6-2, 4-6, 6-4.

It was the start of the Aussie reign of terror: 15 Cups in 18 years, and McGregor had a fine right hand in the first three. He (in the right court) and Sedgman, one of the greatest doubles combos, went together like gin and vermouth, Butch Cassidy and the Sundance Kid. They crafted the lone male Grand Slam in 1951, starting at the Australian by shattering the eight-title procession of Bromwich and Adrian Quist, 11-9, 2-6, 6-3, 4-6, 6-3. Next was the French over Yanks Dick Savitt and Gar Mulloy, 6-2, 2-6, 9-7, 7-5, followed by Wimbledon, over South Africa's Eric Sturgess and Czech Jaroslav Drobny, 3-6, 6-2, 6-3, 3-6, 6-3. To cap it off, they won the U.S. over compatriots Don Candy and Merv Rose, 10-8, 4-6, 6-4, 7-5.

That year in the Davis Cup final, allied with Sedg, Ken was in on the crucial go-ahead point, the doubles, 6-2, 9-7, 6-3, over Tony Trabert and Schroeder, leading to a 3-2 victory over the U.S.

He had been replaced by Rose, loser of both singles, but Ken was back in the singles lineup in, 1952, a treat for his fellow citizens at Memorial Drive in Adelaide, as he beat Trabert, 11-9, 6-4, 6-1, and collaborated with Sedgman in the doubles, 6-3, 6-4, 1-6, 6-3, over Trabert and Vic Seixas that made it 3-0 in the 4-1 victory. That was the end of a brief, resplendent amateur career. He and Sedgman joined the gypsies, the barnstorming pros. Ken played the warmup act against Pancho Segura preceding the feature—Sedgman trying vainly to unseat the king of the hill, Jack Kramer. The first year (a 71-25 beating by the seasoned Segura) was a rude introduction. "Ken was a big-occasion player, not suited to the night-after-night pro grind, mostly at different venues," said historian Joe McCauley.

"I hated to leave Davis Cup," Ken recalled, "but the money [from promoter Jack Kramer] was too good to turn down. We were getting 25 shillings a day as amateurs, and I had a guarantee of about $60,000 for three years."

At 6-3, 180 pounds, a quick, agile and aggressive serve-and-volleyer, McGregor may have been the most athletic of the Australian mob. His sights were on football, but his father, once a pro footballer, thought him too light and guided him toward tennis, saying, "If you don't make the Davis Cup in three years you can go back to footy." Hopman liked his devotion to fitness, and brought him along well. Hall of Famer Ellsworth Vines commented, "Ken was difficult to pass because of his prehensile reach, and he had the most extraordinary overhead of all time."

On the scene barely four years, he won three singles titles and was in the world's Top 10 three times: No. 8 in 1950; No. 7 in 1951; No. 3 in 1952. He lost the 1950 Australian final (to Sedg-

man) and 1951 (to Dick Savitt) before winning in 1952 over Sedgman, 7-5, 12-10, 2-6, 6-2. He also lost to Savitt in the 1951 Wimbledon final, 6-4, 6-4, 6-4.

Born June 2, 1929, at Adelaide, he was elevated to the International Hall in 1999, named to the Australian Tennis Hall of Fame in 2000, and died Dec. 1, 2007, at Myrtle Bank, South Australia.

MAJOR TITLES (9)—Australian singles, 1952; Australian doubles, 1951, 1952; French doubles, 1951, 1952; Wimbledon doubles, 1951, 1952; U.S. doubles, 1951; U.S. mixed doubles, 1950. **DAVIS CUP**—1950, 1951, 1952, 4-3 singles, 2-0 doubles, **SINGLES RECORD IN THE MAJORS**—Australian (14-4). French (11-3), Wimbledon (13-3). U.S. (3-3).

Chuck McKinley
United States (1941–1986)
Hall of Fame—1986

Bubbling with energy and grit, Charles Robert McKinley, Jr., was a tough little guy who hustled every minute and died tragically of a brain tumor shortly after learning, in 1986, that he had been named to the Hall of Fame. But he had achieved his utmost tennis goals, both in 1963—winning Wimbledon, and leading the U.S. to the Davis Cup with a 3-2 victory over the holder, Australia, at Adelaide.

A stubby, chesty, 5-foot-9 Missourian, he learned to play at a St. Louis YMCA, where he was already proficient at table tennis. He was a crowd-wowing player, hurling himself about the court, leaping for smashes at which he was expert since so many opponents tried to lob him. Although favored to win the U.S. Intercollegiate title in 1963 for Trinity in San Antonio, Chuck obtained permission from the college president to go for the larger prize, Wimbledon—"But you'd better win," he insisted. Seeded No. 4, he came through without losing a set or—luck of the draw—without facing a seeded opponent. He beat Fred Stolle in the final, 9-7, 6-1, 6-4, showing that despite limited stature he could serve and volley with anyone.

Curiously, seeded No. 8, he had opposed no other seeds in making his first Wimbledon splash in 1961, until losing the final to No. 2-seeded Rod Laver, 6-3, 6-1, 6-4. As the defender in 1964, he was paid back by Stolle in a four-set semi, 4-6, 10-8, 9-7, 6-4. As the left court player, he blended splendidly with Dennis Ralston in three U.S. doubles championships, 1961, 1963 and 1964. They beat Mexico's Rafe Osuna and Tonio Palafox the first two times, McKinley serving out of two match points in the exciting fifth, 9-7, 4-6, 5-7, 6-3, 11-9, in 1963.

During the long Cup campaign of 1963, he won six of eight singles, all four doubles matches with Ralston. The Cup round was McKinley's tour de force although he lost to Roy Emerson the first day. He and Ralston got the go-ahead point over Emerson and Neale Fraser, 6-3, 4-6, 11-9, 11-9. But after Ralston lost to Emerson on the third day, it "was up to me. That's the way I wanted it, the Cup riding on one match."

It was a rare position for an American. None had (or has since) come through in the Cup-deciding fifth match. McKinley did, despite being down a service break in the fourth to the thunder-serving Aussie rookie John Newcombe, 10-12, 6-2, 9-7,

6-2, as the Memorial Drive stadium rocked with patriotic fervor for Newk. The following year, however, in Cleveland, McKinley couldn't repeat, losing the decisive fifth to Emerson, 3-6, 6-2, 6-4, 6-4, as Australia regained the Cup, 3-2.

More intent on getting a college degree and establishing himself in business, McKinley resisted professional offers, and his career was relatively brief without a great deal of international play. He was ranked seven successive years in the U.S. Top 10 from 1960, No. 1 in 1962 and 1963, and four times in the world's Top 10 from 1961, No. 2 in 1963. The U.S. title eluded him, although he was a semifinalist three straight years, 1962-64, losing to champs, Osuna in 1963, 6-4, 6-4, 10-8; Emerson in 1962, 4-6, 6-4, 6-3, 6-2, and in 1964, 6-4, 11-9, 6-4. But Chuck did win four U.S. titles on two other surfaces: Indoor, 1962 and 1964; Clay, 1962 and 1963.

He was born Jan. 5, 1941, in St. Louis, and died Aug. 10, 1986, in Dallas.

MAJOR TITLES (4)—Wimbledon singles, 1963; U.S. doubles, 1961, 1963, 1964. **OTHER U.S. TITLES** (9)—Indoor singles, 1962, 1964; Clay Court singles, 1962, 1963; Indoor doubles, 1962, with Laver; 1963, 1965, with Ralston; Clay Court doubles, 1961, 1964, with Ralston. **DAVIS CUP**—1960, 1961, 1962, 1963. 1964, 1965, 16-6 singles, 13-3 in doubles, **SINGLES RECORD IN THE MAJORS**—Wimbledon (20-4), U.S. (34-13).

Maurice McLoughlin
United States (1890–1957)
Hall of Fame—1957

He came out of the West with a cannonball serve, spectacular volleys and overhead smashes. He created great excitement in the East and abroad at Wimbledon with the violence of his attack. And more than anything else, Maurice Evans "Red" McLoughlin, known as the "California Comet," opened the eyes of the public to tennis as a demanding game of speed, endurance and skill.

Tennis at the turn of the century was a moderately paced game contested from the back of the court. But McLoughlin, a right-hander, carried this attack forward, projecting the cannonballs and rushing in behind them to meet the return near the net with a cataclysmic overhead or a masterful volley. The volley was not new to the game (it had been used in the first Championship in 1881), but it had not nearly been the finishing stroke that Red Mac made it.

Born Jan. 7, 1890, in Carson City, Nev., McLoughlin polished his game on the public parks courts of northern California, and this in itself was a departure in the direction of democratizing the game. Most of the top-ranking players had developed their games on the turf of exclusive clubs in the East or their own private family courts.

At 19, he had developed sufficiently to be named to the Davis Cup team to play alongside another San Francisco teenager, Melville Long, 19, against Australasia in the 1909 challenge round. They were packed off—just the two of them, McLoughlin the playing captain—as sacrificial lambs for the powerful Australasian lineup of Norman Brookes and Tony Wilding. Whitewashed they were, 5-0, limited to one set for Red, but he absorbed valuable international seasoning.

He enlivened five straight U.S. singles finals, starting in 1911, the 6-4, 6-4, 6-2 victim in Bill Larned's seventh and last title. Red won 1912 and 1913 battles respectively over Wallace Johnson, 3-6, 2-6, 6-2, 6-4, 6-2, and Dick Williams, 6-4, 5-7, 6-3, 6-1. He lost his title to Williams, 6-3, 8-6, 10-8, in the Championships' farewell to Newport in 1914. At the Forest Hills inaugural in an all-San Francisco clash, Mac was beaten by the rising Bill Johnston, 1-6, 6-0, 7-5, 10-8.

His one venture to England in 1913, was an artistic success as the U.S. regained the Davis Cup, and he helped draw unprecedented large crowds to Wimbledon, where he won the all-comers over Aussie Stanley Doust, 6-3, 6-4, 7-5. In the challenge round, he fought defending champ Tony Wilding all the way, but missed a set point at 5-4, 40-30, and was beaten, 8-6, 6-3, 10-8. Then came the Cup tests, shutouts of Germany and Canada, and a 1-1 first day split against Cup-holding Britain. That evolved to a 3-2 U.S. victory as McLoughlin partnered Capt. Harold Hackett to a five-set win over Herbert Roper Barrett and Charles Dixon, 5-7, 6-1, 2-6, 7-5, 6-4. It set up Red for the finisher over Dixon, 8-6, 6-3, 6-2.

McLoughlin reached his peak the next year in the Davis Cup final, even though the Cup was lost. The matching of McLoughlin and Norman Brookes of Australasia brought forth tennis that was a revelation to the thousands who attended at Forest Hills. The match was characterized as "never been equalled." McLoughlin won, 17-15, 6-3, 6-3. The matches attracted 14,000 people daily, and McLoughlin was given much of the credit for the crowds.

After his Davis Cup success, the 1915 *Tennis Guide* said, "In McLoughlin, America undoubtedly has the greatest tennis player of all time." Yet he never again attained that form. Absent from the East for several years, he returned after Army duty in World War I and was hardly recognizable. He had lost his cannonball and his punch. Gone was his whirlwind speed. After he was defeated by Dick Williams decisively in the 1919 quarters, 6-0, 6-3, 6-2, he left the tennis scene for golf, where he soon was shooting in the low 70s. His tennis career had come to a premature end. Some said he was burned out from his violent exertions on the court.

On Dec. 10, 1957, the year of his entry into the Hall of Fame, the Comet died. But in the short time that he had lit up the tennis firmament, as no one before him. He had started the sport on its way to becoming a popular game for Americans. He ranked No. 1 in 1914 and was also in the U.S. Top 10 seven straight years from 1909, No. 1 in 1912-13-14.

MAJOR TITLES (5)—U.S. singles, 1912, 1913: U.S. doubles, 1912, 1913, 1914. **DAVIS CUP**—1909, 1911, 1913, 1914: record 9-4 in singles, 3-4 in doubles. **SINGLES RECORDS IN THE MAJORS**—Wimbledon (7-1), U.S. (49-9)

Frew McMillan
South Africa (1942—)
Hall of Fame—1992

Side by side again, entering the Hall of Fame in 1992, Frew Donald McMillan was reunited with his one-time collaborator on the solid-front team of Hewitt and McMillan. The unorthodox McMillan—stroking with two hands on both sides in the left court—and Bob Hewitt were a dynamite blend, winning five major titles (three Wimbledons) and driving South Africa to the 1974 Davis Cup.

Love was the prime ingredient in bringing them together in 1966. It was Hewitt's romance with his South African wife-to-be that moved the Australian westward to Johannesburg. When he became eligible to play for his new land, Hewitt was yoked to McMillan in 1966, and they were an immediate hit. They won their first start together late that year, and didn't lose until the quarters of the French the following year, a 45-match streak.

In 1967, they won Wimbledon, over Aussies Roy Emerson and Ken Fletcher, 6-2, 6-3, 6-4, and repeated in 1972 over Americans Stan Smith and Erik van Dillen, 6-2, 6-2, 9-7.

A springy 6-foot-1, the slim McMillan was born in Springs, South Africa on May 20, 1942, and grew up there.

"We were touch and thrust," he says of the combination that was so winning over a 15-year period. "Right from the start each of us knew what the other would do. Bob had wonderful returning touch from the first court." McMillan, a right-hander, handled the racket like a cricket bat and could slug or chip. Distinctive beneath a tiny white cap that partially covered his shining dark hair, Frew was the first player of international prominence of two-way, two-fisted swinging.

A straight-set Wimbledon quarterfinal win over five-time champs John Newcombe and Tony Roche en route to the 1978 title showed them at their very best. They continued lethally through the final, 6-1, 6-4, 6-2, over Peter Fleming and John McEnroe. Spanning the amateur and Open eras, they added 60 titles to their five majors. McMillan's individual total of pro doubles titles was 74, fourth on the all-time list behind Tom Okker and McEnroe (78 each) and Todd Woodbridge (83). Frew won two pro singles titles. He also had five major mixed titles, two Wimbledons and two U.S. with Betty Stove for a career total of 10 majors.

MAJOR TITLES (10)—French doubles, 1972; Wimbledon doubles, 1967, 1972, 1978; U.S. doubles, 1977; French mixed, 1966; Wimbledon mixed, 1979, 1981; U.S. mixed, 1977, 1978. **DAVIS CUP**—1965, 1966 1967, 1968, 1969, 1973, 1974, 1975, 1976, 1977, 1978; 2-0 singles, 23-5 doubles. **SINGLES RECORD IN THE MAJORS**—Australian (0-1), French (8-10), Wimbledon (9-17), U.S. (12-10). **MAJOR TITLES WITH HEWITT** (5)—French doubles, 1972; Wimbledon doubles, 1967, 1972, 1978; U.S. doubles, 1977. **DAVIS CUP**—1967, 1968, 1969, 1974, 1978, 16-1 in doubles.

Don McNeill
United States (1918–1996)
Hall of Fame—1965

It was a long way to Paris from Oklahoma, but a tennis court in one place was the same as one in another to a college boy named William Donald McNeill, who became the second American man to win the French title. Doing so in 1939 by beating favorite and world No. 1 Bobby Riggs 7-5, 6-0, 6-3, Don served notice that he would be a thorn in the little hustler's side and intentions.

Though McNeill may have lost his best years to World War II, in which he served as a U.S. Naval intelligence officer, he stands as one of only four Americans to win on the grass at Forest Hills,

the U.S. title (1940), and on the clay at Roland Garros, succeeding Don Budge, and preceding Frank Parker and Tony Trabert.

McNeill, a nimble 5-foot-10, 155 pounds, out of Oklahoma City, with a very sharp backhand, had gone to Europe on a lark. He returned to move unseeded to the U.S. quarterfinals, and give No. 6-seeded Joe Hunt a scare, 6-4, 15-13, 8-10, 4-6, 6-2, in three-plus hours spread over two days. Don felt he could win it one day, and that day wasn't far off. Back to college he went, to graduate and win the Intercollegiate title for tiny Kenyon (Ohio) in 1940, then sting Riggs twice. If beating him in the U.S. Clay Court final, 6-1, 6-4, 7-9, 6-3, wasn't enough, he then completely wrecked defender Bobby's pro plans at Forest Hills. After taking Jack Kramer in the semis, 6-1, 5-7, 6-4, 6-3, Don staged a counterattack against Riggs to seize the U.S. final, 4-6, 6-8, 6-3, 6-3, 7-5. McNeill was the third of five players in the championship round to rebound from two sets down. The victory completed an unusual coupling of headgear: wearing the college and national crowns in the same year, he would have only one such equal, Ted Schroeder of Stanford In 1942.

Don's versatility shows in a record that includes that U.S. Clay Court title of 1940, and as the only man to win the U.S. Indoor before and after the war—a 19-year-old collegian in 1938, over Frank Bowden, 9-7, 3-6, 6-4, 7-5, and in 1950, over Fred Kovaleski, 11-9, 4-6, 6-2, 6-2. He lost his U.S. title in 1941, beaten in the semis by Frank Kovacs, 6-4, 6-2, 10-8. He was in the semis again in 1944, losing to champ Frank Parker, 6-4, 3-6, 6-2, 6-2. He also collected numerous doubles prizes, especially the French of '39, when he and Charlie Harris flinched not at two of the grand old Musketeers, and beat Jacques Brugnon and Jean Borotra for the title, 4-6, 6-4, 6-0, 2-6, 10-8, even though Borotra had four match points on serve at 6-5. McNeill was the first of only two American men to ring up a double in Paris. Tony Trabert emulated by winning both titles in 1954 and 1955.

He ranked in the U.S. Top 10 six times between 1937 and 1946, No. 1 in 1940, world's No. 7 in 1939. On leave from the Navy, he won the U.S. doubles in 1944 with Bob Falkenburg.

"I thought I won it again," he laughed, "several times that afternoon in Boston." He means the titanic U.S. doubles final of 1946 at Longwood. Don and Frank Guernsey had seven match points in the fifth set, but couldn't sway the champs, Bill Talbert and Gardnar Mulloy, 3-6, 6-4, 2-6, 6-3, 20-18. McNeill, born April 30, 1918, at Chickasha, Okla., spent most of his post-college life in New York as an advertising executive, and died Nov. 28, 1996, at Vero Beach, Fla. He was named to the Hall of Fame in 1965.

MAJOR TITLES (4)—French singles, 1939; U.S. singles, 1940; French doubles. 1939; U.S. doubles, 1944. **OTHER U.S. TITLES** (9)-Indoor singles. 1938, 1950; Clay Court singles, 1940; Intercollegiate singles, 1940; Indoor doubles, 1941, 1946 with Frank Guernsey; 1949, 1950. 1951, with Bill Talbert. **SINGLES RECORD IN THE MAJORS**—French (6-0), Wimbledon (1-1), U.S. (27-9).

Helen Wills Moody
United States (1905–1998)
Hall of Fame—1959

It scarcely seems possible that two players of the transcendent ability of Helen Newington Wills Moody Roark and Suzanne Lenglen could have been contemporaries. They were ranked for close to half a century as the two best female tennis players of all time. Their records are unmatched and hardly have been approached.

While indeed contemporaries, they were rivals in only one match, played with international fanfare in 1926 and won by Lenglen, 6-3, 8-6, at Cannes, France. Lenglen, not yet 27, was at the crest of her game, with six Wimbledon championships in her possession. Wills' game at 20 had not quite attained full maturity, though she had been in the Wimbledon final of 1924, and would win eight times. Their rivalry was limited to the single meeting, for later that same year, Wills was stricken with appendicitis and Lenglen turned pro.

It would be difficult to imagine two players of more different personalities and types of game. Between 1919 and 1938, Wills won 52 of 92 tournaments on a 398-35 match record, a .919 average, and had a 158-match winning streak (27 tournaments to the 1933 U.S. final, the only time she lost to Helen Jacobs in 11 meetings). Her 50 straight match wins at Wimbledon and 46 at the U.S. are tournament records. She didn't play the French often enough to hold the record, undefeated but winning only 20 in a row.

Quiet, reserved, and never changing expression, Wills, known as Little Miss Poker Face, played with unruffled poise and never exhibited the style, flair or emotional outbursts that Lenglen did. From her first appearance in the East in 1921, when she was national junior champion, Wills' typical garb on the court was a white sailor suit, white eyeshade and white shoes and stockings.

The game she played right-handed was one of sheer power, which she had developed in practice against men on the West Coast. From both forehand and backhand, she hammered the ball almost the full length of the court regularly, and the speed, pace and depth of her drives, in conjunction with her tactical moves, sufficed to subdue her opponents. She could hit winners as spectacularly from the baseline on the backhand as on the forehand.

She went to the net occasionally, not nearly as often as Lenglen, and Wills was sound in her volleying and decisive overhead with her smash. Her slice service, breaking wide and pulling the receiver beyond the alley, was as good as any female player has commanded.

Her footwork was not so good. She did not move with the grace and quickness of Lenglen, and opponents fared best against her by using the drop shot or changes of length to draw her forward and send her running back. Anchored to the baseline, she could run any opponent into the ground. Because of her sense of anticipation, she seemed to be in the right spot, and it was not often that she appeared to be hurried in her stroking.

She was born Oct. 6, 1905, in Centreville, Calif., and the facts of her invincibility are stark. She won the Wimbledon title a record eight times (surpassed by Martina Navratilova's nine in 1990) in nine tries, her only loss coming in her first appearance, in 1924. From 1927 to 1932, she did not lose a set in singles anywhere. She won seven U.S., five Wimbledon and four French titles without loss of a set until Dorothy Round of Britain extended her to 6-4, 6-8, 6-3 in the 1933 Wimbledon final.

In Wightman Cup play from 1923 to 1938, she won 18 singles matches and lost two, both in 1924. She won the Olympic singles and doubles in Paris in 1924, beating Didi Vlasto of France, 6-2, 6-2, and abetting a mentor, Hazel Wightman to defeat Brits McKane and Phyllis Covell, 7-5, 8-6. When she scored her first Wimbledon victory in 1927, she was the first American woman to be crowned there since May Sutton in 1905.

Two of her three most remarkable matches were her clash with Lenglen in 1926 and her default because of back pain to rival Helen Jacobs when trailing 0-3 in the third set of the 1933 U.S. final. The third remarkable match was in the 1935 Wimbledon final in which Jacobs led, 5-2, in the third set and stood at match point, only to see the-then Mrs. Moody rally and add one more victory to her astounding record.

In 1928, she became the first player to win three majors in the same year—French, Wimbledon and U.S.—and the first American to rule at Stade Roland Garros, where she was unbeaten while winning four titles (1928-29-30, 32). Her total of 19 major singles titles was the record for 32 years, until Margaret Smith Court (24) passed her in 1970. But her success was the most phenomenal ever, considering that she won 19 of 22 entered, winning 126 of 129 matches (.977), never worse than finalist. Nobody has come close to her being involved in 22 major finals in a row—losing the title matches to Jacobs, Molla Mallory in the 1922 U.S. final and Kitty Godfree in the 1924 Wimbledon final—but she was an irregular entrant between 1922 and 1938.

She became Mrs. Aidan Roark in 1939, was considered a fine painter, and was inducted into the Hall of Fame in 1969. She died Jan. 1, 1998 at Carmel, Calif.

MAJOR TITLES (31)—French singles, 1928, 1929, 1930, 1932; Wimbledon singles, 1927, 1928, 1929, 1930, 1932, 1933, 1935, 1938: U.S. singles, 1923, 1924, 1925, 1927, 1928, 1929, 1931; French doubles, 1930, 1932; Wimbledon doubles, 1924, 1927, 1930; U.S. doubles, 1922, 1924, 1925, 1928; Wimbledon mixed 1929; U.S. mixed, 1921, 1928. WIGHTMAN CUP—1923, 1924, 1925, 1927, 1928, 1929, 1930, 1931, 1932, 1938. 18-2 singles, 3-7 doubles. SINGLES RECORD IN THE MAJORS—French (20-0), Wimbledon (55-1), U.S (51-2).

Bessie Moore
United States (1876–1959)
Hall of Fame—1971

Elisabeth "Bessie" Holmes Moore, a New Yorker, was a young champ, winning the first of her U.S. titles at 20 in 1896, over Juliette Atkinson, 6-4, 4-6, 6-2, 6-2. But four years before, she was in the final, losing the first five-set match played by women, 5-7, 6-3, 6-4, 4-6, 6-2, to Ireland's Mabel Cahill. She was the youngest U.S. finalist at 16 until Pam Shriver, a younger 16 in 1978.

Winning four singles titles (1896, 1901, 1903, 1905), she was in four other finals, and though she was eligible for a fifth in 1906 (as the 1905 champ), she did not choose to play in the challenge round, defaulting the title to Helen Homans, the all-comers victor, 6-4, 6-3, over Maud Barger Wallach. Her U.S. total of eight finals was later surpassed by Molla Mallory's 10 and Helen Wills Moody and Chris Evert's nine. Her longevity spread between the finals of 1892 and 1905 is also a U.S. record.

In 1901, she beat Marion Jones in the all-comers final, 4-6, 1-6, 9-7, 9-7, 6-3 (58 games, the longest of all major women's finals), then ousted defender Myrtle McAteer in the challenge round, 6-4, 3-6, 7-5, 2-6, 6-2, to become the lone woman to play five-set matches on successive days.

The 105 games alarmed the men who ran the USTA. They decreed best-of-three-set finals thereafter. Moore and the other women hadn't complained about five-set matches and she said they felt "dissatisfied" by the decision and patronized by the male establishment. Moore, a right-hander, was born March 5, 1876, in Brooklyn, N.Y., and died Jan. 22, 1959, in Starke, Fla. She was elected to the Hall of Fame in 1971.

MAJOR TITLES (8)-U.S. singles, 1896, 1901, 1903, 1905; US doubles, 1896, 1903; U.S. mixed, 1902, 1904, OTHER U.S. TITLES (3)—Indoor singles, 1907; Indoor doubles, 1908, with Helen Pouch; 1909; with Erna Marcus, SINGLES RECORD IN THE MAJORS—U.S. (25-6).

Angela Mortimer
Great Britain (1932—)
Hall of Fame—1993

Turning a physical impairment to her advantage, Florence Angela Margaret Mortimer Barrett capped an excellent career with a rebounding, unexpected Wimbledon triumph in 1961. She was 29 and partially deaf.

"I could hear the applause of the crowd, but not much else," she recalled. "I think it helped me concentrate, shutting out distractions. When I hear players say they have to hear the ball, I smile. I couldn't."

Much applause stirred Centre Court the afternoon that 5-foot-6 Mortimer, the No. 7 seed, overcame the crowd favorite, 6-foot and No. 6-seeded 20-year-old Christine Truman, 4-6, 6-4, 7-5. It was the first all-English finale in 47 years.

Born April 21, 1932, at Plymouth, Mortimer didn't start playing tennis until she was 15. But her resolve, speed and intelligence combined to produce a strong all-round game, with emphasis on groundstrokes, particularly a battering forehand.

Mortimer lost the Wimbledon final to Althea Gibson in 1958, 8-6, 6-2, and was a quarterfinalist in 1953, 1954, 1956, 1959 and 1960. She won the French in 1955 over Dorothty Head Knode, 2-6, 7-5, 10-8, and Australian in 1958 over Lorraine Coghlan, 6-3, 6-4, plus the Wimbledon doubles in 1955.

She played Wightman Cup six years, helping Britain win, 4-3, in 1960 with a critical victory over Janet Hopps, 6-8, 6-4, 6-1, and captained the team seven years (1964-70), piloting the 1968 victory. She was an inhabitant of the world's Top 10 from 1953-62—Nos. 1, 4 and 4 in 1961, 1955 and 1956, respectively.

Following the 1961 season, in which she was a U.S. semifinalist, losing to compatriot Ann Haydon (Jones), 6-4, 6-2, she underwent a stapedectomy, improving her hearing significantly. But she was never again the player of her Wimbledon glory. Angela was a Wimbledon centurion, playing more than 100 matches, 111: 36-11 singles, 35-18 doubles, 5-6 mixed, overall 76-35.

She married broadcaster/journalist John Edward Barrett, former British Davis Cup player and captain.

MAJOR TITLES (4)-Australian singles, 1958; French singles, 1955; Wimbledon singles, 1961; Wimbledon doubles, 1955. **WIGHTMAN CUP**—1953, 1955, 1956, 1959, 1960, 1961. 3-7 singles, 1-4 doubles. **SINGLES RECORD IN THE MAJORS**—Australian (5-0), French (9-2), Wimbledon (36-11). U.S. (10-5).

Gardnar Mulloy
United States (1913—)
Hall of Fame—1972

An eternal beacon in the game, Gardnar Putnam Mulloy held his first U.S. national ranking in 1936 (No. 11 in men's doubles) and continued to play into his 90s, earning at last report a No. 7 singles rankings in 2005 USTA men's 90s singles. He is a man with a complete game, whose volleys and smashes lit up the left court as he and Bill Talbert became one of the finest teams.

They won the U.S. title four times (1942, 1945, 1946, 1948), and were finalists in 1950 and 1953. Probably the one they remembered best almost got away seven times. That was the overblown 1946 final of 74 games as the tourney returned to Boston's Longwood Cricket Club after a wartime stay at Forest Hills, where Bill and Gar won their first two. In the record fifth set for any major, they just said no to seven match points while beating fellow Americans Don McNeill and Frank Guernsey, 3-6, 6-4, 2-6, 6-3, 20-18. Their six final-round appearances are one short of Fred Alexander and Harold Hackett's U.S. team record. He and Talbert won the clinching point in the 1948 Davis Cup victory over Australia at Forest Hills, beating Billy Sidwell and Colin Long, 8-6, 9-7, 2-6, 7-5. Gar was on the team six other years, helping also to win the Cups of 1946 and 1949, and was a winning player-captain in two zone matches, 1952 and 1953. Playing on the 1957 team at 43, he was the oldest U.S. Cupper.

Settling in the U.S. Top 10 14 times between 1939 and 1954, he was No. 1 in 1952, when he was U.S. finalist at Forest Hills, losing to 24-year-old Frank Sedgman, 6-1, 6-2, 6-3. At 38, Mulloy was the oldest to attain that eminence, five weeks older than 38-year-old Bill Lamed in 1911. He ranked in the world's Top 10 four years: No. 8 in 1946; No. 10 in 1947; No. 9 in 1949; No. 7 in 1952. His most startling triumph may have been the Wimbledon doubles in 1957, at 43, joined with Budge Patty, 33. Unseeded, they became the oldest championship team of the post-World War I era by stunning the top-seeded Aussies Lew Hoad, 22, and Neale Fraser, 23, 8-10, 6-4, 6-4, 6-4.

A right-hander, he was born Nov. 22, 1913, in Washington, D.C., but has been a lifelong Miamian, a graduate of the University of Miami and its law school, organizer-coach-leading player of its first tennis team. His first U.S. Championships were the Father and Son doubles with his dad, Robin Mulloy, in 1939, 1941 and 1942, but they have continued to flow from his rackets unceasingly for more than a half-century. Campaigning among the seniors since, he won USTA senior titles year after year through the turn of the century into his 90s.

Serving in the U.S. Navy in World War II, he commanded a landing craft in North African and European invasions.

Major Titles (5)—Wimbledon doubles, 1957; U.S. doubles, 1942, 1945, 1946, 1948. **OTHER U.S. TITLE** (1)—Clay Court doubles, 1946 with Bill Talbert. **DAVIS CUP**—1946,

1948, 1949, 1950, I952, 1953, 1957, 3-0 singles, 8-3 doubles. **SINGLES RECORD IN THE MAJORS**—Australian (3-1), French (13-4), Wimbledon (31-18), U.S. (51-20).

Lindley Murray
United States (1892–1970)
Hall of Fame—1958

A big-serving 6-foot-2 lefty out of California, Robert Lindley Murray was born Nov. 3, 1892, in San Francisco. He had a brief, bright run in the U.S. Championships, losing in the 1916 semis to Bill Johnston, 6-2, 6-3, 6-1, and taking the title in 1917, over figure skating champion, Nat Niles, 5-7, 8-6, 6-3, 6-3, and 1918 over Big Bill Tilden, 6-3, 6-1, 7-5.

He was ranked No. 1 in the U.S. in 1918, No. 4 in 1916 and 1919. A chemical engineer who graduated from Stanford, he was working on explosives production during World War I and had no intention of entering the 1917 Championships, billed as a "patriotic" tournament to raise money for the Red Cross. His tennis fan employer, Elon Hooker of Hooker Chemical in Buffalo, talked Murray into it and he had an explosive tourney, the only one he played that summer.

"My strong points were a vicious serve, a quick dash to the net and the ability to volley decisively anything that came near me," he said.

His serve was lightning on the boards of the Seventh Regiment Armory in New York as Lindley won the 1916 U.S. Indoor over Alrick Man, 6-2, 6-2, 9-7.

He settled in the Buffalo area and died Jan. 17, 1970, in Lewiston Heights, N.Y.

MAJOR TITLES (2)—U.S. singles, 1917-18; **OTHER U.S. TITLES** (1)—Indoor singles, 1916. **SINGLES RECORD IN THE MAJORS**—U.S. (21-3).

Julian Myrick
United States (1880–1969)
Hall of Fame—1963—Administrator

A New Yorker, though born March 1, 1880, in Murfreesboro, N.C., Julian Southall Myrick was inducted into the Hall of Fame in 1963 on the basis of his administrative ability and contributions to the game in the United States. Known as "Uncle Mike" to friends and associates—he was actually an uncle of 1931 Wimbledon champ Sidney Wood—he was president of the USTA 1920-22, and an active committeeman. He was a leader in enlarging the U.S. Championships, influential in construction of the Forest Hills Stadium, at a cost of $300,000 in 1923, and launching the Wightman Cup competition between U.S. and British women, the first edition of which inaugurated the stadium. He died in New York, Jan. 4, 1969.

Ilie Nastase
Romania (1946—)
Hall of Fame—1991

No player in history has been more gifted or mystifying than the Bucharest Buffoon, Ilie Nastase, noted both for his sor-

cery with the racket and his bizarre, even objectionable behavior. He was an entertainer second to none, amusing spectators with his antics and mimicry, also infuriating them with gaucheries and walkouts.

Despite a fragile nervous system and erratic temperament, Nastase, a slender 6-footer, quick, leggy and athletic, could do everything. When his concentration held together he was an artist creating with great originality and panache. His record in the season-closing Masters was spectacular. He won four times, 1971-72-73, 75, and was finalist to Guillermo Vilas in five sets in 1974 on Melbourne grass.

Born July 19, 1946, in Bucharest, he was the greatest of his country, the first Romanian of international prominence. Largely through his play that small country rose to the Davis Cup final on three occasions, 1969, 71-72, losing each time to the United States. At the end of 1985, after playing Davis Cup since 1966, Nastase ranked second behind Italian Nicola Pietrangeli among the busiest players in Cup history, the only men to have won more than 100 matches. Nastase, 11 wins behind, captured 109: 79-22 in singles, 35-15 in doubles for 52 series.

Romania was favored to lift the Cup from the U.S. in the 1972 finale on the friendly slow clay of Nastase's hometown of Bucharest. However, his nervousness combined with an inspired performance by Stan Smith added up to an 11-9, 6-2, 6-3 victory for the American in the crucial opening singles, and the U.S. kept the Cup, 3-2. Nastase's foremost disappointment occurred three months prior, when Smith narrowly defeated him in the Wimbledon final, 4-6, 6-3, 6-3, 4-6, 7-5, one of the most exciting championship matches on Centre Court. Nastase was in another Wimbledon singles final in 1976, but was beaten easily by Bjorn Borg, 6-4, 6-2, 9-7.

Nastase, a right-hander, first came to attention in 1966 when he and his first mentor, countryman Ion Tiriac, reached the final of the French doubles, losing to Clark Graebner and Dennis Ralston.

Romania was a nowhere nation in Davis Cup until Nastase came along to link with the hulking, Draculan ice hockey luminary, Tiriac. The country had entered sporadically since first joining in 1922, winning only one series before 1959. That year Tiriac, from Count Dracula's Transylvanian neighborhood, spurred a couple of wins. Still, Romania had won but nine prior to the 1969 Ilie-Ion splurge of five victories that carried them to the semis against Britain, a 3-2 victory at Wimbledon. There the irrepressible duo, then unknown, flabbergasted everybody, themselves included—"we can't play on this grass," said Tiriac after beating Mark Cox on opening day. It took a fifth match victory by Nastase over Cox to propel them into the final against the U.S. in Cleveland. Another foreign surface, asphalt, plus Arthur Ashe and Stan Smith ended the unfamiliar joyride, 5-0. But they became very familiar figures, getting to the final in the U.S. again in 1971 and getting closer, 3-2. However, it was Ilie's failure against Smith in the opening match (7-5, 6-3, 6-1) that made the difference.

By 1970, Nastase began to assert himself. He won the Italian singles over French Open champ Jan Kodes, 6-3, 1-6, 6-3, 8-6, and jolted Cliff Richey in the U.S. Indoor final from two sets down. Despite Wimbledon and Davis Cup heartaches of 1972, he had the consolation of having won a biggie that year: the U.S. Open from a seeming losing position opposite Arthur Ashe—down 2-4 in the fourth set, and an early break in the fifth. He got out of it, saddening the New York crowd, 3-6, 6-3, 6-7 (1-5), 6-4, 6-3.

His finest season was 1973, when he was regarded as No. 1 in the world after winning the most one-sided Italian final, 6-1, 6-1, 6-1, over Manolo Orantes, the French over Nikola Pilic, 6-3, 6-3, 6-0, and 13 other titles, plus downing Tom Okker in the Masters final, 6-3, 7-5, 4-6, 6-3. That season, one of the stupendous variety, he won 15 of 31 tourneys on a 118-17 match record, also eight doubles for an overall total of 23, tying Rod Laver's Open era record (17 singles, 6 doubles), broken by John McEnroe's 27 in 1979.

Though he provoked controversy, and his career was marred by fines, disqualifications and suspensions, Nastase was good-natured, likeable and friendly off-court. He had a sense of humor and drama in his on-court shenanigans, but frequently did not know when to stop and lost control of himself. "I am a little crazy," he said, "but I try to be a good boy." His comrade, Tiriac, amicably put it this way: "His brain is like a bird in a cage."

He was an expert at putting the ball just beyond an opponent's reach, and applying discomfiting spin. He lobbed and retrieved splendidly, in his prime possibly the fastest player of all, and he could play either baseline or serve-and-volley. In 1976, he was the first European to exceed $1 million in career prize money, and had a career total of $2,076,761. Nastase played World Team Tennis for Hawaii in 1976 and Los Angeles in 1977-78, leading L.A. to the league title in 1978 as player-coach.

Eight times between 1970 and 1977 he was in the world's Top 10, No. 1 in 1973, the year he won the French and Italian back-to-back, an unusual coupling.

In a career begun in the amateur era and continued in the Open era, he was one of five players to win more than 100 pro titles in singles (57) and doubles (51). He was inducted into the Hall of Fame in 1991. He has been Romanian Davis Cup captain and president of the Romanian Tennis Federation, reaping considerable international attention again by running for mayor of Bucharest in 1996, but he was defeated. "Probably a very good thing for him and Bucharest," chuckled Tiriac.

MAJOR TITLES (7)—French singles, 1973; U.S. singles, 1972; French doubles, 1970; Wimbledon doubles, 1973; U.S. doubles, 1975; Wimbledon mixed, 1970, 1972. **DAVIS CUP**—1966-67-68-69-70-71-72-73-74-75-76-77, 79-80, 82-83-84-85, 74-22 singles, 35-15 doubles. **SINGLES RECORD IN THE MAJORS**—Australian (0-1), French (33-13), Wimbledon (35-15) , US. (29-14).

Martina Navratilova
Czechoslovakia/United States (1956—)
Hall of Fame—2000

As the game's most prolific winner of the Open era—probably ever—Martina Navratilova, the puissant left-hander, continued to add to her record totals, as recently as 2006, getting on with her tennis life… indefinitely? Yet a presence in doubles, she won the Wimbledon mixed in 1995 with Jonathan Stark and, incredibly, buoyantly, in 2003, the Australian and Wimbledon mixed with Leander Paes of India. Enough? Not quite. As

the climax of the 2006 U.S. Open, she hitched onto another star American lefty, Bob Bryan, to win the mixed—her 59th major! They beat a pair from Martina's homeland, the Czech Republic, Kveta Peschke and Martin Damm, who probably looked up to her as children, 6-2, 6-3.

She couldn't scale Aussie Margaret Court's Everestian record of 62 singles, doubles and mixed. But Martina gave it a jolly good try through the 32 years from her initial major, the French mixed of 1974 with Colombian lefty Ivan Molina, 6-3, 6-3, over Mexicans Rosie Reyes Darmon and Marcelo Lara. So the supposedly concluding total (59) amounts to 18 singles, 31 doubles, 10 mixed. Through merely 33 years, those are figures for the majors. Career: 168 singles, 177 doubles, 10 mixed—355 championships.

Marvelous Martina may have "retired" from singles at the 1994 year-end WTA Championships at Madison Square Garden, an opening-round defeat by Gabriela Sabatini, 6-4, 6-2, as thousands cheered and wept, saying goodbye and thanks for the memories. After all, she had done so much in New York, winning that prime championship eight times in singles (five times runner-up), 10 times in doubles, plus four singles and 11 doubles titles across the East River at the U.S. Open. But, as it has turned out, nobody wanted her to leave—least of all herself. By the time her second home, Wimbledon, rolled around in 2003, she would catch up with her old pal Billie Jean King's record with a 20th title at the Big W, the mixed with Indian Leander Paes, over Anastasia Rodionova and Andy Ram. She was 49 years, ten months, nine days when she and Bob Bryan won the U.S. Open, obviously the—shall we say?—most experienced personage to grab a major, somewhat longer in the tooth, but with plenty of bite, than the bygone Melburnian, Norman Brookes. He was 46 years, two months, in winning the 1924 Australian doubles. Well, it's certain she's the most prominent mature champ, but it must be pointed out that another Aussie, Horace Rice, was 52 while winning the Australian mixed with Sylvia Lance in 1923. Probably Martina can accept that, and settle for second place.

Nobody, ever, has such a glittering trove of numbers. As a pro since 1973, she played the most singles tournaments (389) and matches (1,661), and won the most titles (168) with a won-loss mark of 1,442-219. She won more prize money, $21,626,089, than all but Ivan Lendl and Pete Sampras.

Her doubles feats, attesting to a grandeur of completeness, were also sparkling: Second most tournaments (347), most matches played (890), most titles (177) and matches won (747), with a won-lost mark of 747-143. Including mixed doubles (27 tournaments played, 10 titles and a 94-19 W-L record), she holds records for most titles (337) and matches won (2,521, against just 353 losses). Thus, she batted .872 in singles, .890 in doubles, .832 in mixed—.877 for everything. It means she won 48.6 per cent of all the tournaments she entered. Whew!

Arguably the greatest player of all time, Martina was born on Oct. 18, 1956, in Prague, Czechoslovakia, and became a U.S. citizen in 1981, after defecting six years earlier. She was raised by her mother, Jana, and stepfather, Mirek Navratil, whose name she took.

Despite her upbringing on slow clay in the small town of Revnice, outside of Prague, she has always been a tornado-like attacker, a net-rusher. She attracted notice at 16 in Paris, the French Open of 1973, by serving-and-volleying a clay specialist, and former champ, No. 5-seeded Nancy Richey to defeat, reaching the quarters unseeded.

Her lustrous 16-year rivalry with Chris Evert was launched that year in Akron, Ohio, an indoor defeat. "She was overweight, but eager and gifted," Evert remembered. "It was a close match [7-6, 6-3]. Even though I'd never heard of her, and couldn't pronounce or spell her name, I could tell she'd be trouble—especially if she got in shape."

She was trouble, and eventually the 5-foot-7-1/2, 140-pound Navratilova made extreme fitness her trademark in overcoming Evert, who became her good friend. Although Evert led in the rivalry, 21-4, at the high point of her dominance, Navratilova won their last encounter, Chicago, in 1988, 6-2, 6-2, to wind up with a 43-37 edge. Four years later, also in Chicago, Martina eclipsed Evert's seemingly unattainable record of 157 pro singles tournament victories. By beating Czech Jana Novotna from two match points down, 7-6 (7-4), 4-6, 7-5, she nailed victory No. 158, and kept going. She had unknowingly begun to stalk Evert at home with her initial title, Pilsen, in 1973.

Her proudest times were spent in the game's temple, Centre Court, Wimbledon, where she became the all-time singles champ by defeating Zina Garrison in 1990, 6-4, 6-1, her ninth championship. The record of eight had been achieved more than a half-century before when Helen Wills Moody beat Helen Jacobs in 1938.

Navratilova began her run at Moody by beating top-seeded Evert in the 1978 final, 2-6, 6-4, 7-5. She repeated over Evert, but was deterred, momentarily, in the 1980 and 1981 semis by Evert and Hana Mandlikova. Rebounding, she reeled off championships in six successive years, snapping Suzanne Lenglen's mark of five straight (1919—23). Driving to the 1988 final, she had rolled up 47 straight match wins, three short of Moody's Wimbledon record streak. But Martina was stopped by the Grand Slammer of that year, Steffi Graf, 5-7, 6-2, 6-1.

Graf beat her for the title in 1989, too, but, when Graf lost to Garrison in the 1990 semis, Martina triumphed again in her eleventh final. There would be one last Centre Court singles final, the twelfth, in 1994, where she lost to Conchita Martinez. The Big M left some lofty records at the Big W for her 22 years besides the titles: Most consecutive finals (nine), most matches (279), singles wins (119), doubles wins (80), overall wins (243). She was 119-13 in singles, 80-14 in doubles, 44-9 in mixed.

Navratilova also won four U.S., three Australian and two French singles. The Australian: 1981 over Evert, 6-7 (4-7), 6-4, 7-5; 1983 over Kathy Jordan; 6-2, 7-6 (7-5); 1985 over Evert, 6-2, 4-6, 6-2. The French: 1982 over Andrea Jaeger 7-6 (8-6), 6-1; 1984 over Evert, 6-3, 6-1. Winning the U.S. was her most frustrating trial. Not until her eleventh try, in 1983 (having lost the 1981 final in a tiebreaker to Tracy Austin) did Navratilova make it: 6-1, 6-3, over Evert. She duplicated the next year over Evert, in a high quality struggle, 4-6, 6-4, 6-4, adding 1986 over Helena Sukova, 6-3, 6-2, and 1987 over Graf, 7-6 (7-4), 6-1. In 1991, almost 35, she was the tourney's oldest losing finalist since 40-year-old Molla Mallory in 1924, bowing to Monica Seles, 7-6 (7-1), 6-1.

Only one prize, a singles Grand Slam, eluded her—barely in 1983 and 1984. Although 1983 was her most overpowering season (16 victories in 17 tournaments on an 86-1 match record), it was 1984 (13 victories in 15 tourneys on 78-2) when the Slam seemed certain. With three of the titles in her satchel, she reached the semis of the last major that year, the Australian, on a pro record 74-match winning streak. However, Sukova, who had ball-chased for her in Prague years before, intervened, 1-6, 6-3, 7-5, snapping her streak of six consecutive major titles. Mandlikova also snipped her second longest streak, 56, in the 1987 Australian final, 7-5, 7-6 (7-1).

Navratilova did, however, register a doubles Grand Slam with Pam Shriver in 1984. Perhaps the greatest of all teams, Navratilova-Shriver won 20 majors (equaling the record total of Americans Louise Brough and Margaret duPont, 1942-57). The Navratilova-Shriver combine produced 79 tournament victories, including 10 season-climaxing Virginia Slims titles, and a record 109-match winning streak between 1983 and a 1985 loss in the Wimbledon final to Liz Smylie and Kathy Jordan, 5-7, 6-3, 6-4.

From 1985 to 1987, she was in the final of all 11 majors (Australian not held in 1986), winning six, a singular feat until Steffi Graf played in 12 straight between 1987, and 1990, winning 10. In 1987 she made a rare triple at the U.S. Open (singles, doubles, mixed), the third of the Open era.

Phenomenally, for almost two decades, 1975-91, Navratilova was no worse than No. 4 in the WTA rankings, seven times attaining No. 1 (1978-79, 82-83-84-85-86). Returning to the top in 1982, she embarked on a record run of 156 weeks into 1987, until supplanted by Graf, who broke the record with 186 straight weeks.

Martina moved to the United States in 1975 after learning that sports federation authorities in the communist Czechoslovak government reportedly planned to curtail her travel because they disapproved of what was called her increasing "Americanization."

"I knew I had to defect," she said. She announced her intention of becoming a U.S. citizen at the 1975 U.S. Open. For years, she was considered a "non-person," her results never printed or announced in Czechoslovakia.

Returning to her homeland in triumph (and to the government's discomfort) as a U.S. citizen in 1986, she led her adopted country's team to a Federation Cup victory, as she had done for Czechoslovakia 11 years before. Playing for the U.S., she was peerless, unbeaten, winning the decisive singles over Mandlikova, 7-5, 6-1 and helped win two other Federation Cups, 1982 and 1989, as well as one Wightman Cup in 1983.

Navratilova credits one of her coaches, pro basketball luminary Nancy Lieberman, for "turning my career around in 1981. Even though I'd won two Wimbledons, she sternly lectured me that I was wasting my talent, needed to work harder than ever, give tennis total commitment. Thanks to her burning me I did."

Oakland was her last tour stop prior to the Garden in 1994, and Martina's last final on her own. She lost narrowly and gamely to Arantxa Sanchez Vicario, 1-6, 7-6 (7-5), 7-6 (7-3). "It would have been nice to have said goodbye to the tour with a win," she sighed after the two-hour, 23-minute test. As it developed, she didn't say goodbye, only "see-ya in a bit." She dabbled in doubles for three tourneys in 1995, got the Wimbledon mixed title, with

Jonathan Stark, reappeared in 2000, and found out she could keep up with the kids, and then some. With Natalia Zvereva in 2002, she resumed adding to her record, winning Madrid over Sanchez Vicario and Rossana Neffa-de los Rios. For a lark, she entered one more singles tournament, Eastbourne. Astoundingly she beat No. 25 Tatiana Panova, then nearly upset Daniela Hantuchova. "What's that lady doing charging the net?" the kids wondered, thinking they'd seen the ghost of championships past. An intelligent, good humored, often opinionated ghost. In 2004, she made more singles cameos, playing five singles tournaments, including the French and Wimbledon. Both majors were ended by Argentinean teenager Gisela Dulko, 6-1, 6-3 in Paris and 3-6, 6-3, 6-3 at Wimbledon. All was in preparation for her clinching a spot on the 2004 U.S. Olympic team. She was an ancient Olympian in Athens—the oldest competitor ever in the tennis competition at age 48—but fell short of medaling with partner Lisa Raymond, losing in the quarterfinals of doubles.

Another of her coaches, Renee Richards, had it right at the Hall of Fame induction in 2000, calling her "Martina the Magnificent."

MAJOR TITLES (59)—Australian singles, 1981, 1983, 1985; French singles, 1982, 1984; Wimbledon singles, 1978, 1979, 1982, 1983, 1984, 1985, 1986, 1987, 1990; U.S. singles, 1983. 1984, 1986, 1987; Australian doubles, 1980, 1982, 1983, 1984, 1985, 1987, 1988, 1989; Australian mixed, 2003; French doubles, 1975. 1982, 1984, 1985, 1986, 1987, 1988; Wimbledon doubles. 1976, 1979, 1981, 1982, 1983, 1984, 1986; U.S. doubles, 1977, 1978, 1980, 1983, 1984, 1986, 1987, 1989, 1990; French mixed, 1974, 1985; Wimbledon mixed, 1985, 1993. 1995; 2003; U.S mixed, 1985, 1987, 2006. **OTHER U.S. TITLES** (8)—Indoor singles, 1975, 1981, 1984, 1986; Indoor doubles, 1979, with Billie Jean King; 1981, 1984, 1985, with Pam Shriver. **FEDERATION CUP**— 1975, 1982, 1986, 1989, 20-0 singles, 16-0 doubles. **WIGHTMAN CUP**—1983, 2-0 singles, 1-0 doubles. **SINGLES RECORD IN THE MAJORS**—Australian (46-7), French (52-10), Wimbledon (120-14), U.S. (89-17).

John Newcombe
Australia (1944—)
Hall of Fame—1986

When good mates John Newcombe and Tony Roche, a potent Australian pair, won the Wimbledon doubles of 1965, it was the start not only of an extraordinary string of major titles for Newcombe but also for the two of them as a unit.

Two years earlier, Newcombe, at 19, attracted international attention as one of the youngest Aussies ever to play Davis Cup. He was selected for the finale to play singles against the United States. Though beaten by both Dennis Ralston and Chuck McKinley during a 3-2 U.S. victory, Newcombe served notice that he was a player to reckon with when he pushed Wimbledon champion McKinley to four hard sets in the decisive fifth match, 10-12, 6-2, 9-7, 6-2.

Newcombe and the left-handed Roche, one of the great doubles teams in history, won five Wimbledons together (1965, 68-69-70, 74) a modern record until countrymen Mark Woodforde and Todd Woodbridge edged ahead of them with six. (The English Doherty brothers won eight between 1897 and 1905, and the English Renshaw brothers won seven between 1880 and 1889.) Newcombe and Roche also won the U.S. in 1967, the French in

1967, 69, and the Australian in 1965, 67, 71, 76, standing as one of only five teams—all Australians—to win all the Big Four titles during a career and leading all teams with 12 majors.

It was in singles, though, that Newcombe made his name. He and Rod Laver are the only players to win the men's singles at Forest Hills and Wimbledon as amateurs and pros: Newcombe, the last amateur champion at Wimbledon, beat Willy Bungert in 1967, 6-3, 6-1, 6-1, and repeated in 1970 over Ken Rosewall, 5-7, 6-3, 6-2, 3-6, 6-1, and 1971 over Stan Smith, 6-3, 5-7, 2-6, 6-4, 6-4.

In all Newcombe, a 6-foot, 170-pound right-hander, won 25 major titles in singles, doubles, and mixed doubles to stand second behind Roy Emerson (28) in the list of all-time male championships.

John David Newcombe was born May 23, 1944, in Sydney, and was more interested in other sports as a youngster. Not until he was 17 did a career in tennis appeal to him. But he was powerful, athletic and extremely competitive, and Australian Davis Cup Captain Harry Hopman was glad when Newcombe turned his full attention to tennis. Newcombe helped Hopman win four Cups, 1964-67. He then returned to Cup play in 1973 for Captain Neale Fraser when all pros were reinstated, joining perhaps the strongest team ever, alongside Laver, Ken Rosewall and Mal Anderson. In the finale that year, Newcombe and Laver were overpowering. Both beat Stan Smith and Tom Gorman in singles, and teamed in crushing Smith and Erik van Dillen, 6-1, 6-2, 6-4, in the doubles during a 5-0 Australian victory that ended the five-year possession of the Cup by the United States. Newk's leadoff taming of Smith, 6-1, 3-6, 6-3, 3-6, 6-4, set the tone, and he and Laver took it out of reach.

Newcombe also played in the World Cup in 1970, the inaugural of the since disbanded team match between the Aussies and the U.S., and helped win five of those Cups for his country.

Newcombe's serve, forehand and volleying were the backbone of his attacking game, which was at its best on grass. His heavy serve was possibly the best of his era. Grass was the setting for his foremost singles wins, the three Wimbledons plus two U.S. Championships at Forest Hills in 1967 and 1973. "You're only as good as your second serve and first volley," was the motto of this intelligent, fun-loving Aussie, and he lived up to it.

Newcombe regretted missing successive Wimbledons of 1972 and 1973 when he felt he might have added to his string. In 1972, he was a member of the World Championship Tennis pro troupe that was banned because of the quarrels between its leader, Lamar Hunt, and the ITF. In 1973, Newcombe was a member of the players union, the ATP, that unselfishly boycotted Wimbledon in another dispute with the ITF. The following year, he stretched his Wimbledon match win streak to 18 before losing to Rosewall in the quarterfinals. That year, Newcombe won the World Championship Tennis singles over an adolescent Bjorn Borg, 4-6, 6-3, 6-2, 6-3.

Newcombe felt, "I'm at my best in a five-set match, especially if I get behind. My adrenaline starts pumping." This was evident in two of his outstanding triumphs, both over Stan Smith, a strong rival for world supremacy in the early 1970s, in the 1971 Wimbledon final and the 1973 Davis Cup finale, rating the latter as his finest performance. Extremely satisfying was his regaining the Aussie title from Jimmy Connors in 1975, 7-5, 3-6, 6-4, 7-6 (7).

In 1967, he was the No. 1 amateur in the world and, in 1970 and 1971, No. 1 of all. He was one of the first to sign a contract to play World Team Tennis (with Houston) in 1974, his presence helping give the new league credibility, although he played just that one season. His best pro season was 1971, when he won five of 19 singles tourneys on a 53-14 march record.

He totaled 73 pro titles—32 in singles, 41 in doubles and won $1,062,408. Overall, amateur and pro, he won 66 singles titles. Newcombe was named to the Hall of Fame, along with Roche, in 1986. He is married to former German player Angelica Pfannenburg and was appointed Australian Davis Cup captain in 1995, winning the 1999 Cup over France, losing the 2000 final to Spain.

MAJOR TITLES (25)—Australian singles, 1973, 1975; Wimbledon singles, 1967, 1970, 1971; U.S. singles, 1967, 1973; Australian doubles, 1965, 1967, 1971, 1973, 1976; French doubles, 1967, 1969, 1973; Wimbledon doubles, 1965, 1966, 1968, 1969, 1970, 1974; U.S. doubles, 1967, 1971, 1973; U.S. mixed, 1964. **DAVIS CUP**–1963-64-65-66-67, 73, 75-76, 16-7 singles, 9-2 doubles. **SINGLES RECORD IN THE MAJORS**—Australian (45-14), French (17-9), Wimbledon (45-11), U.S. (45-9).

Arthur Nielsen
United States (1897–1980)
Hall of Fame—1971—Patron

Arthur Charles Nielsen's name is synonymous with television—the Nielsen Ratings—but he was long an avid player and a generous patron, contributing much time and money to the construction of tennis courts. One such monument to his memory is the Nielsen Center at his alma mater, the University of Wisconsin, where he was captain of the tennis varsity three years, 1916-18.

He continued playing after graduation, teaming with Arthur Nielsen, Jr., to win the U.S. Father and Son doubles titles of 1946 and 1948, and he was good enough to play singles in the U.S. Championships of 1918. A total Chicagoan, he was born there, Sept. 5, 1897, and died there, June 1, 1980. He entered the Hall of Fame in 1971.

Yannick Noah
France (1960—)
Hall of Fame—2005

The kid looked like a tennis prospect, but he was a long way from anywhere that tennis meant anything. And he didn't have a racket. Just a board that he'd fashioned into the shape of a racket. It was 1971 in Yaounde, Cameroon, West Africa, and a lucky day for 11-year-old Yannick Simone Camille Noah because Arthur Ashe was in town, stopping by on a U.S. State Department good will tour.

So here were two future Hall of Famers, meeting for the first time, at a tennis demonstration, Ashe presiding. Learning that Noah was a French citizen, born May 18, 1960, in Sedan, France, of a French mother and a professional soccer-playing Cameroonian father, Ashe was impressed by the very athletic-looking kid. Arthur gave Yannick a racket, wondering if he would like to get some help with his tennis. Yes. Thus, Ashe contacted his friend (also a future Hall of Famer), Philippe Chatrier, head of the French Tennis

Federation, recommending that Noah get proper coaching. Zip! He was whisked off to Paris, eventually to become the most popular French player since the Four Musketeers (Borotra, Brugnon, Cochet, Lacoste) were winning the Davis Cup, 1927-32.

Growing to 6-foot-4, 190 lbs, Yannick was a menacing foe, a carefree, acrobatic volleyer who sought the net regardless of surface. Could he break the overly long French drought in Paris? Oui! After 37 dry years, going back to Marcel Bernard's 1946 triumph over Jaroslav Drobny, Yannick evicted Mats Wilander from the throne room in 1983, 6-2, 7-5, 7-6 (7-3). He was three parts rolled into a delightful one: French, African, the last to win a major with a wooden racket.

An emotional, inspirational figure, he fired France to two Davis Cup finals: first, 1982, as leading player (winning 6 of 8 singles); second, 1991, as captain, convincing left-handed longshots Guy Forget and infirm Henri Leconte that they could upset the U.S. anchored by Pete Sampras and Andre Agassi.

Although John McEnroe was too much for young Noah & Co. to deal with in 1982, Yannick's strong influence fueled the 3-1 ambush of 1991, busting another drought, 59 years between Cups for France. He captained one more Davis Cup in 1996, France over Sweden, 3-2. Then, transferring his leadership talents to his countrywomen, Yannick guided France's first Federation Cup conquest, a 4-1 defeat of Netherlands in the 1997 final.

He is now a well-known singer, composer entertainer in Europe. His 7-foot son, Joakim Noah, was a basketball All-American for the University of Florida (helping the Gators win the NCAA title in 2006 and 2007) and now a member of the NBA's Chicago Bulls.

With Leconte, Yannick won the French doubles in 1984 over Czechs Pavel Slozil and Tom Smid, 6-4, 2-6, 3-6, 6-3, 6-2. But, with Forget, he lost the French of 1987 to Anders Jarryd and Robert Seguso 6-7, 6-7, 6-3, 6-4, 6-2, and, with Leconte, the U.S. of 1986, to Ken Flach and Seguso, 6-7 (5-7), 7-6 (7-1), 7-6 (8-6), 6-0.

Charging and daring would-be passers on clay, as he had at Roland Garros, he won the 1985 Italian over Miloslav Mecir, 6-3, 3-6, 6-2, 7-6 (7-4), and the 1983 German over Jose Higueras, 3-6, 7-5, 6-2, 6-0. On a hard court in 1982, he won Palm Springs [Calif.] by shutting down No. 1 Ivan Lendl's 44-match winning streak, 6-4, 3-6, 6-2.

Noah crashed the world's Top 10 at No. 9 in 1982, and stayed there for five more years straight in this order: Nos. 5, 10, 7, 4, 8. He turned pro in 1978 and won 23 singles titles, 15 doubles titles and $3,440,660 in prize money

MAJOR TITLES (2)—French singles, 1983; French doubles, 1984. **DAVIS CUP**—11 years, 26-15 singles, 13-7 doubles. **SINGLES RECORD IN THE MAJORS**—Australian (11-6), French (40-12), Wimbledon (6-6), U.S. (28-11)

Jana Novotna
Czech Republic (1968—)
Hall of Fame—2005

Jana Novotna would have gotten along well with David Farragut. "Damn the torpedoes—full speed ahead!" cried the victorious Union Admiral Farragut at the Battle of Mobile Bay in 1864

in the U.S. Civil War. That was Jana's style. Throw caution to the winds. Charge!

Serve-and-volley…chip-and-charge…rush-and-crush…slice-and-dice. Shorten the lives of points that way. Let others toil on the baseline. Jana wanted a quick fix, and knew the tricks to get them, one after another. She may have been the last of her kind. But this outlook made her terrific to watch. All aboard—next stop, the net. It also could lead to some awful losses. Remember her letting Chanda Rubin escape from 0-5, 0-40, and nine match points in the third round at the French in 1995, a 7-6 (10-8), 4-6, 8-6, calamity? She was adventurous, and couldn't resist the call of adventure on a tennis court, or resist jangling nerves at times.

Strange for a gal reared on the sluggish clay of Brno, her birthplace on Oct., 2, 1968, in Czechslovakia, baselining territory. But like Martina Navratilova, raised not too far away in Revnice, Novotna had to do it her own unorthodox way—attacking. They would risk the passing torpedoes to launch more of their own. Jana's father wanted her to be a gymnast, but she was going to be too big, 5-foot-10. Nice reach at the net, though. She turned pro in 1987, and began stacking up titles to become that rare paragon of well-roundedness, a centurion—winner of more than 100 singles and doubles crowns. To be exact, 24 singles and 76 doubles: one beautiful Wimbledonian major in singles, 16 majors in doubles.

Wimbledon was a career-long quest. On the lucky 13th try, mellowed out, she hit the jackpot in 1998. At 29 years, nine months, Jana was the oldest winner of a first major during the Open era that was born the same year as she. There was plenty of "she'll never do it" talk around after her first two title round bids went awry: three-set losses that had seemed under control against Steffi Graf in 1993 and Martina Hingis in 1997.

The loss to Graf was a famous fadeaway, 7-6 (8-6), 1-6, 6-4, after solid wins over Gabriela Sabatini, 6-4, 6-3, and nine-time champ Navratilova, 6-4, 6-4. Playing gloriously, Jana served with a 4-1, 40-30 lead in the third set—double faulted and came apart like a paper doll. Against Hingis, a 2-6, 6-3, 6-3, setback, Jana led 2-0 in the third, but got only one more game.

But there was no faltering the following year. She showed fierce resolve as 1997 ended, lighting up Madison Square Garden in a volleying tour de force to win the WTA Tour Championship, 7-6 (7-4), 6-2, 6-3, over Mary Pierce. Novotna shot through the 1998 Wimbledon draw on the loss of one early set, pouncing on future champ Venus Williams in the quarterfinals, 7-5, 7-6 (7-2), paying back No. 1-seeded Hingis, 6-4, 6-4, and firmly downing Nathalie Tauziat of France, 6-4, 7-6 (7-2). In her 45th major tournament, Jana had one all to herself.

Besides her Wimbledon final rounds, she lost one other major final: the Australian in 1991 to Monica Seles, 5-7, 6-3, 6-1.

She won 16 major doubles titles, covering all four—the Australian 1990 (with Helena Sukova), 1995 (with Arantxa Sanchez Vicario); the French 1990 (with Sukova), 1991 (with Gigi Fernandez), 1998 (with Martina Hingis); 1989 (with Sukova), 1990 (with Sukova), 1995 (with Sanchez Vicario); 1998 (with Hingis); U.S., 1994 (with Sanchez Vicario) 1997 (with Davenport) 1998 (with Hingis). She won mixed titles at the Australian 1988 (with Jim Pugh), 1989 (with Pugh); Wimbledon, 1989 (with Pugh); U.S. 1988 (with Pugh). She was also a runner-up in nine major doubles final.

Jana's brilliance at doubles came to light at the 1988 Olympics where she and Sukova won silver, losing the gold to Americans Garrison and Shriver, 4-6, 6-2, 10-8. Two medals were hers in 1996, a silver in doubles, bronze in singles.

In 1990, Jana and Sukova came down the stretch in pursuit of a Grand Slam, but, in possession of the Australian, French, Wimbledon titles, were stopped in the U.S. final by Gigi Fernandez and Navratilova 6-2, 6-4. However, Jana lent a helping right hand to Hingis in her Grand Slam of 1998, sharing the court for the last three titles.

Between 1991 and 1998, she was in the Top 10 seven times, No. 2 in 1997, No. 3 in 1998, No. 4 in 1994, 96. For her career, she won 24 singles titles (568-223 in singles matches), 76 doubles titles and $11,249,284 in prize money.

MAJOR TITLES (17)—Wimbledon singles, 1998; Australian doubles, 1990, 95; French doubles, 1990-91, 98; Wimbledon doubles, 1989-90, 95, 98; U.S. doubles, 1994, 97-98; Australian mixed, 1988-89; Wimbledon mixed.1989; U.S. mixed, 1988 **FEDERATION CUP**—11 years. 22-7 singles, 11-5 doubles. **SINGLES RECORDS IN THE MAJORS**—Australian (23-9), French (41-14), Wimbledon (53-13), U.S. (39-14).

Hans Nusslein
Germany (1910–1991)
Hall of Fame—2006

Although Hans "Hanne" Nusslein, surely one of Germany's greats, had not intended to be a professional tennis player, he had no choice. By age 15 in 1925, he was so skilled that he was able to give lessons, for a pittance. However, learning that he'd been paid a few German marks for instruction, a tennis official saw to it that he was hit with a lifetime ban from amateur competition. No way to protest.

Such was life strictly monitored in some corners of the game in the pre "Open" years. So the game became his living, as a teacher and a highly-respected tournament player at a time when the pros had limited opportunities to compete for modest prize money, overshadowed by the amateur circuits. Nusslein, translated as "little nut," was, indeed a tough little nut, as he became moderately well known in European and American tournaments.

Born on March 31, 1910 in Nuremburg, Germany, right-handed, 5-foot-6, 176 pounds, he was in demand as a Davis Cup coach, advising Netherlands, U.S., Australian, Indian, Swedish and German teams.

Historian Robert Geist writes, "He possessed classic strokes, equal to Hall of Famers Rene Lacoste, Henri Cochet and Karel Kozeluh, as well as excellent volleys, magnificent drop shots and breath-taking half-volleys. As consistent as Ken Rosewall, he was one of the best players during the 1930s."

Big Bill Tilden was the big name among the pros, and Nusslein kept dogging his sneaker steps, winning a goodly share. In 1932, virtually a season-long head-to-head tour of one-nighters, Tilden beat Nusslein approximately 100 to 50 matches.

In the four tournaments that meant the most—the U.S., French, London, World Pro Championships—Nusslein was a man of glowing achievements.

He won nine prominent titles—the 1935 U.S. Pro defeating Karel Kozeluh 6-4, 6-2, 1-6, 7-5; 1937 London Pro, defeating Tilden 6-4, 3-6, 6-3, 2-6, 6-2; 1938 London Pro, defeating Tilden, 7-5, 3-6, 6-3, 3-6, 6-2; 1937 French Pro, defeating Cochet, 6-2, 8-6, 6-3; 1938 French Pro, defeating Tilden, 6-0, 6-1, 6-2; 1932 World Pro, defeating Bruce Barnes, 4-6, 6-1, 6-2, 6-0; 1933 World Pro (round robin), defeating Barnes, 6-3, 6-3, 6-1 defeating Tilden, 1-6, 6-4, 7-5, 6-3, defeating Kozeluh, 6-0, 6-3, 7-5, defeating Roman Najuch of Germany, 6-1, 6-3, 6-2; 1936 World Pro, defeating Cochet; 1937 World Pro, defeating Tilden, 6-2, 7-5, 6-0.

Nusslein served in the German army during World War II, but, highly regarded, he was the first German sportsman invited to England to play after hostilities. He continued to compete to 1957 at age 47. At 43, he gave 25-year-old Pancho Gonzalez a hard time in a 6-4, 6-4, loss in London. He died June 28, 1991 in Altenkirchen, Germany, and entered the Hall in 2006.

Betty Nuthall
Great Britain (1911–1983)
Hall of Fame—1977

Until Betty Kay Nuthall came along from England, no one in the 20th century had taken the women's championship out of the United States. It was a far less widespread and organized game when Irishwoman Mabel Cahill won at Philadelphia in 1891-92. In 1927, the 16-year-old Nuthall, a prodigy who had won the British Hard Court title in the spring (a quarter-finalist there at 14), was not only threatening a long-lived American monopoly at Forest Hills but a precosity record of Bessie Moore, the 16-year-old finalist to Cahill in 1892.

Still serving underhanded, as she had all her life—a habit she would soon change—Betty might have been the youngest of all U.S. champs. but Helen Wills took care of that in the U.S. final, 6-1, 6-4. Nevertheless, Nuthall, exactly the same age to the day as Moore had been, shared the "youngest finalist" record with her until Pam Shriver, a younger 16, displaced them in 1978.

Three years later, 1930, and still a teenager, Nuthall did get the U.S. title, beating in succession the No. 2 and No. 1 seeds, Midge Morrill and Mrs. Anna McCune Harper, 6-1, 6-4. Defending the title, she reached the 1931 semis, losing to Wightman Cup teammate Eileen Bennett Whitingstall. Nuthall again was a semifinalist in 1933, startling onlookers by pushing the champ, Helen Wills Moody, 2-6, 6-3, 6-2. As the youngest to play for Britain when she joined the team in 1927, she was a Wightman Cupper eight years, beating the redoubtable Helen Jacobs in her debut.

She had a fine French in 1931, beating Jacobs before having to contend with the Germans who would clash for the Wimbledon title weeks later. Betty beat Hilde Krahwinkel in the semis to prevent a preview of Wimbledon's all-German final, but lost the title match to the tiny woman who ruled Paris and London, 5-footer Cilly Aussem, 8-6, 6-1. She did, however, win the doubles with Whitingstall.

The main strength of Betty's game was her forehand. Holding the racket out with extended right arm, she used it as a flail, and hit with great power. Speed was the essence of her game; there was no temporizing. She hit with length and discernment, and was resourceful and wise in tactics.

Born May 23, 1911 in Surbiton, Surrey, she took up the game at seven with her father's guidance. She accomplished little in 1928 after her success the previous year, which included beating reigning U.S. champion Molla Mallory at Wimbledon to gain the quarters. It was not until she was bypassed for the Wightman Cup team in 1930 that she decided to take matters into her own hands and campaign alone. Packing her trunk, and accompanied by her brother, Jimmy (the English junior champ), she sailed for the U.S., and her perseverance, initiative and faith in herself were rewarded. This time serving overhand, she came through, the only Brit to rule Forest Hills until Virginia Wade in 1968. Thus she established herself as one of her country's most distinguished performers, ranking in the world's Top 10 five times between 1927 and 1933.

Selected for the Hall of Fame in 1977, she died on Nov. 8, 1983, in New York, where she had been a resident, as Mrs. Franklin Shoemaker.

MAJOR TITLES (9)—U.S. singles, 1930; French doubles, 1931; U.S. doubles 1930-31, 33; French mixed, 1931-32; U.S. mixed, 1929, 1931. **WIGHTMAN CUP**—1927-28-29, 31, 33-34, 39, 3-5 singles, 3-2 doubles. **SINGLES RECORD IN THE MAJORS**—French (13-5), Wimbledon (27-13), U.S. (24-6).

Alex Olmedo
Peru/United States (1936—)
Hall of Fame—1987

Alejandro Olmedo, called "Chief" at the University of Southern California because of his regal bearing at 6-foot-1 and his Incan features, was an aggressive volleyer who constantly sought the net. He fared best on the quickest terrain: Concrete (U.S. Intercollegiate titles in singles and doubles for USC in 1956 and 1958); boards (U.S. Indoor titlist in 1959 over Dick Savitt, 7-9, 6-3, 6-4, 5-7, 12-10) and grass (Wimbledon and Australian chieftain in 1959). His was a quick but huge splash that covered two years.

Born March 24, 1936, in Arequipa, Peru, he picked up the game in his homeland as an extremely agile athlete. But it was refined when he came to USC where he was thrust into the limelight—and controversy—by one of his patrons, Southern California tennis czar Perry Jones. Jones, the U.S. Davis Cup captain in 1958 and 1959, saw in Olmedo the chance for victory after three lean years. Lobbying successfully for Olmedo's inclusion on the basis that the Peruvian was a U.S. resident whose own country had no team, Jones installed him for the semifinal victory over Italy on grass at Perth. Alex won his debut over Nicola Pietrangeli, 5-7, 10-8, 6-0, 6-1. This launched a storm of press criticism over the U.S. using a non-citizen for the only time. Another hassle developed at the Cup round when the No. 1 American, Ham Richardson, was benched in singles in favor of Olmedo. But Jones' policy worked. Olmedo anchored the 3-2 victory over the Aussies at Brisbane by beating Mal Anderson, 8-6, 2-6, 9-7, 8-6, and U.S. champ Ashley Cooper, 6-3, 4-6, 6-4, 8-6, joining his U.S. championship partner, Richardson, in an epic 82-game doubles win over Anderson and Neale Fraser, 10-12, 3-6, 16-14, 6-3, 7-5, saving two match points.

The Chief stuck around to win the Australian title over Fraser, 6-1, 6-2, 3-6, 6-3. A half-year later, Wimbledon belonged to

Olmedo, 6-4, 3-6, 9-7, 7-5, over Rod Laver. Although he beat Laver again in the Cup round the following month, 9-7, 4-6, 10-8, 12-10, the U.S. lost the Cup to Australia, 3-2, at Forest Hills. Fraser, his left-handed conqueror in that series, 8-6, 6-8, 6-4, 8-6, also beat him for the U.S. title, 6-3, 5-7, 6-2, 6-4. In 1960, Olmedo turned pro and joined the nomads on their odyssey of one-night stands, and, in his rookie year, won the U.S. Pro over Tony Trabert, 7-5, 6-4. His brief mentions in the rankings: U.S. Top 10, No. 1 in 1959; No. 2 in 1958; world's Top 10, No. 2 in 1959. His daughter, Amy Olmedo, won the U.S. Public Parks Championship for 12s in 1975. He entered the Hall of Fame in 1987, and became a U.S. citizen in 1999.

MAJOR TITLES (2)—Wimbledon singles, 1959; Australian singles, 1959. **OTHER U.S. TITLES** (11)—Indoor singles, 1959; Pro singles, 1960; Pro doubles, 1960, with Ashley Cooper; Indoor doubles, 1959, with Barry MacKay; Clay Court doubles, 1956;, with Francisco Contreras (MEX); Hard Court singles, 1956; Hard Court doubles, 1957, with Mike Franks; Intercollegiate singles, 1956, 1958; Intercollegiate doubles, 1956 with Contreras; 1958 with Ed Atkinson. **DAVIS CUP**—1958-59, 5-1 singles, 2-1 doubles. **SINGLES RECORD IN THE MAJORS**—Australian (5-0), French (0-2), Wimbledon (10-3), U.S. (15-9).

Margaret Osborne duPont
United States (1918—)
Hall of Fame—1967

One of the most cerebral players, Margaret Evelyn Osborne duPont was a collector of major championships topped only by Margaret Court (62), Martina Navratilova (59) and Billie Jean King (39). In two decades, duPont accumulated 37 championships in singles, doubles and mixed, although never entering the Australian.

Peerless at doubles, she was the canny 5-foot-5-I/2, 145-pound, right-court player, superbly complementing Louise Brough in the most successful team prior to Navratilova and Pam Shriver. Together they won a record 20 major titles: 12 U.S., five Wimbledon, three French—a mark tied by Navratilova and Shriver in 1989. She won the U.S. doubles first with Sarah Palfrey Fabyan (later Cooke) in 1941, and the next time with Brough in a record streak that ran from 1942 through 1950. Their match win streak of 41 ended in the 1951 final, a 6-2, 7-9, 9-7 defeat by Shirley Fry and Doris Hart. As a team in the U.S. Championships, Brough and duPont won 12 of the 14 times they entered and 58 of 60 matches. Mrs. duPont, a right-hander, was the playmaker, utilizing a devilish forehand chop and a variety of other spins that kept the ball low. She lobbed and volleyed excellently, and set up her volley with an effective serve.

Although 31 of her major titles were doubles and mixed doubles, she was just as tough in singles, winning the U.S. thrice in five visits to the final, while she was one-for-three at Wimbledon and two-for-two at the French. Her rivalry with Brough was as close as their friendship and partnership. They split two of the more spectacular finals at the two top championships. Brough won the 1949 Wimbledon final, 10-8, 1-6, 10-8, and duPont won the 1948 U.S. Championships, ducking a match point, 4-6, 6-4, 15-13—48 games, the longest U.S. female final.

She also won the U.S. title in 1949 over Doris Hart, 6-4, 6-1, and again in 1950 over Hart, 6-3, 6-3. She also won at Wimbledon in 1947 over Hart, 6-2, 6-4 and the French in 1946 over Pauline Betz, 1-6, 8-6, 7-5 (saving two match points) and again in 1949, beating Nelly Adamson Landry of France, 7-5, 6-2. In mixed doubles at the U.S. Championships, she set a record by winning nine times: 1943-46 with Bill Talbert; 1950 with Ken McGregor; 1956 with Ken Rosewall and 1958-60 with Neale Fraser. In the 1948 semifinal, she and Talbert won the longest mixed doubles played until 1991—71 games over Gussy Moran and Bob Falkenburg, 27-25, 5-7, 6-1. Forty-three years later, Netherlanders Brenda Schultz-McCarthy and Michael Schapers exceeded that in a 77-game Wimbledon win over Andrea Temesvari and Tom Nijssen, 6-3, 5-7, 29-27.

Born March 4, 1918, in Joseph, Ore., Margaret grew up in San Francisco. She made her initial appearance in the U.S. Top 10 in 1938 at No. 7 and set a longevity record for U.S. females, ranking No. 5 two decades later at age 40 in 1958. Over the 20 years, she was ranked in the U.S. Top 10 14 times, No. 1 from 1948-50. Between 1946 and 1957, she was in the world's Top 10 nine times, including three years as No. 1 (1947-50).

She married William duPont in 1947 and later interrupted her career to give birth to a son. She was one of six women, to win a major title after childbirth.

Hers was one of the finest Wightman Cup records. In nine years of the British-U.S. series, unbeaten in 10 singles and nine doubles, and did not play on a losing side between 1946 and 1962. She also captained the U.S. team nine times, presiding over eight victories.

MAJOR TITLES (37)—French singles, 1946, 1949; Wimbledon singles, 1947; U.S. singles, 1948, 1949, 1950; French doubles. 1946, 1947, 1949; Wimbledon doubles, 1946, 1948, 1949, 1950, 1954; U.S. doubles, 1941, 1942, 1943, 1944, 1945, 1946, 1947, 1948, 1949, 1950, 1955, 1956, 1957; Wimbledon mixed, 1962; U.S. mixed, 1943, 1944, 1945, 1946, 1950, 1956, 1958, 1959, 1960. **OTHER U.S. TITLES** (2)—Hard Court doubles, 1948, with Louise Brough, Hard Court mixed, 1948 with Tom Brown. **WIGHTMAN CUP**—1946, 1947, 1948, 1949, 1950, 1954, 1955, 1957, 1961, 1962, 10-0 singles, 9-0 doubles. **SINGLES RECORD IN THE MAJORS**—French (14-2), Wimbledon (34-8), US (54-14).

Rafael Osuna
Mexico (1938–1969)
Hall of Fame—1979

Mexico's greatest player, Rafael Herrera Osuna, died tragically in an air crash near Monterrey, Mexico on June 6, 1969, shortly after one of his brightest performances. He had spearheaded Mexico's lone Davis Cup triumph over Australia, 3-2, in Mexico City by winning both his singles (the exciting fifth-match clincher over Bill Bowrey, 6-2, 3-6, 8-6, 6-3) as well as the doubles with Vicente Zarazua over John Alexander and Phil Dent. Ironically, it was not only his last match, but the last appearance in the Australian captain's chair of the man whose side he defeated, the legendary Harry Hopman.

Long the anchor of Mexico's team, the super-quick and clever 5-foot-10 Osuna, was the better known half of an extraordinary combine. He and Antonio Palafox showed what two good

men could do for their country in 1962, taking Mexico past the U.S. for the first time, 3-2; followed by wins over Yugoslavia (4-1), Sweden (3-2) and India (5-0) all the way to the finale at Brisbane, where they lost to Cup-holding Australia, 5-0.

During that campaign en route to Australia, Osuna was 5-1 in singles, and with Palafox, 4-0 in doubles. Twice he came through in emotional and decisive fifth sets of fifth matches, beating Jack Douglas of the United States at the wire, 9-7, 6-3, 6-8, 3-6, 6-1, and Jan-Erik Lundquist of Sweden, likewise, 3-6, 6-4, 6-3, 1-6, 6-3, both at Mexico City.

Twice he won the doubles at Wimbledon, his country's only triumphs there, in 1960 and 1963—the first time, at 21, with his University of Southern California pal and partner, Dennis Ralston, 17. They were unseeded and the second-youngest champs, beating Mike Davies and Bobby Wilson of Great Britain 7-5, 6-3, 10-8. In 1963, he and Palafox beat Pierre Darmon and Jean Claude Barclay of France 4-6, 6-2, 6-2, 6-2. The two of them had a terrific series with Ralston and Chuck McKinley in three straight U.S. finals, 1961-63, the Mexicans winning in 1962, 6-4, 10-12, 1-6, 9-7, 6-3, and holding fifth-set match points in 1963.

Ubiquitous on court, confusing to foes, ever seeking the net, he reached a zenith in singles by winning the U.S. title at Forest Hills in 1963, bewildering huge-serving Frank Froehling III, 7-5, 6-4, 6-2, with lobs, chips, angles, flying volleys and footspeed. Slouching, unimposing until his feet and hands whirred into action, he had a beguiling smile and a court manner that endeared him to galleries. At Southern Cal, where he was an All-American, he won the U.S. Intercollegiate singles in 1962 and was the first player since World War I to take the doubles three times: 1961 and 1962 with Ramsey Earnhart and 1963 with Ralston. Osuna was in the world's Top 10 thrice, 1962-64, No. 1 in 1963. He was born Sept. 15, 1938, in Mexico City and he made it into the Hall of Fame in 1979.

MAJOR TITLES (4)—U.S. singles, 1963; U.S. doubles, 1962; Wimbledon doubles, 1960, 1963. **DAVIS CUP**—1958, 1960, 1961, 1962, 1963, 1964, 1965, 1966, 1967 1968, 1969, 23-13 singles, 14-8 doubles. **SINGLES RECORD IN THE MAJORS**—French (2-2), Wimbledon (17-6), U.S. (34-7).

Mary Outerbridge
United States (1852–1886)
Hall of Fame 1981—Innovator

Celebrated as the American "Mother of Tennis" Mary Ewing Outerbridge was undoubtedly one of the pioneers, but the claims by her adherents that she introduced the game to the U.S. are undocumented. The story is that she, a New Yorker, saw soldiers of the British garrison playing tennis in Bermuda, where she was vacationing in 1874, the year of the game's patenting and early marketing. Intrigued, she is said to have taken a set home where her brother, Emilius Outerbridge and friends set up a court at the Staten Island Cricket and Baseball Club.

Tennis was indeed introduced to the U.S. at several locations in 1874, the first documented instance in Arizona. Outerbridge was born March 9, 1852, in Philadelphia, died May 3, 1886 (five years after the first U.S. Championships), on Staten Island, and entered the Hall of Fame in 1981.

Frank Parker
United States (1916–1997)
Hall of Fame—1966

Frank Andrew Parker, a marvelous groundstroker, particularly on the backhand side, was a paragon of durability, ranking in the U.S. Top 10 for 17 straight years (1933-49), a male record until Jimmy Connors surpassed it in 1988. One of the youngest to rank with the elite, 17 in 1933, he was No. 1 in 1944 and 1945, and the oldest ever to play in the U.S. Championships at age 52 in 1968.

He entered in 1968 for fun, this handsome, gracious man who had teamed with Don Budge and Gene Mako to win the Davis Cup for the U.S. in 1937, saying he wanted to be part of yet another era, the "Open." He lost his first match to eventual champion, Arthur Ashe, 6-3, 6-2, 6-2, thus completing a championship career that began with a third-round defeat by No. 4-seeded George Lott, 6-1, 6-4, 4-6, 6-2, at Forest Hills in 1932. In between, as Sgt. Parker, Frankie won the U.S. title on his thirteenth try in 1944, again in 1945, both while on leave from the U.S. Army Air Force during World War II. Based on Guam in 1945, he was ordered to report to New York, 9,000 miles away, to do his duty by defending his title. He beat civilian Bill Talbert both times, 6-4, 3-6, 6-3, 6-3, and 14-12, 6-1, 6-2. A 6-3, 6-4, 6-8 3-6, 6-1 quarterfinal defeat in 1946 by Tom Brown busted his dream of winning three straight. However, he nearly jolted Jack Kramer by winning the first two sets of their 1947 final, 4-6, 2-6, 6-1, 6-0, 6-3. After the 1949 U.S. Championships, his 19th that ended with a semifinal 3-6, 9-7, 6-3, 6-2 loss to champ Pancho Gonzalez, Frankie turned pro to tour with Kramer, Gonzalez and Pancho Segura.

Grass or clay? Didn't matter to 5-foot-8 1/2, 145-pound Frank, at home anywhere, the third of only four American men able to win on the greensward of Forest Hills and the heavy salmon-toned soil of Roland Garros. He won in France in 1948 and 1949—over Jaroslav Drobny, 6-4, 7-5, 5-7, 8-6, then Budge Patty, 6-3, 1-6, 6-1, 6-4—following Don Budge and Don McNeill, and preceding Tony Trabert. But his sure-fire groundies looked especially good in the U.S. Clay Court championship that he won five times between 1933, at age 17, and 1947. His 24-match streak was ended in the 1949 final by Gonzalez, 6-1, 3-6, 8-6, 6-3. Parker built the streak on titles in 1941 (over Bobby Riggs, 6-3, 7-5, 6-8, 4-6, 6-3), 1946 (over Bill Talbert, 6-4, 6-4, 6-2), and 1947 (over Ted Schroeder, 8-6, 6-2, 6-4). Although he and Gonzalez were known primarily for singles, they played a brief but forceful duet on both sides of the English Channel in 1949, winning the French and Wimbledon doubles titles.

Frank won 12 of 14 Davis Cup matches. In 1948, he won both singles in the successful defense, 5-0, against Australia, leading off, 6-4, 6-4, 6-4, over Billy Sidwell. Coupled with his clinching singles win over Charlie Hare 6-2, 6-4, 6-4 while the U.S. heisted the Cup from Britain in 1937, Parker was the only man to help win the Cup with singles victories at either end of World War II.

He was a poor boy who made good. Youngest of five children of a struggling widow, he was born into an unlikely tennis situation, Jan. 31, 1916, in Milwaukee, growing up there. Christened Franciszek Andrzej Paikowski, as a young kid he earned a pittance to help the family as a ballboy at the Town & Tennis Club. Showing a talent for the game, he was encouraged by members, began winning youth tournaments at 11, and was called the "Boy Wonder of Tennis."

He was mentored by a well-known coach, the club's pro, Mercer Beasley, who felt Frankie could become a champion. His mother allowed Frank to live and travel with the Beasleys as his game progressed. Audrey and Mercer regarded him as their own son, overseeing his development as a nationally-ranked junior. However, in 1937, something of a scandal developed—Audrey, 42, and Frank, 21, falling in love. She divorced Beasley, married Frank, and despite their tabloid notices, it worked. They lived, traveling happily together, until her death in 1971.

He was ranked in the world's Top 10 six times between 1937 and 1949, No. 1 in 1948. He entered the Hall of Fame in 1966, and died July 24, 1997 at San Diego.

MAJOR TITLES (6)—French singles 1948, 1949; U.S singles, 1944, 1945; Wimbledon doubles, 1949; French doubles. 1949. **OTHER U.S. TITLES** (7)—Clay Court singles, 1933, 1939, 1941, 1946, 1947; Clay Court doubles, 1939, with Gene Mako; Indoor doubles, 1937, with Greg Mangin. **DAVIS CUP**—1937, 1939, 1946, 1948, 12-2 singles. **SINGLES RECORD IN THE MAJORS**—French (12-1), Wimbledon (12-3), U.S. (60-18).

Gerald Patterson
Australia (1895–1967)
Hall of Fame—1989

A strapping 6-footer, Gerald Leighton Patterson followed Norman Brookes as Australia's second international tennis star. A heroic Military Cross winner with the Australian army in World War I, he played the game with daring, too, charging the net behind an explosive serve, both flat and twisting. His exemplary smash, stiff volleying and good forehand rewarded him with two Wimbledon championships.

An all-or-nothing outlook never was displayed more glaringly than in his Australian championship victory in 1927. Beating lefty Jack Hawkes, 3-6, 6-4, 3-6, 18-16, 6-3, he blasted 29 aces and 29 doubles faults, saving seven match points. In 1919, Patterson took the Wimbledon title with a 6-3, 7-5, 6-2 win over the holder Brookes, who had to wait five years, through World War I to defend in the challenge round. Patterson lost it to Bill Tilden in 1920, 2-6, 6-3, 6-2, 6-4, but with Tilden failing to defend in 1922, he helped christen the new (present) Wimbledon site by defeating Randolph Lycett easily. It was over so fast (6-3, 6-4, 6-2) that no fat lady had a chance to sing. But the world's most famous singer was in the debuting Centre Court, beaming, if not screaming, for her Gerald. That was Dame Nellie Melba, the great Australian diva, Patterson's aunt and No. 1 fan. Patterson was known as the "Human Catapult" at home for his brutal serve, and there were tales that some of his aces were so forceful they bounded into the grandstand.

He spurred Australasia to lost Davis Cup finales in 1922 and 1924 at Forest Hills. In 1925, he was momentarily ahead of his time, using for a while a steel racket strung with wire. He had two U.S. semis apperances, losing to Tilden in 1922, 4-6, 6-4, 6-3, 6-1, and Bill Johnston in 1924, 6-2, 6-0, 6-0, However in 1919, he and Brookes made the first Aussie dent in the Americans that would become a canyon, winning the U.S. doubles over Vinnie

Richards and Tilden, 8-6, 6-3, 4-6, 4-6, 6-2. Sixteen more Australian teams would grab that prize.

Patterson won five Aussie doubles, three with Hawkes, and made the world's Top 10 six years, No. 1 in 1919, No. 3 in 1922. Born Dec. 17, 1895, in Melbourne, he died there June 13, 1967, and was named to the Hall of Fame in 1989.

MAJOR TITLES (9)—Australian singles, 1927; Wimbledon singles, 1919, 22; Australian doubles,1922, 25-26-27; U.S. doubles, 1919; Wimbledon mixed, 1920. **DAVIS CUP**—1919-20, 22, 24, 25, 28, 12-2 singles. **SINGLES RECORD IN THE MAJORS**—Australian (19-4), French (2-1), Wimbledon (17-2), U.S. (10-3)

Budge Patty
United States (1924—)
Hall of Fame—1977

A rare combination for an American male was "Budge" Patty's French-Wimbledon double of 1950. Only Don Budge in 1938 and Tony Trabert in 1955 achieved such a double among Americans.

John Edward Patty was born February 11, 1924, at Ft. Smith, Ark., and grew up in Los Angeles, the tennis vineyard of his youth. He says a brother gave him the nickname "Budge" because "I was so lazy he said I wouldn't budge." It stuck, but he budged gracefully on a tennis court, and graciously in his bearing otherwise, a trim cosmopolitan fellow of 6-foot-1 who preferred to live in Europe after serving there with the U.S. Army in World War II. His smooth groundstroking game played well on the Continent's clay. He won the Italian in 1954. But he was a sharp volleyer, too, a fine doubles player. Seeded fifth, Patty beat second-seeded Bill Talbert in the quarters and top-seeded Frank Sedgman for his 1950 Wimbledon title, 6-1, 8-10, 6-2, 6-3.

At Paris the same year, he overcame lefty Jaroslav Drobny for the title, 6-1, 6-2, 3-6, 5-7, 7-5. Defending in 1951, he was upset by Ham Richardson in the second round at Wimbledon, and by Lennart Bergelin in the fourth round at Paris. Probably his two most renowned matches, both at Wimbledon, were a singles defeat and a doubles victory. In the third round of 1953, despite six match points, he fell to Drobny at dusk in a 93-game, 4-hour-20-minute classic, 8-6, 16-18, 3-6, 8-6, 12-10, despite holding six match points. Four years later, he, 33, and Gar Mulloy, 43—unseeded—were the oldest team of the post-World War I era to win at the Big W, beating top-seeded Lew Hoad, 22, and Neale Fraser, 23, 8-10, 6-4, 6-4, 6-4.

They reached the title round of the U.S. Championships that year, the oldest finalists there, losing to Fraser and Ashley Cooper. Patty is remembered in Paris for an incredible defeat, a 1958 fourth-rounder in which Robert Hailet revived from 5-0, 40-0 down, Patty serving, in the fifth set, to win 5-7, 7-5, 10-8, 4-6, 7-5, saving four match points. Seldom appearing in the U.S., Patty was a quarterfinalist in the 1951 Championships, losing to Dick Savitt, 6-4 in the fifth, and played Davis Cup briefly, to get his only Top 10 ranking, No. 10. But he was ranked seven times in the World Top 10 between 1947 and 1957, No. 1 in 1950. He entered the Hall of Fame in 1977. Over his 15-year amateur career, Patty won 76 singles titles.

MAJOR TITLES (4)—French singles, 1950; Wimbledon singles, 1950; Wimbledon doubles, 1957; French mixed, 1946. **OTHER U.S. TITLES**: (2) Indoor doubles, 1952, Indoor

mixed, 1952. **DAVIS CUP**—1951; 1-0 in singles, 1-0 in doubles. **SINGLES RECORD IN THE MAJORS**—French (44-14), Wimbledon (44-14), U.S. (16-6).

Theodore Pell
United States (1879-1967)
Hall of Fame—1966

Theodore Roosevelt Pell made his mark inside, winning the U.S. Indoor singles in 1907, 1909 and 1911, and the doubles four times between 1905 and 1912. A right-hander, he had a particularly strong backhand, and was ranked in the U.S. Top 10 five times between 1910 and 1918, No. 5 in 1913 and 1915. Pell, a slender 6-foot New Yorker, did have a good time outdoors in 1915 though, in a run to the U.S. semis at Newport, beating two fellow Hall-of-Famers-to-be in straight sets, Watson Washburn and Beals Wright, on the way. But the "Comet" fell on him Maurice McLoughlin, 6-2, 6-0, 7-5. Born in New York, May 12, 1879, he died August 18, 1967, in Sands Point, N.Y.

U.S. TITLES (7)—Indoor singles, 1907, 1909, 1911; Indoor doubles, 1905; 1909, 1911, 1912. **SINGLES RECORDS IN THE MAJORS**—U.S. (21-13)

Fred Perry
Great Britain (1909–1995)
Hall of Fame—1975

It was the technique of one particular stroke that made Fred Perry into a world champion—and probably the best tennis player Great Britain has ever produced.

The knack of making the stroke baffled the promising Briton for so long that he was on the verge of giving up in despair. He had been advised that to get very far, he would have to learn to take the ball early on his continental forehand, the racket making impact instantly as the ball rose from the court.

For months he could not master the timing. Then suddenly, like riding a bicycle, it came to him and he was on his way—on his way to the net on a running forehand, going forward with the swing of the racket to gain good volleying position if the drive did not win outright. It took him to three Wimbledon Championships, three U.S. titles, an Australian and a French title and a lucrative pro career.

Born May 18, 1909, in Stockport, England, the right-handed Frederick John Perry did not take up tennis until he was 18 years old. But he had good coaching and took to the game quickly, for he had been playing table tennis for years and winning tournaments and international recognition.

Perry developed an undercut backhand that came off with surprising pace. He hit the ball smartly with good length and regularity on the serve, was sharp and sound with his smash, perfect in his footwork and timing, and volleyed with dispatch. None of his strokes was overpowering, but his attack was impetuous and relentless, ever challenging, and he ran like a deer in retrieving.

He was the completely equipped and efficient adversary, jaunty, a bit cocky in his breezy self-assurance, with gallery appeal. He could be sarcastic and some thought him egotistical, but it was a pose and he had an ever-ready grin. He cut a handsome figure with his regular features, raven black hair, and phy-

sique that was perfection for the game. Once he developed the stroke that had eluded him, he was virtually unstoppable.

In 1933, Perry led the British to a 4-1 win over the U.S. in the inter-zone final and to the glorious 3-2 victory over France that brought the Davis Cup back to Britain after a wait of 21 years. As Stade Roland Garros boiled with patriotic fervor, and a seventh straight Cup in the balance for the home side, Fred icily erased a set point in the second to take the last match from rookie Andre Merlin, 4-6, 8-6, 6-2, 7-5. It was the climax of the greatest individual season for a Cup winner: 12-1 in singles, 4-2 in doubles.

Britain retained the Cup through 1936 as Perry won every singles match he played in the four challenge rounds. England had not produced a Wimbledon singles champion for a quarter-century, but Perry took care of that, too. He won three straight Wimbledon finals without loss of a set, defeating defender Jack Crawford in 1934, 6-3, 6-0, 7-5, and Gottfried von Cramm in 1935, 6-2, 6-4, 6-4, and again in 1936, 6-1, 6-1, 6-0.

At Forest Hills in 1933, he was the 6-3, 11-13, 4-6, 6-0, 6-1, stopper as Crawford reached the U.S. final with an unprecedented Grand Slam within reach. The next year, Fred might have had the first Slam himself but for a quarterfinal defeat at the French by Italy's Giorgio de Stefani, 6-2, 1-6, 9-7, 6-2.

Perry, a 6-footer, was also impressive elsewhere, winning the U.S. Championship in 1933, 1934 and 1936 (over Don Budge in 1936, 2-6, 6-2, 8-6, 1-6, 10-8, despite two match points), an assault interrupted only in 1935, when he suffered a painful kidney injury in a fall, and lost in the semifinals to Wilmer Allison. In 1934, he won the Australian Championship defeating Crawford 6-3, 7-5, 6-1, and in 1935, he won the French over von Cramm 6-3, 3-6, 6-1, 6-3. Fred was the first player to take all four majors, finishing with a total of eight major singles tites.

When Perry joined the pro tour, he drew huge crowds to see him play Ellsworth Vines and Tilden. Perry won the U.S. Pro Championship in both 1938, over Bruce Barnes, 6-3, 6-2, 6-4, and 1941 over Dick Skeen, 6-4, 6-8, 6-2, 6-3.

After his playing career, he became associated with the manufacturer of tennis clothing that bore his name, was a tennis correspondent for a London newspaper and took part in radio and television coverage of tennis. He was elected to the Hall of Fame in 1975 and died Feb. 2, 1995, in Melbourne. He ranked in the world's Top 10 from 1931 through 1936, No. 1 the last three years.

MAJOR TITLES (14)—Australian singles, 1934; French singles, 1935; Wimbledon singles. 1934-35-36; U.S. singles, 1933-34, 36; Australian doubles, 1934; French doubles, 1933; French mixed, 1932; Wimbledon mixed 1935-36; U.S. mixed. 1932. **DAVIS CUP**—1931-32-33-34-35-36, 34-4 singles, 11-3 doubles. **SINGLES RECORD IN THE MAJORS**—Australian (7-1), French (22-5), Wimbledon (35-5), U.S. (34-4).

Tom Pettitt
Great Britain (1859–1946)
Hall of Fame—1982—Court Tennis

As a youngster, 17, English-born Tom Pettitt emigrated to Boston. He became a wizard at racket sports, and was immensely popular as teaching professional of court tennis at Boston's Tennis & Racquet Club, and that game as well as lawn tennis at The Casino in Newport, Rhode Island, where he was a familiar walrus-mustachioed figure for 65 years until his death in 1946.

He was one of the very first lawn tennis players and instructors, having learned the game in 1876, shortly after its inception. He stopped teaching in 1929, remaining at the Casino as its supervisor. A nimble 5-foot-9, 176 pounder, he could beat any of the members at either lawn or court tennis in his heyday. An old pal, Jimmy Van Alen, liked to tell about Tom using a taped champagne bottle as a bat and winning friendly lawn tennis games. Tom entered the Hall of Fame in 1982 on the basis of his world championship court tennis prowess.

He won the title in a successful 1885 challenge to George Lambert, 7-sets-to-5, at King Henry VIII's old playpen, Hampton Court Palace, outside of London. In an 1890 defense, he turned back challenger Charles Saunders, 7-sets-to-5, at St. Stephens Green, Ireland, later resigning the title, unbeaten.

In 1889, Pettitt faced George Kerr, the Irish professional champ at lawn tennis, in a four-match series in the U.S., stopping at Springfield, Mass., Boston and Newport. Kerr won three matches, but there wasn't much competitive work then for pros. Pettitt was born Dec. 19, 1859, in Beckenham, England, and died Oct. 17, 1946, in Newport, R.I.

Nicola Pietrangeli
Italy (1933—)
Hall of Fame—1986

Nicola "Nicky" Pietrangeli was Signor Davis Cup. That team competition seemed his private preserve, although he won his only Cup from the sidelines as Italy's non-playing captain in 1976. Before that, as a smooth touch operator, twice winner of the French—1959 over Ian Vermaak of South Africa, 3-6, 6-3, 6-4, 6-1, and 1960 over Luis Ayala of Chile, 3-6, 6-3, 6-4, 3-6, 6-3—he had made his name synonymous with Italy. He did it in Davis Cup by playing (164) and winning (120) matches, more than anyone before or since during a Cup career that reached from 1954 through 1972. In 66 series for his country, he was 78-32 in singles, 42-12 in doubles.

Twice he carried Italy all the way to the Cup challenge round, 1960 and 1961, but on alien grass in Australia, and during the reign of Aussie powerhouses. He and 6-foot-6 accomplice Orlando Sirola were unable to come closer to the Cup than a good look. Still, to get there in 1960, they pulled off one of Italy's greatest victories, 3-2 from 0-2 down, over the U.S. in the semifinal at Perth. Despite their discomfort on grass, Pietrangeli—he had squandered eight match points in losing to Barry MacKay, 8-6, 3-6, 8-10, 8-6, 13-11—and Sirola, perhaps the finest doubles team developed in post-World War II Europe, struck back to beat Chuck McKinley and Butch Buchholz, 3-6, 10-8, 6-4, 13-11—seemingly only to prolong their distress. But Pietrangeli stopped Buchholz, 6-1, 6-2, 6-8, 3-6, 6-4, and Sirola clinched, 9-7, 6-3, 8-6, over MacKay.

Pietrangeli was too much for the U.S. to overcome in the following year's semi at Rome as he beat both Whitney Reed, 2-6, 6-8, 6-4, 6-4, 6-4, and Jack Douglas, 9-7, 6-3, 6-2, and also teamed with Sirola again triumphantly in a 4-1 victory. But in the two finales,

only Pietrangeli's meaningless third-day win over Neale Fraser could be salvaged as Australia won, 5-0 and 4-1, respectively.

Solidly built, possessing exceptional instincts for the game and anticipation, 5-foot-11 Nicky was an all-round performer who moved with grace and purpose. He was in four French finals, losing to Manolo Santana in 1961 and 1964, and four Italian, beating countryman Beppe Merlo, 8-6, 6-2, 6-4, in 1957, and Rod Laver, 6-8, 6-1, 6-1, 6-2, in 1961. His best showing away from compatible clay was a 1960 Wimbledon semifinal, losing to Laver, 4-6, 6-3, 8-10, 6-2, 6-4. His was a career of the amateur era during which he won 53 singles titles and was in the world's Top 10 five times between 1957 and 1964, No. 3 in 1959 and 1960. Retired from the court, he captained Italy to the Cup round twice, defeating Chile in 1976 but losing to Australia in 1977.

A right-hander, born Sept. 11, 1933, in Tunis, he is a bon vivant, ever popular with fans and colleagues. He and Sirola were the biggest winners of Cup doubles teams, 34-8.

MAJOR TITLES (4)—French singles, 1959, 1960; French doubles, 1959; French mixed, 1958. **DAVIS CUP**—1954-55-56-57-58-59-60-61-62-63-64-65-66-67-68-69,71-72, 78-32 singles, 42-12 doubles. **SINGLES RECORD IN THE MAJORS**—Australian (2-1), French (46-12), Wimbledon (29-18), US. (5-3).

Adrian Quist
Australia (1913–1991)
Hall of Fame—1984

Elected to the Hall of Fame in 1984 as the left-court half of the great Australian doubles team—Bromwich and Quist, Adrian Karl Quist also won three major singles: the 1936 Australian (over Jack Crawford, 6-2, 6-3, 4-6, 3-6, 9-7), the 1940 Australian (over Crawford, 6-3, 6-1, 7-2) and the 1948 Australian (over the other half, John Bromwich, 6-4, 3-6, 6-3, 2-6, 6-3.) Quist was the only man to win a major before and after World War II, in which he served in the Australian army.

He was also the only man to win a Wimbledon title before and after, doubles with Jack Crawford in 1935, and with Brom in 1950. It seemed fitting that the two old comrades who wreaked so much damage together should meet in the last Aussie singles final with a pre-war flavor, 1948, before the kids led by Frank Sedgman took over. And that it should go to the wire on a sweltering Melbourne afternoon at Kooyong. Quist scraped and scraped to hold onto serve to 3-3 in the fifth, then won the last three games from Brom.

His 13 Australian titles are high for that tournament, ahead of Crawford and partner Brom's 11, and he holds major doubles records: most titles in one tournament, 10, and most with one partner, eight, alongside Bromwich. They won those eight successively (38 straight match wins), also records, between 1938 and 1950. They gave up the title only after an enthralling struggle, 11-9, 2-6, 6-3, 4-6, 6-3, in the 1951 final against youngsters Frank Sedgman, 23, and Ken McGregor, 22. Bromwich was 33, Quist 38. Quist also won in 1936 and 1937 with Don Turnbull for a personal 10 straight (45 match wins), also records.

He and Brom registered a unique triumph in heisting the Davis Cup from the U.S. in 1939. Losing their singles the first day in Phila-

delphia (Quist to Frank Parker, 6-3, 2-6, 6-3, 1-6, 7-5.) They began the unparalleled comeback by beating Jack Kramer and Joe Hunt in doubles, even though they lost the first set and trailed 1-3 in the third. Hunt led 3-2, 30-15 on serve in the third when the turnabout began, 5-7, 6-2, 7-5, 6-2. Quist, a short (5-foot 6-1/2), bouncy right-hander with an all-court game and telling volleys, then hung on after losing the third and fourth sets to beat Wimbledon champ Bobby Riggs, 6-1, 6-4, 3-6, 3-6, 6-4, even though Riggs saved a match point at 5-2 and reached 4-5. Bromwich beat Frank Parker in a groundstroking duel, 6-0, 6-3, 6-1, to ice it in the fifth match.

Quist and Bromwich won the U.S. doubles, too, in 1939, beating Harry Hopman and Jack Crawford, 8-6, 6-1, 6-4. Well beyond expectations, they took their lone Wimbledon crown together in 1950, beating Billy Sidwell and Geoff Brown, 7-5, 3-6, 6-3, 3-6, 6-2—both intramural affairs. Quisty was within a month of his 37th birthday, Brom 31. Having won the French title with Jack Crawford in 1935, Quist won all four major doubles titles and 17 majors altogether. He first appeared in the world's Top 10 in 1936 at No. 4, No. 6 in 1938 and No. 3 in 1939. He was born Aug. 4, 1913, in Medindia, South Australia, and died Nov. 17, 1991, in Sydney.

MAJOR TITLES (17)-Australian singles, 1936, 1940, 1948; Australian doubles. 1936-37-38-39-40, 46-47-48-49-50; French doubles, 1935; Wimbledon doubles, 1935, 50; U.S. doubles, 1939. **DAVIS CUP**—1933-35-36-37-38-39, 46, 48, 24-10 singles, 19-3 doubles. **SINGLES RECORD IN THE MAJORS**—Australian (42-12), French (8-4), Wimbledon (15-6), U.S. (11-4). **MAJOR TITLES WITH BROMWICH** (10)—Australian doubles, 1938-39-40, 46-47-48-49-50; Wimbledon doubles, 1950; U.S. doubles, 1939. **DAVIS CUP**—1938-39, 46, 9-1 doubles.

Pat Rafter
Australia (1972—)
Hall of Fame—2006

It seemed like old times when Patrick Michael Rafter won the 1997 U.S. Open. Aussies all over New York and the rest of the world were raising their glasses of lager to him, the latest nova of their tennis playing tribe. But it had taken a long, long time to restore those old times, an era when Australians treated the U.S. men's championship as their private preserve.

Frank Sedgman in 1951 had started the pirating of the U.S. title. Between him and John Newcombe in 1973 Aussies had won 15 of 23 U.S. singles titles (Americans had won five).

But then Jimmy Connors, John McEnroe, Pete Sampras and Andre Agassi arrived to cheer up the home side and the Aussies descended into a dry spell that was worse than the lament of one of their troubadors, Slim Dusty, crooning "The Pub With No Beer." Twenty-four years passed before a modest country boy, Pat Rafter, seeded No. 13, brought back good old days by serve-and-volleying his way past left-handed Greg Rusedski of Great Britain, 6-3, 6-2, 4-6, 7-5.

Moreover, Pat returned 12 months later to win again, 6-3, 3-6, 6-2, 6-0, over countryman Mark Philippoussis. No Aussie had won two straight in New York since Neale Fraser, 1959-60. Included in that package was a five-set squirmer over the favorite, four-time champ Pete Sampras in the semis, 6-7 (8-10), 6-4, 2-6, 6-4, 6-3. But after two sets of opening his defense, it appeared that Rafter would set a dreadful record: the only U.S. champ to lose in

the first round the following year. Somehow, though he got away from the clever little Moroccan, No. 44 Hicham Arazi, 4-6, 4-6, 6-3, 6-3, 6-1, and it was pretty much serve-and-volley smooth sailing until the struggle with Sampras.

However, poor Pat, seeded No. 4, would get that abysmal record anyway, losing to No. 26 Cedric Pioline for openers in 1999, 4-6, 4-6, 6-3, 7-5, 1-0, ret. as his troublesome right shoulder gave way, causing him to surrender in the fifth set. If that wasn't bad enough, he lost again in the first round of 2000, ranking No. 20, to No. 114, a man sounding like a wine, Galo Blanco of Spain. Bitter wine of a two-point defeat at a few minutes after midnight, 7-6 (7-3), 2-6, 6-3, 1-6, 7-6 (7-5).

Shoulder problems requiring surgery shortened Pat's career, ending at age 29 in 2001. A right-hander born Dec. 28, 1972, at Mt. Isa, Australia, 6-foot-1, 190 lbs. (Mt. Isa, a Queensland outback mining town, also produced champion golfer Greg Norman.)

Pat is the seventh of Jocelyn and Jim Rafter's nine offspring, a dinkum (good old boy) Aussie, noted for his cheerful, sporting manner, named Australian of the Year, 2002.

A humble man known for a gracious manner on the court, great generosity and a gentlemanly demeanor at all times, Rafter carried the hopes of his tennis-mad land for a decade. Nine times he contested the Australian Open and nine times he came away empty-handed, only once reaching the semifinals, in 2001, not quite able to close down the champ, Andre Agassi, 7-5, 2-6, 6-7 (5-7), 6-2, 6-3, in his last, best effort. He did, however, win the homeland doubles in 1999 with Swede Jonas Bjorkman over Indians Leander Paes and Mahesh Bhupathi 6-3, 4-6, 6-5, 6-7 (10), 6-4.

He also failed to win a Davis Cup for his homeland—but that should be qualified. Renewing the game's greatest rivalry, Aussies ventured to a Yanks' lair, Boston (Longwood Cricket Club, host of the original Davis Cup contest in 1900) for the 1999 quarterfinal. In Hadean July heat, Rafter was magnificently just as hot, knocking off Hall of Famer Jim Courier, 7-6 (7-5), 6-4, 6-4, opening day, then rebounding from being down a fifth-set break in the clincher over inspired Todd Martin, 4-6, 5-7, 6-3, 6-2, 6-4. Without those performances, there would have been no Cup for Australia in 1999, when he was absent, hurt, for the final defeat of France.

What would be the last singles match of his career came during the opening day of the Cup final in Melbourne in 2001, when he defeated Sebastien Grosjean of France, 6-3, 7-6 (8-6), 7-5. He was put in the doubles with Lleyton Hewitt to try to get the Aussies to a 2-1 lead, but the Aussie duo fell to Pioline and Fabrice Santoro 2-6, 6-3 7-6 (5), 6-1. His shoulder had nothing left and he could only watch from the sidelines as France took the decisive singles to make off with the Davis Cup, 3-2. Rafter's career record in Davis Cup play was 21-11 (18-10 singles, 3-1 doubles).

His two dramatic Wimbledon title-bout losses were painful, too, but Pat isn't one to brood. In 2000, it seemed that he had Sampras trapped—up a set, leading 4-1 in the second-set breaker with two serves to come. But, he couldn't hang on, and Pete won his seventh Big W at nightfall, 6-7 (10-12), 7-6 (7-5), 6-4, 6-2.

A year later on "Peasants Monday" (brought about by Sunday rain) tickets were first-come-first-served, snapped up by younger fans, mostly Croats and Aussies, who provided a loud, uproarious (but sporting) atmosphere on Centre for the tense five-set duel of Goran Ivanisevic and Rafter. Who could serve and volley better? Wild card wild man Goran not by much—by a hair on his beard, 6-3, 3-6, 6-3, 2-6, 9-7.

To climb into those two Wimbledon finals, Pat had to outscrap Agassi in both tremendous semifinals: 7-5, 4-6, 7-5, 4-6, 6-3, in 2000, and 2-6, 6-3, 3-6, 6-2, 8-6, in 2001.

As the first Aussie to wear the No. 1 ranking since Newcombe in 1971, Pat had it briefly in 1999 (for only one week!), but his three years in the Top 10 were: No. 4 in 1998; No. 2 in 1999; No. 7 in 2001. Despite his preference for quick courts, he volleyed his way to the Italian Open final in 1999, losing to a clay maven, Guga Kuerten, 6-4, 7-5, 7-6 (8-6). No Aussie had gone so far in Rome since Rod Laver won it in 1971.

In a sport with its share of outrageous egos, Rafter was liked for his charm and respected for his politeness. It was his habit to say, "Sorry, mate," when he had to catch his service toss. He was a dream client for sports marketers and is expected to have a public profile long after the end of his professional career.

His Davis Cup captain, John Newcombe, felt Pat's breakthrough was a Cup match against France's Pioline, early in 1997. Sternly trying to rouse his man who had lost the first two sets, Newk got in his face with, "Patrick, this a war of attrition!"

"What's that?" answered Rafter, who nevertheless rebounded to win, 3-6, 6-7 (5-7), 6-4, 7-5, 6-4, and was on his way toward the Hall, arriving 2006.

He won 11 singles (358-191 matches), 10 doubles (214-110) pro titles and earned $11,127,058 in prize money.

MAJOR TITLES (3)—U.S. singles, 1997-98; Australian doubles, 1999. **DAVIS CUP**—1994-95-96-97-98-99-00-01, 18-10 singles, 3-1 doubles. **SINGLES RECORD IN THE MAJORS**—Australian (15-9), French (12-8), Wimbledon (29-9), U.S. (20-7).

Dennis Ralston
United States (1942—)
Hall of Fame—1987

Robert Dennis Ralston was one of those rare men who was a Davis Cup winner both as player and captain. He was considered a stormy figure early in his career although his actions seem tame in comparison with numerous who came after, and he made a name as an outstanding educator and influence while varsity tennis coach at Southern Methodist University.

It was as a doubles player, in the right court alongside Chuck McKinley, that he made his strongest showing. They won the U.S. title thrice (1961, 1963, 1964) and were in the final in 1962. The gem of those victories was 1963 against the sprightly Mexicans, Rafe Osuna and Tonio Palafox, Chuck and Denny slipping out of two match points, 9-7, 4-6, 5-7, 6-3, 11-9.

Wimbledon and the tennis public first heard from him in 1960. As a 17-year-old, joined with his University of Southern California teammate, 21-year-old Rafe Osuna, he took the doubles prize. Unseeded, they were the second-youngest unit to win at the Big W, 7-5, 6-3, 10-8, over Brits Mike Davies and Bobby Wilson, and Ralston was the youngest doubles champ. He suffered many frustrations as a Davis Cup player, but it all came together for him

and McKinley as they pried the peerless punchbowl away from Australia, 3-2, at Adelaide in 1963.

During an arduous Cup campaign, he won six of seven singles and all five doubles, four with McKinley. He led off in a difficult win over rookie John Newcombe, firming up when all seemed lost, 6-4, 6-1, 3-6, 4-6, 7-5, and teamed with McKinley for the go-ahead doubles point, 6-3, 4-6, 11-9, 11-9, over Neale Fraser and Emerson. After Denny lost to Roy Emerson, McKinley clinched against Newcombe, 10-12, 6-2, 9-7, 6-2. They lost the Cup to the Aussies the following year, 3-2, though winning the doubles over Emerson and Fred Stolle. He and McKinley were 8-2 in Cup doubles.

Between 1968 and 1971, he served as coach of winning U.S. teams, and in 1972, became captain for a four-year term. His coolness and calming manner in the face of an uproarious crowd and patriotic local line judges in Bucharest was a highlight of the 1972 Cup victory over Romania.

A slim 6-footer, Ralston was a stylish stroker with a piercing backhand, a fine server and excellent volleyer who was in the U.S. Top 10 for seven straight years from 1960. He was the first to be No. 1 three straight years (1963-65) since Don Budge (1936-38). His career spanned the amateur and Open eras and he also made the world's Top 10: No. 7 in 1963; No. 9 in 1964-65; No. 5 in 1966; No. 8 in 1968. He lost the 1966 Wimbledon final to Manolo Santana, 6-4, 11-9, 6-4.

He had one pro singles title, five in doubles. Denny was an unseeded U.S. semifinalist in 1960, losing to the champ, Neale Fraser, 11-9, 6-3, 6-2. But his best Forest Hills moment was a 7-6 (5-3), 7-5, 5-7, 4-6, 6-3 triumph in 1970 over No. 1 Rod Laver, the defender, to reach the quarters, where he lost to Cliff Richey. He and his dad, Bob Ralston, won the U.S. Father and Son title in 1964.

He was born July 27, 1942, in Bakersfield, Calif., entered the Hall of Fame in 1987. Denny was the first of three men to have won U.S. doubles titles on the four surfaces (grass, clay, indoor, hard), followed by Stan Smith and Bob Lutz. In 1970, Denny won the longest singles match (in games, 93) of the Australian, defeating John Newcombe in the quarterfinals, 19-17, 20-18, 4-6, 6-3, but then lost to champion Arthur Ashe, 6-3, 8-10, 6-3, 2-1 retired.

MAJOR TITLES (5)—French doubles, 1966; U.S. doubles, 1961, 1963, 1964; Wimbledon doubles, 1960. **OTHER U.S. TITLES** (13)—Indoor singles, 1963; Clay Court singles, 1964, 1965; Hard Court singles, 1964, 1965: Indoor doubles, 1963,1965, with Chuck McKinley; Clay Court doubles, 1961, 1964, with McKinley; 1966, with Clark Graebner; Hard Court doubles, 1964, with Bill Bond; 1965, with Tom Edlefsen; Pro doubles, 1967, with Ken Rosewall. **DAVIS CUP**—(As player), 1960-61-62-63-64-65-66, 14-5 singles, 11-4 doubles. **SINGLES RECORD IN THE MAJORS**—Australian, (4-2), French (5-2), Wimbledon (29-13), U.S. (31-13).

Ernest Renshaw
Great Britain (1861–1899)
Hall of Fame—1983

James Ernest Renshaw was the older of the fabled English Renshaw twins by 15 minutes, and he was a half-inch taller at 5-foot-10-1/2. He wasn't, however, as successful in amassing singles titles as brother Willie. The two of them ushered in an attack-

ing era and together were an awesome pair at doubles, winning Wimbledon seven times between 1880 and 1889, a record surpassed by one by the Doherty brothers, Laurie and Reggie.

Ernest, who made the singles title round five times, won in 1888, over Herbert Lawford, 6-3, 7-5, 6-0, and might have done better if his brother hadn't been in the way, losing the prize to Willie three times, 1882, 1883 and 1889, and to Lawford in 1887. Like the Dohertys, the Renshaws were miserable playing against one another. A right-hander, Ernest was born Jan. 3, 1861, in Leamington, England, and died Sept. 2, 1899, in Twyford, England. He entered the Hall of Farne in 1983.

MAJOR TITLES (6)—Wimbledon singles, 1888: Wimbledon doubles, 1884-85-86, 88-89. **SINGLES RECORD IN THE MAJORS**—Wimbledon (32-11)

Willie Renshaw
Great Britain (1861–1904)
Hall of Fame—1983

Bjorn Borg said in 1981, "Yes, I know who Mr. Willie Renshaw was." Few others did. Borg, who had won five straight Wimbledons, was trying to overtake that bygone luminary, but couldn't make it. Not only did William Charles Renshaw, a forceful right-handed aggressor, win an unequaled six straight Wimbledons from 1881, wresting the title from John Hartley, 6-0, 6-2, 6-1, but he added a record seventh title in 1889, defeating older brother (by 15 minutes) Ernest Renshaw, in the title round, 6-4, 6-1, 3-6, 6-0.

In the all-comers final against Harry Barlow, Willie made an all-time recovery. He ducked six match points in the fourth set, trailing 5-2, and came back from 0-5 in the fifth to win, 3-6, 5-7, 8-6, 10-8, 8-6—Willie's longest, toughest match. At match point, 6-7, 30-40 in the fourth Willie was a goner—he had dropped his racket. Staring at an open court and possibly the championship, Barlow, instead of putting the ball away, gave it a soft gallant tap, allowing Willie to recover, eventually saving the day to go after Ernest and the championship. You won't see a Barlow blow today.

England's Renshaw twins (Ernest was also right-handed) were rivals and accomplices. Willie stopped Ernest for the Wimbledon title on three occasions, but five times between 1884 and 1889 they combined for the doubles championship, a record later topped by the Doherty brothers, Laurie and Reggie. The offense-minded Renshaws played doubles as never before, rushing the net and volleying more frequently and effectively than their predecessors, helped by the lowering of the net to its present three feet in 1882.

Willie, noted particularly for his serve and overhead smash, was a third-round loser to D. E. Woodhouse in his Wimbledon debut in 1880. He lost only twice after that, to nemesis Willoby Hamilton in the 1888 quarters, and again in the 1890 challenge round, 6-8, 6-2, 3-6, 6-1, 6-1.

He won 22 of 25 Wimbledon matches in singles, and had a 14-match streak from 1881 to the 1888 defeat by Hamilton, having declined to defend in 1887 because of an elbow injury. That mark wasn't broken until after the challenge round system was abandoned and Fred Perry recorded a 15th straight match win in the first round of his 1936 title.

The Renshaws seemed to be the first to take the game really seriously, playing a full English summer schedule, and then competing on the Riviera during the winter, building a court at Cannes in 1880. Willie was born Jan. 3, 1861, in Leamington, England, and died Aug. 12, 1904, in Swanage, England.

MAJOR TITLES (12)—Wimbledon singles, 1881, 1882, 1883, 1884, 1885, 1886, 1889; Wimbledon doubles, 1884, 1885, 1886, 1888,1889. **SINGLES RECORD IN THE MAJORS**—Wimbledon (22-3).

Vinnie Richards
United States (1903–1959)
Hall of Fame—1959

Vincent Richards was the boy wonder of his day, and hasn't lost that luster: the youngest male to win any of the major championships. A volleying master all his life, he was 15 when Big Bill Tilden, on the verge of greatness, selected the kid as partner in the U.S. doubles championships of 1918 at the Longwood Cricket Club in Boston. They marched through the field, and Vinnie must have felt as though he were in the geriatric ward.

He and Tilden, 25, beat a couple of 38-year-old ex-champs, Fred Alexander and Beals Wright, for the title, 6-3, 6-4, 3-6, 2-6, 6-2. They won twice more in 1921 and 1922, beating Davis Cup teammates Dick Williams and Watson Washburn, 13-11, 12-10, 6-1, then the Australian Davis Cup pair, Gerald Patterson and Pat O'Hara Wood, 4-6, 6-1, 6-3, 6-4. Fittingly, the last national title Richards and Tilden won was a valedictory together, the U.S. Pro doubles 27 years after, in 1945, over Welby Van Horn and Dick Skeen, 7-5, 6-4.

Richards was a pro pioneer, signing on with promoter C.C. Pyle as leading man of the original professional touring troupe in 1926. Of his mates barnstorming across North America during the winter of 1926-27, the star attraction was Suzanne Lenglen. Also along were Paul Feret of France, and fellow Americans Mary K. Browne, Howard Kinsey and Harvey Snodgrass.

It was tough to break into the Davis Cup lineup in singles with Bill Johnston and Tilden around. But Vinnie got his chance in 1924, and beat both Patterson, 6-3, 7-5, 6-4, and O'Hara Wood, 6-3, 6-2, 6-4, during the 5-0 victory over Australia. That year, he won two Olympic golds: beating Henri Cochet, 6-4, 6-4, 5-7, 4-6, 6-2 in singles and uniting in doubles with Frank Hunter to stop Cochet and Jacques Brugnon, 4-6, 6-2, 6-3, 2-6, 6-3. Also a silver in mixed with Marion Zinderstein Jessup in the mixed played at the time. He was on four Cup-winning teams, losing only a doubles with Tilden in 1922. In 1918, Richards was also the youngest ever to play or win a match in the U.S. singles, and he steadily advanced toward the top, a 19-year-old semifinalist in 1922, losing to Johnston, 8-6, 6-2, 6-1. He was back in the semis in 1924, losing to the champ, Tilden, 4-6, 6-2, 8-6, 4-6, 6-4, repeating the result the next year, falling to Big Bill, 6-8, 6-4, 6-4, 6-1. In 1926, he was generally acknowledged as the best American, losing to Jean Borotra in the semis, 3-6, 6-4, 4-6, 8-6, 6-2, while Tilden lost in the quarters to Cochet.

Many felt that 5-foot-10 Richards, who had refined his game well beyond his teen-age volleying skills, deserved the No. 1 U.S. ranking. Instead, because he turned pro, the USTA unfairly

awarded him no ranking for that year when he was No. 6 in the world rankings. He had been in the U.S. and world Top 10 five straight years from 1921, No. 2 in both in 1924.

Once the initial Pyle tour was disbanded, he was active in trying to find other opportunities for the fledgling professionals, no longer welcome at the traditional events. Vinnie, who championed the pros during those difficult years, even after his playing days were over, helped organize the first U.S. Pro Championships in New York in 1927, an event that continued as the longest-running pro tournament through 1999. The purse was $2,000. Richards beat Howard Kinsey, 11-9, 6-4, 6-3, for that title and a first prize of $1,000, and was its singles victor three more times, 1928, 30, 33. He and Kinsey had been the first foreigners to win a French championship, the 1926 doubles over Cochet and Brugnon, 6-4, 6-1, 4-6, 6-4.

Born March 20, 1903, in Yonkers, N.Y., and raised there, he died Sept. 28, 1959, in New York, shortly after entering the Hall of Fame.

MAJOR TITLES (9)—French doubles, 1926; Wimbledon doubles, 1924; U.S. doubles, 1918, 1921, 1922, 1925, 1926; U.S mixed, 1919, 1924. **OTHER U.S TITLES** (20)—Indoor singles, 1919, 1923, 1924; Indoor doubles, 1919, 1920, with Bill Tilden; 1921, with Howard Voshell; 1923, 1924, with Frank Hunter; Clay Court doubles, 1920, with Roland Roberts; Pro singles, 1927, 1928, 1930, 1933; Pro doubles, 1929, with Karel Kozeluh; 1930, 1934, with Howard Kinsey; 1933, with Charles Wood; 1937, with George Lott; 1938, with Fred Perry; 1945, with Bill Tilden. **DAVIS CUP**—1922, 1924, 1925, 1926,. 2-0, singles, 2-1 doubles. **SINGLES RECORD IN THE MAJORS**—French (4-1), Wimbledon (8-3), U.S. (26-9)

Nancy Richey
United States (1942—)
Hall of Fame—2003

To cash in or not to cash in? That was the $1,000 question for Texan Nancy Richey at the French Open in 1968, the first of the majors at which prize money was offered. It was an uncertain time for players, a new beginning for tennis. Nancy, a right-hander, decided to retain her amateur standing (momentarily), and became the only amateur woman to win a major open championship. First prize of $1,000 thus went to Ann Haydon Jones whom Richey beat in the final, 5-7, 6-4, 6-1.

She and Billie Jean King were such close rivals that they were ranked co-No. 1 in the U.S. in 1965. When King bade farewell to amateurism, it was Richey who shoved her out the door painfully, in one of the incredible reversals, 4-6, 7-5, 6-0. The setting was a semifinal of the Madison Square Garden International, the introduction of tennis into the new building. Holding match point at 5-1 in the second, B.J. seemingly had it won with an overhead smash. But Nancy ran deep to field it, raising another lob that her foe bungled. Suddenly it was a new match—Nancy rolled for 12 straight games, 39 of the last 51 points!

Richey won that title over Judy Tegart, 7-5, 7-5, and 68 other singles prizes (25 as a pro), a woman whose illustrious career of 18 years spanned both eras. Her first major in singles was the Australian, 1967, over Lesley Turner, 6-1, 6-4, after a semis defeat of Kerry Melville, 6-4, 6-1.

In 1966, she lost three major finals: Australian to Margaret Smith Court in a walk-over (knee injury in the semis); French to Jones, 6-3, 6-1; U.S. to Maria Bueno, 6-3, 6-1. She also lost the 1969 U.S. final to Court, 6-2, 6-2, the last of her five major title bouts.

Preferring the baseline, she was a flat-stroking blaster with one-handed backhand. No one hit the ball harder in the days of the wooden racket. But she volleyed very well, too, winning four majors in doubles: U.S., 1965, with Bueno; Australian, 1966, with Carole Caldwell Graebner; Wimbledon, 1966, with Bueno; U.S., 1966, with Bueno.

At the U.S. Clay Court Championships, she set a female record, winning six straight titles, 1963-68, covering a 33 match streak. She also won the U.S. Indoor in 1965 and the U.S. Hard Court in 1961.

Slight at 5-6, 130 lbs, she was whippy, finely coordinated, helping win eight Wightman Cups for the U.S., 1962-1970 (9-7 in singles, 4-1 in doubles). In the 1969 Fed Cup final in Athens, a 2-1 U.S. victory over Australia, she beat Melville, 6-4, 6-3, and joined with Peaches Bartkowicz for the decisive 6-4, 6-4 win over Margaret Smith Court and Tegart.

She is the older half (by four years) of the blazing-shotmaking Richeys, the game's most extraordinary sister-brother combo—Nancy Ann and George Clifford, Jr.—schooled in hometown San Angelo, Texas, by teaching pro father, George Richey. She was born Aug. 23, 1942, at San Angelo, (Cliff was born Dec. 31, 1946 at San Angelo) See They Also Served. Both were No. 1 in the U.S. and also placed in the world's Top 10, Nancy eight consecutive years: No. 9 -1963; No. 6—1964; No. 8—1965; No. 5—1966; No. 4—1967, 69-70; No. 3—1968. Nancy was the No. 1 American, 1964-65, 68-69, and in the U.S. Top 10 on 10 other occasions between 1962 and 1976. She played as Mrs. Kenneth Gunter, 1970—75, and entered the Hall in 2003.

MAJOR TITLES (6)—Australian singles, 1967; French singles, 1968; Australian doubles, 1966; Wimbledon doubles, 1966; U.S. doubles, 1965-66. **SINGLES RECORD IN THE MAJORS**—Australian (9-1), French (31-8), Wimbledon (36-11), U.S. (51-18).

Bobby Riggs
United States (1918–1995)
Hall of Fame—1967

Though he had little of the power of Don Budge and Jack Kramer, and though his physique was hardly comparable to that of these six-footers, right-hander Bobby Riggs was one of the smartest, most calculating and resourceful court strategists tennis has seen, particularly in his defensive circumventions. He had a temperament that was unruffled in all circumstances and he hung in the fight without showing a trace of discouragement other than a slight shake of the head. He won the championship at Wimbledon, and twice the U.S. Championships at Forest Hills.

Budge, with his vast power, usually had to work his hardest to turn back the little Californian, whose forte was subduing the fury of the big hitters. Riggs had both the brains and the shots to quell the cannonaders, particularly the drop shot from both forehand and backhand, and a lob matched by few in the way he masked it and his control of its length. Most often Budge required four sets, if not five, to win when they were amateurs.

When they met as pros, Riggs won his full share.

Born Feb. 25, 1918, in Los Angeles, Robert Larimore Riggs first began to make tennis progress at the age of 12, when Dr. Esther Bartosh saw him hitting balls and took over his instruction. In 1934, at 16, he beat Frank Shields, a finalist at Wimbledon and Forest Hills. Two years later, Riggs was ranked No. 4 in the U.S., and he was second to Budge in 1937 and 1938.

Riggs had his best record—the best in the world—in 1939, racking up a triple at Wimbledon the only time he played there, adding the U.S., over Welby Van Horn, 6-4, 6-2, 6-4, while winning nine of 13 tournaments and 54-5 in matches. He said he "scraped up every dime I could find" to bet on himself with a London bookmaker to win the three Wimbledon titles, and came off with $108,000: beating Elwood Cooke, 2-6, 8-6, 3-6, 6-3, 6-2; sharing the doubles with Cooke over Brits Charlie Hare and Frank Wilde, 6-3, 3-6, 6-3, 9-7; and the mixed with Alice Marble over Nina Brown and Wilde, 9-7, 6-1. "I got a little worried about my money when Cooke took me into the fifth set," Bobby said.

After yielding his U.S. title to Don McNeill in the 1940 final, 4-6, 6-8, 6-3, 6-3, 7-5, Bobby regained it in 1941, beating Frank Kovacs, a spectacular shotmaker, 5-7, 6-1, 6-3, 6-3. His career as an amateur soon ended. Riggs was in demand on the pro circuit.

In 1942, he competed in the U.S. Pro Championships and lost the final to all-conquering Budge, 6-2, 6-2, 6-2. But the next time they met, after World War II, in 1946, and this time Riggs beat Budge to take the U.S. Pro at Forest Hills, 6-3, 6-1, 6-1. They went on tour and Riggs won 24 matches to 22. Again in 1947, they met in the final of the U.S. Pro Championships and Riggs won in five long sets, 3-6, 6-3, 10-8, 4-6, 6-3. Late in the year, U.S. champ Jack Kramer made his pro debut at Madison Square Garden in New York and Riggs beat him before a crowd of 15,114 who had plowed through 25 inches of snow in a blizzard. However, Kramer won the tour, 69-20.

After losing to Kramer in the final of the U.S. Pro at Forest Hills and regaining the title in 1949 against Budge, Riggs began to taper off as a player and tried his hand as a promoter when Gussy Moran and Pauline Betz made their debuts as pros in 1950. Years later, in 1973, after fading into virtual obscurity as a senior player who would make a bet on the drop of a hat, Riggs was back, taking on first No. 1 Margaret Smith Court and then No. 2 Billie Jean King in mixed singles matches that gave tennis much publicity. He defeated Court on May 13, 1973 in Ramona, Calif., 6-2, 6-1– it was to became known as "The Mother's Day Massacre." The match was set up to promote a California housing development.

But in what followed on September 20, the high-hyped "Battle of the Sexes," Billie Jean, volleying to the rescue of the young women's pro circuit, made him look like Humpty Dumpty, 6-4, 6-3, 6-3, before a record tennis crowd of 30,472, at Houston's Astrodome. Few things ever fazed Riggs, though, or made him unhappy, and he had a merry time. "When I was the best player in the world, cleaning up at Wimbledon, not many people paid attention," he grinned, "but now, as an old man everybody knows me." And nothing ever made him forget his good manners and sportsmanship of the years when he was playing serious tennis.

He made the world's Top 10 in 1937, 1938 and 1939, No. 1 the last year, and the U.S. Top 10, 1936 through 1941, and was named to the Hall of Fame in 1967. Bobby died Oct. 25, 1995 in Leucadia, Calif., pleased to become a friend of adversary Billie Jean's and knowing they'd advanced their game.

MAJOR TITLES (6)—Wimbledon singles, 1939; U.S. singles, 1939, 1941; Wimbledon doubles, 1939; Wimbledon mixed, 1939; U.S. mixed 1940. **OTHER U.S. TITLES** (12)—Indoor singles, 1940; Clay Court singles, 1936, 1937, 1938; Indoor doubles, 1940, with Elwood Cooke; Clay Court doubles, 1936, with Wayne Sabin; Indoor mixed, 1940, with Pauline Betz; Pro singles, 1946, 1947, 1949; Pro doubles,1942, 1947, with Don Budge. **DAVIS CUP**—1938, 1939, 2-2 singles. **SINGLES RECORD IN THE MAJORS**—French (5-1), Wimbledon (7-1) U.S. (27-4).

Tony Roche
Australia (1945—)
Hall of Fame—1986

With most of a glorious career behind him, it was extremely satisfying for the rugged, self-effacing Anthony Dalton Roche to make his biggest hit for Australia at 31 as a Davis Cup retread in 1977. In 1965 and 1967, alongside John Newcombe, he'd won the Cup-clinching doubles, both years against Spain, over Jose Arilla and Manolo Santana, 6-3, 4-6, 7-5, 6-2; and over Santana and Manolo Orantes, 6-4, 6-4, 6-4. Ten years later, he was recalled for singles duty against Cup-holding Italy before his friends and neighbors in Sydney, and came through. In a stunning opening-day victory, he turned back Adriano Panatta (6-3, 6-4, 6-4), who had led Italy to the 1976 Cup. That set the tone for a 3-1 Australian victory.

His yoking with Newcombe (Roche in the left court) was one of the all-time teams. They won Wimbledon five times (1965, 1968, 1969, 1970, 1974), the best showing of any 20th century male pair until fellow Aussies Mark Woodforde and Todd Woodbridge won a sixth in 1997. Roche, with his wicked left-handed serve and magnificent volleying, took 13 major doubes, 12 with Newcombe, setting a team record.

But Tony, broad-shouldered and barrel-chested, had the groundstrokes to succeed on clay, winning the difficult "Continental Double" in 1966, the Italian and French singles, respectively over home boy Nicola Pietrangeli, 11-9, 6-1, 6-3, and Istvan Gulyas of Hungary, 6-1, 6-4, 7-5. Paradoxically, he lost three major finals on his best surface, grass, and to older countrymen whom he'd idolized: Wimbledon in 1968 to Rod Laver, 6-3, 6-4, 6-2, and the U.S. Open in 1969 to Laver, 7-9, 6-1, 6-2, 6-2; the U.S. Open in 1970, to Ken Rosewall, 2-6, 6-4, 7-6 (5-2), 6-3.

Shoulder and elbow trouble curtailed a career that spanned the amateur and Open eras, but he was in the world's Top 10 in both, six straight years from 1965: No. 7 in 1965; No. 4 in 1966, 68; No. 5 in 1967; No. 2 in 1969; No. 3 in 1970. Tony won 12 pro titles in singles, 27 in doubles. In 1968, he turned pro, signing with World Championship Tennis as one of the so-called "Handsome Eight" along with other rookies Newcombe, Cliff Drysdale, Nikki Pilic and Roger Taylor. His prize money amounted to $529,199. He was a player-coach for Phoenix and Boston in World Team Tennis, and has tutored several pros including Ivan Lendl and Roger

Federer. Roche was a country boy, born in the New South Wales hamlet of Tarcutta on May 17, 1945, a son of the local butcher. He entered the Hall of Fame, along with Newcombe, appropriately, in 1986.

MAJOR TITLES (16)—French singles, 1966; Australian doubles, 1965, 1967, 1971, 1976, 1977; French doubles, 1965, 1967; Wimbledon doubles, 1965, 1968, 1969, 1970, 1974; U.S. doubles, 1967; Australian mixed 1966; Wimbledon mixed, 1976. **DAVIS CUP**—1964, 1965, 1966, 1967, 1974, 1975, 1976, 1977, 1978, 7-3 singles, 7-2 doubles. **SINGLES RECORD IN THE MAJORS**—Australian (33-13), French (23-5), Wimbledon (32-13), U.S. (25-8).

Ellen Roosevelt
United States (1868–1954)
Hall of Fame—1975

The Roosevelt sisters, Ellen, 20, and Grace, 21, first played in the U.S. Championships in 1888, and two years later both were champions. Ellen Crosby Roosevelt won the 1890 singles over defending champ Bertha Townsend, 6-2, 6-2, in the challenge round, and joined with Grace for the doubles championship, 6-1, 6-2, over Townsend and Margarette Ballard.

The Roosevelts, who were born and raised in Hyde Park, N.Y., and were first cousins of U.S. President Franklin D. Roosevelt, were the first sisters to win a major title. They were emulated by Juliette and Kathleen Atkinson at the U.S. Championships of 1897 and 1898, and much later by Serena and Venus Williams. In 1891, however, the Roosevelts were done in by an Irishwoman, Mabel Cahill. Cahill beat Grace, 6-3, 7-5, in the final of the all-comers, then deposed Ellen, 6-4, 6-1, 4-6, 6-3, in the challenge round. In the doubles, Cahill and Emma Leavitt Morgan unseated the sisters, 2-6, 8-6, 6-4.

The only Roosevelt reappearance in the Championships was Ellen's mixed doubles title with Clarence Hobart in 1893. The Roosevelts, reared on a private court at home, may have been the first to be prodded by a tennis parent. Recalled original champ Ellen Hansel: "Their father [John Roosevelt] coached and treated them as if they were a pair of show ponies. We silly, non-serious-minded players giggled at their early-to-bed and careful food habits."

Ellen, a right-hander, was born in August 1868 and died in Hyde Park, Sept. 26, 1954. She entered the Hall of Fame in 1975. Also a right-hander, Grace Walton Roosevelt, who became Mrs. Appleton Clark, was born June 3, 1867, in Hyde Park and died there Nov. 29, 1945.

MAJOR TITLES (3)—U.S. singles, 1890; U.S. doubles, 1890; U.S. mixed 1893. **SINGLES RECORD IN THE MAJORS**—U.S. (5-2).

Merv Rose
Australia (1930—)
Hall of Fame—2001

Mervyn Gordon "Rosie" Rose saw some kids playing tennis in his hometown, Coffs Harbour, New South Wales, liked what he saw, borrowed a pair of sneakers and a racket and won a junior tournament. From that impulsive, humble start grew a man who

would seize major singles titles on clay and grass, help his country win two Davis Cups and land in the Hall in 2001.

An Aussie who went his own way, often to the consternation of tennis officials, he had a carefree nature and a good sense of humor to go along with a mean left-handed serve and "rhythmic game," said Fred Perry. Groundstrokes weren't his forte but, blended with the serve and accurate volleying, they brought him the French title of 1958 over a clay court stalwart, Chilean Luis Ayala, 6-3, 6-4, 6-4. Four years earlier, his serve-and-volleying had outdone that of compatriot Rex Hartwig in the Australian final, 6-2, 0-6, 6-4, 6-2. Rose had lost the 1953 Australian final to Ken Rosewall, 6-0, 6-3, 6-4.

He had taken to clay by winning the German title in 1957, but perhaps a day Rosie will remember more than most occurred in May of 1958 when he entered Rome's Il Foro Italico to face the all-time home hero, Nicola Pietrangeli, for the Italian title. It was the tennis version of Christians at the mercy of lions in the Colosseum. Romans, not very hospitable toward a stranger trying to deprive one of their own, must have wished they could round up some lions to sic on the defiant 6-foot Aussie. They growled and raged themselves, urging Nicola to win for a second straight year. But Rose refused to bend to the virulent chorus or the vibrant Pietrangeli, and won, 5-7, 8-6, 6-4, 1-6, 6-2, with an ultimate set surge. The beer, even if it wasn't good old Aussie beer, tasted mighty good afterwards, the new champ said.

Practically every Aussie lad wants to grow up to have a hand in winning the Davis Cup, and having a swig of beer (or champagne) from it. Rose got his final round chance twice, but the second time, 1957, six years after the first, was better because he was on the court when the 3-2 victory over the U.S. was clinched. In Melbourne's storied Kooyong Stadium, he and Mal Anderson pounded Vic Seixas and Barry MacKay, 6-4, 6-4, 8-6, to give the natives an insurmountable 3-0 lead. While it was a team effort in 1951 at Sydney's White City, Rose, 21, suffered two losses as Australia beat the U.S., 3-2. Seixas beat him in the opener, followed by 30-year-old Ted Schroeder, in his last Cup hurrah, tying the series. Frank Sedgman took Rosie off the hook by beating Seixas.

Five of his seven majors were in doubles, all on grass. His most formidable partner was farm boy Hartwig, with whom he won the Australian and Wimbledon in 1954 and the U.S. in 1953. In 1952 at Longwood, he united with Davis Cup foe Seixas to stop the Aussie juggernaut, Ken McGregor and Sedgman's run at a second successive Grand Slam. Ken and Frank, winners of seven straight majors, were cut down in a massive U.S. final of 73 games, 3-6, 10-8, 10-8, 6-8, 8-6. It was particularly satisfying to Rose because he had lost the Grand Slamming U.S. final 12 months before with another Aussie, Don Candy, 10-8, 6-4, 4-6, 7-5. Rose also won the Wimbledon mixed of 1957 with American Darlene Hard.

For seven years he was among the world's Top 10, as high as No. 3 in 1958. His other 27 singles titles, 12 in 1957, eight in 1958, were racked up on four continents at such way stations as Brisbane, Cuba, Panama, Baranquilla, Dallas and Naples.

He turned pro in 1959 for a brief fling at barnstorming during which he "learned more about tennis from Pancho Gonzalez, Lew Hoad, Ken Rosewall and the rest than I'd ever known." He then became an astute, successful coach. Billie Jean King credits him with reforming her forehand and advancing her game substantially. Rose was born Jan. 23, 1930, at Coff Harbour, Australia.

MAJOR TITLES (7)—Australian singles, 1954; French singles, 1958; Australian doubles, 1954; Wimbledon doubles, 1954; U.S. doubles, 1952, 1953; Wimbledon mixed doubles, 1957. **DAVIS CUP**—1951, 1957, 0-2 singles, 1-0 doubles. **SINGLES RECORD IN THE MAJORS**—Australian (24-8), French (28-7), Wimbledon (26-8), U.S. (12-4).

Ken Rosewall
Australia (1933—)
Hall of Fame—1980

As the Doomsday Stroking Machine, the remarkable, often unbelievable Kenneth Robert "Muscles" Rosewall was a factor in three decades of tennis, winning his first major titles, the Australian and French singles in 1953 as a teen-ager, and continuing as a tournament winner past his 43rd birthday. Probably nobody played better longer. He was yet a tough foe into 1978. At the close of the 1977 season, he was still ranked as one of the top players in the game, No. 12, on the ATP computer, having won two of 24 tournaments on a 44-23 match record.

"It's something I enjoy and find I still do well," was his simple explanation of his prowess in 1977. "But I never imagined myself playing so long when I turned pro in 1957."

The son of a Sydney, Australia, grocer, Rosewall was born in that city Nov. 2, 1934, and grew up there. A natural left-hander, he was taught to play right-handed by his father, Robert Rosewall, and developed a peerless backhand. Some felt his size (5-foot-7, 135 pounds) would impede him, but it was never a problem. He moved quickly, with magnificent anticipation and perfect balance, and never suffered a serious injury. Though his serve wasn't formidable, he placed it well, and backed it up with superb volleying. Rosewall was at home on any surface, and at the baseline or the net. He had an even temperament, was shy and reticent, but good-natured.

Although Rosewall, the little guy, always seemed overshadowed by a rival, first Lew Hoad, then Pancho Gonzalez and Rod Laver, he outlasted them all, and had the last competitive word. Even when Laver was acknowledged as the best in the world, Rosewall could bother him, and twice shocked Rod in the rich World Championship Tennis finals in Dallas (1971 and 1972), snatching the unheard of $50,000 first prize from the favorite's grasp. The latter match, thought by many to be the greatest ever—a 3-1/2 hour struggle watched by millions on TV—went to Rosewall, 4-6, 6-0, 6-3, 6-7 (3-7), 7-6, (7-5), when he stroked two magnificent backhand returns to escape a seemingly untenable position in the decisive tie-breaker (down 5-points-to-4) and win by two points. It was the closest finish of an important championship until Boris Becker beat Ivan Lendl, also 7-5 in a fifth set tie-breaker, for the 1988 Masters title.

Rosewall and Hoad—born only 21 days apart, Ken the elder—were linked as teammates and adversaries almost from their first days on court. In 1952 as 17-year-olds, they made an immediate impact on their first overseas tour, both reaching the quarterfinals of the U.S. Championships at Forest Hills, Ken beat-

ing the No. 1 American, Vic Seixas, 3-6, 6-2, 7-5, 5-7, 6-3. Later the following year (having won the Wimbledon doubles together), shortly after their 19th birthdays, they became the youngest Davis Cup defenders, collaborating for Australia to repel the U.S. challenge in the 1953 finale. Rosewall beat Seixas, 6-2, 3-6, 6-3, 6-4, in the decisive last match to ensure a 3-2 victory.

Though Hoad was considerably stronger physically than Rosewall, who had been given the sardonic nickname, "Muscles" by his mates, Ken always managed to keep up with (and often surpass) him in the early days. Hoad beat Rosewall in the 1956 Wimbledon final, but his bid for a Grand Slam was spoiled when Rosewall knocked him off in the U.S. final at Forest Hills, 4-6, 6-2, 6-3, 6-3.

Linked in doubles as well as the public mind, Ken and Lew might well have made a Grand Slam together in 1953, but came up three wins short. After taking the Australian, French and Wimbledon, they had a bad day in Boston, dropping a close U.S. quarterfinal decision to unseeded Americans Hal Burrows and Straight Clark, 5-7, 14-12, 18-16, 9-7. But they (Kenny unerring of return from the right court) grabbed that title in 1956, over Seixas and Ham Richardson, 6-2, 6-2, 3-6, 6-4.

After helping Australia win the Davis Cup twice more, both 5-0 over the U.S. in 1955 and 1956, winning all four singles and a doubles seemingly effortlessly, Rosewall turned pro to take on the professional king, Pancho Gonzalez. Gonzalez stayed on top, winning their head-to-head tour, 50-26, but it was apparent that Rosewall belonged at the uppermost level. Thus began one of the longest professional careers, certainly the most distinguished in regard to significant victories over so lengthy a span. Rosewall won the first of his three U.S. Pro singles titles over newcomer Laver in 1963, 6-4, 6-2, 6-2, the second by beating in succession, Gonzalez, then and Laver in 1965, 6-4, 6-3, 6-3, and the third over Cliff Drysdale in 1971, 6-4, 6-3, 6-0.

That was one of the three championships that the pros held dearest during their days as outcasts prior to "Open" tennis. The others were the French Pro, won by Rosewall eight times, including seven in a row (1960-66), and Wembley in London, won five times by Rosewall between 1957 and 1968. Memorable battles were the five set, 1963 French Pro final over Laver, 6-8, 6-4, 5-7, 6-3, 6-4, and the 1962 Wembley final over Hoad, 6-4, 5-7, 15-13, 7-5. Ken's sparkling rivalry with Laver stretched over 111 encounters, Rod ahead, 62-49 (6-4 in the Open era). He was 59-101 against Gonzalez and 45-25 over Hoad.

Rosewall holds several longevity records. Fourteen years after his 1956 Forest Hills triumph over Hoad, he beat the favored Tony Roche, 10 years his junior, to win the U.S. Championship again, 2-6, 6-4, 7-6 (5-2), 6-3. Eighteen years after that 1956 final— having beaten favored defender John Newcombe, 6-7 (3-5), 6-4, 7-6 (5-1), 6-3, in the semis—he was crushed in the 1974 windup by Jimmy Connors, 6-1, 6-0, 6-1. Twenty years after appearing in the first of four Wimbledon finals, he lost the 1974 final to Connors, 6-1, 6-1, 6-4. The only big one Rosewall missed out on was Wimbledon singles (finalist 1954, 56, 70, 74), but he won the doubles twice. Nineteen years after his first major title, the Australian, over Mervyn Rose, 6-0, 6-3, 6-4, he won it again, in 1972, over Mal Anderson, 7-6 (7-2), 6-3, 7-5. He also made it to the semis in 1976 and 1977, 24 years after the first time! Twenty years after his first Davis

Cup appearance, he reappeared to help Australia win once again in 1973 (winning the semifinal doubles with Laver over Czechs Jan Kodes and Vladimir Zednik, 6-4, 14-12, 7-9, 8-6). His Davis Cup farewell was 1975, a zone win over New Zealand, in which he won two matches, closing 6-1, 9-11, 7-5, 9-7, over 24-year-old Brian Fairlie, having been in on four Australian Davis Cups and three World Cups, a since disbanded team series against the U.S.

Altogether, Rosewall won 18 major titles in singles, doubles and mixed. In 1974, he served as player-coach of the Pittsburgh Triangles of World Team Tennis. He was the second tennis player to cross one million dollars in prize money, following Laver, and had a career total of $1,600,300.

Like Laver, Gonzalez and Hoad, and a few others, he had one of those rare three-stage careers spanning the amateur era, pro one-night stand years and the Open era. His victories were innumerable, but in the last section, begun at age 33, he won 50 titles, 32 in singles and 18 in doubles. The first of those was the baptismal "Open," the British Hard Court singles at Bournemouth in April of 1968; the second, the initial major Open, the French, a month later— both over Laver, 3-6, 6-2, 6-0, 6-3, and 6-3, 6-1, 2-6, 6-2. His last pro triumph—Hong Kong in 1977 over 30-year-old American Tom Gorman, 6-3, 5-7, 6-4, 6-4— was recorded two weeks after his 43rd birthday, making him the second oldest (just shy of Gonzalez) to win an Open-era title.

Still going, like some super battery, gray but the same in frame and slick of backhand, Ken seemed to be just warming up for the super seniors. He hung out in the world's Top 10 for 12 years: No. 2 in 1953, 55-56, 70, 72; No. 3 in 1954, 68, 71; No. 4 in 1969; No. 5 in 1973; No. 7 in 1974; No. 10 in 1975.

Rosewall was named to the International Tennis Hall of Fame in 1980, and the Australian Tennis Hall of Fame in 1995.

MAJOR TITLES (18)—Australian singles, 1953, 55, 71-72; French singles, 1953, 68; U.S. singles, 1956, 70; Australian doubles, 1953, 56, 72; French doubles, 1953, 68; Wimbledon doubles, 1953, 56; U.S. doubles, 1956, 69; U.S. mixed, 1956. **DAVIS CUP**—1953-54-55-56, 73, 75,. 17-2 singles, 2-1 doubles. **SINGLES RECORD IN THE MAJORS**—Australian (45-10), French (24-3), Wimbledon (47-11), U.S. (57-10).

Dorothy Round
Great Britain (1908–1982)
Hall of Fame—1986

Dorothy Edith Round Little was the leading British female player at the time Helen Wills Moody ruled the courts in the 1930s. Round distinguished herself on several counts, among them that she was the only British player besides Kitty McKane Godfree to win Wimbledon twice since World War I, and in 1935, she was the first woman from overseas to win the Australian Championship, beating Nancy Lyle in an all-English final, 1-6, 6-1, 6-3.

Born July 13, 1908, in Dudley, Worcestershire, England, she developed a right-handed groundstroke game of power and precision and volleying ability equaled by few. She won the Wimbledon crown in 1934 and repeated in 1937. Her play at the net was a factor in her victory over Helen Jacobs in the 1934 final, 6-2, 5-7, 6-3. In the 1937 final, she defeated the strong Polish woman, Jadwiga Jedrzejowska, 6-2, 2-6, 7-5, overcoming a 1-4 deficit in the final set.

To get to the Wimbledon final of 1937, Round defeated Jacobs, 6-4, 6-2, and Simone Mathieu, France's leading player, 6-4, 6-0. Round appeared to rise to her best form when confronted by Jacobs or Moody. In 1933, Round got to the final at Wimbledon and gave Moody one of the most challenging fights of her career, yielding at 6-4, 6-8, 6-3. That same year in the U.S. Championships, she lost to Jacobs in the semifinals, 6-4, 5-7, 6-2.

Round was not as successful, however, in Wightman Cup matches as in major tournaments. She was a member of the defeated British teams from 1931 to 1936. She lost to Jacobs four times before defeating the American 6-3, 6-3 in 1936, in her final appearance in the international team matches. Round (Mrs. Douglas Little in 1937) probably relished that victory particularly, for it was the year Jacobs finally achieved her ambition of winning Wimbledon.

Dorothy was in the world's Top 10 from 1933 through 1937: No. 1 in 1934; No. 3 in 1933, 1936; No. 6 in 1935; No. 2 in 1937, and was named to the Hall of Fame in 1986. She died Nov. 12, 1982, in Kidderminster, England.

MAJOR TITLES (6)—Australian singles, 1935; Wimbledon singles, 1934, 1937. Wimbledon mixed 1934, 1935, 1936. **WIGHTMAN CUP**—1931-32-33-34-35-36, 4-7 singles, 0-2 doubles. **SINGLES RECORD IN THE MAJORS**—Australian (4-0), Wimbledon (35-9), US. (6-2)

Elizabeth Ryan
United States (1892–1979)
Hall of Fame—1972

Elizabeth Montague "Bunny" Ryan, a magnificent doubles player who long held the major tournament record for total championships—19 at Wimbledon between 1914 and 1934—dearly wished to win a major in singles. She missed out, however, in three finals, losing to Suzanne Lenglen (1921), 6-2, 6-0, and Helen Mills Moody (1930), 6-2, 6-2, at Wimbledon, and coming closest in 1926, a heartbreak loss at the U.S. Championships.

In the most elderly of major finals, Ryan, 34, led Molla Mallory, 42, in the third set, 4-0, and had a match point in the thirteenth game only to fall, 4-6, 6-4, 9-7 at Forest Hills.

It may be that she was a bit too stout (at 5-foot-5-1/2, 145 pounds) and slow of foot to equal her doubles success on the singles court. Still, with superb anticipation and tactics, she won numerous singles titles, including the last played in Imperial Russia in 1914. "I got the last train out as the war (World War I) descended," she later recalled. Tennis was her vehicle to travel the glamorous international circuit of the day, playing across the globe with czars, kings, maharajahs, all sorts of royalty on the Riviera.

Her 12 Wimbledon doubles titles (and 13 finals) are tourney records, as are five straight with Lenglen (1919-23), plus 1925. She also won six straight doubles titles (1914-23; no play during World War I, 1915-18). She won a record seven mixed titles (of a record 10 finals) with five different partners, three with Randolph Lycett. Yoked, she and Lenglen never lost (31-0) at the Big W.

Yet standing is Ryan's Wimbledon doubles record of 50 straight match victories from 1914 to the 1928 final. She first played Wimbledon in 1912, reaching the quarters in singles, and

set a championship longevity record: 20 years between first and last titles (1914-34). Only Billie Jean King (224) and Martina Navratilova (293) won more matches at Wimbledon, where Ryan was 190-28: 47-15 in singles, 73-4 in doubles, 70-9 in mixed. A Wimbledon year without a Ryan title was extraordinary. It happened only once, 1928, during her 20-year championship spread.

Ryan, a right-hander with a severe chop, sharp volley and drop shot, was born Feb. 5, 1892, in Anaheim, Calif. While she played for her native land in the 1926 Wightman Cup, she spent most of her life as a London resident. She did work as a teaching pro for a time in the U.S. One of her pupils was Hall of Fame mate Gene Scott.

Intensely protective of her Wimbledon record of 19 titles (of 25 finals), she was uncomfortable sharing it with King when Billie Jean tied her by winning the singles in 1975. Ryan, undoubtedly pleased not to see herself eclipsed, collapsed and died July 8, 1979, at her beloved Wimbledon, the day before King got No. 20 by winning the doubles with Navratilova.

Twice she played enough in the U.S. to make the Top 10 ranking, No. 2 in 1925 and 1926. She was in the world's Top 10 five times between 1925 and 1930: No. 4 in 1925, 30; No. 5 in 1926; No. 3 in 1927; No. 6 in 1928. She entered the Hall of Fame in 1972.

MAJOR TITLES (26)—French doubles, 1930, 31-33-34; Wimbledon doubles, 1914, 1919-20-21-22-23, 25-26-27, 30, 33-34; U.S. doubles, 1926; Wimbledon mixed, 1919, 21, 23, 27-28, 30, 32; U.S. mixed 1926, 33. **WIGHTMAN CUP**—1926, 1-1 singles, 1-0 doubles. **SINGLES RECORD IN THE MAJORS**—French (8-3), Wimbledon (47-15), U.S. 10-3).

Gabriela Sabatini
Argentina (1970—)
Hall of Fame—2006

Which do you prefer? The Divine Argentine? Or Pearl of the Pampas? Descriptive noms de racket befitting a gorgeous gem. Or just plain Gaby, as her friends call her. Doesn't matter. It can only be one person whose name rolls across your tongue like fine wine:

Gabriela Beatrice Sabatini.

As the most extraordinary Latin American lady since Brazilian Maria Bueno was winning Wimbledon and U.S. titles back in the 1960s, making her own way to the Hall of Fame, Gaby had a different style. She adored life at the baseline, her heavy topspinning groundies coming in like a high tide.

"It was so hard, so much work playing against her shots," said Chris Evert. "Gaby was terrific, and so good so young."

As a 14-year-old pro, she made her first impact, playing three matches on the last day at Hilton Head, S.C., in 1985, a tournament backed up by rain. It was a Sunday made for TV drama, and Gaby made the most of it, first finishing up a downpour-interrupted quarterfinal over No. 8 Pam Shriver, 5-7, 7-5, 6-4 then knocking off No. 5 Manuela Maleeva in the semis, 6-1, 7-6(11-9). Evert, No. 2, the defending champ awaited in the final. It was explained to Gaby that the rules allowed her to put it off until Monday and rest.

No thanks, she said. Bring on Evert and the cameras. The kid was sensational for a set, then an empty tank and Chris took over, 6-4, 6-0.

Soon enough, the following year, 1986, she was in the world's Top 10, No. 10, and stayed in that select company for 10 straight years—No. 3 in 1989, 91-92—before retiring in 1996. Everybody liked and respected dark-haired Gaby, a splendid sportswoman in a highly competitive profession. Presenting her for Hall of Fame induction in 2006 was her leading rival, Steffi Graf.

It was Graf whom she beat for her major singles title, the U.S. Open in the 1990 final, 6-2, 7-6 (7-4). "I'll never forget the last shot," she says of a massive forehand passer. "It had been a hot, tiring match. I put everything into that shot…a third set would have been too much for me."

Nobody who was there will forget it either. In a desperate semifinal, she notched a 7-5, 5-7, 6-3 win over Mary Joe Fernandez. She did it by attacking the net and volleying. Continuing that Bueno-like approach, she reached the Wimbledon final in 1991, building a 6-5, 30-15 lead in the third set—two points from the title—but strangely hung back. Graf won, 6-4, 3-6, 8-6 but she and Steffi did collaborate for a major, grabbing the 1988 Wimbledon doubles as teenies away from Natasha Zvereva and Larisa Savchenko Neiland 6-3, 1-6, 12-10.

Rare consistency: from the semifinals of Wimbledon in 1990 through the semifinals of the Australian in 1994, she was no worse than a quarterfinalist in 15 straight majors.

Gaby got a silver at the 1988 Olympics because she couldn't stop golden Steffi, 6-3, 6-3. Steffi got a 1988 Grand Slam because Gaby couldn't win their third set of the U.S. Open final, 6-3, 3-6, 6-1.

A right-hander born May 16, 1970 in Buenos Aires, she grew to 5-foot-9, 130 lbs., spent formative tennis years on Key Biscayne, Florida, coached by Pato Apey. She turned pro in 1985.

Among her prominent titles were the year-end WTA Championships over Shriver, 7-5, 6-2, 6-2, in 1988, and over Lindsay Davenport, 6-3, 6-2, 6-4, in 1994. She also won in Key Biscayne in 1989 over Evert, 6-1, 4-6, 6-2 and the Canadian Open in 1988 over Zvereva, 6-1, 6-2. The Italian Open was a particularly joyful gig. She was in six finals, winning four: 1988 over Canadian Helen Kelesi 6-1, 6-7 (4-7), 6-1; 1989 over Arantxa Sanchez Vicario 6-2, 5-7, 6-4; 1991 over Monica Seles 6-3, 6-2; 1992 over Seles 7-5, 6-4. She lost the 1987 final to Graf, 7-5, 4-6, 6-0; and 1993 to Conchita Martinez 7-5, 6-1.

Gaby was especially adored in Rome where clusters of encouraging signs and banners appeared at Il Foro Italico—even for a few years after she retired. But who wouldn't love her?

She won 27 singles titles (632-189 matches), 12 doubles titles (252-96) and earned $8,785,850 in prize money.

MAJOR TITLES (2)—U.S. singles, 1990; Wimbledon doubles, 1988. **FEDERATION CUP**—1984—87, 95; 13-3 singles, 11-3 doubles. **SINGLES RECORDS IN THE MAJORS**—Australian (29-8), French (42-11), Wimbledon (42-11), U.S. (51-12)

Pete Sampras
United States (1971—)
Hall of Fame—2007

It just happened. He couldn't explain it or understand it. "I didn't know what I was doing. I was just a new kid. Everything I did worked," Pete Sampras would say later, discussing his U.S.

Open triumph of 1990 that anointed him as the youngest of all U.S. champions at 19 years, one month.

He knew what he was doing the rest of the way as "Silky" Sampras, smoothly, uniquely, gliding along a path of greatness in an outwardly unconcerned and effortless manner while mounting a planned and concerted assault on the citadels of the past. Pete knows his tennis history, and was consciously pursuing the man on the spire, Aussie Roy Emerson, who seized 12 major singles championships between 1961 and 1967, the men's record (six Australian, two each French, Wimbledon, U.S.)

Pete razed Emerson's 33-year-old citadel by beating another Queensland country boy, Patrick Rafter, 6-7 (10-12), 7-6 (7-5), 6-4, 6-2, for a thirteenth major at Wimbledon in 2000. New century, new record. But in the shadows of dusk that day he also caught up with an English ghost, Willie Renshaw. Willie had won seven Wimbledons between 1881 and 1889, and this was the seventh for Pete. Emerson sent his congratulations after being eclipsed, laughing that he hadn't even known of holding a record until Sampras began stalking him, and the press picked up on it.

Pete raised his own stronghold higher at 14 by winning the U.S. Open of 2002, even though he was lurching through his worst year, and a spell dryer than the Sahara—33 tournaments without a title. At Wimbledon, he was stung in the second round in what ultimately was his final match at the All England Club, losing to a Swiss stranger, No. 145 George Bastl. At Paris, No. 69 Andrea Gaudenzi booted him from the opening round. He even lost on grass, with a two-set lead, in a Davis Cup match at Houston to turf-wary Spaniard Alex Corretja, 4-6, 4-6, 7-6 (7-4), 7-5, 6-4. Never had he been so down and disregarded.

Yet Pete, ranked and seeded No. 17, was inspired at Flushing Meadow, the scene of his 1989 Open breakthrough. Then he'd knocked off defending champion Mats Wilander, 5-7, 6-3, 1-6, 6-1, 6-4, in the second round. But after suffering final round defeats by 20-year-olds Marat Safin in 2000, 6-4, 6-3, 6-3, and Lleyton Hewitt, 7-6 (7-4), 6-1, 6-1, in 2001, Pete was somehow ready to claim his fifth U.S. title, defeating lifetime rival Andre Agassi in the 2002 finale, 6-3, 6-4, 5-7, 6-4.

It had been a while since Pete had ruled the United States. Squelching the perpetual motion of Michael Chang in the all-Californian Open final of 1996, 6-1, 6-4, 7-6 (7-3), marked his last victory in Flushing, his fourth title. Although he had an off Wimbledon in 1996, losing in the quarters, 7-5, 7-6 (7-3), 6-4, to the new champ Richard Krajicek. Pete was, after all, shooting for his fourth in a row, and had won 25 straight where only Borg (41) and Laver (31) had longer streaks. He would still close out his ninth professional campaign as No. 1 for a fourth consecutive year.

At 6-foot-1, 175 pounds, with a full head of dark hair, the lanky Greek-blooded high school drop-out from Palos Verdes, Calif., was handling his affluence and standing modestly and well. "It's not a good year unless I win two majors. They're what count," he said.

But he was happy to salvage 1996 with one, considering the year's heartaches with the death of his coach and best friend, Tim Gullikson, of a brain tumor, which had been discovered at the Australian Open of 1995. Though unprepared for the French, which followed Gullikson's funeral, he made his finest showing in Paris, the one major that has befuddled him, falling in the

semis to the champ Yevgeny Kafelnikov, 7-6 (7-4), 6-0, 6-2. That was after exciting, draining five-set wins over ex-champs Sergi Bruguera and Jim Courier, as well as Todd Martin.

Born Aug. 1, 1971, in Washington, D.C., the right-hander grew up in Southern California. His older sister, Stella Sampras, played professionally and went on to coach the women's varsity of her alma mater, UCLA. Brother Gus is a player agent. Pete's tennis style was altered at 14 by a pediatrician (and moonlighting tennis pedagogue), Dr. Pete Fisher. Fisher, feeling that Pete's two-handed backhand and baselining were childish, preached volleying, a free-flowing traditional backhand and reverence for the greats of yesteryear in performance and behavior, Rod Laver and Ken Rosewall. As Pete grew, so did his vaunted serve, and everything fell into place. Later it was Gulllkson, Pete said, "who helped me to grow up, compete, focus, learn to play on grass. I owe so much to him."

Rookie pro Pete was out of his first U.S. Open, 1988, almost before it opened, beaten by Jaime Yzaga of Peru in the first round. But he got a footnote in 1989, deposing the champ, Wilander, reaching the fourth round. The next year he was golden, if "unconscious." A long shot, seeded No. 12 and ranked No. 81 when the season commenced, he went through in a spray of aces on a loss of four sets. He showed his mettle by taking out ex-champs back-to-back—Lendl, 6-4, 7-6 (7-3), 3-6, 4-6, 6-2 in the quarterfinals, and McEnroe, 6-2, 6-4, 3-6, 6-3 in the semifinals. Pete demonstrated authenticity and the fact that he was unstoppable, by coolly sealing off canny No. 3-seeded Lendl's counterattack in the quarters, embellishing with 26 aces. "He just kicked my ass," was Andre Agassi's terse summation of unbreakable Pete's 106-minute final round caper, 6-4, 6-3, 6-2. Up jumped the name of Oliver Campbell, dead man dispossessed. He had held the record as youngest champ, 19 years, six months. Pete out-greened him by five months.

A few months later, Pete made a bigger financial splash, collecting a record $2 million for winning the inaugural Grand Slam Cup in Munich over Brad Gilbert 6-3, 6-4, 6-2. Uncomfortable with all the attention brought by these deeds, and rocketing to No. 5 in the rankings, he actually seemed relieved to have the U.S. title lifted from him in the 1991 quarters by Courier, 6-2, 7-6 (7-4), 7-6 (7-5). But he matured, accepted the responsibilities and challenges of life at the top, and became a solid world No. 1 in 1993, repelling all-would-be usurpers for six straight years, copping Jimmy Connors's Open era record of five in a row (1974-78). Nothing as imposing had been seen for almost three-quarters of a century, since Big Bill Tilden's No. 1 parade of six years (1920-25) in the pre-computer days. Though Agassi took it away momentarily by beating Pete in the 1995 Australian Open, 4-6, 6-1 7-6 (8-6), 6-4, Sampras struck back in the U.S. final eight months later, dispiriting Andre, 6-4, 6-3, 4-6, 7-5. Their hot rivalry stood at 20-14 for Pete at his 2002 swan song. Other than the six No. 1's, Pete's 12-year world Top 10 residency: No. 5 in 1990; No. 6 in 1991; No. 3 in 1992, 99-2000; No. 10 in 2001; and the closing entry, No. 13 in 2002.

Davis Cup was not altogether happy for Pete, especially his jitters-wracked debut in the 1991 final. A raucous, nationalistic French crowd in Lyon unnerved him, and Henri Leconte and

Guy Forget pummeled him to defeats, Guy in the clincher, 7-6 (8-6), 3-6, 6-3, 6-4, that gave the French an unexpected Cup, 3-1. He played a winning right-court doubles part (alongside McEnroe) in the 3-1 Cup victory over Switzerland's Jakob Hlasek and Marc Rosset in 1992, 6-7 (5-7), 6-7 (7-9), 7-5, 6-1, 6-2.

In the 1995 final at Moscow, on a clay court spread especially to spread-eagle him within Olympic Stadium, Pete responded by taking charge in the 3-2 victory over Russia in as glorious a weekend triple as performed by any American abroad. First was a five set out-grinding of dirt maven Andrei Chesnokov, 3-6, 6-4, 6-3, 6-7 (5-7), 6-4, immediately after which Pete keeled over, exhausted, cramping. Then came a nifty duet with Todd Martin in the 7-5, 6-4, 6-3, go-ahead flooring of Andrei Olhovskiy and Kafelnikov. Finally, a definitive curtain-lowering riddling of Kafelnikov, 6-2, 6-4, 7-6 (7-4), in a shower of aces (16) and forehand winners (19). All his extraordinary qualities were on display: the grit and stubbornness, fluid groundies, thundering serves, casual yet deadlly volleys and racing forehands.

It all appeared so relaxed and glissando, although his head still slumped in adverse moments. Beneath the calm facade lurked certain physical and emotional frailties, a hereditary blood problem called thalyssemia. This was evident when he collapsed the instant the Chesnokov ordeal ended. And the memorable 1996 afternoon at Flushing where he lost his lunch but not his title in a 7-6 (7-5), 5-7, 5-7, 6-4, 7-6 (9-7) quarterfinal win over Alex Corretja. Ill and vomiting in the conclusive fifth-set tie-breaker, Pete wormed his way out of a match point with a lunging volley. Staggering, he hooked a 90 mph second serve ace—"I don't know where it came from ... I was out of it"—to give himself match point at 8-7. Whereupon, "not wanting to hit another ball," he didn't have to. Corretja lost the only way Pete could win—a double fault. Kismet.

"But that's sweet Pete," says longtime friend and rival, Courier. "Just when you think he's dying, that's when he kills you."

What really killed him was an outlook-changing loss of the 1992 U.S. Open final to Stefan Edberg, 3-6, 6-4, 7-6 (7-5) , 6-2. "For the first time it really hurt to lose, really bothered me. I hadn't been really determined until then," he said. "But I realized that I wasn't going to settle for one major. I had to have more." And so he did.

At the close of 2002, he had won 64 of 265 singles tournaments, losing 24 finals. He'd also won two doubles titles. In the majors, he won 14 of 18 finals. His singles W-L record stands at an impressive 762-222 (.776), 203-39 in the majors (.839). Winning more prize money than anyone else, $43,280,489. His most productive season was 1994, winning 10 of 18 singles tournaments on 77-12. In the 1992 Olympics, he was beaten in the third round by Chesnokov.

Regardless of how long the game is played he will forever be the Big Man of the Big W.

MAJOR TITLES (14)—Australian singles, 1994, 1997; Wimbledon singles, 1993, 1994, 1995; 1997, 1998, 1999, 2000; U.S. singles, 1990, 1993, 1995, 1996, 2002. **OTHER U.S. TITLES** (2)—Hard Court singles, 1991, 1992. **DAVIS CUP**—1991, 1992, 1994, 1995, 1997, 1999, 2000, 2002; 15-8 singles, 4-1 doubles, **SINGLES RECORD IN THE MAJORS**—Australian (45-9), French (24-13), Wimbledon (63-7), U.S. (71-9) **PETE'S**

SWEET FOURTEEN—1990—U.S., d. Andre Agassi (USA), 6-4, 6-3, 6-2; 1993—Wimbledon, d. Jim Courier (USA), 7-6 (7-3), 7-6 (8-6), 4-6, 6-3; 1993—U.S., d. Cedric Pioline (FRA), 6-4, 6-4, 6-3; 1994—Australian, d. Todd Martin (USA), 7-6 (7-4), 6-4, 6-4; 1994—Wimbledon, d. Goran Ivanisevic (CRO), 7-6 (7-2), 7-6 (7-5), 6-0; 1995—Wimbledon, d. Boris Becker (GER), 6-7 (5-7), 6-2, 6-4, 6-2; 1995—U.S., d. Agassi, 6-4, 6-3, 4-6, 7-5; 1996—U.S., d. Michael Chang (USA), 6-1, 6-4, 7-6 (7-3); 1997—Australian, d. Carlos Moya (ESP), 6-2, 6-3, 6-3; 1997—Wimbledon, d. Pioline, 6-4, 6-2, 6-4; 1998—Wimbledon, d. Ivanisevic, 6-7(2-7), 7-6 (11-9), 6-4, 3-6, 6-2; 1999—Wimbledon, d. Agassi, 6-3, 6-4, 7-5; 2000—Wimbledon, d. Pat Rafter (AUS), 6-7 (10-12) 7-6 (7-5), 6-4, 6-2; 2002—U.S., d. Agassi, 6-3, 6-4, 5-7, 6-4

Arantxa Sanchez Vicario

Spain (1971—)
Hall of Fame—2007

Buzzing and flitting the width and breadth of arenas across the planet, the Barcelona Bumblebee—Arantxa Sanchez Vicario—was unceasing in determined pursuit of tennis balls, none seeming too distant to be retrieved in this manner and returned again and again to demoralize opponents. This went on most of her life, more than half of it as a professional, with no reduction in her zest or desire to win.

Long after the glamorous Lili de Alvarez of Madrid enhanced the 1926-27-28 Wimbledon finals, industrious little Sanchez Vicario, a 5-foot-6, 130-pound right-hander, revived female tennis in their country. It happened on a June afternoon in Paris in 1989 as 17-year-old Arantxa faced defeat in the French final. Seeded No. 7, she had done very well to get that far on her third try. She had come to attention the year before by chasing the all-time champ out of town: Chris Evert's last stand, 6-3, 7-6 (7-4). But now Steffi Graf, winner of five consecutive majors, was across the net and serving for the title at 5-4 in the third. Whereupon the intransigent Catalan went into overdrive, punching topspin forehands and two-fisted backhand drives relentlessly, relinquishing only two points and winning, 7-6 (8-6), 3-6, 7-5. Not only the first Spanish woman to take a major, she was the youngest French champ, until Monica Seles weighed in at 16 the following year.

She would become one of 14 women to appear in the finals of all four majors, winning the French again over Mary Pierce, 6-4, 6-4, in 1994, and Seles, 7-6 (7-5), 0-6, 6-2, in 1998. In 1994, she took the U.S. crown from Graf in a tumultuous 1-6, 7-6 (7-3), 6-4, decision and was named the ITF's World Champion. She lost Wimbledon and French finals to Graf in 1995 and 1996, the Australian to Pierce in 1995, 6-3, 6-2.

Perhaps her finest matches were heart-stopping defeats by Graf as they goaded each other to the heights at Wimbledon in 1995, and the French in 1996. Arantxa served for victory at 5-4 and 7-6 in a shotmaking extravaganza in Paris, losing, 6-3, 6-7 (4-7), 10-8 in three hours, three minutes. On Centre Court, they waged a game of games, the 11th of the third set. On it went for 20 minutes and 13 deuces. Serving, Arantxa had eight game points, but couldn't make it, 4-6, 6-1, 7-5, losing the last six points.

Aranzazu Isabel Maria "Arantxa" Sanchez was born Dec. 18, 1971, in Barcelona. The last of a historic tennis-playing Sanchez brood of four, she was a surprise to her non-tennis parents, Emilio and the former Marisa Vicario, whose name Arantxa attached as a tribute, adding it in 1988. Arantxa is also the subject of a family tale. After the births of Marisa (a varsity player at Pepperdine in Santa Monica, Calif.) and Emilio and Javier (both successful pros and Spanish Davis Cuppers), Mama Marisa was told she could have no more children. However, three years later, not long after taking the kids on a roller-coaster ride, she became pregnant. So she has a special place in her heart for that shake-and-rolling rattler at the Tibidabo amusement park overlooking the city. The babe's given name, Aranzazu, is that of a Basque saint.

A woman of sunny nature, Arantxa presented a rather severe look at play, her flowing black hair tightly head-banded above a contentious countenance that conveys her outlook: Surrender never. Ever a hustler on short, spirited legs, she never got enough tennis. Strictly a baseliner at first, she constantly improved her volleying to become one of the finer doubles players. She liked the dual load of singles and doubles, carrying it better than anyone else, usually leading woman in matches played and won. She was one of the few centurions with 100 titles—29 singles, 67 doubles and four mixed. She won 14 majors: four singles, six doubles, four mixed. Her career singles W-L for 329 tournaments: 759-295 (.720); doubles W-L for 298 tournaments: 667-216 (.755). Her most successful doubles partnership, with Jana Novotna, reaped three majors (Australian and Wimbledon, 1995; U.S. 1994) plus the 1995 year-end WTA Championship.

Arantxa represented Spain handsomely in five Olympics (1988, 1992, 1996, 2000, 2004) and 16 years of Federation Cup (1986-98, 2000-02). In 1992, at Barcelona, with her king, Juan Carlos, spectating, she won a bronze in singles, silver in doubles with Conchita Martinez. In 1996, she took silver in singles, losing the final to Lindsay Davenport and bronze, with Martinez in doubles. She and Conchita, the most successful one-two punch in the competition's history wrapped up the Federation Cup five times, 1991, 1993-94-95 and 1998, and attained five other finals, 1989, 1992, 1996, 2000 and 2002. Arantxa holds the records for most years played (16), series (58), total matches (100), wins (72), singles wins (50). She was 18-3 in doubles with Conchita. As a pro 17 years, 1985-2002 (starting at 13 years, six months), she was in the world's Top 10 for 11 years (No. 1 for brief intervals during 1995): No. 5 in 1989, 1991; No. 7 in 1990; No. 4 in 1992, 1998; No. 2 in 1993-94, 1996; No. 3 in 1995; No. 9 in 1997, 2000, retiring at No. 53 in 2002. Her career prize money was $16,917,312.

She was a little lady giving the game a big buzz.

MAJOR TITLES (14)—French singles, 1989, 1994, 1998; U.S. singles, 1994; Australian doubles, 1992, 1995, 1996; Wimbledon doubles, 1995; U.S. doubles, 1993, 1994; Australian mixed, 1993; French mixed, 1990, 1992; U.S. mixed, 2000. **FEDERATION CUP**—1986-87-88-89-90-91-92-93-94-95-96-97-98-99-2000-01-02, 50-22 singles, 22-6 doubles. **SINGLES RECORD IN THE MAJORS**—Australian (41-11), French (72-13), Wimbledon (41-15), U.S. (56-15)

Manolo Santana

Spain (1938—)
Hall of Fame—1984

One of the masters of legerdemain, Manuel Martinez "Manolo" Santana was the first post-World War II European to

gain universal respect because of his ease not only on Continental clay, but the way he took to grass. As well as his winning the most difficult clay event, the French singles in 1961 and 1964—both over Nicola Pietrangeli, 4-6, 6-1, 3-6, 6-0, 6-2; and 6-3, 6-1, 4-6, 7-5—he also captured the greensward gems, Wimbledon of 1966 and the U.S. Championship of 1965 at Forest Hills. In doing so, the engaging Spaniard was the first European champ at Forest Hills since Frenchman Henri Cochet in 1928.

"He was a magician on clay," says Rod Laver. "Manolo could hit the most incredible angles, drive you crazy with topspin lobs or drop shots. And he improved his volleying so that he was dangerous on grass, too. He toyed with me a couple of times in Europe, letting me know I had a lot to learn about clay."

In 1965, Santana became a national hero in Spain and was decorated by the country's dictator, Francisco Franco, with the coveted Medal of Isabella, qualifying for the title *Ilustrissimo*. That year, Santana spearheaded the 4-1 upset of the U.S. at Barcelona during the Davis Cup campaign, and led Spain all the way to the finale for the first time. Although the Spaniards were turned back in Australia, 4-1, Santana gave Roy Emerson his only defeat in 12 title-round singles, 2-6, 6-3, 6-4, 15-13. Two years later, he drove Spain to the finale again, salvaging the only point in a 4-1 defeat by beating John Newcombe, 7-5, 6-4, 6-2.

Only Pietrangeli (164 singles and doubles in 46 series) and Romanian Ilie Nastase played more Davis Cup than Santana. Manolo worked 120 singles (69-17) and doubles (23-11) in 46 series between 1958 and 1973. He set Cup records by winning 13 singles matches in 1967 (equalled by Nastase in 1971), and also by winning 17 singles and doubles in 1965 and 1967 (topped by Nastase's 18 in 1971).

Born May 10, 1938, in Madrid, he worked as a ball boy at a local club and picked up the game. He was very appealing, a slender 5-foot-11 right-hander, who frequently flashed his warm, toothy smile at play, and was an admirable sportsman. His racket control was phenomenal, enabling him to hit with touch and power. He had great flair, the ability to improvise and to inspire himself and his partners and teammates. Never losing heart in the doubles of the 1965 Davis Cup against the U.S., he rallied partner Jose-Luis Arilla as they stormed back to beat Dennis Ralston and Clark Graebner, 4-6, 3-6, 6-3, 6-4, 11-9, in an emotional battle that clinched the decision. Cushions showered down on the two Spaniards as they were carried about the stadium court of the Real Club de Tenis in the manner of bullfighters. Santana and Arilla wept with joy at the most tremendous victory in Spanish tennis annals. Manolo had given the home side a 2-0 lead by beating Frank Froehling, 6-1, 6-4, 6-4, after Juan Gisbert upset Ralston, 3-6, 8-6, 6-1, 6-3.

Less than a month later, a similarly jubilant celebration enveloped Forest Hills after Santana jolted Cliff Drysdale in the U.S. final, 6-2, 7-9, 7-5, 6-1. A troupe of dancers from the World's Fair's Spanish Pavilion toted him from stadium to clubhouse, whereupon they serenaded him.

The following year was Santana's at Wimbledon, where he beat Ralston in the final, 6-4, 11-9, 6-4, and enthralled the gallery with his point and counterpoint thrusts. But 12 months later, beaten by Charlie Pasarell, 10-8, 6-3, 2-6, 8-6, he made an historic

footnote as the lone top-seeded defending champion to lose in Wimbledon's first round—until 2003 when the top-seeded defender Lleyton Hewitt was thusly scrubbed by qualifier Ivo Karlovic.

Beginning in 1961, Santana was in the world's Top 10 seven years: No. 1 in 1966; No. 3 in 1961-62, 67; No. 4 in 1963; No. 6 in 1964; No. 2 in 1965. His career was virtually over when the Open era arrived, but he did elate his countrymen by winning Barcelona in 1970, his last singles victory, plus three pro doubles titles. Overall as amateur and pro, he won 72 singles titles.

Santana came out of retirement briefly in 1973 to play his last season of Davis Cup, and again in 1974 to act as player-coach for New York in the new World Team Tennis league. He was named to the Hall of Fame in 1984, the second Spaniard, following 1977 inductee Manuel Alonso. His successes spurred the rapid development of tennis in Spain, where the sport was not much noticed prior to 1965, but is booming today. His protégé was Manuel Orantes, called Manolito (Little Manolo), who won the U.S. Championship at Forest Hills a decade after his own, beating Jimmy Connors though the surface had by then been transformed to clay.

He spent time as Spain's Davis Cup captain, and has long been a friend to aspiring young players. But despite Spain's important current standing in tennis today, none of its fine players has yet measured up to his four major singles, until the emergence of Rafael Nadal. Call Manolo the Godfather of the Groundstrokes.

MAJOR TITLES (5)—French singles, 1961, 1964; Wimbledon singles, 1966; U.S. singles, 1965; French doubles, 1963. **DAVIS CUP**—1958-59-60-61-62-63-64-65-66-67-68-69-70, 73, 69-17 singles, 23-11 doubles. **SINGLES RECORD IN THE MAJORS**—French (33-6), Wimbledon (12-9), U.S. (25-7)

Dick Savitt
United States (1927—)
Hall of Fame—1976

Only four American men have won the Australian and Wimbledon titles in one year. Richard "Dick" Savitt was the second in 1951 (following Don Budge, 1938, and preceding Jimmy Connors, 1974, and Pete Sampras, 1994). He beat Ken McGregor in both, four sets in the Aussie's lair, 6-3, 2-6, 6-3, 6-1, and straight sets at Wimbledon, 6-4, 6-4, 6-4.

Any hopes he had of a Grand Slam were squelched by champ Jaroslav Drobny, 1-6, 6-8, 6-4, 8-6, 6-3, in a quarterfinal of the French. Defending his Aussie title, Savitt was beaten in the 1952 semis by McGregor, 6-4, 6-4, 3-6, 6-4, and at Wimbledon by Mervyn Rose in a quarterfinal, 6-4, 3-6, 6-4, 4-6, 6-2. In the U.S. Championships, he was a semifinalist in 1950, losing to the champ, Art Larsen, 6-2, 10-8, 7-9, 6-2; while also reaching the Forest Hills Final Four in 1951, losing to Vic Seixas, 6-0, 3-6, 6-3, 6-2. He was also a U.S. quarterfinalist in 1952, 1956 and 1958—in 1956, losing a stirring baseline slugfest to the champ, Ken Rosewall, 6-4, 7-5, 4-6, 8-10, 6-1.

A large, broad-shouldered, dark-haired right-hander, 6-foot-3, 180 pounds, he was a powerful groundstroker and stubborn

competitor. Sav was a king of the Seventh Regiment Armory, a boards runner, in his Manhattan neighborhood, winning the U.S. Indoor thrice. He deposed Bill Talbert in 1952, 6-2, 6-3, 6-4, beat Budge Patty in 1958, 6-1, 6-2, 3-6, 12-10, and, at 34 (no longer ranked), knocked off No. 1 American Whitney Reed, 6-2, 11-9, 6-3, in 1961. But the best remembered of his five finals was a rousing joust he lost to world No. 1 Alex Olmedo, 7-9, 6-3, 6-4, 5-7, 12-10, in 1959. He ranked six times in the U.S. Top 10 between 1950 and 1959, No. 2 in 1951, and four times in the world's Top 10: between 1951 and 1957, No. 2 in 1951.

A Cornell graduate, Dick was born March 4, 1927, in Bayonne, N.J. In 1981, he and his son, Robert, won the U.S. Father and Son doubles title. He was elected to the Hall of Fame in 1976.

MAJOR TITLES (2)—Australian singles, 1951; Wimbledon singles, 1951. **OTHER U.S. TITLES** (3)—Indoor singles, 1952, 1958, 1961. DAVIS CUP—1951, 3-0 singles. **SINGLES RECORD IN THE MAJORS**—Australian (8-1), French (8-2), Wimbledon (11-1), U.S. (29-12)

Ted Schroeder
United States (1921–2006)
Hall of Farne—1966

Emulating Don McNeill in 1940, Frederick Rudolph "Ted" Schroeder out of Stanford became in 1942 only the second player to win the U.S. Intercollegiate and the U.S. singles in the same year. A standout big-situation competitor—especially in Davis Cup—volleying wizard Schroeder, along with his pal, Jack Kramer, recovered the Cup for the U.S. in 1946 after it had spent seven years in Australia during World War II.

Their teammates, Gar Mulloy and Frank Parker, weren't happy when captain Walter Pate selected attack-minded Kramer and Schroeder to play all the way against the favored Aussies in Melbourne. But Schroeder led off by stopping John Bromwich, 3-6, 6-1, 6-2, 0-6, 6-3, and the 5-0 sweep was on. A daring right-hander, Ted helped the U.S. keep the Cup in 1947-48-49 by winning both his singles against Australia each year.

But he was beaten by both Frank Sedgman and Ken McGregor as the Aussies lifted the Cup in 1950. Though he tied the 1951 finale at Sydney, 2-2, by beating Mervyn Rose, 6-4, 13-11, 7-5, the U.S. was tipped, 3-2, by Sedgman's 6-4, 6-2, 6-2, decision over Vic Seixas, and Ted retired. A part-time player, taking vacations from business to compete, Ted rose to his peak in 1949 when he won Wimbledon the only time he entered. That year, Ted not only captured the title with his daring volleying, but he also captivated London with his personality as an outgoing, straightforward Yank smoking a corn-cob pipe. He was known admiringly as "Lucky Ted" for his five-set escapes, four of them, starting with an old antagonist, Mulloy in the first round, 3-6, 9-11, 6-1, 6-0, 7-5, and ending with Jaroslav Drobny in the final, 3-6, 6-0, 6-3, 4-6, 6-4. The last three went the distance—the only such run other than Henri Cochet's in 1927—and he appeared truly lost in the quarters against Sedgman, 3-6, 6-8, 6-3, 6-2, 9-7. Sedg held two match points against serve, one each at 4-5 and 5-6. Ted wriggled free with serve-and-volley—but on a second serve (having footfaulted on the first), the volley clunked off the frame! The second was a backhand passer. He was also behind Eric Sturgess in the semis, 3-6, 7-5, 5-7, 6-1, 6-2. Ted's 29 sets and four five-set matches outdid any other champ in that respect.

Seven years after winning Forest Hills, he reappeared in the U.S. final and seemed the winner after taking the first two sets from Pancho Gonzalez, but faded, 16-18, 2-6, 6-1, 6-2, 6-4. He and Kramer formed one of the great doubles teams, winning the U.S. title thrice, 1940, 1941 and 1947. He refused several offers to join Kramer as a pro. A Californian, he was born July 20, 1921, in Newark, N.J., and was ranked in the U.S. Top 10 nine times between 1940 and 1951—No. 1 in 1942. He was in the world's Top 10 six straight times from 1946—No. 2 the first four years. He served in the U.S. Naval Air Force in World War II and entered the Hall of Fame in 1966. His son, John Schroeder, was an accomplished professional golfer. He died May 26, 2006.

MAJOR TITLES (6)—Wimbledon singles, 1949; U.S singles, 1942; U.S. doubles, 1940, 1941, 1947; U.S. mixed, 1942. **OTHER U.S. TITLES** (9)—Intercollegiate singles. 1942; Intercollegiate doubles, 1942, with Larry Dee; Hard Court singles, 1948, 1949, 1951; Clay Court doubles, 1941, with Jack Kramer; 1947, with Jack Tuero; Hard Court doubles, 1948, with Vic Seixas; 1949, with Eric Sturgess. **DAVIS CUP**—1946-47-48-49-50-51, 11-3 singles, 2-3 doubles. **SINGLES RECORD IN THE MAJORS**—Wimbledon (7-0), U.S. (20-4).

Gene Scott
United States (1937–2006)
Hall of Fame—2008—Contributor

As a skilled and authoritative man-about-everything in tennis, Gene Scott had no equal. He was the game's protean promoter—many times a champion on the court, but also championing the game itself in various roles.

A superb athlete, bright and literate, he was good enough with a racket to play Davis Cup for the United States, and battle to the semifinals of the U.S. Championships at Forest Hills in 1967, as well as the quarterfinals of the French Championships in 1964, beating Marty Mulligan, a three-time Italian champ, probably his best win.

Later, he won 40 U.S. titles in senior age group tournaments, the last in 2004, the 65s, when he also won the world grass court 65's—all this as a veteran of double-hip-replacement surgery. Gene was also a champ at court tennis, the abstruce centuries-old ancestor of today's just-plain tennis, winning the U.S. Open titles, 1973–77.

He cared so much for tennis that he pulled no punches when the people in charge deserved scolding—or lauding. This he did from his bully pulpit, the thoughtful, progressive column ("Vantage Point") he wrote as the 1974 founder-publisher of *Tennis Week* magazine. Some called him the "conscience of tennis," which fit well.

Eugene Lytton Scott was born Dec. 28, 1937, at New York, and grew up at St. James, N.Y. He died March 20, 2006, in Rochester, Minnesota. Attending St. Mark's School, Southborough, Mass., he quickly made his athleticism apparent, playing for the varsities in hockey, track, soccer, tennis. After St Mark's came Yale ('60

where he scored letters in hockey, soccer, lacrosse and tennis. Then it was Virginia Law School ('64), and a brief career as a lawyer. In 1967, his big year at Forest Hills, he tended legal duties during mornings in a Manhattan office, then took the train to the tournament.

He was too broad for that, preferring sports to torts, and entered into managing more than 200 tournaments, the most exotic launched in Moscow, 1990, the Kremlin Cup. With one dial phone in a decrepit office, and a lot of patience and gumption, he showed how it was done to amazed natives just shedding communism. Between 1977 and 1989, he ran the highly successful Masters, the men's year-end championships at Madison Square Garden. He wrote 20 books on tennis, helped grass root programs such as the National Junior Tennis League, was a sharp TV commentator, served on countless administrative committees.

A trim 6-footer who easily made friendships across the planet, he ranked in the U.S. Top 10 five years (1962-63-64, 67-68), No. 4 in 1963. He played Davis Cup in 1963 and 1965, and went 4-0, winning three singles and a doubles, playing in two ties. He won a singles and, with Yale teammate Donald Dell, the doubles against Iran to open the 1963 campaign. Since the U.S. won the Cup that year, Gene played a small part, and was a spare in Australia for the final.

In 1966, Gene teamed with Croat Niki Pilic to set a Wimbledon record, longest doubles match (98 games) in beating Cliff Richey and Torben Ulrich, 19-21, 12-10, 6-4, 4-6, 9-7. (It was broken in 2007.)

Ever ahead of the parade he (along with Billie Jean King, Rosie Casals, Clark Graebner) played the U.S. Championships in 1967 with the strange Wilson T-2000 steel rackets that Jimmy Connors would make famous.

"Wood is dead, will soon be gone," Gene predicted. He learned the game on a public court with chain-link nets, but later took some lessons from Elizabeth "Bunny" Ryan, holder of 19 Wimbledon doubles titles between 1914 and 1934. It seems fitting that he joined her in the International Tennis Hall of Fame in 2008.

Eleo Sears

United States (1881–1968)
Hall of Fame—1968

Eleonora Randolph Sears, though of a proper Bostonian background, was noted for her athleticism and vigor. She was an equestrienne, golfer and determined walker (frequently striding the 40 miles between her Boston home and Providence, R.I.), and maintained a trim, healthful figure into old age.

Right-handed Eleo came from a tennis-playing family. Her father, Fred Sears, was one of the first (if not the first) to play tennis in the U.S., with Dr. James Dwight in 1874. Her uncle, Dick Sears, was the original U.S. champion.

Eleo made it to the U.S. singles final in 1912, losing to Mary K. Browne, 6-4, 6-2. But she won four U.S. doubles: two with Hazel Hotchkiss Wightman, 1911 over Dorothy Green-Florence Sutton, 6-4, 4-6, 6-2, and 1915, over Helen Homans McLean-Mrs. George L. Chapman, 10-8, 6-2. Also two with Molla Bjurstedt Mallory, 1916, over Louise Hammond-Edna Wildey, 4-6, 6-2, 10-8, and 1917, over

Phyllis Walsh-Grace Moore LeRoy, 6-2, 6-4. She had a mixed prize, too, 1916, with Willis Davis over Florence Ballin and a famous-name-to-be, Bill Tilden, 6-4, 7-5.

Eleo made the U.S. Top 10 twice: No. 6 in 1914; and No. 3 in 1916. She was born Sept. 28, 1881, in Boston, died March 16, 1968, in Palm Beach, Fla., and entered the Hall of Fame in 1968.

MAJOR TITLES (5)—U.S. doubles, 1911, 15-16-17; U.S. mixed, 1916. **SINGLES RECORD IN THE MAJORS**—Wimbledon (0-2), U.S. (27-14).

Dick Sears

United States (1861–1943)
Hall of Fame—1955

Never beaten in the U.S. Championships, the original singles champ, Richard Dudley Sears, won his first of seven titles in 1881 while a 19-year-old Harvard ('83) student. As one of 24 entries he, a Bostonian, ventured onto the lawn of the Newport (R.I.) Casino in knickerbockers, long wool socks, a necktie and cap, and wielding a slightly lopsided racket (similar to those for court tennis) that weighed 16 ounces.

Beating first-round opponent, Powell, 6-0, 6-2, Dick was off on an 18-match streak that would carry him through the Championships of 1887, after which he retired from the game. Not until the challenge round format was abandoned and 1920-21 champion Bill Tilden beat Zenzo Shimidzu, 6-2, 6-3, 6-1, to reach the 1922 semis (and register a 19th successive win in the Championships), was Sears' record eclipsed.

Sears later recalled the Championships' launching in 1881: "The nets were four-feet at the posts and three-feet at center. This led to a scheme of attack by playing, whenever possible, across court to avoid lifting drives over the highest part of the net at the sidelines. This method just suited me. I had taken up a mild form of volleying, and all I had to do was to tap the balls, as they came over, first to one side and then to the other, running my opponent all over the court."

A few of the players served underhand, though not the right-handed Sears. In the inaugural final, his fifth match, he beat William Glyn, an Englishman who regularly summered at Newport, 6-0, 6-3, 6-2. During his first three championships, Sears lost no sets, concluding the 1883 tournament with a 6-2, 6-0, 9-7, victory over his mentor, and second cousin, Dr. James Dwight.

In that year, the 5-foot-9, 150-pound Sears began to hit a topspin forehand that he'd seen used in England by the originator, Herbert Lawford. Since the challenge round was instituted in 1884, he had to play but one match, against the victor in the all-comers tournament, to retain the title the last four years. Then he lost one set each to Howard Taylor in 1884, 6-0, 1-6, 6-0, 6-2; Godfrey Brinley in 1885, 6-3, 4-6, 6-0, 6-3; and Livingston Beeckman in 1886, 4-6, 6-1, 6-3, 6-4. His last victim, 6-1, 6-3, 6-2, was Henry Slocum.

Those last four years, Dick used a prized racket given to him in England by the all-time Wimbledon champ, Willie Renshaw, and won four singles and doubles titles with it. He and Dwight won the doubles five times together, 1882-83-84, 86-87, and he won once with Joseph Clark, 1885. Sears was the first of the 19-year-olds to conquer the U.S., slightly older than Oliver

Campbell in 1890, and the very youngest, Pete Sampras, in 1990. He was No. 1 in the U.S. in 1885, 1886 and 1887, the first years of national rankings. Scion of a prominent Boston family, he was born there Oct. 16, 1861, and died there April 8, 1943. His older brother, Fred, played with Dwight, possibly the first tennis in the U.S., in 1874, and a younger brother, Philip, was in the U.S. Top 10 five years, 1887-1891—No. 6 in 1888. A cousin, Eleo Sears, is also in the Hall of Fame. After giving up lawn tennis, Sears won the U.S. Court Tennis singles title in 1892. He served as USTA president in 1887 and 1888 and was elected to the Hall of Fame in 1955.

MAJOR TITLES (13)—U.S. singles, 1881-82-83-84-85-86-87; U.S. doubles, 1882-83-84-85-86-87. **SINGLES RECORD IN THE MAJORS**—U.S. (18-0)

Frank Sedgman
Australia (1927—)
Hall of Fame—1979

The beginning of the most oppressive—yet jolly—dynasty in tennis history was in the strokes of Frank Allan Sedgman, the Australian savior of 1950. He wasn't around long, but he got an awful lot done in a hurry.

Australia was drooping in the Davis Cup after World War II, losing four successive finales to the U.S. Then, in 1950, 22-year-old Sedgman, loser of both his final round singles the previous year, startled crowds at Forest Hills and the favored U.S. team by leading the Cup-snatching gang of Capt. Harry Hopman. Australia, winner of a total of two matches in the four previous beatings, got one right away as Sedgman pounced on Tom Brown, 6-0, 8-6, 9-7. Newcomer Ken McGregor beat Ted Schroeder, and Sedgman returned to the court with 31-year-old John Bromwich to ice it over Gardnar Mulloy and Schroeder, 4-6, 6-4, 6-2, 4-6, 6-4. "At last," enthused Bromwich. The Aussies had the Cup, which Brom had helped win 11 years before during Hopman's first tenure.

Sedg's third-day 6-2, 6-2, 6-2, crunching of Schroeder, a holdover from the 1946 victors, put him in the company of an original, Norman Brookes. Brookes, who spurred the first Cup-napping by the lads from Down Under in 1907, was the most recent Aussie to win three matches in a final. That was in 1911.

The next year was considerably harder, the defense at Sydney, but tripling Sedgman made sure the Cup remained in Australia, 3-2. He beat Schroeder on opening day, 6-4, 6-3, 4-6, 6-4, but Mervyn Rose lost to Vic Seixas. Linked to McGregor in a 6-2, 9-7, 6-3 win over Tony Trabert and Schroeder, Sedg paced a 2-1 lead. But Rose lost again to Schroeder, and it was up to Sedgman. It didn't take long to see he was the master of the situation, beating Seixas, 6-4, 6-2, 6-2. A year later, 1952, virtually the same story at Adelaide: three points for Sedgman, Australia beats the U.S., 4-1. Australia was mad about Sedgman for good reason: Three years, three Cups, 9-for-9 in matches, playing the clincher every year.

Those Cup successes were the start of Capt. Hopman's second stewardship under which Australia won the Davis trophy 15 times between 1950 and 1967, a reign admirable not only for the quality of the tennis but the sportsmanhip and jocular nature of the Aussie oppressors.

There was more for Sedgman, the complete three-way player: Singles, doubles and mixed. In 1951, beating Seixas, 6-4, 6-1, 6-1, he became the first of 13 Aussie men to win U.S. singles championships (18 titles in all). Sedg repeated the following year over Miamian Gardnar Mulloy, 6-1, 6-2, 6-3. For three years (1950-51-52) he was the king, with few slips. He first made a rumbling serve-and-volleying noise in 1949 by beating the venerable Bromwich for the Australian title, 6-3, 6-3, 6-2, sealing a Davis Cup position and finishing No. 4 in the world. Then he posted three supreme years without male equal.

Of the 36 events at the four majors, he was in 23 of the finals, winning 19 titles: four singles (Australian 1950, U.S. 1951-52, Wimbledon 1952); eight doubles (Australian 1951-52, French 1951-52, Wimbledon 1951-52, U.S. 1950-51); seven mixed (Australian 1950, French 1951-52, Wimbledon 1951-52, U.S. 1951-52). In 1952, he was in 11 of the 12 finals, and got the title he most wanted: Wimbledon over crafty lefty Jaroslav Drobny, 4-6, 6-2, 6-3, 6-2. A very busy, energetic guy, indeed. Only the French singles eluded him, in the 1952 final lost to Drobny, 6-2, 6-0, 3-6, 6-4. But Frank took Drob on clay, beating him for the Italian title the same spring, 7-5, 6-3, 1-6, 6-4.

Sedgman, an athletic 5-foot-11, 170-pound right-hander, born Oct. 29, 1927, in Mont Albert, Victoria, Australia, was such an acquisitive winner of major titles during the briefest of stretches, 1949-53, that he stands third among all-time male champions with 22 major victories in singles, doubles and mixed, three behind John Newcombe, six behind Roy Emerson.

In 1951, Sedgman and McGregor scored the only Grand Slam in men's doubles by winning all the majors within a calendar year. They came oh-so-close to Slamming again the following year, going all the way to the U.S. final, where it took another Aussie, Merv Rose, allied with Yank Seixas, to barely beat them, 3-6, 10-8, 10-8, 6-8, 8-6. As it was, Frank and Ken won seven straight major doubles, a male record, and Sedg had eight in a row, having taken the U.S. with John Bromwich in 1950. In his last season as an amateur, Sedgman was the last man to make a rare Wimbledon triple, adding the doubles (with McGregor) and mixed (with Doris Hart) to his singles conquest.

Speed, brilliant volleying and a heavy forehand were his chief assets, plus a fighting-though-good-natured spirit.

Jack Kramer, proprietor of the professional tour and its foremost player, enticed Sedgman to become his challenger in 1953, and they played the customary head-to-head tour between the amateur-king-turned-pro-rookie and the incumbent, Kramer, stayed on top, 54-41.

However, Sedgman's share of the gate was $102,000. He was the first male player to earn more than 100 grand in a season.

Sedgman continued to barnstorm with the pros into the 1960s. He was finalist to Pancho Gonzalez for the U.S. Pro singles championship in 1954, 6-3, 9-7, 3-6, 6-2, and won the U.S. Pro doubles with Andres Gimeno in 1961. Twice he won the pros' highest-regarded championship, Wembley at London—1953 over Gonzalez, 6-1, 6-2, 6-2, and 1958 over Tony Trabert, 6-4, 6-3, 6-4. Keeping himself superbly fit, he was able to launch a second professional career in 1974 when promoter Al Bunis formed the Grand Masters tour for ex-champs over 45. Sedgman won the

Grand Masters championship in a season's-end playoff among the top eight players in 1975, 1977 and 1978, and, in this second phase of professionalism, won more than $250,000 over six seasons.

He made the world's Top 10 in 1949 at No. 4 and reached No. 1 in 1951 and 1952. Altogether, he won 36 amateur and pro singles titles, was named to the International Tennis Hall of Fame in 1979, and the Australian Tennis Hall of Fame in 1996.

MAJOR TITLES (22)—Australian singles, 1949-50; Wimbledon singles, 1952; U.S. singles, 1951, 1952; Australian doubles, 1951-52; French doubles, 1951-52; Wimbledon doubles, 1948, 51-52; U.S. doubles, 1950-51; Australian mixed, 1949-50; French mixed, 1951-52; Wimbledon mixed, 1951-52; U.S. mixed, 1951-52. **DAVIS CUP**—1949-50-51-52, 16-3 singles, 9-0 doubles. **SINGLES RECORD IN THE MAJORS**—Australian (19-5), French (13-4), Wimbledon (26-6), U.S. (20-3).

Pancho Segura
Ecuador (1921—)
Hall of Fame—1984

A curious sight was Francisco Olegario "Pancho" Segura when he appeared on the North American scene in 1941, a mite who began to make a big impression with jarring strokes and jovial personality despite seeming physical limitations. He had won his native Ecuadorian title at 17 in 1938 along with various other Latin American titles, and presently was on his way to big-time tennis in the U.S., riding a tennis scholarship at the University of Miami where his coach was Gardnar Mulloy, his Hall of Fame colleague-to-be. "Mulloy saved me. I didn't have any money, and spoke no English, but he helped me with everything," Segura recalls.

A big smile and a yen for the battle offset what appeared, at first appraisal, to be disadvantages: An unorthodox two-fisted forehand, flimsy-looking bowed legs and a 5-foot-8 frame. Yet his footwork was admirable. He was quick, nimble, extremely effective. By 1942, he had a No. 4 U.S. ranking, and would be the ever-welcome centerpiece at depleted homefront tournaments during World War II, his status as an alien keeping him out of uniform. Over the 1943-45 period, he was the big winner, grabbing 15 of 30 tournaments (7 of 10 in 1943) and 107 of 122 matches. He could never realize his dream of conquering the U.S. at Forest Hills, coming as close as the semis, 1942—45, and the quarters in 1946-47.

Segura was born June 20, 1921, in Guayaquil, Ecuador and was raised there. A childhood attack of rickets deformed his legs but his will was strong, and he drove himself to play tennis well, even though he was so weak at first that he had to grip the racket with both hands. A right-hander, he was likely the first to utilize a two-fisted forehand.

At Miami, he won the National Intercollegiate singles in 1943-44-45, the only man since Malcolm Chace to take three straight—for Brown in 1893, and Yale in 1894-95. Pancho won the U.S. Indoor title of 1946 and the U.S. Clay Court of 1944 and was a member of the U.S. Top 10 six times, No. 3 in 1943-44-45.

But his best days were ahead of him, as a professional. After settling in the U.S., he left the amateurs in 1947, signing on to play mostly the secondary matches on the strung-out worldwide tour of one-nighters. Unfortunately for Segura, he was out of the limelight once he became a professional. While he lost to Aussie Dinny Pails, 41-31 at their end of his first tour (Jack Kramer and Pancho Gonzalez the headliners), he would overcome Frank Parker and Ken McGregor in their series. Sharpening his strokes and tactics and becoming one of the great players, he received little recognition. Kramer and Gonzalez were the stars, but Segura was making his mark in a small circle as a shrewd strategist, a cunning lobber and a killer with that (then) strange forehand.

And Pancho was becoming dangerous for anybody. He prizes a 6-4, 8-10, 1-6, 6-4, 6-3 victory over world-best Kramer in the semis of the U.S. Pro of 1950, a tourney he won over Frank Kovacs, forcing Kovacs to surrender with cramps. That earned Segura a tour against Kramer the following year, but Jack was still too strong, 64-28. Nevertheless, short Pancho was long on endurance. Again he won the U.S. Pro in 1951-52, both times over Gonzalez, seven years his junior—6-3, 6-4, 6-2; and 3-6, 6-4, 3-6, 6-4, 6-0. He then lost the finals to Gonzalez, 1955-56-57, as well as the final of the pros' biggie, Wembley at London, to Gonzalez in 1951, 6-2, 6-2, 2-6, 6-4. There he made the final three more times, 1957, 1959-60, losing to 25-year-old Ken Rosewall in 1960. Segura was 39, and seven years later, he beat Rosewall during a tournament at Binghamton, N.Y. At 41, he lost his last U.S. Pro final, to Butch Buchholz, 6-4, 6-3, 6-4, in 1962. Pancho also won the U.S. Pro doubles with Kramer in 1948 and 1955, and Gonzalez in 1958.

He toured for more than two decades and stands as one of the prominent figures in the history of the pros' days in the wilderness, prior to Open tennis. Hardy and good-natured, Segura was a favorite with crowds. He could always smile and crack a joke, yet was thoroughly professional and a constant competitor. He never made big money. Open tennis arrived too late for him, but he entered the doubles of the first open Wimbledon in 1968 with Alex Olmedo, and in the second round, they won the longest doubles match of Wimbledon's Open era, 94 games, over Abe Segal and Gordon Forbes, 32-30, 5-7, 6-4, 6-4. The 62-game set was the longest ever at Wimbledon.

When his playing career ended, he became one of the best teaching pros, settling in Southern California, and making his mark as one of the sharpest minds in the game. He was instrumental in Jimmy Connors' development, and was elected to the Hall of Fame in 1984.

U.S. TITLES (14)—Intercollegiate singles, 1943, 1994, 1945; Indoor singles, 1946; Clay Court singles, 1944; Pro singles, 1950, 1951, 1952: Clay Court doubles, 1944, 1945 with Bill Talbert; Pro doubles, 1948, 1955 with Jack Kramer; 1954, 1958 with Pancho Gonzalez. **SINGLES RECORD IN THE MAJORS**—French (2-1), Wimbledon (2-2), U.S. (21-7).

Vic Seixas
United States (1923—)
Hall of Fame—1971

When Vic Seixas played—and won—the fifth-longest singles match in tennis history, he was 42. That was in 1966 as Vic went 94

games to beat a 22-year-old Australian Davis Cupper, Bill Bowrey, 32-34, 6-4, 10-8, during the Pennsylvania Grass Championships at Philadelphia. It took nearly four hours.

Elias Victor Seixas, Jr., born Aug 30, 1923, in Philadelphia, played the U.S. Championships at Forest Hills a record 28 times between 1940 and 1969, winning the singles in 1954 over Aussie Rex Hartwig, 3-6, 6-2, 6-4, 6-4. He played more Davis Cup matches than any other American, until John McEnroe, winning 38 of 55 singles and doubles encounters during his seven years on the team between 1951 and 1957. Thirteen times he was ranked in the Top 10 in the U.S. between 1942 and 1966, setting an American longevity record of a 24-year span between his first and last entries (later equaled by Pancho Gonzalez, 1948-72). Vic was No. 1 in 1951, 54, 57; No. 2 in 1952-53, 55.

In 1953, when Seixas won the Wimbledon singles over Kurt Nielsen, 9-7, 6-3, 6-4, and led the U.S. to the Davis Cup final, he was No. 3, high point of his eight years in the world's Top 10 between 1950 and 1957. He was No. 4 in 1951, 54-55-56.

Although he helped the U.S. attain the finale every year he played Davis Cup, the team could win only once, the zenith 1954 when he and Tony Trabert were victorious. After Trabert opened with a win over Lew Hoad, Seixas followed with a stunning 8-6, 6-8, 6-4, 6-3, triumph over his nemesis, Ken Rosewall. That put the U.S. ahead 2-0 on the first day, and Seixas and Trabert clinched the Cup the following day with a doubles victory over Hoad and Rex Hartwig, 6-2, 4-6, 6-2, 10-8, before an outdoor record crowd of 25,578 at Sydney.

Seixas won 15 major titles in singles, doubles and mixed, setting a Wimbledon record by winning the mixed four successive years, 1953, 1954, 1955 with Doris Hart, and 1956 with Shirley Fry.

Among his 13 U.S. titles were the Clay Court singles in 1953, over Ham Richardson, 6-2, 6-4, 6-3, and 1957, 1-6, 8-6, 6-1, 6-3, over Herbie Flam. He also won the Hard Court doubles (with Ted Schroeder) in 1948, and the Indoor doubles (with Trabert) in 1955, making Seixas one of three men to win national titles on all four surfaces. In 1971 he was named to the Hall of Fame.

The 6-foot-1, 180-pound, right-handed Seixas was an attacker who won more on determination and conditioning than on outstanding form. His volleying was exceptional, and he had an excellent match temperament, but a thrashing topspin forehand and sliced backhand were utilitarian. His career was interrupted for three years by World War II, during which he served as a pilot in the U.S. Army Air Force. He graduated from the University of North Carolina. Seixas was one of the few extraordinary amateurs who did not join the pro tour, winning 56 singles titles. Eventually, though, after the age of 50, he did become a pro to compete on the Grand Masters circuit.

MAJOR TITLES (15)—Wimbledon singles, 1953; U.S. singles, 1954; French doubles, 1954-1955; U.S. doubles, 1952, 1954; Australian doubles, 1955: French mixed, 1953; Wimbledon mixed, 1953, 1954, 1955, 1956; U.S. mixed. 1953, 1954, 1955. **OTHER U.S. TITLES** (7)—Clay Court singles, 1953, 1957; Clay Court doubles, 1949, with Sam Match; 1954, with Tony Trabert; Hard Court doubles, 1948, with Ted Schroeder; Indoor doubles, 1955, with Trabert; 1956, with Sam Giammalva. **DAVIS CUP** (As player)—1951, 1952, 1953, 1954, 1955, 1956, 1957, 24-12 singles, 14-5 doubles.

SINGLES RECORD IN THE MAJORS—Australian (4-2), French (17-4), Wimbledon (31-8), U.S. (74-26).

Monica Seles
United States (1973–)
Hall of Fame—2009

How could anybody stop her? An all-time prodigy, a unique No. 1 with her double-barrelled fusillades—both hands on both sides—Monica Seles was a 19-year-old tearing up tennis until that fateful day in Hamburg, April 30, 1993. An allegedly demented German spectator, Guenther Parche, stopped her, struck her down with a knife in the back as she sat beside the court on a changeover.

The quarterfinal match against Maggie Maleeva ended at that abrupt moment, and so did tennis for a kid who seemed destined to be the greatest of all. She had won eight majors (three French, three Australian, two U.S.). After taking the U.S. of 1992 over Arantxa Sanchez Vicario, 6-3, 6-3, she was the youngest ever to hold seven of them (18 years, eight months), undercutting Maureen Connolly by three months. (Curiously, Connolly, who wound up with nine, had been cut off, too, as a teenager, in a traffic accident.) Breaking Steffi Graf's four-year hold on the No. 1 ranking in 1991, Seles had held off Steffi in her last major appearance before her stabbing, to win the Australian, 4-6, 6-3, 6-2.

But putative assassin Parche intervened, claiming he knifed Seles to restore Graf to preeminence, a story the Seles family doubted. It was 28 months before Monica was seen on court again. The psychological damage had been more severe than the physical. She, like everybody else—except, apparently, the judge in Parche's trial and re-trial—wondered why he was not incarcerated. "He's still out there walking the streets," she worried.

Attempting to put it behind her, Monica re-emerged in August 1995, beating Martina Navratilova in an exhibition at Atlantic City, content with the co-No. 1 ranking with Graf granted her by the WTA. Then acting as though nothing had changed, she was back in business—electrifyingly so. Opponents at the Canadian Open in Toronto acted as though they were seeing a ghost. They were—a ghost of championships past—as she marched to the title on a loss of no sets, 12 games in five matches, ripping Amanda Coetzer in the final, 6-0, 6-1.

On to the US Open, where she'd won 14 straight matches. The opposition continued to melt until the final, where Graf ended the streak at 20, fitter in the third set, 7-6 (8-6), 0-6, 6-3. At 6-5 in the tie-breaker, Monica groused at a call of fault on her bid—a fraction wide—for a set-point ace. She lost her composure momentarily, and may have missed the title by a smidgen of an inch.

Her return to Australia, where she'd never been beaten, was triumphant. She won Sydney from match point down over Lindsay Davenport, 4-6, 7-6 (9-7), 6-3, then the Open (Graf was absent) over Anke Huber, 6-4, 6-1, a ninth major title. However, after that, the 1996 season didn't go as well as she and her fans had hoped. Knee and shoulder injuries were bothersome. Her conditioning was suspect; she pulled out of several tourneys. Though she did win three more tournaments and help the U.S. regain the Federation Cup, there was disappointment at the French and Wimbledon. Jana Novotna clipped her Paris streak of 25 in the quarters,

7-6 (9-7), 6-3. More painful perhaps was losing the last four games and a second-rounder at the Big W to an unknown Slovak, No. 59 Katerina Studenikova, 7-5, 5-7, 6-4. "I'm playing too defensively, not attacking the ball the way I used to," Monica said accurately. She was a finalist again at the U.S. Open but was pushed around by a charged-up Graf whose superior quickness showed, 7-5, 6-4.

Seles, a left-hander who has grown to nearly six feet, was born Dec. 2, 1973, of Serbo-Hungarian parentage, at Novi Sad in what was then Yugoslavia. Getting her started, her father, Karolj Seles, a professional cartoonist and keen student of the game, drew faces on the balls for her to hit. He and her mother, Esther, felt her future lay in the United States They moved to Nick Bollettieri's Tennis Academy at Bradenton, Fla., in 1986 when Monica was 12, and headmaster Nick oversaw her early development. Papa took over the coaching again at their Sarasota residence until his death in 1998. Monica became a U.S. citizen in 1995.

Monica sounded the alarm in 1989 as a 15-year-old by spoiling the last final of Chris Everet's illustrious career in. Houston, 3-6, 6-1, 6-4. "She's the next," exulted an overwhelmed witness, historian Ted Tinling. Soon after, "Moanin' Monica" took her bubbly grimacing-and-grunting act to Roland Garros to show Parisians noisy tennis nouvelle: rip-roaring groundies, bludgeoned from. anywhere in a baseball switch-hitting style (the backhand crosshanded). She constantly went for winners, seemingly off-balance and out-of-position but buoyed by excellent footwork and anticipation. Graf barely escaped in the semis. But she wouldn't a year later, in the final, 7-6 (8-6), 6-4. Seles became a major player. She bounded into the world's Top 10 in 1989 (No. 6) and was there through 2002, 13 years, (except for non- ranked 1994): No. 2 in 1990; No. 1 in 1991-92; No. 8 in 1993; co-No. 1 in 1995; co-No. 2 in 1996; No. 5 in 1997; No. 6 in 1998; No. 4 in 1999-2000; No. 10 in 2001; No. 7 in 2002.

For two-and-a-half years Monica was nearly invincible as the titles piled up and her ball-impacting shriek—"Uhh-eee!"—was heard across the globe. She charmed the public with girlish elan and mystified people by vanishing before Wimbledon in 1991 and then resurfacing to win the U.S. Open. She may have been psyched out of a 1992 Grand Slam when complaints about the grunting from Wimbledon victims, Nathalie Tauziat and Martina Navratilova, (leading to a warning from the referee) muted her in the final, where she was destroyed by Graf, 6-2, 6-1. Still, she was the first to win three majors in successive years since Margaret Court (three and four, 1969-70), a feat equaled by Graf in 1995-96. Among her souvenirs was the 1991 U.S. final, when at age 17, she defeated Navratilova, 34, a singular generation gapper, 7-6 (9-7), 6-1. Her brightest seasons of 10 singles titles each were 1991 (winning 74 of 80 matches) and 1992 (70 of 75).

At the close of 2003, after 12 pro seasons, and portions of two others, she had played 177 tournaments and won 53 singles titles with a 595-122 won-loss record (.836); 180-31 in the majors (.861). She has also won six doubles titles with a 89-45 won-loss record and earned $14,891,762 in prize money. She won a singles bronze at the 2000 Olympics, and won her last title, Madrid over Chanda Rubin 6-4, 6-2, in 2002. She was inactive after 2003, and announced her retirement in 2008. An exemplary figure who has coped well with much adversity, including several injuries, she was not the player she might have been, yet is clearly, constantly upbeat, saying, "Tennis will never end for me because I love it so much. When my professional career is over I will continue to play all my life." Monica has put an indelible signature on the game with her style, persona and championships, a woman doubtless on a journey to the Hall of Fame.

MAJOR TITLES (9)—Australian singles, 1991, 1992, 1993, 1996; French singles, 1990, 1991, 1992; US. singles, 1991, 1992. **FEDERATION CUP**—1995-96, 1998, 1999, 2000, 2002 **SINGLES RECORD IN THE MAJORS**— Australian (43-4), French (54-8), Wimbledon (30-9), U.S. (54-10).

Frank Shields
United States (1909–1975)
Hall of Fame—1964

A dashing, handsome performer who spent some time in Hollywood in bit movie roles, unseeded Francis Xavier Shields was the only Wimbledon finalist to lose without going onto the court. Frank defaulted the 1931 final to Sidney Wood beforehand, sidelined by an ankle injury suffered in the semis when he beat Jean Borotra, the 1924 and 1926 champ, 7-5, 3-6, 6-4, 6-4. It wasn't Frank's idea to default. He wanted to play, but was ordered by the U.S. Davis Cup committee to withdraw, in order to be ready for the Cup semifinal against Britain the following weekend. As an amateur, Frank had to abide by the USTA directive. (How times have changed.) The U.S. lost to Britain anyway, 3-2, Shields stopped by Bunny Austin in the decisive fifth match, 8-6, 6-3, 7-5.

The 6-foot-3 right-hander was a came-close guy. As the No. 11 seed, in his first major final, the U.S. of 1930, he had a shot at Johnny Doeg but couldn't connect on a set point against Doeg's rugged lefty serve at 13-14 in the deciding set and lost, 10-8, 1-6, 6-4, 16-14—the longest concluding set of a major singles final. In 1928, an 18-year-old No. 7 seed, he got to the U.S. semis, losing to the champ, Henri Cochet, 6-2, 8-6, 6-4. In 1933, again in the semis as the No. 2 seed, he fell to the top foreign-seeded Wimbledon champ Jack Crawford, 7-5, 6-4, 6-3. A year later at Wimbledon, he came closer as a semifinalist but couldn't hold Crawford down, 2-6, 4-6, 6-4, 6-3, 6-4.

Between 1928 and 1945, he was ranked eight times in the U.S. Top 10, No. 1 in 1933, No. 2 in 1930. Frank made the world's Top 10 five years: No. 5 in 1930-31; No. 7 in 1933, 35; No. 8 in 1934. He was a U.S. Davis Cupper in 1931, 1932 and 1934, and was non-playing captain in 1951 when the team won four series, then lost the finale in Australia, 3-2. In 1934, he sent the U.S. into the finale (a 4-1 loss to Britain) by winning the decisive fifth match, 6-4, 6-2, 6-4, over Viv McGrath to clinch a 3-2 victory over Australia at Wimbledon. It was the only time the U.S. came back from 0-2 to win a Cup series.

Shields was born in New York Nov. 18, 1909, and died there Aug. 19, 1975. Movie and television actress Brooke Shields is his granddaughter.

DAVIS CUP—1931, 1932, 1934, 16-6 singles, 3-0 doubles. **SINGLES RECORD IN THE MAJORS**—French (2-1), Wimbledon (14-3), U.S. (35-17)

Pam Shriver

United States (1962—)
Hall of Fame—2002

Few have made as spectacular a debut in a major championship as 16-year-old Pamela Howard Shriver at the U.S. Open in 1978. A tall schoolgirl amateur with a big racket, big ambition, she had no inhibitions about charging the net and bringing down players such as the Wimbledon champion, Martina Navratilova. She was the first to go to the final in her first U.S. since the champ of 1937, Chilean Anita Lizana.

Pam and Martina—voracious volleyers—would join forces to inscribe the greatest doubles numbers in the history of the female game: A Grand Slam in 1984, 20 major championships, a 109-match winning streak, 79 titles together.

Everything was new in 1978—the USTA National Tennis Center complex in Flushing, hard courts, the oversized Prince racket in her right hand and the 6-foot kid with short curly hair and dimples who was called the "Great Whomping Crane." Ten years before, Arthur Ashe had been the lone amateur to win the Open. Pam, seeded No. 16, the greenest ever to attain the title round (five months younger than 1979 champ Tracy Austin), came within one victory of equaling Ashe, after beating top-seeded Navratilova in the semis, 7-6 (7-5), 7-6 (7-3), a mammoth upset. However, Chris Evert fought off her fast-forward forays in the final, 7-5, 6-4. Lustrous as her 20-year career was, containing 21 singles and 94 doubles titles (one of five women winning more than 100 overall), a position in the world's Top 10 nine times and an Olympic gold medal, Pam never made it to the singles final of a major again.

But she was no stranger to the winners' circle in the highest doubles neighborhoods. Besides the 20 with Navratilova, she won two other majors: the U.S. with Natalia Zvereva in 1991 and the French mixed with Emilio Sanchez in 1987. She and Martina also won the season-ending WTA championship at Madison Square Garden a record 10 times between 1981 and 1991.

An effervescent personality, sharp-witted, Pam was in her element at press conferences as well as on the court, and now makes her mark as a tennis TV commentator. Not an exceptional athlete—"I ran like a duck"—she made up for that with smarts and heart. A preppy in Lutherville, Md., she had her sights on college "with no thought to playing tennis for a living." But one of the old Aussie gang, teaching pro Don Candy, giving her lessons, saw the future when she was 14, and counseled her and her parents to be prepared for everyone's life to change. He was convinced, "She'll make it as a career."

So she did. "After that first Open everything moved so fast. I turned pro in '79. No college plans," she recalls. "I was out in the rough working women's world. I'm glad, but it took a while for me to catch up with myself, to handle the attention, the publicity, travel and injuries."

It was a "startling" phone call from Navratilova in 1980 that would propel her upward among the game's goddesses. "She asked me to be her doubles partner. I couldn't believe it."

They went together like ice cream and cake, Pam in the right court (though occasionally they switched). Their 20 majors between 1981 and 1989 caught up with Margaret Osborne duPont and Louise Brough's record total amassed between 1942

and 1957. First was Wimbledon, 1981, over Anne Smith and Kathy Jordan, 6-3, 7-6 (8-6) where they also ruled in 1982-83-84, 1986. The remainder: Australian, 1982-83-84-85, (no tourney in 1986), 1987-88-89; French, 1984-85, 87-88; U.S., 1983-84, 86-87. They lost two finals, both in 1985, the U.S. and Wimbledon, the latter to Kathy Jordan and Liz Sayers Smylie, 5-7, 6-3, 6-4, concluding their 109-match procession that included 22 wins during their 1984 Slam. Within the streak they won eight successive majors.

Pam, whose career won-loss record in singles was 625-270, treasures most the two wins over Navratilova at the U.S.—the previously mentioned 1978 win and in 1982 (7-6 (7-5), 6-2)—and victories over Chris Evert in the Canadian Open semis of 1987, and Steffi Graf at Madison Square Garden in the season-ending Virginia Slims Championships of 1988, 7-6 (7-3), 7-5. "I was 0-18 against Chrissie before that Canadian win, and I beat Zina Garrison in the final [6-4, 6-1], my biggest title. At the Garden in '88, where I also beat Evert (7-5, 6-4). I was never more focused. It was Steffi's Grand Slam and gold medal year. But I fell to Gabriela Sabatini (7-5, 6-2, 6-2) in the final."

Probably her most emotional triumph was the Olympic gold medal final in Seoul, allied with Garrison in a tremendous battle with Czechs Helena Sukova and Jana Novotna. Winning, 4-6, 6-2, 10-8, Pam and Zina clung to each other weeping elatedly.

She was in the world's Top 10 from 1980 to 1989, reaching No. 4 three times (1983, 1984, 1985) and had career winnings $5,460,566. Her career doubles won-loss record was 622-122. Born July 4, 1962, at Baltimore, she was married to Australian actor and former James "007" Bond George Lazenby, and has three children. She was raised to the Hall in 2002, delighted to return to Newport's Casino where she won two of her singles titles (1986-87), and one doubles on the historic lawn.

MAJOR TITLES (21)—Australian doubles, 1982-83-84-85, 87-88-89; French doubles, 1984-1985, 87, 89; Wimbledon doubles, 1981-82-83-84, 86; U.S. doubles, 1983-84, 86-87, 91. **FEDERATION CUP**—1986-87, 89, 92, 4-0 singles, 14-1 doubles. **SINGLES RECORD IN THE MAJORS**—Australian (31-16), French (2-2), Wimbledon (40-16), U.S. (44-18).

Henry Slocum

United States (1862–1949)
Hall of Fame—1955

A football and tennis player at Yale, Henry Warner Slocum played in the first Intercollegiate Championships, in 1883, as partner of the great footballer, Walter Camp. He took time out from his New York law practice to refine his tennis (to the disapproval of his father), and on his fourth try at the U.S. title in Newport, 1887, he beat Howard Taylor, 12-10, 7-5, 6-4, in the all-comers final, only to become Dick Sears' last championship victim in the challenge round, 6-1, 6-3, 6-2.

But in 1888 he trained harder, and the players showed, he said, "more than the usual keenness" because Sears had announced he wouldn't defend. In the all-comers final, to decide the championship, Slocum, a 5-foot-10, 150-pound right-hander, was sharper against the quick 5-foot-4 Taylor, and became the second champion of the U.S., 6-4, 6-1, 6-0. He successfully defended in 1889 over lefty Quincy Shaw, 6-3, 6-1, 4-6, 6-2.

That year, he and Taylor beat Valentine Hall and Oliver Campbell for the doubles crown, 6-1, 6-3, 6-2. It was Slocum's third time in the doubles final. He lost in 1885 with Percy Knapp and 1887 with Ollie Taylor. But Slocum, 28, was overtaken by collegian Campbell, 19, in the 1890 challenge round, 6-2, 4-6, 6-3, 6-1.

Slocum had realized his tennis ambitions, and immersed himself in law. But he returned to Newport for an 1892 cameo, registering one of the Charnpionships' rare triple bagels—6-0, 6-0, 6-0—over W. N. Ryerson. He was back again 11 years later to play nine times between 1903 and 1913 when he made his last appearance, at 51, beating future World War I flying hero and Massachusetts Congressman Larry Curtis, 6-3, 6-2, 6-3, and losing to future finalist (1921), 24-year-old Wallace Johnson, 6-1, 6-3, 6-3. For his U.S. career, covering 29 years (1884-1913), the remarkably durable Slocum had a 26-14 singles record. In the 1888 quarters, he gave the tennis godfather, James Dwight, 36, his last singles defeat, 4-6, 6-3, 6-0, 6-2. Five straight years, from 1886, he was in the U.S. Top 10, No. 1 in 1888 and 1889. Slocum was born May 28, 1862, died Jan. 22, 1949, and entered the Hall of Fame in 1955. He was president of the USTA, 1892-93.

MAJOR TITLES (3)—U.S. singles, 1888-89; U.S. doubles, 1889. **SINGLES RECORD IN THE MAJORS**—U.S. (26-14).

Stan Smith
United States (1946—)
Hall of Fame—1987

One of the great Davis Cup competitors, Stan Smith added the U.S. (1971) and Wimbledon (1972) titles to his laurels, and, with Bob Lutz, was part of one of the preeminent doubles teams. Smith, who overcame teenage awkwardness to become a feared 6-foot-3 foe with crashing serves and volleys, may have hit his zenith on alien clay. That was in Bucharest in 1972 as the U.S. won a fifth consecutive Cup, and he supplied the clinching victory—the insuperable third point—for a fifth time. That's a Davis Cup record to which he added in 1979, with Lutz, in the 5-0 victory over Italy at San Francisco.

Stan was in on seven Cup-settling victories (1968-69-70-71-72, 78-79), tying him with Bill Tilden (1920-26) for a U.S. high. He also had a smaller share of an eighth Cup in 1981, when he and Lutz took a quarterfinal doubles at Flushing Meadows over Czechs Ivan Lendl and Tom Smid, 9-7, 6-3, 6-2. That was the Cup adieu for Stan and Bob.

A notable sportsman, he had to "concentrate so hard I got a headache," he said after the three-day ordeal at the hands of a loud partisan crowd and overly patriotic line judges in Bucharest. It was an extended, rocky campaign during which Smith won seven of eight singles and, with Erik van Dillen, all five doubles. Stan scored the clinching point in each of five series and nailed down two of the most dramatic singles victories ever by an American in the finale. Romania, loser to the U.S. in the 1969 and 1971 showdowns, appeared the favorite on home earth, but Smith shocked U.S. Open champ Ilie Nastase on the slow court to lead off, 11-9, 6-2, 6-3, and then out-battled the sly, combative Ion Tiriac in a tense five-set struggle, 4-6, 6-2, 6-4, 2-6, 6-0.

Aware that he had to hit outright winners well away from the lines to make sure of the points, Smith did just that to storm through a last-set bagel and send the U.S. safely ahead, 3-1, in the 3-2 victory.

Born Dec. 14, 1946, in Pasadena, Calif., he grew up there and was an All-American at the University of Southern California, where he won the U.S. Intercollegiate singles (1968) and, with Lutz, doubles in 1967 and 1968.

During an 11-year Davis Cup career that began in 1968, embracing 24 engagements, he was on the winning side 22 times, and 16 times provided the clinching point: three times in singles, 13 times in doubles (nine with Lutz, four with van Dillen). He and Lutz won 13 of 14 Cup matches together. As the U.S. ran up a record Cup streak of 17 victories from 1968 to the finale of 1973, Smith was involved in 14, the clincher in 12.

His 1972 Wimbledon triumph over Nastase, 4-6, 6-3, 6-3, 4-6, 7-5, was one of the outstanding finals, and his 1971 defeat of Jan Kodes at Forest Hills, 3-6, 6-3, 6-2, 7-6 (5-3), was the first U.S. final to conclude in a tie-breaker. Smith and Lutz won the U.S. doubles four times and the Australian once (1970) and the U.S. doubles four times (1968, 1974, 1978, 1980). In a career spanning the amateur and Open eras, he was one of five centurions, winning at least 100 pro titles overall in singles and doubles. Stan hit the century with 39 singles, 61 doubles, and won $1,774,881 career prize money. Eleven times between 1967 and 1980, he was in the U.S. Top 10, No. 1 four years (1969, 71-72-73). Six straight times from 1970 he was in the world's Top 10, No. 1 in 1972.

MAJOR TITLES (7)—Wimbledon singles, 1972; U.S. singles, 1971; Australian doubles, 1970; U.S. doubles, 1968, 74, 78, 80. **OTHER U.S. TITLES** (15)—Indoor singles, 1972; Indoor doubles, 1966, 69, with Lutz; 1970, with Arthur Ashe; Clay Court doubles, 1968, with Lutz; Hard Court singles, 1966-67-68; Hard Court doubles, 1966, with Lutz; Pro doubles, 1973, with Erik van Dillen; 1974, 1977, with Lutz; Intercollegiate singles, 1968; Intercollegiate doubles, 1967-68, with Lutz. **DAVIS CUP**—1968-69-70-71-72-73, 75, 77, 79, 81, 15-5 singles, 20-3 doubles. **SINGLES RECORD IN THE MAJORS**—Australian (5-3), French (23-9), Wimbledon (45-17). U.S. (39-19).

Margaret Smith Court
Australia (1942—)
Hall of Fame—1979

For sheer strength of performance and accomplishment there has never been a tennis player to match Margaret Smith Court. As the most prolific winner of major championships, she rolled up 62 titles in singles, doubles and mixed doubles between 1960 and 1975, and took the Australian, French, Wimbledon and U.S. singles all within 1970 for the second female Grand Slam. She is the only player to achieve a Slam in doubles as well as in singles: Margaret and fellow Aussie Ken Fletcher won the four titles in mixed in 1963.

Her closest rivals statistically are not close: Martina Navratilova with 59 majors, and Roy Emerson heading the men with 28. Court has 24 alone in singles, two ahead of Steffi Graf.

From the country town of Albury in New South Wales, where she was born July 16, 1942, Margaret was one of the first Australian notables to be developed outside of the principal cities. Tall

and gangling, nearly six feet, she worked hard in the gym and on the road, as well as on court, to attain coordination and marshal her prodigious strength. She was self-made through determination and training. Her power and incredible reach ("I call her The Arm," said rival Billie Jean King) first paid off and called international attention to her when she won the Australian singles at 18 in 1960, 7-5, 6-2, over countrywoman Jan Lehane. It was the first of her record 11 conquests of her homeland, the first seven in a row.

In 1961, she traveled abroad for the first time and played in her first Wimbledon final, the doubles that she and Lehane lost to Karen Hantze and budding star, Billie Jean.

Margaret was to win three Wimbledon, five French, and five U.S. singles championships, and the greatest of those victories was probably the 1970 Wimbledon final. In considerable pain with a sprained ankle, she held off Billie Jean, 14-12, 11-9, in possibly the finest of female finals there, and certainly the longest in games, 46 (two more than the Suzanne Lenglen-Dorothea Chambers recorded in 1919).

She retired briefly upon marrying Barry Court in 1967, but was soon back on the trail of championships. Margaret was remarkable in that she continued to win major titles, such as the U.S. in 1973, after the birth of her first of three children—the fifth of six women to do so—and was still competing at age 34 in 1977. She was shy and soft-spoken. Late in her career, she became a lay minister.

Court was primarily an attacker, basing her game on a heavy serve and volley, and relying on athleticism and endurance. She could conquer with ground strokes, though, as she demonstrated in stopping clay court terror Chris Evert in the splendid French final of 1973, 6-7 (5-7), 7-6 (8-6), 6-4. Sometimes Court fell prey to nerves, as in her 1971 Wimbledon final defeat by the crowd's favorite, Evonne Goolagong; or the bizarre televised challenge by 55-year-old Bobby Riggs in 1973, which she lost implausibly and badly. She couldn't reach the inspirational heights of her chief foe, King, but held a lifetime edge over Billie Jean, 22-10.

Her Grand Slam year of 1970 makes those of Maureen Connolly, 1953 (12 tournaments), and Steffi Graf, 1988 (14 tournaments), seem almost leisurely. Court won 21 of 27 tournaments on a 104-6 match record, earning $14,800 for the four titles while Graf's prize money take for the four was $877,724. Connolly was an amateur, and certainly several of Court's best years were as such during an 18-year career. As an amateur, she had such years as 1962 (winning 13 of 15 tournaments on a 67-2 match record) and 1964 (13 of 16 on 67-2, including à 39-match winning streak).

She won 92 pro singles titles, had her last sensational season in 1973, winning 18 of 25 tourneys on 102-6, among them the Australian, French and U.S. Altogether, amateur and pro, she won a whopping 194 singles titles, almost beyond imagination. Representing Australia six times in the Federation Cup team competition, she played in the first in 1963 (a final-round defeat by the U.S.), spearheaded Cup victories in 1964-65, 68, 71, and was undefeated in 22 singles.

Tapped for the Hall of Fame in 1979, Court was born a left-hander. She was transformed to a right-handed player (like two other Famers, Maureen Connolly and Ken Rosewall), as frequently happened in that era. She had the best two-season run

in history, 1969-70, with seven majors, missing out only at Wimbledon, 1969, where she lost in the semis to champion Ann Jones, 10-12, 6-3, 6-2. That defeat, as well as a first-round loss at Wimbledon to King in 1962, 1-6, 6-3, 7-5, a final-round loss to Lesley Turner, 6-3, 6-4 at the French in 1965, and a semifinal loss at Wimbledon to Evert, 6-1, 1-6, 6-1 in 1973—her only major losses those years—may have cost her four additional Grand Slams.

She scored triples (singles, doubles, mixed titles) at the Australian in 1963 and Wimbledon and the U.S. in 1970. She won her first major, the Australian singles, in 1960 over Lehane 7-5, 6-2, and last, the U.S. doubles, in 1975, with Virginia Wade over Rosie Casals and King, 7-5, 2-6, 7-6 (7-5). Between 1961 and 1975, she was in the world's. Top 10 for 13 years, No. 1 seven times: 1962-63-64-65, 1969-70, 1973), two behind Helen Wills Moody's record, one behind Steffi Graf. Her career, overlapping the amateur and Open eras, yielded $550,000 in prize money.

MAJOR TITLES (62)—Australian singles, 1960-61-62-63-64-65-66, 69-70-71, 73; French singles, 1962, 64, 69-70, 73; Wimbledon singles, 1963, 65, 70; U.S. singles, 1962, 65, 69-70, 73; Australian doubles, 1961-62-63, 65, 69-70-71, 73; French doubles, 1964-65-66, 73; Wimbledon doubles, 1964, 69; U.S. doubles, 1963, 68, 70, 73, 75; Australian mixed, 1963-64; French mixed, 1963-64-65, 69; Wimbledon mixed, 1963, 65-66, 68, 75; U.S. mixed, 1961-62-63-64-65, 69-70, 72. **FEDERATION CUP**—1963-64-65, 68-69, 71, 22-0 singles, 15-5 doubles. **SINGLES RECORDS IN THE MAJORS**—Australian (60-3), French (20-1), Wimbledon (51-9), U.S. (51-6)

Fred Stolle
Australia (1938—)
Hall of Fame—1985

A loose-limbed, slender 6-foot-3 blond, Frederick Sydney Stolle had his Wimbledon singles frustrations, but overflowed with success everywhere else as one of the overpowering phalanx of Aussies in the 1960s and 1970s. Known as "Fiery Fred" or "Fiery" to his teammates for his outspoken competitiveness, he became also known as the "Old Hacker" at the U.S. Championships of 1966. A proven grass court player for some time, member of winning Australian Davis Cup teams, and thrice Wimbledon runner-up (1963, 1964, 1965), he was outraged on arriving at Forest Hills, fresh from winning the German title, to find himself unseeded.

"I guess they think I'm just an old hacker," said he, almost 28. Then he proceeded to win the title, the second unseeded man to do so, over unseeded John Newcombe, 4-6, 12-10, 6-3, 6-4, chortling, "Well, I guess the Old Hacker can still play a bit." (Unseeded champions Mal Anderson had won in 1957, Andre Agassi, in 1994).

He had won the French in 1965, over teammate Tony Roche, 3-6, 6-0, 6-2, 6-3, showing that he could be patient at the baseline, too, although his strengths were a high-velocity serve, stinging volleys and a splendid backhand. These paid off in his 16 major doubles titles. He won all four major doubles titles and had his greatest success with Bob Hewitt (two Wimbledons, two Australian), Roy Emerson (two U.S. and an Australian), Ken Rosewall (a U.S. and French).

As a member of three victorious Australian Davis Cup teams, 1964, 1965 and 1966, he scored his most memorable win the first

year in the Cup round at Cleveland, 7-5, 6-3, 3-6, 9-11, 6-4, over Dennis Ralston. Down a break in the fifth, with his side trailing the U.S. 2-1, Stolle pulled it out so that Emerson could win the Cup-lifting clincher over Chuck McKinley. Perhaps his lead-off win in the following year's Cup finale meant more since it came in his hometown, Sydney, and he had to dig himself from a very deep hole to beat the Spanish ace, Manolo Santana, 10-12, 3-6, 6-1, 6-4, 7-5, to send the Aussies on their victorious way.

His career spanned the amateur and Open eras, and he was in the world's Top 10 four years, starting with 1963—No. 2 in 1964 and 1966. He turned pro in 1967; as a pro he won two singles and 13 doubles titles, and about $500,000 in career prize money. He had a last U.S. fling in 1972, at 33, beating the No. 5 and No. 11 seeds Newcombe and Cliff Drysdale, respectively, to gain the quarters, where he lost to the champ, Ilie Nastase, 6-4, 3-6, 6-3, 6-2.

Born Oct. 8, 1938, in Hornsby, New South Wales, Fred has worked as a teaching pro, was player-coach of the title-winning New York Apples of World Team Tennis in 1976 and 1977, and of Australia 10 times (5-5) in the since disbanded World Cup against the U.S., 1970-79. His son, Sandon, a pro, played Davis Cup for Australia, won the 1998 U.S. doubles with Czech Cyril Suk. For some time Fred has been a successful television commentator on tennis. He won 31 amateur singles titles.

MAJOR TITLES (18)—French singles, 1965: U.S. singles, 1966; Australian doubles, 1963, 1964, 1966; French doubles, 1965, 1966 Wimbledon doubles, 1962, 1964; U.S. doubles. 1965, 1966, 1969; Australian mixed, 1962; U.S. mixed, 1962, 1965; Wimbledon mixed, 1961, 1964, 1969. **DAVIS CUP**—1964, 1965, 1966, 10-2 singles, 3-1 doubles. **SINGLES RECORD IN THE MAJORS**—Australian (21-9), French (25-8); Wimbledon (31-12), U.S. (25-9).

Bill Talbert
United States (1918–1999)
Hall of Fame—1967

Adapting intelligently and inspiringly to life as a diabetic at a time when a quiet, unstrenuous regimen was prescribed, William Franklin Talbert became a champion. Urbane, immaculately groomed, he represented the game handsomely not only as a winning player but a U.S. Davis Cup captain and thoughtful administrator as director of the U.S. Open. Thwarted twice in U.S. singles finals, 1944 and 1945, by Frank Parker—6-4, 3-6, 6-3, 6-3; and 14-12, 6-1, 6-2—the 5-foot-11, right-handed Talbert made his best showing in doubles in the right court alongside Gardnar Mulloy.

They were in the U.S. final six times, one short of Fred Alexander and Harold Hackett's team record, winning four, 1942, 1945, 1946 and 1948. The 1946 title was the prickliest and most noteworthy, a 74-game drama with Frank Guernsey and Don McNeill, 3-6, 6-4, 2-6, 6-3, 20-18, the longest windup set for any major final. It seemed over numerous times, but Talbert and Mulloy kept shunning match points. Five of them came and went against Mulloy's serve (6-7, 0-40 and 10-11, 15-40). But the sixth at 13-14, 30-40 caused a great furor. Talbert, serving, sent back Guersey's return crosscourt with an angled backhand volley that looked wide to many. Guernsey and McNeill rejoiced, shaking hands. "It

didn't look good for us," Talbert remembered. "But there was no call. The sidelinesman was signaling my shot was good. Barely touched the line, I guess." Play resumed. After losing a point, Talbert saved match point seven with a good serve that Guernsey netted. The next match point, 10 games later, settled it for the comebackers, and the closest of all U.S. finals was over. "There'll never be another one like that because of tie-breakers," said Talbert. He was the most instrumental in the acceptance of the elongated-set-dooming innovation at the Open in 1970, the first of his 10 years in charge. The other majors followed his lead.

Bill himself was in the U.S. doubles final nine times, as was Mulloy. He and Mulloy won the clinching point in the Davis Cup victory over Australia in 1948 at Forest Hills, defeating Billy Sidwell and Colin Long, 8-6, 9-7, 2-6, 7-5. He was on the team six years, winning nine of 10 matches, and captained it to the victory over Australia in 1954, as well as the full seasons of 1955, 1956 and 1957 and portions of 1952 and 1953, compiling a 13-4 record.

A stylish groundstroker and excellent volleyer and tactician, he ranked in the U.S. Top 10 13 times between 1941 and 1954, No. 2 in 1944 and 1945. He was in the world's Top 10 in 1949 and 1950, No. 3 the first year. An Ohioan, born Sept. 4, 1918, at Cincinnati, he grew up there, moving to New York during his playing career. He and Margaret Osborne duPont won the U.S. mixed a record four straight years, 1943-46. He was slick on the slick boards of New York's Seventh Regiment Armory, winning the U.S. Indoor singles in 1948 and 1951, and the doubles five times.

With Bruce Old, Talbert wrote definitive books, *The Game of Singles in Tennis* and *The Game of Doubles in Tennis*. He also wrote an autobiography, *Playing for Life* and a history of the U.S. men's singles championships, *Tennis Observed*. He was involved in the financial printing business for many years, and entered the Hall of Fame in 1967. He died Feb. 28, 1999 in New York City.

MAJOR TITLES (9)—French doubles, 1950; U.S. doubles, 1942, 1945, 1946, 1948; U.S. mixed, 1943, 1944, 1945, 1946. **OTHER U.S. TITLES** (14)—Indoor singles, 1948, 1951; Clay Court singles, 1945; Indoor doubles, 1949, 1950, 1951, with Don McNeill; 1952, with Budge Patty; 1954, with Tony Trabert; Clay Court doubles, 1942, with Bill Reedy; 1944, 1945, with Pancho Segura; 1946, with Gardnar Mulloy; Indoor mixed, 1947, 1948, with Doris Hart. **DAVIS CUP** (As player—1946, 1948, 1949, 1951, 1952, 1953, 2-0 singles, 7-1 doubles. (As captain—1952, 1953, 1954, 1955, 1956 1957: 13-4. **SINGLES RECORD IN THE MAJORS**—Australian (1-1), French (5-1), Wimbledon (4-1), U.S. (46-17).

Bill Tilden
United States (1893–1953)
Hall of Fame—1959

If a player's value is measured by the dominance and influence he exercises over a sport, then William Tatem "Big Bill" Tilden II could be considered the greatest player in the history of tennis.

From 1920 through 1926, he dominated the game as has no player before or since. During those years he was invincible in the United States, won Wimbledon three of the six times he competed there, and captured 13 successive singles matches in the Davis Cup challenge round against the best players from Australia, France and Japan.

With the Bills, Tilden and Johnston, at the core, the U.S. seized the Davis Cup from Australasia in 1920, and kept it a record seven years. But by 1927, the Bills were no longer impervious, and France took over, 3-2, on the last day, in Philadelphia—Rene Lacoste beating Big Bill, 6-3, 4-6, 6-3, 6-2, and Henri Cochet flooring Little Bill, 6-4, 4-6, 6-2, 6-4.

As an amateur (1912-30), Tilden won 138 of 192 tournaments, lost 28 finals and had a 907-62 match record—a phenomenal .936 average. His last major triumph, the Wimbledon singles of 1930, gave him a total of 10 majors, standing as the male high until topped by Roy Emerson (12) in 1967. Bill missed another by two match points he held against René Lacoste in the 1927 French final. He won the U.S. mixed with Mary K. Browne in 1913-14, but had been beaten in the first round of the 1912 singles at Newport by fellow Philadelphian Wallace Johnson (whom he would defeat in the 1921 final). He didn't feel sure enough of his game to try again until 1916, in New York. He was 23, a first-round loser to a kid named Harold Throckmorton. Ignominious, tardy starts in an illustrious career that would contain seven U.S. titles and 69 match victories (a record 42 straight between 1920 and 1926).

By 1918, a war-riddled year, he got to the final, to be blown away by a bullet-serving Lindley Murray, 6-3, 6-1, 7-5. But he'd be back: seven more finals in a row. In 1918, Big Bill's electrifying rivalry with Little Bill Johnston began—six U.S. finals in seven years, more than any other two men skirmished for a major. After losing to Little Bill in 1919, 6-4, 6-4, 6-3, Tilden, disgusted with his puny defensive backhand, hid out all winter at the indoor court of a friend, J.D.E. Jones, in Providence, retooling. He emerged with a brand new, fearsome, multifaceted backhand and complete game, and was ready to conquer the world. He did not lose to Little Bill again in a U.S. final, and held an 11-6 edge in their rivalry. His concentration could be awesome, as during a two-tournament stretch in 1925 when he won 57 straight games at Glen Cove, N.Y., and Providence. Trailing Alfred Chapin, one of few to hold a win over him, 3-4 in the final, he ran it out, 6-4, 6-0, 6-0. Staying in tune on the next stop, he won three straight 6-0, 6-0 matches, then 6-0, 6-1. Another 6-1 set made it 75 of 77 games.

When he first won Wimbledon in 1920, over defender Gerald Patterson 2-6, 6-3, 6-2, 6-4, he was 27 years old, an advanced age for a champion. But he had a long and influential career, and at the age of 52 in 1945, he was still able to push the 27-year-old Bobby Riggs to the limit in a professional match.

Tilden, a right-hander, born Feb. 10, 1893, in Philadelphia, had the ideal tennis build, 6-foot-2, 155 pounds, with thin shanks and big shoulders. He had speed and nimbleness, coordination and perfect balance. He also had marked endurance, despite smoking cigarettes incessantly when not playing. In stroke equipment, he had the weapons to launch an overpowering assault and the resources to defend and confound through a variety of spins and pace when the opponent was impervious to sheer power. Surface didn't matter. He won the U.S. Clay Court singles seven times: 1918 and 1922–27.

Nobody had a more devastating serve than Tilden's cannonball, or a more challenging second serve than his kicking American twist. No player had a stronger combination of forehand and backhand drives, supplemented by a forehand chop and backhand slice. Tilden's mixture of shots was a revelation in his first appearance at Wimbledon. Patterson found his backcourt untenable and was passed over and over when he went to the net behind his powerful serve.

The backcourt was where Tilden played tennis. He was no advocate of the "big game"—the big serve and rush for the net for the instant volley coup. He relished playing tennis as a game of chess, matching wits as well as physical powers. The drop shot, at which he was particularly adroit, and the lob were among his disconcerting weapons.

His knowledge and mastery of spin has hardly ever been exceeded, as evidenced not only on the court but also in his *Match Play and the Spin of the Ball*—a classic written more than half a century ago. Yes, Tilden was a writer, too, but he longed to be an actor above anything else. Unsuccessful in his efforts to the point of sinking most of his family wealth, his tennis earnings and his writing royalties into the theater, he was happiest when playing on the heartstrings of a tennis gallery.

Intelligent and opinionated, he was a man of strong likes and dislikes. He had highly successful friends, both men and women, who were devoted to him, and there were others who disliked him and considered him arrogant and inconsiderate of officials and ball boys who served at his matches. He was constandy wrangling with officers and committeemen of the USTA on Davis Cup policy and enforcement of the amateur rule, and in 1928, he was on the front pages of the American press when he was removed as captain and star player of the Davis Cup team, charged with violating the amateur rule with his press accounts of the Wimbledon Championships, in which he was competing. So angry were the French over the loss of the star member of the cast for the Davis Cup challenge round—the first ever held on French soil—that the American ambassador, Myron T. Herrick interceded for the sake of good relations between the countries, and Tilden was restored to the team.

When Tilden, in the opening match, beat René Lacoste, 1-6, 6-4, 6-4, 2-6, 6-3, the French gallery suffered agony and cursed themselves for insisting that "Teel-den" be restored to the team. It all ended happily for them, however as the French won the other four matches and kept the Davis Cup. On Tilden's return home, he was brought up on the charges of violating the rule at Wimbledon. He was found guilty and was suspended from playing in the U.S. Championships that year.

Eligible for the U.S. title again in 1929, after the lifting of his suspension, he won it for the seventh time, defeating his doubles partner, Frank Hunter, 3-6, 6-3, 4-6, 6-2, 6-4. In 1930, he won Wimbledon for the third time, at the age of 37, over countryman Wilmer Allison, 6-3, 9-7, 6-4. After the U.S. Championships, in which he was beaten in the semis by champion John Doeg 10-8, 6-3, 3-6, 12-10. He notified the USTA of his intention to make a series of motion pictures for profit, thus disqualifying himself for further play as an amateur. He was in the world's Top 10 from 1919 through 1930, No. 1 a record six times (1920-25)—equalled by Pete Sampras in 1998—and in the U.S. Top 10 for 12 straight years from 1918, No. 1 a record 10 times, 1920–29.

In 1931, he entered upon a professional playing career, joining one-time partner Vinnie Richards, Germans Hans Nusslein

and Roman Najuch, and Czech Karel Kozeluh. Tilden's name revived pro tennis, which had languished since its inception in 1926 when Suzanne Lenglen went on tour. His joining the pros paved the way for Ellsworth Vines, Fred Perry and Don Budge to leave the amateur ranks and play for big prize money. Tilden won his pro debut against Kozeluh, 6-4, 6-2, 6-4, before 13,000 fans in Madison Square Garden.

Joining promoter Bill O'Brien, Tilden toured the country in 1932 and 1933, but the Depression was on and new blood was needed. Vines furnished it. Tilden and O'Brien signed him on, and in 1934 Tilden defeated Vines in the younger man's pro debut, 8-6, 6-3, 6-2, before a turnaway crowd of 16,200 at Madison Square Garden. That year, Tilden and Vines went on the first of the great tennis tours, won by Vines, 47-26.

The tours grew in the 1930s and 1940s, and Tilden remained an attraction even though he was approaching the age of 50. For years he traveled across the country, driving by day and sometimes all night and then going on a court a few hours after arriving. At times, when he was managing his tour, he had to help set the stage for the matches.

Tragically, his activity and fortunes dwindled after his conviction on a morals charge (a time less understanding of homosexuality), and imprisonment in 1947, and again in 1949 for parole violation (both terms less than a year). He died of a heart attack under pitiful circumstances, alone and with few resources, on June 5, 1953, in Los Angeles. His bag was packed for a trip to Cleveland to play in the U.S. Pro Championships when perhaps the greatest tennis player of them all was found dead in his room.

MAJOR TITLES (21)—Wimbledon singles. 1920, 1921, 1930; U.S. singles, 1920, 1921, 1922, 1923, 1924, 1925, 1929; Wimbledon doubles, 1927; U.S. doubles, 1918, 1921, 1922, 1923, 1927; French mixed, 1930; U.S. mixed 1913, 1914, 1922, 1923. **OTHER U.S. TITLES** (19)—Indoor singles, 1920; Indoor doubles, 1919, 1920, with Vinnie Richards; 1926, with Frank Anderson; 1929, with Frank Hunter; Indoor mixed, 1921, 1922, with Molla Mallory; 1924, with Hazel Hotchkiss Wightman; Clay Court singles, 1918, 1922, 1923, 1924, 1925, 1926, 1927; Pro singles. 1931, 1935; Pro doubles, 1932, with Bruce Barnes; 1945, with Vinnie Richards. **DAVIS CUP**—1920, 1921, 1922, 1923, 1924, 1925, 1926, 1927, 1928, 1929, 1930, 25-5 singles, 9-2 doubles. **SINGLES RECORD IN THE MAJORS**—French (14-3), Wimbledon (30-3). U.S. (69-7).

Lance Tingay
Great Britain (1915–1990)
Hall of Fame—1982—Journalist

As the dean of a sizeable platoon of British tennis writers of his time, Lance Tingay, friendly, erudite, helpful to colleagues, covered the game for a half-century, present as it evolved from the amateur into the open and highly professional era. He covered his first Wimbledon in 1932 and was the thorough, informed and informative tennis correspondent for *The Daily Telegraph* of London from 1950 to 1980, writing his dispatches from across the world.

Ever good humored, even while pounding his typewriter on deadline, he was a leading historian of the game, the author of *History of Lawn Tennis in Pictures*, *One Hundred Years of Wimbledon*, and *Royalty and Lawn Tennis*, and he wrote for numerous tennis publications and yearbooks. Tingay was born in London

July 15, 1915, and died there March 10, 1990. He was named to the Hall of Fame in 1982.

Ted Tinling
Great Britain (1910–1990)
Hall of Fame—1986—Innovator

The Leaning Tower of Pizzazz, 6-foot-5 Cuthbert Collingwood Tinling entered the Hall of Fame in 1986 as a many-faceted benefactor of the game. Witty and literate, a man who had served as a lieutenant colonel in intelligence for the British army during World War II, a right-hander, was a good enough player to compete on the English circuit after the war. But it was as an involved bystander that he served the game well, first as a teen-ager on the Riviera where he, spending winters for reasons of ill health, umpired matches, including some for the great Suzanne Lenglen.

He was master of ceremonies at Wimbledon until one of his careers, that of designer-dressmaker, made him for a time *persona non grata*. That occurred in 1949 when he scandalously (or so it seemed to the tournament committee) equipped American Gertrude "Gussy" Moran with lace panties that drew hordes of photographers and spectators. Ted made beautiful as well as avant-garde costumes for many female players, including Maureen Connolly, Maria Bueno, Billie Jean King, Rosie Casals, Margaret Court and Evonne Goolagong

He was couturier for the newly formed Virginia Slims circuit, and later the Slimsies' minister of protocol and emcee, a strong advocate of the women's game. An unmistakable bald-headed beacon, he was of immeasurable value late in life as historian and writer who had observed most of the game's luminaries, and as liaison between the players and Wimbledon. Outspoken, generous while informing and counseling newcomers to the game, Ted could make light of his own death, remarking on one of his last days: "Send me a fax to hell to let me know if Jennifer (Capriati) wins Wimbledon." He was born June 23, 1910, in Eastbourne, England, and died May 23, 1990, in Cambridge, England.

Brian Tobin
Australia (1930—)
Hall of Fame—2003—Contributor

Tennis has been a guiding theme far Australian Brian Tobin all his life, from nationally-ranked player to the highest administrative position in the game: President of the ITF (International Tennis Federation) for nine years. During his tenure, the game made tremendous strides, reaching out to more countries and players throughout the world every year, expanding teaching programs and supervising the expansion of the ITF's crown jewels, Davis and Fed Cups.

A Melburnian, born Dec. 5, 1930, he was in his country's Top 10 as an amateur player, No. 8 between 1956 and 1962, and won the U.S. singles championship in the 35-and-over category at Forest Hills in 1967. That year, he captained a traveling squad of world class Aussies, and joined one of them, Davis Cupper Ray Ruffels, to reach the doubles final at the Newport (R.I.) Invitational, where he returned to be anointed for the Hall of Fame in

2003 as an administrator. Tobin captained the victorious Australian Fed Cup team in 1964.

However, the marks he made with executive skills largely earned him his place in the Hall. A long-time volunteer, he became president of the national association, Tennis Australia, in 1983, serving through 1989, formative years during which the Melbourne Park complex came into being as home of the Australian Open, the most modern of the major venues.

After a stint as executive vice president of the ITF from 1989-91, he was elected as president in 1991, and oversaw world-wide expansion of the game.

Bertha Townsend
United States (1869–1909)
Hall of Fame—1974

A Philadelphia-born right-hander, Bertha Louise Townsend appeared in the Championships in her hometown five times. She won in 1888, unseating original champ, Ellen Hansell, in the challenge round, 6-3, 6-5. She fought off the challenge of Lida Vorhees, 7-5, 6-3, to become the first repeating female champ, but then fell to Ellen Roosevelt, 6-2, 6-2, in the 1890 challenge round.

She reappeared, married, in 1894, to reach the final of the all-comers, losing, 6-2, 7-5 to Helen Hellwig, who became champion. The following year, as a semifinalist, her career ended with an 8-3 U.S. singles record. She was born March 7, 1869, died May 12, 1909, at Haverford, Pa., as Mrs. Harry Toulmin, and entered the Hall of Fame in 1974.

MAJOR TITLES (2)—U.S. singles, 1888-89. **SINGLES RECORD IN THE MAJORS—**
U.S. (8-3)

Tony Trabert
United States (1930—)
Hall of Fame—1970

One of the finest seasons ever achieved was the 1955 of Tony Trabert, who won three of the four singles majors—French, Wimbledon and U.S.—and two of the doubles, Australian and U.S., earning the No. 1 peak. Triplers are rare, but none of them won more than 100 singles matches or 30 singles and doubles titles as Tony did that year.

Within the most productive season for an American man were 18 singles triumphs (of 23 tournaments)—106-7, with a 36-match winning streak—plus 12 doubles titles alongside Davis Cup teammate Vic Seixas.

Amassing 13 U.S. titles in singles and doubles, he was one of two Americans (the other, Art Larsen) to win singles championships on all four surfaces. Other than grass at Forest Hills, he won the 1955 Indoor over Ham Richardson, 11-13, 7-5, 9-7, 6-3; the 1953 Hard Court over Tom Brown, 6-4, 11-9, 6-4; the 1951 Clay Court over Larsen, 6-8, 2-6, 6-4, 6-3, 8-6, and, 1955, over Bernard Bartzen, 10-8, 6-1, 6-4. But Tony stands alone in victoriously traveling that surface route in doubles, too. Alas for Trabert, a semifinal defeat by Ken Rosewall at the 1955 Australian may have cost him a Grand Slam.

An exceptional athlete, Marion Anthony Trabert was born Aug. 16, 1930, in Cincinnati where he grew up. He was a standout basketball regular for the University of Cincinnati, for which, as an All-American, he also won the U.S. Intercollegiate singles in 1951.

Traditionally the French Championship has been the most difficult battleground for American men. Tony won five titles at Roland Garros, notably the singles in 1954, over Art Larsen, 6-4, 7-5, 6-1, and 1955, over Swede Sven Davidson, 2-6, 6-1, 6-4, 6-2. He also won the doubles in 1950 (with Bill Talbert) and 1954-55 (with Seixas).

Thirty-four years passed before another American guy followed him, Michael Chang in 1989, and Tony was there as a telecasting witness.

For five years, Trabert was a mainstay of the U.S. Davis Cup team, along with Seixas. In each of those years, 1951-55, the Yanks reached the challenge round final against Australia. Tony's best-remembered match may have been a defeat, a tremendous five-set struggle with Lew Hoad on a rainy afternoon in 1953 at Melbourne. Hoad won out, 13-11, 6-3, 2-6, 3-6, 7-5, to tie the series, 2-2, and Rosewall hung onto the Cup, 6-2, 2-6, 6-3, 6-4, over Seixas.

More determined than ever, Trabert and Seixas, led by Capt. Bill Talbert, returned to Australia a year later, where Trabert beat Hoad, 6-4, 2-6, 12-10, 6-3 on opening day. Seixas bumped Rosewall in four. Then, together Vic and Tony busted an American dry spell of four years by taking the doubles from Lew and Ken, 6-2, 4-6, 6-2, 10-8—the only U.S. seizure of the Cup from the Aussies during an eight-year stretch, 1950-57.

Though an attacker with a powerful backhand and strong volley, competitive right-hander Trabert also had exceptional groundstrokes. In winning the U.S. singles twice, 1953 over Seixas, 6-3, 6-2, 6-3, and 1955 over Rosewall, 9-7, 6-3, 6-3—plus Wimbledon in 1955 over Kurt Nielsen, 6-3, 7-5, 6-1—he did not lose a set. Wow.

Following the custom of the time, Trabert, as the top amateur, signed on with the professionals to challenge the ruler, Pancho Gonzalez, on a head-to-head tour in 1956. Gonzalez won, 74-27. Trabert was runner-up to Alex Olmedo for the U.S. Pro singles title in 1960, having won the doubles with Rex Hartwig in 1956.

When his playing career ended, Trabert worked as a teaching pro, an administrator for the pro tour, as an astute television commentator on tennis as well as the president of the International Tennis Hall of Fame. In 1976, he returned to the Davis Cup scene as the U.S. captain, leading the Cup-winning teams of 1978 and 1979.

He had four years in the U.S. and world's Top 10: 1951, 1953, 1954, 1955—No. 1 in each, respectively 1953 and 1955—before turning pro. His amateur career was interrupted by service in the U.S. Navy.

MAJOR TITLES (10)—French singles 1954, 1955; Wimbledon singles, 1955; U.S. singles, 1953, 1955; Australian doubles, 1955; French doubles 1950, 1954, 1955; U.S. doubles, 1954. **OTHER U.S. TITLES** (13)—Intercollegiate singles, 1951; Indoor singles, 1955; Clay Court singles, 1951, 1955; Hard Court singles, 1953; Indoor doubles, 1954, with Bill Talbert; 1955, with Vic Seixas; Clay Court doubles, 1951, 1955, with

Hamilton Richardson; 1954, with Seixas; Hard Court doubles, 1950, 1953, with Tom Brown; Pro doubles, 1956, with Rex Hartwig. **DAVIS CUP** (As player)—1951, 1952, 1953, 1954, 1955, 16-5 singles, 11-3 doubles; (As Captain)—1953, 1976, 1977, 1978, 1979, 1980. Record 14-3 (2 Cups). **SINGLES RECORD IN THE MAJORS**—Australian (4-2), French (18-2), Wimbledon (13-2), U.S. (23-5).

Lesley Turner Bowrey
Australia (1942—)
Hall of Fame—1997

Although, as an Australian, Lesley Rosemary Turner Bowrey knew her way around extremely well on native grass courts, she achieved her foremost feats far from home, in Paris. Dealing with a surface very foreign to Aussies, she showed superior movement, grit and groundstrokes to triumph twice on clay in the French singles at Stade Roland Garros, 1963 and 1965. She would have owned a trifecta had she cashed a match point against Margaret Smith (Court) in the 1962 final, losing, 6-3, 3-6, 7-5. The next year Lesley won, bouncing back against twice-champ, English lefty Ann Haydon Jones, 2-6, 6-3, 7-5. Two years later, she repeated, this time over countrywoman Smith, 6-3, 6-4, who was by then No. 1. Her fourth time in the final in 1967 was a close-call loss to homebody Françoise Durr, 4-6, 6-3, 6-4. "At least I made the French happy," Lesley says, knowing they hadn't enjoyed one of their own as champion in 38 years (Simone Passemard Mathieu).

On her first trip abroad, an 18-year-old in the spring of 1961, Turner discovered her affinity for continental earth, going to the Italian final, a 6-4, 6-4, defeat by No. 1 Maria Bueno. She and compatriot Jan Lehane won the doubles, an accomplishment she equaled in 1964 with Smith, and 1967 with Rosie Casals. Rome, too, had become a gleeful hunting ground. After losing two more finals, to Smith in 1963 and 1964, Lesley got back at both her conquerors, beating Bueno for the 1967 title, 6-3, 6-3, and Margaret (now Mrs. Court) for the crown in 1968, 2-6, 6-2, 6-3. Her five finals were the tourney record until Chris Evert's sixth and seventh, 1982 and 1984.

But she was unable to win her homeland's title in singles, falling in the 1964 final to Smith and in the final of 1967 to American Nancy Richey. In 1967, Lesley hooked up with Aussie Bill Bowrey to win the Italian mixed over Durr and Frew McMillan, 6-2, 7-5. It was such a good lineup that they decided to make it permanent, marrying the next year. As a wedding present, she won the Italian singles for him, and he reciprocated by winning the Australian singles for her. They stand as the only married couple to win important national titles in the same year. Despite her baseline preference, Lesley was a sharp volleyer, winning 11 of her 13 major championships in doubles. She led off unexpectedly during that initial round-the-world tour with a U.S. title as the pickup partner of American Darlene Hard in Boston. Freshly turned 19, Lesley, having injured her right wrist in a bathtub fall, didn't expect to play. Neither did Hard, the defender, because her usual partner, Bueno, was ill. But they got together and went all the way, beating the Mexican-German alliance of Yola Ramirez and Edda Buding, 6-4, 5-7, 6-0.

Majors in doubles followed at the Australian, 1964 and 1967 (with Judy Tegart Dalton), 1965 (with Smith); French, 1964 and 1965 (with Smith); Wimbledon, 1964 (with Smith); Australian mixed, 1962 (with Fred Stolle) and 1967 (with Owen Davidson); Wimbledon mixed, 1961 and 1964 (with Stolle). She jump-started Davidson's mixed Grand Slam that he completed with Billie Jean King. She was a regular in the world's Top 10 for six years—No. 2 in 1963.

A petite, good-natured but very determined (5-foot-4; 117-pounds) right-hander out of Sydney, where she was born Aug. 16, 1942, Lesley played a strong role in Australia's Federation Cup victories in 1964 and 1965 and reaching the final of 1963. Playing four years and 13 series, she was 7-3 in singles, 6-3 in doubles. Tapped for the International Hall in 1997, she has long been one of Australia's leading coaches. She was named to the Australian Tennis Hall of Fame in 1998. Consistent in the majors, she was a finalist in four, and quarterfinalist or better in 21 of 30 majors she entered.

"A marvelous doubles partner," lauded Stolle. "But here's the odd, funny fact. In 1961, the first year we won the Wimbledon mixed, we were beaten in our local club's tournament."

MAJOR TITLES (13)—French singles, 1963, 1965; Australian doubles. 1964, 1965 1967; French doubles, 1964, 1965; Wimbledon doubles, 1964; U.S. doubles, 1961; Australian mixed, 1962, 1967; Wimbledon mixed 1961, 1964. **FEDERATION CUP**—1963, 1964, 1965 1967; 7-3 singles, 6-3 doubles. **SINGLES RECORD IN THE MAJORS**—Australian (25-4), French (34-6), Wimbledon (29-9), U.S. (11-4)

Jimmy Van Alen
United States (1902–1991)
Hall of Fame—1965—Founder Hall of Fame / Innovator

James Henry Van Alen, born Sept. 19, 1902, in his beloved Newport, R.I., was intimately involved with tennis as player, organizer and—best known—innovator whose pet idea, the tiebreaker, radically altered the game, making it more televisable in the United States. As a U.S. singles champ at court tennis in 1933, 1938 and 1940, he was good enough at that abstruse ancestor of lawn tennis to warrant a Hall of Fame spot as a player. He played tennis well enough to have won his blue at alma mater, Cambridge, appeared in the Wimbledon, French and U.S. Championships, and played in the Newport Casino Invitational, where he had a win over fellow Hall of Famer George Lott.

He would become director of that tournament, a leader in the preservation of the aging wooden Casino (the cradle of U.S. tennis), and, at the instigation of his wife, Candy, the guiding light in founding the Hall of Fame, to which he was elected in 1965.

Feeling the game's scoring should be simplified and deuce done away with, he lobbied tirelessly on behalf of his creation, VASSS: Van Alen Streamlined Scoring System. Among the elements were single-point scoring and 21-point or 31-point matches (a la table tennis), no-ad (games scored 1-2-3-4, maximum 7-points, sudden death at 3-3), medal play (a la golf, based on single point totals for specific numbers of rounds), and, the most celebrated—tie-breakers.

Unveiled in 1965 at the Casino Pro Championships, which he personally sponsored for $10,000 prize money, the seminal tie-breaker needed retooling. That he did with veteran referee

Mike Blanchard, and some counseling by historian Frank Phelps. Eventually, it became sudden death (best-of-9 points).

Amazingly the breaker was accepted by the USTA, and used in U.S. championship events from 1970 through 1974. Thereafter the USTA embraced the current ITF-approved "lingering death" as Van Allen disparagingly called the best-of-12 point version that requires a two-point margin for victory, thus can extend into double figures.

Jimmy would be pleased to know that—tardily, in his view— the ATP and WTA tours have adopted his no-ad scoring (first to four points wins the game) for doubles in 2006 and 2007, respectively.

A man of old family wealth, Jimmy hoped to give the game a common touch, and became an avuncular, almost cherubic figure in planter's straw hat and burgundy blazer at the Casino. His love for tennis was endless, as well as his delight in shaking up the establishment with his brainstorms. He served in the U.S. Navy during World War II, and died July 3, 1991, in Newport. Jimmy would have enjoyed the irony: That semifinal day at Wimbledon Michael Stich deposed champion Stefan Edberg by winning three breakers—4-6, 7-6 (7-5), 7-6 (7-5), 7-6 (7-2)—even though Edberg never lost his serve. Such a tie-breaking match could not have been played before Van Alen's baby was born. A bequest of his wife, Candy, assured that a professional tournament would always continue at the Casino as the Jimmy Van Alen Cup.

John Van Ryn
United States (1905–1999)
Hall of Fame—1963

Allison and Van Ryn were a headline combination during their bright career together between 1929 and 1936 as one of the most formidable U.S. Davis Cup partnerships. Wilmer Allison and John William Van Ryn, Jr. won 14 of 16 Cup matches together, the best for Americans until Peter Fleming and John McEnroe's 14-1.

Their 24 team series (tied with Stan Smith and Vic Seixas) are second only to McEnroe's 30 in U.S. annals. Van Ryn's 24 doubles matches and 22 wins are highs for the U.S. He and Wilmer beat the splendid French teams in Parisian Cup finales (Henri Cochet-Jean Borotra in 1929, Cochet-Jacques Brugnon in 1932), but could do no more than stave off France's successful defenses.

A Princeton man (class of '28), Van Ryn, right-handed, superb at the net, and returning from the right court, won the U.S. Intercollegiate doubles in 1927 with Ken Appel.

Allison and Van Ryn were in the U.S. final six times, one behind Fred Alexander and Harold Hackett's record, winning in 1931 and 1935, the latter over the rising Don Budge and Gene Mako, 6-4, 6-2, 3-6, 2-6, 6-1. They also won Wimbledon in 1929, 1930, beating fellow Yanks Johnny Doeg and George Lott in 1930, 6-3, 6-3, 6-2. "We should've won again in '35," said the engaging Van Ryn, recalling the splendid mixture of himself and Allison, as choice as gin and vermouth. "We had a match point in the fifth set of the final against Jack Crawford and Adrian Quist. They put up a fluky little lob. My ball. Easy. But for some reason I hesitated in starting for it. Wilmer noticed, and decided he'd better take

it—and missed the shot. My fault. All those years together," he smiled, "and we mess up a simple play." Van Ryn, 5-foot-10, 155 pounds, a fluid, well-rounded strokesman, remembered, "My best Wimbledon in singles was '31. I beat [No. 4-seeded] Christian Boussus, got to the quarters, lost to Fred Perry."

In 1931, Van Ryn teamed with Lott to win the French and Wimbledon, a splendid Centre Court triumph over the French whizzes, Brugnon and Cochet, 6-2, 10-8, 9-11, 3-6, 6-3. Thus Johnny was the only American guy to win the Big W three successive times. He ranked in the U.S. Top 10 six times between 1927 and 1932, No. 4 in 1931 when he was a five-set quarterfinal loser at Forest Hills to Lott. He was also a quarterfinalist in 1929 and 1930, losing to Bill Tilden each time in four sets, and 1936 and 1937. In 1929, he was No. 8 in the world's Top 10. Born June 30, 1905, in Newport News, Va., he grew up in Orange, N.J. He was once married to Marjorie Gladman, also an excellent doubles player, and in 1930 and 1931, they were the first of four married couples to be ranked together in the U.S. singles Top 10, he Nos. 9 and 4, she Nos. 7 and 8. Van Ryn went into the Hall of Fame in 1963, and died Aug. 7, 1999, in Palm Beach, Fla.

MAJOR TITLES (6)—French doubles, 1931; Wimbledon doubles, 1929-30-31; U.S. doubles, 1931, 35. **OTHER U.S. TITLES** (2)—Indoor doubles, 1932, with George Lott; Intercollegiate doubles, 1927, with Ken Appel. **DAVIS CUP**—1929-30-31-32-33-34-35-36, 7-1 singles, 22-2 doubles. **SINGLES RECORD IN THE MAJORS**—Australian (1-1), French (4-1), Wimbledon (13-6), U.S. (29-15)

Guillermo Vilas
Argentina (1952—)
Hall of Fame—1991

Seldom has a player found such empathy beyond his own borders as did Guillermo Vilas, the "Young Bull of the Pampas," during his pro career. As the foremost Latin American male, he was the only Argentine to be tapped for the Hall of Fame (1991) until Gabriela Sabatini in 2006, and the first to win major titles (four of them).

The burly 5-foot-11, 175-pound left-hander captivated audiences everywhere with his sportsmanship and sensitivity of a poet, which he is. An appealing head-banded figure of the 1970s and early 1980s, his chestnut hair flowing below his shoulders, Vilas was the epitome of strength and fitness, endurance and patience on court, outlasting opponents from the baseline with his high-rolling top-spinning strokes, hour after hour, a destructive metronome.

His 1977 was a monumental year in the game's history: he won 17 of 33 tournaments (tying Rod Laver's record) on a record of 145 match wins against 14 losses. Among his souvenirs were the French and U.S. Open titles and an Open-era winning streak record of 50 matches—four of these matches from a pre-U.S. Open round-robin event in Harrison, N.Y. were not recognized as official by the ATP and they, subsequently, recognize the streak at only 46 straight matches. The streak, begun after Wimbledon, was stopped at Aix-en-Provence in September by Ilie Nastase, who used one of the controversial "spaghetti" rackets that produced weird strokes and bounces. Vilas quit in disgust. The ban of such

rackets went into effect the day after he lost, sadly too late for Vilas, and the game, as he won his next 26 matches. Seventy-six out of 77 ain't bad.

Although he reveled in the backcourt, Vilas startled Jimmy Connors in the 1977 U.S. Open final with volleying forays that turned the match his way, and set off a wild celebration after he'd won the last championship match in the 54-year-old Forest Hills Stadium, 2-6, 6-3, 7-6 (7-4), 6-0. Joyous fans carried him on victory laps within the concrete arena, as though he were a triumphant matador.

Even if grass seemed anathema to the clay-loving Vilas, he did win the Australian twice—in 1978 over John Marks of Australia 6-4, 6-4, 3-6, 6-3, and 1979 over American John Sadri, 7-6 (7-4), 6-3, 6-2—and the Masters of 1974 on the same turf, Melbourne's Kooyong, over Nastase, 7-6, 6-2, 3-6, 3-6, 6-4. He wasn't a serve-volley smoothie, but his Australian Open record is excellent: two titles plus a final-round loss to missile-serving Roscoe Tanner in 1977, 6-3, 6-3, 6-3, and a 16-match streak to a semis loss to Kim Warwick in 1980, 6-7, 6-4, 6-2, 2-6, 6-4.

As Argentina's foremost Davis Cupper, he took great satisfaction in bulwarking three American Zone wins over the U.S. (1977, 1980, 1983). Vilas won all six of his singles on the Buenos Aires loam, including victories over John McEnroe the last two years, 6-2, 4-6, 6-3, 2-6, 6-4, and 6-4, 6-0, 6-1. In 1981, he led Argentina to the Davis Cup final, a narrow 3-1 defeat by the U.S. in Cincinnati where, in the fifth set, Guillermo actually served for an improbable doubles victory at 7-6, and an unrealized 2-1 lead (with Jose-Luis Clerc) against McEnroe and Peter Fleming. Vilas and Clerc were hardly a team, or doubles players; McEnroe and Fleming were the best. But the match, lost 6-3, 4-6, 6-4, 4-6, 11-9, showed Guillermo's heart and desire on behalf of his homeland.

He was in four French finals, crushing Brian Gottfried in 1977, 6-0, 6-3, 6-0, but couldn't get past the Swedes. He lost to Bjorn Borg in 1975, 6-2, 6-3, 6-4, and 1978, 6-1, 6-1, 6-3 and, wore down before 17-year-old Mats Wilander in 1982, 1-6, 7-6 (8-6), 6-0, 6-4. It was his last major final in a career that landed him in fifth place among the all-time pro winners headed by Connors: 62 singles titles, even with Borg. His career prize money amounted to $4,923,882. It was in Paris, 1973, that he first gained notice, removing defending champ Andres Gimeno from the French in the second round, 6-2, 5-7, 8-6 (best-of-three in early rounds that year). In Paris in 2006, Rafa Nadal erased Vilas' pro era clay court match winning streak of 53, raising it to 81 in 2007. Guillermo was there to congratulate Rafa, also a left-handed Spanish speaker.

Serving as an inspiration for Argentine players as they've developed into a world force, he has guided many who work out at his Buenos Aires club.

Beginning in 1974, Vilas graced the world's Top 10 for nine straight years, No. 2 in 1975, 77: No. 5 in 1974, 80; No. 6 in 1976, 79, 81; No. 3 in 1978; No. 4 in 1982. He was born Aug. 17, 1952, in Mar del Plata, Argentina, where he grew up.

MAJOR TITLES (4)—Australian singles, 1978-1979; French singles, 1977; U.S. singles, 1977. **DAVIS CUP**—1970-71-72-73,75-76-77-78-79-80-81-82-83-84—45-10 singles, 12-14 doubles. **SINGLES RECORD IN THE MAJORS**—Australian (23-3), French (56-17), Wimbledon (15-11), U.S. (43-14).

Ellsworth Vines
United States (1911–1994)
Hall of Fame—1962

One night in 1930, an 18-year-old lad sat in a rocking chair on the porch of the Peninsula Inn in Seabright, N.J., looking out to sea and thinking that his tennis dreams were shattered. "I guess I'm just a flash in the pan like they say," said Henry Ellsworth Vines, Jr.

Weeks earlier, they had been calling him another California Comet, a lanky youth with the kick of a mule in his cannonball serve that terrorized the Eastern grass court circuit. Vines, a right-hander born Sept. 29, 1911 in Los Angeles, ambled along mournfully like slow molasses when he wasn't in hot pursuit of a tennis ball. On the court he was devastating, wherefore came the comparisons to the original California Comet, Maurice McLoughlin.

The Southern California champ, a cornstalk at 6-foot-2, 143 pounds, Vines had easily disposed of two of the better Americans, Frank Hunter and Frank Shields, at Seabright. However, he lost the final to Sidney Wood, unable to cope with Wood's seemingly innocuous game of moderate strokes, and some were saying the new Comet had burned out. It looked that way at Forest Hills, where George Lytleton Rogers beat him in the third round from two sets down.

But Elly went home, won the Pacific Southwest, practiced all winter and spring against slow-ball strategy and came back east in 1931 to take the U.S. title over George Lott, 7-9, 6-3, 9-7, 7-5 winning the last two sets after trailing 5-3 in the third and 5-2 in the fourth.

His 1932 was a splendid campaign that landed him at No. 1 in the world at the age of 20. Vines was the youngest ever on that perch until Aussie Lleyton Hewitt, a younger 20, ascended to the top of the ATP computer ranking 69 years later on winning the year-end Masters of 2001.

Elly was the first man to win both Wimbledon and the U.S. titles in the same year since Bill Tilden in 1920, a man he would face on a head-to-head pro tour in 1934. He seized those two crowns rapaciously, 6-4, 6-2, 6-0, with 30 aces over England's Bunny Austin at the Big W, and, in 59 minutes, over top-seeded Frenchman Henri Cochet, the man he replaced at No. 1, 6-4, 6-4, 6-4 at the U.S. Championships. But he had a dicey semifinal in which he was thrice two points from losing to clever Cliff Sutter, 4-6, 8-10, 12-10, 10-8, 6-1. As a Davis Cup rookie, Vines was 9-1, driving the U.S. to the challenge round, a 3-2 loss to France. He won four of eight tournaments, was 46-5 in matches.

He played on the amateur grass circuit only four years, 1930 through 1933. Besides his No. 1 year in 1932, he was No. 3 in 1931; No. 5 in 1933, in the world's Top 10. His stay in the U.S. Top 10: No. 1 in 1931-32; No. 8 in 1930. Vines established at Forest Hills and Wimbledon that he had an extraordinary serve, perhaps the fastest ever turned loose, with almost no spin. He also had as fast and as risky a forehand as ever seen, a murderous overhead, and outstanding volleying.

Moreover, his disposition and temperament were foolproof. Where others might explode over a line call, Vines would slowly turn his head and grin at the linesman. He was a gambler on the court. He hit his forehand flat, with all his whizzing might, and

closer to the net and the lines than anyone dared. At his best, he was equal to beating any player, but his margin of safety was so thin that on days when he did not have the feel and touch, his errors could be ruinous.

His 1932 Wimbledon triumph ended with his 30th ace. The ball catapulted by Austin so fast that Bunny said he didn't know whether it went by on his left or his right. Don Budge marveled: "Thirty aces in 12 serving games! Considering it was against one of the finest players of the era, and a Wimbledon final, it could be the greatest serving demonstration ever."

But 1933 was a comedown. In a magnificent Wimbledon final, Elly lost his title to Jack Crawford, 4-6, 11-9, 6-2, 2-6, 6-4, falling to cash numerous break points in the second set. Both Austin and Fred Perry beat him as the U.S. lost the Davis Cup semifinal in Paris, a prelude to Britain's seizing the Cup from France. And so did the mite, Bitsy Grant, in the fourth round at Forest Hills, 6-3, 6-3, 6-3. Disgusted, Vines, top seeded in London and New York, couldn't wait to leave for home, his amateur career nearly over.

He signed a professional contract to go on tour with Bill Tilden and lost their opening match, 8-6, 6-3, 6-2, before 16,200 fans at Madison Square Garden. But Vines ultimately carved a 47-26 edge in matches with the aging Tilden. One match in the Garden later between Vines and Fred Perry drew 17,630 spectators. He was the No. 1 pro through 1937, winning the Wembley World Pro title over Tilden, 6-1, 6-3, 5-7, 3-6, 6-3, in 1935 and over Hans Nusslein, 6-4, 6-4, 6-2, in 1936.

Near the end of the decade, Vines' interest in tennis waned. He turned to golf and became the best golfer of top tennis players. For years, he was a teaching pro, one good enough to reach the semifinals of the 1951 PGA Championship.

He was enshrined in the Hall of Fame in 1962, and died March 17, 1994, at LaQuinta, Calif. In 1977, he attended the Wimbledon Centenary as one of the former champions receiving commemorative medals. He had turned out to be much, much more than a flash in the pan.

MAJOR TITLES (6)—Wimbledon singles, 1932; U.S. singles, 1931-32; Australian doubles, 1933; U.S. doubles, 1932; U.S. mixed, 1933. **OTHER U.S. TITLES** (3)—Clay Court singles 1931; Clay Court doubles, 1931, with Keith Gledhill; Pro singles, 1939. **DAVIS CUP**—1932-33, 13-3 singles. **SINGLES RECORD IN THE MAJORS**—Australian (2-1), Wimbledon (13-1), U.S. (16-2).

Baron Gottfried von Cramm
Germany (1909–1976)
Hall of Fame—1977

If any player was the prince charming of tennis, he was Gottfried von Cramm, a baron of the German nobility, 6 feet tall with blond hair, green eyes and a magnetism that, in the words of Don Budge, "made him dominate any scene he was part of." The most accomplished tennis player Germany had known, von Cramm must be one of the finest players never to have won Wimbledon. He was runner-up three years in a row, to Fred Perry in 1935, 6-2, 6-4, 6-4, and 1936, 6-1, 6-1, 6-0, and to Budge in 1937, 6-3, 6-4, 6-2.

Von Cramm, known as "The Baron," was also runner-up to Budge in 1937, 6-1, 7-9, 6-1, 3-6, 6-1 for the U.S. Championship. And

again to Budge in what often has been termed the greatest Davis Cup match ever played, the fifth and deciding one in the 1937 semifinal at Wimbledon. Budge came from 1-4 and had match point five times before he hit the final forehand, racing across the court beyond the alley. Don lay sprawled on the ground as the umpire declared the United States to be winner, 6-8, 5-7, 6-4, 6-2, 8-6.

Said The Baron as he stood at the net waiting for Budge to pick himself up: "Don, this was absolutely the finest match I have ever played in my life. I'm very happy I could have played it against you, whom I like so much. Congratulations." The next moment, their arms were around each other.

Budge often told the story of them walking toward Centre Court for the match, and von Cramm being summoned to a telephone. The caller was the German dictator Hitler, urging him to victory for the fatherland.

Von Cramm, a right-hander, was born July 7, 1909, Nettlingen, Hanover, Germany. He was noted for his endurance and tenacity. In recalling their thrilling Cup match, Budge related how he put four of his best first serves in play, in succession, and all four came back as von Cramm winners.

Few have endured what he did in taking the first of his two French titles in 1934. Five-set matches were the rule and he fought through four of them (of six wins), and snatched a match point away from Aussie Jack Crawford to win the final, 6-4, 7-9, 3-6, 7-5, 6-3. Two years later, another five-setter was his ticket to victory over No. 1 Fred Perry, starting and ending with astounding bagels, 6-0, 2-6, 6-2, 2-6, 6-0. His three straight Wimbledon finals losses, were a record for frustration he shares with Herbert Lawford (1884-86) and Fred Stolle (1963-65). He won six German titles, 1932-35, and two more remarkably after World War II, the last at age 40.

But that wasn't the last that aficionados heard of The Baron. He had always loved representing the fatherland in Davis Cup, was saddened by the Nazi takeover, and elated when the tennis community welcomed back a democratic Germany in 1951. He played three more Cup seasons, leading Germany in 1951 to four wins and the final of the European zone. He was 9-1 in singles, beating men half his age such as Dane Kurt Nielsen, a future Wimbledon runner-up. In 1953, at 44, he returned to Paris to say adieu in defeat by France, registering the last of his 58 Cup singles wins over 30-year-old Paul Remy, 6-4, 6-0, 6-4. He was a Cup centurion, one of only 14 who played more than 100 matches (111). His most productive year was 1935: 11-1 in singles, 4-1 in doubles. In 1937, the year he came so close to winning it, he was 7-2 in singles, 4-1 in doubles.

Popular everywhere he went, von Cramm delighted Americans in 1937 as title runner-up to Budge at Forest Hills and doubles champ with Henner Henkel over Budge and Gene Mako, 6-4, 7-5, 6-4, in Boston.

Von Cramm, at the height of his career when Hitler was preparing Germany to launch World War II, declined to speak for Nazism and was imprisoned by the Gestapo in 1938. Out of favor, he was conscripted for the German army and shipped to probable death on the Russian front. However, he not only suvived but was decorated with an Iron Cross for heroism. After the war, he

had a successful business career and was a tennis administrator. The Baron died in an automobile crash near Cairo, Egypt, Nov. 8, 1976, and a year later was elevated to the Hall of Fame.

MAJOR TITLES (5)—French singles, 1934, 36; French doubles, 1937; U.S. doubles 1937; Wimbledon mixed, 1933. **DAVIS CUP**—1932-33-34-35-36-37, 51-52-53, 58-10 singles, 24-9 doubles). **SINGLES RECORD IN THE MAJORS**—Australian (3-1), French 18-1), Wimbledon (26-7), U.S. (5-1)

Virginia Wade
Great Britain (1945—)
Hall of Fame—1989

If ever a player achieved high drama by winning Wimbledon, it was "Our Ginny"' as her compatriots throughout the United Kingdom called her. It was 1977, Sarah Virginia Wade's 17th try, and the year of the magnificent Wimbledon Centenary. Moreover Queen Elizabeth II appeared for the first time in a quarter- century to present the women's prize. Ginny had set the stage by deposing 1976 champ Chris Evert in the semis, 6-2, 4-6, 6-1.

Attacking incessantly, heedless of whatever mistakes she made, Wade finished strongly to beat Betty Stove for the title, 4-6, 6-3, 6-1, nine days short of her 32nd birthday. An extraordinarily jubilant Centre Court crowd of more than 14,000, unaccustomed to homegrown success, became a chorus in singing *For She's a Jolly Good Fellow*! A tennis queen was saluted by her Queen.

Dark-haired Wade was slender (5-foot-8) and nimble, of elegant bearing. She had the longest and, considering the highly competitive age in which she sparkled, the most fruitful career of any Englishwoman. Her career spanned the amateur and Open eras, and in 1968, she scored two notable firsts. As an amateur, she won the inaugural open, the British Hard Court at Bournemouth, 6-4, 6-1, over Scot Winnie Shaw, turning down the $720 first prize. Five months later, as a pro, she captured the initial U.S. Open (and $6,000), upending the favored defender and Wimbledon champ, Billie Jean King, 6-4, 6-2.

As a pro she won 55 singles titles, eighth among the all-time leaders, and amassed $1,542,278 prize money. She won the Australian title in 1972, over native Evonne Goolagong, 6-4, 6-4, only the third Brit to do so, following Dorothy Round (1935) and Angela Mortimer (1958). With her severely sliced backhand approach and splendid volleying, right-handed Ginny was a natural on grass. But she showed her clay mettle in winning the Italian in 1971, over Helga Niessen Masthoff, 6-4, 6-4. She added doubles majors at the Australian, French and U.S., all with Margaret Court in 1973 plus the U.S. of 1975.

She continued to play Wimbledon through 1987—a record 26 years in all—getting as far as a semifinal defeat by Evert, 8-6, 6-2, in her 1978 defense, and the quarters in 1979 and 1983, when ranked No. 63. Ginny is fifth among all players in matches at the Big W (212): 64-23 in singles, 53-24 in doubles, 24-24 in mixed. She entered the world's Top 10 in 1967 and was there 13 straight years, No. 2 in 1968. She set records for participation in Federation Cup (18 years) and series (57). She played 99 matches and won 66. She was the most persistent Brit in Wightman Cup, playing 21 years.

She was born July 10, 1945 in Bournemouth, England, learned to play tennis in South Africa, where she grew up, and was inducted into the Hall of Fame in 1989.

MAJOR TITLES (7)—Australian singles, 1972; Wimbledon singles, 1977; U.S. singles, 1968; Australian doubles, 1973; French doubles, 1973; U.S. doubles, 1973, 1975. **FEDERATION CUP**—1967-68-69-70-71-72-73-74-75-76-77-78-79, 36-20 singles, 30-13 doubles. **WIGHTMAN CUP**—1965-66-67-68-69-70-71-72-73-74-75-76-77-78-79-80-81-82-83-84-85, 12-23 singles, 7-14 doubles **SINGLES RECORD IN THE MAJORS**—Australian (10-4), French (16-13), Wimbledon (64-23), U.S. (49-19)

Marie Wagner
United States (1883–1975)
Hall of Fame—1969

Queen of the boards, Marie Wagner, a New Yorker, was the scourge of Manhattan's Seventh Regiment Armory where she won the U.S. Indoor singles a record six times: 1908 and 1911, over Mrs. Frederic Schmitz, 6-3, 6-2, and 6-4, 7-9, 6-4; 1909, over Bessie Moore, 6-0, 12-14, 6-0; 1913-14, over Mrs. Charles Beard, 6-1, 6-1, and 6-1, 2-6, 6-4; 1917, over Eleanor Goss, 6-3, 6-1. Marie added four doubles titles: 1910, 13, with Clara Kutroff; 1916, with Molla Bjurstedt (Mallory); 1917 with Margaret Taylor.

She was also singles finalist in 1915 to Mallory. Her best outdoor showing was as the 1914 U.S. finalist to Mary K. Browne, losing, 6-2, 1-6, 6-1.

She ranked No. 6 in 1913 when the U.S. Top 10 was established, and was in that select group every year through 1920: No. 3 in 1914; No. 6 in 1915-16; No. 5 in 1918; No. 8 in 1919; No. 10 in 1920, as well No. 9 in 1922, at age 39. A right-hander, she was born Feb. 2, 1883, in Freeport, N.Y., and died April 1, 1975. She entered the Hall of Fame in 1969.

U.S. TITLES (10)—Indoor singles. 1908, 1909, 1911, 1913, 1914, 1917; Indoor doubles, 1910, 1913 with Clara Kutross; 1916, with Molla Bjurstedt (Mallory); 1917, with Margaret Taylor. **SINGLES RECORD IN THE MAJORS**—U.S. (17-7)

Maud Barger Wallach
United States (1870–1954)
Hall of Fame—1958

A late-in-life tennis success, Maud Barger Wallach—"I started to play at about 30"—became the oldest major champion in 1908. She was 38 when she toppled the defending U.S. champ, lefty Evelyn Sears, 6-3, 1-6, 6-3, in the challenge round, after having beaten Marie Wagner, 4-6, 6-1, 6-3, in the all-comers. Molla Mallory, winning in 1926 at 42, took away Maud's old-age record.

In her first shot at the title, 1906, Maud lost the final to Helen Homans, 6-4, 6-3. Hazel Hotchkiss Wightman, who took the crown from her in the 1909 challenge round, recalled that Mrs. Richard Wallach had a good forehand "but not much of backhand. I concentrated on it until I was well ahead"—winning, 6-1, 6-0.

Maud was a New Yorker, a right-hander, born there June 15, 1870. She was a familiar summer figure at Newport, R.I., generally playing beneath a distinctive wide-brimmed straw hat. "Mine was not a great career," she recalled, "but a long and happy one."

At 46, she made the U.S. quarterfinals of 1916 (losing to runner-up Louise Raymond, 6-1, 6-3) and ranked No. 10, the oldest to do so well in the tournament and the rankings. National rankings for women weren't instituted until 1913, then largely because of her lobbying. But she was No. 5 in 1915. After dying in Baltimore, April 2, 1959, she was buried at Newport, not far from her beloved Casino, and was placed there eternally on her 1958 induction into the Hall of Fame.

MAJOR TITLE—U.S. singles, 1908. **SINGLES RECORD IN THE MAJORS**—U.S. (16-6).

Holcombe Ward
United States (1878–1967)
Hall of Fame—1956

One of the originals, the Harvard Three forming the first U.S. Davis Cup team, Holcombe Ward is also credited with originating the American twist serve which bedeviled the British invaders as the Cup was put into play in 1900. He accompanied donor Dwight Davis to the clinching doubles win over Ernest Black and Herbert Roper Barrett, 6-4, 6-4, 6-4, in the 3-0 victory over the British Isles.

Ward, a 5-foot-9, 135-pound right-hander, played for the Cup-winners again in 1902, and the losers to the Brits in 1905 and 1906. A shrewd, effective doubles player, Holcombe won four national championships linked to sidekick Davis: the Intercollegiate doubles in 1899, and the U.S. crowns of 1899, 1900, and 1901, titles he repeated with Beals Wright in 1904, 1905 and 1906.

But he did figure in singles, too, breaking through as U.S. champ in 1904, over Bill Clothier, 10-8, 6-4, 9-7. However, Wright took the title away from him in the 1905 challenge round, 6-2, 6-1, 11-9. In 1904, he was ranked No. 1, the acme of his seven years in his country's Top 10. In 1922, Ward and Davis reunited to win the U.S. Seniors 45s doubles title. Holcombe served as president of the USTA between 1937 and 1947.

A New Yorker, he was born there Nov. 23, 1878, and died Jan. 23, 1967, in Red Bank, N.J. He was inducted into the Hall of Fame in 1956.

MAJOR TITLES (7)—U.S. singles, 1904; U.S. doubles, 1899, 1900, 1901, 1904, 1905, 1906. **OTHER U.S. TITLES** (2)—Indoor singles, 1901; Intercollegiate doubles, 1899, with Dwight Davis. **DAVIS CUP**—1900, 1902, 1905, 1906, 3-4 singles, 4-3 doubles. **SINGLES RECORD IN THE MAJORS**—Wimbledon (0-1), U.S. (19-8)

Watson Washburn
United States (1894–1973)
Hall of Fame—1965

A New Yorker and a Harvard man, Watson McLean "Watty" Wasburn had a hand in the U.S. record run of seven Davis Cups that began in 1920. Watty played in the first defense, at Forest Hills in 1921, where he and Dick Williams won the cup-clinching match over Japan's Zenzo Shimidzu and Ichiya Kumagae, 6-2, 7-5, 4-6, 7-5.

A 6-foot right-hander who won the US Intercollegiate doubles while at Harvard in 1913, Washburn served in the U.S. army

in World War I. He ranked seven times in the U.S. Top 10 between 1914-1922, No. 5 in 1921, and continued to play extremely well in to his fifties, winning the U.S. 45s singles in 1940, and the doubles in that category thrice, 1940, 42, 44.

He was born June 13, 1894 in New York, was an industrious committee man for the USTA, and died in New York December 2, 1973. He was an uncle of Hall of Famer Sidney Wood, and was inducted in the Hall of Fame in 1965.

U.S. TITLES (2)—Indoor doubles, 1915, with Gus Touchard; Intercollegiate doubles, 1913, with Joe Armstrong. **DAVIS CUP**—1921; 1-0 doubles. **SINGLES RECORDS IN THE MAJORS**—Wimbledon (7-4), U.S. (38-24)

Hazel Hotchkiss Wightman
United States (1886–1974)
Hall of Fame—1957

"Lady Tennis," as she came to be known, remembered herself as a shy, somewhat awed and fascinated college girl when she arrived at the Philadelphia Cricket Club in 1909 for the U.S. Championships. A Californian, Hazel Virginia Hotchkiss hadn't played on grass, but with her attacking style and rock-ribbed volleying—she was the first woman to rely so heavily on the volley—22-year-old Hazel, a right-hander, scythed through the field to lift the title effortlessly (6-0, 6-1) from 39-year-old Maud Barger Wallach in the challenge round, and won the doubles and mixed as well.

Losing only one set (in the all-comers final over Louise Hammond), she was the first of three triple-triple winners in U.S. annals. Repeating singles, doubles and mixed titles in 1910-11, Hazel was emulated by Mary K. Browne (1912-13-14) and Alice Marble (1938-39-40).

Hazel had no trouble with Hammond in the 1910 challenge round, but an old West Coast rival, May Sutton—champion in 1904—pushed her hard in 1911, 8-10, 6-4, 9-7. In 1910, at Seattle, Hazel blitzed a Miss Huiskamp in the only recorded "golden match," 6-0, 6-0, outscoring poor Huiskamp 48-points-to-zero.

Marrying Bostonian George Wightman in 1912, she didn't defend. But, responding to a challenge from her father to win after becoming a mother, a U.S. first. She reappeared in 1915 to lose the singles final to Molla Mallory, and win the doubles and mixed. But papa's wish came true for the spunky 125-pound 5-footer in another comeback in 1919. At 32, she won her fourth singles title. She lost only one set, beating Marion Zinderstein Jessup, 6-1, 6-2, in the final, and reaching the doubles final. Thereafter her long-lived and unapproached success (U.S. adult titles between 1909 and 1943) was confined to doubles, at which she was one of the supremes.

Hazel, devoted to the game in all aspects, generously instructed innumerable players, at no charge, usually in the small garage behind her house, throughout her life. She was able to win important titles with two of her protégés who would join her in the Hall of Fame: Wimbledon, U.S. and Olympic doubles with Helen Wills in 1924; U.S. Indoor doubles with Sarah Palfrey in 1928 through 1931. Her second Olympic gold in 1924 came in the mixed with Dick Williams.

When Williams sprained an ankle in the semis, he suggested they default the final and settle for silver. "Not on her life," he laughed in recounting it later. "Hazel told me to stay at the net and she'd do the running—and we won"—defeating Vinnie Richards and Jessup, 6-2, 6-3.

She envisioned a team tournament for women similar to the Davis Cup, and offered a silver vase as the prize. In 1923, British women were the strongest apart from Americans, and Julian Myrick of the USTA decided that a U.S.-Britain competition would be in order for the Wightman Cup. The event, with Hazel captaining and playing for a winning U.S. side, opened the newly constructed stadium at Forest Hills. A treasured series, it lasted through 1989, disbanded unfortunately with the Brits no longer able to offer competition.

The last of Hazel's record 34 U.S. adult titles was recorded in 1943 as she, 56, and Pauline Betz, 23, won the Indoor doubles over Lillian Lopaus and Judy Atterbury, 7-5, 6-1. Though short, she anticipated and moved extremely well and competed fiercely though undemonstrably. She perfected her volleying early, hitting the ball against the family home in Berkeley, where she grew up and graduated from the University of California. She refused to let the ball bounce because the yard was so uneven. She used to play against her four brothers and then the proud and spiky Sutton sisters, outlasting them by recording 11 U.S. senior (over 40) doubles titles between 1940 and 1954, the last at age 67.

As the Bostonian Mrs. Wightman, she was in the U.S. Top 10 in 1915, 1918 and 1919—No. 1 the last. She was born Dec. 20, 1886, in Healdsburg, Calif., and died Dec. 5, 1974, in Chestnut Hill, Mass. She entered the Hall of Fame in 1956.

MAJOR TITLES (17)—U.S. singles, 1909, 1910, 1911, 1919: Wimbledon doubles, 1924: U.S. doubles, 1909, 1910, 1911, 1915, 1924, 1928; U.S. mixed. 1909, 1910, 1911, 1915, 1918, 1920. **OTHER U.S. TITLES** (18)—Indoor singles, 1919, 1927; Indoor doubles, 1919, 1921, 1924, 1927, with Marion Zinderstein Jessup; 1928, 1929, 1930, 1931, 1933, with Sarah Palfrey; 1943, with Pauline Betz; Indoor mixed, 1923, with Burnham Dell; 1924, with Bill Tilden; 1926, 1927, with G. Peabody Gardner Jr.; 1928, with Henry Johnson. Clay mixed, 1915, with Harry Johnson. **WIGHTMAN CUP**— 1923, 1924, 1927, 1929, 1931; 3-2 doubles. **SINGLES RECORD IN THE MAJORS**— Wimbledon (2-1), U.S. (22-4).

Mal Whitman
United States (1877–1932)
Hall of Fame—1955

One of the Harvard Three, the pioneering U.S. Davis Cup team, Malcolm Douglass Whitman shared leadoff honors with Cup donor Dwight Davis in the initial U.S. vs. British Isles clash in 1900. Playing on side-by-side courts at their club, Boston's Longwood Cricket Club, Whitman beat Arthur Gore, 6-1, 6-3, 6-2, while Davis beat Ernest Black, 4-6, 6-2, 6-4, 6-4. The next day, Holcombe Ward joined Davis for a 6-4, 6-4, 6-4 win over Herbert Roper Barrett and Black to defeat the Brits, 3-0.

A quarterfinalist in the 1896 and 1897 U.S. Championships, Whitman came through at Newport in 1898 with the first of his three straight championships. In the all-comers title match, he beat Davis, 3-6, 6-3, 6-2, 6-1, and was crowned champion because

1897 victor Bob Wrenn, off to the Spanish-American War, didn't defend in the challenge round.

After another successful defense in 1899, 6-1, 6-2, 3-6, 7-5, over Parmly Paret, Whitman had to first win a fight with his father, who wanted him to concentrate on law school (Harvard) and put away his racket. The son won, and that enabled him to put down challenger Bill Larned, 6-4, 1-6, 6-2, 6-2, for his third crown. Whitman had a weirdly bounding reverse twist serve (a stroke no longer seen) and was a sharp volleyer.

He didn't defend in 1901 but returned for a 1902 cameo "to represent my country," helping turn back the British invaders once more, and he reached the U.S. all-comers final, only to be stung by Brit Reggie Doherty, 6-1, 3-6, 6-3, 6-0.

In the Davis Cup in Brooklyn, N.Y., he won both his matches (over Joshua Pim, 6-1, 6-1, 1-6, 6-0, and Reggie Doherty, 6-1, 7-5, 6-4) and the U.S. kept the Cup, 3-2.

Whitman, a handsome 6-foot-2 right-hander, was through after posting an unbeaten Cup record and a 19-3 U.S. match record at Newport. He was in the U.S. Top 10 six times from 1896 in No. 1 1898, 1899, 1900, and No. 2 in 1902. Ever absorbed by the game's history, he wrote *Tennis Origins and Mysteries*, published in 1931. Born March 15, 1877, in New York, he committed suicide there Dec. 28, 1932.

MAJOR TITLES (3)—U.S. singles, 1898, 1899, 1900. **OTHER U.S. TITLES** (3)—Intercollegiate singles, 1896; Intercollegiate doubles, 1897 1898 with Leo Ware. **DAVIS CUP**—1900, 1902; 3-0 in singles. **SINGLES RECORD IN THE MAJOR**—U.S. (19-3).

Mats Wilander
Sweden (1964—)
Hall of Fame—2002

No sooner had Swedes grieved the retirement of Bjorn Borg, and nostalgiously regarded his sixth French title in 1981, than an unheralded young countryman conquered Paris the following year. Unseeded 17-year-old Mats Arne Olof Wilander, a rugged 6-footer, beat powerful one-time champ Guillermo Vilas at his own baseline game 1-6, 7-6 (8-6), 6-0, 6-4 and became the youngest of French champs. It was the first of seven singles majors for Wilander over a seven-year stretch when he competed at the top of the game, reaching No. 1 in 1988.

Although Michael Chang, a younger 17 in 1989, usurped his male precocity record for the majors, Wilander won the French again in 1985 (dethroning Ivan Lendl, 3-6, 6-4, 6-2, 6-2) and 1988 (beating Henri Leconte of France), as well as the Australian, on grass, in 1983, over Lendl, 6-1, 6-4, 6-4, and 1984, over Kevin Curren, 6-7 (5-7), 6-4, 7-6 (7-3), 6-2.

But it was 1988, an all-time season, that stands as his masterpiece. He won three majors, starring with a magnificent five-set Australian final-round victory over hometown hero Patrick Cash in Melbourne's newly opened Flinders Park. It was the Aussie Open's first year on hard courts, and victory—6-3, 6-7 (3-7), 3-6, 6-1, 8-6—meant that Mats was only the second man (emulating Jimmy Connors) to win majors on grass, clay and hard.

While he won the French without much trouble, over Leconte, 7-5, 6-2, 6-1, his dreams of a Grand Slam were pierced by Miloslav

Mecir, 6-3, 6-1, 6-3, in the Wimbledon quarters. An arduous U.S. backcourt duel with Lendl, who'd beaten him for the title in 1987, lasted 4:55 (the longest U.S. final ever) before at last Wilander showed more offensive initiative to win, 6-4, 4-6, 6-3, 5-7, 6-4. As the first winner of three majors in a year since Connors in 1974, he completed 1988 with six victories in 15 tournaments, a 53-11 record, and prize money of $1,726,731.

But after that, having attained the No. 1 ranking, his motivation seemed to disappear. His last of 33 career titles was at Itaparica (Brazil) in 1990, yet in some ways Wilander outdid Borg. Bjorn never won three majors in a year, and he led Sweden to but one Davis Cup. Mats won three. Stunning Connors 6-1, 6-3, 6-3, on opening day in Goteborg in 1984, Wilander launched Sweden to a 4-1 upset of the United States. He backboned a 3-2 win over Germany in 1985 in Munich, winning two singles and a doubles, and a 5-0 win over India in 1987 in Goteborg.

In 1991, he had dropped to No. 157. However, he felt the urge to play again in 1993, and came back to do moderately well, climbing to No. 45 in 1995 and earning about $500,000. He was even selected as a starter for the Davis Cup semifinal against the U.S. in 1995, losing to Andre Agassi and Pete Sampras.

Speedy afoot and an unrelenting competitor through 1988, he was at first a pure top-spinning, grind-it-out baseliner, a right-hander with a two-fisted backhand. But Mats developed attacking skills and a good volley, winning the Wimbledon doubles in 1986 with Joakim Nystrom.

Two memorable matches were Davis Cup losses, two of the longest matches ever played: six hours and 22 minutes against John McEnroe in 1982, 9-7, 6-2, 15-17, 3-6, 8-6; six hours and four minutes against Horst Skoff of Austria in 1989, 6-7 (5-7), 7-6 (9-7), 1-6, 6-4, 9-7. His epic with McEnroe was the longest men's match ever played until Fabrice Santoro and Arnaud Clement played for 6:33 at the 2004 French Open (played, however, over two days).

His career figures are impressive: 33 titles in 220 tournaments; a 524-164 match record, and earnings of $7,976,256.

He was born Aug. 22, 1964, in Vaxjo, Sweden, and grew up there.

MAJOR TITLES (8)—Australian singles, 1983, 1984, 1988; French singles, 1982, 1985, 1988; U.S. singles 1988; Wimbledon doubles, 1986. **DAVIS CUP**—1981, 1982, 1983, 1984, 1985, 1986, 1987, 1988, 1989, 1990; 36-16 singles, 7-2 doubles. **SINGLES RECORD IN THE MAJORS**—Australian (36-7), French (47-9), Wimbledon (25-10), US. (36-11).

Tony Wilding
New Zealand (1883–1915)
Hall of Fame—1978

The British idolized Tony Wilding, a superb figure. His sportsmanship was exemplary, and, besides, he learned his tennis at Cambridge University. Springing from an affluent family that emphasized physical and intellectual achievement, he was a dashing young man in a hurry and often traveled by motorcycle.

Anthony Frederick Wilding, born Oct. 31, 1883, in Christchurch, New Zealand, stood with Aussie Norman Brookes as two of the game's foremost players for nearly a decade. On his sixth try, 1910, Tony won Wimbledon, unseating Arthur Gore in the challenge round, 6-4, 7-5, 4-6, 6-2, and he kept the title through 1913. In that challenge round, he beat Maurice McLoughlin, the formidable California Comet, 8-6, 6-3, 10-8. "He was in prime physical condition," wrote distinguished British tennis authority A. Wallis Myers. "All his best fighting instincts were aroused, his tactics were as sound as his strokes and he won a great victory, the greatest of his career, in three sets."

Wilding, a 6-foot-2, 185-pound right-hander, lost his title to Brookes in 1914, 6-4, 6-4, 7-5, then joined with the "Wizard" to win the Davis Cup back for Australasia, 3-2 over the United States. Tony's triumph over Dick Williams on the first day at Forest Hills was a shock, 7-5, 6-2, 6-3. Williams was one of the most daring and brilliant shotmakers in history, but Wilding played almost unerringly and won in just 29 games. He kept up the pressure alongside Brookes in the vital doubles win over McLoughlin and Tom Bundy, 6-3, 8-6, 9-7, to make it 2-1. Brookes, first day loser to McLoughlin, finished it, 6-1, 6-2, 8-10, 6-3, over Williams.

Tony played the classic game that was in vogue. His drives were the strength of his attack and his defense was outstanding. He could hit with immense pace and over-spin, but when prudence and judgment dictated security of stroke rather than speed, as against a player of Williams' daring, Wilding could temper his drives and play faultlessly from the baseline.

Wilding made his debut on the Australasian Davis Cup team at the age of 21 in 1905. After winning the second Australian Championship in 1906 over a fellow New Zealander, lefty Francis Fisher, 6-0, 6-4, 6-4, his Antipodean partnership with Brookes took off. They stripped the Davis Cup from Britain at Wimbledon in 1907, and though hard-pressed, they kept the trophy the next year at Melbourne, turning back the U.S., 3-2, with Wilding taking the decisive fifth point over Fred Alexander, 6-3, 6-4, 6-1. Then they spanked the U.S. kids, 19-year-olds McLoughlin and Melville Long, 5-0 in 1909, the year Wilding won his second Australian championship, over Ernest Parker, 6-1, 7-5, 6-2. Tony was absent as Australia lost the 1912 Cup showdown to Britain, and his reappearance in the 1914 invasion of New York marked his farewell to tennis.

Following their victory at Forest Hills, he and Brookes went to war. Wilding never came back. At the age of 31, on May 9, 1915, he was killed in action at Neuve Chapelle, France. As world rankings began, he was No. 1 in 1913, and shared No. 2 with Brookes in 1914, and was named to the Hall of Fame in 1978.

MAJOR TITLES (11)—Australian singles, 1906, 1909; Wimbledon singles, 1910, 1911, 1912, 1913; Australian doubles, 1906; Wimbledon doubles, 1907, 1908, 1910, 1914. **DAVIS CUP**—1905, 1906, 1907, 1908, 1910, 1914; 15-6 singles, 6-3 doubles. **SINGLES RECORD IN THE MAJORS**—Australian (10-0), Wimbledon (23-6).

Dick Williams
United States (1891–1968)
Hall of Fame—1957

As the "Miracle Man of Tennis," Richard Norris Williams II (who preferred to be called Dick) survived the sinking of the *Titanic*. After that harrowing experience, tennis seemed child's

play, and he became a risk-taking shotmaker, one of the outstanding players of his time. Born of American parents in Geneva, Switzerland, on January 29, 1891, he departed for the U.S. to enroll at Harvard aboard the ocean liner *Titanic*, which struck an iceberg and sank April 10, 1912.

At the insistence of his infirm father, who perished with the ship, Dick dived from the deck at the last possible moment, swam to a half-submerged lifeboat and clung there in near-freezing water for six hours. When rescued by the *Carpathia*, he was advised by a ship's doctor that amputation of the frozen-stiff, apparently useless legs (common treatment at the time) would save his life. Fortunately, Williams refused, somehow—regardless of intense pain—willing himself to abandon the stretcher and walk the deck. Only months later he was in the quarterfinals of the U.S. Championships, losing in four sets to champion Maurice McLoughlin 6-4, 5-7, 6-4, 3-6, 6-3.

He lived to age 77. For that the tennis world, as well as his hometown, Philadelphia (there a philanthropist and civic leader,) were grateful.

Williams, a 5-foot-11 right-hander, learned to play in Switzerland, using the continental grip and hitting his groundstrokes with underspin. He developed his game as a Harvard undergrad, winning the Intercollegiate championship in 1913 and 1915. During his career, he won 42 singles, 51 doubles and 13 mixed titles.

In 1913, he was runner-up for the U.S. championship to McLoughlin, 6-4, 5-7, 6-3, 6-1. But he reversed that the next year, 6-3, 8-6, 10-8, a stirring final. Throughout the match, Williams maintained a terrific pace and marvelous control, averting the loss of the final set several times with bursts of speed and master strokes that thwarted even so aggressive and gritty a foe as the California Comet.

Occurring during the 1914 tournament was a poignant quarterfinal that could have been called a *Titanic* alumni meeting—Williams beat Karl Behr, who escaped by lifeboat, 6-1, 6-2, 7-5. Neither mentioned it.

In 1916, the second year in the new location, Forest Hills, Dick carried the U.S. again, 4-6, 6-4, 0-6, 6-2, 6-4, this time over Little Bill Johnston, and attained No. 1 ranking.

Beginning in 1913 (a Davis Cup-grabbing 3-2 decision over Britain in which he contributed a singles win), Dick played on five winning Cup teams. After wartime combat service in France with the U.S. Army, a decorated hero (a French Croix de Guerre among his medals), Dick captained six Cup winners, 1921-26, plus the team of 1934.

The 1934 team was unique among U.S. troupes, recovering successfully from a 0-2 deficit to beat Australia, 3-2, thus entering the finale, a defeat by Britain.

Dick was a victorious doubles player in four of those Cup-keeping years (1921, 23, 25-26, notably wins over the French aces, Rene Lacoste-Jean Borotra, 6-4, 6-4, 6-3, in 1925; Henri Cochet-Jacques Brugnon, 6-4, 6-4, 6-2, in 1926). He was a brilliant volleyer whose doubles titles were numerous, including Wimbledon in 1920 with Chuck Garland, and the U.S. in 1925-26, the former with Vinnie Richards over the Aussie champs Gerald Patterson and Jack Hawkes, 6-2, 8-10, 6-4, 11-9. He chuckled about his 1924 Olympic gold medal in mixed doubles alongside Hazel Wightman: "I

had a sprained ankle and suggested to her that we default. Not on your life with Hazel. She told me to stay at the net, and she'd do the running. It worked [over Marion Jessup and Vinnie Richards] even though I was 34 and she 37." He continued playing the U.S. Championships (21 in all, the fifth-highest total) through 1935 when he won a round at age 44. He won 65 of 84 U.S. matches.

Williams had a daring style, taking every possible ball on the rise, when not in volleying position, with hair-trigger timing. He always hit boldly, sharply for the winner, and that included serving for a winner on both the first and second balls. He did not know what it was to temporize. On occasion, his errors caused by his bold tactics might bring defeat by opponents of inferior ability. But it was the commonly held opinion that Williams, on his best days when he had the feel and touch and his breathtaking strokes were flashing on the lines, was unbeatable against any and all. He once won a set over Bill Tilden in five minutes!

He made the world's Top 10 in 1913-14, 1919, 1920, 1921, 1922, 1923 and 1925, was No. 4 in 1923, No. 5 in 1925, and was in the U.S. Top 10 on 12 occassions between 1912 and 1925, No. 1 in 1916. He died June 2, 1968, at Bryn Mawr, Pa.

MAJOR TITLES (6)—U.S. singles, 1914, 1916; Wimbledon doubles, 1926; U.S. doubles, 1925, 1926;. U.S. mixed, 1912. **OTHER U.S. TITLES**—Clay Court singles, 1912, 1915; Intercollegiate singles, 1913, 1915; Intercollegiate doubles, 1914, 1915, with Dick Harte. **DAVIS CUP**—1913, 1914, 1921, 1923, 1925, 1926, 6-3 singles, 4-0 doubles. **SINGLES RECORD IN THE MAJORS**—Wimbledon 10-3, U.S. (65-19).

Major Walter Clompton Wingfield
Great Britain (1833–1912)
Hall of Fame—1997—Contributor

Long overdue for admission to the International Tennis Hall of Fame, Major Walter Clopton Wingfield entered in 1997.

This imaginative Englishman, who had the idea for the modern game of tennis, and patented it in 1874, was born into a well-to-do military family Oct. 16, 1833 at the Old Ruabon Vicarage in Wales, the home of his paternal grandparents. His parents were there on extended leave from Canada, where his father served as a captain of the Sixty-Sixth, the Berkshire Regiment. At three, Walter's mother died in childbirth, and he and his sister were cared for by the mother's father, Col. Michel, who was transferred home having commanded the Royal Artillery in Canada.

In 1838, his father now a major, left the service, returned home and, with his brother, Watkin, raised Walter until the young man, after attending Sandhurst, became an officer in the First Dragoon Guards. Uncle Watkin had served in India where he was renowned as a linguist. He later became an artist and playwright. His play, *The Hidden Treasure*, became the longest running play in London for many years.

Walter served in India during the Sepoy Revolt. From India, his regiment went to China where Wingfield, now a captain, led a British force through some skirmishes with the Chinese. His trophy was a Pekingese dog, a breed he introduced to England. While in India, Wingfield married and soon thereafter, wife and infant son returned to England where he sold his commission. He was 25, had inherited the estate of Rhysnant in Wales, but

preferred the more stimulating life in London, associating with intellectuals and artists.

Wingfield joined the Montgomeryshire Yeomanry as a major. He also was made a Gentleman-at-Arms, the royal guards of the Royal Family. Throughout his life he was an active participant in many sports: court (real) tennis, rackets, bicycling, and was a champion billiards player. From these interests, he saw the need for healthy exercise, as the Industrial Revolution brought thousands from the farms to cities bereft of open fields and woodlands.

Innumerable croquet courts, well cared for but seldom if ever used, were in existence. In a stroke of genius, Wingfield felt those courts could be used for a new racket- ball-and-net game, an outdoor version of court tennis. As many others, he played rackets, an energetic racket-and-ball game played against a wall at numerous taverns. He went about designing portable equipment—net posts and net—that could be installed on a lined court, preferably the lawn of an unused croquet court.

Working in confidence, he conducted several weeks of trials at several country estates. Rackets were designed and made in substantial quantity, as were the several other needs, the equipment fitting into an easily-carried box containing everything required for four to play. The most important aspects, which were novel, were written rules of the game, along with helpful instructions. The rules of *The Major's Game of Lawn Tennis* were printed in December of 1873, not long after his 40th birthday, and entered at Stationers Hall in February of 1874.

Wingfield's gifts to us were not limited to lawn tennis, for with invention of the modern bicycle he designed one called "The Butterfly" and wrote a book on group riding in formation. He devoted many of his later years to food and its preparation.

Such a good man deserved a better life than he was given. His eldest son, a naval midshipman, was lost at sea attempting the rescue of a shipmate. His second son died of disease contracted in an Assam tea plantation, and his last son was killed by an accidental gun shot while in Paris His wife, Alice, afflicted with mental illness and declared insane early in life, never recovered.

Wingfield died April 18, 1912 at the age of 79.

—*George Alexander*

Sidney Wood
United States (1911—)
Hall of Fame—1964

Playing in knickerbockers against the great Frenchman René Lacoste, 15-year-old Sidney Burr Beardsley Wood was the youngest male Wimbledon entrant ever in 1927. Four years later, he became the second-youngest champion of Centre Court, and without stepping onto the hallowed sod. Frank Shields, with an injured ankle, withdrew, the only time Wimbledon has had a defaulted final.

"Frank wanted to play, and so did I," Sidney says. "It was insulting to the fans and the tournament. I didn't want to win that way. But the U.S. Davis Cup committee ordered Frank to withdraw so he'd be ready for Davis Cup the next weekend against Britain, which we lost. It shows you the control the USTA had over us amateurs."

Wood got to the final with a 4-6, 6-2, 6-4, 6-2, decision over Brit Fred Perry, the future champion, and, at 19, became the youngest Wimbledon champ until 17-year-old Boris Becker in 1985.

A sickly child afflicted with tuberculosis, Sidney was born Nov. 1, 1911, in Black Rock, Conn. A 5-foot-9-1/2 right-hander, he never reached the Wimbledon final again, although he did get to play a major final, losing the 1935 U.S. final to Wilmer Allison 6-2, 6-2, 6-3. A slim, nimble blond, he ranked in the U.S. Top 10 on 10 occasions between 1930 and 1945—No. 2 in 1934—and was in the world Top 10 five times between 1931 and 1938—No. 5 in 1938 and No. 6 in 1931.

He was a Davis Cupper in 1931 and 1934 and in the latter year was part of the most astounding U.S. comeback, from 0-2 down against Australia in London at Wimbledon. Having lost to Viv McGrath, Wood was heartened by George Lott and Les Stoefen's holding-action doubles victory over Adrian Quist and Jack Crawford. Then Sidney knocked off 1933 Wimbledon champ Jack Crawford, 6-3, 9-7, 4-6, 4-6, 6-2, to open the third day and tie the score at 2-2. Shields beat McGrath, and the U.S. entered the final, losing, 4-1, to Britain. There, on opening day at Wimbledon, Wood battled the Cup-holder's main man, Fred Perry, losing 6-1, 4-6, 5-7, 6-0, 6-3, and also lost to Bunny Austin on the third day.

An inventive mind, he continued in 2007, at age 96, working on his inventions, one of which was a plastic carpet (Supreme Court), long used for indoor tourneys.

MAJOR TITLE—Wimbledon singles, 1931. **DAVIS CUP**—1931, 1934; 5-6 singles, 3-0 doubles. **SINGLES RECORD IN THE MAJORS**—French (2-1), Wimbledon (21-5), U.S. (42-25).

Bob Wrenn
United States (1873–1925)
Hall of Fame—1955

A four-time U.S. singles champ, Robert Duffield Wrenn won the last of those titles in 1897 before serving in Cuba with Teddy Roosevelt's Rough Riders in the Spanish-American War. One of Bob's comrades in arms was future champion Bill Larned. Unfortunately Wrenn contracted yellow fever during that campaign and never regained pre-war form.

He came from a prominent Chicago family of several fine athletes, and became a topflight football, baseball and tennis player at Harvard. Noted for swiftness and court coverage, a defensive star featuring devilish lobs, he was the first left-hander to win the U.S. singles, appearing in five straight finals. He beat Fred Hovey for the 1893 title, 7-5, 3-6, 6-3, 7-5, and kept it by repelling Irishman Manliffe Goodbody in the 1894 challenge round, 6-8, 6-1, 6-4, 6-4.

Hovey took it from him easily, 6-3, 6-2, 6-4 in 1895. But Bob pulled it back, 7-5, 3-6, 6-0, 1-6, 6-1, in the 1896 challenge round, and fended off Wilberforce Eaves, 4-6, 8-6, 6-3, 2-6, 6-2, in the 1897 challenge round. War service prevented him from defending in 1898.

He did team with his right-handed younger brother, George Lawson Wrenn (born July 2, 1875, died July 29, 1948) as the U.S. Davis Cup doubles pair in 1903. They lost to the British Dohertys,

Laurie and Reggie, 7-5, 9-7, 2-6, 6-3, the only instance of brothers clashing for the Cup. Bob lost the hotly-contested decisive fifth match singles to Reggie, 6-4, 3-6, 6-3, 6-8, 6-4, and the Cup departed the U.S. for the first time.

Bob and George were the first of three brothers to play Davis Cup for the U.S.—later joined by John and Patrick McEnroe (who never played together for the U.S.) and identical twins Bob and Mike Bryan, who began playing doubles together for the U.S. in 2003. Bob and George, however, are the only brothers to rank concurrently in the U.S. Top 10: Bob was No. 1 in 1893, 1894, 1896 and 1897, No. 8 in 1892 and 1900; George four times No. 6 during his five years up there between 1896 and 1900. Another brother, Everts, ranked No. 18 in 1896. In Bob's last thrust for the U.S. singles title, he was beaten by George in a 1900 quarterfinal, 6-4, 6-1, 6-4, the only such brotherly battle at the U.S. Championships until the Spanish Sanchez brothers met in 1992, Emilio beating Javier, 6-4 in the fifth.

After leaving Harvard, Bob became a stockbroker in New York, and was president of the USTA from 1912 through 1915. Born Sept. 20, 1873, in Highland Park, Ill., he died in New York Nov. 12, 1925.

MAJOR TITLES (5)—U.S. singles, 1893, 1894, 1896, 1897; U.S. doubles, 1895. **OTHER U.S. TITLES** (1)-Intercollegiate doubles, 1892, with E B. Winslow. **DAVIS CUP**—1903; 0-2 singles, 0-1 doubles. **SINGLES RECORD IN THE MAJORS**—U.S. (20-3).

Beals Wright
United States (1879–1961)
Hall of Fame—1956

Before the turn of the century, Beals Coleman Wright was a national champion, winning the Interscholastic singles for Boston's Hopkinson School in 1898 at 18, and repeating in 1899 when he made his first of 11 entries in the U.S. Top 10 at No. 8. In 1900, his brother Irving won the Interscholastic for the same school.

In 1905, dethroning Holcombe Ward, Beals was the second lefty to win the U.S. singles, following Bob Wrenn. He had to beat the future champ, Bill Clothier, 9-7, 6-2, 6-2, and an ex-champ, Bill

Larned, 4-6, 6-3, 6-2, 6-2, plus Clarence Hobart, to reach the challenge round and topple Ward, 6-2, 6-1, 11-9. Clothier and Larned got back at him, beating Wright in respective U.S. finals, 1906, 6-3, 6-0, 6-4, and 1908, 6-1, 6-2, 8-6

Beals' biggest year was 1905. It included one of his three U.S. doubles titles (with Ward), and Davis Cup victories over Down Under greats Tony Wilding, 6-3, 6-2, 6-4, and Norman Brookes, 12-10, 5-7, 12-10, 6-4, in London. That launched the foremost tennis rivalry: U.S. against Australia (known as Australasia at that time). However, he didn't play in the next round, the final, and the U.S. was beaten by Britain, 5-0.

In 1908, he beat Wilding and Brookes again, even more stunning victories since it was the Davis Cup finale at Melbourne, their home turf. Australian fans couldn't believe that anybody would turn off both their bright lights. But Wright did, starting with Wilding, 3-6, 7-5, 6-3, 6-1. Out-volleying Brookes was considered impossible, until they saw Beals do it, rescuing two match points, 0-6, 3-6, 7-5, 6-2, 12-10—a wowser during a 100 degree afternoon while knotting the series, 2-2. But it wasn't enough. Wilding won the Cup, 6-3, 6-4, 6-1, over Beals' mate, Fred Alexander. The doubles had been the difference, 6-4, 6-2, 5-7, 1-6, 6-4, for the homeboys.

Wright was a regular in the U.S. Top 10, 10 straight years, 1899-1908, plus 1910. He was No. 1 in 1905; No. 2 in 1901, 07-08; No. 3 in 1902, 06. At the 1904 Olympics in St. Louis, he was double golden, winning the singles over teammate Bob LeRoy, 6-4, 6-4, and the doubles with teammate Edgar Welch. He won the Canadian singles thrice, 1902-04, and brother Irving won it in 1906

The 1956 induction of Beals into the Tennis Hall of Fame was nothing new in the Wright family. Papa George Wright and Uncle Harry Wright had been in the Baseball Hall of Fame for some time, George as a great shortstop, Harry as manager of the Boston Red Stockings. Beals was born Dec. 19, 1879, in Boston, lived in Brookline, Mass., and died Aug. 23, 1961, at Alton, Ill.

MAJOR TITLES (4)—U.S. singles, 1905; U.S. doubles, 1904, 1905, 1906. **DAVIS CUP**—1905, 1907, 1908, 1911; 6-4 singles, 3-3 doubles. **SINGLES RECORD IN THE MAJORS**—Wimbledon (6-2), U.S. (47-11).

En Route to Hall of Fame

Andre Agassi
United States (1970—)

A player of irresistible flair, appeal and shot-making ability since appearing on the professional landscape as a 16-year-old in 1986, Andre Kirk Agassi, was the first Nevadan to make an impact on the game. And what a tremendous impact, although it took longer than expected for him to make the predicted leap to his first major championship, Wimbledon in 1992—and even longer to re-dedicate himself to his profession so that he was solidly established at the heights. At age 33, he was playing better than ever, winning his fourth Australian championship, his eighth major.

Despite a seemingly disastrous slump during which he plummeted to No. 141 in 1997, and finished the year at No. 122, Andre rebounded sensationally to rise to No. 6 in 1998—a record turnaround. He nailed down five of his majors between 1999-2003. The piece de resistance was his French triumph in 1999, evicting the defender Carlos Moya in the fourth round, 4-6, 7-5, 7-5, 6-1, and finishing in a dazzling recovery over Andrei Medvedev, 1-6, 2-6, 6-4, 6-3, 6-4 The win catapulted Agassi into the select company of Fred Perry, Don Budge, Rod Laver and Roy Emerson as only the fifth man to own all four majors.

Andre's first major title, Wimbledon, came after he'd failed as the favorite to beat Pete Sampras for the U.S. Open title in 1990, and Andres Gomez and Jim Courier for the French in 1990 and 1991. After a quick, unhappy thrashing by Henri Leconte, 6-2, 6-1, 6-2, at Wimbledon in 1987, Agassi assiduously avoided the grass until 1991, a successful reappearance ending in a quarterfinal loss to David Wheaton, 6-2, 0-6, 3-6, 7-6 (7-3), 6-2. Realizing the greensward wasn't that forbidding, he returned a year later to take it all, his No. 12 seeding making him among Wimbledon's lowest regarded champions at the starting gate. "This was not the one people looked for me to win," he said correctly, after his buzzing groundies outdid the missile attack of 36-ace-serving Goran Ivanisevic in the final, 6-7 (8-10), 6-4, 6-4, 1-6, 6-4.

Ranked low again in 1994, No. 20, he became only the third non-seed to win the U.S. Championships, taking it on his ninth shot, over German Michael Stich, 6-1, 7-6 (7-3), 7-5 joining Aussies Mal Anderson (1957) and Fred Stolle (1966) in the exclusive unseeded club. He had also made excuses for skipping the long trip to Australia, yet won it on his first try in 1995, spectacularly over Sampras, the defender, 4-6, 6-1, 7-6 (8-6), 6-4.

Following his French title in 1999, Andre won his second U.S.—fifth major—in a five-set battle with Todd Martin, 6-4 6-7 (5-7), 6-7 (2-7), 6-3. 6-2. He then won the 2000 Aussie over Yevgeny Kafelnikov, 3-6, 6-3, 6-2, 6-4, after being two points from defeat in a fourth-set, semifinal tie-breaker against Sampras, 6-4, 3-6, 6-7 (0-7), 7-6 (7-5), 6-1. His third and fourth Aussie titles were both in straight-set finals, over Frenchman Arnaud Clement, 6-4, 6-2, 6-2, in 2001 and German Rainer Schuettler, 6-2, 6-2, 6-1, in 2003. (He missed 2002 with a wrist injury.)

A brilliant shot-maker and thoughtful attacker from the baseline who took the ball so early that he seemed to be playing ping-pong, Agassi needed time to sort out whether being a commercial success was enough. As the most widely marketed player of all-time—"Image is Everything" was one of his sales pitches—he has made more millions off the court than on it. Fortunately, he decided to utilize his gifts to attract as much attention by winning. Never has there been such a controversial figure so broadly associated with the game, thanks to TV commercials, his ever-changing hairstyle, brightly hued attire. Such items as black shoes and denim shorts, considered garish by traditionalists, lured countless buyers as hip or avant-garde. His engagement to actress Brooke Shields (granddaughter of Hall of Famer Frank Shields), whom he married in 1997, didn't hurt. Andre's visibility transcended the sports page. That marriage was short-lived, but he made another high-profile pairing when he wed champion Steffi Graf in 2001 (they have two children, Jaden Gil and Jaz).

But beneath the peacock and the pop idol was a tennis player whose timing, anticipation, coordination and determination enabled him to deliver withering, top-spinning barrages with flicks of the wrist. "When Andre's on, forget it," said Sampras. "He does practically everything better than anybody else."

Agassi, born April 29, 1970 in Las Vegas and grew up there, although he was farmed out to Nick Bollettieri's Tennis Academy at Brandenton, Fla., at age 13. His father, Mike Agassi, an Iranian immigrant and naturalized U.S. citizen, was a strict taskmaster determined that Andre would be a top tennis player. Papa pushed the kid from cradle onward, then gave the prodigy over to surrogate father Bollettieri. An Olympic boxer for Iran in 1952, Mike fell for tennis and taught Andre the new game, "based on the way a fighter throws punches, plus a two-handed backhand for added power." A right-hander, 5-11, Andre played at, 170 pounds.

Andre had his own Olympics in 1996 in Atlanta, where he made off with the gold medal by thumping Spaniard Sergi Bruguera, 6-2, 6-3, 6-1. He and wife Steffi Graf are the only players in tennis history to have all four major championship titles—and a gold medal—in their trophy cases.

By lifting the Australian crown from Sampras in 1995, Agassi also took Pete's No. 1 jersey, and they dueled throughout the year for the top. But Pete ended Andre's excellent summer streak of four tournaments and 26 matches with a 6-4, 6-3, 4-6, 7-5, title-round defeat to regain his U.S. Open title and the top ranking. That loss seemed to deflate Agassi, and 1996—other than the Olympics—was a downer: Ghastly first and second-round losses respectively at Wimbledon (No. 186 Doug Flach) and the French (No. 73 Chris Woodruff), and desultory semifinal losses to Michael Chang at the Australian and the U.S. Opens. His was an uneven course through the first 11 years, up one year, down another (four first-round losses at the U.S. Open for instance), but

the sheer firepower within made him a threat to blast anybody off any court at any time.

A world Top 10 inhabitant 16 times between 1988 and 2005, Agassi finished 1999 as No. 1, and was No. 2 in 1994-95, 2002.

Bollettieri, feeling Andre didn't work hard enough, severed their decade-long relationship in 1993, but he won six majors with Brad Gilbert as coach. Plunging to No. 24, his lowest adult ranking at the time, after losing the first round of the 1993 U.S. Open to No. 61 Thomas Enqvist, he required surgery to repair a damaged wrist—"I thought my career was over." But he came back strong. Aussie Darren Cahill became his coach in 2002, and fitness guru, fellow Las Vegan Gil Reyes, directed Andre's superb physical conditioning.

In 1988, as one of the youngest U.S. Davis Cup rookies at 18, he won all his singles on Latin clay (historic trouble ground for gringos) at Peru and Argentina to spearhead his fallen nation's recovery from the perdition of relegation. He became a valuable hand in the Cup triumphs of 1990, 1992 and 1995, but played sporadically thereafter, a total of 22 ties. Registering four singles wins in 3-2 decisions over Zimbabwe and the Czech Republic in 2000, he sat out Davis Cup play until making a cameo in 2005 against Croatia, losing what became his Cup swan-song to Ivan Ljubicic 6-3, 7-6 (0), 6-3 in the surprising 3-2 U.S. loss. He finished with a 30-6 singles record, representing the U.S. in 1988-1993, 1995, 1997-1998, 2000, 2005.

Andre made his first splash at Stratton Mountain, Vt. in 1986 as a 16-year-old, beating Tim Mayotte en route to the quarterfinals. He won his first title at the end of 1987 in Itaparica (Brazil), over Brazil's Luiz Mattar 7-6, 6-2. The last title (the 60th) was Los Angeles in 2005, 6-4, 7-5, over Gilles Muller of Luxembourg.

His most productive season was 1995: seven titles on a 73-9 match record, but two of his five titles in 1999 were the French and U.S. His feat of playing U.S. Open finals 15 years apart (1990 and 2005) is unequalled. Andre's last genuine hurrah was fending off close defeats. In 2005, he was two sets down and two points from defeat in defeating James Blake in an epic Open quarterfinal 3-6, 3-6, 6-3, 6-3, 7-6(8-6), en route to climbing to the ultimate of his 15th major final, a very combative four-set loss to Roger Federer, 6-3, 2-6, 7-6(7-1), 6-1.

Establishing the Andre Agassi Charitable Foundation, he has shown responsibility and concern, donating millions to such worthy projects as building the Agassi College Preparatory Academy, and the Agassi Boys and Girls Club in the troubled sector of West Las Vegas. Call him a humanitarian champion.

Won eight major singles titles: Australian, 1995, defeating Sampras, 4-6, 6-1, 7-6 (8-6), 6-4; 2000, defeating Yevgeny Kafelnikov, 3-6, 6-3, 6-2, 6-4; 2001, defeating Arnaud Clement, 6-4, 6-2, 6-2; 2003, defeating Rainer Schuettler, 6-2, 6-2, 6-1; French, 1999, defeating Andrei Medvedev, 1-6, 2-6, 6-4, 6-3, 6-4; Wimbledon, 1992, defeating Goran Ivanisevic, 6-7 (8-10), 6-4, 6-4, 1-6, 6-4; U.S., 1994, defeating Michael Stich, 6-1, 7-6 (7-5), 7-5; U.S., 1999, defeating Todd Martin, 6-4, 6-7 (5-7), 6-7 (2-7), 6-3, 6-2.

He lost seven major singles finals: French, 1990, to Andres Gomez, 6-3, 2-6, 6-4, 6-4; 1991, to Jim Courier, 3-6, 6-4, 2-6, 6-1, 6-4; Wimbledon, 1999, to Sampras, 6-3, 6-4, 7-5; U.S., 1990, to Sampras, 6-4, 6-3, 6-2; U.S., 1995, to Sampras, 6-4, 6-3, 4-6, 7-5; U.S., 2002, to

Sampras, 6-3, 6-4, 5-7, 6-5; U.S., 2005, to Roger Federer, 6-3, 2-6, 7-6 (7-1) 6-1.

During a 21-year pro career, ending emotionally at the U.S. Open of 2006, he won 60 singles titles (of 90 finals), one doubles title and $31,152,975 prize money. His career singles won-loss record was 870-274.

MAJOR TITLES (8)—Australian singles, 1995, 2000, 2001, 2003; French singles, 1999; Wimbledon singles, 1992; US singles, 1994, 1999. **DAVIS CUP**—1988, 1989, 1990, 1991, 1992, 1993, 1995, 1997, 1998, 2000, 2005 30-6 in singles. **SINGLES RECORD IN THE MAJORS**—Australian (48-5), French (51-16), Wimbledon (46-13), U.S. (79-19).

Jennifer Capriati
United States (1976—)

Jennifer Marie Capriati, America's tennis prodigy bursting ontp the scene—what a debut!—as a 13-year-old, reached the final of the 1990 Virginia Slims of Florida at Boca Raton. She lost to Gabriela Sabatini, 6-4, 7-5, but had the ladies shaking with her power. A right-hander with a two-fisted backhand, she was the youngest player to reach a tour final, and went on to achieve records as the youngest semifinalist at the French Championships (14 years, two months in 1990) and Wimbledon (15 years, three months 1991), in the latter beating defending champion Martina Navratilova in the quarterfinals, 6-4, 7-5, her earliest Wimbledon loss in 14 years. At the 1991 U.S. Open, she and Monica Seles played one the greatest women's matches in the history of the tournament, Seles winning the hard-smashing semifinal 3-6, 6-3, 7-6 (3). Capriati's most celebrated early triumph came at the 1992 Olympics, where she won the gold medal, defeating Steffi Graf in the final, 3-6, 6-3, 6-4. Born March 29, 1976, in New York and raised in Florida, Capriati faced burn-out after her Olympic triumph. After a first-loss at the 1993 U.S. Open to Leila Meskhi, 1-6, 6-4, 6-4 she dropped off the tour and then faced legal problems with incidents involving shoplifting and marijuana possession. She had a one-match comeback in 1994, losing to Anke Huber in the first round of Philadelphia, 6-4, 3-6, 6-1, before sitting out another 15 months, returning to the tour again full time in 1996. However, despite trials and tribulations, the public forgave, and she was America's tennis sweetheart.

Her dramatic comeback resulted in finally breaking through to win her first major title—the 2001 Australian Open—defeating Martina Hingis, 6-4, 6-3. She repeated as champ in 2002, again defeating Hingis in one of the most dramatic finals ever, in nearly unbearable heat. Capriati, saving four match points—the most ever in a major women's final—defeated Hingis again 4-6, 7-6 (9-7), 6-2. She dramatically won the second leg of a Grand Slam in 2001 at the French, outlasting Belgium's Kim Clijsters, 1-6, 6-4, 12-10. But there was to be no Slam, Jenny upset by Henin-Hardenne in the Wimbledon semifinals 2-6, 6-4, 6-2.

In October of 2001, she earned the momentary world No. 1 ranking. In 2003, she became the only defending Australian champ to lose in the first round (beaten by No. 90 Marlene Weingartner (GER), 2-6, 7-6 (8-6), 6-4. She lost an epic 2003 U.S. Open semifinal with Henin-Hardenne (BEL), 4-6, 7-5, 7-6 (4)—Capriati

merely two points from the final 11 times during the match. In 2004, she lost another squeaky-close U.S. Open semifinal to Elena Dementieva (RUS), again two points away again, 6-0, 2-6, 7-6 (7-5). Besides her Olympic triumph, she also helped bring titles to the U.S. as member of the Wightman Cup in 1989 (in the event's swan song), and the Fed Cup in 1990 and 2000. She also earned "youngest" marks at the Fed Cup (player and winner) in 1990; and the Wightman Cupper (player and winner) in 1989.

She was ranked five times in U.S. Top Three: No. 3, 1990, 2002; No. 2, 1991-92-93, 2001; No. 3, 2002-03. She as also ranked No. 6 in 1996 and in 2000; No. 7 in 1999; No. 4 in 2004. She was in the world's Top 10 for eight years: No. 8 in 1990; No. 6 in 1991 and 2003; No. 7 in 1992; No. 9 in 1993; No. 2 in 2001; No. 3 in 2002; No. 10 in 2004.

She won 13 singles titles (359-146 matches), one doubles title and $10,206,639 prize money in her career. Three shoulder surgeries between 2005 and 2007 sidelined her since 2004.

MAJOR TITLES (3)—Australian singles, 2001, 2002; French singles, 2001 FEDERATION CUP—1990-91, 96, 2000: 10-3 singles, 1-1 doubles WIGHTMAN CUP-1989: 1-0 singles. SINGLES RECORD IN THE MAJORS—Australian (28-6), French (39-10), Wimbledon (38-11), US (35-13).

Justine Henin
Belgium (1982—)

There's not much there, as far as physique goes. But within that 5-foot-5, 120 pound frame churned a highly competitive heart and the flair of an artist who plays the game with superlative grace and style. Flitting across the court quickly, nimbly, Justine Henin was a model of complete greatness, at home anywhere in the rectangle, baseline or net.

However, she is no longer in the game. On May 14, 2008, she stunningly announced her retirement at age 25 (the first No. 1 to do so), and will be sorely missed. She appeared quite satisfied with the decision, having worked tremendously to attain her 20-year goal, and looked forward to the next chapter in her life.

A right-hander with a stunning one-handed backhand drive, she grasped No. 1 for a year (2003), then returned for 2006-07, and would be very difficult to unseat were she still in view.

A brilliant 2007 contained nine titles—among them a fourth French, a second U.S.—and new zest based on heightened happiness in her personal life. Reconnecting with her family after a period of estrangement, and unconnecting with husband Pierre-Yves Hardenne (as Henin-Hardenne she won five of her seven majors), gave Justine an emotional lift. Her dash to the 2007 U.S. title was particularly satisfying since she had to erase the American Williams family in succession, Serena in the quarterfinals, 7-6 (7-3), 6-1, and Venus in the semifinals, 7-6 (7-2), 6-4, before a 6-1, 6-3, crushing of Svetlana Kuznetsova of Russia, who she also beat 6-4, 6-4 in the 2006 French final.

Born June 1, 1982 in Liege, Belgium, she turned pro in 1999 and was coached by Carlos Rodriguez throughout. She played Federation Cup for six years—1999—03, 06 and achieved a 15-1 singles record and 0-2 doubles record and helped win the Cup for Belgium in 2001 and reach the 2006 final. She won the gold medal in women's singles at the 2004 Olympics, defeating Amelie Mauresmo 6-3, 6-3 in the gold-medal match.

She won seven major singles titles—Australian, 2004, defeating countrywomen Kim Clijsters, 6-3, 4-6, 6-3; French, 2003, defeating Clijsters again, 6-0, 6-4; 2005, defeating Mary Pierce of France, 6-1, 6-1; 2006, defeating Svetlana Kuznetsova of Russia, 6-4, 6-4; 2007, defeating Ana Ivanovic of Serbia, 6-1, 6-2; U.S., 2003, defeating Clijsters, 7-5, 6-1; 2007, defeating Kuznetsova, 6-1, 6-3. She lost four major singles finals: Australian, 2006, to Amelie Mauresmo of France, 6-1, 2-0, ret; Wimbledon, 2001, to Venus Williams of the United States, 6-1, 3-6, 6-0; 2006, to Mauresmo, 2-6, 6-3, 6-4; U.S., 2006, to Maria Sharapova of Russia, 6-4, 6-4. Henin also made the semifinals of the Australian, 2003, French, 2001, Wimbledon, 2002-03, 07; the quarterfinals of the Australian, 2002 and 2008. From 2001, she has spent seven straight years in the Top 10: Nos. 7, 5, 1, 8, 6, 1, 1.

She has overcome numerous injuries and illnesses, and the negative publicity that accompanied her quitting the 2006 Australian final to Mauresmo, behind, 6-1, 2-0, claiming a stomach ache. But she showed her spunk during the 2003 U.S. Open. Somehow she beat Jennifer Capriati, 4-6, 7-5, 7-6 (7-4) in the semifinals in 3:03 (ending 12:27AM Saturday morning), even though Capriati was two points from victory 11 times, and served for it at 5-3 in the 2nd and 3rd sets. Justine, cramping in the third set, needed IV attention following the match. Yet later in the day took the championship, beating Clijsters, 7-5, 6-1, avoiding two set points at 4-5, 15-40.

As the first to win three straight French since Monica Seles, 1990-92, Justine revels in the Parisian earth, thrilled as a little girl brought to Roland Garros by her mother. She won two season-ending WTA Tour Championships—2006 defeating Amelie Mauresmo 6-4, 6-3; 2007 defeating Maria Sharapova (3hrs 24min) 5-7, 7-5, 6-3. In 2007, she was the first woman to end a season with more than $5 million in prize money in a season—$5,367,086.

Other prominent singles titles won include the German Open three times—2002, defeating Serena Williams, 6-2, 3-6, 7-6 (7-5), 2003, defeating Clijsters, 6-4, 4-6, 7-5, 2005, defeating Nadia Petrova, 6-3, 4-6, 6-3. She also won the Canadian Open in 2003, defeating. Lina Krasnoroutskaya, 6-1, 6-0 and Indian Wells in 2004, defeating Lindsay Davenport, 6-1, 6-4. During her career, she won 41 singles (489-105 matches), two doubles pro titles and $19,461,375 in prize money.

MAJOR TITLES (7)—Australian singles, 2004; French singles, 2003, 05-06-07; U.S. singles, 2003, 07. FEDERATION CUP—1999-2003, 2006; 15-3 in singles, 0-2 in doubles. SINGLES RECORDS IN THE MAJORS—Australian (30-6); French (35-4), Wimbledon (27-7), U.S. (35-7)

Martina Hingis
Switzerland (1980—)

A child prodigy-with-racket, she fulfilled all heavy expectations, including withstanding the pressure that came with her name. Born Sept. 30, 1980, Kosice, Czechoslovakia (now Slovakia), she was named Martina for Martina Navratilova by mom-coach, Melanie Molitor, expecting the babe to become an internationally famed champion, too.

It worked virtually as scripted. By the time Martina Hingis was 16—she and her mother became Swiss citizens in 1968—she'd been a pro two years, won her first of 42 singles titles (Filderstadt, 1996, over Anke Huber of Germany 6-2, 3-6, 6-3). She was world No. 4 that year, well on her way to No. 1, a position she held in 1997, 99-2000, a member of the Top 10 for eight years. She was No. 2, 1998, No. 4, 2001, No. 10, 2002 as impairing injuries drove her from the tour for three years. A remarkable comeback got her to No. 7 again in 2006, that included winning the Italian Open title, successively beating Venus Williams of the United States, 0-6, 6-3, 6-3 in the semifinals and Dinara Safina of Russia 6-2, 7-5 for the title.

As Wimbledon's second youngest singles victor, 16, in 1997, beating Czech Jana Novotna 2-6, 6-3, 6-3 in the final, she was a bit older than the Wimbledon and majors singles record-holder for precocity, Lottie Dod, 15, in 1887. However, in 1996, Martina, a three-days-younger-15 than Dod, she won the Wimbledon doubles with Czech Helena Sukova, making herself the all-time greenest female to win any major title. Vinnie Richards, 15, was somewhat younger winning the U.S. doubles with Bill Tilden in 1918.

Like namesake Martina—a splendid doubles player, excellent volleyer and tactician—she, 17, ran the quintessential quadrilateral in 1998, posting a Grand Slam in doubles, as a 28-year-old Navratilova had done in 1984 alongside a 22-year-old Pam Shriver. Hingis led off accompanied by Mirjana Lucic of Croatia to win the Australian, and finished off the French, Wimbledon and U.S. aligned with Novotna, all over Lindsay Davenport—Natasha Zvereva. Since Lucic was 15, they are the youngest team (32 years total) to win a major women's doubles, supplanting the 1961 Wimbledon championship feat of Americans Billie Jean King, 17, and Karen Hantze, 18.

Martina is the third female doubles Grand Slammer. Brazil's Maria Bueno, 20 with two partners, was the first in 1960.

A Grand Slam in singles seemed a possibility after Martina won the first of her three Australians in 1997. She tripled that year, but the French Open, you might say, was a horse of a different color. An avid equestrienne, she fell from one of her horses, and wasn't in the best of shape in Paris. Though getting to the final as the No. 1 seed, she was unsaddled, 6-4, 6-2, by No. 9 seed Iva Majoli of Croatia, the longest-shot winner since unseeded Peggy Scriven of Britain won in 1933. Martina added Wimbledon over Novotna, 2-6, 6-3, 6-3, and the U.S. over rookie Venus, 6-0, 7-5, to her purse, and had to settle for one Slam in her life, doubles.

Her best French opportunity, the 1999 final, was derailed by her emotional meltdown and the resistance of 6-time champ Steffi Graf. Hingis led, 6-4, 3-1, then 5-4, 15-0, but could get no closer than three points. Her complaining about line calls got the crowd on her back and behind Steffi. In tears, Martina was beaten, 4-6, 7-5, 6-2. Despite her good fortune at Wimbledon, she was the first top-seeded fall girl in two huge first-round sabotages—qualifier, No. 129, Jelena Dokic of Australia beat her in 1999, 6-2, 6-0, and No. 83 Virginia Ruano Pascual of Spain emulated in 2001, 6-4, 6-2. Such had happened only two other times at Wimbledon.

Melbourne was a happy hunting ground where she graced six straight singles finals, winning three, as well as four doubles. But the most renowned was a loss—the monster 2002 final to Jennifer Capriati, 4-6, 7-6 (9-7), 6-2, in 2:10 of searing heat (125 degrees on court). Requiring a rest period after the second set, it nearly flattened both of them. Hingis led 6-4, 4-0, had it in her hands, four match points in the second set, but Jennifer set a majors record by rescuing each one.

At 5-foot-7, 130 pounds, she is slight of build, but a fighter, crafty, thoughtful, accurate in moving balls to where they cause most difficulty. Right-handed (two-handed backhand), she has battled the bigger, stronger gals such as the Williams Sisters and Davenport gamely and well. She played Federation Cup for four years, 1995–98 and helped Switzerland reach the 1998 final. During her career, she won 43 singles titles, 37 doubles titles and $20,130,657 in prize money

Martina's retirement announcement in November of 2007 was a sad occasion. Of course she's a sure thing to grace the Hall of Fame one day. Hip and back injuries may have made it impossible for her to continue, but she also stated that she had tested positive for cocaine at Wimbledon, a finding that she vehemently denied, and we'd like to believe her. Still it may have had a bearing on her leaving the game and the penalty—a two year suspension seemed harshly unfair.

MAJOR TITLES (15)—Australian singles, 1997-98-99; Wimbledon singles, 1997; U.S. singles, 1997; Australian doubles, 1997-98-99-2002; French doubles, 1998, 2000; Wimbledon doubles, 1996, 1998; U.S. doubles, 1998; Australian mixed, 2006. **FEDERATION CUP**—1995-1996, 1997, 1998; 18-2 in singles, 8-2 in doubles **SINGLES RECORD IN THE MAJORS**—Australian (51-7), French (35-8), Wimbledon (23-8), U.S. (43-9)

Yevgeny Kafelnikov
Russia (1974—)

A smooth, confident right-hander (2-handed backhand), Yevgeny Alexandrevic Kafelnikov of Sochi, was the first Russian to win a major singles title: the French Open in 1996, defeating Michael Stich, 7-6 (7-4), 7-5, 7-6 (7-4). He also won the Australian in 1999, defeating Thomas Enqvist, 4-6, 6-0, 6-3, 7-6 (7-1). He was the best of that territory since Soviet (Georgian) Alex Metreveli (Wimbledon finalist in 1973, world's No. 9 in 1974). He was in the world's Top 10 for six years: No. 6 in 1995; No. 3 in 1996; No. 5 in 1997, 2000; No. 2 in 1999; No. 4 in 2001—and was ranked No. 1 briefly during the 1999 season.

Kafelnikov was born February 18, 1974, in Sochi. A 6-foot-3 blond, he preferred the baseline, though he was a sharp volleyer. He was a rare singles-doubles combiner, also winning four doubles majors—the French in 1996-97 with Daniel Vacek and 2002 with Paul Haarhuis; the U.S. Open in 1997 with Vacek. At the 1996 French, he was the first to score a major singles-doubles double since Ken Rosewall at the 1972 Australian, and the first at the French since Rosewall in 1968.

He lost the Australian final in 2000 to Andre Agassi, 3-6, 6-3, 6-2, 6-4, but won Olympic singles gold "Down Under" in Sydney later in the year, defeating Tommy Haas of Germany, 7-6 (7-4), 3-6,

6-2, 4-6, 6-3. He led Russia to its first Davis Cup final appearance in 1994 (loss to Sweden) and again in 1995 (loss to the United States), but was on the 2002 squad that won the Cup in 2002 (defeating France).

He turned pro in 1992 and won 26 singles titles (609-306 matches), 25 doubles titles (358-213 matches) and $23,883,797 prize money.

MAJOR TITLES (6)—French Open singles, 1996; Australian Open singles 1999, French Open doubles, 1996, 1997, 2002; US Open doubles, 1997; **DAVIS CUP**— 1993-2002; 31-16 singles, 13-12 doubles (1 Cup) **SINGLES RECORD IN THE MAJORS**—Australian (28-7), French (31-10), Wimbledon (16-10), US (24-9).

Gustavo Kuerten
Brazil (1976—)

Gustavo "Guga" Kuerten is clay court royalty. Winning at Roland Garros three times (1997, 2000-01) the skinny, popular Brazilian has joined the French Championships' aristocracy. Only Bjorn Borg has won more times: 1974-75, 78-79-80-81. Not many others have won three: Henri Cochet, 1926, 28, 30; Ivan Lendl, 1984, 86-87; Rafa Nadal, 2005-06-07-08. Guga makes four.

Sadly, Guga wasn't able to add to his triple as a gimpy hip and other health problems hindered him. Following his 2001 win, Brazil issued a postage stamp featuring Kuerten with the Eiffel Tower in the background. Kuerten's toothy smile and outlandishly colored clothes have made him an icon among Brazilian teenagers. Born September 10, 1976, in Florianopolis in the southern state of Santa Catarina, the 6-foot-3, 183 pound Kuerten is the first South American guy to reach the ATP No. 1 ranking (2000) and the biggest tennis star at home since Maria Bueno won three Wimbledon and four U.S. singles championships between 1959 and 1966.

Guga would rather surf than play on turf. He has studiously avoided grass tournaments his game ever suited to clay. His place in Brazilian sporting history was assured in 1997 when he defeated three former champions—Thomas Muster, Yevgeny Kafelnikov, Sergi Bruguera—on his unseeded way to claiming the French Open title. Just 20 years old, he was ranked a lowly No. 66 in the world, the longest shot to go all the way, finishing his first—yes, first in the bigs!—championship by dusting off Bruguera, 6-3, 6-4, 6-2. He followed up in 2000 over Sweden's Magnus Norman, 6-2, 6-3, 2-6, 7-6 (8-6), and the following year over Alex Corretja, 6-7 (3-7), 7-5, 6-2, 6-0, ending 2001 at No. 2.

Kuerten won five titles in 2000, climaxing his No. 1 season by seizing the Masters at Lisbon, getting past two Americans, Pete Sampras in the semis, 6-7 (5-7), 6-3, 6-4 and Andre Agassi in the final, 6-4, 6-4, 6-4. With that, he edged Russia's Marat Safin for the room at the top. In 2001, he lost No. 1 to Aussie Lleyton Hewitt, but by 2002 he was down to No. 37, sliding fast as health problems increased, and hip surgery didn't seem to help.

He might have owned European clay for a while, having done more than capturing Paris. He won the Italian in 1999, Monte Carlo in 1999-2000-01, the German in 2000. The sunny-natured man with the brilliant backhand won 20 singles titles

(358-192 matches), eight doubles titles (107-93) and $14,755,588 in prize money.

MAJOR TITLES (3)— French singles, 1997, 2000, 2001. **DAVIS CUP**—1996-97-98-99-2000-01-02, 21-11 singles, 13-7 doubles, he played 23 ties. **SINGLES RECORD IN THE MAJORS**— Australian (7-8), French (36-7), Wimbledon (7-5), U.S. (15-9).

The Woodies
Australia

Doubles has always been an Australian specialty. Six of the eight top winning men's teams—starting with John Newcombe and Tony Roche's record 12 major titles—have been Aussies. Right behind them with 11 are Todd Andrew Woodbridge and left-handed Mark Raymond Woodforde—The Woodies. You don't have to knock on wood: these guys need no luck to be ushered into the Hall of Fame together. It's as certain as the Australian yen for cold beer. Trying to beat them has been as difficult as a hangover.

Even though attached to others from time to time, they doubled up as a unit in 1991, a nine-year partnership that netted 61 career titles, an "Open era" record, and a pivotal win (2-6, 7-5, 6-2, 6-2, over Olivier Delaitre-Fabrice Santoro) in the 1999 Davis Cup final triumph, 3-2, over France plus Olympic gold in 1996 over Brits Tim Henman-Neil Broad, 6-4, 6-4, 6-2 and Olympic silver in 2000, losing the final to Canada's Sebastien Lareau-Daniel Nestor, 5-7, 6-3, 6-4, 7-6 (7-2).

Of their 11 majors, six were Wimbledons between 1993 and 2000, an "Open era" record, although the English brothers, Laurie and Reggie Doherty, won eight between 1897 and 1908, and Willie and Ernest Renshaw won seven between 1880 and 1889. However, the Woodies set the tournament record of 35 straight match wins from 1993 to the 1998 final, lost to the Dutch pair Jacco Eltingh-Paul Haarhuis, 2-6, 6-4, 7-6 (7-3), 5-7, 10-8. These latter-day Aussies were in 15 major finals as mates.

They won 11 major titles—The Australian, 1997 defeating Alex O'Brien-Lareau, 4-6, 7-5, 7-5, 6-3; in 1992, defeating Americans Kelly Jones-Rick Leach, 6-4, 6-3, 6-4; the French in 2000, defeating Haarhuis-Sandon Stolle, 7-6 (9-7), 6-4; Wimbledon in 2000, defeating Haarhuis-Sandon Stolle, 6-3, 6-4, 6-1; in 1997 defeating Eltingh-Haarhuis, 7-6 (7-4), 7-6 (9-7), 5-7, 6-3; in 1996 defeating Byron Black-Grant Connell, 4-6, 6-1, 6-3, 6-2; in 1995 defeating Leach-Scott Melville, 7-5, 7-6 (10-8), 7-6 (7-5); in 1994 defeating Connell-Pat Galbraith, 7-6 (7-3), 6-3, 6-1; in 1993 defeating Connell-Galbraith, 7-5, 6-3, 7-6 (7-4); the U.S. Open in 1996 defeating Eltingh-Haarhuis, 4-6, 7-6 (7-5), 7-6 (7-2); in 1995 defeating O'Brien-S. Stolle, 6-3, 6-3.

They also lost three other major finals—the Australian in 1998 to Eltingh-Jonas Bjorkman 6-2, 5-7, 2-6, 6-4, 6-3 the French, in 1997 to Yevgeny Kafelnikov-Daniel Vacek, 7-6 (14-12), 4-6, 6-3 and the U.S. Open in 1994 to Eltingh-Haarhuis, 6-3, 7-6 (7-1).

Woodbridge

Born April 2, 1971, in Sydney, Australia, Woodbridge grew up there and turned pro in 1988. He is right-handed, 5 ft-10, 165

lbs., and is regarded as one of greatest at doubles in the right court. A excellent returner and volleying sharpshooter, he was also ranked as high as No. 19 in singles in mid-1997. He won two singles titles—Coral Springs, Fla., in 1995, defeating Greg Rusedski in the final and in 1997 in Adelaide, Australia, defeating Scott Draper in the final. He also lost seven singles finals during his ATP career.

Though best known linked to Woodforde (won 11 majors, ATP Doubles Team of Year, 1992, 95-96-97, 2000), Todd continued three years longer, retiring in 2004. He won four more majors coalescing with Swede Jonas Bjorkman: Australian, 2001, defeating Byron Black and David Prinosil, 6-1, 5-7, 6-4, 6-4. Wimbledon in 2002, defeating Mark Knowles and Nestor, 6-1, 6-2, 6-7 (7-9). 7-5; Wimbledon in 2003, defeating Mahesh Bhupathi and Max Mirnyi, 3-6, 6-3, 7-6 (7-4), 6-3; Wimbledon in 2004, defeating Julian Knowle and Nenad Zimonjic 6-1, 6-4, 4-6, 6-4.

He added six mixed majors for a career total of 21 majors, deadlocking him with Bill Tilden for fourth place on the all-time male honor roll behind three countrymen: Roy Emerson (28), John Newcombe (25), Frank Sedgman (22).

Todd's major mixed titles were the Australian in 1993, with Arantxa Sanchez Vicario; the French in 1992 with Sanchez Vicario; Wimbledon in 1994 with Helena Sukova; the U.S. Open in 1990 with Elizabeth Sayers Smylie; the U.S. Open in 1993 with Sukova; the U.S. Open in 2001 with Rennae Stubbs. He played Davis Cup for 15 years from 1991 and helped Australia win the Cup in 1999 and 2003 and reach the final in 1993, 2000-01. He was 5-4 in singles play and 25-7 in doubles, playing in 32 ties. His career won-loss singles record was (244-236). He won 83 doubles titles (a record) with a 782-260 won-loss record. He earned $10,095,245 in career prize money.

Woodforde

Born September 23, 1965, in Adelaide, Australia, Woodforde grew up there and turned professional in 1984, ending his career in 2000. A slim, six-foot-two, 195-pound left-handed redhead, Woodforde played the left court in doubles and was a clever serve-and-volleyer and master of spin. He connected to fellow Aussie Todd Woodbridge to win 11 major doubles titles, one behind major record-holding team, John Newcombe and Tony Roche.

Apart from Woodbridge, Mark won five more doubles majors for a 16 total, tied for 10th place on the male honor roll with Laurie Doherty and Roche. His other major titles were the U.S. Open in 1989 with John McEnroe, defeating Ken Flach and Robert Seguso, 6-4, 4-6, 6-3, 6-3; Australian mixed in 1992 with Nicole Provis, defeating Sanchez Vicario and Woodbridge, 6-3, 4-6, 11-9; Australian mixed in 1996 with Larisa Savchenko Neiland, defeating Nicole Arendt and Luke Jensen, 4-6, 7-5, 6-0; French mixed in 1995, with Neiland, defeating Jill Hetherington and John Laffnie de Jager, 7-6 (10-8), 7-6 (7-4); the Wimbledon mixed in 1993 with Martina Navratilova, defeating Manon Bollegraf and Tom Nijssen, 6-3, 6-4.

He also won four singles titles: Auckland, 1986, over Bud Schultz, 6-4, 6-3, 3-6, 6-4; hometown Adelaide in 1988, over Wally Masur, 6-2, 6-4 and 1989 over Patrik Kuhnen 7-5, 1-6, 7-5; and Philadelphia, 1993, over Ivan Lendl, 5-4 ret. He also lost five singles finals. His highest singles ranking was No. 27 in 1996.

In Davis Cup, he played 10 years for Australia since 1988, playing 24 ties with an Open record of 4-10 in singles and 17-5 in doubles. He helped Australia win the Cup in 1999 and helped them reach the final in 1993 and 2000. His career won loss record was 319-312 in singles and, in winning 67 career doubles titles, a 647-248 record in doubles. He earned $8,571,605 in career prize money.

Current Elite

Novak Djokovic is a major part of the "Serbian Surge" having won the 2008 Australian Open.

"The Current Elite" are the group of the crème of the crop of professional tennis—the players who consistently contend for major titles and are the personalities that generate the most buzz among fans and media. Many of them have already established Hall of Fame credentials but are not yet finished writing the final lines of the their tennis resumes. We present their tennis credentials as they stand as of the spring of 2008. Roger Federer of Switzerland leads the pack in men's tennis as the "Basel Dazzle" not only battles against the likes of Rafael Nadal of Spain and Novak Djokovic of Serbia for bragging rights in men's tennis, but also stands in competition for the right to be called the greatest of all-time. Venus and Serena Williams—the Sisters Sledgehammer—reign as icons of the current era of women's tennis. Jelena Jankovic and Ana Ivanovic—two members of the "Serbian Surge"—as well as the Siberian siren Maria Sharapova of Russia stand as the sisters' main rivals for supremacy in the ever-changing scope of women's professional tennis.

BIOGRAPHIES

Bryan Twins
United States (1978—)

Michael Carl and Robert Charles: An all-time doubles team, identically devoted to each other and championships. They are the only U.S. team ever to win all four doubles majors and the sixth male team in history to do so, following Australians Frank Sedgman–Ken McGregor (Grand Slam, 1951, total seven), Lew Hoad-Ken Rosewall (total six), Roy Emerson-Neale Fraser (total seven), John Newcombe-Tony Roche (total 12), Todd Woodbridge-Mark Woodforde (total 11). They are also the third twins to win majors, following Willie-Ernest Renshaw (GBR), Wimbledon 1880-81, 84-85-86, 88-89; Wilfred-Herbert Baddeley (GBR), Wimbledon, 1891, 94-95-96. As of July of 2009, they won seven majors—Australian, 2009, Mahesh Bhupathi (IND)-Mark Knowles (BAH), 2007, defeating Max Mirnyi (BLR)-Jonas Bjorkman (SWE), 7-5, 7-5; 2006, defeating Martin Damm (CZE)-Leander Paes (IND), 4-6, 6-3, 6-4; French, 2003, defeating Paul Haarhuis (NED)-Yevgeny Kafelnikov (RUS), 7-6(7-3), 6-3; Wimbledon, 2006, defeating Fabrice Santoro (FRA)-Nenad Zimonjic (SRB), 6-3, 4-6, 6-4, 6-2; U.S. 2008, defeating Lukas Dlouhy (CZE)-Leander Paes (IND), 2005, defeating Mirnyi-Bjorkman, 6-1, 6-4. They also lost eight major finals—Australian, 2004 to Michael Llodra (FRA)-Santoro, 7-6(7-4), 6-3, 2005 to Wayne Black-Kevin Ullyett (ZIM), 6-4, 6-4; French, 2005, to Bjorkman-Mirnyi, 2-6, 6-1, 6-4, 2006, to Bjorkman-Mirnyi, 6-7(5-7), 6-4, 7-5; Wimbledon, 2009, to Daniel Nestor (CAN)-Nenad Zimonjic (SRB) 7-6 (7), 6-7 (3), 7-6 (3), 6-3, 2007 to Arnaud Clement (FRA)-Michael Llodra (FRA) 6-7, 6-3, 6-4, 6-4, 2005, to Stephen Huss (AUS)-Wesley Moodie (RSA), 7-6(7-4), 6-3, 6-7(2-7), 6-3; U.S., 2003, to Bjorkman-Todd Woodbridge (AUS), 5-7, 6-0, 7-5. World Top 10, six years—No. 1, 2005-06-07, No. 2, 2003, 2008, No. 4, 2004, No 7, 2002. Davis Cup six years, 2003–09, 16 ties; 15-2 doubles (through 2009 first round) becoming all-time winningest U.S. Davis Cup doubles pair, surpassing John McEnroe-Peter Fleming and Wilmer Allison-John Van Ryn. Primary goal to play Davis Cup and win Davis Cup, which they clinched against Russia in 2007 Davis Cup final. Born Camarillo, Calif., April 29, 1978 (Mike two minutes older). Won 53 pro doubles titles as team through July 6, 2009. Won two Masters—2004, def. W. Black-Ullyett, 4-6, 7-5, 4-6, 6-2; 2003, def. Llodra-Santoro, 6-7 (6-8), 6-3, 3-6, 7-6 (7-3), 6-4. All-Americans, led Stanford to NCAA team title, 1997-98. Father, Wayne Bryan, teaching pro. Mother, Kathy Blake Bryan, held U.S. national rankings, No. 1, 16s, 1962; No. 13, women, 1964; No. 4 women's doubles and U.S. QF with Kathy Harter, 1965; made third round. Wimbledon singles, 1967.

Bob: Left-handed, 6 ft. 4, 202 lbs., usually plays right court. Scored 1998 NCAA triple (singles, doubles, with Mike, team title). 1-0 Davis Cup singles. Won 53 pro doubles titles and as of July 2009; Won six mixed majors: U.S., 2003 with Katarina Srebotnik (SLO), 2004 with Vera Zvonareva (RUS), 2006 with Martina Navratilova, her 59th and last major title, French Open mixed in 2008/2009 (with Sam Stosur (AUS) and Liezel Huber (USA), respectively) and Wimbledon in 2008 with Victoria Azarenka (BLR).

Mike: Right-handed, 6 ft. 3, 192 lbs., usually plays left court. Won 55 pro doubles titles as of July 6, 2009—two titles without twin brother (Long Island, 2002 with Mahesh Bhupathi (IND);

Nottingham, 2002 with Mark Knowles (BAH); Won two mixed majors: French, 2003, with Lisa Raymond (USA), 2002 U.S. with Raymond.

MAJOR TITLES AS A TEAM (7)—Australian doubles, 2006, 2007, 2009; French doubles, 2003, Wimbledon doubles, 2006, U.S. doubles, 2005, 2008

Lindsay Ann Davenport
United States (1976—)

A winner of six major titles—three in singles—as well as Olympic singles gold in 1996, Lindsay Ann Davenport's brilliant career will assuredly land her in the International Tennis Hall of Fame. Unheralded and seeded No. 9, was the unexpected gold medalist at Atlanta Olympics in 1996, defeating Arantxa Sanchez Vicario (ESP), 7-6 (8-6), 6-2 in final to jump onto the top of the international tennis scene. Born June 8, 1976, Palos Verdes, Calif., into a volleyball family (father, Wink Davenport, a U.S. Olympian, 1968), she broke away to become a tennis great. A big-banging strokeswoman, Lindsay is the tallest (6 ft 3, 175 lbs) ever to play at the female upper level. Turning pro in 1993, proudly as one of the few high school diploma holders, she quickly joined the elite the following year at No. 6, the first of her 10 Top 10 rankings, four times at No. 1. From 1996, they ran: Nos. 9, 3, 1, 2, 2, 1, 12, 5, 1, 1, 25, 73. Owning three of the four singles majors, she started the collection in 1998, deposing Martina Hingis (SUI) in the U.S. Open final, 6-3, 7-5. Next was Wimbledon, 1999. Spoiling the last of 31 major final for seven-time champ Steffi Graf (GER), 6-4, 7-5, Lindsay may have been unique in holding serve throughout against Steffi. Then, the Australian final, 2000, snapping Hingis's three-year, 27-match streak in Melbourne. Running afoul of the Williams Sisters (USA) in 2005 cost her two more. She let a 6-2, 2-2, 15-40 (6 break points) lead slip away against Serena, losing the last nine games, 2-6, 6-3, 6-0. But five months later, possibly her finest start, a war that she and Venus waged in a fit of spectacular driving on Wimbledon's Centre Court. It lasted 2:45, record time for a Wimbledon final. Lindsay came oh-so-close. She served for victory at 6-5 in the second, held a match point at 4-5, 30-40 in the third that vanished with Venus's backhand winner, was two points away four times, but couldn't overcome Sister V's stonewalling, 4-6, 7-6 (7-4), 9-7. Also made the semifinals of the Australian, 1998-99, 01; French, 1998; Wimbledon, 2001, 04; U.S., 1997, 99, 2002-03-04; QF Australian 1994-95, 2004, 06; French 1996, 99, 2005; Wimbledon 1994, 98, 2003; U.S. 2001, 05-06. Played Federation Cup 10 years, 1993–2000, 02, 05, 08—she has played 21 ties; 26-3 singles, 6-0 doubles. Helped U.S. win Cup, 1996, 99-2000, reach final, 1994-95. Her six major titles: Australian singles, 2000, def. Hingis, 6-1, 7-5; Wimbledon singles, 1999, def. Graf, 6-4, 7-5; U.S. singles, 1998, def. Hingis, 6-3, 7-5. French doubles, 1996, with Mary Joe Fernandez (USA), def. Gigi Fernandez (USA)-Natasha Zvereva (BLR), 6-2, 6-2; Wimbledon doubles, 1999, with Corina Morariu (USA), def. Mariaan DeSwardt (RSA)-Elene Tatarkova (UKR), 6-4, 6-4; U.S. doubles, 1997, with Jana Novotna (CZE), def. G. Fernandez-Zvereva, 6-3, 6-4. Lost four major singles finals—Australian, 2005, to S. Williams, 2-6, 6-3, 6-0; Wimbledon, 2000, to V. Williams,

6-3, 7-6 (7-3), 2005, to V. Williams, 4-6, 7-6 (7-4), 9-7; U.S., 2000, to V. Williams, 6-4, 7-5. Won WTA Tour Championship, 1999, def. Hingis, 6-4, 6-2. Lost three WTA Tour Championship finals—1994, to Gabriela Sabatini (ARG), 6-3, 6-2, 6-4; 1998, to Hingis, 7-5, 6-4, 4-6, 6-2; 2001, to S. Williams, walkover, injury. Lost 10 major doubles finals—Australian, 1996, with M.J. Fernandez, to Chanda Rubin (USA)-Arantxa Sanchez Vicario (ESP), 7-5, 2-6, 6-4; 1997, with Lisa Raymond (USA), to Martina Hingis (SUI)-Zvereva, 6-2, 6-2; 1998, with Zvereva, to Hingis-Mirjana Lucic (CRO), 6-4, 2-6, 6-3; 1999, with Zvereva, to Hingis-Anna Kournikova (RUS), 7-5, 6-3; 2001, with Morariu, to S.-V. Williams, 6-2, 4-6, 6-4; 2005, with Morariu, to Svetlana Kuznetsova (RUS)-Alicia Molik (AUS), 6-3, 6-4; French, 1994, with Raymond, to G. Fernandez-Zvereva, 6-2, 6-2; 1998, with Zvereva, to Hingis-Novotna, 6-1, 7-6 (7-4); Wimbledon, 1998, with Zvereva, to Hingis-Novotna, 6-3, 3-6, 8-6; U.S., 1998, with Zvereva, to Hingis-Novotna, 6-3, 6-3. Other prominent singles titles include—Indian Wells, 1997, def. Irina Spirlea, 6-2, 6-1; 2000, def. Hingis, 4-6, 6-4, 6-0. Injuries cluttered her 2006 season as she dropped to No. 25 from No. 1. Pregnancy intervened, she wondered if she should call it a career. She was back in business, the business of winning titles—after she and husband Jonathan Leach (married April 25, 2003) had a son, Jagger Jonathan Leach, born June 10, 2007. She returned to professional tennis in the fall of 2007 and won the title in Bali (over Daniela Hantuchova, (SVK), 6-4, 3-6, 6-2)—two years since her last title (Zurich, 2005, (over Patty Schnyder, (SUI), 7-6 (7-5), 6-3). In her post-pregnancy comeback, she also won titles in Quebec City, Auckland and Memphis—the later being her 55th career singles title, tying her with Virginia Wade for seventh place on the list of most singles titles won in the Open era. On January 14, 2008, Davenport surpassed Steffi Graf in career prize money earned on the women's tour, garnering a total of $21,897,501. She also qualified for the 2008 Olympics—her third Olympiad—and paired with Liezel Huber to reach the quarterfinals of doubles. Dropped off the circuit for a second time due to pregnancy in late 2008 before giving birth to daughter Lauren Andrus Davenport Leach on June 27, 2009. Career: won 55 singles (753-94 matches), 37 doubles (382-115) pro titles, $22,144,735 prize money.

MAJOR TITLES (6)—Australian singles, 2000; Wimbledon singles, 1999; U.S. singles, 1998; French doubles, 1996; Wimbledon doubles, 1999; U.S. doubles, 1997.

Roger Federer
Switzerland (1981—)

As Lord of the Swings, Federer is top of the list in men's tennis as the all-time leader in major singles titles—winning his record-breaking 15th major singles title in dramatic fashion with a 5-7, 7-6 (6), 7-6 (5), 3-6, 16-14 final-round victory over Andy Roddick at Wimbledon in 2009 in the longest Wimbledon final in games and the longest final set in the history of major championship finals. The Wimbledon title moved him past Pete Sampras, a spectator from the Royal Box who held the previous record with 14 majors. The previous month, Federer completed

the "Career Grand Slam"—winning the French Open title, defeating Sweden's Robin Soderling in the final 6-1, 7-6 (1), 6-4—joining Fred Perry, Don Budge, Rod Laver, Roy Emerson and Andre Agassi as only men in tennis history to win all four majors in their career. Federer took over No. 1 in 2004, from Andy Roddick, and held the top spot for a record 237 consecutive weeks. Performing in a smooth, seemingly effortless, style, a right-hander using one-handed backhand, he occupies his status as the best in men's tennis with rare grace and competitive verve, always in the right place to deliver the right shot from his peerless all-court arsenal of angles, spins, volleys, pinpoint serves. Is there a weakness, a flaw? Doubtful. Perhaps only one man has found it: that would be Rafael Nadal of Spain, whose high-rolling topspin and speed afoot has stymied Federer on Parisian clay four straight years—semifinals in 2005, 6-3, 4-6, 6-4, 6-3; finals in 2006, 1-6, 6-1, 6-4, 7-6 (7-4), finals in 2007, 6-3, 4-6, 6-3, 6-4, and finals in 2008 6-1, 6-3, 6-0. Rafa would then end Roger's five-year reign at Wimbledon, beating Federer 6-4, 6-4, 6-7 (5), 6-7 (8), 9-7 in the epic final. Rafa would also snare Roger in an epic Australian Open final in 2009, winning 7–5, 3–6, 7–6(3), 3–6, 6–2. Other than Nadal, Roger has been mistreating his colleagues regularly at the major occasions. He has three major triples (Australian, Wimbledon, U.S.), 2004, 06, 07. Merely eight men in history have tripled: Rod Laver (AUS) twice with Grand Slams in 1962 and 1969; Don Budge (USA) with the original Grand Slam, 1938; Jack Crawford (AUS), 1933; Fred Perry (GBR), 1934, Tony Trabert (USA), 1955; Lew Hoad (AUS), 1956; Ashley Cooper (AUS), 1958; Roy Emerson (AUS), 1964; Mats Wilander (SWE), 1988. But nobody but Roger thrice. After a 2005 French semifinal loss to Nadal, he made it to 10 successive major finals, winning eight. Colossal. Big Bill Tilden (USA) reached 11 straight major finals, winning eight between 1918 and 1927, but there were gaps in his appearances. Federer's triple triples amount to nine of his 15 singles majors as of July of 2009. By reaching the ifnal of Wimbledon in 2009, he reached his 20th major final, breaking Ivan Lendl's record of 19. Roger, who turned pro in 1998, showed an aptitude for Wimbledon's Centre Court greensward as a 19-year-old in 2001, severing Sampras's streak of 31 Wimbledon match wins, 7-6 (9-7), 5-7, 6-4, 6-7 (2-7), 7-5, in the fourth round. He then lost the quarterfinal to Tim Henman (GBR), 7-5, 7-6 (8-6), 2-6, 7-6 (8-6), and, seeded No. 7, was stunned in the 2002 opening round by No. 154 Mario Ancic (CRO), 6-3, 7-6 (7-2), 6-3. A two-match losing streak at the Big W—but he wouldn't lose there again. Near the end of 2007, he lost consecutively to David Nalbandian (ARG) in Paris and Fernando Gonzalez (CHI) in the round robin of the Masters at Shanghai, his longest losing streak four-and-a-half years. Federer says his 2003 first-round loss at the French to No. 88 Luis Horna (PER), 7-6 (8-6), 6-2, 7-6 (7-3), shook him up, made him question his motivation. Bearing down, he was a changed man, won his first major title, Wimbledon seeded No. 4, 7-6 (7-5), 6-2, 7-6 (7-3), over No. 48 Mark Philippoussis (AUS). Won 11 other majors, all singles: Australian, 2004, def. Marat Safin (RUS), 7-6 (7-3), 6-4, 6-2; 2006, def. Marcos Baghdatis (CYP), 5-7, 7-5, 6-0, 6-2; 2007, def. Fernando Gonzalez (CHI), 7-6 (7-2), 6-4, 6-4. French, 2009, def. Robin Soderling (SWE), 6-1, 7-6 (1), 6-4; Wimbledon, 2004, def. Roddick, 4-6, 7-5, 7-6 (7-3),

6-4; 2005, def. Roddick, 6-2, 7-6 (7-2), 6-4; 2006, def. Nadal, 6-0, 7-6 (7-5), 6-7 (2-7), 6-3; 2007, def. Nadal, 7-6 (9-7), 4-6, 7-6 (7-3), 2-6, 6-2; 2009 def. Roddick 5-7, 7-6 (6), 7-6 (5), 3-6, 16-14. U.S., 2004, def. Lleyton Hewitt (AUS), 6-0, 7-6 (7-3); 6-0; 2005; def. Andre Agassi (USA), 6-3, 2-6, 7-6 (7-1), 6-1; 2006, def. Roddick, 6-2, 4-6, 7-5, 6-1; 2007, def. Novak Djokovic (SRB), 7-6 (7-4), 7-6 (7-2), 6-4, 2008, def. Andy Murray (GBR) 6-2, 7-5, 6-2. Masters Cup—Won four titles: 2003, def. Agassi, 6-3, 6-0, 6-4; 2004, def. Hewitt, 6-3, 6-2; 2006, def. James Blake (USA), 6-0, 6-3, 6-4; 2007, def. David Ferrer (ESP). Lost one final: 2005, to Nalbandian, 6-7 (4-7), 6-7 (11-13), 6-2, 6-1, 7-6 (7-3), despite being two sets up and serving at 6-5 in the fifth. Nadal, leading in their rivalry 13-7 as of July of 2009, was the first to push him to five sets in the majors since Roger's defeat of Sampras in 2001. Theirs was a magnificent battle in the 2007 Wimbledon title bout, Roger denying Rafa four break points in the fifth set (two each at 1-2 and 2-3) which could have cost him the championship. His grit showed as he won, 7-6(9-7), 4-6, 7-6(7-3), 2-6, 6-2, and again two months later at the U.S. There Djokovic held five set points on serve (6-5, 40-0, 2 ads) in the first set, and two more set points in the second (5-6, 15-40), but Roger wouldn't budge, 7-6 (7-4), 7-6 (7-2), 6-4. Federer fought back from two-sets down to nearly hold on and win a record sixth straight Wimbledon crown in 2008, falling to Nadal 9-7 in the fifth set. Born Aug. 8, 1981, Basel, Switzerland, where he grew up. Turned pro, 1998, 6 ft. 1, 177 lbs. At the end of 2007, he suffered a case of mononucleosis which hampered his 2008 start. He has a charitable foundation, and is a UNICEF Good Will Ambassador. Career: won 60 singles, seven doubles titles and $ 49,475,219 prize money (as of July of 2009). Played Davis Cup, 1999–2008, he has played 17 ties; 25-6 singles, 10-5 doubles. Fulfilled lifelong dream of winning Olympic gold in Beijing in 2008, pairing with Stan Wawrinka to win doubles gold, defeating Simon Aspelin and Tom Johansson (SWE) 6-3, 6-4, 6-7 (4), 6-3 in the gold medal match. Lost to James Blake of the U.S. in the singles quarterfinals, 6-4, 7-6 (2).

MAJOR TITLES (15)—Australian singles, 2004, 2006, 2007; French singles, 2009, Wimbledon singles, 2003, 2004, 2005, 2006, 2007, 2009; U.S. singles, 2004, 2005, 2006, 2007, 2008.

Lleyton Hewitt
Australia (1981—)

Lleyton Glynn Hewitt is a screaming, fist-pumping, chest-thumping firebrand on court. "C'mon!" he yells at himself, finding inspiration in his obsession with the movie "Rocky" about an underdog boxer. At 5-foot-11, he is a solid 170 pounds. The leanness is deceptive, for he grew up playing breakneck AussieRules Football and hurls his body with abandon at shots others would let pass. Such intensity made him, at 20 in 2001, the youngest men's No. 1 ever, 69 years after Wimbledon champ Ellsworth Vines (USA) was at the top, a slightly older 21 in 1932. He is also the youngest since computer rankings began in 1973. Hewitt has won two major championship singles titles—the 2001 U.S. Open over Pete Sampras (USA), 7-6 (7-4), 6-1, 6-1, and 2002

Wimbledon over David Nalbandian (ARG), 6-1, 6-3, 6-2—as well as the U.S. doubles in 2000 with Max Mirnyi (BLR), as of 2008. He has also won 25 other ATP singles titles since turning pro in 1998 at age 16. He was again No. 1 for 2002. The Australian's passing shots and especially, his return of serve, are strengths. Hewitt himself is enamored with his topspin lob. Critics of Hewitt—and he has many—suggest he lacks the tools to become a dominant player, missing a booming serve, a killer return or a crushing groundstroke. All he does is win. Pat Rafter, his compatriot, called Hewitt a "little mongrel" for his refusal to be beaten. He has also been called an "undersized, overcharged kid," a "racquet-wielding Energizer Bunny," and "Bart Simpson with a Yonex." For his part, Hewitt has called Australian fans "stupid"; called a chair umpire a "spastic"; made an insensitive remark about a black line judge at the U.S. Open; dismissed coaches in controversial fashion; and had a long public spat with the ATP after being fined $103,000 for refusing to do a television interview. Hewitt was born in Adelaide on Feb. 24, 1981. His father Glynn played Australian Rules Football for Richmond and his mother Cherilyn was a professional netballer. Neither sport is for the faint-hearted. Their son learned tennis early, and they took him to his first Australian Open as a spectator at age five. Hewitt qualified for the Australian Open in January, 1997, a month before his 16th birthday, the youngest qualifier in the 108-year-old tournament. He debuted that month on the rankings at No. 797. Four years later, at 20 years, nine months, he was No. 1, undercutting Jimmy Connors (USA), No. 1 on the computer in 1974 at 22 years, three months in 1974. Vines, at 21, was three months older than Lleyton. His precocious talent was displayed at age 16 when he captured his hometown title at Adelaide over Jason Stoltenberg (AUS), 3-6, 6-3, 7-6 (7-4) in 1998. The five men he beat (including Andre Agassi in the semis) had a combined total of 1,108 career victories; Hewitt had none until then. He became the lowest-ranked player, at No. 550, to win in tour history. In 1999, Hewitt won his first clay-court title (Delray Beach), his only victory in four finals. He made his Davis Cup debut that July against the United States, launching the successful drive to the Cup with a leadoff win over Todd Martin, 6-4, 6-7 (1-7), 6-3, 6-0. Russia's Yevgeny Kafelnikov promised to administer a "tennis lesson" to the brash upstart in the semifinal. Instead, the Russian was humbled in straight sets. Lleyton led his nation to three more finals, losing to Spain (2000) and France (2001), defeating Spain in 2003 as he set the pace, downing Juan Carlos Ferrero, 3-6, 6-3, 3-6, 7-6 (7-0), 6-2. Hewitt won four titles in 2000, the first teenager to win that many since Pete Sampras a decade earlier. He got his first major championship title, a doubles at the U.S., youngest male, at 19 years, 6 months, to win a major doubles in the Open era. At Flushing Meadow the following year, he defeated No. 7 seed Kafelnikov in the semis, 6-1, 6-2, 6-1, and Sampras in the final, 7-6 (4-7), 6-1, 6-1, to claim his first singles major championship. Hewitt won five other tournaments in 2001, including the year-end Masters, over Sebastien Grosjean (FRA), 6-3, 6-3, 6-4, appropriately in Sydney, and was at the top of the class. Some thought him a caretaker in the top spot until a more skilled player arrived to succeed the likes of Sampras and Agassi. But not only did he hold the ranking, he added a second

major, Wimbledon, defeating David Nalbandian ARG, 6-1, 6-3, 6-2 and defended his Masters title in Shanghai over Ferrero, 7-5, 7-5, 2-6, 2-6, 6-4. He dropped only two sets at Wimbledon to become the first Australian in 15 years to win on Centre Court. Pat Cash was the last. His dream of being the first Aussie to rule his country since Mark Edmondson in 1976 was squashed in the 2005 final, a 1-6, 6-3, 6-4, 6-4 triumph for Russian Marat Safin. Made semis Wimbledon, 2005; U.S., 2000, 02, 05; quarters French, 2004; U.S., 2003, 06; Wimbledon, 2004, 06. Career (as of May, 2008): won 27 singles, two doubles pro titles, $ $18,094,086 prize money.

MAJOR TITLES (3)— Wimbledon singles, 2002; U.S. singles, 2001; U.S. doubles, 2000.

Svetlana Kuznetsova
Russia (1985—)

Svetlana Kuznetsova was the surprise, first Russian to win U.S. women's singles title in 2004, defeating Elena Dementieva in all-Russian final, 6-3, 7-5. She reached two other major finals—losing the 2007 U.S. final to Justine Henin (BEL), 6-1, 6-3 and the 2006 French final to Henin, 6-4, 6-4, but broke through to win the elusive second singles major at the 2009 French, defeating fellow Russian Dinara Safina 6-4, 6-2 in the final. She won one major doubles title: Australian, 2005, with Alicia Molik (AUS), defeating Lindsay Davenport-Corina Morariu (both USA), 6-3, 6-4. She also lost four major doubles finals: Australian, 2004, with Elena Likhovtseva (RUS), 6-4, 6-3; French, 2004, with Likhovtseva, to Virginia Ruano Pascual (ESP)-Paola Suarez (ARG), 6-0, 6-3; Wimbledon, 2005, with Amelie Mauresmo (FRA), to Cara Black (ZIM)-Liezel Huber (RSA), 6-3, 7-6 (7-5); U.S., 2004, with Likhovtseva, to Pascual-Suarez, 6-4, 7-5. Entering 2009, she played Federation Cup 2004, 2007-2009, posting a 12-4 singles, 4-1 doubles. Won both singles in the 2007 final, including the decisive match over Francesca Schiavone, 4-6, 7-6 (7-5), 7-5, in 4-0 victory over Italy. She also helped win 2004 Cup and represented Russia at the Olympic Games in 2004 and 2008. Born in St. Petersburg, Russia, June 27, 1985, into prominent bicycling family. Father, Alexandr Kuznetsov, coached six Olympic champs. Mother, Galina Tsareva, 6-time world champ. Brother, Nikolai Kuznetsov, Olympic silver medalist, 1996. Robust, strong-legged Sveta nevertheless preferred tennis. Right-handed with a two-handed backhand, 5 ft. 9, 165 lbs, she was in the world's Top 10 for four years—No. 5, 2004; No. 4, 2006; No. 2, 2007, No. 8, 2008. Turned pro 2000, trained in Spain. As of July, 2009, won 11 singles, 14 doubles pro titles, $12,379,668 prize money.

MAJOR TITLES (3)—U.S. singles 2004; French singles 2009; Australian doubles, 2005.

Amelie Mauresmo
France (1979—)

The only French woman to win Wimbledon other than Suzanne Lenglen (1919–23, 25) and the fifth woman of her nation to win a major, Amelie won two majors in 2006—the Australian over Justin Henin (BEL), 6-1, 2-0, ret. and Wimbledon over Henin, 2-6, 6-3, 6-4. Unseeded, she lost the 1999 Australian final to Martina Hingis (SUI), 6-2, 6-3, defeating No. 1 Lindsay Davenport (USA), 6-4, 6-0 in the semifinals. A superb athlete, well-rounded attacking game, she played Federation Cup eight years, 1998-99, 2001–00 played 21 ties, posting a 30-9 singles, 2-2 doubles record through 2009. She led France to the Cup in 2003, winning two singles in 4-1 final-round win over U.S., including the decisive point, 6-2, 6-1, over Meghann Shaughnessy. In 2005 Fed Cup final, lost to Russia 3-2, she lost decisive doubles with Mary Pierce to Elena Dementieva-Dinara Safina, 6-4, 1-6, 6-3. A member of the French Olympic team in 2000, 2004, she won Olympic silver in women's singles in 2004, losing to Justine Henin-Hardenne. World Top 10 for seven years—No. 10, 1999; No. 9, 2001; No, 6, 2002; No. 4, 2003; No. 2, 2004; No. 3, 2005-06 (briefly No. 1, 2004), No. 18, 2007. Made quarterfinals of Australian, 2002, 04-05, French, 2003-04, U.S., 2001, 03-04-05; semifinals of Wimbledon, 2004-05, U.S., 2002, 06., Born in St. Germains en Laye, France on July 5, 1979. A right-hander, 5 ft. 9, 152 lbs, she turned pro in 1993 and was the world junior champ in 1996. Entering 2008, she won 25 singles, three doubles pro titles, $14,955,487 prize money.

MAJOR TITLES (2)—Australian singles, 2006; Wimbledon singles, 2006.

Rafael Nadal
Spain (1986—)

A Herculean figure, power flowing from abundant muscles, and driving his speedy legs, Rafa Nadal became the greatest Spanish player of all time, earning the No. 1 ranking in 2008 and capturing six majors, including epic wins over Roger Federer in the finals of Wimbledon in 2008 and the Australian Open in 2009, to go with his four straight titles on Roland Garros clay from 2005-2008. He hit the game in 2005 like the storm called "El Nino." And he was El Nino, a kid of 19, as he stormed Rome and Paris to become El Rey of Clay. He won nine other titles, skyrocketing from No. 51 in 2004 to No. 2 for three years, right behind Roger Federer (SUI) whom he has bedeviled, leading 8-6 in their head-to-heads entering 2008. Born June 3, 1986, Manacor, Spain, on the isle of Mallorca, the hometown also of 1998 French Open champ, Carlos Moya. They were the guys who put together Spain's Davis Cup triumph of 2004, 3-2 over the U.S. A surprise starter, teen-age lefty Nadal bumped off Andy Roddick, 6-7 (6-8), 6-2, 7-6 (8-6), 6-2, the first day, and Moya clinched over Roddick, 6-2, 7-6 (7-1), 7-6 (7-5). Though 6-1 and 188 pounds, Rafa seems larger and more ominous as heavy, high-bounding topspin roars from his racket and the slice slithers like a rattlesnake. He outruns most shots of his foes, and competes ferociously, though maintaining the spirit of a youngster having gamesplaying fun. A natural right-hander, he started out hitting a two-handed forehand, which became a backhand at the suggestion of his lifelong coach (and uncle) Toni Nadal. Astoundingly, first time around, he won the Italian and French Opens in 2005, and kept the titles in 2006 and 2007. Rafa was the first to hold both since Jim Courier (USA) in 1992. It was super hard going

in Rome in 2005, two points from defeat as he and Guillermo Coria (ARG) slugged it out from sunlight to floodlight for 5:14 hrs, a local record, before Rafa nosed ahead, 6-4, 3-6, 6-3, 4-6, 7-6 (8-6). It was no easier in 2006, another two-point spread in overcoming two match points and Federer in 5:06, 6-7 (0-7), 7-6 (7-5), 6-4, 2-6, 7-6 (7-5). The next year was a breeze, 6-2, 6-2, over Fernando Gonzalez (CHI). He beat Novak Djokovic in the Italian final in 2009, after injury contributing to an early loss to Juan Carlos Ferrero in 2008. Roland Garros, a Spanish playground, is a fun house for Rafa. He had to get rid of Federer in the semifinals of 2005, 6-3, 4-6, 6-3, 6-3, then Mariano Puerta (ARG) for the title, 6-7 (6-8), 6-3, 6-1, 7-5. Federer was the championship obstacle the next two years, but he couldn't handle Rafa in the dirt, 1-6, 6-1, 6-4, 7-6 (7-4), and 2007, too, 6-3, 4-6, 6-3, 6-4. His fourth straight French title was devastating, won without the loss of a set—capped by a 6-1, 6-3, 6-0 rout of Federer in the final. His win streak at Roland Garros ended at 31 in the fourth round of 2009, Robin Soderling of Sweden handing Rafa his first ever loss at the French Open in a 6-2, 6-7 (2), 6-4, 7-6 (2) loss. El Rey of Clay, he set an Open era record of 81 straight wins on clay, erasing the string of 53 in 1977 by Guillermo Vilas (ARG). None other than Federer jammed it at 81 in the Hamburg, 2007 final, 2-6, 6-2, 6-0. Rafa startled everybody (but himself) in overcoming Spanish grass phobia at Wimbledon by 2006 when he rolled to the final, a 6-0, 7-6 (7-5), 6-7 (2-7), 6-3, defeat by Federer. Twelve months later, he nearly stole Federer's front yard in five sets, perhaps the best final since Borg-McEnroe, 1980, 7-6 (9-7), 4-6, 7-6 (7-3), 2-6, 6-2. Holding two break-points at 1-2 and 2-3 in the fifth, he couldn't seize one that might have crowned him. A year later, the Wimbledon title was his in an epic 6-4, 6-4, 6-7 (5), 6-7 (8), 9-7 win over Federer. His best showing at the U.S. Open, however, was a quarterfinal showing in 2006. His major titles—French, 2005, def. Puerta, 6-7 (6-8), 6-3, 6-1, 7-5, 2006, def. Federer, 1-6, 6-1, 6-4, 7-6 (7-4), 2007, def. Federer, 6-3, 4-6, 6-3, 6-4, 2008, def. Federer 6-1, 6-3, 6-0; Wimbledon, 2008, def. Federer 6-4, 6-4, 6-7 (6), 5-7 (8), 9-7; Australian, 2009, def. Federer 7-5, 3-6, 7-6 (3), 3-6, 6-2. Lost two major singles finals—Wimbledon, 2006, to Federer, 6-0, 7-6 (7-5), 6-7 (2-7), 6-3; 2007, to Federer, 7-6 (9-7), 4-6, 7-6 (7-3), 2-6, 6-2. Other prominent titles include—Monte Carlo, 2005, 2006, 2007, 2008, 2009; Italian Open, 2005, def. Coria 6-4, 3-6, 6-3, 4-6, 7-6 (8-6); 2006 def. Federer 6-7 (0-7), 7-6 (7-5), 6-4, 2-6, 7-6 (7-5); 2007 def. F. Gonzalez, 6-2, 6-2; 2009 def. Novak Djokovic 7-6 (2), 6-2. Also won Olympic gold at Beijing Olympics, defeating Gonzalez in gold medal match 6-3, 7-6 (2), 6-3. He turned pro 2001, played Davis Cup, 2004–09, 12-1 in singles, 2-4 in doubles, helping Spain win the Cup, 2004 and in 2008 (but, injured and did not play in the final against Argentina). Knee tendonitis prevented him from playing in 2009 Wimbledon, where he was defending champion. Career as of July of 2009: won 36 singles and 4 doubles pro titles, $ 25,006,295 prize money as of start of July of 2009.

MAJOR TITLES (6)—Australian singles, 2009, French singles, 2005-06-07-08; Wimbledon singles, 2008.

Andrew Stephen Roddick
United States (1982—)

High energy, cyclonic server, Andy holds the 155 mph record set in the 2004 Davis Cup semifinal against Belarus in Charleston, S.C., launching the serve at Vladimir Voltchkov. He won the U.S. Open in 2003, defeating Juan Carlos Ferrero (ESP), 6-3, 7-6 (7-2), 6-3 and became first American to hold world No. 1 since Andre Agassi in 1999. He saved match point with service winner in the Open semifinal win over David Nalbandian (ARG). Won six singles titles that year, had 19-match streak. Fought heroically but lost epic Wimbledon final in 2009, falling to Roger Federer 5-7, 7-6 (6), 7-6 (5), 3-6, 16-14 in longest ever Wimbledon final (in games) and longest fifth set in major tournament final history. He made his first splash at 18, defeating Pete Sampras in the third round, 7-6 (7-2), 6-3, at Key Biscayne in 2001. He broke into world's Top 10 at No. 10 in 2002. Also No. 2, 2004; No. 3, 2005; No. 6, 2006-07; No. 8, 2008. He was the world's No. 1 junior in 2000 and the first U.S. winner of the Australian junior title since Butch Buchholz in 1959. Named to George W. Bush's President's Council on Sports and Fitness in 2006, he is devoted to Davis Cup—nine years, 2001–09 has played 23 ties; 31-11 singles (as of July, 2009). At last rewarded with the 2007 Cup in 4-1 final over Russia, he was 6-0 singles that year, winning two clinchers, defeating Tomas Berdych (CZE), first round, 4-6, 6-3, 6-2, 7-6 (7-4); and defeating Jonas Bjorkman (SWE), semifinal, 6-2, 7-6 (7-3), 6-4. Born Omaha, Nebraska, Aug. 30, 1982, raised mostly in Florida. A right-hander with a two-handed backhand, he is essentially a baseliner with wicked forehand. Frequent coach-changer (Brad Gilbert piloted him to No. 1), also worked with his brother, John Roddick, Dean Goldfine, and, until March 2008, by Hall of Famer Jimmy Connors. Lost two previous (three total) Wimbledon finals to Federer (SUI), 2004, 4-6, 7-5, 7-6 (7-3), 6-4; 2005, 6-2, 7-6 (7-2), 6-4. Lost the U.S. final, 2006, to Federer, 6-2, 4-6, 7-5, 6-1. Won three U.S. Clay Court titles—def. Hyung-Taik Lee (KOR), 7-5, 6-3, 2001; def. Pete Sampras (USA), 7-6 (11-9), 6-3, 2002; def. Sebastien Grosjean (FRA), 6-1, 7-6 (7-5), 2005; He also lost the final in 2003 to Agassi. He made the semifinals of the Australian, 2003, 05, 07, 09; Semifinals at Wimbledon in 2003; Best year: 2003, won six titles, 72-19 won-loss record. Career as of July of 2009, won 27 singles titles, 3 doubles, $ 16,562,109 prize money, as of July, 2009.

MAJOR TITLES (1)—U.S. Open, 2003.

Marat Safin
Russia (1980—)

Big, blazing, bumptious, and sometimes bumbling, excessive in everything he does, 6-4, 195 pound Marat Safin is a good-natured bundle of immense talent waiting to be tamed. Nobody can stop him when he fires on all cylinders, as Pete Sampras learned, swept away, 6-4, 6-3, 6-3, in 2000 U.S. final. Marat, 20 then, first Russian to win the title, appeared to have No. 1 wrapped up that year (won seven titles), but, unraveled at Masters, finished No. 2 behind Guga Kuerten. Blends speed, touch, power; however,

moodiness can transform him into a headless horseman. Fined $2,500 for not tying in a first-round loss to Grant Stafford at the 2000 Australian Open.

A champion racket-smasher, he turned it all around, seeded No. 6 at Flushing during his title run. He turned pro in 1996 and made his first splash in beating Andre Agassi in the first round, defending champion Gustavo Kuerten in the second round at the 1998 French—made the fourth round. Born Jan. 27, 1980 in Moscow of tennis-teaching parentage—Mother, Rausa Islanova, coached him age 6-to-13, then sent him to Valencia, Spain to live under the tutelage Rafael Mensua. Sister Dinara Safina (born April 17, 1986) also world class, top female player, who earned the No. 1 ranking in 2009—making he and Dinara as the only brother-sister combination to earn the top world ranking (Dinara also reached 2008/2009 French and 2009 Australian singles finals). He was a mainstay as Russia won first Davis Cup in 2002, beating France, 3-2 in the final. He was 6-1 singles, 2-2 doubles; won decisive singles over Michel Kratochvil, Switzerland, David Nalbandian, Argentina; and beat Paul-Henri Mathieu, Sebastian Grosjean in the final. Also beat Jose Acasuso of Argentina 6-3, 3-6, 6-3, 7-6 (5) in fifth and decisive match to help Russia win the 2006 Cup in Moscow. He lost the Australian final in 2002 to Tom Johansson, but rebounded in Melbourne in 2005, beating world No. 1 Roger Federer in semifinal, saving a match point in the 5-7, 6-4, 5-7, 7-6 (6), 9-7 win. Beat Lleyton Hewitt for the title, 1-6, 6-3, 6-4, 6-4. He made the semifinals of the French, 2002 and the quarterfinals in 2000; He reached the quarterfinals at Wimbledon, 2001 and the semifinals at the U.S. in 2001. In 2008, he powered to an unexpected semifinal at Wimbledon, defeating Australian Open champion Novak Djokovic en route, losing to Federer. He won 15 singles (380-223 matches), two doubles pro career titles, $14,143,755 in prize money as of July, 2009 he was in the world's Top 10: No. 2, 2000; No. 3, 2002 (No. 11, 2001).

MAJOR TITLES (2)—Australian, 2005, U.S. 2000.

The Serbian Surge

One of the more startling developments in the game's history is the abrupt appearance of championship players in Serbia, a Balkan sliver with a population of 10,150,265—but no tennis tradition, few courts and players. The most recent Serb to be heard from was mammoth server Bobo Zivojinovic, a Wimbledon semifinalist in 1986 (now president of the Serbian Tennis Federation).

Yet at the end of 2007 three young Serbs—Ana Ivanovic, Jelena "Jelly" Jankovic and Novak Djokovic were in the world's Top 10 in singles (Nos. 4-3-3 respectively), and Nenad Zimonjic was No. 5 in doubles. Quite a package from Belgrade.

Why? A mystery? Who knows where talent will surface, but this is obviously a curious Balkan bonanza. Living in Belgrade during the NATO bombing attacks of 1999 was scary, and they had to go elsewhere to nurture their talent: Ivanovic to Switzerland, Djokovic to Germany, Jankovic to the U.S.

Novak Djokovic

He was the first of the quartet to seize a singles major—the Australian of 2008, defeating Jo-Willie Tsonga (FRA), 4-6, 6-4, 6-3, 7-6 (7-2), after deposing Roger Federer in the semis, 7-5, 6-3, 7-6 (7-5). He won the Canadian Open, 2007, by beating Nos. 3-2-1—Andy Roddick, Rafa Nadal, Federer—in succession, then crashed his first major final, the U.S. Open, missing out on five set points in the first, two in the second, succumbing to Federer, 7-6 (7-4), 7-6 (7-2), 6-4. He was a French and Wimbledon semifinalist in 2007, rising from No. 83 in 2005, No. 16 in 2006. Bright, jocular, he was born May 22, 1987, in Belgrade, stands 6-3, weighs 175. Speedy afoot, sensational groundstroker with two-handed backhand, turned pro 2003. First big title came in 2007 at Key Biscayne, beating Willie Canas (ARG), 6-3, 6-2, 6-4. Led Serbia upward into the Davis Cup World Group, 4-1 over Australia, winning two singles and a doubles. He won Olympic bronze in singles at Beijing Games, losing to Rafael Nadal (ESP) in semifinals 6-4, 1-6, 6-4 and beating James Blake (USA) 6-3, 7-6 (4) in bronze medal match. Also won 2008 year-end championships in Shanghai—the Tennis Masters Cup—defeating Nikolay Davydenko of Russia in the final. As of July of 2009, he won 13 titles, including the 2008 Italian Open, and $12,614,868 in prize money.

MAJOR TITLE (1)—Australian singles, 2008.

Ana Ivanovic

First Serb to reach a major singles final, she lost the French in 2007 to Justine Henin (BEL), 6-1, 6-2. Starting 2008, she made the Australian final, losing to Maria Sharapova (RUS), 7-5, 6-3, but beat Daniela Hantuchova (SVK), Venus Williams (USA) on the way. She broke through to win the French title in 2008, defeating Dinara Safina (RUS) in the final 6-4, 6-3 and achieved No. 1 ranking thereafter, becoming the first Serb to hold the top spot. A tall, good-natured beauty, 6-1, 152 pounds, she turned pro in 2003 (No. 705), rising steadily to No. 16, 2005, and No. 14, 2006. A right-hander with strong forehand, two-handed backhand, she was born Nov. 6, 1987, at Belgrade. As of July of 2009, she won eight singles titles and $ 6,753,904 in prize money. She won the Canadian Open in 2006 over Martina Hingis (SUI), 6-2, 6-3, that helped her win the U.S. Open Series as the points-leader in lead-up tournaments to the U.S. Open.

Jelena Jankovic

Mama Snezana knew best. After losing 10 of 11 first round matches in 2006, to dip to No. 34, usually perky Jelly Jankovic was ready to quit and go back to college. But Mama urged her to persist, and by the Italian Open she had straightened her game out, made the quarters, the fourth round at Wimbledon, the semis at the U.S.—beating Nos. 10-7-5 Nicole Vaidisova (CZE), Svetlana Kuznetsova (RUS), Elena Dementieva (RUS) before losing to No. 1 Justine Henin (BEL)—ascending to No. 20, ready to jump up to the Top 10. Born Feb. 28, 1985, at Belgrade, a right-hander with two-handed backhand, she stands 5-10, weighs 135.

Quick legs and fighting spirit set her apart, and returning to Rome in 2007, she won the Italian title over No. 2 Kuznetsova,

7-5, 6-1. That was clay. She also won on hard, Auckland, over Vera Zvonareva (RUS), 7-6 (11-9), 5-7, 6-3, and on grass, Birmingham, over Maria Sharapova, 4-6, 6-3, 7-5. Snaring a first major, she won Wimbledon mixed with Jamie Murray in 2007, and made the semis of the Australian in 2008, losing to champ Sharapova, 6-3, 6-1. her first major singles final came in New York at the 2008 U.S. Open, losing to Serena Williams 6-4, 7-5 in the final. Despite not winning a major title, she followed Ivanovic in the No. 1 ranking on August 10, 2008, holding the top ranking for a total of 17 weeks through the end of 2008 and at the start of 2009.

As of July of 2009, she won 10 singles titles and one doubles pro titles and $7,300,102 in prize money.

MAJOR TITLES (1)—Wimbledon mixed, 2007.

Nenad Zimonjic

Elder of the surging Serbs, born June 4, 1976, at Belgrade, Nenad was the first to win a major—Australian mixed, 2004, with Elena Bovina (RUS). A potent partner, doubles expert, tough at the net, he holds 29 doubles titles, including back-to-back titles at Wimbledon with Daniel Nestor in 2008 and 2009. Also won the French mixed title in 2005 with Katarina Srebotnik (SLO) and the Australian mixed title in 2008 with Sun Tiantian (CHN). Also, twice a runner-up at Wimbledon, 2004, with Mark Knowles (BAH), ands 2006, with Fabrice Santoro (FRA). A right-hander, 6-3, 200 pounds, he turned pro in 1995. As of July of 2009, he won 18 doubles titles and $ 3,907,828 in prize money.

MAJOR TITLE (5)—Wimbledon doubles, 2008, 2009; French mixed, 2005; Australian mixed, 2004, 2008

Maria Sharapova
Russia (1987—)

Dropping onto the world's screen as a teen-ager, Maria Sharapova, the blonde "Siberian Siren," became as well known for her fresh appealing beauty as her punishing groundstrokes and fierce desire to win. The combination makes her face one of the most familiar in sport. A Wimbledon title at 17 assured her of quick wealth as a product endorser.

Living up to the game plan of her ambitious father, Uri Sharapov, the two of them, nearly destitute, daringly departed Russia when she was 9, continuing her tennis education at coach Nick Bollietteri's academy, Bradenton, Fla., eventually turning pro in 2001 at age 14. Success wasn't far behind. At her second Wimbledon in 2004, she went all the way, dethroning Serena Williams (USA), in the final, 6-1, 6-4, from 1-4 in the second set. In the semifinals, she knocked off 1999 champ Lindsay Davenport (USA), 2-6, 7-6 (7-5), 6-1, from 1-3 in the second.

Ranked No. 17, Maria was the longest shot champion at the Big W, and maybe the least experienced, the first since Evonne Goolagong (AUS) in 1971 to win on a second try. Three years later No. 31 Venus Williams (USA) was a longer shot, but it was her 11th Wimbledon and fourth title. Sharapova was also the third youngest to win the oldest championship, a bit older than Martina Hingis, 16, in 1997, and Lottie Dod, 15, in 1887. She wound up 2004 by stopping Serena again, 4-6, 6-2, 6-4, to win the WTA Tour Championship.

In 2006, her fourth time at Flushing, Maria conquered her second major, the U.S. Open, ruthlessly, beating 1-2 to finish: 6-0, 4-6, 6-0, over Australian, Wimbledon champ Amelie Mauresmo (FRA) and French champ Justine Henin-Hardenne (BEL), 6-4, 6-4. She won her third major—the Australian—in 2008, beating Ana Ivanovic of Serbia 7-5, 6-3 in the final.

Russian born in Nyagan, Siberia, April 19, 1987, she is tall (6-2), slim (131 lbs), right-handed (two-handed backhand), has lived in the U.S. most of her life, and loudly goes about her winning business. While her shrieks can be unnerving to viewers, she says it's a lifelong habit. Elegantly attired on court Maria is a couturier's dreamgirl.

Entering the Top 10 at No. 4 in 2004 (from No. 32 in 2003), she resided at Nos. 4, 2, 5 the next three years. She first earned the No. 1 ranking in August of 2005. She also lost a major final at the Australian in 2007 to Serena Williams, 6-1, 6-2. She was an Aussie semifinalist in 2005-06; a French semifinalist in 2007; a Wimbledon semifinalist in 2005-06; and a U.S. semifinalist in 2005; She also was a quarterfinalist at the French in 2004-05; and at Wimbledon in 2007. As of July of 2009, she won 19 singles, three doubles and prize money of $12,383,566 .

MAJOR TITLES (3)—Australian singles, 2008; Wimbledon singles, 2004; U.S singles, 2006.

Williams Sisters
United States

Extraordinary. Phenomenal. Incredible. Fantastic. Unique. Unprecedented.

Take your pick, or lump them all together, the words, of course, fitting Venus and Serena. They stand alone—the Sisters Sledgehammer—in the annals of the game: two all-time greats springing from the same household. Yes, there have been other sensational siblings, such as the English Renshaw and Doherty brothers of early Wimbledon mastery. Or the three world class Maleeva sisters out of Bulgaria. Or Texans Nancy and Cliff Richey, both of whom were in the world Top 10 in the 1970s.

However, none of them come close to the Williams sorority in major accomplishments, triumphs across the planet, brilliance at such tender ages. If there were only one, she would make it to the International Tennis Hall of Fame. But this family will give the Hall a right-handed double dose when their playing days are over. Their bleak background makes the story even more remarkable. Rising from a troubled Los Angeles suburb, Compton, the youngest of five sisters, they were admirably raised and coached by parents (Oracene Price and Richard Williams), who amazingly figured out the game on their own. Presently Venus, then Serena, with little experience in junior competition, made the world their tennis ball. Leaving the difficulties of California, the family moved to Palm Beach Gardens, Fla.

They are the first blacks since Althea Gibson and Arthur Ashe to win majors, and the first siblings in well over a century to oppose one another in major finals—eight times. At long-ago Wimbledons Willie and Ernest Renshaw (thrice) and Laurie and Reggie Doherty (once) had confronted one another in finals. In 1884, Maud Watson beat older sister Lilian, 6-8, 6-3, 6-3, in the inaugural female final. Not until 118 years passed did another similar familial face-off occur at the Big W: Serena over Venus, 7-6 (7-4), 6-3, for the 2002 title. It was so much bigger because by that time the world was watching.

Arriving on the professional scene (Big Sister Venus leading the way in 1994, Little Sister tagging along in 1997), the Sisters soon created an Axis of Anxiety among the opposition. Specializing in baseline barrages with dynamite serves and double-barreled backhands, they were a two-lady tsunami: waves of speed, power, athleticism, competitive fiber such as had never graced the game. As the elder by 15 months, Big Sister, the taller, always looked after Little Sister, the broader, as best-friends closeness developed and solidified.

Much like another heralded world champion, Muhammad Ali, they were going to do it their way. Differently. "I'm not going to be what you want me to be," Ali declared to the public. That was the Sisters' outlook. Reared to be confidently independent, they said they were "different"—and meaning not just complexion. Mysterious in their moves and decisions, following no particular schedule on tour, coming on fiercely to seize huge prizes or at times appearing uninterested, they delighted in turning the game upside down whenever they were being written off. "We have a lot of doubters, but that makes us stronger," says Serena.

A supreme example was 2007. Ranked No. 81, overweight, having played only four tournaments in 2006, Serena bashed her way to her third Australian title. Excepting the feeble Aussie Open of 1978, ruled by No. 111 Chris O'Neil, Serena was the longest shot ever to grab a major, crushing No. 1 Maria Sharapova of Russia, 6-1, 6-2.

Venus, No. 31, in merely her eighth tournament of the year, became the longest shot to capture Wimbledon 2007, her fourth, beating Marion Bartoli of France, 6-4, 6-1.

Serena surprised in 1999 with the family's initial singles major, upstaging Venus by winning the U.S. Open at 17. But Papa Williams had been loudly predicting greatness for them even before they joined the professional circus. He also had tabbed Serena to be the slightly better of his twosome, and only she has ranked No. 1, in 2002, the year Venus was No. 2.

As of July of 2009, the family stash was 31 major titles: 18 singles (11 for Serena), nine doubles majors together and a "Family Slam" in mixed in 1998, each winning two of the four. Singles head-to-head—it's 11-10 in favor of Serena after their meeting in the 2009 Wimbledon final, (Serena leads 7-5 at the majors), although Venus won their maiden head-on crash in a final as pros, 6-1, 4-6, 6-4, the Key Biscayne finale of 1999.

Venus Ebone Starr Williams
(1980—)

At 6-feet-2, Venus is one of the tallest ever female champions, a willowy 160 pound banger of the strongest serve to come along, hitting serves recorded as fast as 128 mph. As a 14-year-old, she made her pro debut in 1994 at Oakland, beating an ex-NCAA champ Shaun Stafford 6-3, 6-4 for starters, and pushing Hall of Famer Arantxa Sanchez Vicario of Spain, the tournament victor and U.S. Open champ, in a second-round loss, 2-6, 6-3, 6-0.

In no rush, paying attention to schoolwork, she wasn't ready for the majors until 1997: a first-round loss at Wimbledon, 4-6, 6-2, 6-4, to No. 91 Magdalena Grzybowska of Poland, but she had a stunning introductory look at the U.S. Open. No debutante has ever come from so far back to attain the final. Ranked No. 66, Venus, blasted groundies and ran down her foes' best shots. She rescued two match points with her two-fisted backhand in the decisive tie-breaker to survive the thrilling semifinal over No. 11, Romanian Irina Spirlea, 7-6 (7-5), 4-6, 7-6 (9-7), in 2:42. However, No. 1 Martina Hingis of Switzerland was too much in the title clash, 6-0, 6-4.

Ending the year at No. 22, she was soon in Top 10 territory, and winning titles, the first of many, Oklahoma City in 1998, 6-3, 6-2, over South Africa's Joanette Kruger. Starting in 1998, she ranked Nos. 5, 3, 3, 3, 2, slipped to No. 11 in 2003, recovered to Nos. 9, 10, took an injuries-riddled tumble to No. 48, then surfaced at No. 8 in 2007. She first attained the No. 1 ranking in February of 2002.

Her breakthrough to major heights came in 2000, on Centre Court, a 6-3, 7-6 (7-3), Wimbledon decision over No. 2 Lindsay Davenport. She had beaten No. 1 Hingis in the quarterfinals, 6-3, 4-6, 6-4, and No. 8 Sister Serena in the semifinals, 6-2, 7-6 (7-3). That pointed the way to a rare triple. She had to beat Nos. 1-2 again to take the U.S. Open: Hingis in the semifinal, 4-6, 6-3, 7-5, from 3-5 in the third, and Davenport, 6-4, 7-5. Soon after came Olympic gold, 6-2, 6-4, over Russia's Elena Dementieva—plus the doubles with Serena, 6-1, 6-1, over the Dutch pair of Kristie Boogert and Miriam Oremans. Not since American Helen Wills in 1924 had a woman taken both golds. She and Serena would also win doubles gold in Beijing in 2008, defeating Anabel Medina Garrigues and Virginia Ruano Pascual of Spain 6-2, 6-0.

Venus maintained her Wimbledon-U.S. supremacy in 2001, stopping a teen-ager, Justine Henin of Belgium, 6-1, 3-6, 6-0, in London and a very familiar face, Serena, at Flushing, 6-2, 6-4. It was their first collision in a major final. Serena would win the next five: 2002 French Open 7-5, 6-3; Wimbledon 7-6 (7-4), 6-3; U.S. Open 6-4, 6-3; 2003 Australian Open 7-5 (7-4), 3-6, 6-4; Wimbledon 4-6, 6-4, 6-2.

After winning only one title in 2003 (Antwerp) and two in 2004 (Charleston, Warsaw)—comedowns from the six title years of 1999-2000-01, and seven in 2002—she appeared to be receding in 2005. Not so. Seeded No. 14, she snared a third Wimbledon by dethroning No. 2 Maria Sharapova of Russia in the semifinals, 7-6 (7-2), 6-1, then beating No. 1 Davenport, 4-6, 7-6 (7-4), 9-7, ducking a match point with a lusty backhand at 4-5 in the third. That took 2:45, the tourney's longest women's final in time. The last title round match point saver had been Wills seven decades previously, defeating Helen Jacobs for the 1935 crown. (In winning the

2001 Key Biscayne final over Jennifer Capriati, 4-6, 6-1, 7-6 (7-4), Venus dodged eight match points against Capriati's serve.)

Fully fit again by 2007, she was primed for a fourth Wimbledon prize. Despite ragged early starts, she found the tune, was too quick and overpowering for four higher seeds, No. 2, No. 5, No. 6, No. 18: 6-1, 6-3, over Sharapova; 6-3, 6-4, over Svetlana Kuznetsova; 6-2, 6-4, over Ana Ivanovic; 6-4, 6-1, over Marion Bartoli.

She lost six major finals, all to Serena: French, 2002, 7-5, 6-3; Wimbledon, 2002, 7-6 (7-4), 6-3; U.S., 2002, 6-4, 6-3; Australian, 2003, 7-6 (7-4), 3-6, 6-4; Wimbledon, 2003, 4-6, 6-4, 6-2; Wimbledon, 2009, 7-6 (3), 6-2.

Born June 17, 1980, at Lynwood, Calif., beyond the court she works at interior and apparel design.

Venus' 19 major titles—Wimbledon singles five times, U.S. singles twice, Australian doubles three times with Serena, French doubles once with Serena, Wimbledon doubles four times with Serena, U.S. Open doubles once with Serena and one French and Australian Open mixed with Justin Gimelstob. As of July of 2009, she has won 41 singles titles, 13 doubles titles and $23,767,663 in prize money.

She played Fed Cup for the U.S. in 1999, 2003-04-05, 07—playing eight ties; posting a 14-2 singles, 3-2 doubles record. Helped the U.S. win the Cup in 1999.

MAJOR TITLES (18) —Wimbledon singles, 2000-01, 2005, 2007-08; U.S. singles, 2000, 2001; Australian doubles, 2001, 2003, 2009; French doubles, 1999, Wimbledon doubles, 2000, 2002, 2008-09; U.S. doubles, 1999; Australian mixed, 1998, French mixed, 1998.

Serena Jamika Williams

(1981—)

Little Sister, always showed the way by Big Sister, wasn't supposed to be the one to take the first huge swing with a racket. But that's what 17-year-old Serena did in 1999, winning the U.S. Open on her second visit to Flushing Meadow while higher ranked No. 3 Venus was relegated to the role of spectator.

After jarring the crown from the head of 1998 queen Lindsay Davenport in the semifinals, 6-4, 1-6, 6-4, Serena, No. 7, got some family revenge in putting down No. 1 Martina Hingis, 6-3, 7-6 (7-4). Hingis had removed Venus in the semifinal, 6-1, 4-6, 6-3. Serena treated champions like dominoes, knocking off four in a row: Conchita Martinez, the Spanish Wimbledon champ of 1994; Monica Seles of the U.S., an Open champion from 1991-1992, plus Davenport and Hingis.

She would have to wait almost three years for the next of her eight singles majors, the French of 2002. But what an extraordinary year that was, victory in every major she entered, and Big Sister as her victim each time: French, 7-5, 6-3; Wimbledon, 7-6 (7-4), 6-3; U.S., 6-4, 6-3. Injuries had kept her out of the Australian. Otherwise, she might have made a Grand Slam. As it was, her triple set her up for an achievement sometimes called the "Serena Slam" since she won the Australian of 2003, a fourth successive major, 7-6 (7-4), 3-6, 6-4, over Venus, becoming the fifth woman to

hold all four titles at once, preceded by Maureen Connolly, Margaret Court, Martina Navratilova, Steffi Graf. In the semifinal of the 2003 Aussie, she ascended from 1-5 in the third, saving two match points to beat Belgium's Kim Clijsters, 4-6, 6-3, 7-5.

Serena's escapist mind-set was on display again in Australia as she won the title of 2005. Maria Sharapova, who had beaten her in the Wimbledon final of 2004, held three match points with serve at 5-4 in the third, but couldn't fell her, in the 2-6, 7-5, 8-6 semifinal. Nor could No. 1 Davenport, despite a 6-2, 2-2 lead, and six break points in the eight-deuce fifth game. Serena hung on, then surged through the last nine games, 2-6, 6-3, 6-0.

But the most unlikely was the Australian of 2007 regardless of the No. 81 ranking, and little preparation. Nevertheless seeds were strewn harmlessly along her way in the last five rounds: No. 5, No. 11, No. 16, No. 10 and No. 1—Nadia Petrova (RUS), Jelly Jankovic (SRB), Shahar Peer (ISR), Nicole Vaidisova (CZE), Sharapova (RUS). Petrova, serving for it at 6-1, 5-4, three points away, was beaten 1-6, 7-5, 6-3. Peer, beaten, 3-6, 6-2, 8-6, was two points away at 6-5, 30-15. But Serena, aflame, was letting no one get closer, least of all Sharapova (6-1, 6-2), from whom she won the first five games. Doubling her enjoyment was beating Sharapova, who had lifted her Wimbledon crown in 2004.

Winning the U.S. in 1999 elevated her to the Top 10 for a stay of six straight years: Nos. 4, 6, 6, 1, 3, 7. She fell off to No. 11, plunged to No. 95 before returning to No. 7 in 2007. After winning the 2008 U.S. Open (d. Jelena Jankovic of Serbia 6-4, 7-5), she returned to the No. 1 ranking and, after losing the ranking to Jankovic for 17 weeks at the end of 2008, beginning of 2009, she regained the top spot again after winning the 2009 Australian Open (d. Dinara Safina of Russia 6-0, 6-3). Curiously, after beating sister Venus, 7-6 (3), 6-2 to win 2009 Wimbledon, she did not overtake Safina in the No. 1 ranking, despite the fact that she won three of the last four majors—and posted a quarterfinal showing at the fourth— the French—and Safina not having won a major.

Born Sept. 26, 1981, Saginaw, Mich.; Serena stands at 5-9, 165 lbs. She won the WTA Year-end Championship in 2001, defeating Davenport, walkover (injury). She lost WTA finals in 2002 to Clijsters, 7-5, 6-3 and in 2004 to Sharapova, 4-6, 6-2, 6-4.

Serena's 22 major titles—four Australian singles; one French singles, three Wimbledon singles, three U.S. singles, three Australian doubles with Venus, one French doubles with Venus, four Wimbledon doubles with Venus, one U.S. doubles with Venus, one Wimbledon mixed with Max Mirnyi and one U.S. Open mixed with Mirnyi. She played Fed Cup for the U.S. in 1999, 2003 and 2007, playing four ties and posting a 4-0 singles and 3-0 doubles record and helped the U.S. to the 1999 Cup. She won Olympic gold in doubles, with Venus in 2000 and 2008. As of May of 2008, she won 34 singles titles, 14 doubles titles and prize money of $25,858,948.

MAJOR TITLES (22)—Australian singles, 2003, 2005, 2007, 2009; French singles, 2002; Wimbledon singles, 2002, 2003, 2009; U.S. singles, 1999, 2002, 2008; Australian doubles, 2001, 2003, 2009; French doubles, 1999; Wimbledon doubles, 2000, 2002, 2008, 2009; U.S. doubles, 1999; Wimbledon mixed, 1998, U.S. mixed 1998.

They Also Served

Anna Kournikova was one of the most popular players on the WTA Tour. Her website always hummed—even when her game did not.

Not everyone can be labeled an all-time great or ascend to the International Tennis Hall of Fame. Nevertheless, numerous others are remembered herein, having made distinctive/unusual marks and contributions. For example, no winner of a major singles title, she or he, is forgotten. You may also find a few rascals, skilled with racket but unlovable such as a homicidal Wimbledon runner-up, Vere "St. Leger" Goold. Whether he hooked a few foes on line calls is unknown, but he thought he could get away with murder.

Abbreviations used: LH, left-hander; RH, right-hander; b., born; d., died; def. defeated. Denoting tournament finish: rd., round; QF, quarterfinal; SF, semifinal; F, final; MP, SP, BP—match points, set points, break points.

AKHURST, Daphne—Daphne Jessie Akhurst Cozens, a tragic Australian RH. Her country's first prolific champ, first female to make world's Top Five (No. 3, 1928), though had short career and life. b. in Sydney, April 22, 1903, d. Jan. 9, 1933, in childbirth in Sydney. Between 1925 and 1931, won 14 majors, all Australian: 5 singles—1925, def. Esna Boyd (AUS), 1-6, 8-6, 6-4; 1926, def. Boyd, 6-1, 6-3; 1928, def. Boyd, 7-5, 6-2; 1929, def. Louie Bickerton (AUS), 6-1, 5-7, 6-2; 1930, def. Sylvia Lance Harper (AUS), 10-8, 2-6, 7-5. Also won 5 doubles: 1924-25, with Harper; 1928, with Boyd; 1929, 31, with Bickerton; 4 mixed: 1924-25, with Jim Willard (AUS); 1928, with Jean Borotra (FRA); 1929, with Gar Moon (AUS). Last doubles, 1931, won as Mrs. Roy Cozens. Made SF, Australian, 1924; Wimbledon, 1928, QF, French, 1928; Wimbledon, 1925, Australian Open women's singles championship trophy named for her.

ALLEN, Leslie—Trailblazer Leslie Allen, first black woman to win a professional singles title—Detroit, 1981, def. Hana Mandlikova (CZE), 6-4, 6-4. Through persistence and a legal victory she uni-sexed the tennis team at Glenville High in hometown, Cleveland, as first female member, No. 1 player. Graduate U. Southern California (1977), helped women's team win NCAA title that year, then turned pro. Strong server, 5 ft 10, 155. Won American Tennis Assn. title, 1977. b. March 12, 1957, Cleveland. Highest ranking, No. 21, 1983. Won 1 singles, 3 doubles pro titles, $334,697 prize money, 10-year career. Now Executive Director Leslie Allen Foundation, New York, aiding kids to develop life skills on and off court.

ALVAREZ, Lili De—Spain's most accomplished female before Arantxa Sanchez Vicario, the chic Lili de Alvarez, later Comtesse de la Valdene, was world No. 2, 1927-28; No. 3, 1926, No. 8, 1930-31. RH, b. May 9, 1905, Rome. Delighted photographers, spectators in avant garde outfits such as culottes, 1931, at Wimbledon. Lost 3 straight Wimbledon F: 1926, to Kitty McKane Godfree (GBR), 6-2, 4-6, 6-3; 1927, to Helen Wills (USA), 6-2, 6-4; 1928, to Wills, 6-2, 6-3. Made French SF 1930-31, QF 1927. Won French doubles, 1929 with Kea Bouman (NED). Tripled at Italian, 1930, winning singles over Lucia Valerio (ITA), 3-6, 8-6, 6-0, doubles, mixed. Lived in Madrid. d. there July 8, 1998.

AMPON, Felicisimo—Felicisimo Hermoso Ampon, speedy, popular miniature, 4 ft 11, 100 pounds, smallest world-class man. Philippines' finest, RH, b. Oct. 27, 1920, Manila. Splendid retriever, made mark at French: QF 1952 (def. Tony Trabert), 1953 (def. Budge Patty). Incredible Davis Cup career over 29-year span (played 16 years; 36 series)—from Philippines' initial team, 1939, to farewell victory, age 47, 1968. Led team to 22-16 record, was 34-26, singles, 6-9 doubles. Nadir: 6-0, 6-0, 6-0, Cup beating by Frank Parker, U.S., 1946. Won 16 post-World War II singles titles.

AMRITRAJ, Vijay, Anand, Ashok—Three rangy, RH brothers, pros, from India with attacking styles, all born, raised in Madras (now Chennai). Vijay and Anand played Davis Cup together 15 years, led India to two title rounds, 1974 and 1987. All live in Los Angeles. Son Prakash (bo. Oct. 1, 1983) a Davis Cupper for India, after playing for Univ. of Southern California.

Vijay Amritraj—b. Dec. 14, 1953, graceful 6 ft 3, superb volleyer, Best world rank, No. 16, 1980. Won 21 singles (384-296 matches), 13 doubles (262-217) career pro titles, $1,331,913. Winning Bretton Woods, N.H., 1973, saved 3 MP each vs. Humphrey Hose (VEN), Rod Laver (AUS), 2 more in F, def. No. 3 Jimmy Connors, 7-5, 2-6, 7-5. Made QF Wimbledon, U.S., 1973 (def. 2nd seed Laver in latter, 7-6, 2-6, 6-4, 2-6, 6-4). Davis Cup: 1970-88, 27-18 singles, 18-10 doubles. A top tennis telecaster.

Anand Amritraj—6 ft 1, b. March 20, 1952. Best World rank, No. 74, 1974. Won 12 pro career doubles titles, 8 with Vijay, $332,133. Davis Cup 1968-88, 11-17 singles, 21-14 doubles. Career: Singles—90-170, Doubles—288-269.

Ashok Amritraj—6 ft 1, b. Feb 22, 1957. Best world rank, No. 201, 1977. Career: Singles—4-26, doubles—20-39.

ANDERSON, J.O.—Australian Davis Cupper, 6 ft 3 RH James Outram "Greyhound" Anderson, always known as J.O. b. Sept. 17, 1895, Enfield, d. July 19, 1960, Sydney. World Top 10; No. 6, 1921; No. 5. 1922; No. 3, 1923-24. Swift afoot, with husky, damaging forehand, poking 'upside-down' backhand (using same racket face as forehand). Won 3 major singles, all Australian: 1922, def. Gerald Patterson (AUS), 6-0, 3-6, 3-6, 6-3, 6-2.; 1924, def. Bob Schlesinger (AUS), 6-3, 6-4, 3-6, 5-7, 6-3; 1925, def. Patterson, 11-9, 2-6, 6-2, 6-3. Also won doubles, 1924, with 46-year-old Norman Brookes (AUS), def. Pat O'Hara Wood-Patterson, 6-2, 6-4, 6-3. Won Wimbledon doubles, 1922, with Randolph Lycett (GBR). Davis Cup, 1919-25, 20-7 singles, 8-1 doubles. Led Aussies to F, 1922-23 (lost to U.S.), gave Bill Johnston, U.S., first Cup defeat, 1923, 4-6, 6-2, 2-6, 7-5, 6-2.

ASBOTH, Joszef—Probably Hungary's finest player, Joszef Asboth was clever performer on clay, won French, 1947, def. Eric Sturgess (RSA), 8-6, 7-5, 6-4. Made Wimbledon SF, 1948. Won 10 post-World War II singles titles. b. Sept. 18, 1917, Szombathely. Davis Cup: 1938-39, 1947-1957; 18-12 singles, 6-5 doubles. World Top 10: No. 8, 1947-48. Turned teaching pro, 1958.

ATKINSON, Kathleen—Kathleen Gill Atkinson, American RH b. Nov. 5, 1875, d. April 30, 1957, Maplewood, N.J. Won 2 U.S. doubles, 1897-98, with Hall of Fame sister, Juliette. In first instance of sisters clashing in U.S. Championships, Juliette beat Kathleen in 1895 SF, 6-1, 6-4, again in 1897 SF, 6-1, 6-3. More than a century later, Manuela beat Maggie in Bulgarian Maleeva sisters meeting, U.S. QF, 1992. Williams sisters (Venus, Serena) were adversaries in 2001-02 U.S. F.

AUSSEM, Cilly—Until Steffi Graf, Cilly Aussem was Germany's most successful woman. Tiny 5-foot RH baseliner. Won 2 major singles, 1931—French, def. Betty Nuthall (GBR), 8-6, 6-1; Wimbledon, def. Hilde Krawinkel, 6-2, 7-5, only all-German female F. Made SF Wimbledon, 1930; French, 1929-30, 34. Won French mixed, 1930, with Bill Tilden (USA), def. Eileen Bennett Whittingstall (GBR)-Henri Cochet (FRA), 6-4, 6-4. World Top 10: No. 7, 1928, No. 2, 1930-31. b. Jan. 4, 1909, Cologne; d., as Countess F. M. della Corte Brae, March 22, 1963, Portofino, Italy.

AUSTIN, Joan—Joan Winifred Austin., b. Jan. 23, 1903, London; d. Apr. 2, 1998, Horley, England. Lost Wimbledon doubles F, 1923, with Evelyn Colyer (GBR). Younger brother, Hall of Famer Henry Wilfred "Bunny" Austin (1906-2000), introduced shorts internationally, 1932, liberating male legs, made singles F Wimbledon, 1932, 38; French, 1937. Joan, a liberator herself, first to play on Centre Court without stockings, 1931. One of her four marriages was to Randolph Lycett, winner Wimbledon doubles, 1921-22-23.

AUSTIN, Tracy, Pam, John & Jeff—Extraordinary California siblings, all played professionally.

Tracy Austin—An all-timer, inducted International Tennis Hall of Fame, 1992. She and John first sister-brother team to win major mixed, Wimbledon, 1980, def. Dianne Fromholtz-Mark Edmondson (both AUS), 4-6, 7-6 (8-6), 6-3. Later Helena Sukova-Cyril Suk (CZE) won French, 1991, Wimbledon, 1996. Cara Black-Wayne Black (ZIM) won French, 2002. See also Hall of Fame section for full bio.

Pamela Jeanne Austin—b. March 12, 1950, Waltham, Mass., RH, 6 ft 1. Played 5 years. Won Ecuador Open, 1972. With brother Jeff, member Denver Racquets, World Team Tennis champs, 1974. Won Pac-8 Doubles for UCLA, 1968; U.S. Amateur doubles with Margie Cooper (USA), 1969; U.S. Amateur Hard Court doubles with Tam O'Shaughnessy (USA), 1969. Highest ranking, U.S. No. 25, 1970.

William Jeffrey Austin—b. July 5, 1951, Waltham, Mass., RH, 5 ft 11, 160. All-American 1972-73, UCLA. Best world ranking: No. 52, 1973.

John Reed Austin—b. July 31, 1957, Torrance, Calif, RH. 6 ft 3, 180. All-American 1977-78, UCLA, helped win NCAA team title, 1976. Won NCAA doubles, 1978, with Bruce Nichols. Best world ranking: No. 97, 1978. Lost F, Columbus, to Brian Teacher, 1983.

A fifth sibling, Douglas Edward Austin, b. Feb. 16, 1954, varsity regular at California State—Long Beach.

AYALA, Luis—Chile's most successful male prior to Marcelo Rios in 1990s. Stocky RH, best on clay, b. Sept. 18, 1932, Santiago. Won Italian, 1959, def. Neale Fraser (AUS), 6-3, 3-6, 6-3, 6-3; lost F, 1960, to Barry MacKay (USA), 7-5, 7-5, 0-6, 0-6, 6-1. Lost 2 French F, 1958, to Merv Rose (AUS), 6-3, 6-4, 6-4; 1960, to Nicola Pietrangeli (ITA), 3-6, 6-3, 6-4, 3-6, 6-3; made SF, 1959. Won French mixed, 1956, with Thelma Coyne Long (AUS). Made QF Wimbledon, 1959, 61; U.S.. 1957, 1959. Davis Cup: 1952-57; 27-6 singles, 10-8 doubles. Captained Chile to F, 1976, lost to Italy. Turned pro, 1961. World Top 10: No. 5, 1958; No. 6, 1959; No. 7, 1960-61. Won 42 amateur singles titles.

BADDELEY, Herbert & Wilfred—English identical twins, Herbert and Wilfred Baddeley, RH, b. Jan. 11, 1872, Bromley. Made names at Wimbledon. In 1891, Wilfred, the better player, 19 years, 5 months, def. Joshua Pim (IRL), 6-4, 1-6, 7-5, 6-0, youngest singles champ for almost a century, until Boris Becker, 17, 1985. Wilfred

made F 6 straight years, winning also 1892, def. Pim, 4-6, 6-3, 6-3, 6-2; 1895, d. Wilberforce Eaves, 4-6, 2-6, 8-6, 6-2, 6-3, eluding a MP. Linked as doubles team, twins made F 6 of 7 years from 1891, winning 1891, 94-95-96. In 1897, they lost to English Dohertys, Laurie and Reggie, for the title, 6-4, 4-6, 8-6, 6-4—only sets of brothers to square off for major title. Herbert made SF, 1895, giving Wilfred a walkover. Wilfred, Irish champ in 1896, d. Jan. 24, 1929, Menton, France; Herbert d. July 20, 1931, Cannes, France.

BARKER, Sue—One of last two Brits to make a major impression (along with Virginia Wade), 5 ft 5 blonde Susan Dorothy Barker Tankard, with forceful RH forehand, won French singles, 1976, def. Renata Tomanova (CZE), 6-2, 0-6, 6-2. Had 3 key singles wins in last British Wightman Cup victories vs. U.S., 1974, 1975, 1978 (def. Jeanne Evert, 4-6, 6-4, 6-1; Janet Newberry, 6-4, 7-5; Tracy Austin, 6-3, 3-6, 6-0). Made Wimbledon SF 1977, QF, 1976; Australian SF 1977, QF 1978. Career: won 15 pro singles titles, $878,701 prize money. Career: Singles—365-208. World Top 10: No. 5, 1976-77, No. 10, 1979. Federation Cup, 1975-82, 15-8 singles, 16-6 doubles; Wightman Cup, 1974-83, 5-13 singles, 4-5 doubles. b. April 19, 1956, Paignton, England. Now a leading BBC telecaster.

BERNARD, Marcel—French LH, Marcel Bernard had no intention of winning the French, 1946. He was 32, rusty, planned to play only doubles, but said OK when they wanted to put him in the draw—startling everyone, including himself, by making F, beating favored Jaroslav Drobny (CZE), 3-6, 2-6, 6-1, 6-4, 6-3. Also won doubles with Yvon Petra (FRA), 11 years after first French titles, mixed, 1935 with Lolette Payot (FRA), 1936 with Billie York (GBR). Davis Cup: 12 years, 1935-39, 1946-56; 13-8 singles, 16-5 doubles. World Top 10: No. 5, 1946. Won 3 other post-World War II singles titles. b. May 18, 1914, La Madeleine, France, d. April 29, 1994, Paris.

BHUPATHI, Mahesh Shrinivas—An Indian All-American (1995 at U. Mississippi, winning NCAA doubles with Ali Hamadeh). Superb at doubles, won titles all 4 majors. b. Madras, India, June 7, 1974, 6 ft 1, 195 lbs, RH (2-handed backhand), turned pro 1995. Played 15 major doubles finals won 11 titles: French, 1999, with Leander Paes (IND), def. Goran Ivanisevic (CRO)-Jeff Tarango (USA), 6-2, 7-5; 2001, with Paes, def. Petr Pala-Pavel Vizner (both CZE), 7-6 (7-5), 6-3; Wimbledon, 1999, with Paes, def. Jared Palmer (USA)-Paul Haarhuis (NED), 6-7 (10-12), 6-3, 6-4, 7-6 (7-4); U.S., 2002, with Max Mirnyi (BLR), def. Jiri Novak-Radek Stepanek (both CZE), 6-3, 3-6, 6-4. Also mixed: Australian, 2006, with Martina Hingis (SUI), d. Elena Likhovtseva (RUS)-Daniel Nestor (CAN), 6-3, 6-3. French, 1997, with Rika Hiraki (JPN), def. Lisa Raymond-Pat Galbraith (both USA), 6-4, 6-1; Wimbledon, 2002, with Likhovtseva, def. Daniela Hantuchova (SVK)-Kevin Ullyett (ZIM), 6-2, 1-6, 6-1; 2005, with Mary Pierce (FRA), def. Tatiana Perebiynis (UKR)-Paul Hanley (AUS), 6-4, 6-2; U.S., 1999, with Ai Sugiyama (JPN), def. Kim Po-Don Johnson (both USA), 6-4, 6-4; 2005, with Hantuchova, def. Katarina Srebotnik (SLO)-Nenad Zimonjic (SRB), 6-4, 6-2. Also won 2009 Australian mixed with countrywoman Sania Mirza Lost 2 Masters doubles F, 2000, with Paes, to Piet Norval (RSA)-Johnson, 7-6 (10-8), 6-3, 6-4; 1999, with Paes, to Sebastien Lareau (CAN)-Alex O'Brien (USA), 6-3,

6-2, 6-2. Highest world singles rank, No. 217, 1998. Davis Cup, 13 years, 8-13 singles, 21-5 doubles. Awarded the Padma Shri, India's highest honor, 2001. As of June of 2009, he won 44 doubles titles and $4,656,405 in prize money.

BJORKMAN, Jonas Lars—Canny, enduring marvel, splendid-volleying Swede, continued dangerous, singles, doubles, touring 17 years. He was an elder among those holding major titles and/ or making SF in singles majors (SF U.S. 1997, Wimbledon 2006); made QF Australian, 1998, 2002; Wimbledon, 2003; U.S., 1994, 98. b. Vaxjo, Sweden, March 23, 1972, RH (2-handed backhand), 6 ft, 180 lbs, turned pro 1991. Highest world singles rank, No. 4, 1997. Played 15 major doubles F, won 9 titles: 3 Australian, 1998 with Jacco Eltingh (NED), def. Todd Woodbridge-Mark Woodforde (both AUS), 6-2, 5-7, 2-6, 6-4, 6-3; 1999, with Pat Rafter (AUS), def. Leander Paes-Mahesh Bhupathi (both IND), 6-3, 4-6, 6-4, 6-7 (10-12), 6-4; 2001, with Woodbridge, d. Byron Black (ZIM)-David Prinosil (GER), 6-1, 5-7, 6-4, 6-4; 2 French, 2005, with Max Mirnyi (BLR) d. Bob-Mike Bryan (USA), 2-6, 6-1, 6-4; 2006 with Mirnyi, def. Bryans, 6-7 (5-7), 6-4, 7-5; 3 Wimbledon, 2002, with Woodbridge, def. Mark Knowles (BAH)-Daniel Nestor (CAN), 6-1, 6-2, 6-7 (7-9), 7-5; 2003, with Woodbridge, def. Bhupathi-Mirnyi, 3-6, 6-3, 7-6 (7-4), 6-3; 2004, with Woodbridge, def. Julian Knowle (AUT)-Nenad Zimonjic (SRB), 6-1, 6-4, 4-6, 6-4; U.S., 2003, with Woodbridge, def. Bryans, 5-7, 6-0, 7-5. Davis Cup, 14 years (Swedish high), 18-11 singles, 21-14 doubles. Prominent in winning Cups 1994, 97-98. Career: 6 singles (414-362 matches), 54 doubles pro titles (709-306), $14,600,323 prize money. Oldies, he, 34, with John McEnroe, 47, won San Jose, 2006, def. Paul Goldstein, 29-Jim Thomas, 31 (both USA), 7-6 (7-2), 4-6, 10-7.

BLACK, Cara, Byron & Wayne—Out of Africa, exceptional siblings, unique world class trio, each representing homeland, Zimbabwe, stalwartly, Byron, Wayne in Davis Cup, Cara (wishing Zimbabwe had another female, thus a Federation Cup team). Short, quick, clever. Brothers 10-5 as partners, Cup doubles. Papa, late Don Black, fine amateur 1950s, made 3rd rd. Wimbledon, 1953, 56; won Monte Carlo, Cannes, 1954. His trio accounted for 10 major doubles titles, winning all 4 majors at least once.

Cara Cavell Black—b. Feb. 17, 1979, Harare, like brothers, grew up barefoot on grass courts in family backyard. A 5 ft 5 RH (2-handed backhand), turned pro 1998. World No. 1 junior 1997, winning Wimbledon, U.S. Open juniors. Doubles maven. Little sister the big winner. Won 8 major doubles titles: 4 Wimbledon titles - 2004, with Rennae Stubbs (AUS), d. Liezel Huber (RSA)-Ai Sugiyama (JPN), 6-3, 7-6 (7-5); 2005, with Huber, def. Svetlana Kuznetsova (RUS)-Amelie Mauresmo (FRA), 6-2, 6-1; 2007, with Huber, def. Katarina Srebotnik (SLO)-Sugiyama, 3-6, 6-3, 6-2; mixed, 2004, with brother, Wayne, def. Alicia Molik-Todd Woodbridge (both AUS), 3-6, 7-6 (10-8), 6-4, saved 6 MP. Also won Australian, 2007, with Huber, def. Chan Yung-Jan-Chia-Jung (both TPE), 6-4, 6-7 (4-7), 6-1 and French mixed, 2002, with brother, Wayne, def. Elena Bovina (RUS)-Mark Knowles (BAH), 6-3, 6-3. (2nd brother-sister to win, following Helena Sukova-Cyril Suk (CZE), 1991) as well as women's and mixed doubles titles at 2008 US Open; defeating Lisa Raymond (USA)-Sam Stosur (AUS) with Huber and with

Leander Paes (IND), def. Huber and Jaime Murray (GBR). Lost 2 major doubles F: French, 2005, with Huber; U.S., 2000, with Elena Likhovtseva (RUS). Lost 5 Year-End WTA F—2001-02, with Likhovtseva; 2004-05-06, with Stubbs, but won titles with Huber in 2007, 2008. Career: won 1 singles (312-239 matches), 50 doubles (586-234 matches) pro titles, $5,575,222 prize money. Made 4th rd. French 2001. Best world singles ranking: No, 43, 2000.

Byron Hamish Black—5 ft 8 RH (2-handed forehand, backhand), b. Oct. 6, 1969, Harare. Splendid college career U. Southern California. All-American 4-times doubles, 3-times singles, a factor in USC winning NCAA team title 1991. Turned pro 1991, retired 2002. Won 2 singles, 22 doubles pro career titles, $5,159,775 prize money. Career: Singles—257-246, Doubles—328-201. Made 4 major doubles F, won 1—French, 1994, with Jonathan Stark (USA), def. Jan Apell-Jonas Bjorkman (both SWE), 6-4, 7-6 (7-5). Lost 3—Australian, 1994, with Stark; 2001, with David Prinosil (GER); Wimbledon, 1996, with Grant Connell (CAN). Made QF U.S., 1995. Best world singles ranking: No. 28, 1998. Davis Cup: 1987-2002, 39-20 singles, 17-8 doubles. Huge Cup upset: Brothers beat home team Australia, 3-2, 1st rd., grass, Mildura, 1998—Byron def. U.S. champ Pat Rafter, 3-6, 6-3, 6-2, 7-6 (7-0), Jason Stoltenberg, 6-3, 6-3, 6-3, 6-4; Wayne def. Mark Woodforde, 6-3, 7-5, 6-7 (6-8), 6-2.

Wayne Hamilton Black—5 ft 7 RH (2-handed backhand), b. Nov. 14, 1973, Harare. Excellent college career Univ. Southern California. All-American 2 times singles, doubles, lost NCAA F 1994 to Mark Merklein, U. Florida. Turned pro 1994, having most success in doubles. Career: won 13 pro doubles titles, (206-137 matches), $3,300,258 prize money. Best world singles ranking, No. 69, 1998. Won 3 major doubles titles: U.S., 2001, with Kevin Ullyett (ZIM), def. Don Johnson-Jared Palmer (both USA). 7-6, 2-6, 6-3; French mixed, 2002, Wimbledon mixed, 2004, mixed with Cara (see above). Lost Australian doubles F, 2000, with Andrew Kratzmann (AUS). Davis Cup, since 1992, 23-18 singles, 17-6 doubles.

BLAKE, James Riley—Biggest win: rebounding from career-threatening maladies, 2004 (broken neck; hearing, sight-impairing, facial paralyzing zoster; death of father, Tom Blake). Dropped to No. 210, fought back through minors to No. 24, 2005. That year def. No. 2 Rafa Nadal (ESP), made QF U.S. 2 pts from beating No. 7 Andre Agassi (USA). Also made U.S. QF, 2006. Then to world Top 10—No. 4, 2006; No. 13 , 2007. b. Yonkers, N.Y., Dec. 28, 1979, raised Fairfield, Conn. RH, 6 ft 1, 183 lbs, turned pro 1999. Davis Cup, 7 years, 18-9 singles, 3-1 doubles; 5-2 singles as U.S. took 2007 Cup, busting 12 year drought. First Harvard man (student 2 years) on Cup winner since Dick Williams, 1926. All-American, 1998-99, lost NCAA F, 1999, to Jeff Morrison, U. Florida, 7-6(7-2), 2-6, 6-4. Wrote well-received memoir (with Andrew Friedman), Breaking Back—How I Lost Everything and Won Back My Life, 2007. Lost F 2006 Masters to Roger Federer (SUI), 6-0, 6-3, 6-4, but beat Federer 6-4, 7-6 (2) in quarterfinals of 2008 Olympic Games in Beijing; lost semifinal to Fernando Gonzalez (CHI) 4-6, 7-5, 11-9 and bronze medal match to Novak Djokovic (SRB) 6-3, 7-6 (4) Career as of June of 2009: won 10 singles pro titles (311-186 matches), $$6,562,998 prize money.

BLOOMER, Shirley—Quick, agile Shirley Juliet Bloomer Brasher, English RH won French 1957, def. Dorothy Head Knode (USA), 6-1, 6-3, lost title, F 1958, to Suzi Kormoczi (HUN), 6-4, 1-6, 6-2. Lost F Wimbledon doubles 1955 with Pat Ward to Angela Mortimer-Anne Shilcock, 7-5, 6-1. Made SF, U.S., 1956; QF, French, 1955-56; Wimbledon, 1956, 58; U.S., 1957. World Top 10: No. 7, 1956; No. 3, 1957; No. 5, 1958. Wightman Cup: 1955-60; 1-6 singles, 2-4 doubles (won 2 Cups). Married, 1959, world-class distance runner Christopher Brasher (Olympic steeplechase gold medalist, 1956). b. June 13, 1934, Grimsby, Lincolnshire, England.

BOLLETTIERI, Nick—Most renowned coach, effervescent Nicholas James Bollettieri, b. July 31, 1931, Pelham, N.Y. Runs assembly line for champs, Bollettieri Sports Academy, Bradenton, Fla. Ex-U.S. Army paratrooper, graduate of Spring Hill (Ala.) College, became teaching pro, 1958. Among pupils to make world Top 10: Andre Agassi, Jimmy Arias, Carling Bassett, Jim Courier, Aaron Krickstein, Monica Seles, Mary Pierce, Iva Majoli, Tommy Haas, Maria Sharapova.

BOOTHBY, Dora—Penelope Dora Harvey Boothby, later Mrs. A.C. Geen, a leading English player of her day. Won Wimbledon singles, 1909, def. Agnes Morton (GBR), 6-4, 4-6, 8-6, and the doubles, 1913, with Winifred McNair. But poor Dora, twice singles finalist (1910-11), to Dolly Douglass Chambers, lost title, 1910, 6-2, 6-2, presently only double-bagel victim, lost 1911 title to Chambers, 6-0, 6-0—two weeks after Chambers double-bageled her in Beckenham F. RH. b. Aug. 2, 1881, Finchley, d. Feb. 22, 1970, London.

BOUMAN, Kea—Only Netherlander to win major women's singles, RH Katerina Cornelia "Kea" Bouman won French, 1927, def. Irene Peacock (RSA), 6-2, 6-4. Also won French doubles, 1929, with Lili de Alvarez (ESP). Took Olympic bronze (mixed with Henk Timmer), 1924. Lauded by Bill Tilden as "very strong with good serve, hard forehand, excellent footwork." b. Nov. 23, 1903, Almeto. Quit to marry Swiss oarsman Alexander Tiedemann, 1931. World Top 10: No. 9, 1927; No. 8, 1928. Made SF French, 1926, 28; QF Wimbledon, 1926; U.S., 1927. d. Nov. 17, 1998.

BOWREY, Bill—Australian RH husband of Hall of Famer Lesley Turner Bowrey. They scored singularly in the year of marriage, 1968, he winning Australian singles, over Juan Gisbert (ESP), 7-5, 2-6, 9-7, 6-4, she Italian, over Margaret Smith Court (AUS), 2-6, 6-2, 6-3. Only husband-wife to hold major singles titles (she won French, 1963, 65) until Steffi Graf married Andre Agassi, 2001. William Walter "Tex" Bowrey, b. Dec. 25, 1943, Sydney. Called "Tex" because he fell off a horse.) Made QF Australian, 1965, 1967; U.S. 1966. Lost 3 major doubles F: Australian, 1967, Wimbledon, 1966, U.S., 1967, all with Owen Davidson (AUS). Davis Cup: 1968-69; 2-2 singles, lost F, 1968.

BOYD, Esna—Try, try again and again did Aussie RH Esna Flora Boyd. Does the 6th time never fail? Lost first 5 Australian singles F, 1922-26, at last won, 1927, 5-7, 6-1, 6-2, over Sylvia Lance Harper (AUS). Then lapsed to second place again, 1928, runner-up to Daphne Akhurst, setting Aussie record for most F lost, 6. Did bet-

ter in Australian doubles, won 4—1922, with Marjorie Mountain (AUS), 1923, with Harper, 1926, with Meryl O'Hara Wood (AUS), 1928, with Akhurst. Lost F 1925, with Kathrine Le Mesurier, 1927, with Harper. Even better in mixed with southpaw Jack Hawkes, winning 1922, 26-27, losing F 1928, totaling 8 Aussie crowns, involved in 17 F. Made QF, Wimbledon, 1925. Won Scottish singles, 1931. Relied on strong flat forehand. b. 21 September 1899, Port Melbourne, Victoria d. in Scotland 1966 as Mrs. Angus Robertson.

BRUGUERA, Sergi—Big, strong (6 ft 2, 167), fast, ungainly Spanish RH (2-handed backhand). Baseliner reveling in Roland Garros soil, won 2 French singles titles with heavy, murderous topspin—1993, dethroned Jim Courier (USA) from a break down in 5th, 6-4, 2-6, 6-2, 3-6, 6-3; 1994, def. countryman Alberto Berasategui, 6-3, 7-5, 2-6, 6-1. Also made F, 1997, lost to Guga Kuerten (BRA), 6-3, 6-4, 6-2, and SF 1995. World Top 10: No. 4, 1993-94; No. 8, 1997. Olympic silver medal, 1996, lost to Andre Agassi (USA), 6-2, 6-3, 6-1. Davis Cup: 1990-96; 11-9 singles, 2-1 doubles. Turned pro 1988. Career: Won 14 singles (447-271 matches), 3 doubles pro titles, $11,632,199 prize money. b. Jan. 16, 1971, Barcelona.

BUTTSWORTH, Coral—Briefly at the heights, Coral Annabel "Corrie" McInnes Buttsworth came out of the bush, Taree, New South Wales, to win 2 Australian singles titles—1931, def. Marjorie Cox Crawford (AUS), 1-6, 6-3, 6-4; 1932, def. Kathrine Le Mesurier (AUS), 9-7, 6-4, relinquishing the crown in 1933 F to Joan Hartigan (AUS), 6-4, 6-3. Coral also won doubles, 1932, with Crawford, whose husband, Jack, would come close to Grand Slamming, 1933. b. 1900, Taree. Married Cecil Buttsworth, 1920. d. December 20, 1985 at Hazelbrook, NSW.

CARILLO, Mary—Mary Jean Carillo, LH, b. March 15, 1957, New York. Played women's tour, collaborated with John McEnroe, his 1st major title, French mixed, 1977, def. Florenta Mihai (ROU)-Ivan Molina (COL), 7-6, 6-3. Best known as broadcaster with wide range; foremost tennis commentator, ESPN, CBS, NBC. Also HBO. Refreshingly informative, uninhibited style. Mother of two.

CASH, Pat—Powerful Aussie RH (6 ft, 185), career shortened by injuries. Strong serve, excellent volleyer, Patrick Hart Cash hit high points—won 1 major singles title: Wimbledon, 1987, def. Ivan Lendl (CZE), 7-6 (7-5), 6-2, 7-5; led Davis Cup victories, 1983, 86, and to F 1990. Lost 2 sensational major F: Australian, 1987, to Stefan Edberg (SWE), 6-3, 6-4, 3-6. 5-7. 6-3 (last Australian on grass); 1988, to Mats Wilander, (SWE), 6-3, 6-7 (3-7), 3-6, 6-1, 8-6 (hard court). Davis Cup, 1983–90, 23-7 singles, 8-3 doubles. Won Cup clinchers over Sweden both years: 1983, beat Joakim Nystrom, 6-4, 6-1, 6-1; 1986, beat Edberg, 13-11, 13-11, 6-4, and, stirringly from 0-2 in sets, Mikael Pernfors, 2-6, 4-6, 6-2, 6-4. 6-3 (called "best Aussie Cup performance" by Capt. Neale Fraser). World Top 10: No. 8 1984; No. 7 1987. b. May 27, 1965, Melbourne. Turned pro 1982. Career: won 7 singles (242-149), 12 doubles (174-110) pro titles, $1,950,345 prize money.

CLIJSTERS, Kim—Quick, solid baseliner. Incredibly good-natured, win or lose. Second Belgian to win U.S. singles, 2005, def. Mary

Pierce (FRA), 6-3, 6-1. Lost 4 major F—French, 2001, to Jennifer Capriati (USA), 1-6, 6-4, 12-10; 2003 to Justine Henin-Hardenne (BEL), 6-0, 6-4; Australian, 2004, to Henin-Hardenne, 6-3, 4-6, 6-3; U.S., 2003, to Henin-Hardenne, 7-5, 6-1. Won 2 major doubles titles—French, 2001, with Ai Sugiyama (JPN), def. Virginia Ruano-Pascual (ESP)-Paola Suarez (ARG), 6-7 (5-7), 6-2, 9-7; Wimbledon, 2003, with Sugiyama, def. Pascual-Suarez, 6-4, 6-4. Lost Wimbledon mixed F, 2000, with Lleyton Hewitt (AUS), to Kim Po-Don Johnson (both USA), 6-4, 7-6 (7-3). Won 2 season–ending WTA Championships—2002, def. Serena Williams (USA), 7-5, 6-3; 2003, def. Amelie Mauresmo (FRA), 6-2, 6-0. b. Bilzen, Belgium, June 8, 1983. RH (2-handed backhand), 5 ft 9, 151 lbs. Turned pro 1997, brief career but won 34 singles (427-104 matches), 11 doubles pro titles, $14,764,296 prize money. World Top 10, 5 years—No. 2, 2003, 06; No. 4, 2002; No. 5, 2001, 06 (Briefly No. 1, 2003). Made SF Australian, 2002-03, 06; French, 2006; Wimbledon, 2006; QF Wimbledon, 2001; U.S., 2001. Best season, 2003: won 9 singles titles of 21 tournaments, 90-12 singles, 47-5 doubles, most singles wins since 90-3 of Martina Navratilova (USA), 1982, first to play more than 100 singles since 107 of Chris Evert (USA), 1979. Federation Cup 7 years, 18-3 singles, 3-1 doubles. Undefeated (4-0) as Belgium (she and Henin, teen-age "Brussels Sprouts") won 2001 Cup; won decisive match, 6-0, 6-4, over Elena Dementieva, in 2-1 F victory over Russia. Sister, Elke Clijsters (b. Bilzen, Belgium, January 18, 1985), played 3 years Federation Cup, Belgium, 0-1 singles, 0-3 doubles. Father, Leo Clijsters, Belgium's pro soccer Player of Year, 1988. Kim retired May 2007, married American pro basketball player, Brian Lynch, soon after, one child.

COSTA, Albert—A happy hunting ground for Spaniards, Roland Garros came under the rule of No. 22 Albert Costa in 2002, the 5th of his country to seize the French championship, Spain's 7th, dating back to Manolo Santana, 1961, 64. It was a 3rd all-Spanish F, def. 11th seeded Juan Carlos Ferrero, 6-1, 6-0, 4-6, 6-3. b. June 25, 1975, Lerida, Spain, stocky 5 ft 11, Costa, never better previously in a major than French QF, 1995. Quick, tireless, turned pro 1993. Career: won 12 pro singles, all clay (385-273 pro record), $7,685,228 prize money. Defending title, 2003, made SF where Ferrero got even, 6-3, 7-6 (7-5), 6-4. Retired 2006. Davis Cup 4 years, 8-5 singles, 0-1 doubles, helped Spain win 2000 Cup. World Top 10: No. 8, 2002 (from No. 40, 2001).

COX, Mark—English LH, Cambridge grad, Mark Cox has niche as first amateur to beat a pro in open competition. On successive April afternoons beat great (but almost 40) Pancho Gonzalez (USA), 0-6, 6-2, 4-6, 6-3, 6-3, then rookie pro Roy Emerson (AUS), 6-0, 6-1, 7-5, gained SF, British Hard Court Championships, Bournemouth 1968, inaugural open. Added another eminent scalp at Australian, 1971, def. 1st seed Rod Laver, 6-3, 4-6, 6-3, 7-6, to make QF. b. July 5, 1943, Leicester. Won 8 singles titles (294-219). Davis Cup 1967-69, 1973, 1978-79, helped Britain reach F, 1978, 15-6 singles, 8-6 doubles.

DALTON, Judy—Judith Anne Marshall Tegart Dalton, Australian RH, b. Dec. 12, 1937, Melbourne. Tall, sturdy, jolly-natured, excellent doubles player, won all major doubles, 8 titles, 5 Australian—1964,

with Lesley Turner (AUS), 1967, with Turner; 1969, with Margaret Smith Court, def. Rosie Casals-Billie Jean King (both USA), 6-4, 6-4; 1970, with Court.; French, 1965, with Court; Wimbledon, 1969, with Court; U.S., 1970, with Court, def. Virginia Wade (GBR)-Casals, 6-3, 6-4. Australian mixed, 1966, with Tony Roche (AUS). Lost 1 major singles F—Wimbledon, 1968, to King, 9-7, 7-5. Made SF Wimbledon, U.S., 1971; QF Australian, 1962, 64-65-66, 68, 70, 74, 77; U.S., 1968. Federation Cup, 1965-67, 69-70 (won Cup 1965, 70). Singles 6-1 doubles 12-3. World Top 10: No. 10, 1967; No. 7, 1968; No. 9, 1971.

DATE, Kimiko—Most successful modern-day Japanese. Quick 5 ft 4 Kimiko "Kid Butterfly" Date with flat groundies (2-handed backhand), excellent anticipation, natural LH transformed to RH. Surprisingly retired at 26, 1996, ranked World No. 8 (also No. 9, 1994; No. 4, 1995). Best win, saved 2 MP, def. Steffi Graf (GER), 7-6 (9-7), 3-6, 12-10, Federation Cup, 1996, led Japan to SF. Made SF Australian, 1994, French, 1995, Wimbledon, 1996; QF, U.S., 1993-94. b. Sept. 28, 1970, Kyoto. Federation Cup, 1989-96, 9-5 singles, 4-3 doubles. Turned pro 1988. Announced a comeback at age 37 in 2008. Qualified for 2009 Australian Open, losing in first round to Kaia Kanepi (HUN) and was awarded a wild card into 2009 Wimbledon, her first visit in 13 years - losing to Caroline Wozniacki in first round Career: won 7 pro singles (235-97 matches) titles, $1,974,253 prize money.

DAVIDSON, Owen—Owen Keir Davidson, LH Australian ladies man: mixed doubles master. b. Oct. 4, 1943, Melbourne. Scored mixed Grand Slam, 1967—Australian, with Lesley Turner (AUS), def. Judy Tegart-Tony Roche (both AUS), 9-7, 6-4; French, with Billie Jean King (USA), def. Ann Haydon Jones (GBR)-Ion Tiriac (ROM), 6-3, 6-1; Wimbledon, with King, def. Maria Bueno (BRA)-Ken Fletcher (AUS), 7-5, 6-2; U.S., with King, def. Rosie Casals-Stan Smith (both USA), 6-3, 6-2. Won 4 other major mixed, all with King: Wimbledon, 1971, def. Margaret Smith Court (AUS)-Marty Riessen (USA) 3-6, 6-2, 15-13; 1973, def. Janet Newberry (USA)-Raul Ramirez (MEX), 6-3, 6-2; U.S., 1971, def. Betty Stove (NED)-Rob Maud (RSA), 6-3, 7-5; 1973, def. Court-Riessen, 6-3, 3-6, 7-6. Also won two major doubles, giving him 10 total: U.S., 1973, with John Newcombe (AUS), def. Rod Laver-Ken Rosewall (both AUS), 7-5, 2-6, 7-5, 7-6. Australian, 1972, with Rosewall, def. Geoff Masters-Ross Case (both AUS), 3-6, 7-6, 6-2. Made SF Wimbledon singles, 1966; QF U.S., 1967. Rookie pro, 1968, as British national coach, played, won very first "open" match, def. amateur John Clifton (GBR), 6-2, 6-3, 4-6, 8-6, inaugural open, British Hard Court, Bournemouth.

DMITRIEVA, Anna—Russian pioneer, Anna Vladimirovna Dmitrieva was first Soviet permitted to play abroad, lost F Wimbledon junior, 1958, to Sally Moore (USA), 6-2, 6-1. LH, b. Dec. 16, 1940, Moscow, 5 ft 4, 126 lbs. Won Soviet title, 1960, 64, also Algerian (over Francoise Durr), 1964; Czechoslovak, 1961; Hungarian, 1962. Now outstanding Russian broadcaster. Federation Cup, 1968, 1-1 singles.

DRYSDALE, Cliff—Eric Clifford Drysdale, best South African male, RH (2-handed backhand). b. May 26, 1941, Nelspruit, Transvaal. Slim 6 ft 2, deceptive groundstroker, good volleyer. First to

use double-handed stroke in U.S. F, 1965, lost to Manolo Santana, 6-2, 7-9, 7-5, 6-1. Second South African to make major F, following Eric Sturgess, U.S., 1948. Won 1 doubles major, U.S. 1972, with Roger Taylor (GBR), d. John Newcombe-Owen Davidson (both AUS), 6-4, 7-6 (7-3), 6-3. Career spanned amateur, open eras. Made SF French, Wimbledon, 1965-66; QF Australian, 1971; French, 1967; U.S., 1968 (beat favorite, No. 1 Rod Laver, 4-6, 6-4, 3-6, 6-1, 6-1). Became pro, 1968, with WCT "Handsome Eight" after winning 28 amateur singles titles, including South African, 1965. Davis Cup, 1962-67, 1974; 30-12 singles, 3-2 doubles, helped South Africa win Cup, 1974. Became U.S. citizen. Career: Won 5 singles (308-186), 6 doubles (189-160) pro titles. World Top 10 for 6 years: No. 4, 1965; No. 9, 1966; No. 10, 1967; No. 9, 1968-69, 71. Now noted TV tennis commentator for ESPN.

EAVES, Wilberforce—An Aussie who got around, Dr. Wilberforce Vaughan Eaves, first of his country to play for major titles abroad. Excellent volleyer. Lost Wimbledon F 1895, 4-6, 2-6, 8-6, 6-2, 6-3, despite holding 1 MP, to Brit Wilfred Baddeley (his lob fell inches long). Lost U.S. F 1897 to Bob Wrenn (USA), 4-6, 8-6, 6-3, 2-6, 6-2. (Also lost Wimbledon all-comers F to eventual champs, 1896, Harold Mahony (IRL), 6-2, 6-2, 11-9; 1897, Reggie Doherty (GBR), 6-3, 7-5, 2-0, ret.). Lost Wimbledon doubles F 1895 with Ernest Lewis. Had 13-6 Wimbledon singles record. Lived in London, won singles bronze medal for Britain, 1908 Olympics. Won Irish title 1895, Welsh 1897, Scottish 1901. Served British army as physician in Boer War. b. Dec. 10, 1867, Melbourne, d. Feb. 2, 1920, London.

EDMONDSON, Mark—Mark Ronald "Eddo" Edmondson, husky 6 ft 1, 190, Aussie RH, longest-shot winner of men's major, Australian, 1976, b. June 28, 1954, Gosford. From obscurity (supported himself as janitor), unseeded, ranked No. 212, won homeland title—beat all-timers, 2-1 seeds, Ken Rosewall, SF, 6-1, 2-6, 6-2, 6-4; John Newcombe, F, 6-7, 6-3, 7-6, 6-1. Thereafter, fine career. Made SF Australian, 1981; Wimbledon, 1982; QF Australian, 1977, 79. Serve-and-volleyer, best at doubles, won 3 majors all with Kim Warwick (AUS)—French, 1985, def. Shlomo Glickstein (ISR)-Hans Simonsson (SWE), 6-3, 6-4, 6-7, 6-3. Australian, 1980, def. Peter McNamara-Paul McNamee (both AUS), 7-5, 6-4; 1981, def. Hank Pfister-John Sadri (both USA), 6-3, 6-7, 6-3. Davis Cup: 1977-85; 11-7 singles, 8-3 doubles, helped win 1983 Cup (4-0 doubles, 2-0 singles). Career: won 6 singles (251-238 matches), 35 doubles (507-258 matches) pro titles, $1,451,680 prize money. Best world rank, No. 15, 1982.

FERNANDEZ, Gigi—Great U.S. doubles performer, acrobatic volleyer (left court), RH beauty, 5'7, 145, Beatriz Cristina "Gigi" Fernandez won 17 major doubles titles, 14 with Natalia Zvereva (BLR): 2 Australian, 1993, def. Pam Shriver (USA)-Elizabeth Sayers Smylie (AUS), 6-4, 6-3; 1994, def. Patty Fendick-Meredith McGrath (both USA), 6-3, 4-6, 6-4. 5 French, 1992, def. Conchita Martinez-Arantxa Sanchez Vicario (both ESP), 6-3, 6-2; 1993, def. Jana Novotna (CZE)-Larisa Savchenko Neiland (LAT), 6-3, 7-5; 1994, def. Lindsay Davenport-Lisa Raymond (both USA), 6-2, 6-2; 1995, def. Novotna-Sanchez Vicario, 6-7 (6-8), 6-4, 7-5; 1997, def. Mary

Joe Fernandez-Raymond (both USA), 6-2, 6-3. 4 Wimbledon, 1992, def. Novotna-Neiland, 6-4, 6-1; 1993, def. Novotna-Neiland, 6-4, 6-7 (4-7), 6-4; 1994, def. Novotna-Sanchez Vicario, 6-4, 6-1; 1997, def. Nicole Arendt (USA)-Manon Bollegraf (NED), 7-6 (7-4), 6-4. 3 U.S., 1992, def. Neiland-Novotna, 7-6 (7-4), 6-1; 1995, def. Brenda Schultz McCarthy (NED)-Rennae Stubbs (AUS), 7-5, 6-3; 1996, def. Novotna-Sanchez Vicario, 1-6, 6-1, 6-4. Gigi's other 3 majors: French, 1991, with Novotna, def. Neiland-Zvereva, 6-4, 6-0; U.S., 1988, with Robin White (USA), def. Jill Hetherington (CAN)-Fendick, 6-4, 6-1; 1990, with Martina Navratilova (USA), def. Helena Sukova (CZE)-Novotna, 6-2, 6-4. Lost 6 major finals—Australian, Wimbledon, 1991, with Novotna; 1995, with Zvereva; French, 1996; Wimbledon, 1995; U.S., 1997, with Zvereva. Also won two Olympic golds, 1992, 1996, with Mary Joe Fernandez (no relation): 1992, def. Martinez-Sanchez Vicario (ESP), 7-5, 2-6, 6-2; 1996, def. Novotna-Sukova (CZE), 7-6 (8-6), 6-4. She and Zvereva, with 14 majors together are in 3rd place behind the 20 of Louise Brough-Margaret Osborne duPont (both USA) and Pam Shriver (USA)-Navratilova. They barely missed Grand Slams, 1993, lost SF, U.S., to Sanchez Vicario-Sukova, 1-6, 6-3, 6-4, ending 40-match major streak, and 1994, lost SF, U.S., to Katerina Maleeva (BUL)-R. White, 7-6 (7-2), 1-6, 6-3. Gigi made Wimbledon singles SF, 1994. Best world singles ranking, No. 22, 1991. b. Feb. 22, 1964, San Juan, Puerto Rico. All-American, Clemson, 1983. Federation Cup, 1988, 90-91-92, 94-95-96; 3-1 singles, 20-2 doubles (won 1990, 1996 Cups). Wightman Cup, 1987-88; 2-0 doubles (won 2 Cups). Turned pro 1983. Career: won 3 singles (270-232 matches), 66 doubles (664-184 matches) pro titles, $4,681,906 prize money.

FERNANDEZ, Mary Joe—U.S. gold medal gal in 2 Olympics, 1992 and 1996, triumphed alongside unrelated Beatriz (Gigi) Fernandez. Won doubles, Barcelona, beat hometowners Arantxa Sanchez Vicario-Conchita Martinez, 7-5, 2-6, 6-2; repeated, Atlanta, def. Jana Novotna-Helena Sukova (CZE), 7-6 (8-6), 6-4. MJ one-up on other U.S. tennis medalists, copping singles bronze, 1992. b. Dominican Republic, Aug. 19, 1971, raised in Miami. RH (2-handed backhand), slim 5 ft 10, 140 lbs. Brainy, poised all-rounder, sharp volleyer. Won top junior tourney, Orange Bowl all 4 divisions: 12s, 1982; 14s, 1983; 16s, 1984; 18s, 1985. Turned pro 1986, youngest, 14 years-8 days, to win U.S. match, def. Sara Gomer (GBR), 6-1, 6-4, 1985. Federation Cup 6 years, 12-8 singles, 4-2 doubles, helped U.S. reach F 1991, 94-95, win 1996 Cup. Lost 3 major F—2 Australian, 1990, to Steffi Graf (GER), 6-3, 6-4; 1992, to Monica Seles (USA), 6-2, 6-3; French, 1993, to Graf, 4-6, 6-2, 6-4, led 3rd set, 4-3, 30-15 with serve. But in QF one of great comebacks, def. Gabriela Sabatini (ARG), 1-6, 7-6 (7-4), 10-8. Trailed 5-1 in 2nd, saved five MP to win, in 3:34. Won 2 major doubles—Australian, 1991, with Patty Fendick (USA), def. G. Fernandez-Novotna, 7-6 (7-4), 6-1; French, 1996 with Lindsay Davenport (USA) def. Natasha Zvereva (BLR)-G. Fernandez, 6-2, 6-1. Also won 1996 WTA Tour Championship doubles, with Davenport, def. Novotna-Arantxa Sanchez Vicario (ESP), 6-3, 6-2. Lost 3 major doubles F—Australian, 1992, with Zina Garrison (USA), 1996, with Davenport; U.S., 1989, with Pam Shriver (USA) World Top 10, 6 years—1990, No. 4; 1991, 95, No. 8; 1992, No. 6; 1993, No. 7; 1997, No. 10. U.S. Top 10, 11 years—1987, No. 6; 1988, No. 5;

1989, 96, No. 4; 1990, No. 2; 1991-92-93, 97, No. 3; 1995, No. 1; 1999, No. 10. Made SF Australian, 1991, 97; French, 1989; Wimbledon, 1991; U.S., 1990, 92; QF Australian, 1993; French, 1986, 90, 97; Wimbledon, 1995-96; U.S., 1995. Career: won 7 singles, (437-203 matches), 19 doubles (485-344 matches) pro titles, $5,258,471 prize money. Husband, tennis agent Tony Godsick, 2 children, Isabella and Nicholas. Now respected TV tennis commentator.

FERRERO, Juan Carlos—Sixth in Spanish line of French champs, 2003 champion def. Martin Verkerk (NED) F, 6-1, 6-3, 6-2; briefly No. 1 that year. Lost F U.S., 2003, to Andy Roddick (USA), 6-3, 7-6 (7-2), 6-3. Lost F, French, 2002 to Albert Costa (ESP), 6-1, 6-0, 4-6, 6-3. Won 2 singles in F as Spain won first Davis Cup, 3-1 over Australia, 2000; def. Lleyton Hewitt, 6-2, 7-6 (7-5), 4-6, 6-4, decisive match. Lost decisive match to Mark Philippoussis, 7-5, 6-3, 1-6, 2-6, 6-0, as Spain lost 2003 F to Australia, 3-1. Davis Cup, 2000–05; 15-7 singles, 0-1 doubles. b. Onteniente, Spain Feb. 12, 1980, RH (2-handed backhand), 6 ft 160 lbs. Turned pro 1998. Won 12 pro singles titles (403-212 matches), $$12,164,134 prize money. World Top 10 for 3 years—No. 3, 2003; No. 1, Sept. 2003; No. 4, 2002; No. 5, 2001. Made QF Australian, 2003; Wimbledon, 2007, SF French, 2000-01.

FIBAK, Wojtek—Best Polish man, Wojtek Fibak, RH, b. Aug. 30, 1952, Poznan. Trained as lawyer. Late starter, first Polish pro, 22, despite opposition of Polish Federation, solid 13-year career. Davis Cup: 1972-92; 19-5 singles, 9-7 doubles. Agile 6 ft, superb volleyer, best at doubles. Career: won 15 singles, 48 doubles pro titles, $2,725,133 prize money. Was in 34 other doubles F. Lost Masters F, 1976, to Manolo Orantes (ESP), 5-7, 6-2, 0-6, 7-6 (7-1), 6-1. Made QF French, 1977, 80; Wimbledon, U.S., 1980. Best world rank, No. 13, 1977. Only Polish male to win a major—Australian doubles, 1978, with Kim Warwick (AUS) d. Paul Kronk-Cliff Letcher (both AUS), 7-6, 7-5. Now proprietor of Warsaw art gallery.

FLEITZ, Beverly—Unique among female major finalists: no backhand. Ambidextrous. (A male ambi, Giorgio de Stefani of Italy, lost French F to Henri Cochet, 1932.) American RH Beverly Joyce Baker Beckett Fleitz hit forehands both sides. No. 1 American, 1959. Lost Wimbledon F, 1955. to Louise Brough (USA), 7-5, 8-6. Lost 1959 Wimbledon doubles F with Christine Truman (GBR) to Jeane Arth-Darlene Hard (both USA), 2-6, 6-2, 6-3. Made SF French, 1955; Wimbledon, 1951; U.S., 1950, 58; QF French, 1951; Wimbledon, 1956; U.S. 1948-49, 54-55. World Top 10: No. 7, 1950, No. 8, 1951; No. 3, 1954-55, 58; No. 4, 1959. U.S. Top 10 7 years: No. 5, 1948, 55; No. 8, 1949; No. 4, 1950; No. 6, 1951; No. 3, 1954; No. 2, 1958. Won 18 singles titles, U.S. Hard Court, 1954, def. Barbara Green (USA) 6-1, 6-3; 1957, def. Mimi Arnold (USA). 6-1, 6-1; 1958, def. Karen Hantze (USA), 6-1, 8-6. Wightman Cup: 1949, 56, 59; 3-0 singles, 1-0 doubles (won 3 Cups). b. March 13, 1930, Providence, R.I.

FLETCHER, Ken—A tremendous bodyguard for Margaret Smith Court was fellow Aussie Ken Fletcher. He chaperoned the all-time champ to 10 major mixed doubles titles—all 4 in 1963 giving themselves grandly a Grand Slam. (Aussie Owen Davidson also had one in 1967, but with 2 partners, Billie Jean King and Lesley Turner). Margaret and Fletch's other mixed titles: Austra-

lian, 1964; French, 1964-65; Wimbledon, 1965-66, 68. "Fletch had a wonderful forehand and imagination for doubles," says Aussie Hall of Famer Ashley Cooper. He won 2 men's doubles majors, French 1964 with Roy Emerson (AUS), Wimbledon 1966 with John Newcombe (AUS), for a majors total of 12. "A very good doubles player—better than anything you'd see today," says Court. At singles, he lost the 1963 Australian F to Emerson, 6-3, 6-3, 6-1. Kenneth Norman Fletcher, b. June 14, 1940, Brisbane, was a rollicking free spirit, a kind man behind the scenes for numerous charities. Their Grand Slam windups: Australian, def. Turner-Fred Stolle (AUS), 7-5, 5-7, 6-4; French, def. Turner-Stolle, 6-1, 6-2; Wimbledon, def. Darlene Hard (USA)-Bob Hewitt (AUS), 11-9, 6-4; U.S., def. Judy Tegart (AUS)-Ed Rubinoff (USA), 3-6, 8-6, 6-2. d. Feb. 11, 2006, Brisbane.

GARRISON, Zina—Zina Lynna Garrison, American RH from Houston public parks, won 1988 Olympic gold (doubles with Pam Shriver, def. Czechs Jana Novotna-Helena Sukova, 4-6, 6-2, 10-8), bronze (singles). Gave Chris Evert her last defeat, QF U.S., 1989, 7-6 (7-1), 6-2. First black woman in major F, Wimbledon, 1990 (as Mrs. Willard Jackson), since Althea Gibson won there, 1958. After tight wins over Monica Seles (USA), 3-6, 6-3, 9-7, saving 1 MP, and Steffi Graf (GER), 6-3, 3-6, 6-4, lost F to Martina Navratilova (USA), 6-4, 6-1. Lost first pro F between two blacks, Largo, Fla., 1986, to childhood pal, Lori McNeil, 2-6, 7-5, 6-2. Aggressive, quick, fine volleyer. b. Nov. 16, 1963, Houston, 5'4, 135 lbs. Made SF U.S., 1988-89; Wimbledon, 1985; QF Wimbledon, 1985, 91; U.S., 1988, 90; World Top 10 for 7 years: No. 10, 1983, 90; No. 9, 1984, 87-88; No. 8, 1985; No. 4, 1989. Turned pro 1982, retired 1997. Federation Cup: 1984-94; 7-4 singles, 15-1 doubles (2 Cups, 1989-90). Wightman Cup: 1987-88; 3-1 singles, 1-1 doubles (2 Cups, captain, 1988). Career: won 14 singles (587-270 matches), 20 doubles (436-231 matches) pro titles, $4,590,816 prize money. Operates youth tennis program, Houston. Coach U.S. Olympic Team, 2004, 2008, Federation Cup, captain, 2004–08.

GARROS, Roland—Big name in the game, but hardly known. In dedicating the new Parisian home of the French Championships in 1928, the sentiment was to honor a fallen hero of World War I. That was Roland Garros, b. 1882, a noted aviator prior to the war—the first to fly across the Mediterranean, from France to Tunisia, 1913 (453 miles, took 8 hours). Became first ace of the French air force. First to mount a machine gun on a plane, downing 5 German planes. Shot down and imprisoned by Germans, 1915. Escaped, 1918, returned to duty against wishes of superiors who felt he'd had enough. Shot down again, fatally, at Vouziers, France, Oct. 5, 1918, 37 days before the war-ending armistice. He had no connection with tennis, but did play some rugby and piano. A dark chapter in a place normally devoted to enjoyment was the transformation of Roland Garros to a prison camp in the early days of World War II. First the French government interned so-called dissidents and undesirables. Among them, prominent author Arthur Koestler, later wrote: "We called ourselves cave dwellers, 600 of us sleeping on wet straw under the stadium, that leaked." Then, when the Nazis occupied Paris, they used RG as a holding pen for Jews and other unfortunates to be sent east to

death camps. But, not up to the invaders' prison standards, it was returned to the French Federation, where the national championships (limited to French, of course) was resumed.

GAUDIO, Gaston—Second Argentine to win French, 2004, unseeded long-shot, No. 44, def. Guillermo Coria (ARG), 0-6, 3-6, 6-4, 6-1, 8-6, saving 2 MP. b. Buenos Aires, Dec. 9, 1978. RH, admirable backhand, 5 ft 9, 155 lbs. Turned pro 1996. World Top 10 for 2 years—No. 10, 2004-05—climbed as high as No. 5 in 2005. Davis Cup, 3 years, 2001–03, 13-3 singles. Won 8 singles (269-190 matches), 3 doubles pro titles, $5,940,239 prize money.

GEMMELL, Rice—Aussie Rice Thomas Hopkins Gemmel, b. 1896, Caulfield, Victoria, was man of the year, 1921, at Australian. A fleeting presence he beat Alf Hedemann for the singles title, 7-5, 6-1, 6-4, collaborated with Sidney H. Eaton for the doubles prize, 7-5, 6-3, 6-3, over N. Brearley-Edward Stokes. None heard from again, and the champ so uncelebrated that he's incorrectly listed as Rhys, not Rice, in some records.

GERULAITIS, Vitas—High-spirited Vitas Kevin Gerulaitis, the "Lithuanian Lion," with flowing golden mane, was a lean, exciting, speedy 6 ft, 155 lbs., RH. A devil-may-care determined attacker, first of 2 American males to win Italian twice—1977, def. Tonino Zugarelli (ITA), 6-2, 7-6 (7-2) 3-6, 7-6 (7-5); 1979, def. Guillermo Vilas (ARG), 6-7 (4-7), 7-6 (7-0), 6-7 (5-7), 6-4, 6-2, in 5:08. (Jim Courier was the other, 1992-93). Won 2 major titles—Australian singles, 1977, def. John Lloyd (GBR), 6-3, 7-6 (7-1), 5-7, 3-6, 6-2; Wimbledon doubles, 1975, with Alex Mayer (USA), def. Colin Dowdeswell (GBR)-Allan Stone (AUS), 7-5, 8-6, 6-4. Lost French F, 1980, to Bjorn Borg (SWE), 6-4, 6-1, 6-2. Made SF or better all majors. Stunning comeback U.S. SF, 1979, def. Roscoe Tanner, 3-6, 2-6, 7-6 (7-5), 6-3, 6-3, service break down, 3rd set. Lost F to John McEnroe, 7-5, 6-3, 6-3, first all-American U.S. male F since Tony Trabert def. Vic Seixas, 1953. Won four of 22 tournaments on 75-21 match record, 1979. Davis Cup: 1977-80, 11-3 singles, 5-1 for Cup winner, 1979, including incredible SF escape from Mark Edmondson at Australia. Down triple MP, 7-8, 0-40 in 3rd, won, 6-8, 14-16, 10-8, 6-3, 6-3. Lost sensational 1977 5-set Wimbledon SF to Borg, 6-4, 3-6, 6-3, 3-6, 8-6. Made SF French, 1979; Wimbledon, 1977, 78; U.S., 1978, 81; QF French, 1982; Wimbledon, 1976, 82. Lost Masters F, 1979, to Borg, 6-2, 6-2; 1981, to Ivan Lendl (CZE), 6-7, 2-6, 7-6, 6-2, 6-4. Career: Won 27 singles (503-216 matches), 9 doubles pro titles, $2,778,748 prize money. World Top 10 for 6 years: No. 4, 1977, 79; No. 5, 1978, 82; No. 9, 1980-81. b. July 26, 1954, Brooklyn, N.Y., d. Sept. 17, 1994, Long Island, NY. Father, Vitas, champion of native Lithuania. Sister, Ruta, was on women's pro tour, No. 31, 1980; French QF, 1979.

GILBERT, Brad—One of most successful coaches of current era, Californian Bradley Nathaniel Joseph Gilbert had fine playing career, highly competitive, shrewd. World Top 10, 1986-87, 89-90, high No. 6 ('89). U.S. Top 10, 1984–93, high No. 2 ('89). U.S. Davis Cup, 5 years, 10-5 singles, helped win 1990 Cup. Won 20 singles titles (519-288 matches), 3 doubles titles, $5,509,260 prize money. Bronze medalist in men's singles, 1988 Olympics, called

medal "the big penny." Had wins over John McEnroe, Jimmy Connors, Boris Becker, Andre Agassi, Pete Sampras during his career. Coached Agassi to 6 major titles 1995-99 (3 Aussie, 2 U.S., 1 French), Olympic gold (1996), No. 1 ranking. Also coached Andy Roddick to U.S. title, No. 1 world ranking in 2003. Wrote books on the game, *Winning Ugly* and *I've Got Your Back*. b. Aug. 9, 1961, Oakland, Calif., lives there, 6-1, 180 lbs. Played for Foothill Junior College, 1980-81; All-American, Pepperdine, 1982, lost NCAA F to Mike Leach, U. Michigan, 7-5, 6-3.

GOMEZ, Andres—"GoGo" was the lone Ecuadoran to win a major, French 1990, beat favored Andre Agassi, 6-3, 2-6, 6-4, 6-4. Won French doubles, 1988, with Emilio Sanchez (ESP), def. John Fitzgerald (AUS)-Anders Jarryd (SWE), 6-3, 6-7 (8-10), 6-4, 6-3. Made QF French, 1984, 86-87; Wimbledon, U.S. 1984. LH, 6 ft 4, 186 lbs. Heavy server, sharp volleyer, smart user of spin, all-rounder. Career: won 21 singles (523-267 matches), 34 doubles (369-194) pro career titles, $4,385,130 prize money. Retired 1993. b. Feb. 27, 1960, Guayaquil. Davis Cup: 1979-93; 31-12 singles, 20-15 doubles. World Top 10: No. 5, 1984; No. 10, 1986; No. 4 then 6, 1990.

GONZALEZ, Fernando—An explosive forehand and one-handed backhand support RH Fernando Francisco Gonzalez, 6 ft, 180 lbs., Chilean b. Santiago July 29, 1980. Yoked to country-man Nico Massu, won gold in doubles at 2004 Olympics, def. Nic Kiefer-Rainer Schuettler, (both GER), 6-2, 4-6, 3-6, 7-6 (9-7), 6-4. Added a bronze in singles, def. Taylor Dent, 6-4, 2-6, 16-14. Added a silver medal to his Olympic resume in 2008, losing singles final to Rafael Nadal (ESP) 6-3, 7-6 (2), 6-3. Turned pro 1999, ranked as high as No. 5, 2007. Career as of June of 2008, won 11 pro singles, 3 in doubles, $$7,799,075. Lost F 2007 Australian to No. 1 Roger Federer (SUI), 7-6(7-2), 6-4, 6-4 after def. No. 2 Rafa Nadal (ESP), 6-2, 6-4, 6-3. Made French SF in 2009, losing to Robin Soderling (SWE) 6-3, 7-5, 5-7, 4-6, 6-4, losing last five games of the match. Made QF Wimbledon 2005. Davis Cup: 11 years, 18-6 singles, 11-6 doubles.

GORE, Spencer—Spencer William Gore, English RH, b. March 10, 1850, Wimbledon; d. April 19, 1906, Ramsgate, England. Game's original champ, Wimbledon, 1877, def. William Marshall, 6-1, 6-2, 6-4, as opportunistic volleyer. Lost F, 1878, to lobbing P. Frank Hadow, 7-5, 6-1, 9-7, walked away forever. Ex-rackets champ, not overly taken by tennis, thought the game tedious.

GOTTFRIED, Brian—Brian Edward Gottfried, hardworking, energetic 6 ft RH. Sound groundstrokes, preferred serve-and-volley. b. Jan. 27, 1952, Baltimore, raised in Florida. All-American, Trinity (Tex.) U., 1971-72, lost NCAA singles, doubles F, 1972. Lost one major F, French, 1977, to Guillermo Vilas (ARG), 6-0, 6-3, 6-0 (fewest games in a F). Won 3 major doubles, with Raul Ramirez (MEX)—French, 1975, def. John Alexander-Phil Dent (both AUS), 6-2, 2-6, 6-2, 6-4; 1977, def. Wojtek Fibak (POL)-Jan Kodes (CZE), 7-6, 4-6, 6-3, 6-4. Wimbledon, 1976, def. Ross Case-Geoff Masters (both AUS), 3-6, 6-3, 8-6, 2-6, 7-5. Lost 4 major doubles F, French, 1976, 80; Wimbledon, 1979; U.S., 1977, all with Ramirez. Davis Cup: 1976-82 (with 1978 winner); 6-7 singles, 1-0 doubles. Made

SF, Wimbledon, 1980; QF, U.S., 1977-78. Heavy-duty 1977, won 5 of 27 tournaments, 108-23 matches. U.S. Top 10, 10 times: No. 2, 1977; No. 3, 1978; No. 5, 1976; No. 6, 1975, 80; No, 8, 1981; No. 9, 1973; No. 10, 1972, 82-83. World Top 10: No. 10, 1976; No. 5, 1977; No. 7, 1978. With Ramirez won 39 doubles, including record 4 straight Italian, 1974-77. Career: Won 25 singles (677-321 matches) 54 doubles (602-245 matches) pro titles, $2,782,514 prize money.

GOOLD, Vere Thomas "St. Leger"—Irish RH, b. Oct. 2, 1853, Waterford. Wimbledon finalist, 1879, lost to John Hartley (GBR), 6-2, 6-4, 6-2, before crowd of 1,100. Personal finale: death in prison, most ignominious for a champ. Won native (Irish) championship, 1879, skilled volleyer. Played as "St. Leger" (pseudonyms not uncommon that time). In 1907, with French wife, Violet Girodin, convicted in French court of murdering Emma Levin, she executed, he given life sentence. d. Sept. 8, 1909, Devil's Island, French Guiana.

GRAEBNER, Carole & Clark—American couple, RH's Carole and Clark Graebner, only husband-wife to rank World Top 10, play major F while married. Fourth couple ranked U.S. Top 10 same years, following Sarah Palfrey and Elwood Cooke (1940, 45), Marjorie "Midge" Gladman and John Van Ryn (1930-31), Virginia Wolfenden and Frank Kovacs (1941). Teammates, Cleveland, World Team Tennis, 1974. However, during divorce proceedings Clark, player-coach, traded her to Pittsburgh for Laura DuPont, a unique divestiture.

Carole Caldwell Graebner—b. June 24, 1943, Pittsburgh, raised in Southern California, d. 19 Nov. 2008 in New York. Baseliner, good volleyer. Lost U.S. F, 1964, to Maria Bueno, 6-1, 6-0 (equaling worst such beating, original F, 1884, Ellen Hansel over Laura Knight). Won 7 amateur singles titles. Won 2 major doubles, with Nancy Richey (USA)—U.S., 1965, def. Billie Jean Moffitt-Karen Hantze Susman (both USA), 6-4, 6-4. Australian, 1966, def. Margaret Smith-Lesley Turner (both AUS), 6-4, 7-5. Also won U.S. Clay doubles, with Richey, 1964-65; U.S. Hard, 1960, with Kathy Chabot; U.S. Hard mixed, with Chris Crawford (USA), 1960. World Top 10: No. 4, 1964; No. 9, 1965. U.S. Top 10 6 years: No. 9, 1961; No. 4, 1962-63; No. 3, 1964-65; No. 6, 1967. Federation Cup: 1963, 66, 2-1 singles, 9-1 doubles (with winner, 1963, 66). Wightman Cup: 1963-64-65, 67, 71, 2-0 singles, 2-2 doubles (won all 5 Cups). d. Nov. 19, 2008.

Clark Edward Graebner—b. Nov. 4, 1943, Cleveland, grew up there, graduate Northwestern U. Strong, 6 ft 2, serve-and-volleyer. Lost U.S. F, 1967, to John Newcombe (AUS), 6-4, 6-4, 8-6. Made SF Wimbledon, U.S., 1968; QF Wimbledon, 1969-70; U.S., 1966. Won 25 amateur singles titles. Won one major doubles, French, 1966, with Dennis Ralston (USA), d. Ilie Nastase-Ion Tiriac (both ROU), 6-3, 6-3, 6-0. Lost F, U.S., 1966, with Ralston. World Top 10: No. 8, 1967; No. 7, 1968. U.S. Top 10 for 8 years: No. 9, 1964; No. 3 1966, 71; No. 4, 1967, 69-70; No. 2, 1968; No. 8, 1972. Davis Cup: 1965-68; 9-2 singles; 5-2 doubles (with 1968 Cup winner). Also won U.S. Indoor, 1971, def. Cliff Richey (USA), 2-6, 7-6, 1-6, 7-6, 6-0; U.S. Clay, 1968, def. Stan Smith (USA), 6-3, 7-5, 6-0; U.S. Hard, 1969, def. Erik Van Dillen (USA), 6-4, 3-6, 4-6, 6-0, 7-5. Won 6 U.S. Clay doubles—3 with Marty

Riessen (USA), 1963, 65, 67; with Ralston, 1966; with Bill Bowrey (AUS), 1969; with Arthur Ashe (USA), 1970.

GREGORY, Colin—Covering remarkable spread of almost 3 decades, Davis Cup career of Dr. John Colin Gregory, English physician, concluded in triumph. He, playing captain, one of oldest to win Cup match: 48 years, 295 days for Britain, with Tony Mottram, def. Josip Pallada-Stevan Laszlo (YUG), 6-4, 1-6, 9-11, 6-2, 6-2, 1952, Belgrade, making the difference in Brits' 3-2 win. Good-humored Yorkshire RH, b. July 28, 1903, Gregory, won a major 23 years before, Australian singles, 1929, def. Bob Schlesinger (AUS), 6-2, 6-2, 5-7, 7-5. Same year lost Wimbledon doubles F with Ian Collins. Davis Cup: 1926–30, 52; 13-9 singles, 8-1 doubles. d. Sept. 10, 1959, Wimbledon.

GULLIKSON, Tim & Tom—Identical twins, RH, 5'11, 175 lbs., Timothy Ernest, LH, 5'11, 170 lbs. Thomas Robert Gullikson, b. Sept. 8, 1951, LaCrosse, Wis., Tom elder by minutes. Graduates, Northern Illinois U. Lost Wimbledon F, 1983, third twins in major F, following English Wimbledonians Renshaws (1884-85-86, 88-89) and Baddeleys (1891, 94-95-96). Sturdy, 5-11, 185, attackers, won 10 pro doubles titles together. Each won singles title at U.S. original site, Newport: Tim, 1977, Tom, 1985.

Tim Gullikson—Best world rank No. 15 Oct, 1979 Career: won 4 singles (269-220 matches) 16 doubles (302-244) pro titles, $1,121,880 prize money. Upset 2nd seed John McEnroe, Wimbledon 4th rd., 1979, 6-4, 6-2, 6-4. Coached Pete Sampras to 6 major singles titles. d. May 3, 1996, Wheaton, Ill.

Tom Gullikson—Best world rank, No. 34, 1984. Career: won 1 singles (218-225 matches), 12 doubles (293-224) pro titles, $889,492 prize money. U.S. Davis Cup captain, 1994—99, (won Cup, 1995).

HADOW, Frank—Patrick Francis Hadow, English RH, b. Jan. 24, 1855, Regents Park; d. June 29, 1946, Bridgewater. Loftiest Wimbledon champ: introduced the lob to thwart, bring down volleyer Spencer Gore, defender, second Wimbledon F, 1878, 7-5, 6-1, 9-7. Lost no sets in tourney, played on holiday from his coffee plantation in Ceylon. Didn't return to defend, may never have played again.

HALL, James Gilbert—After 3 years World War II service, Sgt. U.S. Army, New Yorker Gil, discharged, arrived home for U.S. season, 1944, earning unique eminence: dual U.S. Top 10 rankings—No. 1 seniors (45s), No. 10 men (also No. 8, 1935, made QF U.S.). Won senior title at Longwood, Boston, def. William L. Nassau, Jr. (USA), 6-3, 6-2. Won 4 U.S. Doubles titles: Clay Court, 1929, with Frederic Mercur (USA), def. Ben Gorchakoff-Art Kussman (both USA), 10-12, 3-6, 6-2, 9-7, 6-4; 1930, with Mercur, def. Harris Coggeshall-Wray Brown (both USA), 3-6, 6-3, 7-5, 6-2; 1935, with Berkeley Bell (USA), d. Robert Bryan-John McDiarmid (both USA), 6-4, 6-3, 5-7, 9-11, 6-2 Indoor, 1936, with Kalle Schroder (NOR), def. Greg Mangin-Hall of Famer John Van Ryn (both USA), 6-3, 8-6, 6-2. Lost U.S. Clay Court F, 1929, to Emmett Pare (USA), 6-4, 6-3, 3-6, 4-6, 6-1. Kept U.S. senior singles title 7 straight years through 1950. Also

won 5 U.S. senior doubles titles: 1945-46-47 with Sidney Adelstein (USA), 1949-50 with Hall of Famer Wilmer Allison (USA). b. Springfield, N.J., Sept. 11, 1898, d. New York, Sept. 7, 1977. RH, 5 ft 9, 168 lbs., sturdily built baseliner.

HAMILTON, "Ghost"—Pale, frail-looking Irishman haunted Willie Renshaw by giving him only loss in Wimbledon F, 1890, 6-8, 6-2, 3-6, 6-1, 6-1, depriving Willie of 8th title. RH Willoby James "Ghost" Hamilton from County Kildare made brief mark. Illness (blood poisoning) prevented him from defending. b. Dec. 8, 1864, Monasterevan, County Kildare, Ireland, d. Sept. 27, 1943, Dublin.

HARPER, Sylvia—Single life may have been better for Aussie Sylvia Lance Harper's singles game. She won the Australian title over Esna Boyd (AUS) in 1924, 6-3, 3-6, 8-6, and the doubles as well at age 28, with Daphne Akhurst (AUS). But after becoming Mrs. Harper she lost the F to Boyd, 1927, 5-7, 6-1, 6-2, and Akhurst, 1930, 10-8, 2-6, 7-5. She did win the doubles again, as Mrs. Harper in 1925, repeating with Akhurst, and had won it with Boyd in 1923. An older man suited her in 1923, winning the mixed, with 51-year-old Horrie Rice, def. Mall Molesworth-Bert St. John (both AUS), 2-6, 6-4, 6-4. Thus she had 5 majors, all Australian. b. Oct. 1895, Canterbury, New South Wales.

HARTIGAN, Joan—An international trail-blazer for Aussie women, tall RH Joan Marcia Hartigan reached world Top 10 twice: No. 8, 1934; No. 9, 1935. Made Wimbledon SF both years (lost to 1936 champ Helen Jacobs, 1934, champ Helen Moody, 1935, after beating defender Dorothy Round (GBR), 4-6, 6-4, 6-3). b. 1912, Sydney, d. there Aug. 31, 2000. Rode puissant forehand from baseline to 3 Australian singles titles—1933 d. Coral McInnes Buttsworth (AUS), 6-4, 6-3; 1934 d. Mall Molesworth (AUS), 6-1, 6-4; 1936 d. Nancye Wynne (AUS), 6-4, 6-4. Made Aussie QF, 1937-38, 46; SF, 1939-40. Also won mixed, 1934, with Gar Moon (AUS). Won Scottish singles 1934. Used "upside-down" backhand (same racket face as forehand) Married Hugh Bathurst, 1947.

HARTLEY, John—English clergyman, only such to win major, 2 Wimbledon singles—1879, def. Vere "St. Leger" Goold (IRL), future murderer, 6-2, 6-4, 6-2; 1880, def. Herbert Lawford (GBR), 6-3, 6-2, 2-6, 6-3. Rev. John Thorneycroft Hartley, RH, Oxford grad, extremely steady, unerring, but overwhelmed, 6-0, 6-1, 6-1 in 1881 F as Willie Renshaw (GBR) launched 6-title run. Shares worst F defeat, 2 games, with Gottfried von Cramm (GER), who lost 6-1, 6-1, 6-0, by Fred Perry, 1936. b. Jan. 9, 1849, Tong, England, d. Aug. 21, 1935, Knaresborough, England.

HAWKES, Jack—Unpredictable LH Australian with good twist serve and volley. John Bailey Hawkes won Aussie title 1926, def. Jim Willard (AUS), 6-1, 6-3, 6-1. Also won doubles (left court) with Gerald Patterson (AUS), 1922, 26-27. Had 7 match points but lost longest Aussie F, 1927, to Patterson, 3-6, 6-4, 3-6, 18-16, 6-3—71 games. They lost Wimbledon F, 1928. World No. 10, 1928. Davis Cup 1921–23, 6-7 singles, 5-2 doubles. b. June 7, 1899, Geelong, Australia, d. there, May 31, 1990.

HAWKINS, Paul (Father of Hawk-Eye)—An electronic innovation making an impact on the game is Hawk-Eye. Introduced in 2006 at Key Biscayne, giving players a chance to challenge close, disputed line calls. A series of ball-tracking computers monitor matches and show the ball in question on large screens in the arena, allowing the umpire to overrule or confirm the original call. The young English inventor, Dr. Paul Martin Hawkins (b. April 26, 1974, Bledlow Ridge, Eng.), has a Ph. D. in artificial intelligence, Durham University. His system is useful in cricket telecasts. First challenger was Jamea Jackson (USA) whose forehand down the line was called out. She thought it good, and was proven wrong by the replay. Does the Hawk settle a squawk? Sometimes. But players have a limited number of challenges. A drawback is that the highly-expensive technology is generally used only on an outdoor tournament's principal court, depriving a majority of entrants of its use. Hawk-Eye seems a fitting name for a Hawkins concept.

HEATH, Rod—Wilfrid Rodney Heath, first Australian male champ, RH, won at 21 in hometown, Melbourne, 1905, conquering field of 17 at Warehousemen's Cricket Ground, beating Dr. Arthur H. Curtis's volleying with forehand drives, 4-6, 6-3, 6-4, 6-4. Won again, 1910, def. Horrie Rice (AUS), 6-4, 6-3, 6-2. Davis Cup 1911-1912 (won Cup, 1911); 1-2 singles. After aviation duty, World War I, lost Wimbledon doubles F, 1919, with Randolph Lycett, his SF victim in 1905 Aussie. b. June 15, 1884, Melbourne, d. there Oct. 6, 1936.

HELLWIG, Helen—Helen Rebecca Hellwig, RH out of Brooklyn, 6th to win U.S. singles title, 1894 at 20. Deposed Aline Terry (USA), 7-5, 3-6, 6-0, 3-6, 6-3. With Juliette Atkinson (USA) first team to repeat as U.S. doubles champs, 1894-95. Reappeared 12 years later, made SF, 1907, QF, 1908, as Mrs. William Pouch. Last played 1916 at 42, had 14-8 U.S. singles record. b. March 1874, Brooklyn, d. Nov. 26, 1960, New York.

HENKEL, Henner—The younger of Germany's splendid pre-World War II one-two punch, RH 6 ft Heinrich Ernst Otto "Henner" Henkel was dead at 27, a soldier killed on Stalingrad front, Jan. 13, 1943. He and Gottfried von Cramm nearly won Davis Cup, 1937, 3-2 SF loss to U.S. That year Henkel won French singles, d. Henry "Bunny" Austin (GBR), 6-1, 6-4, 6-3. He and von Cramm, World Nos. 3 and 2, won French and U.S. doubles, 1937, def. Norman Farquharson-Vernon Kirby (both RSA), 6-4, 7-5, 3-6, 6-1; def. Don Budge-Gene Mako (both USA), 6-4, 7-5, 6-4. Also World No. 9, 1936; No. 6, 1939. Davis Cup 1935-39; 33-13 singles, 16-4 doubles (German team also made SF, 1935-36, 38). He made SF Wimbledon, 1938-39; QF, 1937. b. Oct. 9, 1915, Posen, Germany.

HENMAN, Tim—Versatile, all-rounder, solid on all surfaces. Strong serve-and-volleyer, best Brit since Fred Perry, 1936. b. Oxford, England, Sept. 6, 1974. RH, 6 ft 1, 170 lbs. As British No. 1 generated incredible hype and hopes ("Our Tim") at Wimbledon. Made SF 1998-99, 2001-02, losing each time to eventual champion, Pete Sampras, 1998-99; Goran Ivanisevic (CRO), 2001, 2 points from

victory; Lleyton Hewitt (AUS), 2002. Retired end of 2007. First Brit to reach Wimbledon SF since Roger Taylor, 1973. Made SF French, U.S., 2004; QF Wimbledon 1996-97, 2003-04. Decorated with OBE by Queen Elizabeth II. Wimbledon bloodline: Grandfather Henry Billington, first competed at Wimbledon in 1948, won 2 rds. 1948, 50-51. Great-grandmother, Ellen Stawell Brown, possibly first woman to serve overhand, 1901. Won doubles silver medal with Neil Broad, 1996 Olympics. Davis Cup 12 years from 1994, 29-8 singles, 11-6 doubles. World Top 10 for 5 years: No. 7, 1998; No. 10, 2000; No. 9, 2001; No. 8, 2002; No. 6, 2004. Career: won 11 singles (496-274 matches) 4 doubles pro titles, $11,635,542 prize money.

HILLYARD, Blanche Bingley—Hardy, enthusiastic Englishwoman, Blanche Bingley Hillyard played in first female F Wimbledon, 1884, was still around 29 years later, 1913, her last of 17 at age 49. Between 1885 and 1901 (finalist both years), played a majors record 13 Wimbledon F. Won 6, all against compatriots—1885, beat original champ Maud Watson, 6-3, 6-3; 1889, def. Helena Rice, 4-6, 8-6, 6-4; 1894, def. Edith Austin, 6-1, 6-1; 1897, def. Charlotte Cooper (later Mrs. Sterry), 5-7, 7-5, 6-2; 1899, def. Cooper, 6-2, 6-3; 1900, def. Cooper, 4-6, 6-4, 6-4. Had a record 14-year spread from first title, 1886, to last, 1900, at 36, second-oldest female champ. (Charlotte Cooper Sterry was 37, 1908). Blanche's 7 lost F also a record for majors. RH, b. Nov. 3, 1863, Greenford, Middlesex, d. Aug. 6, 1946, Pulborough, Sussex. At Wimbledon, 48-18 in singles. Characterized as "Alert, confident, plucky" by one writer. Best comeback in major F, 1889, def. Rice, 4-6, 8-6, 6-4, from 3-5, 3 MP 2nd set, until Jennifer Capriati saved 4 MP beating Martina Hingis, Australian F 2002, 4-6, 7-6 (9-7), 6-2. At age 48, 1912 (second to last Big W), made SF, lost to champ Ethel Larcombe, 6-1, 6-0. Her last win, the QF, beat future Hall of Famer, 20-year-old "Bunny" Ryan, 3-6, 8-6, 6-3. Lost her farewell, 1913, opening rd., to Ethel Hannam, 4-6, 6-2, 6-0. Set an Eastbourne record, winning 11 singles titles between 1885 and 1905. Also won German, 1897, 1900; Irish, 1888, 1904, 07; Welsh, 1888, singles titles. Married George Hillyard, 1887, he All England Club secretary, 1907-24.

HOMANS, Helen—A New Yorker, Helen Homans started as U.S. champ in doubles, 1905 with Carrie Neely (USA), losing singles F to Bessie Moore, 6-4, 5-7, 6-1. Turned it around, 1906 singles, d. Maud Barger Wallach (USA), 6-4, 6-3, losing doubles with Clover Boldt (USA). Born 1878 or 1879, d. as Mrs. McLean, March 29, 1949, Bronxville, N.Y. Brother, Shep Homans, better known athlete, football All-American, fullback, Princeton, 1890-91.

ISNER, Jonathan Robert—All-time highest-riser Yank, 6 ft 10, 236 lbs, size 15 feet. All-American U. Georgia 2004–07, led Bulldogs to NCAA team title, 2007, won doubles, lost F singles. b. April 26, 1985, Greensboro, N.C. RH (2-handed backhand). Turned pro, 2007, made 3rd rd. U.S., taking set from champ Roger Federer (SUI). Sensational wild card, Washington, with serve called "Big Bertha," 144 aces, won record 5 straight 3rd set tie-breakers, losing F to No. 5 Andy Roddick (USA), 6-4, 7-6 (7-4). Ended year world No. 107, $146,159 prize money.

IVANISEVIC, Goran—All-time Wimbledon long-shot champ, 2001. Arrived as unseeded beggar, pleading for wild card, departed as the king, though ranked No. 125. Spindly yet powerful Croat, Goran Simun Ivanisevic, 6 ft 5, 180 lbs., LH (2-handed backhand). Huge serve, streaky, appealingly jocular. b. Sept. 13, 1971, Split. Only male Croat to win major singles, def. Pat Rafter (AUS) in serve-and-volley thriller, 6-3, 3-6, 6-3, 2-6, 9-7. Served tournament record 213 aces. Unique wild card champ, having lost 3 previous F: 1992, to Andre Agassi (USA); 1994, 98 to Pete Sampras (USA). Second Croat male in major F following fellow townsman, Nikki Pilic, French runner-up to Ilie Nastase (ROU), 1973. Served 206 aces, Wimbledon 1992 (37 vs. Agassi). Holds season ace record, 1,477, 1996. Won Olympic bronzes for Croatia, singles, doubles (with Goran Prpic), 1992. Made SF Wimbledon, 1990, 96; U.S., 1996; QF French, 1990, 92, 94; Australian, 1989, 94, 97. World Top 10 for 6 years: No. 9, 1990; No. 4, 1992, 96; No. 7, 1993; No. 5, 1994 (career high No. 2 in July); No. 10, 1995. Career: won 22 singles (599-333 matches) 9 doubles (263-225) titles, $19,876,579 prize money. Davis Cup 8 years since 1993, 20-6 singles, 12-5 doubles, member of 2005 winning team for Croatia, but did not compete.

JAEGER, Andrea—Peppery, meteoric 5 ft 6, 133 lbs blonde, American prodigy Andrea Jaeger was one of youngest ever ranked in world's Top 10: No. 5 at age 15, 1980. Also No. 6, 1981; No. 3, 1982; No. 4, 1983; then virtually finished by injuries like contemporary rival of similar style, Tracy Austin (USA). Fast, competitive, hard-hitting RH (2-handed backhand), baseliner, youngest champ U.S. Clay Court singles, 1981, def. Virginia Ruzici (ROU), 6-1, 6-0. Lost two major F—to Martina Navratilova (USA), French, 1982, 7-6 (8-6), 6-1 (defeated Chris Evert (USA), SF, 6-3, 6-1); Wimbledon, 1983, 6-0, 6-3 (def. Billie Jean King 6-1, 6-1 in SF). Andrea, 15, Jimmy Arias, 16 (USA), won French mixed, 1981, def. Betty Stove (NED)-Fred McNair (USA), 7-6, 6-4 (youngest team to win major doubles). Made SF, Australian, 1982; French, 1981, 83; U.S., 1980, 82; QF Australian, 1981; Wimbledon, 1980; U.S., 1983. Federation Cup, 2 years (1981 Cup winner), 8-1 singles. Wightman Cup, 1980-81 (both Cup winners), 2-1 singles, 1-0 doubles. b. June 4, 1965, Chicago, raised Lincolnshire, Ill. Career: won 14 pro singles titles (260-85 matches), $1,379,066 prize money. Admirably selfless adult, she fundraises, operates Silver Lining Ranch for terminally ill kids, Aspen, Colorado, became Anglican Dominican nun, Sister Andrea, in 2006.

JAUSOVEC, Mima—Continental clay was the ballroom for nimble, fleet-footed little Mima Jausovec. Winning titles at the French, 1977, def. Florenta Mihai (ROU), 6-2, 6-7 (5-7), 6-1; Italian, 1976, def. Lesley Hunt (AUS), 6-1, 6-3; and German, 1978, def. Virginia Ruzici (ROU), 6-2, 6-3, she stands as the outstanding Slovenian. b. July 20, 1956, Maribor, Yugoslavia (now Slovenia), she also won those 3 titles in doubles, 1978, linked to Ruzici. They lost Wimbledon F, 1978, to Kerry Reid-Wendy Turnbull (both AUS). A factor at all majors, she lost 2 French F, deposed by Ruzici, 1978, 6-2, 6-2; beaten by Chris Evert, 1983, 6-1, 6-2. Made SF Australian, 1980, U.S., 1976; QF French, 1981, Wimbledon, 1978,

81; U.S., 1977, 80. Well-rounded, 5 ft 4 Mima was fine volleyer, also a good skier, growing up in mountainous Maribor. Career: Won 5 singles (351-248 matches), 6 doubles pro career titles, $933,926 prize money. Federation Cup, Yugoslavia, 1973, 75-76, 78-79-80, 84. 7-8 singles, 3-3 doubles. Best world ranking: No. 11, 1977.

JEDRZEJOWSKA, Jadwiga—Chunky "JaJa" Jedrzejowska, best Polish woman, mouthful for umpires, handful for foes. RH, b. Oct. 15, 1912, Krakow; d. Feb. 28, 1980, Katowice. Married Alfred Gallert, 1947. Only Pole in world's Top 10: No. 6, 1936, 38; No. 3, 1937: No. 7, 1939, and major singles F. Lost 3 major singles F—French, 1939, to Simone Mathieu (FRA), 6-3, 8-6; Wimbledon, 1937 (beat Alice Marble (USA), SF, 8-6, 6-2, lost F to Dorothy Round (GBR), 6-2, 2-6, 7-5, led 4-1 3rd); U.S., 1937, lost first all-foreign F to Chilean Anita Lizana, 6-4, 6-2 (def. defender Helen Jacobs (USA), SF, 6-4, 6-4). Won French doubles with Simone Mathieu, 1939. Made SF French, 1937; Wimbledon, 1936; QF U.S., 1938; Wimbledon, 1938-39. Good-natured baseliner with battering forehand.

JENSEN Brothers—Thought of fondly as the wild and crazy guys of the men's tour, and TV personalities, Luke and Murphy Jensen were undoubtedly the greatest players to come out of Ludington, Mich., and are rarities: the 6th set of brothers to win a major doubles—French, 1993, over David Prinosil-Marc Goellner (both GER), 6-4, 6-7 (4-7), 6-4. Followed Gene and Alex Mayer (both USA), French, 1979 as the 2nd fraternal success of the Open era.

Luke Jensen—b. June 18, 1966, Grayling, Mich., 6-3, 190, RH (but ambidextrous, served RH/LH). All-American U. Southern California, 1986-87. Won 10 pro doubles titles, now coach Syracuse U. women's varsity, commentator, ESPN.

Marc Murphy Jensen—b. Oct. 30, 1968, Ludington, 6-4, 180, LH. All-American U. Southern California, 1989, U. Georgia, 1990. Won 4 pro doubles titles, all with Luke. Had singles wins over Andre Agassi (USA), Mats Wilander (SWE). Commentator, Tennis Channel. Younger sisters Rebecca, Rachel Jensen also played pro tour.

JOHANSSON, Tom—One of the more startling champs, 5 ft 11, 176 lbs., RH Thomas Johansson was fifth Swede to win a major, Australian, 2002. Never beyond 3rd rd. in 7 previous tries, never in Top 10, came in at 16th seed but beat favored 9th seed Marat Safin (RUS), 3-6, 6-4, 6-4, 7-6 (7-4) for the title. Made U.S. QF, 1998, 2000 and Wimbledon SF, 2005. Quick, has all-round game. Best world rank, No. 7 June '02, 14 at end 2002. Career: Won 9 pro career singles titles (345-276 matches), 1 doubles, $6,768,644 prize money. Davis Cup, 10 years from 1998, 17-13 singles, 1-3 doubles. b. March 24, 1975, Linkoping, Sweden. Turned pro 1994.

JONES, Henry—Games playing appealed more than medicine to Dr. Henry Jones, English physician who operated only as a sports scribbler for *The Field* (pen name "Cavendish") Smitten by lawn tennis, he proposed its introduction at All England Club, helped organize the original Wimbledon, 1877, ran the show as referee. b. Nov. 2, 1831, London, d. Feb. 10, 1899.

JORDAN, Barbara & Kathy—American sisters, Barbara and higher-ranked Kathy Jordan out of King of Prussia, Pa. RH, All-Americans, Stanford, then winners major titles. First sisters in major singles F (both at Australian) since Maud and Lillian Watson clashed for first Wimbledon title, 1884, and before Williams sisters, Venus and Serena, began their title showdowns at U.S., 2001.

Barbara Jordan—b. April 2, 1957, Milwaukee. Smooth-stroking serve-and-volleyer. Long-shot winner of Australian, 1979 (unseeded, ranked No. 68), def. Sharon Walsh (USA), 6-3, 6-3. Only American champ there 1970s, beat favorite, Czech Hana Mandlikova (1980, 87 champ), QF, 6-2, 6-2, won $10,000, financial high in $135,534 career. Only pro singles title; won two doubles, plus major mixed, French, 1983, with Eliot Teltscher (USA), def. Leslie Allen-Charles Strode (both USA), 6-2, 6-3. Best world rank, No. 37, 1980.

Kathryn "KJ" Jordan—b. Dec. 3, 1959. Bryn Mawr, Pa. Willowy, 5 ft 8, 130 lbs., attacker, awkward-looking but effective stroker, extreme Western forehand, excellent volleyer. Won NCAA singles, doubles, 1979 for Stanford (with Alycia Moulton), then turned pro. Lost F, Australian, 1983, to Martina Navratilova (USA), 6-2, 7-6 (7-5). Made SF Wimbledon, 1984; QF French, 1980; Wimbledon, 1983, beating Chris Evert (USA), 3rd rd., 6-1, 7-6 (7-2), first of 2 times in 19 years Evert failed to make SF. Won all major doubles: Australian, U.S., 1981; French, Wimbledon, 1980, all with Anne Smith (USA). Also Wimbledon, 1985, with Liz Smylie (AUS), 5-7, 6-3, 6-4, ending Navratilova-Pam Shriver (both USA), 109-match streak. Plus Wimbledon mixed, 1986, with Ken Flach (USA). Career: Won 1 singles, Boston, 1982 def. Wendy Turnbull (AUS) 7-5, 1-6, 6-4. (75-54 matches) 41 doubles titles (out of 71 F; 185-50 matches, $1,592,111 prize money. Federation Cup: 1980-85, 6-3 singles, 17-1 doubles (with 1980-81 Cup winners). Wightman Cup: 1979-80; 1-1 singles, 1-0 doubles (both Cup winners). Best world rank: No. 10, 1984; No. 11, 1979; No. 13, 1980.

KARLOVIC, Ivo—"Leaning Tower of Zagreb" (Croatia), b. there Feb. 28, 1979, rising to 6 ft 10 (230 lbs.), tallest player ever. RH, prolific server of aces, average approximately 20 per match. Fired an Open era best 55 aces in his 6-7 (1), 6-7 (4), 7-6 (4), 6-4, 6-3 first-round French Open loss to Lleyton Hewitt (AUS), four shy of all-time record set by Ed Kauder at 1955 U.S. Championships. Turned pro 2000. Pulled an all-time upset, Wimbledon 2003, as qualifier ranked No. 203, beat 1st seeded defending champ Lleyton Hewitt (AUS), 1st rd., 1-6, 7-6(7-5), 6-3, 6-4. No. 18, 2008, No. 22, 2007. Davis Cup, 5-5 singles, 2-2 doubles. As of June of 2009, won 4 singles, 1 doubles titles. $3,025,802 prize money. Made 4th rd. Wimbledon, 2004.

KINGSCOTE, Algie—Algernon Robert Fitzhardinge "Algie" Kingscote, World War I hero, English RH, journeyed Down Under in 1919 to play in F, Britain's losing Davis Cup cause, but won Australian singles, def. Eric Pockley (AUS), 6-4, 6-0, 6-3. Made Wimbledon all-comers F, 1919, lost to champ Gerald Patterson (AUS); QF 1921. Sound all-round. World Top 10: No. 3, 1920; No. 5, 1919. Davis Cup: 7 years from 1919; 7-6 singles, 2-2 doubles. b. 1888, India.

KINSEY, Robert Gladstone—b. May 9, 1897, St. Louis, Mo., raised in San Francisco, d. 1964. RH. 5 ft 11, 140 lbs. Tenacious defender, baseliner with well-placed passing shots. Won 1 major title: U.S. doubles, 1924, with brother, Howard Oreon Kinsey (USA), d. Gerald Patterson-Pat O'Hara Wood (both AUS), 7-5, 5-7, 7-9, 6-3, 6-4. With brother, Howard, won 2 U.S. Clay Court doubles, 1923, d. John Hennessey (USA)-Walter Wesbrook (USA), 6-4, 13-11, 6-3; 1924 def. Bill Tilden-A.L. (Sandy) Wiener (both USA), 6-4, 7-5, 6-2. Davis Cup for Mexico, 1927-28, 0-3 singles, 1-1 doubles. U.S. Top 10, No. 10, 1923.

KORDA, Petr—Gifted skinny Czech LH Petr Korda. 6 ft 3, 160 lbs. Won Australian, 1998, d. Chilean Marcelo Rios, 6-2, 6-2, 6-2. Lost French F, 1992 to Jim Courier (USA), 7-5, 6-2, 6-1. Turned pro 1987. Won Australian doubles, 1996, with Stefan Edberg (SWE), def. Alex O'Brien (USA)-Sebastien Lareau (CAN), 7-5, 7-5, 4-6, 6-1. Lost F French, 1990, with Goran Ivanisevic (CRO). Electrifying, though erratic, all-court shotmaker; knocked Pete Sampras (USA) off U.S. throne, 1997, 4th rd., 6-7 (4-7), 7-5, 7-6 (7-2), 3-6, 7-6 (7-3). b. Jan. 23, 1968. Prague. World's Top 10: No. 9, 1991; No. 7, 1992 (as high as No. 2, Feb., 1998). Made QF Australian, 1993; Wimbledon, 1998; U.S., 1995, 97. Career: Won 10 singles (410-248 matches), 10 doubles (234-160) pro titles, $10,448,900 prize money. Davis Cup 10 years from 1988, 18-9 singles, 11-4 doubles. Ended career in controversy. Suspended after testing positive for anabolic steroid nandralone at Wimbledon, 1998, forfeited $94,529 QF prize money. ITF officials believed "unintentional," but he lost appeal, July 1999, and retired. Wife, Czech Regina Rajchrtova, played WTA Tour; best world ranking No. 39, 1991.

KORMOCZI, Suzi—Hungary's best woman, Suzi Kormoczi was persistent baseliner, patient pursuing success, rose to world No. 2, 1958. RH, b. Aug. 25, 1924, Budapest. First entered French, 1947, won 1958 on 5th try, def. Shirley Bloomer (GBR), 6-4, 1-6, 6-2, becoming oldest champ, almost 34. Oldest champ Italian, 1960, almost 36, def. Ann Haydon (GBR), 6-4, 4-6, 6-1. Lost French title, 1959 F, to Christine Truman (GBR), 6-4, 7-5. Made SF French, 1956, 61; Wimbledon, 1958. World Top 10 for 7 years: No. 7, 1953, 61; No. 10, 1955; No. 5, 1956, 60; No. 2, 1958; No. 8, 1959.

KOURNIKOVA, Anna—Top banana Anna, the game's blonde queen of sexiness, marketability and unrealized potential whose web site (www.kournikova.com) hummed even when her game didn't. From Russia with love she came, 1996, age 15, named WTA's "Most Impressive Newcomer." Ranked No. 13, made 4th rd. U.S. b. Moscow, June 7, 1981. RH (2-handed backhand), 5 ft 8, 125 lbs. Turned pro 1995. Federation Cup, 3 years, 1996-98, 2-5 singles, 10-2 doubles. World Top 10, 1 year, 2000, No. 8. Only Top 10 member not to win a singles title (130 starts), lost 4 F. Excellent volleyer, won 16 pro doubles titles (209-129 matches) including 2 majors: 2 Australian, 2002, with Martina Hingis (SUI), def. Daniela Hantuchova (SVK)-Arantxa Sanchez Vicario (ESP), 6-2, 6-7 (4-7), 6-1; 1999 with Hingis, def. Lindsay Davenport (USA)-Natasha Zvereva (BLR), 7-5, 6-3. Also won 2 WTA Tour Championships: 1999 with Hingis def. Larisa Savchenko Neiland (LAT)-Sanchez Vicario, 6-4, 6-4; 2000 with Hingis def. Nicole Arendt (USA)-Manon Bollegraf

(NED), 6-2, 6-3. Set 2 DF records, 1999 Australian, 31, but def. Miho Saeki (JPN), 1-6, 6-4, 10-8; 73 for tournament. Made QF Australian, 2001; SF Wimbledon, 1997. Also made rare Grand Slump, losing 1st rd. each major, 2002. Career: won $3,584,662 prize money over 8 years, made much more from endorsements.

KRAJICEK, Richard—A fabulous 1996 fortnight was his: Wimbledon's second unseeded champ, Richard Peter Stanislav Krajicek, Netherlands' only winner of a men's singles major. Gangling 6-5 RH, he ranked No. 13 coming in, had a case to dissent to non-seed but let his racket be bombastic mouthpiece, especially with serve, backhand. Romped on loss of one set, ended 25-match Big W streak of No. 1 Pete Sampras (USA), QF, 7-5, 7-6 (7-3), 6-4. Won title fast, def. MaliVai Washington (USA), 6-3, 6-4, 6-3. b. Dec. 6, 1971, Rotterdam, parents defected from Czechoslovakia. Made SF Australian, 1992; French, 1993; QF, French, 1996; Wimbledon, 2002; U.S., 1997, 99-2000. Davis Cup: 1991-95; 4-6 singles, 1-0 doubles. World Top 10: No. 7, 1996; No. 10, 1998-99. Career: Won 17 singles (411-219 matches), 3 doubles pro titles, $10,077,425 prize money.

KRIEK, Johan—Swift, compact, fine volleying 5 ft 9, 168 lbs., RH, Johan Christian Kriek reached peak on Down Under grass, won Australian, 1981-82, def. Steve Denton (USA) in both—6-2, 7-6, 6-7, 6-4; and 6-3, 6-3, 6-2. Made SF Australian, 1984, French, 1986, U.S., 1980; QF Australian, 1983, 85, French, 1981-82; U.S., 1978-79. Won South African, 1983, def. Colin Dowdeswell (GBR), 6-4, 4-6, 1-6, 7-5, 6-3. Won U.S. Indoor, 1982, def. John McEnroe (USA), 6-3, 3-6, 6-4. South African farm boy by birth, April 5, 1958, Pongola. Became U.S. citizen, 1982. Career: won 14 singles (373-220), 8 doubles (206-173) pro titles, $2,383,794 prize money. Best world rank, No. 7 in 1984

KRISHNAN, Ramanathan & Ramesh—Father, son, Ramanathan and Ramesh Krishnan, possibly India's best. Unique, both helping homeland to Davis Cup finales. RH, clever, deceptive. Born, raised in Madras (now Chennai).

Ramanathan Krishnan—b. April 11, 1932, Madras, World Top 10: No. 9, 1959, 62; No, 8, 1960; No. 6, 1961. Davis Cup: 17 years, 1953-69, 1976, 43 ties, 50-19 singles, 19-9 doubles: 97 matches, 12th highest ever. Led India to finale, 1966, lost to Australia, 4-1. Made SF Wimbledon, 1960-61. Career: won 47 amateur singles titles across the globe.

Ramesh Krishnan—b. June 5, 1961, Madras, 5'7, 140 lbs. Turned pro 1976. Best world rank, No. 23, 1985. Made QF, Wimbledon, 1986; U.S., 1981, 87. Davis Cup: 12 years between 1978 and 1992, 24 ties; 23-19 singles, 6-2 doubles (5-3 singles, leading India to 1987 F, lost 5-0 to Sweden). Career: won 8 singles (320-288 matches), 1 doubles pro titles, $1,263,130 prize money.

LANDRY, Nelly—A decade after losing French F, 1938, to Simone Passemard Mathieu (FRA), 6-0, 6-3, French LH Nelly Jeanne Adamson Landry hurdled World War II to win in 1948 at age 31, def. Shirley Fry (USA), 6-2, 0-6, 6-0. b. Dec. 28, 1916, of Belgian

parentage in London. Became French citizen, 1937, marrying French player Paul Landry who made the Wimbledon QF, 1929. Two children. Diminutive 5 ft 3 but excelled as attacker, volleyer. Lost title, 1949 French F, to Margaret Osborne duPont (USA), 7-5, 6-2. Lost 1939 French doubles F with Arlette Halff (FRA) to Billie York (GBR)-Mathieu. Made SF, French, 1954, QF, French 1936, 46, 51, 53; Wimbledon, 1948. World Top 10: No. 7, 1946; No. 10, 1948.

LANGRISHE, May—Mary Isabella Langrishe, original female champ—and youngest, 14, to win national title. Won her own, Irish, 1879, the inaugural, at Dublin's Fitzwilliam Club, first to welcome women. RH, b. Dec. 31, 1864, Ireland. Beat D. Meldon, 6-2, 0-6, 8-6, to rule field of 7. Also won first female doubles title, Northern Championship, Manchester, England, 1882, with older sister. d. Jan. 24, 1939.

LARCOMBE, Ethel—English RH Ethel Warneford Thomson Larcombe jolted Charlotte Cooper Sterry's hopes of 6th Wimbledon title, beat her, 1912 F, 6-3, 6-1. First entered 1902, won on 6th try, age 33. Excellent backhand, last champ to serve underhand. Played at both ends of World War I, losing Wimbledon singles F, 1914, to Dolly Chambers (GBR), 7-5, 6-4. Also lost doubles F, 1914, with Ethel Hannam (GBR), 1919-20, with Chambers. In Wimbledon mixed F, 1913, leading with Jim Parke, was hit in eye by shot, unable to continue, defaulted title to Agnes Tuckey-Hope Crisp (both GBR). Won Irish, 1912, Scottish, 1910, singles titles. Fine athlete, won All England badminton singles 1900-01, 03-04, 06; doubles 1902, 04, 06, mixed 1903, 06. Married Dudley Larcombe, 1906. b. June 8, 1879, Islington, d. Aug. 11, 1965, Budleigh Salterton. Became teaching pro, 1922.

LEACH, Richard David—California vintage, aged very well, 42, retired 2006, after 21 years. Won last (46th) doubles title, Los Angeles, 2005, with Brian MacPhie. Career doubles matches: 648-390. (Briefly retired 2000, assistant coach to father, Dick Leach, their alma mater U. Southern California.) Four-time All-American USC, won NCAA doubles, with Tim Pawsat, 1986; with Scott Melville, 1987. b. Arcadia, Calif., Dec. 28, 1964, LH (2-handed backhand), 6 ft 2, 185 lbs. Turned pro 1987. Sister-in-law, Lindsay Davenport, married brother Jonathan Leach, April 25, 2003. Papa Leach survived most-games-ever match (147), with Dick Dell, def. Len Schloss-Tim Mozur, 3-6, 49-47, 22-20, Newport, R.I., 1967. Rick played 17 major doubles F, won 9 titles: 3 Australian, 1988, with Jim Pugh (USA), def. Jeremy Bates (GBR)-Peter Lundgren (SWE), 6-3, 6-2, 6-3; 1989, with Pugh, def. Darren Cahill-Mark Kratzmann (both AUS), 6-4, 6-4, 6-4; 2000, with Ellis Ferreira (RSA), def. Wayne Black (ZIM)-Kratzmann, 6-4, 3-6, 6-3, 3-6, 18-16. Wimbledon, 1990, with Pugh, def. Danie Visser-Pieter Aldrich (both RSA), 7-6 (7-5), 7-6 (7-4), 7-6 (7-5). U.S., 1993 with Ken Flach (USA), def. Martin Damm-Karel Novacek (both CZE), 6-7 (3-7), 6-4, 6-2. Also 4 mixed: 2 Australian, 1995, with Natasha Zvereva (BLR), def. Gigi Fernandez (USA)-Cyril Suk (CZE), 7-6 (7-4), 6-7 (3-7), 6-4; 1997, with Manon Bollegraf (NED), def. Larisa Savchenko Neiland (LAT)-John-Laffnie de Jager, 6-3, 6-7 (5-7), 7-5; Wimbledon, 1990, with Zina Garrison (USA), def. Elizabeth Sayers Smylie-John Fitzgerald (both AUS), 7-5, 6-2. U.S., 1997, with Bollegraf, d. Mercedes Paz-

Pablo Albano (both ARG), 3-6, 7-5, 7-6 (7-3). Davis Cup, 5 years, 10 ties, 0-1 singles, 7-3 doubles (he and Pugh clinched 1990 Cup, def. Pat Cash-Fitzgerald (AUS), 6-4, 6-2, 3-6, 7-6 (7-2). Career, won 46 (of 82 F) doubles pro titles, $4,293,689 prize money.

LEE, Hyung-Taik—Out of potato fields, Hoingsung, came Korea's finest, turning pro, 1995. b. Hoingsung Jan 3, 1976, lives in Seoul. RH, 5 ft 11, 180 lbs. Davis Cup, 13 years, 40-9 singles, 10-13 doubles, highs for Korea. Olympics, 1996, 2000, 2004, 2008. Highest world singles rank, No. 36, 2007. Made 4th rd., U.S., 2000, 2007. Career, won 1 singles, 1 doubles pro titles, $2,257,901 prize money.

LEHANE, Jan—First woman to utilize a 2-handed backhand at the upper level, RH Jan had bad luck in being a contemporary of fellow Aussie Margaret Smith Court, the all-time champ. She lost 4 straight Australian F to Margaret, 1960-63, the first as teenagers, 7-5, 6-2. Together they made the Wimbledon doubles F, 1961, losing to Billie Jean King-Karen Hantze (both USA), 6-3, 6-4. Jan won the Australian mixed in 1960 with Trevor Fancutt (AUS) and 1961 with Bob Hewitt (AUS), and was a finalist in the 1963 doubles with Lesley Turner (AUS), losing to Robyn Ebbern (AUS) and, of course, Court. But Jan was one of few Aussies to beat Court in singles, F, New South Wales, 1960, 6-1, 6-3. World No. 8, 1960; No. 7, 1963. No. 10, 1964 b. July 9, 1941, Grenfell, NSW.

LIZANA, Anita—Chilean RH Anita Lizana, a significant blip—played U.S. Championships once, 1937, and won, beat Pole Jadwiga Jedrzejowska, 6-4, 6-2, first all-foreign F, 1st Latin American to win a major, and be No. 1 prior to Brazilian Maria Bueno, 1959. Born 1915, Santiago, married Ronald Ellis, settled in England. Made Wimbledon QF, 1936 (led champ Helen Jacobs, 4-2, 30-0 in 3rd), 1937. Short, quick, solid groundstroker with good passing shots, drop shots, admirable footwork. World Top 10: No. 1, 1937; No. 8, 1936.

LJUBICIC, Ivan—Croatian Davis Cup hero, led tiny homeland to Cup, 2005 (3-2 F over Slovak Republic), won 7 of 8 singles, 4 of 4 doubles (with Mario Ancic), decisive singles 3 times: def. Andy Roddick (USA), 4-6, 6-3, 7-6 (13-11), 6-7 (7-9), 6-2; Andrei Pavel (ROM), 6-3, 6-4, 6-3; Nikolay Davydenko (RUS), 6-3, 7-6 (8-6), 6-4. Sparked upsets of U.S., 2003 (4-1), 2005 (3-2), winning 4 singles, 2 doubles. Davis Cup, 10 years, 21 series, 1998-2007, 23-12 singles, 13-6 doubles. b. Banja Luka, Bosnia-Herzegovina, March 19, 1979. Family fled to avoid wartime genocide, 1992, he growing up in Italy, coached by Riccardo Piatti. RH, 6 ft 4, 202 lbs., splendid serve, one-handed backhand. Season leader in aces (929), 2006. World Top 10 for 2 years—No. 3 May 2006, then No. 5 end 2006; No. 9, 2005. Made SF French, QF Australian, 2006. Turned pro 1998. Won 8 pro singles titles (324-214 matches), $$7,546,106 prize money.

LONG, Thelma—Thelma Dorothy Coyne Long, sturdy Australian RH, b. Oct. 14, 1918, Sydney. Had one of longest careers, stretching over 22 years as significant winner, 19 major titles (2-12-5), all Australian except French mixed, 1956, with Chilean Luis Ayala. Fine volleyer, won 1st of record 12 Australian doubles, 1936 (with Nancye Wynne Bolton, her partner in 10 of them), last, 1958. Also

won 2 singles, 1952, def. Helen Angwin (AUS), 6-2, 6-3; 1954, def. Jenny Staley, 6-3, 6-4. Won 4 other mixed 1951-52, 55, with George Worthington (AUS), 1954, with Rex Hartwig (AUS). Lost 4 Australian singles F, 1940, 51, 55-56. Made SF, 1947, 49. Altogether played in 24 Australian F. World Top 10: No. 7, 1952; No.10, 1954. Named to Australian Tennis Hall of Fame, 2002. Won U.S. Hard Court singles, 1952, def. Barbara Davidson (USA), 7-5, 0-6, 9-7.

LOWE, Gordon Arthur—Sir Francis Gordon Lowe, English RH, won last Australian singles title before World War I shut-down, 1915, def. Horrie Rice (AUS), 4-6, 6-1, 6-1, 6-4. b. June 21, 1884, Edgbaston, Cambridge grad, d. May 17, 1972, London. Davis Cup: 1921-25; 8-6 singles. Brother, Arthur Holden Lowe, RH b. Jan. 29, 1886, Edgbaston, Oxford grad, d. Oct. 22, 1958, London. Also British Davis Cup: 1911-19; 9-5 singles. Both World Top 10, 1914: Arthur No. 7, Gordon No. 8. At ages 37 and 35, became 4th of 5 sets of brothers in Wimbledon doubles F, 1921, lost to Max Woosnam-Randolph Lycett (both GBR), 6-3, 6-0, 7-5.

MacKAY, Barry Bruce—Good-natured "Ohio Bear," U.S. amateur mainstay 4 years until turning pro, 1961. Long career, 17 years, winning 24 amateur singles titles, 2 pro, 1970, after opens arrived. Huge serve, adept volleyer. Following playing career founded, promoted tournaments, San Francisco, San Jose. Now TV tennis commentator, b. Cincinnati, Ohio, Aug. 31, 1935. RH, 6 ft 4, 185 lbs., veteran U.S. Air Force, graduate U. Michigan ('57), won NCAA singles, def. Sam Giammalva (Texas), 6-4, 3-6, 6-2, 3-6, 6-3. As U.S. No. 1, 1960, won 11 singles titles. Davis Cup, 4 years, 17-7 singles, 5-2 doubles. Played 3 Cup F vs. Australia, 1957-59, Helped win Cup, 1958. In 1959 def. Rod Laver, 7-5, 6-4, 6-1, but lost decisive match, to Neale Fraser, 8-6, 3-6, 6-2, 6-4. World Top 10—No. 9, 1958; No. 4, 1959-60. U.S. Top 10—No. 5, 1957; No. 3, 1958-59; No. 1, 1960; No. 9, 1970. Won Italian, 1960, def. Luis Ayala (CHI), 7-5, 7-5, 0-6, 0-6, 6-1. Won U.S. Indoor, 1960, def. Dick Savitt (USA), 6-2, 2-6, 10-12, 6-1, 6-4; also won doubles, 1957-58 with Grant Golden (USA), 1959 with Alex Olmedo (PER). Won U.S. Clay Court, 1960, def. Bernard Bartzen (USA), 4-6, 7-5, 6-4, 6-0; also won doubles, 1958, with Giammalva (USA). Made SF Australian, Wimbledon, 1959; QF Wimbledon, 1958, 60; U.S., 1959; French, 1960, SF.

MAHONY, Harold—Tall, quick-tempered but jocular. RH Irishman Harold Segerson Mahony won Wimbledon, 1896, unseating Wilfred Baddeley (GBR), 6-2, 6-8, 5-7, 8-6, 6-3, a fleeting success before Doherty brothers (GBR) took over. Reggie snatched the title, 1897 challenge rd., 6-4, 6-4, 6-3. Made SF Wimbledon, 1891-92, 99, 1901-02. Lost 2 all-comers F, 1893 to Joshua Pim (IRL), 1898 to Laurie Doherty. b. Feb. 13, 1867, Edinburgh, d. June 27, 1904, Caragh Hill, Ireland, falling off his bicycle.

MAIN, Lorne—Lorne Garnet Main was inadvertent father of rare two-way, two-handed style, both forehand and backhand. Foremost proponent was Monica Seles (USA). "Seemed natural to me as a boy since I was a baseball switch-hitter." Canadian RH, 5-8, 145, b. July 9, 1930, Vancouver. No. 1, Canada, 1951-54. Biggest title, Monte Carlo, 1954. Davis Cup, 1949-55, 10-11 singles, 4-3 doubles.

MAJOLI, Iva—Croatian baseliner Iva Majoli, 9th seeded, won French 1997 at 19 over No. 1 Martina Hingis (SUI), 6-4, 6-2, depriving her (winner other 3 majors) of Grand Slam. RH (2-handed backhand). Turned pro 1991. Career: won 8 singles (309-217 matches), 1 doubles pro titles, $4,390,192 prize money. Made QF Australian, 1996; French, 1995-96, 98; Wimbledon, 1997. Federation Cup: 9 years from 1993, 15-12 singles, 5-5 doubles. World Top 10: No. 9, 1995; No. 6, 1997; No. 7, 1996. Won Hopman Cup 1996 with Goran Ivanisevic. b. Aug. 12, 1977, Zagreb.

MALEEVA, Manuela, Katerina & Magdalena—Internationally most exceptional trio of sisters ever, clearly greatest in Bulgarian annals, 41 pro singles titles among them. All three-baselining RH (2-handed backhands), born, brought up in Sofia. Played for Bulgaria, Federation Cup, Olympics, made World Top 10. Mother, Yulia Berberian, champion of Bulgaria 9 years; father, Gyorgy Maleev, Olympic basketball player, 1956. Unique accomplishments, until Williams sisters, Venus and Serena (USA), came along. Katerina, Manuela in world Top 10 together, 1990, have been in QF every major, together at French, 1990, were only sisters to do so pre-Williams. Manuela's 1992 U.S. QF win over Maggie, 6-2, 5-3, ret. (Maggie had beat Martina Navratilova, 6-4, 0-6, 6-3) first such sisterly encounter since 1897, U.S., champ Juliette Atkinson def. sibling, Kathleen, SF, 6-1, 6-3. Manuela, Katerina in 1988 U.S. QF, first sisters there since Atkinsons. Manuela in U.S. QF 5 times (1986, 88-89-90, 93) got there, 1990, by beating Navratilova, 7-5, 3-6, 6-3.

Manuela Maleeva Fragniere—5 ft 8, 127 lbs., b. Feb. 14, 1967, Sofia. Won rain-delayed Italian, 1984, 3 wins last day, F d. Chris Evert (USA), 6-3, 6-3. Won Olympic bronze, singles, 1988. Married Swiss tennis coach Francois Fragniere, 1987, became citizen, played Federation Cup, 1992 Olympics for Switzerland. Retired 1994. Career: won 19 singles (477-187 matches), 4 doubles titles, $3,244,811 prize money. World Top 10 for 9 years: No. 6, 1984, 88; No. 7, 1975; No. 8, 1986-87; No. 9, 1989-90, 92; No. 10, 1991. Federation Cup, 1984-87, 1989, 1991-92, 21-5 singles, 7-10 doubles. Made SF U.S., 1992; QF French, 1984, 87, 89-90; Wimbledon, 1984; Australian, 1985, 94.

Katerina Maleeva—5 ft 6, b. May 7, 1969, Sofia. Career: won 12 singles (369-210 matches), 2 doubles pro titles, $2,220,171 prize money. World Top 10: No. 6, 1990. Federation Cup, 1984-89, 1991-95, 20-9 singles, 9-13 doubles. Made QF Australian, 1990-91; French, 1990; Wimbledon, 1990, 92; U.S., 1993.

Magdalena "Maggie" Maleeva—5 ft 6, 130 lbs., b. April 1, 1975, Sofia. Won first pro title, San Marino, 1992. Career: Won 10 singles (439-290 matches), 2 doubles pro titles, $4,398,582 prize money. World Top 10: No. 6, 1995. Federation Cup, 1991-95, 7-2 singles, 3-3 doubles. Made QF U.S., 1992.

MAO, Zedong (Also Mao Tse-Tung)—Chairman Mao's biographer, Edgar Snow, reported that the chairman enjoyed playing tennis with comrades in Shensi Province after his army had survived the famed, brutal Long March of 6,000 miles in 1935.

Unfortunately his tennis career ended when a goat ate the net. That must have gotten his goat. But he would have been proud of Zi Yan and Jie Zheng, first Chinese ladies to win majors, Australian and Wimbledon doubles, 2006. Mao was born December 26, 1893 in Shaoshan Xiang Tan, Hunan Province, China and died at the age of 82, September 9, 1976 in Beijing.

MARTIN, Todd—Among tallest to play, 6 ft 6, 200 lbs, Todd Christopher Martin was worthy sportsman, member finest U.S. male generation. RH (2-handed backhand), all-rounder, strong serve-volleyer. Ever-willing Davis Cupper, 9 straight years from 1994, 11-8 singles, 5-6 doubles, was instrumental in Cup victory, 1995. In SF won clincher against Sweden, def. Thomas Enqvist, 7-5, 7-5, 7-6 (7-2). In 3-2 F at Moscow, a rock in left court, he and Pete Sampras took pivotal go-ahead point from Russians Yevgeny Kafelnikov-Andrei Olhovskiy, 7-5, 6-4, 6-3. Played 2 major singles F—lost Australian, 1994, to Sampras, 7-6 (7-4), 6-4, 6-4; lost U.S., 1999, narrowly, to Andre Agassi (USA), 6-4, 6-7 (5-7), 6-7 (2-7), 6-3, 6-2. Came close to another, Wimbledon, SF, letting 5th set 5-1 lead slip away to MaliVai Washington (USA), 5-7, 6-4, 6-7 (6-8), 6-3, 10-8. Won Barcelona, 1998, d. Albert Berasategui (ESP), 6-2, 1-6, 6-3, 6-2, first American to win since Herbie Flam, 1956. Born Hinsdale, Ill., July 8, 1970, grew up Lansing, Mich., All-American 2 years at Northwestern U., turned pro 1990. Also made SF at Wimbledon in 1994; U.S., 1994 and 2000; QF Australian, 1999, 2001; Wimbledon, 1993, 99. World Top 10: No. 10, 1994; No. 7, 1999. Also No. 12, 1996; No. 13, 1993. Career, 15 years: won 8 singles titles (411-234 matches) 5 doubles titles (100-85), $8,254,455 prize money.

MARTINEZ, Conchita—Only Spanish woman to win Wimbledon, 1994, thwarted Martina Navratilova's bid for 10th title in F, 6-4, 3-6, 6-3, with top-spinning groundies, backhand passers. Quick, 5 ft 7, 130 lbs., RH, top-notch performer all majors. Lost Australian F, 1998, to Martina Hingis (SUI), 6-3, 6-3; French F, 2000, to Mary Pierce (FRA), 6-2, 7-5. Also made SF Australian, 1995, 2000; French, 1994-95-96; Wimbledon, 1993, 95; U.S., 1995-96; QF Australian, 1994, 96; French, 1989-90-91-92-93, 99; Wimbledon, 2001; U.S, 1991, 95-96. Won record 4 straight Italian—1993, def. Gabriela Sabatini (ARG), 7-5, 6-1; 1994, def. Martina Navratilova (USA), 7-6 (7-5), 6-4; 1995, def. Arantxa Sanchez Vicario (ESP), 6-3, 6-1; 1996, def. Martina Hingis (SUI), 6-2, 6-3. Best year, 1995—won 6 singles titles. With Sanchez Vicario, made Spain dominant in Federation Cup, 1988-96, won 5 Cups (1991, 1993-94-95, 98); 36-7 singles, 15-5 doubles. Olympic silver, 1992, bronze, 1996 (doubles with Sanchez Vicario) and another silver in 2004 with Virginia Ruano-Pascual. b. April 16, 1972, Monzon, Spain. Turned pro 1988. World Top 10 for 9 years: No. 7, 1989; No. 9, 1991; No. 8, 1992; No, 4, 1993; No. 3, 1994; No. 2, 1995; No. 5, 1996, 2000; No. 8, 1998. Career: won 33 singles titles (739-297 matches), 13 doubles titles, $11,527,977 prize money.

MASSU, Nicolas—A twin gold medalist in the 2004 Olympics, 6-footer, 177 lbs. Nicolas Alejandro Massu, b. Oct. 10, 1979, Vina del Mar, Chile, def. Mardy Fish (USA), 6-3, 3-6, 2-6, 6-3, 6-4, for the singles prize, the night before, he teamed with compatriot Fernando Gonzalez for doubles gold, def. Nic Kiefer-Rainer Schuettler (both GER), 6-2, 4-6, 3-6, 7-6 (9-7), 6-4, first ever Olympic golds for Chile in any sport. A pro since 1997, RH (2-handed backhand). Highest world singles rank, No. 12, 2003. Career: won 6 pro titles in singles, 1 in doubles, $4,003,561.

MATSUOKA, Shuzo—Best Japanese male of "Open" era, highest rank No. 46, July 1992. His suffering at U.S. Open, 1st rd., 1995, vs. Petr Korda (CZE), led to change of very old rule regarding cramping, considered "loss of condition," that prohibited aid to a stricken player. As the fallen Matsuoka writhed in obvious pain on court, concerned spectators and officials worried that he might be seriously injured. But no one could help until he was counted out for delay, 10 minutes, and Korda awarded the decision, 7-6 (7-4), 6-7 (4-7), 6-7 (8-10), 6-5, default. Now a similarly wounded player may be assisted by a trainer. b. Tokyo, Japan November 6, 1967. RH 6 ft 1, 176 lbs. Turned pro 1986. Davis Cup 1987-97; 21-10 singles; 2-3 doubles. Career—won 1 singles title (Seoul, 1992), 1 doubles title, $1,117,112 prize money, made Wimbledon QF, 1995.

MAYER, Sandy & Gene—American brothers, Sandy and Gene Mayer, RH, winners of major doubles, one together, French, 1979, def. Ross Case-Phil Dent (both AUS), 6-4, 6-4, 6-4. First brothers to win major since Bob, Howard Kinsey (USA), U.S., 1924. Also, 1983, 1st brothers to rank together in U.S Top 10 since Nos. 1-6 Bob, George Wrenn, 1896, (Gene higher, 4-8). World Top Fifteen, 1981 (Gene higher, 7-14). Only brothers to make Wimbledon QF Open era. Family pro title total: 25 singles, 40 doubles titles. Stanford grads, All-Americans.

Alexander "Sandy" Mayer—b. April 5, 1952, Flushing, N.Y., sleek 5 ft 10, 155 lb. attacker, excellent volleyer, won NCAA singles, 1973, doubles, 1972, (with Roscoe Tanner), 1973 (with Jim Delaney). Made SF Wimbledon, 1973 (rookie pro beat top seed Ilie Nastase (ROU), 4th rd., huge upset, 6-4, 8-6, 6-8, 6-4); QF, 1978, 83. Won Wimbledon doubles, 1975, with Vitas Gerulaitis (USA), def. Colin Dowdeswell (GBR)-Allan Stone (AUS), 7-5, 8-6, 6-4. Best world rank, No. 14, 1981. Career: won 11 singles (332-184 matches), 24 doubles (291-134 matches) pro titles, $1,057,783 prize money. Rare amateur to win open title, Birmingham (Ala.) over pro Charlie Owens, 1973, 6-4, 7-6.

Eugene Mayer—b. April 11, 1956, New York, slender 6-footer, 150 lbs., unorthodox style: both-handed backhand, forehand. Solid groundstroker, good volleyer. Also won French doubles, 1978, with Hank Pfister (USA), def. Jose Higueras-Manolo Orantes (both ESP), 6-3, 6-2, 6-2. Davis Cup: 1982-83; helped win 1982 Cup (3-1, singles). Made QF Wimbledon, 1980, 82; U.S., 1982, 84. World Top 10: No. 4, 1980 (won 5 titles); No. 7, 1981; No. 8, 1982; No. 10, 1983. Career: won 14 singles (316-156 matches), 15 doubles (166-89 matches) pro titles, $1,382,422 prize money.

McATEER, Myrtle—Myrtle McAteer from Pittsburgh was in 6 U.S. women's F, won singles, 1900, def. Edith Parker (USA), 6-2, 6-2, 6-0. Won doubles, 1899, with Jane Craven (USA), 1901, with

Juliette Atkinson (USA). Lost F doubles, 1900, with Marie Wiemer (USA) mixed 1901, with Clyde Stevens. After losing singles title, 1901, 6-4, 3-6, 7-5, 2-6, 6-2, to Bessie Moore (USA), didn't play again. No details known on b. or d. U.S. singles record (5-1).

McGRATH, Viv—Vivian "Viv" McGrath, pronounced "McGraw," Australian original: RH, introduced both-handed backhand to international game (although at Wimbledon, 1911, a native, Harold Bache, used two hands on his backhand in a 1st rd. loss). McGrath's was considered strongest pre-war shot among Aussies. b. Feb. 17, 1916, Mudgee, d. 1978, Buradee. Called "Wonder Boy" at 16, d. world No. 1 Ellsworth Vines (USA), QF, Australian, 1933, 6-3, 2-6, 8-6, 7-5. Won homeland title, 1937, beat another rising double-hander, John Bromwich, 6-3, 1-6, 6-0, 2-6, 6-1. Won Australian doubles, 1935, with Jack Crawford (AUS), def. Fred Perry-Pat Hughes (both GBR), 6-4, 8-6, 6-2 Made SF, Australian, 1934-35, 39-40; QF Australian, 1932, 36, 38; Wimbledon, 1935, 37. Davis Cup, 1933-37 (youngest Aussie, 17), 11-12 singles, 1-2 doubles (4-4 singles, 1933, as team lost European Zone F, 3-2, at Britain, eventual Cup winner). World Top 10: No. 8, 1935; No. 10, 1936. Unable to regain form after army service, World War II.

McENROE, Patrick—A man about many prominent duties, Patrick William McEnroe has won a major title (French doubles, 1989, with Jim Grabb), played Davis Cup for the U.S. (3-1 doubles), later captained the team that busted a 12-year drought, winning the 2007 Cup, his 7th season. Graduate Stanford ('88), All-American. Perceptive TV tennis commentator, named in 2008 to head USTA high performance talent development. b. July 1, 1966, Manhasset, N.Y., RH (2-handed backhand), 5-11 ¾, 170 pounds. (Older brother, John McEnroe, member Hall of Fame. Patrick lost 3 matches to John, 1 F, Chicago, 1991, 3-6, 6-2, 6-4. They won 2 doubles titles together, Richmond, 1984; Paris Indoor, 1992.) Made SF Australian, 1991; QF U.S., 1995. Won one singles title (141-163 matches), 16 doubles titles (310-182 matches) and $3,118,316 prize money. Highest world ranking, No. 28, 1995. Wife, Melissa Errico, a singer and broadway actress.

MECIR, Miloslav—Slovak RH (2-handed backhand) Miloslav "Gattone" Mecir (Big Cat), 6 ft 3, 180 lbs, was a top Czech player, 1985-89. Quick, clever, deceptively mixed speeds, spins, angles. Took Olympic gold, singles, 1988, def. Tim Mayotte (USA), 3-6, 6-2, 6-4, 6-2. Davis Cup: 1983-89, 18-8 singles, 5-1 doubles. Lost 2 Major singles F, both to Ivan Lendl (CZE)—U.S., 1986, 6-4, 6-2, 6-0; Australian, 1989, 6-2, 6-2, 6-2. Made SF French, 1987; Wimbledon, 1988; QF Australian, 1987; U.S., 1987; Turned pro 1982. b. May 19, 1964, Bojnice, Czechoslovakia, career ended 1991 by back problems. Career: won 10 singles titles (262—122 matches), 9 doubles titles (100—53 matches), $2,632,538 prize money.

METREVELI, Alexander—Foremost Soviet man, Alex Metreveli gained prominence in the Open era, beating Pancho Gonzalez (USA), Wimbledon, 1968, 4-6, 6-4, 6-3, 7-5. Georgian RH, b. Feb. 11, 1944, Tblisi. Atypical Soviet, serve-and-volleyer, poised 5 ft 10. Only USSR male in major F, until Russian Yevgeny Kafelnikov (French 1996, Australian, 1999) Lost Wimbledon F 1973, to Jan

Kodes (CZE), 6-1, 9-8 (7-5), 6-3. Also, with Olga Morozova (USSR), lost F Wimbledon mixed, 1968, 70. In career overlapping amateur, open eras, made SF Australian, 1972; French, 1972; QF Australian, 1973, 75; French, 1966; Wimbledon, 1972, 74; U.S., 1974. Davis Cup standout, 14 years, 38 ties, spanning 1963-1980, one of select few to play 100 matches or more (56-14, singles; 24-11, doubles). Best world rank, No. 13, 1974. Won 8 singles, 2 doubles pro titles, 15 amateur singles titles.

MIRNYI, Max—Maxim Nikolaevich Mirnyi was called "Beast of Belarus," 6 ft 5, 205 lbs. Max, assault-minded serve-and-volleyer, his country's all-time best. Davis Cup stalwart. Foremost success at doubles, played 14 major doubles F, won 8 titles: 2 French, 2005, with Jonas Bjorkman (SWE), def. Bob-Mike Bryan (USA), 2-6, 6-1, 6-4; 2006, with Bjorkman, def. Bryans, 6-7 (5-7), 6-4, 7-5; 2 U.S., 2000, with Lleyton Hewitt (AUS), def. Ellis Ferreira (RSA)-Rick Leach (USA), 6-4, 5-7, 7-6 (7-5); 2002, with Mahesh Bhupathi (IND), def. Jiri Novak-Radek Stepanek (both CZE), 6-3, 3-6, 6-4. Also won 3 mixed: 2 U.S., 1998 with Serena Williams, def. Lisa Raymond-Pat Galbraith (both USA), 6-2, 6-2; 2007, with Victoria Azarenka (BLR) def. Meghann Shaughnessy (USA)-Leander Paes (IND), 6-4, 7-6 (8-6); Wimbledon, 1998, with S. Williams, def. Mirjana Lucic (CRO)-Mahesh Bhupathi (IND), 6-4, 6-4. Won Masters doubles, 2006, with Bjorkman, def. Mark Knowles (BAH)-Nestor, 6-2, 6-4. b. Minsk, Belarus, July 6, 1977, moved to Florida, 1992. RH, made QF U.S., 2002. Highest world singles rank, No. 18 Aug 2003, 23 at end 2003. Davis Cup, 14 years, 24-16 singles, 21-9 doubles, led Belarus to SF, 2004, including win over Russia, earning him presidential citation. Career as of March 2008: won 1 singles (239-240 matches), 36 doubles (431-203 matches) pro titles, $8,302,165 prize money.

MIRZA, Sania—Best female emerging from India where such pros are rare. (Trailblazer was Nirupalma Vaidyanathan) b. Nov. 15, 1986, Mumbai, India, resides Hyderabad. Turned pro, 2003. RH (2-handed backhand), 5 ft 8, 127 lbs. Strong forehand, Newcomer of Year, 2006, ranking No. 31. First Indian woman to win pro title, Hyderabad, 2005, def. Alona Bondarenko (UKR), 6-4, 5-7, 6-3. Entering 2008: Won 1 singles, 8 doubles pro titles, $1,437,814 prize money.

MOLESWORTH, Mall—Margaret Mutch "Mall" Molesworth, 1st Australian women's champ, 1922, def. Esna Boyd (AUS), 6-3, 10-8; repeated over Boyd, 1923, 6-1, 7-5. RH, b. 1894, Brisbane; d. July 9, 1985. Might have exceeded 2 singles, 3 doubles titles, 1930, 33-34, with Emily Hood Westacott (AUS), had Championships welcomed women prior to 1922. Won 1st title at 27, with complete game, feared serve. Lost doubles F, 1923, with H. Turner (AUS), Remained factor for some time, made QF 1924, 28-29, 33. Lost singles F, age 40, 1934 to Joan Hartigan (AUS), 6-1, 6-4. Won 29 other singles titles throughout the country, the last in 1935, age 41; also 16 other doubles and 9 mixed. World Top Ten: No. 10, 1922-23; a first for Aussie women.

MOON, Gar—"New star is born—it's a Moon!" declared an Aussie newspaper when Edgar Moon, Queensland RH, beat 1922 Wimbledon champ, 2nd seed Gerald Patterson (AUS), 1st rd. Aus-

tralian, 1926, 6-8, 5-7, 7-5, 6-4, 6-3. He won title, 1930, def. 1st seed Harry Hopman (AUS), 6-3, 6-1, 6-3; def. future champ Jack Crawford (AUS), SF, 7-5, 6-4, 4-6, 6-3. Won Aussie doubles with Crawford, 1932, def. Hopman-Patterson, 12-10, 6-3, 4-6, 6-4. Strong groundies, all-round game. Davis Cup, 1930, 4-0 in singles. b. Dec. 3, 1904, Forest Hill, Australia, d. May 26, 1976.

MOROZOVA, Olga—Pre-eminent Soviet woman, Olga Morozova, RH, b. Feb. 22, 1949, Moscow. Unusual Soviet, preferred serve-and-volley. "Olga the Volga Volleyer." Quick, athletic, 5 ft 7, 132 lbs. Played 8 major F, won 1. Lost 2 major singles F—1974, French, Wimbledon. Only USSR female in Wimbledon singles F, lost to Chris Evert (USA), 6-0, 6-4, beat defender Billie Jean King (USA), QF, 7-5, 6-2. Also lost French F to Evert, 6-1, 6-2. Won French doubles, 1974, with Evert, def. Gail Sherriff (AUS)-Katja Ebbinghaus (GER), 6-4, 2-6, 6-1. Lost 5 other doubles majors—Australian, 1975, with Margaret Smith Court (AUS); French, 1975, with Julie Anthony (USA); U.S., 1976, with Virginia Wade (GBR); Wimbledon mixed, 1968, 70, with Alex Metreveli (USSR). Made SF French, 1975; QF Australian, 1972, 75; French, 1972; Wimbledon, 1973, 75-76; U.S., 1972. Career: won 31 singles, 10 doubles pro titles. World Top 10: No. 10, 1972; No. 8, 1974; No. 7, 1975. First Soviet winner of a U.S. title—Indoor doubles, 1973, with compatriot Marina Kroshina, def. Evonne Goolagong-Janet Young (both AUS), 6-2, 6-4. Federation Cup, 1968, 1978–80, 8-3 singles, 4-1 doubles.

MOTTRAM, Tony, Joy, Buster & Linda—Internationalist English family. Father, Tony; mother, Joy; son, Buster; daughter, Linda. All RH.

Anthony John Mottram—b. June 8, 1920, Coventry. Davis Cup: 1947–1955, 25-13 singles, 11-7 doubles. Made QF Wimbledon 1948; lost doubles F with Bill Sidwell (AUS), 1947, to Jack Kramer-Bob Falkenburg (both USA), 8-6, 6-3, 6-3. Best Brit immediate post-war.

Joy Gannon Mottram—b. March 21, 1928, Enfield. Wightman Cup: 1947-52, 0-1 singles, 0-3 doubles. Won German, 1954. Made Wimbledon 3rd rd., 1946- 47, 49; QF French, 1952.

Christopher John "Buster" Mottram—b. April 25, 1955, Kingston, lanky 6 ft 3, free-swinging big hitter. Made Wimbledon 4th rd., 1982; French 4th rd. 1977. Davis Cup: 1975-83; 27-8 singles, 4-2 doubles (high point, 1978, led Britain to first Davis Cup finale since 1937, 8-2 singles, 1-0 doubles, def. Brian Gottfried, 4-6, 2-6, 10-8, 6-4, 6-3, for lone Brit point in F vs. USA). Career: won 2 singles, (276-176 matches) 5 doubles (120-139) pro titles, about $500,000 prize money. Best world rank, No. 19, 1982, No. 15, Feb. 1983.

Linda Mottram—b. May 17, 1957, Wimbledon. Played Wimbledon 6 straight years from 1974, made 3rd rd., 1975. Won German Indoor, 1976.

MOYA, Carlos—Powerful groundstroking Spaniard (6 ft 3, 185 lbs) Carlos "Charlie" Moya won French 1998, beat compatriot

Alex Corretja, 6-3, 7-5, 6-3. Held No. 1 ranking 2 weeks, 1999. RH (2-handed backhand). Turned pro 1995. Lost 1 major F—Australian, 1997, to Pete Sampras (USA), 6-2, 6-3, 6-3, unseeded beat defender Boris Becker (GER), 1st rd., 5-7, 7-6 (7-4), 3-6, 6-1, 6-4. Lost F Masters, 1998, to Corretja, 3-6, 3-6, 7-5, 6-3, 7-5. Made SF U.S., 1998; QF Australian, 2001; French, 2003, 07; U.S., 2007. As of June, 2009, won 20 singles (573-314 in pro matches) pro titles, $13,382,822 prize money. Davis Cup 7 years from 1996, 20-7 singles. High point—def. Andy Roddick (USA), 6-2, 7-6 (7-1), 7-6, Cup decider, 2004. Also won only point in 3-1 F defeat by Australia, 2003, def. Mark Philippoussis, 6-4, 6-4, 4-6, 7-6 (7-4). World Top 10: No. 7, 1997; No. 6, 1998, No. 5, 2002. b. Aug, 27, 1976, Palma de Mallorca, Spain.

MUSTER, Thomas—Muscular "Moo Man," bellowing bovine noises as he belted at the baseline, Austrian Thomas Muster, 5 ft 11, 165 lbs., LH, seemed indestructible in body and spirit. Sovereign of the soil, strongman of the '90s on clay. Won French singles, 1995, def. Michael Chang (USA), 7-5, 6-2, 6-4. Won 3 Italian—1990, def. Andrei Chesnokov (RUS), 6-1, 6-3, 6-1; 1995, def. Sergi Bruguera (ESP), 3-6, 7-6 (7-5), 6-2, 6-3; 1996, def. Richard Krajicek (NED), 6-2, 6-4, 3-6, 6-3. Astoundingly rehabbed left knee, wrecked in 1989 auto accident, reappearing as a winner in 1990, racking up 37 of 42 career singles titles, 1990-96. Huge year, 1995: won 12 titles on 86-18 (40 straight on clay), saved MP points in 5 wins (def. Boris Becker (GER), 4-6, 5-7, 6-1, 7-6, 6-0, Monte Carlo F, from 2 MP down). On dirt won 44 titles of 55 F, 422-126 matches (.770). World Top 10 for 5 years: No. 7, 1990; No, 9, 1993, 97; No. 3, 1995; No. 5, 1996 (No. 1 for 6 weeks during 1996). Davis Cup: 1984-96; 33-7 singles, 9-9 doubles, nearly beat U.S. single-handed, 1990 SF (3-2), def. Chang, 4-6, 6-2, 6-2, 6-4; Andre Agassi, 6-2, 6-2, 7-6 (7-2). Made SF Australian, 1989; French, 1990; QF Australian, 1994; French, 1998; U.S., 1994-95, 97. Career: won 44 singles (622-271 matches), 1 doubles pro titles, $12,224,410 prize money. b. Oct. 2, 1967, Liebnitz, Austria.

MYSKINA, Anastasia—Slim, slight but quick, clever, determined. Came out of 1st all-Russian major F as 1st of her country to win female major, 2004 French, def. Elena Dementieva, 6-1, 6-2, having def. Venus Williams (USA), 6-3, 6-4, QF, 2001 champ Jennifer Capriati (USA), 6-2, 6-2, SF. b. Moscow, June 8, 1981, RH (2-handed backhand), 5 ft 8, 129 lbs. Turned pro 1999. World Top 10: No. 3, 2004, No. 7, 2003. Career: won 10 singles (355-191 matches), 5 doubles pro titles, $5,606,725 prize money. Made QF Australian, 2003-04, Wimbledon, 2005-06, U.S., 2003. Federation Cup 5 years, 14-5 singles, 4-1 doubles. Helped Russia win 2004-05 Cups over France. Won both singles 2004 F, then decisive doubles with Vera Zvonareva def. Marion Bartoli-Emilie Loit, 7-6 (7-5), 7-5, for 3-2 victory. Finished 4th at 2004 Olympic singles, blowing 5-1 third set lead to gold medalist Justine Henin-Hardenne (BEL) in SF (7-5, 5-7, 8-6), losing bronze to Alicia Molik (AUS) 6-3, 6-4.

O'HARA WOOD, Arthur & Pat—Australian brothers, Arthur and Pat O'Hara Wood, RH, both winners Australian singles title, only brothers to do so. First brothers to win majors since English Wimbledon champs Dohertys, Laurie (1902-03-04-05-06), Reggie (1897-98-99-00).

Dr. Arthur Holroyd O'Hara Wood—b. 1890, Melbourne, d. Oct. 4 or 6, 1918, with Royal Air Force, World War I, shot down over St. Quentin, France. Melbourne physician with all-round game, beat future Hall of Famer Gerald Patterson (AUS) 1914 F, 6-4, 6-3, 5-7, 6-1, then went to war.

Patrick O'Hara Wood—Patrick O'Hara Wood also served militarily, Aussie army. Survived to accumulate 8 major titles, winning Australian singles twice—1920, def. Ron Thomas (AUS), 6-3, 4-6, 6-8, 6-1, 6-3; 1923, def. Bert St. John (AUS), 6-1, 6-1, 6-3. Also won 4 Aussie doubles—1919-20, with Thomas; 1923, with St. John; 1925, with Patterson. Won Wimbledon doubles, 1919, with Thomas; mixed, 1922, with Suzanne Lenglen (FRA). Short, quick, consistent, effortless strokemaker. Davis Cup: 1922, 1924; 9-5 singles, 8-1 doubles, helped Australia gain F both years. b. April 30, 1891. Melbourne; d. there, Dec. 3, 1961. World Top 10: No. 7, 1922. Wife, Meryl Waxman Lister O'Hara Wood, won Australian doubles, 1926, with Esna Boyd (AUS), 1927, with Louie Bickerton (AUS). Lost F, 1924, with Kathrine LeMesurier, 1929, with Sylvia Lance Harper. Also lost 1932 mixed F, with Jiroh Sato (JPN).

OKKER, Tom—Flying Dutchman Tom Samuel Okker, Netherlands' finest male before Wimbledon champ Richard Krajicek. RH, b. Feb. 22, 1944, Amsterdam. Slight (5 ft 10, 145 lbs), speedy, excellent volleyer, one of 5 men to win more than 100 pro titles (31 singles, 78 doubles). Lost F first U.S. Open, 1968, to amateur Arthur Ashe (USA), 14-12, 5-7, 6-3, 3-6, 6-3, taking $14,000 first prize. Made SF all majors: Australian, U.S., 1971; French, 1969; Wimbledon, 1978. Made doubles F all majors—Australian, 1971; Wimbledon, 1969; U.S., 1975. Won French, 1973, with John Newcombe (AUS), def. Jimmy Connors (USA)-Ilie Nastase (ROM), 6-1, 3-6, 6-3, 5-7, 6-4; U.S., 1976, with Marty Riessen (USA), def. Paul Kronk-Cliff Letcher (both AUS), 6-4, 6-4. World Top 10 for 6 years: No. 5, 1968-69; No. 6, 1970; No. 8, 1971-72; No. 7, 1973. Davis Cup: 1964–81, 10-13 singles, 5-7 doubles. Career: won 31 singles (520-216 matches), 78 doubles (550-152 matches) pro titles, $1,257,200 prize money.

O'NEIL, Chris—Tall Aussie, 6-footer Christine Merle O'Neil, RH, was longest shot to win women's major, Australian, 1978. Unseeded, ranked No. 111, she went through weak field, def. No. 68 Betsy Nagelsen (USA), F, 6-3, 7-6 (7-4) on Melbourne grass, winning $6,000, only pro title. b. March 19, 1956, Newcastle, serve-and-volleyer. Highest world rank, No. 80, 1978.

ORANTES, Manolo—Manuel "Manolo" Orantes, stocky, prestidigitating, gracious Spanish LH, master of spin, touch, placement. Won U.S., 1975, sensationally—in succession beat ex-champ, Ilie Nastase (ROM), 6-2, 6-4, 3-6, 6-3; 2nd seed Guillermo Vilas (ARG), defender Jimmy Connors, 6-4, 6-3, 6-3. Great SF comeback over Vilas, 4-6, 1-6, 6-2, 7-5, 6-4—4th set from 0-5, 3 MP, then 5-1, 2 MP. Lost F French, 1974, to Bjorn Borg (SWE), 2-6, 6-7 (1-7), 6-0, 6-1, 6-1; Italian, 1973, to Nastase, 6-1, 6-1, 6-1, tourney's worst F defeat. Won Masters, 1976, def. Wojtek Fibak (POL), 5-7, 6-2, 0-6, 7-6 (7-1), 6-1. Also won U.S. Pro, 1977, def. Eddie Dibbs (USA), 7-6 (7-3), 7-5, 6-4; 1978, def. Harold Solomon (USA), 6-4, 6-3. World Top 10: No. 5, 1975; No. 4, 1976; No. 7, 1977. Made SF French, 1972; QF French,

1976, 78; U.S., 1976-77. b. Feb. 6, 1949, Granada. Davis Cup: 1967-80; 39-19 singles. 21-8 doubles, helped Spain to finale, 1967. Career: 16 years, spanned amateur, open eras, won 32 singles (647-247 matches), 24 doubles (298-155 matches) pro titles, $1,398,303 prize money. Also won 7 amateur singles.

THE ORIGINALS
Suzanne Lenglen (FRA), Mary K. Browne (USA), Vinnie Richards (USA), Howard Kinsey (USA), Paul Feret (FRA), Harvey Snodgrass (USA)—Although coaches and teaching pros had played infrequent tournaments for insignificant payments, the six Originals, fleeing amateurism, were the initial touring pros, ancestors of today's ATP and WTA circuiteers. Assembled by 43-year-old American sports promoter Charles C. "Cash-and-Carry" Pyle in 1926, they traveled by train, playing 40 dates between Oct. 9, 1926 and Feb. 14, 1927, across the U.S., into Canada and (by boat) to Cuba. Leading attraction was the luminous, unbeatable 6-time Wimbledon champ Lenglen. She made $100,000, a fortune at the time, and the others did very well: top American Richards and ex-U.S. champ Browne $35,000 apiece, Kinsey $20,000, Snodgrass $12,000, Feret $10,000. It was a promotional success, Pyle making somewhere between $50,000 and $75,000. But once was enough for him, unable to lure Bill Tilden and Helen Wills away from amateurism.

Suzanne Rachel Flore Lenglen—Was 36-0 over Browne on Originals tour. *(See Hall of Fame section for complete bio)*

Vincent Richards—Was 29-1 singles on Originals tour. *(see Hall of Fame section for complete bio)*

Mary K. Browne—(See Hall of Fame section for complete bio)

Paul Feret—b. Feb. 27, 1901, Paris, d. Feb. 3, 1984, Paris. Davis Cup for France, 1925, 2-0 singles. Made QF French, 1925. Was French No. 4 when turned pro, 3-13 singles on Originals tour. Reinstated as amateur, 1929.

Howard Oreon Kinsey—b. Dec. 3, 1899, St. Louis, Mo., raised in San Francisco, d. July 26, 1966, San Francisco. RH, 5 ft 7, 145 lbs. Baseliner, with variety of off-speed shots, clever lobs. World Top 10—No. 7, 1924; No. 9, 1926. U.S. Top 10—No. 4, 1924; No. 6, 1925. Had rare "cripple" at Wimbledon, lost all 3 F, 1926. Was 3-11 singles on Originals tour. Won 2 major titles—French doubles, 1926, with Vinnie Richards, def. Henri Cochet-Jacques Brugnon (both FRA), 6-4, 6-1, 4-6, 6-4; U.S. doubles, 1924, with brother, Robert Kinsey (USA) def. Gerald Patterson-Pat O'Hara Wood (both AUS), 7-5, 5-7, 7-9, 6-3, 6-4. Lost 3 major F—Wimbledon singles, 1926, to Jean Borotra (FRA), 8-6, 6-1, 6-3 (after saving 5 MP to def. Brugnon (FRA), SF, 6-4, 4-6, 6-3, 3-6, 9-7); Wimbledon doubles, 1926, with Richards, to Brugnon-Cochet, 7-5, 4-6, 6-3, 6-2; Wimbledon mixed, 1926, with Mary K. Browne, to Kitty McKane Godfree-Leslie Godfree (both GBR), husband-wife, 6-3, 6-4. With brother, Robert, won 2 U.S. Clay Court doubles, 1923, def. John Hennessey-Walter Wesbrook (both USA), 6-4, 13-11, 6-3; 1924 def. Bill Tilden-Sandy Wiener (both USA), 6-4, 7-5, 6-2. Made French

QF, 1926; U.S., 1924-25; also QF French mixed with Elizabeth Ryan (USA). Lost F first U.S. Pro Championship, 1927, to Richards, 11-9, 6-4, 6-3.

Snodgrass, Harvey—b. April 29, 1896, Los Angeles, Calif., raised there, d. California, April, 1983. RH. 5 ft 10, 147 lbs., U.S. Top 10—No. 6, 1924; No. 9, 1923. Usually attacker, fine volleyer. Was 4-13 singles on Originals tour. Lost F U.S. Clay Court, 1924, to Bill Tilden (USA), 6-2, 6-1, 6-1. Won U.S. Clay Court doubles, 1925, with Walter Wesbrook (USA), def. Tilden-A.L. "Sandy" Wiener (USA), 6-1, 6-2, 6-1.

Charles C. Pyle—d. 1939, age 56.

PAES, Leander—Quick, clever, excels in doubles, one of India's foremost Davis Cuppers, won singles Olympic bronze, 1996. b. Calcutta, June 17, 1973. RH, 5 ft 10, 170 lbs. Olympic bloodline, father, Vece Paes, field hockey, mother, Jennifer Paes, basketball for India, 1972. Says he "was conceived at that Olympics." Turned pro 1991. Entering 2008, won 1 singles (Newport), 41 doubles (518-269 matches) pro titles, $$5,251,215 prize money. Highest world singles ranking, No. 73, Aug 1998. Played 17 major doubles F, won 9 titles: 3 French, 1999, with Mahesh Bhupathi (IND), def. Goran Ivanisevic (CRO)-Jeff Tarango (USA), 6-2, 7-5; 2001, with Bhupathi def. Petr Pala-Pavel Vizner (both CZE), 7-6 (7-5), 6-3 as well as 2009 with Lukas Dlouhy (CZE) def. Wesley Moodie (RSA)-Dick Norman (BEL) 3-6, 6-3, 6-2; Wimbledon, 1999, with Bhupathi, def. Paul Haarhuis (NED)-Jared Palmer (USA), 6-7 (10-12), 6-3, 6-4, 7-6 (7-4); U.S. 2006 with Martin Damm (CZE) def. Jonas Bjorkman (SWE)-Max Mirnyi (BLR), 6-7 (5-7), 6-4, 6-3. Also 4 mixed: Australian, 2003, with Martina Navratilova (USA) def. Eleni Daniilidou (GRE)-Todd Woodbridge (AUS), 6-4, 7-5; 2 Wimbledon, 2003, with Navratilova, def. Anastassia Rodionova (RUS)-Andy Ram (ISR), 6-3, 6-3; 1999 with Lisa Raymond (USA) def. Anna Kournikova (RUS)-Bjorkman, 6-4, 3-6, 6-3. 2008 U.S .Open with Cara Black (ZIM) def. Liezel Huber (USA)-Jaime Murray (GBR) 7-6, 6-4. Davis Cup—19 years, 45 ties, 48-22 singles, 36-9 doubles. Awarded the Padma Shri, India's highest honor, 2001.

PAILS, Dinny—First of Aussie post-war-developed champs, RH Denis Robert Pails, b. March 4, 1921, Nottingham, England. Won Australian singles, 1947, def. John Bromwich (AUS), 4-6, 6-4, 3-6, 7-5, 8-6. 1947. Lost F, 1946, to Bromwich, 5-7, 6-3, 7-5, 3-6, 6-2. Made SF Wimbledon, 1947; QF Australian, 1940; Wimbledon, 1946. Davis Cup: 1946-47; 3-5 singles. Turned pro, 1947. World No. 6, 1947.

PALFREY, Polly, Lee, Sarah, Mianne & Joey—Five remarkable Bostonians, Palfrey sisters—Joey, Lee, Mianne, Polly, Sarah—all won U.S. junior titles. As adult Sarah won 18 majors (2 U.S. singles), made Hall of Fame. All RH, b. Boston, except Sarah, b. Sharon, Mass.

Margaret Germaine "Polly" Palfrey Woodrow—b. Oct. 7, 1906. Won 1 junior: 18 doubles, 1924, with Fanny Curtis.

Elizabeth Howland "Lee" Palfrey Fullerton—b. Jan. 14, 1909; d. Jan. 5, 1987. Won 1 junior: 18 Indoor doubles, 1926, with Midge Morrill.

Sarah Hammond Palfrey Fabyan Cooke Danzig—b. Sept. 18, 1912, d. Feb. 27, 1996, New York. Won 13 juniors: 18 singles, 1928-29-1930; 18 doubles, 1926, 28-29, with Mianne; 18 Indoor singles, 1927-28, 30; 18 Indoor doubles, 1927-28-29, with Mianne, 1930, with Joey. *See full biography in Hall of Fame Section.*

Mary Ann "Mianne" Palfrey Dexter—b. March 6, 1911, d. Nov. 2, 1993. Won 7 juniors: 18 Indoor singles, 1929; 18 doubles, 1926, 28-29, with Sarah; 18 Indoor doubles, 1927-28-29, with Sarah. Also won adult U.S. Indoor singles, 1930, def. Marion Zinderstein Jessup (USA), 7-5, 6-2.

Joanna "Joey" Oakes Palfrey Brown—b. Jan. 30, 1915, d. Jan. 25, 2002. Won 1 junior; 18 Indoor doubles, 1930, with Sarah.

PANATTA, Adriano—Best Italian in Open era, Adriano Panatta, RH, b. July 9, 1950, Rome. Slick 6 ft god at Il Foro Italico, Rome, responding winningly to feverish chants, "AD-REE-ANNO!" Strong serve, whipping forehand, called "Portiere" (Goaltender) for brilliant volleying saves. Spectacular 1976 (45-15 matches)—Won French singles, def. Harold Solomon (USA), 6-1, 6-4, 4-6, 7-6 (7-3). Won Italian singles, def. Guillermo Vilas (ARG), 2-6, 7-6 (7-5), 6-2, 7-6 (7-1). Lost Italian F, 1978, to Bjorn Borg (SWE) 1-6, 6-3, 6-1, 4-6, 6-3, a tumultuous verbal and tossed-coins assault on Borg. Led Italy to lone Davis Cup, def. Chile, 5-0 (10-1 singles; 5-1 doubles). Also to F, 1977, 79-80. Cup record, 1970–83, 38 ties, 37-26 singles; 27-10 doubles; one of 14 to play 100 matches. MP escapes in big titles, 1976: French, 1 MP, def. Pavel Hutka (CZE), 1st rd., 2-6, 6-2, 6-2, 0-6, 12-10; Italian, 11 MP, def. Kim Warwick (AUS), 1st rd. 3-6, 6-4, 7-6. Best world rank, No. 4 in Aug 1976, 7 at end of 1976. Career: won 10 singles (364-223 matches), 18 doubles (233-152 matches) pro titles, $776,187 prize money. Younger brother, Claudio Panatta (b. Feb. 2, 1960, Rome) played Davis Cup, pro tour.

PARKE, Jim—Sturdy, speedy Irish RH James Cecil Parke, the man of 1912 Australian season. Won singles title, beat Brit teammate Alfred Beamish, 3-6, 6-3, 1-6, 6-1, 7-5. Backboned Davis Cup upset to lift the Cup for Britain, 3-2, stunning Norman Brookes, 8-6, 6-3, 5-7, 6-2, and, clinching, d. Rod Heath, 6-2, 6-4, 6-4. Lost Cup in 1913 F, 3-2, but beat both U.S. starters, Maurice McLoughlin, 8-10, 7-5, 6-4, 1-6, 7-5; Dick Williams, 6-2, 5-7, 5-7, 6-4, 6-2. Made Wimbledon SF 1910; QF 1913-14. World Top 10: No. 4, 1913; No. 6, 1914. Davis Cup: 1908-13, 8-7 singles, 0-5 doubles Also rugby international for Ireland, 1913-18. b. July 26, 1881, Clones County, Ireland, d. Feb.27, 1946, Llandudno, Wales.

PARKER, Ernest—Three champions of Australia were killed in World War I. Two of them met for the 1909 title, Ernest Frederick Parker, a Perth attorney, lost to New Zealander Tony Wilding, 6-1, 7-5, 6-2. But four years later Ernest Parker, 30, beat another New Zealander, 40-yearold Harry Parker (no relation) for the title, 2-6, 6-1, 6-3, 6-2. As he had in 1909, with J.P. Keane, Ernest also won

the doubles, with Alf Hedemann (AUS). Almost five years after that, an artilleryman in the Australian army, Ernest was killed by an enemy shell in France, May 3, 1918. b. Nov. 5, 1883, Perth, he was outstanding, too, at cricket and golf, though slightly built. Ironically turned down twice by the army for weak eyesight, he was finally allowed to join. He played the Championships only twice.

PASARELL, Charlie—World class player who became world class promoter, Charles Manuel Pasarell, Jr., All-American at UCLA, helped U.S. win Davis Cup, 1968, and made life better for players and fans in operating tournaments in the Palm Springs area since 1981. He, a tennis statesman, abetted by close friend-partner, Ray Moore (ex-South African Davis Cupper), was driving force in building Indian Wells Tennis Garden with a 16,100-seat stadium in 2000, the stunning California desert home of one of world's foremost tournaments. A fortnight bash for men and women. b. Feb 12, 1944, San Juan, Puerto Rico, grew up Santurce, P.R. Staunch serve-volleyer, 6 ft 1 ½, 171 lbs. No. 1 U.S., 1967; No. 5, 1965, 69; No. 4, 1966; No. 7, 1968; No. 10, 1970. Won 2 U.S. Indoor, 1966, def. Ron Holmberg (USA), 12-10, 10-8, 8-6; 1967, def. college roommate Arthur Ashe (USA), 13-11, 6-2, 2-6, 9-7 (they won the doubles). Won NCAA, 1966, def. Stan Smith (U. Southern Cal), 6-4, 3-6, 2-6, 6-3, 6-1, (won doubles with Ian Crookenden). Most celebrated matches, Wimbledon—1969, a defeat, by Pancho Gonzalez (USA), 5 hours 12 minutes over 2 days, 22-24, 1-6, 16-14, 6-3, 11-9, had 7 MP; 1967, a win, Pasarell scored an historic first, sabotaging 1st seeded defending champion, No. 1 seed Manolo Santana (ESP), in the opening round, 10-8, 6-3, 2-6, 8-6.

PENROSE, Beryl—Made brief mark, 1955. Won Australian, upset 1st seed Thelma Long (AUS), 6-4, 6-3. Also won German title. Made QF French, Wimbledon, ranked world No. 8. Tall, slender RH, b. 1930, Sydney.

PETRA, Yvon—Yvon Francois Marie Petra, French RH, at 6 ft 5, tallest winner major singles, Wimbledon, 1946, until 6-5 Goran Ivanisevic (CRO) won same title, 2001. A surprise, needing 27 sets, Petra, seeded 5th, def. 1st Dinny Pails (AUS), QF, 7-5, 7-5, 6-8, 6-4; Tom Brown (USA), SF, 4-6, 4-6, 6-3, 7-5, 8-6; 3rd Geoff Brown, (AUS), F, 6-2, 6-4, 7-9, 5-7, 6-4 b. March 8, 1916, Cholon, Indochina (now Vietnam), d. Sept. 12, 1984, Paris. Won 2 French doubles titles—1938, with Bernard Destremau (FRA), d. Don Budge-Gene Mako (both USA), 3-6, 6-3, 9-7, 6-1; 1946, with Marcel Bernard (FRA), d. Pancho Segura (ECU)-Enrique Morea (ARG), 7-5, 6-3, 0-6, 1-6, 10-8. Made SF French, 1946; QF 1937, 47. Davis Cup, 1937-39, 1946-47; 11-3 singles, 4-4 doubles, led France to SF, 1946. Vet French army, wounded, POW in World War II. Turned pro, 1948. Strong server, last man to win a major, Wimbledon, in long trousers. Highest world rank, No. 4, 1946.

PIERCE, Mary—Riding a dynamite forehand, 5 ft 11 Mary Caroline Pierce, Franco-American RH (2-handed backhand) powered her way to 2 major titles—Australian, 1995, def. Arantxa Sanchez Vicario (ESP), 6-3, 6-2; French, 2000, def. Conchita Martinez (ESP), 6-2, 7-5. First French woman to win since Francoise

Durr, 1967. Lost 4 major singles F—Australian, 1997, to Martina Hingis (SUI), 6-2, 6-2; French, 1994, to Sanchez Vicario, 6-4, 6-4 (deposing champ Steffi Graf (GER), SF, 6-2, 6-2); 2005, to Justine Henin (BEL), 6-1, 6-1; U.S., 2005, to Kim Clijsters (BEL), 6-3, 6-1. Made QF Australian, 1993, 98-99; French, 2002; Wimbledon, 1996, 2005; U.S., 1994, 99. b. Jan. 15, 1975, Montreal, Canada, reared in Florida, daughter of French mother, U.S. father, she holds 3 passports, and cast her lot with France, with whom she won 1997, 2003 Federation Cups. Turned pro 1989 at 14 years, 2 months, youngest until Jennifer Capriati at 13 years, 11 months in 1990. Junoesque blonde glamorized return of the tennis dress. Coached by overbearing father, Jim Pierce, until she obtained restraining order, 1993 relationship later restored. Career: Won 18 singles (511-237 matches), 10 doubles pro titles, $9,793,119 prize money. World Top 10 for 6 years: No. 5, 1994-95, 99; No. 7, 1997-98, 2000. Federation Cup, 10 years from 1990; 11-8 singles, 2-2 doubles.

PILIC, Nikki—Nikola "Nikki" Pilic, slim 6-3 Croat, LH, from Split, former-Yugoslavia's best of post-war (until another Split lefty, Goran Ivanisevic). Country's first pro athlete, 1968, with WCT "Handsome Eight." Cause of famous Wimbledon boycott, 1973: most ATP colleagues walked out, protesting Wimbledon's honoring his unfair suspension by Yugoslav Federation. Solidarity on Pilic's behalf was key to establishing the year-old union. b. Aug. 27, 1939, Split. Big serve, forehand. Played 2 major F—Unseeded, lost French singles, 1973, to Ilie Nastase (ROM), 6-3, 6-3, 6-0. Won U.S. doubles, 1970, with Pierre Barthes (FRA), def. Roy Emerson-Rod Laver (both AUS), 6-3, 7-6 (5-4), 4-6, 7-6 (5-2). Made SF Wimbledon, 1967; French, 1967; QF U.S., 1973. Best world rank, No. 7, 1967. Davis Cup: 11 years 1961-77, 27-12 singles, 11-12 doubles. Career: won 4 singles, 7 doubles pro titles. Only man to captain teams winning Davis Cup, 2 countries: Germany, 1988-89, 93; Croatia, 2005.

PIM, Joshua—His cup runneth over with 2 Wimbledon singles titles—1893, def. Wilfred Baddeley (GBR), 3-6, 6-3, 6-1, 6-2; 1894, def. W. Baddeley, 10-8, 6-2, 8-6. Got even with Wilfred, who d. him in 2 F—1891, 6-4, 1-6, 7-5, 6-0; 1892, 4-6, 6-3, 6-3, 6-2. Ireland's Dr. Joshua Pim, RH mustachioed physician with daring netside manner, delighted in difficult volleys, flamboyant shotmaking. Also won 2 Wimbledon doubles—1890, 1893, with Frank Stoker (IRL). After that, retirement to medicine, with a brief losing comeback (0-2) in Davis Cup F, Britain losing to U.S., 3-2, Brooklyn, 1902. Also won Irish singles, 1893-94-95; doubles, 1890-91, 93-94-95. b. May 20, 1869, Bray County, Wicklow Ireland, d. April 15, 1942, Dublin.

RAHIM, Haroon—Foremost player of Pakistan, Haroon Rahim, RH, b. Nov. 12, 1949, Lahore, one of 14 children. Quick, fine volleying All-American, NCAA doubles champ, 1971, UCLA, with Jeff Borowiak. For years, youngest ever Davis Cupper, 15 years, 109 days, 1965, against South Vietnam (beat Vo Van Bay, 6-1 in 5th). Several greener lads, all insignificant otherwise, have lowered the mark since 1990, the youngest being Mohammed-Akhtar Hossain, Bangladesh, 13 years-326 days vs. Myanmar, 2003. Haroon beat Tom Gorman (USA) in closest match ever, 6-7

(3-5), 7-6 (5-1), 7-6 (5-4), Pennsylvania Grass, 1970. Career: Won 1 singles, 6 doubles pro titles, Best world rank, No. 49, 1976.

RAMIREZ, Raul—Raul Carlos Ramirez, Mexico's premier player in the Open era, got tennis education in U.S. All-American, U. Southern California. RH, b. June 20, 1953, Ensenada. Quick 6-footer, 175 lbs., improviser fond of attack, splendid volleyer. Combined with Brian Gottfried (USA) as superb doubles team (39 titles). Won 3 majors—French, 1975, def. John Alexander-Phil Dent (both AUS), 6-2, 2-6, 6-2, 6-4; 1977, def. Wojtek Fibak (POL)-Jan Kodes (CZE), 7-6, 4-6, 6-3, 6-4; Wimbledon, 1976, def. Ross Case-Geoff Masters (both AUS), 3-6, 6-3, 8-6, 2-6, 7-5. Lost 4 major doubles F, French, 1976, 80; Wimbledon, 1979; U.S., 1977. Davis Cup: 1971-82; 22-8 singles, 14-5 doubles. Thorn in U.S. side: Won 4 singles, 2 doubles in 2 Cup early rd. wins, 1975-76. In respective decisive matches, def. Roscoe Tanner, 7-5, 7-9, 6-4, 6-2; Jimmy Connors, 2-6, 6-3, 6-3, 6-4. Best day, won Italian singles, 1975—def. defender Bjorn Borg (SWE), QF, 6-4, 6-3; Ilie Nastase (ROU), SF, 6-2, 5-2, default; Manolo Orantes (ESP), F, 7-6, 7-5, 7-5. Then, with Gottfried, won doubles, def. Jimmy Connors (USA)-Nastase, 6-4, 7-6, 2-6, 6-1. Made SF French, 1976-77; Wimbledon 1976 QF French, 1974-75, 78. Wimbledon, 1978; U.S. 1978. World Top 10: No. 4/5, 1976; No. 8. 1977-78. Career: won 17 (517-254 matches) singles, 62 doubles (569-185 matches) pro titles, $2,217,971 prize money.

RAYMOND, Lisa—Uncommon jumper from campus-to-pro triumphs. All-American NCAA singles champ U. Florida, 1992-93, put volleying expertise to use as big doubles winner, singles standout. Named to U. Florida's 50 Greatest Athletes. b. Norristown, Pa., Aug. 10, 1973, raised Wayne, Pa. RH, turned pro 1993, 5 ft 5, 125 lbs. Federation Cup, 7 years, 3-6 singles, 10-3 doubles. Highest world singles rank, No. 17, 1997. Played 13 major doubles F, won 9 titles: Australian, 2000, with Rennae Stubbs (AUS), d. Martina Hingis (SUI)-Mary Pierce (FRA), 6-4, 5-7, 6-4; French, 2006, with Samantha Stosur (AUS), def. Daniela Hantuchova (SVK)-Ai Sugiyama (JPN), 6-3, 6-2; Wimbledon, 2001, with Stubbs, def. Kim Clijsters (BEL)-Sugiyama, 6-4, 6-3; U.S., 2001, with Stubbs, def. Kim Po-Messerli (USA)-Nathalie Tauziat (FRA), 6-2, 5-7, 7-5; 2005, with Stosur, def. Elena Dementieva (RUS)-Flavia Pennetta (ITA), 6-2, 5-7, 6-3. Also won 4 mixed: French, 2003, with Mike Bryan (USA), def. Elena Likhovtseva (RUS)-Mahesh Bhupathi (IND), 6-3, 6-4; Wimbledon, 1999, with Leander Paes (IND), def. Anna Kournikova (RUS)-Jonas Bjorkman (SWE), 6-4, 3-6, 6-3; U.S., 1996, with Pat Galbraith (USA), def. Manon Bollegraf (NED)-Rick Leach (USA), 7-6 (8-6), 7-6 (7-4); 2002, with M. Bryan, def. Katarina Srebotnik (SLO)-Bob Bryan (USA), 7-6 (11-9), 7-6 (7-1). Won 3 WTA Championships doubles—2001, with Stubbs, def. Cara Black (ZIM)-Likhovtseva, 7-5, 3-6, 6-3; 2005, with Stosur, def. Black-Stubbs, 6-7 (5-7), 7-5, 6-4; 2006, with Stosur, def. Black-Stubbs, 3-6, 6-3, 6-3. Fed Cupper for USA 1997-1998, 2000, 2002-2003, 2004, 2007-2008; (14-9, 11-3 in doubles, 3-6 in singles). 2004 U.S. Olympic team in Athens in singles and doubles, reached QF in doubles with Martina Navratilova. Career as of March 2008: won 4 singles (320-299 matches), 65 doubles (623-208 matches) pro titles, $7,413,509 prize money.

REDL, Hans—Austrian Hans Redl, RH (subsequently only-hander) of extraordinary grit. b. Jan. 19, 1914, Vienna, d. May 26, 1976. Davis Cup, Austria, 1937, then Germany, 1938-39, when his country was annexed. Lost left arm, World War II, fighting with German army in Russia. Amazingly resumed play at upper level, Davis Cup, Austria, 1948-55. Cup record: 2-2 singles with both arms; 3-10 singles, 3-8 doubles, with one arm. Made 4th rd. Wimbledon, 1947. Because of him, rules amended, allow one-armed players to make service toss with racket.

REED, Whitney—Moved like an ape with gout, ever out of position—but reacting swiftly, imaginatively to win points, mostly with volleys, half-volleys. Usually a winner, becoming lone U.S. No. 1 (1961) successfully combining playing with partying. Along his merry way won 28 career amateur singles titles, 6 in 1961. Davis Cup—1958, 61, 2-3 singles, 0-1 doubles. b. Oakland, Calif., Aug. 21, 1932. RH, 6 ft 1, 180 lbs. Won U.S. Hard Court, 1960, def. Bill Hoogs, Jr. (USA), 3-6, 3-6, 7-5, 6-0, 6-1; won doubles with Chris Crawford (USA); also won mixed doubles, 1951, with Anita Kanter (USA), 1959, with Sandra Reynolds (RSA). Won Canadian singles, 1961, def. Mike Sangster (GBR), 3-6, 6-0, 6-4, 6-2; won doubles with Sangster; also won doubles, 1958, with Bob Howe (AUS), mixed doubles, 1958, with Farel Footman (USA). Lost 3 U.S. F, 1959—Indoor, to Dick Savitt (USA); Hard Court to Ramanathan Krishnan (IND); Clay Court, to Bernard Bartzen (USA). Won NCAA singles for San Jose State, 1959, def. Donald Dell (Yale), 7-5, 3-6, 6-2, 4-6, 6-3. U.S. First 10—5 years, 1957, 60, No. 8; 1959, No. 9; 1961, No. 1; 1962, No. 6. Made QF U.S., 1961, 4th rd., 1959.

REID, Kerry—Among very best Aussies, Kerry Anne Melville Reid played 3 major F—won homeland singles (Jan., 1977 version), her 11th try, def. Dianne Fromholtz Balestrat (AUS), 7-5, 6-2. Lost Australian F, 1970, to Margaret Court (AUS), 6-1, 6-3; U.S. F, 1972, to Billie Jean King (USA), 6-3, 7-5. All-rounder with strong forehand, volley. Won 2 major doubles—Wimbledon, 1978, with Wendy Turnbull (AUS), def. Martina Navratilova (USA)-Betty Stove (NED), 4-6, 9-8 (12-10), 6-3, saved 2 MP; Australia (Dec. 1977), with Mona Schallau Guerrant (USA), shared rained-out F with Fromholtz-Helen Gourlay Cawley (AUS). Federation Cup: 1967-79, 20-4 singles, 17-6 doubles (won one Cup, 1968, made 4 F, 1969. 76-77-78) b. Aug. 7, 1947, Mosman, Australia, World Top 10 12 times: No. 5, 1971; No. 10, 1966, 75, 77; No. 9, 1967; No. 7, 1969, 73-74; No. 8, 1970, 72, 76, 78; Made SF all majors: 6 Australian, 1966-67, 69, 73-74, Dec.-1977; French, 1967; Wimbledon, 1974; U.S., 1966; QF French, 1969; Wimbledon, 1971, 73, 76-77; U.S., 1970, 73-74-75, 79. Met American husband Grover "Raz" Reid as teammates on Boston Lobsters, WTT, married 1975. Career: Won 10, singles 10 doubles pro titles, $750,000 prize money. An original "Long Way Baby" of women's pro tour, 1970.

REITANO, Mary—Tiniest Australian champ, 5 ft 2 RH Mary Carter Reitano won title twice—as Carter, 1956, def. Thelma Coyne Long (AUS), 3-6, 6-2, 9-7, saved 1 MP; as newlywed Mrs. Reitano, 1959, def. Renee Schuurman (RSA), 6-2, 6-3. That year, beat all-timer-to-be, Aussie Margaret Smith Court, 16, 2nd rd., 6-4,

7-5, last defeat for Court in nationals until F, 1968, a 39-match streak. Mary lost title, 1960, beat by Margaret, SF, 7-5, 2-6, 6-2. Also made SF 1954-55, 58, 61-62; QF, 1957. Lost 3 Australian doubles F—1956, with Beryl Penrose (AUS); 1959, with Lorraine Coghlan (AUS); 1962, with Darlene Hard (USA). b. Nov. 29, 1934, Sydney, had solid all-court game.

RICE, Horrie—Longest-running Australian, LH Horace Michael "Horrie" Rice, played first interstate match for New South Wales at 22, 1894, last at 53, 1925. Won Australian singles at 35, 1907, def. Harry Parker (AUS), 6-3, 6-3, 6-4. Lost 3 F –1910, to Rod Heath (AUS), 6-4, 6-3, 6-2; 1911, to Norman Brookes (AUS), 6-1, 6-2, 6-3; 1915, to Gordon Lowe (GBR), 4-6, 6-1, 6-1, 6-4. Made SF, 1920, 23, last at age 51. Won Australian doubles, 1915, with Carrie Todd (AUS); Australian mixed, 1923, with Sylvia Lance (AUS), def. Mall Molesworth-Bert St. John (both AUS), 2-6, 6-4, 6-4—at 51, Rice was oldest to win major title. Davis Cup rookie at 39, 1913, 0-2 singles. Eager retriever, distinctive in white knickers, long black sox. Sliced serve, strong backhand, hit with same face of racket as forehand, a stroke described admiringly by Tony Wilding:"Peculiar, one of his own; for ugliness and effectiveness combined I have never seen anything to approach it." b. in Sydney, 1872, d. in Sydney age 78 in 1950.

RICE, Lena—With luck Irishwoman Helena Bertha Grace "Lena" Rice might have been second woman to win successive Wimbledons. Served at 5-3, 40-15 and advantage, 3 match points, 2nd set, but lost 1889 F to Blanche Bingley Hillyard (GBR), 4-6, 8-6, 6-4. Did win title, 1890, beat unknown M. Jacks, 6-4, 6-1; lean year, only 4 entries. Lena did not defend. Won Irish mixed, 1889, with 1890 Wimbledon champ, Willoby Hamilton (IRL). b. June 21, 1866, New Inn, County Tipperary; d. there, June 21, 1907.

RICHARDS, Renee—American LH, 6 ft 1, ophthalmological surgeon, b. Richard Raskind, Aug. 19, 1934, New York. Graduate Yale, Rochester Medical. Unique: Played U.S. as amateur male (1955-56-57, 60), pro female (1977-81). Lost F U.S. doubles, 1977, with Betty Ann Grubb Dent Stuart (USA) to Martina Navratilova (USA)-Betty Stove (NED), 6-1, 7-6. Strong server, clever tactician. Following 1975 sex change surgery, sought to play women's pro tour, faced opposition, resorted to courts of law to gain entry. New York Supreme Court ruling, August 1977, cleared way to enter WTA, USTA events. Age 43, lost 1st rd., U.S., 1977, to Wimbledon champ Virginia Wade (GBR), 6-1, 6-4. Made 3rd rd., 1979, lost to Chris Evert (USA), 6-2, 6-1. Reasonable pro career, five years, winning 1 singles title, def. Caroline Stoll in 1977, Pensacola. Returned to medicine after tennis career. Best world rank, No. 22, 1977. Autobiography, *Second Serve, the Renee Richards Story,* 1983. *No Way Renee,* the second half of the notorious story, written by Renee and published in Feb 2007. Played F of both mens (lost to Gene Scott) and womens (defeated Nancy Richey 7-6, 6-1) US over 35 championships.

RICHARDSON, Hamilton (Ham) Farrar—Overcame diabetes to become outstanding on world scene more than a decade

(1951-65). Cautioned by physicians against playing as diabetic youth, nevertheless continued, brilliantly, never using his difficult condition as excuse. Lean 6-footer, 160 lbs., smooth-flowing strokes, marked by deadly one-handed backhand, crisp volleying. NCAA champ, Tulane, 1953-54. Had memorable days on grass at Boston's Longwood Cricket Club: With father, Roger Richardson, won U.S. Father and Son Doubles, 1953-54. In 1958 U.S. Doubles with Peruvian Alex Omedo—partnering first time—roused Longwood crowd, d. defending champs, Neale Fraser-Ashley Cooper (both AUS), SF, 7-9, 7-5, 6-3, 6-4; won title, d. Sam Giammalva-Barry MacKay (both USA), 3-6, 6-3, 6-3, 6-4. Richardson (left court)-Olmedo continued 1958 success at Brisbane, d. Fraser-Mal Anderson, pivotal win, 10-12, 3-6, 16-14, 6-3, 7-5 as U.S. took Davis Cup from Australia, 3-2. Remarkable rebound, 82 games, longest match in a Cup F. Ham served out of 2 MP 3rd set. Davis Cup 7 years (1952–56, 58, 65). Helped win 1954, 58 Cups, 17-1 singles, 3-1 doubles. World Top 10, 4 years—1954, No. 10; 1955, No. 7; 1956, No. 3; 1958, No. 6. No. 1 U.S., 1956, 58. U.S. Top 10, 9 other years—1951, No. 9; 1952, 55, 63-64, No. 7; 1953, 65, No. 6; 1954, 62, No. 3. Made SF French, 1955; Wimbledon, 1956; U.S. 1952, 54; QF U.S., 1955-56, 60, 62. Made splash Wimbledon, 1951, 17-year-old, ousting defending champ Budge Patty USA), 2nd rd., 4-6, 6-3, 4-6, 10-8, 6-4. Amused at 1955 U.S. 1st rd. win over Ed Kauder (USA), 6-2, 3-6, 9-11, 10-8, 6-0, saving 3 MP. Kauder served majors record 59 aces—But "somehow I got enough of them back to win," Ham laughed. Won 28 amateur singles titles. Unwitting co-instigator of the tie-breaker, winning Newport, R.I., F, 1954, def. Straight Clark (USA), 6-3, 9-7, 12-14, 6-8, 10-8. Their 4 hour, 83 games, infuriated tourney director Jimmy Van Alen. Raging long, loudly at extended deuce sets, overly long matches, Van Alen conceived, introduced the tie-breaker on same court, 1965. b. Aug. 21, 1933, Baton Rouge, La. Gentleman scholar, tennis All-American, Phi Beta Kappa, Tulane, then Rhodes Scholar, Oxford. d. Nov. 5, 2006, New York.

RICHEY, Nancy, Cliff—American brother and sister, Nancy *(See Hall of Fame section for full bio of Nancy)* and Cliff Richey, RH, out of San Angelo, Tex. Attained highest standing for such a family pair. Unique: Both held No. 1 U.S., rank, she 1964-65, 68-69; he, 1970. Both won U.S. Clay Court singles, 1966, played Davis/Federation/Wightman Cup. Careers spanned amateur, Open eras.

RICHEY, George Clifford Jr.—b. Dec. 31, 1946, San Angelo, Tex. Quick, stocky (5 ft 7, 170 lbs): scrappy, hard worker, strong groundstroker, good volleyer. Davis Cup, 1966-67, 70, 10-3 singles. He, Arthur Ashe led U.S. to Cup, 1970, def. Germany, 5-0. Cliff def. Christian Kuhnke, 6-3, 6-4, 6-2; Wilhelm Bungert, 6-4, 6-4, 7-5. Best season, 1970, 28 tournaments, won 8 singles titles, 93-19 (.830) record. Won U.S. Clay, def. Stan Smith (USA), 6-2, 10-8, 3-6, 6-1. Lost U.S. Indoor F to Ilie Nastase (ROU), 6-8, 3-6, 6-4, 9-7, 6-0. Made SF, French, 1970, U.S., 1970, 72; QF Australian, 1967; Wimbledon, 1971. World Top 10: No. 7, 1970. Took U.S. No. 1 rank, 1970, by narrowest margin: 1-point victory. His def. No. 2 Smith in 5-4 5th set tie-breaker, Pacific Coast SF, decided order of rank, 7-6, 6-7, 6-4, 4-6, 7-6 (5-4). Also won U.S. Clay, 1966, def. Frank Froehling

(USA) 13-11, 6-1, 6-3. Career, spanning open, amateur eras, won 10 singles (349-184 matches) and 1 doubles pro titles; also 18 amateur singles titles. Wrote a memoir about his battle with depression with his daughter Hilaire called *Acing Depression: A Tennis Champion's Toughest Match.*

ROBB, Muriel—An intruding champ, 1902 Wimbledon, English RH Muriel Evelyn Robb interrupted title monopolies of countrywomen Charlotte Cooper Sterry, Blanche Hillyard and Dorothea Douglass Chambers. She beat defending champ Sterry in a one-and-only two-part F. Muriel had to work harder than most, 4 sets. A downpour halted F at 1 set apiece. Losing the 1st set, 6-4, but hanging in by winning the second, 13-11, Muriel was ready for the unique reprise when it was decided to play the whole thing over again next day. Then she won, 7-5, 6-1. Sweet revenge. Sterry had double-bageled her in the 1901 QF. b. May 13, 1878, Newcastle-upon-Tyne, she had brief British celebrity, winning Welsh, 1899, Irish, Scottish titles, 1901. And briefest life of any champ. Less than five years after Wimbledon triumph she was dead, age 28, Feb. 12, 1907, town of her birth.

ROPER, Herbert Barrett—Herbert Roper Barrett, English RH, b. Nov. 24, 1873, Upton, d. July 27, 1943, Horsham. An original Davis Cupper with losing British, 1900. Also played 1907, 12-13-14; 0-2 singles, 4-4 doubles. Captained British Cup winners, 1933-1936. Had good long run, lost 2 Wimbledon singles F—1908 to Arthur Gore (GBR), 6-3, 6-2, 4-6, 3-6, 6-4; 1911 to Tony Wilding (NZL), 6-4, 4-6, 2-6, 6-2, ret. (exhaustion). Won 3 Wimbledon doubles, 1909, with Arthur Gore (GBR), def. Harry Parker-Stanley Doust (both AUS), 6-2, 6-1, 6-4; 1912, with Charles Dixon (GBR), d. Max Decugis-Andre Gobert (both FRA), 3-6, 6-3, 6-4, 7-5; 1913, with Dixon, def. Friedrich Rahe-Heinrich Kleinschroth (both GER), 6-2, 6-4, 4-6, 6-2. Lost 3 F—1908, 10 with Gore; 1914 with Dixon. In 1926, age 48, with Gore, 54, won historic 1st rd. over Duke of York (future King George VI) and Louis Grieg (GBR), 6-1, 6-3, 6-2, only appearance of royalty on court. (Apparently George was more comfortable in a court with a throne instead of a net.).

RUANO, Virginia Pascual And SUAREZ, Paola—Muy favuloso Spanish-speaking Spain-Argentina coalition, Virginia Ruano Pascual of Madrid and Paolo Suarez of Munro, Argentina., 3rd leading team Open era, altogether won 32 doubles titles. Played 13 major doubles F, won 8 titles: Won Australian, 2004, def. Svetlana Kuznetsova-Elena Likhovtseva (both RUS), 6-4, 6-3; French, 2001, def. Jelena Dokic (AUS)-Conchita Martinez (ESP), 6-2, 6-1; 2002, def. Lisa Raymond (USA)-Rennae Stubbs (AUS), 6-4, 6-2; 2004, def. Kuznetsova-Likhovtseva, 6-0, 6-3; 2005, def. Black (ZIM)-Liezel Huber (RSA), 4-6, 6-3, 6-3; U.S., 2002, def. Elena Dementieva (RUS)-Janette Husarova (SVK), 6-2, 6-1; 2003, def. Martina Navratilova (USA)-Kuznetsova, 6-2, 6-3; 2004, def. Kuznetsova-Likhovtseva, 6-4, 7-5. Also won WTA Championship, 2003, def. Kim Clijsters (BEL)-Ai Sugiyama (JPN), 6-4, 3-6, 6-3.

Ruano Pascual—b. Madrid, Sept. 21, 1973, RH, 5 ft 7, 132 lbs., turned pro 1992. Federation Cup—13 years from 1992, helped Spain win Cup, 1993-94-95, 0-4 singles, 14-13 doubles. Made QF Australian, 2004; French, 1996. Highest world singles ranking, No. 32, 1998. Big Wimbledon upset, 2001, as No. 83, def. 1st seed Martina Hingis (SUI), 1st rd., 6-4, 6-2. Won 9th major, French mixed, 2001, with Tomas Carbonell (ESP), def. Suarez-Jamie Oncins (BRA), 7-5, 6-3. Won silver medal in 2004 Olympics with Conchita Martinez in women's doubles. Career won 3 singles (382-325 matches), 39 doubles (527-229 matches) pro titles, $5,064,299 prize money.

Paola Suarez—b. Pergamino, Argentina, June 23, 1976, RH (2-handed backhand), 5 ft 7, 141 lbs., turned pro 1994. Made SF French, 2004; QF French, 2002; Wimbledon, 2004; U.S., 2003. Highest world singles ranking, No. 14, 2003. Lost 2 mixed major final, Australian mixed, 2002, with Gaston Etlis (ARG), to Daniela Hantuchova (SVK)-Kevin Ullyett (ZIM), 6-3, 6-2; 200 French mixed with Jaime Oncins (BRA) (see above). Career: won 4 singles (371-239 matches), 44 doubles pro (497-179 matches) titles, $5,134,870 prize money.

RUZICI, Virginia—Romania's standout woman, Virginia Ruzici, b. Jan. 31, 1955, Cimpa-Turzil, grew up in Bucharest. 5 ft 8, RH, baseliner with lusty forehand. Played 6 major F—Won French singles, 1978, def. Mima Jausovec (YUG), 6-2, 6-2; lost French singles, 1980, to Chris Evert (USA), 6-0, 6-3. Won French doubles, 1978, with Jausovec, def. Lesley Turner Bowrey (AUS)-Gail Sherriff Lovera (FRA), 5-7, 6-4, 8-6. Lost French mixed, 1978, with Patrice Dominguez (FRA), 1979, with Ion Tiriac (ROU); Lost Wimbledon doubles, 1978, with Jausovec. Won U.S. Clay, 1982, def. Helena Sukova (CZE), 6-2, 6-0. Best world rank: No. 11, 1980; No. 12, 1978, 82. Made SF French, 1976, 80; QF Australia, 1980; French, 1979, 81-82; Wimbledon, 1978, 81; U.S., 1976, 78. Federation Cup, 1973-77, 80-81, 83; 12-6 singles, 8-4 doubles. Career: over 13-years won 14 singles, 8 doubles pro titles, $1,184,228 prize money.

SANCHEZ, Arantxa, Emilio & Javier—Probably most accomplished family combination ever at uppermost level: Arantxa Sanchez Vicario *(See Hall of Fame section for complete bio)* and her older brothers, Emilio and Javier, all RH from Barcelona, represented Spain, Davis/Federation Cup, Arantxa, Emilio in Olympics.

Emilio Sanchez—Quick, smooth-stroking, sharp volleyer, 5 ft 10, 164 lbs., b. May 29, 1965, Madrid. Won Italian singles, 1991, d. Alberto Mancini (ARG), 6-3, 6-1, 3-0, ret. Excellent at doubles, won 4 major titles—U.S., 1988, with Sergio Casal (ESP), d. Rick Leach-Jim Pugh (both USA), walkover; French, 1990, with Casal, def. Goran Ivanisevic (CRO)-Petr Korda (CZE), 7-5, 6-3; French mixed, 1987, with Pam Shriver (USA), def. Lori McNeil-Sherwood Stewart (both USA), 6-3, 7-6 (7-4); U.S. mixed, 1987, with Martina Navratilova (USA) def. Betsy Nagelsen-Paul Annacone (both USA), 6-4, 6-7 (6-8), 7-6 (14-12). Won Olympic silver, 1988, with Casal. Davis Cup: 1984-95, 18-14 singles, 14-9 doubles. Made QF U.S., 1988. Career: won 15 singles (428-292 matches), 50 dou-

bles (44 with Casal, 3 with brother Javier, 532-273 matches) pro titles, $5,339,395 prize money. Best world rank, No. 7 April 1990, 8 at end 1990. Captained Spain to Davis Cup title in 2008.

Javier Sanchez—Speedy, 5 ft 10, 155 lbs., b. Feb. 1, 1968, Pamplona, Spain. Consistent winner singles, doubles. Made QF U.S. 1991, 96. Davis Cup, 1987–89, 3-2 singles. Career: won 4 singles (327-335 matches), 20 doubles (3 with brother Emilio) pro titles (379-311 doubles) $4,427,811 prize money. Best world rank, No. 23, 1994.

SANTORO, Fabrice Vetea—Clever, unorthodox (both hands both sides), "Monsieur Legerdemain" with wide array of speeds, spins, angles, "The Magician." Drives big hitters bonkers. Excels singles, doubles. Won 3 doubles majors—Australian, 2003, with Michael Llodra (FRA), def. Mark Knowles (BAH)-Daniel Nestor (CAN), 6-4, 3-6, 6-3; 2004, with Llodra, def. Bob-Mike Bryan (USA), 7-6 (7-4), 6-3. French mixed, 2005, with Daniela Hantuchova (SVK), def. Martina Navratilova (USA)-Leander Paes (IND), 3-6, 6-3, 6-2. Lost 2 major doubles F—Australian, 2002, with Llodra; French, 2004, with Llodra. 2008 Australian Open set a new record for most majors played, his 62nd. Davis Cup, 7 years between 1991 and 2002, 6-6 singles, 9-5 doubles. Helped France win 2001 Cup over Australia, won go-ahead doubles in F with Cedric Pioline, def. Lleyton Hewitt-Patrick Rafter, 2-6, 6-3, 7-6 (7-5), 6-1. Also won doubles with Nico Escude in F loss to Russia, 2002. Won longest singles match ever, 6:33 (over 2 days), def. Arnaud Clement (FRA), 6-4, 6-3, 6-7 (5-7), 3-6, 16-14, saved 2 MP, 1st rd., French, 2004. Born Tahiti Dec. 9, 1972. RH, 5 ft 10, 163 lbs. Highest world rank, No. 22, 2001. Made Australian QF 2006. Turned pro 1989. Career as of June 2009: won 6 singles, 24 doubles pro titles, $9,828,843 prize money.

SATOH, Jiro—Highest ranking Japanese ever—yet tragic. World No. 3, 1933, also No. 9, 1931, 5 ft 5 RH Jiro Satoh killed himself at age 26, having thrice led Japan to Davis Cup SF. b. Jan. 5, 1908, Tokyo, all-rounder, nifty touch. Adept on clay, grass: Made SF Australian, 1932; French, 1931, 33; Wimbledon, 1933 (lost both, 1933, to champ, Aussie Jack Crawford); QF Wimbledon, 1931. Lost Wimbledon doubles F, 1933, with Ryosuki Nunoi (JPN). Had wins over Hall of Famers Jack Crawford (AUS), Fred Perry (GBR), Elly Vines (USA). Despondent over 3-2 loss to Australia, 1933, feeling pressure of leading team—"I would have been unable to help..." said suicide note. He leaped from shipboard into Strait of Malacca. April 5, 1939, on the way to Cup opener in England. Davis Cup: 1931–33, 14-4 singles, 8-2 doubles.

SAWAMATSU, Kazuko & Junko—Sisters, Kazuko and Junko Sawamatsu, RH (2-handed backhands), 1st Japanese women to make mark on pro tour. Federation Cup together, 1970-71. Kazuko 1st Japanese woman to win major, Wimbledon doubles, 1975, with Ann Kiyomura (USA), unseeded def. Francoise Durr (FRA)-Betty Stove (NED), 7-5, 1-6, 7-5. Only tourney together. Made QF with Junko, 1970.

Kazuko Sawamatsu—Sturdy 5 ft 7, b. Jan. 5, 1951, Nishinomiya. Solid groundstroker, won Japan Open, 1968, 72, 75. Made SF Australian, 1973 (beat Virginia Wade); QF French, 1975; Won Japanese National, 1967, 72; Wimbledon, French Junior, 1969. Federation Cup, 6 years from 1970, 30 series, 25-5 singles, 19-5 doubles, Japanese highs. Won 3 singles titles.

Junko Sawamatsu—b. April 10, 1998, Nishinomiya. Made Australian QF 1973. Federation Cup, 2 years, 1-2 doubles. Daughter, Naoko Sawamatsu (RH, 2-handed backhand), b. March 23, 1973, Nishinomiya, on WTA tour 10 years, made QF Australian, 1995 Career: won 4 singles pro titles, $1,107,264 prize money. Best world rank, No. 17, 1995.

SCRIVEN, Peggy—First of five LH to win French singles, only unseeded champ, England's Margaret Croft "Peggy" Scriven was 20, beat Simone Passemard Mathieu (FRA) 1933 F, 6-2, 4-6, 6-4. Repeated, 1934, d. Helen Jacobs (USA), 7-5, 4-6, 6-1. Made SF 1935, a Paris winning streak of 14 matches ended by Mathieu, 8-6, 6-1. Made QF French, 1936; Wimbledon, 1931, 33-34, 37. Won French doubles, 1935, with Kay Stammers (GBR), def. Ida Adamoff (FRA)-Hilde Krahwinkel Sperling (GER) 6-4, 6-0. World Top 10: No. 5, 1933-34, No. 10, 1935. Wightman Cup: 1933-34; 0-4 singles. b. Aug 17, 1912, Leeds, Yorkshire, England, d. Jan. 25, 2001 as Mrs. F. H. Vivian, Haslemere, Surrey, England.

SEARS, Evelyn—Evelyn Georgianna Sears of Waltham, Mass., Longwood Cricket Club member, first LH to win U.S. titles—singles 1907, def. Carrie Neely (USA), 6-3, 6-2; doubles, 1908, with Margaret Curtis (USA), d. Marion Steever (USA)-Neely, 6-3, 5-7, 9-7. Didn't venture to Philadelphia until 1907, won impressively at 32, losing no sets, 17 games in 5 matches. As defender, lost challenge round, 1908, to Maud Barger Wallach (USA), 6-2, 1-6, 6-3. Tried again, 1916, made SF. Good tennis bloodline, cousin of initial U.S. champ, Richard Sears. b. March 9, 1875, Waltham, d. there, Nov. 10, 1966.

SHIMIDZU, Zenzo—Zenzo "Shimmy" Shimidzu, first Japanese of note, attained highest male level. b. March 25, 1891, Tokyo; d. April 12, 1977, Amagaski City, Japan. Self-taught, 5 ft 6, quick-footed, unorthodox RH. Clever tactician. Weird stroker, heavy topspin; same face of racket, forehand, backhand, yet effective on grass. Lost Wimbledon F (all-comers), 1920, to champ Bill Tilden (USA), 6-4, 6-4, 13-11; SF (all-comers), 1921, to Manuel Alonso (ESP), 3-6, 7-5, 3-6, 6-4, 8-6. Davis Cup 1921-25, 9-8 singles, 3-5 doubles. In Japan's Davis Cup debut year, 1921, he, with Ichiya Kumagae (b. Sept. 10, 1891; d. Aug. 16, 1968), def. India, 5-0, upset Australia, 4-1 in SF, took homeland to Cup zenith, the challenge round vs. defender, U.S., Forest Hills. Astoundingly Shimidzu came within two points, 3rd set, of beating Tilden first day, losing, 5-7, 4-6, 7-5, 6-2, 6-1, stricken by cramps in 3rd set. Though beaten, 5-0, the Japanese were competitive. World Top 10: No. 9, 1920; No. 4. 1921. Working in the U.S., Shimidzu and Kumagae had Top 10 U.S. rankings: Shimidzu (No. 7, 1922), Kumagae (No. 5, 1916; No. 6, 1918; No. 3, 1919; No. 4, 1920; No. 7, 1921).

SIROLA, Orlando—Gaunt, towering Italian RH Orlando Sirola, tallest (6 ft 6) to play in Davis Cup F (1960-61 defeats by Australia), major F prior to Todd Martin (USA), also 6 ft 6, in Cup F, 1995/1997. With Nicola Pietrangeli (ITA), Sirola won French doubles, 1959, def. Roy Emerson-Neale Fraser (both AUS), 6-3, 6-2, 14-12; lost Wimbledon doubles, 1956, French, 1955. Won Italian doubles, 1960; lost 6 F, 1955-56-57, 59, 61, 63. b. April 30, 1928, Fiume; d. Nov. 13, 1995, Bologna. Self-taught, late starter, 1950. Huge serve, overhead, good volleyer, streaky. Joined Cup team, 1953, aligned with Pietrangeli, 1955, playing, winning as pair most doubles in Cup annals (34-8). Among most active Cuppers: 22-25 singles, 35-8 doubles. High point, 1960 Cup SF, 3-2 comeback, from 0-2 over U.S. Won pivotal doubles, def. Butch Buchholz-Chuck McKinley, 3-6, 10-8, 6-4, 13-11. Sirola won decider, def. Barry MacKay, 9-7, 6-3, 8-6.

SPERLING, Hilde—Tall, slim German RH, Hilde Krahwinkel Sperling was strong presence for decade. World Top 10 for 10 straight years: No. 10, 1930; No. 6, 1931; No. 5, 1932; No. 4, 1933, 35, 37-38-39; No. 3, 1934; No. 2, 1936. Won 3 straight French singles 1935-37, def. Simone Passemard Mathieu (FRA) in each, 6-2, 6-1; 6-3, 6-4; 6-2, 6-4, tying 1928-30 run of Helen Wills Moody (USA), equalled by Monica Seles (USA), 1990-92, Justine Henin (BEL), 2005–07. Lost only all-German female Wimbledon F to Cilly Aussem, 1931, 6-2, 7-5; also F to Helen Jacobs (USA), 1936, 6-2, 4-6, 7-5. Won Wimbledon mixed, 1933, with Gottfried von Cramm (GER); lost F, 1930, with Daniel Prenn (GER). Lost Wimbledon doubles, 1935, with Mathieu. Total 8 major F. b. March 26, 1908, Essen, Germany, became Danish citizen (marrying Svend Sperling, 1933), d. March 7, 1981, Halsingborg, Sweden.

SRICHAPHAN, Paradorn—First Thai male prominent on world scene, leading Asian, turned pro 1997. b. Bangkok June 14, 1979. RH, 6 ft 1, 180 lbs. Davis Cup, 9 years, 31-10 singles, 2-3 doubles, Thai highs. Highest world singles rank, No. 11, 2003. Made 4th rd. Australian, 2004; U.S., Wimbledon, 2003, def. No. 3 Andre Agassi (USA), 2d rd. Wimbledon, 2002. Olympics, 2004. Career: won 5 singles (239-193 matches) pro titles, $3,458,330 prize money.

STERRY, Charlotte—English RH Charlotte Reinagle Cooper Sterry, consistent factor at Wimbledon over extraordinary period of 21 years and two centuries with 43-13 match W-L, 11 F. Big W's oldest female champ, 37, 1908; oldest finalist, 41, 1912. Played 18 times between 1893–1919. Made run of 8 straight F (1895-92), the record until 9 straight of Martina Navratilova (USA), 1982–90. Won 5 singles titles at Wimbledon—1895, def. Helen Jackson (GBR), 7-5, 8-6; 1896, d. Alice Simpson Pickering (GBR), 6-2, 6-3; 1898, def. Louise Martin (GBR), 6-4, 6-4; 1901, def. Blanche Bingley Hillyard (GBR), 6-2, 6-2; 1908, def. Agnes Morton (GBR), 6-4, 6-4 (last 3 as Mrs. Rex Sterry). Lost doubles F 1913, with Dolly Chambers. Won Olympic singles, 1900, def. Helene Prevost (FRA), 6-1, 6-4. Also mixed with Reggie Doherty, first woman gold medalist any sport. Won Scottish, 1895, Irish, 1895, 98, singles titles. b. Sept. 22, 1870, Ealing; d. Oct. 10, 1966, Helensburgh, Scotland. Daughter, Gwendolyn Sterry, 1-0 Wightman Cup doubles, 1927; made Wimbledon 3rd rd., 1926.

STICH, Michael—Spindly 6 ft 4, 175 lbs., RH, fluid stroker, attacker with big serve, Michael Stich dethroned countryman Boris Becker, Wimbledon, 1991, 6-4, 7-6 (7-4), 6-4, only all-German male F. Lost 2 major singles F—U.S. 1994 to Andre Agassi (USA), 6-1, 7-6 (7-5), 7-5; French, 1996, to Yevgeny Kafelnikov (RUS), 7-6 (7-4), 7-5, 7-6 (7-4). Made SF Australian, 1993; French, 1991; Wimbledon, 1997; QF Australia, 1992; Wimbledon, 1992-93; U.S., 1991. Davis Cup: 1990–95, 21-9 singles, 14-2 doubles. Led Germany to 1993 Cup, 4-1 over Australia, rare triple with series alive: won both singles, def. Jason Stoltenberg, 6-7 (2-7), 6-3, 6-1, 4-6, 6-3, and clincher, def. Richard Fromberg, 6-4, 6-2, 6-2, plus doubles with Patrik Kuhnen. World Top 10: No. 4, 1991; No. 2, 1993; No. 9, 1994. Turned pro 1988. Career: won 18 singles (385-176 matches), 10 doubles (165-110 matches) pro titles, $12,592,483 prize money. b. Oct. 18, 1968, Pinneberg, Germany.

ST. JOHN, Bert—Extraordinary one-handed athlete at upper level of Australian sport, LH Queenslander Cecil Bertram Vernon St. John, only man thus impaired to reach major F. At 44, oldest Australian singles finalist, lost, 1923, to Pat O'Hara Wood (AUS), 6-1, 6-1, 6-3. Earlier, 1915, lost doubles F with Gordon Lowe (GBR) to Horrie Rice-Clairie Todd (both AUS), 8-6, 6-4, 7-9, 6-3. Also made SF, 1915. Exceptional at cricket.

STOVE, Betty—Netherlands' Betty Flippina Stove, 6 ft RH, her country's foremost woman. Powerful server, fine volleyer, erratic. Only female Hollander in major singles F—lost Wimbledon, 1977, to Virginia Wade (GBR), 4-6, 6-3, 6-1. Country's leading player in major F (1 singles, 24 doubles). Won 10—French, 1972, with Billie Jean King (USA), 1979, with Wendy Turnbull (AUS); Wimbledon, 1972, with King; U.S., 1972, with Francoise Durr (FRA); 1977, with Martina Navratilova (USA), 1979, with Turnbull; Wimbledon mixed, 1978, 81; U.S. mixed, 1977-78, all with Frew McMillan (RSA). Lost 15 F—French, 1973, with Durr; 8 Wimbledon, 1973, 75, with Durr, 1976, with King, 1977, with Navratilova, 1979, with Turnbull, 1975 mixed, with Allan Stone (AUS), 1977, 79, with McMillan; 6 U.S., 1974, with Durr; 1980, with Pam Shriver (USA); mixed, 1971, with Rob Maud (RSA), 1976-79-80, with McMillan. Rarity: Lost all 3 Wimbledon F, 1977. Made singles SF U.S., 1977; QF Wimbledon, 1975. b. June 24, 1945, Rotterdam. Federation Cup: 1966–76, 20-4 singles, 20-8 doubles. World Top 10: No. 7, 1976-77, No. 9, 1978. Career: won 1 singles title and $1,047,356 prize money.

SUK/SUKOVA, Vera, Helena & Cyril—Great name in Czechoslovak game. Mother, Vera; son, Cyril; daughter, Helena, all RH major champions. Played for country in Federation/Davis Cup. Only mother, daughter in major singles F, world Top 10. Father, Cyril Suk, ex-president Czechoslovak Federation.

Vera Puzejova Sukova—b. June 13, 1931, Uherske Hradiste; d. May 13, 1982, Prague. Married Suk, 1961. Unimpressive serve, strokes, but strong, persistent, competitive. Stolid baseliner, retriever, fine passing shots: Made SF French, 1957, lost to champ Shirley Bloomer (GBR), 6-4, 2-6, 6-4; QF 1959-60, 63-64.

Unseeded, had stunning Wimbledon, 1962, def. 6th, 2nd, 3rd seeds—defender Angela Mortimer (GBR), 1-6, 6-4, 6-3, Darlene Hard (USA), 6-4, 6-3, ex-champ Maria Bueno (BRA), 6-4, 6-3, lost F to 8th Karen Susman (USA), 6-4, 6-4. Also made QF, U.S., 1962. World Top 10: No. 6, 1957; No. 5, 1962; No. 10, 1963. Federation Cup, 1963, 1-0 singles, 0-1 doubles. Was Czechoslovak national coach, early tutor of Martina Navratilova.

Helena Sukova—b. Feb. 23, 1965, Prague. At 6-2, tallest female players of consequence, until 6 ft 3 Lindsay Davenport (USA) won Olympic gold, 1996. Standout serve-and-volleyer, possessing sound groundies. Lost 4 major F—Australian, 1984 to Chris Evert (USA), 6-7 (4-7), 6-1, 6-3; 1989, to Steffi Graf (GER), 6-4, 6-4; U.S., 1986, to Martina Navratilova (USA), 6-3, 6-2 (def. Evert, SF, 6-2, 6-4) and 1993, to Graf, 6-3, 6-3. Ended Navratilova's pro record 74-match streak and Grand Slam bid, SF, Australian, 1984, 1-6, 6-3, 7-5. Made SF French, 1986, U.S., 1987; QF French, 1988; Wimbledon, 1985, 88; U.S., 1984-85, 89. World Top 10 for 6 years: No. 7, 1984, 87; No. 9, 1985; No. 5, 1986; No, 8, 1988-89. Superior at doubles, won 14 majors—Australian, 1990, with Jana Novotna (CZE), 1992, with Arantxa Sanchez Vicario (ESP); French, 1990, with Novotna; Wimbledon, 1987, with Claudia Kohde-Kilsch (GER), 1989-90, with Novotna, 1996, with half-her-age Swiss Martina Hingis, 15; U.S., 1985, with Kohde-Kilsch, 1993, with Sanchez Vicario; French mixed, 1991, with Cyril Suk (1st brother-sister to win in Paris, equaled by Cara-Wayne Black, 2002); Wimbledon, 1994, with Todd Woodbridge (AUS); U.S., 1993, with Woodbridge; Wimbledon, 1996-97, with Cyril. Missed Grand Slam with Novotna, 1990, lost U.S. F to Navratilova-Gigi Fernandez (USA), 6-2, 6-4. Federation Cup all-timer, 13 years from 1981, 54 series, 45-11 singles, 12-5 doubles (with four Cup winners, 1983-84-85, 88). Career: won 10 singles (614-307 matches), 68 doubles (752-220 matches) pro titles, $6,391,245 prize money. Olympic silver, doubles, 1988, 1996, with Novotna.

Cyril Suk—b. Jan. 19, 1967, Prague. Quick, clever, 6 ft 2, 150 lbs. Singles (best world rank, No. 184, 1988) over-shadowed by doubles expertise. Davis Cup: 1992–96, 6-4 doubles. Career: won 32 career pro doubles (488-412 matches) titles, $3,651,530 prize money. Won 5 majors—U.S. doubles, 1998, with Sandon Stolle (AUS); French mixed, 1991, with sister, Helena; Wimbledon mixed, 1996-97, with Helena, 1992, with Larisa Savchenko Neiland (LAT). Lost 4 major F—Australian mixed, 1995, with Gigi Fernandez (USA), 1998, with Helena; Wimbledon mixed, 1995, with G. Fernandez; U.S. mixed, 1995, with G. Fernandez. World Top 10, 8 years: 1992, No. 5, with Tom Nijssen (NED); 1993-94, No. 7, with Nijssen; 1995, No. 4, with Daniel Vacek (CZE); 1998, No. 7, with Stolle; 2002, 04, No. 7, with Martin Damm (CZE), 2003, No. 8, with Damm, 2004.

SUGIYAMA, Ai—Miniscule (5 ft 4, 121 lbs) but mighty competitor over longest Japanese career and the iron-man of professional tennis. b. Tokyo, July 5, 1975, RH (2-handed backhand), turned pro 1992. At 2009 Wimbledon, played her 61st straight main draw of a major–a new standard for men and women.

Previous record was held by Wayne Ferreira, who played 56 straight majors. Made QF Australian, 2000; Wimbledon, 2004. Incredible Sunday, 2003, morning-to-night, 1-day-4 match-2 title ordeal (6:18 on court), winning Scottsdale (Ariz.) singles, doubles, both SF and F, between 10:10 and 20:30. Saved 3 MP, def. Alexandra Stevenson (USA) SF, then, with Kim Clijsters (BEL) def. Marion Bartoli (FRA)-Stephanie Cohen-Aloro (FRA), SF. Then def. Clijsters, 3-6, 7-5, 6-4, F, plus, with Clijsters, def. Lindsay Davenport-Lisa Raymond (both USA), 6-1, 6-4. Ai means love in Japanese—she loved that day. Quick, cheerful, excellent at doubles. Coached by mother, Fusako, at their Palm International Tennis Academy. Played 9 major doubles F, won 4 titles: French, 2003, with Clijsters, def. Virginia Ruano Pascual (ESP)-Paola Suarez (ARG), 6-7 (5-7), 6-2, 9-7; Wimbledon, 2003, with Clijsters, def. Ruano Pascual-Suarez, 6-4, 6-4; U.S., 2000, with Julie Halard-Decugis (FRA) def. Cara Black (ZIM)-Elena Likhovtseva (RUS), 6-0, 1-6, 6-1. Also won 1 mixed, U.S., 1999, with Mahesh Bhupathi (IND), def. Kim Po (USA)-Don Johnson (USA), 6-4, 6-4. Highest world singles rank, No. 10, 2003. Federation Cup, 10 years, 13-17 singles, 12-5 doubles, helped Japan reach SF, 1996. Career: won 6 singles, 38 doubles pro titles, $7,952,156 prize money.

SUSMAN, Karen—Lovely, free-flowing, 5 ft 7. Brilliant RH serve-and-volleyer out of Chula Vista, Calif., Karen Janice Hantze was 1961 unseeded surprise, Wimbledon champ, 18, alongside Billie Jean Moffitt (King) (USA), 17. Youngest doubles winners, def. Margaret Smith (Court)-Jan Lehane (both AUS), 6-3, 6-4. Again surprising, 1962, as Mrs. Rod Susman, seeded 8th, won singles, def. Vera Sukova (CZE), 6-4, 6-4. Repeated with BJ in doubles, 1962, def. Sandra Reynolds-Renee Schuurman (both RSA), 5-7, 6-3, 7-5; lost F, 1964. Won U.S. doubles, 1964, def. Smith-Lesley Turner (both AUS), 3-6, 6-2, 6-4; lost F, 1962, 65. Didn't defend Wimbledon, 1963, gave birth to daughter. Made QF, Wimbledon, 1961; U.S., 1959. World Top 10: No. 10, 1961, No. 4, 1962, No. 8, 1964. U.S. Top 10: No. 6, 1959; No. 2, 1960-61-62; No. 4, 1964. Wightman Cup, 1960-62, 1965, 3-3 singles, 3-0 doubles (won 3 Cups). Federation Cup, 1964: 4-0 doubles. Won 13 amateur singles titles. b. Dec. 11, 1942, San Diego.

TANNER, Roscoe—Tennessean Roscoe Leonard Tanner, b. Oct. 15, 1951 in Chattanooga, grew up Lookout Mountain. Extraordinarily swift server nicknamed "Bullet Man." LH, 6 feet, 170 pounds. Graduate Stanford ('73), All-American, won NCAA doubles with Alex Mayer, 1972. Won 16 singles titles (582-282 matches), 13 doubles titles (272-182 matches) titles, $1,696,198 prize money. Davis Cup, 4 years, 9-4 singles. Helped U.S. win Cup, 1981. Won Australian, 1977, d. Guillermo Vilas (ARG), 6-3, 6-3, 6-3; lost F Wimbledon, 1979, sensational battle to Bjorn Borg (SWE), 6-7 (4-7), 6-1, 3-6, 6-3, 6-4. Made SF Wimbledon, 1975-76; U.S., 1974, 79; QF Wimbledon, 1980, 83; U.S., 1980, 83. World Top 10: No. 5, 1979; No. 9, 1975. Widely-publicized post career difficulties: imprisoned thrice, crimes of financial manipulations, indiscretions, irregularities, outlined in autobiog, *Double Fault: My Rise and Fall and My Road Back*.

TAPSCOTT, Billie—South African Ruth Daphne Tapscott, b. May 31, 1903, Kimberly, d. 1970. Emancipated female legs, shocked Wimbledon, 1927, appearing without stockings. Hose goes. "It's just the way we do it at home." With bared gams, made QF, probably inspired Joan Austin Lycett, first bold peeler of hose for Centre Court match, 1931, as stockings, went the way of corsets. RH, won South African singles, 1930. Married South African player Collin John James Robbins, 1930.

TEACHER, Brian—Long-armed lightning server from San Diego, 6 ft 3, 175 lbs., RH Brian David Teacher seized his monumental prize, Australian singles, 1980, on cruise control, lost 3 sets, beat homeboy Kim Warwick quick, 7-5, 7-6 (7-4), 6-3. Made QF Australian, Wimbledon, 1982. UCLA grad, 4 years All-American. Best World Rank, No. 12, 1980; No. 16, 1981. Career: Won 8 singles (335-236 matches), 16 doubles (220-172 matches) pro titles, $1,426,514 prize money. b. Dec. 23, 1959, San Diego.

TERRY, Aline—Mystery woman of U.S. Championships. Came from Princeton, N.J., becoming 5th to win singles, def. Augusta Schultz (USA), 6-1, 6-3. Also won doubles, 1893, with Hattie Butler (USA). Lost both, 1894, singles to Helen Hellwig (USA) in 5-set challenge round struggle, 7-5, 3-6, 6-0, 3-6, 6-3. Never heard from again. Age unknown, no details b. or d. Called "lithe, feline, leaped at balls like a tiger" by 1895, 97-98 champ Juliette Atkinson.

TIRIAC, Ion—First prominent Romanian of Open era, Ion Ioan Tiriac, b. May 9, 1939, Brasov. Hulking, glowering, ungainly 6 ft RH, excellent athlete, fierce competitor. Played Olympic ice hockey prior late start in tennis. Played almost 2 decades, spanned amateur, Open eras. Shrewd polyglot, tactician: "I am best tennis player who cannot play tennis." Davis Cup: 1959-77; led way for protégé Ilie Nastase. Together carried Romania to three F, all lost to U.S., 1969, 71-72. Sixth in all-time Cup matches played, 109 (40-28, singles: 30-11, doubles). Highest ATP ranking No. 72, 1974 (best years were pre-computer). Career: won 2 singles, 27 doubles (294-141 matches) pro titles. Won 19 amateur singles titles. Entrepreneur in variety of businesses. Tournament promoter, managed champs Guillermo Vilas, Boris Becker.

TODD, Pat—Mary Patricia Canning Todd, 5 ft 8 California RH, says she "got by on a backhand and guts," made fine immediate post-war record. Won French singles, 1947, d. Doris Hart (USA), 6-3, 3-6. 6-4. Lost F, 1950, played despite blood poisoning, to Hart, 6-4, 4-6, 6-2 then hospitalized. World Top 10 for 7 years: No. 5, 1946-47-48-49, 52; No. 4, 1950; No. 9, 1951. Made SF French, 1948; Wimbledon, 1948-49-50, 52; U.S., 1946, 48; QF Wimbledon, 1947; U.S. 1945, 47, 49-50. Only 3-times winner over world's No. 1 Mo Connolly, 1952. Won French doubles, 1948, with Hart, d. Shirley Fry-Mary Arnold Prentiss (both USA), 6-4, 6-2; lost; F, 1947, with Hart; won mixed, 1948, with Jaroslav Drobny (CZE) Might have tripled, 1948, defaulted SF to champ-to-be Nelly Adamson Landry (FRA): referee unfairly advanced starting time to "now" while she ate lunch. Wightman Cup, 1947-51, 4-1 doubles (won Cup every year). b. July 22, 1922, San Francisco.

TRUMAN, Chris—Darling of homeland fans from teen-age years onward, English 6 ft blonde RH Christine Clara Truman, all-rounder. Won 1959 French singles at 18 years, 4 months, def. Suzi Kormoczi (HUN), 6-4, 7-5, youngest until Steffi Graf (GER), just 18, 1987. Lost 2 major F—U.S., 1959 to Maria Bueno (BRA), 6-1, 6-4; Wimbledon, 1961 heart-breaker to Angela Mortimer (GBR), 4-6, 6-4, 7-5. Made SF Australian, 1960; French, 1963; Wimbledon, 1957, 60, 65; U.S., 1960; QF French, 1958, 61, 64; U.S., 1958, 61, 63. World Top 10 for 6 years: No. 9, 1957; No. 6. 1958; No. 2, 1959; No. 4, 1960; No. 7, 1961, 65. Was 34-14 at Wimbledon. At 17, Chris electrified compatriots, terminating U.S. Wightman Cup winning streak at 21, at Wimbledon, 4-3. She def. Dorothy Head Knode, 6-4, 6-4, world No. 1 Althea Gibson, 2-6, 6-3, 6-4, won decisive doubles with Shirley Bloomer, def. Karol Fageros-Knode, 6-2, 6-3. As Mrs. Gerry Janes, with sister, Nell Truman, 1968, won decisive doubles in 4-3 victory, def. Stephanie DeFina-Kathy Harter, 5-7, 6-4, 6-3. Federation Cup, 1963, 65, 68, 6-3 singles, 2-2 doubles. Wightman Cup, 1957-71, 6-12 singles, 5-4 doubles (won Cups, 1958, 60, 68). Lost longest female singles set ever played, 1963 Wightman, to Billie Jean King, 6-4, 19-17. b. Feb. 16, 1941, Loughton, England.

TURNBULL, Wendy—All-time Aussie Wendy May "Rabbit" Turnbull, 5 ft 3 RH was noted for speed, exceptional volley. Only woman of her country other than Margaret Court, Evonne Goolagong to make three major Open era singles F—Lost Australian, 1980, to Hana Mandlikova (CZE), 6-0, 7-5; French, 1979, to Chris Evert (USA), 6-2, 6-0; U.S., 1977, to Evert, 7-6 (7-3), 6-2 (def. 2nd seed Martina Navatilova (USA), SF, 2-6, 7-5, 6-4.) Played 22 major F. Made SF Australian, 1980-81, 84; U.S., 1978, 84; QF Australian, 1982-83-84 French 1980; Wimbledon, 1979-80-81; U.S., 1986. Won 9 major doubles—French, 1979, with Betty Stove (NED); Wimbledon, 1978, with Kerry Melville (AUS); U.S., 1979, with Stove, 1982, with Rosie Casals (USA). Plus 5 mixed, French, 1979, with Bob Hewitt (RSA), 1982, with John Lloyd (GBR); Wimbledon, 1983-84, with J. Lloyd; U.S., 1980, with Marty Riessen (USA). Lost 11 major doubles F—Australian, 1983, with Anne Hobbs (GBR), 1988, with Evert; French, 1982, with Casals; 4 Wimbledon, 1979, with Stove, 1980, 83, with Casals, 1986, with Hana Mandlikova (CZE); 4 U.S., 1978, with Kerry Melville Reid, 1981, with Casals, 1984, with Hobbs, 1986, with Mandlikova. World Top 10 for 8 years: No. 9, 1977; No. 7, 1978-79; No. 8, 1980-81, 83; No. 5, 1982, 84. Federation Cup, 1977-88, most Aussie wins, 17-8 singles, 29-8 doubles (made 4 F). Career: Won 13 singles (577-318 matches), 55 doubles (352-130 matches) pro titles, $2,769,024 prize money. b. Nov. 25, 1952, Brisbane. Olympic bronze, 1988, doubles with Liz Smylie.

ULRICH, Einer, Torben & Jorgen—Davis Cup workhorses for Denmark. Father, Einer, two sons, Torben and Jorgen Ulrich, all b. in Copenhagen, played 230 Cup matches between 1924 and 1978.

Einer Ulrich—RH, b. May 6, 1896. Davis Cup, 1924–38, 23-23 singles, 16-12 doubles.

Torben Ulrich—Free-spirited, bearded LH, b. Oct. 4, 1928; family's most prominent, strong serve, delicate touch. Career spanned

amateur, Open eras. Made 4th rd. French, 1959; 3rd rd., U.S., 1969, at 40. Davis Cup, 1948-61, 1964-68, 1978; one of few in over 100 matches; 31-35 singles, 15-21 doubles. 7th oldest of all Cuppers, 48 years, 11 months. Last match, 1978. Son Lars, is drummer for rock band Metallica.

Jorgen Ulrich—RH, b. Aug. 21, 1935. Davis Cup, 1955, 1958-71; 18-18 singles, 8-10 doubles, 3-3 with Torben.

WASHINGTON, Malivai, Mashiska, Mashona & Micheala—

Exceptional siblings from Swartz Creek, Mich., all RH (2-handed backhands); all played pro tour, coached by father, William Washington.

MaliVai Onyeaka—Most successful MaliVai Onyeaka, b. June 20, 1969, Glen Cove, N.Y., sinewy 5 ft 11, well-rounded game. 1st black U.S. Davis Cupper since Arthur Ashe, 1993, 96-97 (3-2 singles). Wrecked left knee beating Gustavo Kuerten, 3-6, 7-6 (8-6), 7-6 (7-3), 6-3, Cup victory at Brazil, 1997, led to 1999 retirement. Unseeded, made Wimbledon F, 1996, lost to Richard Krajicek (NED), 6-3, 6-4, 6-3; incredible SF comeback from 1-5 in the 5th, def. Todd Martin, 5-7, 6-4, 6-7 (6-8), 6-3, 10-8. Made Australian QF, 1994; Olympic QF, 1996. Best world rank, No. 11, 1992. All-American, U. Michigan, 1987-88. Career: won 4 pro singles (matches 254-184) titles, $3,239,865 prize money.

Mashiska Isabelita Washington—b. Dec. 19, 1979, Flint, Mich., 5 ft 11. All-American, Michigan State, 1994. Best world ranking: No. 290, 1999. Won $143,963 prize money.

Mashona Lakuta Washington—b. May 31, 1976, Flint, Mich. Won U.S. 18 Indoor singles, 1992. Best world ranking: No. 50, 2004. Turned pro 1995. Reached third round of 2005 Wimbledon. U.S. Fed Cup Team in 2005, 2006 (0-2 in singles). Won $917,666 prize money as of June, 2009.

Micheala Bharati Washington—b. Jan. 27, 1966, Carbondale, Ill. Played 1 year as pro. World ranking No. 81, 1984. Won $30,525 prize money.

WATSON, Maud—First lady of Wimbledon, Englishwoman Maud Edith Eleanor Watson, 19, won intramural battle, becoming pioneer among major champs. def. sister, Lillian Mary Watson, 6-8, 6-3, 6-3 as Wimbledon introduced female tourney (13 entered), 1884. Also won Irish, 1889-85; Welsh, 1887, titles. RH (served overhand, could volley), b. Oct. 9, 1864, Harrow; d. June 6, 1946, Charmouth. (Lillian b. Sept. 17, 1857, Harrow; d. May 27, 1918, Berkswell, England.) Maud retained title, 1885, def. future champ Blanche Bingley Hillyard, 6-1, 7-5, but fell to Hillyard, 6-3, 6-3, 1886 F, said farewell to the Big W. Decorated with MBE for nursing work in World War I.

WEIR, Reginald—Racial pioneer, New York physician, Dr. Reginald S. Weir, overcame early discrimination to win U.S. titles. Though Althea Gibson received much attention entering U.S. at Forest Hills, 1950, RH Weir was 1st black to play national cham-

pionship sanctioned by USTA: U.S. Indoor, 1948, New York. Also 1st to win U.S. title, Senior (over 45) Indoor singles, 1956, def. Ed Tarangioli, 5-7, 6-3, 6-1. Also won, 1957, 59 (plus doubles, 1961-62), at 7th Regiment Armory, New York, gratifying turnaround where he'd been refused entry U.S. Junior Indoor, 1929. b. 1911; d. Aug. 21, 1987, Fairlawn, N.J.

WESTACOTT, Emily—Unorthodox Queenslander, using same racket face for backhand and forehand, RH Emily Jane Lucy Harding Hood Westacott was baseline banger patiently, but exuberantly pursuing Australian title. After QF finishes 1932-33-34, SF 1935, lost F to Nancye Wynne (AUS) 1937, 6-3, 5-7, 6-4. Then went all the way, 1939, def. Nell Hall Hopman (AUS), 6-1, 6-2. Won Aussie doubles 1933-34 with Mall Molesworth (AUS), lost F, 1937, with Hopman; 1939, with May Hardcastle (AUS). b. May 6, 1910, Brisbane, married Clyde Westacott Aug. 20, 1930; d. Oct. 9, 1980.

ZI, Yan & JIE, Zheng—The startling break-through gals of China, gave People's Republic first major titles, Australian, Wimbledon doubles, 2006. Won 6 doubles titles, 2006, made SF French, QF U.S. A hot year for Jie and Zi, from hot food territory, Cheng Du in Sichuan. Won Australian, beat 1st seeded Lisa Raymond (USA)-Samantha Stosur (AUS), 2-6, 7-6 (9-7), 6-3, saved 3 MP in breaker. Won Wimbledon, def. Virginia Ruano Pascual (ESP)-Paolo Suarez (ARG), 3-6, 6-3, 6-2. Also, paired to win women's doubles Olympic bronze at 2008 Beijing Games.

Yan Zi—b. Cheng Du, Nov. 12, 1984, RH (2-handed backhand), 5 ft 7 1/2, 121 lbs, turned pro 2003. Entering 2008 highest world singles rank, No. 58, 2007. Federation Cup, 6 years, 1-4 singles, 3-2 doubles. Career: won 1 singles, 15 doubles, $1,315,100 prize money.

Zheng Jie—b. Cheng Du, July 5, 1983, RH (2-handed backhand), 5 ft 4 1/2, 126 lbs, turned pro 2003. Entering 2008 highest world singles rank, No. 15, 2009; doubles No. 3 in 2009. Federation Cup, 5 years, 15-7 singles, 5-2 doubles. Career: won 3 singles (216-124 matches), 11 doubles (242-94 matches) pro titles, $$2,630,794 prize money. Upset No. 1 seed Ana Ivanovic (SRB) in third round of Wimbledon en route to semifinals, best ever Chinese performance at All England Club. Lost to Serena Williams (USA), 6-2, 7-6. Coached by husband, Li Chen.

ZVEREVA, Natalia—Mother Freedom of Soviet tennis, demanded full prize money, 1989, at a time country's players received meager subsidy from national federation, a portion of the prize money they won. Her dissent was risky business then, earned public disapproval—but she got her way, benefitting colleagues. Nimble, sharp volleying RH Belarussian, leggy 5 ft 8, b. April 16, 1971, Minsk. Often called Natasha. Upset No. 2 Martina Navratilova (USA) 4th rd., 6-3, 7-6 (7-5), but nervously lost only singles major F, French, 1988, fast, 6-0, 6-0, to Steffi Graf (GER). Made SF Wimbledon, 1998 (def. Graf, 6-4, 7-5, 3rd rd., 1st time in 19 tries); QF Australian, 1995; French, 1992; Wimbledon, 1990, 92-93; U.S., 1993. Two-way toiler, won 1,148 matches, singles and doubles.

Became doubles great (right court), won 20 majors, 14 with Gigi Fernandez (USA)—2 Australian, 1993-94; 5 French, 1992-93-94-95, 97; 4 Wimbledon, 1992-93-94, 97; 3 U.S., 1992, 95-96. Second all-time team total, behind 20, Louise Brough-Margaret Osborne duPont (both USA) and Navratilova-Pam Shriver (USA). Twice they narrowly missed Grand Slam, 1993, lost SF, U.S., to Arantxa Sanchez Vicario (ESP)-Helena Sukova (CZE), 1-6, 6-3, 6-4, ending 40-match majors streak, and 1994, lost SF, U.S., to Katerina Maleeva (BUL)-Robin White (USA), 7-6 (7-2), 1-6, 6-3. First Soviets to win major, French, 1989, she and Larisa Savchenko (Neiland), def. Gabriela Sabatini (ARG)-Graf, 6-4, 6-4. Other 3 doubles majors: Australian, 1997, with Martina Hingis (SUI); Wimbledon, 1991, with Neiland; U.S. 1991, with Shriver. Also Australian mixed, 1995, with Rick Leach (USA); 1990, with Jim Pugh (USA). World Top 10: No. 7, 1988; No. 10, 1994. Federation Cup (USSR/Belarus), 1986-96, 23-11 singles, 18-4 doubles: Made Olympics, QF, 1988, 3rd rd., 1992; won doubles bronze with Leila Meskhi, 1992, also played 1996, 2000. Turned pro, 1988. Career: won 4 singles (434-252 matches), 82 doubles (714-170 matches) pro titles, $7,792,503 prize money.

Rankings, Tours and Other Championships

SECTION V

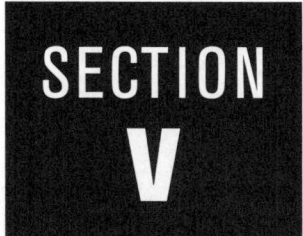

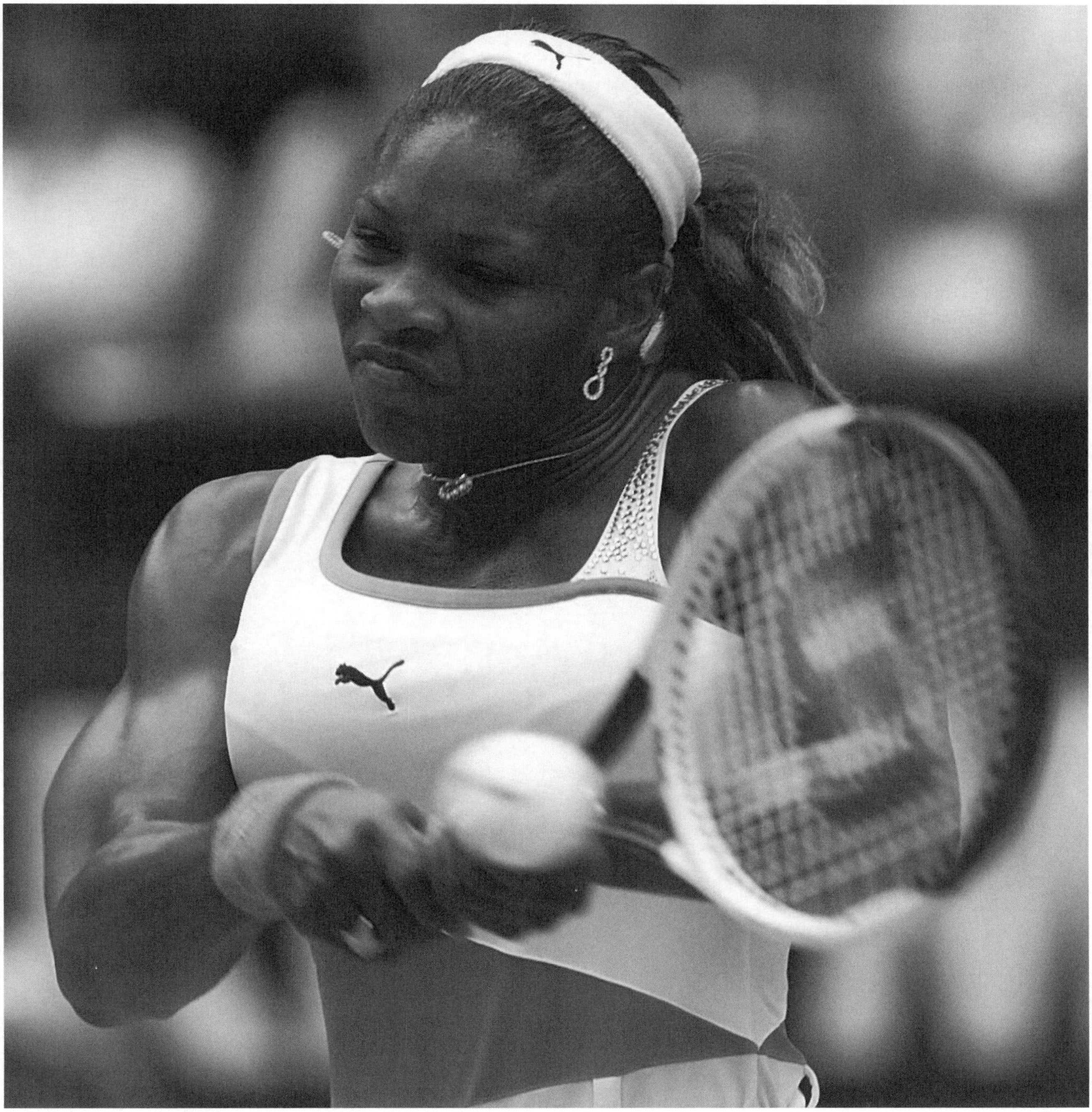

In 2003, **Serena Williams** won the Australian Open women's singles title to complete the "Serena Slam" as she became only the fifth player in the history of women's tennis to hold all four major titles at the same time, joining Maureen Connolly, Margaret Court, Steffi Graf and Martina Navratilova.

Ranking Histories CHAPTER 17

Stefan Edberg finished as the world's No. 1 ranked player in 1990 and 1991.

For decades, world singles rankings were often controversial, sometimes amusingly so. However, in 1973, the ATP (Association of Tennis Professionals), then in 1975 the WTA (Women's Tennis Association) entered the computer age. Since then, "Blinky," the ATP computer, and "Medusa," the WTA computer, have issued weekly rankings based on results to see who's who, and as guides to tournament seedings.

National associations/federations have ranked their own players since the 19th century, by committee judgements, starting with the USTA's first Top 10s in 1885 (men) and 1913 (women).

Pre-computer world rankings, a matter of judgement and opinion, usually made by astute tennis journalists, have appeared since 1913 (men) and 1921 (women). We have used those of the well-traveled, keen-eyed authorities of London's *Daily Telegraph* (with time-outs for World Wars I and II): Wallis Myers, 1913–38; John Olliff, 1939–51; Lance Tingay, 1952–67. Rankings since the advent of the Open era in 1968 and prior to computers (1973 for men, 1975 for women) are those of Bud Collins, *Boston Globe*/ESPN/Tennis Channel.

The longest uninterrupted reigns as the year's No. 1 are these—Helen Wills Moody (USA), seven years, 1927–33; Bill Tilden (USA), six years, 1920–25; Pete Sampras (USA), six years, 1993–98; Suzanne Lenglen (FRA), six years, 1921–26; Martina Navratilova (USA), five years, 1982–86; Jimmy Connors (USA), five years, 1974–78.

World Top 10 Rankings

Men

1913

1. Tony Wilding (NZL)
2. Norman Brookes (AUS)
   Maurice McLoughlin (USA)
4. Jim Cecil Parke (IRL)
5. Dick Williams (USA)
6. Charles Dixon (GBR)
7. Otto Froitzheim (GER)
8. Stanley Doust (AUS)
9. Andre Gobert (FRA)
10. Max Decugis (FRA)

1914

1. Maurice McLoughlin (USA)
2. Norman Brookes (AUS)
   Tony Wilding (NZL)
4. Otto Froitzheim (GER)
5. Dick Williams (USA)
6. Jim Cecil Parke (IRL)
7. Arthur Lowe (GBR)
8. F. Gordon Lowe (GBR)
9. Heinrich Klienschroth (GER)
10. Max Decugis (FRA)

1919

1. Gerald Patterson (AUS)
   Bill Johnston (USA)
3. Andre Gobert (FRA)
4. Bill Tilden (USA)
5. Norman Brookes (AUS)
6. Algernon Kingscote (GBR)
7. Dick Williams (USA)
8. Percival Davson (GBR)
9. Will Davis (USA)
10. William Laurentz (FRA)

1920

1. Bill Tilden (USA)
2. Bill Johnston (USA)
3. Algernon Kingscote (GBR)
4. Jim Cecil Parke (IRL)
5. Andre Gobert (FRA)
6. Norman Brookes (AUS)
7. Dick Williams (USA)
8. William Laurentz (FRA)
9. Zenzo Shimidzu (JPN)
10. Gerald Patterson (AUS)

1921

1. Bill Tilden (USA)
2. Bill Johnston (USA)
3. Vinnie Richards (USA)
4. Zenzo Shimidzu (JPN)
5. Gerald Patterson (AUS)
6. James Anderson (AUS)
7. Brian Norton (RSA)
8. Manuel Alonso (ESP)
9. Dick Williams (USA)
10. Andre Gobert (FRA)

1922

1. Bill Tilden (USA)
2. Bill Johnston (USA)
3. Gerald Patterson (AUS)
4. Vinnie Richards (USA)
5. Jim Anderson (AUS)
6. Henri Cochet (FRA)
7. Pat O' Hara Wood (AUS)
8. Dick Williams (USA)
9. Algernon Kingscote (GBR)
10. Andre Gobert (FRA)

1923

1. Bill Tilden (USA)
2. Bill Johnston (USA)
3. Jim Anderson (AUS)
4. Dick Williams (USA)
5. Frank Hunter (USA)
6. Vinnie Richards (USA)
7. Brian Norton (RSA)
8. Manuel Alonso (ESP)
9. Jean Washer (BEL)
10. Henri Cochet (FRA)

1924

1. Bill Tilden (USA)
2. Vinnie Richards (USA)
3. Jim Anderson (AUS)
4. Bill Johnston (USA)
5. Rene Lascoste (FRA)
6. Jean Borotra (FRA)
7. Howard Kinsey (USA)
8. Gerald Patterson (AUS)
9. Henri Cochet (FRA)
10. Manuel Alonso (ESP)

1925

1. Bill Tilden (USA)
2. Bill Johnston (USA)
3. Vinnie Richards (USA)
4. Rene Lacoste (FRA)
5. Dick Williams (USA)
6. Jean Borotra (FRA)
7. Gerald Patterson (AUS)
8. Manuel Alonso (ESP)
9. Brian Norton (RSA)
10. Takeichi Harada (JPN)

1926

1. Rene Lacoste (FRA)
2. Jean Borotra (FRA)
3. Henri Cochet (FRA)
4. Bill Johnston (USA)
5. Bill Tilden (USA)
6. Vinnie Richards (USA)
7. Takeichi Harada (JPN)
8. Manuel Alonso (ESP)
9. Howard Kinsey (USA)
10. Jacques Brugnon (FRA)

1927

1. Rene Lacoste (FRA)
2. Bill Tilden (USA)
3. Henri Cochet (FRA)
4. Jean Borotra (FRA)
5. Manuel Alonso (ESP)
6. Frank Hunter (USA)
7. George Lott (USA)
8. John Hennessey (USA)
9. Jacques Brugnon (FRA)
10. Jan Kozeluh (CZE)

1928

1. Henri Cochet (FRA)
2. Rene Lacoste (FRA)
3. Bill Tilden (USA)
4. Frank Hunter (USA)
5. Jean Borotra (FRA)
6. George Lott (USA)
7. Bunny Austin (GBR)
8. John Hennessey (USA)
9. Umberto de Morpurgo (ITA)
10. John Hawkes (AUS)

1929

1. Henri Cochet (FRA)
2. Rene Lacoste (FRA)
3. Jean Borotra (FRA)
4. Bill Tilden (USA)
5. Frank Hunter (USA)
6. George Lott (USA)
7. John Doeg (USA)
8. John Van Ryn (USA)
9. Bunny Austin (GBR)
10. Umberto de Morpurgo (ITA)

1930

1. Henri Cochet (FRA)
2. Bill Tilden (USA)
3. Jean Borotra (FRA)
4. John Doeg (USA)
5. Frank Shields (USA)
6. Wilmer Allison (USA)
7. George Lott (USA)
8. Umberto de Morpurgo (ITA)
9. Christian Boussus (FRA)
10. Bunny Austin (GBR)

1931

1. Henri Cochet (FRA)
2. Bunny Austin (GBR)
3. Ellsworth Vines (USA)
4. Fred Perry (GBR)
5. Frank Shields (USA)
6. Sidney Wood (USA)
7. Jean Borotra (FRA)
8. George Lott (USA)
9. Jiro Satoh (JPN)
10. John Van Ryn (USA)

1932

1. Ellsworth Vines (USA)
2. Henri Cochet (FRA)
3. Jean Borotra (FRA)
4. Wilmer Allison (USA)
5. Cliff Sutter (USA)
6. Daniel Prenn (GER)
7. Fred Perry (GBR)
8. Gottfried von Cramm (GER)
9. Bunny Austin (GBR)
10. Jack Crawford (AUS)

1933

1. Jack Crawford (AUS)
2. Fred Perry (GBR)
3. Jiro Satoh (JPN)
4. Bunny Austin (GBR)
5. Ellsworth Vines (USA)
6. Henri Cochet (FRA)
7. Frank Shields (USA)
8. Sidney Wood (USA)
9. Gottfried von Cramm (GER)
10. Lester Stoefen (USA)

1934

1. Fred Perry (GBR)
2. Jack Crawford (AUS)
3. Gottfried von Cramm (GER)
4. Bunny Austin (GBR)
5. Wilmer Allison (USA)
6. Sidney Wood (USA)
7. Roderich Menzel (CZE)
8. Frank Shields (USA)
9. Giorgio de Stefani (ITA)
10. Christian Boussus (FRA)

1935

1. Fred Perry (GBR)
2. Jack Crawford (AUS)
3. Gottfried von Cramm (GER)
4. Wilmer Allison (USA)
5. Bunny Austin (GBR)
6. Don Budge (USA)
7. Frank Shields (USA)
8. Viv McGrath (AUS)
9. Christian Boussus (FRA)
10. Sidney Woods (USA)

1936

1. Fred Perry (GBR)
2. Gottfried von Cramm (GER)
3. Don Budge (USA)
4. Adrian Quist (AUS)
5. Bunny Austin (GBR)
6. Jack Crawford (AUS)
7. Wilmer Allison (USA)
8. Bryan Grant (USA)
9. Henner Henkel (GER)
10. Viv McGrath (AUS)

1937

1. Don Budge (USA)
2. Gottfried von Cramm (GER)
3. Henner Henkel (GER)
4. Bunny Austin (GBR)
5. Bobby Riggs (USA)
6. Bryan Grant (USA)
7. Jack Crawford (AUS)
8. Roderich Menzel (CZE)
9. Frank Parker (USA)
10. Charlie Hare (GBR)

1938

1. Don Budge (USA)
2. Bunny Austin (GBR)
3. John Bromwich (AUS)
4. Bobby Riggs (USA)
5. Sidney Wood (USA)
6. Adrian Quist (AUS)
7. Roderich Menzel (CZE)
8. Jiro Yamagishi (JPN)
9. Gene Mako (USA)
10. Franjo Puncec (YUG)

1939

1. Bobby Riggs (USA)
2. John Bromwich (AUS)
3. Adrian Quist (AUS)
4. Franjo Puncec (YUG)
5. Frank Parker (USA)
6. Henner Henkel (GER)
7. Don McNeill (USA)
8. Elwood Cooke (USA)
9. Welby Van Horn (USA)
10. Joe Hunt (USA)

1946

1. Jack Kramer (USA)
2. Ted Schroeder (USA)
3. Jaroslav Drobny (CZE)
4. Yvon Petra (FRA)
5. Marcel Bernard (FRA)
6. John Bromwich (AUS)
7. Tom Brown (USA)
8. Gardnar Mulloy (USA)
9. Frank Parker (USA)
10. Geoff Brown (AUS)

1947

1. Jack Kramer (USA)
2. Ted Schroeder (USA)
3. Frank Parker (USA)
4. John Bromwich (AUS)
5. Jaroslav Drobny (CZE)
6. Dinny Pails (AUS)
7. Tom Brown (USA)
8. Budge Patty (USA)
9. Joszef Asboth (HUN)
10. Gardnar Mulloy (USA)

1948

1. Frank Parker (USA)
2. Ted Schroeder (USA)
3. Pancho Gonzalez (USA)
4. John Bromwich (AUS)
5. Jaroslav Drobny (CZE)
6. Eric Sturgess (RSA)
7. Bob Falkenburg (USA)
8. Joszef Asboth (HUN)
9. Lennart Bergelin (SWE)
10. Adrian Quist (AUS)

1949

1. Pancho Gonzalez (USA)
2. Ted Schroeder (USA)
3. Bill Talbert (USA)
4. Frank Sedgman (AUS)
5. Frank Parker (USA)
6. Eric Sturgess (RSA)
7. Jaroslav Drobny (CZE)
8. Budge Patty (USA)
9. Gardnar Mulloy (USA)
10. Billy Sidwell (AUS)

1950

1. Budge Patty (USA)
2. Frank Sedgman (AUS)
3. Art Larsen (USA)
4. Jaroslav Drobny (EGY)
5. Herbie Flam (USA)
6. Ted Schroeder (USA)
7. Vic Seixas (USA)
8. Ken McGregor (AUS)
9. Bill Talbert (USA)
10. Eric Sturgess (RSA)

1951

1. Frank Sedgman (AUS)
2. Dick Savitt (USA)
3. Jaroslav Drobny (EGY)
4. Vic Seixas (USA)
5. Tony Trabert (USA)
6. Ted Schroeder (USA)
7. Ken McGregor (AUS)
8. Herbie Flam (USA)
9. Art Larsen (USA)
10. Mervyn Rose (AUS)

1952

1. Frank Sedgman (AUS)
2. Jaroslav Drobny (EGY)
3. Ken McGregor (AUS)
4. Mervyn Rose (AUS)
5. Vic Seixas (USA)
6. Herbie Flam (USA)
7. Gardnar Mulloy (USA)
8. Eric Sturgess (RSA)
9. Dick Savitt (USA)
10. Ken Rosewall (AUS)
    Lew Hoad (AUS)

1953

1. Tony Trabert (USA)
2. Ken Rosewall (AUS)
3. Vic Seixas (USA)
4. Jaroslav Drobny (EGY)
5. Lew Hoad (AUS)
6. Mervyn Rose (AUS)
7. Kurt Nielsen (DEN)
8. Budge Patty (USA)
9. Sven Davidson (SWE)
10. Enrique Morea (ARG)

1954

1. Jaroslav Drobny (EGY)
2. Tony Trabert (USA)
3. Ken Rosewall (AUS)
4. Vic Seixas (USA)
5. Rex Hartwig (AUS)
6. Mervyn Rose (AUS)
7. Lew Hoad (AUS)
8. Budge Patty (USA)
9. Art Larsen (USA)
10. Enrique Morea (ARG)
    Ham Richardson (USA)
    Sven Davidson (SWE)

1955

1. Tony Trabert (USA)
2. Ken Rosewall (AUS)
3. Lew Hoad (AUS)
4. Vic Seixas (USA)
5. Rex Hartwig (AUS)
6. Budge Patty (USA)
7. Ham Richardson (USA)
8. Kurt Nielsen (DEN)
9. Jaroslav Drobny (EGY)
10. Sven Davidson (SWE)
    Mervyn Rose (AUS)

1956

1. Lew Hoad (AUS)
2. Ken Rosewall (AUS)
3. Ham Richardson (USA)
4. Vic Seixas (USA)
5. Sven Davidson (SWE)
6. Neale Fraser (AUS)
7. Ashley Cooper (AUS)
8. Dick Savitt (USA)
9. Herbie Flam (USA)
10. Budge Patty (USA)
    Nicola Pietrangeli (ITA)

1957

1. Ashley Cooper (AUS)
2. Mal Anderson (AUS)
3. Sven Davidson (SWE)
4. Herbie Flam (USA)
5. Neale Fraser (AUS)
6. Mervyn Rose (AUS)
7. Vic Seixas (USA)
8. Budge Patty (USA)
9. Nicola Pietrangeli (ITA)
10. Dick Savitt (USA)

1958

1. Ashley Cooper (AUS)
2. Mal Anderson (AUS)
3. Mervyn Rose (AUS)
4. Neale Fraser (AUS)
5. Luis Ayala (CHI)
6. Ham Richardson (USA)
7. Nicola Pietrangeli (ITA)
8. Ulf Schmidt (SWE)
9. Barry MacKay (USA)
10. Sven Davidson (SWE)

1959

1. Neale Fraser (AUS)
2. Alex Olmedo (PER)
3. Nicola Pietrangeli (ITA)
4. Barry MacKay (USA)
5. Rod Laver (AUS)
6. Luis Ayala (CHI)
7. Roy Emerson (AUS)
8. Bernard Bartzen (USA)
9. Ramanathan Krishnan (IND)
10. Ian Vermaak (RSA)

1960

1. Neale Fraser (AUS)
2. Rod Laver (AUS)
3. Nicola Pietrangeli (ITA)
4. Barry MacKay (USA)
5. Butch Buchholz (USA)
6. Roy Emerson (AUS)
7. Luis Ayala (CHI)
8. Ramanathan Krishnan (IND)
9. Jan-Erik Lundquist (SWE)
10. Dennis Ralston (USA)

1961

1. Rod Laver (AUS)
2. Roy Emerson (AUS)
3. Manolo Santana (ESP)
4. Nicola Pietrangeli (ITA)
5. Chuck McKinley (USA)
6. Ramanathan Krishnan (IND)
7. Luis Ayala (CHI)
8. Neale Fraser (AUS)
9. Jan-Erik Lundquist (SWE)
10. Ulf Schmidt (SWE)

1962

1. Rod Laver (AUS)
2. Roy Emerson (AUS)
3. Manolo Santana (ESP)
4. Neale Fraser (AUS)
5. Chuck McKinley (USA)
6. Rafael Osuna (MEX)
7. Marty Mulligan (AUS)
8. Bob Hewitt (AUS)
9. Ramanathan Krishnan (IND)
10. Wilhelm Bungert (GER)

1963

1. Rafael Osuna (MEX)
2. Chuck McKinley (USA)
3. Roy Emerson (AUS)
4. Manolo Santana (ESP)
5. Fred Stolle (AUS)
6. Frank Froehling III (USA)
7. Dennis Ralston (USA)
8. Boro Jovanovic (YUG)
9. Mike Sangster (GBR)
10. Marty Mulligan (AUS)

1964

1. Roy Emerson (AUS)
2. Fred Stolle (AUS)
3. Jan-Erik Lundquist (SWE)
4. Wilhelm Bungert (GER)
5. Chuck McKinley (USA)
6. Manolo Santana (ESP)
7. Nicola Pietrangeli (ITA)
8. Christian Kuhnke (GER)
9. Dennis Ralston (USA)
10. Rafael Osuna (MEX)

1965

1. Roy Emerson (AUS)
2. Manolo Santana (ESP)
3. Fred Stolle (AUS)
4. Cliff Drysdale (RSA)
5. Marty Mulligan (AUS)
6. Jan-Erik Lundquist (SWE)
7. Tony Roche (AUS)
8. John Newcombe (AUS)
9. Dennis Ralston (USA)
10. Arthur Ashe (USA)

1966

1. Manolo Santana (ESP)
2. Fred Stolle (AUS)
3. Roy Emerson (AUS)
4. Tony Roche (AUS)
5. Dennis Ralston (USA)
6. John Newcombe (AUS)
7. Arthur Ashe (USA)
8. Istvan Gulyas (HUN)
9. Cliff Drysdale (RSA)
10. Ken Flecther (AUS)

1967

1. John Newcombe (AUS)
2. Roy Emerson (AUS)
3. Manolo Santana (ESP)
4. Marty Mulligan (AUS)
5. Tony Roche (AUS)
6. Bob Hewitt (RSA)
7. Nikki Pilic (YUG)
8. Clark Graebner (USA)
9. Arthur Ashe (USA)
10. Jan Leschly (DEN)
    Wilhelm Bungert (GER)
    Cliff Drysdale (RSA)

1968

1. Rod Laver (AUS)
2. Arthur Ashe (USA)
3. Ken Rosewall (AUS)
4. Tony Roche (AUS)
5. Tom Okker (NED)
6. John Newcombe (AUS)
7. Clark Graebner (USA)
8. Dennis Ralston (USA)
9. Cliff Drysdale (RSA)
10. Pancho Gonzalez (USA)

1969

1. Rod Laver (AUS)
2. Tony Roche (AUS)
3. John Newcombe (AUS)
4. Ken Rosewall (AUS)
5. Tom Okker (NED)
6. Pancho Gonzalez (USA)
7. Stan Smith (USA)
8. Arthur Ashe (USA)
9. Cliff Drysdale (RSA)
10. Andres Gimeno (ESP)

1970

1. John Newcombe (AUS)
2. Ken Rosewall (AUS)
3. Tony Roche (AUS)
4. Rod Laver (AUS)
5. Ilie Nastase (ROM)
6. Tom Okker (NED)
7. Cliff Richey (USA)
8. Stan Smith (USA)
9. Arthur Ashe (USA)
10. Andres Gimeno (ESP)

1971

1. John Newcombe (AUS)
2. Stan Smith (USA)
3. Ken Rosewall (AUS)
4. Rod Laver (AUS)
5. Jan Kodes (CZE)
6. Arthur Ashe (USA)
7. Ilie Nastase (ROM)
8. Tom Okker (NED)
9. Cliff Drysdale (RSA)
10. Marty Riessen (USA)

1972

1. Stan Smith (USA)
2. Ken Rosewall (AUS)
3. Ilie Nastase (ROM)
4. Rod Laver (AUS)
5. Arthur Ashe (USA)
6. John Newcombe (AUS)
7. Bob Lutz (USA)
8. Tom Okker (NED)
9. Marty Riessen (USA)
10. Andres Gimeno (ESP)

1973 (computer rankings begin)

1. Ilie Nastase (ROM)
2. John Newcombe (AUS)
3. Jimmy Connors (USA)
4. Tom Okker (NED)
5. Stan Smith (USA)
6. Ken Rosewall (AUS)
7. Manuel Orantes (ESP)
8. Rod Laver (AUS)
9. Jan Kodes (CZE)
10. Arthur Ashe (USA)

1974

1. Jimmy Connors (USA)
2. John Newcombe (AUS)
3. Bjorn Borg (SWE)
4. Rod Laver (AUS)
5. Guillermo Vilas (ARG)
6. Tom Okker (NED)
7. Arthur Ashe (USA)
8. Ken Rosewall (AUS)
9. Stan Smith (USA)
10. Ilie Nastase (ROM)

1975

1. Jimmy Connors (USA)
2. Guillermo Vilas (ARG)
3. Bjorn Borg (SWE)
4. Arthur Ashe (USA)
5. Manuel Orantes (ESP)
6. Ken Rosewall (AUS)
7. Ilie Nastase (ROM)
8. John Alexander (AUS)
9. Roscoe Tanner (USA)
10. Rod Laver (AUS)

1976

1. Jimmy Connors (USA)
2. Bjorn Borg (SWE)
3. Ilie Nastase (ROM)
4. Manuel Orantes (ESP)
5. Raul Ramirez (MEX)
6. Guillermo Vilas (ARG)
7. Adriano Panatta (ITA)
8. Harold Solomon (USA)
9. Eddie Dibbs (USA)
10. Brian Gottfried (USA)

1977

1. Jimmy Connors (USA)
2. Guillermo Vilas (ARG)
3. Bjorn Borg (SWE)
4. Vitas Gerulaitis (USA)
5. Brian Gottfried (USA)
6. Eddie Dibbs (USA)
7. Manuel Orantes (ESP)
8. Raul Ramirez (MEX)
9. Ilie Nastase (ROM)
10. Dick Stockton (USA)

1978

1. Jimmy Connors (USA)
2. Bjorn Borg (SWE)
3. Guillermo Vilas (ARG)
4. John McEnroe (USA)
5. Vitas Gerulaitis (USA)
6. Eddie Dibbs (USA)
7. Brian Gottfried (USA)
8. Raul Ramirez (MEX)
9. Harold Solomon (USA)
10. Corrado Barazzutti (ITA)

1979

1. Bjorn Borg (SWE)
2. Jimmy Connors (USA)
3. John McEnroe (USA)
4. Vitas Gerulaitis (USA)
5. Roscoe Tanner (USA)
6. Guillermo Vilas (ARG)
7. Arthur Ashe (USA)
8. Harold Solomon (USA)
9. Jose Higueras (ESP)
10. Eddie Dibbs (USA)

1980

1. Bjorn Borg (SWE)
2. John McEnroe (USA)
3. Jimmy Connors (USA)
4. Gene Mayer (USA)
5. Guillermo Vilas (ARG)
6. Ivan Lendl (CZE)
7. Harold Solomon (USA)
8. Jose-Luis Clerc (ARG)
9. Vitas Gerulaitis (USA)
10. Eliot Teltscher (USA)

1981

1. John McEnroe (USA)
2. Ivan Lendl (CZE)
3. Jimmy Connors (USA)
4. Bjorn Borg (SWE)
5. Jose-Luis Clerc (ARG)
6. Guillermo Vilas (ARG)
7. Gene Mayer (USA)
8. Eliot Teltscher (USA)
9. Vitas Gerulaitis (USA)
10. Peter McNamara (AUS)

1982

1. John McEnroe (USA)
2. Jimmy Connors (USA)
3. Ivan Lendl (CZE)
4. Guillermo Vilas (ARG)
5. Vitas Gerulaitis (USA)
6. Jose-Luis Clerc (ARG)
7. Mats Wilander (SWE)
8. Gene Mayer (USA)
9. Yannick Noah (FRA)
10. Peter McNamara (AUS)

1983

1. John McEnroe (USA)
2. Ivan Lendl (CZE)
3. Jimmy Connors (USA)
4. Mats Wilander (SWE)
5. Yannick Noah (FRA)
6. Jimmy Arias (USA)
7. Jose Higueras (ESP)
8. Jose-Luis Clerc (ARG)
9. Kevin Curren (RSA)
10. Gene Mayer (USA)

1984

1. John McEnroe (USA)
2. Jimmy Connors (USA)
3. Ivan Lendl (CZE)
4. Mats Wilander (SWE)
5. Andres Gomez (ECU)
6. Anders Jarryd (SWE)
7. Henrik Sundstrom (SWE)
8. Pat Cash (AUS)
9. Eliot Teltscher (USA)
10. Yannick Noah (FRA)

1985

1. Ivan Lendl (CZE)
2. John McEnroe (USA)
3. Mats Wilander (SWE)
4. Jimmy Connors (USA)
5. Stefan Edberg (SWE)
6. Boris Becker (GER)
7. Yannick Noah (FRA)
8. Anders Jarryd (SWE)
9. Miloslav Mecir (CZE)
10. Kevin Curren (USA)

1986

1. Ivan Lendl (CZE)
2. Boris Becker (GER)
3. Mats Wilander (SWE)
4. Yannick Noah (FRA)
5. Stefan Edberg (SWE)
6. Henri Leconte (FRA)
7. Joakim Nystrom (SWE)
8. Jimmy Connors (USA)
9. Miloslav Mecir (CZE)
10. Andres Gomez (ECU)

1987

1. Ivan Lendl (CZE)
2. Stefan Edberg (SWE)
3. Mats Wilander (SWE)
4. Jimmy Connors (USA)
5. Boris Becker (GER)
6. Miloslav Mecir (CZE)
7. Pat Cash (AUS)
8. Yannick Noah (FRA)
9. Tim Mayotte (USA)
10. John McEnroe (USA)

1988

1. Mats Wilander (SWE)
2. Ivan Lendl (CZE)
3. Andre Agassi (USA)
4. Boris Becker (GER)
5. Stefan Edberg (SWE)
6. Kent Carlsson (SWE)
7. Jimmy Connors (USA)
8. Jakob Hlasek (SUI)
9. Henri Leconte (FRA)
10. Tim Mayotte (USA)

1989

1. Ivan Lendl (CZE)
2. Boris Becker (GER)
3. Stefan Edberg (SWE)
4. John McEnroe (USA)
5. Michael Chang (USA)
6. Brad Gilbert (USA)
7. Andre Agassi (USA)
8. Aaron Krickstein (USA)
9. Alberto Mancini (ARG)
10. Jay Berger (USA)

1990

1. Stefan Edberg (SWE)
2. Boris Becker (GER)
3. Ivan Lendl (CZE)
4. Andre Agassi (USA)
5. Pete Sampras (USA)
6. Andres Gomez (ECU)
7. Thomas Muster (AUT)
8. Emilio Sanchez (ESP)
9. Goran Ivanisevic (CRO)
10. Brad Gilbert (USA)

1991

1. Stefan Edberg (SWE)
2. Jim Courier (USA)
3. Boris Becker (GER)
4. Michael Stich (GER)
5. Ivan Lendl (CZE)
6. Pete Sampras (USA)
7. Guy Forget (FRA)
8. Karel Novacek (CZE)
9. Peter Korda (CZE)
10. Andre Agassi (USA)

1992

1. Jim Courier (USA)
2. Stefan Edberg (SWE)
3. Pete Sampras (USA)
4. Goran Ivanisevic (CRO)
5. Boris Becker (GER)
6. Michael Chang (USA)
7. Petr Korda (CZE)
8. Ivan Lendl (USA)
9. Andre Agassi (USA)
10. Richard Krajicek (NED)

1993

1. Pete Sampras (USA)
2. Michael Stich (GER)
3. Jim Courier (USA)
4. Sergi Bruguera (ESP)
5. Stefan Edberg (SWE)
6. Andrei Medvedev (UKR)
7. Goran Ivanisevic (CRO)
8. Michael Chang (USA)
9. Thomas Muster (AUT)
10. Cedric Pioline (FRA)

1994

1. Pete Sampras (USA)
2. Andre Agassi (USA)
3. Boris Becker (GER)
4. Sergi Bruguera (ESP)
5. Goran Ivanisevic (CRO)
6. Michael Chang (USA)
7. Stefan Edberg (SWE)
8. Alberto Berasategui (ESP)
9. Michael Stich (GER)
10. Todd Martin (USA)

1995

1. Pete Sampras (USA)
2. Andre Agassi (USA)
3. Thomas Muster (AUT)
4. Boris Becker (GER)
5. Michael Chang (USA)
6. Yevgeny Kafelnikov (RUS)
7. Thomas Enqvist (SWE)
8. Jim Courier (USA)
9. Wayne Ferreira (RSA)
10. Goran Ivanisevic (CRO)

1996

1. Pete Sampras (USA)
2. Michael Chang (USA)
3. Yevgeny Kafelnikov (RUS)
4. Goran Ivanisevic (CRO)
5. Thomas Muster (AUT)
6. Boris Becker (GER)
7. Richard Krajicek (NED)
8. Andre Agassi (USA)
9. Thomas Enqvist (SWE)
10. Wayne Ferreira (RSA)

1997

1. Pete Sampras (USA)
2. Patrick Rafter (AUS)
3. Michael Chang (USA)
4. Jonas Bjorkman (SWE)
5. Yevgeny Kafelnikov (RUS)
6. Greg Rusedski (GBR)
7. Carlos Moya (ESP)
8. Sergi Bruguera (ESP)
9. Thomas Muster (AUT)
10. Marcelo Rios (CHI)

1998

1. Pete Sampras (USA)
2. Marcelo Rios (CHI)
3. Alex Corretja (ESP)
4. Patrick Rafter (AUS)
5. Carlos Moya (ESP)
6. Andre Agassi (USA)
7. Tim Henman (GBR)
8. Karol Kucera (SVK)
9. Greg Rusedski (GBR)
10. Richard Krajicek (NED)

1999

1. Andre Agassi (USA)
2. Yevgeny Kafelnikov (RUS)
3. Pete Sampras (USA)
4. Thomas Enqvist (SWE)
5. Gustavo Kuerten (BRA)
6. Nicolas Kiefer (GER)
7. Todd Martin (USA)
8. Nicola Lapentti (ECU)
9. Marcelo Rios (CHI)
10. Richard Krajicek (NED)

2000

1. Gustavo Kuerten (BRA)
2. Marat Safin (RUS)
3. Pete Sampras (USA)
4. Magnus Norman (SWE)
5. Yevgeny Kafelnikov (RUS)
6. Andre Agassi (USA)
7. Lleyton Hewitt (AUS)
8. Alex Corretja (ESP)
9. Thomas Enqvist (SWE)
10. Tim Henman (GBR)

2001

1. Lleyton Hewitt (AUS)
2. Gustavo Kuerten (BRA)
3. Andre Agassi (USA)
4. Yevgeny Kafelnikov (RUS)
5. Juan Carlos Ferrero (ESP)
6. Sebastien Grosjean (FRA)
7. Patrick Rafter (AUS)
8. Tommy Haas (GER)
9. Tim Henman (GBR)
10. Pete Sampras (USA)

2002

1. Lleyton Hewitt (AUS)
2. Andre Agassi (USA)
3. Marat Safin (RUS)
4. Juan Carlos Ferrero (ESP)
5. Carlos Moya (ESP)
6. Roger Federer (SUI)
7. Jiri Novak (CZE)
8. Tim Henman (GBR)
9. Albert Costa (ESP)
10. Andy Roddick (USA)

2003

1. Andy Roddick (USA)
2. Roger Federer (SUI)
3. Juan Carlos Ferrero (ESP)
4. Andre Agassi (USA)
5. Guillermo Coria (ARG)
6. Rainer Schuettler (GER)
7. Carlos Moya (ESP)
8. David Nalbandian (ARG)
9. Mark Philippoussis (AUS)
10. Sebastian Grosjean (FRA)

2004

1. Roger Federer (SUI)
2. Andy Roddick (USA)
3. Lleyton Hewitt (AUS)
4. Marat Safin (RUS)
5. Carlos Moya (ESP)
6. Tim Henman (GBR)
7. Guillermo Coria (ARG)
8. Andre Agassi (USA)
9. David Nalbandian (ARG)
10. Gaston Gaudio (ARG)

2005

1. Roger Federer (SUI)
2. Rafael Nadal (ESP)
3. Andy Roddick (USA)
4. Lleyton Hewitt (AUS)
5. Nikolay Davydenko (RUS)
6. David Nalbandian (ARG)
7. Andre Agassi (USA)
8. Guillermo Coria (ARG)
9. Ivan Ljubicic (CRO)
10. Gaston Gaudio (ARG)

2006

1. Roger Federer (SUI)
2. Rafael Nadal (ESP)
3. Nikolay Davydenko (RUS)
4. James Blake (USA)
5. Ivan Ljubicic (CRO)
6. Andy Roddick (USA)
7. Tommy Robredo (ESP)
8. David Nalbandian (ARG)
9. Mario Ancic (CRO)
10. Fernando Gonzalez (CHI)

2007

1. Roger Federer (SUI)
2. Rafael Nadal (ESP)
3. Novak Djokovic (SRB)
4. Nikolay Davydenko (RUS)
5. David Ferrer (ESP)
6. Andy Roddick (USA)
7. Fernando Gonzalez (CHI)
8. Richard Gasquet (FRA)
9. David Nalbandian (ARG)
10. Tommy Robredo (ESP)

2008

1. Rafael Nadal (ESP)
2. Roger Federer (SUI)
3. Novak Djokovic (SRB)
4. Andy Murray (GBR)
5. Nikolay Davydenko (RUS)
6. Jo-Wilfried Tsonga (FRA)
7. Gilles Simon (FRA)
8. Andy Roddick (USA)
9. Juan Martin del Potro (ARG)
10. James Blake (USA)

Women

1921

1. Suzanne Lenglen (FRA)
2. Molla Bjurstedt Mallory (USA)
3. Mary K. Browne (USA)
4. Elizabeth Ryan (USA)
5. Kitty McKane (GBR)
6. May Sutton Bundy (USA)
7. Irene Peacock (RSA)
8. Geraldine Beamish (GBR)
9. Eleanor Goss (USA)
10. Marlon Zinderstein Jessup (USA)

1922

1. Suzanne Lenglen (FRA)
2. Molla Bjurstedt Mallory (USA)
3. Helen Wills (USA)
4. Kitty McKane (GBR)
5. Geraldine Beamish (GBR)
6. Irene Peacock (RSA)
7. Elizabeth Ryan (USA)
8. Marlon Zinderstein Jessup (USA)
9. May Sutton Bundy (USA)
10. Margaret Molesworth (AUS)

1923

1. Suzanne Lenglen (FRA)
2. Kitty McKane (GBR)
3. Helen Wills (USA)
4. Geraldine Beamish (GBR)
5. Molla Bjurstedt Mallory (USA)
6. Eleanor Goss (USA)
7. Elizabeth Ryan (USA)
8. Didi Vlasto (FRA)
9. Leslie Bancroft (USA)
10. Margaret Molesworth (AUS)

1924

1. Suzanne Lenglen (FRA)
2. Kitty McKane (GBR)
3. Helen Wills (USA)
4. Molla Mallory (USA)
5. Mary K. Browne (USA)
6. Eleanor Goss (USA)
7. Elizabeth Ryan (USA)
8. Phyllis Satterthwaite (GBR)
9. Marlon Zinderstein Jessup (USA)
10. Sylvia Lance (AUS)

1925

1. Suzanne Lenglen (FRA)
2. Helen Wills (USA)
3. Kitty McKane (GBR)
4. Elizabeth Ryan (USA)
5. Molla Bjurstedt Mallory (USA)
6. Eleanor Goss (USA)
7. D. Douglas Chambers (GBR)
8. Joan Fry (GBR)
9. Marguerite Billout (FRA)
10. Marlon Zinderstein Jessup (USA)

1926

1. Suzanne Lenglen (FRA)
2. Kitty McKane Godfree (GBR)
3. Lili de Alvarez (ESP)
4. Molla Bjurstedt Mallory (USA)
5. Elizabeth Ryan (USA)
6. Mary K. Browne (USA)
7. Joan Fry (GBR)
8. Phoebe Holcroft Watson (GBR)
10. Marlon Zinderstein Jessup (USA)
    Didi Vlasto (FRA)

1927

1. Helen Wills (USA)
2. Lili de Alvarez (ESP)
3. Elizabeth Ryan (USA)
4. Molla Bjurstedt Mallory (USA)
5. Kitty McKane Godfree (GBR)
6. Betty Nuthall (GBR)
7. Bobbie Heine (RSA)
8. Joan Fry (GBR)
9. Kea Bouman (NED)
10. Charlotte Hosmer Chapin (USA)

1928

1. Helen Wills (USA)
2. Lili de Alvarez (ESP)
3. Daphne Akhurst (AUS)
4. Eileen Bennett (GBR)
5. Phoebe Holcroft Watson (GBR)
6. Elizabeth Ryan (USA)
7. Cilly Aussem (GER)
8. Kea Bouman (NED)
9. Helen Jacobs (USA)
10. Esna Boyd (AUS)

1929

1. Helen Wills (USA)
2. Phoebe Holcroft Watson (GBR)
3. Helen Jacobs (USA)
4. Betty Nuthall (GBR)
5. Bobbie Heine (RSA)
6. Simone Passermard Mathieu (FRA)
7. Eileen Bennett (GBR)
8. Paula von Reznicek (GER)
9. Peggy Saunders Michell (GBR)
10. Elsie Goldsack (GBR)

1930

1. Helen Wills Moody (USA)
2. Cilly Aussem (GER)
3. Phoebe Holcroft Watson (GBR)
4. Elizabeth Ryan (USA)
5. Simone Passermard Mathieu (FRA)
6. Helen Jacobs (USA)
7. Phyllis Mudford (GBR)
8. Lili de Alvarez (ESP)
9. Betty Nuthall (GBR)
10. Hilde Krahwinkel (GER)

1931

1. Helen Wills Moody (USA)
2. Cilly Aussem (GER)
3. E. Bennett Whittingstall (GBR)
4. Helen Jacobs (USA)
5. Betty Nuthall (GBR)
6. Hilde Krahwinkel (GER)
7. Simone Passermard Mathieu (FRA)
8. Lili de Alvarez (ESP)
9. Phyllis Mudford (GBR)
10. Elsie Goldsack Pittman (GBR)

1932

1. Helen Wills Moody (USA)
2. Helen Jacobs (USA)
3. Simone Passermard Mathieu (FRA)
4. Lolette Payot (SUI)
5. Hilde Krahwinkel (GER)
6. Mary Heeley (ENG)
7. E. Bennett Whittingstall (GBR)
8. Marie Luise Horn (GER)
9. Kay Stammers (GBR)
10. Josane Sigart (BEL)

1933

1. Helen Wills Moody (USA)
2. Helen Jacobs (USA)
3. Dorothy Round (GBR)
4. Hilde Krahwinkel (GER)
5. Margaret Scriven (GBR)
6. Simone Passermard Mathieu (FRA)
7. Sarah Palfrey (USA)
8. Betty Nuthall (GBR)
9. Lolette Payot (SUI)
10. Alice Marble (USA)

1934

1. Dorothy Round (GBR)
2. Helen Jacobs (USA)
3. Hilde Krahwinkel Sperling (DEN)
4. Sarah Palfrey (USA)
5. Margaret Scriven (GBR)
6. Simone Passermard Mathieu (FRA)
7. Lolette Payot (SUI)
8. Joan Hartigan (AUS)
9. Cilly Aussem (GER)
10. Carolin Babcock (USA)

1935

1. Helen Wills Moody (USA)
2. Helen Jacobs (USA)
3. Kay Stammers (GBR)
4. Hilde Krahwinkel Sperling (DEN)
5. Sarah Palfrey Fabyan (USA)
6. Dorothy Round (GBR)
7. Mary Arnold (USA)
8. Simone Passermard Mathieu (FRA)
9. Joan Hartigan (AUS)
10. Margaret Scriven (GBR)

1936

1. Helen Wills Moody (USA)
2. Hilde Krahwinkel Sperling (DEN)
3. Dorothy Round (GBR)
4. Alice Marble (USA)
5. Simone Passermard Mathieu (FRA)
6. Jadwiga Jedrzejowska (POL)
7. Kay Stammers (GBR)
8. Anita Lizana (CHI)
9. Sarah Palfrey Fabyan (USA)
10. Carolin Babcock (USA)

1937

1. Anita Lizana (CHI)
2. Dorothy Round Little (GBR)
3. Jadwiga Jedrzejowska (POL)
4. Hilde Krahwinkel Sperling (DEN)
5. Simone Passermard Mathieu (FRA)
6. Helen Jacobs (USA)
7. Alice Marble (USA)
8. Marie Luise Horn (GER)
9. Mary Hardwick (GBR)
10. Dorothy Bundy (USA)

1938

1. Helen Wills Moody (USA)
2. Helen Jacobs (USA)
3. Alice Marble (USA)
4. Hilde Krahwinkel Sperling (DEN)
5. Simone Passermard Mathieu (FRA)
6. Jadwiga Jedrzejowska (POL)
7. Sarah Palfrey Fabyan (USA)
8. Bobby Heine Miller (RSA)
9. Kay Stammers (GBR)
10. Nancye Wynne (AUS)

1939

1. Alice Marble (USA)
2. Kay Stammers (GBR)
3. Helen Jacobs (USA)
4. Hilde Krahwinkel Sperling (DEN)
5. Simone Passermard Mathieu (FRA)
6. Sarah Palfrey Fabyan (USA)
7. Jadwiga Jedrzejowska (POL)
8. Mary Hardwick (GBR)
9. Valerie Scott (GBR)
10. Virginia Wolfenden (USA)

1946

1. Pauline Betz (USA)
2. Margaret Osborne (USA)
3. Louise Brough (USA)
4. Doris Hart (USA)
5. Pat Canning Todd (USA)
6. Dorothy Bundy (USA)
7. Nelly Adamson Landry (FRA)
8. Kay Stammers Menzies (GBR)
9. Shirley Fry (USA)
10. Virginia Wolfenden Kovacs (USA)

1947

1. Margaret Osborne duPont (USA)
2. Louise Brough (USA)
3. Doris Hart (USA)
4. Nancye Wynne Bolton (AUS)
5. Pat Canning Todd (USA)
6. Sheila Piercey Summers (RSA)
7. Jean Bostock (GBR)
8. Barbara Krase (USA)
9. Betty Hilton (GBR)
10. Madga Rurac (ROM)

1948

1. Margaret Osborne duPont (USA)
2. Louise Brough (USA)
3. Doris Hart (USA)
4. Nancye Wynne Bolton (AUS)
5. Pat Canning Todd (USA)
6. Jean Bostock (GBR)
7. Sheila Piercey Summers (RSA)
8. Shirley Fry (USA)
9. Madga Rurac (ROM)
10. Nelly Adamson Landry (FRA)

1949

1. Margaret Osborne duPont (USA)
2. Louise Brough (USA)
3. Doris Hart (USA)
4. Nancye Wynne Bolton (AUS)
5. Pat Canning Todd (USA)
6. Betty Hilton (GBR)
7. Sheila Piercey Summers (RSA)
8. Annelies Ullstein Bossi (ITA)
9. Joan Curry (GBR)
10. Jean Walker-Smith (GBR)

1950

1. Margaret Osborne duPont (USA)
2. Louise Brough (USA)
3. Doris Hart (USA)
4. Pat Canning Todd (USA)
5. Barbara Scofield (USA)
6. Nancy Chaffee (USA)
7. Beverly Baker (USA)
8. Shirley Fry (USA)
9. Annelies Ullstein Bossi (ITA)
10. Maria Weiss (ARG)

1951

1. Doris Hart (USA)
2. Maureen Connolly (USA)
3. Shirley Fry (USA)
4. Nancy Chaffee Kiner (USA)
5. Jean Walker-Smith (GBR)
6. Jean Quertier (GBR)
7. Louise Brough (USA)
8. Beverly Baker Fleitz (USA)
9. Pat Canning Todd (USA)
10. Kay Tuckey Maule (GBR)

1952

1. Maureen Connolly (USA)
2. Doris Hart (USA)
3. Louise Brough (USA)
4. Shirley Fry (USA)
5. Pat Canning Todd (USA)
6. Nancy Chaffee Kiner (USA)
7. Thelma Coyne Long (AUS)
8. Jean Walker-Smith (GBR)
9. Jean Quertier-Rinkel (USA)
10. Dorothy Head Knode (USA)

1953

1. Maureen Connolly (USA)
2. Doris Hart (USA)
3. Louise Brough (USA)
4. Shirley Fry (USA)
5. Margaret Osborne duPont (USA)
6. Dorothy Head Knode (USA)
7. Suzi Kormoczi (HUN)
8. Angela Mortimer (GBR)
9. Helen Fletcher (GBR)
10. Jean Quertier-Rinkel (USA)

1954

1. Maureen Connolly (USA)
2. Doris Hart (USA)
3. Beverly Baker Fleitz (USA)
4. Louise Brough (USA)
5. Margaret Osborne duPont (USA)
6. Shirley Fry (USA)
7. Betty Rosenquest Pratt (USA)
8. Helen Fletcher (GBR)
9. Angela Mortimer (GBR)
10. Ginette Bucaille (FRA)
   Thelma Coyne Long (AUS)

1955

1. Louise Brough (USA)
2. Doris Hart (USA)
3. Beverly Baker Fleitz (USA)
4. Angela Mortimer (GBR)
5. Dorothy Head Knode (USA)
6. Barbara Breit (USA)
7. Darlene Hard (USA)
8. Beryl Penrose (AUS)
9. Pat Ward (GBR)
10 . Suzi Kormoczi (HUN)
   Shirley Fry (USA)

1956

1. Shirley Fry (USA)
2. Althea Gibson (USA)
3. Louise Brough (USA)
4. Angela Mortimer (GBR)
5. Suzi Kormoczi (HUN)
6. Angela Buxton (GBR)
7. Shirley Bloomer (GBR)
8. Pat Ward (GBR)
9. Betty Rosenquest Pratt (JAM)
10. Darlene Hard (USA)
   Margaret Osborne duPont (USA)

1957

1. Althea Gibson (USA)
2. Darlene Hard (USA)
3. Shirley Bloomer (GBR)
4. Louise Brough (USA)
5. Dorothy Head Knode (USA)
6. Vera Puzejova (CZE)
7. Ann Haydon (GBR)
8. Yola Ramirez (MEX)
9. Christine Truman (GBR)
10. Margaret Osborne duPont (USA)

1958

1. Althea Gibson (USA)
2. Suzi Kormoczi (HUN)
3. Beverly Baker Fleitz (USA)
4. Darlene Hard (USA)
5. Shirley Bloomer (GBR)
6. Christine Truman (GBR)
7. Angela Mortimer (GBR)
8. Ann Haydon (GBR)
9. Maria Bueno (BRA)
10. Dorothy Head Knode (USA)

1959

1. Maria Bueno (BRA)
2. Christine Truman (GBR)
3. Darlene Hard (USA)
4. Beverly Baker Fleitz (USA)
5. Sandra Reynolds (RSA)
6. Angela Mortimer (GBR)
7. Ann Haydon (GBR)
8. Suzi Kormoczi (HUN)
9. Sally Moore (USA)
10. Yola Ramirez (MEX)

1960

1. Maria Bueno (BRA)
2. Darlene Hard (USA)
3. Sandra Reynolds (RSA)
4. Christine Truman (GBR)
5. Suzi Kormoczi (HUN)
6. Ann Haydon (GBR)
7. Angela Mortimer (GBR)
8. Jan Lehane (AUS)
9. Yola Ramirez (MEX)
10. Renee Schuurman (RSA)

1961

1. Angela Mortimer (GBR)
2. Darlene Hard (USA)
3. Ann Haydon (GBR)
4. Margaret Smith (AUS)
5. Sandra Reynolds (RSA)
6. Yola Ramirez (MEX)
7. Christine Truman (GBR)
8. Suzi Kormoczi (HUN)
9. Renee Schuurman (RSA)
10. Karen Hantze (USA)

1962

1. Margaret Smith (AUS)
2. Maria Bueno (BRA)
3. Darlene Hard (USA)
4. Karen Hantze Susman (USA)
5. Vera Puzejova Sukova (CZE)
6. Sandra Reynolds Price (RSA)
7. Lesley Turner (AUS)
8. Ann Haydon (GBR)
9. Renee Schuurman (RSA)
10. Angela Mortimer (GBR)

1963

1. Margaret Smith (AUS)
2. Lesley Turner (AUS)
3. Maria Bueno (BRA)
4. Billie Jean Moffitt (USA)
5. Ann Haydon Jones (GBR)
6. Darlene Hard (USA)
7. Jan Lehane (USA)
8. Renee Schuurman (RSA)
9. Nancy Richey (USA)
10. Vera Puzejova Sukova (CZE)

1964

1. Margaret Smith (AUS)
2. Maria Bueno (BRA)
3. Lesley Turner (AUS)
4. Carole Caldwell Graebner (USA)
5. Helga Schultze (GER)
6. Nancy Richey (USA)
7. Billie Jean Moffitt (USA)
8. Karen Hantze Susman (USA)
9. Robyn Ebbern (AUS)
10. Jan Lehane (AUS)

1965

1. Margaret Smith (AUS)
2. Maria Bueno (BRA)
3. Lesley Turner (AUS)
4. Billie Jean King (USA)
5. Ann Haydon Jones (ENG)
6. Annette van Zyl (RSA)
7. Christine Truman (GBR)
8. Nancy Richey (USA)
9. Carole Caldwell Graebner (USA)
10. Francoise Durr (FRA)

1966

1. Billie Jean King (USA)
2. Margaret Smith (AUS)
3. Maria Bueno (BRA)
4. Ann Haydon Jones (GBR)
5. Nancy Richey (USA)
6. Annette van Zyl (RSA)
7. Norma Baylon (ARG)
8. Francoise Durr (FRA)
9. Rosie Casals (USA)
10. Kerry Melville (AUS)

1967

1. Billie Jean King (USA)
2. Ann Haydon Jones (GBR)
3. Francoise Durr (FRA)
4. Nancy Richey (USA)
5. Lesley Turner (AUS)
6. Rosie Casals (USA)
7. Maria Bueno (BRA)
8. Virginia Wade (GBR)
9. Kerry Melville (AUS)
10. Judy Tegart (AUS)

1968

1. Billie Jean King (USA)
2. Virginia Wade (GBR)
3. Nancy Richey (USA)
4. Margaret Smith Court (AUS)
5. Maria Bueno (BRA)
6. Ann Haydon Jones (GBR)
7. Judy Tegart (AUS)
8. Lesley Turner Bowrey (AUS)
9. Annette Van Zyl duPlooy (RSA)
10. Rosie Casals (USA)

1969

1. Margaret Smith Court (AUS)
2. Ann Haydon Jones (GBR)
3. Billie Jean King (USA)
4. Nancy Richey (USA)
5. Julie Heldman (USA)
6. Rosie Casals (USA)
7. Kerry Melville (AUS)
8. Mary Ann Eisel (USA)
9. Virginia Wade (GBR)
10. Lesley Turner Bowrey (AUS)

1970

1. Margaret Smith Court (AUS)
2. Billie Jean King (USA)
3. Rosie Casals (USA)
4. Nancy Richey (USA)
5. Virginia Wade (GBR)
6. Helga Niessen Masthoff (GER)
7. Ann Haydon Jones (GBR)
8. Kerry Melville (AUS)
9. Karen Krantzcke (AUS)
10. Francoise Durr (FRA)

1971

1. Billie Jean King (USA)
2. Evonne Goolagong (AUS)
3. Margaret Smith Court (AUS)
4. Rosie Casals (USA)
5. Kerry Melville (AUS)
6. Francoise Durr (FRA)
7. Virginia Wade (GBR)
8. Helga Niessen Masthoff (GER)
9. Judy Tegart (AUS)
10. Chris Evert (USA)

1972

1. Billie Jean King (USA)
2. Margaret Smith Court (AUS)
3. Nancy Richey Gunter (USA)
4. Chris Evert (USA)
5. Virginia Wade (GBR)
6. Evonne Goolagong (AUS)
7. Rosie Casals (USA)
8. Kerry Melville (AUS)
9. Francoise Durr (FRA)
10. Olga Morozova (USSR)

1973

1. Margaret Smith Court (AUS)
2. Billie Jean King (USA)
3. E. Goolagong Cawley (AUS)
4. Chris Evert (USA)
5. Rosie Casals (USA)
6. Virginia Wade (GBR)
7. Kerry Melville (AUS)
8. Nancy Richey Gunter (USA)
9. Julie Heldman (USA)
10. Helga Niessen Masthoff (GER)

1974

1. Billie Jean King (USA)
2. E. Goolagong Cawley (AUS)
3. Chris Evert (USA)
4. Virginia Wade (GBR)
5. Julie Heldman (USA)
6. Rosie Casals (USA)
7. Kerry Melville (AUS)
8. Olga Morozova (USSR)
9. Lesley Hunt (AUS)
10. Francoise Durr (FRA)

1975 (Computer rankings begin)

1. Chris Evert (USA)
2. Billie Jean King (USA)
3. E. Goolagong Cawley (AUS)
4. Martina Navratilova (CZE)
5. Virginia Wade (GBR)
6. Margaret Smith Court (AUS)
7. Olga Morozova (USSR)
8. Nancy Richey Gunter (USA)
9. Francoise Durr (FRA)
10. Rosie Casals (USA)

1976

1. Chris Evert (USA)
2. E. Goolagong Cawley (AUS)
3. Virginia Wade (GBR)
4. Martina Navratilova (CZE)
5. Sue Barker (GBR)
6. Betty Stove (NED)
7. Dianne Fromholtz (AUS)
8. Mima Jausovec (YUG)
9. Rosie Casals (USA)
10. Francoise Durr (FRA)

1977

1. Chris Evert (USA)
2. Billie Jean King (USA)
3. Martina Navratilova (CZE)
4. Virginia Wade (GBR)
5. Sue Barker (GBR)
6. Rosie Casals (USA)
7. Betty Stove (NED)
8. Dianne Fromholtz (AUS)
9. Wendy Turnbull (AUS)
10. Kerry Melville Reid (AUS)

1978

1. Martina Navratilova (CZE)
2. Chris Evert (USA)
3. E. Goolagong Cawley (AUS)
4. Virginia Wade (GBR)
5. Billie Jean King (USA)
6. Tracy Austin (USA)
7. Wendy Turnbull (AUS)
8. Kerry Melville Reid (AUS)
9. Betty Stove (NED)
10. Dianne Fromholtz (AUS)

1979

1. Martina Navratilova (CZE)
2. Chris Evert Lloyd (USA)
3. Tracy Austin (USA)
4. E. Goolagong Cawley (AUS)
5. Billie Jean King (USA)
6. Dianne Fromholtz (AUS)
7. Wendy Turnbull (AUS)
8. Virginia Wade (GBR)
9. Kerry Melville Reid (AUS)
10. Sue Barker (GBR)

1980

1. Chris Evert Lloyd (USA)
2. Tracy Austin (USA)
3. Martina Navratilova (CZE)
4. Hana Mandlikova (CZE)
5. E. Goolagong Cawley (AUS)
6. Billie Jean King (USA)
7. Andrea Jaeger (USA)
8. Wendy Turnbull (AUS)
9. Pam Shriver (USA)
10. Greer Stevens (RSA)

1981

1. Chris Evert Lloyd (USA)
2. Tracy Austin (USA)
3. Martina Navratilova (CZE)
4. Andrea Jaeger (USA)
5. Hana Mandlikova (CZE)
6. Sylvia Hanika (GER)
7. Pam Shriver (US)
8. Wendy Turnbull (AUS)
9. Bettina Bunge (GER)
10. Barbara Potter (USA)

1982

1. Martina Navratilova (USA)
2. Chris Evert Lloyd (USA)
3. Andrea Jaeger (USA)
4. Tracy Austin (USA)
5. Wendy Turnbull (AUS)
6. Pam Shriver (USA)
7. Hana Mandlikova (CZE)
8. Barbara Potter (USA)
9. Bettina Bunge (GER)
10. Sylvia Hanika (GER)

1983

1. Martina Navratilova (USA)
2. Chris Evert Lloyd (USA)
3. Andrea Jaeger (USA)
4. Pam Shriver (USA)
5. Sylvia Hanika (GER)
6. Jo Durie (GBR)
7. Bettina Bunge (GER)
8. Wendy Turnbull (AUS)
9. Tracy Austin (USA)
10. Zina Garrison (USA)

1984

1. Martina Navratilova (USA)
2. Chris Evert Lloyd (USA)
3. Hana Mandlikova (CZE)
4. Pam Shriver (USA)
5. Wendy Turnbull (AUS)
6. Manuela Maleeva (BUL)
7. Helena Sukova (CZE)
8. Claudia Kohde-Kilsch (GER)
9. Zina Garrison (USA)
10. Kathy Jordan (USA)

1985

1. Martina Navratilova (USA)
2. Chris Evert Lloyd (USA)
3. Hana Mandlikova (CZE)
4. Pam Shriver (USA)
5. Claudia Kohde-Kilsch (GER)
6. Steffi Graf (GER)
7. Manuela Maleeva (BUL)
8. Zina Garrison (USA)
9. Helena Sukova (CZE)
10. Bonnie Gadusek (USA)

1986

1. Martina Navratilova (USA)
2. Chris Evert Lloyd (USA)
3. Steffi Graf (GER)
4. Hana Mandlikova (CZE)
5. Helena Sukova (CZE)
6. Pam Shriver (USA)
7. Claudia Kohde-Kilsch (GER)
8. Manuela Maleeva (BUL)
9. Kathy Rinaldi (USA)
10. Gabriela Sabatini (ARG)

1987

1. Steffi Graf (GER)
2. Martina Navratilova (USA)
3. Chris Evert (USA)
4. Pam Shriver (USA)
5. Hana Mandlikova (CZE)
6. Gabriela Sabatini (ARG)
7. Helena Sukova (CZE)
8. Manuela Maleeva (BUL)
9. Zina Garrison (USA)
10. Claudia Kohde-Kilsch (GER)

1988

1. Steffi Graf (GER)
2. Martina Navratilova (USA)
3. Chris Evert (USA)
4. Gabriela Sabatini (ARG)
5. Pam Shriver (USA)
6. M. Maleeva Fragniere (BUL)
7. Natalia Zvereva (USSR)
8. Helena Sukova (CZE)
9. Zina Garrison (USA)
10. Barbara Potter (USA)

1989

1. Steffi Graf (GER)
2. Martina Navratilova (USA)
3. Gabriela Sabatini (ARG)
4. Zina Garrison (USA)
5. Arantxa Sanchez (ESP)
6. Monica Seles (YUG)
7. Conchita Martinez (ESP)
8. Helena Sukova (CZE)
6. M. Maleeva Fragniere (BUL)
10. Chris Evert (USA)

1990

1. Steffi Graf (GER)
2. Monica Seles (YUG)
3. Martina Navratilova (USA)
4. Mary Joe Fernandez (USA)
5. Gabriela Sabatini (ARG)
6. Katerina Maleeva (BUL)
7. Arantxa Sanchez Vicario (ESP)
8. Jennifer Capriati (USA)
9. M. Maleeva Fragniere (SUI)
10. Zina Garrison (USA)

1991

1. Monica Seles (YUG)
2. Steffi Graf (GER)
3. Gabriela Sabatini (ARG)
4. Martina Navratilova (USA)
5. Arantxa Sanchez Vicario (ESP)
6. Jennifer Capriati (USA)
7. Jana Novotna (CZE)
8. Mary Joe Fernandez (USA)
9. Conchita Martinez (ESP)
10. M. Maleeva Fragniere (SUI)

1992

1. Monica Seles (YUG)
2. Steffi Graf (GER)
3. Gabriela Sabatini (ARG)
4. Arantxa Sanchez Vicario (ESP)
5. Martina Navratilova (USA)
6. Mary Joe Fernandez (USA)
7. Jennifer Capriati (USA)
8. Conchita Martinez (ESP)
9. M. Maleeva Fragniere (SUI)
10. Jana Novotna (CZE)

1993

1. Steffi Graf (GER)
2. Arantxa Sanchez Vicario (ESP)
3. Martina Navratilova (USA)
4. Conchita Martinez (ESP)
5. Gabriela Sabatini (ARG)
6. Jana Novotna (CZE)
7. Mary Joe Fernandez (USA)
8. Monica Seles (YUG)
9. Jennifer Capriati (USA)
10. Anke Huber (GER)

1994

1. Steffi Graf (GER)
2. Arantxa Sanchez Vicario (ESP)
3. Conchita Martinez (ESP)
4. Jana Novotna (CZE)
5. Mary Pierce (FRA)
6. Lindsay Davenport (USA)
7. Gabriela Sabatini (ARG)
8. Martina Navratilova (USA)
9. Kimiko Date (JPN)
10. Natalia Zvereva (BLR)

1995

1. Steffi Graf (GER)
   Monica Seles (USA)
2. Conchita Martinez (ESP)
3. Arantxa Sanchez Vicario (ESP)
4. Kimiko Date (JPN)
5. Mary Pierce (FRA)
6. Magdalena Maleeva (BUL)
7. Gabriela Sabatini (ARG)
8. Mary Joe Fernandez (USA)
9. Iva Majoli (CRO)
10. Anke Huber (GER)

1996

1. Steffi Graf (GER)
2. Monica Seles (USA)
   Arantxa Sanchez Vicario (ESP)
3. Jana Novotna (CZE)
4. Martina Hingis (SUI)
5. Conchita Martinez (ESP)
6. Anke Huber (GER)
7. Iva Majoli (CRO)
8. Kimiko Date (JPN)
9. Lindsay Davenport (USA)
10. Barbara Paulus (AUT)

1997

1. Martina Hingis (SUI)
2. Jana Novotna (CZE)
3. Lindsay Davenport (USA)
4. Amanda Coetzer (RSA)
5. Monica Seles (USA)
6. Iva Majoli (CRO)
7. Mary Pierce (FRA)
8. Irina Spirlea (ROM)
9. Arantxa Sanchez Vicario (ESP)
10. Mary Joe Fernandez (USA)

1998

1. Lindsay Davenport (USA)
2. Martina Hingis (SUI)
3. Jana Novotna (CZE)
4. Arantxa Sanchez Vicario (ESP)
5. Venus Williams (USA)
6. Monica Seles (USA)
7. Mary Pierce (FRA)
8. Conchita Martinez (ESP)
9. Steffi Graf (GER)
10. Nathalie Tauziat (FRA)

1999

1. Martina Hingis (SUI)
2. Lindsay Davenport (USA)
3. Venus Williams (USA)
4. Serena Williams (USA)
5. Mary Pierce (FRA)
6. Monica Seles (USA)
7. Nathalie Tauziat (FRA)
8. Barbara Schett (AUT)
9. Julie Halard-Decugis (FRA)
10. Amelie Mauresmo (FRA)

2000

1. Martina Hingis (SUI)
2. Lindsay Davenport (USA)
3. Venus Williams (USA)
4. Monica Seles (USA)
5. Conchita Martinez (ESP)
6. Serena Williams (USA)
7. Mary Pierce (FRA)
8. Anna Kournikova (RUS)
9. Arantxa Sanchez Vicario (ESP)
10. Nathalie Tauziat (FRA)

2001

1. Lindsay Davenport (USA)
2. Jennifer Capriati (USA)
3. Venus Williams (USA)
4. Martina Hingis (SUI)
5. Kim Clijsters (BEL)
6. Serena Williams (USA)
7. Justine Henin (BEL)
8. Jelena Dokic (AUS)
9. Amelie Mauresmo (FRA)
10. Monica Seles (USA)

2002

1. Serena Williams (USA)
2. Venus Williams (USA)
3. Jennifer Capriati (USA)
4. Kim Clijsters (BEL)
5. Justine Henin (BEL)
6. Amelie Mauresmo (FRA)
7. Monica Seles (USA)
8. Daniela Hantuchova (SVK)
9. Jelena Dokic (AUS)
10. Martina Hingis (SUI)

2003

1. Justine Henin-Hardenne (BEL)
2. Kim Clijsters (BEL)
3. Serena Williams (USA)
4. Amelie Mauresmo (FRA)
5. Lindsay Davenport (USA)
6. Jennifer Capriati (USA)
7. Anastasia Myskina (RUS)
8. Elena Dementieva (RUS)
9. Chanda Rubin (USA)
10. Ai Sugiyama (JPN)

2004

1. Lindsay Davenport (USA)
2. Amelie Mauresmo (FRA)
3. Anastasia Myskina (RUS)
4. Maria Sharapova (RUS)
5. Svetlana Kuznetsova (RUS)
6. Elena Dementieva (RUS)
7. Serena Williams (USA)
8. Justine Henin-Hardenne (BEL)
9. Venus Williams (USA)
10. Jennifer Capriati (USA)

2005

1. Lindsay Davenport (USA)
2. Kim Clijsters (BEL)
3. Amelie Mauresmo (FRA)
4. Maria Sharapova (RUS)
5. Mary Pierce (FRA)
6. Justine Henin-Hardenne (BEL)
7. Patty Schnyder (SUI)
8. Elena Dementieva (RUS)
9. Nadia Petrova (RUS)
10. Venus Williams (USA)

2006

1. Justine Henin-Hardenne (BEL)
2. Maria Sharapova (RUS)
3. Amelie Mauresmo (FRA)
4. Svetlana Kuznetsova (RUS)
5. Kim Clijsters (BEL)
6. Nadia Petrova (RUS)
7. Martina Hingis (SUI)
8. Elena Dementieva (RUS)
7. Patty Schnyder (SUI)
10. Nicole Vaidisova (CZE)

2007

1. Justine Henin-Hardenne (BEL)
2. Jelena Jankovic (SRB)
3. Svetlana Kuznetsova (RUS)
4. Ana Ivanovic (SRB)
5. Serena Williams (USA)
6. Anna Chakvetadze (RUS)
7. Venus Williams (USA)
8. Daniela Hantuchova (SVK)
9. Maria Sharapova (RUS)
10. Marion Bartoli (FRA)

2008

1. Jelena Jankovic (SRB)
2. Serena Williams (USA)
3. Dinara Safina (RUS)
4. Elena Dementieva (RUS)
5. Ana Ivanovic (SRB)
6. Venus Williams (USA)
7. Vera Zvonareva (RUS)
8. Svetlana Kuznetsova (RUS)
9. Maria Sharapova (RUS)
10. Agnieszka Radwanska (POL)

No. 1 ATP Ranking History

Since the ATP computer ranking was adopted in 1973, 23 different players have held the top spot, as follows:

Weeks No.1

Pete Sampras (USA)	286
Ivan Lendl (CZE)	270
Jimmy Connors (USA)	268
Roger Federer (SUI)	238*
John McEnroe (USA)	170
Bjorn Borg (SWE)	109
Andre Agassi (USA)	101
Lleyton Hewitt (AUS)	80
Stefan Edberg (SWE)	72
Jim Courier (USA)	58
Rafael Nadal (ESP)	46
Gustavo Kuerten (BRA)	43
Ilie Nastase (ROM)	40
Mats Wilander (SWE)	20
Andy Roddick (USA)	13
Boris Becker (GER)	12
Marat Safin (RUS)	9
John Newcombe (AUS)	8
Juan Carlos Ferrero (ESP)	8
Yevgeny Kafelnikov (RUS)	6
Thomas Muster (AUT)	6
Marcelo Rios (CHI)	6
Carlos Moya (ESP)	2
Patrick Rafter (AUS)	1

As of July 6, 2009

No. 1 History

Player	Weeks	Date
Ilie Nastase (1)	**40**	**Aug. 23, 1973**
John Newcombe (2)	**8**	**June 3, 1974**
Jimmy Connors (3)	**160**	**July 29, 1974**
Bjorn Borg (4)	**1**	**Aug. 23, 1977**
Connors	84	Aug. 30, 1977
Borg	6	Apr. 9, 1979
Connors	7	May 21, 1979
Borg	34	July 9, 1979
John McEnroe (5)	**3**	**Mar. 3, 1980**
Borg	20	Mar. 24, 1980
McEnroe	1	Aug. 11, 1980
Borg	46	Aug. 18, 1980
McEnroe	2	July. 6, 1981
Borg	2	July. 20, 1981
McEnroe	58	Aug. 3, 1981
Connors	7	Sept. 13, 1982
McEnroe	1	Nov. 1, 1982
Connors	1	Nov. 8, 1982
McEnroe	11	Nov. 15, 1982
Connors	1	Jan. 31, 1983
McEnroe	1	Feb. 7, 1983
Connors	2	Feb. 14, 1983
Ivan Lendl (6)	**11**	**Feb. 38, 1983**
Connors	3	May 16, 1983
McEnroe	1	June 6, 1983
Connors	3	June 13, 1983
McEnroe	17	July 4, 1983
Lendl	6	Oct. 31, 1983
McEnroe	4	Dec. 12, 1983
Lendl	9	Jan. 9, 1984
McEnroe	13	May 12, 1984
Lendl	1	June 11, 1984
McEnroe	3	June 18, 1984
Lendl	5	July 9, 1984
McEnroe	53	Aug. 13, 1984
Lendl	1	Aug. 19, 1985
McEnroe	2	Aug. 26, 1985
Lendl	157	Sept. 9, 1985
Mats Wilander (7)	**20**	**Sept. 9, 1985**
Lendl	80	Jan. 30, 1989
Stefan Edberg (8)	**24**	**Aug. 13, 1990**
Boris Becker (9)	**3**	**Jan. 28, 1991**
Edberg	20	Feb. 18, 1991
Becker	9	July 8, 1991
Edberg	22	Sept. 9, 1991
Jim Courier (10)	**6**	**Feb. 10, 1992**
Edberg	3	Mar. 23, 1992
Courier	22	Apr. 13, 1992
Edberg	3	Sept. 14, 1992
Courier	27	Oct. 5, 1992
Pete Sampras (11)	**19**	**Apr. 12, 1993**
Courier	3	Aug. 23, 1993
Sampras	82	Sept. 13, 1993
Andre Agassi (12)	**30**	**Apr. 10, 1995**
Sampras	12	Nov. 6, 1995
Agassi	2	Jan. 29, 1996
Thomas Muster (13)	**1**	**Feb. 12, 1996**
Sampras	3	Feb. 19, 1996
Muster	5	Mar. 11, 1996
Sampras	102	Apr. 15, 1996
Marcelo Rios (14)	**4**	**Mar. 30, 1998**
Sampras	15	Apr. 27, 1998
Rios	2	Aug. 10, 1998
Sampras	20	Aug. 24, 1998
Carlos Moya (15)	**2**	**Mar. 15, 1999**
Sampras	5	Mar. 29, 1999
Yevgeny Kafelnikov (16)	**6**	**May 3, 1999**
Sampras	3	June 14, 1999
Agassi	3	July 5, 1999
Patrick Rafter (17)	**1**	**July 26, 1999**
Sampras	6	Aug. 2, 1999
Agassi	52	Sept. 13, 1999
Sampras	10	Sept. 11, 2000
Marat Safin (18)	**2**	**Nov. 20, 2000**
Gustavo Kuerten (19)	**8**	**Dec. 4, 2000**
Safin	4	Jan. 29, 2001
Kuerten	5	Feb. 26, 2001
Safin	3	Apr. 2, 2001
Kuerten	30	Apr. 22, 2001
Lleyton Hewitt (20)	**75**	**Nov. 19, 2001**
Agassi	2	Apr. 28, 2003
Hewitt	5	May 12, 2003
Agassi	12	June 16, 2003
Juan Carlos Ferrero (21)	**8**	**Sept. 8, 2003**
Andy Roddick (22)	**13**	**Nov. 3, 2003**
Roger Federer (23)	**237***	**Feb. 2, 2004**
Rafael Nadal (24)	**46**	**Aug. 18, 2008**
Federer	1*	July 6, 2009

As of July 6, 2009

No. 1 WTA Ranking History

Since the WTA computer ranking was adopted in 1975, 17 different players have held the top spot, as follows:

Weeks No. 1

Steffi Graf (GER)	377
Martina Navratilova (USA)	332
Chris Evert (USA)	260
Martina Hingis (SUI)	209
Monica Seles (USA)	178
Justine Henin (BEL)	117
Lindsay Davenport (USA)	98
Serena Williams (USA)	72
Amelie Mauresmo (FRA)	39
Tracy Austin (USA)	21
Kim Clijsters (BEL)	19
Maria Sharapova (RUS)	19
Jelena Jankovic	18
Jennifer Capriati (USA)	17
Dinara Safina	13*
Ana Ivanovic (SRB)	12
A. Sanchez Vicario (ESP)	12
Venus Williams (USA)	11
Evonne Goolagong (AUS)	2

As of July 6, 2009

No. 1 Ranked Players

Player	Weeks	Date
Chris Evert (1)	**26**	**Nov 3, 1975**
Evonne Goolagong (2)	**2**	**Apr 26, 1976**
Evert	112	May 10, 1976
Martina Navratilova (3)	**27**	**Jul 10, 1978**
Evert	2	Jan 14, 1979
Navratilova	4	Jan 28, 1979
Evert	7	Feb 25, 1979
Navratilova	10	Apr 16, 1979
Evert	11	Jun 25, 1979
Navratilova	30	Sep 10, 1979
Tracy Austin (4)	**2**	**Apr 07, 1980**
Navratilova	10	Apr 21, 1980
Austin	20	Jul 01, 1980
Evert	76	Nov 18, 1980
Navratilova	2	May 03, 1982
Evert	4	May 17, 1982
Navratilova	156	Jun 14, 1982
Evert	18	Jun 10, 1985
Navratilova	2	Oct 14, 1985
Evert	4	Oct 28, 1985
Navratilova	90	Nov 25, 1985
Steffi Graf (5) Record	**186**	**Aug 17, 1987**
Monica Seles (6)	**21**	**Mar 11, 1991**
Graf	1	Aug 05, 1991
Seles	1	Aug 12, 1991
Graf	3	Aug 19, 1991
Seles	91	Sep 09, 1991
Graf	87	Jun 07, 1993
Arantxa Sanchez Vicario (7)	**2**	**Feb 06, 1995**
Graf	1	Feb 20, 1995
Sanchez Vicario	6	Feb 27, 1995
Graf	5	Apr 10, 1995
Sanchez Vicario	4	May 15, 1995
Graf	9	Jun 12, 1995
Graf & Seles	64	Aug 15, 1995
Graf	2	Nov 04, 1996
Graf & Seles	1	Nov 18, 1996
Graf	18	Nov 25, 1996
Martina Hingis (8)	**80**	**Mar 31, 1997**
Lindsay Davenport (9)	**17**	**Oct 12, 1998**
Hingis	21	Feb 08, 1999
Davenport	5	Jul 05, 1999
Hingis	34	Aug 09, 1999
Davenport	5	Apr 03, 2000
Hingis	1	May 08, 2000
Davenport	1	May 15, 2000
Hingis	73	May 22, 2000
Jennifer Capriati (10)	**3**	**Oct 15, 2001**
Davenport	10	Nov 05, 2001
Capriati	6	Jan 14, 2002
Venus Williams (11)	**3**	**Feb 25, 2002**
Capriati	5	Mar 18, 2002
Venus Williams	4	Apr 22, 2002
Capriati	3	May 20, 2002
Venus Williams	4	Jun 10, 2002
Serena Williams (12)	**57**	**Jul 08, 2002**
Kim Clijsters (13)	**10**	**Aug 11, 2003**
Justine Henin (14)	**1**	**Oct 20, 2003**
Clijsters	2	Oct 27, 2003
Henin	44	Nov 10, 2003
Amélie Mauresmo (15)	**5**	**Sep 13, 2004**
Davenport	44	Oct 18, 2004
Maria Sharapova (16)	**1**	**Aug 22, 2005**
Davenport	2	Aug 29, 2005
Sharapova	6	Sep 12, 2005
Davenport	14	Oct 24, 2005
Clijsters	7	Jan 30, 2006
Mauresmo	34	Mar 20, 2006
Henin	11	Nov 13, 2006
Sharapova	7	Jan 29, 2007
Henin	61	Mar 19, 2007
Sharapova	4	May 19, 2008
Ana Ivanovic (17)	**9**	**June 9, 2008**
Jelena Jankovic (18)	**1**	**Aug 10, 2008**
Ivanovic	**12**	**Sep 7, 2008**
Serena Williams	4	Sep 8, 2008
Jankovic	17	Oct 6, 2008
Serena Williams	11	Feb 2, 2009
Dinara Safina (19)	13*	Apr 20, 2009

As of July 6, 2009

General Records

Martina Navratilova is a record holder in many categories, including most singles titles won (167) and most doubles titles won (177).

Are all records made to be broken? Perhaps, but some marks achieved and documented in the pages to follow will take Herculean efforts to overcome. For example, will anyone ever win 182 matches in a row as Suzanne Lenglen did in the 1920s? Will a man ranked as low as No. 212 win a major singles title as Mark Edmondson did at the 1976 Australian Open? Can anyone match the 167 singles titles and 177 doubles titles won by Martina Navratilova? They will need a lot of talent—and a rather large trophy case.

SINGLES TOURNAMENTS WON – CAREER
Open Era (Since 1968)
Men (as of July 6, 2009)

109	Jimmy Connors	1971-1989
94	Ivan Lendl	1980-1994
77	John McEnroe	1978-1992
64	Pete Sampras	1990-2002
62	Guillermo Vilas	1973-1986
62	Bjorn Borg	1974-1981
60	Roger Federer	2001–
60	Andre Agassi	1987-2005
57	Ilie Nastase	1970-1981
54	Rod Laver	1968-1973
49	Boris Becker	1985-1996

Women (as of July 6, 2009)

167	Martina Navratilova	1973-2008
154	Chris Evert	1971-1989
107	Steffi Graf	1986-1999
92	Margaret Smith Court	1968-1977
68	Evonne Goolagong Cawley	1970-1980
67	Billie Jean King	1968-1983
55	Lindsay Davenport	1993–
55	Virginia Wade	1968-1978
53	Monica Seles	1989-2002
43	Martina Hingis	1996-2004
41	Justine Henin	1999-2008
41	Venus Williams	1998–

DOUBLES TOURNAMENTS WON CAREER – TEAM
Open Era
Men

61	Mark Woodforde and Todd Woodbridge	1991-2000
57	John McEnroe and Peter Fleming	1978-1986
	Bob Hewitt and Frew McMillan	1970-1980
53*	Bob and Mike Bryan	2001–
44	Sergio Casal and Emilio Sanchez	1985-1995

Women

79 Martina Navratilova and Pam Shriver——(matches won-lost, 390-25), played 101 tournaments together

56 Rosie Casals and Billie Jean King——(matches won-lost, 294-41), played 98 tournaments together 1971-1992

As of July 6, 2009

DOUBLES TOURNAMENTS WON CAREER – INDIVIDUAL
Open Era
Men

83	Todd Woodbridge	1990-2005
78	Tom Okker	1968-1980
78	John McEnroe	1978-2006
74	Frew McMillan	1970-1982
67	Mark Woodforde	1988-2000
66	Peter Fleming	1978-1987
65	Bob Hewitt	1970-1980
62	Raul Ramirez	1973-1983
61	Stan Smith	1968-1984
60	Marty Riessen	1968-1981

Women

177	Martina Navratilova	1974-2006
112	Rosie Casals	1968-1988
106	Pam Shriver	1978-1994
101	Billie Jean King	1968-1983
80	Natasha Zvereva	1988-2002
76	Jana Novotna	1987-1999
68	Gigi Fernandez	1995-1997
	Helena Sukova	1984-1998
67	Arantxa Sanchez Vicario	1986-2004
66	Larisa Savchenko Neiland	985-1999

MOST DOUBLES FINALS PLAYED – CAREER
Men

125	Tom Okker	1968-1980
119	Frew McMillan	1970-1980
114	Todd Woodbridge	1990-2005

Women

210	Martina Navratilova	1974-2006

SINGLES TOURNAMENT FINALS – CAREER
Men

158	Jimmy Connors	1971-1989
144	Ivan Lendl	1979-1994

Women

239	Martina Navratilova	1974-1994
227	Chris Evert	1972-1989

SINGLES TOURNAMENTS WON – SEASON
Men

17	Rod Laver	32 entered, 1969
17	Guillermo Vilas	33 entered, 1977
15	Ivan Lendl	23 entered, 1982
15	Ilie Nastase	31 entered, 1973

Women

21	Margaret Smith Court	1970
18	Margaret Smith Court	1973
17	Billie Jean King	1971
16	Martina Navratilova	1983

DOUBLES TOURNAMENTS WON – SEASON
Men

17	John McEnroe	1979

Women

21	Billie Jean King	1971
21	Rosie Casals	1971

DOUBLES TOURNAMENTS WON – TEAM – SEASON
Men

15	John McEnroe and Peter Fleming	1979

Women

19	Rosie Casals and Billie Jean King	1971

CONSECUTIVE SINGLES MATCH VICTORIES

Men

98	Bill Tilden	1924-1925
92	Don Budge	1937-1938
55	Roy Emerson	1964
50**	Guillermo Vilas	1977
44	Ivan Lendl	1981-1982
42	John McEnroe	1984
41	Roger Federer	2006-2007
41	Bjorn Borg	1978

Women

182	Suzanne Lenglen	1921-1926
158	Helen Wills Moody	1926-1933
116	Suzanne Lenglen	1919-1921
111	Alice Marble	1938-1940
74	Martina Navratilova	1984
66	Steffi Graf	1990
58	Martina Navratilova	1985-1987

** Includes four match victories at an event in Rye, NY in August of 1977 not recognized by the ATP, but counted by Bud Collins and other historians

CONSECUTIVE DOUBLES MATCH VICTORIES – TEAM

109   Martina Navratilova and Pam Shriver (1984-1985)

SINGLES MATCHES PLAYED – SEASON

Men

159	Guillermo Vilas	1977
142	Ivan Lendl	1980
135	Ilie Nastase	1973
123	Arthur Ashe	1975

Women

126	Billie Jean King	1971
116	Rosie Casals	1971
110	Margaret Smith Court	1970
108	Margaret Smith Court	1973
	Chris Evert	1974
103	Martina Navratilova	1981
102	Martina Navratilova	1979

SINGLES MATCHES WON – SEASON

Men

145	Guillermo Vilas	159 matches played–1977
118	Ilie Nastase	135 matches played–1973
113	Ivan Lendl	142 matches played–1980
107	Ivan Lendl	116 matches played–1982
106	Rod Laver	122 matches played–1969

Women

112	Billie Jean King	126 matches played–1971
104	Margaret Smith Court	110 matches played–1970
102	Margaret Smith Court	108 matches played–1973
100	Chris Evert	108 matches played–1974
90	Martina Navratilova	102 matches played–1979

SINGLES TOURNAMENTS PLAYED IN A SEASON

Men

40	Ross Case	1973
	Onny Parun	1973
39	Dick Crealy	1974
38	Bob Carmichael	1973
	Frew McMillan	1973
36	Gerald Battrick	1973
	Barry Phillips-Moore	1974
	Ray Moore	1975
	Javier Sanchez	1994

Women

31	Billie Jean King	1971
30	Kim Steinmetz	1985
29	Camille Benjamin	1985
28	Camille Benjamin	1986
	Jelena Jankovic	2007

DOUBLES MATCHES PLAYED – SEASON

Men

86	John McEnroe	1979
86	Bob Bryan	2007
86	Mike Bryan	2007

Women

99	Rosie Casals	1982

DOUBLES MATCHES WON – SEASON

Men

83	John McEnroe	1979

Women

82	Rosie Casals	1971

DOUBLES TOURNAMENTS PLAYED – TEAM – SEASON

Men

21	Bob and Mike Bryan	2007, 2008

Women

24	Rosie Casals and Billie Jean King	1971

DOUBLES MATCHES PLAYED – TEAM – SEASON

Men

86	Bob and Mike Bryan	2007

Women

78	Rosie Casals and Billie Jean King	1971

DOUBLES MATCHES WON – TEAM – SEASON

Men

86	Bob and Mike Bryan	2007

Women

73	Rosie Casals and Billie Jean King	1971

MOST SINGLES AND DOUBLES TOURNAMENTS PLAYED – SEASON

Men

44	Guillermo Vilas	1977

Women

60	Rosie Casals	1971

MOST SINGLES AND DOUBLES TITLES WON – COMBINED – SEASON

Men

27   John McEnroe   10 singles, 17 doubles, 1979

Women

38   Billie Jean King   17 singles, 21 doubles, 1971

MOST SINGLES AND DOUBLES MATCHES PLAYED – COMBINED – SEASON

Men

221   Guillermo Vilas   159 singles, 62 doubles, 1977
192   John McEnroe   106 singles, 86 doubles, 1979

Women

210   Billie Jean King   1971

MOST SINGLES AND DOUBLES MATCHES WON – COMBINED – SEASON

Men

187   Guillermo Vilas   145 singles, 42 doubles, 1977

Women

192   Billie Jean King   1971

DOUBLES TOURNAMENTS PLAYED IN A SEASON

Men

41   Libor Pimek   1994

Women

30   Rosie Casals   1982

SINGLES TOURNAMENTS PLAYED – CAREER

Men

410   Jimmy Connors   1974-1996
348   Ivan Lendl   1978-1994

Women

389   Martina Navratilova 1972-2004
315   Rosie Casals   1968-1986
303   Chris Evert   1970-1989

SINGLES MATCHES PLAYED – CAREER

Men

1,622   Jimmy Connors   1971-1994
1,310   Ivan Lendl   1978-1994

Women

1,661   Martina Navratilova   1972-2004
1,448   Chris Evert   1970-2004

SINGLES MATCHES WON – CAREER

Men

1,337   Jimmy Connors   (1970-1996)
1,072   Ivan Lendl   (1978-1994)

Women

1,442   Martina Navratilova   (1972-2004)
1,304   Chris Evert   (1970-1989)

MATCH WINNING PERCENTAGE – SEASON

Men

.987 Bill Tilden   1925   (78-1)
.965 John McEnroe   1984   (82-3)

Women

1.000   Alice Marble   1939, 1940   (45-0)

(Suzanne Lenglen and Helen Wills Moody also had undefeated seasons, but fewer match victories)

.981 Martina Navratilova   1983   (86-1)

LOWEST-RANKED MAJOR FINALISTS

Men

No. 212   Mark Edmondson   1976 Australian Open champion
No. 188   John Marks   1978 Australian Open finalist
No. 125   Goran Ivanisevic   2001 Wimbledon champion
No. 100   Andrei Medvedev   1999 French Open finalist
No. 91   Chris Lewis   1983 Wimbledon finalist
No. 86   Marat Safin   2004 Australian Open finalist
No. 66   Gustavo Kuerten   1997 French Open champion
No. 22*   Mark Philippoussis   1998 US Open finalist

* Lowest-ranked men's singles finalist at the US Open

Women

Not Ranked   Evonne Goolagong   1977 Australian Open champion
No. 111   Chris O'Neil   1978 Australian Open champion
No. 81   Serena Williams   2007 Australian Open champion
No. 68   Barbara Jordan   1979 Australian Open champion
No. 66   Venus Williams   1997 US Open finalist
No. 31   Venus Williams   2007 Wimbledon champion

MOST MAJOR TOURNAMENTS PLAYED – CAREER

Men Singles

68   Fabrice Santoro   1989 - 2009*
61   Andre Agassi   1986 - 2006

Women's Singles

71   Amy Frazier   1987- 2006

* Through 2009 Wimbledon

CONSECUTIVE MAJOR TOURNAMENTS PLAYED

Men Singles

56   Wayne Ferreira   (1991 Australian Open – 2004 US Open)

Women Singles

61   Ai Sugiyama   (1994 Wimbledon – 2009 Wimbledon*)

* Through 2009 Wimbledon

OLDEST PLAYERS TO WIN A SINGLES TITLE

Men

Pancho Gonzalez—43 years, 9 months, 1972 Des Moines
Ken Rosewall—43 years, 11 days, 1977 Hong Kong

Women

Billie Jean King—39 years, 7 months, 23 days, 1983 Birmingham
Martina Navratilova—37 years, 4 months, 2 days, 1994 Paris Indoors

YOUNGEST PLAYERS TO WIN A SINGLES TITLE

Men

Aaron Krickstein—16 years, 2 months, 1983 Tel Aviv

Michael Chang—16 years, 7 months, 1988 San Francisco

Lleyton Hewitt—16 years, 10 months, 1998 Adelaide

Women

Tracy Austin—14 years, 28 days, 1977 Portland

Andrea Jaeger—14 years, 7 months, 14 days, 1980 Las Vegas

Kathy Rinaldi—14 years, 6 months, 24 days, 1981 Kyoto

LOWEST RANKED PLAYERS TO WIN A SINGLES TITLE

Men

Lleyton Hewitt, No. 550, Adelaide, Australia, 1998

Women

Angelique Widaja, No. 579, Bali, Indonesia, 2001

LONGEST MATCHES – GAMES

Men's Singles

126 games Roger Taylor of Great Britain d. Wieslaw Gasiorek of Poland, 27-29, 31-29, 6-4; Kings Cup match, Warsaw, 1966

Women's Singles

62 games Kathy Blake of the United States d. Elena Subirats of Mexico 12-10, 6-8, 14-12, first round, Piping Rock Invitational, Locust Valley, N.Y., 1966

Men's Doubles

147 games Dick Leach and Dick Dell d. Len Schloss and Tom Mozur, 3-6, 49-47, 22-20, second round, Newport (R.I.), Casino Invitation, 1967

Women's Doubles

81 games Nancy Richey and Carole Graebner, d. Carol Hanks and Justina Bricka, 31-33, 6-1, 6-4, semifinal, Eastern Grass Championships, South Orange, N.J., 1964

Mixed Doubles

77 games Brenda Schultz and Michiel Schapers d. Andrea Temesvari and Tom Njissen, 6-3, 5-7, 29-27, Wimbledon, mixed doubles, first round, 1991

OTHER "CENTURY" (100 GAME) MATCHES

Men's Singles

112 games Pancho Gonzalez d. Charlie Pasarell 22-24, 1-6, 16-14, 6-3, 11-9, first round, Wimbledon, 1969

107 games Dick Knight d. Mike Sprengelmeyer, 32-30, 3-6, 19-17; qualifying, Southampton (N.Y.), 1967

100 games F.D. Robbins d. Dick Dell, 22-20, 9-7, 6-8, 8-10, 6-4; first round, U.S. Open, 1969

100 games Harry Fritz d. Jorge Andrew, 16-14, 11-9, 9-11, 4-6, 11-9; America Zone Davis Cup, Canada at Venezuela, 1982

Men's Doubles

144 games Bobby Wilson and Mark Cox d. Ron Holmberg and Charlie Pasarell, 26-24, 17-19, 30-28; QF, US Indoor, Salisbury, MD, 1968

135 games Ted Schroeder and Bob Falkenburg d. Pancho Gonzalez and Hugh Stewart, 36-34, 2-6, 4-6, 6-4, 19-17; Final, Southern California, Los Angeles, 1949

122 games Stan Smith and Erik van Dillen d. Jaime Fillol and Patricio Cornejo, 7-9, 37-39, 8-6, 6-1, 6-3; Davis Cup USA vs. Chile, America Zone match, Little Rock Ark., 1973

106 games Len Schloss and Tom Mozur d. Chris Bovett and Butch Seewagen, 7-5, 48-46; 2nd rd., Southampton, NY, 1967

105 games Cliff Drysdale and Ray Moore d. Roy Emerson and Ron Barnes, 29-31, 8-6, 3-6, 8-6, 6-2; QF, US Doubles, Boston, 1967

105 games Jim Orborne and Bill Bowrey d. Terry Addison and Ray Keldie, 3-6, 43-41, 7-5; Pennsylvania Grass, Phildelphia, SF, 1969

105 games Joaquin Loyo-Mayo and Marcelo Lara d. Manolo Santana and Luis Garcia, 10-12, 24-22, 11-9, 3-6, 6-2; 3rd rd., US Doubles, Boston, 1966

102 games Don White and Bob Galloway d. Hugh Sweeney and Lamar Roemer, 6-4, 17-15, 4-6, 18-20, 7-5; 1st rd, US Doubles, Boston, 1964

100 games Cliff Sutter and Gene McAuliff d. Frank Shields and George Lott; 12-14, 14-12, 25-23; SF, Buffalo Indoor, 1934

100 games Bob Lutz and Joaquin Loyo-Mayo d. Bill Bond and Dick Leach; 19-17, 33-31; QF, Phoenix,1969

LONGEST MATCHES – TIME

Men's Singles

6:33   Fabrice Santoro d. Arnaud Clement 6-4, 6-3, 6-7 (5), 3-6, 16-14, 2004 French Open first round

6:22   John McEnroe d. Mats Wilander 9-7, 6-2, 15-17, 3-6, 8-6, 5th rubber, Davis Cup Quarterfinal, St. Louis, Mo, 1982

6:20   Boris Becker d. John McEnroe 4-6, 15-13, 8-10, 6-2, 6-2, Davis Cup, Qualifying Round, Hartford, 1987

Women's Singles

6:31   Vicki Nelson Dunbar d. Jean Hepner, 6-4, 7-6 (13-11), 1984, Richmond, Va., first round (tie-breaker alone lasted 1 hour and 47 minutes, one point lasted 29 minutes, a rally of 643 strokes)

4:07   Virginie Buisson d. Noelle Van Lottum 6-7 (3), 7-5, 6-2, 1995 French Open first round

3:55   Kerry Melville Reid d. Pam Teeguarden 7-6 (7), 4-6, 16-14, 1972 French Open third round

Men's Doubles

6:20   Lucas Arnold and David Nalbandian d. Yevgeny Kafelnikov and Marat Safin, 2003 Davis Cup semifinals 6-4, 6-4, 5-7, 3-6, 19-17, 2002 Davis Cup Semifinal, Moscow

LONGEST TIE-BREAKERS

Men's Singles

38 – (20-18)   Roger Federer d. Marat Safin 6-3, 7-6 (20-18), semifinal, 2004 Tennis Masters Cup, Houston

38 – (20-18)   Bjorn Borg d. Premjit Lall 6-3, 6-4, 9-8 (20-18), first round, 1973 Wimbledon

38 – (20-18)   Andy Roddick d. Jo-Wilfried Tsonga 6-7 (18-20), 7-6 (7-2), 6-2, 6-3, first round, 2007 Australian Open

38 – (20-18)   Goran Ivanisevic d. Daniel Nestor 6-4, 7-6 (5), 7-6 (20-18), first round, 1993 US Open

| 38 – (20-18) | Jose Acasuso d. Bjorn Phau 7-5 7-6 (20-18), first round, Toronto, 2006 |
| 38 – (20-18) | Goran Ivanisevic d. Greg Rusedski, 4-6, 6-4, 7-6 (20-18), semifinal, Queens Club, 1997 |

Women's Singles

| 40 – (21-19) | Emmanuelle Gagliardi d. Tara Snyder 6-7 (19-21), 6-1, 6-1, second round, Madrid, 1999 |

Men's Doubles

| 50 – (26-24) | Michael Mortensen and Jan Gunnarson d. John Frawley and Victor Pecci 6-4, 6-4, 3-6, 7-6 (26-24), first round, Wimbledon, 1985 |

Women's Doubles

| 42 – (22-20) | Nicole Pratt and Bryanne Stewart d. Corina Morariu and Rennae Stubbs 7-6 (5), 7-6 (22-20), first round, 2006 Amelia Island |

LONGEST MATCH TIE-BREAKER

(Played in lieu of a third set, best of 10 points)

| 44 – (23-21) | Albert Montanes and Ruben Ramirez-Hidalgo d. Simon Aspelin and Frantisek Cermak 7-6 1-6, 23-21 (Match Tie-Break), first round, Estoril, 2007 |

TIE-BREAKERS WON FROM 0-6 DOWN

Paul McNamee and Peter Doohan d. Ken Flach and Robert Seguso, 6-2, 3-6, 7-6 (8-6), 1st rd., Ft. Myers, Fla., 1986 (saved 6 match points)

Jan Siemerink lost to Richard Krajicek, 7-6 (7-2), 6-4, 6-7 (2-7), 6-7 (8-10), 6-4, 1st rd, 1994 U.S. Open (saved 7 match points in 4th set but lost)

Nathalie Tauziat d. Tamarine Tanasugarn, 4-6, 7-6 (8-6), 6-3, 2nd rd., 1996 Birmingham, England, (saved 6 match points)

Mary Pierce d. Elena Likhovtseva, 7-5, 4-6, 7-6 (8-6), QF, 2005, Moscow, (saved 6 match points)

LONGEST TIE BREAKER – TIME

| 1 hour, 47 minutes | 2nd set, Vicki Nelson-Dunbar d. Jean Hepner, 6-4, 7-6(13-11), 1st round, Virginia Sims of Richmond, Virginia, 1984. One point of the tie-breaker lasted 29 minutes, with the ball crossing the nest 643 times |

LONGEST GAME

Men

| 31 minutes | The longest known singles game consisted of 37 deuces (80 points) played between Anthony Fawcett of Rhodesia and Keith Glass of Great Britain in the first round of the Surbiton Championships in Surrey, England on May 25, 1975. The game lasted 31 minutes |

Women

| 52 minutes | Noelle van Lottum and Sandra Begijn played a game that lasted 52 minutes in the semifinals of the Dutch Indoor Championships at Ede, Gelderland on February 12, 1984 |

LONGEST POINT

| 29 minutes | 2nd set, Vicki Nelson-Dunbar, d. Jean Hepner, 6-4, 7-6(13-11), 1st rd., Virginia Slims of Richmond, Virginia, 1984. One point in the TB lasted 29 minutes with the ball going over the net 643 times |

WINNING STREAKS PER SURFACE

Men's Singles

Clay

| 81 | Rafael Nadal | 2005–2007 |

Hard Court

| 56 | Roger Federer | 2004–2006 |

Grass

| 65 | Roger Federer | 2003–2008 |

Indoor Carpet

| 66 | John McEnroe | 1983–85 |

Women Singles

Clay

| 125 | Chris Evert | August 12,1973–May 12,1979 |

Hard Court

| 82 | Steffi Graf | March, 1988–September, 1990 |

Grass

| 47 | Martina Navratilova | June, 1985–January, 1987 |

Indoor Carpet

| 48 | Martina Navratilova | March, 1986–November, 1987 |

LATEST FINISHES AT MAJOR CHAMPIONSHIPS

(US Open and Australian Open are only majors with night play)

Australian Open

| 4:34 am | Lleyton Hewitt d. Marcos Baghdatis 4-6, 7-5, 7-5, 6-7 (4), 6-3 in the 2008 third round |

| 3:34 am | Andreas Seppi d. Bobby Reynolds 6-1, 6-7 (4), 6-7 (5), 7-6 (3), 6-3 in the 2007 first round |

US Open

| 2:26 am | Mats Wilander d. Mikael Pernfors 6-1, 6-7 (4), 6-7 (5), 7-6 (3), 6-3 in the 1993 second round |

| 2:14 am | Younes El Aynaoui d. Wayne Ferreira 3-6, 7-5, 7-5, 7-6 (3) in the 2002 fourth round |

| | The latest recorded start of a match at a major tournament came in 1987, when shortly after midnight, Gabriela Sabatini and Beverly Bowes took the court for a first round match, following a four-hour Boris Becker-Tim Wilkison match. Sabatini won 6-3, 6-3 in a match that ended at 1:30 am |

Wimbledon

| 10:39 pm | Andy Murray d. Stanislas Wawrinka 2-6, 6-3, 6-3, 5-7, 6-3 in 2009 fourth round (In the first ever Wimbledon night match and the first complete match played under the retractable roof on Centre Court) |

OTHER LATE FINISHES

| 2:51 am | Nicolas Massu and Fernando Gonzalez of Chile defeated Nicolas Kiefer and Rainer Schuettler of Germany 6-2, 4-6, 3-6, 6-7 (7), 6-4 in the gold medal match in men's doubles at the 2004 Olympic Games in four hours and 43 minutes |

| 3:24 am | Benjamin Becker of Germany defeated Jiri Novak of the Czech Republic 6-3, 3-6, 7-6 (4) in the round of 16, AIG Open in Tokyo, Oct. 5, 2006 |

LARGEST CROWDS

30,492   1973 "Battle of the Sexes" – Billie Jean King USA d. Bobby Riggs USA, 6-4, 6-4, 6-3, Houston Astrodome, Houston, Texas, September 20, 1973

27,200   2004 Davis Cup Final – USA vs. Spain, Spain d. USA 3-2, Estadio Olympico, Seville, Spain, December 3-5, 2004

26,578   1954 Davis Cup Challenge Round – USA vs. Australia (USA d. Australia 3-1, White City Courts, Sydney, Australia), Dec. 27-29, 1954

25,250   2007 US Open men's singles final – Roger Federer d. Novak Djokovic, 7-6 (4), 7-6 (2), 6-4

ACES IN A SEASON

Men

1,477   1996 Goran Ivanisevic

ACES IN A MATCH

Men

59   Ed Kauder (lost to Ham Richardson, 6-2, 3-6, 9-11, 10-8, 6-0 1st. rd., US Championships, 1955)

55   Ivo Karlovic (lost to Lleyton Hewitt 6-7 (1), 6-7 (4), 7-6 (4), 6-4, 6-3 1st rd, French Open, 2009

54   Gary Muller (d. Peter Lundgren 4-6, 7-6, 20-18 Wimbledon qualifying, Roehampton, 1993)

51   Joachim Johansson (lost to Andre Agassi, 6-7 (4), 7-6 (5), 7-6 (3), 6-4 Australian Open, 4th rd., 2005)

51   Ivo Karlovic (lost to Daniele Bracciali, 6-7 (4), 7-6 (8), 3-6, 7-6 (5), 12-10 Wimbledon, 1st rd., 2005)

50   Roger Federer (defeated Andy Roddick 5-7, 7-6 (6), 7-6 (5), 3-6, 16-14 Wimbledon F, 2009

50   Chris Guccione (lost to Olivier Patience, 4-6, 7-6 (7-3), 23-21 Wimbledon qualifying, 2005)

49   Richard Krajicek (lost to Yevgeny Kafelnikov, 6-7 (0), 6-7 (4), 6-3, 6-1, 7-6 (5) US Open QF, 1999)

48   Marc Rosset (lost to Arnaud Clement, 6-3, 3-6, 7-6 (4), 6-7 (6), 15-13 2001 Davis Cup, Neuchatel Switzerland)

Women

22   Brenda Schultz-McCarthy (d. Iva Majoli 6-4, 5-7, 6-0 Birmingham, QF, 1994)

20   Serena Williams (d. Elena Dementieva 6-7 (4), 7-5, 8-6, Wimbledon, SF, 2009)

19   Meghann Shaughnessy (d. Nuria Llagostera Vives 6-4, 4-6, 10-8, Wimbledon, 2nd rd., 2004)

18   Samantha Stosur (d. Kristina Brandi, 4-6, 6-2, 6-2, Wimbledon, 1st rd., 2007)

18   Julie Coin (lost to Dominika Cibulkova 6-4, 3-6, 6-3, Wimbledon, 1st rd, 2009)

18   Venus Williams (d. Amy Frazier, 6-7 (5), 6-4, 7-6 (5) Stanford, QF, 2000) she also served 20 double faults in the match.

FASTEST SERVES

Men

155 mph Andy Roddick (vs. Vladimir Voltchkov, USA vs. Belarus Davis Cup SF, Charleston, S.C., 2004)

Women

130 mph Brenda Schultz-McCarthy (vs. Julia Cohen, 1st rd., of qualifying, Cincinnati, 2006)

FOOT FAULTS IN A MATCH

26   Stefan Edberg (vs. Aaron Krickstein, 1st rd., US Open, 1983)

22   Yevgeny Kafelnikov (vs. Mark Philippoussis, 1st rd., Wimbledon, 1998)

DOUBLE FAULTS IN A MATCH

Men

30   Marc Rosset (in a 6-3, 3-6, 7-6 (4), 6-7 (6), 15-13 loss to Arnaud Clement in 5:47 in the 2001 Davis Cup QF between Switzerland and France in Neuchatel, Switzerland Rosset also served 48 aces)

26   Marc Rosset (vs. Michael Joyce in a 6-0, 6-7 (10), 7-5, 6-2, 1st rd., loss at Wimbledon in 1995)

23   Guillermo Coria vs. Nicolas Kiefer in a 6-7, 6-4, 6-3 win in the 3rd. rd., of Monte Carlo, 2006 (three-set match record)

Women

31   Anna Kournikova vs. Miho Saeki in a 1-6, 6-4, 10-8, 2nd rd., win at the 1999 Australian Open. In her 1st rd., win in that tournament over Jill Craybas, Kournikova served 23 double faults

20   Venus Williams (vs. Amy Frazier, quarterfinals, Stanford, 2000)

19   Debbie Graham (vs. Martina Navratilova, Oakland, 1994)

CONSECUTIVE DOUBLE FAULTS

17   Consecutive double faults in a 1st rd. Wimbledon match 1957, which were made by Maria de Amorin of Brazil in her loss to Berna Thung of The Netherlands, 6-3, 4-6, 6-1. (*Wimbledon Compendium*)

CONSECUTIVE ACES

10   Sam Querry d. James Blake, 7-6(8-6), 6-7(4-7), 7-6(7-4), quarterfinals, Indianapolis 2007. He served 34 aces in the match

CONSECUTIVE MATCH LOSSES

Men

21	Vince Spadea	1999-2000
20	Gary Donnelly	1986-1987

Other Big Events

Kim Clijsters won two WTA Tour year-end championships in 2002 and 2003 and is one of 17 women to earn the No. 1 world ranking. The Belgian also won an Italian singles title and two titles in both Indian Wells and Key Biscayne, including the "Coast-to-Coast Double" in 2005..

There is a lot more to tennis than the majors and Cup play. The Sony Ericsson Open in Key Biscayne, Fla., and the BNP Paribas Open in Indian Wells, Calif., are seen by many as the two biggest events in the sport outside of the major championships. Outside of the French Championships, the Italian Championships is celebrated as the biggest event in continental Europe. During the 1970s and early 1980s, the event was celebrated in some circles as a bigger and more prestigious title than the Australian Open. Winning Wimbledon, the French and the Italian Championships in the same year has been referred to as the "Old World Triple." World Team Tennis and the Hopman Cup are unique to team tennis—and sports—in their co-ed formats with men and women competing with and against each other.

The Coast to Coast Double: Indian Wells and Key Biscayne

Other than the U.S. Open, the successive springtime fortnights of Indian Wells, Calif., and Key Biscayne, Fla., blending men and women, are the foremost tournaments in North America, probably a dead heat behind the four majors in world prominence. Moving from the California desert to the Florida seaside, the pair provide a solid month of solid hard court tennis.

In 2000, two men who played Davis Cup, Charlie Pasarell for the United States, and Ray Moore for South Africa, built the Indian Wells Tennis Garden, a beautifully landscaped plot amid mountains anchored by a lighted 16,000 seat center court, the largest in the U.S. apart from Arthur Ashe Stadium at the USTA Billie Jean King National Tennis Center.

Pasarell began promoting tournaments in the neighborhood in 1981 at La Quinta, eventually settling in at Indian Wells. He and Moore have been partners since 1987.

Butch Buchholz, also an ex-U.S. Davis Cupper (and member of the International Tennis Hall of Fame), and his brother, Clifford, overcame numerous Floridian trials to establish what is now the Sony Ericsson Open at Crandon Park on an isle, Key Biscayne, across Biscayne Bay from Miami. Opening business in 1985 at Delray Beach, Fla., the brothers moved south to Boca Raton the next year, and farther south to the Key the year after that, finally feeling at home among the palms and mangrove. Their floodlit center court, holding 13,800 and replacing bleachers, was ready in 1994. With 18 tennis courts, the record attendance was made in 2008.

Serena Williams won the Sony Ericsson Open in Key Biscayne for a fifth time in 2008.

BNP Paribas Open

Men's Singles

Year	Champion	Runner-up	Score in final
Palm Springs, California			
1976	Jimmy Connors (USA)	Roscoe Tanner (USA)	6-4, 6-4
1977	Brian Gottfried (USA)	Guillermo Vilas (ARG)	2-6, 6-1, 6-3
1978	Roscoe Tanner (USA)	Raúl Ramírez (MEX)	6-1, 7-6
Rancho Mirage, California			
1979	Roscoe Tanner (USA)	Brian Gottfried (USA)	6-4, 6-2
1980	final canceled (rain)		
La Quinta, California			
1981	Jimmy Connors (USA)	Ivan Lendl (CZE)	6-3, 7-6
1982	Yannick Noah (FRA)	Ivan Lendl (CZE)	6-4, 2-6, 7-5
1983	José Higueras (ESP)	Eliot Teltscher (USA)	6-4, 6-2
1984	Jimmy Connors (USA)	Yannick Noah (FRA)	6-2, 6-7, 6-3
1985	Larry Stefanki (USA)	David Pate (USA)	6-1, 6-4, 3-6, 6-3
1986	Joakim Nyström (SWE)	Yannick Noah (FRA)	6-1, 6-3, 6-2
Indian Wells, Calif.			
1987	Boris Becker (GER)	Stefan Edberg (SWE)	6-4, 6-4, 7-5
1988	Boris Becker (GER)	Emilio Sánchez (ESP)	7-5, 6-4, 2-6, 6-4
1989	Miloslav Mecír (CZE)	Yannick Noah (FRA)	3-6, 2-6, 6-1, 6-2, 6-3
1990	Stefan Edberg (SWE)	Andre Agassi (USA)	6-4, 5-7, 7-6, 7-6
1991	Jim Courier (USA)	Guy Forget (FRA)	4-6, 6-3, 4-6, 6-3, 7-6
1992	Michael Chang (USA)	Andrei Chesnokov (RUS)	6-3, 6-4, 7-5
1993	Jim Courier (USA)	Wayne Ferreira (RSA)	6-3, 6-3, 6-1
1994	Pete Sampras (USA)	Petr Korda (CZE)	4-6, 6-3, 3-6, 6-3, 6-2
1995	Pete Sampras (USA)	Andre Agassi (USA)	7-5, 6-3, 7-5
1996	Michael Chang (USA)	Paul Haarhuis (NED)	7-5, 6-1, 6-1
1997	Michael Chang (USA)	Bohdan Ulihrach (CZE)	4-6, 6-3, 6-4, 6-3
1998	Marcelo Ríos (CHI)	Greg Rusedski (GBR)	6-3, 6-7, 7-6, 6-4
1999	Mark Philippoussis (AUS)	Carlos Moyà (ESP)	5-7, 6-4, 6-4, 4-6, 6-2
2000	Àlex Corretja (ESP)	Thomas Enqvist (SWE)	6-4, 6-4, 6-3
2001	Andre Agassi (USA)	Pete Sampras (USA)	7-6, 7-5, 6-1
2002	Lleyton Hewitt (AUS)	Tim Henman (GBR)	6-1, 6-2
2003	Lleyton Hewitt (AUS)	Gustavo Kuerten (BRA)	6-1, 6-1
2004	Roger Federer (SUI)	Tim Henman (GBR)	6-3, 6-3
2005	Roger Federer (SUI)	Lleyton Hewitt (AUS)	6-2, 6-4, 6-4
2006	Roger Federer (SUI)	James Blake (USA)	7-5, 6-3, 6-0
2007	Rafael Nadal (ESP)	Novak Djokovic (SRB)	6-2, 7-5
2008	Novak Djokovic (SRB)	Mardy Fish (USA)	6-2, 5-7, 6-3
2009	Rafael Nadal (ESP)	Andy Murray (GBR)	6-1, 6-2

Women's Results

Year	Champion	Runner-up	Score
1989	Manuela Maleeva Fragniere (BUL)	Jenny Byrne (AUS)	6-4, 6-1
1990	Martina Navrátilová (USA)	Helena Suková (CZE)	6-2, 5-7, 6-1
1991	Martina Navrátilová (USA)	Monica Seles (YUG)	6-2, 7-6(6)
1992	Monica Seles (YUG)	Conchita Martínez (ESP)	6-3, 6-1
1993	Mary Joe Fernández (USA)	Amanda Coetzer (RSA)	3-6, 6-1, 7-6(6)
1994	Steffi Graf (GER)	Amanda Coetzer (RSA)	6-0, 6-4
1995	Mary Joe Fernández (USA)	Natasha Zvereva (BLR)	6-4, 6-3
1996	Steffi Graf (GER)	Conchita Martínez (ESP)	7-6(5), 7-6(5)
1997	Lindsay Davenport (USA)	Irina Spîrlea (ROM)	6-2, 6-1
1998	Martina Hingis (SUI)	Lindsay Davenport (USA)	6-3, 6-4
1999	Serena Williams (USA)	Steffi Graf (GER)	6-3, 3-6, 7-5
2000	Lindsay Davenport (USA)	Martina Hingis (SUI)	4-6, 6-4, 6-0
2001	Serena Williams (USA)	Kim Clijsters (BEL)	4-6, 6-4, 6-2
2002	Daniela Hantuchová (SVK)	Martina Hingis (SUI)	6-3, 6-4
2003	Kim Clijsters (BEL)	Lindsay Davenport (USA)	6-4, 7-5
2004	Justine Henin-Hardenne (BEL)	Lindsay Davenport (USA)	6-1, 6-4
2005	Kim Clijsters (BEL)	Lindsay Davenport (USA)	6-4, 4-6, 6-2
2006	Maria Sharapova (RUS)	Elena Dementieva (RUS)	6-1, 6-2
2007	Daniela Hantuchová (SVK)	Svetlana Kuznetsova (RUS)	6-3, 6-4
2008	Ana Ivanovic (SRB)	Svetlana Kuznetsova (RUS)	6-4, 6-3
2009	Vera Zvonareva (RUS)	Victoria Azarenka (BLR)	6-3, 6-3

Sony Ericsson Open
Key Biscayne, Fla.

Men's Singles

Year	Champion	Runner-up	Score in final
1985	Tim Mayotte (USA)	Scott Davis (USA)	4-6, 4-6, 6-3, 6-2, 6-4
1986	Ivan Lendl (CZE)	Mats Wilander (SWE)	3-6, 6-1, 7-6, 6-4
1987	Miloslav Mecír (CZE)	Ivan Lendl (USA)	7-5, 6-2, 7-5
1988	Mats Wilander (SWE)	Jimmy Connors (USA)	6-4, 4-6, 6-4, 6-4
1989	Ivan Lendl (USA)	Thomas Muster (AUT)	w/o (injury)
1990	Andre Agassi (USA)	Stefan Edberg (SWE)	6-1, 6-4, 0-6, 6-2
1991	Jim Courier (USA)	David Wheaton (USA)	4-6, 6-3, 6-4
1992	Michael Chang (USA)	Alberto Mancini (ARG)	7-5, 7-5
1993	Pete Sampras (USA)	MaliVai Washington (USA)	6-3, 6-2
1994	Pete Sampras (USA)	Andre Agassi (USA)	5-7, 6-3, 6-3
1995	Andre Agassi (USA)	Pete Sampras (USA)	3-6, 6-2, 7-6
1996	Andre Agassi (USA)	Goran Ivanievic (CRO)	3-0 (retired)
1997	Thomas Muster (AUT)	Sergi Bruguera (ESP)	7-6, 6-3, 6-1
1998	Marcelo Ríos (CHI)	Andre Agassi (USA)	7-5, 6-3, 6-4
1999	Richard Krajicek (NED)	Sébastien Grosjean (FRA)	4-6, 6-1, 6-2, 7-5
2000	Pete Sampras (USA)	Gustavo Kuerten (BRA)	6-1, 6-7, 7-6, 7-6
2001	Andre Agassi (USA)	Jan-Michael Gambill (USA)	7-6, 6-1, 6-0

Year	Champion	Runner-up	Score in final
2002	Andre Agassi (USA)	Roger Federer (SUI)	6-3, 6-3, 3-6, 6-4
2003	Andre Agassi (USA)	Carlos Moyà (ESP)	6-3, 6-3
2004	Andy Roddick (USA)	Guillermo Coria (ARG)	6-7, 6-3, 6-1 (retired)
2005	Roger Federer (SUI)	Rafael Nadal (ESP)	2-6, 6-7, 7-6, 6-3, 6-1
2006	Roger Federer (SUI)	Ivan Ljubicic (CRO)	7-6, 7-6, 7-6
2007	Novak Djokovic (SRB)	Guillermo Cañas (ARG)	6-3 6-2 6-4
2008	Nikolay Davydenko (RUS)	Rafael Nadal (ESP)	6-4, 6-2
2009	Andy Murray (GBR)	Novak Djokovic (SRB)	6-2, 7-5

Women's Singles

Year	Champion	Runner-up	Score in final
1985	Martina Navrátilova (USA)	Chris Evert Lloyd (USA)	6-2, 6-4
1986	Chris Evert-Lloyd (USA)	Steffi Graf (GER)	6-4, 6-2
1987	Steffi Graf (GER)	Chris Evert Lloyd (USA)	6-1, 6-2
1988	Steffi Graf (GER)	Chris Evert (USA)	6-4, 6-4
1989	Gabriela Sabatini (ARG)	Chris Evert (USA)	6-1, 4-6, 6-2
1990	Monica Seles (YUG)	Judith Wiesner (AUT)	6-1, 6-2
1991	Monica Seles (YUG)	Gabriela Sabatini (ARG)	6-3, 7-5
1992	Arantxa Sánchez Vicario (ESP)	Gabriela Sabatini (ARG)	6-1, 6-4
1993	Arantxa Sánchez Vicario (ESP)	Steffi Graf (GER)	6-4, 3-6, 6-3
1994	Steffi Graf (GER)	Natasha Zvereva (BLR)	4-6, 6-1, 6-2
1995	Steffi Graf (GER)	Kimiko Date (JPN)	6-1, 6-4
1996	Steffi Graf (GER)	Chanda Rubin (USA)	6-1, 6-3
1997	Martina Hingis (SUI)	Monica Seles (YUG)	6-2, 6-1
1998	Venus Williams (USA)	Anna Kournikova (RUS)	2-6, 6-4, 6-1
1999	Venus Williams (USA)	Serena Williams (USA)	6-1, 4-6, 6-4
2000	Martina Hingis (SUI)	Lindsay Davenport (USA)	6-3, 6-2
2001	Venus Williams (USA)	Jennifer Capriati (USA)	4-6, 6-1, 7-6 (7-4)
2002	Serena Williams (USA)	Jennifer Capriati (USA)	7-5, 7-6 (7-4)
2003	Serena Williams (USA)	Jennifer Capriati (USA)	4-6, 6-4, 6-1
2004	Serena Williams (USA)	Elena Dementieva (RUS)	6-1, 6-1
2005	Kim Clijsters (BEL)	Maria Sharapova (RUS)	6-3, 7-5
2006	Svetlana Kuznetsova (RUS)	Maria Sharapova (RUS)	6-4, 6-3
2007	Serena Williams (USA)	Justine Henin (BEL)	0-6, 7-5, 6-3
2008	Serena Williams (USA)	Jelena Jankovic (SRB)	6-1, 5-7, 6-3
2009	Victoria Azarenka (BLR)	Serena Williams (USA)	6-3, 6-1

Italian Championships

Although the Italian International Championships was launched in Milan in 1930, where American Big Bill Tilden captured one of his last amateur titles, the dictator Mussolini wanted the event in his capital, Rome, and directed that Il Foro Italico, be constructed to accommodate the tournament. (Mussolini, strictly a hacker, had a private court and pro, Mario Belardinelli.)

The Foro, originally named for Mussolini, a handsome clay court complex beside the Tiber, boasts a marble arena surrounded by sporting statuary, and terraced outer courts ringed by Respighi's Pines of Rome. It welcomed the Championships in 1935, the men's title won by another American, Wilmer Hines. Subsequently shut down by political uncertainties in 1936, then World War II, the tournament didn't resume until 1950, missing four post-war years as punishment by the International Tennis Federation for Italy's wartime role as an Axis nation. From 1980-84, the women's tournament was exiled to Perugia, then Taranto in 1985, abandoned in 1986, but restored to Rome in 1987. The Championships, becoming "open" in 1969, is now a two-week event divided separately between the men and women.

The Tennis Club Milano was the original home of the event before the move to Rome. In 1961, for just one year, the tournament was shifted to Sporting Club Torino. The only unseeded champions of the event were Marty Mulligan (AUS) in 1963; Julie Heldman (USA) in 1969; Felix Mantilla (ESP) in 2003; Martina Hingis (SUI) in 2006. The tie-breaker was adopted in 1971. One peculiar trans-Atlantic match was the 1976 men's doubles final. Rained out in Rome, it was later played in Houston, Texas.

Men's Singles Finals

Year	Champion	Runner-up	Score in final
1930	Bill Tilden (USA)	Umberto de Morpurgo (ITA)	6-1, 6-1, 6-2
1931	George Hughes (GBR)	Henri Cochet (FRA)	6-4, 6-3, 6-2
1932	Andre Merlin (FRA)	George Hughes (GBR)	6-1, 5-7, 6-0, 8-6
1933	Emanuele Sartorio (ITA)	Martin Legeay (FRA)	6-3, 6-1, 6-3
1934	Giovanni Palmieri (ITA)	Giorgio de Stefani (ITA)	6-3, 6-0, 7-5
1935	Wilmer Hines (USA)	Giovanni Palmieri (ITA)	6-3, 10-8, 9-7
1936–49 not held			
1950	Jaroslav Drobny (EGY)	William Talbert (USA)	6-4, 6-3, 7-9, 6-2
1951	Jaroslav Drobny (EGY)	Gianni Cucelli (ITA)	6-1, 10-8, 6-0
1952	Frank Sedgman (AUS)	Jaroslav Drobny (EGY)	7-5, 6-3, 1-6, 6-4
1953	Jaroslav Drobny (EGY)	Lew Hoad (AUS)	6-2, 6-1, 6-2
1954	Budge Patty (USA)	Enrique Morea (ARG)	11-9, 6-4, 6-4
1955	Fausto Gardini (ITA)	Giuseppe Merlo (ITA)	1-6, 6-1, 3-6, 6-6 (retired)
1956	Lew Hoad (AUS)	Sven Davidson (SWE)	7-5, 6-2, 6-0
1957	Nicola Pietrangeli (ITA)	Giuseppe Merlo (ITA)	8-6, 6-2, 6-4
1958	Mervyn Rose (AUS)	Nicola Pietrangeli (ITA)	5-7, 8-6, 6-4, 1-6, 6-2
1959	Luis Ayala (CHI)	Neale Fraser (AUS)	6-3, 3-6, 6-3, 6-3
1960	Barry MacKay (AUS)	Luis Ayala (CHI)	7-5, 7-5, 0-6, 0-6, 6-1
1961	Nicola Pietrangeli (ITA)	Rod Laver (AUS)	6-8, 6-1, 6-1, 6-2

Year	Champion	Runner-up	Score in final
1962	Rod Laver (AUS)	Roy Emerson (AUS)	6-2, 1-6, 3-6, 6-3, 6-1
1963	Marty Mulligan (AUS)	Boro Jovanovic (YUG)	6-2, 4-6, 6-3, 8-6
1964	Jan-Erik Lundquist (SWE)	Fred Stolle (AUS)	1-6, 7-5, 6-3, 6-1
1965	Marty Mulligan (AUS)	Manuel Santana (ESP)	1-6, 6-4, 6-3, 6-1
1966	Tony Roche (AUS)	Nicola Pietrangeli (ITA)	11-9, 6-1, 6-3
1967	Marty Mulligan (AUS)	Tony Roche (AUS)	6-3, 0-6, 6-4, 6-1
1968	Tom Okker (NED)	Bob Hewitt (RSA)	10-8, 6-8, 6-1, 1-6, 6-0
1969	John Newcombe (AUS)	Tony Roche (AUS)	6-3, 4-6, 6-2, 5-7, 6-3
1970	Ilie Nastase (ROU)	Jan Kodes (CZE)	6-3, 1-6, 6-3, 8-6
1971	Rod Laver (AUS)	Jan Kodes (CZE)	7-5, 6-3, 6-3
1972	Manuel Orantes (ESP)	Jan Kodes (CZE)	4-6, 6-1, 7-5, 6-2
1973	Ilie Nastase (ROU)	Manuel Orantes (ESP)	6-1, 6-1, 6-1
1974	Bjorn Borg (SWE)	Ilie Nastase (ROU)	6-3, 6-4, 6-2
1975	Raul Ramirez (MEX)	Manuel Orantes (ESP)	7-6, 7-5, 7-5
1976	Adriano Panatta (ITA)	Guillermo Vilas (ARG)	2-6, 7-6, 6-2, 7-6
1977	Vitas Gerulaitis (USA)	Antonio Zugarelli (ITA)	6-2, 7-6, 3-6, 7-6
1978	Bjorn Borg (SWE)	Adriano Panatta (ITA)	1-6, 6-3, 6-1, 4-6, 6-3
1979	Vitas Gerulaitis (USA)	Guillermo Vilas (ARG)	6-7, 7-6, 6-7, 6-4, 6-2
1980	Guillermo Vilas (ARG)	Yannick Noah (FRA)	6-0, 6-4, 6-4
1981	Jose-Luis Clerc (ARG)	Victor Pecci (PAR)	6-3, 6-4, 6-0
1982	Andres Gomez (ECU)	Eliot Teltscher (USA)	6-2, 6-3, 6-2
1983	Jimmy Arias (USA)	Jose Higueras (ESP)	6-2, 6-7, 6-1, 6-4
1984	Andres Gomez (ECU)	Aaron Krickstein (USA)	2-6, 6-1, 6-2, 6-2
1985	Yannick Noah (FRA)	Miloslav Mecir (CZE)	6-3, 3-6, 6-2, 7-6
1986	Ivan Lendl (CZE)	Emilio Sanchez (ESP)	7-5, 4-6, 6-1, 6-1
1987	Mats Wilander (SWE)	Martin Jaite (ARG)	6-3, 6-4, 6-4
1988	Ivan Lendl (CZE)	Guillermo Perez-Roldan (ARG)	2-6, 6-4, 6-2, 4-6, 6-4
1989	Alberto Mancini (ARG)	Andre Agassi (USA)	6-3, 4-6, 2-6, 7-6, 6-1
1990	Thomas Muster (AUT)	Andrei Chesnokov (USSR)	6-1, 6-3, 6-1
1991	Emilio Sanchez (ESP)	Alberto Mancini (ARG)	6-3, 6-1, 3-0 (retired)
1992	Jim Courier (USA)	Carlos Costa (ESP)	7-6, 6-0, 6-4
1993	Jim Courier (USA)	Goran Ivanievic (CRO)	6-1, 6-2, 6-2
1994	Pete Sampras (USA)	Boris Becker (GER)	6-1, 6-2, 6-2
1995	Thomas Muster (AUT)	Sergi Bruguera (ESP)	3-6, 7-6, 6-2, 6-3
1996	Thomas Muster (AUT)	Richard Krajicek (NED)	6-2, 6-4, 3-6, 6-3
1997	Alex Corretja (ESP)	Marcelo Rios (CHI)	7-5, 7-5, 6-3
1998	Marcelo Ríos (CHI)	Albert Costa (ESP)	w/o (injury)
1999	Gustavo Kuerten (BRA)	Patrick Rafter (AUS)	6-4, 7-5, 7-6
2000	Magnus Norman (SWE)	Gustavo Kuerten (BRA)	6-3, 4-6, 6-4, 6-4
2001	Juan Carlos Ferrero (ESP)	Gustavo Kuerten (BRA)	3-6, 6-1, 2-6, 6-4, 6-2
2002	Andre Agassi (USA)	Tommy Haas (GER)	6-3, 6-3, 6-0
2003	Felix Mantilla (ESP)	Roger Federer (SUI)	7-5, 6-2, 7-6
2004	Carlos Moya (ESP)	David Nalbandian (ARG)	6-3, 6-3, 6-1
2005	Rafael Nadal (ESP)	Guillermo Coria (ARG)	6-4, 3-6, 6-3, 4-6, 7-6
2006	Rafael Nadal (ESP)	Roger Federer (SUI)	6-7, 7-6, 6-4, 2-6, 7-6
2007	Rafael Nadal (ESP)	Fernando Gonzalez (CHI)	6-2, 6-2
2008	Novak Djokovic (SRB)	Stanislas Wawrinka (SUI)	4-6, 6-3, 6-3
2009	Rafael Nadal (ESP)	Novak Djokovic (SRB)	7-6 (2), 6-2

Women's Singles Finals

Year	Champion	Runner-up	Score in final
1930	Lili de Alvarez (ESP)	Lucia Valerio (ITA)	3-6, 8-6, 6-0
1931	Lucia Valerio (ITA)	Dorothy Andrus (USA)	2-6, 6-2, 6-2
1932	Ida Adamoff (FRA)	Lucia Valerio (ITA)	6-4, 7-5
1933	Elizabeth Ryan (USA)	Ida Adamoff (FRA)	6-1, 6-1
1934	Helen Jacobs (USA)	Lucia Valerio (ITA)	6-3, 6-0
1935	Hilde Krahwinkel-Sperling (DEN)	Lucia Valerio (ITA)	6-4, 6-1
1936–49 not held			
1950	Annelies Ullstein-Bossi (ITA)	Joan Curry (GBR)	6-4, 6-4
1951	Doris Hart (USA)	Shirley Fry (USA)	6-3, 8-6
1952	Susan Partridge (GBR)	Pat Harrison (GBR)	6-3, 7-5
1953	Doris Hart (USA)	Maureen Connolly (USA)	4-6, 9-7, 6-3
1954	Maureen Connolly (USA)	Patricia Ward GBR)	6-3, 6-0
1955	Patricia Ward (GBR)	Erika Vollmer (GER)	6-4, 6-3
1956	Althea Gibson (USA)	Zsuzsa Kormoczy (HUN)	6-3, 7-5
1957	Shirley Bloomer (GBR)	Dorothy Head Knode (USA)	1-6, 9-7, 6-2
1958	Maria Bueno (BRA)	Lorraine Coghlan (AUS)	3-6, 6-3, 6-3
1959	Christine Truman (GBR)	Sandra Reynolds (RSA)	6-0, 6-1
1960	Zsuzsi Kormoczy (HUN)	Ann Haydon (GBR)	6-4, 4-6, 6-1
1961	Maria Bueno (BRA)	Lesley Turner (AUS)	6-4, 6-4
1962	Margaret Smith (AUS)	Maria Bueno (BRA)	8-6, 5-7, 6-4
1963	Margaret Smith (AUS)	Lesley Turner (AUS)	6-3, 6-4
1964	Margaret Smith (AUS)	Lesley Turner (AUS)	6-1, 6-1
1965	Maria Bueno (BRA)	Nancy Richey (USA)	6-1, 1-6, 6-3
1966	Ann Haydon Jones (GBR)	Annette Van Zyl (RSA)	8-6, 6-1
1967	Lesley Turner (AUS)	Maria Bueno (BRA)	6-3, 6-3
1968	Lesley Turner Bowrey (AUS)	Margaret Court (AUS)	2-6, 6-2, 6-3
1969	Julie Heldman (USA)	Kerry Melville (AUS)	7-5, 6-3
1970	Billie Jean King (USA)	Julie Heldman (USA)	6-1, 6-3
1971	Virginia Wade (GBR)	Helga Niessen-Masthoff (GER)	6-4, 6-4
1972	Linda Tuero (USA)	Olga Morozova (USSR)	6-4, 6-3
1973	Evonne Goolagong (AUS)	Chris Evert (USA)	7-6, 6-0
1974	Chris Evert (USA)	Martina Navratilova (CZE)	6-3, 6-3
1975	Chris Evert (USA)	Martina Navratilova (CZE)	6-1, 6-0
1976	Mima Jauovec (YUG)	Lesley Hunt (AUS)	6-1, 6-3
1977	Janet Newberry (USA)	Renata Tomanova (CZE)	6-3, 7-6
1978	Regina Marsikova (CZE)	Virginia Ruzici (ROU)	7-5, 7-5
1979	Tracy Austin (USA)	Sylvia Hanika (GER)	6-4, 1-6, 6-3
1980	Chris Evert Lloyd (USA)	Virginia Ruzici (ROU)	5-7, 6-2, 6-2
1981	Chris Evert Lloyd (USA)	Virginia Ruzici (ROU)	6-1, 6-2
1982	Chris Evert Lloyd (USA)	Hana Mandlíkova (CZE)	6-0, 6-2
1983	Andrea Temesvari (HUN)	Bonnie Gadusek (USA)	6-1, 6-0
1984	Manuela Maleeva (BUL)	Chris Evert Lloyd (USA)	6-3, 6-3
1985	Raffaella Reggi (ITA)	Vicki Nelson-Dunbar (USA)	6-4, 6-4
1986	not held		
1987	Steffi Graf (GER)	Gabriela Sabatini (ARG)	7-5, 4-6, 6-0
1988	Gabriela Sabatini (ARG)	Helen Kelesi (CAN)	6-1, 6-7, 6-1
1989	Gabriela Sabatini (ARG)	Arantxa Sanchez (ESP)	6-2, 5-7, 6-4

Year	Champion	Runner-up	Score in final
1990	Monica Seles (YUG)	Martina Navratilova (USA)	6-1, 6-1
1991	Gabriela Sabatini (ARG)	Monica Seles (YUG)	6-3, 6-2
1992	Gabriela Sabatini (ARG)	Monica Seles (YUG)	7-5, 6-4
1993	Conchita Martinez (ESP)	Gabriela Sabatini (ARG)	7-5, 6-1
1994	Conchita Martinez (ESP)	Martina Navratilova (USA)	7-6, 6-4
1995	Conchita Martinez (ESP)	Arantxa Sanchez Vicario (ESP)	6-3, 6-1
1996	Conchita Martinez (ESP)	Martina Hingis (SUI)	6-2, 6-3
1997	Mary Pierce (FRA)	Conchita Martinez (ESP)	6-4, 6-0
1998	Martina Hingis (SUI)	Venus Williams (USA)	6-3, 2-6, 6-3
1999	Venus Williams (USA)	Mary Pierce (FRA)	6-4, 6-2
2000	Monica Seles (USA)	Amelie Mauresmo (FRA)	6-2, 7-6
2001	Jelena Dokic (AUS)	Amelie Mauresmo (FRA)	7-6, 6-1
2002	Serena Williams (USA)	Justine Henin-Hardenne (BEL)	7-6, 6-4
2003	Kim Clijsters (BEL)	Amélie Mauresmo (FRA)	3-6, 7-6, 6-0
2004	Amelie Mauresmo (FRA)	Jennifer Capriati (USA)	3-6, 6-3, 7-6
2005	Amelie Mauresmo (FRA)	Patty Schnyder (SUI)	2-6, 6-3, 6-4
2006	Martina Hingis (SUI)	Dinara Safina (RUS)	6-2, 7-5
2007	Jelena Jankovic (SRB)	Svetlana Kuznetsova (RUS)	7-5, 6-1
2008	Jelena Jankovic (SRB)	Alize Cornet (FRA)	6-2, 6-2
2009	Dinara Safina (RUS)	Svetlana Kuznetsova (RUS)	6-3, 6-2

Hopman Cup

Prior to the Australian Open, the Hopman Cup, a mixed team event, is played indoors at Perth, Australia. It is named appropriately for Australian Harry Hopman, (1906-1985), an International Tennis Hall of Famer who excelled in team competition, captaining his homeland to 16 Davis Cups between 1939 and 1967. Involving national teams of one man and one woman, the format is best-of-three matches: women's and men's singles, and mixed doubles. Launched in 1989, it was approved as an official ITF event in 1997. The United States and the Slovak Republic have won the most Hopman Cup titles—both winning the championship four times.

Serena Williams (left) and **Mardy Fish** won the Hopman Cup for the United States in 2008.

Hopman Cup Champions

1989

Czechoslovakia def. Australia 2-0

Helena Sukova (CZE) def. Hana Mandlikova (AUS) 6-4, 6-3

Miloslav Mecir–Sukova (CZE) def. Pat Cash–Mandlikova (AUS) 6-2, 6-4

1990

Spain def. United States 2-1

Emilio Sanchez (ESP) def. John McEnroe (USA) 5-7, 7-5, 7-5

Arantxa Sanchez Vicario (ESP) def. Pam Shriver (USA) 6-3, 6-3

McEnroe–Shriver def. Sanchez–Sanchez Vicario (ESP) 6-3, 6-2

1991

Yugoslavia def. United States 3-0

Monica Seles (YUG) def. Zina Garrison (USA) 6-1, 6-1

Goran Prpic (YUG) def. David Wheaton (USA) 4-6, 6-3, 7-5

Prpic–Seles (YUG) def. Wheaton–Garrison (USA) 8-3*

shortened to pro-set

1992

Switzerland def. Czechoslovakia 2-1

Manuela Maleeva-Fragniere (SUI) def. Helena Sukova (CZE) 6-2, 6-4

Jakob Hlasek (SUI) def. Karel Novacek (CZE) 6-4, 6-4

Novacek-Sukova (CZE) def. Hlasek–Maleeva-Fragniere (SUI) 8-4*

shortened to pro-set

1993

Germany def. Spain 2-1

Steffi Graf (GER) def. Arantxa Sanchez Vicario (ESP) 6-4, 6-3

Michael Stich (GER) def. Emilio Sanchez (ESP) 7-5, 6-3

Sanchez–Sanchez Vicario (ESP) def. Stich–Graf (GER) w/o

1994

Czech Republic def. Germany 2-1

Jana Novotna (CZE) def. Anke Huber (GER) 1-6, 6-4, 6-3

Petr Korda (CZE) def. Bernd Karbacher (GER) 6-3, 6-3

Karbacher–Huber (GER) def. Korda–Novotna (CZE) 8-3 *

shortened to pro-set

1995

Germany def. Ukraine 3-0

Anke Huber (GER) def. Natalia Medvedeva (UKR) 6-4, 3-6, 6-4

Boris Becker (GER) def. Andrei Medvedev (UKR) 6-3, 6-7, 6-3

Becker–Huber (GER) def. Medvedev–Medvedeva (UKR) w/o

1996

Croatia def. Switzerland 2-1:

Martina Hingis (SUI) def. Iva Majoli (CRO) 6-3, 6-0

Goran Ivanisevic (CRO) def. Marc Rosset (SUI) 7-6, 7-5

Ivanisevic–Majoli (CRO) def. Rosset–Hingis (SUI) 3-6, 7-6, 5-5, ret.

1997

United States def. South Africa 2-1

Chanda Rubin (USA) def. Amanda Coetzer (RSA) 7-5, 6-2

Wayne Ferreira (RSA) def. Justin Gimelstob (USA) 6-4, 7-6(4)

Gimelstob–Rubin (USA) def. Ferreira–Coetzer (RSA) 3-6, 6-2, 7-5

1998

Slovak Republic def. France 2-1

Mary Pierce (FRA) def. Karina Habsudova (SVK) 6-4, 7-5

Karol Kucera (SVK) def. Cedric Pioline (FRA) 7-6 (7), 6-4

Habsudova–Kucera (SVK) def. Pierce–Pioline (FRA) 6-3, 6-4

1999

Australia def. Sweden 2-1

Jelena Dokic (AUS) def. Asa Carlsson (SWE) 6-2, 7-6 (8)

Mark Philippoussis (AUS) def. Jonas Bjorkman (SWE) 6-3, 7-6 (6)

Bjorkman–Carlsson (SWE) def. Philippoussis/Dokic (AUS) 8-6 *

* shortened to pro-set

2000

South Africa def. Thailand 3-0

Amanda Coetzer (RSA) def Tamarine Tanasugarn (THA) 3-6, 6-4, 6-4

Wayne Ferreira (RSA) def. Paradorn Srichaphan (THA) 7-6, 6-3

Ferreira–Coetzer (RSA) def. Srichaphan–Tansugarn (THA) 8-1*

* shortened to pro-set

2001

Switzerland def. United States 2-1

Martina Hingis (SUI) def. Monica Seles (USA) 7-5, 6-4

Roger Federer (SUI) def. Jan-Michael Gambill (USA) 6-4, 6-3

Gambill–Seles (USA) def. Federer–Hingis (SUI), 2-6, 6-4, 7-6

2002

Spain def. United States 2-1

Monica Seles (USA) def Aranxta Sanchez Vicario (ESP) 6-1, 7-6

Tommy Robredo (ESP) def. Jan-Michael Gambill (USA) 6-3, 2-6, 7-6 (7-2)

Robredo–Sanchez Vicario (ESP) def. Gambill–Seles (USA) 6-4, 6-2

2003

United States def. Australia 3-0

Serena Williams (USA) def. Alicia Molik (AUS) 6-2, 6-3

James Blake (USA) def. Lleyton Hewitt (AUS) 6-3, 6-4

Blake–Williams (USA) def. Hewitt–Molik (AUS) 6-3, 6-2

2004

United States def. Slovak Republic 2-1

Lindsay Davenport (USA) def. Daniela Hantuchova (SVK) 6-3, 6-1

Karol Kucera (SVK) def. James Blake (USA) 4-6, 6-4, 7-6 (5)

Davenport–Blake (USA) def. Hantuchova–Kucera (SVK) 6-2, 6-3

2005

Slovak Republic def. Argentina 3-0

Daniela Hantuchova (SVK) def. Gisela Dulko (ARG) 1-6, 6-4, 6-4

Dominik Hrbaty (SVK) def. Guillermo Coria (ARG) 6-4, 6-1

Hantuchova–Hrbaty (SVK) def. Dulko–Coria (ARG), w/o

2006

United States def. Netherlands 2-1

Michaella Krajicek (NED) def. Lisa Raymond (USA) 6-4, 7-6 (4)

Taylor Dent (USA) def. Peter Wessels (NED) 6-1, 6-4

Dent–Raymond (USA) def. Wessels–Krajicek (NED) 4-6, 6-2, 7-6 (7)

2007

Russia def. Spain 2-0

Nadia Petrova (RUS) def. Annabel Medina Garrigues (ESP) 6-0, 6-4

Dmitry Tursunov (RUS) def. Tommy Robredo (ESP) 6-4, 7-5

2008

United States def. Serbia 2-1

Serena Williams (USA) def. Jelena Jankovic (SRB) w/o

Novak Djokovic (SRB) def. Mardy Fish (USA) 6-2, 6-7 (4), 7-6 (4)

Williams–Fish (USA) def. Jankovic–Djokovic (SRB) 7-6(4), 6-2

2009

Slovak Republic def. Russia 2-0

Dominika Cibulkova (SVK) d. Dinara Safina (RUS) 6-7 (3), 6-1, 6-4

Dominik Hrbaty (SVK) d. Marat Safin (RUS) 6-7, (5), 7-5, 7-6 (3)

World Team Tennis

City team franchises, the foundation of major pro sports in the United States, came to tennis with the establishment of World Team Tennis in 1973. The original league lasted five years, folding because of large financial losses after the 1978 season. Founded by Dennis Murphy, Jordan Kaiser and Larry King (then husband of Billie Jean King), the WTT operated with 16 cities between Boston and Honolulu in 1974, a high point, and involved most of the game's leading players during its lifespan. They were well paid to ignore the summer season and play team tennis, a new concept in which teams had both male and female players. It was single-set tennis, five sets (men's and women's singles and doubles plus mixed doubles) constituting a match, the score based on total games won. Fearing the summer competition, the International Tennis Federation railed against WTT, and the French Open barred players from the league in 1974, a move which deprived Jimmy Connors, who won the other three majors, a shot at a Grand Slam.

A feature of the first season was the unprecedented appearance of women coaching professional teams containing men—Billie Jean King led the Philadelphia Freedoms, Rosie Casals the Detroit Loves.

Billie Jean King revived the concept modestly under the masthead of Team Tennis in 1981, with a shorter season, and few big-name players, although Connors and Martina Navratilova came aboard in 1991 with Los Angeles and Atlanta respectively. In 1992, Team Tennis resumed using its old name, World Team Tennis.

A number of big names have participated in WTT over the past few years including, Andre Agassi, Lindsay Davenport, Monica Seles, Andy Roddick, Martina Navratilova and the Williams sisters. The championship trophy is called the King Trophy in honor of founder Billie Jean King.

World Team Tennis Champions

Year	WTT Championships	Score
1974	Denver d. Philadelphia	27-21, 28-24
1975	Pittsburgh d. Oakland-San Francisco	25-26, 28-25, 21-14
1976	New York d. Oakland-San Francisco	31-23, 29-21, 31-13
1977	New York d. Phoenix	27-22, 28-17
1978	Los Angeles d. Boston	24-21, 30-20, 26-27, 28-25
1981	Los Angeles finished first	
1982	Dallas finished first	
1983	Chicago d. Los Angeles	26-30
1984	San Diego d. Long Beach	30-13
1985	San Diego d. St. Louis	25-24
1986	San Antonio d. Sacramento	25-23
1987	Charlotte d. San Antonio	25-20
1988	Charlotte d. New Jersey	27-22
1989	San Antonio d. Sacramento	27-25
1990	Los Angeles d. Raleigh	27-16
1991	Atlanta d. Los Angeles	27-16
1992	Atlanta d. Newport Beach	30-17
1993	Wichita d. Newport Beach	26-23
1994	New Jersey d. Idaho	28-25
1995	New Jersey d. Atlanta	28-20
1996	St. Louis d. Delaware	27-16
1997	Sacramento finished first	
1998	Sacramento d. New York	30-13
1999	Sacramento d. Springfield	23-15
2000	Sacramento d. Delaware	21-20
2001	Philadelphia d. Springfield	20-18
2002	Sacramento d. New York	21-13
2003	Delaware Smash d. Sacramento Capitals	21-14
2004	Newport Beach Breakers d. Delaware Smash	23-17
2005	New York Sportimes d. Newport Beach Breakers	21-18
2006	Philadelphia Freedoms d. Newport Beach Breakers	21-14
2007	Sacramento Capitals d. New York Buzz	24-20
2008	New York Buzz d. Kansas City Explorers	21-18

Chris Evert (middle) and **Ilie Nastase** (right) led the Los Angeles Strings to the World Team Tennis title in 1978.

Year-End Championships

In 2007, **Roger Federer** won the year-end Tennis Masters Cup for a fourth time.

Ever since Jack Kramer envisioned and implemented the Grand Prix structure in the early days of the Open era, professional tennis has featured year-end championships —and in some years, multiple season-closing events. Men's tennis featured the year-end "Masters"—best known during its 13-year run at Madison Square Garden in New York —held in December, and, curiously—from January, 1978 to January, 1986—in the next calendar year. In the 1970s and 1980s, World Championship Tennis concluded its slate of events with its WCT Finals in Dallas in March. When WCT was phased out of the game in the late 1980s, and the International Tennis Federation and the ATP Tour were at odds over the control of the men's game, two year-end men's events were staged from 1990 to 1999. The "Masters" was still contested—although moved from New York to locations elsewhere in the world and renamed—and the International Tennis Federation and the four major championships combined to stage the Grand Slam Cup. The women have been less complicated than the men, staging its year-end WTA Championships as the pre-eminent year-end event since 1972.

Grand Prix Masters/ATP World Championship/Tennis Masters Cup

The Grand Prix Masters was a playoff for the top eight players at of a year-long series of Grand Prix tournaments. The players earned the right to play the Masters by accumulating points in tournaments throughout the year. It became a prestigious event from the time the first Masters was played under the sponsorship Pepsi in 1970.

Other sponsors included Commercial Union 1972-76, Colgate 1977-79, Volvo 1980-1984, and Nabisco 1985-1989. When the MIPTC (Men's International Professional Tennis Council) disbanded at the end of 1989, the ATP (Association of Tennis Professionals) took over their own tour with IBM as the sponsor from 1990-1992. When the Transition occurred, the ATP moved the eight-player, round robin event from Madison Square Garden in New York (where it had been since 1977) to the Festhalle in Frankfurt. The event was held in Germany for the 1990s, moving from Frankfurt to Hannover for the 1997-1999 championships. In 2000, the event was re-branded the Tennis Masters Cup and was played in Lisbon, Portugal in 2000, Sydney, Australia in 2001, Shanghai, China in 2002, 2005, 2006, 2007 and in Houston, Texas in 2003 and 2004.

Grand Prix Masters

1970 (Tokyo) Stan Smith won a round-robin among six players with 4-1 record

1971 (Paris) Ilie Nastase won a round-robin among seven players with 6-0 record

1972 (Barcelona) Ilie Nastase d. Stan Smith 6-3, 6-2, 3-6, 2-6, 6-3

1973 (Boston) Ilie Nastase d. Tom Okker 6-3, 7-5, 4-6, 6-3

1974 (Melbourne) Guillermo Vilas d. Ilie Nastase 7-6, 6-2, 3-6, 3-6, 6-4

1975 (Stockholm) Ilie Nastase d. Bjorn Borg 6-2, 6-2, 6-1

1976 (Houston) Manuel Orantes d. Wojtek Fibak 5-7, 6-2, 0-6, 7-6 (7-1), 6-1

1977 (New York) Jimmy Connors d. Bjorn Borg 6-4, 1-6, 6-4

1978 (New York) John McEnroe d. Arthur Ashe 6-7, 6-3, 7-5

1979 (New York) Bjorn Borg d. Vitas Gerulaitis 6-2. 6-2

1980 (New York) Bjorn Borg d. Ivan Lendl 6-4, 6-2, 6-2

1981 (New York) Ivan Lendl d. Vitas Gerulaitis 6-7 (5-7), 2-6, 7-6 (8-6), 6-2, 6-4

1982 (New York) Ivan Lendl d. John McEnroe 6-4, 6-4, 6-2

1983 (New York) John McEnroe d. Ivan Lendl 6-3, 6-4, 6-4

1984 (New York) John McEnroe d. Ivan Lendl 7-5, 6-0, 6-4

1985 (New York) Ivan Lendl d. Boris Becker 6-2, 7-6 (7-1), 6-3

1986 (New York) Ivan Lendl d. Boris Becker 6-4, 6-4, 6-4

1987 (New York) Ivan Lendl d. Mats Wilander 6-2, 6-2, 6-3

1988 (New York) Boris Becker d. Ivan Lendl 5-7, 7-6 (7-5), 3-6, 6-2, 7-6 (7-5)

1989 (New York) Stefan Ebberg d. Boris Becker 4-6, 7-6 (8-6), 6-3, 6-1

ATP World Championships

1990 (Frankfurt) Andre Agassi d. Stefan Edberg 5-7, 7-6 (7-5), 7-5, 6-2

1991 (Frankfurt) Pete Sampras d. Jim Courier 3-6, 7-6 (7-5), 6-3, 6-4

1992 (Frankfurt) Boris Becker d. Jim Courier 6-4, 6-3, 7-5

1993 (Frankfurt) Michael Stich d. Pete Sampras 7-6 (7-3), 2-6, 7-6 (9-7), 6-2

1994 (Frankfurt) Pete Sampras d. Boris Becker 4-6, 6-3, 7-5, 6-4

1995 (Frankfurt) Boris Becker d. Michael Chang 7-6 (7-3), 6-0, 7-6 (7-5)

1996 (Hanover) Pete Sampras d. Boris Becker 3-6, 7-6 (7-5), 7-6 (7-4), 6-7 (11-13), 6-4

1997 (Hannover) Pete Sampras d. Yevgeny Kafelnikov 6-3, 6-2, 6-2

1998 (Hannover) Alex Corretja d. Carlos Moya 3-6, 3-6, 7-5, 6-3, 7-5

1999 (Hannover) Pete Sampras d. Andre Agassi 6-1, 7-5, 6-4

Tennis Masters Cup

2000 (Lisbon) Gustavo Kuerten d. Andre Agassi 6-4, 6-4, 6-4

2001 (Sydney) Lleyton Hewitt d. Sebastian Grosjean 6-3, 6-3, 6-4

2002 (Shanghai) Lleyton Hewitt d. Juan Carlos Ferrero 7-5, 7-5, 2-6, 2-6, 6-4

2003 (Houston) Roger Federer d. Andre Agassi 6-3, 6-0, 6-4

2004 (Houston) Roger Federer d. Lleyton Hewitt 6-3, 6-2

2005 (Shanghai) David Nalbandian d. Roger Federer 6-7(4), 6-7(11), 6-2, 6-1, 7-6(3)

2006 (Shanghai) Roger Federer d. James Blake 6-0, 6-3, 6-4

2007 (Shanghai) Roger Federer d. David Ferrer 6-2, 6-3, 6-2

2008 (Shanghai) Novak Djokovic d. Nikolay Davydenko, 6-1, 7-5

WTA Championships

The WTA season-ending championships are perhaps best known as The Virginia Slims Championships (the company sponsoring the year-end championships from 1972-1978 and from 1983 to 1994). Avon, Corel, Chase and Sony Ericsson have also sponsored the event through the years.

After the modern day WTA was founded in 1970 by nine pioneering women players, led by Billie Jean King and Rosie Casals, the first season-ending tournament for the top qualifying players was played in 1972 in Boca Raton, Fla. The event's best known site is Madison Square Garden in New York, where it was held from 1979 to 2000. Since 2000, the event has been held in Munich, Los Angeles, Madrid and Doha. From 1984 to 1998, the event featured a best-of-five-set women's final.

Virginia Slims Championships

1972	(Boca Raton, Fla.) Chris Evert d. Kerry Melville 7-5, 6-4
1973	(Boca Raton, Fla.) Chris Evert d. Nancy Richey 6-3, 6-3
1974	(Los Angeles) Evonne Goolagong d. Chris Evert 6-3, 6-4
1975	(Los Angeles) Chris Evert d. Martina Navratilova 6-4, 6-2
1976	(Los Angeles) Evonne Goolagong d. Chris Evert 6-3, 5-7, 6-3
1977	(New York) Chris Evert d. Sue Barker 2-6, 6-1, 6-1
1978	(Oakland) Martina Navratilova d. Evonne Goolagong 7-6, 6-4

Avon Championships

1979	(New York) Martina Navratilova d. Tracy Austin 6-3, 3-6, 6-2
1980	(New York) Tracy Austin d. Martina Navratilova 6-2, 2-6, 6-2
1981	(New York) Martina Navratilova d. Andrea Jaeger 6-3, 7-6 (7-3)
1982	(New York) Svlvia Hanika d. Martina Navratilova 1-6, 6-3, 6-4

Virginia Slims Championships

1983	(New York) Martina Navratilova d. Chris Evert 6-2, 6-0
1984	(New York) Martina Navratilova d. Chris Evert Lloyd 6-3, 7-5, 6-1
1985	(New York) Martina Navratilova d. Helena Sukova 6-3, 7-5, 6-4
1986	(spring) (New York) Martina Navratilova d. Hana Mandlikova 6-2, 6-0, 3-6, 6-1
1986	(fall) (New York) Martina Navratilova d. Steffi Graf 7-6 (7-1), 6-3, 6-2
1987	(New York) Steffi Graf d. Gabriela Sabatini 4-6, 6-4, 6-0, 6-4
1988	(New York) Gabriela Sabatini d. Pam Shriver 7-5, 6-2, 6-2
1989	(New York) Steffi Graf d. Martina Navratilova 6-4, 7-5, 2-6, 6-2
1990	(New York) Monica Seles d. Gabriela Sabatini 6-4, 5-7, 3-6, 6-4, 6-2
1991	(New York) Monica Seles d. Martina Navratilova 6-4, 3-6, 7-5, 6-0
1992	(New York) Monica Seles d. Martina Navratilova 7-5, 6-3, 6-1
1993	(New York) Steffi Graf d. Arantxa Sanchez Vicario 6-1, 6-4, 3-6, 6-1
1994	(New York) Gabriela Sabatini d. Lindsay Davenport 6-3, 6-3, 6-4

Corel Championships

1995	(New York) Steffi Graf d. Anke Huber 6-1, 2-6, 6-1, 4-6, 6-3

Chase Championships

1996	(New York) Steffi Graf d. Martina Hingis 6-3, 4-6, 6-0, 4-6, 6-0
1997	(New York) Jana Novotna d. Mary Pierce 7-6, 6-2, 6-3
1998	(New York) Martina Hingis d. Lindsay Davenport 7-5, 6-4, 4-6, 6-2
1999	(New York) Lindsay Davenport d. Martina Hingis 6-4, 6-2
2000	(New York) Martina Hingis d. Monica Seles 6-7 (5), 6-4, 6-4

Sanex Championships

2001	(Munich) Serena Williams d. Lindsay Davenport, walkover

Home Depot Championships

2002	(Los Angeles) Kim Clijsters d. Serena Williams 7-5, 6-3

WTA Tour Championships

2003	(Los Angeles) Kim Clijsters d. Amelie Mauresmo 6-2, 6-0
2004	(Los Angeles) Marina Sharapova d. Serena Williams 4-6, 6-2, 6-4

Sony Ericsson Championships

2005	(Los Angeles) Amelie Mauresmo d.Mary Pierce 5-7, 7-6 (3), 6-4
2006	(Madrid) Justine Henin d. Amelie Mauresmo 6-4, 6-3
2007	(Madrid) Justine Henin d. Maria Sharapova 5-7, 7-5, 6-3
2008	(Doha) Venus Williams d. Vera Zvonareva 6-7 (5), 6-0, 6-2

Year-End Doubles Championships

ATP Tour Year-End Doubles Championships

1970   (Tokyo) Arthur Ashe and Stan Smith won in round robin play with a 2-0 record

1971   Not played

1972   Not played

1973   Not played

1974   Not played

1975   (Stockholm) Juan Gisbert and Manuel Orantes won in round robin play with a 2-1 record

1976   (Houston) Sherwood Stewart and Fred McNair def. Brian Gottfried and Raul Ramirez, 6-3, 5-7, 5-7, 6-4, 6-4

1977   (New York) Bob Hewitt and Frew McMillan def. Bob Lutz and Stan Smith, 7-5, 7-6, 6-3

1978   (New York) John McEnroe and Peter Fleming def. Wojtek Fibak and Tom Okker, 6-4, 6-2, 6-4

1979   (New York) John McEnroe and Peter Fleming def. Wojtek Fibak and Tom Okker, 6-3, 7-6, 6-1

1980   (New York) John McEnroe and Peter Fleming def. Peter McNamara and Paul McNamee, 6-4, 6-3

1981   (New York) John McEnroe and Peter Fleming def. Steve Denton and Kevin Curren, 6-3, 6-3

1982   (New York) John McEnroe and Peter Fleming def. Sherwood Steward and Ferdi Taygan, 7-5, 6-3

1983   (New York) John McEnroe and Peter Fleming def. Pavel Slozil and Tomas Smid, 6-2, 6-2

1984   (New York) John McEnroe and Peter Fleming def. Mark Edmondson and Sherwood Stewart, 6-3, 6-1

1985   (New York) Stefan Edberg and Anders Jarryd def. Joakim Nystrom and Mats Wilander, 6-1, 7-6

1986   (London) Stefan Edberg and Anders Jarryd def. Yannick Noah and Guy Forget, 6-3, 7-6, 6-3

1987   (London) Miloslav Mecir and Tomas Smid def. Ken Flach and Robert Seguso, 6-4, 7-5, 6-7, 6-3

1988   (London) Rick Leach and Jim Pugh def. Sergio Casal and Emilio Sanchez, 6-4, 6-3, 2-6, 6-0

1989   (London) Jim Grabb and Patrick McEnroe def. Anders Jarryd and John Fitzgerald, 7-5, 7-6, 5-7, 6-3

1990   (Sanctuary Cove, Australia) Guy Forget and Jacob Hlasek def. Sergio Casal and Emilio Sanchez, 6-4, 7-6 (5), 5-7, 6-4

1991   (Johannesburg) Anders Jarryd and John Fitzgerald def. Ken Flach and Robert Seguso, 6-4, 6-4, 2-6, 6-4

1992   (Johannesburg) Todd Woodbridge and Mark Woodforde def. John Fitzgerald and Anders Jarryd, 6-2, 7-6 (4), 5-7, 3-6, 6-3

1993   (Johannesburg) Jacco Eltingh and Paul Haarhuis def. Todd Woodbridge and Mark Woodforde, 7-6 (4), 7-6 (5), 6-4

1994   (Jakarta, Indonesia) Jan Apell and Jonas Bjorkman def. Todd Woodbridge and Mark Woodforde 6-4, 4-6, 4-6, 7-6 (5), 7-6(6)

1995   (Eindhoven, Netherlands) Grant Connell and Pat Galbraith def. Jacco Eltingh and Paul Haarhuis, 7-6 (6), 7-6 (6), 3-6, 7-6 (2)

1996   (Hartford, USA) Todd Woodbridge and Todd Woodforde def. Sebastien Lareau and Alex O'Brien, 6-4, 5-7, 6-2, 7-6 (3)

1997   (Hartford, USA) Rick Leach and Jonathan Stark def. Mahesh Bhupathi and Leander Paes, 6-3, 6-4, 7-6 (3)

1998   (Hartford, USA) Jacco Eltingh and Paul Haarhuis def. Daniel Nestor and Mark Knowles, 6-4, 6-2, 7-5

1999   (Hartford, USA) Sebastien Lareau and Alex O'Brien def. Mahesh Bhupathi and Leander Paes, 6-3, 6-2, 6-2

2000   (Bangalore, India) Don Johnson and Piet Norval def. Mahesh Bhupathi and Leander Paes, 7-6 (8), 6-3, 6-4

2001   Not played

2002   Not played

2003   (Houston) Bob Bryan and Mike Bryan def. Michael Llodra and Fabrice Santoro, 6-7 (6), 6-3, 3-6, 7-6 (3), 6-4

2004   (Houston) Bob Bryan and Mike Bryan def. Wayne Black and Kevin Ullyett, 4-6, 7-5, 6-4, 6-2

2005   (Shanghai) Michael Llodra and Fabrice Santoro def. Leander Paes and Nenad Zimonjic, 6-7 (6), 6-3, 7-6 (4)

2006   (Shanghai) Jonas Bjorkman and Max Mirnyi def. Daniel Nestor and Mark Knowles, 6-2, 6-4

2007   (Shanghai) Daniel Nestor and Mark Knowles def. Simon Aspelin and Julien Knowle, 6-2, 6-3

2008   (Shanghai) Daniel Nestor and Nenad Zimonjic def. Bob Bryan and Mike Bryan, 7-6 (3), 6-2

WTA Tour Year-End Doubles Championships

1972   Not played

1973   (Boca Raton) Rosie Casals and Margaret Court def. Francoise Durr and Betty Stove, 6-2, 6-4

1974   (Los Angeles) Rosie Casals and Billie Jean King def. Francoise Durr and Betty Stove, 6-1, 6-7 (2-5), 7-5

1975   Not played

1976   Not played

1977   Not played

1978   Not played

1979   (New York) Francoise Durr and Betty Stove def. Sue Barker and Ann Kiyomura, 6-4, 6-2

1980   (New York) Billie Jean King and Martina Navratilova def. Rosie Casals and Wendy Turnbull, 6-3, 4-6, 6-3

1981   (New York) Martina Navratilova and Pam Shriver def. Barbara Potter and Sharon Walsh, 6-0, 7-6 (6)

1982   (New York) Martina Navratilova and Pam Shriver def. Kathy Jordan and Anne Smith, 6-4, 6-3

1983   (New York) Martina Navratilova and Pam Shriver def. Claudia Kohde Kilsch and Eva Pfaff, 7-5, 6-2

1984   (New York) Martina Navratilova and Pam Shriver def. Jo Durie and Ann Kiyomura, 6-3, 6-1

1985   (New York) Martina Navratilova and Pam Shriver def. Claudia Kohde Kilsch and Helena Sukova, 6-7 (4), 6-4, 7-6 (5)

1986   (New York - March) Hana Mandlikova and Wendy Turnbull def. Claudia Kohde Kilsch and Helena Sukova, 6-4, 6-7 (4), 6-3

1986   (New York - November) Martina Navratilova and Pam Shriver def. Claudia Kohde Kilsch and Helena Sukova, 7-6 (1), 6-3

1987   (New York) Martina Navratilova and Pam Shriver def. Claudia Kohde Kilsch and Helena Sukova, 6-1, 6-1

1988   (New York) Martina Navratilova and Pam Shriver def. Larisa Savchenko Neiland and Natasha Zvereva, 6-3, 6-4

1989   (New York) Martina Navratilova and Pam Shriver def. Larisa Savchenko Neiland and Natasha Zvereva, 6-3, 6-2

1990   (New York) Kathy Jordan and Elizabeth Smylie def. Mercedes Paz and Arantxa Sanchez Vicario, 7-6 (4), 6-4

1991   (New York) Martina Navratilova and Pam Shriver def. Gigi Fernandez and Jana Novotna, 4-6, 7-5, 6-4

1992   (New York) Arantxa Sanchez Vicario and Helena Sukova def. Larisa Savchenko Neiland and Jana Novotna, 7-6 (4), 6-1

1993   (New York) Gigi Fernandez and Natasha Zvereva def. Larisa Savchenko Neiland and Jana Novotna, 6-3, 7-5

1994   (New York) Gigi Fernandez and Natasha Zvereva def. Jana Novotna and Arantxa Sanchez Vicario, 6-3, 6-7 (4), 6-3

1995   (New York) Jana Novotna and Arantxa Sánchez Vicario def. Gigi Fernandez and Natasha Zvereva, 6-2, 6-1

1996   (New York) Lindsay Davenport and Mary Joe Fernandez def. Jana Novotna and Arantxa Sanchez Vicario, 6-3, 6-2

1997   (New York) Lindsay Davenport and Jana Novotna def. Alexandra Fusai and Nathalie Tauziat, 6-7 (5), 6-3, 6-2

1998   (New York) Lindsay Davenport and Natasha Zvereva def. Alexandra Fusai and Nathalie Tauziat, 6-7 (6), 7-5, 6-3

1999   (New York) Martina Hingis and Anna Kournikova def. Larisa Savchenko Neiland and Arantxa Sanchez Vicario, 6-4, 6-4

2000   (New York) Martina Hingis and Anna Kournikova def. Nicole Arendt and Manon Bollegraf, 6-2, 6-3

2001   (Munich) Lisa Raymond and Rennae Stubbs def. Cara Black and Elena Likhovtseva, 7-5, 3-6, 6-3

2002   (Los Angeles) Elena Dementieva and Janette Husarova def. Cara Black and Elena Likhovtseva, 4-6, 6-4, 6-3

2003   (Los Angeles) Virginia Ruano Pascual and Paola Suarez def. Kim Clijsters and Ai Sugiyama, 6-4, 3-6, 6-3

2004   (Los Angeles) Nadia Petrova and Meghann Shaughnessy def. Cara Black and Rennae Stubbs, 7-5, 6-2

2005   (Los Angeles) Lisa Raymond and Samantha Stosur def. Cara Black and Rennae Stubbs, 6-7 (5), 7-5, 6-4

2006   (Madrid) Lisa Raymond and Samantha Stosur def. Cara Black and Rennae Stubbs, 3-6, 6-3, 6-3

2007   (Madrid) Cara Black and Liezel Huber def. Katarina Srebotnik and Ai Sugiyama, 5-7, 7-3, (10-8 Champions Tie-Break)

2008   (Doha) Cara Black and Liezel Huber def. Kveta Peschke and Rennae Stubbs, 6-1, 7-5

World Championship Tennis (WCT) Finals

The Dallas-based World Championship Tennis (WCT) was the first solid promoter of the Open era. The 1967 brainchild of Dave Dixon of New Orleans soon had to be bailed out and taken over by his partners Lamar Hunt and Al Hill, Jr., in Dallas. Dixon and aide Bob Briner hastened the advent of opens by skimming the cream of amateurism late in 1967, signing John Newcombe, Tony Roche, Cliff Drysdale, Nikki Pilic and Roger Taylor to pro contracts. Adding pros Dennis Ralston, Pierre Barthes, Butch Buchholz to a mix called the "Handsome Eight," WCT began as a small circuit in 1968, but expanded under the guidance of Hunt and his director, Mike Davies, to a global operation, attracting TV and substantial sponsorship dollars.

The tour climaxed with the season-ending playoffs for the eight top finishers in Dallas. Starting in 1971, with an astounding first prize of $50,000, by far the richest (won by Ken Rosewall), it became a focal point of the year every May through 1989. WCT alternately battled and integrated with the ITF's Grand Prix circuit until 1990. That year, the Grand Prix and WCT were killed by Hamilton Jordan, new chief of the ATP, who rearranged male tennis in establishing the ATP Tour.

WCT Finals—Dallas

Year	Champion	Runner-up	Score in final
1971	Ken Rosewall	Rod Laver	6-4, 1-6, 7-6, 7-6
1972	Ken Rosewall	Rod Laver	4-6, 6-0, 6-3, 6-7, 7-6
1973	Stan Smith	Arthur Ashe	6-3, 6-3, 4-6, 6-4
1974	John Newcombe	Björn Borg	4-6, 6-3, 6-3, 6-2
1975	Arthur Ashe	Björn Borg	3-6, 6-4, 6-4, 6-0
1976	Björn Borg	Guillermo Vilas	1-6, 6-1, 7-5, 6-1
1977	Jimmy Connors	Dick Stockton	6-7, 6-1, 6-4, 6-3
1978	Vitas Gerulaitis	Eddie Dibbs	6-3, 6-2, 6-1
1979	John McEnroe	Björn Borg	7-5, 4-6, 6-2, 7-6
1980	Jimmy Connors	John McEnroe	2-6, 7-6, 6-1, 6-2
1981	John McEnroe	Johan Kriek	6-1, 6-2, 6-4
1982	Ivan Lendl	John McEnroe	6-2, 3-6, 6-3, 6-3
1983	John McEnroe	Ivan Lendl	6-2, 4-6, 6-3, 6-7, 7-6
1984	John McEnroe	Jimmy Connors	6-1, 6-2, 6-3
1985	Ivan Lendl	Tim Mayotte	7-6, 6-4, 6-1
1986	Anders Järryd	Boris Becker	6-7, 6-1, 6-1, 6-4
1987	Miloslav Mecír	John McEnroe	6-0, 3-6, 6-2, 6-2
1988	Boris Becker	Stefan Edberg	6-4, 1-6, 7-5, 6-2
1989	John McEnroe	Brad Gilbert	6-3, 6-3, 7-6

The Grand Slam Cup

The Grand Slam Cup was organized by the ITF in 1990 to compete with the ATP Championships as a year-end attraction, continuing the divisive rivalry of the two governing bodies. Containing a similar cast of players, it brought together in Munich the top 16 in finishers during the four major championships. It offered $6 million in prize money and the largest prize money (varying according to a bonus scheme). The winners the first three years (Pete Sampras, David Wheaton and Michael Stich) got a flat $2 million first prize. In 1998, the event added a women's event, but it was only held for two years. After the 1999 event, the men's tournament was discontinued when a compromise was made between the ITF and the ATP and both men's events were merged into the year-end Tennis Masters Cup.

Grand Slam Cup

Year	Champion	Runner-up	Score in final
Men			
1990	Pete Sampras	Brad Gilbert	6-3, 6-4, 6-2
1991	David Wheaton	Michael Chang	7-5, 6-2, 6-4
1992	Michael Stich	Michael Chang	6-2, 6-3, 6-2
1993	Petr Korda	Michael Stich	2-6, 6-4, 7-6, 2-6, 11-9
1994	Magnus Larsson	Pete Sampras	7-6, 4-6, 7-6, 6-4
1995	Goran Ivanisevic	Todd Martin	7-6, 6-3, 6-4
1996	Boris Becker	Goran Ivanisevic	6-3, 6-4, 6-4
1997	Pete Sampras	Patrick Rafter	6-2, 6-4, 7-5
1998	Marcelo Rios	Andre Agassi	6-4, 2-6, 7-6, 5-7, 6-3
1999	Greg Rusedski	Tommy Haas	6-3, 6-4, 6-7, 7-6
Women			
1998	Venus Williams	Patty Schnyder	6-2, 3-6, 6-2
1999	Serena Williams	Venus Williams	6-1, 3-6, 6-3

Pro Tennis in the Pre-Open Era

In addition to being a member of Charles C. Pyle's first tour of professional players in 1926, **Vinnie Richards** won the first two editions of the U.S. Pro Championships. As an amateur, Richards won the gold medal in singles and doubles at the 1924 Olympic Games and was a five-time winner of the U.S. doubles title.

Prior to the start of the Open era in 1968, mainstream tournaments were limited only to amateurs, which left minimal playing opportunities for players who wanted to be paid for playing tennis. Head-to-head tours—barnstorming from city to city—started in 1926 when Suzanne Lenglen took her show on the road alongside Mary K. Browne, Vinnie Richards and Howard Kinsey, Harvey Snodgrass and Paul Feret. Bill Tilden, Ellsworth Vines, Fred Perry, Don Budge, Jack Kramer, Bobby Riggs, Pancho Gonzalez and other tennis greats also later joined the "play for pay" group after conquering the amateur game. Professional tournaments, starting with the U.S. Pro Championships in 1927, also came into existence with the U.S., French Pro and London Pro Indoor Championships being the three most prestigious events during this era.

U.S. Pro Championships

Although there were earlier instances of professional tournaments offering prize money, particularly in France and Britain, with teaching professionals/coaches as entries, the U.S. Pro Championships stood, until it ceased in 2000, as the oldest continuous played pro event. It began in 1927 on courts of the small, since vanished, Notlek Tennis Club on the West Side of Manhattan, starring the newly-avowed touring pros, Vinnie Richards and Howard Kinsey, from the Pyle troupe, and was played for a $2,000 purse. Richards won first prize, $1,000 as the initial champion. The tournament, ever very healthy financially, somehow kept going, often changing surfaces and locations, surviving indoors (1955-1962) in Cleveland as the "World Pro Championships." In 1963 at Forest Hills it went bankrupt (only Pancho Gonzalez, who negotiated a prior guarantee, got paid), and seemed finished at last. The tournament was revived at Boston's Longwood Cricket Club in 1964 and continued there until its demise following the 1999 event.

Karel Kozeluh won the U.S. Pro Championships in 1929, 1932 and 1937.

Year	Winner	Runner-up	Score	Site
1927	Vinnie Richards	Howard Kinsey	11-9, 6-4, 6-3	Brooklyn, N.Y.
1928	Vinnie Richards	Karel Kozeluh	8-6, 6-3, 0-6, 6-2	West Side Tennis Club, Forest Hills, Queens, N.Y.
1929	Karel Kozeluh	Vinnie Richards	6-4, 6-4, 4-6, 4-6, 7-5	West Side Tennis Club
1930	Vinnie Richards	Karel Kozeluh	2-6, 10-8, 6-3, 6-4	West Side Tennis Club
1931	Bill Tilden	Vinnie Richards	7-5, 6-2, 6-1	West Side Tennis Club
1932	Karel Kozeluh	Hans Nusslein	6-2, 6-3, 7-5	South Shore Country Club, Chicago, Ill.
1933	Vinnie Richards	Frank Hunter	6-3, 6-0, 6-2	Rye, New York
1934	Hans Nusslein	Karel Kozeluh	6-4, 6-4, 1-6, 7-5	South Shore Country Club
1935	Bill Tilden	Karel Kozeluh	0-6, 6-1, 6-4, 0-6, 6-4	Terrace Club, Brooklyn, N.Y.
1936	Joe Whalen	Charles Wood	4-6, 4-6, 6-3, 6-2, 6-3	Tudor City Courts, New York
1937	Karel Kozeluh	Bruce Barnes	6-2, 6-3, 4-6, 4-6, 6-1	Greenbrier Golf and Tennis Club, White Sulfur Springs, West Virginia
1938	Bruce Barnes	Karel Kozeluh	5-7, 6-2, 6-4, 3-6, 6-4	Chicago Arena, Chicago
1939	Ellsworth Vines	Fred Perry	8-6, 6-1, 20-18	Beverly Hills Tennis Club, Los Angeles
1940	Don Budge	Bruce Barnes	6-3, 5-7, 6-4, 6-3	Chicago Town and Tennis Club, Chicago
1941	Fred Perry	Dick Skeen	6-4, 6-8, 6-2, 6-3	Chicago Town and Tennis Club
1942	Don Budge	Bobby Riggs	6-2, 6-2, 6-2	West Side Tennis Club
1943	Bruce Barnes	John Nogrady	6-1, 7-9, 7-5, 4-6, 6-3	Officer's Club, Ft. Knox, Ky.
1944	not held			
1945	Welby Van Horn	John Nogrady	6-4, 6-2, 6-2	Rip's Courts – New York, N.Y.
1946	Bobby Riggs	Don Budge	6-3, 6-1, 6-1	West Side Tennis Club
1947	Bobby Riggs	Don Budge	3-6, 6-3, 10-8, 4-6, 6-3	West Side Tennis Club
1948	Jack Kramer	Bobby Riggs	14-12, 6-2, 3-6, 7-5	West Side Tennis Club
1949	Bobby Riggs	Don Budge	9-7, 3-6, 6-3, 6-3	West Side Tennis Club
1950	Pancho Segura	Frank Kovacs	6-4, 1-6, 8-6, 4-4, ret	Cleveland, Ohio
1951	Pancho Segura	Pancho Gonzalez	6-3, 6-4, 6-2	West Side Tennis Club
1952	Pancho Segura	Pancho Gonzalez	3-6, 6-4, 3-6, 6-4, 6-0	Cleveland, Ohio, Lakewood Public Courts
1953	Pancho Gonzalez	Don Budge	4-6, 6-4, 7-5, 6-2	Cleveland, Ohio
1954	Pancho Gonzalez	Frank Sedgman	6-3, 9-7, 3-6, 6-2	Cleveland Arena, Cleveland
1955	Pancho Gonzalez	Pancho Segura	**21-16, 19-21, 21-8, 20-22, 21-19	Cleveland Arena
1956	Pancho Gonzalez	Pancho Segura	**21-15, 13-21, 21-14, 22-20	Cleveland Arena
1957	Pancho Gonzalez	Pancho Segura	6-3, 3-6, 7-5, 6-1	Cleveland Arena

	Winner	Runner-up	Score	Site
1958	Pancho Gonzalez	Lew Hoad	3-6, 4-6, 14-12, 6-1, 6-4	Cleveland Arena
1959	Pancho Gonzalez	Lew Hoad	6-4, 6-2, 6-4	Cleveland Arena
1960	Alex Olmedo	Tony Trabert	7-5, 6-4	Cleveland Arena
1961	Pancho Gonzalez	Frank Sedgman	6-3, 7-5	Cleveland Arena
1962	Butch Buchholz	Pancho Segura	6-4, 6-3, 6-4	Cleveland Arena
1963	Ken Rosewall	Rod Laver	6-4, 6-2, 6-2	West Side Tennis Club
1964	Rod Laver	Pancho Gonzalez	4-6, 6-3, 7-5, 6-4	Longwood Cricket Club, Brookline, Mass.
1965	Ken Rosewall	Rod Laver	6-4, 6-3, 6-3	Longwood Cricket Club
1966	Rod Laver	Ken Rosewall	6-4, 4-6, 6-2, 8-10, 6-3	Longwood Cricket Club
1967	Rod Laver	Andres Gimeno	4-6, 6-4, 6-3, 7-5	Longwood Cricket Club
1968	Rod Laver	John Newcombe	6-4, 6-4, 9-7	Longwood Cricket Club
1969	Rod Laver	John Newcombe	7-5, 6-2, 4-6, 6-1	Longwood Cricket Club
1970	Tony Roche	Rod Laver	3-6, 6-4, 1-6, 6-2, 6-2	Longwood Cricket Club
1971	Ken Rosewall	Cliff Drysdale	6-4, 6-3, 6-0	Longwood Cricket Club
1972	Bob Lutz	Tom Okker	6-4, 2-6, 6-4, 6-4	Longwood Cricket Club
1973	Jimmy Connors	Arthur Ashe	6-3, 4-6, 6-4, 3-6, 6-2	Longwood Cricket Club
1974	Björn Borg	Tom Okker	7-6, 6-1, 6-1	Longwood Cricket Club
1975	Björn Borg	Guillermo Vilas	6-3, 6-4, 6-2	Longwood Cricket Club
1976	Björn Borg	Harold Solomon	6-7, 6-4, 6-1, 6-2	Longwood Cricket Club
1977	Manuel Orantes	Eddie Dibbs	7-6, 7-5, 6-4	Longwood Cricket Club
1978	Manuel Orantes	Harold Solomon	6-4, 6-3	Longwood Cricket Club
1979	Jose Higueras	Hans Gildemeister	6-3, 6-1	Longwood Cricket Club
1980	Eddie Dibbs	Jose-Luis Clerc	6-2, 6-1	Longwood Cricket Club
1981	Jose-Luis Clerc	Hans Gildemeister	0-6, 6-2, 6-2	Longwood Cricket Club
1982	Guillermo Vilas	Mel Purcell	6-4, 6-0	Longwood Cricket Club
1983	Jose-Luis Clerc	Jimmy Arias	6-3, 3-6, 6-0	Longwood Cricket Club
1984	Aaron Krickstein	Jose-Luis Clerc	7-6, 3-6, 6-4	Longwood Cricket Club
1985	Mats Wilander	Martín Jaite	6-2, 6-4	Longwood Cricket Club
1986	Andrés Gómez	Martín Jaite	7-5, 6-4	Longwood Cricket Club
1987	Mats Wilander	Kent Carlsson	7-6, 6-1	Longwood Cricket Club
1988	Thomas Muster	Lawson Duncan	6-2, 6-2	Longwood Cricket Club
1989	Andrés Gómez	Mats Wilander	6-1, 6-4s	Longwood Cricket Club
1990	Martín Jaite	Libor Nemecek	7-5, 6-3	Longwood Cricket Club
1991	Andrés Gómez	Andrei Cherkasov	7-5, 6-3	Longwood Cricket Club
1992	Ivan Lendl	Richey Reneberg	6-3, 6-3	Longwood Cricket Club
1993	Ivan Lendl	Todd Martin	5-7, 6-3, 7-6	Longwood Cricket Club
1994	Ivan Lendl	MaliVai Washington	7-5, 7-6	Longwood Cricket Club
1995	not completed due to rain			Longwood Cricket Club
1996	not held			
1997	Sjeng Schalken	Marcelo Rios	7-5, 6-3	Longwood Cricket Club
1998	Michael Chang	Paul Haarhuis	6-3, 6-4	Longwood Cricket Club
1999	Marat Safin	Greg Rusedski	6-4, 7-6(11)	Longwood Cricket Club

** VASSS Scoring

London Pro and French Pro Championships

Besides the U.S. Pro, the highest regarded tournaments among the pros prior to Open tennis were the London Indoor Pro Championships and the French Pro Championships. The French Pro Championships was held in Paris, mostly at Stade Roland Garros, but from 1963-1967 at Stade Coubertin. The London event, usually known as Wembley, was played at the Empire Pool.

London Indoor Pro

Year	Winner	Runner-Up	Score
1934	Ellsworth Vines	Hans Nusslein	round robin
1935	Ellsworth Vines	Bill Tilden	6-1, 6-3, 5-7, 3-6, 6-3
1936	Ellsworth Vines	Hans Nusslein	6-4, 6-4, 6-2
1937	Hans Nusslein	Bill Tilden	6-4, 3-6, 6-3, 2-6, 6-2
1938	Hans Nusslein	Bill Tilden	7-5, 3-6, 6-3, 3-6, 6-2
1939	Don Budge	Hans Nusslein	round robin
1940–48 not held			
1949	Jack Kramer	Bobby Riggs	6-4, 6-2, 6-3
1950	Pancho Gonzalez	Welby Van Horn	6-3, 6-2, 6-4
1951	Pancho Gonzalez	Pancho Segura	6-2, 6-2, 2-6, 6-4
1952	Pancho Gonzalez	Jack Kramer	3-6, 3-6, 6-2, 6-4, 7-5
1953	Frank Sedgman	Pancho Gonzalez	6-1, 6-2, 6-2
1954–55 not held			
1956	Pancho Gonzalez	Frank Sedgman	4-6, 11-9, 11-9, 9-7
1957	Ken Rosewall	Pancho Segura	1-6, 6-3, 6-4, 3-6, 6-4
1958	Frank Sedgman	Tony Trabert	6-4, 6-3, 6-4
1959	Mal Anderson	Pancho Segura	4-6, 6-4, 3-6, 6-3, 8-6
1960	Ken Rosewall	Pancho Segura	5-7, 8-6, 6-1, 6-3
1961	Ken Rosewall	Lew Hoad	6-3, 3-6, 6-2, 6-3
1962	Ken Rosewall	Lew Hoad	6-4, 5-7, 15-13, 7-5
1963	Ken Rosewall	Lew Hoad	6-4, 6-2, 4-6, 6-3
1964	Rod Laver	Ken Rosewall	7-5, 4-6, 5-7, 8-6, 8-6
1965	Rod Laver	Andres Gimeno	6-2, 6-3, 6-4
1966	Rod Laver	Ken Rosewall	6-2, 6-2, 6-3
1967	Rod Laver	Ken Rosewall	2-6, 6-1, 1-6, 8-6, 6-2
1968	Ken Rosewall	John Newcombe	6-4, 4-6, 7-5, 6-4

French Pro Championships

Year	Winner	Runner-Up	Score
1930	Karel Kozeluh	Albert Burke	6-1, 6-2, 6-1
1931	Martin Plaa	Robert Ramillon	6-3, 6-1, 3-6, 6-2
1932	Robert Ramillon	Martin Plaa	6-4, 3-6, 8-6, 6-4
1933	Bill Tilden	Henri Cochet	6-2, 6-4, 6-2
1934	Bill Tilden	Martin Plaa	6-2, 6-4, 7-5
1935	Ellsworth Vines	Hans Nusslein	10-8, 6-4, 3-6, 6-1
1938	Henri Cochet	Robert Ramillon	6-3, 6-1, 6-1
1939	Don Budge	Ellsworth Vines	6-2, 7-5, 6-3
1940–1952 not held			
1953	Frank Sedgman	Pancho Gonzalez	6-1, 6-3
1954–1955 not held			
1956	Tony Trabert	Pancho Gonzalez	6-3, 4-6, 5-7, 8-6, 6-2
1957	not held		
1958	Ken Rosewall	Lew Hoad	3-6, 6-2, 6-4, 6-0
1959	Tony Trabert	Frank Sedgman	6-4, 6-4, 6-4
1960	Ken Rosewall	Lew Hoad	6-2, 2-6, 6-2, 6-1
1961	Ken Rosewall	Pancho Gonzalez	2-6, 6-4, 6-3, 8-6
1962	Ken Rosewall	Andres Gimeno	3-6, 6-2, 7-5, 6-2
1963	Ken Rosewall	Rod Laver	6-8, 6-4, 5-7, 6-3, 6-4
1964	Ken Rosewall	Rod Laver	6-3, 7-5, 3-6, 6-3
1965	Ken Rosewall	Rod Laver	6-3, 6-2, 6-4
1966	Ken Rosewall	Rod Laver	6-3, 6-2, 14-12
1967	Rod Laver	Andres Gimeno	6-4, 8-6, 4-6, 6-2
1968	Rod Laver	John Newcombe	6-2, 6-2, 6-3

One-Night Stands of the Bygone Pros

Until the dawn of Open tennis in 1968, the usual format for the handful of playing pros—outlaws beyond the boundaries of traditional amateur tourneys—was a tour of one-night stands, indoors on a portable canvas court, across the United States, and sometimes other countries as well. The champion of the previous tour went head-to-head against a challenger, most often the leading amateur who had turned pro, as during the winter of 1934, when rookie Ellsworth Vines, 23, brought down the biggest name, Bill Tilden, 41, by 47 matches to 26.

After resisting promoters for several years, Tilden finally turned pro in 1931, having failed to extricate the Davis Cup from France or win a long-desired eighth U.S. title. He then toured victoriously against the Czech master, Karel Kozeluh, and repeated the next winter against German Hans Nusslein. Nusslein had the edge in 1933, but since Tilden had the drawing power, he was the rookie Vines' opponent. Vines' triumphant campaign over Tilden, his senior by 18 years, left him in charge to fend off Fred Perry in 1937. Tilden stuck around, as did a few others, to play secondary roles.

Whoever the promoter, he lured the leading amateur with a guarantee against a percentage of gate receipts, making a similar type of deal with the champion, and generally paying the others' salaries. It all began in November 1926 as promoter Charles C. Pyle transformed the first troupe—Suzanne Lenglen, Mary K. Browne, Vinnie Richards, Howard Kinsey, Harvey Snodgrass, Paul Feret—from amateurs to pros en masse, principally to capitalize on Lenglen's gate appeal on a North American tour. The last challenge tour, 1963, was Australian-dominated as pros Ken Rosewall and Lew Hoad personally guaranteed 1962 Grand Slammer Rod Laver $125,000 over three years to give up his amateur status, and put them back in business.

Although the pros grew slightly in numbers and began leaning toward tournament formats in 1964, hastening the day of opens, tours continued into 1968, but merely as exhibitions, lacking the king-of-the-hill aspect. Pancho Gonzalez, the losing challenger in his first tour against player/promoter Jack Kramer in 1949-1950, later became the most successful king-of-the-canvas. Here are the best-documented tours:

1926–27	Suzanne Lenglen d. Mark K. Browne, 38-0
1928	Karel Kozeluh d. Vinnie Richards, 13-7
1931	Bill Tilden d. Karel Kozeluh, 63-13; Tilden d. Richards, 4-0
1932	Bill Tilden d. Hans Nusslein and Vinnie Richards
1933	Hans Nusslein d. Bill Tilden
1934	Ellsworth Vines d. Bill Tilden, 47-26
1935	Ellsworth Vines d. Lester Stoefen, Bruce Barnes, Bill Tilden, others
1935	Bill Tilden d. George Lott, 73-27; Ellsworth Vines d. Tilden, Lester Stoefen, Bruce Barnes and others
1936	Bill Tilden d. Bruce Barnes and others; Ellsworth Vines d. Lester Stoefen, Bill Tilden and others; Ethel Burkhardt Arnold d. Jane Sharp
1937	Ellsworth Vines d. Fred Perry, 32-29; Perry d. Bill Tilden, 4-3
1938	Ellsworth Vines d. Fred Perry, 49-35
1939	Don Budge d. Ellsworth Vines, 21-18; Don Budge d. Fred Perry, 18-11
1941	Don Budge d. Bill Tilden, 51-7; Alice Marble d. Mary Hardwick, 17-3
1942	Don Budge won a round-robin tour with a 54-18 record, 15-10 over Bobby Riggs. Others; Bobby Riggs, 36-36; Frank Kovacs, 25-26; Fred Perry, 25-30
1946–47	Bobby Riggs d. Don Budge, 23-21
1947	Pauline Betz d. Sarah Palfrey Fabyan Cooke
1947–48	Jack Kramer d. Bobby Riggs, 69-20
1949–50	Jack Kramer d. Pancho Gonzalez, 96-27
1950-51	Jack Kramer d. Pancho Segura, 64-28; Pauline Betz d. Gussy Moran
1953	Jack Kramer d. Frank Sedgman, 54-41; Pancho Segura d. Ken McGregor
1954	Pancho Gonzalez d. Frank Sedgman and Pancho Segura, round-robin, both, 30-21; Segura d. Sedgman, 23-22
1955–56	Pancho Gonzalez d. Tony Trabert, 74-27
1957	Pancho Gonzalez d. Ken Rosewall, 50-26
1958	Pancho Gonzalez d. Lew Hoad, 51-36
1959	Pancho Gonzalez d. Lew Hoad, Mal Anderson and Ashley Cooper, round-robin
1959–60	Althea Gibson d. Karol Fageros, 114-4
1959–60	Pancho Gonzalez d. Alex Olmedo, Ken Rosewall and Pancho Segura, round-robin
1961	Pancho Gonzalez leading winner in tour involving Butch Bucholz, Barry MacKay, Andres Gimeno, Lew Hoad, Alex Olmedo, Frank Sedgman, Tony Trabert, Ashley Cooper
1963	Ken Rosewall, Rod Laver finished 1-2 on tour also including Luis Ayala, Butch Buchholz, Andres Gimeno, Barry MacKay

Index

Austin, John Reed (Austin siblings) (USA), 664
1980: Wimbledon mixed title with sister Tracy, 201, 202
Austin, Pamela Jeanne (Austin siblings), 155, 664
Austin, Tracy (Austin siblings) (USA), 211, 215, 533, 664
1977: 14-year-old at Wimbledon, 187, 189. See Klima, Mita
1978: asserting herself, 191; in victorious Federation Cup team, 194
1979: youngest U.S. champion, 96, 171, 196, 199; in team play, 197, 316
1980: banked $500,000, 201, 202, 203
1981: added a second U.S. title, 204, 207; on Wightman Cup team, 208
1984: chronic back ailments, 220
Austin, William Jeffrey (Austin siblings), 664
Australia
first Victorian Championship in 1879, 10
Australian Championships
1970: became "Open," 157. See Australian Open
Australian Open, 351-376
1905: third major championships, 15
1915: continued, 15
1922: women's singles championships started, 25
1927: new venue, Kooyong, Melbourne, 36
1977: Australian Open twice in one year, 188
1988: new venue Flinders Park, now Melbourne Park, 36, 240
results: 1919, 19; 1920, 21; 1921, 23; 1922, 25; 1923, 27; 1924, 29; 1925, 31; 1926, 34; 1927, 36; 1928, 38; 1929, 40; 1930, 42; 1931, 44; 1932, 47; 1933, 50; 1934, 52; 1935, 54; 1936, 57; 1937, 60; 1938, 63; 1939, 66; 1940, 68; 1946, 82; 1947, 82; 1948, 88; 1949, 91; 1950, 94; 1951, 97; 1952, 99; 1953, 102; 1954, 104; 1955, 106; 1956, 108; 1957, 111; 1958, 114; 1959, 116; 1960, 119; 1961, 122; 1962, 125; 1963, 128; 1964, 131; 1965, 134; 1966, 137; 1967, 141; 1968, 148; 1969, 152; 1970, 157; 1971, 162; 1972, 166; 1973, 171; 1974, 175; 1975, 180; 1976, 185; 1977, 190; 1978, 195; 1979, 199; 1980, 203; 1981, 208; 1982, 213; 1983, 218; 1984, 223; 1985, 228; 1986, 233; 1987, 238; 1988, 243; 1989, 248; 1990, 253; 1991, 258; 1992, 263; 1993, 267; 1994, 271; 1995, 276; 1996, 281; 1997, 284; 1998, 288; 1999, 293; 2000, 297; 2001, 301; 2002, 306; 2003, 307; 2004, 315; 2005, 320; 2006, 324; 2007, 329
Austria, 189, 250, 280, 314
1913: as a founding member of ITF, 14
one of nine entries for Davis Cup, 15
Avis Challenge Cup, 183
Avon Championships, 196, 197, 199, 201, 202, 203, 207, 208, 213, 726
1978: new sponsor for WTA, 195
1982: withdrew sponsorship, 210
Ayala, Luis (Chilean), 110, 113, 664
1959: Italian title, 115
1960: runner-up in French singles, 118
1961: Kramer failed to lure Ayala, 120, 121
1968: a coach in Puerto Rico, went to Bournemouth, 145. See Bournemouth.

B

Babcock, Carolin (USA)
1932: U.S. women's singles finalist, 47
1936: on Wightman Cup winning team, 57
Bad Homburg, Gemany
venue of 1973 Federation Cup, 171
Baddeley, Herbert (Baddeley twins) (English), 664
Baddeley, Wilfred (Baddeley twins) (English), 252
1891: youngest Wimbledon champion, 10. See Becker, Boris; Sampras, Pete
bagel, zero
credited to Eddie Dibbs, 4
Baghdatis, Marcos (CYP)
2006: Australian finalist, 322, 323
Bagnal-Wild, R. B.
proposed match byes in 1883; accepted in 1885, 6
Baker, Josephine
the toast of Paris, 62
Baker, Larry (administrator), 533-534
Balcells, Juan (ESP)
2000: in victorious Spanish Davis Cup team, 296, 297
Baldwin, Baldwin
wealthy American lover, 33
Ball, Syd (AUS)
1974: with Bob Giltinan, lost doubles to Ross Case–Geoff Masters, 175
Baltimore Banners
a team under World Team Tennis, 173
Barazzutti, Corrado (ITA), 202
1976: in Italy's Davis Cup team winner over Chile, 183
1977: in Italy's Davis Cup showdown with Australia, 187, 188

1979: in Davis Cup final against U.S., 199
2006: as victorious Fed Cup captain, 324
Barcelona Bumblebee. See Sanchez Vicario, Arantxa
Barcelona, Spain, 177, 249, 260, 295, 317
venue for Spain's Davis Cup, 199
1972: venue for the Commercial Union Masters, 165
1988: ITF include pros for 1992 Barcelona Games, 239
Barclay, Jean Claude 148, 152, 157, 162, 166, 171
1963: with Pierre Darmon, lost Wimbledon doubles, 127
Barker, Sue (GBR), 197, 203, 212, 664
1975: in Italian doubles finals, 179, 180
1976: in Wightman Cup team, 184; won the German and the French titles, 185
1977: 0-1 against Billie Jean King, 189
1978: in victorious Wightman Cup team, 194, 195
1981: in Wightman Cup and Federation Cup teams, 208
1983: in Wightman Cup team, 216
Barlow, Harry (British)
1889: lost to Willie Renshaw at Wimbledon finals, 7
Barnes, Bruce (Texan)
1937: U.S. Pro finalist, 60
1938: U.S. Pro finalist, 63
1943: U.S. Pro champion; Navy lieutenant, 74
Barnes, Ronnie (BRA)
1963: U.S. semifinalist, 127
1967: with Roy Emerson in 105 games, 140
Barron, Dorothy Shepherd, 34
1929: in Wightman Cup challenge, 40
Barthes, Pierre, 168, 729
1967: signed with Dave Dixon, Bob Briner, 141
Bartkowicz, Jane "Peaches" (USA)
1967: two-handed backhand, 140
1969: in victorious Wightman Cup and Federation Cup team, 152
1970: signed with Gladys Heldman, 155, 157
Bartoli, Marion
2002: beat Arantxa Sanchez Vicario in first round, 305
Bartzen, Bernard "Tut" 122
1944: lost to Bob Falkenburg, 75
1959: U.S. men's singles semifinalist, 116
1961: in State Department tour, 122
Basel, Switzerland, 250, 287
Bassett, Carling (Canadian)
1983: Australian quarterfinalist, 216
1984: stopped by Manuela Maleeva at Italian Open, 220, 222, 262
Bassi, Lucia (ITA)
1960: lost in French first round to Betty Abbas, 118
Bastad, Sweden, 179
Bastl, George
2002: beats Pete Sampras at Wimbledon, 304
Beamish, Alfred (Britain)
in British Isle Davis Cup team, 12
Beamish, Winifred Ramsey
1925: Wimbledon finalist, 30
Becker, Benjamin
2006: in Andre Agassi's last show at U.S. Open, 324
Becker, Boris (West Germany), 264, 265, 266, 269, 270, 274, 275, 282, 328, 534-535
1985: at 17 youngest ever Wimbledon champion, 10, 43, 224, 225; on Davis Cup team, 226; lost Grand Prix Masters, 227
1986: Wimbledon title, 230, 232
1987: in Davis Cup relegation playoff, 235, 237
1988: tie-breaker at Masters, 163, 240; on Davis Cup team, 243
1989: one-sided 22 games, 65; wins first U.S. Open crown, 244; wins third Wimbledon title, 245, 247
1990: French Open finalist, 250, 252
1991: won Australian Open title, 255, 256
1992: Wimbledon quarterfinalist, 261; in Olympics, 262
1996: sixth major title at Australian Open, 277, 280
1998: Wimbledon quarterfinalist, 283
1999: career ends at Wimbledon, 291
Behr, Karl (USA), 12, 535
Belardinelli, Mario (pro), 719
Belgium, 15, 288, 301, 309, 310, 321, 324
1913: founding member of ITF, 14
Bellamy, Rex (writer), 108, 121, 145, 226
Bender, Richard
1944: lost to senior Gil Hall, 75
Bengtson, Ove (Swede)
1975: as Bjorn Borg's second in Davis Cup victory over Czechoslovakia, 178
1978: in Davis Cup loss to U.S., 193
Benjamin, Camille (American)
1985: beaten by Gabriela Sabatini, 227
Bennett, Arnold (writer), 155

Bennett, Eileen (Mrs. Eileen Bennett Whittingstall) (GBR), 36
1928: French finalist; on Wightman Cup winning team, 38, 40
1930: wore an open-backed tennis dress, 42
1931: as U.S. singles finalist, 44
1932: in Wightman Cup team, 47
Bennett, Paul
1942: Seymour Greenberg's coach, 72
Benny, Jack (American show–business celebrity)
1937: infuriated in Davis Cup match, 59
Bentley, Rita (GBR)
1966: in Wightman Cup team, 137
Berasategui, Alberto (ESP)
1994: in French finals, 269
1998: ended run at Australian quarterfinals, 286
Berdych, Tomas (Czech)
2004: knocked out Roger Federer, 312, 313
2005: beaten at U.S. Open, 318
2007: in Czech Davis Cup team, 326
Bergelin, Lennart (Swede)
1948: conqueror over top-seeded Frank Parker, 87
Berger, Jay (USA)
1988: in Davis Cup team, 240
1991: defeated by John McEnroe, 256
Bernard, Marcel (FRA), 47, 54, 57, 664
1946: knocked out Jaroslav Drobny in French finals; French doubles title with Yvon Petra, 80, 82
Bertolucci, Paolo (ITA)
1976: in Italy's victorious Davis Cup team against Chile, 183
1979: in Davis Cup campaign against U.S., 199
1980: in Davis Cup campaign against Czechoslovakia, 202
Betz, Pauline (USA), 77, 78, 535
1940: lost to Mary Hardwick, 67
1941: won six titles, 69, 70
1942: "…we got more attention," won U.S. singles title, 72
1943: won U.S. triple, 74
1944: third U.S. title, 76
1946: in Wightman Cup, 81
1947: suspended, 84
1950: pro debut; married Bob Addie, 94
Bhupathi, Mahesh (IND), 665
2003: in French mixed doubles finals, 310
Bickerton, Louie (AUS), 40
1930: Australian finalist, 42
Big Bill. See Tilden, Bill
Billington, Henry (GBR)
1939: doubles with Pat Hughes in quarterfinal lost to Bobby Riggs–Elwood Cooke, 65
Bingley, Blanche (Mrs. George Hillyard), 673
a champion six times, 13, 303
Bjorkman, Jonas Lars (Swede), 275, 280, 313, 326, 665
1994: in Swedish victorious Davis Cup team against Russia, 271
1997: on victorious Davis Cup team, 283, 284
1998: in successive Davis Cup champion team, 285, 288
2003: won doubles at Wimbledon and U.S., 310
Bjurstedt, Molla (Mrs. Franklin Mallory), 19, 31, 38, 588
1912: Norwegian Olympian, 14
1917–18: U.S. champion, 15
1921: sixth title, 23
1922: seventh title, age disparity, 25
1923: inaugural Wightman Cup champion team, 26
1924: in Wightman Cup challenge team, 28, 29
1926: U.S. champion, eight titles, oldest, 14, 33
1927: on Wightman Cup winning team, 36
1929: U.S. semifinalist, 45 years old, 40
Black, Byron (brother to Wayne) (ZIM), 665
2000: in Davis Cup Zimbabwe vs. U.S., 296
Black, Cara (younger sister to Wayne and Byron) (ZIM), 320, 665
2004: doubles title, 313, 314
Black, Wayne (brother to Byron) (ZIM), 665
2000: in Davis Cup Zimbabwe vs. U.S., 296
2004: beaten by the Bryan twins at doubles, 314
Black, Ernest (Scot), 486
1900: in Davis Cup challenge team, 11
Blackbutt, Queensland, 126
Blackman, Jill (AUS)
1966: in Australian doubles finals with Fay Toyne, 136
Blake, James (USA), 665
2003: on U.S. Davis Cup team, 310
2005: in second-round defeat, 317; in dramatic U.S. quarterfinal game, 318
2006: flattened at Masters, 321, 323; in Davis Cup team semifinal vs. Russia, 324
2007: in Davis Cup team, 325, 326, 328
a Harvardian, 326

Burton, Veronica
    1973: on British Wightman Cup 50th anniversary
        team, 171
Buttsworth, Coral McInnes, 666
    1931: Australian title, 44
    1932: second Australian title, 47
    1933: lost Australian title to Joan Hartigan, 49
Buxton, Angela (GBR)
    1955: on Wightman Cup team, 106

C

Caesars Palace, 260
Cahill, Mabel (Irish), 543-544
    1891-92: U.S. champ, 10
Cahill, Mike
    1987: in lengthiest tiebreaker, 238
Cairnes, J. J. (Irish)
    1881: Ladies Cup, winner over Dick Sears, 10
Calleri, Augustin (ARG)
    2006: in Davis Cup Argentina vs. Russia match, 324
Campbell, Oliver, 544
    1889: 18 years old, entered U.S. championships, 10
    1890: U.S. youngest champion, 10
Canadian Championships
    1890: founding of, 15
    1890: men's championships, 15
    1892: women's championsips, 15
Canadian Open, 178, 201, 203, 207, 216, 219, 221, 222,
    236, 237, 270, 272, 273, 274, 308, 318, 328
Canas, Willy "Willie" (ARG)
    2002: removed Lleyton Hewitt in French fourth
        round, 303
    2005: lost to Mariano Puerta in French quarters, 317
    2007: beat Roger Federer at Indian Wells and Key
        Biscayne, 327
Candy, Don (AUS), 98, 101
    1951: with Mervyn Rose won U.S. doubles, 96
    1956: Candy–Bob Perry won French doubles, 108
    1957: Candy–Rose as French runners-up, 110
    1959: Candy–Bob Howe lost at Australian doubles,
        115
Cane, Paolo (ITA)
    1987: five-set challenge to Ivan Lendl at Wimbledon,
        237
Cano, Ricardo (ARG)
    1977: in Argentina's Davis Cup victory over U.S., 188
Capriati, Jennifer (USA), 265, 294, 303, 304, 305, 309, 312,
    313, 314, 647-648
    1989: a 13-year-old in Wightman Cup, 245
    1990: cracks Top Ten, 189, 207; in Federation Cup
        team success, 249, 250, 251
    1991: stunned Martina Navratilova, 255; in U.S.
        Federation Cup finals, 256
    1992: in Olympics, 260; shocked, 262
    2001: won French title, 62, 299; claimed Australian
        title, 298, 299, 300, 301
    2002: triumphed at the Australian, 302
Caratti, Cristiano (ITA), 256
Carillo, Mary (USA), 190, 666
Carroll, Lewis (Charles L. Dodgson)
    Alice in Wonderland, Lawn Tennis Tournaments, 6
    envisioned seeding in 1883, implemented in 1922, 6
Cartwright, Bec
    wife of Lleyton Hewitt, 317
Casale, Pam
    1986: won a set from Chris Evert Lloyd, 231
Casals, Pablo (cellist), 62
Casals, Rosie "Rosemary," 145, 146, 147, 148, 160, 166,
    179, 197, 203, 334, 544-545, 723, 726
    "Rosebud," 155
    1966: 17-year-old, in U.S. doubles finals, 136, 137
    1967: at Australian semifinals, 139; on Federation
        Cup team, 140; signed with MacCall's troupe, 141
    1970: won Wimbledon doubles, 154; part of
        "Houston Nine," 155
    1971: Rosie–Billie Jean King in Wimbledon doubles
        title, 161
    1973: took biggest check, 171
    1974: Rosie–King won U.S. doubles, 175
    1975: Rosie–Marty Riessen runners-up at Spalding
        Mixed Doubles Classic, 177
    1976: in Federation Cup, 184
    1977: Rosie–Dick Stockton won Spalding Mixed
        Doubles, 188; ranked No. 1 with Chris Evert in
        doubles, 189
    1983: Rosie–Wendy Turnbull Wimbledon finalist,
        216
Case, Ross 166, 183, 185, 187, 190
    "Snake," 173
    1974: lost to Phil Dent at Australian semis, 175
    1976: Case–Geoff Masters Australian finalist; Case–
        Masters Wimbledon finalist, 183
    1977: Case–Masters won Wimbledon, 187
    1979: Case–Masters lost French title, 197

Cash, Pat "Patrick" (AUS), 231, 232, 245, 261, 666
    1983: on Australian Davis Cup team, 218
    1984: lost to John McEnroe at Wimbledon, 221
    1985: Cash–John Fitzgerald Wimbledon finalist, 225
    1987: won Wimbledon crown, 235, 304, 317; jolted
        by India in Davis Cup, 237
    1988: won South African title, 242, 317
    1990: on Australia's Davis Cup team, 250
Castano, Catalina, 270
Catt, Deirde (GBR) 131
    1960: with Ann Haydon, lost U. S. doubles, 118
    1961: Catt–Christine Truman clobbered in
        Wightman Cup play, 121
    1962: Catt–Liz Starkie in Wightman Cup defeat, 124
    1963: pushed off Billie Jean King in U.S. fourth
        round, 127
Cavendish. See Jones, Henry
Cawley, Roger (Englishman)
    1976: married Evonne Goolagong, 202
Cecchini, Sandra (ITA), 232
Cepkova, Slenca (Czech)
    1935: won the first set against Helen Wills Moody, 53
Chace, Malcolm, 545
    1895: represented America, 10. See Davis Cup, 1895
Chaffee, Nancy (USA)
    1951: U.S. doubles finalist with Pat Canning Todd, 96
Chambers, Dolly
    Douglass Chambers. See Douglass, Dorothea
        "Dolly"
Chanfreau, Mme. Jean Baptiste, 139. See Sheriff, Gail
    Chanfreau, Gail Sheriff
    Lovera, Gail Sheriff Chanfreau
Chang, Michael (USA), 251, 252, 256, 257, 275, 277, 279,
    282, 283, 284, 546
    1972: born in, 244
    1987: 15, defeated in U.S. second round, 238
    1988: won San Francisco, 240
    1989: at 17, won French over Stefan Edberg, 246,
        316
    1990: took possession of Davis Cup with Andre
        Agassi, 250
    1992: Olympic third round exit; in epic match
        against Edberg at U.S. Open, 262
    1994: knocked out by Agassi at U.S. Open, 270
    1995: at French finals, 274
    2001: exit at French second round, 299
Chapacu, Hugo (Paraguayan), 235
Chapin, Charlotte Hosmer, 36
Charles, Goodyear
    inventor of vulcanized rubber, 6
Charles, Lesley, 171
Chase Championship, 280, 281, 284, 288, 292, 293, 296,
    297, 726
Chatrier, Philippe (future head of French Federation
    and ITF), 546
    1940: new balls from USLTA, 67
    1974: barred World Team Tennis league players, 173
    1990: row with Andre Agassi, 250
Chatrier, Susan Patridge. See Patridge, Susan
Chela, Juan Ignacio (ARG)
    2004: French quarterfinalist, 312
    2006: lost in Davis Cup Argentina vs. Russia match,
        324
Cheney, "Dodo" Bundy. See Bundy, Dodo
    Hall of Famer, 13
Chesnokov, Andrei
    1986: stunned Mats Wilander at French third round,
        231
    1989: exit at French round, 246
Chipp, Herbert, 7
Cincinnati, 74, 77, 93, 105, 171, 197, 202, 205, 206, 219,
    221, 252, 274, 291, 308
Carlsbad, California, 197, 212
Clapp, Mrs. Louise Brough. See Brough, Louise
Clark, Clarence (brother to Joseph), 7, 547
    1881: MCC's secretary–treasurer, 9
Clark, Georgina (referee), 290
Clark, Joseph (brother to Clarence), 7, 9, 547
Clark, Nigel (Englishman)
    1981: journalist dialogue with Charlie Steiner, 205
Clark, Straight (USA)
    1953: with Hal Burrows at U.S. doubles, 101
Clavet, Francisco, 292
Clement, Arnaud (FRA), 220, 290, 308
    2001: crushed by Andre Agassi at Australian finals,
        298, 299
Clerc, Jose–Luis (ARG), 210, 216
    1980: lost in Davis Cup Argentina vs.
        Czechoslovakia match, 202
    1981: four U.S. Clay court titles, 205; lost in Davis
        Cup Argentina vs. U.S. clincher, 206
    1983: on Davis Cup winning team against U.S., 218,
        240
Clerici, Gianni Emilio (journalist), 547-548

Cleveland, Ohio, 99, 102, 114, 116, 119, 122, 124, 130,134,
    138, 140, 150, 151, 152, 156, 161, 162, 166, 175
Clijsters, Kim (BEL), 296, 300, 303, 305, 309, 310, 322,
    327, 666-667
    1999: defeated by Serena Williams at U.S. third
        round, 292
    2001: lost to Jennifer Capriati at French Open, 292,
        298, 299; with Justine Henin, captured the Fed
        Cup for Belgium, 301
    2003: year-end No. 2, 307
    2004: Australian finalist, 312
    2005: won U.S. jackpot over Mary Pierce, 319. See
        Fayat, Serge
Clothier, Bill, 548
Cochet, Henri (FRA), 52, 60, 177, 333, 548-549
    "The Ballboy of Lyon," musketeer, 28
    1925: Wimbledon comeback win over John
        Hennessey, 31
    1926: U.S. champion; French champion; Wimbledon
        champion, 35
    1927: on Davis Cup wining team, 36
    1928: U.S. champion; French champion; in Davis
        Cup defense, 37, 38
    1929: French title, 39; in Davis Cup defense, 40
    1930: French title, 41; in Davis Cup defense, 42
    1931: in Davis Cup defense, 44; Pete Sampras
        compared, 275
    1932: never returned to Forest Hills, 38, 46; fourth
        French title, 47
    1933: turns pro; lost to Bill Tilden in Paris, 50
    1934: Madison Square Garden, lost to Bill Tilden, 52
    1943: appeared in Wimbledon finals, 41 years old,
        67. See Robert, Abdesselam
    1977: honored at Wimbledon's Centenary
        celebrations, 186
Code of Conduct, 183
Coetzer, Amanda (RSA), 278
    1993: with Ines Gorochategui, lost U.S. doubles, 267
    1995: lost to Monica Seles at Canadian Open, 273
    1997: beat Steffi Graf at Australian fourth round,
        282, 283
Clinton, Bill (former U.S. President), 299
Coghlan, Lorraine (Lorraine Coghlan Robinson) (AUS),
    117, 139
    1958: Australian finalist, 113
    1959: with Mary Carter Reitano, Australian doubles
        finalist, 116
Coleman, Patricia (AUS)
    1973: on Fed Cup team, 171
Coles, Glynis (GBR), 175, 180, 203
    1975: with Sue Barker, Italian doubles finalist, 179
Colgate Company (sponsor), 183, 184, 186, 188, 189,
    192, 201, 725
Collins, Bud (announcer), 549, 695
    1979: "Breakfast at Wimbledon," 198
    1981: "...call him McEnroney," 205
Collins, Ian (GBR), 46
Colonel Merryboy (Maureen Connolly's horse), 103
Colwell, Robert (USLTA president)
    1972: changed Davis Cup Challenge Round venue,
        165
Colyer, Evelyn (GBR)
    1923: Wimbledon doubles finalist, 27
    1924: as Wightman Cup champions, 29
    1925: in Wightman Cup defense, 31
    1926: French doubles finalist; in Wightman
        challenge, 34
Coman, John (umpire), 182
Combe, R. T., 5
    lawn tennis court in 1881, 5
Comer, Sara, 76
Commercial Union (sponsor), 160, 165, 170, 173, 174,
    177, 178, 182, 183, 725
Commonwealth Caribbean, 164
Conlin, Edward (umpire), 21
Connell, Grant (CAN), 257
    1991: lost at Wimbledon first round, 257
    1993: with Pat Galbraith, Wimbledon doubles
        finalists, 267
Connolly, Maureen "Little Mo" (USA), 124, 146, 154, 161,
    165, 174, 189, 194, 199, 215, 222, 236, 239, 283, 309,
    334, 549-550
    1951: 16, in Wightman Cup competition; U.S. singles
        title, 96
    1952: Wimbledon singles champion, 99. See Tingay,
        Lance
    1953: swept Australian, French, Wimbledon, and
        U.S. singles, 101
    1954: French triple; struck by a truck, 104
        died at 34, 100
Connors, Brett David (son of Jimmy and Patti), 196
Connors, Jimmy (USA), 160, 165, 196, 197, 199, 255, 257,
    268, 285, 323, 328, 311, 312, 316, 326, 550-552, 723
    1970: U.S. doubles with Pancho Gonzalez, 156

Ireland
Fitzwilliam Club, Dublin in 1877, 10
Irish Championship
in 1879 Dublin, 9
Isner, John "Long John" (USA), 673
2007: exit at U.S. third round, 328
Italian Open (Championships), 41, 92, 98, 99, 101, 103, 105, 107, 110, 113, 115, 116, 120, 121, 123, 124, 127, 130, 133, 135, 136, 139, 141, 144, 152, 155, 156, 159, 160, 161, 164, 168, 170, 171, 173, 174, 176, 178, 179, 182, 185, 188, 189, 192, 196, 197, 202, 205, 215, 216, 219, 220, 231, 236, 237, 245, 246, 249, 250, 255, 269, 271, 273, 317, 323, 326, 719-720
Italy, 37, 83, 152, 175, 183, 188, 199, 202, 232, 275, 280, 288, 321, 324
first courts in 1878, 10
Itaparica, Brazil, 240
Ivanisevic, Goran (Croat), 251, 252, 253, 262, 274, 276, 279, 310, 673
"Incendiary I," 261
1994: Wimbledon finalist, 269, 270, 271
1998: Wimbledon finalist again, 286, 288
2001: won Wimbledon crown, 299, 300, 301
2004: bids adieu, 313
Ivanovic, Anna (Serb), 318, 658-659
2007: French finalist, 327, 329

J

Jacobs, Helen (USA), 42, 57, 575-576
1927: U.S. semifinalist, 36
1928: in Wightman Cup challenge, 38
1928: U.S. finalist, 38
1929: on Wightman Cup winning team, 40
1939: in Wimbledon doubles finals with Billie Yorke, 65, 66
Jackson, Willard, 251
Jaeger, Andrea (USA), 194, 199, 201, 203, 211, 213, 220, 260, 280, 673-674
1981: won French mixed doubles, 207, 208
1983: youngest Wimbledon finalist, 215, 216, 218
Jaggard–Lai, Michelle (Australian), 266
Jaite, Martin (Argentine), 230, 237, 240
Jamaica, 14
first club in 1883, 10
James, Freda (Freda James Hammersley) (GBR), 50, 54
1936: Wimbledon women's doubles title, 56, 57
1939: U.S. women's doubles finalist, 66
James, Ted (umpire), 205
Janes, Christine Truman. See Truman, Christine
Jankovic, Jelena "Jelly" (Serb), 303, 329, 659
Japan Open, 242
Jarryd, Anders 212, 218, 225, 230, 233, 235, 238, 242, 243, 247, 248, 258, 259, 263
1984: Swedish Davis Cupper, 220, 223
1993: knocked out Boris Becker at Australian Open, 264, 267
Jausovec, Mima (Yugoslav), 194, 195, 207, 215, 218, 674
1976: won Italian title, 184, 185
1977: won French crown, 189, 190
Javorsky, Jim (CZE), 111, 122
Jedrzejowska, Jadwiga (Polish), 57, 68, 674
1937: Wimbledon women's finalist, 59, 60
1938: U.S. women's doubles finalist, 62, 63
1939: French doubles title, 65, 66
Jelen Eric (West German), 231, 235, 247, 258
1988: in Davis Cup vs. Sweden, 243
Jensen, Luke (brother to Murphy) (USA), 281, 674
1993: with Murphy, won French doubles title, 267, 310
Jensen, Murphy (brother to Luke) (USA), 267, 310, 674
Jessup, Mrs. Marion Zinderstein. See Zinderstein, Marion
jeu de paume (Fr), 4
Jie Zheng (CHN), 691
2006: won the Australian and Wimbledon doubles with Zi Yan, 691
Johannesburg, South Africa, 130, 140, 150, 161, 258, 263
Johansson, Joachim "Pim Pim" (Swede), 314, 317, 326
Johansson, Kjell (Swede), 193
Johansson, Thomas "Tom" (Swede), 318, 326, 674
2002: first major title, 302, 303, 306
John, Elton, 170
Johnson, Melissa, 277
Johnson, Reid (net judge), 192
Johnson, Robert Walter, 674
Johnson, Wallace, 13, 19
1921: U.S. finalist, lost to Bill Tilden, 19, 23
Johnston, Bill, 19, 29, 576-577
1920: U.S. doubles champion with Clarence Griffins, 21
1922: U.S. finalist, 25
1923: Wimbledon champion over Frank Hunter; in U.S. Davis Cup defense, 27
1925: U.S. finalist; tuberculosis, 31

1926: U.S. quarterfinalist, 33, 34
Johnston, William
See also Johnston, Bill: Little Bill
Jones, Arnold (son of J. D. E.) sparring partner, 21
Jones, Henry (Cavendish), 674
in 1877 committee for new rules; co-founder of All England Club. 6. See Heathcote, Charles G.: Marshall, Julian: Walsh, John
Jones, J. D. E. (father of Arnold)
indoor court training, 21
Jones, Kelly (USA), 243
1992: Australian doubles finalist with Rick Leach, 263
Jones, Marion (American), 577
1905: first American entry at Wimbledon, 13
Jones, Mrs. Phillip "Pip". See Haydon, Ann
Jones, Perry T., 82, 113, 578
1959: U.S. Davis Cup captain, 115
Jordan, Barbara (sister to Kathy) (USA), 179, 218, 283, 674
Jordan, Hamilton, 729
1990: new executive director, 250
Jordan, Kathy (sister to Barbara) (USA), 199, 203, 208, 213, 215, 216, 218, 220, 223, 225, 228, 233, 235, 238, 252, 253, 674-675
Jorgensen, Gordon (USTA president), 239
Jovanovic, Boro (Yugoslav)
1962: Wimbledon men's doubles finalist, 124, 125
Juan Carlos (King of Spain), 296
Juliette, (Roger Federer's cow), 308, 313, 323
Jusserand, J. J. (French ambassador), 4

K

Kafelnikov, Yevgeny (RUS), 225, 273, 282, 284, 294-297, 299, 300, 306, 310, 649-650
in Russian Davis Cup team, 271, 275
1996: French title; won French doubles with Daniel Vacek, 278, 279, 281
1999: Australian title, 289, 290, 292, 293
Kaiser, Jordan, 723
Kamrath, Bob, 62
Kansas City, Missouri, 183, 188, 193, 258
Karatancheva, Sesil (BUL), 318
Karbacher, Bernd, (GER), 268, 287
Kardon, Craig, 251
Karlovic, Ivo (Croat), 139, 675
2003: undreamed of debut, 308
Karlsson, Carina (Swede), 215
Kauder, Ed, 292
Keldie, Ray (AUS), 148, 169
Kelleher, Bob (USLTA President), 128, 144, 578
Kendrick, Robert (American), 323
Kerr, George
Irish professional champ, 10
Key Biscayne, Florida, 227, 236, 237, 245, 249, 272, 309, 317, 323, 327, 717
Kiefer, Nicolas (GER), 318, 319
1999: lost to Boris Becker at Wimbledon, 291
2004: with Rainer Schuettler, in Olympics, 313
2006: took a set from Federer at Australian semis, 323
Kieran, John (New York Times columnist), 49, 333
Kijimuta, Akiko (Japanese), 260
King Roger I, 311. See Roger Federer
King Trophy, 723
King, Billie Jean (Bille Jean Moffitt) (USA), 19, 52, 121, 578-580, 723, 726
1959: a 15-year-old at Forest Hills, 116
1965: married Larry King, 133
1967: Woman of the Year, triples, 140
1967: in Federation Cup, 140
1970: Houston Nine formed, 155. See Gray, David: Heldman, Gladys
1972: wins the French, 165; wins all four majors, 305
1973: president of WTA, 170
1975: Wimbledon title, 179
1979: wins 20th title, 198, 199
1980: U.S. doubles title with Navratilova, 203
King, Larry, 723
married Billie Jean Moffitt, 133
Kingscote, Algernon (British), 19, 21, 675
1922: opening match at new All England Club venue, 25
Kingsley, Charles (British), 44
Kingsley, Frank (GBR), 25
Kinsey, Howard (USA), 25, 29, 33, 197, 682, 731, 734
1926: joined Charles C. Pyle troupe, 33; rare "cripple," 34
1927: U.S. Pro Championships finalist, 36
Kinsey, Robert "Bob" (USA), 29, 197, 675
Kirby, Venon (South African), 52
Kirk, Brenda (South African), 161, 171
Kiyomura, Ann (American), 203
1975: unlikely Wimbledon doubles winner, 179, 180

Kleinschroth, Heinrich (German), 15
Klima, Mita (Austrian), 187
Kloss, Ilana (RSA)
1976: won U.S. doubles title with Delina "Linky" Boshoff, 184
Klosterkemper, Horst (referee), 178
Knight, Billy (GBR), 111, 116
Knight, Dick (American), 140
Knight, Laura, 10, 130
Knode, Dorothy Head (USA), 99, 101, 106, 118
1956: French doubles finalist with Darlene Hard, 107
1957: Italian finalist, 110
Knowle, Julian (Austrian)
2007: with Simon Aspelin, in Tennis Masters, 326
Knowles, Mark (Bahamian)
2007: with Daniel Nestor, in Tennis Masters, 326
Knowles, Mark (BAH), 266, 276, 288, 306, 310, 314, 315, 326, 329
Koch, Thomaz "Tom" (BRA), 136, 139, 148, 180
Kodes, Jan (CZE), 164, 167, 173, 178, 188, 190, 580
1970: French title, 155, 156, 157
1971: second title, 159, 162
1973: another title, 168, 169, 171
Kohde Kilsch, Claudia (GER), 212, 213, 216, 220, 223, 231, 236, 238, 240, 241, 243
"Twin Towers" with Helena Sukova, 225
1985: won U.S. doubles title over Martina Navratilova–Pam Shriver, 225, 227, 228
Kohlschreiber, Philipp (GER), 326
Koslowski, Lars (German), 261
Korda, Petr (CZE), 250, 253, 259, 261, 263, 267, 280, 281, 283, 675
1998: surprise winner, 285, 287, 288
Korff, John (promoter)
1991: paid fine, 256
Kormoczi, Suzi (Hungarian), 113, 114, 116, 118, 121, 675
1956: Italian finalist, 107
Kournikova, Anna (RUS), 283, 293, 297, 305, 306, 675
"Russian pin-up," 309
Kovac, Hella (YUG)
1939: in French doubles finals, 65, 66
Kovacs, Frank (American), 62
1941: won four titles, 70
1942: turns pro, 72
1950: in U.S. Pro finals, 94
Kovacs, Virginia Wolfenden, 76
Kozeluh, Karel (Czech), 54, 60, 580-581, 734
1928: pro-tour winner, 38
1929: won U.S. Pro title, 40
1932: another title, 47
Krahwinkel, Hilde Sperling. See Sperling, Hilde
Krajicek, Michaella, 322
Krajicek, Richard (Dutchman), 262, 270, 274, 286, 287, 292, 296, 675
1996: a major title, 277, 278, 279, 281
Kramer, Jack (USA) 65, 79, 104, 108, 114, 115, 119, 120, 124, 126, 153, 161, 202, 581-582, 734
1943: in U.S. singles final, 74; in Coast Guard, 76
1946: assumed the crown, 82. See Coons, Hannibal
1947: signed with promoter Jack Harris, 84. See Olliff, John; Sports Illustrated
1948: pro debut, 86, 87
1949: winner over Gonzalez, 91
1950: still king, 94
1952: as player–promoter, 99
1953: arthritic back, 102
1957: signs Hoad to challenge Pancho Gonzalez, 110
1962: quits, 125
1964: enlisted to contact the pros, 131
1970: idea for Grand Prix, 153, 154, 155
1972: ATP executive director, 164, 165
1974: lawsuit from Bill Riordan, 173
1975: lawsuit quietly dropped, 177
1989: last of Grand Prix, 248
Krantzcke, Karen (USA), 148, 151, 154, 157, 166, 174, 175
Krasnoroutskaya, Lina (RUS), 310
Krickstein, Aaron (USA), 217, 219, 226, 235, 240, 247
"Kricker," 250, 257
1990: in U.S. Davis Cup quarterfinal match vs. Czech Milan Srejber, 250
Kriek, Johan (formerly South African), 192, 201, 208, 217, 222, 224, 240, 675-676
1981: naturalized U.S. citizen 206
1982: won title, 210, 213
Krishnan, Ramanathan (IND), 121, 122, 135, 147, 235, 676
Krishnan, Ramesh (son of Ramanathan) (IND), 205, 213, 245, 676
Kronk, Paul (AUS)
1976: Paul Kronk–Cliff Letcher in U.S. Open, 183
Kucera, Karol, 285, 287, 295, 320
Kuerten, Gustavo "Guga" (BRA), 290, 299, 301, 303, 308, 312, 313, 650
1997: first major title, 282, 284
2000: captured French title, 294, 295, 297

INDEX

INDEX

Australian Championships

Men's Singles Finals

Year	Winner	Defeated	S1	S2	S3	S4	S5
1905	Rodney Heath (AUS)	Arthur Curtis (AUS)	4-6	6-3	6-4	6-4	
1906	Anthony Wilding (NZL)	Francis Fisher (AUS)	6-0	6-4	6-4		
1907	Horrie Rice (AUS)	Harry Parker (AUS)	6-3	6-4	6-4		
1908	Fred Alexander (USA)	Alfred Dunlop (AUS)	3-6	3-6	6-0	6-2	6-3
1909	Anthony Wilding (NZL)	Ernest Parker (AUS)	6-1	7-5	6-2		
1910	Rodney Heath (AUS)	Horrie Rice (AUS)	6-4	6-3	6-2		
1911	Norman Brookes (AUS)	Horrie Rice (AUS)	6-1	6-2	6-3		
1912	Jim Parke (IRL)	Alfred Beamish (GBR)	3-6	6-3	1-6	6-1	7-5
1913	Ernest Parker (AUS)	Harry Parker (AUS)	2-6	6-1	6-3	6-2	
1914	Arthur O'Hara Wood (AUS)	Gerald Patterson (AUS)	6-4	6-3	5-7	6-1	
1915	Gordon Lowe (GBR)	Horrie Rice (AUS)	4-6	6-1	6-1	6-4	
1916-18	Not held—WW I						
1919	Algernon Kingscote (GBR)	Eric Pockley (AUS)	6-4	6-0	6-3		
1920	Pat O'Hara Wood (AUS)	Ron Thomas (AUS)	6-3	4-6	6-8	6-1	6-3
1921	Rice Gemmell (AUS)	Alf Hedemann (AUS)	7-5	6-1	6-4		
1922	James Anderson (AUS)	Gerald Patterson (AUS)	6-0	3-6	3-6	6-3	6-2
1923	Pat O'Hara Wood (AUS)	Bert St. John (AUS)	6-1	6-1	6-3		
1924	James Anderson (AUS)	Bob Schlesinger (AUS)	6-3	6-4	3-6	5-7	6-3
1925	James Anderson (AUS)	Gerald Patterson (AUS)	11-9	2-6	6-2	6-3	
1926	Jack Hawkes (AUS)	Jim Willard (AUS)	6-1	6-3	6-1		
1927	Gerald Patterson (AUS)	Jack Hawkes (AUS)	3-6	6-4	3-6	18-16	6-3
1928	Jean Borotra (FRA)	Jack Cummings (AUS)	6-4	6-1	4-6	5-7	6-3
1929	Colin Gregory (GBR)	Bob Schlesinger (AUS)	6-2	6-2	5-7	7-5	
1930	Gar Moon (AUS)	Harry Hopman (AUS)	6-3	6-1	6-3		
1931	Jack Crawford (AUS)	Harry Hopman (AUS)	9-4	6-2	2-6	6-1	
1932	Jack Crawford (AUS)	Harry Hopman (AUS)	4-6	6-3	3-6	6-3	6-1
1933	Jack Crawford (AUS)	Keith Gledhill (USA)	2-6	7-5	6-3	6-2	
1934	Fred Perry (GBR)	Jack Crawford (AUS)	6-3	7-5	6-1		
1935	Jack Crawford (AUS)	Fred Perry (GBR)	2-6	6-4	6-4	6-4	
1936	Adrian Quist (AUS)	Jack Crawford (AUS)	6-2	6-3	4-6	3-6	-97
1937	Viv McGrath (AUS)	John Bromwich (AUS)	6-3	1-6	6-0	2-6	6-1
1938	Don Budge (USA)	John Bromwich (AUS)	6-4	6-2	6-1		
1939	John Bromwich (AUS)	Adrian Quist (AUS)	6-4	6-1	6-2		
1940	Adrian Quist (AUS)	Jack Crawford (AUS)	-63	6-1	6-2		
1941-45	Not held —WW II						
1946	John Bromwich (AUS)	Dinny Pails (AUS)	5-7	6-3	7-5	3-6	**6-2**
1947	Dinny Pails (AUS)	John Bromwich (AUS)	4-6	6-4	3-6	7-5	**8-6**
1948	Adrian Quist (AUS)	John Bromwich (AUS)	6-4	3-6	6-3	2-6	**6-3**
1949	Frank Sedgman (AUS)	John Bromwich (AUS)	6-3	6-2	6-2		
1950	Frank Sedgman (AUS)	Ken McGregor (AUS)	6-3	6-4	4-6	6-1	
1951	Richard Savitt (USA)	Ken McGregor (AUS)	6-3	2-6	6-3	6-1	
1952	Ken McGregor (AUS)	Frank Sedgman (AUS)	7-5	12-10	2-6	6-2	
1953	Ken Rosewall (AUS)	Merv Rose (AUS)	6-0	6-3	6-4		
1954	Merv Rose (AUS)	Rex Hartwig (AUS)	6-2	0-6	6-4	6-2	
1955	Ken Rosewall (AUS)	Lew Hoad (AUS)	9-7	6-4	6-2		
1956	Lew Hoad (AUS)	Ken Rosewall (AUS)	6-4	3-6	6-4	7-5	
1957	Ashley Cooper (AUS)	Neale Fraser (AUS)	6-3	9-11	6-4	6-2	
1958	Ashley Cooper (AUS)	Mal Anderson (AUS)	7-5	6-3	6-4		
1959	Alex Olmedo (PER)	Neale Fraser (AUS)	6-1	6-2	3-6	6-3	
1960	Rod Laver (AUS)	Neale Fraser (AUS)	5-7	3-6	6-3	8-6	8-6
1961	Roy Emerson (AUS)	Rod Laver (AUS)	1-6	6-3	7-5	6-4	
1962	Rod Laver (AUS)	Roy Emerson (AUS)	8-6	0-6	6-4	6-4	
1963	Roy Emerson (AUS)	Ken Fletcher (AUS)	6-3	6-3	6-1		
1964	Roy Emerson (AUS)	Fred Stolle (AUS)	6-3	6-4	6-2		
1965	Roy Emerson (AUS)	Fred Stolle (AUS)	7-9	2-6	6-4	7-5	6-1
1966	Roy Emerson (AUS)	Arthur Ashe (USA)	6-4	6-8	6-2	6-3	
1967	Roy Emerson (AUS)	Arthur Ashe (USA)	6-4	6-1	6-4		
1968	Bill Bowrey (AUS)	Juan Gisbert (ESP)	7-5	2-6	9-7	6-4	
1969	Rod Laver (AUS)	Andres Gimeno (ESP)	6-3	6-4	7-5		
1970	Arthur Ashe (USA)	Dick Crealy (AUS)	6-4	9-7	6-2		
1971	Ken Rosewall (AUS)	Arthur Ashe (USA)	6-1	7-5	6-3		
1972	Ken Rosewall (AUS)	Mal Anderson (AUS)	7-6(2)	6-3	7-5		
1973	John Newcombe (AUS)	Onny Parun (NZL)	6-3	6-7	7-5	6-1	
1974	Jimmy Connors (USA)	Phil Dent (AUS)	7-6(7)	6-4	4-6	6-3	
1975	John Newcombe (AUS)	Jimmy Connors (USA)	7-5	3-6	6-4	7-6(7)	
1976	Mark Edmondson (AUS)	John Newcombe (AUS)	6-7	6-3	7-6	6-1	
1977 (Jan)	Roscoe Tanner (USA)	Guillermo Vilas (ARG)	6-3	6-3	6-3		
1977 (Dec)	Vitas Gerulaitis (USA)	John Lloyd (GBR)	6-3	7-6(1)	5-7	3-6	6-2
1978	Guillermo Vilas (ARG)	John Marks (AUS)	6-4	6-4	3-6	6-3	
1979	Guillermo Vilas (ARG)	John Sadri (USA)	7-6(4)	6-3	6-2		
1980	Brian Teacher (USA)	Kim Warwick (AUS)	7-5	7-6(4)	6-3		
1981	Johan Kriek (RSA)	Steve Denton (USA)	6-2	7-6(1)	6-7(1)	6-4	
1982	Johan Kriek (RSA)	Steve Denton (USA)	6-3	6-3	6-2		
1983	Mats Wilander (SWE)	Ivan Lendl (CZE)	6-1	6-4	6-4		
1984	Mats Wilander (SWE)	Kevin Curren(RSA)	6-7(5)	6-4	7-6(3)	6-2	
1985	Stefan Edberg (SWE)	Mats Wilander (SWE)	6-4	6-3	6-3		
1987	Stefan Edberg (SWE)	Pat Cash (AUS)	6-3	6-4	3-6	5-7	6-3
1988	Mats Wilander (SWE)	Pat Cash (AUS)	6-3	6-7(3)	3-6	6-1	8-6
1989	Ivan Lendl (CZE)	Miloslav Mecir (CZE)	6-2	6-2	6-2		
1990	Ivan Lendl (CZE)	Stefan Edberg (SWE)	4-6	7-6(3)	5-2	(ret. inj.)	
1991	Boris Becker (GER)	Ivan Lendl (CZE)	1-6	6-4	6-4	6-4	
1992	Jim Courier (USA)	Stefan Edberg (SWE)	6-3	3-6	6-4	6-2	
1993	Jim Courier (USA)	Stefan Edberg (SWE)	6-2	6-1	2-6	7-5	
1994	Pete Sampras (USA)	Todd Martin (USA)	7-6(4)	6-4	6-4		
1995	Andre Agassi (USA)	Pete Sampras (USA)	4-6	6-1	7-6(5)	6-4	
1996	Boris Becker (GER)	Michael Chang (USA)	6-2	6-4	2-6	6-2	
1997	Pete Sampras (USA)	Carlos Moya (ESP)	6-2	6-3	6-3		
1998	Petr Korda (CZE)	Marcelo Rios (CHI)	6-2	6-2	6-2		
1999	Yevgeny Kafelnikov (RUS)	Thomas Enqvist (SWE)	4-6	6-0	6-3	7-6(1)	
2000	Andre Agassi (USA)	Yevgeny Kafelnikov (RUS)	3-6	6-3	6-2	6-4	
2001	Andre Agassi (USA)	Arnaud Clement (FRA)	6-4	6-2	6-2		
2002	Thomas Johansson (SWE)	Marat Safin (RUS)	3-6	6-4	6-4	7-6(4)	
2003	Andre Agassi (USA)	Rainer Schuettler (GER)	6-2	6-2	6-1		

Year	Winner	Defeated	S1	S2	S3	S4	S5
2004	Roger Federer (SUI)	Marat Safin (RUS)	7-6(3)	6-4	6-2		
2005	Marat Safin (RUS)	Lleyton Hewitt (AUS)	1-6	6-3	6-4	6-4	
2006	Roger Federer (SUI)	Marcos Baghdatis (CYP)	5-7	7-5	6-0	6-2	
2007	Roger Federer (SUI)	Fernando Gonzalez (CHI)	7-6(2)	6-4	6-4		
2008	Novak Djokovic (SRB)	Jo-Wilfried Tsonga (FRA)	4-6	6-4	6-3	7-6(2)	
2009	Rafael Nadal (ESP)	Roger Federer (SUI)	7-5	3-6	7-6(3)	3-6	6-2

Women's Singles Finals

Year	Winner	Defeated	S1	S2	S3
1922	Mall Molesworth (AUS)	Esna Boyd (AUS)	6-3	10-8	
1923	Mall Molesworth (AUS)	Esna Boyd (AUS)	6-1	7-5	
1924	Sylvia Lance (AUS)	Esna Boyd (AUS)	6-3	3-6	6-4
1925	Daphne Akhurst (AUS)	Esna Boyd (AUS)	1-6	8-6	6-4
1926	Daphne Akhurst (AUS)	Esna Boyd (AUS)	6-1	6-3	
1927	Esna Boyd (AUS)	Sylvia Lance Harper (AUS)	5-7	6-1	6-2
1928	Daphne Akhurst (AUS)	Esna Boyd (AUS)	7-5	6-2	
1929	Daphne Akhurst (AUS)	Louie Bickerton (AUS)	6-1	5-7	6-2
1930	Daphne Akhurst (AUS)	Sylvia Lance Harper (AUS)	10-8	2-6	7-5
1931	Coral McInnes Buttsworth (AUS)	Marjorie Cox Crawford (AUS)	1-6	6-3	6-4
1932	Coral McInnes Buttsworth (AUS)	Kathrine Le Mesurier (AUS)	9-7	6-4	
1933	Joan Hartigan (AUS)	Coral McInnes Buttsworth (AUS)	6-4	6-3	
1934	Joan Hartigan (AUS)	Mall Molesworth (AUS)	6-1	6-4	
1935	Dorothy Round (GBR)	Nancy Lyle (GBR)	1-6	6-1	6-3
1936	Joan Hartigan (AUS)	Nancye Wynne (AUS)	6-4	6-4	
1937	Nancye Wynne (AUS)	Emily Hood Westacott (AUS)	6-3	5-7	6-4
1938	Dorothy Bundy (USA)	Dorothy Stevenson (AUS)	6-3	6-2	
1939	Emily Hood Westacott (AUS)	Nell Hall Hopman (AUS)	6-1	6-2	
1940	Nancye Wynne (AUS)	Thelma Coyne Long (AUS)	5-7	6-4	6-0
1941-45 Not held —WWII					
1946	Nancye Wynne Bolton (AUS)	Joyce Fitch (AUS)	6-4	6-4	
1947	Nancye Wynne Bolton (AUS)	Nell Hall Hopman (AUS)	6-3	6-2	
1948	Nancye Bolton (AUS)	Marie Toomey (AUS)	6-3	6-1	
1949	Doris Hart (USA)	Nancye Bolton (AUS)	6-3	6-4	
1950	Louise Brough (USA)	Doris Hart (USA)	6-4	3-6	6-4
1951	Nancye Bolton (AUS)	Thelma Long (AUS)	6-1	7-5	
1952	Thelma Long (AUS)	Helen Angwin (AUS)	6-2	6-3	
1953	Maureen Connolly (USA)	Julia Sampson (USA)	6-3	6-2	
1954	Thelma Long (AUS)	Jenny Staley (AUS)	6-3	6-4	
1955	Beryl Penrose (AUS)	Thelma Long (AUS)	6-4	6-3	
1956	Mary Carter (AUS)	Thelma Long (AUS)	3-6	6-2	9-7
1957	Shirley Fry (USA)	Althea Gibson (USA)	6-3	6-4	
1958	Angela Mortimer (GBR)	Lorraine Coghlan (AUS)	6-3	6-4	
1959	Mary Carter Reitano (AUS)	Renee Schuurman (RSA)	6-2	6-3	

Year	Winner	Defeated	S1	S2	S3
1960	Margaret Smith (AUS)	Jan Lehane (AUS)	7-5	6-2	
1961	Margaret Smith (AUS)	Jan Lehane (AUS)	6-1	6-4	
1962	Margaret Smith (AUS)	Jan Lehane (AUS)	6-0	6-2	
1963	Margaret Smith (AUS)	Jan Lehane (AUS)	6-2	6-2	
1964	Margaret Smith (AUS)	Lesley Turner (AUS)	6-3	6-2	
1965	Margaret Smith (AUS)	Maria Bueno (BRA)	5-7	6-3	5-2(retired)
1966	Margaret Smith (AUS)	Nancy Richey (USA)	(walkover)		
1967	Nancy Richey (USA)	Lesley Turner (AUS)	6-1	6-4	
1968	Billie Jean King (USA)	Margaret Smith Court (AUS)	6-1	6-2	
1969	Margaret Smith Court (AUS)	Billie Jean King (USA)	6-4	6-1	
1970	Margaret Smith Court (AUS)	Kerry Melville (AUS)	6-1	6-3	
1971	Margaret Smith Court (AUS)	Evonne Goolagong (AUS)	2-6	7-6(0)	7-5
1972	Virginia Wade (GBR)	Evonne Goolagong (AUS)	6-4	6-4	
1973	Margaret Smith Court (AUS)	Evonne Goolagong (AUS)	6-4	7-5	
1974	Evonne Goolagong (AUS)	Chris Evert (USA)	7-6(5)	4-6	6-0
1975	Evonne Goolagong (AUS)	Martina Navratilova (CZE)	6-3	6-2	
1976	Evonne Goolagong Cawley (AUS)	Renata Tomanova (CZE)	6-2	6-2	
1977 (Jan)	Kerry Melville Reid (AUS)	Dianne Fromholtz (AUS)	7-5	6-2	
1977 (Dec)	Evonne Goolagong Cawley (AUS)	Helen Gourlay Cawley (AUS)	6-3	6-0	
1978	Chris O'Neill (AUS)	Betsy Nagelsen (USA)	6-3	7-6(4)	
1979	Barbara Jordan (USA)	Sharon Walsh (USA)	6-3	6-3	
1980	Hana Mandlikova (CZE)	Wendy Turnbull (AUS)	6-0	7-5	
1981	Martina Navratilova (USA)	Chris Evert Lloyd (USA)	6-7(4)	6-4	7-5
1982	Chris Evert Lloyd (USA)	Martina Navratilova (USA)	6-3	2-6	6-3
1983	Martina Navratilova (USA)	Kathy Jordan (USA)	6-2	7-6(5)	
1984	Chris Evert Lloyd (USA)	Helena Sukova (CZE)	6-7(4)	6-1	6-2
1985	Martina Navratilova (USA)	Chris Evert Lloyd (USA)	6-2	4-6	6-2
1987	Hana Mandlikova (CZE)	Martina Navratilova (USA)	7-5	7-6(2)	
1988	Steffi Graf (GER)	Chris Evert (USA)	6-1	7-6(3)	
1989	Steffi Graf (GER)	Helena Sukova (CZE)	6-4	6-4	
1990	Steffi Graf (GER)	Mary Joe Fernandez (USA)	6-3	6-4	
1991	Monica Seles (YUG)	Jana Novotna (CZE)	5-7	6-3	6-1
1992	Monica Seles (YUG)	Mary Joe Fernandez (USA)	6-2	6-3	
1993	Monica Seles (YUG)	Steffi Graf (GER)	4-6	6-3	6-2
1994	Steffi Graf (GER)	Arantxa Sanchez Vicario(ESP)	6-0	6-2	
1995	Mary Pierce (FRA)	Arantxa Sanchez Vicario(ESP)	6-3	6-2	
1996	Monica Seles (USA)	Anke Huber (GER)	6-4	6-1	
1997	Martina Hingis (SUI)	Mary Pierce (FRA)	6-2	6-2	
1998	Martina Hingis (SUI)	Conchita Martinez (ESP)	6-3	6-3	
1999	Martina Hingis (SUI)	Amelie Mauresmo (FRA)	6-2	6-3	
2000	Lindsay Davenport (USA)	Martina Hingis (SUI)	6-1	7-5	
2001	Jennifer Capriati (USA)	Martina Hingis (SUI)	6-4	6-3	
2002	Jennifer Capriati (USA)	Martina Hingis (SUI)	4-6	7-6(7)	6-2
2003	Serena Williams (USA)	Venus Williams (USA)	7-6(4)	3-6	6-4
2004	Justine Henin-Hardenne (BEL)	Kim Clijsters (BEL)	6-3	4-6	6-3
2005	Serena Williams (USA)	Lindsay Davenport (USA)	2-6	6-3	6-0
2006	Amelie Mauresmo (FRA)	Justine Henin-Hardenne (BEL)	6-1	2-0 (retired)	
2007	Serena Williams (USA)	Maria Sharapova (RUS)	6-1	6-2	
2008	Maria Sharapova (RUS)	Ana Ivanovic (SRB)	7-5	6-3	
2009	Serena Williams (USA)	Dinara Safina (RUS)	6-0	6-3	

French Championships

Men's Singles Finals

Rd	Winner	Defeated	S1	S2	S3	S4	S5
1925	Rene Lacoste (FRA)	Jean Borotra (FRA)	7-5	6-1	6-4		
1926	Henri Cochet (FRA)	Rene Lacoste (FRA)	6-2	6-4	6-3		
1927	Rene Lacoste (FRA)	Bill Tilden (USA)	6-4	4-6	5-7	6-3	11-9
1928	Henri Cochet (FRA)	Rene Lacoste (FRA)	5-7	6-3	6-1	6-3	
1929	Rene Lacoste (FRA)	Jean Borotra (FRA)	6-3	2-6	6-0	2-6	8-6
1930	Henri Cochet (FRA)	Bill Tilden (USA)	3-6	8-6	6-3	6-1	
1931	Jean Borotra (FRA)	Christian Boussus (FRA)	2-6	6-4	7-5	6-4	
1932	Henri Cochet (FRA)	Giorgio de Stefani (ITA)	6-0	6-4	4-6	6-3	
1933	Jack Crawford (AUS)	Henri Cochet (FRA)	8-6	6-1	6-3		
1934	Gottfried von Cramm (GER)	Jack Crawford (AUS)	6-4	7-9	3-6	7-5	6-3
1935	Fred Perry (GBR)	Gottfried von Cramm (GER)	6-3	3-6	6-1	6-3	
1936	Gottfried von Cramm (GER)	Fred Perry (GBR)	6-0	2-6	6-2	2-6	6-0
1937	Henner Henkel (GER)	Bunny Austin (GBR)	6-1	6-4	6-3		
1938	Don Budge (USA)	Roderich Menzel (CZE)	6-3	6-2	6-4		
1939	Don NcNeill (USA)	Bobby Riggs (USA)	7-5	6-0	6-3		
1940-45 Not held—WW II							
1946	Marcel Bernard (FRA)	Jaroslav Drobny (CZE)	3-6	2-6	6-1	6-4	6-3
1947	Joszef Asboth (HUN)	Eric Sturgess (RSA)	8-6	7-5	6-4		
1948	Frank Parker (USA)	Jaroslav Drobny (CZE)	6-4	7-5	5-7	8-6	
1949	Frank Parker (USA)	Budge Patty (USA)	6-3	1-6	6-1	6-4	
1950	Budge Patty (USA)	Jaroslav Drobny (CZE)	6-1	6-2	3-6	5-7	7-5
1951	Jaroslav Drobny (CZE)	Eric Sturgess (RSA)	6-3	6-3	6-3		
1952	Jaroslav Drobny (CZE)	Frank Sedgman (AUS)	6-2	6-0	3-6	6-4	
1953	Ken Rosewall (AUS)	Vic Seixas (USA)	6-3	6-4	1-6	6-2	
1954	Tony Trabert (USA)	Art Larsen (USA)	6-4	7-5	6-1		
1955	Tony Trabert (USA)	Sven Davidson (SWE)	2-6	6-1	6-4	6-2	
1956	Lew Hoad (AUS)	Sven Davidson (SWE)	6-4	8-6	6-3		
1957	Sven Davidson (SWE)	Herbie Flam (USA)	6-3	6-4	6-4		
1958	Merv Rose (AUS)	Luis Ayala (CHI)	6-3	6-4	6-4		
1959	Nicola Pietrangeli (ITA)	Ian Vermaak (RSA)	3-6	6-3	6-4	6-1	
1960	Nicola Pietrangeli (ITA)	Luis Ayala (CHI)	3-6	6-3	6-4	4-6	6-3
1961	Manolo Santana (ESP)	Nicola Pietrangeli (ITA)	4-6	6-1	3-6	6-0	6-2
1962	Rod Laver (AUS)	Roy Emerson (AUS)	3-6	2-6	6-3	9-7	6-2
1963	Roy Emerson (AUS)	Pierre Darmon (FRA)	3-6	6-1	6-4	6-4	
1964	Manolo Santana (ESP)	Nicola Pietrangeli (ITA)	6-3	6-1	4-6	7-5	
1965	Fred Stolle (AUS)	Tony Roche (AUS)	3-6	6-0	6-2	6-3	
1966	Tony Roche (AUS)	Istvan Gulyas (HUN)	6-1	6-4	7-5		
1967	Roy Emerson (AUS)	Tony Roche (AUS)	6-1	6-4	2-6	6-2	
1968	Ken Rosewall (AUS)	Rod Laver (AUS)	6-3	6-1	2-6	6-2	
1969	Rod Laver (AUS)	Ken Rosewall (AUS)	6-4	6-3	6-4		
1970	Jan Kodes (CZE)	Zeljko Franulovic (YUG)	6-2	6-4	6-0		
1971	Jan Kodes (CZE)	Ilie Nastase (ROU)	8-6	6-2	2-6	7-5	
1972	Andres Gimeno (ESP)	Patrick Proisy (FRA)	4-6	6-3	6-1	6-1	
1973	Ilie Nastase (ROU)	Nikki Pilic (YUG)	6-3	6-3	6-0		
1974	Bjorn Borg (SWE)	Manolo Orantes (ESP)	2-6	6-7(1)	6-0	6-1	6-1
1975	Bjorn Borg (SWE)	Guillermo Vilas (ARG)	6-2	6-3	6-4		
1976	Adriano Panatta (ITA)	Harold Solomon (USA)	6-1	6-4	4-6	7-6(3)	
1977	Guillermo Vilas (ARG)	Brian Gottfried (USA)	6-0	6-3	6-0		
1978	Bjorn Borg (SWE)	Guillermo Vilas (ARG)	6-1	6-1	6-3		
1979	Bjorn Borg (SWE)	Victor Pecci (PAR)	6-3	6-1	6-7(6)	6-4	
1980	Bjorn Borg (SWE)	Vitas Gerulaitis (USA)	6-4	6-1	6-2		
1981	Bjorn Borg (SWE)	Ivan Lendl (CZE)	6-1	4-6	6-2	3-6	6-1
1982	Mats Wilander (SWE)	Guillermo Vilas (ARG)	1-6	7-6(6)	6-0	6-4	
1983	Yannick Noah (FRA)	Mats Wilander (SWE)	6-2	7-5	7-6(3)		
1984	Ivan Lendl (CZE)	John McEnroe (USA)	3-6	2-6	6-4	7-5	7-5
1985	Mats Wilander (SWE)	Ivan Lendl (CZE)	3-6	6-4	6-2	6-2	
1986	Ivan Lendl (CZE)	Mikael Pernfors (SWE)	6-3	6-2	6-4		
1987	Ivan Lendl (CZE)	Mats Wilander (SWE)	7-5	6-2	3-6	7-6(3)	
1988	Mats Wilander (SWE)	Henri Leconte (FRA)	7-5	6-2	6-1		
1989	Michael Chang (USA)	Stefan Edberg (SWE)	6-1	3-6	4-6	6-4	6-2
1990	Andres Gomez (ECU)	Andre Agassi (USA)	6-3	2-6	6-4	6-4	
1991	Jim Courier (USA)	Andre Agassi (USA)	3-6	6-4	2-6	6-1	6-4
1992	Jim Courier (USA)	Petr Korda (CZE)	7-5	6-2	6-1		
1993	Sergi Bruguera (ESP)	Jim Courier (USA)	6-4	2-6	6-2	3-6	6-3
1994	Sergi Bruguera (ESP)	Alberto Berasategui (ESP)	6-3	7-5	2-6	6-1	
1995	Thomas Muster (AUT)	Michael Chang (USA)	7-5	6-2	6-4		
1996	Yevgeny Kafelnikov (RUS)	Michael Stich (GER)	7-6(4)	7-5	7-9(4)		
1997	Gustavo Kuerten (BRA)	Sergi Bruguera (ESP)	6-3	6-4	6-2		
1998	Carlos Moya (ESP)	Alex Corretja (ESP)	6-3	7-5	6-3		
1999	Andre Agassi (USA)	Andrei Medvedev (UKR)	1-6	2-6	6-4	6-3	6-4
2000	Gustavo Kuerten (BRA)	Magnus Norman (SWE)	6-2	6-3	2-6	7-6(6)	
2001	Gustavo Kuerten (BRA)	Alex Corretja (ESP)	6-7(3)	7-5	6-2	6-0	
2002	Albert Costa (ESP)	Juan Carlos Ferrero (ESP)	6-1	6-0	4-6	6-3	
2003	Juan Carlos Ferrero (ESP)	Martin Verkerk (NED)	6-1	6-3	6-2		
2004	Gaston Gaudio (ARG)	Guillermo Coria (ARG)	0-6	3-6	6-4	6-1	8-6
2005	Rafael Nadal (ESP)	Mariano Puerta (ARG)	6-7(6)	6-3	6-1	7-5	
2006	Rafael Nadal (ESP)	Roger Federer (SUI)	1-6	6-1	6-4	7-6(4)	
2007	Rafael Nadal (ESP)	Roger Federer (SUI)	6-3	4-6	6-3	6-4	
2008	Rafael Nadal (ESP)	Roger Federer (SUI)	6-1	6-3	6-0		
2009	Roger Federer (SUI)	Robin Soderling (SWE)	6-1	7-6(1)	6-4		

Women's Singles Finals

Rd	Winner	Defeated	S1	S2	S3
1925	Suzanne Lenglen (FRA)	Kitty McKane (GBR)	6-1	6-2	
1926	Suzanne Lenglen (FRA)	Mary Kendall Browne (USA)	6-1	6-0	
1927	Kea Bouman (NED)	Irene Bowder Peacock (RSA)	6-2	6-4	
1928	Helen Wills (USA)	Eileen Bennett (GBR)	6-1	6-2	
1929	Helen Wills (USA)	Simone Passemard Mathieu (FRA)	6-3	6-4	
1930	Helen Wills Moody (USA)	Helen Jacobs (USA)	6-2	6-1	
1931	Cilly Aussem (GER)	Betty Nuthall (GBR)	8-6	6-1	
1932	Helen Wills Moody (USA)	Simone Passemard Mathieu (FRA)	7-5	6-1	
1933	Margaret Scriven (GBR)	Simone Passemard Mathieu (FRA)	6-2	4-6	6-4
1934	Margaret Scriven (GBR)	Helen Jacobs (USA)	7-5	4-6	6-1
1935	Hilde Krahwinkel Sperling (DEN)	Simone Passemard Mathieu (FRA)	6-2	6-1	
1936	Hilde Krahwinkel Sperling (DEN)	Simone Passemard Mathieu (FRA)	6-3	6-4	

Rd	Winner	Defeated	S1	S2	S3
1937	Hilde Krahwinkel Sperling (DEN)	Simone Passemard Mathieu (FRA)	6-2	6-4	
1938	Simone Passemard Mathieu (FRA)	Nelly Adamson Landry (FRA)	6-0	6-3	
1939	Simone Passemard Mathieu (FRA)	Jadwiga Jedrzejowska (POL)	6-3	8-6	
1940-45 Not held—WW II					
1946	Margaret Osborne (USA)	Pauline Betz (USA)	1-6	8-6	7-5
1947	Pat Canning Todd (USA)	Doris Hart (USA)	6-3	3-6	6-4
1948	Nelly Adamson Landry (FRA)	Shirley Fry (USA)	6-2	0-6	6-0
1949	Margaret Osborne duPont (USA)	Nelly Adamson Landry (FRA)	7-5	6-2	
1950	Doris Hart (USA)	Pat Canning Todd (USA)	6-4	4-6	6-2
1951	Shirley Fry (USA)	Doris Hart (USA)	6-3	3-6	6-3
1952	Doris Hart (USA)	Shirley Fry (USA)	6-4	6-4	
1953	Maureen Connolly (USA)	Doris Hart (USA)	6-2	6-4	
1954	Maureen Connolly (USA)	Ginette Bucaille (FRA)	6-4	6-1	
1955	Angela Mortimer (GBR)	Dorothy Head Knode (USA)	2-6	7-5	10-8
1956	Althea Gibson (USA)	Angela Mortimer (GBR)	6-0	12-10	
1957	Shirley Bloomer (GBR)	Dorothy Head Knode (USA)	6-1	6-3	
1958	Zsuzsi Kormoczy (HUN)	Shirley Bloomer (GBR)	6-4	1-6	6-2
1959	Christine Truman (GBR)	Zsuzsi Kormoczy (HUN)	6-4	7-5	
1960	Darlene Hard (USA)	Yola Ramirez (MEX)	6-3	6-4	
1961	Ann Haydon (GBR)	Yola Ramirez (MEX)	6-2	6-1	
1962	Margaret Smith (AUS)	Lesley Turner (AUS)	6-3	3-6	7-5
1963	Lesley Turner (AUS)	Ann Haydon Jones (GBR)	2-6	6-3	7-5
1964	Margaret Smith (AUS)	Maria Bueno (BRA)	5-7	6-1	6-2
1965	Lesley Turner (AUS)	Margaret Smith (AUS)	6-3	6-4	
1966	Ann Haydon Jones (GBR)	Nancy Richey (USA)	6-3	6-1	
1967	Francoise Durr (FRA)	Lesley Turner (AUS)	4-6	6-3	6-4
1968	Nancy Richey (USA)	Ann Haydon Jones (GBR)	5-7	6-4	6-1
1969	Margaret Smith Court (AUS)	Ann Haydon Jones (GBR)	6-1	4-6	6-3
1970	Margaret Smith Court (AUS)	Helga Niessen-Masthoff (GER)	6-2	6-4	
1971	Evonne Goolagoong (AUS)	Helen Gourlay (AUS)	6-3	7-5	
1972	Billie Jean King (USA)	Evonne Goolagong (AUS)	6-3	6-3	
1973	Margaret Smith Court (AUS)	Chris Evert (USA)	6-7(5)	7-6(6)	6-4
1974	Chris Evert (USA)	Olga Morozova (USSR)	6-1	6-2	
1975	Chris Evert (USA)	Martina Navratilova (CZE)	2-6	6-2	6-1

Rd	Winner	Defeated	S1	S2	S3
1976	Sue Barker (GBR)	Renata Tomanova (CZE)	6-2	0-6	6-2
1977	Mima Jausovec (YUG)	Florenta Mihai (ROU)	6-2	6-7(5)	6-1
1978	Virginia Ruzici (ROU)	Mima Jausovec (YUG)	6-2	6-2	
1979	Chris Evert Lloyd (USA)	Wendy Turnbull (AUS)	6-2	6-0	
1980	Chris Evert Lloyd (USA)	Virginia Ruzici (ROU)	6-0	6-3	
1981	Hana Mandlikova (CZE)	Sylvia Hanika (GER)	6-2	6-4	
1982	Martina Navratilova (USA)	Andrea Jaeger (USA)	7-6(6)	6-1	
1983	Chris Evert Lloyd (USA)	Mima Jausovec (YUG)	6-1	6-2	
1984	Martina Navratilova (USA)	Chris Evert Lloyd (USA)	6-3	6-1	
1985	Chris Evert Lloyd (USA)	Martina Navratilova (USA)	6-3	6-7(4)	7-5
1986	Chris Evert Lloyd (USA)	Martina Navratilova (USA)	2-6	6-3	6-3
1987	Steffi Graf (GER)	Martina Navratilova (USA)	6-4	4-6	8-6
1988	Steffi Graf (GER)	Natalia Zvereva (BLR)	6-0	6-0	
1989	Arantxa Sanchez Vicario (ESP)	Steffi Graf (GER)	7-6(6)	3-6	7-5
1990	Monica Seles (YUG)	Steffi Graf (GER)	7-6(6)	6-4	
1991	Monica Seles (YUG)	Arantxa Sanchez Vicario (ESP)	6-3	6-4	
1992	Monica Seles (YUG)	Steffi Graf (GER)	6-2	3-6	10-8
1993	Steffi Graf (GER)	Mary Joe Fernandez (USA)	4-6	6-2	6-4
1994	Arantxa Sanchez Vicario (ESP)	Mary Pierce (FRA)	6-4	6-4	
1995	Steffi Graf (GER)	Arantxa Sanchez Vicario (ESP)	7-5	4-6	6-0
1996	Steffi Graf (GER)	Arantxa Sanchez Vicario (ESP)	6-3	6-7(4)	10-8
1997	Iva Majoli (CRO)	Martina Hingis (SUI)	6-4	6-2	
1998	Arantxa Sanchez Vicario (ESP)	Monica Seles (USA)	7-6(5)	0-6	6-2
1999	Steffi Graf (GER)	Martina Hingis (SUI)	4-6	7-5	6-2
2000	Mary Pierce (FRA)	Conchita Martinez (ESP)	6-2	7-5	
2001	Jennifer Capriati (USA)	Kim Clijsters (BEL)	1-6	6-4	12-10
2002	Serena Williams (USA)	Venus Williams (USA)	7-5	6-3	
2003	Justine Henin-Hardenne (BEL)	Kim Clijsters (BEL)	6-4	6-0	
2004	Anastasia Myskina (RUS)	Elene Dementieva (RUS)	6-1	6-2	
2005	Justine Henin-Hardenne (BEL)	Mary Pierce (FRA)	6-1	6-1	
2006	Justine Henin-Hardenne (BEL)	Svetlana Kuznetsova (RUS)	6-4	6-4	
2007	Justine Henin (BEL)	Ana Ivanovic (SRB)	6-1	6-2	
2008	Ana Ivanovic (SRB)	Dinara Safina (RUS)	6-4	6-3	
2009	Svetlana Kuznetsova (RUS)	Dinara Safina (RUS)	6-4	6-2	

Wimbledon

Men's Singles Finals

Rd	Winner	Defeated	S1	S2	S3	S4	S5
1877	Spencer Gore (GBR)	William Marshall (GBR)	6-1	6-2	6-4		
1878	Frank Hadow (GBR)	Spencer Gore (GBR)	7-5	6-1	9-7		
1879	John Hartley (GBR)	Vere "St. Leger" Goold (GBR)	6-2	6-4	6-2		
1880	John Hartley (GBR)	Herbert Lawford (GBR)	6-3	6-2	2-6	6-3	
1881	Willie Renshaw (GBR)	John Hartley (GBR)	6-0	6-1	6-1		
1882	Willie Renshaw (GBR)	Ernest Renshaw (GBR)	6-1	2-6	4-6	6-2	6-2
1883	Willie Renshaw (GBR)	Ernest Renshaw (GBR)	2-6	6-3	6-3	4-6	6-3
1884	Willie Renshaw (GBR)	Herbert Lawford (GBR)	6-0	6-4	9-7		

Rd	Winner	Defeated	S1	S2	S3	S4	S5
1885	Willie Renshaw (GBR)	Herbert Lawford (GBR)	7-5	6-2	4-6	7-5	
1886	Willie Renshaw (GBR)	Herbert Lawford (GBR)	6-0	5-7	6-3	6-4	
1887	Herbert Lawford (GBR)	Ernest Renshaw (GBR)	1-6	6-3	3-6	6-4	6-4
1888	Ernest Renshaw (GBR)	Herbert Lawford (GBR)	6-3	7-5	6-0		
1889	Willie Renshaw (GBR)	Ernest Renshaw (GBR)	6-4	6-1	3-6	6-0	
1890	Ghost Hamilton (GBR)	Willie Renshaw (GBR)	'6-8	6-2	3-6	6-1	6-1
1891	Wilfred Baddeley (GBR)	Ghost Hamilton (GBR)	(walkover)				
1892	Wilfred Baddeley (GBR)	Joshua Pim (GBR)	4-6	6-3	6-3	6-2	

Rd	Winner	Defeated	S1	S2	S3	S4	S5
1893	Joshua Pim (GBR)	Wilfred Baddeley (GBR)	3-6	6-1	6-3	6-2	
1894	Joshua Pim (GBR)	Wilfred Baddeley (GBR)	10-8	6-2	8-6		
1895	Wilfred Baddeley (GBR)	Wilberforce Eaves (GBR)	4-6	2-6	8-6	6-2	6-3
1896	Harold Mahony (GBR)	Wilfred Baddeley (GBR)	6-2	6-8	5-7	8-6	6-3
1897	Reggie Doherty (GBR)	Harold Mahony (GBR)	6-4	6-4	6-3		
1898	Reggie Doherty (GBR)	Laurie Doherty (GBR)	6-3	6-3	2-6	5-7	6-1
1899	Reggie Doherty (GBR)	Arthur Gore (GBR)	1-6	4-6	6-3	6-3	6-3
1900	Reggie Doherty (GBR)	Sidney H. Smith (GBR)	6-8	6-3	6-1	6-2	
1901	Arthur Gore (GBR)	Reggie Doherty (GBR)	4-6	7-5	6-4	6-4	
1902	Laurie Doherty (GBR)	Arthur Gore (GBR)	6-4	6-3	3-6	6-0	
1903	Laurie Doherty (GBR)	Frank Riseley (GBR)	7-5	6-3	6-0		
1904	Laurie Doherty (GBR)	Frank Riseley (GBR)	6-1	7-5	8-6		
1905	Laurie Doherty (GBR)	Norman Brookes (AUS)	8-6	6-2	6-4		
1906	Laurie Doherty (GBR)	Frank Riseley (GBR)	6-4	4-6	6-2	6-3	
1907	Norman Brookes (AUS)	Arthur Gore (GBR)	6-4	6-2	6-2		
1908	Arthur Gore (GBR)	Herbert Roper Barrett (GBR)	6-3	6-2	4-6	3-6	6-4
1909	Arthur Gore (GBR)	Josiah Ritchie (GBR)	6-8	1-6	6-2	6-2	6-2
1910	Tony Wilding (NZL)	Arthur Gore (GBR)	6-4	7-5	4-6	6-2	
1911	Tony Wilding (NZL)	Herbert Roper Barrett (GBR)	6-4	4-6	2-6	6-2	(retd)
1912	Tony Wilding (NZL)	Arthur Gore (GBR)	6-4	6-4	4-6	6-4	
1913	Tony Wilding (NZL)	Maurice McLoughlin (USA)	8-6	6-3	10-8		
1914	Norman Brookes (AUS)	Tony Wilding (NZL)	6-4	6-4	7-5		
1915 - 18 Not held - WW I							
1919	Gerald Patterson (AUS)	Norman Brookes (AUS)	6-3	7-5	6-2		
1920	Bill Tilden (USA)	Gerald Patterson (AUS)	2-6	6-3	6-2	6-4	
1921	Bill Tilden (USA)	Brian Norton (RSA)	4-6	2-6	6-1	6-0	7-5
1922	Gerald Patterson (AUS)	Randolph Lycett (AUS)	6-3	6-4	6-2		
1923	Bill Johnston (USA)	Frank Hunter (USA)	6-0	6-3	6-1		
1924	Jean Borotra (FRA)	Rene Lacoste (FRA)	6-1	3-6	6-1	3-6	6-4
1925	Rene Lacoste (FRA)	Jean Borotra (FRA)	6-3	6-3	4-6	8-6	
1926	Jean Borotra (FRA)	Howard Kinsey (USA)	8-6	6-1	6-3		
1927	Henri Cochet (FRA)	Jean Borotra (FRA)	4-6	4-6	6-3	6-4	7-5
1928	Rene Lacoste (FRA)	Henri Cochet (FRA)	6-1	4-6	6-4	6-2	
1929	Henri Cochet (FRA)	Jean Borotra (FRA)	6-4	6-3	6-4		
1930	Bill Tilden (USA)	Wilmer Allison (USA)	6-3	9-7	6-4		
1931	Sidney Wood (USA)	Francis Shields (USA)	(walkover)				
1932	Ellsworth Vines (USA)	Bunny Austin (GBR)	6-4	6-2	6-0		
1933	Jack Crawford (AUS)	Ellsworth Vines (USA)	4-6	11-9	6-2	2-6	6-4
1934	Fred Perry (GBR)	Jack Crawford (AUS)	6-3	6-0	7-5		
1935	Fred Perry (GBR)	Gottfried von Cramm (GER)	6-2	6-4	6-4		
1936	Fred Perry (GBR)	Gottfried von Cramm (GER)	6-1	6-1	6-0		
1937	Don Budge (USA)	Gottfried von Cramm (GER)	6-3	6-4	6-2		
1938	Don Budge (USA)	Bunny Austin (GBR)	6-1	6-0	6-3		
1939	Bobby Riggs (USA)	Elwood Cooke (USA)	2-6	8-6	3-6	6-3	6-2
1940 - 1945 Not held - WW II							
1946	Yvon Petra (FRA)	Geoff Brown (AUS)	4-6	4-6	6-3	7-5	8-6
1947	Jack Kramer (USA)	Tom Brown Jr. (USA)	6-1	6-3	6-2		
1948	Bob Falkenburg (USA)	John Bromwich (AUS)	7-5	0-6	6-2	3-6	7-5
1949	Ted Schroeder (USA)	Jaroslav Drobny (EGY)	3-6	6-0	6-3	4-6	6-4
1950	Budge Patty (USA)	Frank Sedgman (AUS)	6-1	8-10	6-2	6-3	
1951	Dick Savitt (USA)	Ken McGregor (AUS)	6-4	6-4	6-4		
1952	Frank Sedgman (AUS)	Jaroslav Drobny (EGY)	4-6	6-2	6-3	6-2	
1953	Viv Seixas (USA)	Kurt Nielsen (DEN)	9-7	6-3	6-4		
1954	Jaroslav Drobny (EGY)	Ken Rosewall (AUS)	13-11	4-6	6-2	9-7	
1955	Tony Trabert (USA)	Kurt Nielsen (DEN)	6-3	7-5	6-1		
1956	Lew Hoad (AUS)	Ken Rosewall (AUS)	6-2	4-6	7-5	6-4	
1957	Lew Hoad (AUS)	Ashley Cooper (AUS)	6-2	6-1	6-2		
1958	Ashley Cooper (AUS)	Neale Fraser (AUS)	3-6	6-3	6-4	13-11	
1959	Alejandro Olmedo (USA)	Rod Laver (AUS)	6-4	6-3	6-4		
1960	Neale Fraser (AUS)	Rod Laver (AUS)	6-4	3-6	9-7	7-5	
1961	Rod Laver (AUS)	Chuck McKinley (USA)	6-3	6-1	6-4		
1962	Rod Laver (AUS)	Marty Mulligan (AUS)	6-2	6-2	6-1		
1963	Chuck McKinley (USA)	Fred Stolle (AUS)	9-7	6-1	6-4		
1964	Roy Emerson (AUS)	Fred Stolle (AUS)	6-4	12-10	4-6	6-3	
1965	Roy Emerson (AUS)	Fred Stolle (AUS)	6-2	6-4	6-4		
1966	Manolo Santana (ESP)	Dennis Ralston (USA)	6-4	11-9	6-4		
1967	John Newcombe (AUS)	Wilhelm Bungert (GER)	6-3	6-1	6-1		
1968	Rod Laver (AUS)	Tony Roche (AUS)	6-3	6-4	6-2		
1969	Rod Laver (AUS)	John Newcombe (AUS)	6-4	5-7	6-4	6-4	
1970	John Newcombe (AUS)	Ken Rosewall (AUS)	5-7	6-3	6-3	3-6	6-1
1971	John Newcombe (AUS)	Stan Smith (USA)	6-3	5-7	2-6	6-4	6-4
1972	Stan Smith (USA)	Ilie Nastase (ROU)	4-6	6-3	6-3	4-6	7-5
1973	Jan Kodes (CZE)	Alex Metreveli (USSR)	6-1	9-8(5)	6-3		
1974	Jimmy Connors (USA)	Ken Rosewall (AUS)	6-1	6-1	6-4		
1975	Arthur Ashe (USA)	Jimmy Connors (USA)	6-1	6-1	5-7	6-4	
1976	Bjorn Borg (SWE)	Ilie Nastase (ROU)	6-4	6-2	9-7		
1977	Bjorn Borg (SWE)	Jimmy Connors (USA)	3-6	6-2	6-1	5-7	6-4
1978	Bjorn Borg (SWE)	Jimmy Connors (USA)	6-2	6-2	6-3		
1979	Bjorn Borg (SWE)	Roscoe Tanner (USA)	6-7(4)	6-1	3-6	6-3	6-4
1980	Bjorn Borg (SWE)	John McEnroe (USA)	1-6	7-5	6-3	6-7(16)	8-6
1981	John McEnroe (USA)	Bjorn Borg (SWE)	4-6	7-6(1)	7-6(4)	6-4	
1982	Jimmy Connors (USA)	John McEnroe (USA)	3-6	6-3	6-7(2)	7-6(5)	6-4
1983	John McEnroe (USA)	Chris Lewis (AUS)	6-2	6-2	6-2		
1984	John McEnroe (USA)	Jimmy Connors (USA)	6-1	6-1	6-2		
1985	Boris Becker (GER)	Kevin Curren (USA)	6-3	6-7(4)	7-6(3)	6-4	
1986	Boris Becker (GER)	Ivan Lendl (CZE)	6-4	6-3	7-5		
1987	Pat Cash (AUS)	Ivan Lendl (CZE)	7-6(5)	6-2	7-5		
1988	Stefan Edberg (SWE)	Boris Becker (GER)	4-6	7-6(2)	6-4	6-2	
1989	Boris Becker (GER)	Stefan Edberg (SWE)	6-0	7-6(1)	6-4		
1990	Stefan Edberg (SWE)	Boris Becker (GER)	6-2	6-2	3-6	3-6	6-4
1991	Michael Stich (GER)	Boris Becker (GER)	6-4	7-6(4)	6-4		
1992	Andre Agassi (USA)	Goran Ivanisevic (CRO)	6-7(8)	6-4	6-4	1-6	6-4
1993	Pete Sampras (USA)	Jim Courier (USA)	7-6(3)	7-6(6)	3-6	6-3	
1994	Pete Sampras (USA)	Goran Ivanisevic (CRO)	7-6(2)	7-6(5)	6-0		
1995	Pete Sampras (USA)	Boris Becker (GER)	6-7(5)	6-2	6-4	6-2	
1996	Richard Krajicek (NED)	MaliVai Washington (USA)	6-3	6-4	6-3		
1997	Pete Sampras (USA)	Cedric Pioline (FRA)	6-4	6-2	6-4		
1998	Pete Sampras (USA)	Goran Ivanisevic (CRO)	6-7(2)	7-6(9)	6-4	3-6	6-2
1999	Pete Sampras (USA)	Andre Agassi (USA)	6-3	6-4	7-5		
2000	Pete Sampras (USA)	Patrick Rafter (AUS)	6-7(10)	7-6(5)	6-4	6-2	
2001	Goran Ivanisevic (CRO)	Patrick Rafter (AUS)	6-3	3-6	6-3	2-6	9-7
2002	Lleyton Hewitt (AUS)	David Nalbandian (ARG)	6-1	6-3	6-2		
2003	Roger Federer (SUI)	Mark Philippoussis (AUS)	7-6(5)	6-2	7-6(3)		
2004	Roger Federer (SUI)	Andy Roddick (USA)	4-6	7-5	7-6(3)	6-4	
2005	Roger Federer (SUI)	Andy Roddick (USA)	6-2	7-6(2)	6-4		
2006	Roger Federer (SUI)	Rafael Nadal (ESP)	6-0	7-6(5)	6-7(2)	6-3	
2007	Roger Federer (SUI)	Rafael Nadal (ESP)	7-6(7)	4-6	7-6(3)	2-6	6-2
2008	Rafael Nadal (ESP)	Roger Federer (SUI)	6-4	6-4	6-7(5)	6-7(8)	9-7
2009	Roger Federer (SUI)	Andy Roddick (USA)	5-7	7-6(6)	7-6(5)	3-6	16-14

Women's Singles Finals

Rd	Winner	Defeated	S1	S2	S3
1884	Maud Watson (GBR)	Lillian Watson (GBR)	6-8	6-3	6-3
1885	Maud Watson (GBR)	Blanche Bingley (GBR)	6-1	7-5	
1886	Blanche Bingley (GBR)	Maud Watson (GBR)	6-3	6-3	
1887	Charlotte Dod (GBR)	Blanche Bingley Hillyard (GBR)	6-2	6-0	
1888	Charlotte Dod (GBR)	Blanche Bingley Hillyard (GBR)	6-3	6-3	
1889	Blanche Bingley Hillyard (GBR)	Helena Rice (GBR)	4-6	8-6	6-4
1890	Helena Rice (GBR)	M. Jacks (GBR)	6-4	6-1	
1891	Charlotte Dod (GBR)	Blanche Bingley Hillyard (GBR)	6-2	6-1	
1892	Charlotte Dod (GBR)	Blanche Bingley Hillyard (GBR)	6-1	6-1	
1893	Charlotte Dod (GBR)	Blanche Bingley Hillyard (GBR)	6-8	6-1	6-4
1894	Blanche Bingley Hillyard (GBR)	Edith Austin (GBR)	6-1,	6-1,	
1895	Charlotte Cooper (GBR)	Helen Jackson (GBR)	7-5	8-6	
1896	Charlotte Cooper (GBR)	Alice Simpson Pickering (GBR)	6-2	6-3	
1897	Blanche Bingley Hillyard (GBR)	Charlotte Cooper (GBR)	5-7	7-5	6-2
1898	Charlotte Cooper (GBR)	Louisa Martin (GBR)	6-4	6-4	
1899	Blanche Bingley Hillyard (GBR)	Charlotte Cooper (GBR)	6-2	6-3	
1900	Blanche Bingley Hillyard (GBR)	Charlotte Cooper (GBR)	4-6	6-4	6-4
1901	Charlotte Cooper Sterry (GBR)	Blanche Bingley Hillyard (GBR)	6-2	6-2	
1902	Muriel Robb (GBR)	Charlotte Cooper Sterry (GBR)	7-5	6-1	
1903	Dorothea Douglass (GBR)	Ethel Thomson (GBR)	4-6	6-4	6-2
1904	Dorothea Douglass (GBR)	Charlotte Cooper Sterry (GBR)	6-0	6-3	
1905	May Sutton (USA)	Dorothea Douglass (GBR)	6-3	6-4	
1906	Dorothea Douglass (GBR)	May Sutton (USA)	6-3	9-7	
1907	May Sutton (USA)	D. Douglass Chambers (GBR)	6-1	6-4	
1908	Charlotte Cooper Sterry (GBR)	Agnes Morton (GBR)	6-4	6-4	
1909	Dora Boothby (GBR)	Agnes Morton (GBR)	6-4	4-6	8-6
1910	Dorothea Douglass Chambers (GBR)	Dora Boothby (GBR)	6-2	6-2	
1911	Dorothea Douglass Chambers (GBR)	Dora Boothby (GBR)	6-0	6-0	
1912	Ethel Thomson Larcombe (GBR)	Charlotte Cooper Sterry (GBR)	6-3	6-1	
1913	Dorothea Douglass Chambers (GBR)	Winifred Slocock McNair (GBR)	6-0	6-4	
1914	Dorothea Douglass Chambers (GBR)	Ethel Thomson Larcombe (GBR)	7-5	6-4	
1915 - 1918 Not held -- WW I					
1919	Suzanne Lenglen (FRA)	Dorothea Douglass Chambers (GBR)	10-8	4-6	9-7
1920	Suzanne Lenglen (FRA)	Dorothea Douglass Chambers (GBR)	6-3	6-0	
1921	Suzanne Lenglen (FRA)	Elizabeth Ryan (USA)	6-2	6-0	
1922	Suzanne Lenglen (FRA)	Molla Bjurstedt Mallory (USA)	6-2	6-0	
1923	Suzanne Lenglen (FRA)	Kitty McKane (GBR)	6-2	6-2	
1924	Kitty McKane (GBR)	Helen Wills (USA)	4-6	6-4	6-4
1925	Suzanne Lenglen (FRA)	Joan Fry (GBR)	6-2	6-0	
1926	Kitty McKane Godfree (GBR)	Lili de Alvarez (ESP)	6-2	4-6	6-3
1927	Helen Wills (USA)	Lili de Alvarez (ESP)	6-2	6-4	
1928	Helen Wills (USA)	Lili de Alvarez (ESP)	6-2	6-3	
1929	Helen Wills (USA)	Helen Jacobs (USA)	6-1	6-2	
1930	Helen Wills Moody (USA)	Elizabeth Ryan (USA)	6-2	6-2	
1931	Cilly Aussem (GER)	Hilde Krahwinkel (GER)	6-2	7-5	
1932	Helen Wills Moody (USA)	Helen Jacobs (USA)	6-3	6-1	
1933	Helen Wills Moody (USA)	Dorothy Round (GBR)	6-4	6-8	6-3
1934	Dorothy Round (GBR)	Helen Jacobs (USA)	6-2	5-7	6-3
1935	Helen Wills Moody (USA)	Helen Jacobs (USA)	6-3	3-6	7-5
1936	Helen Jacobs (USA)	Hilde Krahwinkel Sperling (DEN)	6-2	4-6	7-5
1937	Dorothy Round (GBR)	Jadwiga Jedrzejowska (POL)	6-2	2-6	7-5
1938	Helen Wills Moody (USA)	Helen Jacobs (USA)	6-4	6-0	
1939	Alice Marble (USA)	Kay Stammers (GBR)	6-2	6-0	
1940 - 1945 Not held - WW II					
1946	Pauline Betz (USA)	Louise Brough (USA)	6-2	6-4	
1947	Margaret Osborne (USA)	Doris Hart (USA)	6-2	6-4	
1948	Louise Brough (USA)	Doris Hart (USA)	6-3	8-6	
1949	Louise Brough (USA)	Margaret Osborne duPont (USA)	10-8	1-6	10-8
1950	Louise Brough (USA)	Margaret Osborne duPont (USA)	6-1	3-6	6-1
1951	Doris Hart (USA)	Shirley Fry (USA)	6-1	6-0	
1952	Maureen Connolly (USA)	Louise Brough (USA)	7-5	6-3	
1953	Maureen Connolly (USA)	Doris Hart (USA)	8-6	7-5	
1954	Maureen Connolly (USA)	Louise Brough (USA)	6-2	7-5	
1955	Louise Brough (USA)	Beverly Beverly Fleitz (USA)	7-5	8-6	
1956	Shirley Fry (USA)	Angela Buxton (GBR)	6-3	6-1	
1957	Althea Gibson (USA)	Darlene Hard (USA)	6-3	6-2	
1958	Althea Gibson (USA)	Angela Mortimer (GBR)	8-6	6-2	
1959	Maria Bueno (BRA)	Darlene Hard (USA)	6-4	6-3	
1960	Maria Bueno (BRA)	Sandra Reynolds (RSA)	8-6	6-0	
1961	Angela Mortimer (GBR)	Christine Truman (GBR)	4-6	6-4	7-5
1962	Karen Hantze Susman (USA)	Vera Sukova (CZE)	6-4	6-4	
1963	Maria Bueno (BRA)	Billie Jean Moffitt (USA)	6-3	6-4	
1964	Maria Bueno (BRA)	Margaret Smith (AUS)	6-4	7-9	6-3
1965	Margaret Smith (AUS)	Maria Bueno (BRA)	6-4	7-5	
1966	Billie Jean King (USA)	Maria Bueno (BRA)	6-3	3-6	6-1
1967	Billie Jean King (USA)	Ann Haydon Jones (GBR)	6-3	6-4	
1968	Billie Jean King (USA)	Judy Tegart (AUS)	9-7	7-5	
1969	Ann Haydon Jones (GBR)	Billie Jean King (USA)	3-6	6-3	6-2
1970	Margaret Smith Court (AUS)	Billie Jean King (USA)	14-12	11-9	
1971	Evonne Goolagong (AUS)	Margaret Smith Court (AUS)	6-4	6-1	
1972	Billie Jean King (USA)	Evonne Goolagong (AUS)	6-3	6-3	
1973	Billie Jean King (USA)	Chris Evert (USA)	6-0	7-5	
1974	Chris Evert (USA)	Olga Morozova (USSR)	6-0	6-4	
1975	Billie Jean King (USA)	Evonne Goolagong Cawley (AUS)	6-0	6-1	
1976	Chris Evert (USA)	Evonne Goolagong Cawley (AUS)	6-3	4-6	8-6
1977	Virginia Wade (GBR)	Betty Stove (NED)	4-6	6-3	6-1
1978	Martina Navratilova (CZE)	Chris Evert Lloyd (USA)	2-6	6-4	7-5
1979	Martina Navratilova (CZE)	Chris Evert Lloyd (USA)	6-4	6-4	
1980	Evonne Goolagong Cawley (AUS)	Chris Evert Lloyd (USA)	6-1	7-6(4)	
1981	Chris Evert Lloyd (USA)	Hana Mandlikova (CZE)	6-2	6-2	
1982	Martina Navratilova (USA)	Chirs Evert Lloyd (USA)	6-1	3-6	6-2
1983	Martina Navratilova (USA)	Andrea Jaeger (USA)	6-0	6-3	
1984	Martina Navratilova (USA)	Chris Evert Lloyd (USA)	7-6(5)	6-2	
1985	Martina Navratilova (USA)	Chris Evert Lloyd (USA)	4-6	6-3	6-2
1986	Martina Navratilova (USA)	Hana Mandlikova (CZE)	7-6(1)	6-3	
1987	Martina Navratilova (USA)	Steffi Graf (GER)	7-5	6-3	
1988	Steffi Graf (GER)	Martina Navratilova (USA)	5-7	6-2	6-1
1989	Steffi Graf (GER)	Martina Navratilova (USA)	6-2	6-7(1)	6-1
1990	Martina Navratilova (USA)	Zina Garrison (USA)	6-4	6-1	
1991	Steffi Graf (GER)	Gabriela Sabatini (ARG)	6-4	3-6	8-6
1992	Steffi Graf (GER)	Monica Seles (YUG)	6-2	6-1	
1993	Steffi Graf (GER)	Jana Novotna (CZE)	7-6(6)	1-6	6-4
1994	Conchita Martinez (ESP)	Martina Navratilova (USA)	6-4	3-6	6-3
1995	Steffi Graf (GER)	Arantxa Sanchez Vicario (ESP)	4-6	6-1	7-5
1996	Steffi Graf (GER)	Arantxa Sanchez Vicario (ESP)	6-3	7-5	
1997	Martina Hingis (SUI)	Jana Novotna (CZE)	2-6	6-3	6-3

Rd	Winner	Defeated	S1	S2	S3
1998	Jana Novotna (CZE)	Nathalie Tauziat (FRA)	6-4	7-6(2)	
1999	Lindsay Davenport (USA)	Steffi Graf (GER)	6-4	7-5	
2000	Venus Williams (USA)	Lindsay Davenport (USA)	6-3	7-6(3)	
2001	Venus Williams (USA)	Justine Henin (BEL)	6-1	3-6	6-0
2002	Serena Williams (USA)	Venus Williams (USA)	7-6(4)	6-3	
2003	Serena Williams (USA)	Venus Williams (USA)	4-6	6-4	6-2

Rd	Winner	Defeated	S1	S2	S3
2004	Maria Sharapova (RUS)	Serena Williams (USA)	6-1	6-4	
2005	Venus Williams (USA)	Lindsay Davenport (USA)	4-6	7-6(4)	9-7
2006	Amelie Mauresmo (FRA)	Justine Henin-Hardenne (BEL)	2-6	6-3	6-4
2007	Venus Williams (USA)	Marion Bartoli (FRA)	6-4	6-1	
2008	Venus Williams (USA)	Serena Williams (USA)	7-5	6-4	
2009	Serena Williams (USA)	Venus Williams (USA)	7-6(3)	6-2	

U.S. Championships

Men's Singles Finals

Rd	Winner	Defeated	S1	S2	S3	S4	S5
1881	Richard Sears (USA)	William Glyn (USA)	6-0	6-3	6-2		
1882	Richard Sears (USA)	Clarence Clark (USA)	6-1	6-4	6-0		
1883	Richard Sears (USA)	James Dwight (USA)	6-2	6-0	9-7		
1884	Richard Sears (USA)	Howard Taylor (USA)	6-0	1-6	6-0	6-2	
1885	Richard Sears (USA)	Godfrey Brinley (USA)	6-3	4-6	6-0	6-3	
1886	Richard Sears (USA)	Livingston Beeckman (USA)	4-6	6-1	6-3	6-4	
1887	Richard Sears (USA)	Henry Slocum (USA)	6-1	6-3	6-2		
1888	Henry Slocum (USA)	Howard Taylor (USA)	6-4	6-1	6-0		
1889	Henry Slocum (USA)	Quincy A. Shaw (USA)	6-3	6-1	4-6	6-2	
1890	Oliver Campbell (USA)	Henry Slocum (USA)	6-2	4-6	6-3	6-1	
1891	Oliver Campbell (USA)	Clarence Hobart (USA)	2-6	7-5	7-9	6-1	6-2
1892	Oliver Campbell (USA)	Fred Hovey (USA)	7-5	3-6	6-3	7-5	
1893	Robert Wrenn (USA)	Fred Hovey (USA)	6-4	3-6	6-4	6-4	
1894	Robert Wrenn (USA)	Manliffe Goodbody (USA)	6-8	6-1	6-4	6-4	
1895	Fred Hovey (USA)	Robert Wrenn (USA)	6-3	6-2	6-4		
1896	Robert Wrenn (USA)	Fred Hovey (USA)	7-5	3-6	6-0	1-6	6-1
1897	Robert Wrenn (USA)	Wilberforce Eaves (GBR)	4-6	8-6	6-3	2-6	6-2
1898	Malcolm Whitman (USA)	Dwight Davis (USA)	3-6	6-2	6-2	6-1	
1899	Malcolm Whitman (USA)	Parmly Paret (USA)	6-1	6-2	3-6	7-5	
1900	Malcolm Whitman (USA)	Bill Larned (USA)	6-4	1-6	6-2	6-2	
1901	Bill Larned (USA)	Beals Wright (USA)	6-2	6-8	6-4	6-4	
1902	Bill Larned (USA)	Reggie Doherty (GBR)	4-6	6-2	6-4	8-6	
1903	Laurie Doherty (GBR)	Bill Larned (USA)	6-0	6-3	10-8		
1904	Holcombe Ward (USA)	Bill Clothier (USA)	10-8	6-4	9-7		
1905	Beals Wright (USA)	Holcombe Ward (USA)	6-2	6-1	11-9		
1906	Bill Clothier (USA)	Beals Wright (USA)	6-3	6-0	6-4		
1907	Bill Larned (USA)	Bob LeRoy (USA)	6-2	6-2	6-4		
1908	Bill Larned (USA)	Beals Wright (USA)	6-1	6-2	8-6		
1909	Bill Larned (USA)	Bill Clothier (USA)	6-1	6-2	5-7	1-6	6-1
1910	Bill Larned (USA)	Tom Bundy (USA)	6-1	5-7	6-2	6-8	6-1
1911	Bill Larned (USA)	Maurice McLoughlin (USA)	6-4	6-4	6-2		
1912	Maurice McLoughlin (USA)	Wallace Johnson (USA)	3-6	2-6	6-2	6-4	6-2
1913	Maurice McLoughlin (USA)	Dick Williams (USA)	6-4	5-7	6-3	6-1	
1914	Dick Williams (USA)	Maurice McLoughlin (USA)	6-3	8-6	10-8		
1915	Bill Johnston (USA)	Maurice McLoughlin (USA)	1-6	6-0	7-5	10-8	
1916	Dick Williams (USA)	Bill Johnston (USA)	4-6	6-4	0-6	6-2	6-4
1917	Lindley Murray (USA)	Nathaniel Niles (USA)	5-7	8-6	6-3	6-3	
1918	Lindley Murray (USA)	Bill Tilden (USA)	6-3	6-1	7-5		
1919	Bill Johnston (USA)	Bill Tilden (USA)	6-4	6-4	6-3		
1920	Bill Tilden (USA)	Bill Johnston (USA)	6-1	1-6	7-5	5-7	6-3
1921	Bill Tilden (USA)	Wallace Johnson (USA)	6-1	6-3	6-1		
1922	Bill Tilden (USA)	Bill Johnston (USA)	4-6	3-6	6-2	6-3	6-4
1923	Bill Tilden (USA)	Bill Johnston (USA)	6-4	6-1	6-4		
1924	Bill Tilden (USA)	Bill Johnston (USA)	6-1	9-7	6-2		
1925	Bill Tilden (USA)	Bill Johnston (USA)	4-6	11-9	6-3	4-6	6-3
1926	Rene Lacoste (FRA)	Jean Borotra (FRA)	6-4	6-0	6-4		
1927	Rene Lacoste (FRA)	Bill Tilden (USA)	11-9	6-3	11-9		
1928	Henri Cochet (FRA)	Frank Hunter (USA)	4-6	6-4	3-6	7-5	6-3
1929	Bill Tilden (USA)	Frank Hunter (USA)	3-6	6-3	4-6	6-2	6-4
1930	Johnny Doeg (USA)	Francis Shields (USA)	10-8	1-6	6-4	16-14	
1931	Ellsworth Vines (USA)	Frank Hunter (USA)	7-9	6-3	9-7	7-5	
1932	Ellsworth Vines (USA)	Henri Cochet (FRA)	6-4	6-4	6-4		
1933	Fred Perry (GBR)	Jack Crawford (AUS)	6-3	11-13	4-6	6-0	6-1
1934	Fred Perry (GBR)	Wilmer Allison (USA)	6-4	6-3	3-6	1-6	8-6
1935	Wilmer Allison (USA)	Sidney Wood (USA)	6-2	6-2	6-3		
1936	Fred Perry (GBR)	Don Budge (USA)	2-6	6-2	8-6	1-6	10-8
1937	Don Budge (USA)	Gottfried von Cramm (GER)	6-1	7-9	6-1	3-6	6-1
1938	Don Budge (USA)	Gene Mako (USA)	6-3	6-8	6-2	6-1	
1939	Bobby Riggs (USA)	Welby Van Horn (USA)	6-4	6-2	6-4		
1940	Don McNeill (USA)	Bobby Riggs (USA)	4-6	6-8	6-3	6-3	7-5
1941	Bobby Riggs (USA)	Frank Kovacs (USA)	5-7	6-1	6-3	6-3	
1942	Ted Schroeder (USA)	Frank Parker (USA)	8-6	7-5	3-6	4-6	6-2
1943	Joseph R. Hunt (USA)	Jack Kramer (USA)	6-3	6-8	10-8	'6-2	
1944	Frank Parker (USA)	Bill Talbert (USA)	6-4	3-6	6-3	6-3	
1945	Frank Parker (USA)	Bill Talbert (USA)	14-12	6-1	6-2		
1946	Jack Kramer (USA)	Tom Brown Jr. (USA)	9-7	6-3	6-0		
1947	Jack Kramer (USA)	Frank Parker (USA)	4-6	2-6	6-1	6-0	6-3
1948	Pancho Gonzalez (USA)	Eric Sturgess (USA)	6-2	6-3	14-12		
1949	Pancho Gonzalez (USA)	Ted Schroeder (USA)	16-18	2-6	6-1	6-2	6-4
1950	Art Larsen (USA)	Herbie Flam (USA)	6-3	4-6	5-7	6-4	6-3
1951	Frank Sedgman (AUS)	Vic Seixas (USA)	6-4	6-1	6-1		
1952	Frank Sedgman (AUS)	Gardnar Mulloy (USA)	6-1	6-2	6-3		
1953	Tony Trabert (USA)	Vic Seixas (USA)	6-3	6-2	6-3		
1954	Vic Seixas (USA)	Rex Hartwig (AUS)	3-6	6-2	6-4	6-4	

Rd	Winner	Defeated	S1	S2	S3	S4	S5
1955	Tony Trabert (USA)	Ken Rosewall (AUS)	9-7	6-3	6-3		
1956	Ken Rosewall (AUS)	Lew Hoad (AUS)	4-6	6-2	6-3	6-3	
1957	Mal Anderson (AUS)	Ashley Cooper (AUS)	10-8	7-5	6-4		
1958	Ashley Cooper (AUS)	Mal Anderson (AUS)	6-2	3-6	4-6	10-8	8-6
1959	Neale Fraser (AUS)	Alex Olmedo (PER)	6-3	5-7	6-2	6-4	
1960	Neale Fraser (AUS)	Rod Laver (AUS)	6-4	6-4	9-7		
1961	Roy Emerson (AUS)	Rod Laver (AUS)	7-5	6-3	6-2		
1962	Rod Laver (AUS)	Roy Emerson (AUS)	6-2	6-4	5-7	6-4	
1963	Rafael Osuna (MEX)	Frank Froehling III (AUS)	7-5	6-4	6-2		
1964	Roy Emerson (AUS)	Fred Stolle (AUS)	6-4	6-1	6-4		
1965	Manolo Santana (ESP)	Cliff Drysdale (RSA)	6-2	7-9	7-5	6-1	
1966	Fred Stolle (AUS)	John Newcombe (AUS)	4-6	12-10	6-3	6-4	
1967	John Newcombe (AUS)	Clark Graebner (USA)	6-4	6-4	8-6		
1968	Arthur Ashe (USA)	Tom Okker (NED)	14-12	5-7	6-3	3-6	6-3
1968 amat	Arthur Ashe (USA)	Bob Lutz (USA)	4-6	6-3	8-10	6-0	6-4
1969	Rod Laver (AUS)	Tony Roche (AUS)	7-9	6-1	6-2	6-2	
1970	Ken Rosewall (AUS)	Tony Roche (AUS)	2-6	6-4	7-6(2)	6-3	
1971	Stan Smith (USA)	Jan Kodes (CZE)	3-6	6-3	6-2	7-6(3)	
1972	Ilie Nastase (ROU)	Arthur Ashe (USA)	3-6	6-3	6-7(5)	6-4	6-3
1973	John Newcombe (AUS)	Jan Kodes (CZE)	6-4	1-9	4-6	6-2	6-3
1974	Jimmy Connors (USA)	Ken Rosewall (AUS)	6-1	6-0	6-1		
1975	Manolo Orantes (ESP)	Jimmy Connors (USA)	6-4	6-3	6-3		
1976	Jimmy Connors (USA)	Bjorn Borg (SWE)	6-4	3-6	7-6(9)	6-4	
1977	Guillermo Vilas (ARG)	Jimmy Connors (USA)	2-6	6-3	7-6(4)	6-0	
1978	Jimmy Connors (USA)	Bjorn Borg (SWE)	6-4	6-2	6-2		
1979	John McEnroe (USA)	Vitas Gerulaitis (USA)	7-5	6-3	6-3		
1980	John McEnroe (USA)	Bjorn Borg (SWE)	7-6(4)	6-1	6-7(5)	5-7	6-4
1981	John McEnroe (USA)	Bjorn Borg (SWE)	4-6	6-2	6-4	6-3	
1982	Jimmy Connors (USA)	Ivan Lendl (CZE)	6-3	6-2	4-6	6-4	
1983	Jimmy Connors (USA)	Ivan Lendl (CZE)	6-3	6-7(2)	7-5	6-0	
1984	John McEnroe (USA)	Ivan Lendl (CZE)	6-3	6-4	6-1		
1985	Ivan Lendl (CZE)	John McEnroe (USA)	7-6(1)	6-3	6-4		
1986	Ivan Lendl (CZE)	Miloslav Mecir (CZE)	6-4	6-2	6-0		
1987	Ivan Lendl (CZE)	Mats Wilander (SWE)	'6-7(7)	6-0	7-6(4)	6-4	
1988	Mats Wilander (SWE)	Ivan Lendl (CZE)	6-4	4-6	6-3	5-7	6-4
1989	Boris Becker (GER)	Ivan Lendl (CZE)	7-6(2)	1-6	6-3	7-6(4)	
1990	Pete Sampras (USA)	Andre Agassi (USA)	6-4	6-3	6-2		
1991	Stefan Edberg (SWE)	Jim Courier (USA)	6-2	6-4	6-0		
1992	Stefan Edberg (SWE)	Pete Sampras (USA)	3-6	6-4	7-6(5)	6-2	
1993	Pete Sampras (USA)	Cedric Pioline (FRA)	6-4	6-4	6-3		
1994	Andre Agassi (USA)	Michael Stich (GER)	6-1	7-6(5)	7-5		
1995	Pete Sampras (USA)	Andre Agassi (USA)	6-4	6-3	4-6	7-5	
1996	Pete Sampras (USA)	Michael Chang (USA)	6-1	6-4	7-6(3)		
1997	Patrick Rafter (AUS)	Greg Rusedski (GBR)	6-3	6-2	4-6	7-5	
1998	Patrick Rafter (AUS)	Mark Philippoussis (AUS)	6-3	3-6	6-2	6-0	
1999	Andre Agassi (USA)	Todd Martin (USA)	6-4	6-7(5)	6-7(2)	6-3	6-2
2000	Marat Safin (RUS)	Pete Sampras (USA)	6-4	6-3	6-3		
2001	Lleyton Hewitt (AUS)	Pete Sampras (USA)	7-6(4)	6-1	6-1		
2002	Pete Sampras (USA)	Andre Agassi (USA)	6-3	6-4	5-7	6-4	
2003	Andy Roddick (USA)	Juan Carlos Ferrero (ESP)	6-3	7-6(2)	6-3		
2004	Roger Federer (SUI)	Lleyton Hewitt (AUS)	6-0	7-6(3)	6-0		
2005	Roger Federer (SUI)	Andre Agassi (USA)	6-3	2-6	7-6(1)	6-1	
2006	Roger Federer (SUI)	Andy Roddick (USA)	6-2	4-6	7-5	6-1	
2007	Roger Federer (SUI)	Novak Djokovic (SRB)	7-6(4)	7-6(2)	6-4		
2008	Roger Federer (SUI)	Andy Murray (GBR)	6-2	7-5	6-2		

Women's Singles Finals

Rd	Winner	Defeated	S1	S2	S3	S4	S5
1887	Ellen Hansell (USA)	Laura Knight (USA)	6-1	6-0			
1888	Bertha Townsend (USA)	Ellen Hansell (USA)	6-3	6-5			
1889	Bertha Townsend (USA)	Lida Voorhees (USA)	7-5	6-2			
1890	Ellen Roosevelt (USA)	Bertha Townsend (USA)	6-2	6-2			
1891	Mabel Cahill (GBR)	Ellen Roosevelt (USA)	6-4	6-1	4-6	6-3	
1892	Mabel Cahill (GBR)	Elisabeth Moore (USA)	5-7	6-3	6-4	4-6	6-2
1893	Aline Terry (USA)	Augusta Schultz (USA)	6-1	6-3			
1894	Helen Hellwig (USA)	Aline Terry (USA)	7-5	3-6	6-0	3-6	6-3
1895	Juliette Atkinson (USA)	Helen Hellwig (USA)	6-4	6-2	6-1		
1896	Elisabeth Moore (USA)	Juliette Atkinson (USA)	6-4	4-6	6-2	6-2	
1897	Juliette Atkinson (USA)	Elisabeth Moore (USA)	6-3	6-3	4-6	3-6	6-3
1898	Juliette Atkinson (USA)	Marion Jones (USA)	6-3	5-7	6-4	2-6	7-5
1899	Marion Jones (USA)	Maud Banks (USA)	6-1	6-1	7-5		
1900	Myrtle McAteer (USA)	Marion Jones (USA)	(default)				
1901	Elisabeth Moore (USA)	Myrtle McAteer (USA)	6-4	3-6	7-5	2-6	6-2

USLTA adopts 3-set format

Rd	Winner	Defeated	S1	S2	S3
1902	Marion Jones (USA)	Elisabeth Moore (USA)	6-1	1-0 (default)	
1903	Elisabeth Moore (USA)	Marion Jones (USA)	7-5	8-6	
1904	May Sutton (USA)	Elisabeth Moore (USA)	6-1	6-2	
1905	Elisabeth Moore (USA)	Helen Homans (USA)	6-4	5-7	6-1
1906	Helen Homans (USA)	Maud Barger Wallach (USA)	6-4	6-3	
1907	Evelyn Sears (USA)	Carrie Neely (USA)	6-3	6-2	
1908	Maud Barger Wallach (USA)	Evelyn Sears (USA)	6-3	1-6	6-3
1909	Hazel Hotchkiss (USA)	Maud Barger Wallach (USA)	6-0	6-1	
1910	Hazel Hotchkiss (USA)	Louise Hammond (USA)	6-4	6-2	
1911	Hazel Hotchkiss (USA)	Florence Sutton (USA)	8-10	6-1	9-7
1912	Mary K. Browne (USA)	Eleonora Sears (USA)	6-4	6-2	
1913	Mary K. Browne (USA)	Dorothy Green (USA)	6-2	7-5	
1914	Mary K. Browne (USA)	Marie Wagner (USA)	6-2	1-6	6-1
1915	Molla Bjurstedt (NOR)	Hazel Hotchkiss Wightman (USA)	4-6	6-2	6-0
1916	Molla Bjurstedt (NOR)	Louise Hammond Raymond (USA)	6-0	6-1	
1917	Molla Bjurstedt (NOR)	Marion Vanderhoef (USA)	4-6	6-0	6-2
1918	Molla Bjurstedt (NOR)	Eleanor Goss (USA)	6-4	6-3	
1919	Hazel Hotchkiss Wightman (USA)	Marion Zinderstein (USA)	6-1	6-2	
1920	Molla Bjurstedt Mallory (USA)	Marion Zinderstein (USA)	6-3	6-1	
1921	Molla Bjurstedt Mallory (USA)	Mary K. Browne (USA)	4-6	6-4	6-2
1922	Molla Bjurstedt Mallory (USA)	Helen Wills (USA)	6-3	6-1	
1923	Helen Wills (USA)	Molla Bjurstedt Mallory (USA)	6-2	6-1	
1924	Helen Wills (USA)	Molla Bjurstedt Mallory (USA)	6-1	6-3	
1925	Helen Wills (USA)	Kitty McKane (GBR)	3-6	6-0	6-2
1926	Molla Bjurstedt Mallory (USA)	Elizabeth Ryan (USA)	4-6	6-4	9-7
1927	Helen Wills (USA)	Betty Nuthall (GBR)	6-1	6-4	
1928	Helen Wills (USA)	Helen Jacobs (USA)	6-2	6-1	
1929	Helen Wills Moody (USA)	Phoebe Holcroft Watson (GBR)	6-4	6-2	
1930	Betty Nuthall (GBR)	Anna McCune Harper (USA)	6-1	6-4	
1931	Helen Wills Moody (USA)	Eileen Bennett Whittingstall (GBR)	6-4	6-1	
1932	Helen Jacobs (USA)	Carolin Babcock (USA)	6-2	6-2	
1933	Helen Jacobs (USA)	Helen Wills Moody (USA)	8-6	3-6	3-0
1934	Helen Jacobs (USA)	Sarah Palfrey (USA)	6-1	6-4	
1935	Helen Jacobs (USA)	Sarah Palfrey Fabyan (USA)	6-2	6-4	
1936	Alice Marble (USA)	Helen Jacobs (USA)	4-6	6-3	6-2

Rd	Winner	Defeated	S1	S2	S3
1937	Anita Lizana (CHI)	Jadwiga Jedrzejowska (POL)	6-4	6-2	
1938	Alice Marble (USA)	Nancye Wynne (AUS)	6-0	6-3	
1939	Alice Marble (USA)	Helen Jacobs (USA)	6-0	8-10	6-4
1940	Alice Marble (USA)	Helen Jacobs (USA)	6-2	6-3	
1941	Sarah Palfrey Cooke (USA)	Pauline Betz (USA)	7-5	6-2	
1942	Pauline Betz (USA)	Louise Brough (USA)	4-6	6-1	6-4
1943	Pauline Betz (USA)	Louise Brough (USA)	6-3	5-7	6-3
1944	Pauline Betz (USA)	Margaret Osborne (USA)	6-3	8-6	
1945	Sarah Palfrey Cooke (USA)	Pauline Betz (USA)	3-6	8-6	6-4
1946	Pauline Betz (USA)	Doris Hart (USA)	11-9	6-3	
1947	Louise Brough (USA)	Margaret Osborne duPont (USA)	8-6	4-6	6-1
1948	Margaret Osborne duPont (USA)	Louise Brough (USA)	4-6	6-4	15-13
1949	Margaret Osborne duPont (USA)	Doris Hart (USA)	6-4	6-1	
1950	Margaret Osborne duPont (USA)	Doris Hart (USA)	6-3	6-3	
1951	Maureen Connolly (USA)	Shirley Fry (USA)	6-3	1-6	6-4
1952	Maureen Connolly (USA)	Doris Hart (USA)	6-3	7-5	
1953	Maureen Connolly (USA)	Doris Hart (USA)	6-2	6-4	
1954	Doris Hart (USA)	Louise Brough (USA)	6-8	6-1	8-6
1955	Doris Hart (USA)	Pat Ward (GBR)	6-4	6-2	
1956	Shirley Fry (USA)	Althea Gibson (USA)	6-3	6-4	
1957	Althea Gibson (USA)	Louise Brough (USA)	6-3	6-2	
1958	Althea Gibson (USA)	Darlene Hard (USA)	3-6	6-1	6-2
1959	Maria Bueno (BRA)	Christine Truman (GBR)	6-1	6-4	
1960	Darlene Hard (USA)	Maria Bueno (BRA)	6-3	10-12	6-4
1961	Darlene Hard (USA)	Ann Haydon (GBR)	6-3	6-4	
1962	Margaret Smith (AUS)	Darlene Hard (USA)	9-7	6-4	
1963	Maria Bueno (BRA)	Margaret Smith (AUS)	7-5	6-4	
1964	Maria Bueno (BRA)	Carole Caldwell Graebner (USA)	6-1	6-0	
1965	Margaret Smith (AUS)	Billie Jean Moffitt (USA)	8-6	7-5	
1966	Maria Bueno (BRA)	Nancy Richey (USA)	6-3	6-1	
1967	Billie Jean King (USA)	Ann Haydon Jones (GBR)	11-9	6-4	
1968	Virginia Wade (GBR)	Billie Jean King (USA)	6-4	6-2	
1969	Margaret Smith Court (AUS)	Nancy Richey (USA)	6-2	6-2	
1970	Margaret Smith Court (AUS)	Rosie Casals (USA)	6-2	2-6	6-1
1971	Billie Jean King (USA)	Rosie Casals (USA)	6-4	7-6(2)	
1972	Billie Jean King (USA)	Kerry Melville (AUS)	6-3	7-5	
1973	Margaret Smith Court (AUS)	Evonne Goolagong (AUS)	7-6(2)	5-7	6-2
1974	Billie Jean King (USA)	Evonne Goolagong (AUS)	3-6	6-3	7-5
1975	Chris Evert (USA)	Evonne Goolagong (AUS)	5-7	6-4	6-2
1976	Chris Evert (USA)	Evonne Goolagong (AUS)	6-3	6-0	
1977	Chris Evert (USA)	Wendy Turnbull (AUS)	7-6(3)	6-2	
1978	Chris Evert (USA)	Pam Shriver (USA)	7-5	6-4	
1979	Tracy Austin (USA)	Chris Evert Lloyd (USA)	6-4	6-3	
1980	Chris Evert Lloyd (USA)	Hana Mandlikova (CZE)	5-7	6-1	6-1
1981	Tracy Austin (USA)	Martina Navratilova (USA)	1-6	7-6(4)	7-6(1)
1982	Chris Evert Lloyd (USA)	Hana Mandlikova (CZE)	6-3	6-1	
1983	Martina Navratilova (USA)	Chris Evert Lloyd (USA)	6-1	6-3	
1984	Martina Navratilova (USA)	Chris Evert Lloyd (USA)	4-6	6-4	6-4
1985	Hana Mandlikova (CZE)	Martina Navratilova (USA)	7-6(3)	1-6	7-6(2)
1986	Martina Navratilova (USA)	Helena Sukova (CZE)	6-3	6-2	
1987	Martina Navratilova (USA)	Steffi Graf (GER)	7-6(4)	6-1	
1988	Steffi Graf (GER)	Gabriela Sabatini (ARG)	6-3	3-6	6-1
1989	Steffi Graf (GER)	Martina Navratilova (USA)	3-6	7-5	6-1
1990	Gabriela Sabatini (ARG)	Steffi Graf (GER)	6-2	7-6(4)	
1991	Monica Seles (YUG)	Martina Navratilova (USA)	7-6(1)	6-1	
1992	Monica Seles (YUG)	Arantxa Sanchez Vicario (ESP)	6-3	6-3	
1993	Steffi Graf (GER)	Helena Sukova (CZE)	6-3	6-3	
1994	Arantxa Sanchez Vicario (ESP)	Steffi Graf (GER)	1-6	7-6(3)	6-4
1995	Steffi Graf (GER)	Monica Seles (USA)	7-6(6)	0-6	6-3
1996	Steffi Graf (GER)	Monica Seles (USA)	7-5	6-4	
1997	Martina Hingis (SUI)	Venus Williams (USA)	6-0	6-4	
1998	Lindsay Davenport (USA)	Martina Hingis (SUI)	6-3	7-5	
1999	Serena Williams (USA)	Martina Hingis (SUI)	6-3	7-6(4)	
2000	Venus Williams (USA)	Lindsay Davenport (USA)	6-4	7-5	
2001	Venus Williams (USA)	Serena Williams (USA)	6-2	6-4	
2002	Serena Williams (USA)	Venus Williams (USA)	6-4	6-3	
2003	Justine Henin-Hardenne (BEL)	Kim Clijsters (BEL)	7-5	6-1	
2004	Svetlana Kuznetsova (RUS)	Elena Dementieva (RUS)	6-3	7-5	
2005	Kim Clijsters (BEL)	Mary Pierce (FRA)	6-3	6-1	
2006	Maria Sharapova (RUS)	Justine Henin-Hardenne (BEL)	6-4	6-4	
2007	Justine Henin (BEL)	Svetlana Kuznetsova (RUS)	6-1	6-3	
2008	Serena Williams (USA)	Jelena Jankovic (SRB)	6-4	7-5	

Also From New Chapter Press

On This Day In Tennis History
BY RANDY WALKER

Fun and fact-filled, this compilation offers anniversaries, summaries, and anecdotes of events from the world of tennis for every day in the calendar year. Presented in a day-by-day format, the entries into this mini-encyclopedia include major tournament victory dates, summaries of the greatest matches ever played, trivia, and statistics as well as little-known and quirky happenings. Easy-to-use and packed with fascinating details, this compendium is the perfect companion for tennis and general sports fans alike.

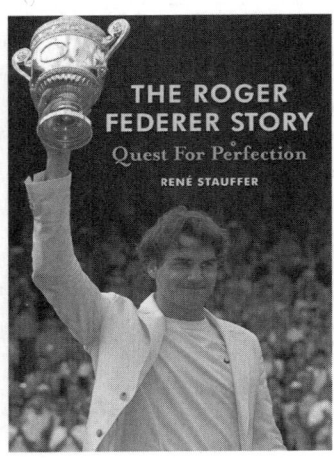

The Roger Federer Story, Quest For Perfection
BY RENE STAUFFER

Regarded by many as the greatest tennis player in the history of the sport, this authoritative biography is based on many exclusive interviews with Federer and his family as well as the author's experience covering the international tennis circuit for many years. Completely comprehensive, it provides an informed account of the Swiss tennis star from his early days as a temperamental player on the junior circuit, through his early professional career, to his winning major tennis tournaments, including the U.S. Open and Wimbledon. Readers will appreciate the anecdotes about his early years, revel in the insider's view of the professional tennis circuit, and be inspired by this champion's rise to the top of his game.

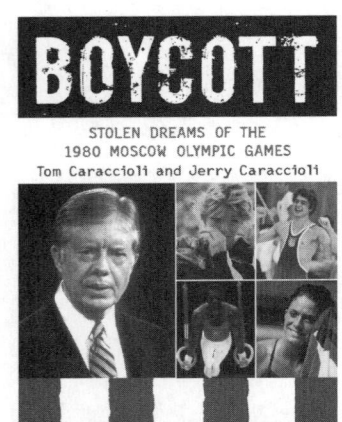

BOYCOTT:
Stolen Dreams of the 1980 Moscow Olympic Games
BY TOM AND JERRY CARACCIOLI

With a thorough exploration of the political climate of the time and the Soviet Union's invasion of Afghanistan, this book describes the repercussions of Jimmy Carter's American boycott of the 1980 Olympic Games in Moscow. Despite missing the games they had trained relentlessly to compete in, many U.S. athletes went on to achieve remarkable successes in sports and overcame the bitter disappointment of a once-in-a-lifetime opportunity dashed by geopolitics.

www.newchapterpressmedia.com